PAUL KANE'S FRONTIER

Special Acknowledgment

This book, which contains a new and greatly enriched edition of Paul Kane's classic *Wanderings of an Artist*, has been made possible through the generous aid and cooperation of Mrs. Nelda C. Stark and the Nelda C. and H. J. Lutcher Stark Foundation of Orange, Texas. Original watercolours and paintings from Kane's western travels are reproduced from collections in the Stark Foundation. Two manuscript versions of *Wanderings of an Artist*, also in the Stark Foundation collections, were used by the editor in preparing the present text.

Plate I. Paul Kane, a self-portrait, painted during his western trip, 1846–48. Stark wwc103; crIV-597.

Paul Kane's Frontier

INCLUDING *Wanderings of an Artist among the Indians of North America* BY PAUL KANE

EDITED WITH A BIOGRAPHICAL INTRODUCTION
AND A CATALOGUE RAISONNÉ BY

J. Russell Harper

PUBLISHED FOR THE AMON CARTER MUSEUM, FORT WORTH, AND THE

NATIONAL GALLERY OF CANADA, OTTAWA, BY THE UNIVERSITY OF TORONTO PRESS, TORONTO

International Standard Book Number 0–8020–1734–7
Library of Congress Catalog Card Number 79–146522
© 1971 by the Amon Carter Museum of Western Art
All Rights Reserved
Manufactured in the United States of America
Composition, Printing, and Binding: Kingsport Press, Kingsport, Tennessee
Illustrations: The Meriden Gravure Company, Meriden, Connecticut
Published in Canada by University of Toronto Press 1971

CONTENTS

Introduction ix

Acknowledgments xiii

Illustrations xv

A Note on Names 2

PART ONE   Paul Kane: His Life and Career as an Artist . . . 3

   I Early Years 5

   II Sketching among the Indians, 1845–1848 14

   III A Trip to the Red River, 1849 30

   IV One Hundred Western Canvases 32

   V *Wanderings of an Artist* 38

   VI The Later Years 42

PART TWO   *Wanderings of an Artist among the Indians of North America from Canada to Vancouver's Island and Oregon through the Hudson's Bay Company's Territory and Back Again,* a reprint of the edition of 1859 47

PART THREE   Paul Kane's Sketches and Paintings . . . 159

PART FOUR   A *Catalogue Raisonné* 267

Appendices 311

Bibliography 341

Index 343

INTRODUCTION

Paul Kane was fortunate enough to receive national acclaim during his own lifetime. It was his large canvases of the western Indians and their romantic land, and his book *Wanderings of an Artist,* which were known then and these have remained the basis of his reputation. But he also left many hundreds of small sketches, which have been virtually unknown for well over a century. This study of Kane and his activities has its origin in the sketches as well as his canvases and his book, and also in his journals, letters and other material not previously made public. The large number of sketches shown here increase his importance immeasurably: they are significant historically, they have a freshness not found in many canvases, and they are altogether more exciting as paintings than his elaborated works. Paul Kane now emerges as a giant among North American artists of his period.

From 1845 to 1848 Kane travelled through the western spaces of America. First he journeyed alone, then in the brigades of the Hudson's Bay Company fur traders, and always he sketched as he went. His trip from Toronto to the Pacific was one of the longest and most adventurous sketching trips in the story of painting. On it he covered many thousands of miles, through high mountain passes in icy weather and across deserts in the blazing sun, hungry and thirsty; he descended torrents in frail canoes; he worked constantly among not always friendly native people. He recorded the Indians in detail, their homes, their ceremonials and their customs, first in the Great Lakes region and then across the western plains, through the Oregon country and along the Pacific northwest coast when these were still unknown regions.

Kane was a remarkable man who lived at a remarkable time. He was very much a man of that time, and his career as an artist-explorer is typical of the story of these years in Canada. Many Canadians, like Kane, were then probing into a variety of facets of their surroundings and seeing their world with a new keenness. Some pursued an interest in natural history, and laid the foundations for the study in Canada of its flora and fauna. Many became restless and dissatisfied with inadequacies in government; the aftermath of rebellion in 1837 was the gradual creation of a whole new political structure. Others, concerned about knowledge for their sons and daughters, instituted new elementary and secondary school systems and founded the great universities of McGill, Queen's and Toronto. Farmers, not content with the results of their labour, organized societies to promote better farming methods and the importation of pure-bred livestock. Business men saw a need for more means of transportation as an impetus to industrial expansion; they commenced the building of new roads, of canals and railways. Writers became more aware of the society about them and penned the first novels and stories based on the Canadian environment.

Paul Kane gave to the subjects of his brush that same appraising look which other Canadians were giving to many aspects of their life and surroundings. He set out on a search for truth, and it was this determination that he claimed always to be at the centre of his work and art.

This volume has grown out of an idea for a major book on Paul Kane which originated with Mitchell A. Wilder, Director of the Amon Carter Museum of Western Art, Fort Worth, Texas. He secured the co-operation of Mrs. Nelda C. Stark, whose late husband had purchased a superb collection of Kane's sketches and manuscripts; she generously agreed to make all her material available to the public for the first time. Mr. Wilder then approached Dr. Jean Sutherland Boggs, Director of the National Gallery of Canada, Ottawa, who at once agreed that the Gallery would become co-sponsor with the Amon

Carter Museum of a study of Kane and a major exhibition of his paintings. This co-operation between Canada and the United States is particularly appropriate since almost half of Kane's paintings are related to areas in what is now American territory. In all he spent approximately nine years south of the present border.

The research recorded in this volume on Paul Kane and his paintings, which survive in astonishing numbers, was begun by the author late in 1967. It has had much of the excitement of discovery which Kane himself experienced during his four years of seeking subject-matter among the Indians of the frontier. A number of approaches to a study of Kane's life and works suggested themselves. Each was bewildering in its possibilities. From a practical point of view it was necessary to restrict the undertaking to two essential aspects. One would be concerned directly with the artist himself, that is with the events of his career, his philosophical approach as a painter to his subject-matter, and his importance in the world of art. The second aspect would be the recording and documenting of the over eight hundred known paintings and sketches, chiefly from his trips on the western frontier. These works are mainly in several collections. Two large and magnificent accumulations are held by the Royal Ontario Museum, Toronto, and the Nelda C. and H. J. Lutcher Stark Foundation, Orange, Texas. Twelve items each are in the National Gallery of Canada, Ottawa, and the Bushnell Collection of the Peabody Museum, Harvard University; there are smaller numbers in other places. No attempt has been made here to analyse the ethnological significance of Kane's many records of Indian life; the subject would be a study in itself and one that invites exploration now. Even the limited objectives chosen have necessitated protracted detective work. In it has been combined luck, disappointment, sidetracking, and discovery, and it has meant a search that has taken me from Ontario to Victoria on the Pacific, over much of the historic terrain covered by Kane, and even to England.

Kane died nearly a century ago, and the attempt to collect information which would make him into an individual rather than just a name presented problems. During his lifetime he had been particularly reticent in speaking of himself beyond matters relating to his Indian paintings, and as close a friend as Sir Daniel Wilson had the greatest difficulty in compiling a biography at the time of the artist's death. It seemed possible that, despite the lapse of time, descendants of his family or of friends or associates might still have material. This was indeed the case. His grandchildren were found to be living in Winnipeg; they had many personal papers, paintings and sketches, portions of his library, and memorabilia of great value in documenting his career. At an early stage I also compiled a list of the people and places mentioned in Kane's book, *Wanderings of an Artist,* and in other published literature on him. Armed with this list as a starting point, I made a systematic check of the principal archives, manuscript collections and libraries from Ontario to British Columbia in Canada, in the northwestern United States, in Alabama and in England. Inquiries were made about possible papers referring to Kane himself or to men of some historical significance in my list. The co-operation in answer to my queries from archivists and librarians was most generous; many who had nothing relevant suggested other possible sources, and some put me directly in touch with various specialists who were of great assistance. The results were in sum most gratifying. The papers of Sir George Simpson, Kane's first patron, were seen in the Hudson's Bay Company archives; these, and the journals kept at the Company's posts at the time of Kane's visits, yielded many useful references. Papers in the Royal Ontario Museum provided both clarification and further leads. Diaries of several missionaries, such as the Rev. John Hunter of Cumberland House and Mrs. Mary Walker of the Walker and Eells mission in the Oregon Territory, contained interesting observations on the man. Descendants of the Honourable George W. Allan, Kane's second patron, had several paintings, and their papers referred to Kane's trip to Fort Garry in 1849 with Sir Edward Poore. This allusion to Poore led to the unexpected discovery of letters among the Poore family papers which completely documented this episode. Thus each discovery generated its own excitement as the picture of Kane gradually developed, and often also suggested new avenues of research.

During the search for original letters and other manuscript material, several publications about Kane were located which, curiously, had previously missed the attention of art historians. Of particular interest were an informative biography published in the *Anglo-American Magazine* of 1856, a unique printed catalogue of the 1848 exhibition in the Toronto City Hall of Kane's sketches during his four years in the west, personal recollections of Kane published by W. H. G. Kingston in 1856, and two letters from Kane to Lord Strathcona published in the latter's biography by Beckles Willson. Contemporary newspaper articles brought a sense of immediacy and vitality to the story. Toronto papers recorded Kane's visit to the theatre during his youth, devoted several columns to the local reaction to his 1848 exhibition, and gave him an obituary. Papers published in Mobile, Alabama, in 1841 and 1843 and in Oregon City in 1846 added more material. Reviews of Kane's *Wanderings of an Artist* were most illuminating about attitudes then current towards the threatened extinction of the American Indian; a critique in the *Revue des deux mondes*, the most scholarly of all, had not previously been used by writers.

Needless to add, all previously listed publications on Kane were checked, a study was made of the literature of the mid 19th century fur trade and particularly of the Hudson's Bay Company's operations, and publications describing affairs in the Oregon Territory during the crucial 1840s were examined. Reference points for the assessment of Kane's contribution and stature were provided by a study of George Catlin, John Mix Stanley, Henry J. Warre and other painters of Indians and western scenery at the time. One of the most significant discoveries was that of a documented link between Kane and Catlin and various references to his knowledge of Stanley's activities as a painter in the Oregon.

The second aspect of my task, one which appeared to be of formidable complexity, was the preparation of a *catalogue raisonné*. The hundreds of sketches in the Royal Ontario Museum and the Stark Foundation collections, as well as others scattered throughout Canada and the United States were, with but a few exceptions, unknown to the general public and indeed had been seen by comparatively few people. The awesome task of identifying these was simplified in an unexpected way. Many sketches bore numbers, some having as many as seven of these inscribed on them. The numbers appeared to refer to various series. Keys to five of these series were actually discovered, and three series proved to relate to material prepared by Kane himself and thus of primary importance. This first-hand information was in the landscape and portrait logs which the artist kept on his western trip, and in the list of 240 sketches published in the 1848 catalogue. By checking inscribed numbers in these sources, it was possible to identify the bulk of the material. A few items were not clearly identifiable, but most of them seem to be of secondary interest. Some sketches bear ancient identification inscriptions; they proved to be not in Kane's hand and many were quite incorrect. If proof had been needed of the value of Kane's lists, it came when three of the twelve sketches carefully studied by D. I. Bushnell without their aid proved to be misidentified. Surprisingly, most of the sketches listed in the three series have been located. The whole collection, geographically arranged, unites to present a spectacular panorama of the western frontier during the 1840s: the west's celebrated men, its places of historic interest, its way of life which is now strange to us, and an ethnologically rich series of paintings of Indians from a day when their culture was still comparatively pure. A list of the later canvases purchased in 1856 by George W. Allan was in the Royal Ontario Museum collection; by checking it and the subject-matter of the sketches identified, several new identifications of canvases have been made.

Every writer about Kane points out that he was a professional portrait painter before turning to the western landscape and the Indians. Surprisingly little is known of his portraits. As a result of the work for this volume some positive identifications have been possible, some myths have been destroyed, and certain stylistic traits have been isolated. Much remains to be discovered, and it is hoped that the publication of this volume may itself lead to new sources of information.

One gratifying result of this research has been the discovery of Kane as a man with a humanitarian viewpoint unusual in his day and age. His stature as an artist also grows immeasurably from an examination of his field sketches. His journey over many thousands of miles of the difficult western frontier is unequalled by any other artist on the continent of his time, and he had a superb eye for recording the historically important. Certainly he is the equal of and in many respects superior to any other 19th century painter of the North American Indian.

The selection of the illustrations to be included in this book was a delightful exercise since the number of both colour and black-and-white plates to be included permitted generous visual demonstration of Kane's many interests and of various aspects of his work as a creative artist. The choice was guided by several considerations.

The Indians and their life were, of course, Kane's most absorbing interest as an artist. From his western travels it has been possible to include not only portraits of Big Snake, the famous prairie warrior, and of other celebrated chiefs whom he met, but also some of the compelling studies of less exalted Indian men and women from many tribes. Sketches of houses, clothing, canoes, weapons and artefacts from many tribes give a brief look at the material culture of the Indians, and others record such unique ceremonials as the Chualpays scalp dance at Fort Colvile, secret society dances of Vancouver Island, and Blackfoot medicine pipe-stem dances in Saskatchewan. Naturally, with the Hudson's Bay Company as his host, Kane left a visual record of their posts; included is at least one illustration of each of the posts he visited, the tangible symbols of British sovereignty and trade in the wilderness. The westward move of American settlers stirred his imagination; studies of Oregon City, the new metropolis of the west, of mission posts, and of the Puget Sound settlement echo his excitement at this turn of events. Many pure landscape studies have been included; travelling by canoe on rivers and lakes, Kane had full opportunity to appreciate the majesty of the western reaches of the continent. I have included his views of such striking natural phenomena as the Grand Coulee, the Chimney Rocks, waterfalls and erupting Mount St. Helens, as well as quieter autumn pastorals on the North Saskatchewan River and the picturesque Thirty Thousand Islands of Georgian Bay. The illustrations of his journeys have been arranged geographically from east to west, and they are thus a visual travelogue of the area over which he wandered.

A few illustrations of Kane's student works and of portraits painted in Ontario and the midwestern and southern United States are included. No exhaustive research has been done on phases of his career other than his western tour. Hopefully the examples selected will aid in identifying other Kane portraits, particularly in Ontario and Alabama.

On the technical side, illustrations have been selected to demonstrate Kane's procedures and his merits and shortcomings as an artist. Several reproductions demonstrate how *Winter Travelling in Dog Sleds* evolved, originating in small sketch studies, worked out in a pencilled composition, and ending as a canvas. Other illustrations indicate something of the loss of immediacy when he moved from sketch to canvas, his tendency to fumble in establishing proportions, his occasional reliance on earlier sources. Some of his canvases echo popular taste of the time, but anyone studying these illustrations will be very much aware of the fact that when Kane followed his own inclinations, particularly in working on his small field sketches, he was able to give a freshness and brilliance extraordinary for the years preceding impressionism.

A word should be said here about the structure of this book and how the reader might approach it. It has four main parts, which are both independent and interlocking. The first presents an account of Paul Kane's life and work, with special attention to the significant years of his career and to the period of his travels in the west, including references to information from other sources which give contemporary context to his journey; cross-references are made specifically to plates and figures of this book which reproduce works discussed in this biographical account, and references to *Wanderings of an Artist* are implicit. The second part of the book is a reprinting of the text of the first edition of *Wanderings*, which enables the reader to follow Kane's great journey as told in his own words; in this text have been interpolated references to the illustrations in the present volume and to all the items in sections III and IV of the *catalogue raisonné* so that the reader has constantly available to him a visual and a documentary accompaniment to Kane's narrative of his search for artistic subject-matter. The third part is made up of 205 black-and-white figures; their captions direct the reader to the corresponding items in the fourth part, the *catalogue raisonné*, which lists all Kane's work so far as it is known. Its sections III and IV organize the canvases and sketches of the frontier geographically from east to west, and by kinds of subjects within the various geographical areas; they also provide cross-references to relevant remarks by Kane in *Wanderings*, give background information about places and individuals and Indian tribes which Kane sketched, and indicate which items of the *catalogue* are reproduced in the present volume.

This description will indicate that the reader, depending on his interest, can begin his examination with any one of the four parts and consult the others both simultaneously and later. The appendices provide documents related to the three parts of text, and the index is a guide to the various references in all divisions of the book to individuals, places, and topics.

ACKNOWLEDGMENTS

Generous assistance in preparing this volume has been given by innumerable individuals scattered over two continents. To all I should like to express my warmest thanks. Particular mention must be made first of those who made available the artist's paintings and sketches and hitherto unpublished papers, without which this task would have been redundant. Mrs. Nelda C. Stark has graciously opened for publication the Stark Foundation's unrivalled collection of Kane material; it has made an absolutely essential contribution to the volume. My thanks go also to the artist's descendants: to his grandson's widow, Mrs. Paul Kane III, and to his granddaughters, Mrs. T. M. Willet and Mrs. R. W. Thurston, for the use which they have kindly permitted of their material. Their unflagging interest has been a source of real inspiration. Nothing would have been possible without the planning of Mitchell Wilder of the Amon Carter Museum of Western American Art, Fort Worth, and Jean Sutherland Boggs of the National Gallery of Canada, Ottawa. Their enthusiasm has remained constant, they have put the resources of their institutions behind the project, and both have laboured long in bringing the work to fruition. Through the splendid co-operation of Peter C. Swann and his staff at the Royal Ontario Museum, Toronto, its superb holdings of Kane canvases and sketches were made available for study and reproduction; they have aided in innumerable other ways. The Canada Council has kindly provided assistance so that cleaning of Kane's works in the Museum's collections might be undertaken.

Many other institutions and individuals have helped either by opening their collections for study or by supplying information. My thanks go to the following: Mrs. P. E. Anderson and Mrs. K. B. Edsall, Peabody Museum of Archaeology and Ethnology, Harvard University; David J. Armour, Mackinac Island State Commission; Mrs. Ralph D. Baker; John A. Bovey and Miss E. Blight, Provincial Library and Archives of Manitoba; Clyde N. Bowden, Inland Rivers Library, Cincinnati; Mrs. E. Collard; Alan Cooke, Scott Polar Research Institute, Cambridge, Eng.; Earle Connette, Washington State University Library; Joseph P. Donnelly, S.J.; Mrs. E. Ediger, Glenbow Foundation; John C. Ewers, Smithsonian Institution; Miss Linda Francis, Education Centre Library, Toronto; Miss Edith Firth and A. Suddon, Metropolitan Toronto Central Library; Rev. F. A. Garrett; Mrs. Jas. A. Grant; Frank L. Green, Washington State Historical Society; Edwin C. Guillet; Mr. and Mrs. Leslie Haslett; John Herapath; J. H. Herbert and Richard G. Conn, Manitoba Museum of Science and History; Mrs. Mary Hicky; E. J. Holmgren, Provincial Librarian of Alberta; Mrs. Tom Horst, Historic Mobile Preservation Society; John A. Hussey, Historian, National Park Service, United States Department of the Interior; R. E. Hutchison, Scottish National Portrait Gallery; Willard Ireland and Mrs. Dorothy Blakey Smith, Provincial Archives, British Columbia; the staff of the Hudson's Bay Company Archives, London, Eng. (Miss Alice Johnson was especially helpful); Miss Rosemary Keen, Church Missionary Society Archives, London, Eng.; Kenneth E. Kidd; John H. Kuony, Oshkosh Public Museum; Glenn Lucas, United Church of Canada Archives; C. M. McAllister; P. L. McNair, British Columbia Provincial Museum; Mrs. B. B. McNaughton; Methodist Missionary Society Archives, London, Eng.; H. R. Milner; New York Public Library; Murrough O'Brien; J. E. O'Flaherty, S.J.; Robin Poore; Robert Porter, Peterborough Public Library; Léon Pouliot, S.J.; Mrs. W. Punch, Sault Ste Marie Public Library; M. Ruggles, National Gallery of Canada; Mrs. V. Rust, Henry E. Huntington Library and Art Gallery; Martin Schmitt, University of Oregon; W. I. Smith and staff, Public Archives of Canada; Mrs. Frances K. Smith, Agnes Etherington Art Centre, Kingston,

Ont.; Stuart A. Smith, Beaverbrook Art Gallery; Eric J. Spicer, Parliamentary Librarian, Ottawa; Dr. Jean Stephenson; Franz Stenzel; Wm. E. Taylor and G. M. Day, National Museum of Canada; Peter C. Swann, E. S. Rogers, Mrs. E. A. Phillimore and Mrs. M. Allodi, Royal Ontario Museum; G. P. H. Vernon; Mrs. E. S. Watson; Samuel E. Weir; Wm. J. Withrow and staff, Art Gallery of Ontario; Ross Woodbridge; the Hon. John Yaremko; R. Mackworth Young, Royal Archivist, Windsor. In addition my thanks go to a large number of other people who have generously supplied information.

Finally I should like to express a special debt of gratitude to the staff of the University of Texas Press and the University of Toronto Press, and particularly to Miss Francess Halpenny whose keen observation, depth of perception, and long experience and understanding have prevented many errors and smoothed many rough patches.

J. Russell Harper

Alexandria, Ontario
January 1970

ILLUSTRATIONS

COLOUR PLATES

Following page

Plate I.   Paul Kane, a self-portrait, made during his travels in the west (*frontispiece*)   iv

Plate II.   Brayley Norton (Mrs. H. R. Norton), a portrait . .   6

Plate III.   French River rapids   14

Plate IV.   Ojibwa Camp (Georgian Bay)   22

Plate V.   Sault Ste Marie   22

Plate VI.   Two portrait studies of Indians; sketched probably at Manitowaning or Sault Ste Marie   30

Plate VII.   Mani-tow-wah-bay or "He-Devil," an Ojibwa from Lake Michigan   38

Plate VIII.   Now-on-dhu-go, an Ottawa chief from Lake Michigan   38

Plate IX.   Coe-coosh or "The Hog," a Potawatomi   46

Plate X.   Sioux Scalp Dance   54

Plate XI.   Chief from Fort William (Maydoc-game-kinungee or "I hear the Noise of the Deer," an Ojibwa)   54

Plate XII.   The Mountain Portage (west of Fort William) . .   62

Plate XIII.   White Mud Portage, Winnipeg River   70

Plate XIV.   An encampment on the Winnipeg River   70

Plate XV.   Two portraits of Sioux (south of Fort Garry?) . . .   78

Plate XVI.   A camp on the prairies   86

Plate XVII.   Panoramic view of Métis chasing a buffalo herd . .   86

Plate XVIII.   Norway House   94

Plate XIX.   Muck-Cranium, a Cree from Fort Carlton . . .   102

Plate XX.   The Man that Always Rides (seen at Fort Carlton?) .   102

Plate XXI.   Otisskun or "The Horn," a Cree chief, near Fort Pitt   110

Plate XXII.   Cree Indian, near Fort Pitt   118

Plate XXIII.   Medicine pipe-stem dance of the Blackfoot, east of Fort Pitt   118

Plate XXIV.   A lake in the plains   126

Plate XXV.   Fort Edmonton   134

Plate XXVI.   Winter Travelling (a wedding party, Fort Edmonton)   134

Plate XXVII.   François Lucie, a Cree half-breed guide, Fort Edmonton   142

Plate XXVIII.   Assiniboin chiefs at Rocky Mountain House: Mah-Min or "The Feather" and Wah-he-joe-tass-e-neen or "The half-white Man"   142

Plate XXIX.   Boat Encampment, Columbia River   150

Plate XXX.   Kettle Falls, Fort Colvile   150

Plate XXXI.   Drying salmon at the Dalles, Columbia River, with Indian lodges   164

Plate XXXII.   Sketch on the Spokane River   164

Plate XXXIII.   Tum-se-ne-ho or "The Man without Blood," a Spokan chief, Spokane River   170

Plate XXXIV.   The Pelouse River, with basaltic rock . . .   182

Plate XXXV.   Falls on the upper Pelouse River   188

Plate XXXVI.   Casanov, a Chinook (?) chief, Fort Vancouver . .   188

Plate XXXVII.   Indian ceremonial lodge, Columbia River . . .   194

Plate XXXVIII.   The mills of Oregon City   206

Plate XXXIX.   St. Paul's Mission, Willamette valley . . .   212

Plate XL.   Clackama Indians, with painted faces   212

Plate XLI.   Mount St. Helens   218

Plate XLII.   Chinook grave, Cowlitz River   230

Plate XLIII.   Northwest canoes   236

Plate XLIV.   Medicine masks of the northwest coast tribes . .   236

Plate XLV.   Clallam woman weaving a basket, and other studies (Vancouver Island)   242

Plate XLVI.   Clallam travelling lodges, Vancouver Island . . .   254

Plate XLVII.   Culchillum wearing a medicine cap; a Cowichan from the Strait of Georgia   260

Plate XLVIII.   A Ucaltas man and a Nisqually girl   260

BLACK-AND-WHITE PLATES

Fig. 1.   Paul Kane, a photograph   161

Fig. 2.   Mrs. W. S. Conger, a portrait painted *c.* 1834 . . .   162

Fig. 3.   Eliza (Clench) Armour, sister-in-law of Paul Kane, a portrait painted *c.* 1836   162

Fig. 4. The riverboat *Norma* (New Orleans), with her captain, painted *c.* 1839–41 162

Figs. 5, 6. Sketches from Kane's European travels, 1841–43: Roman youth; trees in a Roman landscape 163

Fig. 7. Kane's pencil copy of a self-portrait by Peter Paul Rubens in the Uffizi gallery, Florence, done in 1842 163

Fig. 8. George Gurnett, mayor of Toronto, a portrait probably painted 1844–46 164

Fig. 9. James Richardson, of Cobourg and St. Catharines, a portrait 164

Fig. 10. Bloor's Brewery, Toronto 165

Fig. 11. Thomas Daly, city clerk of Toronto, a pencil sketch . . 165

Fig. 12. Niagara Falls, a pencil sketch 166

Fig. 13. Homewood, the early residence of the Hon. G. W. Allan, Toronto, a painting *c.* 1849 166

The Expedition of 1845

Fig. 14. Kwa-qua-dah-bon-niva-skung or "Dawn of Day," a chief of the Saugeen, Lake Huron 167

Fig. 15. Maska-nonga or "Big Fish," an Ojibwa, Saugeen village . 167

Fig. 16. Sketches made on Georgian Bay, Lake Huron . . . 168

Fig. 17. An Ojibwa chief's daughter, from Lake St. Clair; sketched at Saugeen village 168

Fig. 18. Wappoose (Wah-pus or "The Rabbit"), Saugeen village . 168

Fig. 19. Indian encampment on Big Bay, Owen Sound, Lake Huron 169

Fig. 20. An Indian Encampment on Lake Huron 169

Fig. 21. Indian Bivouac (Georgian Bay region) 170

Fig. 22. French River Rapids 170

Fig. 23. Ojibwa grave house, Georgian Bay 171

Figs. 24, 25. Manitowaning, Manitoulin Island: Indians assembled for the receipt of presents from the government. . . 171

Fig. 26. Shawwanossoway or "One with his Face towards the West," Ojibwa medicine man; at Manitowaning 172

Fig. 27. Indian from Michipicoten; at Manitowaning . . . 172

Fig. 28. Muck-koze or "Young Bear," Ottawa chief, Manitoulin Island 173

Fig. 29. Awbonwaishkum, Ottawa chief; at Manitowaning . . 174

Fig. 30. Stone pipe carved by Awbonwaishkum 174

Fig. 31. Captain George Ironsides, a Wyandot; Indian agent, Manitowaning 174

Fig. 32. Sketches of a pipe and a club; at Manitowaning (?) . . 175

Fig. 33. Asabonish or "The Raccoon," and his daughter; Ottawa Indians, at Wikwemikong, Manitoulin Island 175

Fig. 34. Sault Ste Marie 175

Figs. 35, 36. Mackinac: fort and Indian village; natural bridge (Arch Rock) 176

Fig. 37. Mackinac: rocky headland with wigwams 177

Fig. 38. Wampum belts, from Mackinac 177

Fig. 39. Ke-wah-ten or "The North Wind" (?), Lake Winnebago 178

Fig. 40. Iwa-toke or "The Serpent," a Menominee, Lake Winnebago 179

Fig. 41. Fishing by Torch Light (Fox River) 179

Fig. 42. Oscosh or "The Bravest of the Brave," Menominee chief, Fox River 180

Fig. 43. Match-o-kee-maw or "Big Chief," Menominee chief, Fox River 180

Figs. 44, 45. Muck-a-ta, Fox River 181

Fig. 46. Mauza-pau-Kan or "Brave Soldier," Winnebago chief, Fox River 181

The Expedition of 1846–48

Fig. 47. Kakabeka Falls, northern Ontario 182

Fig. 48. Pin Portage, northern Ontario 182

Figs. 49, 50. Fort Frances 183

Fig. 51. Slave Falls, Winnipeg River 184

Fig. 52. Winnipeg River 184

Fig. 53. Cash-a-cabut and Each-a-quip: Saulteaux, region of Fort Frances 185

Fig. 54. Sho-ne-ah or "Silver," a Saulteaux chief, Fort Alexander. 185

Fig. 55. Peter Jacobs, Wesleyan Indian missionary 185

Figs. 56, 57. Red River Settlement 186

Fig. 58. A Sioux Indian; sketched south of Fort Garry (?) . . 187

Fig. 59. Na-taw-waugh-cit or "The Man that was born," a Saulteaux; south of Fort Garry 187

The Buffalo Hunt, south of Fort Garry

Fig. 60. Half Breeds Travelling 188

Fig. 61. Red River cart and ox 189

Fig. 62. Dog with travois 189

Fig. 63. Métis setting up camp 189

Figs. 64, 65. Half Breed Encampment 190

Fig. 66. Métis camp and hunters 191

Fig. 67. Half Breeds Running Buffalo 191

Figs. 68, 69. Wounded buffalo bull 192

Fig. 70. Donald Ross, chief factor, Norway House 193

Fig. 71. Wesleyan mission station, Jack River 193

Fig. 72. A Saulteaux girl (Red River) and an Assiniboin . . . 194

Fig. 73. Brigade of boats, near Le Pas 194

Fig. 74. Brigade of Boats 195

Fig. 75. Fort Carlton 196

Fig. 76. Ogemawwah Chack or "The Spirit Chief," an Eskimo, Norway House 196

Fig. 77. The buffalo hunt near Fort Carlton 196

Fig. 78. A Buffalo Pound 197

Fig. 79. "The Man that Shot the Wolf with an Arrow," a Cree, Fort Carlton 198

Fig. 80. Cree Indians travelling 198

Figs. 81, 82. Saskatchewan River: Serpentine Valley; Golden Valley 199

Fig. 83. Fort Pitt 200

Fig. 84. Prairie antelope 200

Figs. 85, 86. Kee-a-kee-ka-sa-coo-way or "The Man who gives the War-whoop," a Cree, Fort Pitt 201

Figs. 87, 88. Cree pipe-stems 202

Fig. 89. Indian Horse Race 203

Fig. 90. The Death of Big Snake; a contemporary print . . . 204

Fig. 91. Wah-nis-stow or "The White Buffalo," a Sarsi chief; sketched near Fort Pitt 204

Fig. 92. Big Snake, a Blackfoot Chief, recounting his War Exploits 205

Fig. 93. Medicine Pipe Stem Dance (Blackfoot) 206

Fig. 94. Jacket ornamented with a crow 206

Fig. 95. Buffalo robe, painted with adventures of a Blood Indian . 207

Figs. 96, 97. Studies of buffalo, near Fort Pitt 208

Fig. 98. Buffalo Bulls Fighting 209

Fig. 99. A Prairie on Fire (near Fort Edmonton?) 210

Fig. 100. Sled dogs of the plains 210

Figs. 101, 102, 103. A wedding party, Fort Edmonton: studies of sled, sled dogs, snow on trees 211

Fig. 104. Catching Wild Horses 212

Figs. 105, 106. Assiniboine Hunting Buffalo; Italian print used by Kane for this subject 213

Fig. 107. Cunnawa-bum or "One that looks at the stars" (Cree half-breed girl, Fort Edmonton) 214

Fig. 108. Rocky Mountain House 215

Fig. 109. Mah-Min or "The Feather" (Assiniboin chief, Rocky Mountain House) 216

Fig. 110. Buffaloes at Sunset (west of Fort Edmonton) . . . 217

Fig. 111. Jasper House 217

Figs. 112, 113, 114. Sketches of animals, Rocky Mountains: pack horses, Bighorn ram, goat 218

Fig. 115. Athabasca River in the mountains 219

Fig. 116. The Committee's Punch Bowl, Rocky Mountains . . 219

Figs. 117, 118. Mountain peaks, Boat Encampment, Columbia River; with a photograph of the same view 220

Fig. 119. The Little Dalles, Columbia River 221

Fig. 120. Studies among the Kutenai Indians, Columbia River . 222

Fig. 121. Columbia River, near Grand Rapids 222

Fig. 122. Ask-a-weelish and See-pays ("Chief of the Waters"), Indians from the region of Fort Colvile 223

Fig. 123. Catching salmon, Columbia River 223

Fig. 124. Smoking salmon, Columbia River 224

Figs. 125, 126. Chualpays Indians playing the game of Al-kol-lock, Fort Colvile 224, 225

Figs. 127-30. Chualpays scalp dance, Fort Colvile . . 226, 227

Fig. 131. Mission station, Tshimakain 228

Fig. 132. Lower falls, Pelouse River 228

Figs. 133, 134. Fort Walla Walla: a river view and the post . . 229

Fig. 135. Chimney Rocks, Columbia River 230

Fig. 136. Landscape; near Fort Walla Walla (?) 230

Figs. 137, 138. The Whitman mission, Waiilatpu; Mrs. Whitman's fan 231

Figs. 139, 140. Cayuse Indians, at the Whitman mission: To-ma-kus; Til-au-kite or "Act of Lightning" 232

Fig. 141. Nez Percé Indian 232

Figs. 142, 143. Walla Walla Indians: Peo-Peo-mox-mox or "The Yellow Serpent," a chief; son of Peo-Peo-mox-mox . . . 233

Figs. 144, 145. The Cascades, Columbia River 234

Fig. 146. Below the Cascades, with Indian fishing 235

Fig. 147. Tomaquin, a chief of the Cascade, Columbia River . 235

Fig. 148. Mancemuckt, a chief of the Skinpah, Columbia River . 235

Fig. 149. A Cascade Indian, Columbia River 236

Figs. 150, 151. Fort Vancouver 237

Figs. 152, 153. Fort Vancouver: handbill of a theatrical performance; sketch of man with saddle horse 238

Fig. 154. Old Cox, a Sandwich Islander of the Hudson's Bay Company 238

Figs. 155, 156. Near Fort Vancouver: a well in the woods: Indian (girl?) on a race course 239

Figs. 157, 158. Chinook lodges, Fort Vancouver: rushes used in building an interior 240

Fig. 159. A Klikitat lodge, Fort Vancouver 241

Fig. 160. A Chinook travelling lodge, with a view of Mount Hood 241

Fig. 161. Oregon City 242

Fig. 162. Falls near Oregon City 242

Fig. 163. Willamette valley at Champoeg 243

Figs. 164, 165. Mount St. Helens 243, 244

Fig. 166. Coffin Rock, lower Columbia River 244

Figs. 167, 168. Indian burials: King Comcomly's burial canoe; graves on the Cowlitz River 245

Fig. 169. Flathead woman, Cowlitz River 246

Fig. 170. A child having its head flattened 246

Fig. 171. Flathead Woman and Child, Caw-wacham 247

Fig. 172. Prairie de Bute, near the Nisqually River 248

Fig. 173. Nisqually, a village on Puget Sound 248

Fig. 174. Indian lodge, Nisqually 249

Fig. 175. Lock-hi-num, a chief of Whidbey Island 249

Fig. 176. Toanichum, an Indian village, Whidbey Island . . . 250

Figs. 177, 180. Battle between Clallam and Makah, at I-eh-nus, Strait of Juan de Fuca; a sketch and a painting . . . 250, 251

Fig. 178.   Chaw-u-wit, a chief's daughter, Strait of Juan de Fuca .   251
Fig. 179.   Indian graves at I-eh-nus   251
Fig. 181.   Shawstun, a Snohomish chief, from Puget Sound . .   252
Fig. 182.   Salmon trap, Suck, Strait of Juan de Fuca   252
Fig. 183.   Crossing the Strait of Juan de Fuca in a storm . . .   253
Fig. 184.   An Indian village, Esquimalt   254
Fig. 185.   War party, Juan de Fuca   254
Fig. 186.   Canoes returning with camas, Esquimalt   255
Fig. 187.   Northwest canoes   255
Figs. 188, 189.   Fort Victoria   256
Fig. 190.   Medicine man with mask, from Strait of Juan de Fuca .   257
Fig. 191.   Medicine Mask Dance (northwest coast)   258
Fig. 192.   Interior of a Winter Lodge of the Clallams (Vancouver
    Island)   259

Fig. 193.   Indian medicine rattle, northwest coast   260
Fig. 194.   A Clallam lodge, Vancouver Island   260
Fig. 195.   Carved house post, Fort Victoria (?)   260
Figs. 196, 197.   Fort Victoria: woman weaving a blanket; woman
    spinning yarn   261
Fig. 198.   Fort Victoria: figures inside a lodge   262
Fig. 199.   Game of lehallum, Vancouver Island   262
Fig. 200.   Saw-se-a (a Cowichan chief, Strait of Georgia) . .   263
Fig. 201.   A Nootka chief, northern Vancouver Island . . .   264
Fig. 202.   Ma-cheek-e-a-wis, a Chimmesyan Indian (British Co-
    lumbia)   264
Fig. 203.   A Babbine Chief (British Columbia)   265
Figs. 204, 205.   A Babine woman; Babine pipe-stem   266

PAUL KANE'S FRONTIER

A NOTE ON NAMES

The names of places, Indian tribes, and individuals as given by Paul Kane in his manuscripts and his published book, by Kane and others in inscriptions on his works, and in catalogues or other records of his paintings, show considerable variation in spelling. Names of tribes and places are also often not those used today. In the reprinting of Kane's *Wanderings* in this book, the spellings of names in his first edition (1859) have been followed faithfully. The forms he gives there to names of particular Indians are used in Part One and in the *catalogue raisonné* of Part Four when sketches are identified. The names of tribes, place names and other personal names are given in Part One, in the notes to Part Two and in Part Four in accepted modern forms. In this connection, guidance has been sought from *Handbook of American Indians North of Mexico*, edited by F. W. Hodge.

PART ONE   Paul Kane: His Life and Career as an Artist

I. Early Years

York was the town in British North America to which Paul Kane came by sailing ship as an Irish immigrant boy about 1819.[1] It was the little capital of Upper Canada,[2] a province which only 28 years earlier had been carved out of the wilderness won by Britain from France during the Seven Years' War. Captain Francis Hall, who visited the province about the time of Kane's arrival, noted a blending of American and British qualities, a character very different from that of older French Quebec:

The system of farming is here altogether English, or American. The low, deep-roofed Canadian dwelling [of older French Canada] gives place to the English farm-house, or Yankey fir-boarded mansion, with a dozen sash windows in its front. Instead of churches, we have taverns; gaols, and assembly-rooms, for convents; and a half sulky nod for a French bow. . . . when the American or Englishman nods, 'tis like the growling salutation of a mastiff, who has not quite leisure enough to turn and quarrel with you.[3]

The province's first English-speaking settlers had been some 7,000 Americans, who in a single year, 1784, were given land within its borders. These were mostly families of soldiers in regiments which had been loyal to the British crown during the Revolutionary War and were disbanded at its end. Former officers originally received up to 1,000 acres and the grants descended to 100 acres for privates. The new settlers formed groups dissatisfied with and dispossessed by the new republican government to the south of the border, and in recognition of their fidelity to the crown the king bestowed on them and their descendants a proud title, United Empire Loyalists. The emergence of a province largely created by the Loyalists was formally recognized in 1791 when Upper Canada was set up as a separate entity and elected a first parliament composed almost entirely of former regimental officers. The prospect of land above the lakes later brought a steady influx of other settlers from the United States and also from England, Scotland and Ireland, men full of optimism for the future and looking forward to a free and full life for themselves and their children. By 1812 the population had increased to 75,000. Then the future of British North America had been threatened by war with the United States and possible disaffection within, but from 1812 to 1814 the militia had supported the British redcoats in defence of the realm and the result had instilled a new feeling of self-confidence. Houses and farms were being built, and the forest back of the lakes and the great river St. Lawrence was gradually changing into a succession of scattered free holdings linked by stage roads with villages and towns at strategic points. Optimism was everywhere, even despite the problems of a post-war depression.[4]

York itself, where the Kanes settled, had only been founded in 1793. Although it was Upper Canada's seat of government, mean buildings, muddy streets and a few precarious sidewalks gave a miserable air to the place. The forest crowded in on every side. Visiting York just three years before the Kanes arrived, Captain Hall had not been complimentary:

[It] is a place of considerable importance in the eyes of its inhabitants; to a stranger, however, it presents little more than about 100 wooden houses, several of them conveniently, and even elegantly built, and I think one, or perhaps two, of brick. The public buildings were destroyed by the Americans [during its capture in 1813]; but as no ruins of them are visible, we must conclude, either, that the destruction exceeded the desolation of Jerusalem, or that the loss to the arts is not quite irreparable: I believe that they did not leave one stone upon another, for they did not find one.[5]

John Howison came the same year as the Kanes, after a visit in Kingston at the eastern end of Lake Ontario. Kingston he had admired but he found the little capital so dull that after walking the streets for about an hour he returned to the comforts of the steamship *Frontenac* on which he was travelling up the lakes.[6]

But there was another side to York's story and this was its prospects for the future. Some of the immigrants who, after the Napoleonic Wars, were crossing the Atlantic in slow, unsanitary

---

[1] "York" became "Toronto" after its incorporation as a city in 1834.

[2] "Upper Canada" was given a new name, "Canada West," as part of the united province of Canada, 1840–67, and became the province of "Ontario" after Confederation in 1867.

[3] Francis Hall, *Travels in Canada and the United States in 1816 and 1817* (London 1819), pp. 123–24.

[4] Historical background may be found in Gerald M. Craig, *Upper Canada: The Formative Years: 1784–1841* (Toronto 1963), and in J. M. S. Careless, *The Union of the Canadas: 1841–1857* (Toronto 1967).

[5] Hall, *Travels*, pp. 168–69.

[6] John Howison, *Sketches of Upper Canada* (Edinburgh 1821), p. 72.

ships settled in the town instead of a forest clearing and increased its population. Among these newcomers was Michael Kane, the artist's father, with his family.

York was a town with two faces. New legislative buildings were under construction in Simcoe Square near the lakeshore, and the governor's residence close by was being enlarged. Some twenty families, mostly government officials, lived in substantial houses. These were the people who really "mattered." A few, like W. W. Baldwin, had set their homes well back from the waterfront and they had almost the air of estates. Baldwin himself had cut an avenue from his home through the forest so that he could see the harbour shipping. Clustered around these larger houses were the dwellings of the bulk of the citizenry—labourers, tinsmiths, cabinet-makers and tradespeople—men who supported the five York breweries in operation or under construction. It was to this more humble part of the population that Michael Kane belonged. He set up as a "wine and spirits merchant" with his vaults at the corner of present-day Yonge and Adelaide streets. The settlement might be without distinction now, but it would soon be transformed into a city of importance, and the growth of the city would parallel the development of Michael's son Paul from a local amateur into a recognized professional artist.

Mystery shrouds certain aspects of Paul Kane's life. It obscures also some of the life of his father Michael. One fanciful story about the elder Kane, entirely without foundation, describes how he served with Governor Simcoe's troops in Upper Canada in 1794 and helped to lay out York.[7] Certainly he served in the British army, but there is no record that his regiment was ever in America. Michael Kane was born in Preston, Lancashire, and enlisted in the Royal Artillery at Mansfield, Nottinghamshire, in 1793 at the age of 18; almost immediately he transferred to the more glamorous Royal Horse Artillery. He was duly promoted to corporal in 1798 and was discharged from Captain G. W. Dixon's company in 1801.[8] Meanwhile he had been in Ireland. There he married Frances Loach, a girl from Mallow, County Cork, because of "an unfortunate circumstance." Paul's parentage thus combined a conservative and objective English spirit with the spark of a warmer, more romantic Irish temperament. For a year after leaving the army, Michael rented a house in Fermoy, County Cork, but moved from there to Mallow. Tradition says that it was in 1819 that he emigrated with his wife and family to York.[9] There he lived for the balance of his life.

Nothing is known of Michael Kane's personal life and atti-

tudes except what can be gleaned by reading between the lines of a letter to his son.[10] This expresses a fierce adherence to the new world and an aversion to marriage before such a step had been well considered. One senses a practical man. By rumour, he had little interest in the arts or artists. He advanced money several times to his son Paul, but always in the form of loans and not as gifts to subsidize a struggling painter. No one mentions the artist's mother; he had four sisters; one brother died and the others became tradesmen.[11] Michael Kane was buried in 1851 in old St. James's churchyard, Toronto.

Paul Kane himself set up puzzles as if to confuse his biographers. He considered himself very much a Canadian and was determined that he should be remembered as one. On various occasions he stated that he was a native of York, and he wrote in his 1861 census return that he was a Torontonian by birth—but people have for a long time taken liberties in their reports to government. An obituary in a Toronto newspaper, which his grandchildren say was probably composed by his widow, repeats this claim. Friends, all prominent local Toronto citizens, re-echoed his assertion of Canadian origins. He was actually baptized at the parish church, Mallow, Ireland, on September 16, 1810. In the register his surname was written as "Keane" which is how "Kane" is pronounced in that part of Ireland.

The boy was presumably enrolled at one of York's few schools immediately after his arrival in the town; these could have offered little to someone who wanted to become an artist. Most writers assume that he studied in the ugly little frame building of the York District Grammar School, to which the petty government officials sent their sons.[12] If so, the school's much publicized virtue, teaching by a system of constant repeti-

---

[7] Nicholas Flood Davin, *The Irishman in Canada* (London 1877), p. 211. The statement is repeated by other writers.

[8] British war records show that Michael Kane (enlisted Cane) was recruited to the 1st Battalion, Royal Artillery, 1793. His name was spelled Cain when he transferred to the Royal Horse Artillery in July of that year. His service record (W.O. 69/1) reads: "Gunner Michael Cain, aged 18, height 5.7½. / Enlisted 2 February 1793 at Mansfield [Notts]. / Born Preston, Lancs. / Trade Labourer. / Can read and write. / Colouring dark, hair dark, eyes gray. / Bombardier 6 November 1794. Corporal 5 April 1798. / Discharged 30 September 1801."

[9] Metropolitan Toronto Central Library, Manuscript Division, has lists of early York householders. Kane's name does not appear in the list for 1819. Those for 1820 and 1821 are missing, but in that of 1822 his name is given.

[10] Appendix 10, Letter 1.

[11] The children of Michael Kane are as follows: James, born 1799; Mary 1801; Julia 1803; Frederick 1806; Oliver 1807; Paul 1810; Charlotte 1811; Harriet 1813. Not all of them reached maturity.

[12] The York District Grammar School records are not to be found so that it is impossible to confirm whether Kane attended or the names of instructors he might have had. Kane's association with the school was first mentioned by Davin (*The Irishman in Canada*, p. 611). Davin gives no source. No biography of Kane published during his lifetime makes any reference to the school.

Plate II. Brayley Norton (Mrs. H. R. Norton). ROM L965.1.2; CRI-20.

tion which would bring perfection, had little effect. The diary he wrote while travelling among the Indians is phonetic in its spelling, and he dictated his western letters to Hudson's Bay company scribes. The first draft of *Wanderings of an Artist* is in his wife's hand. His prose is factual and straightforward without any of the Greek and Latin phraseology which would permit colonial graduates to hold their heads high among the cultivated overseas. One wonders if perhaps he attended some more humble school than Bishop John Strachan's renowned establishment. He is alleged to have been a pupil until he was sixteen. This hardly seems likely, but possibly, as a contemporary biographer wrote,[13] he idled away his time in drawing rather than applying himself to the more academic subjects.

York's frontier environment helped to turn Kane's thoughts during boyhood towards the native people and the Northwest. He wrote that the subject of Indians "was one in which I felt a deep interest in my boyhood. I had been accustomed to see hundreds of Indians about my native village, then Little York. . . ."[14] For the town's recalcitrant youths, the Northwest was a romantic goal. Dr. Scadding, an early Toronto antiquarian, recounted, in an often quoted passage, how it beckoned to adventurous souls:

A sporting ramble through the woods, a fishing excursion on the waters, could not be undertaken without communications with Indians and half-breeds and bad specimens of the French *voyageur*. It was from such sources that a certain idea was derived which, as we remember, was in great vogue among the more fractious of the lads at the school at York. The proposition circulated about, whenever anything went counter to their notions, always was "to run away to the Nor'-West." What the process really involved, or where the "Nor'-West" precisely was, were things vaguely realized. A sort of savage "land of Cockaigne," a region of perfect freedom among the Indians, was imagined; and to reach it Lakes Huron and Superior were to be traversed.[15]

But a curiosity about Indians might have more in it than the restlessness of youth. Kane's boyhood coincided with the rise of an interest in Indians by an increasing number of perceptive people, as part of the new concern with man's surroundings which became apparent at that time. Mists of disinterest after the fierce initial clash between Indians and Europeans during early settlement days along the Atlantic had so hidden the aborigines that many Canadians were only dimly aware that these original residents were still in the background of their life in the east. Now these mists began to roll away, and the Indians to emerge as humans. At the same time philosophers in Europe, and especially in France, were examining Indians and other primitive peoples for lessons to remedy the decadence they felt in their own sophisticated society.

As part of this new interest, Adam Kidd published at Montreal in 1830 a long epic poem *The Huron Chief*.[16] He pictured the Indian as a man with hopes, fears, sorrows and joys—not the cruel warrior who was an ever present threat to the settler's home. In 1836 appeared in Toronto a book by J. Mackintosh dealing with the American Indian tribes and their life and customs.[17] Kane was to own a copy. In New Brunswick, Abraham Gesner, a lawyer, geologist, scientist and inventor, one of the "universal men" found in this age, saw the abject poverty of the Micmac and Malecite Indians of the Saint John River and sought ways to restore them to the dignified, independent life they had known as hunters. He instituted schemes for the sale of Indian handicrafts. He also gathered Indian artefacts so that Canadians generally could appreciate the culture of these forgotten peoples, and from this collection the New Brunswick Museum has grown.

A few Canadian artists also displayed an awakening interest in Indians during the 1820s and 1830s. J. D. Wells, to name one, hung a study of Indians at the exhibition of the Toronto Society of Artists and Amateurs in 1834, a show in which Kane himself was to have paintings. An anonymous New Brunswick or Nova Scotia artist painted superb decorative canvases and water colours of Micmac hunters, with their canoes, trophies of the hunt, wigwams, and unique costumes.[18] Full of detail, these have a feeling of intimacy and the artist seems much more involved with his subjects than in most contemporary paintings in which Indians appear. For instance, J. P. Cockburn, like several British army officers in Canada on garrison duty, regarded the Indians whom he painted merely as curious native peoples in one part of the growing British Empire overseas. Many local painters also introduced them simply as an element in the landscape: in numerous stereotyped views of Halifax Citadel, for example, wigwams are romanticized additions in the foreground

[13] Henry J. Morgan, *Sketches of Celebrated Canadians and Persons Connected with Canada* (Quebec 1862), p. 731.

[14] *Wanderings of an Artist*, p. 51 below.

[15] Henry Scadding, *Toronto of Old* (Toronto 1872), p. 163.

[16] Adam Kidd, *The Huron Chief, and Other Poems* (Montreal 1830).

[17] J. Mackintosh, *The Discovery of America, by Christopher Columbus; and the Origin of the North American Indians* (Toronto 1836).

[18] Typical of paintings by this anonymous artist are one in the National Gallery of Canada, Ottawa, Cat. no. 663, "Micmac Indians," and two in the Beaverbrook Art Gallery, Fredericton, N.B., "Indian Voyageurs: Hunting" and "Indian Voyageurs: Returning from the Hunt." The National Gallery painting is reproduced in J. Russell Harper, *Painting in Canada* (Toronto 1966), Plate 98.

without a hint that the Indians who lived in them might have personalities.[19]

One Canadian commentator, however, went so far as to think of the western Indian as part of the Canadian environment which he was proposing as a central theme in a national art. Kane's paintings seem like the fulfilment of a prophecy made by Philippe Aubert de Gaspé, a Quebec lawyer, politician, and man of letters, whose interests extended to art. In 1833 he recorded his impressions of studios which he had been visiting in Quebec. He was greatly elated with the studio of Joseph Legaré. The exact canvases he saw in it we do not know, but he mentions being excited by paintings of local landscapes and contemporary events. Legaré's canvases generally pictured such newsworthy happenings as rock slides and the fires which were the scourge of 19th century Canadian cities and towns. A cholera epidemic in his native Quebec appears in one canvas, where smudge pots line the streets to kill impure vapours while death wagons and funeral processions circulate through the streets bathed weirdly in moonlight.[20] Such an involvement in his immediate surroundings by a man locally born was a new note in Canadian art.

Aubert de Gaspé's fertile mind was touched by Legaré's renditions of contemporary life and his imagination conjured up other local yet romantic subjects which native Canadians could paint.

. . . it has often excited my wonder that our native painters have not devoted some part of their time and study to the scenery of Canada—and to their shame be it spoken they have not; and truly they have neglected a field from which rare laurels will yet be won. . . . Our winter views —breaking through the ice—Indian camps by night—the mounted Sioux, Chief of the western wilderness, and the bivouacs on the Prairies—Hillock —and the chase of the buffalo—the council tent—the savage and his forest wigwam.[21]

This is the first recorded suggestion by a Canadian that the Indian could be a major subject for a painter. Kane would concentrate his efforts for four years on the very themes which Aubert de Gaspé had mentioned, and he was to picture the Sioux, chieftains of the west, the buffalo hunt, the prairies and the Rockies, and other scenes of which the Quebecker had no knowledge. This achievement would bring him "rare laurels" as the first Canadian artist really to use the Indian's world. Thus a subject which had presented itself to him as a boy was to become his life's work.

During his younger days Kane is mentioned once in York newspapers, in connection with his attendance at Toronto's first

"theatre" just after he had left school. This modest affair was operated in the ballroom on the second floor of Frank's Hotel, King Street, from 1820 to 1829. A single violinist, shade over one eye, substituted for a full orchestra. Dr. Scadding, who often attended, recounted that at the performances

Pizarro, Barbarossa or the Siege of Algiers, Ali Baba or the Forty Thieves, the Lady of the Lake, the Miller and his Men, were among the pieces here represented. The body-guard of the Dey of Algiers, we remember, consisted of two men, who always came in with military precision just after the hero, and placed themselves in a formal manner at fixed distances behind him, like two sentries. They were in fact soldiers from the garrison, we think. All this appeared very effective.[22]

Dr. Scadding pointed out, however, that this humble place had the same magic as Drury Lane for young Londoners. Here Kane was introduced to the theatre, which seems to have been a life-long interest. In the library he had as an older man was a six-volume set of Shakespeare's plays and an eleven-volume collection of Bell's *British Theatre*. The fact is significant because Kane's years of development coincided with an era when play-acting was enjoying a revival everywhere. Shakespearean drama, stage tableaux, the whole world of make-believe, constituted one aspect of the new romanticism sweeping Europe and America. The theatre was patronized by no group more than artists and became a major factor in directing them towards romantic concepts in painting.

The details of Kane's attendance at the theatre on that night of June 4, 1828, are perhaps of more antiquarian than artistic interest. *Tom and Jerry* or *Life in London* was scheduled for performance at Frank's. The raising of the old baize curtain, called for 7 o'clock, was delayed repeatedly. Near Kane in the pit as the audience waited sat Charles French and several rowdy youths who frequently adjourned to the outside staircase for drinks before the play actually began between 9 and 10 o'clock. They went out again to the tavern in the interval. When they finally left the theatre, they were in such an ugly mood that French picked a quarrel with Isaac Jones, an Uxbridge Quaker, and killed him. Kane saw the fight from across the street and gave evidence at the inquest. A murder conviction was handed down at the October assizes, and the guilty French was hanged

[19] The point is well illustrated in a canvas by John Poad Drake, "Port of Halifax," c. 1820; National Gallery of Canada, Cat. no. 9978; it appears in Harper, *Painting in Canada*, as Plate 100.
[20] See Harper, *Painting in Canada*, pp. 80–82 for details of the life and work of Joseph Legaré.
[21] *Quebec Gazette* (Quebec), December 13, 1833.
[22] Scadding, *Toronto of Old*, p. 110.

publicly the following week. He had been an apprentice in the printing house of the controversial William Lyon Mackenzie, soon to lead a rebellion in Upper Canada (a century later his grandson was Canada's prime minister). A spectator in the great crush about the scaffold reported that Mackenzie stood beside the accused at the Court House steps when the noose was lowered, and cried until the tears rolled down his cheeks and made his starched white collar soggy. Assuredly Paul Kane would also have been in that huge crowd.

The incident at the theatre is tantalizingly lonely. Kane's life from 1826, when he was certainly no longer a school boy, until 1836, when he left Canada for the United States and Europe, must be pieced together from fact, tradition and speculation. During these ten years he turned into a young painter with a serious ideal of art as his objective. He was to dedicate himself to a life of artistic work at a time when there were few professionals in the newly emerging Canada although there were numerous amateurs.

For part of this decade Kane worked as a decorative furniture painter. He was apprenticed to W. S. Conger, owner of a furniture factory on Front Street, York. Conger was sympathetic to his ambitions, and is said to have bought him his first canvas, brushes and paints in New York. The date on which Kane ceased to work for the Conger factory is uncertain. Conger moved from York to Cobourg in 1829 although his York shop evidently continued in operation. An entry in the Toronto directory for 1833–34 names Paul "Cane" as a coach, sign and house painter on King Street. Does this indicate that he had gone into business on his own? Sign painting was a customary way for young men on the American frontier to launch themselves into the art world.

The statement has been made several times that Kane studied painting with Toronto's eccentric art master, Thomas Drury, while he was attending the York District Grammar School. This cannot be verified, and there is, in fact, no certain proof that Drury lived in York before 1830.[23] Without instruction, models or any of the other accepted prerequisites of art, Kane had made much headway on his own. Then in 1830, "Having acquired a respectable knowledge of perspective, he felt emboldened to wait upon Mr. Drury, the then drawing master of Upper Canada College, with some of his attempts at delineation. This gentleman at once recognized the marks of original genius, and the germs of future excellence in these essays, and promptly enrolled the young artist in the number of his pupils." [24] Upper Canada College is Toronto's oldest and best-

known grammar school for boys. It would seem that Kane must have studied privately with the master for he was now a young adult and certainly would not have been a regular pupil. Drury was a landscape painter who, like Cornelius Krieghoff in Quebec a few years later, taught by having his pupils copy his own works.

A canvas survives from the years when Kane was just beginning to receive instruction. It is a naïve three-quarter length portrait of a young lady, large and ambitious in conception. She sits theatrically, before a background of blue and red drapes, and the canvas is sufficiently "primitive" in style to have a certain appeal. It is the effort of an ambitious youth who wants to run before he can walk. Kane kept it, and it is still the property of a descendant. Did he use Conger's gift of painting supplies for this canvas? Another early portrait is of a young friend, Michael Peter Empey; it has a more accomplished manner and stylistically foreshadows a portrait of Mayor Gurnett of Toronto which seems to have been painted years later (Fig. 8). It is significant that both canvases are portraits, the most difficult of all subject-matter; they are indicative of the young man's practical bent since portrait commissions were the only paintings which had any real commercial sale in Upper Canada.

Kane's development as a painter must have been stimulated by the rapid growth of artistic interest in York, which became the city of Toronto in 1834. Even if standards generally were low, there were enough professional and amateur painters that leading citizens supported formation of the Society of Artists and Amateurs for exhibition purposes. The Society's influential backers were given permission to hold their first show in the province's legislative buildings, and 24 exhibitors hung 196 pictures. There were works by a few professional portrait painters and by architects who sent in architectural and topographical renderings. Military men submitted their coloured drawings, and both lady and gentlemen amateurs a variety of flower studies.[25] Disaster ensued. The cholera epidemic which

[23] The claim that Kane studied at the York District Grammar School under Drury originated in Daniel Wilson's eulogy following Kane's death in 1871 ("Paul Kane, the Canadian Artist," *Canadian Journal*, Toronto, May 1871, p. 67). Wilson realized that he knew little about Kane's early life in spite of their friendship—Kane talked rarely about himself—and had to write to the Hon. George Allan for details. In preparing his text, Wilson in some way altered Kane's contacts with Drury, which had taken place at Upper Canada College, to appear as having occurred at the York District Grammar School.

[24] *Anglo-American Magazine* (Toronto), May 1855, p. 401.

[25] *Catalogue of the First Exhibition of the Society of Artists & Amateurs of Toronto, 1834* (Toronto 1834).

Legaré had painted in Quebec struck Toronto during the exhibition. Few ventured out to pay the admission fee and buy catalogues. Monetary losses were large. John G. Howard, a prominent Toronto architect and art enthusiast, paid much of the deficit from his own pocket, and another decade was to pass before anyone dared suggest a second local art exhibition.

Kane entered nine paintings in the 1834 exhibition. Eight were copies, seven from prints and the eighth after a landscape by his teacher, Drury. A view of John Gamble's house at Mimico was his only original work. Toronto art critics of the time knew little about reviewing exhibitions: the man for the *Patriot* eloquently noted that one of Kane's paintings possessed much truth to nature and was tenderly pencilled; another's merit lay in the fact that the "distances are actually a good way off, and the figures are alive and busy in their several vocations." The reviewer concludes on a moralizing note: "practice and study should make Mr. Kane an artist of name." [26]

Kane had several artists among his friends in Toronto. Samuel Bell Waugh (1814–1885) was one. An American from Mercer, Pennsylvania, and Kane's junior by four years, he lived in Toronto during 1834 and 1835. He then moved on to Montreal for a short time, and by mid-century had become a well-known artist in Philadelphia. James Bowman (1793–1842), another American, was in Toronto at the same time as Waugh, and the two of them made a pact with Kane to study in Italy together at some future date. Bowman had previously been in Lower Canada, where his career had been by no means placid. The artist Antoine Plamondon had almost literally driven him out of Quebec City in 1833, and the next year in Montreal his murals for Notre Dame Church had been much criticized. His reception in Toronto in October 1834 was more cordial. He had arrived with impressive samples of his own canvases for publicity purposes, such as his portrait of the Danish sculptor, Thorwaldsen, a painting of the Capuchin chapel in Rome, and an interior view of the Indian chapel at Two Mountains near Montreal.[27] Bowman had studied in Rome and under Sir Thomas Lawrence. The laudatory editorial in a Toronto newspaper in December 1834 must have appealed to a young artist like Kane: "Mr. Bowman presents a fine subject for moral reflection; he was lately a Backwoods-man of America, and in the recesses of the forest [he] became fired with the noble ambition to rival the first in the Arts. What a stimulus to youthful ambition." [28] Shortly after this notice was published, the governor-general gave Bowman a portrait commission. Certain local "patriots" objected to the choice of an American, but

the *Patriot* saw nothing unusual in it. The paper pointed out in a reply that Mr. Bowman was British by training although "an American artist," and "to use a musty phrase, *'a man is not abase for being born in a stable.'* " The article concludes: "Mr. Bowman could not have attained his excellence in America—who there could have taught him?" [29]

Despite the attractions of friendship, Kane, who seems to have been a restless and impatient youth, followed Conger from Toronto to Cobourg in 1834. Cobourg was an established and prosperous town on Lake Ontario, with many well-known families, and it did not have a resident professional artist. Presumably Kane decorated furniture there. For whom is uncertain. Conger, his old employer, is said to have had a financial interest with Henry Richard Norton in a cabinet-making firm in Cobourg. F. S. Clench, Kane's future father-in-law, was, however, the best cabinet-maker in that town. Clench's staff must have lived in, judging from the number he indicates as dwelling in his house in a census return in the 1830s; if Kane was one of them, he would have had plenty of opportunity to meet the daughter, Harriet. But although there may be some doubt about whether he painted furniture in Cobourg, there is ample evidence that he was spending much time painting portraits of the town's leading citizens. Conger and his wife are said to have been his first Cobourg subjects; their portraits, done about 1834, demonstrate a beginner's clumsiness (Fig. 2). Later came members of the Clench family (Fig. 3), Conger's business partner, Henry Richard Norton, and his wife, and other local people. Kane's portraits are difficult to identify. He never signed them, and his style varied. One group, obviously by the same hand, are primitive in style with the faces treated in broad planes; they have a direct appeal and warm colouring. An example is the portrait of Mrs. Norton (Plate II); photographs of the portraits of Mrs. Clench and of Mrs. Weller, wife of a celebrated early Canadian stage coach operator, show the same characteristics. All of the group must date from his Cobourg days.[30] They rank in quality with many contemporary primitives from Quebec and the Maritimes, and are part of a phase of primitivism which was widely followed in 19th century Canada and

[26] *Patriot* (Toronto), July 8, 1834.

[27] *Ibid.*, October 21, 1834. According to the newspaper, the Indians intended to present the picture of the chapel to the Pope.

[28] *Ibid.*, December 5, 1834.

[29] *Ibid.*, December 23, 1834.

[30] For information about Kane's portraits in the Cobourg area and illustrations of a number, see Edwin C. Guillet, *The Valley of the Trent* (Toronto 1957), p. lvii and Figs. 99–104.

which produced some of the most appealing among early Canadian canvases.

Kane left Cobourg because of his friendship with James Bowman, and the move was another turning point in his life. According to the *Patriot*, Bowman and Waugh, "who has given many proofs of much genius," were to go to Rome in the spring of 1835.[31] Instead Bowman went to Detroit, and towards the end of 1836 Kane went there also, expecting to meet his two friends and proceed with them to Rome. At Detroit he met a disappointment. Bowman had just been married and cancelled his trip. Kane apparently wrote to his father about his situation, and Michael Kane, not wholly sympathetic to his son's ambitions, replied on November 4, 1836:

You say that Mr. Bowman has got married and that in all probability will prevent your Italian excursion. This I take to be a fortunate circumstance first in keeping you on the Continent where you ought to remain and Secondly Mr. B. has given you a precedent which you would do well to imitate Viz—acquire long experience before you attempt the blind hazard of marriage.[32]

Waugh went on to Rome alone, where Kane met him several years later. Meanwhile, postponing his own trip, he reported to his father that he was doing well with portrait commissions in the United States; actually he was probably short of money and timid about setting out alone for foreign countries.

Knowledge of Kane's movements for the next five years is sketchy. He painted some portraits in Detroit, where he lived in the American Hotel and had a studio in the Desnoyers Building. At this time he probably met John Mix Stanley, who was then studying with Bowman. Stanley was to become a celebrated painter of Indians and would work in the Oregon country at the same time as Kane. One writer mentions that Kane did some painting in Saint Louis. There is much more information about his activities in Mobile, Alabama, to which he went early in 1840. There he had painting rooms in the town's Corinthian Hall, and his reputation was high enough to prompt a feature article on the fine arts in a local newspaper.[33] The columnist, after proudly describing American progress during his generation in literature, sculpture and other arts, comments on Kane's contribution. He had just finished a striking full-length canvas of Queen Victoria based on one by the English artist, Chalon. Its regal magnificence was enhanced by a brilliance of colour, but sketchily painted areas in it offended the critic's taste; this was a decade when figurative precision and finish were new virtues. Diplomatically, Kane had also painted a portrait of General Harrison immediately preceding his inauguration to a

brief presidency. The writer, like Kane's personal friends in Toronto, Rome, the Oregon, or wherever he travelled, concludes by calling him a "gentleman and very clever fellow."

An article appeared during 1855 in the *Anglo-American Magazine* which, though not always accurate in reporting Kane's activities, gives the most complete summary of these American years which can be found:

Accordingly in 1836, he removed to Detroit, and having there executed some "counterfeit presentments,"—as Hamlet hath it—travelled over the principal cities of the United States, in the exercise of his profession. Sailing down the Mississippi, he landed at New Orleans in the fall of 1838, literally without one shilling in his exchequer, having been robbed on board the steam-boat of everything he possessed, except his garmenture. In order to pay for his passage, he was constrained to transfer the gruff features of the skipper to canvas.

By painting a few portraits in New Orleans, Kane was enabled to accumulate sufficient means to carry him to Mobile, where he became a favourite, and met with considerable success. At the expiration of two years, he had by prudence and unflagging industry, realized funds sufficient to carry him to Italy, a consummation which had long been the cherished dream of his existence.[34]

The only known American canvas, done some time after 1839, pictures the captain or owner of the river steamer *Norma* (Fig. 4). Many others must hang unrecognized on the walls of homes in Mobile and elsewhere. English travellers in the United States in these years noted that portraits were being painted everywhere, and Kane obviously shared in this lucrative activity before photography virtually wiped it out little more than a decade later.

Kane's eagerness for study abroad was that of every young painter on the American continent who wished to advance in his profession. He was expected to make a European tour; on it he would copy Old Masters, contemplate the great canvases of the Renaissance and later painters, and receive instruction in the noted galleries. Many aspiring artists in the United States were accordingly making this European pilgrimage; before Kane, Théophile Hamel had gone from Quebec to Rome, and Antoine Plamondon had studied in Paris. The dream which Kane had cherished for several years presumably became possible with his earnings in Mobile, and he sailed for Europe on June 18, 1841.

[31] *Patriot*, December 5, 1834.
[32] Appendix 10, Letter 1.
[33] For his rooms, see *Mobile Advertiser for the County* (Mobile), April 18, 1843. The article appeared in the *Commercial Register* (Mobile), March 20, 1841, and is given in full below, Appendix 11.
[34] *Anglo-American Magazine*, May 1855, pp. 401–2.

Kane's passport survives. He crossed the Atlantic on the American sailing ship *Paetobus* from New Orleans, and after a voyage of nearly three months arrived at Marseilles on September 14. He hastened to Genoa for his first look at a great European art gallery, then went on to Rome. Through that majestic city passed every young gentleman from England on the Grand Tour; there Keats and other poets of romanticism had lived. Hamel had written home about the gay times he had had dancing with belles from Edinburgh and London, but Kane apparently allowed himself no such frivolities.

The winter in Rome was spent in serious study, copying paintings by Murillo, Andrea del Sarto and Raphael "to improve his colouring." Strangely, portraits painted after his return to North America, such as that of James Richardson (Fig. 9), lack the warmth noticeable in some of his primitives, like that of Mrs. Norton, but they do have a unity of tone which bespeaks acquaintance with the greater sophistication of European painting. Many of the copies Kane made in Italy are of single heads. His portrait of Pope Gregory XV after Busato, for example, is merely the head from the larger composition which had been painted shortly before and was then a local sensation. Again, as a practical man, Kane realized that the single portrait was the prevalent fashion in Canada to which he would return, and the study of these in Europe would eventually be more useful than tackling elaborate and time-consuming compositions. As he worked in Rome's academies alongside students from the British Isles and elsewhere, he made casual friendships with them,[35] but also impressed acquaintances in high places. One gave him an introduction for presentation to the Bishop of Cincinnati after his return home. Another gave him a diamond stick-pin. Generally, however, it was a winter of concentrated hard work. When funds were low, he sold the occasional copy of an Old Master.

The spring of 1842 brought relaxation. Kane and an Edinburgh artist whom he had met in Rome, Hope James Stewart, walked together to Naples. This was a "noisy and *favourite* place" after the quiet of Rome, and they remained during March and April. One writer asserts that they made out-of-town jaunts to see the antiquities at Herculaneum and Pompeii.[36] Another claims that from Naples Kane went much farther afield and crossed the Mediterranean. He

availed himself of an offered passage in a Levantine cruiser, and visited the coasts both of Asia and Africa. He joined a party of Syrian explorers, and was already on his way to Jerusalem, when they were deserted by their Arab guides, and, after being exposed to great danger, were compelled to

return to the coast, and abandon the attempt. This failure to accomplish a visit to the most sacred scenes of the ancient historic world was always a subject of mortifying reflection to him. It was on his return from this unsuccessful pilgrimage that he landed on some part of the African shore; and so was able to say, on regaining his Canadian home, that he had been in every quarter of the globe.[37]

There are no stamps in Kane's passport to indicate that he left Naples for a visit to a foreign state, yet such stamps would have been a legal necessity. How to reconcile this account of his trip with his passport is a conundrum.

The two artist friends left Naples in May 1842 and until October hiked through northern Italy. Their longest stop was in Florence. Kane received permission to draw and to paint in the Pitti Palace and in the Uffizi where he copied Raphael's *Pope Julius II*. He lost his Neapolitan and one of his Roman sketchbooks and notes, but returned home with three volumes of sketches. One has principally views of Rome (Figs. 5, 6). A second contains numerous pencil studies of the self-portraits of Rubens (Fig. 7), Dolci and others and of paintings in the great Florentine collections. Close examination of these copies of Old Masters demonstrates Kane's tendency to misjudge proportions, a weakness he had to struggle against throughout his painting career. Sometimes a neck is seen to be too thick when checked against the original, or heads may be proportionately too large or too small. Years later, when he was painting canvases based on sketches from his western tours in North America, the judging of proportions must have been a constant nightmare; continual adjustments can still be detected through the layers of paint (see Fig. 65). A third surviving sketchbook of that summer, filled in Florence and Venice, has much architectural detail together with sketches of Donatello's statues for Or San Michele, Italian furniture and landscape. Kane's official pass to sketch in the Accademia in Venice still survives, but he seems to have made little use of it; instead he spent much time "scouting" with an English art student named Salter.

The Italian tour ended after thirteen months. Kane's canvases from Rome and Florence were boxed and shipped to London, and Kane himself left the country for Switzerland by way of the Brenner Pass. Another young painter, who was to contribute greatly to the art of Canadian landscape and still life, had crossed the same pass in 1834 after study in Italy; this was

[35] A letter to Kane (Appendix 10, Letter 2) names a number of art students whom he had met in Italy.

[36] *Anglo-American Magazine*, May 1855, p. 402.

[37] Daniel Wilson, "Paul Kane, the Canadian Artist," *Canadian Journal*, May 1871, pp. 68–69.

Daniel Fowler, born, in England, the same year as Kane, who came to Canada in 1843. The brilliance of the sun on the snow in the high Alps unfortunately harmed Kane's eyes, and the effects were to trouble him in later life. A brief stop was made in Paris. On October 20, 1842, he sailed from Calais for a winter in London. His friend Stewart accompanied him but continued on by ship to Edinburgh.[38]

Kane's stay in London proved to be another crucial step in shaping his career. It was at this point that his interests shifted from commissioned portraits to the painting of the western Indians. He was spending a pleasant winter in London with another artist friend, Stewart Watson. The only shadow was illness brought on by the notoriously foul English weather. Then, late that winter, George Catlin reopened his exhibition of American Indian paintings in Piccadilly. It made a profound impression on Kane.

George Catlin had, from 1830 to 1836, lived and painted among no fewer than 48 Indian tribes scattered over the American plains to the foothills of the Rocky Mountains. The clash of cultures between red and white with increasing immigration from the eastern seaboard was then creating an acutely tense situation. Propagandists described the aborigines in darkest terms, but Catlin held them in high regard. He had seen them deprived of their natural life as free hunters on the plains through the expansion of European civilization, and he spoke of them with real anguish of spirit:

I love a people who have always made me welcome to the best they had . . . who are honest without laws, who have no jails and no poor-house . . . who never take the name of God in vain . . . who worship God without a Bible, and I believe that God loves them also . . . who are free from religious animosities . . . who have never raised a hand against me, or stolen my property, where there was no law to punish either . . . who never fought a battle with white men except on their own ground . . . and oh! how I love a people who don't live for the love of money.[39]

With firm devotion to these wronged Indian tribes, Catlin began a crusade on their behalf at Albany during 1837. He visited many eastern American cities where exhibitions of his Indian paintings were held and where he gave lectures on the Red Man. Concurrently he waged a campaign to urge the Congress to purchase his record of a people whom he believed would soon be extinct as a result of its contact with whites. This was unsuccessful. A disappointed man, he packed for overseas 600 canvases and several thousand ethnological items which he had collected, intending to display them in European capitals.

Kane must surely have learned of Catlin's work while he was in the United States, but was in no city there in which the Indian paintings were displayed and certainly could not have seen them. His direct association with the painter could only have been in England.

The London exhibition of Catlin's Indian paintings had opened in Egyptian Hall, Piccadilly, on February 1, 1840, two years before Kane's arrival in the city. The official opening was preceded by three days of private viewing when the Duke of Cambridge, the Duke and Duchess of Sutherland, the Duke of Wellington, the Bishop of London, and many other notables attended. Catlin became a London celebrity, and crowds flocked to see his show. His book, *Letters and Notes on the Manners, Customs, and Condition of the North American Indians*, published in October 1841, was an immediate success.[40] When Kane arrived in London a year later, however, interest had waned to such a point that Catlin was making a provincial tour of Liverpool, Edinburgh and Manchester. He returned to London in the early months of 1843 and formed what was to prove an unhappy partnership with Arthur Rankin, who had brought nine Ojibwa to the city for display. The two men signed a new lease for Egyptian Hall. There was a command performance before Queen Victoria and the Prince Consort in Buckingham Palace; it was widely publicized and the attention it drew must have impressed Kane. The Catlin-Rankin partnership broke up after three months, and ruined the prospect of further financial success. A tragic figure, Catlin wandered around Europe for the next ten years, then slipped away for a long South American tour among almost unknown tribes before returning finally to further travels in the American West. He died in 1872.

Sometime early in 1843 a friendship appears to have developed between Catlin and Kane. The only direct reference to this friendship is in a letter of 1847 from Peter Skene Ogden to Kane in which Ogden speaks of "Catlin, a friend of yours."[41] At no other time than 1843 could the paths of Kane and Catlin have crossed. Kane must have attended an exhibition of Catlin's work either in London or in one of the provincial cities, and undoubtedly had read and familiarized himself that winter with Catlin's

[38] It has been suggested that Stewart emigrated to Canada as a farmer in 1847 but this cannot be confirmed.
[39] George McCracken, *George Catlin and the Old Frontier* (New York 1959), p. 4; ellipses are in the original.
[40] George Catlin, *Letters and Notes on the Manners, Customs, and Condition of the North American Indians* (London 1841). There were a number of reprints, the best known being that of 1876 by Chatto and Windus, London.
[41] Appendix 10, Letter 10.

recently published book. It became a guide to certain phases of his own painting, and indeed portions of his own book, *Wanderings of an Artist*, were obviously inspired by Catlin's volume. An interest in the same subject-matter was felt by Stewart Watson, with whom Kane shared quarters in London; he too wanted to paint North American aborigines, and he wrote to Kane in 1844: "I am still in the determination to come to Canada and to paint Indians, and hope that I'll meet you and work together. . . ." [42] Unquestionably the two must have discussed painting Indians while Kane was still in London; they may have met Catlin together.

There is no clear evidence to explain Kane's almost instant conversion at this time to the cause of painting Indians. A cynic might suggest that he saw a good thing and anticipated fame and fortune coming to him by means of a gallery of Canadian Indians. Or had he unconsciously been rebelling against a career devoted to portraiture, in which he had not so far displayed any outstanding ability, and now found a theme that intrigued him? Did he perhaps foresee what the introduction of cheap, popular photography would do to the kind of portraiture in which he had been engaged? Or was it that his contacts with Catlin and his work suddenly revived and focussed his own interest in Indians, latent since his boyhood? One wonders if, as he turned to them, he realized that he was embarking on a career of such absorption and excitement that it would last his life long.

Kane left London to recross the Atlantic in the early months of 1843, firmly intending to paint a gallery of Canadian Indians which would be similar to Catlin's of Indians in the United States.[43] But there was to be a delay. He sailed from Liverpool for the southern United States and by April 1843 was back in Mobile, advertising his return to his old painting rooms, formerly the parlour of the Corinthian Hall.[44] His name is listed in the Mobile directory for the following year.[45] Stewart Watson addressed a letter to him on June 4, 1844, as "Portrait Painter, Toronto," but at that date he was still in the south. Again the *Anglo-American Magazine* gives the only lucid account of the two-year interval after Kane left London:

[42] Appendix 10, Letter 2.
[43] *Ibid.*
[44] *Mobile Advertiser for the County*, April 18, 1843.
[45] The Mobile *Directory* for 1844 lists Kane at the southeast corner of Royal and Dauphin Streets.
[46] The date should be 1843. Curiously, Kane seems to have attempted deliberately to conceal the two years he spent in Mobile on his return from Europe. He stated repeatedly that he had been overseas for four years when he had actually only been there for two.
[47] *Anglo-American Magazine*, May 1855, p. 402.

Having resolved to return to this continent, Kane repaired to Liverpool, but found when he got there, that he lacked funds sufficient to pay his passage over the Atlantic. He was fortunate enough, however, to fall in with the master of a United States vessel, who consented to give him a berth on credit. Arriving safely at Mobile, in the spring of 1845 [*sic* [46]], after, however, nearly suffering shipwreck, he was enabled to procure a loan from an old acquaintance, and discharged his debt to the honest skipper.

Remaining in Mobile only long enough to accumulate sufficient funds to repay his friend, and furnish the means of locomotion, he returned to Toronto after an absence of nearly nine years.[47]

Kane's card case has survived in his family's collection. It still contains two calling cards of John Warburton Womack. Womack was a remarkable Southerner who was speaker of the Alabama legislature when only 21 and was nominated for the vice-presidency of the United States at 26 (he declined to run because if the president had died in office he could not have succeeded because of his age). He married a wealthy young widow and was known as a kind and generous man. Did he help Kane financially at this time, or was he merely a possibility for a portrait commission?

Kane returned to Toronto in the spring of 1845. He was now 35. His formative years as student and youthful painter were over. He had found his subject-matter and had dedicated himself also to a philosophical ideal. His life's work was about to begin.

II. Sketching among the Indians, 1845–1848

Kane spent little time in his "native" Toronto before leaving for the wide western spaces on June 17, 1845. As he himself tells us, he took no companion but his portfolio, paint box, gun and ammunition. He had no money, no resources, no promises of assistance,[1] knew nothing of the west to which he was going, and had had no contacts with Indians except for casual meetings years earlier. What Paul Kane did have was determination, keenness of spirit supported by an indomitable will, and an intrepid devotion to an ideal. They proved sufficient.

A sense of urgency was not far from the surface despite the calm of Kane's outward manner, which had all the Indian's equanimity. He was convinced that the red man was disappearing everywhere as a result of the disease and dislocation caused

[1] He seems to have made some inquiries about means of travel in the west before he left Toronto; see below for his discussion with Angus Bethune, late of the North West Company.

French River Rapids
Paul Kane 1845

Plate III. French River rapids. Stark POP22; crIII-25.

by the incursion of whites into all the western reaches of North America. The natives who commonly wandered York's streets in his boyhood had already vanished. He owned John Tanner's story which declared that there would be a speedy and utter extinction of the natives unless a new approach was taken towards them.[2] Like Catlin, Kane felt impelled to preserve for posterity a record of the Indian chieftains, the customs of the tribes and the lands where they lived before change had made such a record impossible.

Kane himself gives an account of his adventurous travels in the great wilderness of the Northwest throughout the next four years. This account is reprinted below, and there is thus no need to follow the route of his journeys in detail here. Briefly, Kane spent the 1845 season around the Great Lakes, chiefly among the Ojibwa. For the next three years he travelled westward among the plains tribes and over the Rockies and western plateau region to the lower Columbia River; from Fort Vancouver on that river he went up the Pacific coast to Vancouver Island. His homeward journey took more than twelve months. The years were full of incident, and he came back with a bulging portfolio of sketches.

A pattern for work was established during the 1845 season and continued in the travels that followed. Kane moved from one centre to another where he knew that Indians congregated. Whenever possible he sketched the principal chiefs—notable men such as the celebrated Menominee of Wisconsin, Oscosh, or a descendant of Tecumseh. His method, he said, was simply to walk up to an Indian, sit down, and begin to sketch his portrait without saying a word. The subject objected quickly if he disapproved. At times Kane was regarded as a medicine man because of his cleverness in producing a "second self"; indeed some were fearful that his possession of this other self could put them in his power. Once he even put such fear to work for him; in his journal for May 20, 1847, appears this anecdote:

A man followed me to-day from lodge to lodge and told the Indians that they would die if I sketched them, which annoyed me very much. I tried to get rid of him but could not until I hit on an expedient, which was to sketch him, which was successful. He told me if I would stop, he would go away and not trouble me more. [See also *Wanderings*, p. 101, below.]

Occasionally he used flattery to overcome qualms, declaring that he intended to show the picture to the Indians' "great mother, the Queen," who would be most anxious to see it. Once he broke off making a sketch because of the chatter of the eight distracted wives of a Vancouver Island chieftain who felt that some harm would befall their husband through the sketch; he himself sat all the while like a "Grand Turk," flattered by the attention paid to him. Kane went further, sketching pipes, ceremonial articles of all kinds, tools of daily life, and houses and villages. Constantly he sought for the strange and uncommon in native customs, such as the more spectacular Indian rituals: medicine pipe ceremonials on the prairies, scalp dances on the upper Columbia River, coffin burials on the lower Columbia. He found few remains of the ancient rites in the Great Lakes region; already acculturation had suppressed many of the old ways and replaced them with a kind of apathy. Finally, Kane recorded the striking features of the landscapes he encountered. His first year he made sketches of Mackinac's tourist attraction of that time, a great natural bridge. Later he would set down the open prairies, swirling fires, towering snow-capped peaks, waterfalls twice the height of Niagara, and the rocky inlets of the far Northwest.

Sketching materials were light and compact. Some of his books for pencil and water colour studies are no more than ten inches across; a larger one, 10 by 14 inches, with marbled cover, contains Whatman paper watermarked 1843. Reference sketches are in pencil; portraits and landscapes in water colour are fresh, direct drawings. For more important works he carried oiled paper (possibly prepared pages from the larger sketchbook) on which he sketched using oil paints. These oil sketches on paper were light and could be packed into a much smaller space than either canvases or paintings on board. A century and a quarter later, they have unfortunately become exceedingly fragile. Many of Kane's oil sketches were taken from life. Preliminary studies in water colour exist for others, and presumably he transcribed them into oil at the first available moment while the immediate mood was still upon him. Sometimes the fur trade brigade with which he travelled halted for so brief a stop that he was forced to work in the faster water colour. Perhaps he had also to conserve his supply of oil colours. Where could they be replenished? Sketches from the last few weeks of travel are all in water colour: had some of the oil pigments been exhausted?

Like any artist, Kane had his less successful moments. Some of the sketches are certainly dull and undistinguished. Yet despite the hardships of travel and the necessity of working under the most trying and difficult circumstances, he returned with an incredible number of sketches in which the quality is generally

---

[2] *A Narrative of the Captivity and Adventures of John Tanner*, ed. Edwin James (New York 1830), p. 20.

high. In fact the collection is unsurpassed for that period by any other painter of Indians in America.

The first months of travel and sketching were spent around Georgian Bay. From Saugeen village he went to Manitowaning on Manitoulin Island where Ojibwa, Ottawa and Wyandot had gathered for the annual ceremony of the giving of presents by the British government.[3] Here were Indians from the shores of Lakes Huron, Nipissing and Superior and all the adjoining islands. Indeed so many prominent chiefs were available to him as subjects that he went on to similar gatherings at Mackinac Island and on the Fox River of Ojibwa, Menominee and Pota- watomi; bands were to receive payment for lands sold to the American government. In no other way could Kane have assem- bled in one short summer such a varied gallery of Indian personages representative of a number of tribes. Most of his studies are simply portrait busts, a form he preferred. Occasion- ally he did a full-length work, such as the superb sketch of Mani-tow-wah-bay or "He-Devil" at Mackinac (Plate VII).

At Sault Ste Marie that first summer, Kane's fortunes changed through an unexpected offer of help from John Ballen- den, the local Hudson's Bay Company factor. This company has had a history which matches the immensity of the country in which it has performed its operations. It was given exclusive trading privileges in the regions whose waters drained into Hudson Bay in 1670. Thereafter the Company effectually ruled the whole area stretching across to the Pacific, and, at Kane's time, from the Arctic south to the northern American border. For years the Company also controlled the Oregon territory, but this would change with its approaching transfer from British to American jurisdiction.[4]

The real head of the Hudson's Bay Company empire in these years was an energetic Scot, Sir George Simpson. An illegitimate child, he had entered the Company's service at an early age to seek fame and fortune. Forceful, self-confident and shrewd, he had become both governor of Rupert's Land (the Company's territory), and general superintendent of all company affairs in North America. This made him the virtual monarch of vast regions. He travelled from place to place in his special canoe to direct the Company's business transactions and to administer justice. In this canoe Sir George took his own private piper whose skirling bagpipes echoed through the woods and over the plains as he travelled up and down rivers and lakes. Simpson's powers were enormous and no one could travel easily in com- pany territory if he willed otherwise. On the other hand, his

help could make all things possible for visitors to regions under his control.

Kane showed John Ballenden his newly completed sketches and described his hopes for painting a cycle of Indians and also the western landscape. He outlined plans to travel next year with two companions by way of Fort William and the Rainy River to the Red River Settlement. Eventually he hoped to go on to the Pacific. Kane also told Ballenden of his discussion of this project with Angus Bethune in Toronto before setting out. Bethune had discouraged Kane's hopes of receiving help during the trip from Hudson's Bay Company posts, stressing the inhos- pitality of its local officials. He had helped arrange the merger of the North West Company with the Hudson's Bay Company in 1821 and the former Nor'Wester had little affection for the new masters. This judgment by Bethune may have piqued Ballenden, or he may simply have been impressed with Kane's plans. At any rate he wrote to Sir George Simpson on October 29, 1845, praising Kane's sketches and devotion to his profession and assuring Sir George that Kane was prepared for the hard- ships of travel in the west.[5] Simpson, impressed, nevertheless wanted assurance that Kane was a British subject before he would even consider helping him.[6] Kane was.

Negotiations between Sir George and Kane continued throughout the ensuing winter after the artist's return to Toronto. Kane arranged to meet Simpson at Montreal, and J. H. Lefroy wrote an introduction for him. Lefroy, a British army officer then doing scientific work at the magnetic observa- tory in Toronto, was an intimate of leading families both in Canada and in Britain. His name carried respect. He pointed out to Simpson that Kane's pictures would be not only vivid but also "faithful" sketches of the novelties of the west, and that he would prove an interesting visitor for company gentlemen at various posts. Following Kane's visit to Montreal, Lefroy wrote a second time, on March 30, 1846, expressing satisfaction that the superintendent had promised his help. He also assured Sir George that Kane would travel alone the next year, and no doubt would return from the west with a portfolio of sketches not much inferior to Catlin's in variety and greatly superior in

---

[3] For a detailed account of the treaty ceremony at this place in 1838 see Anna Jameson, *Sketches in Canada and Rambles among the Red Men* (London 1852), pp. 276–87.

[4] On the Hudson's Bay Company see E. E. Rich, *The Hudson's Bay Company, 1660–1870*, 3 vols. (Toronto 1960) and *The Fur Trade and the Northwest to 1857* (Toronto 1967).

[5] Hudson's Bay Company Archives, D5/15, Ballenden to Simpson, October 29, 1845.

[6] *Ibid.*, D4/67, Simpson to Ballenden, November 17, 1845.

truth. He assessed Kane as a modest and respectable man.[7]

Sir George Simpson wrote Kane's final letter of authorization only after reaching Rainy River in northern Ontario on May 31, 1846. Simpson and Kane had been travelling west from Toronto at the same time, and Sir George had had an opportunity to gauge the artist's fierce determination. Left behind at Mackinac when he missed the steamboat, Kane had gone to fantastic lengths to overtake Simpson. He set a new and amazing local record for speed by setting off in a skiff with three boys, the eldest an eighteen-year-old stripling, and covering 90 miles of lake and river in less than 24 hours. He had caught up with the amazed Sir George at Sault Ste Marie. At Fort Frances Simpson wrote a circular letter to all Hudson's Bay Company officers in "Ruperts Land and Elsewhere," directing that the artist be given free transportation on company boats and "hospitalities" at all posts (see Appendix 10). Kane, a guest of the Hudson's Bay Company, could go without cost anywhere within the vast territories it controlled.

There were no more colourful men than the crews of the fur trade brigades of the Hudson's Bay Company, who linked all parts of the northern half of the continent. Kane had been introduced to this method of canoe travelling in May when he had joined the brigade going westward from Fort William on Lake Superior to the Red River. He would see much more of it before his return. It was a genuinely romantic experience to be in the great decorated canoes which were like living things as they leaped under the paddles of the voyageurs. Many of these specially selected young men were French-Canadians from the St. Lawrence, others were half-breeds and Indians born in the west. Lithe and bronzed, they were a colourful lot, with handkerchiefs twisted around their heads and sashes at their waists, and spoke in a unique accent. Washington Irving described them in *Astoria:*

The dress of these people is generally half civilized, half savage. They wear a capot or surcoat, made of a blanket, a striped cotton shirt, cloth trowsers, or leather leggins, moccasons of deer-skin, and a belt of variegated worsted, from which are suspended the knife, tobacco-pouch, and other implements. Their language is of the same piebald character, being a French patois, embroidered with Indian and English words and phrases.[8]

These voyageurs, carefree, good-natured, almost always singing, had much of the gaiety and lightness of heart of their French ancestry, were full of anecdote, and were ever ready for a dance. Kane called them amphibious water dogs, for after two thousand miles of paddling they would still wade cheerfully for

sixteen hours at a time in the cold northern Ontario rivers where the rapids were difficult and the task of dragging canoes against the current was formidable. The steersman of the canoe, most experienced of all, stood at the prow, "turning and twisting himself with the lithe agility of a snake, and striking first on one side then on the other, . . . very graceful and picturesque." [9]

The voyageurs travelled by "pipes," pausing to smoke for a brief five minutes and then paddling on at a rate of 50 strokes to the minute which made their canoes "absolutely seem to fly over the water." Normally three pipes marked about twelve miles of travel.[10] They ran even dangerous rapids and, when portages were necessary, carried the canoes and heavy bales often over difficult terrain. Kane meanwhile took advantage of halts to sketch the scenery of northern Ontario or the Columbia River. Day started at three or four o'clock in the morning with some five hours of paddling before breakfast, and camp was made at night only in time for Kane to paint the occasional sunset. It was a gruelling ordeal experienced by these proud and free men of the fur trade brigades.

Sir George Simpson's suggestions were to influence some of Kane's choices of subject-matter. Simpson urged Kane, for example, to go with the half-breeds (or, more correctly, Métis) on the annual buffalo hunt south from the Red River Settlement. That Kane should have made his trip in 1846 is one of the fortunate quirks of fate which repeatedly arranged that he be in the west to record important events at critical moments. The great hunt of 1846 was one of the last on the Winnipeg prairies: wanton slaughter of the buffalo had brought them nearly to extermination. After an hour's chase, Kane writes, 500 dead and dying animals covered from five to six square miles. Up to that time, buffalo had been the bulwark of Fort Garry's economy, and hunters made as much in a few weeks as farmers did in a whole year. Figures give life to this story. The number of carts in the annual hunt had increased from 540 in 1820 to 1,210 in 1840. During the latter year, 620 hunters, 650 women and 360 boys and girls went out in one party.[11] Between 1820 and 1840 hunters had killed an incredible 650,000 buffalo during these annual expeditions in the west, and this was not the total for there was additional slaughter by smaller parties.[12] Little won-

[7] *Ibid.,* D5/15, Lefroy to Simpson, March 30, 1846.

[8] Washington Irving, *Astoria; or, Anecdotes of an Enterprise beyond the Rocky Mountains* (author's rev. ed.; New York 1849), p. 47.

[9] Anna Jameson, *Sketches in Canada,* pp. 296–98.

[10] *Ibid.*

[11] Alexander Begg, *History of the North-West* (Toronto 1894), I, 299.

[12] E. Douglas Branch, *The Hunting of the Buffalo* (Lincoln, Neb., 1962), p. 83.

der that no buffalo herds were found south of Red River after 1847. If Kane had made his western trip two years later, he could not have pencilled his historic panoramas (Plate XVII, Fig. 67) of huntsmen riding pell-mell into a herd of from four to five thousand bulls, an episode of blood and carnage, and of danger as horses tripped in gopher holes and their thrown riders were pursued by wounded animals. It was, as Kane describes it, a scene "of intense excitement" and reckless confusion.

Buffalo would occupy Kane's mind that whole summer during his crossing of the plains, and he was indeed to be the outstanding painter of the vast buffalo herds on the Canadian prairie during their last phase. He sketched the buffalo pound at Fort Carlton, and made studies of an Indian high in a tree waving his feather-decked medicine pipe at the entrance so that its magical powers would send many and fat buffalo into the drive (Figs. 77, 78). Exotic touches delighted him, even if the slaughter was painful. When he was beyond Fort Pitt he was amazed by the vast buffalo herds which covered the prairie "as far as the eye could reach." At Fort Edmonton he saw the mounted Assiniboin chasing buffalo with piercing iron-tipped arrows and spears (Fig. 105). But, strangely, during the homeward trip he completely ignored as subject-matter the largest herd of all, 10,000 buffalo, which he saw wallowing in the snow. All phases of the buffalo hunt as it was practised throughout the seasons were pictured by Kane, except that he did no scenes of the animals struggling through deep snow; by contrast, this phase was one which Catlin seemed to find most picturesque. Kane was only interested during a winter hunt in the fact that he shot one of the largest buffalo bulls he had ever seen. He kept the head, a massive 202 pounds in weight, and repeatedly painted it.

The character of the faces and the dress of Kane's Indians change perceptibly in his sketches as he moves westward. On the prairies they are no longer pictured wearing clothing with European additions or with government medals around their necks. These men of the plains have not the quiet submissive air of the men of Manitowaning who had been in contact with Europeans for generations and foresaw the end of their free native life as hunters. Instead, his Sioux chieftain (Fig. 58), the Assiniboin named Mah-Min (Plate XXVIII, Fig. 109) or the Blackfoot, Big Snake (Fig. 92), are noble beings. Muck-Cranium, the Cree from Fort Carlton (Plate XIX), is above all the haughty Indian looking far out over the plains which are his empire. Here is the proud savage, not beaten down by Europeans, the kind of man for whom Catlin had such regard. Kane finally had

met the Indians he really wanted to paint and through his pictures of them he rendered an unsurpassed tribute to the first residents of this continent.

Kane did paintings of virtually all the Hudson's Bay Company posts he visited, from Fort Frances (Figs. 49, 50) to Fort Victoria (Figs. 188, 189). Fort Garry (Figs. 56, 57), Norway House (Plate XVIII), Fort Carlton (Fig. 75), Fort Pitt (Fig. 83), Fort Edmonton (Plate XXV) and Rocky Mountain House (Fig. 108) were links in the chain across the prairies. Others like Jasper House (Fig. 111), Fort Walla Walla (Fig. 134), and Fort Vancouver (Figs. 150, 151) led across the mountains to the Pacific. These squat bastions in the wilderness spaces spelled safety and comfort when travellers saw them from a distance, and this was the way Kane preferred to sketch them. He could thus present them in their natural surroundings, which close-up studies would not have allowed. Such a panoramic view of the Hudson's Bay Company's empire impressively documents its presence throughout these far-flung regions.

One regret might nevertheless be expressed. Kane painted no close-up of the exterior of Fort Edmonton or of a renowned audience room inside the fort. These features have been graphically described by other travellers:

The fort was painted inside and out, with devices to suit the taste of the savages who frequented it. Over the gateway were a fantastic pair of vanes, and the ceilings and walls of the hall presented gaudy colors and queer sculptures for the admiration of the Indians, the buildings, for the same reason, being painted red.[13]

True, there is a suggestion of the weather-vane over the fort entrance in Kane's canvas, but the exterior must have needed repainting at the time of his visit for there is no suggestion of the appealing red.

Yet a complaint is churlish perhaps. Kane was back at the fort for Christmas in 1847 and as if to atone vividly describes in prose the festive dinner in that same room. Its decorations were the "awe and wonder" of the natives but "were [the artist] to attempt a repetition of the same style in one of the rooms of the Vatican, it might subject him to some severe criticisms from the fastidious."[14] Here at Christmas, with the temperature registering from 40 to 50 degrees below zero outside, the Europeans, including the Rev. Mr. Rundle whose name is commemorated in a mountain peak, ate boiled buffalo hump and buffalo calf,

---

[13] Begg, *History of the North-West*, I, 212.
[14] *Wanderings of an Artist*, p. 138 below.

dried moose nose, white fish browned in buffalo marrow, buffalo tongue, beaver tails, roast wild goose, and piles of turnips and potatoes. That same evening everyone at the fort, white, Métis and Indians alike, joined in festivities in the "Great House." At the gala ball they dressed with bright sashes and ornamented mocassins, and spoke a babble of tongues. Highland reels were squeaked out by a fiddler. One of Kane's partners was a young Cree girl, "who sported enough beads round her neck to have made a pedlar's fortune," and as they danced she kept jumping up and down with a grave face, both feet off the ground at once "as only an Indian can." Kane painted another girl he met at the dance, a half-breed Cree named Cun-ne-wa-bum (Fig. 107). She looks out demurely enough from beneath a fan made of a white swan's wing, and wears a beaded dress which he later obtained for his ethnological collection.

From Fort Edmonton, Kane had set out on October 6, 1846, for the most harrowing phase of his journey, a crossing of the Rockies in early winter by a pass at over 5,000 feet. It was essential that the Hudson's Bay Company men get through. They carried with them packs of otter skins brought from York Factory which were destined for the Russians on the upper northwest coast of the Pacific: the company's annual rental for trading rights in lands owned by the Russians in that region. Horses stuck in deep snow drifts on the way over, and finally had to be given up for snow-shoes. The party had frequently to wade in rivers choked with floating blocks of ice. When the Columbia was reached, some boats upset in its dangerous rapids. But men and furs reached their destination.

Kane arrived at Fort Vancouver on December 8, 1846, and the relaxation was welcome after the arduous trip across the continent. The fort was the centre of the Hudson's Bay Company's west coast operations, and two of its principal men in that area, James Douglas and Peter Skene Ogden, already famed as fur traders, were hospitable to Kane. The Company needed its shrewdest and most reliable factors for such critical posts. The name "Kane" meant nothing to the men at the fort, however. Thomas Lowe, a company employee, was much more interested in the new bride whom Richard Lane, in charge of the brigade, had brought with him. Kane's intention, to paint the Indians and the local scenery as a record for posterity, was not grasped immediately by the staff despite Simpson's introduction. Lowe wrote:

It is supposed that [he's] taking views and sketches of the most remarkable places on the route, in order to embellish the work about to be published by Sir George Simpson; and it is thought that he intends to go over the same route as Sir George took in the years 1841 and '42, by the Sandwich Islands and through Siberia. . . .[15]

Sir George's book was published in London, the very next year, without illustrations, so that Lowe was evidently wrong in the first of his assumptions.[16]

Kane had arrived at Fort Vancouver in time for the festive Christmas season of 1846 at this far west post. Hudson's Bay Company men on the frontiers kept up their spirits with lusty celebrations and dinners were eaten in the best style. Both Fort Vancouver and Fort Walla Walla had imported English bone china, and the finest of oriental ware was brought carefully to posts which in some ways were havens of English-style living.[17]

Kane made a firm and fast friend of Peter Skene Ogden during these winter months. Ogden had spent most of his life on the Pacific coast from 1818. No man knew the west better than he, and his knowledge of the Indians was unrivalled.[18] He had studied for the law, and on the frontier, where there was no written law and no legal tribunal to appeal to, performed in his own part the acts of "summary legislation, [and] sometimes [. . .] the parts of judge, jury, sheriff, hangman, gallows and all!"[19] He has been presumed to be the anonymous author of *Traits of Indian Life and Character* published in London during 1853. Kane and Ogden passed convivial evenings with married couples at homes in the village area around the fort.[20] Obviously there was much banter about ladies, a good deal of laughter, and general gossip about all and sundry over games of backgammon.

The winter weather was extremely bad for outdoor sketching but Kane dutifully, if without much interest, recorded the fort. He showed more enthusiasm in painting the Indians of the neighbourhood. He mentions particularly the venerable old chief Casanov (Plate XXXVI), who in his days of greatest power could muster 1,000 warriors and had had 10 wives and 18 slaves. During the interlude at Fort Vancouver Kane took time

[15] British Columbia, Provincial Archives, Thomas Lowe's journals kept at Fort Vancouver, Columbia River.
[16] Sir George Simpson, *Narrative of a Journey round the World during the Years 1841 and 1842* (London 1847).
[17] See John A. Hussey, *The History of Fort Vancouver and Its Physical Structure* (Portland, Washington State Historical Society, n.d.), especially Plates XLV, XLVI, XLVII, XLVIII.
[18] On Ogden's life see T. C. Elliott, "Peter Skene Ogden, Fur Trader," *Oregon Historical Quarterly*, 1910, and E. E. Rich, *The Hudson's Bay Company*, II.
[19] Ross Cox, *The Columbia River; or Scenes and Adventures during a Residence of Six Years on the Western Side of the Rocky Mountains among Various Tribes of Indians Hitherto Unknown*, ed. Edgar I. and Jane R. Stewart (Norman, Okla., 1957), p. 308.
[20] See Appendix 10, Letter 10.

for a day's outing, cantering to the plains behind the fort with friends and sketching them in humorous vein while they were resting before the return gallop (Fig. 153). This mood was a relaxation from the serious studies he had been doing for two years. H.M.S. *Modeste* was anchored in the river by the fort and there was a social going and coming between officers and men of the Royal Navy and the Company's gentlemen and other employees. Kane spent much time with the officers in horse-racing and chasing wild calves. But he found himself in Oregon when more serious events were the preoccupation. The ship was there to maintain law and order at a difficult moment and tension was high.

A treaty of June 15, 1846, had fixed the western boundary between British and American territory to the Pacific and de-creed that from June 1846 all lands south of the 49th parallel would be United States soil. A first American provisional gov-ernment had already been established at Champoeg in 1843. The Hudson's Bay Company foresaw an end to its operations on the Columbia and planned a move for its headquarters north to Fort Victoria within continuing British territory. In these years, too, colonists, weary with the roughness and heat of a long journey, were coming in covered wagons over the mountains by the old Oregon trail at an incredible rate. Kane, astonished at their numbers, compiled a table of annual arrivals: 5 people had arrived from the eastern states during 1834; in 1844, it was 1,475 who crossed over the trail; 3,000 in 1845; and in 1846 between 800 and 900 "souls" arrived in the settlement with another 1,000 going to California.[21] The Indians were dis-traught. The white man's diseases accompanied the settlers and were killing them off in tremendous numbers. So many died in one Columbia River village that no one was left to bury the dead; their bones lay scattered amid its deserted dwellings. Violence would soon erupt at the Whitman Mission (Fig. 137) near Fort Walla Walla. And the appalling destruction of the Indians would continue. In March 1848 Ogden reported the arrival of 4,000 emigrants with "their pleasant travelling com-panions the Measles, Dysentry and Typhus Fever." Deaths among the whites totalled 119 that year "but the Indian popula-tion as usual shared most conspicuous": on the Columbia River alone, 1,500 Indians died during the summer.[22]

Tension, however, did not lessen the camaraderie which came from the presence of H.M.S. *Modeste* in harbour. The ship's officers, like others on ships held fast in the Arctic ice or docked elsewhere for long periods, organized its company into a theatri-cal group as an aid to morale. A play-bill, probably unique among

relics of the west coast's early theatrical events, was kept by Kane (Fig. 152). This handwritten broadside records the com-pany's performance at Fort Vancouver harbour on January 5, 1847. The group offered the farces "High Life below Stairs" and "The Deuce is in him" and as a conclusion "the laughable Comedy of 'The Irish Widow.'" Songs interspersed made it a full evening. That Kane saved this play-bill speaks eloquently of his continuing interest in theatricals, first noted in muddy little York years before. Various pencil doodles among his sketches are obviously theatrical characters: a dandy poses with his cane as he declaims his lines, and there are children dressed in pixy hats. These sketches are mixed in with those from the west coast, although there is nothing definitely to connect them with the performance described in the play-bill.

The theatrical evening attended by Kane actually was only one in a long series by the *Modeste*'s crew during Oregon's first "season." Captain Henry J. Warre, who travelled on the Pacific coast in 1845–46 as part of his mission to investigate defence of the international boundary, attended performances three times and gives more information about them. The first of his visits was on January 8, 1846, and Kane must have witnessed a similar scene when he attended just a year later.

This was the day fixed for the performance of the first Play, ever performed in Oregon—on board the "Modeste" for which great prepara-tions had been for some time going forward—the Stage was rigged on the deck, which was covered in with sails & flags, &c. The façade was really beautifully painted by the sailors themselves. We dined on board. The play commenced at 7 oC. All the H.B. Company's officers & their Ladies attended from the Fort; as also several Americans from the Settlements.— numbering nearly 300 persons, including the Officers & crew of the Ship. The "Mayor of Garrati" & "The deuce is in him" were the pieces selected & were performed inimitably; particularly by the "Ladies" who looked and acted their parts to perfection; the sailor boys made rather large Women & had (as was remarked by a nice little girl of Mr. Douglas) "very red necks." Some of the ladies (nearly all of whom are half-breeds) wondered that they were not before aware that "*any Women lived on board*"—So that the deception was perfect. Between the plays, the Glee Singers gave some excellent songs, which were repeatedly encored, & the play concluded with "God Save the Queen" by the whole Corps Dramatique.

Warre reports that rain nearly ruined the second performance for which a sailor wrote and delivered the prologue: it was undoubtedly earthy but wholesome. Some settlers from the Twality Plains nearby were in the audience and found the

21 Kane family papers.
22 Appendix 10, Letter 14.

man-of-war almost as novel as the plays. Highly excitable nationalism nearly ruined the third evening, in March, when another double bill was enthusiastically received:

Fortunately for the Amateurs on board the Modeste, the 10th March proved a lovely day for the third representation of their Theatricals.—Numbers of Settlers and their families arrived to witness the performance & all the Officers returned to be present.—The Plays chosen were "She Stoops to Conquer" & "Miss in her Teens"—both of which were exceedingly well performed and with great applause.—There were several Americans present who were delighted with the plays, but made some objection to the National Songs for which some of them were nearly fittingly [sic] thrashed by the "Tars"—after they had gone on shore.—However, every thing went off well [&] the Yankees made a sort of apology for their dissent.[23]

New immigrants to Oregon brought other innovations to the west. The *Oregon Spectator* of Oregon City commenced publication in 1846, and Kane seems to have been intrigued with the newspaper. He purchased four issues to send to friends in the east so that they could better understand local conditions. Its editor, awake to everything novel, reported Kane's visit to Oregon City in the issue of February 10, 1847. Kane was then on his way to sketch at Champoeg, and during the visit he had made "faithful and beautiful" pictures of the new town and the falls (Plate XXXVIII; Figs. 161, 162). His paintings captivated the editor, and he saw them as a way of giving a true account of the far west: "Our countrymen on the eastern slope of the Rocky Mountains entertain imperfect notions, doubtless, of the appearance of Oregon and the Settlements, but we can assure them that in the achievements of Mr. Kane, they may behold correct delineations of the country." Kane himself was much concerned throughout his travels that easterners should accept his sketches as being truthful.

A Jesuit, Father Michael Acolti, escorted Kane from Oregon City through the Willamette valley to Champoeg and *en route* they visited two Catholic mission stations. Many early residents in the region were former Hudson's Bay Company employees with French-Canadian Catholic backgrounds, men who had settled on the plains after retirement from company service.[24] Kane was particularly interested in the St. Paul Mission.[25] Here children, red and white, were taught by a staff of nuns from Quebec, timid women, separated from their homes by a continent. Father De Smet had sketched their convent school, but his crude efforts have little historical value. By contrast Kane made a superb rendering of the mission (Plate XXXIX). Prominent is the new church with a steeple which had been built for the

sisters. It is reputedly the first brick building erected on the Pacific coast and no other accurate picture of it seems to exist.

Kane's second sketching expedition from Fort Vancouver was up the Pacific coast in the region of the Canadian northwest then known as New Caledonia. He left on March 25, 1847, with the good wishes of James Douglas who had assured him that he would find much both beautiful and sublime at Nisqually and beyond. The next day Kane met with another of his pieces of luck: when he reached the mouth of the "Kattleputal" (Lewis) River, he saw Mount St. Helens erupting smoke in the distance. This was one of the last of North America's active volcanoes, and had created whole chapters of the Indian myths and legends that fascinated Kane. Many stories linked Mount St. Helens with Mount Hood, which Kane had painted repeatedly from Fort Vancouver. One, for example, described the two peaks as a married couple, Hood being the husband and St. Helens the wife. They quarrelled fiercely and threw fire at each other. St. Helens was victor; Hood, being afraid of her, has since kept quiet and the wife, "having a stout heart, still burned."[26] Kane tried to hire Indian guides to ascend Mount St. Helens with him. It had never been climbed and he was told stories of "Skoocooms," evil genii who had eaten a man visiting it, and of a lake at the base with fish having heads like those of bears. No one would go with him and his only accomplishment was gathering another legend.

Mount St. Helens' most violent eruption had occurred in 1842. A Methodist missionary, Josiah L. Parrish, saw an unusual sight. Smoke and fire shot up, and the smoke spread out at a certain point in a line parallel to the horizon, looking like a vast table supported by immense pillars of flame and smoke. Kane saw and sketched a similar smoke ring, but his picture lacks some of the drama of the more violent eruption five years earlier (Plate XLI). When he painted a canvas of Mount St. Helens (Fig. 164) he chose to show a lurid scene of an eruption by night. After Kane's visit sporadic bursts of activity occurred for some ten years with smoke pouring from crevasses in the ice-capped mountain. Since then the volcano has been completely dormant.

[23] The two descriptions by Warre are in the Henry J. Warre Papers, Public Archives of Canada, MG24F71. See also *Oregon Spectator*, August 20, 1846; January 21, 1847.
[24] See John A. Hussey, *Champoeg: Place of Transition* (Portland, Oregon Historical Society, 1967).
[25] For an account of the mission see [Carl Landerholm], *Notices & Voyages of the Famed Quebec Mission to the Pacific Northwest . . . 1838 to 1847* (Portland, Oregon Historical Society, 1956).
[26] For further details see Kenneth L. Holmes, "Mount St. Helens' Recent Eruptions," *Oregon Historical Quarterly*, 1955, pp. 197–209.

Nearly a hundred sketches survive from the three months during which Kane worked on the southern tip of Vancouver Island, along the adjoining coasts of British Columbia and in the state of Washington. These are of the greatest ethnological and historical interest, and some are among his finest artistic productions. Their subject-matter has no parallel in the work of any other 19th century artist in the same region. Kane was attracted by the number and variety of tribes and no better place existed than Fort Victoria for sketching them. Locally there were Clallam, Sanetch, Makah and others, and farther afield such peoples as the northerly Chimmesyan, Kwakiutl and Haida. Indians from up and down the coast came to the post in large numbers, and a short canoe journey could take him to the homes of others.

Kane was struck by the facial characteristics of the individual tribes and by the head deformations many of them practised. He recorded their boats, both the great decorated war canoes and the less ostentatious craft of the camas-gathering fleet (Figs. 185, 186, 187). He pictured women spinning the wool which they rubbed on their thighs and weaving with primitive looms, the small white dogs raised for wool, and the domestic activities inside the large houses grouped into villages at Fort Victoria, Esquimalt and Suck (for example, Plate XLV, Figs. 196, 197).

In these villages Kane also sketched ornately carved masks with moon-faces and other visages, elaborate rattles, house posts carved to honour ancestral animals, and figures which were grave guardians (Plate XLIV, Figs. 190, 191, 193, 195). Here were the spectacular art forms of a native people whose material culture was more advanced than that of any other Canadian aborigines. Kane does not seem, however, to have been invited to attend the secret society meetings where the elaborately painted ritual masks which he sketched were worn. These ghostly dances were usually held at night when the red of fires piercing its gloom added mystery and drama. Kane's re-creation of such a dance shows masked figures performing in full day-light on a sunny slope, and he omits any suggestion of the excited and often terrified circle of spectators.

No artist of the Victorian period attempted to picture the west coast Indians as Kane had done. In the present century, Emily Carr, who was born in Victoria, in her turn became fascinated with the Indians of this region. She painted various tribes over many years with profound humanity, with humility, under-standing and love, and her paintings revealed the religious concepts central in the Indian's art, especially in his great carved totem poles, into which the native sculptor breathed vitality and

strength. Hers was a remarkable insight into the simple and honest ways which she found lingering among these once-proud people. Her dedication is one end of a thread which stretches back to Catlin and Kane, even if her painting has the artistic qualities of a later generation.

Events were occurring in this region which would be significant for British Columbia's future, just as farther south in Oregon a future destiny was being worked out. James Douglas had directed the erection of Fort Victoria towards the southern end of Vancouver Island just four years earlier. He named it in honour of Britain's queen, and she was to knight him in 1863 as the virtual founder of a new Canadian province. Kane and Captain Warre, a visitor during 1846, both set down views of this new bastion of British interests on the Pacific.

The Hudson's Bay Company was in these years making a vigorous effort to sell shares in an agricultural development company for Puget Sound where they envisioned a rich new farming community. Promotional circulars were distributed widely, forecasting wealth for investors in this new Pacific Coast enterprise. One went to the bishop at St. Boniface in the Red River Settlement, and he carefully filed it away. As usual alert to history in the making, Kane sketched the newsworthy little village of Nisqually then receiving much attention (Fig. 173).

At last Kane felt his work along the Pacific was finished. He had sketched in all the parts of the far west which were then being talked about and his thoughts turned to his homeward trip. He left Fort Vancouver on July 1, 1847.

It was proposed that Kane would call on the missionaries in the interior of Oregon on his return trip. At the Dalles of the upper Columbia River he was travelling quickly and did not have time to stop at the Methodist mission nearby. It was not, however, so important for him to halt there since he had been able to view numbers of Indians in that particular sector of the Columbia and had made many sketches. His chief interest in the missionaries was really the means of introduction they provided to the Indians in their particular region. Their usefulness is well illustrated by an incident on his westward trek. The fur trade brigade in which he was travelling had stopped at Cumberland House (Le Pas). The Rev. J. Hunter, a local Church of England missionary, wrote on August 25, 1846, in his diary:

The Saskatchewan Brigade arrived here to-day from York Factory in charge of Mr. Rowand. Distributed tracts among the men in the boat. Accompanied Mr. Cain [*sic*], an Artist proceeding with the Brigade, to the tent of Mistahpa'oo to inspect his drums, Medicine Bags, etc. Mr. Cain

Plate IV. Ojibwa Camp (Spider Islands, Georgian Bay). ROM912.1.3; crIII-28.

Plate V. Sault Ste Marie (Ojibwa village). ROM912.1.9; crIII-65.

took a sketch of his drum and the grotesque figures portrayed on it. The principal figure was a man surrounded with a number of tents, over which Mistahpa'oo described him as presiding and protecting.[27]

Although he missed the Methodist mission in 1847, Kane did stop to sketch at Walla Walla as he moved east and also in the strange and romantic Pelouse River valley where the "magnificent scenes" tempted his curiosity. His route led him on July 18 to the American Protestant mission among the Cayuse Indians at Waiilatpu. Evidently he hoped Dr. Marcus Whitman, who was in charge, would introduce him to the local natives. They had a reputation for being aggressive. At this very time they were seething with anger and their bad feelings would soon reach a boiling point. Dr. Whitman, his wife Narcissa, and others had crossed on the Oregon Trail in 1836 to found the first Protestant mission in Oregon. They had laboured among the Cayuse when they first arrived, but had had to undertake additional duties when in 1843 the great wagon trains of immigrants arrived over the Trail. These new arrivals were welcomed and helped at the mission house, a T-shaped adobe building built by the missionaries themselves, who had smoothed and white-washed the walls with a solution from river mussel shells. Paint bought from the Hudson's Bay Company brightened the building with green doors and window frames, grey interior wood-work, and yellow pine floors.[28] The increasing immigration of succeeding years was reflected in the necessity to give homes to children, half-breed and white, who became orphans on the Trail. Seven Sager children, whose parents had died while coming west, were adopted in 1844.

Kane was at the Whitman mission July 18 to 22, 1847. He describes graphically how the doctor took him to a Cayuse lodge, where he evidently made two sketches of To-ma-kus (Fig. 139). The Indian attempted to throw one sketch in the fire, but Kane snatched it from him. "He glanced at me like a fiend, and appeared greatly enraged, but before he had time to recover from his surprise I left the lodge and mounted my horse, not without occasionally looking back to see if he might not send an arrow after me."[29] Chief Til-au-kite was also sketched here (Fig. 140). Whitman's adopted daughter, one of the Sager children, recalled Kane's visit years later, describing how he had made pictures at the mission. She relates that she and the other children were cleaning up the yard and relaxed from their labour by trying to balance the rake on their finger. Mrs. Whitman reproved them and told them she did not want such frivolity in a picture.[30] Kane's pencil sketch, the only known view of the mission (Fig. 137), omits the children completely,

but in the foreground is a man leading a horse on the old Oregon Trail. When Kane returned to Walla Walla, he undertook to carry a little dog for Mr. Whitman, but in that inhospitable country the heat was so intense that the animal died of prostration on the way.

The second visit of Kane to an Oregon mission, in September, required a detour from Fort Colvile to Tshimakain some seventy miles away. From 1838 to 1849 the Rev. Elkanah Walker and the Rev. Cushing Eells with their wives maintained an establishment among the Spokan Indians. Kane was a guest of the Walkers and visited the Eells for dinner; both had comfortable log houses. One day he and Walker roamed about admiring the impressive scenery. Another day he went with an Indian hoping to visit some celebrated caves but failed to find them. Walker reported to him that there had been fighting at the Dalles between whites and Indians and two on each side had been killed. Tension in the region was obviously mounting. Kane's water-colour sketch (Fig. 131) shows the mission post in its last phase before its abandonment because of the Indian wars which were threatening even during his visit.

The diary of Mrs. Walker under date of September 11 makes a personal reference to Kane. His rough manners after exposure through three years of rugged travel on the frontier, his wild hair and great beard, must have intimidated a woman of the manse. "I think Mr. K[ane] a clever artist but an ungodly man, of not much learning. He gave me considerable information about birds."[31] Her reference to the birds is reinforced by the fact that Kane had several books on nature study in his library, and his son was a great lover of birds in his student days at Trinity College School, Port Hope.

In *Wanderings of an Artist* Kane records for September 21 the arrival of a messenger sent from Walla Walla to Fort Colvile, bringing news of an Indian uprising at the Whitman mission. Kane is curiously in error about the date for the tragedy took place on November 29, and just when he did hear of it is obscure: by November he was up on the Athabasca River. Til-au-kite and To-ma-kus, goaded to fury, had murdered Dr.

[27] Church Missionary Society Archives, London, journal of Archdeacon J. Hunter 1844–1865, ref. C C1/037.

[28] For the mission's history and its buildings see Erwin N. Thompson, *Whitman Mission, National Historic Site* (National Park Service Historical Handbook Series no. 37; Washington 1964).

[29] *Wanderings of an Artist*, p. 116 below.

[30] Matilda J. Sager Delaney, *The Whitman Massacre* (Spokane, Ethel Reed Chapter of the Daughters of the American Revolution, 1920).

[31] Henry E. Huntington Library and Art Gallery, diary of Elkanah Walker and Mary Richardson Walker.

Whitman and a general massacre followed. There had been a measles epidemic among the Indians and malcontents spread word that the doctor was poisoning them. Thirteen mission people were killed, several escaped, and 49 were held captive as hostages until released by Peter Skene Ogden who presented the Indians with company guns, blankets and ammunition in exchange for the prisoners.[32] The slayers had split the skulls of the missionaries before abandoning the bodies so that the evil spirits would escape. The mission of Henry Spalding at Lapwai was immediately discontinued, and Walker and Eells closed their mission the following March. The Whitman massacre was one of the most famous and unhappy episodes of the old west.

Though Kane, throughout his wanderings, was greatly concerned that people would later accept his sketches as being true portrayals of the regions he had seen, he was more worried about those of the Northwest coast and the Oregon, then almost unknown in the east, than he was about those of the prairies since Canadians did have some knowledge of the plains. An obvious solution was to secure certificates of authenticity from well-known Hudson's Bay Company men. James Douglas wrote the first of these at Fort Vancouver in June, the day before Kane left for the east.[33] With as much excitement as that grave man could muster, Douglas described the sketches as "faithful and spirited," "masterly" in delineation, an assurance he could give as he had known the places himself for the twenty years he had spent on the Columbia and in the Northwest. Farther up the Columbia, at Walla Walla, William McBean wrote another statement and John Lee Lewes a third at Fort Colvile in September.[34] Kane had been Lewes's guest for six weeks while he had painted portraits (Fig. 122), fishing scenes (Plate XXX; Figs. 123, 124), and the weird Chualpays scalp dance studies (Figs. 127–30). Not to be outdone by Douglas, Lewes pointed out that he had been in the west for forty years among the North American Indians, and emphasized that Kane's pictures of manners and customs had "a correctness, that none but a Master hand could accomplish." No Torontonian was going to think Kane an imposter.

Several other artists were painting in the Oregon and other parts of the regions covered by Kane during that same decade, and some of their pictures are identical in subject-matter with those by Kane. He was thus only one of a group of painters with similar interests. This influx of artists is understandable. The slow but irresistible movement west of American immigrants was taking them across the plains and mountains to the Colum-

bia; "Go west, young man" had become a popular phrase. Inevitably clashes with Indians occurred on the frontier, and word of these went back to the older parts of the United States. The transference of Oregon to the United States and the new provisional governments were feature stories in eastern newspapers. Books on the region were for sale in many stores, a response to the tremendous interest in the newly opening Northwest. In a day when cameras were not yet effective as tourist gadgets, only an artist's sketch could picture these new frontiers for those at home. "Go West" became a fashionable directive for artists as well as immigrants.

John Mix Stanley, the most important of these artists from the eastern United States who painted the Indians and local scenery in the Oregon, arrived during July 1847.[35] It is just possible that he reached Fort Vancouver before Kane left for the east on the first day of the month. Certainly Kane knew of Stanley's arrival shortly after his departure from Fort Vancouver. Kane received sporadic reports of the progress through Oregon of his old friend from the Detroit days of 1836 and followed his work with the greatest interest.

Stanley had first painted Indians on a visit to Galena and Fort Snelling in 1838.[36] Many sketching trips to the plains had followed, in imitation of those of Catlin. He was named official draughtsman for General S. W. Kearny's army expedition to California in 1846. On his discharge, he travelled north to sketch in the Oregon, and began painting Chinook Indians and tribes of the Willamette and Clackamas rivers. Peter Skene Ogden wrote Kane on September 2, 1847, saying that Stanley was then preparing to leave for the interior "in quest of scenery," and that Indian chiefs were "in great demand with him." He went on in the same letter to complain about the changing times on the Columbia with the influx of people: "What with Artists, Archbishops, Bishops, Priests, Nuns, Deacons and Fathers, 22 having lately arrived direct from Brest the country will be lost forever." He refers to one group of religious which had only lately come to Fort Vancouver; it included nuns who "for the salvation of the morals of the Country have been selected with more than usual precautions, being composed of old Women pass'd forty and beauty at a very low discount." However Ogden was

[32] See Thompson, *Whitman Mission*, pp. 66, 72.
[33] Appendix 10, Letter 7.
[34] Appendix 10, Letters 9, 11.
[35] Stanley's arrival was reported in the *Oregon Spectator*, July 8, 1847.
[36] For Stanley's career and his Oregon expedition see Nellie B. Pipes, "John Mix Stanley, Indian Painter," *Oregon Historical Quarterly*, 1932, pp. 250–58.

quite willing that one of the artists, Stanley, paint his portrait during the spring of 1847.[37]

Stanley went directly from Fort Vancouver to visit the Walker and Eells Mission, but arrived after Kane's departure. He sketched it from the identical spot at which Kane had sat, but the result is rather more awkward than Kane's sketch. Stanley went on to Fort Colvile and from there retraced his steps down river, intending to paint Dr. Whitman's portrait at Waiilatpu. When he was only a few miles from his destination, he heard of the slaughter on November 29, just two days earlier. He himself nearly lost his life with some Cayuse Indians, but escaped to Walla Walla when an Indian confused his identity, and then returned to Fort Vancouver.[38] He sketched both portraits and scenery in the interior. At Walla Walla he painted Peo-Peo-mox-mox and "Telo-kit," and at Fort Vancouver "Casino"; Kane had painted all three (Figs. 142, 140, Plate XXXVI).[39] Repeatedly Stanley sketched views from the same vantage points as had Kane, for instance Coffin Rock (Fig. 166), the Fort Colvile salmon fisheries (Plate XXX; Figs. 123, 124), the Pelouse and Willamette falls (Plate XXXV; Figs. 132, 162), and others. Stanley then left the Oregon for the Hawaiian Islands. After his return to the United States he exhibited his paintings in New York and throughout the New England area during 1850–51. Efforts were made to persuade the government to buy his collections for the Smithsonian Institution, and Stanley actually deposited all of his Oregon canvases there in 1853. A fire in 1865 unfortunately burned the majority of them, and many of those destroyed were the duplicates in subject-matter of works by Kane. (The collection, incidentally, had not yet been purchased.)

Captain Henry J. Warre shared with Kane more than an interest in the theatre. With his fellow officer on the defence mission, he had taken the same route as Kane from Fort Carlton to Fort Victoria just a year before Kane's arrival in the far west and had also sketched many identical subjects. The captain was a trained observer and set the landscape down in remarkable detail. British army and navy tradition held that sketching should be a gentleman officer's avocation, and indeed many, as did Warre, achieved excellence. In addition to water colours, he made on occasion detailed pencil or pen studies in his journal.[40] Hudson's Bay Company officials apparently pointed out the "tourist sights" to Warre as he passed through, just as they did for Kane and Stanley. Warre travelled up the Willamette valley, saw Indian canoe burials on the lower Columbia, and was impressed by Mount Hood. He sketched the new Fort Victoria, Fort Vancouver, the strange Kutenai canoes, and many views of the Rockies and the plains. Back in England, he took advantage of British concern for the ownership of the Oregon and published his choicest subjects as coloured lithographs.[41] Today they are collector's items.

There were still other artists in the Oregon during those years. Young Gustavus Sohon, who arrived at a slightly later date, deserves mention. A German immigrant, he had joined the American army in 1852 when little more than a boy, and then went with an exploration party to the upper Columbia River. Sohon was referred to by one of the party as "the artist, barometer-carrier, and observer . . . an intelligent German, a clever sketcher, and competent to take instrumental observations." [42] He was at the great Walla Walla council six miles from the site of the Whitman mission when in 1855 the United States negotiated the cession of 60,000 square miles of land by the Indians and set aside reservations for them. The Walla Walla, Cayuse, Nez Percé, Umatilla and other nations were represented by their chieftains and braves, and Sohon sketched the events in detail, adding portraits of the principal participants.

When Kane's work is assessed against that of other artists who worked in Oregon, his is seen to be the most complete of all the records. Similarly, the number and variety of the subjects he painted as he crossed the Canadian prairies are not equalled by any other artist of those times, by Warre or by Peter Rindisbacher, who painted at the Red River twenty years earlier, or by William G. R. Hind in his superb water colours of his trip across the prairies and over the mountains to the Cariboo golddigging with the Overlanders of '62.

A Hudson's Bay Company's autumn brigade left Fort Colvile

---

[37] Appendix 10, Letter 10. The portrait is now in the Provincial Archives of British Columbia, Victoria.

[38] For two versions of this episode see Appendix 10, Letter 14, and Nellie B. Pipes, "John Mix Stanley," p. 252.

[39] For Stanley's Oregon paintings see *Smithsonian Miscellaneous Collections* (Washington), II, 1862, 60–72.

[40] The collections of the Public Archives of Canada include the journals of Warre, in which are drawings and several water colour sketches, and also some individual water colours.

[41] Henry James Warre, *Sketches in North America and the Oregon Territory* (London 1848).

[42] For Sohon and his western sketches see John C. Ewers, *Gustavus Sohon's Portraits of Flathead and Pend d'Oreille Indians, 1854* (Washington, Smithsonian Institution, 1948).

late in September 1847 with Kane in temporary charge until the canoes got to Boat Encampment. They reached the appointed place on October 10, expecting to meet the horses from the east with the furs for the Russians for that year, but one of the delays followed which were especially irritating to brigade men accustomed to fast travel. They waited three weeks. Bored, Kane entered in his daily journal such innocuous memoranda as "Nothing of importance," "Nothing," or "Rained all day." One sunny afternoon he sketched the encampment with his tent and luggage in the foreground, and, to assist him in painting it up later as a canvas, he made a detailed study of the distant mountain peaks (Plate XXIX, Fig. 117). The brigade men varied the monotony on the 12th by paying special tribute to Kane, the "good companion" of the voyage. They made a "lobstick." A tall pine (Kane says in his diary that it was 111 feet high) was trimmed of its lower branches. On one side a smooth surface was cut and he was invited to carve his name on it. The men fired three rounds and gave three hearty cheers in his honour, and the place was thereafter to be named after him.[43] A trapper along the Columbia River rediscovered the tree in 1934. It still bore the carved words: "P. Kane, Oct. 12, 1847," and the section bearing this inscription was cut out and sent to the British Columbia Museum.

"Kane's Encampment" is no longer to be found on the map but the artist's name is commemorated in another way, in the name of a mountain peak to the east of the point where he was camping. Kane, on the arrival of the brigade from the east, went back with a small party and some of the horses to winter east of the Rockies. He says that they left Boat Encampment on October 31, but actually it may have been somewhat later because of his miscalculation of dates. Snow and cold made travelling incredibly difficult. They reached the Committee's Punch Bowl (Fig. 116) on November 2; Kane says about this lake in his journal, "Rather cold punch at present." That night was the coldest on which Kane had ever camped out, the thermometer dropping to more than 56 degrees below zero. As he attempted to wash, the water froze in a solid mass in his hair and beard and he could only thaw it out by standing so close to the fire that it scorched his face. The sun had shone brightly during the afternoon of this day in which he experienced the greatest discomfort in all his years of wanderings. He afterwards blamed the glare of the sun on the snow in the Rockies for contributing to the

[43] See note 6 to chapter XXI of *Wanderings of an Artist*, below.
[44] Cox, *The Columbia River*, p. 144, makes the same complaint.

weakness of his eyes.[44] Presumably he was so taken up with the hardships of the trail that he did not see or did not bother to mention a mountain peak just northeast of the Committee's Punch Bowl. This was named Mount Kane in his honour by the Canadian government in 1912.

Fort Edmonton was reached early in December. Kane was exhausted from exposure and hunger and was suffering not only from snow blindness but also from *mal de racquet*, the severe muscular pains experienced by those not accustomed to wearing snow-shoes. He had had to wear a pair during the later stages of the journey. But once back in the comfort of the fort, he looked forward to six months of painting on the western prairies centring his activities on Forts Edmonton and Pitt and Rocky Mountain House.

The rule of sketching only Indians was perforce relaxed shortly after he reached Fort Edmonton. A young Hudson's Bay Company man had come from Fort Pitt to claim his bride, the factor's daughter, and a gala occasion was proclaimed. The Reverend Mr. Rundle performed the marriage; the bride's father had forgotten that a minister was necessary until just a few hours before the ceremony and Rundle had been approached at the last minute. He remained to indulge in the sumptuous banquet which Mr. Harriott provided that night. Kane, who went with the couple to Fort Pitt, sketched both the gay turn-out of the teams of dogs (Fig. 101), the bride's having been purchased in Quebec and brought by the groom over thousands of miles for the occasion, and her newly decorated cariole (Fig. 103). From these sketches was painted the well-known canvas of the wedding party's departure, enigmatically titled *Winter Travelling in Dog Sleds* (Plate XXVI). Yet scratch the brusqueness which went to the point of not mentioning that the subject of the painting was a wedding party and Kane would turn out to be a very human person.

The sketches of the Assiniboin Kane was able to make by a trip to Rocky Mountain House in April gave him much satisfaction. The old head chief, Mah-Min (Plate XXVIII, Fig. 109), was so impressed that he took off his great bear's claw collar and presented it to the artist; a second chief, Wah-he-joe-tass-e-neen, feeling rather left out, requested that his portrait be taken; Kane graciously acceded (Plate XXVIII). On their return journey to Edmonton Kane and his companion were counting on a good meal at one of the food caches which, scattered about the prairies, were intended for travellers who found themselves short of supplies. They found inside it a wolverine, so fat from eating food that he could no longer squeeze between the logs to escape. The food was almost destroyed, but Kane sketched the cache in memory of a lost dinner.

Studies of unusual pipe-stems gave him even greater satisfaction. Ritual pipes were smoked by the Plains Indians before going into battle and they regarded them with the greatest awe and respect. A Cree chieftain, Kee-a-kee-ka-sa-coo-way, who arrived at Fort Pitt during Kane's visit, had been elected the tribe's pipe bearer for four years (Fig. 85). His effects in this office were carried by two horses and the pipe-stem itself was in the custody of his favourite wife but was well wrapped since no woman must see it. This was a golden opportunity to sketch just such a Plains ritual as had been suggested by Sir George Simpson. The Cree chief had pipe-stems of other chiefs which he was carrying on a war mission, and with great ceremony each was revealed to Kane who made individual sketches. Largest and finest was one ornamented with both an eagle head and several woodpecker skins attached to the stem (Fig. 88). Kane sketched the chief holding it (Fig. 86), and by some unknown means (such sacred objects were not disposed of lightly) secured an almost identical specimen for his own collection.

The wanderings on the plains were drawing to their close. Kane travelled eastward with the fur brigade down the Saskatchewan River towards Norway House where he would again meet Sir George Simpson before going on to Toronto. Near Fort Pitt came a fitting conclusion to the tour when early in June the brigade met a great party of 1,500 warriors from 1,200 lodges, members of the fierce Blackfoot, the nation best known of all Plains warriors; with them were their allies, the Blood, Sarsi, Gros Ventres and Piegan. One of the leaders of the band was Big Snake himself, a celebrated Blackfoot warrior who strode up and down cracking his whip, singing war songs and spoiling for a fight. Kane's sketch of Big Snake's brother was pronounced so lifelike that he was considered to be a medicine man and was given free entry to all the activities of the Blackfoot camp. He saw a race by naked youth on horseback (Fig. 89). He sketched Big Snake, Little Horn and the other principal chieftains (Figs. 91, 92). A Blood Indian gave his decorated shirt and trousers to his old friend Mr. Harriott, who in turn handed them over to Kane for his collection, not particularly wanting to wear them himself. Kane's final success was receipt of an invitation to attend a medicine pipe-stem dance by the assembled warriors before they continued on their war tour; his own magical powers were expected to increase the ritual's effectiveness. A good viewing place was picked for him and he made an oil sketch of the scene (Plate XXIII). Brilliant sunshine high-

lights the Indian dancers who gesticulate with their colourful feather-trimmed pipes, while onlookers, gathered before their tents, are absorbed by the ceremony. This, unique among Kane's field sketches, and the most effective of all, was a noble conclusion to his western Indian series.

Various incidents enlivened the remainder of the journey. Out from Le Pas Kane was able to move ahead in a lighter craft and could sketch the approaching brigade of 24 boats; in one of them he had travelled many miles. Their loads, which had in them pemmican, grease, buffalo skins and other cargo, were less than they should have been because the Blackfoot had done no trading that year.[45] At Le Pas Dr. John Rae and Sir John Richardson had passed them, going to the northwest in search of Sir John Franklin, who was lost in the Arctic, and about whom even Queen Victoria was worrying. They made more impression on Kane then he did on them; Rae's journal mentions meeting the brigade, but has no reference to Kane.[46] Kane's travelling companion at this time was the Rev. J. Hunter who had taken him to visit Indian lodges during the westward trip. There was a delay at Norway House before the final dash through to Upper Canada, and Kane spent his time in shooting and fishing for sturgeon and Winnipeg gold-eye. He did not cook the latter since a company man had said "They eat like mud." He often had with him an 110-year-old Eskimo about whom a strange story was told. Kane repeats it in *Wanderings*. When his wife died during childbirth, the Eskimo gave suck to his starving infant. Milk flowed from his nipple after a few days and the baby was saved. One reader of the 1859 edition of Kane's book has written in the margin: "Cum grano salis." (Fig. 76)

Kane crossed what is now northern Ontario with a swiftly moving band of canoes but had another delay at Fort Frances. He sketched Indians and portages at every opportunity, realizing that he might never again have the opportunity. His last field sketch pictures the old Ojibwa chieftain, Maydoc-game-kin-ungee (Plate XI), proudly wearing the scarlet coat given by the Hudson's Bay Company to those natives whom they wished especially to honour and a chief's medal as the Queen's loyal subject. Sault Ste Marie was reached on October 1, 1848, and Kane went from there to Toronto by comfortable Great Lakes steamer.

No artist ever travelled and lived for three years more cheaply than Kane had done on his 1846–48 wanderings. He

[45] Journal of Archdeacon J. Hunter (see note 27), June 12, 1848.
[46] See, however, Earl of Southesk, *Saskatchewan and the Rocky Mountains . . .* (new ed., Edmonton 1969), p. 5.

had had free hospitality and travelling privileges with the Hudson's Bay Company men, but he was nevertheless a frugal man with simple needs. A clay pipe of tobacco and a quart of rum were his occasional concessions to good living. These were drawn from company stores at various posts. Clothes wore out; he needed, for example, two new shirts, a new Scotch bonnet, a pair of blankets, and the combs so necessary for sanitary reasons when living with the Indians. He anticipated the necessity of making small gifts to the Indians as token payment for posing and bartering for specimens to be added to his collection: for these purposes he had glass beads, scarlet and blue cloth, looking glasses and other minor items. For his Babine blanket he paid "five pounds of tobacco, ten charges of ammunition, one blanket, one pound of beads, two check shirts, and one ounce of vermilion." [47] His carved mask cost him a pound of tobacco. Some items were bought from the Company: a northwest coast cedar hat was purchased at Fort Victoria for 1/1; a "raincoat" made from seal intestine by the Aleuts had come from the store at Fort Simpson. A painted buffalo robe to which he refers was bought for him at a price of 15/- from the store at York Factory to which it had been brought from the prairies (Fig. 95). In payment for goods advanced from company stores, he turned in skins of buffalo shot on the prairies at 3/9 each and moose skins at 6/- each. Thus on reaching Toronto he only owed the Company £14/6/9 for his transcontinental journey. He remitted it promptly to Sir George Simpson.

Kane reached Toronto on October 13, 1848. He intended to start painting canvases from his sketches at once but could not since some pictures intended for Sir George Simpson had been damaged in transit and these had to be repaired. Rumours circulated about his remarkable journey and his sketches, and he was induced to exhibit the whole collection publicly in Toronto's "Old" City Hall on Front Street for a small entrance fee. The building was then being used as a market, new quarters having been erected for council meetings in the 1830s. The mayor and city clerk may have backed the exhibition, since Kane had painted a portrait of the mayor, George Gurnett, who was editor of the Toronto *Courier* (Fig. 8). Thomas Daly, the clerk, was an amateur artist and Kane had done a profile drawing of him one day (Fig. 11) while in a discussion with him. The catalogue of the show (see Appendix 3) lists 240 sketches. Indian souvenirs provided another curiosity for the exhibition, which opened on November 9, 1848. Kane regretted that he

[47] *Wanderings of an Artist*, p. 107 below.

had no large canvases; these he felt would have made the show truly a success.

Only visitors who would have been impressed by mere size, however, might have considered that the showing would have been improved by the addition of canvases. Kane had lavished the greatest care on both his water colour and his oil sketches during the western trip. Landscapes bloom with the glow of the clear Canadian atmosphere. Drawings of heads are masterpieces in miniature with a careful expression of character, luminous backgrounds, and appealing colour. All of the sketches in the exhibition were painted with a factual and objective approach which could not fail to speak directly to those who saw them. By contrast, a similar show of Catlin's works would have revealed a nervous, romantic air. Curiously, when Kane painted up his sketches into canvases, he altered his approach, losing the lucid freshness of his first impressions by introducing subjective overtones. These were intended to make his canvases into more profound works of art, but by present-day standards they quite failed to do so.

The newspapers gave the artist an ovation. Hugh Scobie, a local journalist who had published the catalogue, had made a few preliminary references to the show in his *British Colonist* by way of publicity, but printed a more extensive commentary on November 17, 1848. As was typical of mid 19th century reviewers, he paid little attention to the aesthetic qualities in the paintings but much to subject-matter and treatment. His facts were not always strictly accurate, but the review demonstrates the high regard in which Kane's sketches were held by his contemporaries and the sense Torontonians had of the uniqueness of this first great vista of the west. The review is entitled "Kane's Indian Gallery," and reads in part:

The difficulty is, to select a number among so many that are interesting, for the first attention. Perhaps a spirited sketch portrait of a Blackfoot chief, on a grey horse, in all the pride and picturesque splendor of the Indian hunter, is the favorite with most visitors [presumably this is a lost sketch from which was painted Plate XX, "The Man that Always Rides"]; but we do not see that it does more credit to his artistic powers than some very beautiful sketches near it, of scenery on the western prairies, some of which, we are informed, have been requested by Sir George Simpson, than whom there must not be a better judge of the fidelity of Mr. Kane's pencil. A striking characteristic of Mr. Kane's paintings, particularly in their present state, is the truthfulness. Nothing has been sacrificed to effect —no exaggerated examples of costumes—no incredible distortions of features—are permitted to move our wonder, or exalt our conceptions of what is sufficiently wild and striking without improvements. In this respect he contrasts very favorably with Mr. Catlin, who certainly indulged in artistic license to the utmost extent; but in no respect, as an artist, do we think him inferior to his predecessor—in some respects he is superior. There is extraordinary spirit in most of his sketches, whether in water colour or in oil, particularly in the figures, and when we consider that many of them were finished on the spot as we see them, frequently under the most unfavorable circumstances, it is difficult to speak in too high terms of the energy, enterprise and skill of our young fellow townsman. The sketches on the western side of the Rocky Mountains, ground scarcely trodden by any traveller before Mr. Kane, and certainly never before made known to us through the medium of the pencil, are exceedingly interesting. We have here, for the first time, some of the most picturesque scenes of that region; those mysterious "Shining Mountains" of Jonathan Carver, and the older travellers, which are environed to this day by scarcely less romance and interest, than they were invested with by his imagination. We see here the wild natives of Paget's [sic] Sound and its environs, the most barbarous and debased of the Indian tribes, and, at the same time, by a singular anomaly, the most advanced in regular trade, and even manufacture. . . . We think that every mother in this favored city will be interested in a sketch of a poor little infant undergoing the barbarous and preposterous process of having its skull flattened [Fig. 170]. To the portraits of individuals are added sketches of their habitations, their canoes, their methods of the chase, and of the wild scenery of New Caledonia, including the most valuable of our possessions on that coast—Vancouver's Island. Mr. Kane has also made a very extensive and curious collection of specimens of the arts and manufactures of the natives—one, we must say, which gives the visitor a high opinion of their ingenuity and their capabilities of future civilization. The present exhibition contains 240 sketches of persons and scenes belonging to the most interesting regions on both sides of the Rocky Mountains, and these are, we are informed, but part of the contents of Mr. Kane's portfolio. As his absence from the city has not much exceeded two years, in which time he has journeyed many thousands of miles, and twice crossed the Continent, he must have laboured with a degree of diligence and industry deserving of the highest commendation. . . .

Other Toronto newspapers also commented. George Brown's *Globe* for November 15 noted with typical Scottish reticence and scepticism that it had "no doubt" that the Indian portraits and northwestern scenes were "particularly accurate," but its reporter was much more impressed with Kane's large stuffed buffalo head, also on display. The *Christian Guardian* (November 15) and the *Patriot* (November 13) both mentioned individual works. François Lucie's portrait (Plate XXVII), the Blackfoot on horseback, and the view of Mount St. Helens with the smoke cone (Plate XLI) drew their special admiration. One sketch of Mount Hood was described as "perhaps the most perfect picture in the room" (this sketch has not been located). Toronto in the 1840s lacked an art school and the learning

process was almost wholly the copying of available paintings. Most of the newspapers admonished young artists to seize the unusual opportunity of Kane's exhibition to learn something of their craft. Scobie noted:

The sketches are of varied degrees of forwardness from the first outlines in the artist's pocket-book to the more careful and finished oil painting—a circumstance that makes the whole collection particularly interesting to all who study art.

The *Patriot* made a similar recommendation:

Those of our young friends particularly, who may be seeking instruction in the art of drawing, we strongly advise to study these sketches closely, to mark well their simplicity and *elegance*, to note how free they are from exaggeration of tone or colour, and how truly the *perspective* is maintained throughout. We advise the young draftsman or draftswoman to observe all this, and then go, follow Mr. Kane's example, and copy from nature, for there is a harmony in nature not to be found elsewhere.

The philosophy closely parallels that of Emerson and the artists of the Hudson River School south of the border who found in the natural world a perfect harmony.

Kane abruptly closed the exhibition. He was impatient to begin painting his canvases. But the showing had given Torontonians their first comprehensive look at the west and it must have been a factor in turning thoughts in Upper Canada to the promise of that region, then much neglected. But this period of unawareness was coming to an end and men like William Hamilton Merritt would shortly be visiting Chicago and the American west to assess progress there. Kane's exhibition may even have been, ironically, an indirect cause of stirring up the resentment against the Hudson's Bay Company which was the result of the turning of hungry eyes in Canada West towards the great land mass of the prairies as a place for future expansion. There would come a time when the pressure of the Canadian government would result in the Company's having to surrender its control and open the Northwest for development.

So successful had been Kane's Toronto showing that Sir George Simpson offered his patronage for a similar exhibition in Montreal.[48] Kane declined by saying that "unfortunately my circumstances at present do not permit it." His canvases were exhibited at the Art Association of Montreal shortly after 1900. The only time when the sketches seem again to have been put on public view was at the Winnipeg Board of Trade in 1922.

One jarring note resulted from the 1848 exhibition. Captain

---

[48] Appendix 10, Letter 17.

John O'Brien, whose son was to be the first president of the Royal Canadian Academy, wrote to the newspapers about it and his excess of enthusiasm and praise displeased Sir George Simpson. It caused a first break in the cordial relations between Simpson and Kane. But there were compensations. The artist met his second patron, George W. Allan, probably at the exhibition. Kane had breakfast with Allan on a morning in December and a close friendship between the two persisted thereafter.

Kane's field sketches were split into two groups during his lifetime and many still remain in two collections although items were occasionally sold and have thus become separated from the main bodies. One group, comprising over three hundred pencil and water colour sketches, passed with a number of canvases into the ownership of the Hon. George W. Allan and eventually to a descendant, Major R. Willis. He presented them to the Royal Ontario Museum in 1946 where, with Kane's canvases already in that institution, they formed an amazingly rich collection.

Other sketches, many in oil on paper and others in water colour and pencil, were in Kane's studio at his death and passed to his widow who kept them as poignant reminders of her husband's adventures. A son, Paul Kane II, moved as a homesteader to Manitoba, a part of Canada in which his father had played such an illustrious role as a painter. The sketches were sent to him after his mother's death in 1892. He kept this pictorial record of his father's frontier for years in a small walnut box in the spare bedroom at Rathwell, Manitoba. These western sketches, unmounted and so fragile that they could hardly be handled without damage, were unknown to Canadians generally but on wet Sunday afternoons they were brought out and examined on the parlour table to the delight of Kane's grandchildren. Paul Kane III, in ailing health, sold a group of over two hundred sketches in 1957 to H. J. Lutcher Stark. His wife has turned them over to the Stark Foundation, and this unusual collection is thus available for study for the first time.

III. A Trip to the Red River, 1849

While Kane was working on his final four paintings for Sir George Simpson, an opportunity came for another western trip. Sir Edward Poore, 23 years old, a restless young officer of the Scots Fusilier Guards with a hankering for adventure and excitement, was contemplating a two-year journey through the Rockies and on to the Sandwich Islands. He offered Kane £200 a year plus expenses as "conductor, guide and interpreter" to him and his party.[1] The artist accepted and wrote to Sir George Simpson on the eve of his departure saying that it would afford him "the opportunity of greatly enlarging my present collection." Then, as if with a twinge of conscience about not having completed his undertaking, he promised to take his sketches along with him to the Red River and there finish his copying on canvas for Sir George.[2]

Sir Edward Poore, who signed his letters to his mother as "(the wild) E. Poore," had come from England to America in 1846. It was rumoured that a young English lady had refused his advances. He visited old friends in Cobourg, probably two brothers-in-law; then he hastened to see the wild west at St. Louis where he hunted buffalo, elk, deer, antelope, grouse, raccoons, turkeys, bears and wolves. A month later he was back again in Cobourg; his jacket and money had been stolen on the return journey, he had had to pawn his pistols in Buffalo, and he arrived with just $1 left in his pocket. The young baronet bought a house at nearby Grafton, and there he played polo with friends.[3] But adventure seemed a necessity to him and the far west beckoned again; a trip across the Rockies with some friends was the answer he found this time for a periodic outburst of energy. Companions on the trip were to be a Mr. Franklin and Charles Philips. He had probably met or heard of Kane in Cobourg where the artist was courting Miss Harriet Clench, and he actually purchased a number of his western paintings which were sent home to England. (Their whereabouts today are unknown.) He seems to have had aspirations of becoming a western painter himself since Kane was to be cast in the roles of tutor and guide.

George Allan gave one of his breakfast parties in Kane's honour on April 13, 1849, the day before the departure. Captain and Mrs. J. H. Lefroy (Mrs. Allan's sister), and a Mr. Heath were also guests. The party was, unhappily, a prelude to frustration.

Poore chose to travel through the United States to the Red River rather than by the difficult Lake Superior route. From Buffalo the party went to Sandusky, and then embarked at Cincinnati on the steamer *Dr. Franklin II* which carried them down the Ohio, up the Mississippi through St. Louis, and on to Galena, Illinois, which they reached on May 2. Cholera on

---

[1] Royal Ontario Museum, Reminiscences of Paul Kane by Mrs. [Allan] Cassels. For letters relating to Sir Edward Poore see Appendix 10.

[2] Hudson's Bay Company Archives, D5/25, Kane to Simpson, April 13, 1849.

[3] Information supplied by Mr. E. C. Guillet.

Plate VI. Sketchbook page: Indian youth wearing chief's medal and Indian girl with beads. ROM946.15.35; CrIII-77.

board the ship gave them a bad scare but they reached Saint Peter unscathed and there they disembarked. They started overland for the Red River on May 15 with one cart, five horses, five mules, and a guide with his own horse. On the way they bought still another cart and horse, and a canoe for crossing the many streams they were likely to meet. Bad luck dogged their heels, and relations grew more and more tense as feelings were aroused by the frustrations from the variety of difficulties they encountered. Poore wrote to his mother:

Philips one morn tied his horse up to the cart with the canoe on it (the canoe is to cross the rivers with, many very bad), some thing frightened him & he threw his head up & broke about 4 ft. off the end of it. All the way we have had mud, water, etc. for it has been a very wet season & the carts would stick & we had to get into the water—Frank, the Guide & myself often up to our waists in water, a thing Kane or Philips would never do if it was possible to avoid.[4]

On another day a cart upset and most of the provisions were lost in the water. Four horses and two pack mules bolted for freedom before it had been righted. Poore and Franklin had to pursue the runaways over treacherous ground, and did not return with the missing animals until late in the evening, only to find that Kane and Philips had eaten the last of their supplies. The two made "supper off *Tea leaves they had used and sugar.*" On yet another occasion a horse kicked Poore in the mouth; two teeth were lost, and after this injury he mailed a section of his upper jaw-bone to his mother. Philips almost cut his foot off with an axe. Kane evidently must have considered these young gentlemen as greenhorns and perhaps treated them accordingly.

Furious with the world, Poore dismissed Kane at Fort Garry as impertinent, overbearing and incapable of fulfilling his contract; Kane, he said, could not speak the Indian dialects or act as a guide since he had travelled west before by the easier means of the Hudson's Bay Company's fur brigades. In fact Poore also accused Kane of telling tales to the officials of the Company, with the result that passage was refused to these dashing young gentlemen. Actually Lord Elgin had written Sir George Simpson requesting assistance for Poore before he had set out, and Sir George had granted hospitality at company posts in view of the high quarters from which the request had come, but he had made no promise about passage with the brigades.

The party arrived at Fort Garry on June 18. Philips went to bed, an invalid, and spent two months there recuperating. While they were waiting for Philips, Poore and Franklin went on a three-week buffalo hunt along the Red River, but shot

nothing; the buffalo had already vanished from the Winnipeg prairies. The two then departed for the Pacific on July 27, leaving behind Philips and Kane. They hired an Indian and a half-breed, and they took along seven horses and eight mules. At one point Franklin shot a buffalo; Poore had just taken aim at the same animal but his horse had tripped in a gopher hole at that moment and he had not had time to pull the trigger. Poore drew a caricature of the incident in a letter to his mother, seemingly the only art work he attempted on the journey. Hudson's Bay Company officials were much concerned about the inexperienced travellers when they reached Fort Edmonton and decided to allow them to go with the brigade across the Rockies. Poore was involved in an escapade at Mountain Portage during the crossing, and the result was the accidental shooting of a company employee by one of the men in the party.

Poore and Franklin arrived at Fort Vancouver in November; the company officials there found them "harmless creatures [who] take life easily, giving no trouble."[5] Kane had been much perturbed about the whole frustrating trip and wrote about it to his old friend, Peter Skene Ogden. Ogden's reply from Fort Vancouver in March 1851 reads in part:

I was disappointed in not seeing you here with Sir Edward. The latter did not make a *deep* impression with the *Vancouvery Dandys* and still less with the military who often remarked he could be no Gent., having no regard to dress—so you see the external garment is their criterion of a Gent.—although I am not overfond of dress, still I am of opinion that rules of propriety should in all things be strictly observed which I must say Sir Edward lost sight of. What has become of the Man and friend Franklin, truly a free young Man.[6]

Poore, by his own account, wore "*long hair, earrings,* leather trousers fringed & all the other fixings belonging to a half breed" when he was at Fort Garry; evidently the "hippy" garb was retained for the rest of his journey. He and Franklin continued on to Fort Victoria in December. Then word is said to have come from England that the young lady on whom Poore had set his affections was ready to receive his advances.[7] The young baronet hurried home, married, and was back in Cobourg in 1851 where his son was born two years later. Shortly afterwards, Sir Edward took his family back to England. There he left them while he rushed off to Australia; he lived out the rest of his life on the sub-continent as a wandering expatriate, having

[4] Appendix 10, Letter 19.
[5] *Eden Colvile's Letters, 1849–1852,* ed. E. E. Rich (Hudson's Bay Record Society Publications, vol. XIX, 1956), p. 190.
[6] Appendix 10, Letter 22.
[7] Mrs. Cassels, Reminiscences.

completely broken his family ties. He died in Adelaide in 1893, a penniless miner, on his way to the gold fields.[8]

Philips, left behind at Fort Garry in 1849, recovered. He, Kane and the retiring factor, James Sinclair, left the Red River for Canada on August 30, travelling by the United States. John Ballenden, Kane's old friend from Sault Ste Marie, who had been transferred to Fort Garry, kept Sir George Simpson informed about developments. The departure of Philips was advisable, he reported, since he had given indiscreet attentions to ladies who were rather beneath his station, and they might have become troublesome.[9]

No sketches were made by Kane during this visit to Fort Garry, so far as is known. The governor-general, the Earl of Elgin, scion of an ancient Scottish family, whose father had brought the Elgin Marbles to England from the Parthenon, called with the Countess of Elgin at Kane's Toronto studio a year later, on August 16, 1850. They came to see his "pictures taken while travelling in the West with Sir E. Poore."[10] Presumably they actually looked at sketches brought back from the 1845–48 expeditions.

IV. One Hundred Western Canvases

Kane had rented a studio on King Street, Toronto, after he returned from his western wanderings. W. H. G. Kingston, the English novelist, and his bride, on their wedding trip to Canada, found the artist at work in it during 1853, the year of his own marriage, and described him in his studio surroundings. That morning, as they recalled, "We found our way up a steep, high stair to an apartment at the top of the house, more like a poet's chamber than a painter's studio, where we found the artist at work." Here, Kane reminisced genially with his guests about his adventures, and attracted Kingston's goodwill:

His appearance, though roughish from the style of life he had led, much prepossessed me in his favour, and still more did his manners, which were truly pleasing and courteous. He is more like a real old master of the genuine art-loving, gain-scorning, fame-desiring stamp, than one expects to

meet in these utilitarian, gold-seeking days. He works hard, but steadily. . . .[1]

The tools of the artist's craft were around the studio. There was, for instance, a highly prized mahogany paint box. When the top was lifted access could be had to the upper section with its storage for bottles: these square glass bottles were filled with his pigments, ochre, vermilion, blues, lamp black and others, and his mediums.[2] Beneath, sliding from the box's front, was a drawer filled with fine stubble and sable brushes. Among the Kane family papers are receipts of the mid 1850s for his painting supplies—stretching frames for the canvas at 15/- a half dozen, canvas at 5/6 a yard, and sable brushes at 6/3 a dozen. Most of the supplies were bought from A. J. Pell, a famous old Toronto firm of art suppliers. Kane's manual when he needed technical advice was F. T. Burton's *The Artist's Ascunum*.[3]

Kane's method of working up his canvases was discovered only recently during the course of restoration of one of the Hon. George W. Allan's pictures; it was found to be backed by an unfinished painting. Kane had applied a priming coat of white lead on the canvas. This was his usual practice with undercoating for his oils; in a similar way he had applied a coat of white lead to his paper before painting oil sketches during his transcontinental tour.[4] After the priming coat, he had washed in his sky in pale blue and his land area in a greenish tone. He then drew in his subject-matter with a fine brush in burnt umber as a guide for the more detailed painting in richer pigment and full colour.[5]

It was the artist's plan that his studio works should be a cycle of the round number of one hundred, made up of canvases based on his western sketches and covering all phases of Indian life and the landscape in the territories where they lived. The cycle was to provide a panorama from the Great Lakes to the Pacific, and be a memorial to the frontier and its Indian peoples. The preservation of his work for Canadians was Kane's fondest wish, just as Catlin and Stanley in the United States hoped that their paintings would be purchased for posterity.

Kane had commenced painting his western canvases immedi-

[8] An obituary appeared in *The Age* (Melbourne, Australia), December 21, 1893, under the heading "A Strange Career."

[9] Hudson's Bay Company Archives, D5/25, Ballenden to Simpson, August 29, 1849.

[10] Kane family papers, letter from F. A. Grant, aide-de-camp to the Earl of Elgin, to Kane, August 16, 1850.

[1] W. H. G. Kingston, *Western Wanderings; or, A Pleasure Trip in the Canadas* (London 1856), I, 44.

[2] Appendix 8 gives an analysis of these bottles.

[3] F. T. Burton, *The Artist's Ascunum; or, The Essence of a Variety of Useful and Entertaining Arts Carefully and Perspicaciously Laid Down, the Greater Part from Actual Experiment* (Stamford, England, 1812).

[4] Information supplied by F. duPont Cornelius.

[5] Information supplied by Mrs. E. Phillimore, Royal Ontario Museum.

ately after returning to Toronto in 1848. He nevertheless had to regret that his exhibition of sketches at the City Hall that year included no large works; they had not yet been completed. His first duty had been to paint fourteen canvases for Sir George Simpson, but they were only one step towards the hundred works since they were preliminary studies to be copied in replica later. The Simpson group was evidently finished at the close of 1849.[6]

By 1851 Kane had finished some of his planned group and eight canvases were exhibited that autumn at the Upper Canada Provincial Exhibition, in Brockville. He attended in person. Visitors picked him out as a celebrity wherever his striking face was seen in the crowds. The reviews were lengthy and lauded his work. One commented on the unique character of the Indian customs displayed, and on Kane's superb compositions which were sometimes "a little similar to some of Poussins." His inclusion of intriguing details, such as the prairie rose—an unfamiliar and "pretty wild flower"—in the foreground of the picture of the Indian horse race (Fig. 89), was a virtue. Above all, the fact that "there is not a fold of the robe, or plait of the dress, which has not been sketched from nature" was commendable.[7] Another writer, supporting acquisition of these canvases for future viewers, contributed this paragraph: "It is hoped that Canada may at some future day possess the entire collection of this great artist, which must be of great importance in a national point of view, as well as be the means of preserving memorials of these interesting tribes when they have entirely disappeared before the face of the white men."[8] This hope that his canvases would be purchased for the Canadian people was echoed in an article in the *Journal of Education for Upper Canada* the following spring. The author was almost certainly the journal's editor, Egerton Ryerson, a respected educationist who would be known as the father of a new provincial school system. This second comment went even further than had the previous one by suggesting that the paintings should form the nucleus for a "national picture gallery"; it would thus be possible to "secure them to the country, as well as gratify the patriotic desire of the talented artist."[9] The government showed no inclination to make a move in the direction suggested. It was already giving help to Kane.

This assistance by the government involved dealings which were to drag on for years. On July 26, 1850, a petition had been presented to the House of Assembly by Kane asking for financial aid so that he might paint up canvases from his hundreds of sketches; it would eliminate the necessity of his interrupting his painting of the west to undertake commissions and teaching in order to keep solvent.[10] Although such help was rather radical at the time, government subsidy to the arts and letters was not unknown. Kane probably was aware of Théophile Hamel's commission from the Canadian government to prepare portraits of leading legislative figures. It also granted money later to Abbé Léon Provancher to assist him with a first scientific illustrated work on Canadian flora (published in 1862). Similar assistance to scholars in the United States had been given by Congress and almost certainly Kane knew that Henry Schoolcraft had received money to prepare and publish his books on North American Indians. Kane had, indeed, purchased Schoolcraft's first volume. Catlin had made repeated attempts to persuade Congress to buy his Indian paintings. There was thus more than enough precedent for Kane's request for help.

Governments are not noted for hasty action. There was no decision about his petition. Next year it was revived under the joint sponsorship of J.-C. Taché and a Mr. Uniacke, and presented again on June 4, 1851.[11] Taché reported to Kane on the night of August 5 that the petition had been debated that day and he waxed eloquent about the praise which had been heaped on the artist:

This day, mark it, is a day of reward for your exertions as an artist. The Legislature of your country have eulogized you, the most eminent men have praised your talents. Two hours have been expended in exalting your talents and your energy. This is not flattery, this is the truth.[12]

Surely on no other occasion has a Canadian parliament spent two hours in eulogizing an artist. The grant was referred to a committee for consideration, and a parliamentary delegation which then called at Kane's studio was duly impressed by his work. Being of a practical turn characteristic of a legislature where prudent farmers and tradespeople held much power, members were aghast at paying out money without tangible return. (The Canada Council was still a century in the future.)

---

[6] See Appendix 10, Letter 17. The Simpson collection was later dispersed and the fate of the pictures is not known although it is thought the Coe Collection may have some.

[7] *Anglo-American Magazine* (Toronto), I, July–Dec. 1852, 371–74.

[8] *Canadian Agriculturist* (Toronto), III, 1851, 228.

[9] *Journal of Education for Upper Canada* (Toronto), V, June 1852, 95.

[10] Province of Canada, Legislative Assembly, *Journals*, 1850, p. 194. A letter of 1851 in the Kane family papers refers to his teaching.

[11] Province of Canada, Legislative Assembly, *Journals*, 1851, p. 49.

[12] Appendix 10, Letter 24.

The committee recommended that, instead of making an outright gift, the government should purchase twelve paintings for £500. They actually talked about half of this sum, but finally the larger amount was set aside by the Assembly. Lord Mark Kerr, Lord Elgin's aide, and himself an artist of some ability, called at Kane's studio with two other gentlemen. They chose twelve subjects, evidently from canvases already painted, and it was agreed that the artist should paint replicas for the government. The matter was settled by August 30 and Kane continued painting the hundred canvases of his western cycle without monetary worries.

Delivery of the canvases to the government was, however, delayed repeatedly. These were the years of wandering parliaments in the united province. Shortly after the commission had been given, the whole administration moved to Quebec, and without a reminder on his door step as it were, Kane did nothing about fulfilling his obligations. A note came in 1853 requesting that the canvases be sent to Quebec. Nothing was done. The government returned to Toronto in 1855: still no pictures had been sent. The Canadian commissioners for the great world's fair to be held in Paris during that year wanted the works commissioned by the government to hang in the Canadian displays, but, not having them, they were forced to borrow several from George Allan. He had purchased and received the entire set of one hundred canvases, which Kane had considered his primary task.

The selection of Kane's paintings for the Paris showing gave satisfaction in Canada although the rest of the Canadian display was bitterly criticized. One satirical reviewer pointed out that it might have been more appropriate to send a rural "outhouse" to Paris as a sample of Canada's architecture than to provide a vaunted model of Brock's Monument at Queenston as a sample of her progress in the arts. But the same reviewer felt: "It is a redeeming mercy that Paul Kane's fine pictures, have not been rejected by the 'inquest of taste.' He is almost the only artist, in the proper sense of the word, that Canada boasts of, and I cherish strong hopes that he is destined at once to immortalize himself, and do honour to the land of his nativity." [13] Better still, the canvases were well received by French critics. We do not know which paintings were sent to Paris except for the group portrait of the Blackfoot chiefs, which was singled out for special comment (Fig. 92 is a replica). Kane must have been highly gratified; he secured and kept the book published by the Canadian government which dealt with its participation at the fair and mentioned his canvases. [14]

The government, exasperated at what seemed to be deliberate stalling, now threatened to sue Kane for non-delivery. The artist appeared in person during May 1856 before a committee of the legislature and requested that it not resort to a lawsuit. He repeated his verbal representations in a letter dated May 21, admitting that he had anticipated that the commission would come up again, stating that he had begun the twelve works, and promising that he would soon have them completed. In justification of his actions he wrote that under a private agreement with the committee of 1851 he was excused from delivery of the paintings before he had published his book since any display of them would probably infringe his copyright. [15] Delivery of the canvases was indeed made shortly after this intervention by the government and Kane supplied extensive notes on the paintings. [16]

The twelve canvases hung in the Library of Parliament until 1879, when they were transferred to the Speaker's Chambers. By 1900 the collection was reduced to eleven. [17] Five were delivered to the National Gallery of Canada about that time and the balance were transferred to its collection in 1956. [18] Hamel's paintings have, however, been retained for display in the halls of the Houses of Parliament. The Kane canvases were thus among the first bought for what became the national collection and in a sense their purchase met Egerton Ryerson's suggestion although the group was only given to the National Gallery after many years.

George William Allan, who was Kane's patron and close friend in these years, had first met him in 1848. He was then a young lawyer, son of a leading Canadian capitalist and a man of broad interests. The breakfasts at which he was accustomed to entertain were famous and he indulged his more personal interests at the pleasant morning hour before commencing the day's business activities. He had studied art when he was a boy at Upper Canada College under Thomas Drury, Kane's old master, and his interest in art persisted; he was for a time president of the Ontario Society of Artists. Other activities mark him out as having been a remarkable man. He later became a fellow of the Royal Geographical Society of England, president of the

[13] *Anglo-American Magazine* (Toronto), VI, Jan.–June 1855, 298.

[14] *Canada at the Universal Exhibition of 1855,* printed by order of the Legislative Assembly (Toronto 1856).

[15] See Appendix 12.

[16] See Appendix 6.

[17] The canvas showing Boat Encampment had been lost. It has been stated that it was burned in a fire in the Parliament Buildings at Quebec in 1860.

[18] National Gallery of Canada, *Catalogue of Paintings and Sculptures*, III, 152–56.

Horticultural Society of Toronto, the Upper Canada Bible Society, the Toronto Conservatory of Music, and the Historical Society of Ontario. He was a Canadian senator from 1867 and Speaker of the Senate from 1888 to 1891.

Mrs. Allan Cassels, Allan's daughter, recalled Kane had been depressed in 1851 when the government agreed to buy no more than a few canvases, and threatened to set out again for the Pacific; he was only restrained by his coming marriage to Harriet Clench.[19] But his luck was about to change. Allan, who had been abroad for some time and had lost his young wife in Italy, returned to Canada in July 1852. Three months later his father also died and he inherited a sizeable fortune. Alone in the world, Allan now set out to indulge his interests. He commissioned family portraits from George-Théodore Berthon, the respected French painter then living in Toronto; he purchased water colours from Lucius O'Brien, a rising young artist who like Allan had attended Upper Canada College; and he came to Kane's rescue. He bought the entire cycle of one hundred western paintings on which Kane had been working so diligently and which were evidently virtually completed at this time,[20] together with the Indian curiosities which Kane had put in storage. The paintings cost $20,000 and this sum the artist frugally saved; his wife had a small inheritance on which they were able to live.

It was 1853 when Kane married and gave up his roamings. He was 44, and must have felt that he had spent long enough in contemplating his father's instructions not to take such a step until he had considered it thoroughly. His bride, Harriet Clench of Cobourg, was the daughter of F. S. Clench, the cabinet-maker whom Kane had known before he went to the United States in 1836. She must have been sympathetic to his work, since she was herself an artist of some quality who painted flower studies and occasional landscapes illustrating Ontario's pioneer period. With her she brought a substantial dowry, and evidently her father gave the young couple as a wedding present sufficient furniture from the Clench factory for their home. Much of it was black walnut. The artist's house was furnished with it at the time of his death, and it still graces the homes of the Kanes' grandchildren.

The paintings Kane sold to Allan hung at Moss Park, the stately Georgian home in Toronto into which Allan had moved following his father's death. There they remained until after his own death in 1901. Allan maintained a keen interest in Kane's paintings and ethnological material, and he himself gathered a number of objects of natural history and curios. These objects were all arranged in the hall of his home and a large room known as "The Museum." The Indian artefacts and stuffed birds were a special concern, and when he was away he sent messages back from Ottawa and other places to Wiggins and Hogarth, his gardener and coachman. "Please see that they put camphor in the buffalo case and into the boxes with Paul Kane's things." "I hope the Indian dresses have been thoroughly overhauled. I am very much afraid of those confounded moths getting among my birds." "Has the Museum been smoked yet?" The Museum, as Mrs. Cassels recalls, was a constant source of pleasure to Allan and his family:

The extra fire, blazing in the Museum on a wintry Sunday afternoon, was a treat to all of us. While the elders gathered around the hearth, the children played together, inspecting "things" which were really a fearful joy when faced alone, such as the Indian scalp, or the flathead skull Paul Kane had risked his life to get. I am certain we were far more interested in the Indian portraits than in any of our forebears. And to be told off to "show the Museum" to a visitor was a matter of pride, and when it proved to be a good-natured, long-suffering one, a pleasure, at all events for us.[21]

Financial difficulties for the Allan family following the death of the Hon. George W. forced the sale of many assets. The Kane paintings were purchased by Sir Edmund Osler, who donated them in 1912 to the Royal Ontario Museum; its great collections were then being amassed with extraordinary speed by Dr. C. T. Currelly. Kane's dream that his paintings might be preserved intact in a public collection for the nation was thus partly realized. The ethnological collections were donated later by the Allan family to the Manitoba Museum of Science and History, and so these artefacts are now on the prairies where many of them had been collected.

Of the 100 canvases, 41 are single portraits of Indians representative of tribes scattered from the Great Lakes area to Fort Victoria on the distant Pacific. The heads are those of men and women about whom Kane tells dramatic tales—and they look the part. A second group illustrate Indian life and customs. The more colourful sides of the Indian culture are shown in pictures of the ritual pipe-stem dance on the prairies (Plate XXIII), the chaos of the buffalo hunt (Plate XVII), or the strange incantations of medicine men in the Pacific northwest (Figs. 190, 191). A third group is made up of landscapes, showing majestic scenes of nature and also forts and towns on the wilderness frontier.

[19] Royal Ontario Museum, Reminiscences of Paul Kane by Mrs. Cassels.
[20] Appendix 5 gives a list of the canvases turned over to Allan in 1856. Some substitutions were evidently made later.
[21] Reminiscences by Mrs. Cassels.

Kane's landscapes are never quiet pastorals suitable for dreaming poets, but rather depict settlements made famous by the activities of Hudson's Bay Company fur traders, or places with lively visual interest, such as the Kakabeka Falls portage (Plate XII), the storied rocks of the "Ki-use" maidens (Fig. 135), or Mount St. Helens in mysterious eruption (Plate XLI).

These canvases are based on the sketches completed in his four years of travel. Some are simply enlargements of them. Other, more elaborate compositions are assemblages created from several small sketches re-grouped for a large scene. *Winter Travelling* (Plate XXVI), for example, is based on studies of elaborately decorated dogs and of the new sled, and of trees heavily laden with snow (Figs. 100–103). All these elements were combined into a trial pencil sketch before the canvas was begun.

To appreciate the canvases fully, they must be contrasted with the preliminary studies in the sketches. It will be seen at once that the qualities of the sketches are not the same as those of the canvases painted from them. In the sketches picturesque subject-matter has been rendered with fidelity, and his honesty made a direct and forceful appeal to Kane's contemporaries, as has already been noted. Yet in painting the canvases Kane tried to make improvements over the sketches, and the result was a dichotomy between study and finished work.

The Chualpays scalp dance may serve as an example. The sketch (Fig. 127), despite its dramatic overtones, is handled with great objectivity. It has spontaneity and an immediacy of time and place. The approach is not photographic, but it is direct and perceptive, and results in what must have been an accurate picture of the event. The canvas based on the sketch (Fig. 129) has completely new subjective overtones which dissipate the compelling quality of the original. The many new elements introduced into the finished oil accentuate drama at the expense of truth. Camp fires cast a weird red glow over the ritual. Kane, as in other instances, has turned day into night. Overhead a crescent moon, with a wisp of cloud over its face, looks down on the frenzied dance. The shapes of houses, illuminated by unnatural light, provide an atmospheric stage set. The artist has accentuated stripes painted on the medicine man's body, and highlighted the dresses of the attendant maidens with additional colour touches. At one side is a group of friendly and evidently local Indians, who have brought the scalp of a Blackfoot as a present to the dancer. One of these men wears a Plains Indian jacket. Strangest of all, a beaded medallion on the breast of one man, which certainly accentuates the picturesque effect, seems to be the design of a medallion of a Blackfoot who should be a thousand miles away from the spot. The ritual is actually celebrating the murder of one of his tribal brothers in a revenge slaying.

Further comparison of field sketches and canvases demonstrates that the fresh colouring which is one of the glories of the former is lost. Several reasons have been suggested for the lowering of the colour key in the transcription. An easy explanation would be that the duller powdered pigment Kane used in his studio could not match the brilliance of the tube colours he presumably carried on his travels. Or, when he was working indoors, did he forget how vivid the light effects could be in the clear Canadian atmosphere? Possibly he could not really credit the brilliance of his own field sketches. The French River canvas (Fig. 22) is dull indeed when placed beside the lively sketch (Plate III). What a sparkling canvas Norway House (Plate XVIII) could have made! Or, again, did Kane perhaps have some preconceived idea that great pictures were solid and dark like those of the old masters he had seen in Italian galleries, their surfaces subdued by layers of varnish? The uninspired colouring of Kakabeka Falls (Fig. 47) may be understandable; it was worked up from a pencil sketch without colour notes. The Allan family certainly regretted sometimes that Kane's trees were not greener and his skies bluer, and also noted that his browns and yellows did not improve with age.

Into many canvases Kane deliberately introduced neutral greys. Did he feel that grey would give a sense of unity and order to the finished canvas, that it would hold every element in its proper place and prevent any one colour from jumping out of the picture frame? We can only wish that he had transcribed to his canvas the colours used in certain portrait sketches so that we could assess the results. He did a series of striking head studies during his first year of field work in the Great Lakes region, and the backgrounds are in stimulating yellow, orange, rich brown and green. These are not backgrounds based on nature directly but are suggestive of sun on landscape. The broken but brilliant splashes of colour have much emotional appeal. The study of Now-on-dhu-go (Plate VIII), an Ottawa Indian from Lake Michigan, is particularly noteworthy. The background sparkles with the pure atmospheric colours of the Impressionists; if the technique had been followed on a large scale, it could have catapulted Kane into the ranks of those preparing for the Impressionist movement soon to sweep France. But instead, in most of his portrait canvases, he preferred to substitute a neutral grey or another dull tone for the colours of his sketches.

And why are there so many cloud banks in the landscape canvases? They hide the clear and exhilarating blue prairie sky. Had Kane seen too many Dutch marines in Europe?

However we must not be too unkind. The Canadian art critic of Kane's day would have found his canvases eminently satisfactory, and indeed an improvement over the field studies. Tastes change, and although today we demand the fresh and colourful, a direct copy of nature was not completely satisfactory to the mid 19th century connoisseur. Then taste demanded that nature should be reconstituted to give a "breadth of effect," an attitude which is well stated by a critic writing about the exhibition of the Ontario Society of Artists held in 1873. He notes:

Some . . . were charming studies, evidently finished on the spot. Though in reference to this it may not be out of place to remark that, while the study of nature cannot be too strongly inculcated, yet a sketch from nature, and a finished picture embodying the earnest and oft renewed study of nature, are not to be confounded without misleading results. . . . But we may remark that some of the larger water-colour drawings betrayed only too much evidence of being done on the spot. They had plenty of accuracy of detail, very valuable as artistic study; but wanted the breadth of effect which is needed to make a picture. Photography will give the detail of the landscape under any light and shade, and from any point of view; but the art of the true artist is required to bring his accumulated study of nature to bear on this subject; just as the poet makes "a thing of beauty" out of what seems homely and prosaic to the common eye.[22]

Kane, by his own standards, felt that his canvases were factually truthful, yet certain embellishments he added to the subject-matter shown in the sketches can cause some dismay. His oil sketch of Coe-coosh or "The Hog" (Plate IX), a Fox River Potawatomi, emphasizes the Indian's painted face, his ugly scowl and his disreputable robes. In the canvas, Coe-coosh has the same red face, but is wearing an elaborate roach on his head (which, indeed, Potawatomi sometimes wore), brooches of trade silver in his hair (and many Indians of the Fox River did wear such brooches), and has a quite respectable buttoned jacket. The old scoundrel has become rather a romantic individual, and his appeal to the eye has been enhanced. Is Kane being completely truthful? Certainly all of the articles added come from the Fox River region, but is this canvas still Coe-coosh?

Variations of this kind between sketches and canvases are numerous. There is an exquisite and refined water colour sketch of a Sioux chieftain (Plate XV). In the canvas (Fig. 58) he dons a handsome embroidered robe which he had not worn in the water colour study. Some stage props came from the artist's ethnological collection and whether this is really a Sioux robe is

problematical. Mah-Min, chief of the Assiniboin, met at Rocky Mountain House, is dressed up for the canvas (Fig. 109) with another roach, a club which may not even come from the prairies, a quiver slung over his back, and a beaded jacket. The bear's claw necklace, which was in the sketch and which he gave to Kane, is still around his neck. How does the Otisskun of the canvas acquire his red calumet pipe? Such elaborations add to the picturesque and romantic effect of the larger paintings; yet despite the fact that Kane had seen all these articles at some time in his wanderings, his re-assembly for artistic effect creates conundrums for ethnologists.

Kane's old difficulty in judging proportions correctly reappears in the canvases and was the reason for numerous alterations. One Métis woman in his *Half Breed Encampment* (Fig. 64) he reduced from an eight-foot Amazon to more reasonable proportions. Canvases at Moss Park were retouched frequently. Kane called, usually during breakfast, to take one after another away for alteration; this activity caused continual anxiety to the owner who was apprehensive as to whether the retouching would result in a real improvement.

A number of commentators, including Charles W. Jefferys, have condemned Kane's fine blood horses, descendants of Arabian stallions, suggesting that more lowly beasts would be in keeping with the probable mounts of prairie Indians.[23] On the other hand, some suggest that a certain elegant bearing for prairie horses is correct since they descend from horses imported by the Spanish into Mexico. Indian chiefs were proud of their special horses. Catlin describes how a chief overheard a man criticizing one of his horses in a painting for not having more common lines; the Indian was enraged, saying his horse was of excellent breeding; he would not ride except on the best of steeds.

Kane had constant trouble in sketching moving objects, and so seemed unable to set down wildly charging horses or buffalo while the action occurred. Yet hunting scenes, horseback races, even armed fights, were among the most colourful subjects in the west, and so, feeling obliged to include them, he fell back at times on the ready-made compositions of others. He describes in his book two Assiniboin whom he had seen riding across the prairie in hot pursuit of a buffalo, but apparently he did not sketch them at the time. Back in Toronto he looked at a book of Italian engravings, which had a plate picturing Italian youths

[22] *Canadian Magazine and National Review* (Toronto), III, 1873, 545.
[23] See *Wanderings of an Artist* (1968 ed.), pp. xliii–xliv.

on superb steeds chasing an Italian bull, with their lances raised. By transforming the young Italians into Assiniboin Indians, the bull into a buffalo, and putting open prairie beneath the horses' feet, Kane recreated with great *éclat* the hunt he had seen south of Edmonton. (See Figs. 105, 106.) Ironically this apocryphal composition has been the favourite of ethnologists when choosing illustrations demonstrating Indians hunting on the prairie.

A few, possibly not more than half a dozen, other paintings by Kane are based on engravings or paintings of other artists. "The Man that Always Rides" (Plate XX) has a pose used repeatedly by Catlin but whether Catlin's work suggested the rearing horse is uncertain. The same stance was used by Velazquez long before and by Gros and Delacroix in Kane's own era. Most strange and interesting of all Kane's borrowings is his first attempt in the series on the great buffalo hunt. He had not previously dealt with any subject on this scale, and in any case had no time to set down the hunt directly for he was on a horse revelling in the chase. When he did tire of riding and got out his sketchbook, it was to make quick pencil notes of a single dangerously wounded bull, and he nearly lost his life doing so (Fig. 68). He later searched for some kind of precedent to help him record the crowded and busy scene. His first interpretation (Plate XVII), which he must have made on his return to camp that evening, is related to an English sporting print where horses are riding to hounds. This obviously would not quite do! He tried again from another angle. The new sketch (now lost) went off to Sir George Simpson, who wrote to him about it disapprovingly:

In taking the sketch of the buffalo hunt you were good enough to send me last year, you must have stood in the rear of the herd; a side view would have given a better idea of the appearance of the animals, as from the hind view, it required a little explanation to make a stranger understand that the mass of dark objects before him, were intended either for buffalo or any other living animals.[24]

Kane repainted the subject. This time his composition is a detail of the herd viewed from the side (Fig. 67). The whole could be handled more successfully in that way in order to give an immediate feeling of the drama in the swiftly moving mass.

Whatever regrets we may have about Kane's departure from his sketches in painting his canvases, it is still true that they are an important contribution to our knowledge of the frontier of his day. Together, the sketches and canvases form an immense

and striking panorama of the west and present the Indian and his life in all their variety. That panorama made an impression on everyone who saw it: the man in the street, a newspaper editor, a contemporary Canadian artist. The *Anglo-American Magazine* published in 1853 a view by Lucius O'Brien of an Indian scene at Twelve Mile Creek between Hamilton and Niagara Falls. In explanation, the magazine noted: "We give this plate for the double purpose of illustrating a scene in Indian life and of laying before Canadian readers of the present generation a glimpse of the past, a sight which, though now rare to their eyes, was to their fathers common." [25] Kane's depiction of the frontier west fulfilled both these purposes for succeeding generations.

V. *Wanderings of an Artist*

Kane was penniless and hungry for acclaim when he returned to Toronto from his western explorations. He needed money simply for food and he also wanted recognition for his four years of hardship in the wilderness. His paintings would be admired and discussed in due course, but a book about his travels might bring in royalties and would also tell a wider public about his exploits and the Indians whom he held in such high regard. George Catlin's *Letters and Notes on the Manners, Customs, and Condition of the North American Indians* had been a phenomenal success. By 1848 it had already been reprinted several times, had made for Catlin a good deal of money, and had secured his niche in history.

Within a week after reaching home, Kane wrote to Sir George Simpson in Montreal about how best to publish such a book. Presumably one reason for approaching Sir George was that he had recently published an account of his own voyage around the world. Simpson replied, recommending the subscription method as a good one, and promising to persuade his friends to subscribe for copies. He offered some additional practical advice, suggesting that Kane visit nearby towns, obtain portrait commissions to assist with his expenses, and at the same time secure signatures for copies of the projected volume.[1] Kane would have none of this; he was determined to devote all the time he had for painting to completing his Indian canvases.

Sir George went further. By means of a friend, he arranged

[24] Appendix 10, Letter 12.
[25] *Anglo-American Magazine* (Toronto), III, 1853, 17.

[1] Appendix 10, Letter 16.

Plate VII. Mani-tow-wah-bay or "He-Devil," an Ojibwa, Lake Michigan. Glenbow-Alberta Institute, Calgary; crIII-88.

Now - on - du - go -

Ottowa Tribe
Lake Michigan

81

Plate VIII. Now-on-dhu-go, Ottawa chief, Lake Michigan. Stark EOP27; CRIII-89.

for John Russell Bartlett to write to Kane from New York. Bartlett, an American, had spent much time in the southwest and knew many people interested in science. He suggested that Kane approach the Smithsonian Institution in Washington which would probably print his book and engrave the plates for illustrations. The Smithsonian paid nothing for manuscripts but allowed authors a handsome fee for supervising publication of their own books. *Ancient Monuments of the Mississippi Valley*, he said, had been printed in this way. Kane's book would then be distributed free to all parts of the world and he would become a celebrated personality. The Smithsonian even gave the used type to authors for publication of a second edition at the author's expense, and writers often made a good thing out of sale of the reprints.[2] But Kane did nothing about these various proposals. The book after all had not yet even been begun.

The writing of *Wanderings of an Artist* apparently proceeded hand in hand with his painting. The first evidence that part of it had been completed came in 1855 when on March 14 Kane delivered a paper on the Chinook Indians before the Canadian Institute, of which he was a member. This paper, virtually unaltered, became a chapter of his book. Two other papers were read at Institute meetings in 1855 and 1856. The three lectures, and supplementary material for the first one, were published by the Institute in its journal and that on the Chinook Indians also appeared in the *Daily Colonist*.[3]

Kane's narrative is based on his field notes which at times he follows word for word.[4] Personal spellings in the original were, however, corrected judiciously for publication with, for instance, "ice" replacing "ise," "fright" for "frite" and "country" for "cuntry." But the original diary has been expanded with extracts from his field logs of landscapes and portraits and by numerous stories and legends about various Indians he had met. Some of these are involved tales and it seems curious that he made no notes in reference to them while he was travelling; one might even wonder whether a few may have been taken from other books (no borrowings have been traced). Several travel books dealing with the American Indians were gathered by Kane, presumably for research purposes but also probably to give him some idea of the style of writing he should use; a few dealt with tribes he had visited.[5] His book when completed was a straightforward narrative depending for interest on its information and description rather than on literary pretensions. On at least one occasion he seems to have taken liberties with fact. This was in connection with the buffalo hunt near Fort Garry in June 1846, and concerns an incident between the Métis and Sioux. Kane's

field journal puts it two years before his trip, an early manuscript version of the book says that it occurred a year before; in the printed book Kane sees it happen.[6]

Whether Kane approached a publisher before 1858 is uncertain, but in that year he decided to go in person to London. George W. Allan was visiting there at the time, and Allan's brother-in-law, John Henry Lefroy, who had returned from duty in Canada, was in England too. Both offered to assist in arranging details with a publisher. Kane also approached Sir George Simpson at Lachine before he sailed. Sir George sent a letter to William G. Smith, secretary to the Hudson's Bay Company, asking Smith to introduce Kane to various members of its board with the request that they give him all possible help. In doing so, he noted that Kane had not only always been personally grateful for assistance given him, but had also defended the Company against the many attacks being made on it in these years; it could be anticipated that his book, which would likely appeal to a wide audience because of its illustrations, would similarly favour the Company.[7] Board minutes of the Hudson's Bay Company during March 1858 do indeed note that "Mr Paul Kane" should be "cordially received and encouraged."[8] A famous Company man, "Bear" Ellice, formerly a Montrealer, evidently was particularly helpful to him.

Frederick A. Verner, who would later paint the west, and Kane's portrait, and who was an admirer and friend of the

[2] Kane family papers, Bartlett to Kane, October 25, 1848.

[3] Paul Kane, "Incidents of Travel on the North-West Coast, Vancouver's Island, Oregon &c.: The Chinook Indians," *Canadian Journal* (Toronto), July 1855, pp. 273–80; "Notes of a Sojourn among the Half-Breeds, Hudson Bay Company's Territory, Red River," *ibid.*, 1856, pp. 128–38; "Notes of Travel among the Walla-Walla Indians," *ibid.*, pp. 417–24; "The Chinook Indians," *ibid.*, 1857, pp. 11–30. "The Chinook Indians," *Daily Colonist* (Toronto), August 6–9, 1855.

[4] Kane kept a journal during his 1846–48 expedition. It commences with an entry dated May 9, 1846, and ends on September 12, 1848. He evidently intended that it should be a daily diary, but there are gaps, some of them for weeks at a time, for instance when he was staying at Fort Vancouver in the winter of 1846–47. This journal contains much of what is now in *Wanderings*, with variations in minor details; significant variations are given below in the notes to the text of that book.

[5] Books which he owned personally include: Ross Cox, *Adventures on the Columbia River* (New York 1832); *A Narrative of the Captivity and Adventures of John Tanner* (New York 1830); J. Mackintosh, *The Discovery of America, by Christopher Columbus; and the Origin of the North American Indians* (Toronto 1836); Henry Schoolcraft, *The Indian and the Wigwam: Personal Memoirs of a Residence of Thirty Years with the Indian Tribes on the American Frontiers* (Philadelphia 1851); Sir George Simpson, *Narrative of a Journey round the World during the Years 1841 and 1842* (London 1847); Sir John Richardson, *An Arctic Searching Expedition* (London 1851); Sir George Back, *Narrative of the Arctic Land Expedition to the Mouth of the Great Fish River . . . 1833, 1834 and 1835* (London 1836); W. L. Stone, *Life of Joseph Brant* (New York 1838).

[6] *Wanderings of an Artist*, p. 70 below.

[7] Hudson's Bay Company Archives, D4/54, Simpson to Smith, February 25, 1858.

[8] L. J. Burpee gives an account of Kane's activities in London in his introduction to the 1925 edition of *Wanderings of an Artist*; see the 1968 reprint, p. xl.

pioneer artist, recalled when himself an old man the troubles which Kane had in arranging publication.[9] It has to be remembered, of course, that he wrote about them more than half a century after the incidents he was recalling and his memory was possibly no longer as sharp as it might have been. Verner asserted that immediately on his arrival in London Kane took his manuscript to the Longman firm. He also said that twelve paintings (perhaps those bought by Sir George Simpson, although the number is neither the fourteen ordered by him nor the ten listed as delivered) were exhibited for the Royal Family at Buckingham Palace during 1858. True, it was quite usual for exhibitions of colonial paintings to be arranged for the monarch. Commander Inglefield's water colours of the Canadian Arctic with his little ship dwarfed by great icebergs were viewed by Queen Victoria at Windsor, the collection being arranged in the corridor for her inspection after lunch. But the daily diary at Buckingham Palace for 1858 contains no reference to such an exhibition and it seems a bit of fantasy.

Verner stated that six months after Kane arrived overseas he was still waiting for a decision about acceptance from the publisher. He then called at the Longman office for what he thought would be the last time. Longman opened a large room, its shelves filled with manuscripts, and remonstrated: " 'How is it that you expect me to look over yours when none in this collection is looked at yet?' Kane's reply was, 'I am independent of the world. Give me my manuscript. I am returning to Canada.' " But the fame of Kane's paintings had now reached high places in London. The publisher had by this time heard independently of his celebrated expedition. Kane was asked to return the following day, and publication was then arranged. The final version of his manuscript was retained by the publishers, only to be burned during the London blitz of 1940. An early version was kept in Toronto and it is this version which is now held by the Stark Foundation.

Wanderings of an Artist among the Indians of North America appeared in 1859, the British price being 25/–. James Bain, Toronto bookseller, was the Canadian agent, and his prospectus, dated January 3, offered copies at $5.50 each. It gave details of the chapter headings and described the twenty-one illustrations, eight of them chromo-lithographs. It suggested that the mass of information on the western Indians would be doubly welcome and valuable "in view of their hunting grounds being broken up by the whistle of the locomotive, as it opens up a highway between East and West." [10]

The book was an immediate success, not least because of the coloured lithographs made from Allan's canvases and the wood engravings from sketches which were scattered through the text. The principal reviews dwelt at length on the assumption that the Indians would soon be extinct through contact with Europeans.

Daniel Wilson praised the volume in a Toronto publication. He commented that although the work was not strictly a literary creation it presented a "soul-stirring journal of adventures and strange perils" recorded in a way which brought out all the writer's striking detail, his "discriminating perception," "the felicitous pencillings of his sketch-book, and all the rich colouring of his portfolio." Naturally, since he was himself interested in ethnology, Wilson emphasized the account of aboriginal characteristics in the life of these primitive peoples as an important aspect of the work. He castigates the publisher, however, for the chromo-lithograph *Half-Breed Cree Girl* which appeared as a frontispiece (this was Cun-ne-wa-bum whom Kane had met in Fort Edmonton at the Christmas dance); he had noted in the original canvas an exceedingly interesting illustration of the blending of white and Indian features, but reproduction removed every trace of the Indian features in a desire to produce the engraver's idea of a pretty face. Wilson adds that it might just as well have been the face of a wax doll.[11]

The London *Athenaeum* noted that the author of the book, an "American," had devoted himself to an American purpose, sketching and recording the deeds and outward form of an unhappily vanishing race.[12] Then this over-romantic reviewer changed to a poetic vein, likening the Indian to the snowdrift which melts and disappears forever. It is a typical touch of heavy Victorian sentiment. The reviewer hoped that Kane's example would be followed: "It is well that ere it fade, some lover of the Red Man who, like Mr. Kane, can strap his portfolio and paint-box on his back, should fill a bullock's horn with powder, and taking his rifle in his firm hand, stride on board the snorting steam-packet at Sturgeon Bay in Lake Huron." Kane's allusions to the Flatheads struck the reviewer as a happy opportunity for criticizing a London monument he evidently disliked: the Flathead chief, he said, must have somewhat resembled the statue of George III in Cockspur Street.

The most scholarly review occupied an impressive twenty-

[9] *Ibid.*, p. xli.
[10] Ontario Archives, *Prospectus of Wanderings of an Artist among the Indians of North America, by Paul Kane* (Toronto, January 3, 1859).
[11] *Canadian Journal* (Toronto), 1859, pp. 186–94.
[12] *Athenaeum* (London), July 2, 1859, pp. 14–15.

three pages in the *Revue des deux mondes*, reflecting the interest of a large number of French scholars and philosophers at this time in primitive peoples.[13] Lavollée, the author of the review, introduced his essay with yet another dissertation on the vanishing American Indian.

One must make haste to visit the Red Men. Their tribes, not long since still masters of a whole world, are disappearing rapidly, driven back and destroyed by the inroads of the white race. Their future is inevitable. Perhaps before a century has passed, the last Indian of North America will have returned to the abode of the Great Spirit: an unfortunate race which, after having lived and multiplied in barbarism, has been stricken to death by contact with civilization! In the United States, the territories assigned to the Indians are being depopulated on a frightening scale; it is the same in British North America. It is not that the white race wishes at any price to dominate and exist alone on these immense regions, which could easily support both the old and the new masters of the American continent. Originally, in the first keenness of conquest, when the European pioneers were bent upon acquiring land, there were undoubtedly numerous acts of violence; but today, inspired by more humane ideas, the administration of the United States and the British government are making praiseworthy efforts to maintain the Red Men, to civilize them by religion and by work. Honour and interest alike bid them protect the tribes, who have been successively deprived of vast spaces, sterile in their hands. Unfortunately there are inexorable laws. The Indians are doomed; their fate will be that of so many primitive races now gone. Let us leave to the ethnographers and the philosophers the task of learned discourse on these great human revolutions and of pronouncing the funeral oration for peoples who have disappeared. On this occasion it is a question simply of describing from nature, while there is still time, some of the features of the life and character of the Red Men, of making a short excursion into the midst of tribes who live, under English rule, in the territories between Canada and the Pacific Ocean.

Lavollée goes on, after a brief reference to Chateaubriand and Cooper, to give a detailed summary of Kane's book, which he describes as not being a literary or scientific work, but valuable as a record of all the artist had seen. The reviewer mentions especially the gathering of the tribes for the treaty ceremonies on the Great Lakes, the portages across to the prairies (with the wistful reminder in their place names of the era of the French), the Métis, the great buffalo hunt, Kane's ways of securing the portraits he wanted, the rigours of the mountain passes, the customs of the Flatheads and Chinooks, the salmon fishing on the Columbia River, the holiday festivities at Fort Edmonton and the wedding, the efforts of a variety of missionaries to spread their faiths. He gives a full rendition of the mournful and romantic tale of the Indian chief who having lost his last

and most loved son asked to be buried alive with him. His abridgement of the book concludes with an elegy for the Indian which, like the one in the *Athenaeum* review, makes use of the snows of the northern world for an analogy. Now that the railway and the search for gold are going to bring more and more whites to the west, he writes, the Indian will be driven far to the north, to the eternal ice of the pole:

there, having cast aside his useless snares and shot his last arrow into empty space, hoping only for the hospitality of the Great Spirit, he will lie down upon the snow, which will soon cover him as with a shroud, and, with him, a whole race will have disappeared forever from the face of the earth.

The English language edition of *Wanderings of an Artist* sold out completely, and within the next four years three foreign language editions appeared. A French edition, evidently pirated, was printed in 1861; it omits Kane's name as author and is without illustrations. A Danish edition was published in Copenhagen in 1861. The most elaborate of the foreign editions, in German, was issued in parts beginning in 1860; later these parts were reissued as a complete volume,[14] with 4 new colour plates and 62 black-and-white illustrations; many of these 62 engravings were fantasies of some romantic European artist's imagination. All the early editions are now collectors' items, with the foreign language copies scarce indeed. The English edition was not reprinted until the twentieth century.[15]

An unfortunate rupture in the friendship of Sir George Simpson and Paul Kane resulted from the publication of his book. The author chose to dedicate *Wanderings of an Artist* to the Honourable George Allan in tribute to his benefactions. Simpson was highly offended, demonstrating a rather petty annoyance and even a certain vindictiveness. In 1861 Kane was considering a sketching trip to the Labrador. Possibly he may have

[13] Charles-Hubert Lavollée, "Un artiste chez les Peaux-rouges," *Revue des deux mondes* (Paris), 1859, pp. 963–86; translation by present author. The original French text for the two quotations from Lavollée's review will be found in an addendum at the end of this section of Part One.

[14] *Les Indiens de la baie d'Hudson, promenades d'un artiste parmi les Indiens de l'Amérique du Nord . . .* (Paris, Amyot, 1861), trans. Edouard Delessert. Paul Kane, *En Kunstners Vandringer blandt Indianerne i Nordamerika fra Canada til Vancouvers O og Oregon, gjennem Hudsons-Bai-Kompagniets Territorium* (Kjobenhavn, F. H. Eibes Forlag—Louis Kleins Bogtryferi, 1863), trans. J. K. Paul Kane, *Wanderungen unter den Indianern Nordamerikas von Canada nach der Vancouvers Insel und Oregon* (Leipzig, Schrader, 1860); *Wanderungen eines Kunstlers unter den Indianern Nordamerikas von Canada nach der Vancouvers Insel und nach Oregon* (Leipzig 1862), trans. Luise Hauthal.

[15] See the introductory note to the text of *Wanderings* reprinted below. Some Canadian schoolchildren learned Kane's name. Lesson LXXII on pp. 194–96 of J. Douglas Borthwick's *The British American Reader* (Montreal 1860) was "The Flat-Head Indians" by Paul Kane.

been planning to accompany Henry Youle Hind as artist in his proposed expedition to that region, which took place the next year.[16] Kane's old spirit was revived with the thoughts of sketching other Indian tribes "in their native habitat" and on March 21 he wrote to Donald Smith (later Lord Strathcona), then a Hudson's Bay Company factor at the north shore post of Mingan along the Gulf of St. Lawrence. Kane asked whether Smith would make any facilities available to him, adding that "as I had the misfortune to incur the Governor's displeasure, I understand that he has given orders that I was not to be countenanced by any officers in the service."[17] He explained that his offence was in neither giving paintings to Simpson (actually Simpson had requested an account from Kane for the pictures), nor dedicating his book to him. Kane did not go with Hind; instead Hind took with him next spring his brother, William G. R. Hind, whose superb illustrations decorate the book in which Henry describes the Labrador.

Kane contemplated one further publication: a book of illustrations which would include both landscapes and studies of Indians. The idea probably came again from one of Catlin's volumes, for the latter had brought out a book of magnificently engraved plates of North American Indians in 1844.[18] Kane proposed as his title "Pictorial sketches with Historical notices taken during two journeys across the continent of America to the Columbia River and North West Coast of the Pacific in the years 1845, 1846, 1847 and 1848, by Paul Kane." He started work on the text, which he evidently intended should consist solely of explanatory notes, a paragraph accompanying each plate. Much of the material in the text he prepared is simply a duplication of what had already been published in *Wanderings of an Artist*.[19] The book was never published.

Addendum: Passages from Lavollée's review of *Wanderings of an Artist*

Il faut se hâter de visiter les peaux-rouges. Ces tribus, naguère encore maîtresses de tout un monde, disparaissent rapidement refoulées et anéanties par l'invasion de la race blanche. Leurs destins sont marqués. Avant un

[16] Henry Youle Hind, *Explorations in the Interior of the Labrador Peninsula, the Country of the Montagnais and Nasquapee Indians* (London 1863).

[17] Beckles Willson, *The Life of Lord Strathcona and Mount Royal* (London 1915), pp. 108–09.

[18] George Catlin, *Catlin's North American Indian Portfolio: Hunting Scenes and Amusements of the Rocky Mountains and Prairies of America* (London 1844).

[19] The manuscript which Kane prepared for this second volume is in the collection of the Nelda C. and H. J. Lutcher Stark Foundation. Much of it merely duplicates portions of *Wanderings of an Artist*. An occasional note about sketches is new, and appropriate additions from this new material have been made in Appendices 1 and 2.

siècle peut-être, le dernier Indien de l'Amérique du Nord aura regagné le séjour du Grand-Esprit: race malheureuse qui, après avoir vécu en se multipliant dans la barbarie, s'éteint frappée de mort au contact de la civilisation! Dans les États-Unis, les territoires assignés aux Indiens se dépeuplent dans des proportions effrayantes; il en est de même dans l'Amérique anglaise. Ce n'est point que la race blanche veuille à tout prix dominer et exister seule sur ces immenses régions, qui pourraient aisément nourrir les anciens et les nouveaux maîtres du continent américain. Dans l'origine, aux premières ardeurs de la conquête, lorsque les pionniers européens se sont précipités sur le sol, il y eut sans doute de nombreux actes de violence; mais aujourd'hui, sous l'inspiration d'idées plus humaines, l'administration des États-Unis et le gouvernement britannique tentent de louables efforts pour conserver les peaux-rouges, pour les civiliser par la religion et par le travail. L'honneur et l'intérêt leur commandent de protéger ces tribus, qui ont été successivement expropriées des vastes espaces demeurés stériles entre leurs mains. Malheureusement il y a des lois fatales. Les Indiens sont condamnés; ils auront le destin de tant de races primitives aujourd'hui disparues. Laissons aux ethnographes et aux philosophes le soin de disserter savamment sur ces grandes révolutions humaines et de prononcer l'oraison funèbre des peuples qui s'en vont. Il s'agit simplement ici de décrire d'après nature, quand il en est temps encore, quelques traits de la vie et du caractère des peaux-rouges, de faire une courte excursion au milieu des tribus qui habitent, sous la domination anglaise, les territoires compris entre le Canada et l'Océan-Pacifique.

Repoussé par l'invasion européenne, abruti par les spiritueux que lui apporteront les blancs, l'Indien remontera vers le nord, il fuira jusqu'à ce qu'il se trouve acculé aux glaces éternelles du pôle; là, après avoir jeté ses inutiles filets et lancé dans le vide sa dernière flèche, n'espérant plus que dans l'hospitalité promise par le Grand-Esprit, il se couchera sur la neige, qui l'aura bientôt couvert de son linceul, et, avec lui, toute une race aura disparu à jamais de la surface de la terre.

VI. The Later Years

Kane's days as a wanderer sketching in far places were not to be repeated. He settled down in Toronto, meeting occasionally with friends and leading generally a sedentary life. The Honourable George Allan described him as being at this time 5 feet 11 inches tall, with a particularly keen memory, vivid in description of the curious and distant things he had seen, and with "somewhat of the quiet, unimpressible manner of the Indians, among whom he had spent some of the most eventful years of his life."[1] He had a dignity about him that even a child could

[1] Daniel Wilson, "Paul Kane, the Canadian Artist," *Canadian Journal* (Toronto), May 1871, p. 72. This article is based largely on a memorandum supplied by Allan to Wilson.

feel, and he made a strong impression on one of the Allan children. "There was still that look of observation in his eyes, as he turned them upon you, and I remember well the tones of his gentle, rather grunty voice, saying what he had to say, with few words, in a very pleasant cultivated accent." [2] His face, pockmarked since youth, was a kind face. He was much respected by all who met him.

The Kanes lived during their early married years on Jarvis Street in Toronto and then built a house for themselves at 56 Wellesley Street (the location is marked today with an official plaque); it was named "Miss-qua-Kany Lodge," and Mrs Kane lived here until her death in 1892. Across the street lived Captain O'Brien, father of the artist Lucius O'Brien. The Kane home, graced with fine solid furniture, had engravings on the walls, and Kane's own copies of paintings by Murillo, Leonardo da Vinci and Raphael, and of a martyrdom of St. John the Baptist, and a copy too of the portrait of himself by his friend Verner. His large library displayed a remarkable breadth of interest.[3] Kane had become a man of standing in Toronto, then a busy young city. He had four children, two sons and two daughters. The younger boy attended Trinity College School, Port Hope, where Ontario's leading citizens sent their sons. Young Kane and the Honourable George Allan's son were companions, with a common interest in natural history. The older son, Paul, moved to Manitoba in the 1880s.

Remarkably few canvases other than compositions based on his western sketches were painted after Kane's return to the east in 1848. His canvas self-portrait, showing a cultivated young man, has the pinkish flesh tones of a face that has not been exposed for four years in the wilds and it must date from just before he set out for the west. Portraits of James Richardson (Fig. 9), a newspaper editor originally from Cobourg, of Mayor George Gurnett of Toronto (Fig. 8) and of one or two others can be no later than 1851 and must have been painted during the years when he was worrying about finances and before he received the government commission. He considered Joseph Brant's portrait as one of his obligatory hundred subjects; it may be based on an engraving of an A. E. Ames portrait of Brant used as a frontispiece in W. L. Stone's *Life of Brant* [4] (Kane owned this book); on the other hand, it may be based on a portrait by Catlin who in turn seems to have based his work on the engraving. Curiously, Kane copied a Cornelius Krieghoff painting of a French-Canadian notary that had been done in 1848; are there perhaps circulating today other copies by Kane of canvases which masquerade as Krieghoff originals? An oil of

Niagara Falls, probably from some sketch made on a holiday excursion (Fig. 12), is the single known canvas with local subject-matter.

Most unusual of all his later canvases (it can no longer be located) was a re-creation of *Columbus Meeting the Indians on His Landing at San Salvador*. Three ships are in the harbour and the woods are alive with hundreds of Indians peering from every forest tree at the white man as he sets foot on the soil of the New World for the first time.[5] He has departed from his usual factual approach, with his painting based solidly on his own experience, and moved into the realm of imagination. There is one possible explanation for such a radically new direction. Kane had exhibited some paintings of the west at the Upper Canada Provincial Exhibition in 1852. These were entered for competition as "historical" works but the judges contended that on the contrary they were "contemporary" in subject-matter. One reviewer, probably Henry Youle Hind, in discussing the question reiterated the current belief that historical paintings were the highest form of art:

It was clearly a misapprehension of the nature of the subject matter required, and not a want of power, which occasioned this disappointment —we shall hope to see, upon a future occasion, that the spirit stirring incidents of the last war,[6] and the great events which have marked the social progress and constitutional history of the country, have found their fitting expositor in the first native artist of Canada. Considering, however, that historical painting is the highest branch of art, we must remark that the prizes offered are wholly insufficient to tempt an artist capable of executing such a subject to sacrifice time which might be given to easier and more romantic employment.[7]

Is the "Columbus" perhaps Kane's answer to Hind's comments? If so, he remains consistent with his interests by conjuring up a historical painting in which Indians appear, and indeed setting them in the context of the event from which the troubles of the American natives arose.

A remarkable aspect of Kane's later years was the degree of his devotion from 1849 to 1859 to cultivation of his western

[2] Mrs. Cassels, in her Reminiscences of Paul Kane, in the collection of the Royal Ontario Museum.
[3] See Appendix 9.
[4] W. L. Stone, *Life of Joseph Brant—Thayendanegea* (New York 1838), frontispiece.
[5] The painting may be based on a description of the landing of Columbus in a book owned by Kane: J. Mackintosh, *The Discovery of America, by Christopher Columbus; and the Origin of the North American Indians* (Toronto 1836).
[6] The reviewer is presumably referring to the War of 1812–14 rather than the rebellion of 1837 in the Canadas.
[7] *Canadian Journal* (Toronto), 1852, p. 52.

project through painting and writing. Nothing whatever was allowed to interfere. The Toronto Society of Artists, on the president's motion, invited him to become a member in March 1849. Three days later, signing himself somewhat facetiously as "Paolo Canoe," he declined the honour; since "all my time and means are devoted to one particular object, it is impossible for me to give that attention to the interests of the Society which it deserves without great personal inconvenience to myself." [8] Sir Sandford Fleming, inventor of standard time and promoter of intellectual and scientific interests in Toronto, invited him to design a vignette for the new Canadian Institute; he did not reply to the invitation. His only indulgence was to accept an appointment in 1852 as a lieutenant in the Second Toronto Independent Artillery Company of the militia. Paintings were sent to the Upper Canada Provincial Exhibitions from 1850 to 1857, but possibly only to help the promotion of his book and to present to the public some visible results of his travels. Then, with his main body of works completed and his book published, and his eye trouble beginning, he lost interest in promotion and ceased exhibiting. He apparently even refused to talk about subjects that did not interest him, although on matters with which he was familiar he was a lively conversationalist. To be photographed in front of his ethnological specimens delighted him; he even dressed in some of the costumes he had collected and, holding his gun, took up somewhat romantic poses.

This routine of living was interrupted when in 1856 the short-lived lithographic firm, Fuller and Benecke, was established at the Victoria House, Toronto. Kane supervised in that year the colour work for the firm's reproduction of "The Death of Big Snake," said to be the first large coloured lithograph made in Canada (Fig. 90). It was printed at a time when Cornelius Krieghoff was bemoaning the lack of high quality prints in Canada. Krieghoff had sent his own paintings for lithographic reproduction to Munich in 1849, and to Philadelphia in 1866. He complained about the high tariff and wrote to the Canadian minister of finance requesting its removal as an incentive to greater importation of quality prints. He deplored the country's lack of good drawing masters and of collections of good prints and ornaments; as a result, he wrote, no wonder that "our young men should be drunkards and our girls flirts." [9] The lithograph of Kane's work was evidently not a commercial success; the experiment was not repeated.

During these years Kane developed an intimate friendship with Daniel Wilson who in 1853 had been appointed Professor of History and English Literature at University College, To-

ronto. In his native Scotland Wilson had been interested in Scottish archaeology, but in Toronto his attention turned to prehistory in general. Wilson's *Prehistoric Man* is a pioneer Canadian ethnological study. [10] Repeatedly and at length the author drew from Kane's experiences among western primitive peoples, and on them based many of his conclusions. He paid handsome tribute to Kane's help in the book. Throughout it he also introduced illustrations based on Kane's sketches, and on at least one other occasion, in a book on Indian pipes, had used sketches for reproduction. [11] Good friends, Wilson and Kane conversed on matters in which they had "mutual interest."

Tragically, Kane did not develop a new approach to painting with the passage of time. *Wanderings of an Artist* appeared in 1859 and the consuming fire which had burned in him for fifteen years died down. He scarcely touched a brush after that date. Kane had had his due of praise, and without new paintings to maintain their interest, the public gradually began to lose sight of him in the bustle of Canadian expansion. Possibly his thought of a Labrador trip was his last struggle to reawaken his creative urge. He began to complain that "Canada was no place for an artist." It seems quite likely that his health was beginning to fail, and there is a comment that as a result the good companion of the hearthside was beginning to "turn into a bear with a sore head." He gave up his studio in the 1860s. Growing blindness, first noticeable in 1859, began to cut him off from other people. Smallpox had left his eyes weak, but he felt that snow blindness suffered during the crossing of the Brenner Pass in Switzerland and the glare of the sun in the high passes of the Rocky Mountains during his western tour were contributing factors. The loss of sight increased his sense of isolation.

Frederick Verner, who would assume Kane's mantle as a painter of the prairie Indians and the buffalo, was a companion during this time. Years before, when Verner was merely a boy, he had knocked at Kane's studio door; he had requested drawing lessons, and the door closed abruptly in his face without a word of explanation. Now, after Verner had returned to Canada from Italy in 1862, he struck up a friendship with the aging artist. Verner had had his own adventures, as a red shirt in Garibaldi's army assisting in the liberation of Italy. He painted a portrait of Kane and later made two replicas. Kane is pictured

[8] Kane family papers, Kane to John Johnson, March 6, 1849.
[9] J. Russell Harper, *Painting in Canada: A History* (Toronto 1966), pp. 129, 130.
[10] Daniel Wilson, *Prehistoric Man* (Cambridge 1862). Wilson became Sir Daniel in 1888.
[11] *Pipes and Tobacco, an ethnological sketch* (Toronto 1857).

as a rather venerable old man with reddish hair and beard, and wearing the diamond stickpin given to him as a young man by some close friend when he was in Rome. Those who knew Kane declared that he was a much more attractive individual than the rather flat "Cossack" face painted by Verner would indicate. Certainly he is not, in this painting, anything like the colourful man of the Toronto photographs (Fig. 1).

Paul Kane died on February 20, 1871. An obituary preserved by his family has in its conclusion an attractive picture of his later years:

During the last few years Mr. Kane had led a very retiring life. He was very fond, however, of the water, and during the summer months seldom failed to make a daily visit to the island, returning regularly by the last ferry boat in the evening. He was a general favourite with all those who had the pleasure of his acquaintance, and he will be long remembered not only on account of his great talents as an artist, but on account of his goodness of heart and upright character as a man. He was only a few hours ill—having been out of the city on the morning of the day he died.

In her bereavement, his widow borrowed some of her husband's sketches from Mr. Allan, "for sentimental reasons." They were returned later and are a part of those in the Royal Ontario Museum.

Daniel Wilson paid eloquent tribute to Kane in the detailed biographical study which he prepared for the *Canadian Journal*.[12] He mentions how unusual Kane's career had been for its day:

In the midst of this conflict between the artless rudeness of savage life, and the progressive energy of the Anglo-Saxon colonist, young Paul grew up from boyhood, with few external influences calculated in the slightest degree to stimulate artistic tastes, or to direct his attention to the study of Indian manners and customs.

He points out also that despite the fact that the Indian, in debasement, now haunts the new centres of civilization, Kane

had felt an intense interest in his life as a free man and had devoted much of his career to recording that life. In conclusion Wilson comes back to the perseverance with which Kane had pursued his laudable ambition:

His published narrative is a modest, but interesting and vivid description of novel scenes and incidents of travel; and his career is a creditable instance of the pursuit of a favourite art, by a self-taught artist, in spite of the most discouraging impediments to success.

In 1882, thirty-two years after Kane's western travels concluded, Lucius O'Brien was travelling with his brother Henry in the foothills of the Rockies. He had become the first president of the new Royal Canadian Academy in 1880. The railway predicted by reviewers of Kane's book in 1859 had not yet completely linked the east with the west but it was under construction. The O'Briens had gone to Chicago by rail and then went on by horseback to the mountains. Lucius had been much interested in Kane during his youth. He himself had painted Indians both as "Lords of the Forest" and in other roles. Here in the Rockies, he and Henry, a mission worker, were travelling from one Indian camp to another. On August 7 they were proceeding up Rosebud Creek when they met an old chief. As they had done at many another such meeting, they inquired whether he had known Paul Kane. The old chief, after a pause, said he remembered the painter of the past and described him correctly.[13] The man with the fierce red beard had made a deep impression on the memory of the Indians, and the sketching hand which had given him in their eyes something of the power of a medicine man had in turn ensured that many of them would not be forgotten far into the future.

[12] "Paul Kane, the Canadian Artist," *Canadian Journal* (Toronto), May 1871, pp. 66–72.
[13] Henry O'Brien, manuscript journal for the Rockies, 1882, collection of Mrs. J. A. Grant.

20.

Paul Kane
1846

Coo-Coosh

a Potawatami Indian

The Hog Potawatami

Plate IX. Coe-coosh or "The Hog," a Potawatomi, Fox River. Stark EOP30; crIII-126.

PART TWO   *Wanderings of an Artist*

A NOTE ON THE TEXT

The text of *Wanderings of an Artist* printed here is that of the original edition published in London, England, in 1859 by Longman, Brown, Green, Longmans, and Roberts, except that it omits the Appendix; this was the only complete edition published in English in Paul Kane's lifetime. A second edition, in which the text differs from that of the first edition in minor details, was published by the Radisson Society of Canada in 1925; it contained an "Editor's Foreword" by John W. Garvin, and Introduction and Notes by Lawrence J. Burpee, and two lists ("Catalogue of Paintings by Paul Kane in the Royal Ontario Museum of Archaeology, in Toronto" and "List of Pictures Purchased for the Legislative Council"). This second edition, reprinted by offset, was published again in 1968 by the Charles E. Tuttle Company, Inc., and M. G. Hurtig Ltd., with an "Introduction to the New Edition" by J. G. MacGregor.

Enclosed within square brackets at relevant points in the text are cross-references to plates and figures printed in the present volume and to entries in its *catalogue raisonné* (thus the reference crIII-2 indicates item 2 in section III of the *catalogue raisonné*). The 1859 edition had 21 illustrations to which Kane refers in his narrative; the *catalogue raisonné* identifies these.

The footnotes to the text are intended to serve two purposes. Some identify persons mentioned by Paul Kane in the text or provide further information about events recorded there. The majority present variations from the printed text of *Wanderings* which are to be found in two manuscripts, in the possession of the Nelda and H. J. Lutcher Stark Foundation of Orange, Texas. These manuscripts are (1) a journal, in Kane's hand, which he kept from 1846 to 1848 and on which a part of the published text is based; (2) a version of the *Wanderings*, in his wife's hand, which was revised further before publication. Both manuscripts show numerous minor variations from the printed version, but only significant ones are recorded here. References to the journal are introduced by the abbreviation "kj" and to the manuscript version of *Wanderings* by "kwms." The 1859 edition of *Wanderings* had three footnotes, and these are incorporated into the present numbering system and identified by the abbreviation "w59." Kane's spelling in kj has been modernized.

Wanderings of an Artist

AMONG THE INDIANS OF NORTH AMERICA
FROM CANADA TO VANCOUVER'S ISLAND
AND OREGON THROUGH THE HUDSON'S
BAY COMPANY'S TERRITORY
AND BACK AGAIN

By Paul Kane

TO

GEORGE WILLIAM ALLAN, ESQ.

OF MOSS PARK, TORONTO, CANADA WEST

This Work

DESIGNED TO ILLUSTRATE THE MANNERS AND CUSTOMS OF THE

INDIAN TRIBES OF BRITISH AMERICA

Is Respectfully Dedicated

AS A TOKEN OF GRATITUDE FOR THE KIND AND GENEROUS INTEREST

HE HAS ALWAYS TAKEN IN THE AUTHOR'S LABOURS,

AS WELL AS A SINCERE EXPRESSION OF ADMIRATION OF THE

LIBERALITY WITH WHICH, AS A NATIVE CANADIAN,

HE IS EVER READY TO FOSTER CANADIAN TALENT AND ENTERPRISE.

Toronto: July 9, 1858.

Preface.

On my return to Canada from the continent of Europe, where I had passed nearly four years in studying my profession as a painter, I determined to devote whatever talents and proficiency I possessed to the painting of a series of pictures illustrative of the North American Indians and scenery. The subject was one in which I felt a deep interest in my boyhood. I had been accustomed to see hundreds of Indians about my native village, then Little York, muddy and dirty, just struggling into existence, now the City of Toronto, bursting forth in all its energy and commercial strength. But the face of the red man is now no longer seen. All traces of his footsteps are fast being obliterated from his once favourite haunts, and those who would see the aborigines of this country in their original state, or seek to study their native manners and customs, must travel far through the pathless forest to find them. To me the wild woods were not altogether unknown, and the Indians but recalled old friends with whom I had associated in my childhood, and though at the commencement of my travels I possessed neither influence nor means for such an undertaking, yet it was with a determined spirit and a light heart that I had made the few preparations which were in my power for my future proceedings.

The principal object in my undertaking was to sketch pictures of the principal chiefs, and their original costumes, to illustrate their manners and customs, and to represent the scenery of an almost unknown country. These paintings, however, would necessarily require explanations and notes, and I accordingly kept a diary of my journey, as being the most easy and familiar form in which I could put such information as I might collect. The following pages are the notes of my daily journey, with little alteration from the original wording, as I jotted them down in pencil at the time; and although without any claim to public approbation as a literary production, still I trust they will possess not only an interest for the curious, but also an intrinsic value to the historian, as they relate not only to that vast tract of country bordering on the great chain of American lakes, the Red River settlement, the valley of Sascatchawan, and its boundless prairies, through which it is proposed to lay the great railway connecting the Atlantic and Pacific Oceans, through the British possessions; but also across the Rocky Mountains down the Columbia River to Oregon, Puget's Sound, and Vancouver's Island, where the recent gold discoveries in the vicinity have drawn thousands of hardy adventurers to those wild scenes amongst which I strayed almost alone, and scarcely meeting a white man or hearing the sound of my own language.

The illustrations—executed from my sketches, or finished paintings, for the purpose of illustrating the present work—constitute only a few specimens of the different classes of subjects which engaged my pencil during a sojourn of nearly four years among the Indians of the North-west. In that period I executed numerous portraits of chiefs, warriors, and medicine-men of the different tribes among whom I sojourned, and also of their wives and daughters. The Indian fishing and hunting scenes, games, dances, and other characteristic customs, also occupied my pencil; while I was not forgetful of the interest which justly attaches to the scenery of a new and unexplored country, and especially to such parts of it as were either intimately associated with native legends and traditions, or otherwise specially connected with the native tribes—as their favourite fishing or hunting grounds, the locations of their villages, or the burying-places of the tribes. The whole of these sketches are now in my possession, and I have already been honoured by a commission to execute a series of paintings from them for the Legislature of the Province of Canada, which now have a place in the Library of the Provincial Parliament. A much more extensive series of oil paintings had been executed by me, from my sketches, for George W. Allan, Esq., of Moss Park, the liberal patron of Canadian art; and I would gladly indulge the hope that the present work will not prove the sole published fruits of my travels among the Indian tribes of North America, but that it will rather be a mere illustration of the novelty and interest which attach to those rarely explored regions, and enable me to publish a much more extensive series of illustrations of the characteristics, habits, and scenery of the country and its occupants.

PAUL KANE

Chapter I.

Departure from Toronto.—An Indian Village.—The "Big Pike's" Likeness.—The Chiefs of Saugeen.—An Island Labyrinth.—The Encampment.—An Indian Kettle of Fish.—The Household Drudge. —Manetouawning.—Anecdote of the Chief Sigennok.—The Egyptian Sphynx on Indian Pipes.—A Serenade.—The Conjuror.—The Power of Love.—The Escape.—Heraldic Devices.—Departure for the Sault St. Marie.

I left Toronto on the 17th of June 1845, with no companions but my portfolio and box of paints, my gun, and a stock of ammunition, taking the most direct route to Lake Simcoe. Thence I took the steamboat for Orillia; and crossed over to Sturgeon Bay on Lake Huron, where I had to hire an Indian with a canoe, the packet having left for Penetanguishene a few hours before I reached "Cold Water." After paddling all night, we overtook her the next morning at Penetanguishene, or the "Rolling Sand Bank," which is seated in a deep bay, forming a secure harbour for vessels of any amount of tonnage: it has been so named by the Indians from a high bank of rolling sand at the entrance of the bay. There is a small naval depôt here, and a steamer is employed in making trips of inspection round the lake and its shores. A larger one has been for some years laid up in ordinary, and is no doubt now unfit for use. Besides this depôt, there is a village inhabited by a few whites and half-breeds.

We left Penetanguishene on the 20th, and arrived at Owen's Sound the same evening. I here met with three men bound for Saugeen, about thirty-five or forty miles west of this place, where a council of chiefs was to meet for the purpose of negotiating the sale of a tract of land to the Provincial Government.[1] After engaging an Indian to carry my pack and act as guide, I started in company with them on foot. Our journey was a disagreeable one, through woods and swamps, the rain all the time coming down in torrents. We had to encamp at night supperless, and without shelter of any kind, in our wet clothes, as we had omitted to bring blankets or provisions under the expectation of reaching Saugeen the same evening. We made an early start the next morning, and arrived there about noon, where we found a large assemblage of Indians holding a camp meeting, with its usual accompaniments of boisterous singing and praying, under the superintendence of six or seven Methodist preachers.

The Indian village of Saugeen, meaning "the Mouth of a River," contains about 200 inhabitants (Ojibbeways). It is the site of a former battleground between the Ojibbeways, as usually pronounced, or Chippawas, and the Mohawks. Of this, the mounds erected over the slain afford abundant evidence in the protrusion of the bones through the surface of the ground. The land hereabouts is excellent, but only a small part is cultivated, as the inhabitants subsist principally on fish, which are taken in great abundance at the entrance of the river. They also kill hundreds of deer by erecting a fence of brushwood many miles in extent, behind which the Indians conceal themselves; and as the deer, in their annual migrations, are seeking an opening through this fence, they fall a prey to the unerring aim of the red man. I sketched the principal chief, named Maticwaub, or "the Bow." [2] [crIII-1] The band of which he is the head chief forms a part of the great nation of the Ojibbeways, which still inhabits the shores of Lakes Huron, Michigan, and Superior. [Fig. 14; crIII-2, 3] There is also another large band of them on the upper Mississippi, 90 or 100 miles above the falls of Saint Anthony; they speak the same language; their medicine dances, called Matayway, and their feasts are in every respect the same, identifying them as one and the same people, although scattered so widely apart. Another branch of them, called the Pilleurs, is found some 200 or 300 miles farther north. They derive their name from their thievish propensities, and richly deserve it, as I unfortunately experienced some few years afterwards on visiting their country.

I also took a sketch of a chief named Maskuhnoonjee, or the "Big Pike." [Figs. 15, 16; crIII-4, 5, 6] This man was very proud of having his likeness taken, and put on his chief's medal presented by the Government to those they acknowledge as chiefs. I have never known a chief to barter away one of these marks of distinction, which they seldom wear on unimportant occasions. An interesting girl, the daughter of a chief from Lake St. Clair, gave me much trouble in prevailing on her to sit for her likeness, although her father insisted upon it; her repugnance proceeded from a superstitious belief that by so doing she would place herself in the power of the possessor of what is regarded by an Indian as a second self. [Fig. 17; crIII-7, 8,

[1] According to the report of the Indian Commissioner for 1845 (in the Public Archives of Canada, RG10, vol. 612), chieftains from St. Clair, Huron, Ontario, Simcoe, Rice and Mud lakes attended the Saugeen meeting; the purpose of the meeting differs from that assigned by Kane. The objective of the Indians is given as formulation of plans by which the Saugeen lands could be held for the sole benefit of the "Ojibwa Nation," the petitioning of the government for aid in establishing a manual labour school, and the sounding out of chieftains about formation of one large settlement at Owen Sound for the various groups. The Bruce Peninsula, in which Saugeen was located, was to be ceded to the British government on October 31, 1854.
[2] KWMS states that Kane sketched not only Maticwaub but also three or four subordinate chiefs and other members of the tribe.

8a] Wāh-pūs, "the Rabbit," also permitted me to take his portrait. [Fig. 18; crIII-9, 10, 11] He resides at Owen's Sound, and was formerly as much renowned for his unconquerable fierceness and intemperance as he is now for his temperance and wisdom. This change in his character is attributable to the influence of the Methodist missionaries, whose church he has joined. He was the first Indian I had seen whose hair had been pulled out, all except the scalp-lock; this custom is common amongst many tribes of Indians, though not universal amongst any.

I remained at Saugeen about ten days,[3] residing in the family of an Indian who had been educated as a Wesleyan missionary.[4] I then returned to Owen's Sound, accompanied by a young man named Dillon, who was extremely desirous of joining in my excursion. [Fig. 19; crIII-12] On arriving at the Sound I bought a canoe and a stock of provisions, and embarked with my new companion for Penetanguishene in our route for the Manitoulin Islands. On the fourth day we passed Christian Island, on which are still standing the ruins of a fort, said to have been built by two Jesuit priests who took refuge on the island with a large band of Hurons, after they had been defeated by the Iroquoisin. They defended the fort until they were nearly all destroyed by hunger and disease, when the missionaries led the survivors to Quebec.[5] The day after passing this island we again reached Penetanguishene, where we obtained a fresh supply of provisions, after which we threaded a labyrinth of islands of every size and form, amounting, as is said, to upwards of 30,-000;[6] and both being strangers to the navigation, we continually lost ourselves in its picturesque mazes, enchanted with the beauty of the ever-varying scenery, as we glided along in our light canoe. We fished and hunted for fouteen days, almost unconscious of the lapse of time so agreeably spent. We saw only two or three Indians, the greater part of them having preceded us to Manetouawning to receive their presents.

Sketch No. 1 [crIII-18] represents an Indian encampment amongst the islands of Lake Huron; the wigwams are made of

[3] KJ says he remained for a week.
[4] This was Richard Conway, an Indian born on the Rice Lake reservation near Peterborough, Ont.
[5] KJ gives what was evidently a local legend: that the Chippewa had been attacked by the Potawatomi and 8,000 Chippewa had gone to the island. The published version has the correct story.
[6] KJ puts the number at 2,700.
[7] W59: "It would be as well to note here that the word *"Portage"* is applied to such places as require the canoes to be taken bodily out of the water and carried up the ascent by the men, and *"Discharge"* to such shallows or rapids as will not allow the canoes to pass without being considerably lightened or entirely emptied, and then pulled or dragged by cord over the difficulty."

birch-bark, stripped from the trees in large pieces and sewed together with long fibrous roots; when the birch tree cannot be conveniently had, they weave rushes into mats, called Apuckway, for covering, which are stretched round in the same manner as the bark, upon eight or ten poles tied together at the top, and stuck in the ground at the required circle of the tent, a hole being left at the top to permit the smoke to go out. The fire is made in the centre of the lodge, and the inmates sleep all round with their feet towards it. [Fig. 20; crIII-13 to 21] These lodges are much more comfortable than one would at first suppose from their loose appearance—that is, as far as warmth is considered. The filth, stench, and vermin make them almost intolerable to a white man; but Indians are invariably dirty, and it must be something very terrible indeed which will induce them to take half an hour's trouble in moving their lodge. As to removing the filth, that is never done. Their canoes are also made of birch-bark stretched over a very light frame of split cedar laths; the greatest attention being paid to symmetry and form. [crIII-23] They travel a great deal and are often exposed to rough weather in these boats, which, being extremely light, are carried across "portages" with ease.[7] They make their mohcocks, or kettles, of birch-bark, in which they cook fish and game. This is done by putting red hot stones into the water, and it is astonishing how quickly an Indian woman will boil a fish in this way. The Indians round Lake Huron raise a good deal of corn, which is dried and then pounded in a sort of mortar, made out of a hollow log, as represented in the sketch. [crIII-22]

The Indians in this neighbourhood having a direct communication with the whites, use guns and other weapons of civilized manufacture, bows and arrows being seldom seen except with the children. [Fig. 21; crIII-24] As amongst all other tribes of North American Indians, the women do all the household work, carrying wood, putting up lodges, and cooking. I here noticed a custom amongst the women bearing a curious resemblance to the ancient usages of the Jews. At certain stated periods they are not allowed the slightest intercourse with the rest of the tribe, but are obliged to build a little hut for themselves a short distance from the camp, where they live entirely secluded until their return to health.

[French River: Pl. III, Fig. 22; crIII-25, 26]

Previous to entering the bay of Manetouawning, we put ashore on one of the Spider Islands, to escape from a heavy shower, where we found a single lodge. [Pl. IV; crIII-27 to 31] A woman and her two children were there, but the men were off in the distance fishing, which is the principal occupation of the Indians hereabouts in summer, there being very little game, except occasionally a bear or deer, and, at particular seasons, ducks. The afternoon being clear, I had a fine view of the La Cloche Mountains, and spent the remainder of the evening in sketching. [Fig. 23; crIII-32 to 37]

Manetouawning is situated at the extremity of a bay six miles long, in the great Manetoulin Island, and is 200 miles distant from Penetanguishene by the route we took.

The word Manetouawning signifies "the Spirit Hole." The village consists of forty or fifty log-houses built by the Provincial Government for the Indians. [crIII-38] There is a mission, with a church and pastor, an Indian agent, a doctor, and a blacksmith, all paid by the Government. I found nearly 2000 Indians here,[8] waiting the arrival of the vessel that was freighted with their annual presents, comprising guns, ammunition, axes, kettles, and other implements useful to the Indian. [Fig. 24; crIII-39, 40]

The principal chief here is Sigennok; he is an acute and intelligent Indian; he is appointed to distribute to his tribe their due share of the presents annually consigned to them. [crIII-42] He receives a salary from the British Government as interpreter. This is paid him from policy, for although useless as an interpreter, from not speaking the English language, his natural eloquence is such that he possesses great influence over his tribe; indeed, it is to the untiring volubility of his tongue that he owes his name, which signifies "The Blackbird." The following anecdote, illustrative of character, was related to me by Captain Anderson, now superintendent of Indian affairs:—Sigennok was, in his younger days, in the continual habit of drinking to excess, and when under the influence of his potations was a perfect maniac, and only to be controlled by main force; but as the attempt to place him under due restraint was attended with no small personal danger, on account of his Herculean strength, it was the custom of his attendants to increase the amount of stimulus, and ply him with it until he became insensible, rather than expose themselves to danger from his ungovernable violence. One day, when in this state of drunken stupor, Captain Anderson—who at that time filled the post of Indian agent,—saw him lying in front of his lodge in one of these fits of oblivion, and bound him hand and foot with strong cords, placing a sickly decrepit boy to watch

over him, with instructions to hasten to him (Captain Anderson) the moment the sleeper should awake, and by no means to let him know who it was that had bound him. After some hours he revived, and angrily demanded of the boy, who had dared to treat him with such indignity. The little fellow, without replying to the inquiry, hobbled away to the captain: he at once hastened to his prisoner, who put the same interrogatory to him as he had before done to the boy, and furiously demanded his instant liberation. The captain replied that the boy had bound him by his own orders, and that he had lain for hours exposed to the derision of the whole camp. He took the opportunity also of commenting forcibly on the disgrace to which so great a warrior had thus subjected himself, merely to gratify a vile and disgusting propensity, which reduced him manifestly beneath the level of the brute beast, which never sacrificed its reason, or the power to protect itself from annoyance or insult from its fellows.

Sigennok, his pride humbled, and greatly mortified at the degraded position in which he had placed himself—in the power, as it were, of the most helpless of his tribe—formed the prompt resolution of at once and for ever abandoning his favourite habit, and promised Captain Anderson that if he would release him from his bonds, he would never again taste ardent spirits. The captain took him at his word, and unbound him. Twenty-three years had elapsed since the occurrence, during which Sigennok had never been known to violate the promise then made.

Sketch No. 2 [Fig. 29] represents Awbonwaishkum. [crIII-53, 54] This head possesses the characteristics of the Indian to a striking degree: the small piercing eyes, high cheekbones, large mouth, protuberant and hanging lips, are strongly indicative of the race. This chief is a man of great ingenuity and judgment. The sketch No. 3 [Fig. 30] is that of a pipe carved by Awbonwaishkum out of a dark-coloured stone, his only tools being an old knife and broken file. [crIII-55] I leave it to antiquaries to explain how the bowl of this pipe happens to bear so striking a resemblance to the head of the Egyptian sphinx. I questioned Awbonwaishkum as to whether he knew of any tradition connected with the design, but the only explanation he could offer was, that his forefathers had made similar pipes with the same shaped head for the bowl, and that he therefore supposed the model had always existed among the Indians.

Strolling one evening in the vicinity of the camp, I heard the sound of some musical instrument, and upon approaching the performer, who was lying under a tree, I found that he was playing on an instrument resembling a flageolet in construction,

Plate X. Sioux Scalp Dance (Fort Snelling). ROM912.1.15; CRIII-144.

Plate XI. Chief from Fort William (Maydoc-game-kinungee, an Ojibwa). ROM 912.1.16; CRIV-2.

but much softer in tone. This instrument is principally used by lovers, who play for hours in the vicinity of their mistress's lodge. I have often listened with pleasure to this music, as its simple and plaintive notes stole through the stillness of the forest. The lover made no secret of his object, but conversed with me freely upon the subject of his love.

The Indians assemble annually at Manetouawning from all parts of the shores of Lakes Huron, Nipissing, and Superior, as well as from all the neighbouring islands. [Figs. 27, 28; crIII-43, 46 to 52, 57 to 60] On the arrival of the presents, the Indians, male and female, accompanied by their children, immediately seated themselves in rows on the grass, each chief heading his own little band, and giving in their number and names to Sigennok, who here appears in his proper element, dividing the goods among them with great impartiality. [Fig. 25; crIII-41] He is really a very useful man. His voice is heard everywhere above the universal din of tongues, his native eloquence is unceasing, and seems to have the effect of allaying every envious and unpleasant feeling, and keeping all in good humour and proper order.[9]

Among the numerous Indians assembled here, was one that particularly attracted my attention from his venerable and dignified appearance. In reply to my inquiry, as to who he was, I learned that he was called Shawwanossoway, or "One with his Face towards the West," and that he was a great medicine-man, skilled in the past, present and future. [Fig. 26; crIII-44, 45] As I happened to lose, some days previously, some articles from my tent, I resolved, for the sake of an introduction, and the gratification of my curiosity, to apply to the seer. On laying my case before him, he told me that his power was of no avail wherever the pale faces were concerned, and, notwithstanding my offer of a very liberal remuneration, I could not prevail upon him to put his incantations into practice. He had been, I was told, a celebrated warrior in his youth, but that owing to a romantic incident, he had abandoned the tomahawk and scalping-knife for the peaceable profession of the medicine-man, or, in common parlance, the necromancer or conjuror, in which he has obtained great repute among his people.

[9] According to the report of the Indian commissioner (see note 1), the following presents were handed out on this occasion: 149 yards of blue and grey cloth, 227½ yards of caddies, 942½ yards molton, 747½ yards blue or grey ratteen, 1,975⅓ yards stroud, 102 yards Irish linen, 2,630 yards printed calico, 570 one-point blankets, 240 one and half-point blankets, 250 two-point blankets, 794 two and half-point blankets, 646 three-point blankets, 22 twilled cotton shawls, 1,128 oz. sewing thread, 5,760 sewing needles, 1,440 horn combs, 1,440 awls, 1,440 butcher knives, 1,360 lb. tobacco, 1,326 lb. ball, 4,590 lb. shot, 1,972 lb. gunpowder, 2,652 flints.

There dwelt many years before, on the shores of one of the great lakes, a band of Ojibbeways. Among them was a family consisting of a father and mother, with a grown-up son and daughter, the latter named Awh-mid-way, or, "There is music in her footsteps:" she exceeded in beauty the rest of the tribe, and was eagerly sought in marriage by all the young warriors of her nation. It was not long before Muck-e-tick-enow, or, "Black Eagle," renowned for his prowess in battle and the chase, had, by his assiduities, won her undivided affections; nor did she conceal from him this favourable state of her feelings, but, in accordance with the customs of her people, she had unhesitatingly extinguished the blazing bark which he had sent floating down the stream that glided past her lodge, and thus acknowledged him as her accepted lover. Confident of possessing her heart, he directed all his endeavours to the propitiation of her parents, and eagerly sought how to compensate them for the loss they would undergo in relinquishing a daughter so dearly loved. For this purpose he departed on a long and distant hunt, and while straining every faculty of his mind and body in collecting trophies and presents wherewith to conciliate them, and show his entire devotion to the object of his adoration, their evil destiny brought Shawwanossoway, then a great war chief, in all the pride of manly strength and vigour, to their camp, on his return from a war excursion, in which he had greatly distinguished himself, and spread his fame far and wide, as the terror of his enemies and the boast of his friends.

Having heard of the transcendent charms of Awh-mid-way, he presented himself before her, girded with the scalps of his enemies, and loaded with other trophies of victory. No sooner did he behold her, than, overcome by her charms, he devoted himself to her service and endeavoured, by every art that the most passionate love could dictate, to win her regard. He recounted the numerous battles he had won, the enemies he had slain: he displayed the reeking scalps he had torn from the defeated enemy,—warriors who had been the terror of his nation: he named the many chiefs who had sued to him for peace, and at the same time plied every artifice to win the good-will of her parents, who, proud of what they considered their daughter's superb conquest, listened to him with delight, and urged her, by every persuasive argument, to accept so distinguished a chief as her husband, expatiating on the honour such an alliance would confer on their family. Constant, however, to her first love, she turned a deaf ear to all the protestations of his rival, whose tales of conquest and bloody trophies only excited her abhorrence.

But, nothing daunted, and determined to win her, either by fair means or by foul, Shawwanossoway persevered in his suit, trusting to time and accident to attain his object. The poor girl, now made truly wretched by his undeviating persecution, accompanied by the menaces of her parents, who were determined to conquer what they regarded as the rebellious obstinacy of their child, at length came to the resolution of appealing to the generosity and honour of her persecutor, and, in the hope of propitiating his forbearance, in an evil hour she confessed her long-cherished affection for Muck-e-tick-enow. He no sooner discovered the cause of her rejection of his suit, than rage and jealousy took full possession of his heart, and plans of vengeance rapidly succeeded each other, until he decided on the assassination of his rival. Having learned from his unsuspecting charmer the route her lover had taken, he tracked him, and came up with his camp, and, concealing himself from observation, crawled towards the fire, where his victim sat alone preparing his evening repast, and shot him from behind a tree. Hiding the body among some brushwood, he took possession of the game of his murdered rival as a means of accounting for his own absence, and hastened back to the village, where he renewed his suit more ardently than before, to the utter disappointment and distress of Awh-mid-way who still rejected all his overtures with indignation, until, urged by the positive commands and threats of her parents, she at last, hoping by some artifice still to put off the evil day, consented to name a time when she would receive him as her husband, trusting that her lover would in the meantime return and rescue her from the impending sacrifice, and concealing, as well as she could, her increasing aversion to her persecutor.

The dreaded day at last, however, arrived, but no lover of course returned. Little did she think that his mangled remains had fallen a prey to the ravenous beasts of the forest—for still hope fondly directed her gaze in the direction she had seen him take at his departure, when all was sunshine and prospective happiness. With aching eyes and a bursting heart she saw the evening approach that was to bind her irrevocably to one she abhorred.

The bridal canoe which, according to the Indian custom, had been prepared with all the necessary stores to convey the betrothed pair on a month's excursion together, which is, in fact, the only marriage ceremony, was already lying upon the beach. Night had come—the nuptial feast was prepared—the last she was to partake of in her father's lodge—when lo! the bride was missing, and consternation usurped the place of gaiety in the

bridal throng. Eagerly did they seek her with torches and shouts through the neighbouring forests, but no answering sound met their ears, although the search was continued with untiring eagerness till daylight. Then, for the first time, it was discovered that the bridal canoe was gone, and, concluding that the bride had availed herself of it to aid her escape, Shawwanossoway, accompanied by her brother, started in pursuit on foot, following the direction of the shore.

After proceeding for several hours, they caught sight of the canoe and its fair occupant in the distance. Increasing their speed, they reached a point which the canoe must necessarily pass round. Here the lover swam out, hoping to intercept it. In vain did he endeavour, by every means he could devise, to induce her to stop and take him on board. Defeated by her resolute refusal and the vigour and skill with which she plied her paddle, he was obliged to relinquish the pursuit and return to the shore. He had scarcely landed, when a violent storm, accompanied with thunder, lightning, and heavy rain, compelled the pair to encamp for the night. Notwithstanding the tempest, she continued her efforts until the shades of night hid her from their view. The clouds dispersed with the dawning day, and they continued their pursuit until they at length espied the canoe lying on the shore. Thinking they had at last attained their object, they quickened their steps; but, on coming up to it, they encountered a troop of wolves, and their horror may well be conceived on discovering the remains of the being they loved almost wholly devoured, and only to be recognised by her torn and scattered garments. With aching hearts, they carefully gathered her cherished remains, and, placing them in the canoe, returned to the camp, where she was wept and mourned over for many weeks by her disconsolate relatives and friends, and buried with all the ceremonies of her tribe.

It was evident that the heavy storm had driven the canoe ashore, and it is probable that her materials for kindling a fire having become soaked with water, she had been debarred the only means of protecting herself from these ravenous animals.

Shawwanossoway was so much grieved at the misery which his ungovernable passions had brought upon the object of his warmest love, that he formed the resolution of abandoning his warlike pursuits; and, throwing up the tomahawk to the Great Spirit, that it might be employed only as an instrument of justice, he took in its stead the rattle of the medicine-man; nor did he ever after act inconsistently with his altered character.

Six miles from Manetouawning is another village called Wequimecong, comprising fifty or sixty houses, and a Catholic mission with a church.[10] I made a sketch of the principal chief, named Asabonish, "the Racoon," and his daughter. [Fig. 33; crIII-63] He belongs to the tribe of Ahtawwah Indians. This tribe is now scarcely distinct from the Ojibbeways, with whom they have numerously intermarried, and speak the same language. The Indians of this village subsist chiefly on salmon and white fish, which they take in such quantities as to be able to barter away a surplus beyond their own wants for other necessaries. The inhabitants also make abundance of maple sugar, which they sell to the traders; nor are they so very deficient in agricultural skill and industry, having, under the able and kind guidance of the missionary, cultivated many patches of wheat, corn, and potatoes, as well as erected a neat little church.

While I was at Manetouawning, the successor of Mr. Anderson, Captain Ironsides, arrived there; and as he was a half-breed and chief of the Wyandots, I have introduced him among my Indian sketches. [Fig. 31; crIII-56] His name signifies, "Walk in the water:" he is a descendant of Tecumseh, and uses the same *to-tem,* a turtle, each Indian family having a sort of heraldic device, which they use as a signature on important occasions. Sometimes a family passing through the woods will cut a chip out of a tree, and mark their to-tem on the fresh surface, so that the next may know who passed; or should a chief wish to send to a post for any articles, he draws the articles on a piece of birch-bark, and puts his to-tem, a fox, a dog, a bear, or whatever it may be, at the bottom; these are perfectly well understood, and answer every purpose of a written order. [Fig. 32; crIII-61, 62]

I remained at the Manitoulin Island a fortnight, parting with Mr. Dillon, who returned in the schooner that brought the presents. I left for the Sault St. Marie on board the steamer "Experiment," a Government vessel; Captain Harper, who commanded, kindly taking my canoe on board, and giving me a passage. At the Sault St. Marie I made the acquaintance of Mr. Ballantyne, the gentleman in charge of the Hudson Bay Company's Post, who was exceedingly kind.[11] [Pls. V, VI; Fig. 34; crIII-64 to 77] He strongly advised me against attempting to penetrate into the interior, except under the auspices of the Company, representing it as almost impossible and certainly very dangerous; but urged me to apply to Sir George Simpson,

the Governor of the Company at Lachine, who, he thought, when aware of the object I had in view, would send me forward with the spring brigade of canoes next year. Hoping that, by following this advice, I should be able to travel further, and see more of the wilder tribes, I determined upon confining my travels for the present to a mere summer campaign.

Chapter II.

Mackenaw, the "Turtle Island."—Famished Dogs.—The Chief He-Devil.—Green Bay, a Commercial Port.—Consolation in Sorrow.—An Indian Council.—Gambling Habits.—Illicit Traffic in Spirits.—Anecdote of Revenge.—A young Assassin.—Day of Reckoning.—Scenes of Drunkenness.

As it is my intention to speak of the Sault St. Marie in my next trip, I will pass over any mention of it here. After remaining a few days, I embarked on board a steamer[1] for Mackenaw, a distance of ninety miles. There I found a large band of Indians to the number of 2600, who had come from all quarters to receive their pay of $25,000 for land ceded to the United States;[2] these Indians were also Ojibbeways and Ottawas. On arriving among them, I at once pitched my tent in their midst, and commenced to sketch their most remarkable personages. [Pl. VIII; crIII-89 to 94] I soon had to remove my tent, from the circumstance that their famishing dogs, which they keep for the purpose of hunting and drawing their sleds in winter, contrived to carry off all my provisions, and seemed likely to serve me in the same way. This will appear by no means improbable, when I state that, while I was one evening finishing a sketch, sitting on the ground alone in my tent, with my candle stuck in the earth at my side, one of these audacious brutes unceremoniously dashed in through the entrance, seized the burning candle in his jaws and bolted off with it, leaving me in total darkness.

The next day, as I approached my tent, I saw a dog running away from it, and thinking it probably the same rascal that had stolen my candle, I thought to inflict summary justice upon the marauder, and fired the contents of my pistol into his carcase. Beyond my expectations, which had only been to wound, I saw that I had killed him, and was immediately assailed with a

---

[10] According to the report of the Indian commissioner (see note 1), the church maintained a school with a Catholic schoolmaster, Charles Lamorandière. Attendance in 1845 ranged from 32 to 35 boys and 24 to 26 girls.

[11] This is John Ballenden, a well-known Hudson's Bay Company factor, who was subsequently chief factor of the Red River post.

[1] KJ says the vessel was the *General Scott.*

[2] KJ states that nearly 3,000 Indians were waiting to receive payments of $25 each.

demand, from the owner of the dog and his wife, for payment for the loss of his services, which I agreed to liquidate on their paying me for the losses I had sustained in hams and other provisions which their dog had stolen from me. Hereupon they balanced accounts, and considered that we were about even, giving me an invitation to join them at supper, and partake with them of the slaughtered animal, in which operation I afterwards saw them happily engaged.

The Indian name of the island is Mitchi-mac-inum, or, "the Big Turtle," to which animal it bears a strong resemblance in form when seen from a certain point.

It is situated in the straits between Lakes Huron and Michigan [Fig. 37; crIII-84 to 87]; it contains some picturesque spots, one in particular, a natural bridge, which all strangers visit. [Fig. 36; crIII-79 to 83] There is a garrison on the island, consisting of a company of soldiers. [Fig. 35; crIII-78] The inhabitants support themselves chiefly by fishing, the straits here yielding an immense supply of large salmon and white fish. [crIII-97 to 105] Many traders assemble at Mackenaw, at the periods of payment, bringing with them large quantities of spirituous liquors, which they sell clandestinely to these poor creatures, it being prohibited by Government; and many an Indian who travels thither from a long distance returns to his wigwam poorer than he left it, his sole satisfaction being that he and his family have enjoyed a glorious bout of intoxication.

I took the likeness of a chief named Mani-tow-wah-bay, or, "He-Devil." [Pl. VII; crIII-88] He anxiously inquired what I wanted the likenesses for. In order to induce him to sit, I told him that they were going home to his great mother, the Queen. He said that he had often heard of her, and was very desirous of seeing her, and that had he the time and means, he would pay her a visit. It pleased him much that his second self would have an opportunity of seeing her. He told me, with much pride that he had been a successful warrior, and had taken nine scalps in his warfare. He was very fond of liquor, and, when under its influence, was one of the most violent and unmanageable among them.

[Wampum belts: Fig. 38; crIII-95, 96]

Having remained at Mackenaw for three weeks, I left for Green Bay, which is well situated for a commercial port, and must eventually become a place of importance, from the rich farming country in its vicinity; but owing to over speculation in every way in the years 1836 and 1837, it has been paralysed, and houses might now be obtained for the keeping them in repair. Here I amused myself with shooting snipe, which are

met with in abundance. In about a week I left in company with three gentlemen going to Fox River to see the Manōmanee Indians, who were now assembling to receive their payment for lands sold to the United States Government in the vicinity of Lake Winebago. We embarked in my little canoe, and proceeded up stream, arriving on the second night about 11 o'clock at an Indian log-house on the shore of Lake Winebago, or, "Muddy Lake." Two Indian girls, sisters, reside here alone. I remained with them the next day, and took their likenesses; the elder was named Iwa-toke, or, "the Serpent," the younger was called Ke-wah-ten, "the North Wind." [Fig. 39, crIII-107; Fig. 40, crIII-106, 108] We then proceeded up the lake to Fox River, entering which we found an Indian trading-house, round about which a number of idlers were pledging everything they possessed for liquor, under the influence of which dozens were lying about in a state of beastly intoxication.

An Indian called Wah-bannim, or, "the White Dog," sat to me for his likeness. [crIII-109, 110] He was in mourning for his wife, who had died some three months before; the mourning suit consisting of a coat of black paint with which he had smeared his face. He apologised for not appearing in full mourning costume to have his likeness taken, lamenting that a part of the paint had worn off; he was eagerly seeking to obtain whisky to console him for his loss. We gladly quitted this disgusting scene of dissipation, and continued our course up the monotonous stream. After paddling for two days, we reached the Monōmanee camp.

The evening previous to our arrival, we saw some Indians spearing salmon; by night, this has always a very picturesque appearance, the strong red glare of the blazing pine knots and roots in the iron frame, or light-jack, at the bow of the canoe throwing the naked figures of the Indians into wild relief upon the dark water and sombre woods. Great numbers of fish are killed in this manner. As the light is intense, and being above the head of the spearsman, it enables him to see the fish distinctly at a great depth, and at the same time it apparently either dazzles or attracts the fish. In my boyish days I have seen as many as a hundred light-jacks gliding about the Bay of Toronto, and have often joined in the sport. This, I suppose, gave me additional interest in the scene; and although very tired with my long day's paddling, I sat down by the fire, and while my companion was cooking some fish in a moh-cock, Indian fashion (for we had lost our kettle), I made the sketch No. 4. [Fig. 41; crIII-111, 112]

Here we found about 3000 Indians assembled, anxiously

awaiting the arrival of the agent with their money [3] [crIII-124, 130–40]; there was also a large number of traders collected, all busily occupied in the erection of booths for the display of their finery. In about a week the bank of the river wore the aspect of a little town; the booths, placed in rows, presented a scene of bustle and animation: the finery was, of course, all displayed to the best advantage on the outsides of the booths. On the arrival of the Indian agent a council was immediately called in a place erected for the occasion, in which thirty chiefs assembled. I attended in compliance with an invitation I had received from the head chief, Oscosh, or, "the Bravest of the Brave." [Fig. 42; crIII-113, 114]

He opened the council by lighting a pipe, and handing it to all present, each person taking a whiff or two, and passing it to the next. [crIII-116] The mingling clouds of smoke raised by each are supposed to ascend to the Great Spirit, in token of the harmony that pervades the assembly, and to attest the purity of their intentions. After this ceremony the main business of the council began: it almost exclusively consisted of complaints to be forwarded to the Government. After several of the minor chiefs had delivered their sentiments, Oscosh himself rose, and spoke for about an hour, and a finer flow of native eloquence—seasoned with good sense—I never heard, than proceeded from the lips of this untutored savage. Although a small man, his appearance, while speaking, possessed dignity; his attitude was graceful, and free from uncouth gesticulation. He complained of numerous acts of injustice which he supposed their great father, the President, could not possibly know, and which he desired might be represented to him, through the agent, accompanied with a pipe-stem of peace richly ornamented. [crIII-115]

One of the grievances he specified was, that their money passed through too many hands before it reached them, and that a great part of it was thus lost to them. He wound up his long harangue by descanting upon the narrow limits in which they were pent up, which did not allow them sufficient hunting grounds without encroaching upon the rights of other tribes. He said that, like the deer chased by the dogs, they would have to take to the water.

When Oscosh aspired to the dignity of head chief, his election was opposed in the council by another chief, who insisted on contesting the post of honour with him. Oscosh replied, that as there could be only one head chief, he was quite willing on the

instant to settle the dispute with their knives by the destruction of one or the other. This proposal was declined, and his claim has never since been disputed. This tribe is remarkably partial to gaudy decorations, and ornament themselves with great quantities of beads, silver ornaments, and feathers. This passion for display is confined chiefly to the men.

[crIII-118, 119, 121]

They are much addicted to gambling, and I have seen them commence playing, covered with highly-prized decorations, which have gradually changed hands, as the game proceeded, until its close has left the original possessor without a blanket to cover him. The principal despoilers of the Manōmanees are the Pottowattomies, some of whom make it their business to visit the Manōmanee camp on a regular black-leg expedition at the time the latter receive their Government pay, in order to fleece them of whatever they can, and they generally return home laden with booty. Liquor, whenever they can obtain it, is their chief bane, and lays them more open to the fraudulent schemes of their despoilers.

I made a sketch of Coe-coosh, "the Hog," one of these Pottowattomie black-legs, whom I saw intently engaged in gambling. [Pl. IX; crIII-126] The introduction of spirits among the Indians is, as before mentioned, prohibited under severe penalties by the laws of the United States, and with the greatest propriety, as an Indian, when under its influence, is one of the most dangerous animals in existence, and there being so few whites to control them at the period of payment, we should have been in no small danger of losing our lives had it been readily attainable.

I was myself, on this occasion, called up in the dead of the night by the United States' marshal, who had been commissioned to prevent its introduction among them; he required my assistance, in common with all the other whites on the spot, in order to make a search throughout the camp to detect the person who was selling liquor, as some of the Indians were already drunk. Having a suspicion that a half-breed was engaged in the illicit traffic, we all proceeded to his tent. Although we plainly smelt the liquor in his tin pots, not a single keg was to be found in spite of the most vigilant search, carried even to the extent of digging up the earth in his tent. When I was leaving the neighbourhood, I got him to confess that he had sunk several kegs, with buoys attached to them, in the middle of the river. By keeping watch by turns through the night, it fortunately passed over without mischief.

["Pine Tree" (?), crIII-127, 128]

[3] In 1845 the United States Treasury provided $6,000 for payments to the Menominee. National Archives, "Letters Sent by the Superintendent and Agent of the Office of Indian Affairs, Mackinac Agency, 1833–1851," letter of July 4, 1845.

Among other Indians whose likeness I took, is that of Kit-chie-ogi-maw, or, "the Great Chief," a Manōmanee, who was celebrated among his tribe for many acts of daring, one of which was narrated to me by his half brother: it occurred eight or ten years previously. [Fig. 43; crIII-117, 120]

His maternal uncle, who was then at Mackenaw, chanced to be present in a grocery store, where ardent spirits were sold, when two soldiers entered, one of whom treated him with so much indignity, that, seizing him in his powerful grasp, and being the stronger and more active man, he threw the soldier down with great violence on the ground upon his back, and planting his knee upon his breast, assured him that he would do him no further injury, if he would behave himself properly. This assurance, given in his own language, was, unfortunately, not understood by either of the soldiers; the second of whom, seeing his comrade in the power of a savage, and his life, as he thought, in peril, instantly drew his side-arms and stabbed the ill-fated Indian to the heart. No punishment of any importance followed the commission of this crime; the offender was merely sent away from Mackenaw to escape the vengeance of the relatives of the murdered man.

A year or two subsequently to this unhappy occurrence, as two white men, a Mr. Clayman and a Mr. Burnett, were coming down the Fox River in a canoe, they chanced to pass the lodge of Kitchie-ogi-maw's father, the brother-in-law of the deceased Indian, who, with his family, was camped on the banks of the river. They were noticed by the squaw, the dead man's sister, who called to her husband that now had arrived the opportunity of revenging her brother's death, and that it was his duty, as a man, not to let so good a chance escape him; but her husband, unwilling to risk so hazardous an encounter without other aid than that of his son, Kitchie-ogi-maw, then a stripling of only fourteen years, hesitated to comply with her request. On which, in order to show her contempt of what she considered his pusillanimity, she hastily divested herself of the breech cloth usually worn by Indian women, and, throwing it insultingly in his face, told him to wear it, for that he was no man. The husband, stung by the opprobrious imputation, caught up his gun, and commanded his son to follow him. The boy declined having any concern in killing the white men, but consented to accompany him for his protection.

The two Americans had now landed and were preparing their camp for the night; one of them was upon his knees engaged in kindling a fire, the other approaching at a distance with an armful of wood; the father raised his gun, but dropped it again to his side in evident agitation; the boy thereupon turned to him, saying, "Father, you tremble too much; give me the gun, and let me do it," and, taking the weapon from his father's hands, he approached the kneeling man from behind, and shot him dead; the other one, hearing the report and catching sight of the Indians, threw down the wood he had collected and ran for his life; the boy seeing a double-barrelled gun lying on the ground near the man he had killed, seized it and followed the fugitive, telling his father to assist in the pursuit, as if this man escaped they might be punished through his evidence for killing the other.

The father was unable to keep up with the boy, who gained on the white man, and, when within twenty or thirty yards of him, took aim and endeavoured to fire; but being unused to the double trigger, and not having cocked both locks, he pulled the wrong one: determined to make sure of his next aim, he cocked both and pulled the two triggers together; part of the charge entered the victim's shoulder, but the recoil of the two barrels going off at once, knocked the boy backwards on the ground. He was, however, only stunned for the moment, and soon recovered his feet; drawing his scalping knife, the young assassin continued his pursuit of the now almost exhausted man, who, in endeavouring to leap over a log lying on the ground, stumbled and fell.

The bloody young wretch now made sure of his victim, and before the latter could recover his feet, had come up within a few yards of him. The white man seeing that the youngster was alone, and the father not within sight, faced his pursuer, armed likewise with a knife, and resolved to grapple with him. But the boy dexterously kept out of his reach, dodging him round the fallen log, until his father should come up when they could unitedly overpower him. The wounded fugitive having now recovered breath, and noticing the father in the distance, took to flight once more, dogged by his indefatigable tormentor, and continued his speed till the morning dawned, when he fell in with some friendly Indians, who protected him and dressed his wounds, none of which were mortal: they supplied all his wants, until he was strong enough to return to his home. Kitchie-ogi-maw now deemed it the safest plan to keep away from any of the White Settlements, and he continues still to observe the same precaution.

I found some Indians of the Winebago tribe at the camp on a visit. The word Winebago signifies "dirty water;" and they are so called from living on the margin of a lake of that name. They are easily distinguished from other tribes, as they have the custom of pulling out their eyebrows.

I took the likeness of their chief, Mauza-pau-Kan, or the "Brave Soldier." [Fig. 46; crIII-129] I remained here for three weeks, and received much kindness and attention from the Manōmanees. Hearing that I was taking sketches of the most noted Indians in the camp, a fellow named Muck-a-ta paid me a visit. He was one of the most ill favoured of any that had been the subjects of my pencil, and by all accounts his physiognomy did not belie his character. [Figs. 44, 45; crIII-122, 123]

The Indians had no sooner received their money than a scene ensued that baffles description. Large quantities of liquor immediately found their way into the camp from some unknown quarter, and the sad effect was almost instantaneous. There was scarcely a man, woman, or child, old enough to lift the vessel to its mouth, that was not wallowing in beastly drunkenness; and we gladly availed ourselves of the arrival of a small steamer that plies on Lake Winebago and the Fox River to make our escape from the disgusting and dangerous scene of singing and dancing and fighting going on around us. We disembarked at a place called "Fond du Lac," where we hired a waggon, and crossed over to the Sheboygan on Lake Michigan, and embarked on board another steamer for Buffalo, which I left again on the 30th of November and arrived the day following at Toronto.

[Fort Snelling: Pl. X; crIII-141 to 144]

Chapter III.

Sir George Simpson.—My Start.—Difficulties of the Route.—The Sault St. Marie.—The "White Fish" and "Thunder Point."—A Day behind the Fair.—Pulling against Stream.—Mangeurs du Lard.—The Lost Men's Portage.—The Blanket of the Dead.—A Compliment from Sir George.—Running from a Bear.

In the ensuing March I repaired to Lachine to seek an interview with Sir George Simpson.[1] Having exhibited to him the sketches which I had made, and explained the nature of the objects which I had in view,[2] Sir George entered cordially into my plans; and, in order to facilitate them, ordered a passage in the spring brigade of canoes.

Accordingly, on the 9th of May, 1846, I left Toronto in company with Governor Simpson for the Sault St. Marie, in order to embark in the brigade of canoes which had left Lachine some time previously, taking the route of the Ottawa and Lake Huron.[3]

On my arrival at Mackenaw in the evening, I was informed by the master of the steamboat that he would not leave until 9 o'clock next morning. Trusting to this assurance, I went on shore for the night; but on coming down to the wharf on the following day, I found that the vessel with Sir George Simpson had departed about twenty minutes previously.[4] This was indeed a damper of no ordinary magnitude, as, should I fail in seeing Sir George before he left the Sault, I should not be able to accompany the canoes. I was aware, likewise, that the governor would not remain longer than a few hours; but how to overtake him was the difficulty, as no boat would leave for four days.

Determined, however, not to be disappointed in my proposed expedition, I used every exertion to procure a mode of conveyance.[5] Walking along the beach, I saw a small skiff lying, and having found the owner, inquired if I could hire it, and whether there was any chance of procuring a crew. The man strongly advised me not to attempt such a perilous voyage, as it was blowing hard, and that it was not in mortal power to reach the Sault by daylight next morning. Resolved, however, to make the attempt, I at length succeeded in chartering the skiff and engaging a crew, consisting of three boys, the eldest being under nineteen years of age.[6] It must be added that they were all well acquainted with boating. The striplings held out no hopes of being able to accomplish the undertaking within the given time, and were only induced to make the attempt by the offer of a high reward. Thus, in a tiny skiff, with a blanket for a sail, and a

[1] KWMS states that Kane left Toronto for Lachine on March 25.
[2] KWMS reads: "My object in taking this journey was to obtain Sir George's permission to accompany the brigade of canoes which annually leaves Lachine for the North-west passing up the Ottawa into Lake Huron."
[3] KWMS reads: "I was apprehensive of not being able to reach this place till the Brigade had passed as I had been informed that they had left Lachine this season five days before the usual period, the ice of the Ottawa having broken up earlier this season than ordinary. I arrived at 4 P.M. at Buffalo on the same day having stopped a short time on our way up to admire for the hundredth time the Falls of Niagara. At Buffalo we embarked at 7 P.M. on board an American steamer bound for Mackinaw, on the 10th at Cleveland, on the 11th at Detroit, and on the 12th landed at Mackinaw."
[4] KWMS reads: "As I unwisely decided to breakfast there [the hotel where Kane had spent the night], I found on my arrival at the wharf that I was half an hour too late. The steamer had carried off my baggage."
[5] KWMS states that the steamer would not return for two days.
[6] KWMS describes how Kane gave a man $10 to find a crew to take him to Sault St. Marie and then promised the boys $20 if they could reach there in time to catch Sir George Simpson.

single loaf of bread along with a little tea and sugar for stores, we launched out in the lake to make a traverse of forty-five miles.[7]

The wind being favourable, the boat shot ahead with tremendous rapidity, but the danger was imminent and continuous from the moment we left the shore until we reached the mouth of the river of St. Marie, which we did at sunset.

Here we remained about twenty minutes, and discussed our tea and bread with appetites sharpened to intensity. But now commenced another difficulty, the navigation of forty-five miles of a river with which we were totally unacquainted, in a dark night against the current and through a channel dotted with numerous islands. All this was to be accomplished by daylight, or the toil and anxiety would be of no avail.

We however set forth unflinchingly; and after a night of the most violent exertion, after running into all sorts of wrong places and backing out again, after giving up half a dozen times in despair, and as often renewing the struggle, our exertions were crowned with success. When morning dawned, there lay the eagerly looked-for steamer not two miles from us.[8]

On getting up in the morning, Sir George Simpson was astonished at seeing me; and his amazement was not lessened when he learned the mode of my conveyance.[9] The voyage on no former occasion had been performed in so short a time under corresponding circumstances, and to this day the undertaking is still talked of as a rather notable adventure in Mackenaw and the Sault.

The Sault St. Marie is situated at the lower extremity of Lake Superior, where it debouches into the river St. Marie, in its course to Lake Huron: having in this part of the river a considerable fall, for about a mile and a half in length, it soon becomes a foaming torrent, down which, however, canoes, steered by practised guides, ordinarily descend safely, although with terrific violence. Sometimes, indeed, the venture is fatal to the bark and its occupants. A short time before our arrival on the present occasion, a canoe, in running down the rapid, had struck upon a sunken rock that made a hole through her bottom. She instantly filled, but, owing to the extreme buoyancy of the

birch-bark these canoes are made of, the men, by balancing themselves adroitly in her, and squatting up to their necks in the water, thereby lessening their weight materially, were enabled to steer her with safety down the foaming billows, and run her on the shore in an eddy at the foot of the rapids.

I took a sketch of the rapids above alluded to, from the American side. [CRIII-71] There is a small town called the Sault St. Marie, on the American side, containing 700 or 800 inhabitants, with a well-built garrison, prettily situated on the river's bank. On the Canadian side, about half a mile direct across, the Hudson's Bay Company have a trading establishment, and the Custom House officer, Mr. Wilson, a tolerably handsome house. With these two exceptions, the British side presents to the traveller a collection of poor miserable hovels, occupied solely by half-breeds and Indians. In strolling among these hovels, I made a sketch of a good-looking half-breed girl, whose sudden appearance, emerging from such a wretched neighbourhood, took me by surprise. [CRIII-75]

As the brigade of canoes had passed up two days before my arrival at the Sault, and Sir George's canoes were too heavily laden, he was unable to give me a passage. My only alternative was to wait until the "White Fish," a small schooner belonging to the Company, and lying at the upper end of the portage, was unloaded, and trust to the chance of her intercepting the canoes at Fort William. This was very doubtful, depending, as it entirely did, upon the wind; but I had no alternative. Sir George had embarked on the 14th in his canoe, leaving me to follow in the way above named. It took four days to unload the schooner, so that she was not ready to leave before the 20th of May. We had a fair wind at starting, which continued until the night of the 23rd, when it came to blow a gale off "Thunder Point." The night being very dark, we were apprehensive of driving on the rocks at the base of this formidable mountain—Thunder Point, as it is called, being in fact, a perpendicular rock of twelve or fifteen hundred feet high. Seeing it, as I then did, for the first time, by the glare of the almost incessant flashes of lightning, it presented one of the grandest and most terrific spectacles I had ever witnessed. As our crew consisted of only two men, I was under the necessity of assisting to work the vessel, so that all hope of a comfortable sleep in my warm hammock had to be abandoned, and I was obliged to remain the whole night on deck.

At daybreak we succeeded in rounding this dangerous point, and soon passed El Royal, which island is supposed to contain valuable mineral wealth, and cast anchor near the mouth of the

---

[7] KWMS says they left at 10 A.M.

[8] KJ says the voyage was made in 20 hours and KWMS says 21 hours: an example of the many small inconsistencies in the various versions.

[9] KWMS reads: "We encountered Sir George Simpson at the Hudson's Bay Co. post as he was leaving his chamber. As the possibility of our having made the voyage in the way I have described had not once occurred to him, Sir George's first enquiry was 'What other steamer could have arrived?' In explanation I showed him our boat and my three companions all by this time soundly sleeping on the beach."

Plate XII. The Mountain Portage (Kakabeka Falls). ROM912.1.18; CRIV-6.

Kaministaqueah River, which we ascended about two miles to Fort William, in a small boat. This fort, during the existence of the North-west Company, was one of considerable importance as a depôt for all the trade carried on in furs, &c. This importance it has lost, in consequence of the goods which formerly passed by the route of Lake Superior, now passing by Hudson's Bay since the two rival companies have merged into one; but as it possesses the best land in the vicinity of Lake Superior, it might still be made a place of much consideration in an agricultural point of view.

On delivering my letter of introduction to Mr. Mackenzie, the gentleman in charge of the fort, I learned, to my great disappointment, that the brigade had passed up the river the day before. I was compelled, in this dilemma, to trespass on the kindness of this gentleman for the supply of a light canoe and three men, in order to overtake them if possible before they reached the mountain portage, forty miles in advance. In the course of half an hour, thanks to Mr. Mackenzie's kindness, we were straining at the paddles, and, ten hours afterwards, had the satisfaction of coming up with the brigade about thirty-five miles from our starting point.

I found a gentleman named Lane [10] in charge of the brigade, which consisted of three canoes with eight men in each. We all camped immediately, and at 3 o'clock next morning were again *en route* in our canoes. These are constructed of the bark of the birch tree, and are about twenty-eight feet long and four to five feet beam, strong, and capable of carrying, besides their crew of eight men, twenty-five pieces; but at the same time so light as to be easily carried on the shoulders of two men. All goods taken into the interior, and all peltries brought out, are made into packs of 90 lbs. each, for the purpose of easy handling at the frequent *portages* and *discharges*; these packs are called pieces.

After pulling our canoes up a rapid current, we arrived about 8 o'clock at the mountain portage, whose falls surpass even those of Niagara in picturesque beauty; for, although far inferior in volume of water, their height is nearly equal, and the scenery surrounding them infinitely more wild and romantic. Whilst the men were engaged in making the portage, I took advantage of the delay to make a sketch. [Fig. 47; crIV-3, 4, 5]

I have since been informed that the large flat rock which divided the torrent in the centre has fallen in. The interruption thus caused by the falls is about two miles of very steep ascent, up which the men have to carry the canoes and baggage, the

[10] Burpee, in the 1925 edition of *Wanderings*, identifies him as "W. D. Lane." Could he have been W. F. Lane?

former on their shoulders, the latter on their backs, by means of what is technically named a portage-strap, both ends of which are attached to the load of two pieces, while the middle of the strap goes round the forehead, which thus supports the principal part of the burden. [Pl. XII; crIV-6] The men who usually work this brigade of canoes are hired at Lachine, and are called by the uncouth name of *Mangeurs du Lard*, or pork-eaters, among the old hands in the interior, to whom they are unequal in encountering the difficulties incident to a voyage from Lachine to the mouth of the Columbia, whither some of them are sent, and become almost skeletons by the time they reach their destination, through the unavoidable privations and hardships they have to undergo.

Launching our canoes again, we proceeded for about a mile, and made another portage called "The Lost Men's Portage," owing to three men having lost themselves in the woods in crossing it. [crIV-6A] I very nearly met with the same fate myself; for, having gone up to the rapids to take a sketch, I endeavoured, when I had finished, to find my way back, and spent two hours in an unsuccessful attempt to gain the path. I then fortunately thought of discharging my fowling-piece as a signal, and had the pleasure of immediately hearing an answering shot, which guided my steps to the party who were anxiously awaiting my return to embark.

Proceeding a few miles up the stream, we reached the "Pin Portage," so called from the rocks over which we had to carry the canoes being so sharp as actually to cut the feet of the men, who usually go barefooted or only wearing light mocassins. [Fig. 48; crIV-7] We made, in all, six portages in one day, viz., "Ecarté," "Rose Décharge," and "De l'Isle," and the three before named, travelling a distance of forty-three miles: the current was so impetuous, even where we could avail ourselves of our canoes, that the men found the greatest difficulty in forcing up against it with poles.

On the 26th of May we journeyed twenty-six miles, making the following portages and discharges, viz.:—"Recousi Portage," "Couteau Portage," "Belanger Décharge," "Mauvais Décharge," "Tremble Décharge," "Penet Décharge," "Maître Portage," "Little Dog Portage," "Dog Portage [crIV-8]," and the "Big Dog Portage;" the latter affords a splendid view from its summit of the Kaministaqueah river, meandering in the distance, as far as the eye can reach, through one of the loveliest valleys in nature. This view I wished much to have sketched, but time is of so much importance in the movements of these brigades, that I did not consider myself justified in waiting.

The "Big Dog Portage" derives its name from an Indian tradition that a big dog once slept on the summit, and left the impression of his form on the highest point of land, which remains to this present time. The length of this portage is two miles; we camped at the upper end; and while here I made a sketch of the fall, during one of the heaviest showers of rain I ever experienced.

One of our *Mangeurs du Lard* presenting himself at the camp fire in a handsome rabbit-skin blanket, was asked by Mr. Lane where he had obtained it. He replied that he had found it among the bushes. Mr. Lane, knowing that it is customary among the Indians to place offerings of all descriptions upon the graves of their deceased relatives, first rendering them unserviceable to any evil disposed persons in this world, under the idea that the Great Spirit will repair them on the arrival of the deceased in the next, and that they hold in the greatest abhorrence, and never fail to punish, any one who sacrilegiously disturbs them, ordered him immediately to return to the place whence he took it, and replace it exactly as he had found it, unless he wished to have us all murdered. When the man understood what he had done, he replaced the blanket immediately.

On the 27th, Sir George Simpson passed us with his two canoes, accompanied by his secretary Mr. Hopkins. Sir George only stopped a few minutes to congratulate me on my having overcome the difficulties of my starting: he seemed to think that the perseverance and determination I had shown augured well for my future success, and as his canoes were much lighter and better manned than ours, he passed on rapidly in advance. As there were no more currents to overcome, the men this day threw away their poles as useless, and started on a race with their paddles for about fifteen miles through "Dog Lake" and entered "Dog River." We now had to make a long portage of three miles over a high mountain into a small lake.[11] At the upper end of this portage we again overtook Sir George, and were invited to dine with him at the next, some four or five miles further on, but we unluckily could not again come up with him.

On inquiring the cause of some loud shouting that I heard in the woods, I was told that some of our men had surrounded a bear which had given them battle, but that, unarmed as they were, they had deemed discretion the better part of valour, and sounded a retreat. We camped on the banks of a small river. We

[11] KJ names it the "Little Dog Portage" and gives the length as four miles (another example of the minor variations in the various accounts).

had hitherto stemmed against the stream of waters that emptied itself into the Atlantic; but we had now reached streams that flowed at a much more rapid rate, and coursed on to Hudson's Bay. At the close of this day we had accomplished a distance of thirty-three miles, having made the following portages, viz.:— "Barrière Portage," "Joudain Portage," and "Prairie Portage."

Chapter IV.

Four Miles of Swamp.—Lake of a Thousand Isles.—Virtue of a Silver Bullet.—A wild Tale.—Living One upon Another.—The Great Medicine-Man.—A Timid "Little Rat."—A Caterpillar Plague.—Butter in the Wilderness.—A Leap into the Grave.—Going down the Winnipeg.—A novel Viameter.

May 28*th.*—To-day we passed over one of the largest and most difficult portages in the whole route, it is called the "Savan Portage;" it passes through about four miles of swamp. It formerly had logs laid lengthwise, for the convenience of the men carrying the loads; but they are now for the most part decayed, so that the poor fellows had sometimes to wade up to the middle in mud and water. In all, we made to-day about thirty miles, including the following portages, viz.:—"Milieu Portage" and "Savan Portage," from whence we went twenty miles down the Savan River, and camped near its mouth, where it empties into "Mille Lacs."

On the 29th, we passed through the Lake of the Thousand Islands, thirty-six miles long, a name it well deserves. The scenery surrounding us was truly beautiful; the innumerable rocky islands varying from several miles in length to the smallest proportions, all covered with trees, chiefly pine. [crIV-9] This lake is filled with innumerable ducks, which the Indians entice in the following curious manner:—A young dog is trained by dragging a piece of meat attached to a string up and down the edge of the shore several times, and putting the dog on the scent, who follows it rapidly, wagging his tail. After the dog has followed it for some time, he is given the meat; this is done repeatedly until the dog will do so whenever he is ordered, and his motions attract the ducks swimming in the distance to within reach of the Indian, who lies concealed on the banks. The flock of ducks is so crowded and numerous, that I have known an Indian kill forty ducks by firing at them whilst in the water, and rapidly loading and firing again whilst the same flock was circling above his head. Our first portage after leaving this lovely lake was "Portage de Pente." We camped at the end of the next portage, called "Little Discharge," having made a distance altogether of fifty-six miles.

May 30th.—We made an early start, reaching the "French Portage" by breakfast-time.[1] Here we lightened the canoes of the principal part of the baggage, and carried it across the portage, a distance of three miles, in order that we might be able to send the canoes round by the river, which had now become very shallow, to meet us at the further end of the portage. We camped this evening at a small lake called Sturgeon Lake, having come a distance of forty-eight miles, passing "French Portage," and "Portage de Morts."

May 31st.—We passed down the "Rivière Maligne"[2] until we came to what are termed the First, Second, and Third portages, and, making the portage "De l'Isle" and "Du Lac," camped near "Lac la Croix Traverse," accomplishing a distance of only twenty-seven miles.

June 1st.—We passed down the river "Macau," where there are some beautiful rapids and falls.[3] Here we fell in with the first Indians we had met since leaving the Lake of the Thousand Islands; they are called "Saulteaux," being a branch of the Ojibbeways, whose language they speak with very slight variation. We purchased from an Indian man and woman some dried sturgeon. The female wore a rabbit-skin dress: they were, as I afterwards learned, considered to be cannibals, the Indian term for which is *Weendigo*, or "One who eats Human Flesh." There is a superstitious belief among Indians that the Weendigo cannot be killed by anything short of a silver bullet. I was informed, on good authority, that a case had occurred here in which a father and daughter had killed and eaten six of their own family from absolute want. The story went on to state, that they then camped at some distance off in the vicinity of an old Indian woman, who happened to be alone in her lodge, her relations having gone out hunting. Seeing the father and daughter arrive unaccompanied by any other members of the family, all of whom she knew, she began to suspect that some foul play had taken place, and to feel apprehensive for her own safety. By way of precaution, she resolved to make the entrance to her lodge very slippery, and as it was winter, and the frost severe, she poured water repeatedly over the ground as fast as it froze, until it was covered with a mass of smooth ice; and instead of going to bed, she remained sitting up in her lodge, watching

[1] In KJ Kane records sketching the French Portage.
[2] In KJ Kane records sketching Rivière Maligne.
[3] In KJ Kane records sketching the falls on the "Macau" River.

with an axe in her hand. When near midnight, she heard steps advancing cautiously over the crackling snow, and looking through the crevices of the lodge, caught sight of the girl in the attitude of listening, as if to ascertain whether the inmate was asleep; this the old woman feigned by snoring aloud. The welcome sound no sooner reached the ears of the wretched girl, than she rushed forward, but, slipping on the ice, fell down at the entrance of the lodge, whereupon the intended victim sprang upon the murderess and buried the axe in her brains: and not doubting but the villainous father was near at hand, she fled with all her speed to a distance, to escape his vengeance. In the meantime, the Weendigo father, who was impatiently watching for the expected signal to his horrid repast, crept up to the lodge, and called to his daughter; hearing no reply, he went on, and, in place of the dead body of the old woman, he saw his own daughter, and hunger overcoming every other feeling, he saved his own life by devouring her remains.

The *Weendigoes* are looked upon with superstitious dread and horror by all Indians, and any one known to have eaten human flesh is shunned by the rest; as it is supposed that, having once tasted it, they would do so again had they an opportunity. They are obliged, therefore, to make their lodges at some distance from the rest of the tribe, and the children are particularly kept out of their way; however, they are not molested or injured in any way, but seem rather to be pitied for the misery they must have endured before they could be brought to this state. I do not think that any Indian, at least none that I have ever seen, would eat his fellow-creature, except under the influence of starvation; nor do I think that there is any tribe of Indians on the North American continent to whom the word "cannibal" can be properly applied.

We traversed to-day a distance of forty-one miles, passing four portages before entering Lake Meican, which is nine miles long, to "Portage Neuf," entering the "Lac la Pluie," where we camped; its name did not seem inappropriate, for we were detained here two days by the incessant torrents of rain that poured down. It took us until the evening of the 4th to reach Fort Francis, at the lower end of the lake, a distance of fifty miles, where I found a letter from Sir George Simpson, enclosing a circular.

There is a beautiful fall of water here within sight of the fort, at the commencement of the river which runs from Lac la Pluie to the Lake of the Woods. Vast quantities of white fish and sturgeon are taken at the foot of the rapids, with which our mess-table at the fort was abundantly supplied; indeed, the chief food here consists of fish and wild rice, with a little grain grown in the vicinity of the fort, this being the first land I had seen fit for agricultural purposes since I had left Fort William. We continued at the fort until the morning of the 5th. There was a large camp of Salteaux Indians in the immediate vicinity: a considerable party of them came to the establishment in the morning to see the "great medicine-man" who made Indians,[4] Mr. Lane having given them to understand that my object in travelling through the country was to paint their likenesses.

I applied to the head chief, Waw-gas-kontz, "the Little Rat," to take his likeness, but was refused, on the grounds that he feared something bad would result to him; but after Iacaway, "the Loud Speaker," had sat for his [crIV-29], Waw-gas-kontz seemed ashamed of his cowardice, and became very anxious to have it done, following me down to the canoe. I had not time, however, to do so; but I could not get rid of him until I promised to take his likeness on my return.

June 5th.—We left the fort at 10 this morning; the rain continued all day, and obliged us to camp at 4 in the afternoon, the distance we went being about thirty miles.

June 6th.—It was a remarkable fact that the trees on each side of the river, and part of the Lake of the Woods, for full 150 miles of our route, were literally stripped of foliage by myriads of green caterpillars, which had left nothing but the bare branches; and I was informed that the scourge extended to more than twice the distance I have named, the whole country wearing the dreary aspect of winter at the commencement of summer.

As it was impossible to take our breakfast on land, unless we made up our minds to eat them, dropping incessantly as they did from the trees among our food, and the ground everywhere covered with them *en masse,* we were compelled to take it in our canoes. We met some Indians, from whom we purchased seven fine sturgeons, each weighing perhaps forty or fifty pounds. We paid for the whole one cotton shirt. We next entered the Lake of the Woods, and camped on a beautiful rocky island, having made fifty-three miles in one day.

June 7th.—We passed through the above lake, sixty-eight miles long. When passing a small island about the middle of it, the steersman of my canoe put ashore on this island, and running to a clump of bushes returned with a small keg of butter, which he told us he had left hidden, or, as they call it, *en cache,* the year before: it proved an acquisition to our larder, although its age had not improved its flavour. We next made the "Rat Portage," at the foot of which is the fort, a small establishment

where they were so badly supplied with provisions as to be able to afford us only two white fish. We consequently thought it advisable to leave the place, although late in the evening, and camped a few miles lower down the Winnipeg River; having travelled to-day a distance of seventy-two miles.

June 8th.—We continued our course down the river Winnipeg, which is broken by numerous beautiful rapids and falls, being indeed one of the most picturesque rivers we had passed in the whole route. Our bowsman caught a pike, which in appearance had two tails, one at each end; but we found on examination that the tail and part of the body of another fish or sucker, nearly as large as himself, which he had tried to swallow, was protruding from his mouth, evidencing the extreme voracity of this species. We passed to-day a Catholic missionary station called "Wabassemmung" (or White Dog) [crIV-13?], which, on my return, two years and a half afterwards, I found deserted, from the circumstance that the Indians of this quarter did not prove very willing converts. We camped for the night a few miles below this station, and still found the caterpillars before alluded to extremely annoying, covering as they did completely our blankets and clothing. We had passed the following places, viz.: "the Dalles," "Grand Décharge," "Terre jaune Portage," "the Charrette Portage," "Terre blanche Portage," "Cave Portage," and Wabassemmung, a distance of seventy-one miles.

June 9th.—We passed the "Chute de Jaques,"[5] so called from a man thus named, who, being dared by one of his companions to run his canoe over a fall of fifteen or twenty feet, an exploit never attempted before or since, unhesitatingly essayed the bold feat, and pushing off his frail bark, jumped into it, and on rounding a small island darted down the main sheet, his companions meanwhile anxiously watching for his safety from the shore. As might have been expected, he was dashed to pieces and no more seen. [crIV-18] We camped this evening, after completing a distance of sixty miles, and making the following portages, viz.: "Portage de l'Isle," "Chute de Jaques," "Point des Bois" (the Indian name of this fall is Ka-mash-aw-aw-sing, or, "the Two Carrying-Places"); "Rochers Boules," "the Slave Falls," which is the highest of all the falls of the Winnipeg River; I never heard the reason of its bearing this name. At "Barrière Portage" we found the black flies and mosquitoes so annoying all night, as to deprive us entirely of sleep.

[4] w 59: "The Indians attach a mysterious meaning to the word 'medicine,' applying it to almost everything they cannot clearly understand."

[5] kj records that Kane sketched the Chute de Jacques.

June 10th.—We ran three or four beautiful rapids to-day in our canoes, the men showing great expertness in their management, although so much risk attends it that several canoes have been lost in the attempt. We made about sixty miles to-day down the Winnipeg [Fig. 52; crIV-24, 26–28], passing the following places, viz.: the "Grand Rapid," six portages, all within sight of each other, and about five miles in length inclusively: they are known collectively by the name of "The Six Portages"—the first and second portage of the "Bonnet," "the Grand Bonnet," "Petits Rochers," and "Terre Blanche." We encamped about a couple of miles below the rapids at 5 o'clock —earlier than usual, as our canoes had received some little injury and required repairs. It is usual to start every morning between 3 and 4 o'clock and proceed till 8 for breakfast, then continue steadily on until an hour before dark, just so as to give the men time to prepare for the night. The only rest allowed being at intervals of about an hour, when all hands stop two or three minutes to fill their pipes. It is quite a common way of expressing the distance of one place to another to say that it is so many pipes; and this, amongst those who have travelled in the interior gives a very good idea of the distance. The evening was very beautiful, and soon after we had pitched our tents and lighted our fires, we were visited by some Saulteaux Indians. As I had plenty of time, I sketched the encampment.[6] Our visitors, the clear stream reflecting the brilliant sky so peculiar to North America, the granite rocks backed by the rich foliage of the woods with Indians and voyageurs moving about, made a most pleasing subject. [Pl. XIV; crIV-22, 23]

Chapter V.

Fort Alexander.—Mr. Lane.—A Western Career.—Value of Bark to the Indian.—The Medicine Lodge.—A Double Shot.—Fort Garry. —The nearest Market Town.—Red River Settlement.—White Horse Plain.—Hunting the Buffalo.

June 11th.—We made an early start with a fine breeze, filling our sail,[1] and arrived at Fort Alexander to breakfast, a distance of seventeen or eighteen miles including the three portages: "First Eau Qui Merit," "Second Eau Qui Merit," "Third Eau

Qui Merit." Fort Alexander is situated on Winnipeg River, about three miles above where it disembogues into Lake Winnipeg, and has some good farming land in its vicinity. I here took my farewell of Mr. Lane with great regret, and left the brigade of canoes, which proceeded with him to Norway House, on his route to Mackenzie River. Mr. Lane had entered the Hudson's Bay Company's service when very young, and having served for twenty-six years, he became dissatisfied with the slowness of his promotion, and determined to resign and return to Ireland, his native land. However, on his return home, he found himself lost in civilised life, and quite unable to occupy himself with any business pursuits there; and when I met him, he was again in the employment of the Company, at a lower salary than he had before received, and was going to Mackenzie River, one of the most remote and bleak posts in the whole region, accompanied by his wife, a half-breed. The last that I heard of him was that he had arrived at his post almost starved to death, after travelling about 700 miles on snow shoes through the depth of winter.

Hearing that a camp of Indians lay within a few miles, I requested a Mr. Setler, in charge of the establishment, to procure me a guide to them. I found it indispensably necessary to wear a veil all the way, as a protection from the mosquitoes, which I had never before seen so numerous. I found a very large camp of Saulteaux Indians assembled. [Fig. 54; crIV-32] They have a medicine lodge erected in the centre of their encampment, to which I at once directed my steps. It was rather an oblong structure, composed of poles bent in the form of an arch, and both ends forced into the ground, so as to form, when completed, a long arched chamber, protected from the weather by a covering of birch bark. This bark is one of the most valuable materials that nature supplies to the Red-man, as by its friendly aid he is enabled to brave the inclemency of the weather on land, and float lightly and safely over the vast inland seas that so abound in his wild domain; and when any transient impediments present themselves to his using it on water, so light is its weight, that he easily carries it on his shoulder. Such also is its compactness and closeness of texture, that he forms his culinary and other utensils of it, and, as it is quite impervious to water, he is able, by the aid of heated stones, to boil his fish in them. It also serves for a material or papyrus on which to transmit his hieroglyphic correspondence.

On my first entrance into the medicine lodge—(the reader is already apprised of the mysterious meaning the Indian attaches

---

[6] KWMS has a longer description of the camp site, which is interesting since Kane sketched the camp. It reads: "Mr. Lane's tent and mine are at the edge of the woods. Some of the men are bringing fuel to cook and keep off mosquitoes, while others are putting pitch on the large painted Hudson's Bay canoe."

[1] KJ says they travelled at seven or eight miles an hour.

to the term "medicine")—I found four men, who appeared to be chiefs, sitting upon mats spread upon the ground gesticulating with great violence, and keeping time to the beating of a drum. Something, apparently of a sacred nature was covered up in the centre of the group, which I was not allowed to see. They almost instantly ceased their "pow-wow," or music, and seemed rather displeased at my intrusion, although they approached, and inquiringly felt the legs of my fustian pantaloons,[2] pronouncing me a chief on account of their fineness.

On looking around me, which I now ventured to do, I saw that the interior of their lodge or sanctuary was hung round with mats constructed with rushes, to which were attached various offerings consisting principally of bits of red and blue cloth, calico, &c., strings of beads, scalps of enemies, and sundry other articles beyond my comprehension. Finding they did not proceed with their "pow-wow," I began to think I was intruding, and retired. But no sooner had I emerged from the lodge, than I was surrounded by crowds of women and children, whom nothing would satisfy short of examining me from head to foot, following me in swarms through the camp, not apparently with any hostile intentions, but for the mere gratification of their curiosity. I passed a grave surmounted with a scalp hung on a pole, torn, doubtless, from an enemy by the warrior buried beneath. I now returned to the fort, first engaging six of the Indians to proceed with me to Red River. We left at four o'clock in the afternoon in a small boat, accompanied by Mr. Setler, and camped on the shore of Lake Winnipeg.

June 12th.—I wrote this part of my journal by the light of a blazing fire in the above encampment, surrounded by my six painted warriors sleeping in the front of the tent, their hideous faces gleaming in the fire-light: a head wind all day had prevented our making any great progress.

June 13th.—We entered the mouth of the Red River about ten this morning. The banks of this river, which here enters the lake, are for five or six miles low and marshy. After proceeding up stream for about twenty miles, we arrived at the Stone Fort, belonging to the Company, where I found Sir George Simpson and several of the gentlemen of the Company, who assemble here annually for the purpose of holding a council for the transaction of business. I remained here until the 15th, and left for the Upper Fort, about twenty miles higher up. We rode on horseback, accompanied by Mr. Peter Jacobs, Wesleyan Indian missionary [Fig. 55; crIV-33, 34], and arrived there in about four hours, after a pleasant ride of eighteen or twenty miles through a considerable part of Red River Settlement. Here

there are a judge and a court house. A Saulteaux Indian was hung here last year for shooting a Sioux Indian and another of his own tribe at one shot, the ball having passed through the Sioux and entered the Saulteaux's body: his intention was to kill the Sioux only, with whom his tribe then was, and had been from time immemorial, at war, so that the killing of the Saulteaux was accidental. The country here is not very beautiful; a dead level plain with very little timber, the landscape wearing more the appearance of the cultivated farms of the old country with scarcely a stick or stump upon it.

This settlement is the chief provision depôt of the Hudson's Bay Company, and it is also here that large quantities of pimmi-kon [pemmican] are procured from the half-breeds, a race who, keeping themselves distinct from both Indians and whites, form a tribe of themselves; and, although they have adopted some of the customs and manners of the French voyageurs, are much more attached to the wild and savage manners of the Red-man. Fort Garry, one of the most important establishments of the Company, is erected on the forks of the Red River and the Assiniboine, in long. 97° W., and in lat. 50° 6' 20" N., as will be seen in sketch No. 5. [Figs. 56, 57; crIV-35 to 38] On the opposite side of the river is situated the Roman Catholic church,[3] and two or three miles further down there is a Protestant church.[4] The settlement is formed along the banks of the river for about fifty miles, and extends back from the water, according to the original grant from the Indians, as far as a person can distinguish a man from a horse on a clear day.

Lord Selkirk first attempted to form a settlement here in 1811, but it was speedily abandoned. A few years afterwards several Scotch families, including some from the Orkney Islands, emigrated under the auspices of the Hudson's Bay Company, and now number about 3000, who live as farmers, in great plenty so far as mere food and clothing are concerned.[5] As for the luxuries of life, they are almost unattainable, as they have no market nearer than St. Paul's, on the Mississippi River, a distance of nearly 700 miles over a trackless prairie. The half-

---

[2] KJ states that the trousers are moleskin.

[3] Bishop Joseph-Norbert Provencher built the first Roman Catholic church at the settlement between 1818 and 1820. The church to which Kane refers and shows in the sketch was commenced in 1829 and used until rebuilt in 1908.

[4] The Rev. John West arrived in the 1820s and founded a Protestant church. Services were conducted in a log building from 1831 to 1849 when it was replaced by the present St. Andrews-on-the-Red.

[5] Kane seems to have had trouble in ascertaining the population of the Red River Settlement. KJ gives 1,000 whites and 2,000 half-breeds, and KWMS gives 2,000 whites and 4,000 half-breeds.

breeds are more numerous than the whites, and now amount to 6000. These are the descendants of the white men in the Hudson's Bay Company's employment and the native Indian women. They all speak the Cree language and the Lower Canadian patois; they are governed by a chief named Grant, much after the manner of the Indian tribes. He has presided over them now for a long period, and was implicated in the disturbances which occurred between the Hudson Bay and North-West Companies. He was brought to Canada charged with the murder of Governor Semple, but no sufficient evidence could be produced against him.[6]

The half-breeds are a very hardy race of men, capable of enduring the greatest hardships and fatigues: but their Indian propensities predominate, and consequently they make poor farmers, neglecting their land for the more exciting pleasures of the chase. Their buffalo hunts are conducted by the whole tribe, and take place twice a year, about the middle of June and October, at which periods notice is sent round to all the families to meet at a certain day on the White Horse Plain, about twenty miles from Fort Garry. Here the tribe is divided into three bands, each taking a separate route for the purpose of falling in with the herds of buffaloes. These bands are each accompanied by about 500 carts, drawn by either an ox or a horse. [Fig. 61; crIV-55] Their cart is a curious-looking vehicle, made by themselves with their own axes, and fastened together with wooden pins and leather strings, nails not being procurable. The tire of the wheel is made of buffalo hide, and put on wet; when it becomes dry, it shrinks, and is so tight that it never falls off, and lasts as long as the cart holds together.

Chapter VI.

Plain of Roses.—A Desert Filter.—Making Pimmi-kon.—Canine Camp-followers.—Dry Dance Mountain.—Vigils of the Braves.— Death at the Feast.—Successful Ambush.—The Scalp Dance.—A Hunter's Appetite.—The Grand Chase.—Marking the Game.— Head over Heels.—Sketching under Difficulties.—A Troublesome Tenant.

[6] Cuthbert Grant (1796?–1854) was the colourful half-breed son of a prominent trader of the North West Company, who had assumed leadership of the half-breeds of the Red River during uprisings in 1815 and 1816. Later he co-operated with the Hudson's Bay Company, and was named Warden of the Plains in 1828. Year by year he was appointed leader of the buffalo hunt by the other half-breeds. He was made a member of the Council of Assiniboia. See E. E. Rich, *The Hudson's Bay Company, 1660–1870* (Toronto 1960), vol. II.

I arrived at Fort Garry about three days after the half-breeds had departed; but as I was very anxious to witness buffalo hunting, I procured a guide, a cart for my tent, &c., and a saddle horse for myself, and started after one of the bands.[1] We travelled that day about thirty miles, and encamped in the evening on a beautiful plain covered with innumerable small roses.[2] [Pl. XVI; crIV-52] The next day was anything but pleasant, as our route lay through a marshy tract of country, in which we were obliged to strain through a piece of cloth all the water we drank, on account of the numerous insects, some of which were accounted highly dangerous, and are said to have the power of eating through the coats of the stomach, and causing death even to horses.

The next day I arrived at the Pambinaw River [crIV-53], and found the band cutting poles, which they are obliged to carry with them to dry the meat on [crIV-56], as, after leaving this, no more timbered land is met with until the three bands meet together again at the Turtle Mountain, where the meat they have taken and dried on the route is made into pimmi-kon. This process is as follows:—The thin slices of dried meat are pounded between two stones until the fibres separate; about 50lbs. of this are put into a bag of buffalo skin, with about 40lbs. of melted fat, and mixed together while hot, and sewed up, forming a hard and compact mass; hence its name in the Cree language, *pimmi* signifying meat, and *kon*, fat. Each cart brings home ten of these bags, and all that the half-breeds do not require for themselves is eagerly bought by the Company, for the purpose of sending to the more distant posts, where food is scarce. One pound of this is considered equal to four pounds of ordinary meat, and the pimmi-kon keeps for years perfectly good exposed to any weather.[3]

I was received by the band with the greatest cordiality. They numbered about two hundred hunters, besides women and children.[4] [Fig. 62; crIV-57 to 62] They live, during these hunting excursions, in lodges formed of dressed buffalo skins. They

[1] KJ states that he had trouble in securing a man to go with him since the Sioux and half-breeds were then at war. He left Fort Garry on June 18.

[2] KJ refers to Kane's sketching the sight.

[3] KJ states that the Hudson's Bay Company took part of the dried meat and all of the fat after it was rendered.

[4] KJ describes the party of hunters more fully, stating that they were divided into two parties, of 250 men each, with their wives and children. In all there were about 1,500 carts, drawn by oxen or horses, to carry the meat home. When it was dried, each cart could carry 1,000 pounds. It took 10 buffalo to load a cart. There were about 2,000 half-breeds in all. "They are a distinct class of themselves. They live at the Red River, speak the Indian language, and live by hunting, going out to the Plains twice a year to hunt the buffalo."

are always accompanied by an immense number of dogs, which follow them from the settlements for the purpose of feeding on the offal and remains of the slain buffaloes. These dogs are very like wolves, both in appearance and disposition, and, no doubt, a cross breed between the wolf and dog. A great many of them acknowledge no particular master, and are sometimes dangerous in times of scarcity. I have myself known them to attack the horses and eat them.[5]

Our camp broke up on the following morning, and proceeded on their route to the open plains.[6] [Fig. 60; crIV-54] The carts containing the women and children, and each decorated with some flag, or other conspicuous emblem, on a pole, so that the hunters might recognise their own from a distance, wound off in one continuous line, extending for miles, accompanied by the hunters on horseback. During the forenoon, whilst the line of mounted hunters and carts were winding round the margin of a small lake, I took the opportunity of making a sketch of the singular cavalcade. [crIV-63, 64]

The following day we passed the Dry Dance Mountain, where the Indians, before going on a war party, have a custom of dancing and fasting for three days and nights. This practice is always observed by young warriors going to battle for the first time, to accustom them to the privations and fatigues which they must expect to undergo, and to prove their strength and endurance. Should any sink under the fatigue and fasting of this ceremony, they are invariably sent back to the camp where the women and children remain.[7] [Figs. 63, 64, 65; crIV-65 to 68]

After leaving this mountain, we proceeded on our route without meeting any buffalo, although we saw plenty of indications of their having been in the neighbourhood a short time previously. On the evening of the second day we were visited by twelve Sioux chiefs, with whom the half-breeds had been at war for several years. [Pl. XV; Fig. 58; crIV-40 to 42] They came for the purpose of negotiating a permanent peace, but, whilst smoking the pipe of peace in the council lodge, the dead body of a half-breed, who had gone to a short distance from the camp,

was brought in newly scalped, and his death was at once attributed to the Sioux. The half-breeds, not being at war with any other nation, a general feeling of rage at once sprang up in the young men, and they would have taken instant vengeance, for the supposed act of treachery, upon the twelve chiefs in their power, but for the interference of the old and more temperate of the body, who, deprecating so flagrant a breach of the laws of hospitality, escorted them out of danger, but, at the same time, told them that no peace could be concluded until satisfaction was had for the murder of their friend.[8]

Exposed, as the half-breeds thus are, to all the vicissitudes of wild Indian life, their camps, while on the move, are always preceded by scouts, for the purpose of reconnoitring either for enemies or buffaloes. If they see the latter, they give signal of such being the case, by throwing up handfuls of dust; and, if the former, by running their horses to and fro.

Three days after the departure of the Sioux chiefs, our scouts were observed by their companions to make the signal of enemies being in sight. Immediately a hundred of the best mounted hastened to the spot, and, concealing themselves behind the shelter of the bank of a small stream, sent out two as decoys, who exposed themselves to the view of the Sioux. The latter, supposing them to be alone, rushed upon them, whereupon the concealed half-breeds sprang up, and poured in a volley amongst them, which brought down eight. The others escaped, although several must have been wounded, as much blood was afterwards discovered on their track.[9] Though differing in very few respects from the pure Indians, they [the half-breeds] do not adopt the practice of scalping; and, in this case, being satisfied with their revenge, they abandoned the dead bodies to the malice of a small party of Saulteaux who accompanied them.

The Saulteaux are a band of the great Ojibbeway nation, both words signifying "the Jumpers," and derive the name from their expertness in leaping their canoes over the numerous rapids which occur in the rivers of their vicinity. [Fig. 59; cr-IV-43, 44 and 48–51?]

I took a sketch of one of them, Peccothis, "the Man with a Lump on his Navel." [crIV-45, 46, 47] He appeared delighted with it at first; but the others laughed so much at the likeness, and made so many jokes about it, that he became quite irritated, and insisted that I should destroy it, or, at least, not show it as long as I remained with the tribe.

The Saulteaux, although numerous, are not a warlike tribe, and the Sioux, who are noted for their daring and courage, have long waged a savage war on them, in consequence of which the

[5] KJ notes that on this day the party did not move since it was Sunday.

[6] KJ for June 22 refers to sketching the break-up of the camp and the manner of "catching refractory horses."

[7] KJ for June 23 refers to his seeing "a beautiful antelope."

[8] KJ for June 18 describes the incident reported here as occurring two years earlier when twelve Sioux came to a half-breed camp to make peace. If it did not occur during Kane's visit, he seems to have been attempting to make the printed book more vivid by changing the time to the present. However, if the incident had indeed occurred two years earlier, one wonders if Kane actually met, and sketched, Sioux when he was on this hunting trip.

[9] According to the sense of KJ, Kane is again intimating that this next incident occurred two years earlier; it also says that not two decoys but one were sent out.

Paul Kane 1846

White Mud Portage Winnepeg R.

Plate XIII. White Mud Portage, Winnipeg River. Stark pwc7; crIV-19.

Encampment River Winnipeg Paul Kane 1846

Plate XIV. Encampment, Winnipeg River. Stark POP15;CRIV-22.

Saulteaux do not venture to hunt in the plains except in company with the half-breeds. Immediately on their getting possession of the bodies, they commenced a scalp dance, during which they mutilated the bodies in a most horrible manner. One old woman, who had lost several relations by the Sioux, rendered herself particularly conspicuous by digging out their eyes and otherwise dismembering them.

The following afternoon, we arrived at the margin of a small lake, where we encamped rather earlier than usual, for the sake of the water. Next day [10] I was gratified with the sight of a band of about forty buffalo cows in the distance, and our hunters in full chase; they were the first I had seen, but were too far off for me to join in the sport.[11] They succeeded in killing twenty-five, which were distributed through the camp, and proved most welcome to all of us, as our provisions were getting rather short, and I was abundantly tired of pimmi-kon and dried meat. The fires being lighted with the wood we had brought with us in the carts, the whole party commenced feasting with a voracity which appeared perfectly astonishing to me, until I tried myself, and found by experience how much hunting on the plains stimulates the appetite.

The upper part of the hunch of the buffalo, weighing four or five pounds, is called by the Indians the little hunch. This is of a harder and more compact nature than the rest, though very tender, and is usually put aside for keeping. The lower and larger part is streaked with fat and is very juicy and delicious. These, with the tongues, are considered the delicacies of the buffalo. After the party had gorged themselves with as much as they could devour, they passed the evening in roasting the marrow bones and regaling themselves with their contents.

For the next two or three days we fell in with only a single buffalo, or small herds of them; but as we proceeded they became more frequent.[12] At last our scouts brought in word of an immense herd of buffalo bulls about two miles in advance of us. They are known in the distance from the cows, by their feeding singly, and being scattered wider over the plain, whereas the cows keep together for the protection of the calves, which are always kept in the centre of the herd. A half-breed, of the name of Hallett, who was exceedingly attentive to me, woke me in the morning, to accompany him in advance of the party, that I might have the opportunity of examining the buffalo whilst feeding, before the commencement of the hunt. Six hours' hard riding brought us within a quarter of a mile of the nearest of the herd. The main body stretched over the plains as far as the eye could reach. Fortunately the wind blew in our faces: had it blown towards the buffaloes, they would have scented us miles off. I wished to have attacked them at once, but my companion would not allow me until the rest of the party came up, as it was contrary to the law of the tribe. We, therefore, sheltered ourselves from the observation of the herd behind a mound, relieving our horses of their saddles to cool them. In about an hour the hunters came up to us, numbering about one hundred and thirty, and immediate preparations were made for the chase. Every man loaded his gun, looked to his priming, and examined the efficiency of his saddle-girths. [Fig. 66; crIV-69, 70]

The elder men strongly cautioned the less experienced not to shoot each other; a caution by no means unnecessary, as such accidents frequently occur. Each hunter then filled his mouth with balls, which he drops into the gun without wadding; by this means loading much quicker and being enabled to do so whilst his horse is at full speed. It is true, that the gun is more liable to burst, but that they do not seem to mind. Nor does the gun carry so far, or so true; but that is of less consequence, as they always fire quite close to the animal.

Everything being adjusted, we all walked our horses towards the herd. By the time we had gone about two hundred yards, the herd perceived us, and started off in the opposite direction at the top of their speed. We now put our horses to the full gallop, and in twenty minutes were in their midst. There could not have been less than four or five thousand in our immediate vicinity, all bulls, not a single cow amongst them.

The scene now became one of intense excitement; the huge bulls thundering over the plain in headlong confusion, whilst the fearless hunters rode recklessly in their midst, keeping up an incessant fire at but a few yards' distance from their victims. [Pl. XVII; Fig. 67; crIV-71 to 75] Upon the fall of each buffalo, the successful hunter merely threw some article of his apparel—

[10] KJ for June 24 reads: "Made a sketch of the carts in motion. Got ahead of the party when an Indian called out that there were buffalo to the right of me. I ascended a small hill when I" etc.

[11] KJ records that Kane himself joined the chase: "I was not long in turning my horse's head in the direction of the chase. After running about 3 miles, I came nearly up to a cow. My horse became afraid. After beating for about 2 miles more, I came close enough for a shot when I found I had no ball. I fired a shot but without effect."

[12] KJ for June 25 reads: "This morning I took good care that I had plenty of balls. Left with Mr. Hallet [*sic*] and the hunters. All started ahead of the carts hearing that there were buffalo not far off. Saw the buffalo about 7 miles ahead but when we came up within a short distance, we found that they were on the other side of the lake (Lake de Roche), so I did not get a chance to run them. Some of the hunters got across and killed about 60." He continues by noting that the hunt when the immense herd was sighted was the next day.

often carried by him solely for that purpose—to denote his own prey, and then rushed on to another. These marks are scarcely ever disputed, but should a doubt arise as to the ownership, the carcase is equally divided among the claimants.

The chase continued only about one hour, and extended over an area of from five to six square miles, where might be seen the dead and dying buffaloes, to the number of five hundred. In the meantime my horse, which had started at a good run, was suddenly confronted by a large bull that made his appearance from behind a knoll, within a few yards of him, and being thus taken by surprise, he sprung to one side, and getting his foot into one of the innumerable badger holes, with which the plains abound, he fell at once, and I was thrown over his head with such violence, that I was completely stunned, but soon recovered my recollection. Some of the men caught my horse, and I was speedily remounted, and soon saw reason to congratulate myself on my good fortune, for I found a man who had been thrown in a similar way, lying a short distance from me quite senseless, in which state he was carried back to the camp.

I again joined in the pursuit; and coming up with a large bull, I had the satisfaction of bringing him down at the first fire. Excited by my success, I threw down my cap and galloping on, soon put a bullet through another enormous animal. He did not, however, fall, but stopped and faced me, pawing the earth, bellowing and glaring savagely at me. The blood was streaming profusely from his mouth, and I thought he would soon drop. The position in which he stood was so fine that I could not resist the desire of making a sketch. I accordingly dismounted, and had just commenced, when he suddenly made a dash at me.[13] I had hardly time to spring on my horse and get away from him, leaving my gun and everything else behind. [Figs. 68, 69; crIV-76 to 80]

When he came up to where I had been standing, he turned over the articles I had dropped, pawing fiercely as he tossed them about, and then retreated towards the herd. I immediately recovered my gun, and having reloaded, again pursued him, and soon planted another shot in him; and this time he remained on his legs long enough for me to make a sketch. This done I returned with it to the camp, carrying the tongues of the animals I had killed, according to custom, as trophies of my success as a hunter.

I have often witnessed an Indian buffalo hunt since, but never

[13] KJ states that he laid his gun on the pommel of his saddle before dismounting, and took out his sketchbook.
[14] Here again Kane seems to have moved the past to the present. KJ states that the buffalo's rampage had taken place the previous spring.

one on so large a scale. In returning to the camp, I fell in with one of the hunters coolly driving a wounded buffalo before him. In answer to my inquiry why he did not shoot him, he said he would not do so until he got him close to the lodges, as it would save the trouble of bringing a cart for the meat. He had already driven him seven miles, and afterwards killed him within two hundred yards of the tents. That evening, while the hunters were still absent, a buffalo, bewildered by the hunt, got amongst the tents, and at last got into one, after having terrified all the women and children, who precipitately took to flight. When the men returned they found him there still, and being unable to dislodge him, they shot him down from the opening in the top.[14]

Chapter VII.

Camping amongst the Slain.—Wholesale Slaughter.—A Sick Guide. —Parting from the Half-breeds.—A False Alarm.—Dismal Night's Lodging.—Dreadful Position.—Stinking River.—Death of the Guide.—Paternal Government.—The Fire-Water Curse.

Our camp was now moved to the field of slaughter, for the greater convenience of collecting the meat. However lightly I wished to think of my fall, I found myself the next day suffering considerably from the effects of it, and the fatigue I had undergone. The man whom I had brought with me as a guide was also suffering much from an attack of the measles. Next day our hunters sighted and chased another large band of bulls with good success. At night we were annoyed by the incessant howling and fighting of innumerable dogs and wolves that had followed us to the hunt, seemingly as well aware of the feast that was preparing for them as we could be ourselves. The plain now resembled one vast shambles: the women, whose business it is, being all busily employed in cutting the flesh into slices, and hanging them in the sun on racks, made of poles tied together. In reference to the immense number of buffaloes killed, I may mention that it is calculated that the half-breeds alone destroy thirty thousand annually.

Having satisfied myself with buffalo hunting amongst the half-breeds, I was anxious to return to the settlement, in order to prosecute my journey. On proposing to set out I found my guide so unwell, that I feared he would not be able to travel. I tried to procure one of the hunters to take his place and return with me, but none of them would consent to travel alone over so large a tract of country, from fear of the Sioux, in whose territory we then were; and who they dreaded, from the late occurrence, would be watching to cut off any stragglers. Being unable to procure a fresh man, I was about to start alone, when my guide, who thought himself better, proposed to accompany me, on condition that he should ride in the cart, and not be expected to attend to the horses or cooking. This I readily agreed to, as his services as guide were of the utmost importance.

We started next morning for the settlement,[1] a distance which I supposed to be somewhat over two hundred miles. A party of twenty of the hunters escorted us for eight or ten miles, to see that there were no Sioux in the immediate vicinity. We then parted, after taking the customary smoke on separating from friends. I could not avoid a strong feeling of regret at leaving them, having experienced many acts of kindness at their hands, hardly to be expected from so wild and uncultivated a people. We found a great scarcity of water on our return, most of the swamps that had supplied us on our way out being now dried up by the heat of the season.

We fell in with a great many stray dogs and wolves, which appeared to be led on by the scent of the dead carcasses. After hobbling the horses, putting up my tent, and cooking the supper, I then turned in for the night, not without some apprehensions of a hostile visit from the Sioux, as we were still on their hunting grounds, and in the territory of the United States, being still a few miles south of the boundary line. During the night my guide, who was very ill and feverish, cried out that the Sioux were upon us. I started up with my gun in my hand, for I slept with it by my side, and rushing out in the dark, was near shooting my own horse, which, by stumbling over one of the tent pins, had alarmed my companion.

We travelled on the next day with as great rapidity as the ill health of my guide would permit, and on the evening of the 30th of June, we encamped on the bank of the Pambinaw. I lost considerable time next morning in catching the horses, as they are able from habit to run a considerable distance, and pretty fast, in spite of their hobbles.[2] In the afternoon we arrived at the Swampy Lake, about fourteen miles across. A little before sunset we reached about the middle of it, but my guide complained so much that I could not proceed further.

I succeeded in finding a small dry spot above water large enough for me to sit on, but not affording room for my legs,

which had to remain in the water, there being no more room in the small cart than was necessary for the sick man. Having no means for cooking, I was compelled to eat my dried meat raw. I tried to compose myself to sleep, but found it impossible, from the myriads of mosquitoes which appeared determined to extract the last drop of blood from my body. After battling with them until 4 o'clock next morning, my eyes almost blinded by their stings, I went in search of the horses, which had strayed away to some distance into deeper water, tempted by some sort of flags growing there. I had to wade up to my middle in pursuit of them, and it was not until 9 o'clock that we were able to proceed.

After leaving this dismal swamp we were within a day's march of the settlement; and my guide, believing himself to be much better, insisted upon my leaving him to drive the cart, whilst I proceeded at a more rapid rate on horseback. This, however, I would not do until I had seen him safe across Stinking River, which the horses had almost to swim in crossing. Having got him over safely, I left him, and proceeded onwards in the direction of the fort. But I had not gone far before I encountered one of the numerous swampy lakes that abound in this region, and render travelling extremely difficult. I had no doubt got on a wrong track, for in endeavouring to cross, my horse quickly sank up to his neck in mud and water. Seeing that I could neither advance nor recede, I dismounted, and found myself in the same predicament, scarcely able to keep my head above the surface. I managed, however, to reach the dry land; and, with the lasso, or long line, which every voyageur in these parts invariably has attached to his horse's neck, succeeded in getting the animal out. I remounted, and endeavoured to cross in another direction, but with no better success. I now found myself surrounded on all sides, as far as I could see, with nothing but swamp. My horse refused to be ridden any further. I had therefore, to dismount, and drag him along as best I could, wading up to my very middle in mud and water abounding with reptiles.

That I had lost my way was now certain; and as it was raining hard, I could not see the sun, nor had I a compass. I, however, determined to fix upon one certain course, and keep that at all hazards, in hopes that I might reach the Assiniboine River, by following which I could not fail to reach the settlement. After travelling in uncertainty for ten or twelve miles, I had at length the satisfaction of reaching the river, and in two hours afterwards I arrived safe at Fort Garry. The next morning I learned that my guide had been brought in by two men

---

[1] KJ states that they left on June 29.
[2] KJ states that here Kane saw a large wolf, tried to get a shot at it, but found it too wild.

who were looking for stray horses. The poor fellow had got rapidly worse after my leaving, and had only proceeded a short distance when he was compelled to stop. He only survived two days after his arrival.[3]

Fort Garry is one of the best built forts in the Hudson's Bay territory. It has a stone wall, with bastions mounted with cannon, inclosing large storehouses and handsome residences for the gentlemen of the establishment. Its strength is such that it has nothing to fear from the surrounding half-breeds or Indians. The gentleman in charge was Mr. Christie, whose many acts of kindness and attention I must ever remember with feelings of grateful respect.[4]

The office of Governor of the Red River Settlement is one of great responsibility and trouble, as the happiness and comfort of the whole settlement depend to a great extent upon the manner in which he carries out his instructions. The half-breeds are much inclined to grumbling, and although the Company treat them with great liberality, they still ask almost for impossibilities; indeed, as far as the Company is concerned, I cannot conceive a more just and strict course than that which they pursue in the conduct of the whole of their immense traffic. In times of scarcity they help all around them, in sickness they furnish them with medicines, and even try to act as mediators between hostile bands of Indians. No drunkenness or debauchery is seen around their posts, and so strict is their prohibition of liquor, that even their officers can only procure a small allowance, which is given as part of their annual outfit on voyages.

Without entering into the general question of the policy of giving a monopoly of the fur trade to one company, I cannot but record, as the firm conviction which I formed from a comparison between the Indians in the Hudson's Bay Company territories and those in the United States, that opening up the trade with the Indians to all who wish indiscriminately to engage in it, must lead to their annihilation. For while it is the interest of such a body as the Hudson's Bay Company to improve the Indians and encourage them to industry, according to their own native habits in hunting and the chase, even with a view to their own profit, it is as obviously the interest of small companies and private adventurers to draw as much wealth as they possibly can from the country in the shortest possible time, although in doing so the very source from which the wealth springs should

be destroyed. The unfortunate craving for intoxicating liquor which characterises all the tribes of Indians, and the terrible effects thereby produced upon them, render it a deadly instrument in the hands of designing men.

It is well known that, although the laws of the United States strictly prohibit the sale of liquor to the Indians, it is impossible to enforce them, and whilst many traders are making rapid fortunes in their territories, the Indians are fast declining in character, numbers, and wealth, whilst those in contact with the Hudson's Bay Company maintain their numbers, retain native characteristics unimpaired, and in some degree share in the advantages which civilisation places within their reach.

Chapter VIII.

Catching the Boat.—Queer Fish.—Fatal Thunder-bolt.—Killing Portraits.—Raising the Wind.—An Island with Wings.—Norway House.—Playgreen Lake.—Bound to the Rock.—A Model Athlete. —Shooting a Buck Moose.—Luxury of a Clean Shirt.—Life for Life. —A Violent Puss.—Buffalo Pounds.—A Perfect Centaur.

Hearing that two small sloops belonging to the Company which ply between the Red River and Norway House would leave the Lower, or Stone Fort, immediately, I rode down on the 5th of July, in company with Mr. W. Simpson, a brother-in-law of Sir George's, and reached our destination in about three hours. This establishment is larger than the Upper Fort, and built with still greater strength, but not so neatly arranged in the interior. We rested about an hour, and then embarked in one of the sloops; two Catholic missionaries, Mr. Le Fleck and Mr. Taché, who were bound for Isle La Croix, occupying the other.[1] We dropped down the river a few miles, and cast anchor in front of the residence of Mr. Smithers, the Episcopalian missionary,[2] and his larder and cellar being well supplied, we passed a most agreeable evening, notwithstanding the mosquitoes, which were very troublesome. Early next morning we went round his very

---

[3] KJ states that the name of his guide who died was Francis de Gourlay (or Gurlay).

[4] This is Alexander Christie (fl. 1809–1849), member of a family prominent in the fur trade. He was governor of Assiniboia in 1833–39 and 1844–48, then he retired and returned to his native Scotland.

[1] Kane refers to the Rev. Louis-François-Richer Laflèche (1818–1898) who had gone to the Red River mission in 1844 and who with Father Taché organized the Isle-à-la-Crosse mission. He was coadjutor Bishop of St. Boniface before returning to Canada in 1854. The Rev. Alexandre-Antonin Taché (1823–1894) went to St. Boniface in 1845. He later became first archbishop of St. Boniface.

[2] The Rev. John Smithurst (1807–1867), to whom Kane refers as "Smithers," was a cousin of Florence Nightingale. He was engaged to her but their marriage was forbidden because of their relationship. He went as a Church of England missionary to the Saulteaux and Swampy Cree at the Indian settlement below Selkirk, Man., where he served from 1839 to 1851.

extensive farm, which seemed to be in a high state of cultivation. He works it principally by Indians, who receive a share of the produce according to their labour.

After a hearty breakfast, we bid a reluctant farewell to our kind host, and drifted down the current, there not being enough wind to fill our sails. When night had set in, I distinctly heard the noise made by the Red River sun-fish, which I have only noticed in this river. The fish resemble our Canadian black bass, weighing from two to three pounds, and during the night they make a singular noise, resembling a person groaning; how they produced these sounds, I was unable to ascertain. We proceeded only a short distance to-day, the current running very slow. After casting anchor for the night, the mosquitoes became so troublesome on board, that Mr. Simpson and I took our blankets on shore and went to an Indian lodge within a short distance of the river, the smoke which pervades these places generally keeping them free from the nuisance. There were three or four families of women and children in the lodge, but the men were all absent hunting. They cleared a corner for us to sleep in, but one of the most awful thunder storms, accompanied by heavy rain, that I had ever witnessed, set in, and effectually prevented our repose. Such tempests are here of frequent occurrence; so vivid was the lightning, and so near the rattling and crashing of the thunder, that I fancied several times during the night that I heard our vessels dashed to pieces by it. The missionaries on board were much terrified, and spent, I believe, the whole night in prayer. A short time previously a lodge containing seven persons was struck by the electric fluid; four of them were immediately killed, the other three were much injured, but recovered. These accidents are of very frequent occurrence about Red River.

July 7th.—We embarked in the morning, and proceeded at a slow rate. On arriving at the mouth of the river we were obliged to cast anchor, as it still remained a dead calm.

July 8th.—This morning we had a strong head wind, putting a stop to our further progress for the present. Mr. Simpson and I took a small boat, and returned up the river to an Indian camp of Saulteaux which we had passed the day before. The Indians crowded round the boat on our arrival, inquiring what we wanted. Our interpreter told them that I had come to take their likenesses. One of them, a huge ugly-looking fellow, entirely naked, stepped up telling me to take his, as he was just as the Great Spirit had made him. I declined, however, as I wanted to sketch one of the females, but she refused, as she could not dress herself suitably for such an occasion, being in mourning for

some friends she had lost, and therefore only wearing her oldest and dirtiest clothes.

After some difficulty, I succeeded in getting a young girl to sit in the costume of this tribe, although her mother was very much afraid it might shorten her life. But on my assuring her that it was more likely to prolong it, she seemed quite satisfied. [Fig. 72; crIV-86] After finishing my sketch, which they all looked at with great astonishment, a medicine-man stepped up and told us that he would give us three days' fair wind for a pound of tobacco. As the demand was so enormous for so small a supply of wind, we declined the bargain, whereupon he hesitatingly reduced his price, offering a greater quantity of wind for a smaller amount of tobacco, till at length, having reduced his price to a small plug for six days, we closed the bargain, declining his invitation to stay and partake of a large roasted dog, which we had seen slaughtered on our arrival. We returned to our vessel to pass another uncomfortable night, tormented by the mosquitoes, which all our efforts at smoking failed to drive out of our hot little cabin.

July 9th.—Hauled up our anchor and left the mouth of the river with a fair wind, and proceeded up Lake Winnipeg.

July 10th.—To-day we were wind-bound under the lee of a low rocky island, and although the surf ran very high on the beach, we determined to explore it as a relief to the monotony of our voyage. [crIV-81?] The attempt furnished us with plenty of excitement, as the boat filled before we reached the shore. We, however, arrived safe, and walked across the island about half a mile. It was literally covered with gulls and pelicans, which were hatching, and all rose in one body on our approach in such a dense mass as to give the appearance of the island itself taking wings.[3] The rocks were so covered with eggs and young birds, that it was difficult to tread without crushing them. Wearied with the discordant screeching of the birds over our heads, and the smell from their dung being very offensive, we soon returned to our vessels. Large quantities of eggs are collected on this island by the voyageurs and Indians, gull's eggs being considered a great delicacy at certain seasons. There did not appear to be any considerable collection of guano here, as probably the island is washed almost clean by the high water and heavy rains in the spring of the year.

July 11th.—We entered the Straits between Lake Winnipeg and Playgreen Lake. The lake derives its name from a green plain which the Indians frequent to play their great game of

[3] KJ notes the Indian saying that the pelicans are the birds that make the thunder.

ball. We cast anchor here, and having a small net on board, we set it, and caught a great number of jack-fish or pike, which we found excellent eating.

July 12*th.*—Sailed on through Playgreen Lake, a distance of twenty-five miles, the channel lying between numerous small rocky islands, some of them so near that we could easily have sprung on shore from the vessel; from Playgreen Lake we entered Jack-fish River, and the current soon carried us to Norway House, a distance of nine miles, where we arrived in the afternoon. [Pl. XVIII; crIV-82, 83] Mr. Ross, the gentleman in charge, received us with great kindness and hospitality. [Fig. 70; crIV-89] Notwithstanding the barrenness of the soil and the severity of the cold in this region, which prevents all hope of deriving any advantage from agricultural pursuits, a Wesleyan Methodist mission is established within a few miles of the fort. [Fig. 71; crIV-84, 85] It is under the superintendence of the Reverend Mr. Mason, and consists of about thirty small log houses, with a church and dwelling-house for the minister. It is supported by the Company with the hope of improving the Indians; but, to judge from appearances, with but small success, as they are decidedly the dirtiest Indians I have met with, and the less that is said about their morality the better.

The Indians belong to the Mas-ka-gau tribe, or "Swamp Indians," so called from their inhabiting the low swampy land which extends the whole way from Norway House to Hudson's Bay. This race is rather diminutive in comparison with those who inhabit the plains, probably from their suffering often for want of food; and instances of their being compelled by hunger to eat one another are not uncommon. Their language somewhat resembles the Cree, but is not so agreeable in sound. I made a sketch of one of them, called the I-ac-a-way, "the Man who is gone on a Hunt without raising his Camp." [4]

I remained at Norway House until the 14th of August, waiting for the brigade of boats which had gone down in the Spring to York Factory, in Hudson's Bay, with the furs, and was now expected back on their return with the outfit of goods for the interior trade. [5] Our time passed very monotonously until the 13th, when Mr. Rowand, chief factor, arrived with six boats: one of the boats under the charge of a clerk, Mr. Lane,

was entirely devoted to the carriage of the furs paid annually by the Hudson's Bay Company to the Russian Government, for the privilege of trading in their territory. [6] These consisted of seventy pieces or packs, each containing seventy-five otter skins of the very best description. They are principally collected on the Mackenzie River, from whence they are carried to York Factory, where they are culled and packed with the greatest care; they have then to be carried up the Saskatchawan, across the Rocky Mountains, down the Columbia River, to Vancouver's Island, and then shipped to Sitka. I mention these furs particularly here, as they were the source of much trouble to us in our future progress.

On the morning of the 14th we left Norway House, in the boats, for Playgreen Lake. These boats are about twenty-eight feet long, and strongly built, so as to be able to stand a heavy press of sail and rough weather, which they often encounter in the lakes: they carry about eighty or ninety packs of 90 lbs. each, and have a crew of seven men, a steersman and six rowers. Mr. Lane was accompanied by his wife, a half-breed, who travelled with us all the way to Fort Vancouver, on the Columbia. We had scarcely got into Playgreen Lake when a heavy gale separated the boats and drove ours on to a rock in the lake. Here we were compelled to remain two nights and a day, without a stick to make a fire, and exposed to the incessant rain, as it was not possible to raise our tents. In the distance we could perceive our more fortunate companions, who had succeeded in gaining the mainland, comfortably under canvas, with blazing fires; but so terrific was the gale that we dared not venture to leave the shelter of the rock.

On the 16th, the wind having somewhat abated, we were enabled to join the rest of the party, when the blazing fires and comfortably cooked food soon restored our spirits. Being sufficiently recruited, and the wind being fair, we again embarked, although the lake was still very rough.

This lake is about 300 miles long, but so shallow, that in high winds the mud at the bottom is stirred up, from which it derives the name of Winnipeg, or Muddy Lake. On the present occasion the waves rose so high that some of the men became sick, and we were obliged to put into a lee shore, not being able to find a landing-place. On nearing the shore some of the men jumped into the water and held the boats off, whilst the others unloaded them and carried the goods on their heads through the dashing surf. When the boats were emptied, they were then enabled to drag them up on the beach. Here we were compelled to remain until the 18th, occupying ourselves in shooting ducks and gulls,

---

[4] This would seem to be the sketch, unlocated, referred to in item 8 of Kane's portrait log. The name "I-ac-a-way" also appears for another Indian; see crIV-29.

[5] KJ refers here specifically to Mr. Ross, factor at Norway House, as a "very kind and good man."

[6] This is Richard Lane. See *Dictionary of Canadian Biography*, vol. X.

which we found in great abundance, and which proved capital eating.

The waves having abated on the morning of the 18th, we made an early start, and arrived in the afternoon at the mouth of the Saskatchawan River. The navigation is here interrupted by what is called the Grand Rapid, which is about three miles long, one mile of which runs with great rapidity, and presents a continual foamy appearance, down which boats are able to descend, but in going up are obliged to make a portage.

I was told a story of one of the steersmen of our brigade, named Paulet Paul, who in steering his boat down by an oar passed through a ring in the stern of the boat, fell overboard, from the oar, on which he was leaning with his whole force, suddenly breaking. His great bodily strength enabled him to gain a footing, and to stand against the rapid until the boat following came past, into which he sprang, and urging the men to pull, he eventually succeeded in jumping into his own boat and guiding her safely down, thereby saving the valuable cargo which might have otherwise been lost. He was a half-breed, and certainly one of the finest formed men I ever saw, and when naked, no painter could desire a finer model. We encamped on the shore, and were obliged to remain here till the third day, for the purpose of getting the goods across, as it required the crews of all the boats to haul each over in succession. There are usually Indians to be met at this portage, who assist the men for a small consideration, but on this occasion they were unfortunately absent.

August 21st.—Embarked in the afternoon, and on the 22nd passed through Cedar Lake, and again entered the Saskatchawan River; the land in the neighbourhood of which is very flat and marshy, innumerable small lakes being scattered over the whole region. We met with nothing worth recording till the 25th, when we arrived at the "Pau," a Church of England missionary station, occupied by the Rev. Mr. Hunter.[7] He resides in a neat house most brilliantly decorated inside with blue and red paint, much to the admiration of his flock, which consists of only a small band of the same tribe of Indians as are met with about Norway House. Mr. Hunter and his amiable lady invited us to their table, where we found some bread made from wheat of their own raising, ground in a hand-mill, and they spared no exertions to make us as comfortable as possible.[8]

Mr. Hunter accompanied me to a medicine-man's lodge, a short distance from his own residence. Seeing a very handsomely worked otter-skin bag, apparently well filled, hanging up in the lodge, I inquired as to its purpose, when the Indian

informed me it was his medicine-bag, but would not let me examine its contents until he had seen some of my sketches, and was informed that I was a great medicine-man myself, upon which he opened it for my inspection. The contents consisted of bits of bones, shells, minerals, red earth, and other heterogeneous accumulations, perfectly incomprehensible to my uninitiated capacity.

Aug. 26th.[9]—We left the hospitable mansion of Mr. Hunter with many kind wishes for our safety and success, and continued our journey along the low and swampy banks of the river. On the 28th, we passed the mouth of the Cumberland River. Here the men had to harness themselves to the boats with their portage straps and drag the boats up the river for several days. We passed a large quantity of the bones of buffaloes which had been drowned in the preceding winter in attempting to cross the ice. The wolves had picked them all clean.

On the 29th I fired both barrels loaded with ball at a large buck moose, which was swimming across the river. He, however, arrived at the other side and trotted up the bank. Thinking I had missed him, I went on, but on my return the following year, two Indians, who had been attracted by the shots, told me that he had dropped 200 yards from the river.

Aug. 30th.—We this day fell in with a small band of Crees, from whom we procured some buffalo meat, tongues, and beaver tails; the last is considered a great delicacy. It is a fat, gristly substance, but to me by no means palatable; the rest of our party, however, seemed to enjoy it much. The tongues were decidedly delicious; they are cured by drying them in the smoke of the lodges.

The river as we ascended presented a more inviting appearance, the banks becoming bolder and covered principally with pine and poplar, the latter trees springing up wherever the former are burned off. The men suffered severely from the heat, which was very oppressive.

September 6th.—We were within about eighteen or twenty miles of Carlton, when about dark in the evening we heard a tremendous splashing in the water, but so far off that we could not see the cause. Mr. Rowand at once conjectured it to be a large party of Blackfeet swimming their horses across the river, which they do by driving the horse into the water till he loses

---

[7] James Hunter had taken over Cumberland Station mission in 1844 and, with the co-operation of the Hudson's Bay Company, it was speedily enlarged to a place of importance.

[8] KJ records that Hunter "killed a small pig which we feasted on for a day." The missionary evidently regarded the arrival of the brigade as a gala occasion.

[9] KJ records the date as August 28, not 26.

his footing, when the rider slips off and seizes the tail of the animal, and is thus towed to the opposite shore. We were somewhat alarmed, and immediately loaded our guns, the Blackfeet being the most hostile tribe on the continent; but on coming up to the spot, we found it was the horsekeeper of Fort Carlton, who was swimming his horses across to an island in the middle of the river to save them from the wolves, which had killed several of them, owing to the scarcity of buffaloes. As we had but a short distance to travel next day we encamped for the night.

Sept. 7th.—When we arrived within a couple of miles of Carlton, we halted for the purpose of arranging our toilets previous to presenting ourselves at the establishment. This consisted chiefly of a thorough washing; some, indeed, put on clean shirts, but few, however, could boast of such a luxury. This compliment to the inhabitants was by no means unnecessary, as we were in a most ragged and dirty condition.

The country in the vicinity of Carlton, which is situated between the wooded country and the other plains, varies much from that through which we had been travelling. Instead of dense masses of unbroken forest, it presents more the appearance of a park; the gently undulating plains being dotted here and there with clumps of small trees. The banks of the river rise to the height of 150 or 200 feet in smooth rolling hills covered with verdure. The fort, which is situated about a quarter of a mile back from the river, is enclosed with wooden pickets, and is fortified with blunderbusses on swivels mounted in the bastion. [Fig. 75; crIV-96] This fort is in greater danger from the Blackfeet than any of the Company's establishments, being feebly manned and not capable of offering much resistance to an attack. Their horses have frequently been driven off without the inmates of the fort daring to leave it for their rescue. The buffaloes are here abundant, as is evident from the immense accumulation of their bones which strew the plains in every direction. [Saskatchewan River: Fig. 81; crIV-110 to 119, 178, 179]

The whole of the boats not having yet arrived, we remained here for several days. On the second evening after our arrival we were rather alarmed by the rapid approach of fire, which had originated far off to the west on the prairies. Fortunately, when within about half a mile of the fort, the wind changed, and it turned to the south. We, however, remained up nearly all night for fear of accidents. There were some Cree Indians about the fort, which is one of the trading ports of that nation who extend along the Saskatchawan to the Rocky Mountains, and is one of

the largest tribes of Indians in the Hudson's Bay Company's dominions. [Pl. XIX; Fig. 80; crIV-103, 106 to 109] This tribe has been from time immemorial at war with the Blackfeet, whom they at one time conquered and held in subjection: even now the Crees call the Blackfeet slaves, although they have gained their independence, and are a fierce and warlike tribe. These wars are kept up with unremitting perseverance from year to year; and were they as destructive in proportion to the numbers engaged as the wars of civilised nations, the continent would soon be depopulated of the whole Indian race; but, luckily, Indians are satisfied with small victories, and a few scalps and horses taken from the enemy are quite sufficient to entitle the warriors to return to their friends in triumph and glory. [Pl. XX; crIV-105?]

I made a sketch of Us-koos-koosish, "Young Grass," a Cree brave.[10] [crIV-102] He was very proud of showing his many wounds, and expressed himself rather dissatisfied with my picture, as I had not delineated all the scars, no matter what was their locality. He had a younger brother killed by one of his own tribe in a quarrel; this he considered incumbent on him to revenge, and tracked the offender for upwards of six months before he found an opportunity of killing him, which he however effected at last.

This custom of taking life for life is universal amongst all Indians; and the first death often leads to many, until the feud is stayed either by the intervention of powerful friends, or by one party paying the other a satisfaction in horses or other Indian valuables. An Indian, however, in taking revenge for the death of a relative does not in all cases seek the actual offender; as should the party be one of his own tribe any relative will do, however distant. Should he be a white man, the Indian would most probably kill the first white man he could find.

Mr. Rundell,[11] a missionary, whose station was at Edmonton, was at Carlton awaiting our arrival, for the purpose of returning in company with us. He had with him a favourite cat which he had brought with him in the canoes from Edmonton, being afraid to leave her behind him, as there was some danger of her being eaten during his absence. This cat was the object of a good deal of amusement among the party, of great curiosity amongst

---

[10] KJ states that Kane made a sketch of Fort Carlton and of two Cree Indians, one being a great warrior who had been wounded by the Blackfoot. The latter was evidently Us-koos-koosish.

[11] The Rev. Robert Terrill Rundle (1811–1896), a Methodist, was the first Protestant missionary in Alberta (1840–48). Mount Rundle in Banff National Park is named after him.

Plate XV. Two portrait heads, Sioux; south of Fort Garry(?). ROM946.15.57; CrIV-40.

the Indians, and of a good deal of anxiety and trouble to its kind master.

Mr. Rowand, myself, and Mr. Rundell, having determined to proceed to Edmonton on horseback, as being the shortest and most agreeable route, we procured horses and a guide and, on the morning of the 12th September, we arose early for our start. The Indians had collected in numbers round the fort to see us off, and shake hands with us, a practice which they seem to have taken a particular fancy for. No sooner had we mounted our rather skittish animals than the Indians crowded around, and Mr. Rundell, who was rather a favourite amongst them, came in for a large share of their attentions, which seemed to be rather annoying to his horse. His cat he had tied to the pummel of his saddle by a string, about four feet long, round her neck, and had her safely, as he thought, concealed in the breast of his capote. She, however, did not relish the plunging of the horse, and made a spring out, utterly astonishing the Indians, who could not conceive where she had come from. The string brought her up against the horse's legs, which she immediately attacked. The horse now became furious, kicking violently, and at last threw Mr. Rundell over his head, but fortunately without much injury. All present were convulsed with laughter, to which the Indians added screeching and yelling as an accompaniment, rendering the whole scene indescribably ludicrous. Puss's life was saved by the string breaking; but we left her behind for the men to bring in the boats, evidently to the regret of her master, notwithstanding the hearty laugh which we had had at his expense.

We were accompanied by a party of hunters proceeding to a buffalo pound about six miles off. These pounds can only be made in the vicinity of forests, as they are composed of logs piled up roughly, five feet high, and enclose about two acres. At one side an entrance is left, about ten feet wide, and from each side of this, to the distance of half a mile, a row of posts or short stumps, called dead men, are planted, at the distance of twenty feet each, gradually widening out into the plain from the entrance. [crIV-97] When we arrived at the pound we found a party there anxiously awaiting the arrival of the buffaloes, which their companions were driving in. This is accomplished as follows:—A man, mounted on a fleet horse, usually rides forward till he sees a band of buffaloes. This may be sixteen or eighteen miles distant from the ground, but of course the nearer to it the better. The hunter immediately strikes a light with a flint and steel, and places the lighted spunk in a handful of dried grass, the smoke arising from which the buffaloes soon

smell and start away from it at the top of their speed. The man now rides up alongside of the herd, which, from some unaccountable propensity, invariably endeavour to cross in front of his horse. I have had them follow me for miles in order to do so. The hunter thus possesses an unfailing means, wherever the pound may be situated, of conducting them to it by the dexterous management of his horse. Indians are stationed at intervals behind the posts, or dead men, provided with buffalo robes, who, when the herd are once in the avenue, rise up and shake the robes, yelling and urging them on until they get into the enclosure, the spot usually selected for which is one with a tree in the centre. On this they hang offerings to propitiate the Great Spirit to direct the herd towards it. A man is also placed in the tree with a medicine pipe-stem in his hand, which he waves continually, chaunting a sort of prayer to the Great Spirit, the burden of which is that the buffaloes may be numerous and fat. [Figs. 77, 78; crIV-98 to 101]

As soon as all the herd are within the pound, the entrance is immediately closed with logs, the buffaloes running round and round one after another, and very rarely attempting to break out, which would not be difficult, from the insufficiency of the structure. Should one succeed in doing so the whole herd immediately follow. When once in the enclosure the Indians soon despatch them with their arrows and spears.

Whilst the buffaloes were being driven in, the scene was certainly exciting and picturesque; but the slaughter in the enclosure was more painful than pleasing. This had been the third herd that had been driven into this pound within the last ten or twelve days, and the putrefying carcases tainted the air all round. The Indians in this manner destroy innumerable buffaloes, apparently for the mere pleasure of the thing. I have myself seen a pound so filled up with their dead carcases that I could scarcely imagine how the enclosure could have contained them while living. It is not unusual to drive in so many that their aggregate bulk forces down the barriers. There are thousands of them annually killed in this manner; but not one in twenty is used in any way by the Indians, so that thousands are left to rot where they fall. I heard of a pound, too far out of my direct road to visit, formed entirely of the bones of dead buffaloes that had been killed in a former pound on the same spot, piled up in a circle similarly to the logs above described. This improvidence, in not saving the meat, often exposes them to great hardships during the seasons of the year in which the buffalo migrates to the south.

As is frequently the case on buffalo hunts, a large band of

wolves hovered round us in expectation of a feast, and a young Indian, for the purpose of showing his dexterity, galloped off towards them mounted on a small Indian horse. He succeeded in separating one from the pack, and notwithstanding all the dodging of the wolf, managed to drive him quite close to us. As he approached he entirely abandoned his bridle, and to look at them, one would imagine, from the rapid turnings of the horse without the apparent direction of the rider, that he was as eager in the pursuit as his master. When he had succeeded in getting the wolf close to us, he transfixed him with an arrow at the first shot. [Fig. 79; crIV-104?] We selected a comfortable place on the banks of the river, and, on the boats coming up, we formed our encampment for the night.

Sept. 13*th.*—In the morning we passed a small island on which we saw a herd of eighteen deer. [crIV-125] Our hunter went round to the other side, the water being shallow enough to wade across, and, getting behind the bushes, fired twice at them before they could escape, and brought down two. The rest crossed over to our side of the river, and, as a noble buck was ascending the bank, we all fired at him. He escaped, notwithstanding, into the woods, and I hobbled my horse and pursued him on foot, tracking him readily by the blood which flowed from his wounds. I soon saw him lying down, apparently so exhausted that I forbore to fire again. This forbearance cost me the deer, for on my coming up, he made a sudden plunge into the thicket and escaped. I followed his track a long distance, but could not come up to him. On my return I found two wolves making a dead set at my poor horse, who was trembling with fear. One of them was in the act of springing at him. It was impossible for him to get away, as his fore feet were tied together. I instantly levelled my double-barrelled gun and killed both, one after the other.

Chapter IX.

Beautiful Valley.—Crossing the Water.—The curious Cabree.—A shouting Aide-de-Camp.—Strange Memento Mori.—The Love of Indian Mothers.—No Coat, no Fire.—The "Little Slave."—A Voyageur's Trust.—Surrounded by Beef.—A spirited Cow.

On my coming back to the party, I found them hanging up the two deer for the use of the crews of the boats, having taken what they wanted for themselves. This they did by forming a triangle with poles about twelve feet high in a conspicuous place on the bank, so that the wolves could not reach the meat, and fastening a red handkerchief above it to keep off the crows. Towards evening, as we were approaching the place where we were to cross the river, I saw some buffaloes idly grazing in a valley, and as I wished to give a general idea of the beauty of the scenery which lies all along the banks of the Saskatchawan from this point to Edmonton, I sat down to make a sketch, the rest of the party promising to wait for me at the crossing place. It was the commencement of Indian summer; the evening was very fine, and threw that peculiar soft, warm haziness over the landscape, which is supposed to proceed from the burning of the immense prairies. The sleepy buffaloes grazing upon the undulating hills, here and there relieved by clumps of small trees, the unbroken stillness, and the approaching evening, rendered it altogether a scene of most enchanting repose. [crIV-165 to 170]

On coming up to Mr. Rowand, we prepared to cross for the purpose of avoiding a strong bend in the river. Our ammunition, and other things that required to be kept dry, were put into a sort of basket made of a few willow twigs, with a buffalo skin drawn by a running string over them, something in the form of large bowls. This basket was floated in the water, and dragged by a string held in the teeth. The horse was then driven in, and the traveller, holding on by his tail, was safely ferried to the other side with his baggage.

Sept. 14*th.*—Saw an immense number of cabrees, or prairie antelopes. [Fig. 84; crIV-123] These are the smallest of the deer tribe, amazingly fleet, and very shy, but, strange to say, possessed of great curiosity, apparently determined to look at everything they do not understand, so long as they do not scent it. Our hunter set off into the valley, to show me the manner of shooting them, while I made a sketch. A small stream wound its way through this most beautiful and picturesque valley in a course unusually tortuous, and was fringed on each side by a border of small, dense, and intensely green and purple bushes, contrasting beautifully with the rich yellow grass of the gradually sloping banks, about 200 feet in height, and the golden hues of the few poplars which had just begun to assume the autumnal tints. [Fig. 82; crIV-120, 121]

The hunter stole forward and hid himself behind a small bush, so as to have the wind blowing from them, and gently waved a piece of rag tied to his ramrod; as soon as the cabrees perceived this, they gradually came up to him, until within shot, when he knocked one over; this was of course all he could expect, as the rest were off in an instant.

In the evening we saw smoke in the distance, which we supposed to proceed from a camp of Indians; we waited, therefore, till the boats arrived, with a view to our mutual protection, should they prove to be a hostile tribe. The boats arrived after a short time, and we remained with them all night without molestation.

Sept. 15th.—About an hour after leaving our encampment, we crossed the river again in our boat, and found a large camp of Cree Indians. They came down to us in great numbers. Mr. Rowand, being acquainted with their chiefs, they were very friendly with us, and we bought a large quantity of dried meat from them. About a year and a half after this, on my return, I met the head chief, Kee-a-kee-ka-sa-coo-way, or the "Man who gives the War-whoop," and learned something of his history, which will be introduced in the latter part of my journal. When I was in his company for some time at Fort Pitt, in January 1848, the second chief, Muck-e-too, or "Powder," acted as a sort of aide-de-camp to the other, the head chief issuing his commands in a low tone, while the other mounted his horse and delivered them to the rest of the camp in a loud commanding manner. Muck-e-too is a great warrior and horse thief, the two most important qualifications for a chief, skill in stealing horses being regarded with as much respect as taking scalps. We had much difficulty in getting away from them, as they wished to have a long talk, but our time not permitting, we resumed our journey. They, however, adroitly detained a boat that had not yet come up, and the persons in charge had to give them some tobacco before they would allow them to proceed.

Sept. 16th.—We rode on till the middle of the day through a most delightful country, covered with luxuriant herbage, the plains being enamelled with flowers of various kinds, presenting more the aspect of a garden than of uncultivated land. While roasting some meat before the fire for our breakfast, and allowing our horses to feed, we espied a party of Indians on the opposite side of the river, who were evidently making signals to another party in our rear whom we did not see.[1] Upon this, eight of their young men came down to reconnoitre, and finding we were friends, kindly conducted us to their camp. We bartered with them for some horses.

I made a sketch of one of their chiefs, Otisskun, or "The Horn," or rather I made a sketch of his back. I did this for the purpose of showing his war-cap, and also to delineate the bag

[1] KJ refers to the Indians sketched here as Assiniboin; a list of canvases given by Burpee in the 1925 edition of *Wanderings* refers to Otisskun, one of several men whom Kane sketched here, as a Cree; see also crIV-127.

which he carries at his back. [Pl. XXI; crIV-127, 128, 129] These bags are constantly worn, and contain some of the bones or hair of their deceased relatives. These relics they regard with the greatest veneration, and make them their constant companions, whether riding, walking, or sleeping. They are generally worn for a period of three years. Not only amongst this tribe, but also amongst others, the affection for their relatives is very remarkable, though of course sometimes exhibited in a strange manner, as appears to us. As an instance of this, I may mention the universal custom of Indian mothers eagerly seeking another child, although it may be of an enemy, to replace one of her own, whom she may have lost, no matter how many other children she may have. This child is always treated with as great, if not greater, kindness than the rest; but all the mother's care evidently arises from, and has reference to, the love which she bore to the departed.

I had an unexpected trouble to catch my horse, which had got loose, in consequence of the hungry Indian dogs having eaten the lasso of raw hide with which I had fastened him.

Sept. 17th.—We were aroused in the night by our hunter, who told us that the horses were stolen, and as he would not leave the fire unless we accompanied him, we all started in pursuit. After a run of about a mile, we came up with the horses pursued by a band of wolves; the billets of wood attached to their lassoes having retarded their further escape; the wolves were loth to leave their expected prey, but after a shot or two they took to flight. The horses were evidently much terrified, as they showed by remaining close to the camp-fires all night afterwards. [crIV-124]

In the course of our ride to-day we killed a cabree, which was fortunate, as Mr. and Mrs. Lane arrived at our camp fire in the evening in a state of severe exhaustion, having left the boats in the morning and walked the whole day without tasting food. The boats had reached the other side of the river, and, for want of a channel, had been unable to cross over and take them in. It was unfortunately a very cold night, and very little wood could be procured; besides which, we were unprovided with either tents or blankets, having dispensed with these luxuries since we left Carlton, where we began our journey on horseback. The greatest sufferer probably from the cold of the night was a young clerk who had walked with them, and left his coat and waistcoat in the boat.

Sept. 19th.—The boats this morning found a channel and crossed over to take in the party, who had left them the morning before. We reached Fort Pitt in the evening. It is a neat and compact little fort, and is, like all the rest of the forts except those at Red River, constructed of wood. [Fig. 83; crIV-122] The country here abounds in buffalo; grain and other produce might be raised plentifully here if cultivated. We remained till the 23rd, and I took a sketch of Chimaza, the "Little Slave," a Chippewayeen Indian. [crIV-126] He was the only one of that tribe I ever saw, as they live far north of Fort Pitt, on the Athabasca Lake; his prowess and dexterity in hunting won him a degree of notoriety amongst the traders. He had, when I saw him, upwards of a hundred moose skins, besides furs to a considerable amount, which he had brought to the fort to trade with.

Sept. 23rd.—I left the fort on horseback, accompanied by Mr. Rowand, Mr. Rundell, an Indian boy, and a fresh hunter; on reaching the river we crossed in a boat, and swam our horses by the bridle. We left this establishment in true voyageur style, unburthened with food of any kind, and, although contemplating a journey of 200 miles, trusting solely to our guns, having not even a grain of salt. After leaving the boat, we saddled our horses, and had not proceeded more than ten miles, when we fell in with immense numbers of buffaloes.

During the whole of the three days that it took us to reach Edmonton House, we saw nothing else but these animals covering the plains as far as the eye could reach, and so numerous were they, that at times they impeded our progress, filling the air with dust almost to suffocation. We killed one whenever we required a supply of food, selecting the fattest of the cows, taking only the tongues and boss, or hump, for our present meal, and not burdening ourselves unnecessarily with more. Mr. Rowand fired and wounded a cow, which made immediately for a clump of bushes; he followed it, when the animal turned upon him, and bore him and his horse to the ground, leaping over them, and escaping among the rest. Fortunately, he received no hurt beyond the mortification of being thrown down and run over by an animal which he felt assured he should see roasting at our evening camp fire.

Chapter X.

Long Grass Prairie.—An obstinate Bear.—Abandoning a tired Horse.—Dried-up Lakes.—Shooting wild Geese.—A dangerous Swim.—Boat-building.—The blazing Prairie.—Setting Fire to fight Fire.—A cool Confession.—Indian want of Gallantry.—An Indian Strongbow.

Sept. 24th.—We passed through what is called the Long Grass Prairie. [crIV-172] The bones of a whole camp of Indians, who were carried off by that fatal scourge of their race, the small-pox, were here bleaching on the plains, having fallen from the platforms and trees on which it is their custom to suspend their dead, covered with skins,—which latter, as well as the supports, time had destroyed. An immense grisly bear was drinking out of a pond, and our hunter went ahead of the party to try and get a shot at him. The bear quietly awaited his attack, and the Indian, seeing him so cool, rather hesitated to advance, not deeming it prudent or safe to depend on the fleetness of his horse unless he had a good start of the bear. He fired, therefore, at too great a distance for his shot to tell. The bear rose up very composedly on his hind legs, and regarding the hunter for a moment, turned about and walked away. I then determined to try my luck. As I was very well mounted, I rode up to within forty or fifty yards of him, and as he turned to look at me, I discharged both barrels; one wounded him in the shoulder, and, with a savage growl, he turned and pursued me. I set off at full gallop towards Mr. Rowand, who waited till he came within shot, when he put another ball into him,—but still the bear advanced.

In the meantime, the Indian and I had both managed to reload, and, as the bear came forward, the Indian fired, and must have hit, as the bear again rose on his hind legs; when, taking deliberate aim, I lodged a ball in his heart, and the huge monster fell to the ground. The Indian now skinned him and cut off his paws, which we found most delicious picking when roasted in the evening. The claws, which I preserved, measured four and a half inches. There is no animal on the whole continent that the Indians hold in so much dread as the grisly bear, and few will attack one of them when alone, unless with a very fleet horse under him.

We had much difficulty that evening in finding a place to encamp away from the immense number of buffaloes that surrounded us, and we found it necessary to fire off our guns during the night to keep them away. [Figs. 96, 97, 98; crIV-171, 173 to 177] We passed through a spot covered with great quantities of shed antlers of the deer. We had ridden so fast as to knock up Mr. Rowand's horse, but, having driven several loose horses with us, to provide against such emergencies, we were not inconvenienced, leaving the poor brute a prey to the wolves, which were constantly hovering about us.

We encamped this evening on the borders of a very beautiful fresh water lake. [Pl. XXIV; crIV-181?] We had passed in our route daily many *dried-up* lakes, principally small, the basins covered with an incrustation of sub-carbonate of soda. [crIV-180] Many of these are bordered with a dense growth of plants resembling in structure the well-known marine production called samphire, but of a rich purple colour. So unbroken is the incrustation of soda, as to give the spots the appearance of being covered with snow.

[Prairie landscapes: crIV-182, 183, 184]

Sept. 26th.—Mr. Rundell remained at the encampment this morning with the Indian boy, being completely knocked up by the hard riding of the preceding days. We were reluctant to leave him, but were under the necessity of going on as fast as possible, as I had still a long journey before me, and the season was drawing to a close. Mr. Rowand and myself, therefore, left the camp at half-past 3 A.M., and pursued our journey almost at a gallop the whole way, having stopped only once for about an hour, for breakfast and to breathe our horses.

About 5 o'clock in the afternoon, when about eight or ten miles from Fort Edmonton, we were met by a party of gentlemen from the fort, who were out shooting wild geese, in which they had been very successful, and on seeing the jaded condition of our horses, they were kind enough to exchange with us, so that we started off for the remaining distance at a round gallop.

On getting to the edge of the river, which it was necessary to cross to reach the fort, Mr. Rowand, having a fine large horse under him, plunged in. Though my horse was very small, I did not hesitate in following him. Mr. Rowand's horse carried him over in fine style, but mine, not being equal to the task, sank under me; still, however, I held firmly on to him, till, drifting into the rapid, he struck a sunken rock in striving to obtain a footing, on which he nearly brought me under him; but, on drifting a little further down, he fortunately found footing in a more shallow part, and was able to ford across, Mr. Rowand appearing greatly to enjoy the scene from his safe position on the shore. We were greeted by the occupants of the fort in their gayest attire, the day being Sunday.

Edmonton is a large establishment: as it has to furnish many other districts with provisions, a large supply is always kept on hand, consisting entirely of dried meat, tongues, and pimmi-kon. There are usually here a chief factor and a clerk, with forty or fifty men with their wives and children, amounting altogether to about 130, who all live within the pickets of the fort. [Pl. XXV; crIV-188 to 191] Their employment consists chiefly in building boats for the trade, sawing timber, most of which they raft down the river from ninety miles higher up, cutting up the small poplar which abounds on the margin of the river for fire-wood, 800 cords of which are consumed every winter, to supply the numerous fires in the establishment. The employment of the women, who are all, without a single exception, either squaws or half-breeds, consists in making moccasins and clothing for the men, and converting the dried meat into pimmi-kon.

On the night of our arrival at Edmonton, the wind increased to a perfect hurricane, and we had reason to be thankful to Providence for our timely escape from the awful scene we now witnessed from our present place of safety, for, had we been one day later, we might have been involved in its fiery embrace. The scene on which our attention was now riveted, was the conflagration of the prairie through which we had passed but a few hours before. The scene was terrific in the extreme; the night being intensely dark gave increased effect to the brilliancy of the flames. [Fig. 99; crIV-185, 186, 187] We were apprehensive at one time of its crossing the river to the side on which the fort is situated, which must in that case have been destroyed. Our fears, too, for Mr. Rundell, whom we had left behind with the boys, were only relieved three days afterwards, when he arrived in safety. It appeared that he had noticed the fire at a long distance off, and immediately started for the nearest bend in the river, which with great exertions he reached in time, and succeeded in crossing. The mode resorted to by the Indians, when in the immediate vicinity of a prairie on fire, is to set fire to a long patch in front of them, which they follow up, and thus depriving the fire in the rear of fuel, escape all but the smoke, which, however, nearly suffocates them.

[Saskatchewan River: crIV-192, 193]

As we had to remain here until the arrival of the boat with Mr. Lane and the Russian packs of otters, I took a sketch of the fort, and having leisure, I went a good deal amongst the Indians, who are constantly about the fort for the purpose of trading; they were principally Crees [crIV-211] and Assiniboines: Potika-poo-tis, the "Little Round Man," an Assiniboine chief, sat for me. He was well known about the fort, and was commonly called the Duke of Wellington, I suppose from his small person and his warlike feats. [crIV-207] He was on one occasion set upon by a party of Blackfeet, and, while in the act of discharging his gun, received a wound, which he showed me, of rather a remarkable nature. The ball entered his wrist, passed through the arm, entered the neck, and came out near the upper part of the spine. He had received several wounds, but none that seemed seriously to endanger his life, as at the time I saw him he was in good health.

After relating various stories of his war and hunting exploits, he, to my great astonishment, told me that he had killed his own mother. It appears that, while travelling, she told him that she felt too old and feeble to sustain the hardships of life, and too lame to travel any further, and asked him to take pity on her, and end her misery, on which he unhesitatingly shot her on the spot. I asked him whereabouts he had directed his ball. His reply was, "Do you think I would shoot her in a bad place? I hit her there;" pointing his finger to the region of the heart. "She died instantly, and I cried at first; but after I had buried her, the impression wore off."

It must not be supposed that Indians look on the softer sex with feelings at all resembling those entertained towards them in civilised life; in fact, they regard them more in the light of slaves than as companionable beings. As might be expected, this is most evident in their treatment of aged women, whom they consider as scarcely fit to live.

Some of the Company's servants were going up the Saskatchawan river on the ice in the winter, with a sledge of dogs drawing a load, comprising, among other things, an eight-gallon keg of spirits; and in crossing over a piece of bad ice, the dogs went through sledge and all, and were instantly carried under by the force of the current. In the following summer, some Indians, while bathing near the shore, picked up the cask safe and sound; and finding, on examination, that it was full of rum, made up their minds to have a booze. One of them, however, suggested the possibility that the white men had put poison in it, to be revenged on them for having fired on the inland brigade of canoes while going up the river the year before. This deterred them from drinking any until they had tested its quality. For this purpose they selected eight of the oldest women in the camp to try the experiment on. The women fell into the snare; and, becoming intoxicated, commenced singing with great glee. But an old chief soon put a stop to their potations, saying there could be no poison in it, and that it was far too good to be thrown away upon old women. The whole tribe then set to, and were not long in draining the cask.

One day, whilst wandering some distance to the south of the fort, I saw two Assiniboine Indians hunting buffaloes. One was armed with a spear, formed of an ashpole about ten feet long, ornamented with tufts of hair, and having an iron head, which is procured from the trading posts; the other with a bow formed of ash, with the sinews of a buffalo gummed to the back of it. These they use with great dexterity and force; I have known an instance of the arrows passing through the body of the animal,

and sticking in the ground at the opposite side. [Fig. 105; crIV-208, 209, 210]

[Indian studies: crIV-228 to 239]

Chapter XI.

Leaving Fort Edmonton.—The Last of the Buffaloes.—Sir George's Highland Piper.—An Indian Delicacy.—Freak of an Evil Spirit.—Singular Cradle.—Jasper's House.—The Snow and the Cold.—First-steps in Snow Shoes.—Nearly Roasted Alive.—Going down Hill.—Wading an Icy Torrent.—Making up for lost Time.—Shooting the Dalle de Mort.—A Narrow Escape.—A Wet Voyage.

We remained at Edmonton till the morning of the 6th, preparing for the arduous journey which now lay before us. On that morning we started at daybreak. Our party consisted of Mr. Lane and his wife, a young man named Charles, a clerk, who was going to a post on the west side of the Rocky Mountains, a person of the name of M'Gillveray, and sixteen men. We had with us sixty-five horses to carry our baggage and provisions. This seems a large supply of horses for so small a party; but it must be taken into consideration that Edmonton is the last post at which we could get a supply of provisions on this side of the mountains; so that we were necessarily obliged to carry a large quantity with us, owing to the difficulty which always arises in getting the men away from comfortable quarters to commence a long and difficult journey, coupled with the wildness of the horses on a first day's march. We only succeeded in reaching Sturgeon Creek, a distance of about sixteen miles, on the first day. Seeing a group of buffaloes reposing near a small lake, I took a sketch (No. 6). They were the last that I should see for some time; and it was easy for me to keep up with the party at the slow rate at which they proceeded. [Fig. 110; crIV-240 to 244]

Oct. 7th.—The prairies were now fast receding behind us, our course lying to the northward. The track became almost impassable, being wet and swampy; and the horses often stuck fast, and threw off their loads in their struggles to extricate themselves from the mire. We were lucky enough to vary our provisions by killing a great many geese of the kind called "wavy." Could we have procured a little salt, I should have found them more palatable.

Oct. 8th.—The tremendous hurricane above alluded to had torn up immense trees by the roots, and scattered them in piles one on another in all directions, detaining us sometimes for hours, while the men cut a path through them for the horses. Our progress through the thick woods, which we had now fairly entered, was necessarily very slow and fatiguing.

Oct. 9th.—The track still continued bad, and we saw no game; so that our time passed very monotonously, as we had to keep pace with the loaded horses. A Highlander of the name of Colin Frazer had joined our party. He was on his way to a small post, of which he had the charge, at the head of the Athabasca River, in the Rocky Mountains, where he had resided for the last eleven years. He had been brought to the country by Sir George Simpson, in the capacity of his piper, at the time when he explored Frazer's River, and made an extensive voyage through a country hitherto little known, and among Indians who had seen few or no white men. He carried the pipes with him, dressed in his Highland costume; and when stopping at forts, or wherever he found Indians, the bagpipes were put in requisition, much to the astonishment of the natives, who supposed him to be a relation of the Great Spirit, having, of course, never beheld so extraordinary a looking man, or such a musical instrument, which astonished them as much as the sound produced. One of the Indians asked him to intercede with the Great Spirit for him; but Frazer remarked, the petitioner little thought how limited his influence was in that quarter.

Oct. 10th.—I left the party this morning and proceeded on, and at two o'clock in the afternoon, after a smart ride, I arrived at Fort Assiniboine, on the Athabasca River. This establishment, although honoured with the name of a fort, is a mere post used for taking care of horses, a common man or horsekeeper being in charge of it. The rest of the party arrived late the same evening.

Oct. 11th.—We found two boats here, which our men immediately overhauled and set to work to repair and pitch. At 2 o'clock P.M. we embarked, and continued travelling slowly on, against a very strong current, for five days. The water was very low, which added greatly to our difficulties. We saw no game nor Indians to break the monotony of our labour, and the nights and mornings were becoming very cold.

Oct. 15th.—When we stopped to take breakfast, it was very cold and snowing. We held a council, and it was determined that, as the weather had set in so bad, five men and one boat, with the clerk Charles, should return back to Fort Assiniboine with the Russian packs of otter skins.[1] We were now all obliged to crowd into one boat, the others having gone back; and were frequently obliged to disembark and lighten the boat, owing to the unusual lowness of the river. We had almost continually to drag the boat onwards with a line, the men waist deep in the water. One of them slipped off a log into deep water, and it was with no small difficulty we saved him from being drowned. We had not extricated him from the river five minutes before his clothes were stiff with ice. I asked him if he was not cold, and his reply was characteristic of the hardihood of the Iroquois, of which tribe our party principally consisted, "My clothes are cold, but I am not."

Oct. 16th.—The weather had now set in so cold that we began to doubt the possibility of crossing the mountains this season. The line by which the men dragged the boat broke twice to-day in the rapids, and our boat was nearly dashed to pieces among the rocks. Had this misfortune happened, we should have lost all our provisions, and had a great chance of perishing with hunger.

Oct. 17th and 18th.—Weather fine. This is the most monotonous river that ever I have met with in my travels. Nothing but point after point appearing, all thickly covered with pine, any extensive view being entirely out of the question. The course of the river, although tortuous, is rapid, but unbroken by falls, running at the rate of six or seven miles an hour on an average.

Oct. 19th.—We fell in with an Indian hunter and his family. He had two bark canoes; he sold one of them to Colin Frazer, in which he embarked with four men, for the purpose of lightening our boat, and proceeded on in advance of us. We traded with them for some beaver meat and moose noses; the latter is the most delicate eating I ever met with, and is valued amongst the Indians beyond all other food.

Oct. 20th and 21st.—The weather was fine, and we made good progress.

Oct. 22nd.—The men were in extraordinarily good spirits.[2] I measured a tree lying on the ground, which had been cut down by the beaver; it was seven feet in circumference. We found three bears left *en cache* by Colin Frazer, an old one and two cubs. He told me afterwards that he had killed the two cubs at one shot, while one was climbing over the back of the other to ascend a bank. The cubs proved fine eating, and were much relished, as our fresh provisions had been long exhausted.

Oct. 23rd.—We passed a camp fire still burning that had been left by Frazer the night previously.

---

[1] KJ mentions 40 packs of otter, and notes that at the meeting of the men to decide what they should do because of the bad travelling conditions it was agreed that 4 men should go back and 12 go on. Kane says that as a mere passenger he did not have a vote.

[2] KJ notes the men's exuberance: "Men singing. Had for breakfast moose meat and beaver tails."

Oct. 24th.—We passed the Rapids de Mort. The men had great difficulty in getting the boat up; we, of course, had all to walk. All the ponds and still water were frozen hard enough to bear. The rapidity of the current, however, prevented ice forming in the river. A small bag of pimmi-kon made in the usual way, except that it contained Sasketome berries, was stolen, and a search being made for its recovery, a part of it was found in one of the men's bags. The only temptation to the theft could have been that it was more palatable than his own. M'Gillveray, being one of the most powerful men of the party, was called upon to administer the punishment, which he did by repeatedly knocking the delinquent down. This severity of punishment was called for by the fact, that the most disastrous consequences might arise on a journey through these desolate regions, if the most rigid care were not taken of the provisions.

Oct. 25th to 27th.—There was no change in the general aspect of the country; the same monotonous scenery still surrounded us.

Oct. 28th.—We passed the mouth of the Old Man's River. The Indians say that an evil spirit once came down this river—which is so rapid that no canoe can ascend it—and that having reached its mouth, where it enters the Athabasca, he made five steps down, leaving a rapid at every step. These rapids are a mile apart. After which he returned and went up his own river, and has not since been heard of. The river now became so shallow, that we were obliged to make two discharges.

Oct. 29th.—The bank of the river being very high, I ascended it, and saw for the first time the sublime and apparently endless chain of the Rocky Mountains. The outline was scarcely perceptible in the distance through the intervening smoky atmosphere, which is caused by the almost invariable conflagration of the woods at this season of the year. M'Gillveray wounded a moose while out with his gun. The deer took to the water, and swam across to the opposite side. I took the boat and followed him, and brought him down at the first shot. He was a fine large buck. It being nearly night, we encamped on the spot, and supped heartily off him, carrying his remains with us next morning.

Oct. 30th.—We had a fine view of the mountains from the boat for the first time; the men greeted them with a hearty cheer.

Oct. 31st.—The atmosphere clear but very cold. I made a sketch of the river and the mountains in the distance. [crIV-245, 246, 247]

Nov. 1st.—We entered Jasper's Lake in the morning. This lake is about twelve miles long, and from three to four miles wide, but at this season of the year very shallow, on account of its sources in the mountains being frozen. We had to land three men on the south shore for the purpose of decreasing the draft of our boat; but even then we proceeded with great difficulty. Shortly after we had put them on shore, it began to blow a perfect hurricane, which drove us to the north side, and a snow storm coming on, we were compelled to encamp. This was unfortunate, as it was impossible to communicate with the men whom we had left at the other side, and who were without either provisions or blankets, and we knew from the intense cold that they must be suffering severely.

Nov. 2nd.—We were now close upon the mountains, and it is scarcely possible to conceive the intense force with which the wind howled through a gap formed by the perpendicular rock called "Miëtte's Rock," 1500 feet high, on the one side, and a lofty mountain on the other. [crIV-249] The former derives its appellation from a French voyageur, who climbed its summit and sat smoking his pipe with his legs hanging over the fearful abyss. M'Gillveray and the guide went on to Colin Frazer's, distant about fourteen or fifteen miles, to procure horses, as we found that further progress in the boat was impossible, both on account of the shallowness of the water and the violence of the wind.

Nov. 3rd.—The hurricane still continued, accompanied by very heavy snow; indeed, from what I heard, I believe it is always blowing at this place. The forest is composed entirely of very high pine trees, small in circumference, and growing thickly together; these had a very curious appearance in the storm, as they waved in the wind like a field of grain. The immense long roots seemed to be especially provided them by nature to prevent their being blown over; and, as the soil is very light, and upon a rocky foundation, these roots formed a net work near the surface, which was in constant motion, and rocked us to sleep as we lay round our camp fires.

Meanwhile, our guide returned from Jasper's House with several horses. We found our boat blown out of the water, and lying fifteen feet distant from it on the shore although its weight was so great, that the strength of our remaining nine men could not return it to its element.

I selected a horse, and, taking the guide with me, started for the establishment in advance of the rest of the party. After a severe ride of four hours, and having forded the river four times, dangerously crowded with drift ice borne down by a rapid current, sometimes coming over the saddle, I arrived at Jasper's

Plate XVI. Camping on the prairies (Kane and a companion). Stark POP18; crIV-52.

Paul Kane 1846

Half-breeds running Buffalo

Plate XVII. Métis chasing a buffalo herd. Stark pwc16; crIV-71.

House cold, wet, and famished. [crIV-248] But I was soon cheered by a blazing fire and five or six pounds of mountain sheep, which I certainly then thought far more delicious than any domestic animal of the same species. About 10 o'clock that evening, to our great joy, the three men whom we had left on the south shore, came in. Their sufferings had been very great, as they had been wandering through the woods for three days without food, endeavouring to find the house, which none of them had been at before. One of them had not even taken his coat with him, and it was only by lying huddled together at night that they escaped being frozen. Another suffered dreadfully from the swelled state of his legs, caused by the strings usually tied round their leggings being too tight, and which, owing to his benumbed condition, he did not perceive. We had some difficulty in cutting them off, as they were buried in the swollen flesh.

Nov. 4th.—Mr. Lane and party arrived safe in the evening with the loaded horses. Jasper's House consists of only three miserable log huts. The dwelling-house is composed of two rooms, of about fourteen or fifteen feet square each. One of them is used by all comers and goers: Indians, voyageurs, and traders, men, women, and children being huddled together indiscriminately; the other room being devoted to the exclusive occupation of Colin and his family, consisting of a Cree squaw, and nine interesting half-breed children. One of the other huts is used for storing provision in, when they can get any, and the other I should have thought a dog-kennel had I seen many of the canine species about. This post is only kept up for the purpose of supplying horses to parties crossing the mountains. I made a sketch of the establishment (No. 7). [Fig. 111; crIV-250]

Nov. 5th.—We started with a cavalcade of thirteen loaded horses, but as we did not expect to be able to get the horses across the mountains, I got an Indian to make me a pair of snow shoes. The Indians about here do not number above fifteen or twenty; they are the Shoo-Schawp[3] tribe, and their chief, of whom I made a sketch, is called "Capote Blanc" by the voyageurs—in their own language it is Assannitchay, but means the same. [crIV-251] His proper location is a long distance to the north-east; but he had been treacherously entrapped, whilst travelling with thirty-seven of his people, by a hostile tribe, which met him and invited him to sit down and smoke the pipe of peace. They unsuspectingly laid down their arms, but before they had time to smoke, their treacherous hosts seized their

[3] The "Shoo-Schawp" or Shuswap Indians lived to the southwest rather than the northeast of this spot, their lands lying between the Columbia and Fraser rivers.

arms and murdered them all except eleven, who managed to escape, and fled to Jasper's House, where they remained, never daring to return to their own country through the hostile tribe. Capote Blanc was a very simple, kind-hearted old man, with whom I became very friendly.

[Carrier Indian: crIV-252]

We left this inhospitable spot about noon, and crossed the river in a small canoe to where the men were waiting for us, with the horses, which they had swam across the river in the morning. [Figs. 112, 115; crIV-253, 254, 264, 265] We rode on till 4 o'clock, and encamped in a small prairie, of which I made a sketch. [crIV-263?]

Nov. 6th.—We made but few miles of progress to-day, being obliged to encamp at La Row's [LaRocque's] Prairie in order to pasture our horses, our next stopping place being too distant to reach that evening. [crIV-255]

Nov. 7th.—We made a *long day*; our route lay sometimes over almost inaccessible crags, and at others through gloomy and tangled forest; as we ascended, the snow increased in depth, and we began to feel the effects of the increasing cold and rarefaction of the atmosphere.

Nov. 8th.—We saw two mountain goats looking down on us from a lofty and precipitous ledge of rock, not exceeding, to all appearance, a few inches in width. [Fig. 114; crIV-258 to 262] One of the Indians who accompanied us from Jasper's House to take back the horses, started to attain a crag above them, as these animals cannot be approached near enough to shoot them from below, their gaze being always directed downwards. They chanced, however, to see him going up, and immediately escaped to an inaccessible height.

Nov. 9th.—Finding the snow so deep, and knowing, not only that we were late, but that our further progress must be slow, we became apprehensive that the party who should be waiting for us with boats and provisions from Fort Vancouver, at the other side of the mountains, would give up all hopes of meeting us and might leave. This would have entailed the most fearful hardships upon us, if it did not produce actual destruction, as we should have had to recross the mountains with scarcely any or no provisions. We, therefore, despatched the guide and M'Gillveray, to hasten on to Boat Encampment. We encamped at the "Grand Batteur," where we found some snow shoes, which had been hidden by the party that had come out in the spring.

Nov. 10th.—We had not proceeded far before the horses stuck fast in the snow, and we were obliged to encamp on the spot to give those men who were unprovided time to make snow shoes, without which they could not proceed. [CRIV-266, 267, 268] We remained here all day, and sent the horses back with everything we could dispense with, our provisions and blankets being quite as much as the men could carry; and some of the new hands, who had only come into the country that year, were now so knocked up by their long and fatiguing voyage from Montreal, which they had left in the spring, as to be quite useless.

Nov. 11th.—We sent two experienced men in advance to beat the track for the new beginners, and made our first essay on snow shoes. Some of our men succeeded but indifferently in the attempt, having never used them before; and the shoes, which we made the day before not being of the best description, materially impeded our progress. The shoes which the Indian had made for me at Jasper House were particularly good ones, and I found little difficulty in their use. Mrs. Lane had also taken the precaution to bring a pair with her, and as she had been accustomed to them from her childhood at Red River, where they are a great deal used, she proved one of our best pedestrians. We encamped early, making for the first time what is called a regular winter encampment. This is only made where the snow is so deep that it cannot be removed so as to reach the ground. The depth to which the snow attains can be calculated by the stumps of the trees cut off at its former level for previous camp fires; some of these were twelve or fifteen feet above us at the present time, and the snow was nine or ten feet deep under us. Some of the old voyageurs amused themselves by telling the new hands or *Mangeurs du Lard*, that the Indians in those parts were giants from thirty to forty feet high, and that accounted for the trees being cut off at such an unusual height.

It is necessary to walk repeatedly with snow shoes over the place chosen for the encampment until it is sufficiently beaten down to bear a man without sinking on its surface. Five or six logs of green timber, from eighteen to twenty feet long, are laid down close together, in parallel lines, so as to form a platform. The fire of dry wood is then kindled on it, and pine branches are spread on each side, on which the party, wrapped in their blankets, lie down with their feet towards the fire. The parallel logs rarely burn through in one night, but the dropping coals and heat form a deep chasm immediately under the fire, into which the logs are prevented from falling by their length. Into this hole an Iroquois, who had placed himself too near the fire, rolled a depth of at least six or seven feet, the snow having

melted from under him while asleep. His cries awoke me, and after a hearty laugh at his fiery entombment, we succeeded in dragging him out.

Nov. 12th.—To-day we attained what is called the Height of Land. There is a small lake at this eminence called the Committee's Punch-bowl; this forms the head waters of one branch of the Columbia River on the west side of the mountains, and of the Athabasca on the east side. It is about three quarters of a mile in circumference, and is remarkable as giving rise to two such mighty rivers; the waters of the one emptying in the Pacific Ocean, and of the other into the Arctic Sea. We encamped on its margin, with difficulty protecting ourselves from the intense cold. [Fig. 116; CRIV-269]

Nov. 13th.—The lake being frozen over to some depth, we walked across it, and shortly after commenced the descent of the grand côte, having been seven days continually ascending. The descent was so steep, that it took us only one day to get down to nearly the same level as that of Jasper's House. The descent was a work of great difficulty on snow shoes, particularly for those carrying loads; their feet frequently slipped from under them, and the loads rolled down the hill. Some of the men, indeed, adopted the mode of rolling such loads as would not be injured down before them. On reaching the bottom, we found eight men waiting, whom M'Gillveray and the guide had sent on to assist us to Boat Encampment, and we all encamped together.

Nov. 14th.—I remained at the camp fire finishing one of my sketches, the men having made a very early start in order to reach Boat Encampment, where they would get a fresh supply of provisions, ours being nearly exhausted. [CRIV-270 to 274] As soon as I had finished my sketch I followed them, and soon arrived at a river about seventy yards across, and with a very rapid current.

Having followed their track in the snow to the edge of the river, and seeing the strength of the current, I began to look for other tracks, under the impression that they might possibly have discovered a way to get round it. But I was soon undeceived by seeing in the snow on the other side the path they had beaten down on the opposite bank; nothing, therefore, remained but for me to take off my snow shoes, and make the traverse. The water was up to my middle, running very rapidly, and filled with drift ice, some pieces of which struck me, and nearly forced me down the stream. I found on coming out of the water my capote and leggings frozen stiff. My difficulties, however, were only beginning, as I was soon obliged to cross again four times, when, my legs becoming completely benumbed, I dared not venture on the fifth, until I had restored the circulation by running up and down the beach. I had to cross twelve others in a similar manner, being seventeen in all, before I overtook the rest of the party at the encampment. The reason of these frequent crossings is, that the only pass across the mountains is the gorge formed by the Athabasca at one side, and the Columbia at the other; and the beds of these torrents can only be crossed in the spring before the thaws commence, or in the fall after the severe weather has set in. During the summer the melting of the mountain snow and ice renders them utterly impracticable.

Nov. 15th.—It will be easily imagined with what regret we left a warm fire and comfortable encampment, to plunge at once into one of the deepest crossings we had yet encountered, covered like the preceding with running ice. Here, as in many other of the crossings, our only means of withstanding the force of the current was for all to go abreast shoulder to shoulder, in a line parallel with it, each man being supported by all below him. Mrs. Lane, although it was necessary to carry her in the arms of two powerful men across the river, acquitted herself in other respects as well as any of us. One of the greatest annoyances accompanying the use of snow shoes, is that of having to take them off on entering a river, and replacing them over the wet and frozen moccasins on coming out of it.

Before stopping to breakfast this morning, we crossed the river twenty-five times, and twelve times more before camping; having waded it thirty-seven times in all during the day.

The Columbia here makes long reaches, to and fro, through a valley, in some parts three miles wide, and backed with stupendous mountains, rearing their snowy tops above the clouds, and forming here and there immense glaciers, reflecting the rays of the sun with extreme brilliancy and prismatic beauty. The last part of the route lay through a slimy lake or swamp, frozen over, but not with sufficient solidity to bear us, so that we had to wade above our knees in a dense mass of snow, ice, and mud, there being no such thing as a dry spot to afford a moment's respite from the scarcely endurable severity of the cold, under which I thought I must have sunk exhausted.

At length, however, we arrived at Boat Encampment, about 5 P.M., almost perishing with cold and hunger, having tasted nothing since what I have already termed breakfast, which consisted only of a small supply of soup made of pemmi-kon, this being the mode of making the most of a small quantity of it.

On our arrival we found a good fire blazing, and some soup made from pork and corn, brought from Fort Vancouver, boiling in the pot, which I attacked with so much avidity, that one of the men, fearing I might take too much in my present exhausted state, politely walked off with the bowl and its contents.[4]

The men had been here waiting our arrival for thirty-nine days, and would have returned to Fort Vancouver the next day, had not the guide and M'Gillveray opportunely arrived in time to prevent them, as they thought we had either been cut off by the Indians, or that we had found it impossible to cross the mountains. In fact, they were clearing the snow out of the boats preparatory to starting. Had our messengers not arrived in time, it would most likely have proved fatal to us all, as we could not have re-crossed the mountains without provisions.

On leaving Boat Encampment, I did not take any sketches, although the scenery was exceedingly grand; the rapidity with which we now travelled, and the necessity for doing so owing to the lateness of the season, prevented me; and as I was determined to return by the same route, I knew that I should then have plenty of time and opportunity. I shall therefore give a mere outline of my rapid journey to Fort Vancouver, a distance of 1200 miles down the Columbia River, which we accomplished in fifteen days, and which afterwards took me four months to ascend.

[Indians in the mountains: crIV-280, 281]

Nov. 16th.—Our two boats were by this time ready; they were formed canoe fashion, with round bottoms of boards, clinker built. On leaving Boat Encampment the scene is exceedingly grand; immense mountains receding further and further in the distance on every side. Few who read this journal, surrounded by the comforts of civilised life, will be able to imagine the heartfelt satisfaction with which we exchanged the wearisome snow-shoe for the comfortable boats, and the painful anxiety of half-satisfied appetites for a well-stocked larder. True it was, that the innumerable rapids of the Columbia were filled with dangers of no ordinary character, and that it required the constant exercise of all our energy and skill to escape their perils, but we now had health and high spirits to help us. We no longer had to toil on in clothes frozen stiff from wading across torrents, half-famished, and with the consciousness ever before us, that

---

[4] KJ: "The men were so glad to see us that they sang and danced and cut up all manner of capers."

whatever were our hardships and fatigue, rest was sure destruction in the cold solitudes of those dreary mountains.

About three hours after our departure, we shot the celebrated "Dalle de Mort." It is about three miles long and is the most dangerous of all the rapids on the Columbia.[5]

17th and 18th.—We passed through the two lakes, and were obliged to work night and day to avail ourselves of the calm weather, although the snow fell without ceasing.

19th.—We again entered the current of the river, where the men were enabled to rest for a few hours.

Nov. 20th.—About noon we ran through the Little Dalle, which, though short, is a series of dangerous whirlpools, which can only be passed with the greatest precaution, and arrived safe at Colville at 6 o'clock in the evening. Colville is beautifully situated about a mile above the falls of the Chaudière or Kettle Falls; it exceeds in height any other fall on the Columbia, and derives its name from the round holes that the water has hollowed out in the rocks, resembling cauldrons of various sizes. Here we were most hospitably entertained by Mr. Lewis, who was in charge. To avoid this fall we had to carry our boats a distance of two miles over a hill two or three hundred feet high. We remained here three days, during which time the men did little else but eat and sleep. The rapidity with which they changed their appearance was astonishing. Some of them became so much improved in looks, that it was with difficulty we could recognise our voyageurs.

Nov. 23rd.—We encamped in the evening a few miles below the falls. During the night some Indians, who had been prowling about, crept into the boats and stole some wearing apparel, which proved very annoying to us, as our wardrobes were rather limited.

Nov. 24th.—We arrived at the Grand Rapid, which the boats were obliged to run. I, however, preferred getting out to walk, with the object of making some sketches. [Fig. 121; crIV-290] I had proceeded nearly three miles along the shore, and felt somewhat astonished at not seeing the boats following, when I observed something in the water, which I at first took to be the head of an Indian swimming across. I accordingly prepared my gun in case of an attack, as the Indians about here are considered some of the worst on the Columbia. On close observation, however, I made out the object to be the hood which I had noticed Mrs. Lane to wear in the morning, and soon afterwards I perceived the paddles and oars of one of the boats. I now began to feel alarmed for the safety of some of the party, and immediately returned to the rapid as fast as possible. There I saw one

of the boats, in which Mr. and Mrs. Lane were, in a most dangerous situation, having struck in the midst of the rapids upon a rock, which had stove in her side. The conduct of the men evinced great presence of mind. The instant she struck, they had sprung on the gunwale next the rock, and by their united weight kept her lying upon it. The water foamed and raged around them with fearful violence. Had she slipped off, they must all have been dashed to pieces amongst the rocks and rapids below; as it was, they managed to maintain their position, until the crew of the other boat, which had run the rapids safely, had unloaded and dragged the empty boat up the rapids again. They then succeeded in throwing a line to their hapless companions. But there was still considerable danger, lest in hauling the empty boat towards them they might pull themselves off the rock; they at length, however, succeeded by cautious management in getting the boat alongside, and in embarking in safety. In a moment afterwards their own boat slipped from the rock, and was dashed to pieces. Everything that floated we picked up afterwards, but still we lost a great many useful and necessary articles. We had, in consequence of this mishap, to send back overland to Colville for another boat. This detained us until the morning of the 26th. We now continued our journey rapidly and safely, and arrived at Okanagan on the evening of the 28th November. Our provisions had run short, and we were compelled to shoot one of the horses of the establishment, which we roasted, and found very palatable. In our emergency the men partook of it so voraciously that some of them were unable to work the next day.

Nov. 29th.—We continued our course, and in four days arrived at Fort Walla-Walla. Here we remained till December 4th, when we entered that part of the country which is annually visited by an almost continuous rain for five months of the year, and during the remainder of our voyage to Fort Vancouver, which we reached on the 8th December, we were exposed in our open boats to an incessant shower. Mr. Douglas and Mr. Ogden,[6] the two chief factors in charge of the fort, came down to

[5] KJ: "There were 2 men killed and eaten here from starvation, their canoe having been lost and their provisions run out. One killed two of his companions and the fourth one escaped. Our guide's father was one of the men killed. About 8 years ago there was [*sic*] 14 passengers drowned here by the upsetting of a canoe."

[6] Sir James Douglas (1803–1877), a British Guianan, joined the North West Company in 1820, then transferred to the Hudson's Bay Company, and retired as a chief factor in 1858. He was appointed governor of Vancouver Island in 1851 and of British Columbia in 1858. See *Dictionary of Canadian Biography*, vol. X.

Peter Skene Ogden (1794–1854), a Quebecker, had joined the North West Company in 1811 and became a chief trader of the Hudson's Bay Company in 1823 and chief factor in 1835. Most of his life after 1818 was spent on the Pacific slope, and he died in Oregon City.

the landing, a distance of about half a mile, to welcome us on our arrival, all hopes of which they had given up, and conducted us up to the fort, where we were entertained with the most liberal hospitality.[7]

Chapter XII.

Fort Vancouver.—The Flatheads.—Hereditary Names.—Casanov. —Ravages of Fever.—The Evil Genius.—How to flatten the Head. —The Sign of a Slave.—An impracticable Tongue.—"Clark, how are you?"—Revolting Habits.—Chinook Costume.—Baskets Watertight.—How they cook the Camas.—Chinook Olives.—Chinook Lodges.—Good-tempered Gamblers.

Fort Vancouver, the Indian name of which is Katchutequa, or "the Plain," is the largest post in the Hudson's Bay Company's dominions, and has usually two chief factors, with eight or ten clerks and 200 voyageurs, residing there. [Figs. 150, 151; crIV-397 to 401] Our society was also enlivened by the addition of the officers of Her Majesty's ship of war the "Modeste," which had been on this station for two years, and lay in the river opposite the establishment. The buildings are enclosed by strong pickets about sixteen feet high, with bastions for cannon at the corners. The men, with their Indian wives, live in log huts near the margin of the river, forming a little village—quite a Babel of languages, as the inhabitants are a mixture of English, French, Iroquois, Sandwich Islanders [Fig. 154; crIV-416, 417], Crees and Chinooks.

The Columbia is here, ninety miles from its mouth, a mile and a quarter wide; the surrounding country is well wooded and fertile, the oak and pine being of the finest description. [Fig. 155; crIV-409 to 413, and ? 441, 442] A large farm is cultivated about eight miles up the river, producing more grain than the fort consumes; the surplus being sent to the Sandwich Islands and the Russian dominions. They have immense herds of domestic horned cattle, which run wild in unknown numbers; and sheep and horses are equally numerous. [crIV-406] When first introduced from California, Dr. M'Laughlin, the gentle-

man then in charge, would not allow any of the horned cattle to be killed for the use of the establishment until their numbers had reached 600, by which means they have multiplied beyond calculation. During the five months' autumn and winter, it rains almost continuously, with very little frost or snow. The river, however, was frozen over for a short time during the winter I spent there, but it was remarked as the coldest season ever experienced; during the other seven months the weather is dry and sultry.

[Mount Hood: crIV-402 to 405]

The Flat-Head Indians are met with on the banks of the Columbia River, from its mouth eastward to the Cascades, a distance of about 150 miles; they extend up the Walhamette River's mouth, about thirty or forty miles, and through the district between the Walhamette and Fort Astoria, now called Fort George. To the north they extend along the Cowlitz River, and the tract of land lying between that and Puget's Sound. About two-thirds of Vancouver's Island is also occupied by them, and they are found along the coasts of Puget's Sound and the Straits of Juan de Fuca. The Flatheads are divided into numerous tribes, each having its own peculiar locality, and differing more or less from the others in language, customs, and manners. Those in the immediate vicinity of the fort are principally Chinooks and Klickataats, and are governed by a chief called Casanov. This name has no translation, the Indians on the west side of the Rocky Mountains differing from those on the east in having hereditary names, to which no particular meaning appears to be attached, and the origin of which is in many instances forgotten.

Casanov is a man of advanced age, and resides principally at Fort Vancouver. I made a sketch (No. 8) of him while staying at the fort. [Pl. XXXVI; crIV-418, 419] Previously to 1829 Casanov was considered a powerful chief, and could lead into the field 1000 men, but in that year the Hudson's Bay Company and emigrants from the United States introduced the plough for the first time into Oregon; and the locality, hitherto considered one of the most healthy, was almost depopulated by the fever and ague. His own immediate family, consisting of ten wives, four children, and eighteen slaves, were reduced in one year to one wife, one child, and two slaves. Casanov is a man of more than ordinary talent for an Indian, and he has maintained his great influence over his tribe chiefly by means of the superstitious dread in which they held him. For many years, in the early period of his life, he kept a hired assassin to remove any obnoxious individual against whom he entertained personal

---

[7] KJ contains at this point an insertion evidently intended as an appendix: "This winter so cold in Oregon that 317 horses died at Colvil out of 320 leaving only 3 alive. Horned cattle not so great a proportion of deaths. The Indians suffered greatly. Some of the chiefs owned as much as 1000 to 1500 horses.

"Accidents on the Columbia River: Drowned at the Rapid St. Martin 2 / Dalles des Morts 2 / 2 grose point [*sic*] 11 / Rappid de Prate 5 / La Shute 1 / Little Dalles 26 / Grand Dalles 15 / Cascades 4 / Portage New 2 / [Total:] 68."

enmity. This bravo, whose occupation was no secret, went by the name of Casanov's scoocoom, or, "the Evil Genius." He finally fell in love with one of Casanov's wives, who eloped with him. Casanov vowed vengeance, but the pair for a long time eluded his search; until one day he met his wife in a canoe near the mouth of the Cowlitz River, and shot her on the spot, and at last procured also the assassination of the lover.

A few years before my arrival at Fort Vancouver, Mr. Douglass, who was then in charge, heard from his office the report of a gun inside the gates. This being a breach of discipline he hurried out to inquire the cause of so unusual a circumstance, and found one of Casanov's slaves standing over the body of an Indian whom he had just killed, and in the act of reloading his gun with apparent indifference, Casanov himself standing by. On Mr. Douglass arriving at the spot, he was told by Casanov, with an apology, that the man deserved death according to the laws of the tribe, who as well as the white man inflicted punishment proportionate to the nature of the offence. In this case the crime was one of the greatest an Indian could be guilty of, namely, the robbing the sepulchre canoes. Mr. Douglass, after severely reprimanding him, allowed him to depart with the dead body.

Sacred as the Indians hold their burial places, Casanov himself, a short time after the latter occurrence, had his only son buried in the cemetery of the Fort. He died of consumption—a disease very common amongst all Indians—proceeding no doubt from their constant exposure to the sudden vicissitudes of the climate. The coffin was made sufficiently large to contain all the necessaries supposed to be required for his comfort and convenience in the world of spirits. The chaplain of the Fort read the usual service at the grave, and after the conclusion of the ceremony, Casanov returned to his lodge, and the same evening attempted, as narrated below, the life of the bereaved mother, who was the daughter of the great chief generally known as King Comcomly, so beautifully alluded to in Washington Irving's "Astoria." She was formerly the wife of a Mr. McDougall,[1] who bought her from her father for, as it was supposed, the enormous price of ten articles of each description, guns, blankets, knives, hatchets, &c., then in Fort Astoria. Comcomly, however, acted with unexpected liberality on the occasion by carpeting her path from the canoe to the Fort with sea otter skins, at that time numerous and valuable, but now scarce, and presenting them as a dowry, in reality far exceeding in value the articles at which she had been estimated. On Mr. McDougall's leaving the Indian country she became the wife of Casanov. [Fig. 167; crIV-478]

It is the prevailing opinion of the chiefs that they and their sons are too important to die in a natural way, and whenever the event takes place, they attribute it to the malevolent influence of some other person, whom they fix upon, often in the most unaccountable manner, frequently selecting those the most dear to themselves and the deceased. The person so selected is sacrificed without hesitation. On this occasion Casanov selected the afflicted mother, notwithstanding she had during the sickness of her son been one of the most assiduous and devoted of his attendants, and of his several wives she was the one he most loved; but it is the general belief of the Indians on the west side of the mountains, that the greater the privation they inflict on themselves the greater would be the manifestation of their grief, and the more pleasing to the departed spirit. Casanov assigned to me an additional motive for his wish to kill his wife, namely, that as he knew she had been so useful to her son and so necessary to his happiness and comfort in this world, he wished to send her with him as his companion on his long journey. She, however, escaped into the woods, and next morning reached the Fort imploring protection; she was accordingly secreted for several days until her own relations took her home to Chinook Point. In the meantime a woman was found murdered in the woods, and the act was universally attributed to Casanov or one of his emissaries.

I may here mention a painful occurrence which took place on Thompson's River, in New Caledonia, as illustrative of this peculiar superstition.

A chief dying, his widow considered a sacrifice as indispensable, but having selected a victim of rather too much importance, she was unable for some time to accomplish her object; at length the nephew of the chief, no longer able to bear the continual taunts of cowardice which she unceasingly heaped upon him, seized his gun and started for the Company's Fort on the river, about twenty miles distant. On arriving he was courteously received by Mr. Black,[2] the gentleman in charge of the Fort, who expressed great regret at the death of his old friend the chief. After presenting the Indian with something to eat and giving him some tobacco, Mr. Black turned to leave the room, and while opening the door was shot from behind by his treacherous guest and immediately expired. The murderer succeeded

---

[1] Duncan McDougall was a fur trader working with the Pacific Fur Company of John Jacob Astor as a partner in 1810. He joined the Nor'Westers and died at Fort William after 1817.

[2] Samuel Black (c. 1785–1841) was a Nor'Wester but joined the Hudson's Bay Company in 1823. He had been in charge of Walla Walla and Kamloops before his murder by the Indian.

in escaping from the Fort, but the tribe, who were warmly attached to Mr. Black, took his revenge upon themselves and hunted him down. This was done more to evince their high esteem for Mr. Black than from any sense of impropriety in the customary sacrifice.

Amongst the Chinooks I have never heard any traditions as to their former origin, although such traditions are common amongst those on the east side of the Rocky Mountains. They do not believe in any future state of punishment, although in this world they suppose themselves exposed to the malicious designs of the scoocoom or evil genius, to whom they attribute all their misfortunes and ill luck. The Good Spirit is called the *Hias Soch-a-li Ti-yah*, that is the Great High Chief from whom they obtain all that is good in this life, and to whose happy and peaceful hunting grounds they will all eventually go, to reside for ever in comfort and abundance.

The Chinooks and Cowlitz Indians carry the custom of flattening the head to a greater extent than any other of the Flathead tribes. The process is as follows:—The Indian mothers all carry their infants strapped to a piece of board covered with moss or loose fibres of cedar bark, and in order to flatten the head they place a pad on the infant's forehead, on the top of which is laid a piece of smooth bark, bound on by a leathern band passing through holes in the board on either side, and kept tightly pressed across the front of the head,—a sort of pillow of grass or cedar fibres being placed under the back of the neck to support it. This process commences with the birth of the infant, and is continued for a period of from eight to twelve months, by which time the head has lost its natural shape, and acquired that of a wedge: the front of the skull flat and higher at the crown, giving it a most unnatural appearance. [Fig. 170; crIV-490]

It might be supposed, from the extent to which this is carried, that the operation would be attended with great suffering to the infant, but I have never heard the infants crying or moaning, although I have seen the eyes seemingly starting out of the sockets from the great pressure. But on the contrary, when the lashings were removed, I have noticed them cry until they were replaced. From the apparent dulness of the children whilst under the pressure, I should imagine that a state of torpor or insensibility is induced, and that the return to consciousness occasioned by its removal, must be naturally followed by the sense of pain.

This unnatural operation does not, however, seem to injure the health, the mortality amongst the Flathead children not being perceptibly greater than amongst other Indian tribes; nor does it seem to injure their intellect. On the contrary, the Flatheads are generally considered fully as intelligent as the surrounding tribes, who allow their heads to preserve their natural shape, and it is from amongst the round heads that the Flatheads take their slaves, looking with contempt even upon the white for having round heads, the flat head being considered as the distinguishing mark of freedom.

The Chinooks, like all other Indians, pluck out the beard at its first appearance. Slavery is carried on to a great extent among them, and considering how much they have themselves been reduced, they still retain a large number of slaves. These are usually procured from the Chastay tribe, who live near the Umqua, a river south of the Columbia, emptying near the Pacific. They are sometimes seized by war parties, but children are often bought from their own people. They do not flatten the head, nor is the child of one of them (although by a Chinook father) allowed this privilege. Their slavery is of the most abject description. The Chinook men and women treat them with great severity, and exercise the power of life and death at pleasure. I took a sketch of a Chastay female slave, the lower part of whose face, from the corners of the mouth to the ears and downwards, was tattooed of a blueish colour. [crIV-440] The men of this tribe do not tattoo, but paint their faces like other Indians.

I would willingly give a specimen of the barbarous language of this people, were it possible to represent by any combination of our alphabet the horrible, harsh, spluttering sounds which proceed from their throats, apparently unguided either by the tongue or lip. It is so difficult to acquire a mastery of their language that none have been able to attain it, except those who have been born among them. They have, however, by their intercourse with the English and French traders, succeeded in amalgamating, after a fashion, some words of each of these tongues with their own, and forming a sort of patois, barbarous enough certainly, but still sufficient to enable them to communicate with the traders. This patois I was enabled after some short time to acquire, and could converse with most of the chiefs with tolerable ease; their common salutation is Clak-hoh-ah-yah, originating, as I believe, in their having heard in the early days of the fur trade, a gentleman named Clark [3] frequently addressed by his friends, "Clark, how are you?" This salutation is now applied to every white man, their own language affording no

[3] John Clarke (1781–1852), a fur trader born in Montreal, had worked for the North West Company in 1800–10, for the Pacific Fur Company of John Jacob Astor in 1810–14, and as a factor of the Hudson's Bay Company in 1821–30.

appropriate expression. Their language is also peculiar in containing no oaths, or any words conveying gratitude or thanks.

Their habits are extremely filthy, their persons abounding with vermin, and one of their chief amusements consists in picking these disgusting insects from each other's heads and eating them. On my asking an Indian one day why he ate them, he replied that they bit him, and he gratified his revenge by biting them in return. It might naturally be supposed that they are thus beset from want of combs, or other means of displacing the intruders; but this is not the case, as they pride themselves on carrying such companions about them, and giving their friends the opportunity of amusing themselves by hunting and eating them.

The costume of the men consists of a musk-rat skin robe, the size of our ordinary blanket, thrown over the shoulder, without any breech-cloth, moccasins, or leggings. The dress which Casanov is represented as wearing, in the picture, being one that was presented to him by a friend from Walla-Walla. Painting the face is not much practised amongst them, except on extraordinary occasions, such as the death of a relative, some solemn feast, or going on a war party. The female dress consists of a girdle of cedar-bark round the waist, with a dense mass of strings of the same material hanging from it all round, and reaching almost to the knees. This is their sole summer habiliment. They, however, in very severe weather, add the musk-rat blanket. They also make another sort of blanket from the skin of the wild goose, which is here taken in great abundance. The skin is stripped from the bird with the feathers on and cut in strips, which they twist so as to have the feathers outwards. This makes a feathered cord, and is then netted together so as to form a blanket, the feathers filling up the meshes, rendering it a light and very warm covering. In the summer these are entirely thrown aside, not being in any case worn from feelings of delicacy. The men go quite naked, though the women always wear the cedar petticoat. [crIV-437]

The country which the Chinooks inhabit being almost destitute of furs, they have little to trade in with the whites. This, coupled with their laziness, probably induced by the ease with which they procure fish, which is their chief subsistence, prevents their obtaining ornaments of European manufacture, consequently anything of the kind is seldom seen amongst them.

The Chinooks evince very little taste, in comparison with some of the tribes on the eastern side of the Rocky Mountains, in ornamenting either their persons, or their warlike or domestic implements. The only utensils I saw at all creditable to their decorative skill were carved bowls and spoons of horn, and baskets made of roots and grass, woven so closely, as to serve all the purposes of a pail, in holding and carrying water. In these they even boil their fish. This is done by immersing the fish in one of the baskets filled with water, into which they throw red hot stones until the fish is cooked; and I have seen fish dressed as expeditiously by them in this way, as if done in a kettle over the fire by our own people. The only vegetables in use among them are the camas and wappatoo. The camas is a bulbous root, much resembling the onion in outward appearance, but is more like the potato when cooked, and is very good eating. The wappatoo is somewhat similar, but larger, and not so dry or delicate in its flavour. They are found in immense quantities in the plains in the vicinity of Fort Vancouver, and in the spring of the year present a most curious and beautiful appearance, the whole surface presenting an uninterrupted sheet of bright ultramarine blue, from the innumerable blossoms of these plants. They are cooked by digging a hole in the ground, then putting down a layer of hot stones, covering them with dry grass, on which the roots are placed, they are then covered with a layer of grass, and on the top of this they place earth, with a small hole perforated through the earth and grass down to the vegetables. Into this water is poured, which, reaching the hot stones, forms sufficient steam to completely cook the roots in a short time, the hole being immediately stopped up on the introduction of the water. They often adopt the same ingenious process for cooking their fish and game.

There is another article of food made use of amongst them, which, from its disgusting nature, I should have been tempted to omit, were it not a peculiarly characteristic trait of the Chinook Indian, both from its extraordinary character and its use, being confined solely to this tribe. The whites have given it the name of Chinook olives, and it is prepared as follows:—About a bushel of acorns are placed in a hole dug for the purpose close to the entrance of the lodge or hut, covered over with a thin layer of grass, on the top of which is laid about half a foot of earth. Every member of the family henceforth regards this hole as the special place of deposit for his urine, which is on no occasion to be diverted from its legitimate receptacle. In this hole the acorns are allowed to remain four or five months before they are considered fit for use. However disgusting such an odoriferous preparation would be to people in civilised life, the product is regarded by them as the greatest of all delicacies.

During the season the Chinooks are engaged in gathering camas and fishing, they live in lodges constructed by means of a

Norway House Paul Kane
1846

Plate XVIII. Norway House. Stark POP14;CRIV-83.

few poles covered with mats made of rushes, which can be easily moved from place to place [Figs. 157, 160; crIV-426, 427, 429 to 432], but in the villages they build permanent huts of split cedar boards. Having selected a dry place for the hut, a hole is dug about three feet deep, and about twenty feet square. Round the sides square cedar boards are sunk and fastened together with cords and twisted roots, rising about four feet above the outer level; two posts are sunk at the middle of each end with a crotch at the top, on which the ridge pole is laid, and boards are laid from thence to the top of the upright boards fastened in the same manner. Round the interior are erected sleeping places, one above another, something like the berths in a vessel, but larger. In the centre of this lodge the fire is made, and the smoke escapes through a hole left in the roof for that purpose. [Pl. XXXVII; Figs. 158, 159; crIV-424, 425, 428]

The fire is obtained by means of a small flat piece of dry cedar, in which a small hollow is cut, with a channel for the ignited charcoal to run over; this piece the Indian sits on to hold it steady, while he rapidly twirls a round stick of the same wood between the palms of his hands, with the point pressed into the hollow of the flat piece. In a very short time sparks begin to fall through the channel upon finely frayed cedar bark placed underneath, which they soon ignite. There is a great deal of knack in doing this, but those who are used to it will light a fire in a very short time. The men usually carry these sticks about with them, as after they have been once used they produce the fire more quickly.

The only native warlike instruments I have seen amongst them were bows and arrows; these they use with great precision. Their canoes are hollowed out of the cedar by fire, and smoothed off with stone axes. Some of them are very large, as the cedar grows to an enormous size in this neighbourhood. They are made very light, and from their formation, are capable of withstanding very heavy seas.

The principal amusement of the Chinooks is gambling, which is carried to great excess amongst them. [crIV-433] You never visit the camp but you hear the eternal gambling song of *"he hah ha,"* accompanied by the beating of small sticks on some hollow substance. Their games are few. The one most generally played amongst them consists in holding in each hand a small stick, the thickness of a goose quill, and about an inch and a half in length, one plain, and the other distinguished by a little thread wound round it, the opposite party being required to guess in which hand the marked stick is to be found. A Chinook will play at this simple game for days and nights together, until

he has gambled away everything he possesses, even to his wife. They play, however, with much equanimity, and I never knew any ill feeling evinced by the loser against his successful opponent. They will cheat if they can, and pride themselves on its success; if detected, no unpleasant consequence follows, the offending party being merely laughed at, and allowed to amend his game. They also take great delight in a game with a ball, which is played by them in the same manner as the Cree, Chippewa, and Sioux Indians. Two poles are erected about a mile apart, and the company is divided into two bands, armed with sticks, having a small ring or hoop at the end, with which the ball is picked up and thrown to a great distance; each party then strives to get the ball past their own goal. There are sometimes a hundred on a side, and the play is kept up with great noise and excitement. At this game they bet heavily, as it is generally played between tribes or villages. The Chinooks have tolerably good horses, and are fond of racing, at which they also bet considerably. They are expert jockeys, and ride fearlessly.

[Indians: crIV-422, 423, 434 to 439]

Chapter XIII.

Leaving Fort Vancouver.—Seven degrees below Zero.—The Magic Bullet.—A Match for the Indians.—A Jesuit Mission.—Harmonious Gamesters.—A Wild Calf Chase.—The Swallow-tailed Coat.—The Haunted Volcano.—The Cocked Hat.—Dead Men's Canoes.—Filching a Good Name.—The Prairie de Bute.

I continued at Fort Vancouver for about a month, and left on the 10th of January 1847, with Mr. Mackenlie, a chief trader, for Oregon City, where the company has an establishment. After going down the Columbia about five miles, we entered the mouth of the Walhamette River, and ascended it twenty-five miles to Oregon City, passing two cities that are to be. One of them contained but two houses, and the other was not much more advanced. Oregon City contains about ninety-four houses, and two or three hundred inhabitants. There are a Methodist and a Roman Catholic church, two hotels, two grist mills, three saw mills, four stores, two watchmakers, one gunsmith, one lawyer, and doctors *ad libitum*. [Pl. XXXVIII; Fig. 161; crIV-443 to 450] The city stands near the Falls of the Walhamette which is here about thirty-two feet high. [Fig. 162; crIV-451, 452, 453]

The water privileges are of the most powerful and convenient description. Dr. M'Laughlin, formerly a chief factor in the Hudson's Bay Company, first obtained a location of the place, and now owns the principal mills. A great drawback, however, to its prosperity, is, that vessels cannot ascend the river nearer to it than fifteen miles, on account of the rapids. At the head of the navigation a city is building, which must eventually rival, if not eclipse Oregon in commercial prosperity. The morning after our arrival the thermometer stood at 7° below zero. Such intense cold had not been felt by the oldest inhabitants of these regions. It had the effect of killing nearly all the cattle that had become acclimated, as they are never housed. The Columbia, too, was frozen over, an unprecedented circumstance, so that my travels were for a time interrupted. I was, however, very comfortably quartered at Mr. Mackenlie's residence, who amused me in the long winter evenings over a good fire by his interesting tales of Indian life, with which he was well conversant. I will relate a couple of his anecdotes.

While he was in charge of a fort in New Caledonia, which is situated south of the Columbia River, he had a carat of tobacco, or three pounds, stolen from him. It was all that he had at that time, and of course was a serious loss. Supposing it to have been taken by some of the Indians, who were trading in large numbers about the establishment at that time, he requested the chief to call a council of all the tribe, as he had something to say to them. On this they all assembled and squatted down, leaving an open space in the centre, into which he walked with his fowling piece; this he loaded with two balls in the presence of the assembly, after which he related the circumstance of his loss, and stated his belief that some one of the Indians then present had taken it. He then told them that he wished that every one present would place his mouth to the muzzle of the gun, and blow into it, assuring them that it would injure no one innocent of the theft; but, on the other hand, if the guilty party should attempt to do so, it would inevitably kill him. He himself set the example of blowing into the piece, standing muzzle upwards on the ground; the chief followed, as well as the whole tribe, with the exception of one man, who sat hanging down his head, and when called upon by the chief to follow the example of the rest refused, saying, that he would not tempt the Great Spirit, for that he had taken the tobacco, and would return it, which he accordingly did.

Whilst Mr. Mackenlie was in charge of Walla-Walla he exhibited an instance of great presence of mind under very trying circumstances. His clerk had a quarrel and fight with the son of the chief, whom he beat. The Indian thereupon collected a large party of the tribe, and rushed with them into the yard of the fort, and attempted to seize the offender for the purpose of taking his life. Mr. Mackenlie kept them off for some time, but finding he could do so no longer, he ordered one of the men to bring him out a keg of powder, the head of which he knocked in, and taking a flint and steel from his pocket, he stood over it as if about to ignite it, telling the Indians that if they did not immediately depart he would show them how a white chief could die and destroy his enemies. The Indians took the alarm, and fled through the gates, which he immediately barred against them, secretly sending the clerk the next day to another post out of their reach.

After remaining at Mr. Mackenlie's house for about three weeks, I ascended the Walhamette River, in company with Father Acolti, a Jesuit missionary, for about thirty miles. We then disembarked and proceeded on horseback about eight miles to the Roman Catholic mission, where there is a large establishment of religieuses for the purposes of education, as well as a good brick church, situated in a beautiful prairie, surrounded with woods. [Pl. XXXIX; crIV-454] It has also a nunnery occupied by six Sisters of Charity, who employ themselves in teaching the children, both white and red, amounting to forty-two pupils.

Father Acolti's residence is three miles from here, the Jesuit mission being distinct from the Roman Catholic; at least they are under separate authorities. Besides this one under Father Acolti, there are three Jesuit missions near the Rocky Mountains, and one in New Caledonia. This part of the country contains the largest tract of good land that is to be met with in Oregon. I enjoyed the hospitality of Père Acolti's establishment for three or four days, when I again returned to the Walhamette; and previously to embarking in the canoe, I ascended a high mountain, and made a sketch of the windings of the river, with the Umqua Mountains, where it takes its rise, in the distance. [Fig. 163; crIV-455, 456, 457]

After visiting Mr. Mackenlie at Oregon City for a few days, I once more started for Fort Vancouver. About four miles below Oregon the Klackamuss enters the Walhamette; and, seated on the banks at its mouth, I saw a party of Indians of the Klackamuss tribe, and I put ashore for the purpose of taking a sketch of them. [Pl. XL; crIV-458, 459] They were busy gambling at one of their favourite games. Two were seated together on skins, and immediately opposite to them sat two others, several trinkets and ornaments being placed between them, for which they played. The game consists in one of them having his hands covered with a small round mat resting on the ground. He has four small sticks in his hands, which he disposes under the mat in certain positions, requiring the opposite party to guess how he has placed them. If he guesses right, the mat is handed round to the next, and a stick is stuck up as a counter in his favour. If wrong, a stick is stuck up on the opposite side as a mark against him. This, like almost all the Indian games, was accompanied with singing; but in this case the singing was peculiarly sweet and wild, possessing a harmony I never heard before or since amongst Indians.

This tribe was once very numerous; but owing to their close vicinity to Oregon City, and the ease with which they can procure spirits, they have dwindled down to six or eight lodges.

We arrived late that evening at Fort Vancouver, having paddled on all day through heavy rain and cold. This, however, is thought little of in the Columbia during the rainy seasons, as no one troubles himself with making vain attempts to avoid wet at these periods. I remained here until the 25th of March; and although the weather was very wet, I found plenty of amusement with the officers of the "Modeste," who had built stables, and selected some very good horses. [Fig. 153; cRIV-407, 408, 465?, 466?] With these we ran races, and chased the wild calves; the object of which latter exercise consisted principally in showing the dexterity of the rider, in stooping from his saddle and throwing the calf head-over-heels by the tail.

[Theatrical entertainments: Fig. 152; cRIV-414, 415?]

These sports we occasionally varied by shooting and fishing, ducks and geese and seal being in great quantities in the neighbourhood of the fort. One day, a tall, large-boned Indian came on board the "Modeste" while I was sitting below with some of the officers. The Indian was dressed, as usual, in full costume, as they would call it in California (where, it is said, a shirt collar and spurs are considered the only clothing indispensably necessary); that is to say, he had his paddle in his hand, and walked about the deck with great gravity, examining the cannon, and other things equally incomprehensible to him, much to the amusement of the idle sailors. The purser, no doubt from a feeling of delicacy, took the Indian below, and gave him an old swallow-tailed coat of his, which was adorned with numerous brass buttons. The Indian, highly delighted, struggled into the garment with the greatest difficulty, as it was infinitely too small for him, the cuffs reaching but little below the elbow, and the front not meeting within a foot. Having, however, succeeded in getting into it, he perambulated the deck with tenfold dignity,

and the whole ship's crew yelled with laughter. The extraordinary noise brought us all on deck, and, amongst others, the captain came up. Even his dignity could not withstand the absurdity of the figure, to which he immediately added, by sending his steward down for an old cocked hat of his, which was given to the Indian. When this was mounted the figure was complete; and seldom has the deck of one of Her Majesty's ships been the scene of such uproarious and violent laughter. I made several efforts to make a sketch of the Indian before I could succeed; and though I at length did so, yet I fear that the picture would give but a faint idea of the cause of all our merriment. [cRIV-415?]

March 25th.—I started from the Fort for Vancouver's Island in a small wooden canoe, with a couple of Indians, and encamped at the mouth of the Walhamette.[1]

March 26th.—When we arrived at the mouth of the Kattlepoutal River, twenty-six miles from Fort Vancouver, I stopped to make a sketch of the volcano, Mount St. Helen's, distant, I suppose, about thirty or forty miles. This mountain has never been visited by either Whites or Indians; the latter assert that it is inhabited by a race of beings of a different species, who are cannibals, and whom they hold in great dread; they also say that there is a lake at its base with a very extraordinary kind of fish in it, with a head more resembling that of a bear than any other animal. These superstitions are taken from the statement of a man who, they say, went to the mountain with another, and escaped the fate of his companion, who was eaten by the "Skoocooms," or evil genii. I offered a considerable bribe to any Indian who would accompany me in its exploration, but could not find one hardy enough to venture. It is of very great height, and being eternally covered with snow, is seen at a great distance. There was not a cloud visible in the sky at the time I commenced my sketch, and not a breath of air was perceptible: suddenly a stream of white smoke shot up from the crater of the mountain, and hovered a short time over its summit; it then settled down like a cap. This shape it retained for about an hour and a-half, and then gradually disappeared. [Pl. XLI; Figs. 164, 165; cRIV-460 to 464, 467]

About three years before this the mountain was in a violent state of irruption for three or four days, and threw up burning stones and lava to an immense height, which ran in burning torrents down its snow-clad sides.[2] About ten miles lower down

---

[1] KJ states that they left at 4 P.M. and only travelled five miles the first day.
[2] KJ records Kane's making a sketch of the mountain from "Chalifour's Lake."

we encamped for the night near Coffin Rock,[3] much against the inclination of my men, whose superstition would have led them to avoid such a place. This rock gets its name from its being the place in which the Indians deposit their dead. I took a sketch of the rock before the night set in. [Fig. 166; crIV-470 to 473]

There is another rock lower down, on which were deposited two or three hundred of their burial canoes; but Commodore Wilkes having made a fire near the spot, it communicated to the bodies, and nearly the whole of them were consumed. The Indians showed much indignation at the violation of a place which was held so sacred by them, and would no doubt have sought revenge had they felt themselves strong enough to do so. [See p. 99, note 6.]

March 27th.—As usual, the rain came down in torrents. As we neared one of the points on the river, we perceived a naked Indian watching us; as we came up he ran away to his lodge, and, to my astonishment, reappeared in the cocked hat and purser's coat aforesaid. He received me with great friendship, having recognised me, before landing, as one of the party he had seen on board the "Modeste." He took me to his lodge and gave me some boiled salmon. He seemed to take great care of his uniform; but, unfortunately, the coat would not stretch, and it now burst wide open all the way up the back, which, I have no doubt, added considerably to his comfort. [Chinook: crIV-468, 469] After leaving him we entered the Cowlitz River, and proceeded up about eight miles and encamped on its banks. We saw a family of emigrants winding their toilsome way in quest of a spot to make their home. Their condition appeared miserable in the extreme.[4]

March 28th.—One of my Indians falling sick here, I procured another Indian and proceeded up the river at a very slow rate, owing to the rapidity of the current. The pine trees here are the largest I have ever seen. I measured one, which had drifted down the stream, and which had apparently a third of its length broken off. It was still 180 feet long, and 26 feet in circumference 5 feet from its root. [Trees with moss: crIV-482 to 487]

March 29th.—We came to another Indian burial ground, which seemed to be highly decorated. I wished my Indians to put ashore, but they would not do so. I was obliged, therefore, to put them out of the canoe on the opposite side of the river, and paddle the canoe over by myself. I have no doubt that they would have opposed my doing so had it not been for the name

[3] KJ says that Coffin Rock is four miles above the entrance to the Cowlitz River.
[4] KJ adds that the pines at the camping place were very large, and that the emigrant family was bound for Nisqually.

which I had already acquired amongst the Indians, of being a great medicine-man, on account of the likenesses which I had taken. My power of pourtraying the features of individuals was attributed entirely to supernatural agency, and I found that, in looking at my pictures, they always covered their eyes with their hands and looked through the fingers; this being also the invariable custom when looking at a dead person. On arriving at the place I found it lavishly decorated with numerous articles, of supposed utility and ornament, for the convenience of the defunct in the journey to the world of spirits. These articles consisted of blankets, tin cups, pots, pans, kettles, plates, baskets, horn bowls, and spoons, with shreds of cloth of various colours. One canoe, which was decorated more highly than the rest, I examined particularly. All the articles appended to it were rendered useless for this world by either tearing, breaking, or boring holes in them, the Indians believing that they would be made whole again by the Great Spirit. On examining the interior of a canoe I found a great number of ioquas and other shells, together with beads and rings: even the mouth of the deceased was filled with these articles. The body itself was carefully enveloped in numerous folds of matting made of rushes. At the bottom of the canoe lay a bow and arrow, a paddle, a spear, and a kind of pick, made of horn, for digging the camas roots; the top of the canoe, immediately over the body, had a covering of bark, and holes were bored in the bottom to allow the water to run out. These canoes are always placed on wooden supports, suspended in the branches of trees, or placed upon isolated rocks in the river, to keep them beyond the reach of ravenous animals. Sketch No. 9 represents this burial place. [Pl. XLII; Figs. 167, 168; crIV-474 to 478]

During my stay the Indians watched me closely from the opposite bank, and, on my return, they examined me as minutely as they well could with their eyes to see that I had not brought anything away with me. Had I been so imprudent as to have done so I should probably have answered for the sacrilege with my life, death being the certain penalty to the most trifling violation of the sanctity of a coffin canoe. I endeavoured to discover who was buried in the richly decorated canoe, but the only information I could get from them was that the deceased was the daughter of a Chinook chief. The Indians here have a superstitious dread of mentioning the name of any person after death, nor will they tell you their own names, which can only be found out from a third party. One of the men asked me if my desire to know his name proceeded from a wish to steal it. It is not an uncommon thing for a chief, when he wishes to pay you a very high compliment, to give and call you by his own name, and adopt some other for himself.

March 30th.—We landed at the Cowlitz farm, which belongs to the Hudson's Bay Company.[5] Large quantities of wheat are raised at this place. I had a fine view of Mount St. Helen's throwing up a long column of dark smoke into the clear blue sky. Here I remained until the 5th of April, and took the likeness of Kiscox, the chief of the Cowlitz Indians, a small tribe of about 200. [crIV-488] They flatten their heads and speak a language very similar to the Chinooks. They were very friendly to me and I was a good deal amongst them. [crIV-479, 480, 481] Sketch No. 10 is Caw-wacham, a woman of the tribe, with her child under the process of having its head flattened. It was with some difficulty that I persuaded her to sit, as she seemed apprehensive that it would be injurious to her. [Figs. 169, 170, 171; crIV-489 to 493] On the 5th of April I procured horses to cross to Nasquala at Puget's Sound, and rain poured down in torrents the whole day, making the swamps nearly impassable. We encamped in the evening near a small village of Cowlitz Indians, whom we found unusually kind and civil.

April 6th.—We passed over what is called the Mud Mountain. The mud is so very deep in this pass that we were compelled to dismount and drag our horses through it by the bridle; the poor beasts being up to their bellies in mud of the tenacity of bird-lime. This evening we encamped in the Prairie de Bute. This is remarkable for having innumerable round elevations, touching each other like so many hemispheres, of ten or twelve yards in circumference, and four or five feet in height. I dug one of them open, but found nothing in it but loose stones, although I went four or five feet down.[6] The whole surface is thickly covered with coarse grass. I travelled twenty-two miles through this extraordinary looking prairie. [Fig. 172; crIV-494 to 497]

April 7th.—We found some difficulty in crossing the Nasqually River, as the rains had flooded it, and we were obliged to adopt the usual plan where canoes cannot be obtained, that is,

swimming at our horses' tails, and floating our things over in skin baskets. A couple of hours brought us to Nasqually,[7] which was established by a company called the Puget's Sound Company, for grazing and farming.[8] When I visited it, it had about 6000 sheep and 2000 horned cattle. Its site is beautiful, on the banks of the eastern end of Puget's Sound. [Fig. 173; crIV-498] The land is inferior to that in some other parts of the same district, the soil being gravelly; the grass, however, grows luxuriantly, and the mildness of the climate adapts it well for grazing purposes, as it is never necessary to house the animals. The wool, which is good, finds its way to the English market by the Company's ships, and the cattle are slaughtered and salted for the Sandwich Islands and the Russian dominions. The Indians about here are of very large stature; indeed, the largest that I have met with on the continent. The women are particularly large and stout. The tribe numbers between five or six hundred. They flatten their heads, but use a language different from the Chinooks. [Fig. 174; crIV-499, 500] I made a sketch of Lach-oh-lett, their head chief, and his daughter, who wore a cap made of grass of different colours, much used by the women. [Pl. XLVIII; crIV-501, 502]

Chapter XIV.

Fort Victoria.—Accidental Clover.—Blankets of Dog's Hair.—Aprons of Bark.—A Chief's Inauguration.—Monstrous Sturgeon.—Crows which Feed on Fish.—The Domestic Institution.—The Dead Slave.—Frightening a Native.—Washing the Dead.—The Game of Lehallum.—An Expensive Feast.—Medicine Caps.

April 8th.—I left Nasqually this morning with six Indians in a canoe, and continued paddling on the whole day and the following night, as the tide seemed favourable, not stopping till 2 P.M., when we reached Fort Victoria on Vancouver's Island, having travelled ninety miles without stopping.[1] Fort Victoria stands upon the banks of an inlet in the island about seven miles long and a quarter of a mile wide, forming a safe and convenient harbour, deep enough for any sized vessel. [Figs. 188, 189; crIV-535, 536, 537] Its Indian name is the Esquimelt, or, Place for gathering Camas, great quantities of that vegetable

[5] Burpee, in the 1925 edition of *Wanderings,* gives this note: "Simon Plomondeau was advised by McLoughlin to settle on Cowlitz Prairie. Others followed, and in 1839 a large farm was surveyed by Charles Ross, John Work and James Douglas as a company settlement." KJ notes that there was a Catholic mission here.

[6] KJ notes that the "Wilks Party" dug into some of the mounds but found nothing but round stones. This is a reference to Lt. Charles Wilkes who led an expedition in the west in 1838–42.

[7] KJ notes here that a canoe and six Indians awaited Kane at Nisqually to take him to Fort Victoria.

[8] KJ names the farm superintendent as "Dr. Tolmey." This would be William Fraser Tolmie (1812–1886).

[1] The Fort Victoria "Journal" (Hudson's Bay Co. Archives B226a) states for April 8 that about 5 P.M. Mr. Côté arrived with a canoe which had left the fort with the English packet on March 23 and that it brought Mr. Sangster and Kane as passengers from Nisqually.

being found in the neighbourhood. On my arrival I was kindly welcomed by Mr. Finlayson, the gentleman in charge. He gave me a comfortable room, which I made my headquarters during the two months I was occupied in sketching excursions amongst the Indians in the neighbourhood and along the surrounding coasts.

The soil of this locality is good, and wheat is grown in considerable abundance. Clover grows plentifully, and is supposed to have sprung from accidental seeds which had fallen from the packages of goods brought from England; many of which are made up in hay.

The interior of the island has not been explored to any extent except by the Indians, who represent it as badly supplied with water in the summer, and the water obtained from a well dug at the fort was found to be too brackish for use. The appearance of the interior, when seen from the coast, is rocky and mountainous, evidently volcanic; the trees are large, principally oak and pine. The timbers of a vessel of some magnitude were being got out. The establishment is very large, and must eventually become the great depôt for the business of the Company. They had ten white men and forty Indians engaged in building new stores and warehouses. On the opposite side of the harbour, facing the fort, stands a village of Clal-lums Indians. [Pl. XLIII; Figs. 184, 185, 186, 187; crIV-526? to 534] They boast of being able to turn out 500 warriors, armed chiefly with bows and arrows. The lodges are built of cedar like the Chinook lodges, but much larger, some of them being sixty or seventy feet long. [Pl. XLV; Figs. 192, 194, 195, 198; crIV-545 to 551, 555, 557]

The men wear no clothing in summer, and nothing but a blanket in winter, made either of dog's hair alone, or dog's hair and goosedown mixed, frayed cedar-bark, or wildgoose skin, like the Chinooks. They have a peculiar breed of small dogs with long hair of a brownish black and a clear white. These dogs are bred for clothing purposes. [crIV-558, 559] The hair is cut off with a knife and mixed with goosedown and a little white earth, with a view of curing the feathers. This is then beaten together with sticks, and twisted into threads by rubbing it down the thigh with the palm of the hand, in the same way that a shoemaker forms his waxend, after which it undergoes a second twisting on a distaff to increase its firmness. [Fig. 197; crIV-553, 554] The cedar bark is frayed and twisted into threads in a similar manner. These threads are then woven into blankets by a very simple loom of their own contrivance. A single thread is wound over rollers at the top and bottom of a square frame, so

as to form a continuous woof through which an alternate thread is carried by the hand, and pressed closely together by a sort of wooden comb; by turning the rollers every part of the woof is brought within reach of the weaver; by this means a bag is formed, open at each end, which being cut down makes a square blanket. [Fig. 196; crIV-552, 556] The women wear only an apron of twisted cedar-bark shreds, tied round the waist and hanging down in front only, almost to the knees. They however, use the blankets more than the men do, but certainly not from any feeling of delicacy.

This tribe flatten the head, but their language varies very much from the Chinook; however, the same patois used on the Columbia is spoken by many of them, and I was thus enabled to communicate easily with them. I took a sketch of Chea-clach, their head chief [crIV-566, 567], of whose inauguration I heard the following account from an eye-witness. On his father becoming too old to fulfil the duties of head chief, the son was called upon by the tribe to take his place; on which occasion he left [for?] the mountains for the ostensible purpose of fasting and dreaming for thirty days and nights; these Indians, like all other tribes, placing great confidence in dreams, and believing that it is necessary to undergo a long fast whenever they are desirous of inducing one of any importance. At the end of the period assigned, the tribe prepared a great feast. After covering himself with a thick covering of grease and goosedown, he rushed into the midst of the village, seized a small dog, and began devouring it alive, this being a customary preliminary on such occasions. The tribe collected about him singing and dancing in the wildest manner, on which he approached those whom he most regarded and bit their bare shoulders or arms, which was considered by them as a high mark of distinction, more especially those from whom he took the piece clean out and swallowed it. Of the women he took no notice.

I have seen many men on the North-west coast of the Pacific who bore frightful marks of what they regarded as an honourable distinction; nor is this the only way in which their persons become disfigured. I have myself seen a young girl bleeding most profusely from gashes inflicted by her own hand over her arms and bosom with a sharp flint, on the occasion of losing a near relative. After some time spent in singing and dancing, Chea-clach retired with his people to the feast prepared inside a large lodge, which consisted principally of whale's blubber, in their opinion the greatest of all delicacies, although they have salmon, cod, sturgeon, and other excellent fish in great abundance.

All the tribes about here subsist almost entirely upon fish, which they obtain with so little trouble during all seasons of the year, that they are probably the laziest race of people in the world. Sturgeon are caught in considerable numbers, and here attain an enormous size, weighing from four to six hundred weight; this is done by means of a long pointed spear handle seventy to eighty feet in length, fitted into, but not actually fastened to, a barbed spear-head, to which is attached a line, with which they feel along the bottom of the river where the sturgeon are found lying at the spawning season. Upon feeling the fish the barbed spear is driven in and the handle withdrawn. The fish is then gradually drawn in by the line, which being very long, allows the sturgeon to waste his great strength, so that he can with safety be taken into the canoe or towed ashore. Most of their fishing lines are formed of a long seaweed, which is often found 150 feet long, of equal thickness throughout the whole length, and about as thick as a black-lead pencil; while wet it is very strong. Their fish-hooks are made of pine-roots, made something in the shape of our ordinary hooks, but attached differently to the line; the barb is made of bone.

Clams are in great plenty, and are preyed on in great numbers by the crows, who seize them in their claws and fly up with them to some height, and then let them drop on the rocks, which of course smashes the shell to pieces. I have watched dozens of them at this singular employment. A small oyster of a fine flavour is found in the bays in great plenty. Seal, wild ducks and geese, are also in great numbers.

The Indians are extremely fond of herring-roe, which they collect in the following manner:—Cedar branches are sunk to the bottom of the river in shallow places by placing upon them a few heavy stones, taking care not to cover the green foliage, as the fish prefer spawning on anything green. The branches are all covered by the next morning with the spawn, which is washed off into their waterproof baskets, to the bottom of which it sinks; it is then squeezed by the hand into small balls and dried, and is very palatable.

The only other vegetable besides the camas and wappatoos that the Indians use, are the roots of fern roasted, which here grow to a very large size.

[Clallam travelling lodges: Pl. XLVI; crIV-560 to 563]

Slavery in its most cruel form exists among the Indians of the whole coast, from California to Behring's Straits, the stronger tribes making slaves of all the others they can conquer. In the interior, where there is but little warfare, slavery does not exist. On the coast a custom prevails which authorises the seizure and enslavement, unless ransomed by his friends, of every Indian met with at a distance from his tribe, although they may not be at war with each other. The master exercises the power of life and death over his slaves, whom he sacrifices at pleasure in gratification of any superstitious or other whim of the moment.

One morning while I was sketching, I saw upon the rocks the dead body of a young woman, thrown out to the vultures and crows, whom I had seen a few days previously walking about in perfect health. Mr. Finlayson, the gentleman in charge of Fort Victoria, accompanied me to the lodge she belonged to, where we found an Indian woman, her mistress, who made light of her death, and was doubtless the cause of it. She told us that a slave had no right to burial, and became perfectly furious when Mr. Finlayson told her that the slave was far better than herself. "I," she exclaimed, "the daughter of a chief, no better than a dead slave!" and bridling up with all the dignity she could assume, she stalked out, and next morning she had up her lodge and was gone. I was also told by an eye-witness, of a chief, who having erected a colossal idol of wood, sacrificed five slaves to it, barbarously murdering them at its base, and asking in a boasting manner who amongst them could afford to kill so many slaves.

These Indians also flatten their heads, and are far more superstitious than any I have met with. They believe, for instance, that if they can procure the hair of an enemy and confine it with a frog in a hole, the head from which it came will suffer all the torments that the frog endures in its living grave. They are never seen to spit without carefully obliterating all traces of their saliva. This they do lest an enemy should find it, in which case they believe he would have the power of doing them some injury. They always spit on their blankets, if they happen to wear one at the time.

I was indebted to the superstitious fears which they attached to my pictures for the safety and ease with which I mingled amongst them. One of them gave me a great deal of annoyance by continually following and watching me wherever I went, for the purpose of warning the other Indians against my sketching them, telling them that it would expose them to all sorts of ill luck. I repeatedly requested him to desist, but in vain. At last I bethought me of looking steadily at himself, paper and pencil in hand, as if in the act of taking his likeness; when he became greatly alarmed, and asked me what I was about. I replied, "I am taking a sketch of you." He earnestly begged of me to stop, and promised never to annoy me again.

These Indians have a great dance, which is called "The

Medicine Mask Dance;" this is performed both before and after any important action of the tribe, such as fishing, gathering camas, or going on a war party, either for the purpose of gaining the goodwill of the Great Spirit in their undertaking, or else in honour of him for the success which has attended them. Six or eight of the principal men of the tribe, generally medicine-men, adorn themselves with masks cut out of some soft light wood with feathers, highly painted and ornamented, with the eyes and mouth ingeniously made to open and shut. In their hands they hold carved rattles, which are shaken in time to a monotonous song or humming noise (for there are no words to it) which is sung by the whole company as they slowly dance round and round in a circle. [Pl. XLIV; Figs. 190, 191, 193; crIV-538 to 544]

Among the Clal-lums and other tribes inhabiting this region, I have never heard any traditions as to their former origin, although such traditions are common amongst those on the east side of the Rocky Mountains. They do not believe in any future state of punishment, although in this world they suppose themselves exposed to the malicious designs of the skoocoom, or evil genius, to whom they attribute all their misfortune and ill luck.

The good spirit is called Hias-Soch-a-la-Ti-Yah, that is, the great high chief, from whom they obtain all that is good in this life, and to whose happy and peaceful hunting-grounds they will all eventually go to reside for ever in comfort and abundance. The medicine-men of the tribe are supposed to possess a mysterious influence with these two spirits, either for good or evil. They form a secret society, the initiation into which is accompanied with great ceremony and much expense. The candidate has to prepare a feast for his friends and all who choose to partake of it, and make presents to the other medicine-men. A lodge is prepared for him which he enters, and remains alone for three days and nights without food, whilst those already initiated keep dancing and singing round the lodge during the whole time. After this fast, which is supposed to endue him with wonderful skill, he is taken up apparently lifeless and plunged into the nearest cold water, where they rub and wash him until he revives: this they call "washing the dead." As soon as he revives, he runs into the woods, and soon returns dressed as a medicine-man, which generally consists of the light down of the goose stuck all over their bodies and heads with thick grease, and a mantle of frayed cedar bark, with the medicine rattle in his hand. He now collects all his property, blankets, shells, and ornaments, and distributes the whole amongst his friends, trusting for his future support to the fees of his profession. The

dancing and singing are still continued with great vigour, during the division of the property, at the conclusion of which the whole party again sit down to feast, apparently with miraculous appetites, the quantity of food consumed being perfectly incredible.

Their lodges are the largest buildings of any description that I have met with amongst Indians. They are divided in the interior into compartments, so as to accommodate eight or ten families, and are well built, considering that the boards are split from the logs with bone wedges; but they succeed in getting them out with great smoothness and regularity. I took a sketch one day while a party were engaged in gambling in the centre of the lodge. The game is called lehallum, and is played with ten small circular pieces of wood, one of which is marked black; these pieces are shuffled about rapidly by the player between two bundles of frayed cedar bark. His opponent suddenly stops his shuffling, and endeavours to guess in which bundle the blackened piece is concealed. They are so passionately fond of this game that they frequently pass two or three consecutive days and nights at it without ceasing. [Fig. 199; crIV-564, 565]

Saw-se-a the head chief of the Cowitchins,[2] from the Gulf of Georgia, an inveterate gambler, was engaged at the game. [Fig. 200; crIV-568, 569] He had come to the Esquimelt on a friendly visit. This chief was a great warrior in his younger days, and received an arrow through the cheek in one of his battles. He took many captives, whom he usually sold to the tribes further north, thus diminishing their chance of escaping back through a hostile country to their own people, the northern tribes making slaves only of those living south of them. He possessed much of what is considered wealth amongst the Indians, and it gradually accumulated from tributes which he exacted from his people. On his possessions reaching a certain amount it is customary to make a great feast, to which all contribute. The neighbouring chiefs with whom he is in amity are invited, and at the conclusion of the entertainment, he distributes all he has collected since the last feast, perhaps three or four years preceding, among his guests as presents. The amount of property thus collected and given away by a chief is sometimes very considerable. I have heard of one possessing as many as twelve bales of blankets, from twenty to thirty guns, with numberless pots, kettles, and pans, knives, and other articles of cutlery, and great quantities of beads, and other trinkets,

[2] The Victoria "Journal" for May 20 states: "A large number of Indians are now encamped in the vicinity, some of whom arrived in the course of the day, but traded little or no furs."

Plate XIX. Muck-Cranium, a Cree from Fort Carlton. Stark POP6; CRIV-103.

Plate XX. The Man that Always Rides. ROM912.1.44; CRIV-105.

as well as numerous beautiful Chinese boxes, which find their way here from the Sandwich Islands. The object in thus giving his treasures away is to add to his own importance in the eyes of others, his own people often boasting of how much their chief had given away, and exhibiting with pride such things as they had received themselves from him.

I also took a sketch of his son, No. 11, Culchillum. He had a medicine cap on, to which he attached great importance. It was made of human hair, taken from the heads of persons killed in battle, and ornamented with feathers. This, he told me, he only wore on great occasions, such as his present visit to the Clal-lums. On my expressing a wish to purchase it, he told me that he valued it too highly to part with it; nor would he allow me to take it to my tent to finish this sketch without himself accompanying it, for fear it might be deprived of some of its magical properties. [Pl. XLVII; crIV-570, 571]

[Mount Baker: crIV-525]

Chapter XV.

A Coasting Trip.—Indian Curiosity.—Rather Violent Quacks.—An Awkward Hint.—Fighting for a Whale.—A Warm Siege.—Running a Deadly Muck.—Catching Wild Ducks.—A Great Unknown.—The Fate of the "Tonquin."—Fishing for Money.—Shawstun the Ugly. —Caledonian Suttee.—Beautiful Biglips.—Price of a Second Spouse.

As I was desirous to coast round the Straits of De Fuca and visit the tribes on its shores, I employed Chea-clach the head chief and four of his people to take me and the interpreter of the fort round the straits in his canoe; and on the morning of the 6th of May we started about 10 o'clock, running up the east side of Vancouver's Island, and crossed the canal De Aro to the main land.[1] On nearing an Indian village, which contained, as I afterwards found, between five or six hundred Indians, they came rushing down to the beach in an attitude apparently hostile, and as the boats of the exploring expedition had been attacked the year before at the same place, we naturally felt some apprehensions for our safety.

We had no sooner approached the shore than a dense crowd surrounded us, wading up to their middles in water, and seizing our canoe dragged us all high and dry upon the shore, and inquired what we wanted. I replied, that I would explain my business to their chief, who immediately stepped forward in a friendly manner. Having told him that my business was to visit all the Indians, and to take likenesses of the head chiefs and

great warriors, he took me to his lodge, where I seated myself on a mat with him in front of me and commenced my drawing. [crIV-503] In a few minutes the place was crowded, and when it could hold no more, the people clambered to the top of the lodge and tore off the mats from the supports, to which they clung, one upon another, like a swarm of bees, peering down upon us. Look which way I could it seemed one solid mass of hideous faces, daubed with red and white mud.

I hastily finished my sketch and hurried away, first giving the chief a plug of tobacco for his civility. His name was Chea-clach, chief of the Clallums.[2] On coming over I found the wind so strong that I thought it advisable to risk an encampment, and pitched my tent about two hundred yards from the village. We were soon surrounded by hundreds of Indians, the chief among the rest. I gave the latter some supper, and all the news, which he eagerly inquired after, and on my telling him I was tired and wished to go to sleep, which I could not do while so many of his people were about, he instantly arose and desired them to retire, which was promptly obeyed, he going away with them.

About 10 o'clock at night I strolled into the village, and on hearing a great noise in one of the lodges I entered it, and found an old woman supporting one of the handsomest Indian girls I had ever seen. She was in a state of nudity. Cross-legged and naked, in the middle of the room sat the medicine-man, with a wooden dish of water before him; twelve or fifteen other men were sitting round the lodge. The object in view was to cure the girl of a disease affecting her side. As soon as my presence was noticed a space was cleared for me to sit down. The officiating medicine-man appeared in a state of profuse perspiration from the exertions he had used, and soon took his seat among the rest as if quite exhausted; a younger medicine-man then took his place in front of the bowl, and close beside the patient. Throwing off his blanket he commenced singing and gesticulating in the most violent manner, whilst the others kept time by beating with little sticks on hollow wooden bowls and drums, singing continually. After exercising himself in this manner for about half an hour, until the perspiration ran down his body, he darted

[1] The Fort Victoria "Journal" states that Kane with the fort's interpreter crossed the straits on the morning of April 23 to the "Tlalum" (Clallam) village in a "Sangh" canoe. It records that he returned about 10 A.M. on the 30th. *Wanderings* gives May 6 as date of departure and May 14 as date of return.
KJ states that the crossing was 10 miles and that the village at which he arrived was "Cawa Chin" (Cowichan). The published version states that it was Clallam (see note 2). KJ does not have the phrase "to the main land."
[2] The preceding sentence does not occur in KJ or KWMS. The introduction of it here in the published version bestows on the chief the name Chea-clach which has already been given as the name of Kane's guide on the tour of the straits.

suddenly upon the young woman, catching hold of her side with his teeth and shaking her for a few minutes, while the patient seemed to suffer great agony. He then relinquished his hold, and cried out he had got it, at the same time holding his hands to his mouth; after which he plunged them in the water and pretended to hold down with great difficulty the disease which he had extracted, lest it might spring out and return to its victim.

At length, having obtained the mastery over it, he turned round to me in an exulting manner, and held something up between the finger and thumb of each hand, which had the appearance of a piece of cartilage, whereupon one of the Indians sharpened his knife, and divided it in two, leaving one end in each hand. One of the pieces he threw into the water, and the other into the fire, accompanying the action with a diabolical noise, which none but a medicine-man can make. After which he got up perfectly satisfied with himself, although the poor patient seemed to me anything but relieved by the violent treatment she had undergone.

[Straits Indians: crIV-504, 505, 506, 572?, 573]

May 7th.—We this morning left our encampment before daylight, without waiting to pay our respects to the chief. In the afternoon we touched at Whitby's Island, which divides the Straits of De Fuca from Puget's Sound. [crIV-507] A Catholic mission had been established on the island some few years before, but was obliged to be given up, owing to the turbulent disposition of the Indians, who, though friendly to the Hudson Bay Company as traders, look with great suspicion upon others who attempt to settle there, fearing that the whites would attempt to dispossess them of their lands.

On approaching the village of Toanichum, we perceived two stout bastions of logs, well calculated for defence in Indian warfare, and built with considerable skill. As our canoe neared the land, I observed them hurrying towards these bastions, and shortly afterwards we heard several shots. Supposing this to be intended as a salute, we drew still nearer, and were astonished at hearing more discharges, and seeing the balls fall near our canoe. My Indians immediately ceased paddling, and it was with the utmost difficulty that I could prevail on them to proceed. Had we shown the least inclination to retreat, I have no doubt that the firing would have been continued, and with better aim. However, on my landing and asking what they meant, they said it was only done for the purpose of letting me know that they were in the possession of fire-arms. [Fig. 176; crIV-511]

They afterwards treated me very hospitably. Lock-hi-num, the chief, offered us all the supplies at his command. It was, however, with the greatest difficulty that I could prevail on him to let me take his likeness; but at last I succeeded, by showing him the likenesses of several other chiefs, and telling him that they were intended to be shown to his Great Mother, the Queen, who no doubt would be much disappointed if his was not amongst the rest. [Fig. 175; crIV-508] I remained amongst them two or three hours, and sketched the village. I also succeeded in getting a very good-looking woman, the wife of the second chief, to sit for me. [crIV-509, 510] She had the flattest head of any I had seen in that vicinity. We then crossed over to the south side of the strait, and encamped for the night.

May 8th.—Proceeded up the south side of the straits in our canoe, and encamped on a long sand spit, projecting into the straits three or four miles.

May 9th.—Made a portage across the spit, and by the evening reached I-eh-nus, a Clallum village or fort. It was composed of a double row of strong pickets, the outer ones about twenty feet high, and the inner row about five feet, enclosing a space of 150 feet square. The whole of this inner space is roofed in, and divided into small compartments, or pens, for the use of each separate family. There were about 200 of the tribe in the fort at the time of my arrival. Their chief, Yates-sut-soot, received me with great cordiality. [crIV-514?] I remained with them three days, and all the tribe treated me with kindness, with one solitary exception, proceeding from a superstitious fear that the presence of a white man in a lodge would produce sickness in the family. Yates-sut-soot was very apprehensive of an attack from the Macaw Indians, and believing my powers and influence as a medicine-man to be of much importance, eagerly asked me which side I would take, in the event of their coming. I replied, that as long as they treated me well I would be their friend.

A few months before my arrival a great battle had been fought with the Macaws, in which the Clallums had suffered very severely. It originated in the Clallums having taken possession of the body of a whale which had been killed by the Macaws, but had got away, and was drifted by the current to the village. The Macaws demanded a share of the spoil, and also the return of their spears, some fifteen or twenty in number, which were sticking in the carcase; both demands were refused, and a feeling of animosity sprang up beween the tribes.

There are few whales now caught on the coast, but the Indians are most enthusiastic in the hunt, and the blubber is highly prized amongst them; it is cut into strips about four inches wide and two feet long, and eaten generally with dried fish.

Their manner of catching the whale is ingenious, and from the description which I received of the hunt must be very exciting. Upon a whale being seen blowing in the offing, they rush down to their large canoes, and push off with ten or twelve men in each. Each canoe is furnished with a number of strong seal-skin bags filled with air, and made with great care and skill, capable of containing about ten gallons each. To each bag is attached a barbed spear-head, made of bone or iron, when they can get it, by a strong string, eight or nine feet long, and in the socket of the spear-head is fitted a handle, seven or eight feet in length. Upon coming up with the whale, the barbed heads with the bags attached are driven into him and the handles withdrawn. The attack is continually renewed, until the whale is no longer able to sink from the buoyancy of the bags, when he is despatched and towed ashore. They are sometimes led twenty or thirty miles out to sea in the chase, but such is the admirable construction of their canoes, and so skilfully are they managed, that an accident rarely happens.

A few months after the quarrel about the whale, the brother of Yellow-cum, the head chief of the Macaws, went to Fort Victoria to trade for ammunition and other necessaries, and on his return was attacked by the Clallums. He and one of his men were killed, but three others escaped, and succeeded in getting to Cape Flattery, where Yellow-cum resided. Immediately upon hearing of the death of his brother, Yellow-cum fitted out twelve of his largest canoes, with twenty warriors in each, and made a sudden descent upon I-eh-nus; but he soon perceived that he had little chance of success while the Clallums remained within their enclosure completely protected by the logs, while his men were exposed without any shelter to the galling fire which was kept up through the openings between the pickets. He accordingly sent some of his party to the westward side of the fort, who set fire to the grass and wood, which soon communicated with the buildings, while he and the rest of his party kept watch to prevent any from escaping. The Clallums were soon forced to rush out and cover the retreat of their women and children into the mountains. Yates-sut-soot and Yellow-cum fought with great bravery hand to hand, with nothing but their knives, until they were separated in the mêlée. I saw one of the Clallums who had been shockingly gashed in the battle, having had to run through a long line of the Macaws, each of whom made a cut at him as he passed. The buildings were only partly

consumed. Yellow-cum took eighteen prisoners, mostly females, who were made slaves, and he had eight heads stuck on poles placed in the bows of the canoes on his return. These heads are carried to their village, and placed in front of the lodge of the warriors who had killed them as trophies. These Indians do not scalp their enemies. [Figs. 177, 180; crIV-515, 517]

Near the village are numerous singular graves with different erections over them, on which the Indians place the offerings for the dead. [Fig. 179; crIV-516]

May 12th.—We left with the intention of returning to Vancouver's Island, but the wind being very violent we had to put back to the shore, which we coasted for twelve or fourteen miles, until we came to the mouth of a river. The land to the south of us rises in one continuous range of high mountains far as the eye can reach, the peaks of many of which are covered with snow, even at this period of the year. We ascended the river about a mile to an Indian fishing station called Suck. The whole breadth of the stream is obstructed by stakes and open work of willow and other branches, with holes at intervals leading into wicker compartments, which the fish enter in their way up the river from the sea. Once in they cannot get out, as the holes are formed with wicker work inside shaped something like a funnel or a wire mouse-trap. In this preserve they are speared without trouble when required, and the village has thus a constant supply of food. They were catching great quantities at the time of my arrival, and we obtained an abundant supply for a small piece of tobacco. [Fig. 182; crIV-520, 521, 522]

These Indians also take a great many ducks by means of a fine net stretched between two posts about thirty feet high, and fifty or sixty feet apart. This is erected in a narrow valley through which the ducks fly in the evening. A smoky fire is made at the bottom of the net, which prevents the ducks from seeing it, and when they fly against it they become confused and fall down, when they are seized by the Indians.

The wind being still too strong for us to venture, we remained until the 14th. Chaw-u-wit, the chief's daughter, allowed me to take her likeness. Whilst she was sitting a great many of the Indians surrounded us, causing her much annoyance, as their native bashfulness renders all squaws peculiarly sensitive to any public notice or ridicule. She was, perhaps, about the best-looking girl I had seen in the straits, which is certainly no very high compliment to the rest of the female population. [Fig. 178; crIV-518, 519]

Chea-clack considering that our canoe was too small, succeeded in changing it for a larger one, and at 3 o'clock A.M. we embarked and proceeded to make a traverse of thirty-two miles in an open sea. When we had been out for about a couple of hours the wind increased to a perfect gale, and blowing against an ebb tide caused a heavy swell. We were obliged to keep one man constantly baling to prevent our being swamped. [Fig. 183; crIV-524]

The Indians on board now commenced one of their wild chants, which increased to a perfect yell whenever a wave larger than the rest approached; this was accompanied with blowing and spitting against the wind as if they were in angry contention with the evil spirit of the storm. It was altogether a scene of the most wild and intense excitement: the mountainous waves roaming round our little canoe as if to engulph us every moment, the wind howling over our heads, and the yelling Indians, made it actually terrific. I was surprised at the dexterity with which they managed the canoe, all putting out their paddles on the windward side whenever a wave broke, thus breaking its force and guiding the spray over our heads to the other side of the boat.

It was with the greatest anxiety that I watched each coming wave as it came thundering down, and I must confess that I felt considerable fear as to the event. However, we arrived safely at the fort at 2 P.M., without further damage than what we suffered from intense fatigue, as might be expected, from eleven hours' hard work, thoroughly soaked and without food; but even this soon passed away before the cheerful fire and "hearty" dinner with which we were welcomed at Fort Victoria. One of the Indians told me he had no fear during the storm, except on my account, as his brethren could easily reach the shore by swimming, even should the distance have been ten miles.

[Olympics: crIV-523]

A couple of days after my arrival at the fort, I was engaged in taking the likeness of an Indian. The door of my room was suddenly thrown open, and an Indian entered of a very plain and unprepossessing appearance. As I was unwilling to be disturbed, I rather unceremoniously dismissed the intruder, and closed the door on him, supposing him to be some common Indian; for were I to admit all comers, I should have been annoyed from morning till night. About half an hour afterwards, Mr. Finlayson came in, and told me that the great Yellow-cum, the head chief of the Macaws at Cape Flattery, had arrived at the fort. I had heard so much of this chief, both from his enemies, the Clallums at I-eh-nus, and the Indians at

Fort Vancouver, that I had determined to go to Cape Flattery, a distance of sixty miles, to see him. I was therefore very glad of his coming, as it would save me the journey; and I immediately went out in search of him, and was not a little astonished and vexed to find in him the visitor I had so rudely sent out of my room. I of course apologised, by stating my ignorance of who he was, and told him how anxious I had been to see him, and of my intention of going to Cape Flattery for that purpose. He said that he willingly acquitted me of any intentional insult; but he had felt extremely mortified at being treated so before so many Indians.

He accompanied me to my room, where I made a sketch of him, and had from him a recital of much of his private history. [crIV-580?] Yellow-cum's father was the pilot of the unfortunate "Tonquin," the vessel sent out by John Jacob Astor to trade with the Indians north of Vancouver's Island, mentioned in Washington Irving's "Astoria." He was the only survivor who escaped from the vessel previous to her being blown up, the rest of the unfortunate crew having been butchered on board, or blown up with the ship. It was impossible to obtain a clear narrative of this melancholy event, as no white man lived to tell the tale.

Yellow-cum is the wealthiest man of his tribe. His property consists principally of slaves and ioquas, a small shell found at Cape Flattery, and only there, in great abundance. These shells are used as money, and a great traffic is carried on among all the tribes by means of them. They are obtained at the bottom of the sea, at a considerable depth, by means of a long pole stuck in a flat board about fifteen inches square. From this board a number of bone pieces project, which, when pressed down, enter the hollow ends of the shells, which seem to be attached to the bottom by their small ends. The shells stick on the pieces, and are thus brought to the surface. They are from an inch and a half to two inches in length, and are white, slender, and hollow, and tapering to a point; slightly curved, and about the size of an ordinary tobacco-pipe stem. They are valuable in proportion to their length, and their value increases according to a fixed ratio, forty shells being the standard number to extend a fathom's length; which number, in that case, is equal in value to a beaver skin; but if thirty-nine be found large enough to make the fathom, it would be worth two beavers' skins; if thirty-eight, three skins; and so on, increasing one beaver skin for every shell less than the standard number.

Yellow-cum presented me with a pair of ear ornaments of

these shells, consisting of seventy or eighty shells in each. His wealth also partly consisted of sea otter skins, which are the most valuable fur found on the North American coast, their usual value in the tariff being twelve blankets; two blankets being equal to a gun; tobacco and ammunition and other things in proportion. The blanket is the standard by which the value of all articles on the north-west coast is calculated. Independent of his wealth, he possesses vast influence over all the tribes, and has become head chief from his own personal prowess and ability, and not from any hereditary claim to that dignity. It may be adduced, as a proof of the courage of this chief, and of his personal confidence, that I saw him at the fort surrounded by, and in cheerful conversation with, several of the chiefs of the Clallums, with whom he had often been engaged in deadly conflict. His prudence, however, led him to remain inside the fort after nightfall.

I visited the lodges of the Eus-ā-nich Indians, who were on a visit. The chief was very rich, and had eight wives with him. I made him understand, by showing him some sketches, that I wished to take his likeness. This was, however, opposed so violently by his ladies, that I was glad to escape out of reach of their tongues, as they were all chattering together, while he sat like a Grand Turk, evidently flattered by the interest they showed for his welfare. A few days afterwards, I met the chief some distance from his camp, and alone, when he willingly consented to let me take his likeness upon my giving him a piece of tobacco. [crIV-574?]

In one of my daily excursions, I was particularly struck by the ugliness of an Indian whom I met. Upon inquiry, I found he was Shawstun, the head chief of the Sinahōmās. He inquired very earnestly if my sketching him would not involve the risk of his dying; and after I had finished the sketch, and given him a piece of tobacco, he held it up for some moments, and said it was a small recompense for risking his life. He followed me afterwards for two or three days, begging of me to destroy the picture; and at last, to get rid of him, I made a rough copy of it, which I tore up in his presence, pretending that it was the original. [Fig. 181; crIV-512, 513]

I remained on Vancouver's Island until the 10th of June; and perhaps it would be as well, before my taking leave of it, to give a general summary of the information I acquired, from personal observation, and from the gentlemen of the Hudson's Bay Company, respecting the characteristics of the different tribes inhabiting these regions.

The Indians south of the Columbia River tattoo themselves below the mouth, which gives a light blue appearance to the countenance. Those at the mouth of the Columbia, and for a hundred miles up it, as well as those at Puget's Sound, and the Straits of De Fuca, and at the southern part of Vancouver's Island, have their heads flattened down in their infancy, as represented in the sketches of the Chinook tribe. [crIV-579] Those inhabiting the north part of the island have their heads compressed into a conical shape during infancy. This is done by means of a bandage, which is wound round the forehead, and gradually tightened, until the head becomes of the required shape. [Fig. 201; crIV-575 to 578]

The next tribe lying north of these on the continent are called by the voyageurs "Babines," or Big-lips, from the fact of the females having their under lips enlarged by the insertion of a piece of wood. [Figs. 203, 204, 205; crIV-585, 586, 587, 589, 590] A small, slender piece of bone is inserted through the under lip of the infant, from below upwards, and is gradually enlarged, until a flat piece of wood three inches long, and an inch and a half wide, has caused the lip to protrude to a frightful extent, the protrusion increasing with age. Great importance is attached to the size of the lip, as it constitutes the standard of female beauty; it also marks the difference between native free women and their slaves.

When the stick is removed on any occasion the lip drops down to the chin, presenting one of the most disgusting spectacles imaginable.

The men sometimes wear a ring through the nose, formed of bone, or brass if they can get it; but the practice is not universal. [Fig. 202; crIV-583, 584] They wear a cap made of the fibres of cedar-bark, woven very finely together, and a blanket made from the wool of the mountain sheep; they are very valuable, and take years in making. For one [blanket] which I procured with great difficulty, I had to pay five pounds of tobacco, ten charges of ammunition, one blanket, one pound of beads, two check shirts, and one ounce of vermilion. [crIV-588]

The next tribes, still more north than the last, insert beads of various colours, two-thirds of their depth, into the whole length of the upper lip, giving it the appearance of so much bead work. [Haida: crIV-581. Kwakiutl: Pl. XLVIII; crIV-582]

In the interior of New Caledonia, which is east of Vancouver's Island and north of the Columbia, among the tribe called "Taw-wa-tins," who are also Babines, and also among other tribes in their neighbourhood, the custom prevails of burning the bodies, with circumstances of peculiar barbarity to the widows of the deceased. The dead body of the husband is laid naked upon a large heap of resinous wood, his wife is then placed upon the body and covered over with a skin; the pile is then lighted, and the poor woman is compelled to remain until she is nearly suffocated, when she is allowed to descend as best she can through the smoke and flames. No sooner, however, does she reach the ground, than she is expected to prevent the body from becoming distorted by the action of the fire on the muscles and sinews; and whenever such an event takes place she must, with her bare hands, restore the burning corpse to its proper position; her person being the whole time exposed to the scorching effects of the intense heat. Should she fail in the due performance of this indispensable rite, from weakness or the intensity of her pain, she is held up by some one until the body is consumed. A continual singing and beating of drums is kept up throughout the ceremony, which drowns her cries. Afterwards she must collect the unconsumed pieces of bone and ashes and put them into a bag made for the purpose, which she has to carry on her back for three years; remaining for the time a slave to her husband's relations, and being neither allowed to wash nor comb herself for the whole time, so that she soon becomes a most disgusting object. At the expiration of the three years, a feast is given by her tormentors, who invite all the friends and relations of her and themselves. At the commencement they deposit with great ceremony the remains of the burnt dead in a box, which they affix to the top of a high pole, and dance around it. The widow is then stripped naked and smeared from head to foot with fish oil, over which one of the by-standers throws a quantity of swan's down, covering her entire person. She is then obliged to dance with the others. After all this is over she is free to marry again, if she have the inclination, and courage enough to venture on a second risk of being roasted alive and the subsequent horrors. [crIV-591]

It has often happened that a widow who has married a second husband, in the hope perhaps of not outliving him, committed suicide in the event of her second husband's death, rather than undergo a second ordeal. I was unable to learn any explanation of the motive for these cruel rites, and can only account for them in the natural selfishness, laziness, and cruelty of the Indians, who probably hope by these means to render their wives more attentive to their personal ease and comfort; whilst, at the same time, it secures them from assassination either by a jealous or an errant spouse.

Chapter XVI.

Searching for a lost Wife.—A simple Ruse.—A Harvest of Fish.—The Legend of the Rock.—The little Fisherman.—Battle of the Dwarfs and Geese.—A Ride on a Whale.—An Indian Niobe.—Naming the Dead.—Licensed to get Drunk.—Settling old Scores.—Stealing a Skull.—Punishing Deserters.—An Amateur Surgeon.—Scarcity of Wood.—Rattlesnakes in Plenty.—The Grasshopper and Wolf.—The Magic Salmon Leap.

June 9th.—The Company's vessel which annually brings out goods and despatches for the interior having arrived, Mr. Finlayson was anxious to forward the letters on, and knowing that I was soon to start on my return, he asked me if I would take them to Fort Vancouver.[1] I was very anxious to do anything in my power in return for the hospitality and kindness I had received, and accordingly commenced my preparations for starting on the following morning. An old Nasqually chief had come down to the coast to look for a favourite wife who had been carried off by some of his predatory neighbours, and, as he supposed, had been sold somewhere in Vancouver's Island. But not being successful in his search, he was now returning, and I engaged to go with him. He was very glad of my company, as my being the bearer of despatches would be a certain protection for the whole party from whatever Indians we might meet. I asked him how he had managed to escape on coming down, and he showed me an old piece of newspaper, which he said he held up whenever he met with strange Indians, and that they, supposing it to be a letter for Fort Victoria, had allowed him to pass without molestation.

The gentlemen in charge of the various posts, have frequent occasion to send letters, sometimes for a considerable distance, when it is either inconvenient or impossible for them to fit out a canoe with their own men to carry it. In such cases the letter is given to an Indian, who carries it as far as suits his convenience and safety. He then sells the letter to another, who carries it until he finds an opportunity of selling it to advantage; it is thus passed on and sold until it arrives at its destination, gradually increasing in value according to the distance, and the last possessor receiving the reward for its safe delivery. In this manner

[1] The Fort Victoria "Journal" for June 5, 1847, records the departure of Kane, bearing a packet of letters received from England by the *Mary Dare*, for Nisqually in the company of Indians from that area who had been visiting. This date differs from the date in *Wanderings*, above.

letters are frequently sent with perfect security, and with much greater rapidity than could be done otherwise.

June 10th.—Early in the morning I embarked with the chief, a wife he had brought with him, and two slaves: we paddled on all day, and made good progress. In the evening we encamped under a high rock, where we found some goose eggs, of which we made a hearty supper.

June 11th.—We came to a rocky island, which was covered with thousands of seal, playing and basking in the sun. We shot several of them, as the Indians highly prize the blubber as food; but it was far too oily for my stomach. I, however, shot a white-headed eagle, and roasted him for my supper, and found him particularly good eating.

June 12th.—In the evening we arrived at an Indian village, where we stopped for the night; the whole surface of the water at this place seemed to be alive with the gambles of a small silvery fish, dancing and glistening in the rays of the setting sun. This fish is about the size of our sardines, and is caught in immense numbers; it is called there ulé kun, and is much prized on account of its delicacy and extraordinary fatness. When dried this fish will burn from one end to the other with a clear steady light like a candle.

There were several canoes out fishing in the evening, and they caught them with astonishing rapidity: this is done by means of an instrument about seven feet long, the handle is about three feet, into which is fixed a curved wooden blade about four feet, something the shape of a sabre, with the edge at the back. In this edge, at the distance of about an inch and a half, are inserted sharp bone teeth, about an inch long. The Indian stands in the canoe and, holding it as he would a paddle, draws it edgeways with both hands rapidly through the dense mass of fish, which are so thick that every tooth will strike a fish. One knock across the thwarts safely deposits them in the bottom of the canoe. This is done with such rapidity that they never use nets for this description of fishing.

June 13th.—To-day as we neared the shore we perceived two deer grazing, which the Indians were anxious to go after, but as we had already lost some time on the way I was more anxious to proceed. While at a very long distance I fired my double-barrelled gun at them, more in the hopes of driving them away than of killing them, when, much to the astonishment of both myself and the Indians, one of them fell dead. The chief looked very hard at me and then examined the gun, apparently in doubt whether the magic was in the gun or myself. I said

nothing, but took it all as a matter of course, whilst the Indians evidently looked upon me as a person not to be trifled with. We had a splendid supper that evening on our venison, and I took good care not to test the qualities of my gun again before them, although they often asked me.

June 14th.—Whilst passing an isolated rock, standing six or seven feet high above the water, and a little more than four feet in circumference, the old chief asked me if I knew what it had originally been. On my replying in the negative, he told me the following legend:—

"It is many moons since a Nasqually family lived near this spot. It consisted of a widow with four sons,—one of them was by her first husband, the other three by the second. The three younger sons treated their elder brother with great unkindness, refusing him any share of the produce of their hunting and fishing; he, on the contrary, wishing to conciliate them, always gave them a share of his spoils. He, in fact, was a great medicine-man, although this was unknown to them, and, being tired of their harsh treatment, which no kindness on his part seemed to soften, he at length resolved to retaliate. He accordingly one day entered the lodge, where they were feasting, and told them that there was a large seal a short distance off. They instantly seized their spears and started in the direction he pointed out, and, coming up to the animal, the eldest drove his spear into it. This seal was 'a great medicine,' a familiar of the elder brother, who had himself created him for the occasion. The foremost of them had no sooner driven in his spear than he found it impossible to disengage his hand from the handle, or to draw it out; the two others drove in their spears with the like effect. The seal now took to the water, dragging them after it, and swam far out to sea. Having travelled on for many miles they saw an island in the distance, towards which the seal made. On nearing the shore they found, for the first time, they could remove their hands from their spears. They accordingly landed, and supposing themselves in some enemy's country, they hid themselves in a clump of bushes from observation. While lying concealed, they saw a diminutive canoe coming round a point in the distance, paddled by a very little man, who, when he came opposite to where they were, anchored his boat with a stone attached to a long line, without perceiving them. He now sprang over the side, and diving down, remained a long time under water. At length he rose to the surface, and brought with him a large fish, which he threw into the boat: this he repeated several times, each time looking in to count the fish he had caught. The three brothers being very hungry, one of them offered to swim out while the little man was under water, and steal one of the fish. This he safely accomplished before the return of the fisherman; but the little fellow no sooner returned with another fish than he discovered that one of those already caught was missing, and, stretching out his hand, he passed it slowly along the horizon, until it pointed directly to their place of concealment. He now drew up his anchor and paddled to the shore, and immediately discovered the three brothers, and being as miraculously strong as he was diminutive, he tied their hands and feet together and, throwing them into his canoe, jumped in and paddled back in the direction from whence he had come. Having rounded the distant point, where they had first descried him, they came to a village inhabited by a race of people as small as their captor, their houses, boats, and utensils being all in proportion to themselves.

"The three brothers were then taken out and thrown, bound as they were, into a lodge, while a council was convened to decide upon their fate. During the sitting of the council an immense flock of birds, resembling geese, but much larger, pounced down upon the inhabitants, and commenced a violent attack. These birds had the power of throwing their sharp quills like the porcupine, and although the little warriors fought with great valour, they soon became covered with the piercing darts and all sunk insensible on the ground. When all resistance had ceased the birds took to flight and disappeared.

"The brothers had witnessed the conflict from their place of confinement, and with much labour had succeeded in releasing themselves from their bonds, when they went to the battle ground, and commenced pulling the quills from the apparently lifeless bodies; but no sooner had they done this, than all instantly returned to consciousness. When all of them had become well again they wished to express their gratitude to their preservers, and offered to grant whatsoever they should desire. The brothers requested to be sent back to their own country. A council was accordingly called to decide on the easiest mode of doing so, and they eventually determined upon employing a whale for the purpose. The brothers were then seated on the back of the monster, and proceeded in the direction of Nasqually. However, when they had reached about half way, the whale began to think what a fool he was for carrying them instead of turning them into porpoises, and letting them swim home themselves. Now the whale is considered as a 'Soch-a-li-ti-yah,' or Great Spirit, although not the same as the 'Hias-Soch-a-li-ti-yah,' or Great High Spirit, possessing greater powers than all

other animals put together, and no sooner had he thought upon the matter than he carried it into effect. This, accordingly, is the way that the porpoises first came into existence, and accounts for their being constantly at war with the seals, one of which species was the cause of their misfortunes. After the three brothers had so strangely disappeared, their mother came down to the beach and remained there for days, watching for their return and bewailing their absence with tears. Whilst thus engaged one day the whale happened to pass by, and, taking pity on her distress, turned her into that stone."

I could not observe any very special peculiarity in the formation of this rock while paddling past it in a canoe; and, at least from the points of observation presented to my eye, no resemblance to the human figure, such as the conclusion of the legend might lead us to anticipate, appeared to be traceable. Standing, however, as this rock does, entirely isolated, and without any other being visible for miles around, it has naturally become an object of special note to the Indians, and is not uncalculated, from its solitary position, to be made the scene of some of the fanciful creations of their superstitious credulity.

June 15th.—We arrived at Nasqually, where I procured horses to take me to the Cowlitz River. I again crossed Prairie de Bute and Mud Mountain, and arrived at my old friend Kiscox's lodge on the evening of the third day; but, to my astonishment, I found him and his family unusually distant in their manners, and the children even running away from me and hiding. At last he asked if I had not taken the likeness of a woman when last among them. I said that I had, and mentioned her name, Caw-wacham, alluding to the portrait of a woman and child, No. 10 [crIV-491]; a dead silence ensued, nor could I get the slightest answer to my inquires. Upon leaving the lodge, I met a half-breed, who told me that Caw-wacham was dead, and that I was supposed to be the cause of her death. The silence was occasioned by my having mentioned a dead person's name, which is considered disrespectful to the deceased, and unlucky.

I immediately procured a canoe, and started for Fort Vancouver, down the river, paddling all night, well knowing the danger that would result from my meeting with any of her relations, and arrived safely at Fort Vancouver on the 20th of June,[2] with my budget of news from the civilised world. Here I had to remain until the 1st of July, waiting for the boats, which were daily arriving from New Caledonia and the Upper Columbia with furs, and reloading again with their winter outfits

---

[2] KJ states that Kane arrived at Fort Vancouver on June 11 after a nine-day passage from Fort Victoria.

a Cree War cap.

Paul Kane - 1846

Plate XXI. Otisskun or "The Horn," a Cree, Fort Pitt. Stark POP17; CrIV-127.

for their posts in the interior. During this time I amused myself in hunting and sketching. I took a sketch of a Chinook boy with a singular headdress of beads; the design seemed to be entirely original with him, as I had never before met with any resembling it. [Fig. 156; crIV-420, 421]

July 1st.—The nine boats composing the brigade had now completed their outfit, and were all prepared for their different destinations. Mr. Lewis [3] was to command until he arrived at his own post, Colville; but we had great difficulty in collecting the men, between sixty and seventy in number: some wanted their allowance of rum, or regale, before they started, given to the Company's men only preparatory to a long voyage. Others were bidding farewell to their Indian loves, and were hard to be found; in fact, all hesitated to give up the life of idleness and plenty in which they had been luxuriating for the last two or three weeks, for the toils and privations which they well knew were before them. However, towards evening we succeeded in collecting our crews, and Mr. Lewis promised them their regale on the first fitting opportunity. The fort gave us a salute of seven guns, which was repeated by the Company's ship lying at the store-house. The occupants of the fort crowded round us; and at last, amidst cheers and hearty wishes for our safety, we pushed off. Owing to the lateness of the hour at which we started, we only got to the Company's mills, eight miles from the fort, that evening.

July 2nd.—We started very early this morning, and the men plied their oars with unusual vigour, as they were to get their regale this evening. [crIV-389, 390] By 2 o'clock P.M. we had reached the Prairie de Thé, a distance of twenty-eight miles. Here we landed to let the men have their customary debauch. In the Hudson's Bay Company's service no rations of liquor are given to the men, either while they are stopping in fort or while travelling, nor are they allowed to purchase any; but when they are about commencing a long journey, the men are given what is called a regale, which consists of a pint of rum each. This, however, they are not allowed to drink until they are some distance from the post, where those who are entitled to get drunk may do so without interfering with the resident servants of the establishment.

Immediately on landing, the camp was made, fires lit, and victuals cooked; in short, every preparation for the night was completed before the liquor was given out. As soon as the men got their allowance, they commenced all sorts of athletic games; running, jumping, wrestling, &c. We had eight Sandwich Islanders amongst the crews, who afforded great amusement by a

sort of pantomimic dance accompanied by singing. The whole thing was exceedingly grotesque and ridiculous, and elicited peals of laughter from the audience; gradually, as the rum began to take effect, the brigades, belonging to different posts, began to boast of their deeds of daring and endurance. This gradually led on to trying which was the best man. Numberless fights ensued; black eyes and bloody noses became plentiful, but all terminated in good humour.[4] The next day the men were stupid from the effects of drink, but quite good-tempered and obedient; in fact, the fights of the previous evening seemed to be a sort of final settlement of all old grudges and disputes. We did not get away until 3 o'clock P.M., and only made a distance of about fourteen miles.[5] We encamped at the foot of the Cascades, where the first portage in ascending the Columbia commences. [Figs. 146, 149; crIV-388, 396]

July 4th and 5th.—We were engaged both days in carrying the parcels of goods across the portage, and dragging the empty boats up by lines.[6] This is a large fishing station, and immense numbers of fish are caught by the Hudson's Bay Company and the Cascade Indians, who congregate about here in great numbers at the fishing season, which happened at the time of our passing. They gave us a good deal of trouble and uneasiness, as it was only by the utmost vigilance that we could keep them from stealing. On the evening of the 5th we got over the portage; and, although the men were tired, we proceeded seven miles further up the river before we encamped, so as to get clear of the Indians. [Fig. 145; crIV-384 to 387]

In strolling about while the men were engaged in carrying the goods across the Cascades, I discovered a large burying-ground of Flatheads, and I was very anxious to procure a skull. To do this, however, I had to use the greatest precaution, and ran no small risk, not only in getting it, but in having it in my possession afterwards; even the voyageurs would have refused to travel with me, had they known that I had it in my collection, not only on account of the superstitious dread in which they hold these burial-places, but also on account of the danger of discovery, which might have cost the lives of the whole party. I, however, took advantage of the men being busy watching the Indians to keep them from stealing, and the Indians being

---

[3] John Lewes, chief trader and chief factor of the Hudson's Bay Company, who was active in the Columbia Department, and whom Kane had already met on his outward trip; see also Appendix 10, Letter 11. KJ states that Donald Manson, then stationed in New Caledonia, was second in command of the party.

[4] In KJ Kane complains that the noise kept him awake all night.

[5] KJ states that they travelled three, not fourteen, miles.

[6] KJ notes that they carried 450 parcels each weighing 65 pounds across the portage.

equally busy in watching for an opportunity to steal, and succeeded in getting a very perfect skull smuggled in among my traps without the slightest suspicion.

At the place where we encamped on the evening of the 5th, there were a great many stumps of trees standing in the river; it is supposed to be a landslip. I made a sketch of it. [Fig. 144; crIV-382, 383]

During the night, two of our Sandwich Islanders deserted. A boat was immediately unloaded, and sent back, with the view of intercepting them at the Cascades. They had received 10l. sterling each in goods as their outfit, and, in passing the Cascades, had hid their bags in the woods, and hoped to get back again to the coast with their booty. Their pursuers, however, discovered their track, and found the goods, though they did not find the men; but knowing they must be near the place, they got Tomaquin to look after them. [Fig. 147; crIV-391] The next morning, Tomaquin with three of his tribe, brought them in: each of the Indians, while paddling, carried his knife in his mouth, ready to strike should the Islanders make any resistance. It appeared that they had visited his camp in the night, on which he assembled his tribe and surrounded them; when the Islanders, thinking they were going to be killed, surrendered and begged for mercy. Tomaquin was rewarded with four blankets and four shirts.[7] The next thing was to punish the deserters, and very little time was wasted in either finding a verdict or carrying it out. Our guide, a tall powerful Iroquois, took one of them, and Mr. Lewis seized the other, as they stepped from the canoe: the punishment consisted in simply knocking the men down, kicking them until they got up, and knocking them down again until they could not get up any more, when they finished them off with a few more kicks. Mr. Lewis, although a very powerful man, had only his left hand, a gun having exploded in his right, shattering it so dreadfully that he was obliged to have it cut off at the wrist; but the operation having been performed in the roughest backwood fashion, it often pained him, and the doctors wanted him to let them cut it off again, so as to make a good stump, but he would not let them. On this stump he usually wore a heavy wooden shield, but, luckily for the poor Islanders, it was not on when they landed, or, as he said himself, he might have killed them. The punishment of those men must of course appear savage and severe to persons in civilised life, but it is only treatment of this kind that will keep this sort of men in order; and desertion or insubordination, on journeys through the interior, is often attended by the most dangerous consequences to the whole party.

July 6th.—It rained heavily all day, and the wind became so high, that we were obliged to put ashore, although the ground was very low and swampy, and the mosquitoes were in myriads.

July 7th.—Passed a Methodist mission,[8] and came to the Portage of the Dalles. We employed the Indians here to make the portage, thirty to each boat, for which each man receives five balls and powder. The Indians at the Dalles do not distort the head. The country begins to look barren, and is entirely destitute of wood. Salmon in great abundance is caught in these rapids. [crIV-392]

July 8th.—Arrived at the Chutes: we found no difficulty as to the carriage of our boats, as the Indians were very numerous and willing to be employed. In former times these people were more troublesome than any other tribes on the Columbia River. In making this portage, it was then necessary to have sixty armed men for the protection of the goods. It was here that the man with the tin box was shot, mentioned in Washington Irving's "Astoria." We were on the present occasion obliged to buy wood from the Indians, to cook our supper, not a tree nor even a bush being visible in any direction. The Indians, who obtain drift-wood for their own use when the river is high and brings it within their reach, of course prize it highly from its scarcity. The Indians who reside and congregate about the Chutes for the purpose of fishing, are called the Skeen tribe; they do not flatten their heads, and appear to be a hardy, brave people, at this time particularly friendly to the Hudson's Bay Company people, and at peace with their Flathead neighbours. The Indians hereabouts catch a few deer and some other game, out of whose skins they make whatever dresses they wear, which are, however, very scanty. I give, in Sketch No. 12, the likeness of Mancemuckt, the chief; he wore a fox-skin cap and a leather deerskin shirt at the time. [Fig. 148; crIV-393, 394, 395]

July 9th.—Left the Chutes with a strong fair wind, running up the rapids under sail, while the water curled over the bows of the boats, which we only prevented from filling by shortening the sail. We encamped in the neighbourhood of a very thievish tribe of Indians, according to report, and were obliged to make

---

[7] KJ recounts that Kane asked Tomaquin if he were not afraid of the Sandwich Islanders. Tomaquin replied that it was only the whites of whom he was afraid.

[8] The Methodist station at the Dalles had been founded among the Wasco Indians in April 1838 by the Rev. H. K. W. Perkins at a place called Wascopam. It was under the auspices of the Oregon Missionary Society, a Methodist organization. The mission was taken over by the American Board of Commissioners for Foreign Missions in 1847. See Gustavus Hines, *Oregon, Its History, Conditions and Prospects* (New York 1859), pp. 30–31.

use of one of the burial canoes for fuel, taking the bones out and depositing them carefully near some of the others. We had not got our pot to boil, before some of the tribe made their appearance, and gave us to understand that we had destroyed the grave of a relative of one of the men. After a great deal of arguing and trouble, and our party being too strong for the Indians to attempt any open violence, this man consented, at last, to receive some tobacco, ammunition, and other little presents, as an indemnity for our sacrilege. This we willingly gave him, as, had we not done so, in all probability they would have killed the first white man they could have laid their hands on with impunity; having, however, received compensation for the insult, there was no fear of anything further being done about it.

July 10th.—Saw great quantities of rattlesnakes to-day, some few of which we killed; the men, while tracking (that is hauling the boats along the edge of the shore by a line, in places where the river is too rapid to row), were in great dread of them as they had no shoes, but fortunately no one was bitten. It is said by the Indians, that salt applied plentifully and immediately to the wound will effect a cure, also that drinking copiously of ardent spirits as soon as the bite has been inflicted will avert the danger. I have, however, never seen either of them tried, and should much suspect the latter cure to be merely a piece of Indian cunning, to overcome the great difficulty of getting liquor, on any terms, from the Company's servants and officers.

July 11th.—Many Indians followed us for a long distance on horseback along the shore. I obtained one of their horses, and, accompanied by an Indian, took a gallop of seven or eight miles into the interior, and found the country equally sterile and unpromising as on the banks of the stream. The bend in the river, which the boats were, of course, obliged to follow, enabled me to come up with them a very few miles further; the ride, although uninteresting as regarded landscape—for not a tree was visible as far as the eye could reach—was still a delightful change to me from the monotony of the boats. As we approached the place where the Walla-Walla debouches into the Columbia river, we came in sight of two extraordinary rocks projecting from a high steep cone or mound about 700 feet above the level of the river. These are called by the voyageurs the Chimney Rocks, and from their being visible from a great distance, they are very serviceable as landmarks. Sketch No. 13 represents one of them and the cone, but, owing to the position in which I stood while taking the sketch, the other rock or chimney is not visible, being immediately in rear of the one represented. [Fig. 135; crIV-358 to 361]

The Walla-Walla Indians call these the "Rocks of the Ki-use girls," of which they relate the following legend, which was told to me by an Indian, whilst I was sketching this extraordinary scene. It must be borne in mind that all Indian tribes select some animal to which they attribute supernatural, or, in the language of the country, *medicine* powers: the whale, for instance, on the north-west coast; the kee-yeu, or war eagle, on the east side of the Rocky Mountains, supposed to be the maker of thunder; and the wolf on the Columbia River. Now the great medicine wolf of the Columbia River—according to the Walla-Walla tradition, the most cunning and artful of all manitous—having heard that a great medicine grasshopper was desolating the whole of the country which of right belonged to himself, and was especially under his protection, immediately resolved to trace him out, and have a personal encounter with him. With this view, he proceeded down the banks of the river, and soon fell in with the object of his search. Each of these formidable manitous thought it best to resort to stratagem to overcome his opponent. Being afraid of each other's "medicine" powers, they accordingly commenced by exchanging civilities, and then, with a view of terrifying each other, began boasting of their wonderful exploits, and the numbers they had killed and eaten. The grasshopper said to the wolf that the best way to ascertain who had devoured the largest numbers would be to vomit up the contents of their respective stomachs, and he who threw up the most hair—that being an indigestible substance—by showing who had swallowed the most animals, should be considered as the superior. To this proposal the wolf consented, and they commenced retching and vomiting up all in their stomachs. The grasshopper, in the violence of his exertions, naturally closed his eyes, and the wolf, perceiving this, adroitly drew a great part of his opponent's share over to his own side without being detected. The grasshopper, when he perceived how much larger the pile before the wolf was than his own, gave up the contest, and proposed to the wolf an exchange of shirts in token of amity and forgiveness. To this also the wolf consented, but requested the grasshopper to take off his shirt first as he was the first proposer; but the grasshopper refused, and wished the wolf to commence the ceremony.

The wolf finally even agreed to this, and striking himself suddenly on the breast, his shirt immediately flew off; the grasshopper was greatly astonished, and not being possessed of any charm by which he could strip himself so expeditiously, was obliged to take off his shirt in the common way of drawing it over his head; the wolf now watched his opportunity, and while the grasshopper had his head and arms entangled in the shirt, he killed him.

The wolf having thus got rid of his troublesome and dangerous rival, commenced his return home. On arriving within a few miles of the Walla-Walla, he saw three beautiful Ki-use girls, with whom he fell desperately in love: they were engaged in carrying stones into the river, in order to make an artificial cascade or rapid, to catch the salmon in leaping over it. The wolf secretly watched their operations through the day, and repaired at night to the dam and entirely destroyed their work: this he repeated for three successive evenings. On the fourth morning, he saw the girls sitting weeping on the bank, and accosted them, inquiring what was the matter: they told him they were starving, as they could get no fish for want of a dam. He then proposed to erect a dam for them, if they would consent to become his wives, to which they consented sooner than perish from the want of food. A long point of stones running nearly across the river is to this day attributed to the magic of the wolf-lover.

For a long time he lived happily with the three sisters (a custom very frequent amongst Indians, who marry as many sisters in a family as they can, and assign as a reason that sisters will naturally agree together better than strangers); but at length the wolf became jealous of his wives, and, by his supernatural power, changed two of them into the two basalt pillars, on the south side of the river, and then changed himself into a lark rock, somewhat similar to them, on the north side, so that he might watch them for ever afterwards. I asked the narrator what had become of the third sister. Says he, "Did you not observe a cavern as you came up?" I said that I had. "That," he replied, "is all that remains of her!"

Chapter XVII.

Fort Walla-Walla.—Salmon the Staff of Life.—Burrows for the Winter.—Ride to see a Cataract.—Splendid Fall of Water.—Desert of burning Sand.—A jealous Spouse.—Respect to a dead Chief.

July 12th.—I arrived at Walla-Walla. It is a small fort, built of *dobies*, or blocks of mud baked in the sun, which is here intensely hot. Fort Walla-Walla is situated at the mouth of the river of the same name, in the most sandy and barren desert that can be conceived, and is about 500 miles from the mouth of the Columbia. Little or no rain ever falls here, although a few miles

lower down the river it is seen from hence to pour down in torrents. Owing to its being built at the mouth of a gully, formed by the Columbia River through high mountainous land leading to the Pacific Ocean, it is exposed to furious gales of wind, which rush through the opening in the hills with inconceivable violence, and raise the sand in clouds so dense and continuous as frequently to render travelling impossible. I was kindly received by Mr. M'Bain, a clerk in the Hudson's Bay Company's service, who, with five men, had charge of the fort. The establishment is kept up solely for trading with the Indians from the interior, as those about the post have few or no peltries to deal in. [Figs. 134, 136; crIV-354 to 356, 357?]

The Walla-Walla Indians live almost entirely upon salmon throughout the whole year. In the summer season they inhabit lodges made of mats of rushes spread on poles. [crIV-374] Owing to the absence of trees in their vicinity, they have to depend for the small quantity of fuel which they require, upon the drift-wood, which they collect from the river in the spring. In the winter they dig a large circular excavation in the ground, about ten or twelve feet deep, and from forty to fifty feet in circumference, and cover it over with split logs, over which they place a layer of mud collected from the river. A hole is left at one side of this roofing, large enough for one person to enter at a time. A stick with notches reaches to the bottom of the excavation, and serves as a ladder, by means of which they ascend and descend into the subterranean dwelling. Here twelve or fifteen persons burrow through the winter, having little or no occasion for fuel; their food of dried salmon being most frequently eaten uncooked, and the place being excessively warm from the numbers congregated together in so small and confined a space. They are frequently obliged, by the drifting billows of sand, to close the aperture, when the heat and stench become insupportable to all but those accustomed to it. The drifting of the sand is a frightful feature in this barren waste. Great numbers of the Indians lose their sight, and even those who have not suffered to so great an extent have the appearance of labouring under intense inflammation of these organs. The salmon, while in the process of drying, also become filled with sand to such an extent as to wear away the teeth of the Indians, and an Indian is seldom met with over forty years of age whose teeth are not worn quite to the gums.

July 13th.—Procured three horses and a man, and left for the Paluce or Pavilion River; traversed a sandy country, where we could find no water until we arrived at the Fouchay River, when we met with Pere José, a Jesuit missionary, who had left

Walla-Walla on the night before, on the way to his mission of the Cœur de Laine.[1] Here we encamped.

July 14th.—Started at five o'clock in the morning. Weather intensely hot, and no water procurable all day.[2] Found some Indians, who ferried ourselves and baggage over the Nezperees River, in a canoe, which is here about 250 yards wide. We swam our horses at the mouth of the Pelouse River, where it empties itself into the Nezperees. The Chief of this place is named Slo-ce-ac-cum. [crIV-353] He wore his hair divided in long masses, stuck together with grease. The tribe do not number more than seventy or eighty warriors, and are called Upputup-pets. He told me that there was a fall up the Pelouse that no white man had ever seen, and that he would conduct me up the bed of the river, as it was sufficiently shallow for our horses. I accepted his proposal, and rode eight or ten miles through a wild and savage gorge, composed of dark brown basaltic rocks, heaped in confusion one upon another to the height of 1000 and 1500 feet, sometimes taking the appearance of immense ruins in the distance. [Pl. XXXIV; crIV-341, 351?, 352?] At one place the strata assumed the circular form, and somewhat the appearance, of the Colosseum at Rome. [crIV-338, 339, 340] Our path, at the bottom of this gorge, was very difficult, as it lay through masses of tangled brush and fallen rocks.

The chief now halted,[3] and refused to go further unless I gave him a blanket in payment; but as this was unreasonable I urged on my horse, desiring my own man, who accompanied me, to follow with the jaded nag. I had not advanced more than a mile when the chief came up to us and guided us to the falls through one of the boldest and most sublime passes the eye ever beheld. At the foot of the falls we made our encampment, and our guide left us, quite satisfied with his present of tobacco and ammunition. The water falls in one perpendicular sheet of about 600 feet in height, from between rocks of a greyish-yellow colour, which rise to about 400 feet above the summit of the fall. The water tumbles into a rocky basin below, with a continuous hollow echoing roar, and courses with great velocity along its bed, until it falls into the Nezperees. There was a constant current of air around our encampment, which was delightfully cool and refreshing. When I was there it was low water, and the

Indian told me, that during the rainy season the falls were much increased in volume, and of course in grandeur of effect. [Fig. 132; crIV-342 to 346]

July 15th.—Having finished my sketches of this magnificent scene, we left our encampment for a fall fifteen or twenty miles higher up the river, and it was necessary for us to leave the bed of the river and attain the top of the banks, which being at least 1000 feet above us, would have been impracticable, had we not found a ravine, which, although steep and difficult, we managed to lead our horses up. In this hollow we found great quantities of wild currants, of delicious flavour, which proved most refreshing. [cr-IV-347]

At length we gained the summit. The country around, as far as the eye could reach, seemed to be a perfect desert of yellow, hot sand, with immense masses of broken rock jutting up abruptly here and there over the surface. No trees or shrubs of any kind relieved the monotony of the barren waste. A few patches of tuft-grass, thinly scattered here and there, were the only representatives of vegetation, while animal life seemed to be entirely extinct, and during my whole journey through this place I never met with an animal or bird,—not even a mosquito or a snake.

We now followed the course of the river, and encamped at the upper fall, where I remained until the 17th sketching, much gratified with the surrounding magnificent scenes. The fall of water is only about fifteen feet. Along the margin of the river high bushes and grass grow, whose bright green contrasts vividly with the high hills of yellow sand which enclose them. [Pl. XXXV; crIV-348, 349]

I was anxious to have remained in this neighbourhood for a week or ten days longer, to have made some more sketches of the curious and strange region in which I found myself, but the half-breed whom I had with me became so anxious to return, and so importunate and sulky about it, that he made me quite uncomfortable, and I consented to return. I found out afterwards that it was on account of his wife, of whom he was jealous, being left at the fort. Had I known this sooner I would have chosen another man; as it was, it was with great regret that I commenced retracing my steps down the river on the 17th, and in the evening again encamped on the banks of the Nezperees.

During the day we saw a large band of fine horses running wild; they had belonged to a chief who was much honoured by his tribe, and as a mark of respect, at his death, they determined not to use or touch his horses, which had, accordingly, kept

---

[1] Father Joseph Joset came to America in 1843 and went directly to the far west where he spent the balance of his life. Cœur d'Alene mission was founded in 1843 on the Spokane River in what is now upper Idaho.

[2] KJ: "14th. Left at 5 this morning for the River Nez Perces and arrived at 12, a distance of 30 m. No water all day. A good place for a person with the hydrophobia."

[3] The chief had halted at a ford. KJ notes that the chief thought he had Kane in his power and that Kane could not find his way out.

increasing in numbers. I took a sketch of the Nezperees, near the mouth of the Pelouse River, showing the singular formation of the basaltic rocks. [Fig. 133; crIV-350]

Chapter XVIII.

The Stream dried up.—American Presbyterian Mission.—A perfect Savage.—Scorched to death by the Sun.—Disastrous Expedition.— The Messenger of Woe.—The "Yellow Serpent."—A Father of Sorrow.—A Grave-side Address.—The Living and the Dead.—The lost Cup.—Taken for a Scoocoom.—A dreadful Disappointment.

July 18th.—Started for Dr. Whitman's mission, a distance of sixty miles, neither myself nor my man knowing anything of the road. I inquired of one of the Indians here: he pointed out the direction, but told us that we would be sure to die before we reached it for want of water; nor could we prevail on any of them to guide us. However, we started in the direction pointed out: the weather was intensely hot, and we had nothing to shelter us from the scorching rays of the sun, which were reflected back by the hot yellow sand.[1] Towards the middle of the day we observed a bush in the distance, and in our line of march; we eagerly rushed forward, hoping to find water, for want of which both ourselves and our horses were now suffering severely; but had the mortification to find the stream dried up, if ever there had been one there. Our only hope was now to struggle on as fast as possible, but our horses soon began to fail, and we were obliged to lead them many a weary mile tottering with exhaustion, before we arrived at the mission house. This we at length accomplished about 6 o'clock in the evening, and I was received very kindly by the missionary and his wife. [Figs. 137, 138; crIV-362, 363]

Dr. Whitman's duties included those of superintendent of the American Presbyterian missions on the west side of the Rocky Mountains. He had built himself a house of unburnt clay, for want of timber, which, as stated above, is here extremely scarce. He had resided at this locality, on the banks of the Walla-Walla River, upwards of eight years, doing all in his power to benefit the Indians in his mission. He had brought forty or fifty acres of land in the vicinity of the river under cultivation, and had a great many heads of domestic cattle, affording greater comfort to his family than one would expect in such an isolated spot. I remained with him four days, during which he kindly accompanied me amongst the Indians. These Indians, the Kye-use, resemble the Walla-Wallas very much. They are always allies in war, and their language and customs are almost identical, except that the Kye-use Indians are far more vicious and ungovernable.

Dr. Whitman took me to the lodge of an Indian called To-ma-kus, that I might take his likeness. We found him in his lodge sitting perfectly naked. His appearance was the most savage I ever beheld, and his looks, as I afterwards heard, by no means belied his character. He was not aware of what I was doing until I had finished the sketch. He then asked to look at it, and inquired what I intended doing with it, and whether I was not going to give it to the Americans, against whom he bore a strong antipathy, superstitiously fancying that their possessing it would put him in their power. I in vain told him that I should not give it to them; but not being satisfied with this assurance, he attempted to throw it in the fire, when I seized him by the arm and snatched it from him. He glanced at me like a fiend, and appeared greatly enraged, but before he had time to recover from his surprise I left the lodge and mounted my horse, not without occasionally looking back to see if he might not send an arrow after me. [Fig. 139; crIV-364?, 365, 366]

Usually, when I wished to take the likeness of an Indian, I walked into the lodge, sat down, and commenced without speaking, as an Indian under these circumstances will generally pretend not to notice. If they did not like what I was doing they would get up and walk away; but if I asked them to sit they most frequently refused, supposing that it would have some injurious effect upon themselves. In this manner I went into the lodge of Til-au-kite, the chief, and took his likeness without a word passing between us. [Fig. 140; crIV-367, 368, 369]

[Plateau Indian: crIV-370]

Having enjoyed the kind hospitality of Dr. Whitman and his lady for four days, on

July 22nd[2] I left for Walla-Walla, after breakfast, taking with me, at the Doctor's desire, a dog belonging to Mr. M'Bain. The weather continued intensely hot, and I had not ridden more than an hour when I observed the poor animal in a state of such extreme exhaustion that I requested my man to place him on his horse, but the man, feeling inconvenienced by him, put him down on the ground, and in a few minutes afterwards the poor brute lay down and died, actually scorched to death by the burning sand.

On the day after my arrival at the fort, a boy, one of the sons of Peo-Peo-mox-mox, the chief of the Walla-Wallas, arrived at

---

[1] KJ says that they went 30 miles without water, rested at the "Tuchay" (Fuchay?) for an hour, and then went another 20 miles.
[2] KJ gives the date of departure as July 20.

the camp close to the fort. [Fig. 143; crIV-377] He was a few days in advance of a war party headed by his father, and composed of Walla-Walla and Kye-use Indians, which had been absent eighteen months, and had been almost given up by the tribes. This party, numbering 200 men, had started for California for the purpose of revenging the death of another son of the chief, who had been killed by some Californian emigrants; and the messenger now arrived bringing the most disastrous tidings, not only of the total failure of the expedition, but also of their suffering and detention by sickness. Hearing that a messenger was coming in across the plains, I went to the Indian camp and was there at his arrival. No sooner had he dismounted from his horse than the whole camp, men, women, and children, surrounded him, eagerly inquiring after their absent friends, as they had hitherto received no intelligence, beyond a report, that the party had been cut off by hostile tribes. His downcast looks and silence confirmed the fears that some dire calamity must have happened, and they set up a tremendous howl, while he stood silent and dejected, with the tears streaming down his face. At length, after much coaxing and entreaty on their part, he commenced the recital of their misfortunes.

After describing the progress of the journey up to the time of the disease (the measles) making its appearance, during which he was listened to in breathless silence, he began to name its victims one after another. On the first name being mentioned, a terrific howl ensued, the women loosening their hair and gesticulating in a most violent manner. When this had subsided, he, after much persuasion, named a second and a third, until he had named upwards of thirty. The same signs of intense grief followed the mention of each name, presenting a scene which accustomed as I was to Indian life, I must confess, affected me deeply. I stood close by them on a log, with the interpreter of the fort, who explained to me the Indian's statement, which occupied nearly three hours. After this the excitement increased, and apprehensions were entertained at the fort that it might lead to some hostile movement against the establishment. This fear, however, was groundless, as the Indians knew the distinction between the Hudson's Bay Company and the Americans. They immediately sent messengers in every direction on horseback to spread the news of the disaster among all the neighbouring tribes, and Mr. M'Bain and I both considered that Dr. Whitman and his family would be in great danger. I, therefore, determined to go and warn him of what had occurred. It was six o'clock in the evening when I started, but I had a good horse, and arrived at his house in three hours. I told him of the arrival

of the messenger, and the excitement of the Indians, and advised him strongly to come to the fort, for a while at least, until the Indians had cooled down; but he said he had lived so long amongst them, and had done so much for them, that he did not apprehend they would injure him. I remained with him only an hour, and hastened back to the fort, where I arrived at one o'clock, A.M. Not wishing to expose myself unnecessarily to any danger arising from the superstitious notions which the Indians might attach to my having taken some of their likenesses, I remained at Fort Walla-Walla four or five days, during which the war party had returned, and I had an opportunity of taking the likeness of the great chief Peo-Peo-mox-mox, or, "the Yellow Serpent," who exercises great influence, not only over his own people, but also among the neighbouring tribes.[3] [Fig. 142; crIV-375, 376]

While at the fort one of the gentlemen of the establishment, who had been amongst the Indians for forty years, and who had resided for the most part of that time amongst the Walla-Wallas, related to me the following story, which I shall introduce, as nearly as possible, in the manner in which it was told to me; as it is strongly illustrative of the Indian character, of their love for their children, and the firmness with which they meet the approach of death, and their belief in a future state.

Several years back, when the Walla-Wallas used to go in annual buffalo hunts, and herds of these immense animals frequented the west side of the mountains, though now rarely seen, the tribe was governed by a chief adored by his own people, and respected and feared by all the surrounding tribes for his great wisdom and courage. This chief had many sons, who, in childhood, all promised to resemble their father both in mind and body, but one by one, as they arrived at manhood, and as the proud father hoped to see them take their place amongst the warriors and leaders of the tribe, they withered and sank into untimely graves, and as each loved one passed away, the stern chief soothed his silent sorrow with hopes of those still left. At last his hair grew white with sorrow and with age, and he had but one boy left—his youngest—but apparently the strongest, the bravest, and the best: at least to the old warrior's heart he was all this; for in him still seemed to live all the most cherished virtues of his dead brothers.

The old man now devoted his whole time to the instruction of this boy: he taught him to hunt the buffalo and the moose, to

---

[3] For Peo-Peo-mox-mox, see Richard Dillon, *Fool's Gold: The Decline and Fall of John Sutter of California* (New York 1967).

snare the lynx and trap the bear, to draw the bow and poise the spear with unerring aim. Young as the boy was, he yet made him head the warriors of his tribe, and led him on himself, the foremost to surprise the enemy and secure the bloody trophies of victory; already had he become the theme of the war-chant, and his name was known far and wide for all the virtues that could adorn an Indian brave.

But the Great Spirit took this one too; and the lonely and desolate father shut himself up in the solitude of his lodge, and no one saw him nor spoke to him, nor was there any sound of wailing or of grief heard from that sad abode. At length the appointed day arrived upon which the body was to be laid in its last resting-place, where the chief had ordered a large grave to be made; and the funeral procession being formed, the chief came forth and placed himself at their head, but, to the astonishment of all, instead of being dressed in the shabby garments indicative of mourning, he came forth arrayed in full war costume, fully equipped as if for some distant hostile excursion, painted with the most brilliant war paints, and hung round with the trophies of his many bloody and successful wars.

Calmly and sternly he marched to the grave, and the body of his loved son having been laid in it, with all the Indian treasures supposed to be useful to him in the next world, the bereaved father stood on the verge, and addressed his tribe: "From my youth upwards I have ever sought the honour and welfare of my tribe, and have never spared myself either in the battle or the chase. I have led you from victory to victory, and, instead of being surrounded by hostile tribes, you are now feared by all, and your friendship is sought, and your enmity dreaded, wherever the hunters of the tribe may roam. I have been a father to you, and ye have been as children to me, for more moons than I am able to count, until my hairs have become as hoar frost upon the mountains. You have never withheld your obedience from me, nor will you deny it to me now. When the Great Spirit was pleased to call my children one by one, to His blessed hunting grounds, I saw them borne to the sepulchre of their fathers without murmuring against His will, so long as one was left me. I toiled on for him, taking pride in his pride, glorying in his glory, and living in his life, fondly hoping that when I should go to join his loved brothers in the other world that I should leave him to perpetuate my deeds amongst you; but the Great Spirit hath called him also,—this last prop of my declining years,—this hope of my old age,—endeared to me by so many fond recollections of his worth, his manly strength, his courage, skill, and prowess in war. Alas! he lies in the cold ground, and I

am left alone, like the sapless trunk of a tree whose branches have been scathed by the lightning. I tracked that loved form, now cold, from its childhood's gambols to its manly acts of daring. I it was who first placed in his hands the bow and the tomahawk, and taught him how to use them; and often have you witnessed and praised his skill and courage in wielding them. And shall I now forsake him, and leave him alone and unaided, to take the long and toilsome journey in the Spirit's hunting grounds? No! his spirit beckons me to follow, and he shall not be disappointed; the same grave shall contain us, the same earth shall cover us; and as in this world, his father's arm was ever near to assist him in every toil and danger, so shall his spirit find him by his side in the long and toilsome journey to the plenteous and everlasting hunting grounds of the Great Spirit. You, my people, have never disobeyed me, and will not fail to fulfil my last commands. I now leave you, and when I lie extended at his side[,] heap the earth over us both: nothing can change my purpose." He then descended into the grave, and clasped the corpse in his arms. His people, after in vain endeavouring to change his resolution, obeyed his commands, and buried the living and the dead. A stick, with a piece of ragged red cloth, was the only monument erected over the warriors, but their names will form the theme of many an Indian *talk* as long as the Walla-Walla tribe exists.

July 29th.—I had determined to go to Colville by the Grand Coulet: this, from the appearance of the two extremities, seemed to have been a former bed of the Columbia River, but no person could tell me anything about it, nor could I hear of any one, either Indian or White, who had penetrated any considerable distance up it; the place was, however, so much talked of as the abode of evil spirits and other strange things, that I could not resist the desire of trying to explore it. I accordingly sent on everything by the boats, except what I usually carried about my own person, but I could not get an Indian guide, as none of them would venture an encounter with the evil spirits.

At last a half-breed, called Donny, although ignorant of the route, agreed to accompany me. We procured two riding horses, and one to carry our provisions, consisting of two fine hams, which had been sent to me from Fort Vancouver, and a stock of dried salmon, cured by the Indians. About ten miles from the fort, we swam our horses across the Nezperees River, where it enters the Columbia, and then proceeded along the banks of the Columbia, about ten miles further, where we encamped for the night.

During the day we passed a large encampment of Nezperees,

A Cree Indian from
Edmonton — 79
79.

Plate XXII. Cree Indian. Stark POP16; crIV-139.

Plate XXIII. Medicine pipe-stem dance (Blackfoot). Stark POP10; CRIV-157.

who were very kind to us, but stole a tin cup (a valuable article in that part of the world) I suppose as a souvenir of my visit. I took a sketch of a man, and might have frightened the chief into getting the cup restored to me by means of this sketch, but I had been so warned of the treachery and villany of these Indians, that I considered it too dangerous an experiment. [Fig. 141; crIV-371 to 373]

July 30th.—Proceeded along the shore for eight or ten miles,[4] when I discovered that I had left my pistols and some other articles at our last night's encampment. I had, therefore, to send my man back for them, while I sat by the river, with horses and baggage, under a burning sun, without the slightest shelter. Whilst sitting there, a canoe approached with four Indians, streaked all over with white mud (the ordinary pipe-clay). On landing, they showed much surprise, and watched very cautiously at a distance, some creeping close to me, and then retreating. This continued for about three hours, during which not a sound broke through the surrounding stillness. I had commenced travelling very early, and this, combined with the heat and silence, made me intensely drowsy. Even the danger I was in scarcely sufficed to keep my eyes open, but the Indians were evidently at fault as to what to make of me.

As I sat upon the packs taken from the horse, nodding in silence, with a fixed stare at them whichever way they turned, my double-barrelled gun, cocked, across my knees, and a large red beard (an object of great wonder to all Indians) hanging half way down my breast, I was, no doubt, a very good embodiment of their ideas of a scoocoom, or evil genius. To this I attributed my safety, and took good care not to encourage their closer acquaintance, as I had no wish to have my immortality tested by them.

At length my man returned with the missing articles, and the Indians hastily took to their canoe and crossed the river. We now continued our course along the river until evening, when we encamped, and as we were very hungry, and expected a hard journey next day, we determined upon attacking one of our hams. I accordingly seized hold of the bone to pull it from the bag with which it was covered, when, alas! the bare bone slipped out, leaving a living mass of maggots, into which the heat had turned the flesh, behind. Upon examination, we found the other in the same state, and had to satisfy our hunger on the salmon, which, as usual, was full of sand.

---

[4] KJ states that he went 30 miles, not eight or ten, before he missed his pistols.

Chapter XIX.

The Horrors of Thirst.—The Lake of Pelicans.—A queer Bedfellow. —Steering by the Sun.—Sweet Water at Last.—Rather a hardy Horse.—Losing each Other.—Wonderful natural Walls.—The Grand Coulet.—A Great Treat.—The River Columbia.—Indians again.

July 31st.—Owing to the great bend which the Columbia takes to the northward, I thought I should save a considerable distance by striking across the country, and intersecting the Grand Coulet at some distance from its mouth. We accordingly left the river early in the morning, and travelled all day through a barren, sandy desert, without a drop of water to drink, a tree to rest under, or a spot of grass to sit upon. Towards evening, we saw in the distance a small lake, and to this we accordingly pushed forward: as soon as our horses perceived it, wearied and exhausted as they were, they rushed forward and plunged bodily into the water. No sooner, however, had they tasted it, than they drew their heads back, refusing to drink. On alighting, I found the water was intensely salt, and never shall I forget the painful emotion which came over me, as it became certain to my mind that I could not satisfy my thirst. Our horses were too weary, after our long and rapid ride, to proceed further; and though it was tantalising to look at the water which we could not drink, the vegetation which surrounded it was refreshing to the horses, and we remained here all night, though we enjoyed scarcely any sleep owing to our thirst.

August 1st.—We started at 4 o'clock this morning, and travelled steadily on without getting water, until about noon, when we fell in with a narrow lake, about a mile long, very shallow, and swarming with pelicans, whose dung had made the water green and thick. Bad as this was, added to its being also rather salt, yet our thirst was so great, that we strained some through a cloth and drank it. Leaving this Lake of Pelicans, we now entered upon a still more discouraging route: the country, as far as the eye could reach, was covered with loose fine sand, which the violent winds of this region had drifted into immense mounds, varying from 80 to 120 feet in height. [crIV-378] This was very toilsome to us, as our horses had become so exhausted that we were obliged to lead them, and we sank deep at every step in the hot sand. Had the wind risen while we were crossing this place, we must have been immediately buried in the sand. Towards evening we arrived at a rock, and in a small cleft we discovered three or four gallons of water almost as black as ink, and abounding in disgusting animalcula. The horses no sooner saw it, than they made a spring towards it, and it was with the greatest difficulty we drove them back, fearing that they would drink all, and leave us to our misery. After satisfying our thirst, we strained a kettleful for our supper, and allowed the horses to drink up the remainder, which they did to the last drop, showing how necessary was the precaution we had taken. Here we passed the night.

Aug. 2nd.—I awoke in the morning, and felt something cold and clammy against my thigh, and on throwing off my blanket, perceived a reptile of the lizard species, eight or ten inches long, which had been my companion during the night. I cannot say whether it was venomous or not, but I found no ill effects from it. We proceeded on, and about noon emerged from these mountains of sand; the country was still sandy and barren, but here and there we found tufts of grass sufficient to support our horses. The country was intersected with immense walls of basaltic rock, which continually threw us out of our direct course, or rather the course I had determined on, for of the actual route I had no information. These interruptions added considerably to our difficulties, as I had no compass, and it was only by noticing the sun at mid-day by my watch, and fixing on some distant hill, that I guided my course. We still suffered from the want of water, and my man was getting disheartened at our wandering thus almost at random through this trackless desert.

Aug. 3rd.[1]—After riding a few hours, we came to an immense gully or dried-up water-course crossing our route. The banks rose seven or eight hundred feet high from the bottom on each side, and its width was nearly half a mile. At first it seemed impossible to pass it; however, after many difficulties, we succeeded in leading our horses to the bottom, which we crossed, and clambered up the rocks on the opposite side for about 200 feet, when we came to one of the most beautiful spots that can well be conceived: at least, it appeared to us all that was beautiful, amongst the surrounding desolation.

It was a piece of table land, about half a mile in circumference, covered with luxuriant grass, and having in its centre a small lake of exquisitely cool fresh water. The basaltic rock rose like an amphitheatre, from about three-quarters of its circuit to the height of about 500 feet, while the precipice up which we had toiled sank down at the other side. We remained here three hours, luxuriating in the delicious water, so sweet to us after suffering the torments of thirst for so long. My man seemed as

if he never could have enough of it, for when he could swallow no more, he walked in, clothes and all, and actually wallowed in it, the horses following his example. How much longer we might have been tempted to stay here, it is impossible to say, but we accidentally set fire to the grass and were obliged to decamp; this was accomplished with considerable difficulty, and in getting up the precipitous rocks, the pack-horse lost his footing and fell to the bottom, but pitching, fortunately, on his back with the packs under him, he escaped with a few cuts on his legs only. Had he been anything but an Indian horse, he would doubtless have paid the forfeit of his life for the insecurity of his feet.

As soon as I arrived at the level of the country once more, I saw in the distance another vast wall of rock, and leaving my man to bring up the unfortunate pack-horse, I rode briskly forward to endeavour to find a passage over this formidable barrier, considering it to be like many others that we had already passed, an isolated wall of basalt. I therefore rode backwards and forwards along its front, exploring every part that presented any opening, but without finding one that our horses could traverse. At last I came to the conclusion that we must go round it, but my man not having come up, it was necessary for me to return and seek him, which proved for several hours unavailing, and I began to fear that he and my provisions were inevitably lost; however, after riding a long way back, I fell upon his track, which I followed up with care.

I soon perceived that he had taken a wrong direction. After some time, I saw him mounted on a high rock in the distance, shouting and signalling with all his might till I got up to him: he was very much frightened, as he said that if he had lost me he never could have got on. Though the day was by this time pretty far advanced, we succeeded in making a circuit of the basaltic wall, and struck a deep ravine which in the distance so much resembled the banks of the Columbia, that I at first thought I had missed my way, and had come upon the river.

When we reached the edge, I saw that there was no water at the bottom, and that there could be no doubt of my having at last arrived at the Grand Coulet.[2] With great difficulty we descended the bank, 1000 feet; its width varies from one mile to a mile and a half; and there can be no doubt of its having been previously an arm of the Columbia, which now flows four or five hundred feet below it, leaving the channel of the Coulet dry,

---

[1] kj gives the date as August 2.
[2] kj states that they went through the Grand Coulee for ten miles, and went in all 35 miles.

and exposing to view the bases of the enormous rocky islands that now stud its bottom, some of them rising to the elevation of the surrounding country. [CRIV-379, 380, 381]

This wonderful gully is about 150 miles long, and walled-in in many places with an unbroken length twenty miles long of perpendicular basalt 1000 feet high.[3] The bottom of this valley is perfectly level, and covered with luxuriant grass, except where broken by the immense rocks above mentioned: there is not a single tree to be seen throughout its whole extent, and scarcely a bush; neither did we see any insects, reptiles, or animals. Having found a beautiful spring of water gushing from the rocks, we encamped near it. After we had rested ourselves, we commenced an examination of our provisions of dried salmon, for we saw no chance of adding anything to our larder, and of course what we had was of great importance. Much to our regret, we found that it was perfectly alive with maggots, and every mouthful had to be well shaken before eating; so full of life indeed had the fish become, that my man proposed tying them by the tails to prevent their crawling away. Bad as the salmon was, our prospects were made still more gloomy by the fact that there was but a very small supply left, and that we had a long and unknown road to travel before we could hope for any help. A thunderstorm came on during the night, and in the whole course of my life I never heard any-thing so awfully sublime as the endless reverberations amongst the rocks of this grand and beautiful ravine. There is hardly another spot in the world that could produce so astounding an effect.

Aug. 4th.—We followed the course of the Coulet, lost in admiration of its beauty and grandeur assuming a new aspect of increased wildness and magnificence at every turn. I shot the first bird we had seen since leaving Walla-Walla, except the pelicans, which are never eaten, even by the Indians, who are far from particular. This bird proved to be what is here called a wild turkey, but resembling in nothing the wild turkeys of the south. Its plumage resembles that of a pheasant, it is not larger than a domestic hen, and its flesh, though very white, is dry and unpalatable; to us, however, it proved a great treat, as we were enabled to make one meal without the usual accompaniments of sand and maggots. Our journey now would have been delight-

ful, if we had anything like good food. We had plenty of grass of the best quality for our horses, delicious springs gushing from the rocks at every mile or two, and camping grounds which almost tempted us to stay at the risk of starvation.

Aug. 5th.[4]—Towards evening we began to see trees, princi-pally pine, in the heights and in the distance, and I concluded that we were now approaching the Columbia River. I now pressed forward and before sundown emerged from the gorge of this stupendous ravine, and saw the mighty river flowing at least 500 feet below us, though the banks rose considerably more than that height above us on each side. This river exceeds in grandeur any other perhaps in the world, not so much from its volume of water, although that is immense, as from the romantic wilderness of its stupendous and ever-varying surround-ing scenery, now towering into snow-capped mountains thou-sands of feet high, and now sinking in undulating terraces to the level of its pellucid waters.

Two Indians were floating down the river, on a few logs tied together. They were the first we had encountered for many days[5]; and on our hailing them, they landed, and climbed up to us. They told me we were ten days' journey from Colville. This I did not believe, although I could not tell why they wished to deceive me. I gave them a little tobacco, and hoped to get some provisions from them, but they said they had none, so we were obliged to make our supper on the salmon as usual. We de-scended the bank, and camped for the night on the margin of the river.

Chapter XX.

A Dangerous Path.—Incredible Sagacity.—Levying Black Mail.—Fort Colville.—Hiding-Places of the Indians.—Indian Baptism.—The Kettle Falls.—Tilting at the Ring.—Chief of the Waters.—Dead Salmon by Thousands.—Dislike to Salt Meat.—A Widow's Consolation.—A Wife for the Woods.

August 6th.[1]—We continued along the shore for twelve or fifteen miles, under the rocky banks, which towered over our heads fourteen or fifteen hundred feet. In some places, immense ledges hung over our path, seemingly ready to crush all beneath them. At length we came to a high perpendicular rock jutting out into the river; and as the water was too deep and too rapid to allow us to wade round its base, we attempted to ascend the

---

[3] KJ: "Every 5 or 6 miles I found a cold spring of water, quite refreshing after what I had suffered. My man set fire to the prairie where we had breakfasted which came very near burning our horses had we not got it under control. We were at the time walled in by high rocks and only one narrow pass to get out."

[4] KJ reads August 3.

[5] KJ mentions four days.

[1] KJ reads August 4.

bank over loose rocks and stones that slipped from under us at every step, and rolled thundering to the bottom. Having led our horses up about three hundred feet, I stopped, and sent Donny a-head on foot to seek for an opening to the top. The pack-horse could with great difficulty preserve his footing under his load. One of the other horses, with incredible sagacity, now walked up past me, until he reached his burdened companion; and, putting his shoulder under one side of the load, actually assisted him in sustaining it, until the man's return. Finding that we could not possibly ascend, we were obliged to turn back; and we did not find a practicable place to ascend until we had nearly reached the place from which we had started in the morning.

At last, with great difficulty, we succeeded in gaining the upper bank, and entered upon a wild and romantic district, studded here and there with small clumps of trees, which gradually increased in thickness, until we became surrounded with dense woods, having made a circuit of about twenty-five miles, traversing gullies of prodigious depth and steepness. We again struck the river opposite the mouth of a small stream, on whose banks we saw a couple of Indians. As soon as we were perceived, they sent a canoe over to us, offering to assist in swimming the horses across, as they assured us that the shortest and best route to Colville was on the other side. We accepted their friendly offer, and camped alongside them on the other side. Both Donny and myself were dreadfully fatigued from the length of our day's travel, the labour we had gone through, and the weakness under which we suffered from the want of sufficient food. These Indians, as I afterwards learned, were generally very unfriendly to the whites, and had often given trouble to small parties passing, generally levying a pretty heavy toll for a free passage through their territory. But to me they were all kindness, presenting me with plenty of fresh salmon and dried berries, which were most acceptable, after the disgusting fare on which we had been so long struggling to support life; and one of them proposed to accompany me as a guide to Colville. My last day's experience made me gladly accept of this offer; and long before darkness set in, I found myself as sound asleep as the most weary of dyspeptic patients could wish himself to be.

August 7th.—Started very early in the morning with the guide, and made, what is called in those parts, a long day. We were continually ascending and descending, and found it very fatiguing. It was quite dark when we encamped on the banks of the river.

August 8th.—Started again very early for the purpose of reaching Colville before night. Came to a high hill overlooking

the Columbia for many miles of its course, and sat down on its summit to enjoy the magnificent prospect, and give a short rest to the horses. [crIV-332?] As I was lying under the trees, the wind sprang up, and, much to my astonishment, I felt the whole sod moving under me. At first I imagined it to be an earthquake, and expected to see the whole hillside move off; but on examination, I found that it proceeded from the roots of the immense trees being interlaced one within another in the shallow soil. This alone prevented their being blown over, as the rocks are everywhere close to the surface; and as the wind bends the tops of the trees, the roots rise and fall with the surface in a rolling motion like a dead swell. We proceeded on until we were within a mile of Kettle Falls, where we swam across in the usual way, holding on by the tails of our horses; and just at dusk we were kindly received by Mr. Lewis.

Fort Colville stands in the middle of a small prairie, about one mile and a half wide by about three miles long, surrounded by high hills. This little prairie is extremely valuable for agricultural purposes, as it is, in fact, an island of fertility, surrounded by barren rocks, sandy plains, and arid mountains, to the distance of three or four hundred miles along the river, the Spokan valley to the south being the nearest land fit for cultivation. [crIV-330] I remained here until the 9th of September, when I made an excursion of sixty miles, accompanied by Mr. Lewis, to Walker and Eales' [Eells'] Presbyterian mission, where I was most hospitably received by these worthy people. [Fig. 131; crIV-336]

Each of the missionaries had a comfortable log-house, situated in the midst of a fertile plain, and, with their wives and children, seem to be happily located. There are numerous Indian *caches* of dried salmon in the vicinity, which are very seldom robbed, although left in isolated spots for months without any person in charge. I enjoyed for a week the kind hospitality of my hosts, who were most attentive in accompanying me in my visits to the Spokan River and the Indians in the vicinity. [Pl. XXXII; crIV-334, 335]

The Spokan Indians are a small tribe, differing very little from the Indians at Colville either in their appearance, habits, or language. They all seemed to treat the missionaries with great affection and respect; but as to their success in making converts, I must speak with great diffidence, as I was not sufficiently acquainted with the language to examine them, even had I wished to do so. I have no doubt that a great number have been baptised; but I also am aware that almost all Indians will take a name from a man whom they esteem, and give him one in return; and the more ceremony there is about the transaction, the more importance will be attached to it, and the greater the inducement to others to be equally honoured. No influence, however, seems to be able to make agriculturists of them, as they still pursue their hunting and fishing, evincing the greatest dislike to anything like manual labour. [Pl. XXXIII; crIV-331, 337]

On the 17th [2] of September I returned again to Colville. The Indian village is situated about two miles below the fort, on a rocky eminence overlooking the Kettle Falls. These are the highest in the Columbia River. They are about one thousand yards across, and eighteen feet high. The immense body of water tumbling amongst the broken rocks renders them exceedingly picturesque and grand. [Plate XXX; crIV-297, 298, 299, 307] The Indians have no particular name for them, giving them the general name of Tum-tum, which is applied to all falls of water. The voyageurs call them the "Chaudière," or "Kettle Falls," from the numerous round holes worn in the solid rocks by loose boulders. These boulders, being caught in the inequalities of rocks below the falls, are constantly driven round by the tremendous force of the current, and wear out holes as perfectly round and smooth as in the inner surface of a cast-iron kettle. The village has a population of about five hundred souls, called, in their own language, Chualpays. [crIV-294?] They differ but little from the Walla-Wallas. The lodges are formed of mats of rushes stretched on poles. A flooring is made of sticks, raised three or four feet from the ground, leaving the space beneath it entirely open, and forming a cool, airy, and shady place, in which to hang their salmon to dry. [Pl. XXXI; Fig. 124; crIV-308 to 312, 315]

These people are governed by two chiefs, Allam-māk-hum Stole-luch, the "Chief of the Earth." [*sic*] This chief exercises great power over the tribe except as regards the fishing, which is under the exclusive control of See-pays, the "Chief of the Waters." He [Allam-mak-hum Stole-luch] dispenses justice strictly, and punishes with rigour any cheating or dishonesty among his subjects. [crIV-295] He opposes the gambling propensities of his tribe to the utmost, even depriving the victorious gamblers of their share of the fish received annually from the Chief of the Waters; but still the passion for gambling continues, and an instance occurred during my stay here of a young man committing suicide by shooting himself, having lost everything he possessed by indulging in this habit. I may here remark

that suicide prevails more among the Indians of the Columbia River than in any other portion of the continent which I have visited.

A curious case occurred, about a year before my visit, of two sisters, wives of one man, each jealous of the other, who went into the woods and hung themselves, as was supposed, unknown to each other, as they were found dead a long distance apart.

The principal game played here is called Al-kol-lock, and requires considerable skill. A smooth level piece of ground is chosen, and a slight barrier of a couple of sticks placed lengthwise, is laid at each end of the chosen spot, being from forty to fifty feet apart and only a few inches high. The two players, stripped naked, are armed each with a very slight spear about three feet long, and finely pointed with bone; one of them takes a ring made of bone, or some heavy wood, and wound round with cord; this ring is about three inches in diameter, on the inner circumference of which are fastened six beads of different colours at equal distances, to each of which a separate numerical value is attached. The ring is then rolled along the ground to one of the barriers, and is followed at the distance of two or three yards by the players, and as the ring strikes the barrier and is falling on its side, the spears are thrown, so that the ring may fall on them. If only one of the spears should be covered by the ring, the owner of it counts according to the coloured bead over it. But it generally happens, from the dexterity of the players, that the ring covers both spears, and each counts according to the colour of the beads above his spear; they then play towards the other barrier, and so on until one party has attained the number agreed upon for game. [Figs. 125, 126; crIV-316 to 321]

The other chief is called See-pays, the "Chief of the Waters," or the "Salmon Chief." [Fig. 122; crIV-292, 293, 296?] No one is allowed to catch fish without his permission. His large fishing basket or trap is put down a month before anyone is allowed to fish for themselves. This basket is constructed of stout willow wands woven together, and supported by stout sticks of timber, and is so placed that the salmon, in leaping up the falls strike against a stick placed at the top, and are thrown back into the confined space at the bottom of the trap, which is too narrow to allow them to attempt another jump.

The salmon commence their ascent about the 15th of July, and continue to arrive in almost incredible numbers for nearly two months; in fact, there is one continuous body of them, more resembling a flock of birds than anything else in their extraordinary leap up the falls, beginning at sunrise and ceasing at the

[2] kj gives the date as 16th, not 17th.

approach of night. The chief told me that he had taken as many as 1700 salmon, weighing on an average 30 lbs. each, in the course of one day. Probably the daily average taken in the chief's basket is about 400. The chief distributes the fish thus taken during the season amongst his people, everyone, even to the smallest child, getting an equal share.

By the time the salmon reach the Kettle Falls, after surmounting the numerous rapids impeding their journey from the sea, a distance of between 700 and 800 miles, they become so exhausted, that in their efforts to leap these falls, their strength often proves unequal to the task, and striking against the projecting rocks they batter their noses so severely, that they fall back stunned and often dead, and float down the river, where they are picked up some six miles below by another camp of Indians, who do not belong to the Salmon Chief's jurisdiction, and of course have no participation in the produce of his basket. None of these salmon coming up from the sea ever return, but remain in the river and die by thousands; in fact, in such numbers that in our passage down the river in the fall, whenever we came to still water, we found them floating dead or cast up along the shore in such vast numbers as literally to poison the atmosphere.

The young fish return to the sea in the spring. Strange to say, nothing has ever been found in the stomachs of the salmon caught in the Columbia River; and no angler, although frequent trials have been made by the most expert in the art, has yet succeeded in tempting them to take any description of fly or other bait.

After the expiration of one month, the Salmon Chief abandons his exclusive privilege, as the fish are then getting thin and poor, and allows all who wish it to take them. For this purpose some use smaller baskets made like the chief's; others use the spear, with which they are very expert, and an ordinary spearsman will take easily as many as 200 in a day; others use a small hand-net in the rapids, where the salmon are crowded together and near the surface. These nets are somewhat like our common landing-nets, but ingeniously contrived, so that when a fish is in them, his own struggles loosen a little stick which keeps the mouth of the net open while empty; the weight of the salmon then draws the mouth close like a purse, and effectually secures the prey.

Salmon is almost the only food used by the Indians on the Lower Columbia River, the two months' fishing affording a sufficient supply to last them the whole year round. The mode in which they cure them is by splitting them down the back,

after which each half is again split, making them sufficiently thin to dry with facility, a process occupying in general from four to five days.[3] The salmon are afterwards sewed up in rush mats, containing about ninety or one hundred pounds, and put up on scaffolds to keep the dogs from them. Infinitely greater numbers of salmon could be readily taken here, if it were desired; but, as the chief considerately remarked to me, if he were to take all that came up, there would be none left for the Indians on the upper part of the river; so that they content themselves with supplying their own wants. [Fig. 123; crIV-300 to 306, 313, 314]

A few days before leaving Colville I was informed that the Chualpays were about to celebrate a scalp dance, and accordingly I took my sketch-book and went down to their encampment, where I learned that a small party had returned from a hunting expedition to the mountains, bringing with them, as a present from a friendly tribe, the scalp of a Blackfoot Indian. This to them was a present of inestimable value, as one of their tribe had been killed by a Blackfoot Indian two or three years before, and they had not been able to obtain any revenge for the injury. This scalp, however, would soothe the sorrows of his widow and friends. Accordingly, it was stretched upon a small hoop, and attached to a stick as a handle, and thus carried by the afflicted woman to a place where a large fire was kindled: here she commenced dancing and singing, swaying the scalp violently about and kicking it, whilst eight women, hideously painted, chanted and danced round her and the fire. The remainder of the tribe stood round in a circle, beating drums, and all singing. [Figs. 127 to 130; crIV-322 to 329]

Having witnessed the performance for about four or five hours, seeing no variation in it, nor any likelihood of its termination, I returned, deeply impressed with the sincerity of a grief which could endure such violent monotony for so long a period. My kind host, Mr. Lewis, was now obliged to give up rambling about with me, as he had to see to the preparations for the further progress of the return brigade. Both himself and his Cree wife were most attentive in adding every little thing to my outfit which they could supply. Mrs. Lewis was a most excellent wife for a trader, possessing great energy and decision, combined with natural kindness of disposition. Several years before I became acquainted with her she had amputated her husband's arm, a little below the elbow, with a common knife, and tied it up so well, that he soon recovered without any other assistance.

[3] w59: "I have never seen salt made use of by any tribe of Indians for the purpose of preserving food, and they all evince the greatest dislike to salt meat."

Her surgical aid had been called in requisition by the accidental discharge of his gun, which had shattered the limb so much that it was hopeless to try and save it.

[Chinewoss: CRIV-333]

Chapter XXI.

Dreadful Tidings.—Horrible Tragedy.—A devoted Husband.—A joyful Surprise.—Perilous Pass.—Walk on Shore.—The Rapid of the Dead.—The detected Cannibal.—A Western Honeymoon.—The Last Embrace.—Capote Blanc.—Boat Encampment.—A bothered Steed.—Forest swept away.—The Flooded Athabasca.—Shoes long as yourself.—Crossing Jasper's Lake.—In for it everyway.—Rising of the River.—Starving of the Dogs.—Waiting for a Frost-Bridge.—Too Thin to be Eaten.—Fort Assiniboine.—Pleasure after Pain.

Sept. 21*st.*—This evening two men arrived from Walla-Walla, and my grief and horror can be well imagined when they told me the sad fate of those with whom I had so lately been a cherished guest.[1] It appeared that the war party before mentioned had brought the measles back with them, and that it spread with fearful rapidity through the neighbouring tribe, but more particularly among the Key-uses. Dr. Whitman, as a medical man, did all he could to stay its progress; but owing to their injudicious mode of living, which he could not prevail on them to relinquish, great numbers of them died. At this time the doctor's family consisted of himself, his wife, and a nephew, with two or three servants, and several children whom he had humanely adopted, left orphans by the death of their parents who had died on their way to Oregon, besides a Spanish half-breed boy, whom he had brought up for several years. There were likewise several families of emigrants staying with him at the time, to rest and refresh themselves and cattle.

The Indians supposed that the doctor could have stayed the course of the malady had he wished it; and they were confirmed in this belief by the Spanish half-breed boy, who told some of them that he had overheard the doctor say to his wife after they had retired for the night, that he would give them bad medicine, and kill all the Indians, that he might appropriate their

land to himself. They accordingly concocted a plan to destroy the doctor and his wife, and all the males of the establishment. With this object in view, about sixty of them armed themselves and came to his house. The inmates, having no suspicion of any hostile intention, were totally unprepared for resistance or flight. Dr. and Mrs. Whitman and their nephew, a youth about seventeen or eighteen years of age, were sitting in their parlour in the afternoon, when Til-au-kite, the chief, and To-ma-kus entered the room, and, addressing the doctor, told him very coolly that they had come to kill him. The doctor, not believing it possible that they could entertain any hostile intentions towards him, told them as much; but while in the act of speaking, To-ma-kus drew a tomahawk from under his robe and buried it deep in his brain. The unfortunate man fell dead from his chair. Mrs. Whitman and the nephew fled up stairs, and locked themselves into an upper room.

In the meantime Til-au-kite gave the war whoop, as a signal to his party outside to proceed in the work of destruction, which they did with the ferocity and yells of so many fiends. Mrs. Whitman, hearing the shrieks and groans of the dying, looked out of the window, and was shot through the breast by a son of the chief, but not mortally wounded. A party then rushed up stairs, and, despatching the nephew on the spot, dragged her down by the hair of her head, and, taking her to the front of the house, mutilated her in a shocking manner with their knives and tomahawks.

There was one man who had a wife bedridden. On the commencement of the affray he ran to her room, and, taking her up in his arms, carried her, unperceived by the Indians, to the thick bushes that skirted the river, and hurried on with his burden in the direction of Fort Walla-Walla. Having reached a distance of fifteen miles, he became so exhausted, that, unable to carry her further, he concealed her in a thick hummock of bushes on the margin of the river, and hastened to the fort for assistance. On his arrival, Mr. M'Bain immediately sent out men with him, and brought her in. She had fortunately suffered nothing more than fright. The number killed, including Dr. and Mrs. Whitman, amounted to fourteen. The other females and children were carried off by the Indians, and two of them were forthwith taken as wives by Til-au-kite's son and another. A man, employed in a little mill, forming a part of the establishment, was spared to work the mill for the Indians.

The day following this awful tragedy, a Catholic priest, who had not heard of the massacre, stopped, on seeing the mangled corpses strewn round the house, and requested permission to

[1] Kane's date for receiving word of the Whitman massacre is curious. The incident actually occurred on November 27–29. His memory must have been faulty when he came to set down the date of the event itself and a date and place for receipt of the news. KJ makes no mention of the receipt of news of the massacre; it also refers to Kane's party reaching Boat Encampment in October 1847, thus long before the date of the massacre.

bury them, which he did with the rites of his own church. The permission was granted the more readily as these Indians are friendly towards the Catholic missionaries. On the priest leaving the place, he met, at a distance of five or six miles, a brother missionary of the deceased, a Mr. Spalding, the field of whose labours lay about a hundred miles off, at a place on the River Coldwater.[2] He communicated to him the melancholy fate of his friend, and advised him to fly as fast as possible, or in all probability he would be another victim. He gave him a share of his provisions, and Mr. Spalding hurried homeward full of apprehensions for the safety of his own family; but unfortunately his horse escaped from him in the night, and, after a six days' toilsome march on foot, having lost his way, he at length reached the banks of the river, but on the opposite side to his own house.

In the dead of the night, and in a state of starvation, having eaten nothing for three days, everything seeming to be quiet about his own place, he cautiously embarked in a small canoe and paddled across the river. But he had no sooner landed than an Indian seized him and dragged him to his house, where he found all his family prisoners, and the Indians in full possession. These Indians were not of the same tribe with those who had destroyed Dr. Whitman's family, nor had they at all participated in the outrage; but having heard of it, and fearing that the whites would include them in their vengeance, they had seized on the family of Mr. Spalding for the purpose of holding them as hostages for their own safety. The family were uninjured, and he was overjoyed to find that things were no worse.

Mr. Ogden, the chief factor of the Hudson's Bay Company on the Columbia, immediately on hearing of the outrage, came to Walla-Walla, and, although the occurrence took place in the territory of the United States, and of course the sufferers could have no further claim to the protection of the Company than such as humanity dictated, he at once purchased the release of all the prisoners, and from them the particulars of the massacre were afterwards obtained. The Indians, in their negotiations with Mr. Ogden, offered to give up the prisoners for nothing, if he would guarantee that the United States would not go to war with them; but this, of course, he could not do.

On the 22nd September our two boats, with their crews of

six men each, being all ready, we bade farewell to our kind host and his family and again embarked on the river.[3] As usual, on leaving a fort, we did not start till evening, and stopped again for the night at ten miles distant, at Day's Encampment. We had no regale, as these men were not going into the interior. They only carried the express to Boat Encampment, where they exchange boxes with the express from the east side of the mountains, with whom I was to recross.

Sept. 23rd.—To-day we succeeded in getting past the Little Dalles in safety. They are about twenty miles from Kettle Falls, and are the narrowest part of the Columbia River for full one thousand miles. It is here contracted into a passage of one hundred and fifty yards by lofty rocks on each side, through which it rushes with tremendous violence, forming whirlpools in its passage capable of engulphing the largest forest trees, which are afterwards disgorged with great force. This is one of the most dangerous places that the boats have to pass. In going up the river the boats are all emptied, and the freight has to be carried about half a mile over the tops of the high and rugged rocks. One man remains in each boat with a long pole to keep it off from the rocks, whilst the others drag it by a long tow-rope up the torrent. [Fig. 119; crIV-286, 287]

Last year a man, who was on the outside of the rope, was jerked over the rocks by some sudden strain, and was immediately lost. In coming down, however, all remain in the boats; and the guides in this perilous pass, display the greatest courage and presence of mind at moments when the slightest error in managing the frail bark would hurl its occupants to certain destruction. On arriving at the head of the rapids, the guide gets out on to the rocks and surveys the whirlpools. If they are filling in "or making," as they term it, the men rest on their paddles until they commence throwing off, when the guides instantly re-embark, and shove off the boat, and shoot through this dread portal with the speed of lightning. Sometimes the boats are whirled round in the vortex with such awful rapidity that it renders the management impossible, and the boat and its hapless crew are swallowed up in the abyss.

Sept. 24th.—We had fine weather and made good progress. I shot the largest wolf to-day I had ever seen; he was swimming away from us across the river.

Sept. 25th.—The morning broke dark and cloudy, and soon turned to heavy rain; but the wind was fair, so we hoisted our sail, and soon scudded into an open lake, about three miles wide and twelve long.

Sept. 26th.—It continued raining heavily all night, and heavy

---

[2] The Rev. Henry Spalding came with his wife to the Oregon in 1836 along with the Whitmans, but established his mission station at Lapwai Creek two miles from its junction with the Clearwater River among the Nez Percé Indians.

[3] KJ states that Kane was placed in charge of the two Hudson's Bay Company boats with instructions to meet the express coming from the other side of the mountains.

Plate XXIV. A lake in the plains, between Fort Pitt and Fort Edmonton. ROM946.15.138; CRIV-181.

mists hung over us during the day; but we continued our journey and got into what is called another lake.

Sept. 27th.—Still in the lakes. The day was clearer, and we could distinguish the surrounding scenery, which seemed to consist of immense mountains, towering peak on peak above the clouds. The land appeared barren and unfit for cultivation. The cedars are of enormous magnitude, some of them measuring not less than thirty or forty feet in circumference. I was told of one fifty feet, but did not see it. I attempted to reach the upper side of one which had been uprooted and lay on the ground, with the end of my gun stretched out at arm's length, and could but just attain it. [Fig. 122; crIV-283 to 285, 288, 289]

Sept. 28th.—We had an exciting chase after a mountain goat, which showed himself in the distance, on a point of land jutting out into the lake. Putting the boat ashore, I started in pursuit, accompanied by three or four Indians, and after a long hunt succeeded in killing him. He afforded us a most delicious repast. In size and shape he somewhat resembled the domestic goat, but was covered with white wool resembling that of a sheep; the horns are straight, small, pointed, and black.

Sept. 29th.—Got through the lakes by 5 o'clock P.M., and again entered into what may be more properly called the river. The rain was pouring heavily on us almost all day, whilst in the distance we could see the tops of the mountains becoming white with snow down to a well-defined line, where it seemed to change to rain.

Sept. 30th.—Started at 6 A.M., during a pouring rain, which soon soaked us to the skin. We stopped here to make some paddles,[4] in a forest abounding with birch, the only wood fit for this purpose, and which is not met with lower down the Columbia; large cedar-trees were also very abundant.

Oct. 1st.—The morning was fine and clear, and the temperature was agreeable: I was enabled to leave the boat for a walk for a few miles along the shore, much to the relief of my legs. The place is a sandbank, extending for miles in a direction parallel with the shore, and generally but a few furlongs from it; it is called the "Grand Batteur." The steepness of the banks of the river, and the density of the under-brushwood, had confined us to the boats for the last three days; it was therefore no wonder that I should enjoy a walk. We saw some very large piles of drift-wood, called by the Canadians "Aumbereaux." These piles consist of trees of all sizes, but usually very large, which are drifted down the river, and are piled high up upon one another by the force of the ice when they meet with any obstruction. I amused myself by setting fire to some of them *en*

passant, and leaving an immense fire burning, the smoke of which we could see for days in our rear.

Oct. 2nd.—It again rained heavily all day. Towards the evening we encamped. It is difficult to imagine the pleasure of an encampment round a large fire, after sitting in an open boat on the Columbia River, with the rain pouring down in torrents all day; but though the rain may not have ceased, yet the cheerful warmth of the fire dispels all the annoyance of mere moisture in this uncivilised state of life. We passed the Upper Little Dalle, a very long and rapid shoot of three or four miles. One of the Indians brought in some white berries, which he ate eagerly, but which I found very nauseous. I never saw any berry in the course of my travels which the Indians scruple to eat, nor have I seen any ill effect result from their doing so.

Oct. 3rd.—Saw four carriboos, a species of deer of the ordinary size, which we followed, but without success, as they got the wind of us before we could approach them within gunshot. We fell in with the Indian chief of the lakes, and procured some bear's and deer's meat from him, of which he seemed to possess a plentiful supply.[5] A small species of dog was tied to the bushes near his lodge, to prevent them from hunting on their own account, and driving away all the deer. The chief told me that when disposed to hunt with them, he had only to find a fresh deer-track, set his dogs on it and lie down to sleep, as they never fail to find the deer, and turn them back to the place where they had left him lying. We saw some of these dogs, apparently on the track of some deer, full twelve or fifteen miles from the chief's lodge.

Oct. 4th.—The chief, with wife and daughter, accompanied us in their canoe, which they paddled with great dexterity, from ten to fifteen miles. They make their canoes of pine bark, being the only Indians who use this material for the purpose; their form is also peculiar and very beautiful. These canoes run the rapids with more safety for their size, than those of any other shape. The chief and his ladies breakfasted with us, and then bid us good bye. [Figs. 120, 121; crIV-290, 291]

We camped at night below the "Dalle des Morts," or the Rapid of the Dead, so called from the following circumstance. About twenty-five or thirty years ago, an Iroquois, a half-breed, and a French Canadian, having charge of a boat, had to descend this frightful rapid. Fearful of running it, they affixed a long

---

[4] KJ mentions stopping for six hours to make paddles, the first time that the crews had had an opportunity to walk for three days.

[5] KJ: The chief "had a long range to hunt in—from Colville to Boat Encampment. I admired his dogs. . . . I saw that at all the lodges that they kept their dogs tied for fear that they will go hunting on their own account."

line to the bow, and being themselves on the shore, they attempted to lower her gradually by means of it down the foaming torrent. The boat took a sheer and ran outside of a rock, and all their efforts to get her back, or reach the rock themselves through the boiling surge were unavailing. The rope, chafing on the sharp edge of the rock, soon broke, and she dashed down among the whirling eddies, and broke to pieces, with their whole stock of provisions on board.

They then continued to follow on foot, along the rugged and difficult banks of the river, without food, guns, or ammunition; nor had they been able to save even a blanket, to protect them from the inclement weather. At night they encamped in a shivering and famishing condition, not having been able to surmount more than three miles of the obstacles that obstructed their passage at every step along the banks. The next day they proceeded with no better success. They well knew that if they constructed a raft it would not live an hour in this part of the Columbia River, owing to the quick succession of rapids that here beset the navigation. In this starving condition they continued their slow progress till the third day, when the half-breed, fearing his companions would kill him for their food, left them, and was never after heard of, falling, in all probability, a prey to the wolves. The other two lay down, and the Iroquois watching his opportunity, got up at night, and beat his companion's brains out with a stick, and going to work in a methodical manner, after first satisfying his craving hunger with a portion of the body, cut the remainder in thin slices and dried them in the sun, after the manner in which buffalo meat is prepared. Here he remained three days drying his meat, which he made into a pack, and continued his journey with it down the river bank, until he came to the commencement of the Upper Lake, where he made a raft, on which he placed his dried meat, and covered it over with pine-bark, seating himself upon it, and paddling down the lake.

He had not proceeded very far, before he met a canoe, which had been sent from one of the forts below, on the Spokan River, in quest of them, owing to their long absence. The new comers immediately inquired what had become of his two companions; he replied, that they had deserted him, giving at the same time an account of the loss of the boat. They took him on board their canoe, and one of the men seeing the bark on the raft, and desirous of getting it to place under him in the canoe, the Iroquois shoved off the raft, with evident signs of confusion, on which the man, who noticed his embarrassment, paddled up to it, and lifting the bark, discovered the dried meat beneath it,

among which was a human foot. He was asked how he had obtained the dried meat, and replied, that he had killed a wolf, swimming across the river.

The foot with the meat was slyly deposited in a bag, belonging to one of the men, but not without the act being perceived by the murderer, who, while they were asleep during the night, threw the bag and its contents into the river. Appearing not to notice its loss, they went on to Fort Spokan, and delivered him up to Mr. M'Mullan, the person in charge, detailing the particulars. The Indian was shortly afterwards sent to a distant post in New Caledonia, both as a punishment, and also in order to get rid of him, as no voyageur will willingly associate with any one known to have eaten human flesh. I had previously travelled several hundreds of miles with the son of this very man, who always behaved well, although there certainly was something repulsive in his appearance, which would have made me dislike to have had him for a companion in a situation such as above described.

Oct. 5th.—It rained so hard throughout the day and night, and the river was swollen so much, that we despaired of hauling the boats up the rapids, and therefore remained until the following morning at our encampment.

Oct. 6th.—It was a lovely morning. Saw some carriboos, but could not approach them near enough for a shot. We had a magnificent view of the Rocky Mountains in the distance, in all their azure grandeur. The flood soon subsided sufficiently to allow our ascending the rapids, although it took us the whole day to haul the boats up—the distance is not more than three miles—but the boats were so strained and tossed about in the operation, that we were obliged to haul them ashore and grease their bottoms with the resin which exudes from the pine.

Whilst the men were engaged in these operations, I took advantage of the delay, and made a sketch, looking down the rapids. [crIV-282] As I was sketching, our steersman, who was present at the time, told me a melancholy occurrence, which took place at this spot, and which I will give as nearly as possible in his own words. "About four years ago," said he, "I crossed the Rocky Mountains with a party of forty. When we got to Boat Encampment, we embarked in two boats; the one which I was steering had twenty-two on board, amongst whom was a gentleman sent into the interior for the purpose of botanical research. On his way to Saskatchawan, he had fallen in with a young lady, a half-breed, who was travelling to cross the mountains and go down the Columbia on a visit to some of her friends. They had not travelled far, before a mutual attachment induced them to become man and wife, at Edmonton, though few couples, I think, in the world would choose a trip across the mountains for a honeymoon excursion; but they bore all their hardships and labours cheerfully, perfectly happy in helping each other, and being kind to their companions.

"We had two or three other women with us, and I had my own daughter, about ten years old, whom I was taking home to my wife at Fort Vancouver. I had left her two or three years before, on the east side of the mountains, with some of her relations, as I was unable to bring her over at the time I had come with my wife. We had also a young man of the name of M'Gillveray, belonging to the Company, with a small dog; the remainder was principally voyageurs.

"When I came to the head of the rapids, I found that the other boat, which contained the principal guide, had passed on, and I thought, therefore, that the rapids were in a proper state for running them, that is, that the whirlpools were throwing out and not filling, which they do alternately. I therefore went on without stopping, and when in the midst of the rapids, where there was no possibility of staying the downward course of the boat, I discovered to my dismay that the whirlpools were filling. One moment more and the water curled over the sides of the boat, immediately filling her. I called out for all to sit still and hold on steadily to the seats, as the boat would not sink entirely owing to the nature of the cargo, and that I could guide them to shore in this state. We ran more than a mile in safety, when the boat ran close by a ledge of rocks. The botanist, who held his wife in his arms, seeing the boat approach so near the rock, made a sudden spring for the shore; but the boat filled with water, yielded to the double weight of himself and wife, and they sank clasped in each other's arms. The boat was suddenly turned completely bottom upwards; but I and another man succeeded in getting on the top of her, and were thus carried down safely. We thought we heard some noise inside the boat, and the man who was with me, being a good swimmer, dived under, and soon, to my unexpected joy, appeared with my little daughter, who almost miraculously had been preserved by being jammed in amongst the luggage, and supported by the small quantity of air which had been caught by the boat when she turned over. We soon got ashore: M'Gillveray and four others saved themselves by swimming, the remaining fourteen were drowned; we immediately commenced searching for the bodies, and soon recovered all of them, the unfortunate botanist and his wife still fast locked in each other's arms,—an embrace which we had not the hearts to unclasp, but buried them as we found them, in one grave. We afterwards found M'Gillveray's little dog thrown up dead on a sandbank, with his master's cap held firmly between his teeth."

Oct. 7th.—We embarked in the morning, and continued our journey through a continual drizzle of rain, which was anything but pleasant.

Oct. 8th.—The weather cleared up, and we saw carriboos in great numbers; but, as usual, they were too wary for us to get a shot at them. Passed the rapids of St. Martin before night.

Oct. 9th.—Travelled but a short distance to-day, having to cut our way through the numerous fallen trees which, projecting into the stream, obstructed the course close to the shore, which we were obliged to take owing to the violence of the current in mid-channel.

Oct. 10th.—In the forenoon we perceived tracks of human feet in the sand on the shore, which astonished us very much, as no Indians come near these parts; and on approaching Boat Encampment, which we did about 2 P.M., we perceived smoke rising, which made us hope that the brigade from the east with the express had arrived, but were much disappointed at finding that it was only my old friend Capote Blanc, the Sho-shawp chief from Jasper's House, and two Indians who had come over to hunt. Here we made a suitable encampment, and hauled up our boats high and dry on the sand. Capote Blanc had been very successful in his hunt, and had a large stock of dried moose meat and beavers' tails, with which he supplied us abundantly, receiving a few small articles and ammunition in exchange.

We now had nothing to do but to try and pass the time pleasantly as we could under the circumstances, until the arrival of the brigade from the east side of the mountains. [Pl. XXIX; Figs. 117, 118; crIV-275 to 279] The men spent the day principally in gambling, and performing charms which they supposed would hasten the arrival of the brigade, such as erecting crosses, with one of the arms pointing to the direction from which it was expected. They also prepared what they call a "lobstick." [6] For this purpose a high tree is chosen which has thick branches at the top, and all the lower limbs are carefully trimmed off; a smooth surface is then cut on one side of the tree, on which the person in whose honour it has been trimmed is invited to cut his name; this being done, three rounds of blank-charges are fired, and three cheers given, and the spot

---

[6] KJ for October 12 reads: "The men cut a lobstick of 111 feet and I am requested to put my name on it as it was intended for me. Our little party then turned out and fired 3 rounds, and gave 3 cheers in honour of their Bushway as I was called." "Bushway" is a version of *bourgeois*, and evidently a term applied to a leader of a party in the fur trade; see Richard Dillon, *Fool's Gold*, p. 45.

afterwards bears the name of his encampment. On this occasion I had the honour of carving my name upon the "lobstick." We had almost constant rain, accompanied by immense snow-flakes, which obscured our view of the mountains nearly the whole time of our remaining here. I, however, managed to pick out some few bright hours for sketching.

We found very little game about here; the men only succeeded in trapping a few martens, and we began to be very uneasy, fearing that some disaster must have befallen the brigade which was to meet us.[7] I endeavoured to prevail on some of the men to accompany me across the mountains; but they would not go with me, so that I was forced to stay with the rest. Boat Encampment derives its name from its being the head of the navigable water. Three rivers here unite, forming the commencement of the north branch of the Columbia, so that the enlargement of the river is very sudden.

Oct. 28th.—About three o'clock in the afternoon a clerk in the company's service arrived,[8] and announced that he had come in advance of the eastern brigade, which would arrive next day under the command of Mr. Low: this was indeed joyful news to us, as we were all heartily tired of our gloomy situation.

Oct. 29th.—Mr. Low and party arrived this morning with between fifty and sixty horses loaded with provision, and the furs destined for Russia. They had been nine days crossing from Jasper's House. Mr. Low seemed doubtful about our being able to recross with the horses; but I cared little whether we had horses or not, so that I got away, for I was completely wearied with my long inaction. My provisions, too, were getting short, and the person in charge did not offer to replenish my stock, so that I had no choice but to cross as quickly as possible.

Oct. 30th.—This day Mr. Low left for Fort Vancouver with the boats[9] which had brought me up, leaving me with four Indians[10] who had accompanied him from the east side for the purpose of taking the horses back, and of guiding me over the mountains.

Oct. 31st.—It was a beautiful morning, and we started about ten o'clock, after loading fifteen horses out of the fifty-six which Mr. Low had brought with him, and got the first day as far as the Grande Batture, where we encamped.

Nov. 1st.—We passed through the Pointe des Bois, a distance of ten miles, by about the worst road I had ever travelled, it being cut up by so many horses having passed it a short time previously. My horse stuck in a mud hole until he sank up to his head, and it was with the greatest difficulty that one of the men and myself extricated him alive. What with the horses sticking

in the mud, the packs falling off, the shouting to the animals in Cree, and swearing at them in French, there being no oaths in the Indian languages, I never passed such a busy, tiresome, noisy, and disagreeable day in my life. This was in a great measure owing to having so few men to look after so large a number of horses, which would not keep the road, but ran helter skelter through the thick woods. At last we arrived at the bottom of the Grande Côte, and there encamped for the night, thoroughly wearied out and disgusted with horse-driving.

Nov. 2nd.—We started an hour before daybreak to ascend the stupendous Grande Côte, and soon found the snow becoming deeper at every step. One of our horses fell down a declivity of twenty-five to thirty feet with a heavy load on his back, and, strange to say, neither deranged his load nor hurt himself. We soon had him on the track again as well as ever, except that he certainly looked a little *bothered*. The snow now reached up to the horses' sides as we slowly toiled along, and reached the summit just as the sun sank below the horizon; but we could not stop here, as there was no food for the horses, we were therefore obliged to push on past the Committee's Punch Bowl,[11] a lake I have before described.

It was intensely cold, as might be supposed, in this elevated region. Although the sun shone during the day with intense brilliancy, my long beard became one solid mass of ice. It was long after dark before we arrived at the Campment de Fusei, having met with no other place which afforded any food for the horses,[12] and even here they had to dig the snow away with their hoofs to enable them to get at it.

A distressing occurrence took place here some years previously. Whilst a party were ascending this mountain, a lady, who was crossing to meet her husband, was in the rear, and it was not noticed until the party had encamped that she was not come up. Men were instantly sent back to seek her. After some

---

[7] There are many indications of frustration in the KJ entries. Those for October 24–26 read:

"24th: Prew, Sanslay and Le Frambeys agree to start with me to-morrow across the mountains on foot.

"25th: The men have declined to start for want of moccasins.

"26th: Cold ice made two inches in the night. The men have tried every expedient to bring the brigade such as making a cross and directing its arms in the way they are expected. Another sign, if the moon passes close to such and such a star, the brigade will be here tomorrow and according to the distance so they gauge the time they will arrive."

[8] KJ identifies the new arrivals as Mr. Mackenzie and a guide.

[9] KJ reads that they left with four boats.

[10] KJ calls the men who were left with Kane half-breeds and not Indians.

[11] KJ adds ironically: "Rather cold punch at present."

[12] KJ says the snow was too deep higher up for the horses to get food.

hours' search, they found her tracks in the snow, which they followed until they came to a perpendicular rock overhanging a roaring torrent; here all traces of her were lost, and her body was never found, notwithstanding every exertion was made to find it. Little doubt, however, could exist but that she had lost her way, and had fallen over the precipice into the torrent, which would have quickly hurried her into chasms where the foot of man could not reach.

Nov. 3rd.—Last night was the coldest (according to my feelings) that I had ever experienced; [13] but not having a thermometer with me, I do not know what was the intensity. I am, however, confident that it was colder on that night than it was on a subsequent night, when the spirit thermometer indicated *56° below zero,* a temperature at which mercury would have become frozen and useless. I endeavoured to thaw myself by melting some snow over the fire; but the water froze upon my hair and beard, although I stood as close as I well could to a blazing fire, and I actually had to scorch my face before I could thaw the ice out. We now passed through the Grande Batture, and, much to our relief, found the snow decreasing in depth as we descended. We succeeded in reaching the Campment de Regnalle in the evening, and camped there for the night.

Nov. 4th.—We got our breakfast and started long before day.[14] We made good progress until about noon, when we came to a wild tract of country which appeared to have been visited years before by some terrible hurricane, which had uprooted the whole forest for miles round, not leaving a tree standing; a younger growth of trees were now pushing their heads up through the fallen timber of the ancient forest. We all got so hungry with our violent exercise in such a cold clear atmosphere, that we could not resist the temptation of stopping and cooking something to eat, before we entered the tangled maze before us. This was the first time we had done so, as daylight was too valuable to be wasted in sitting down, and the danger of being caught in one of the tremendous snow storms, which are so frequent in these regions, was too imminent for us not to push on to the utmost of our power. The snow often lies here to the depth of twenty or thirty feet, and one storm might have caused us the loss of the horses and baggage at least, even if we had been able to save ourselves by making snow shoes. It was, therefore, no slight temptation which could induce the men who knew the country to stop for dinner; but hunger is a good persuader, and carried the question. After dinner we pushed on with renewed strength; but it was with great difficulty that we were enabled to get the horses through the fallen and tangled woods, and it was not until after nightfall that we reached the "Grand Traverse," where we found three men, who had been sent out to meet us and assist in driving in our sixty horses, which were as yet all safe.

Nov. 5th.—In the morning we found the Athabasca River in a flooded state, and a heavy snow storm had set in; we, however, proceeded to ford the rapid stream, although the snow was driving with such fury in our faces that we could not distinguish the opposite bank. The water almost covered the backs of the horses, and my pack, containing sketches and curiosities, &c., had to be carried on the shoulders of the men riding across, to keep them out of the water. After fording the river we crossed La Rouge's Prair[i]e, and encamped on the very spot that I had slept at exactly a year previously, to the very day.

Nov. 6th.—The wind blew intensely cold, and we had to pass along the margin of a frozen lake, seven or eight miles long, over which the snow drifted furiously in our faces. It became so cold that we could no longer sit on the horses, but were obliged to dismount and drive them on before us. My beard, the growth of nearly two years, gave me great trouble, as it became heavy with ice from the freezing of my breath; even my nostrils became stopped up, and I was forced to breathe through my mouth.

Fortunately I fell in with an Indian lodge,[15] and had an opportunity of thawing myself, so that I rode the remainder of the way to Jasper's House with comparative comfort. There we soon forgot our trouble over a good piece of mountain sheep, which is really delicious, even when not seasoned by such hardships as we had undergone.

This place is completely surrounded by lofty mountains, some of them close to the house, others many miles distant, and is subject to violent tornadoes, which sweep through the mountain gorges with terrific fury. A great number of mountain sheep had been driven down into the valleys by the intensity of the cold, which had set in this winter with unusual severity. I have counted as many as five large flocks of these animals grazing in different directions from the house at one time, and the Indians brought them in every day, so that we fared most sumptuously. These sheep are those most commonly called the "big horn." [crIV-257, 263]

---

[13] KJ reads that this was the coldest night in which Kane had ever camped out rather than the coldest he had ever experienced.

[14] KJ reads: "It is strange I have not taken a meal in daylight since leaving Boat Encampment. We have to travel both late and early for fear of being set fast by the snow as it sometimes falls to a depth of 25 feet."

[15] KJ points out that the lodge belonged to one of the men in Kane's party.

I made a sketch of a ram's head of an enormous size; [16] his horns were similar in shape to those of our domestic ram, but measured forty-two inches in length. [Fig. 113; crIV-256] They are considerably larger than our domestic sheep; their coat somewhat resembles in texture and colour the red deer, but a little darker. We were now obliged to set our men to work to make snow-shoes, as our further journey had to be made over deep snow. The birch wood of which they are made does not grow near Jasper's House, and the men had to go twenty miles off to get it. At last, by the 14th, our snow shoes and a sledge were completed, and with much difficulty I obtained two wretched dogs from the Indians, and one Mr. Colin Frazer lent me, to drag the sledge with my packs, provisions, and blankets. I had two men, one an Indian, the other a half-breed. They had come with Mr. Low from Edmonton, with seven others, and ought to have waited for me; but we had been so long coming, and the weather had got so cold, that the seven got afraid of waiting any longer, and departed without me. Had these two followed the example of their companions, I should have been obliged to spend a most dreary winter in the wretched accommodation which Jasper's House afforded.

Nov. 15th.—Early in the morning we equipped ourselves for the journey, putting on snow shoes between five and six feet long,—the pair I wore were exactly my own height, five feet eleven inches. Owing to our having so few dogs, we could not carry many provisions, but trusted to our guns to provide more on the way.

About fifteen or sixteen miles from Jasper's House, we came to an Indian lodge, which we found tenanted by a woman and her five children, her husband being out on a hunt. She was so civil and kind, and the lodge was so comfortable, that we were induced to stop, particularly as it was our first day on snow shoes, and stopping there saved us the trouble of making a camp for ourselves. The hunter returned late in the evening, having killed four sheep, one of which he brought home on his back. This we all set to work to cook, the squaw boiling as much as her kettle would hold, and the men sticking the rest upon sticks and roasting it. The whole party then set resolutely to work, and ate the whole sheep, and it was not a small one either. The hunter told us that he had seen thirty-four sheep that day, and that he never remembered a winter in which so many sheep had come down from the mountains. He proved a most agreeable host,

[16] The sketch is evidently crIV-256; it is now in the Stark Collection. kj notes that he intended the sketch for Sir George Simpson. The Simpson collection has been dispersed and no trace of a painting based on this sketch has been found.

and entertained me with stories of his hunting exploits during the whole evening. My kind hostess prepared me a bed of sheep skins for the night, the most comfortable bed I had slept in for many months.

Nov. 16th.—At an early hour before daylight we got our breakfast and harnessed our dogs, and made our way through some very thick woods. We entered on Jasper's Lake, twelve miles long, the wind blowing a perfect hurricane, as it always does here when it blows at all. Fortunately the wind always comes from the mountains: had it been otherwise, we should not have been able to pass along the lake on the glare ice against such a storm of wind and sleet; as it was, we were blown along by the wind, and could only stop ourselves by lying down; our sledge sometimes flying in front of the dogs, while we were enveloped in a cloud of snow that prevented our seeing more than a few yards before us.

When we were about half way over the lake, we perceived two Indians, who were making their way across in a course intersecting our own route, and evidently had hard work to keep in the right direction. On coming up to them, we all sat down and had a smoke. The Indians, when they come to ice or hard frozen snow, where the snow shoe has to be taken off, always take off their moccasins also, and travel barefooted; by this means they preserve their moccasins, and when they sit down they put them on dry and wrap their feet in their furs. This walking barefooted on ice in such intense cold would seem dangerous to the inexperienced, but, in fact, the feet of those who are accustomed to it suffer less in this way than they do from the ice which always forms on the inside of the moccasin in long and quick travelling, as the ice thus formed cracks into small pieces and cuts the feet. After we had crossed the lake, we proceeded about five miles down the river, and encamped.

Nov. 17th.—The night had been intensely cold, but all felt well and in high spirits when we started in the morning. These feelings were, however, soon damped by the painful difficulties which we soon encountered. Where the river is rapid, the ice becomes rough, craggy, and unsafe, and is raised in hillocks to a considerable height, by the masses being forced by the current on the top of each other. Some of those hillocks we met were so formidable, that we at first doubted the possibility of surmounting them; even in the hollows we were obliged to move slowly, feeling our way with long sticks, to ascertain if the ice was solid. This was rendered necessary by the frequent occurrence of flat fields of ice, which, being formed high above the usual level of the water, and having nothing to support them underneath, easily give way, and the traveller falls either into the torrent far below, or upon another layer of ice. These dangerous places are formed by the large masses of ice getting jammed together against the rocks, or in some bend of the river, and damming the water up, on the top of which a thin coating is formed. As soon as the weight of water becomes too heavy for the dam, it is carried away, and the water sinks, leaving the coat formed on the top without support from beneath, which, when covered with snow, it is impossible to distinguish from good ice, except by feeling it with a stick.

We had not proceeded very far, before one of the men fell through one of these places; luckily he did not come to water, and we soon got him out. Our dogs were now almost useless, as they were unable to drag the sledge over the uneven surface, and we were obliged to push the sledge after them with our poles, and often to lift the dogs, sledge, and baggage up and down the perpendicular ice ridges (or *bourdigneaux*, as the voyageurs call them) with which our path was constantly intersected. At this place it was impossible to leave the river, as the ground on both sides was so broken, and the forest was so dense and tangled, that we should have starved long before we could have made our way through it. About an hour before sundown I unfortunately broke through, and it was with the utmost difficulty that I saved myself from being carried under by the current, which here ran with the velocity of a mill race: happily, I neither lost my pole nor my presence of mind, so the men had time to come up and help me out; but the moment I was out of the water my clothes became perfectly stiff, and we were obliged to make a fire and encamp for the night.

Nov. 18*th.*—Our trials seemed now to be increasing at every step, but the struggle was not optional now; so cheering ourselves with the idea that none know what they can bear until they are tried, we prepared for an early start. Our first trouble was that the dog Mr. Frazer lent me (the best dog we had) was gone; he had gnawed the cord asunder with which he was tied, and bolted off home.[17] This was a serious loss, as besides his use in drawing the sledge, we did not know but that we might want to eat him, our provisions were getting so scarce, and we met with very few rabbits, the only thing to be found on the route at this season.

Our next difficulty was to pass the Grand Rapid, where we found the river obstructed for nearly four miles by bourdigneaux, from ten to fourteen feet high. Over this continuous mass

[17] KJ emphasizes Kane's concern at the loss of the dog: it resulted in his trunk having to be left behind to be sent on later.

of icy pinnacles we scrambled with incredible labour, our limbs bruised with repeated falls, and our feet wounded and cut by treading on the sharp edges of fractured ice. At last, overpowered by fatigue and pain, we made our camp for the night, almost disheartened with our slow progress, as we had not made more than ten or twelve miles through the whole day.

During the night we were awoke by a tremendous roaring amongst the masses of ice, caused by a rising in the river. I could not help feeling apprehensive lest we should be crushed amongst it, from our camp being so near; but the men were too tired to move, and I was too tired to argue with them; so we slept on.

Nov. 19*th.*—When we got up in the morning, we found that the water had overflowed the ice, and we were compelled to make a circuit through the woods. We found the brush and fallen timber so thick, that we had to cut a road through it to enable our two dogs and the sledge to get along. It took us three hours to make an advance of one mile, before we again got back to the bourdigneaux, glad even to get to them, in preference to the tangled and almost impassable growth of trees and underwood which follows the course of the river through its whole length. This day I suffered a great deal; my feet were so severely cut by the frozen strings of my snow-shoes, that I left a track of blood behind me on the snow at every step. At night, when we encamped, it became so cold that we could only sleep for a few minutes at a time: no matter how large we made the fire, it would only keep that part warm which was immediately next to it, so that we were obliged to keep turning round and round to save ourselves from freezing.

Nov. 20*th.*—This morning I found I had what the voyageurs call *mal de racquet.* This complaint attacks those who are unaccustomed to the use of snow-shoes, if they walk far on them at first. It is felt at the instep. I do not know how to convey an idea of the intense pain, except by saying that it feels as if the bones were broken, and the rough edges were grinding against each other at every motion.

Nov. 21*st.*—In the morning we found that the river had become dammed up a short distance below our encampment, and was throwing the ice up in mountainous heaps with tremendous noise. This forced us again to make a short détour through the woods, which we effected with a great deal of trouble. By the time we got to the river again it snowed very hard, and continued without intermission all day; notwithstanding all this, and the mal de racquet, from which I suffered very severely, we pushed on, and, impelled by dire necessity, for our supply of food was fast diminishing, we made rather a good day's journey. We had, up to this, always given our dogs food every day, but my guide advised us not to do so any more, as he had known dogs travel twenty days without food, and every ounce we now had was too precious to give to them, even if they died; so the poor brutes were tied up supperless, and we tried to content ourselves with about half of what was our usual allowance.

Nov. 22nd.—The snow still continued, and was getting very deep and light, adding considerably to the labour of our journey; but we toiled on manfully, and succeeded in getting across Baptiste River before we stopped for the night, which did not seem to me as cold as usual, I suppose on account of the falling snow and stillness of the atmosphere.

Nov. 23rd.—The snow had ceased falling, but lay very deep and feathery on the ground, so that it fell over on to the snow-shoes, adding to their weight. This to me became very distressing, after two or three hours' walking, owing to the state of my ankles; but the weather was clear and fine, and the bright sun, while it lasted, seemed to cheer us on, so that at night, when we stopped, we calculated that we had made at least thirty-five miles. Not having met with any rabbits, we were obliged to stint ourselves in food, and starve our dogs.

Nov. 24th.—To-day we again came to open water, and had to make another détour through the woods of about a mile and a half, but it was not such a bad place as we had encountered before, the woods being a little more open. When we came to the river again, we found ourselves on the top of a high bank, down which we lowered our sledge and baggage, and then pitched the poor dogs after. As for ourselves, we scrambled at the commencement of the descent, then rolled a little by way of variety, and fell the rest of the way; however, the snow was so deep, that we did not get hurt, and after some trouble in unburying ourselves at the bottom, we continued our route along the river.

Nov. 2[5]th.—We had not travelled more than twenty miles, when we came to a part of the river in which the current was so rapid, that the ice was all tumbling about in broken masses. On each side we were encompassed by high banks rising into hills, which it was impossible for us to ascend; and as it is a rule, in travelling in the interior, never to go back, we had nothing for it but to encamp under the shelter of the hill, in hopes that the intense cold of the night would sufficiently unite the masses of ice to enable us to cross in the morning.

After our camp was made, the men, seeing me suffer so much from the mal de racquet, recommended me to scarify my in-steps, and kindly offered to perform the operation, which is done with a sharp gun-flint; but I was afraid of the frost getting into the wounds, and refused, although I had every confidence in their knowledge of what would be the best remedy in a case like mine. We had not succeeded in shooting a single animal on our route, and it was with melancholy forebodings we looked at our diminished stock of provisions. Our poor dogs looked so savage and starved, that we had to tie their heads close up to the trees, fearing lest they might gnaw the strings, and make off.

Nov. 26th.—In the morning we found the ice sufficiently strong to induce us to proceed, but we had to use great caution, as it was still very weak. Our long snow shoes covering such a large surface, supported us safely; but the ice was so thin, that the dogs and sledge went through, and we should have lost everything we had, had not the Indian held a string fastened to the sledge, and by this means hauled them up. When we surmounted this difficulty, we found the ice better than usual, and were enabled to make in all forty miles before we encamped.

Nov. 27th.—We got on to-day very well till about noon, when the mal de racquet became so painful to me, that I thought I would try to walk without my snow-shoes. But I had not waded through the snow very far before I fell through the ice. Luckily, I got out easily enough, but I was wet through; and as our provisions were nearly all gone, and we were all hungry, I pushed on in my wet clothes, trusting to the violent exercise to keep me warm. I certainly did not suffer from cold, but the freezing of my leathern trowsers chafed my legs and made me very uncomfortable. We encamped after a very hard day's work, and as we were in great hopes of reaching Fort Assiniboine next day, we finished the last of our provisions.

Nov. 28th.—We started early in the morning, about three o'clock: this was an hour earlier than we usually got away, but we had nothing to cook and no breakfast to eat. I began to feel that my hardships were telling seriously on me. The mal de racquet tortured me at every step; the soles of my feet were terribly cut and wounded from the ice, which formed inside of my stockings as much as an eighth of an inch thick every day, occasioned by the freezing of the perspiration. It breaks in small pieces, and is like so much sharp gravel in the shoes; and I was weak from the want of food: but the hope of reaching a place of safety kept me up, and I toiled on over the bourdigneaux, which were very numerous to-day, steadily but slowly. At last, overcome with fatigue and weakness we had to encamp still far from the fort. We had a long consultation over our camp fire, as to whether we should eat the dogs or not, but their thinness saved

Edmonton House

Paul Kane
1846

Plate XXV. Fort Edmonton. Stark pwc22; crIV-188.

Plate XXVI. Winter Travelling (a wedding party leaving Fort Edmonton). ROM912.1.48; crIV-201.

them—the two would not have furnished us with a sufficient meal; besides, they could draw the sledge still, and that was a great consideration to us in our weak state; and we knew that if we met with no accident, we must reach the fort next day; still, if the dogs had been young, and in anything like condition, they would most assuredly have gone into the pot.

Nov. 29th.—We again started very early in the morning, hunger waking us up earlier than usual. It is the general rule of travelling in these northern regions, to start as soon as awake, and to continue until fagged out. Daylight is of such short duration (not more than four or five hours) at this time of the year, that it is taken little into account, the light of the snow and the Aurora enabling the traveller to see at all hours. Our way was not very bad, in comparison with what we had come over; still we had to move on slowly from weakness, and it was not until four o'clock P.M., that we arrived at Fort Assiniboine, having travelled 350 miles in fifteen days.

No sooner had we arrived, than all hands set to work cooking; luckily for us, this post is plentifully supplied with white fish—indeed, it is almost the only thing they ever have to eat here—which are caught in immense numbers in a small lake near the fort, called M'Leod's Lake.[18] I never saw such large ones as those caught here. They average six and seven pounds; and one of them which I saw weighed had actually attained to the enormous weight of eighteen pounds.

Whether it was the hunger from which I was suffering, or the real goodness of the fish, I know not now; but certainly they seemed to be the most delicious I had ever tasted, and the memory of that feast hung over me, even in my dreams, for many a day afterwards. One of the women devoted herself to the rather arduous task of satisfying my appetite, whilst my two men cooked on their own account, thinking that nobody else would do it quick enough; and no cook who cared for his reputation would have dished-up fish in the raw state in which they devoured the first two or three. I, however, controlled myself, and gave the woman a little time to prepare mine. Having wrapped my feet up in clean pieces of blanket (the only stockings worn in the interior) and put on a pair of clean dry moccasins, I bethought me of the poor dogs, and taking down some raw fish, went out to feed them. It was almost miraculous to see the big lumps of fish which they gulped down, without even an attempt at mastication. Their appearance after the repast was singularly ridiculous, as their bellies were paunched

out like full bladders, whilst the rest of their bodies retained still all the scraggy symptoms of prolonged hunger.

On returning from my charitable errand, I found that the good woman had lost no time, and soon, seated on a pile of buffalo skins before a good fire, I commenced the most luxurious repast of which it had ever been my fate to partake. I had no brandy, spirits, nor wine, neither had I tea, or coffee—nothing but water to drink. I had no Harvey's sauce, or catsup, or butter, or bread, or potatoes, or any other vegetable. I had nothing but fish; no variety, save that some were broiled on the hot coals and some were boiled. But I had been suffering for days from intense cold, and I now had rest; I had been starving, and I now had food; I had been weary and in pain, without rest or relief, and I now had both rest and ease. But, to sum up all, I had come through a long and serious peril, where for days I had been haunted with the idea that I must camp alone in that solitary forest, and let the men go on, with no food to support me but what I might obtain by the chance snaring of rabbits. It was, in fact, the dread of this almost hopeless alternative, that urged me to exertions upon which I cannot look back except with wonder, and thus brought me at last to the safety and comfort in which I now luxuriated. How many fish the men ate, I do not know; but having satiated themselves, they all lay down to sleep. In the middle of the night they woke me up, to ask me if I would not join them in another feast, but I did not; much to their astonishment, as the woman had told them that she was afraid I was sick, as I only ate four fish out of the seven she had prepared for me. However, in the morning, about five o'clock, I commenced again, and made another hearty meal; and then how happy I was when I lay down and slept again, instead of clambering over the rugged bourdigneaux!

Chapter XXII.

An easy Time.—Clever Rabbit-snare.—Fort Edmonton.—Buffalo Ice-pits.—The Horse and its Keeper.—A tame Battue.—Saving the Credit of the Herd.—Harnessing the Dogs.—My Big Head.—Sober Mirth.—Christmas-day in the Wilds.—Our Fare.—The Feast and the Dance.—"One that looks at the Stars."—Fighting to the Death. —The better part of Valour.—Making a Calf.—An affectionate Bull. —The Aurora Borealis.

Nov. 30th and Dec. 1st.—I remained at Fort Assiniboine to allow my feet to recover, which they did rapidly, as I did little

---

[18] KJ adds: "Made a hearty meal on white fish which Mrs. Brazeau got ready for us."

135

but sleep before the fire and eat fish. On the evening of the 1st we all felt so well, that we prepared to proceed next morning to Edmonton, which we calculated to reach easily in four days.

Dec. 2nd.—We started early in the morning on snow-shoes,[1] taking with us very little provisions, as we were assured that we should find plenty of rabbits on the road. Our route lay through the woods, which were very thick and encumbered with fallen trees: this rendered our progress slow and very fatiguing; but our renewed strength, and the certainty of a good supper when we stopped kept up our spirits and enabled us to make a very good day's journey.[2] When we encamped for the night, we set to work cooking the rabbits which we had killed on the way, of which we had more than enough. The whole evening they were running across our path. This year they were much more numerous than had been remembered for a long time previously, and the woods were filled with traps set by the Indians, from which we might have helped ourselves if we pleased; but this would not have been considered right as long as we had our guns to shoot them. These snares are fastened to the top of young saplings in such a manner as to spring up when the rabbit is caught, and so suspend him in the air; if this was not done, the wolves and the lynxes, who always follow the rabbits in great numbers, and whose tracks we perceived all round us, would eat them as fast as they were caught.

The lynx is caught by a slip noose made of sinew, simply fastened to a small movable log, which the ensnared animal can drag with difficulty after him. Strange to say, they never attempt to gnaw the string which holds them, although, from the shape of their teeth, they evidently could do so with the greatest ease.

Dec. 3rd, 4th, and 5th.—Our route was mostly through woods, but the weather was pleasant, and we had abundance of rabbits, so that the journey seemed like a mere pleasure trip in comparison with what we had gone through.

On the evening of the 5th we arrived at Fort Edmonton, where I was most kindly received by Mr. Harriett,[3] and provided with a comfortable room to myself—a luxury I had not known for many months. This was to be my head-quarters for the winter; and certainly no place in the interior is at all equal to it, either in comfort or interest. All the Company's servants,[4] with their wives and children, numbering about 130, live within the palings of the fort in comfortable log-houses, supplied with abundance of fire-wood.

Along the banks of the river in the vicinity of the fort, about twenty feet below the upper surface, beds of hard coal are seen protruding, which is, however, not much used, except in the blacksmith's forge, for which purpose it seems to be admirably adapted. The want of proper grates or furnaces in those distant regions, where iron is at present so scarce, prevents its general use as fuel.

Provisions are in the greatest plenty, consisting of fresh buffalo meat, venison, salted geese, magnificent white fish, and rabbits in abundance, with plenty of good potatoes, turnips, and flour. The potatoes are very fine, and the turnips do well here. Of wheat, they can of course have only one crop; but with very indifferent farming they manage to get from twenty to twenty-five bushels per acre. The crop, however, is sometimes destroyed by early frost. The corn is ground in a windmill, which had been erected since my last visit, and seemed to make very good flour. Indian corn has been tried, but it did not succeed, owing to the very short summer.[5]

Outside, the buffaloes range in thousands close to the fort; deer are to be obtained at an easy distance; rabbits run about in all directions, and wolves and lynxes prowl after them all through the neighbouring woods. As for seeing aborigines, no place can be more advantageous. Seven of the most important and warlike tribes on the continent are in constant communication with the fort, which is situated in the country of the Crees and Assiniboines, and is visited at least twice in the year by the Blackfeet, Sur-cees, Gros-Vents, Pay-gans, and Blood Indians, who come to sell the dried buffalo meat and fat for making pemmi-kon, which is prepared in large quantities for the supply of the other posts.

The buffaloes were extremely numerous this winter, and several had been shot within a few hundred yards of the fort. The men had already commenced gathering their supply of fresh meat for the summer in the ice-pit. This is made by digging a square hole, capable of containing 700 or 800 buffalo carcases. As soon as the ice in the river is of sufficient thickness, it is cut into square blocks of a uniform size with saws; with these blocks the floor of the pit is regularly paved, and the blocks cemented together by pouring water in between them, and allowing it to freeze solid. In like manner, the walls are solidly built up to the surface of the ground. The head and feet of the buffalo, when

---

[1] KJ states that he left for Edmonton by horseback, not snowshoe.
[2] KJ notes that they found the road very thick despite the fact that sleds had passed a few days before.
[3] This is John Edward Harriott, appointed a chief factor of the Hudson's Bay Company in 1846.
[4] KJ puts the number of the Company's servants in the fort at 50.
[5] KJ adds: "It supplies to other forts about 1000 bags of pemmican."

killed, are cut off, and the carcase, without being skinned, is divided into quarters, and piled in layers in the pit as brought in, until it is filled up, when the whole is covered with a thick coating of straw, which is again protected from the sun and rain by a shed. In this manner the meat keeps perfectly good through the whole summer, and eats much better than fresh killed meat, being more tender and better flavoured.

Shortly after my arrival, Mr. Harriett, myself, and two or three gentlemen of the establishment, prepared for a buffalo hunt. We had our choice of splendid horses, as about a dozen are selected and kept in stables for the gentlemen's use from the wild band of 700 or 800, which roam about the fort, and forage for themselves through the winter, by scraping the snow away from the long grass with their hoofs. [Fig. 104; crIV-203] These horses have only one man to take care of them, who is called the horsekeeper; he follows them about and encamps near them with his family, turning the band should he perceive them going too far away. This would appear to be a most arduous task; but instinct soon teaches the animals that their only safety from their great enemies, the wolves, is by remaining near the habitations of man; and by keeping in one body they are enabled to fight the bands of wolves, which they often drive off after severe contests. Thus they do not stray far away, and they never leave the band. These horses are kept and bred there for the purpose of sending off the pemmi-kon and stores to other forts during the summer; in winter they are almost useless, on account of the depth of snow.

In the morning we breakfasted most heartily on white fish and buffalo tongues, accompanied by tea, milk, sugar, and *galettes*, which the voyageurs consider a great luxury. These are cakes made of simple flour and water, and baked by clearing away a place near the fire; the cake is then laid on the hot ground, and covered with hot ashes, where it is allowed to remain until sufficiently baked. They are very light and pleasant, and are much esteemed. We then mounted our chosen horses, and got upon the track the men had made on the river by hauling wood. This we followed for about six miles, when we espied a band of buffaloes on the bank; but a dog, who had sneaked after us, running after them, gave the alarm too soon, and they started off at full speed, much to our disappointment. We caught the dog, and tied his legs together, and left him lying in the road to await our return.

After going about three miles further, we came to a place where the snow was trodden down in every direction, and on ascending the bank, we found ourselves in the close vicinity of an enormous band of buffaloes, probably numbering nearly 10,000. An Indian hunter started off for the purpose of turning some of them towards us; but the snow was so deep, that the buffaloes were either unable or unwilling to run far, and at last came to a dead stand. We therefore secured our horses, and advanced towards them on foot to within forty or fifty yards, when we commenced firing, which we continued to do until we were tired of a sport so little exciting; for, strange to say, they never tried either to escape or to attack us.

Seeing a very large bull in the herd, I thought I would kill him, for the purpose of getting the skin of his enormous head, and preserving it. [crIV-204, 205, 206] He fell; but as he was surrounded by three others that I could not frighten away, I was obliged to shoot them all before I could venture near him, although they were all bulls, and they are not generally saved for meat. The sport proving rather tedious, from the unusual quietness of the buffaloes, we determined to return home, and send the men for the carcases, and remounted our horses. But, before we came to the river, we found an old bull standing right in our way, and Mr. Harriett, for the purpose of driving him off, fired at him and slightly wounded him, when he turned and made a furious charge. Mr. Harriett barely escaped by jumping his horse on one side. So close, indeed, was the charge, that the horse was slightly struck on the rump. The animal still pursued Mr. Harriett at full speed, and we all set after him, firing ball after ball into him, as we ranged up close to him, without any apparent effect than that of making him more furious, and turning his rage on ourselves. This enabled Mr. Harriett to reload, and plant a couple more balls in him, which evidently sickened him. We were now all close to him, and we all fired deliberately at him. At last, after receiving sixteen bullets in his body, he slowly fell, dying harder than I had ever seen an animal die before.

On our return, we told the men to get the dog-sledges ready to go in the morning to bring in the cows we had killed, numbering twenty-seven, with the head of the bull I wanted; whereupon the squaws and half-breed women, who have always this job to do, started off to catch the requisite number of dogs. About the fort there are always two or three hundred who forage for themselves like the horses, and lie outside. These dogs are quite as valuable there as horses, as it is with them that everything is drawn over the snow. Two of them will easily draw in a large cow; yet no care is taken of them, except that of beating them sufficiently before using them, to make them quiet for the time they are in harness.

It would be almost impossible to catch these animals, who are almost as wild as wolves, were it not for the precaution which is taken in the autumn of catching the dogs singly by stratagem, and tying light logs to them, which they can drag about. By this means the squaws soon catch as many as they want, and bring them into the fort, where they are fed—sometimes—before being harnessed. This operation is certainly (if it were not for the cruelty exhibited) one of the most amusing scenes I had witnessed. Early next morning I was roused by a yelling and screaming that made me rush from my room, thinking that we were all being murdered; and there I saw the women harnessing the dogs. Such a scene! The women were like so many furies with big sticks, threshing away at the poor animals, who rolled and yelled in agony and terror, until each team was yoked up and started off.

During the day the men returned, bringing the quartered cows ready to be put in the ice-pit, and my big head, which, before skinning, I had put in the scales, and found that it weighed exactly 202 lbs. The skin of the head I brought home with me.

The fort at this time of the year presented a most pleasing picture of cheerful activity: every one was busy; the men, some in hunting and bringing in the meat when the weather permitted, some in sawing boards in the saw-pit, and building the boats, about thirty feet long and six feet beam, which go as far as York Factory, and are found more convenient for carrying goods on the Saskatchawan and Red River than canoes. They are mostly built at Edmonton, because there are more boats required to take the peltries to York Factory than is required to bring goods back; and more than one-half of the boats built here never return. This system requires them to keep constantly building.

The women find ample employment in making mocassins and clothes for the men, putting up pemmi-kon in ninety-pound bags, and doing all the household drudgery, in which the men never assist them. The evenings are spent round their large fires in eternal gossiping and smoking. The sole musician of the establishment, a fiddler, is now in great requisition amongst the French part of the inmates, who give full vent to their national vivacity, whilst the more sedate Indian looks on with solemn enjoyment.

No liquor is allowed to the men or Indians; but the want of it did not in the least seem to impair their cheerfulness. True, the gentlemen of the fort had liquor brought out at their own expense; but the rules respecting its use were so strict and so well known, that none but those to whom it belonged either expected, or asked, to share it.

On Christmas-day the flag was hoisted, and all appeared in their best and gaudiest style, to do honour to the holiday. Towards noon every chimney gave evidence of being in full blast, whilst savoury steams of cooking pervaded the atmosphere in all directions. About two o'clock we sat down to dinner. Our party consisted of Mr. Harriett, the chief, and three clerks, Mr. Thebo,[6] the Roman Catholic missionary from Manitou Lake, about thirty miles off, Mr. Rundell, the Wesleyan missionary, who resided within the pickets, and myself, the wanderer, who, though returning from the shores of the Pacific, was still the latest importation from civilised life.

The dining-hall in which we assembled was the largest room in the fort, probably about fifty by twenty-five feet, well warmed by large fires, which are scarcely ever allowed to go out. The walls and ceilings are boarded, as plastering is not used, there being no limestone within reach; but these boards are painted in a style of the most startling barbaric gaudiness, and the ceiling filled with centre-pieces of fantastic gilt scrolls, making altogether a saloon which no white man would enter for the first time without a start, and which the Indians always looked upon with awe and wonder.

The room was intended as a reception room for the wild chiefs who visited the fort; and the artist who designed the decorations was no doubt directed to "astonish the natives." If such were his instructions, he deserves the highest praise for having faithfully complied with them, although, were he to attempt a repetition of the same style in one of the rooms of the Vatican, it might subject him to some severe criticisms from the fastidious. No table-cloth shed its snowy whiteness over the board; no silver candelabra or gaudy china interfered with its simple magnificence. The bright tin plates and dishes reflected jolly faces, and burnished gold can give no truer zest to a feast.

Perhaps it might be interesting to some dyspeptic idler, who painfully strolls through a city park, to coax an appetite to a sufficient intensity to enable him to pick an ortolan, if I were to describe to him the fare set before us, to appease appetites nourished by constant out-door exercise in an atmosphere ranging at 40° to 50° below zero. At the head, before Mr. Harriett, was a large dish of boiled buffalo hump; at the foot smoked a boiled buffalo calf. Start not, gentle reader, the calf is very

---

[6] The Rev. Jean-Baptiste Thibault (1810–1879), who became vicar-general of the diocese of St. Boniface in 1843. See *Dictionary of Canadian Biography*, vol. X.

small, and is taken from the cow by the Cæsarean operation long before it attains its full growth. This, boiled whole, is one of the most esteemed dishes amongst the epicures of the interior. My pleasing duty was to help a dish of mouffle, or dried moose nose; the gentleman on my left distributed, with graceful impartiality, the white fish, delicately browned in buffalo marrow. The worthy priest helped the buffalo tongue, whilst Mr. Rundell cut up the beavers' tails. Nor was the other gentleman left unemployed, as all his spare time was occupied in dissecting a roast wild goose. The centre of the table was graced with piles of potatoes, turnips, and bread conveniently placed, so that each could help himself without interrupting the labours of his companions. Such was our jolly Christmas dinner at Edmonton; and long will it remain in my memory, although no pies, or puddings, or blanc manges, shed their fragrance over the scene.

In the evening the hall was prepared for the dance to which Mr. Harriett had invited all the inmates of the fort, and was early filled by the gaily dressed guests. Indians, whose chief ornament consisted in the paint on their faces, voyageurs with bright sashes and neatly ornamented mocassins, half-breeds glittering in every ornament they could lay their hands on; whether civilised or savage, all were laughing, and jabbering in as many different languages as there were styles of dress. English, however, was little used, as none could speak it but those who sat at the dinner-table. The dancing was most picturesque, and almost all joined in it. Occasionally I, among the rest, led out a young Cree squaw, who sported enough beads round her neck to have made a pedlar's fortune, and having led her into the centre of the room, I danced round her with all the agility I was capable of exhibiting, to some highland-reel tune which the fiddler played with great vigour, whilst my partner with grave face kept jumping up and down, both feet off the ground at once, as only an Indian can dance. I believe, however, that we elicited a great deal of applause from Indian squaws and children, who sat squatting round the room on the floor. Another lady with whom I sported the light fantastic toe, whose poetic name was Cun-ne-wa-bum, or "One that looks at the Stars," was a half-breed Cree girl; and I was so much struck by her beauty, that I prevailed upon her to promise to sit for her likeness, which she afterwards did with great patience, holding her fan, which was made of the tip end of swan's wing with an ornamental handle of porcupine's quills, in a most coquettish manner. [Fig. 107; crIV-212, 213, 214]

After enjoying ourselves with such boisterous vigour for several hours, we all gladly retired to rest about twelve o'clock, the guests separating in great good humour, not only with themselves but with their entertainers.

A few days afterwards, when we had recovered from the effects of our Christmas festivities, I went out with François Lucie, the half-breed voyageur [Pl. XXVII; crIV-215, 216], of whom Sir George Simpson, in his "Journey round the World," tells the following story:—

"A band of Assiniboines had carried off twenty-four horses from Edmonton, and, being pursued, they were overtaken at the small river Boutbière. One of the keepers of the animals, a very courageous man, of the name of François Lucie, plunged into the stream, grappling in the midst with a tall savage, and, in spite of his inferiority of strength, he kept so close that his enemy could not draw his bow; still, however, the Indian continued to strike his assailant on the head with the weapon in question, and thereby knocked him off his horse into the water. Springing immediately to his feet, Lucie was about to smite the Assiniboine with his dagger, when the savage arrested his arm by seizing a whip, which was hanging to his wrist by a loop, and then turning round the handle, with a scornful laugh, he drew the string so tight as to render the poor man's hand nearly powerless. François continued nevertheless to saw away at the fellow's fingers with his dagger till he had nearly cut them off, and when at length the Assiniboine of necessity relaxed his grasp, François, with the quickness of thought, sheathed the weapon in his heart." François told me the story himself, much as related above, except, he said, that the savage did not die immediately, although he had ripped his breast so open that he could see his heart throbbing, and that he never let go the lasso of the stolen horses until it ceased, which was for some minutes, though he tried to pull it from his hand.

We had not left the fort more than five or six miles behind us, when we fell in with an enormous grisly bear, but François would not fire at him, nor allow me to do so, although I told him I had helped to kill one before. A younger man than he, who had his character to make, might have been foolish enough to have run the risk, for the sake of the standing it would have given him amongst his companions; but François had a character established, and would not risk attacking so formidable an animal with only two men. In fact, their enormous strength, agility, and wonderful tenacity of life, make them shunned even by large numbers, and few are killed, except by young men, for the sake of proudly wearing the claws—one of the most esteemed ornaments to an Indian chief—round their necks.

The bear walked on, looking at us now and then, but seeming

to treat us with contempt. My fingers were itching to let fly at him: it seemed so easy, and his skin was in such fine condition. But though my gun had two barrels, and François was by my side, with the almost certainty of putting three balls well in; yet we well knew that it was ten chances to one that three balls would [not] kill him quick enough to prevent a hand-to-hand encounter, a sort of amusement that neither were Quixotic enough to desire. After we had proceeded a few miles further, we fell in with a small band of buffaloes, and François initiated me into the mysteries of "making a calf."

This ruse is generally performed by two men, one covering himself with wolf skin, the other with buffalo skin. They then crawl on all fours within sight of the buffaloes, and as soon as they have engaged their attention, the pretended wolf jumps on the pretended calf, which bellows in imitation of a real one. The buffaloes seem to be easily deceived in this way. As the bellowing is generally perfect, the herd rush on to the protection of their supposed young with such impetuosity that they do not perceive the cheat until they are quite close enough to be shot; indeed, François' bellowing was so perfect, that we were nearly run down. As soon, however, as we jumped up, they turned and fled, leaving two of their number behind, who paid the penalty of their want of discernment with their lives.

We shortly afterwards fell in with a solitary bull and cow, and again "made a calf." The cow attempted to spring towards us, but the bull seeming to understand the trick, tried to stop her by running between us: the cow, however, dodged and got round him, and ran within ten or fifteen yards of us, with the bull close at her heels, when we both fired and brought her down. The bull instantly stopped short, and bending over her, tried to raise her up with his nose, evincing the most persevering affection for her in a rather ridiculous manner; nor could we get rid of him so as to cut up the cow, without shooting him also, although bull flesh is not desirable at this season of the year, when the female can be procured.

Having loaded our horses with the choice parts of the three cows we had killed, we proceeded home, François having taken particular care to secure the mesenteries or monyplies, as he called them, a part much esteemed in the interior, although I must confess I did not like it myself.

Another mode of hunting buffaloes, which we often practised with great success at Edmonton, was accompanied however with considerable fatigue: it consisted in crawling on our bellies and dragging ourselves along by our hands, being first fully certain that we were to the leeward of the herd, however light the wind, lest they should scent us until we came within a few yards of them, which they would almost invariably permit us to do. Should there be twenty hunters engaged in the sport, each man follows exactly in the track of his leader, keeping his head close to the heels of his predecessor: the buffaloes seem not to take the slightest notice of the moving line, which the Indians account for by saying that the buffalo supposes it to be a big snake winding through the snow or grass.

Tired as I was at night after my day's hunt, I was kept long from my bed, fascinated by the appearance of the heavens, which presented to the view one of the most splendid meteoric phenomena I had ever witnessed. Soon after dark a zone of light began to appear, increasing rapidly in brilliancy until about nine or ten o'clock, when it attained its greatest intensity. It was about four degrees in breadth, and extended from the east to the west across the zenith. In its centre, immediately overhead, appeared a blood-red ball of fire, of greater diameter than the full moon rising in a misty horizon; from the ball emanated rays of crimson light, merging into a brilliant yellow at the northern edges. The belt also on the northern side presented the same dazzling brightness; while the snow and every object surrounding us was tinted by the same hues. I continued lost in admiration of this splendid phenomenon until past one in the morning, when it still shone with undiminished, if not increased, brilliancy. Tired out at last, I was compelled to retire to bed, but those who still sat up told me that it faded away about three o'clock in the morning, without varying its position or form. The Indians have a poetical superstition in regard to the Aurora Borealis, which is in this high latitude remarkably brilliant, shooting up coruscations of surprising splendour. These, they think, are "the spirits of the dead dancing before the Manitou, or Great Spirit."

Chapter XXIII.

A pleasant Wedding.—Sledges and Carioles.—Useful but Dangerous Dogs.—The Hunter's Bravado.—Journey through the Snow.—An unwilling Chase.—A Tumble in a Drift.—Indian Etiquette.—The Spotted Leg.—The Indian in Heaven.—Battle of the Dogs.—Arrival at Fort Pitt.—The Medicine Pipe-stem and its Carrier.—Ceremony of opening Pipe-stems.—Exhibition of Medicine Dresses.—Digging up the Hatchet.—Crying for War.—Invoking the Great Spirit.— Preparing for the March.—Eating a Warrior's Heart.

On the 6th of January 1848, we had a wedding at Edmonton; the bride was the daughter of the gentleman in charge, the bridegroom Mr. Rowand, junior, who resided at Fort Pitt, a distance of 200 miles from the establishment. [crIV-202?] After the ceremony, which was performed by the Rev. Mr. Rundell, the Methodist missionary, we spent a pleasant evening, feasting and dancing until midnight. Having received an invitation to accompany the happy pair on the journey home, I gladly accepted it, as I began to find my amusements rather monotonous. Next morning I was awoke by the yelping of the dogs and the ringing of the bells on the dog-collars, accompanied by the shouts of the men thrashing the brutes into something like discipline, as they harnessed them to the sledges and carioles. [Fig. 100; crIV-195] On coming out into the yard, I found our party nearly ready to start. It consisted of Mr. Rowand and his bride, with nine men.[1] We had three carioles and six sledges, with four dogs to each, forming when on route a long and picturesque cavalcade: all the dogs gaudily decorated with saddle-cloths of various colours, fringed and embroidered in the most fantastic manner, with innumerable small bells and feathers, producing altogether a pleasing and enlivening effect (sketch No. 14).

Our carioles were also handsomely decorated, the bride's more particularly, which had been made expressly for the occasion, and was elaborately painted and ornamented, and was drawn by a set of dogs recently imported from Lower Canada by Mr. Rowand. The cariole is intended for carrying one person only; it is a thin flat board, about eighteen inches wide, bent up in front, with a straight back behind to lean against; the sides are made of green buffalo hide, with the hair scraped completely off and dried, resembling thick parchment; this entirely covers the front part, so that a person slips into it as into a tin bath. [Pl. XXVI; Figs. 101 to 103; crIV-194, 196 to 201]

We started as the day dawned, the dogs running at a furious rate, as they invariably do at first starting, and require all the strength and agility of the men to keep the sledges and carioles from upsetting, which they manage to do as well as they can by holding on to a cord attached to each side from behind. Two men go before on the run in snow shoes to beat a track, which the dogs instinctively follow: these men are relieved every two hours, as it is very laborious. The dogs generally used are of a breed peculiar to the country, and partake largely of the character and disposition of the wolf, which they often so resemble in appearance as sometimes to have been shot in mistake. Their ferocity is so great that they are often dangerous. Some of them

this winter attacked a horse belonging to Mr. Harriett, harnessed to a sledge. Mr. Harriett had tied him to a stake and left him; on his return, in about half an hour, he found the dogs tearing him to pieces; nor would the dogs leave their prey until he had shot five of them: the horse died almost immediately.

Mr. Rundell was himself attacked one evening, while walking a short distance from the fort, by a band of these brutes belonging to the establishment; they got him down, and, but for his cries bringing the assistance of a squaw, they would have served him in a similar manner.

Immediately on leaving the fort, we got on the ice of the Saskatchawan River, and travelled down it all day, having, in the true voyageur style, trusted to our prowess as hunters for a supply of food on our journey, although of 200 miles; and, having literally brought nothing with us but the kettles,[2] we were unable to break our fast until we had killed a fat cow, which was soon demolished by ourselves and the dogs. This apparent absence of foresight is, in reality, often affected by the voyageurs out of bravado, for they are quite as much disinclined to hunger and abstinence as other people. In our case we might certainly have brought plenty of food if we liked, but, on the other hand, buffaloes were plentiful, and there was almost a certainty of obtaining them.[3]

Jan. 9th.—Left our encampment three hours before day, and about daylight we killed two buffaloes and stopped to breakfast. The wind blew very cold and strong all day, with continued snow. After breakfast we left the circuitous windings of the river, and the friendly shelter of its banks and woods, to cut across the bleak and open plains, where we were exposed to the full fury of the chill blast; but this shortened our journey by many miles. In the evening we killed two more buffaloes, and encamped in a clump of pines, the last sheltered spot we might expect on our journey.

Jan. 10th.—Our spirit thermometer stood this morning at 47° below zero, Fahr.[4] Finding it impossible to keep myself warm in my cariole, in spite of plenty of skins and blankets, I put on a pair of snow shoes and walked all day. The snow was three feet deep on an average, and was drifted by the wind with such

---

[1] KJ says that the party which left on January 8 was accompanied for the first day by Mr. Prudence, the bride's uncle, and François Lucie on sleds. The number of dogs with the party is given as 46.

[2] KJ adds: "Not even a pinch of salt. This family think it quite unvoyageurlike to travel with anything like comfort." There was plenty of food to be had for the hunting since they saw six large herds of buffalo on the first day.

[3] KJ: "We camped early as we had had no breakfast on leaving the fort."

[4] KJ notes that the reason it was so cold was because there were no woods to protect them.

violence in our faces as to nearly blind us; notwithstanding which our guides seemed to find no difficulty in pursuing their course—such is the instinctive faculty of these men in tracing their way over this trackless desert, where not a stick or a shrub is to be met with to guide them. Towards evening we arrived at a sort of enclosure, which had evidently been erected by the Blackfoot Indians as a protection from the Crees, whose country this is, but where the Blackfeet sometimes come to steal horses. In the evening we only got one cow, which seemed barely to satisfy our dogs.[5]

Jan. 11*th.*—Started as usual this morning three hours before daylight, the days being short: this early starting is necessary to allow the men to stop and make the encampment before dark. We met two of the Company's men on their way from Carlton to the place we had so recently left. We killed only one buffalo to-day, and were obliged to sleep on the snow, no pine branches being within reach to make our beds.[6] These we missed much, as they add much to the comfort of an encampment.

Jan. 12*th.*—We again got on the river. Having brought a small quantity of meat from our last night's supper with us, but not sufficient for all, some of our party went on in advance to hunt, whilst we stopped to take a scanty breakfast. About two hours afterwards we came up to them, sitting round a good fire cooking a fine fat cow, the delicate pieces of which they were demolishing with considerable rapidity, owing to the lateness of their meal.

During the day a diverting occurrence took place, although it might have turned out very serious. A herd of buffaloes had come down the bank on to the ice, and did not perceive our approach until the foremost sledge was so near them as to excite the dogs, who rushed furiously after them, notwithstanding all the efforts of the men to stop them. The spirit of the hunt was at once communicated through the whole line, and we were soon all, carioles and sledges, dashing along at a furious rate after the buffaloes. The frightened animals made a bold dash at last through a deep snow bank, and attempted to scramble up the steep bank of the river, the top of which the foremost one had nearly reached, when, slipping, he rolled over and knocked those behind, one on top of another, down into the deep snow-drift amongst the men and dogs, who were struggling in it. It would be impossible to describe the wild scene of uproar and confusion that followed. Some of our sledges were smashed, and one of the men was nearly killed; but at last we succeeded in getting clear and repairing damages. We continued on our wedding tour.

Jan. 13*th.*—Started at half-past 1 A.M. We followed a buffalo track along the river, in the deep ruts of which our carioles were frequently upset, rolling us into the snow. Having killed three buffaloes on the banks of the river, we stopped to breakfast; two calves, evidently belonging to the slaughtered animals, remained within a hundred yards of our fire the whole time.[7]

Leaving the river, we passed over a succession of hills and valleys until dark, when we arrived at a camp of Cree Indians, consisting of about forty lodges. We went to the lodge of the chief named "Broken Arm," who received us very kindly, spreading buffalo robes in the best part of his tent for us to sit on, and placing before us the best his stock afforded. After supper, the chief having cut some tobacco and filled a handsome stone pipe, took a few whiffs from it himself, and then presented it to me. On my doing the same, and offering it to him again, as is the custom, he told me that he wished me to accept it as a gift.

The lodge was soon filled with Indians, anxious to learn the news, which they are always eager to hear from strangers. Amongst our visitors was the son-in-law of the chief; and, according to the Indian custom, he took his seat with his back towards his father and mother-in-law, never addressing them but through the medium of a third party, and they preserving the same etiquette towards him. This rule is not broken through until the son-in-law proves himself worthy of personally speaking to him, by having killed an enemy with white hairs; they then become entitled to wear a dress trimmed with human hair, taken from the scalps of their foes. I remarked that one of the leggings of the young man was spotted with some red earth, and the other not: on inquiring the reason, I was told that the spotted leg had been wounded, and the red earth was intended to indicate blood.

We sat up very late, talking to the chief, who seemed to enjoy our society very much. Amongst other topics of discourse, he began talking about the efforts of the missionaries amongst his people, and seemed to think that they would not be very successful; for though he did not interfere with the religious belief of any of his tribe, yet many thought as he did; and his idea was, that as Mr. Rundell had told him that what he preached was the only true road to heaven, and Mr. Hunter told him the same thing, and so did Mr. Thebo, and as they all three said that the other two were wrong, and as he did not know which was right, he thought they ought to call a council amongst

---

[5] KJ states that they killed three buffalo all day without leaving their straight course.
[6] KJ notes that they slept on dry willows.
[7] KJ says that the dogs were tied at the time.

Plate XXVII. François Lucie, a Cree half-breed guide, Fort Edmonton. Stark POP9; CRIV-215.

Plate XXVIII. Assiniboin chiefs, Rocky Mountain House. *Left:* Mah-Min or "The Feather," head chief. *Right:* Wah-he-joe-tass-e-neen or "The half-white Man," second chief. Stark PWC1; CRIV-221.

themselves, and that then he would go with them all three; but that until they agreed he would wait. He then told us that there was a tradition in his tribe of one of them having become a Christian, and was very good, and did all that he ought; and that when he died he was taken up to the white man's heaven, where everything was very good and very beautiful, and all were happy amongst their friends and relatives who had gone before them, and where they had everything that the white man loves and longs for; but the Indian could not share their joy and pleasure, for all was strange to him, and he met none of the spirits of his ancestors, and there was none to welcome him, no hunting nor fishing, nor any of those joys in which he used to delight, and his spirit grew sad. Then the Great Manitou called him, and asked him, "Why art thou sad in this beautiful heaven which I have made for your joy and happiness?" and the Indian told him that he sighed for the company of the spirits of his relations, and that he felt lone and sorrowful. So the Great Manitou told him that he could not send him to the Indian heaven, as he had, whilst on earth, chosen this one, but that as he had been a very good man, he would send him back to earth again, and give him another chance.

Jan. 14th.—We travelled to-day through a hilly country until we arrived at another encampment of about thirty lodges. Our dogs rushed down amongst the lodges, dragging the sledges and carioles after them, and were immediately attacked by all the dogs in the Indian camp, barking, howling, and fighting, until all the sledges were upset, and some of them broken to pieces. It was half an hour before we could separate the enraged brutes.[8]

These Indians had a buffalo pound within a short distance of their encampment, which was literally crammed with the dead frozen carcases they had slaughtered in it. On nearing Fort Pitt we fell in with two buffaloes, immediately in our track, and as we did not want the meat, they might have been allowed to escape, but for the large development of the bump of destructiveness in our men's heads.

We reached the fort soon after dark, having been seven days on our route from Edmonton. We had killed seventeen buffaloes in this journey, for feeding ourselves and dogs. The animals had, we were told, never appeared in such vast numbers, nor shown themselves so near the Company's establishments; some have even been shot within the gates of the fort. They killed with their horns twenty or thirty horses in their attempt to drive them off from the patches of grass which the horses had pawed the snow from with their hoofs for the purpose of getting at the grass, and severely gored many others, which eventually recovered.

These remarks convey but a faint idea of the astonishing numbers of these animals: within the whole distance we had travelled on this journey we were never out of sight of large herds of them, and we had not found it necessary to go a step out of our direct course to find more than we required for our use. They were probably migrating northwards, to escape from the human migrations which are so rapidly filling up the southern and western regions, which were formerly their pasture grounds.

I spent a very pleasant and interesting month at Fort Pitt,[9] surrounded by Cree Indians, this being one of their principal places of resort, and had ample opportunity of studying their habits and manners. [Pl. XXII; crIV-139 to 142] I took an elaborate sketch of a pipe-stem carrier with his medicine pipe-stem. The pipe-stem carrier is elected every four years by the band of the whole tribe to which he belongs, and is not allowed to retain the distinction beyond that period, all being eligible for the situation who have sufficient means to pay for it. But the expense is considerable, as the new officer elect has to pay his predecessor for the emblems of his dignity, which frequently are valued at from fifteen to twenty horses. Should he not possess sufficient means, his friends usually make up the deficiency, otherwise the office would in many cases be declined. It is, however, compulsory upon the person elected to serve if he can pay. The official insignia of the pipe-stem carrier are numerous, consisting of a highly ornamental skin tent, in which he is always expected to reside; a bear's skin upon which the pipe-stem is to be exposed to view when any circumstance requires it to be taken out from its manifold coverings in which it is usually wrapped up, such as a council of war, or a medicine pipe-stem dance, or on a quarrel taking place in the tribe, to settle which the medicine-man opens it for the adverse parties to smoke out of,—their superstitions leading them to fear a refusal of the reconciling ceremony, lest some calamity should be inflicted on them by the Great Spirit for their presumption;—a medicine rattle, which is employed in their medicine dances, and a wooden bowl, from which the dignitary always takes his food,—this he always carries about his person, sometimes in his hand, and often on his head;—besides numerous small articles.

It requires two horses to carry them when on the move. The pipe-stem itself is usually carried by the favourite wife of the

[8] KJ estimates that there were in all about 200 dogs.
[9] KJ states that Kane remained at Fort Pitt for 20 days.

official, and should it under any circumstances fall on the ground, it is regarded as a bad omen, and many ceremonies must be gone through to reinstate it. A young man, a half-breed, assured me that he had once a pipe-stem committed to his charge by an official who had gone out on a hunting excursion, and that being well aware of the sanctity attributed to it by the Crees, he was determined to try himself the effect of throwing it down and kicking it about, and that shortly after this act of desecration, as it would be considered, the pipe-stem carrier was killed by the Blackfeet. From that time he became a firm believer in the sanctity of the pipe-stem, and, as may be supposed, told me this story as a great secret.

A pipe-stem carrier always sits on the right side of his lodge as you enter, and it is considered a great mark of disrespect to him if you pass between him and the fire, which always occupies the centre of the lodge. He must not condescend to cut his own meat, but it is always cut for him by one of his wives, of whom he usually has five or six, and placed in his medicine bowl, which, as before said, he has always with him. One of the greatest inconveniences attached to the office, particularly to an Indian, who has always innumerable parasitical insects infesting his person, is, that the pipe-stem carrier dares not scratch his own head without compromising his dignity, without the intervention of a stick, which he always carries for that purpose. The pipe-stem, enclosed in its wrappers, always hangs in a large bag, when they can procure it, of party-coloured woollen cloth, on the outside of the lodge, and is never taken inside either by night or by day, nor allowed to be uncovered when any woman is present.

About a fortnight after my arrival, Kee-a-kee-ka-sa-coo-way, "the Man who gives the War-whoop," whom I mentioned before as having met on the Saskatchawan on my journey out, arrived at Fort Pitt with his sub-chief, Muck-e-too, "Powder." [crIV-133?]

Kee-a-kee-ka-sa-coo-way is the head chief of all the Crees, and was now travelling through all their camps to induce them to take up the tomahawk and follow him on a war excursion in the following spring. He had eleven medicine pipe-stems with him, ten of which belonged to inferior chiefs, who had already consented to join in the expedition. Being curious to witness the opening of these pipe-stems and see the ceremonial accompanying it, I travelled with him to the camp, situated a few miles from Fort Pitt. On our arrival, the wrappers of the stems were removed and carried in procession, headed by the chief in person, through the camp. The procession, halted in front of nearly

every lodge, where he delivered a continuous harangue, the burden of which was to rouse them to take up arms and revenge the death of the warriors who had been killed in former wars. During the whole of this address the tears continued to stream down his face as if at his entire command. This the Indians call crying for war.

The weather was most intensely cold, notwithstanding which, and his being half naked, so strongly was every feeling concentrated on the subject, that he appeared altogether insensible to its severity, although the thermometer must have indicated at least thirty to forty degrees below zero. On the day following, I endeavoured to prevail on him to open the pipe-stems, in order that I might sketch some of them; this he at first declined, until he had been told that I was a great medicine-man, and that my sketching them would very much increase their efficiency when opened on the field of battle. He thereupon opened them with the following ceremonies. He first took a coal from the fire, and sprinkled upon it the dried leaves of a plant collected on the Rocky Mountains, the smoke of which filled the place with a fragrant odour resembling that of the incense burned in Catholic churches; while this was burning, he filled the bowls of these pipes with tobacco and some other weed, after which he took off all his clothes, with the exception of the breechcloth.

On my looking rather suspiciously at the clothes he had taken off, seeing they were rather old and filthy, he took notice of my doing so, and remarked, that although he possessed better, he was not allowed by the customs of his tribe to wear them, as he was then mourning the death of four of his relations who had been killed by the Blackfeet the year before. (He, however, put on his good clothes for me afterwards, when I took sketch No. 15, as I told him that the picture would be shown to the queen.) [Figs. 85, 86; crIV-130, 131, 132] He then threw over his shoulders the skin of a wolf highly ornamented after the Indian fashion, and immediately removed the wrappers of leather, &c., that covered one of the stems, and inserting it into one of the bowls he had previously filled with tobacco, commenced a song which I could not understand.

On finishing, he lighted the pipe, and inhaled a mouthful of smoke; then turning his face upwards and pointing in the same direction with the stem, he blew upwards a long stream of smoke, and called on the Great Spirit to give them success in war, to enable them to take many scalps, and set their enemies asleep whilst they carried off their horses; that their own wives might continue virtuous and never grow old. He then turned the stem to the earth, after blowing out another puff of smoke, and called upon the earth to produce abundance of buffalo and roots for the coming season. He then pointed the stem towards me, and requested that, if I possessed any influence with the Great Spirit, I would intercede with him for the supply of all their wants. A half-breed woman happening to look into the lodge at this moment, the ceremony was instantly suspended, and she as instantly shrunk back; a woman never being allowed to be present when the medicine pipe-stem is exposed to view.

After some little prolonged ceremony, consisting principally of all present smoking from each stem as it was opened, he permitted me to sketch them, but never left the lodge until I had finished and he had carefully recovered and removed them. He told me he had been on this war mission to nearly every camp in his tribe, and intended to visit the whole of them; the distance he would have to travel in snow shoes to accomplish this would not be less than six or seven hundred miles. It is the custom of the Indians after such a call to assemble at a place appointed on the Saskatchawan River, where they continue feasting and dancing three days previously to their starting for the enemy's country. Here all their pipe-stems and medicine dresses are exhibited, and they decorate themselves with all the finery they can command, in which they continue their advance until they reach the enemy. But no sooner are they in view, than their ornaments and their whole clothing are hastily thrown aside, and they fight naked. [Figs. 87, 88; crIV-134 to 138]

A year before my arrival amongst them, a war party of 700 left for the Blackfeet country, which nation the Crees regard as their natural enemies, and are never at peace with them. After travelling for some fifteen or twenty days, a sickness broke out among them, affecting numbers and carrying off a few. This was considered by some of their great men a judgment upon them from the Great Spirit for some previous misconduct, and they, therefore, returned home without having accomplished anything. On another occasion a similar party fell in with a great warrior among the Blackfeet, named "Big Horn," and six of his tribe, who were out on the legitimate calling of horse stealing, —for the greater the horse thief the greater the warrior. This small band, seeing their inferiority to their enemies, attempted flight; but finding escape impossible, they instantly dug holes sufficiently deep to intrench themselves, from which they kept up a constant fire with guns and arrows, and for nearly twelve hours held at bay this large war party, bringing down every man who ventured within shot, until their ammunition and arrows were entirely exhausted, when they of course fell an easy prey to their enemies, thirty of whom had fallen before their

fire. This so enraged the Crees that they cut them in pieces, and mangled the dead bodies in a most brutal manner, and carried their scalps back as trophies.

It is said that Big Horn frequently sprang out from his intrenchment, and tried to irritate his foes by recounting the numbers of them he had destroyed, and boasting his many war exploits, and the Cree scalps that then hung in his lodge. So exasperated were they against him, that they tore out his heart from his quivering body, and savagely devoured it amongst them.

I returned to Edmonton by the same route, and in the same manner I had come from it,[10] and as nothing material occurred in the route, I omit the details.

Chapter XXIV.

Departure from Edmonton.—Taming a Wild Calf.—A Raft of Ice. —Rocky Mountain Fort.—Stuffing a Dead Foe.—A Token of Friendship.—A Lecture on Lying.—Honest Thieves.—"I can't get out."—Start for Norway House.—Drowned Buffaloes.—Meeting a War Party.—Smoking with "Big Snake."—Camping with the Braves. —Avenging a Slight.—A Cowardly Shot.—The Olive-branch refused.—A Busy Pencil.—Disinterested Kindness.

I remained at Edmonton until the 12th of April, when, having heard that a large band of Blackfeet were shortly expected to visit Rocky Mountain House, situated about 180 miles south-west of Edmonton, on the Saskatchawan, for the purpose of trading, and being anxious to see them, I started with a small party of six men and about twenty horses, ten of which were loaded with goods. The snow had not left the ground, and our horses were in very bad condition, from living out all the winter, except the one which I rode, which had been kept in, and was the most vicious brute I ever met. When I dismounted from him the first evening, he tried to get away from me, and when he found that I held on to the lasso, he attacked me with open mouth, and had not one of the men knocked him down with a stick, he might have seriously injured me. Our progress was, therefore, necessarily slow, as I would not ride away from the party.

We found buffaloes in places where the Indians said they had never been seen before, and remained two days at a place called

---

[10] KJ notes that on this occasion he was at Fort Edmonton for six days.

Battle River, to rest our horses, as we had plenty of food for ourselves and grass for the horses. I went out with an Indian and killed a cow, which was followed by her calf. Wishing to take the calf alive, so that it might carry itself to the camp, I pursued and caught it, and, tying my sash round its neck, endeavoured to drag it along; but it plunged and tried so violently to escape that I was about to kill it, when the Indian took hold of its head, and turning up its muzzle, spat two or three times into it, when, much to my astonishment, the animal became perfectly docile, and followed us quietly to the camp, where it was immediately cooked for supper.

Finding three of the rivers in our route much flooded, we were obliged to make rafts to cross upon, so as to keep the goods dry. At the fourth river we were fortunate to find a raft formed by nature, in the shape of a large mass of floating ice, which one of the men swimming out dragged ashore. It was sufficiently buoyant to support two or three men, and by attaching our lassoes to it, and drawing it backwards and forwards, we soon got all our goods over dry. The horses we made swim.

Some of the men suffered severely from what is called "snow blind," which is a species of inflammation, brought on by the strong glare of the sun reflected from the snow. The pain in the eyeballs is excessive, and resembles the feeling produced by having sand in the eyes; the sufferers are sometimes blinded by it for weeks. This can be prevented by wearing a veil, which I did, and is generally adopted when they can be procured.

We arrived at Rocky Mountain Fort on the 21st of April. This fort is beautifully situated on the banks of the Saskatcha-wan, in a small prairie, backed by the Rocky Mountains in the distance. In the vicinity was a camp of Assiniboine lodges, formed entirely of pine branches. [Fig. 108; crIV-217, 218, 220?] It [Rocky Mountain House] was built for the purpose of keeping a supply of goods to trade with the Blackfoot Indians, who come there every winter, and is abandoned and left empty every summer. It is built like most of the other forts, of wood, but with more than ordinary regard to strength, which is thought necessary on account of the vicious disposition of the Blackfoot tribe, who are, without exception, the most warlike on the northern continent. I may state that beds of coal are seen protruding here along the banks of the river, similar to that of Edmonton.

[Cree: crIV-227]

There is also a small band of Assiniboines in the neighbour-hood of the fort. The Blackfeet attacked them last year, and carried off two girls captives. One of them, after having been carried away a long distance, was stripped naked, and told to find her way back as best she could, and as she was never heard of afterwards, it was supposed that she perished from cold and hunger; the other girl was taken charge of by a chief, who sent her relations word that she should be returned safe, which promise he fulfilled.

We found a man at the establishment, called Jemmy Jock, a Cree half-breed, who had temporary charge of it; he had obtained much Blackfoot celebrity. He was sent out when a clerk of Hudson's Bay Company, by them, to the Blackfoot Indians, in order to learn their language, for the purpose of facilitating the trade with them. He then married a daughter of one of their chiefs, and taking a fancy to their mode of life, he left the Company's service, and stayed with them. He afterwards became one of their chiefs, and being a man of singular acuteness, soon acquired great influence. The missionaries entertained very little respect for him, and have spoken very badly of him throughout the whole country; but as far as my intercourse with him went, I always found him trustworthy and hospitable. I learned much from him relative to the customs of the Blackfoot tribe, of which, owing to his long residence amongst them, thirty or forty years, he possessed a greater knowledge probably than any other man with the same education.

Shortly after my arrival a report was brought in that the Blackfoot Indians had killed a party of Crees, and that amongst the slain was a pipe-stem carrier, whom they had skinned and stuffed with grass; the figure was then placed in a trail which the Crees were accustomed to pass in their hunting excursions. The Assiniboines, who reside in the vicinity of this fort, I found the most kind and honourable of any tribe that I met with. They constitute a very small part (say forty or fifty families) of a very large tribe who live in a more easterly direction. Mah-Min, "The Feather," their head chief, permitted me to take his likeness, and after I had finished it, and it was shown to the others, who all recognised and admired it, he said to me, "You are a greater chief than I am, and I present you with this collar of grizzly bear's claws, which I have worn for twenty-three summers, and which I hope you will wear as a token of my friendship." This collar I have, of course, brought home with me. [Pl. XXVIII; Fig. 109; crIV-221 to 224]

The second chief, Wah-he-joe-tass-e-neen, "The half-white Man," seeing that I was so successful with his head chief's likeness, and probably feeling a little jealous, came and requested me to take his also, which I willingly did, as he had one of the most extraordinary countenances I had met with for some time. [Pl. XXVIII; CRIV-221, 225, 226] He was a man, however, noted as a great hunter, and as an evidence of his tremendous powers of endurance, it was related to me that one morning he had started on snow shoes in pursuit of two moose, and pursued them until they separated. He then followed one track until he killed his prey, cut it up, and put it on scaffolding to secure it from the wolves. He then returned to where the tracks separated, and followed the other; this he also killed, and placed, as he had done the former, returning to his lodge late in the evening. In the morning he sent off three men with dog sledges to bring in the game, and they were three days following his tracks before they got home.

Mah-Min gave one of the missionaries who was up here last summer a very long and serious lecture upon lying. It seems the missionary, who did not smoke himself, had brought with him a carat of tobacco for the purpose of purchasing horses and food from the Indians, should he require them. Immediately on his arrival, the Indians, who had exhausted their stock, eagerly inquired if he had any tobacco, but he was afraid that if he acknowledged he had any they would want it all, and leave him without anything to barter with them, and denied that he had any. Shortly afterwards, when he was about to return, he went to Mah-Min, and told him that he wanted horses and some provisions to return, and that he would pay him for them in tobacco, when Mah-Min said to him, "You preach to the Indians many things, and tell them not to steal or lie; how can they believe or listen to you? You are the father of lies. You said you had no tobacco, and now you say you have plenty."

We had nothing to eat at Rocky Mountain House but rabbits, and even of those we could not get as much as we wanted; this was in consequence of the *cache*, in which the dried meat was placed, having been robbed by the Assiniboines, who, if they could not be honest against the temptations of hunger, at least tried to be as much so as they could, for they placed furs of considerable value in the place of the meat they had stolen. This was the second year they had played the same game; but however satisfactory the arrangement might be to the Hudson's Bay Company, it certainly was anything but pleasant either to their servants or myself; so that after being half starved for ten days, and seeing no signs of the Blackfoot Indians coming in, I persuaded Jemmy Jock to come back with me to Edmonton. This he agreed to do, and he said he had a *cache* of dried meat on the road which would supply us with plenty, so that all we had to do was to ride fast until we came to it.

Early in the morning, we started, taking four extra horses with us as relays. This is done by one man riding in front, then the loose horses, and the other man follows and drives them on; the horses seldom stray or give trouble in this way, and, as they carry no weight, are comparatively fresh when the horse you ride has broken down. We rode the whole day at a tremendous pace, stimulated by hunger, and arrived at the *cache* towards dusk. Having tied our horses, Jemmy went to the *cache*, which was made of logs built together, something like a loghouse, but not very closely fitted together, and began throwing off the heavy logs which covered the top and concealed it. [CR-IV-219] He heard a regular rumpus within, so he called to me to fetch the guns; when I got up, he removed part of the top, and a fine fat wolverine jumped out, which I immediately shot down. The brute must have been starved and desperately thin to have squeezed himself through the openings between the logs, and no doubt impelled by hunger, and the smell of the meat inside, had not thought much of a slight squeeze. However, when he was once in, and had had a good meal, he could not get out again, and the idea of starving himself as long as the meat lasted, did not seem to have occurred to him. This was a great disappointment to us, as there was very little left, and that mangled, torn, and tossed about in the dirt by the animal. We, however, contrived to make a supper, and saved some for the future; but it was so little, that instead of taking our time on the road as we had intended, we had nothing for it but to ride as fast as we could.

The next day was most uncomfortable, as we had a heavy snow storm blowing in our faces the whole day; but we pushed on gallantly, and finished our provisions between supper and breakfast next morning, and on the afternoon of the third day we got into Edmonton, but only with two horses, the others having been fagged out and left behind.

May 22nd.—Mr. Low arrived from the east side of the Rocky Mountains, in company with Mr. de Merse,[1] the Roman Catholic Bishop of Vancouver, and Mr. Paul Frazer. The boats and their cargoes had been long prepared, and we only waited for a favourable break in the weather to commence our journey home.

May 25th.—The weather having cleared up, we embarked with the before-mentioned gentlemen for Norway House. We had twenty-three boats, and 130 men, with Mr. Harriett as our chief. We saw great numbers of dead buffaloes along the shore of the river, which, from the long continuance of the snow

[1] Modeste Demers (1809–1871), appointed first bishop of Victoria in 1847. See *Dictionary of Canadian Biography*, vol. X.

covering the herbage, had become so exhausted, that they were drowned in attempting to swim across the river, in their accustomed migration to the south every spring, and now lay in thousands along the banks.[2] At night we drifted down with the current, the men tying several boats together, so as to be under the guidance of one man, whilst the rest lay down and slept.

May 26th.—We saw several large herds of buffaloes swimming across the river, all going south.[3]

May 27th.—What with the strong current, the men pulling all day, and our drifting all night, we again arrived at Fort Pitt, where we got an addition to our party of two more boats. These boats are all loaded with the furs and pimmi-kon of the Saskatchawan district. The furs are taken down to York Factory, in the Hudson's Bay, where they are shipped to Europe; the pimmi-kon is intended for those posts where provisions are difficult to be procured. We remained at Fort Pitt for two days whilst the other boats were getting ready, and I took advantage of the delay to sketch a Cree chief. He was dressed in full costume, with a pipe-stem in his hand. [See pp. 143–45, above]

May 29th.—We left Fort Pitt, quite filling the river with our fleet of boats, presenting a most imposing and animated appearance, considering that we were navigating inland waters so far from the boundaries of civilisation. We saw great numbers of wolves busily employed in devouring the carcases of the drowned buffaloes, and had some amusing hunts with our boats after them, our men greatly enjoying the sport.[4] We continued our course in great humour and comfort, without meeting with anything which I considered particularly worthy of recording at the time, until

June 1st, when we saw a large party of mounted Indians, riding furiously towards us. On their nearer approach they proved to be a large war party, consisting of Blackfoot Indians, Blood Indians, Sur-cees, Gros Ventres, and Pay-gans.[5] We had a Cree Indian in one of our boats, whom we had to stow away under the skins which covered the goods, lest he should be discovered by the party, who were expressly bound on an expedition against his tribe, and whom our disproportionate number could not have opposed had they sought to take him from us. We instantly put ashore to meet them, and Mr. Harriett and myself met them on the banks of the river, leaving strict orders

with the men to keep the boats afloat sufficiently near the shore for us to re-embark promptly in case of danger. They received Mr. Harriett, however, in a most friendly manner, he being personally known to numbers of them. They immediately spread a buffalo skin for us to sit down upon, depositing all their arms, consisting of knives, guns, and bows and arrows, on the ground in front of us, in token of amity.

There was, however, one exception to this pacific demonstration, in the case of an Indian I had frequently heard spoken of before, named Omoxesisixany, "Big Snake." [crIV-146, 147] This chief walked round the party, cracking and flourishing a whip, and singing a war song, evidently desirous of getting up a fight, and refusing to lay down his arms with the rest, although frequently requested to do so. At length, however, he put them down, and sat with the rest, and taking (though with evident reluctance) a few puffs from the pipe which was going the round of the party, in token of peace, he turned to Mr. Harriett and said, that as he had smoked with the white man, he would present him with his horse, at the same time leading up a beautiful brown animal which I had seen him alight from on our arrival, he handed Mr. Harriett the lasso. Mr. Harriett declined his gift, explaining that it was impossible for him to take it with him in the boats.

They told us they were a party of 1500 warriors, from 1200 lodges, who were then "pitching on" towards Fort Edmonton; that is, they were making short journeys, and pitching their tents on towards Edmonton, leaving few behind capable of bearing arms. They were in pursuit of the Crees and Assiniboines, whom they threatened totally to annihilate, boasting that they themselves were as numerous as the grass on the plains. They were the best mounted, the best looking, the most warlike in appearance, and the best accoutred of any tribe I had ever seen on the continent during my route. As Mr. Harriett was very anxious to cultivate the acquaintance and friendship of such questionable characters, he accepted of their invitation to "camp" with them until the following morning, which was exceedingly acceptable to me, as it enabled me to make several sketches, and to hear something about them. After our smoke several of the young Braves engaged in a horse race, to which sport they are very partial, and at which they bet heavily; they generally ride on those occasions stark naked, without a saddle, and with only a lasso fastened to the lower jaw of the horse as represented in Sketch No. 16. [Fig. 89; crIV-143, 144, 145] I had some difficulty at first in getting the chiefs to let me take

---

[2] KJ notes: "Thousands died of starvation. I counted in sight at one time no less than 18."

[3] KJ adds: "As they do every spring and return in fall to the woods."

[4] KJ notes that they shot several wolves swimming across the river.

[5] KJ places the number in the party at 500.

their likenesses, but after they comprehended what I wanted, they made no objections.

Big Snake's brother was the first who sat to me [crIV-153], and while I was sketching, he told me the following anecdote of his brother, of whom he seemed to be very proud. Mr. Harriett understood the language and acted as interpreter. Some time back, Big Snake had the free admission to one of the American forts near the Rocky Mountains. Coming up one day with two other Indians, to enter the gate, it was shut rudely in his face by the orders of the commander, who had only lately arrived in the country. This his pride led him to regard as a direct insult; he rode away, and falling in with some cattle that he knew belonged to the fort, he commenced firing on them, and killed thirteen. As soon as the sentinel, who had given the offence, heard the shots, he suspected the reason, and informed the superintendent, who immediately collected his men, and sallied out with them well armed, in the direction of the firing. Big Snake being on the watch, hid himself with his two companions behind a small hill.

The party from the fort apprehending there might be a large number of Indians hid, hesitated to advance within gun-shot; but a negro of the party offered to proceed and reconnoitre. Approaching the hill with great caution, and seeing no one, he began to think they had escaped; but, when within about twenty yards of the top, Big Snake sprang up from his lair and fired, bringing him down, and the next moment bore off his scalp, and waved it in derision towards the Americans.

A short time afterwards Big Snake met a large party of Blackfeet, "pitching" towards the fort on a trade. On his arrival amongst them, he stated what he had done, and dared any one to censure his conduct on peril of making him his enemy. Although the band well knew that what he had done amounted to an open declaration of war, and would of course cut off any communication or trade with the establishment, unless they actually gave up Big Snake as a prisoner, yet they suffered their disappointment in silence rather than incur the anger of one whom they so much feared. Another band of the same tribe, ignorant of the circumstance, arrived at the fort a few days afterwards. The Americans, thinking this a good opportunity of chastising the aggressors, loaded one of their cannons with musket-balls, and while the unsuspecting Indians were standing huddled together at the gate, waiting for admittance, applied the fusee. Fortunately it did not explode, and the Indians, seeing the unusual stir and the flash, became alarmed, and fled.

On a second application of the fusee, it discharged its murderous projectiles amongst the fugitives, and killed ten persons, principally women and children.

Some time after, Big Snake heard that one of the most influential Indians of the tribe had blamed him, in a speech, for involving the tribe in much inconvenience and destroying their trade. On hearing these remarks, he directly went in search of the censurer, armed with a scalping-knife, and, on coming up with him, attempted to stab him; his foot, however, slipped in the attempt, which saved the other's life, although he received a severe wound in the side. These two continued for some time after in a state of deadly hostility, until Big Snake was persuaded by many of his friends to make peace, to which he at length consented, and proceeded towards his lodge for that purpose. In the meantime he had told his wife, if she saw any disturbance, to move her lodge instantly to the top of a small hill, a few hundred yards distant, which might be more easily defended. On his arrival at the man's lodge, he found him seated with his wife and children around him, and, taking up one of the children, he began to caress it, and asked it to intercede with its father for the injury he had done him. The man, however, moodily held down his head without any reply, whilst Big Snake again asked the child to take pity on him still. The father remained silent. On which Big Snake, getting enraged at the rejection of the friendly overtures he had condescended to make to one whom he regarded so much as an inferior, and feeling himself humiliated by the refusal, rushed from the tent, seized his gun, which he had taken the precaution of placing within reach in case of emergency, and commenced firing through the skin covering of the tent, killing two of its inmates, and wounding a third; after which he returned to the hill, where his wife was pitching the tent, according to his orders, where he remained and defied the whole camp to molest him.

After I had finished this picture, and the others had examined it with great attention, a general impression seemed to prevail amongst them all that I must be a great medicine-man. And as we encouraged the idea, which afforded us no inconsiderable protection from any treachery on their part, I had no trouble in getting as many sitters as I could possibly manage. Amongst others, I sketched group No. 17 [Fig. 92; crIV-154, 155, 156], consisting of Big Snake, the centre figure; Mis-ke-me-kin, "The Iron Collar," a Blood Indian chief, with his face painted red [crIV-149]; to the extreme left of the picture, is a chief called "Little Horn," with a buffalo robe draped round him, and between him and Big Snake is Wah-nis-stow, "The White Buffalo," principal chief of the Sur-cee tribe. [Fig. 91; crIV-150, 151] In the background stand two chiefs of inferior quality, one of them has his face painted half black, being in half-mourning for some friend. [crIV-152?] As they were expecting to have a fight with the Crees next day, they got up a medicine dance in the afternoon, and I was solemnly invited to attend, that I might add my magical powers in increasing its efficacy. Amongst all the tribes here assembled, the sacredness of the medicine pipe-stem is held in very high estimation, and it was with much solemnity that I was placed in the best position, to work my incantations; that is to say, to make the sketch No. 18. [Plate XXIII; Figs. 93, 94, 95; crIV-157 to 164]

Next morning we embarked, after having presented the chiefs with eight or ten pounds of tobacco [6] to be distributed amongst the rest, and had not proceeded many miles, when we had to put ashore again [7] to gratify an old Blood Indian chief, who had arrived at the camp shortly after our departure, and had galloped immediately after us, for the purpose of having a talk with Mr. Harriett, whom he had known many years before, and for whom he entertained the warmest friendship. After the talk, he stripped himself naked, excepting his breech-cloth. Mr. Harriett, not to be behindhand with him, gave him everything but his shirt and pantaloons: it was rather a losing operation for him; although the chief's leather shirt and leggings were quite new and highly ornamented, yet they were not exactly what Mr. Harriett would like to wear, so he gave them to me to add to my stock of Indian costumes. One of the Indians who had accompanied the old chief, noticing I had a new capote on, thought he would try what could be done by an interchange of civilities with me. He accordingly took off a dirty old greasy shirt he had on, and laid it down before me; but as I had no other clothes with me but what I had on, I was forced to decline this most endearing mark of friendship, much to his disappointment, although the scamp could not help grinning as I shook my head in token of refusal.

June 3rd.—We were obliged to lie by the whole of this day, on account of the violence of the wind and snow, which rendered any attempt at proceeding very uncomfortable, and almost useless.

June 4th.—Early in the forenoon, we arrived at Carlton,

[6] kj describes the gift as 25 or 30 pounds of tobacco.
[7] kj states that they put ashore to meet another party of Indians that had been following them about 20 miles behind.

and Bishop De Merse immediately took horses to cross by land to Red River Settlement, a distance of sixteen days' journey.

Chapter XXV.

Fort Carlton.—Battle of the Indians.—Death of a Hero.—Cumberland House.—An Unwieldy Wife.—Shooting the Grand Rapids.—Norway House.—Child Suckled by a Man.—"Big Snake's" Fate.—Storm on the Winnipeg.—"The Constant Sky."—A Midnight Incantation.—Powers of the Medicine.—Fort Alexander.—The Grand Bonnet.—The Plague of Mosquitoes.—Stopped by a Fog.—Deserted Mission.—Two Days' Feast.—The Lake of the Woods.—Watermen indeed.—Fort Frances.—An Express Canoe.—Lake Superior.—Sault St. Marie.—Conclusion.

The Crees around this post all took to the woods on hearing of the large party of Blackfeet in their vicinity, and, as we heard, were collecting in large numbers in a camp, about fourteen miles off, for the purpose of opposing the invasion of the hostile tribes.

June 5th.—We remained at Carlton during the day, as Mr. Harriett was anxious to hear of the proceedings of the hostile tribes; indeed, he felt rather apprehensive of the treachery of the Blackfeet, and knew that the large numbers of our party would check them from attempting anything which might hereafter call for redress.

June 6th.—In the morning a fugitive arrived, bringing news of a battle between the hostile Indians. It appears that the Crees had a medicine dance, and had, according to their custom, erected an ornamental pole, around which they hang their medicine bags, &c., whilst dancing. After the conclusion of their dance, they returned to their camp, a distance of about three miles, which consisted of ninety lodges, leaving the medicine pole standing; shortly after, the invading war party we had met discovered the pole, and on one of their number climbing to the top, to tear off the ornaments, he from the height perceived the Cree camp in the distance, upon which the party prepared themselves for battle.

One of the Cree scouts had also perceived them, but had formed a very erroneous idea of their numbers, and had mentioned them only as a small party. Upon this the Crees immediately proceeded to the attack, thinking to overwhelm them by their superior numbers, and did not discover their error until

Encampment Foot of the Rocky Mountains

Plate XXIX. Boat Encampment, Columbia River. Stark wwc100; crIV-276.

Plate XXX. Kettle Falls, Fort Colvile. Stark woP19; crIV-298.

they were actually engaged. When they perceived that they were so much outnumbered, they retreated to their camp; all but one chief, Pe-ho-this, who, disdaining to fly, dashed madly into the midst of his enemies, dealing death around him with his poke-a-mau-gun or war club. On every side, bullet and arrow pierced his body; but he continued the unequal conflict, until his bridle arm was shattered by a ball, when his wounded and frightened horse, no longer under control, dashed with him from the tumult, and carried him still living to his lodge, but with only just sufficient strength to enable him to beg his tribe to take care of his wives and children for his sake, when he fell dead from his charger.

The whole camp now fled with their women and children, leaving their lodges standing; except two old and enfeebled chiefs, who, as is not unusual amongst Indians under such circumstances, remained in the best lodge, and having dressed themselves in their gayest clothes and ornaments, painted their faces, lit their pipes, and sat singing their war songs, until the Blackfeet came up and soon despatched them.

The Crees had nineteen killed and forty wounded, besides losing their lodges and a good deal of property, which they could not carry with them. The Sur-cees lost Wah-nis-stow, before mentioned, and having taken six scalps, thought they had done enough, and returned from the battle to have a dance with the scalps. The Blood Indians, after losing three of their party, also retired after taking a few scalps, leaving the Blackfeet, who had lost six, to bear the brunt of the battle; the Pay-gans and Gros Ventres not having arrived until the fight was over, of course suffered no loss.

Immediately after hearing this, Mr. Harriett ordered us to embark, as he knew that the Blackfeet and their allies would immediately return to their own country after meeting with any success, and having a few scalps to take home, according to the invariable custom of the Indians. We embarked early in the forenoon, and glided quickly down the rapid stream, aided by our oars. We now were out of the buffalo country altogether, and had no fresh meat but some little that we had brought with us for the use of the gentlemen of the party; the men, however, were plentifully supplied with pemmi-kon.

June 10th.—We arrived at Cumberland House, which we left next morning, having received an addition to our party of three more boats and their crews.[1]

June 12th.—We arrived at the Paw, where my old friend Mr. Hunter gave me a most hearty welcome. Mrs. Hunter had died during my absence, and he had been waiting for us for the purpose of going down to Norway House. We met here Sir John Richardson and Dr. Rae, *en route* to Mackenzie River, with two canoes in search of Sir John Franklin. From them we first heard of the events that had recently occurred in Europe, the flight of Louis Philippe from Paris, and the revolutionary movements then agitating the Continent.

Whilst walking past the small trading post established here, Mr. Hunter asked me to go in, and we were received very kindly by a little shrivelled up French Canadian, married to a Cree squaw, one of the most extraordinary looking women I had ever seen. She was so fat that she was obliged to sit on a small waggon, in which they drew her about, and her mode of going to bed was by rolling off this on to a buffalo skin. She had not been able to use her legs for many years. I have generally noticed that all Indian women, when brought into the forts, and when relieved from the toils and exposures of their native life, become fat, lazy, and unwieldy.

We left the same evening, bringing Mr. Hunter with us. Few incidents worth noticing occurred on our route. Mr. Harriett's boat, in which I sat, was generally a-head of the party, being lighter and rather better built than the rest. One evening we got to the place Mr. Harriett selected for encampment considerably before any of the others, and I got out my drawing materials and took a sketch of the brigade, as it was coming up with a fair breeze, crowding on all sail to escape a thunder storm rolling fast after them. [Figs. 73, 74; cRIV-92 to 95]

June 17th.—We arrived at the Grand Rapids, and the whole brigade shot down them, a distance of three and a half miles; this is the same rapid where Paulet Paul achieved his herculean feat before mentioned. No rapid in the whole course of the navigation on the eastern side of the mountains is at all to be compared to this in point of velocity, grandeur, or danger to the navigator. The brigade flies down as if impelled by a hurricane, many shipping a good deal of water in the perpendicular leaps which they often had to take in the descent. The whole course is one white sheet of foam, from one end to the other.

We passed here the brigade of boats[2] bound upwards for Mackenzie River; they were laboriously making the portage up, whilst we were shooting down with lightning speed. The heavily laden men, as they toiled along the banks, cast many an

---

[1] KJ for June 10: "Cumberland, crossed over 3 miles to see the Fort. Got a keg of beer from Mr. de Shambo [?] which [I] passed. Soon left on the same day."
[2] KJ identifies Mr. Kinsey as being in charge of the brigade.

envious look at our flying company, who yelled and shouted with excitement whilst plunging down the foaming cataract. Having run the rapids in safety, we arrived in a few minutes more at Lake Winnipeg, and encamped on the shore, where we cooked and ate our supper. From this point we had to make a traverse of seventy miles as the crow flies to Mossy Point, the entrance to Jack Fish River; but as the wind was against us, we lay down to sleep.

About 1 o'clock in the morning we were all aroused, and found the wind blowing fresh and fair, so that we put off immediately to take advantage of the fortunate occurrence. I was soon asleep again in the boat, and did not awake till after sunrise, when I found we were far out of sight of land and the wind blowing a heavy gale. About 2 o'clock P.M. we rounded Mossy Point, and at 5 o'clock arrived at Norway House, where the brigade left me, they going on to York Factory, and I remaining to meet Major McKenzie, who was expected soon to pass on his way to Fort Francis.

The annual council of chief factors, which is usually held at Red River, was this year held at Norway House, and I had the pleasure of again meeting with Sir George Simpson, and several gentlemen to whose kindness I had before been deeply indebted. I was detained here for more than a month, and though the weather was clear and fine, yet we could not sit in the house in comfort without having the stove lighted. I amused myself in fishing and shooting. I speared a good many sturgeon, which are here very fine and numerous, and also great lots of gold eyes, which are a peculiar species of fish, like the herring, though larger and thicker, but not worth catching. Mr. Rowand said that they eat like mud. I certainly never tasted them but once, and I was not tempted to repeat the experiment.

I was often accompanied in the canoe by Ogemawwah Chack, "The Spirit Chief" (sketch No. 19), an Esquimaux from the Hudson's Bay who had attained to an extreme old age. [Fig. 76; crIV-90, 91] According to received opinion, he was 110 years old, and the events which he related as having witnessed seemed to warrant the belief. He had an only son, whom I often met, quite elderly in appearance. The mother of this boy had died very shortly after his birth, and there being no woman giving suck near at the time, the father, to soothe the cries of the starving infant, placed the child's mouth to his own breast, and finding that the child derived some benefit from it, he continued the practice for some days, and, strange to say, milk flowed from his nipple, and he brought up the child without the assistance of any woman.

Before leaving Norway House, some Cree Indians arrived, and boasted that one of their war chiefs had vanquished the great Blackfoot chief, Big Snake, in single combat. [Fig. 90; crIV-148] Big Snake had ridden away from the main body of his tribe, in hopes of stealing some horses, as he thought that the Crees in their precipitate flight were likely to have left them behind; and, hoping to have all he got for himself, he took no comrades with him. The Cree chief discovered him from behind a hill, riding alone on the plain beneath, and, burning with vengeance, rushed at him, without waiting for his other warriors, who were not, however, far off. Big Snake did not see the others, and disdaining to fly from a single foe, he boldly galloped to meet his enemy; but the fight was short, as the Cree succeeded in piercing him with his spear at the first meeting, and he was scalped and dead before the others came up.

July 24th.—Major McKenzie at last arrived with five boats, manned principally with Indians; he only remained a few hours, when I embarked with him; but we only proceeded about six miles when it became dark, and we encamped for the night.

July 25th.—We stopped to breakfast at a picturesque little island near the outlet of Lake Winnipeg, after which we passed the Spider Islands, so called from the countless myriads of these insects which infest them. In the evening we encamped at Point de Tremble, on Poplar Point.

July 26th.—We left in the morning with a strong breeze, which changed into a perfect gale, making many of our Indians sea-sick. The swells of Lake Winnipeg, from the shallowness of this wide expanse of water when set in motion by a heavy wind, are far more abrupt and dangerous for boats than those of the Atlantic; and I could not but feel very apprehensive for our safety,—a feeling which was evidently shared by Major McKenzie, for he kept a signal flying from his mast-head, which the guide well knew meant for him to put ashore, but which he would not obey, as he considered it a most dangerous alternative to change his course; and the shore, from its rocky character, being very difficult of approach in stormy weather.[3] We, however, by dint of constant baling, continued our course in safety until we arrived at the mouth of Behring's River, which we entered in safety, much to the relief of the Major's anxiety for both cargoes and crews. Here we remained windbound for the rest of the day and part of the following.

By way of passing the time, I took my gun and strolled up

[3] KJ notes that Major McKenzie had been able to stand the battle of Corunna when he was wounded, but that the swells of Lake Winnipeg completely upset him.

the river, accompanied by the guide, and fell in with a solitary Sotto woman and child sitting under a tree. She was quite alone, as her husband had gone up the river fishing in the morning. She did not appear to be at all alarmed or confused at our approach, and freely entered into conversation with the guide, to whom she told her name, Caw-kee-ka-keesh-e-ko, "The Constant Sky." Tempted by the beauty of the scene, and she seeming to be in no wise unwilling, I sketched her likeness and the surrounding landscape with considerable care. [CRIV-87, 88]

July 27th.—We started rather late,[4] and being only able to make Rabbit Point, we encamped. We here found immense flocks of wild pigeons, and killed a good supply. Our Indians killed several skunks, which they prize very much as delicate eating, preferring them to the pigeons, although the bare smell of them in our vicinity almost took away my appetite for the former.

July 28th.—About 2 o'clock P.M., we endeavoured to proceed, but only got as far as the Dog's Head, the wind being so strong and unfavourable, that it was thought useless to run any risk for the short distance that we would be able to make against it. In the evening our Indians constructed a jonglerie, or medicine lodge, the main object of which was to procure a fair wind for next day. For this purpose they first drive ten or twelve poles, nine or ten feet long, into the ground, enclosing a circular area of about three feet in diameter, with a boat sail open at the top. The medicine-man, one of whom is generally found in every brigade, gets inside and commences shaking the poles violently, rattling his medicinal rattle, and singing hoarse incantations to the Great Spirit for a fair wind. Being unable to sleep on account of the discordant noises, I wrapped a blanket round me, and went out into the woods, where they were holding their midnight orgies, and lay down amongst those on the outside of the medicine lodge, to witness the proceedings. I had no sooner done so than the incantations at once ceased, and the performer exclaimed that a white man was present. How he ascertained this fact I am at a loss to surmise, as it was pitch dark at the time, and he was enclosed in the narrow tent, without any apparent opening through which he could espy me, even had it been light enough to distinguish one person from another.

The Major, who, with many other intelligent persons, is a firm believer in their medicine, told me that a Canadian once had the temerity to peep under the covering which enclosed the jonglerie, but that he got such a fright that he never fairly recovered from it, nor could he ever be prevailed upon to tell what it was that had so appalled him. After about two hours'

shaking and singing, the medicine-man cried out that he saw five boats with the sails set running before the wind, which communication was greeted by the whole party with their usual grunt of satisfaction and assent.

After this, many questions were asked him by the Indians, some inquiring after the health of their families at home, whom they had not seen for many months. Upon putting the question, the inquirer threw a small piece of tobacco over the covering of the tent, upon which the medicine-man agitated the tent, and shook his rattle violently, and then replied that he saw one family enjoying themselves over a fat sturgeon, another engaged in some pleasing employment, &c., &c. I then put a question to him myself, accompanying it with a double portion of tobacco, for which I got a double portion of noise. I asked about my curiosities which I had left at Norway House (for want of room in our boats), to be brought on by the canoes which had taken up Sir John Richardson on their return, they not being engaged to carry him further than Prairie River. The medicine-man told me that he saw the party with my baggage encamped on a sandy point, which we had ourselves passed two days before.

However singular the coincidence may appear, it is a fact, that on the next day we had a fair wind, for which the medicine-man of course took all the credit; and it is no less true, that the canoes with my baggage were on the sandy point on the day stated, for I inquired particularly of them when they came up to us.

July 29th.—We started very early in the morning, with a fair wind, and stopped to breakfast at the Loon Narrows. We reached Otter Head [5] in the evening, and then encamped.

July 30th.—We breakfasted at Point Mille-lac, and arrived at 10 o'clock A.M. at Fort Alexander, where we found a great number of Saulteaux Indians, who come in large numbers about this season of the year, and disperse themselves among the small lakes, where they gather great quantities of wild rice, resembling our own in taste, but much larger and black.[6] The scarcity of other provisions in these parts renders the rice very valuable, but the Indians are so lazy, that they will not collect much more than they want for themselves without being bribed to do so, and the clerk in charge of the establishment is obliged to give

---

[4] KJ: "They breakfasted at Sturgeon River."

[5] KJ reads Buffalo Head.

[6] KJ notes that they purchased 250 bushels from the Indians. The price was one-third of a pint of rum for a bushel of rice. Kane adds that rice cannot be got without rum.

them, for that purpose, a certain quantity of rum to induce them to go to collect rice for the establishment, and also to give them some on their return, besides paying them in goods for the quantity they bring in. Major McKenzie here met his wife and two daughters, who had been on a visit to Red River. We remained at Fort Alexander four days, changing our crews, the Indians who had been with us belonging here.

Before leaving Lake Winnipeg, I would remark that the whole of its eastern shore, which I had just coasted, presented a most wild, rocky, rough, hilly, and almost impassable country, and several of the Indians who had been through, described it as being of the same character far back from the lake, and interspersed with innumerable lakes and swamps.

August 3rd.—We left with four boats, manned with thirty men, twenty-seven of whom were Indians, two French Canadians, and one Orkney man, and commenced the ascent of the Winnipeg River. Mrs. McKenzie and her two daughters were to follow us in a light canoe, with a crew of Indians. We had to make several portages during the day, and in the evening got over the portage of the Prancing Horses, a cascade about twenty feet high. We had a whole fleet of light canoes following us, containing the Indian wives and children. Two of them contained brides, who had been married in the morning without any ceremony that I heard of.

Aug. 4th.—In the morning,[7] we made the White Mud Portage, which was very picturesque, and of which I took a sketch, No. 20, with the Indians and squaws who were following us, carrying their canoes across [Pl. XIII; crIV-19, 20, 21]; and in the course of the day made another called Little Rock, about seven feet high, and camped at the upper end of it.

Aug. 5th.—Left at 4 o'clock A.M., and arrived at the Grand Bonnet, a portage of a mile in length, which it took us the whole day to drag the boats across; the weather was burning hot, and the mosquitoes in legions. The canoes, containing the women and children, kept close at our heels, and always came up to our encampment for provisions; this so reduced our stock, that out of regard to our own safety, we were obliged to put them upon short allowance.[8]

Aug. 6th.—We crossed the Second Bonnet, and met some Indians, who sold us a few sturgeon, and crossing Lac de Bonnet, where several of our Indian followers left us for the rice-grounds, we encamped for the night on the banks of the river Malaine. Owing to the low marshy state of the country hereabouts, we were dreadfully tormented with mosquitoes. The poor Orkney man, in particular, seemed to be an especial fa-

vourite, and there had been evidently an attempt made to eat him up altogether. In the morning, his face presented the appearance of a person in the smallpox.

Aug. 7th.—Passed six portages to-day, one of which is called the Wooden Horse, and encamped at the Grande Gullete. The chief's son,[9] of Rat Portage, who was one of our engaged men, here deserted us, and stole off in a canoe with his two wives. [Fig. 53; crIV-30, 31]

Aug. 8th.—To-day we had to make several portages,[10] and in the evening encamped three miles above the Grand Rapid of this river, having still thirteen canoes of Indians paddling in our wake. This evening we found some smooth flat rocks, which the voyageurs always prefer to grass or earth to make their bed on, and I can say, from experience, that they have formed a judicious estimate of the superior comfort they afford after a hard day's travel; for grass or sand is certainly the worst surface to sleep upon, however soft it may feel at first.

Aug. 9th.—We breakfasted at the Barrière Portage, and arrived about noon at the Slave Falls, of which I made a sketch. [Fig. 51; crIV-14 to 17] Three military officers, Captain Moody, Mr. Brown, and Mr. Constable, caught up to us in their light canoes; they were on their way from Red River to Canada, and pushed on after a very short stay. We had hardly bid them good-bye, when Mrs. McKenzie and her two lovely daughters came up, and stayed with us until next morning. Our Indians now refused to proceed further, unless they received an allowance of rum; and the Major was obliged to promise them a supply as soon as he arrived at Rat Portage.

Aug. 10th.—Our starting[11] was delayed this morning in consequence of a dense fog, and we only got as far as the Rochers Boules before breakfast; after which, the ladies left us for their residence at Rat Portage. During the day we passed the Aux Chênes, and encamped about four miles below the Point of Woods.

Aug. 11th.[12]—Our provisions were now getting very low, and we had still further to restrict our distributions to the women

[7] KJ notes that they made a portage of the Silver Falls before the portages of the White Mud Falls and the Little Rock Falls. They thus made three portages in one day. He notes the second falls were ten feet high.

[8] KJ states that they crossed both the First and the Second Bonnet. The weather was intensely hot and the mosquitoes were in myriads.

[9] KJ identifies the chief's son as Cashi-Cabit, the Long Tooth, or "The Tooth of the Glutton."

[10] KJ adds: "One of the 2 women that got married at Fort Alexander had fits. I gave her some peppermint and told her sister to rub her. She had eaten too much."

[11] KJ notes that they had to wait until 6 A.M. before setting out.

[12] KJ for August 11 states that they made an early start and breakfasted at Chute à Jacques. He adds that canoes were leaving for Winnipeg.

and children. On each side of the river for a long distance are innumerable small shallow lakes, bearing usually large quantities of rice; but the water in them had sunk so low this season, that the Indians were apprehensive of a failure in the crop, which would be attended with the most serious consequences, as upon it was placed their whole dependence for food. When we arrived at the Grand Equerre we stopped for the night.

Aug. 12th.—We passed to-day the deserted Catholic mission called Wabe-samung, "White Dog," from the name of the portage next above it. This was established by Mr. Belcour,[13] a Catholic priest, but he had left it the year before, as he found there was not enough of land near it that would pay for cultivation. The whole country between this and Fort Alexander was rocky and barren, so that no mission could hope to get any Indians to settle permanently near it. In the evening we encamped at the White Dog Portage.[14]

Aug. 13th.—We got to the Yellow Mud Portage by breakfast-time, and afterwards crossed the "Grande Décharge," so called from its being the place where the boats are hauled up after the goods are discharged from them, in distinction from a portage, at which latter place, as I have already observed, it is necessary to carry the boats as well as the cargoes. In the evening we encamped at what is called the Fishery, or the place where the people from Rat Portage come to fish. It was with great difficulty we could find a place to sleep on free from ants, whose hillocks we disturbed at every step. I made several attempts to lie down, but they annoyed me so much, that at last I got into one of the boats.[15]

Aug. 14th.—Left our encampment at 3 A.M., and arrived at Rat Portage at 10, where we were received by Mrs. McKenzie with the greatest hospitality and kindness. The Indians here subsist on sturgeon and white fish in the summer, and rice and rabbits in the winter. We rested ourselves here two days, and employed ourselves principally in feasting on white fish, to make up for the short allowance of food under which we had lately been suffering.

Aug. 16th.—It was with great regret that I parted with the kind Major and his family. The men having made the portage from which this post is named, we left about 2 in the afternoon, and soon entered the Lake of the Woods, where we chose a comfortable little island, and encamped for the night.

Aug. 17th.—We threaded our way among innumerable islands, many of them thickly covered with woods, from which circumstance the lake takes its name. We saw on one of them about five acres of cultivated corn, the only instance of the kind

I had seen since I left Norway House. There is another island called Garden Island, which lay to the west of our route, about six miles long and about three wide, on which I was told some Indians raised yearly a few bushels of corn and potatoes. At night we again chose an island for our resting place.

Aug. 18th.—We were wind-bound until 5 P.M., during which time we were visited by a large party of Saulteaux Indians; we embarked in the evening, but only succeeded in getting on about six miles before we were again obliged to stop, and remained all the next day.

Aug. 20th.—Made an early start with a fair wind, which carried us into the mouth of the River La Pluie. Here we found some Indians who were gathering snow-berries and sand-berries; the latter are the size of large grapes, of a reddish blue colour. They grow on long vines trailing upon the sand, and are very good eating when washed free of the particles which adhere to them. We encamped about four miles up the river, and were again tortured by our old enemies the mosquitoes, aided by detachments of black flies.

Aug. 21st.—Roused by the flies, we started early.[16] Our route up the river was much enlivened by the antics of the Indians when tracking, that is, hauling the boats up the current, which they do for days together whenever the banks, or indeed the bed of the river, will admit of it; for they seemed to be perfectly amphibious, wading about in the water, and swimming from side to side as a matter of course, without thinking of getting into the boat, and making great fun of one of our Canadians who had got into a canoe with two squaws, to cross.[17]

Aug. 22nd.—The men woke me up at 2 o'clock in the morning from my warm blankets, for the purpose of getting under way; but when just ready to start, we were prevented by a violent storm of rain, which continued until about 6 o'clock, when we immediately set off. The country about here is very swampy, but, from its height, I think much of it might be drained, and adapted for cultivation. I noticed all along the banks of this river, that wherever pine trees had been burned

[13] The Rev. Georges-Antoine Bellecourt (1803–1874) served as a missionary in the northwest from 1831 to 1858. He operated the mission of Notre Dame de Merci at Wabassimong in 1843–44. See *Dictionary of Canadian Biography*, vol. X.

[14] KJ states that they camped at the White Mud Portage. He had mentioned it earlier, and evidently corrected his entry for the book.

[15] KJ: "We received the Chief of Rat Portage on board while his 2 wives paddled a canoe alongside. He seemed rather proud of sitting with white chiefs. We took them to Rat Portage."

[16] Kane was a great admirer of the canoemen. He entered in his journal: "Never saw such water dogs as our men."

[17] KJ notes of the one exception, "a small Canadian who would not risk it."

down, poplars invariably sprung up in their places, although no other poplars could be seen in the vicinity.

Aug. 23rd.—We left our encampment at 1 A.M., so as to make sure of arriving at Fort Frances before night. The Indians tracked with the line the whole day, frequently up to their middles in the water, and often swimming; this wearisome toil they kept up for sixteen hours, with the exception of one hour, during which we stopped for breakfast, never for one moment losing their cheerfulness and good humour. I scarcely think that any other race of people could go through such fatigue with the same alacrity and energy.[18]

At 5 o'clock P.M. we reached Fort Frances, so named after the sister of Lady Simpson. [Figs. 49, 50; crIV-10, 11] Here the annual three months' voyage terminates, that being the time which it takes to convey the furs to York Factory, in Hudson's Bay, and bring back the outfit of goods.[19] The fort is situated near where Rainy Lake disembogues into a river of the same name, forming a beautiful cascade. [crIV-12] The Indians catch great quantities of sturgeon at the foot of these falls in the month of June.[20] The sturgeon here are very small—seldom weighing more than 40 or 50 lbs.—at least in comparison with those taken at the mouth of Frazer's River on the west side of the mountains, which often weigh from 5 to 7 cwt.

Fort Frances has usually about 250 Indians in its neighbourhood, who have a half-breed missionary of the Methodist church resident amongst them;[21] but I understood he was about to leave them, disheartened by the small success attendant upon his exertions. The Indians live here as at Rat Portage, on rice, fish, and rabbits. The last are so numerous in the winter, that one man caught eighty-six in one night, being only unsuccessful with fourteen snares out of the 100 he had set in the evening.

The skins, like the Canadian, are far inferior to the European rabbits': the only use to which I have seen them applied has been in the manufacture of rabbit-skin robes, which are made by cutting the skin with the hair on into strips, which are twisted and netted together in such a manner as to keep the hair outwards on both sides of the robe. The people of the fort grow some wheat and potatoes, but though there is some very good land about, they find it impossible to induce the Indians to cultivate it. The crop of wheat which they got in while I was there, was almost entirely spoiled by smut, and they were obliged to wash it before they could turn it to any account. I remained here eighteen days waiting for the passing of the express canoe which annually carries the letters from the interior posts to Lachine.

Sept. 10th.—The express canoe arrived in the evening with Mr. M'Tavish.[22] He was come direct from York Factory, where he had been stationed for fourteen years, and gave a most dismal account of the climate and country; he was now going to the Sault St. Marie, to the charge of which post he had been recently appointed by way of giving him a little taste of civilisation, of which he rather stood in need.

Sept. 11th.—We started at 6 o'clock in the morning, and got through Lac la Pluie by 5 in the afternoon; after this we had to make two portages, and encamped just before dark at the second.

Sept. 12th.—Started at 3 o'clock A.M., the morning was very cold and foggy; and we had a severe frost during the night. We breakfasted at the Grand Chute, and had a very severe day's work afterwards, as we had to make four bad portages, and did not encamp until 9 o'clock at night; the men having worked eighteen hours steadily. We were lucky enough to meet some Indians after dark,[23] from whom we obtained a good supply of delicious white fish. We now exerted all our energies to hasten our journey as the danger of ice setting in was becoming imminent, and with great labour we arrived at the Mountain Portage on the evening of the 18th.

Sept. 19th.—I got up at the first appearance of day, that I might have the opportunity whilst the men were making the portage, of again visiting the Kakabakka falls. As the day dawned the magnificent spectacle gradually cleared to my view in all its mighty grandeur and magnificence, and I felt more impressed than ever with the opinion that these falls far surpass the Niagara in beauty and picturesque effect, and would have much liked to have taken another sketch of them; but my admiring contemplations were hastily cut short by a peremptory summons from the canoes, which were waiting for me. I hastily

[18] KJ, noting that they went until 5 P.M., says: "There are not many men in the world that could stand it."

[19] KJ states that when the men had carried their packs to the stores, their three month's voyage was over.

Kane was wrong about the naming of Fort Frances, which commemorates Lady Simpson herself.

[20] KJ goes into detail about obtaining caviar from the sturgeon at this place, stating: "They have received 18 packs of sturgeon sands [caviar] in one year, 90 pounds per pack, 12½ sands to the pound. There will be 20,450 sands in the 18 packs, and as there is but one sand taken from a sturgeon, there will be 20,450 sturgeon caught here in the month of June."

[21] The missionary was the Rev. Peter Jacobs, who was highly critical of the Hudson's Bay Company management at the Fort Frances post.

[22] With them as passenger was William Mactavish (d. 1870), at the time a Hudson's Bay Company clerk, but appointed a chief factor in 1851, Governor of Assiniboia in 1858, and Governor of Rupert's Land in 1864.

[23] According to KJ, the Indians were met at Grand Rapids.

rejoined them, and we dashed down the uninterrupted current forty miles to Fort William, where we arrived early in the afternoon. On leaving Fort William, we suffered a great deal the next five days from the high cold wind, which frequently stopped our progress.

Sept. 24th.—We were wind-bound at the mouth of a small river, and as there seemed no prospect of a change, I followed the stream up about ten miles until I came to a cascade. The interior of the country as far as I went seemed to be of the same character as the coast, high mountain rocks, interspersed with a few trees of stunted growth and scanty herbage. I was lucky enough to shoot four ducks, which proved a most acceptable addition to the pemmi-kon and fish which we had brought with us. We got off next day, although the weather was still bad, but we were anxious to get to Michipicoton, as there is a post there, and we might obtain some little comfort at least, if we were detained.

Sept. 27th.—We arrived at the post about 9 o'clock in the evening, and remained there the whole of next day. The post is situated in a deep bay at the mouth of the river, and is sur-rounded by some of the best land to be found on the British shores of Lake Superior. The head chief of the Ojibbeways, who resides near the post, sat for me in his red coat trimmed with gold lace. These coats are given by the Company to such Indian chiefs as have been friendly and serviceable to them, and are very highly prized by their possessors. His name was Maydoc-game-kinungee, "I hear the Noise of the Deer." [Pl. XI; crIV-1, 2]

Sept. 29th.—We started very early in the morning, and encamped that evening opposite to Montreal Island.

Sept. 30th.—We got to Montreal River, where we stopped for two hours for breakfast, passed Micah Bay at 1 o'clock, and encamped at night at the Isle aux Sables.

Oct. 1st.—We stopped to breakfast at 4 o'clock near Gros-Cap, a porphyry rock rising 1500 feet above the level of the lake, and got to the post at Sault St. Marie by 2 o'clock P.M. Here I consider that my Indian travels finish, as the rest of my journey home to Toronto was performed on board steam-boats; and the greatest hardship I had to endure, was the difficulty I found in trying to sleep in a civilised bed.

PART THREE   Paul Kane's Sketches and Paintings

For an explanation of the capitalization and spelling used in the captions, please refer to the introduction to Part Four, where a list of abbreviations for the collections will also be found.

Fig. 1. Paul Kane, a photograph. Collection of Mrs. Paul Kane III.

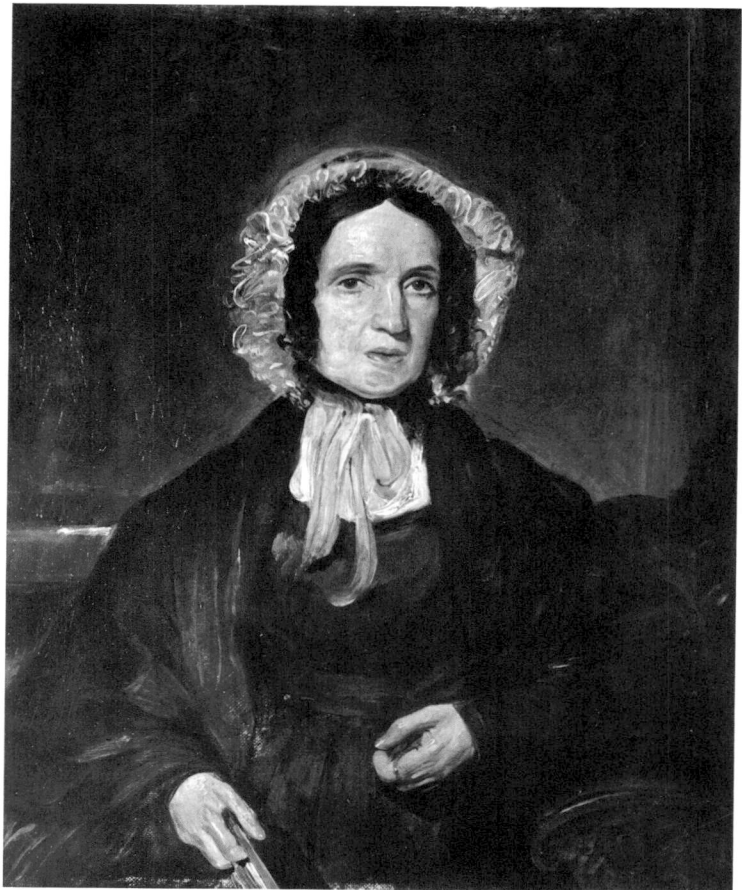

Fig. 2. Mrs. W. S. Conger, painted *c.* 1834. Collection of S. E. Weir; CRI-13.

COURTESY STARK FOUNDATION, ORANGE, TEXAS

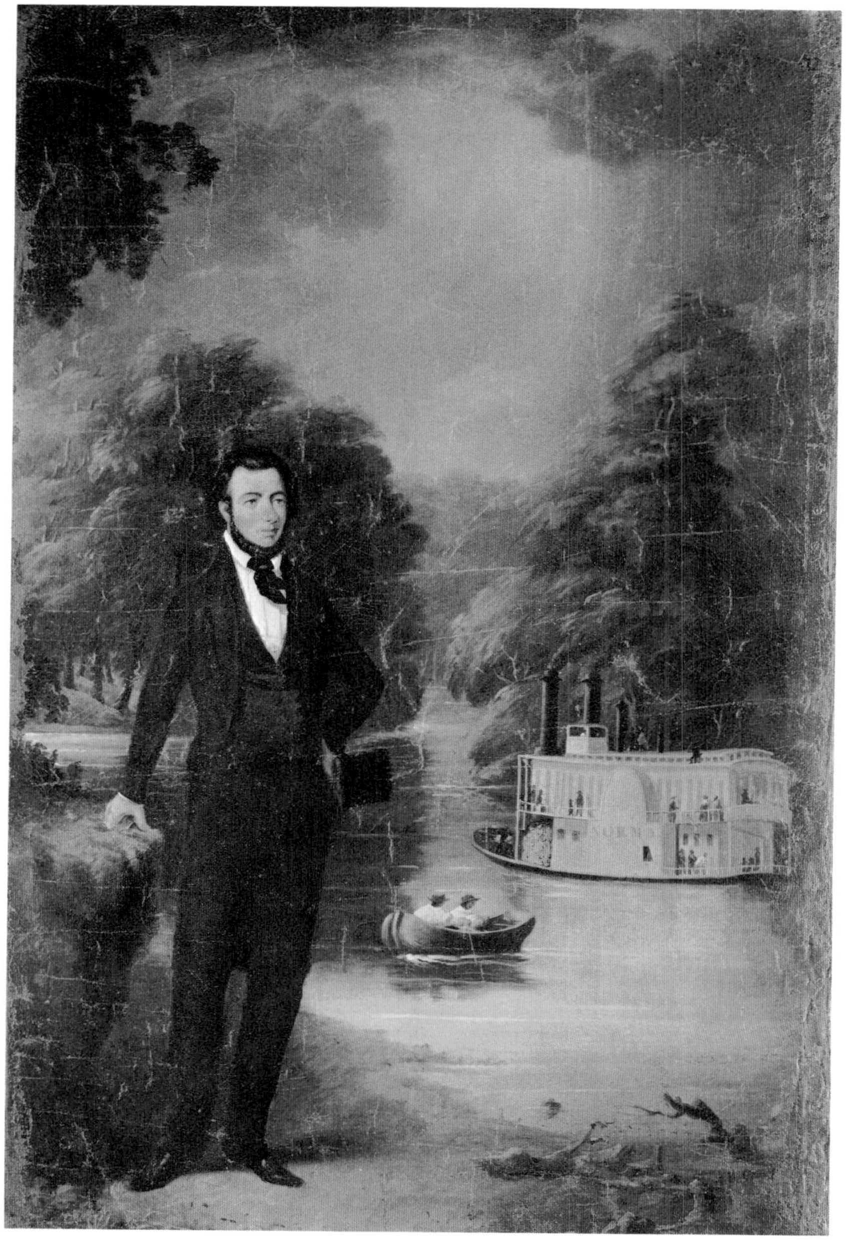

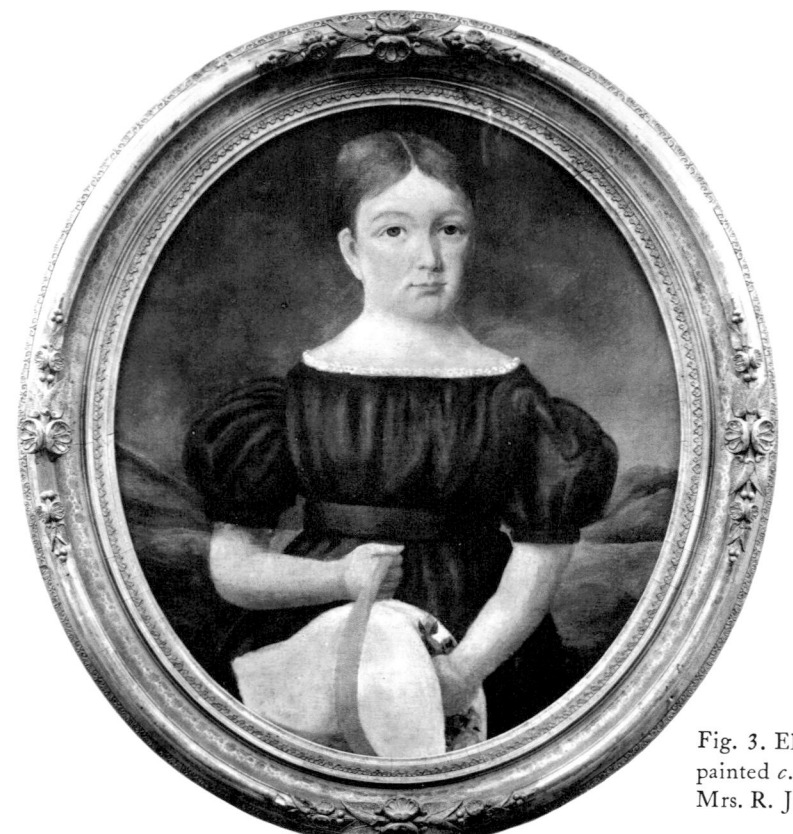

Fig. 4. The riverboat *Norma* with her captain. Stark OP26; CRI-25.

Fig. 3. Eliza (Clench) Armour, painted *c.* 1836. Collection of Mrs. R. J. Shirley; CRI-24.

Fig. 5. Roman youth, from one of Kane's European sketchbooks.
Collection of Mrs. T. M. Willet; CRII-6.

Fig. 6. Trees in a Roman landscape, from one of Kane's European sketchbooks.
Collection of Mrs. T. M. Willet; CRII-6.

Fig. 7. Rubens, self-portrait, as copied
by Kane. Private collection; CRII-9.

163

Fig. 8. Mayor George Gurnett of Toronto. Corporation of the City of Toronto; crV-26.

Fig. 9. James Richardson, of Cobourg and St. Catharines. ROM964.185; crV-28.

Plate XXXI. Drying salmon at the Dalles, Columbia River. Stark wwc50; crIV-310.

Plate XXXII. Spokane River. ROM946.15.189; crIV-334.

COURTESY ROYAL ONTARIO MUSEUM, TORONTO

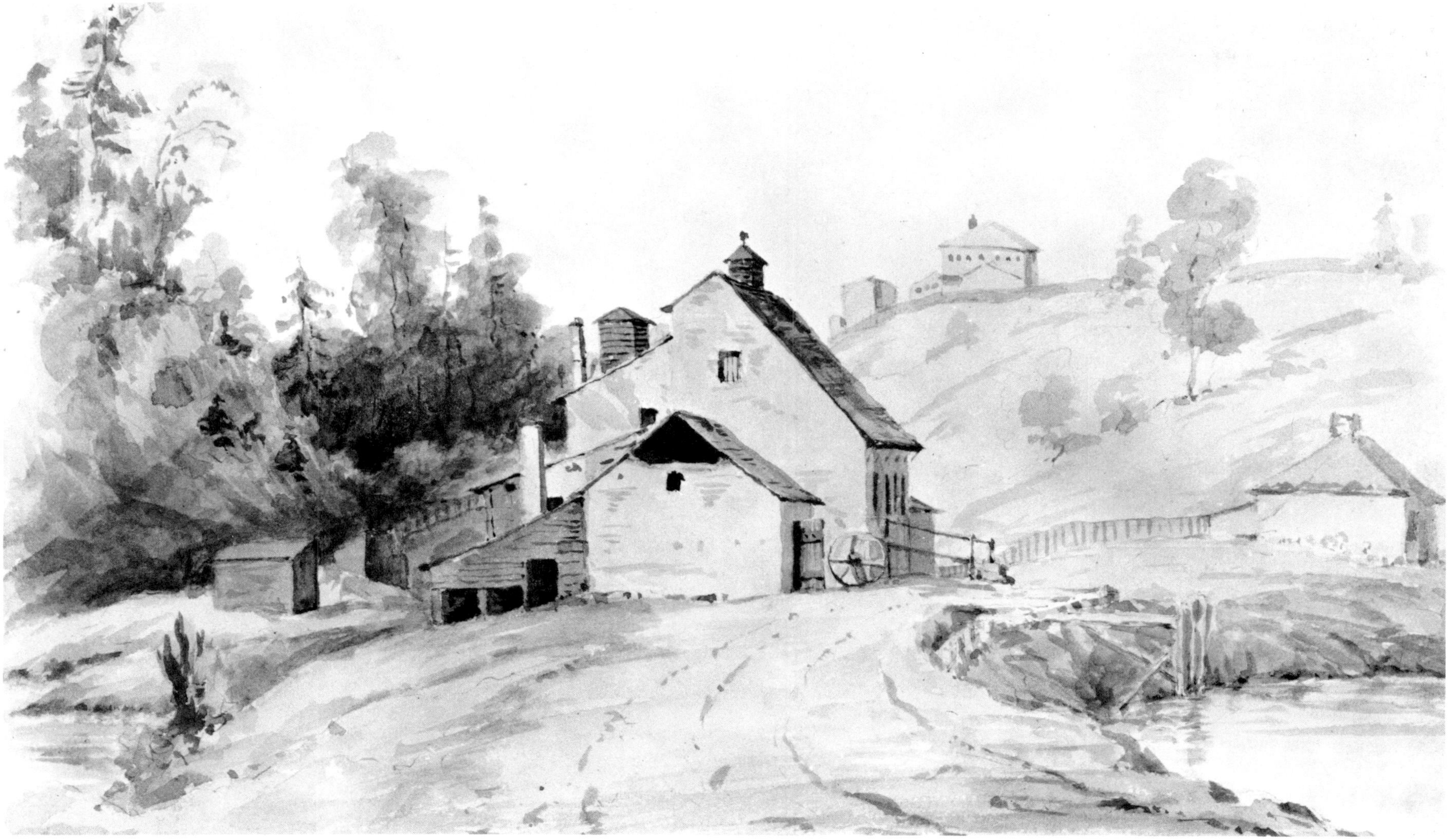

Fig. 10. Bloor's Brewery, Toronto. ROM946.15.254; CRV-12.

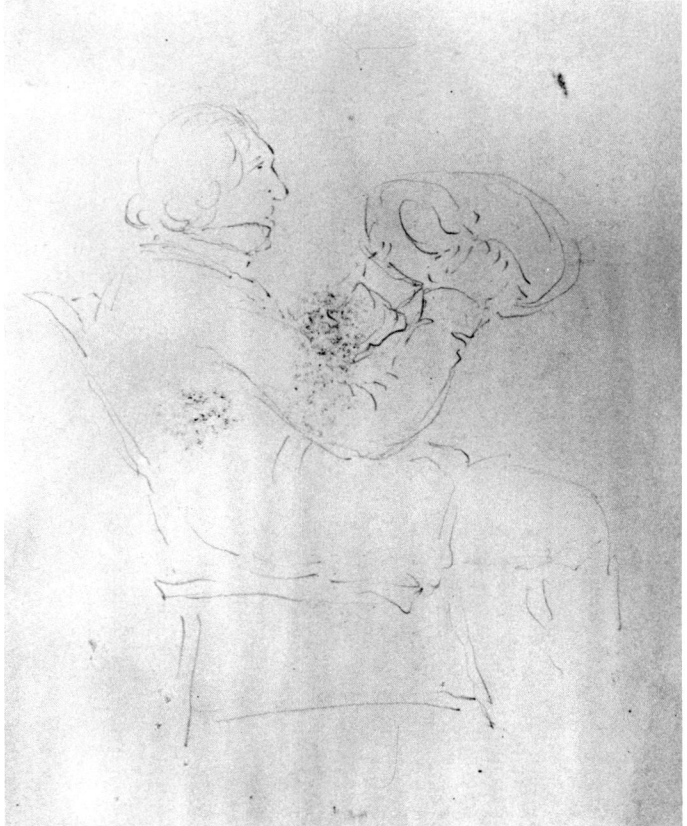

Fig. 11. Thomas Daly, city clerk of Toronto, an artist. ROM946.15.142; CRV-33.

COURTESY ROYAL ONTARIO MUSEUM, TORONTO

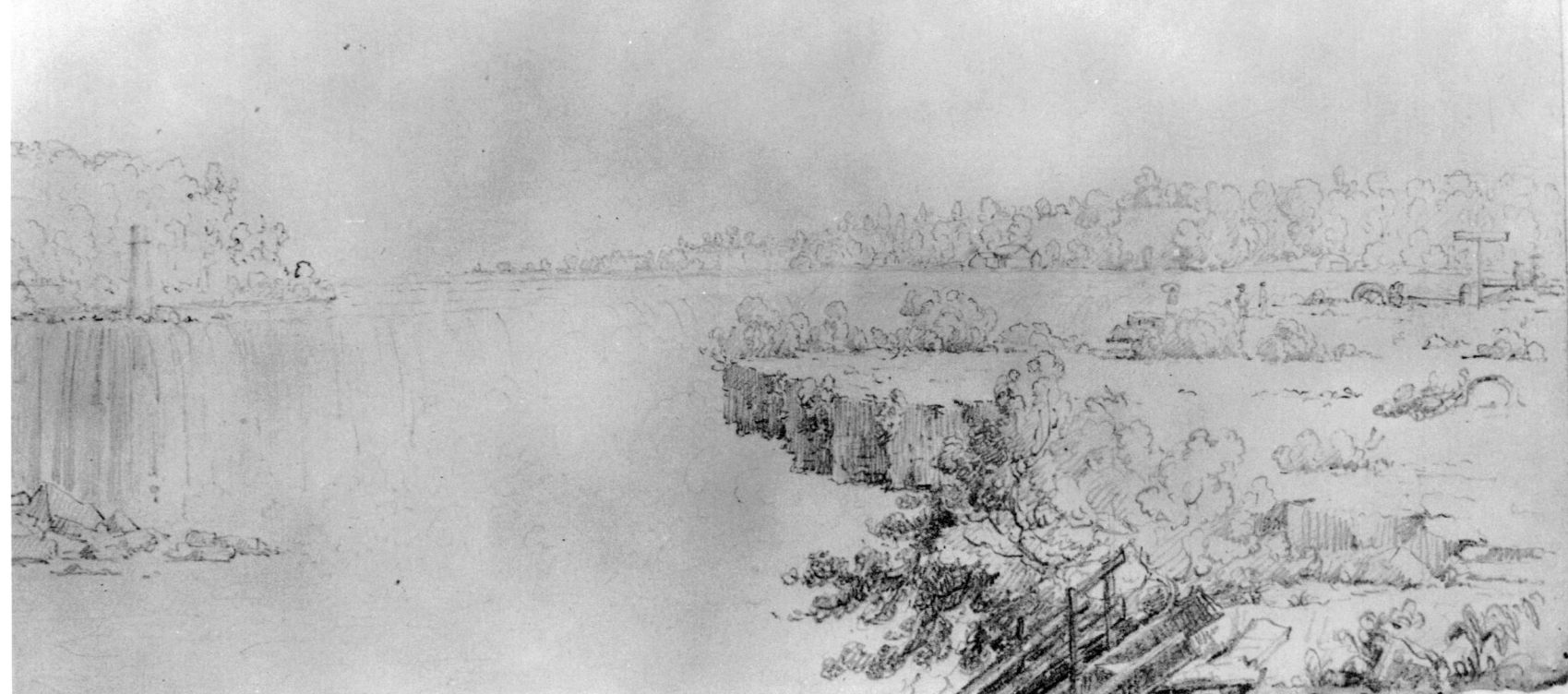

Fig. 12. Niagara Falls. ROM946.15.335; CRV-3.

COURTESY ROYAL ONTARIO MUSEUM, TORONTO

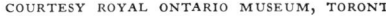

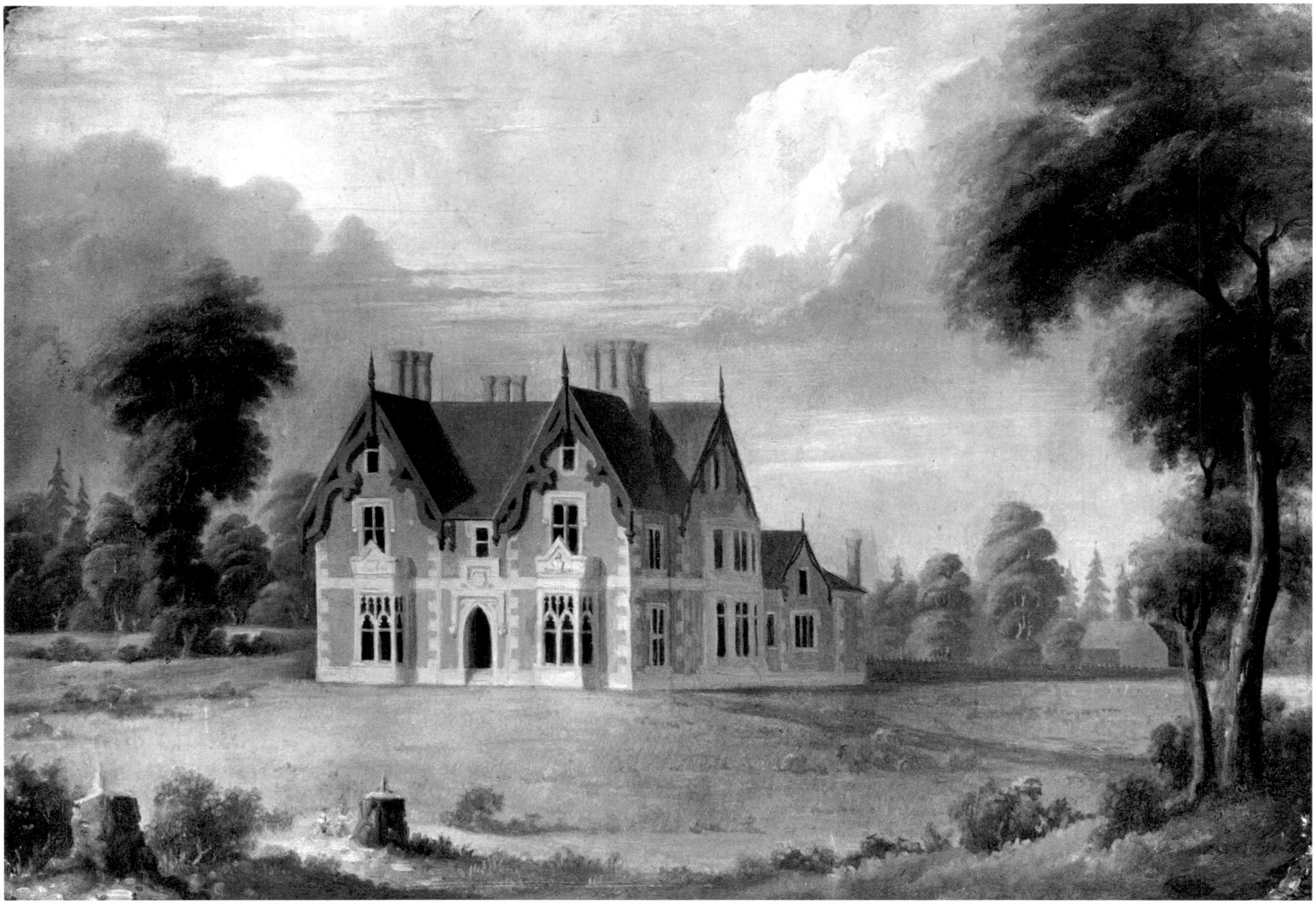

Fig. 13. Homewood, the early residence of the Hon. G. W. Allan. Collection of G. P. H. Vernon; CRV-13.

Fig. 14. Kwa-qua-dah-bon-niva-skung or "Dawn of Day," a chief of the Saugeen.
Stark EOP9; CRIII-3.

Fig. 15. Maska-nonga or "Big Fish," an Ojibwa, Saugeen village.
Stark EOP19; CRIII-5.

167

Fig. 16. A page of sketches made on Georgian Bay. ROM946.15.53; crIII-6.

Fig. 17. An Ojibwa chief's daughter from Lake St. Clair. Stark EOP5; crIII-7.

Fig. 18. Wappoose (Wah-pus or "The Rabbit"), Saugeen village. ROM912.1.1; crIII-11.

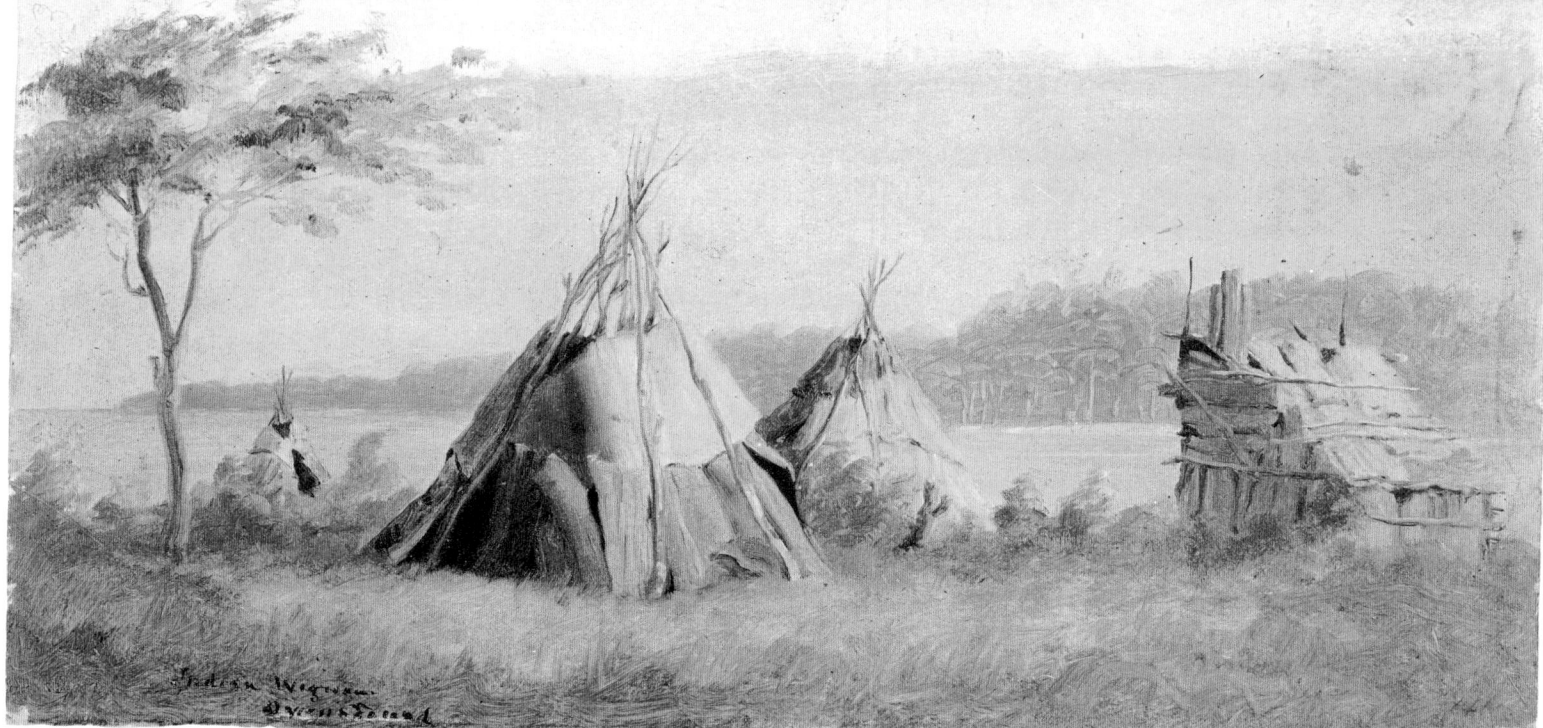

Fig. 19. Indian encampment on Big Bay, Owen Sound. Stark EOP13; CRIII-12.

COURTESY STARK FOUNDATION, ORANGE, TEXAS

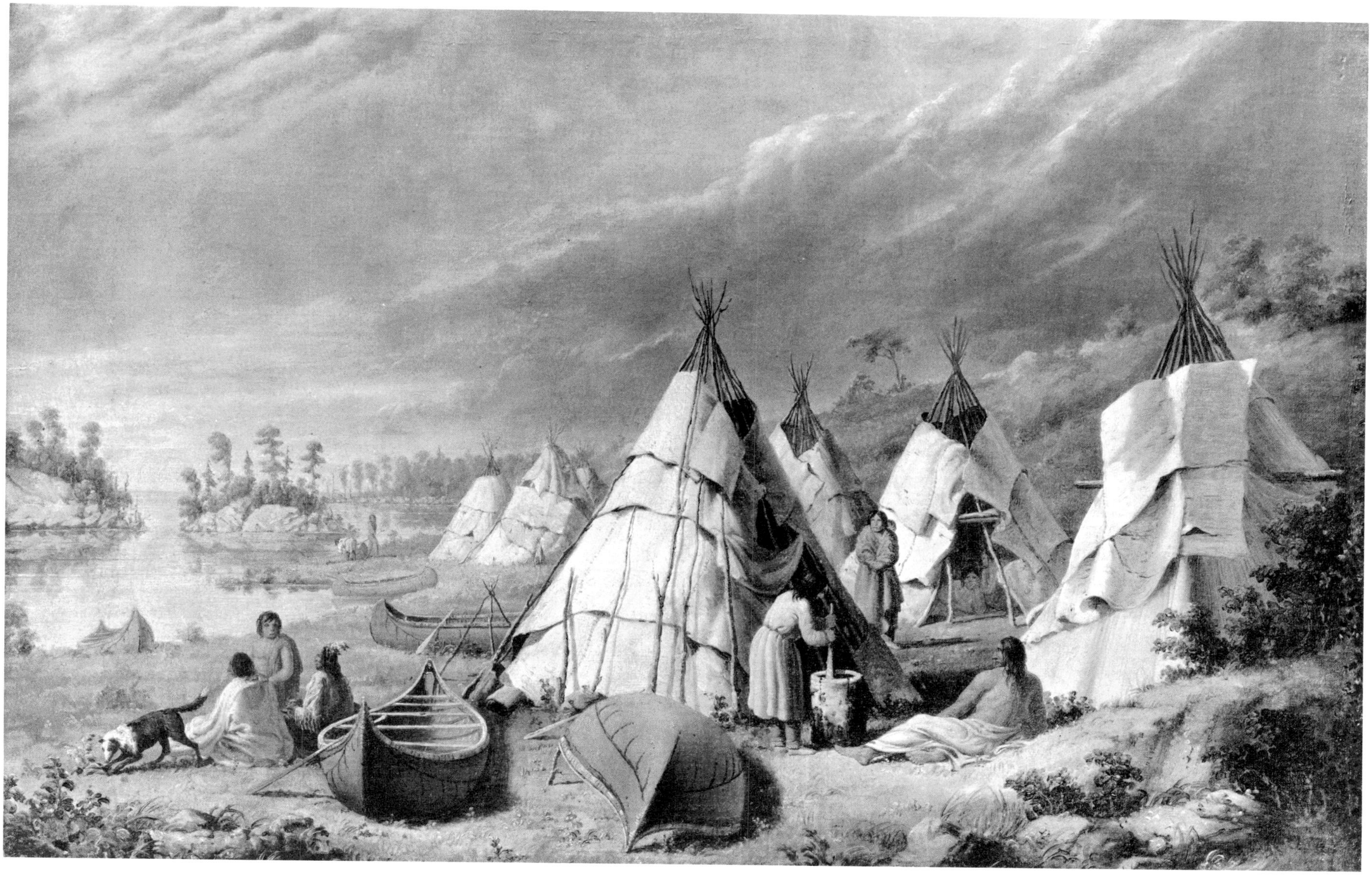

Fig. 20. An Indian Encampment on Lake Huron. Art Gallery of Ontario 2121; CRIII-19.

COURTESY ART GALLERY OF ONTARIO, TORONTO

Fig. 21. Indian Bivouac. Public Archives of Canada, Kane I-1; crIII-24.

Fig. 22. French River Rapids. rom912.1.2; crIII-26.

COURTESY ROYAL ONTARIO MUSEUM, TORONTO

Spokan Chief Spokan River

90.

202

Plate XXXIII. Tum-se-ne-ho or "The Man without Blood," a Spokan chief. Stark wwc43; crIV-337.

COURTESY DAVID MITCHELL GALLERY, TORONTO

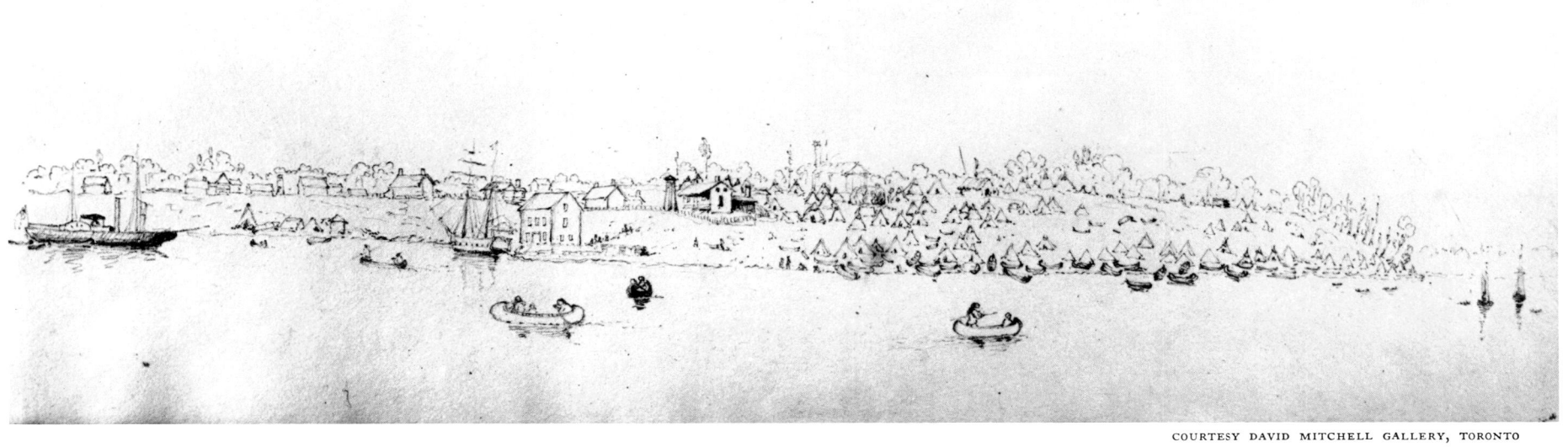

Fig. 24. Manitowaning, with wigwams of Indians assembled for the receipt of presents. David Mitchell Gallery; CRIII-39.

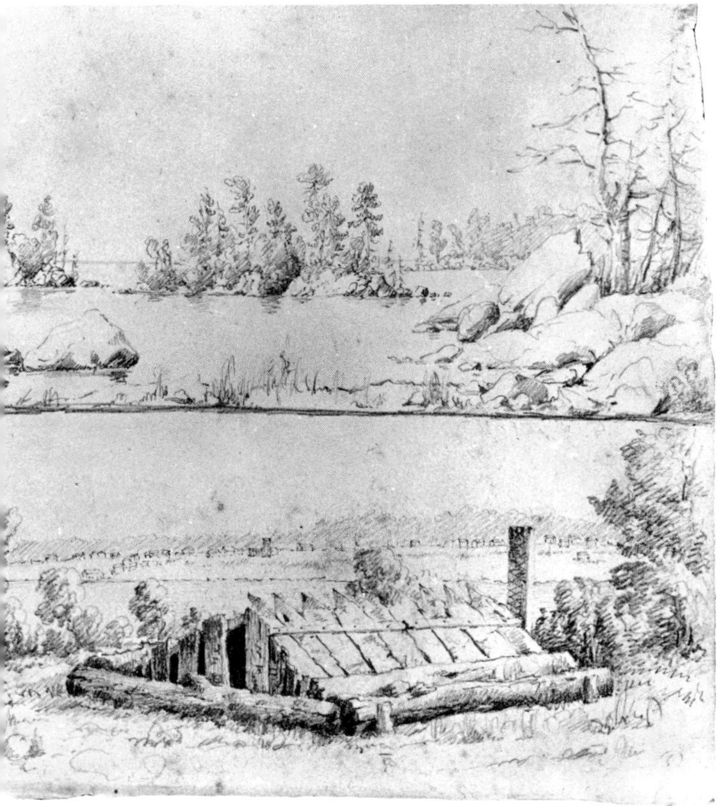

COURTESY ROYAL ONTARIO MUSEUM, TORONTO

Fig. 23. From a page of sketches, Georgian Bay. *Upper*, rocky islands; *lower*, Ojibwa grave house opposite Manitowaning. ROM946.15.51; CRIII-36.

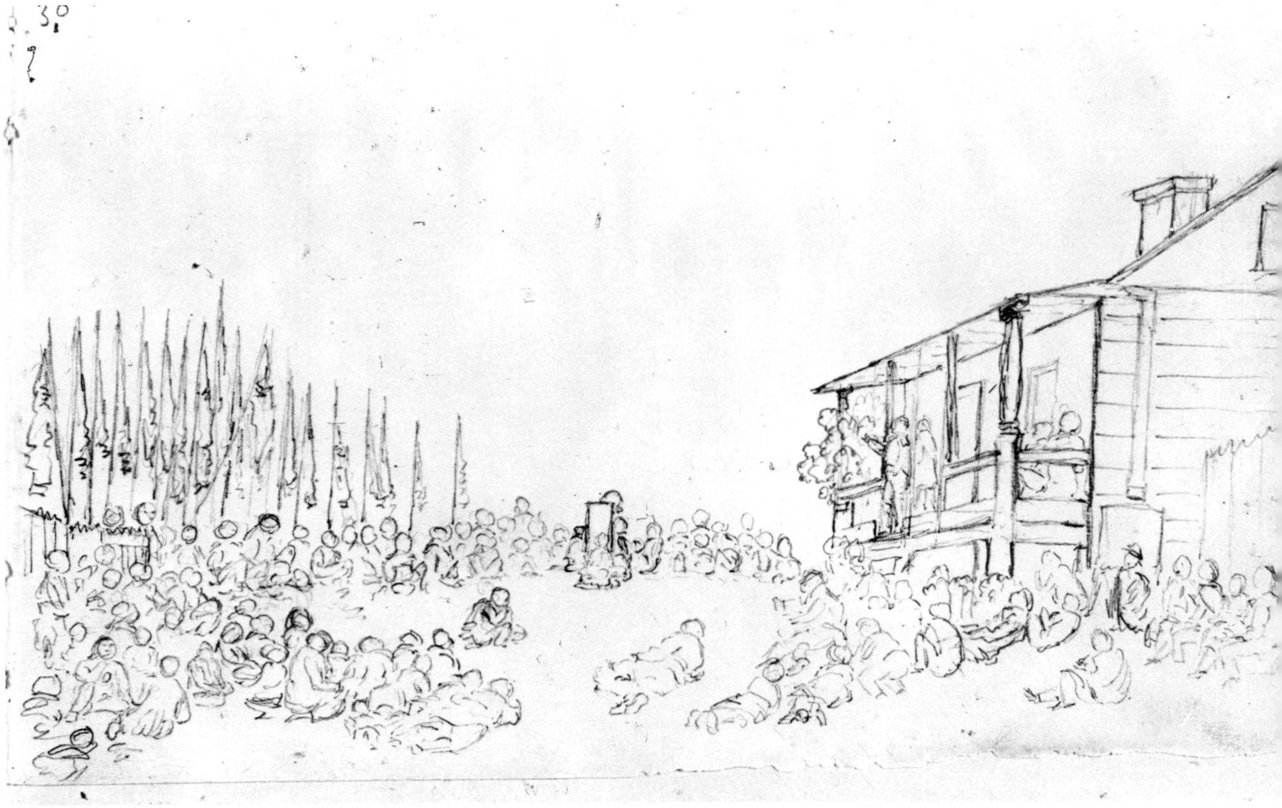

COURTESY ROYAL ONTARIO MUSEUM, TORONTO

Fig. 25. Manitowaning and the assembly of tribes for the receipt of presents. ROM946.15.30; CRIII-41.

Fig. 26. Shawwanossoway or "One with his Face towards the West," an Ojibwa medicine man sketched at Manitowaning. Stark EOP2; CRIII-44.

Fig. 27. Indian from Michipicoten. Stark EOP6; CRIII-50.

Much-kose
Young Bear
Ah-taw-wah Chief

Fig. 28. Muck-koze or "Young Bear," Ottawa chief, Manitoulin Island. Stark EOP24; crIII-52.

Fig. 29. Awbonwaishkum, Ottawa chief, Manitowaning. Stark EOP12; crIII-53.

Fig. 31. Captain George Ironsides or "Walk on the Water," Indian agent, Manitowaning. Stark EOP16; crIII-56.

Fig. 30. Stone pipe carved by Awbonwaishkum. Stark EOP21; crIII-55.

COURTESY STARK FOUNDATION, ORANGE, TEXAS

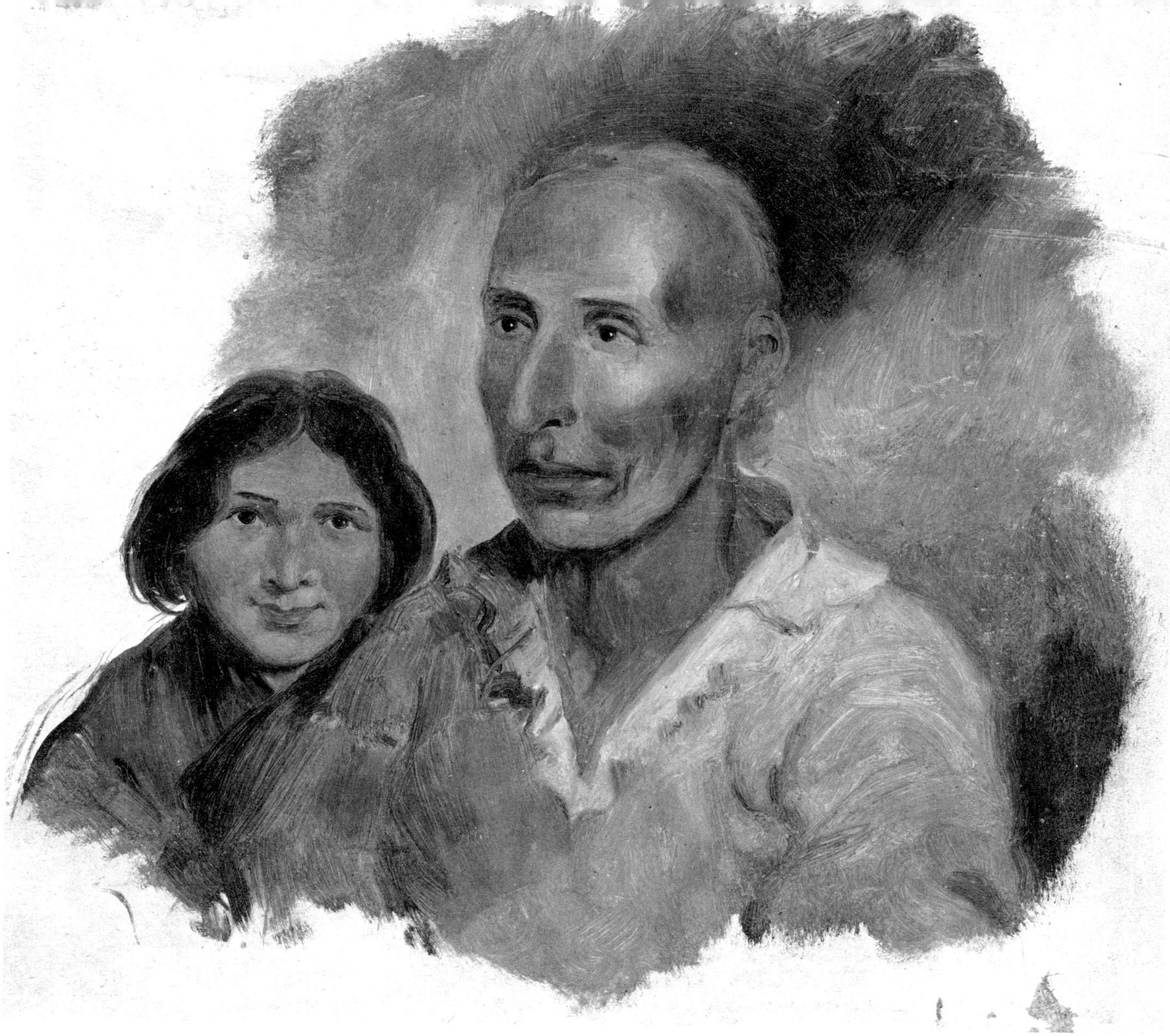

Fig. 33. Asabonish or "The Raccoon," Ottawa chief, with his daughter, sketched at Wikwemikong. Stark EOP28; CRIII-63.

COURTESY ROYAL ONTARIO MUSEUM, TORONTO

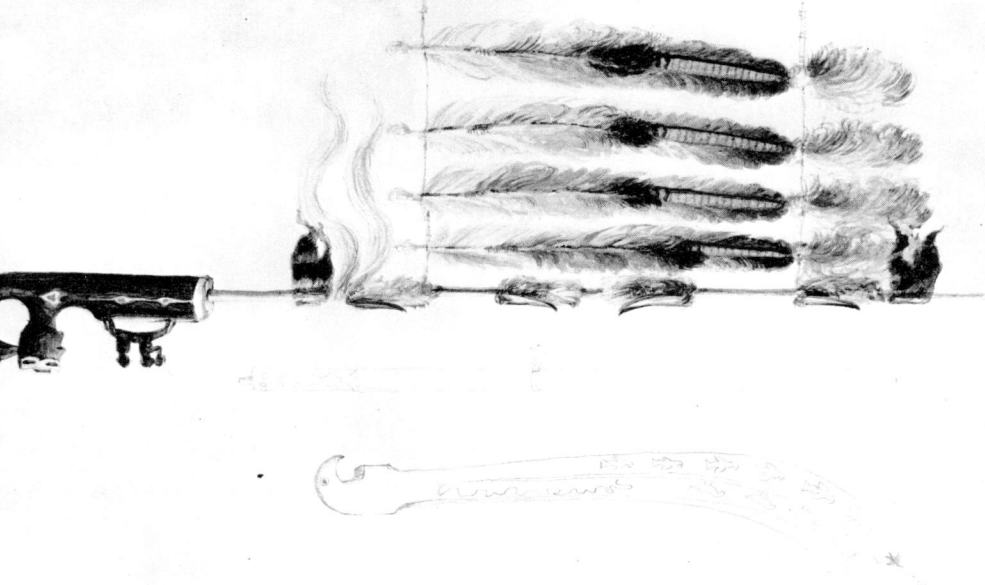

Fig. 32. Pipe and club, sketched at Manitowaning(?). ROM946.15.33; CRIII-62.

COURTESY ROYAL ONTARIO MUSEUM, TORONTO

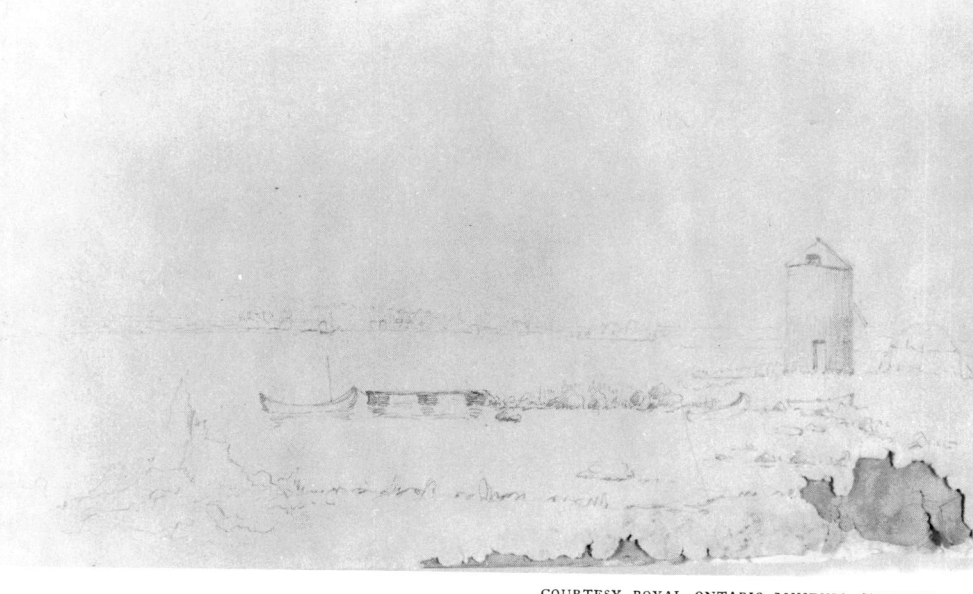

Fig. 34. Sault Ste Marie, with the Ermatinger grist mill. ROM946.15.25; CRIII-74.

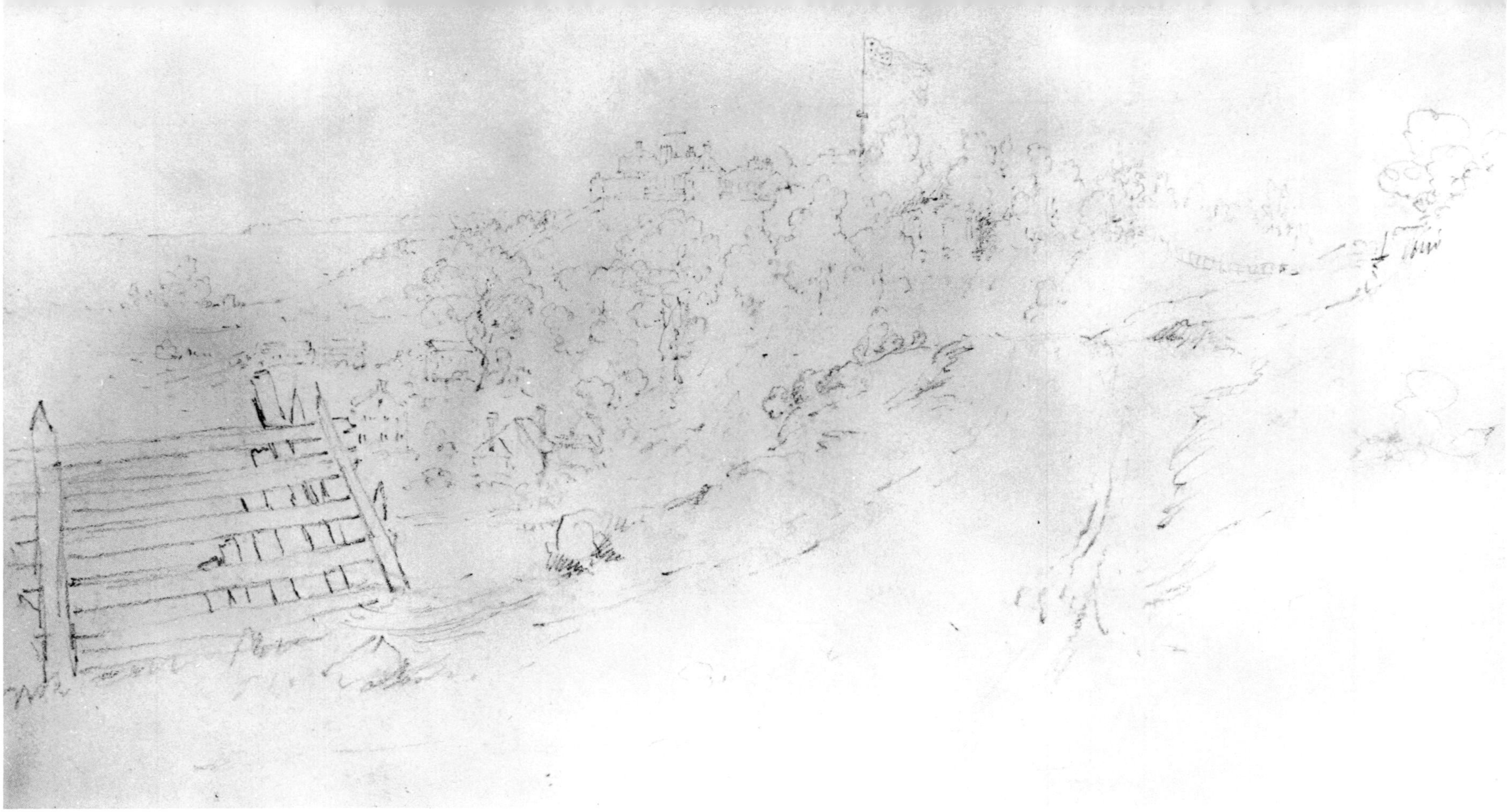

COURTESY ROYAL ONTARIO MUSEUM, TORONTO

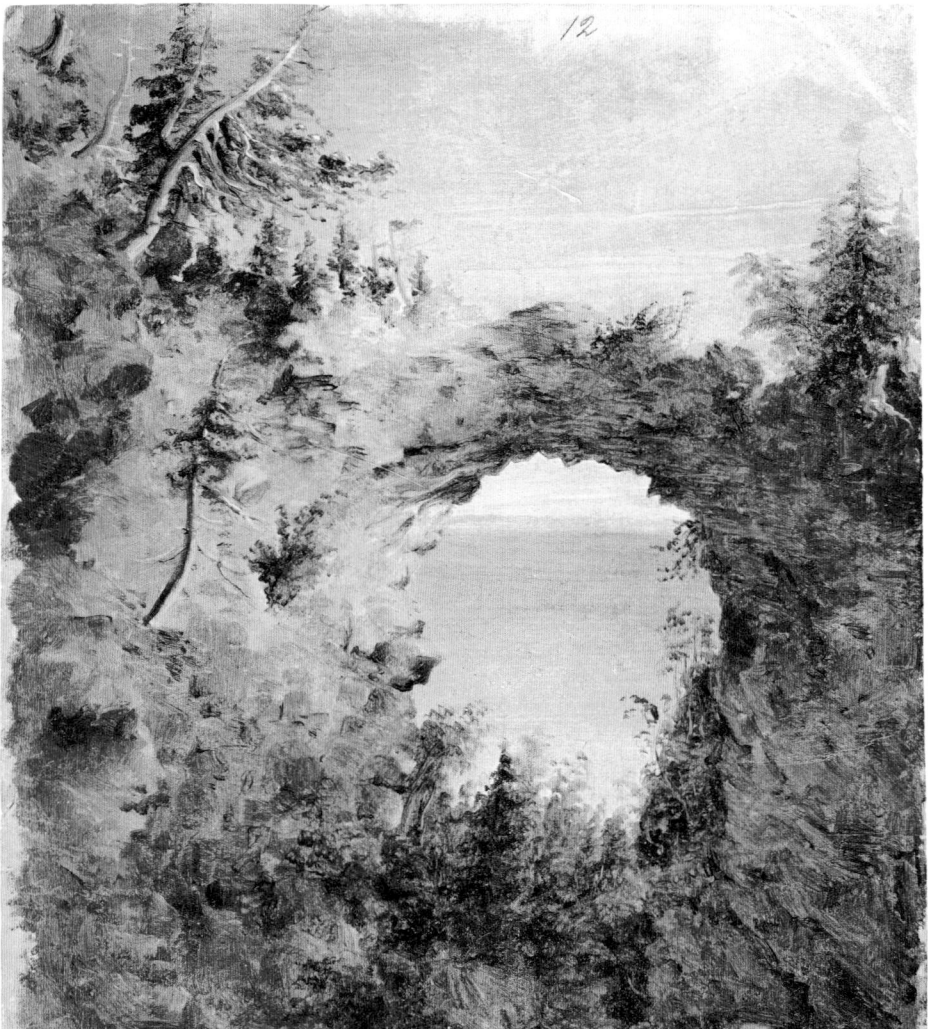

Fig. 35. Fort and Indian village at Mackinac. ROM946.15.255; CRIII-78.

COURTESY STARK FOUNDATION, ORANGE, TEXAS

Fig. 36. The natural bridge at Mackinac. Stark EOP20; CRIII-82.

Fig. 37. Rocky headland with wigwams, Mackinac.
Stark EOP29; CrIII-84.

Fig. 38. Wampum belts, from Mackinac.
Stark A4-43; CrIII-95.

177

Fig. 39. Ke-wah-ten or "The North Wind"(?). Stark POP3; CRIII-107.

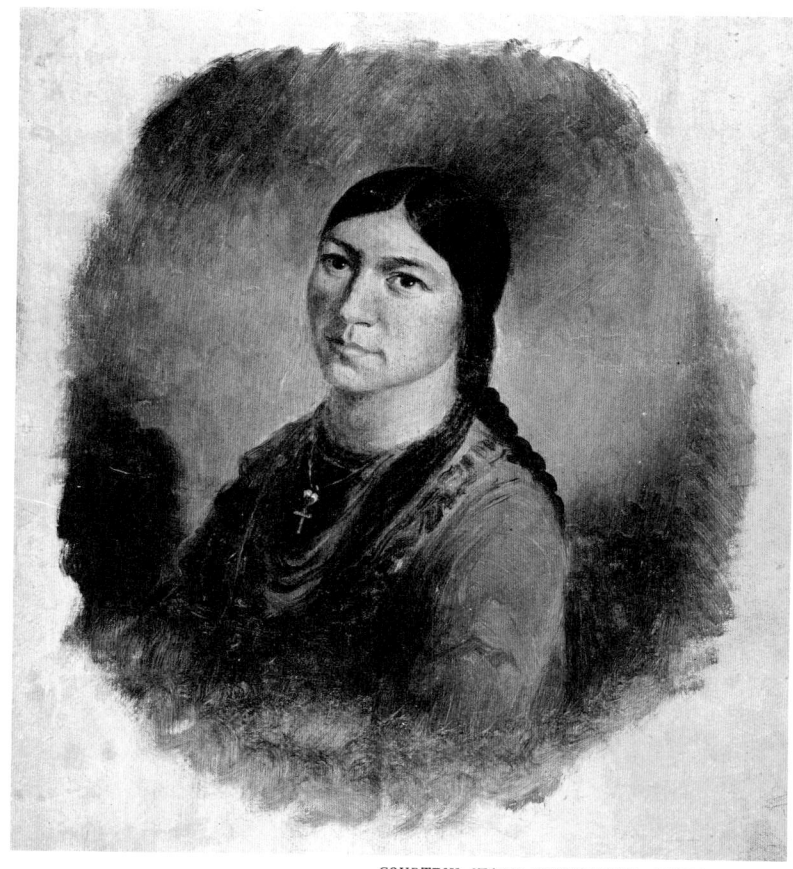

Fig. 40. Iwa-toke or "The Serpent,"
a Menominee, Lake Winnebago.
Stark EOP26; CRIII-106.

COURTESY STARK FOUNDATION, ORANGE, TEXAS

Fig. 41. Fishing by Torch Light (Fox River).
ROM912.1.10; CRIII-112.

COURTESY ROYAL ONTARIO MUSEUM, TORONTO

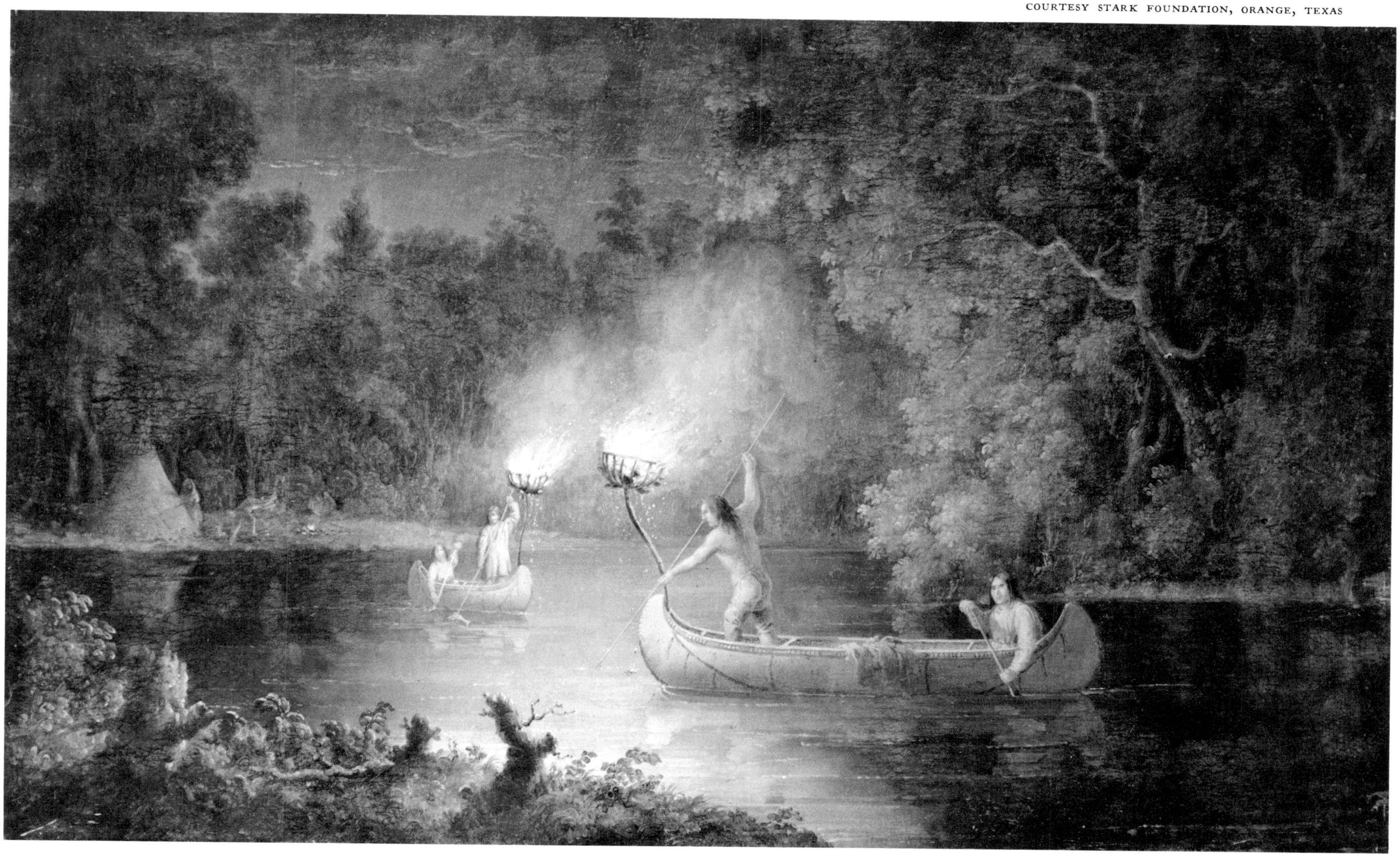

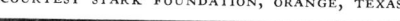

Fig. 42. Oscosh or "The Bravest of the Brave," Menominee chief, Fox River.
Stark A4-38; crIII-113.

Fig. 43. Match-o-kee-maw or "Big Chief," Menominee chief, Fox River.
Stark pop4; crIII-117.

COURTESY STARK FOUNDATION, ORANGE, TEXAS

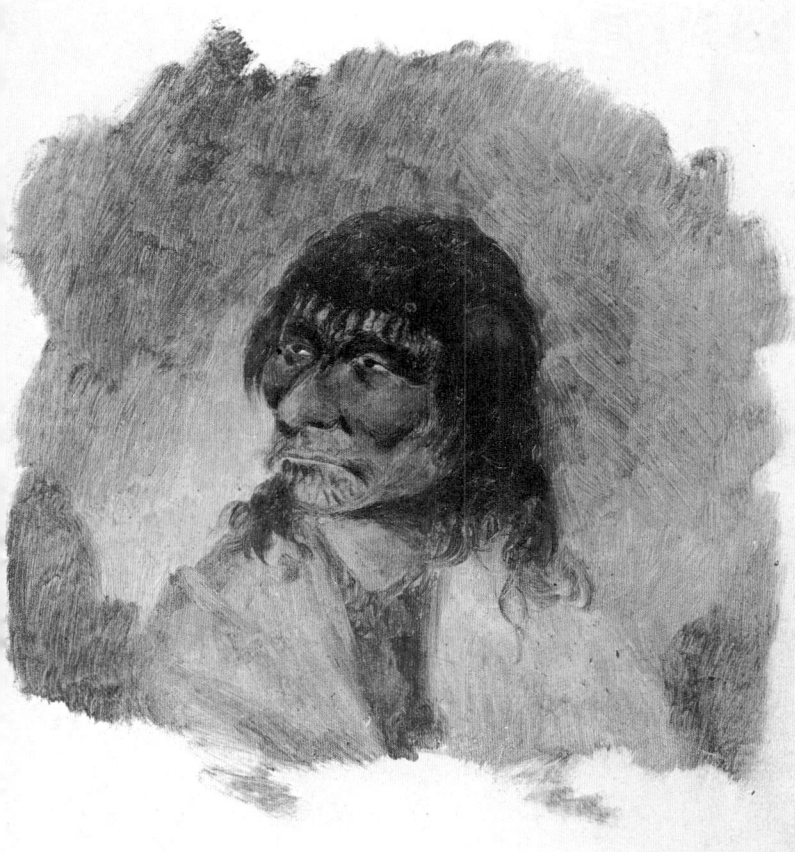

Fig. 44. Muck-a-ta, Fox River. Stark EOP17; CRIII-122.

COURTESY ROYAL ONTARIO MUSEUM, TORONTO

Fig. 45. Muck-a-ta, Fox River. ROM912.1.12; CRIII-123.

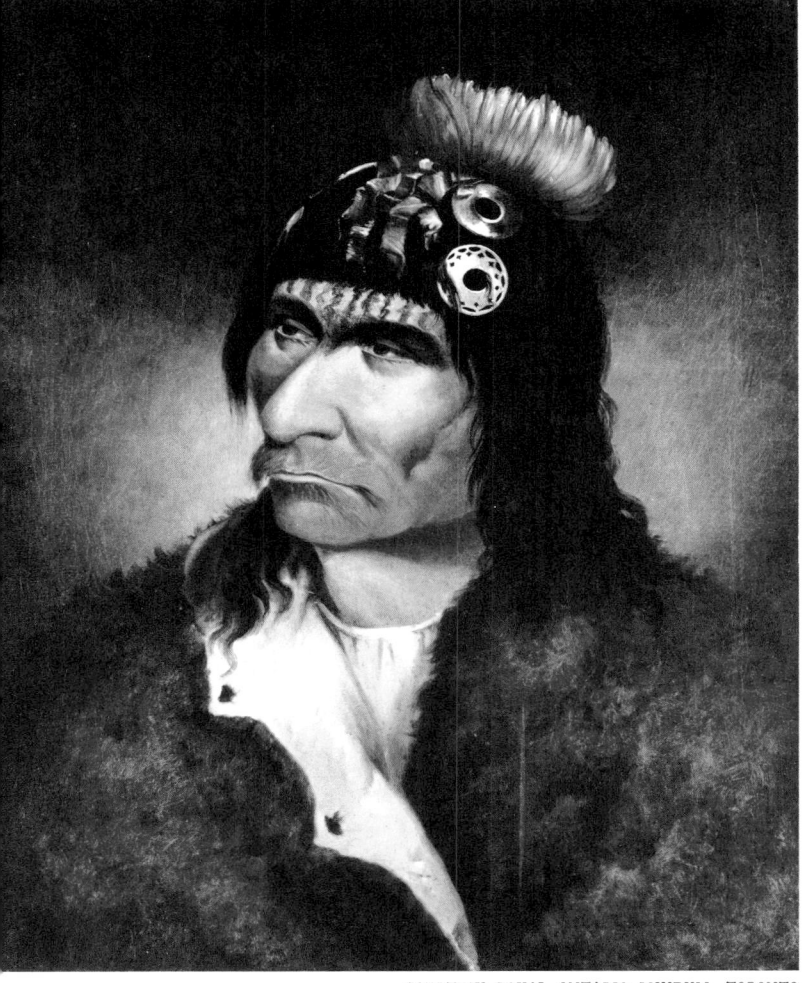

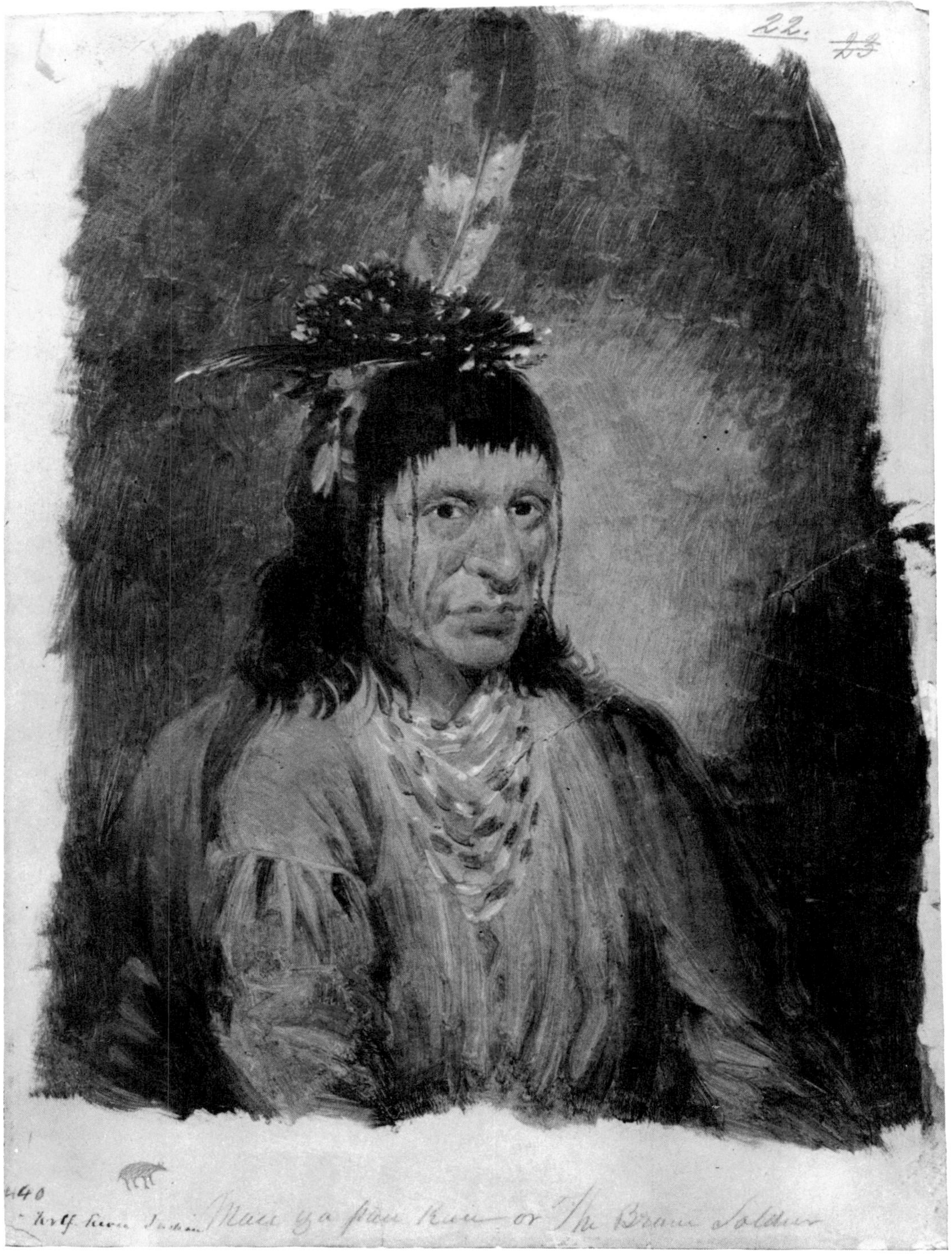

COURTESY NATIONAL GALLERY OF CANADA, OTTAWA

Fig. 46. Mauza-pau-Kan or "Brave Soldier," a Winnebago chief, Fox River. National Gallery of Canada 6457; CRIII-129.

COURTESY ROYAL ONTARIO MUSEUM, TORONTO

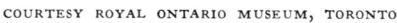

Fig. 47. Kakabeka Falls. ROM946.15.66; CRIV-3.

COURTESY STARK FOUNDATION, ORANGE, TEXAS

Fig. 48. Pin Portage. Stark POP25; CRIV-7.

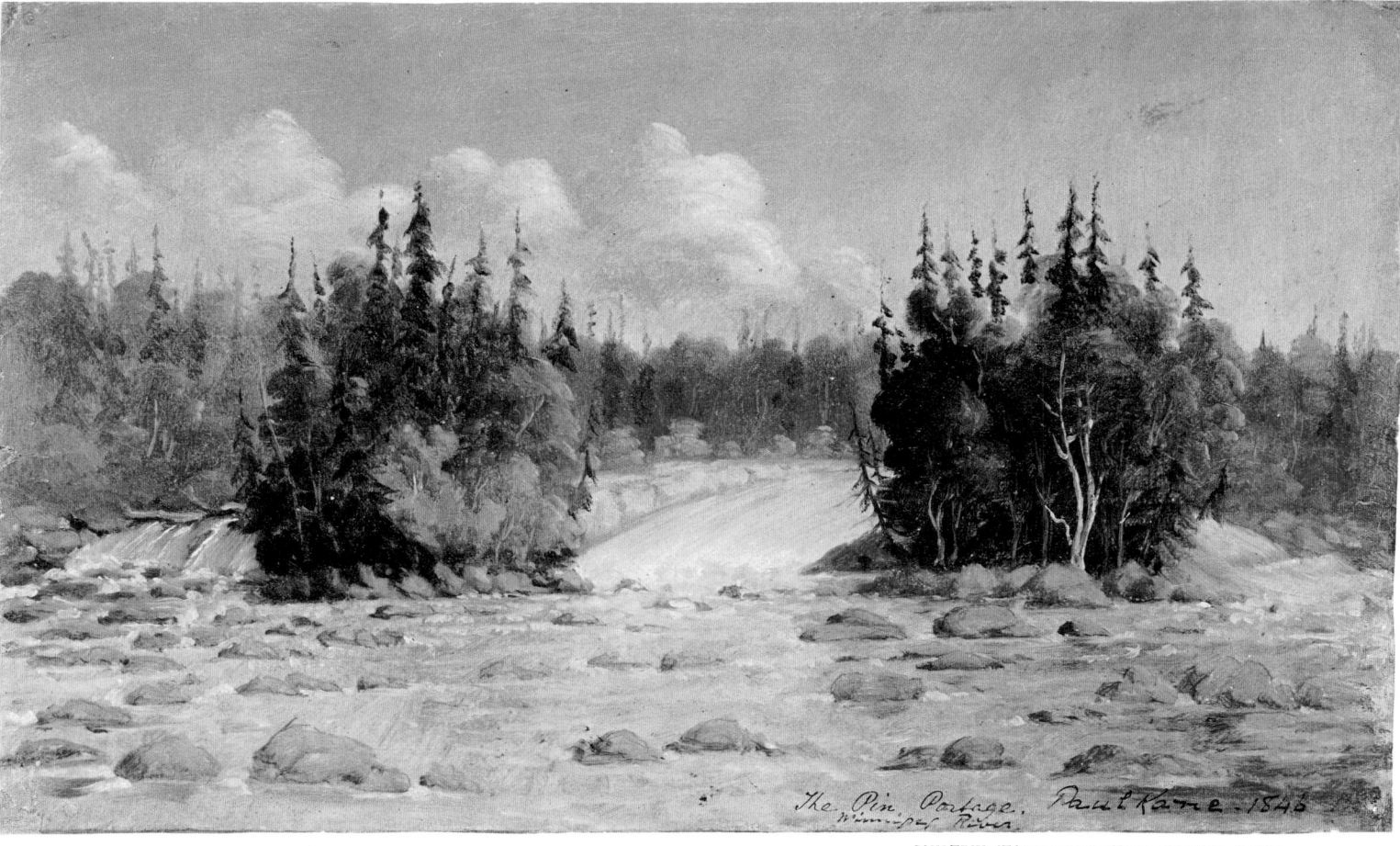

Plate XXXIV. Looking down the Pelouse River. ROM946.15.182; CrIV-341.

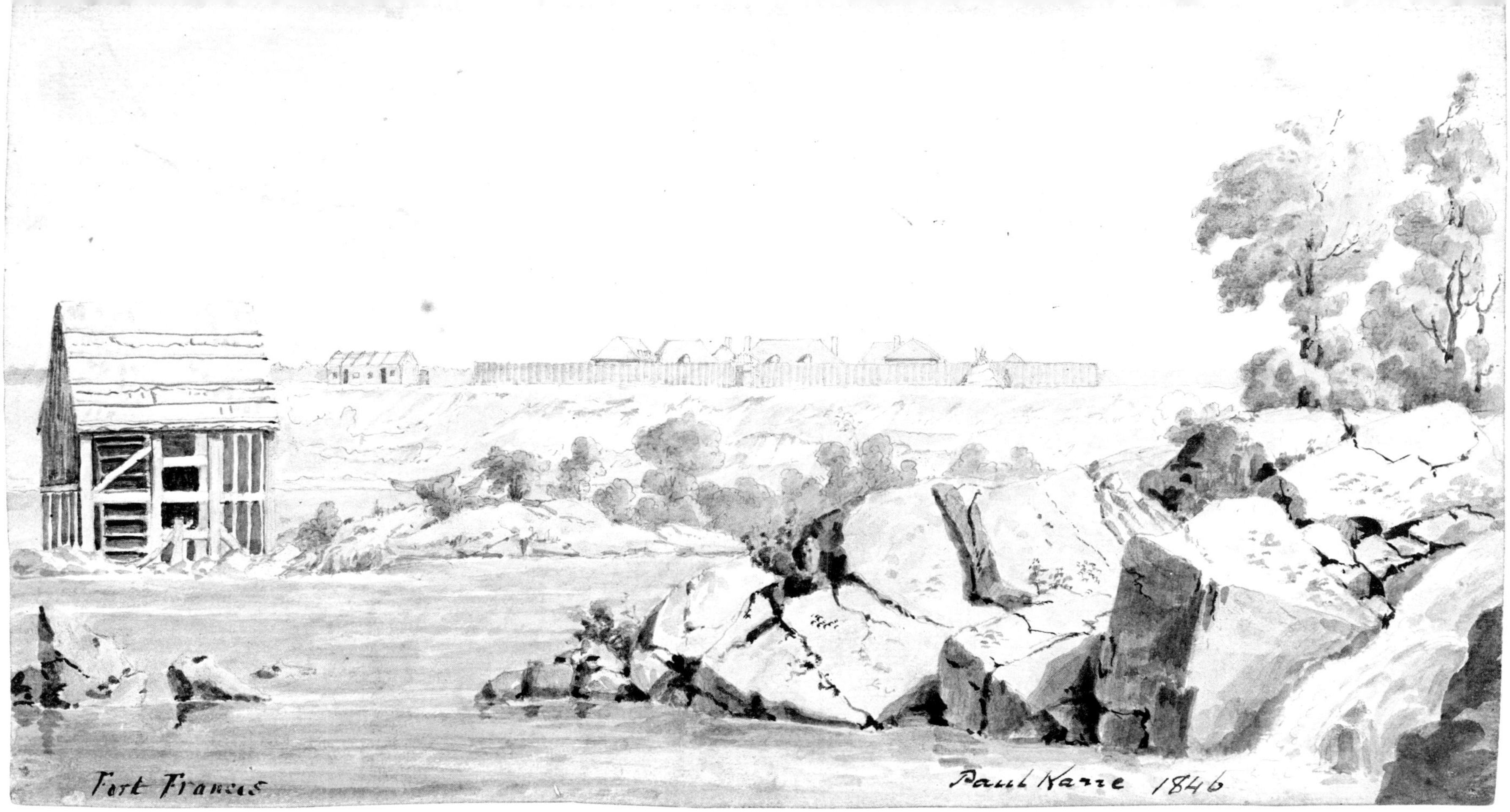
Fort Frances
Paul Kane 1846

COURTESY STARK FOUNDATION, ORANGE, TEXAS

Fig. 49. Fort Frances. Stark PWC2; CRIV-10.

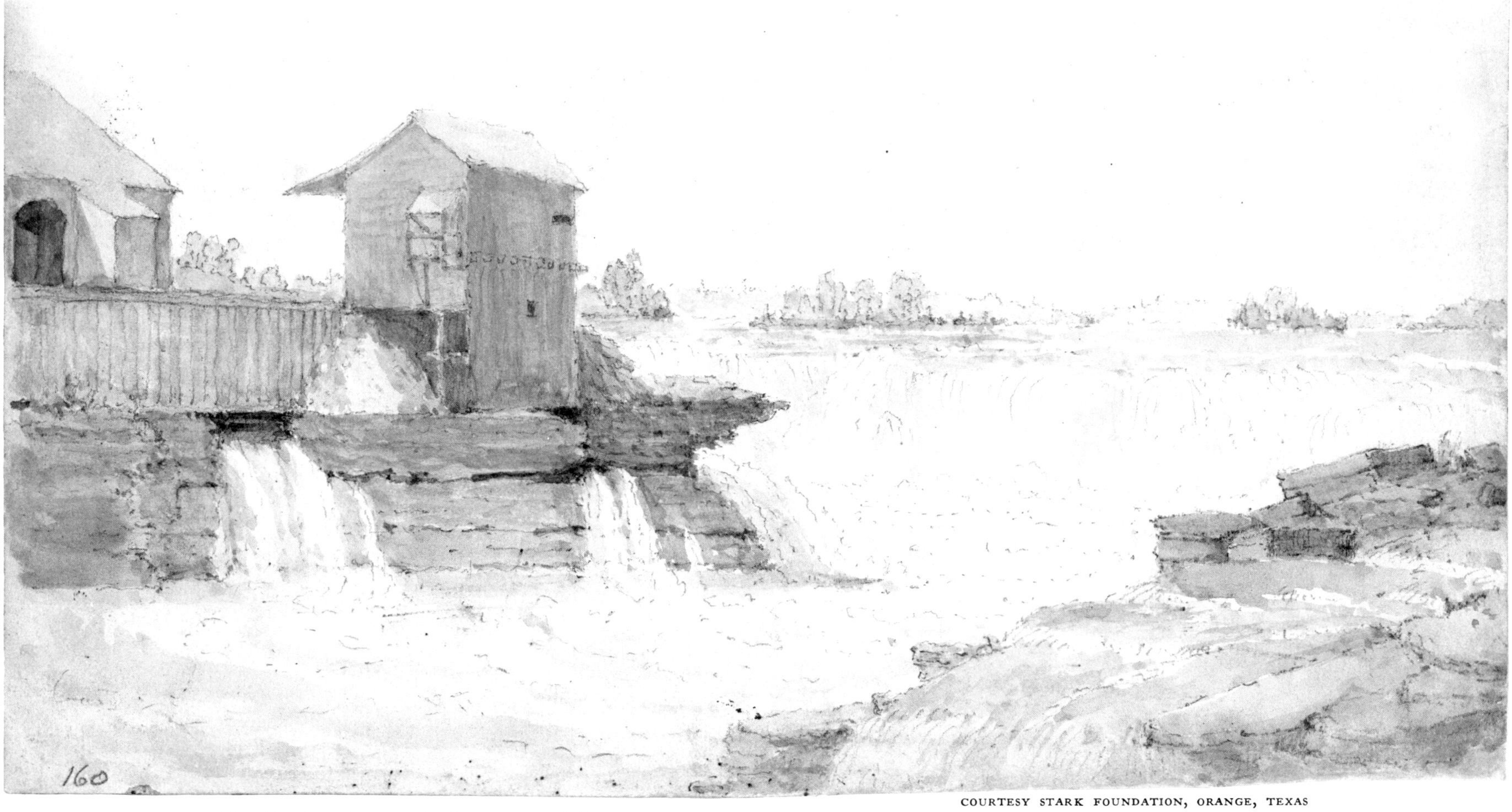
160

COURTESY STARK FOUNDATION, ORANGE, TEXAS

Fig. 50. Fort Frances. Stark PWC3; CRIV-11.

Fig. 51. Slave Falls, Winnipeg River. Stark wwc19; crIV-15.

184

Fig. 52. Winnipeg River. Stark pop13; crIV-24.

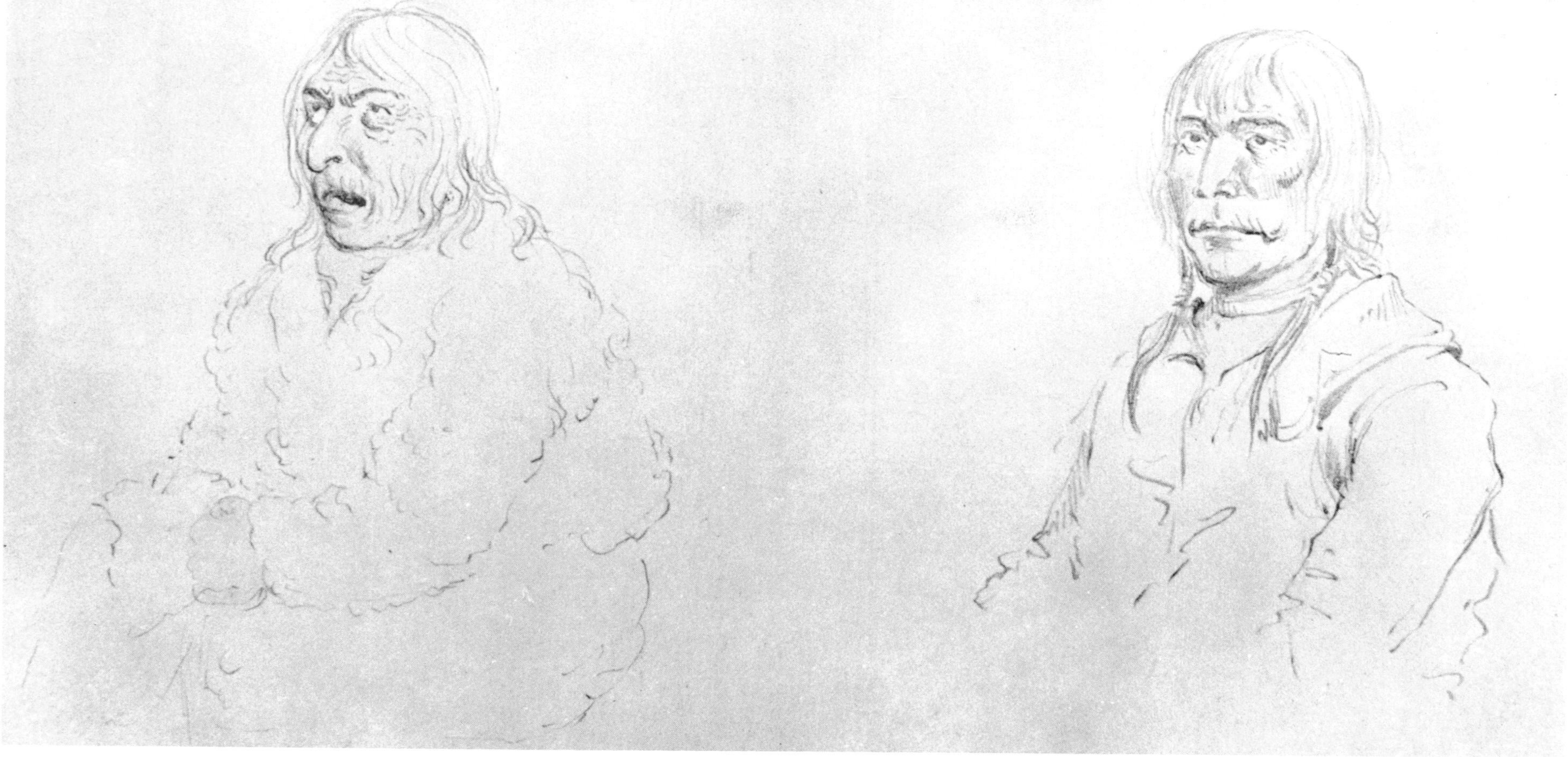

COURTESY ROYAL ONTARIO MUSEUM, TORONTO

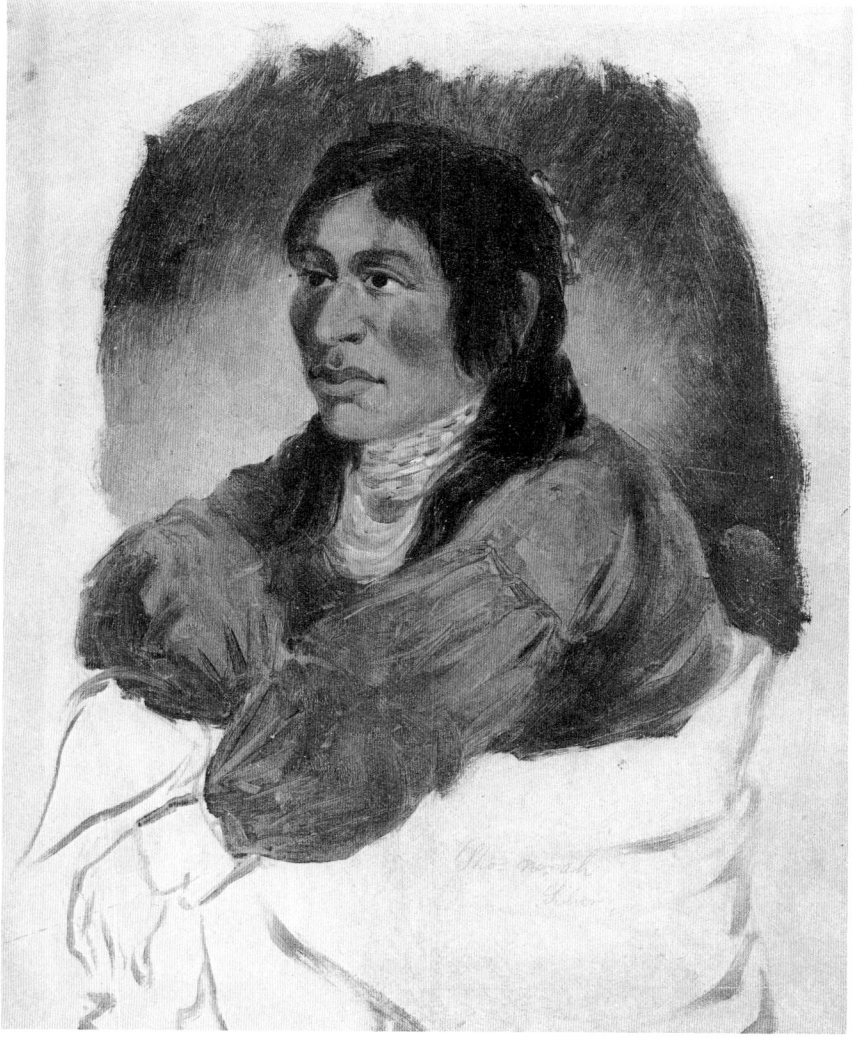

Fig. 53. Two Indian heads, Cash-a-cabut (*left*) and Each-a-quip (*right*), Saulteaux from the Fort Frances region. ROM946.15.273; CRIV-30.

COURTESY STARK FOUNDATION, ORANGE, TEXAS

Fig. 54. Sho-ne-ah or "Silver," a Saulteaux chief, Fort Alexander. Stark POP5; CRIV-32.

COURTESY STARK FOUNDATION, ORANGE, TEXAS

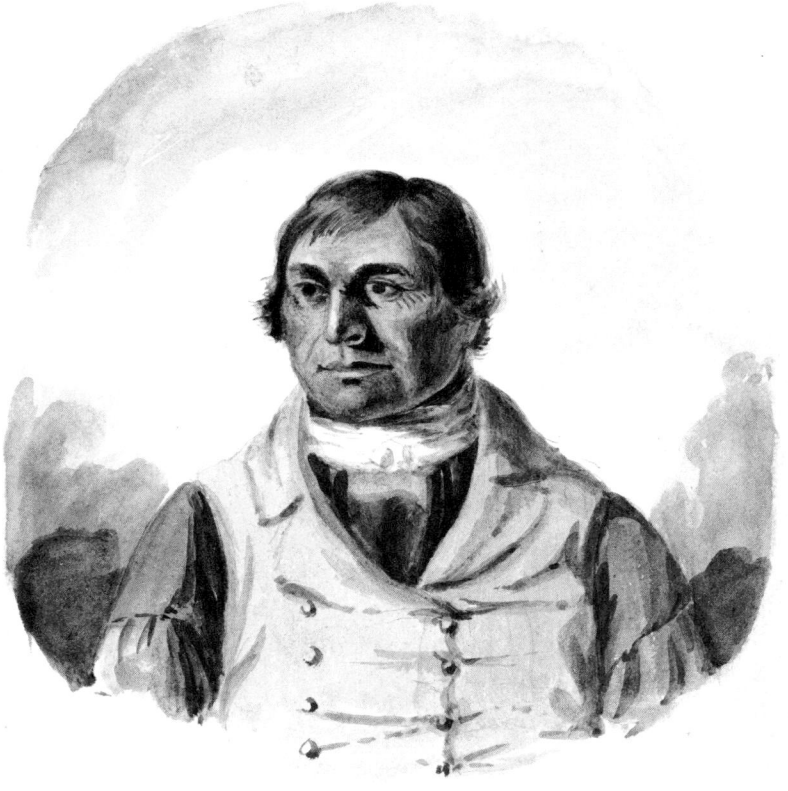

Fig. 55. Peter Jacobs, Wesleyan Indian missionary. Stark PWC14; CRIV-33.

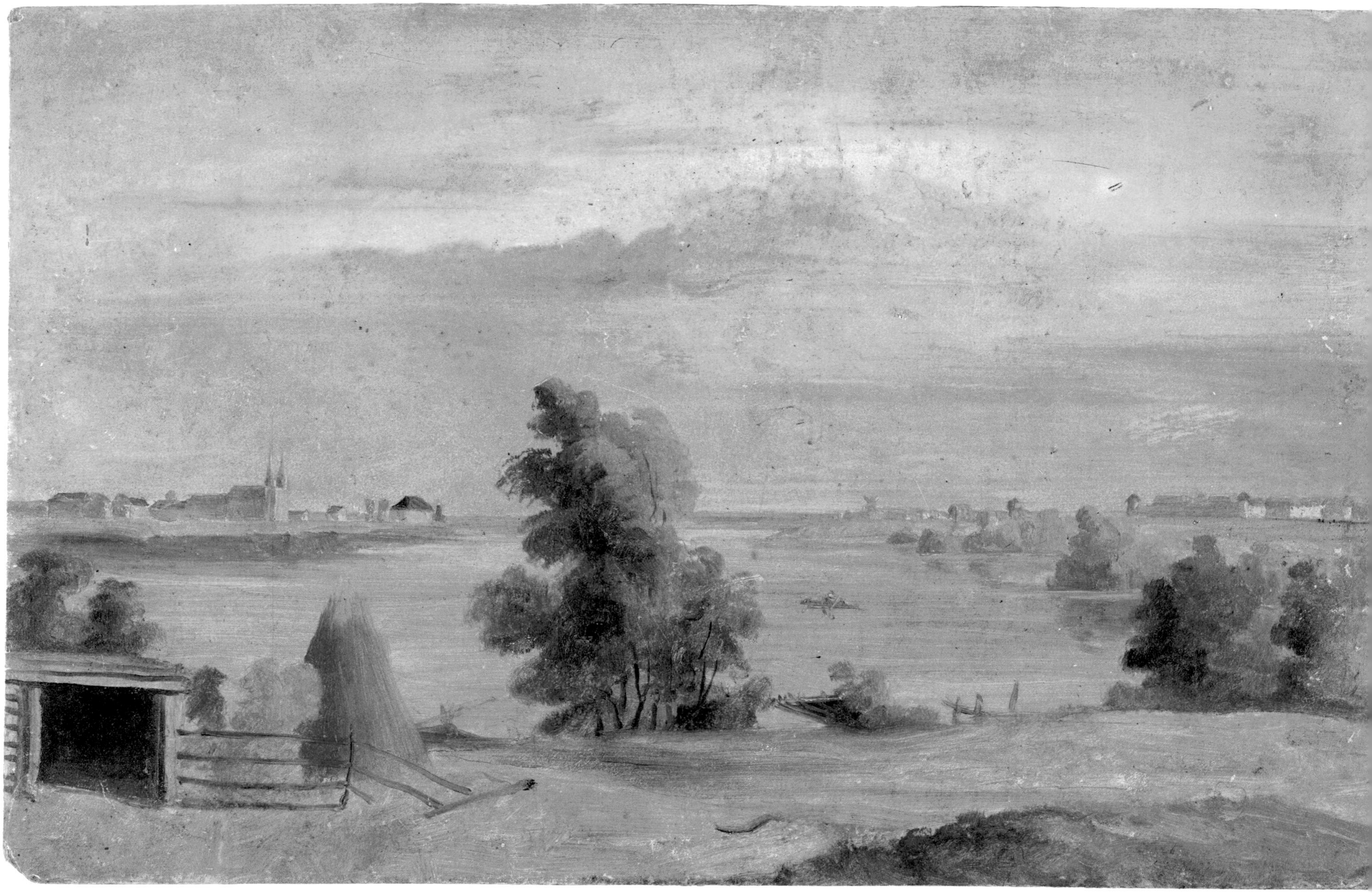

COURTESY STARK FOUNDATION, ORANGE, TEXAS

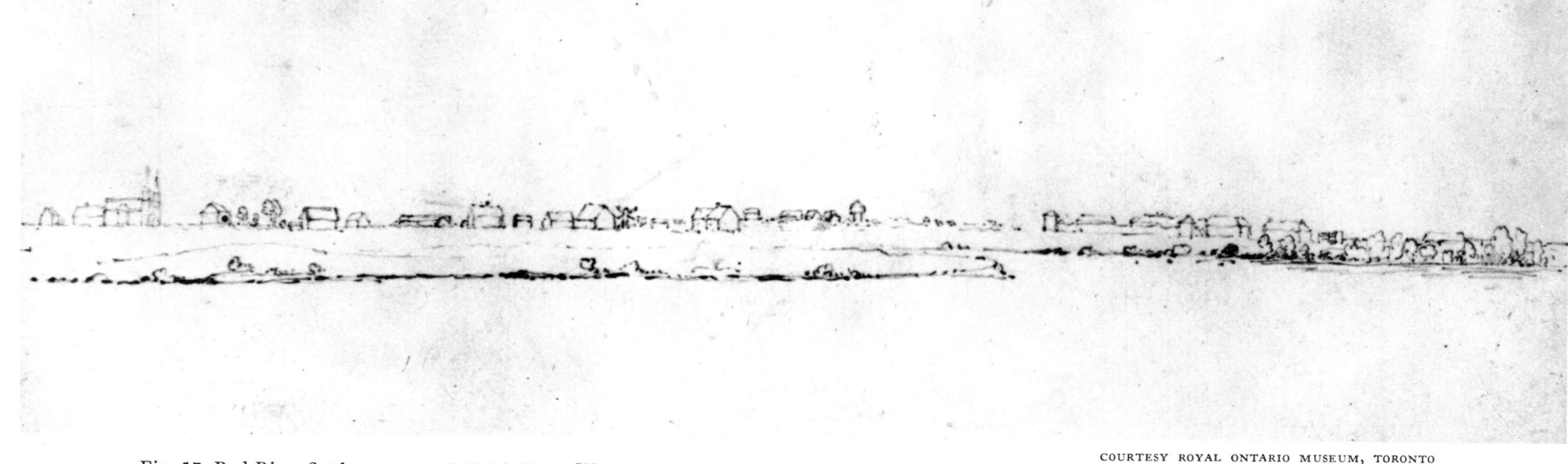

Fig. 56. Red River Settlement. Stark POP1; CRIV-36.

COURTESY ROYAL ONTARIO MUSEUM, TORONTO

Fig. 57. Red River Settlement. ROM946.15.68; CRIV-35.

Fig. 58. A Sioux Indian (apparently sketched south of Fort Garry). ROM912.1.29; crIV-41.

Fig. 59. Na-taw-waugh-cit or "The Man that was born," Saulteaux, sketched south of Fort Garry. Stark EOP22; crIV-43.

Fig. 60. Half Breeds Travelling. ROM912.1.24; crIV-54.

Paul Kane 1847
Upper Pelouse Falls
128

Plate XXXV. Falls, upper Pelouse River. Stark WOP22; CRIV-349.

Chinook Indian — Columbia River

93.

Plate XXXVI. Casanov, noted warrior, Fort Vancouver. Stark WOP4; CRIV-418.

COURTESY ROYAL ONTARIO MUSEUM, TORONTO

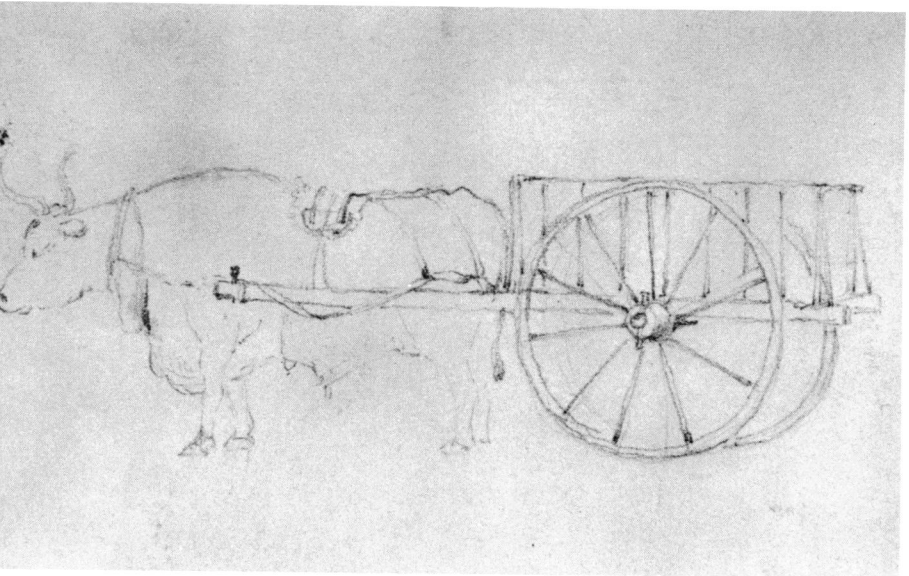

Fig. 61. Red River cart and ox. ROM946.15.74; CRIV-55.

COURTESY ROYAL ONTARIO MUSEUM, TORONTO

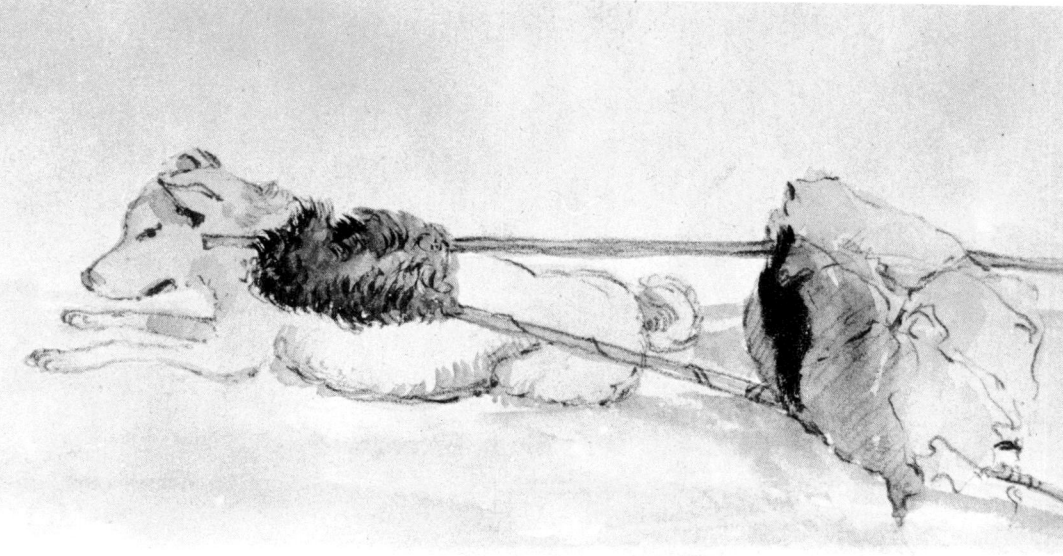

Fig. 62. Dog with travois. ROM946.15.84; CRIV-58.

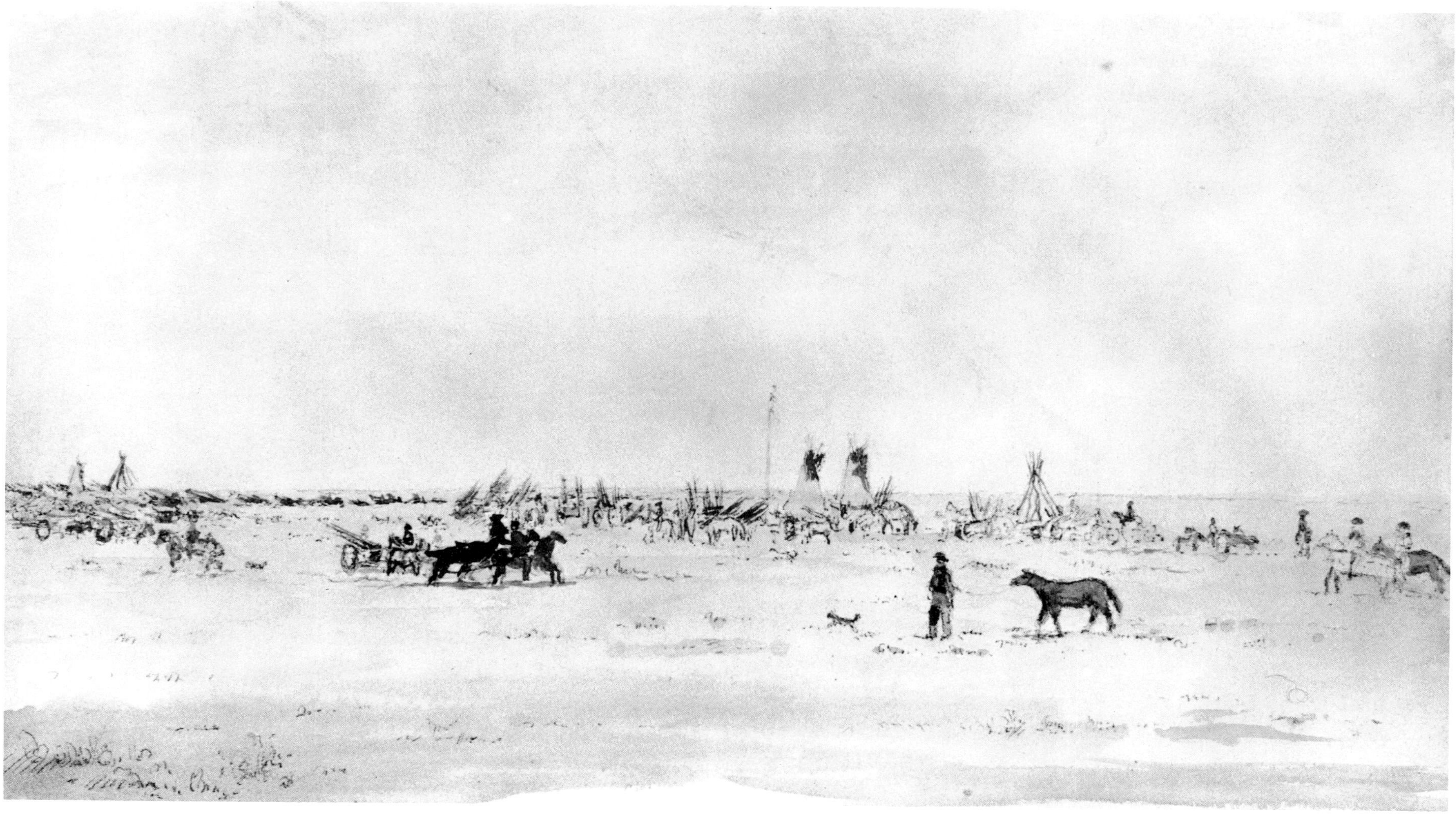

Fig. 63. Métis setting up camp on the prairies. ROM946.15.71; CRIV-66.

COURTESY ROYAL ONTARIO MUSEUM, TORONTO

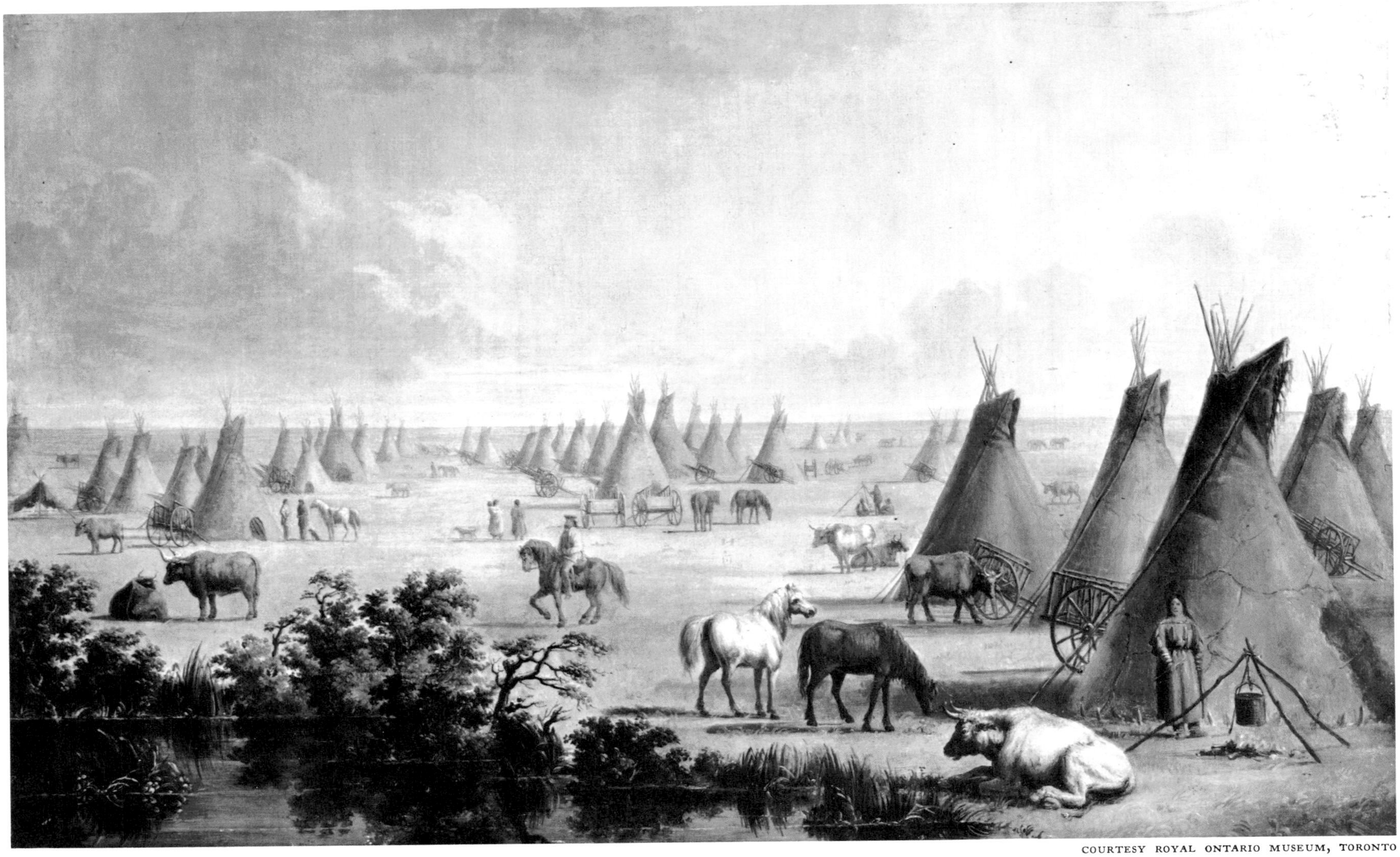

COURTESY ROYAL ONTARIO MUSEUM, TORONTO

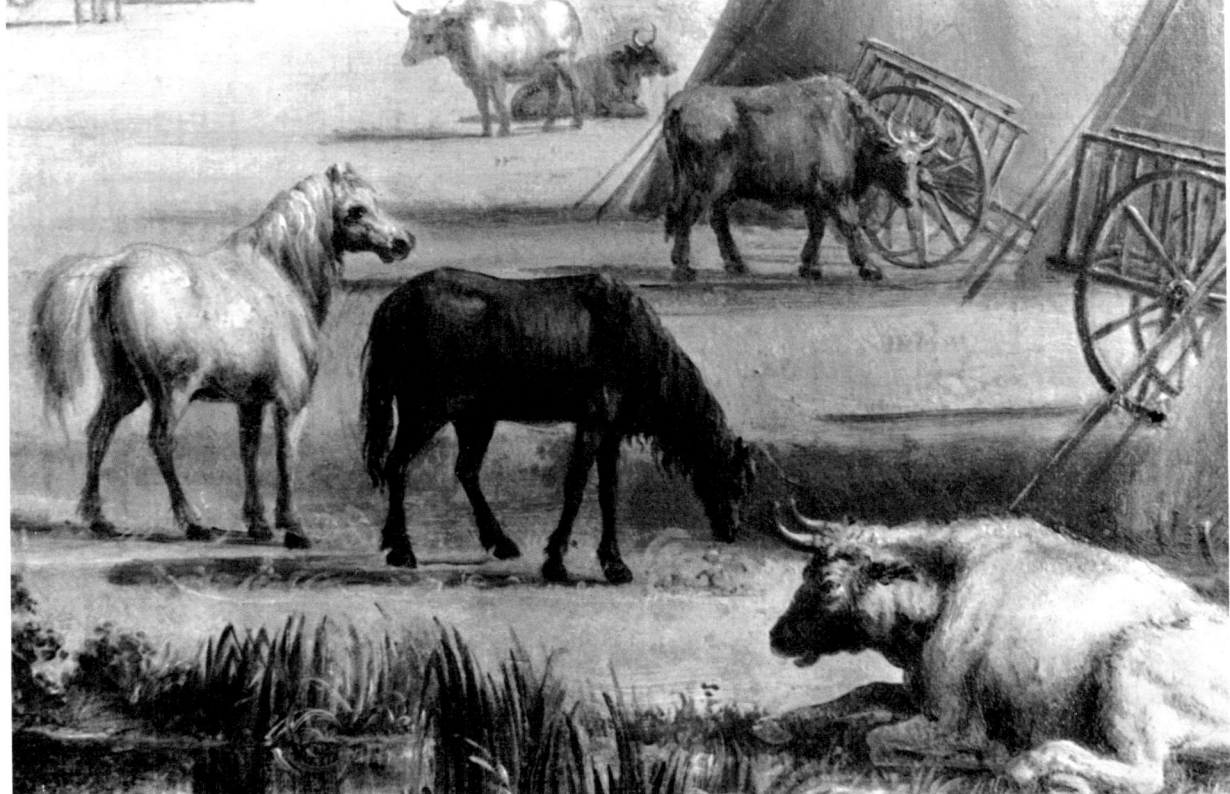

Fig. 64. Half Breed Encampment.
ROM912.1.25; CRIV-68.

Fig. 65. Half Breed Encampment
(a detail of Fig. 64).

COURTESY ROYAL ONTARIO MUSEUM, TORONTO

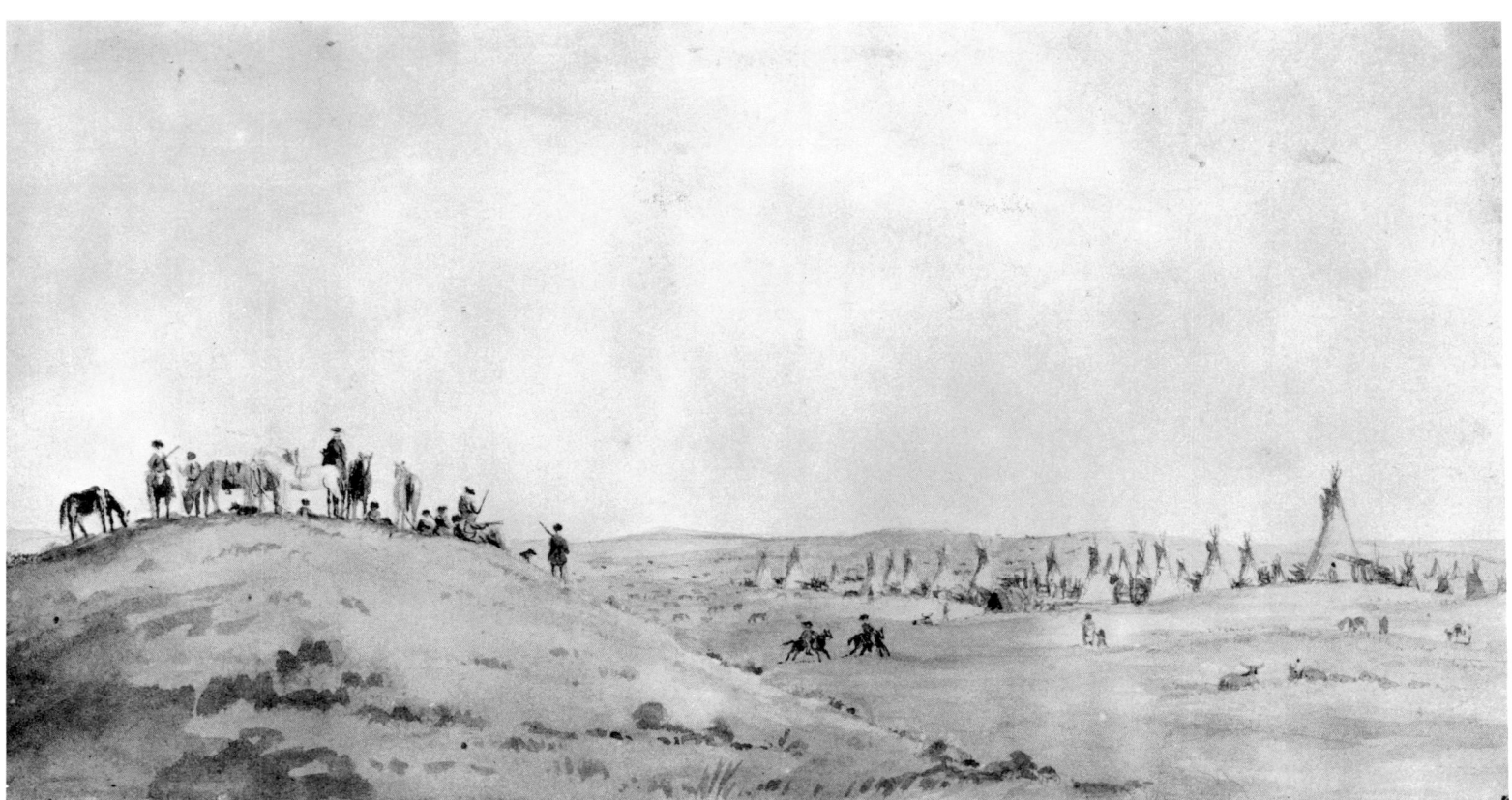

Fig. 66. Métis camp and hunters. ROM946.15.70; CRIV-69.

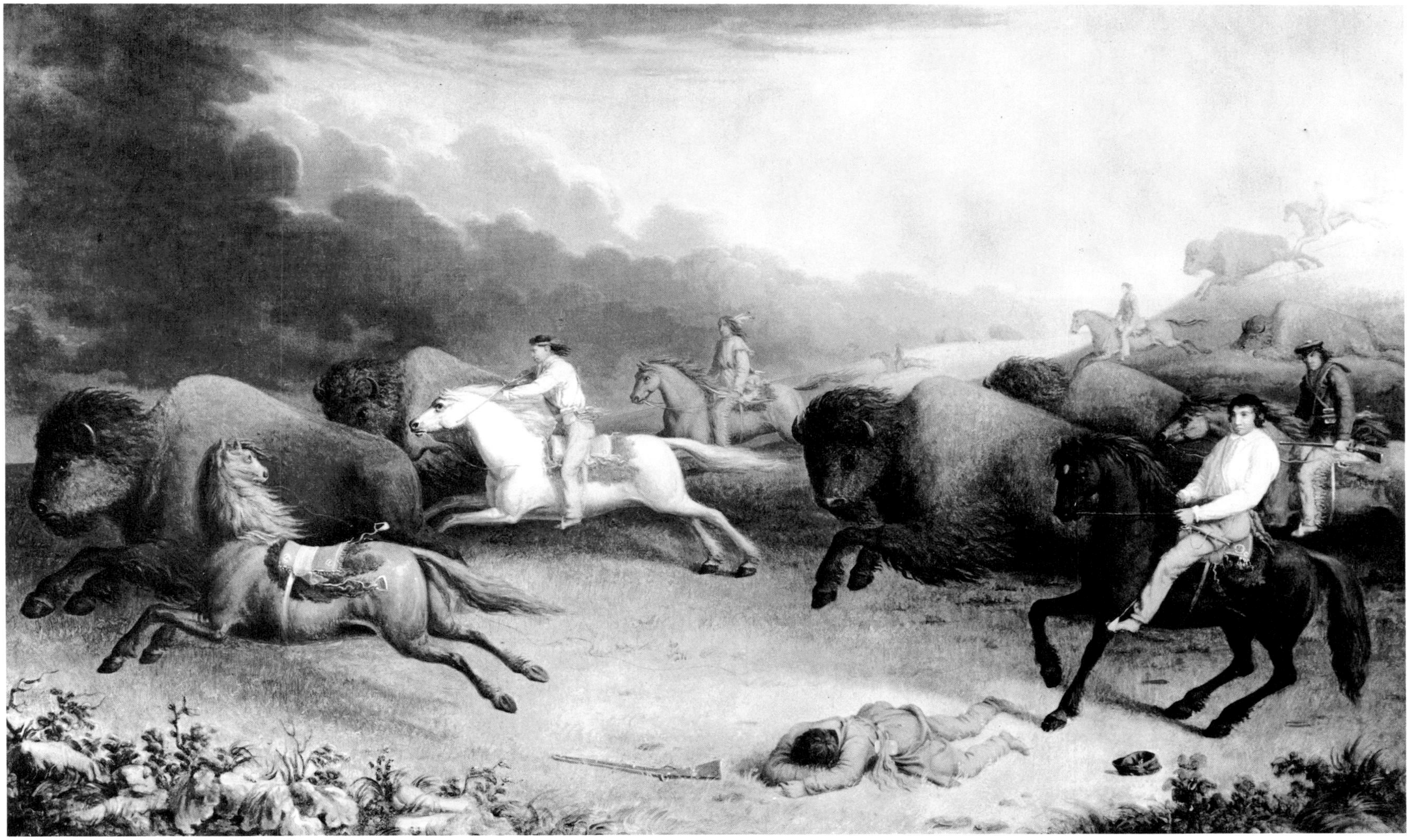

COURTESY ROYAL ONTARIO MUSEUM, TORONTO

Fig. 67. Half Breeds Running Buffalo. ROM912.1.26; CRIV-73.

Fig. 68. Wounded buffalo bull, shot by Kane. ROM946.15.87; crIV-78.

Fig. 69. Wounded buffalo bull, shot by Kane. Stark PWC8; crIV-79.

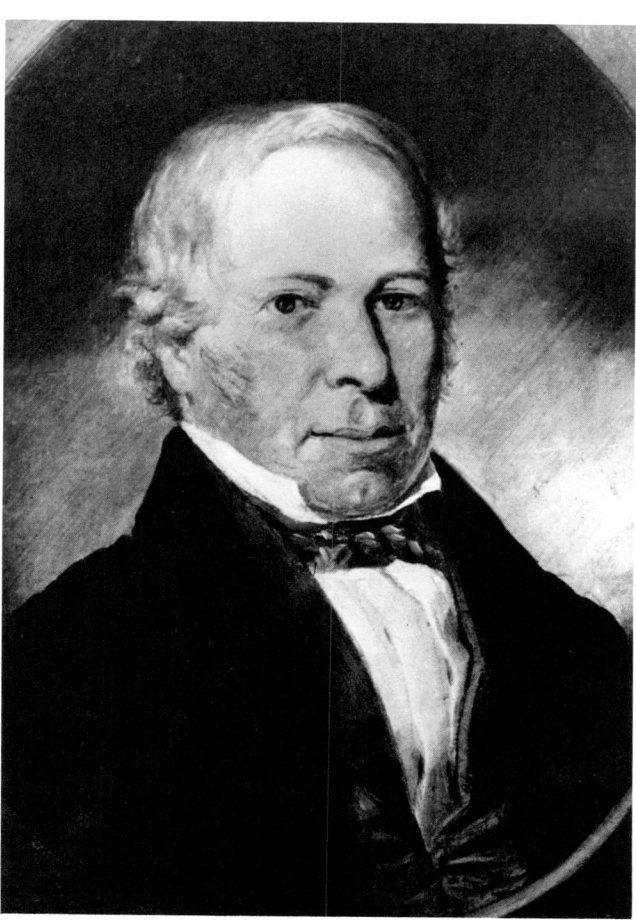

Fig. 70. Donald Ross, Chief Factor, Norway House. Provincial Archives, British Columbia, 3760; CRIV-89.

Fig. 71. Wesleyan mission station, Jack River. Stark PWC17; CRIV-84.

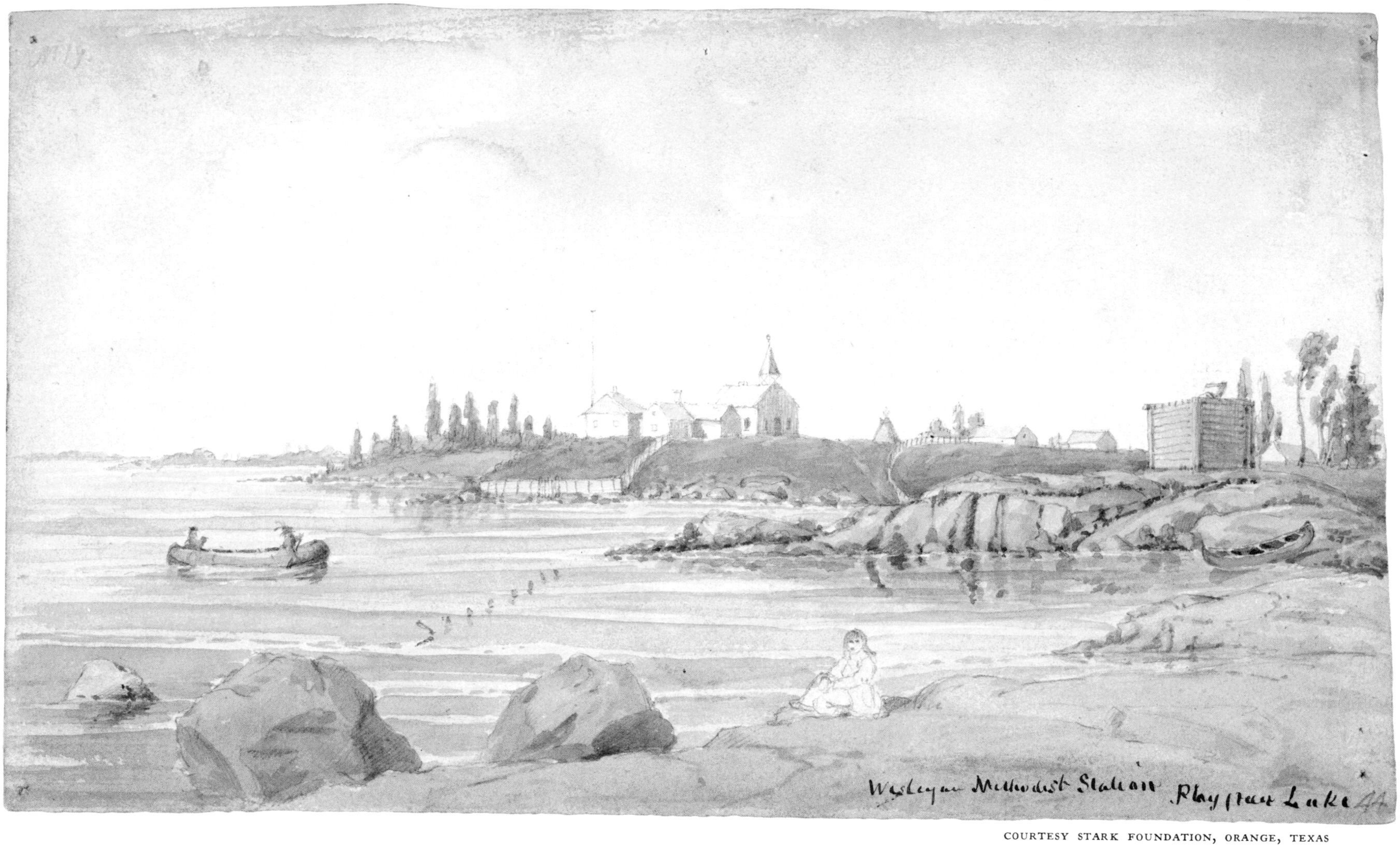
Wesleyan Methodist Station Playgreen Lake

COURTESY STARK FOUNDATION, ORANGE, TEXAS

Fig. 72. Two portrait studies: a Saulteaux girl and an Assiniboin. ROM946.15.61; CRIV-86.

Fig. 73. Brigade of boats, near Le Pas. ROM946.15.83; CRIV-92.

Plate XXXVII. Interior of a ceremonial lodge, Columbia River. Stark WOP13; crIV-425.

Fig. 74. Brigade of Boats. ROM 912.1.31; CRIV-95.

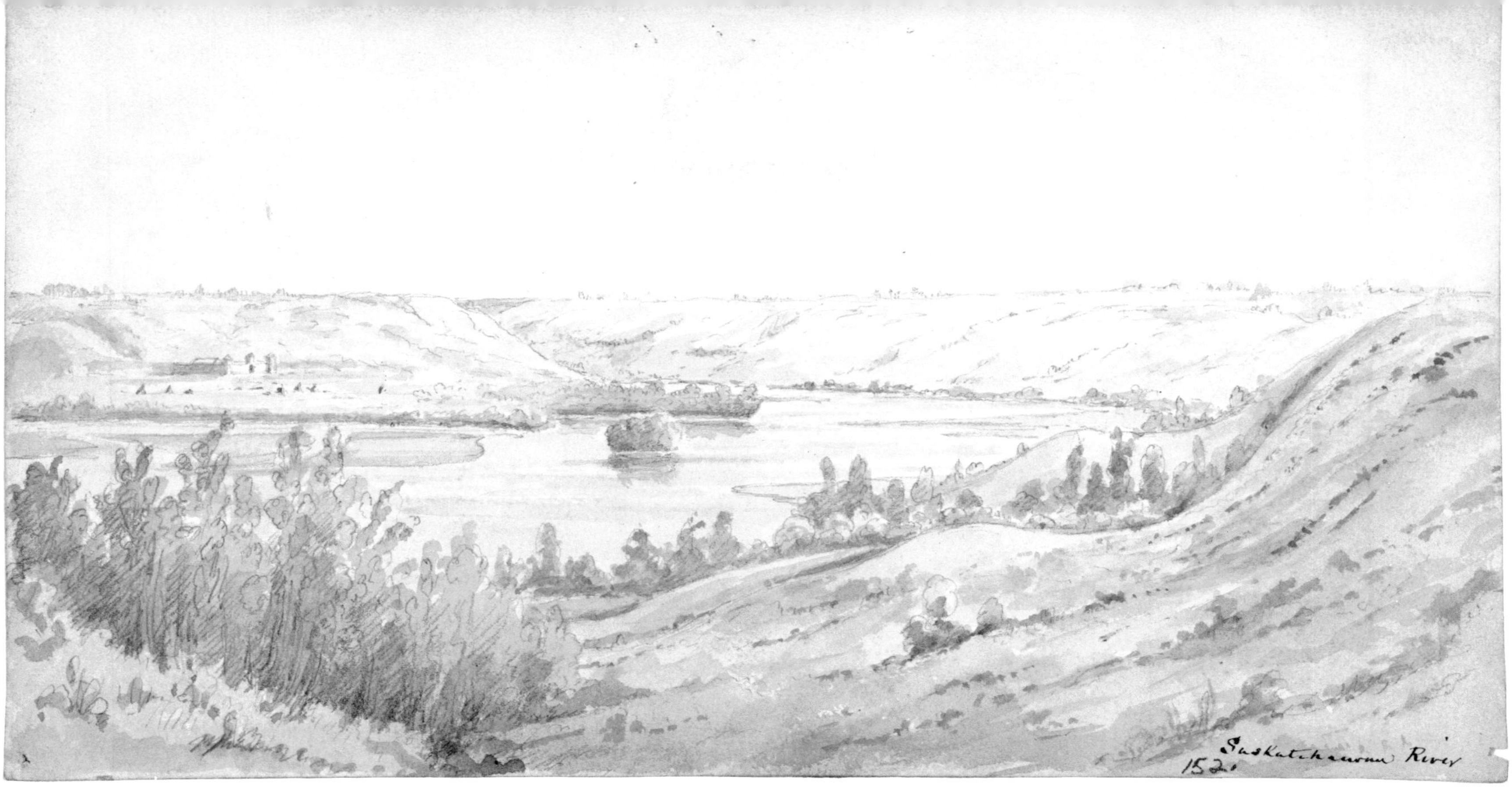

COURTESY STARK FOUNDATION, ORANGE, TEXAS

Fig. 75. Fort Carlton from a distance. Stark PWC18; CRIV-96.

COURTESY STARK FOUNDATION, ORANGE, TEXAS

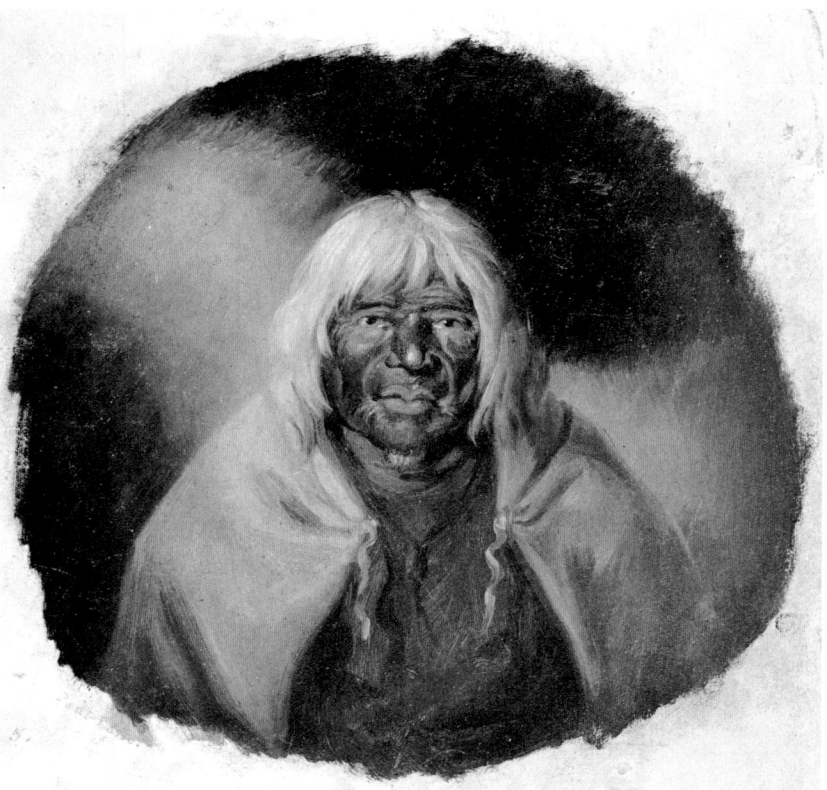

Fig. 76. Ogemawwah Chack or "The Spirit Chief," an Eskimo, Norway House. Stark WOP2; CRIV-90.

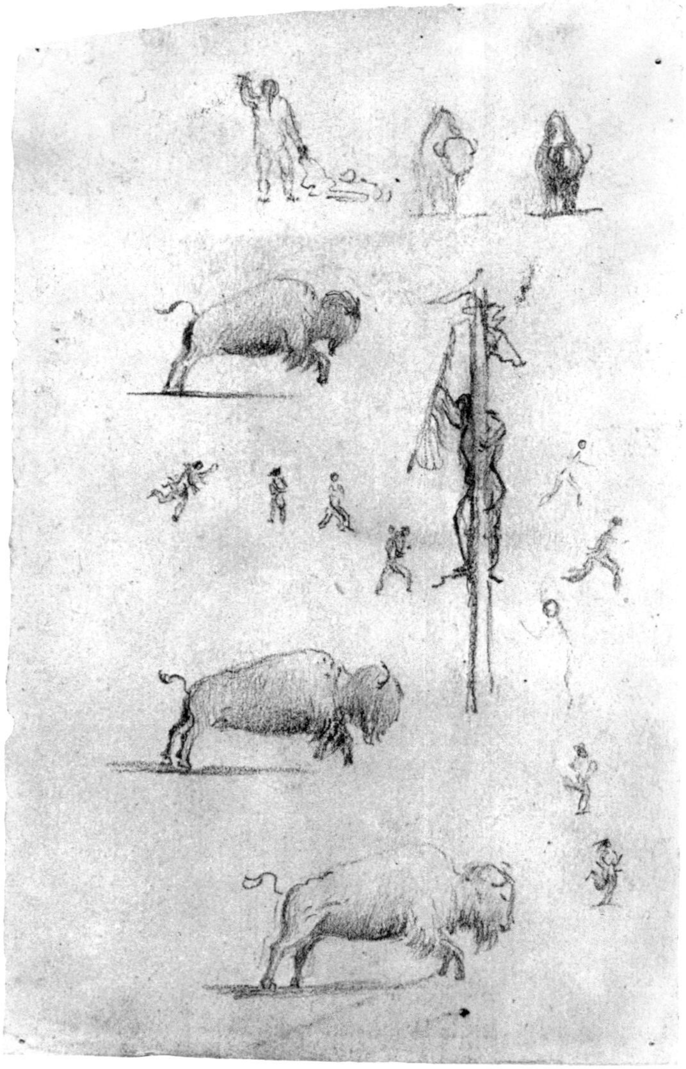

Fig. 77. Studies of the buffalo hunt near Fort Carlton. ROM946.15.103; CRIV-99.

COURTESY ROYAL ONTARIO MUSEUM, TORONTO

Fig. 78. A Buffalo Pound. ROM912.1.33; CRIV-101.

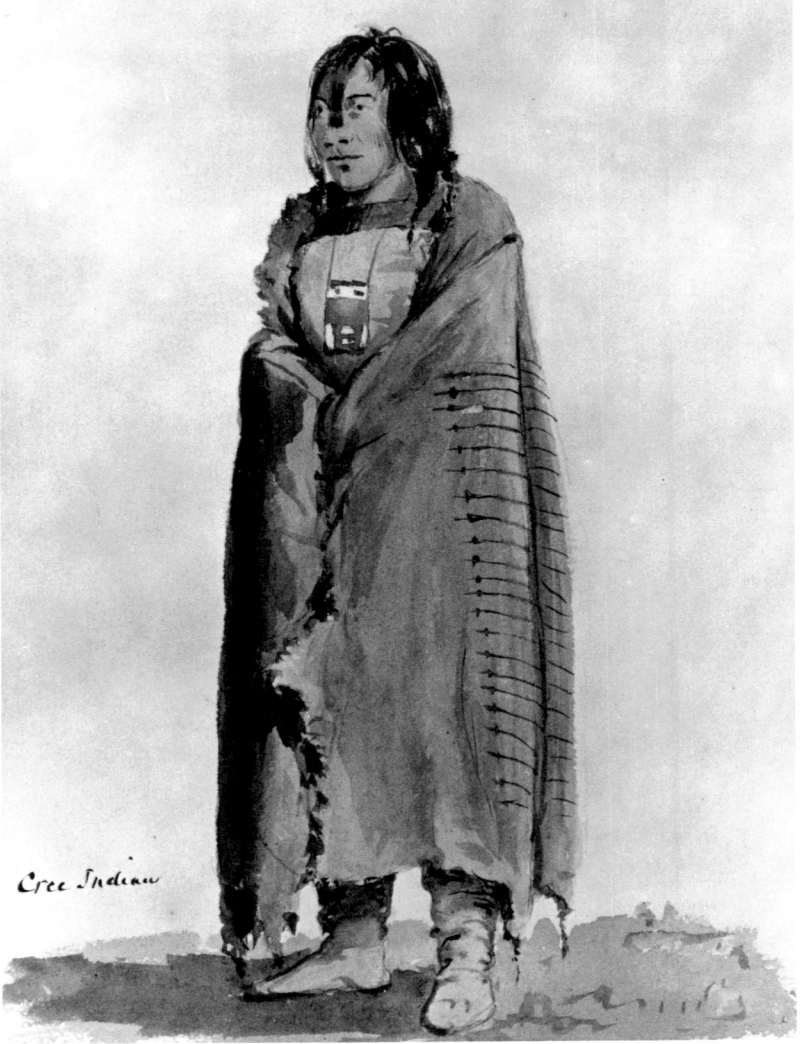

Fig. 79. "The Man that Shot the Wolf with an Arrow," a Cree, Fort Carlton. ROM946.15.96; CRIV-104.

COURTESY ROYAL ONTARIO MUSEUM, TORONTO

Fig. 80. Cree Indians travelling. ROM946.15.102; CRIV-106.

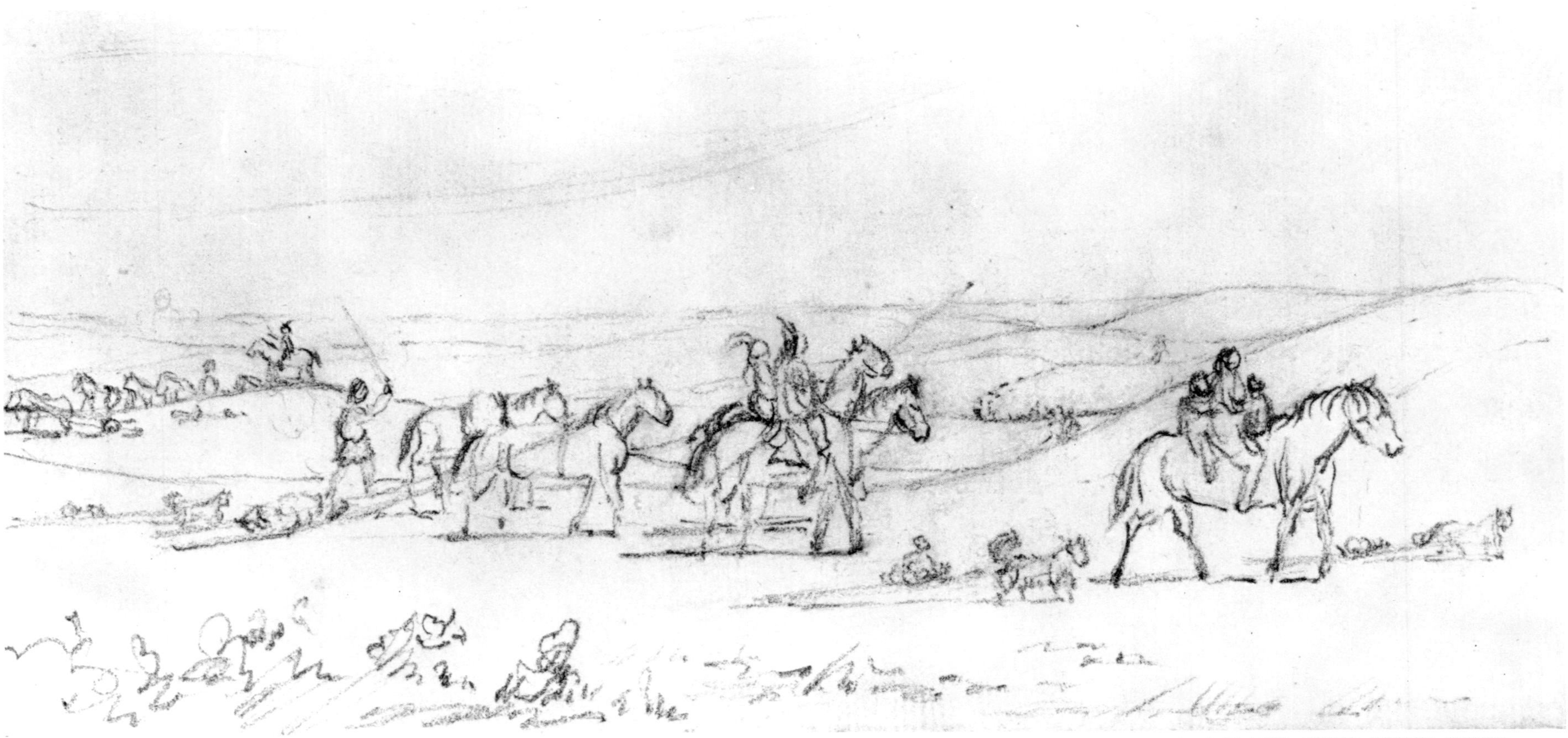

COURTESY ROYAL ONTARIO MUSEUM, TORONTO

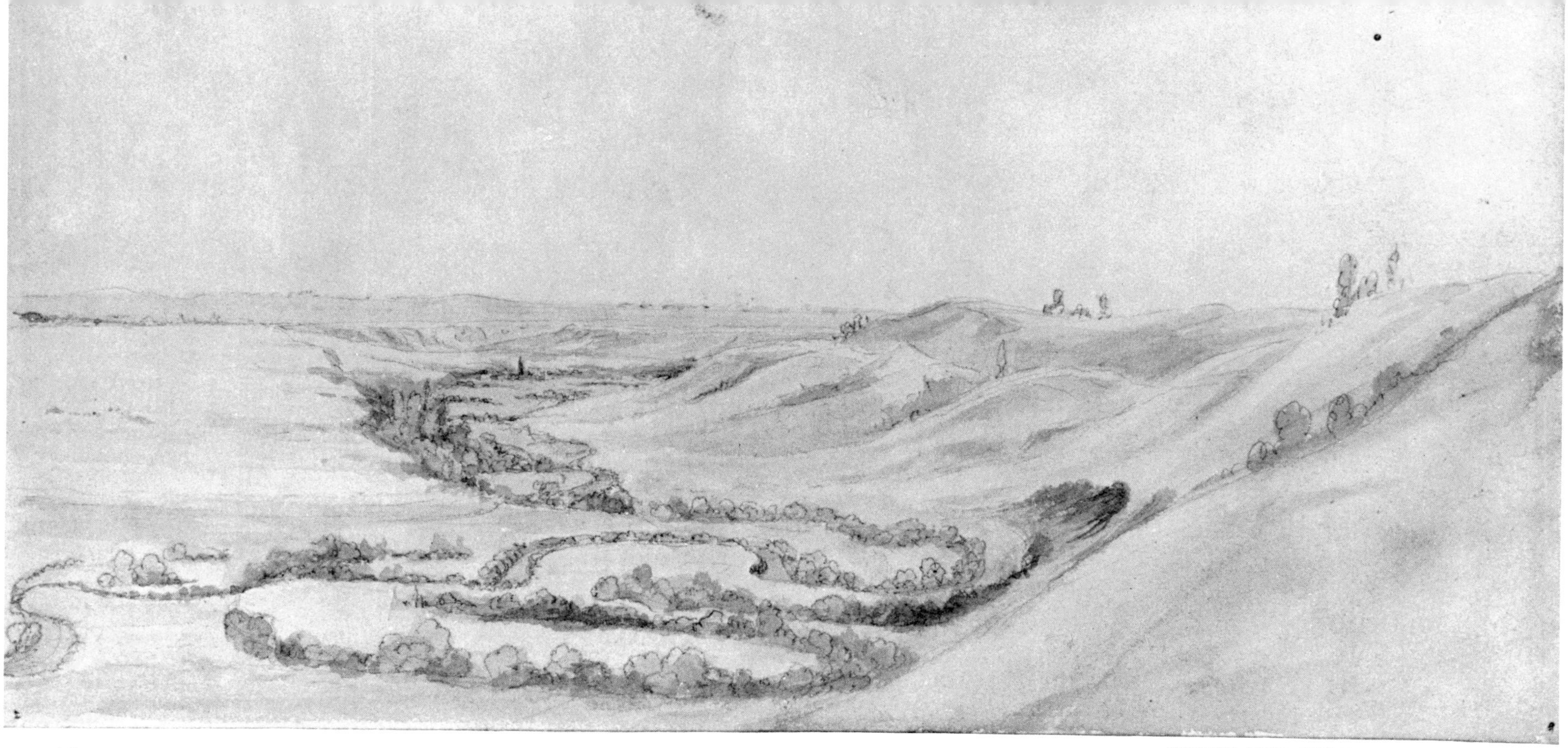

Fig. 81. The Serpentine Valley, Saskatchewan River. ROM946.15.139; CRIV-119.

COURTESY ROYAL ONTARIO MUSEUM, TORONTO

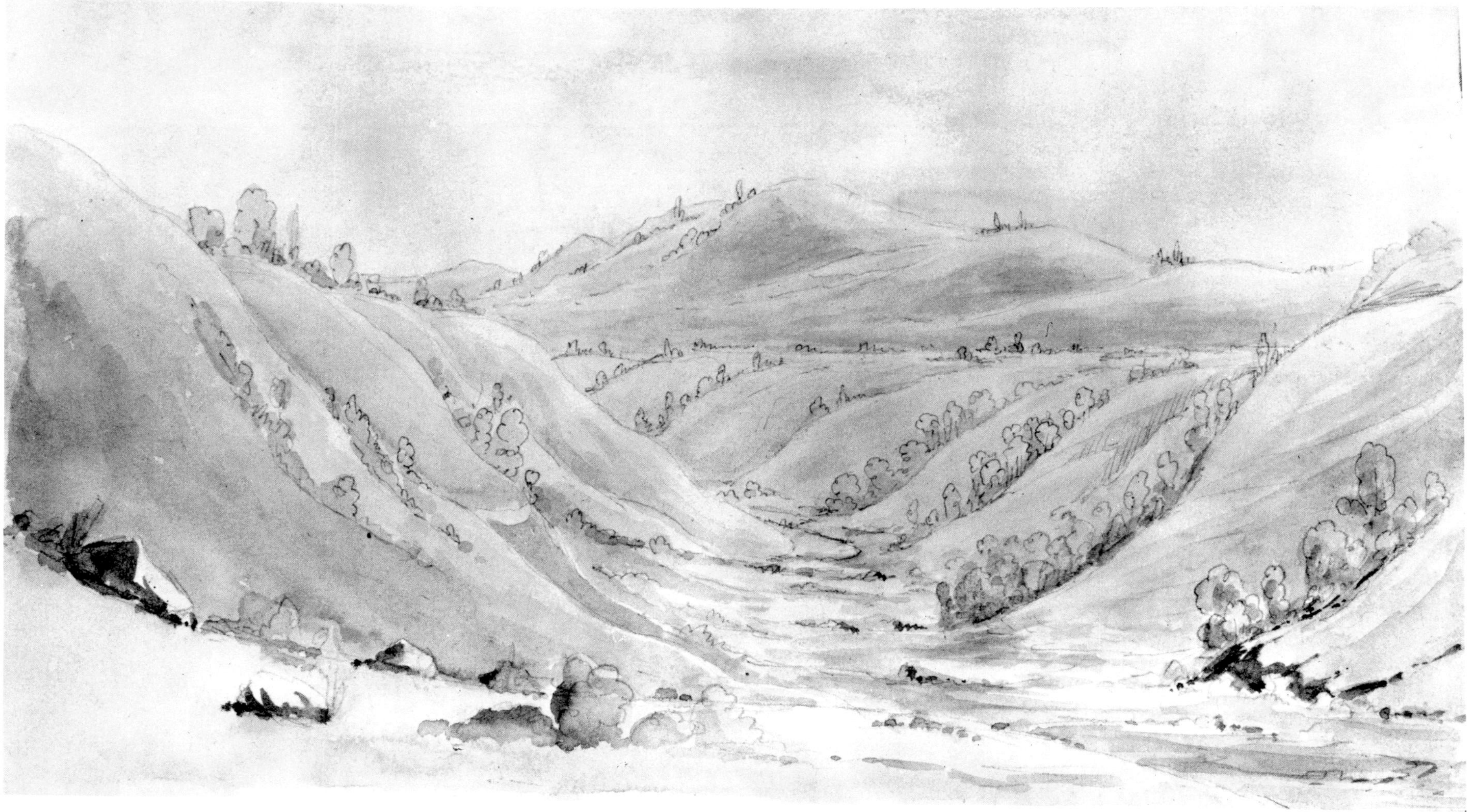

Fig. 82. The Golden Valley, Saskatchewan River. ROM946.15.108; CRIV-120.

COURTESY ROYAL ONTARIO MUSEUM, TORONTO

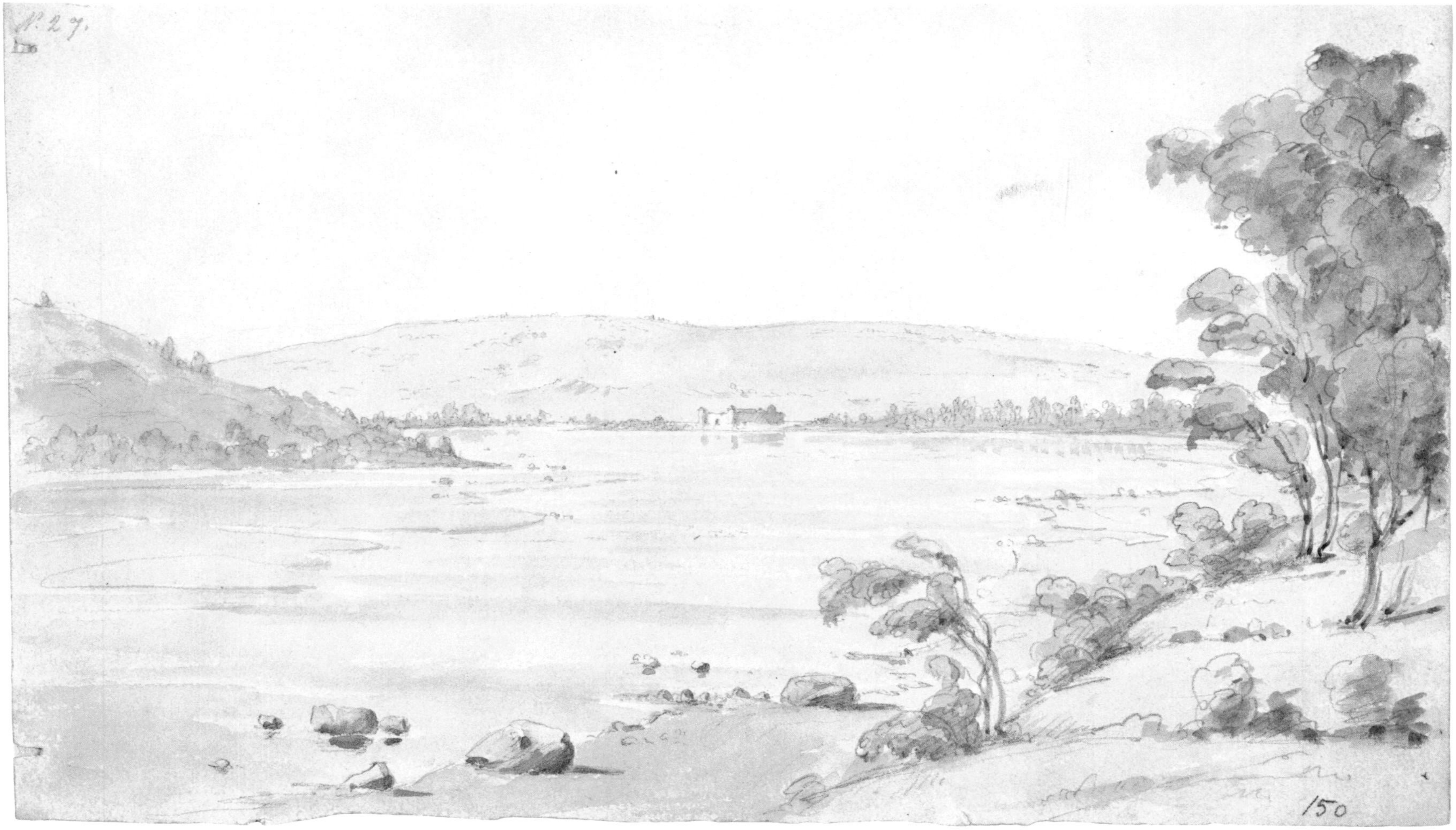

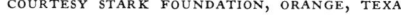

Fig. 83. Fort Pitt, with bluff. Stark pwc23; crIV-122.

COURTESY STARK FOUNDATION, ORANGE, TEXAS

Fig. 84. Prairie antelope.
Stark pwc11; crIV-123.

COURTESY STARK FOUNDATION, ORANGE, TEXAS

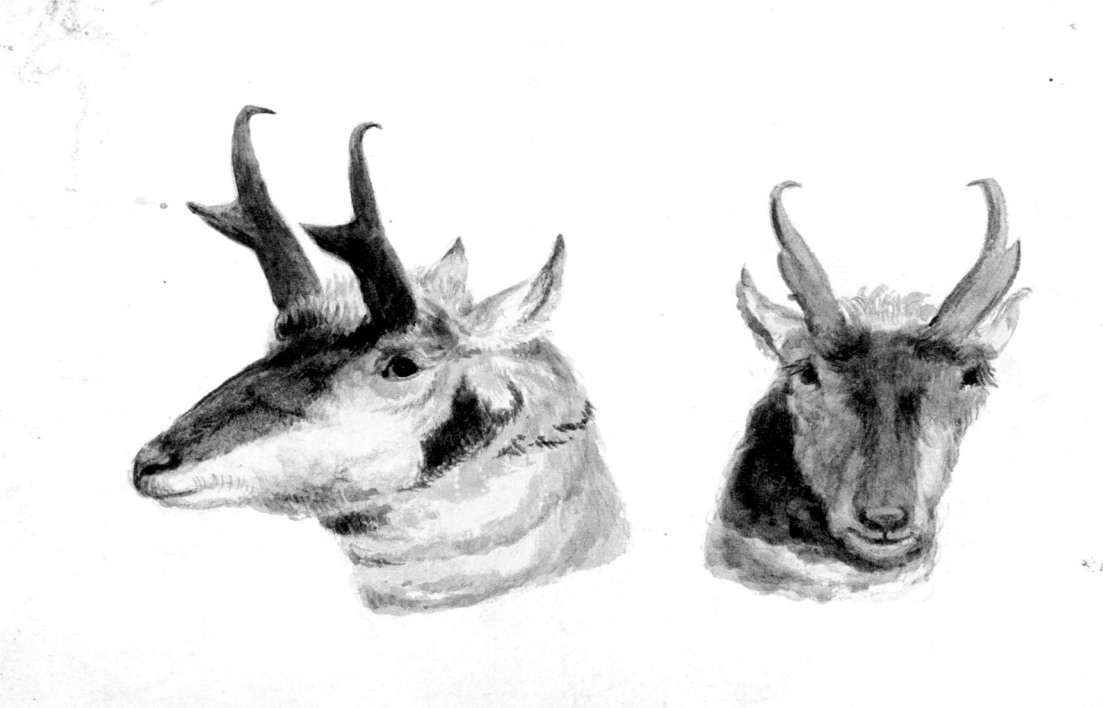

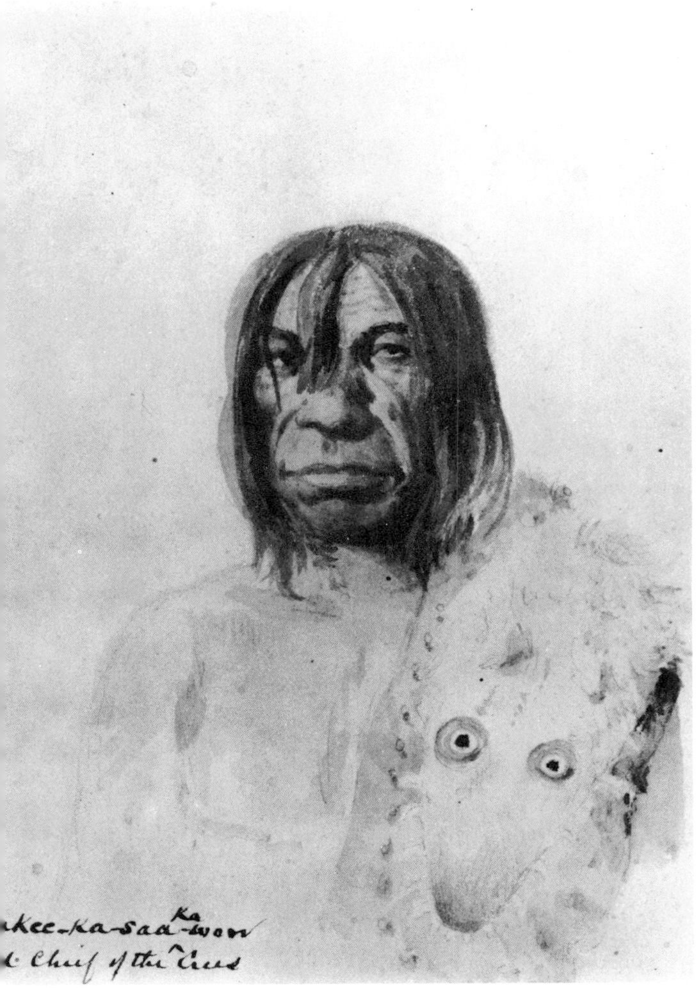

Fig. 86. Kee-akee-ka-saa-ka-wow, "The Man that gives the War Whoop" (Fort Pitt). ROM912.1.42; crIV-132.

akee-ka-saa-ka-wow
Chief of the Crees

Fig. 85. Kee-a-kee-ka-sa-coo-way or "The Man who gives the War-whoop," a Cree, Fort Pitt. Peabody Museum, Harvard University—Bushnell 41-72/395; crIV-131.

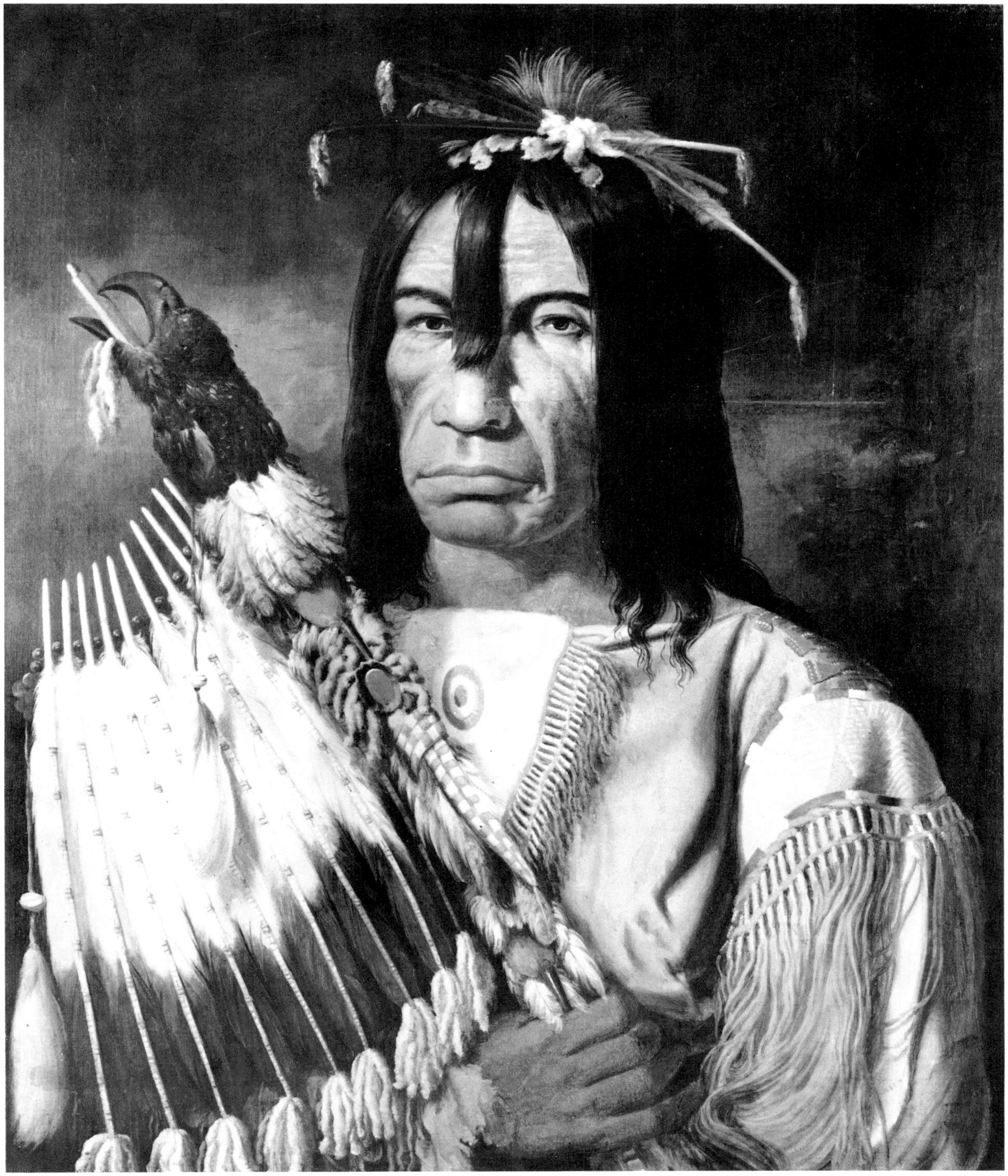

COURTESY ROYAL ONTARIO MUSEUM, TORONTO

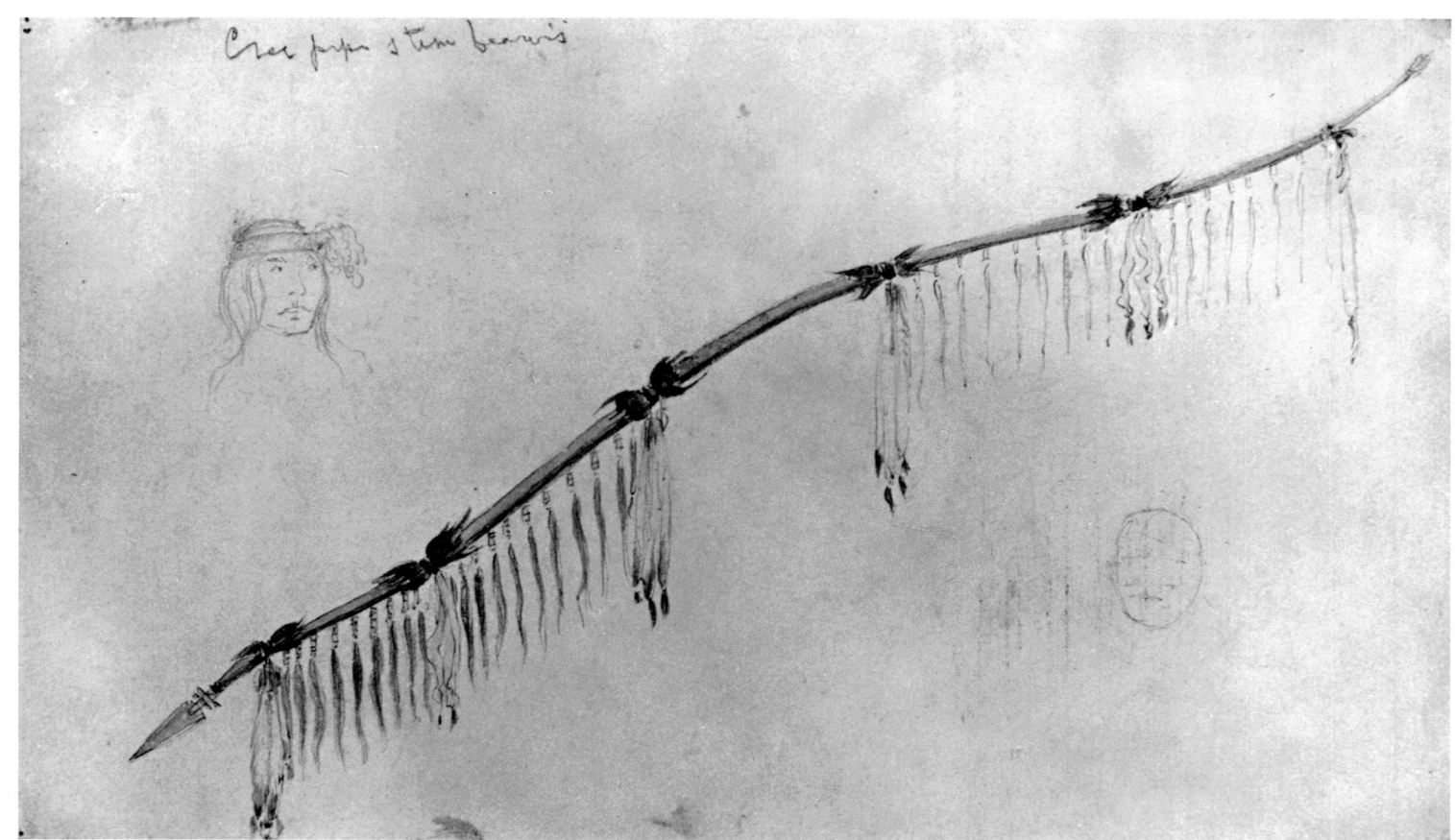

Fig. 87. Cree pipe-stem. ROM946.15.99; CRIV-135.

COURTESY ROYAL ONTARIO MUSEUM, TORONTO

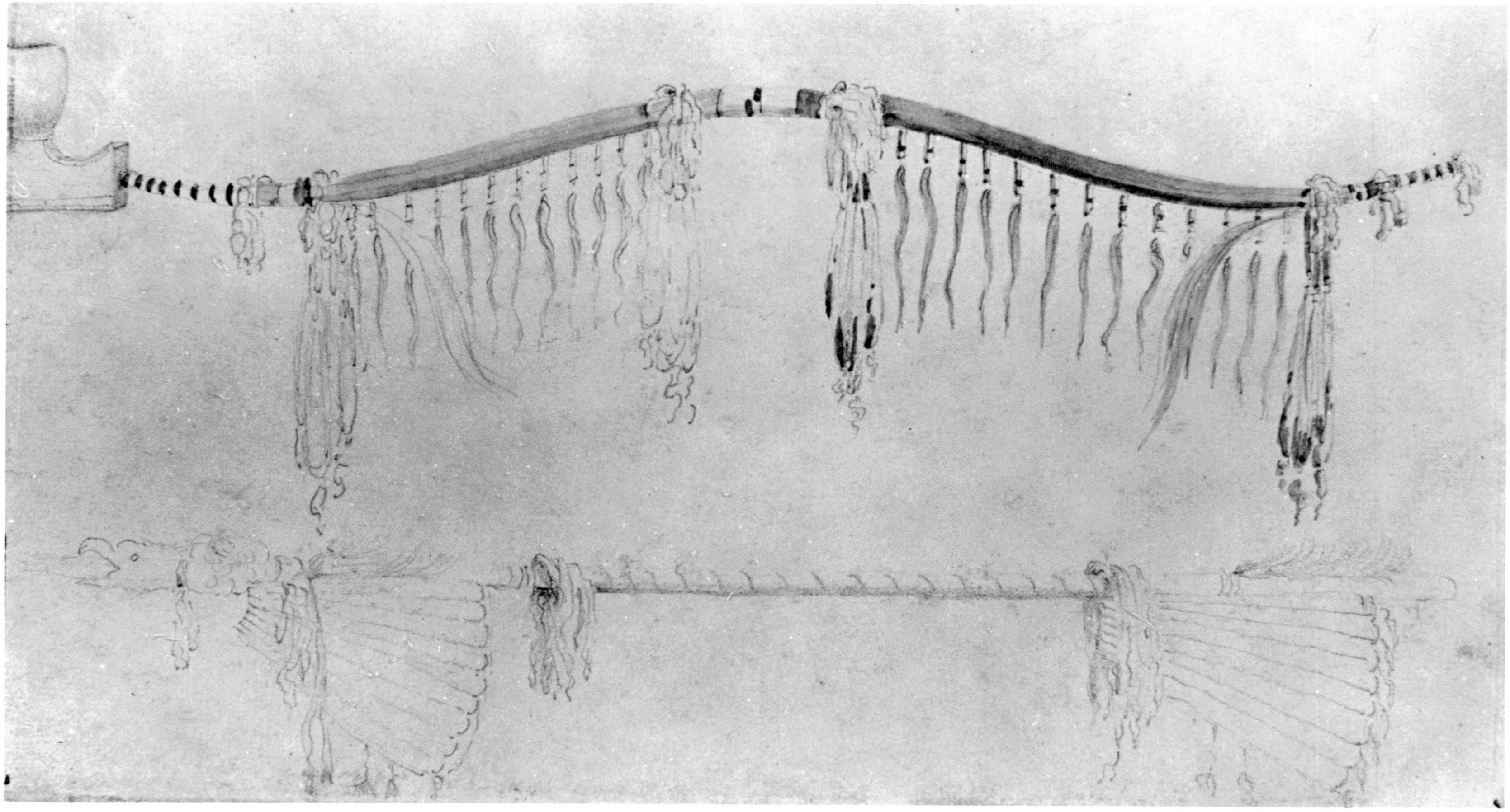

Fig. 88. Cree pipe-stems. ROM946.15.100; CRIV-136.

Fig. 89. Indian Horse Race. National Gallery of Canada 6921; crIV-145.

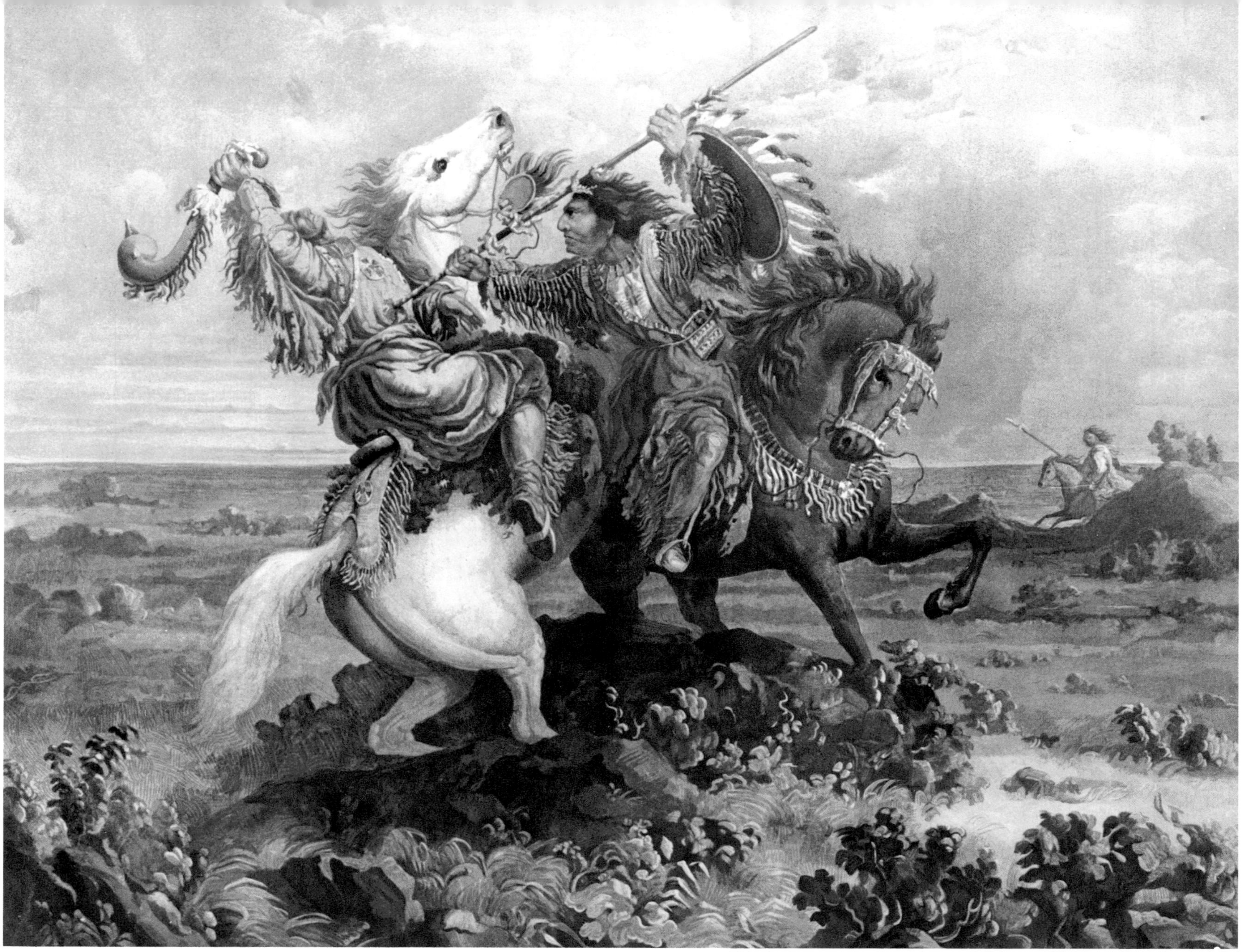

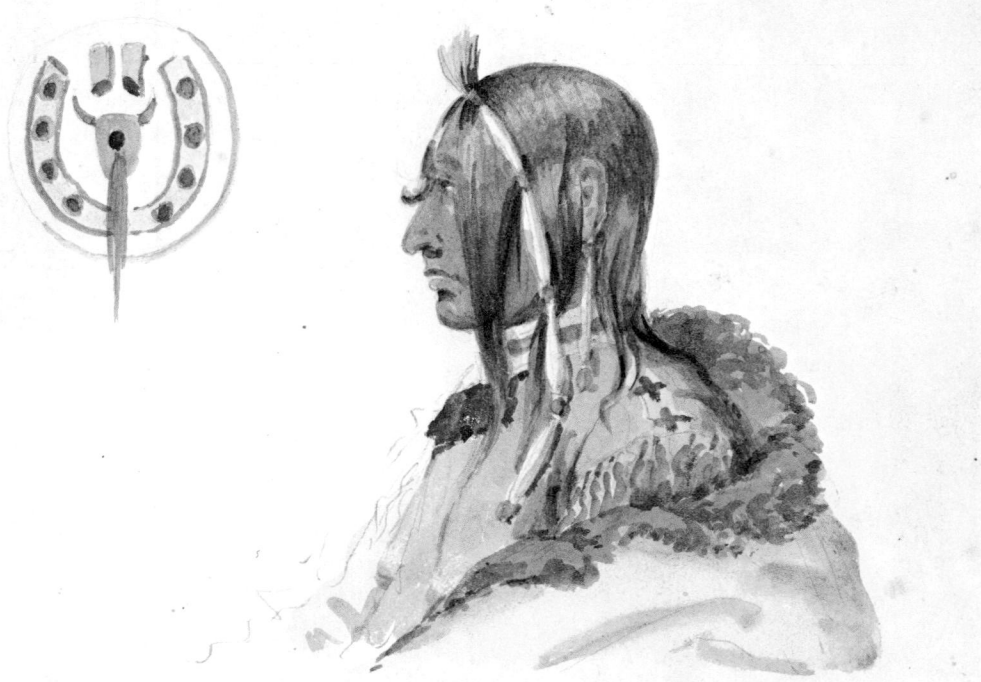

Fig. 90. The Death of Big Snake; contemporary print made in Toronto. Collection of A. A. H. Vernon; crIV-148.

COURTESY STARK FOUNDATION, ORANGE, TEXAS

Fig. 91. Wah-nis-stow or "The White Buffalo," a Sarsi chief, sketched near Fort Pitt. Stark pwc5; crIV-150.

Fig. 92. Big Snake, a Blackfoot Chief, recounting his War Exploits. National Gallery of Canada 22; crIV-155.

Fig. 93. Medicine Pipe Stem Dance (Blackfoot). ROM912.1.56; crIV-158.

Fig. 94. Jacket ornamented with a crow (military society regalia). ROM946.15.313; crIV-162.

Plate XXXVIII. The mills of Oregon City. Stark WOP16; CRIV-449.

Fig. 95. Buffalo robe depicting adventures of Sa-co or "The Sinew Piece," a Blood. Stark wwc82; cr-164.

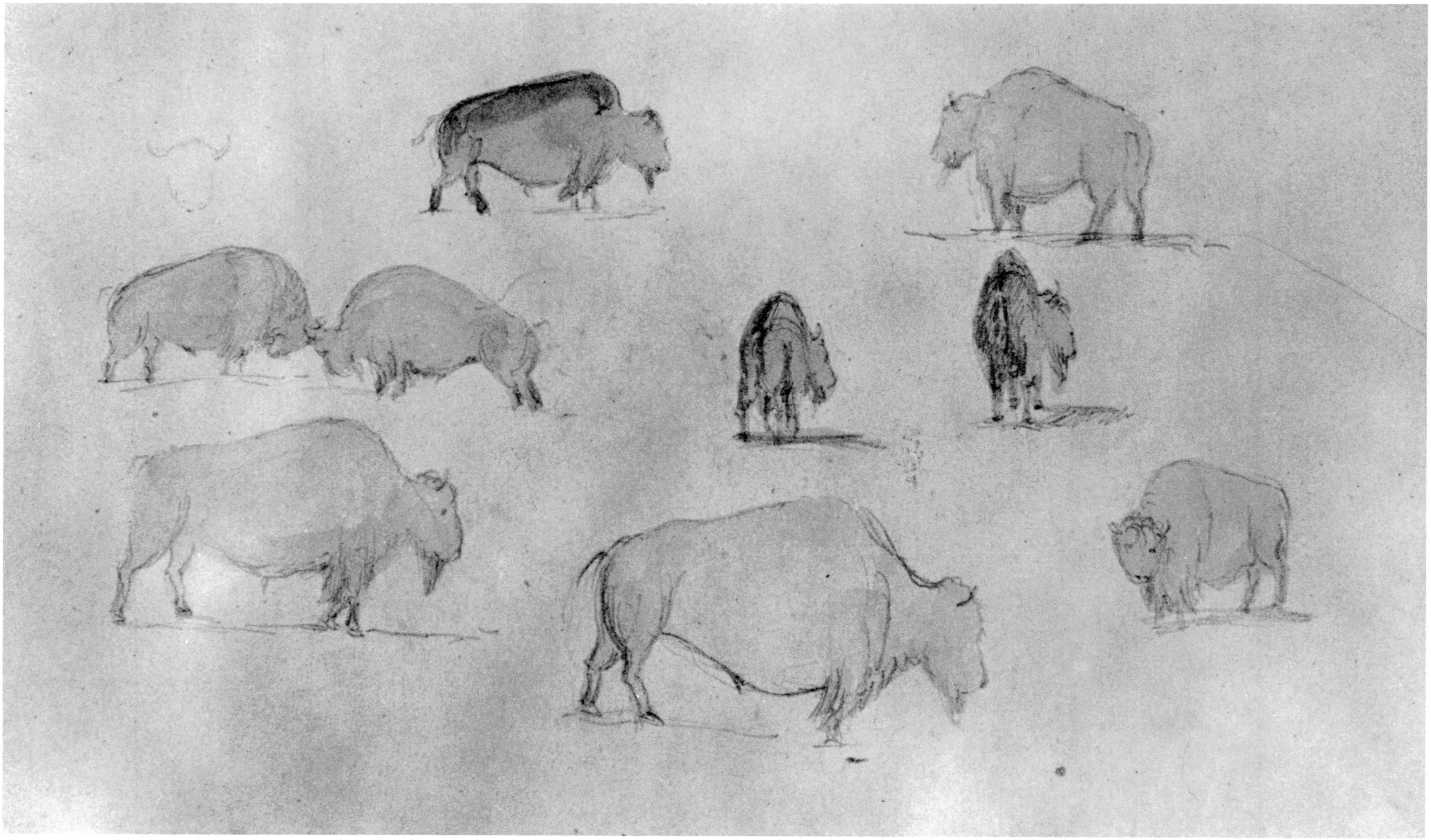

COURTESY ROYAL ONTARIO MUSEUM, TORONTO

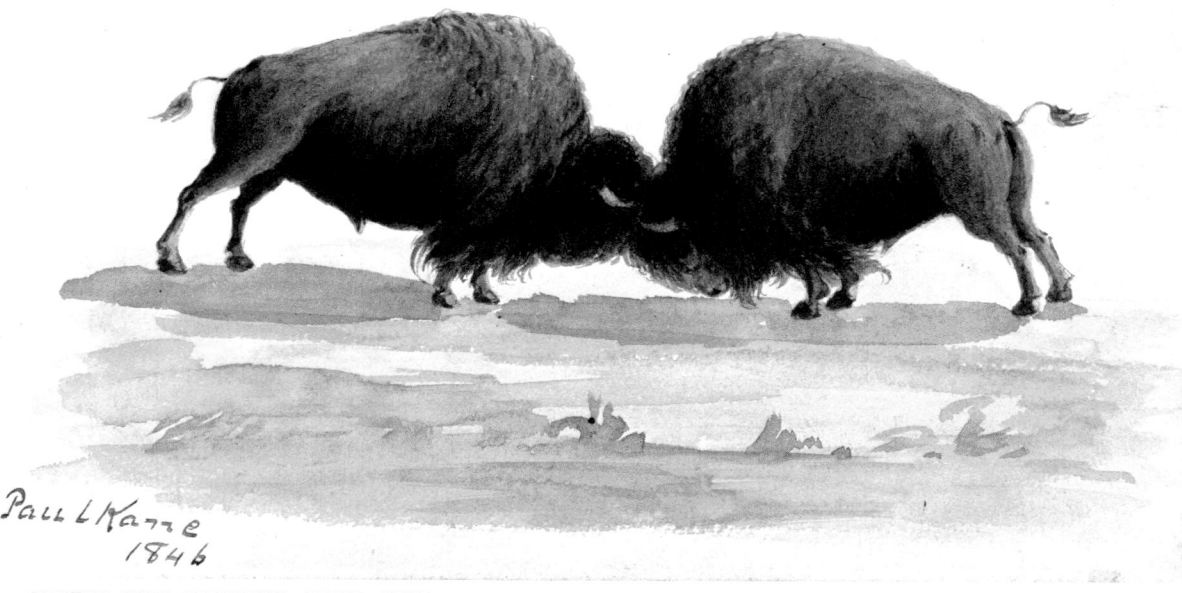

Fig. 96. Studies of buffalo, near Fort Pitt.
ROM946.15.90; CRIV-174.

Paul Kane
1846

COURTESY STARK FOUNDATION, ORANGE, TEXAS

Fig. 97. Buffalo bulls fighting, near Fort Pitt.
Stark PWC9; CRIV-175.

Fig. 98. Buffalo Bulls Fighting. ROM912.1.28; CRIV-176.

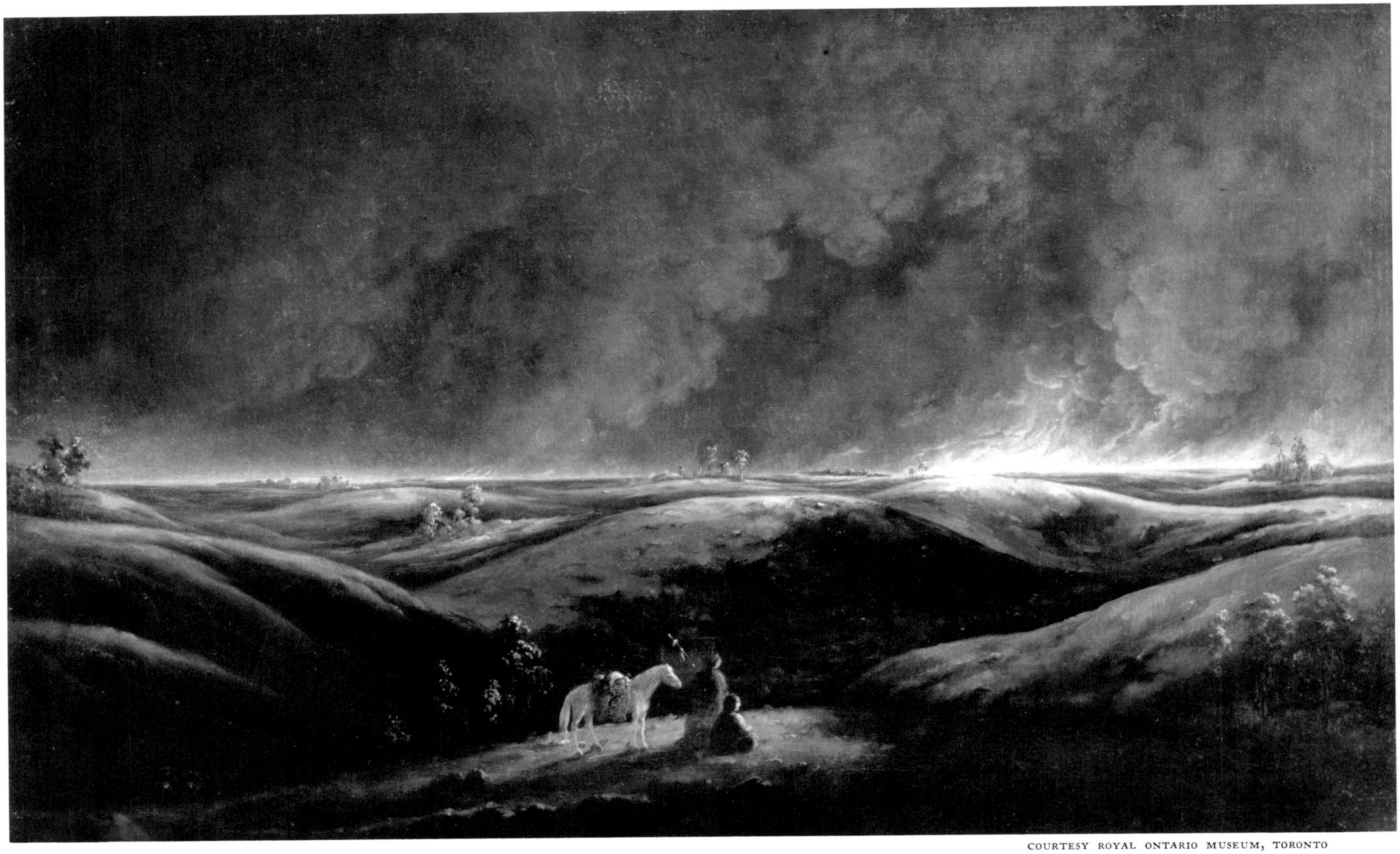

COURTESY ROYAL ONTARIO MUSEUM, TORONTO

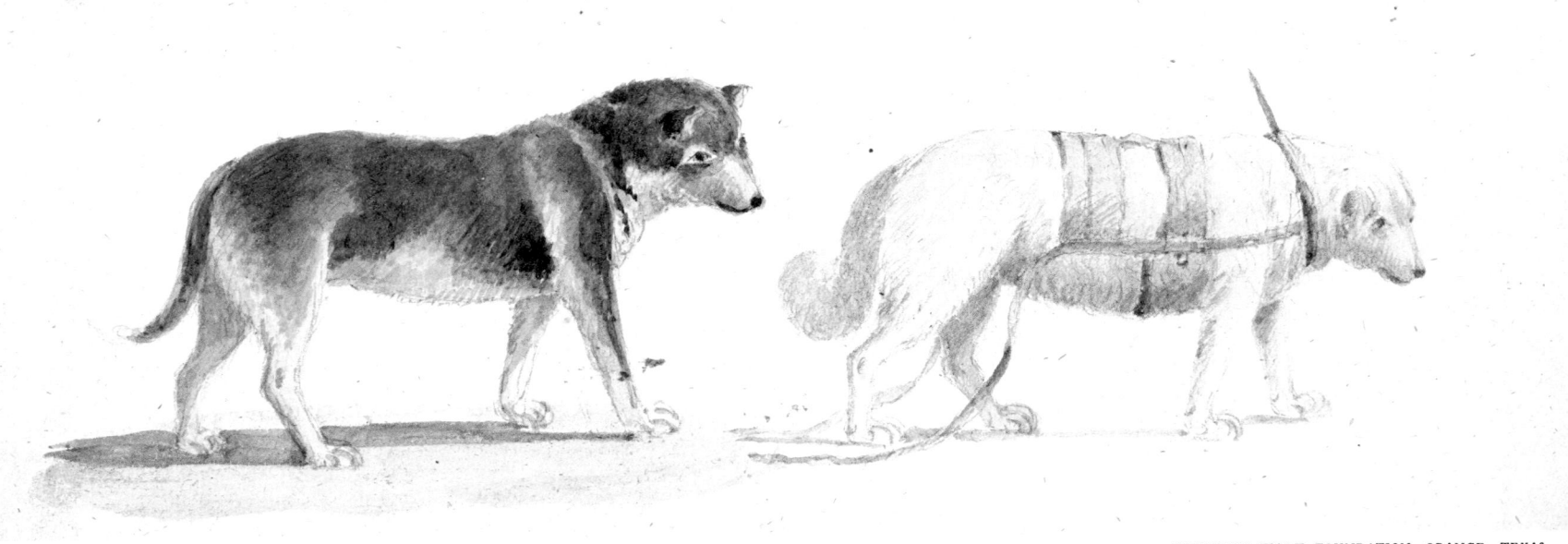

Fig. 99. A Prairie on Fire. ROM912.1.39; CRIV-187.

COURTESY STARK FOUNDATION, ORANGE, TEXAS

Fig. 100. Sled dogs of the plains. Stark PWC13; CRIV-195.

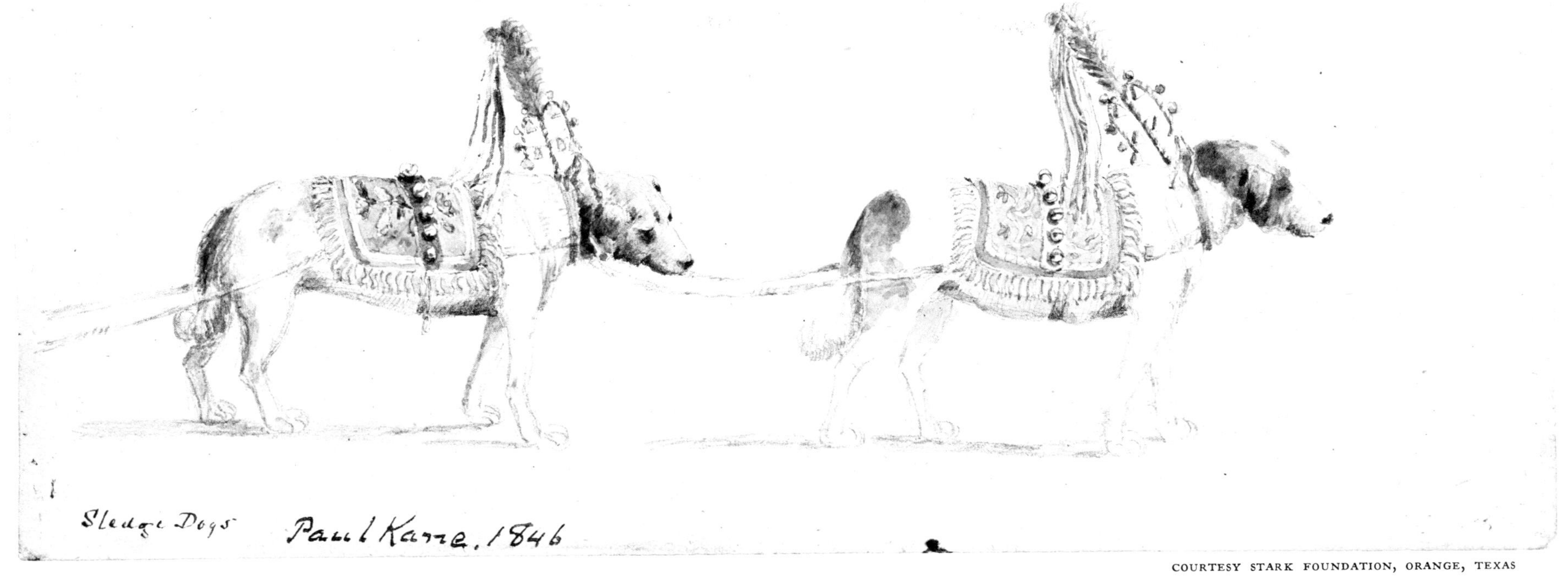
Sledge Dogs
Paul Kane, 1846

COURTESY STARK FOUNDATION, ORANGE, TEXAS

Fig. 101. Sled dogs decorated for a wedding party, Fort Edmonton.
Stark PWC12; CRIV-194.

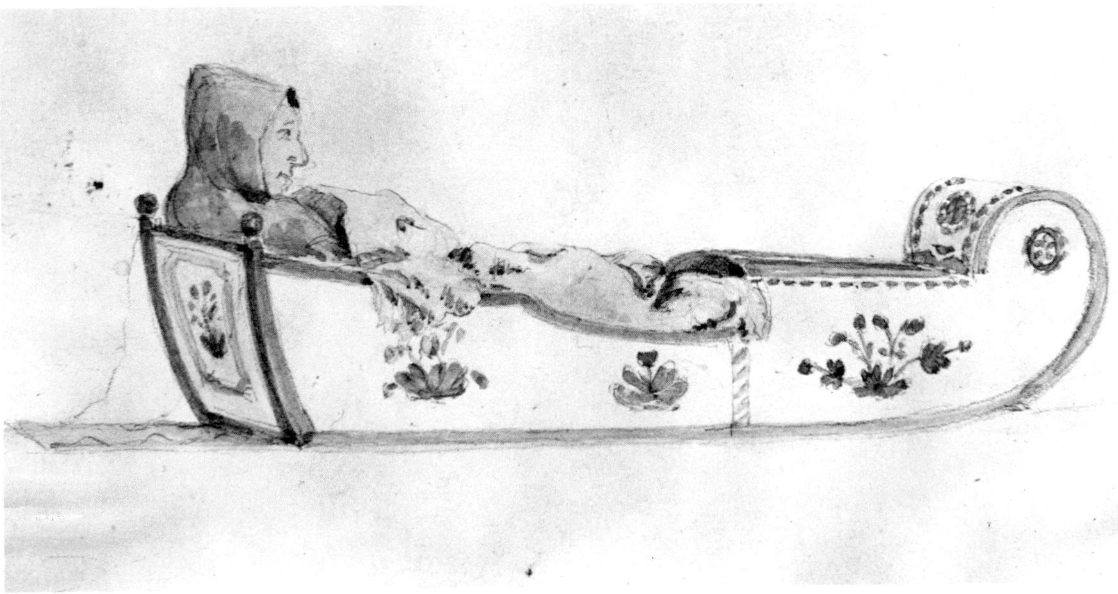

COURTESY ROYAL ONTARIO MUSEUM, TORONTO

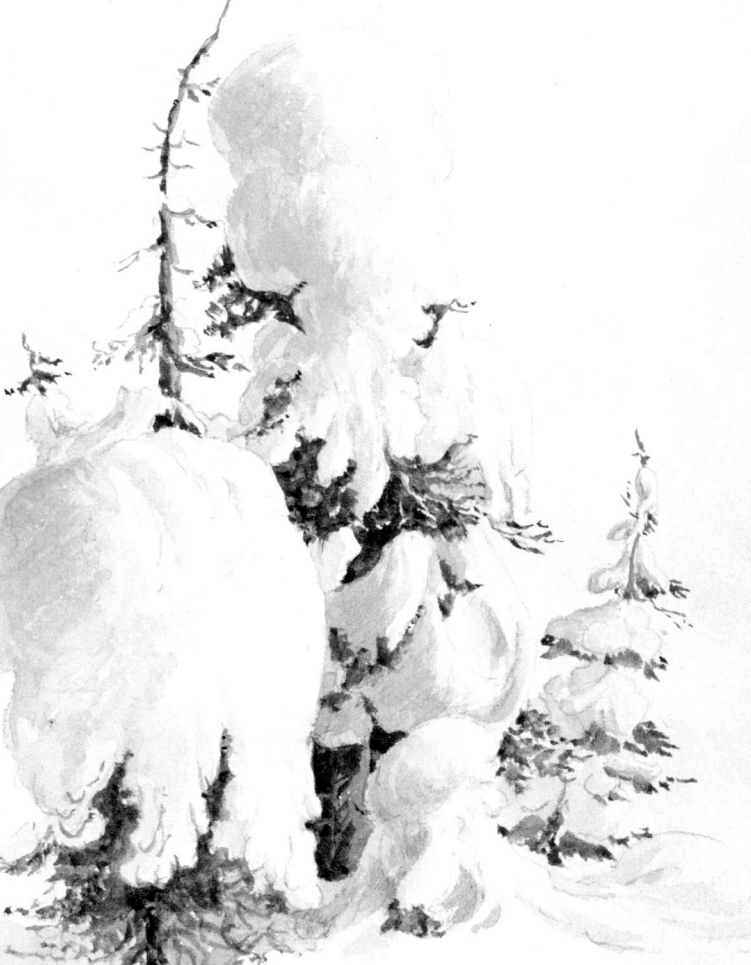

Fig. 103. Decorated sled for wedding party, Fort Edmonton. ROM946.15.129; CRIV-199.

COURTESY STARK FOUNDATION, ORANGE, TEXAS

Fig. 102. Snow on trees.
Stark WWC40; CRIV-196.

Fig. 104. Catching Wild Horses. ROM912.1.45; CRIV-203.

Plate XXXIX. St. Paul's Mission, Willamette valley. ROM946.15.264; CRIV-454.

Willamette Indians

Plate XL. Clackama Indians, Willamette valley. Stark wop11; crIV-459.

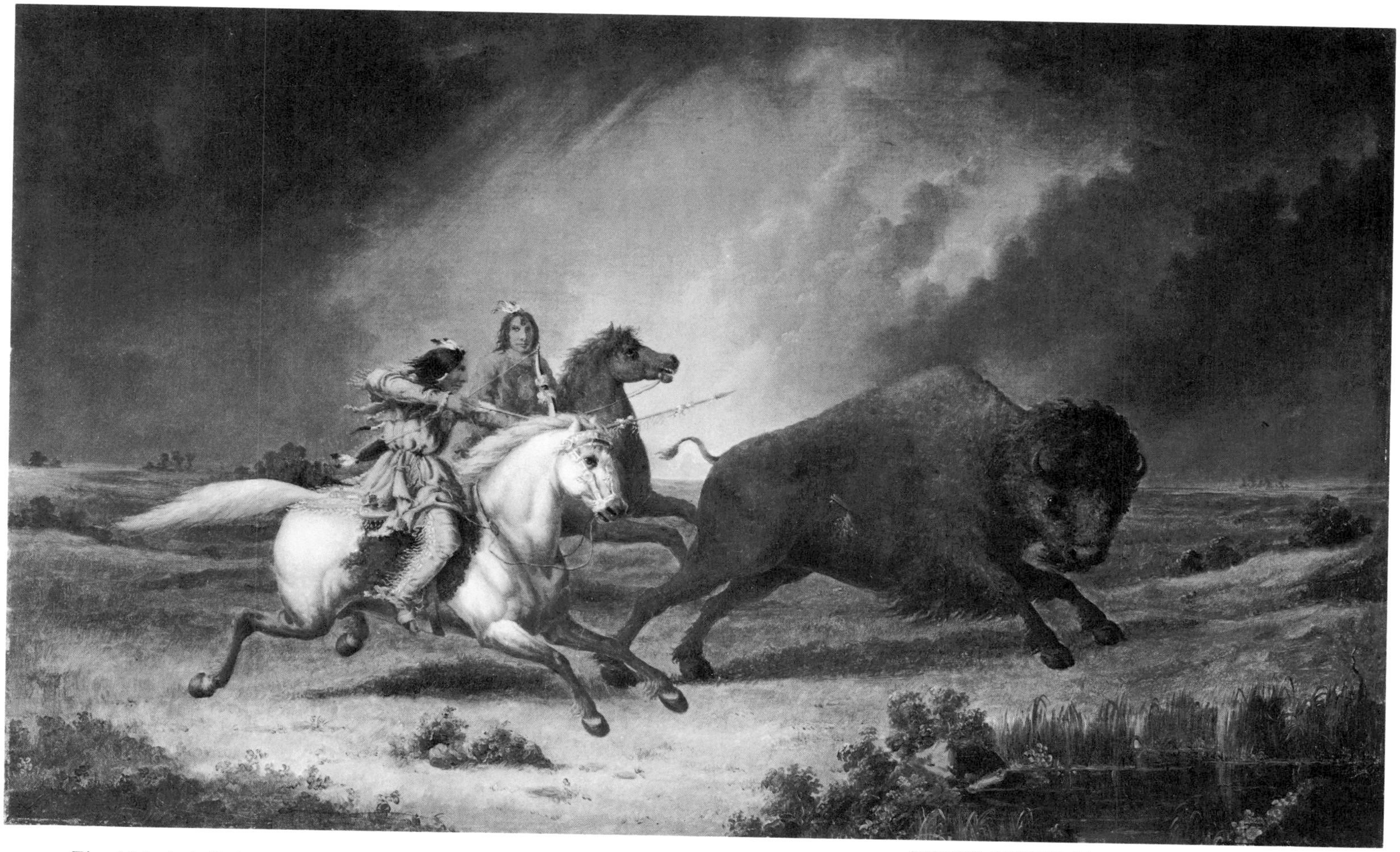

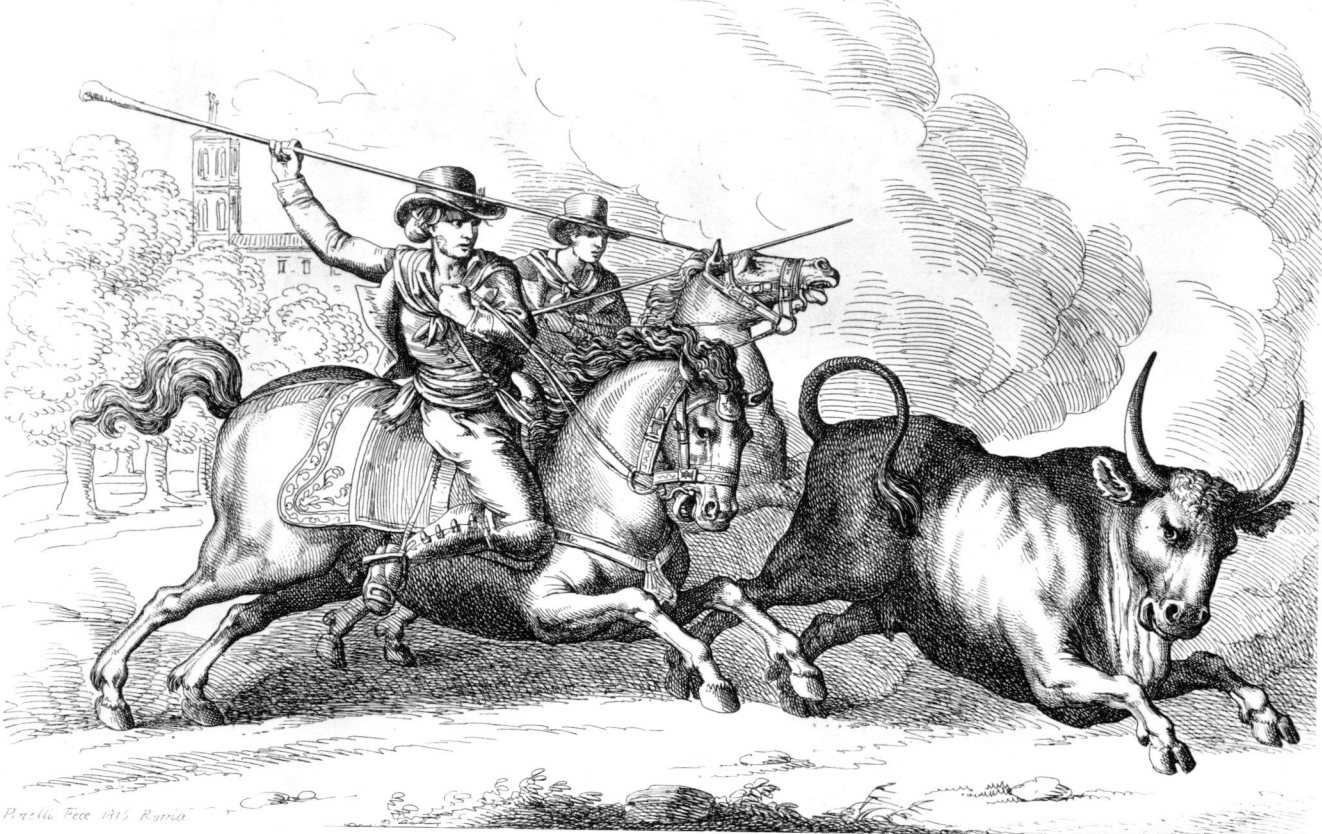

Fig. 105. Assiniboine Hunting Buffalo. National Gallery of Canada 6920; crIV-209.

COURTESY NATIONAL GALLERY OF CANADA, OTTAWA

Fig. 106. Italian youths chasing a bull, a print used by Kane in painting the canvas of which Fig. 105 is a replica. Collection of Mrs. Paul Kane III; crIV-208.

Fig. 107. Cunnawa-bum or "One that looks at the stars" (Cree half-breed girl, Fort Edmonton). ROM912.1.41; CRIV-214.

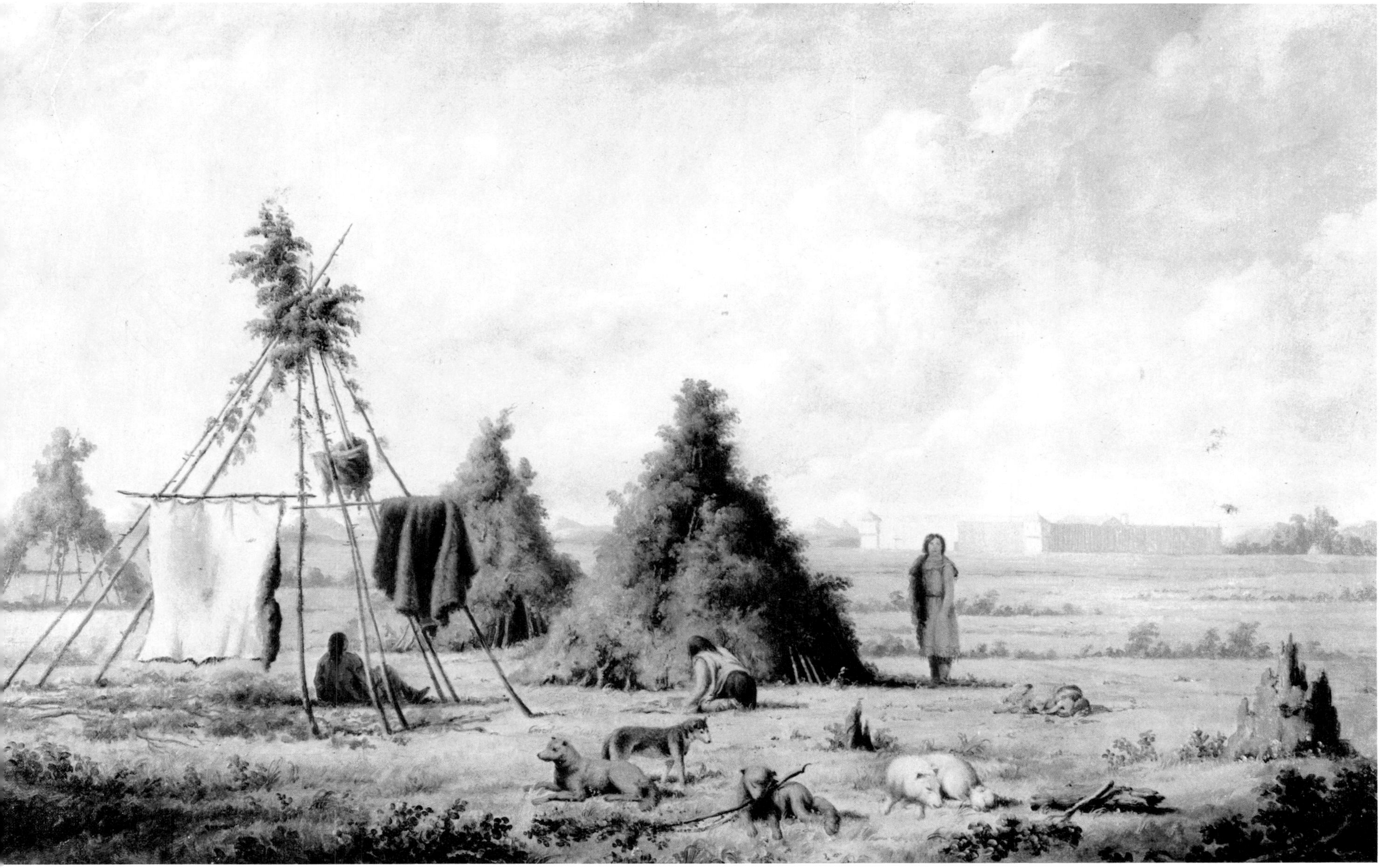

COURTESY ROYAL ONTARIO MUSEUM, TORONTO

Fig. 108. Rocky Mountain House. ROM912.1.57; CRIV-218.

Fig. 109. Mah-Min or "The Feather" (Assiniboin chief, Rocky Mountain House). Montreal Museum of Fine Arts 47.992; crIV-223.

Fig. 110. Buffaloes at Sunset. National Gallery of Canada 6919; crIV-243.

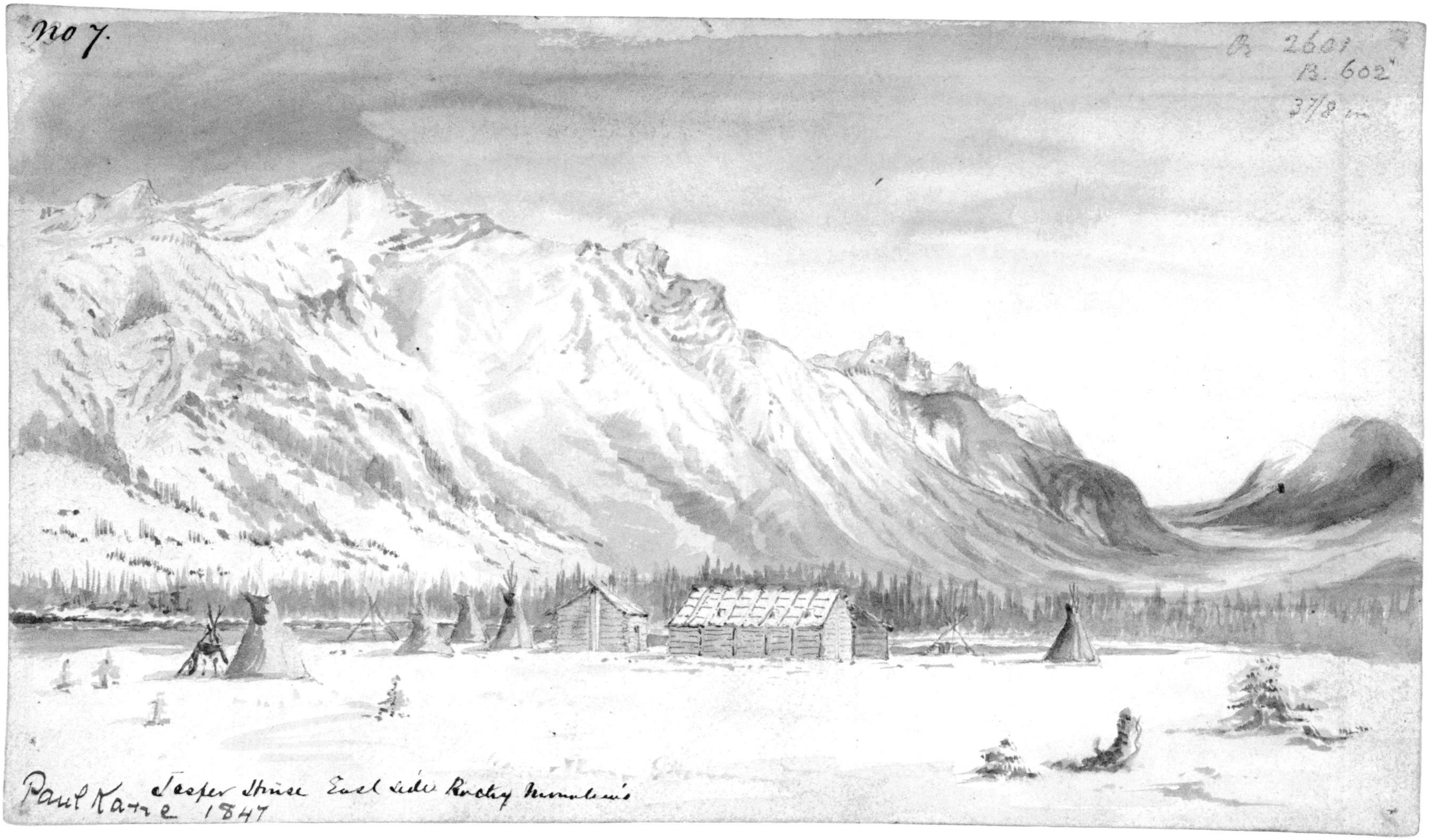

no 7.

Paul Kane Jasper House East side Rocky Mountain's 1847

Fig. 111. Jasper House. Stark pwc25; crIV-250.

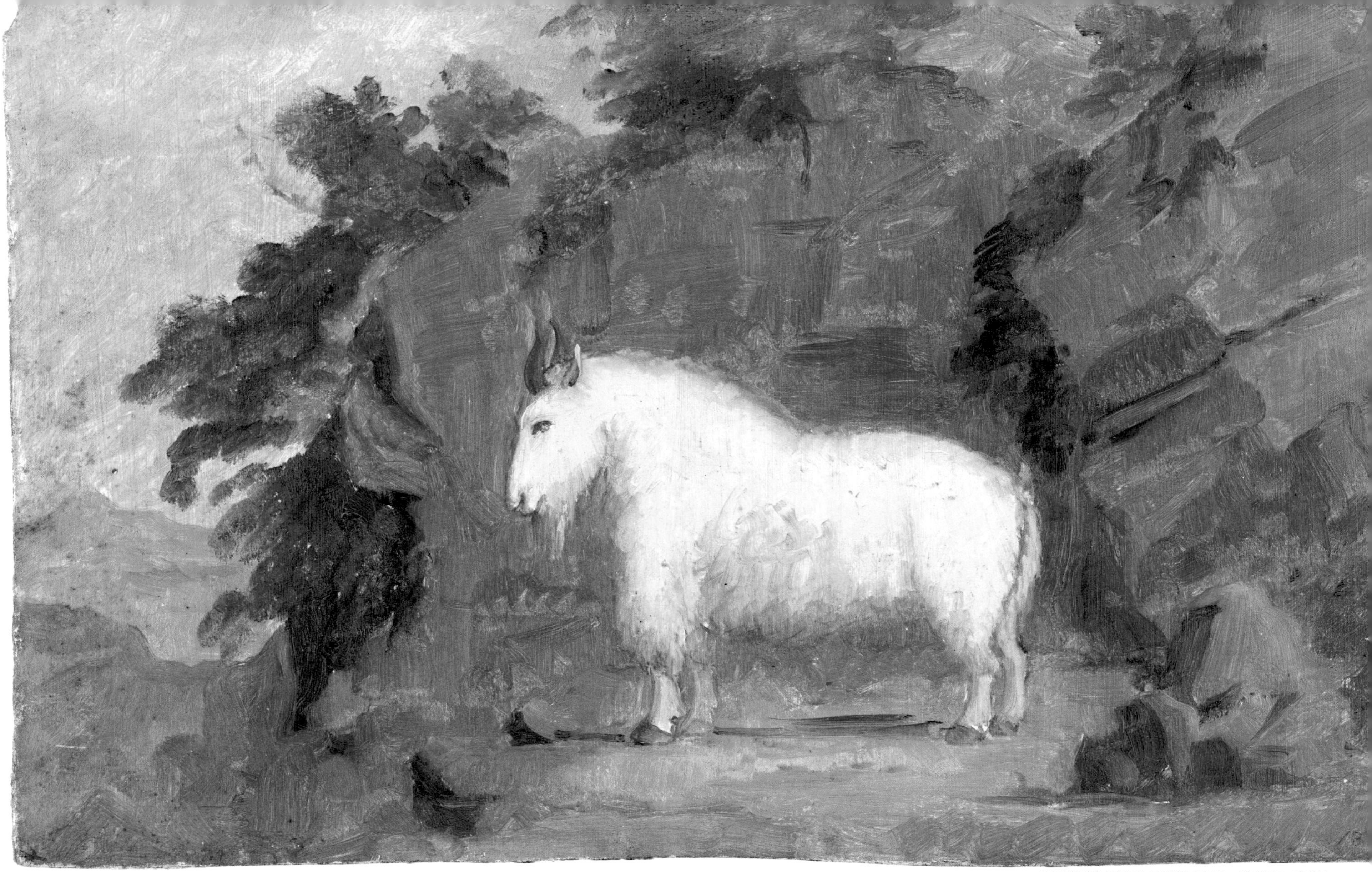

Fig. 114. Rocky Mountain goat. Stark wop18; crIV-262.

Fig. 112. Pack horses, in the mountains. rom946.15.133; crIV-253.

Rocky Mountain Sh

Fig. 113. Bighorn Rocky Mountain ram. Stark wwc98A; crIV-256.

Mount St. Helens with smoke from
the crater hovering in a peculiar form
over the top of the mountain

Plate XLI. Mount St. Helens, with smoke cone. Stark wop10; crIV-461.

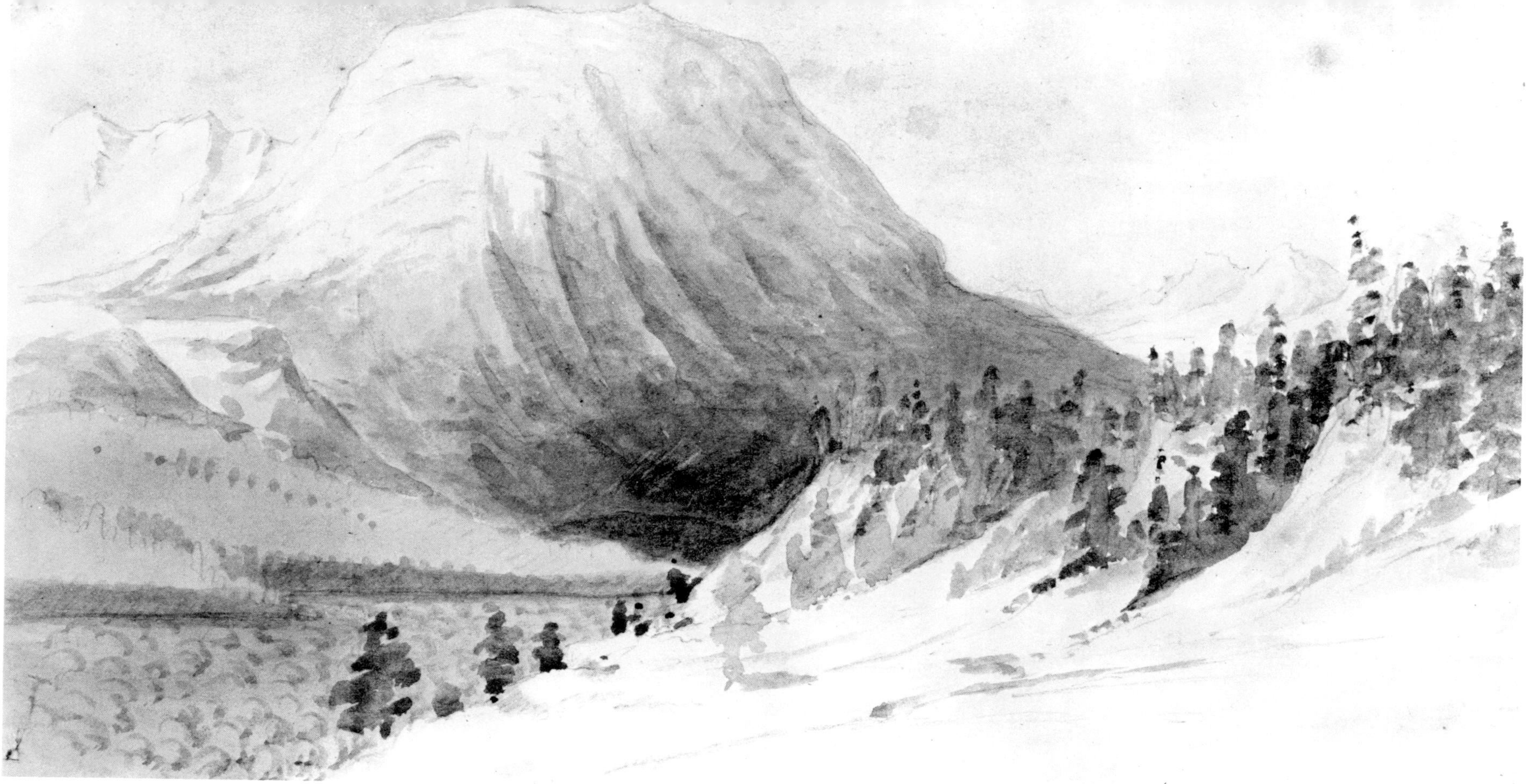

Fig. 115. Athabasca River in the mountains. ROM946.15.238; CRIV-264. COURTESY ROYAL ONTARIO MUSEUM, TORONTO

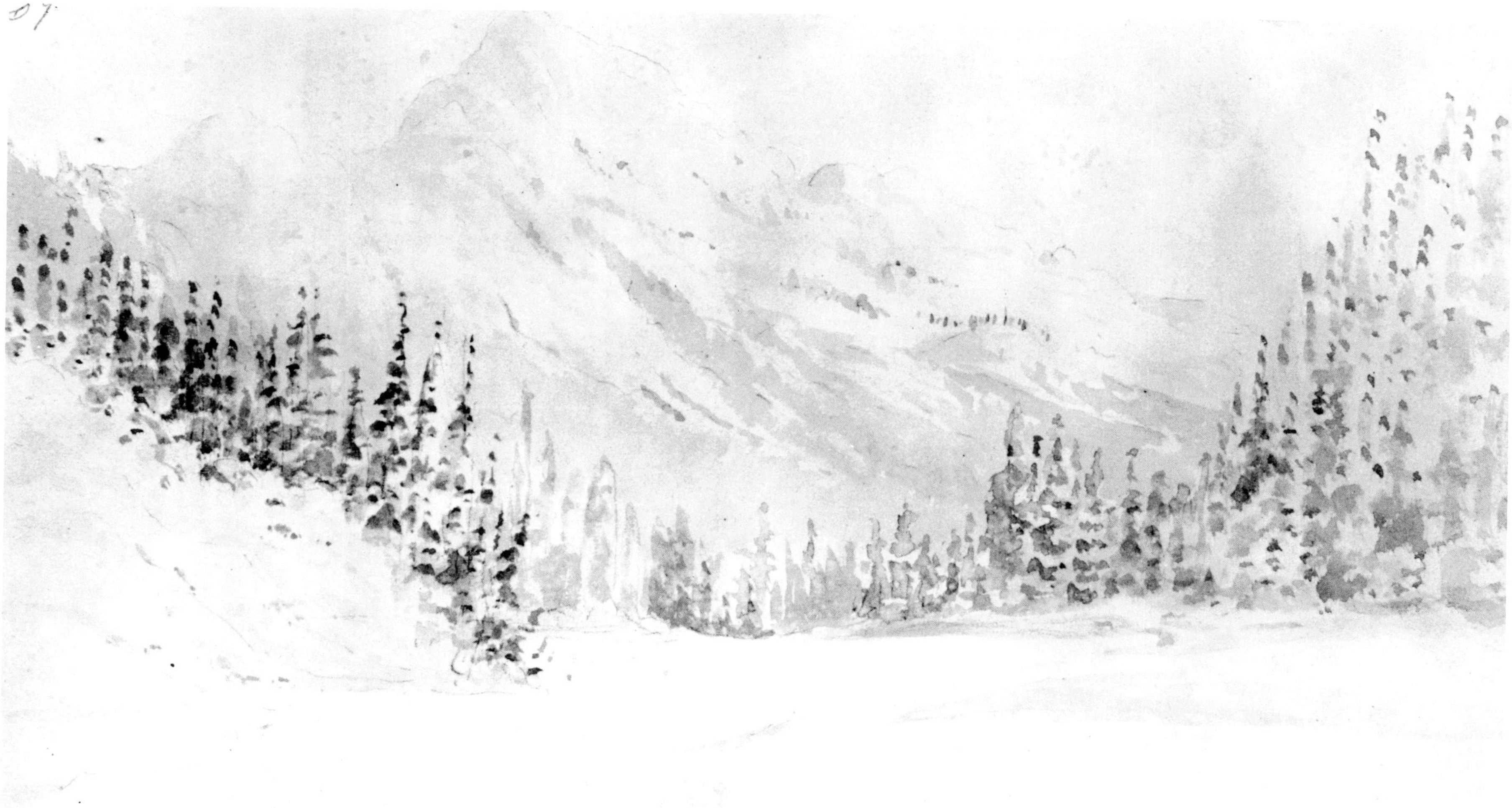

Fig. 116. The Committee's Punch Bowl, Rocky Mountains. ROM946.15.239; CRIV-269. COURTESY ROYAL ONTARIO MUSEUM, TORONTO

COURTESY ROYAL ONTARIO MUSEUM, TORONTO

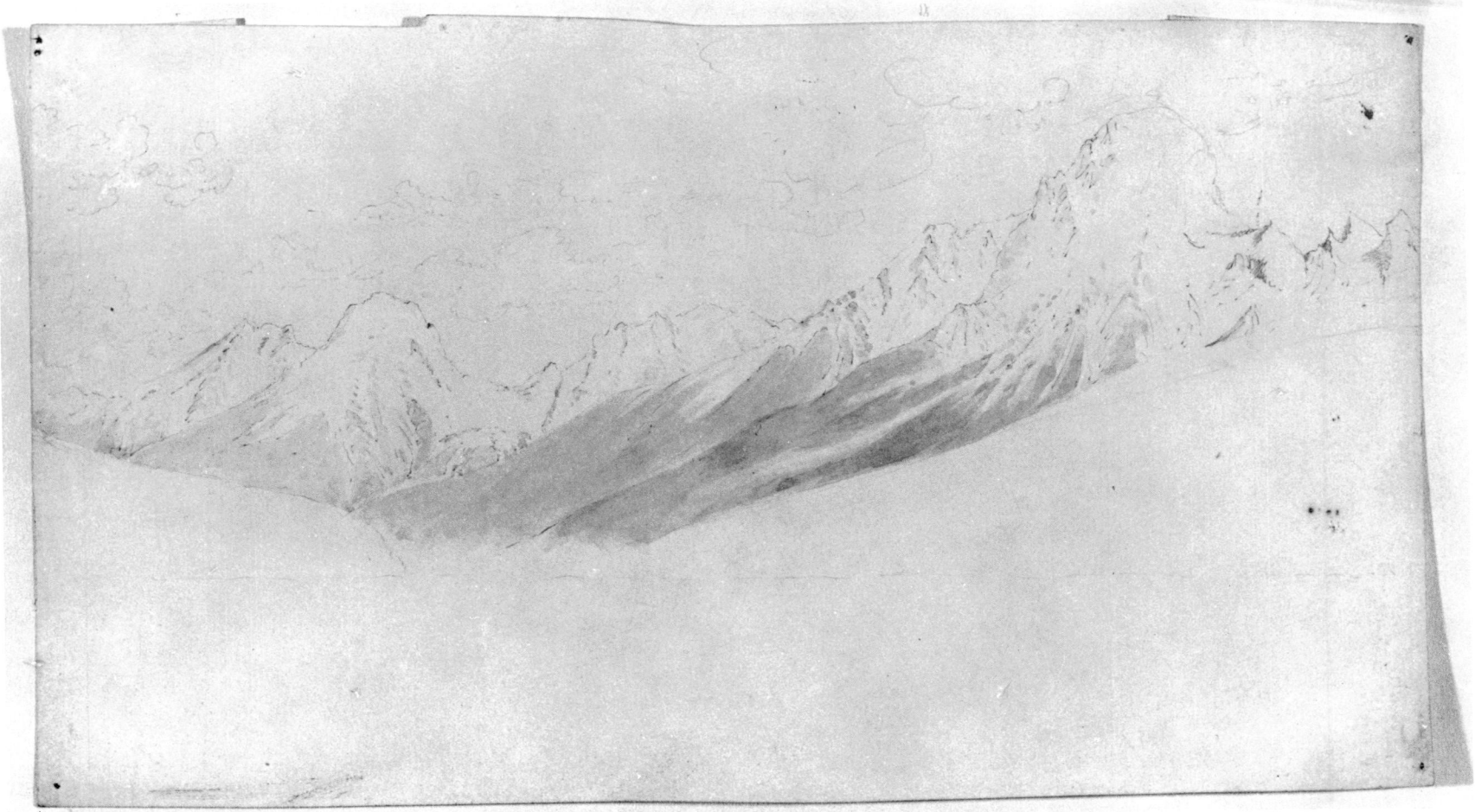

Fig. 117. Mountain peaks as seen from Boat Encampment, Columbia River. ROM946.15.236; CRIV-277.

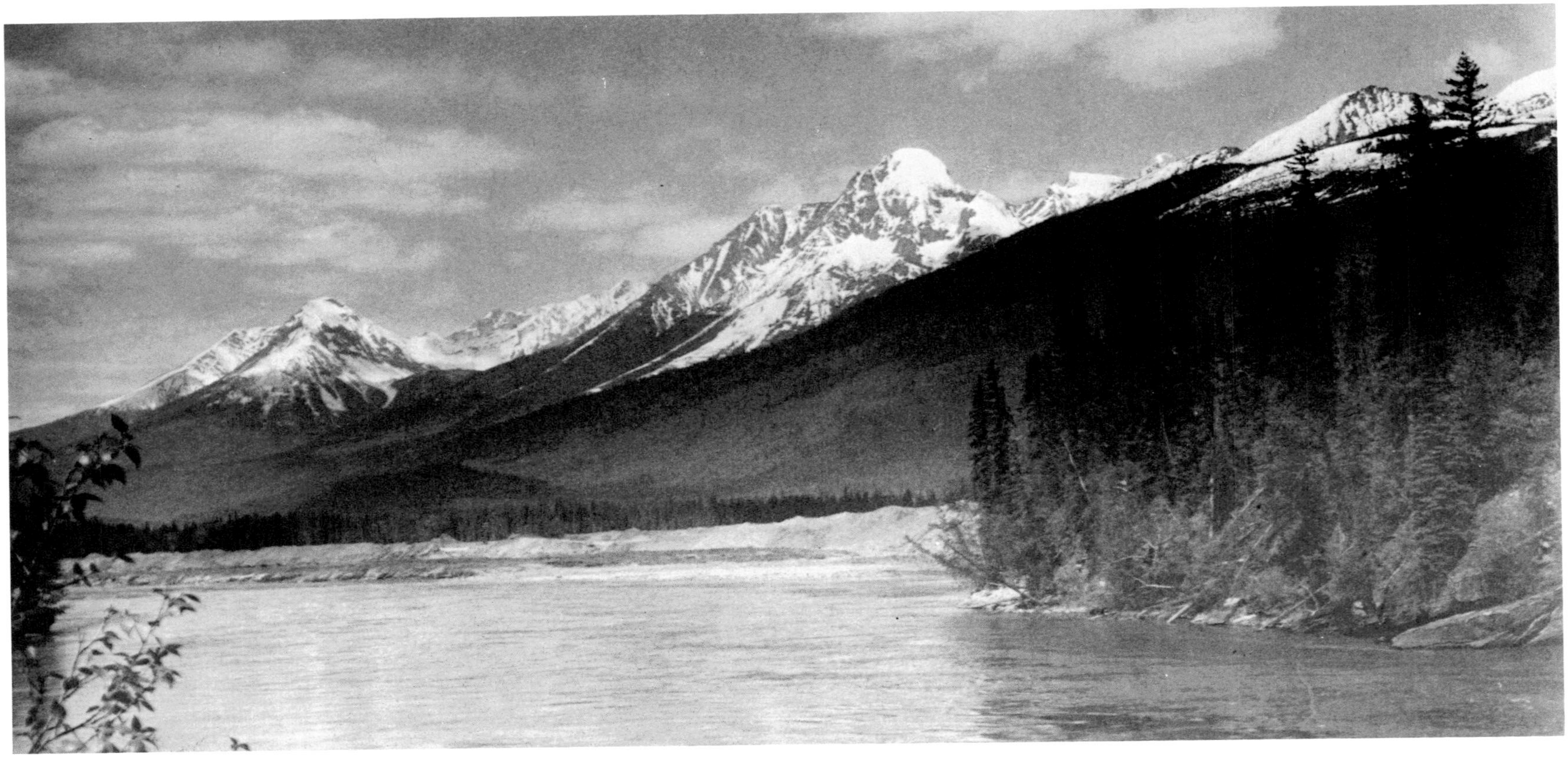

Fig. 118. A photograph of the view sketched by Kane in Fig. 117. Photograph by Mrs. E. Dickey, Revelstoke, B.C.

Fig. 119. The Little Dalles, Columbia River. Stark wwc6; crIV-286.

COURTESY ROYAL ONTARIO MUSEUM, TORONTO

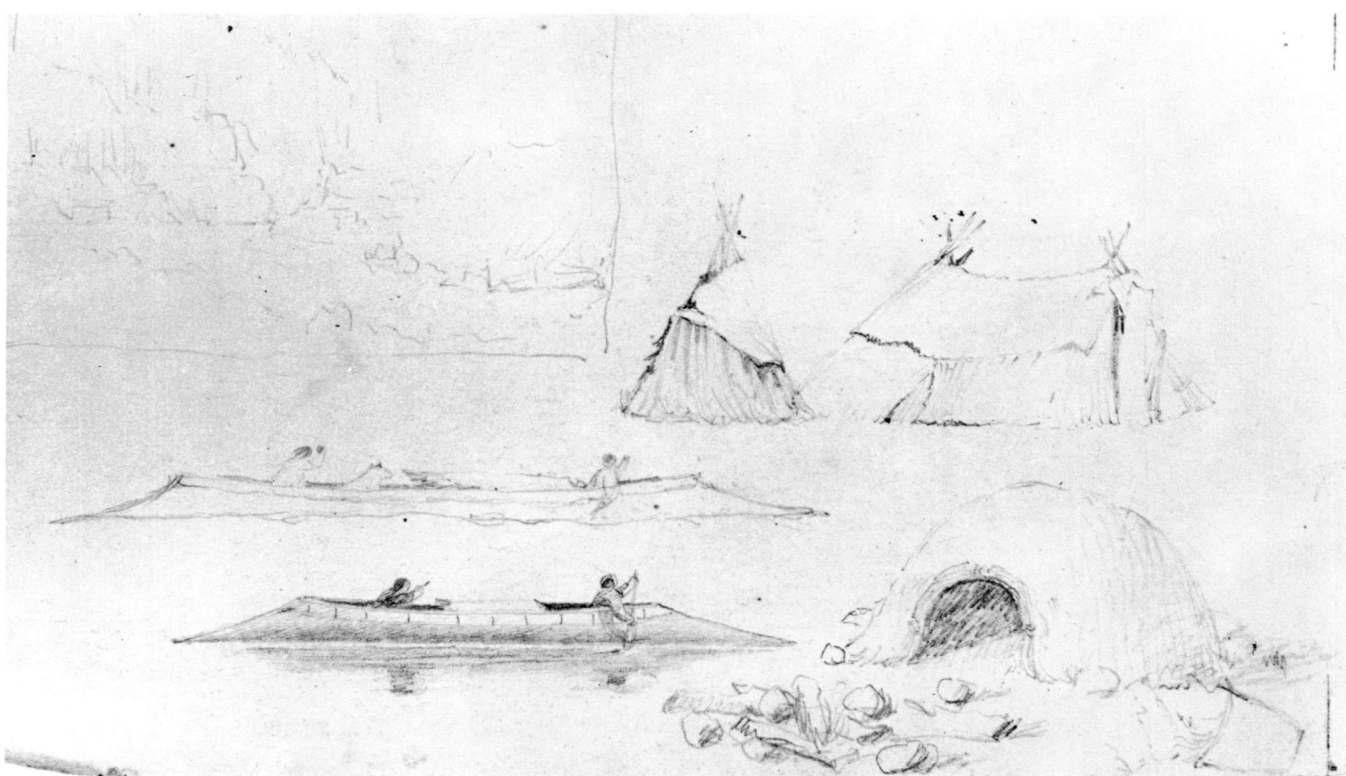

Fig. 120. Studies among the Kutenai Indians, Columbia River. ROM946.15.202; CRIV-291.

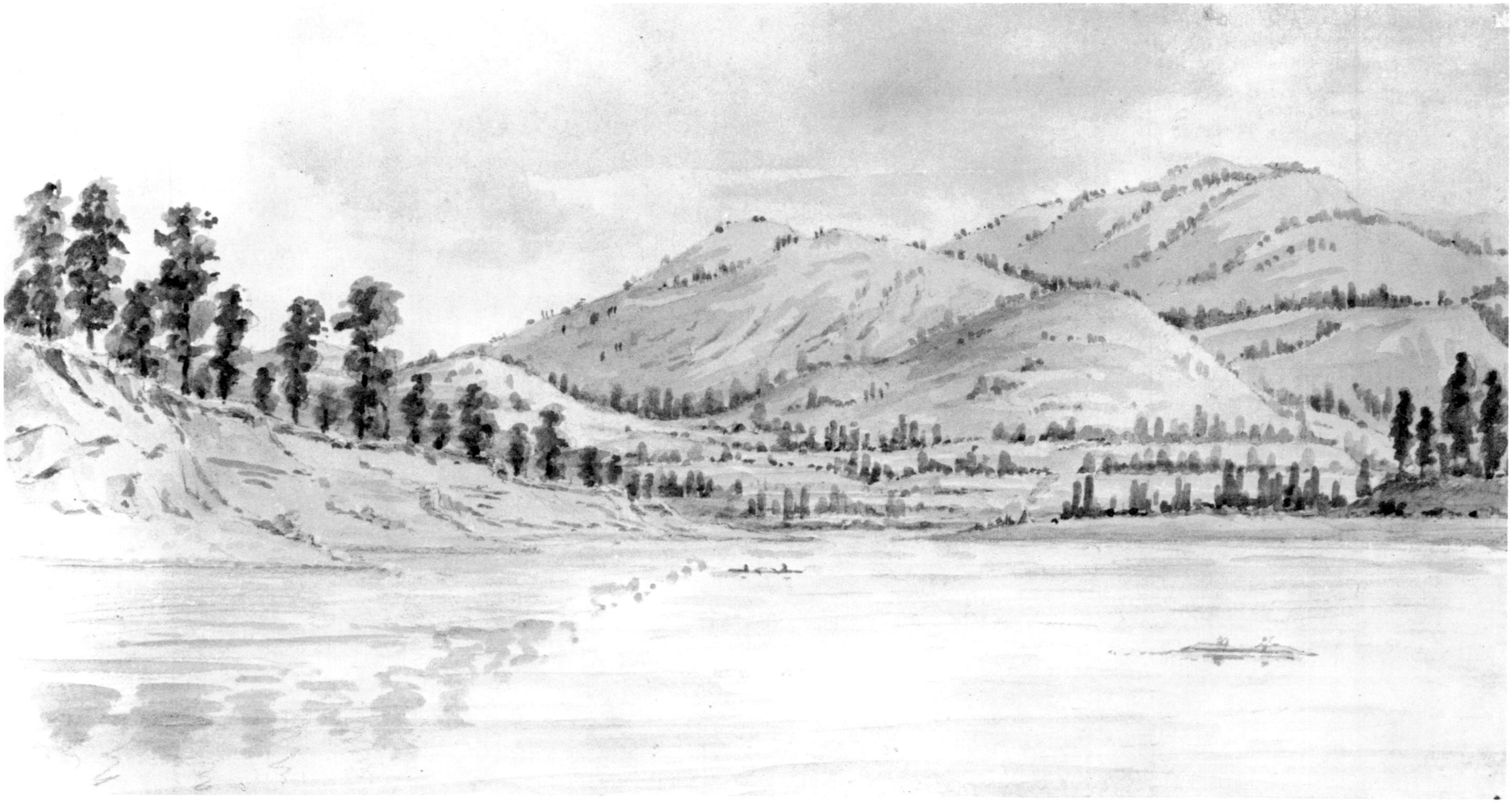

COURTESY ROYAL ONTARIO MUSEUM, TORONTO

Fig. 121. Columbia River near Grand Rapids. ROM946.15.174; CRIV-290.

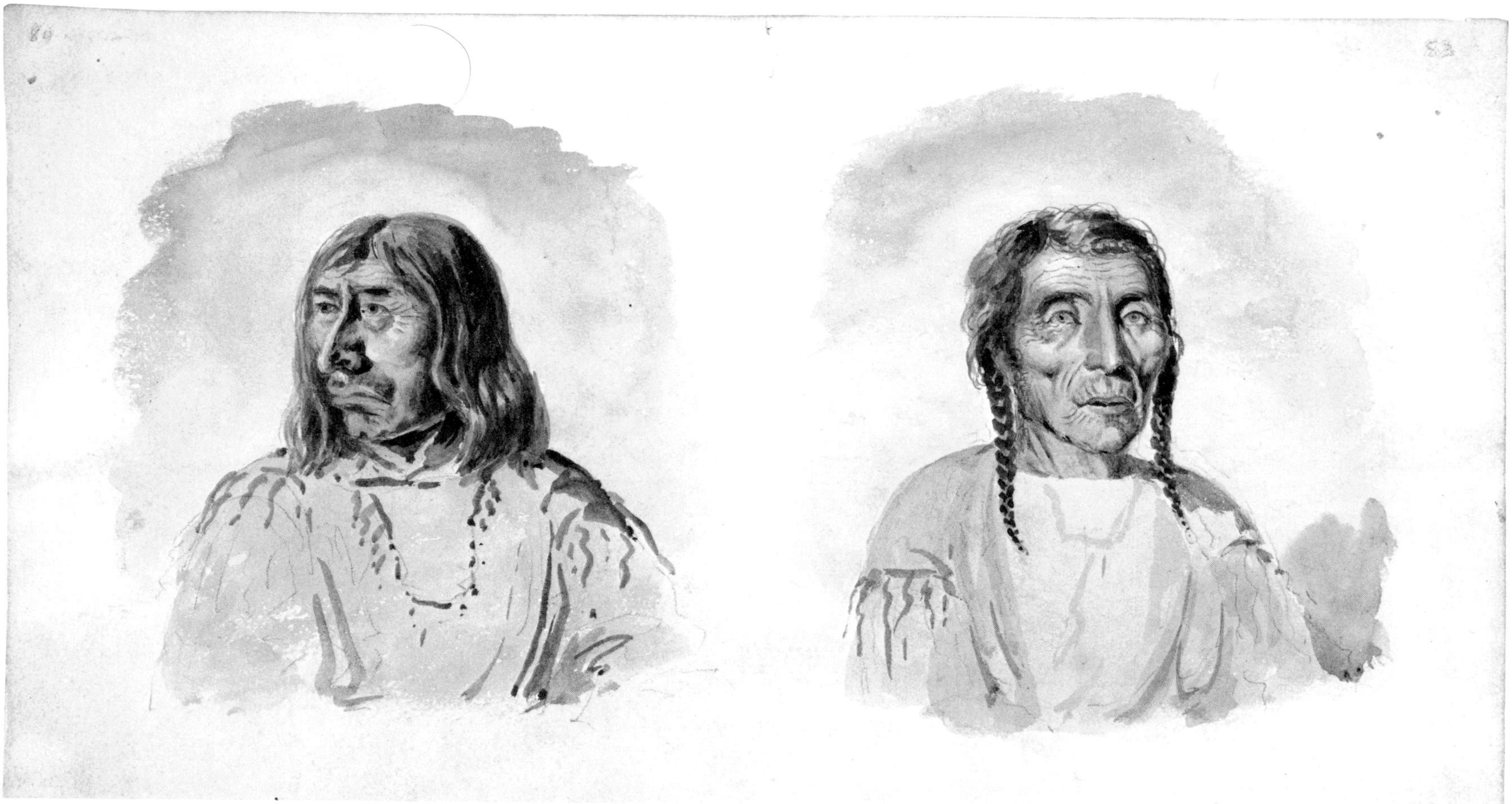

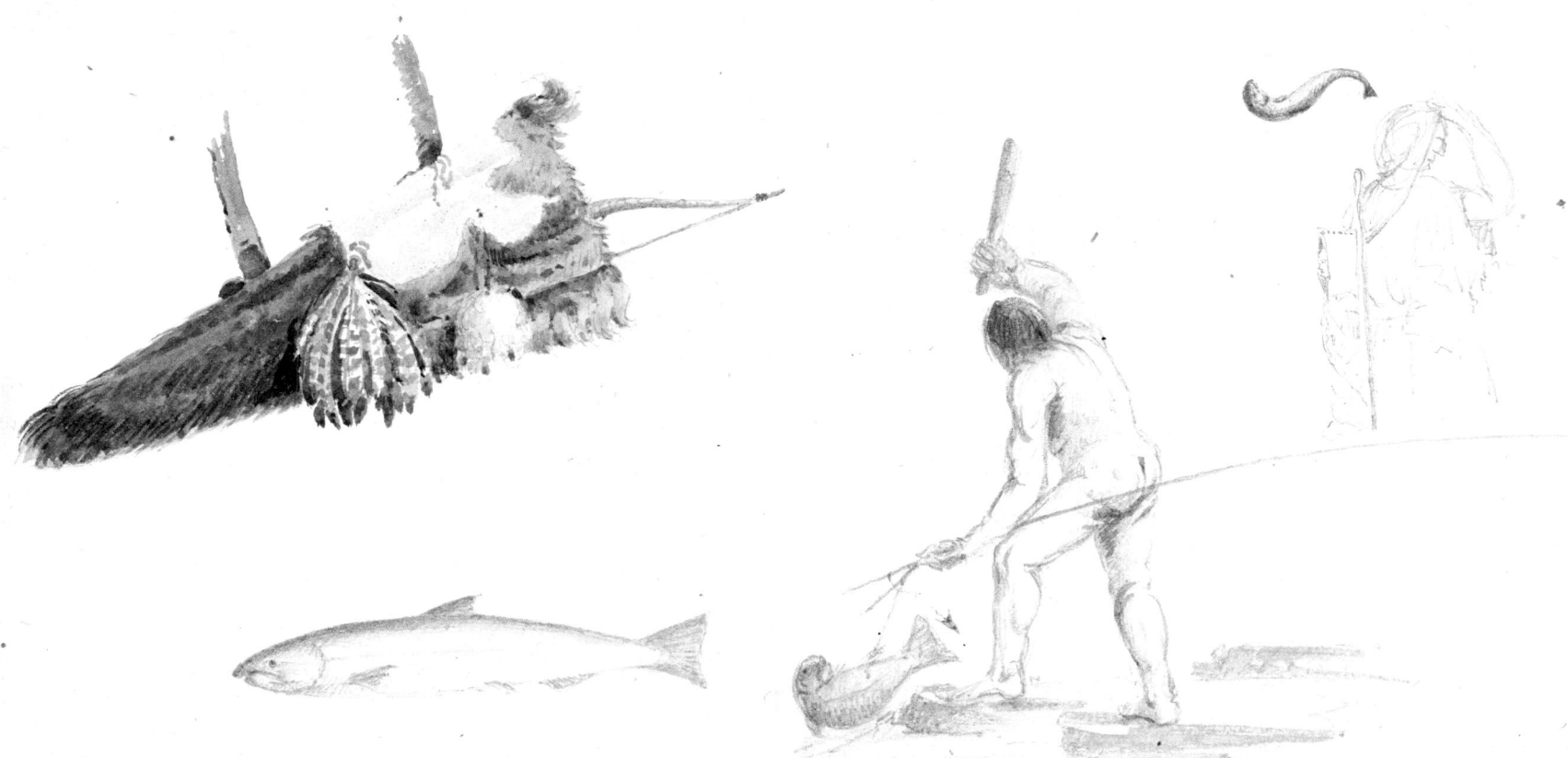

Fig. 122. Ask-a-weelish (*left*) and See-pays or "Chief of the Waters" (*right*), Fort Colvile. Stark WWC80; CRIV-288, 292.

COURTESY STARK FOUNDATION, ORANGE, TEXAS

Fig. 123. Catching salmon on the Columbia River. Stark WWC87; CRIV-306.

COURTESY STARK FOUNDATION, ORANGE, TEXAS

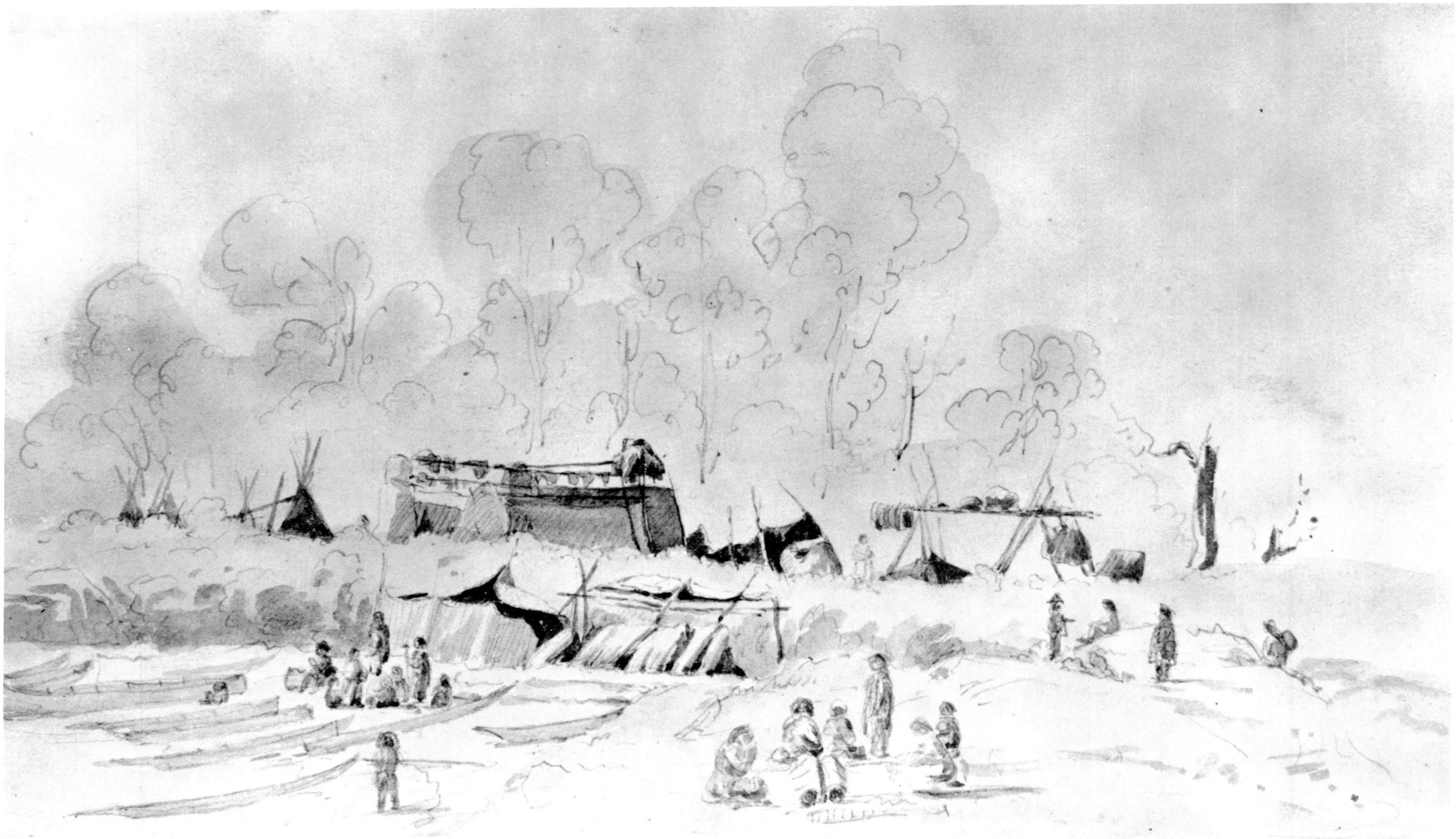

COURTESY ROYAL ONTARIO MUSEUM, TORONTO

Fig. 124. Indians smoking salmon near the Columbia River. ROM946.15.206; CRIV-309.

COURTESY NATIONAL GALLERY OF CANADA, OTTAWA

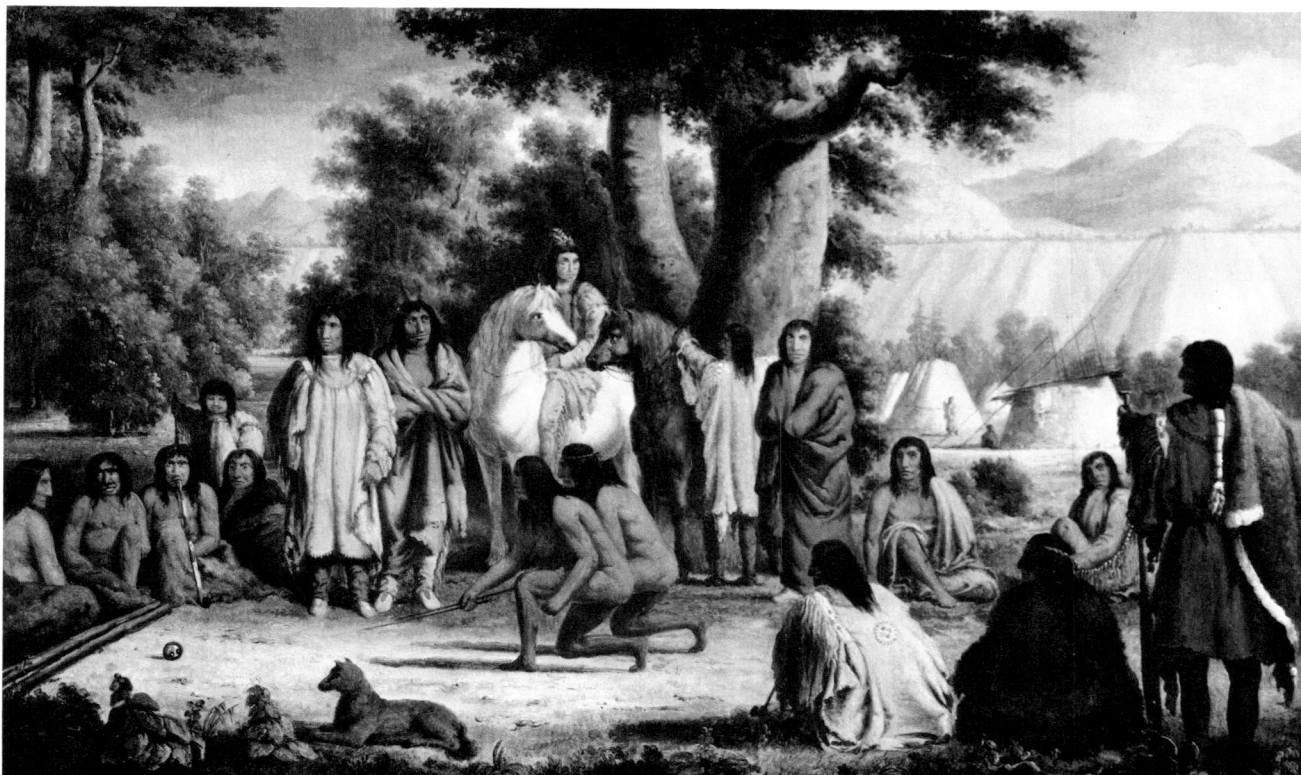

COURTESY STARK FOUNDATION, ORANGE, TEXAS

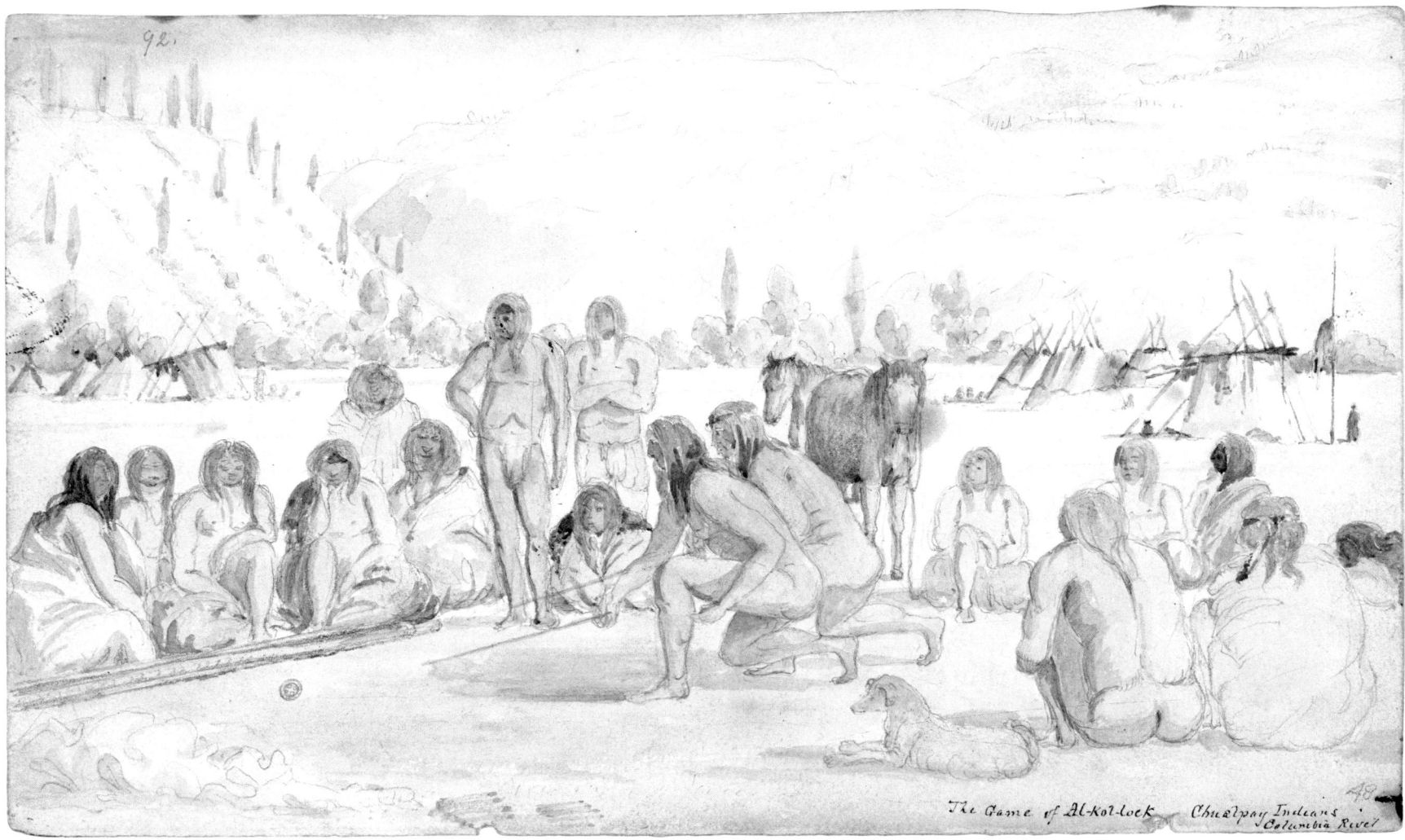

Fig. 125. The Chualpays game of Al-kol-lock, Fort Colvile. Stark wwc78; crIV-316.

Fig. 126. Indians Playing at Alcoloh (Al-kol-lock).
National Gallery of Canada 60; crIV-321.

Fig. 127. Chualpays scalp dance, Fort Colvile. Stark wwc31; crIV-322.

COURTESY STARK FOUNDATION, ORANGE, TEXAS

Fig. 128. Painted faces of Chualpays women dancers, Fort Colvile. Stark wwc72; crIV-324.

COURTESY STARK FOUNDATION, ORANGE, TEXAS

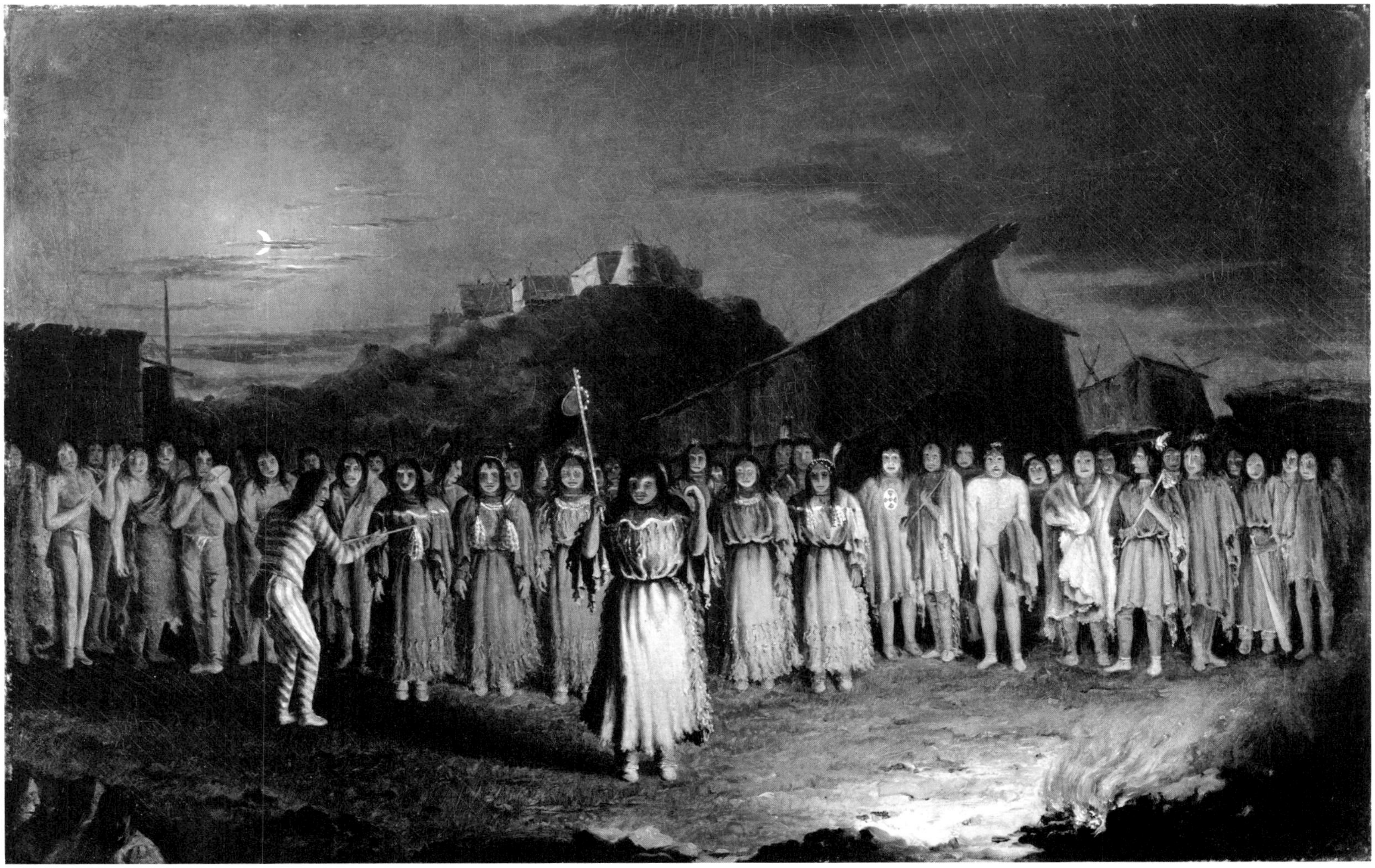

COURTESY NATIONAL GALLERY OF CANADA, OTTAWA

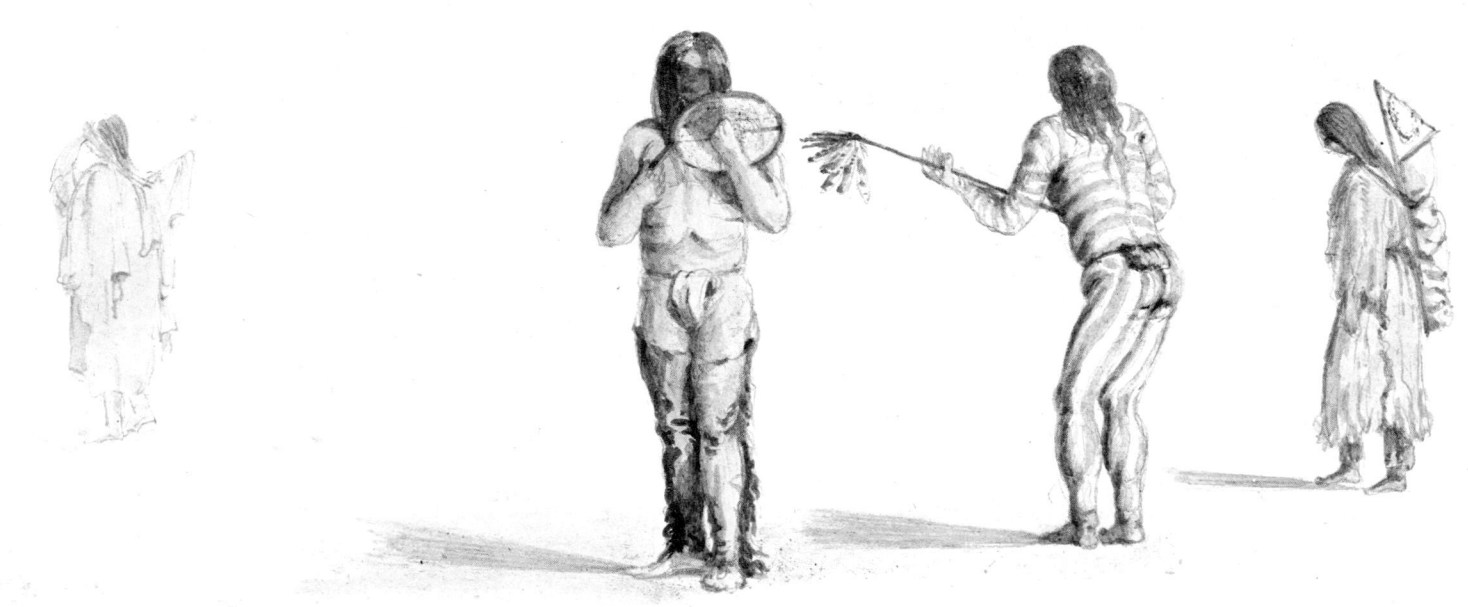

Fig. 129. Scalp Dance by Spokane (?) Indians. National Gallery of Canada 103; CRIV-329.

COURTESY STARK FOUNDATION, ORANGE, TEXAS

Fig. 130. Studies of a Chualpays scalp dance, with a medicine man. Stark WWC63; CRIV-327.

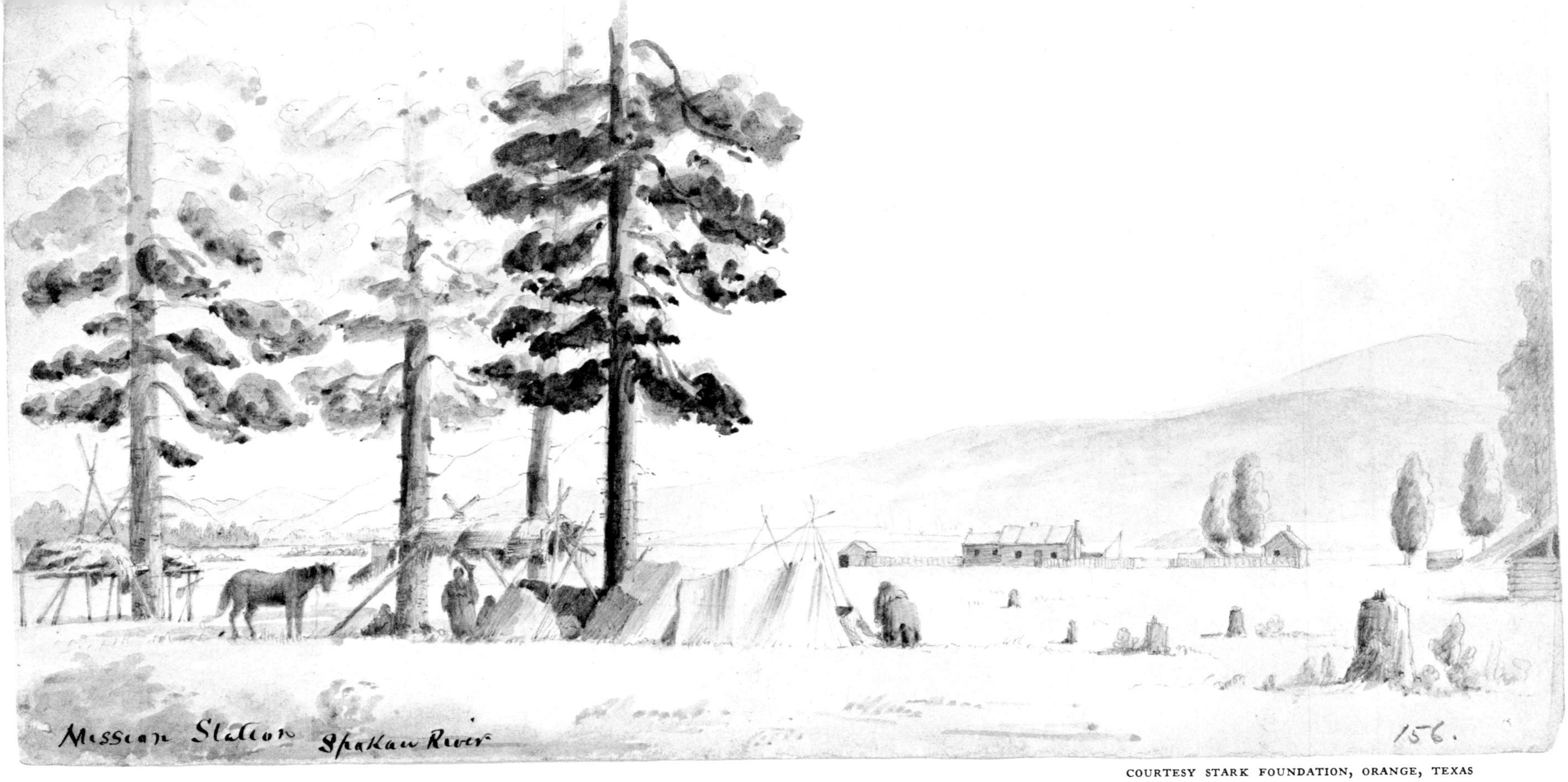

Mission Station Spokan River

156.

Fig. 131. Mission station of the Rev. Elkanah Walker and the Rev. Cushing Eells, Tshimakain. Stark wwc69; crIV-336.

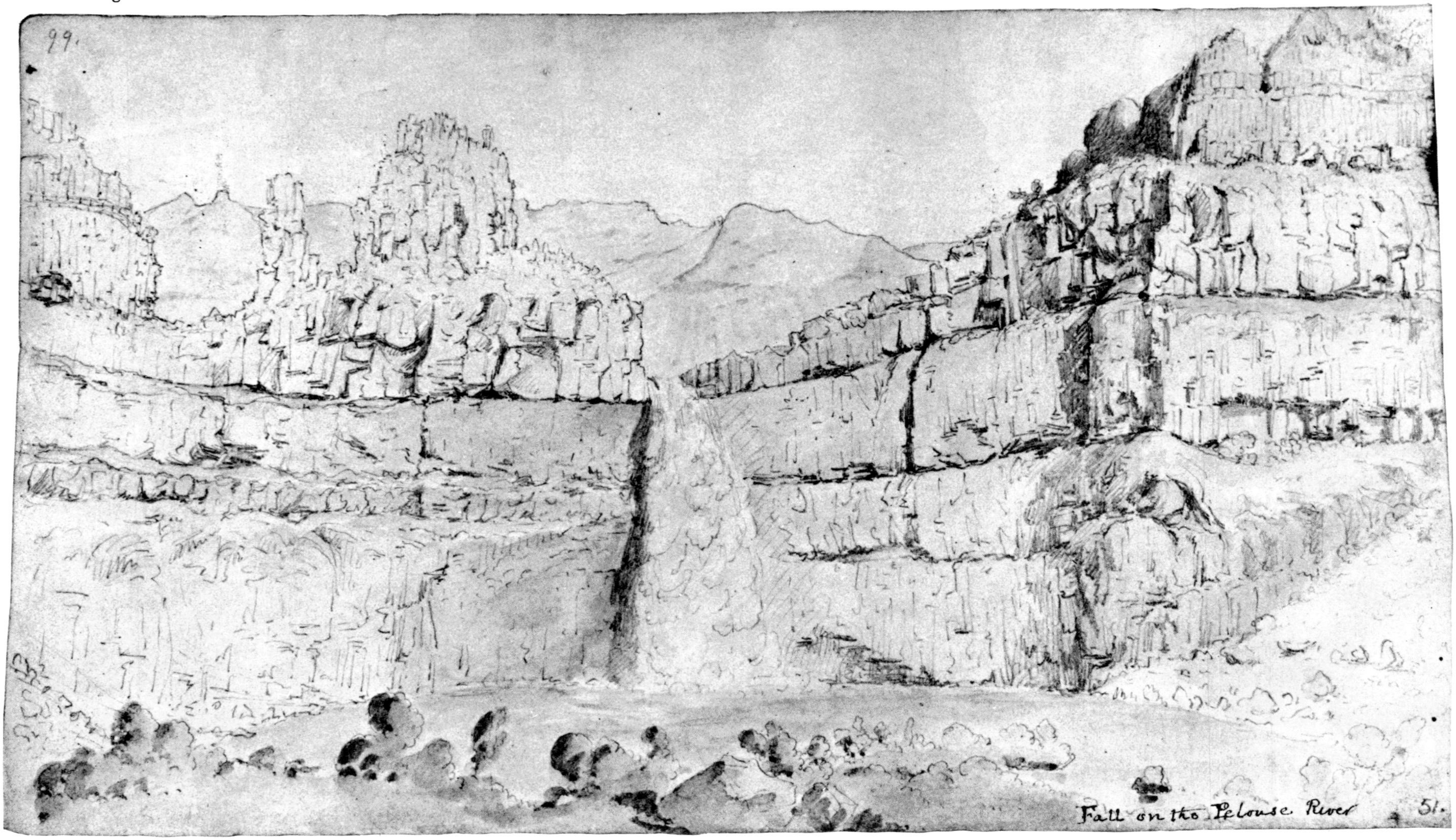

99.

Fall on the Pelouse River

51.

Fig. 132. Lower falls, Pelouse River. Stark wwc49; crIV-343.

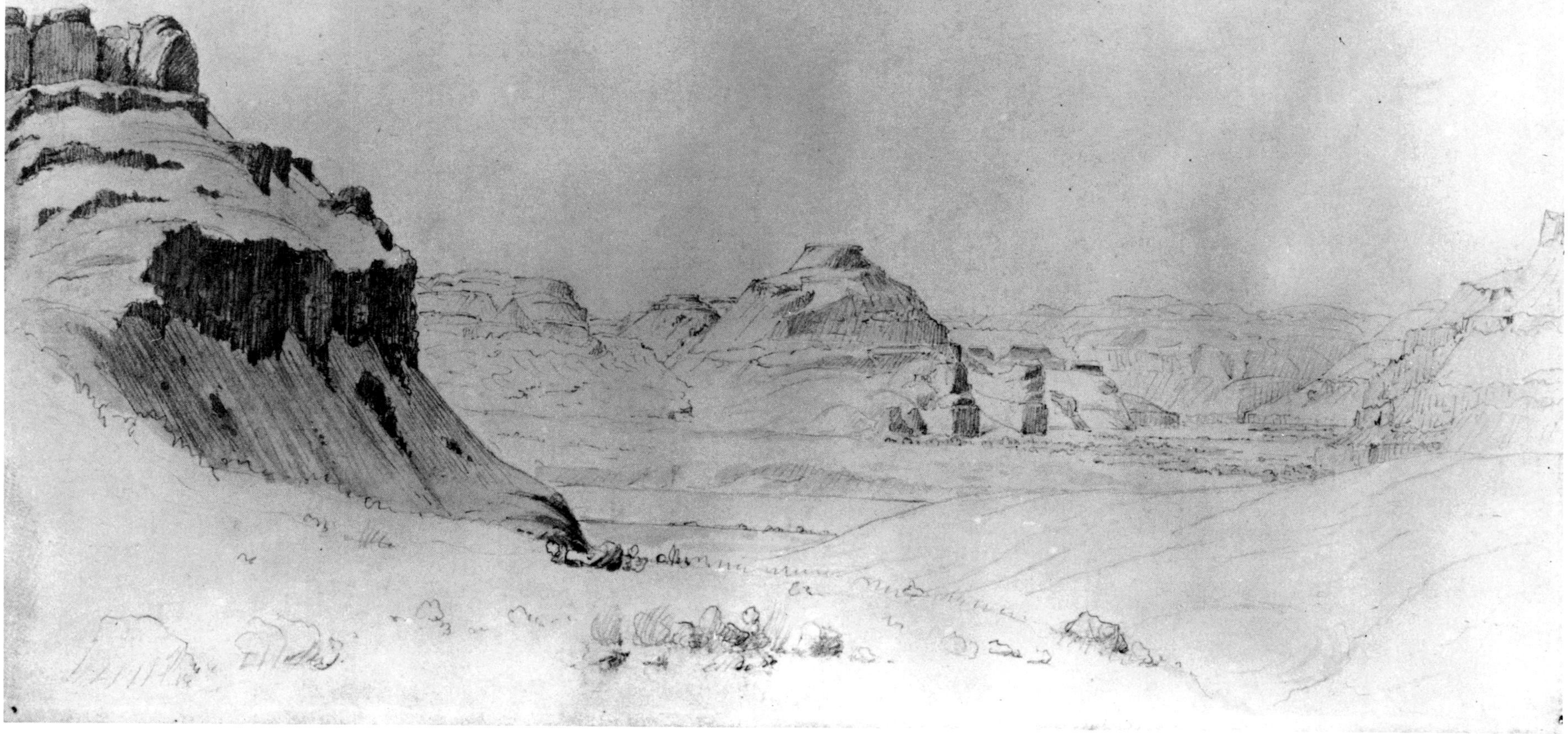

COURTESY ROYAL ONTARIO MUSEUM, TORONTO

Fig. 133. A river view near Fort Walla Walla. ROM946.15.186; CRIV-350.

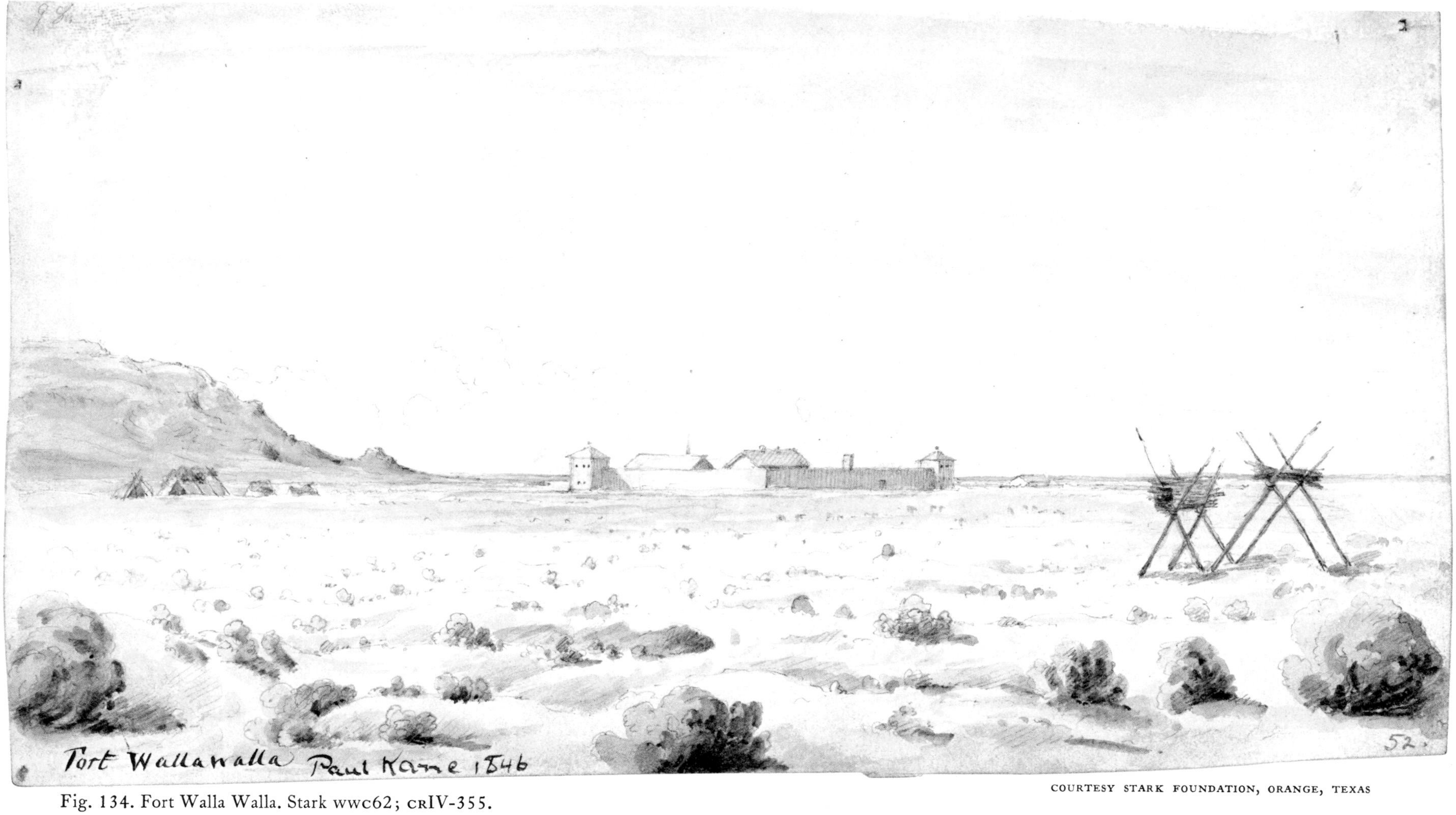
Fort Wallawalla Paul Kane 1846
52

COURTESY STARK FOUNDATION, ORANGE, TEXAS

Fig. 134. Fort Walla Walla. Stark WWC62; CRIV-355.

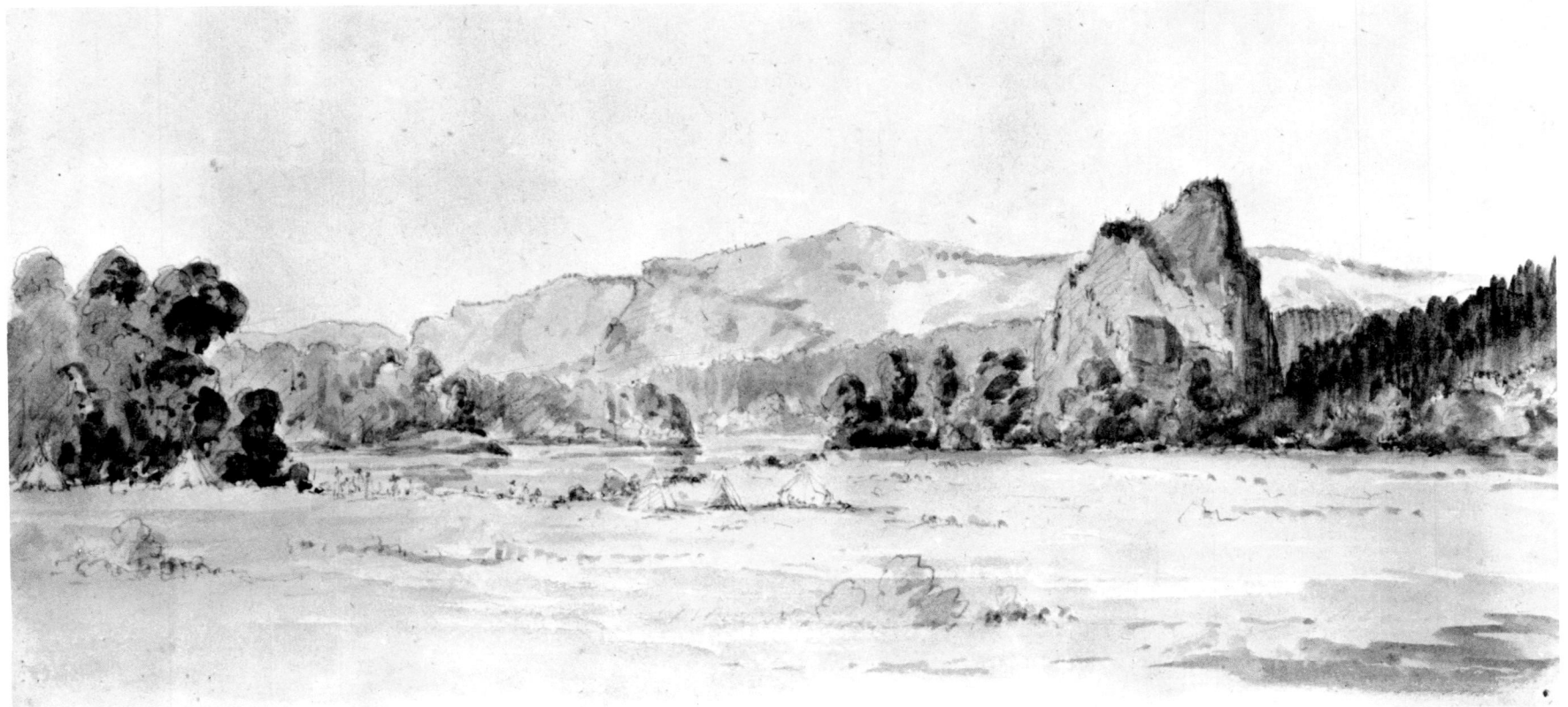

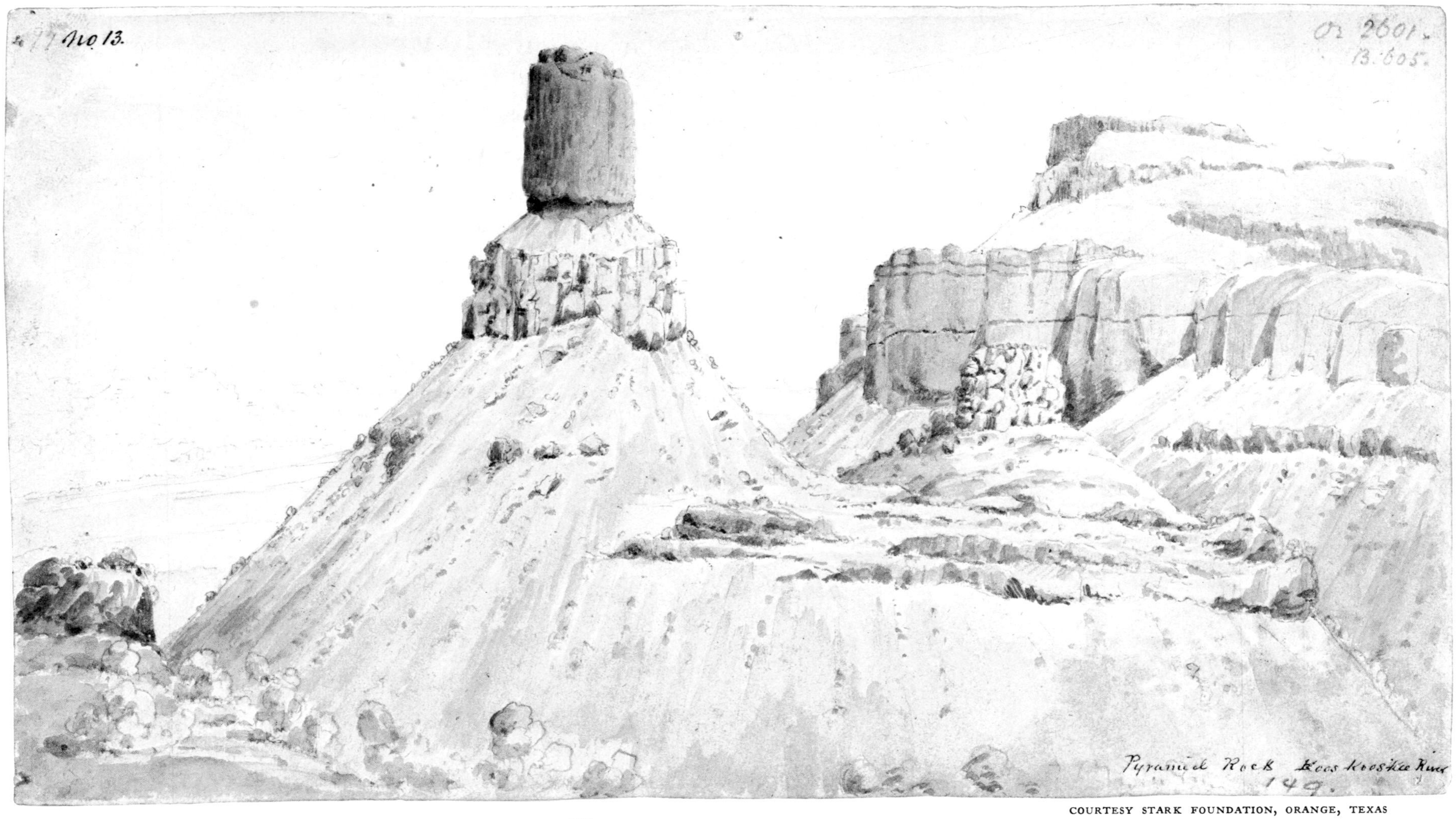
no 13.
Pyramid Rock Koos Kooskee River
149.

COURTESY STARK FOUNDATION, ORANGE, TEXAS

Fig. 135. Chimney Rocks, Columbia River. Stark WWC65; CRIV-358.

COURTESY ROYAL ONTARIO MUSEUM, TORONTO

Fig. 136. Landscape, near Fort Walla Walla (?). ROM946.15.173; CRIV-357.

Burial Canoes

170

Plate XLII. Chinook grave, Cowlitz River. Stark wwc29; crIV-475.

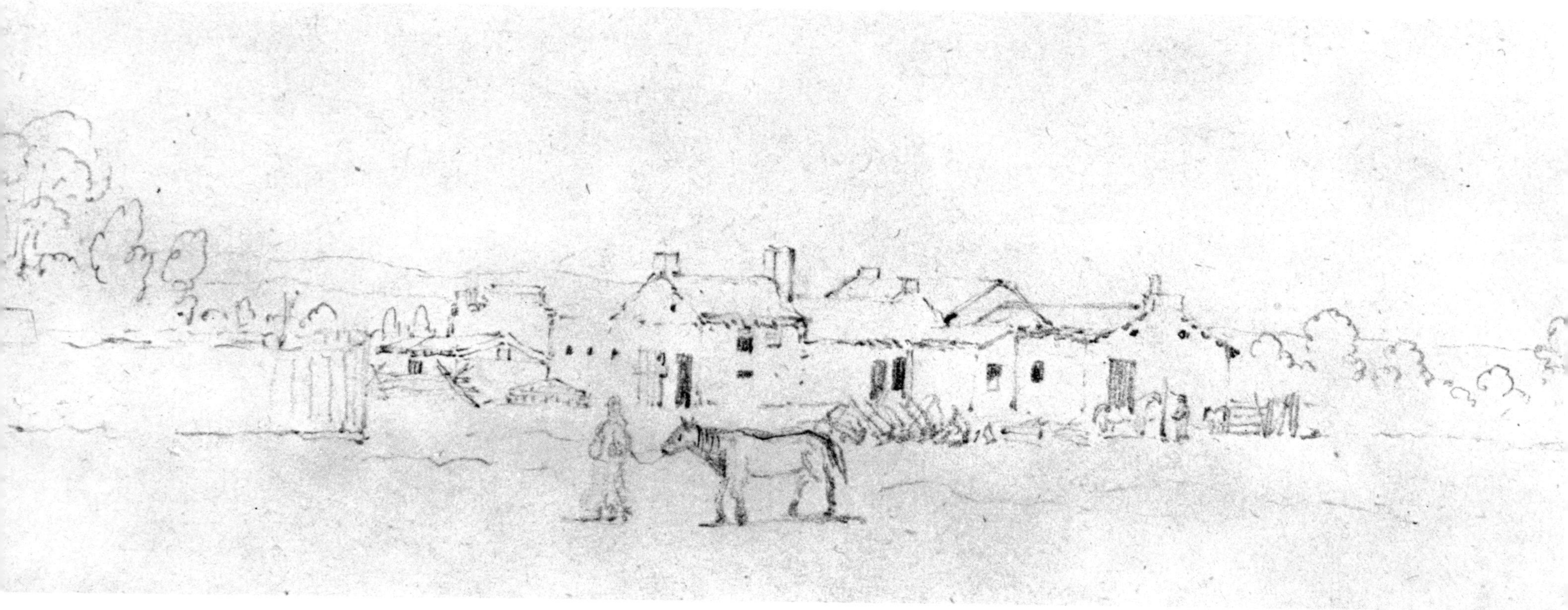

Fig. 137. The Whitman Mission, Waiilatpu. ROM946.15.318; CRIV-362.

COURTESY ROYAL ONTARIO MUSEUM, TORONTO

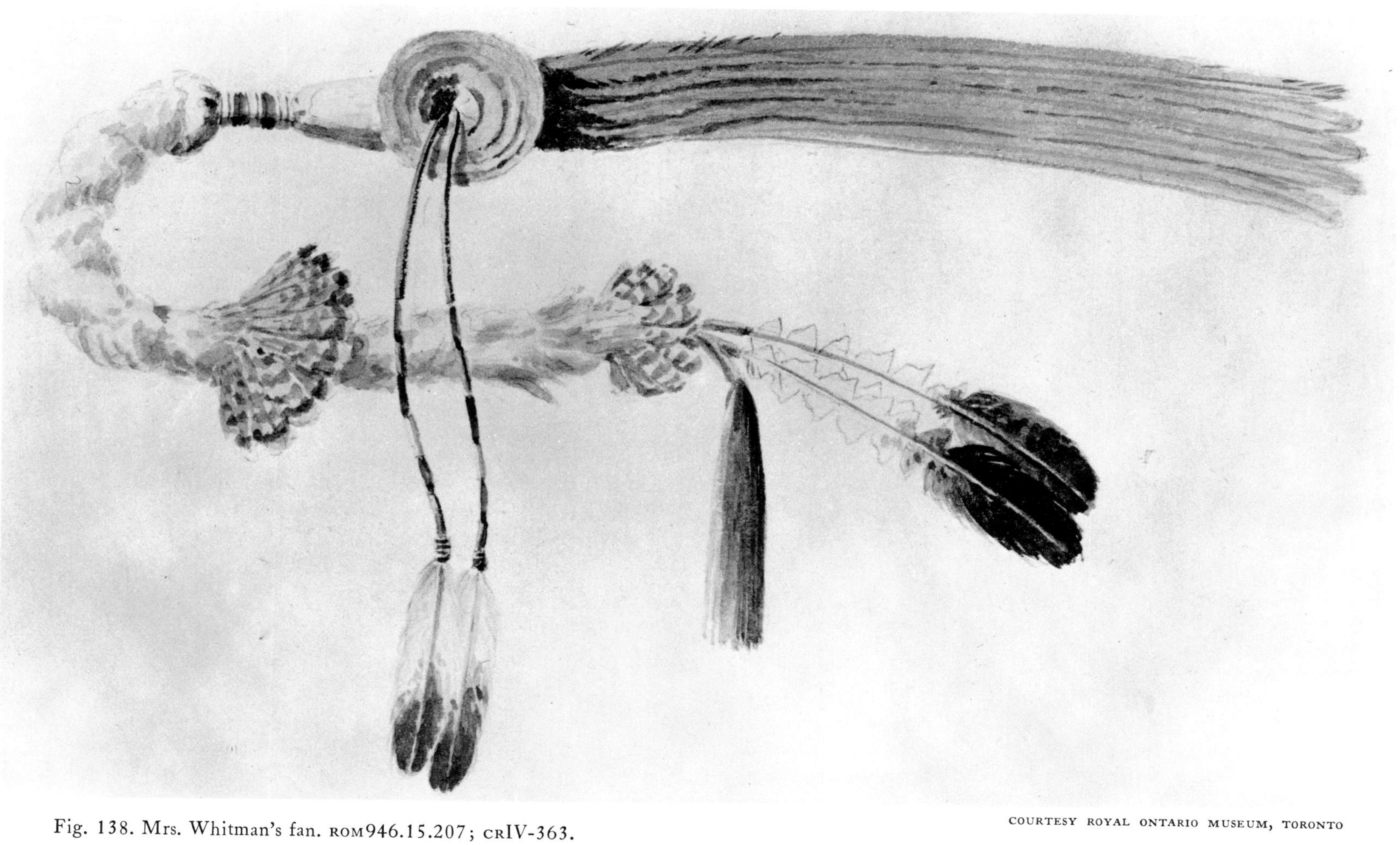

Fig. 138. Mrs. Whitman's fan. ROM946.15.207; CRIV-363.

COURTESY ROYAL ONTARIO MUSEUM, TORONTO

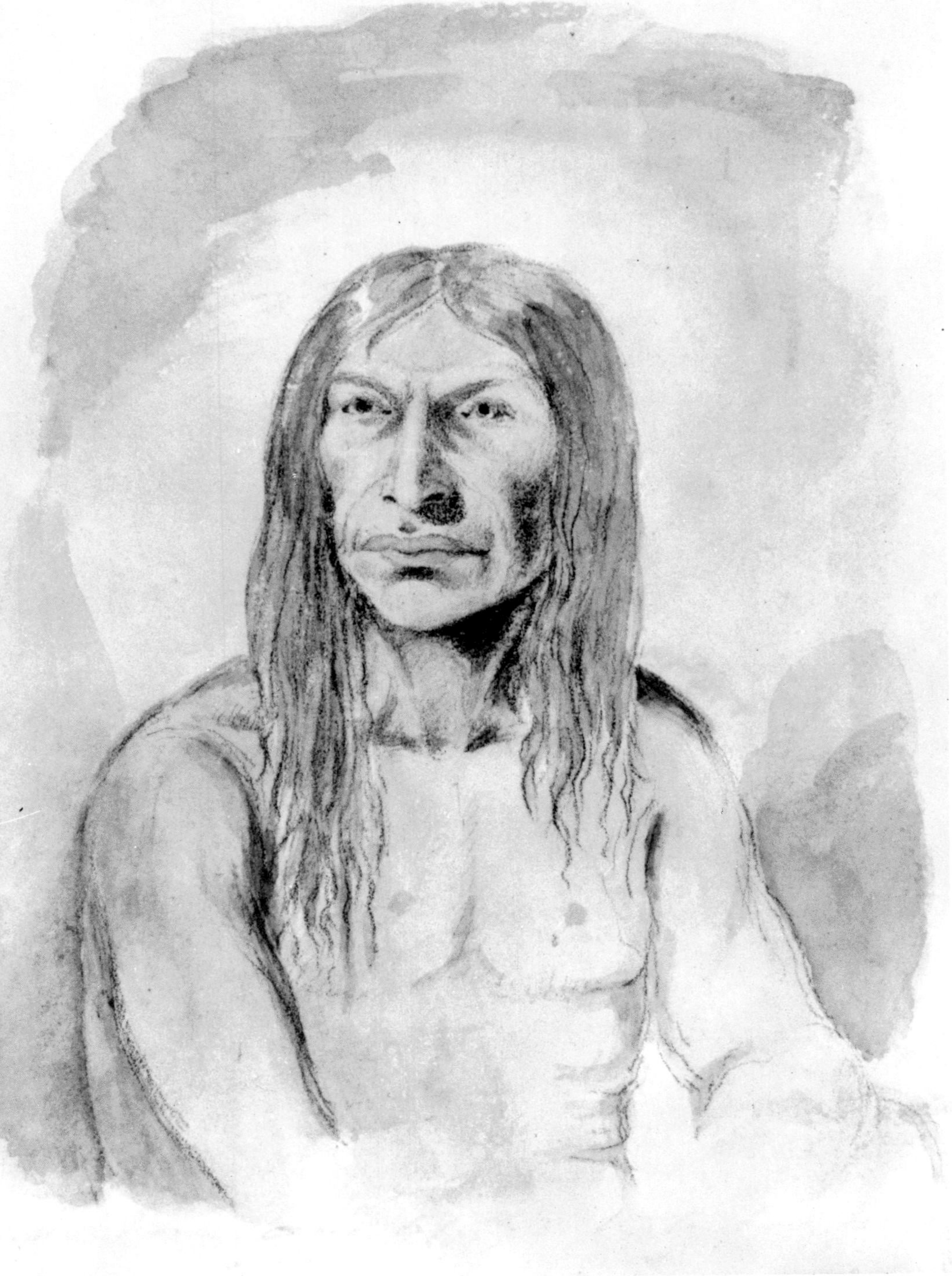

COURTESY PEABODY MUSEUM, HARVARD UNIVERSITY

Fig. 139. To-ma-kus, a Cayuse, at the Whitman Mission. Peabody Museum, Harvard University—Bushnell 41-72/393; CRIV-365.

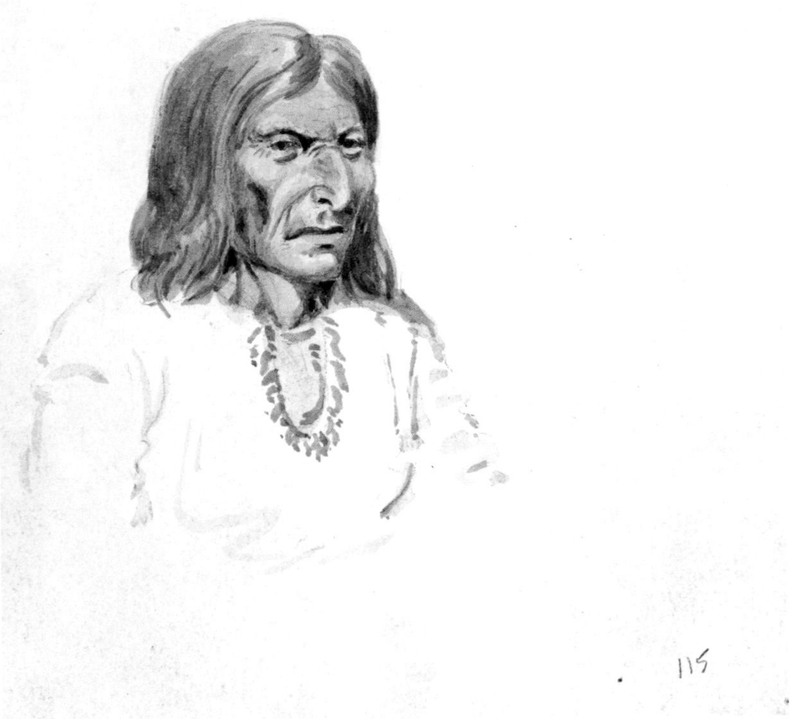

COURTESY STARK FOUNDATION, ORANGE, TEXAS

Fig. 140. Til-au-kite or "Act of Lightning," a Cayuse, Whitman Mission. Stark WWC59; CRIV-367.

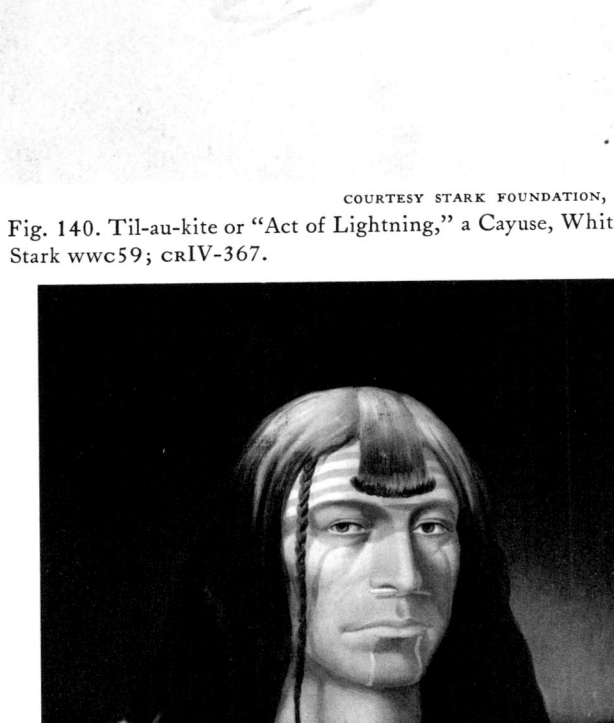

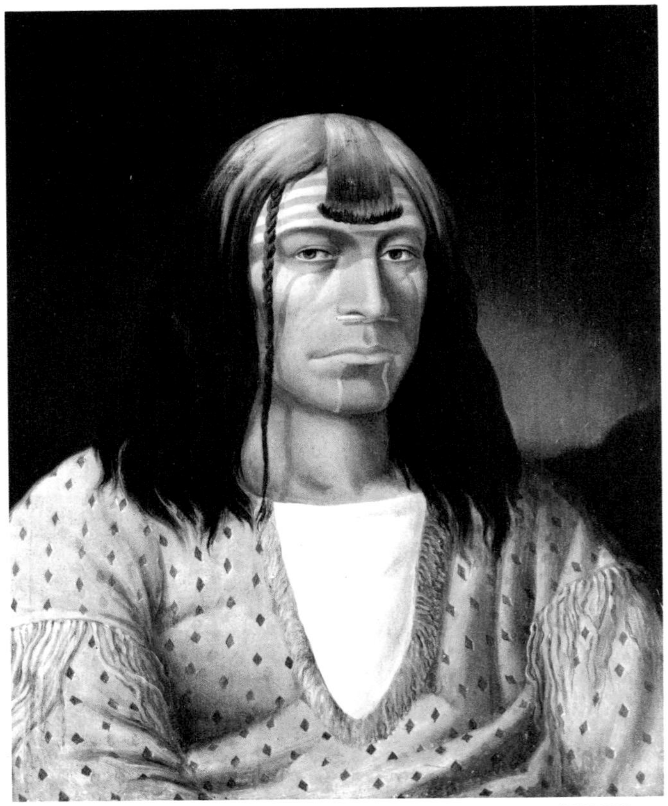

COURTESY ROYAL ONTARIO MUSEUM, TORONTO

Fig. 141. Nez Percé Indian. ROM912.1.72; CRIV-372.

Fig. 142. Peo-Peo-mox-mox (or "The Yellow Serpent"; a Walla Walla chief). ROM912.1.69; crIV-376.

Fig. 143. Son of Peo-Peo-mox-mox, a Walla Walla. ROM946.15.196; crIV-377.

233

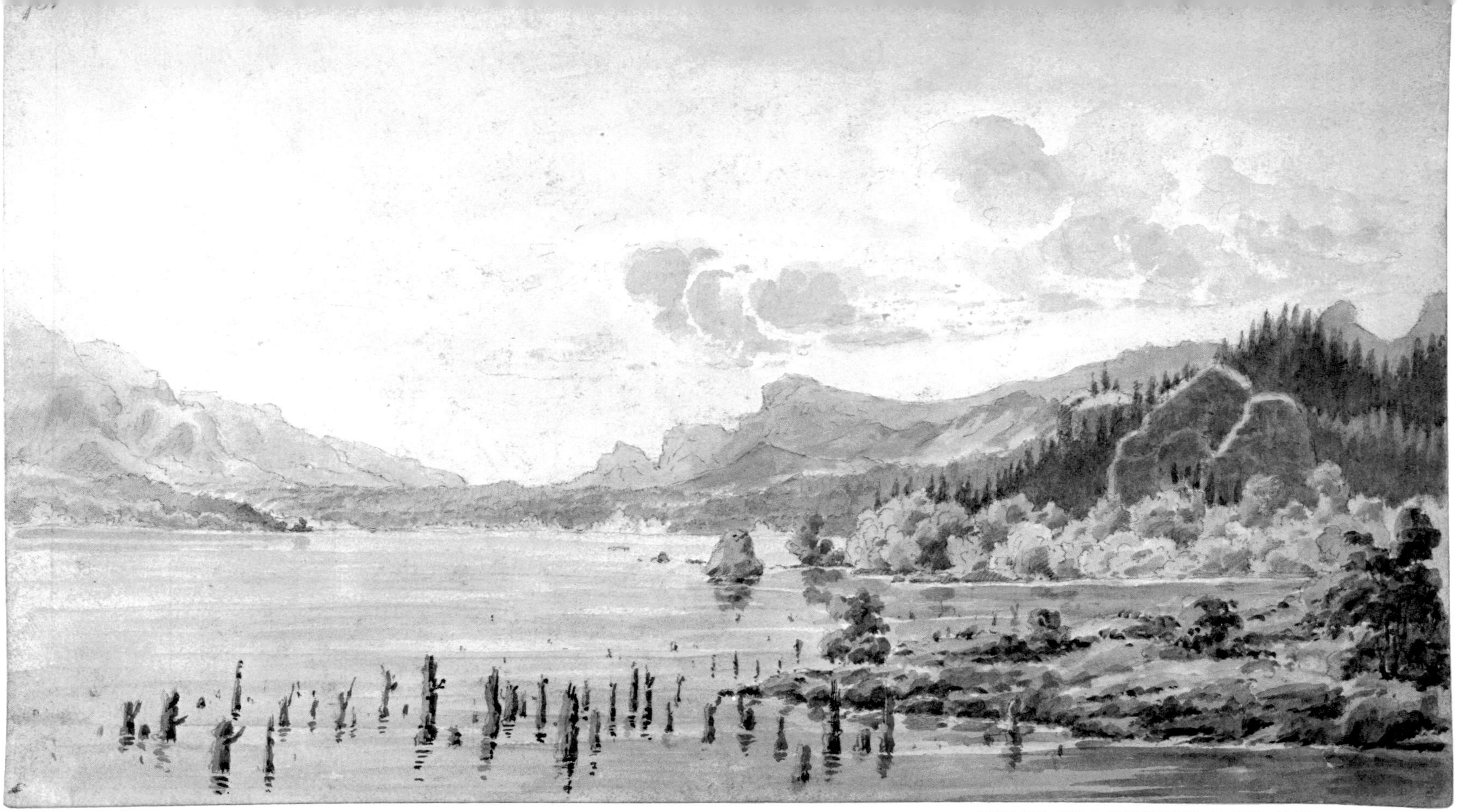

COURTESY STARK FOUNDATION, ORANGE, TEXAS

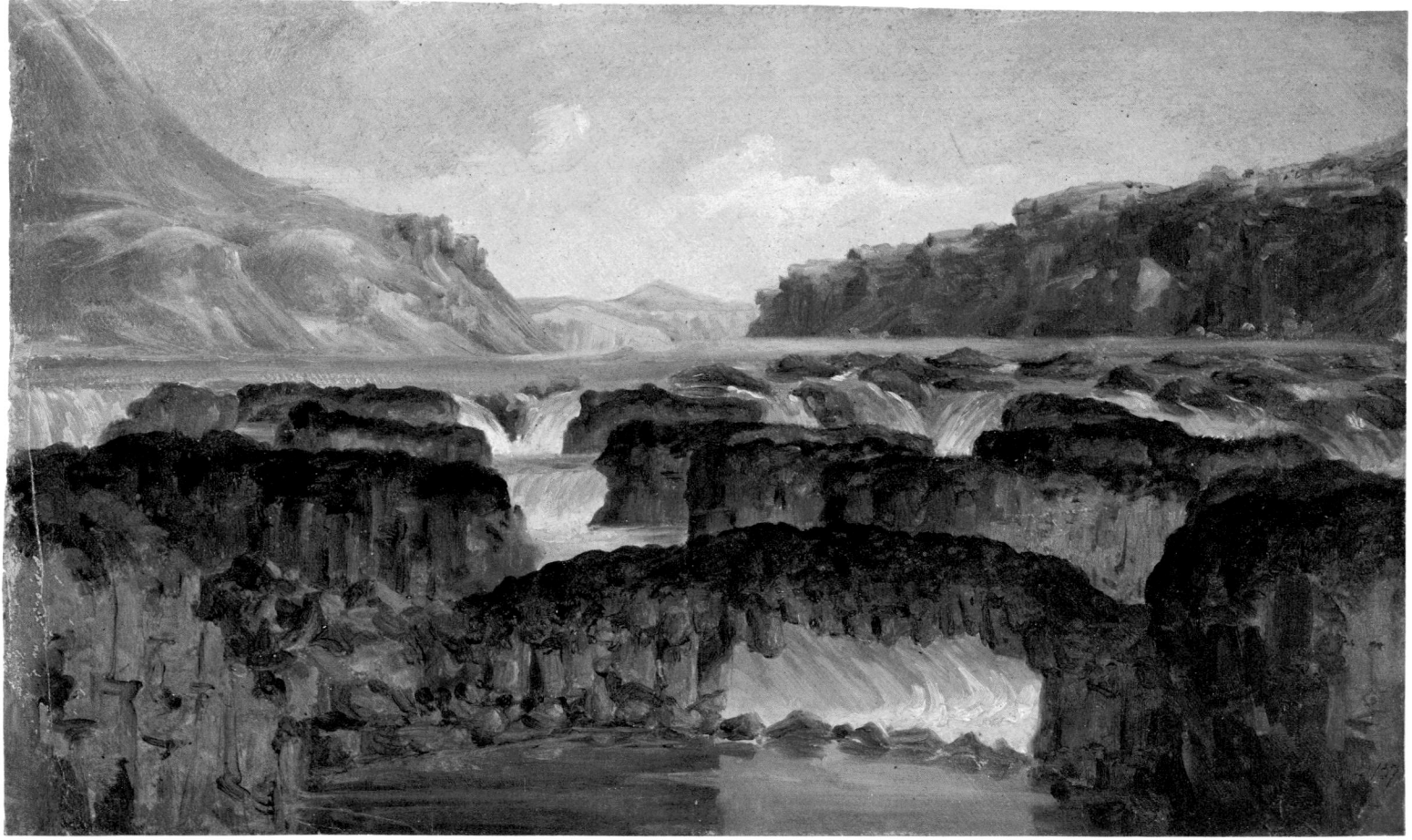

Fig. 144. Landslip above the Cascades, Columbia River. Stark wwc30; crIV-382.

COURTESY STARK FOUNDATION, ORANGE, TEXAS

Fig. 145. The Cascades, Columbia River. Stark wop9; crIV-387.

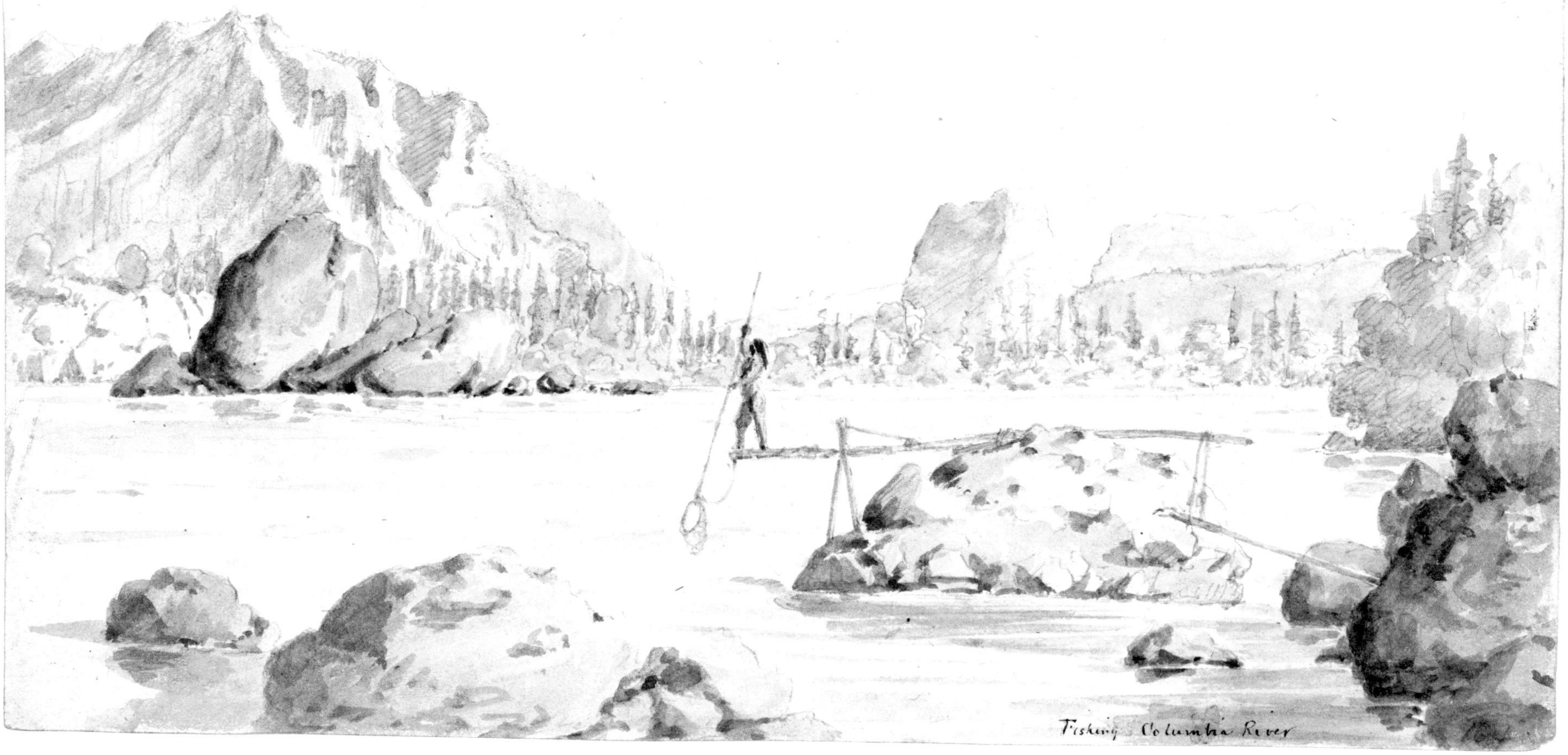

COURTESY STARK FOUNDATION, ORANGE, TEXAS

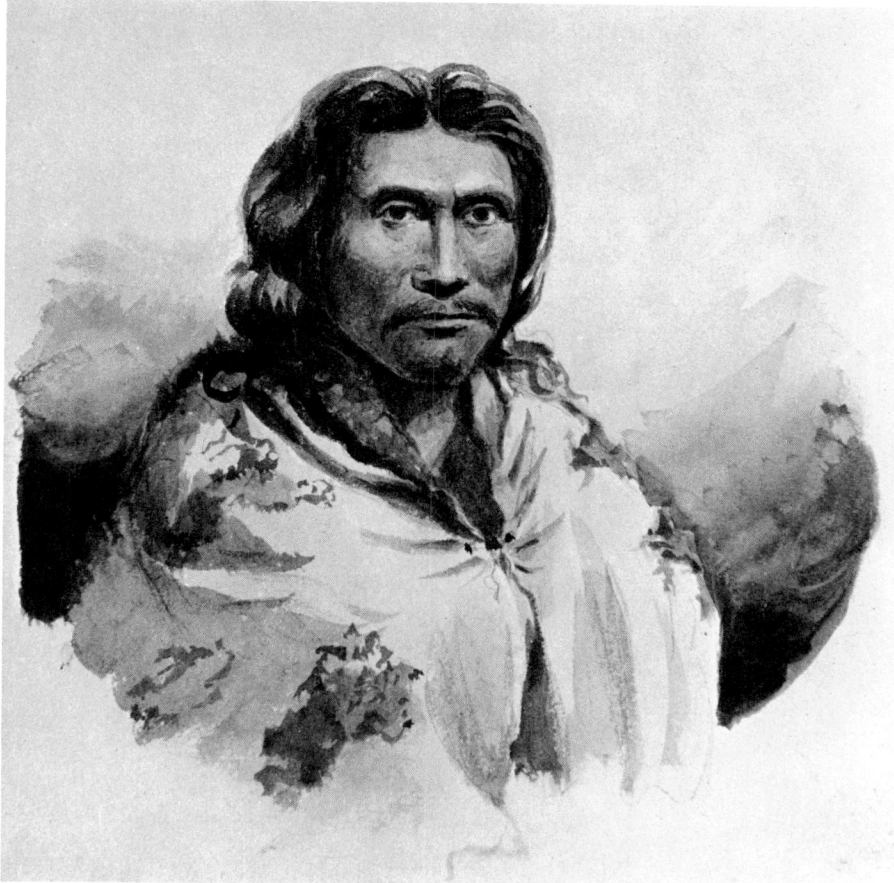

Fig. 146. Below the Cascades, Columbia River, with Indian fishing. Stark WWC92; CRIV-388.

COURTESY ROYAL ONTARIO MUSEUM, TORONTO

Fig. 147. Tomaquin, Cascade chief, Columbia River. ROM946.15.195; CRIV-391.

COURTESY STARK FOUNDATION, ORANGE, TEXAS

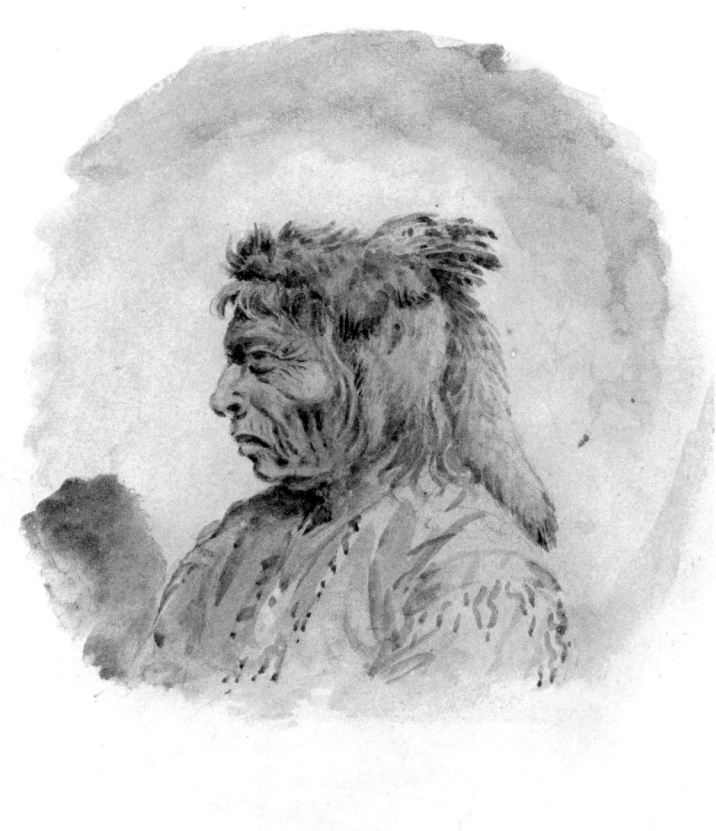

Fig. 148. Mancemuckt, chief of the Skinpah, Columbia River. Stark WWC102-I; CRIV-393.

Fig. 149. A Cascade Indian, Columbia River. Stark wwc55; crIV-396.

Plate XLIII. Northwest canoes. ROM946.15.231; crIV-531.

Medicine Masks North West Coast B.C.

Paul Kane
1847

Plate XLIV. Medicine masks of the northwest coast tribes. Stark wwc27; crIV-538.

COURTESY ROYAL ONTARIO MUSEUM, TORONTO

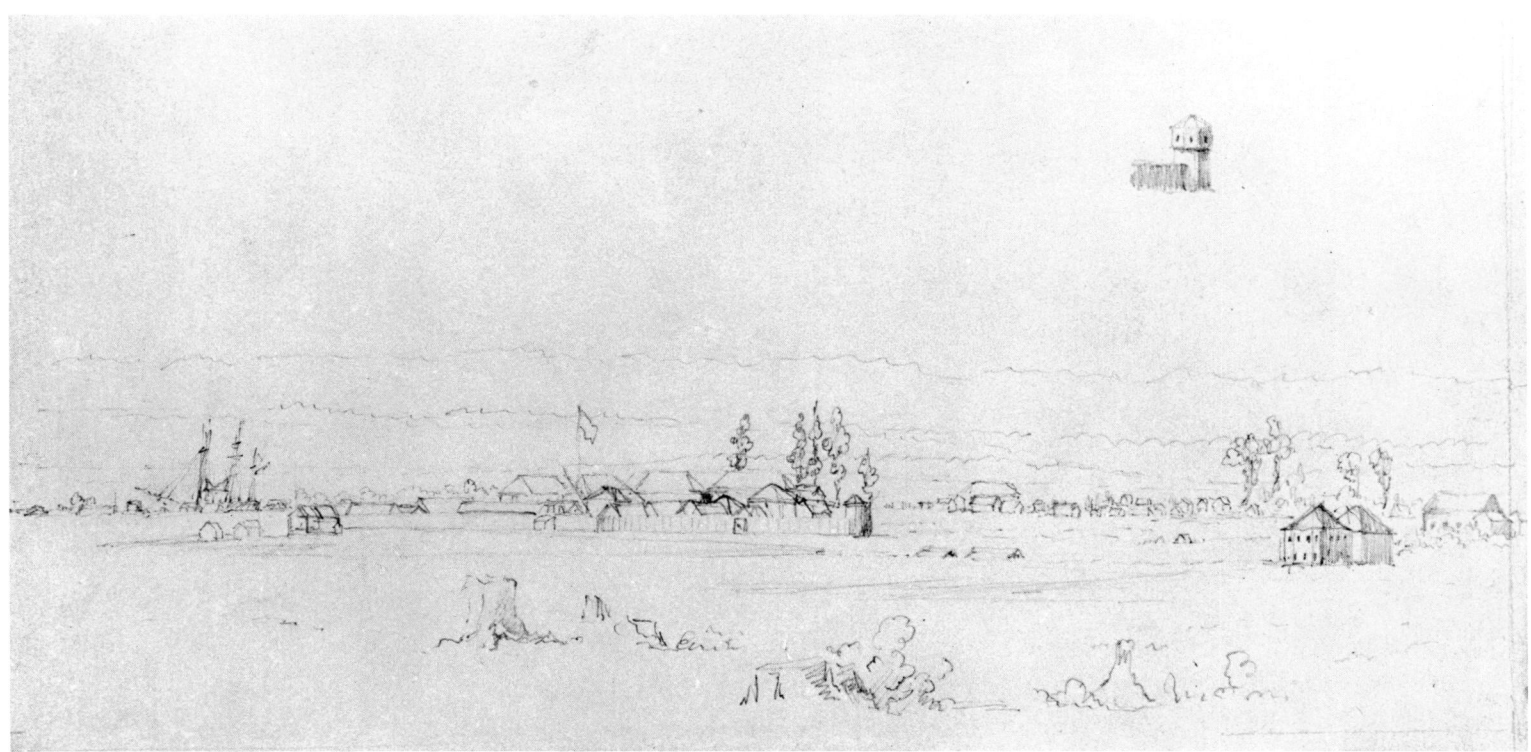

Fig. 150. Fort Vancouver. ROM946.15.211; CRIV-397.

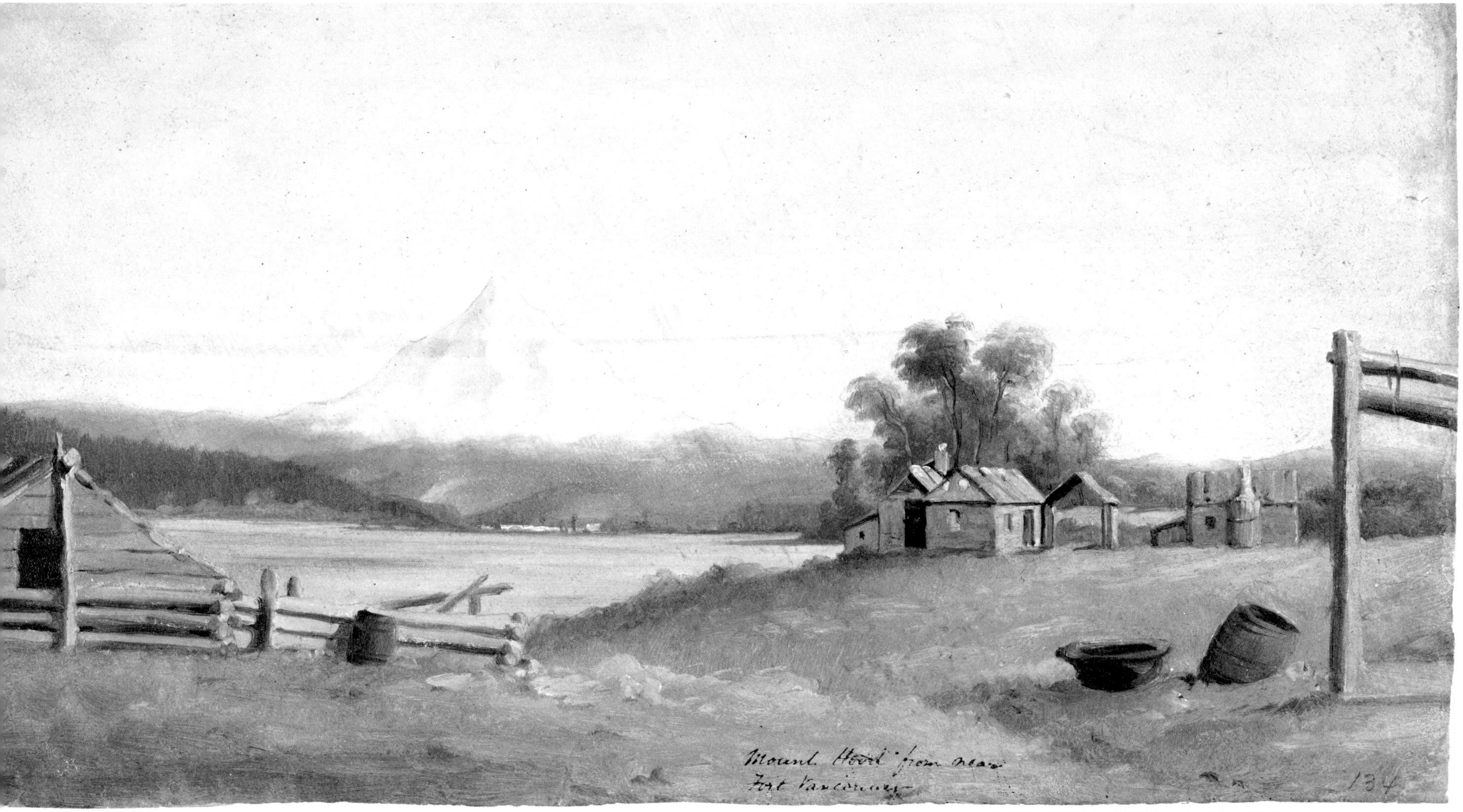

COURTESY STARK FOUNDATION, ORANGE, TEXAS

Fig. 151. Fort Vancouver, west end. Stark WOP17; CRIV-400.

Fig. 154. Old Cox, a Sandwich Islander of the Hudson's Bay Company. ROM946.15.271; crIV-416.

Fig. 152. A handbill for a theatrical performance at Fort Vancouver, a souvenir kept by Kane. Collection of Mrs. Paul Kane III.

238

Fig. 153. Man with saddle horse, near Fort Vancouver. ROM946.15.251; crIV-408.

Fig. 155. Well in the woods, near Fort Vancouver.
Stark WOP8; CRIV-409.

Fig. 156. Indian (girl?) on a race course near Fort Vancouver. Stark WWC35; CRIV-420.

239

COURTESY ROYAL ONTARIO MUSEUM, TORONTO

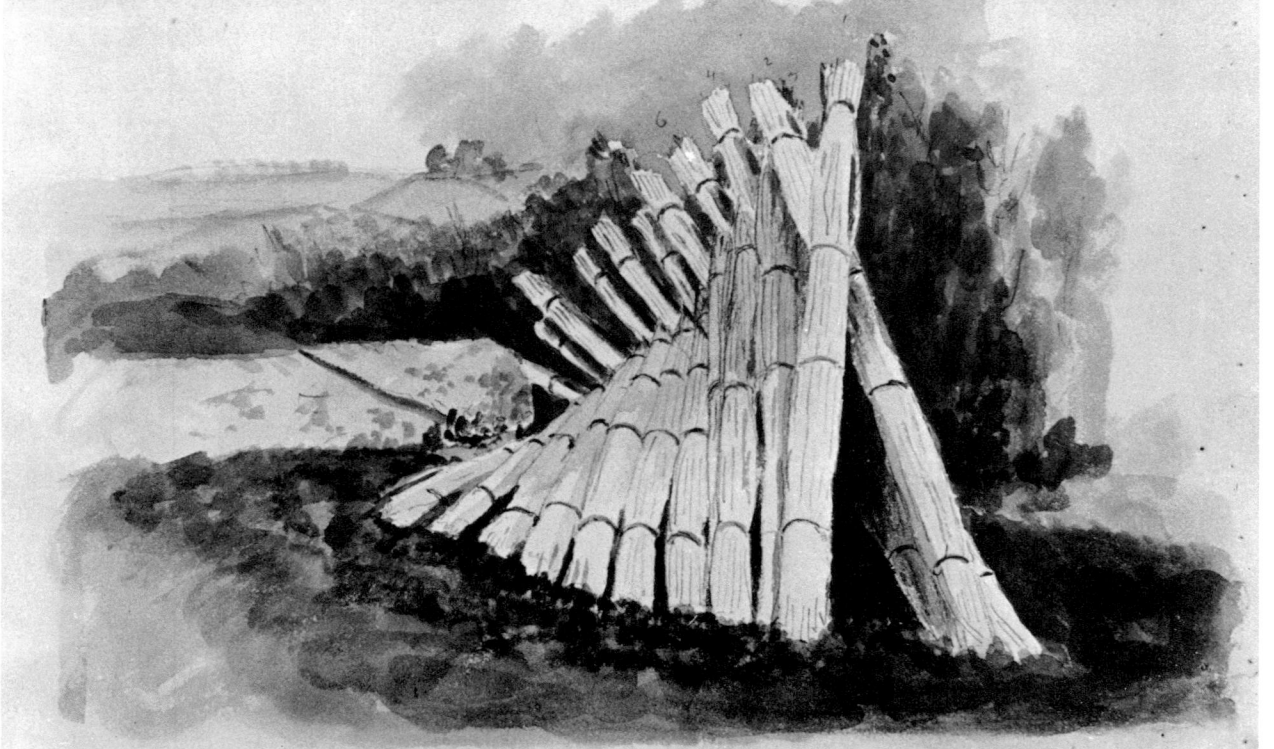

Fig. 157. Bundle of rushes used for making mats. ROM946.15.321; CRIV-427.

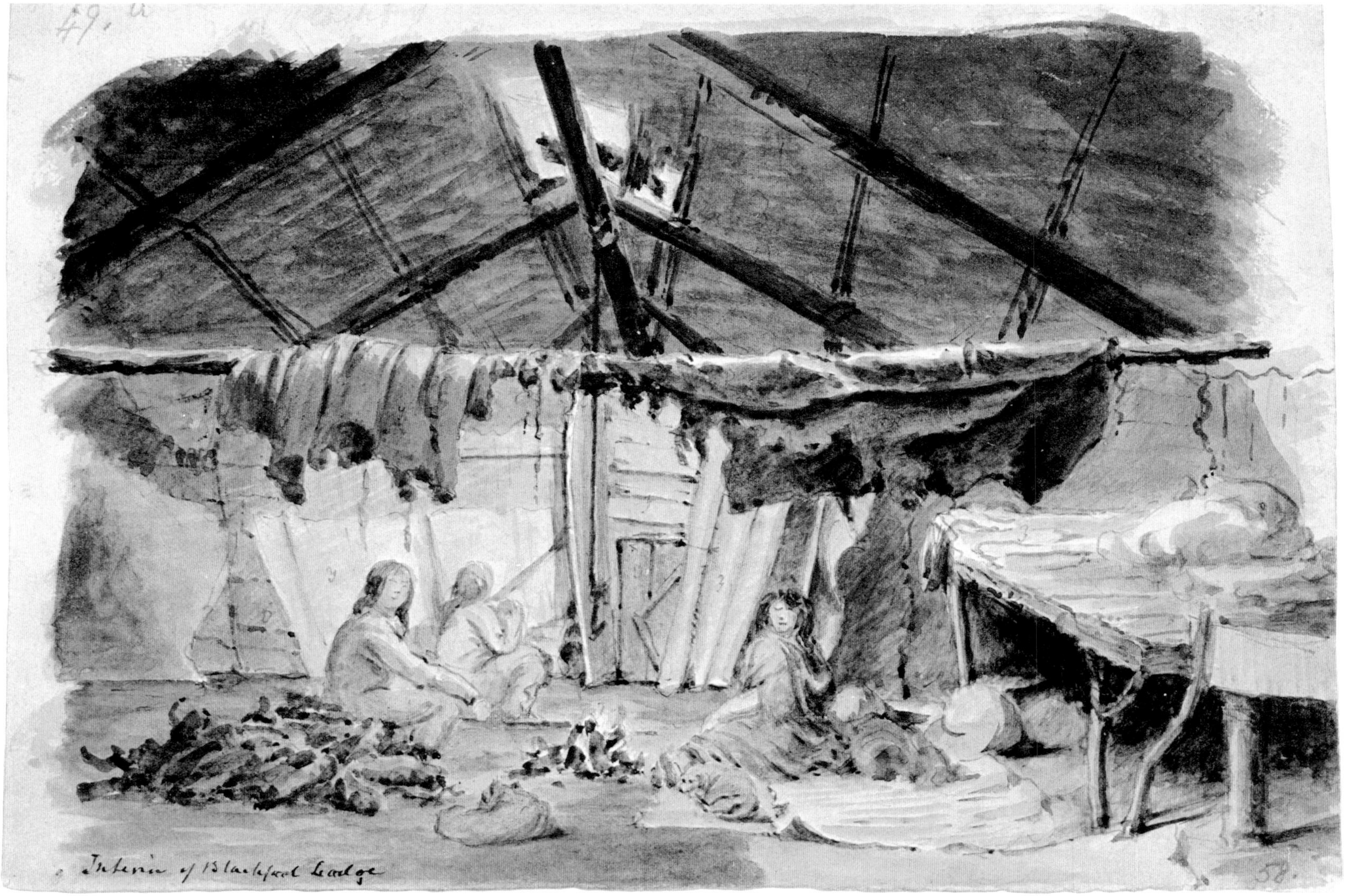

COURTESY STARK FOUNDATION, ORANGE, TEXAS

Fig. 158. Interior of a Chinook lodge, Fort Vancouver. Stark WWC41; CRIV-424.

Fig. 159. A Klikitat lodge, Fort Vancouver. ROM946.15.221; CRIV-428.

Chinook Lodge - Mount Hood in the distance

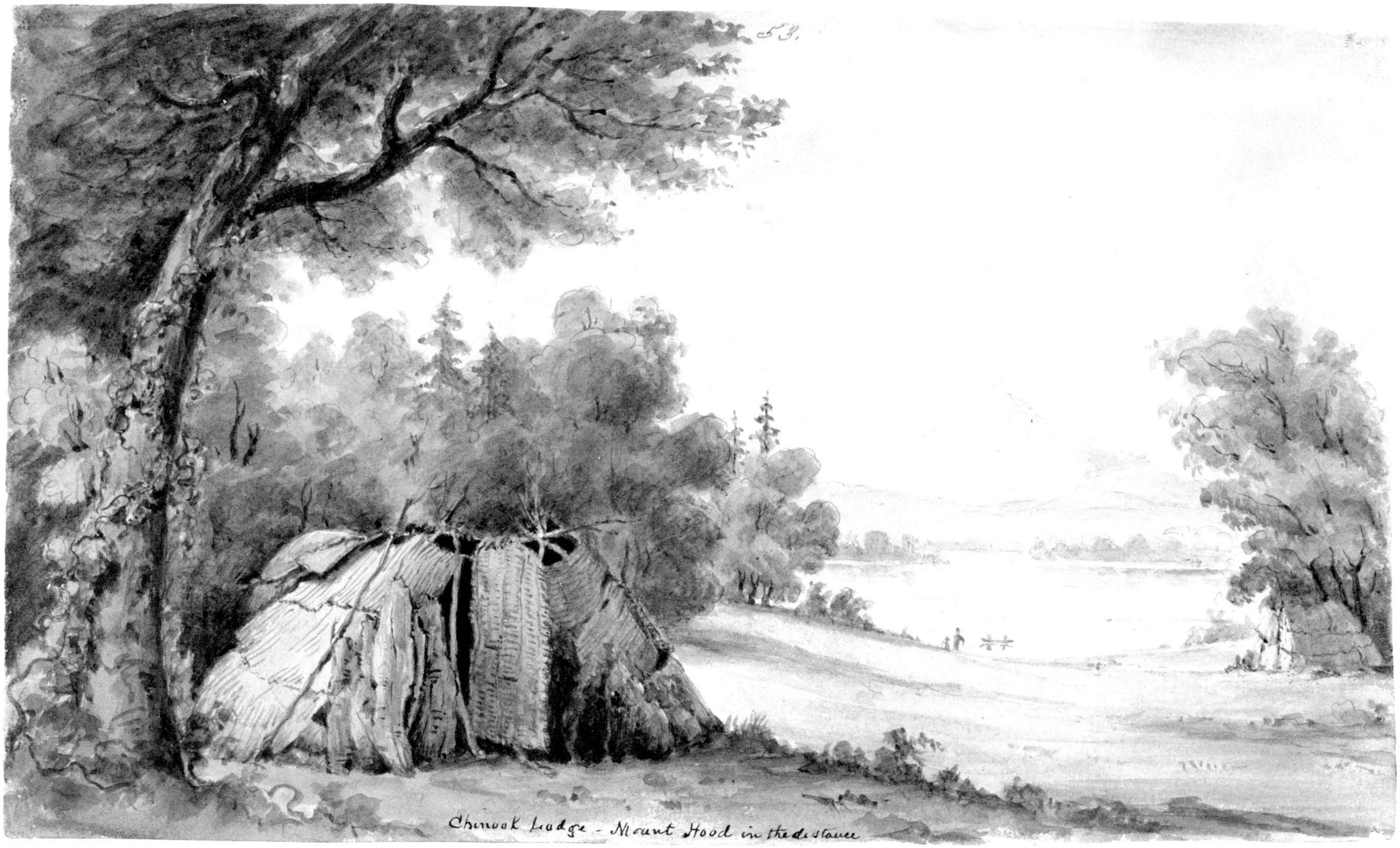

Fig. 160. A Chinook travelling lodge, with a view of Mount Hood. Stark WWC101; CRIV-429.

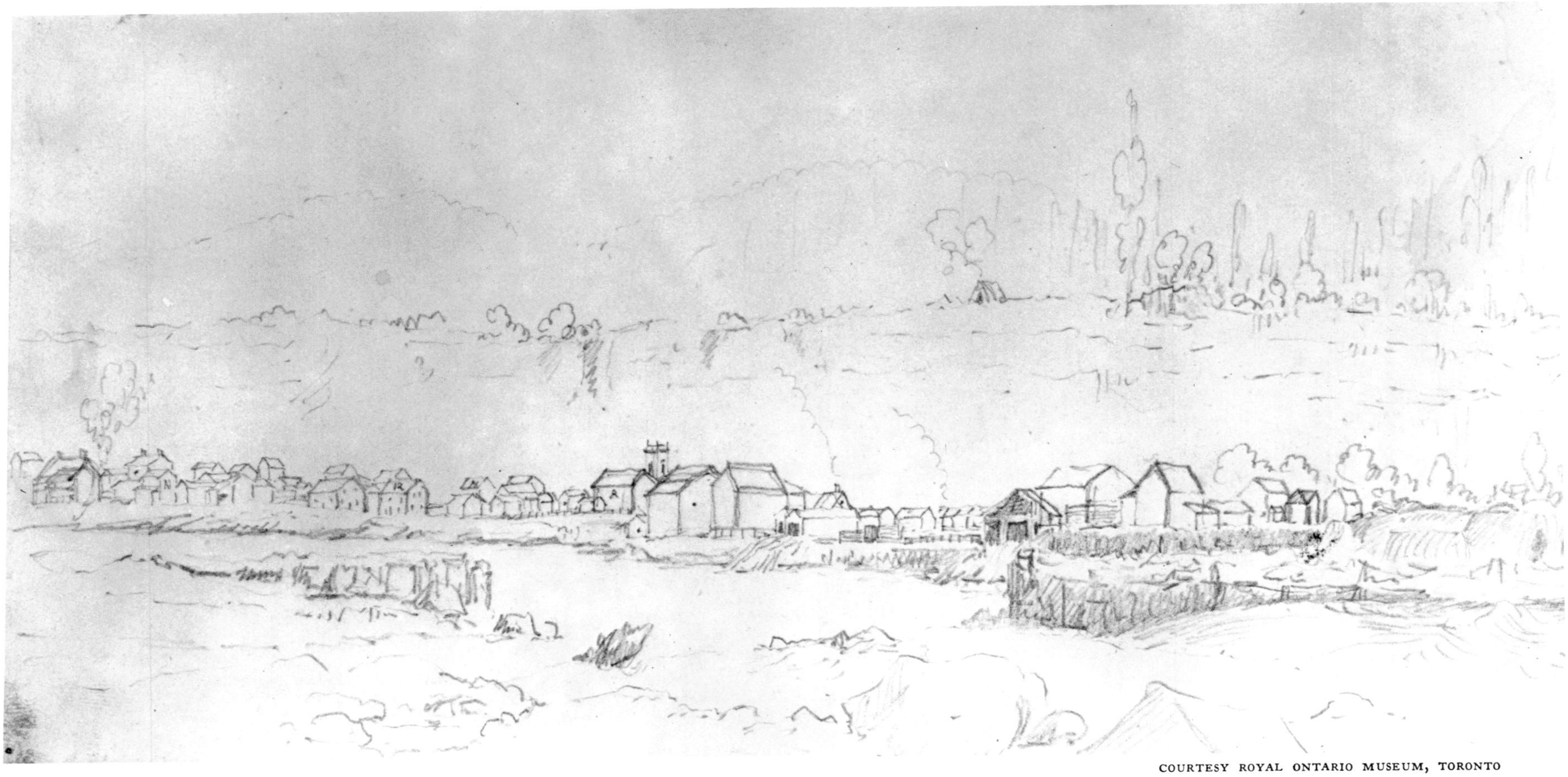

COURTESY ROYAL ONTARIO MUSEUM, TORONTO

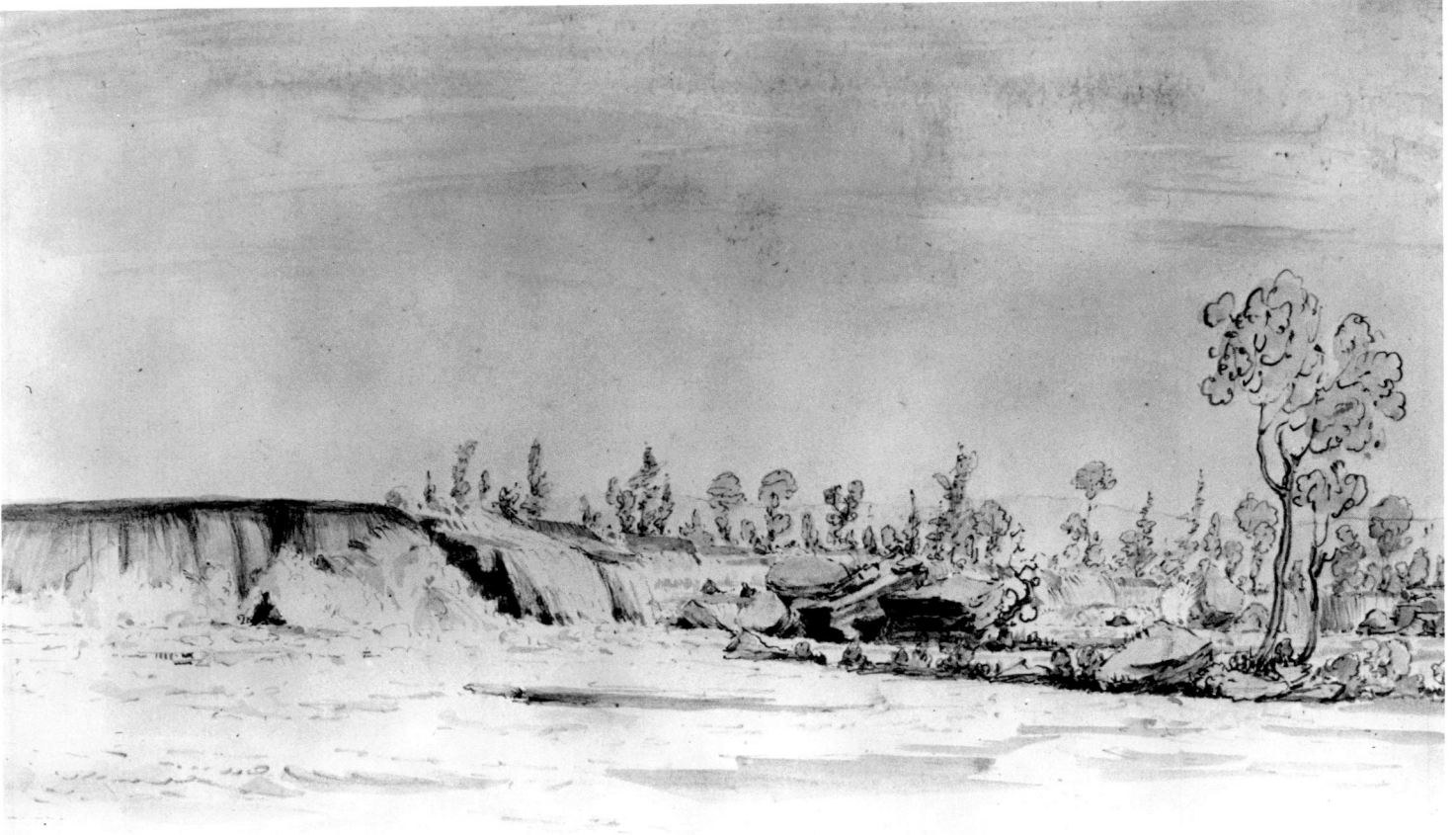

Fig. 161. Oregon City. ROM946.15.164; CRIV-448.

COURTESY ROYAL ONTARIO MUSEUM, TORONTO

Fig. 162. Falls near Oregon City. ROM946.15.269; CRIV-452.

Clalam Indian woman basket making

Plate XLV. Clallam woman weaving basket, and other studies. Stark wwc45; crIV-555.

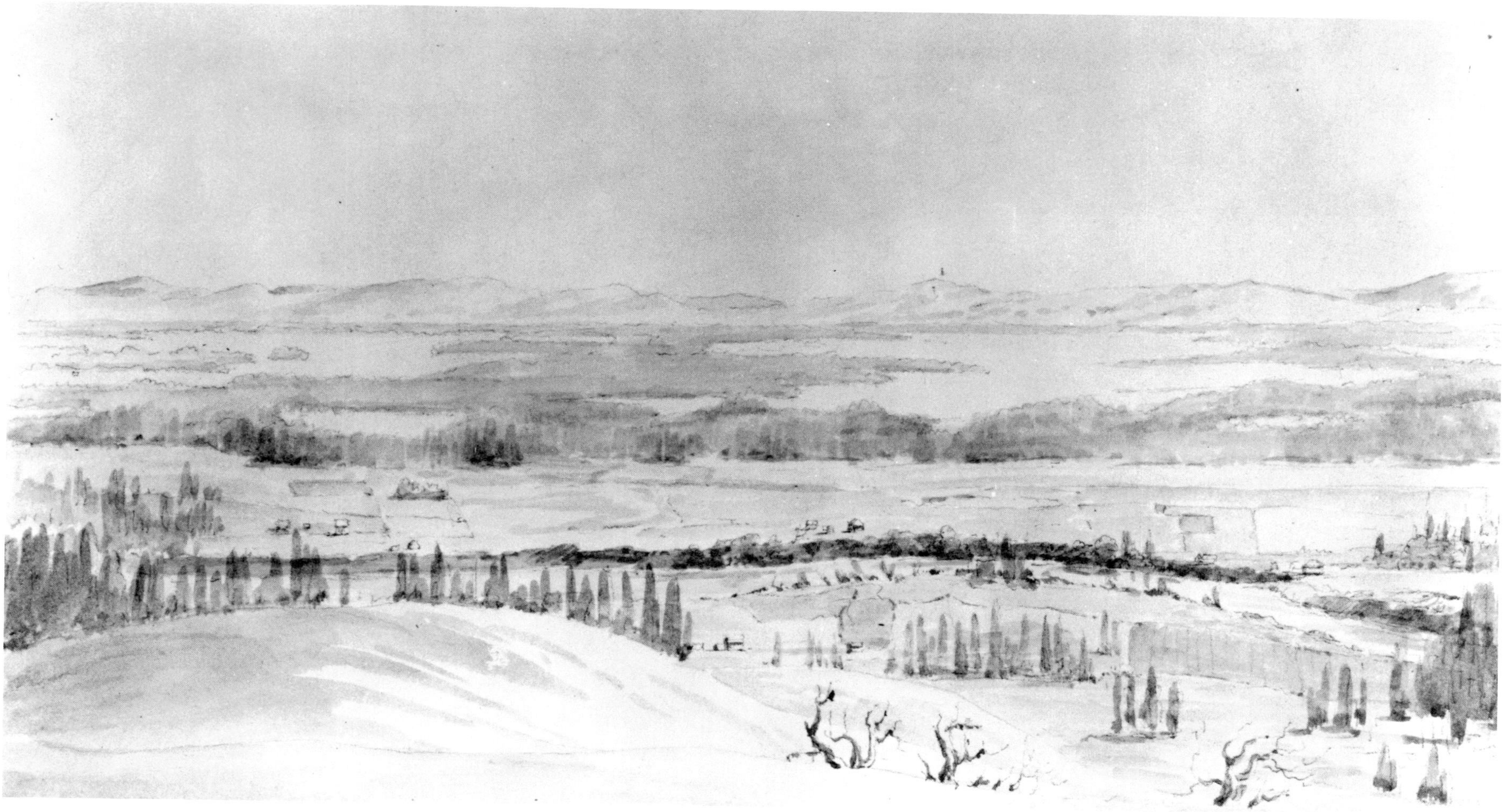

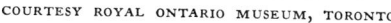

Fig. 163. Willamette valley at Champoeg. ROM946.15.193; CRIV-455.

COURTESY ROYAL ONTARIO MUSEUM, TORONTO

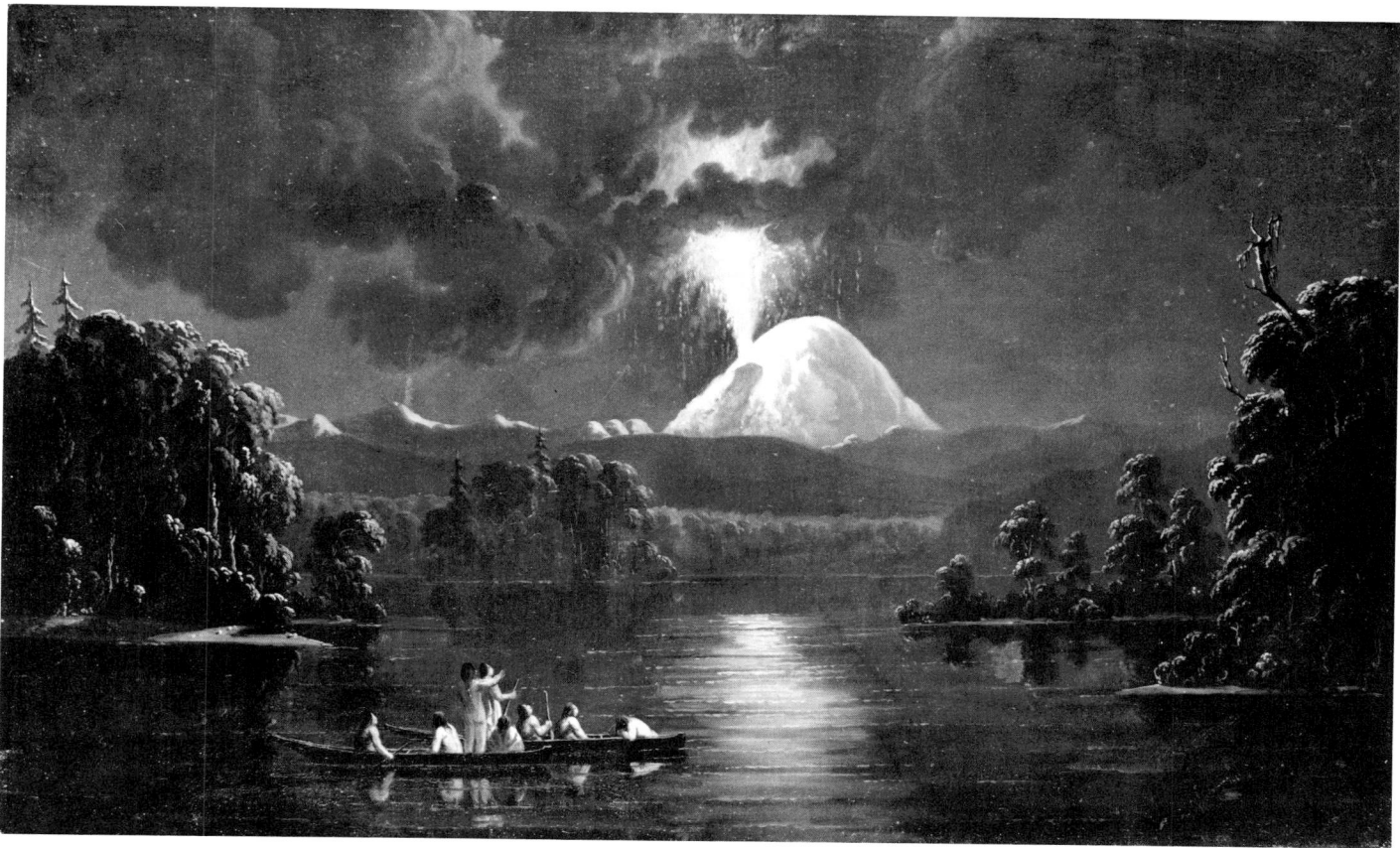

Fig. 164. Mount St. Helens erupting. ROM912.1.78; CRIV-462.

COURTESY ROYAL ONTARIO MUSEUM, TORONTO

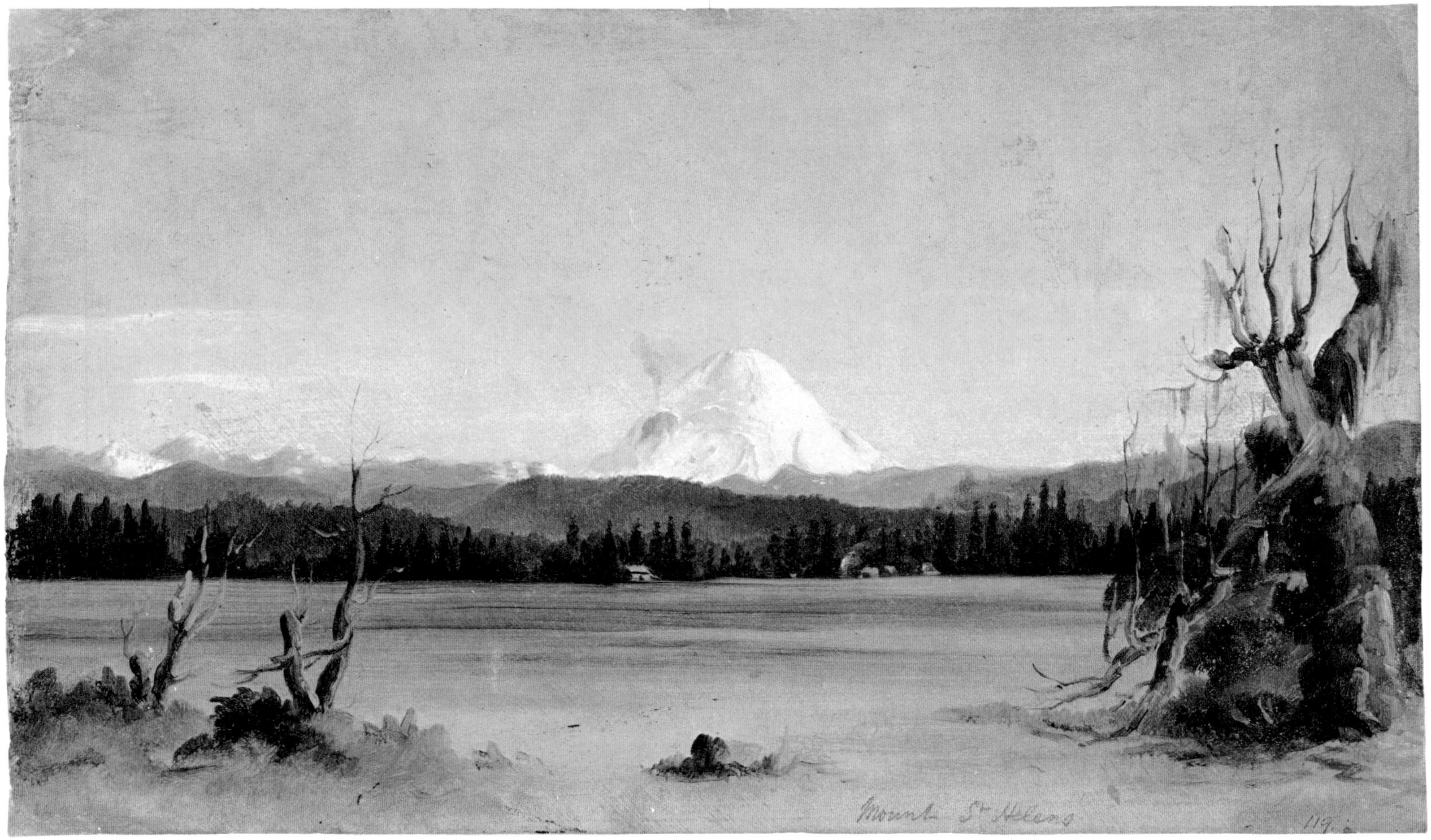

COURTESY STARK FOUNDATION, ORANGE, TEXAS

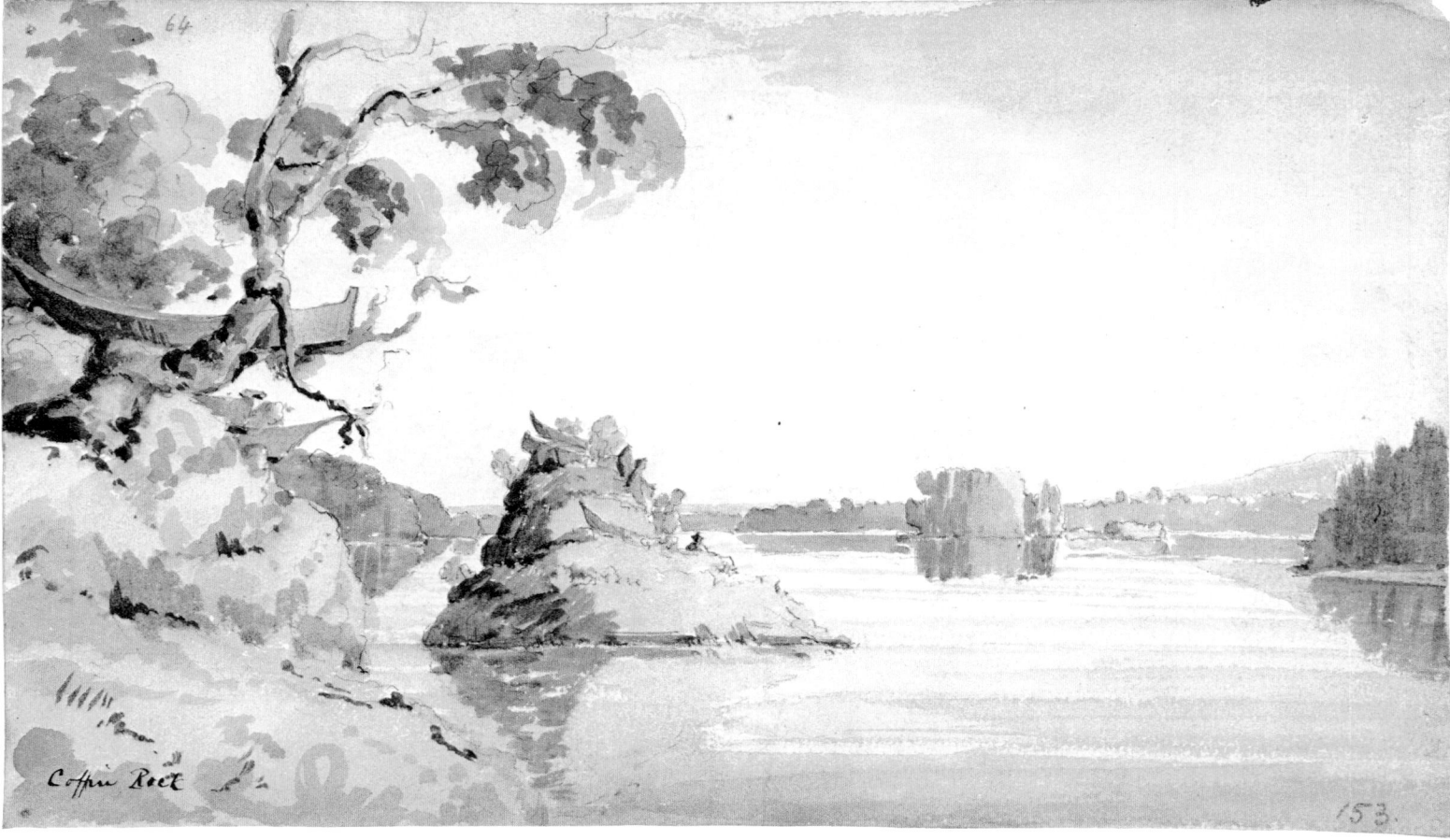

Fig. 165. Mount St. Helens. Stark wop21; crIV-464.

COURTESY STARK FOUNDATION, ORANGE, TEXAS

Fig. 166. Coffin Rock, lower Columbia River. Stark wwc91; crIV-470.

COURTESY STARK FOUNDATION, ORANGE, TEXAS

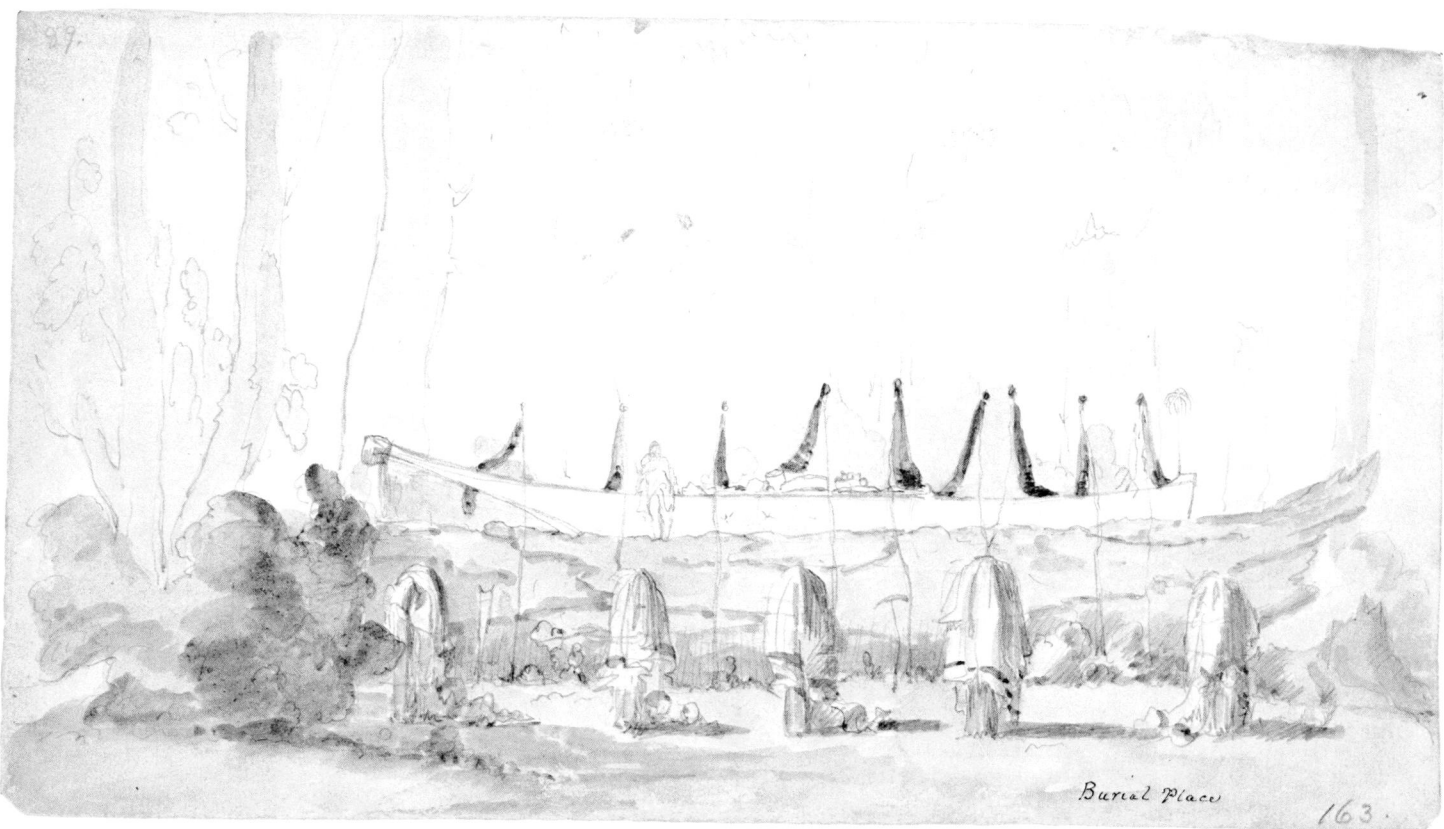

Fig. 167. King Comcomly's burial canoe. Stark wwc86; crIV-478.

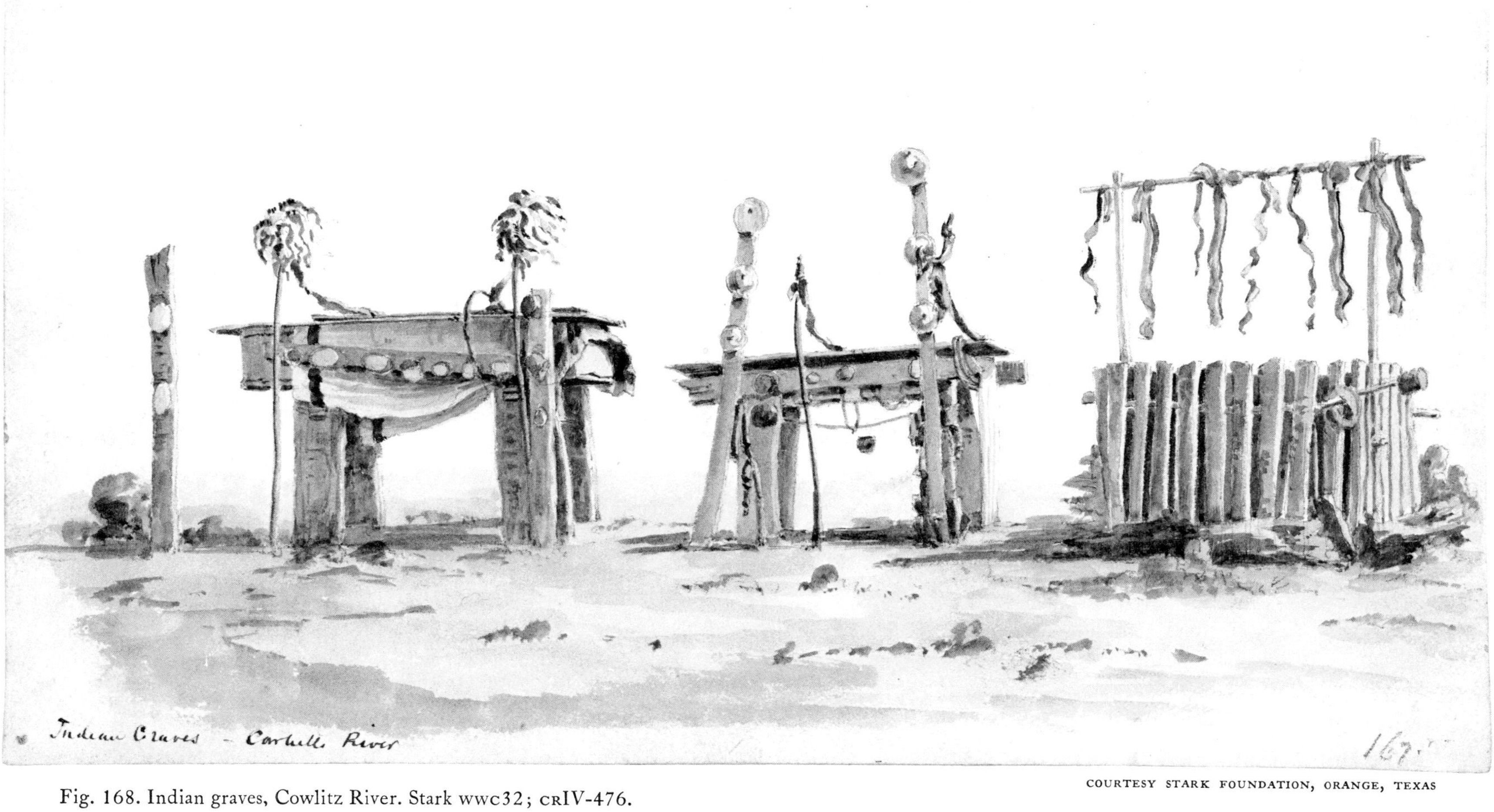

COURTESY STARK FOUNDATION, ORANGE, TEXAS

Fig. 168. Indian graves, Cowlitz River. Stark wwc32; crIV-476.

Fig. 169. Flathead woman, Cowlitz River.
Stark wwc102G; crIV-489.

Fig. 170. A child having its head flattened.
Stark wwc10; crIV-490.

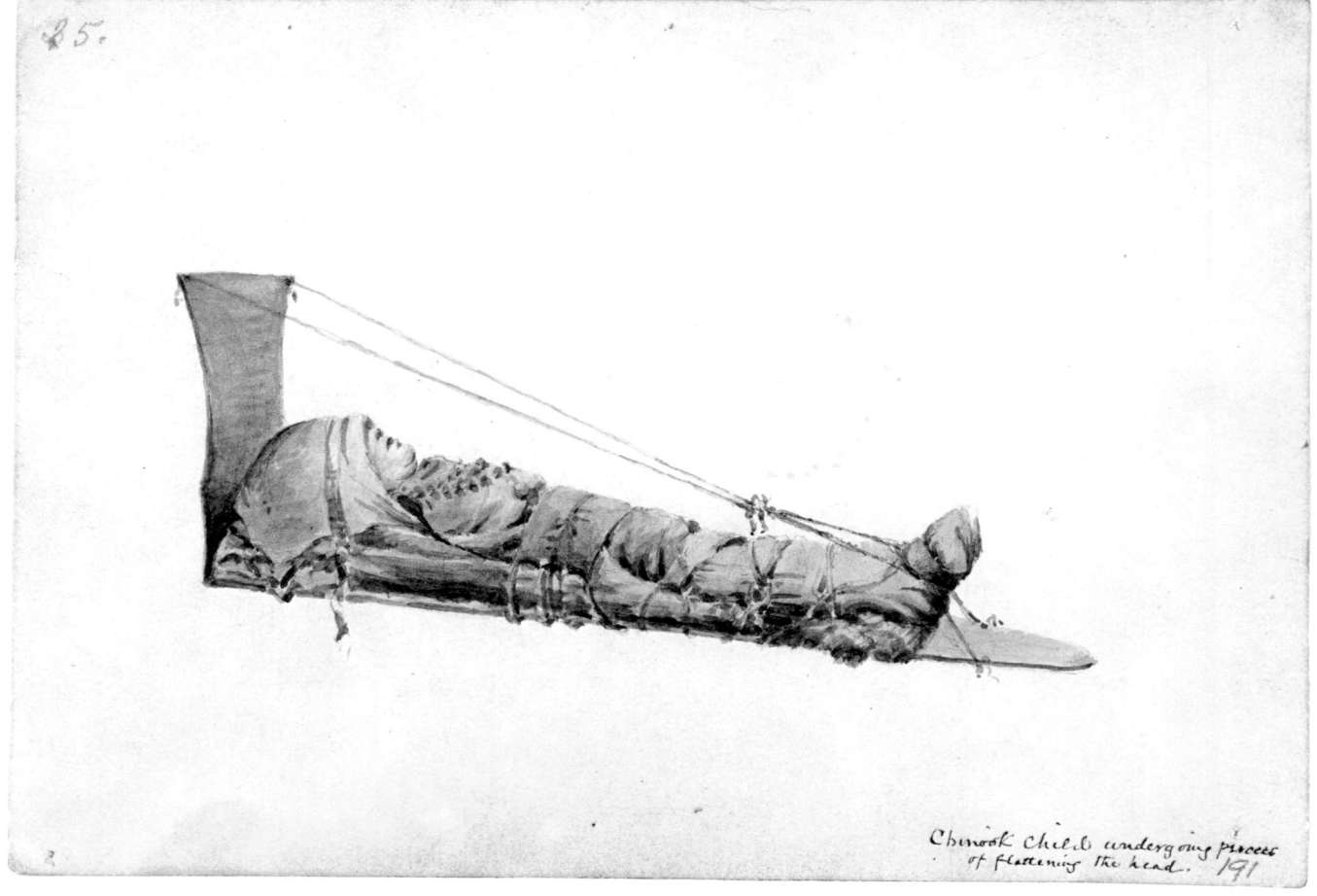

Chinook Child undergoing process
of flattening the head. 191

Fig. 171. Flathead Woman and Child, Caw-wacham. Montreal Museum of Fine Arts 47.991 crIV-492.

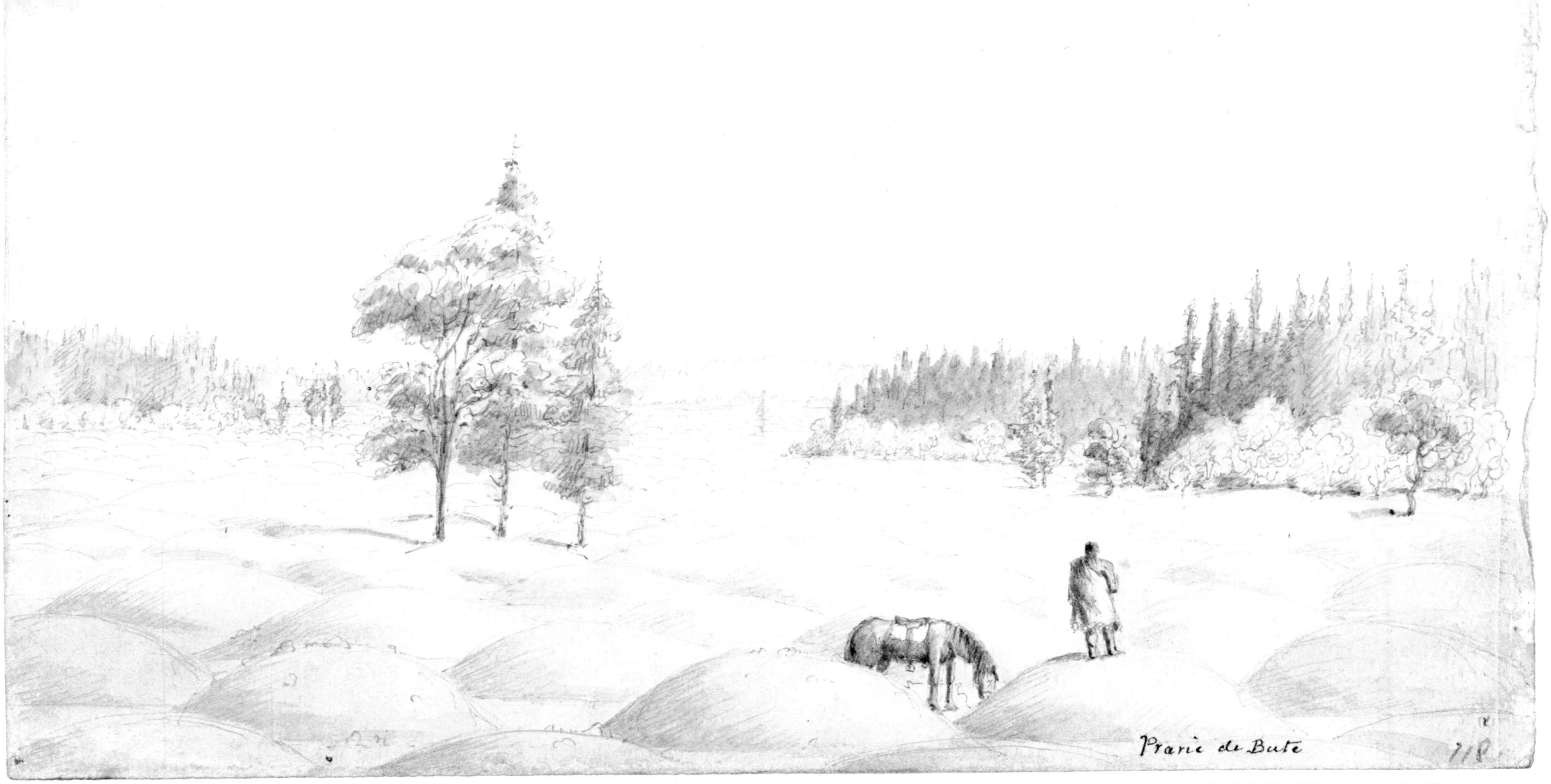

COURTESY STARK FOUNDATION, ORANGE, TEXAS

Fig. 172. Prairie de Bute. Stark wwc64; crIV-494.

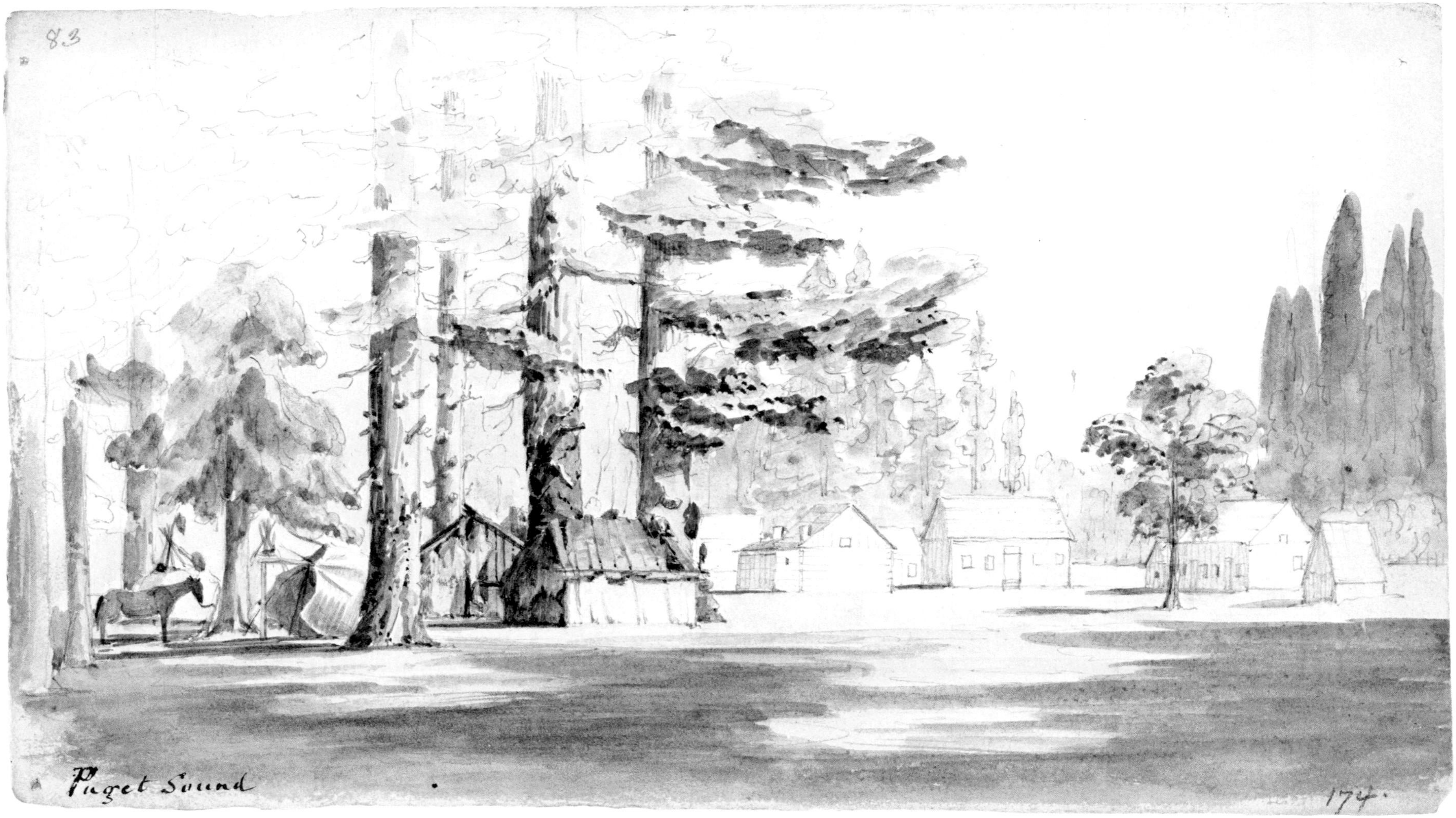

COURTESY STARK FOUNDATION, ORANGE, TEXAS

Fig. 173. Nisqually, a village on Puget Sound. Stark wwc47; crIV-498.

Fig. 174. Indian lodge at Nisqually.
ROM946.15.322; CRIV-499.

Fig. 175. Lock-hi-num, a chief of Whidbey Island.
Stark WWC56; CRIV-508.

Indian Chief Puget Sound.

207

249

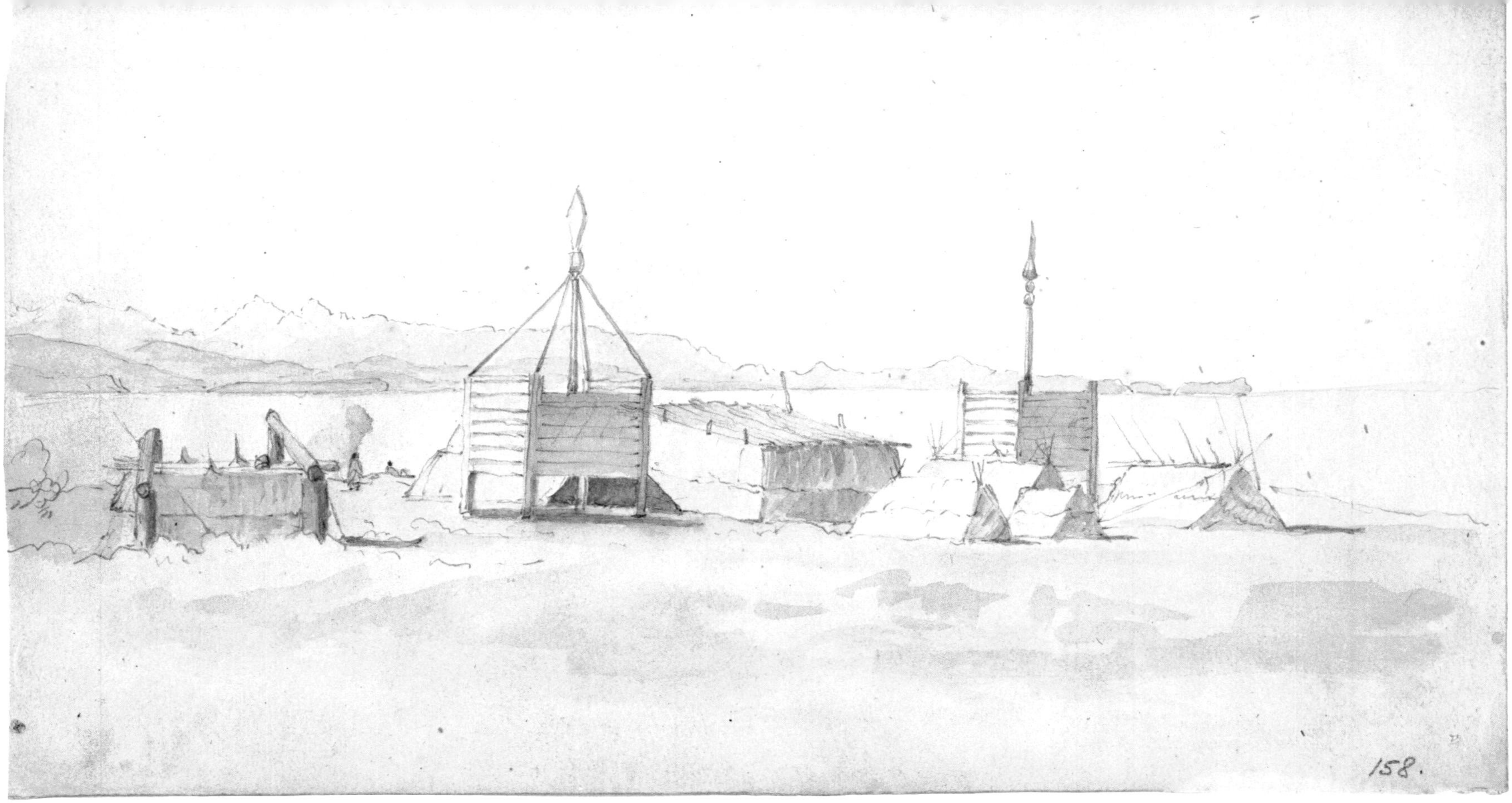

COURTESY STARK FOUNDATION, ORANGE, TEXAS

Fig. 176. Indian village of Toanichum, Whidbey Island. Stark wwc3; crIV-511.

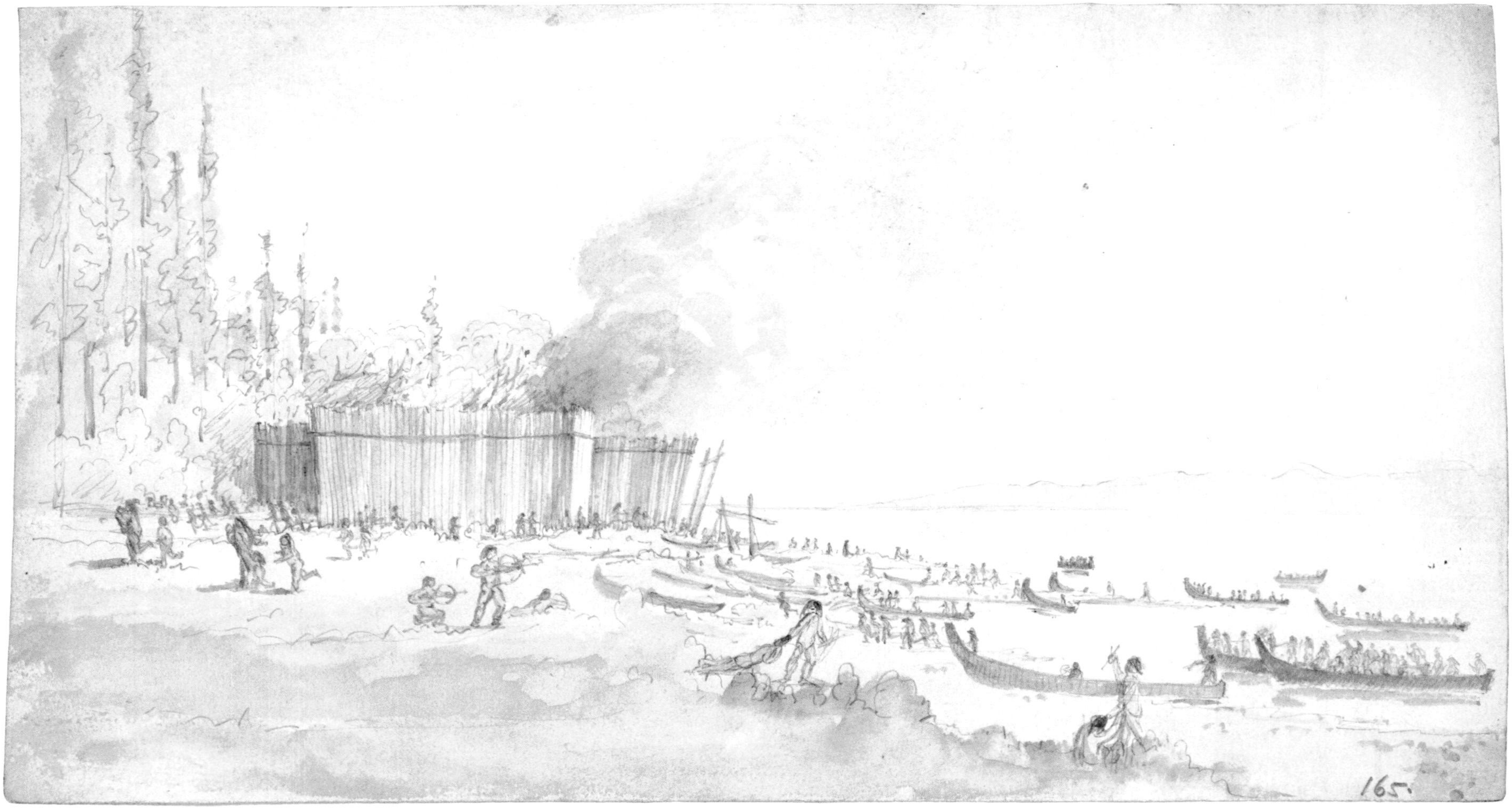

COURTESY STARK FOUNDATION, ORANGE, TEXAS

Fig. 177. Battle between Clallam and Makah at I-eh-nus, Strait of Juan de Fuca. Stark wwc54; crIV-515.

COURTESY STARK FOUNDATION, ORANGE, TEXAS

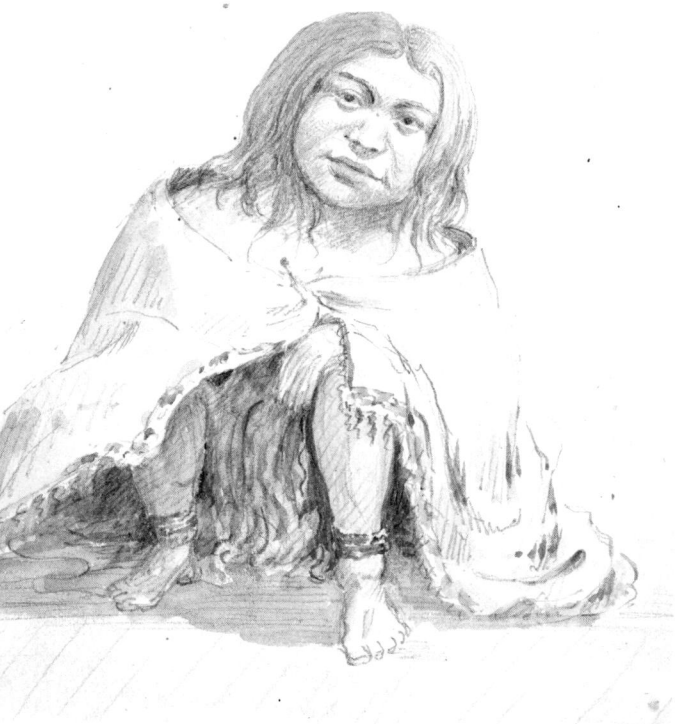

Fig. 178. Chaw-u-wit, daughter of the chief at Suck, Strait of Juan de Fuca. Stark WWC8; CRIV-518.

COURTESY ROYAL ONTARIO MUSEUM, TORONTO

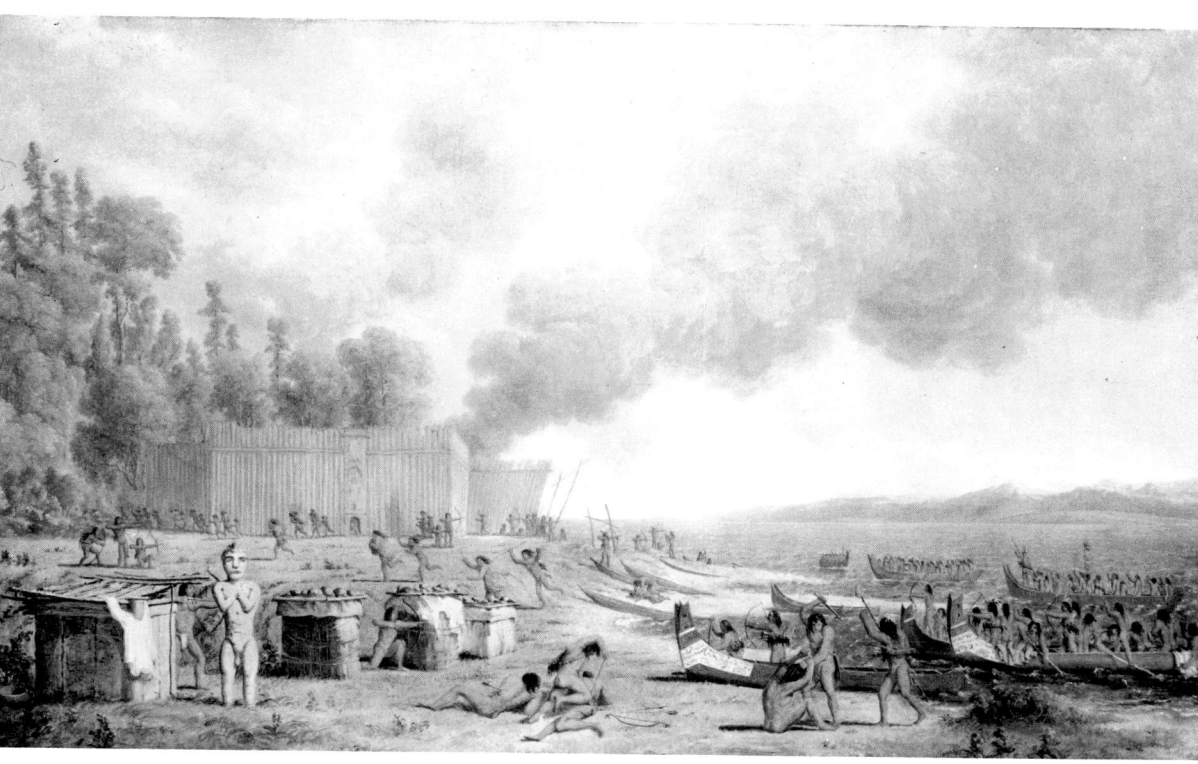

Fig. 180. A Battle of I-eh-nus. ROM912.1.84; CRIV-517.

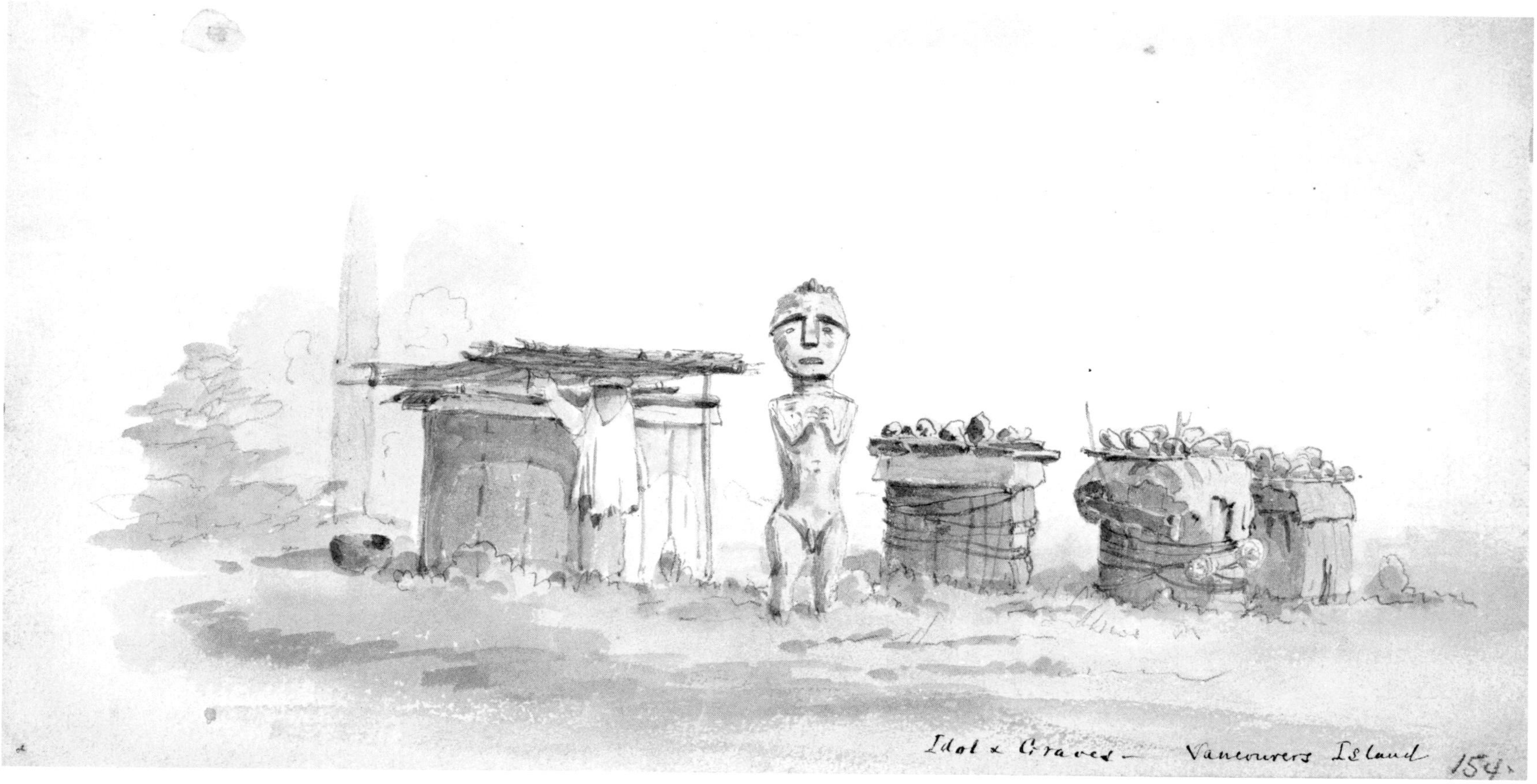

Fig. 179. Graves at I-eh-nus, Strait of Juan de Fuca. Stark WWC89; CRIV-516.

COURTESY STARK FOUNDATION, ORANGE, TEXAS

Fig. 181. Shawstun, Snohomish chief from Puget Sound. Stark wwc37; crIV-512.

Fig. 182. Salmon trap at Suck. Stark wwc26; crIV-520.

Salmon Trap   Du Fuca Strats 1847

Paul Kane

Crossing the Shade of de Fuca
Paul Kane 1847

Fig. 183. Crossing the Strait of Juan de Fuca in a storm. Stark wwc70; crIV-524.

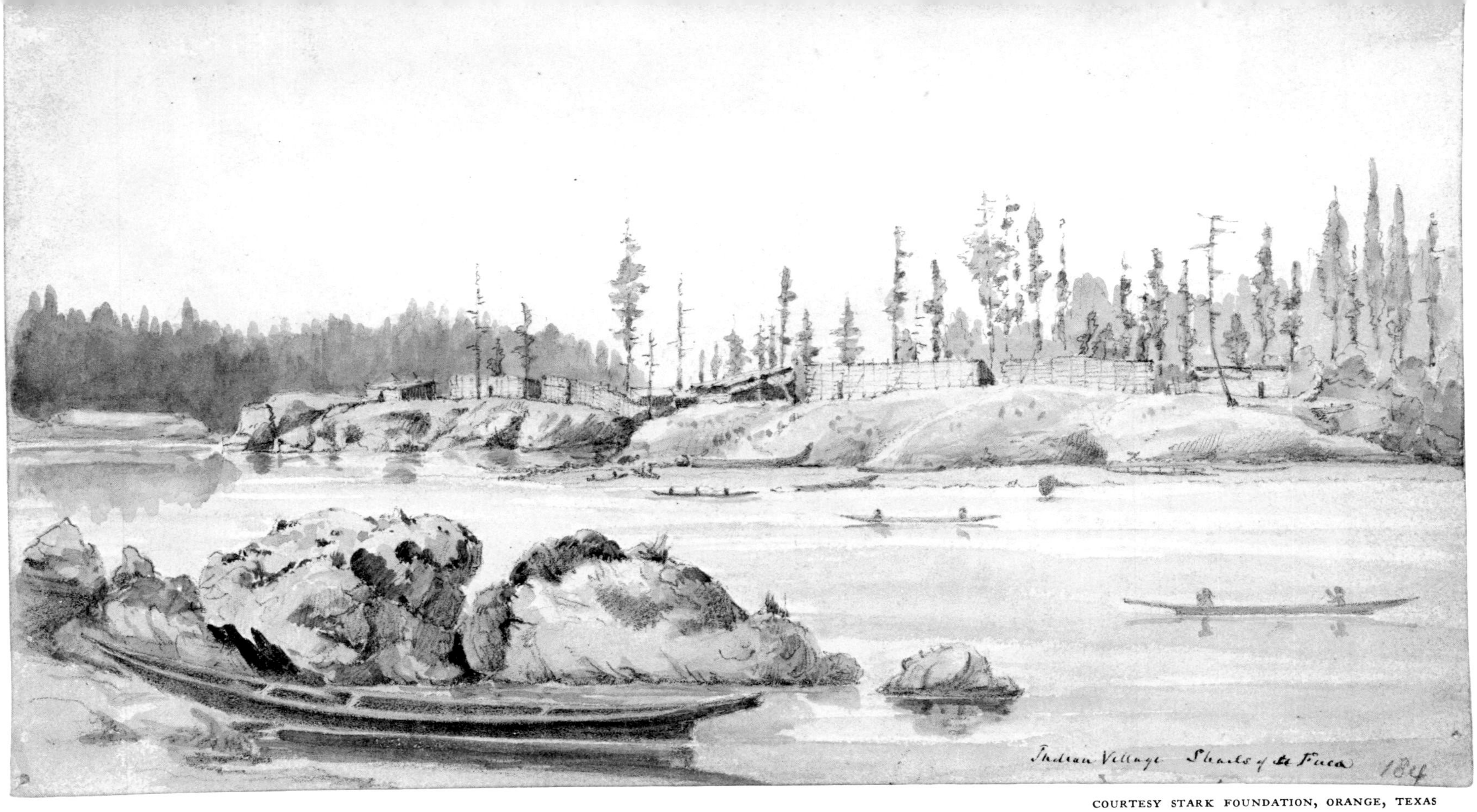

COURTESY STARK FOUNDATION, ORANGE, TEXAS

Fig. 184. An Indian village, Esquimalt. Stark wwc66; crIV-526.

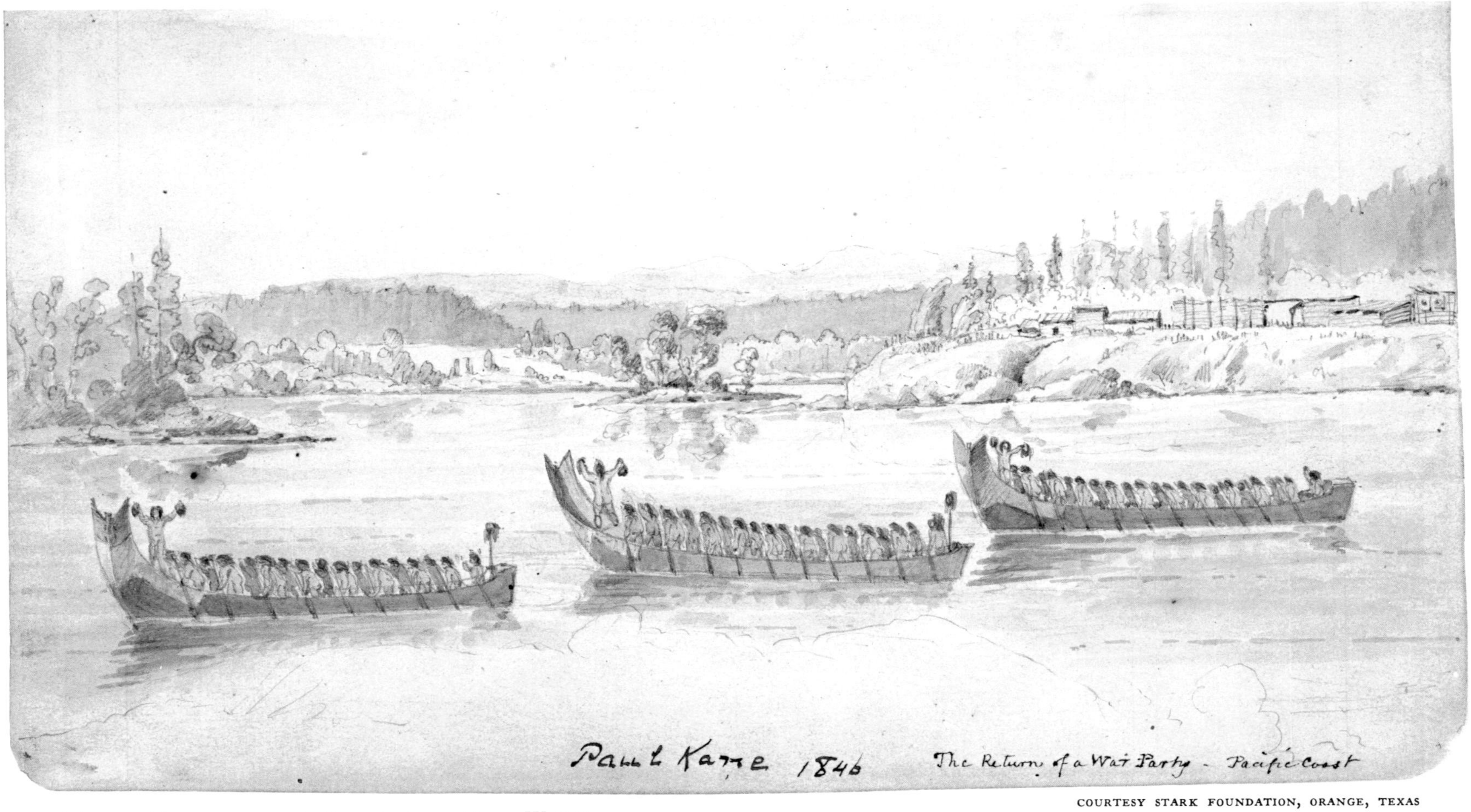

COURTESY STARK FOUNDATION, ORANGE, TEXAS

Fig. 185. War party, Juan de Fuca. Stark wwc90; crIV-527.

Plate XLVI. Clallam travelling lodges. Stark wwc4; crIV-560.

Fig. 186. An Indian village, Esquimalt, with canoes returning from gathering camas. Stark wwc58; crIV-529.

Fig. 187. Northwest canoes. Stark wwc71A; crIV-533.

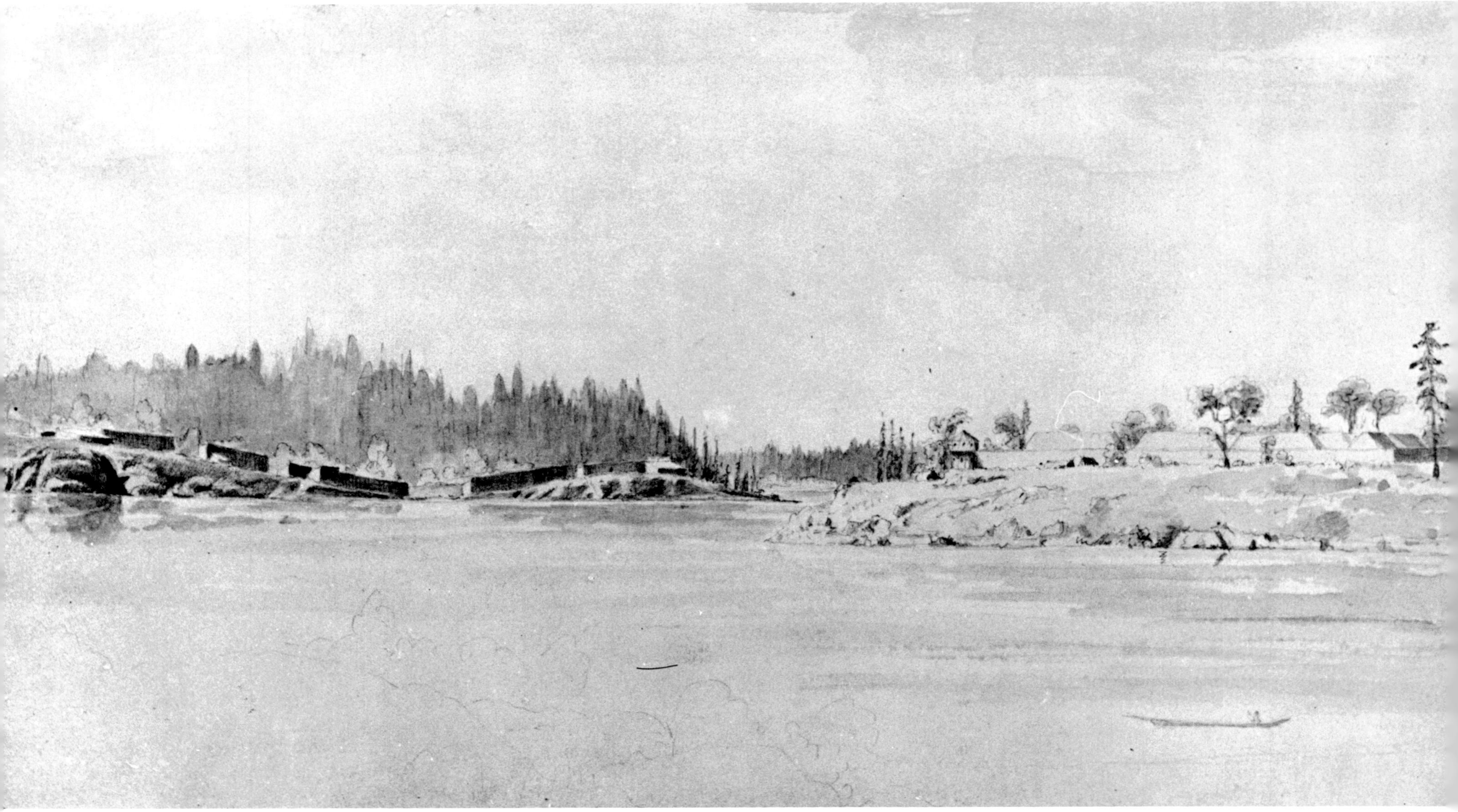

COURTESY ROYAL ONTARIO MUSEUM, TORONTO

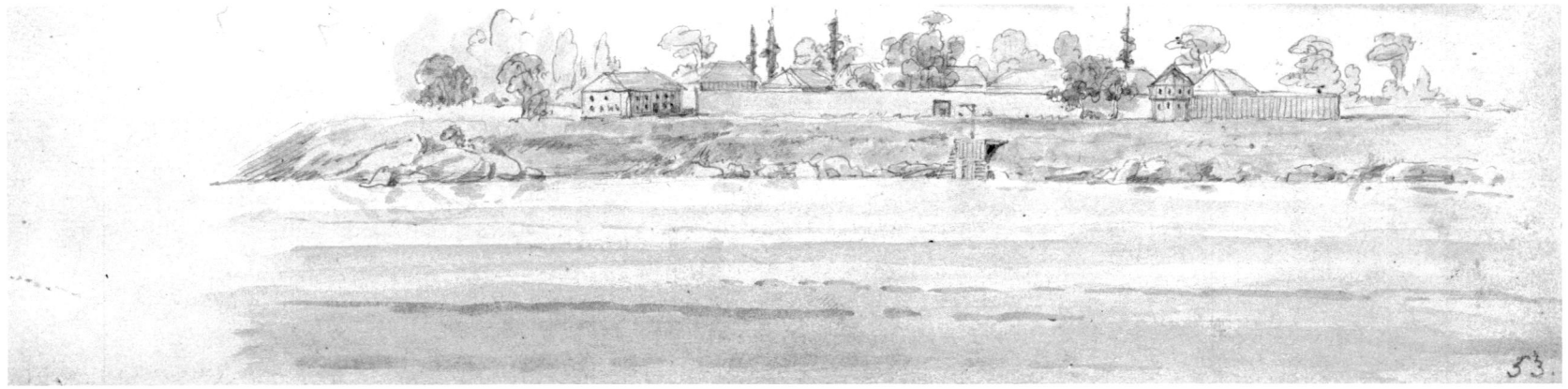

Fig. 188. Fort Victoria, with an Indian village. ROM946.15.212; CRIV-535.

COURTESY STARK FOUNDATION, ORANGE, TEXAS

Fig. 189. Fort Victoria. Stark WWC104; CRIV-536.

Fig. 190. Medicine man with mask, from Strait of Juan de Fuca. Stark woᴘ7; cʀIV-539.

Fig. 191. Medicine Mask Dance. ROM912.1.92; CRIV-541.

Fig. 192. Interior of a Winter Lodge of the Clallams. National Gallery of Canada 6923; crIV-550.

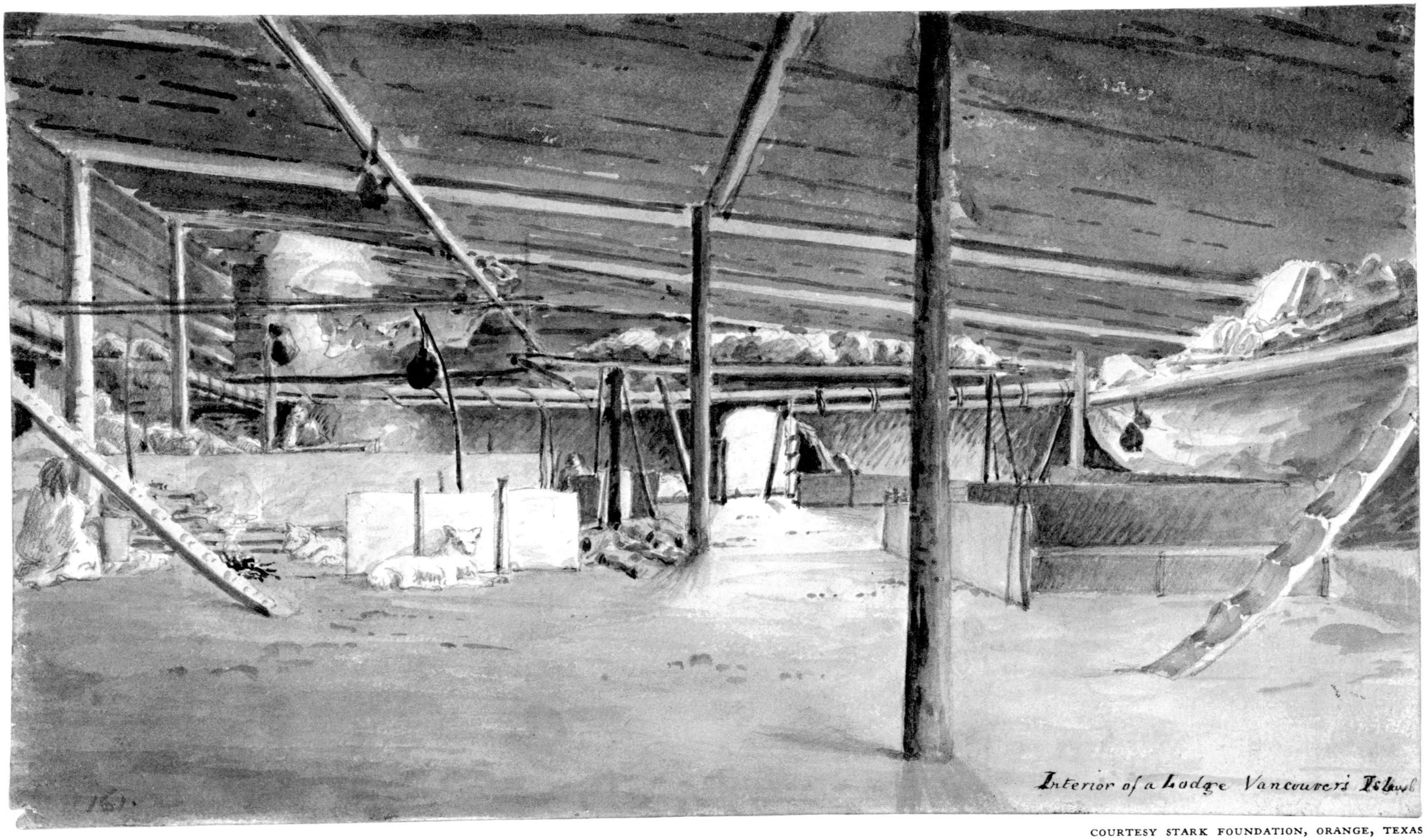

COURTESY STARK FOUNDATION, ORANGE, TEXAS

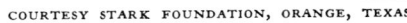

Fig. 194. Interior of a Clallam lodge, Vancouver Island. Stark wwc81; crIV-545.

COURTESY STARK FOUNDATION, ORANGE, TEXAS

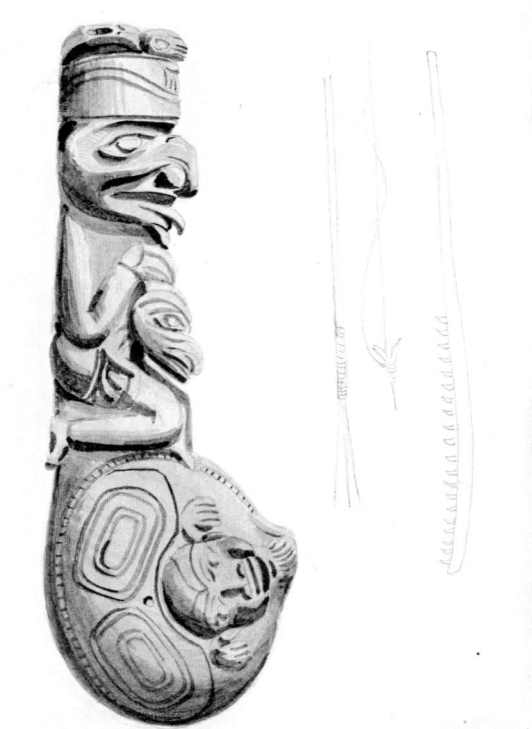

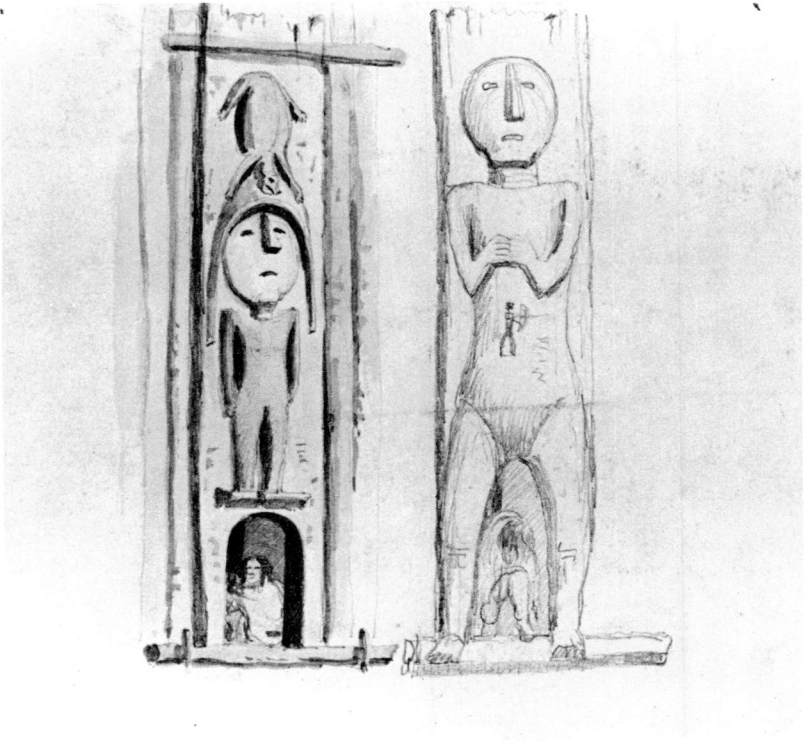

Fig. 193. Indian medicine rattle, northwest coast. Stark wwc99A; crIV-544.

COURTESY ROYAL ONTARIO MUSEUM, TORONTO

Fig. 195. Carved house post, Fort Victoria (?). ROM946.15.248; crIV-551.

Plate XLVII. Culchillum, a Cowichan, wearing a medicine cap, Fort Victoria. Stark wwc102H; crIV-570.

66
67.

Indians of Johnsons Straits

20d

Plate XLVIII. A Ucaltas man and a Nisqually girl. Stark wwc83; crIV-582, 502.

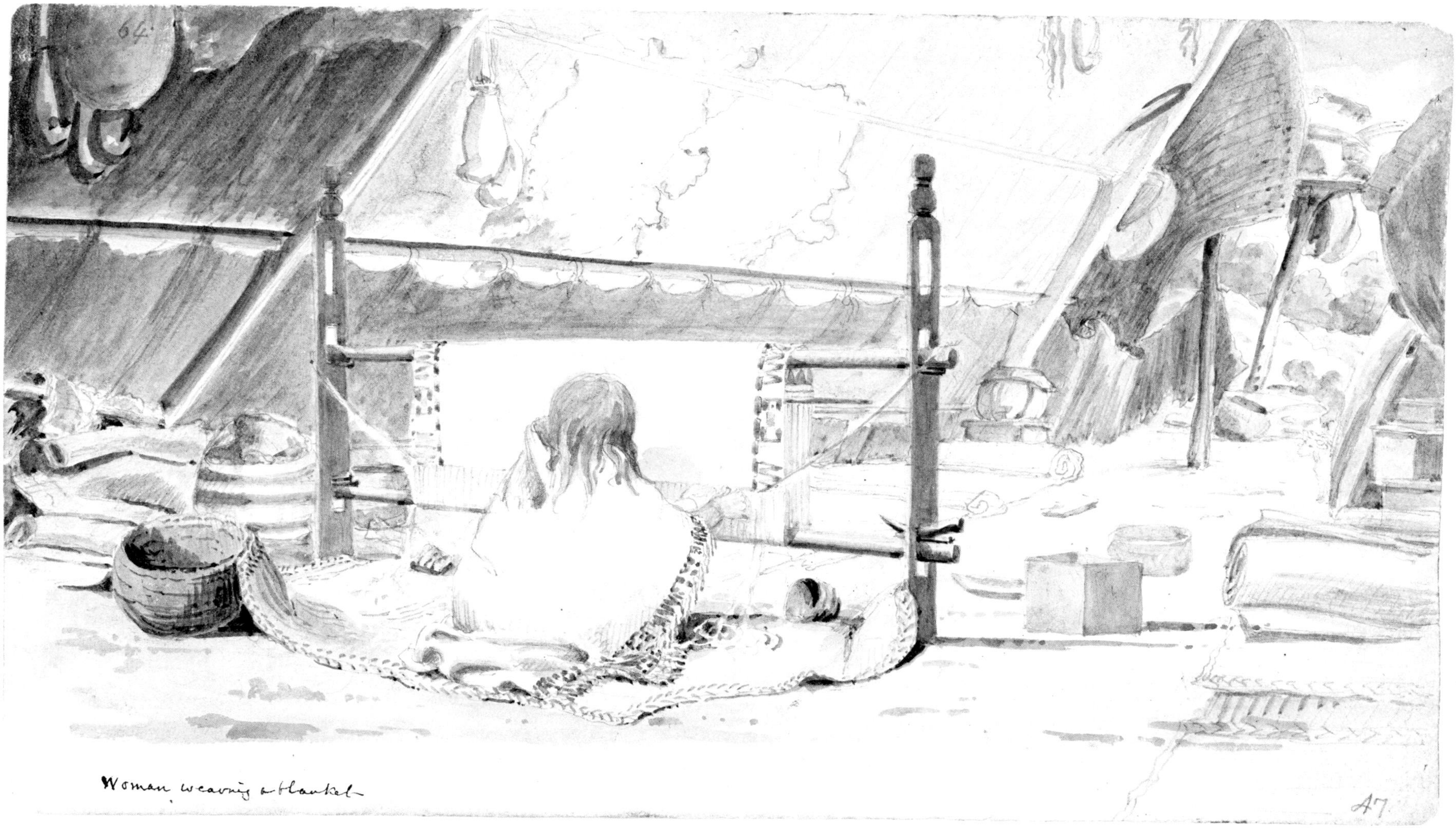

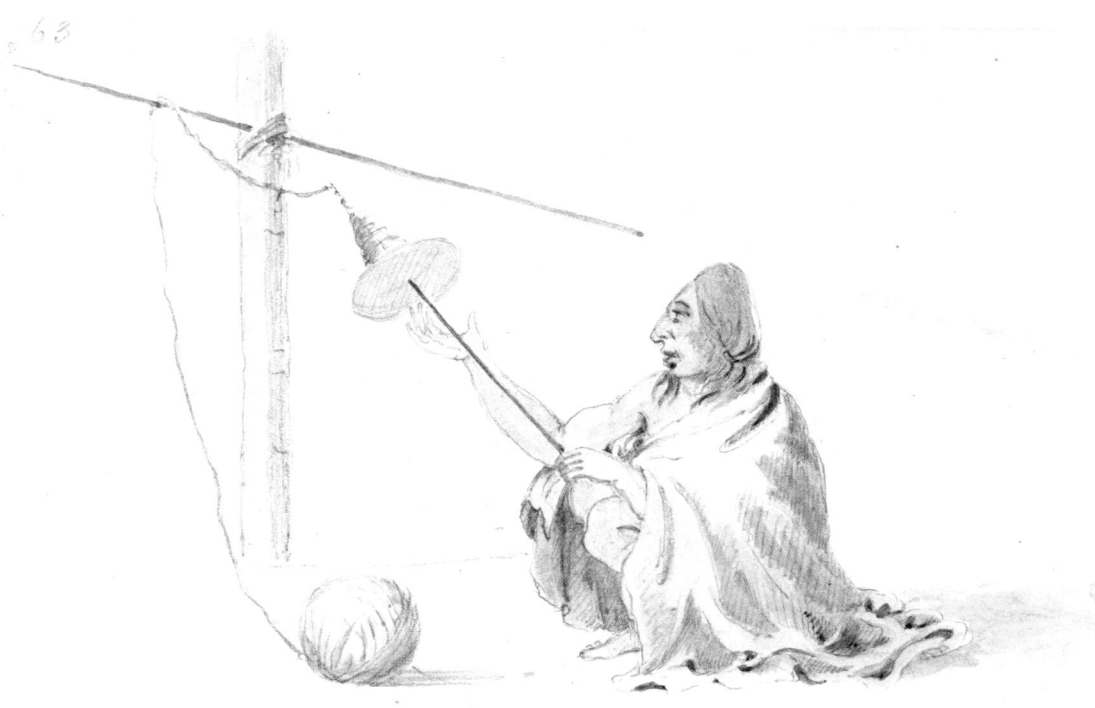

Fig. 196. Indian woman weaving a blanket, Fort Victoria. Stark wwc73; crIV-552.

COURTESY STARK FOUNDATION, ORANGE, TEXAS

COURTESY STARK FOUNDATION, ORANGE, TEXAS

Fig. 197. Woman spinning yarn, Fort Victoria. Stark wwc97; crIV-553.

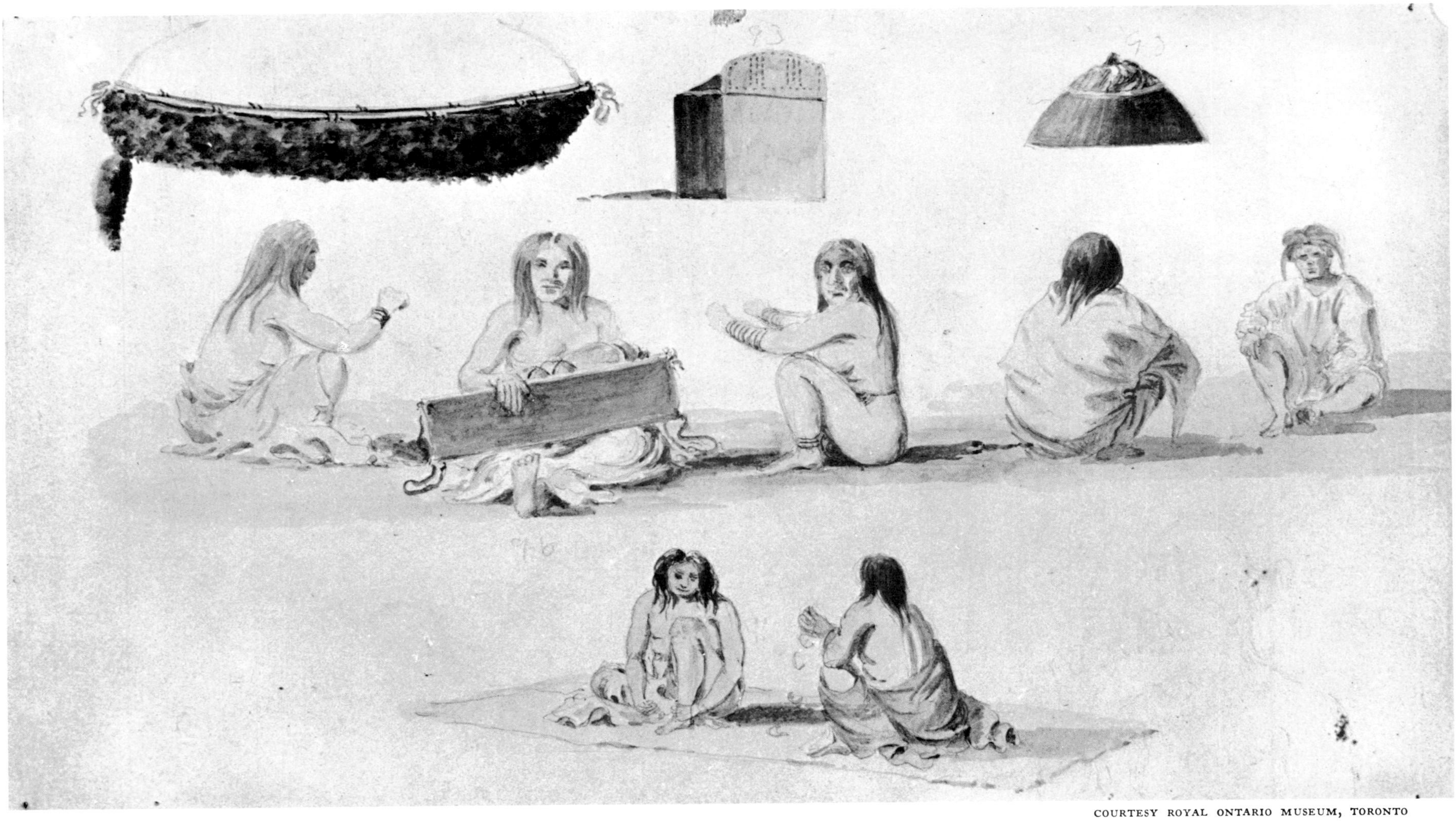

COURTESY ROYAL ONTARIO MUSEUM, TORONTO

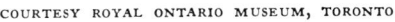

Fig. 198. Studies of figures inside a lodge, Fort Victoria. ROM946.15.227; CRIV-557.

COURTESY STARK FOUNDATION, ORANGE, TEXAS

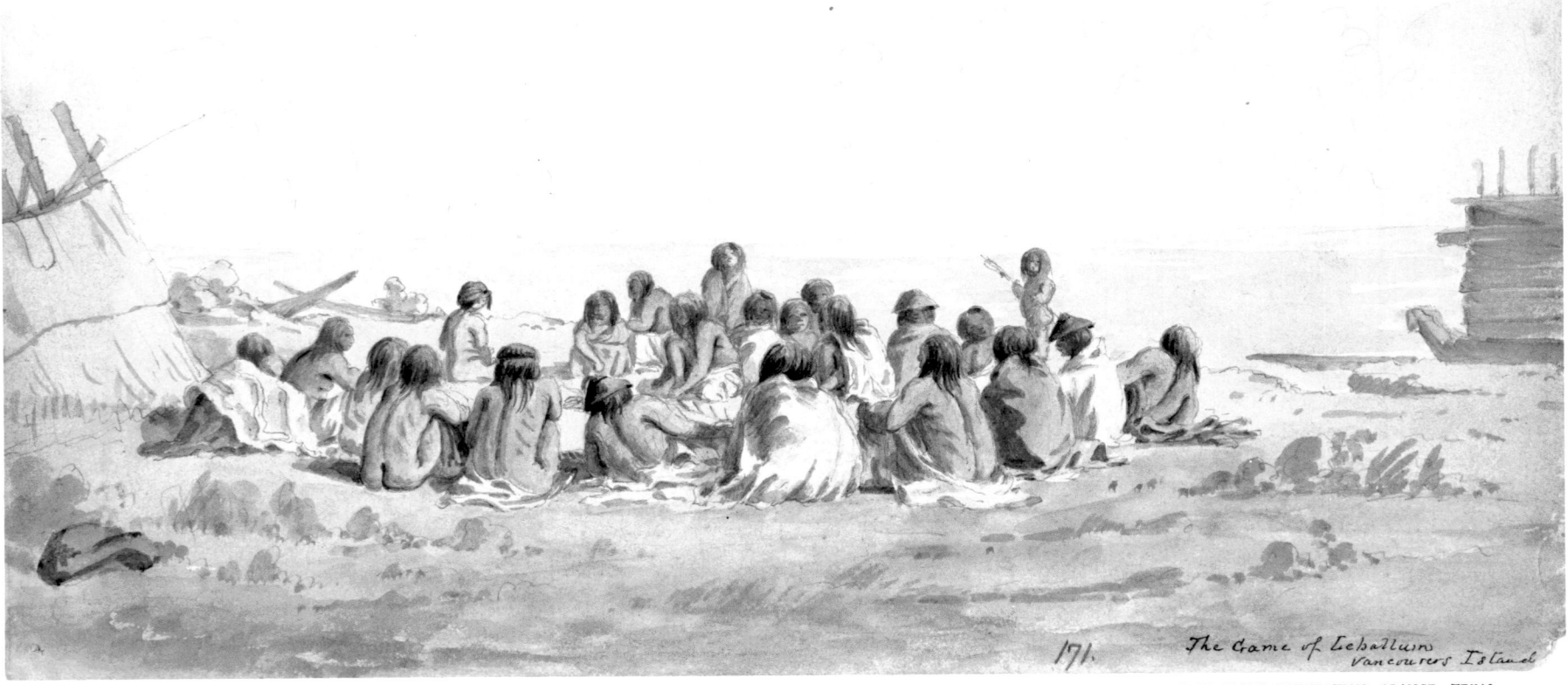

Fig. 199. Game of lehallum, Vancouver Island. Stark WWC25; CRIV-564.

Fig. 200. Saw-se-a (a Cowichan chief, Strait of Georgia). ROM912.1.94; CRIV-569.

Fig. 201. A Nootka chief, northern Vancouver Island. Stark wwc16; crIV-575.

Fig. 202. Ma-cheek-e-a-wis, a Chimmesyan Indian. Stark wop6; crIV-584.

Fig. 203. A Babbine Chief. ROM912.1.87; crIV-587.

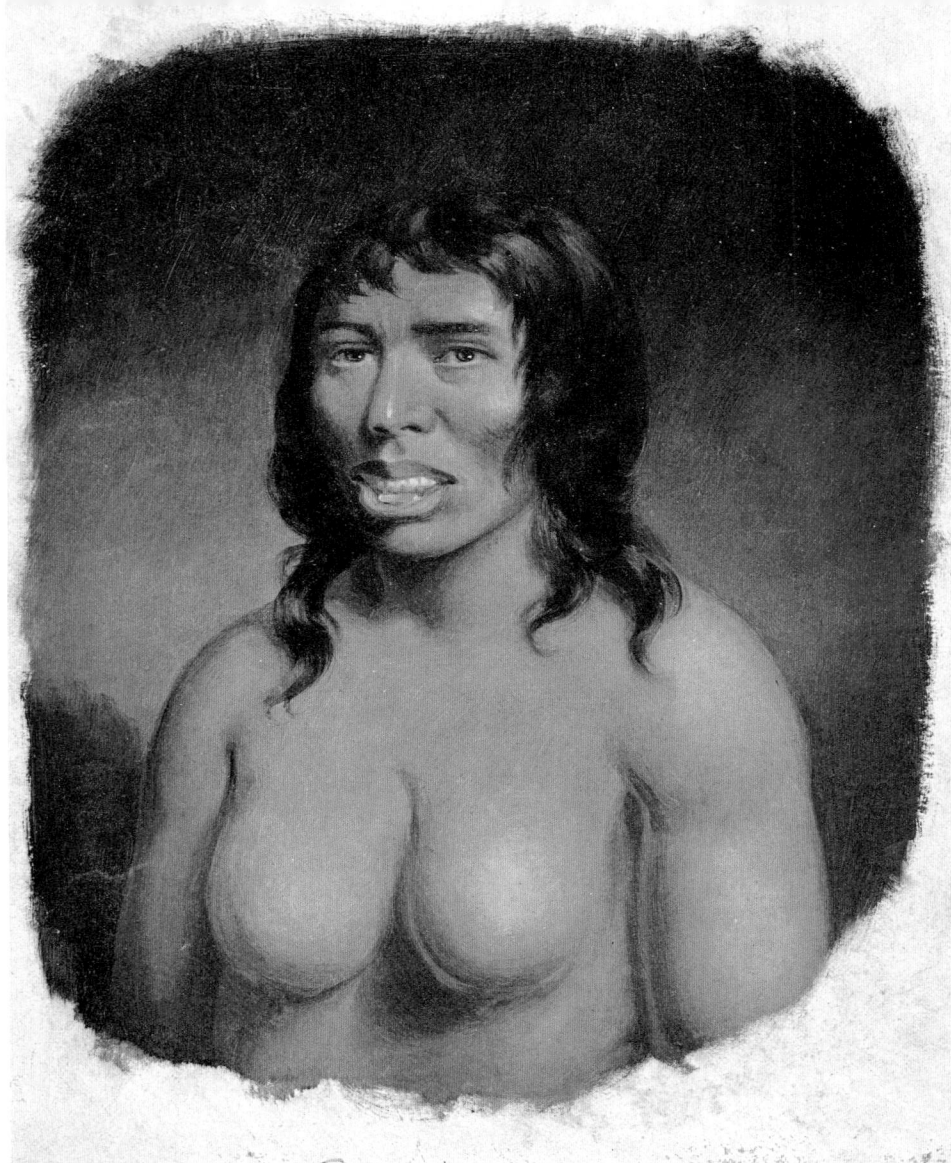

Fig. 204. A Babine woman. Stark woₚ12; crIV-585.

Fig. 205. Babine pipe-stem. Stark wwc1; crIV-589.

PART FOUR   A *Catalogue Raisonné*

Introduction

Paul Kane's works divide themselves logically into several groups. These are made up of works he painted before going to Europe; sketches and canvases from the years of his study in Europe, 1841–43; works relating to his Indian travels in the Great Lakes region during 1845; those relating to his travels between Lake Superior and the Pacific during 1846–48; and works completed in the Toronto area, both portraits and landscapes, after 1845. The *catalogue raisonné* has therefore been divided into the following sections:

I: Works done before 1841.
II: Works done in Europe 1841–43.
III: Portraits and landscapes of the Great Lakes region, 1845.
IV: Portraits and landscapes of the west, 1846–48.
V: Portraits and landscapes, done chiefly in the Toronto region, following 1845.

Within each of these sections works are grouped in various ways to provide a pattern for the presentation. In sections III and IV, for instance, there are subordinate headings for stages of the western travels; the divisions they introduce may originate in his visits at Hudson's Bay Company posts, in routes of travel from post to post, etc. These divisions are often broken into sub-groups for such subject-matter as landscape, portraits of Indians from particular tribes, ceremonials, and hunting scenes, the works within a sub-group relating to the stage of the journey indicated by the heading for the division. Within any group are listed canvases, sketches on which they were based, and sketches of related subjects. For example, all sketches and canvases of the buffalo hunt south of Fort Garry have been placed in one sub-group; studies and canvases for the encampment of the Métis buffalo hunters in another. Sub-groups usually have a preliminary paragraph intended to provide identification or background information for them.

Within each item in the *catalogue,* whether it is sketch or canvas, are included: (1) title, if any has been assigned previously to the picture (in capital and lower-case letters), or a phrase (in lower-case letters) briefly identifying the subject-matter; (2) explanatory notes if required; (3) reference to a list or lists in which the work may have been noted at some time (i.e. Kane's own logs, an exhibition list, a collector's list); (4) the medium in which the work was done; (5) its over-all size; (6) plate or figure number if it is illustrated in this book; (7) the collection in which it is now held. References to *Wanderings of an Artist* give page numbers of the text reprinted here; they also indicate when an item has appeared as an illustration in the 1859 edition.

As has been noted in the preliminary pages of this book, Kane's spelling of names of Indians and their tribes varies considerably. In this *catalogue raisonné* names of individual Indians are normally given in the spelling used by Kane in the printed version of *Wanderings of an Artist;* alternative spelling found in his manuscripts or elsewhere appears in a following parenthesis. Names of tribes and geographical names are in modern style, but where Kane's spelling may be significant it is provided.

The titles by which Kane's Indian canvases have been known have varied through the years. The earliest complete listing of his much publicized cycle of one hundred Indian works is that in the hand of the Honourable George W. Allan, made when they were turned over to him by Kane in 1856 (see Appendix 5). The title of 1856 has been assigned here to the appropriate works. The majority of these canvases are, however, now in the Royal Ontario Museum collections, and have been entered in several previously published lists; the first was a catalogue published about 1903 when the canvases were the property of E. B. Osler, and another list appeared in the Radisson Society edition of *Wanderings* (1925; reprinted 1968). Later titles by which these canvases are known follow the original titles, within brackets. For other collections, the titles given are those by which the owner now knows the paintings.

Abbreviations

A4	Stark Foundation Collection, Paul Kane, Artifact no. 4
AG	Allan Gift: Sketches given by the Allan family to Mrs. Paul Kane following the artist's death in 1871 (see Appendix 7)
Bushnell	David I. Bushnell Collection, Peabody Museum, Harvard University
Coe	Coe Collection, Yale University
CR	*Catalogue raisonné*
Glenbow	Glenbow–Alberta Institute, Calgary
GS	Paintings delivered by Kane to Sir George Simpson (see Appendix 4)
GWA	Paintings delivered by Kane to the Honourable George W. Allan, 1856 (see Appendix 5)
KLL	Kane's landscape log kept on his 1846–48 travels, now in the Stark Foundation (see Appendix 1)
KPL	Kane's portrait log kept on his 1846–48 travels, now in the Stark Foundation (see Appendix 2)

LP   Paintings delivered by Kane to the Parliament of Canada, 1855 (see Appendix 6) for its Library

NGC   National Gallery of Canada collections, Ottawa

PAC   Public Archives of Canada, Ottawa

ROM   Royal Ontario Museum (Ethnology Department) collections, Toronto

Stark   Nelda C. and H. J. Lutcher Stark Foundation collections, Orange, Texas

TCH   *Catalogue of Sketches of Indians, and Indian Chiefs, Landscapes, Dances, Costumes, &c, &c by Paul Kane;* for the exhibition at the Toronto City Hall, 1848 (see Appendix 3)

*   An asterisk indicates the item has not been seen by the present author.

Section I

Paintings and sketches executed by Kane before he went to Europe in 1841

LANDSCAPES

Kane exhibited nine paintings, principally copies, at the exhibition in Toronto of the Society of Artists and Amateurs, 1834. None has been traced. The following list has been extracted from the printed catalogue, and follows its wording.

I-1   Harlech Castle and distant view of Snowdon, North Wales, copy. SAAT 1834, no. 112.*

I-2   Lake George, after (Thomas) Drury. SAAT 1834, no. 113.*

I-3   Residence of John Gamble, Esq., Mimico Creek. SAAT 1834, no. 116.* There is a remote possibility that this landscape is the one listed as V-14.

I-4   Elm Park, from a print. SAAT 1834, no. 121.*

I-5   View of Niagara Falls, from a print. SAAT 1834, no. 140.*

I-6   Falls of Tivoli, from a print. SAAT 1834, no. 151.*

I-7   A Mameluke, from a print. SAAT 1834, no. 152.*

I-8   Hardraw Force, from a print. SAAT 1834, no. 173.*

I-9   Landscape, from a print. SAAT 1834, no. 174.*

PORTRAITS

The following portraits have been attributed to Kane. Not all have been located and examined by the author.

I-10   Young girl (naïve style). Possibly c. 1830. Oil on canvas. 2'10" x 2'7". (Colln Mrs. Paul Kane III)

I-11   Michael Peter Empey. The subject, who was a friend of Kane, was born c. 1811 and lived at Bradford, Ont. The painting must date from the early 1830s. Oil on paper mounted on wooden panel. 8" x 7¼". (Colln Mrs. S. Trivett)

I-12   W. S. Conger. For a biography of the subject see G. W. Craw, *The Peterborough Story* (Peterborough 1967). Illustrated in E. C. Guillet's *The Valley of the Trent* (Toronto 1957), Plate 103. Painted c. 1834. Oil on canvas. 12" x 10". (Colln Peterborough Centennial Museum) *

I-13   Mrs. W. S. Conger. Painted c. 1834. Oil on canvas. 12" x 9⅞". Fig. 2. (Colln S. E. Weir) *

I-14   F. S. Clench (Kane's father-in-law). Illustrated in Guillet, *The Valley of the Trent*, Plate 102. Possibly c. 1836. Oil on canvas. (Private colln) *

I-15   Mrs. F. S. Clench (Kane's mother-in-law). Illustrated in Guillet, *The Valley of the Trent*, Plate 101. Possibly c. 1836. Oil on canvas. (Private colln)*

I-16   William Weller. Illustrated in Guillet, *The Valley of the Trent*, Plate 99. Oil on canvas. (Private colln) *

I-17   Mercy (Willcox) Weller. Illustrated in Guillet, *The Valley of the Trent*, Plate 100. Oil on canvas. (Private colln) *

I-18   The Hon. Henry Ruttan (1791–1871). For a biography of the subject see *Dictionary of Canadian Biography*, vol. X. Illustrated in Guillet, *The Valley of the Trent*, Plate 104. Oil on canvas. (Private colln) *

I-19   Henry Richard Norton. Norton was a partner of W. S. Conger (see I-12), and operated a cabinet-making shop in Cobourg, Ont. See also K. E. Kidd, "Notes on scattered works of Paul Kane," in the 1962 *Annual* of the Art and Archaeology Division, Royal Ontario Museum, Toronto. Oil on wooden panel. 1'11½" x 1'7". (ROM L965.1.1)

In this same article Kidd attributes a portrait of Charles Fothergill, now in the collection of the ROM, to Kane. Information which has come to light subsequently proves that this portrait is the work of George S. Gilbert.

I-20   Brayley Norton (wife of H. R. Norton). See Kidd, 1962 *Annual*, Art and Archaeology Division, ROM. Oil on wooden panel. 1'11½" x 1'7". Plate II. (ROM L965.1.2) This portrait, on loan to the Sigmund Samuel Gallery of Canadiana of the ROM through the courtesy of Mr. E. C. Guillet, is reproduced with his kind approval.

I-21   The Hon. Zaccheus Burnham (1777–1857). Burnham, born at Dumbarton, N.J., lived in Cobourg and its district. He was a militia captain in charge of shipping on Lake Ontario, 1812, a member of both the Legislative Assembly and the Legislative Council, and treasurer of the Newcastle District. Oil on canvas. 2'6¼" x 2'2¼". (Colln N. Nickels) *

I-22   George Hetherington. Exhibited at the Art Gallery of Toronto in 1934, and then the property of T. S. Lawson.*

I-23   Mrs. Perry (sister of Mrs. W. S. Conger). Referred to in the notes on Kane made by F. S. Challener, now in the Art Gallery of Ontario.*

I-24 Eliza (Clench) Armour, younger sister of Harriet (Clench) Kane. Born in Cobourg 1831. Painted *c.* 1836. Oil on canvas. (Oval) 2′ x 1′8″. Fig. 3. (Colln Mrs. R. J. Shirley)

I-25 The riverboat *Norma* with captain (or owner). This ship was built at Louisville, Ky., 1839, 188 44/95 tons, and then transferred to New Orleans. The figure is probably that of George Washington Haygood of New Orleans, at various times both master and part owner. Probably painted at New Orleans 1839–41. Oil on canvas. 2′10½″ x 1′9½″. Fig. 4. (Stark OP26)

I-26 Queen Victoria. Full length portrait copied from an engraving of a portrait by H. B. Chalon. Painted 1840–41. Not located; referred to in the *Commercial Register* (Mobile, Alabama), March 20, 1841.* (See Appendix 11.)

I-27 President Harrison. Portrait, probably half length. Painted 1840–41. Not located. Referred to in the *Commercial Register* (Mobile, Alabama), March 20, 1841.* (See Appendix 11.)

Section II

Paintings and sketches executed in Europe 1841–1843

Kane regretted having lost some of the notes and sketches completed in Italy, particularly sketchbooks of the work done in Rome and Naples. These appear to have been lost before his return to Canada in 1845. Section II contains some paintings which he is known to have executed but which have since disappeared.

ROMAN PERIOD

Kane was in Rome from September 17, 1841, to February 17, 1842, when he left for Naples. He seems to have spent much of his time in the Borghese Gallery copying paintings. The following are works known to have been copied or sketched in Rome.

II-1 A Madonna, by Murillo (1617–1682). The title appears on a shipping list but the work has not been located. Owned by Kane at his death, 1871.*

II-2 A Mary Magdalene, by Andrea del Sarto (1486–1531). The title appears on a shipping list but the work has not been located.*

II-3 A head, by Raphael (1483–1520). There are two Raphael heads in the Borghese Gallery. The title appears on a shipping list but the work has not been located.*

II-4 A head, by J. Palma Il Vecchio (1480–1528). There is such a portrait in the Borghese Gallery. The title appears on a shipping list but the work has not been located.*

II-5 A portrait of Gregory XV, by Giovanni Busato (1806–1886). The head has been taken as a detail from a celebrated picture of the time. Oil on canvas. (Colln Mrs. Paul Kane III)

II-6 A Roman sketchbook. This book has 23 pages with pencil sketches of Roman views including the Claudian Aquaduct and tombs of the emperors, and 3 pages with sepia water-colour figure studies. 5½″ x 4″. Figs. 5, 6. (Colln Mrs. T. M. Willet)

FLORENTINE PERIOD

Kane was in Florence from May 27 to August 12, 1842, when he left for Venice. He made application on June 14 to paint in the Pitti Palace. He seems to have worked chiefly among the self-portraits now in the Uffizi Collection.

II-7 Pope Julius II, by Raphael. Copy of a portrait now in the Uffizi Collection. Oil on canvas. (Colln Mrs. R. W. Thurston)

II-8 A Florentine sketchbook. In this book are 28 pencil sketches, including landscapes, architectural subjects, Ariosto's chair, and studies of paintings in the Uffizi including the self-portraits of C. Dolci and F. Lippi, and the portrait of Daniel Barbaro by Veronese. 4″ x 5½″. (Colln Mrs. Paul Kane III)

II-9 Self-portrait, by Peter Paul Rubens (1577–1640), from the painting in the Uffizi. Originally part of sketchbook, II-8. Pencil. 5½″ x 4″. Fig. 7. (Private colln)

II-10 Self-portrait, by Rembrandt (1609–1669). Copy of a portrait in the Uffizi Collection. The title appears on a shipping list but the work has not been located. Owned by Kane at his death, 1871.*

II-11 Portrait, by Leonardo da Vinci (1452–1519). Copy of a portrait, probably in the Uffizi. The title appears on a shipping list but the work has not been located. Owned by Kane at his death, 1871.*

FLORENTINE AND VENETIAN PERIODS

Kane reached Venice from Florence about August 15, 1842, and remained until September 28, 1842, when he left for France and England via Milan. He received a permit to sketch in the Accademia, Venice, on September 15, 1842.

II-12 A section of a sketchbook. The Italian section comprises 15 sketches in pencil completed in Florence and Venice. (The balance of the book includes studies of Indians made on Georgian Bay, which are entered in CRIII.) Italian studies include those of the marble statue of St. George by Donatello from Or San Michele, Florence, architectural details, chairs, a bridge over a Venetian canal, a gondola, and a general view of Venice. 5¾″ x 8¾″. (ROM946.15.3 to ROM946.15.17)

MISCELLANEOUS PAINTINGS

II-13 Italian youth. Oil on paper. (Colln Mrs. R. W. Thurston)

II-14 Pilgrims at a Shrine. Oil on canvas. (Colln M. O'Brien, on loan to ROM)

II-15 "Una Donna alla Fontana (Girl at Fountain)." Sketch, probably a copy of a painting in Rome or Florence. The title appears on a shipping list but the work has not been located.*

II-16 "Piperani." Sketch, probably a copy of a painting in Rome or Florence. The title appears on a shipping list but the work has not been located.*

II-17 "Donna di Frescati." Sketch, probably a copy of a painting in Rome or Florence. The title appears on a shipping list but the work has not been located.*

II-18 "Donna di Mola de Gaeta." Sketch, probably a copy of a painting in Rome or Florence. The title appears on a shipping list but the work has not been located.*

II-19 Martyrdom of St. John the Baptist. Original not located; owned by Kane at his death in 1871.*

Section III

Paintings, sketches and drawings of Indians and landscapes relating to the 1845 expedition to Georgian Bay, Lakes Huron and Michigan, and adjoining regions

Kane left Toronto on June 17, 1845. He travelled to the Saugeen Indian reservation on Lake Huron where he made his first Indian sketches. From there he passed through the Thirty Thousand Islands of Georgian Bay to Manitoulin Island, Sault Ste Marie and Mackinac Island at the entrance to Lake Michigan. Proceeding down Lake Michigan to Green Bay, he visited the Lake Winnebago and Fox River regions in Wisconsin. He executed no sketches on his return journey to Toronto that autumn. Sketches made on the trip and paintings based on them have been arranged geographically following the route of his travels.

No log of Kane's 1845 sketches has been located, making identification of several particularly difficult. It seems fairly certain that a log for some of these sketches once existed. Identification has been based principally on the catalogue of the 1848 exhibition in the Toronto City Hall, in which many were shown, on notes made either by a member of the George W. Allan family or possibly by Kane's grandson, and on references to sketches in *Wanderings*. Identification of a number is tentative; fortunately most of these are of minor importance.

Kane's tribal designations have been followed. Chippewa and Ojibwa are actually synonomous terms which apply to one large tribal group. This can be subdivided into the Ojibwa of Lake Superior, the Missisauga of Manitoulin Island and the mainland around the Mississaga River, the Ottawa of Georgian Bay and the Potawatomi of Michigan. Missisauga are not mentioned in Kane's writings.

SAUGEEN

Kane remained at the Saugeen Indian village from June 22 to June 30. It is situated near Chief's Point on Lake Huron towards the base of the Bruce Peninsula. The Saugeen were settled in two bands, one at the mouth of the Saugeen River and the other on Sydenham Bay. They moved to these sites after surrendering their territories by treaty to the British government in 1836. Kane refers to them as "Saugeens," "Saguenays," and "Ojibwas."

III-1 Ojibwa (Ojibbeway) Chief (?). It has been suggested that this is Maticwaub or "The Bow," principal Saugeen chief, whom Kane mentions sketching (*Wanderings*, p. 52). No field sketch has been located. No such title or name appears in the list of canvases turned over by Kane to Allan; however GWA 70, designated as a portrait of "Maun-qua-dous," is apparently this canvas. Oil on canvas. 2'3" x 1'8½". (ROM912.1.4)

III-2 Kwa-qua-dah-bon-niva-skung or "Dawn of Day," chief of the "Saguenays" (Saugeen). This is possibly one of three or four lesser chieftains subsidiary to Maticwaub (see III-1). Sketched June 24, 1845. (See III-3.) w.c. 5¾" x 8¾". (ROM946.15.56)

III-3 Kwa-qua-dah-bon-niva-skung or "Dawn of Day." Identification has been based on an inscription, pre-dating Kane's death, on the sketch. (See III-2; see also IV-394.) AG72. Oil on paper. 12⅛" x 9¾". Fig. 14. (Stark EOP9)

III-4 An Ojibwa chief. It has been suggested, without apparent foundation, that this is a portrait of Maskuhnoonjee or "Big Pike" (*Wanderings*, p. 52). The chieftain bears no resemblance to the one in III-5, also identified as Maskuhnoonjee (but note change in spelling). See also III-6 for another sketch identified as of "The Pike." AG90. Oil on paper. 8⅛" x 6⅞". (Stark EOP4)

III-5 Sketch bearing double inscription of Maska-nonga or "Big Fish" and Shewans-u-ne-bin or "Alias 8 Summers." It is evidently a portrait of Maskuhnoonjee or "Big Pike," an Ojibwa: it was so exhibited in 1848 and so listed after Kane's death. (See III-4 and III-6.) TCH2. AG76. Oil on paper. 12⅜" x 9¾". Fig. 15. (Stark EOP19)

III-6 Page of studies. *Top* (left to right): 1/ Indian head in profile; 2/ European wearing beaver hat; 3/ Indian head inscribed Oogemsh-wah-be-zee or "Chief Young Swan"; 4/ Indian head inscribed Mus-Kosh or "Pike" (see III-4 and III-5). *Bottom* (left to right): 1/ overturned canoe; 2/ standing woman holding child; 3/ two standing women holding children. The inscriptions are evidently in Kane's hand. Pencil. 5¾" x 8¾". Fig. 16. (ROM946.15.53)

III-7 A chief's daughter from Lake St. Clair. An early inscription on the sketch, not in Kane's hand, identifies her as an Ojibwa. Kane refers to her (*Wanderings*, pp. 52–53). TCH238. AG6. Oil on paper. 9⅝" x 6⅛". Fig. 17. (Stark EOP5)

III-8 A Woman from Manitooawning (The Daughter of Asabonish). This canvas is obviously based on III-7, a portrait of a chief's daughter from Lake St. Clair, rather than on the girl in III-63, as has been claimed. GWA85. Oil on canvas. 2'1" x 1'10". (ROM912.1.7)

III-8A The Daughter of Asabonish. Replica of III-8. Oil on canvas. (Oval) 1'11½" x 1'6¼". (Colln Mr. and Mrs. Jules Loeb)

III-9 Wah-pus (Waugh-bi-see) or "The Rabbit," an Indian chieftain from Owen Sound who was at Saugeen during Kane's visit (*Wanderings*, p. 53). Crude sketches of canoes in margin. Pencil. 4¾" x 3". (Stark A4-1)

III-10 Sketches of Wah-pus or "The Rabbit" (three-quarter view), and (on reverse) white woman wearing bonnet. Pencil. 3" x 4". (ROM946.15.311)

III-11 Wappoose (Wah-pus or "The Rabbit"). Painting based probably on III-9. GWA76. Oil on canvas. 2'1" x 1'8". Fig. 18. (ROM912.1.1)

OWEN SOUND

Kane visited this town both in going to and in returning from Saugeen.

III-12 Indian encampment on Big Bay at Owen Sound. Identified from an early inscription, not in Kane's hand. AG8. Oil on paper. 6¾" x 11⅛". Fig. 19. (Stark EOP13)

GEORGIAN BAY

Thirty Thousand Islands

Kane and a companion, Dillon, canoed for two weeks among these islands. Locale of the sketches is not documented, but all evidently relate to the canvas of an Indian village (III-18 and III-19) which Kane says is among the islands.

III-13 Indian encampment with four bark wigwams and canoe. Pencil. 5¾" x 8¾". (ROM946.15.37)

III-14 Indian encampment of bark wigwams. Pencil. 5¾" x 8¾". (ROM946.15.39)

III-15 Indian encampment with ten bark wigwams and eight canoes in foreground. Pencil. 5¾" x 8¾". (ROM946.15.40)

III-16 Indian encampment with two bark wigwams. Pencil. 5¾" x 8¾". (ROM946.15.43)

III-17 Indian encampment with three bark wigwams and tent (possibly that of Kane). w.c. 5¾" x 8¾". (ROM946.15.32)

III-18 A Sketch on Lake Huron (Encampment among the Islands of Lake Huron). No sketch of this village has been located and the canvas is based presumably on sketches III-13 to III-17. (*Wanderings*, p. 53; woodcut, Fig. 1.) GWA42. Oil on canvas. 1'6" x 2'5". (ROM912.1.8)

III-19 An Indian Encampment on Lake Huron. Replica of III-18. Oil on canvas. 1'7" x 2'5". Fig. 20. (Art Gallery of Ontario 2121)

GEORGIAN BAY REGION

Conical Ojibwa wigwams

Conical wigwams of poles covered with birch bark appear in a number of sketches such as III-12 to III-19. The following isolated sketches cannot

be assigned to any particular locale but are presumably from the Georgian Bay region.

III-20 Wigwam, evidently covered with matting. Sketch has inscription, not in Kane's hand, reading "Indian wigwam on Lake Ontario"; it is more probably from Georgian Bay. AG35. Oil on paper. 9⅝" x 11⅝". (Stark EOP15)

III-21 Wigwam, evidently covered with matting and birch bark. Bears an inscription, not in Kane's hand, reading "Wigwam, Lake Huron." TCH43. AG42. Oil on paper. 9¾" x 12⅛". (Stark EOP32)

Indian life

III-22 Page of studies: Indian head with feather in hair; two Indians grinding corn in mortar (see *Wanderings*, p. 53); fishing net; dog; tripod of oars. Pencil. 5¾" x 8⅞". (ROM946.15.1)

III-23 Page of studies, principally of Indians reclining and of canoes. Pencil. 5¾" x 8¾". (ROM946.15.2)

III-24 Indian Bivouac. Painting of romantic character incorporating items from III-22 and III-23 including tripod of paddles, mortar, dog, reclining figure and canoes, and introducing a gun as mentioned by Kane (*Wanderings*, p. 53). Oil on canvas. 2'2⅞" x 3'2⅛". Fig. 21. (PAC Kane I-1)

See also III-128

FRENCH RIVER

Although his narrative does not mention the French River, Kane presumably visited it while canoeing through the Thirty Thousand Islands.

III-25 French River rapids. A party of military men or fur traders halt along the river. KLL7. TCH50. AG14. Oil on paper. 8⅛" x 13½". Plate III. (Stark POP22)

III-26 French River Rapids. Painting based on III-25. GWA19. Oil on canvas. 1'8" x 2'5". Fig. 22. (ROM912.1.2)

SPIDER ISLANDS

Kane reports the breaking of a sudden thunderstorm when he was approaching Manitowaning Bay, Manitoulin Island, from the northeast. He went ashore on an island where he found a single lodge and an Indian woman with two children (*Wanderings*, p. 53). The following works cannot all be assigned with certainty to Spider Islands but were evidently sketched either there or nearby.

III-27 Tent pitched beneath pine tree on island. Pencil. 5¾" x 8¾". (ROM946.15.46)

III-28 Ojibwa Camp (Ojibwa Camp on Spider Islands). Painting based on III-27 but substituting wigwam for tent. GWA2. Oil on canvas. 1'¾" x 1'7". Plate IV. (ROM912.1.3)

III-29 Conical wigwam beneath trees on island. By report the locale is Spider Islands. Pencil. 5¾" x 8¾". (ROM946.15.47)

III-30 Ojibwa Camp. Painting based on III-29. Oil on canvas. 1'5½" x 2'4½". (Colln Mrs. T. M. Willet)

III-31 Ojibwa camp, Spider Islands. Bushnell identified this sketch without stating reasons (see D. I. Bushnell, *Sketches by Paul Kane in the Indian Country*, Smithsonian Institution 1940, pp. 4–5). Oil on paper. 8½" x 14". (Bushnell 41-72/391)

III-32 Shoreline and islands, probably either Spider Islands or Thirty Thousand Islands. Pencil. 5¾" x 8¾". (ROM946.15.48)

III-33 Small rocky islands and wigwam, probably either Spider Islands or Thirty Thousand Islands. Pencil. 5¾" x 8¾". (ROM946.15.50)

III-34 Small rocky islands, probably either Spider Islands or Thirty Thousand Islands. Pencil. 5¾" x 8¾". (ROM946.15.49)

III-35 Indian standing on rocky headland. Georgian Bay region. Pencil. 5¾" x 8¾". (ROM946.15.52)

III-36 Page of sketches. *Upper:* rocky shoreline, designated as "Rock 1." *Centre:* rocky islands. *Bottom:* Indian grave house of Ojibwa type on shoreline. The landscape is that of the Georgian Bay region, distant village in lower frame is Manitowaning. Pencil. 5¾" x 8¾". Fig. 23. (ROM946.15.51)

III-37 Two low-lying islands. Pencil. 3" x 4¾". (Stark A4-2)

MANITOULIN ISLAND

Manitowaning

Manitowaning (spelled "Manetouawning" by Kane), an Indian village situated on Manitowaning Bay towards the western end of Manitoulin Island, was visited by Kane during July 1845 (*Wanderings*, p. 54). At this time Indians of several tribes had gathered at Manitowaning to receive presents (*Wanderings*, p. 55). Settlement of Manitoulin Island by the Indians began in 1836; by 1844 the population on the whole island, chiefly Ottawa and Chippewa, numbered some 700. Distribution of presents by the British government began in 1836; it was discontinued in 1860.

TOPOGRAPHY

III-38 Manitowaning as seen from across Manitowaning Bay. Pencil. 5¾" x 8¾". (ROM946.15.45)

III-39 View of Manitowaning with Indian wigwams during the 1845 assembly for the receipt of presents. Pencil. 8¼" x 1'2". Fig. 24. (Colln David Mitchell Gallery)

III-40 View of Manitowaning with Indian wigwams and groups of Indians during the assembly of tribes. Pencil. 8¼" x 1'2". (Colln David Mitchell Gallery)

III-41 View of bands arranged for receipt of presents. Pencil. 5¾" x 8¾". Fig. 25. (ROM946.15.30)

OJIBWA

Kane took the assembly of tribes for receipt of presents as an opportunity to sketch Indian chiefs from the whole region. The MS of *Wanderings*

before revision for publication indicates that, in addition to the individuals whom he mentions as having sketched, there were "many other chiefs of lesser note, of most of whom I made sketches." Evidently among these were a number of Ojibwa chieftains from Lake Superior. The following sketches are apparently of Ojibwa at Manitowaning.

III-42 Sigennok or "The Blackbird," head chief. He was paid by the British government as an "interpreter" (*Wanderings*, pp. 54, 55). (See III-58.) Presumably this is the same individual as "As,si,ke,nack (The Blackbird)" described by Anna Jameson as a remarkable man and the most celebrated orator of his nation when she met him in 1838. She quotes his translation of the governor's address at Manitowaning during the treaty ceremony in that year. (See Mrs. Anna Jameson, *Sketches in Canada and Rambles among the Red Men*, London 1852, part II, pp. 276, 278–82.) TCH1. AG82. Oil on paper. 9¾" x 6¼". (Stark EOP14)

III-43 Page of portrait studies. *Left:* profile head inscribed "Now-qua-ke-glick, Noon day." *Centre:* boy, head and shoulders, inscribed "Sig-in-nock-ence" (son of Sigennok, III-42). *Right:* head in profile, unidentified. Pencil. 5¾" x 8¾". (ROM946.15.44)

III-44 Shawwanossoway or "One with his Face towards the West." Kane points out that he was a great medicine man (*Wanderings*, pp. 55–56). TCH16. Oil on paper. 12¼" x 95/8". Fig. 26. (Stark EOP2)

III-45 Shah-wah-nas-ha-wa (Shaw-wan-osso-way). Painting based on sketch III-44. GWA99. Oil on canvas. 2'1" x 1'8". (ROM912.1.6)

III-46 Ojibwa from Lake Superior. Probably sketched at Manitowaning. TCH5. AG59. Oil on paper. 11½" x 9¼". (Stark EOP23)

III-47 Ojibwa Indian boy from Lake Superior. Probably sketched at Manitowaning. TCH6. AG10. Oil on paper. 6¾" x 55/8". (Stark EOP3)

III-48 She-bah-ke-zhick or "Hole in the Sky," an Ojibwa chief from Lake Superior (Fort William?). Probably sketched at Manitowaning. (See also IV-45, 47.) TCH3. Oil on paper. 113/8" x 9¼". (Stark EOP33)

III-49 Indian from Michipicoten. Probably an Ojibwa, sketched at Manitowaning. TCH 10. AG78. Oil on paper. 11" x 6½". (Stark EOP18)

III-50 Indian from Michipicoten. Probably an Ojibwa, sketched at Manitowaning. TCH9. Oil on paper. 12¼" x 9¾". Fig. 27. (Stark EOP6)

III-51 Saw-gun. Probably an Ojibwa, sketched at Manitowaning. TCH7. Oil on paper. c. 5" x 5". (Colln Mrs. T. M. Willet)

See also IV-1, 2.

OTTAWA

Five or six wandering families of the Ottawa tribe, originally from Lake Michigan, lived on Manitoulin Island in 1835. Others who had been living on lands in the United States arrived shortly after, and evidently by 1844 a sizeable number of Ottawa Indians were among the 700 residents of the island.

III-52   Muck-koze or "Young Bear," chief of the Ottawa of Manitoulin Island. His Anglicized name is sometimes given as "Black Bear." (See IV-133.) TCH13. AG87. Oil on paper. 12⅜″ x 9⅝″. Fig. 28. (Stark EOP24)

III-53   Awbonwaishkum, Ottawa chief from Manitowaning. (*Wanderings*, p. 54; woodcut, Fig. 2.) TCH12. AG45. Oil on paper. 9¾″ x 7¾″. Fig. 29. (Stark EOP12)

III-54   Awbonwaishkum. Painting based on III-53. Oil on canvas. (Over-all) 2′1″ x 1′8″; (oval) 2′ x 1′6½″. (ROM912.1.5)

III-55   Stone pipe carved by Awbonwaishkum. Sketch of a pipe now in the ROM collections. It has been stated, without supporting evidence, that this pipe comes from Lake Superior. (*Wanderings*, p. 54; woodcut, Fig. 3). Oil on paper. 7¼″ x 12¼″. Fig. 30. (Stark EOP21)

WYANDOT

A group of Huron Indians known as Wyandot moved about 1750 to the Ohio valley and there exerted considerable influence. They were always pro-British in their dealings.

III-56   Captain George Ironsides or "Walk on the Water." Kane states that he was a descendant of Tecumseh, a Shawnee chief from the Ohio River valley killed by the Americans in a bloody battle on the Thames River in Upper Canada (Ontario), 1812. Ironsides arrived in Manitowaning during Kane's visit to take over as Indian agent for the British (*Wanderings*, p. 57). Oil on paper. 11⅝″ x 9⅜″. Fig. 31. (Stark EOP16)

NO TRIBAL DESIGNATION

The following sketches of Indians, presumably either Ojibwa or Ottawa, were made at Manitowaning.

III-57   Sha-nu-oh-ke-zhick or "Against the Heavens" (an inscription on the sketch, not in Kane's hand, reads Sha-Neu-Oh-Rigits or "The Heron"), an Indian from Lake Nipissing. TCH8. AG21. Oil on paper. 11¼″ x 9½″. (Stark EOP11)

III-58   Ma-cheek-e-wis. This portrait was formerly identified as that of Sigennok (III-42). The new attribution is based on the TCH catalogue. It should be noted that the man in III-42 wears an Indian chief's medal, appropriate to Sigennok. TCH4 (see IV-584). Oil on paper. 10⅞″ x 8¼″. (Stark EOP1)

III-59   Two Indian portrait heads. *Left:* man wearing chief's medal and identified by totem of a catfish. *Right:* man identified by inscription Cath-a-nish-a-na-bay or "Black Indian." These sketches are tentatively assigned to Manitowaning, but it is possible the subjects were Saulteaux from the Fort Frances area. w.c. 5¾″ x 8¾″. (ROM946.15.19)

III-60   Page of sketches. *Left:* studies of two carved stone pipes. *Right:* full-face portrait head of Indian. Possibly sketched at Manitowaning. Pencil and w.c. 5¾″ x 8¾″. (ROM946.15.36)

See also III-76, 77.

ARTEFACTS

The following sketches have been assigned provisionally to Manitowaning but with little supporting evidence.

III-61   Sketches of drums. *Left:* drums with insignia of pair of facing animals and figure above. *Right:* unfinished sketch of drum. w.c. and pencil. 5¾″ x 8¾″. (ROM946.15.31)

III-62   Sketch of pipe and club. *Upper:* club with bird's head finial on grip. *Lower:* black stone pipe with lead inlay and elaborate feather decoration on stem. Pencil and w.c. 5¾″ x 8¾″. Fig. 32. (ROM946.15.33)

Wikwemikong (Wequimecong)

Wikwemikong is a village six miles from Manitowaning (*Wanderings*, pp. 56–57). The manuscript version of Kane's book states that he remained there for a fortnight and "made sketches of the two principal chiefs of this village and many others." It is possible that some portraits here assigned to Manitowaning may actually have been sketched at Wikwemikong.

OTTAWA

III-63   Asabonish or "The Raccoon," principal Ottawa chief at Wikwemikong, with his daughter (*Wanderings*, p. 57). Burpee states that the daughter is the subject of a canvas, III-8. However III-8 is obviously based on III-7 rather than on the girl's head in this sketch, despite the fact that GWA85 lists the III-8 canvas as "A Woman from Manitooawning." TCH11. AG49. Oil on paper. 12¼″ x 9¾″. Fig. 33. (Stark EOP28)

SAULT STE MARIE

Sault Ste Marie straddles the international boundary on the St. Mary's River. Kane visited the place during August 1845, May 1846 and October 1848. He states in *Wanderings* (p. 57) that in 1845 he remained a few days (the manuscript version states two weeks). He sketched on both the American and the Canadian side of the river. All sketches executed at Sault Ste Marie are included here in the 1845 section; it is possible a few were done during later visits.

Indian village on American shore

III-64   Indian encampment with two domed wigwams, Ojibwa type, covered with matting and birch bark. Pencil. 5¾″ x 8¾″. (ROM946.15.21)

III-65   Sault Ste Marie. Painting based on III-64 but with an added wigwam. GWA30. Oil on canvas. 1′7″ x 2′6″. Plate V. (ROM912.1.9)

III-66 Dome-shaped wigwam with three birch-bark canoes. Pencil and w.c. 5¾″ x 8¾″. (ROM946.15.22)

III-67 Dome-shaped wigwam. Pencil. 5¾″ x 8¾″. (ROM946.15.27)

III-68 Dome-shaped wigwam with camp-fire shelter. Pencil. 5¾″ x 8¾″. (ROM946.15.34)

III-69 Two dome-shaped wigwams with fish net. Pencil. 5¾″ x 8¾″. (ROM946.15.24)

III-70 Dome-shaped wigwam. Pencil. 5¾″ x 8¾″. (ROM946.15.28)

St. Mary's River

III-71 Two Indians in a canoe paddling in rapids. View from the American shore. (*Wanderings*, p. 62.) Pencil. 5¾″ x 8¾″. (ROM946.15.29)

III-72 Two Indians with fish net paddling a canoe in rapids. View from the Canadian shore. Pencil. 5¾″ x 8¾″. (ROM946.15.38)

III-73 Two Indians with fish net paddling a canoe in rapids. View from the American shore. Pencil. 5¾″ x 8¾″. (ROM946.15.26)

III-74 View of the Canadian shore with ruined grist mill and dome-shaped wigwam. The former is the remains of a mill built by Charles Oakes Ermatinger (1780–1853), an Indian trader who was agent of the North West Company at Sault Ste Marie for several years. Through construction of the mill at what became known as Windmill Point he hoped to encourage wheat growing in the area. Pencil. 5¾″ x 8¾″. Fig. 34. (ROM946.15.25)

Portraits

A locale for III-76 and III-77 cannot be ascertained with any certainty. It is probable they were executed at either Manitowaning or Sault Ste Marie.

III-75 Susan Belo, a half-breed girl (*Wanderings*, p. 62). TCH17. AG23. Oil on paper. 12⅛″ x 9¾″. (Stark EOP8)

III-76 Page of studies including five heads, standing figure of a woman and an Indian spear. Pencil. 5¾″ x 8¾″. (ROM946.15.23)

III-77 Two Indian portrait studies. *Left:* young man wearing Indian chief's medal; inscribed C-dah-mak-Skuash. *Right:* girl wearing beads. Pencil and w.c. 5¾″ x 8¾″. Plate VI. (ROM946.15.35)

MACKINAC

Kane visited Mackinac Island, at the entrance to the straits leading from Lake Huron to Lake Michigan, in 1845. As at Manitowaning, he found many Indians assembled here to receive treaty money and presents, this time from the United States government (*Wanderings*, pp. 57–58). He used the opportunity to make several portrait sketches. The published *Wanderings* states that he remained at Mackinac for three weeks; his manuscript version reads six weeks.

Topography

III-78 General view of the fort and Indian village. A fort was built on the island by Capt. Patrick Sinclair of the American army in 1780–81. It was the scene of considerable action between the Americans and British during the war of 1812–14, and was captured by the British on July 27, 1812. The fort was responsible for the development of Mackinac Island as a fur-trading centre. Pencil. 7″ x 9¾″. Fig. 35. (ROM946.15.255)

III-79 The natural bridge at Mackinac. Kane points out that this picturesque spot (known today as Arch Rock) was visited by "all strangers" (*Wanderings*, p. 58). Pencil. 5¼″ x 8¾″. (ROM-946.15.20)

III-80 The natural bridge at Mackinac. Pencil. 4¾″ x 3″. (Stark A4-13)

III-81 The natural bridge at Mackinac. Pencil. 4¾″ x 3″. (Stark A4-14)

III-82 The natural bridge at Mackinac. TCH45(?). AG1. Oil on paper. 12⅜″ x 9⅞″. Fig. 36. (Stark EOP20)

III-83 The natural bridge at Mackinac. TCH47. AG66. Oil on paper. 11½″ x 9⅝″. (Stark EOP31)

III-84 Rocky headland with wigwams in foreground. This sketch has been described as a "Landscape near Spider Island, Lake Superior" and as "Lake Superior." Colouring and terrain are similar to those in III-82 and III-83. It is almost certainly one of the Mackinac Island sketches exhibited in 1848. TCH46(?). Oil on paper. 12¼″ x 9⅝″. Fig. 37. (Stark EOP29)

III-85 Wooded shoreline, possibly on Mackinac Island. Pencil. 3″ x 4¾″. (Stark A4-12)

III-86 Sketch of rocky pinnacle on Mackinac Island (now known as Sugar Loaf). Pencil. 8¼″ x 1′2″. (Private colln)

III-87 Page of studies, probably made on Mackinac Island. *Left:* seated Indian. *Right:* rocky headland. Pencil. 5¾″ x 8¾″. (ROM-946.15.41)

Ojibwa and Ottawa

III-88 Mani-tow-wah-bay (Man-a-to-wa-bay) or "He-Devil," an Ojibwa from Lake Michigan (*Wanderings*, p. 58). TCH239. Oil on paper. 11¾″ x 8⅞″. Plate VII. (Glenbow)

III-89 Now-on-dhu-go, an Ottawa chief from Lake Michigan. TCH15. AG22. Oil on paper. 11⅝″ x 9⅜″. Plate VIII. (Stark EOP27)

III-90 Page of studies. *Left:* birch-bark box decorated with quill work (see IV-88, 469). *Centre:* head of Indian wearing medal around neck. *Right:* rocky headland suggesting Mackinac Island landscape. Pencil. 5¾″ x 8¾″. (ROM946.15.42)

Potawatomi

The following sketches may well be associated with the Mackinac Island material, judging from their position in the sketchbook (an uncertain criterion). Kane also met Potawatomi at Fox River.

III-91 Studies of three Indian heads in profile; labelled "Potawatomi." Pencil. 3″ x 4¾″. (Stark A4-4)

III-92 Studies of three Indian heads in profile and a horse. One head is obviously that of the individual pictured in III-90. Pencil. 3″ x 4¾″. (Stark A4-5)

III-93 Two Indian heads, with silver ornaments, in profile. Pencil. 4¾″ x 3″. (Stark A4-3)

III-94 Page of studies. *Left:* group of standing figures. *Right:* head in profile. Pencil. 3″ x 4¾″. (Stark A4-11)

Wampum belts

III-95 Sketches of four wampum belts evidently associated with the Indians at Mackinac: 1/ belt with inscription dated 1764 (possibly a wampum belt given by Sir William Johnson to the Indians at the Niagara conference of 1764); 2/ belt, undated; 3/ belt with inscription STTIB 1786; 4/ belt with inscription LIEUT COL. R. MC DOUALL COMM. MACKINAC (McDouall was British commander at Fort Mackinac during the war of 1812–14). Pencil. 3″ x 4¾″. Fig. 38. (Stark A4-43)

III-96 Sketches of three wampum belts (a fourth roughed in), evidently associated with the Indians of Mackinac. These are a second version of nos. 1, 2 and 3 in III-95. Pencil. 4½″ x 1′2″. (Private colln)

Studies of Indian life

Locale of the following sketches is uncertain. Association in the sketchbook with other Mackinac Island material seems to indicate that they were done there, but the subjects are typical of the whole general region.

III-97 Page of studies: group of Indians by wigwam, group of five Indians, and a large canoe with nine passengers. Pencil 4¾″ x 3″. (Stark A4-6)

III-98 Page of studies: seated figure, with boat under sail. Pencil. 3″ x 4¾″. (Stark A4-7)

III-99 Shoreline with birch-bark canoe and domed wigwam. Pencil. 3″ x 4¾″. (Stark A4-8)

III-100 Studies of two wigwams and overturned canoe. Pencil. 3″ x 4¾″. (Stark A4-9)

III-101 Studies of two wigwams. Pencil. 3″ x 4¾″. (Stark A4-10)

III-102 Studies of shoreline with domed wigwam, canoe and standing figure. Pencil. 3″ x 4¾″. (Stark A4-15)

III-103 Study of an adult figure and a boy holding bow. Pencil. 4¾″ x 3″. (Stark A4-16)

III-104 Sketch of birch-bark canoe. Pencil. 4¾″ x 3″. (Stark A4-17)

III-105 Bay with low shoreline and domed wigwam in foreground. Pencil. 3″ x 4¾″. (Stark A4-18)

LAKE WINNEBAGO

Kane visited Lake Winnebago during the autumn of 1845 while travelling along the Fox River (in the state of Wisconsin). From Green Bay he accompanied three American government officials on their way to pay treaty moneys to Indians living west of Lake Michigan.

Menominee

Kane sketched two sisters living on the lakeshore (*Wanderings*, p. 58); this is traditionally Winnebago territory, but Kane specifically states in the catalogue of 1848 that the girls were Menominee.

III-106 Iwa-toke or "The Serpent." (See also IV-251.) TCH20. AG86. Oil on paper. 12¼″ x 9⅝″. Fig. 40. (Stark EOP26)

III-107 Ke-wah-ten or "The North Wind." This sketch was exhibited at the Toronto City Hall in 1848 as a portrait of Iwa-toke's sister. It bears a notation, not in Kane's hand, "Menomenee Tribe, Lake Winnebago." It has also been described as a portrait of "Kee-wa-a-tin 'North Wind,' an Indian girl from the Menomenee tribe on Winnipeg River." Unlike Iwa-toke, this girl is decked out with elaborate silver ornaments and ear-rings. (See also III-108.) TCH21. AG61. Oil on paper. 12¼″ x 9½″. Fig. 39. (Stark POP3)

III-108 Portrait of a girl, bearing an inscription, not in Kane's hand, reading "Indian Woman, Fox River, Winnebago." The sketch is so similar in feeling to that of Iwa-toke, III-106, that one would assume that this girl was Iwa-toke's sister rather than the girl in III-107 who has been called Ke-wah-ten. AG50. Oil on paper. 12⅛″ x 9⅞″. (Stark EOP25)

Winnebago(?)

III-109 Wah-bannim (Wah-bo-nim) or "The White Dog." This sketch bears an inscription, not in Kane's hand, reading "Indian from Lake Winnebago." Kane describes Wah-bannim as wearing black paint in mourning for his wife (*Wanderings*, p. 58). (See also IV-365.) TCH22. AG4. Oil on paper. 12¼″ x 10″. (Stark POP21)

III-110 Waugh-be-nim (Wah-bannim). Painting based on III-109. Face is painted black for mourning and eyebrows are plucked. This painting has been described as that of a Menominee Indian but there is no documentary evidence as to tribe and the area is traditionally Winnebago. GWA98. Oil on canvas. 2′1″ x 1′8″. (ROM912.1.13)

FOX RIVER

Spearing fish

The evening before Kane reached a Menominee camp on Fox River (*Wanderings*, p. 58) he watched Indians spearing fish by torch light as he had himself done in "boyish days" on Toronto Bay. Kane states that the fish were salmon. In this he was mistaken; no salmon were known in the Great Lakes above Niagara Falls.

III-111 Spearing by torch light on Fox River (*Wanderings*; woodcut, Fig. 4). Oil on paper. (Colln Major R. W. Willis)

III-112 Fishing by Torch Light (Spearing salmon by torch light). Painting based on III-111. GWA39. Oil on canvas. 1′6″ x 2′5″. Fig. 41. (ROM912.1.10)

Menominee

Kane made a two-day journey up the Fox River from Lake Winnebago to visit a Menominee camp. He found 3,000 Indians assembled for the annual payment of treaty moneys by the American government (*Wanderings*, pp. 59–61). The site is known today locally as the "Poygan" Pay Ground. As at Manitowaning and Mackinac, Kane used the opportunity to sketch various Indians.

III-113 Oscosh (Oshkosh) or "The Bravest of the Brave." Kane describes him as head chief of the Menominee (*Wanderings*, p. 59). Oscosh (1795–1850) as a young man assisted the British in capturing Michilimackinac in the war of 1812. He represented his people in negotiations with the Americans in 1827; they recognized him on that occasion as head chief of the Menominee. An extant portrait by Samuel M. Brookes shows him in European garb. His name is perpetuated in that of the town of Oshkosh, Wisconsin. Pencil. 4¾″ x 3″. Fig. 42. (Stark A4-38)

III-114 Two sketches of portrait heads. *Upper:* Indian with silver hair ornaments, braided hair queues on side of face, and feather hair ornament. *Lower:* Sketch labelled "O" with a figure identical to that in III-113 except for a head ornament. Pencil. 4¾″ x 3″. (Stark A4-22)

III-115 Pipe of Peace. Evidently this is the pipe which, Kane says, Oscosh was sending to President John Tyler of the United States (*Wanderings*, p. 59). Two figures hold hands in friendship at the base of the richly decorated stem. Pencil. 4¾″ x 3″. (Stark A4-23)

III-116 Pipe of Peace. This is possibly the pipe used at the opening of the annual treaty money ceremony; Kane describes how Oscosh first lit it and then passed it on to the other chieftains. Pencil. 3″ x 4¾″. (Stark A4-24)

III-117 Match-o-kee-maw or "Big Chief"; inscription, possibly in Kane's hand. This may be a form of the name of an Indian Kane sketched whom he refers to as Kitchie-ogi-maw or "the Great Chief" (*Wanderings*, p. 60). See III-120. AG62. Oil on paper. 12⅜″ x 9¾″. Fig. 43. (Stark POP4)

III-118 Three studies of Indian heads. *Upper:* slight sketch with head dress. *Lower left:* three-quarter head with face painting similar to that in III-117; *Lower right:* full-face head with single-feather head dress. Pencil. 4¾″ x 3″. (Stark A4-25)

III-119 Study of head with face painting and features similar to those in III-117 and III-118. 4¾″ x 3″. (Stark A4-27)

III-120 Kitchie-ogi-maw. It is difficult to reconcile this portrait with the sketches III-117 to III-119. The roach, feather in hair and sheathed knife around the neck are similar to those pictured in III-121. GWA90. Oil on canvas. 2′6″ x 2′1″. (ROM912.1.11)

III-121 Page of sketches: profile head with elaborate head ornament; detached head ornament; knife in suspended sheath; head with knife in sheath suspended around neck. The knife is similar to that in III-120. Pencil. 4¾″ x 3″. (Stark A4-37)

III-122 Muck-a-ta. The TCH catalogue describes him as a Menominee although the sketch bears an inscription "Potowattamie." Kane refers to a visit from him (*Wanderings*, p. 61). TCH23. AG43. Oil on paper. 12¼″ x 9⅝″. Fig. 44. (Stark EOP17)

III-123 Muck-a-ta. Painting based on III-122 but with embellishments. This canvas does not appear in the list of Kane's paintings received by Allan in 1856. Presumably it was delivered later and substituted for a canvas which Kane took back. Oil on canvas. 2′1″ x 1′8″. Fig. 45. (ROM912.1.12)

III-124 Muck-e-tah-kin-ne-u, or "Black Eagle." TCH19. AG38. 12¼″ x 9¾″. (Stark EOP10)

[There is no III-125.]

Potawatomi

III-126 Coe-coosh or "The Hog," described by Kane as a Potawatomi "black-leg" (*Wanderings*, p. 59). A sketch IV-225 and a canvas IV-226 have been identified incorrectly as of Coe-coosh, a mistake which resulted from a framing error. TCH14. Oil on paper. 11¾″ x 9½″. Plate IX. (Stark EOP30)

III-127 A Potawatomi Indian. This painting has generally been known as a portrait of Coe-coosh, but the face in it does not correspond in any particular with the features in III-126. It has also been published incorrectly as a portrait of Wah-he-joe-tass-e-neen (IV-226), a mistake resulting from a framing error. (See also III-128.) GWA75. Oil on canvas. 2′1″ x 1′8″. (ROM912.1.14)

III-128 "Pine Tree." Replica of III-127. This replica was identified in recent years by an Indian of the Lake Huron–Georgian Bay region as a portrait of his grandfather. Oil on canvas. 2′6″ x 2′1″. (ROML957.11)

Winnebago

III-129 Mauza-pau-Kan, or the "Brave Soldier." Chief of the Winnebago. Kane refers to making his portrait (*Wanderings*, p. 61; it seems clear from the sketch and the context in the book that the sentence referring to Mauza-pau-Kan actually belongs at the end of the preceding paragraph). TCH18 (where the subject is designated as from Wolf River). Oil on paper. 12⅜″ x 9″. Fig. 46. (NGC6457)

Unidentified Indians, chiefly Menominee

III-130 Page of sketches. Three heads, two in profile, and one full face with face painted in quarter segments. Pencil. 3″ x 4¾″. (Stark A4-21).

III-131 Page of studies. Five heads and a leg. Pencil 4¾″ x 3″. (Stark A4-26)

III-132   Oke-a-sa. Study of head, full face, with painted cheeks and cheek ornaments, silver ear decorations, roach and many strands of beads. Pencil. 4¾″ x 3″. (Stark A4-28)

III-133   Page of four head studies, some with silver ornaments. Pencil. 4¾″ x 3″. (Stark A4-30).

III-134   Page with two portrait studies. *Upper:* full-face head study with hair ornamentation, painted face and strands of beads; inscribed Ac-o-namy. *Lower:* profile head inscribed In-na-quwa. Pencil. 4¾″ x 3″. (Stark A4-31)

III-135   Page with six head studies. Pencil. 4¾″ x 3″. (Stark A4-33)

III-136   Page with three head studies. *Upper:* painted face with head ornament. *Lower left:* profile head with feather head dress. *Lower right:* unfinished sketch. Pencil. 4¾″ x 3″. (Stark A4-34)

III-137   Profile study of head with single-feather head dress, silver hair ornaments and silver ear ornament. Pencil. 4¾″ x 3″. (Stark A4-35)

III-138   Two profile head studies. *Upper:* head with elaborate facial painting and two braided queues on each side of face. *Lower:* head with silver ornaments, elaborate silver ear ornaments and three feathers in roach. Pencil. 4¾″ x 3″. (Stark A4-36)

III-139   Studies of two heads. *Upper:* three-quarter view. *Lower:* profile head with hair queue and feather head dress. Pencil. 4¾″ x 3″. (Stark A4-39)

III-140   Sketch of single head. Pencil. 4¾″ x 3″. (Stark A4-40)

FORT SNELLING

Sioux scalp dance

There is no evidence that Kane visited For Snelling, site of Minneapolis, while he was in the region west of Lake Michigan in 1845. He probably went through Minneapolis on his westward trip to Fort Garry in 1849, at which time he may have seen the fort. However his preliminary studies for a canvas showing a Sioux scalp dance and the fort do not appear to have been made on the site. Bushnell (*Sketches*, p. 24) quotes a letter from Henry Lewis to Kane from Montreal July 4 (1850?), in which Lewis sends Kane a sketch of Fort Snelling.

III-141   Sketch of figure bearing scalp trophies in each hand. Pencil. 5½″ x 9½″. (ROM946.15.58)

III-142   Standing figure with robe falling on ground. 5″ x 8″. (ROM946.15.276)

III-143   Pencil study for Sioux scalp dance. Presumably the Lewis sketch of the fort was used in preparing the background for this study. Pencil. 5½″ x 9″. (ROM946.15.155)

III-144   Sioux Scalp Dance. Fort Snelling is in the background. Painting is based on studies III-141 to III-143. GWA50. Oil on canvas. 4′ x 2′5″. Plate X. (ROM912.1.15)

Section IV

Paintings, sketches and drawings relating to Kane's 1846–48 expedition from Toronto to Fort Victoria by the Hudson's Bay Company routes across the Canadian plains and through the Oregon territory

Kane left Toronto for his second major sketching trip among the Indians on May 9, 1846. He joined the Hudson's Bay Company spring brigade beyond Fort William, travelling with it by way of Norway House and Fort Edmonton, crossing the Rockies and reaching Fort Vancouver in the Oregon territory, on the Columbia River, December 8, 1846. *En route* he made a detour to Fort Garry to observe the annual spring buffalo hunt of 1846. Kane sketched during the winter of 1846–47 in the Fort Vancouver region and during the following spring at Fort Victoria and its environs. Leaving Fort Vancouver on July 1, 1847, he started eastward on his homeward trip, halting to do much sketching in the plateau region of the Oregon country. He reached Fort Edmonton on December 5. Using this post as his base of operations, he sketched extensively on the western plains during the first months of 1848. Kane left Fort Edmonton with a returning fur trade brigade on May 25, 1848, travelling by way of Norway House and reaching Toronto the following October.

This section has been arranged geographically, moving from east to west. Divisions within it include works related to both the outward and the return journey.

SAULT STE MARIE

Sault Ste Marie material has been listed in section III. Despite Kane's remarks in *Wanderings* (p. 62), it is clear from other evidence, including his sketchbook, that most if not all of it was executed in 1845 rather than in 1846 or 1848.

MICHIPICOTEN

Ojibwa

This Lake Superior island is traditionally Ojibwa territory. Items III-46 to III-51 are portraits of Ojibwa evidently from this island and its adjacent regions but they were sketched at Manitowaning in 1845. Kane visited Michipicoten September 27–29, 1848, on his return trip to Toronto.

IV-1   Maydoc-game-kinungee or "I hear the Noise of the Deer." This Ojibwa chief was painted on Michipicoten Island but may have been there on a visit from the Kaministiquia River (*Wanderings*, p. 157). TCH81. w.c. 4½″ x 5¼″. (Bushnell H-72/402)

IV-2   Chief from Fort William (Maydoc-gan-kinungee). Painting based on IV-1. GWA91. Oil on canvas. 2′6″ x 2′1″. Plate XI. (ROM12.1.16)

FORT WILLIAM TO LAKE WINNIPEG

On May 24, 1846, Kane joined the Hudson's Bay Company fur brigade under Mr. Lane 35 miles beyond Fort William. He accompanied it as far as Fort Alexander which was reached June 11. He retraced this route in 1848, with Major McKenzie's party from Norway House, leaving Fort Alexander on August 3 and reaching Fort William September 19, 1848.

Topography

IV-3 Kakabeka Falls. Kane describes making a sketch of it on May 25, 1846 (*Wanderings*, p. 63). He points out that the table rock had fallen some time between 1848 and the date of the publication of *Wanderings*, 1859. Pencil. 5¼″ x 8½″. Fig. 47. (ROM946.15.66)

IV-4 Kakabeka Falls (Kakkabakka Falls). Painting based on IV-3. GWA53. Oil on canvas. 1′9½″ x 2′5½″. (ROM912.1.17)

IV-5 Kakabeka Falls. Replica of IV-4. GS12 (?). Oil on canvas. 12⅛″ x 18¼″. (Coe)

IV-6 The Mountain Portage. This has sometimes been referred to as "The By-pass at Kakabeka Falls." Kane sketched Kakabeka Falls while the men were portaging (*Wanderings*, p. 63). No preliminary sketch has been located for this painting. Possibly it was inspired by some European painting or engraving; the composition is unusual for Kane. GWA54. Oil on canvas. 2′1½″ x 1′8″. Plate XII. (ROM912.1.18)

IV-6A Lost Men's Portage, west of Kakabeka Falls, sketched May 25, 1846 (*Wanderings*, p. 63). The sketch is on the same sheet as IV-301, at the upper right. KLL5. w.c. 5″ x 7¼″. (ROM946.15.-332)

IV-7 Pin Portage. Kane describes passing over the portage on May 25, 1846; this sketch was probably executed then rather than on the return journey (*Wanderings*, p. 63). TCH49. AG30. Oil on paper. 8⅛″ x 13¼″. Fig. 48. (Stark POP25)

IV-8 Dog Portage. Kane reports making a sketch of the waterfall at the upper end of Big Dog Portage on May 26, 1846 (*Wanderings*, p. 63). This sketch was probably made at that portage rather than at Dog Portage proper. KLL1. AG41. TCH48. Oil on paper. 8″ x 13⅜″. (Stark POP24)

IV-9 Hunting Ducks (at Lake of the Thousand Islands, Winnipeg River). Kane describes in detail the hunting methods witnessed here May 29, 1846 (*Wanderings*, p. 64). The painting is probably based on a sketch, not located. GWA40. Oil on canvas. 1′6″ x 2′5″. (ROM912.1.22)

IV-10 Fort Frances. General view with water mill in foreground and fort in rear. Kane was at Fort Frances from August 23 to September 11, 1848, at which time this sketch was probably executed. (*Wanderings*, p. 156.) TCH199. AG131. w.c. 5½″ x 9¼″. Fig. 49. (Stark PWC2)

IV-11 Fort Frances. View of the water mill from the fort. (See IV-10.) AG152. w.c. 5½″ x 9⅛″. Fig. 50. (Stark PWC3)

IV-12 Falls near Fort Frances. Kane seems to have made two sketches of these falls, either between June 1 and June 5, 1846, or between August 30 and September 10, 1848. He refers in his manuscript journal to sketching rapids, where Rainy River empties out of Rainy Lake on its way to the Lake of the Woods, during the 1846 trip (also *Wanderings*, p. 65); the resulting sketch, unlocated, may have been the one exhibited as TCH198. The second sketch, IV-12, was made on the same spot; it has been exhibited as "Coffin Rock" (see IV-470). (See *Wanderings*, p. 156.) TCH180. AG170. w.c. 5½″ x 9⅛″. (Stark PWC4)

IV-13 Unidentified view. There is a slight possibility that this is the mission post of Wabassimong seen by Kane on June 8, 1846, and August 12, 1848 (*Wanderings*, pp. 66, 155). Pencil. 5½″ x 6½″. (ROM946.15.317)

IV-14 Slave Falls, Winnipeg River. Sir George Simpson had particularly requested Kane to note this, the highest falls on the Winnipeg River (letter of May 31, 1846; Appendix 10, Letter 3). Evidently Kane made not only this sketch but also IV-15 and IV-16 on August 9, 1848 (*Wanderings*, p. 154). Pencil. 5″ x 7½″. (ROM946.15.67)

IV-15 Slave Falls, Winnipeg River. Sketch formerly identified as of "Dalles des Morts." AG179. w.c. 5½″ x 9⅜″. Fig. 51. (Stark WWC19)

IV-16 Slave Falls, Winnipeg River. (See IV-14 and IV-15.) TCH200. AG158. w.c. 5⅜″ x 9½″. (Stark PWC20)

IV-17 Slave Falls, Winnipeg River. Painting based on IV-16. GWA17. Oil on canvas. 1′6″ x 2′5″. (ROM912.1.20)

IV-18 Chute-de-Jacques, Winnipeg River. Kane was here on June 9, 1846, and August 11, 1848 (*Wanderings*, pp. 66, 154). KLL2. TCH52. Oil on paper. 8″ x 13⅜″. (Stark POP19)

IV-19 White Mud Portage, Winnipeg River. This sketch was made on August 4, 1848 (*Wanderings*, p. 154). TCH201. AG97. w.c. 5¼″ x 9⅜″. Plate XIII. (Stark PWC7)

IV-20 White Mud Portage. Painting based on IV-19. (*Wanderings*; coloured litho.) GWA6. Oil on canvas. 1′6″ x 2′5″. (ROM912.1.21)

IV-21 White Mud Portage. Replica of IV-20. LP10. Oil on canvas. 1′5½″ x 2′4½″. (NGC138). A second replica of IV-20 was sold by Knoedler & Co., New York, in 1952 *; see R. H. Hubbard, *The National Gallery of Canada: Catalogue of Paintings and Sculptures*, vol. III.

IV-22 An encampment on the Winnipeg River. Sketched June 10, 1846 (*Wanderings*, p. 67). Kane reports that the visiting Indians were Saulteaux. KLL8. TCH51. Oil on paper. 8⅛″ x 13⅜″. Plate XIV. (Stark POP15)

IV-23 Encampment, River Winnipeg. Painting based on IV-22. GWA31. Oil on canvas. 1′7″ x 2′6″. (ROM912.1.19)

IV-24   Winnipeg River. KLL4. AG92. Oil on paper. 8″ x 13⅜″. Fig. 52. (Stark POP13)

[There is no IV-25.]

IV-26   Large Smith's Rock Portage. Identified from an inscription, not in Kane's hand. w.c. 5½″ x 9¼″. (ROM946.15.257)

IV-27   Oke Falls. Identified from an inscription, not in Kane's hand. w.c. 5½″ x 9¼″. (ROM946.15.258)

IV-28   Two canoes on a rocky shoreline. Topography is similar to that in the region but the locale has not been identified. Pencil. 4⅞″ x 7¼″. TCH202. AG204. (Stark 3)

Saulteaux

"Saulteaux" is a term given occasionally to the Ojibwa of the Lake Superior region. Kane refers to them also as "Soto" and mentions meeting a number between Fort William and Lake Winnipeg. In addition to the following sketches, he pictures Saulteaux in IV-19 to IV-23.

IV-29   Iacaway (Ias-a-way), or "The Loud Speaker." Sketched at Fort Frances June 4, 1846 (*Wanderings*, p. 66). This sketch was formerly published as one of "Little Rat," Rainy River (see also IV-46, 221); no sketch of Little Rat (or Waw-gas-kontz), KPL2, has been located. (See also IV-130.) Probably KPL1. TCH24. Oil on paper. 8″ x 7″. (Agnes Etherington Art Gallery, Kingston, 0-89).

IV-30   Two Indian portrait heads. Inscription on reverse reads: (*left*) Cash-a-cabut or "Greedy Tooth"; (*right*) Each-a-quip or "One who sits with his feathers on." The names are in the Ojibwa tongue. Sketched in the Fort Frances region. (*Wanderings*, p. 154) Pencil. 5½″ x 9¼″. Fig. 53. (ROM946.15.273)

IV-31   Head-and-shoulder portrait study of Indian. An inscription in Ojibwa, evidently referring to this sketch, reads: Tipich-la-ga-sheck or "The Spirit Sky." Probably sketched at the same time as IV-30. Pencil. 4½″ x 5½″. (ROM946.15.274)

IV-32   Sho-ne-ah or "Silver." A Saulteaux chief from Fort Alexander. Kane visited his village June 11, 1846 (*Wanderings*, pp. 67–68). AG46. Oil on paper. 12¼″ x 9¾″. Fig. 54. (Stark POP5)

LAKE WINNIPEG TO FORT GARRY

Kane left Fort Alexander on June 11, 1845, and arrived at Lower Fort Garry two days later. He went to Upper Fort Garry on June 15 in the company of the Rev. Peter Jacobs (*Wanderings*, p. 68).

IV-33   Peter Jacobs, Wesleyan Indian missionary. AG161. w.c. 5″ x 4⅝″. Fig. 55. (Stark PWC14)

IV-34   Peter Jacobs, Wesleyan Indian missionary. Oil sketch based on IV-33. 8⅝″ x 6⅞″. (Colln S. E. Weir)

FORT GARRY

Upper Fort Garry (built 1835, demolished 1882) was the Hudson's Bay Company's headquarters in western Canada and its chief provision depot. It formed the focal point of a settlement on the Red River which grew up in the area following the first arrival of Lord Selkirk's Highland immigrants in 1812. Kane spent a short time here on his arrival June 15, 1845, leaving almost immediately for the Métis buffalo hunt. He remained for a few days at the upper fort on his return from the hunt before leaving from the lower fort for Norway House on July 5. (*Wanderings*, pp. 68–69, 74.)

Topography

IV-35   Red River Settlement. General view. *Left to right:* St. Boniface Cathedral, blockhouse, Upper Fort Garry. Pencil. 5½″ x 9″. Fig. 57. (ROM946.15.68)

IV-36   Red River Settlement. General view. *Left to right:* Bishop's palace, cathedral and Grey Sisters' Hospital in St. Boniface, and the windmill and Upper Fort Garry across the river. TCH210. AG88. Oil on paper. 9″ x 13⅞″. Fig. 56. (Stark POP1)

IV-37   Red River Settlement. Painting based on IV-36. (*Wanderings*; woodcut, Fig. 5). GWA3. Oil on canvas. 1′6″ x 2′5″. (ROM912.-1.23)

IV-38   Red River Settlement. Replica of IV-37. LP9. Oil on canvas. 1′6″ x 2′5″. (NGC102)

IV-39   River scenery. Possibly a view along the Red or the Saskatchewan River. 5″ x 6½″. (ROM946.15.118)

SOUTH OF FORT GARRY

Kane spent the latter part of June 1846 with Métis hunters on their annual buffalo hunt southwest of Fort Garry. (*Wanderings*, pp. 69–72.) He made sketches of Indians he met on the way, of the landscape, the Métis hunters, and various phases of the buffalo hunt proper. Items IV-40 to IV-80 all relate to this expedition.

Sioux

The Sioux or Dakota, a large tribe, occupied territory from east of the Mississippi River to the head of Green Bay, and north beyond the Canadian border towards Lake Winnipeg. Kane says he met twelve Sioux chieftains after passing Dry Dance Mountain (*Wanderings*, p. 70). He makes no mention of sketching them, but at no other time in his journeys does he appear to have met members of this tribe; see, however, note 9 to chapter VI of *Wanderings*. His paintings of Sioux at Fort Snelling (III-140 to III-143) were not done from life.

IV-40   Two portraits. w.c. 5¼″ x 8¼″. Plate XV. (ROM946.15.57)

IV-41   A Sioux Indian. Painting is based on the sketch of a Sioux in IV-40 (*left side*). The robe seems to be based on a specimen in Kane's ethnological collection. GWA87. Oil on canvas. 2′8″ x 1′8″; (oval) 2′ x 1′7″. Fig. 58. (ROM912.1.29)

IV-42   Three portrait studies. Pencil. 5½″ x 8½″. (ROM946.15.64)

Saulteaux

A small band of Saulteaux accompanied the Métis during the buffalo hunt. Evidently the following sketches were made during the hunt.

IV-43 Na-taw-waugh-cit (Na-too-waw-sit) or "The Man that was born." Full figure portrait with an otter robe. KPL4. TCH240. Oil on paper. 11¼″ x 7¾″. Fig. 59. (Stark EOP22)

IV-44 Na-taw-waugh-cit or "The Man that was born." KPL4. w.c. 7″ x 5″. (ROM946.15.277)

IV-45 Peccothis (Pe-ca-dhis) or "The Man with a Lump on his Navel." Profile study. Kane describes sketching him (*Wanderings*, p. 70). This item was formerly identified as a portrait of She-bah-ke-zhick or "Hole in the Sky" (see III-48). KPL3. Pencil. 5″ x 3″. (ROM946.15.63)

IV-46 Peccothis (Pe-ca-dhis) or "The Man with a Lump on his Navel." Formerly this sketch was identified as one of Waw-gas-kontz (see IV-29). KPL3. TCH25. AG89. Oil on paper. 8⅛″ x 6½″. (Stark POP2)

IV-47 Two portrait studies. The one at the left seems to relate to KPL3, "Peccothis" (IV-45, 46) but this is conjectural: Kane used, it would appear, three different number series and the "3" may relate to a lost series. This person has also been identified as She-bah-ke-zhick (III-48 and see IV-45), but without supporting evidence. The figure on the right is unidentified. w.c. 5¼″ x 7¼″. (ROM946.15.62)

See also IV-48 to IV-51.

Unidentified Indians

A group of sketches for which there is no documentary identification were evidently completed at this time. A roach suggests that the subjects may be Saulteaux, but this suggestion is without substantiation.

IV-48 Unidentified head. Oil on paper. 8″ x 9½″. AG51. (Stark WWC74)

IV-49 Unidentified head. This is the same individual as the one in IV-48. w.c. 3¾″ x 4½″. (ROM946.15.78)

IV-50 Unidentified head. w.c. 3¾″ x 4½″. (ROM946.15.79)

IV-51 Unidentified head. w.c. 3¾″ x 4½″. (ROM946.15.80)

Camp scenes

IV-52 Sketch on the prairies. Kane describes camping with a companion 30 miles south of Fort Garry *en route* to the hunt (*Wanderings*, p. 69). This sketch has been inscribed, but not in Kane's hand, as "Scratching River." TCH209. Oil on paper. 8⅛″ x 11⅜″. Plate XVI. (Stark POP18)

IV-53 Pembina River. Kane reported finding the main body of hunters along this river, a two-day journey from Fort Garry (*Wanderings*, p. 69). TCH233. AG167. w.c. 5¼″ x 8⅞″. (Stark PWC 15)

IV-54 Half Breeds Travelling. Painting is possibly based on an unlocated sketch which Kane mentions as having made three days after he left Fort Garry (*Wanderings*, p. 70). GWA35. Oil on canvas. 1′6″ x 2′5″. Fig. 60. (ROM912.1.24)

IV-55 Red River cart and ox. Kane describes the cart's construction (*Wanderings*, p. 69). Pencil. 5″ x 7″. Fig. 61. (ROM946.15.74)

IV-56 Page of sketches, showing Red River cart and ox; standing Métis smoking; Métis loading poles on cart. Described by Kane (*Wanderings*, p. 69). Pencil. 5″ x 7″. (ROM946.15.75)

IV-57 Baby in dog travois. w.c. 5″ x 6½″. (ROM946.15.85)

IV-58 Dog with travois. w.c. 4¾″ x 6½″. Fig. 62. (ROM946.15.84)

IV-59 Dog with travois. Pencil. 5″ x 6½″. (ROM946.15.146)

IV-60 Packhorse and drag. Pencil. 4¾″ x 6½″. (ROM946.15.144)

IV-61 Cow with pack on back. Pencil. 4¾″ x 6½″. (ROM946.15.144)

IV-62 Study of dog and bird. Pencil. 5½″ x 9¼″. (ROM946.15.83)

IV-63 Panoramic view of Métis travelling on prairie with camping equipment (*Wanderings*, p. 70). Pencil. 5½″ x 9″. (ROM946.15.69)

IV-64 Panoramic view of Métis travelling on prairie with equipment (*Wanderings*, p. 70). Pencil. 5″ x 7″. (ROM946.15.76)

IV-65 Métis encampment. This has also been described as an Ojibwa encampment. TCH208. AG181. w.c. 5¼″ x 8⅞″. (Stark PWC6)

IV-66 Panoramic view of Métis setting up camp on the prairies. w.c. 5½″ x 9″. Fig. 63. (ROM946.15.71)

IV-67 View of section of a Métis encampment. w.c. 5″ x 7″ (ROM946.15.72)

IV-68 Half Breed Encampment. Composite painting, evidently based on IV-65 to IV-67 and other studies. GWA27. Oil on canvas. 1′6″ x 2′5″. Figs. 64, 65. (ROM912.1.25)

The buffalo hunt

IV-69 Métis camp and hunters on hilltop. This scene is probably that described by Kane when the group were waiting for the hunt to begin (*Wanderings*, p. 71). w.c. 5¼″ x 8¾″. Fig. 66. (ROM946.15.70)

IV-70 Studies of Métis hunters on hilltop awaiting signal to charge the buffalo herd, and a downed buffalo. Pencil. 5″ x 7″. (ROM946.15.77)

IV-71 Panoramic view of Métis chasing the main buffalo herd (*Wanderings*, pp. 71–72). w.c. 5⅛″ x 8⅞″. Plate XVII. (Stark PWC16)

IV-72 Panoramic view of Métis chasing the main buffalo herd. A second and unfinished version of IV-71. AG74. Oil on paper. 8½″ x 13¾″. (Stark POP23)

IV-73 Half Breeds Running Buffalo. No preliminary study seems to have been executed for this work. Note remarks by Sir George Simpson advising adjustment of Kane's original version (Appendix 10, Letter 12). GWA34. Oil on canvas. 1′6″ x 2′5″. Fig. 67. (ROM912.1.26)

IV-74 Half Breeds Running Buffalo. Replica of IV-73. Probably GS13. Oil on canvas. 12⅛″ x 18¼″. (Coe)

IV-75 Page of buffalo hunt studies: Métis slaughtering buffalo, standing buffalo, buffalo head. Pencil and w.c. 5″ x 7″. (ROM946.15.93)

Wounded buffalo

While Kane was sketching during the hunt on June 26, 1845, a wounded buffalo charged him (*Wanderings*, p. 72). Kane shot him.

IV-76   Standing buffalo bull. Pencil. 5½″ x 6½″. (ROM946.15.86(1))

IV-77   Standing buffalo bull. Pencil. 5½″ x 6½″. (ROM946.15.86(2))

IV-78   Standing buffalo bull, wounded. Pencil. 5½″ x 6½″. Fig. 68. (ROM946.15.87)

IV-79   Wounded buffalo bull. TCH172. AG106. w.c. 4⅛″ x 5⅜″. Fig. 69. (Stark PWC8)

IV-80   Wounded Buffalo Bull. Painting based on IV-79. GWA43. Oil on canvas. 1′6″ x 2′5″. (ROM912.1.27)

FORT GARRY TO NORWAY HOUSE

Kane left Fort Garry July 5, 1846, arriving at Norway House July 12. He was forced to remain at Norway House until August 14. The brigade with which he was to travel was bringing trade goods from York Factory for the interior and otter skins which were to be carried to the Pacific as annual payment for the Russians (*Wanderings*, p. 76). On his return Kane retraced part of this ground, leaving Norway House July 24, 1848, and arriving at Fort Alexander on the 30th.

Topography

IV-81   Lake with rocky shoreline. It has been suggested, without supporting evidence, that this is a shore on Lake Winnipeg. w.c. 5″ x 6″. (ROM946.15.95)

IV-82   Norway House. Norway House, on Little Playgreen Lake at the north end of Lake Winnipeg, was established in 1814 as a staging post on the road from York Factory to the Red River Settlement. The first building was burned in 1824 and it was immediately reconstructed on a modest scale. A new and more extensive fort was commenced in 1831, which gradually assumed greater importance as a stopping place for traffic going to the Red River and for the fur brigades using the Saskatchewan River. It was this fort which Kane visited; parts of it still stand today (*Wanderings*, pp. 74, 152). (See W. B. Ready, "Norway House," *The Beaver*, Winnipeg, March 1949, pp. 30–34.) Pencil. 5½″ x 9″. (ROM946.15.213)

IV-83   Norway House. KLL9. TCH78. Oil on paper. 8″ x 13½″. Plate XVIII. (Stark POP14)

IV-84   Wesleyan mission station, Jack River (Playgreen Lake). Kane visited the station July 12, 1846 (*Wanderings*, p. 76). The Rev. Wm Mason, resident missionary, reported from this place (known at the time as Rossville) on August 20, 1844, stating that the church, then under construction and shown in the sketch, soon would be finished. (Methodist Missionary Society Archives, London, Eng.) Mason had arrived in 1843; by 1847 he had established a printing press where he was publishing tracts in Cree, and in 1848 the *Rules of the Methodist Missionary Society*.

KLL19. TCH196. AG182. w.c. 5⅜″ x 8⅞″. Fig. 71. (Stark PWC17)

IV-85   Wesleyan mission station, Jack River. Pencil. 5″ x 7″. (ROM946.15.73)

Saulteaux

IV-86   Two portrait studies. *Right:* young girl. In his portrait log Kane refers to a sketch of a Saulteaux girl whose mother "wanted to know if it would hurt her to sit for her picture." The same incident is recorded in *Wanderings* (p. 75) as occurring on his outward journey. In the log Kane calls this girl Caw-ce-cu-che-cock (Cawkeekaikeedje-ekoke), "Constant Sky." However, in the published book he uses this name for a woman met on his return journey; see IV-87, 88. KPL5. *Left:* Portrait study with note in Kane's hand "Assinboine." w.c. 5¼″ x 7¼″. Fig. 72. (ROM946.15.61)

IV-87   Caw-kee-ka-keesh-e-ko or "The Constant Sky." Kane sketched this woman at the mouth of Behring River, Lake Winnipeg, on July 26, 1848, and he gives this name to her in *Wanderings* (p. 153). (See also IV-237.) Probably TCH26. Oil on paper. *c.* 5½″ x 5½″. (Colln Paul Kane IV)

IV-88   The Constant Sky (Caw-kee-kee-keesh-e-ko). Painting evidently based on IV-87. The quillwork box on which the woman rests her hand is based on one in a sketch, III-90, and reappears in IV-469. GWA59. Oil on canvas. 2′1″ x 2′6″. (ROM912.1.30)

NORWAY HOUSE

Portraits

IV-89   Donald Ross, Chief Factor, Norway House (*Wanderings*, p. 76). Mrs. R. B. Ross, a member of the subject's family, wrote in 1920 of this painting: "This picture was painted by the artist PAUL KANE 13th August 1846 and is a portrait of DONALD ROSS, Esq., Chief Factor of the Hudson's Bay Co. (and founder of Norway House). . . . Mr. Kane was to leave Norway House the next day. He met Mr. Ross going to hold service in the big hall (on Sunday) and said that if he wanted his portrait painted he (Mr. Kane) must do it that day. Mr. Ross agreed and it was painted on Sunday and is a very good likeness. . . ." Oil on paper. 7″ x 6″. Fig. 70. (Provincial Archives, British Columbia, 3760)

IV-90   Ogemawwah Chack (Oke-maw-wah-jack) or "The Spirit Chief." This Eskimo went out with Kane from Norway House to fish and shoot in 1848 (*Wanderings*, p. 152). Formerly this sketch was identified as that of Tomaquin, chief of the Cascade, Columbia River (see IV-391). TCH33. AG58. Oil on paper. 10⅛″ x 9⅛″. Fig. 76. (Stark WOP2)

IV-91   An Esquimaux (Oge-maw-waw-chawk). Painting based on IV-90 and probably using an Eskimo fur jacket from Kane's ethnological collection. (*Wanderings*; coloured litho.) GWA89. Oil on canvas. 2′6″ x 2′1″. (ROM912.1.32)

NORWAY HOUSE TO FORT CARLTON

Kane left Norway House with the fur trade brigade under the charge of Mr. Rowand on August 14, 1846, arriving at Fort Carlton, on the North Saskatchewan River, September 7. On his return journey in 1848, he left Fort Carlton June 6 and reached Norway House June 18.

Topography

IV-92   Brigade of boats. Kane completed this sketch on his return journey in 1848 when he hurried ahead of the brigade near Le Pas to sketch it; as he was doing so, a sudden thunderstorm threatened (*Wanderings*, p. 151). Pencil. 5½″ x 9¼″. Fig. 73. (ROM-946.15.83)

IV-93   Brigade of boats. Study of three boats. Pencil. 4″ x 5″. (ROM-946.15.334)

IV-94   York boats on the river. This is evidently the study for IV-95. AG206. Pencil. 5⅜″ x 9⅜″. (Stark 4)

IV-95   Brigade of Boats. Painting based on IV-93 and IV-94. GWA1. Oil on canvas. 1′6″ x 2′5″. Fig. 74. (ROM912.1.31)

IV-96   Fort Carlton from a distance (*Wanderings*, p. 78). When Henry J. Warre visited the fort a year before Kane's outward trip, he wrote: it "is miserable as a defensive building—is octagonal & built of wood, at every angle two large Blunderbusses are mounted and kept ready loaded to intimidate the enemy (on the Chinese plan I suppose). The numbers of Dogs, Children, Indians and cattle around make the place very dirty, and the mosquitoes are more troublesome than I ever remember them. The Valley of the River is wild and pretty and in winter the Buffalo surround the Fort. Bears are very abundant, also Elk. . . ." (Public Archives of Canada, Henry J. Warre Papers.) KLL20. TCH231. AG202. w.c. 5⅜″ x 8⅞″. Fig. 75. (Stark PWC18)

FORT CARLTON

A buffalo pound

Kane accompanied Indians, almost certainly Cree, on a buffalo hunt on September 12, 1846. This hunt took place six miles from Fort Carlton, which he had been visiting (*Wanderings*, p. 79).

IV- 97   Buffalo pound as prepared for the hunt by Indians. Sketch shows pound with funnel-like entrance of sticks and brush. Pencil. 5½″ x 9½″. (ROM946.15.104)

IV- 98   Driving buffalo into pound. General view of the hunt with mounted rider leading buffalo into pound, men rising behind posts ("dead men") to wave buffalo robes as the buffalo approach, and various gifts to the Great Spirit hanging in tall trees at the entrance to the pound. Pencil. 5⅜″ x 9¼″. AG208. (Stark 1)

IV- 99   Page of buffalo hunt studies: Indian standing with buffalo robe; hunters running buffalo into pound; running buffalo, Indian in tree waving medicine pipe-stem at entrance to pound. Pencil. 3″ x 5″. Fig. 77. (ROM946.15.103)

IV-100   Prairie landscape. This view has been introduced into the background of the canvas IV-101. w.c. 5″ x 7″. (ROM946.15.107)

IV-101   A Buffalo Pound. Painting based on IV-97 to IV-100. GWA7. Oil on canvas. 1′6″ x 2′5″. Fig. 78. (ROM912.1.33)

Cree

The Cree, an important Algonquian tribe, lived in Manitoba and Saskatchewan between the Red and Saskatchewan rivers. They were much reduced by smallpox in 1786 and 1838. The tribe, split into bands, had dispersed to many parts of the prairies for the purpose of trading with the Hudson's Bay Company.

Kane spent much time with the Cree. He first encountered them during the several days after his arrival at Fort Carlton on September 7, 1846. He sketched Cree also at Fort Pitt, Fort Edmonton, Rocky Mountain House and intermediate points.

IV-102   Us-koos-koosish (Uskoosekoosis/ Hus-kus-coo-sish) or "Young Grass." Kane sketched this Cree brave at Fort Carlton (*Wanderings*, p. 78). KPL7. TCH29. Oil on paper. 11¾″ x 8¼″. (Colln C. M. McCallister)

IV-103   Muck-Cranium, a Cree from Fort Carlton. AG52. Oil on paper. 11⅛″ x 6¾″. Plate XIX. (Stark POP6)

IV-104   "The Man that Shot the Wolf with an Arrow," a Cree sketched at Fort Carlton. Kane describes an incident which appears to relate to this man (*Wanderings*, p. 80) and refers to him as "A Perfect Centaur" (*Wanderings*, p. 74). Burpee follows a catalogue of the Allan collection canvases published *c*. 1900 in identifying this description with the canvas IV-105. KPL11. TCH86. w.c. 5½″ x 9″. Fig. 79. (ROM946.15.96)

IV-105   The Man that Always Rides. This man's identity is uncertain. A possibility for an identification is a man whom Kane lists in his notes as Eikutope, "The man that always rides," and whom he describes as a Blackfoot (later killed by a Cree in one of their forays); a sketch has not been found. (See also IV-104.) As in other cases, the composition for this canvas would appear to have a European prototype (or possibly to be after a painting by George Catlin). GWA79. Oil on canvas. 2′ x 1′6¼″. Plate XX. (ROM912.1.44)

IV-106   Cree Indians travelling. A note on the reverse, not in Kane's hand, reads: "Cree Indians on the March, Fort Carlton." Pencil. 4½″ x 8¾″. Fig. 80. (ROM946.15.102)

IV-107   Cree Indians Travelling. Painting based on IV-106. GWA49. Oil on canvas. 1′6″ x 2′5″. (ROM912.1.49)

IV-108   Cree tent with women gambling, Fort Carlton. KLL10. Pencil. 5″ x 6½″. (ROM946.15.152)

IV-109   Two portrait studies of Cree. *Right:* Pe-pa-ka-chos-a (Pe-pa-ka-chos). *Left:* Achu-wish-a-ma-hy or "The Grizzly Bear Standing." Probably sketched at Fort Carlton. TCH87 and TCH88. 5½″ x 9″. (ROM946.15.97)

FORT CARLTON TO FORT PITT

Kane, in company with the Rev. Mr. Rundle and Mr. Rowand, left Fort Carlton on September 12, 1846. On September 19 they reached Fort Pitt, on the North Saskatchewan River, encountering numerous Cree on the way. Kane remained at Fort Pitt until September 23. In 1848 he was again in Fort Pitt for a month after January 14, and from May 27 to 29 during his return journey to Toronto.

Topography

The exact location for most of the sketches of the North Saskatchewan valley has not been determined. All have been entered here although some may actually be of landscapes beyond Fort Pitt.

IV-110 Scene on the Saskatchewan River. Formerly identified as a view near Lethbridge, Alta., or on the Belly River. KLL13. w.c. 5½″ x 9″. (ROM946.15.119)

IV-111 Scene on the Saskatchewan River. Formerly identified as a view near Lethbridge, Alta., or on the Belly River. KLL14. w.c. 5½″ x 9″. (ROM946.15.125)

IV-112 Scene on the Saskatchewan River. A second version of IV-111. Formerly identified as Bow River valley. w.c. 5½″ x 9″. (ROM946.15.126)

IV-113 Scene on the Saskatchewan River. KLL15. Pencil. 5½″ x 8¾″. (ROM946.15.110)

IV-114 Scene on the Saskatchewan River. A second version of IV-113. Pencil. 5½″ x 9″. (ROM946.15.111)

IV-115 Scene on the Saskatchewan River. Formerly identified as possibly the Belly River. KLL16. w.c. 5½″ x 9″. (ROM946.15.120)

IV-116 Scene on the Saskatchewan River. On the reverse is a small sketch of a tent and a Red River cart. KLL17. AG160. w.c. 5½″ x 9⅞″. (Stark PWC19)

IV-117 Scene on the Saskatchewan River. KLL18. w.c. 5″ x 7″. (ROM946.15.109)

IV-118 Scene on the Saskatchewan River. On the reverse is a slight sketch of a horse drawing poles. Pencil. 5″ x 6½″. (ROM946.15.116)

IV-119 The Serpentine Valley. KLL25. w.c. 5½″ x 9″. Fig. 81. (ROM946.15.139)

IV-120 The Golden Valley. Kane describes making this sketch on September 14, 1846 (*Wanderings*, p. 80). KLL26. w.c. 4½″ x 9″. Fig. 82. (ROM946.15.108)

IV-121 A Valley in the Plains. Painting based on IV-120. GWA57. Oil on canvas. 1′6″ x 2′5″. (ROM912.1.34)

IV-122 Fort Pitt, with bluff. Warre, on a visit to Fort Pitt in 1845, wrote: "it is beautiful; as we ascended the north branch of the river the Fort appears like a Gentleman's seat surrounded by magnificent [*sic*] timber, but alas! The reality disappointed our expectations. The trees dwindled into small poplars and the fort itself is a mere wooden building 120 ft square with walls 20 ft high and two blockhouses at the angles of the river front

and one in the rear. As at Carlton, Blunderbusses are kept ready loaded and if we may believe the account given by the Interpreter in charge of the fort, not without some reason [because of the Blackfoot]. . . . The interior of the Fort is crowded with wooden buildings, rendering fire extremely probable, and almost impossible to put a stop to should it once gain a head." (Public Archives of Canada, Henry J. Warre Papers.) (See *Wanderings*, pp. 81–82.) KLL27. TCH205. AG218. w.c. 5⅜″ x 9″. Fig. 83. (Stark PWC23)

FORT PITT

Wild life

IV-123 Heads of prairie antelope (*Wanderings*, pp. 80, 81). TCH171. AG186. w.c. 4⅞″ x 7″. Fig. 84. (Stark PWC11)

IV-124 Wolf's head (*Wanderings*, p. 81). An inscription, not in Kane's hand, describes this animal as Mah-i-cum or Prairie Dog. TCH237. AG91. Oil on paper. 6½″ x 8⅛″. (Stark POP11)

IV-125 Deer (*Wanderings*, p. 80). Pencil. 5″ x 6½″. (ROM946.15.59)

Chipewyan

The Chipewyan lived in the Lake Athabasca region. In September 1846 Kane discovered a single member of this tribe living at Fort Pitt.

IV-126 Chimaza (Chin-i-a-sa) or "The Little Slave" (*Wanderings*, p. 82). KPL12. TCH92. w.c. 7″ x 4⅞″. (Stark PWC21)

Cree

Kane met Cree at Fort Pitt and vicinity on three different occasions. Most of the following group were apparently sketched during the month after January 14, 1848 (other times for sketches are noted). Kane's manuscript journal states that the Indians sketched at Fort Pitt were Assiniboin; this is evidently an error on his part.

IV-127 Otisskun (O-this-skun) or "The Horn." A Cree chieftain with war-cap and bag sketched September 16, 1846 (*Wanderings*, p. 81). An inscription, not in Kane's hand, calls him a Cree. KPL15. TCH28. Oil on paper. 13¼″ x 8⅛″. Plate XXI. (Stark POP17)

IV-128 The War Cap (The War Cap of Otiskun). Painting based on IV-127 but with a ceremonial pipe, based on IV-135, added. GWA97. Oil on canvas. 2′6″ x 2′1″. (ROM912.1.35)

IV-129 Studies of two figures. *Left:* seated figure, inscribed in Kane's hand "The Horn, U-thay-skun." *Right:* standing figure. KPL15. w.c. and pencil. 5″ x 6½″. (ROM946.15.151)

IV-130 Kee-a-kee-ka-sa-coo-way (Caw-ke-ka-saw-k-way) or "The Man who gives the War-whoop." Kane mentions meeting this man at Fort Pitt during January 1848 (*Wanderings*, pp. 81, 144–45). Sketch is inscribed in Kane's hand "The man that always speaks," and his journal gives the same English equivalent. This sketch was identified formerly as one of Iacaway, Saulteaux chieftain at

Fort Frances (see IV-29). KPL14. w.c. 5″ x 6½″. (ROM-946.15.60)

IV-131 Kee-a-kee-ka-sa-coo-way (Ka-ah-ke-ka-sahk-a-wa-ow), or "The Man who gives the War-whoop." A portrait study of the individual pictured in IV-130. (See Bushnell, *Sketches*, pp. 12–14.) KPL14. TCH84. w.c. Fig. 85. (Bushnell 41-72/395)

IV-132 Kee-akee-ka-saa-ka-wow, "The Man that gives the War Whoop" (Kee-a-kee-ka-sa-coo-way). The facial features are evidently based on IV-131. An elaborate hair ornament may be inspired by hair pins collected by Kane (now in Manitoba Museum of Science and History). Although the chief's medicine pipe-stem is similar to the one on the left in IV-136, it is more probably based on an actual specimen collected by Kane (also in Manitoba Museum of Science and History). (See *Wanderings*, p. 144; coloured litho.) GWA69. Oil on canvas. 2′6″ x 2′1″. Fig. 86. (ROM912.1.42)

IV-133 Muck-e-too or "Powder"(?) second chief of the Cree, met at Fort Pitt. Kane mentions meeting this man with Kee-a-kee-ka-sa-coo-way (IV-130). (*Wanderings*, pp. 81, 144.) The sketch itself has been identified as of Muck-koze or "Young Bear," an Ottawa chieftain (III-52). Both IV-133 and III-52 have been keyed to TCH13. KPL13. w.c. 3½″ x 4¾″. (ROM946.15.54)

IV-134 Cree pipe-stem. Presumably this is one of eleven pipe-stems which Kane saw in the possession of Kee-a-kee-ka-sa-coo-way (*Wanderings*, p. 145). w.c. 5½″ x 9½″. (ROM946.15.101)

IV-135 Cree pipe-stem (see IV-134) and pencil studies of two Indian heads. w.c. 5½″ x 9¼″. Fig. 87. (ROM946.15.99)

IV-136 Two Cree pipe-stems (see IV-134). *Left:* pipe-stem with golden eagle head. *Right:* decorated pipe-stem. Pencil and w.c. 5¾″ x 9½″. Fig. 88. (ROM946.15.100)

IV-137 Cree pipe-stems (see IV-134). (See Bushnell, *Sketches*, p. 14). w.c. 9¼″ x 5½″. (Bushnell 41-72/396)

IV-138 Cree pipe-stem (see IV-134). TCH41? (which states, incorrectly, that this pipe-stem is from the Pacific coast near the Strait of Juan de Fuca; see also IV-160). AG15. Oil on paper. 11⅝″ x 9¼″. (Stark POP7)

IV-139 Cree Indian. This sketch was exhibited in Toronto in 1848 as that of an Indian of the Cree tribe from the Saskatchewan River near Fort Pitt. Subsequently it was listed, without apparent basis, as "Cree Indian, Edmonton." TCH27. AG73. Oil on paper. 12¼″ x 9¾″. Plate XXII. (Stark POP16)

IV-140 Cree Pipe-Stem Bearer. Painting based on IV-139 (for face) and IV-135 (for pipe-stem). (See *Wanderings*, pp. 143–44.) The painting does not appear to have been turned over by Kane to Allan in 1856 and was probably given to him at a later date. Oil on canvas. 2′6″ x 2′1″. (ROM912.1.36)

IV-141 A Cree woman. Probably sketched at Fort Pitt. KPL18. w.c. 5½″ x 2¾″. (ROM946.15.300)

IV-142 Five standing figures, almost certainly sketched at Fort Pitt. *Upper:* Three-quarter view of standing male, tribe not specified; standing woman with child on back, labelled "Cree"; back view of standing woman, labelled "Cree." *Lower:* standing figure, Musk-ku-thay-ka-ou-mu-thay or "The man that always runs in the plains," an Assiniboin; seated figure, Mis-cu-pa-puck-we or "Red Shirt," an Assiniboin. KPL16 and KPL17. w.c. 5″ x 7″. (ROM946.15.150)

Blackfoot and allies

During the 18th century the Blackfoot were the strongest and most aggressive of all prairie tribes. Their territory extended from present-day Saskatchewan to the Rockies and from the North Saskatchewan River to the upper Missouri. They were divided into three tribal units, each under its own chieftain: the Blackfoot proper, the Blood, and the Piegan. The Sarsi, who originally occupied territory from the Peace River to the Red Deer River, affiliated themselves wholeheartedly with the Blackfoot.

On his return trip to Toronto, Kane left Fort Pitt with the Hudson's Bay Company fur brigade on May 29, 1848. They met a large party of Indians east of the fort on June 1 (*Wanderings*, pp. 148–50), and camped with them for a day during which Kane made several sketches. The party consisted of Blackfoot and their allies, from the Blood, Sarsi, Gros Ventres and Piegan.

IV-143 Indian Horse Race. Kane describes the race (*Wanderings*, p. 148; woodcut, Fig. 16). No preliminary sketches have been located. GWA9. Oil on canvas. 1′6″ x 2′5″. (ROM912.1.51)

IV-144 Indian Horse Race. Replica of IV-143. Oil on canvas. (Colln Mrs. James A. Grant)

IV-145 Indian Horse Race. Replica of IV-143. LP11. Oil on canvas. 1′6½″ x 2′5¼″. Fig. 89. (NGC6921)

IV-146 Omoxesisixany or "Big Snake" (*Wanderings*, pp. 148–50). An identification has evidently been based on an inscription not in Kane's hand. (See Bushnell, *Sketches*, pp. 20–21.) TCH90(?). w.c. 4½″ x 5½″. (Bushnell 41-72/399)

IV-147 Big Snake, Blackfoot Chief from the Western Prairies. Painting is supposedly based on IV-146. GWA73. Oil on canvas. 2′1″ x 1′8″. (ROM912.1.52)

IV-148 The Death of Big Snake. Kane heard an erroneous report of the death of Big Snake when he got to Norway House in June 1848 (*Wanderings*, p. 152). Big Snake actually died in 1858. Kane painted this imaginary view of the incident after reaching Toronto. No preliminary sketches have been located and the composition suggests that the canvas was based on a European prototype. The painting was made into a large coloured lithograph in Toronto *c.* 1856 (Fig. 90). GWA41. Oil on canvas. 1′8″ x 2′1¼″. (ROM912.1.53)

IV-149 Mis-ke-me-kin or "The Iron Collar." Kane says that this Blood Indian had his face painted red (*Wanderings*, p. 149). (See Bushnell, *Sketches*, pp. 20–21). TCH89. w.c. (Bushnell 41-72/400)

IV-150 Wah-nis-stow or "The White Buffalo"; according to Kane's narrative, principal chief of the Sarsi (*Wanderings*, p. 150). This sketch was labelled as that of a Blackfoot when exhibited in Toronto in 1848. TCH91. AG192. w.c. 5¼″ x 5¼″. Fig. 91. (Stark PWC5)

IV-151 Insignia. Study of a detail introduced into IV-150. Pencil. 5¼″ x 7¼″. (ROM946.15.272)

IV-152 Indian chieftain. No certain identification has been established for this figure. Kane refers to a lesser chieftain at the Blackfoot camp with his face partially painted black for mourning (*Wanderings*, p. 150). Evidently the face in this sketch was introduced into IV-154; however, the figure with the blackened face in IV-154 does not wear the same clothing as the man in this sketch. An inscription on the sketch, not in Kane's hand, identifies the subject as Red Vest or "The Feather," a Cree. 11″ x 8¼″. AG57. (Stark POP26)

IV-153 Big Snake's Brother. Kane mentions sketching this man (*Wanderings*, p. 149). No preliminary sketch for this canvas has been located. GWA65. Oil on canvas. 2′6″ x 2′1″. (ROM912.1.54)

IV-154 Six Blackfoot Chiefs (Six Indian Chiefs). Kane describes making the original sketches for this group portrait (*Wanderings*, pp. 149–50; coloured litho.). He identifies the chieftains (*left to right*) as Little Horn; a lesser chieftain; Wah-nis-tow; Big Snake; another lesser chieftain; Mis-ke-me-kin. Three of the portraits are presumably based on sketches IV-146, IV-149, IV-150 and possibly IV-152, but there is little actual resemblance. The clothes are seemingly based on items in Kane's ethnological collection, but there are variations from surviving specimens. GWA72. Oil on canvas. 2′1″ x 2′6″. (ROM912.1.50)

IV-155 Big Snake, a Blackfoot Chief, recounting his War Exploits to Five of His Subordinate Chiefs (Blackfoot Chief and Subordinates). Replica of IV-154. LP1. Oil on canvas. 2′1″ x 2′6″. Fig. 92. (NGC22)

IV-156 Staff of Big Snake. Study for IV-154 and IV-155. Pencil, 4½″ x 7½″. (ROM946.15.105)

IV-157 Medicine pipe-stem dance. Kane says that the Indians assigned him a good position for viewing the ritual while he was executing his sketch (*Wanderings*, p. 150). TCH59. Oil on paper. 9¾″ x 12¼″. Plate XXIII. (Stark POP10)

IV-158 Medicine Pipe Stem Dance. Painting based on IV-157. The eagle head pipe-stem is probably sketched from a specimen (now in Manitoba Museum of Science and History) similar to one drawn by Kane earlier; see IV-132, 136 left. (*Wanderings*;

coloured litho.). GWA37. Oil on canvas. 2′5″ x 4′7″. Fig. 93. (ROM912.1.56)

IV-159 Blackfoot pipe-stem carrier. Single figure holding eagle head pipe-stem in the reverse position to that in IV-132. Pencil. 7½″ x 5½″. (ROM946.15.106A)

IV-160 Blackfoot pipe-stem (fragment of original sketch). Detail study. This object was at one time described as the feathers of an Indian ceremonial head dress. The sketch has been inscribed TCH41 (see also IV-138). AG54. Oil on paper. 9⅝″ x 8″. (Stark EOP7)

IV-161 Blackfoot Pipe Stem Carrier. Painting based on IV-159 and IV-160. GWA80. Oil on canvas. 1′8″ x 1′2″. (ROM912.1.55)

IV-162 Jacket ornamented with a crow. Evidently part of a military society regalia. w.c. 5″ x 7¼″. Fig. 94. (ROM946.15.313)

IV-163 Head dress ornamented with a weasel. Evidently part of a military society regalia. Pencil. 5¾″ x 9½″. (ROM946.15.314)

IV-164 Painted buffalo robe recording the adventures of Sa-co or "The Sinew Piece," a Blood Indian. KLL30. TCH148. AG210. 5⅜″ x 8⅞″. Fig. 95. (Stark WWC82)

Buffalo

Kane describes seeing many buffalo on the prairie before he reached Fort Pitt on his westward trip during 1846; he continued to see these animals until he reached Fort Edmonton. Studies, evidently of this region, are grouped together here, but the majority cannot be dated.

IV-165 Studies of two buffalo. Pencil. 5¼″ x 6½″. (ROM946.15.92)

IV-166 Studies of three buffalo. Pencil. 5¼″ x 6½″. (ROM946.15.88)

IV-167 Studies of three buffalo. Pencil. 5″ x 7¼″. (ROM946.15.89)

IV-168 Studies of three buffalo. Pencil. 5¼″ x 6½″. (ROM946.15.91)

IV-169 Buffalo skull on the prairies. w.c. 2¾″ x 5½″. (ROM-946.15.153)

IV-170 Indian Summer on the Saskatchewan. Evidently painted from a sketch, unlocated, made September 13, 1846 (*Wanderings*, p. 80). Details have been introduced from IV-166 to IV-169. GWA44. Oil on canvas. 1′6″ x 2′5″. (ROM912.1.37)

IV-171 Buffalo trail. w.c. 5½″ x 9″. (ROM946.15.147)

IV-172 Long Grass Valley with dead man's hill in the distance. This was possibly sketched in the region of Long Grass Prairie (*Wanderings*, p. 82), where, Kane reports on September 24, 1846, buffalo were so numerous as to impede progress. KLL28. w.c. 5½″ x 9″. (ROM946.15.148)

IV-173 Buffalo in the Saskatchewan River valley. Pencil. 5″ x 4″. (ROM946.15.334)

IV-174 Page of studies of buffalo. These include a preliminary study of two fighting bulls (see also IV-175 to IV-177). w.c. 5″ x 6½″. Fig. 96. (ROM946.15.90)

IV-175 Buffalo bulls fighting. Painting study based on sketch in IV-174. w.c. 4⅞″ x 6½″. Fig. 97. (Stark PWC9)

IV-176 Buffalo Bulls Fighting. Painting based on IV-175. GWA10. Oil on canvas. 1′6″ x 2′5″. Fig. 98. (ROM912.1.28)

IV-177 Buffalo Bulls Fighting. Replica of IV-176. (Colln Mrs. Ralph D. Baker)

FORT PITT TO FORT EDMONTON

Topography

In 1846 Kane, accompanied by the Rev. Mr. Rundle and Mr. Rowand, left Fort Pitt on September 23 and arrived in Fort Edmonton September 26. The following sketches form an extension of the series IV-110 to IV-121; it is possible that some were executed before Kane reached Fort Pitt.

IV-178 Scene on the Saskatchewan River. KLL22. Pencil. 5½″ x 9″. (ROM946.15.114)

IV-179 Scene on the Saskatchewan River. Pencil. 5½″ x 9.″ (ROM946.15.115)

IV-180 Salt lake. Described by Kane (*Wanderings*, pp. 82–83). Probably sketched September 24, 1846. KLL23. w.c. 5¾″ x 6½″. (ROM946.15.149)

IV-181 A lake in the plains. This may be the lake beside which Kane says he camped on the evening of September 24, 1846 (*Wanderings*, p. 82). KLL24. TCH204. w.c. 5¼″ x 9″. Plate XXIV. (ROM946.15.138)

IV-182 Prairie landscape. Pencil. 5½″ x 9″. (ROM946.15.121)

IV-183 Prairie landscape. Locale said to be between Edmonton and Prince Albert. w.c. 5½″ x 9¼″. (ROM946.15.140)

IV-184 Rolling hillside and prairie. Pencil. 5½″ x 9.″ (ROM946.15.-143)

IV-185 Prairie fire. This is presumably the fire seen by Kane on September 26, 1846, from Fort Edmonton (*Wanderings*, p. 83). Unfinished w.c. 7½″ x 12″. (ROM946.15.319)

IV-186 A prairie on fire. Presumably another view of the fire sketched in IV-185. KLL21. TCH203. w.c. 5½″ x 9″. (ROM946.15.124)

IV-187 A Prairie on Fire. Painting based on IV-186 but changed from a day to a night view. GWA55. Oil on canvas. 1′6″ x 2′5″. Fig. 99. (ROM912.1.39)

FORT EDMONTON

Kane was at Fort Edmonton from September 26 to October 6, 1846, when he left for the Pacific. He returned December 5, 1847, remaining until January 7, 1848, when he left for a visit to Fort Pitt. He returned again during February, leaving on April 12 for Rocky Mountain House. He went back to Fort Edmonton, and left there for Norway House with the spring fur brigade on May 25, 1848. (*Wanderings*, pp. 83, 136, 138–39.)

Fort and environs

Fort Edmonton, on the North Saskatchewan River, was the Hudson's Bay Company's principal post on the western prairies. The building pictured in IV-188 is the last of several built by the Company. The first was erected at Sturgeon River in 1795. A second stood within the limits of the present city of Edmonton from 1802 to 1810. Concurrently the North West Company had a fort nearby. A new main fort was built after the union of the two companies in 1821, but in 1830 floods forced its abandonment as it stood on low ground. The final Fort Edmonton, visited by Kane, was built betwen 1830 and 1832. This stood until 1915 when it was dismantled for the construction of the Legislative Building of the Province of Alberta.

IV-188 Fort Edmonton. KLL29. TCH206. AG183. w.c. 5⅜″ x 9″. Plate XXV. (Stark PWC22)

IV-189 Edmonton. Painting based on IV-188. GWA20. Oil on canvas. 1′6″ x 2′5″. (ROM912.1.38)

IV-190 Fort Edmonton. General view of the high ground overlooking the plain and the fort. Pencil. 5½″ x 9″. (ROM946.15.122)

IV-191 Fort Edmonton. Pencil. 2½″ x 5¾″. (ROM946.15.113)

IV-192 Eroding banks of the Saskatchewan River, evidently in the vicinity of Fort Edmonton. Pencil. 2½″ x 5¾″. (ROM946.15.112)

IV-193 View of the Saskatchewan River, evidently upstream from Fort Edmonton. Unfinished w.c. 5″ x 6½″. (ROM946.15.117)

Wedding party

Kane describes the wedding of Miss Harriott, daughter of John Edward Harriott, the chief factor at Fort Edmonton, to Mr. Rowand Jr., "who resided at" Fort Pitt. This took place on January 6, 1848 (*Wanderings*, p. 141). Kane recounts that he accompanied the bridal party which left the fort the next day and travelled in their company to Fort Pitt.

IV-194 Sled dogs decorated for the wedding party. Described on reverse as "Contines dogs." Kane points out that the bride's cariole was pulled by dogs brought recently from Lower Canada (Quebec) (*Wanderings*, p. 141). TCH174. w.c. 5½″ x 9½″. Fig. 101. (Stark PWC12)

IV-195 Sled dogs of the plains (Indian dogs). Kane makes particular reference to their ferocity (*Wanderings*, p. 141). TCH156. AG164. w.c. 5½″ x 9½″. Fig. 100. (Stark PWC13)

IV-196 Study of snow on trees. This sketch is included here because it was incorporated into the composite painting of the wedding party, IV-201, although there is no proof that it was done at Fort Edmonton. TCH146. AG140. w.c. 6⅞″ x 4⅞″. Fig. 102. (Stark WWC40)

IV-197 Evergreen laden with snow, a sketch included here because of its similarity to IV-196. w.c. 5″ x 7″. (ROM946.15.286)

IV-198 Evergreen laden with snow, a sketch included here because of its similarity to IV-196. w.c. 5″ x 7″. (ROM946.15.287)

IV-199 Decorated sled. Kane says that it was especially ornamented for the bride (*Wanderings*, p. 141). w.c. 5¼″ x 9¼″. Fig. 103. (ROM946.15.129)

IV-200   Winter travelling with dog sleds. Preliminary study for IV-201. Pencil. 5⅝″ x 9¼″. (Stark 2).

IV-201   Winter Travelling (Winter Travelling in Dog Sleds). View of the Rowand wedding party leaving Edmonton for Fort Pitt on January 7, 1848 (*Wanderings*, p. 141; woodcut Fig. 14). The painting is based on the studies in IV-194, IV-196, IV-199, IV-200. GWA38. Oil on canvas. 1′7″ x 2′5″. Plate XXVI. (ROM912.1.48)

IV-202   Sketch of young man and woman. There is no documentary identification of this couple, but it seems possible that they may be Miss Harriott and Mr. Rowand Jr. at the time of the wedding in Fort Edmonton. Pencil. (Stark, sketch in Kane's journal)

Catching wild horses

IV-203   Catching Wild Horses. No preliminary sketches exist for this painting nor does Kane make direct reference to the incident. He does refer to roaming bands of horses in the Edmonton area during December 1847, and this painting probably pictures a locale west of the city (*Wanderings*, p. 137). GWA11. Oil on canvas. 1′6″ x 2′5″. Fig. 104. (ROM912.1.45)

Gigantic buffalo head

Kane killed an enormous buffalo for its head while hunting near Fort Edmonton *c*. December 5, 1847 (*Wanderings*, p. 137). This trophy is now in the Manitoba Museum of Science and History. The following sketches appear to be studies of it.

IV-204   Buffalo head. Pencil. 4¾″ x 5½″. (ROM946.15.94)

IV-205   Buffalo head. TCH55. AG68. Oil on paper. 6½″ x 8″. (Stark POP12)

IV-206   Two buffalo heads. AG178. w.c. 4⅞″ x 6⅞″. (Stark PWC10)

Assiniboin

The Assiniboin, a branch of the Sioux, lived during the 17th century in the Lake of the Woods region. They had moved into the central prairies by the mid 19th century, but introduction of firearms drove them even farther west. The tribe had divided into two groups by the 1860s. The northern Assiniboin, with whom Kane came in contact, were on the western branches of the Saskatchewan and Assiniboine rivers towards the Rocky Mountains. The southern group were in American territory. The tribe, who were nomads, were closely allied to the Cree.

IV-207   Potika-poo-tis or "The Little Round Man," nicknamed "The Duke of Wellington." Kane sketched him at Fort Edmonton in September 1846 (*Wanderings*, p. 83), and calls him an Assiniboin chief. This sketch has been referred to, incorrectly, as "Cree Chief from Fort Edmonton." KPL10. AG83. Oil on paper. 11⅜″ x 9½″. (Stark POP8)

IV-208   Running Buffalo (Two Assiniboine Indians Running a Buffalo). Kane describes how he saw Assiniboin hunting while he was at Fort Edmonton (*Wanderings*, p. 84). He makes no mention of sketching them at the time, and no sketches have been located. The painting is based on an Italian print by Pinelli engraved in Rome in 1815, entitled "Cavalcatura che conducona le bestie bovine in Rome per macellare." The print comes from a volume *Nuova Raccolta di cinquanta Costumi pittoreschi incisi all' acqua forte da Bartolomeo Pinelli* (Roma 1816), which was in Kane's library (Fig. 106). GWA58. Oil on canvas. 1′6″ x 2′5″. (ROM-912.1.46). A replica of this painting was sold by Knoedler & Co. in New York in recent years; it has not been traced.*

IV-209   Assiniboine Hunting Buffalo. Replica of IV-208. LP6. Oil on canvas. 1′6½″ x 2′5¾″. Fig. 105. (NGC6920)

IV-210   Assiniboine Running Buffalo. Replica of IV-209. Oil on canvas. 1′5½″ x 2′4″. (Colln H. R. Milner)

Cree

IV-211   A Cree from Edmonton. No preliminary sketches for this painting have been located. GWA71. Oil on canvas. 2′6″ x 2′1″. (ROM912.1.43)

IV-212   Cun-ne-wa-bum. Four compositional studies for IV-214. Pencil. 3¾″ x 4½″. (ROM946.15.79)

IV-213   Cun-ne-wa-bum. Three compositional studies for IV-214. Pencil. 3¾″ x 4½″. (ROM946.15.80)

IV-214   Cunnawa-bum (Cun-ne-wa-bum) or "One that looks at the stars." Half-breed Cree girl who danced with Kane at the 1847 Christmas evening ball at Fort Edmonton (*Wanderings*, p. 139; coloured litho., frontispiece). The dress is in the Manitoba Museum of Science and History. IV-212 and IV-213 are compositional studies for this painting, but no actual study for the head has been located. GWA60. Oil on canvas. 2′1″ x 1′8″; (oval) 2′ x 1′7″. Fig. 107. (ROM912.1.41)

IV-215   François Lucie, a Cree half-breed guide. Kane hunted with him and refers to him on several occasions (*Wanderings*, p. 139 *et al.*). TCH31. AG16. Oil on paper. 10⅞″ x 8¾″. Plate XXVII. (Stark POP9)

IV-216   François Lucie. Painting based on IV-215. GWA100. Oil on canvas. 2′6″ x 2′1¾″. (ROM912.1.40)

ROCKY MOUNTAIN HOUSE

Kane left Fort Edmonton April 12, 1848, and reached Rocky Mountain House on the 21st. He returned to Fort Edmonton early in May. Much of his stay at Rocky Mountain House was spent in sketching Assiniboin and Cree.

Topography

Rocky Mountain House had been established as a post by the North West Company in 1799, and was chosen by the Hudson's Bay Company to replace its own post after the union of the two companies in 1821. It was operated from 1828 to 1861 as a winter post only. This fort was completely rebuilt in 1864 but abandoned in 1875 in favour of the Calgary post.

IV-217   Rocky Mountain House with Assiniboin lodges in the foreground. (*Wanderings*, p. 146.) (Bushnell, *Sketches*, p. 15.) TCH211. w.c. 5½" x 9⅛". (Bushnell 41-72/397)

IV-218   Rocky Mountain House. Painting based on IV-217. GWA48. Oil on canvas. 1'6" x 2'5". Fig. 108. (ROM912.1.57)

IV-219   Log cache for food storage between Rocky Mountain House and Fort Edmonton. Kane describes finding a wolverine in it (*Wanderings*, p. 147). Pencil. 5½" x 9". (ROM946.15.302)

Assiniboin

IV-220   Assiniboin lodge at Rocky Mountain House (?). This lodge resembles those pictured in IV-217 and IV-218, but evergreen lodges are known to have existed in other parts of the west. This particular lodge appears to be of birch bark with a covering of evergreen. w.c. 5½" x 9½". (ROM946.15.217)

IV-221   Assiniboin chiefs at Rocky Mountain House. *Left:* Mah-Min or "The Feather," head chief. *Right:* Wah-he-joe-tass-e-neen or "The half-white man," second chief. (*Wanderings*, pp. 146–47.) Formerly these sketches were incorrectly identified as portraits of Iacaway and Little Rat (see IV-29). TCH82 and TCH83. AG100. w.c. 5¼" x 8⅞". Plate XXVIII. (Stark PWC1)

IV-222   Head Chief of the Assiniboins (Mah-Min). The portrait is based on that in IV-221, but there are variations in the dress. The club, roach and quiver were evidently suggested by those in IV-224 (which have not definitely been established as Assiniboin). GWA62. Oil on canvas. 2'6" x 2'1". (ROM912.1.58)

IV-223   Mah-Min or "The Feather" (Head Chief of the Assiniboine). Replica of IV-222. This portrait has on occasion been referred to as that of a Blackfoot. Oil on canvas. 2'6" x 2'1". Fig. 109. (Montreal Museum of Fine Arts 47.992)

IV-224   War clubs. Evidently these clubs and a quiver have been introduced into IV-222 and IV-223, but there is no documentary proof that they are Assiniboin. TCH155. AG125. w.c. 5¼" x 9½". (Stark WWC75)

IV-225   Wah-he-joe-tass-e-neen or "The half-white man." This is evidently a preliminary sketch. It was formerly identified as a sketch of Coe-coosh (see III-126). w.c. 4½" x 5". (ROM-946.15.55)

IV-226   Second Chief of the Assiniboins (Wah-he-joe-tass-e-neen). Painting based on IV-221, and formerly identified as a portrait of Coe-coosh (III-127). GWA63. Oil on canvas. 2'6" x 2'1". (ROM912.1.59)

Cree

IV-227   Pe-a-pus-qua-hum or "One that passes through the sky." This Cree lived among the Assiniboin at Rocky Mountain House.

(See Bushnell, *Sketches*, pp. 17–18.) TCH85. w.c. 5½" x 4½". (Bushnell 41-72/398)

PRAIRIE INDIAN ENCAMPMENTS

No locale or tribe can be identified for the following sketches. A number of the figures are evidently Cree but lack of documentary evidence would make any attribution conjectural.

IV-228   Group of Plains Indians with tepee and horse. Pencil. 4½" x 6½". (ROM946.15.308)

IV-229   Group of Plains Indians with tepee and horse. Pencil. 4½" x 6". (ROM946.15.309)

IV-230   Group of three seated women. w.c. 5½" x 9". (ROM946.15.-312)

IV-231   Seated woman. It has been suggested that she is an Ojibwa girl from the Georgian Bay Region (Kathleen Wood, "Paul Kane Sketches," *Rotunda*, Winter 1969, p. 9, illus.). It seems equally possible that she is related to the group pictured in IV-230. Pencil. 5" x 7½". (ROM946.15.291)

IV-232   Group of Plains Indians smoking. Pencil. 3¾" x 5½". (ROM-946.15.315)

IV-233   Seated Indian with pipe. Evidently this is a more detailed study of one of the group in IV-232. Pencil. 3¾" x 5½". (ROM-946.15.316)

IV-234   Two standing figures: man with trade gun, possibly a Hudson's Bay Company employee, and an Indian. Pencil. 6½" x 10". (ROM946.15.303)

IV-235   Page of sketches, probably all completed on the plains. *Left to right:* standing European boy holding spear; profile head of Indian with forelock similar to that worn by the Cree at Fort Carlton (see, e.g., IV-103); profile head of Indian with beads on side of face. Numbers have been associated with each of the three sketches in a recent hand; they do not correspond with Kane's log. Pencil. 5½" x 6½". (ROM946.15.294)

IV-236   Indian woman with papoose and cradle board on her back. An inscription on the reverse, possibly in Kane's hand, reads: "Bay-je-gi-she-quish, The Striped Cloud," and "Og-sah-wah-nah-quoch-ogue, The Golden Cloud." Pencil. 4" x 4¾". (ROM-946.15.154)

IV-237   Seated Indian girl leaning on a post. It has been suggested, without confirmation, that this is a crude study of the Saulteaux girl in IV-87. w.c. 5" x 7¼". (ROM946.15.81)

IV-238   Indians grouped around a tepee; a crude sketch. Pencil. 5½" x 9¼". (ROM946.15.219)

IV-239   Indian encampment on shoreline. An inscription in sepia ink on the reverse, possibly in Kane's hand, reads: "Edmonton, Mar. 5th." The paper is watermarked Whatman 46. Pencil. 3½" x 5". (ROM946.15.123)

FORT EDMONTON TO FORT ASSINIBOINE

Kane left Fort Edmonton for the Pacific on October 6, 1846, and arrived at Fort Assiniboine, Athabasca River, on the 10th. He notes seeing buffalo on this outward journey. He retraced the route during the late autumn of 1847, but does not mention sketching on the return journey.

IV-240   Group of Buffalo. Kane describes sketching a group at "Sturgeon Creek" sixteen miles west of Fort Edmonton (*Wanderings*, p. 84; woodcut, Fig. 6). No preliminary sketches have been located. GWA32. Oil on canvas. 1′7½″ x 2′5″; (oval) 1′5½″ x 2′3¼″. (ROM912.1.47)

IV-241   Buffaloes at Sunset. Replica of IV-240. Oil on canvas; (oval) 1′4½″ x 2′½″. (Colln Mr. and Mrs. Jules Loeb)

IV-242   Buffaloes reposing near Sturgeon Creek. Replica of IV-240. Oil on canvas; (oval) 1′2¾″ x 2′1″. (Glenbow)

IV-243   Buffaloes at Sunset. Replica of IV-240. LP4. Oil on canvas; (oval) 1′4½″ x 2′3½″. Fig. 110. (NGC6919)

IV-244   Buffaloes at Sunset. Replica of IV-240. The Coe collection, which contains this replica, allegedly came from Sir George Simpson's collection, but this canvas is not in the list of paintings ordered by Sir George from Kane. Oil on canvas. 10¾″ x 16½″. (Coe)

FORT ASSINIBOINE TO JASPER HOUSE

Kane left Fort Assiniboine October 11, 1846, and arrived at Jasper House November 3, where he remained for two days. On his return journey, he was at Jasper House November 5–15, 1847, and reached Fort Assiniboine on November 29. He encountered many difficulties on his return journey; the sketches in this group were probably all completed on the outward trip.

Jasper House, on the Athabasca River, was an important supply depot for horses and canoes carrying freight to the west coast by way of the Athabasca and Yellowhead passes. A post was built by the North West Company at Jasper, near the outlet of Brulé Lake, about 1813. It was rebuilt by the Hudson's Bay Company between 1827 and 1829 near the mouth of the Miette River and was maintained until 1884. (*Wanderings*, p. 87.)

IV-245   Athabasca River with mountains in the distance. Probably sketched October 31, 1846 (*Wanderings*, p. 86). An inscription on the reverse reads "Jasper's Lake." KLL31. w.c. 5″ x 7″. (ROM946.15.131)

IV-246   Athabasca River with mountain in the distance. Close-up view of terrain in IV-245. Pencil. 5″ x 6½″. (ROM946.15.268)

IV-247   Athabasca River. Pencil. 5″ x 6½″. (ROM946.15.234)

IV-248   Jasper House and Jasper Lake. Pencil. 5″ x 6½″. (ROM-946.15.267)

IV-249   Jasper Lake with Miette's Rock. KLL32. TCH190. w.c. 5″ x 7″. (ROM946.15.130)

IV-250   Jasper House. (*Wanderings*; woodcut, Fig. 7.) KLL33. TCH189. AG139. w.c. 5¼″ x 8⅞″. Fig. 111. (Stark PWC25)

JASPER HOUSE

Shuswap and Carrier

The Shuswap were the most important of the Salishan tribes in British Columbia; they held much territory between the Columbia and Fraser rivers including the basin of the Thompson River above Ashcroft. The Carrier (their formal name is Takulli) were a tribe of British Columbia living on the upper Fraser and the Blackwater rivers and in the vicinity of Stuart and Babine lakes.

IV-251   As-in-a-chap (Assannitchay) or "Capote Blanc." Kane met this Shuswap at Jasper on November 5, 1846, and again at Boat Encampment on October 10, 1847 (*Wanderings*, pp. 87, 129). This sketch was identified formerly as one of Iwa-toke, the Menominee from Lake Winnebago (III-106). (See Bushnell, *Sketches*, p. 6.) KPL20. w.c. 5½″ x 4½″. (Bushnell 41-72/392)

IV-252   A-chis-a-lay or "The Call of the Wind." This sketch was evidently made at Jasper House. Kane describes the man in his log as a member of the "As-ick-an-a" tribe from the Peace River, and says Sir Alexander Mackenzie called its people the "Carriers." KPL21. TCH93. AG216. w.c. 5⅜″ x 9″. (Stark PWC24)

JASPER TO BOAT ENCAMPMENT

Kane left Jasper on November 5, 1846. He crossed over to Boat Encampment on the Columbia River by way of the Committee's Punch Bowl and reached it on November 14. Returning a year later, he left Boat Encampment on October 31 and arrived at Jasper on November 6, 1847.

IV-253   Four pack horses. These are probably horses in the cavalcade which was with Kane's party when it left Jasper on November 5, 1846 (*Wanderings*, p. 87). Pencil. 5¼″ x 6½″. Fig. 112. (ROM946.15.133)

IV-254   Sketch of pack horse and detail study of horse's head. Pencil. 5″ x 7″. (ROM946.15.249)

IV-255   LaRocque's Prairie with wild horses. Kane camped at this spot on the night of November 6, 1846, and exactly a year later on his way home (*Wanderings*, pp. 87, 131). The sketch was formerly identified incorrectly as of "The Cascade Mountains, B. Columbia." KLL35. TCH191. w.c. 5½″ x 8¾″. (Stark WWC79)

IV-256   Bighorn Rocky Mountain ram. Kane made this sketch on November 6, 1847, just before reaching Jasper on his homeward journey, and reports the horns as having a length of 42 inches (*Wanderings*, pp. 131–32). TCH175. AG103. w.c. 5″ x 7¼″. Fig. 113. (Stark WWC98A)

IV-257   Bighorn Rocky Mountain sheep (ewe). w.c. 5″ x 7″. (ROM-946.15.135)

IV-258   Rocky Mountain goat (*Wanderings*, pp. 87, 127). Pencil. 5″ x 7″. (ROM946.15.136)

IV-259 Rocky Mountain goat. Pencil. 5″ x 7″. (ROM946.15.137)

IV-260 Rocky Mountain goat (head). Pencil. 5″ x 7″. (ROM-946.15.134)

IV-261 Rocky Mountain goat. TCH145. AG201. w.c. 5″ x 7¼″. (Stark wwc94)

IV-262 Rocky Mountain goat. Presumably this is the sketch for a canvas, unlocated, painted for Sir George Simpson (GS14). AG96. Oil on paper. 9″ x 14″. Fig. 114. (Stark wop18)

IV-263 Prairie with mountain sheep. KLL34. w.c. 5½″ x 9″. (ROM946.15.237)

IV-264 Athabasca River in the mountains. KLL37. TCH194. w.c. 5½″ x 9″. Fig. 115. (ROM946.15.238)

IV-265 Athabasca River in the mountains. KLL36. w.c. 5½″ x 9″. (ROM-946.15.328)

IV-266 A winter scene in the Rockies: Athabasca River. KLL36. w.c. 5¼″ x 9″. (Stark wwc18)

IV-267 Snow in the Rockies. Possibly painted November 10–12, 1846, when Kane experienced very heavy snow in the mountains (*Wanderings*, p. 88). w.c. 5″ x 7″. (ROM946.15.132)

IV-268 Tree laden with snow. w.c. 5½″ x 4½″. (ROM946.15.289)

IV-269 The Committee's Punch Bowl. Probably sketched November 12, 1846 (*Wanderings*, p. 88). KLL39. w.c. 5½″ x 9″. Fig. 116. (ROM946.15.239)

IV-270 A sketch of the falls at the headwaters of the Columbia River. This is probably the sketch Kane refers to under the date November 14, 1846 (*Wanderings*, p. 88). KLL40. w.c. 5″ x 7″. (ROM946.15.278)

IV-271 A sketch on the upper Columbia River (?). Pencil. 5½″ x 9″. (ROM946.15.241)

IV-272 A sketch on the upper Columbia River (?). Pencil. 5½″ x 9″. (ROM946.15.240)

IV-273 Mountain landscape. An earlier suggestion that this is a view of Mount St. Helens is incorrect. Pencil. 5¼″ x 9″. (ROM-946.15.160)

IV-274 A river in the mountains, possibly the Columbia River. AG150. w.c. 4⅞″ x 7″. (Stark wwc12)

IV-275 Camping scene in the woods, possibly near Boat Encampment. Pencil. 5″ x 7″. (ROM946.15.296)

IV-276 Boat Encampment. Sketch with Kane's tent and luggage. Kane was here on November 15, 1846, and October 10–31, 1847 (*Wanderings*, pp. 89, 129–30). TCH230. w.c. 5¼″ x 8¾″. Plate XXIX. (Stark wwc100)

IV-277 Study of mountain peaks as seen from Boat Encampment. w.c. 5½″ x 9½″. Fig. 117. (ROM946.15.236)

IV-278 Boat Encampment. Painting based on IV-276 and IV-277. GWA26. Oil on canvas. 1′6″ x 2′5″. (ROM912.1.60)

IV-279 Boat Encampment. Replica of IV-278. Oil on canvas. 1′1¾″ x 1′8¼″ (Glenbow)

MOUNTAINS

Plains Indians

IV-280 Party of three Indians in birch-bark canoe. Pencil. 5½″ x 9½″. (ROM946.15.301)

IV-281 Party of Indians in two canoes on mountain lake. Evidently this is a representation of an Indian legend. IV-280 is possibly a preliminary sketch. Oil on canvas. 1′6″ x 2′5″. (Colln P. Winkworth)

BOAT ENCAMPMENT TO FORT COLVILE

IV-282 Dalles des Morts, or the Rapid of the Dead (probably based on a sketch to which Kane refers in *Wanderings*, p. 128). GWA13. Oil on canvas. 1′6″ x 2′5″. (ROM912.1.61)

IV-283 Sailing on Upper Arrow Lakes. Probably sketched September 25–29, 1847 (*Wanderings*, p. 127). Pencil. 5″ x 7″. (ROM946.15.82)

IV-284 Shoreline of Upper Arrow Lakes. Formerly described as "View on the Columbia River." Pencil. 5″ x 6¼″. (ROM946.15.333)

IV-285 Shoreline of Upper Arrow Lakes. Pencil. 5½″ x 9″. (ROM-946.15.176)

IV-286 The Little Dalles, twenty miles above Kettle Falls near Fort Colvile. Probably sketched September 23, 1847 (*Wanderings*, p. 126). KLL115. AG209. wc.. 5½″ x 9½″. Fig. 119. (Stark wwc6)

IV-287 The Little Dalles. Painting based on IV-286. Oil on canvas. 1′7¾″ x 2′5″. (Stark wop24)

COLUMBIA RIVER

Kutenai

The Kutenai Indians, of a distinct linguistic stock, lived in the southeastern part of British Columbia and on the lakes near the source of the Columbia River. The lower Kutenai group in particular were distinguished for their unusual bark canoes. (*Wanderings*, p. 127)

IV-288 Ask-a-weelish. A chief of the lakes 60 miles above Colvile. TCH95. AG99. w.c. 5¼″ x 8⅞″. Fig. 122. (Stark wwc80, left)

IV-289 An Indian of the lakes above Colvile. KPL22. TCH106. AG185. w.c. 4⅞″ x 3⅝″. (Stark wwc38)

IV-290 Columbia River near Grand Rapids. A Kutenai-type canoe is in the water. KLL41. w.c. 5½″ x 9″. Fig. 121. (ROM946.15.174)

IV-291 Page of sketches: Kutenai canoe, sweathouse, tepee, and a mat lodge of the upper Columbia River. Pencil. 5½″ x 9½″. Fig. 120. (ROM946.15.202)

FORT COLVILE

Chualpays

Kane identifies the Indians whom he met at Fort Colvile as Chualpays and remarks that they are similar to the Spokan and not much different from the Walla Walla. A division of Salish, they are referred to in modern terminology as "Colville." (The Hudson's Bay Company post on the Columbia had been named "Colvile" for a governor of the Company and this spelling is used in the present book where appropriate.)

IV-292 See-pays, or "Chief of the Waters." Sketch was probably made September 17, 1847 (*Wanderings*, p. 123). KPL83. TCH96. AG99. w.c. 5¼″ x 8⅞″. Fig. 122. (Stark wwc80, right)

IV-293 Chief of the Salmon (See-pays). Painting based on IV-292. GWA92. Oil on canvas. 2′6″ x 2′1″. (ROM912.1.63)

IV-294 El-ko-ka-shin, a "Shawalloway Indian, from the Cascades." This designation, from the TCH catalogue, evidently refers to this sketch. An inscription on it, not in Kane's hand, reads "The Blue Jay from Kettle Falls." Both names may apply to this individual. A "Blue Jay" is a man set apart among Salishan tribes because of his dealings with the supernatural; see R. G. Conn, "The Rarest Kind of Blue Jay," *Blue Jay* (Regina, Sask.), XXV, 1, March 1967. TCH98. AG104. w.c. 5¼″ x 8⅞″. (Stark wwc20, left)

IV-295 Allam-mak-hum Stole-luch (Elle-a-ma-cum-stuck) or "Chief of the Earth." Kane describes him in his book as a Chualpays (*Wanderings*, p. 123), but in his manuscript portrait log as a Spokan. It was formerly suggested that this sketch might be a portrait of Casanov (seeIV-418). KPL23. w.c. 7″ x 5″. (ROM-946.15.215)

IV-296 Unidentified portrait. The treatment of hair is similar to that for See-pays, chief of the Chualpays (see IV-293). AG159. w.c. 4¾″ x 3¾″. (Stark wwc39)

SALMON FISHING

Kane discusses in detail the methods used by Chualpays in salmon fishing near Fort Colvile, which he observed on his return trip across the continent (*Wanderings*, pp. 123–24). Sketches associated with this type of fishing are gathered together below, although some may have originated at other points along the Columbia since Kane mentions salmon fishing at Fort Walla Walla and Fort Vancouver; only those sketches which can definitely be associated with other areas are not included here.

IV-297 Kettle Falls, Spokane River. KLL112. TCH182. AG151. w.c. 5⅜″ x 9½″. (Stark wwc68)

IV-298 Kettle Falls. KLL111. AG7. Oil on paper. 8⅛″ x 13⅜″. Plate XXX. (Stark wop19)

IV-299 Kettle Falls. Inscribed, but not in Kane's hand, "Salmon Falls, Koos-koos-kia River." AG156. w.c. 5½″ x 9⅞″. (Stark wwc46)

IV-300 Weir on Columbia River at Colvile. Pencil. 5¼″ x 9½″. (ROM946.15.161)

IV-301 Platform for fishermen at Kettle Falls. (In the upper right is a small landscape, Lost Men's Portage; see IV-6a). w.c. 5″ x 7¼″. (ROM946.15.332)

IV-302 Indian with fish spear poised on platform. Pencil 5¼″ x 9½″. (ROM946.15.203)

IV-303 Salmon weir at Kettle Falls. Study of the central portion of the waterfalls. w.c. 5½″ x 9⅜″. (ROM946.15.205)

IV-304 Indians spearing salmon on the Columbia River. TCH166. AG133. w.c. 5½″ x 9½″(Stark wwc84)

IV-305 Indians spearing salmon. AG168. w.c. 5⅜″ x 9½″. (Stark wwc85)

IV-306 Catching salmon on the Columbia River. *Left:* elaborately decorated quiver with bow. *Lower right:* Indian with speared fish and club; study of woman with tump line and a papoose on her back. AG105. w.c. 5⅜″ x 9½″. Fig. 123. (Stark wwc87)

IV-307 Falls at Colville. Painting based on sketches IV-299 to IV-306. GWA5. Oil on canvas. 1′7″ x 2′5″. (ROM912.1.64)

IV-308 Fish houses, Columbia River. Indian lodges: 1/ the head chief's lodge; 2/ the second chief's; 3/ the salmon chief's. (See IV-310, 328.) The third lodge is evidently that of See-pays (IV-292). KLL114. AG191. w.c. 5½″ x 9⅜″. (Stark wwc60)

IV-309 Indians smoking salmon near the Columbia River. On reverse, seated woman. w.c. and pencil. 5½″ x 9″. Fig. 124. (ROM946.15.206)

IV-310 Drying salmon at the Dalles, Columbia River. Indian lodges: 1/ the head chief's lodge; 2/ the second chief's. (See IV-308.) KLL113. AG180. w.c. 5½″ x 9¼″. Plate XXXI. (Stark wwc50)

IV-311 Indian Camp, Colville. Painting based on IV-310. The woman with tump line and papoose has probably been suggested by the sketch in IV-306, and the horse with woman's saddle by IV-370. GWA15. Oil on canvas. 1′7″ x 2′5½″. (ROM912.1.62)

IV-312 Drying salmon at the Dalles, Columbia River. Oil version of IV-310. Oil on paper. 8½″ x 13½″. (Colln H. R. Milner)

IV-313 Three standing fishermen with dip nets. Pencil. 5½″ x9″. (ROM946.15.325)

IV-314 Spearing fish. Pencil. 5¼″ x 10½″. (ROM946.15.244)

IV-315 Fish-drying camp on the Columbia River. Pencil. 6¾″ x 9¾″. (ROM946.15.198)

GAME OF AL-KOL-LOCK

Kane witnessed this game of the Chualpays during his stay at Fort Colvile September 17–22, 1847 (*Wanderings*, p. 123). He describes the method of playing; a ring falls on thrown spears and scores are determined by means of coloured balls on the ring, each of which has a different value.

IV-316 Game of Al-kol-lock, Columbia River. AG116. w.c. 5½″ x 9″. Fig. 125. (Stark wwc78)

IV-317 Study of the ring used in Al-kol-lock; it includes colour notations for beads. Pencil. 5½″ x 9½″. (ROM946.15.204)

IV-318 Study of ring and of bone-tipped wand used in the game of Al-kol-lock. w.c. 4½″ x 6½″. (ROM946.15.210)

IV-319 Study of two figures playing Al-kol-lock, and the backs of two observers seated on right. Pencil. 5½″ x 9½″. (ROM-946.15.209)

IV-320 Game of Alcoloh (Al-kol-lock). Painting based on IV-316, and with background based on IV-332. GWA21. Oil on canvas. 1′6″ x 2′5″. (ROM912.1.65)

IV-321 Indians Playing at Alcoloh. Replica of IV-320. LP12. Oil on canvas. 1′6″ x 2′5″. Fig. 126. (NGC60)

SCALP DANCE

Kane witnessed a scalp dance during his stay at Fort Colvile, September 17–22, 1847 (*Wanderings*, p. 124). He sketched various aspects of the ritual.

IV-322 Chualpays scalp dance. TCH60. AG115. w.c. 5⅜″ x 9½″. Fig. 127. (Stark wwc31)

IV-323 Studies of the scalp dance. *Left:* medicine man and widow holding hoop with Blackfoot scalp. *Right:* eight faces of women dancers, with colour notations. Pencil. 5½″ x 9½″. (ROM-946.15.230)

IV-324 Painted faces of eight attendant women dancers. TCH94. AG127. w.c. 5½″ x 9⅜″. Fig. 128. (Stark wwc72)

IV-325 Sketches of two standing figures. *Left:* medicine man. *Right:* figure holding hoop. Pencil. 5½″ x 9½″. (ROM946.15.229)

IV-326 Studies of scalp dance. *Left:* three heads with painted faces, and details of scalp attached to stick held by the widow. *Centre:* medicine man with body painting. *Right:* two studies of widow holding scalp. Pencil. 5½″ x 9¼″. (ROM946.15.208)

IV-327 Studies of scalp dance. *Left:* unidentified figure of an Indian. *Centre:* standing figure holding hoop and a medicine man with painted stripes on body. *Right:* woman with cradle board. AG165. w.c. 5⅜″ x 9½″. Fig. 130. (Stark wwc63)

IV-328 Scalp Dance, Colville. Painting based on sketches IV-322 to IV-327, and on buildings in IV-308. GWA22. Oil on canvas. 1′7″ x 2′5″. (ROM912.1.66)

IV-329 Scalp Dance by Spokane [*sic*] Indians. Replica of IV-328. LP5. Oil on canvas. 1′7″ x 2′5″. Fig. 129. (NGC103)

Miscellaneous sketches

IV-330 Hudson's Bay mill, Fort Colvile. Pencil. 5¼″ x 9″. (ROM-946.15.159)

IV-331 Painted horse, Colvile. This has been described incorrectly as a Blackfoot horse (see Bushnell, *Sketches*, pp. 18–19). KLL116. TCH154. w.c. 5⅜″ x 9⅛″. (Bushnell 41-72/401)

IV-332 Sketch on the Columbia River 50 miles below Colvile. Identified from a notation on the sketch, not in Kane's hand. (See IV-320.) AG145. w.c. 5⅜″ x 9½″. (Stark wwc42)

See also IV-290.

Flathead

Authorities usually describe this tribe as living in the western part of what is now the state of Montana; their formal name is given as Salish, and they are placed as a division of the Salishan family. There were small bodies of Salish in the area around the Spokane River, and they are usually identified as Spokan.

It is not clear to what group Kane is referring in connection with the sketch listed below. He points out in a manuscript note related to it that the Flatheads were closely related to the Spokan (see IV-337). He also says that the name Flathead is a misnomer as the heads of these Indians were not artificially flattened like those of the Chinook. (The name likely arises because their heads were not distorted but left flat on top.) He refers elsewhere (*Wanderings*, p. 111) to a Flathead burial ground at the Cascades on the Columbia River.

IV-333 Chinewoss, a Flathead or "Sheach-a-way" Indian from west of the Rockies. Identification has been made from an inscription on the reverse. KPL Addendum. TCH97. AG104. w.c. 5¼″ x 8⅞″. (Stark wwc20, right)

SPOKANE RIVER

Topography

IV-334 Sketch on the Spokane River. KLL117. TCH216. w.c. 5½″ x 9″. Plate XXXII. (ROM946.15.189)

IV-335 Falls on the Spokane River (?). This highly tentative identification has been made from a recent inscription on the reverse of the sketch. Pencil. 5½″ x 9″. (ROM946.15.190)

IV-336 Mission station of Walker and Eells, Spokane River. Kane arrived at the mission for a week's visit on September 9, 1847 (*Wanderings*, p. 122). The station had been established by the Rev. Elkanah Walker and the Rev. Cushing Eells as a mission to the Spokan Indians at Tshimakain in 1834, and was abandoned in 1848; it was supported by the American Board of Commissioners for Foreign Missions. KLL118. TCH197. AG187. w.c. 5⅜″ x 9⅜″. Fig. 131. (Stark wwc69)

Spokan

The Spokan were Salish Indians living in several small groups on and near the Spokane River in the northeastern part of what is now the state of Washington. Kane, in company with Mr. Walker and Mr. Eells, the Presbyterian missionaries, visited there between September 9 and 17, 1847 (*Wanderings*, pp. 122–23).

IV-337 Tum-se-ne-ho, or "The Man without Blood," a Spokan chief of the Spokane River. TCH109. w.c. 9⅜″ x 5½″. Plate XXXIII. (Stark wwc43)

PELOUSE RIVER

Topography

Kane left Walla Walla on July 13, 1847, to visit the Pelouse River. He was particularly impressed by its upper and lower falls.

IV-338   Coliseum-like formation near the lower falls. Sketch formerly identified as "Walls of the Columbia." Kane saw the formation on July 14, 1847 (*Wanderings*, p. 115). KLL101. w.c. 5½″ x 9½″. (ROM946.15.180)

IV-339   Coliseum-like formation near the lower falls, a second view, w.c. 5½″ x 9½″. (ROM946.15.181)

IV-340   The amphitheatre near the lower falls. Sketched July 14, 1847 (*Wanderings*, p. 115). An inscription on the sketch, not in Kane's hand, reads: "Grand Coulee near Walla-Walla River." KLL100. w.c. 5½″ x 9⅜″. (Stark wwc5)

IV-341   Looking down the Pelouse River with its basaltic rock. Sketched July 14, 1847 (*Wanderings*, p. 115). KLL104. w.c. 5½″ x 9½″. Plate XXXIV. (ROM946.15.182)

IV-342   Rocky gorge. It has been suggested that this is the entrance to the lower falls region. Pencil. 5″ x 7¼″. (ROM946.15.187)

IV-343   The lower falls on the Pelouse River. Sketched July 14, 1847 (*Wanderings*, p. 115). KLL99. TCH220. AG146. w.c. 5½″ x 9½″. Fig. 132. (Stark wwc49)

IV-344   The lower falls on the Pelouse River, the same view as in IV-343. AG75. Oil on paper. 9⅛″ x 14″. (Stark wop20)

IV-345   Peluce [Pelouse] Falls. Painting based on sketches IV-343 and IV-344. GWA16. Oil on canvas. 1′6″ x 2′5¼″. (ROM912.1.70)

IV-346   Pelouse Falls. Replica of IV-345. GS11. Oil on canvas. 11¾″ x 18¼″. (Coe)

IV-347   A Sketch on the Peluce [Pelouse]. Possibly this is the ravine which Kane ascended July 15, 1847 (*Wanderings*, p. 115). GWA56. Oil on canvas. 1′7¼″ x 2′6″. (ROM912.1.71)

IV-348   Falls on the upper Pelouse River. Visited by Kane July 15 to 17, 1847 (*Wanderings*, p. 115). KLL102. AG163. w.c. 5½″ x 9¾″. (Stark wwc44)

IV-349   Falls on the upper Pelouse River. TCH61. Oil on paper. 8⅛″ x 13⅜″. Plate XXXV. (Stark wop22)

IV-350   Nez Percé River or south branch of the Columbia River or Snake River (*Wanderings*, p. 116). The locale was identified formerly as "Rock called the Too-He-Pu-See-Girls" (see IV-358). KLL105. w.c. 5½″ x 9½″. Fig. 133. (ROM-946.15.186)

IV-351   River scenery. It has been suggested, but without supporting evidence, that the river is the Pelouse. w.c. 5½″ x 9″. (ROM-946.15.188)

IV-352   River scenery. It has been suggested, but without supporting evidence, that the river is the Pelouse. w.c. 5″ x 7¼″. (ROM946.15.179)

Paloos Indians

The Paloos are a Shahaptian tribe who occupied the Pelouse River valley in the present states of Washington and Idaho, and the north bank of the Snake River as far as its junction with the Columbia River. They numbered 500 in 1854. The tribe has always had close relations with the Nez Percé Indians.

IV-353   Slo-ce-ac-cum, chief of the "Upputuppets." Sketched July 14, 1847 (*Wanderings*, p. 115). Reverse bears an inscription, not in Kane's hand, reading "How-e-ago-sun-upet-uppet." KPL73. w.c. 5″ x 7″. (ROM946.15.197)

FORT WALLA WALLA

Kane visited Fort Walla Walla on July 12, 1847, and again on the 22nd after returning from a visit to the Pelouse River and the Whitman Mission (*Wanderings*, pp. 114, 117). Fort Walla Walla, often called Fort Nez Percé, comprised the following buildings in 1847: 1 dwelling house 38′ x 28′; 1 range of houses occupied by men of the establishment 48′ x 18′; 1 dwelling house 17′ x 18′; 1 range of stores 46′ x 21′; a second 40′ x 13′; 1 powder magazine 7′ x 10′; 1 pigeon house 9′ x 7′; 1 poultry house 10′ x 9′; 2 stone bastions each 16′ x 16′; wall of fort 12′ high, 1½′ thick, 113′ x 113′, with stone foundations. Outbuildings comprised 1 stable 33′ x 18′; 1 house 14′ x 10′ for smoking meat; 1 root house 20′ x 15′; 1 pig sty 30′ x 16′; 1 horse park 56′ x 54′, 6′ high. A farm had a dwelling 20′ x 15′, 1 dairy built of logs 20′ x 15′, with 30 acres of cultivated land. The buildings were all of adobe construction except the dairy. (Hudson's Bay Company Archives, London, D5/18.) The fort was abandoned in 1856 as a result of the Indian wars.

Topography

IV-354   Fort Walla Walla. Pencil. 5½″ x 9½″. (ROM946.15.172)

IV-355   Fort Walla Walla. KLL98. TCH183. AG47. w.c. 5⅜″ x 9½″. Fig. 134. (Stark wwc62)

IV-356   The Rock of the Nez Percé Girl (Scene near Walla Walla). View as described by Kane, with Indian fishing (*Wanderings*, p. 114). No preliminary sketch has been located. GWA33. Oil on canvas. 1′6″ x 2′5″. (ROM912.1.68)

IV-357   Landscape. It is said to be near Walla Walla, according to a recent notation which is not confirmed. w.c. 5½″ x 9½″. Fig. 136. (ROM946.15.173)

Chimney Rocks

Kane arrived on July 11, 1847, at the junction of the Columbia and Walla Walla rivers and was much impressed by the "Chimney Rocks," a formation known to the Walla Walla Indians as the "Rocks of the Ki-use Girls" (*Wanderings*, pp. 113–14).

IV-358   Chimney Rocks (*Wanderings*, p. 113; woodcut, Fig. 13). KLL97. TCH185. AG162. w.c. 5⅜″ x 9½″. Fig. 135. (Stark wwc65)

IV-359 Chimney Rocks. A detail study. Pencil. 5½″ x 9″. (ROM-946.15.177)

IV-360 Chimney Rocks. A detail study. Pencil. 5″ x 6½″. (ROM-946.15.245)

IV-361 Castle Rocks, Columbia River (Chimney Rocks). The painting is based on IV-358. GWA14. Oil on canvas. 1′6″ x 2′5¼″. (ROM912.1.67)

WHITMAN MISSION

Kane visited the mission July 18–22, 1847 (*Wanderings*, p. 116). It had been founded at Waiilatpu among the Cayuse in 1836 by Marcus and Narcissa Whitman. They carried on mission work there under the auspices of the American Board of Commissioners for Foreign Missions for eleven years. They were massacred shortly after Kane's visit.

IV-362 The Whitman Mission. This building was finished in 1839. It was a T-shaped structure with a wooden frame, walls of adobe bricks, and a roof of poles, straw and earth. The walls were smoothed and whitewashed with a solution made from river mussel shells; later the Hudson's Bay Company supplied green paint for the doors and window frames, grey for the interior woodwork, and yellow for the pine floors. The main section of the house was at first of a storey-and-a-half construction with three rooms on the ground floor and space for bedrooms above. A long single-storey wing contained a kitchen, a bedroom and a classroom. To this an out-kitchen, storeroom and other facilities were added at a later date. The house was burned in 1872. (E. N. Thompson, *Whitman Mission, National Historic Site*, National Park Service, Historical Handbook Series no. 37, Washington, 1964.) This sketch by Kane is the only known surviving view of the mission. Pencil. 5½″ x 9½″. Fig. 137. (ROM946.15.318)

IV-363 Mrs. Whitman's fan. TCH153. w.c. 5½″ x 9½″. Fig. 138. (ROM946.15.207)

Cayuse

At the time of Kane's trip, the Cayuse, a Waiilatpuan tribe, occupied territory in the present-day states of Washington and Oregon around the headwaters of the Walla Walla, Umatilla and Grand Ronde rivers. In the mid-1830s they numbered 400 individuals and were noted horse traders. They were always closely associated with the Nez Percé tribe, and by 1851 had so intermarried with them that there were few remaining pure-blood members of the tribe.

IV-364 To-ma-kus, an Indian at Dr. Whitman's mission (?). Kane describes sketching the man after his arrival on July 18, 1847; he found him sitting naked in his lodge (*Wanderings*, p. 116). Kane reports later that he was the murderer of Dr. Whitman (*Wanderings*, p. 125). This tentative identification has been made from an inscription on the sketch, not apparently in Kane's hand. AG118. w.c. 7⅛″ x 5⅛″. (Stark wwc77)

IV-365 To-ma-kus, the murderer of Dr. Whitman (see IV-364). This sketch was formerly identified as one of Wah-bannim (III-109) (see Bushnell, *Sketches*, p. 6). The new attribution is made on the basis of Kane's portrait log. KPL79. TCH101(?). w.c. 4½″ x 5½″. Fig. 139. (Bushnell 41-72/393)

IV-366 Tomakus. Portrait based on IV-365. GWA82. Oil on canvas. 2′ x 1′7″; (oval) 1′8″ x 1′2″. (ROM912.1.73)

IV-367 Til-au-kite (Te-law-cite-an) or "Act of Lightning." This man was a chief of the Cayuse and one of Dr. Whitman's murderers. Sketched between July 19 and 21, 1847 (*Wanderings*, p. 116). KPL78. TCH99. AG177. w.c. 5¼″ x 4⅜″. Fig. 140. (Stark wwc59)

IV-368 Tilli-koit (Til-au-kite). This canvas does not appear to be based on IV-367. GWA78. Oil on canvas. 2′1″ x 1′8″. (ROM-912.1.74)

IV-369 The wife of Til-au-kite. KPL74. TCH100. w.c. 7¼″ x 5¼″. (Stark wwc28)

IV-370 Page with two sketches. *Right:* woman wearing hat of the Plateau region. *Left:* study of a woman's saddle of this general region (see also IV-311). Tribe unidentified. Possibly sketched either among the Cayuse or at Fort Colvile. w.c. 5½″ x 9½″. (ROM946.15.162)

WALLA WALLA REGION

Nez Percé

The Nez Percé, or Sahaptin as they were later called, lived in the early 19th century in what is now western Idaho, northeastern Oregon, and in southeastern Washington, on the lower Snake River and its tributaries. They were neighbours of the Cayuse and Walla Walla on several branches of the Snake.

IV-371 Nez Percé Indian. Bushnell considers that this is the sketch Kane refers to as having made on July 29, 1847 (*Sketches*, pp. 9–11; see *Wanderings*, p. 119). w.c. 4½″ x 5½″. (Bushnell 41-72/394)

IV-372 Nez Percé Indian. Painting based on IV-371, but with variations. GWA74. Oil on canvas. 2′1″ x 1′8″. Fig. 141. (ROM912.1.72)

IV-373 Nach-a-wish, a Nez Percé Indian. This attribution is made on the basis of an entry in Kane's portrait log. The sketch bears an inscription "Portrait of the Indian who murdered Dr. Whitman" but this is not in Kane's hand. KPL77. AG130. w.c. 5¼″ x 4½″. (Stark wwc36)

Walla Walla

The Walla Walla Indians, a Shahaptian tribe, lived on the lower Walla Walla River and the eastern bank of the Columbia River from the Snake River to the Umatilla River in the present states of Washington and Oregon. They are closely related to the Nez Percé but have a distinct dialect. Kane was in contact with them during his stay at Fort Walla Walla in July 1847.

IV-374 A Walla Walla lodge. KLL52. TCH179. w.c. 5″ x 7″. (ROM-946.15.222)

IV-375 Tam-at-a-pa, brother of Chief Peo-Peo-mox-mox of the Walla Walla Indians. KPL76. TCH103. w.c. 5¼″ x 8⅞″. (Stark wwc15, left)

IV-376 Peo-Peo-mox-mox (or "The Yellow Serpent"), chief of the Walla Walla Indians. Kane sketched him at Fort Walla Walla between July 22 and 26, 1847 (*Wanderings*, p. 117). No sketch for this painting has been located. GWA94. Oil on canvas. 2′1″ x 1′8″. Fig. 142. (ROM912.1.69)

IV-377 Son of Peo-Peo-mox-mox. Kane has numbered this sketch as KPL80, but the numbering evidently relates to a lost portion of the log. TCH102. w.c. 4½″ x 5¼″. Fig. 143. (ROM-946.15.196)

GRAND COULEE REGION

Kane left Fort Walla Walla on July 29, 1847, and travelled by way of the Grand Coulee to Fort Colvile which he reached on August 8, 1847 (*Wanderings*, pp. 118–22). The following sketches were evidently completed during this trip.

IV-378 Sketch of sand dune country. Inscription on the reverse, not in Kane's hand, reads "Alakpowa, a tributary of the Columbia R." The locale is possibly the sand dune country described by Kane (*Wanderings*, p. 119). w.c. 5½″ x 9″. (ROM946.15.192)

IV-379 Grand Coulee. KLL107. TCH218. AG157. w.c. 5⅜″ x 9½″. (Stark wwc51)

IV-380 Grand Coulee. KLL108. w.c. 5½″ x 9½″. (ROM946.15.178)

IV-381 Grand Coulee. KLL109. TCH219. w.c. 5⅜″ x 9½″. (Stark wwc7)

LOWER COLUMBIA RIVER

Topography

On his return journey in 1847, Kane describes passing the portages of the Cascades, the Dalles, and the Chutes on July 3 to July 8 (*Wanderings*, pp. 111–12). These sketches were probably completed at that time. When he had descended the Columbia River late in 1846 the brigade was moving quickly and he does not mention this region.

IV-382 "Landslip" six miles above the Cascades on the Columbia River (*Wanderings*, p. 112). KLL95. TCH186. AG33. w.c. 5¼″ x 8⅞″. Fig. 144. (Stark wwc30)

IV-383 "Landslip" six miles above the Cascades on the Columbia River. Rough sketch for IV-382. Pencil. 4″ x 5¼″. (ROM946.15.297)

IV-384 At the head of the Cascades. KLL94. w.c. 5″ x 7¼″. (ROM-946.15.331)

IV-385 The Cascades. This sketch was earlier identified as a sketch on the Spokane River. KLL93. TCH187. AG149. w.c. 5⅜″ x 9½″. (Stark wwc53)

IV-386 The Cascades. KLL42. Pencil study. 5½″ x 9″. (ROM-946.15.183)

IV-387 The Cascades. Sketch based on IV-386. AG32. Oil on paper. 8¼″ x 13¼″. Fig. 145. (Stark wop9)

IV-388 Below the Cascades. Indian fishing on the Columbia River (*Wanderings*, p. 111). KLL92. AG169. w.c. 5½″ x 9½″. Fig. 146. (Stark wwc92)

IV-389 Cape Horn, twenty miles above Fort Vancouver, 200 feet high and subject to high winds. Pencil. 5½″ x 9½″. (ROM-946.15.266)

IV-390 Cape Horn. Same view as in IV-389. KLL90. TCH184. AG184. w.c. 5⅜″ x 9¼″. (Stark wwc67)

Cascade, Dalles, Skinpah, Tenino

The Cascade (the formal name is Watlala) were a division of the Chinookan family, who lived at the Cascades or farther up the Columbia River towards the Dalles. The Dalles Indians were Chinookan tribes who lived at the Dalles and on the opposite side of the Columbia River. The Tenino, a Shahaptian tribe, inhabited the valley of the Deschutes River in what is now the state of Oregon, and their dialect was spoken on the Columbia from the Dalles to the Umatilla River. The Skinpah (or Skeen, Skein, Shutes), for example, who lived on the north bank of the Columbia opposite the mouth of the Deschutes, spoke the Tenino dialect. Distinctions among the tribes of this region were not easy for white observers and were further complicated by seasonal visits of other Indians on fishing expeditions.

IV-391 Tomaquin (Tamaquin), chief of the Cascade on the Columbia River (*Wanderings*, p. 112). (See also IV-90.) KPL24. TCH110. w.c. 7″ x 5″. Fig. 147. (ROM946.15.195)

IV-392 So-wall-o-way (Saw-wollo-wa), "a Dall or Tenimo Indian," a chief of the Dalles. KPL70. TCH108. AG109. w.c. 7⅛″ x 5″. (Stark wwc9)

IV-393 Mancemuckt, chief of the Skeen or Shutes. Sketched on July 8, 1847 (*Wanderings*, p. 112). KPL72. w.c. 5½″ x 3⅞″. Fig. 148. (Stark wwc102-I)

IV-394 Mancemuckt, chief of the Skeen or Shutes. Formerly this sketch was identified as one of Kwa-qua-dah-bon-niva-skung, a chief of the Saugeen Indians (see III-2, 3). KPL72. w.c. 7½″ x 5″. (ROM946.15.56)

IV-395 An Indian of the Dalles, Columbia River (Mancemuckt). Painting is based on IV-393 (*Wanderings*; coloured litho.). GWA77. Oil on canvas. 2′1″ x 1′8″, (oval) 2¼″ x 1′7½″. (ROM912.1.75)

IV-396 A Cascade Indian, sketched about 40 miles above Fort Vancouver. KPL34. w.c. 7″ x 5″. Fig. 149. (Stark wwc55)

FORT VANCOUVER

The Fort and environs

Fort Vancouver was founded by the Hudson's Bay Company in 1825–26 as a fur-trade supply depot, and for at least twenty years was headquarters for its operations west of the Rockies and its principal centre in the Pacific Northwest. The original fort had been erected a mile back from the Columbia River. It was rebuilt on the final site closer to the river in 1829. This second structure was the one which Kane visited and where he lived intermittently from December 8, 1846, to July 1, 1847. The fort was abandoned by the Hudson's Bay Company in 1860 as a result of American penetration into the area, which had become part of the United States in June 1846.

At the time of Kane's visit (*Wanderings*, p. 91), there were from 60 to 75 buildings in the village west of the fort's stockade where lesser employees of the fort such as tradesmen, artisans, boatmen and labourers lived. North of the stockade the framework for two new schoolhouses, each measuring 50 by 40 feet, had been erected in 1844; in 1848 they were said to be without floors and to be used for shearing sheep. The first large-scale agricultural operations had been begun in 1826 on 300 acres. (See John A. Hussey, *A History of Fort Vancouver and its Physical Structure*, Washington State Historical Society, 1957, for a detailed history of the fort.)

IV-397 Fort Vancouver. General view in 1847 looking south towards the Columbia River. *At left*, two unfinished school buildings; *at right*, village outside the stockade; *centre*, the fort proper, with the east and south stockade walls; *in left distance*, ship in dock, almost certainly H.M.S. *Modeste*; *at upper right*, detail of redoubt at southeastern angle of the bastion. This view is similar to that in an oil painting of *c.* 1845 in the Coe Collection, Yale University, by an unidentified artist (see Hussey, *History of Fort Vancouver*, frontispiece). Kane's sketch was formerly identified as one of Fort Victoria. Pencil. 5½″ x 9″. Fig. 150. (ROM946.15.211)

IV-398 Fort Vancouver. General view in 1847 looking southeast towards the west and south walls of the stockade, and with Mount Hood on the horizon. Pencil. 5½″ x 9″. (ROM946.15.141)

IV-399 Fort Vancouver. Village area to the west of the fort proper, looking south towards Mount Hood. *Upper right:* detail of log building and fence. Pencil. 5½″ x 9″. (ROM946.15.169)

IV-400 Fort Vancouver. A sketch taken from the west end of the plain in front of the fort. The same view as in IV-399 but with additional details. KLL57. TCH62. AG95. Oil on paper. 8″ x 13⅜″. Fig. 151. (Stark WOP17)

IV-401 Fort Vancouver. Corner of stockade with tepee. Pencil. 5″ x 7″. (ROM946.15.270)

IV-402 Mount Hood. View from north bank of the Columbia River near Fort Vancouver. Buildings in foreground. Pencil. 5½″ x 9″. (ROM946.15.167)

IV-403 Mount Hood. View from north bank of the Columbia River near Fort Vancouver. Pencil. 5½″ x 9″. (ROM946.15.168)

IV-404 Mount Hood. View from north bank of the Columbia River, probably near Fort Vancouver. Trees in foreground. Pencil. 5¼″ x 9″. (ROM946.15.199)

IV-405 Mount Hood. View from north bank of the Columbia River, probably near Fort Vancouver. Pencil. 5½″ x 9½″. (ROM946.15.185)

IV-406 Studies of pasturing cattle. They are possibly part of the herds of cattle at Fort Vancouver (*Wanderings*, p. 91). Pencil. 4¾″ x 7¼″. (ROM946.15.256)

IV-407 Groups around a camp fire. Possibly at Fort Vancouver. Pencil. 8″ x 9½″. (ROM946.15.259)

IV-408 Man with saddle horse. A semi-caricature. Probably one of Kane's friends at Fort Vancouver. (*Wanderings*, p. 97.) w.c. 5″ x 7″. Fig. 153. (ROM946.15.251)

IV-409 Well in the woods (a burned-out tree stump) northeast of Fort Vancouver. KLL59. TCH72. AG79. Oil on paper. 11½″ x 9¼″. Fig. 155. (Stark WOP8)

IV-410 Well in the woods. Another version of IV-409. w.c. 5″ x 7″. (ROM946.15.285)

IV-411 Stump with whimsical doodle. Another version of IV-409. w.c. 5½″ x 3″. (ROM946.15.284)

IV-412 Mud puppy. w.c. 5½″ x 9½″. (ROM946.15.265)

IV-413 Valley with fields. No definite locale has been determined for this sketch. The neighbourhood of Fort Vancouver has been suggested. The sketch bears a number 48, which in KLL is the number assigned to the falls of the Willamette at Oregon City. Could this possibly be a view of the new farms at Champoeg? It is also possible that the sketch is a view in southern Ontario and has no connection with Kane's western tour. AG81. w.c. 5¾″ x 11⅛″. (Stark PWC26)

See also IV-429, 430, 431, 450, 465 for other sketches related to Mount Hood.

Theatrical studies

The crew of H.M.S. *Modeste* presented a series of theatrical evenings during 1846–47. Kane attended on at least one occasion. The following were possibly sketched at one of these performances.

IV-414 Heads of two harlequins. Pencil. 5″ x 7¼″. (ROM946.15.263)

IV-415 Military figure with tricorne hat and gun. (*Wanderings*, p. 97?) Pencil. 5¼″ x 6½″. (ROM946.15.294, reverse).

Sandwich Islanders

Sandwich (Hawaiian) Islanders were among the staff at various Hudson's Bay Company establishments on the Pacific coast. The Company maintained a post in the Sandwich Islands, and there was considerable traffic back and forth between it and the west coast of the American continent. Kane refers to eight Islanders in the party with which he started up the Columbia in July 1847, two of whom tried to desert on one occasion (*Wanderings*, pp. 111, 112).

IV-416   Old Cox, Sandwich Islander. KPL39. TCH122. w.c. 5″ x 7″. Fig. 154. (ROM946.15.271)

IV-417   Study of a head, possibly that of a Sandwich Islander, and a parrot. Pencil. 5″ x 6½″. (ROM946.15.235)

Chinook, Klikitat and Calapooya

Kane points out that the Indians living in the vicinity of Fort Vancouver were chiefly "Chinooks and Klickataats" (*Wanderings*, p. 91). Tribes of the Chinookan linguistic family lived on the Columbia River from the Dalles to the coast, and on the Willamette River as far up as the present site of Oregon City; it is probable that Kane is referring to these tribes when he uses the term "Chinook." The Chinook proper claimed territory on the north side of the Columbia River for about fifteen miles from its mouth and north along the seacoast as far as the northern part of Shoalwater Bay.

The Klikitat were of the Shahaptian linguistic stock and lived at the headwaters of the Cowlitz, Lewis, White Salmon and Klickitat rivers, north of the Columbia. The Calapooya (the name is given to a division of the Kalapooian family but the term often means the whole family) occupied a large territory in the present state of Oregon running south from that of the Chinook and cut off from the sea by the coastal tribes, but extending east to the Deschutes River.

IV-418   Casanov (Ca-is-no-of), noted warrior chief from Fort Vancouver. Kane states in his log that the man was a "Kalupanet" (Calapooya) chief but in the TCH catalogue he is identified as a Chinook. *Wanderings*, p. 91, states that Casanov governed the Indians in the region of Fort Vancouver, mainly "Chinooks and Klickataats." (*Wanderings*; woodcut, Fig. 8). (See also IV-295.) KPL29. TCH34. AG17. Oil on paper. 9⅝″ x 8⅛″. Plate XXXVI. (Stark WOP4)

IV-419   Casanov. Painting based on IV-418. GWA67. Oil on canvas. 2′6″ x 2′1″. (ROM912.1.76)

IV-420   Indian on a race course near Fort Vancouver, sketched with a head dress of beads. Identified as a boy in the TCH catalogue, this figure is more probably a girl wearing a special band to hide her eyes during menstruation. The belief that it was harmful magic for her to look at people during this particular time necessitated this precaution. (See *Wanderings*, p. 111.) KPL38. TCH116. AG138. w.c. 4⅞″ x 7″. Fig. 156. (Stark WWC35)

IV-421   Study of figure in IV-420. Pencil. 5″ x 7¼″. (ROM946.15.323)

IV-422   Klikitat Indian. KPL26. TCH117. AG174. w.c. 7″ x 4⅞″. (Stark WWC13)

IV-423   Indian head. Possibly sketched at Fort Vancouver. Pencil. 5″ x 7″. (ROM946.15.330)

Indian lodges

IV-424   Lodge interior. Kane describes this as the interior of a Chinook lodge at Fort Vancouver; the lodge appears to be constructed of split cedar boards (*Wanderings*, pp. 94–95), and matting is hung in the interior. This was formerly identified, incorrectly, as a Blackfoot lodge. KLL49. TCH159. AG69. w.c. 5″ x 7″. Fig. 158. (Stark WWC41)

IV-425   Lodge interior, described as being on the Columbia River. This is evidently a ceremonial lodge, with a special screen at one end. Oil on paper. 9½″ x 11½″. Plate XXXVII. (Stark WOP13)

IV-426   Temporary lodge of the Chinook, covered with woven rush mats, probably on the Columbia River (*Wanderings*, p. 95). A note on the reverse, not in Kane's hand, suggests that the lodge was on Vancouver Island. Pencil. 4¾″ x 6¾″. (ROM946.15.223)

IV-427   Bundle of rushes. These are evidently rushes cut for the construction of lodges (*Wanderings*, p. 95). w.c. 5″ x 7¼″. Fig. 157. (ROM946.15.321)

IV-428   Klikitat lodge. KLL44. TCH214. w.c. 5″ x 7″. Fig. 159. (ROM-946.15.221)

IV-429   Chinook travelling lodge with view of Mount Hood. These lodges were used while fishing and gathering camas (*Wanderings*, p. 95). TCH177. 5½″ x 9″. Fig. 160. (Stark WWC101)

IV-430   Chinook Lodge, Mount Hood in the distance. Painted from sketch IV-429, but with additional figures. GWA24. Oil on canvas. 1′6″ x 2′5″. (ROM912.1.99)

IV-431   Mount Hood. Replica of IV-430. This version was delivered to the Library of Parliament early in 1856, at which time Kane described it as a painting of "Chinooks, a Branch of the Flat Head Tribes of the N.W. Coast." The painting is entered in volume III of the *Catalogue* of the National Gallery of Canada as "Mount Hood with Spokane Indians," but there is no apparent reason for the alteration from "Chinook" to "Spokane." LP3. Oil on canvas. 1′7″ x 2′6″. (NGC6918)

IV-432   West Coast Indian Encampment. Replica of IV-430. Oil on canvas. 1′5½″ x 2′4½″. (Beaverbrook Art Gallery)

Indian groups

Locale of the following cannot be determined conclusively. Possibly they are sketches of Chinook at Fort Vancouver.

IV-433   Lodge interior with six Indians seated in foreground, presumably gambling, and two others reclining in background (*Wanderings*, p. 95). Pencil. 5″ x 7″. (ROM946.15.246)

IV-434   Indian head. Pencil. 5″ x 8″. (ROM946.15.276)

IV-435   Three nude figures dancing. 5″ x 8″. Pencil. (ROM946.15.275)

IV-436   Studies of figures from Columbia River region, executed either at Fort Vancouver or near Fort Colvile. The sketch is numbered "87," the number referring, presumably, to a lost portion of Kane's log which seems to have covered the upper Columbia

River region. TCH112. AG176. w.c. 5⅜″ x 9½″. (Stark wwc61)

IV-437 Group of seated and standing Indians. These include a woman with cedar-bark string skirt (*Wanderings*, p. 94). Probably sketched at Fort Vancouver. Pencil. 6½″ x 8½″. (ROM-946.15.306)

IV-438 Three Indians holding dip nets, sketched at Fort Vancouver or Fort Colvile. Pencil. 5½″ x 9″. (ROM946.15.325)

IV-439 Indian, identified by inscription, not in Kane's hand, as "Cowlitz Indian." w.c. 5⅛″ x 4¼″. (Stark wwc102D)

Chasta

Kane describes the prevalence of slavery among the Indians of the Fort Vancouver region (*Wanderings*, p. 93). The Chasta were probably an Athapascan tribe: in 1867 they resided on the Siletz Reservation in Oregon. Kane says that they lived near the Umpqua River, and others mention the Rogue River.

IV-440 A slave of the Chasta tribe, found among the Chinook of the Fort Vancouver region (*Wanderings*, p. 93). TCH121. AG107. w.c. 6⅞″ x 4⅞″. (Stark wwc57)

COLUMBIA RIVER VALLEY (?)

IV-441 Sketch of lake with low shoreline. Pencil. 5″ x 6½″. (ROM-946.15.145)

IV-442 Sketch of lake surrounded by evergreens. Pencil. 5″ x 7″. (ROM946.15.295)

WILLAMETTE VALLEY

Kane left Fort Vancouver on January 10, 1847, with Mr. Mackenlie, a chief trader, for Oregon City. He remained with him at Oregon City for three weeks, during which time there was unprecedented frost (*Wanderings*, pp. 95–96). From Oregon City he continued on up the river with Father Acolti to visit the Roman Catholic mission of St. Paul (*Wanderings*, p. 96). On his return he again stayed with Mr. Mackenlie for a few days (*Wanderings*, p. 96) before setting out for Fort Vancouver. He stopped to sketch some Clackamas River Indians about four miles below Oregon City on this journey.

Topography

IV-443 Oregon City. Upper end, showing mills and Methodist church from the opposite shore of the river. Pencil. 5½″ x 9″. (ROM-946.15.163)

IV-444 Oregon City. Kane's landscape log notes: "Oregon from below: it has 2 watch makers, 1 blacksmith, 1 gunsmith, 1 tailor, 3 saw mills and 2 grist mills." KLL56. TCH66. AG11. Oil on paper. 8⅛″ x 13½″. (Stark wop14)

IV-445 Oregon City. Painting executed from IV-444. Oil on canvas. GWA4. 1′6″ x 2′5″. (ROM912.1.82)

IV-446 Oregon City. Two views from the shore. *Upper:* general view of town with details of buildings. *Lower:* general view. Pencil. 5½″ x 9″. (ROM946.15.326)

IV-447 Oregon City: a second view. KLL45. TCH67(?). AG44 (incorrectly given as "Mackinaw"). Oil on paper. 8″ x 13¼″. (Stark wop15)

IV-448 Oregon City. General view looking downstream from shore opposite the town and beside waterfall. Pencil. 5½″ x 9″. Fig. 161. (ROM946.15.164)

IV-449 The mills of Oregon City. KLL47. TCH65. AG94. Oil on paper. 8½″ x 13⅜″. Plate XXXVIII. (Stark wop16)

IV-450 Oregon City (?) Two sketches of groups of buildings, presumably at the lower end of Oregon City; one has Mount Hood in the distance. Alternatively, these may possibly be buildings in the environs of Fort Vancouver. Pencil. 5½″ x 9″. (ROM-946.15.171)

IV-451 Falls near Oregon City. Kane exhibited several sketches of waterfalls in this area; TCH68 and TCH69 are described as "Falls near Oregon City," and TCH212 as "Falls on the Wilhamet River." This sketch does not seem to be any of the items exhibited. Pencil. 5½″ x 9″. (ROM946.15.175)

IV-452 Falls near Oregon City. Possibly TCH68 or TCH69. w.c. 5½″ x 8½″. Fig. 162. (ROM946.15.269)

IV-453 Falls near Oregon City (?). Pencil. 5½″ x 8½″. (ROM-946.15.65)

See also IV-413.

IV-454 St. Paul de Wallamette, Willamette valley. Kane describes visiting the mission with Father Acolti (*Wanderings*, p. 96). It was about 32 miles from Oregon City, and was established early in the decade by a group of nuns from Quebec who opened classes immediately on their arrival for Indian and white children. The brick chapel was under construction in February 1845 and was evidently completed at the time of Kane's visit; it is said to have been the first brick building erected on the upper Pacific coast. (For details of mission work in the area see *Notices & Voyages of the famed Quebec Mission to the Pacific Northwest . . . 1838 to 1847*, Portland, Oregon Historical Society, 1956.) TCH195. w.c. 5½″ x 9½″. Plate XXXIX. (ROM946.15.264)

IV-455 Willamette valley from the high hill in front of Champoeg (*Wanderings*, p. 96). Champoeg, site of an Indian village and a trading post of the Astor company, was settled by farmers in the 1830s. The first organized government in the region was set up here in 1843. Buildings pictured in Kane's sketch include the Hudson's Bay Company house and store, the André Longtain and Robert Newell properties and others. Several residents were former Hudson's Bay Company employees. (For full details of the Champoeg settlement see J. A. Hussey, *Champoeg: Place of*

Transition, Portland, Oregon Historical Society, 1967.) KLL62. w.c. 5¼″ x 8¾″. Fig. 163. (ROM946.15.193)

IV-456 Willamette valley. Presumably this is KLL62, but the mission to which the artist makes reference in his log cannot be distinguished. TCH213. AG190. w.c. 5½″ x 9⅜″. (Stark WWC24)

IV-457 The Willamette River from the Mountain (The Walhamette River from a Mountain). Painting based on IV-455. GWA52. Oil on canvas. 2′4½″ x 1′6″. (ROM912.1.81)

Clackama

Kane visited this tribe during early February 1847 (*Wanderings*, pp. 96–97). The Clackama were a Chinookan tribe occupying several villages on the Clackamas River in Oregon. Their entire population was said to be only 88 in 1851, whereas in 1806 they had numbered 1,800.

IV-458 Indian head in profile. KPL28. w.c. 5⅞″ x 4¼″. (Stark WWC102(A))

IV-459 Four Clackama Indians with painted faces. Kane points out that they had been gambling when he met them. The face in IV-458 is that of one of the group. KPL28. TCH36. AG63. Oil on paper. 11½″ x 9⅜″. Plate XL. (Stark WOP11)

MOUNT ST. HELENS

Mount St. Helens, a 9,671 foot peak, is approximately 50 miles northeast of present-day Portland, Oregon. Although its volcano is now dormant, it erupted from vents in the sides between 1841 and 1857. Kane sketched the erupting volcano in March 1847, while *en route* from Fort Vancouver to Fort Victoria (*Wanderings*, p. 97). (See Kenneth L. Holmes, "Mount St. Helens' Recent Eruptions," *Oregon Historical Society Quarterly*, LVI, 3, 1955, 197–200.)

IV-460 View of Mount St. Helens from the mouth of what Kane calls the "Cattlepoutal" or "Kattlepoutal" River. Evidently this is the field sketch which Kane describes having made on March 26, 1847 (*Wanderings*, p. 97). Holmes (p. 206) points out that the sketch was made from the mouth of the Lewis River. KLL63. w.c. 5″ x 7″. (ROM946.15.329)

IV-461 View of Mount St. Helens with smoke cone. The foreground of the sketch is evidently based on IV-460. Kane reports watching this phenomenon for an hour and a half (*Wanderings*, p. 97). Holmes (p. 205) notes that Josiah L. Parrish, a Methodist missionary, saw a similar phenomenon in 1842. TCH63. AG19. Oil on paper. 8⅛″ x 13⅜″. Plate XLI. (Stark WOP10)

IV-462 Mount St. Helens. This night view is evidently based on IV-460 for foreground and on IV-463 for the erupting volcano in the distance. GWA18. Oil on canvas. 1′6″ x 2′5″. Fig. 164. (ROM-912.1.78)

IV-463 View of Mount St. Helens from the Cowlitz farm. Kane made this sketch on March 30, 1847 (*Wanderings*, p. 99). KLL69. w.c. 5½″ x 9″. Fig. 165. (ROM946.15.184)

IV-464 View of Mount St. Helens erupting. Presumably this sketch is based on IV-463, but a more elaborate foreground has been added. KLL69. TCH64. AG37. Oil on paper. 8″ x 13⅜″. Fig. 164. (Stark WOP21)

IV-465 Fourth plain, to the rear of Fort Vancouver, with three saddle horses and riders resting. Presumably this sketch shows the north side of Mount St. Helens although it has been suggested that the mountain is Hood. KLL51. 3½″ x 5″. (ROM946.15.165)

IV-466 Fourth plain, to the rear of Fort Vancouver. A second version of IV-465, with one horse. Pencil. 5″ x 6¼″. (ROM946.15.166)

IV-467 Mouth of "Cattlepoutal" (Lewis) River. Sketch of the foreground of IV-460, but omitting the mountain. Pencil. 7″ x 10″. (ROM946.15.298)

FORT ASTORIA

Chinook

Astoria, located on the south side of the Columbia River, was adjacent to the territory of the Chinook on the north side at the river's mouth. The post had originally been established by Astor's Pacific Fur Company in 1811 for trading purposes, and was re-established in 1843 by overlanders. Kane makes no reference to visiting Astoria either during his trip from Fort Vancouver to Fort Victoria, when he came down the Columbia River to the mouth of the Cowlitz River, or while he was staying at Fort Vancouver during the winter of 1846–47. However, he specifies that the two following sketches portray women from Fort Astoria and his log states that IV-478 was done there.

IV-468 A Chinook woman from Astoria. KPL36. w.c. 7″ x 5″. (Stark WWC21)

IV-469 Chinook girl from Fort Astoria. No sketch for this girl has been located. The box she holds is apparently based on a sketch executed at Mackinac (III-90; see also IV-88). Oil on canvas. 2′6″ x 2′1″. (Stark WOP23)

LOWER COLUMBIA AND COWLITZ RIVERS

Indian burials

Kane visited several canoe burial grounds, examining the first of them on March 29, 1847. He discusses the practice at length (*Wanderings*, p. 98).

IV-470 Coffin Rock. Kane writes that this site is on the Columbia River ten miles downstream from the mouth of the "Kattlepoutal" (Lewis) River, which in turn is 26 miles from Fort Vancouver. He camped there on the night of March 26, 1847 (*Wanderings*, p. 98). KLL64. AG119. w.c. 5¼″ x 8⅞″. Fig. 166. (Stark WWC-91)

IV-471 Coffin Rock. Painting based on IV-470. GWA12. Oil on canvas. 1′6″ x 2′5″. (ROM912.1.77)

IV-472 Rocky shoreline. This landscape is similar to the shoreline in the vicinity of Coffin Rock. Pencil. 5½″ x 9″. (ROM946.15.191)

IV-473 Shoreline similar to that in the region of Coffin Rock. Unfinished w.c. 5½″ x 9″. (ROM946.15.170)

IV-474 Chinook canoe grave on the Cowlitz River. Presumably this is the burial place Kane saw March 29, 1847 (*Wanderings*, p. 98; woodcut, Fig. 9). KLL66. TCH161. AG132. w.c. 5″ x 7″. (Stark wwc22)

IV-475 Chinook grave on the Cowlitz River. KLL65. TCH163. AG193. w.c. 5¼″ x 8⅞″. Plate XLII. (Stark wwc29)

IV-476 Graves near the farm on the Cowlitz River. These may be near the group pictured in IV-475. KLL68. TCH164. AG207. w.c. 5¼″ x 8⅞″. Fig. 168. (Stark wwc32)

IV-477 Burying Place on the Cowlitz River. Painting is based on sketches IV-473 and IV-474, and possibly also on other sketches not located. GWA47. Oil on canvas. 1′6″ x 2′5″. (ROM912.1.79)

IV-478 King Comcomly's burial canoe. Although Kane, as noted above, makes no mention of visiting Astoria in his published narrative or manuscript diary, his landscape log specifies that this is "the grave of Com-comly at Astoria, Chief of the Chinooks." Comcomly received the Lewis and Clark expedition in 1805. After the Astoria expedition arrived at the mouth of the Columbia River to commence a permanent fur trade, he gave his daughter in 1813 as a bride to Duncan McDougall, the Canadian then at their head; she married Casanov, IV-418, when McDougall left the area (*Wanderings*, p. 92). Comcomly is said to have been preceded by 300 slaves when he visited Fort Vancouver. KLL89. AG110. w.c. 5⅜″ x 9¼″. Fig. 167. (Stark wwc86)

Canoes

IV-479 Cowlitz canoe. Identified from an inscription in Kane's hand. This canoe has a vertical prow and stem. It is ornamented with two carved animal heads, one attached to the prow facing forward and the other attached to the inside of the stern, similarly facing forward. Paddle above. This form of canoe is similar to the one in IV-480 which bears an identification, uncorroborated, on the mat reading "Klick-a-tat." Pencil. 3½″ x 12″. (ROM-946.15.201)

IV-480 Three canoes and paddles of the Columbia River. The canoes have been identified, but by a hand other than Kane's, as: *upper*, Klick-a-tat; *centre*, Chinook; *lower*, Cowlitz. However the upper of these three canoes is identical with the one pictured in IV-479, which is labelled as "Cowlitz" in Kane's hand. AG120. w.c. 5⅜″ x 9″. (Stark wwc2)

IV-481 Two canoes of the Columbia River region. The upper is identical to the lower of the three in IV-480, which is identified as "Cowlitz" (but see note on IV-480). The lower canoe has a shark's head painted on the prow and is identical with the centre canoe of the three in IV-480, identified as "Chinook." Pencil. 5½″ x 9″. (ROM946.15.200)

Tree studies

It has been suggested that Kane made these sketches while travelling from Fort Vancouver to Puget Sound during April 1847. They were obviously done in the Pacific coast region.

IV-482 Study of tree covered with moss. TCH170. w.c. 5½″ x 9½″. (ROM946.15.279)

IV-483 Study of tree covered with moss. TCH158. w.c. 9½″ x 5½″. (ROM946.15.280)

IV-484 Tree stump and windfall. w.c. 3¾″ x 7″. (ROM946.15.281)

IV-485 Study of a tree covered with moss. w.c. 5″ x 7¼″. (ROM-946.15.282)

IV-486 Study of a tree covered with moss. w.c. 5½″ x 3″. (ROM-946.15.283)

IV-487 Study of a tree covered with moss. w.c. 5½″ x 3″. (ROM-946.15.284, reverse).

COWLITZ RIVER

Cowlitz

The Cowlitz Indians were a Salish tribe living on the Cowlitz River in the southwestern portion of the present state of Washington. Once powerful, their numbers in 1847 were, Kane states, 200. Kane made the following sketches when he met members of the tribe during his visit to the Cowlitz farm which was operated by the Hudson's Bay Company. He was there from March 30 to April 5, 1847, on his way to Fort Victoria. He encountered members of the tribe on his return journey to Fort Vancouver between June 15 and June 20, but did not linger because of their hostility. He says that the tribe spoke a language similar to that of the Chinook, and flattened their heads.

IV-488 Kiscox (Kiss-cox), a Cowlitz River chief (*Wanderings*, p. 99). KPL40. TCH119. AG102. w.c. 7″ x 4⅞″. (Stark wwc11)

IV-489 A Flathead woman. She is possibly Caw-wacham, referred to by Kane (*Wanderings*, pp. 99, 110) and listed as KPL33. w.c. 5¾″ x 4¼″. Fig. 169. (Stark wwc102G)

IV-490 A child in the process of having its head flattened (*Wanderings*, pp. 93, 99). This sketch was used by Daniel Wilson in the preparation of a coloured lithograph of a "Flathead Woman and Child" (*Prehistoric Man*, 1862, II, frontispiece). KPL35. TCH167. AG114. 4⅞″ x 7″. Fig. 170. (Stark wwc10)

IV-491 Flathead Woman and Child, Caw-wacham (Caw-wacham). Painting based on sketches IV-489 and IV-490 (*Wanderings*; coloured litho.). GWA68. Oil on canvas. 2′6″ x 2′1″. (ROM-912.1.80)

IV-492 Flathead Woman and Child, Caw-wacham. Replica of IV-491. Oil on canvas. 2′6″ x 2′1″. Fig. 171. (Montreal Museum of Fine Arts 47.991)

IV-493 Flathead child. No documentation has been found for this sketch. It may have been made in the Cowlitz area, or it may be

TCH115, described as "Child's head—Chinook." w.c. 5½″ x 4″. (Stark wwc102F)

See also IV-439.

PRAIRIE DE BUTE

Kane passed over a 22-mile stretch of plain on his way from the Cowlitz farm to the Nisqually River. It was dotted with peculiar mounds, and he describes seeing them on April 6, 1847, and again on June 15, 1847, when he was returning to Fort Vancouver (*Wanderings*, pp. 99, 110).

IV-494   Prairie de Bute. KLL70. TCH217. w.c. 5⅜″ x 9⅜″. Fig. 172. (Stark wwc64)

IV-495   Prairie de Bute. Pencil. 4¾″ x 7″. (ROM946.15.156)

IV-496   Prairie de Bute. Pencil. 5″ x 6½″. (ROM946.15.158)

IV-497   Prairie de Bute. Painting based on IV-494. GWA36. Oil on canvas. 1′6″ x 2′5″. (ROM912.1.83)

PUGET SOUND

Topography

IV-498   Nisqually, a village on Puget Sound. The Hudson's Bay Company had formed the Puget's Sound Agricultural Company to promote land settlement. Kane visited the area on April 7, 1847 (*Wanderings*, p. 99). KLL83. TCH215. AG166. w.c. 5⅜″ x 9¼″. Fig. 173. (Stark wwc47)

Nisqually

Kane refers to the Nisqually Indians at the time of his visit to the Nisqually area on April 7, 1847 (*Wanderings*, p. 99).

IV-499   Indian lodge at Nisqually. KLL71. w.c. 3¾″ x 7″. Fig. 174. (ROM946.15.322)

IV-500   Indian lodge of Lach-oh-lett, head chief of the Nisqually. KLL72. w.c. 5″ x 7″. (ROM946.15.324)

IV-501   Lach-oh-lett (Lach-a-lit), a Nisqually chief living on the shores of Puget Sound. KPL41. w.c. 5″ x 7″. (ROM946.15.277)

IV-502   Nisqually girl. KPL67. TCH125. AG142. w.c. 5¼″ x 8⅞″. Plate XLVIII. (Stark wwc83, right; see also IV-582)

STRAITS OF GEORGIA AND JUAN DE FUCA

In his published narrative (p. 103) Kane says he hired five natives from the Indian village adjoining Fort Victoria to accompany him on a tour of the straits region. He also took with him the fort's interpreter. According to *Wanderings*, they departed May 6 and returned to Fort Victoria on May 15, 1847; Kane notes that he left again for Fort Vancouver on June 10. From Fort Victoria he and his party travelled east around the lower end of Vancouver Island and through the Haro Strait. On "the main land" they visited a village apparently near the mouth of the Fraser River. Subsequently they travelled southwest along the mainland and called at "Toanichum" on Whidbey Island, and at "I-eh-nus" and "Suck" on the south shore of Juan de Fuca. They returned to Fort Victoria by canoe

across the open straits. (The notes provided for chapters XIV, XV, and XVI of *Wanderings*, above, record variations elsewhere in some details of this itinerary.)

Sketches IV-503 to IV-524 were almost all completed on this tour.

Mainland village

Kane stopped on May 6 at a village he describes as occupied by the Clallam. They are a Salish tribe closely related to the Songish. In *Wanderings* this village is sited on the mainland, but see note 1 for chapter XV of *Wanderings*.

IV-503   Cloll-uck, chief of the Clallam, "entrance to the Canal de Arrow" (Haro Strait). KPL47 (Kane's additional notes identify him as the Indian referred to in *Wanderings*, p. 103; see also note 2 for *Wanderings*, chapter XV). w.c. 5″ x 7″. (ROM946.15.98, left)

IV-504   E-a-cle, "a Cathi chief on the south side of the straits." Kane reports that he came from a neighbouring village, which Kane apparently did not visit. KPL48. 5″ x 7″. (ROM946.15.98, right)

IV-505   Rough sketch of a woman with a bowl and a fire-making stick, inscribed "south side of strait." Probably sketched in the region of Haro Strait. Pencil. 5″ x 7″. (ROM946.15.224)

IV-506   "A Quatlin from the mouth of Fraser's River." "Quatlin" refers to Kwantlen, who were a Cowichan tribe in the area at the mouth of the south Fraser River (see also IV-568 to IV-573). KPL52. TCH141. AG144. w.c. 7″ x 5⅛″. (Stark wwc33)

Skagit River or Whidbey Island: Skagit

Kane uses a variety of names (Shatchet, Sca-chet, Suchet) for what is evidently the Skagit, a Salish group. Their lands were at the mouth of the Skagit River in the present state of Washington and on the central part of Whidbey Island.

IV-507   A "Shatchet" Indian. This man is referred to in the catalogue of the 1848 exhibition, evidently incorrectly, as being from the Fraser River. KPL43. TCH142. AG175. w.c. 7″ x 5″. (Stark wwc76)

Whidbey Island, Toanichum: Clallam (?)

Kane visited this village on May 7 (*Wanderings*, p. 104). He identifies the village by name but not by tribe. It is in the traditional territory of the Clallam.

IV-508   Lock-hi-num, a chief of Whidbey Island (*Wanderings*, p. 104). KPL42. TCH123. AG199. w.c. 7″ x 4⅞″. Fig. 175. (Stark wwc56)

IV-509   A Flathead woman, wife of a Clallam chief, Whidbey Island. Evidently this is the wife of the second chief of Toanichum whom Kane mentions sketching (*Wanderings*, p. 104). TCH134. w.c. 6⅛″ x 4¼″. (Stark wwc102G)

IV-510   A Flathead Woman, Whidbey Island (A Flathead Woman).

Painting based on IV-509. GWA93. Oil on canvas. 2′1″ x 1′8″. (ROM912.1.85)

IV-511   Indian village of Toanichum, Whidbey Island. KLL73. TCH223. AG211. w.c. 5⅜″ x 9″. Fig. 176. (Stark WWC3)

Puget Sound: Snohomish

The Snohomish were a Salish tribe who lived on Whidbey Island, and on the mainland at the mouth of the Snohomish River.

IV-512   Shawstun (Shouts-ton), head chief of the "Sinna-hamus" Indians. Sketched at Fort Victoria (*Wanderings*, p. 107). Kane points out in his log that this man's tribe lived on Puget Sound. KPL55. TCH129. AG197. w.c. 6¾″ x 4¾″. Fig. 181. (Stark WWC37)

IV-513   Ona-put (Onepa), a "Sinna-hamus chief," Puget Sound. KPL54. TCH133. w.c. 5¼″ x 4½″. (Stark WWC102E)

South shore of Juan de Fuca

I-EH-NUS: CLALLAM

Kane remained at I-eh-nus village May 9 to May 12 (*Wanderings*, pp. 104–5).

IV-514   Probably Yates-sut-soot (Yeats-sut-sute), chief of the Clallam at I-eh-nus. Formerly this portrait was identified as that of "Old Bear," a Spokan Indian. It was exhibited by Kane in 1848 as of a "Chinook" Indian. KPL49. TCH120. AG123. w.c. 7″ x 4⅞″. (Stark WWC52)

IV-515   Battle between Clallam and Makah at I-eh-nus. The Makah were a Nootka tribe living at Cape Flattery to the west of I-eh-nus. This is evidently an imaginary sketch based on an account of the battle (*Wanderings*, p. 104). The sketch was formerly identified as the "Battle of Walula encampment." KLL77. AG155. w.c. 5¼″ x 9⅜″. Fig. 177. (Stark WWC54)

IV-516   Graves at I-eh-nus (*Wanderings*, p. 105). KLL78. TCH152. AG194. w.c. 5¼″ x 8⅞″. Fig. 179. (Stark WWC89)

IV-517   A Battle of I-eh-nus (A Battle). Painting based on sketches IV-515, IV-516, IV-551. GWA23. Oil on canvas. 1′6″ x 2′5″. Fig. 180. (ROM912.1.84)

SUCK: CLALLAM

Strong winds forced Kane and his party to remain at Suck, which he states is west of I-eh-nus, from May 12 to 14. Did he confuse the name of this village with that of Sooke on the south end of Vancouver Island? Or did the inhabitants of this village migrate to Sooke shortly after Kane's visit? Suttles ("Economic Life of the Coast Salish of Haro and Rosaria Straits," Ph.D. thesis, University of Washington, 1951) refers to Sooke Indians of Sooke Bay making a treaty with Sir James Douglas in 1850 and implies that they were then newly arrived at that village site.

IV-518   Chaw-u-wit, daughter of the chief at Suck (*Wanderings*, p.

105). KPL50. TCH137. AG173. w.c. 7″ x 4¾″. Fig. 178. (Stark WWC8)

IV-519   A Clallum Girl (Chau-u-wit). Burpee and others have identified this painting as a portrait of Chaw-u-wit. It is not based on the sketch of her (IV-518) nor on any other sketch which has been located. There is always the possibility that it is from a lost sketch. GWA88. Oil on canvas. 2′1″ x 1′8″. (ROM912.1.86)

IV-520   Salmon trap at Suck (*Wanderings*, p. 105). TCH224. AG124. w.c. 5¼″ x 8⅞″. Fig. 182. (Stark WWC26)

IV-521   A Weir for Catching Salmon. Painting based on IV-520. Originally this canvas was in the Allan collection, and presumably was given back to Kane in return for another canvas. GWA51. Oil on canvas. 1′6″ x 2′5″. (Stark WOP25)

IV-522   Landscape, with bundles of sticks marked as being four feet long. Evidently these stakes were prepared for use in the construction of the salmon trap at Suck. w.c. 7½″ x 10¼″. (ROM-946.15.320)

IV-523   Mountain landscape. Tentatively this landscape has been identified as a view of the Olympics seen from Beecher Bay near Race Rocks. Pencil. 5″ x 6½″. (ROM946.15.242)

Strait of Juan de Fuca

IV-524   Crossing the Strait of Juan de Fuca. Apparently this sketch, which shows Kane and his party returning to Fort Victoria by canoe in a storm, was completed from memory (*Wanderings*, p. 106). KLL79. TCH229. AG111. w.c. 5½″ x 9⅜″. Fig. 183. (Stark WWC70)

MOUNT BAKER

This prominent peak is in the state of Washington south of the 49th parallel and due east of Victoria.

IV-525   Mount Baker from Gordon Head, Vancouver Island, with the mountain rising above San Juan Island. This sketch was formerly known as one of Mount Hood. KLL76. TCH228. AG135. w.c. 5½″ x 9¼″. (Stark WWC48)

ESQUIMALT, INDIAN VILLAGE

The sketches in this group seem all to be associated with an Indian village which was on the east side of the Esquimalt harbour. Kane's published narrative does not mention an Indian village by this name specifically, but it is referred to in his manuscript notes.

IV-526   A "Sangeys Village on the Esquimault"(?) This was formerly known as a sketch of the village of Sooke, and in fact the topography is similar to that at Sooke. The Songish were a Salish tribe of the southern end of Vancouver Island, around Victoria. KLL84. TCH225. AG200. w.c. 5¼″ x 8⅞″. Fig. 184 (Stark WWC66)

IV-527   War party, Juan de Fuca. The sketch pictures the upper reaches of Esquimalt harbour with the rocky area called Gibraltar Point. (See also IV-537.) KLL87. TCH151. AG134. w.c. 5½″ x 8⅞″. Fig. 185. (Stark wwc90)

IV-528   Details of canoe in IV-527. Pencil. 4¾″ x 7¼″. (ROM-946.15.250)

IV-529   Indian village at Esquimalt with canoes returning from gathering camas. Apparently this is the village pictured in IV-526 and IV-527. KLL80. TCH226. AG113. w.c. 4⅞″ x 7″. Fig. 186. (Stark wwc58)

IV-530   Northwest canoes. KLL85. TCH149. AG188. w.c. 5⅜″ x 9½″. (Stark wwc93)

IV-531   Northwest canoes. KLL85. TCH150. w.c. 5½″ x 9½″. Plate XLIII. (ROM946.15.231)

IV-532   Northwest canoes. w.c. 5½″ x 9″. (ROM946.15.232)

IV-533   Northwest canoes. AG153. w.c. 4⅞″ x 7″. Fig. 187. (Stark wwc71A)

IV-534   The Esquimalt, Indian Village (The Esquimalt). Composite painting with a village and canoes in left foreground based on IV-529, and a village on the distant shore suggested by IV-526 and IV-527. Early sources record only one Indian village at Esquimalt, indicating that Kane may have introduced two villages for compositional reasons. There are records of two Indian villages adjoining Fort Victoria before 1861; however this painting is said to be a view of Esquimalt rather than Fort Victoria. GWA45. Oil on canvas. 1′6″ x 2′5″. (ROM912.1.90)

FORT VICTORIA

The Fort

Kane stayed at Fort Victoria intermittently between April 8 and June 9, 1847. Fort Victoria was established by the Hudson's Bay Company as a base for fur trade operations in New Caledonia. The original fort was built by a party of 50 men and 3 officers under James (later Sir James) Douglas. Construction was started on March 16, 1843. The work was especially urgent since the new fort was expected to replace Fort Vancouver as the centre for the Company's operations on the Pacific; from 1840 on, the Company was much aware of the imminent transfer of the Oregon territory to the United States. The fort straddled the present Fort Street in Victoria. Its bastions were destroyed in 1861, and the fur storehouse, constructed in 1846, was then turned into the Theatre Royal; this, the last of the fort's buildings left standing, was destroyed in 1892.

IV-535   Fort Victoria with Indian village (*Wanderings*, pp. 99–100). The Indian village was on Singhees Road, Victoria West, until 1911 when the residents were moved to the Esquimalt Reserve. w.c. 5½″ x 9¼″. Fig. 188. (ROM946.15.212)

IV-536   Fort Victoria, sketched from a spot called today Hospital Rock on the Industrial Reserve, the site of the Indian village during Kane's visit. *Upper:* whimsical portrait sketch and interior of

an Indian house. AG128. w.c. 5½″ x 8⅞″. Fig. 189. (Stark wwc104)

IV-537   The Return of a War Party. Painting based on sketch of Fort Victoria (IV-535) and with two war canoes suggested by the sketch of the war party in IV-527. GWA46. Oil on canvas. 1′6″ x 2′5″. (ROM912.1.91)

Northwest dance rituals

All the principal tribes of the northwest Pacific Coast organized their society according to social rank. The elaborate activities of the potlach were centred around the establishment of social claims and marked by the ceremonial distribution of hospitality and gifts. At certain times totem poles would be erected and there were dances, songs and theatrical performances, designed to demonstrate the special privileges of those giving the potlach. These performances were witnessed by invited guests. Masks and rattles played a large part in the performances, and were among the most elaborate art work of these peoples.

Kane makes no attempt to distinguish the masks and rattles of the different tribes; those he sketches are evidently representative of a variety of tribal groups. Most sketches were probably made at Fort Victoria where members of a number of west coast tribes came as visitors.

IV-538   Medicine masks of the northwest coast tribes. Presumably this sketch was made at Fort Victoria but presents masks of different tribes. In the Kane papers there is, for instance, a reference to a male mask from Fort Simpson (farther up the mainland of British Columbia). The mask at the upper left of this sketch is similar to the "Man with a moustache" mask collected in 1806 by the Russians along the Pacific northwest coast. (Erna Siebert and Werner Forman, *North American Indian Art*, London, 1967, Plates 25 and 30.) The mask in the centre of the upper row is a "Moon Mask," possibly carved by a member of the Bellacoola tribe. KLL86. TCH165. w.c. 5½″ x 8¾″. Plate XLIV. (Stark wwc27)

IV-539   Medicine man with mask from Strait of Juan de Fuca. TCH37. AG53. Oil on paper. 7¾″ x 5½″. Fig. 190. (Stark wop7)

IV-540   Medicine man with mask. TCH38. Oil on paper. 12½″ x 9¾″. (Stark wop5)

IV-541   Medicine Mask Dance. Such dances were normally performed at night in special houses rather than outdoors by daylight. The painting incorporates three of the masks pictured in IV-538. (According to Kenneth Kidd, a version of this subject, probably the sketch for the painting, is in the Eberstadt Collection of Western American Art, New York.*) GWA8. Oil on canvas. 1′6″ x 2′5″. Fig. 191. (ROM912.1.92)

IV-542   Medicine Mask Dance. Replica of IV-541. Said to be in a private Toronto collection.*

IV-543   Carved west coast mask and war club. Pencil. 5¾″ x 9½″. (ROM946.15.128)

IV-544 Indian medicine rattle with west coast motif. AG212. w.c. 5″ x 7″. Fig. 193. (Stark wwc99A)

Domestic life of Clallam and other Indians

Kane is the principal authority for the Clallam having a village in the Fort Victoria region. A few evidently found their way to the southern end of Vancouver Island. Kane, who met and sketched members of the tribe on his tour of the straits, states that they had a large village on Victoria harbour (*Wanderings*, p. 100). In connection with this group of sketches there are references to the Songish (see also IV-526) and to the Sanetch (Eus-a-nich), a Salish tribe occupying the Saanich peninsula adjoining the present city of Victoria (see also IV-574).

IV-545 Interior of a Clallam lodge, Vancouver Island (*Wanderings*, pp. 100, 102). KLL88 (?). TCH169. AG108. w.c. 5¼″ x 8⅞″. Fig. 194. (Stark wwc81)

IV-546 Interior of a lodge with a family group and dogs arranged around a camp fire. The sketch evidently shows a unit in a multiple family dwelling. AG172. w.c. 5½″ x 9¼″. (Stark wwc88)

IV-547 Interior of a lodge, Vancouver Island. Family group arranged around a camp fire, and baby suspended in a cradle. A marginal note, not in Kane's hand, states that this is a Clallam travelling lodge. AG203. w.c. 5″ x 7⅛″. (Stark wwc96)

IV-548 Indian cradle. AG219. w.c. 4⅞″ x 6¾″. (Stark wwc95)

IV-549 Interior of a Lodge, Vancouver's Island (Interior of a Lodge). This composite painting is based on IV-545, IV-546 (for the group in the right middle distance), IV-548 (for suspended cradle). GWA29. Oil on canvas. 1′7″ x 2′6″. (ROM912.1.97)

IV-550 Interior of a Winter Lodge of the Clallams. Replica of IV-549. LP9. Oil on canvas. 1′6½″ x 2′5¼″. Fig. 192. (NGC6923)

IV-551 Carved house post. Probably sketched at Fort Victoria. w.c. 5″ x 7″. Fig. 195. (ROM946.15.248)

IV-552 Interior of a lodge with Indian woman weaving a blanket (*Wanderings*, p. 100). Kane in his log refers to the woman as being a "Eus-a-nich." KPL64. TCH168. AG141. w.c. 5½″ x 9¼″. Fig. 196. (Stark wwc73)

IV-553 Woman spinning yarn (*Wanderings*, p. 100). Kane calls her a "Sangas" in his log. KPL63. TCH144. AG220. w.c. 4⅞″ x 7″. Fig. 197. (Stark wwc97)

IV-554 Girl spinning in a lodge. Kane's log describes her as a "Sangeys." KPL45. w.c. 5″ x 7″. (ROM946.15.226)

IV-555 Clallam woman weaving a basket, and studies of carved argillite dish, storage box, and white-haired dog. AG117. w.c. 5⅜″ x 8⅞″. Plate XLV. (Stark wwc45)

IV-556 A Woman Weaving a Blanket (Clal-lum Woman Weaving a Blanket). Composite painting based on IV-552, IV-553 and IV-555. GWA28. Oil on canvas. 1′6″ x 2′5″. (ROM912.1.93)

IV-557 Page of studies of figures inside a lodge. *Upper, left to right:* suspended cradle covered with bear skin, storage box, woven hat.

Centre: five seated figures, one a mother feeding a child on cradle board. *Lower:* two women gambling. w.c. 5½″ x 9½″. Fig. 198. (ROM946.15.227)

IV-558 Sketch of dog after being clipped for wool (*Wanderings*, p. 100), and of a canoe being launched. Pencil. 4¾″ x 7″. (ROM946.15.157)

IV-559 Study of two dogs, and of a bed shelf in a lodge interior. Pencil. 5″ x 7″. (ROM946.15.225)

IV-560 Clallam travelling lodges. KLL74. AG122. w.c. 5¼″ x 9⅞″. Plate XLVI. (Stark wwc4).

IV-561 Lodges on Vancouver's Island (Fishing Lodges of the Clallams). Painting based on IV-560. GWA25. Oil on canvas. 1′6″ x 2′5″. (ROM912.1.96)

IV-562 Fishing Lodges of the Clallums. Replica of IV-561. LP8. Oil on canvas. 1′6½″ x 2′5¼″. (NGC6922)

IV-563 Clallam Indian Travelling Lodges. Painting with same subject-matter as IV-561. Probably TCH77. Oil on paper. 8½″ x 13½″. (Colln H. R. Milner)

IV-564 The game of lehallum, Vancouver Island (*Wanderings*, p. 102). TCH227. AG136. w.c. 5⅜″ x 9⅜″. Fig. 199. (Stark wwc25)

IV-565 Study of a group in a lodge interior, probably gambling. Pencil. 4⅞″ x 7″. (Stark wwc71B)

IV-566 Chea-clach, head chief of the Clallam. He accompanied Kane on a tour of the region and the Strait of Juan de Fuca (*Wanderings*, pp. 100, 103). KPL44. TCH35. AG56. Oil on paper. 12¼″ x 9⅞″. (Stark wop3)

IV-567 Chee-ah-clak (Chea-clach). Portrait based on IV-566. GWA83. Oil on canvas. 2′6″ x 2′1¼″. (ROM912.1.89)

Indian visitors to the Fort

Many visitors at Fort Victoria belonged to other tribes of the northwest coast area and came to the Hudson's Bay Company post to trade. Kane used the opportunity to augment his collection of paintings of the various Indian tribes. Portraits he secured in this way would appear to be IV-568 to IV-590. See also IV-512.

COWICHAN

Kane was in the territory of this tribe during his tour of the straits (see IV-506), but the following sketches were of visitors to Victoria.

IV-568 Saw-se-a, head chief of the Cowichan, from the Gulf of Georgia (*Wanderings*, pp. 102–3). KPL60. TCH139. w.c. 5¼″ x4⅛″. (Stark wwc102C)

IV-569 Saw-se-a (San-ce-a). Painting based on IV-568. GWA95. Oil on canvas. 2′1″ x 1′8″. Fig. 200. (ROM912.1.94)

IV-570 Culchillum, the son of Saw-se-a, wearing a medicine cap (*Wanderings*, p. 103; woodcut, Fig. 11). KPL61. TCH140. w.c. 5¼″ x 4½″. Plate XLVII. (Stark wwc102H)

IV-571 Medicine Man, Vancouver's Island (Culchillum). Painting based on IV-570. GWA64. Oil on canvas. 2′6″ x 2′1″. (ROM912.1.95)

IV-572 A "Whellamay" girl. Exhibited in 1848 as a Cowichan Indian from the Strait of Juan de Fuca. KPL58. TCH127. w.c. 5″ x 7″. (Stark WWC23, left)

IV-573 A Cowichan woman. KPL59. TCH127. w.c. 5″ x 7″. (Stark WWC23, right)

SANETCH

Kane visited their lodges to make sketches while they were visiting at Fort Victoria (*Wanderings*, p. 107). (See also IV-552 and heading above it.)

IV-574 A "U-Saanich"; from Haro Strait. KPL51. TCH131. w.c. 5″ x 7″. (ROM946.15.194)

NOOTKA

Nootka was a term originally applied to a tribe of Nootka Sound on the west coast of Vancouver Island, but eventually it was extended to all tribes speaking the same language. They occupied the island's west coast with the exception of the northerly tip. The Makah (see IV-515, 580) are sometimes included as part of the Nootka group. (*Wanderings*, p. 107)

IV-575 A New-a-tay (Nootka) chief. Kane would seem to be incorrect in stating in his log that the chief is from the north end of Vancouver Island; the extreme northern tip is Kwakiutl territory (see Wilson, *Prehistoric Man*, 1862, II, 317). KPL65. TCH143. AG198. w.c. 7″ x 4⅞″. Fig. 201. (Stark WWC16)

IV-576 A Conical Shaped Headed Indian (A New-a-tee). It has been suggested that this is the same man as the one in IV-575. The two are not strikingly similar, but the painting was probably inspired by the sketch. GWA86. Oil on canvas. 2′1″ x 1′8″. (ROM912.1.98)

IV-577 Page of five studies demonstrating conical head deformations. These Indians are possibly Nootka. Pencil. 5½″ x 2¼″. (ROM946.15.217)

IV-578 Indian child with head deformation, evidently of a conical type. w.c. 7″ x 5″. (ROM946.15.216)

IV-579 Indian child from south of Juan de Fuca. Inscription, not in Kane's hand, reads "Chinook Child." (See Wilson, *Prehistoric Man*, 1862, II, 320.) KPL68. AG213. w.c. 5″ x 3½″. (Stark WWC14)

MAKAH

The Makah (Macaw) belong to the Nootka group and live on Cape Flattery, in the present state of Washington.

IV-580 Cape Flattery Indian. The inscription on the sketch is not in Kane's hand. Kane describes sketching Yellow-cum, wealthiest of the Cape Flattery Indians (*Wanderings*, pp. 106–7), and records his sketch as KPL53. No such sketch has been positively identified. This is possibly the item in question. KPL53(?). TCH132(?). w.c. 5¼″ x 4⅝″. (Stark WWC102J)

See also IV-515.

HAIDA

Haida is the native and popular name for the Indians of the Queen Charlotte Islands and for those from the southern end of Prince of Wales Island. Cumshaw was a Haida town at the northern entrance to Cumshaw Inlet, Queen Charlotte Islands. Its population in 1836–41 was estimated at 286 people, living in 20 houses.

IV-581 Slum-a-chusset, a Cumshaw chief. KPL57. TCH130. w.c. 5″ x 7″. (ROM946.15.214)

KWAKIUTL

The Kwakiutl, a group of closely related tribes, lived in the neighbourhood of Prince Rupert, B.C. During the 1850s and 1860s a large tribe of the group, the Lekwiltok (or Ucaltas), lived between Knight and Bute inlets.

IV-582 A "You-call-tee" (Ucaltas) Indian. KPL66. TCH126. AG142. w.c. 5¼″ x 8⅞″. Plate XLVIII. (Stark WWC83, left; see also IV-502)

CHIMMESYAN

The Chimmesyan (Tsimshian), a small linguistic family, lived on the Nass and Skeena rivers and the neighbouring coast to the south. A number of remote groups moved to the vicinity of Fort Simpson when it was built by the Hudson's Bay Company in 1834 on the mainland opposite the Queen Charlotte Islands. Members of the tribe were periodic visitors to Fort Victoria.

Evidently Kane confused the Chimmesyan and the Babine (Big Lips), a branch of the Takulli living in the interior of British Columbia north of Babine Lake. Babine were known to have copied the customs of the coastal tribes, including use of labrets (*Wanderings*, pp. 107–8). The following entries seem to refer to Chimmesyan rather than to the Babine.

IV-583 Chief of the Chimmesyan Indians with a ring in his nose. Queen Charlotte Islands, Chatham Sound. (For the custom of the ring in the nose see *Wanderings*, p. 107.) KPL69. TCH136. AG129. w.c. 7″ x 5″. (Stark WWC34)

IV-584 Ma-cheek-e-a-wis, Chimmesyan Indian. KPL69. TCH4(?). There may be an error in the TCH catalogue, since another sketch also bears the number TCH4. AG48. Oil on paper. 10⅛″ x 9½″. Fig. 202. (Stark WOP6)

IV-585 A Babine woman. TCH80. Oil on paper. 11½″ x 9¼″. Fig. 204. (Stark WOP12)

IV-586 A Babbine Woman (A Babbine or Big-lip Woman). The woman in this painting is evidently based on the sketch IV-585, with the child added. GWA84. Oil on canvas. 2′6″ x 2′1″. (ROM912.1.88)

IV-587 A Babbine Chief. This canvas is probably based on an unlocated sketch. When lithographed for the frontispiece in the Wilson book, *Prehistoric Man*, the title was changed to "Chimseyan Chief." GWA61. Oil on canvas. 2′6″ x 2′1″. Fig. 203. (ROM-912.1.87)

IV-588 Chimmesyan (or Babine) blanket. This is probably the blanket which Kane says he bought (*Wanderings*, p. 107). It was used as an accoutrement in the painting IV-587. On occasion, it has been described, but incorrectly, as Clallam. w.c. 5½″ x 9″. (ROM946.15.228)

IV-589 Babine pipe-stem of carved slate. TCH173. AG147. w.c. 4⅜″ x 8⅞″. Fig. 205. (Stark WWC1)

IV-590 Babine pipe-stem of carved slate. AG148. w.c. 5½″ x 9″. (Stark WWC17)

TAUTIN

Kane refers to the "Taw-wa-tin" (Tautin), who are a branch of the Takulli living on the mainland, opposite Vancouver Island. Kane may be confused in the tribal terminology.

IV-591 Cremation rites, evidently drawn from imagination (*Wanderings*, pp. 107–8). Pencil. 5½″ x 9″. (ROM946.15.327)

UNIDENTIFIED LOCALE

Gambling scenes

A wide range of suggestions have been advanced about the locale for the following group of sketches. They include the Georgian Bay region, Rocky Mountain House (Assiniboin), and Fort Vancouver or Fort Victoria. The bear's claw collar suggests the figures may be Assiniboin, but of course other tribes also wore these collars.

IV-592 Group of three seated Indians gambling. Pencil. 5″ x 7″. (ROM-946.15.260)

IV-593 Group of seven Indians gambling. Pencil. 5″ x 7″. (ROM-946.15.261)

IV-594 Group of five seated Indians gambling. Pencil. 5″ x 7″. (ROM-946.15.262)

GUIDES AND VOYAGEURS

IV-595 Tommskarrohoto, an Iroquois guide from Caughnawaga near Montreal. This identification is tentative. The sketch was previously identified as that of a Kwantlen chief. KPL87(?). AG44. Oil on paper. 9⅓″ x 5⅞″. (Stark WOP1)

IV-596 A voyageur. This sketch has been identified, without firm evidence, as the head of Sir George Simpson; the identification is obviously incorrect. w.c. 6½″ x 5″. (ROM946.15.252)

PERSONAL SKETCHES

IV-597 Self-portrait made during the course of his western tour. Oil on paper. 8⅛″ x 6⅝″. Plate I. (Stark WWC103)

IV-598 Sketch of a house inscribed "Paul Kane's Wigwam," and with an Indian head inscribed "Design for Knocker." w.c. 8″ x 12½″. (ROM946.15.253)

IV-599 Architectural design of a cottage, and an Indian caricature. Pencil. 8″ x 10″. (ROM946.15.259)

PORTRAITS OF WHITES FROM KANE'S WESTERN TOURS

No identification in Kane's notes has been made for the following sketches. He mentions a number of people whom he met during the tour including missionaries, Hudson's Bay Company officials and (in letters) local residents of Fort Vancouver.

IV-600 Bust of woman. Pencil. 5″ x 7″. (ROM946.15.247)

IV-601 Bearded man's head. Pencil. 5″ x 7″. (ROM946.15.288).

IV-602 Head of woman in a classical pose. Pencil. 4½″ x 5½″. (ROM-946.15.290)

IV-603 Head of bearded man wearing a hat. Pencil. 5″ x 3½″. (ROM-946.15.292)

IV-604 Head of a woman with kerchief tied over her head. This sketch and IV-603 appear to be a pair. Pencil. 5″ x 3½″. (ROM-946.15.293)

IV-605 Three-quarter length sketch of woman seated at a table. Pencil. 4″ x 5¼″. (ROM946.15.299)

IV-606 Profile study of head of woman wearing a sunbonnet. Pencil. 3″ x 4″. (ROM946.15.311)

Section V

Landscapes, portraits and other sketches and paintings executed by Kane following his return to Canada in 1845 but evidently not related to his travels in western North America

NIAGARA FALLS AND DISTRICT

Kane frequently visited Niagara Falls, which could be reached easily by means of the steamer running from Toronto to Queenston. On May 6, 1846, he halted at Niagara Falls while travelling west with Sir George Simpson, "to admire for the hundredth time the Falls of Niagara." His drawing master, Thomas Drury, spent much time in sketching at Niagara. The following undated sketches and paintings were probably executed after 1845.

V-1 Niagara Falls. Panoramic view of the Canadian and American falls from the heights on the Canadian side. AG154. w.c. 5½″ x 9⅛″. (Stark EWC1)

V-2 Niagara Falls. Panoramic view identical to that in V-1 but with suggestions of autumn colouring. Oil on canvas. (Oval) 1′6″ x 2′5″. (Colln Mrs. Paul Kane III)

V-3 Niagara Falls. The Canadian falls from the edge of the ravine on the Canadian side. Pencil. 5½″ x 9″. Fig. 12. (ROM946.15.335)

V-4 Niagara Falls. The American falls from the edge of the ravine on the Canadian side. Pencil. 5½″ x 9″. (ROM946.15.336)

V-5 Niagara Falls. The Canadian falls from the Canadian shore. Pencil. 2½″ x 5½″. (ROM946.15.337)

V-6 Niagara Falls. The 45-foot tower was built on the American side of the Canadian falls in 1833. It was joined to Goat Island by the Terrapin Bridge. Pencil. 5½″ x 9″. (ROM946.15.338)

V-7 Niagara Falls. The American falls from the shoreline on the American side. Pencil. 5½″ x 9″. (ROM946.15.339)

V-8 Niagara Falls. The Canadian falls from the edge of the ravine on the Canadian side. Pencil. 3″ x 5½″. (ROM946.15.340)

V-9 Niagara Falls. The brow of the Falls. Attributed to Kane. w.c. (Colln Maj.-Gen. M. P. Bogart)*

V-10 Queenston. View of the ruins of Brock's Monument after being blown up by a sympathizer with William Lyon Mackenzie, in 1840. The monument had been erected to commemorate Sir Isaac Brock, British general, who was killed during the battle in which American forces were defeated in their attack on the heights, October 13, 1812. The monument was rebuilt in 1854. Pencil. 5½″ x 9″. (ROM946.15.341)

V-11 Sketch of a stereoscopic view for tourist entertainment, probably at Niagara Falls. Pencil. 5½″ x 9″. (ROM946.15.342)

TORONTO

V-12 Bloor's Brewery, Rosedale Ravine. The brewery was established by Joseph Bloor in 1830, and he eventually turned it over to John Rose. The latter operated it as Castle Frank Brewery until 1864. The building was torn down in 1875. The blockhouse on the hill to the right stood in the middle of Bloor Street at the head of Sherbourne Street. It had been built to protect Toronto from the north during the 1837–38 uprising and was torn down in the same year as the brewery, 1875. w.c. 5½″ x 9″. Fig. 10. (ROM946.15.254)

V-13 "Homewood," first residence of George W. Allan, Toronto (built 1846, demolished in 1940s). Mrs. Allan's diary reads in an entry of February 9, 1849: "I went to George's office and we went to Kane's rooms, to see his sketches and a view he is taking of 'Homewood.'" Oil on canvas. 10⅞″ x 15¾″. Fig. 13. (Colln G. P. H. Vernon)

LANDSCAPES, MISCELLANEOUS

V-14 Rural Ontario farmhouse with bridge. There is a remote possibility that this is the residence of John Gamble (see I-3). w.c. 5½″ x 9″. (ROM946.15.310)

V-15 Rural landscape with autumn colouring. w.c. (Oval) 3½″ x 4½″. (ROM946.15.304)

V-16 Church spire, unidentified; (on reverse) man with curling broom. Pencil. (Oval) 4½″ x 3½″. (ROM946.15.305)

See also IV-413.

PAINTINGS RELATING TO INDIANS

V-17 Joseph Brant. This painting is identical in subject-matter to a painting by George Catlin also in the ROM collections. Both are evidently based on a portrait of Brant by Ezra Ames, an engraved reproduction of which was used as the frontispiece in a two-volume work by W. L. Stone, *Life of Joseph Brant—Thayendanegea* (New York 1838). The book was in Kane's library. GWA66. Oil on canvas. 2′6″ x 2′1″. (ROM912.1.100)

V-18 Columbus Meeting the Indians at His Landing at San Salvador. Formerly in the Perkins Bull Collection, Brampton, and sold in Montreal in 1953.*

V-19 Portrait of an Indian. Said to have been in the collection of a Toronto mayor c. 1870. Oil on canvas. (Colln Harold E. Groves) *

V-20 Scene in the Northwest, a Portrait. Unlocated, this portrait may actually have been a painting, done in the winter of 1845–46 from a sketch executed during the previous summer, which entered the Allan collection. Shown at the exhibition of the Toronto Society of Artists, 1847, no. 26.*

V-21 Indian Summer on Lake Superior. (See remarks on V-20.) Shown at the exhibition of the Toronto Society of Artists, 1847, no. 88.*

V-22 Group of Indians. Said to have been suggested by a plate in a book by Sir John Richardson, *Arctic Searching Expedition* (London 1851), vol. I, Plate IX. w.c. 5¼″ x 9¼″. (ROM946.15.218)

PORTRAITS

It is virtually impossible to determine whether certain portraits were executed by Kane before or after his European tour. The following, for documentary or stylistic reasons, are presumed to date from after 1844. There are likely a number of portraits of the pre-1841 and post-1843 period which have survived unidentified in the region of Mobile, Alabama.

V-23 Self-Portrait. Probably executed immediately after Kane's return from Europe. Used as a frontispiece in the 1925 edition of *Wanderings of an Artist*. Oil on canvas. (Colln S. E. Weir) *

V-24 Unidentified man. Oil on canvas. 2′5″ x 2′. (Colln Mrs. Paul Kane III, 49/PK)

V-25 Portrait of a mother and child. Unlocated work, shown in Toronto at the exhibition of the Society of Artists, 1847, no. 24.*

V-26 George Gurnett (1792?–1861). Gurnett was Mayor of Toronto 1837, 1848 and 1849. See W. S. Wallace, *Macmillan Dictionary of Canadian Biography*. Shown in Toronto at the exhibition of the Toronto Society of Artists, 1847, no. 39. This painting was presumably done in the 1844–46 period although the style is tight and it has an archaic character which is related to that of I-11. Oil on paper. 2'10" x 2'2". Fig. 8. (Colln of mayors' portraits, Corporation of the City of Toronto)

V-27 Portrait of a Gentleman. Shown in Toronto at the exhibition of the Society of Artists, 1847, no. 117.*

V-28 James Richardson (d. 1853). As a young man, Richardson lived in Cobourg; he edited the *St. Catharines Constitutional*, 1850–53. Oil on canvas. 29¼" x 24¾". Fig. 9. (ROM964.185)

V-29 Allan MacNab (presumably Sir Allan MacNab, 1798–1862, although there is some controversy as to whether this may actually be a portrait of Sir Allan's father; see K. E. Kidd, ROM, Art and Archaeology Division, *Annual*, 1962, pp. 64–73). In reference to the attribution to Kane, it should be noted that James Bowman, Kane's artist friend, painted Sir Allan MacNab, Sir Allan's mother-in-law, and other members of the family in 1831; could this canvas and V-30 actually be by Bowman rather than Kane? Oil on canvas. (ROM, on loan to Dundurn Castle Museum, Hamilton) *

V-30 Archibald MacNab, brother of Sir Allan MacNab. (See K. E.

Kidd, and V-29 above.) Oil on canvas. (ROM, on loan to Dundurn Castle Museum, Hamilton) *

V-31 A French-Canadian Notary. This is a copy of a portrait by Cornelius Krieghoff dated 1848 (Beaverbrook Art Gallery). Oil on canvas. 2'3" x 1'9". (Colln Mrs. Paul Kane III, 55/PK)

V-32 Study of the back of a girl. Oil on canvas. 2'¼" x 1'7". (Stark OP27)

V-33 Thomas Daly, Toronto city clerk and an amateur artist. Kane may have done this sketch at the time he was exhibiting his western sketches late in 1848 in the old Toronto City Hall at the request of the Toronto City Council. Pencil. 5½" x 9". Fig. 11. (ROM946.15.142)

V-34 Mackenzie through the Mountains. This is an imaginary sketch of Sir Alexander Mackenzie, famous trader and explorer, going across the Rocky Mountains to the Pacific in 1793. Pencil and ink. 5¼" x 10½". (ROM946.15.243)

APPENDICES

1   Paul Kane's Landscape Log, Kept on His 1846–48 Journey
2   Paul Kane's Portrait Log, Kept on His 1846–48 Journey
3   Catalogue for Paul Kane's Exhibition, 1848
4   Paintings delivered by Paul Kane to Sir George Simpson, 1849
5   Canvases Sent by Paul Kane to George W. Allan, 1856
6   Paul Kane's Draft of Notes for Paintings Delivered to the Parliament of Canada, 1856
7   Works of Paul Kane Given to Mrs. Kane by the Allan Family, 1871
8   Pigments and Mediums Used by Paul Kane
9   Books in the Library of Paul Kane at His Death, 1871
10 Letters, Principally to and from Paul Kane
11 Paul Kane in Alabama, 1841
12 Paul Kane before the Parliament of Canada, 1856

Appendix 1

Paul Kane's Landscape Log, Kept on His 1846–48 Journey *

No. 1. The Dog Portage on the Dog Ravene.

No. 2. Portage de Gock. It derives its name from the following circumstance. There is an Indian by the name of Gock who was taunted by one of his companions to run it with his canoe. He went round the small island and took the shote but was dashed to pieces, canoe and all.

No. 3. Portage de Boar on the R. Winnipeg. Its Indian name is Carneshawsing the two carrying places.

No. 4. Is a sketch on the R. Winnipeg.

No. 5. The Lost Man's Portage on the Fort William R. 2 men lost themselves for 4 days.

No. 6. A carrying place, Fort William R.

No. 7. The brigade stopping to have breakfast at French R. Rapids.

No. 8. Visited by a party of Sotos at our evening encampment.

No. 9. Norway House.

No. 10. A Cree Tent with woman gaming. Carlton.

No. 11. See notes on Saw-waughten.

No. 12. Ft. Garry, Red River.

No. 13, 14, 15, 16, 17, 18 are sketches on the Saskatchewan.

No. 19. The Methodist Mission at Jack River.

No. 20. Carlton.

No. 21. Burnt Prairie.

No. 22 and 23. Salt Lakes.

No. 24. A Lake in the Planes.

No. 25. The Serpentine Valley.

No. 26. The Golden Valley.

No. 27. Fort Pitt with Bluff. Also crossing the river.

No. 28. Long Grass Valley with the Dead Men's Hill in the distance. Buffalo feeding.

No. 29. Edmonton.

No. 30. A Buffalo robe with the war adventures of Sa-Co—the Sinnew. Piece. A Blood Indian.

No. 31. Athabaska River with the Rocky Mountains in the distance.

No. 32. Jasper's Lake with Miette's Rock.

33. Jasper's House.

34. A prairie with mountain sheep.

35. Le Rocque's prairie with wild horses.

36. The Athabaska in the Mountains.

37. A sketch in the mountains.

38. A snow scene in the mountains.

39. The committee's punch bowl.

40. A sketch of a fall at the head waters of the Columbia.

41. Columbia River, the grand rapid.

42. The Cascades.

43. No. 1. Click-a-tat. 2. Chinook. No. 3. Cowlitz Canoe.

44. Click-a-tat lodge.

45. Oregon the City. There is about 94 houses and 200 inhabitants. The Hudson's Bay Co. has an establishment here. There are 4 other stores here, 2 hotels and 2 churches, Catholic and Methodist.

46. Main Street in Oregon City.

47. The mills of Oregon.

48. Falls of the Willamette, 30 feet high.

49. A Chinook Lodge interior painted at Vancouver. These lodges are made of split cedar and mats.

50. Click-a-tat lodge on the Columbia near Vancouver.

51. The Fourth plain eight miles back of Vancouver.

52. A Walla Walla Lodge.

53. The lower plain near Vancouver with Mount Hood in the distance.

54. A sketch of Mount Hood above Vancouver.

56. Oregon from below. It has 2 watch makers, 1 blacksmith, 1 gunsmith, 1 tailor, 3 saw mills and 2 grist mills.

57. A sketch taken from the west end of the plain in front of Fort Vancouver.

58. A Cascade Indian lodge taken on the south side of the Columbia.

59. The well in the woods, a hollow burnt stump which keeps water good for a long time from the wood being charred. No water near this spot. It is north east from Ft. Vancouver.

60. Fort Vancouver, one of the largest forts in the H. B. Co. territory, it has 2 chief factors, 14 clerks and 200 men. Keep a large stock of cattle.

61. The Catholic mission about 32 miles above Oregon City. Mr. Demers, Superior, Mr. Bolduc, Assistant. It has a nunnery attached to it with 6 Nuns or Sisters of Charity. They have 42 pupils. It is near the River Willamette. There is near here also a Jesuit Mission, Father Acolti, Superior. They have 3 Missions in the Rocky Mountains and one in New Caledonia. I was treated with a great deal of kindness here by Father Acolti.

* The Landscape Log is preserved as a manuscript held by the Nelda C. and H. J. Lutcher Stark Foundation, Orange, Texas. The wording and spelling of Kane's original are followed; material in the log which appears in *Wanderings of an Artist* has been omitted. Kane prepared a manuscript for a second book which would be largely illustrations (see section VI of Part One); much of the text merely duplicates *Wanderings of an Artist*; the occasional note about a sketch is new, and this material has been added at appropriate points in this appendix and in Appendix 2.

62. 2 sketches taken from the top of a high hill in front of **Champoeg** showing the country for 20 miles with Champoeg in the foreground of one and the mission in the other. This is the character of the country in this part of Oregon.

63. The mouth of the Cattle-putle River with Mount St. Helens in the distance, a cloud on top of it, and the sky clear in every direction. Taken from the Columbia.

64. Coffin Rock. This is the mode of burial in this part of the Columbia down to the mouth of the river.

65. A Chinook grave on the Cowlitz River. . . .

66. A Chinook grave on the Cowlitz.

67. A Cowlitz grave.

68. Graves near the farm on the Cowlitz. They bury in canoes also.

69. Mount St. Helens as seen from the Cowlitz farm. This is a burning mountain about 40 miles from the farm. . . .

70. Prairie de Bute or Hill Prairie between the Cowlitz and Nisqually. These hills were thought to be the burial place of the Indians but on examination they were found to contain nothing but stones. Commodore Wilkes examined some of them. It is 20 miles from Nisqually.

71. A Nisqually Indian lodge.

72. The lodge of Loch-o-let at Nisqually.

73. The Indian village of To-an-e-chum on Whidbey's Island in the Straits. When we arrived near here, the Indians flew to their bastions and fired off several guns to intimidate us from landing if we were hostile and to let us know that they had guns. When we got on shore they treated us with much kindness. They live here in constant fear of one another for if an unfortunate individual is caught out alone, he is made a slave of by the next tribe though they are not at war with one another.

74. Clallum travelling lodges. These are only used when they go fishing for a short time.

75. A place for catching salmon on the south side of the S. called Suck. . . .

76. Mount Baker taken from Vancouver's Island looking across the Canal de Arrow.

77. The battle of I. Eanus on the south side of the straits. . . . They do not scalp the dead here as in other parts. They cut off the head and stick it on a pole which they place in front of their canoes or near their lodges.

78. Graves at I Enis.

79. Crossing the Dungeness in the Straits of De Fuca to Vancouver's Island in a heavy blow. . . . [The crew] kept up their medicine song all the time. The old man in the stern kept up one continual howl like a dog but when one wave bigger than the rest would threaten to engulf us, then there was one great shout to drive it back and stay its progress. . . .

80. The canoes returning from gathering camas to the Esquimault.

81. Canal de Arow.

82. Fort Victoria.

83. Nisqually.

84. Sangeys Village on the Esquimault.

85. North West Canoes.

86. North West Masks.

87. A war party in the Straits of de Fuca.

88. The inside of a Clallum Lodge.

89. The grave of Com-comly at Astoria, Chief of the Chinooks.

90. Cape Horn, 20 m. above Vancouver on the Columbia, 200 feet high and subject to high winds.

91. The Grand Prairie and big rock some call the Castle.

92. Below the Cascades 3 m.

93. The Cascades.

94. At the head of the Cascades.

95. The land slip. Some suppose these trees to have grown where they are and the water to have risen from an avalanche of rock falling across the Cascade 6 m. below. This is incorrect as the rocks are worn smooth by the action of the water at the Cascades.

96. The Shutes where the man with the tin box was shot (Astoria).

97. The Rocks of the 2 Crausegeeves near Walla Walla. . . .

98. Fort Walla Walla.

99. The Pelouse Falls 400 feet. The rock is about 650 feet composed of basalt.

100. The amphitheatre near the lower falls.

101. The Coliseum near the lower falls.

102. The upper fall 15 feet.

103. A front view of the same.

104. Looking down the Pelouse River, the rocks all basaltic.

105. The Nezperse or south branch of the Columbia or Snake River.

106. Kause [Cayuse?] fan given to Mrs. Whitman at an Indian feast.

107. The Grand Coulee.

108 and 109. Grand Coulee.

110. A sketch on the Columbia 50 m. below Colville.

111. The Kettle Falls. 1700 salmon have been taken from this basket in one day. I weighed three. One was 35, the other 2, 32 pounds each. One man has the whole of control of this fishery. There is one spot where if a basket was placed they might catch 3 or 4000 a day. It is called the Kettle Falls by the whites from the water coming round holes in the rocks. This sketch is from the south side of the river.

112. A sketch of the Kettle Falls from the north shore. . . . The fall is about 19 feet. . . .

113 and 114. Indian lodges. No. 1, the Head Chief's lodge. 2. The Second Chief's. 3. The Salmon Chief's in Sketch No. 113 at Colville.

115. The Little Falls 20 m. above Colville. . . . The lives of 14 persons out of 30 were lost near here. . . .

116. A painted horse, Colville. The Indians are very fond of painting their horses before going to run a race.

117. A sketch on the Spokane.

118. Walker and Eells mission with cachés in the foreground. . . .

Appendix 2

Paul Kane's Portrait Log, Kept on His 1846–48 Journey *

1. I-as-a-way (Iacaway). The Loud Speaker. A Soto chief taken at Fort Frances on Rainy Lake.

2. Wayus-Rons (Wawgaskontz). The Little Rat. A chief taken at the same place.

3. Pe-ca-dhis (Peccondiss). The man with the lump on his navel. Taken on the Plains with the half breeds. A Soto.

4. Na-taw-waugh-cit (Natawassit). A Soto. The man that was born. This man wanted 2 horses for his robe.

5. Caw-ce-cu-che-cock (Cawkeekaikeedje-ekoke). A Soto. The Constant Sky. Her mother wanted to know if it would hurt her to sit for her picture. (I saw at this camp a rather good-looking girl whom I tried to persuade to wash the grease and dirt from her face and sit to me. With this however the customs of the tribe forbade her acquiescence as she was then in mourning for the loss of a relative and not allowed to cleanse her person or apparel for a year. She had not then washed herself for 3 months. Although her then apparel was disgustingly filthy she showed me a number of handsome Indian female dresses.)

6. Ogemaw-waugh-juck. The Spirit Chief. He is so old that he remembers when the French took Churchill.

7. Hus-Kuss-coo-sish (Uskoosekoosish). Young Grass. A Cree who has been in a great many battles with the Blackfeet. He has a ball through the shoulder and was shot in the belly.

8. Nicaway (Nickaway). The man that goes on a hunting party without rousing camp. A Musk-e-gaw (Muskaigow or Swampy Indian) from Norway House.

9. Do. (Musk-e-gaw from Norway House). Young woman.

10. An Assiniboine. Pe-tic-o-low-this. The little round man. . . . A bear was in the practice of coming to his tent to steal meat. He made a stage and put some meat under it and laid down on top in the night. The bear came and he shot him. . . . He was painted at Edmonton.

11. A Cree taken at Carlton, name not known. This is the man that shot the wolf with an arrow.

12. Chiniaza. The little slave. A Chipeway-an. Taken at Fort Pitt. (This tribe lives near the Athabasca lake. His prowess and dexterity in hunting wild animals of all kinds won him a degree of notoriety among the traders. He had when I saw him a hundred moose skins besides furs to a considerable amount.)

13. Muck-e-too.

14. Caw-Ke-Ka-saw-K-Way. For these two look at the journal.

15. O-this-skun. The Horn. He carries the bones of his brother in a bag on his back, handsomely ornamented.

16. Musk-ku-thay-ka-ou-mu-thay (Muskoothay-Capoomonthay). The man that always runs in the Plains. (An Asnaboyne or Stonee Indian so called from the river Asnaboyne which has a very rocky channel.)

17. Mis-cu-pa-puck-we (Mascoupay Pochawyon). Red Shirt. Assiniboine.

18. A Cree Woman.

19. Ka-Kee-se-guce-na-may-ed (Cawkeesaykeijenawmeed). The man that gives the day. (This man is a Cree and a great warrior.) He wished to know why I did not show the place in his shoulder where the Blackfeet wounded him.

20. As-in-a-chu. The white cappa or Waugh-be-gin-a. A Shuswap chief. Taken at Jaspers.

21. A·Chis·a·lay (Atchisalay). The Call of the Wind. The As-ick-an-a tribe from Peace River, called by Sir A. Mackenzie the Carriers (for their carrying great burthens on their backs having no beasts of burthen to substitute). Their teeth are worn down by eating dried salmon, his food being full of sand.

22. Taken on the lakes above Colville. (A boy paddling a canoe sketched on one of the Columbia Lakes.)

23. Elle-a-ma-coum-staluck (Allamahkum Stoolach). The Chief of the Earth. A Spokane Chief. (The head chief of the Shooalpay tribe at the Kettle Falls.) A Man of a great deal of influence.

24. Ta-ma-quin-a-tum (Tamaquin). Water Chief of Cascade Indians with a beard which you seldom see. These Indians live on fish (salmon) caught in great abundance on the Columbia. Waugh-Cla-Ca is the name of this tribe. They take their name from a lake that is near their village.

25. A Chinook woman taken at Vancouver. (This was a large tribe and the locality healthy previous to 1829 in which year the plow was first introduced by the Hudson's Bay Co. and immigrants from the United States. In that year fever and ague first made its appearance among them and depopulated large tracts of country, nearly all the following villages which previous to that time contained a large population are now extinct. Their principal settlement is Chinook Point at the mouth of the Columbia River, where King Cumcumly ruled in 1810. The Clatsup village contains very small remnant of its former inhabitants. Wasiackum is entirely extinct. Catlamut is the same. Kullowith the same, and the mouth of the Cowletts River the same. Kullimo, Katlepootle and Walkumup are also in the same condition. On Sovey's Island there were formerly four villages viz—Namenum, Mucknoma, Mamme-with and Naquaick—and at the present day scarcely a lodge remains on the island. They died of this disease in such numbers that their bodies lie unburied on the river's bank by scores—and numbers were met with floating down the river. The Hudson's Bay Company supplied the sick liberally with Quinine and other appropriate medicines, but their efforts were counteracted by the Indian mode of living, and the injurious system they obstinately pursued of treating the complaint—this consisted

---

* See note for Appendix 1, which applies also to Appendix 2. In the Portrait Log manuscript there are jottings of names of Indians whom Kane had sketched in 1845, but these scrawled names are omitted here. He also made some small identification sketches of heads and landscapes; these have been listed in the *catalogue raisonné* and their source given as Stark A4.

principally in flinging into the river without reference to the particular periods of the disease at which only cold bathing could be beneficial or safe.)

26. A Click-a-tat taken at Vancouver. This is the manner that they wear their hair when they are offended. (The Sotos on the contrary loosen their hair from all confinement and allow it to fall down over the face when they wish to evince a similar irritated feeling. The Klickatats most generally reside at the Cascades.)

27. A woman of the Chai-to tribe near the Umqua.

28. 4 Clackamus Indians taken on the Clackamus River near the City of Oregon. (Their lodges were formerly very numerous, but owing to the fatal effects of ardent spirits, which in spite of prohibition and fines against selling it to the Indians, they manage to obtain from their close vicinity to Oregon City where whiskey or a poisonous compound called there blue ruin, is illicitly distilled. Their numbers have so greatly diminished that there are not now more than 6 or 8 lodges in this river, and little doubt can be entertained that in a few years these also will melt away.)

29. Casenove, Chief of the Kalupanet Nation.

30. Waslameth (the only remaining) wife of Casenove, Kalapanet tribe, belonging to the neighborhood of Vancouver.

[There is no number 31 in Kane's log.]

32. Chief by the name of Cut-tell-tow (Kutteltoo) lives near the Pisk-ca-kuse River between Wallawalla and Okanagon. This is one of the most celebrated thieves (of horses) in the country. He is commonly known as the tall young man. (Chief of the Piscocoose Indians.)

33. Caw-we-chum (Cawitcham), a woman of the Caw-we-litcks (Cowlitz), on Cowlitz River that flows into the Columbia 60 miles below Vancouver on the south side.

34. Cascade Indian about 40 miles above Vancouver.

35. A child (Chinook) under the process of having its head flattened.

36. A Chinook woman from Astoria.

37. A Masset (Shatchet) Indian from Queen Charlotte Islands.

38. An Indian taken on the Indian race course near Vancouver taken with a head dress of beads.

39. Old Cox from the Sandwich Islands who was present at the death of Capt. Cook. He does not know his age. (He accompanied Prince Tamihami to England, and after his death returned to the Sandwich Islands and from there he came to the Columbia River in one of the Hudson's Bay Co. ships and entered their service. I met him as well as many of his countrymen at Fort Vancouver where they were employed in the company's service.)

40. Ciss-Cox (Kisscox), a Cowlitz Chief lives on a river of the same name. Amount to about 200. Live on camess and fish. Flatten their heads and wear the rat blanket.

41. Loch-o-let (Lacholett), Nisqually Chief, lives on the shores of Puget's Sound. These are the largest Indians I have ever met with. (The women are particularly tall and stout.)

42. Loch-hinum (Lochinum), Chief of the Tu-an-a-chun, on Whidbey's

Island. I had some difficulty in getting him to set until he heard that all the other chiefs had set.

43. A Shatchet Indian.

44. Che-a-clack, Chief of the Sangeys, number about 500 warriors, live on the south end of Vancouver's Island in the Straits of de Fuca.

45. A Sangeys girl spinning. (A Songas girl twisting yarn.)

46. Ska-tel-san—a Samas tillacum with a (grass) hat that is much worn here south of de Fuca.

47. Cloll-uck (Claluch). Chief of the Clallums, entrance to the Canal de Arrow. There are about 20 lodges here. This man was a chief of a good deal of influence among his people.

48. E·a-cle-a (Eaclach), a Cath-i (Cathay) chief on the south side of the straits. I met him in his canoe with 3 of his wives. He wanted me to go to his village where he said he had plenty of salmon and good things to eat. I made a sketch of him while in his canoe.

49. Yeats-sut-sute (Yates-sut-sook). Chief of the Clallums. The name of the village is I·Eanus (Hienus), population 500, with 40 large canoes.

50. Chaw-you-wit (Chawuwit), the daughter of a chief of a place called Suck, the handsomest girl I have ever seen on the coast south side of the straits.

51. A U-Sanich (Eusanitch) Indian . . . Canal de Arrow.

52. A Quatlin from the mouth of Fraser's River. This tribe is at war with the Sangeys. He had some beautiful shells in his ears. (The favourite food of this tribe is the sturgeon which here attain an enormous size, some having been taken of 700 lbs. weight.) . . .

53. Yellow-cum or Cape Flattery Jack.

54. Ona-put-a—Sinna-hamus chief lives in Puget's Sound. His tribe is war like.

55. Head chief of the Sinna-hamus Indians. This is a large tribe and lives in Puget's Sound. His name is Shouts-ton (Shawtstun).

56. A Clallum woman making a basket which they make very handsome. (These baskets are made like those of the Chinooks to hold water and are handsomely formed of grass dyed of different colors.)

57. Slam-a-chusset (Slamahkusset), a Cum-shaw chief. I could not find out where his tribe lived. Taken at F. Victoria.

58. A Whellamay (Walmah) girl.

59. A Cawitchen woman.

60. Saw-see-a, head chief of the Cawitchans. He is a great gambler at the game called le-halem and lives in the Gulf of Georgia.

61. Cull-chillam, the son of Saw-see-a, with a medicine cap on.

62. The wife of a Clallum chief on Whidby's Island.

63. A Sangas woman twisting yarn.

64. A You-Sanish (Eusanitch) woman weaving a blanket.

65. A New-a-tay Chief. (This tribe lives on the north end of Vancouver's Island and compress the head in infancy into a conical shape bringing the vertex nearly to a point. . . .)

66. A You-calltee (Eucaltee) Indian. These Indians are the dread of all the neighbouring tribes. They live in Johnston's St. They watch their opportunity and when the Indians of the Gulf of Georgia entered for

the purpose of fishing, they pounce upon them and woe be to the poor devil that is caught alone. They frighten their children with the name of a You-call-tee.

67. A Nesqually girl with (coloured) grass cap on her head.

68. Child of the S. of De Fuca.

69. Chim-see-an (Chimseyan). Slaves are not allowed to wear a ring in their nose. Rings in the nose is a mark of freedom.

70. Saw-wollo-wa (Soowallowa). A Dall or Tenimo Indian. (An Indian of the Tenimo.)

71. Qua-w-tus (Kuatus). A Wishcum Indian (living in the vicinity of the Dalls).

72. Mani-nucht (Mancemuckt) the chief of the Skene or Shutes.

73. Slam-e-ass-sun (Slooassun). The Chief of the Pelouse or Pavilion River. The name of this tribe is the Uppet Uppets and but small (not numbering more than 70 or 80 warriors).

74. The wife of Tilaukaikt. A (head chief) Waulupu or Kyuse Chief, a man of influence and lived near Dr. Whitman's Mission and are a large tribe, 1,000.

75. I-e-ash-an (Ieash) the foolish, a Cham-nass-am (Chamnapam), at the mouth of the Nezperce River. A small tribe, a branch of the Nezperces.

76. Tam-at-a-pa, a brother of the great Walla Walla Chief Pe-a-pe-o-macks-macks (Peo-peo-mox-mox) or the Yellow Serpent, a man of great influence in his tribe. He is feared for he will horsewhip a man for the most trifling offence. This tribe numbers 3,500 (Mr. McKinley). (I took a sketch of the boy, son of Peo-peo-mox-mox, whose name was Tuchnoot or the Man without Medicine.)

77. Nach-a-wish, a Nezpercé Indian. This tribe is large and live on the Nezperce River.

78. Te-law-cite-an (Teilochikt), the man that is in the act of lighting. The head chief of the Waulpa Kyuse lives near Dr. Whitman's and has given him a great deal of trouble. He has slapped his face and pulled his ears which the Dr. took without a murmur.

79. Ta-mach-hus (Tamakus). The greatest savage I have ever met with. (I had no sooner finished the sketch than Tamakus asked to look at it, and enquired what I intended doing with it, whether I was not going to give it to the Americans against whom he bore a strong antipathy and superstitiously fancied that their possessing it would put him in their power. I in vain told him that I should not give it to them, but not being satisfied with this assurance, he was going to throw it in the fire when I seized his arm and snatched it from him. He glared at me like a fiend and appeared greatly annoyed but before he had time to recover from his surprise, I left the lodge and mounted my horse, not without occasionally looking behind to see if he were following.)

80. Keishawellish, Head Chief of the Senechastey Indians, living on the lakes on the Columbia River 60 miles above the Kettle Falls, numbering 300 souls. These people hunt between this and the Rocky Mountains, where game is abundant, particularly the Cariboo, a species of deer. They occupy the whole range between here and the Rocky Mountains.

81. Achewishamahigh, or "The Grisly Bear Standing," head chief of the Callaspellums living on a lake of the same name, south of the Columbia River. Their numbers are about 650. There is a Jesuit mission established among the Indians.

82. Tumsinniho, "The man without blood," a Spokane Indian living on the Spokan River.

83. A Spokan Indian.

84. A Sketch of Indians playing the game of Alkoloch. This game is one of skill and more difficult to acquire than any Indian game I have seen. . . . This game is played by all the Indians on the Columbia River, and the present sketch was taken among the Scualpees. The stakes were played for two horses.

85. Paikachose, a Cree, a most expert horse thief, having just brought in 7 of these animals which he has taken from the Blackfeet.

86. Eikeetopee, "The man that always rides," a Blackfoot Indian, who I afterwards learned was killed by the Crees in one of their excursions.

87. Tommskarrohoto, an Iroquois. He has been a guide in the employ of the Hudson's Bay Company for the last 25 or 30 years. This tribe resides principally at Cochnawaga (Caughnawaga) near Montreal. This man I met with on Lake Winnipeg on his return from accompanying Sir John Richardson into the interior in the capacity of a guide. There are no people perhaps so dextrous in the management of a canoe as the Iroquois. Nearly all the guides on the Columbia River and other waters in the Hudson's Bay territory belong to this tribe.

88. Maydoigamekinungee, "I hear the noise of the deer," is head chief of the Ojibbeways on the Camonanestaquay river.

Appendix 3

Catalogue for Paul Kane's Exhibition, 1848 *

1 Sig-in-nock—Blackbird—Head Chief of Ma-ni-too-awning, Ojibwah tribe.

2 Mas-kuh-noon-ge—Big Fish—An Indian of the Ojibwah tribe.

3 She-bah-ke-zhick—Hole in the Sky—An Indian Chief of Ojibwah tribe, from Lake Superior.

4 Ma-cheek-e-wis.

5–6 Indians of the same tribe from Lake Superior.

7 Saw-gun.

8 Sha-nu-oh-ke-zhick—Against the Heavens—from Lake Nipissing.

9–10 Indians from Michipicaton.

11 As-a-bo-nish—Racoon—Indian Chief of the Attawah tribe, from the Manitoulin Islands.

* *Catalogue of Sketches of Indians, and Indian Chiefs, Landscapes, Dances, Costumes, &c. &c. by Paul Kane.* Toronto: Printed by Scobie and Balfour, Adelaide Buildings, King Street. November, 1848.

A copy of this *Catalogue* is in the Metropolitan Toronto Central Library. It is referred to as TCH in the *catalogue raisonné* above.

12 Indian from Manitooawning.

13 Muck-koze—The Young Bear—Chief of Ottawah tribe, from the Manitoulin Islands.

14 Co-cosh—The Hog—a Pot-a-wat-o-me Indian.

15 Now-on-dhu-go—of Attawah tribe from Lake Michigan.

16 Shaw-way-nos-soway—a great Medicine Man, from the Manitoulin Islands.

17 A half-breed Indian Girl, from the Sault St. Mary.

18 Maw-za-pau-kau—The Brave Soldier—from Wolf River.

19 Muck-e-tah-kin-ne-u—Black Eagle—Manomone tribe, from Fox River, Lake Winnibago.

20 I-o-we-to-ke—The Serpent—an Indian Woman of the Manomone tribe, from Fox River, Lake Winnibago.

21 Ke-wah-tin—The North Wind—Man[o]mone tribe, Lake Winnibago.

22 Wah-bo-nim—The White Dog—Manomone tribe, Lake Winnibago.

23 Muck-a-too—same as above.

24 I-a-co-way—The Loud Speaker—Chief of the Soto Indians, from Fort Francis lac la pluie.

25 Pe-co-dhis—same as above.

26 Ka-ke-ka-ki-ji-koe—The Constant Sky—a Soto girl from the Red River Settlement.

27 ⎫ Indians of the Cree tribe, from the Saskachawan River, near
28 War Cap. ⎭ Fort Pitt.

29 Hus-kus-coo-sish—The Young Grass—of the Cree tribe, on the Saskachawan River.

30 Pe-tic-o-paw-this—The Little Round Man—of the Cree tribe, on the Saskachawan River, near Carlton.

31 Francis Lucie—a half-breed Cree, from Edmonton House.

32 A blood Indian Chief—from the Western prairies.

33 Oke-maw-wah-jack—The Spirit Chief—an Esquimaux.

34 Ca-is-no—of the Chi[n]ook tribe, from Columbia River.

35 Chi-a-clah—Chief of the Songes, from Vancouver's Island.

36 Wilhamet Indians.

37–8–9–40 Medicine Men on the Pacific Coast, near the Straits de Fuca.

41 A Medicine Pipe, do. do.

42–3–4 Indian Wigwams.

45–6–7 Sketches on the Island of Mackinaw.

48 The Dog Portage.

49 The Pin Portage.

50 French River Rapids.

51 Encampment on River Winnipeg.

52 Chûte à Jacko, on do. do.

53 Pointe des Bois, do. do.

54 Blackfoot Chief, from the Western prairies.

55 Buffalo head.

56 Group of Buffaloe.

57 Saskachawan River.

58 A Buffalo Pound.

59 A Medicine Pipe Stem Dance.

60 A Scalp Dance.

61 Falls on the Peluce River.

62 View near Fort Vancouver (Mount Hood)

63–4 Sketches of Mount St. Helen, near Fort Vancouver.

65 Mills in Oregon City.

66 Oregon City.

67 Main Street, Oregon City.

68–9 Falls near Oregon City.

70 Fort Vancouver.

71 Interior of a Click-a-tat Lodge on Columbia River.

72 A Well in the Woods.

73 Lodges on the Columbia River—drying Salmon.

74 Catching Salmon on the Falls near Colville, Columbia River.

75 Castle Rock, Columbia River.

76 Sketch of Mount Hood, Columbia River.

77 Lodges on Vancouver's Island.

78 Norway House.

79 Sketch on River Winnipeg.

80 Babeen Woman, North West Coast.

Sketches in Water Colours.

81 May-dwi-ga-mi-ki-nun-ge—I hear the noise of the deer—The head chief of the Ojibwah tribe, on the Kaministaquoiah River.

82 Mah-min—The Feather—Head Chief of the Asseneboine tribe, Rocky Mountain House.

83 Wah-ke-jo-e-tass-a-neen—The white half man—second chief of the Asseneboine tribe, Rocky Mountain House.

84 Ka-ah-ke-ka-sahk-a-wa-ow—The man that gives the war whoop—The head chief of the Cree tribe.

85 Pe-a-pus-qua-hum—One that passes through the sky—a Cree Indian living among the Asseneboines, Rocky Mountain House.

86 A Cree Indian.

87 Pe-pa-ka-chos—A Cree Indian.

88 Achu-wish-a-ma-hy—The Grisly Bear standing—a Cree Indian.

89 Iron Collar—Blood Indian Chief from the Western prairies.

90 Big Snake—Blackfoot Chief from do.

91 White Buffalo Calf—Blackfoot Indian do.

92 Chin-i-a-sa—The Little Slave—a Chippawayan Indian, on the Athabasca River.

93 Achi-sa-lay—The call of the Wind—of the Assickanay tribe, on the Rocky Mountains.

94 Collection of Painted Heads.

95 A Chief of the Lakes, Columbia River.

96 See-pase—Chief of the Salmon, Columbia River.

97 Chin-oo-as—A Flathead Indian, from the West side of the Rocky Mountains.

98 El-ko-ka-shin—A Shawalloway Indian, from the Cascades.

Appendices

99 Tillu-ko-ikt—A Chief of the Kyoos tribe. This man was one of the party of Indians who murdered Dr. & Mrs. Whitman, and 12 other individuals of the Missionary Station at Wy-al-poo, on the Walla Walla River.

100 The Wife of Tillu-ko-ikt.

101 Tamachus—also one of Dr. W.'s murderers.

102 Son of the great Walla Walla Chief, Pe-o-pe-o-maux-maux.

103 Brother to the same.

104–5 Nepersee Indians, Nepersee River.

106 Indian of the Lakes.

107 Ku-ar-tos—An Indian of the Wishkum tribe, from the Shoots on the Columbia River.

108 So-wall-o-way—a Chief of the Dalles.

109 Tum-se-ne-ho—The Man without Blood—a Spokan Chief, on the Spokan River.

110 To-ma-quin—a Cascade Chief, Columbia River.

111 A Cascade Indian, Columbia River.

112 Studies of Figures, do.

113–14 Chin-ook Women, from Astoria.

115 Child's head—Chinook, do.

116 Boy with head dress, do.

117 A Click-a-tat Indian, Columbia River.

118 Cow-we-cham—Cow-we-litcks—River Cow-we-litcks.

119 Kiss-cox—Chief of do. do.

120 A Chinook Indian.

121 A Slave of the Chastay tribe, south of the Columbia River, on the Sea Coast.

122 Old Cox—a Sandwich Islander, who was present at the murder of Capt. Cook.

123 Law-hi-num—Chief of Whidbey's Island, Paget Sound.

124 Sca-tel-son—a Songhes Indian, Vancouver's Island.

125 A Girl from Pagit Sound.

126 Ukultee Indian, Johnson's Straits.

127 A Cow-i-chin Indian, from the Straits de Fuca.

128 Yate-sut-soot—Chief of the Chalms, south side of the Straits de Fuca.

129 A Chief of the Sin-no-ho-mas, Puget Sound.

130 Slam-ma-hur-set—Chief of the Cum-sin-no-ho—taken at Fort Victoria, Vancouver's Island.

131 A U-sa-nich Indian, from the Gulf of Georgia.

132 Yallocum, Chief of Cape Flattery.

133 Onepa—A Sinnohomas, Puget Sound.

134 Wife of Clalm Chief, Whidbey Island.

135–6 Chiefs of the Chimpseyans, Chatham Sound.

137 A daughter of a Clalm Chief, south of the Straits de Fuca.

138 A Clalm Woman making a basket.

139 Saw-sea-a, the Head Chief of the Cow-i-chin tribe.

140 Son of Saw-se-a—Medicine Man—north of Fraser's River.

141 A Quat-lin Indian, on Fraser's River.

142 A Sca-chet Indian, do.

143 A Nu-et-tee Chief, north end of Vancouver's Island. The Nuettee Indians have conical-shaped heads.

144 A Songhes Woman twisting yarn.

145 A Mountain Goat.

146 Study of Snow on a tree.

147 Study of a Carved Stone Pipe.

148 Buffalo War Robe.

149–50 North West Canoes.

151 War Party in Canoes, in the Esquimelt.

152 Indian Graves—Puget's Sound.

153 Sketch of Indian Fan—belonged to the late Mrs. Whitman, murdered by Tillukoikt, Tamachus and others.

154 A Painted Horse.

155 War Clubs.

156 Indian Dogs.

157 A Sketch.

158 Moss Tree.

159 Interior of Lodge.

160 Canoes on Columbia River.

161–2–3 Indian Graves on Columbia River.

164 Indian Graves on Cowlet's River.

165 Medicine Masks—North West Coast.

166 Indians spearing Fish—Columbia River.

167 Method of flattening the head among the Chinook Indians.

168 Indian Woman weaving a blanket.

169 Interior of a Clalm Lodge.

170 Pine Tree.

171 Heads of Prairie Antelopes.

172 A Buffalo Bull.

173 Carved Stone Pipe.

174 Sled Dogs.

175 A Mountain Ram's Head.

Sketches on the Columbia River.

176 Dalle des Morts.

177 Mount Hood.

178 Columbia River.

179 Indian Lodge.

180 Coffin Rock.

181 The Little Dalles.

182 The Kettle Falls.

183 Fort Walla-Walla.

184 Cape Horn.

185 Rock called the Too-ne-per-see-girls.

186 Supposed Land Slip.

187 Cascades.
188 Sketch near Fort Vancouver.

Sketches in the Rocky Mountains.

189 Jasper's House.
190 Jasper's Lake.
191 Laroque's Prairie.
192 Snow Scene in the Mountains.
193–4 Mountain Scenery.
195 Roman Catholic Mission Station, near the Wilhamet River, 30 miles from Oregon City.
196 Wesleyan Methodist Station, Play Green Lake.
197 Presbyterian Mission Station, near the Spokan River.
198 Falls near Fort Francis—Rainy Lake.
199 Fort Francis.
200 Slave Falls.
201 White Mud Portage.
202 Canoes.
203 Prairie on Fire.
204 Lake in the Prairie.
205 Fort Pitt.
206 Edmunton House.
207 Indian Grave.
208 Encampment of Half-breeds, near Red River Settlement.
209 Sketch in the Prairie.
210 Fort Gary, Red River.
211 Rocky Mountain House.
212 Falls on the Wilhamet River.
213 Bird's Eye View of Wilhamet River.
214 A Click-a-tat Lodge.
215 Puget Sound Establishment.
216 Sketch on Spokan River.
217 Prairie de Bute.
218–19 Sketches on the Grande Coulé south of the Columbia River.
220–1–2 Sketches on the Peluce River, a branch of the Nepersee River.
223 Indian Forts on Whidbey's Island.
224 A Barrière for catching salmon, south of the Straits de Fuca.
225 A Songhes village at the Straits de Fuca.
226 Indians returning from gathering Camas, Vancouver's Island.
227 Indians gambling—the game of Le-hal-lum.
228 Mount Baker, from Vancouver's Island.
229 Crossing the Straits de Fuca.
230 Boat Encampment, head of the North Branch of the Columbia River.
231–2 Carlton, Saskachawan River.
233 Pambino River.
234 Columbia River.

235 Lodges on Prairie, near Fort Vancouver.
236 Carved Pipe.
237 A wolf's head.
238 A Chief's Daughter from Lake St. Clair.
239 Man-a-to-wa-bay—The *He-devil*—Ojibwah tribe, Lake Michigan.
240 Na-too-waw-sit—The man that was born—a Soto Indian.

Appendix 4

Paintings Delivered by Paul Kane to Sir George Simpson, 1849 *

1. A buffalo Pound; 2. An Indian Lodge near Fort Vancouver, Mount Hood in the Distance; 3. Catching Salmon at Colville; 4. Indian Lodges near Colville; 5. Castle Rock on the Columbia River; 6. Indian Lodges on Vancouver Island; 7. A Scalp Dance near Colville; 8. A Sketch on the Saskatchewan; 9. Portrait of a Cree taken at Edmonton; 10. A Blackfoot on Horseback.

[Kane states that an injury to his hand has prevented him from completing an additional four sketches, namely, The Falls of Pelouse, The Kaministaquoiah Falls, A Buffalo Hunt, and Mountain Goat. For Sir George's acknowledgment see Appendix 10, Letter 17.]

* This list is referred to in the *catalogue raisonné* as GS.

Appendix 5

Canvases Sent by Paul Kane to George W. Allan, 1856 *

Brigade of boats	1
Ojibbeway Camp	2
Red River Settlement	3
Oregon City	4
Falls at Colville	5
White Mud Portage	6
A Buffalo pound	7
Medicine Mask dance	8
Indian Horse race	9
Buffalo bulls fighting	10

* The original of this list is in the collections of the Royal Ontario Museum, Toronto. It is referred to in the *catalogue raisonné* as GWA.

Appendices

Catching Wild Horses	11
Coffin Rock	12
Dalle des Morts, or the Rapid of the dead	13
Castle rock, Columbia River	14
Indian Camp, Colville	15
Peluce Fall	16
Slave Fall	17
Mount St. Helens	18
French River Rapids	19
Edmonton	20
Game of Alcoloh	21
Scalp dance, Colville	22
A battle of I-eh-nus	23
Chinook Lodge, Mount Hood in the distance	24
Lodges on Vancouver's Island	25
Boat Encampment	26
Half breed Encampment	27
A Woman Weaving a Blanket	28
Interior of a Lodge, Vancouvers Island	29
Sault Ste. Marie	30
Encampment, River Winipeg	31
Group of Buffalo	32
The Rock of the Nesperses Girl	33
Half breeds running Buffalo	34
Half breeds travelling	35
Prairie des Butes	36
Medicine Pipe Stem dance	37
Winter travelling	38
Fishing by Torch Light	39
Hunting ducks	40
The death of Big Snake	41
A Sketch on Lake Huron	42
Wounded Buffalo bull	43
Indian Summer on the Saskatchewan	44
The Esquimalt, Indian village	45
The return of a War Party	46
Burying place on the Cowlitz River	47
Rocky Mountain House	48
Cree Indians travelling	49
Sioux Scalp dance	50
A Ware for catching salmon	51
The Wilhamet River from a Mountain	52
The Cackabakah Falls	53
The Mountain Portage	54
A Prairie on fire	55
A Sketch on the Peluce	56
A Valley in the Plains	57
Running Buffalo	58

Portraits

The Constant Sky	59
Cunnawa-bum	60
A Babbine Chief	61
Head Chief of the Assineboins	62
Second Chief of the Assineboins	63
Medicine Man, Vancouvers Island	64
Big Snake's Brother	65
Brant	66
Casan-ov	67
Flat Head woman and child, Caw-wacham	68
Kee-akee-ka-sac-ka-wow (The Man that gives the War Whoop, Head chief of the Crees)	69
Maun-qua-dous	70
A Cree from Edmonton	71
Six Black feet Chiefs	72
Big Snake, Blackfoot Chief from the Western Prairies	73
A Nesperces Indian	74
A Pottowattome Indian	75
Wappoose	76
An Indian of the Dalles, Columbia River	77
Tilli-koit	78
The man that always rides	79
Blackfoot Pipe Stem Carrier	80
The Midday Woman	81
Tomakus	82
Chee-ah-clak	83
A Babbine Woman	84
A Woman from Manitooawning	85
A conical shaped headed Indian	86
A Sioux Indian	87
A Clallum girl	88
An Esquimaux	89
Kitche-ogi-maw	90
Chief from Fort William	91
Chief of the Salmon	92
A Flat Head Woman, Whitby's Island	93
Peo-peo-mox-mox	94
San-ce-a	95
Yallicum	96
The War Cap	97
Waugh-be-nim	98
Shah-wah-nas-ha-wa	99
François Lucie	100

follow it throw each a dart under it, the object being that the ring should fall and rest upon the darts & the beads which happen to rest on the darts count towards the game according to their color. This game is played by all the Indians on the Columbia River.

Appendix 6

Paul Kane's Draft of Notes for Paintings Delivered to the Parliament of Canada, 1856 *

1. Big Snake, A Blackfoot Chief, recounting his war exploits to 5 of his subordinate chiefs.
2. *"Boat Encampment,"* situated at the head of the N. Branch of the navigable waters of the Columbia River (for canoes). Derives its name from its being the terminus of all boat navigation & the commencement of the land carrier across the Mountains, consequently the spot at which all parties going or returning must necessarily encamp.
3. *"Mount Hood"*—A Mountain about 7000 feet high situated near the South side of the Columbia River & at about 120 yards from its mouth. The figures in the foreground are "Chinooks," a Branch of the Flat Head Tribes of the N.W. Coast.
4. *Buffaloes at Sunset*—taken near Edmonton at a small lake near the Saskatchewan River.
5. *Scalp Dance*—by a party of "Spokane" Indians taken on the Upper Columbia.
6. "Assineboines" Indians—hunting or "running Buffalo" on horseback —taken in the plains situate on the East of the Rocky Mts. & in their vicinity.
7. *Fishing Lodges of the "Clallums"*—on Vancouver's Island. These Lodges are constructed of a coarse description of matting which is taken down and carried in Canoes when travelling.
8. *Interior of a Winter Lodge* of "Clallums" on Vancouver's Island. These lodges are constructed of split cedar & are consequently not portable—are frequently large enough to accommodate 100 *individuals*.
9. *Part of Red River Settlement* with a view of Fort Garry on the right & the Catholic Church at the left of the River.
10. *The White Mud Portage*—situate on River Winnipeg. The picture represents "Saulteaux" Indians carrying their canoes & baggage, called *"Making the Portages."*
11. *A Horse Race*—Among the Blackfeet Indians on the Prairies. An amusement of very frequent occurrence & consists generally of a 4 mile Race, viz: two miles to & from a given point.—the Riders being invariably in a state of nudity.
12. Two Indians playing the Game "Alcoloh." This sketch was taken among the Shualpees near the Falls of the Columbia.—The game consists in rolling a ring of iron 3 inches in diameter with 6 beads of different colors bound by strings to the inner edge of the circle. The Ring is rolled along the ground until it strikes agst. a stick intercepting its progress.—At the moment of its devolution the two competitors who

* The original of this draft is in the Kane family papers. It is referred to in the *catalogue raisonné* as LP.

Appendix 7

Works of Paul Kane Given to Mrs. Kane by the Allan Family, 1871 *

1. Mackinaw.
2. Upper Pelluce Falls.
3. River Scene.
4. Wah-Be-Num (White Dog), Lake Winebago.
5. Vue d'un Belvidere.
6. An Ojjibeway Girl from St. Claire.
7. Salmon Spearing.
8. Wigwams, Owen Sound.
9. Scene near Fort Vancouver.
10. Ojibiway Indian Boy Lake Superior.
11. Oregon City.
12. Norway House.
13. Chute à Jacque, Winnipeg River.
14. French River Rapids.
15. Medicine Pipe Stem.
16. François Lucie.
17. Chinook Indian, Columbia River.
18. She-bah-ke-zhick—Hole in the Sky. Ojibwah Indian, Ft. William, Lake Superior.
19. Mt. St. Helens with smoke from crater.
20. Indian Boy.
21. Sha-new-di-kigik—The Heavens. Indian, Lake Nipissing.
22. Ottawa Tribe, Lake Nipigne, Naw-on-do-go.
23. Susan Belo, Half Breed Girl, Sault de St. Marie.
24. Coo-Coosh, The Hog. Potawatamie Indian.
25. Sig-in-nock—Black Bird, Ojibwah Chief.
26. Encampment, Winnipeg River.
27. Cree War Cap.
28. Medicine Man with Mask, Vancouver Island.
29. Soto Indian.
30. Pin Portage.
31. Babbene Woman, Pacific Coast.
32. Waterfall.
33. River Scene.

* The list is available in the collections of the Royal Ontario Museum. It is referred to in the *catalogue raisonné* as AG.

34. Mackinaw.
35. Wigwam.
36. Prairie de Bute.
37. Mt. St. Helens.
38. Muck-e-tah-kin-new, Black Eagle, Fox River, Lake Winnipeg.
39. Interior of Lodge, Columbia River.
40. Pointe aux Bois.
41. Dog Portage.
42. Wigwam, Lake Huron.
43. Muck-a-ta, Potawatamee Indian.
44. Indian man.
45. Aw-bon-wuish-kum, Indian from Manitowaning.
46. Sho-ne-ah, Silver.
47. Ft. Walla Walla.
48. Mo-chuke-e-nis, Indian Portrait.
49. Indian Chief, Manitoulin Island.
50. Indian Girl.
51. Indian Boy.
52. Indian Man.
53. Medicine Men, Straits de Fuca.
54. Indian Pipe.
55. Prairie Encampment.
56. Chee-u-clak, Head Chief of the Songees, Vancouver Is.
57. Indian Portrait.
58. Indian Portrait.
59. Indian from Lake Superior.
60. Cottage Scene.
61. Ke-wah-tin, The North Wind, Manamane Tribe, Lake Winnipeg.
62. Match-o-ke-man, Big Chief.
63. Group of Willamette Indians.
64. Paul Kane.
65. Indian Girl.
66. Mackinaw.
67. Cashto.
68. Buffalo Head.
69. Interior of Blackfoot Lodge.
70. Medicine Pipe Stem Dance, Blackfeet & Blood Indians.
71. Indian from Michipicoten.
72. Kaw-qua-dab-bow-nwa-skung, Dawn of Day, Chief of Saugene Indians, July 24, 45.
73. Cree Indian, Edmonton.
74. Buffalo Hunting.
75. Grand Coulet.
76. Mus-kuh-now-je, Big Fish, Ojjibewah Tribe.
77. River Scene.
78. Michipicoten Indian from Lake Superior.
79. A Well in the Woods.
80. Shah-wuk-nahsoowa, Great Medicine Man, Manitoulin.
81. Prairie Scene.
82. Head Chief, Ojibwah Indian, Manitowaning.
83. Cree Indian Chief.
84. Captain Ironside, descendent of Tecumseh.
85. Sabo(?).
86. Io-we-toke, Indian Woman, Fox River, Winnebago.
87. Muckose, Young Bear, Ahtaw-wah Chief.
88. River Scene.
89. Chief of Seto Indians, Fort Frances, Lake LePluie.
90. Ojibwah Indian.
91. Mah-he-cum, Indian Dog.
92. Winnipeg River.
93. Pipe from Lake Superior.
94. Part of Oregon City.
95. Mt. Hood from near Fort Vancouver.
96. Rocky Mountain Goat.
97. White Mud Portage, Winnipeg River.
98. Medicine Masks, North West Coast, B.C.
99. Columbia River Indians.
100. Indians.
101. Indians.
102. Indian.
103. Rocky Mt. Sheep head.
104. Indians.
105. Catching Salmon, Columbia River.
106. Wounded Buffalo.
107. Slave of the Chastay tribe, Pacific Coast.
108. Interior of Lodge, Vancouver Island.
109. Indian.
110. Burial Place.
111. Crossing the Straits of de Fuca.
112. Sledge Dogs.
113. Vancouver Island.
114. Chinook Child undergoing process of flattening the head.
115. Dance of the Women.
116. Game of Al-Kol-lock, Chucepay Indians, Columbia River.
117. Chalur Indian Woman basket making.
118. Indian.
119. Coffin Rock.
120. Canoes of Columbia.
121. Tilanpoikt Indian.
122. Wigwams, B. Columbia.
123. Indian.
124. Salmon Trap, de Fuca Straits.
125. Quivers, Pipes, &c.
126. Buffalos Fighting.
127. Indian heads.
128. Fort and interior of hut.

129. Chief of Chimpseyans, Chatham Sound.
130. Indian.
131. Windmill & Fort.
132. Burial Canoe, Cowlitzs Indians.
133. Indians spearing fish, Columbia River.
134. Return of War Party, Pacific Coast.
135. Mount Hood.
136. Game of Lihallum, Vancouver Island.
137. Fort Frances.
138. Chinook Indian Boy.
139. Jasper House, East side Rocky Mts.
140. Winter Scene.
141. Woman weaving a blanket.
142. Indians of Johnson's Straits.
143. Grand Coulet and near Walla Wallah River.
144. Fraser River Indian.
145. River Sketch.
146. Fall on Peluse River.
147. Pipe Stems.
148. Pipe Stem.
149. Water Fall.
150. River Scene.
151. Kettle Falls.
152. Water Fall.
153. Canoes.
154. Falls of Niagara.
155. Walulah Encampment.
156. Salmon Falls, Koos-koos-Kia River.
157. Upper Columbia.
158. Falls on Slave River.
159. Indian.
160. View of Saskatchewan.
161. Peter Jacobs.
162. Pyramid Rock, Koos-Koos-Kia River.
163. Falls on Upper Pelouse.
164. Dogs of the Plains.
165. Medicine Men.
166. Puget Sound.
167. Pembina River.
168. Spearing Salmon.
169. Fishing Columbia River.
170. Falls near St. Frances, Rainy Lake.
171. Wedding Party Travelling by Dog Sledge.
172. Interior of hut.
173. Indian.
174. Indian.
175. Suchal Indian.

176. Columbia River Indians.
177. Indian.
178. Buffalo Head.
179. Dalle des Meurtes.
180. Drying Salmon at the Dalles, Columbia River.
181. Ojibbeway Camp.
182. Wesleyan Methodist Station, Playfair Lake.
183. Edmonton House.
184. Cape Horn.
185. Indian of the Lakes.
186. Antelope Heads.
187. Mission Station, Spokane River.
188. Canoes, Pacific Coast.
189. Cascade Mts., B. Columbia.
190. Willamette River.
191. Fish House, B.C.
192. Blackfoot Indian.
193. Burial Canoes.
194. Idol & Graves, Vancouver Island.
195. Cowichin Indians, Straits of Fuca.
196. Half breeds running buffalo.
197. Indian Chief, Puget Sound.
198. Indian.
199. Indian Chief, Puget Sound.
200. Indian Village, Straits de Fuca.
201. Rocky Mountain Goat.
202. Saskatchewan River.
203. Lodge, Vancouver Island.
204. Canoe.
205. Study of Snow on Trees.
206. Naval Scene.
207. Indian Graves Calulle River.
208. Driving Buffalo into a pound.
209. The Little Dalles.
210. Picture writing on skin.
211. Huts.
212. Pipe Stem.
213. Chinook Child.
214. Chippeweyan Indian, Athabasca River.
215. Flathead Woman.
216. A-ches-a-lay, Call of the Wind, of the Asichuna Tribe of Peace River called by Mr. A. Mackenzie Carrier Indian.
217. ———
218. River Scene.
219. Indian Cradle.
220. Flathead Woman spinning yarn.
221. Prairie Scene.

Appendix 8

Pigments and Mediums Used by Paul Kane

The following analysis of pigments and mediums in Kane's studio sketch box (Colln Mrs. Paul Kane III) has been prepared by M. Ruggles, R. Boyer, J. Childs and J. Hanlan of the Conservation Laboratories of the National Gallery of Canada (November 1969)

Sample	Result of analysis	Method of analysis
1, White	White lead, $2\ PbCO_3 \cdot Pb(OH)_2$	X-ray diffraction
2, Red	Gypsum, $CaSO_4 \cdot 2H_2O$	X-ray diffraction
	Alizarin	Infra-red spectroscopy
3, Blue	Prussian Blue, $Fe_4\ (Fe(CN)_6)_3$	X-ray diffraction
	Alunite $(K,Na)\ Al_3(OH)_6(SO_4)_2$	X-ray diffraction
4, Pink	Calcium carbonate, $CaCO_3$	X-ray diffraction
	Alizarin	Infra-red spectroscopy
5, Brown	Hematite, $\times\ Fe_2O_3$	X-ray diffraction
	Magnesioferrite, $MgFe_2O_4$	X-ray diffraction
6, Blue	Cf. no. 3	
7, Brown	Van Dyck Brown	Infra-red spectroscopy
8, Red	Vermilion, HgS	X-ray diffraction
	Probably alizarin	
9, Brown	Mixed with sand and oxidized linseed oil	Infra-red spectroscopy
	Hematite, $\times\ Fe_2O_3$	X-ray diffraction
	Magnesioferrite, $MgFe_2O_4$	
10, Yellow	Yellow ochre	X-ray diffraction
11, Brown	Goethite, $Fe_2O_3 \cdot H_2O$	X-ray diffraction
	Arsenic impurity	X-ray fluorescence
12, Black	Bone or Ivory black	X-ray diffraction
	Calcium phosphate, $Ca_3(PO_4)_2$	
13, Yellow	White lead, $2PbCO_3 \cdot Pb(OH)_2$, and partially oxidized white lead, probably $2PbO \cdot PbCO_3$, which can be produced by calcination	X-ray diffraction
14, Dark brown resin	Mixture of Batavia Damar resin and Mastic resin most probable	Infra-red spectroscopy
15, Viscous amber liquid	Mastic resin	Infra-red spectroscopy
	Turpentine	Odour
16, Viscous yellowish brown liquid	Linseed oil	Infra-red spectroscopy
17, Red (plus medium)	Vermilion, HgS	X-ray diffraction
18, Not original	(not investigated)	
19, Amber pellets	Mastic resin	Infra-red spectroscopy

Appendix 9

Books in the Library of Paul Kane at His Death, 1871 *

Two years of "Illustrated Magazine of Art"
11 vols. Bell's British Theatre
6 vols. Shakespeare
3 vols. Waverley Novels
Italian Dictionary
Nugent's French-English Dictionary
2 vols. Pain's Sketchbook
1 vol. Polar Seas & regions
Diary of a late Physician
Remarks on Italy
The Sketchbook of Geoffrey Crayon, Esq.
Daily Communication with God
Matthew Henry
Tales from Blackwood
The Last Days of Pompeii
Life of Archbishop Cranmer
Prismatics
History of England—Macaulay
Sparks from a Locomotive
Book of 1000 Anecdotes
Queen of Hearts. Wilkie Collins
Life of Benvenuto Cellini
Michael Angelo & Raphael
Richardson's Arctic Expedition
Geographical view of the world
The Sparrowgrass Papers—Cozzens
Stack's Italy
Scenes and adventures as a soldier & settler—Moodie
Woman's right to labour—Mrs. Dall
9 vols. Chambers Journal
Dr. Chase's Receipts
Journal of Devotions
John Bull
Pollock's Course of Time
Young's Night Thoughts
Mason's Select Remains
Sheridan's Dictionary
Lemprieces(?) Classical dictionary

* This list was obtained from the Surrogate Court Office, County of York, Ontario. It has been reproduced without change.

Walke's Dictionary
India and its inhabitants
The Indian in his Wigwam, Schoolcraft
Report of the Commissioner of Indian Affairs
Powell on evidence
Aeroleuchius (?) in the principles of Composition
Prof. Wilson—2 vols. Prehistoric Man
2 vols. Life of Brant
Edmund Burke
4 vols. Animal Kingdom
Bacon Currier (?)
Burns' Works
Adams Geography
Cyclopedia of Medicine and Surgery
Culpepper's Herbal
Appleton's Cyclopedia of Biography
Byron's Works
Captain Back's Arctic Land Expedition
Tanner's Narrative
Thirty Years among the Indians
Canada at the Universal Exposition
Valentine McClutchy, The Fish Agent
The Comic History of Rome
Captain Ross's Second Voyage
Rennie's Supplement to the Shakespeare
Locke On the Understanding
3 vols. Otis
Cox's Adventures
Simpson's Journey Around the World
Good's Book of Nature
Origin of the North American Indians
4 vol. Wanderings of an Artist, Paul Kane
2 vols. Italian Costume, Camille Bonnard
Olieeve de Raphael 152 plates

Appendix 10
Letters, Principally to and from Paul Kane

Letter 1: Michael Kane, Toronto, to Paul Kane, Detroit

Toronto 4th Novr. 1836

My Dear Paul,

Yours of the 22nd ultimo I received on the 2nd Inst—The statement of your advantageous removal from hence is most gratifying—as you have begun, so I hope you will continue prosperous—

You say that Mr. Bowman has got married and that in all probability will prevent your Italian excursion. This I take to be a fortunate circumstance first in keeping you on the Continent where you ought to remain and

Secondly Mr. B. has given you a precedent which you would go well to imitate Viz—acquire long experience before you attempt the blind hazard of marriage.

Frederick has not been with me since you left Toronto—Dan and family are well and I remain

Dear Paul
Your Father
Michael Kane

[Kane family papers]

Letter 2: Stewart Watson, London, to Paul Kane, Toronto

My Dear Kane.

If I were near you I should see whether the length of my *cane* could measure your Kane. What a long time has passed since you left us and not one line of remembrance. I will not accuse you either of neglect nor forgetfulness for it is more in nature to deny the possession of these evil qualities to the friends we regard than to bring them in array against them as excuse for what after all may have been unavoidable. So I will not blame you but gratify my vanity by thinking that as I have a kindly recollection of you that sometimes you will think so of us. I wrote you a very long letter to the care of your father at Toronto and therein gave you a sort of statement of my hopes and prospects. In it I said that much would depend on the success of my picture of St. Peters in the Exhibition of the Royal Academy and if it sold. My cattle pictures sold in Edinburgh and since that time I have sold other two fancy Italian subjects. This together with painting some Portraits has been my means of living but just as I had placed my picture of St. Peters in the Exhibition and had the satisfaction to see it well hung and in the expectation of selling it, the Art Unions were declared illegal and fourteen thousand pounds which had been collected this year for the purchase of pictures to have been disposed of by lottery so I have no hopes from that quarter. Our friend Stewart was here last year and we had many delightful talk of Italy and our good friend Paul Kane. He is settled in Edinburgh and had some good pictures in the last Exhibition. Syme has been ill again and wrote me that he thought of going to the Water Doctor in Germany to be healed in His "seat of honour." Kennedy's large picture was quite a failure, a horrid thing. The Academy talk of doing away entirely with the sending out a pensioner to Italy as Kennedy and the three before him came home worse than they went out. Salter wrote me two or three months ago from Rome. He was scouting about as he was wont with you in Venice, and was to return to England this fall. Dunbar had married a girl in Trastevarino, so he is settled for life in Rome. There was a good joke happened with him and White and a young Italian, the result was a challenge from Dunbar and he was put in jail, but he said "I am of an English Noble family and claim the privilege of being placed in St. Angelo." Here he had to pay about ten times as much as he would have done in the other jail, so he now boasts of the last year being the most eventful of his life. He turned Catholic—was a week in jail and married. Since writing this, Mrs. Watson hints that *you* told us this piece of news of Dunbar, if so, you'll excuse it. Our old friend, a Mr. Handyside, arrived here from Montreal shortly after your departure. He came on business with the Secretary of the Colonies here about the cause of Canada. He was very anxious that we should come out to Canada and settle. Now I do not think either it or the States a good place for us artists, but I have a very warm side to your side of the water, and particularly to a Canadian comfortable country house with plenty of wood and freedom. It is an up hill business in this country to be an artist and there [is] so much opposition. The artists here have all got fresco mad from the idea that the government intend to decorate the new Houses of Parliament. My friend Newcombe of New York wrote me some time ago. He gives a sad picture of America. Henry Inman has sold off and come to London where Mr. Huntingdon (who was in Italy shortly before you came), has also come to settle. Waugh is *married* and settled in *Philadelphia*, and Paul Kane is where? Do write soon and tell me. I have commenced my costumes. They are splendidly published by Akerman in the Strand but they do not yield me much. I think I have done pretty well thus far and will not give you any further news till you write me. I hope you will continue in your promise to give me free quarters if and when we arrive. I am still in the determination to come to Canada and to paint Indians and hope that I'll meet you and work together for in truth I am tired of England. Mrs. Watson desires to be kindly remembered to you and with my best regards believe me ever your affectionate friend,

> Stewart Watson,
> 91 Dean Street, Soho Square, London,
> 4 June 1844.

Mr. Martin with whom we staid at Russell St. was lost with his little son in a Steam Boat coming from Scotland.

[Kane family papers]

Letter 3: Sir George Simpson to Paul Kane

> Fort Frances, Lac à la Pluie,
> 31 May 1846.

My dear sir,

I enclose, according to promise, a Circular to the gentlemen of the H.B. Co's. Service which will secure you every assistance & attention throughout the country.—As there will be a boat or canoe sent from Ft. Alexander to Red River Settlement as soon as you arrive there, I think a visit to that place might be agreeable to you, especially as I might be able to put you in the way of being a spectator of the grand Buffalo hunts made in the plains in that vicinity. Wishing you a safe and pleasant voyage, I am

> My dear sir,
> Yours truly,
> G. Simpson.

P.S. I would strongly recommend you paying attention to the magnificent falls on the Winnipeg River.

> P. Kane, Esq.,
> En Route,
> Lac à la Pluie.

[Kane family papers]

Letter 4: Sir George Simpson to Hudson's Bay Co. Posts

> Fort Frances—Lac à la Pluie,
> 31 May 1846.

Gentlemen,

I have the pleasure to introduce to you the bearer hereof Mr. P. Kane an Artist, who has come to the country on a professional tour; and I have to request the favor of your showing that gentleman your kind attentions and the hospitalities of such of the Company's posts as he may visit; and you will be pleased to afford Mr. Kane passages from post to post in the Company's craft—free of charge.

> I am,
> Gentlemen,
> Your very obedt. sevt.,
> G. Simpson.

The Gentlemen of the
Hon. Hudsons Bay Co's. Service,
Ruperts Land and Elsewhere.

[Kane family papers]

Letter 5: Robert Cluston, Fort Garry, to Paul Kane

> Fort Garry, R. R. Settmts,
> 15 Decr. 1846.

Mr. Kane,
Edmonton House,
Sir,

While at St. Peter's last autumn I met Sir George Simpson on his way to Canada, and was requested by him to say that you would much oblige him, if you could send him a *Side* view of the Buffalo hunt, to match the one he has already got.—

> Believe me,
> Yours very truly,
> Robt. Cluston.

[Kane family papers]

Letter 6: James Douglas, Fort Vancouver, to Paul Kane

Fort Vancouver 31 May 1847.

Paul Kane Esquire,

My Dear Sir

As there is an Express about to start for Victoria, I do myself the pleasure of dispatching a note, in quest of you, which will I presume find you somewhere on the road, safe and well.

I hope you have had a useful, if not over agreeable journey, and that you have been as well rewarded, for all your trouble, as you expected when you left this place.

I have no doubt you have found much of the beautiful and the sublime in the scenery of Nisqually and the Sound beyond, which it will be a great pleasure to see, in all the freshness of nature, indelibly fixed, on the glowing canvas. I hope you have met with every assistance and attention from the gentlemen at the several establishments you have visited in course of your present journey, and I beg to mention that the canoe, which takes the present express to Victoria, will return immediately to Nisqually, and is wholly at your service, if you wish to take a passage by it on your way home. The Cadboro, Modeste and Cowilitz are unfortunately all wind bound in Baker's Bay and it is quite uncertain when they may get to sea, as the weather continues unfavourable. We have had no foreign arrivals since your departure.

Wishing you a safe and pleasant return,
Yours very truly,
James Douglas.

[Kane family papers]

*Letter 7: Certificate by Sir James Douglas respecting
Kane's sketches*

I have seen Mr. Kane's faithful and spirited sketches of Oregon Scenery, and have been perfectly delighted with these masterly delineations of places, rendered familiar by a residence of 20 years on the banks of the Columbia and N. West Coast.

The Indian Portraits and Costumes are perfect and it is impossible to give a better idea, than they Convey, of the dress and appearance of the Native inhabitants of this Country.

James Douglas,
C. Factor, Hudsons Bay Co.

Fort Vancouver,
30th June '47.

[Kane family papers]

Letter 8: Paul Kane to Peter S. Ogden, Fort Vancouver

Fort Colville, 20th 7 47

My dear Mr. Ogden,

I have just arrived from Mr. Walker & Eells where I have been most kindly received and hospitably entertained which I partly attribute to your letter having preceded me. I have to thank you for this, and many other marks of your kindness, which will be duly remembered and properly appreciated. I have made some valuable sketches on the Pavellion and in the Grand Coulie, the latter surpasses in grandeur and sublimity my fondest expectations. I thank you for your letter of the 2nd and the 4 Spectators. I am just packing up for my departure. Give my respects to Mr. Ogden, Mr. Cory and Mr. Douglas and all my old Friends. You will hear more from me the next time.

I remain,
Yours truly,
Paul Kane.

P.S. I am sorry you have not heard from Mr. Work. I hope in the Spring you may find it convenient to send me if not all at least a part of the Articles expected, Yours &.&. P. Kane.

[Kane family papers]

*Letter 9: Certificate by William McBean respecting
Kane's sketches*

I have been favoured with the sight of Mr. Kane's Sketches of Landscapes and Portraits, some of which he drew while passing a few days here, and am happy to remark that the whole is admirably and happily executed —with an exact and strong similitude to the Original.

Heartily wishing him every success and with sentiments of the greatest possible Respect and Esteem, I beg to subscribe myself,
and am, his Most Obt. Hum. Servant,

William McBean.
In charge of Fort Nez Perces or Wallawalla.
30th July 1847.

[Kane family papers]

Letter 10: Peter S. Ogden, Fort Vancouver, to Paul Kane

Oregon,
Vancouver, September 2nd, 1847.

My dear Kain:

Since you took your departure little has taken place here to vary the dull monotony with the exception of a visit of four Americans, 1 East Indian and one French ship, the latter loaded with one Archbishop and 21

Priests, Fathers & Nuns, the latter for the salvation of the morals of the Country have been selected with more than usual precautions, being composed of old Women pass'd forty and beauty at a very low discount. We are indebted to the Oregon Spectator in being visited by so many Ships, but I regret to say they left the Settlement with only half loads. We have also had a reinforcement of two Missionary Methodist Gent. to replace those on hand who have been ordered home and have obeyed orders. But now comes sad news indeed alas poor *Mrs. Corry* has been entirely eclipsed and thrown into the *shade*. You artists understand the meaning of this latter word better than I can describe it and shall leave it to you, know then that Capt. Drury of the East India Ship was accompanied by Mrs. Drury and the all-beautiful and accomplished Miss D. aged 18[;] altho' invited and passed and repassed the Ship twice could not muster sufficient resolution to pay my respects, not so with David McLoughlin, he did and at first sight fell a victim. It is no exaggeration, she is all I can assure you as I have described her, in this one and all who have seen her fully agree in opinion. Proposals have been duly and *regularly* made, the Lady, her Father and Mother, have all duly given their consent, but the old Gent has enacted such I consider most *cruel* terms and that no Father has a right to demand, that before marriage they both become Members of the R.C. Church and take the Sacrament prior to being united, you perhaps differ in opinion with me in regard to a Father's rights. I should certainly like to argue the point with you, but knowing you so well scarcely suppose there would be a difference. However, let all this remain for the present undecided and let me tell you the Ship and the young Lady have now gone to California and will return in November when David's fate will be decided. Now from what I have stated do you not think with the assistance of the imagination there is a *sublime* field for a sketch and you who have already done so much justice to the wild scenery of Oregon in this quarter and in the N. West Coast, could easily assert one with your pencil and indeed for the benefit of your friends and no doubt the Public also—It is to be doubly regretted that the weather during the winter was so unfavourable to your pursuits and your stay so short in the Interior country. You have no doubt added largely to your stock and I trust one day and that not far distant I shall have the pleasure of seeing them—This indeed has been a very warm summer and to convey to you some idea from the 17 August to 21 the Thermometer in the shade averaged 106 and May, June, & July a fair average was 95. What then must it have been in the Interior Country in these arid Plains. I expect to hear you have been almost burned alive. I hope you have however succeeded in making a large collection of Sketches and that they will reach their destination in safety. Mr. & Mrs. Corry still continue to reside within our Stockades in the same house (East End) that you so often visited and would from what I have heard be inclined to remain for the winter and no doubt will as their new House is far, very far from being completed.

Mr. Stanley is now going up to the Interior in quest of Scenery. What with Artists, Archbishops, Bishops, Priests, Nuns, Deacons and Fathers, 22 having lately arrived direct from *Brest* the country will be lost forever. At the Dalles a few days since the Americans, say seven in number, had a squabble, one of the seven killed and two nearly murdered and one slightly —the Indians one killed and two slightly wounded. The Gov. has gone to settle this affair, he will I fear make bad worse. 500 Waggons are on their way here and 500 waggons of Mormons have commenced a location at the South side of Great Salt Lake. Many parts of this letter will be almost unintelligible to you, but in the tedious passages you will have in ascending the Columbia you will have full time to decipher it and I only wish I were with you to assist you. Thank God the time is drawing night and before I bid you a safe passage across the Mountains and a pleasant winter, let me add, remember your promise—I shall write you in the Spring. Our ship is not yet arrived from the Coast, altho it has been expected the last ten days, but rest assured I shall not forget my promise in sending you whatever may come from Work.

Yours sincerely and truly,
Peter Skeen Ogden.

Mr. Graham is to be married this week to Miss Susan Birnier. Stanley is employed by Catlin, a friend of yours, to sketch for him. Indian Chiefs are in great demand with him.

[Kane family papers]

Letter 11: Certificate by John Lee Lewes respecting Kane's sketches

Fort Colvile, Columbia River,
September 16th, 1847.

Mr. Paul Kane during a residence of about six weeks with me, at Fort Colvile, Columbia River, several times let me have the opportunity of examining the many Sketches he had taken West of the Rocky Mountains, consisting of Landscape scenery, Groups of Indian figures, and individual likenesses of many Aboriginees of these parts. A residence of four Years on the Banks of the Columbia in the Service of the Hudson's Bay Company and thirty six Years in the same Employment, East of the Rocky Mountains, making a total of Forty Years constant intercourse with the many different Tribes of Natives who inhabit these vast regions, has given me many opportunities of seeing Indian life as it actually exists among them, and from a perfect knowledge I have of them, I here beg leave to testify that the sketches which Mr. Kane has taken, representing Indian Groups are most true and striking, their manners and customs are depicted with a correctness, that none but a Master hand could accomplish.

The individual likenesses are also of a first rate class, personal acquaintance with the greater portion of the Individuals from whom these Sketches were taken, enables me to vouch for their correctness, which are most striking and perfect likenesses of the living Originals.

The Landscape Scenery representing many parts of the Columbia River, with which I am well acquainted are also most correctly delineated, and from their truth to nature, well adapted to convey a Just Idea of the many Picturesque and romantic spots of the Columbia.

John Lee Lewes,
Chief Factor of the Hudson's Bay Comp.

[Kane family papers]

Letter 12: Sir George Simpson to Paul Kane

[undated; 1847?]

Mr. Kane,
My dear Sir,

I am disappointed in not hearing from you by the Spring express but was glad to learn that you were well and hope to hear that you have passed an agreeable time of it across the mountains.

I understand you are expected back to this side the mountains in the Autumn, with the intention of passing the winter in the Saskatchewan: while there I should feel greatly obliged if you would take for me some sketches of buffalo hunts, Indian camps, Councils, feasts, Conjuring matches, dances, warlike exhibitions or any other scenes of savage life that you may consider likely to be attractive or interesting, with a view to their being coloured and framed, &, of equal size so as to match each other.—As you are likely to have a long winter before you, perhaps you could prepare a dozen and upon as large a scale in point of size as possible. In taking the sketch of the buffalo hunt you were good enough to send me last year, you must have stood in the rear of the herd; a side view would have given a better idea of the appearance of the animals, as from the hind view, it required a little explanation to make a stranger understand that the mass of dark objects before him, were intended either for buffalo or any other living animals.

I shall expect the pleasure of seeing you at Norway House next spring, meantime believe me,

My dear Sir,
Truly yours,
G. Simpson.

P.S. I intend the sketches applied for, if you would be good enough to provide them, to be framed and hung up in a room I design as a museum for Indian curiosities.

[Kane family papers]

Letter 13: Paul Kane to John Lee Lewes

Edmonton House, March 2nd, 1848

My Dear Sir;

You are aware before this that you are expected on this side of the Mountains. Had you come you would have had to walk to Fort Assiniboine or remain at Jaspers all winter, as the river set fast before I arrived there. I was fourteen days, and suffered a good deal from "Mal des rakettes" and want of provisions. I arrived at Edmonton on the 6th December, being 75 days from your hospitable mansion. I left the two Boys to rusticate at Jaspers as it was impossible for them to walk so far, especially the fat one who got still fatter on the voyage. Your keg of sugar I left with Mr. Fraser in good order. I intended to open your Cassette at Fort Assinboine and found that the Keys you gave me which I enclose, would not fit the Lock. It was apparently dry and uninjured, so I left it. We had had a Wedding here lately, a Daughter of Mr. Harriott's by a former wife, to Mr. John Rowand. I accompanied them to Fort Pitt and have just returned.

Give my best respects to Mrs. Lewes, Frederick and Mr. McArthur.

I remain,
Yours truly,
Paul Kane.

To John Lee Lewes
Colville.

[Kane family papers]

Letter 14: Peter S. Ogden to Paul Kane

Vancouver, March 12, 1848

My dear Kane,

Many thanks for your friendly *notice* of me in yours from Colville which reached here on the 20th Nov. earlier than the year preceding as you can truly vouch for. Now friend before I proceed further I give you fair warning I am writing by candle light and intend to inflict on you a long letter and as my writing is at the best very unintelligible if you have not a good stock of patience, had better throw this sheet in the fire without even giving it a perusal or your patience a severe trial for only on it both must go through the ordeal so God help and assist and grant you a safe deliverance.—I was indeed glad to hear the wild scenery of the Interior of Oregon far exceeded your expectations and your time was amply repaid. In this opinion you agree with Stanley who has gone over from what he tells me privately the same Country and will now shortly leave this Country for the Islands. The only difference between your two cases, on his return to Walla Walla had a most narrow escape of his life but more of this before I finish my letter and let me in the interim proceed to transact business together. The memo. of curiosities you requested from the Coast came duly in the Fall 15th Oct. but by no means so complete as I had expected but my friend Work excuses himself on the plea of want of sufficent time to obtain more and this I verily believe to be true. I now forward you a copy of what was received and what is now forwarded and from the precautions I have taken trust will reach you in safety and shall only regret if they do not as I verily believe you did not expect I would have taken any interest in your affairs after you were gone, and so long as I remain shall be most happy to render you all the assistance in my power to promote your views.

We have had very dull and gloomy times since the Fall.—The American Immigration consisting four thousand Souls if they have any, brought in with them their pleasant travelling companions the Measles, Dysentry and Typhus Fever. All these found a fair field to employ themselves in, soon lost fourteen men. In this number was the Guide who you must have seen last Summer in Mr. Lewis boat, about forty Americans, Sixty five individuals in the French Settlement, but the Indian population as usual shared most conspicuous. On the occasion from the Col[umbia] River alone fifteen hundred died. You will remark this, the Cowlitz, Nisqually and Pugets Sound are not included but I am still in hopes to receive a report from them before the Express starts and if I do, you shall have it—The last account we had the Measles had reached Whidby Island and I presume will travel all over the Coast and you may easily imagine the Indians residing in villages what destruction it will make—At Walla Walla the Cayuse imputed their deaths to Dr. Whitman's medicines and in retaliation murdered not only him but his worthy wife and twelve Americans. This indeed was a cruel deed and [they] retained including Spalding Mission upwards of sixty Individuals, Men, Women and Children in captivity to redeem their unfortunate fellow beings, and fortunately surrendered. I made a trip to Walla Wala but you will find all particulars connected with this affair in the Paper I now forward you. I had rather an unpleasant trip but humanity dictated the propriety of going to their relief—and has also enabled me to write a sketch on this melancholy subject and as I *felt* the subject those who have perused it agree in saying I have done it every justice, even your particular friend Mrs. Corry agrees in opinion even as well as *Richard*—and I can assure you pleases *self*. Stanley has also employed his talents on the same subject which accompanies my sketch and also tends greatly to improve mine. I have already alluded to Stanley's *narrow* escape—two days after the Massacre on his return from Mr. Spaldings and when within five miles of the Drs. Mission an Indian from the latter place met him (a Cayuse) and with a Pistol cocked presented at his head in a threatening wise demanded to know if he was an American or French. Fortunately Stanley did not understand him but still more so he replied he was an Il lyena (A Frenchman), when he was ordered to lose no time in reaching the Fort, which advice he readily followed, and escaped a cruel death. Poor Barclay lost his eldest son, a most severe blow to them. This was the only death inside the Pickets. At one time for nearly four weeks there were not including Gent. six that were not laid low. During this period the Doctor's berth was no sinecure. As for myself I was about at the time and only came in for a slight attack of Dysentry. Mr. and Mrs. Corry still continue to occupy the same house and fill the most important situation. In April they propose leaving us as they have made *some* progress with their house. It is *now sound*. This has occupied the little Man's attention since you left this and he thinks he has made real progress. At present War is raging in the Interior. Four Hundred Americans have gone up to Walla Wala and we are uneasy about getting the Express up. It goes by a new *route* and Love has charge of it. The present War has already cost two hundred and fifty six thousand dollars and its present daily expense is equal to fifteen hundred per day. Do you think Uncle Sam will consent to all this? There are a variety of opinions on the subject—May I hope to hear from you. Recollect your promise. I know I can depend on you. May we hope to meet again in 49. I am making every preparation for it—

Yrs. Truly and Sincerely,
Peter Skeen Ogden.

[Kane family papers]

Letter 15: Hector E. McKenzie to Paul Kane

Lesser Slave Lake, March 24th, 1848

My Dear Sir,

I must now redeem the promise that I gave you in parting and endeavour to give you an account of our trip, altho this trip was like other trips in this country with the possession of little or no interest.—We found Mr. Brazeau with whom we remained for two and a half days, recounting the extraordinary success he had had in the way of being a Lynx catcher together with sundry other matters. The Weather for Voyaging was tolerably fine till we reached this Lake when a Storm caught us on the middle of a traverse accompanied by snow that you could not see the length of your nose if you were to be paid a thousand dollars more or less. The snow was so thick that we could not see land in any direction so that we did not know which way to go—for instead of going straight we were going in an opposite direction until Belleface undertook to guide up to the place we intended to reach, and performed it satisfactorily of which he was not a little vain. I must give the poor devil his due, there was not one of us who could have found the place we intended to cross to until the storm had been over. We reached this place on the 22nd Inst. and found Mr. McDougall together with the Mrs. & Miss with the rest of the bantlings in good Health. We are to start for Dunvegan tomorrow and Mr. McDougall is providing everything for our comfort for the journey because he wants us away from here. That accounts for the milk &—For I am persuaded that he would not have been so attentive to our comfort En Route to Dunvegan if the circumstances were otherwise—Mr. Priest Bourrassa come from Dunvegan on our arrival there and perhaps you will have the pleasure of seeing him at Edmonton.—He is another Beauty and will no doubt afford you a good subject for your art—How goes the *Backgammon Board* science versus Luck & *vice versa*.

I still remember the promise I made you of getting a Bow &c when I get to McKenzie River. Let me know what will be your address when you will be locating at Toronto—I have nothing particular to add more to this scroll so I will conclude in wishing you every blessing,

I am,
My Dear Sir
Your most obedient & Grateful Servt.
Hector E. McKenzie.

P.S. Please send me a copy of "Poor Lucy Neale".

H. McK.

Mr. Paul Kane,
Edmonton.

[Kane family papers]

Letter 16: Sir George Simpson to Paul Kane

Hudson's Bay House,
Lachine 9 Nov. 1848.

My dear Sir,

The pressure of business has prevented my earlier acknowledging receipt of your letter of 22 October, by which I was happy to learn that you had reached home in safety, after your extended wanderings in the Indian country.

With reference to the mode of bringing out your proposed publication. I think the best plan would be to do it by subscription, and as it would be necessary to travel about to collect subscribers, you might, by giving attention to the portrait painting branch of your art in the principal towns you would visit, I should think make sufficient to clear your expenses.—I naturally feel a great interest in your undertaking, and if you decide on adopting the plan of publishing by subscription, I should do my best towards inducing my friends to enter their names upon your list.

I am sorry to hear that some of your paintings were damaged on the way down; I hope however, your collection has not sustained any material injury, which would indeed have been mortifying, after having expended so much time and labour upon them.

Your account which reached me by the last Canoe from the interior, is enclosed, showing a balance against you of £-14.6.9 Cy.

I remain,
My dear sir,
Yours very faithfully,
G. Simpson.

Paul Kane, Esq.,
Toronto.

[Kane family papers]

Letter 17: Sir George Simpson to Paul Kane

Hudson's Bay House,
Lachine, 19 January
1849.

My dear Sir,

I have to acknowledge your letter of 3 inst. accompanying the ten sketches [see Appendix 4], which came safely to hand and for which I am much obliged. I shall be glad to receive at your convenience the remaining 4 sketches you are preparing for me, accompanied by a Memo of what I am indebted to you for these pictures, which I prize very highly.

I am happy to hear your exhibition at Toronto fully answered your expectation. I think that the present would be a favourable time for you to open a similar exhibition in Montreal, when the town is full of strangers, owing to the meeting of Parliament—and I should have much pleasure in promoting your views here by any means in my power.—

The amount enclosed in your note was quite correct and has squared your little account from the interior.

I remain,
My dear Sir,
Yours very faithfully,
G. Simpson.

Paul Kane, Esq.,
Toronto.

[Kane family papers]

Letter 18: Sir E. Poore to Lady Poore

Datestamp: Galena, Illinois, May 4

Up the Mississippi,
May 2, 1849.

Dear Mother,

Here we are all safe and sound as yet, about 250 miles above St. Louis. On the Steamer Dr. Franklin No. 2 (coming down from Cincinnati) one man died on board of the cholera and we had 5 other cases of it. Philips has been very much frightened about it and was wishing every day to get away from St. Louis. We were 6 days getting down from Buffalo to Sandusky a 3 day passage, but taking the journey altogether we have got on very well. I expect I shall not be able to write to you again till we get to Vancouver's Island.

I called on the American Fur Company but I could not see them. This will be mailed at Galena, the great Lead mines of the West. It was a miserable thing to see a man die as that one I spoke of did away from home. He had left from home with $5000 to buy cattle, was taken sick and did not tell any one of it till 2 days after and in the middle of the 2nd day he died. They made a kind of a coffin for him and when about 7 miles above Cairo cut a cross on a tree and buried him under it, some kind of parson said a kind of a sermon over him and we left again. I should think we met and passed about 70 or 80 men going to California, everyone seemed to be mad after gold. Tell Stew I paid Kane for his pictures. Love to all.

Aff. Love,
E. Poore

[Poore family papers]

Letter 19: Sir E. Poore to Lady Poore

Red River,
June 18, [1849]

Dear Mother,

Since we left St. Peaters we have had nothing but bad luck. We left there on the 15 of May with one cart, 5 mules & 5 horses & one guide & his horse. On the road we got another cart & horse & a canoe. Philips one morn tied his horse up to the cart with the canoe on it (the canoe is to cross the rivers with, many very bad), some thing frightened him & he threw his head up & broke about 4 ft. off the end of it. All the way we have had mud, water, etc. for it has been a very wet season & the carts would stick & we had to get off into the water—Frank, the Guide, & myself often up to our waists in water, a thing Kane or Philips would never do if it was possible to avoid. I wish so much F. & I had come alone as we first intended. One evening we came to a large village of Indians who would not let us pass for some time so we made as tho we would camp but told the Chief that we had got a lot of papers &c which some of them were about them. & that they *might* be about presents which if they kept us *might be* withheld from them (They have only had presents once). In about 2 hours we were allowed to pass & we went on till 11 P.M. Two days after as we were helping the carts thro a river (Rice R.) the guide said he heard a shout, the horses and two pack mules with all our provisions (except tea) were over on this side the Hs., tied up; when we got the carts thro we went to get on our horses, my 3, the guides & the two pack mules were *gone*, hunted about for the trail, found it. I got on a black pony, took my rifle & F. his & off we started after them. Kane was on the pony but would not go because we thought the horses had been stolen by Indians & we might if we came up to them have to fight. I had run a stick up into my foot which was the reason I rode. F & I found the h[orses] had gone off full gallop, in going they had kept bushes between us & them the whole way & had gone nearly in a direct line E.N.E. The ground was in many places very swampy & full of rabbit holes in others, but they had not gone into a single swamp nor over one rabbit hole. In going on we thought we heard a hollow & when we came up to the place found the horses had stopped & walked about 100 yds. & started again full jump proving, all things taken together, no doubt they were in the hands of Indians. Left the trail at dark, got back to camp & as the rest had eaten what they could lay their hands on F. & I made supper off *Tea leaves they had used and sugar*. Started on next day. On the 5th of this month as I was driving one of the carts (we had to get on as we best could) now & eat what we could kill (i.e. such birds &c no large animals) I was turned out by having the horses hind foot put in my mouth (i.e. kicked). I spit out at once the tooth on the right side of the front ones & the front one next it was driven at an angle of 45 in my mouth, broke the roof & split my upper lip about an inch and a half down towards my chin right thro. F. & I started to ride here (it was about 60 miles from this). That night we swam one river (Rat R.) so I was wet all night having

got ½ dry by a fire we made. When we arrived here (started next morn at 4 A.M. and here at 10) the Dr. was sick with the gout & ten miles off so I doctored myself & am nearly well now. Philipps after we left him in trying to cut down a tree the axe slippped & he cut his foot ½ off & is now in bed. F. & I are going to start tomorrow on a buffalo hunt *by ourselves*. I suppose we will be away about 3 weeks, hope P. will be fit to go on by that time.

Affte. Love,
E. Poore

I shall not have another chance of writing till I get to the Columbia. I am going to send 2 Boxes from here with 150 Buffalo tongues & Bosses which will arrive in London about the end of September & be directed to you Care of the Hudson Bay Co. & you must send & fetch it.

[Poore family papers]

Letter 20: Sir E. Poore to Lady Poore

Fort Garry, Ruperts Land (i.e. Red River)

Dear Mother,

This morn Frank & myself start for the Columbia with *one old Indian & a half breed* of the place. Charley stays the winter here & I had intended to do so also but then I thought it would be a waste of time & money. Kane we found out is a regular imposter or humbug, he has only crossed the *mountains* in the *company's boats*, i.e. they go nearly all the way in them. Tell George that by incessant practice I can use the lasso like an Indian. When you get this send *Bill* down to the H'ble Hudsons Bay House (I think it is in Fenchurch Street No. 4 or 5) and ask for 3 boxes directed to you at Inverness Road to be left there till called for, one of them with myne & Frank's watch which have got broken. Will you have them mended & send them to Stuarts by the first opportunity. There is also all the odds and ends I could pick up in so short a time, in the nest of boxes there is a small piece of paper with Lady Poore on it in which is contained 3 pieces of E. Poore's upper jaw which have come out since his teeth were kicked by the pony's foot; the other two are full of Buffalo tongues and Bosses, they *must be soaked in water* 24 hours before being boiled to be good. The hair line in the small box is an Indian bridle and bit just like the one I use. I would have sent a saddle to match but it is too good a one to ride on but I will bring it or send it home some day. You ought to see me now with *long hair, earrings,* leather *trousers fringed* & all the other fixings belonging to a half breed. Kane we are going to send back for he is *of no use whatever* so I *suppose* all the drawing I shall ever do you might stick in your eye. It is likely when I get to Cali[fornia] that I shall try a little in the cattle line as I know a man that is there in it and I think I should make a very good *riding partner*. Tell George I think I have at last found a place for him to emigrate to *Pugets Sound*, no winter in fact everything he could want but more of that when I have seen to it. I will write an account of it from Fort Vancouver. We shall have to pass through the Black feet country, *the* worst

333

in all America but I hope we shall get on all right (not get our hair lifted). Frank I like *more & more*. We pull so well together & I believe he would go thro thick & thin with me. With best love to all believe me dear Mother,

to be yr aff
Son (the wild)
E. Poore.

[Poore family papers]

Letter 21: Sir Edward Poore to Lady Poore

Fort Vancouver,
Nov. 19, 1849.

Dear Mother,

I suppose you will be anxious to here how yr. hopeful gets on so here he is in a state of high preservation but *very thin*, Do. Franklin. After I wrote to you finding Kane such a very disagreeable person, we gave him money to quit & poor Philip's foot was not in a fit state to travel (We waited 50 days) so I told him F & I had made up our minds to start. We had tried hard to get a passage by the boats but Sir G. Simpson would not give in and I found out after it was because of Kane. F. & I started from Red R. on the 27th of July with 7 horses, 8 mules, an Indian & a half breed (i.e. half Ind.). Mosquitoes very bad, in fact we and the poor animals were nearly eaten up with them. After various adventures not good enough to write here except our guide (the Ind.) lost the way twice, as we were riding along we saw a *Buffalo Bull*, didn't I feel queer just kind of all overish, changed horses on to *My Hunter*, a little blue poney, one that had come from the Blackfeet Ind., very fast, Do. F. & off we started. The beast had got scent of us & had started but we were bound to catch him. They have a most extraordinary gallop. After a long race I suppose it must have been 5 miles, I was about 100 yds. in front of F. I was putting in the best licks to get alongside to fire, the poney put his foot in a badger hole (it is quite extraordinary the number of them & their formation. They are made first by the ground squirrel and dug out & eaten by the badgers. They are about a foot over & 3 to 5 ft. deep straight down) & came over such a buster his nose was the first part that came to the ground & then his ears & then his tail. F. came up. Are you hurt? No, says I, go on. Got up & when I came up to him again he had fired & broke his shoulder. Two more shots finished him. The guide had told us to take the tenderloin & tongue out. The next thing was to do it. After cutting about ½ an hour got out about 20 lb. of meat which I thought was the loin & F. tried the tongue. He got hold of what we thought was the wind pipe but turned out to be the tongue. Next thing, where were the rest. Looked around for the tracks & when we came to them there were Crees with them. Went to their camp & found 30 tents of them, 14 Stonees & 10 Chipeways & stayed with them that night & next day. I felt very much shook when I got cool. Two days after we had to cross the South Branch R. We came and nooned there. The

Ind. went down to a point to bind some willows together in that [oval framework] shape. The things were then put on the top & the oil clothes under & the ends or the sides brought to the top & drawn together with a string. It makes a first rate boat. Goulat said, well something is wrong for old hog back is running (he had not hurried himself before). When he came he said that he had seen eight Indian tracks & he said that he thought they were an advance guard of a party of B[lack]feet Indians. We expected them to fire on us as soon as we were in the water. We then made the oil cloth boats striped & tied the two boats to *2 horses tails* to swim over, but after three trials we found it would not act, so made two paddles and got on over and Goulat on the other. We then (the Ind. and me) swam the horses over. I got on one but he rolled so he struck my foot so I left him and swam on my own hook. It was a long swim & water *very* cold. By the time I got over I had had as much as I wanted & shook as if I had the ague. The next day July 14 we came to Carlton House, a dirty little fort. From there we took 6 fresh horses, left the Ind. & took 2 other men. Fort Pitt without anything of consequence. From there to Edmonton House saw plenty of buffalo. Great fun running them. I wrote to Philips who intended to stay at R. R. till next spring & come up by the boats. This country is *not what it is cracked up to be*. We were very nearly turning back from this to go back from this & I really did not think it was worth the trouble so far to see. Hunting there is next to none & little excitement excepting driving 10 loose & pack horses if that is any. About 300 B[lack]feet Ind. had just left. Some of them had fallen in with two tents of Crees & wounded two. If we had fallen in then it would have been bad for our health. They were so frightened at this that we could not get a guide across the mountains so we had to wait there 26 days for the boats. In going up the Athabasca R. one of the men fell in the water & I was the only one that went in after him. The water was bitter cold & current strong. Two days after F. shot two red deer. The day before I had had a little pain in my chest & that morn it was so bad I could hardly get to the place. It was about a mile from the R. It has worn nearly off now. In crossing the mountain portage a most melancholy accident happened the gentleman in charge, a very agreeable person by the name of Charles. One even after camp a raven came & set on a tree close by. F. took his rifle and missed it. I laughed at him when he said he could drive in any knot in a tree you like to show. I pointed out one. No, stop said Charles, let us all have a shot for a shilling apiece, the best to win. There was an oldish man of the name of Young who had an American rifle I had warned him as being a very dangerous one & apt to go off. C. said to him, come out & bring yr. old rifle (F. & I had plugged up the nipple partly thro fun & danger but he had got it off) & have a shot. He came out and fired & returned into the tent loaded. They were standing round the fire, C. with his back to it, F. with his face facing two other young clerks & the cook. I had been to make a mark. As Young came out of the tent the rifle went off and shot poor Charles in the right breast (F. was singed). He fell nearly into the fire which we put out and got the tent over him. He never spoke after. Once he appeared to be sensible but directly after his face resumed the same stupid look. He was in great pain, said "let me go" twice & "mercy" once.

He also spoke of what we took to be some words of Cree but we could not make them out. The only sentence he spoke was "that was well done, Mr. Young." He then sat up & looked round wildly & banged down & died. He suffered about two hours. Next morning we rolled him in 3 blankets & buried him making after a small log house over him.

At Boat Encampment we took the boats to come down the Columbia. Arrived at Colvil safe, started again & two days after running a rapid ours was the 2nd boat (there were two) we ran up agst. a rock and smashed, scrambled on the rock 10 of us. The boat broke in two and two persons sat on the part of the boat that was left. It was as much as the 10 of us could do to stand on the rock it was so small. The other boat knocked a hole in herself & was just sinking when she got to land. There we were for nearly 4 hours, the water nearly up to my knees, all the time very cold & the current about 15 miles per hr. They mended the other boat and with difficulty took us off. At Walla Walla they fired twice out of a cannon & the second time as the man was ramming down, it went off & nearly took his head off. It was an awful sight, the hand was only hanging by a few cords. I told them they had better cut it off, but none of them would do it. The Dr. here has taken his arm off today at the elbow. He is a Sandwich Islander. Fancy a common teamster or carter gets here *now $125 per month,* sailors $150, cook & steward $200, mate $350, capt. $500. By these you may judge of wages. The commonest board in California is from *$5 to $7 a day* cord trousers here $10, 3 point blanket $10, etc. potatoes $3 & 4 the bushel. What direction we are going now, dear mother, I do not know. They say here we ought to go back by Mexico but time will show. Give my best love to all the sisters at home '& abroad. The cholera is not in California yet. Tell Stewart when you write to him that we have often wished he could have seen us when we have been in a fix, how he would have laughed at us in many places. Over 3,000 people have come *over land across the Interior* to California. One man told me they had passed on an average 10 graves a day on the road. Nearly one half the people at the diggings have died & there they lay unburied, all are in such a hurry for gold. The seeds are small shrubs they grow in a sandy soil. I have not read this over. You must forgive mistakes.

Love,
E. Poore.

[Poore family papers]

Letter 22: James Douglas to Paul Kane

Fort Victoria,
16th Jany. 1851.

My dear Sir,

I had the pleasure of your communication from Toronto, in November last by our Express from York Factory. I was truly happy to hear of your welfare and of the great encouragement you had received both at home and from abroad, in publishing your Indian sketches, a work which I

trust may prove as profitable in a pecuniary way, as I have no doubt, it will be honourable to your talents, as an artist.

I shall be very happy to contribute my mite towards the success and completeness of your work, though I am rather at a loss how articles of dress could be forwarded from this country to Canada without putting you to a serious expense. Probably the least objectionable plan would be to ship them to England by the Company's annual vessel—from thence to be forwarded to Canada. Pray inform me if that would answer. I regret that you have not received the Kodiak dress, which according to promise, I left at Vancouver, on my appointment to Fort Victoria, with Mr. Ogden, to forward by the express in the autumn. It must have remained by the way, as I have no doubt Ogden sent it on—and it may probably yet reach you. [The Kodiak dress must have, in fact, reached Kane. It is now in the collections of the Manitoba Museum of Science and History, Winnipeg.]

Sir Edward Poore spent the greater part of last winter at this place and left us in spring to recross the mountains. He was not much edified nor greatly charmed with his north western journey; our country in fact possesses few attractions except to men of business, and it is not likely to please the mere pleasure hunter.

I am sorry to observe that the fatal spirit of disunion has not yet been suppressed in Canada—there may be grievances as there must necessarily be imperfections in all human institutions, but it is not in annexation that I would seek for relief were I a Canadian. Had you as much of Yankee justice and liberality as we have in this quarter, the idea of annexation would soon lose its charm.

I shall be happy to hear from you as often as convenient.

With best wishes,
I remain,
Dear Sir,
Yours truly,
James Douglas.

[Kane family papers]

Letter 23: Peter S. Ogden to Paul Kane

Vancouver, March 18th, 1851.

My dear Kane,

Many thanks for your friendly letter dated Toronto March 26th 1850 which the Fall express safely delivered me at least six weeks earlier than you arrived here. I was disappointed in not seeing you here with Sir Edward. The latter did not make a *deep* impression with the *Vancouver Dandys* and still less with the military who often remarked he could be no Gent., having no regard to dress—so you see the external garment is their criterion of a Gent.—altho I am not overfond of dress, still I am of opinion the rules of propriety should in all things be strictly observed which I must say Sir Edward lost sight of. What has become of the Man and friend Franklin, truly a free young Man. Now Kane let me give you a little Vancouver news—Two years since Douglas was appointed to Vancouver's

Island & Depy. Governor Richard Blows Lane, appointed by the Queen. Did you ever read of [undecipherable] being Governor of [undecipherable], something very similar to the situation they hold there and so long as Gold Mines are in existence no one will be so rash as to land and settle there. In fact here the Oregonians are constantly in motion and their eyes and ears are open and at the slightest report all are ready to start. I regretted much to learn the fate of the curiosities. I had taken great care in packing them and strongly recommended the parcel to Mr. Lane who promised fair. I had also taken the same precaution with the Guide but as the latter is dead we cannot well call him to an account and as Love is no longer in the Company's service it is useless to say a word to him on the subject. Had they been in time to forward by the Fall Express would have reached you in safety. They were a fine collection—it is not impossible but I pay you a visit before many years. We have now regular Mails via Panama and we have monthly news from England and the States. This is a great change for the better but it adds greatly to my labours. Thank God for all, and except the fever I have no cause to complain on the score of health. Glad to learn your paintings and sketches give you full employment. I hope they may prove lucrative. I hear Stanley is massing a rich harvest from his travels in Oregon, the Islands and California. He did not visit Vancouver's Island so there in regard to wild scenery and Rocky Mountains you have decidedly the advantage over him. He is a worthy young Man and I heartily wish *you* every success. Mr. and Mrs. Compton reside at 4th Plain about seven Miles from this place. He finds farming on a gravelly soil not very lucrative and is gaining a livelihood by painting and Mrs. C. teaches the young ideas [?] how to shoot. She is as fascinating as ever and much admired by the Officers. Amongst the latter here there's one a great favourite of mine. Bales & Scriven are the order of the day. They have a splendid Brass band and good German musicians—we have (officers) a good billiard table—have Parties nightly in fact as gay as we would be if in Toronto for we have a Gov., also Judges, Atty. General, Sectys. Lawyers and Doctors by the Gross. In fact we have a general assortment but I trust you will make no further enquiries as to what kind of Gents they are. Should your inclination and interest ever again lead you again to this place rest assured of a hearty welcome from

Yrs. Truly and Sincerely,
Peter Skeen Ogden.

Write me when your inclination leads your thoughts towards an Exile. Lane, Mackinlay, Law & Allen have all become merchants on their own accounts.

[Kane family papers]

Letter 24: J. C. Taché to Paul Kane

5 Aoust, 1851.

My Dear Sir,

I am infinitely glad to inform you that Mr. Uniacke and me having brought your case before the House, we have entirely succeeded. Now no doubt will remain in one way or another you'll get at least £250. This day, mark it, is a day of reward for your exertions as an artist. The Legislature of your country have eulogized you, the most eminent men have praised your talents. Two hours have been expended in exalting your talents and your energy. This is not flattery, this is the truth.

Here are the names of the Gentlemen that have spoken with the more warmth in your favor, MM. Uniacke, Elmslie, Baldwin, Sherwood, Chairman, and

Your friend,
J. C. Taché.

Paul Kane, Esqr.
  Toronto.
[Kane family papers]

Appendix 11
Paul Kane in Alabama, 1841

"THE FINE ARTS—MR. KANE"

Commercial Register (Mobile, Alabama), March 20, 1841

Every body recollects the sneering remark of a Scotch reviewer, made twenty years since, "Who reads an American book?" The coxcomb would be mortified (were he alive) by being asked, "Who does not read American books?" Then, both literature and art, on this western continent, were in their infancy, now there is a hopeful prospect that we shall be able to pay back with interest, our obligations to Great Britain for the loan of her genius. In science and mechanics, she boasts little advantage of us. In literature we may not yet have sowed our wild oats. Like lusty youth, we often violate all rules, and begin to teach before we have learned anything ourselves; nevertheless we have names which will be coeval with the memory of English genius. Our greatest deficiency is in imaginative literature, or rather we are more prolific in imaginative trash, than our European mother:—but who is unwise enough to expect poetry from a nation in its apprenticeship? From men who are placed in a field where every thing invites them to labor for a competency, and among whom there is little of aristocratic habit and wealth, and none of that condition of society which marked the Augustan, Medicean and Elizabethan ages of literature! A nation must have some experience in luxury; the descent of property must be such as to ensure its accumulation and stability, giving leisure for idleness and engendering a habit of magnificence and display, before any adequate patronage can be imparted to literature and the fine arts. Either men must be liberally paid for their genius or society must be so constituted as to oblige genius to spin its silken web or languish in want and starve in obscurity. This was the condition of England when a hot roll secured, simultaneously, death, immortality, and a tomb in Westminster abbey to Otway.

In this country, if a genius cannot live by his poetry, he can learn a trade, serve as a clerk, or go out into the new country, seize the plough, and, like Cincinnatus "greatly independent live." Poetry is a starving and contemptible business among a hard working nation, and that is the main reason why it is so badly followed here.

In art we may soon be able to show John Bull specimens that will put Sir Arthur Shea and the whole Royal Academy to the blush. Sully has borne the palm from the best English portrait painters, and Alston, in Boston, is now engaged on a historical picture which is likely to rival Martin or Dubuffe's most celebrated works. In sculpture, Cincinatti has nourished artists who, although mere boys, have given a tone to our national character in Europe. The genius of Power, now languishing in poverty among the classical sculpture of Italy, has excited the wonder and admiration of the best European critics; and Greenough has just shipped from Florence a colossal statue of Washington, which probably could not be surpassed or reached by Thorwaldsen, the most eminent sculptor now living. We may yet (who knows?) rival Apelles and Praxiteles.

This, however, is a wandering from my purpose.—My object is to direct public attention to the paintings of Mr. PAUL KANE, an artist who has lived among us some ten or twelve months. This gentleman's full length VICTORIA, after the picture by *Chalons* [*sic.*] of the Royal Academy, is indicative of a high degree of talent. In point of merit, the work approaches that of the original artist from the fact that it is a full length copy of a *miniature engraving.** The colouring and tone, with the masses of light and shade, are peculiar to himself. The drapery is so disposed as always to present, no matter how frequently examined, the most graceful and easy curvatures, and its tints are gorgeous and brilliant in the extreme. The flesh is clear and transparent, while the limbs and immediate adjuncts of the figure, are presented to the eye through a purity and silvery clearness of tone, which gives to them almost the distinctness of *bas relief*. There are besides, a dignity and a sort of aristocratic self-possession about the whole which one naturally expects to find in everything connected with royalty. This quality is by no means the least difficult part of the art. How far the work is a correct likeness, I am unable to judge; but it seems to me to embody my idea of Her Majesty, as drawn from reading the best descriptions of her personal appearance. Without much sweetness of character or femininity of expression, there is a great deal of benevolence of feeling in her portrait, resulting one would suppose, while looking at the round, lusty, rather Dutch-built figure, as much from high health and the activity of vivativeness, as from native disposition. The stock whence her Majesty comes was never remarkable for loftiness of character or genius, and Victoria seems to be no exception to the rule.

There is one objection in my mind to this picture, and that is the want of finish in the less essential parts of the work. I hold this to be a defect, although in a measure recommended by that great master, Sir Joshua Reynolds, with Northcote among many other eminent men among his pupils.—Modern critics on the art, among whom is the acute Hazlett, have attributed a very prejudiced influence to this error. The most celebrated pictures of the greatest artists are those which are the most finished—in which the details are as complete as the superior parts of the work. A good painter, by a proper disposition of his details and the use of colors which heighten the contrast while preserving the harmony of the parts, need apprehend little danger of the less essential destroying the effect of the more essential parts. The theory of Reynolds has made many a man of genius a slovenly, careless dauber.

In half-length figures, Mr. Kane excels. His portraits are very striking, as much from their correct likeness as from the baldness of their outline, their softness and dignity, and the transparency of their coloring. His picture of General Harrison, painted at a very short notice, is exceedingly life-like, and the masses of light and shade and depth of coloring are as much like those described of Rembrandt as the works of any young artist I have seen. If there is any objection to his portraits, it is a little stiffness, which I am disposed to attribute to the constrained posture that most sitters maintain, rather than to the artist. Ease and grace are everything in a portrait. Even negligence is better than stiffness. This, however, will be found a capital defect, in almost all portraiture—a defect which can only be readily observed by seeing a great number of pictures together. There is a sameness in the attitude—a sort of holiday or Sunday appearance about the figures as though they had put on their best looks to suit the occasion. Variety in this department of the art is a great excellence and deserves a more attentive study from the fact that there is so little scope for its exertion.

Mr. Kane, however, has other merits beside those of an artist. He is a gentleman and a very clever fellow, and is always happy to see visitors to his studio, whether they come from mere curiosity or as visitors.

B.

---

* NOTE. Although the copy of an engraving, I am assured that Mr. Kane's Victoria is as correct a likeness as the original painting itself. It differs somewhat from that of Sully in portraiture, and in attitude, is, as a picture (not a work of art), infinitely more imposing and interesting.

Appendix 12
Paul Kane before the Parliament of Canada, 1856

(*Journals* of the Legislative Assembly of Canada, 1856, pp. 556–57)

Mr. *Paul Kane* begs leave to bring under the notice of the Contingent Committee the following circumstances connected with his agreement to furnish the House of Assembly with twelve Paintings, in consideration of receiving £500, which was paid to him in 1851:—

In the first place, Mr. *Kane* begs to state that the understanding arrived at between Mr. *Hincks*, Mr. *Malcolm Cameron*, and the other Gentlemen with whom he was in communication when the grant referred to was made, was that the Paintings should only be supplied to the House after Mr. *Kane* had finished his complete series, which he has now been exclusively engaged at for eleven years and has not yet accomplished. The object of his application to the House was for a gratuity to enable him to devote himself entirely to that work with a view to the publication of his Pictures, in illustration of a narrative of his travels and adventures in the North-West, which he intended, and still intends giving to the Press. It will be obvious to the Committee, and this view was at once admitted to be reasonable by the Committee in 1851, that out of a series of Paintings intended for publication under copyright, to make twelve choice selections and expose them in an apartment public as the Library of the Legislature, would effectively destroy his right, and in fact the necessity of securing such copyright, as nothing could prevent the public from obtaining access to them for any purpose they might desire. The arrangement, therefore, was that these Paintings should be presented to the House as soon as it could be done without any such danger.

In explanation of the period elapsed since the arrangement was effected, Mr. *Kane* begs the Members of the Committee to consider that he has been many years engaged at the work in question in his own interest, and that no delay that was not absolutely indispensable in so voluminous a work can reasonably be supposed to have been voluntarily incurred.

These remarks Mr. *Kane* offers in justification of himself and of the time transpired since he undertook that engagement; he has now, however, to inform the Committee that, anticipating the return of the Government to *Toronto* would be immediately followed by a demand of the nature now made upon him, he waived the consideration above set forth, and has now been for some months occupied in preparing the series intended for the House, which he hopes to complete by the close of the Summer. He, therefore, requests that the Committee will be good enough to withdraw their Report, which was prepared and presented without his being called upon to offer any explanations, and suspend action in the matter until the opening of the next Session, when Mr. *Kane* will be prepared to place the twelve Paintings in the hands of the proper Officer of the House, on the understanding that such precautions as he may suggest will be adopted to prevent his prospective copyright being infringed, in furtherance of the understanding on which was based as well Mr. *Kane*'s original application, as the liberal action of the Committee upon it.

BIBLIOGRAPHY AND INDEX

BIBLIOGRAPHY

This bibliography lists works directly related to the life and career of Paul Kane. The notes to Part One and Part Two contain references (with bibliographical information) to other works which have provided background for the present study; the names of their authors appear in the index.

WRITINGS BY THE ARTIST

Paul Kane, "The Chinook Indians," *Canadian Journal*, new ser., II (1857), 11–30.

———, "The Chinook Indians," *Daily Colonist* (Toronto), August 6, 7, 8, 9, 1855.

———, "Incidents of Travel on the North-West coast, Vancouver's Island, Oregon, etc.: The Chinook Indians," *Canadian Journal*, III (1854–55), 273–79.

———, "Notes of a Sojourn among the Half-Breeds, Hudson's Bay Company's territory, Red River," *Canadian Journal*, new ser., I (1856), 128–38.

———, "Notes of Travel among the Walla-Walla Indians," *Canadian Journal*, new ser., I (1856), 417–24.

———, *Wanderings of an Artist among the Indians of North America from Canada to Vancouver's Island and Oregon through the Hudson's Bay Company's Territory and Back Again* (London 1859); re-published with introduction and notes by L. J. Burpee (Master-works of Canadian authors, ed. J. W. Garvin, VII, Toronto 1925; repub. with intro. by J. G. MacGregor, Edmonton 1968).

Les Indiens de la baie d'Hudson, promenades d'un artiste parmi les Indiens de l'Amérique du Nord . . . , trans. by Edouard Delessert (Paris 1861).

Wanderungen eines Künstlers unter den Indianern Nordamerikas . . . , trans. by Louise Hauthal (Leipzig 1862).

En Kunstners Vandringer blandt Indianerne i Nordamerika . . . , by J. K. (Copenhagen 1863).

REVIEWS OF KANE'S WRITINGS

Charles Lavollée, "Un artiste chez les Peaux-Rouges," *Revue des deux mondes* (Paris), XXII (1859), 963–86.

Daniel Wilson, "*Wanderings of an Artist*," *Canadian Journal*, new ser., IV (1859), 186–94.

Athenaeum (London), July 2, 1859, pp. 14–15.

CATALOGUES IN WHICH KANE'S WORK IS MENTIONED

Catalogue of the First Exhibition of the Society of Artists and Amateurs of Toronto (Toronto 1834).

Catalogue of Sketches and Paintings by Paul Kane (Winnipeg 1922).

Catalogue, Pictures of Indians and Indian Life by Paul Kane (property of E. B. Osler, n.p., [1904]).

Paul Kane, *Catalogue of Sketches of Indians, Chiefs, Landscapes, Dances, Costumes, etc.* (Toronto 1848).

National Gallery of Canada, *Catalogue of Paintings and Sculpture*, ed. R. H. Hubbard (3v., Ottawa, 1959–61), III, *The Canadian School*, 151–56.

Toronto Society of Arts (Toronto 1847).

PUBLICATIONS WHICH DISCUSS KANE'S SKETCHES AND PAINTINGS

Anglo-American Magazine (Toronto), I, 1852, 372–74 (review of Kane's paintings at the Upper Canada Provincial Exhibition, 1852).

B., "The Fine Arts—Mr. Kane," *Commercial Register* (Mobile, Alabama), March 20, 1841.

D. I. Bushnell, Jr., *Sketches by Paul Kane in the Indian Country, 1845–1848* (Smithsonian Miscellaneous Collections, XCIX, Washington 1940).

Canadian Agriculturist (Toronto), III (1851), 228; IV (1852), 292–93.

W. G. Colgate, "An Early Portrait by Paul Kane," *Ontario History*, XL (1948), 23–25.

E. C. Guillet, *The Valley of the Trent*, Champlain Society, Ontario Series (Toronto 1957).

J. R. Harper, "Ontario Painters 1846–1867," National Gallery of Canada, *Bulletin*, I (Ottawa 1963), 16–31.

K. E. Kidd, "Notes on Scattered Works of Paul Kane," Royal Ontario Museum, Art and Archaeology Division, *Annual*, 1962, 64–73.

————, "Paul Kane—A Sheaf of Sketches," *Canadian Art* (Ottawa), VIII (1950–51), 166–67.

E. S. Rogers, *Paul Kane Sketch Pad* (Toronto 1969).

Kathleen Wood, "Paul Kane Sketches," *Rotunda* (Toronto), II (1969), 4–15.

PRINCIPAL PUBLICATIONS DEALING WITH KANE'S CAREER

W. G. Colgate, *Canadian Art, its Origin and Development* (Toronto 1943).

E. A. Corbett, "Paul Kane in Western Canada," *Geographical Magazine* (London), July 1947, 94–103.

N. F. Davin, *The Irishman in Canada* (London and Toronto 1877), 611–17.

J. R. Harper, *Painting in Canada, a History* (Toronto 1966).

————, "Paul Kane," *Dictionary of Canadian Biography*, vol. X (Toronto 1971).

Bertha L. Heilbron, "Artist as Buffalo Hunter: Paul Kane and the Red River Half-Breeds," *Minnesota History*, XXXVI (8), December 1959, 309–14.

K. E. Kidd, "Paul Kane, Painter of Indians," Royal Ontario Museum of Archaeology, *Bulletin* 23 (Toronto 1955), 9–13.

————, "The Wanderings of Kane," *Beaver*, Outfit 277 (December 1946), 3–9.

W. H. G. Kingston, *Western Wanderings; or, A Pleasure Tour in the Canadas* (2v., London 1856), II, 39, 42–47.

H. J. Morgan, *Sketches of Celebrated Canadians* (Quebec 1862), 731–33.

"Paul Kane," *Anglo-American Magazine* (Toronto), VI (May 1855), 401–6.

A. H. Robson, *Paul Kane* (Toronto 1938).

Daniel Wilson, "Paul Kane, the Canadian Artist," *Canadian Journal*, new ser., XIII (1871–73), 66–72.

————, *Prehistoric Man: Searches into the Origin of Civilization in the Old and the New World* (2v., Cambridge and London 1862).

INDEX

NOTE: K.: Kane; HBC: Hudson's Bay Company. Identification of place names is by present-day nomenclature: for example, the provinces of Ontario, Manitoba, Saskatchewan, Alberta, and British Columbia; the states of Oregon and Washington

Accademia (Venice), 12, 271
A-chis-a-lay, 291
Achu-wish-a-ma-hy, 284
Acolti, Father Michael, 21, 96, 300
"Act of Lightning," *see* Til-au-kite
Adelaide (Australia), 32
Africa, K. in (?), 12
"Against the Heavens," *see* Sha-nu-oh-ke-zhick
agents, to the Indians: Capt. Anderson, 54, 57; Capt. Ironsides, 57, 275; at Fox River, 59
"Alakpowa" River (Columbia River area), 297
Aleuts (Aleutian Islands), 28
"Alias 8 Summers," *see* Shewans-u-ne-bin
Al-kol-lock, game of, 123, 293–94
Allam-mak-hum Stole-luch, 123, 293
Allan, George W.: friendship with K., 9, 30, 34, 42, 43, 309; collection of K.'s works, 30, 32, 34, 35, 36, 37, 45, 51, 272, 278, 284, 286, 304, 309, App. 5, 7; life of, 30, 34–35, 309; and *Wanderings*, 39, 40, 41
Allan, Mrs. George W., 309
Ames, A. E., 43, 309
Ancient Monuments of the Mississippi Valley, 39
Anderson, Thomas Gummersall, 54, 57
Anglo-American Magazine, 11, 12, 14, 33, 34, 38
antelope, 70, 80, 285
Arctic Ocean, 88
Armour, Eliza (Clench), 10, 271
Arrow Lakes (Columbia River), 90, 126–27, 128, 292
Asabonish, 57, 272, 275; daughter of, 57, 272, 275
Asia, K. in (?), 12
As-in-a-chap, *see* Capote Blanc
Ask-a-weelish, 292
"Assannitchay," *see* Capote Blanc
As,si,ke,nack, *see* Sigennok

Assiniboia (territory), 156
Assiniboin (Indians), 18, 26, 37, 38, 81, 83, 136, 139, 146, 147, 148, 289; sketches of, 283, 285, 286, 289, 290, 308
Assiniboine River, 68, 73, 289
Astor, John Jacob, 92, 93, 106, 300, 301, 302
Astoria (Irving), 17, 92, 106, 112
Athabasca, Lake, 82, 285
Athabasca River, 23, 85–88, 89, 131, 132–35, 291, 292
Athenaeum (London), 40, 41
Atlantic Ocean (and coast), 51, 64, 152
Aubert de Gaspé, Philippe, 8
aurora borealis, 140
Awbonwaishkum, 54, 275

Babine, "Babbine" (Indians), 28, 107, 307, 308
Babine Lake (B.C.), 291, 307
Back, Sir George, 39
Bain, James, 40
Baldwin, W. W., 6
Ballenden, John, 16, 32, 57
Barbaro, Daniel, 271
Bartlett, John Russell, 39
Bay-je-gi-she-quish, 290
bear, 85; grizzly, 82, 139–40, 146
beaver, 139, 272
Beaverbrook Gallery (Fredericton, N.B.), 7, 310
Begg, Alexander, 17, 18
Behring River (Man.), 152, 283
Belcourt, Rev. Georges-Antoine, 155
Bell, ed. (*British Theatre*), 8
Bellacoola (Indians), 305
Belly River (Alta.), 285
Belo, Susan, 62, 276
Bering Strait, 101
Berthon, George-Théodore, **35**
Bethune, Angus, 16
Big Bay (Owen Sound, Ont.), 273

"Big Chief," *see* Match-o-kee-maw
Big Dog Portage (Kaministiquia River), 63, 280
"Big Fish," *see* Maska-nonga
"Big Horn," 145
"Big Pike," *see* Maskuhnoonjee
"Big Snake," *see* Omoxesisixany
birch bark, uses of, 67; *see also* Indians, domestic life; water transportation
Black, Samuel, 92–93
"Black Bear," *see* Muck-koze
"Black Eagle," *see* Muck-e-tah-kin-ne-u; Muck-e-tick-enow
"Black Indian," *see* Cath-a-nish-a-na-bay
"Blackbird, The," *see* Sigennok
Blackfoot (Indians), 145, 147; K.'s illustrations of, 18, 27, 28, 29, 34, 36, 149, 284, 286–87, 290, 294, 299; description of, 27, 77, 78, 136, 142, 146, 148–50, 287; warfare of, 78, 83, 124, 144, 145, 146, 148, 149, 150–51, 152, 284, 294
Blood (Indians), 27, 136, 148, 149, 150, 151, 286–87
Bloor, Joseph, brewery of, 309
"Blue Jay," *see* El-ko-ka-shin
Boat Encampment (Columbia River), 26, 87, 88, 89, 125, 126, 127, 128, 129–30, 131, 291; sketches of, 26, 34, 130, 292
Bonnet, Lac de (Ont.), 154
Borghese Gallery (Rome), 271
Borthwick, J. Douglas, 41
"Bow, The," *see* Maticwaub
Bow River (Alta.), 285
Bowman, James, 10, 11, 310
Bradford (Ont.), 270
Branch, E. Douglas, 17
Brant, Joseph, 43, 309
"Brave Soldier," *see* Mauza-pau-Kan
"Bravest of the Brave, The," *see* Oscosh
Brazeau, Mrs. (Fort Assiniboine), 135
brigades, of fur trade: travel of, 17, 26, 63, 67, 76, 82, 85–90, 111–13, 126–35, 138, 147–48, 151, 152, 153–57, 291; de-

scription of, 17, 27, 63, 76, 111, 129, 138, 139, 141, 152, 153, 154, 155–56, 299; discipline in, 86, 111, 128; sketches of, 273, 284, 308
British Colonist, 28
British Columbia, 22, 26, 291, 292; Indians of, 304–8; *see also* New Caledonia
Brock, Sir Isaac, monument to, 34, 309
Brockville (Ont.), 33
"Broken Arm," 142
Brookes, Samuel M., 278
Brown, Mr. ("military officer," met on Winnipeg River), 154
Bruce Peninsula (Ont.), 52
Buckingham Palace, 40
Buffalo (city), 30, 61
buffalo: herds of, 18, 31, 71, 78, 82, 84, 117, 137, 143, 147–48; eating of, 77, 136–37, 138–39, 141–43; sketches of, 287, 291
buffalo, hunting of, 31, 39, 41, 79; by K., 8, 28, 29, 35, 140, 146, 279, 283, 289; description of, 17–18, 69–72, 137–38; sketches of, 37–38, 282–83, 284, 289; *see also* Métis
Burnham, Hon. Zaccheus, 270
Burpee, L. J., 63, 81, 99, 275, 284, 304
Burton, F. T., 32
Busato (painter), 12, 271
Bushnell, D. I., 274, 279, 286, 287, 290, 291, 294, 296
"Bushway" (Kane), 129

cache (of food), 147, 290
Calapooya (Indians), 299
California, 20, 91, 97, 101, 117
"Call of the Wild, The," *see* A-chis-a-lay
camas (for food), 94, 99, 101, 102, 299, 305
Canada, Province of, 308; assistance to Kane, 33–34, 51, App. 10, 12
Canada East, *see* Quebec

Canada West (part of united province), 5; *see also* Ontario; Upper Canada
Canadian Agriculturist, 33
Canadian Institute, 39, 43
Canadian Journal (Canadian Institute), 39, 40, 43, 45
Canadian Magazine and National Review, 37
Canadian Pacific Railway, 51
Cape Flattery (Wash.), 105, 106, 304, 307
Cape Horn (Columbia River), 297
"Capote Blanc," 87, 129, 291
Careless, J. M. S., 5
Cariboo (B.C.), 25
carioles (for travelling), 141, 288–89
Carr, Emily, 22
Carrier (Indians), 291
cart, Red River, 69, 282, 285
Carver, Jonathan, 29
Casanov, 19, 25, 91–92, 94, 293, 299, 302
Cascade (Indians), 111, 112, 283, 297
Cascade Mountains, 291
Cascades (Columbia River), 111, 112, 293, 294, 297
Cash-a-cabut (Cash-i-Cabit), 154, 281
Cassels, Mrs. A. (née Allan), 31, 35, 42–43
Castle Rocks, *see* Chimney Rocks
caterpillars, scourge of, 66
Cath-a-nish-a-na-bay, 275
Catlin, George: his life and paintings, 13, 18, 32, 33, 37, 309; *Letters . . . on North American Indians*, 13, 38; and K., 13–14, 284; work compared to K.'s, 16, 18, 22, 28, 38, 43; and J. M. Stanley, 24; *Catlin's Portfolio*, 42
cattle, domestic, 91, 99, 116, 298
Caughnawaga (Que.), 308
Caw-kee-ka-keesh-e-ko, 153, 283, 290
Caw-wacham, 99, 110, 302
Cayuse (Indians), 23, 25, 116, 117, 125–26, 296
C-dah-mak-skuash, 276
cedar: for clothing, 94, 100, 300; for canoes, 95
Challener, F. S., 270
Chalon, H. B., 11, 271
Champoeg (Ore.), 20, 21, 298, 300
Charles, Mr. (HBC clerk), 84, 85
Chasta (Indians), 93, 300
Chateaubriand, F. R., 41
Chaw-u-wit, 105, 304
Chea-clach (Clallam, Vancouver Island), 100, 103, 105, 306; *see also* Cloll-uck
Chicago, 29
"Chief of the Earth," *see* Allam-mak-hum Stole-luch
"Chief of the Waters," *see* See-pays
"Chief Young Swan," *see* Oogemsh-wah-be-zee
Chimaza, 81, 285
Chimmesyan (Indians), 307, 308

Chimney Rocks (Columbia River), 36, 113, 295, 296
Chinewoss, 294
Chinook (Indians), 24, 39, 41, 91, 93–95, 98, 99, 100, 107, 111, 294, 299–300, 301–2, 303, 304, 307
Chipewyan (Indians), 82, 285
Chippewa (Indians), 52, 53, 272, 274
cholera, epidemic of, 8, 9–10, 30
Christian Guardian, 29
Christian Island (Georgian Bay), 53
Christie, Alexander, 74
Christmas: at Fort Edmonton (1847), 18–19, 138–39, 289; at Fort Vancouver (1846), 19
Chualpays (Indians), 24, 36, 123–24, 292–94
Chute-de-Jacques (Winnipeg River), 66, 154, 280
Chutes (Columbia River), 112, 297
Cincinnati, 30
Clackama (Indians), 96–97, 301
Clackamas River (Ore.), 24, 300, 301
Clallam (Indians), 22, 100–2, 103, 104, 105, 106, 107, 303–4, 306, 308
Clark, John, 93
Clark, William, 302
Clench, Eliza, *see* Armour
Clench, F. S., 10, 35, 270
Clench, Mrs. F. S., 10, 270
Clench, Harriet, *see* Kane
Cleveland, 61
Cloll-uck, 303
Cluston, Robert, App. 10
coal, beds of, 136, 146
Cobourg (Ont.), 9, 10, 11, 30, 31, 35, 43, 270, 271, 310
Cockburn, J. P., 7
Coe Collection (Yale University), 33, 291, 298, App. 4
Coe-coosh, 37, 59, 278, 290
Coeur d'Alene mission, 115
Coffin Rock (Columbia River), 25, 97, 280, 301, 302
Coldwater (Ont.), 52
Columbia River, 15, 17, 19, 24, 25, 26, 42, 63, 76, 87, 88, 93, 107, 110, 295; Indians of, 20, 22, 93–95, 96–97, 98–99, 100, 107, 112, 113, 122–25, 283, 291, 292–94, 296, 297, 299–300, 301; settlement of area, 20, 24, 91, 98, 125, 300; canoe burials of, 25, 98–99, 301–2; fishing on, 41, 111, 112, 123–24; K.'s travels on, 51, 89–91, 95, 111–14, 118, 119, 120–22, 126–30, 279, 291; descriptions of, 89, 91, 96, 97, 112, 113, 114, 119, 120, 121–22, 126, 127, 130; sketches of, 292, 294, 295, 297, 298, 300, 301–2
Columbus, Christopher, 43, 309
Colvile, Eden, 31, 293
Colville (Indians), *see* Chualpays
Comcomly, King, 92, 302

Commercial Register (Mobile), 11, 271, App. 11
Committee's Punch Bowl (Rocky Mountains), 26, 88, 130, 291, 292
Confederation (of Canada, 1867), 5
Conger, W. S., 9, 10, 270
Conger, Mrs. W. S., 10, 270
Conn, R. G., 293
Constable, Mr. ("military officer," met on Winnipeg River), 154
"Constant Sky, The," *see* Caw-kee-ka-keesh-e-ko
Conway, Richard, 53
Cooper, James Fenimore, 41
Copenhagen, 41
Cornelius, F. duPont, 32
Corunna, battle of, 152
Courier (Toronto), 28
Cowichan (Indians), 102, 103, 303, 306, 307
Cowlitz (Indians), 99, 300, 302
Cowlitz River, 91, 92, 98, 99, 110, 299, 301, 302, 303
Cox, Ross, 19, 26, 39
Craig, Gerald M., 5
Craw, G. W., 270
Cree (Indians): K.'s illustrations of, 18, 19, 81, 143, 144, 148, 284, 289, 290; at Fort Edmonton, 19, 83, 136, 139, 284, 289; at other HBC posts, 69, 76, 283, 290; of prairies, 77, 78, 81, 142, 143–45, 146, 148, 150, 151, 152, 284, 285–86, 287; description of, 78, 91, 95, 143–45, 151; and fur trade, 124, 130, 146, 284
Culchillum, 103, 306, 307
Cumberland House, 22, 77, 151; *see also* Le Pas
Cumberland River (Man.), 77
Cumshaw (Queen Charlotte Islands), 307
Cun-ne-wa-bum, 19, 40, 139, 289
Currelly, Dr. C. T., 35

Daily Colonist (Toronto), 39
Dalle(s) de(s) Mort(s) (Columbia River), 90, 127–28, 280, 292
Dalles (Indians), 112, 297
Dalles, The (Columbia River), 22, 23, 90, 112, 126, 127, 292, 293, 297, 299
Daly, Thomas, 28, 310
Davin, Nicholas Flood, 6
"Dawn of Day," *see* Kwa-qua-dah-bon-niva-skung
De Smet, Father Pierre Jean, 21
deer, hunting of, 80, 109, 127, 136, 285
Delacroix, F. V. E., 38
Delaney, Matilda J. (Sager), 23
Demers, Modeste, 147, 150
Deschutes River (Ore.), 297, 299
Detroit, K. in, 11, 61
Dillon, Mr. (companion, 1845 trip), 53, 57, 273
Dillon, Richard, 117, 129
discharge (décharge), meaning of, 64, 155

Dixon, Capt. G. W., 6
Dog Portage (Kaministiquia River), 63, 280
dogs: for travelling, 26, 36, 57, 81, 132–35, 141–43, 282, 288–89; in hunting, 64, 70, 73, 127, 137–38; for wool, 100, 306
Dolci, C., 12, 271
Donatello, 12, 271
"Donna alla Fontana" (sketch), 271
"Donna di Frescati" (sketch), 271
"Donna di Mola de Gaeta" (sketch), 271
Donny (half-breed guide), 118–22
Douglas, James, 19, 21, 90, 92, 304, 305, App. 10
Drake, John Poad, 8
Drury, Thomas, 9, 10, 34, 270, 308
Dry Dance Mountain (south of Fort Garry), 70, 281
ducks, hunting of, 54, 64, 105, 157, 280
"Duke of Wellington," *see* Potika-poo-tis

Each-a-quip, 281
E-a-cle, 303
Eberstadt Collection (N.Y.), 305
Edinburgh, 12
Eells, Rev. Cushing, 23, 24, 25, 122, 294
Eikutope, 284
Elgin, James Bruce, 8th Earl of, 31, 32, 34
Elgin, Countess of, 32
El-ko-ka-shin, 293
Elle-a-ma-cum-stuck, *see* Allam-mak-hum Stole-luch
Ellice, Edward ("Bear"), 39
Elliott, T. C., 19
Elm Park (painting), 270
Emerson, Ralph Waldo, 29
Empey, Michael Peter, 9, 270
England, K. in, 13, 14, 271
Ermatinger, Charles Oakes, 276
Eskimo, 27, 152, 283
Esquimalt (B.C.), 22, 99, 102, 304–5; *see also* Fort Victoria
Europe, 8, 148, 151; K. in, 11–13
"Eus-a-nich," *see* Sanetch

"Feather, The," *see* Mah-Min; "Red Vest"
Fermoy (County Cork), 6
Finlayson, Roderick, 100, 101, 106, 108
fire, on prairies, 78, 83, 288
Flathead (Indians), 40, 41, 91, 93, 111, 112, 294, 299, 302, 303
Fleming, Sir Sandford, 44
Florence (Italy), 12, 271
Fond du Lac (Wisc.), 61
Forman, Werner, 305
Fort Alexander, 67, 153, 154, 155, 280, 281, 283
Fort Assiniboine, 85, 134, 135, 291
Fort Astoria, 91, 92, 301, 302
Fort Carlton, 18, 25, 77, 78, 81, 142, 150, 284, 285
Fort Colvile, 23, 25, 111, 118, 121, 127, 292; sketches of, 24, 293–94, 296, 299,

Index

300; Indian salmon fisheries at, 25, 123–24, 293; K. at, 90, 122, 123–24, 293–94, 297
Fort Edmonton, 18, 26, 31, 78, 79, 80, 82, 83, 129, 132, 139, 143, 148, 286, 287, 288, 290, 291; K.'s depiction of, 18–19, 83, 136, 138–39, 146, 288; K. at, 26, 37, 40, 41, 83–84, 136–40, 145, 147, 279, 284, 288–89, 290; wedding at (1848), 26, 141, 288–89
Fort Frances, 17, 18, 27, 65, 66, 152, 156, 275, 280, 281, 285
Fort Garry, 17, 18, 31, 32, 39, 68–69, 74, 279, 281, 283
Fort George, see Fort Astoria
Fort Okanagan, 90
Fort Pitt, 18, 26, 27, 141, 286; K. at, 27, 81, 82, 143–45, 148, 285, 286, 287, 288, 289
Fort Simpson, 28, 305, 307
Fort Snelling, 24, 279, 281
Fort Spokane, 128
Fort Vancouver, 15, 24, 25, 31, 76, 87, 89, 96, 106, 108, 305; sketches of, 18, 19, 25, 297, 298–300, 301, 302; K. at, 19, 22, 39, 90, 91, 95, 97, 110, 118, 130, 279, 293, 298, 300, 301, 303, 308; life at, 19–21, 91, 92, 94, 111, 129, 298; Indians at, 299–300
Fort Victoria, 22, 25, 28, 31, 99, 101, 105; sketches of, 18, 25, 298, 305; and HBC, 20, 22, 100; K. at, 100, 102, 103, 106, 108, 279, 301, 303, 304; Indians at, 304–8
Fort Walla Walla, 19, 20, 23, 24, 25, 93, 94, 96, 115, 125, 126; depiction of, 18, 25, 295; K. at, 90, 114, 116, 293, 295, 297
Fort William, 16, 17, 62, 63, 66, 157, 274, 279, 280, 281
Fothergill, Charles, 270
Fowler, Daniel, 13
Fox River, 16, 37, 58–61, 272, 277–79
France, 271; interest in Indians, 7, 41
Franklin, Mr. (on Poore expedition), 30, 31
Franklin, Sir John, 27, 151
Frank's Hotel (York), 8
Fraser, Colin, 85, 86, 87, 132, 133
Fraser, Paul, 147
Fraser River, 85, 87, 156, 291, 303
French, Charles, 8–9
French Portage (northwestern Ont.), 65
French River (Ont.), 36, 273
Fuchay River (Ore.), 114, 116
Fuller and Benecke (lithographic firm), 44

Galena (Ill.), 24, 30
"galettes" (cakes), 137
Gamble, John, 10, 270, 309
Garibaldi, 44
geese, wild, 83, 84, 136, 139
Genoa (Italy), 12
George III, King, 40

George, Lake (painting), 270
Georgia, Gulf of, 102, 303, 306
Georgian Bay (Lake Huron), 16; K. on, 53–54; 271, 275; sketches of, 273–74, 278, 290, 308
Gesner, Abraham, 7
Gilbert, George S., 270
Globe (Toronto), 29
goats, mountain, 87, 127, 292
"Golden Cloud, The," see Og-sah-wah-nah-quoch-ogue
Golden Valley (Sask.), 285
goldeyes (fish), 152
Gourlay, Francis de (guide), 69, 72–74
Grafton (Ont.), 30
Grand Batteur (Columbia River), 127; (Rocky Mountains), 87, 130, 131
Grand Bonnet portage (Winnipeg River), 154
Grand Coulee, 118, 119–21, 297
Grand Rapids (Columbia River), 90; (Saskatchewan River), 77, 151
Grand Tour, of Europe, 12
Grand Côte (Rocky Mountains), 130
Grande Décharge (west of Lake of the Woods), 155
Grant, Cuthbert, 69
"Great Chief, The," see Kitchie-ogi-maw
Great Lakes, 15, 27, 32, 36, 41, 51, 277; see also Lakes Huron, Michigan, Ontario, Superior
"Greedy Tooth," see Cash-a-cabut
Green Bay (Mich.), 58, 272, 277, 281
Gregory XV, Pope, 12, 271
"Grizzly Bear Standing, The," see Achu-wish-a-ma-hy
Gros, A. J., Baron, 38
Gros Ventres (Indians), 27, 136, 148, 151, 286
Guillet, Edwin C., 10, 30, 270
gulls (Lake Winnipeg), 75
Gurnett, George, 9, 28, 43, 309

Haida (Indians), 22, 307
"Half-white Man, The," see Wah-he-joe-tass-e-neen
Halifax, 7–8
Hall, Capt. Francis, 5
Hamel, Théophile, 11, 12, 33, 34
Hamilton (Ont.), 38
Hardraw Force (painting), 270
Harlech Castle (painting), 270
Haro Strait, 103, 303, 307
Harper, Capt. (on Great Lakes), 57
Harper, J. Russell, 7, 8
Harriott, Miss, 141, 288, 289
Harriott, John Edward, 141; at Fort Edmonton, 26, 136–39, 141, 288; relations with Indians, 27, 148, 149, 150; on 1848 brigade, 147–51
Harrison, William Henry (President), 11, 271
Hawaiian Islands, 25
Haygood, George Washington, 271

Heath, Mr. (friend of G. W. Allan), 30
"He-Devil," see Mani-tow-wah-bay
Height of Land (Rocky Mountains), 88
Herculaneum, 12
"Heron, The," see Sha-Neu-Oh-Rigits
Hetherington, George, 270
Hind, Henry Youle, 41, 42, 43
Hind, William G. R., 25, 42
Hines, Gustavus, 112
Historical Society of Ontario, 35
historical subjects, in painting, 43
"Hog, The," see Coe-coosh
"Hole in the Sky," see She-bah-ke-zhick
Holmes, Kenneth L., 21, 301
"Homewood" (residence of G. W. Allan), 309
Hopkins, Mr. (Sir G. Simpson's secretary), 64, 156
Hopkins, Frances Ann, 156
"Horn, The," see Otisskun; U-thay-skun
horses: and hunting the buffalo, 71–72, 137, 283; on plains, 73, 77, 79, 80, 81, 82, 83, 84, 137, 143, 145, 147, 284, 289; in mountains, 87, 88, 130–31, 291; on west coast, 99, 115, 122; see also Indians, horses of
Horticultural Society of Toronto, 35
Howard, John G., 10
How-e-ago-sun-upet-uppet, see Slo-ce-ac-cum
Howison, John, 5
Hubbard, R. H., 280
Hudson Bay, 16, 63, 64, 76, 148, 152, 156
Hudson River School (painters), 29
Hudson's Bay Company: assistance to K. in travelling, 7, 16–17, 25, 26, 27–28, 31, 42, 57, 61, 99, 103, 107, 136, 152, 279; in Oregon, 16, 19, 20, 23, 96, 111, 126, 298, 305; history of, 16, 29, 63, 93, 96, 298, 299, 305; western brigades, 17, 19, 63, 67, 76, 82, 85–90, 111–13, 126–35, 138, 147–48, 151, 153–56, 273, 284, 286, 288, 299; posts of, 18, 19–21, 36, 62, 63, 68, 74, 78, 83, 91, 99–100, 111, 114, 122, 135, 136, 138–39, 146, 152, 153–54, 156, 157, 281, 283, 284, 288, 289, 290, 291, 293, 294, 295, 298, 305, 307; and Russians on west coast, 19, 26, 76, 83, 85, 91, 99, 130, 302; agricultural activities of, 22, 91, 99, 136, 139, 156, 301, 302, 303; relations with Indians, 27, 74, 76, 78, 92, 96, 104, 108, 112, 113, 117, 126, 138, 146, 147, 148, 150, 157, 284, 295, 306; and trip of Sir Edward Poore (1849–50), 31; and Wanderings, 39; and North West Company, 63; relations with its men, 67, 74, 138; and missionaries, 76, 77, 138, 156, 296; see also Cumberland House; Fort Alexander; Fort Assiniboine; Fort Carlton; Fort Colvile; Fort Edmonton; Fort Frances; Fort Garry; Fort Okanagan; Fort Pitt; Fort Simpson; Fort Spokane; Fort Van-

couver; Fort Victoria; Fort Walla Walla; Fort William, Ile-à-la Crosse; Jasper House; Le Pas; Michipicoten; Norway House; Rat Portage; Rocky Mountain House; Sault Ste Marie; York Factory
Hunter, Rev. J., 22, 27, 77, 142, 151
Hunter, Mrs. J., 151
Huron (Indians), 53, 275
Huron, Lake, 7, 16, 40, 52, 53, 55, 58, 61, 62; sketches of, 272–75
Huron Chief, The (Kidd), 7
Hussey, John A., 19, 21, 298, 300

"I hear the Noise of the Deer," see Maydoc-game-kin-ungee
Iacaway ("The Loud Speaker"), 66, 76, 281, 285, 290; I-ac-a-way ("The Man who is gone on a Hunt"), 76
ice, in river travel, 133–34, 146
Idaho (state), 295, 296
I-eh-nus (Juan de Fuca), 104–5, 106, 303, 304
Ile-à-la-Crosse (Sask.), 74
Impressionist painters, 36
Indians, North American
agriculture of: Lake Huron, 52, 53, 57; among Spokan, 123
attitudes of: to K., 15, 27, 45, 58, 65, 75, 98, 99, 103, 104, 107, 116, 117, 119, 122; to Europeans, 18, 20, 59, 60, 85, 92–93, 98, 104, 106, 149; to missionaries, 24, 77, 79, 104, 117, 122, 125–26, 142–43, 147, 155
attitudes towards: in 19th century, 7–8, 13, 29, 33, 40–41, 43, 45; of K., 13–15, 18, 35–36, 38, 51; of missionaries, 76, 116, 142–43, 146, 147; see also Carr, Emily; Catlin, George; Hudson's Bay Company; Wilson, Daniel
burial practices of, 15, 22, 52, 64, 92, 97, 98, 105, 111, 113, 274, 294, 302–3, 304
clothing of: European elements, 18, 27, 28, 97, 98, 157, 278; chief's medals, 18, 27, 52, 275, 276; bear's claw collars, 26, 139, 146, 308; decorations, 37, 59, 94, 107, 276, 277, 278, 279, 281, 282, 286, 290, 299, 307; robes, 37, 156, 279, 281, 282, 287; garments, 38, 94, 99, 107, 132, 139, 145, 287, 296, 300, 306; blankets, 100, 106, 107, 306, 308; feather head dress, 273, 278, 279, 287
customs of, 92, 123, 124, 142, 144; romance, 55; to-tem, 57, 275; mourning, 58, 75, 100, 108, 117–18, 150, 287; vengeance, 60, 78, 92, 117; cannibalism, 65, 76, 128; nomenclature, 91, 122; wampum, 277
diseases of, 20, 24, 83, 91, 103–4, 117, 125, 145, 284
domestic life of, 67, 84; spinning and

345

weaving, 22, 306; utensils, 53, 59, 94, 306; corn, 53, 155, 273; camas, 94, 99, 101, 102, 299, 305; food, 94, 100, 101, 127, 155; fire making, 95, 303; rice gathering, 153–54, 155, 156
eloquence of, 54, 55, 59, 274
feasts of, 52, 100, 102, 145
fishing by: Lake Huron, 52, 53, 57, 58, 273; Fox River, 58, 277; Lake of the Woods, 66; Vancouver Island, 101; northwest coast, 102, 105, 109, 304, 306; Columbia River, 111, 112, 114, 123–24, 293, 295, 297, 299, 300; Sault Ste Marie, 276
habits of, personal, 53, 76, 93, 139, 144
horses of, 37, 77, 79, 81, 95, 115, 139, 143, 144, 145, 148, 277, 284, 290, 293, 294
houses of: Great Lakes area, 53, 273–74, 275–76, 277; west coast, 95, 114, 123, 292, 293, 299, 303, 305; Clallam, 100, 102, 104, 306; plains, 146, 290
hunting by: buffalo, 8, 18, 35, 37, 79, 146, 285; deer, 52, 53, 112; ducks, 54, 64, 105, 280; gulls' eggs, 75; bear, 82; mountain sheep, 87, 131, 132; whale, 100, 105
language of, 93, 100, 139; see also eloquence
legends of, 21, 39, 86, 97, 109–10, 113–14, 292
liquor and, 54, 58, 59, 61, 74, 97, 113, 138, 154
masks of, 22, 102, 305
medicine dances of, 27, 52, 102, 150, 299, 305
medicine men of, 23, 35, 55, 67–68, 75, 77, 102, 103, 103–4, 143–44, 153, 293, 294, 306, 307
music of, 54, 68, 102, 124, 144
physiognomy of, 22, 37, 53, 54, 59, 60, 61, 105, 107, 114, 115, 116, 139, 149, 150, 277, 290; head deformations, 22, 29, 93, 99, 100, 101, 104, 107, 112, 294, 302, 307; face painting, 68, 278, 279, 287, 301
pipe ceremonials of, 15, 18, 35, 54, 59, 275, 278, 308; Cree, 27, 79, 142, 143–45, 148, 284, 285, 286; Blackfoot, 27, 148, 150, 287
recreations of: horse racing, 27, 33, 95, 148, 286; gambling, 59, 95, 96–97, 102, 123, 284, 299, 301, 306, 308; ball, 76, 95; Al-kol-lock, 123, 293–94
religion of, 59, 64, 79, 85, 93, 98, 102, 110, 117, 140, 142–43, 143–45, 153, 284
scalp dances of, 15, 24, 36, 71, 124, 151, 279, 294
slavery among, 91, 92, 93, 101, 102, 105, 106, 300, 302
superstitions of, 5, 21, 53, 65, 81, 97,

98, 100, 101, 113, 118, 140; and K. as artist, 15, 66, 75, 98, 99, 101, 107, 116, 149, 150
tobacco, uses of, 81, 103, 105, 107, 142, 144, 147, 150, 153
treaty agreements with, 25, 68, 104; Mackinac, 15, 16, 276; Manitowaning, 16, 54, 55, 274; Fox River, 16, 58, 277, 278; Saugeen, 52, 272
villages or camps of: Saugeen, 16, 52–53, 272–73; Manitowaning, 16, 54, 274; Vancouver Island, 22, 100, 303, 304–5, 306, 307; B.C. straits, 22, 103, 104, 105, 106, 109, 303–4; Georgian Bay Islands, 53, 273–74; Wikwemikong, 57, 275; Mackinac, 57–58, 276–77; Fox River, 58–59, 61, 278; Sault Ste Marie, 62, 275–76; Fort Frances, 66, 156; Fort Alexander, 67–68, 281; Red River, 75; Saskatchewan River, 81; Fort Walla Walla, 114, 117; Nez Percé camp, 119; Fort Colvile, 123–24; Cree (near Fort Pitt), 142–45; Assiniboin (Rocky Mountain House), 146, 290; Blackfoot (Saskatchewan River), 148–50; Fort Vancouver, 299–300; B.C. mainland, 303, 307
warfare of, 70, 78, 81, 87, 102, 144–45; Huron and Iroquois, 53; Saulteaux and Sioux, 68; Sioux and Métis, 69, 70; Cree and Blackfoot, 78, 83, 142, 144, 145, 146, 148, 150–51, 152, 284; Clallam and Makah, 104–5, 304, 305; Cayuse and Walla Walla against whites, 117; Assiniboin and Blackfoot, 146, 148
water transportation of, 67, 106, 304; northwest canoes, 22, 302, 305; birch-bark canoes, 53, 70, 272, 273, 275–76, 277; cedar canoes, 95; pine bark canoes, 127, 292; in Rocky Mountains, 292
wealth of, 106, 106–7; see also horses
weapons of: guns, 53, 54, 104, 105, 145, 148; bow and arrow, 80, 84, 95, 100, 145, 148, 277, 290, 293; spear, 84, 276; knives, 105, 148; clubs, 290, 305
women, role of, 105; domestic activity, 53, 137–38, 306; and children, 81, 290, 293, 294, 306, 307; in old age, 84; relation to husband, 92, 108, 308; and ceremonials, 124, 144, 145, 294
See also Assiniboin; Babine; Bellacoola; Blackfoot; Blood; Calapooya; Carrier; Cascade; Cayuse; Chasta; Chimmesyan; Chinook; Chipewyan; Chippewa; Chualpays; Clackama; Clallam; Colville; Cowichan; Cowlitz; Cree; Dalles; Flathead; Gros Ventres; Haida; Huron; Iroquois; Klikitat; Kutenai; Kwakiutl; Kwantlen; Makah; Malecite; Menominee; Micmac;

Missisauga; Mohawk; Nez Percé; Nisqually; Nootka; Ojibwa; Ottawa; Paloos; Piegan; Plains; Salish; Sanetch; Sarsi; Saugeen; Saulteaux; Shuswap; Sioux; Skagit; Skinpah; Snohomish; Songish; Spokan; Takulli; Tautin; Tenino; Ucaltas; Umatilla; Walla Walla; Winnebago; Wyandot
Indians, unnamed, in K.'s works: Sioux chieftain, 18, 281; girl from Lake St. Clair, 52, 272; Saulteaux girl (Red River), 75, 283; man in naval coat and cocked hat (Fort Vancouver), 97, 98, 298; chief's wife, Whidbey Island, 104, 303, 304; Chinook boy (?), 111, 299; Blackfoot chiefs, 150, 287; groups, 282, 290, 299–300, 308, 309; Nez Percé (girl), 295, (man), 296; Cascade Indian, 297
Inglefield, Sir E. A., 40
Ireland, 5, 6
"Iron Collar, The," see Mis-ke-me-kin
Ironsides, Capt. George, 57, 275
Iroquois (Indians), 53, 85, 88, 91, 112, 127, 128, 308
Irving, Washington, 17, 92, 106, 112
Italian youth (painting), 271
Italy, 44; K.'s travels in, 10, 11–12, 36, 271; borrowings from, by K., 37–38, 271
Iwa-toke, 58, 277, 291

Jack River, 76, 152, 283
Jacobs, Rev. Peter, 68, 156, 281
Jameson, Mrs. Anna, 16, 17, 274
Jasper House, 18, 86, 87, 88, 129, 130, 131, 132, 291
Jasper Lake, 86, 132, 291
Jefferys, Charles W., 37
Jemmy Jock, 146, 147
John the Baptist, St. (painting), 43, 271
Johnson, Sir William, 277
Jones, Isaac, 8
"jonglerie" (medicine lodge), 153
Joset, Father Joseph, 114–15
Journal of Education for Upper Canada, 33
Juan de Fuca, Strait of, 91, 103, 104, 105, 106, 107, 286, 303–4, 305, 306, 307
Julius II, Pope, 12, 271

Kakabeka Falls (Ont.), 36, 63, 156, 280
"Kalupanet," see Calapooya
Kaministiquia River (Ont.), 63, 279
Kane, Michael, 6, 11, App. 10
Kane, Mrs. Michael (Frances Loach), 6
Kane, Paul, life of
1810–1845: birth, 6; boyhood, 6–7, 9, 15, 277; relations with father, 6, 11, App. 10; development of interest in Indians, 7, 8, 13, 14, 15, 32; and the theatre, 8–9, 20; early painting, 9–10, 12, 14, 270; artist friends in

Toronto (1830s), 10; in Cobourg (1830s), 10–11, 35; in United States (1836–41, 1843–45), 11, 14, 35, 309, App. 11; personality and appearance, 11, 14, 23, 26, 28, 31, 33 (see also below); in Europe and England (1841–43), 11–13, 13–14, 36, 37, 271–72; and John Mix Stanley, 11, 24–25; qualities as a painter, 12, 15–16, 22, 25, 27, 28–29 (see also below); and George Catlin, 13–14, 16, 28; problem of eyesight, 13, 26, 44, 146; painting tools, 15, 32, 36, App. 8; desire for authenticity, 21, 24, 28, 36, 37; interest in birds, 23; and Henry J. Warre, 25
shows of work: (1834), 7, 10, 270; (1847), 309, 310; (1848), 28–29, 33, 272, 286, 310, App. 3; (1850–57), 33, 43, 44; (1855, Paris), 34; (1900), 29; (1922), 29
western travels, 1845–49 (see also individual place names): K. a witness of historic scenes, 7, 21, 22, 23, 71, 97; purpose of, 14–15, 32, 51, 65; sketching on, 15, 16, 17, 22–23, 28, 41, 51, 58, 63, 72, 75, 98, 99, 101, 103, 104, 116, 144, 146, 149, 150, 153; methods of travel, 16–17, 26, 27, 28, 31, 52, 61, 82, 86–90, 103, 106, 107, 111, 116, 130–31, 135, 141, 282, 292; hunting on, 17–18, 27, 28, 29, 31, 38, 59, 69–73, 80, 82, 97, 137–38, 140, 283, 289; K.'s view of Indians, 18, 35–36, 51, 117; friendship with Peter Skene Ogden, 19, App. 10; interest in Indian legends, 21, 39, 41; importance of sketches (on northwest coast), 22, (on prairies), 25, 27, 38; collection of artefacts, 27, 28, 29, 35, 37, 44, 146, 153, 281, 283, 286, 287, 308; dispersal of sketches and paintings, 30, 34, 35; trip with Sir Edward Poore (1849), 30–32, 279, App. 10; K.'s field logs, 39, App. 1, 2; self-portrait on, 282, 308
1849–1871: journal, keeping of, 7, 34, 39, 51; in Toronto (after 1845), 11, 13, 14, 16, 28, 32, 309, 310; marriage, 32, 35; cycle of western canvases, 32, 35, 43, 44, 51; technique in working up canvases, 32, 36–38, 280, 284, 286, 289, App. 8; qualities of canvases, 33, 35–38; commission from government, 33–34, 35, 43, 51, 299, App. 6, 10, 12; relations with George W. Allan, 34–35, 37, 42, 309, App. 5, 7; use of engravings as models, 37–38; K.'s library, 39, 43, 309, App. 9; preparing manuscript of Wanderings, 38–39, 44, 51; publication of, 38–40, 44, 309; papers to Canadian Institute, 39; reception of

book, 40–41, 45; friendship with Verner, 40, 44–45; interest in Labrador, 41–42, 44; possible second book, 42; personality and appearance, 42–43, 44, 45, 119; family life, 43; later painting, 43, 44, 309–310; in militia, 44; friendship with Daniel Wilson, 44, 45; experiment with lithography, 44, 286; death, 45
Kane, Paul, II (son), 30, 43
Kane, Paul, III (Grandson), 30, 272
Kane, Mrs. Paul (Harriet Clench), 10, 30, 35, 43, 271
Kattlepoutal River, *see* Lewis River
Kearny, General S. W., 24
Keats, John, 12
Kee-a-kee-ka-sa-coo-way, 27, 81, 144, 285, 286
Kerr, Lord Mark, 34
Kettle Falls (Fort Colvile), 90, 122–24, 126, 292, 293
Ke-wah-ten, 58, 277
Kidd, Adam, 7
Kidd, K. E., 270, 305, 310
Kingston, W. H. G., 32
Kingston (Ont.), 5
"Kinsey," Mr. (1848 brigade), 151
Kiscox, 99, 110, 302
Kitchie-ogi-maw, 60, 278
Klikitat (Indians), 91, 299, 302
"Koos-koos-kia" River (Ore.?), 293
Krieghoff, Cornelius, 9, 43, 44, 310
Kutenai (Indians), 25, 127, 292
Kwakiutl (Indians), 22, 307
Kwantlen (Indians), 303, 308
Kwa-qua-dah-bon-niva-skung, 272, 297

La Cloche Mountains (Lake Huron), 54
La Rocque's Prairie, 87, 131, 291
Labrador, 41, 42, 44
Lac la Pluie, *see* Rainy Lake
Lachine (Que.), 39, 57, 61, 63, 156
Lach-oh-lett, 99, 303
lacrosse, game of, 95
Laflèche, the Rev. L.-F.-R., 74
Lake of the Woods, 65, 66, 155, 280, 289
Landerholm, Carl, 21, 300
landscapes of K., unidentified, 270, 280, 283, 285, 288, 295, 300, 309
Lane, Mr. (1845 brigade), 63, 64, 66, 67, 280
Lane, Richard (and wife), 19, 76, 83, 84, 87, 88, 89, 90
Lapwai Creek (Ore.), 24, 126
"Large Smith's Rock Portage" (northern Ont.), 281
Lavollée, Charles-Hubert, 41, 42
Lawrence, Sir Thomas, 10
Le Pas (Man.), 22, 27, 77, 151, 284
Lefroy, J. H., 16, 30, 39
Lefroy, Mrs., 30
Legaré, Joseph, 8, 10
lehallum, game of (Clallam), 102, 306
Leonardo da Vinci, 43, 271

Lethbridge (Alta.), 285
letters, carrying of, in northwest, 108, 156
Letters . . . on the Manners . . . of the North American Indians (Catlin), 13, 38
Lewes, John Lee, 24, 90, 111, 112, 122, 124, App. 10
Lewes, Mrs. John Lee, 124
Lewis, Henry, 279
Lewis, Meriwether, 302
Lewis River (Ore.), 21, 97, 299, 301
Lippi, Fra F., 271
Little Dalle(s), *see* Dalles, The
"Little Horn," 27, 149, 287
"Little Rat, The," *see* Waw-gas-kontz
Little Rock Falls (Winnipeg River), 154
"Little Round Man, The," *see* Potika-pootis
"Little Slave, The," *see* Chimaza
Loach, Frances, *see* Kane
lobstick, made for K., 26, 129
Lock-hi-num, 104, 303
London (England), 39, 40
Long Grass Prairie (Saskatchewan River), 82, 287
"Long Tooth," *see* Cash-a-cabut
Longman, Mr. (publisher), 40
Lost Men's Portage (Kaministiquia River), 63, 280, 293
"Loud Speaker, The," *see* Iacaway
Louis Philippe (France), 151
Louisville (Ky.), 271
Lowe, Thomas, 19, 130, 132, 147
Lower Canada, *see* Quebec
Lower Fort, *see* Fort Garry
Lucie, François, 29, 139, 141, 289
lynx, 136

"Macau" River (northern Ont.), 65
McBain, Mr. (Fort Walla Walla), 114, 116, 117, 125
McBean, William, 24, App. 10
McCracken, George, 13
McDouall, Col. R., 277
McDougall, Ducan, 92, 302
McGillveray (*sic*), Mr. (HBC), 84, 85, 86, 87, 88, 89
Ma-cheek-e-(a)-wis, 275, 307
Mackenlie (*sic*) Mr. (Oregon City), *see* McKinlay, A.
Mackenzie, Mr. (Fort William), 63
McKenzie, Major, 152, 153, 154, 155; wife of, 154, 155
Mackenzie, Sir Alexander, 291, 310
McKenzie, Hector E., App. 10
Mackenzie, William Lyon, 9, 309
Mackenzie River, 67, 76, 151
Mackinac, 15, 16, 17, 57–58, 60, 61, 62, 272, 276–77, 278, 301; natural bridge (Arch Rock), 15, 58, 276; Sugar Loaf, 276
McKinlay, A., 95, 96, 300
Mackintosh, J., 7, 39, 43
McLoughlin, Dr. John, 91, 96

"McMullan," Mr. (Fort Spokane), 128
MacNab, Allan, 310
MacNab, Sir Allan, 310
MacNab, Archibald, 310
Mactavish, William, 156
Mah-i-cum (Prairie Dog), sketch, 285
Mah-Min, 18, 26, 37, 146, 147, 290
Makah (Indians), 22, 104, 105, 304, 307
Malecite (Indians), 7
"Maligne," "Malaine" River (northern Ont.), 65, 154
Mallow (County Cork), 6
Mameluke (painting), 270
"Man that Always Rides, The," 28, 29, 38, 284; *see also* Eikutope
"Man that always runs in the plains, The," 286
"Man that always speaks, The," *see* Kee-a-kee-ka-sa-coo-way
"Man that Shot the Wolf with an Arrow, The," 284
"Man that was Born, The," *see* Na-taw-waugh-cit
"Man who gives the War-whoop, The," *see* Kee-a-kee-ka-sa-coo-way
"Man who is gone on a Hunt without raising his Camp, The," *see* I-ac-a-way
"Man with a Lump on his Navel, The," *see* Peccothis
"Man without Blood, The," *see* Tum-se-ne-ho
Mancemuckt, 112, 297
mangeurs du lard, 63, 88
Manitoba, 30, 43
Manitoba Museum of Science and History, 35, 286, 287, 289
Manitoulin Island, 16, 53, 54–55, 56–57, 272, 274–75
Manitowaning (Manitoulin Island), 16, 18, 53–55, 56, 57, 273–75, 278, 279
Mani-tow-wah-bay, 16, 58, 276
Mansfield (Nottinghamshire), 6
Marseilles, 12
Maska-nonga, 272
Maskuhnoonjee, 52, 272
Mason, Rev. William, 76, 283
Match-o-kee-maw, 278
Maticwaub, 52, 272
Maun-qua-dous, 272
Mauza-pau-Kan, 61, 278
Maydoc-game-kin-ungee, 27, 157, 279
"Meican," Lake (northern Ont.), 65
Menominee (Indians), 15, 16, 58, 61, 277, 278, 279, 291
Merritt, William Hamilton, 29
Métis, 19, 37, 39, 41, 68, 69, 74, 83, 289; buffalo hunt of, 17, 41, 69–73, 281, 282–83; and Sioux, 70–71
Mexico, 37
Michigan, Lake, 36, 52, 58, 61, 271, 274, 276, 279
Michilimackinac, 278
Michipicoten, 157, 274, 279
Micmac (Indians), 7

Miëtte's Rock (Jasper), 86, 291
Milan (Italy), 271
Mille Lacs, Lac de (Port Savanne, Ont.), 64
Mimico (Ont.), 10, 270
Mingan (Que.), 42
Minneapolis (Minn.), 279
Mis-cu-pa-puck-we, 286
Mis-ke-me-kin, 149, 287
missions, 41
    Catholic: Oregon, 22, 24, 95, 96, 99, 115, 125, 300; Lake Huron, 23, 53, 57; Wabassimong, 66, 155; prairies, 68, 75, 138; west coast, 104
    Church of England, 22, 74, 77
    Protestant: Oregon, 22–24, 95, 112, 116, 122, 125–26, 294, 296, 300; Lake Huron, 52, 53; prairies, 68, 76, 78, 138, 141, 283; Fort Frances, 156
Missisauga (Indians), 272
Mississippi River, 11, 30, 52, 68, 281
Missouri River, 286
Miss-qua-Kany Lodge (Toronto), 43
Mistahpa'oo, 22, 23
Mobile (Alta.), K. in, 11, 14, 271, 309, App. 11
Mobile Advertiser for the County, 11, 14
moccasins, 132, 138
Modeste, H.M.S., 20–21, 91, 97, 98, 298
Mohawk (Indians), 52
Montreal, 7, 10, 16, 29, 38, 88, 308, 309
Moody, Capt. (met on Winnipeg River), 154
moose, hunting of, 77, 82, 85, 86, 139, 147
Morgan, Henry J., 7
mosquitoes, problem of, 66, 67, 75, 112, 154, 155
Moss Park (Allan home), 35, 37, 51
Mount Baker, 304
Mount Hood, 21, 25, 29, 298, 299, 300, 301, 304
Mount Kane, 26
Mount St. Helens, 21, 29, 36, 97, 99, 292, 301
Mountain Portage (Fort William), 156
Muck-a-ta, 61, 278
Muck-Cranium, 18, 284, 290
Muck-e-tah-kin-ne-u, 278
Muck-e-tick-enow, 55, 56
Muck-e-too, 81, 144, 286
Muck-koze, 275, 286
Mud Mountain (Ore.), 99, 110
Munich, 44
Murillo, B. E., 12, 43, 271
Musk-ku-thay-ka-ou-mu-thay, 286
Mus-Kosh, 272

Nack-a-wish, 296
Naples, K. in, 12, 271
Napoleonic Wars, 5
Narrative of a Journey . . . (Simpson), 19, 38, 39
Na-taw-waugh-cit, 282

National Gallery of Canada, 7, 8, 34, 299
New Brunswick, 7
New Brunswick Museum, 7
New Caledonia, 21, 29, 92, 96, 107, 110, 128, 305; see also British Columbia
New Orleans, 11, 12, 271
New York City, 9, 25, 39
Nez Percé (Indians), 25, 118, 126, 295, 296, 297
Nez Percé River, 115, 116, 118, 295
Niagara Falls (Can., U.S.A.), 15, 38, 61, 63, 156, 277; paintings of, 43, 270, 308–9
Nipissing, Lake, 16, 55, 275
Nisqually (Indians), 99, 108, 303
Nisqually (Wash.), 21, 22, 99, 108, 110, 303
Nisqually River, 99
"Noon day," see Now-qua-ke-glick
Nootka (Indians), 107, 304, 307
Nootka Sound (Vancouver I.), 307
Norma (steamer), 11, 271
North West Company, 16, 63, 69, 92, 93, 276, 288, 289, 291
"North Wind, The," see Ke-wah-ten
Norton, Brayley (Mrs. Henry Richard Norton), 10, 12, 270
Norton, Henry Richard, 270
Norway House, 27, 67, 74, 76, 77, 147, 151, 152, 153, 155, 279, 280, 281, 284, 286, 288; sketches of, 18, 36, 283
Notre Dame Church (Montreal), 10
Nova Scotia, 7
Now-on-dhu-go, 36, 276
Now-qua-ke-glick, 274

O'Brien, Henry, 45
O'Brien, Capt. John, 29, 43
O'Brien, Lucius, 29, 35, 38, 43, 45
Ogden, Peter Skene, 13, 19, 20, 24, 25, 31, 90, 126, App. 10
Ogemawwah Chack, 27, 152, 283
Og-sah-wah-nah-quoch-ogue, 290
Ohio River, 30, 275
Ojibwa (Indians), 13, 15, 52, 55, 57, 65, 70, 157; sketches of, 16, 27, 52–53, 157, 272–76, 279, 281, 282, 290
Oke Falls (northern Ont.), 281
Oke-a-sa, 279
"Old Bear," 304
Old Cox, 299
Old Man's River (Athabasca country), 86
Olympic Mts. (Wash.), 304
Omoxesisixany, 18, 27, 44, 148–50, 152, 286–87; brother of, 27, 149, 150, 287
Ona-put, 304
"One that looks at the stars," see Cun-ne-wa-bum
"One that passes through the sky," see Pe-a-pus-qua-hum
"One who sits with his feathers on," see Each-a-quip
"One with his Face towards the West," see Shawwanossoway

Ontario, 5, 17, 21; sketches of, 298, 309; see also Upper Canada
Ontario, Lake, 5, 10, 52
Ontario Society of Artists, 34, 37
Oogemsh-wah-be-zee, 272
Oregon, 11, 296, 299; artists in, 11, 24–25; K. in, 11, 51, 91, 95–99, 110, 111–28, 279, 300; possession of, 16, 20, 22, 24, 25, 298, 300, 305; settlers in, 20, 21, 23, 24, 91, 98, 125, 300; K.'s sketches of, 21, 24, 292–302; missions in, 22–23, 95, 96, 112, 115, 116, 125–26, 300
Oregon City, 21, 95–96, 298, 299, 300
Oregon Spectator, 21, 24
Oregon Trail, 20, 23
Orillia (Ont.), 52
Orkney Islands, 68, 154
Oscosh, 15, 59, 278
Oshkosh (Wisc.), 278
Osler, Sir Edmund, 35
Otisskun, 37, 81, 285
Ottawa (Indians), 16, 36, 57, 272, 274–75, 276, 286
Ottawa River, 61
Overlanders (1862), 25
Owen Sound (Ont.), 52, 53, 273

Pacific Fur Company, 92, 93, 300, 301, 302
Pacific Ocean (and coast), 32, 35, 51, 88, 93, 114, 138, 288, 291, 298, 302, 305, 310
Palma, J., Il Vecchio, 271
Paloos (Indians), 115, 295
Paris (France), 11, 13, 151; exhibition of 1855, 34
Parrish, Josiah L., 21, 301
Patriot (Toronto), 10, 11, 29
Paulet Paul, 77, 151
Peace River, 291
Pe-a-pus-qua-hum, 290
Peccothis, 70, 282
Pe-ho-this, 151
pelicans, 119, 121
Pell, A. J., 32
Pelouse River, 23, 25, 115, 116, 295
Pembina River, 69, 73, 282
pemmican, 69, 136, 137, 138, 148, 151, 157
Penetanguishene (Ont.), 52, 53, 54
Peo-Peo-mox-mox, 25, 117, 297; son of, 117, 297
Pe-pa-ka-chos-a, 284
Perkins, H. K. W., 112
Perry, Mrs. (painting), 270
Peterborough (Ont.), 53
Philadelphia, 10, 44
Philips, Charles, 30–32
Phillimore, Mrs. E., 32
Piegan (Indians), 27, 136, 148, 151, 286–87
pigeons, wild, 153
"Pike," see Mus-Kosh

Pilgrims at a shrine (painting), 271
"Pilleurs" (Ojibwa), 52
Pin Portage (Kaministiquia River), 63, 280
"Pine Tree," 278
Pinelli, Bartolomeo, 289
"Piperani" (sketch), 271
Pipes, Nellie B., 24, 25
Pitti Palace (Florence), 12, 271
Plains (Indians), 27, 36, 290, 292; see also prairies
Plamondon, Antoine, 10, 11
Playgreen Lake, 75, 76, 283
Pompeii, 12
Poore, Sir Edward, 30–32, App. 10
Port Hope (Ont.), 43
portages: meaning of, 64, 155; between Lakes Superior and Winnipeg, 63–67, 154–57, 280–81; on Columbia River, 111, 126, 128–29; on Saskatchewan River, 151
Portland (Ore.), 301
portraits: fashion for, 9, 11, 12, 14; by K., not identified, 308, 309, 310
Potawatomi (Indians), 16, 37, 53, 59, 272, 276–77, 278
Potika-poo-tis, 83, 289
potlach ceremony, 102–3, 305
"Powder," see Muck-e-too
Prairie de Bute (Ore.), 99, 110, 303
prairies: Métis of, 17–18, 68, 69, 282–83, 289; Indians of, 18, 26–27, 36, 44, 282, 284, 285–87, 289, 290; depicted by artists, 25, 29; K.'s sketches of, 37, 284, 285, 287, 288, 290; K. describes, 78, 80, 81, 82–83
Prehistoric Man (Wilson), 44, 302, 307, 308
Preston (Lancashire), 6
primitives, painting of, 9, 10, 12
Prince Albert (Sask.), 288
Prince Rupert (B.C.), 307
Provancher, Abbé Léon, 33
Provencher, Joseph-Norbert, 68
Prudence (sic), Mr. (Fort Edmonton), 141
Puget Sound: agriculture on, 22, 99, 303; Indians of, 29, 91, 99, 107, 303; K.'s travels on, 51, 99, 104, 302, 303, 304
Puget's Sound Agricultural Company, 99, 303

"Quatlin," see Kwantlen
Quebec (city), 8, 9, 10, 11, 34
Quebec (province), 5, 10, 21, 26, 53, 141, 288, 300
Queen Charlotte Islands, 307
Queenston (Ont.), 308, 309

"Rabbit, The," see Wah-pus
rabbits, 136, 147, 155, 156
"Raccoon, The," see Asabonish
Rae, Dr. John, 27, 151
Rainy Lake, 65, 156, 280

Rainy River, 16, 17, 155, 156, 280, 281
Rankin, Arthur, 13
Raphael Santi, 12, 43, 271
Rat Portage (Kenora, Ont.), 66, 154, 155, 156
Rathwell (Man.), 30
rattlesnakes, 113
Ready, W. B., 283
Rebellion (Canada's), 9, 43, 309
Red River, 17, 18, 25, 30, 31, 32, 68, 74, 75, 138, 281, 282, 283, 284
Red River Settlement, 16, 17, 22, 51, 68–69, 74, 82, 88, 150, 152, 154, 283; illustrations of, 68, 281
"Red Shirt," see Mis-cu-pa-puck-we
"Red Vest," 287
Rembrandt, 271
Revolution (American), 5
Revue des deux mondes, 40–41
rice, wild, 153–54, 155, 156
Rice Lake (Ont.), 52, 53
Rich, E. E., 16, 19, 31, 69
Richardson, James, 12, 43, 310
Richardson, Sir John, 27, 39, 151, 153, 309
Rindisbacher, Peter, 25
"Rock called the Too-He-Pu-See-Girls," see Chimney Rocks
"Rocks of the Ki-use girls," see Chimney Rocks
Rocky Mountain House: K. at, 18, 26, 37, 145, 146, 147, 284, 288; sketches at, 18, 289–90, 308
Rocky Mountains, 13, 21, 26, 29, 30, 31, 44, 45, 76, 85, 91, 93, 113, 116, 128, 144, 146, 147, 149, 286, 289, 294, 298; K.'s sketches in, 8, 15, 29, 87, 88, 130, 291–92, 310; K.'s crossing of, 19, 41, 51, 84, 86–89, 129–32, 279; Warre's sketches of, 25
Rome, 10, 11, 289; K. in, 11, 12, 271
Rose, John, 309
Ross, Donald, 76, 283
Ross, Mrs. R. B., 283
Rowand, John, 22, 76, 79, 80, 81, 82, 83, 152, 284, 285, 288
Rowand, Mr., Jr. (Fort Pitt), 141, 288, 289
Royal Artillery, 6
Royal Canadian Academy, 29, 45
Royal Horse Artillery, 6
Royal Navy, 20
Royal Ontario Museum, 30, 35, 45
Rubens, Peter Paul, 12, 271
Rundle, Rev. T. R., 18, 26, 78, 79, 82, 83, 138, 139, 141, 142, 285, 288
Rupert's Land, 16, 17, 156
Ruttan, Hon. Henry, 270
Russia, 305; relations with HBC, 19, 26, 76, 83, 85, 91, 99, 130, 283
Ryerson, Egerton, 33, 34

Sa-co, 287
Sager, see Delaney

Index

Sahaptin, see Nez Percé
St. Boniface, 22, 138, 281
St. Clair, Lake, 52, 272
St. John River (N.B.), 7
St. Lawrence, Gulf of, 42
St. Lawrence River, 5, 17
Saint Louis (Mo.), 11, 30
St. Mary's River, 62, 276
St. Paul de Wallamette mission, 21, 300
St. Paul (Minn.), 68
St. Peter (U.S.A.), 30
Salish (Indians), 293, 294, 304, 305, 306
salmon: fishery, Columbia River, 41, 112, 123–24, 293; spearing for (Fox River), 58, 277; at Suck, 304
"Salmon Chief," see See-pays
salt lakes, Saskatchewan River, 82–83, 288
Salter, Mr. (English art student), 12
San Juan Island, 304
Sandusky (Ohio), 30
Sandwich Islands, 30, 91, 99, 103, 111, 112, 298–99
Sanetch (Indians), 22, 107, 306, 307
Sarsi (Indians), 27, 136, 148, 150, 151, 286, 287
Sarto, Andrea del, 12, 271
Saskatchewan River, 22, 27, 51, 76, 77–84, 128, 138, 141, 144, 145, 146, 148, 283, 284, 286, 289; sketches of, 80, 281, 285, 287, 288
Saugeen (Indians), 272–73, 297
Saugeen village (Georgian Bay), 16, 52–53, 272–73
Sault Ste Marie (Can., U.S.A.), 16, 17, 27, 32, 57, 61, 62, 156, 157, 272, 275–76, 279
Saulteaux (Indians), 65, 66, 67, 68, 70, 71, 75, 153, 155, 275, 280–82, 283, 285, 290
Saw-gun, 274
Saw-se-a, 102, 306
Scadding, Henry, 7, 8
Schoolcraft, Henry, 33, 39
Scobie, Hugh, 28, 29
Scotland, 5
"Scratching River" (Man.), 282
seal, hunting of, 109
Second Toronto Independent Artillery Company, 44
See-pays, 123–24, 293
Selkirk, Lord, 68, 281
Semple, Governor Robert, 69
"Serpent, The," see Iwa-toke
Serpentine Valley (Sask.), 285
"Setler," Mr. (Fort Alexander), 67, 68
Seven Years' War, 5
Shakespeare, William, K. and, 8
Sha-Neu-Oh-Rigits, 275
Sha-nu-oh-ke-zhick, 275
Shawstun, 107, 304
Shawwanossoway, 55–56, 274
She-bah-ke-zhick, 274, 282
sheep, mountain, 87, 131, 132, 291, 292
shells, as currency, 106

Shewans-u-ne-bin, 272
Sho-ne-ah, 281
Shuswap (Indians), 87, 129, 291
Shutes, see Skinpah
Siebert, Erna, 305
Sigennok, 54–55, 274, 275
Sig-in-nock-ence, 274
"Silver," see Sho-ne-ah
Simcoe, John Graves, 6
Simcoe, Lake, 52
Simpson, Lady Frances, 156
Simpson, Sir George, 75, 308; life of, 16, 68, 85; assistance to K., 16–17, 19, 28, 29, 30, 42, 57, 61, 62, 64, 65, 152, 308, App. 10; suggestions re sketching, 17, 27, 38, 280, 282, App. 10; Narrative of a Journey, 19, 38, 39, 139; K.'s pictures for, 28, 30, 33, 40, 42, 132, 291, 292, App. 4, 10; and Sir Edward Poore, 31, 32; and K.'s Wanderings, 38–39, 42
Simpson, W., 74, 75
Sinclair, James, 32
"Sinew Piece, The," 287
Sioux (Indians), 8, 18, 37, 39, 68, 95, 279, 281, 289; warfare of, 70, 71, 72, 73
Sitka (Alaska), 76
Skagit, "Shatchet" (Indians), 303
Skagit River (Wash.), 303
Skeen, see Skinpah
Skinpah, Shutes, Skeen (Indians), 112, 297
skunk, as food, 153
Slave Falls (Winnipeg River), 66, 154, 280
sleds (travelling), 141, 288–89
Slo-ce-ac-cum, 115, 295
Slum-a-chusset, 307
Smith, Donald (Lord Strathcona), 42
Smith, William G., 39
Smithurst, the Rev. John, 74
Smithsonian Institution, 25, 39
Snake River (northwest), 295, 296; see also Lewis River
Snohomish (Indians), 107, 304
Snohomish River (Wash.), 304
snow blindness, 13, 26, 44, 146
snowshoes, travel on, 26, 67, 87, 88, 89, 131, 132–35, 141, 145
Society of Artists and Amateurs (Toronto), 7, 9–10, 43, 270, 309, 310
Sohon, Gustavus, 25
Songish, "Sangeys" (Indians), 103, 303, 304, 306
Sooke (Vancouver I.), 304
Southesk, Earl of, 27
So-wall-o-way, 297
Spalding, Henry, 24, 126
Spider Islands (Lake Huron), 53, 273–74; (Lake Winnipeg), 152
"Spirit Chief, The," see Ogemawwah Chack
"Spirit Sky, The," see Tipich-la-ga-sheck

Spokan (Indians), 23, 123, 292, 293, 294, 299, 304
Spokane River, 122, 128, 293, 294, 297
Stanley, John Mix: acquaintance with K., II, 24; painting in northwest, 24–25, 32
Stark, H. J. Lutcher, 30, 40, 42
Stark, Mrs. Lutcher, 30
Stark Foundation, 30, 40
Stewart, Hope James, 12, 13
Stone, W. L., 39, 43, 309
Stone Fort (Red River), 68, 74
Strachan, Bishop John, 7
"Striped Cloud, The," see Bay-je-gi-she-quish
sturgeon, 156
Sturgeon Bay (Lake Huron), 40, 52
Sturgeon Creek (west of Edmonton), 84, 291
Sturgeon Lake (northwestern Ont.), 65
Suck (Juan de Fuca), 22, 105, 303, 304
Superior, Lake, 7, 16, 17, 30, 52, 55, 62, 63, 157, 272, 274, 275, 276, 279, 281, 309
Suttles, Wayne, 304
Switzerland, 13

Taché, Rev. A.-A., 74
Taché, J. C., 33, 74, App. 10
Takulli (Babine, Carrier, Tautin) (Indians), 291, 307, 308
Tam-at-a-pa, 297
Tanner, John, 15, 39
Tautin (Indians), 107–8, 308
Tecumseh, 15, 57, 275
Tenino (Indians), 297
Terrapin Tower (Niagara Falls), 309
theatre, 19th-century interest in, 8
Thibault ("Thebo"), Rev. Jean-Baptiste, 138, 142
Thirty Thousand Islands, see Georgian Bay
Thompson, Erwin N., 23, 24, 296
Thompson River (B.C.), 92, 291
Thorwaldsen, A. B., 10
Thousand Islands, Lake of the, 64, 65, 280
Thunder Point (Lake Superior), 62
Til-au-kite, 23, 35, 116, 125, 296; son of, 125; wife of, 296
Tipich-la-ga-sheck, 281
Tivoli (painting), 270
Toanichum (Whidbey Island), 104, 303, 304
Tolmie, William Fraser, 99
To-ma-kus, 23, 116, 125, 296
Tomaquin, 112, 283, 297
Tommskarrohoto, 308
Tonquin (ship), 106
"Tooth of the Glutton, The," see Cash-a-cabut
Toronto, 5, 9, 16, 17, 27, 28, 34, 37, 38, 40, 42, 43, 45, 51, 52, 61, 157; K.'s life in, 6, 11, 14, 16, 28, 32, 33, 38, 42–45, 58; interest in art, 9–10, 28, 29,

270; sketches in, 309, 310; see also York
Toronto, streets in: Adelaide, 6; Bloor, 309; Front, 9, 28; Jarvis, 43; King, 8, 9, 32; Sherbourne, 309; Wellesley, 43; Yonge, 6
Toronto Conservatory of Music, 35
Traits of Indian Life and Character (Ogden?), 19
trees: pine forest, Jasper, 86; west coast, 94, 95, 98, 100, 121, 122, 127, 298, 300, 302; Rocky Mountains, 131, 146, 292; prairies, 141, 142, 288
Trinity College School (Port Hope), 23, 43
Tshimakain (Wash.), 23, 294
Tum-se-ne-ho, 294
turkeys, wild, 121
Turtle Mountain (south of Fort Garry), 69
Twelve Mile Creek (Ont.), 38
Two Mountains (Que.), 10
Tyler, John, 278

Ucaltas, "You-call-tee" (Indians), 307
Uffizi gallery (Florence), 12, 271
Umatilla (Indians), 25
Umatilla River (Ore.), 296, 297
Umpqua Mountains, 96
Umpqua River (Ore.), 93, 300
Uniacke, Mr. (petitioner on K.'s behalf), 33
United Empire Loyalists, 5
United States, 5, 25, 32, 42, 73; artists of, 11; K. in, 11, 13, 14; territory in northwest, 20, 24, 91, 126, 298, 305; and Indians, 25, 74, 126, 149, 278; see also Indians, treaty agreements with
Upper Canada (province), 5, 6, 9, 12, 27, 28–29, 154; see also Ontario
Upper Canada Bible Society, 35
Upper Canada College (Toronto), 9, 34, 35
Upper Fort, see Fort Garry
"Upputuppets," see Paloos
Us-koos-koosish, 78, 284
U-thay-skun, 285

Vancouver Island, 15, 22, 76, 97, 101, 103, 105, 106, 107, 108, 147; K.'s travels on, 22, 29, 51, 99, 100, 106, 303, 308; Indians of, 91, 100–2, 107, 299, 304–5, 305–7
Vatican, 138
Velazquez, 38
Venice, 12, 271
Verner, Frederick A., 39, 40, 43, 44, 45
Veronese, 271
Victoria, Queen, 11, 13, 27, 40, 58, 104, 144, 271

Wabassimong (northern Ont.), 66, 155, 280
Wah-bannim, 58, 277, 296

Wah-he-joe-tass-e-neen, 26, 146, 278, 290
Wah-nis-stow, 150, 151, 287
Wah-pus (Wappoose), 53, 273
Waiilatpu (Ore.), 23, 25
"Walk in the water," see Ironsides, Capt.
Walker, Rev. Elkanah, 23, 24, 25, 122, 294
Walker, Mary Richardson (Mrs. Elkanah), 23
Walla Walla (Indians), 25, 39, 113, 116–18, 123, 126, 293, 295, 296–97
Walla Walla River, 113, 114, 116, 295, 296
Wallace, W. S., 309
"Walula encampment, Battle of," 304
War of 1812, 5, 43, 276, 277, 278
Warre, Captain Henry J., 20–21, 22, 25, 284, 285
Wasco (Indians), 112
Washington (state), 22, 294, 295, 296, 302–3, 304, 307
Washington, D.C., 39

Watlala, see Cascade
Watson, Stewart, 13, 14, App. 10
Waw-gas-kontz, 66, 281, 282, 290
Waugh, Samuel Bell, 10, 11
Weendigo ("One who eats Human Flesh"), 65
Weller, William, 10, 270
Weller, Mrs. William (Mercy Willcox), 10, 270
Wells, J. D., 7
whale, hunting of, 100, 105
"Whellamay" girl, 307
Whidbey Island (Strait of Juan de Fuca), 104, 303, 304
"White Buffalo, The," see Wah-nis-stow
"White Dog, The," see Wah-bannim
White Mud Portage (Winnipeg River), 154, 280
whitefish, 135, 136, 137, 139, 155
Whitman, Dr. Marcus: massacre, 20, 23–24, 25, 125–26, 296; mission of, 23, 25, 116–17, 295, 296

Whitman, Narcissa, 23, 125, 296
Wikwemikong, "Wequimecong" (Manitoulin Island), 56, 275
Wilkes, Lt. Charles, 98, 99
Willamette River, 21, 91, 97, 299; sketches of, 24, 25, 298, 300–1; K.'s travels on, 95–96
Willis, Major R., 30
Willson, Beckles, 42
Wilson, Mr. (Sault Ste Marie), 62
Wilson, Daniel: articles on K., 9, 12, 40, 45; friendship with K., 44; use of K.'s sketches, 302, 307, 308
Windsor (England), 40
Winnebago (Indians), 60, 277, 278
Winnebago, Lake, 58, 60, 61, 277, 291
Winnipeg, 17, 29, 31, 154
Winnipeg, Lake, 67, 68, 77, 152–4, 281, 283
Winnipeg River, 66, 67, 154, 155, 277, 280, 281
Wolverine, 147, 290

wolves, on prairies, 77, 78, 80, 81, 82, 136, 137, 141, 148, 285
Womack, John Warburton, 14
Wood, Kathleen, 290
Wyandot (Indians), 16, 57, 275

Yates-sut-soot, 104, 105, 304
"Yellow Serpent, The," see Peo-Peo-mox-mox
Yellow-cum, 105, 106–7, 307
Yellowhead Pass, 291
York (Upper Canada), description of (c. 1819), 5, 6, 7, 9, 10; K.'s life in, 7, 9, 15, 20, 51, 277; see also Toronto
York boats, 138, 148, 152, 284
York District Grammar School, 6, 7, 9
York Factory, 22, 28, 76, 138, 148, 152, 156, 283
"Young Bear," see Muck-koze
Young girl (naïve style painting), 9, 270
"Young Grass," see Us-koos-koosish

PRINCIPLES OF
ENGINEERING
GRAPHICS

Books by the Authors

Basic Technical Drawing, rev. ed., by H. C. Spencer and J. T. Dygdon (Glencoe Publishing Company, 1980)

Basic Technical Drawing Problems by H. C. Spencer and J. T. Dygdon (Macmillan Publishing Company, 1972)

Descriptive Geometry, 8th ed., by E. G. Paré, R. O. Loving, I. L. Hill, and R. C. Paré (Macmillan Publishing Company, 1991)

Descriptive Geometry Worksheets, Series A, 8th ed., by E. G. Paré, R. O. Loving, I. L. Hill, and R. C. Paré (Macmillan Publishing Company, 1991)

Descriptive Geometry Worksheets, Series B, 8th ed., by E. G. Paré, R. O. Loving, I. L. Hill, and R. C. Paré (Macmillan Publishing Company, 1991)

Engineering Graphics, 5th ed., by F. E. Giesecke, A. Mitchell, H. C. Spencer, I. L. Hill, R. O. Loving, J. T. Dygdon, and J. E. Novak (Macmillan Publishing Company, 1993)

Engineering Graphics Problems, Series 1, 5th ed., by H. C. Spencer, I. L. Hill, R. O. Loving, J. T. Dygdon, and J. E. Novak (Macmillan Publishing Company, 1993)

Principles of Engineering Graphics, 2nd ed., by F. E. Giesecke, A. Mitchell, H. C. Spencer, I. L. Hill, R. O. Loving, J. T. Dygdon, and J. E. Novak (Macmillan Publishing Company, 1994)

Technical Drawing, 9th ed., by F. E. Giesecke, A. Mitchell, H. C. Spencer, I. L. Hill, J. T. Dygdon, and J. E. Novak (Macmillan Publishing Company, 1991)

Technical Drawing Problems, Series 1, 9th ed., by F. E. Giesecke, A. Mitchell, H. C. Spencer, I. L. Hill, J. T. Dygdon, and J. E. Novak (Macmillan Publishing Company, 1991)

Technical Drawing Problems, Series 2, 9th ed., by H. C. Spencer, I. L. Hill, J. T. Dygdon, and J. E. Novak (Macmillan Publishing Company, 1991)

Technical Drawing Problems, Series 3, 9th ed., by H. C. Spencer, I. L. Hill, J. T. Dygdon, and J. E. Novak (Macmillan Publishing Company, 1991)

PRINCIPLES OF

ENGINEERING GRAPHICS

SECOND EDITION

FREDERICK E. GIESECKE
Late Professor Emeritus of Drawing
Texas A&M University

ALVA MITCHELL
Late Professor Emeritus of Engineering Drawing
Texas A&M University

HENRY CECIL SPENCER
Late Professor Emeritus of Technical Drawing
Formerly Director of Department
Illinois Institute of Technology

IVAN LEROY HILL
Late Professor Emeritus of Engineering Graphics
Formerly Chairman of Department
Illinois Institute of Technology

ROBERT OLIN LOVING
Professor Emeritus of Engineering Graphics
Illinois Institute of Technology

JOHN THOMAS DYGDON
Professor of Engineering Graphics,
Chairman of Department,
and Director of the Division of Academic Services
and Office of Educational Services
Illinois Institute of Technology

JAMES E. NOVAK
Associate Director/Executive Officer, Office of Educational Services
Illinois Institute of Technology

PRENTICE HALL
Englewood Cliffs, NJ 07632

Library of Congress Cataloging-in-Publication Data

Principles of engineering graphics / Frederick E. Giesecke ... [et al.] - 2nd ed.
    p. cm.
    Portions of this book are reprinted from Engineering graphics, 5th ed.
     and from Principles of engineering graphics problems.
    Includes index.
    ISBN 0-02-342820-1
    1. Engineering graphics.   I. Giesecke, Frederick Ernest.
T353.P847   1994
604.2-dc20   93-16447
                        CIP

Editor: John Griffin
Production Supervisor: Elisabeth Belfer
Production Manager: Paul Smolenski
Test Designer: Patrice Fodero
Cover Designer: Russ Maselli
Cover photograph: Stephen Webster

This book was set in Caledonia by York Graphic Services, Inc.

 © 1994 by Prentice-Hall, Inc.
A Simon & Schuster Company
Englewood Cliffs, New Jersey 07632

Copyright ©1994 by Macmillan Publishing Company, a division of Macmillan, Inc.

Printed in the United States of America

10 9 8 7 6

ISBN 0-02-342820-1

Prentice-Hall International (UK) Limited, *London*
Prentice-Hall of Australia Pty. Limited, *Sydney*
Prentice-Hall Canada Inc., *Toronto*
Prentice-Hall Hispanoamericana, S.A., *Mexico*
Prentice-Hall of India Private Limited, *New Delhi*
Prentice-Hall of Japan, Inc., *Tokyo*
Simon & Schuster Asia Pte. Ltd., *Singapore*
Editora Prentice-Hall do Brasil, Ltda., *Rio de Janeiro*

This Edition of the Book
is Dedicated to the Memory
of our Friend and Colleague

IVAN L. HILL

Preface

Principles of Engineering Graphics is our response to the latest developments in engineering and technical education. Our goals in writing this new text were to

1. Produce a concise and affordable textbook that can be used for either a one- or a two-semester course in technical drawing and design, descriptive geometry, graphs and diagrams, and computer graphics.
2. Include worksheets with the text rather than as a supplement.
3. Include a thorough introduction to computer graphics.
4. Retain the high standard of accuracy and excellence established in nine editions of *Technical Drawing* and five editions of *Engineering Graphics*.
5. Provide the student with a text that will cover the foundations of the subject and serve as a valuable reference book long after graduation.

For those instructors teaching an introductory course on the theory of engineering graphics including manual and computer graphics techniques, the contents of this text will be sufficient. For those wishing to spend additional time developing the manual or computer drafting skills of their students, the book has been priced so a supplemental manual workbook or computer software manual may be required without imposing too great a financial burden.

Principles of Engineering Graphics meets the needs of today's curriculum. Much of this text is adapted or condensed from *Engineering Graphics*, 5th Edition, by the same authors and published by Macmillan Publishing Company. The purpose of this book is *to teach the language of the engineer*. This goal has prompted the authors to illustrate and explain the basic principles from the standpoint of the student—that is, to present each principle so clearly that the student is certain to understand it, and to make the text interesting enough to encourage all students to read and study on their own initiative. By this means the authors hope to free the instructor from the repetitive labor of teaching each student individually the subject matter that the textbook can teach. Thus more class time can be given to the special requirements of individual programs—such as explaining the features of your school's brand of computer graphics software—or in giving more attention to those students having real difficulties.

Features of This Text/Workbook

A unique feature of this book is the combination of the textbook and workbook. By including worksheets in the same volume, we are able to provide a more convenient learning tool at an affordable paperback price.

A long-standing feature is the emphasis on technical sketching throughout the text as well as in an early chapter devoted specifically to sketching. This chapter is unique in integrating the basic concepts of views with freehand sketching so that the subject of multiview drawing can be introduced through the medium of sketches.

The increased use of computer technology for drafting, design work, and manufacturing processes is reflected in many chapters. Two chapters are specifically devoted to this new technology. Chapter 3 presents a generic introduction to computer-aided design and drafting and a survey of computer equipment, or hardware, of current CAD systems. Chapter 8 includes a general discussion of the use and operation of a CAD system focusing on computer graphics programs, or software. Rather than describing one particular software package, examples are given showing how several popular programs can be applied by the user. In addition, relevant material has been added to the other chapters with examples of how computer graphics may be used in particular applications. Many illustrations of computer-generated drawings and the equipment used to make them have been included. These discussions emphasize the relationship between traditional drafting techniques and computer graphics. A comprehensive glossary of CAD/CAM terms and concepts is given in the Appendix.

The growing importance of the engineer's design function is emphasized, especially in the chapter on design and working drawings. The chapter is designed to give the student an understanding of the fundamentals of the design process.

The book consistently reflects the latest trends and practices in education, industry, and especially the various current sections of the ANSI Y14 *American National Standard Drafting Manual* and other relevant ANSI standards.

The chapters on manufacturing processes, dimensioning, tolerancing, and threads and fasteners have been extensively reviewed to ensure their conformity with the latest ANSI standards. Every effort has been made to ensure that this book is completely abreast of the many technological developments of recent years.

The high quality of drafting in the illustrations and problems that appear in *Engineering Graphics*, 5th Edition, has been maintained in *Principles of Engineering Graphics*. A large number of drawings include the approved system of metric dimensions, now that the metric system is more widely used internationally. The current editions of ANSI standards also indicate a preference for the use of metric units. Many problems, especially in the chapter on design and working drawings, provide an opportunity for the student to convert dimensions to either the decimal-inch system or the metric system.

It is expected that the instructor who uses this text/workbook will supplement the worksheet problems with assignments from the text, to be drawn on blank paper. Many of the text problems are designed for Size A4 or Size A sheets, the same size as the easily filed worksheets. A supply of blank sheets and cross section sheets, both rectangular and isometric, is provided on the reverse sides of the worksheets.

Acknowledgments

The authors wish to express their thanks to the many individuals and companies who so generously contributed their services and materials to the production of this text. We are especially indebted to Mr. E. J. Mysiak, Engineering Product Manager, Pyle

National, Inc.; Mr. Stephen A. Smith, Manager, Product Design and Development, Packaging Corporation of America; the late Mr. Byron Urbanick, Vice President, Instructional Design Systems; and Mr. James W. Zagorski, Kelly High School, Chicago Public Schools. The authors also express their thanks to Mr. Gary W. Rybicki and Mr. William T. Briggs Jr., Department of Engineering Graphics, Illinois Institute of Technology, for their helpful suggestions and cooperation.

Special thanks are due to our editor John Griffin and to our production supervisor Elisabeth Belfer.

Students, teachers, engineers, designers, and drafters are invited to write concerning any questions that may arise. All comments and suggestions will be welcomed.

Robert O. Loving
Evergreen Park IL

John Thomas Dygdon
Illinois Institute of Technology
Chicago IL

James E. Novak
Illinois Institute of Technology
Chicago IL

Contents

1. The Graphic Language and Design 1
2. Instrumental Drawing 11
3. Introduction to CAD 55
4. Lettering 87
5. Geometric Constructions 109
6. Sketching and Shape Description 149
7. Multiview Projection 179
8. Using a CAD System 225
9. Sectional Views 257
10. Auxiliary Views 285
11. Revolutions 309
12. Manufacturing Processes 323
13. Dimensioning 341
14. Tolerancing 379
15. Thread, Fasteners, and Springs 411
16. Design and Working Drawings 447
17. Axonometric Projection 499
18. Oblique Projection 531
19. Points, Lines, and Planes 547
20. Parallelism and Perpendicularity 581
21. Intersections and Developments 597
22. Line and Plane Tangencies 625
23. Graphs and Diagrams 639

Appendix A·1

Index I·1

Worksheets W·1

CHAPTER
1

The Graphic Language and Design

The old saying "necessity is the mother of invention" continues to hold, and a new machine, structure, system, or device is the result of that need. If the new device, machine, system, or gadget is really needed or desired, people will buy it, providing it does not cost too much. Then, naturally, these questions may arise: Is there a wide potential market? Can this device or system be made available at a price that people are willing to pay? If these questions can be answered satisfactorily, then the inventor, designer, or officials of a company may elect to go ahead with the development of production and marketing plans for the new project or system.

A new machine, structure, or system, or an improvement thereof, must exist in the mind of the engineer or designer before it can become a reality. This original concept or idea is usually placed on paper, or as an image on a computer screen, and communicated to others by the way of the *graphic language* in the form of freehand *idea sketches*, Figs. 1.1 and 6.1. These idea or design sketches are then followed by other sketches, such as *computation sketches*, for developing the idea more fully.

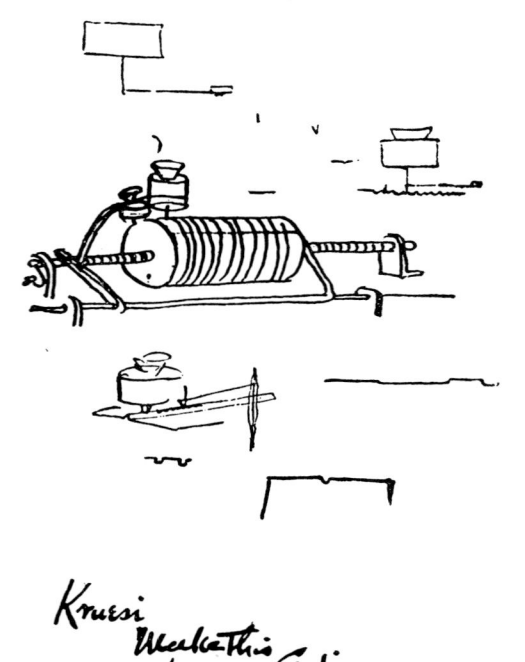

1.1 The Young Engineer*

The engineer or designer must be able to create idea sketches, calculate stresses, analyze motions, size the parts, specify materials and production methods, make design layouts, and supervise the preparation of drawings and specifications that will control the numerous details of production, assembly, and maintenance of the product. In order to perform or supervise these many tasks, the engineer makes liberal use of freehand sketches. He or she must be able to record and communicate ideas quickly to associate and support personnel. Facility in freehand sketching (Chapter 6) or the ability to work with computer-controlled drawing techniques, §16.27, requires a thorough knowledge of the graphic language. The engineer or designer who

*Henceforth in this text, all conventional titles such as student, drafter, designer, engineer, engineering technician, engineering technologist, and so on are intended to refer to all persons, male and female.

Fig. 1.1 Edison's Phonograph. *Original sketch of Thomas A. Edison's first conception of the phonograph; reproduced by special permission of Mrs. Edison.*

Fig. 1.2 Computer-Aided Design and Drafting Section of an Engineering Department. *Courtesy of Jervis B. Webb Co.*

Fig. 1.3 Engineering Drafting Department. *Courtesy of AT&T Bell Laboratories.*

uses a computer for drawing and design work must be proficient in drafting, designing, and conceptualizing.

Typical engineering and design departments are shown in Figs. 1.2 and 1.3. Many of the staff have considerable training and experience; others are recent graduates who are gaining experience. There is much to be learned on the job, and it is necessary for the inexperienced person to start at a low level and advance to more responsibility as experience is gained.

1.2 The Graphic Language

Although people around the world speak different languages, a universal graphic language has existed since the earliest of times. The earliest forms of writing were through picture forms, such as the Egyptian hieroglyphics, Fig. 1.4. Later these forms were simplified and became the abstract symbols used in our writing today.

A drawing is a *graphic representation* of a real thing, an idea, or a proposed design for later manufacture or construction. Drawings may take many

Fig. 1.4 Egyptian Hieroglyphics.

forms, but the graphic method of representation is a basic natural form of communication of ideas that is universal and timeless in character.

1.3 Two Types of Drawings

Graphic representation has been developed along two distinct lines, according to the purpose: (1) artistic and (2) technical.

From the beginning of time, artists have used drawings to express aesthetic, philosophic, or other abstract ideas. People learned by listening to their elders and by looking at sculptures, pictures, or drawings in public places. Everybody could understand pictures, and they were a principal source of information. The artist was not just an artist in the

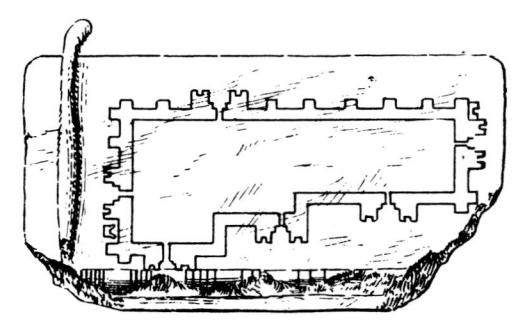

Fig. 1.5 Plan of a Fortress. This stone tablet is part of a statue now in the Louvre, in Paris, and is classified in the earliest period of Chaldean art, about 4000 B.C. *From Transactions ASCE, May 1891*

aesthetic sense, but also a teacher or philosopher, a means of expression and communication.

The other line along which drawing has developed has been the technical. From the beginning of recorded history, people have used drawings to represent the design of objects to be built or constructed. Of these earliest drawings no trace remains, but we definitely know that drawings were used, for people could not have designed and built as they did without using fairly accurate drawings.

1.4 Earliest Technical Drawings
Perhaps the earliest known technical drawing in existence is the plan view for a design of a fortress drawn by the Chaldean engineer Gudea and engraved upon a stone tablet, Fig. 1.5. It is remarkable how similar this plan is to those made by modern architects, although "drawn" thousands of years before paper was invented.

In museums we can see actual specimens of early drawing instruments. Compasses were made of bronze and were about the same size as those in current use. As shown in Fig. 1.6, the old compass resembled the dividers of today. Pens were cut from reeds.

The theory of projections of objects upon imaginary plans of projection (to obtain *views*, Chapter 7) apparently was not developed until the early part of the fifteenth century—by the Italian architects Alberti, Brunelleschi, and others. It is well known that Leonardo da Vinci used drawings to record and transmit to others his ideas and designs for mechanical constructions, and many of these drawings are still in existence, Fig. 1.7. It is not clear whether Leonardo ever made mechanical drawings showing orthographic views as we now know them, but it is probable that he did. Leonardo's treatise on painting, published in 1651, is regarded as the first book ever printed on the theory of projection drawing; however, its subject was perspective and not orthographic projection.

The scriber-type compass gave way to the compass with a graphite lead shortly after graphite pencils were developed. At Mount Vernon we can see the drawing instruments used by the great civil engineer George Washington, bearing the date 1749. This set, Fig. 1.8, is very similar to the conventional drawing instruments used today, consisting of a divider and a compass with pencil and pen attachments plus a ruling pen with parallel blades similar to the modern pens.

1.5 Early Descriptive Geometry
The beginnings of descriptive geometry are associated with the problems encountered in designs for building construction and military fortifications of France in the eighteenth century. Gaspard Monge (1746–1818) is considered the "inventor" of descrip-

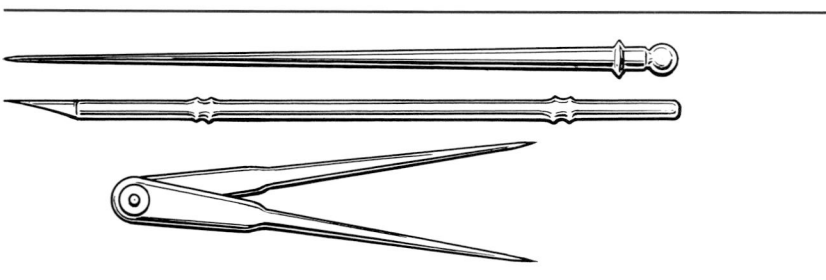

Fig. 1.6 Roman Stylus, Pen, and Compass. *From Historical Note on Drawing Instruments, published by V & E Manufacturing Co.*

Fig. 1.7 An Arsenal, by Leonardo da Vinci. *The Bettmann Archive*

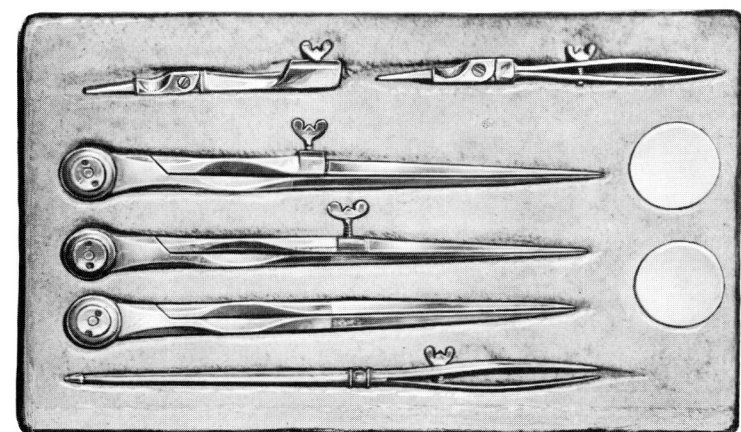

Fig. 1.8 George Washington's Drawing Instruments. *From Historical Note on Drawing Instruments, published by V & E Manufacturing Co.*

tive geometry, although his efforts were preceded by publications on stereotomy, architecture, and perspective in which many of the principles were used. It was while he was a professor at the Polytechnic School in France near the close of the eighteenth century that Monge developed the principles of projection that are now the basis of our technical drawing. These principles of descriptive geometry were soon recognized to be of such military importance that Monge was compelled to keep his principles secret until 1795, following which they became an important part of technical education in France and Germany and later in the United States. His book, *La Géométrie Descriptive*, is still regarded as the first text to expound the basic principles of projection drawing.

Monge's principles were brought to the United States from France in 1816 by Claude Crozet, an alumnus of the Polytechnic School and a professor at the United States Military Academy at West Point. He published the first text on the subject of descriptive geometry in the English language in 1821. In the years immediately following, these principles became a regular part of early engineering curricula at Rensselaer Polytechnic Institute, Harvard University, Yale University, and others. During the same period, the idea of manufacturing interchangeable parts in the early arms industries was being developed, and the principles of projection drawing were applied to these problems.

1.6 Modern Technical Drawing

Perhaps the first text on technical drawing in this country was *Geometrical Drawing*, published in 1849 by William Minifie, a high school teacher in Baltimore. In 1850 the Alteneder family organized the first drawing instrument manufacturing company in the United States (Theo. Alteneder & Sons, Philadelphia). In 1876 the blueprint process was introduced at the Philadelphia Centennial Exposition. Up to this time the graphic language was more or less an art, characterized by fine-line drawings made to resemble copper-plate engraving, by the use of shade lines, and by the use of water color "washes." These techniques became unnecessary after the introduction of blueprinting, and drawings gradually were made less ornate to obtain the best results from this method of reproduction. This was the beginning of modern technical drawing. The graphic language now became a relatively exact method of representation, and the building of a working model as a regular preliminary to construction became unnecessary.

Up to about 1900, drawings everywhere were generally made in what is called first-angle projection, §7.38, in which the top view was placed under the front view, the left-side view was placed at the right of the front view, and so on. At this time in the United States, after a considerable period of argument pro and con, practice gradually settled on the present *third-angle projection* in which the views are situated in what we regard as their more logical or natural positions. Today, third-angle projection is standard in the United States, but first-angle projection is still used throughout much of the world.

During the early part of the twentieth century, many books were published in which the graphic language was analyzed and explained in connection with its rapidly changing engineering design and industrial applications. Many of these writers were not satisfied with the term "mechanical drawing" because they recognized that technical drawing was really a graphic language. Anthony's *An Introduction to the Graphic Language*, French's *Engineering Drawing*, and Giesecke et al., *Technical Drawing* were all written with this point of view.

1.7 Drafting Standards

In all of the previously mentioned books there has been a definite tendency to standardize the characters of the graphic language, to eliminate its provincialisms and dialects, and to give industry, engineering, and science a uniform, effective graphic language. Of prime importance in this movement in the United States has been the work of the American National Standards Institute (ANSI) with the American Society for Engineering Education, the Society of Automotive Engineers, and the American Society of Mechanical Engineers. As sponsors they have prepared the *American National Standard Drafting Manual—Y14*, which is comprised of several separate sections that were published as approved standards as they were completed over a period of years. See Appendix 1.

These sections outline the most important idioms and usages in a form that is acceptable to the majority and are considered the most authoritative guide to uniform drafting practices in this country today. The Y14 Standard gives the characters of the graphic language, and it remains for the textbooks to explain the grammar and the penmanship.

Fig. 1.9 CAD Workstation. *Courtesy of Control Data Corporation*

1.8 Definitions

After this brief survey of the historical development of the graphic language, and before we begin a serious study of theory and applications, a few terms need to be defined.

Descriptive geometry. The grammar of the graphic language; it is the three-dimensional geometry forming the background for the practical applications of the language and through which many of its problems may be solved graphically.

Instrumental or ***mechanical drawing.*** Properly applies only to a drawing made with drawing instruments. The use of "mechanical drawing" to denote all industrial drawings is unfortunate not only because such drawings are not always mechanically drawn but also because that usage tends to belittle the broad scope of the graphic language by naming it superficially for its principal mode of execution.

Computer graphics. The application of conventional computer techniques with the aid of one of many graphic data processing systems available to the analysis, modification, and the finalizing of a graphical solution. The use of computers to produce technical drawings is called computer-aided design or computer-aided drafting (CAD) and also computer-aided design and drafting (CADD). A typical CAD workstation is shown in Fig. 1.9.

Engineering drawing and ***engineering drafting.*** Broad terms widely used to denote the graphic language. However, since the language is used not only by engineers but also by a much larger group of people in diverse fields who are concerned with technical work or with industrial production, these terms are still not broad enough.

Technical drawing. A broad term that adequately suggests the scope of the graphic language. It is rightly applied to any drawing used to express technical ideas. This term has been used by various writers since Monge's time at least and is still widely used, mostly in Europe.

Engineering graphics or ***engineering design graphics.*** Generally applied to drawings for technical use and has come to mean that part of technical drawing that is concerned with the graphical representation of designs and specifications for physical objects and data relationships as used in engineering and science.

Technical sketching. The freehand expression of the graphic language, whereas ***mechanical drawing*** is the instrumental expression of it. Technical sketching is a most valuable tool for the engineer and others engaged in technical work because through it most technical ideas can be expressed quickly and effectively without the use of special equipment.

Blueprint reading. The term applied to the "reading" of the language from drawings made by others. Actually, the blueprint process is only one of many forms by which drawings are reproduced today, but the term "blueprint reading" has been accepted through usage to mean the interpretation of all ideas expressed on technical drawings, whether or not the drawings are blueprints.

1.9 What Engineering, Science, and Technology Students Should Know

From the dawn of history the development of technical knowledge has been accompanied, and to a large extent made possible, by a corresponding graphic language. Today the intimate connection between engineering and science and the universal graphic language is more vital than ever before, and the engineer, scientist, or technician who is ignorant of or deficient in the principal mode of expression in his or her technical field is professionally illiterate. Thus, training in the application of technical drawing is required in virtually every engineering school in the world.

The old days of fine-line drawings and of shading and "washes" are gone forever; artistic talent is no longer a prerequisite to learning the fundamentals of the graphic language. Instead, today's student of graphics needs precisely the aptitudes, abilities, and computer skills that will be needed in the science and engineering courses that are studied concurrently and later.

The well-trained engineer, scientist, or technician must be able to make and read correct graphical representations of engineering structures, designs, and data relationships. This means that the individual must understand the fundamental principles, or the *grammar*, of the language and be able to execute the work with reasonable skill, which is *penmanship*.

Graphics students often try to excuse themselves for inferior results (usually caused by lack of application) by arguing that after graduation they do not expect to do any drafting at all; they expect to have others make any needed drawings under their direction. Such a student presumptuously expects, immediately after graduation, to be the accomplished engineer concerned with bigger things and forgets that a first assignment may involve working with drawings and possibly revising drawings, either on the board or with computerized aids, under the direction of an experienced engineer. Entering the engineering profession via graphics provides an excellent opportunity to learn about the product, the company operations, and the supervision of others.

Even a young engineer who has not been successful in developing a skillful penmanship in the graphic language will have use for its grammar, since the ability to *read* a drawing will be of utmost importance. See Chapter 16.

Furthermore, the engineering student is apt to overlook the fact that, in practically all the subsequent courses taken in college, technical drawings will be encountered in most textbooks. The student is often called upon by instructors to supplement calculations with mechanical drawings or sketches. Thus, a mastery of a course in technical drawing utilizing both traditional methods and computer systems (CAD) will aid materially not only in professional practice after graduation but more immediately in other technical courses, and it will have a definite bearing on scholastic progress.

Besides the direct values to be obtained from a serious study of the graphic language, there are a number of very important training values that, though they may be considered by-products, are as essential as the language itself. Many students learn the meaning of neatness, speed, and accuracy for the first time in a drawing course. These are basic habits that every successful engineer, scientist, and technician must have or acquire.

All authorities agree that the ability to *think in three dimensions* is one of the most important requisites of the successful scientist and engineer. This training to visualize objects in space, to use the constructive imagination, is one of the principal values to be obtained from a study of the graphic language. The ability to *visualize* is possessed to an outstanding degree by persons of extraordinary creative ability. It is difficult to think of Edison, De Forest, or Einstein as being deficient in constructive imagination.

With the increase in technological development and the consequent crowding of drawing courses by the other engineering and science courses in our colleges, it is doubly necessary for students to make the most of the limited time devoted to the language of the profession, to the end that they will not be professionally illiterate, but will possess an ability to express ideas quickly and accurately through the correct use of the graphic language.

1.10 Projections

Behind every drawing of an object is a space relationship involving four imaginary things.

1. The *observer's eye*, or the *station point*.

2. The *object*.

3. The *plane* or *planes of projection*.

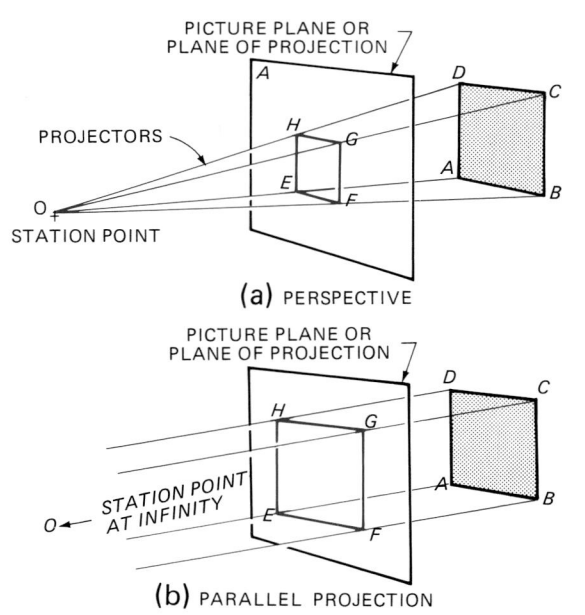

(a) PERSPECTIVE

(b) PARALLEL PROJECTION

Fig. 1.10   Projections.

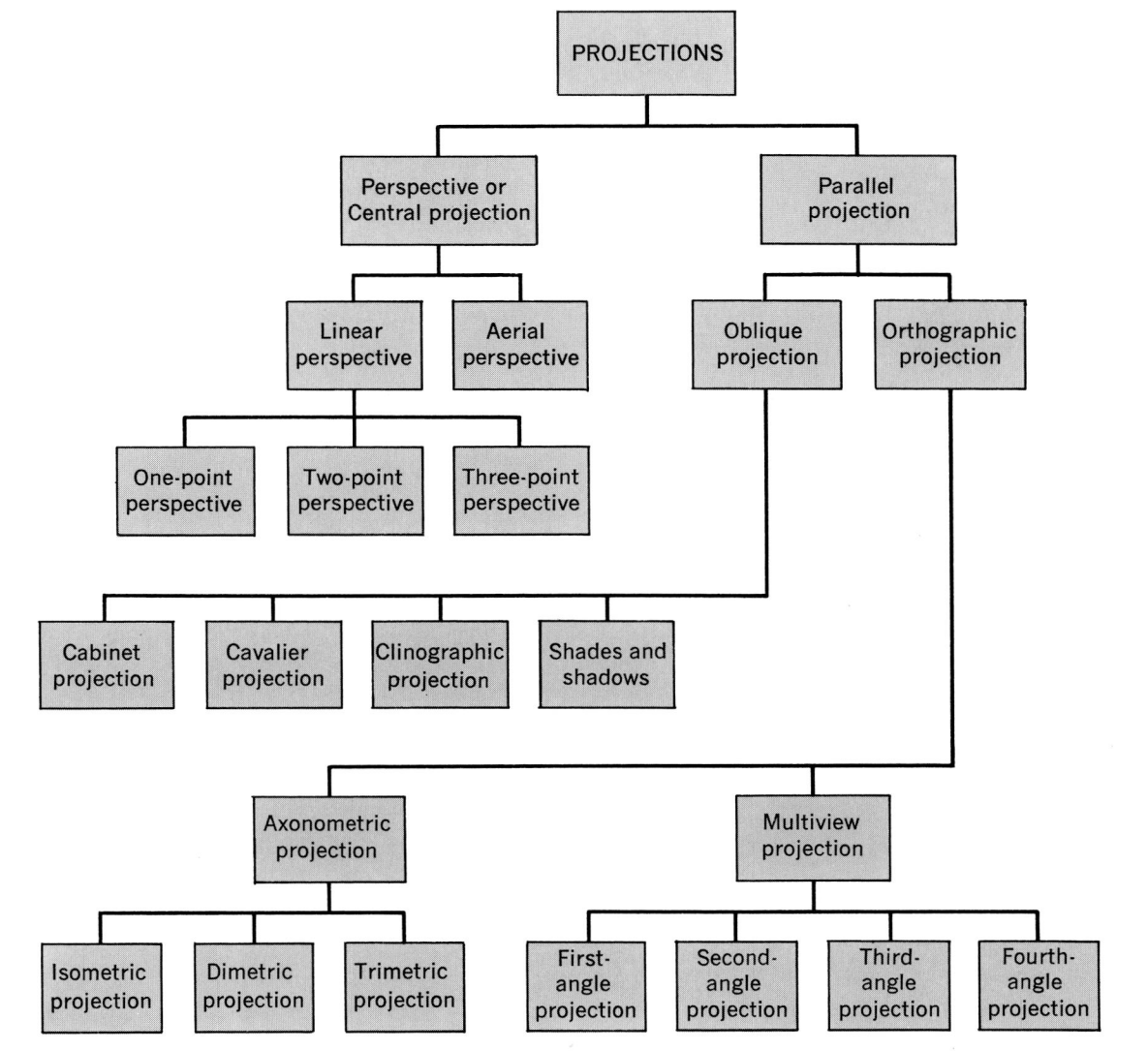

Fig. 1.11 Classification of Projections.

4. The *projectors*, also called visual rays and lines of sight.

For example, in Fig. 1.10 (a) the drawing EFGH is the projection, on the plane of projection A, of the square ABCD as viewed by an observer whose eye is at the point O. The projection or drawing upon the plane is produced by the points where the projectors pierce the plane of projection (piercing points). In this case, where the observer is relatively close to the object and the projectors form a "cone" of projectors, the resulting projection is known as a perspective.

If the observer's eye is imagined as infinitely distant from the object and the plane of projection, the projectors will be parallel, as shown in Fig. 1.10 (b); hence, this type of projection is known as a *parallel* projection. If the projectors, in addition to being parallel to each other, are perpendicular (normal) to the plane of projection, the result is an *orthographic*, or right-angle, projection. If they are parallel to each other but oblique to the plane of projection, the result is an *oblique* projection.

These two main types of projection—perspective and central or parallel projection—are further broken down into many subtypes, as shown in Fig. 1.11,

Table 1.1   *Classification by Projectors*

Classes of Projection	Distance from Observer to Plane of Projection	Direction of Projectors
Perspective	Finite	Radiating from station point
Parallel	Infinite	Parallel to each other
Oblique	Infinite	Parallel to each other and oblique to plane of projection
Orthographic	Infinite	Perpendicular to plane of projection
Axonometric	Infinite	Perpendicular to plane of projection
Multiview	Infinite	Perpendicular to planes of projection

and will be treated at length in the various chapters that follow.

A classification of the main types of projection according to their projectors is shown in Table 1.1.

Instrumental Drawing

For many years the items of equipment essential to students in technical schools, and to engineers and designers in professional practice, remained unchanged. One needed a drawing board, T-square, triangles, an architects' or engineers' scale, and a professional quality set of drawing instruments. Recently, however, there has been a shift toward greater use of the drafting machine, the parallel-ruling straightedge, the technical fountain pen, and other modern equipment—not to mention the significant increase in the use of the computer as a drafting tool.

The basic items of equipment are shown in Fig. 2.1. To secure the most satisfactory results, the drawing equipment should be of high grade. When drawing instruments (item 3) are to be purchased, the advice of an experienced drafter or designer, or a reliable dealer,* should be sought because it is difficult for beginners to distinguish high-grade instruments from those that are inferior.

*Keuffel & Esser Co., Rockaway, NJ; Dietzgen Corp., Des Plaines, IL; AM International–Bruning Div., Itasca, IL; Teledyne Post, Des Plaines, IL; Vemco Corp., San Dimas, CA; Staedtler Mars, Elk Grove Village, IL; Koh-I-Noor Rapidograph, Inc., Bloomsbury, NJ; are some of the larger distributors of this equipment; their products are available through local dealers.

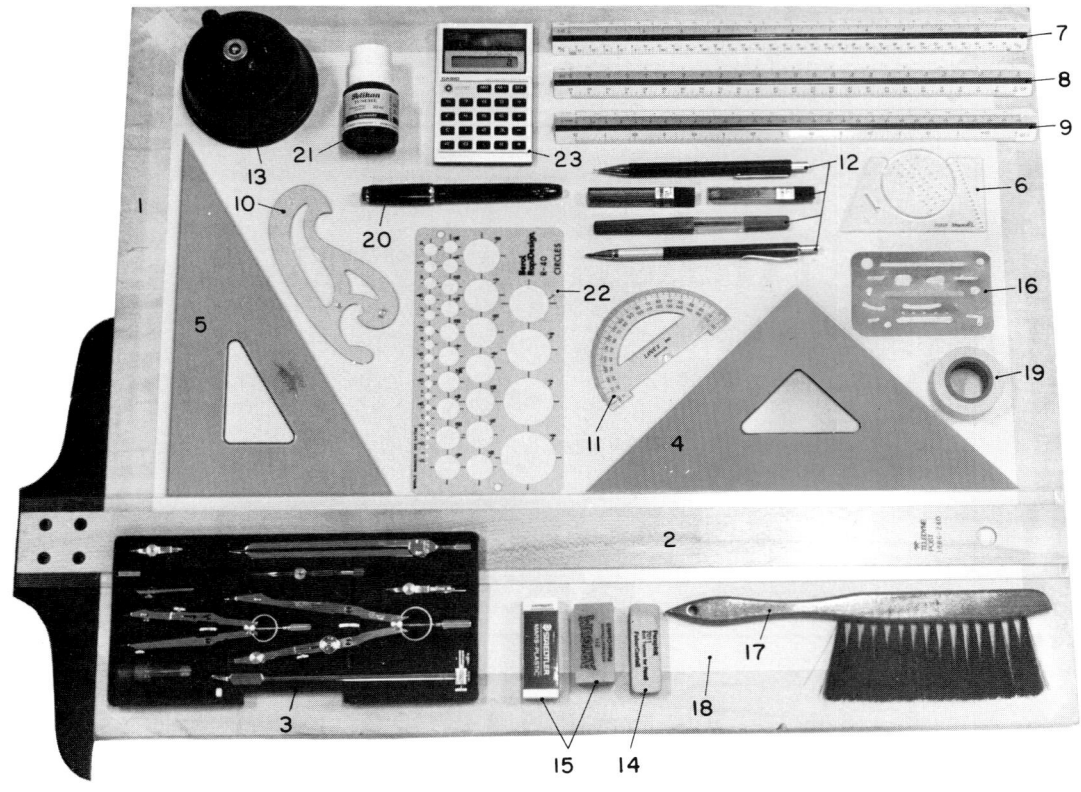

Fig. 2.1　Principal Items of Equipment.

2.1 Typical Equipment

A complete list of equipment for students of technical drawing follows. The numbers refer to the equipment illustrated in Fig. 2.1.

1. Drawing board (approx. 20″ × 24″), drafting table, or desk, §2.4.

2. T-square (24″, transparent edge), drafting machine, or parallel ruling edge, §§2.5, 2.56, and 2.57.

3. Set of instruments, §§2.33 and 2.34.

4. 45° triangle (8″ sides), §2.16.

5. 30° × 60° triangle (10″ long side), §2.16.

6. Ames Lettering Guide or lettering triangle, §4.16.

7. Architects' triangular scale, §2.28.

8. Engineers' triangular scale, §2.27.

9. Metric triangular scale, §2.25.

10. Irregular curve, §2.53.

11. Protractor, §2.18.

12. Mechanical pencils and/or thin-lead mechanical pencils and HB, F, 2H, and 4H to 6H leads, or drawing pencils. See §§2.8 and 2.9.

13. Lead pointer and sandpaper pad, §2.10.

14. Pencil eraser, §2.12.

15. Plastic drafting eraser or Artgum cleaning eraser, §2.12.

16. Erasing shield, §2.12.

17. Dusting brush, §2.12.

18. Drawing paper, tracing paper, tracing cloth, or films as required. Backing sheet (drawing paper—white, cream, or light green) to be used under drawings and tracings.

19. Drafting tape, §2.7.

20. Technical fountain pens, §2.48.

21. Drawing ink, §2.50.

22. Templates, §2.55.

Fig. *2.2* Orderliness Promotes Efficiency and Accuracy.

23.   Calculator.

24.   Cleansing tissue or dust cloth (not shown).

2.2 Objectives in Drafting

On the following pages, the correct methods to be used in instrumental drawing are explained. The student who practices and learns correct manipulation of the drawing instruments will eventually be able to draw correctly by habit, thus giving his or her full attention to the problems at hand.

The following are the important objectives the student should strive to attain:

1.   *Accuracy.* No drawing is of maximum usefulness if it is not accurate. The student cannot achieve success in a college career or later in professional employment if the habit of accuracy is not acquired.

2.   *Speed.* "Time is money" in industry, and there is no demand for the slow drafter, technician, or engineer. However, speed is not attained by hurrying; it is an unsought by-product of *intelligent and continuous work*. It comes with study and practice.

3.   *Legibility.* The drafter, technician, or engineer should remember that the drawing is a means of communication to others, and that it must be clear and legible in order to serve its purpose well. Care should be given to details, especially to lettering, Chapter 4.

4.   *Neatness.* If a drawing is to be accurate and legible, it must also be clean; therefore, the student should constantly strive to acquire the habit of neatness. Untidy drawings are the result of sloppy and careless methods, §2.13, and will be unacceptable to an instructor or employer.

2.3 Drafting at Home or School

In the school drafting room, as in the industrial drafting room, the student is expected to give thoughtful and continuous attention to the problems at hand.

Technical drawing requires headwork and must be done in quiet surroundings without distractions. The efficient drafting student sees to it that the correct equipment is available and refrains from borrowing—a nuisance to everyone. While the student is drawing, the textbook—the chief source of information—should be available and in a convenient position, Fig. 2.2.

When questions arise, first use the index of the text and endeavor to find the answer for yourself.

Try to develop self-reliance and initiative, but when you really need help, ask your instructor. Students who go about their work intelligently, with a minimum waste of time, first study the assignment carefully to be sure that they understand the principles involved; second, make sure that the correct equipment is in proper condition (such as sharp pencils); and third, make an effort to dig out answers for themselves (the only true education).

One of the principal means of promoting efficiency in drafting is orderliness. Efficiency, in turn, will produce accuracy in drawing. All needed equipment and materials should be placed in an orderly manner so that everything is in a convenient place and can readily be found when needed, Fig. 2.2. The drawing area should be kept clear of equipment not in direct use. Form the habit of placing each item in a regular place outside the drawing area when it is not being used.

When drawing at home, if possible work in a room by yourself. Place a book under the upper portion of the drawing board to give the board a convenient inclination, or you can pull out the study table drawer and use it to support the drawing board at a slant.

It is best to work in natural north light coming from the left and slightly from the front. Never work on a drawing in direct sunlight or in dim light, as either may be injurious to the eyes. If artificial light is needed, the light source should be such that shadows are not cast where lines are being drawn and that there will be as little reflected glare from the paper as possible. Special fluorescent drafting lamps are available with adjustable arms so that the light source may be moved to any desired position. Drafting will not hurt eyes that are in normal condition, but the exacting work will often disclose deficiencies not previously suspected.

Left-handers   Place the head of the T-square on the right, and have the light come from the right and slightly from the front.

2.4 Drawing Boards

If the left edge of the drafting table top has a true straightedge and if the surface is hard and smooth (such as masonite), a drawing board is unnecessary, provided that drafting tape is used to fasten the drawings. It is recommended that a backing sheet of heavy drawing paper be placed between the drawing and the table top.

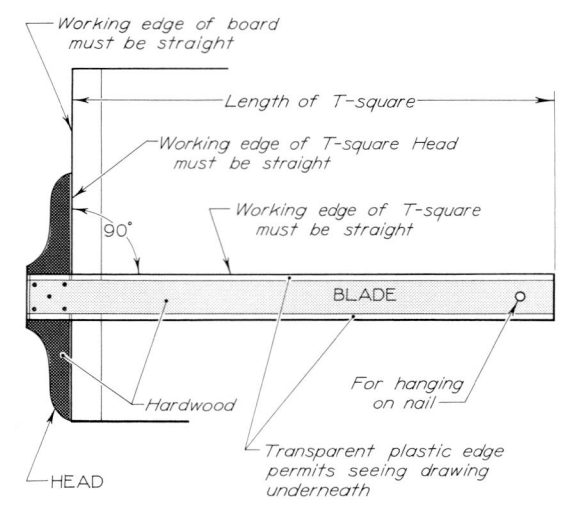

Fig. 2.3   The T-square.

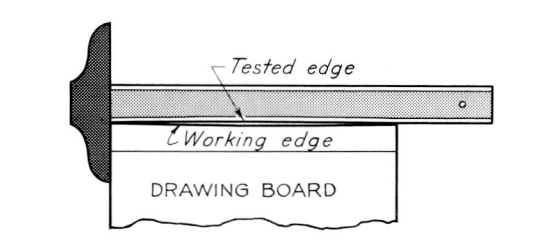

Fig. 2.4   Testing the Working Edge of the Drawing Board.

However, in most cases a drawing board will be needed. These vary from 9″ × 12″ (for sketching and field work) up to 48″ × 72″ or larger. The recommended size for students is 20″ × 24″, Fig. 2.1, which will accommodate the largest sheet likely to be used.

Drafters use drafting tape, which in turn permits surfaces such as hardwood, masonite, or other materials to be used for drawing boards.

The left-hand edge of the board is called the *working edge* because the T-square head slides against it, Fig. 2.3. This edge must be straight, and you should test the edge with a T-square blade that has been tested and found straight, Fig. 2.4. If the edge of the board is not true, it should be replaced.

2.5 T-square

The T-square, Fig. 2.3, is composed of a long strip, called the *blade*, fastened rigidly at right angles to a shorter piece called the *head*. The upper edge of the blade and the inner edge of the head are *working edges* and must be straight. The working edge of the head must not be convex or the T-square will rock when the head is placed against the board. The blade should have transparent plastic edges and should be free of nicks along the working edge. Transparent edges are recommended, since they permit the drafter to see the drawing in the vicinity of the lines being drawn.

Do not use the T-square for any rough purpose. Never cut paper along its working edge, as the plastic is easily cut and even a slight nick will ruin the T-square.

2.6 Testing and Correcting the T-square

To test the working edge of the head, see if the T-square rocks when the head is placed against a straight edge, such as a drawing board working edge that has already been tested and found true. If the working edge of the head is not straight, the T-square should be replaced.

To test the working edge of the blade, Fig. 2.5, draw a sharp line very carefully with a hard pencil along the entire length of the working edge; then turn the T-square over and draw the line again along the same edge. If the edge is straight, the two lines will coincide; otherwise, the space between the lines will be twice the error of the blade.

It is difficult to correct a crooked T-square blade, and if the error is considerable, it may be necessary to discard the T-square and obtain another.

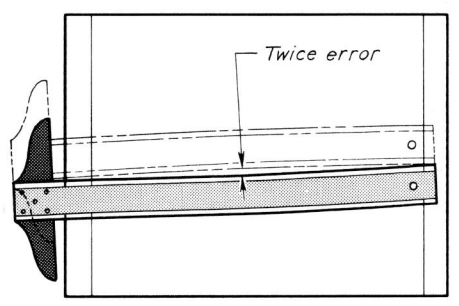

Fig. 2.5   Testing the T-square.

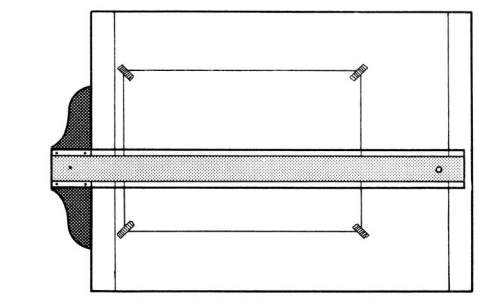

Fig. 2.6   Placing Paper on Drawing Board.

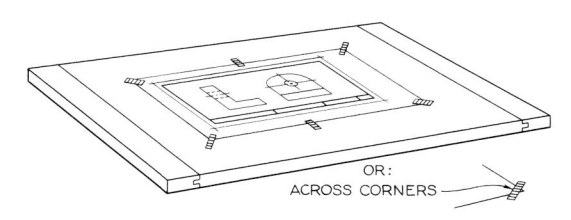

Fig. 2.7   Positions of Drafting Tape.

2.7 Fastening Paper to the Board

The drawing paper should be placed close enough to the working edge of the board to reduce to a minimum any error resulting from a slight "give," or bending of the blade of the T-square, and close enough to the upper edge of the board to permit space at the bottom of the sheet for using the T-square and supporting the arm while drawing, Fig. 2.6.

Drafting tape is preferred for fastening the drawing to the board, Fig. 2.7, because it does not damage the board and it will not damage the paper if it is removed by *pulling it off slowly toward the edge of the paper.*

To fasten the paper in place, press the T-square head firmly against the working edge of the drawing board with the left hand, while the paper is adjusted with the right hand until the top edge coincides with the upper edge of the T-square. Then move the T-square to the position shown and fasten the upper left corner, then the lower right corner, and finally the remaining corners. Large sheets may require additional fastening, whereas small sheets may require fastening only at the two upper corners.

Tracing paper should not be fastened directly to the board because small imperfections in the surface

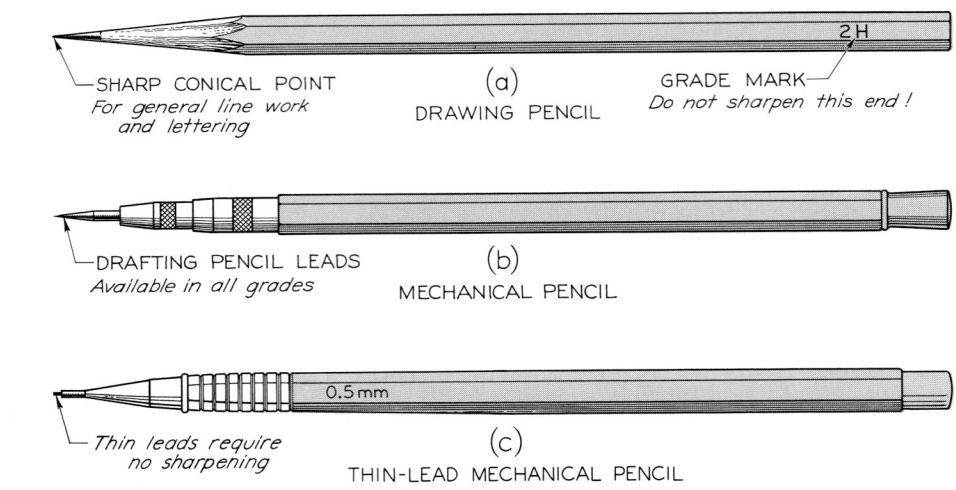

Fig. 2.8   Drawing Pencils.

of the board will interfere with the line work. Always fasten a larger backing sheet of heavy drawing paper on the board first, then fasten the tracing paper over this sheet.

2.8 Drawing Pencils

High-quality drawing pencils, Fig. 2.8 (a), should be used in technical drawing—never ordinary writing pencils.

Many makes of mechanical pencils are available, Fig. 2.8 (b), together with refill drafting leads of conventional size in all grades. Choose the holder that feels comfortable in the hand and that grips the lead firmly without slipping. Mechanical pencils have the advantages of maintaining a constant length of lead while permitting the use of a lead practically to the end, of being easily refilled with new leads, of affording a ready source for compass leads, of having no wood to be sharpened, and of easy sharpening of the lead by various mechanical pencil pointers now available

Thin-lead mechanical pencils, Fig. 2.8 (c), are available with 0.3, 0.5, 0.7, or 0.9 mm diameter drafting leads in several grades. These thin leads produce uniform width lines without sharpening, providing both a time savings and a cost benefit.

Mechanical pencils are recommended as they are less expensive in the long run.

2.9 Choices of Grade of Pencil

Drawing pencil leads are made of graphite with the addition of a polymer binder or of kaolin (clay) in varying amounts to make 18 grades from 9H, the hardest, down to 7B, the softest. The uses of these different grades are shown in Fig. 2.9. Note that small diameter leads are used for the harder grades, whereas large diameter leads are used to give more strength to the softer grades. Hence, the degree of hardness in the wood pencil can be roughly judged by a comparison of the diameters.

Specifically formulated leads of carbon black particles in a polymer binder are also available in several grades for use on the polyester films now found quite extensively in industry. See §2.61.

To select the grade of lead, first take into consideration the type of line work required. For light construction lines, guide lines for lettering, and for accurate geometrical constructions or work where accuracy is of prime importance, use a hard lead, such as 4H to 6H.

For mechanical drawings on drawing paper or tracing paper, the lines should be **black,** particularly for drawings to be reproduced. The lead chosen must be soft enough to produce jet black lines, but hard enough not to smudge too easily or permit the point to crumble under normal pressure. The same comparatively soft lead is preferred for lettering and arrowheads.

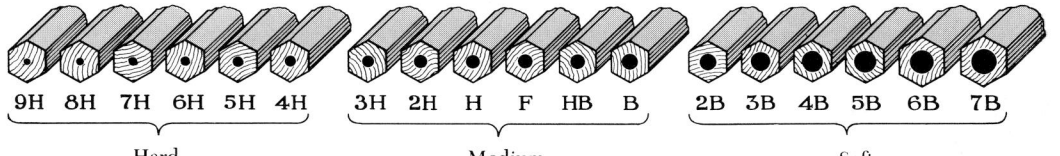

9H 8H 7H 6H 5H 4H	3H 2H H F HB B	2B 3B 4B 5B 6B 7B
Hard	**Medium**	**Soft**
The hard leads in this group (left) are used where extreme accuracy is required, as on graphical computations and charts and diagrams. The softer leads in this group (right) are used by some for line work on engineering drawings, but their use is restricted because the lines are apt to be too light.	These grades are for general purpose work in technical drawing. The softer grades (right) are used for technical sketching, for lettering, arrowheads, and other freehand work on mechanical drawings. The harder leads (left) are used for line work on machine drawings and architectural drawings. The **H** and **2H** leads are widely used on pencil tracings for reproduction.	These leads are too soft to be useful in mechanical drafting. Their use for such work results in smudged, rough lines that are hard to erase, and the lead must be sharpened continually. These grades are used for art work of various kinds, and for full-size details in architectural drawing.

Fig. 2.9 Lead Grade Chart.

This lead will vary from F to 2H, roughly, depending on the paper and weather conditions. If the paper is hard, it will be necessary generally to use harder leads. For softer surfaces, softer leads can be used. The weather factor to consider is the humidity. On humid days the paper absorbs moisture from the atmosphere and becomes soft. This can be recognized because the paper expands and becomes wrinkled. It is necessary to select softer leads to offset the softening of the paper. If you have been using a 2H lead, for example, change to an F until the weather clears up.

2.10 Sharpening the Pencil

Keep your lead sharp! This is certainly the instruction needed most frequently by the beginning student. A dull lead produces fuzzy, sloppy, indefinite lines. Only a sharp lead is capable of producing clean-cut black lines that sparkle with clarity.

If a good mechanical pencil, Fig. 2.8 (b), is used, much time may be saved in sharpening, since the lead can be fed from the pencil as needed. Two excellent lead pointers for mechanical pencils are shown in Fig. 2.10. Each has the advantage of one-hand manipulation, and of collecting the loose graphite particles inside, where they cannot soil the hands, the drawing, or other equipment.

If thin-lead mechanical pencils are used, Fig. 2.8 (c), no sharpening is required since the lead di-

(a) TRU-POINT

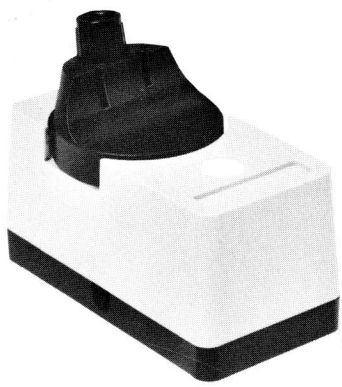

(b) BEROL TURQUOISE

Fig. 2.10 Pencil Lead Pointers. *Courtesy of Keuffel & Esser Co.*

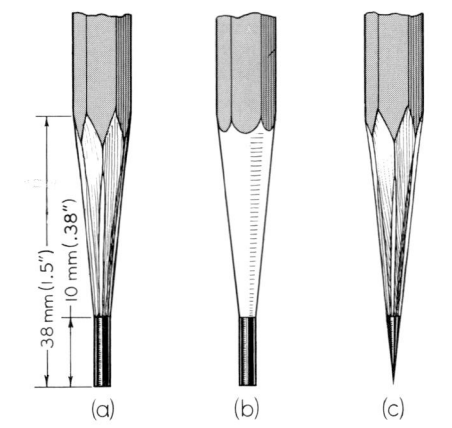

Fig. 2.11   Pencil Points.

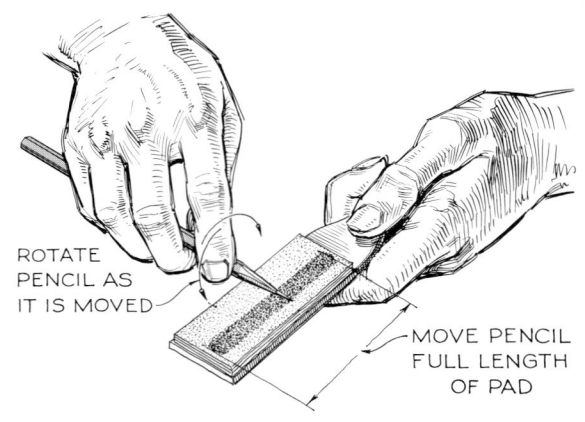

Fig. 2.13   Shaping the Lead.

ameter determines the line width. Hence, several thin-lead mechanical pencils are required for the various line widths used in technical drawing. Each thin-lead mechanical pencil will accommodate only one diameter of lead.

If a wood drawing pencil is used, Fig. 2.8 (a), sharpen the unlettered end in order to preserve the identifying grade mark. First, the wood is removed with a knife or a special drafting pencil sharpener starting about 38 mm (1.5") from the end and about 10 mm (.38") of uncut lead is exposed, Fig. 2.11 (a) or (b). Next the lead is shaped to a sharp conical point, and the point is wiped clean with cloth or paper tissue to remove loose particles of graphite.

Mechanical devices for removal of the wood are shown in Fig. 2.12 (a) and (b). The procedures for shaping the lead are illustrated in Fig. 2.13.

Never sharpen your pencil over the drawing or any of your equipment.

Keep the pencil pointer close by, as frequent pointing of the pencil will be necessary.

When the sandpaper pad is not in use, it should be kept in a container, such as an envelope, to prevent the particles of graphite from falling upon the drawing board or drawing equipment, Fig. 2.12 (c).

Many drafters burnish the point on a piece of hard paper to obtain a smoother, sharper point. However, for drawing visible lines the point should not be needle-sharp, but very slightly rounded. First sharpen the lead to a needle point, then stand the pencil vertically, and with a few rotary motions on the paper, wear the point down slightly to the desired shape.

2.11 Alphabet of Lines

Each line on a technical drawing has a definite meaning and is drawn in a certain way. The line conventions endorsed by the American National Standards Institute, ANSI Y14.2M–1979 (R1987), are presented in Fig. 2.14, together with illustrations of various applications.

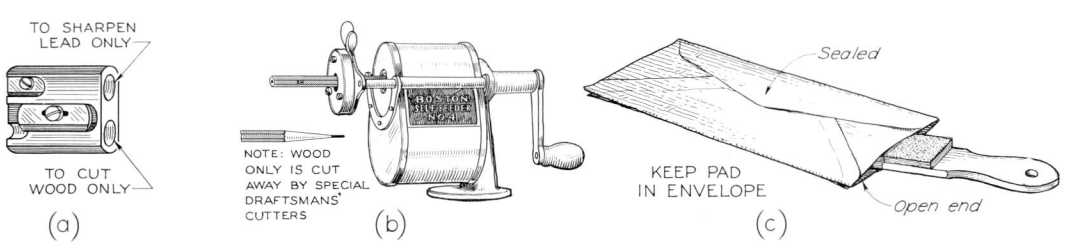

Fig. 2.12   Pencil Sharpeners.

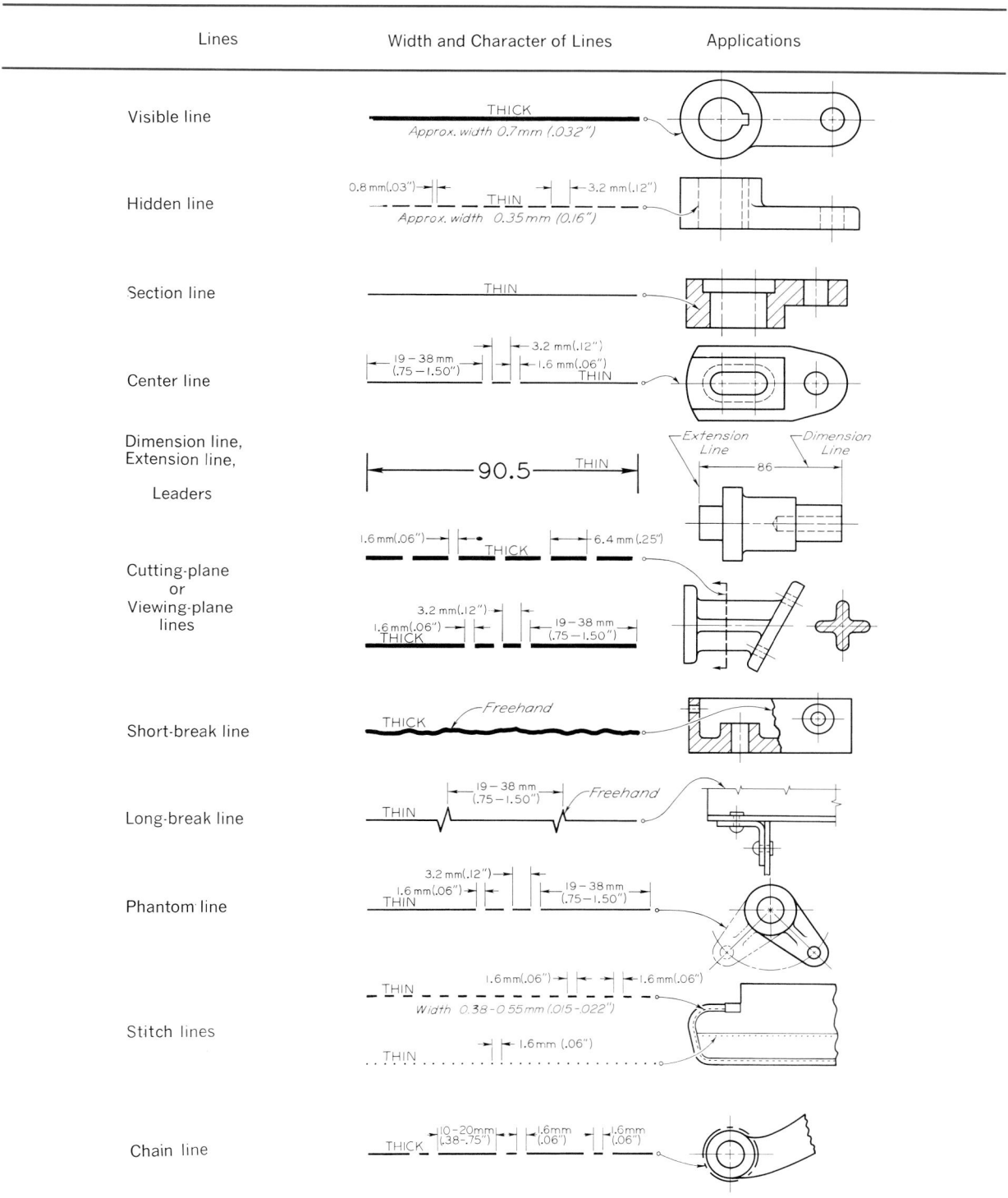

Lines	Width and Character of Lines	Applications

Fig. 2.14 Alphabet of Lines (Full Size).

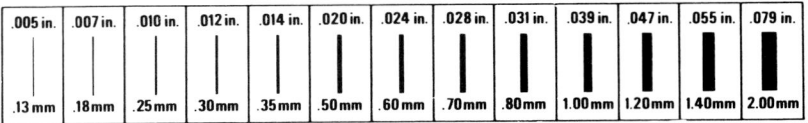

.005 in.	.007 in.	.010 in.	.012 in.	.014 in.	.020 in.	.024 in.	.028 in.	.031 in.	.039 in.	.047 in.	.055 in.	.079 in.
.13 mm	.18 mm	.25 mm	.30 mm	.35 mm	.50 mm	.60 mm	.70 mm	.80 mm	1.00 mm	1.20 mm	1.40 mm	2.00 mm

Fig. 2.15   Line Gage. *Courtesy of Koh-I-Noor Rapidograph, Inc.*

Two widths of lines are recommended for use on drawings. All lines should be clean-cut, dark, uniform throughout the drawing, and properly spaced for legible reproduction by all commonly used methods. Minimum spacing of 1.5 mm (.06″) between parallel lines is usually satisfactory for all reduction and/or reproduction processes. The size and style of the drawing and the smallest size to which it is to be reduced govern the actual width of each line. The contrast between the two widths of lines should be distinct. Pencil leads should be hard enough to prevent smudging, but soft enough to produce the dense black lines so necessary for quality reproduction.

When photoreduction and blowback are not necessary, as is the case for most drafting laboratory assignments, three weights of lines may improve the appearance and legibility of the drawing. The "thin lines" may be made in two widths—regular thin lines for hidden lines and stitch lines and a somewhat thinner version for the other secondary lines such as center lines, extension lines, dimension lines, leaders, section lines, phantom lines, and long-break lines.

For the "thick lines"—visible, cutting plane, and short break—use a relatively soft lead such as F or H. All thin lines should be made with a sharp medium-grade lead such as H or 2H. All lines (except construction lines) must be *sharp* and *dark*. Make construction lines with a sharp 4H or 6H lead so thin that they barely can be seen at arm's length and need not be erased.

The high-quality photoreduction and reproduction processes used in the production of this book permitted the use of three weights of lines in many illustrations and drawings for increased legibility.

In Fig. 2.14, the ideal lengths of all dashes are indicated. It would be well to measure the first few hidden dashes and center-line dashes you make and then thereafter to estimate the lengths carefully by eye.

The line gage, Fig. 2.15, is a convenient reference for lines of various widths.

2.12 Erasing

Erasers are available in many degrees of hardness and abrasiveness. For general drafting the Pink Pearl or the Mars-Plastic is suggested, Fig. 2.16. These erasers are suitable for erasing pencil or ink line work. Best results are obtained if a hard surface, such as a triangle is placed under the area being erased. If the surface has become badly grooved by the lines, the surface can be improved by burnishing the back side with a hard smooth object or with the back of the fingernail.

The erasing shield, Fig. 2.17, is used to protect the lines near those being erased.

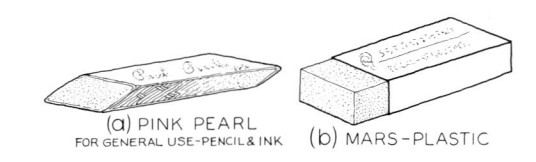

(a) PINK PEARL
FOR GENERAL USE-PENCIL & INK   (b) MARS-PLASTIC

Fig. 2.16   Erasers.

Fig. 2.17   Using the Erasing Shield.

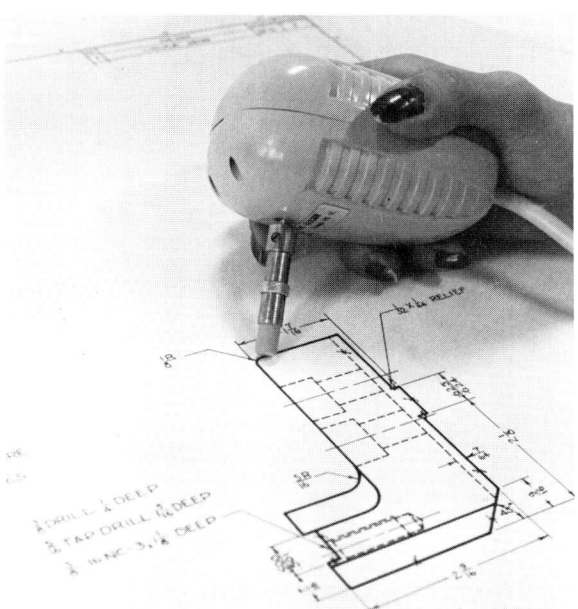

Fig. 2.18   Electric Erasing Machine.

Fig. 2.19   Dusting Brush.

The electric erasing machine, Fig. 2.18, saves time and is essential if much drafting is being done.

A dusting brush, Fig. 2.19, is useful for removing eraser crumbs without smearing the drawing.

2.13 Keeping Drawings Clean

Cleanliness in drafting is very important and should become a habit. Cleanliness does not just happen; it results only from a conscious effort to observe correct procedures.

First, the drafter's hands should be clean at all times. Oily or perspiring hands should be frequently washed with soap and water. Talcum powder on the hands tends to absorb excessive perspiration.

Second, all drafting equipment, such as drawing board, T-square, triangles, and scale, should be wiped frequently with a clean cloth. Water should be used sparingly and dried off immediately. A soft eraser may also be used for cleaning drawing equipment.

Third, the largest contributing factor to dirty drawings is *not dirt, but graphite* from the pencil; hence, the drafter should observe the following precautions:

1. Never sharpen a lead over the drawing or any equipment.

2. Always wipe the lead point with a clean cloth or cleansing tissue, after sharpening or pointing, to remove small particles of loose graphite.

3. Never place the sandpaper pad or file in contact with any other drawing equipment unless it is completely enclosed in an envelope or similar cover, Fig. 2.12 (c).

4. Never work with the sleeves or hands resting upon a penciled area. Keep such parts of the drawing covered with clean paper (not a cloth). In lettering a drawing, always place a piece of paper under the hand.

5. Avoid unnecessary sliding of the T-square or triangles across the drawing. Pick up the triangles by their tips and tilt the T-square blade upward slightly before moving. A very light sprinkling of powdered Artgum or drafting powder on the drawing helps to keep the drawing clean by picking up the loose graphite particles as you work. It should be brushed off and replaced occasionally.

6. Never rub across the drawing with the palm of the hand to remove eraser particles; use a dust brush, Fig. 2.19, or flick—don't rub—the particles off with a clean cloth.

If the foregoing rules are observed, a completed drawing will not need to be cleaned. The practice of making a pencil drawing, scrubbing it with a soft eraser, and then retracing the lines is poor technique. It is also a waste of time and a habit that should not be acquired.

At the end of the period or of the day's work, the drawing should be covered with paper or cloth to protect it from dust.

If the drawing must be removed from the board before it is complete, it can be carried flat in a draw-

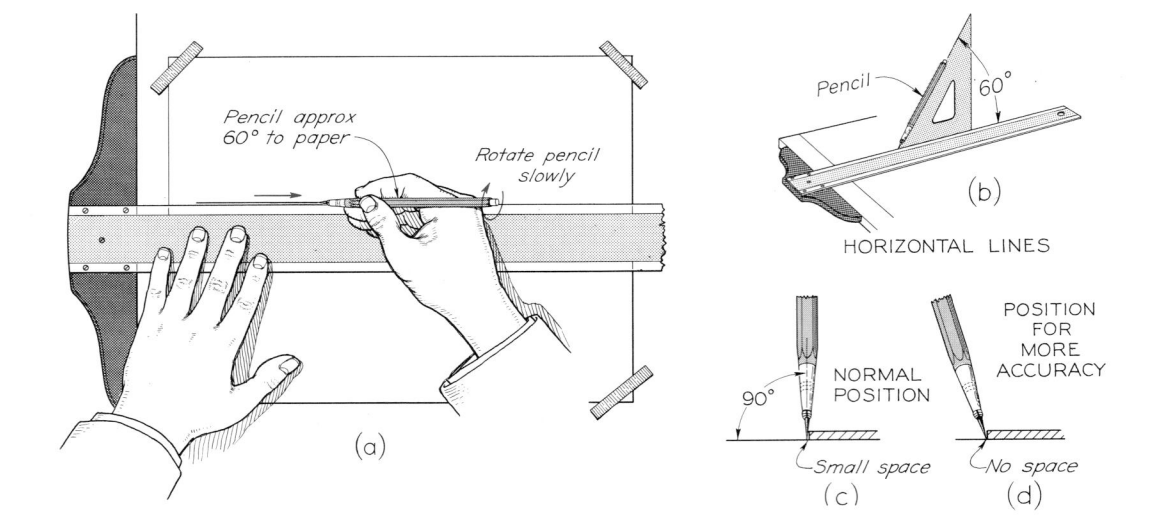

Fig. 2.20   Drawing a Horizontal Line.

ing portfolio or gently rolled and carried in a card-board or plastic tube, preferably one with ends that can be closed.

2.14 Horizontal Lines

To draw a horizontal line, Fig. 2.20 (a), press the head of the T-square firmly against the working edge of the board with the left hand; then slide the left hand to the position shown, so as to press the blade tightly against the paper. Lean the pencil in the direction of the line at an angle of approximately 60° with the paper, (b), and draw the line from left to right. Keep the pencil in a vertical plane, (b) and (c); otherwise, the line may not be straight. While drawing the line, let the little finger of the hand holding the pencil glide lightly on the blade of the T-square, and rotate the pencil slowly, except for the thin-lead pencils, between the thumb and forefinger so as to distribute the wear uniformly on the lead and maintain a symmetrical point.

When great accuracy is required, the pencil may be "toed in" as shown at (d) to produce a perfectly straight line.

Thin-lead pencils should be held nearly vertical to the paper and not rotated. Also, pushing the thin-lead pencil from left to right, rather than pulling it, tends to minimize lead breakage.

Left-handers   In general, reverse the procedure just outlined. Place the T-square head against the right edge of the board, and with the pencil in the left hand, draw the line from right to left.

2.15 Vertical Lines

Use either the 45° triangle or the 30° × 60° triangle to draw vertical lines. Place the triangle on the T-square with the *vertical edge on the left* as shown in Fig. 2.21 (a). With the left hand, press the head of the T-square against the board, then slide the hand to the position shown where it holds both the T-square and the triangle firmly in position. Then draw the line upward, rotating the pencil slowly between the thumb and forefinger.

Lean the pencil in the direction of the line at an angle of approximately 60° with the paper and in a vertical plane, (b). Meanwhile, the upper part of the body should be twisted to the right as shown at (c).

See §2.14 regarding the use of thin-lead pencils.

Left-handers   In general, reverse the above procedure. Place the T-square head on the right and the vertical edge of the triangle on the right; then, with the right hand, hold the T-square and triangle firmly together, and with the left hand draw the line upward.

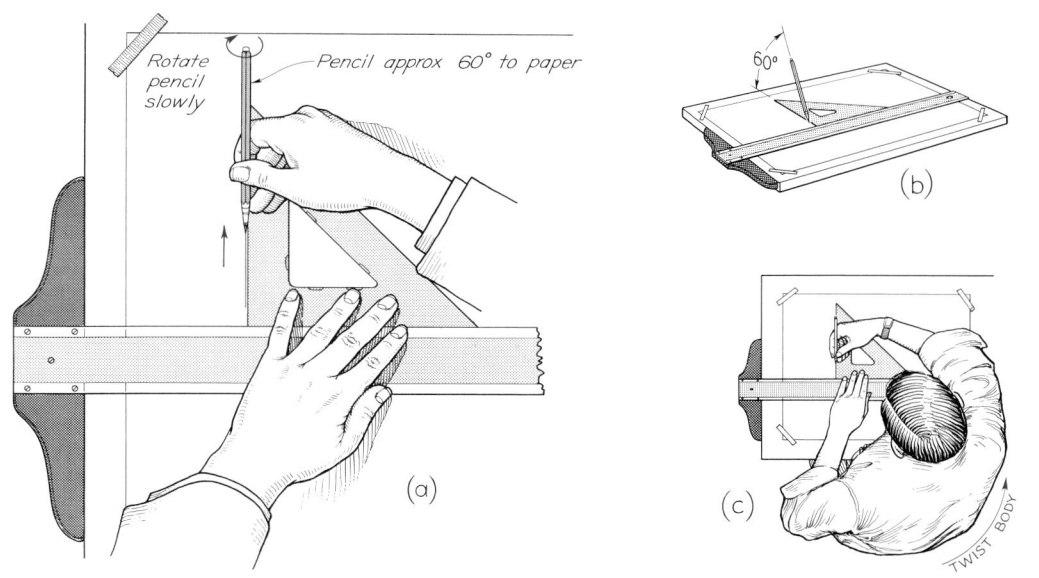

Fig. 2.21   Drawing a Vertical Line.

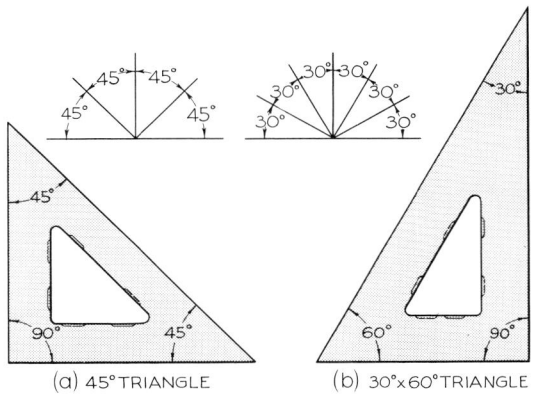

(a) 45° TRIANGLE   (b) 30° x 60° TRIANGLE

Fig. 2.22   Triangles.

The only time it is advisable for right-handers to turn the triangle so that the vertical edge is on the right is when drawing a vertical line near the right end of the T-square. In this case, the line would be drawn downward.

2.16 The Triangles

Most inclined lines in mechanical drawing are drawn at standard angles with the *45° triangle* and the *30° × 60° triangle*, Fig. 2.22. The triangles are made of transparent plastic so that lines of the draw-ing can be seen through them. A good combination of triangles is the 30° × 60° triangle with a long side of 10″ and a 45° triangle with each side 8″ long.

2.17 Inclined Lines

The positions of the triangles for drawing lines at all of the possible angles are shown in Fig. 2.23. In the figure it is understood that the triangles in each case are resting upon the blade of the T-square. Thus, it is possible to divide 360° into twenty-four 15° sectors with the triangles used singly or in combination.

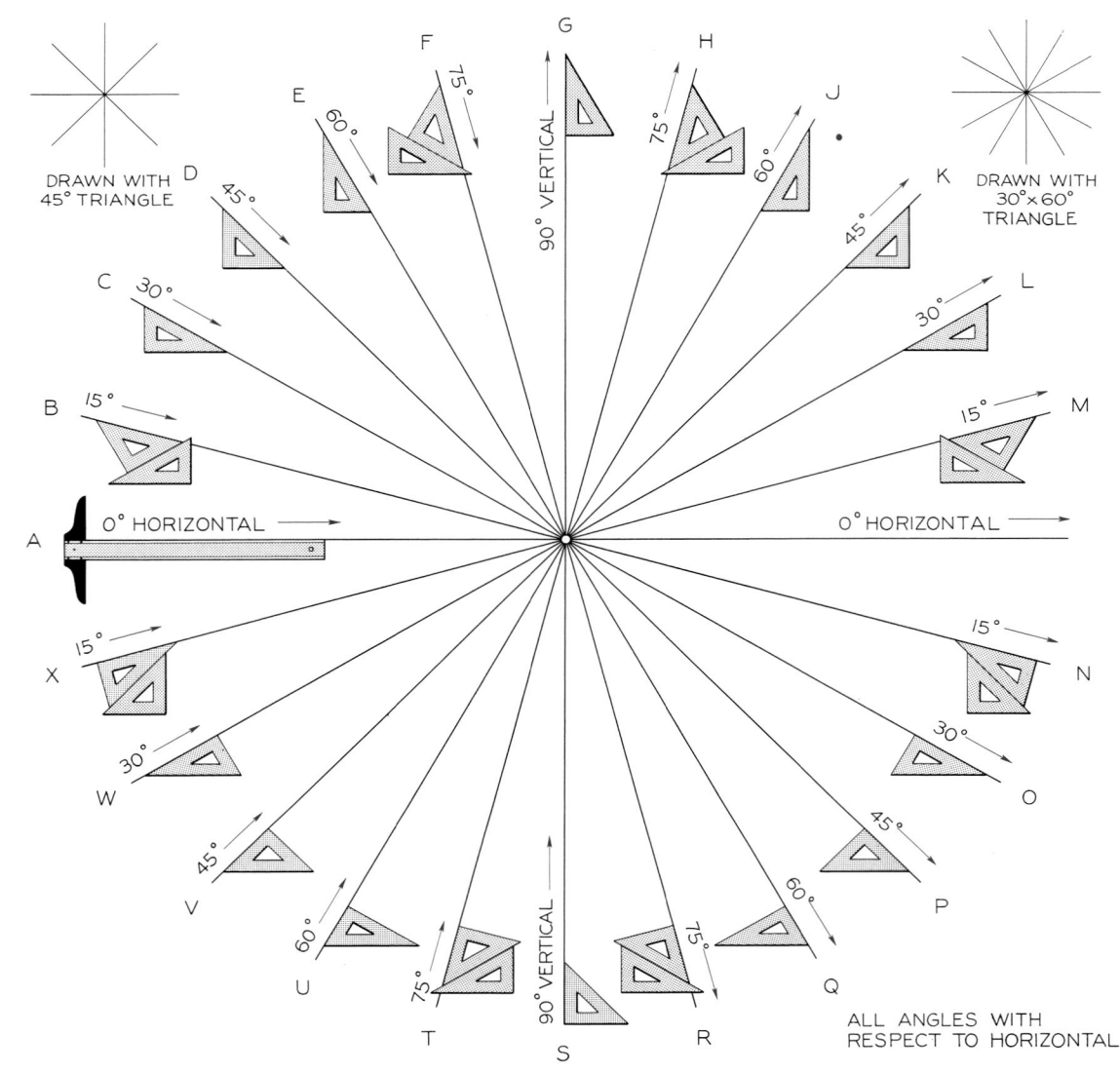

Fig. 2.23 The Triangle Wheel.

Note carefully the directions for drawing the lines, as indicated by the arrows, and that all lines in the left half are drawn *toward the center*, while those in the right half are drawn *away from the center*.

2.18 Protractors

For measuring or setting off angles other than those obtainable with the triangles, the *protractor* is used. The best protractors are made of nickel silver and are capable of most accurate work, Fig. 2.24 (a). For ordinary work the plastic protractor is satisfactory

and much cheaper, (b). To set off angles with greater accuracy, use one of the methods presented in §5.20.

2.19 Drafting Angles

A variety of devices combining the protractor with triangles to produce great versatility of use are available, one type of which is shown in Fig. 2.25.

2.20 To Draw a Line Through Two Points

To draw a line through two points, Fig. 2.26, place the pencil vertically at one of the points, and move

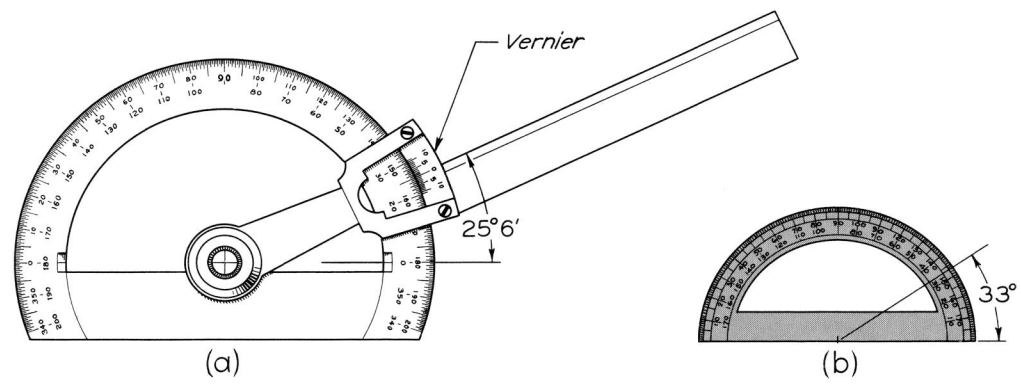

Fig. 2.24 Protractors.

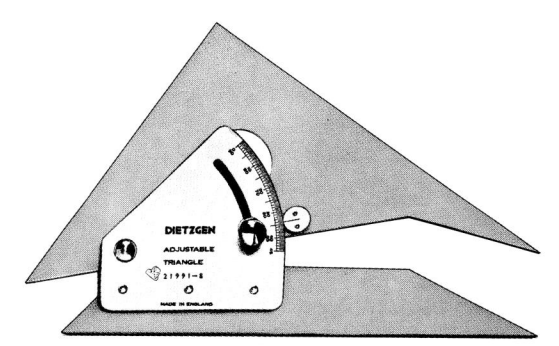

Fig. 2.25 Adjustable Triangle.

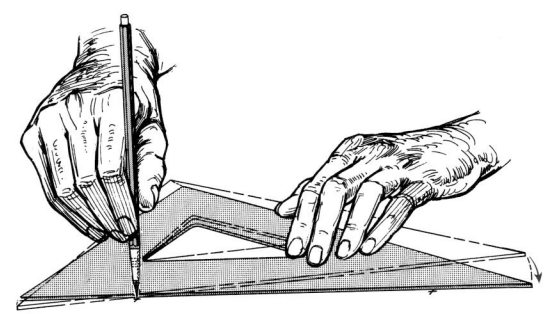

Fig. 2.26 To Draw a Pencil Line Through Two Points.

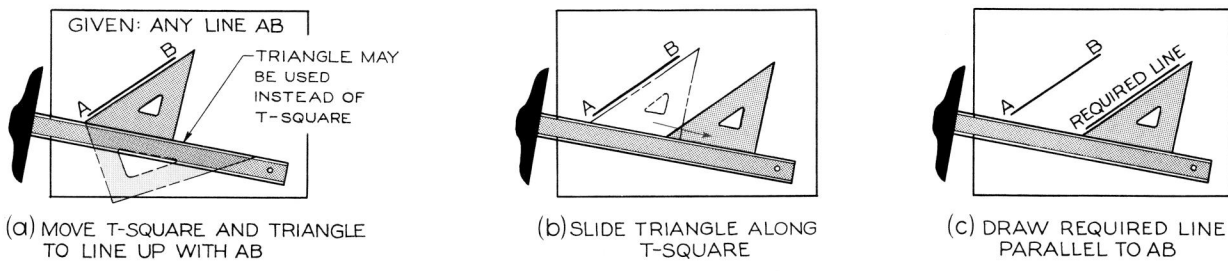

Fig. 2.27 To Draw a Line Parallel to a Given Line.

the straightedge about the pencil point as a pivot until it lines up with the other point; then draw the line along the edge.

2.21 Parallel Lines

To draw a line parallel to a given line, Fig. 2.27, move the triangle and T-square as a unit until the

hypotenuse of the triangle lines up with the given line, (a); then, holding the T-square firmly in position, slide the triangle away from the line, (b), and draw the required line along the hypotenuse, (c).

Obviously any straightedge, such as one of the triangles, may be substituted for the T-square in this operation, as shown at (a).

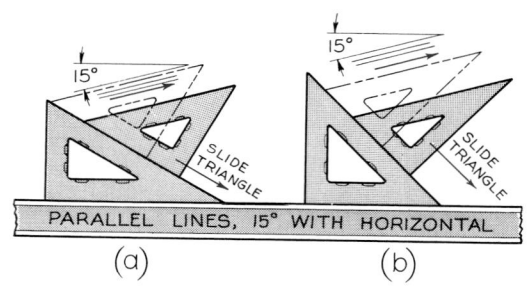

Fig. 2.28   Parallel Lines.

To draw parallel lines at 15° with horizontal, arrange the triangles as shown in Fig. 2.28.

2.22 Perpendicular Lines

To draw a line perpendicular to a given line, move the T-square and triangle as a unit until one edge of the triangle lines up with the given line, Fig. 2.29 (a); then slide the triangle across the line, (b), and draw the required line, (c).

To draw perpendicular lines when one of the lines makes 15° with horizontal, arrange the triangles as shown in Fig. 2.30.

2.23 Lines at 30°, 60°, or 45° with Given Line

To draw a line making 30° with a given line, arrange the triangle as shown in Fig. 2.31. Angles of 60° and 45° may be drawn in a similar manner.

2.24 Scales

A drawing of an object may be the same size as the object (full size), or it may be larger or smaller than the object.

The ratio of reduction or enlargement depends upon the relative sizes of the object and of the sheet of paper upon which the drawing is to be made. For example, a machine part may be half size; a building may be drawn $\frac{1}{48}$ size; a map may be drawn $\frac{1}{1200}$ size; or a printed circuit board, Fig. 2.32, may be drawn four times size.

Scales, Fig. 2.33, are classified as the *metric scale* (a), the *engineers' scale* (b), the *decimal scale* (c), the *mechanical engineers' scale* (d), and the *architects' scale* (e).

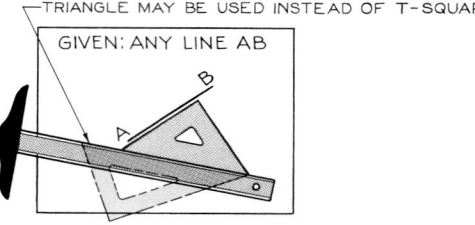

(a) MOVE T-SQUARE AND TRIANGLE TO LINE UP WITH AB

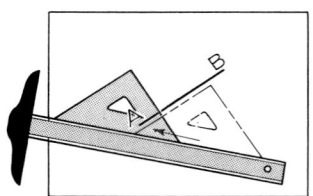

(b) SLIDE TRIANGLE ALONG T-SQUARE

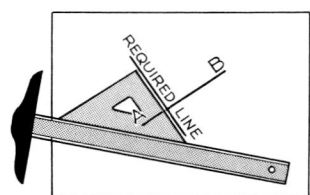

(c) DRAW REQUIRED LINE PERPENDICULAR TO AB

Fig. 2.29   To Draw a Line Perpendicular to a Given Line.

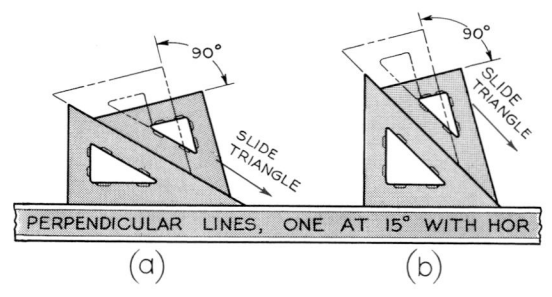

Fig. 2.30   Perpendicular Lines.

A full-divided scale is one in which the basic units are subdivided throughout the length of the scale. Only the lower scale at (e) is an open divided scale, one in which only the end unit is subdivided.

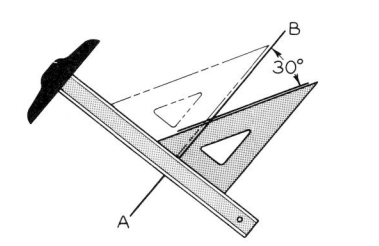

Fig. 2.31   Line at 30° with Given Line.

Fig. 2.32   Printed Circuit Board. *United Nations/ Guthrie.*

Scales are usually made of plastic or boxwood. The better wood scales have white plastic edges. Scales are either triangular, Fig. 2.34 (a) and (b), or flat, (c) to (f). The triangular scales have the advantage of combining many scales on one stick, but the user will waste much time looking for the required scale if a *scale guard*, (g), is not used. The flat scale is almost universally used by professional drafters because of its convenience, but several flat scales are necessary to replace one triangular scale, and the total cost is greater.

2.25 Metric Scales Fig. 2.33 (a)

The metric system is an international language of measurement that, despite modifications over the past 200 years, has been the foundation of science and industry and is clearly defined. The modern form of the metric system is the International System of Units, commonly referred to as SI (from the French name, Le Système International d'Unités). It is important to remember that SI differs in several respects from former metric systems. For example, cc was previously an accepted abbreviation for cubic centimeter; in SI the symbol used is cm^3. In the past, degree centigrade was accepted as an alternative name for degree Celsius; in SI only degree Celsius is used. Probably the most important characteristic of SI is that it is a unique system; each quantity has only one unit. The SI system was established in 1960 by international agreement and is now considered the standard international language of measurement.

The metric scale is used when the meter is the standard for linear measurement. The meter was established by the French in 1791 with a length of one ten-millionth of the distance from the Earth's equator to the pole. The meter is equal to 39.37 inches or approximately 1.1 yards.

The metric system for linear measurement is a decimal system similar to our system of counting money. For example,

$$
\begin{aligned}
1 \text{ mm} &= 1 \text{ millimeter } (\tfrac{1}{1000} \text{ of a meter}) \\
1 \text{ cm} &= 1 \text{ centimeter } (\tfrac{1}{100} \text{ of a meter}) \\
&= 10 \text{ mm} \\
1 \text{ dm} &= 1 \text{ decimeter } (\tfrac{1}{10} \text{ of a meter}) \\
&= 10 \text{ cm } = 100 \text{ mm} \\
1 \text{ m} &= 1 \text{ meter } = 100 \text{ cm } = 1000 \text{ mm} \\
1 \text{ km} &= 1 \text{ kilometer } = 1000 \text{ m} \\
&= 100\,000 \text{ cm } = 1\,000\,000 \text{ mm}
\end{aligned}
$$

The primary unit of measurement for engineering drawings and design in the mechanical industries is the millimeter (mm). Secondary units of measure are the meter (m) and the kilometer (km). The centimeter (cm) and the decimeter (dm) are rarely used.

In recent years, the auto and other industries have used a dual dimensioning system of millimeters and inches; see Fig. 16.22. The large agricultural machinery manufacturers have elected to use all metric dimensions with the inch equivalents given in a table on the drawing, Fig. 16.22.

Many of the dimensions in the illustrations and the problems in this text are given in metric units. Dimensions that are given in the customary units (inches and feet, either decimal or fractional) may be converted easily to metric values. In accordance with standard practice, the ratio 1 in. = 25.4 mm is

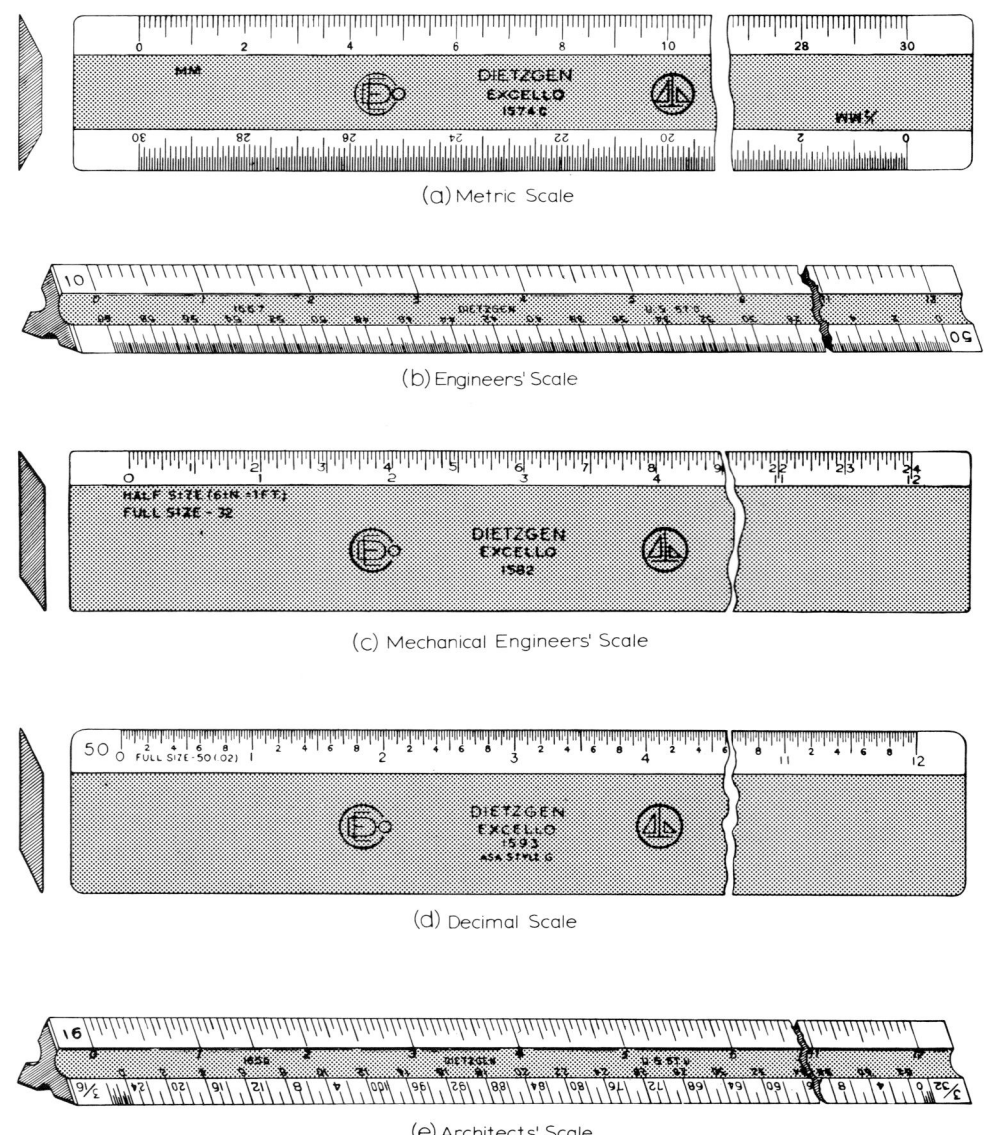

(a) Metric Scale

(b) Engineers' Scale

(c) Mechanical Engineers' Scale

(d) Decimal Scale

(e) Architects' Scale

Fig. 2.33   Types of Scales.

used. Decimal equivalents tables can be found inside the front cover, and conversion tables are given in Appendix 31.

Metric scales are available in flat and triangular styles with a variety of scale graduations. The triangular scale illustrated in Fig. 2.35 has one full-size scale and five reduced-size scales, all full divided. By means of these scales a drawing can be made full size, enlarged size, or reduced size. To specify the scale on a drawing, see §2.31.

Full Size Fig. 2.35 (a)

The 1 : 1 scale is full size, and each division is actually 1 mm in width with the numbering of the calibrations at 10 mm intervals. The same scale is convenient also for the ratios of 1 : 10, 1 : 100, 1 : 1000, and so on.

Half Size Fig. 2.35 (a)

The 1 : 2 scale is one-half size, and each division equals 2 mm with the calibration numbering at 20-

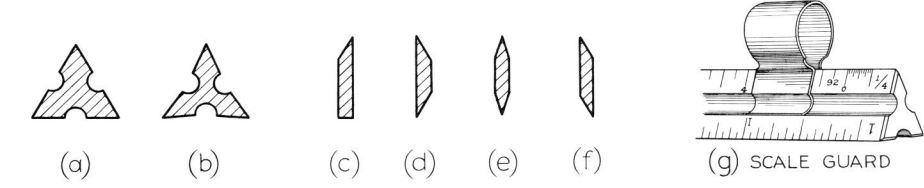

Fig. 2.34 Sections of Scales and Scale Guard.

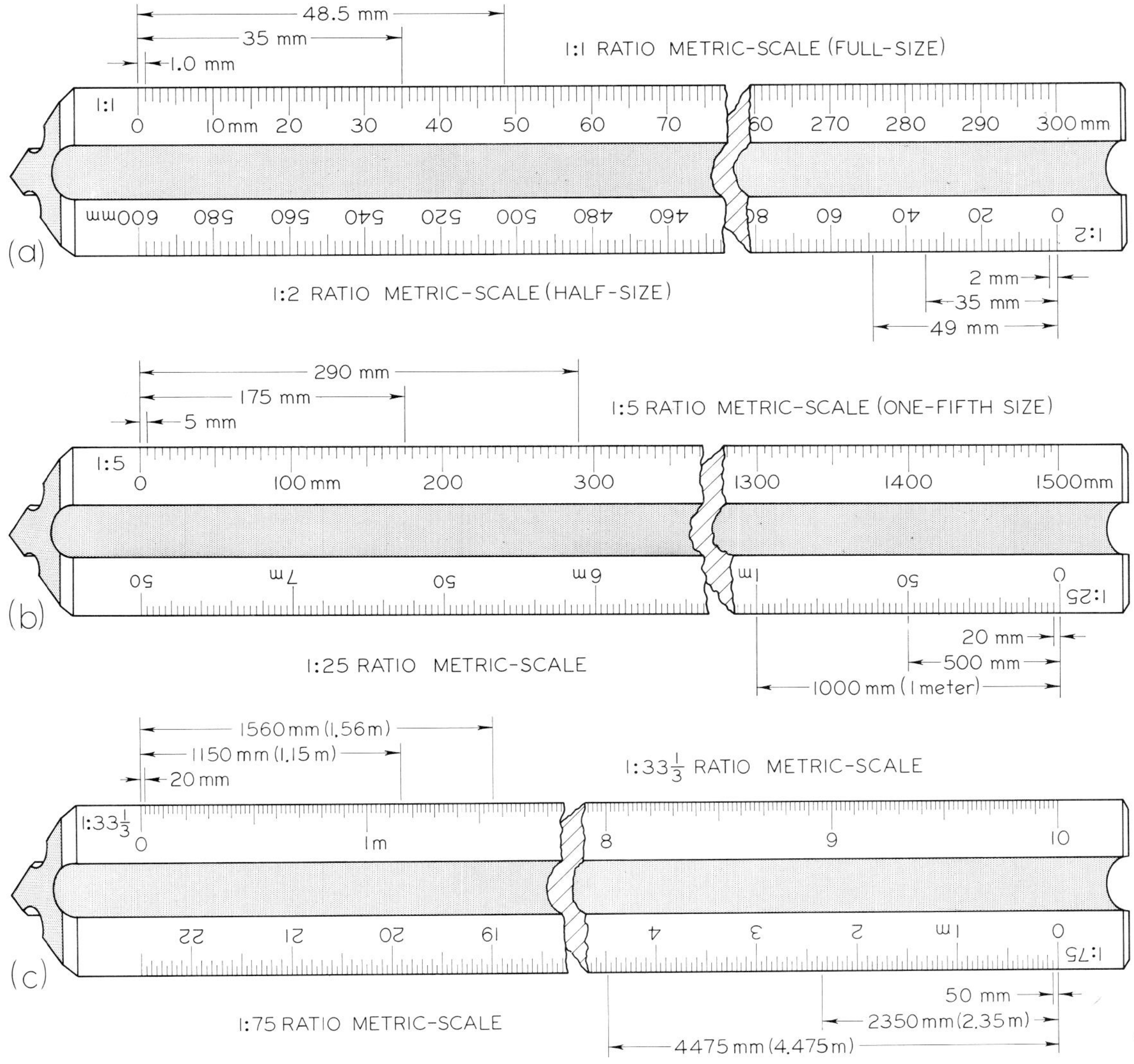

Fig. 2.35 Metric Scales.

unit intervals. In addition, this scale is convenient for ratios of 1 : 20, 1 : 200, 1 : 2000, and so on.

The remaining four scales on this triangular metric scale include the typical scale ratios of 1 : 5, 1 : 25, 1 : 33⅓, and 1 : 75, as illustrated at (b) and (c). These ratios also may be enlarged or reduced as desired by multiplying or dividing by a factor of 10. Metric scales are also available with other scale ratios for specific drawing purposes.

The metric scale is also used in map drawing and in drawing force diagrams or other graphical constructions that involve such scales as 1 mm = 1 kg and 1 mm = 500 kg.

2.26 Inch-Foot Scales

Several scales that are based upon the inch-foot system of measurement continue in domestic use today along with the metric system of measurement that is accepted worldwide for science, technology, and international trade.

2.27 Engineers' Scale   Fig. 2.33 (b)

The *engineers' scale* is graduated in the decimal system. It is also frequently called the *civil engineers' scale* because it was originally used mainly in civil engineering. The name *chain scale* also persists because it was derived from the surveyors' chain composed of 100 links, used for land measurements. The name "engineers' scale" is perhaps best, because the scale is used generally by engineers of all kinds.

The engineers' scale is graduated in units of one inch divided into 10, 20, 30, 40, 50, and 60 parts. Thus, the engineers' scale is convenient in machine drawing to set off dimensions expressed in decimals. For example, to set off 1.650″ full size, Fig. 2.36 (a), use the 10-scale and simply set off one main division plus 6½ subdivisions. To set off the same dimension half size, use the 20-scale, (b), since the 20-scale is exactly half the size of the 10-scale. Similarly, to set off a dimension quarter size, use the 40-scale.

The engineers' scale is used also in drawing maps to scales of 1″ = 50″, 1″ = 500′, 1″ = 5 miles, and so on and in drawing stress diagrams or other graphical constructions to such scales as 1″ = 20 lb and 1″ = 4000 lb.

2.28 Architects' Scale   Fig. 2.33 (e)

The *architects' scale* is intended primarily for drawings of buildings, piping systems, and other large

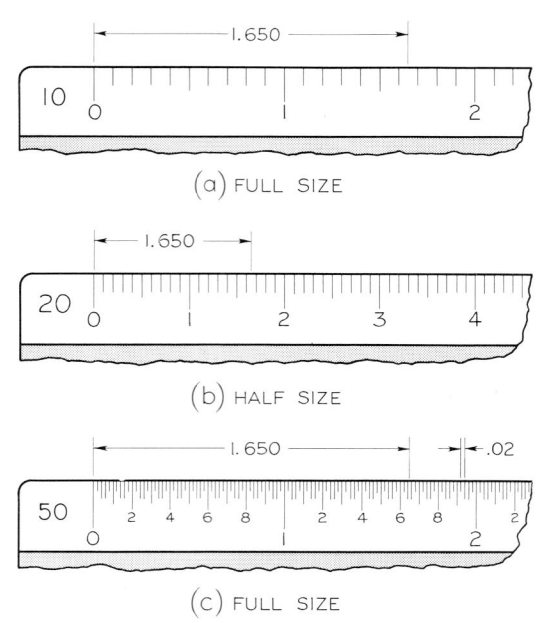

Fig. 2.36   Decimal Dimensions.

structures that must be drawn to a reduced scale to fit on a sheet of paper. The full-size scale is also useful in drawing relatively small objects, and for that reason the architects' scale has rather general usage.

The architects' scale has 1 full-size scale and 10 overlapping reduced-size scales. By means of these scales a drawing may be made to various sizes from full size to 1/128 size. *Note particularly, in all of the reduced scales the major divisions represent feet, and their subdivisions represent inches and fractions thereof.* Thus, the scale marked ¾ means ¾ inch = 1 foot, not ¾ inch = 1 inch; that is, one-sixteenth size, not three-fourths size. And the scale marked ½ means ½ inch = 1 foot, not ½ inch = 1 inch, that is, one-twenty-fourth size, not half-size.

All of the scales, from full size to 1/128 size, are shown in Fig. 2.37. Some are upside down, just as they may occur in use. These scales are described as follows:

Full Size   Fig. 2.37 (a)

Each division in the full-size scale is 1/16″. Each inch is divided first into halves, then quarters, eighths, and finally sixteenths, the division lines diminishing in length with each division. To set off 1/32″, estimate

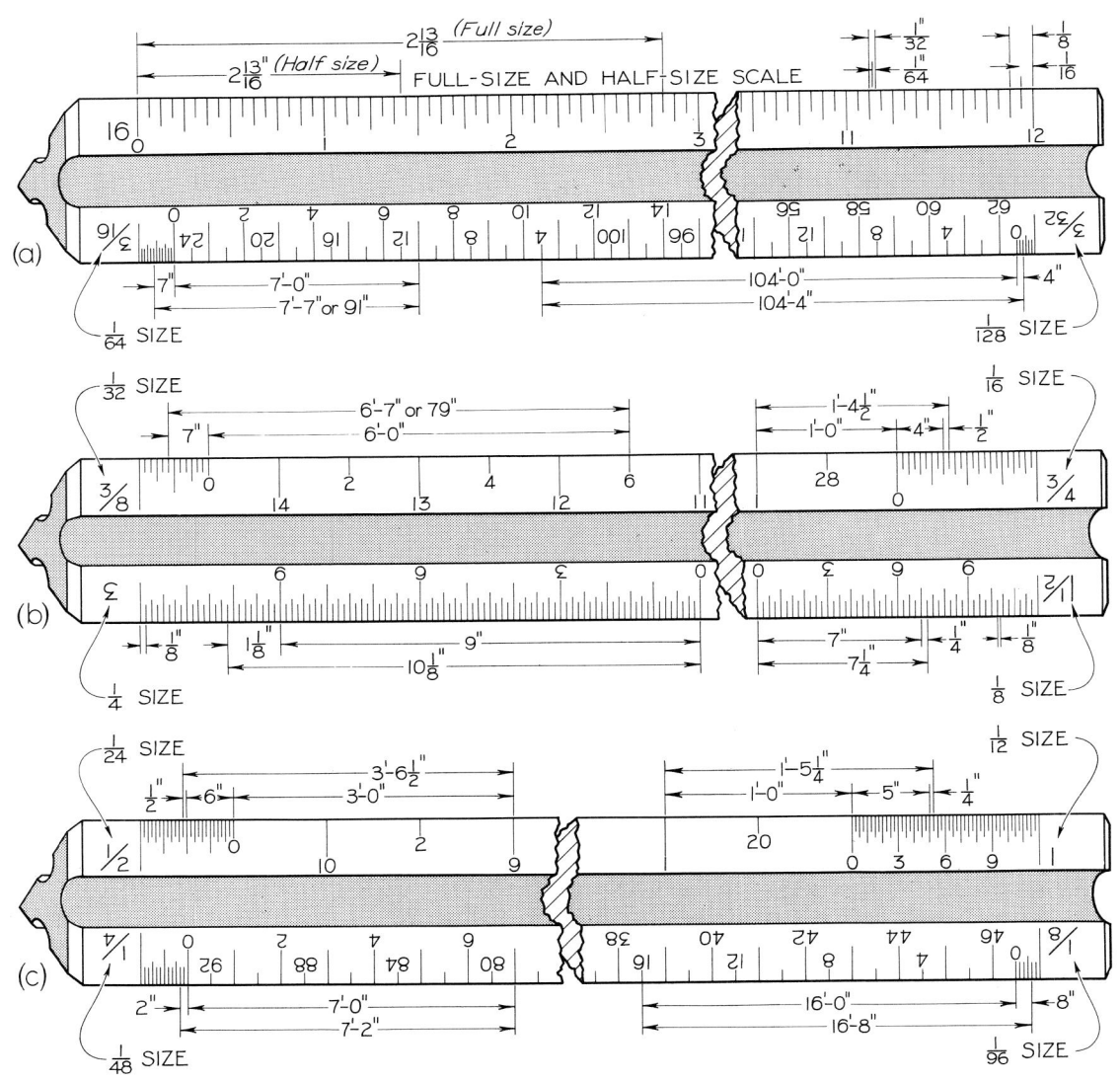

Fig. 2.37 Architects' Scales.

visually one half of $\frac{1}{16}''$; to set off $\frac{1}{64}''$, estimate one-fourth of $\frac{1}{16}''$.

Half Size Fig. 2.37 (a)
Use the full-size scale, and divide every dimension mentally by two (do not use the $\frac{1}{2}$ scale, which is intended for drawing to a scale of $\frac{1}{2}'' = 1'$, or one-twenty-fourth size). To set off 1″, measure $\frac{1}{2}''$; to set off 2″, measure 1″; to set off $3\frac{1}{4}''$, measure $1\frac{1}{2}''$ (half of 3″), then $\frac{1}{8}''$ (half of $\frac{1}{4}''$); $6\frac{1}{2}$ to set off $2\frac{13}{16}''$ (see figure), measure 1″, then $\frac{13}{32}''$ ($6\frac{1}{16}''$ or half of $\frac{13}{16}''$).

Quarter Size Fig. 2.37 (b)
Use the 3″ scale in which 3″ = 1′. The subdivided portion to the left of zero represents 1 foot compressed to actually 3″ in length and is divided into inches, then half inches, quarter inches, and finally eighth inches. Thus the entire portion representing 1 foot would actually measure 3 inches; therefore, 3″ = 1′. To set off anything less than 12″, start at zero and measure to the left.

To set off $10\frac{1}{8}''$, read off 9″ from zero to the left, and add $1\frac{1}{8}''$ and set off the total $10\frac{1}{8}''$, as shown. To set off more than 12″, for example, $1'-9\frac{3}{8}''$ (see your scale), find the 1′ mark to the right of zero and the 9⅜″ mark to the left of zero; the required distance is the distance between these marks and represents 1′–9⅜″.

Eighth Size Fig. 2.37 (b)

Use the 1½″ scale in which 1½″ = 1′. The subdivided portion to the right of zero represents 1′ and is divided into inches, then half inches, and finally quarter inches. The entire portion, representing 1′, actually is 1½″; therefore, 1½″ = 1′. To set off anything less than 12″, start at zero and measure to the right.

Double Size

Use the full-size scale, and multiply every dimension mentally by 2. To set off 1″, measure 2″; to set off 3¼″, measure 6½″; and so on. The double-size scale is occasionally used to represent small objects. In such cases, a small actual-size outline view should be shown near the bottom of the sheet to help the shop worker visualize the actual size of the object.

Other Sizes Fig. 2.37.

The other scales besides those just described are used chiefly by architects. Machine drawings are customarily made only double size, full size, half size, one-fourth size, or one-eighth size.

2.29 Decimal Scale Fig. 2.33 (d)

The increasing use of decimal dimensions has brought about the development of a scale specifically for that use. On the full-size scale, each inch is divided into fiftieths of an inch, or .02″, as shown in Fig. 2.36 (c), and on the half- and quarter-size scales, the inches are compressed to half size or quarter size, and then are divided into 10 parts, so that each subdivision stands for .1″.

The complete decimal system of dimensioning, in which this scale is used, is described in §13.10.

2.30 Mechanical Engineers' Scale
Fig. 2.33 (c)

The objects represented in machine drawing vary in size from small parts, an inch or smaller in size, to machines of large dimensions. By drawing these objects full size, half size, quarter size, or eighth

size, the drawings will readily come within the limits of the standard-size sheets. For this reason the mechanical engineers' scales are divided into units representing inches to full size, half size, quarter size, or eighth size. To make a drawing of an object to a scale of one-half size, for example, use the mechanical drafter's scale marked half size, which is graduated so that every ½″ represents 1″. Thus, the half-size scale is simply a full-size scale compressed to one-half size.

These scales are also very useful in dividing dimensions. For example, to draw a 3 11/16″ diameter circle full size, we need half of 3 11/16″ to use as radius. Instead of using arithmetic to find half of 3 11/16″, it is easier to set off 3 11/16″ on the half-size scale.

Triangular combination scales are available that include the full- and half-size mechanical engineers' scales, several architects' scales, and an engineers' scale.

2.31 To Specify the Scale on a Drawing

For machine drawings the scale indicates the ratio of the size of the drawing of the part or machine to its actual size irrespective of the unit of measurement used. The recommended practice is to letter FULL SIZE or 1:1; HALF SIZE or 1:2; and similarly for other reductions. Expansion or enlargement scales are given as 2 : 1 or 2×; 3 : 1 or 3×; 5 : 1 or 5×; 10 : 1 or 10×; and so on.

The various scale calibrations available on the metric scales and the engineers' scale provide almost unlimited scale ratios. The preferred metric scale ratios appear to be 1 : 1, 1 : 2, 1 : 5, 1 : 10, 1 : 20, 1 : 50, 1 : 100, and 1 : 200. For examples of how scales may be shown on machine drawings, see Figs. 16.24 and 16.25.

Map scales are indicated in terms of fractions, such as Scale $\frac{1}{62500}$, or graphically, such as 400 0   400   800 Ft.

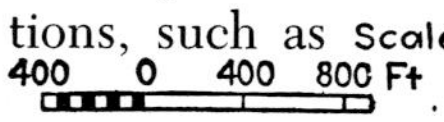

2.32 Accurate Measurements

Accurate drafting depends considerably upon the correct use of the scale in setting off distances. Do not take measurements directly off the scale with the dividers or compass, as damage will result to the scale. Place the scale on the drawing with the edge parallel to the line on which the measurement is to be made and, with a sharp pencil having a conical point, make a short dash at right angles to the scale

Fig. 2.38 Accurate Measurements.

and opposite the correct graduation mark, as shown in Fig. 2.38 (a). If extreme accuracy is required, a tiny prick mark may be made at the required point with the needle point or stylus, as shown at (b), or with one leg of the dividers.

Avoid cumulative errors in the use of the scale. If a number of distances are to be set off end-to-end, all should be set off at one setting of the scale by adding each successive measurement to the preceding one, if possible. Avoid setting off the distances individually by moving the scale to a new position each time, since slight errors in the measurements may accumulate and give rise to a large error.

2.33 Drawing Instruments

Drawing instruments are generally sold in sets, in cases, but they may be purchased separately. The principal parts of high-grade instruments are usually made of nickel silver, which has a silvery luster, is corrosion-resistant, and can be readily machined into desired shapes. Tool steel is used for the blades of ruling pens, for spring parts, for divider points, and for the various screws.

In technical drawing, accuracy, neatness, and speed are essential, §2.2. These objectives are not likely to be obtained with cheap or inferior drawing instruments. For the student or the professional drafter, it is advisable, and in the end more economical, to purchase the best instruments that can be afforded. Good instruments will satisfy the most rigid requirements, and the satisfaction, saving in time, and improved quality of work that good in-

struments can produce will more than justify the higher price.

Unfortunately, the qualities of high-grade instruments are not likely to be recognized by the beginner, who is not familiar with the performance characteristics required and who is apt to be attracted by elaborate sets containing a large number of shiny low-quality instruments. Therefore, the student should obtain the advice of the drafting instructor, of an experienced drafter, or of a reliable dealer.

2.34 Giant Bow Set

Formerly it was general practice to make pencil drawings on detail paper and then to make an inked tracing from it on tracing cloth. As reproduction methods and transparent tracing papers were improved, it was found that a great deal of time could be saved by making drawings directly in pencil with dense black lines on the tracing paper and making prints or photocopies therefrom, thus doing away with the preliminary pencil drawing on detail paper. Today, though inked tracings are still made when a fine appearance is necessary and where the greater cost is justified, the overwhelming proportion of drawings are made directly in pencil on tracing paper, vellum, polyester films, or pencil tracing cloth.

These developments have brought about the present giant bow sets that are offered now by all the major manufacturers, Fig. 2.39. The sets contain various combinations of instruments, but all feature a large bow compass in place of the traditional large compass. The large bow instrument is much sturdier and is capable of taking the heavy pressure neces-

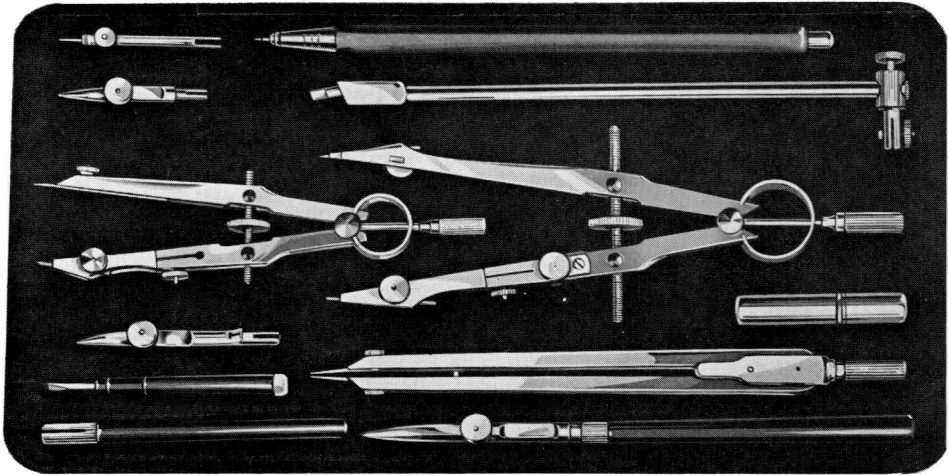

Fig. 2.39 Giant Bow Set. *Courtesy of Frank Oppenheimer*

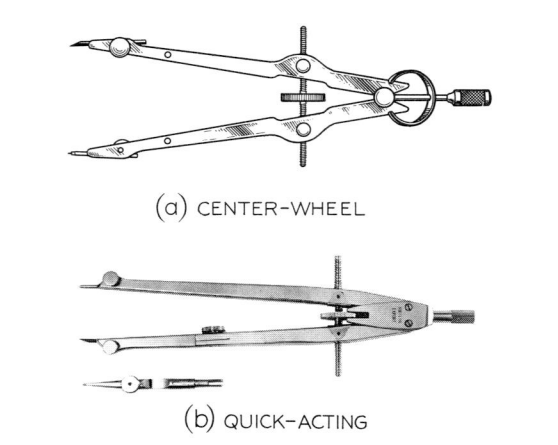

(a) CENTER-WHEEL

(b) QUICK-ACTING

Fig. 2.40 Giant Bow Compass. *(b) Courtesy of Frank Oppenheimer*

sary to produce dense black lines without losing the setting.

Most of the large bows are of the center-wheel type, Fig. 2.40 (a). Several manufacturers now offer different varieties of quick-acting bows. The large bow compass shown at (b) can be adjusted to the approximate setting by simply opening or closing the legs in the same manner as for the other bow-style compass.

2.35 The Compass

The giant bow compass, Figs. 2.39–2.41, has a socket joint in one leg that permits the insertion of either pencil or pen attachments. A *lengthening bar* or a *beam attachment* is often provided to increase the radius. For production drafting, in which it is necessary to make dense black lines to secure clear legible reproductions, the giant bow, or an appropriate template, Figs. 2.68 and 2.69, is preferred.

2.36 Using the Compass

These instructions apply generally both to the old style and the giant bow compasses. The compass, with pencil and inking attachments, is used for drawing circles of approximately 25 mm (1″) radius or larger, Fig. 2.41. Most compass needle points have a plain end for use when the compass is converted into dividers and a shoulder end for use as a compass. Adjust the needle point with the shoulder end out and so that the small point extends *slightly* farther than the pencil lead or pen nib, Fig. 2.43 (d).

To draw a penciled circle, Fig. 2.41: (1) set off the required radius on one of the center lines, (2) place the needle point at the exact intersection of the center lines, (3) adjust the compass to the required radius (25 mm or more), and (4) lean the compass forward and draw the circle clockwise while rotating the handle between the thumb and fore-

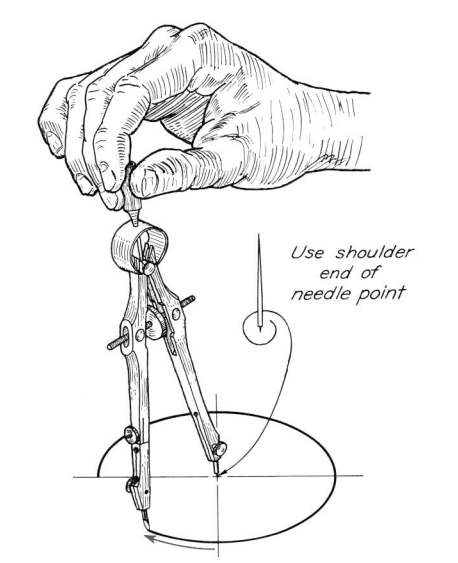

Use shoulder end of needle point

Fig. 2.41   Using the Giant Bow Compass.

finger. To obtain sufficient weight of line, it may be necessary to repeat the movement several times.

Any error in radius will result in a doubled error in diameter, so, it is best to draw a trial circle first on scrap paper or on the backing sheet and then check the diameter with the scale.

On drawings having circular arcs and tangent straight lines, draw the arcs first, whether in pencil or in ink, as it is much easier to connect a straight line to an arc than the reverse.

For very large circles, a beam compass, §2.38, is preferred, or use the lengthening bar to increase the compass radius. Use both hands, as shown in Fig. 2.42, but be careful not to jar the instrument and thus change the adjustment.

When using the compass to draw construction lines, use a 4H to 6H lead so that the lines will be very dim. For required lines, the arcs and circles must be black, and softer leads must be used. However, since heavy pressure cannot be exerted on the compass as it can on a pencil, it is usually necessary to use a compass lead that is one or two grades softer than the pencil used for the corresponding line work. For example, if a 2H lead is used for visible lines drawn with the pencil, then an F lead might be found suitable for the compass work. The hard leads supplied with the compass are usually unsatisfactory for most line work except construction lines. In summary, use leads in the compass that will produce arcs and circles that *match* the straight pencil lines.

It is necessary to exert pressure on the compass to produce heavy "reproducible" circles, and this tends to enlarge the compass center hole in the paper, especially if there are a number of concentric circles. In such cases, use a horn center, or center tack, in the hole, and place the needle point of the compass in the center of the tack.

Fig. 2.42   Drawing a Circle of Large Radius with the Beam Compass.

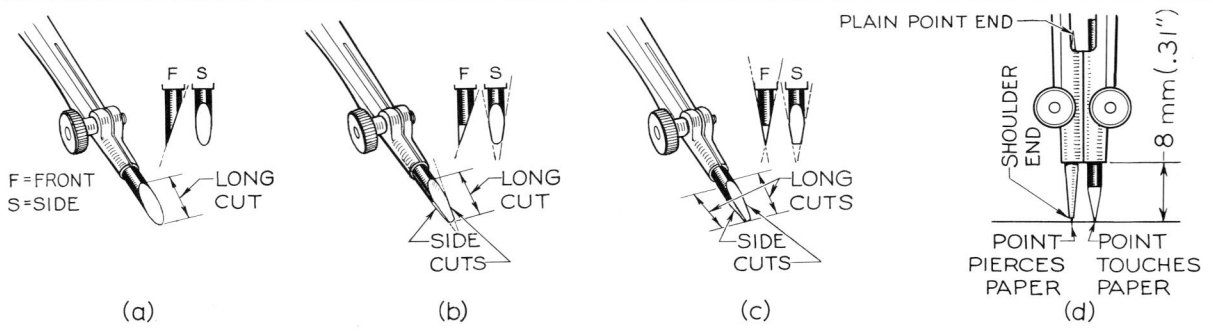

Fig. 2.43 Compass Lead Points.

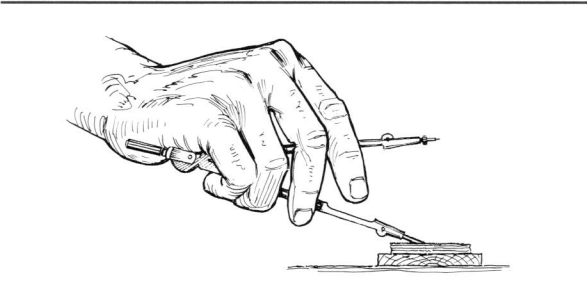

Fig. 2.44 Sharpening Compass Lead.

2.37 Sharpening the Compass Lead

Various forms of compass lead points are illustrated in Fig. 2.43. At (a), a single elliptical face has been formed by rubbing on the sandpaper pad, as shown in Fig. 2.44. At (b), the point is narrowed by small side cuts. At (c), two long cuts and two small side cuts have been made so as to produce a point similar to that on a screwdriver. At (d), the cone point is prepared by chucking the lead in a mechanical pencil and shaping it in a pencil pointer. Avoid using leads that are too short to be exposed as shown.

In using the compass, *never use the plain end of the needle point*. Instead, use the shoulder end, as shown in Fig. 2.43 (d), adjusted so that the tiny needle point extends about halfway into the paper when the compass lead just touches the paper.

2.38 Beam Compass

The beam compass, or trammel, Fig. 2.45, is used for drawing arcs or circles larger than can be drawn with the regular compass and for transferring distances too great for the regular dividers. Besides steel points, pencil and pen attachments are provided. The beams may be made of nickel silver, steel, aluminum, or wood and are procurable in var-

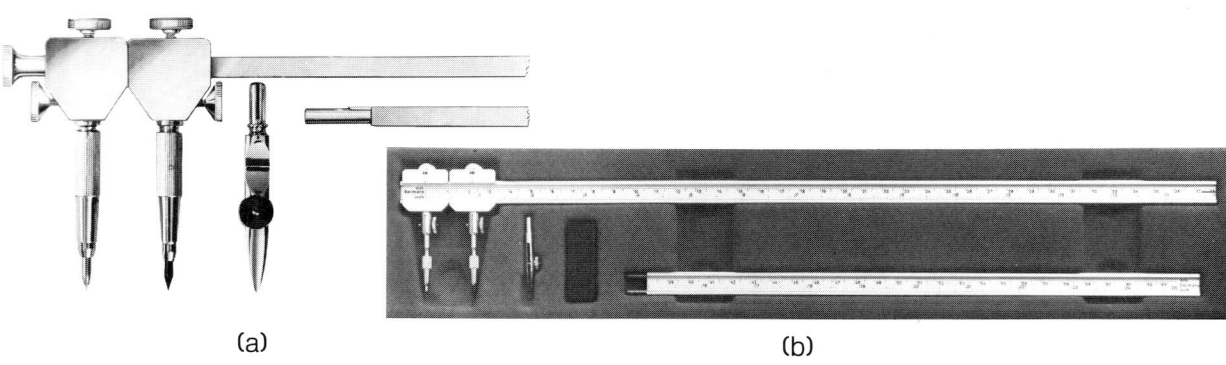

Fig. 2.45 Beam Compass Sets. *(a) Courtesy of Frank Oppenheimer; (b) Courtesy of Tacro, Div. of A&T Importers, Inc.*

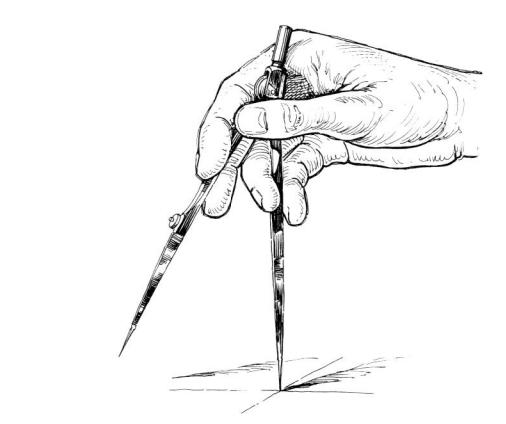

Fig. 2.46   Adjusting the Dividers.

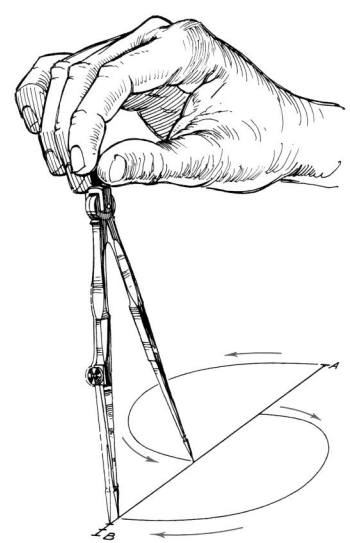

Fig. 2.47   Using the Dividers.

ious lengths. A square nickel silver beam compass set is shown in Fig. 2.45 (a), and at (b) a set with the beam graduated in millimeters and inches.

2.39 Dividers

The dividers are similar to the compass in construction and are made in square, flat, and round forms.

The friction adjustment for the pivot joint should be loose enough to permit easy manipulation with one hand, as shown in Fig. 2.46. If the pivot joint is too tight, the legs of the compass tend to spring back instead of stopping at the desired point when the pressure of the fingers is released. To adjust tension, use a small screwdriver.

Many dividers are made with a spring and thumbscrew in one leg so that minute adjustments in the setting can be made by turning the small thumbscrew.

2.40 Using the Dividers

The dividers, as the name implies, are used for *dividing* distances into a number of equal parts. They are used also for *transferring distances* or for *setting off* a series of equal distances. The dividers are used for spaces of approximately 25 mm (1″) or more. For less than 25 mm spaces, use the bow dividers, Fig. 2.50 (a). *Never use the large dividers for small spaces*

when the bow dividers can be used; the latter are more accurate.

To divide a given distance into a number of equal parts, Fig. 2.47, the method is one of trial and error. Adjust the dividers with the fingers of the hand that holds them, to the approximate unit of division, estimated by eye. Rotate the dividers counterclockwise through 180°, and so on, until the desired number of units has been stepped off. If the last prick of the dividers falls short of the end of the line to be divided, increase the distance between the divider points proportionately. For example, to divide the line AB, Fig. 2.47, into three equal parts, the dividers are set by eye to approximately one-third the length AB. When it is found that the trial radius is too small, the distance between the divider points is increased by one-third the remaining distance. If the last prick of the dividers is beyond the end of the line, a similar decreasing adjustment is made.

The student should avoid *cumulative errors,* which may result when the dividers are used to set off a series of distances end to end. To set off a large number of equal divisions, say, 15, first set off 3 equal large divisions and then divide each into 5 equal parts. Wherever possible in such cases, use the scale instead of the dividers, as described in §2.32, or set off the total and then divide into the parts by means of the parallel-line method, §§5.14 and 5.15.

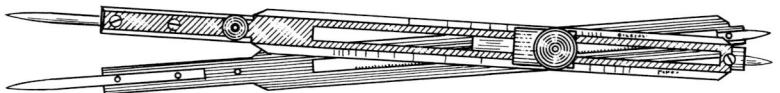

Fig. 2.48 Proportional Dividers.

2.41 Proportional Dividers

For enlarging or reducing a drawing, proportional dividers, Fig. 2.48, are convenient. They may be used also for dividing distances into a number of equal parts, or for obtaining a percentage reduction of a distance. For this purpose, points of division are marked on the instrument so as to secure the required subdivisions readily. Some instruments are calibrated to obtain special ratios, such as $1 : \sqrt{2}$, the diameter of a circle to the side of an equal square, and feet to meters.

2.42 The Bow Instruments

The bow instruments are classified as the *bow dividers*, *bow pen*, and *bow pencil*. A combination pen and pencil bow, usually with center-wheel adjustment, Fig. 2.49, and separate instruments with either side-wheel or center-wheel adjustment, Fig. 2.50, are available. The choice is a matter of personal preference.

2.43 Using the Bow Instruments

The bow pencil and bow pen are used for drawing circles of approximately 25 mm (1″) radius or smaller. The bow dividers are used for the same purpose as the large dividers, but for smaller (approximately 25 mm or less) spaces and more accurate work.

Whether the center-wheel or side-wheel instrument is used, the adjustment should be made with the thumb and finger of the hand that holds the instrument, Fig. 2.51 (a). The instrument is manipulated by twirling the head between the thumb and fingers, (b).

The lead is sharpened in the same manner as for the large compass, §2.37, except that for small radii, the inclined cut may be turned *inside* if preferred, Fig. 2.52 (a). For general use, the lead should be turned to the outside, as shown at (b). In either case, always keep the compass lead sharpened. *Avoid stubby compass leads,* which cannot be properly sharpened. At least 6 mm (¼″) of lead should extend from the compass at all times.

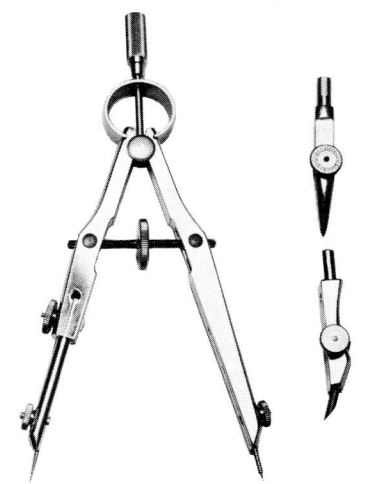

Fig. 2.49   Combination Pen and Pencil Bow.
Courtesy of Frank Oppenheimer

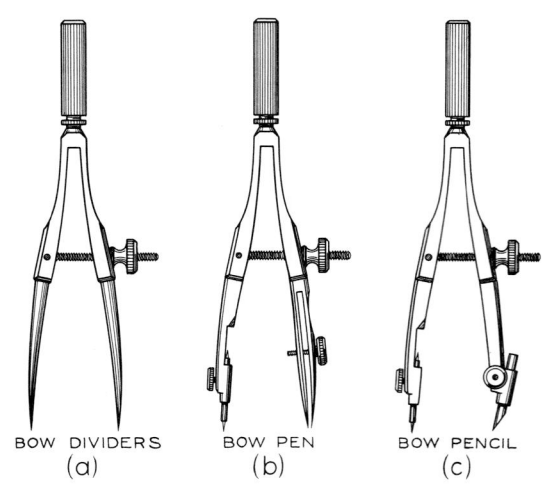

BOW DIVIDERS   BOW PEN   BOW PENCIL
(a)   (b)   (c)

Fig. 2.50   Bow Instruments with Side Wheel.

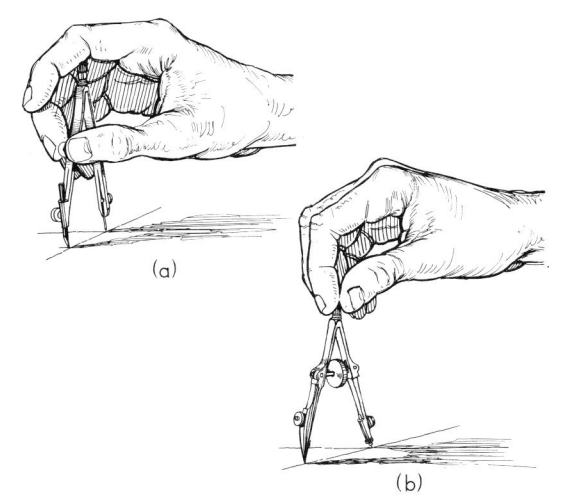

Fig. 2.51 Using the Bow Instruments.

In adjusting the needle point of the bow pencil or bow pen, be sure to have the needle extending slightly longer than the pen or the lead, Fig. 2.43 (d), the same as for the large compass.

In drawing small circles, greater care is necessary in sharpening and adjusting the lead and the needle point, and especially in accurately setting the

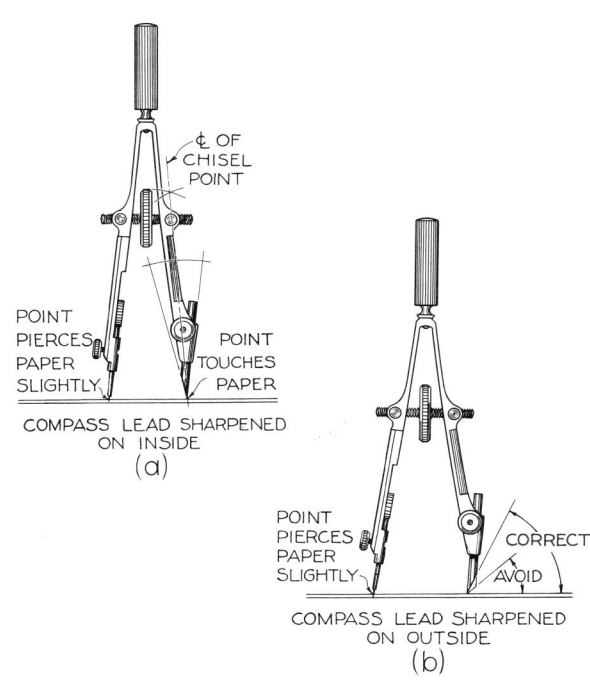

Fig. 2.52 Compass-Lead Points.

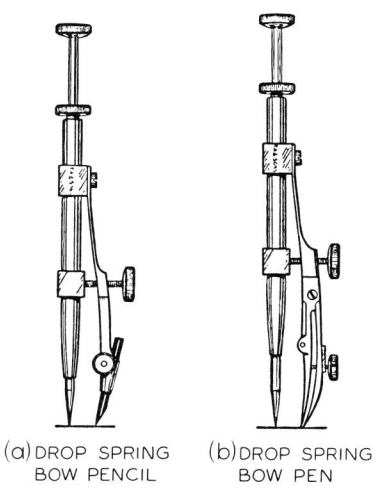

Fig. 2.53 Drop Spring Bow Instruments.

desired radius. If a 6.35 mm ($\frac{1}{4}$ ″) diameter circle is to be drawn, and if the radius is "off" only 0.8 mm ($\frac{1}{32}$ ″) the total error on diameter is approximately 25 percent, which is far too much error.

Appropriate templates may be used also for drawing small circles. See Figs. 2.68 and 2.69.

2.44 Drop Spring Bow Pencil and Pen

These compasses, Fig. 2.53, are designed for drawing multiple identical small circles, such as drill holes or rivet heads. A central pin is made to move easily up and down through a tube to which the pen or pencil unit is attached. To use the instrument, hold the knurled head of the tube between the thumb and second finger, placing the first finger on top of the knurled head of the pin. Place the point of the pin at the desired center, lower the pen or pencil until it touches the paper, and twirl the instrument clockwise with the thumb and second finger. Then lift the tube independently of the pin, and finally lift the entire instrument.

2.45 To Lay Out a Sheet

After the sheet has been attached to the board, as explained in §2.7, proceed as follows, Fig. 2.54 (see also Layout A–2, inside back cover).

I. Using the T-square, draw a horizontal *trim line* near the lower edge of the paper, and then using the triangle, draw a vertical trim line near the left

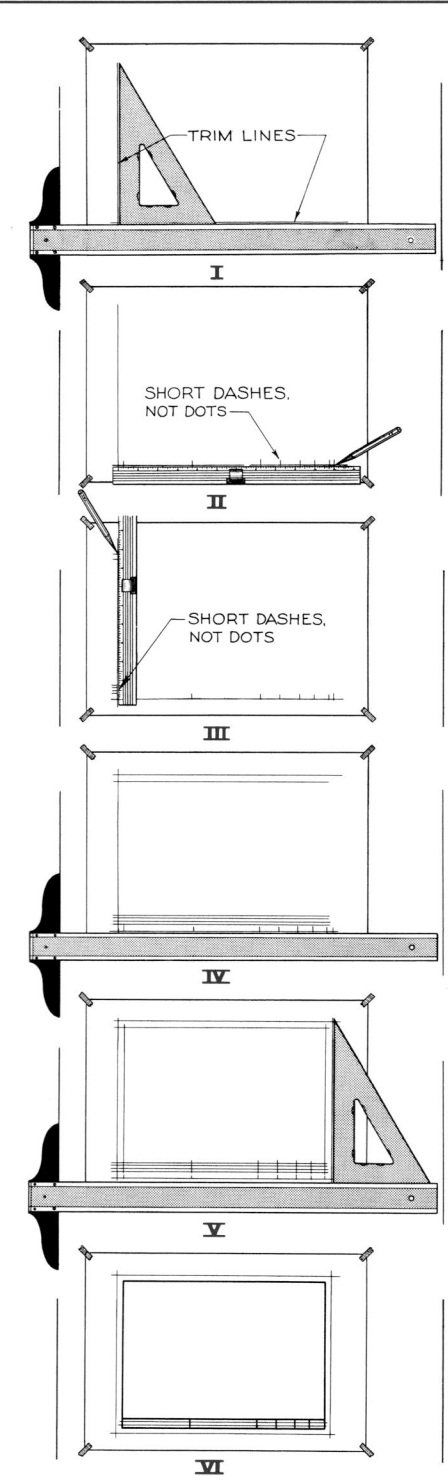

Fig. 2.54 To Lay Out a Sheet.
Layout A–2; see inside back cover.

edge of the paper. Both should be *light construction lines.*

II.   Place the scale along the lower trim line with the full-size scale up. Draw short light dashes *perpendicular* to the scale at the required distances. See Fig. 2.38 (a).

III.   Place the scale along the left trim line with the full-size scale to the left, and mark the required distances with short light dashes perpendicular to the scale.

IV.   Draw horizontal construction lines with the aid of the T-square through the marks at the left of the sheet.

V.   Draw vertical construction lines, *from the bottom upward,* along the edge of the triangle through the marks at the bottom of the sheet.

VI.   Retrace the border and the title strip to make them heavier. Notice that the layout is made independently of the edges of the paper.*

2.46 Technique of Pencil Drawing

By far the greater part of commercial drafting is executed in pencil. Most prints or photocopies are made from pencil tracings, and all ink tracings must be preceded by pencil drawings. It should therefore be evident that skill in drafting chiefly implies skill in pencil drawing.

Technique is a style or quality of drawing imparted by the individual drafter to the work. It is characterized by crisp black linework and lettering. Technique in lettering is discussed in §4.12.

Dark Accented Lines

The pencil lines of a finished pencil drawing or tracing should be very dark, Fig. 2.55. Dark crisp lines are necessary to give punch or snap to the drawing. Ends of lines should be accented by a little extra pressure on the pencil, (a). Curves should be as dark as other lines, (b). Hidden-line dashes and center-line dashes should be carefully estimated as to length and spacing and should be of uniform width throughout their length, (c) and (d).

Dimension lines, extension lines, section lines, and center lines also should be dark. The difference

*In industrial drafting rooms the sheets are available, cut to standard sizes, with border and title strips already printed. Drafting supply houses can supply such papers, printed to order, to schools for little extra cost.

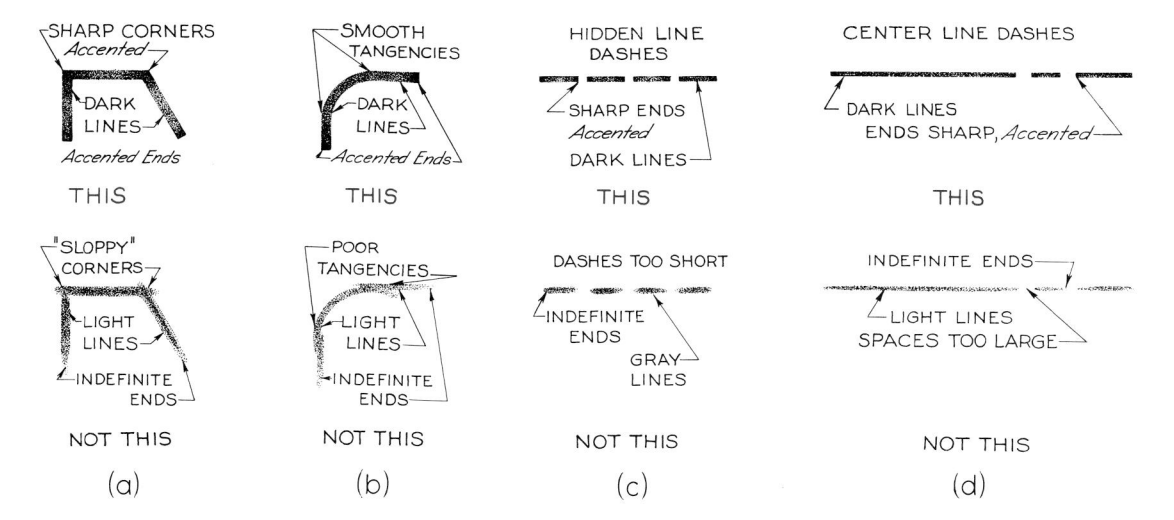

Fig. 2.55 Technique of Lines (Enlarged).

between these lines and visible lines is mostly in width—there is very little difference, if any, in blackness.

A simple way to determine whether your lines on tracing paper or cloth are dense black is to hold the tracing up to the light. Lines that are not opaque black will not print clearly by most reproduction processes.

Construction lines should be made with a sharp, hard lead and *should be so light that they need not be erased* when the drawing is completed.

Contrast in Lines

Contrast in pencil lines should be similar to that of ink lines; that is, the difference beween the various lines should be mostly in the *widths* of the lines, with little if any difference in the degree of darkness, Fig. 2.56. The visible lines should contrast strongly with the thin lines of the drawing. If necessary, draw over a visible line several times to get the desired thickness and darkness. A short retracing stroke backward (to the left), producing a jabbing action, results in a darker line.

2.47 Pencil Tracing

While some pencil tracings are made of a drawing placed underneath the tracing paper (usually when a great deal of erasing and changing is necessary on the original drawing), most drawings today are made directly in pencil on tracing paper, pencil tracing cloth, films, or vellum. These are not tracings but pencil drawings, and the methods and technique are the same as previously described for pencil drawing.

In making a drawing directly on a tracing medium, a smooth sheet of heavy white drawing

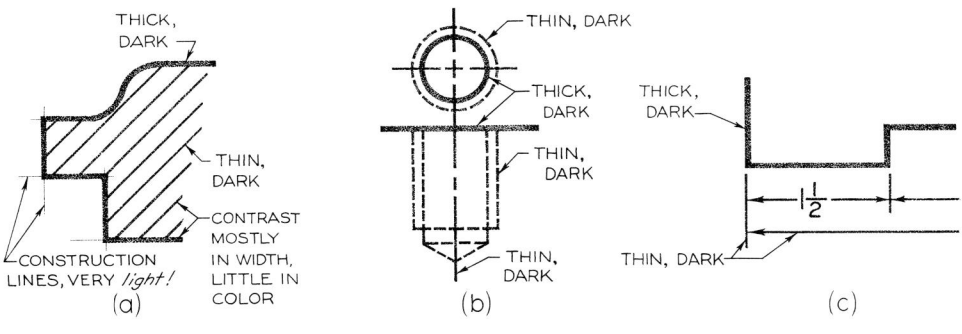

Fig. 2.56 Contrast of Lines (Enlarged).

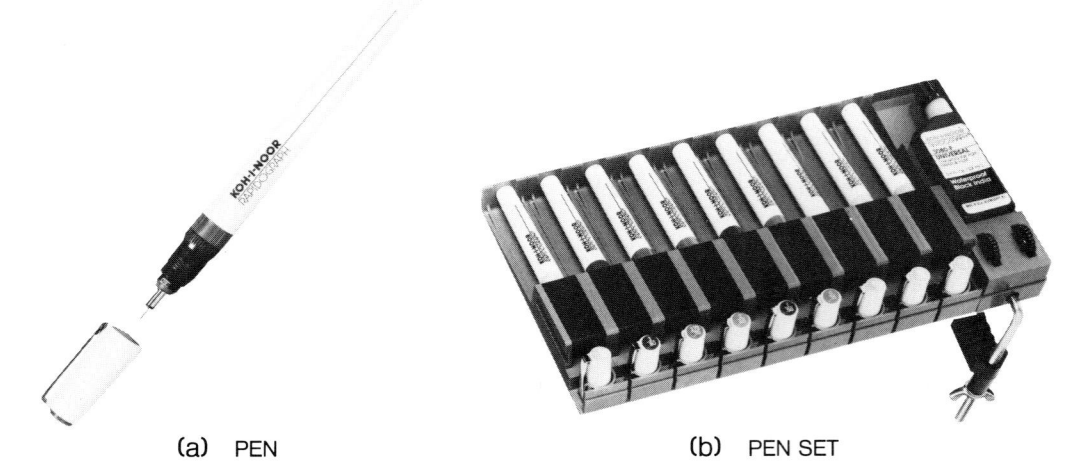

(a) PEN   (b) PEN SET

Fig. 2.57   Technical Fountain Pen and Pen Set. *Courtesy of Koh-I-Noor Rapidograph, Inc.*

paper, a backing sheet, should be placed underneath. The whiteness of the backing sheet improves the visibility of the lines, and the hardness of the surface makes it possible to exert pressure on the pencil and produce dense black lines without excessive grooving of the paper.

All lines must be dark and cleanly drawn when drawings are intended to be reproduced.

2.48 Technical Fountain Pens

The technical fountain pen, Figs. 2.57 and 2.58, with the tube and needle point, is available in several line widths. Many prefer this type of pen, for the line widths are fixed and it is suitable for freehand or mechanical lettering and line work. The pen requires an occasional filling and a minimum of skill to use. For uniform line work, the pen should be used perpendicular to the paper. For best results, follow the manufacturer's recommendations for operation and cleaning.

2.49 Ruling Pens

The ruling pen, Fig. 2.59, should be of the highest quality, with blades of high-grade tempered steel sharpened properly at the factory. The nibs should be sharp, but not sharp enough to cut the paper.

The *detail pen*, capable of holding a considerable quantity of ink, is extremely useful for drawing long

Fig. 2.58   Using the Technical Fountain Pen.

heavy lines, (b). This type of pen is preferred for small amounts of ink work as the pen is easily adjusted for the desired line width and is readily cleaned after use.

For methods using the ruling pen, see §2.51.

2.50 Drawing Ink

Drawing ink is composed chiefly of carbon in colloidal suspension and gum. The fine particles of carbon give the deep, black luster to the ink, and the

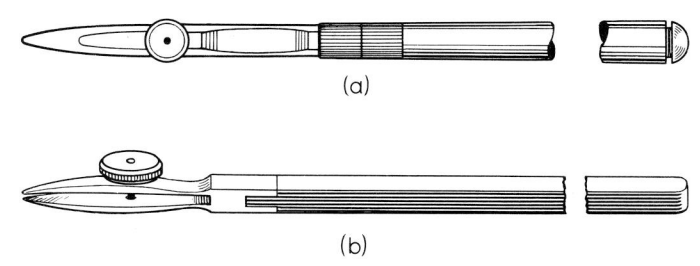

Fig. 2.59   Ruling Pens.

gum makes it waterproof and quick to dry. The ink
bottle, or flask, should not be left uncovered, as
evaporation will cause the ink to thicken.

Special drawing ink is available for use on acetate
and polyester films. Such inks should not be used in
technical fountain pens unless the pens are specifically made for acetate-based inks.

For removing dried waterproof drawing ink from
pens or instruments, pen-cleaning fluids are available at dealers.

2.51 Use of the Ruling Pen

The ruling pen, Fig. 2.59, is used to ink lines drawn
with instruments, never to ink freehand lines or
freehand lettering. The proper method of filling the
pen is shown in Fig. 2.60.

The pen should lean at an angle of about 60° with
the paper in the direction in which the line is being
drawn and in a vertical plane containing the line,
Fig. 2.61.

The ruling pen is used in inking irregular curves,

Fig. 2.60   Filling the Ruling Pen.

as well as straight lines, as shown in Figs. 2.65 and
2.66. The pen should be held more nearly vertical
when used with an irregular curve than when used
with the T-square or a triangle. The ruling pen
should lean only slightly in the direction in which
the line is being drawn.

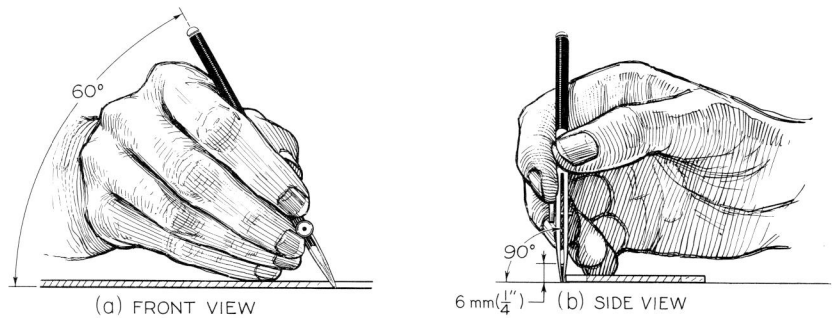

Fig. 2.61   Position of Hand in Using the Ruling Pen.

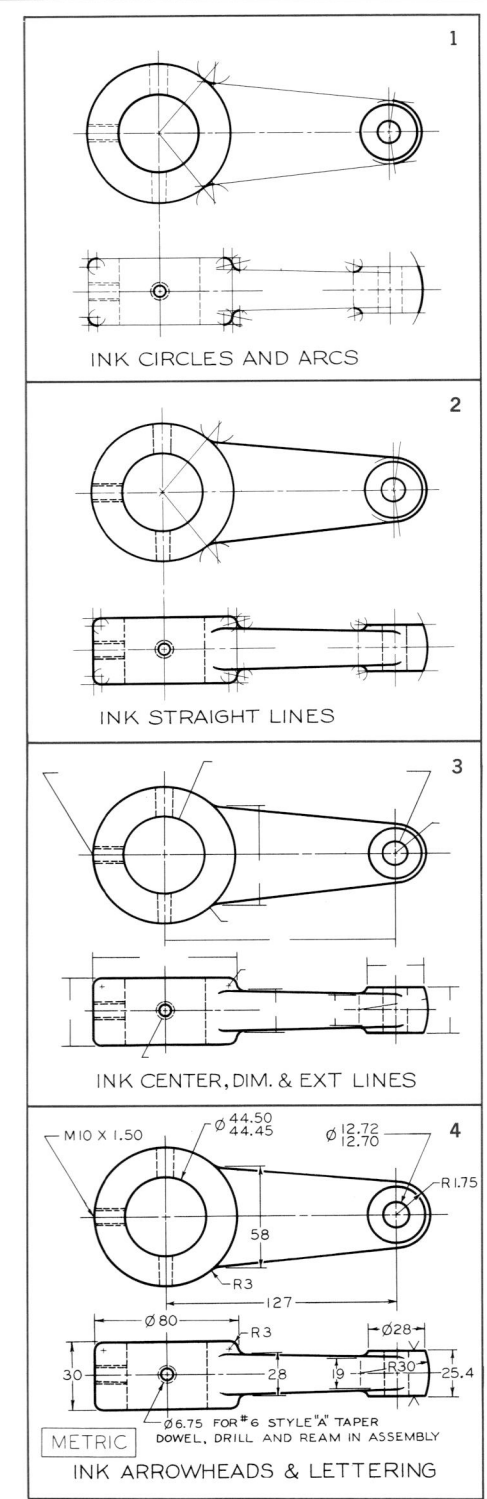

INK CIRCLES AND ARCS

INK STRAIGHT LINES

INK CENTER, DIM. & EXT LINES

INK ARROWHEADS & LETTERING

Fig. 2.62 Order of Inking.

2.52 Order of Inking Fig. 2.62

A definite order should be followed in inking a drawing or tracing, as follows.

1. (a) Mark all tangent points in pencil directly on the drawing or tracing.
   (b) Indent all compass centers (with pricker or divider point).
   (c) Ink visible circles and arcs.
   (d) Ink hidden circles and arcs.
   (e) Ink irregular curves, if any.

2. (1st: horizontal; 2nd: vertical; 3rd: inclined)
   (a) Ink visible straight lines.
   (b) Ink hidden straight lines.

3. (1st: horizontal; 2nd: vertical; 3rd: inclined) Ink center lines, extension lines, dimension lines, leader lines, and section lines (if any).

4. (a) Ink arrowheads and dimension figures.
   (b) Ink notes, titles, etc. (pencil guide lines directly on tracing.)

Some drafters prefer to ink center lines before indenting the compass centers because ink can go through the holes and cause blots on the back of the sheet.

When an ink blot is made, the excess ink should be taken up with a blotter, or smeared with the finger if a blotter is not available, and not allowed to soak into the paper. When the spot is thoroughly dry, the remaining ink can be erased easily.

For cleaning untidy drawings or for removing the original pencil lines from an inked drawing, the Pink Pearl or the Mars-Plastic eraser is suitable if used lightly. Pencil lines or dirt can be removed from tracing cloth by rubbing lightly with a cloth moistened with carbon tetrachloride or benzine. Use either with care in a well-ventilated area.

When erasure on cloth damages the surface, it may be restored by rubbing the spot with soapstone and then applying pounce or chalk dust. If the damage is not too great, an application of the powder will be sufficient.

When a gap in a thick ink line is made by erasing, the gap should be filled in with a series of fine lines that are allowed to run together. A single heavy line is difficult to match and is more likely to run and cause a blot.

In commercial drafting rooms, the electric erasing machine, Fig. 2.18, is usually available to save the time of the drafter.

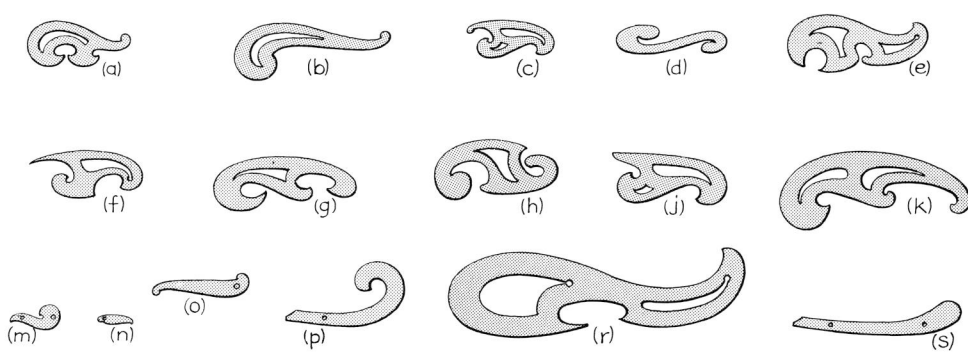

Fig. 2.63 Irregular or French Curves.

2.53 Irregular Curves

When it is required to draw mechanical curves other than circles or circular arcs, an irregular or French curve is generally employed. Many different forms and sizes of curves are manufactured, as suggested by the more common forms illustrated in Fig. 2.63.

The curves are composed largely of successive segments of the geometric curves, such as the ellipse, parabola, hyperbola, and involute. The best curves are made of highly transparent plastic. Among the many special types of curves that are available are hyperbolas, parabolas, ellipses, logarithmic spirals, ship curves, and railroad curves.

Adjustable curves, Fig. 2.64, are also available. The curve shown at (a) consists of a core of lead, enclosed by a coil spring attached to a flexible strip. The one at (b) consists of a spline, to which "ducks" (weights) are attached. The spline can be bent to form any desired curve, limited only by the elasticity of the material. An ordinary piece of solder wire

can be used very successfully by bending the wire to the desired curve.

2.54 Using the Irregular Curve

The irregular curve is a device for the *mechanical drawing of curved lines and should not be applied directly to the points* or used for purposes of producing an initial curve. The proper use of the irregular curve requires skill, especially when the lines are to be drawn in ink. After points have been plotted through which the curve is to pass, a light pencil line should be sketched freehand smoothly through the points.

To draw a mechanical line over the freehand line with the aid of the irregular curve, it is only necessary to match the various segments of the irregular curve with successive portions of the freehand curve and to draw the line with pencil or ruling pen along the edge of the curve, Fig. 2.65. It is very important

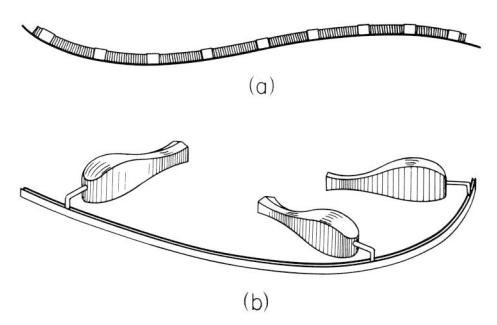

Fig. 2.64 Adjustable Curves.

Fig. 2.65 Using the Irregular Curve.

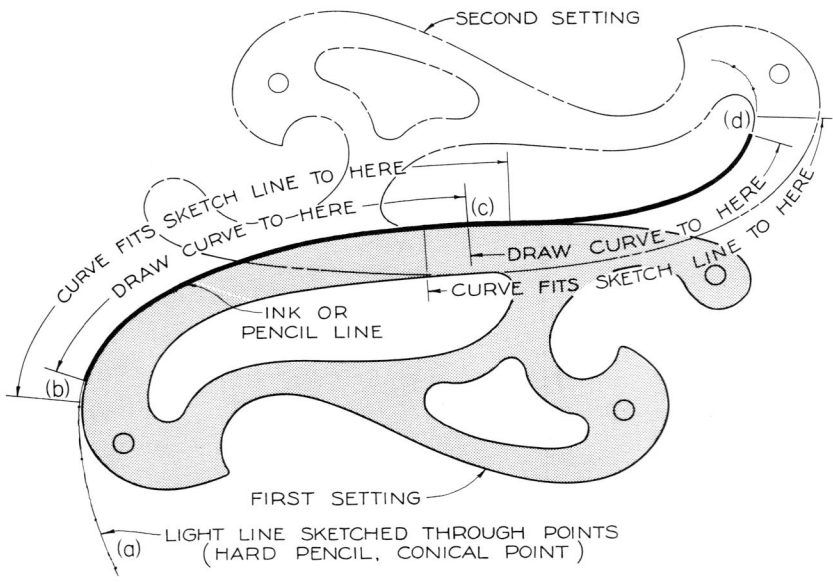

Fig. 2.66   Settings of Irregular Curve.

that the irregular curve match the curve to be drawn for some distance at each end beyond the segment to be drawn for any one setting of the curve, as shown in Fig. 2.66. When this rule is observed, the successive sections of the curve will be tangent to each other, without any abrupt change in the curvature of the line. In placing the irregular curve, the short-radius end of the curve should be turned toward the short-radius part of the curve to be drawn; that is, the portion of the irregular curve used should have the same curvilinear tendency as the portion of the curve to be drawn. This will prevent abrupt changes in direction.

The drafter should change position with the drawing when necessary, to avoid working on a near side of the curve.

When plotting points to establish the path of a curve, it is desirable to plot more points, and closer together, where sharp turns in the curve occur.

Free curves may also be drawn with the compass, as shown in Fig. 5.42.

For symmetrical curves, such as an ellipse, Fig. 2.67, use the same segment of the irregular curve in two or more opposite places. For example, at (a) the irregular curve is matched to the curve and the line drawn from 1 to 2. Light pencil dashes are then drawn directly on the irregular curve at these points (the curve will take pencil marks well if it is lightly "frosted" by rubbing with a hard pencil eraser). At (b) the irregular curve is turned over and matched so that the line may be drawn from 2 to 1. In similar manner, the same segment is used again at (c) and

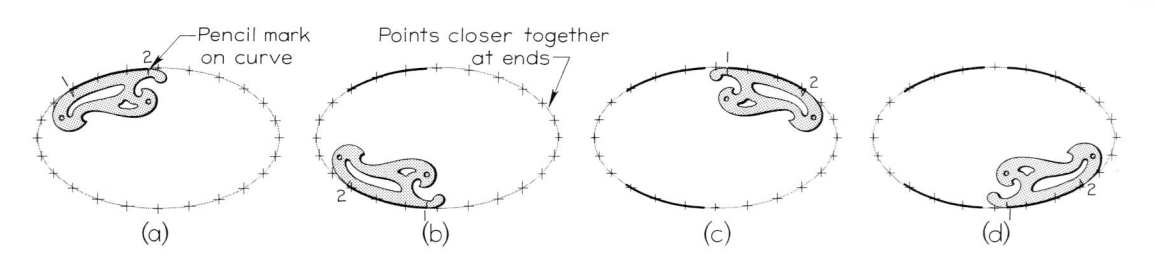

Fig. 2.67   Symmetrical Figures.

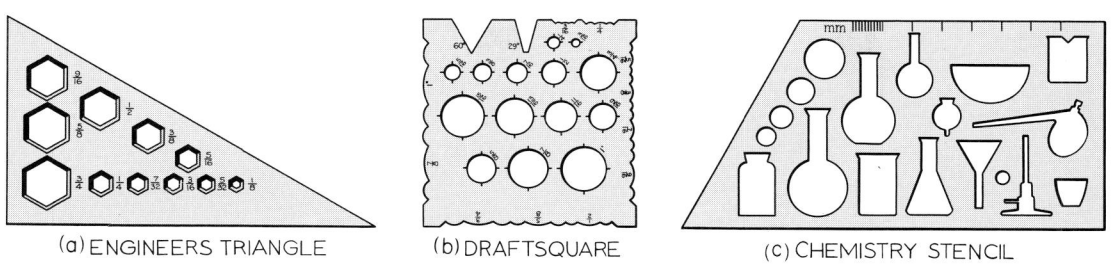

(a) ENGINEERS TRIANGLE (b) DRAFTSQUARE (c) CHEMISTRY STENCIL

Fig. 2.68 Drafting Devices.

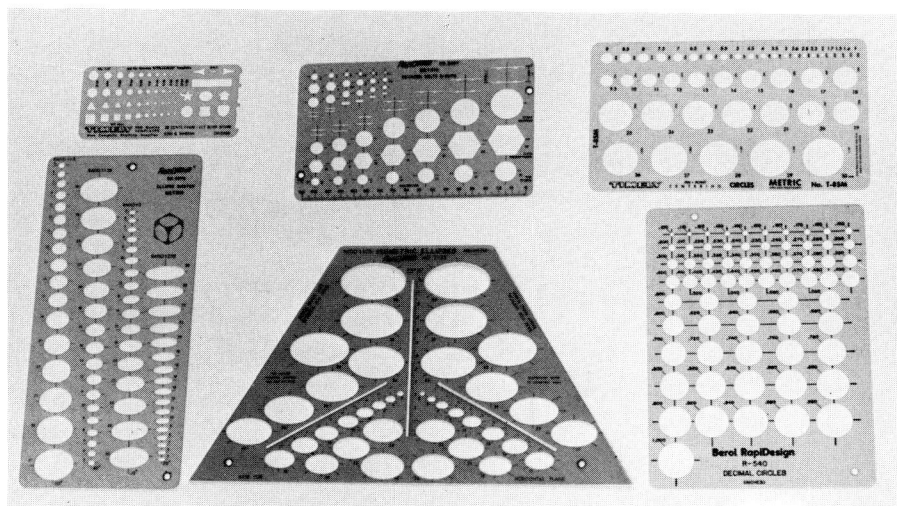

Fig. 2.69 Templates.

(d). The ellipse is completed by filling in the gaps at the ends by using the irregular curve or, if desired, the compass.

2.55 Templates

Templates are available for a great variety of specialized needs. A template may be found for drawing almost any ordinary drafting symbols or repetitive features. The engineers' triangle, Fig. 2.68 (a), is useful for drawing hexagons or for bolt heads and nuts; the draftsquare, (b), is convenient for drawing the curves on bolt heads and nuts, for drawing circles, thread forms, and so forth; and the chemistry stencil, (c), is useful for drawing chemical apparatus in schematic form.

Ellipse templates, §5.56, are perhaps more widely used than any other type. Circle templates are useful for drawing small circles quickly and for drawing fillets and rounds, and are used extensively in tool and die drawings. Some of the more commonly used templates are shown in Fig. 2.69.

2.56 Drafting Machines

The drafting machine, Fig. 2.70, is an ingenious device that replaces the T-square, triangles, scales, and protractor. The links, or bands, are arranged so that the controlling head is always in any desired fixed position regardless of where it is placed on the board; thus, the horizontal straightedge will remain horizontal if so set. The controlling head is graduated in degrees (including a vernier on certain machines), which allows the straightedges, or scales, to

Fig. 2.70   Drafting Machine. *Courtesy of Keuffel & Esser Co.*

be set and locked at any angle. There are automatic stops at the more frequently used angles, such as 15°, 30°, 45°, 60°, 75°, and 90°.

Drafting machines and drafting tables, Fig. 2.71, have been greatly improved in recent years. The chief advantage of the drafting machine is that it

Fig. 2.71   Adjustable Drafting Table with Track Drafting Machine. *Courtesy of Keuffel & Esser Co.*

speeds up drafting. Since its parts are made of metal, their accurate relationships are not subject to change, whereas T-squares, triangles, and working edges of drawing boards must be checked and corrected frequently. Drafting machines for left-handers are available from the manufacturers.

2.57 Parallel-Ruling Straightedge

For large drawings, the long T-square becomes unwieldy, and considerable inaccuracy may result from the "give" or swing of the blade. In such case the parallel-ruling straightedge, Fig. 2.72, is recommended. The ends of the straightedge are controlled by a system of cords and pulleys which permit the straightedge to be moved up or down on the board while maintaining a horizontal position.

2.58 Drawing Papers

Drawing paper, or *detail paper,* is used whenever a drawing is to be made in pencil but not for reproduction. For working drawings and for general use, the preferred paper is light cream or buff in color, and it is available in rolls of widths 24″ and 36″ and in cut sheets of standard sizes such as 8.5″ × 11″, 11″ × 17″, 17″ × 22″, and so on. Most industrial drafting rooms use standard sheets, §2.62, with printed borders and title strips, and since the cost for printing adds so little to the price per sheet, many schools have also adopted printed sheets.

The best drawing papers have up to 100 percent pure rag stock; have strong fibers that afford superior erasing qualities, folding strength, and toughness; and will not discolor or grow brittle with age. The paper should have a fine grain or tooth that will pick up the graphite and produce clean, dense black lines. However, if the paper is too rough, it will wear down the pencil excessively and will produce ragged, grainy lines. The paper should have a hard surface so that it will not groove too easily when pressure is applied to the pencil.

For ink work, as for catalog and book illustrations, white papers are used. The better papers, such as Bristol Board and Strathmore, come in several thicknesses such as 2-ply, 3-ply, and 4-ply.

2.59 Tracing Papers

Tracing paper is a thin transparent paper upon which drawings are made for the purpose of reproducing by blueprinting or by other similar

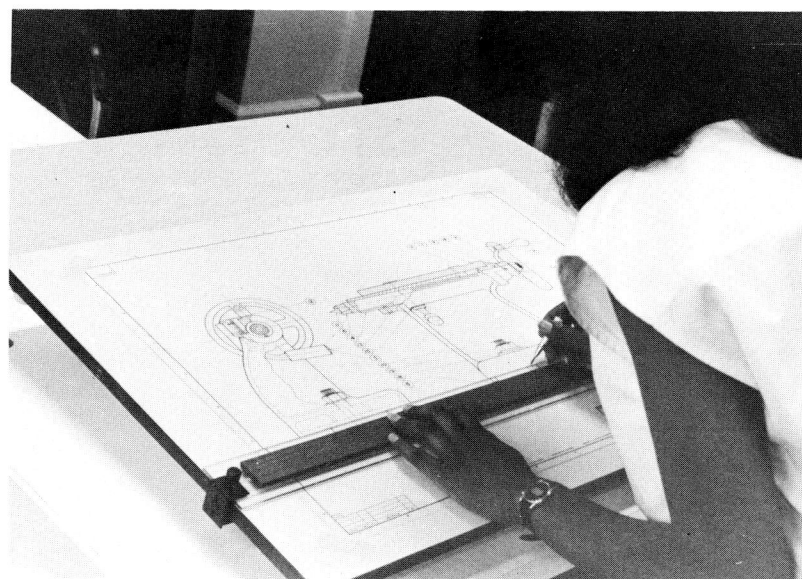

Fig. 2.72 Parallel-Ruling Straightedge.

processes. Tracings are usually made in pencil, but may be made in ink. Most tracing papers will take pencil or ink, but some are especially suited to one or to the other.

Tracing papers are of two kinds: (1) those treated with oils, waxes, or similar substances to render them more transparent, called *vellums;* (2) those not so treated, but which may be quite transparent, owing to the high quality of the raw materials and the methods of manufacture. Some treated papers deteriorate rapidly with age, becoming brittle in many cases within a few months, but some excellent vellums are available. Untreated papers made entirely of good rag stock will last indefinitely and will remain tough.

2.60 Tracing Cloth
Tracing cloth is a thin transparent muslin fabric (cotton, not "linen" as commonly supposed) sized with a starch compound or plastic to provide a good working surface for pencil or ink. It is much more expensive than tracing paper. Tracing cloth is available in rolls of standard widths, such as 30″, 36″, and 42″, and also in sheets of standard sizes, with or without printed borders and title forms.

For pencil tracings, special pencil tracing cloths are available. Many concerns make their drawings in pencil directly on this cloth, dispensing entirely

with the preliminary pencil drawing on detail paper, thus saving a great deal of time. These cloths generally have a surface that will produce dense black lines when hard pencils are used. Hence, these drawings do not easily smudge and will stand up well with handling.

2.61 Polyester Films and Coated Sheets
The polyester film is a superior drafting material available in rolls and sheets of standard size. It is made by bonding a mat surface to one or both sides of a clear polyester sheet. The transparency and printing qualities are very good, the mat drawing surface is excellent for pencil or ink, erasures leave no ghost marks, and the film has high dimensional stability. Its resistance to cracking, bending, or tearing makes it virtually indestructible, if given reasonable care. The film has rapidly replaced cloth and is competing with vellum in some applications. Some companies have found it more economical to make their drawings directly in ink on the film.

Large coated sheets of aluminum, which provides a good dimensional stability, are often used in the aircraft and auto industry for full-scale layouts that are scribed into the coating with a steel point rather than a pencil. The layouts are reproduced from the sheets photographically.

2.62 Standard Sheets

Two systems of sheet sizes together with length, width, and letter designations are listed by ANSI as follows.

Nearest International Size[a] (millimeter)	Standard USA Size[a] (inch)
A4 210 × 297	A 8.5 × 11.0
A3 297 × 420	B 11.0 × 17.0
A2 420 × 594	C 17.0 × 22.0
A1 594 × 841	D 22.0 × 34.0
A0 841 × 1189	E 34.0 × 44.0

[a]ANSI Y14.1–1980 (R1987).

The use of the basic sheet size, 8.5″ × 11.0″ or 210 mm × 297 mm and multiples thereof, permits filing of small tracings and of folded prints in standard files with or without correspondence. These sizes can be cut without waste from the standard rolls of paper, cloth, or film.

For layout designations, title blocks, revision blocks, and list of materials blocks, see inside the back cover of this book. See also §16.12.

2.63 The Computer as a Drafting Tool

The development of CAD workstations and the availability of drafting software have made the computer a valuable drafting instrument. The use of the computer in drafting began in 1963 when Ivan Sutherland, of M.I.T., developed "Sketchpad," a pro-

Fig. 2.73 Computer-Aided Drafting System. *Courtesy Bausch & Lomb*

gram for engineers and drafters. The use of the computer continued to grow and by the late 1970s was widespread. All drafters and engineers today need to become familiar with computer systems in drafting and design.

Most CAD systems, regardless of their size, Fig. 2.73, consist of an input device such as a joystick or digitizer pad, a cathode-ray tube (CRT—much like a television screen) on which to "build" the drawing, and a plotter that prints the final results. These devices are shown and discussed in Chapters 3 and 8. It is appropriate to point out that this new approach is developing rapidly and that much routine drafting can be done on CAD systems.

It should be noted that a student will need to learn the basic concepts of orthographic and pictorial projections as well as dimensioning before a CAD system can be effectively used.

Instrumental Drawing Problems

All of the following constructions, Figs. 2.74–2.84, are to be drawn in pencil on Layout A–2 (see inside the back cover of this book). The steps in drawing this layout are shown in Fig. 2.54. Draw all construction lines *lightly*, using a hard lead (4H to 6H), and all required lines dense black with a softer lead (F to H). If construction lines are drawn properly—that is, *lightly*—they need not be erased.

If the layout is to be made on the A4 size sheet, width dimensions for title-strip forms will need to be adjusted to fit the available space.

The drawings in Figs. 2.79–2.84 are to be drawn in pencil, preferably on tracing paper or vellum; then prints should be made to show the effectiveness of the student's technique. If ink tracings are required, the originals may be drawn on film or on detail paper and then traced on vellum or tracing cloth. For any assigned problem, the instructor may require that all dimensions and notes be lettered in order to afford further lettering practice.

The problems at the end of Chapter 5, "Geometric Constructions," provide excellent additional practice to develop skill in the use of drawing instruments.

Since many of the problems in this chapter are of a general nature, they can also be solved on most computer graphics systems. If a system is available, the instructor may choose to assign specific problems to be completed by this method.

Additional problems in convenient form for solution are presented in the worksheets at the back of this book. Refer to Drawings 2-1 and 2-2 and accompanying instructions.

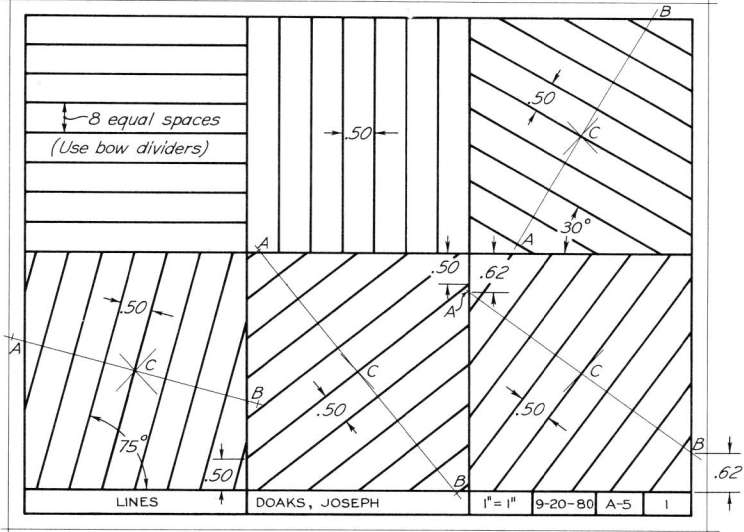

Fig. 2.74 Using Layout A–2 or A4–2 (adjusted), divide working space into six equal rectangles, and draw visible lines, as shown. Draw construction lines **AB** through centers **C** at right angles to required lines; then along each construction line, set off 0.50″ spaces and draw required visible lines. Omit dimensions and instructional notes.

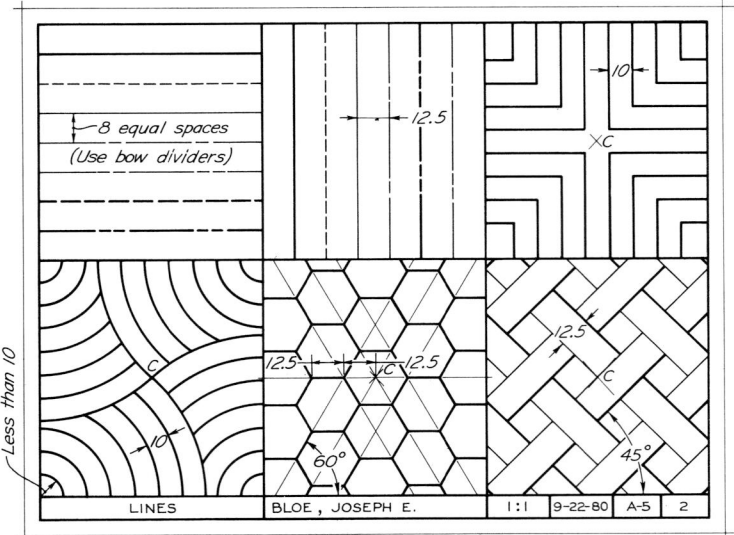

Fig. 2.75 Using Layout A–2 or A4–2 (adjusted), divide working space into six equal rectangles, and draw lines as shown. In first two spaces, draw conventional lines to match those in Fig. 2.14. In remaining spaces, locate centers **C** by diagonals, and then work constructions out from them. Omit the metric dimensions and instructional notes.

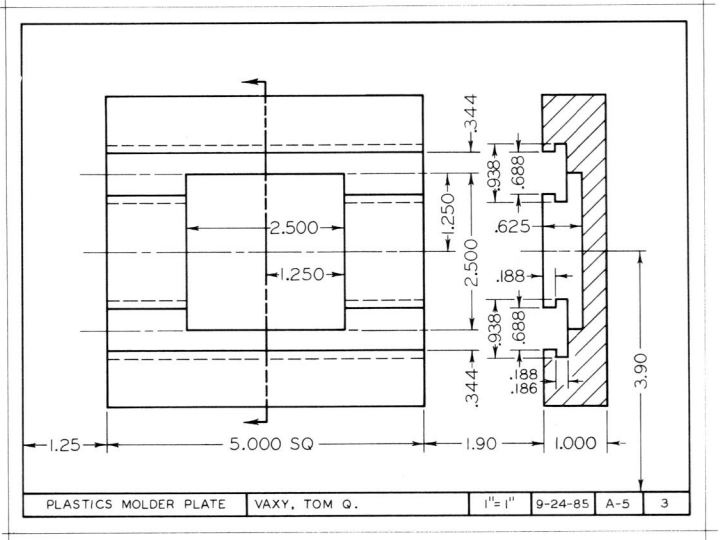

Fig. 2.76 Using Layout A–2 or A4–2 (adjusted), draw views in pencil, as shown. Omit all dimensions.

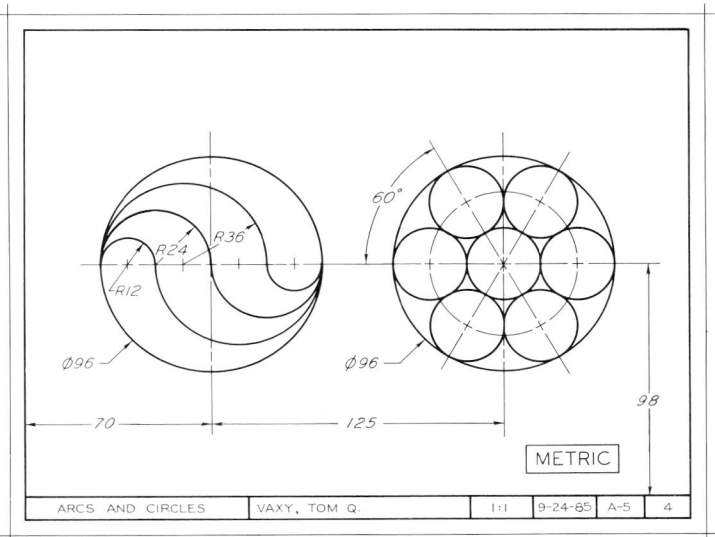

Fig. 2.77 Using Layout A–2 or A4–2 (adjusted), draw figures in pencil, as shown. Use bow pencil for all arcs and circles within its radius range. Omit all dimensions.

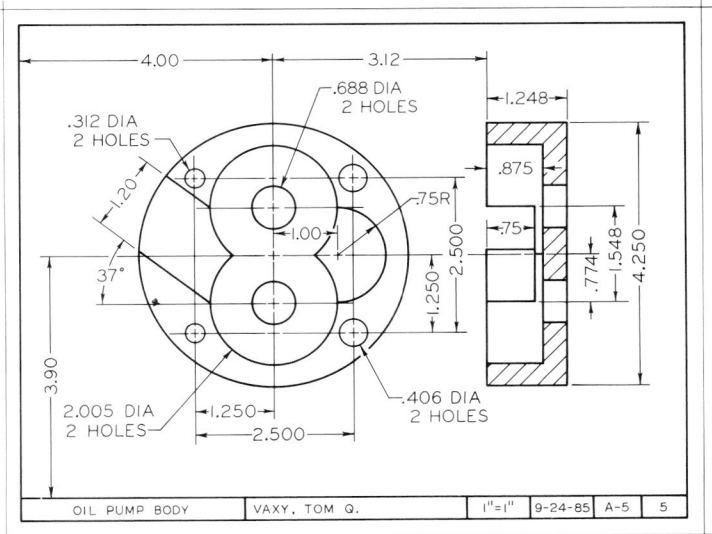

Fig. 2.78 Using Layout A–2 or A4–2 (adjusted), draw views in pencil, as shown. Use bow pencil for all arcs and circles within its radius range. Omit all dimensions.

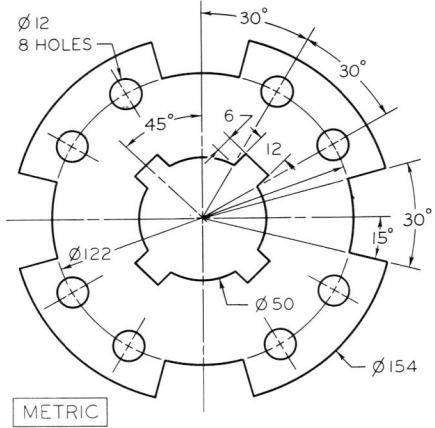

Fig. 2.79 Friction Plate. Using Layout A–2 or A4–2 (adjusted), draw in pencil. Omit dimensions and notes.

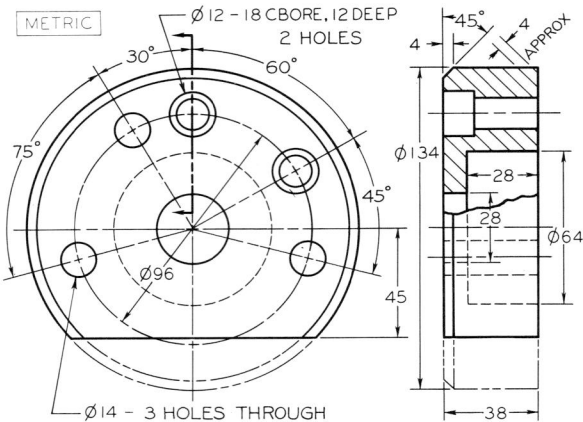

Fig. 2.80 Seal Cover. Using Layout A–2 or A4–2 (adjusted), draw views in pencil. Omit dimensions and notes. See §9.8.

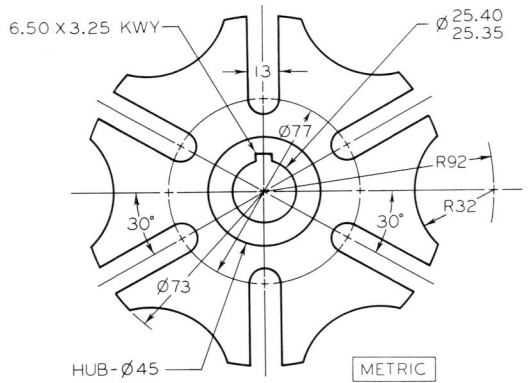

Fig. 2.81 Geneva Cam. Using Layout A–2 or A4–2 (adjusted), draw in pencil. Omit dimensions and notes.

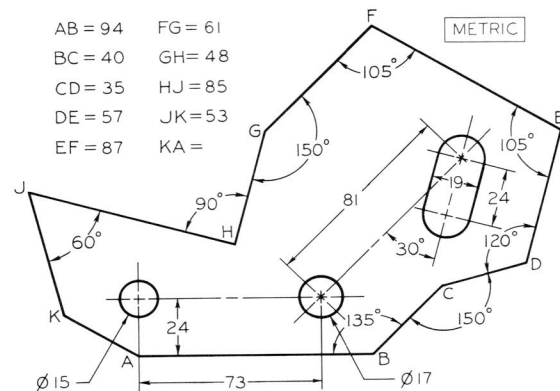

Fig. 2.82 Shear Plate. Using Layout A–2 or A4–2 (adjusted), draw accurately in pencil. Give length of **KA**. Omit other dimensions and notes.

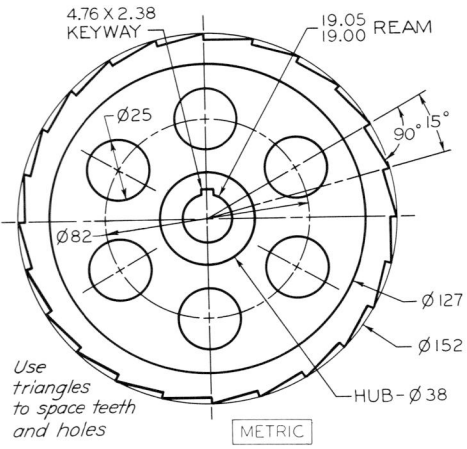

Fig. 2.83 Ratchet Wheel. Using Layout A–2 or A4–2 (adjusted), draw in pencil. Omit dimensions and notes.

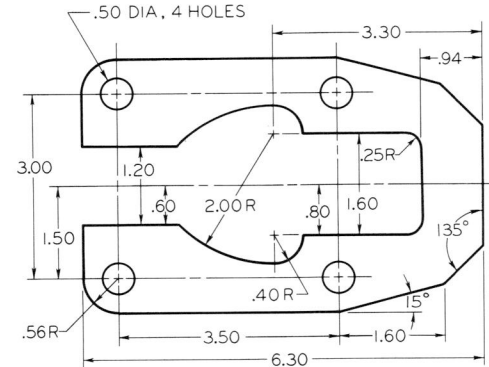

Fig. 2.84 Latch Plate. Using Layout A–2 or A4–2 (adjusted), draw in pencil. Omit dimensions and notes.

CHAPTER

3

Introduction to CAD

By James W. Zagorski*

The use of electronic computers today in nearly every phase of engineering, science, business, and industry is well known. The computer has altered accounting and manufacturing procedures, as well as engineering concepts. The integration of computers into the manufacturing process, from design to marketing, is changing the methods used in the training of technicians, drafters, designers, and engineers.

Engineering, in particular, is a constantly changing field. As new theories and practices evolve, more powerful tools must be developed and perfected to allow the engineer and designer to keep pace with the expanding body of technical knowledge. Modern computers are capable of carrying out long and complex sequences of operations, manipulating and storing information, and making logical comparisons and routine decisions, if properly programmed, all at tremendous speed and with very little human intervention. The computer has become an indispensable and effective tool for design and practical problem solving. New methods for analysis and design, the creation of technical drawings, and the solving of engineering problems, as well as the development of new concepts in automation and robotics, are the result of the influence of the computer on current engineering and industrial practices.

One simple fact that is frequently overlooked is that computers are not new. Charles Babbage, an English mathematician, developed the idea of a mechanical digital computer in the 1830s, and many of the principles used in Babbage's design are the basis of today's computers. The computer is only a highly sophisticated electronic tool. It is capable of data storage, basic logical functions, and mathematical calculations, but not without a human interface to give it instructions. Because of the phenomenal technological advancements during the last decade, the term *computer* has become a part of everyone's vocabulary. Computer applications have expanded human capabilities to such an extent that virtually every type of business and industry utilizes a computer directly or indirectly.

*Instructor, Kelly High School, Chicago Public Schools.

3.1 Computer Systems and Components

Engineers and drafters have used computers for many years to perform the mathematical calculations required in their work. Only recently, however, has the computer been accepted as a valuable tool in the preparation of technical drawings. Traditionally, drawings were made by using drafting instruments and applying ink, or graphite, to paper or film. Revisions and reproductions of these drawings were time consuming and often costly. Now the computer is used to produce, revise, store, and transmit original drawings. This method of producing drawings is called *computer-aided design* or *computer-aided drafting* (CAD) and also *computer-aided design and drafting* (CADD). Since these and other comparable terms are used synonymously, and since industry and software creators are beginning to standardize, they will be referred to throughout this chapter simply as CAD.

Other terms such as *computer-aided manufacturing* (CAM) or *computer integrated manufacturing* (CIM) are often used in conjunction with the term CAD. CAD/CAM refers to the integration of computers into the design and production process. See Fig. 3.1. CAD/CAM/CIM is used to describe the use of computers in the total manufacturing process, from design to production, publishing of technical material, marketing, to cost accounting. The single concept that these processes refer to is the use of a computer and software to aid the designer or drafter in the preparation and completion of a task.

Computer graphics is a very broad field and is another term that is frequently used—and often misused. It covers the creation and manipulation of computer-generated images and may include areas in photography, business, cartography, animation, and publication, as well as drafting and design.

A complete computer system consists of *hardware* and *software*. The various pieces of physical equipment that comprise a computer system are known as hardware. The programs, instructions, and other documentation that permit the computer system to operate are classified as software. Computer programs are categorized as either application programs or operating system programs. Operating system programs are sets of instructions that control the operation of the computer and peripheral devices as well as the execution of specific programs and data flow to and from peripheral devices. This type of program may also provide support for activities and programs such as input/output control, editing, storage assignment, data management, diagnostics; assign drives for I/O devices; and support standard system commands and networking. Application programs are the link between specific system use and its related tasks—design, drafting, desktop publishing, etc.—and the general operating system program. All computer-aided drafting systems consist of similar hardware components, Fig. 3.2, such as input devices, a central processing unit, data storage devices, and output devices. For input devices, Fig. 3.3, the system may have one or more of the follow-

Fig. 3.1 Typical CAD/CAM Application. Chrysler CAD/CAM (computer-aided design, computer-aided manufacturing) locates the positions where robots spot weld body sections in the company's U.S. assembly plants. Weld positions on Chrysler LeBaron side body section shown on the CAD/CAM computer screen *(left)* become a reality in the St. Louis assembly plant *(right)*. *Courtesy of Control Data Corporation.*

Fig. 3.2 Typical CAD Workstation. *Courtesy of Hewlett-Packard Company.*

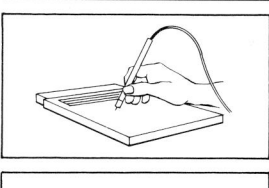

Digitizer is the most widely used input device because of its versatility in many applications. Cursor cross-hairs on the screen follow the movement of a stylus or a puck on an electronic tablet.

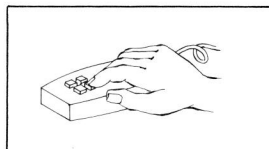

Mouse can be used on ordinary surfaces such as a desktop, but slippage often causes inaccuracies.

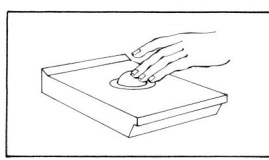

Trackball gives good tactile feedback and provides for precise cursor positioning on the screen through fairly large ball displacements.

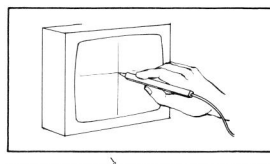

Lightpen is inexpensive and interacts directly with the screen for a natural drawing interface. But operation for long periods can produce arm fatigue.

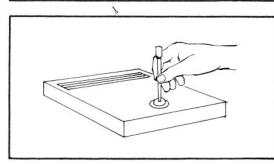

Joystick performs graphics operations quickly by providing rapid cursor movement for relatively small device displacement.

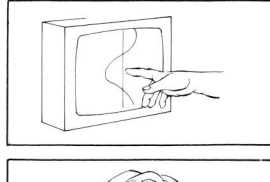

Touch-sensitive screen allows a direct interface with the screen and requires no external pointing device. But arm fatigue is a problem, and accuracy is limited.

Voice-data entry can provide for rapid entry of commands. But software must be refined before this technology gains widespread use.

Fig. 3.3 Graphic Input Devices. *Courtesy of* Machine Design.

ing: a keyboard terminal, mouse, digitizer/graphics tablet, and light pen.

Output devices the CAD system may include would be a plotter, an alphanumeric/graphics character printer, and some type of *cathode ray tube* (CRT) or monitor, Fig. 3.4.

Frequently, some devices are combined. For example, a terminal or workstation can contain the typewriter keyboard, CRT, data storage device, and possibly a processing unit all in the same cabinet. Such a combined device is known as an I/O device because its input and output functions are no longer considered separately and is often called a *workstation*, Fig. 3.5.

The system must have a data storage device, Fig. 3.6, such as a tape drive, a hard (fixed) or soft (floppy) disk drive, or an optical disk drive (CD-ROM).

Finally, a computer or central processing unit (CPU), Fig. 3.7, is needed to do all the numerical manipulations and to control all the other devices connected to the system.

The system itself may be interactive or passive. An interactive system allows for data input to be viewed and modified as the commands are entered.

In a passive system, the program, must be run to completion before the results can be viewed.

A CAD system configuration could include a single terminal, called a standalone workstation, or a group of terminals sharing the same storage and processing capabilities, known as a network. It is not uncommon to have several persons working on different tasks sharing the same system of storage and

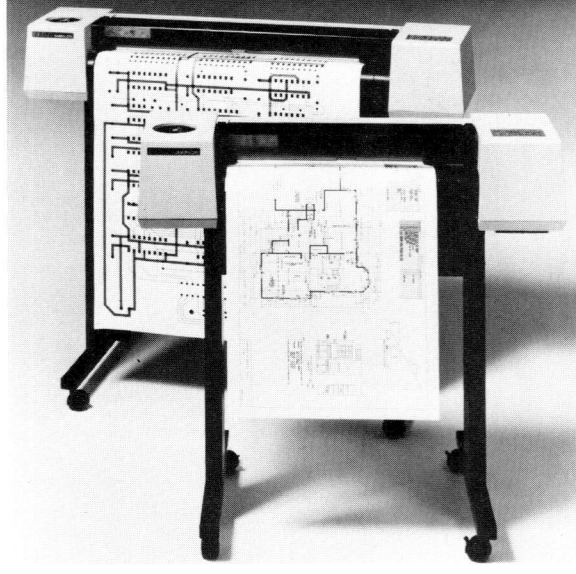

(a) PLOTTER

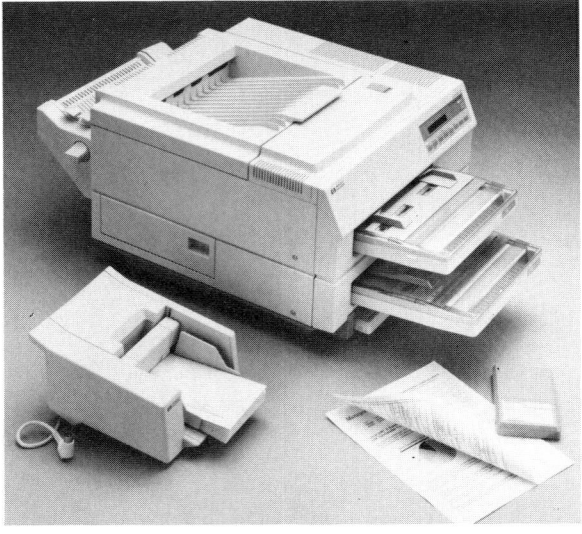

(b) LASER PRINTER

(c) MONITOR

Fig. 3.4 Output Devices. *(a), (b) courtesy of Hewlett-Packard Company; (c) courtesy of California Computer Products, Inc.*

processing. The end product of any CAD system is still a set of specifications, working drawings, and, in some cases, numerical control tapes.

3.2 Computer Types

Computers may be classified as one of two distinct types, *analog* or *digital*. An analog computer measures continuously without steps, whereas the digital computer counts by digits, going from one to two, three, and so on, in distinct steps. A slide rule, an electric wall clock with minute and hour hands, and the radial speedometer on a car are all examples of analog devices. An abacus and a digital watch are examples of digital devices. Digital computers are more widely used than analog computers because they are more flexible and can do a greater variety of jobs.

Analog computers are generally used for mathematical problem solving and usually are not found outside of an educational institution or research facility. This type of computer, which measures con-

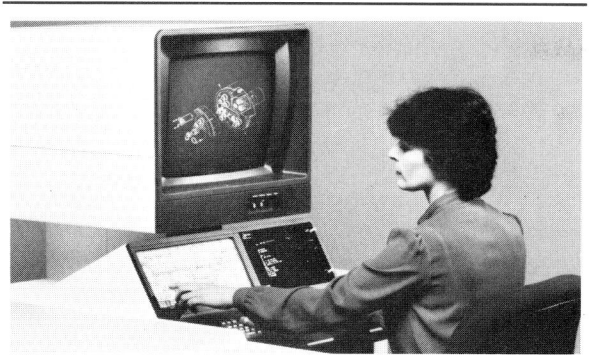

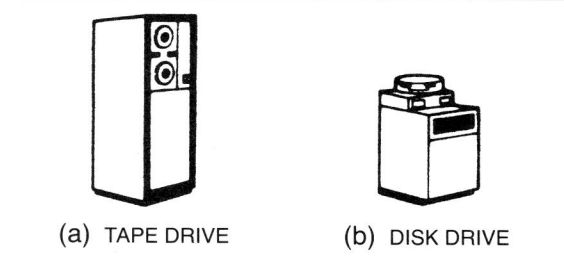

Fig. 3.6   Data Storage Devices.

Fig. 3.5   CAD Workstation. *Courtesy of Auto-trol Technology Corporation.*

Fig. 3.7   Central Processing Unit with CAD Workstation. *Courtesy of Computervision Corporation, a subsidiary of Prime Computer, Inc.*

tinuous physical properties, is often used to monitor and control electronic, hydraulic, or mechanical equipment. Digital computers have extensive applications in business and finance, engineering, numerical control, and computer graphics.

Both types of computers have undergone great changes in appearance and in operation. Equipment that once filled the greater part of a large room has now been replaced by machines that occupy small desktop areas. This new generation of computers can do more operations in less time with less human input than did their ancestors. The single most important advancement in computer technology has been the development of the *integrated circuit* (IC). The IC chip has replaced thousands of components on the *printed circuit* (PC) board and made possible

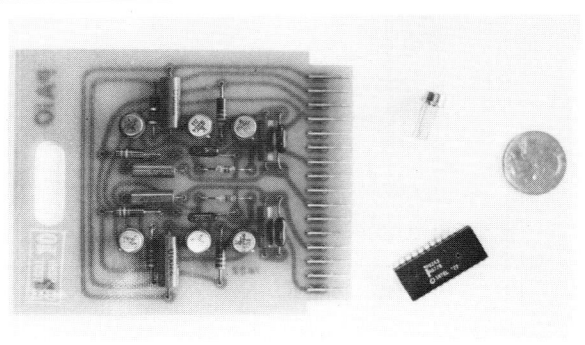

Fig. 3.8 Size Comparison of a PC Board and an IC Chip.

the development of microprocessors. The microprocessor is the processing unit of a computer. The difference in size between a PC board with individual components and an IC chip is shown in Fig. 3.8. The term *microminiaturization* is applied to advanced integrated circuit chip technology. The evolution of IC chip technology has led to the increased production of low-cost microcomputers. Microcomputers are largely responsible for the increase in use of computer-aided drafting systems in industry. Low-cost microcomputer CAD systems can now be cost-justified by industrial users.

3.3 Computer-Aided Drafting

The traditional tools of the designer or engineer have been the drawing board, an array of drawing instruments, and the slide rule. In recent years templates have been developed for certain symbols that have to be drawn frequently and the slide rule has been replaced by an electronic calculator. Conventional drafting equipment is now being replaced by another tool called a computer.

The first demonstration of the computer as a design and drafting tool was given at the Massachusetts Institute of Technology, in 1963, by Dr. Ivan Sutherland, with his system called "Sketch-pad," which used a cathode ray tube and a light pen for graphic input to a computer. The first commercial computer-aided drafting system was introduced in 1964 by International Business Machines. Many changes in CAD systems have taken place since the introduction of the first system. The changes in the systems are due to the advent of the microprocessor, more sophisticated software (programs), and new industrial applications. In most cases, the drafter/engi-

neer can create, revise, obtain prints (hard copy), and store drawings with relative ease, utilizing less space. CAD was originally developed to aid in creating production drawings. The advent of three-dimensional CAD software made it apparent that a 3D computer model could assist not only in the manufacture of the part but also, together with the three-dimensional database, in testing the design with finite element analysis programs, in developing technical manuals and other documentation that combine illustrations of the design with text from word processing programs, and in marketing where the 3D solid models can be used with a rendering and animation program. Increases in productivity and cost effectiveness are two advantages constantly stressed by CAD advocates. In addition, CAD stations can be linked directly or through a *local area network* (LAN) to the manufacturing or production equipment, or with *numerical control* (NC) equipment to automatically program a tape that can be used on NC machines in manufacturing operations or in robotics, Fig. 3.9.

The primary uses of CAD are in mechanical engineering and electronic design, civil engineering, and cartography. The design and layout of printed circuits are a principal application of CAD in the electronics industry, which, prior to 1976, was the largest CAD user. Mechanical engineering has since overtaken electronics and continues to expand its CAD applications and use. Continued expansion in mechanical design applications is expected because the design, analysis, and numerical control capabilities of CAD can be applied to such a varied range of products and processes. Cartography, seismic data display, demographic analysis, urban planning, piping layouts, and especially architectural design also show growth in CAD use. A relatively new area in computer graphics is *image processing*. Image processing includes animation, 35-mm slide preparation, photocolor enhancement, and font and character generation used in television broadcasting and the graphic arts industry.

It should not be assumed that all drawings in the future will be made by computers and that engineers, designers, and drafters will no longer be needed. A computer is capable of doing a great many things, but in reality it is an electronic device with no brain. It cannot think and will not do anything more, or anything less, than the human operator instructs it to do. Drafters will continue to be the backbone of the design or drafting department, although now their work will be more creative as many

Fig. 3.9 Computer-Controlled and -Programmed Robot Welding Line at Chrysler Corporation's Jefferson Assembly Plant. *Courtesy of Control Data Corporation.*

of the tedious and repetitive tasks are automated. A CAD system is not creative, but it can assist the individual to be more productive. The creation of a drawing will continue to be of prime importance; CAD simply provides the means for replacing technique in the preparation of a drawing to save time. Although CAD will continue to be an important part of engineering work in the future, a knowledge of the principles of technical drawing will still be a prime requisite for engineers, designers, and drafters engaged in this activity; if anything, additional training in this subject will be necessary.

3.4 CAD System Configurations

A CAD system, Fig. 3.10, will contain all of the components of a traditional computer system, with additional components for graphical data input, display generation, and graphical output. As stated previously, a complete CAD system will include various pieces of physical equipment called hardware and CAD software. The computer, or central processing unit (CPU), controls all functions of the system and processes all data from input devices. Since graphics programs on the computer are so mathematics intensive, the CPU usually requires the help of an additional IC chip called a math coprocessor to speed up the drawing process.

There are many devices that can feed data into the CPU. Entering data into the computer is called input. Input devices commonly used in a CAD system are the keyboard, mouse, graphics tablet, digitizing table, or menu pad. With the exception of the keyboard and menu pad, most graphical input devices are pointing devices, in that they use electronic signals to transfer movements of the device by the operator's hand to a cursor that moves about the display screen in corresponding fashion to a specific location.

After the computer has processed the data, it will generate the results through an output device. An

Fig. 3.10 CAD Workstation with Keyboard and Keypad. *Courtesy of Hewlett-Packard Company.*

output device may be a cathode ray tube (CRT or monitor), a printer, or a plotter. While the monitor will only display the design on the screen, printers and plotters will generate original drawings on paper or film. These drawings are called hard copy.

Internal and auxiliary storage devices are also considered part of the system hardware. These devices may be a tape drive, hard disk drive, soft or floppy disk drive, or an optical disk drive. Each of these can store the necessary data for later retrieval.

Programs, computer language codes, and other documents are considered part of the system of software. Hardware and software together make up the complete CAD system.

3.5 Central Processing Unit

The central processing unit (CPU), or computer, receives all data and manages, manipulates, and controls all functions of the CAD system. CAD systems used digital computers, which receive input in the form of numbers (digits) and letters or special characters that represent predetermined combinations of numbers or digits. All data must be converted into a binary form or code for the computer to understand and accept it. This is known as digitizing the information. This code is called *binary coded decimal instructions* (BCDI). This binary code uses a two-digit system, 1 and 0, to transmit all data through the circuits. The number 1 is the "on" signal; the 0, the "off" signal. A *bit* is a binary digit (*b*inary dig*it*). Bits are grouped, or organized, into larger units called words to be accessed by computer instructions. Word length, which is expressed as bits, differs with various computers. The most common word lengths are 8, 16, and 32 bits. The word length indicates the maximum word size that can be processed, as a unit, during an instruction cycle. Often, computers are categorized by their word length, such as 8-bit, 16-bit, or 32-bit computers. The number of bits in the word length indicates the processing power of the computer (the larger the word length, the greater the processing power). A sequential group of adjacent bits in a computer is called a *byte*. The current industry standard is 8 bits equal 1 byte. A byte represents a character that is operated on as a unit by the CPU. The length of a word on a majority of computer systems currently is 4 bytes. This means that each word in any one of these systems occupies a 32-bit storage location. The memory capacity of a computer is therefore expressed as a number of bytes rather than bits.

Computers use two types of memory. Permanent memory, called ROM (read only memory), is encoded into a microprocessor chip and is not lost when the computer is turned off. ROM, coordinated with the disk operating system (DOS), performs a diagnostic check of the system to insure all circuits are operational when the computer is turned on. Random access memory (RAM) is considered temporary memory. Any program or file stored in RAM is lost when the computer is turned off. A computer's memory capacity is based on its RAM, or temporary memory.

Since CAD systems utilize digital computers, we will restrict our discussion of computer types to digital computers. Digital computers are commonly divided into three classes: *mainframe, mini,* and *micro.* The difference between the three classes is essentially word length (capacity). The largest CPU's are called mainframes, Fig. 3.11. A mainframe computer will have internal memory measured in megabytes (1 MB = 1 million bytes), usually word lengths of 32 bits or more, and multimegabyte or gigabyte (GB, 1000 million bytes) disks, and high-speed tape drives for external data storage. Instruction times for these machines are measured and expressed in *nanoseconds* (thousandths of a microsecond) or in *mips* (millions of instructions per second). Mainframes are usually general-purpose computers; they can be used for a variety of functions within a company, such as accounting and inventory control, and as the core of a CAD system.

Minicomputers, Fig. 3.12, began as smaller size mainframes. The development of the microprocessor chip has lessened the distinction between the

Fig. 3.11   Mainframe Computer System. *Courtesy of Control Data Corporation.*

Fig. 3.12 Minicomputer Workstation. *Courtesy of Hewlett-Packard Company.*

mainframe computer and the minicomputer. The minicomputer's internal memory is smaller, its speed of operation is somewhat slower, and it is somewhat limited in flexibility of use. Two desirable features of a minicomputer are real-time operation (immediate response to an alarm or command) and

lower cost systems and peripherals. It is generally accepted that the development of the minicomputer was the beginning of the great demand for CAD systems.

Microcomputers, Fig. 3.13, basically composed of a CPU combined with a memory and control features, were originally single-purpose machines. Microcomputers are currently lower cost equivalents of full-scale minicomputers, often equalling the computational power and speed of many minicomputers. New microcomputer system architecture allows for internal memory expansion of up to 32 MB and internal data storage devices in excess of 100 MB. Microcomputers in use today are 8-bit, 16-bit, or 32-bit systems. Microcomputers currently used for CAD tend to require more internal memory, 640 kilobytes (1 kB = 1000 bytes) to 10 MB, because of the mathematical computations involved with CAD programs. Originally, CAD programs developed primarily for microcomputers were two-dimensional and used for production drawings only. CAD programs today can be used to create complete three-dimensional models, analyze the design, optimize the design, and generate all necessary data used in the production of the model. The wide variety of peripherals and CAD software now available makes these microsystems cost effective for smaller firms.

Fig. 3.13 Four Microcomputers Linked to Control Data's CYBERNET Data Services Network to Take Advantage of Large-System Computing Power and Applications Software. *Courtesy of Control Data Corporation.*

3.6 Display Devices

Another major reason for the rapid growth in CAD systems is the further development of display devices. These display devices, commonly referred to as monitors, utilize a wide variety of imaging principles. Each device has definite characteristics with regard to brightness, clarity, resolution, response time, and color. The purpose of any graphics display is to project an image on a screen. The image that is displayed may be alphanumeric (text symbols, letters, and/or numerals) or graphical (pictorial symbols and/or lines). Users of interactive CAD systems communicate directly or indirectly through graphics terminals. The information requested by the user may be displayed as animated figures, graphs, color-coded diagrams, or simply a series of lines. Most interactive CAD systems use one of three main types of display devices—the storage tube, Fig. 3.14 (a), the vector refresh, (b), and the raster scan, (c)—all of which produce images through the basic cathode ray tube (CRT) principle.

A storage tube CAD monitor, also called a direct view storage tube (DVST), was the most popular computer display device for many years. In a storage tube, flood guns constantly blanket the entire CRT screen with electrons that alone do not have the energy to illuminate the phosphor on the screen. A focused writing beam produces a visible track or line by electron bombardment. The screen grid becomes positively charged in the area where the tightly focused beam strikes it, allowing electrons from the flood gun to be accelerated onto the screen and cause the phosphor to glow. The image is constantly displayed without the need for any retacing of the writing beam, and the image is stored on the screen, thus making very little demand on the computer. The major advantage of storage tubes is that large amounts of graphics data can be stored on the screen without the need to be constantly refreshed from the computer memory. Other advantages of the storage tube are its excellent flicker-free resolution, high display capacity, and moderate cost. The limitation of storage tube devices is lack of dynamic capability. Once an image is created and stored, lines cannot be selectively erased, and the image cannot be changed without *repainting* (redrawing) the entire image, so that interactive display manipulation is not possible. In addition, storage tubes have low brightness and contrast. They are also monochromatic (single color), usually green. Despite their limitations, the high resolution and high data storage capacity of

(a) STORAGE TUBE

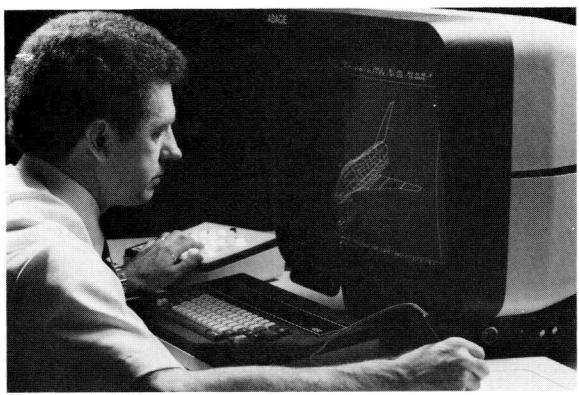

(b) VECTOR REFRESH

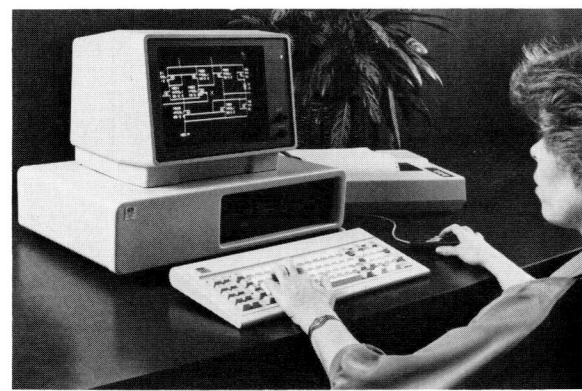

(c) RASTER SCAN

Fig. 3.14 Display Devices. *(b) courtesy of Adage, Inc.; (c) courtesy of Control Data Corporation.*

DVSTs make them well suited for presenting analysis results in the form of contour plots and other drawing formats.

Vector refresh monitors (also called stroke writing, random scan, or calligraphic system) use an electron writing beam to directly trace out the image lines on the CRT screen in a continuous sweep similar to oscilloscopes. After the beam has generated a complete image or line, it constantly retraces, or refreshes, the image before the phosphor fades. Because the displayed image is stored in memory, the need for additional hardware and memory for image storage and refreshing increases system complexity, making this monitor one of the most expensive. The advantages of vector refresh monitors are the ability to display motion or animation, high brightness level, high resolution, and selective erasing. These features make this display device an excellent monitor to use for complex geometric modeling and finite element analysis. The major disadvantages of vector refresh technology are the limited color capabilities and the flicker encountered when there is a large amount of information on the screen; complex images reduce the refresh rate below a frequency of 30 hertz, which appears to the human eye as a flicker.

Raster scan devices are similar to conventional television screens. These devices produce an image with a matrix of picture-element dots within a grid called *pixels*. Each pixel is either a light or dark image that falls within a square area on the grid and appears on the screen as a dot. As in conventional television, an electron beam is swept across the entire screen, line by line, top to bottom. This process is called raster scanning. A signal turns on or illuminates a pixel according to a pattern stored in memory, which is referred to as a bit map. The screen is scanned 60 times a second to update the image before the phosphor dims. Recent advances in raster scan technology have increased the resolution of these devices and decreased system cost through "intelligent" graphics monitors. The majority of new graphics systems being marketed contain raster scan devices. The advantages of this type of device are the wide range of colors that can be simultaneously displayed on the screen, the ability to show motion, high brightness level, and selective erasing. The major disadvantage of this technology is the high memory and processing requirements that result in higher cost.

There are several other types of graphic display devices in use, including the gas plasma, electroluminescent, and liquid crystal displays, that fall into the flat screen technology area. Each has greater limitations and associated problems than the devices mentioned, so that they are much less extensively used for graphics than other display devices.

3.7 Input Devices

The graphical display of data was available on first generation computers, but the process was time consuming. Programs had to be written and data entered by means of batch mode processing. A system developed in the 1950s for the Air Defense Command called SAGE used the light pen for data input. Further development of an interactive method of data input by Dr. Ivan Sutherland with his "Sketchpad" system increased the usage and popularity of computer-generated graphics. Since then, many diverse types of input devices have been developed. A CAD system may use one or a combination of input devices to create images on the display screen. Graphic input devices may be grouped into three categories: (1) *keyboard* and *touch-sensitive,* (2) *time-dependent,* and (3) *coordinate-dependent* devices.

The alphanumeric keyboard is the universal input device by which data and commands are entered. A typical keyboard consists of alpha-numeric character keys for keying in letters, numbers, and common symbols such as #, &, and %; cursor control keys with words or arrows printed on them indicating directional movement of the screen cursor; and special function keys that are used by some software programs for entering commands with a single keystroke. Many large mainframe-based CAD systems have used a special function keypad, or menu pad, that allows access to a command with a single keystroke, Fig. 3.15 (a). Single stroke command selection was considered so essential for cost effectiveness and ease of use that developers of mini- and microcomputer-based CAD systems included this feature of single and double keystroke command access into their program utilizing the CTRL, ALT, SHIFT, and function keys. Typically, a CAD system will use a keyboard for inputting commands and text, and another input device for cursor control.

Digitizing tablets are one of the most commonly used input devices. They can be used to create an original CAD drawing or to convert an existing pen or pencil and paper drawing into a CAD drawing.

(a) MENU PAD, LIGHT PEN, AND KEYBOARD

(b) KEYBOARD AND MOUSE

(c) KEYBOARD, THUMBWHEEL, AND GRAPHICS TABLET

(d) KEYBOARD, JOYSTICK, AND GRAPHICS TABLET

Fig. 3.15   Graphic Input Devices. *(a) courtesy of Jervis B. Webb Co.; (b) courtesy of Hewlett-Packard Company; (c) courtesy of Bausch & Lomb; (d) courtesy of California Computer Products, Inc.*

Digitizing tablets range in size from $8\frac{1}{2}'' \times 11''$ to $36'' \times 48''$. Tablets larger than $36'' \times 48''$, called digitizing tables, are used primarily for converting existing drawings to a CAD system format. The *resolution* of digitizing tablets is important. This determines how small a movement the input device can detect, usually expressed in thousandths of an inch, and depends on the number of wires per inch in the tablet's grid system. The working area on a tablet can be divided up into smaller sections. One section could then contain system control features; another, command functions; another, screen control commands; and so on. A much smaller area on the tablet then remains to represent the screen's

working area. Attached to the tablet will be either a puck or a stylus. A *puck* is a small, hand-held, box-like device with a clear plastic extension, or window, containing crosshairs, that transfers the location of the puck on the tablet grid to the relative location on the screen. Single or multiple buttons on top of the puck are used to select points and/or commands for input to the system. A *stylus* appears to be a ball-point pen with an electronic cable attached to it. The tip of the stylus senses the position on the tablet grid and relays these coordinates to the computer. When the stylus is moved across the tablet, the screen cursor moves correspondingly across the screen. The stylus also contains a pressure-sensitive tip that enables the user to select points or commands by pressing down on the stylus.

An input device that has gained in popularity and use with both large and small CAD systems is called a *mouse,* Fig. 3.15 (b). A mouse may be of the mechanical type or the optical type. Both are similar in appearance to a puck without the plastic extension and crosshairs. A mechanical mouse uses a roller, or ball, on the underside of the device to detect movement. An optical mouse senses movement and position by bouncing a light off a special reflective surface. Both types of these devices will have from one to three buttons on top of them to select positions or commands. The advantages of this type of device are that it is easy to use, requires a very small working area, and is relatively inexpensive. A mouse cannot, however, be used to digitize existing drawings into a CAD format.

One of the oldest input devices used on CAD systems is the *trackball,* Fig. 3.15 (c). Trackballs were used on many large mainframe-based CAD systems and were often incorporated into the keyboard. A trackball consists of a ball nested in a holder, or cup, much like the underside of a mechanical mouse, and from one to three buttons for entering coordinate data into the system. Within the holder are sensors that pick up the movement of the ball. The ball is moved in any direction with the fingers or hand to control cursor movement on the CRT screen. Cursor speed and button function can be set by the user.

A *joystick,* Fig. 3.15 (d), is an input device more commonly used with video games today than with CAD systems. This device looks like a small rectangular box with a lever extending vertically from the top surface. This hand-controlled lever is used to manipulate the screen cursor and manually enter coordinate data. Buttons on the device can be used to enter coordinate location or specific commands. This device is inexpensive and requires a very small working area, but sometimes presents a problem when very precise cursor positioning is important.

The *light* pen, next to the keyboard, is the oldest type of CAD input device currently in use, Fig. 3.15 (a). It looks much like a ballpoint pen or the stylus on a digitizing tablet. A light pen is a hand-held, photosensitive device, which works only with raster scan or vector refresh monitors, that is used to identify displayed elements of a design or to specify a location on the screen where an action is to take place. The pen senses light created by the electron beam as it scans the surface of the CRT. When the pen is held close to or touches the CRT screen, the computer can determine its location and position the cursor under the pen. Because this input device more closely emulates the traditional drafter's pencil or pen than other devices, it quickly gained popularity. Its decline in popularity resulted from studies that showed it was tiring to use and therefore cut the productivity of the user.

Touch-panel displays, though not widely used with CAD systems, are another type of input device. These devices allow the user to touch an area on the screen with a finger to activate commands or functions. This area on the screen contains a pressure-sensitive mesh that picks up the location of the finger and transfers it to the computer, which activates the command associated with that specific location. These devices work well with function or command entry but are inaccurate for CAD coordinate entry.

One of the most recent developments in data input is *voice recognition* technology. This technology utilizes a combination of specialized integrated circuits and software to recognize spoken words. The system itself must first be "trained" by repeating commands into a microphone. The computer converts the operator's oral commands to digital form and then stores the characteristics of the operator's voice. Once trained, when the operator gives an oral command, the system will check the sound against the words stored in its memory and then execute the command. Since this technology is new, it has several distinct disadvantages for CAD users. The vocabulary supported by the system is limited. The memory required for storing complex sound or voice patterns is extremely large. Access time, or time between the spoken word and command activation, may be several seconds. Finally, if the operator's voice changes in some manner or words have similar voice patterns, the system may not recognize the oral input at all.

3.8 Output Devices

In most instances, the user of a CAD system will need a record of images that are stored on database files or displayed on the CRT. When an image is placed on paper, film, or other media, it is then referred to as *hard* copy. This hard copy can be produced by one of several types of output devices.

The device most commonly used for the reproduction of computerized drawings is the *pen plotter,* Fig. 3.16. A pen plotter is an electro-mechanical graphics output device. Pen plotters may be classi-

(a) DRUM

(b) MICROGRIP

(c) FLATBED

(d) MICROGRIP

Fig. 3.16 Plotters. *(a) courtesy of California Computer Products, Inc.; (b) courtesy of Control Data Corporation; (c) courtesy of Versatec, Inc.; (d) courtesy of Hewlett-Packard Company.*

fied as drum, flatbed, or microgrip. The *drum plotter*, (a), utilizes a long narrow cylinder in combination with a movable pen carriage. The medium to be drawn on (paper, vellum, or film) is mounted curved rather than flat and conforms to the shape of the cylinder drum. The drum rotates, moving the drawing surface, and provides one axis of movement, while the pen carriage moves the pens parallel to the axis of the cylinder and provides the other axis of movement. The combined movement of drum and pen allows circles, curves, and inclined lines to be

drawn. The pen carriage on a drum plotter typically holds more than one pen so that varied line weights or multicolor plots can be drawn. These plotters accept up to E size paper in single sheets or in a roll that is then cut after the drawing is plotted.

Flatbed plotters, Fig. 3.16 (c), differ from drum plotters in that the medium to be drawn on is mounted flat and held stationary by electrostatic or vacuum attraction while the pen carriage controls movement in box axes. The area of these plotters may be as small as A size ($8\frac{1}{2}'' \times 11''$) or larger than E size (34″ × 44″), and from one to eight pens may be used for varied line weights and multicolor plots.

Microgrip plotters, Fig. 3.16 (b) and (d), have become one of the most widely used types of output devices. Their popularity is due to their adaptability to all types of computers, size ranges, low maintenance, and relatively inexpensive pricing. Microgrip plotters are similar to drum plotters in that the medium to be drawn on is moved in one axis while the pen moves along the other axis. These plotters get their name from the small rollers that grip the edges of the medium and move it back and forth under the pen carriage. These plotters range from A to E size, with single or multiple pen carriages, and may accept cut sheets or rolls.

All pen plotters are rated according to specified standards for accuracy, acceleration, repeatability, and speed. Accuracy is the amount of deviation in the geometry it is supposed to draw, usually ranging from .001″ to .005″. Acceleration is the rate at which the pen attains plotting speed and is expressed in *Gs* (for gravitational force). Pen speed is important because slower speeds usually produce darker lines. The faster the pen attains a constant speed, the more consistent the linework will be. The ability of a plotter to retrace the same drawing over and over again is called repeatability. The deviation of the pen in redrawing the same line is the measure of repeatability and usually varies from .001″ to .005″. Plotter pen speed determines how fast the pen moves across the drawing medium. Pen speed may range up to 22″ per second on some plotters. Most CAD software also allows the operator to set the speed at which drawings will be plotted to achieve maximum line quality and consistency. Slow pen speeds normally produce better quality plots than high pen speeds.

Other factors help determine the quality of a pen-plotted drawing. The variety of pens, inks, and drawing media available allows the operator to coordinate pen, ink, and paper to produce the most desirable hard copy.

Dot matrix plotting is another method by which hard copy can be produced. This technology, in use for some time, has typically been associated with printing devices that were not suitable for producing quality hard copy. Recent technology, however, has permitted the development of devices that can produce accurate, industrial quality dot matrix plots. These devices use a process called rasterization to convert images to a series of dots. The image is transferred optically (or sometimes by a laser) to the surface of the medium on a selenium drum that is elec-

trostatically charged. Sometimes the image may be created by an array of nibs that electrically charge small dots on the medium. The drum, with the addition of a toner, usually a very fine carbon powder that adheres to the surface of the drum only in places where there is an image, then transfers that image to the surface of the paper. A high-quality raster scan plotter can produce an image so fine and of such quality that it is not obvious how the image was produced unless examined under a magnifying glass.

Electrostatic plotters, Fig. 3.17, produce hard copy by placing an electrostatic charge on specially coated paper and having a toner, or ink, adhere to the charged area. Drawing geometry is converted through rasterization into a series of dots. These dots represent the charged area. Resolution of these plotters is determined by the number of dots per inch (dpi), usually ranging from 300 to 600 dpi. This type of plotter produces hard-copy drawings in single or multicolors much faster than pen plotters, but the cost, power, and environment requirements are also much greater.

Dot matrix technology has produced machines

Fig. 3.17 Electrostatic Plotter. *Courtesy of Hewlett-Packard Company.*

Fig. 3.18 Ink Jet Printer. *Courtesy of Hewlett-Packard Company.*

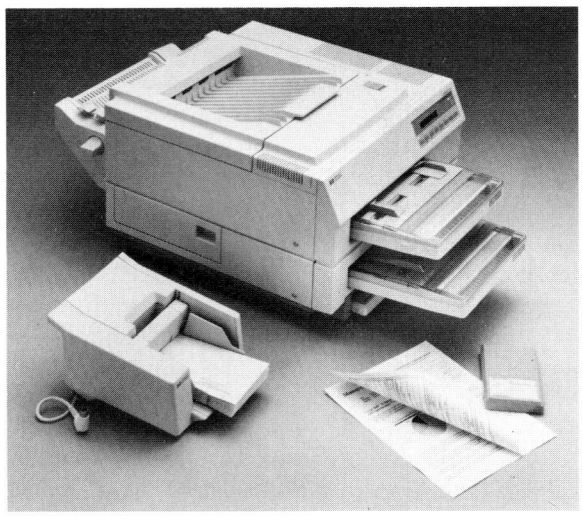

Fig. 3.19 Laser Printer. *Courtesy of Hewlett-Packard Company.*

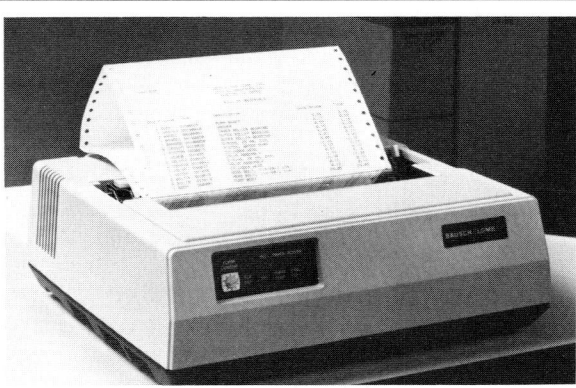

Fig. 3.20 Dot Matrix Printer. *Courtesy of Bausch & Lomb.*

that are now dual purpose, although not originally designed as such. These machines were originally designed as printers to handle word processing and spreadsheet programs using alphanumeric characters. With the increasing popularity and use of CAD and other graphics software, manufacturers have improved the technology of these devices so that they can now create graphic hard copy close or equivalent to true plotter quality. The device can now be classified as a printer/plotter.

An *ink jet printer/plotter*, Fig. 3.18, produces images by depositing droplets of ink on paper. These droplets correspond to the dots created by the rasterization process. This device places a charge on the ink rather than the paper, as in the electrostatic process. Ink jet plotters can produce good quality color-rendered images in addition to standard technical drawings.

Laser technology represents the newest evolution in plotter technology. A *laser printer/plotter*, Fig. 3.19, uses a beam of light to create images. This device utilizes electrostatic charging and raster scanning to produce a plotted image.

Dot matrix printers, Fig. 3.20, produce images by one of two processes. They can produce images through impact on carbon or ink ribbon, or they may use a heat (thermal) process. Each method uses a number of pins in a specific configuration, such as 5×7, 7×9, or 9×9, set in the printer head. Machine commands control the sequence in which the pins strike the medium to produce an image.

3.9 Data Storage Devices

Since all data kept in RAM (random access memory) will be lost when the computer is turned off, it must be saved, or stored, before the power is off. Data storage devices provide a place to save information permanently for later use. CAD programs, for exam-

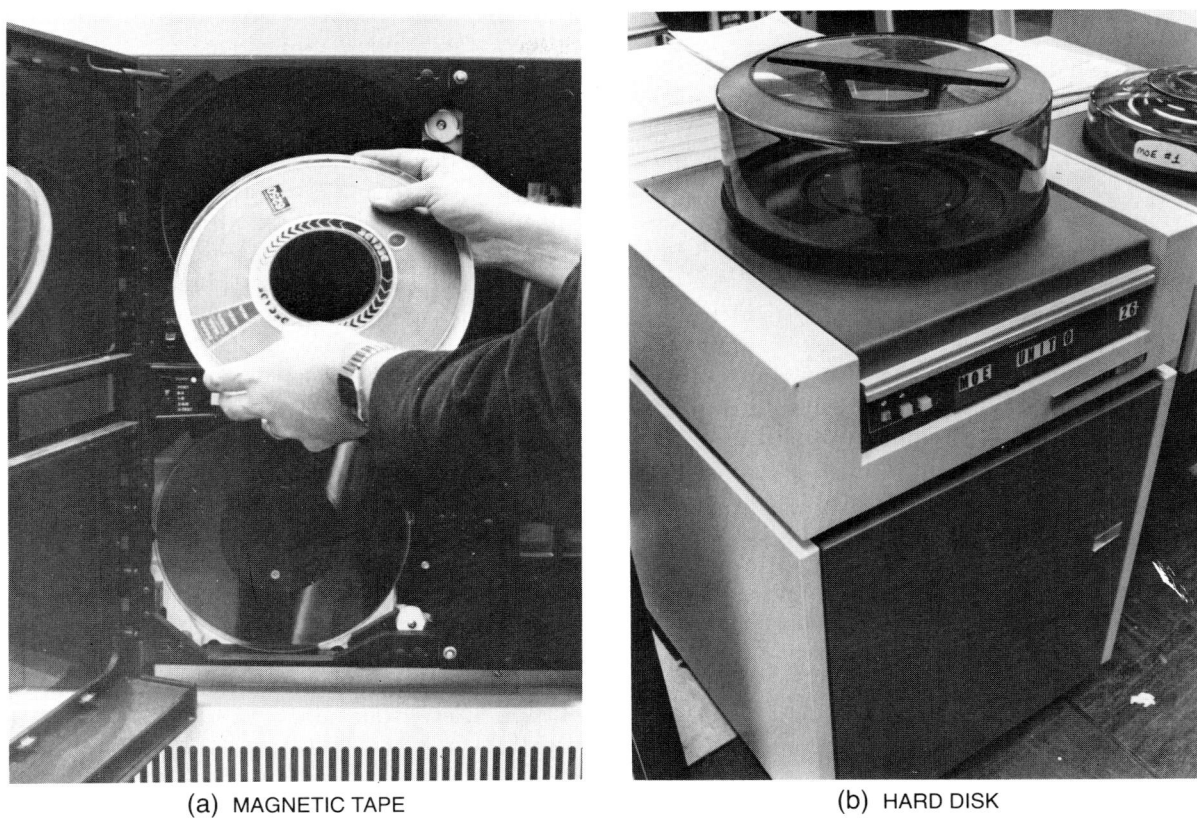

(a) MAGNETIC TAPE   (b) HARD DISK

Fig. 3.21   Storage Devices.

ple, are stored on a disk or tape and when loaded (or activated), portions of the program go into RAM, which is temporary memory. While a drawing is being worked on, all data associated with that drawing is kept in the same temporary memory. When the drawing is completed, or the operator must stop, that drawing and all the associated data must be saved, or directed to a storage device, before the program is exited or the power shut off. Otherwise all accumulated data from that work session will be lost. These storage devices can be considered electronic file cabinets.

Magnetic tape drives and disk drives, Fig. 3.21, are two distinct categories of storage devices. *Magnetic tape* storage, (a) uses plastic tape coated with magnetic particles. When data is sent from the computer for storage on the tape, these particles are charged by a read/write head in the tape drive. The data being sent is recorded as a series of charges along the tape. Once these particles are charged, they will remain charged until the head writes over them or they are demagnetized. Tape drives file and

read data in sequential order. This means they must look through data in the order that the tape is wound and unwound. This is similar to forwarding or rewinding a video tape to look for a specific scene, or an audio tape to play a particular song. Magnetic tape drives may be either reel to reel or cassette type. Reel to reel tape drives consist of two reels and a drive controller. One reel is used for tape storage and the second reel as a take-up reel. These tape reels may vary in size from 6″ to 12″ in diameter. The longer the tape, the more data that can be stored on it. Over a gigabyte of data may be stored on some reel to reel tape systems. Cassette tape storage devices were originally created to back-up microcomputer systems. These cassettes were slow and did not hold the amount of data that can be found on current microcomputers. Recent technology, however, has produced tape cassettes that are high speed and can store over a gigabyte of data. These cassettes resemble audio cassettes in both size and appearance. Tape storage is essentially used for backing up data from a hard drive, or for archival purposes, since the tapes can be removed and stored for later use.

Disk storage devices are the most commonly used method of data storage. *Disk drives* may be of fixed (hard disk) variety, flexible (floppy) variety, or optical type. Disk drives file and read data in random order. This means that the device writes data to any portion of the disk that is empty, and is able to locate data almost instantly, because it has access to the whole disk at once. Disk drives are rated according to their type, access time, capacity, and transfer rate.

The *fixed disk drive*, or hard disk, Fig. 3.21 (b), is the most common method of data storage. This type of drive uses an aluminum disk as the medium for storage. These drives may be internal, attached inside the computer case, or external, in a separate case or cabinet. A disk controller or controller card must be installed in the computer to allow the computer and drive to communicate or interface with each other. The storage capacity of these drives will range from 10 MB to several hundred megabytes. Access time is expressed in milliseconds (ms) and will range from 18 to 80 ms. The lower the number in milliseconds, the faster the access time. Transfer rate is the speed at which the drive can send data to the CPU and is expressed in bytes per second (bps). The higher the number in bytes per second, the faster the data can be sent.

Floppy disk drives, Fig. 3.22, derive their name from the removable flexible plastic disks used in this device. The disks used in this drive are available in three sizes, $3\frac{1}{2}''$, $5\frac{1}{4}''$, and $8''$ in diameter. All three sizes come in either high density or low density formats. The density of a disk refers to the amount of magnetic particles on the disk. This helps to determine the amount of data the disk will hold. Disks will also be classified as single sided or double sided, depending on whether data can be stored on one or both surfaces of the disk. Typically, a $3\frac{1}{2}''$ disk, called micro-diskette, will hold 720 kB of data in double-sided low-density format or 1.44 MB of data in double-sided high-density format. A $5\frac{1}{4}''$ disk will hold 360 kB in double-sided low-density format, and 1.2 MB in double-sided high-density format. The floppy disk is inexpensive and convenient to use but holds less data and is slower than fixed disk drives.

The ever-increasing need for larger storage capacity has spurred the development of new technologies. The newest technology in data storage is *optical disk drives*. Optical disks are removable, like floppy disks, and capable of holding many gigabytes of data. These drives use a laser to read and write data to a chemically coated aluminum disk, Fig. 3.23. The original optical disk drive was a read only device and was called a *compact disk read only memory* (CD-ROM) drive. Each disk normally contained a program that could be read or accessed, but no data could be written on it after installation.

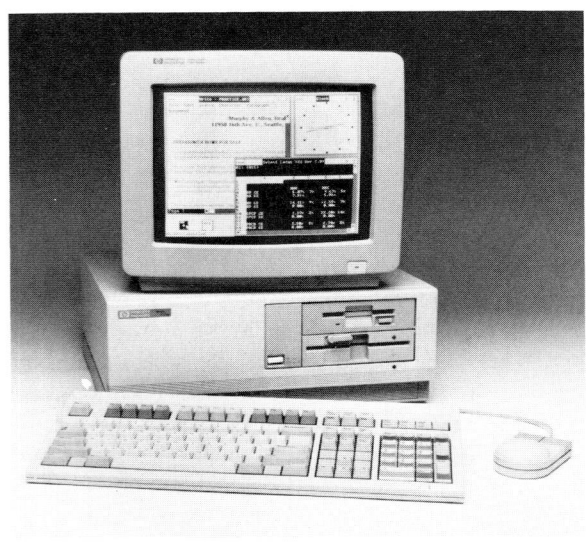

Fig. 3.22 Microcomputer with Two Flexible (Floppy) Disk Drives. *Courtesy of Hewlett-Packard Company.*

Fig. 3.23 Optical Disk. *Courtesy of Hewlett-Packard Company.*

Further developments produced a *write once read many* (WORM) drive. This device allows data to be written on it, but the data becomes permanent on the disk and cannot be erased. This storage device is especially suited for archival purposes. The data is "burned" into the disk surface by a laser so the information becomes more permanent than magnetic storage, and the disk is removable. A third generation optical disk drive, write many read many, currently in its infancy, allows data to be erased and written over.

3.10 Operating System Programs

As previously stated, the term *software* refers to all programs that are written to be performed on a computer. Operating system programs are the code (the written set of instructions) that the system follows to handle input, operate the system, and output data. They translate user programs into machine language programs and may be written in a variety of standard computer languages. Regardless of which language is used, drafters and designers need not be proficient in programming, for they will be users rather than developers of the programs. A computer *operating system* (OS) is the program that manages the operation of the physical equipment and controls the execution of other programs on the system. The speed at which a CAD system can interact with an application program depends on how efficiently the operating system manages the various tasks. Operating systems may be designated as *multiprocessing* or *multiprogramming*. Some operating systems can do both multiprocessing and multiprogramming but require large memory. Real-time multiprocessing operating systems are usually prefered over multiprogramming systems. Operating system software is completely hardware dependent.

3.11 Application Programs

The computer programs designed to perform specific tasks in response to a particular user's requirements are called *application programs*. When a user enters variables into a CAD system, for example, the application program is responsible for producing images on the display and completing any required calculations. Application programs are expensive to develop, and it is considered more economical to purchase existing software than to develop new programs. Application software is written for specific operating system software and can be used with any computer system that has the same operating system and therefore can be considered hardware independent.

A complete computer-aided drafting system is capable of a variety of operations and can produce many different types of drawings. Examples of some of the operations performed and drawings created are shown in Figs. 3.24–3.35.

3.12 Using a CAD System

After a CAD system has been installed, the beginning user must become thoroughly familiar with it and learn how to use it effectively. This will require learning some new skills as well as a different vocabulary. All CAD systems create drawings using basic geometric entities that are selected and placed on a screen by the CAD operator. The method and number of operations that are required to activate the various commands differ from one system to another.

Most CAD manufacturers offer training programs and tutorials that will make the learning process much easier. They will provide instruction and training manuals that give information and details about the operation of the system. These manuals can be used not only during the initial training period but also for reference purposes during later operation of the system.

All basic geometric entities are drawn in the same manner; for example, certain parameters must be set prior to the construction of an entity, such as line style, density, and position on the drawing. Some systems require that other parameters be established prior to drawing, such as conventional English or metric (ISO) paper size and pen type.

Most experienced drafters have developed shorter or simpler methods for creating a drawing, such as using overlays or templates. CAD systems also have simplified methods for drawing. Some systems have symbol libraries that contain many of the frequently used symbols, such as electrical relays, switches, transformers, resistors, bolts, nuts, keys, piping, and architectural symbols. These symbols may be in a symbol library, Fig. 3.36, or the symbol may be located on one of the templates in the library of templates. Some CAD systems allow the users to customize their symbol libraries. The desired symbols must first be drawn by the user on the CAD system the same as they would appear on a drawing board. This process may initially take as much time as it would manually, but once the image has been

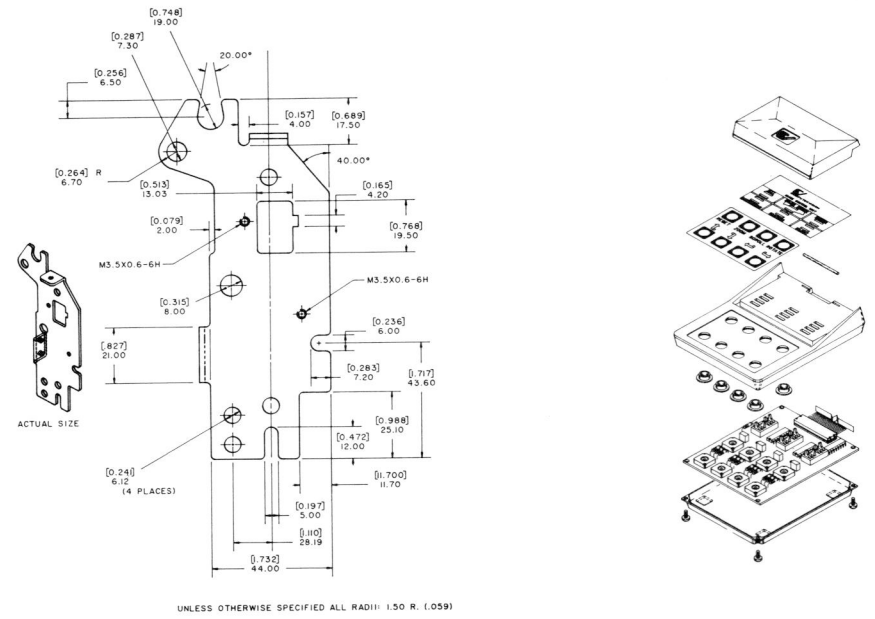

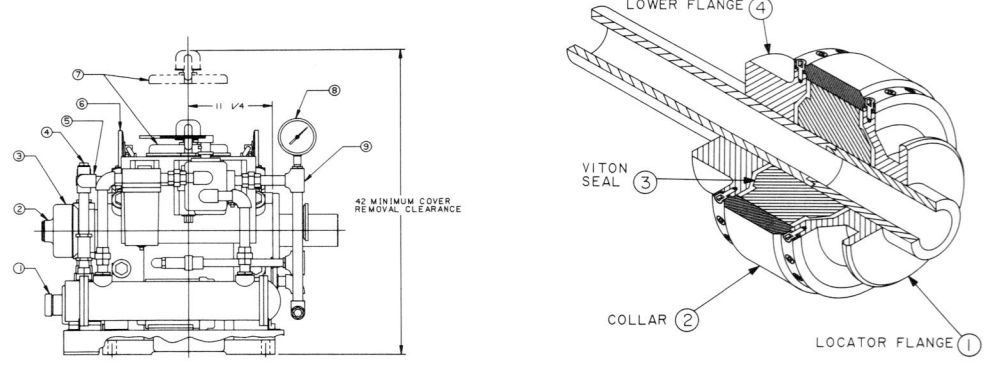

Fig. 3.24 Computer-Generated Drawings. *Courtesy of Computervision Corporation, a subsidiary of Prime Computer, Inc.*

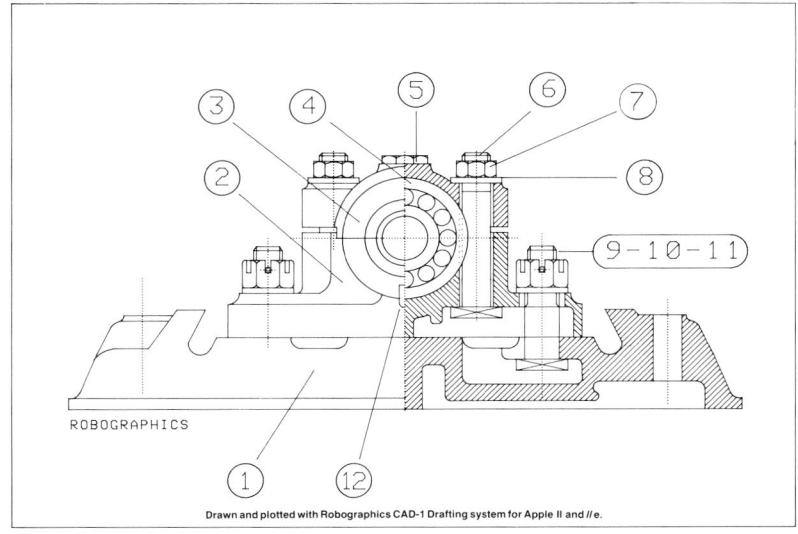

Fig. 3.25   Computer-Generated Assembly Drawing in Half Section. *Courtesy of Chessel-Robocom Corporation.*

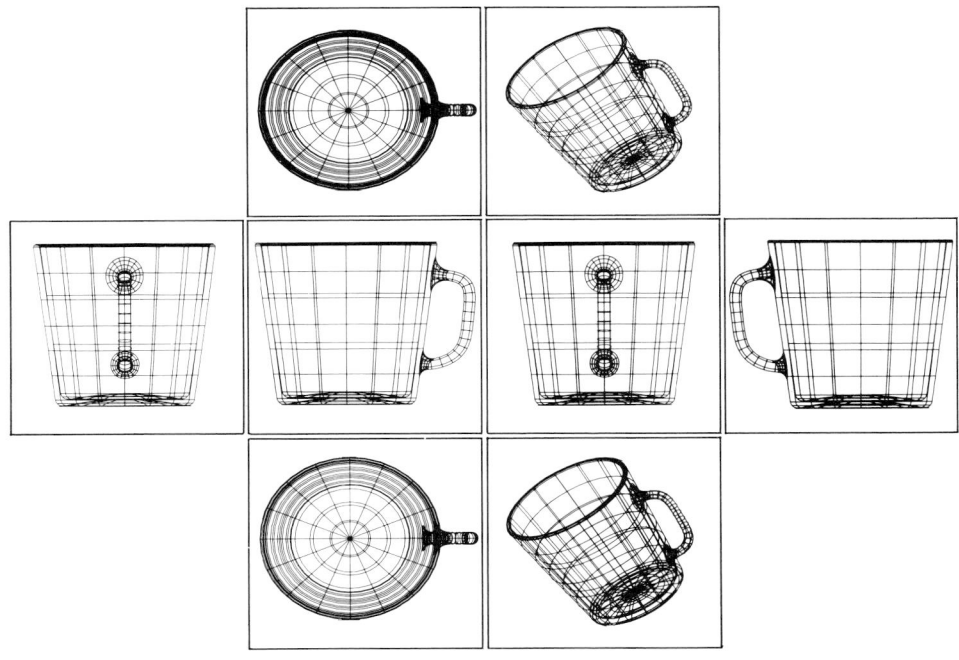

Fig. 3.26   Mold Design and Production. With the Auto-trol AD/380 automated design and drafting system, a part can be displayed in multiple views so the mold designer can see the part from all angles. *Courtesy of Auto-trol Technology Corporation.*

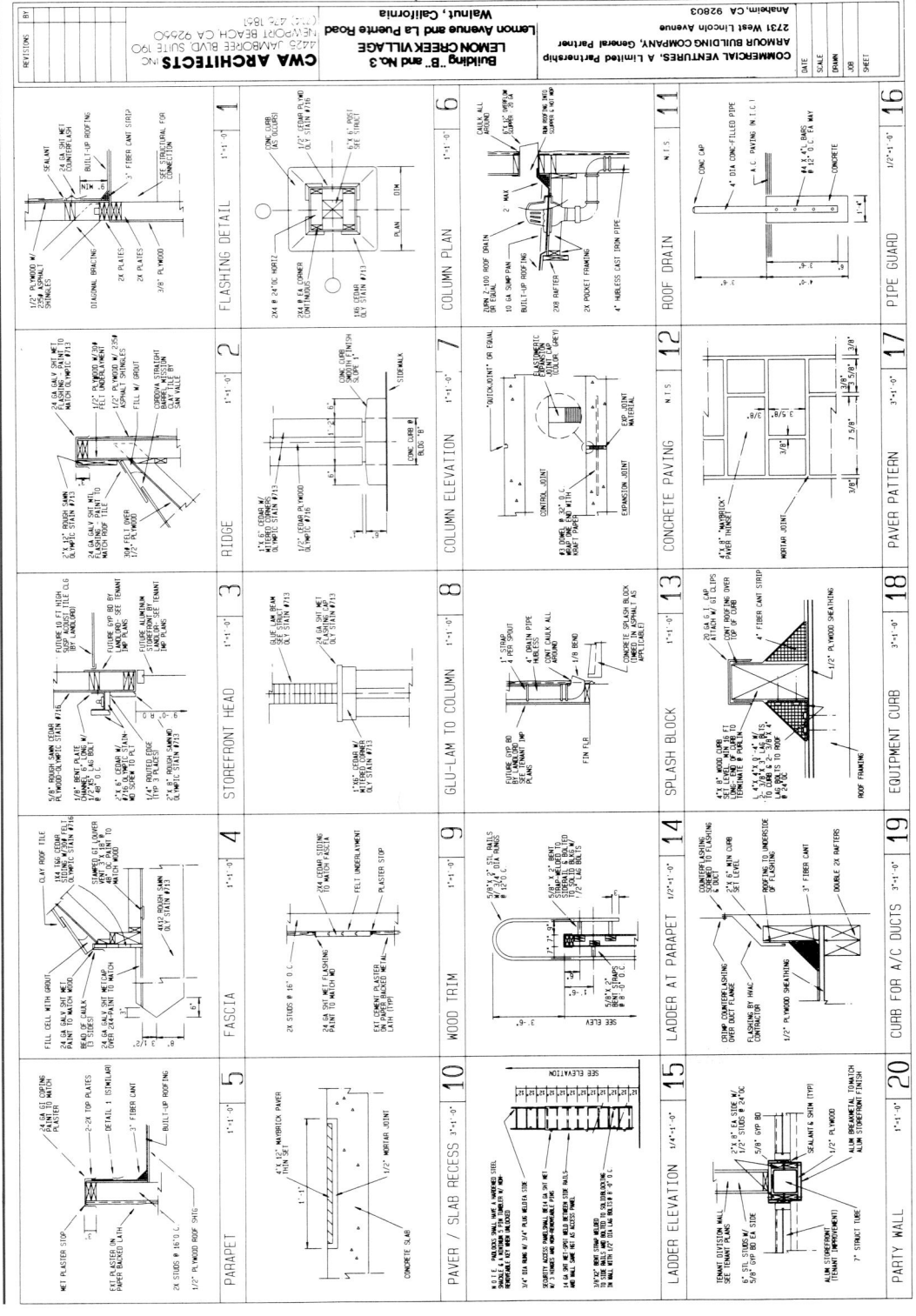

Fig. 3.27 Architectural Details Produced by Using the VersaCAD System. *Courtesy of VersaCAD, Inc.*

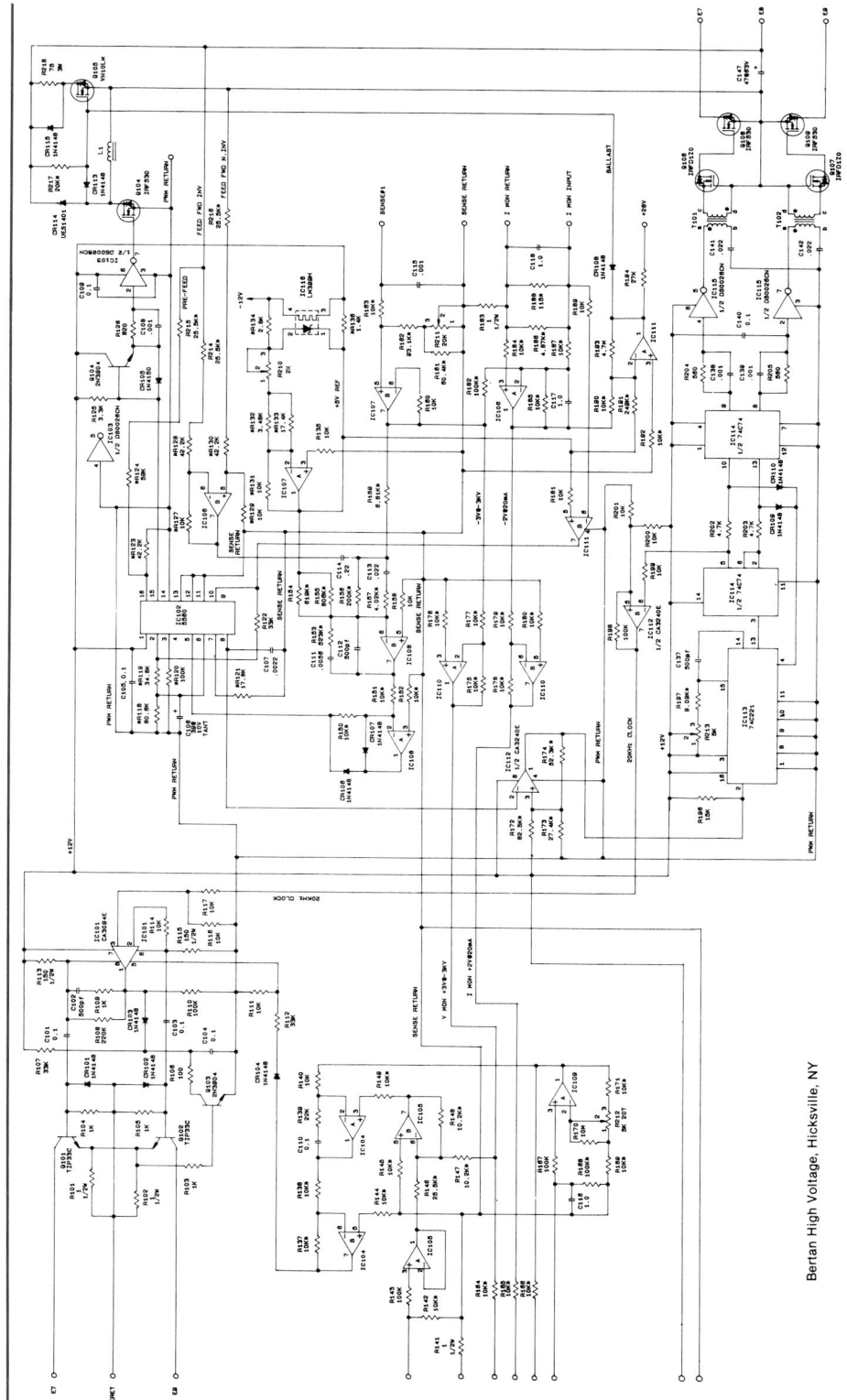

Fig. 3.28 Electronic Diagram Produced by Using the VersaCAD System. *Courtesy of VersaCAD, Inc.*

Bertan High Voltage, Hicksville, NY

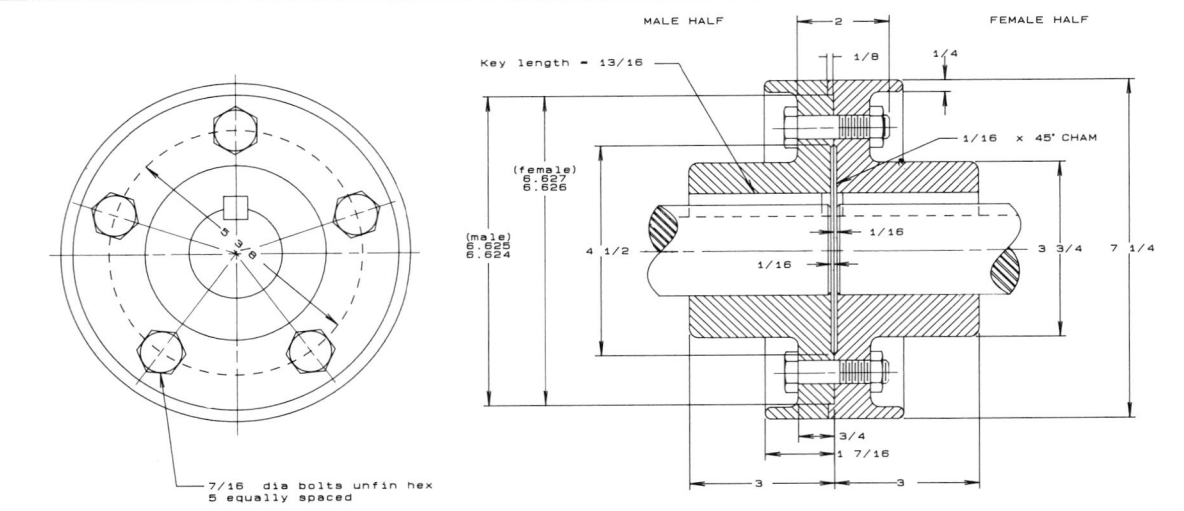

Fig. 3.29 Assembly Drawing in Section Produced by Using the VersaCAD Advanced System. *Courtesy of VersaCAD, Inc.*

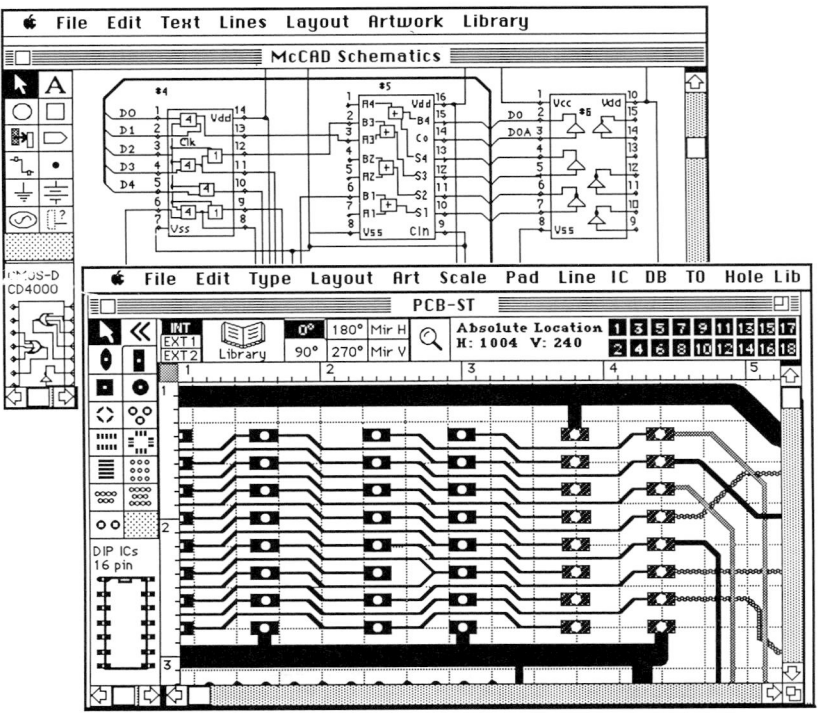

Fig. 3.30 Electronic Schematic Diagram and Printed Circuit Board Layout Generated on a Macintosh Computer with McCAD Software. *Courtesy of VAMP, Inc.*

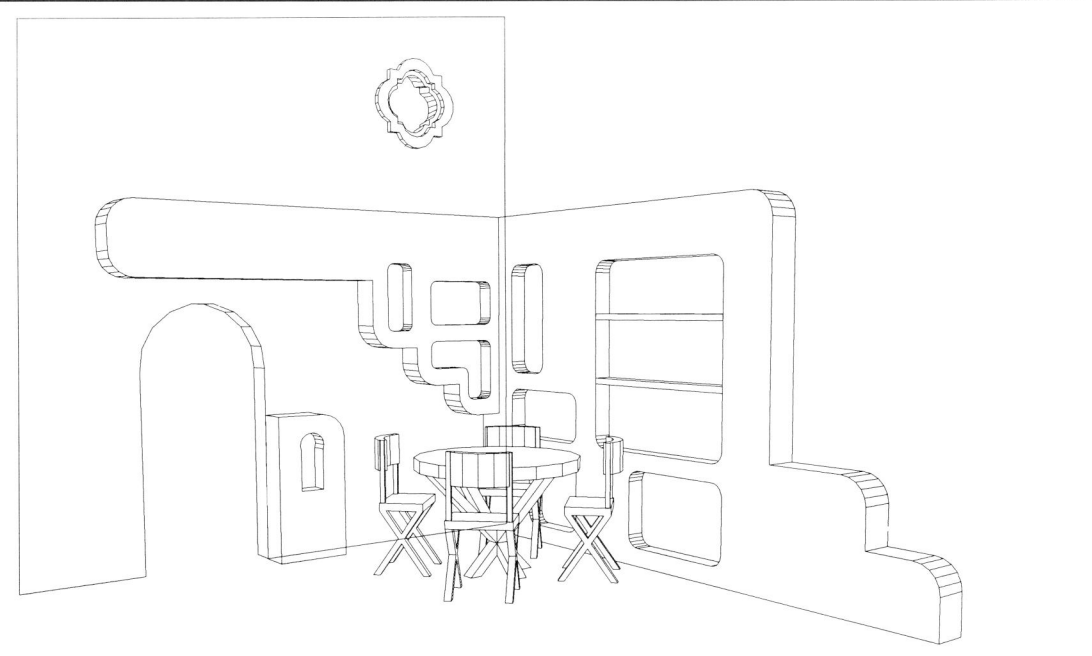

Fig. 3.31 Computer-Generated Perspective of Interior Room Detail Produced by Using SilverScreen CAD Program. *Courtesy of Schroff Development Corp.*

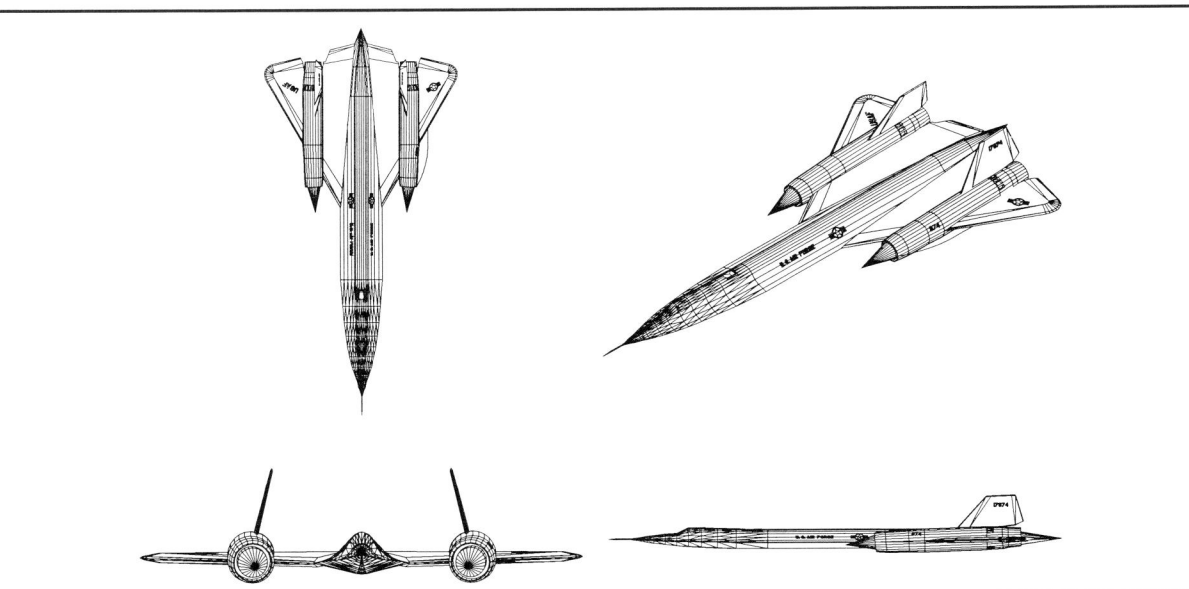

Fig. 3.32 Computer-Generated Multiview and Pictorial Drawing of U.S. Air Force SR-71 Reconnaissance Plane Produced by Using SilverScreen CAD Program. *Courtesy of Schroff Development Corp.*

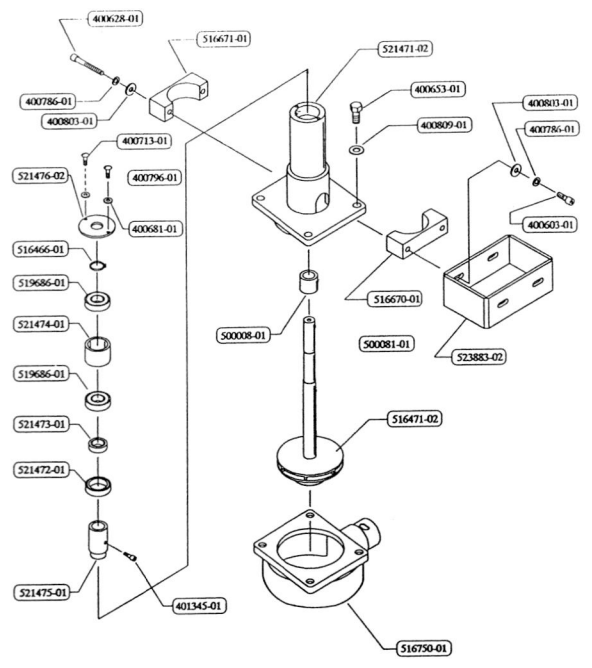

Fig. 3.33 Computer-Generated Isometric Exploded Assembly Drawing Produced by Using TRI-CAD Software. *Courtesy of Cadgrafix, Inc.*

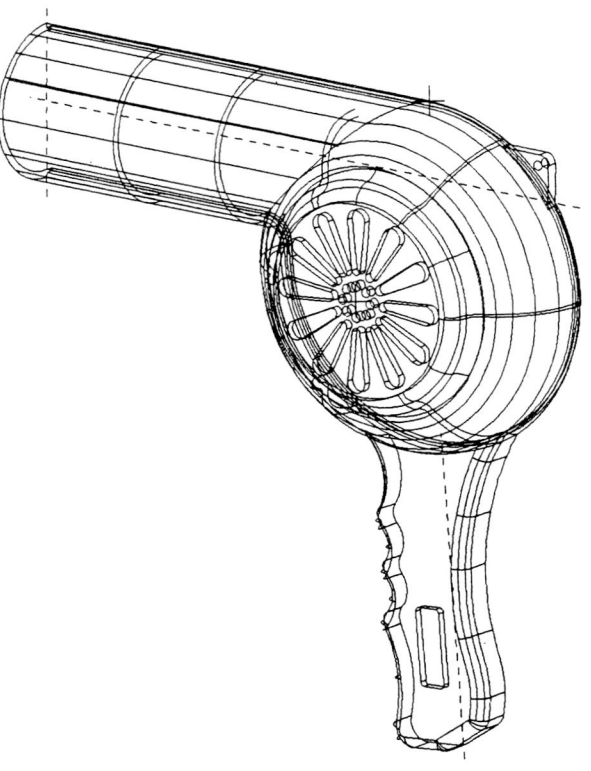

Fig. 3.34 Computer-Generated Wireframe Pictorial of Hair Dryer Produced by Using **CADKEY** Software. *Courtesy of CADKEY, Inc.*

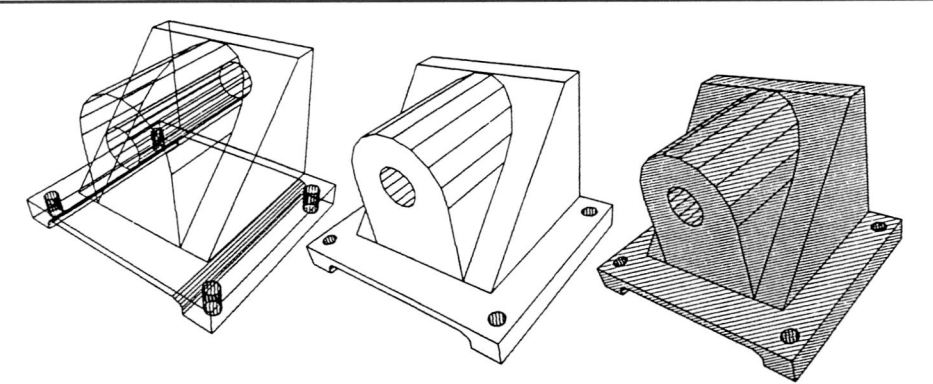

Fig. 3.35 Example of Wireframe, Solid, and Shaded Solid Pictorials Produced Using SilverScreen CAD Program. *Courtesy of Schroff Development Corp.*

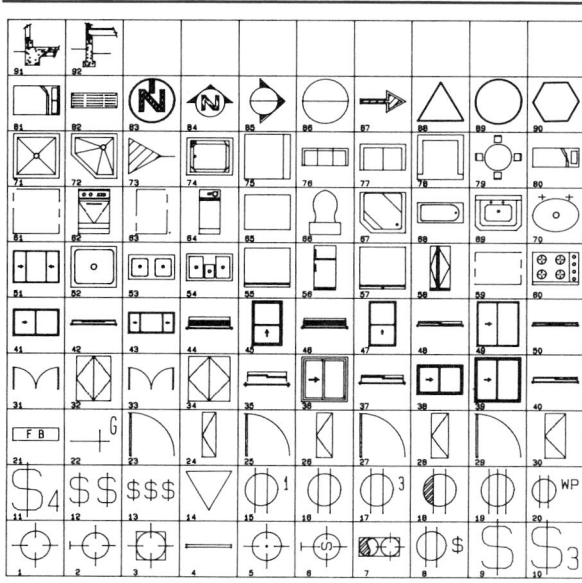

Fig. 3.36 Symbol Library. *Courtesy of T&W Systems, Inc.*

entered in the computer database, it need never be drawn again. The symbol can easily be retrieved from the symbol library whenever required.

Any CAD system function can be classified as entity creation, manipulation, or storage. Once a drawing has been created, it can be manipulated on the screen by the CAD operator. Some commonly used commands to manipulate an image are MOVE, ROTATE, COPY, PAN, ZOOM, SCALE, DELETE, and LAYER.

After the CAD operator completes a drawing, it can then be placed in the computer's storage on a disk or tape. The command, and even the method, to perform this function may differ from one system to another. The terms SAVE and QUIT are frequently used for data storage, but the computer receiving this command may automatically transfer the data from its main memory to a soft disk in one system and to a hard disk on another system.

It is not possible to list all commands for every CAD system in a single chapter of a textbook. Every CAD system manufacturer does, however, provide a user's manual for its system that contains this information. To become proficient in the use of any system, it is imperative that the user be aware of, and frequently refer to, the user's manual. See Appendix 3 for a glossary of CAD terms and definitions.

3.13 Selecting a CAD System

As the number of manufacturers of computer system equipment has increased, there has been a corresponding decrease in the cost of these systems. Some CAD systems may contain only those features necessary to produce simple two-dimensional entities, while others have the capability to create true three-dimensional views automatically. The manufacturers of some of these systems are eager to promote new or improved functions that may not be found on other systems. Almost daily the computer industry announces amazing advances.

Since the newer CAD systems are generally easier to operate, the words *user friendly* now are frequently used by manufacturers to promote their systems. There has, however, been a tendency by some to exaggerate what their particular systems can do. A prospective user should therefore view all claims with some skepticism, until proved, for they can be misleading and often lead to disappointment. Unfortunately, many firms have purchased a system only to discover later that it did not perform as expected.

Before purchasing a CAD system, it is highly recommended that a careful, well-thought-out plan for selecting a system be developed and followed. This plan can be divided into five phases:

I. Establish the need for a CAD system.

II. Survey and select system features.

III. Request CAD system demonstrations.

IV. Review selected systems.

V. Select, purchase, and install a CAD system.

Let us now discuss each of these phases in greater detail.

I. Establish the Need for a CAD System

The first consideration in the selection process is to determine whether a CAD system is needed at all. All potential users of the CAD system should be consulted as to how, when, and where a system would be used and whether it would be cost effective in their particular operations. Never purchase a system simply because it may be considered a first step into the future and your firm wants to project a progressive image. It is important to investigate and evaluate the time- and cost-saving claims of manufacturers by contacting firms that have CAD systems in operation. Contact as many firms as possible, especially those with a wide range of experience. Prepare a brief questionnaire to survey these firms asking questions regarding costs, training periods, system operation, and so on. Also ask at what point after installation the system became cost effective. Evaluate the responses to these questions and compare them with your specific requirements. This information will assist you in deciding if a CAD system can be beneficial to your firm at the present time.

Undoubtedly, you will hear many spectacular claims about the productivity of CAD systems. The productivity, however, will depend on the type of engineering operation. For example, among the first companies to introduce and use CAD systems were the electronic industry manufacturers. They found that drafters were constantly redrawing many symbols (resistor, transistor, etc.) and standard hardware parts (nuts, screws, etc.). Although they used plastic templates, common in all drafting departments, a considerable amount of time was spent doing tedious, repetitive drawing tasks. Since much of the time was devoted to tracing or redrawing something that was previously drawn, it was determined that a CAD system would save as much as 50 percent of the drafting time compared to using traditional methods. It is important to remember that with CAD it is only necessary to draw something once, even though initially it may take as long, or perhaps longer, to create it on the system as on the drawing board. From that point on, however, you need only to recall this information from data storage, which a CAD system can do with amazing speed. In this example, the benefits of CAD are obvious.

The process of determining the need for a CAD system can be time consuming and frustrating. Nevertheless, speed should be sacrificed to careful deliberation in this phase.

II. Survey and Select System Features

It is generally agreed that software should be selected before hardware. However, some CAD systems are *turnkey* systems, that is, a total system with software and hardware combined and inseparable. Therefore, you should examine all the features of any given system very carefully before being attracted by spectacular hardware. For example, some systems have two cathode ray display screens. The chance of being impressed by this feature may overshadow the question of whether one really needs the two CRT screens.

Consider whether the system will be multipurpose or used strictly for CAD. Will other office operations such as word processing or accounting be done on this machine? The answer to this question may add or eliminate CAD programs based on their operating system software.

Investigate how well a system will exchange information or interface with other CAD or CAM systems. Many systems do not have this capability. One mechanism the industry is trying to standardize on for exchanging information with other CAD systems is known as initial graphics exchange specification (IGES), and if a system has it, this can be a definite advantage.

It is suggested that you survey the people who will use the system to determine what they think is desirable in a CAD system. From this survey, develop a checklist of hardware and software features that your future system should have.

III. Request CAD System Demonstrations

After the checklist has been created and approved by all parties concerned, make arrangements to see the various CAD systems in operation. A list of vendors can be compiled from advertisements in trade journals, magazines, and so on, or from the various directories of computer graphics manufacturers that are published. Contact the vendors to arrange demonstrations. Explain to them exactly what you expect the system to do. If the vendors are completely aware of your requirements, they will be able to give a more realistic presentation. Most of all, be prepared to ask questions. With each succeeding demonstration your questions will also be more effective. Moreover, the answers that you receive will be more meaningful.

Some of the questions that you should ask are

1. What are the brand names of the equipment used?

2. Are service contracts available? If so, what are the details and the cost of the contract? In most instances, it is highly unlikely that your own staff will be able to repair the complicated equipment; therefore, a service contract is advisable. It is also possible in some situations to obtain service contracts from third parties that specialize in this type of business. The service provided by these firms for preventive and downtime maintenance may even be less costly than that offered by the original manufacturer.

3. What is the warranty period, or periods, if parts of the system are furnished by different vendors? Also, is the warranty paid for by the origi-

nal vendor or is the cost shared by the user and vendor?

4. What types of CAD software are provided, and what operations can be performed?

5. What kind and length of training will be provided to the user staff? How long after installation will it take for the staff to be proficient enough for the system to be cost effective?

6. Does the vendor issue software updates? If so, how often is this done and what is the cost?

7. What is the reputation of the vendor for providing user support in the form of toll-free telephone assistance or other methods of communication? Is the vendor readily available when the user encounters software and/or hardware problems and requires assistance?

8. Who currently uses the particular system? Will the vendor provide a list of current users? Users that have several months experience with a CAD system are best qualified to answer question 7.

A CAD system analysis worksheet can be very helpful when demonstrations are presented. Items to be included on the worksheet may be arranged according to hardware and software specifications. The hardware features that should be listed will generally be included in the following five categories: (1) central processor, (2) data input devices, (3) display monitors, (4) data storage, and (5) output devices.

1. *Central Processor.* When gathering information about a central processor, five areas that are common to computers should be investigated. These are (a) word size, (b) memory, (c) storage, (d) execution rate, and (e) operating system. Each of these areas should be carefully considered prior to the purchase of any software separate from the hardware. If, however, a turnkey system is being considered, then you have no choice, since the manufacturer has built the system centered on a central processor. A brief definition of each of these terms follows.

(a) Word size. A term used to indicate the microprocessor capability, usually expressed as 8 bit, 16 bit, dual 16 bit, and 32 bit. Computers process information in words; the larger the word, the faster the processing.

(b) Memory (or RAM, random access memory). RAM indicates how many bytes (1 byte = 8 bits) of temporary memory can be utilized by the CPU. For example, 64 kB means 64,000 bytes, and 10 MB means 10 million bytes, and so on. Most CPUs have expansion slots where additional memory cards can be inserted. This fact is significant when you wish to expand the system or create a network by adding workstations at a later date. If you add more workstations to any system without expanding the memory, you will notice a definite degrading of the system's performance. The system will be slow in movement and response.

(c) Execution rate. This is the rate at which the computer acts on information entered, and it is usually expressed in nanoseconds (millionth of a second) per event, or operation. Frequently, this rate is a function of word size and main memory size. Or to explain it in terms of operation: a 32-bit word size CPU with 10 MB of main memory will produce a system capable of operating at an incredible speed.

(d) Operating system programs. These programs control the computer's method of processing data (different from applications software) and are usually supplied by the computer manufacturer. If the software is purchased separately, it is important to know whether or not it will function properly with the CPU's operating system and other hardware peripherals connected to the system.

2. *Data Input Devices.* A variety of the devices available for data entry also allow the user to communicate with the CAD system. A keyboard is normally the standard device included with a system. Other devices may be a graphics tablet, mouse, light pen, thumbwheel(s), trackball, and so on. One or more of these devices may be included with a turnkey system or may be offered as an optional feature. The higher quality graphics devices have finer resolution (expressed in thousandths of an inch) and greater accuracy. The higher the quality, the greater the cost of the device.

3. *Display Monitors.* All interactive (CAD) systems have display monitors: vector refresh, raster scan, or direct view storage tube (DVST). In turnkey systems the monitor is included as part of the workstation. Raster scan monitors are categorized as monochrome or color, and according to their resolution and number of colors they can display. The industry has now standardized classifications of monitors as

1. Monochrome.
2. Color graphics array (CGA).
3. Enhanced color graphics array (EGA).
4. Video graphics array (VGA).

5. Super VGA.

6. Professional graphics array (PGA).

The following features should be considered in selecting a monitor.

(a) Single or dual display monitors. Does the system use one or two screens? If two screens are used, how are they formulated? Is one screen for graphics and the other for text and menu display, or are both screens for graphics display? Although two screens may be an impressive attraction, many CAD systems operate very well with one graphic display screen and are far less expensive.

(b) Resolution. Resolution is the smallest spacing between two display elements that permits the elements to be distinguished on the terminal. It indicates the clarity of display and usually is expressed as pixels (picture elements), or lines, such as 1024 × 1024. The higher the numbers, the better the definition of lines, circles, arcs, and so on.

(c) Monochrome or color. Monochrome means single color only, such as green, amber, or white lines on a dark background. Color refers to a display containing a full spectrum of colors such as that on the screen of a color television set. Although a color display may be an attractive optional feature, a CAD system will function very well with a monochrome display and will be less costly.

(d) Screen size. The size of the viewing area (12″, 14″, or 19″) is measured diagonally across the screen. If the resolution is coarse, not much will be gained by using a large screen, but with fine resolution a larger screen will produce a clearer display.

4. *Storage.* The manner in which the computer system accumulates and retains information for future use is called storage. When reviewing these specifications carefully consider these features.

(a) Storage type. Storage is typically in the form of hard or soft disk, magnetic tape, and so on.

(b) Capacity. The amount of system storage is called capacity and is expressed (measured) in bytes, such as 712 kB or 40 MB. A larger number indicates a greater capacity.

(c) Access time. The speed at which the computer retrieves information is called access time. It is one measure of system response.

(d) Removable or nonremovable. Ascertain if data can be removed from the drive and stored elsewhere, such as on tape, disk packs, or floppy disks.

(e) Expandable. Determine if the storage capac-

ity of the system can be expanded. If it can, to what extent?

5. *Output Devices.* The end result of any computer system is output. In a CAD system the output is usually in the form of hard-copy drawings, although mathematical calculations may also be part of the output. Two common devices that are used to create hard copy on a CAD system are plotters and printers. Several issues that should be considered regarding output devices are

(a) Will the device be included in the system price or do you purchase it separately?

(b) Is the device manufactured by a recognized company with an established reputation for quality, service, and so on?

(c) What is the maximum size of drawing that the device can generate?

(d) How fast does the device operate?

(e) What is the resolution and accuracy of the completed drawing, usually expressed in thousandths of an inch?

(f) If a plotter is used, what different types and sizes of pens and colors of ink can be used?

(g) If a printer is used, what type is it—ink jet, dot matrix, laser, and so on?

The questions and information provided in each of the preceding five categories pertaining to hardware features are offered as a guide to assist the prospective buyer and user in the comparison and evaluation of CAD systems. The worksheet may be expanded, or modified, to reflect particular requirements. A similar worksheet should also be developed listing CAD system software feature requirements.

With the completion of this phase you will have achieved several important goals. Your knowledge and understanding of CAD systems will have increased, and you will be in a position to identify those system features that you require and can afford. In addition, you will have assembled a list of current users of CAD systems for future reference or exchange of information.

IV. Review Selected Systems
It is important at this stage that all of the collected information be organized and carefully reviewed. A list should be made now of only those systems that merit further serious consideration. You may wish to request another demonstration of the particular systems that are on your revised list and to request additional information from current users regarding

equipment performance, staff training, vendor support, and so on. Remember, if you select a system made by a reputable and financially stable manufacturer, and purchase it from a dependable retailer, you will sacrifice nothing in terms of service and support. Throughout this chapter we have made every effort to feature or illustrate systems and equipment made by such firms.

V. Final Selection, Purchase, and Installation of a CAD System

This last phase occurs when the final decision will be made as to whether or not to purchase a CAD system. The decision invariably will depend on how you plan to use the system and how much you can afford to pay for it. If the decision is made to acquire a system, determine costs, choose a delivery date, and arrange for installation and training.

3.14 Summary

The information presented in this chapter is intended to familiarize the student with the basic "generic" concepts, hardware, peripherals, and systems in CAD. It is not possible, nor was it intended, to present programs, subroutines, or all the commands used on CAD systems.

When possible, the instructor should arrange for students to visit nearby engineering and drafting departments that have CAD systems in operation. Those students who wish to obtain additional information on this subject should consult their school or local library.

Introduction to CAD Problems

The following problems are given to examine your retention and understanding of the subject matter presented in this chapter. When necessary, refer to the appropriate sections of the chapter to check your answers.

___

Prob. 3.1 Define the following terms: computer system, hardware, software, analog, digital, computer graphics, CAD, CADD, and CAM.

Prob. 3.2 What are the principal components of a computer system? A CAD system? Draw a systems flowchart that illustrates the sequence of operations for each of the systems.

Prob. 3.3 Prepare a list of CAD system hardware components and give examples of each.

Prob. 3.4 List and describe the main types of graphics monitors.

Prob. 3.5 Arrange a visit to the computer center at your school, or to a local engineering design office, and prepare a written report on the use of computers in design and drafting at these facilities.

CHAPTER

4

Lettering

The designs of modern alphabets had their origin in Egyptian hieroglyphics, Fig. 1.4, which evolved over time into a cursive hieroglyphic or hieratic writing. This writing was adopted by the Phoenicians who developed it into an alphabet of 22 letters. The Greeks later adopted the Phoenician alphabet but it evolved into two distinct types in different sections of Greece: an Eastern Greek type, used also in Asia Minor, and a Western Greek type, used in the Greek colonies in and near Italy, which became the Latin alphabet about 700 B.C. The Latin alphabet came into general use throughout the Old World.

Originally, the Roman capital alphabet consisted of 22 characters, and these have remained practically unchanged to this day. The numerous modern styles of letters were derived from the design of the original Roman capitals.

4.1 Lettering* Styles

Before the invention of printing by Gutenberg in the fifteenth century, all letters were made by hand, and their designs were modified and decorated according to the individual writer's taste. In England these letters became known as Old English. The early German printers adopted the Old English letters, and they are still in limited use.

The early Italian printers used Roman letters, which were later introduced into England and gradually replaced the Old English letters. The Roman

Lettering, not "printing," is the correct term for making letters by hand. *Printing* means the production of printed material on a printing press.

capitals have come down to us virtually in their original form. A general classification of letter styles is shown in Fig. 4.1.

4.2 Roman Letters

The term *Roman* refers to any letter that has wide downward strokes and thin connecting strokes, as would result from the use of a wide pen, and the ends of the strokes are terminated with spurs called *serifs*. Roman letters include the Old Roman and Modern Roman and may be vertical or inclined. Inclined letters are also referred to as *italic*, regardless of the letter style; those shown in Fig. 4.1 are inclined Modern Roman.

Fig. 4.1   Classification of Letter Styles.

Fig. 4.2   Old Roman Capitals, with Numerals and Lowercase of Similar Design.

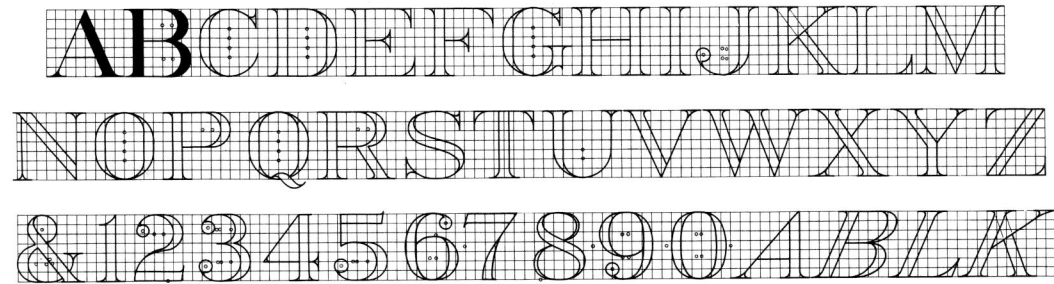

Fig. 4.3 Modern Roman Capitals and Numerals.

Fig. 4.4 Lowercase Modern Roman Letters.

Old Roman Letters Fig. 4.2

The Old Roman letter is the basis of all our letters and is still regarded as the most beautiful. This letter is employed mostly by architects. Because of its great beauty, it is used almost exclusively on buildings and for inscriptions on bronze or stone.

Modern Roman Letters Figs. 4.3 and 4.4

The Modern Roman, or simply "Roman," letters were developed during the eighteenth century by the type founders; the letters used in most modern newspapers, magazines, and books are of this style. The text of this book is set in Modern Roman capital and lowercase letters. These letters are often used on maps, especially for titles. They may be drawn in outline and then filled in, as shown in Fig. 4.3, or

they may be produced with one of the broad-nib pens shown in Fig. 4.13.

A typical example of the use of Modern Roman in titles is shown in Fig. 4.43. Their use on maps is discussed in §4.27.

4.3 Gothic Letters

The *Text* letters shown in Fig. 4.1 are often loosely referred to as Old English, although these and other similar letters, such as German Text, are actually Gothic. German Text is the only form of medieval Gothic in commercial use today.

Commercial Gothic is a relatively modern development that originated from the earlier Gothic forms. Also called sans-serif Gothic, this letter is the

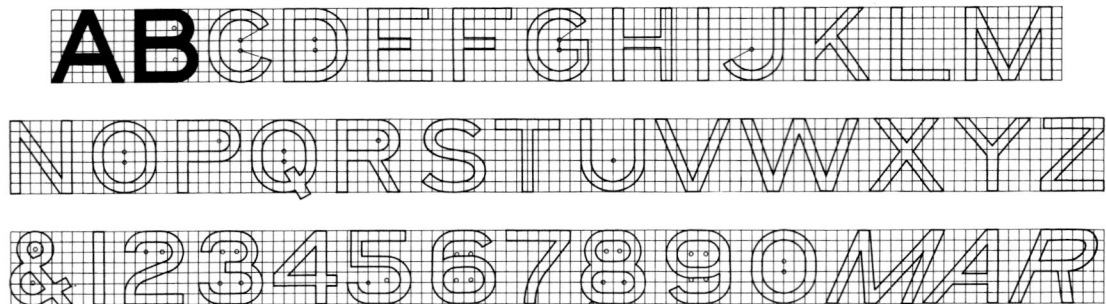

Fig. 4.5   Gothic Capital Letters.

CONDENSED LETTERS

EXTENDED LETTERS

Condensed Letters

Extended Letters

Fig. 4.6   Condensed and Extended Letters.

only one of interest to engineers, Fig. 4.5. It is the plainest and most legible style and is the one from which our single-stroke engineering letters are derived. While admittedly not as beautiful as many other styles, sans-serif letters are very legible and comparatively easy to make. They may also be drawn in outline and filled in, Fig. 4.5.

Extended and Condensed Letters Fig. 4.6
To meet design or space requirements, letters may be narrower and spaced closer together, in which case they are called compressed or condensed letters. If the letters are wider than normal, they are referred to as extended letters.

Lightface and Boldface Letters Fig. 4.7
Letters also vary as to the thickness of the stems or strokes. Letters having very thin stems are called

LIGHTFACE

BOLDFACE

Fig. 4.7   Lightface and Boldface Letters.

LIGHTFACE, while those having heavy stems are called **BOLDFACE.** As the preceding sentence demonstrates, Modern Roman also exists as lightface and boldface.

4.4 Greek Alphabet
Greek letters are often used as symbols in both mathematics and technical drawing by the engineer. A Greek alphabet, showing both uppercase and lowercase letters, is given for reference purposes in Fig. 4.8.

4.5 Single-Stroke Gothic Letters
During the latter part of the nineteenth century the development of industry and of technical drawing in the United States made evident a need for a simple legible letter that could be executed with single strokes of an ordinary pen. To meet this need, C. W. Reinhardt, formerly chief draftsman for *Engineering News*, developed alphabets of capital and lowercase inclined and "upright" letters,* based on the old

*Published in *Engineering News* in about 1893 and in book form in 1895.

A α	alpha	I ι	iota	P ρ	rho
B β	beta	K κ	kappa	Σ s	sigma
Γ γ	gamma	Λ λ	lambda	T τ	tau
Δ δ	delta	M μ	mu	Υ υ	upsilon
E ϵ	epsilon	N ν	nu	Φ ϕ	phi
Z ζ	zeta	Ξ ξ	xi	X χ	chi
H η	eta	O o	omicron	Ψ ψ	psi
Θ θ	theta	Π π	pi	Ω ω	omega

Fig. 4.8 Greek Alphabet.

Gothic letters. For each letter he worked out a systematic series of strokes. The single-stroke Gothic letters used on technical drawings today are based on Reinhardt's work.

4.6 Standardization of Lettering

Reinhardt's development of single-stroke letters was the first step toward standardization of technical lettering. Since that time, however, there has been an unnecessary and confusing diversity of lettering styles and forms. In 1935 the American National Standards Institute suggested letter forms that are now generally considered as standard. The lettering forms given in the present standard [ANSI Y14.2M–1979 (R1987)] are practically the same as those given in 1935 except that lowercase forms have since been added.

The letters in this chapter and throughout this text conform to the American National Standard. Vertical letters are perhaps slightly more legible than inclined letters, but they are more difficult to execute. Both vertical and inclined letters are standard, and the engineer or drafter may be called on to use either.

Lettering on drawings must be legible and suitable for easy and rapid execution. The single-stroke Gothic letters shown in Figs. 4.25 and 4.26 meet these requirements. Either vertical or inclined letters may be used, but only one style should appear on any one drawing. Background areas between letters in words should appear approximately equal, and words should be clearly separated by a space equal to the height of the lettering. Only when special emphasis is necessary should the lettering be underlined.

It is not desirable to vary the size of the lettering according to the size of the drawing except when a drawing is to be reduced in reproduction.

Drawings for microfilm reproduction require well-spaced lettering to prevent "fill-ins." The microfont alphabet, Fig. 4.9, is an adaptation of the single-stroke Gothic characters developed by the National Microfilm Association. Only the vertical style is shown.

4.7 Uniformity

In any style of lettering, uniformity is essential. Uniformity in height, proportion, inclination, strength of lines, spacing of letters, and spacing of words insures a pleasing appearance, Fig. 4.10.

Uniformity in height and inclination is promoted by the use of light guide lines, §4.14. Uniformity in strength of lines can be obtained only by the skilled use of properly selected pencils and pens, §§4.10 and 4.11.

4.8 Optical Illusions

Good lettering involves artistic design, in which the white and black areas are carefully balanced to produce a pleasing effect. Letters are designed to *look* well, and some allowances must be made for errors in perception. Note that in Fig. 4.25 the width of the standard H is less than its height to eliminate a square appearance, the numeral 8 is narrower at the top to give it stability, and the width of the letter W is greater than its height, for the acute angles in the W give it a compressed appearance. Such acute angles should be avoided in good letter design.

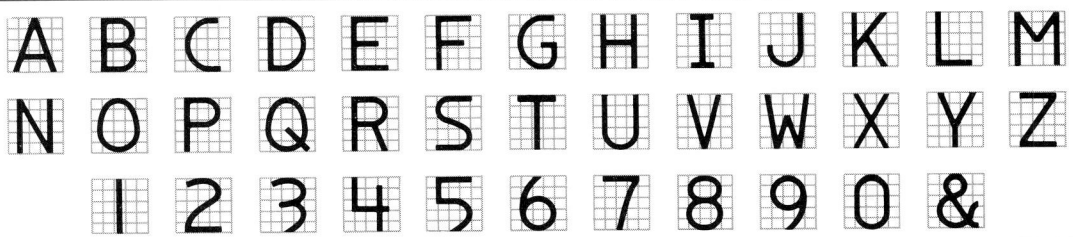

Fig. 4.9 Microfont Alphabet.

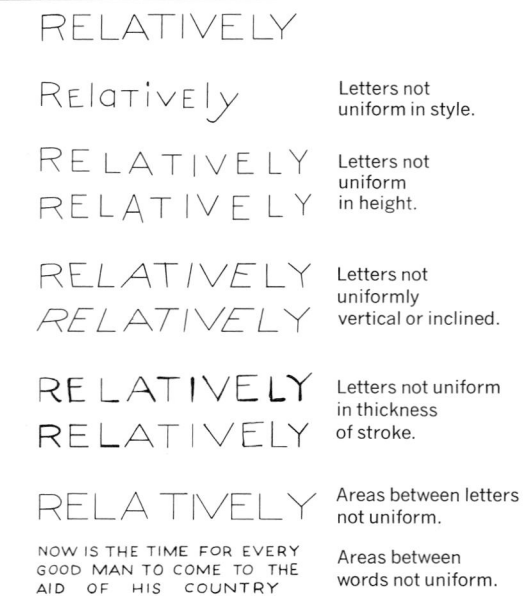

RELATIVELY	
Relatively	Letters not uniform in style.
RELATIVELY	Letters not uniform
RELATIVELY	in height.
RELATIVELY	Letters not uniformly
RELATIVELY	vertical or inclined.
RE LATIVELY	Letters not uniform in thickness
RELATIVELY	of stroke.
RELA TIVELY	Areas between letters not uniform.
NOW IS THE TIME FOR EVERY GOOD MAN TO COME TO THE AID OF HIS COUNTRY	Areas between words not uniform.

Fig. 4.10   Uniformity in Lettering.

4.9 Stability

If the upper portions of certain letters and numerals are equal in width to the lower portions, the characters appear top-heavy. To correct this, the upper portions are reduced in size where possible, thereby producing the effect of stability and a more pleasing appearance, Fig. 4.11.

If the central horizontal strokes of the letters B, E, F, and H are placed at midheight, they will appear to be below center. To overcome this optical illu-

sion, these strokes should be drawn slightly above the center.

4.10 Lettering Pencils

Pencil letters are best made with a medium-soft lead with a conical point, Fig. 2.11 (c), or with a suitable thin-lead pencil, Fig. 2.8 (c).

Today the majority of drawings are finished in pencil and reproduced. To reproduce well by any process, the pencil lettering must be dense black, as should all other final lines on the drawing. The right lead to use depends largely on the amount of tooth or grain in the paper, the rougher papers requiring the harder pencils. The lead should be soft enough to produce jet black lettering, yet hard enough to prevent excessive wearing down of the point, crumbling of the point, and smearing of the graphite.

4.11 Lettering Pens

The choice of a pen for lettering is determined by the size and style of the letters, the thickness of stroke desired, and the personal preference of the drafter. Fig. 4.12 shows a variety of the best pen points in a range from the *tit quill*, the finest, to the *ball-pointed*, the coarsest. The widths of the lines made by the several pens are shown full size. Letters more than $\frac{1}{2}''$ (12.7 mm) in height generally require a special pen, Fig. 4.13.

The technical fountain pen, Fig. 4.14, is a newer instrument that drafters now use for lettering and line work. The point is a small tube in which an

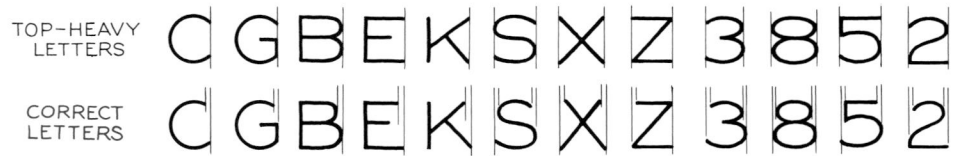

TOP-HEAVY LETTERS   CGBEKSXZ 3852

CORRECT LETTERS   CGBEKSXZ 3852

Fig. 4.11   Stability of Letters.

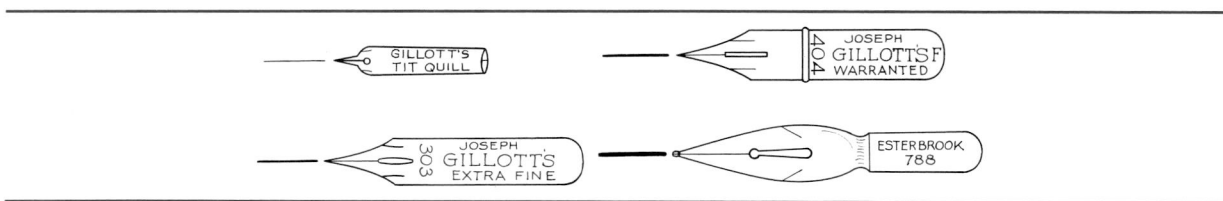

Fig. 4.12   Pen Points (Full Size).

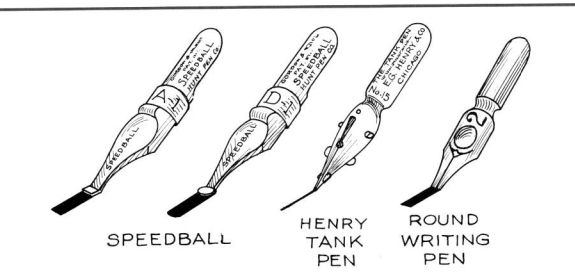

Fig. 4.13 Special Pens for Freehand Lettering.

Fig. 4.14 Technical Fountain Pen. *Courtesy of Keuffel & Esser Co.*

automatic plunger rod keeps the ink flowing, and the pen has a reservoir cartridge for the storage of ink. The pen point produces a uniform thickness of line and makes the task of inking much simpler. These pens are available in sets of different point sizes and may be used with lettering instruments and templates.

Any lettering pen must be kept clean. All these pens should be frequently cleaned with cleaning fluid to keep them in service.

4.12 Technique of Lettering

Any normal person can learn to letter if a persistent and intelligent effort is made. Although it is true that "practice makes perfect," it must be understood that practice alone is not enough; it must be accompanied by *continuous effort to improve.*

Lettering is freehand drawing and not writing. Therefore, the six fundamental strokes and their direction for freehand drawing are basic to lettering, Fig. 4.15. The horizontal strokes are drawn to the right, and all vertical, inclined, and curved strokes are drawn downward.

Good lettering is always accomplished by conscious effort and is never done well otherwise,

though good muscular coordination is of great assistance. Ability to letter has little relationship to writing ability; excellent letterers are often poor writers.

There are three necessary aspects of learning to letter.

1. Knowledge of the proportions and forms of the letters and the order of the strokes. No one can make a good letter who does not have a clear mental image of the correct form of the letter.

2. Knowledge of composition—the spacing of letters and words. Rules governing composition should be thoroughly mastered, §4.24.

3. Persistent practice, with *continuous effort to improve.*

First, sharpen the pencil to a needle point; then dull the point *very slightly* by marking on paper while holding the pencil vertically and rotating the pencil to round off the point.

Pencil lettering should be executed with a fairly soft pencil, such as an F or H for ordinary paper; the strokes should be *dark* and *sharp*, not gray and blurred. In order to wear the lead down uniformly and thereby keep the lettering sharp, turn the pencil frequently to a new position.

The correct position of the hand in lettering is shown in Fig. 4.16. In general, draw vertical strokes downward or toward you with a finger movement, and draw horizontal strokes from left to right with a wrist movement without turning the paper.

Since practically all pencil lettering will be reproduced, the letters should be dense black. Avoid hard pencils that, even with considerable pressure, produce gray lines. Use a fairly soft pencil and keep it sharp by frequent dressing of the point on the sandpaper pad or file. An example (full size) of pencil lettering exhibiting correct technique is shown in Fig. 4.17.

4.13 Left-handers

All evidence indicates that the left-handed drafter is just as skillful as the right-hander, and this includes

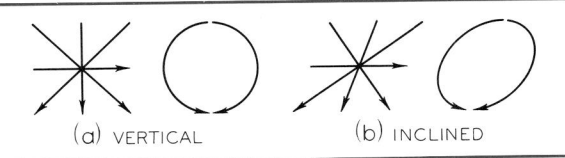

(a) VERTICAL   (b) INCLINED

Fig. 4.15 Basic Lettering Strokes.

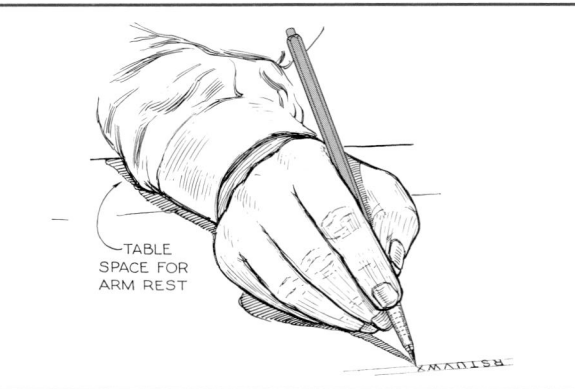

Fig. 4.16   Position of Hand in Lettering.

skill in lettering. The most important step in learning to letter is learning the correct shapes and proportions of letters, and these can be learned as well by the left-hander as by anyone else. The left-hander does have a problem of developing a system of strokes that seems personally most suitable. The strokes shown in Figs. 4.25 and 4.26 are for right-handers. The left-hander should experiment with each letter to find out which strokes are best. The

habits of left-handers vary so much that it is futile to suggest a standard system of strokes for all left-handers.

4.14 Guide Lines Fig. 4.18
Extremely light horizontal guide lines are necessary to regulate the height of letters. In addition, light vertical or inclined guide lines are needed to keep the letters uniformly vertical or inclined. Guide lines are absolutely essential for good lettering and should be regarded as a welcome aid, not as an unnecessary requirement.

4.15 Guide Lines for Capital Letters
Guide lines for vertical capital letters are shown in Fig. 4.19. On working drawings, capital letters are commonly made $\frac{1}{8}''$ (3.2 mm) high, with the space between lines of lettering from three-fifths to the full height of the letters. See Table 16.1 for ANSI-recommended minimum letter heights on drawings. The vertical guide lines are not used to space the letters—this should always be done by eye while

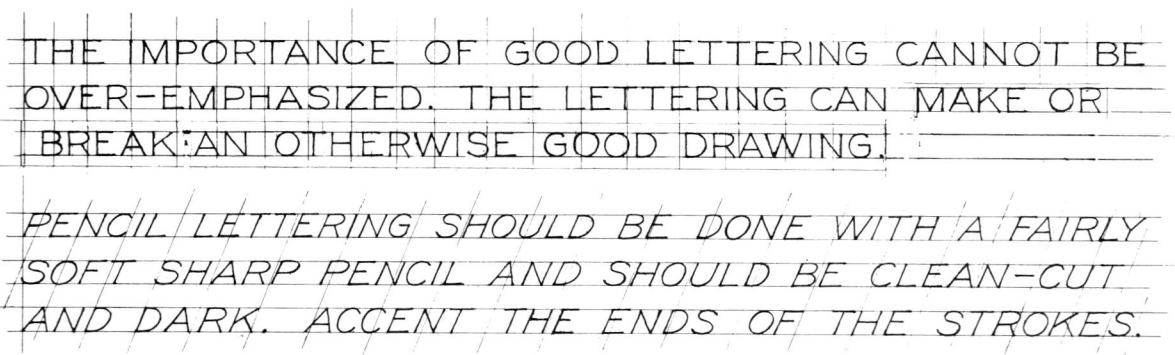

Fig. 4.17   Pencil Lettering (Full Size).

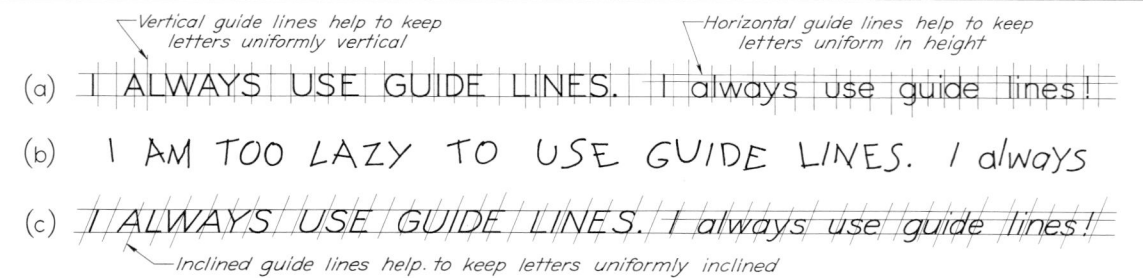

Fig. 4.18   Guide Lines.

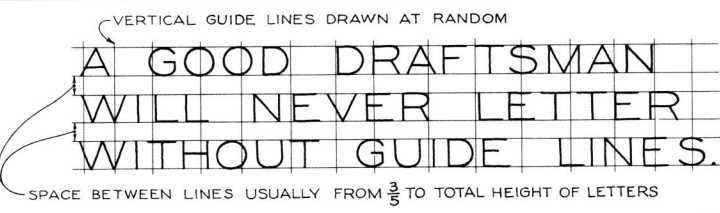

Fig. 4.19 Guide Lines for Vertical Capital Letters.

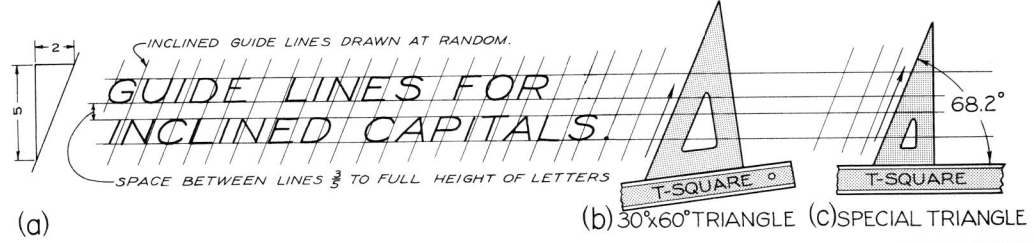

Fig. 4.20 Guide Lines for Inclined Capital Letters.

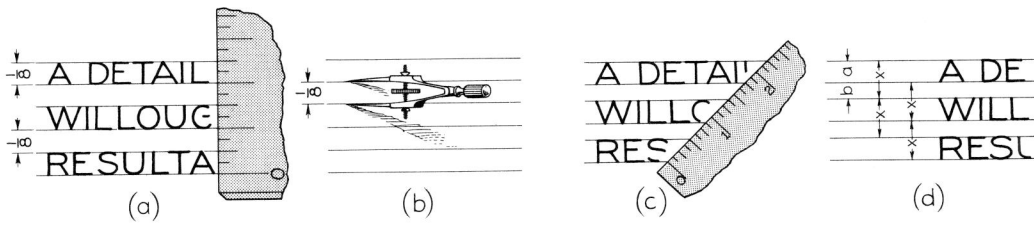

Fig. 4.21 Spacing of Guide Lines.

lettering—but only to keep the letters uniformly vertical. Accordingly, they should be drawn at random. Where several lines of letters are to be made, these vertical guide lines should be continuous from top to bottom of the lettered area, as shown.

Guide lines for inclined capital letters are shown in Fig. 4.20. The spacing of horizontal guide lines is the same as for vertical capital lettering. The American National Standard slope of 2 in 5 (or 68.2° with horizontal) may be established by drawing a "slope triangle," as shown at (a), and drawing the guide lines at random with the T-square and triangle, as shown at (b). Special triangles for the purpose may be used, as shown at (c), or the lines may be drawn with the Braddock–Rowe Lettering Triangle, Fig. 4.23, or the Ames Lettering Guide, Fig. 4.24.

A simple method of spacing horizontal guide lines is to use the scale, as shown in Fig. 4.21 (a), and merely set off a series of $\frac{1}{8}''$ spaces, making both the letters and the spaces between lines of letters $\frac{1}{8}''$

high. Another method of setting off equal spaces, $\frac{1}{8}''$ or otherwise, is to use the bow dividers, as shown at (b).

If it is desired to make the spaces between lines of letters less than the height of the letters, the methods shown at (c) and (d) will be convenient. At (c) the scale is placed diagonally, the letters in this case being four units high and the spaces between lines of lettering being three units. If the scale is rotated clockwise about the zero mark as a pivot, the height of the letters and the spaces between lines of letters diminish but remain proportional. If the scale is moved counterclockwise, the spaces are increased. The same unequal spacing may be accomplished with the bow dividers, as shown at (d). Let distance $x = a + b$, and set off x-distances, as shown.

When large and small capitals are used in combination, the small capitals should be three-fifths to two-thirds as high as the large capitals, Fig. 4.22.

Fig. 4.22   Large and Small Capital Letters.

This is in conformity with the guideline devices described in §§4.16 and 4.17.

4.16 Lettering Triangles

Lettering triangles, which are available in a variety of shapes and sizes, are provided with sets of holes in which the pencil is inserted and the guide lines are produced by moving the triangle with the pencil point along the T-square. The Braddock-Rowe Lettering Triangle, Fig. 4.23, is convenient for drawing guide lines for lettering and dimension figures as well as for drawing section lines. In addition, the triangle is used as a utility 45° triangle. The numbers at the bottom of the triangle indicate heights of letters in thirty-seconds of an inch. Thus, to draw guide lines for $\frac{1}{8}''$ (3.2 mm) capitals, use the No. 4 set of holes. For lowercase letters, draw guide lines from every hole; for capitals, omit the second hole in each group. The spacing of holes is such that the lower portions of lowercase letters are two-thirds as high as the capitals, and the spacing between lines of lettering is also two-thirds as high as the capitals.

The column of holes at the extreme left is used to draw guide lines for dimension figures $\frac{1}{8}''$ (3.2 mm) high and fractions $\frac{1}{4}''$ (6.4 mm) high and also for section lines $\frac{1}{16}''$ (1.6 mm) apart.

4.17 Ames Lettering Guide Fig. 4.24

The Ames Lettering Guide is an ingenious transparent plastic device composed of a frame holding a disk with three columns of holes. The vertical distances between the holes may be adjusted quickly to the desired spacing for guide lines or section lines by simply turning the disk to one of the settings indicated at the bottom of the disk. These numbers indicate heights of letters in thirty-seconds of an inch. Thus, for $\frac{1}{8}''$ high letters, the No. 4 setting would be used. The center column of holes is used primarily to draw guide lines for numerals and fractions, the height of the whole number being two units and the height of the fraction four units. The No. 4 setting of the disk will provide guide lines for $\frac{1}{8}''$ whole numbers, with fractions twice as high, or $\frac{1}{4}''$, as shown at (a). Since the spaces are equal, these holes can also be used to draw equally spaced guide lines for lettering or to draw section lines. The Ames Lettering Guide is also available with metric graduations for desired metric spacing.

The two outer columns of holes are used to draw guide lines for capitals or lowercase letters, the column marked three-fifths being used where it is desired to make the lower portions of lowercase letters three-fifths the total height of the letters and the column marked two-thirds being used where the lower portion is to be two-thirds the total height of the letters. In each case, for capitals, the middle hole of each set is not used. The two-thirds and three-fifths also indicate the spaces between lines of letters.

The sides of the guide are used to draw inclined or vertical guide lines, as shown at (b) and (c).

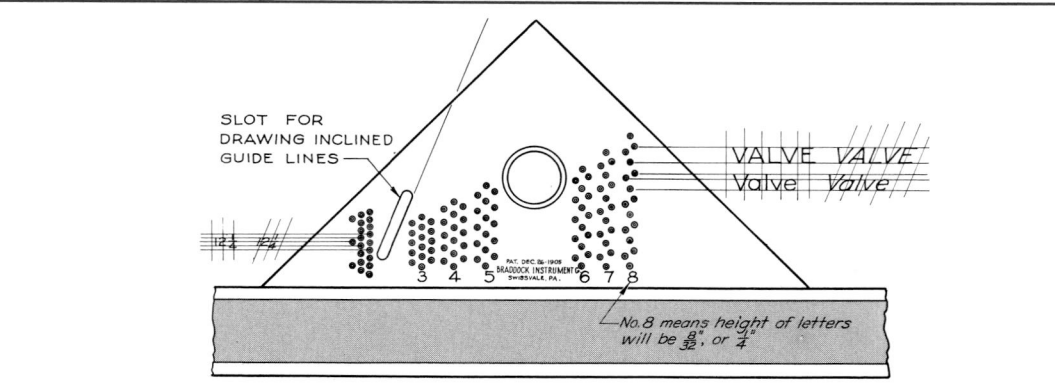

Fig. 4.23   Braddock-Rowe Lettering Triangle.

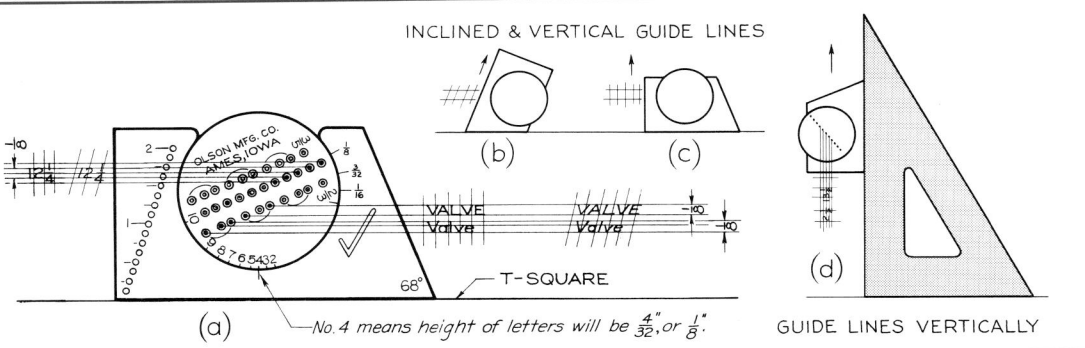

Fig. 4.24   Ames Lettering Guide.

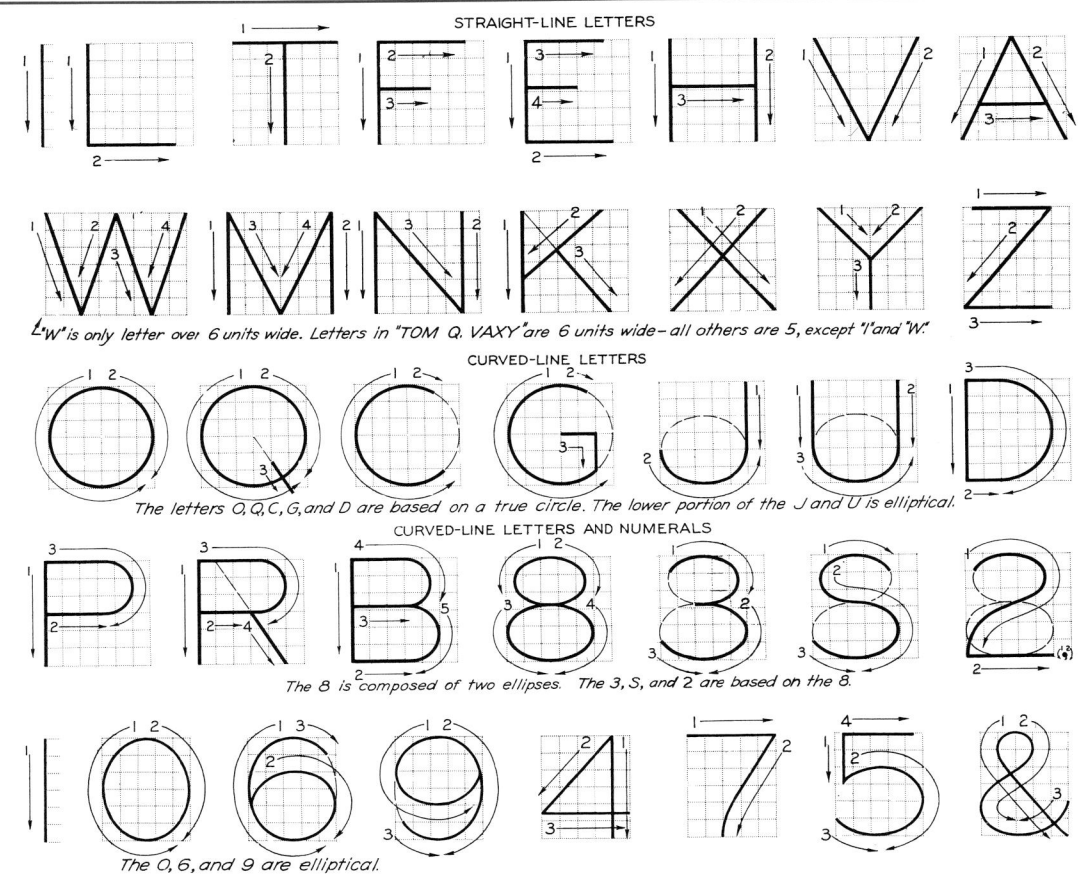

Fig. 4.25   Vertical Capital Letters and Numerals.

4.18 **Vertical Capital Letters and Numerals** Fig. 4.25

For convenience in learning the proportions of the letters and numerals, each character is shown in a grid 6 units high. Numbered arrows indicate the order and direction of strokes. The widths of the letters can be easily remembered. The letter I or the numeral 1 has no width. The W is 8 units wide ($1\frac{1}{3}$ times the height) and is the widest letter in the alphabet. All the other letters or numerals are either 5 or 6 units wide, and it is easy to remember the 6-unit letters because when assembled they spell TOM Q. VAXY. All numerals except the 1 are 5 units wide.

All horizontal strokes are drawn to the right, and all vertical, inclined, and curved strokes are drawn downward, Fig. 4.15.

As shown in Fig. 4.25, the letters are classified as *straight-line letters* or *curved-line letters*. On the third row the letters O, Q, C, and G are all based on the circle. The lower portions of the J and U are semiellipses, and the right sides of the D, P, R, and B are semicircular. The 8, 3, S, and 2 are all based on the figure 8, which is composed of a small ellipse over a larger ellipse. The 6 and 9 are based on the elliptical zero. The lower part of the 5 is also elliptical in shape.

4.19 Inclined Capital Letters and Numerals Fig. 4.26

The order and direction of the strokes and the proportions of the inclined capital letters and numerals are the same as those for the vertical characters. The methods of drawing guide lines for inclined capital letters are given in §4.15, and for numerals in §4.20. Inclined letters are also classified as straight-line or curved-line letters, most of the curves being elliptical in shape.

4.20 Guide Lines for Whole Numbers and Fractions

Complete guide lines should be drawn for whole numbers and fractions, especially by beginners. This

Fig. 4.26   Inclined Capital Letters and Numerals.

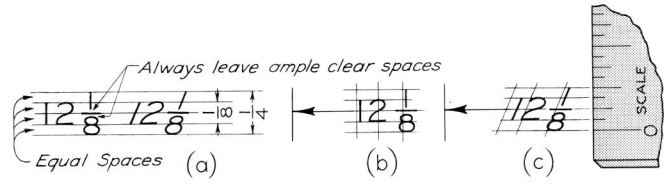

Fig. 4.27   Guide Lines for Dimension Figures.

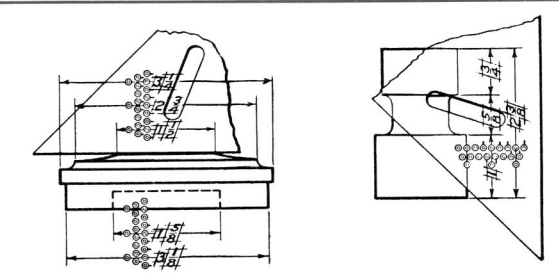

Fig. 4.28   Use of Braddock-Rowe Triangle.

means that both horizontal and vertical guide lines, or horizontal and inclined guide lines, should be drawn.

Draw five equally spaced guide lines for whole numbers and fractions, Fig. 4.27. Thus, fractions are twice the height of the corresponding whole numbers. Make the numerator and the denominator each about three-fourths as high as the whole number to allow ample clear space between them and the fraction bar. For dimensioning, the most commonly used height for whole numbers is $\frac{1}{8}''$ (3.2 mm), and for fractions $\frac{1}{4}''$ (6.4 mm), as shown.

If the Braddock-Rowe Triangle is used, the column of holes at the left produces five guide lines $\frac{1}{16}''$ (1.6 mm) apart, Fig. 4.28.

If the Ames Lettering Guide, Fig. 4.24, is used with the No. 4 setting of the disk, the same five guide lines, $\frac{1}{16}''$ (1.6 mm) apart, may be drawn from the central column of holes.

Some of the most common errors in lettering fractions are illustrated in Fig. 4.29. Never let numerals touch the fraction bar, (a). Center the denominator under the numerator, (b). Never use an inclined fraction bar, (c), except when lettering in a narrow space, as in a parts list. Make the fraction bar slightly longer than the widest part of the fraction, (d).

4.21 Guide Lines for Lowercase Letters

Fig. 4.30

Lowercase letters have four horizontal guide lines, called the cap line, waist line, base line, and drop line. Strokes of letters that extend up to the cap line are called ascenders, and those that extend down to the drop line, descenders. Since only five letters have descenders, the drop line is little needed and is usually omitted. In spacing horizontal guide lines, space a may vary from three-fifths to two-thirds of space b. Spaces c are equal, as shown.

If it is desired to set off guide lines for letters $\frac{3}{16}''$ (4.8 mm) high with the scale (using two-thirds ratio), it is only necessary to set off equal spaces each $\frac{1}{16}''$ (1.6 mm), Fig. 4.31 (a). The lower portion of the letter thus would be $\frac{1}{8}''$ (3.2 mm), and the space between lines of letters would also be $\frac{1}{8}''$ (3.2 mm). If the scale is placed at an angle, the spaces will diminish but remain equal, (b). Thus, this method may be easily used for various heights of lettering.

The Braddock-Rowe Triangle, Fig. 4.23, and the Ames Lettering Guide, Fig. 4.24, produce guide

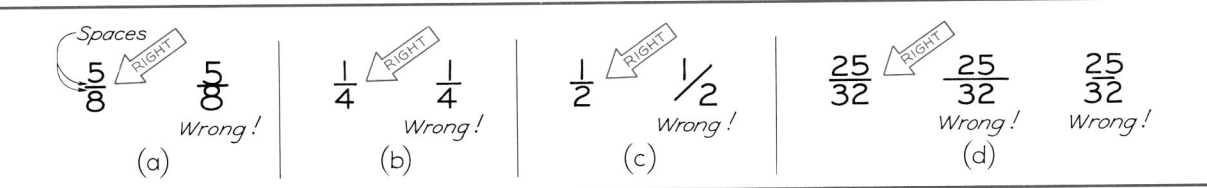

Fig. 4.29   Common Errors.

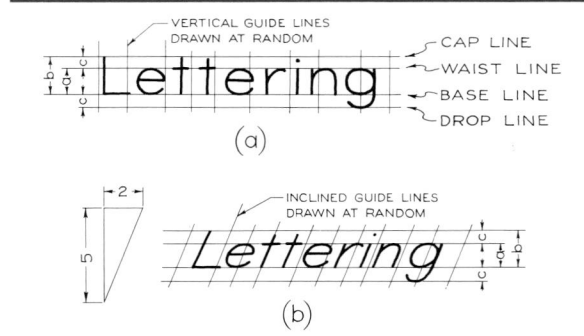

(a)

(b)

Fig. 4.30   Guide Lines for Lowercase Letters.

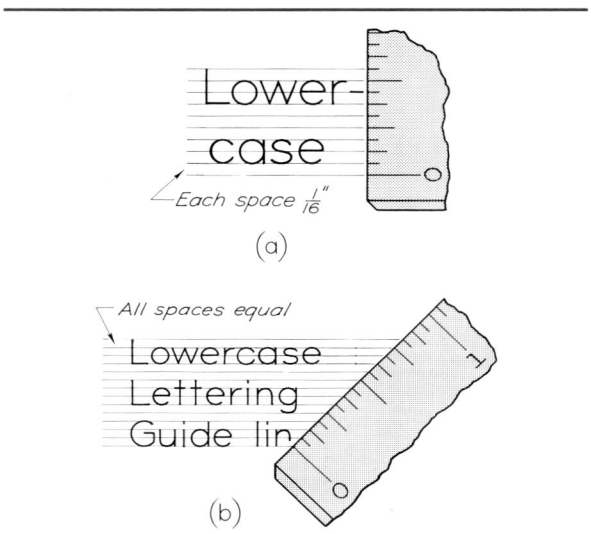

(a)

(b)

Fig. 4.31   Spacing with the Scale.

lines for lowercase letters as described here and are highly recommended.

4.22 Vertical Lowercase Letters Fig. 4.32
Vertical lowercase letters are used largely on map drawings and very seldom on machine drawings. The shapes are based on a repetition of the circle or circular arc and the straight line, with some variations. The lower part of the letter is usually two-thirds the height of the capital letter.

4.23 Inclined Lowercase Letters Fig. 4.33
The order and direction of the strokes and the proportions of inclined lowercase letters are the same as those of vertical lowercase letters. The slope of the letters is the same as for inclined capitals, or 68.2° with horizontal. The slope may be determined by drawing a "slope triangle" of 2 in 5, as shown in Fig. 4.30 (b), or with the aid of the inclined slot in the Braddock-Rowe Triangle, Fig. 4.23, or with the Ames Lettering Guide, Fig. 4.24 (b).

4.24 Spacing of Letters and Words
Fig. 4.34
Uniformity in spacing of letters is a matter of equalizing spaces by eye. *The background areas between letters, not the distances between them, should be approximately equal.* In (a) the actual distances are equal, but the letters do not appear equally spaced. At (b) the distances are intentionally unequal, but the background areas between letters are approximately equal, and the result is an even and pleasing spacing.

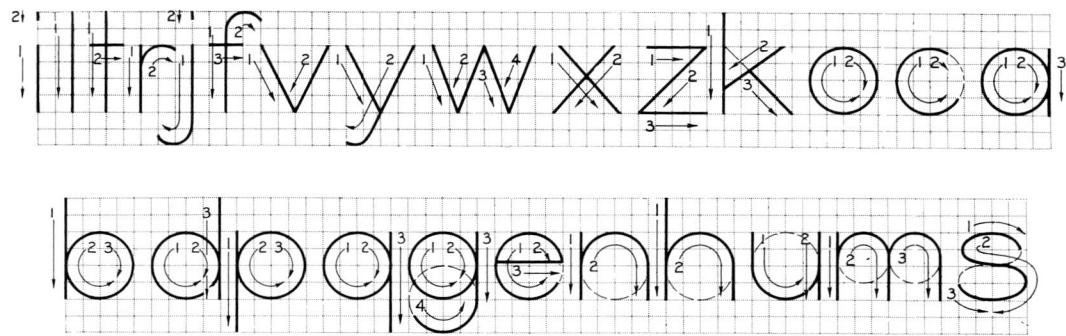

Fig. 4.32   Vertical Lowercase Letters.

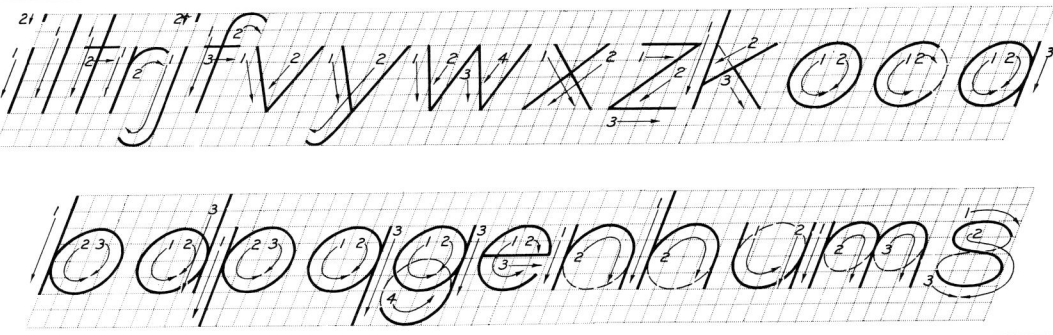

Fig. 4.33   Inclined Lowercase Letters.

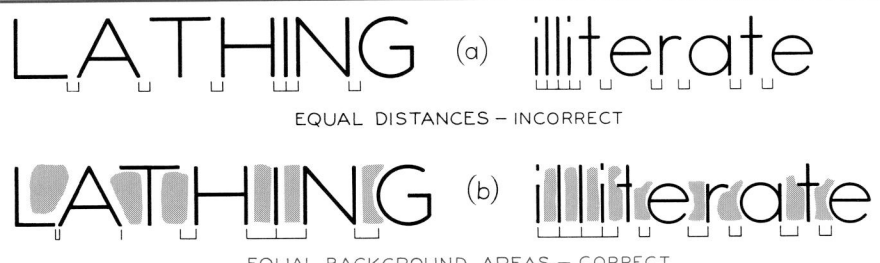

Fig. 4.34   Spacing Between Letters.

Some combinations, much as LT and VA, may even have to be slightly overlapped to secure good spacing. In some cases the width of a letter may be decreased. For example, the lower stroke of the L may be shortened when followed by A.

Space words well apart, but space letters closely within words. Make each word a compact unit well separated from adjacent words. For either upper-case or lowercase lettering, make the spaces between words approximately equal to a capital O, Fig. 4.35. Avoid spacing letters too far apart and words

too close together, as shown at (b). Samples of good spacing are also shown in Fig. 4.17.

When it is necessary to letter to a stop line as in Fig. 4.36 (a), space each letter from *right to left,* as shown in step II, estimating the widths of the letters by eye. Then letter from *left to right,* as shown at III, and finally erase the spacing marks.

When it is necessary to space letters symmetrically about a center line, Fig. 4.36 (b), which is frequently the case in titles, Figs. 4.43–4.45, number the letters as shown, with the space between words

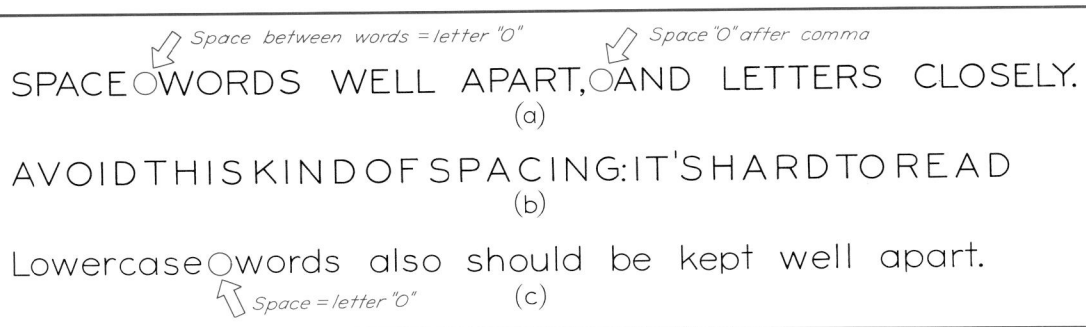

Fig. 4.35   Spacing Words.

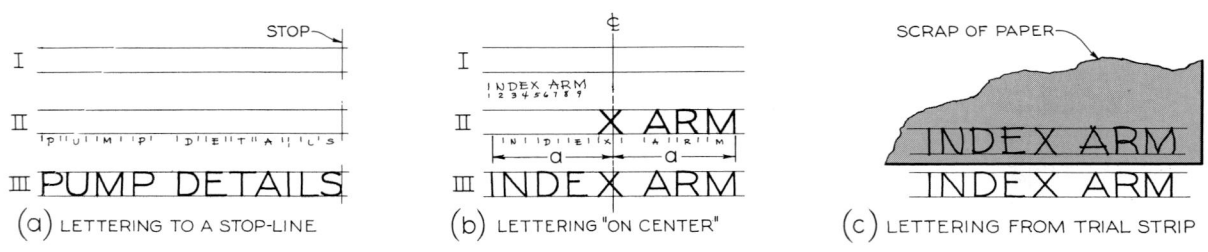

(a) LETTERING TO A STOP-LINE   (b) LETTERING "ON CENTER"   (c) LETTERING FROM TRIAL STRIP

Fig. 4.36   Spacing to a Stop Line and "on Center."

considered as one letter. Then place the middle letter on center, making allowance for narrow letters (Is) or wide letters (Ws) on either side. The X in Fig. 4.36 (b) is placed slightly to the left of center to compensate for the letter I, which has no width. Check with the dividers to make sure that distances *a* are exactly equal.

Another method is to letter roughly a trial line of lettering along the bottom edge of a scrap of paper, place it in position immediately above, as shown at (c), and then letter the line in place. Be sure to use guide lines for the trial lettering.

4.25 Lettering Devices

The Leroy Standard Lettering Instrument, Fig. 4.37, is perhaps the most widely used lettering device. A guide pin follows grooved letters in a template, and the inking point moves on the paper. By adjusting the arm on the scriber, the letters may be made vertical or inclined. A number of templates and pen sizes for letters and symbols are available, including templates for a wide variety of "builtup" letters similar to those made by the Varigraph and Letterguide, described shortly. Inside each pen is a cleaning pin used to keep the small tube open. These pins are easily broken, especially the small ones, when the pen is not promptly cleaned. To clean a pen, draw it across a blotter until all ink has been absorbed; then insert the pin and remove it and wipe it with a cloth. Repeat this until the pin remains clean. If the ink has dried, the pens may be cleaned with Leroy pen-cleaning fluid, available at dealers. Leroy lettering sets, Fig. 4.38, are available as standard or metric sets. Both have the same style and features except for pen size designations. Leroy pens are also available in various sizes in standard or reservoir types.

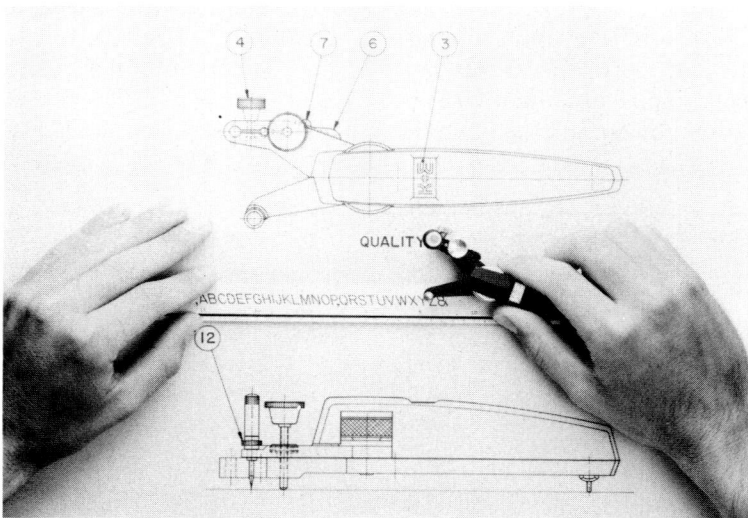

Fig. 4.37   Leroy Standard Lettering Instrument. *Courtesy of Keuffel & Esser Co.*

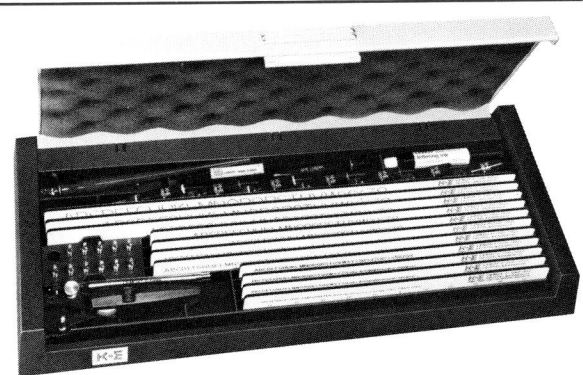

Fig. 4.38 Leroy Standard Lettering Set. *Courtesy of Keuffel & Esser Co.*

Fig. 4.39 Wrico Lettering Guide. *Courtesy of Wood-Regan Instrument Co., Inc.*

The Wrico Lettering Guide, Fig. 4.39, consists of a scriber and templates similar to the Leroy system. Wrico letters more closely resemble American National Standard letters than do those of other sets.

The Varigraph is a more elaborate device for making a wide variety of either single-stroke letters or "builtup" letters. As shown in Fig. 4.40, a guide pin is moved along the grooves in a template, and the pen forms the letters.

The Letterguide scriber, Fig. 4.41, is a much simpler instrument, which also makes a large variety of styles and sizes of letters when used with the various templates available. It also operates with a guide pin moving in the grooved letters of the template, while the pen, which is mounted on an adjustable arm, makes the letters in outline.

The Kroy Lettering Machine, Fig. 4.42, is a unique lettering machine that creates type on tape which can then be applied on drawings, artwork, posters, and the like. Lettering is produced by dialing the type disk to the desired character and pressing the print button. Spacing is automatic and adjustable. The machine is available in electric or manual models that use either 61- or 80-character type disks. Several type styles and sizes are available.

Various forms of press-on lettering and special lettering devices (typewriters, etc.) are available. In addition, the various computer-aided drafting sys-

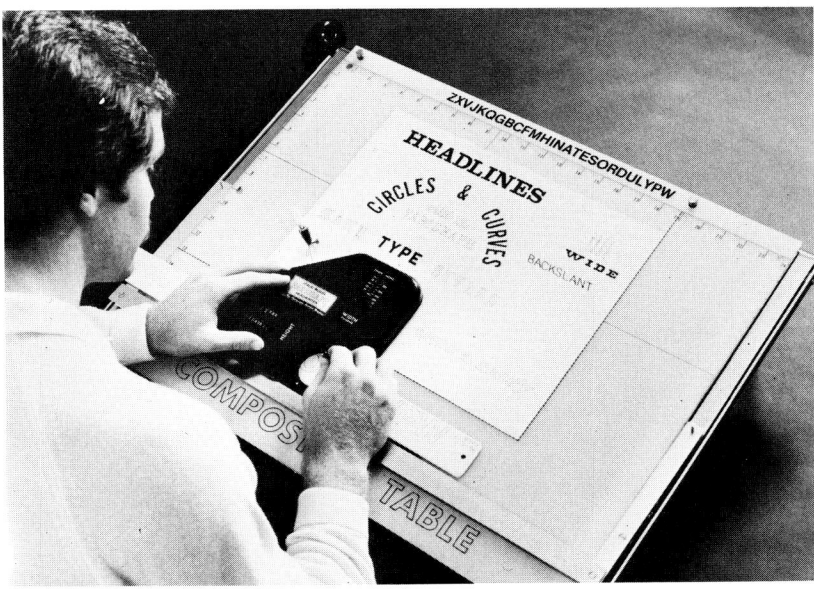

Fig. 4.40 The Varigraph Machine and Table. *Courtesy of Varigraph, Inc.*

Fig. 4.41   Letterguide. *Courtesy of Letterguide Co.*

tems have the capability to produce letters of different heights and styles and to make changes as required. In whatever way the lettering is applied to the drawing and whatever style of lettering is used, the lettering must meet the requirements for legibility and microfilm reproduction.

4.26 Titles

The composition of titles on machine drawings is relatively simple. In most cases, the title and related information are lettered in "title boxes" or "title strips," which are printed directly on the drawing paper, tracing paper, tracing cloth or polyester film. See, for example, Figs. 16.24–16.26. The main drawing title is usually centered in a rectangular space. This may be done by the method shown in Fig. 4.36 (b); or, if the lettering is being done on tracing paper or cloth, the title may be lettered first on scrap paper and then placed underneath the tracing, as shown in Fig. 4.43, and then lettered directly over.

If a title box is not used, the title of a machine drawing may be lettered in the lower right corner of the sheet as a "balanced title," Fig. 4.44. A balanced title is simply one that is arranged symmetrically about an imaginary center line. These titles take such forms as the rectangle, the oval, the inverted pyramid, or any other simple symmetrical form.

On display drawings, or on highly finished maps or architectural drawings, titles may be composed of filled-in letters, usually Gothic or Roman, Fig. 4.45.

In any kind of title, the most important words are given most prominence by making the lettering larger, heavier, or both. Other data, such as scale and date, may be displayed smaller.

4.27 Lettering on Maps

Modern Roman letters are generally used on maps, as follows.

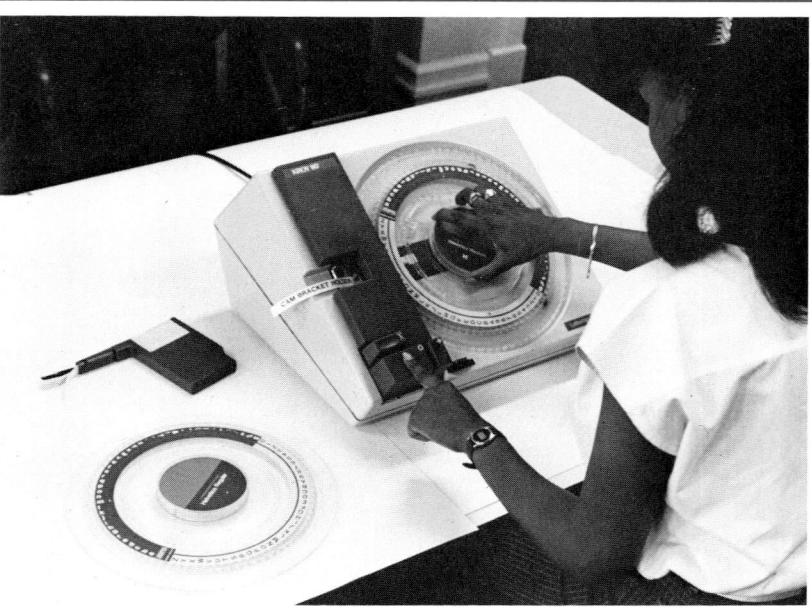

Fig. 4.42   Kroy Lettering Machine.

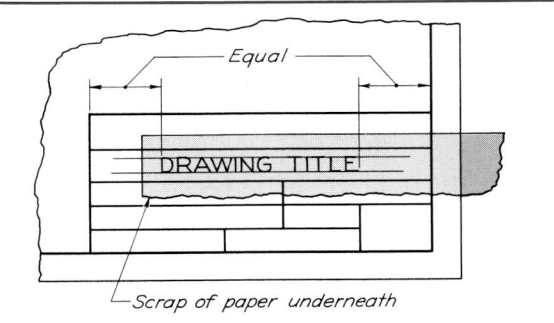

Fig. 4.43   Centering Title in Title Box.

TOOL GRINDING MACHINE
TOOL REST SLIDE
SCALE : FULL SIZE
AMERICAN MACHINE COMPANY
NEW YORK CITY

DRAWN BY ____   CHECKED BY ____

Fig. 4.44   Balanced Machine-Drawing Title.

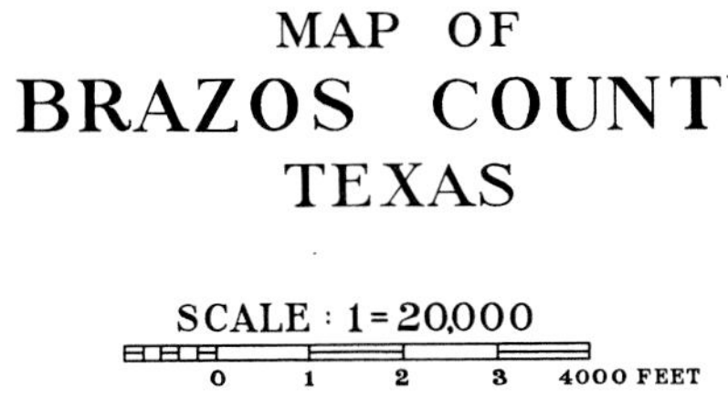

MAP OF
BRAZOS COUNTY
TEXAS

SCALE : 1=20,000

0   1   2   3   4000 FEET

Fig. 4.45   Balanced Map Title.

1. *Vertical capitals.* Names of states, countries, townships, capital cities, large cities, and titles of maps.

2. *Vertical lowercase* (first letter of each word a capital). Names of small towns, villages, post offices, etc.

3. *Inclined capitals.* Names of oceans, bays, gulfs, sounds, large lakes, and rivers.

4. *Inclined lowercase* or "stump" letters (first letter of each word a capital). Names of rivers, creeks, small lakes, ponds, marshes, brooks, and springs.

Gothic letters are used as follows.

1. *Vertical capitals.* Names of prominent land features such as mountains, plateaus, and canyons.

2. *Vertical lowercase.* Names of small land features such as small valleys, islands, and ridges.

3. *Inclined capitals.* Names of railroads, tunnels, highways, bridges, and other public structures.

4.28 Computer Graphics

Lettering is a standard feature available in computer graphics programs. Using CAD software, the drafter or designer can add titles, notes, and dimensioning information to a computer-generated drawing. Several fonts, Figs. 4.46 and 4.47, and a variety of sizes may be selected. When modifications are required, it is easy for the CAD operator to make appropriate lettering changes on the drawing.

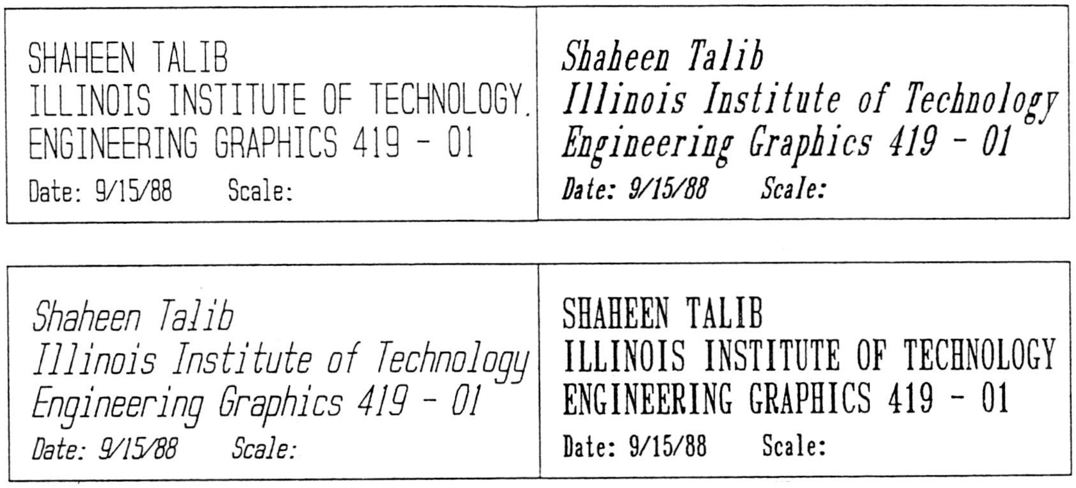

SHAHEEN TALIB
ILLINOIS INSTITUTE OF TECHNOLOGY
ENGINEERING GRAPHICS 419 - 01
Date: 9/15/88   Scale:

Shaheen Talib
Illinois Institute of Technology
Engineering Graphics 419 - 01
Date: 9/15/88   Scale:

Shaheen Talib
Illinois Institute of Technology
Engineering Graphics 419 - 01
Date: 9/15/88   Scale:

SHAHEEN TALIB
ILLINOIS INSTITUTE OF TECHNOLOGY
ENGINEERING GRAPHICS 419 - 01
Date: 9/15/88   Scale:

Fig. 4.46   CAD Lettering Examples. *Courtesy of Department of Engineering Graphics, Illinois Institute of Technology.*

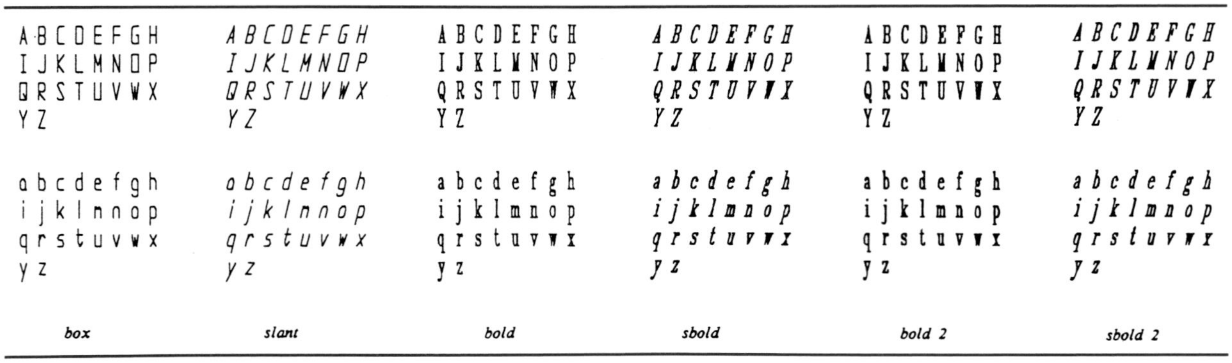

A·BCDEFGH IJKLMNOP QRSTUVWX YZ	ABCDEFGH IJKLMNOP QRSTUVWX YZ	ABCDEFGH IJKLMNOP QRSTUVWX YZ	ABCDEFGH IJKLMNOP QRSTUVWX YZ	ABCDEFGH IJKLMNOP QRSTUVWX YZ	ABCDEFGH IJKLMNOP QRSTUVWX YZ
abcdefgh ijklnnop qrstuvwx yz	abcdefgh ijklnnop qrstuvwx yz	abcdefgh ijklmnop qrstuvwx yz	abcdefgh ijklmnop qrstuvwx yz	abcdefgh ijklmnop qrstuvwx yz	abcdefgh ijklmnop qrstuvwx yz
box	*slant*	*bold*	*sbold*	*bold 2*	*sbold 2*

Fig. 4.47 Typical CAD Type Fonts. *Courtesy of CADKEY.*

Lettering Exercises

Layouts for lettering practice are given in Figs. 4.48–4.51. Draw complete horizontal and vertical or inclined guide lines *very lightly.* Draw the vertical or inclined guide lines through the full height of the lettered area of the sheet. For practice in ink lettering, the last two lines and the title strip on each sheet may be lettered in ink, if assigned by the instructor. Omit all dimensions.

Additional problems in convenient form for solution are presented in the worksheets at the back of this book. Refer to Drawings 4-1 to 4-6 and accompanying instructions.

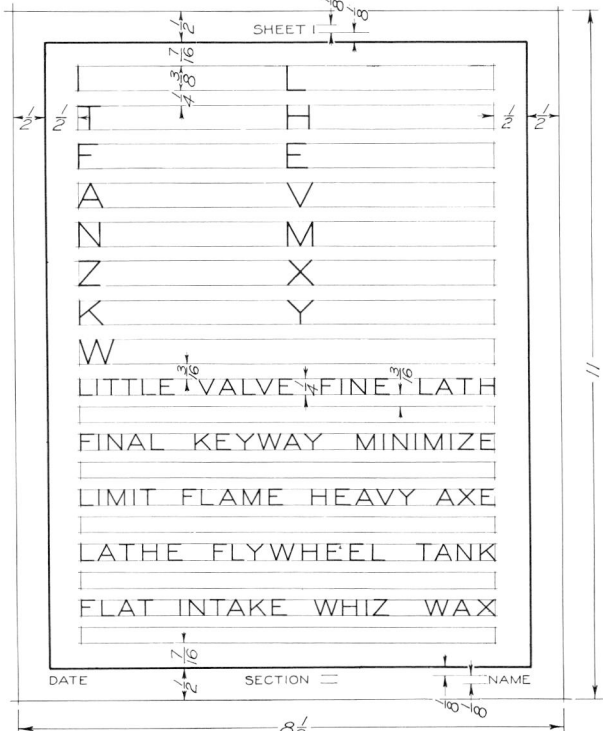

Fig. 4.48 Lay out sheet, add vertical or inclined guide lines, and fill in vertical or inclined capital letters as assigned. For decimal-inch and millimeter equivalents of given dimensions, see table inside of front cover.

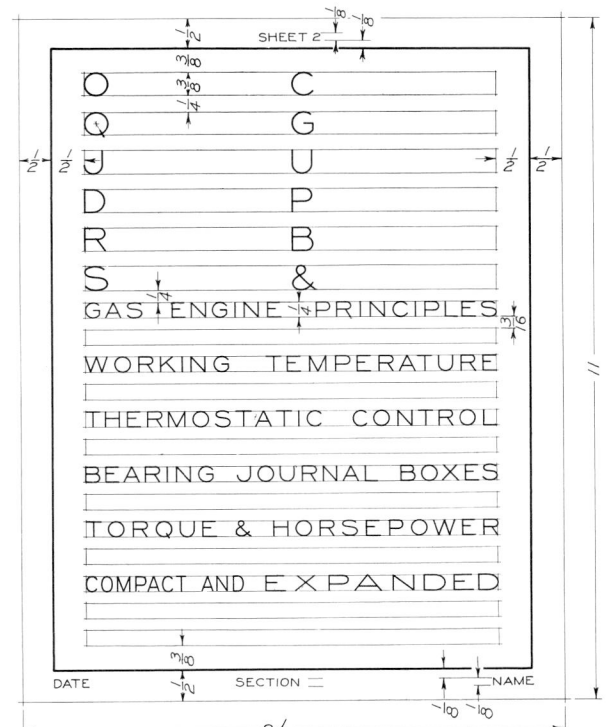

Fig. 4.49 Lay out sheet, add vertical or inclined guide lines, and fill in vertical or inclined capital letters as assigned. For decimal-inch and millimeter equivalents of given dimensions, see table inside of front cover.

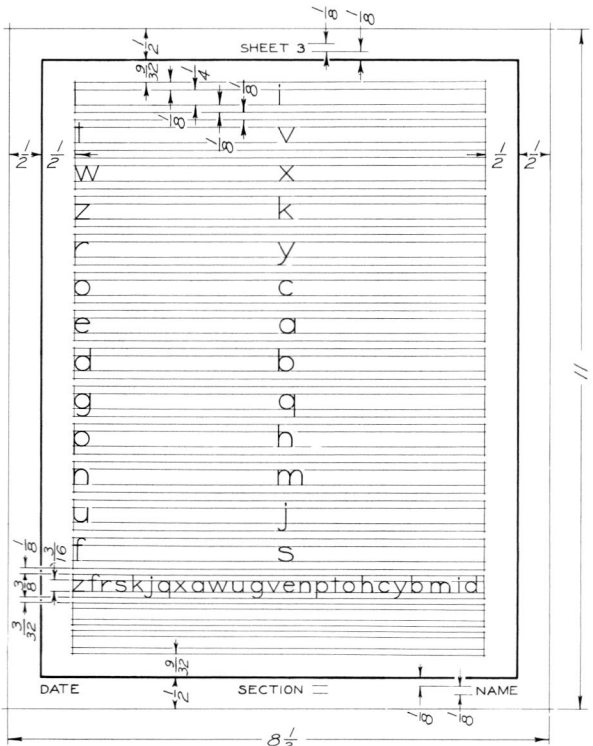

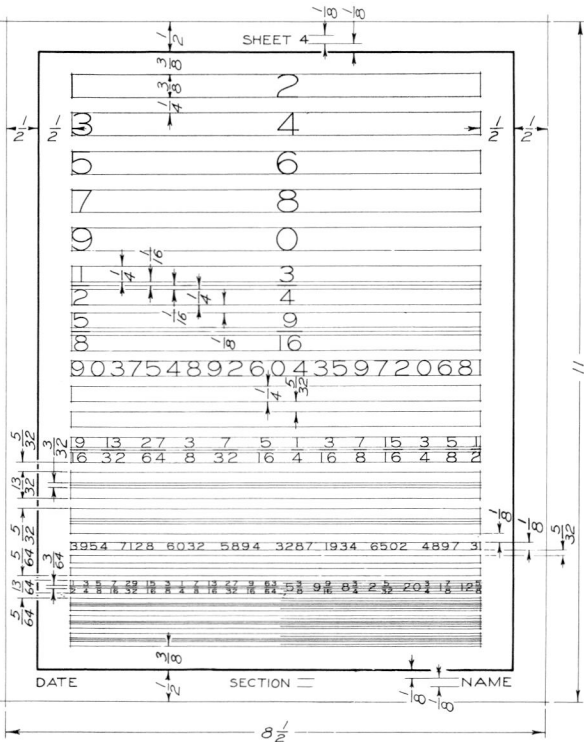

Fig. 4.50 Lay out sheet, add vertical or inclined guide lines, and fill in vertical or inclined lowercase letters as assigned. For decimal-inch and millimeter equivalents of given dimensions, see table inside of front cover.

Fig. 4.51 Lay out sheet, add vertical or inclined guide lines, and fill in vertical or inclined numerals as assigned. For decimal-inch and millimeter equivalents of given dimensions, see table inside of front cover.

Geometric Constructions

Many of the constructions used in technical design drawings are based upon plane geometry, and every drafter, technician, or engineer should be sufficiently familiar with them to be able to apply them to the solutions of problems. Pure geometry problems may be solved only with the compass and a straightedge, and in some cases these methods may be used to advantage in technical drawing. However, the drafter or designer has available the T-square,* triangles, dividers, and other equipment, such as drafting machines, that in many cases can yield accurate results more quickly by what we may term "preferred methods." Therefore, many of the solutions in this chapter are practical adaptations of the principles of pure geometry.

This chapter is designed to present definitions of terms and geometric constructions of importance in technical drawing, suggest simplified methods of construction, point out practical applications, and afford opportunity for practice in accurate instrumental drawing. The problems at the end of this chapter may be regarded as a continuation of those at the end of Chapter 2.

In drawing these constructions, accuracy is most important. Use a sharp medium-hard lead (H to 3H) in your pencil and compasses. Draw construction lines extremely light—so light that they can hardly be seen when your drawing is held at arm's length. Draw all final and required lines medium to thin but dark.

*Hereafter, reference to the T-square could also refer to the parallel straightedge or drafting machine.

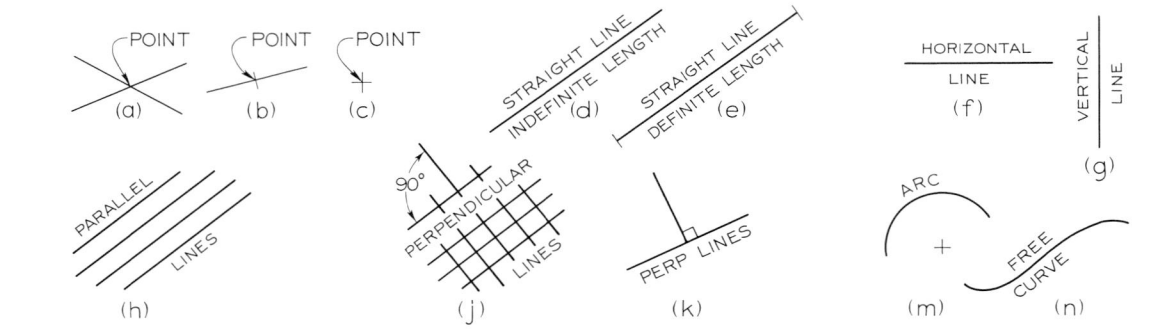

Fig. 5.1   Points and Lines.

5.1 Points and Lines Fig. 5.1

A *point* represents a location in space or on a drawing, and has no width, height, or depth. A point is represented by the intersection of two lines, (a), by a short crossbar on a line, (b), or by a small cross, (c). Never represent a point by a simple dot on the paper.

A line is defined by Euclid as "that which has length without breadth." A *straight line* is the shortest distance between two points and is commonly referred to simply as a "line." If the line is indefinite in extent, the length is a matter of convenience, and the endpoints are not fixed, (d). If the endpoints of the line are significant, they must be marked by means of small mechanically drawn crossbars, (e). Other common terms are illustrated from (f) to (h). Either straight lines or curved lines are parallel if the shortest distance between them remains constant. The common symbol for parallel lines is ∥, and for perpendicular lines it is ⊥ (singular) or ⊥s (plural). Two perpendicular lines may be marked with a "box" to indicate perpendicularity, as shown at (k). Such symbols may be used on sketches, but not in production drawings.

5.2 Angles Fig. 5.2

An angle is formed by two intersecting lines. A common symbol for angle is ∠ (singular) or ∠s (plural). There are 360 degrees (360°) in a full circle, as shown at (a). A degree is divided into 60 minutes (60′), and a minute is divided into 60 seconds (60″). Thus, 37° 26′ 10″ is read: 37 degrees, 26 minutes, and 10 seconds. When minutes alone are indicated, the number of minutes should be preceded by 0°, as 0° 20′.

The different kinds of angles are illustrated in (b) to (e). Two angles are *complementary*, (f), if they total 90°, and are *supplementary*, (g), if they total 180°. Most angles used in technical drawing can be drawn easily with the T-square or straightedge and triangles, Fig. 2.23. To draw odd angles, use the protractor, Fig. 2.24. For considerable accuracy, use a *vernier protractor*, or the tangent, sine, or chord methods, §5.20.

5.3 Triangles Fig. 5.3

A triangle is a plane figure bounded by three straight sides, and the sum of the interior angles is always 180°. A right triangle, (d), has one 90° angle, and the square of the hypotenuse is equal to the

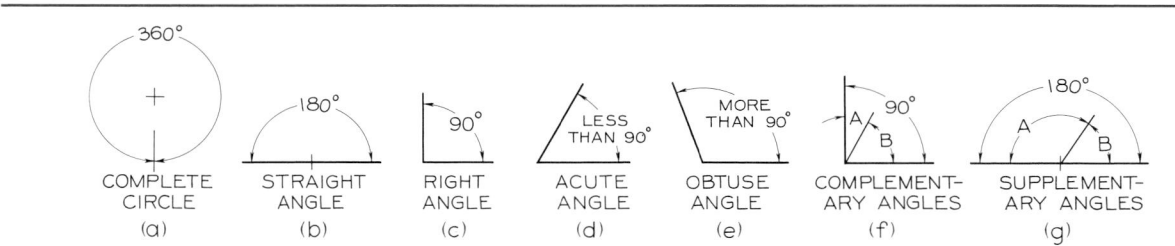

Fig. 5.2   Angles.

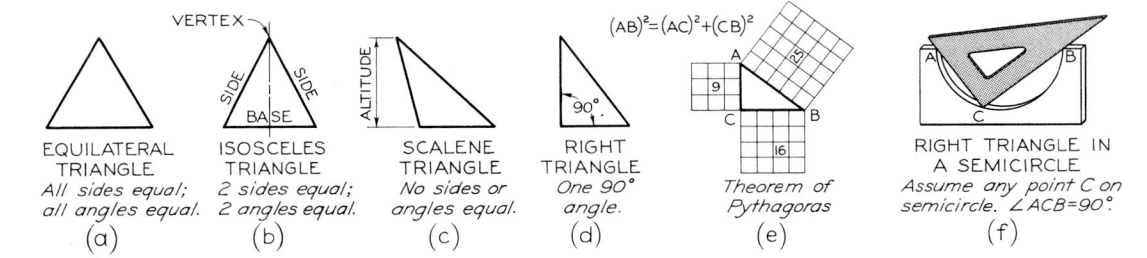

Fig. 5.3 Triangles.

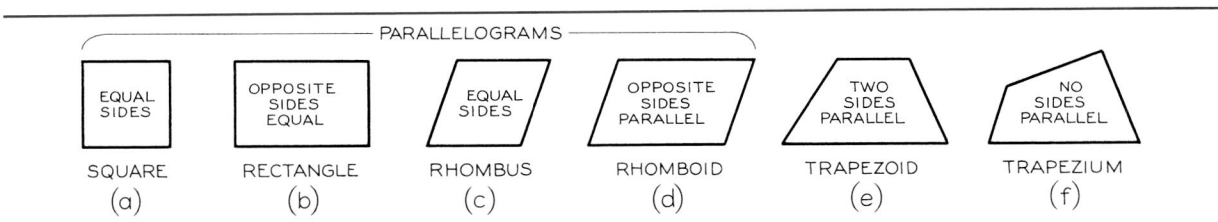

Fig. 5.4 Quadrilaterals.

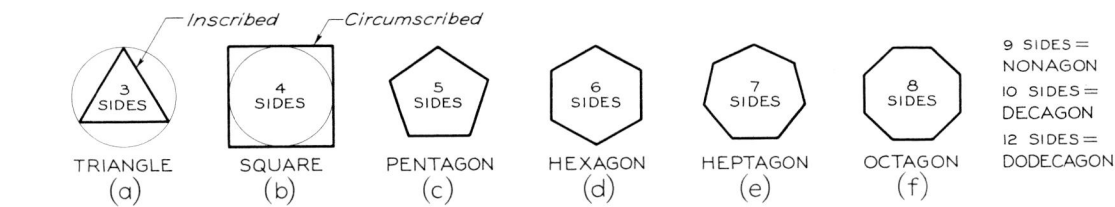

Fig. 5.5 Regular Polygons.

sum of the squares of the two sides, (e). As shown
at (f), any triangle inscribed in a semicircle is a
right triangle if the hypotenuse coincides with the
diameter.

5.4 Quadrilaterals Fig. 5.4
A quadrilateral is a plane figure bounded by four
straight sides. If the opposite sides are parallel, the
quadrilateral is also a parallelogram.

5.5 Polygons Fig. 5.5
A polygon is any plane figure bounded by straight
lines. If the polygon has equal angles and equal
sides, it can be inscribed in or circumscribed around
a circle and is called a *regular polygon.*

5.6 Circles and Arcs Fig. 5.6
A circle, (a), is a closed curve all points of which are
the same distance from a point called the center.
Circumference refers to the circle or to the distance

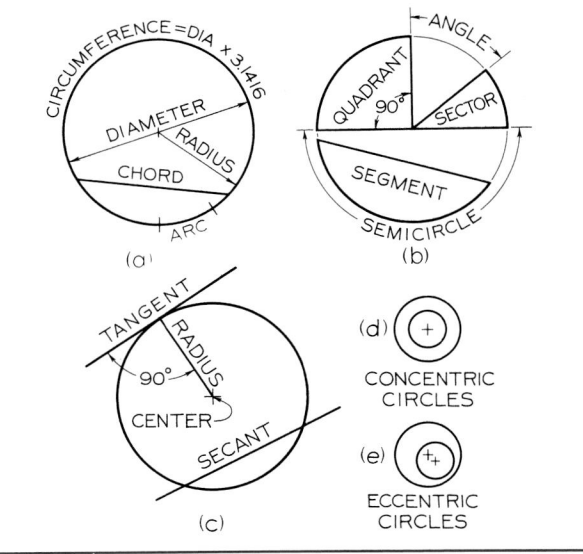

Fig. 5.6 The Circle.

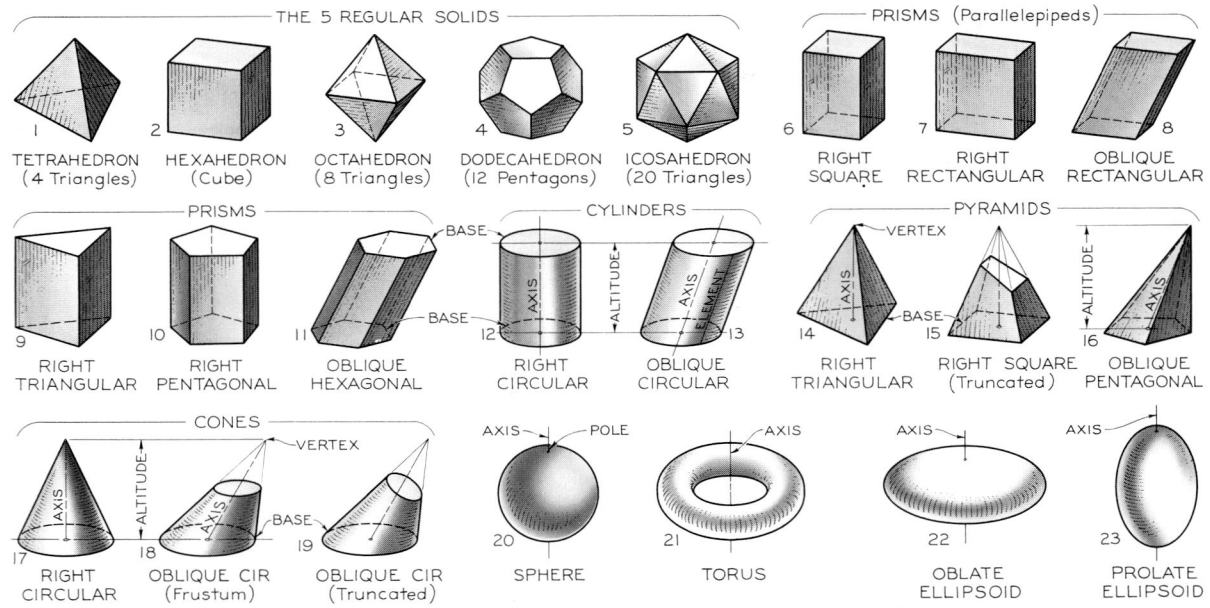

Fig. 5.7 Solids.

around the circle. This distance equals the diameter multiplied by π (called pi) or 3.1416. Other definitions are illustrated in the figure.

5.7 Solids Fig. 5.7

Solids bounded by plane surfaces are *polyhedra*. The surfaces are called faces, and if these are equal regular polygons, the solids are regular polyhedra.

A *prism* has two bases, which are parallel equal polygons, and three or more lateral faces, which are parallelograms. A triangular prism has a triangular base; a rectangular prism has rectangular bases; and so on. If the bases are parallelograms, the prism is a parallelepiped. A right prism has faces and lateral edges perpendicular to the bases; an oblique prism has faces and lateral edges oblique to the bases. If one end is cut off to form an end not parallel to the bases, the prism is said to be truncated.

A *pyramid* has a polygon for a base and triangular lateral faces intersecting at a common point called the vertex. The center line from the center of the base to the vertex is the axis. If the axis is perpendicular to the base, the pyramid is a right pyramid; otherwise it is an oblique pyramid. A triangular pyramid has a triangular base; a square pyramid has a square base, and so on. If a portion near the vertex has been cut off, the pyramid is truncated, or referred to as a frustum.

A *cylinder* is generated by a straight line, called the generatrix, moving in contact with a curved line

and always remaining parallel to its previous position or to the axis. Each position of the generatrix is called an element of the cylinder.

A *cone* is generated by a straight line moving in contact with a curved line and passing through a fixed point, the vertex of the cone. Each position of the generatrix is an element of the cone.

A *sphere* is generated by a circle revolving about one of its diameters. This diameter becomes the axis of the sphere, and the ends of the axis are poles of the sphere.

A *torus* is generated by a circle (or other curve) revolving about an axis that is eccentric to the curve.

5.8 To Bisect a Line or a Circular Arc
Fig. 5.8

Given line or arc AB, as shown at (a), to be bisected.

I. From A and B draw equal arcs with radius greater than half AB.

II. and III. Join intersections D and E with a straight line to locate center C.

5.9 To Bisect a Line with Triangle and T-square Fig. 5.9

From endpoints A and B, draw construction lines at 30°, 45°, or 60° with the given line; then through their intersection, C, draw a line perpendicular to the given line to locate the center D, as shown.

To divide a line with the dividers, see §2.40.

To Transfer an Angle

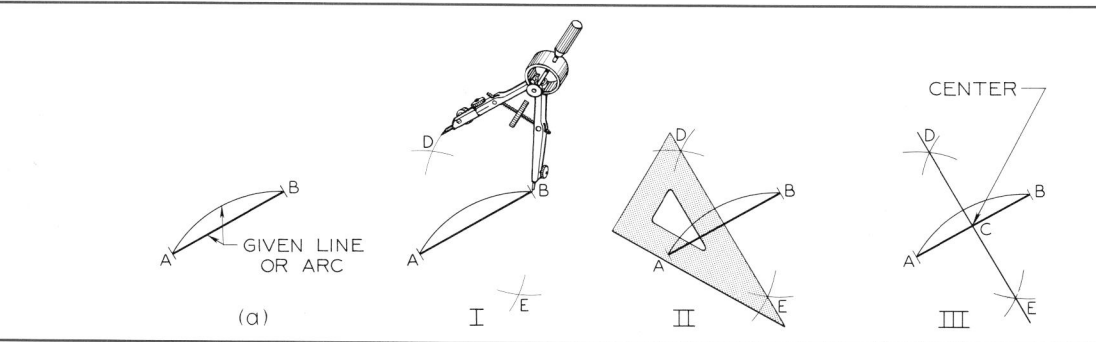

Fig. 5.8 Bisecting a Line or a Circular Arc (§5.8).

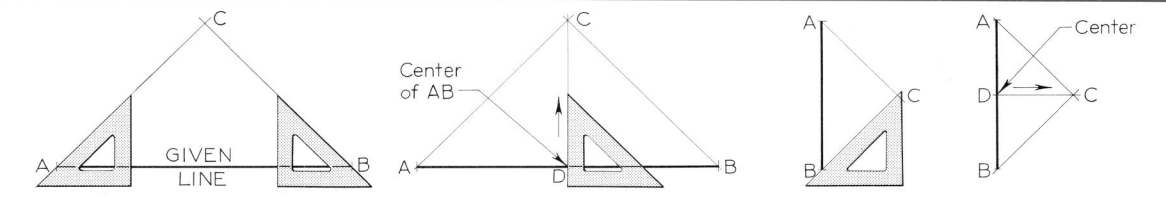

Fig. 5.9 Bisecting a Line with Triangle and T-square (§5.9).

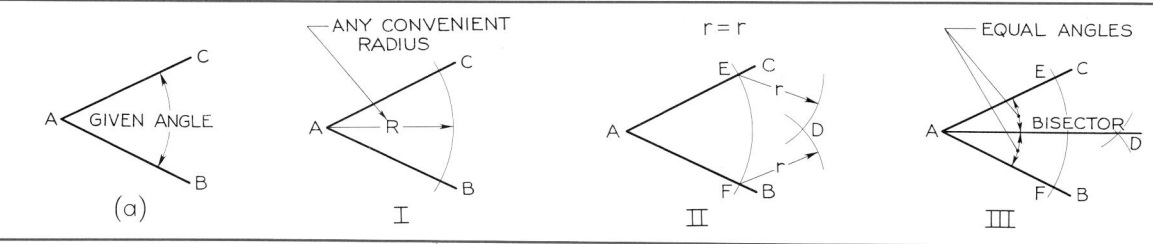

Fig. 5.10 Bisecting an Angle (§5.10).

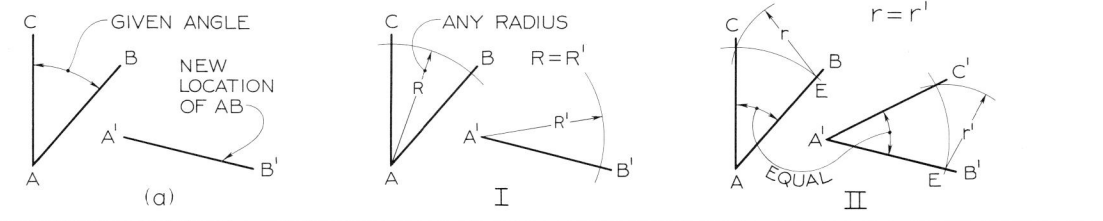

Fig. 5.11 Transferring an Angle (§5.11).

5.10 To Bisect an Angle Fig. 5.10

Given angle BAC, as shown at (a), to be bisected.

  I.   Strike large arc R.

  II.   Strike equal arcs r with radius slightly larger than half BC, to intersect at D.

III.   Draw line AD, which bisects angle.

5.11 To Transfer an Angle Fig. 5.11

Given angle BAC, as shown at (a), to be transferred to the new position at A′B′.

  I.   Use any convenient radius R, and strike arcs from centers A and A′.

  II.   Strike equal arcs r, and draw side A′C′.

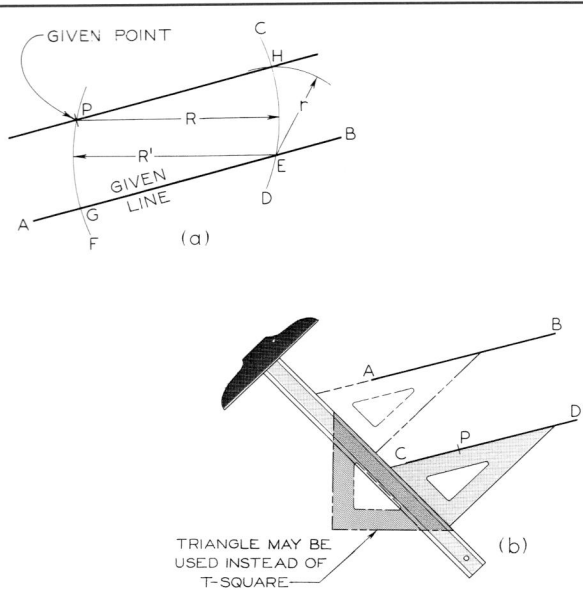

(a)

Fig. 5.12 Drawing a Line Through a Point Parallel to a Line (§5.12).

5.12 To Draw a Line Through a Point and Parallel to a Line

Fig. 5.12 (a) With given point P as center, and any convenient radius R, strike arc CD to intersect the given line AB at E. With E as center and the same radius, strike arc R′ to intersect the given line at G. With PG as radius, and E as center, strike arc r to locate point H. The line PH is the required line.

Fig. 5.12 (b) *Preferred Method* Move the triangle and T-square as a unit until the triangle lines up with given line AB; then slide the triangle until its

edge passes through the given point P. Draw CD, the required parallel line. See also §2.21.

5.13 To Draw a Line Parallel to a Line and at a Given Distance

Let AB be the line and CD the given distance.

Fig. 5.13 (a) With points E and F near A and B, respectively, as centers, and CD as radius, draw two arcs. The line GH, tangent to the arcs, is the required line.

Fig. 5.13 (b) *Preferred Method* With any point E of the line as center and CD as radius, strike an arc JK. Move the triangle and T-square as a unit until the triangle lines up with the given line AB; then slide the triangle until its edge is tangent to the arc JK, and draw the required line GH.

Fig. 5.13 (c) With centers selected at random on the curved line AB, and with CD as radius, draw a series of arcs; then draw the required line tangent to these arcs as explained in §2.54.

5.14 To Divide a Line into Equal Parts

Fig. 5.14

I.   Draw a light construction line at any convenient angle from one end of line.

II. With dividers or scale, set off from intersection of lines as many equal divisions as needed, in this case, three.

III. Connect last division point to other end of line, using triangle and T-square, as shown.

IV. Slide triangle along T-square and draw parallel lines through other division points, as shown.

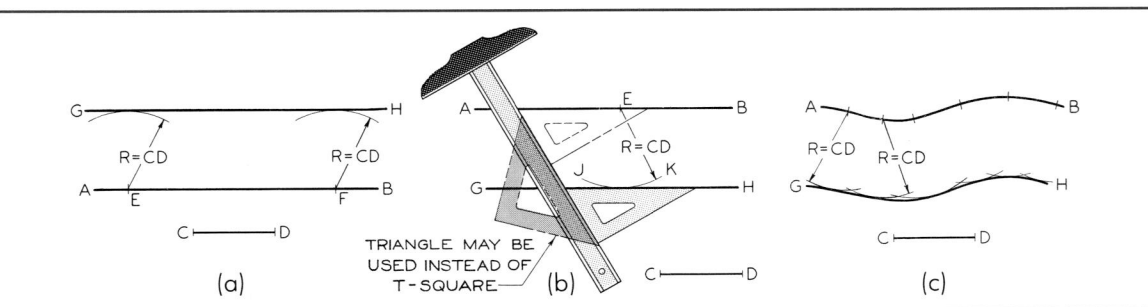

Fig. 5.13 Drawing a Line Parallel to a Line at a Given Distance (§5.13).

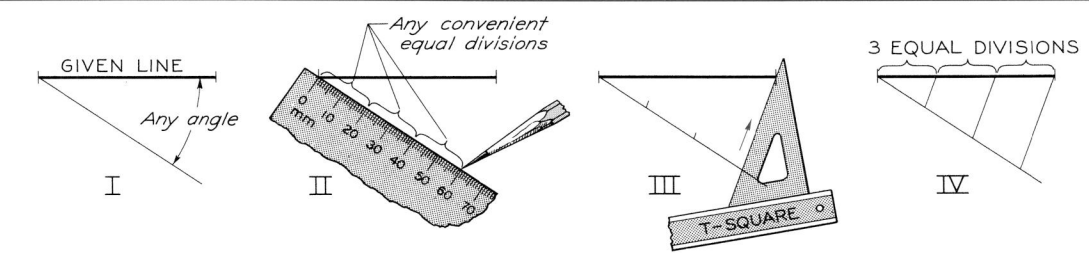

Fig. 5.14   Dividing a Line into Equal Parts (§5.14).

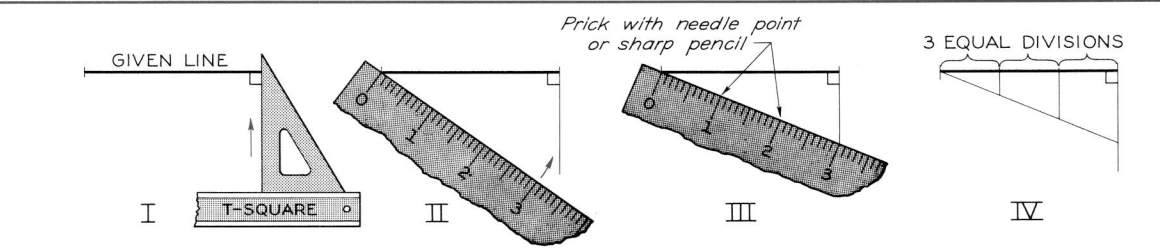

Fig. 5.15   Dividing a Line into Equal Parts (§5.15).

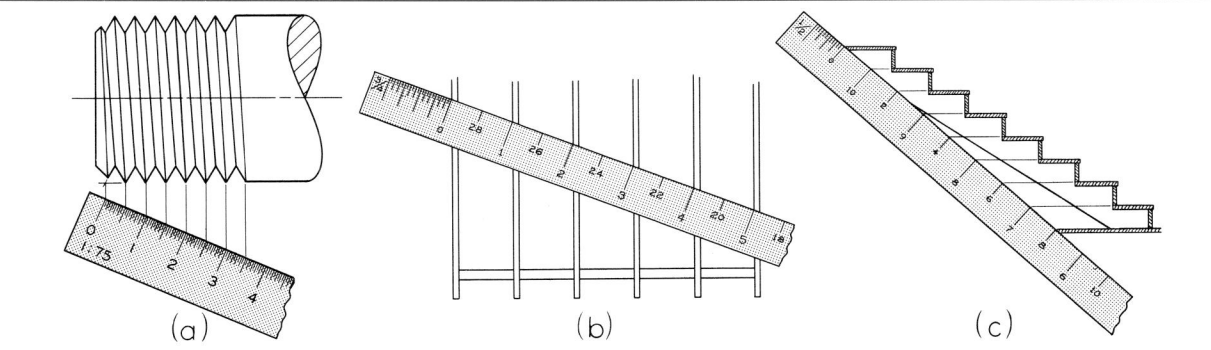

Fig. 5.16   Practical Applications of Dividing a Line into Equal Parts (§5.15).

5.15 To Divide a Line into Equal Parts
Fig. 5.15

I.   Draw vertical construction line at one end of given line.

II.   Set zero of scale at other end of line.

III.   Swing scale up until third unit falls on vertical line, and make tiny dots at each point, or prick points with dividers.

IV.   Draw vertical construction lines through each point.

Some practical applications of this method are shown in Fig. 5.16.

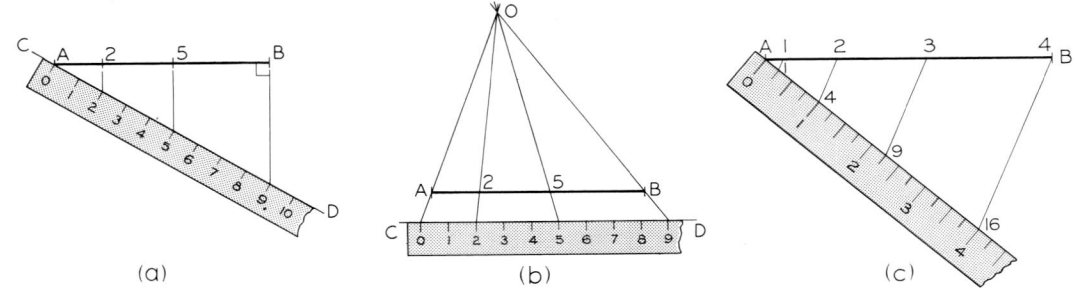

Fig. 5.17   Dividing a Line into Proportional Parts (§5.16).

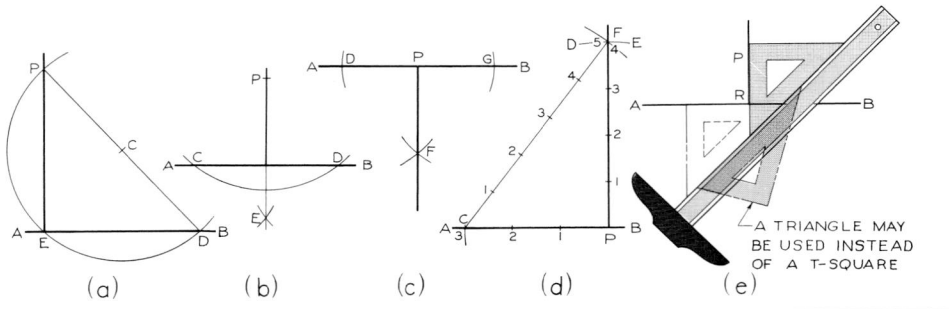

Fig. 5.18   Drawing a Line Through a Point and Perpendicular to a Line (§5.17).

5.16 **To Divide a Line into Proportional Parts** Fig. 5.17

Let it be required to divide the line **AB** into three parts proportional to 2, 3, and 4.

Fig. 5.17 (a)   *Preferred Method*   Draw a vertical line from point **B**. Select a scale of convenient size for a total of nine units and set the zero of the scale at **A**. Swing the scale up until the ninth unit falls on the vertical line. Along the scale, set off points for 2, 3, and 4 units, as shown. Draw vertical lines through these points.

Fig. 5.17 (b)   Draw a line **CD** parallel to **AB** and at any convenient distance. On this line, set off 2, 3, and 4 units, as shown. Draw lines through the ends of the two lines to intersect at the point **O**. Draw lines through **O** and the points 2 and 5 to divide **AB** into the required proportional parts.

     Constructions of this type are useful in the preparation of graphs (Chapter 23).

Fig. 5.17 (c)   Given **AB**, to divide into proportional parts, in this case proportional to the square of *x*, where $x = 1, 2, 3, \ldots$. Set zero of scale at end of

line and set off divisions 4, 9, 16, ... Join the last division to the other end of the line, and draw parallel lines as shown. This method may be used for any power of *x*.

5.17 **To Draw a Line Through a Point and Perpendicular to a Line** Fig. 5.18

Given the line **AB** and a point **P**.

When the Point Is Not on the Line
Fig. 5.18 (a)

From **P** draw any convenient inclined line, as **PD**. Find center **C** of line **PD**, and draw arc with radius **CP**. The line **EP** is the required perpendicular.

Fig. 5.18 (b)   With **P** as center, strike an arc to intersect **AB** at **C** and **D**. With **C** and **D** as centers, and radius slightly greater than half **CD**, strike arcs to intersect at **E**. The line **PE** is the required perpendicular.

When the Point Is on the Line Fig. 5.18 (c)
With **P** as center and any radius, strike arcs to intersect **AB** at **D** and **G**. With **D** and **G** as centers, and radius slightly greater than half **DG**, strike equal

arcs to intersect at F. The line PF is the required perpendicular.

Fig. 5.18 (d)   Select any convenient unit of length, for example, 6 mm or $\frac{1}{4}''$. With P as center, and 3 units as radius, strike an arc to intersect given line at C. With P as center, and 4 units as radius, strike arc DE. With C as center, and 5 units as radius, strike an arc to intersect DE at F. The line PF is the required perpendicular.

This method makes use of the 3–4–5 right triangle and is frequently used in laying off rectangular foundations of large machines, buildings, or other structures. For this purpose a steel tape may be used and distances of 30, 40, and 50 feet measured as the three sides of the right triangle.

Fig. 5.18 (e) *Preferred Method*   Move the triangle and T-square as a unit until the triangle lines up with AB; then slide the triangle until its edge passes through the point P (whether P is on or off the line), and draw the required perpendicular.

5.18 To Draw a Triangle with Sides Given Fig. 5.19
Given the sides A, B, and C, as shown at (a).

I.   Draw one side, as C, in desired position, and strike arc with radius equal to given side A.

II.   Strike arc with radius equal to given side B.

III.   Draw sides A and B from intersection of arcs, as shown.

5.19 To Draw a Right Triangle with Hypotenuse and One Side Given Fig. 5.20
Given sides S and R. With AB as a diameter equal to S, draw semicircle. With A as center, and R as radius, draw an arc intersecting the semicircle at C. Draw AC and CB to complete the right triangle.

5.20 To Lay Out an Angle Fig. 5.21
Many angles can be laid out directly with the triangle, Fig. 2.23, or they may be laid out with the protractor, Fig. 2.24. Other methods, where considerable accuracy is required, are as follows:

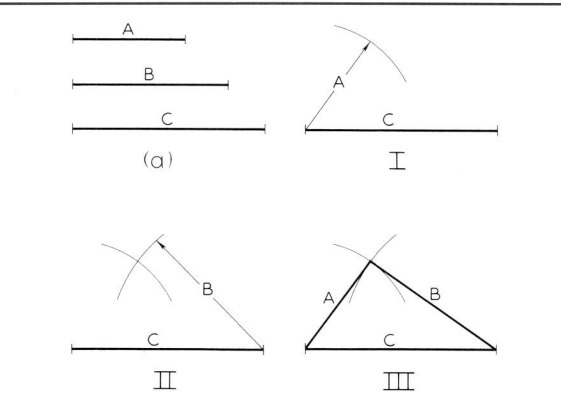

Fig. 5.19   Drawing a Triangle with Sides Given (§5.18).

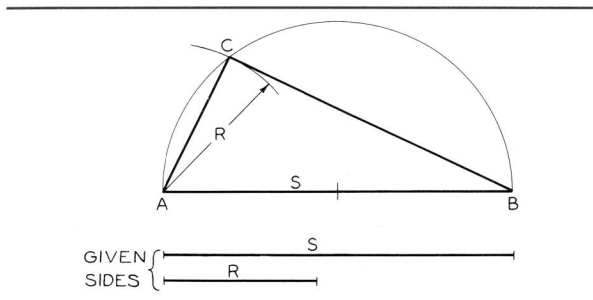

Fig. 5.20   Drawing a Right Triangle (§5.19).

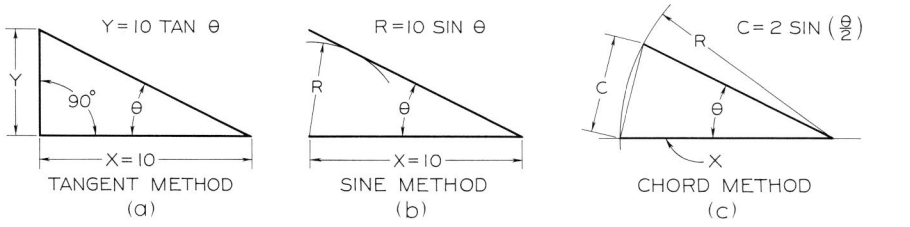

Fig. 5.21   Laying Out Angles (§5.20).

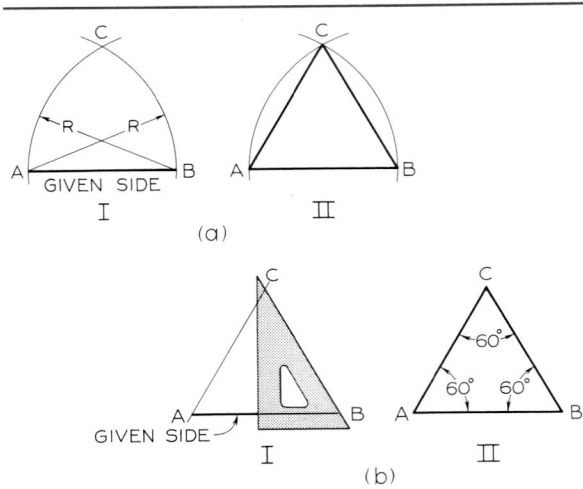

Fig. 5.22   Drawing an Equilateral Triangle (§5.21).

Tangent Method Fig. 5.21 (a)

The tangent of angle θ is $\frac{y}{x}$, and $y = x \tan \theta$. To construct the angle, assume a convenient value for x, preferably 10 units of convenient length, as shown. (The larger the unit, the more accurate will be the construction.) Find the tangent of angle θ in a table of natural tangents, multiply by 10, and set off $y = 10 \tan \theta$.

EXAMPLE   To set off $31\frac{1}{2}°$, find the natural tangent of $31\frac{1}{2}°$, which is 0.6128. Then

$$y = 10 \text{ units} \times 0.6128 = 6.128 \text{ units}$$

Sine Method Fig. 5.21 (b)

Draw line x to any convenient length, preferably 10 units as shown. Find the sine of angle θ in a table of natural sines, multiply by 10, and strike arc $R = 10 \sin \theta$. Draw the other side of the angle tangent to the arc, as shown.

EXAMPLE   To set off $25\frac{1}{2}°$, find the natural sine of $25\frac{1}{2}°$, which is 0.4305. Then

$$R = 10 \text{ units} \times 0.4305 = 4.305 \text{ units}$$

Chord Method Fig. 5.21 (c)

Draw line x to any convenient length, draw arc with any convenient radius R, say, 10 units. Find the chordal length C in a table of chords (see a machinists' handbook), and multiply the value by 10, since the table is made for a radius of 1 unit.

EXAMPLE   To set off 43° 20′, the chordal length C for 1 unit radius, as given in a table of chords = 0.7384, and if $R = 10$ units, then $C = 7.384$ units.

If a table is not available, the chord C may be calculated by the formula $C = 2 \sin \frac{\theta}{2}$.

EXAMPLE   Half of 43° 20′ = 21° 40′. The sine of 21° 40′ = 0.3692. $C = 2 \times 0.3692 = 0.7384$ for a 1 unit radius. For a 10 unit radius, $C = 7.384$ units.

5.21 To Draw an Equilateral Triangle
Given side AB.

Fig. 5.22 (a)   With A and B as centers and AB as radius, strike arcs to intersect at C. Draw lines AC and BC to complete the triangle.

Fig. 5.22 (b)   Preferred Method   Draw lines through points A and B making angles of 60° with the given line and intersecting at C, as shown.

5.22 To Draw a Square
Fig. 5.23 (a)   Given one side AB. Through point A, draw a perpendicular, Fig. 5.18 (c). With A as center, and AB as radius, draw the arc to intersect the

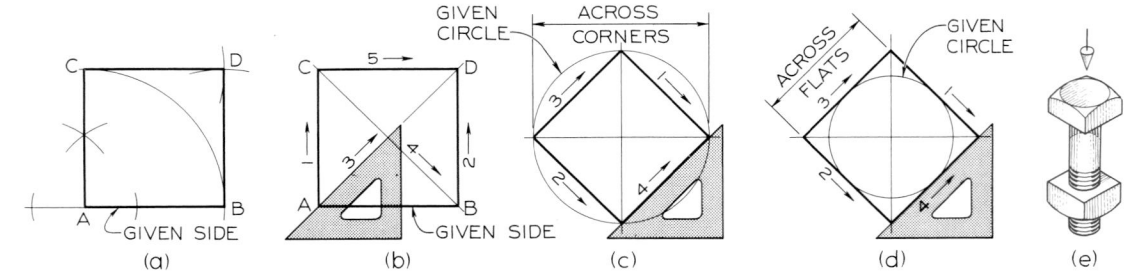

Fig. 5.23   Drawing a Square (§5.22).

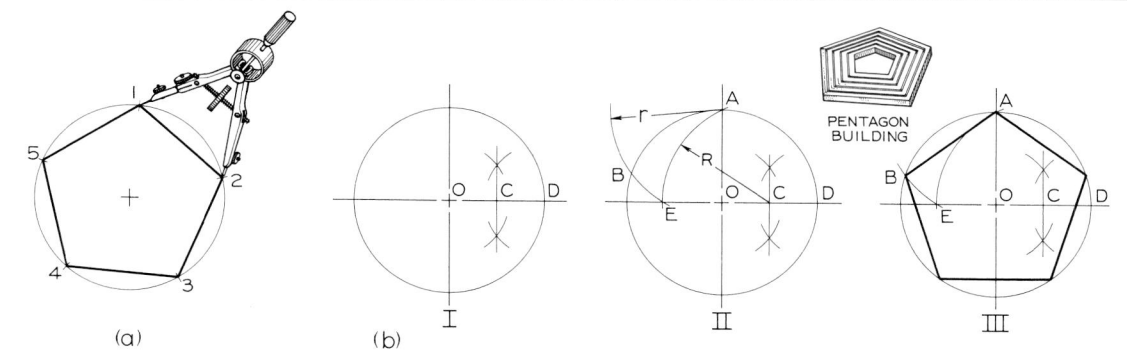

Fig. 5.24 Drawing a Pentagon (§5.23).

perpendicular at C. With B and C as centers, and AB as radius, strike arcs to intersect at D. Draw lines CD and BD.

Fig. 5.23 (b) Preferred Method Given one side AB. Using the T-square or parallel straightedge and 45° triangle, draw lines AC and BD perpendicular to AB and the lines AD and BC at 45° with AB. Draw line CD.

Fig. 5.23 (c) Preferred Method Given the circumscribed circle (distance "across corners"), draw two diameters at right angles to each other. The intersections of these diameters with the circle are vertexes of an inscribed square.

Fig. 5.23 (d) Preferred Method Given the inscribed circle (distance "across flats," as in drawing bolt heads), use the T-square (or parallel straightedge) and 45° triangle and draw the four sides tangent to the circle.

5.23 To Draw a Regular Pentagon
Given the circumscribed circle.

Fig. 5.24 (a) Preferred Method Divide the circumference of the circle into five equal parts with the dividers, and join the points with straight lines.

Geometrical Method Fig. 5.24 (b)
 I.   Bisect radius OD at C.

 II.   With C as center, and CA as radius, strike arc AE. With A as center, and AE as radius, strike arc EB.

 III.   Draw line AB; then set off distances AB around the circumference of the circle, and draw the sides through these points.

5.24 To Draw a Hexagon
Given the circumscribed circle.

Fig. 5.25 (a) Each side of a hexagon is equal to the radius of the circumscribed circle. Therefore, using the compass or dividers and the radius of the circle, set off the six sides of the hexagon around the circle, and connect the points with straight lines. As a check on the accuracy of the construction, make sure that opposite sides of the hexagon are parallel.

Fig. 5.25 (b) Preferred Method This construction is a variation of the one shown at (a). Draw vertical and horizontal center lines. With A and B as centers

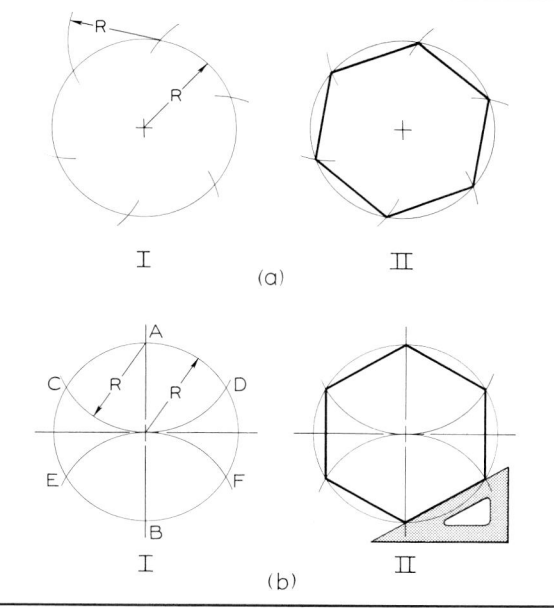

Fig. 5.25 Drawing a Hexagon (§5.24).

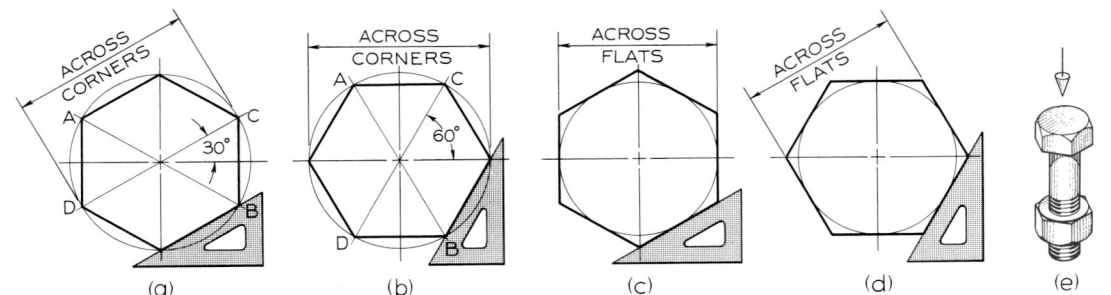

Fig. 5.26   Drawing a Hexagon (§5.25).

and radius equal to that of the circle, draw arcs to intersect the circle at C, D, E, and F, and complete the hexagon as shown.

5.25 To Draw a Hexagon
Given the circumscribed or inscribed circle. *Both Acceptable Methods.*

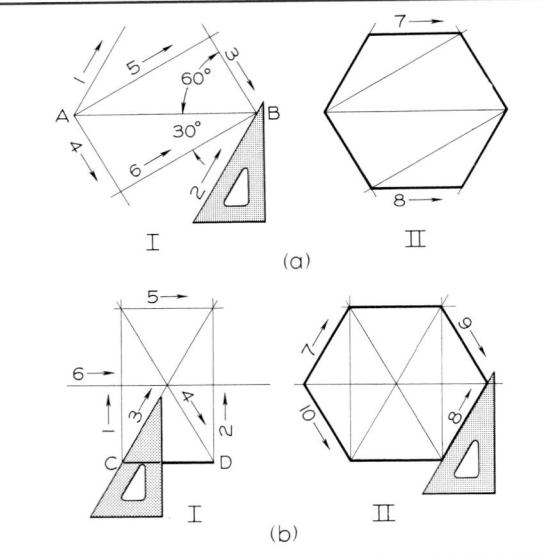

Fig. 5.27   Drawing a Hexagon (§5.26).

Fig. 5.26 (a) and (b)   Given the circumscribed circle (distance "across corners"). Draw vertical and horizontal center lines, and then diagonals AB and CD at 30° or 60° with horizontal; then with the 30° × 60° triangle and the T-square, draw the six sides as shown.

Fig. 5.26 (c) and (d)   Given the inscribed circle (distance "across flats"). Draw vertical and horizontal center lines; then with the 30° × 60° triangle and the T-square or straightedge draw the six sides tangent to the circle. This method is used in drawing bolt heads and nuts. For maximum accuracy, diagonals may be added as at (a) and (b).

5.26 To Draw a Hexagon Fig. 5.27
Using the 30° × 60° triangle and the T-square or straightedge, draw lines in the order shown at (a) where the distance AB ("across corners") is given, or as shown at (b) where a side CD is given.

5.27 To Draw an Octagon
Fig. 5.28 (a)   Preferred Method   Given inscribed circle, or distance "across flats." Using the T-square or straightedge and 45° triangle, draw the eight sides tangent to the circle, as shown.

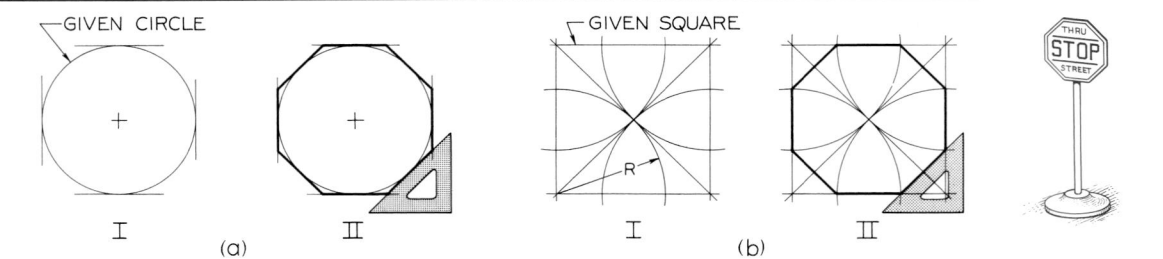

Fig. 5.28   Drawing an Octagon (§5.27).

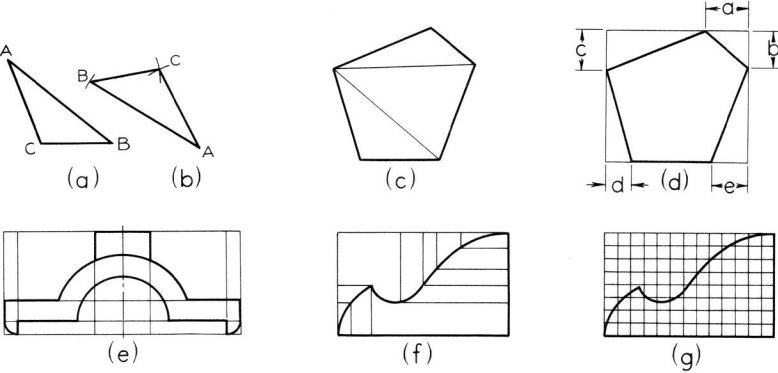

Fig. 5.29 Transferring a Plane Figure (§5.28).

Fig. 5.28 (b) Given circumscribed square, or distance "across flats." Draw diagonals of square; then with the corners of the given square as centers, and with half the diagonal as radius, draw arcs cutting the sides as shown at I. Using the T-square and 45° triangle, draw the eight sides as shown at II.

5.28 To Transfer Plane Figures by Geometric Methods

To Transfer a Triangle to a New Location Fig. 5.29 (a) and (b)

Set off any side, as AB, in the new location, (b). With the ends of the line as centers and the lengths of the other sides of the given triangle, (a), as radii, strike two arcs to intersect at C. Join C to A and B to complete the triangle.

To Transfer a Polygon by the Triangle Method Fig. 5.29 (c)

Divide the polygon into triangles as shown, and transfer each triangle as explained previously.

To Transfer a Polygon by the Rectangle Method Fig. 5.29 (d)

Circumscribe a rectangle about the given polygon. Draw a congruent rectangle in the new location and locate the vertexes of the polygon by transferring location measurements a, b, c, and so on, along the sides of the rectangle to the new rectangle. Join the points thus found to complete the figure.

To Transfer Irregular Figures Fig. 5.29 (e)

Figures composed of rectangular and circular forms are readily transferred by enclosing the elementary features in rectangles and determining centers of arcs and circles. These may then be transferred to the new location.

To Transfer Figures by Offset Measurements Fig. 5.29 (f)

Offset location measurements are frequently useful in transferring figures composed of free curves. When the figure has been enclosed by a rectangle, the sides of the rectangle are used as reference lines for the location of points along the curve.

To Transfer Figures by a System of Squares Fig. 5.29 (g)

Figures involving free curves are easily copied, enlarged, or reduced by the use of a system of squares. For example, to enlarge a figure to double size, draw the containing rectangle and all small squares double their original size. Then draw the lines through the corresponding points in the new set of squares. See also Fig. 6.18.

5.29 To Transfer Drawings by Tracing-Paper Methods

To transfer a drawing to an opaque sheet, the following procedures may be used.

Prick-Point Method

Lay tracing paper over the drawing to be transferred. With a sharp pencil, make a small dot directly over each important point on the drawing. Encircle each dot so as not to lose it. Remove the tracing paper, place it over the paper to receive the transferred drawing, and maneuver the tracing paper into the desired position. With a needle point (such as a point of the dividers), prick through each

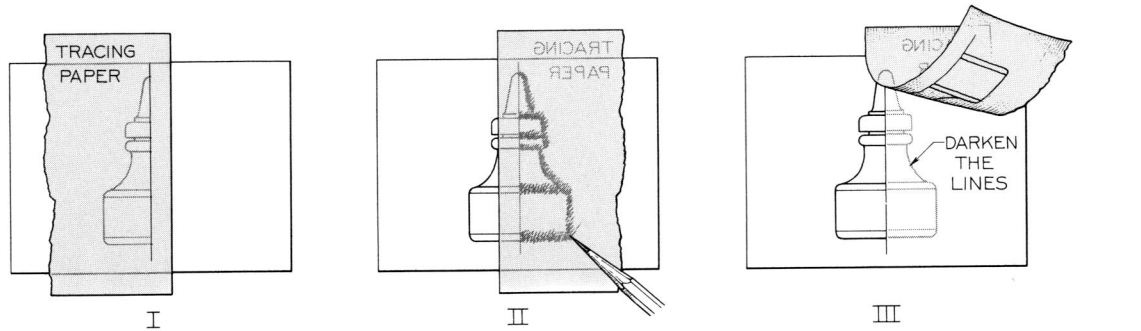

Fig. 5.30   Transferring a Symmetrical Half (§5.29).

dot. Remove the tracing paper and connect the pricked points to reproduce the lines of the original drawing.

To reproduce arcs or circles, it is only necessary to transfer the center and one point on the circumference. To duplicate a free curve, transfer as many pricked points on the curve as desired.

Tracing Method

Lay tracing paper over the drawing to be transferred, and make a pencil tracing of it. Turn the tracing paper over and mark over the lines with short strokes of a soft pencil so as to provide a coating of graphite over every line. Turn tracing face up and fasten in position where drawing is to be transferred. Trace over all lines of the tracing, using a hard pencil. The graphite on the back acts as a carbon paper and will produce dim but definite lines. Heavy in the dim lines to complete the transfer.

Fig. 5.30   If one-half of a symmetrical object has been drawn, as for the ink bottle at I, the other half may be easily drawn with the aid of tracing paper as follows.

I.   Trace the half already drawn.

II.   Turn tracing paper over and maneuver to the position for the right half. Then trace over the lines freehand or mark over the lines with short strokes as shown.

III.   Remove the tracing paper, revealing the dim imprinted lines for the right half. Heavy in these lines to complete the drawing.

5.30 To Enlarge or Reduce a Drawing

Fig. 5.31 (a)   The construction shown is an adaptation of the parallel-line method, Figs. 5.14 and 5.15, and may be used whenever it is desired to enlarge or reduce any group of dimensions to the same ratio. Thus if full-size dimensions are laid off along the vertical line, the enlarged dimensions would appear along the horizontal line, as shown.

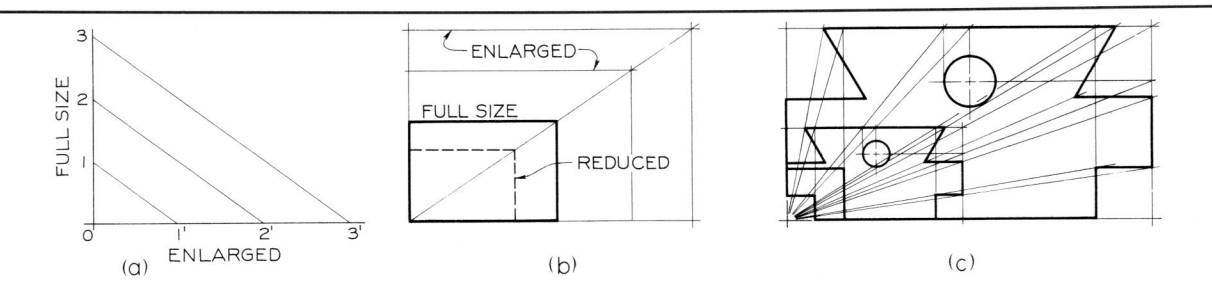

Fig. 5.31   Enlarging or Reducing (§5.30).

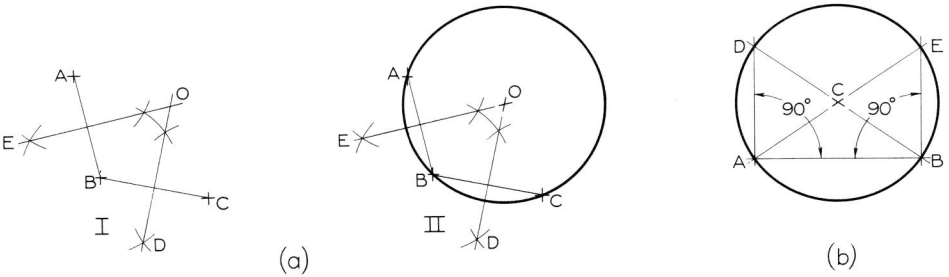

Fig. 5.32 Finding Center of Circle (§§5.31 and 5.32).

Fig. 5.31 (b) To enlarge or reduce a rectangle (say, a photograph), a simple method is to use the diagonal, as shown.

Fig. 5.31 (c) A simple method of enlarging or reducing a drawing is to make use of radial lines, as shown. The original drawing is placed underneath a sheet of tracing paper, and the enlarged or reduced drawing is made directly on the tracing paper.

5.31 To Draw a Circle Through Three Points Fig. 5.32 (a)

I. Let A, B, and C be the three given points not in a straight line. Draw lines AB and BC, which will be chords of the circle. Draw perpendicular bisectors EO and DO, Fig. 5.8, intersecting at O.

II. With center at O, draw required circle through the points.

5.32 To Find the Center of a Circle
Fig. 5.32 (b)

Draw any chord AB, preferably horizontal as shown. Draw perpendiculars from A and B, cutting circle at D and E. Draw diagonals DB and EA whose inter-

section C will be the center of the circle. This method uses the principle that any right triangle inscribed in a circle cuts off a semicircle, as was shown earlier, in Fig. 5.3 (f).

Another method, slightly longer, is to reverse the procedure of Fig. 5.32 (a). Draw any two non-parallel chords and draw perpendicular bisectors. The intersection of the bisectors will be the center of the circle.

5.33 To Draw a Circle Tangent to a Line at a Given Point Fig. 5.33
Given a line AB and a point P on the line, as shown at (a).

I. At P erect a perpendicular to the line.

II. Set off the radius of the required circle on the perpendicular.

III. Draw circle with radius CP.

5.34 To Draw a Tangent to a Circle Through a Point
Fig. 5.34 (a) Preferred Method Given point P on the circle. Move the T-square and triangle as a unit until one side of the triangle passes through the

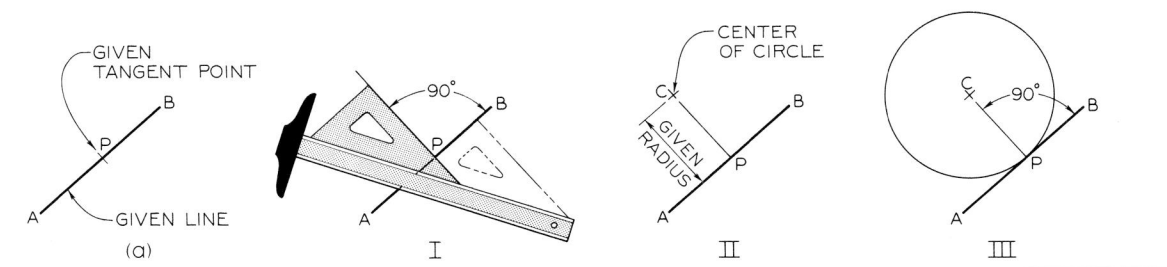

Fig. 5.33 Drawing a Circle Tangent to a Line (§5.33).

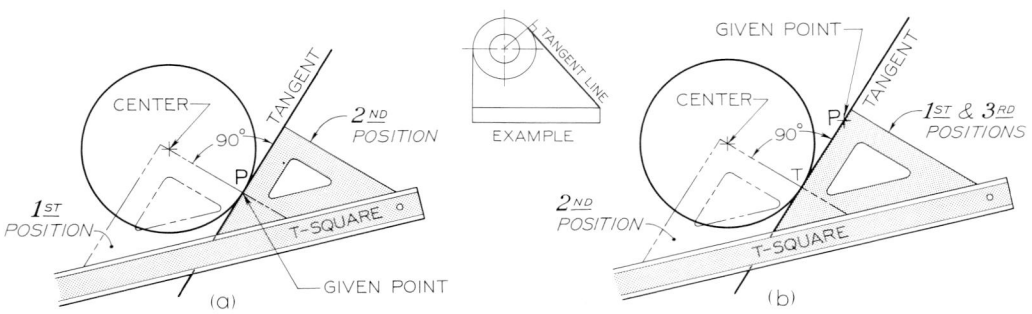

Fig. 5.34   Drawing a Tangent to a Circle Through a Point (§5.34).

point P and the center of the circle; then slide the triangle until the other side passes through point P, and draw the required tangent.

Fig. 5.34 (b)   Given point P outside the circle. Move the T-square and triangle as a unit until one side of the triangle passes through point P and, by inspection, is tangent to the circle; then slide the triangle until the other side passes through the center of the circle, and lightly mark the point of tangency T. Finally move the triangle back to its starting position, and draw the required tangent.

In both constructions either triangle may be used. Also, a second triangle may be used in place of the T-square.

5.35 To Draw Tangents to Two Circles
Fig. 5.35 (a) and (b)
Move the triangle and T-square as a unit until one side of the triangle is tangent, by inspection, to the two circles; then slide the triangle until the other side passes through the center of one circle, and lightly mark the point of tangency. Then slide the triangle until the side passes through the center of the other circle, and mark the point of tangency. Finally, slide the triangle back to the tangent position, and draw the tangent lines between the two points of tangency. Draw the second tangent line in a similar manner.

5.36 To Draw an Arc Tangent to a Line or Arc and Through a Point
Fig. 5.36 (a)   Given line AB, point P, and radius R. Draw line DE parallel to given line and distance R from it. From P draw arc with radius R, cutting line DE at C, the center of the required tangent arc.

Fig. 5.36 (b)   Given line AB, with tangent point Q on the line, and point P. Draw PQ, which will be a chord of the required arc. Draw perpendicular bisector DE, and at Q erect a perpendicular to the line to intersect DE at C, the center of the required tangent arc.

Fig. 5.36 (c)   Given arc with center Q, point P, and radius R. From P strike arc with radius R. From Q strike arc with radius equal to that of the given arc plus R. The intersection C of the arcs is the center of the required tangent arc.

5.37 To Draw an Arc Tangent to Two Lines at Right Angles Fig. 5.37 (a)

I.   Given two lines at right angles to each other.

II.   With given radius R, strike arc intersecting given lines at tangent points T.

III.   With given radius R again, and with points T as centers, strike arcs intersecting at C.

IV.   With C as center and given radius R, draw required tangent arc.

For Small Radii Fig. 5.37 (b)
For small radii, such as $\frac{1}{8}$R for fillets and rounds, it is not practicable to draw complete tangency constructions. Instead, draw a 45° bisector of the angle and locate the center of the arc by trial along this line, as shown.

Note that the center C can be located by intersecting lines parallel to the given lines, as shown in

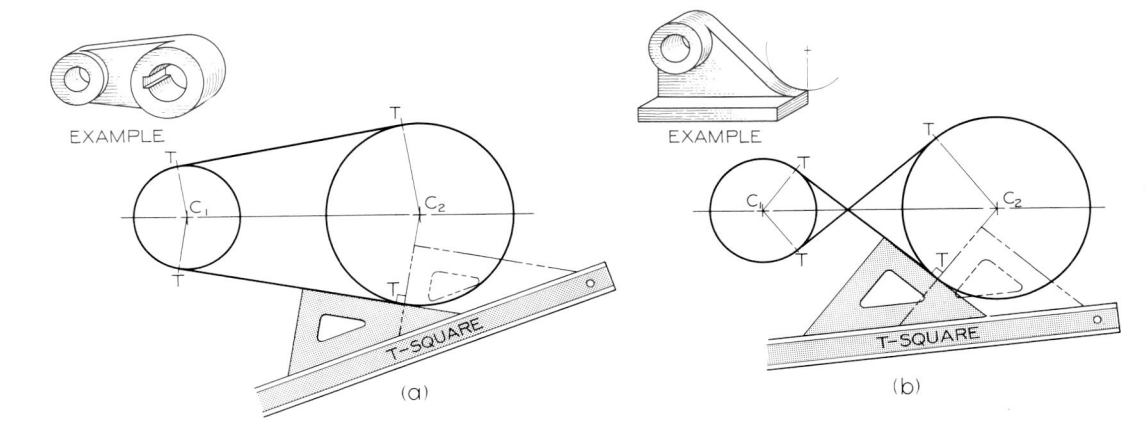

Fig. 5.35   Drawing Tangents to Two Circles (§5.35).

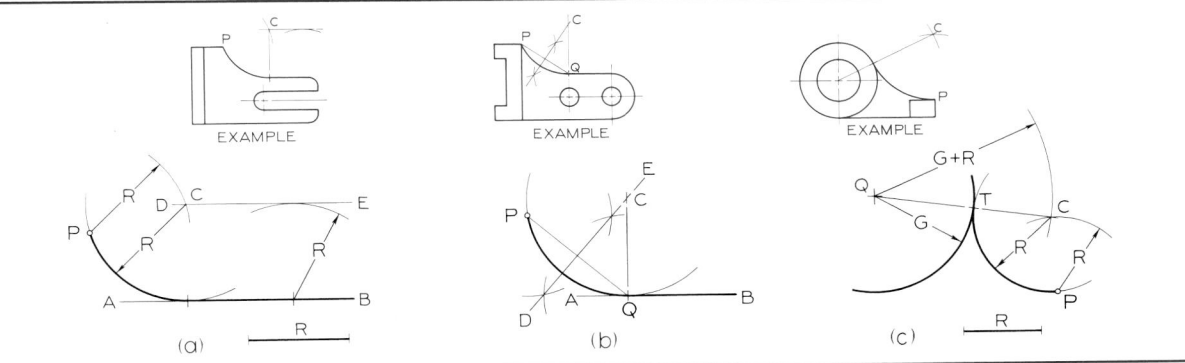

Fig. 5.36   Tangents (§5.36).

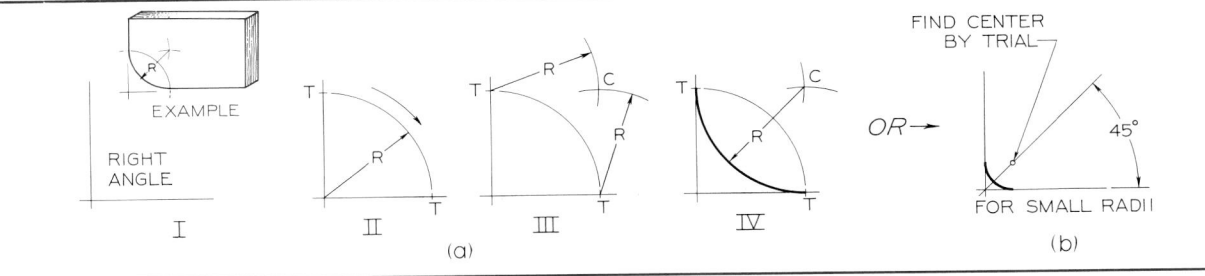

Fig. 5.37   Drawing a Tangent Arc in a Right Angle (§5.37).

Fig. 5.13 (b). The circle template can also be used to draw the arcs R for the parallel line method of Fig. 5.13 (b). While the circle template is very convenient to use for small radii up to about $\frac{5}{8}''$ or 16 mm, it is necessary that the diameter of a circle on the template precisely equals twice the required radius.

5.38 To Draw an Arc Tangent to Two Lines at Acute or Obtuse Angles Fig. 5.38 (a) or (b)

I.   Given two lines not making 90° with each other.

II.   Draw lines parallel to given lines, at distance R from them, to intersect at C, the required center.

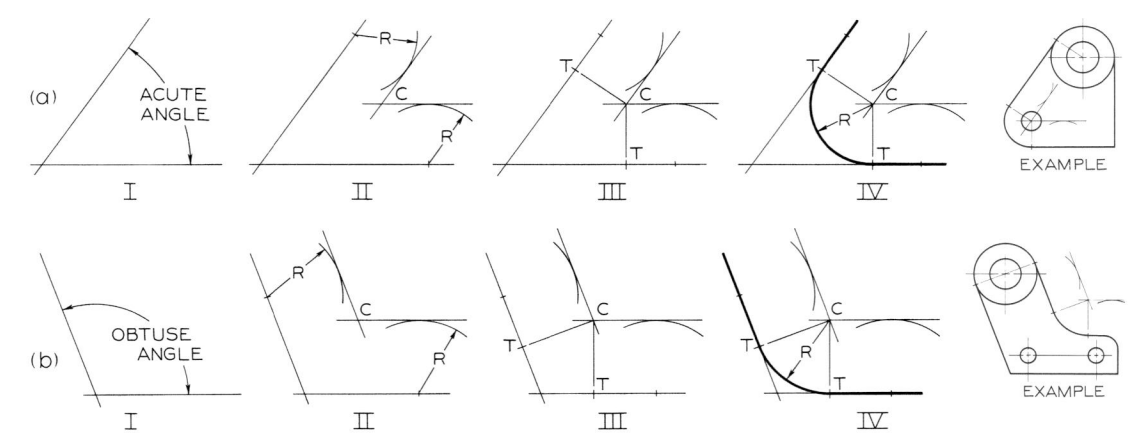

Fig. 5.38   Drawing Tangent Arcs (§5.38).

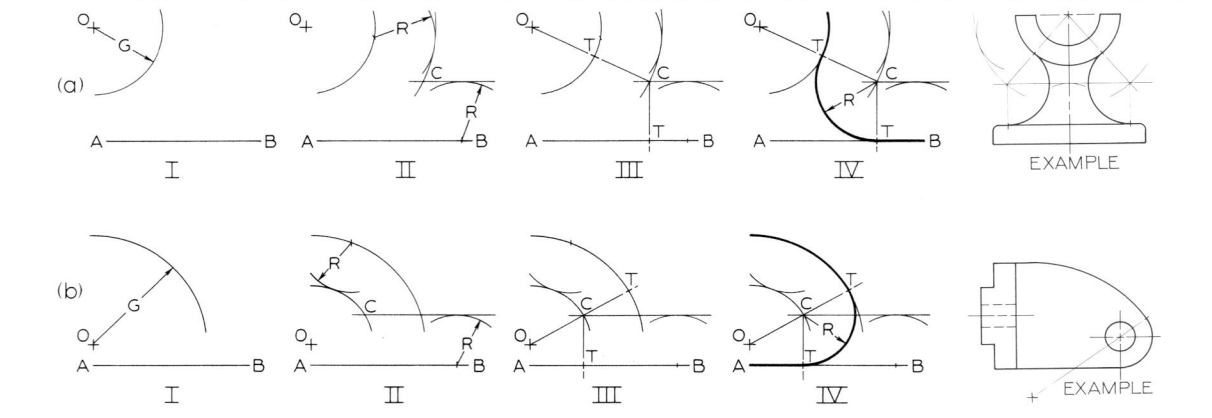

Fig. 5.39   Drawing Tangent Arcs (§5.39).

III.   From **C** drop perpendiculars to the given lines respectively to locate tangent points **T**.

IV.   With **C** as center and with given radius **R**, draw required tangent arc between the points of tangency.

5.39 To Draw an Arc Tangent to an Arc and a Straight Line Fig. 5.39 (a) or (b)

I.   Given arc with radius **G** and straight line **AB**.

II.   Draw straight line and an arc parallel, respectively, to the given straight line and arc at the required radius distance **R** from them, to intersect at **C**, the required center.

III.   From **C** drop a perpendicular to the given straight line to obtain one point of tangency **T**. Join the centers **C** and **O** with a straight line to locate the other point of tangency **T**.

IV.   With center **C** and given radius **R**, draw required tangent arc between the points of tangency.

5.40 To Draw an Arc Tangent to Two Arcs Fig. 5.40 (a) or (b)

I.   Given arcs with centers **A** and **B**, and required radius **R**.

II.   With **A** and **B** as centers, draw arcs parallel to the given arcs and at a distance **R** from them; their

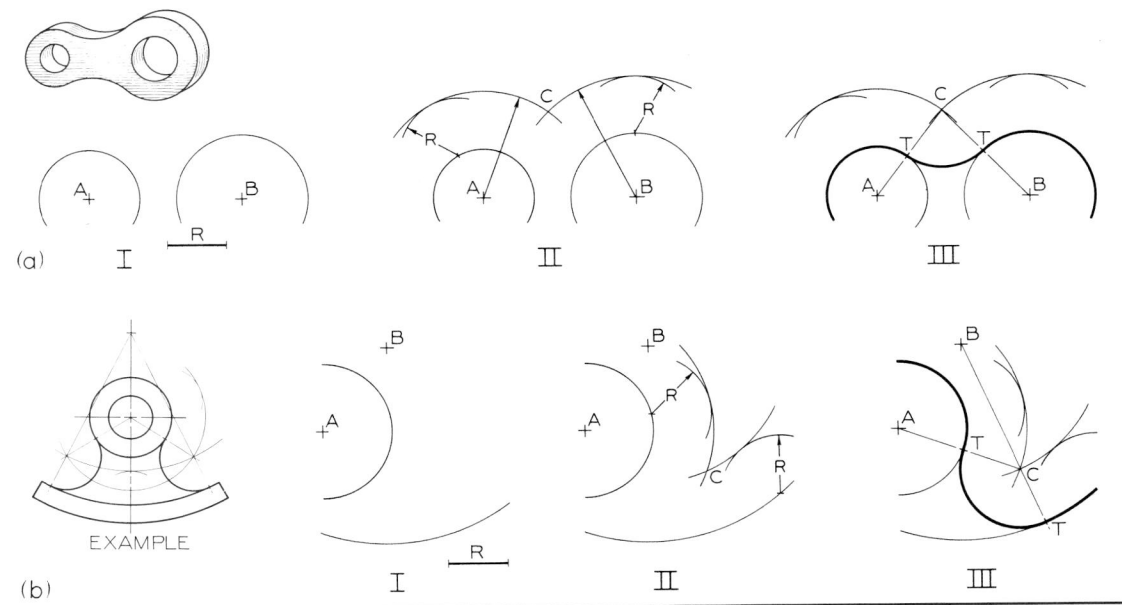

Fig. 5.40 Drawing an Arc Tangent to Two Arcs (§5.39).

intersection **C** is the center of the required tangent arc.

III. Draw lines of centers **AC** and **BC** to locate points of tangency **T**, and draw required tangent arc between the points of tangency, as shown.

5.41 To Draw an Arc Tangent to Two Arcs and Enclosing One or Both

The Required Arc Encloses Both Given Arcs Fig. 5.41 (a)

With A and B as centers, strike arcs **HK − r** (given radius minus radius of small circle) and **HK − R** (given radius minus radius of large circle) intersecting at **G**, the center of the required tangent arc. Lines of centers **GA** and **GB** (extended) determine points of tangency **T**.

The Required Arc Encloses One Given Arc Fig. 5.41 (b)

With C and D as centers, strike arcs **HK + r** (given radius plus radius of small circle) and **HK − R** (given radius minus radius of large circle) intersecting at **G**, the center of the required tangent arc. Lines of centers **GC** and **GD** (extended) determine points of tangency **T**.

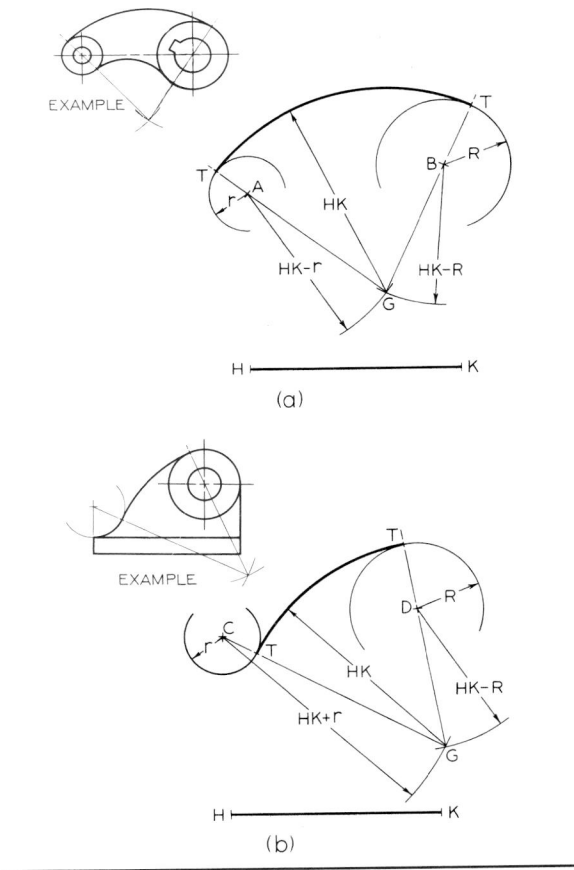

Fig. 5.41 Drawing Tangent Arcs (§5.41).

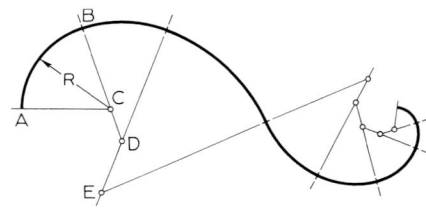

Fig. 5.42   A Series of Tangent Arcs (§5.42).

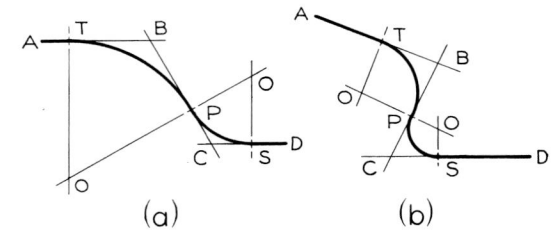

Fig. 5.44   Tangent Curves (§5.44).

5.42 To Draw a Series of Tangent Arcs Conforming to a Curve Fig. 5.42

First sketch lightly a smooth curve as desired. By trial, find a radius R and a center C, producing an arc AB that closely follows that portion of the curve. The successive centers D, E, and so on, will be on lines joining the centers with the points of tangency, as shown.

5.43 To Draw an Ogee Curve

Connecting Two Parallel Lines Fig. 5.43 (a)

Let NA and BM be the two parallel lines. Draw AB, and assume inflection point T (at midpoint if two equal arcs are desired). At A and B erect perpendiculars AF and BC. Draw perpendicular bisectors of AT and BT. The intersections F and C of these bisectors and the perpendiculars, respectively, are the centers of the required tangent arcs.

Fig. 5.43 (b)   Let AB and CD be the two parallel lines, with point B as one end of the curve and R the given radii. At B erect perpendicular to AB, make BG = R, and draw arc as shown. Draw line SP parallel to CD at distance R from CD. With center G, draw arc of radius 2R, intersecting line SP at O. Draw perpendicular OJ to locate tangent point J, and join centers G and O to locate point of tangency

T. Using centers G and O and radius R, draw the two tangent arcs as shown.

Connecting Two Nonparallel Lines
Fig. 5.43 (c)

Let AB and CD be the two nonparallel lines. Erect perpendicular to AB at B. Select point G on the perpendicular so that BG equals any desired radius, and draw arc as shown. Erect perpendicular to CD at C and make CE = BG. Join G to E and bisect it. The intersection F of the bisector and the perpendicular CE, extended, is the center of the second arc. Join centers of the two arcs to locate tangent point T, the inflection point of the curve.

5.44 To Draw a Curve Tangent to Three Intersecting Lines

Fig. 5.44 (a) and (b)   Let AB, BC, and CD be the given lines. Select point of tangency P at any point on line BC. Make BT equal to BP, and CS equal to CP, and erect perpendiculars at the points P, T, and S. Their intersections O and Q are the centers of the required tangent arcs.

5.45 To Rectify a Circular Arc

To *rectify* an arc is to lay out its true length along a straight line. The constructions are approximate, but

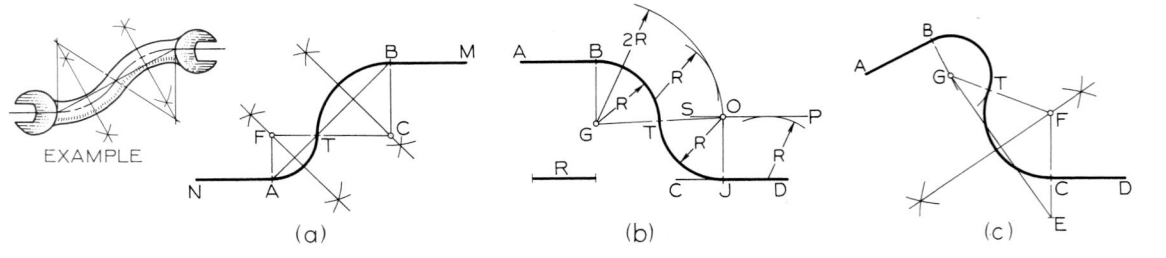

Fig. 5.43   Drawing an Ogee Curve (§5.43).

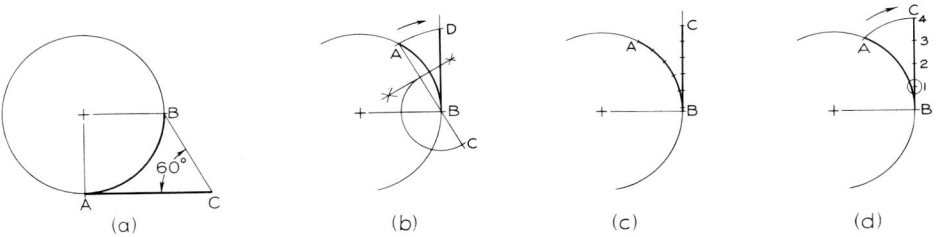

Fig. 5.45 Rectifying Circular Arcs (§§5.45 and 5.46).

well within the range of accuracy of drawing instruments.

To Rectify a Quadrant of a Circle, AB
Fig. 5.45 (a)
Draw AC tangent to the circle and BC at 60° to AC, as shown. The line AC is almost equal to the arc AB, the difference in length being about 1 in 240.

To Rectify Arc AB Fig. 5.45 (b)
Draw tangent at B. Draw chord AB and extend it to C, making BC equal to half AB. With C as center and radius CA, strike the arc AD. The tangent BD is slightly shorter than the given arc AB. For an angle of 45° the difference in length is about 1 in 2866.

Fig. 5.45 (c) Use the bow dividers, and beginning at A, set off equal distances until the division point nearest to B is reached. At this point, reverse the direction and set off an equal number of distances along the tangent to determine point C. The tangent BC is slightly shorter than the given arc AB. If the angle subtended by each division is 10°, the error is approximately 1 in 830.

NOTE   If the angle θ subtending an arc of radius R is known, the length of the arc is $2\pi R \dfrac{\theta}{360°} = 0.01745R\theta$.

5.46 To Set Off a Given Length Along a Given Arc
Fig. 5.45 (c) Reverse the preceding method so as to transfer distances from the tangent line to the arc.

Fig. 5.45 (d) To set off the length BC along the arc BA, draw BC tangent to the arc at B. Divide BC into four equal parts. With center at 1, the first division point, and radius 1–C, draw the arc CA. The arc BA is practically equal to BC for angles less than 30°. For 45° the difference is approximately 1 in 3232, and for 60° it is about 1 in 835.

5.47 The Conic Sections Fig. 5.46
The conic sections are curves produced by planes intersecting a right circular cone. Four types of

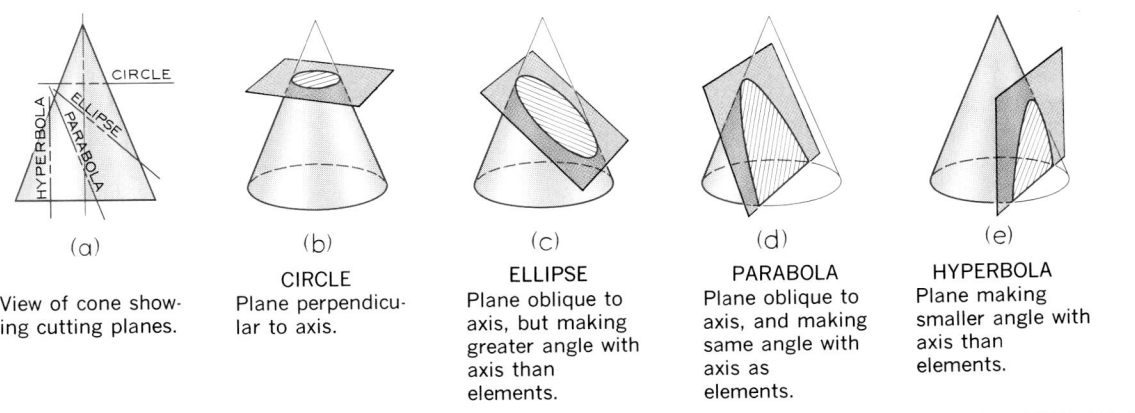

(a)	(b)	(c)	(d)	(e)
	CIRCLE	ELLIPSE	PARABOLA	HYPERBOLA
View of cone showing cutting planes.	Plane perpendicular to axis.	Plane oblique to axis, but making greater angle with axis than elements.	Plane oblique to axis, and making same angle with axis as elements.	Plane making smaller angle with axis than elements.

Fig. 5.46 Conic Sections (§5.47).

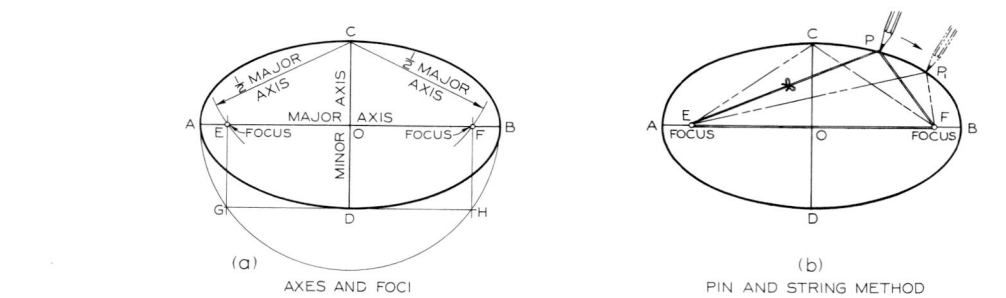

Fig. 5.47   Ellipse Constructions (§5.48).

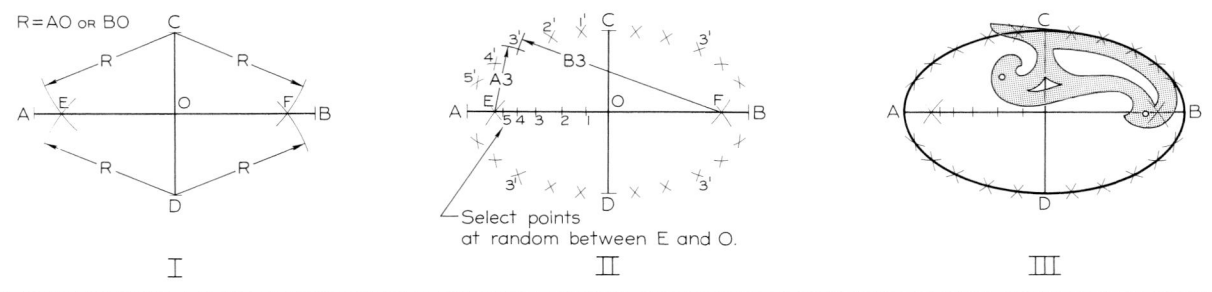

Fig. 5.48   Drawing a Foci Ellipse (§5.49).

curves are produced: the *circle, ellipse, parabola,* and *hyperbola,* according to the position of the planes, as shown. These curves were studied in detail by the ancient Greeks, and are of great interest in mathematics, as well as in technical drawing. For equations, see any text on analytic geometry.

5.48 Ellipse Construction

The long axis of an ellipse is the major axis, and the short axis is the minor axis, Fig. 5.47 (a). The foci E and F are found by striking arcs with radius equal to half the major axis and with center at the end of the minor axis. Another method is to draw a semicircle with the major axis as diameter, then to draw GH parallel to the major axis and GE and HF parallel to the minor axis, as shown.

An ellipse is generated by a point moving so that the sum of its distances from two points (the foci) is constant and equal to the major axis. For example, Fig. 5.47 (b), an ellipse may be constructed by placing a looped string around the foci E and F, and around C, one end of the minor axis, and moving the pencil point P along its maximum orbit while the string is kept taut.

5.49 To Draw a Foci Ellipse Fig. 5.48

Let **AB** be the major axis and **CD** the minor axis. This method is the geometrical counterpart of the pin-and-string method. Keep the construction very light, as follows.

I.   To find foci **E** and **F**, strike arcs **R** with radius equal to half the major axis and with centers at the ends of the minor axis.

II.   Between **E** and **O** on the major axis, mark at random a number of points (spacing those on the left more closely), equal to the number of points desired in each quadrant of the ellipse. In this figure, five points were deemed sufficient. For large ellipses, more points should be used—enough to insure a smooth, accurate curve. Begin construction with any one of these points, such as **3**. With **E** and **F** as centers and radii A–3 and B–3, respectively (from the ends of the major axis to point **3**), strike arcs to intersect at four points **3′**, as shown. Using the remaining points **1**, **2**, **4**, and **5**, for each find four additional points on the ellipse in the same manner.

III.   Sketch the ellipse lightly through the points;

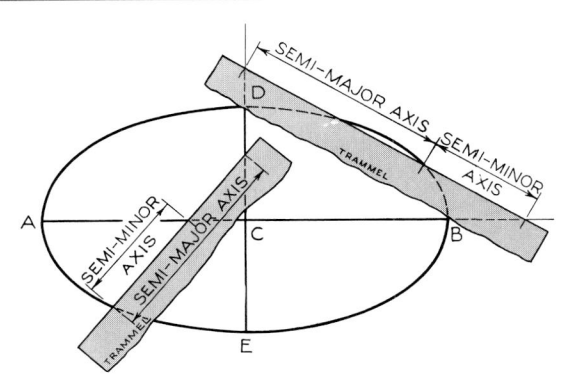

Fig. 5.49 Drawing a Trammel Ellipse (§5.50).

then heavy in the final ellipse with the aid of the irregular curve. Fig. 2.66.

5.50 To Draw a Trammel Ellipse Fig. 5.49

A "long trammel" or a "short-trammel" may be prepared from a small strip of stiff paper or thin cardboard, as shown. In both cases, set off on the edge of the trammel distances equal to the semimajor and semiminor axes. In one case these distances overlap; in the other they are end to end. To use either method, place the trammel so that the two of the points are on the respective axes, as shown; the third point will then be on the curve and can be marked with a small dot. Find additional points by moving the trammel to other positions, always keeping the two points exactly on the respective axes. Extend the axes to use the long trammel. Find enough points to insure a smooth and symmetrical ellipse. Sketch the ellipse lightly through the points; then heavy in the ellipse with the aid of the irregular curve, Fig. 2.66.

5.51 To Draw a Concentric-Circle Ellipse
Fig. 5.50

If a circle is viewed so that the line of sight is perpendicular to the plane of the circle, as shown for the silver dollar at (a), the circle will appear as a circle, in true size and shape. If the circle is viewed at an angle, as shown at (b), it will appear as an ellipse. If the circle is viewed edgewise, it appears as a straight line, as shown at (c). The case shown at (b) is the basis for the construction of an ellipse by the concentric-circle method, as follows (keep the construction very light).

I. Draw circles on the major and minor axes using them as diameters and draw any diagonal XX through center O. From the points X, in which the diagonal intersects the large circle, draw lines XE parallel to the minor axes, and from points H, in which it intersects the small circle, draw lines HE parallel to the major axis. The intersections E are points on the ellipse. Two additional points, S and R, can be found by extending lines XE and HE, giving a total of four points from the one diagonal XX.

II. Draw as many additional diagonals as needed to provide a sufficient number of points for a smooth and symmetrical ellipse, each diagonal accounting for four points on the ellipse. Notice that where the curve is sharpest (near the ends of the ellipse), the points are constructed closer together to better determine the curve.

III. Sketch the ellipse lightly through the points, then heavy in the final ellipse with the aid of the irregular curve.

NOTE It is evident at I, Fig. 5.50, that the ordinate EZ of the ellipse is to the corresponding ordinate XZ of the circle as b is to a, where b represents the semiminor axis and a the semimajor axis.

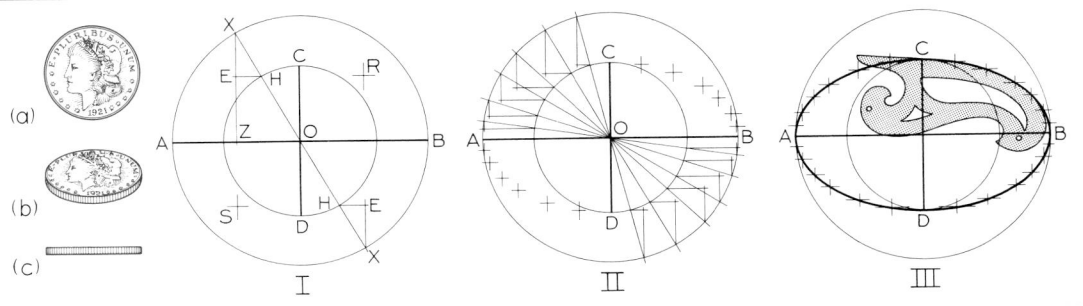

Fig. 5.50 Drawing a Concentric-Circle Ellipse (§5.51).

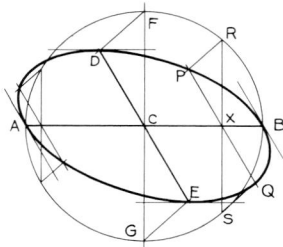

Fig. 5.51 Oblique-Circle Ellipse (§5.52).

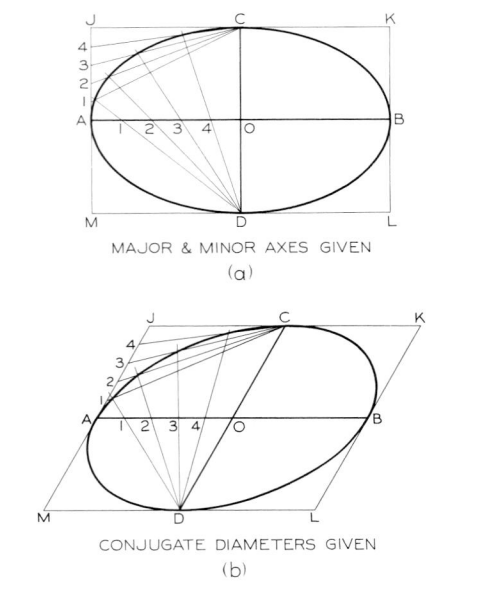

MAJOR & MINOR AXES GIVEN
(a)

CONJUGATE DIAMETERS GIVEN
(b)

Fig. 5.52 Parallelogram Ellipse (§5.53).

Thus, the area of the ellipse is equal to the area of the circumscribed circle multiplied by $\frac{b}{a}$; hence, it is equal to πab.

5.52 To Draw an Ellipse on Conjugate Diameters—Oblique-Circle Method
Fig. 5.51

Let AB and DE be the given conjugate diameters. *Two diameters are conjugate when each is parallel to the tangents at the extremities of the other.* With center at C and radius CA, draw a circle; draw the diameter GF perpendicular to AB, and draw lines joining points D and F and points G and E.

Assume that the required ellipse is an oblique projection of the circle just drawn; the points D and E of the ellipse are the oblique projections of the points F and G of the circle, respectively; similarly, the points P and Q are the oblique projections of the points R and S, respectively. The points P and Q are determined by assuming the point X at any point on AB and drawing the lines RS and PQ, and RP and SQ, parallel, respectively, to GF and DE and FD and GE.

Determine at least five points in each quadrant (more for larger ellipses) by assuming additional points on the major axis and proceeding as explained for point X. Sketch the ellipse lightly through the points; then heavy in the final ellipse with the aid of the irregular curve, Fig. 2.66.

5.53 To Draw a Parallelogram Ellipse
Fig. 5.52 (a) and (b)

Given the major and minor axes, or the conjugate diameters AB and CD, draw a rectangle or parallelogram with sides parallel to the axes, respectively. Divide AO and AJ into the same number of equal parts, and draw *light* lines through these points from

the ends of the minor axis, as shown. The intersection of like-numbered lines will be points on the ellipse. Locate points in the remaining three quadrants in a similar manner. Sketch the ellipse lightly through the points; then heavy in the final ellipse with the aid of the irregular curve, Fig. 2.66.

5.54 To Find the Axes of an Ellipse, with Conjugate Diameters Given
Fig. 5.53 (a) Conjugate diameters AB and CD and the ellipse are given. With intersection O of the conjugate diameters (center of ellipse) as center, and any convenient radius, draw a circle to intersect the ellipse in four points. Join these points with straight lines, as shown; the resulting quadrilateral will be a rectangle whose sides are parallel, respectively, to the required major and minor axes. Draw the axes EF and GH parallel to the sides of the rectangle.

Fig. 5.53 (b) Ellipse only is given. To find the center of the ellipse, draw a circumscribing rectangle or parallelogram about the ellipse; then, draw diagonals to intersect at center O as shown. The axes are then found as shown at (a).

Fig. 5.53 (c) Conjugate diameters AB and CD only are given. With O as center and CD as diameter, draw a circle. Through center O and perpendicular

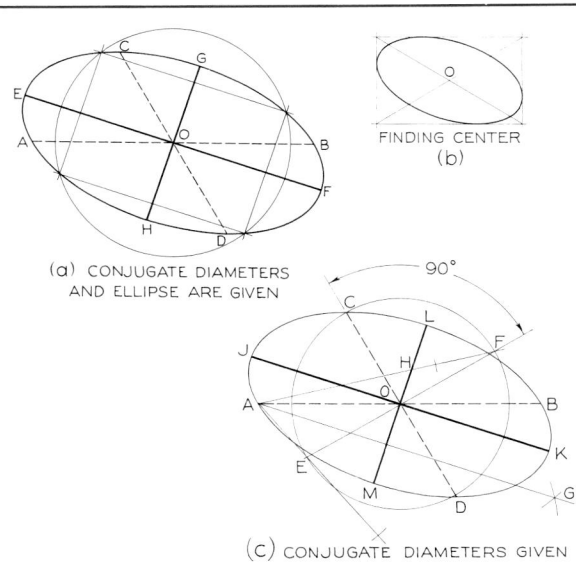

(a) CONJUGATE DIAMETERS
AND ELLIPSE ARE GIVEN

FINDING CENTER
(b)

(c) CONJUGATE DIAMETERS GIVEN

Fig. 5.53 Finding the Axes of an Ellipse (§5.54).

to CD, draw line EF. From points E and F, where this perpendicular intersects the circle, draw lines FA and EA to form angle FAE. Draw the bisector AG of this angle. The major axis JK will be parallel to this bisector, and the minor axis LM will be perpendicular to it. The length AH will be one half the

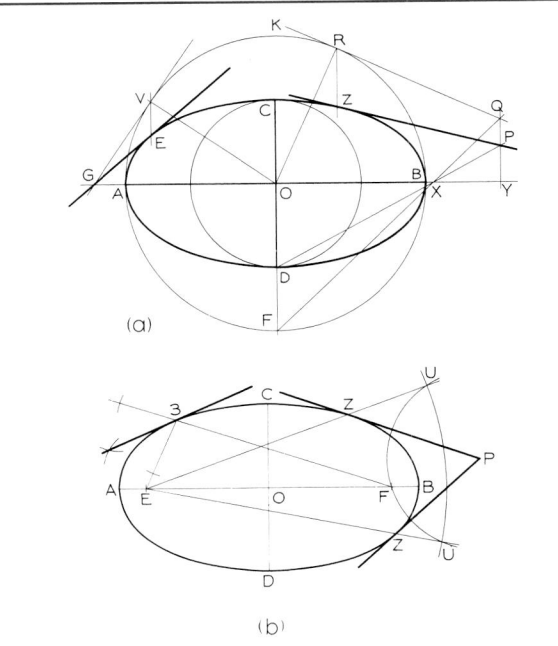

(a)

(b)

Fig. 5.54 Tangents to an Ellipse (§5.55).

major axis, and HF one half the minor axis. The resulting major and minor axes are JK and LM, respectively.

5.55 To Draw a Tangent to an Ellipse

Concentric Circle Construction Fig. 5.54 (a)
To draw a tangent at any point on the ellipse, as E, draw the ordinate at E to intersect the circle at V. Draw a tangent to the circle at V, §5.34, and extend it to intersect the major axis extended at G. The line GE is the required tangent.

To draw a tangent from a point outside the ellipse, as P, draw the ordinate PY and extend it. Draw DP, intersecting the major axis at X. Draw FX and extend it to intersect the ordinate through P at Q. Then, from similar triangles, QY:PY = OF:OD. Draw tangent to the circle from Q, §5.34, find the point of tangency R, and draw the ordinate at R to intersect the ellipse at Z. The line ZP is the required tangent. As a check on the drawing, the tangents RQ and ZP should intersect at a point on the major axis extended. Two tangents to the ellipse can be drawn from point P.

Foci Construction Fig. 5.54 (b)
To draw a tangent at any point on the ellipse, such as point 3, draw the focal radii E–3 and F–3, extend one, and bisect the exterior angle, as shown. The bisector is the required tangent.

To draw a tangent from any point outside the ellipse, such as point P, with center at P and radius PF, strike an arc as shown. With center at E and radius AB, strike an arc to intersect the first arc at points U. Draw the lines EU to intersect the ellipse at the points Z. The lines PZ are the required tangents.

5.56 Ellipse Templates

To save time in drawing ellipses, and to insure uniform results, ellipse templates, Fig. 5.55 (a), are often used. These are plastic sheets with elliptical openings in a wide variety of sizes, and usually come in sets of six or more sheets.

Ellipse guides are usually designated by the ellipse angle, the angle at which a circle is viewed to appear as an ellipse. In Fig. 5.55 (b) the angle between the line of sight and the edge view of the plane of the circle is found to be about 49°; hence, the 50° ellipse template is indicated. Ellipse templates are generally available in ellipse angles at 5° intervals, as 15°, 20°, 25°, and so on. On this 50°

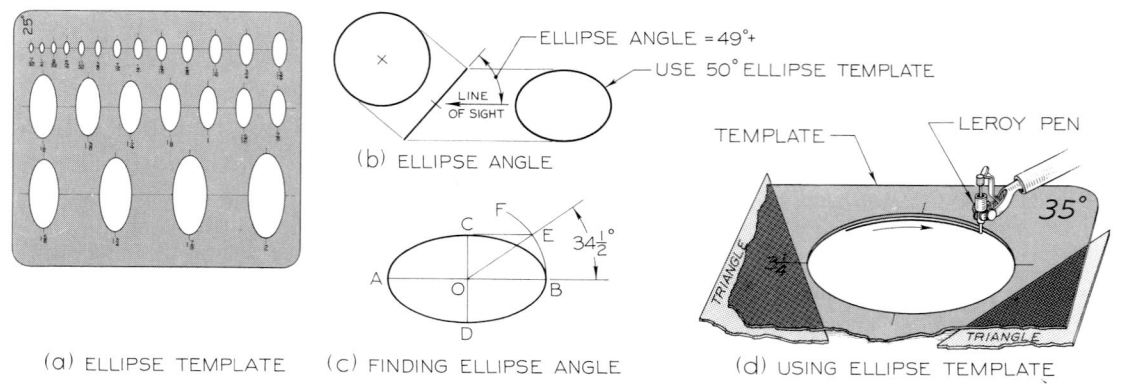

Fig. 5.55   Using the Ellipse Template (§5.56).

template a variety of sizes of 50° ellipses is provided, and it is only necessary to select the one that fits. If the ellipse angle is not easily determined, you can always look for the ellipse that is approximately as long and as "fat" as the ellipse to be drawn.

A simple construction for finding the ellipse angle when the views are not available is shown at (c). Using center **O**, strike arc **BF**; then draw **CE** parallel to the major axis. Draw diagonal **OE**, and measure angle **EOB** with the protractor, §2.18. Use the ellipse template nearest to this angle; in this case a 35° template is selected.

Since it is not feasible to have ellipse openings for every exact size that may be required, it is often necessary to use the template somewhat in the manner of an irregular curve. For example, if the opening is too long and too "fat" for the required ellipse, one end may be drawn and then the template shifted slightly to draw the other end. Similarly, one long side may be drawn and then the template shifted slightly to draw the opposite side. In such cases, leave gaps between the four segments, to be

filled in freehand or with the aid of an irregular curve. When the differences between the ellipse openings and the required ellipse are small, it is only necessary to lean the pencil slightly outward or inward from the guiding edge to offset the differences.

For inking the ellipses, the Leroy, Rapidograph, or Wrico pens are recommended. The Leroy pen is shown in Fig. 5.55 (d).

5.57 To Draw an Approximate Ellipse
Fig. 5.56
For many purposes, particularly where a small ellipse is required, the approximate circular-arc method is perfectly satisfactory. Such an ellipse is sure to be symmetrical and may be quickly drawn.

Given axes **AB** and **CD**.

I.   Draw line **AC**. With **O** as center and **OA** as radius, strike the arc **AE**. With **C** as center and **CE** as radius, strike the arc **EF**.

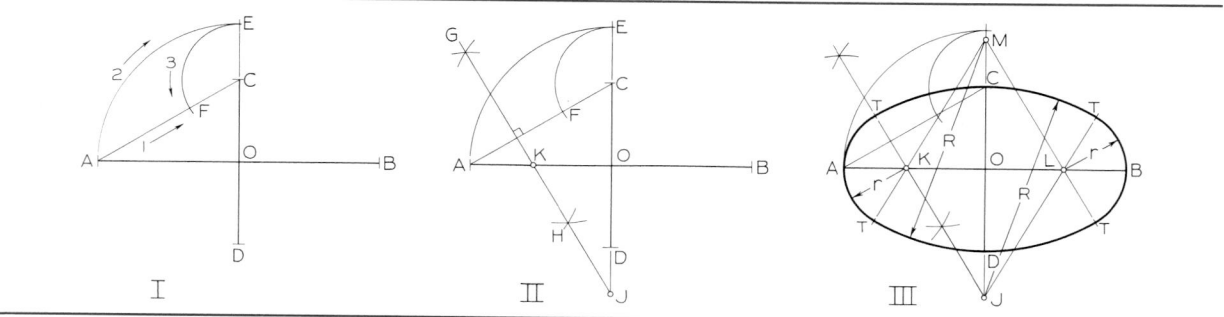

Fig. 5.56   Drawing an Approximate Ellipse (§5.57)

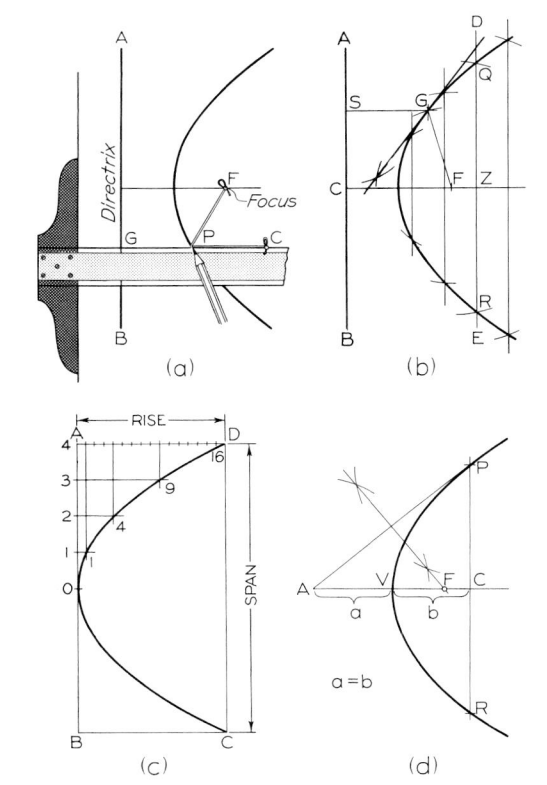

Fig. 5.57 Drawing a Parabola (§5.58).

II.   Draw perpendicular bisector **GH** of the line **AF**; the points **K** and **J**, where it intersects the axes, are centers of the required arcs.

III.   Find centers **M** and **L** by setting off **OL** = **OK** and **OM** = **OJ**. Using centers **K**, **L**, **M**, and **J**, draw circular arcs as shown. The points of tangency **T** are at the junctures of the arcs on the lines joining the centers.

5.58 To Draw a Parabola
The curve of intersection between a right circular cone and a plane parallel to one of its elements, Fig. 5.46 (d), is a parabola. *A parabola is generated by a point moving so that its distances from a fixed point, the focus, and from a fixed line, the directrix, remain equal.* For example:

Fig. 5.57 (a)   Given focus **F** and directrix **AB**: A parabola may be generated by a pencil guided by a string, as shown. Fasten the string at **F** and **C**; its length is **GC**. The point **C** is selected at random, its

distance from **G** depending on the desired extent of the curve. Keep the string taut and the pencil against the T-square, as shown.

Fig. 5.57 (b)   Given focus **F** and directrix **AB**: Draw a line **DE** parallel to the directrix and at any distance **CZ** from it. With center at **F** and radius **CZ**, strike arcs to intersect the line **DE** in the points **Q** and **R**, which are points on the parabola. Determine as many additional points as are necessary to draw the parabola accurately, by drawing additional lines parallel to line **AB** and proceeding in the same manner.

   A tangent to the parabola at any point **G** bisects the angle formed by the focal line **FG** and the line **SG** perpendicular to the directrix.

Fig. 5.57 (c)   Given the rise and span of the parabola: Divide **AO** into any number of equal parts, and divide **AD** into a number of equal parts amounting to the square of that number. From line **AB**, each point on the parabola is offset by a number of units equal to the square of the number of units from point **O**. For example, point **3** projects **9** units (the square of **3**). This method is generally used for drawing parabolic arches.

Fig. 5.57 (d)   Given points **P**, **R**, and **V** of a parabola, to find the focus **F**: Draw tangent at **P**, making a = b. Draw perpendicular bisector of **AP**, which intersects the axis at **F**, the focus of the parabola.

Fig. 5.58 (a) or (b)   Given rectangle or parallelogram **ABCD**: Divide **BC** into any even number of equal parts, and divide the sides **AB** and **DC** each into half as many parts, and draw lines as shown. The intersections of like-numbered lines are points on the parabola.

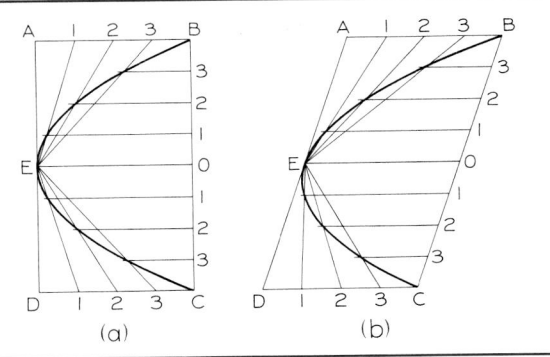

Fig. 5.58 Drawing a Parabola (§5.58).

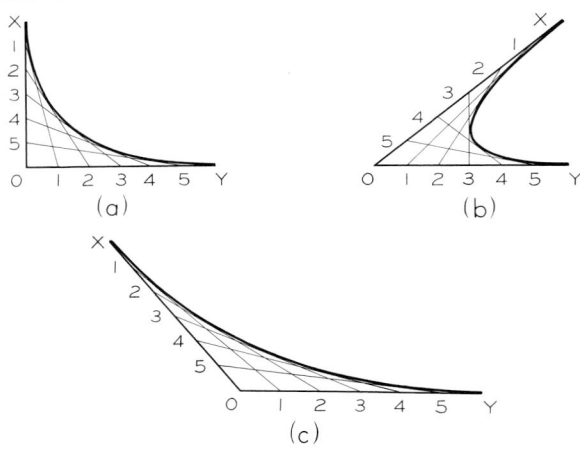

Fig. 5.59   Parabolic Curves (§5.59).

Practical Applications

The parabola is used for reflecting surfaces for light and sound, for vertical curves in highways, for forms of arches, and approximately for forms of the curves of cables for suspension bridges. It is also used to show the bending moment at any point on a uniformly loaded beam or girder.

5.59 To Join Two Points by a Parabolic Curve Fig. 5.59

Let X and Y be the given points. Assume any point O, and draw tangents XO and YO. Divide XO and YO into the same number of equal parts, number the division points as shown, and connect corresponding points. These lines are tangents of the required parabola and form its envelope. Sketch a light smooth curve, and then heavy in the curve with the aid of the irregular curve, §2.54.

These parabolic curves are more pleasing in appearance than circular arcs and are useful in machine design. If the tangents OX and OY are equal, the axis of the parabola will bisect the angle between them.

5.60 To Draw a Hyperbola

The curve of intersection between a right circular cone and a plane making an angle with the axis smaller than that made by the elements, Fig. 5.46 (e), is a hyperbola. *A hyperbola is generated by a point moving so that the difference of its distances from two fixed points, the foci, is constant and equal to the transverse axis of the hyperbola.*

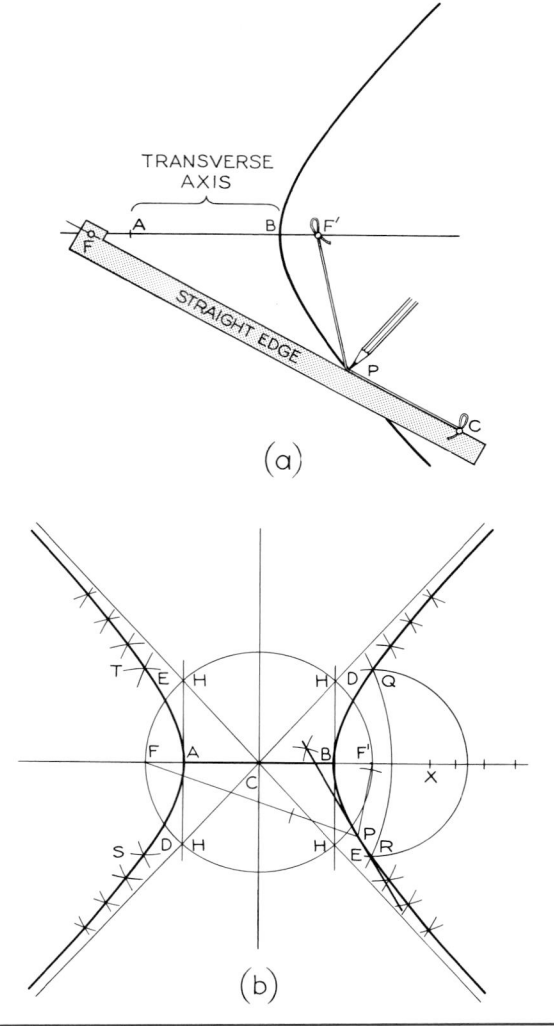

Fig. 5.60   Drawing a Hyperbola (§5.60).

Fig. 5.60 (a)   Let F and F′ be the foci and AB the transverse axis. The curve may be generated by a pencil guided by a string, as shown. Fasten a string at F′ and C; its length is FC minus AB. The point C is chosen at random; its distance from F depends on the desired extent of the curve.

Fasten the straightedge at F. If it is revolved about F, with the pencil point moving against it and with the string taut, the hyperbola may be drawn as shown.

Fig. 5.60 (b)   To construct the curve geometrically, select any point X on the transverse axis produced. With centers at F and F′ and BX as radius, strike the arcs DE. With the same centers, F and F′, and AX as radius, strike arcs to intersect the arcs first drawn in the points Q, R, S, and T, which are points of the required hyperbola. Find as many additional points as are necessary to draw the curves accurately by selecting other points similar to point X along the transverse axis, and proceeding as described for point X.

To draw the tangent to a hyperbola at a given point P, bisect the angle between the focal radii FP and F'P. The bisector is the required tangent.

To draw the asymptotes HCH of the hyperbola, draw a circle with the diameter FF' and erect perpendiculars to the transverse axis at the points A and B to intersect the circle in the points H. The lines HCH are the required asymptotes.

5.61 To Draw an Equilateral Hyperbola
Fig. 5.61
Let the asymptotes OB and OA, at right angles to each other, and the point P on the curve be given.

Fig. 5.61 (a) In an equilateral hyperbola the asymptotes, at right angles to each other, may be used as the axes to which the curve is referred. If a chord of the hyperbola is extended to intersect the axes, the intercepts between the curve and the axes are equal. For example, a chord through given point P intersects the axes at points 1 and 2, intercepts P–1 and 2–3 are equal, and point 3 is a point on the hyperbola. Likewise, another chord through P provides equal intercepts P–1' and 3'–2', and point 3' is a point on the curve. Not all chords need be drawn through given point P, but as new points are established on the curve, chords may be drawn through them to obtain more points. After enough points are found to insure an accurate curve, the hyperbola is drawn with the aid of the irregular curve, §2.54.

Fig. 5.61 (b) In an equilateral hyperbola, the coordinates are related so that their products remain constant. Through given point P, draw lines 1–P–Y and 2–P–Z parallel, respectively, to the axes. From the origin of coordinates O, draw any diagonal intersecting these two lines at points 3 and X. At these points draw lines parallel to the axes, intersecting at point 4, a point on the curve. Likewise, another diagonal from O intersects the two lines through P at points 8 and Y, and lines through these points parallel to the axes intersect at point 9, another point on the curve. A third diagonal similarly produces point 10 on the curve, and so on. Find as many

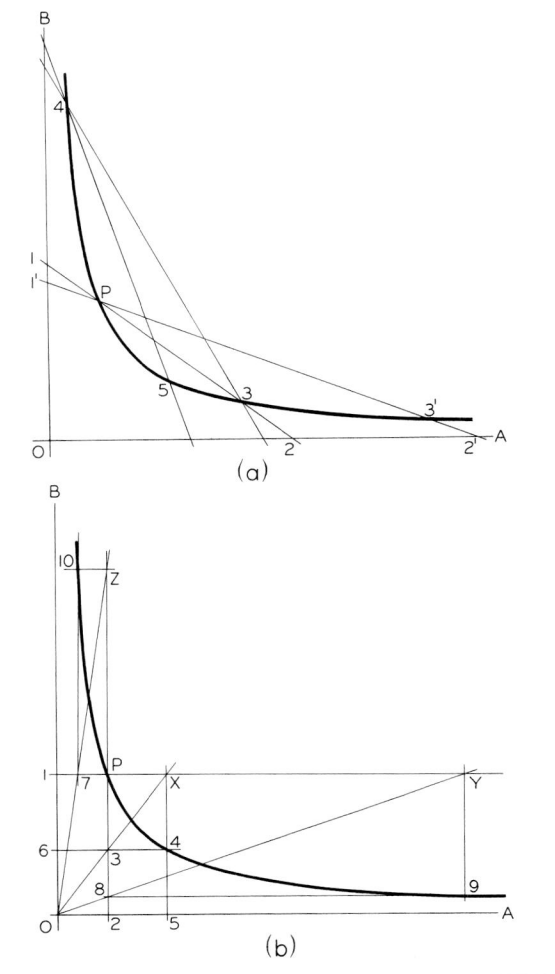

Fig. 5.61 Equilateral Hyperbola (§5.61).

points as necessary for a smooth curve, and draw the parabola with the aid of the irregular curve, §2.54. It is evident from the similar triangles O–X–5 and O–3–2 that lines P–1 × P–2 = 4–5 × 4–6.

The equilateral hyperbola can be used to represent varying pressure of a gas as the volume varies, since the pressure varies inversely as the volume; that is, pressure × volume is constant.

5.62 To Draw a Spiral of Archimedes
Fig. 5.62
To find points on the curve, draw lines through the pole C, making equal angles with each other, such as 30° angles, and beginning with any one line, set off any distance, such as 2 mm or $\frac{1}{16}$"; set off twice that distance on the next line, three times on the

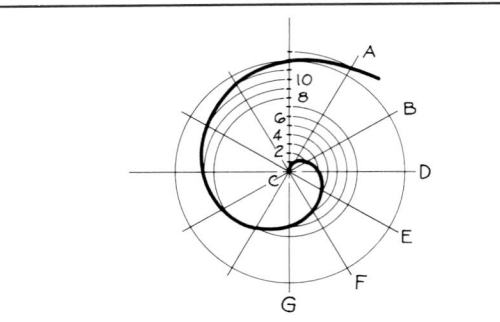

Fig. 5.62 Spiral of Archimedes (§5.62).

third, and so on. Through the points thus determined, draw a smooth curve, using the irregular curve, §2.54.

5.63 To Draw a Helix Fig. 5.63

A helix is generated by a point moving around and along the surface of a cylinder or cone with a uniform angular velocity about the axis, and with a uniform linear velocity in the direction of the axis. A cylindrical helix is generally known simply as a helix. The distance measured parallel to the axis traversed by the point in one revolution is called the lead.

If the cylindrical surface upon which a helix is generated is rolled out onto a plane, the helix becomes a straight line as shown in Fig. 5.63 (a), and

the portion below the helix becomes a right triangle, the altitude of which is equal to the lead of the helix and the length of the base equal to the circumference of the cylinder. Such a helix can, therefore, be defined as the shortest line that can be drawn on the surface of a cylinder connecting two points not on the same element.

To draw the helix, draw two views of the cylinder upon which the helix is generated, (b), and divide the circle of the base into any number of equal parts. On the rectangular view of the cylinder, set off the lead and divide it into the same number of equal parts as the base. Number the divisions as shown, in this case 16. When the generating point has moved one-sixteenth of the distance around the cylinder, it will have risen one-sixteenth of the lead; when it has moved halfway around the cylinder, it will have risen half the lead; and so on. Points on the helix are found by projecting up from point 1 in the circular view to line 1 in the rectangular view, from point 2 in the circular view to line 2 in the rectangular view, and so on.

The helix shown at (b) is a right-hand helix. In a left-hand helix, (c), the visible portions of the curve are inclined in the opposite direction, that is, downward to the right. The helix shown at (b) can be converted into a left-hand helix by interchanging the visible and hidden lines.

The helix finds many applications in industry, as in screw threads, worm gears, conveyors, spiral stairways, and so on. The stripes of a barber pole are helical in form.

The construction for a right-hand conical helix is shown at (d).

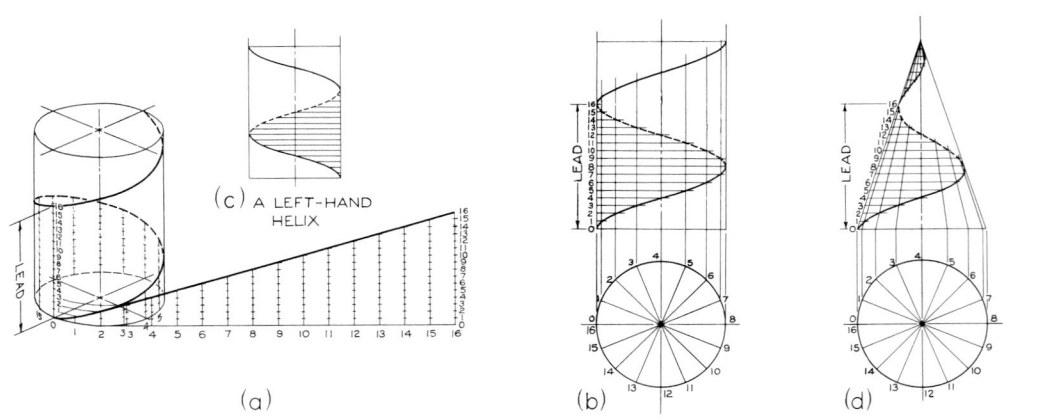

Fig. 5.63 Helix (§5.63).

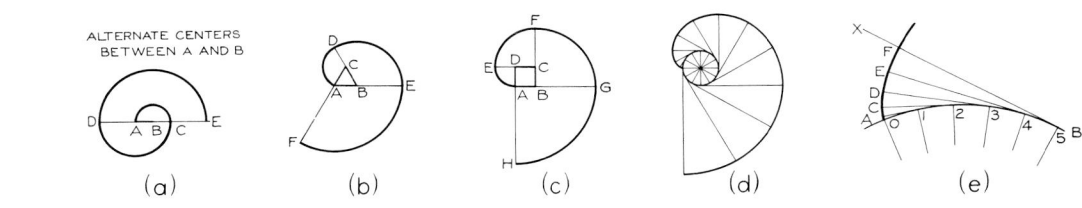

Fig. 5.64 Involutes (§5.64).

5.64 To Draw an Involute Fig. 5.64

The path of a point on a string, as the string unwinds from a line, a polygon, or a circle, is an involute.

To Draw an Involute of a Line Fig. 5.64 (a)

Let AB be the given line. With AB as radius and B as center, draw the semicircle AC. With AC as radius and A as center, draw the semicircle CD. With BD as radius and B as center, draw the semicircle DE. Continue similarly, alternating centers between A and B, until a figure of the required size is completed.

To Draw an Involute of a Triangle

Fig. 5.64 (b)

Let ABC be the given triangle. With CA as radius and C as center, strike the arc AD. With BD as radius and B as center, strike the arc DE. With AE as radius and A as center, strike the arc EF. Continue similarly until a figure of the required size is completed.

To Draw an Involute of a Square

Fig. 5.64 (c)

Let ABCD be the given square. With DA as radius and D as center, draw the 90° arc AE. Proceed as for the involute of a triangle until a figure of the required size is completed.

To Draw an Involute of a Circle Fig. 5.64 (d)

A circle may be regarded as a polygon with an infinite number of sides. The involute is constructed by dividing the circumference into a number of equal parts, drawing a tangent at each division point, setting off along each tangent the length of the corresponding circular arc, Fig. 5.45 (c), and drawing the required curve through the points set off on the several tangents.

Fig. 5.64 (e) The involute may be generated by a point on a straight line that is rolled on a fixed circle. Points on the required curve may be determined by setting off equal distances 0–1, 1–2, 2–3, and so forth, along the circumference, drawing a tangent at each division point, and proceeding as explained for (d).

The involute of a circle is used in the construction of involute gear teeth. In this system, the involute forms the face and a part of the flank of the teeth of gear wheels; the outlines of the teeth of racks are straight lines.

5.65 To Draw a Cycloid Fig. 5.65

A cycloid may be generated by a point P in the circumference of a circle that rolls along a straight line.

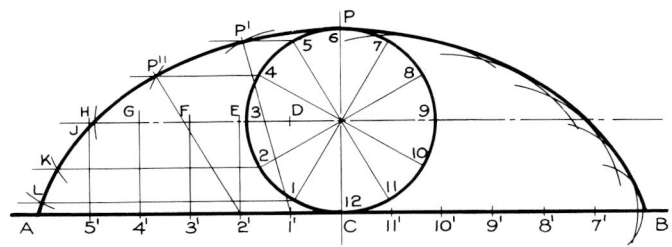

Fig. 5.65 Cycloid (§5.65).

Given the generating circle and the straight line AB tangent to it, make the distances CA and CB each equal to the semicircumference of the circle, Fig. 5.45 (c). Divide these distances and the semicircumference into the same number of equal parts, six, for instance, and number them consecutively as shown. Suppose the circle to roll to the left; when point 1 of the circle reaches point 1′ of the line, the center of the circle will be at D, point 7 will be the highest point of the circle, and the generating point 6 will be at the same distance from the line AB as point 5 is when the circle is in its central position. Hence, to find the point P′, draw a line through point 5 parallel to AB and intersect it with an arc drawn from the center D with a radius equal to that of the circle. To find point P″, draw a line through point 4 parallel to AB, and intersect it with an arc drawn from the center E, with a radius equal to that of the circle. Points J, K, and L are found in a similar manner.

Another method that may be employed is shown in the right half of the figure. With center at 11′ and the chord 11–6 as radius, strike an arc. With 10′ as center and the chord 10–6 as radius, strike an arc. Continue similarly with centers 9′, 8′, and 7′. Draw the required cycloid tangent to these arcs.

Either method may be used; however, the second is the shorter one and is preferred. It is evident, from the tangent arcs drawn in the manner just described, that the line joining the generating point and the point of contact for the generating circle is a normal of the cycloid; the lines 1′–P′ and 2′–P″, for instance, are normals; this property makes the cycloid suitable for the outlines of gear teeth.

5.66 To Draw an Epicycloid or a Hypocycloid Fig. 5.66

If the generating point P is on the circumference of a circle that rolls along the convex side of a larger circle, (a), the curve generated is an epicycloid. If the circle rolls along the concave side of a larger

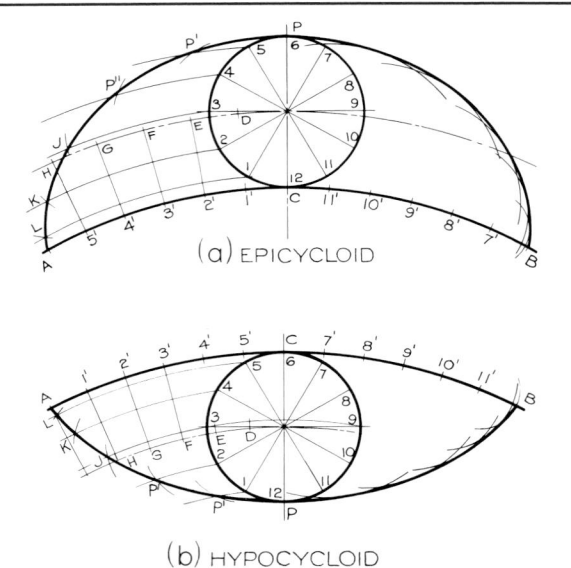

(a) EPICYCLOID

(b) HYPOCYCLOID

Fig. 5.66   Epicycloid and Hypocycloid (§5.66).

circle, (b), the curve generated is a hypocycloid. These curves are drawn in a manner similar to the cycloid, Fig. 5.65. These curves, like the cycloid, are used to form the outlines of certain gear teeth and are, therefore, of practical importance in machine design.

5.67 Computer Graphics

Through the use of various application programs and routines available in computer graphics, it is possible to accurately establish the various geometric constructions shown in Chapter 5. CAD programs are particularly well suited for repetitive operations such as dividing a line into a number of equal parts, and for generating lines representing mathematical curves such as the hyperbola and parabola. Examples of CAD-produced geometric shapes and surfaces are shown in Fig. 5.67.

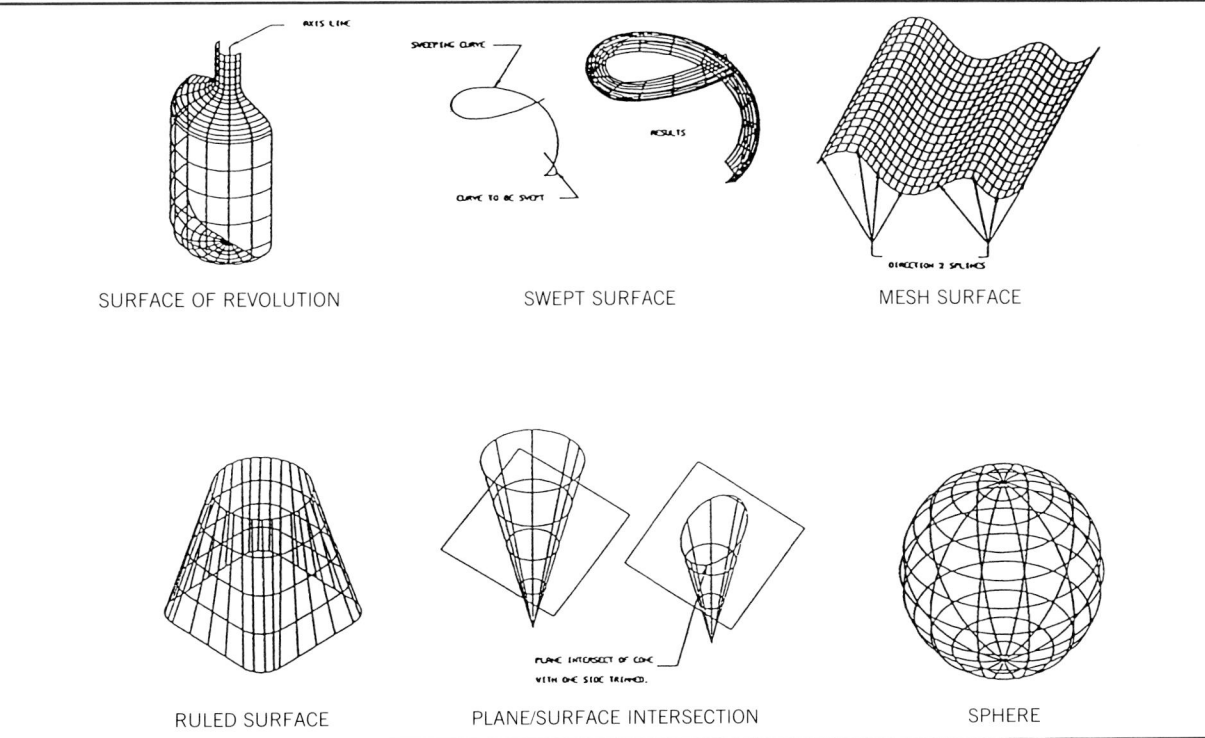

SURFACE OF REVOLUTION   SWEPT SURFACE   MESH SURFACE

RULED SURFACE   PLANE/SURFACE INTERSECTION   SPHERE

Fig. 5.67 Geometric Shapes and Surfaces Produced with TRI-CAD System. *Courtesy of Cadgrafix, Inc.*

Geometric Construction Problems

Geometric constructions should be made very accurately, with a hard pencil (2H to 4H) having a long, sharp, conical point. Draw given and required lines dark and medium in thickness, and draw construction lines *very light*. Do not erase construction lines. Indicate points and lines as described in §5.1.

The instructor will make assignments from the many problems that follow. Use Layout A–2 (see inside of back cover) divided into four parts, as shown in Fig. 5.68, or Layout A4–2 (adjusted). Additional sheets with other problems selected from Figs. 5.69 to 5.80 and drawn on the same sheet layout, may be assigned by the instructor.

Many problems are dimensioned in the metric system. The instructor may assign the student to convert the remaining problems to metric measure. See inside front cover for decimal and millimeter equivalents.

The student should exercise care in setting up each problem so as to make the best use of the space available, to present the problem to best advantage, and to produce a pleasing appearance. Letter the principal points of all constructions in a manner similar to the various illustrations in this chapter.

Since many of the problems in this chapter are of a general nature, they can also be solved on most computer graphics systems. If a system is available, the instructor may choose to assign specific problems to be completed by this method.

Additional problems in convenient form for solution are presented in the worksheets at the back of this book. Refer to Drawings 5–1 to 5–3 and accompanying instructions.

The first four problems are shown in Fig. 5.68.

Prob. 5.1 Draw an inclined line **AB** 65 mm long and bisect it, Fig. 5.8.

Prob. 5.2 Draw any angle with vertex at **C**. Bisect it, Fig. 5.10, and transfer one half in new position at **D**, Fig. 5.11.

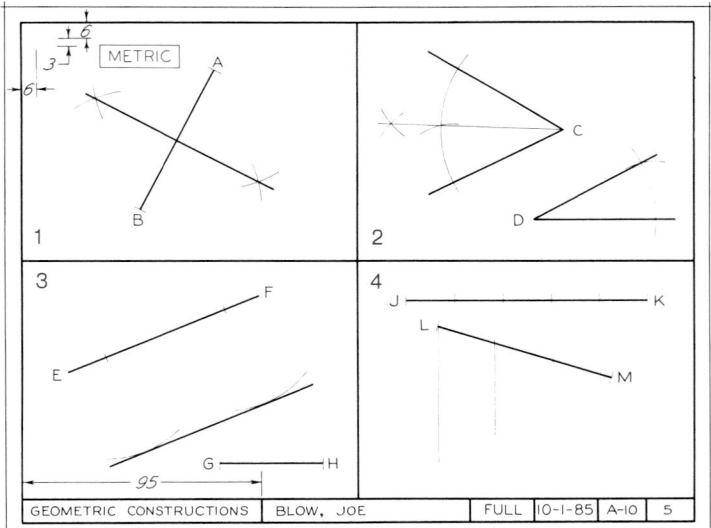

Fig. 5.68 Geometric Constructions.
Layout A–2 or A4–2 (adjusted). (Probs. 5.1 to 5.4)

Prob. 5.3 Draw an inclined line EF and assume distance GH = 42 mm. Draw a line parallel to EF and at the distance GH from it, Fig. 5.13 (a).

Prob. 5.4 Draw the line JK 95 mm long and divide it into five equal parts with the dividers, §2.40. Draw a line LM 58 mm long and divide it into three equal parts by the parallel-line method, Fig. 5.15.

Prob. 5.5 Draw a line OP 92 mm long and divide it into three proportional parts to 3, 5, and 9, Fig. 5.17 (a).

Prob. 5.6 Draw a line 87 mm long and divide it into parts proportional to the square of x where $x = 1$, 2, 3, and 4, Fig. 5.17 (c).

Prob. 5.7 Draw a triangle having sides 76 mm, 85 mm, and 65 mm, Fig. 5.19. Bisect the three interior angles, Fig. 5.10. The bisectors should meet at a point. Draw the inscribed circle with the point as center.

Prob. 5.8 Draw a right triangle having the hypotenuse 65 mm and one leg 40 mm, Figs. 5.3 and 5.20, and draw a circle through the three vertexes, Fig. 5.32.

Prob. 5.9 Draw an inclined line QR 84 mm long. Select a point P on the line 32 mm from Q, and erect a perpendicular, Fig. 5.18 (c). Assume a point S about 45.5 mm from the line, and erect a perpendicular from S to the line, Fig. 5.18 (b).

Prob. 5.10 Draw two lines making an angle of $35\frac{1}{2}°$ with each other, using the tangent method, Fig. 5.21 (c). Check with protractor, §2.18.

Prob. 5.11 Draw two lines making an angle of $33°16'$ with each other, using the sine method, Fig 5.21 (c). Check with protractor, §2.18.

Prob. 5.12 Draw an equilateral triangle, Fig. 5.3 (a), having 63.5 mm sides, Fig. 5.22 (a). Bisect the interior angles, Fig. 5.10. Draw the inscribed circle, using the intersection of the bisectors as center.

Prob. 5.13 Draw inclined line TU 55 mm long, and then draw a square on TU as a given side, Fig. 5.23 (a).

Prob. 5.14 Draw a 54 mm diameter circle (lightly); then inscribe a square in the circle and circumscribe a square on the circle, Fig. 5.23 (c) and (d).

Prob. 5.15 Draw a 65 mm diameter circle (lightly), find the vertexes of a regular inscribed pentagon, Fig. 5.24 (a), and join the vertexes to form a five-pointed star.

Prob. 5.16 Draw a 65 mm diameter circle (lightly), inscribe a hexagon, Fig. 5.25 (b), and circumscribe a hexagon, Fig. 5.26 (d).

Prob. 5.17 Draw a square (lightly) with 63.5 mm sides, Fig. 5.23 (b), and inscribe an octagon, Fig. 5.28 (b).

Prob. 5.18 Draw a triangle similar to that in Fig. 5.29 (a), having sides 50 mm, 38 mm, and 73 mm long, and transfer the triangle to a new location and turned 180° similar to that in Fig. 5.29 (b). Check by pricked point method, §5.29.

Prob. 5.19 In center of space, draw a rectangle 88 mm wide and 61 mm high. Show construction for reducing this rectangle to 58 mm wide and then to 70 mm wide, Fig. 5.31 (b).

Prob. 5.20 Draw three points arranged approximately as in Fig. 5.32 (a), and draw a circle through the three points.

Prob. 5.21   Draw a 58 mm diameter circle. Assume a point **S** on the left side of the circle and draw a tangent at that point, Fig. 5.34 (a). Assume a point **T** to the right of the circle 50 mm from its center, and draw two tangents to the circle through the point, Fig. 5.34 (b).

Prob. 5.22   Through center of space, draw horizontal center line; then draw two circles 50 mm diameter and 38 mm diameter, respectively, with centers 54 mm apart. Locate the circles so that the construction will be centered in the space. Draw "open-belt" tangents to the circles, Fig. 5.35 (a).

Prob. 5.23   Same as Prob. 5.21, except draw "crossed-belt" tangents to the circle, Fig. 5.35 (b).

Prob. 5.24   Draw vertical line **VW** 33 mm from left side of space. Assume point **P** 44 mm farther to the right and 25 mm down from top of space. Draw a 56 mm diameter circle through P, tangent to VW, Fig. 5.36 (a).

Prob. 5.25   Draw vertical line **XY** 35 mm from left side of space. Assume point **P** 44 mm farther to the right and 25 mm down from top of space. Assume point **Q** on line XY and 50 mm from P. Draw a circle through P and tangent to XY at Q, Fig. 5.36 (b).

Prob. 5.26   Draw a 64 mm diameter circle with center **C** 16 mm directly to left of center of space. Assume point **P** at the lower right and 60 mm from C. Draw an arc with 25 mm radius through P and tangent to the circle, Fig. 5.36 (c).

Prob. 5.27   Draw a vertical line and a horizontal line, each 65 mm long, Fig. 5.37 (I). Draw an arc with 38 mm radius, tangent to the lines.

Prob. 5.28   Draw a horizontal line 20 mm up from bottom of space. Select a point on the line 50 mm from the left side of space, and through it draw a line upward to the right at 60° to horizontal. Draw arcs with 35 mm radius within obtuse angle and acute angle, respectively, tangent to the two lines, Fig. 5.38.

Prob. 5.29   Draw two intersecting lines making an angle of 60° with each other similar to Fig. 5.38 (a). Assume a point **P** on one line at a distance of 45 mm from the intersection. Draw an arc tangent to both lines with one point of tangency at **P**, Fig. 5.33.

Prob. 5.30   Draw vertical line **AB** 32 mm from left side of space. Draw an arc of 42 mm radius with center 75 mm to right of line and in lower right portion of space. Draw arc of 25 mm radius tangent to **AB** and to the first arc, Fig. 5.39.

Prob. 5.31   With centers 20 mm up from bottom of space, and 86 mm apart, draw arcs of radii 44 mm and 24 mm, respectively. Draw arc of 32 mm radius tangent to the two arcs, Fig. 5.40.

Prob. 5.32   Draw two circles as in Prob. 5.22. Draw arc of 70 mm radius tangent to upper sides of, and enclosing, the circles, Fig. 5.41 (a). Draw an arc of 50 mm radius tangent to the circles but enclosing only the smaller circle, Fig. 5.41 (b).

Prob. 5.33   Draw two parallel inclined lines 45 mm apart. Choose a point on each line and connect them with an ogee curve tangent to the two parallel lines, Fig. 5.43 (a).

Prob. 5.34   Draw an arc of 54 mm radius that subtends an angle of 90°. Find the length of the arc by two methods, Fig. 5.45 (a) and (c). Calculate the length of the arc and compare with the lengths determined graphically. See note at end of §5.45.

Prob. 5.35 Draw a major axis 102 mm long (horizontally) and minor axis 64 mm long, with their intersection at the center of the space. Draw ellipse by foci method with at least five points in each quadrant, Fig. 5.48.

Prob. 5.36 Draw axes as in Prob. 5.35, and draw ellipse by trammel method, Fig. 5.49.

Prob. 5.37 Draw axes as in Prob. 5.35, and draw ellipse by concentric-circle method, Fig. 5.50.

Prob. 5.38 Draw axes as in Prob. 5.35, and draw ellipse by parallelogram method, Fig. 5.25 (a).

Prob. 5.39 Draw conjugate diameters intersecting at center of space. Draw 88 mm diameter horizontally, and 70 mm diameter at 60° with horizontal. Draw oblique-circle ellipse, Fig. 5.51. Find at least 5 points in each quadrant.

Prob. 5.40 Draw conjugate diameters as in Prob. 5.39, and draw ellipse by parallelogram method, Fig. 5.52 (b).

Prob. 5.41 Draw axes as in Prob. 5.35, and draw an approximate ellipse, Fig. 5.56.

Prob. 5.42 Draw a parabola with a vertical axis, and the focus 12 mm from the directrix, Fig. 5.57 (b). Find at least nine points on the curve.

Prob. 5.43 Draw a hyperbola with a horizontal transverse axis 25 mm long and the foci 38 mm apart, Fig. 5.60 (b). Draw the asymptotes.

Prob. 5.44 Draw horizontal line near bottom of space, and vertical line near left side of space. Assume point P 16 mm to right of vertical line and 38 mm above horizontal line. Draw equilateral hyperbola through P and with reference to the two lines as asymptotes. Use either method of Fig. 5.61.

Prob. 5.45 Using the center of the space as the pole, draw a spiral of Archimedes with the generating point moving in a counterclockwise direction and away from the pole at the rate of 25 mm in each convolution, Fig. 5.62.

Prob. 5.46 Through center of space, draw horizontal center line, and on it construct a right-hand helix 50 mm diameter, 64 mm long, and with a lead of 25 mm, Fig. 5.63. Draw only a half-circular end view.

Prob. 5.47 Draw the involute of an equilateral triangle with 15 mm sides, Fig. 5.64 (b).

Prob. 5.48 Draw the involute of a 20 mm diameter circle, Fig. 5.64 (d).

Prob. 5.49 Draw a cycloid generated by a 30 mm diameter circle rolling along a horizontal straight line, Fig. 5.65.

Prob. 5.50 Draw an epicycloid generated by a 38 mm diameter circle rolling along a circular arc having a radius of 64 mm, Fig. 5.66 (a).

Prob. 5.51 Draw a hypocycloid generated by a 38 mm diameter circle rolling along a circular arc having a radius of 64 mm, Fig. 5.66 (b).

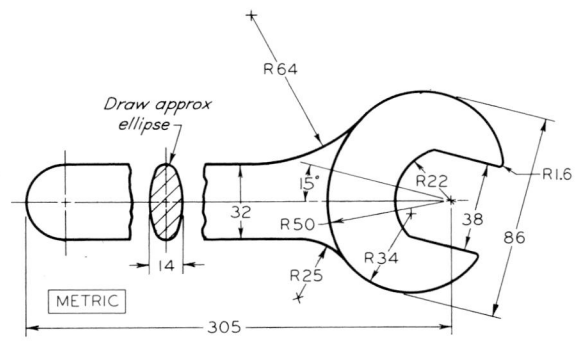

Fig. 5.69   Spanner.*

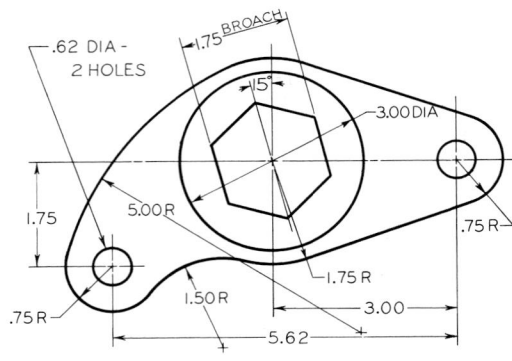

Fig. 5.70   Rocker Arm.*

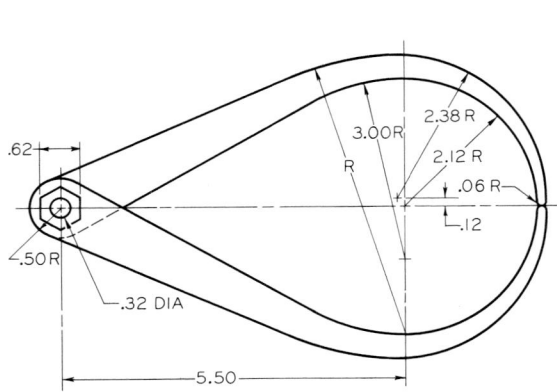

Fig. 5.71   Outside Caliper.*

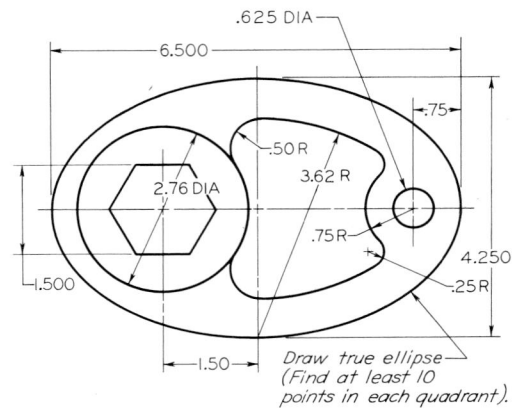

Fig. 5.72   Special Cam.*

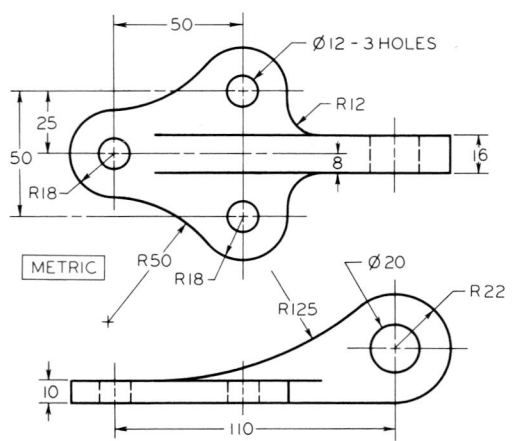

Fig. 5.73   Boiler Stay.*

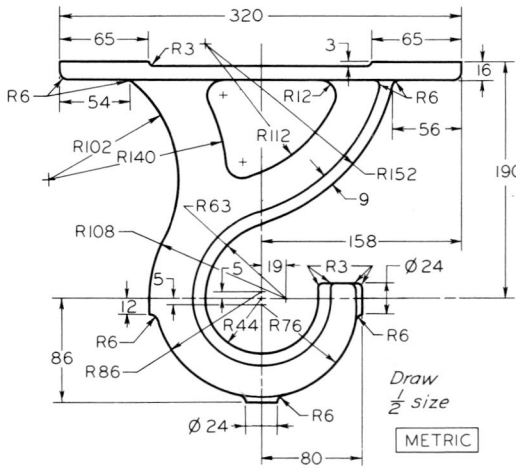

Fig. 5.74   Shaft Hanger Casting.*

*Using Layout A–2 or A4–2 (adjusted), draw assigned problem with instruments. Omit dimensions and notes unless assigned by instructor.

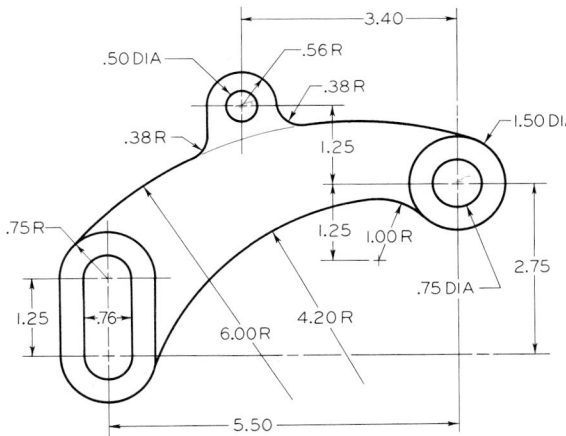

Fig. 5.75   Shift Lever.*

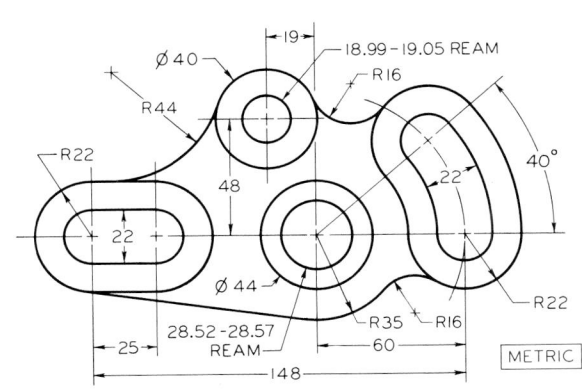

Fig. 5.76   Gear Arm.*

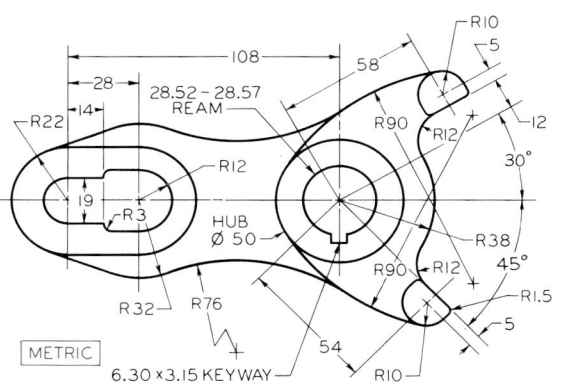

Fig. 5.77   Form Roll Lever.*

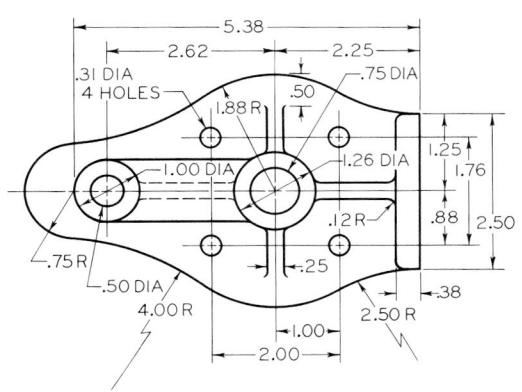

Fig. 5.78   Press Base.*

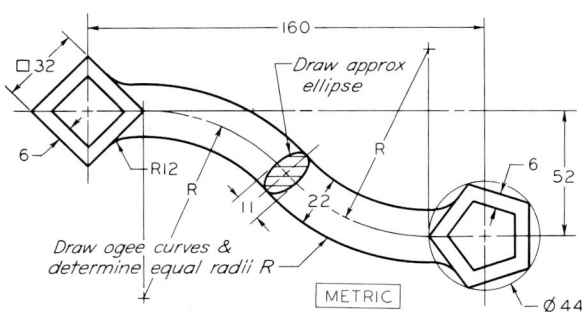

Fig. 5.79   Special S-Wrench.*

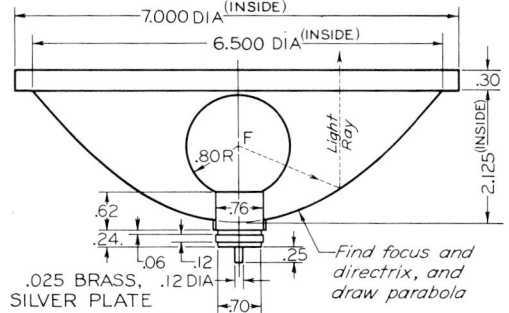

Fig. 5.80   Auto Headlight Reflector.*

*Using Layout A–2 or A4–2 (adjusted), draw assigned problem with instruments. Omit dimensions and notes unless assigned by instructor.

CHAPTER

6

Sketching and Shape Description

The importance of freehand drawing or sketching in engineering, design, and technical communications cannot be overestimated. To the person who possesses a complete knowledge of drawing as a language, the ability to execute quick, accurate, and clear sketches of ideas and designs constitutes a valuable means of expression. The old Chinese saying that "one picture is worth a thousand words" is not without foundation.

Most original design ideas find their first expression through the medium of a freehand sketch, §16.2. Freehand sketching is a valuable means of amplifying and clarifying, as well as recording, verbal explanations. Executives sketch freehand daily to explain their ideas to subordinates. Engineers often prepare their designs and turn them over to their detailers or designers in this convenient form as shown in the well-executed sketch of details for a steam locomotive, Fig. 6.1.

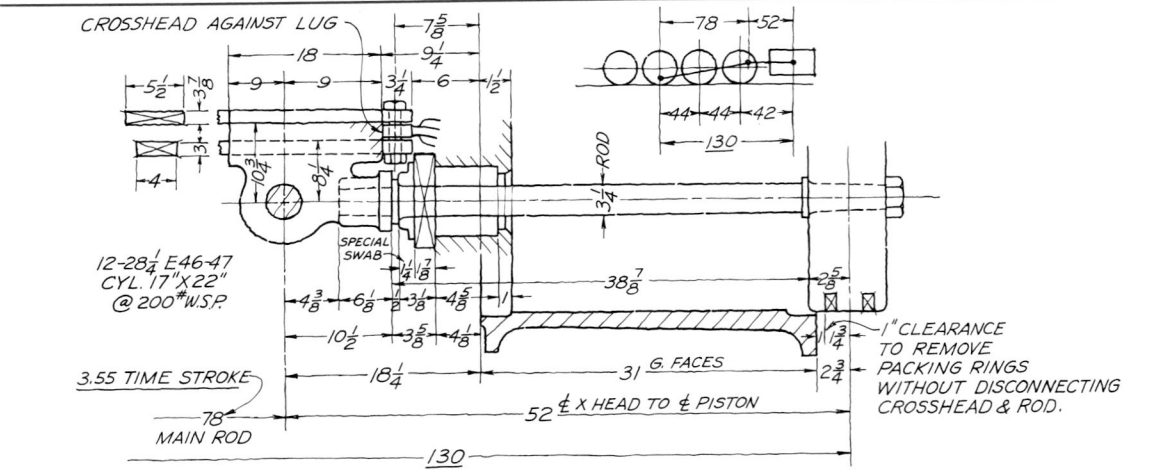

Fig. 6.1 Typical Design Sketch.

6.1 Technical Sketching

Freehand sketches are of great assistance to designers in organizing their thoughts and recording their ideas. Sketching is an effective and economical means of formulating various solutions to a given problem so that a choice can be made between them at the outset. Often much time can be lost if the designer starts his or her scaled layout before adequate preliminary study with the aid of sketches. Information concerning changes in design or covering replacement of broken parts or lost drawings is usually conveyed through sketches. Many engineers consider the ability to render serviceable sketches of greater value to them than skill in instrument drawing. The designer, technician, or engineer will find daily use for this valuable means of formulating, expressing, and recording ideas.

The degree of perfection required in a given sketch depends upon its use. Sketches hurriedly made to supplement oral description may be rough and incomplete. On the other hand, if a sketch is the medium of conveying important and precise information to engineers, technicians or skilled workers, it should be executed as carefully as possible under the circumstances.

The term "freehand sketch" is too often understood to mean a crude or sloppy freehand drawing in which no particular effort has been made. On the contrary, a freehand sketch should be made with care and with attention to proportion, clarity, and correct line widths.

6.2 Sketching Materials

One advantage of freehand sketching is that it requires only pencil, paper, and eraser—items that anyone has for ready use.

When sketches are made in the field, where an accurate record is required, a small notebook or sketching pad is frequently used. Often clipboards are employed to hold the paper. Graph paper is helpful to the sketcher, especially to the person who cannot sketch reasonably well without guide lines. Paper with 4, 5, 8, or 10 squares per inch is recommended. Such paper is convenient for sketching to scale since values can be assigned to the squares, and the squares counted to secure proportional distances, as shown in Fig. 6.2.

Sketching pads of plain tracing paper are available, accompanied by a master cross-section sheet. The drafter places a blank sheet over the master grid and can see the grid through the transparent sheet.

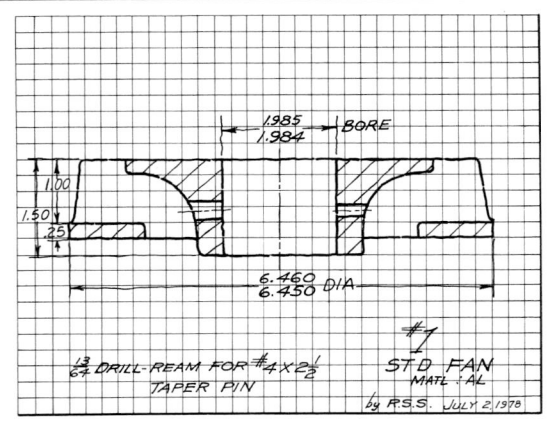

Fig. 6.2 Sketch on Graph Paper.

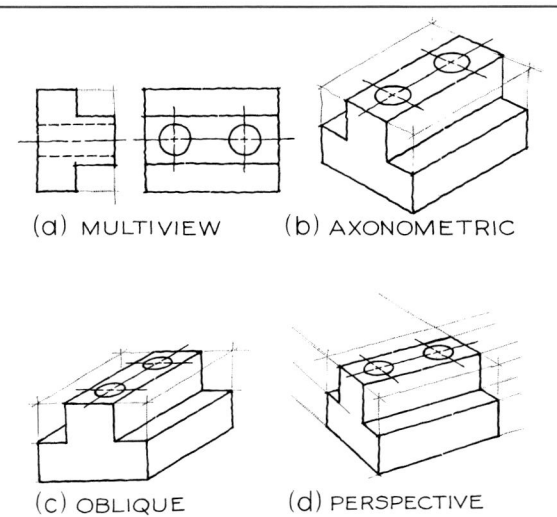

Fig. 6.3   Types of Projection.

(a) MULTIVIEW   (b) AXONOMETRIC

(c) OBLIQUE   (d) PERSPECTIVE

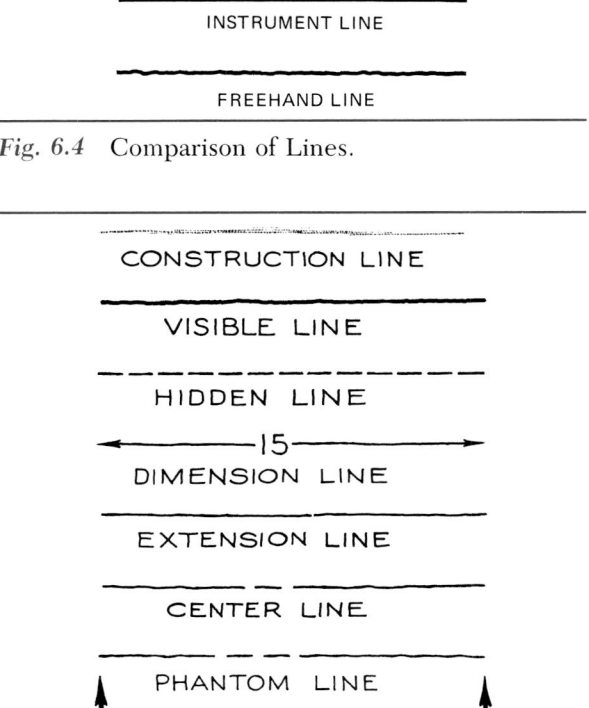

Fig. 6.4   Comparison of Lines.

INSTRUMENT LINE

FREEHAND LINE

CONSTRUCTION LINE

VISIBLE LINE

HIDDEN LINE

|←————— 15 ————→|
DIMENSION LINE

EXTENSION LINE

CENTER LINE

PHANTOM LINE

CUTTING-PLANE LINES

Fig. 6.5   Sketch Lines.

An alternate procedure is to draw, with instruments, a master cross-section sheet, using ink, making the squares either 10 mm or .25″ as desired. Ordinary bond typewriter paper is then placed over the master sheet and the sketch made thereon. Such a sketch is not only more uniform and "true" but shows up better because the cross-section lines are absent.

For isometric sketching, a specially ruled isometric paper is available, Fig. 6.26.

Soft pencils, such as HB or F, should be used for freehand sketching. For carefully made sketches, two soft erasers are recommended, a Pink Pearl and a Mars-Plastic, Fig. 2.16.

6.3 Types of Sketches

Since technical sketches are made of three-dimensional objects, the form of the sketch conforms approximately to one of the four standard types of projection, as shown in Fig. 6.3. In *multiview* projection, (a), the object is described by its necessary views, as discussed in §§6.11–6.24. Or the object may be shown pictorially in a single view, by *axonometric (isometric)*, *oblique*, or *perspective sketches*, (b), (c), and (d), as discussed in §§6.11–6.17.

6.4 Scale

Sketches usually are *not made to any scale*. Objects should be sketched in their correct proportions as accurately as possible, by eye. However, cross-section paper provides a ready scale (by counting squares) that may be used to assist in sketching to

correct proportions. The size of the sketch is purely optional, depending upon the complexity of the object and the size of paper available. Small objects are often sketched oversize so as to show the necessary details clearly.

6.5 Technique of Lines

The chief difference between an instrument drawing and a freehand sketch lies in the character or *technique* of the lines. A good freehand line is not expected to be rigidly straight or exactly uniform, as an instrument line. While the effectiveness of an instrument line lies in exacting uniformity, the quality of a freehand line lies in its *freedom* and *variety*, Figs. 6.4 and 6.7.

Conventional lines, drawn instrumentally, are shown in Fig. 2.14, and the corresponding freehand renderings are shown in Fig. 6.5. The freehand construction line is a very light rough line in which some strokes may overlap. All other lines should be dark and clean-cut. Accent the ends of all dashes, and maintain a sharp contrast between the line

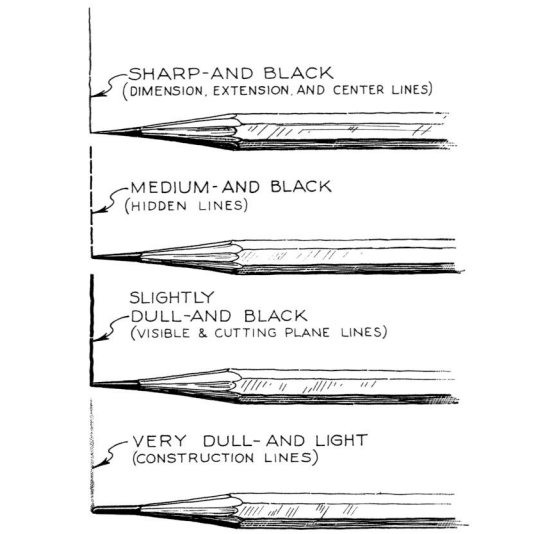

Fig. 6.6 Pencil Points.

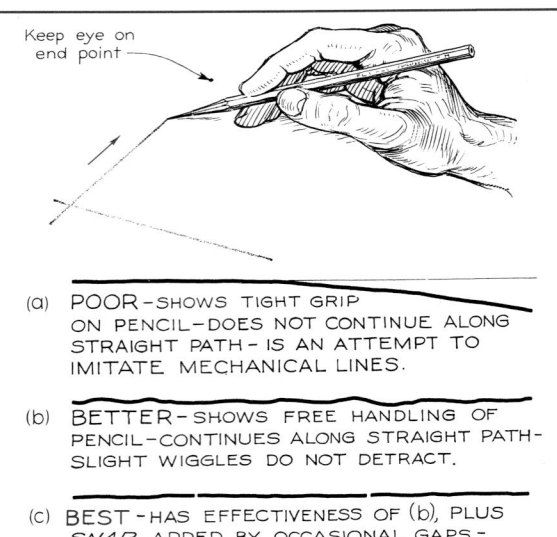

(a) POOR—SHOWS TIGHT GRIP ON PENCIL—DOES NOT CONTINUE ALONG STRAIGHT PATH—IS AN ATTEMPT TO IMITATE MECHANICAL LINES.

(b) BETTER—SHOWS FREE HANDLING OF PENCIL—CONTINUES ALONG STRAIGHT PATH—SLIGHT WIGGLES DO NOT DETRACT.

(c) BEST—HAS EFFECTIVENESS OF (b), PLUS *SNAP* ADDED BY OCCASIONAL GAPS—EASIER TO DRAW STRAIGHT.

Fig. 6.7 Drawing Horizontal Lines.

thicknesses. In particular, make visible lines **heavy** so the outline will stand out clearly, and make hidden lines, center lines, dimension lines, and extension lines *thin*.

6.6 Sharpening Sketching Pencils

For sketching, use a mechanical pencil with a soft lead, such as HB or F, and sharpen it to a conical point, as shown in Fig. 2.11 (c). Use this sharp point for center lines, dimension lines, and extension lines. For visible lines, hidden lines, and cutting-plane lines, round off the point slightly to produce the desired thickness of line, Fig. 6.6. Make all lines dark, with the exception of construction lines, which should be very light.

The use of thin-lead mechanical pencils with suitable diameters and grades of leads minimizes the need for sharpening and point dressing.

6.7 Straight Lines

Since the majority of lines on the average sketch are straight lines, it is necessary to learn to make them well. Hold the pencil naturally, about 1½″ back from the point, and approximately at right angles to the line to be drawn. Draw horizontal lines from left to right with a free and easy wrist-and-arm movement, Fig. 6.7. Draw vertical lines downward with finger and wrist movements, Fig. 6.8.

Inclined lines may be made to conform in direction to horizontal or vertical lines by shifting position with respect to the paper or by turning the paper slightly; hence, they may be drawn with the same general movements, Fig. 6.9.

In sketching long lines, mark the ends of the line with light dots, then move the pencil back and forth between the dots in long sweeps, keeping the eye always on the dot toward which the pencil is moving, the point of the pencil touching the paper lightly, and each successive stroke correcting the defects of the preceding strokes. When the path of the line has been established sufficiently, apply a little more pressure, replacing the trial series with a distinct line. Then, dim the line with a soft eraser and draw the final line clean-cut and dark, keeping the eye now on the point of the pencil.

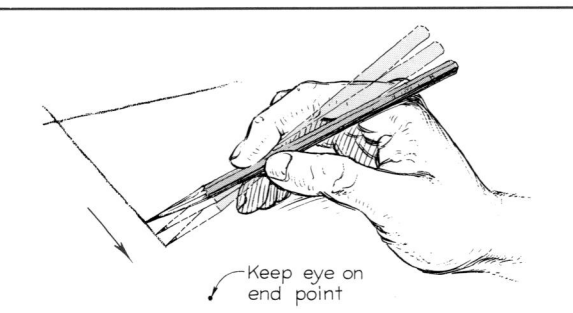

Fig. 6.8 Drawing Vertical Lines.

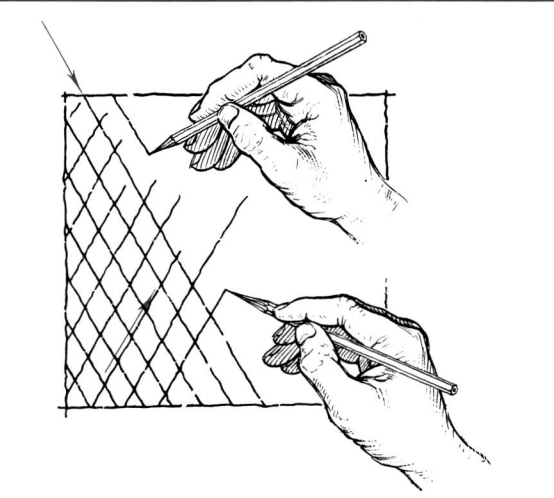

Fig. 6.9 Drawing Inclined Lines.

An easy method of blocking in horizontal or vertical lines is to hold the hand and pencil rigidly and glide the fingertips along the edge of the pad or board, as shown in Fig. 6.10 (a).

Another method, (b), is to mark the distance on the edge of a card or a strip of paper and transfer this distance at intervals, as shown; then draw the final line through these points. Or the pencil may

be held as shown at the lower part of (b), and distance marks made on the paper at intervals by tilting the lead down to the paper. It will be seen that both methods of transferring distances are substitutes for the dividers and will have many uses in sketching.

A common method of finding the midpoint of a line AB, shown at (c), is to hold the pencil in the left hand with the thumb gaging the estimated half-distance. Try this distance on the left and then on the right until the center is located by trial, and mark the center C, as shown. Another method is to mark the total distance AB on the edge of a strip of paper and then to fold the paper to bring points A and B together, thus locating center C at the crease. To find quarter points, the folded strip can be folded once more.

6.8 Circles and Arcs

Small circles and arcs can be easily sketched in one or two strokes, as for the circular portions of letters, without any preliminary blocking in.

One method of sketching a larger circle, Fig. 6.11, is first to sketch lightly the enclosing square, mark the midpoints of the sides, draw light arcs tangent to the sides of the square, and then heavy in the final circle.

Another method, Fig. 6.12, is to sketch the two

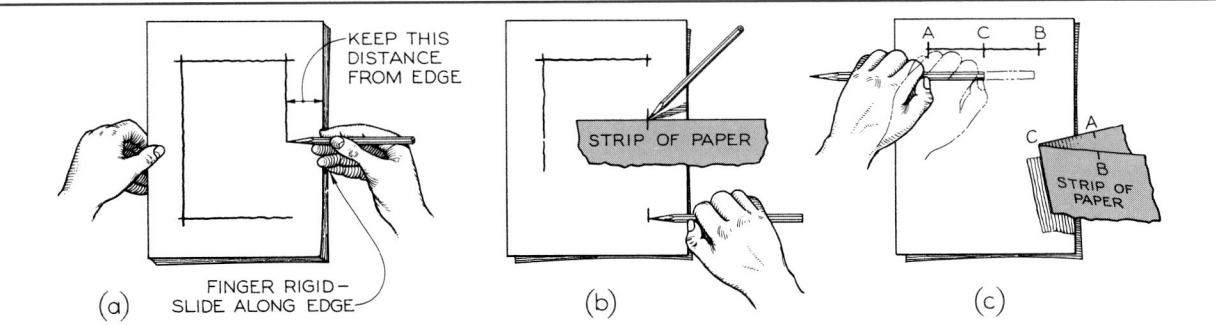

Fig. 6.10 Blocking in Horizontal and Vertical Lines.

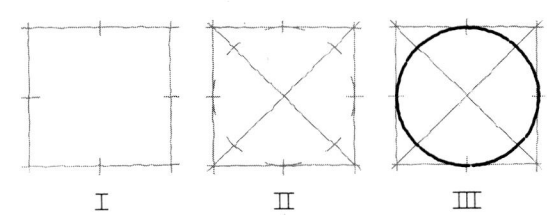

Fig. 6.11 Sketching a Circle.

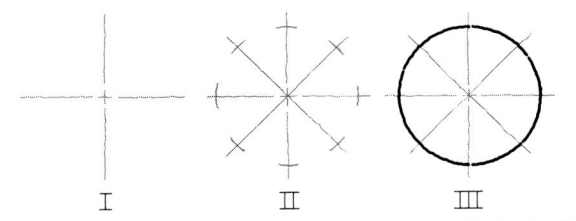

Fig. 6.12 Sketching a Circle.

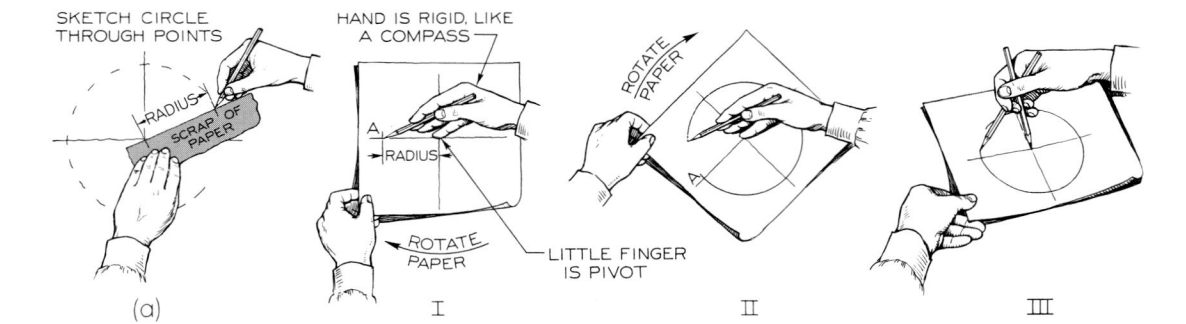

Fig. 6.13   Sketching Circles.

center lines, add light 45° radial lines, sketch light arcs across the lines at the estimated radius distance from the center, and finally sketch the required circle heavily. Dim all construction lines with a soft eraser before heavying in the final circle.

An excellent method, particularly for large circles, Fig. 6.13 (a), is to mark the estimated radius on the edge of a card or scrap of paper, to set off from the center as many points as desired, and to sketch the final heavy circle through these points.

The clever drafter will prefer the method at I and II, in which the hand is used as a compass. Place the tip of the little finger, or the knuckle joint of the little finger, at the center; "feed" the pencil out to the desired radius, hold this position rigidly, and carefully revolve the paper with the other hand, as shown. If you are using a sketching pad, place the pad on your knee and revolve the entire pad on the knee as a pivot.

At III, two pencils are held rigidly like a compass and the paper is slowly revolved.

Methods of sketching arcs, Fig. 6.14, are adaptations of those used for sketching circles. In general, it is easier to sketch arcs with the hand and pencil on the concave side of the curve. In sketching tangent arcs, always keep in mind the actual geometric constructions, carefully approximating all points of tangency.

6.9 Ellipses

If a circle is viewed obliquely, Fig. 5.50 (b), it appears as an ellipse. With a little practice, you can learn to sketch small ellipses with a free arm movement, Fig. 6.15 (a). Hold the pencil naturally, rest the weight on the upper part of the forearm, and move the pencil rapidly above the paper in the elliptical path desired; then lower the pencil so as to describe several light overlapping ellipses, as shown

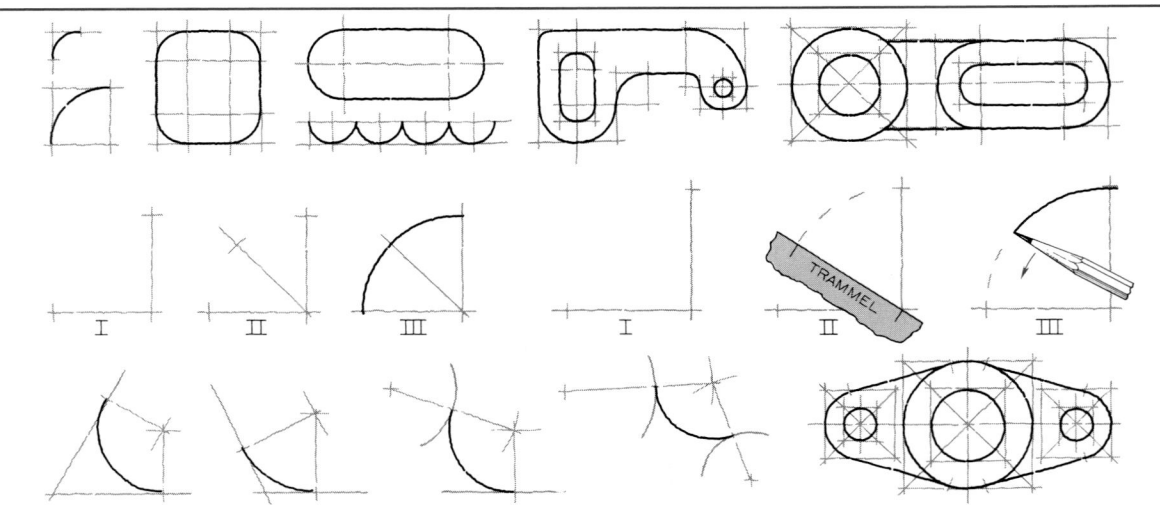

Fig. 6.14   Sketching Arcs.

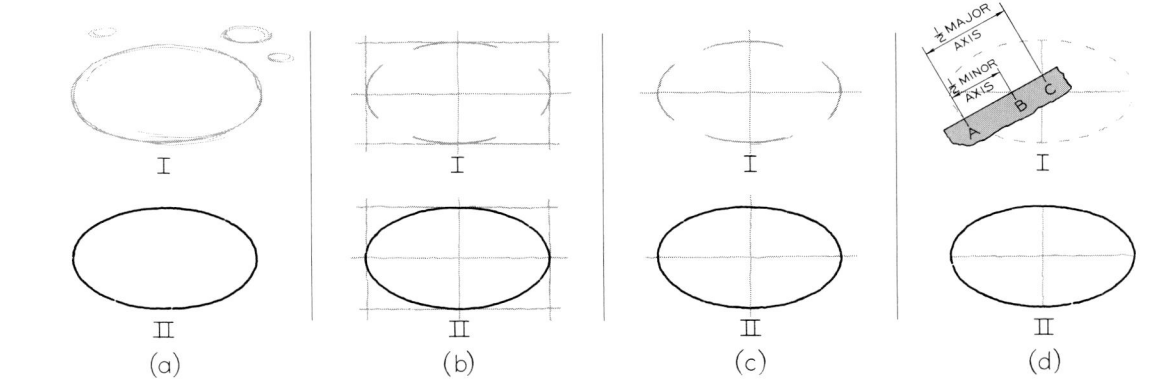

Fig. 6.15 Sketching Ellipses.

at I. Dim all lines with a soft eraser and heavy in the final ellipse, II.

Another method, (b), is to sketch lightly the enclosing rectangle, I, mark the midpoints of the sides, and sketch light tangent arcs, as shown. Then, II, complete the ellipse lightly, dim all lines with a soft eraser, and heavy in the final ellipse.

The same general procedure shown at (b) may be used in sketching the ellipse upon the given axes, as shown at (c).

The trammel method, (d), is excellent for sketching large ellipses. Prepare a "trammel" on the edge of a card or strip of paper, move it to different positions, and mark points on the ellipse at A. The trammel method is explained in §5.50. Sketch the final ellipse through the points, as shown. For sketching isometric ellipses, see §6.13.

6.10 **Proportions**

The most important rule in freehand sketching is *keep the sketch in proportion.* No matter how brilliant the technique or how well the small details are drawn, if the proportions—especially the large overall proportions—are bad, the sketch will be bad. First, the relative proportions of the height to the width must be carefully established; then as you proceed to the medium-sized areas and the small details, constantly compare each new estimated distance with already established distances.

If you are working from a given picture, such as the utility cabinet in Fig. 6.16 (a), it is first necessary to establish the relative width compared to the height. One way is to use the pencil as a measuring stick, as shown. In this case, the height is about $1\frac{3}{4}$ times the width. Then

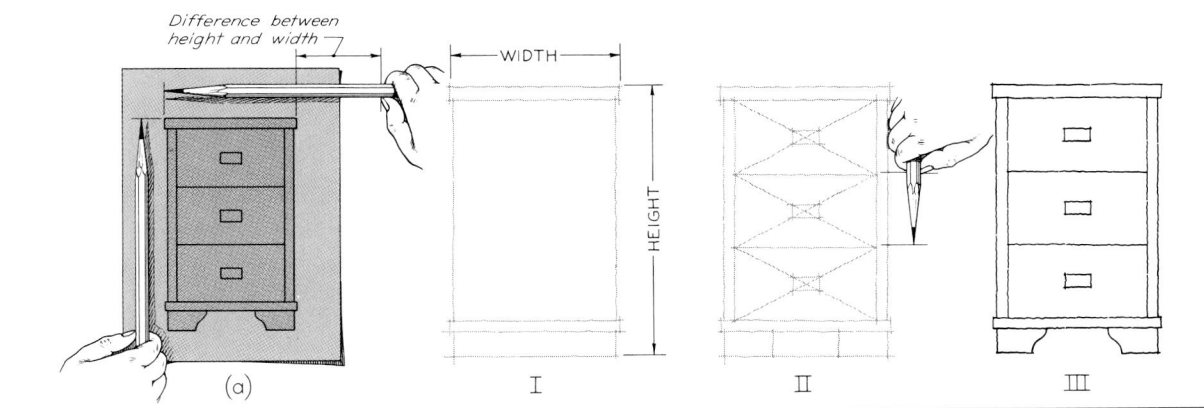

Fig. 6.16 Sketching a Utility Cabinet.

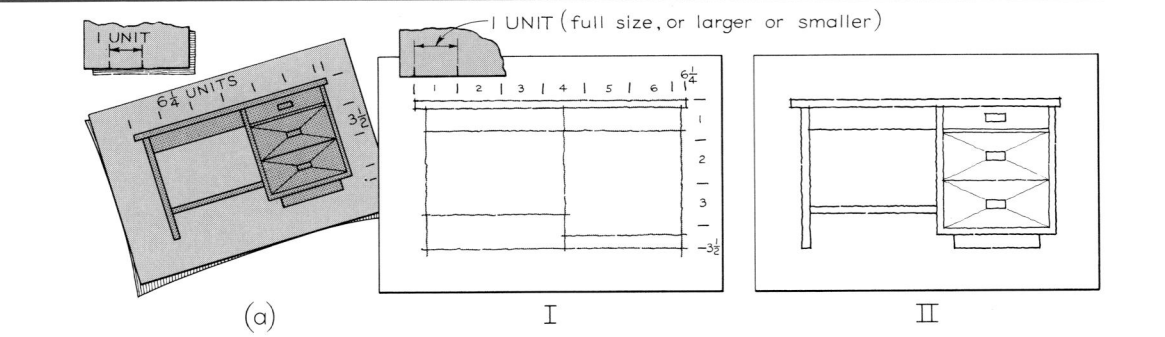

Fig. 6.17   Sketching a Desk.

I.   Sketch the enclosing rectangle in the correct. proportion. In this case, the sketch is to be slightly larger than the given picture.

II.   Divide the available drawer space into three parts with the pencil by trial, as shown. Sketch light diagonals to locate centers of drawers, and block in drawer handles. Sketch all remaining details.

III.   Dim all construction with a soft eraser, and heavy in all final lines.

Another method of estimating distances is illustrated in Fig. 6.17. On the edge of a card or strip of paper, mark an arbitrary unit. Then see how many units wide and how many units high the desk is. If you are working from the actual object, you can use a scale, a piece of paper, or the pencil itself as a unit to determine the proportions.

To sketch an object composed of many curves to the same scale or to a larger or smaller scale, the method of "squares" is recommended, Fig. 6.18. On the given picture, rule accurate grid lines to form squares of any convenient size. It is best to use a scale and some convenient spacing, such as either .50″ or 10 mm. On the new sheet rule a similar grid, making the spacing of the lines proportional to the original, but reduced or enlarged as desired. Make the final sketch by drawing the lines in and across the grid lines as in the original, as near as you can estimate by eye.

In sketching from an actual object, you can easily compare various distances on the object by using the pencil to compare measurements, as shown in Fig. 6.19. While doing this, do not change your position, and always hold your pencil at arm's length. The length sighted can then be compared in similar manner with any other dimension of the object. If the object is small, such as a machine part, you can compare distances in the manner of Fig. 6.16, by actually placing the pencil against the object itself.

In establishing proportions, the blocking-in method is recommended, especially for irregular

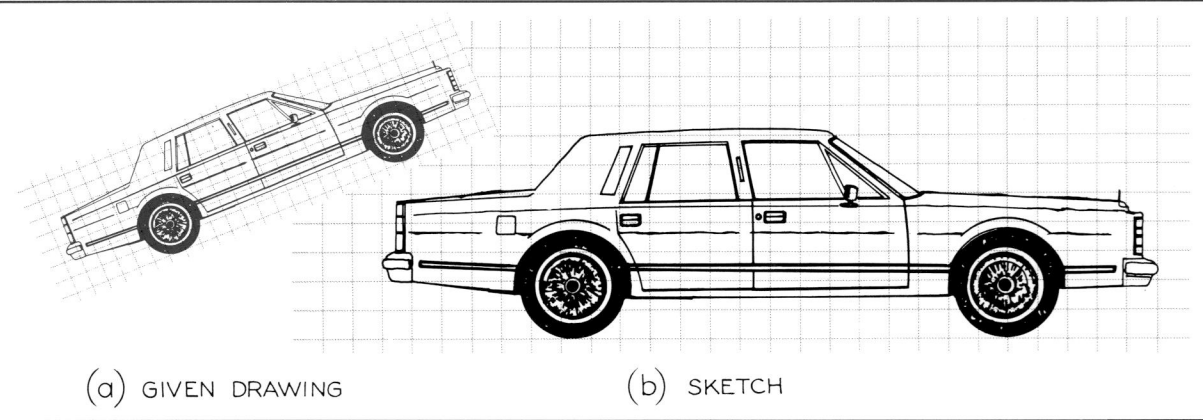

(a) GIVEN DRAWING   (b) SKETCH

Fig. 6.18   Squares Method.

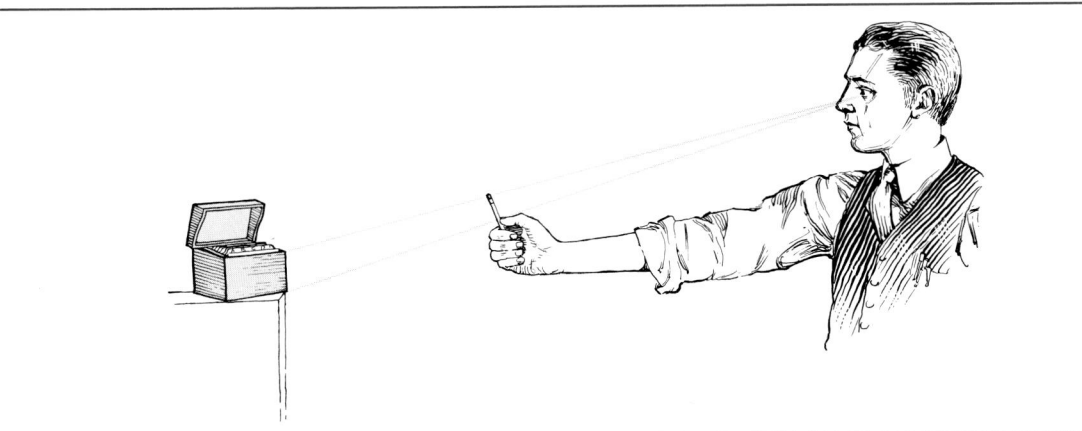

Fig. 6.19 Estimating Dimensions.

shapes. The steps for blocking in and completing the sketch of a Shaft Hanger are shown in Fig. 6.20. As always, first give attention to the main proportions, next to the general sizes and direction of flow of curved shapes, and finally to the snappy lines of the completed sketch.

In making sketches from actual machine parts, it is necessary to use the measuring tools used in the shop, especially those needed to determine dimensions that must be relatively accurate. For a discussion of these methods, see Chapter 12.

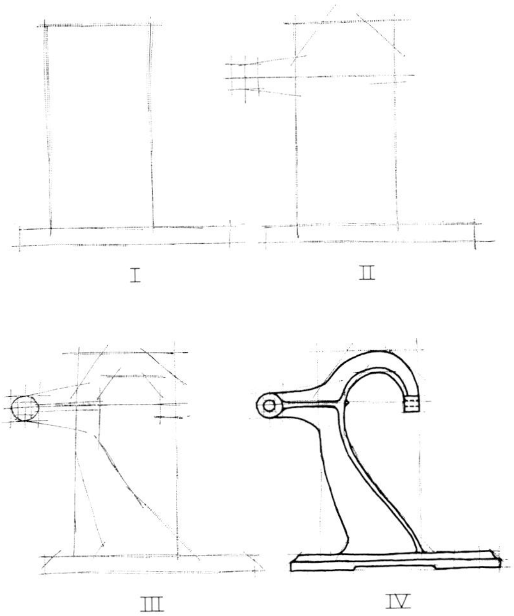

6.11 Pictorial Sketching

We shall now examine several simple methods of preparing pictorial sketches that will be of great assistance in learning the principles of multiview projection. A detailed and more technical treatment of pictorial drawing is given in Chapters 17 and 18.

6.12 Isometric Sketching

To make an isometric sketch from an actual object, hold the object in your hand and tilt it toward you, as shown in Fig. 6.21 (a). In this position, the front

Fig. 6.20 Blocking in an Irregular Object (Shaft Hanger).

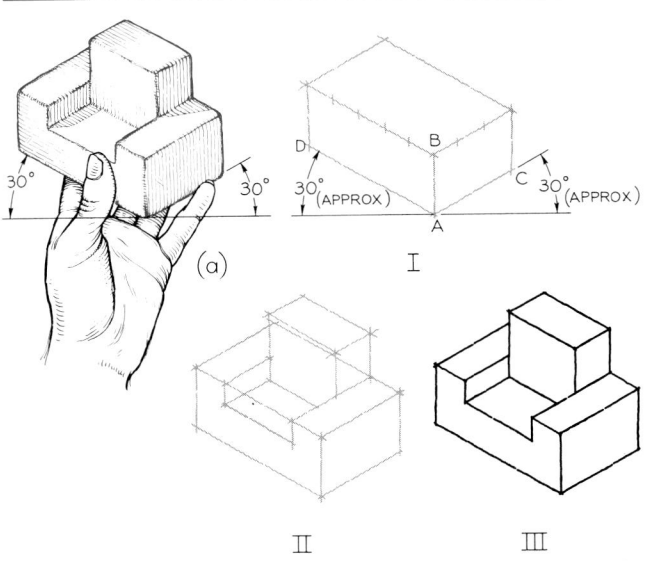

Fig. 6.21 Isometric Sketching.

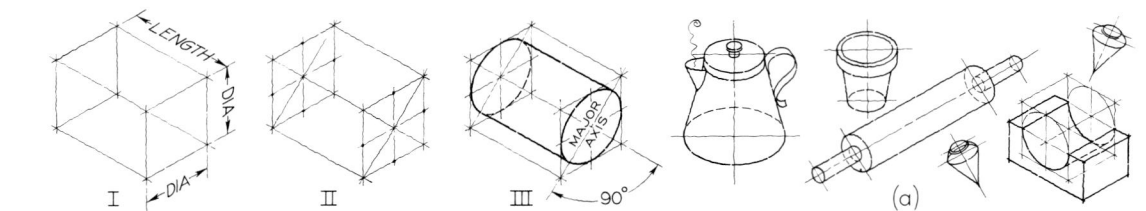

Fig. 6.22   Isometric Ellipses.

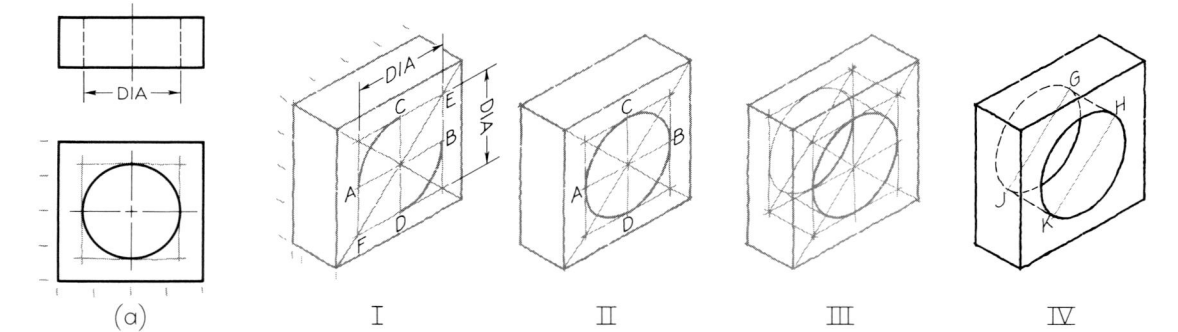

Fig. 6.23   Isometric Ellipses.

corner will appear vertical, and the two receding bottom edges and those parallel to them, respectively, will appear at about 30° with horizontal, as shown. The steps in sketching are

I.   Sketch the enclosing box lightly, making **AB** vertical and **AC** and **AD** approximately 30° with horizontal. These three lines are the *isometric axes*. Make **AB**, **AC**, and **AD** approximately proportional in length to the actual corresponding edges on the object. Sketch the remaining lines parallel, respectively, to these three lines.

II.   Block in the recess and the projecting block.

III.   Dim all construction lines with a soft eraser, and heavy in all final lines.

NOTE   The angle of the receding lines may be less than 30°, say, 20° or 15°. Although the result will not be an isometric sketch, the sketch may be more pleasing and effective in many cases.

6.13 Isometric Ellipses
As shown in Fig. 5.50 (b), a circle viewed at an angle appears as an ellipse. When objects having cylindrical or conical shapes are placed in the isometric or other oblique positions, the circles will be viewed at an angle and will appear as ellipses, Fig. 6.22.

The most important consideration in sketching isometric ellipses is: *The major axis of the ellipse is always at right angles to the center line of the cylinder, and the minor axis is at right angles to the major axis and coincides with the center line.*

Two views of a block with a large cylindrical hole are shown in Fig. 6.23 (a). The steps in sketching the object are

I.   Sketch the block and the enclosing parallelogram for the ellipse, making the sides of the parallelogram parallel to the edges of the block and equal in length to the diameter of the hole. Draw diagonals to locate the center of the hole, and then draw center lines **AB** and **CD**. Points **A**, **B**, **C**, and **D** will be midpoints of the sides of the parallelogram, and the ellipse will be tangent to the sides at those points. The major axis will be on the diagonal **EF**, which is at right angles to the center line of the hole, and the minor axis will fall along the short diagonal. Sketch long, flat elliptical sides **CA** and **BD**, as shown.

II.   Sketch short small-radius arcs **CB** and **AD** to complete the ellipse. Avoid making the ends of the ellipse "squared off" or pointed like a football.

III.   Sketch lightly the parallelogram for the ellipse that lies in the back plane of the object, and sketch the ellipse in the same manner as the front ellipse.

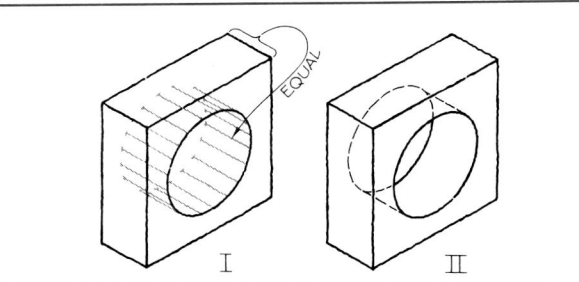

Fig. 6.24 Isometric Ellipses.

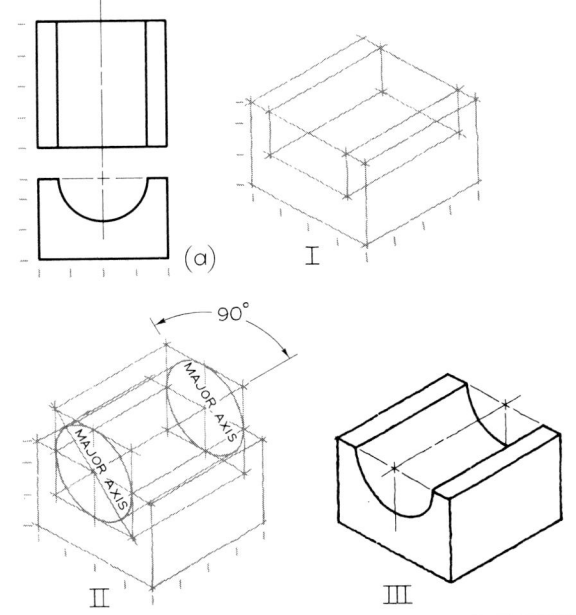

Fig. 6.25 Sketching Semiellipses.

IV. Draw lines **GH** and **JK** tangent to the two ellipses. Dim all construction with a soft eraser, and heavy in all final lines.

Another method for determining the back ellipse is shown in Fig. 6.24.

I. Select points at random on the front ellipse and sketch "depth lines" equal in length to the depth of the block.

II. Sketch the ellipse through the ends of the lines, as shown.

Two views of a bearing with a semicylindrical opening are shown in Fig. 6.25 (a). The steps in sketching are

I. Block in the object, including the rectangular space for the semicylinder.

II. Block in the box enclosing the complete cylinder. Sketch the entire cylinder lightly.

III. Dim all construction lines, and heavy in all final lines, showing only the lower half of the cylinder.

6.14 Sketching on Isometric Paper

Two views of a guide block are shown in Fig. 6.26 (a). The steps in sketching illustrate not only the use of isometric paper but also the sketching of individual planes or faces in order to build up a pictorial visualization from the given views.

I. Sketch isometric of enclosing box, counting off the isometric grid spaces to equal the corresponding squares on the given views. Sketch surface **A**, as shown.

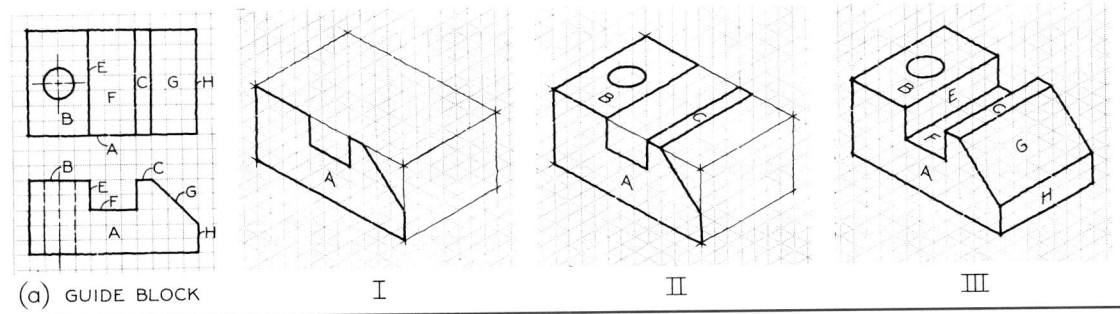

Fig. 6.26 Sketching on Isometric Paper.

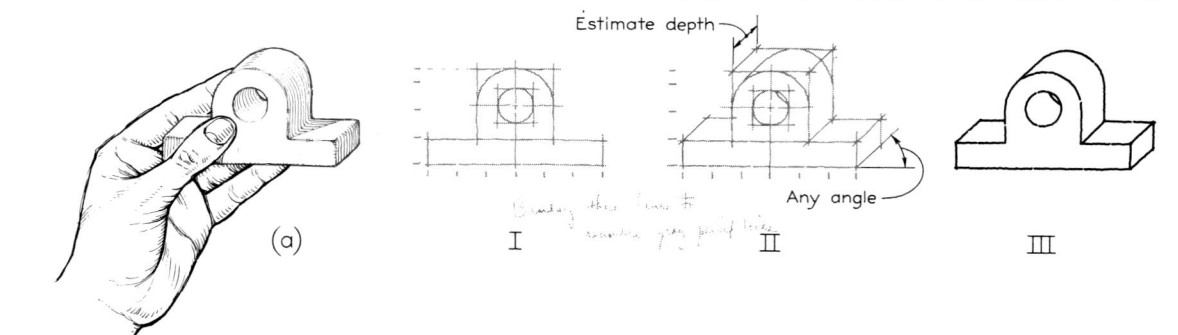

Fig. 6.27   Sketching in Oblique.

II.   Sketch additional surfaces **B** and **C** and the small ellipse.

III.   Sketch additional surfaces **E**, **F**, **G**, and **H** to complete the sketch.

6.15 Oblique Sketching

Another simple method for sketching pictorially is oblique sketching, Fig. 6.27. Hold the object in your hand, as shown at (a).

I.   Block in the front face of the bearing, as if you were sketching a front view.

II.   Sketch receding lines parallel to each other and at any convenient angle, say, 30° or 45° with horizontal, approximately. Cut off receding lines so that the depth appears correct. These lines may be full length, but a more natural appearance results if they are cut to three-quarters or one-half size, approximately. If they are full length, the sketch is a *cavalier* sketch. If half size, the sketch is a *cabinet* sketch. See §18.4.

III.   Dim all construction lines with a soft eraser and heavy in the final lines.

NOTE   Oblique sketching is a less suitable method for any object having circular shapes in or parallel to more than one plane of the object, because ellipses result when circular shapes are viewed obliquely. Therefore, place the object with most or all of the circular shapes toward you, so that they will appear as true circles and arcs in oblique sketching, as in Fig. 6.27.

6.16 Oblique Sketching on Graph Paper

Ordinary graph paper is suitable and convenient for oblique sketching. Two views of a bearing bracket are shown in Fig. 6.28 (a). The dimensions are determined simply by counting the squares.

I.   Sketch lightly the enclosing box construction. Sketch the receding lines at 45° diagonally through the squares. To establish the depth at a reduced scale, sketch the receding lines diagonally through

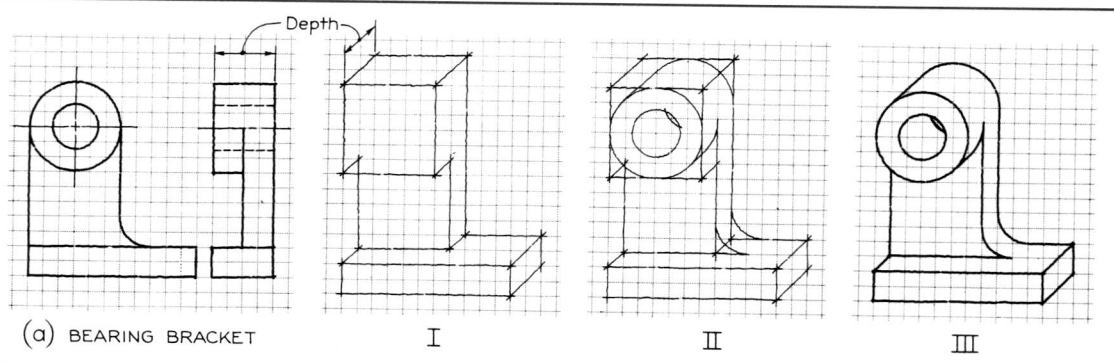

(a) BEARING BRACKET   I   II   III

Fig. 6.28   Oblique Sketching on Cross-section Paper.

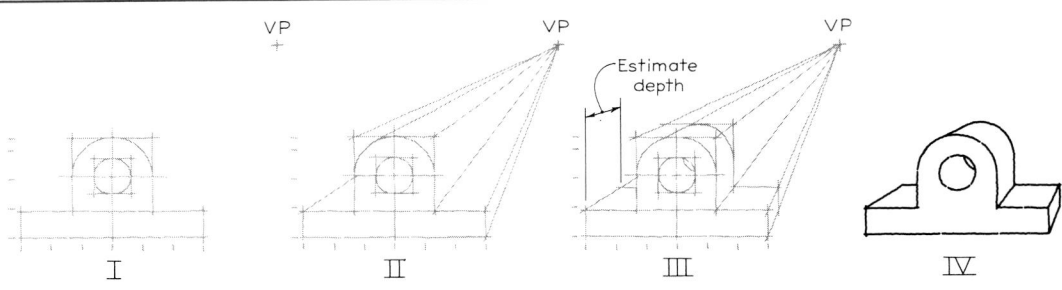

Fig. 6.29 Sketching in One-Point Perspective.

half as many squares as the given number shown at (a).

II.   Sketch all arcs and circles.

III.   Heavy in all final lines.

6.17 Perspective Sketching

The bearing sketched in oblique in Fig. 6.27 can easily be sketched in *one-point perspective* (one vanishing point), as shown in Fig. 6.29.

I.   Sketch the true front face of the object, just as in oblique sketching. Select the vanishing point (VP) for the receding lines. In most cases, it is desirable to place VP above and to the right of the picture, as shown, although it can be placed anywhere in the vicinity of the picture. But if it is placed too close to the center, the lines will converge too sharply, and the picture will be distorted.

II.   Sketch the receding lines toward VP.

III.   Estimate the depth to look well, and sketch in the back portion of the object. Note that the back circle and arc will be slightly smaller than the front circle and arc.

IV.   Dim all construction lines with a soft eraser, and heavy in all final lines. Note the similarity between the perspective sketch and the oblique sketch in Fig. 6.27.

Two-point perspective (two vanishing points) is the most true to life of all pictorial methods, but it requires some natural sketching ability or considerable practice for best results. The simple method shown in Fig. 6.30 can be used successfully by the nonartistic student.

I.   Sketch front corner of desk in true height, and locate two *vanishing points* (VPL and VPR) on a *horizon* line (eye level). The distance CA may vary—

the greater it is, the higher the eye level will be and the more we will be looking down on top of the object. A good rule of thumb is to make C–VPL one-third to one-fourth of C–VPR.

II.   Estimate depth and width, and sketch enclosing box.

III.   Block in all details. Note that all parallel lines converge toward the same vanishing point.

IV.   Dim the construction lines with a soft eraser as necessary, and heavy in all final lines. Make the outlines thicker and the inside lines thinner, especially where they are close together.

6.18 Views of Objects

A pictorial drawing or a photograph shows an object as it *appears* to the observer, but not as it *is*. Such a picture cannot describe the object fully, no matter from which direction it is viewed, because it does not show the exact shapes and sizes of the several parts.

In industry, a complete and clear description of the shape and size of an object to be made is necessary, to make certain that the object will be manufactured exactly as intended by the designer. In order to provide this information clearly and accurately, a number of *views*, systematically arranged, are used. This system of views is called *multiview projection*. Each view provides certain definite information if the view is taken in a direction perpendicular to a principal face or side of the object. For example, as shown in Fig. 6.31 (a), an observer looking perpendicularly toward one face of the object obtains a true view of the shape and size of that side. This view as seen by the observer is shown at (b). (The observer is theoretically at an infinite distance from the object.)

An object has three principal dimensions: *width*, *height*, and *depth*, as shown at (a). In technical draw-

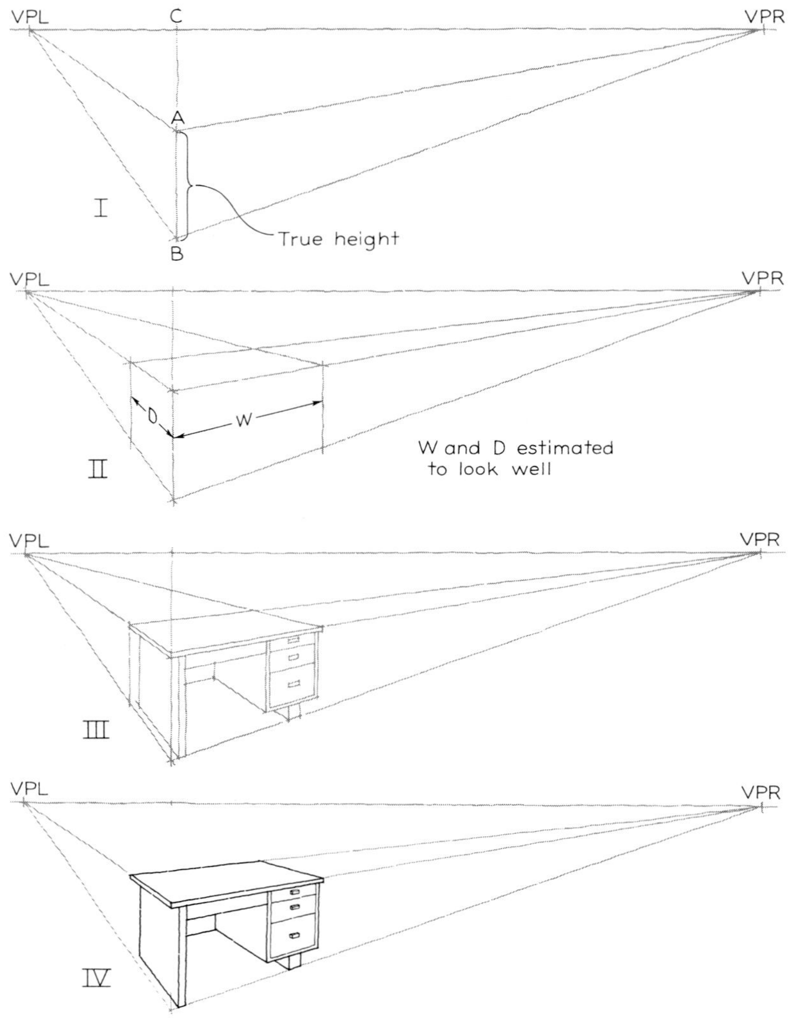

VPL
C
VPR
A
I
B
True height
VPL
VPR
D
W
W and D estimated
to look well
II
VPL
VPR
III
VPL
VPR
IV

Fig. 6.30 Two-Point Perspective.

HEIGHT
WIDTH
DEPTH
(a)
FRONT VIEW
HEIGHT
WIDTH
(b)

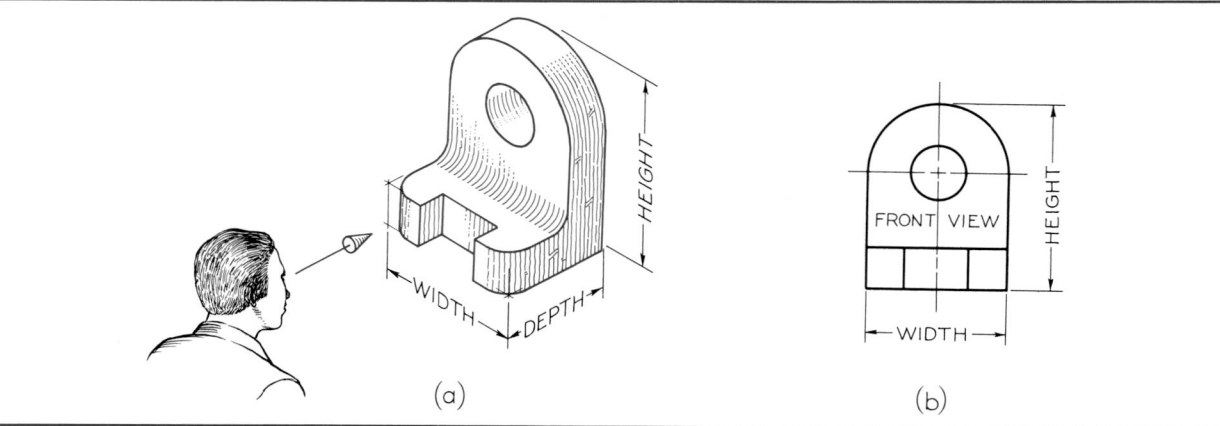

Fig. 6.31 Front View of an Object.

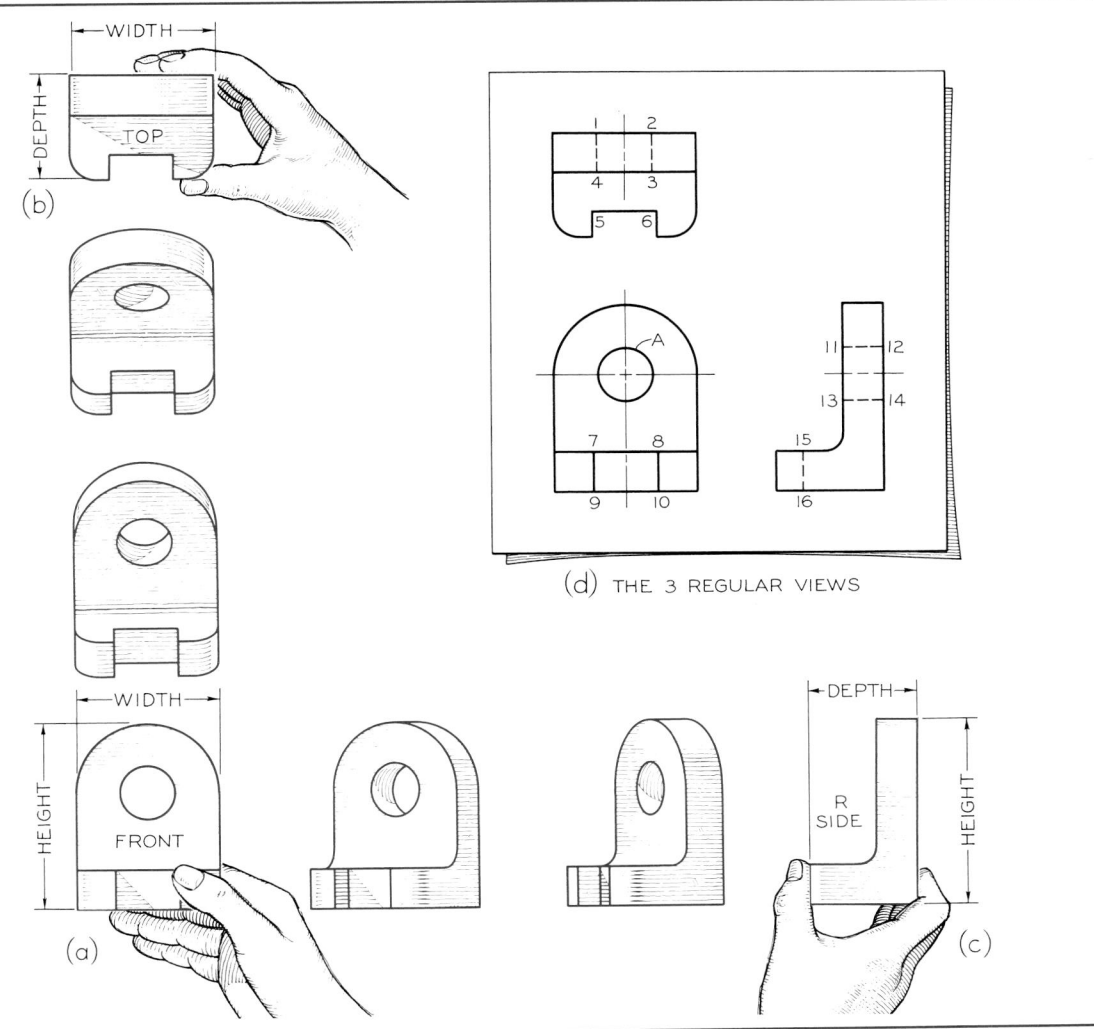

Fig. 6.32 The Three Regular Views.

ing, these fixed terms are used for dimensions taken in these directions, regardless of the shape of the object. The terms "length" and "thickness" are not used because they cannot be applied in all cases. Note at (b) that the front view shows only the height and width of the object and not the depth. In fact, *any one view of a three-dimensional object can show only two dimensions; the third dimension will be found in an adjacent view.*

6.19 Revolving the Object

To obtain additional views, revolve the object as shown in Fig. 6.32. First, hold the object in the front-view position, as shown at (a).

To get the *top view*, (b), revolve the object so as to bring the *top of the object up and toward you.* To get the *right-side view*, (c), revolve the object so as to bring the *right side to the right and toward you.* To obtain views of any of the other sides, merely turn the object so as to bring those sides toward you.

The top, front, and right-side views, arranged closer together, are shown at (d). These are called the *three regular views* because they are the views most frequently used.

At this stage we can consider spacing between views as purely a matter of appearance. The views should be spaced well apart and yet close enough to appear related to each other. The space between

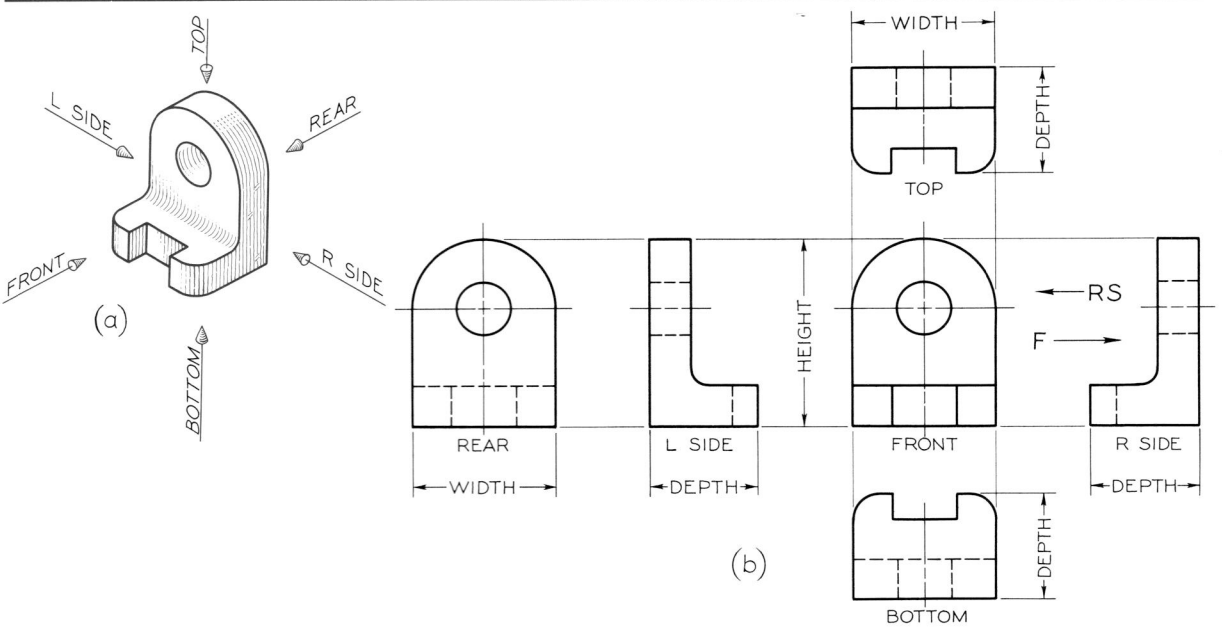

Fig. 6.33   The Six Views.

the front and top views may or may not be equal to the space between the front and side views. If dimensions (Chapter 13) are to be added to the sketch, sufficient space for them between views will have to be allowed.

An important advantage that a view has over a photograph of an object is that hidden features can be clearly shown by means of *hidden lines*, Fig. 2.14. In Fig. 6.32 (d), surface 7–8–9–10 in the front view appears as a visible line 5–6 in the top view and as a hidden line 15–16 in the side view. Also, hole A, which appears as a circle in the front view, shows as hidden lines 1–4 and 2–3 in the top view, and 11–12 and 13–14 in the side view. For a complete discussion of hidden lines, see §6.25.

Note, too, the use of center lines for the hole in Fig. 6.32 (d). See §6.26.

6.20 The Six Views

Any object can be viewed from six mutually perpendicular directions, as shown in Fig. 6.33 (a). Thus, six views may be drawn if necessary, as shown at (b). Except as explained in §7.8, these six views are always arranged as shown, which is the American National Standard arrangement of views. The *top*, *front*, and *bottom views* line up vertically, whereas the *rear*, *left-side*, *front*, and *right-side views* line up

horizontally. To draw a view out of place is a serious error, generally regarded as one of the worst mistakes one can make in this subject. See Fig. 6.47.

Note that the height is shown in the rear, left-side, front, and right-side views; the width is shown in the rear, top, front, and bottom views; and the depth is shown in the four views that surround the front view, namely, the left-side, top, right-side, and bottom views. In each view, two of the principal dimensions are shown, and the third is not shown. Observe also that in the four views that surround the front view, the front of the object is faced toward the front view.

Adjacent views are reciprocal. If the front view, Fig. 6.33, is imagined to be the object itself, the right-side view is obtained by looking toward the right side of the front view, as shown by the arrow RS. Likewise, if the right-side view is imagined to be the object, the front view is obtained by looking toward the left side of the right-side view, as shown by the arrow F. The same relation exists between any two adjacent views.

Obviously, the six views may be obtained either by shifting the object with respect to the observer, as we have seen, Fig. 6.32, or by shifting the observer with respect to the object, Fig. 6.33. Another illustration of the second method is given in Fig. 6.34, showing six views of a house. The observer can

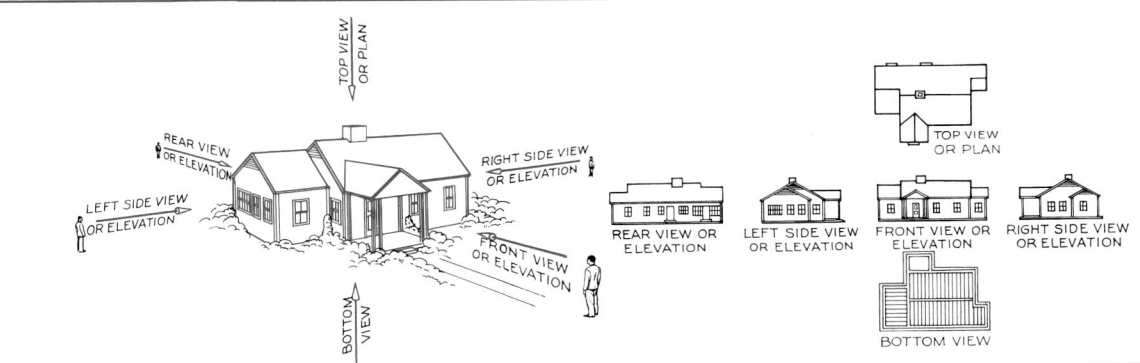

Fig. 6.34   Six Views of a House.

walk around the house and view its front, sides, and rear and can imagine the top view as seen from an airplane and the bottom or "worms's-eye view" as seen from underneath.* Notice the use of the terms *plan*, for the top view, and *elevation*, for all views showing the height of the building. These terms are regularly used in architectural drawing and, occasionally, with reference to drawings in other fields.

6.21 Orientation of Front View

Six views of a compact automobile are shown in Fig. 6.35. The view chosen for the front view in this case is the side, not the front of the automobile. In general, the front view should show the object in its operating position, particularly of familiar objects

*Architects frequently draw the views of a building on separate sheets because of the large sizes of the drawings.

such as the house shown above and the automobile. A machine part is often drawn in the position it occupies in the assembly. However, in most cases this is not important, and the drafter may assume the object to be in any convenient position. For example, an automobile connecting rod is usually drawn horizontally on the sheet, Fig. 16.30. Also, it is customary to draw screws, bolts, shafts, tubes, and other elongated parts in a horizontal position, not only because they are usually manufactured in this position but also because they can be presented more satisfactorily on paper in this position.

6.22 Choice of Views

A drawing for use in production should contain *only those views* needed for a clear and complete shape description of the object. These minimum required views are referred to as the *necessary views*. In se-

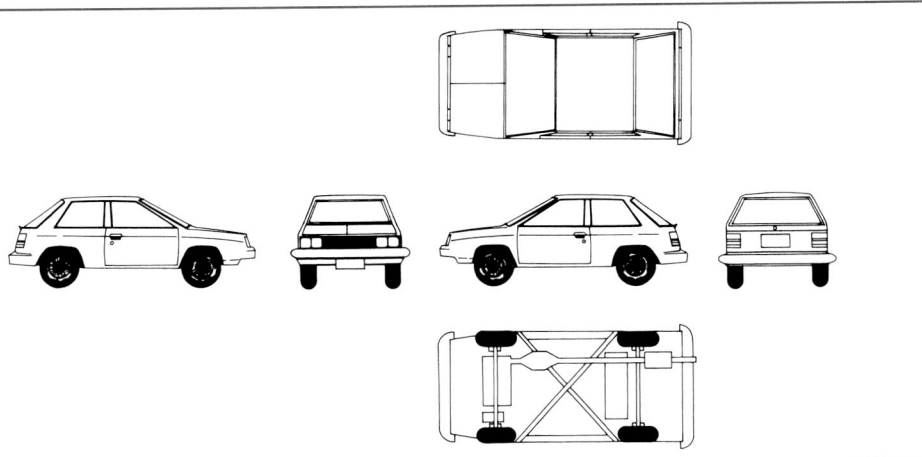

Fig. 6.35   Six Views of a Compact Automobile.

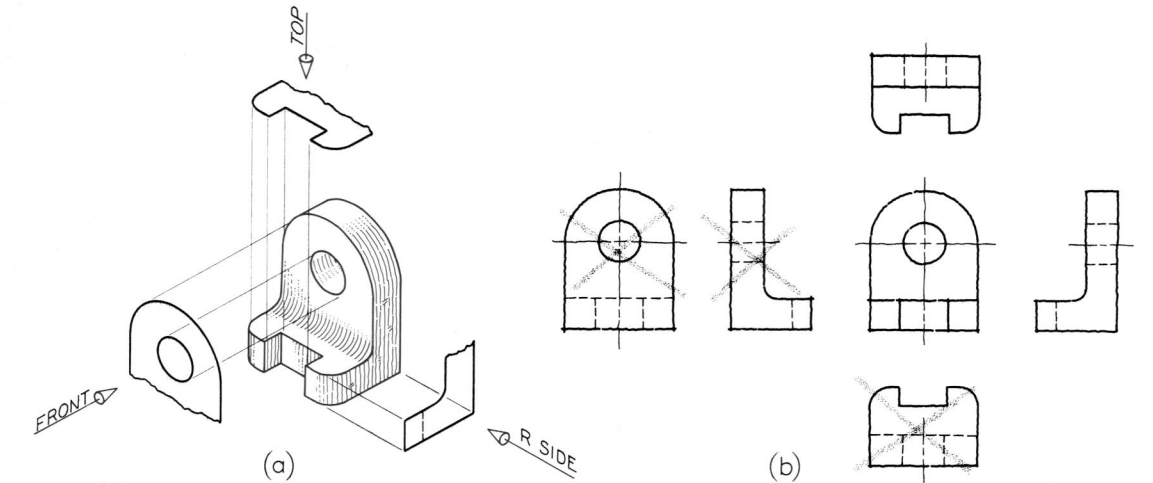

Fig. 6.36   Choice of Views.

lecting views, the drafter should choose those that show best the essential contours or shapes and should give preference to those with the least number of hidden lines.

As shown in Fig. 6.36 (a), three distinctive features of this object need to be shown on the drawing.

1. Rounded top and hole, seen from the front.

2. Rectangular notch and rounded corners, seen from the top.

3. Right angle with filleted corner, seen from the side.

Another way to choose necessary views is to eliminate unnecessary views. At (b) a "thumbnail sketch" of the six views is shown. Both the front and rear views show the true shapes of the hole and the rounded top, but the front view is preferred because it has no hidden lines. Therefore, the rear view (which is seldom needed) is crossed out.

Both the top and bottom views show the rectangular notch and rounded corners, but the top view is preferred because it has fewer hidden lines.

Both the right-side and left-side views show the right angle with the filleted corner. In fact, in this case the side views are identical, except reversed. In such instances, it is customary to choose the right-side view.

The necessary views, then, are the three remaining views: the top, front, and right-side views. These are the three regular views referred to in connection with Fig. 6.32.

More complicated objects may require more than three views or special views such as partial views, §7.9; sectional views, Chapter 9; auxiliary views, Chapter 10.

6.23 Two-View Drawings

Often only two views are needed to describe clearly the shape of an object. In Fig. 6.37 (a), the right-side view shows no significant contours of the object,

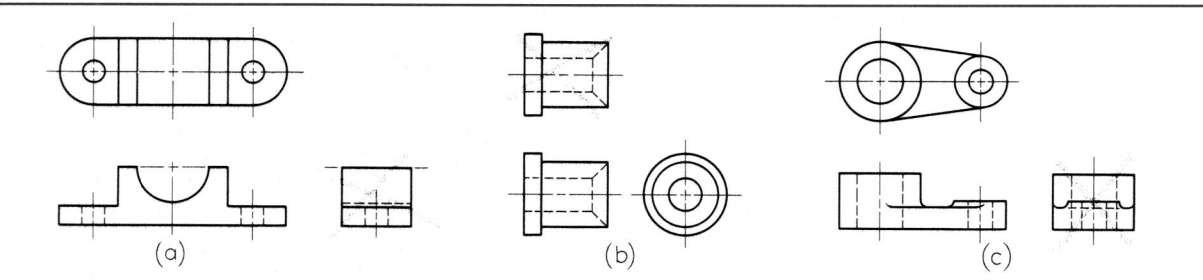

Fig. 6.37   Two Necessary Views.

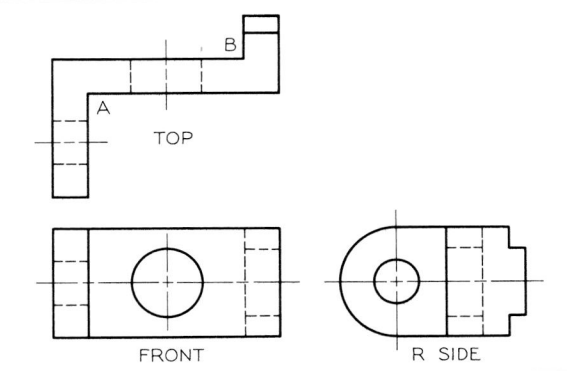

Fig. 6.38   Three Views.

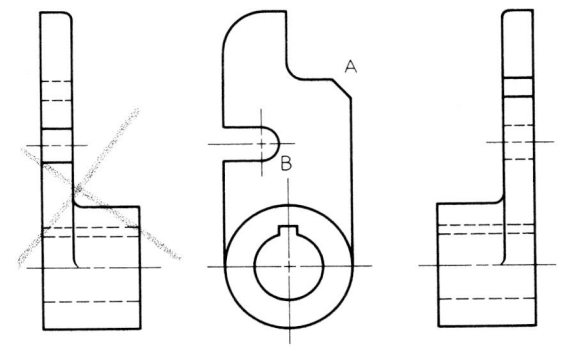

Fig. 6.39   Choice of Right-Side View.

and is crossed out. At (b) the top and front views are identical, so the top view is eliminated. At (c), no additional information not already given in the front and top views is shown in the side view, so the side view is unnecessary.

The question often arises: What are the absolute minimum views required? For example, in Fig.

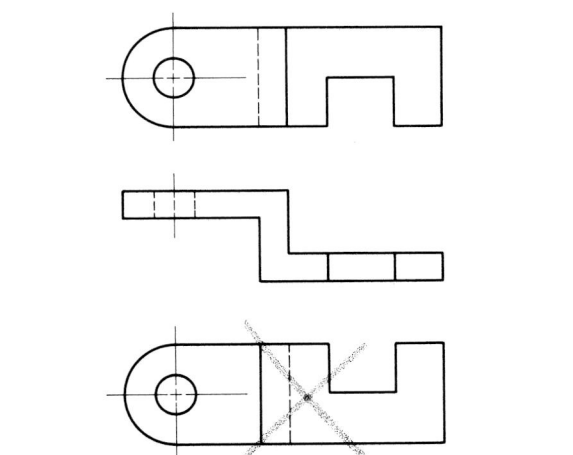

Fig. 6.40   Choice of Top View.

6.38, the top view might be omitted, leaving only the front and right-side views. However, it is more difficult to "read" the two views or visualize the object, because the characteristic "Z" shape of the top view is omitted. In addition, one must assume that corners A and B (top view) are square and not filleted. In this example, all three views are necessary.

If the object requires only two views, and the left-side and right-side views are equally descriptive, the right-side view is customarily chosen, Fig. 6.39. If contour A were omitted, then the presence of slot B would make it necessary to choose the left-side view in preference to the right-side view.

If the object requires only two views, and the top and bottom views are equally descriptive, the top view is customarily chosen, Fig. 6.40.

If only two views are necessary, and the top view and right-side view are equally descriptive, the combination chosen is that which spaces best on the paper, Fig. 6.41.

6.24 One-View Drawings
Frequently a single view supplemented by a note or lettered symbols is sufficient to describe clearly the shape of a relatively simple object. In Fig. 6.42

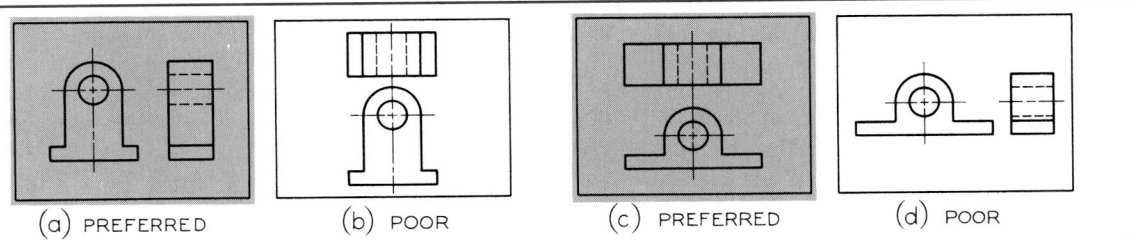

| (a) PREFERRED | (b) POOR | (c) PREFERRED | (d) POOR |

Fig. 6.41   Choice of Views to Fit Paper.

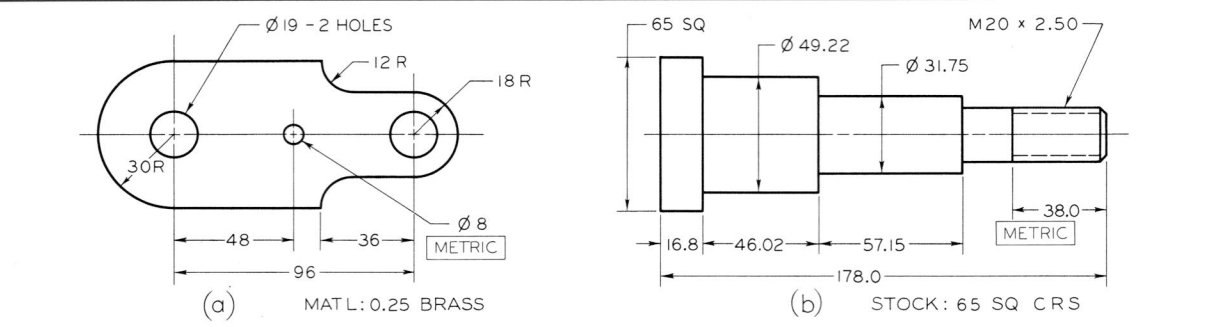

Fig. 6.42 One-View Drawings.

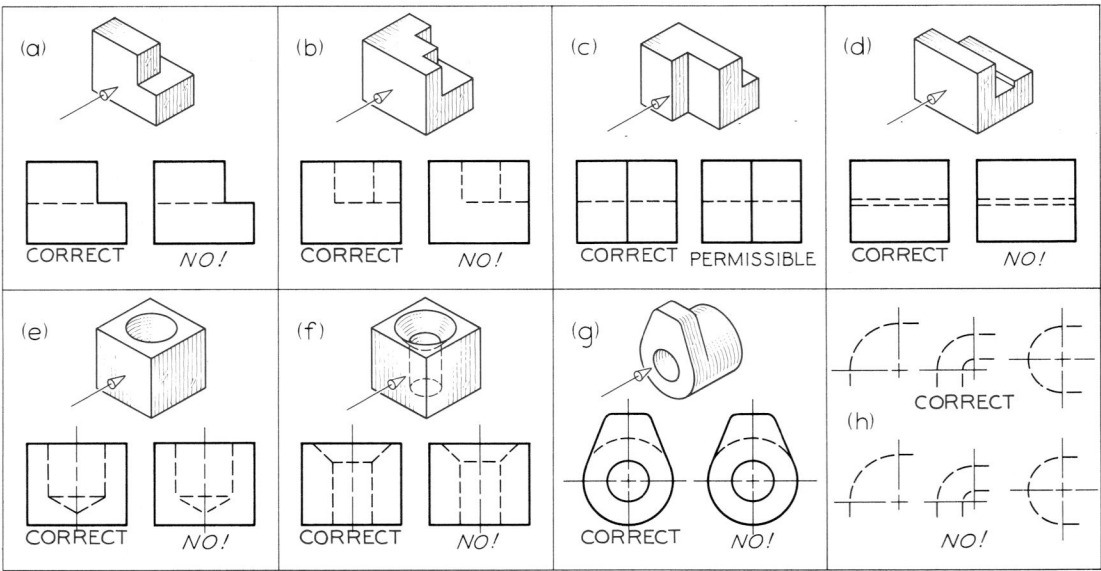

Fig. 6.43 Hidden-Line Practices.

(a), one view of the Shim, plus a note indicating the thickness as 0.25 mm, is sufficient. At (b), the left end is 65 mm square, the next portion is 49.22 mm diameter, the next is 31.75 mm diameter, and the portion with the thread is 20 mm diameter, as indicated in the note. Nearly all shafts, bolts, screws, and similar parts should be represented by single views in this manner.

6.25 Hidden Lines

Correct and incorrect practices in drawing hidden lines are illustrated in Fig. 6.43. In general, a hidden line should join a visible line except when it causes the visible line to extend too far, as shown at (a). In other words, *leave a gap whenever a hidden-line dash forms a continuation of a visible line.* Hidden lines should intersect to form L and T corners, as shown at (b). A hidden line preferably should "jump" a visible line when possible, (c). Parallel hidden lines should be drawn so that the dashes are staggered, in a manner similar to bricklaying, as at (d). When two or three hidden lines meet at a point, the dashes should join, as shown for the bottom of the drilled hole at (e), and for the top of a countersunk hole, (f). The example at (g) is similar to (a) in that hidden lines should not join visible lines when it makes the visible line extend too far. Correct and incorrect methods of drawing hidden arcs are shown at (h).

Poorly drawn hidden lines can easily spoil a drawing. Each dash should be carefully drawn about 5 mm long and spaced only about 1 mm apart, by eye. Accent the beginning and end of each dash by

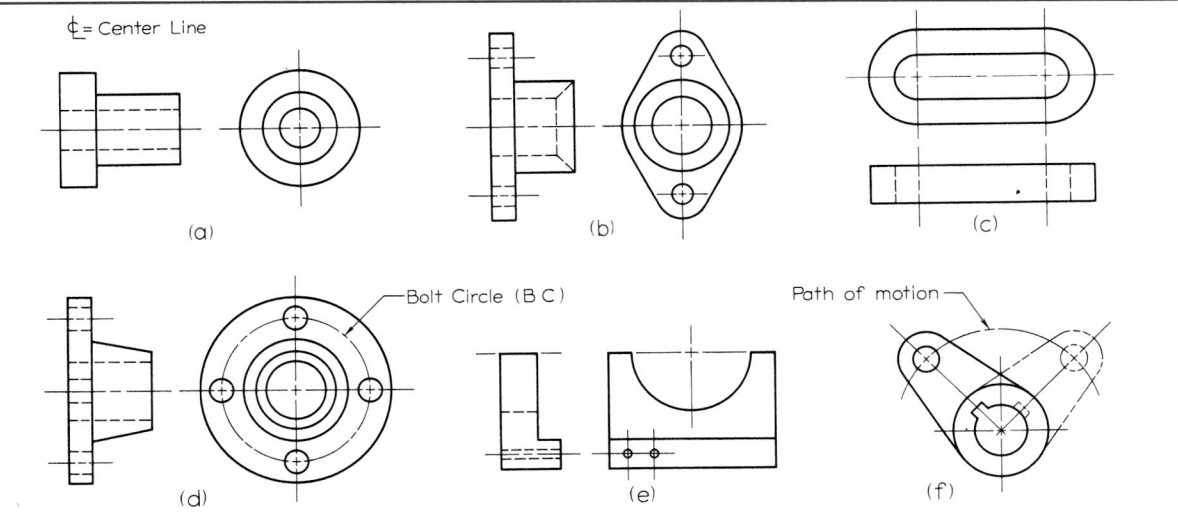

Fig. 6.44 Center-Line Applications.

pressing down on the pencil, whether drawn free-hand or mechanically.

In general, views should be chosen that show features with visible lines, so far as possible. After this has been done, hidden lines should be used wherever necessary to make the drawing clear. Where they are not needed for clearness, hidden lines should be omitted, so as not to clutter the drawing any more than necessary and in order to save time. The beginner, however, would do well to be cautious about leaving out hidden lines until experience shows when they can be safely omitted.

6.26 Center Lines

Center lines (symbol: ₵) are used to indicate axes of symmetrical objects or features, bolt circles, and paths of motion. Typical applications are shown in Fig. 6.44. As shown at (a), a single center line is drawn in the longitudinal view and crossed center lines in the circular view. The small dashes should cross at the intersections of center lines. Center lines should extend uniformly about 8 mm outside the feature for which they are drawn.

The long dashes of center lines may vary from 20 to 40 mm or more in length, depending upon the size of the drawing. The short dashes should be about 5 mm long, with spaces about 2 mm. Center lines should always start and end with long dashes. Short center lines, especially for small holes, as at (e), may be made solid as shown. Always leave a gap as at (e) when a center line forms a continuation of

a visible or hidden line. Center lines should be thin enough to contrast well with the visible and hidden lines but dark enough to reproduce well.

Center lines are useful mainly in dimensioning and should be omitted from unimportant rounded or filleted corners and other shapes that are self-locating.

6.27 Sketching Two Views

The Support Block in Fig. 6.45 (a) requires only two views. The steps in sketching are

I. Block in lightly the enclosing rectangles for the two views. Sketch horizontal lines **1** and **2** to establish the height of the object, while making spaces **A** approximately equal. Sketch vertical lines **3**, **4**, **5**, and **6** to establish the width and depth in correct proportion to the already established height, while making spaces **B** approximately equal, and space **C** equal to or slightly less than space **B**.

II. Block in smaller details, using diagonals to locate the center, as shown. Sketch lightly the circle and arcs.

III. Dim all construction lines with a soft eraser, and heavy in all final lines.

6.28 Sketching Three Views

A Lever Bracket requiring three views is shown in Fig. 6.46 (a). The steps in sketching the three views are as follows.

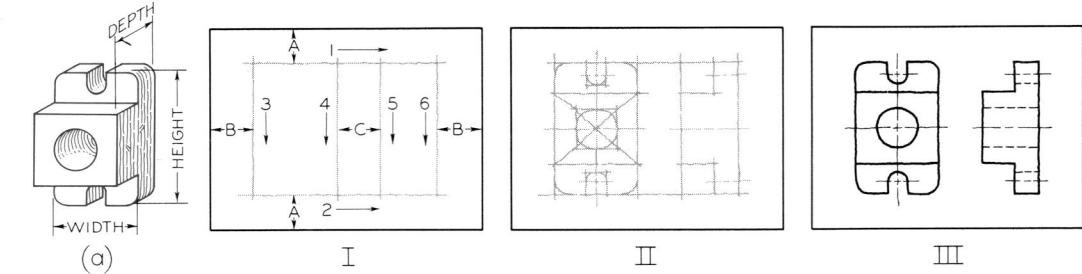

Fig. 6.45 Sketching Two Views of a Support Block.

I.   Block in the enclosing rectangles for the three views. Sketch horizontal lines 1, 2, 3, and 4 to establish the height of the front view and the depth of the top view, while making spaces A approximately equal and space C equal to or slightly less than space A. Sketch vertical lines 5, 6, 7, and 8 to establish the width of the top and front views, and the depth of the side view. Make sure that this is in correct proportion to the height, while making spaces B approximately equal and space D equal to or slightly less than one space B. Note that spaces C and D are not necessarily equal, but are independent of each other. Similarly, spaces A and B are not necessarily equal. To transfer the depth dimension from the top view to the side view, use the edge of a card or strip of paper, as shown, or transfer the distance by using the pencil as a measuring stick, as shown in Fig. 6.10 (b) and (c). Note that *the depth in the top and side views must always be equal.*

II.   Block in all details lightly.

III.   Sketch all arcs and circles lightly.

IV.   Dim all construction lines with a soft eraser.

V.   Heavy in all final lines so that the views will stand out clearly.

6.29 Alignment of Views

Errors in arranging the views are so commonly made by students that it is necessary to repeat: The views must be drawn in accordance with the American National Standard arrangement, Fig. 6.33. In

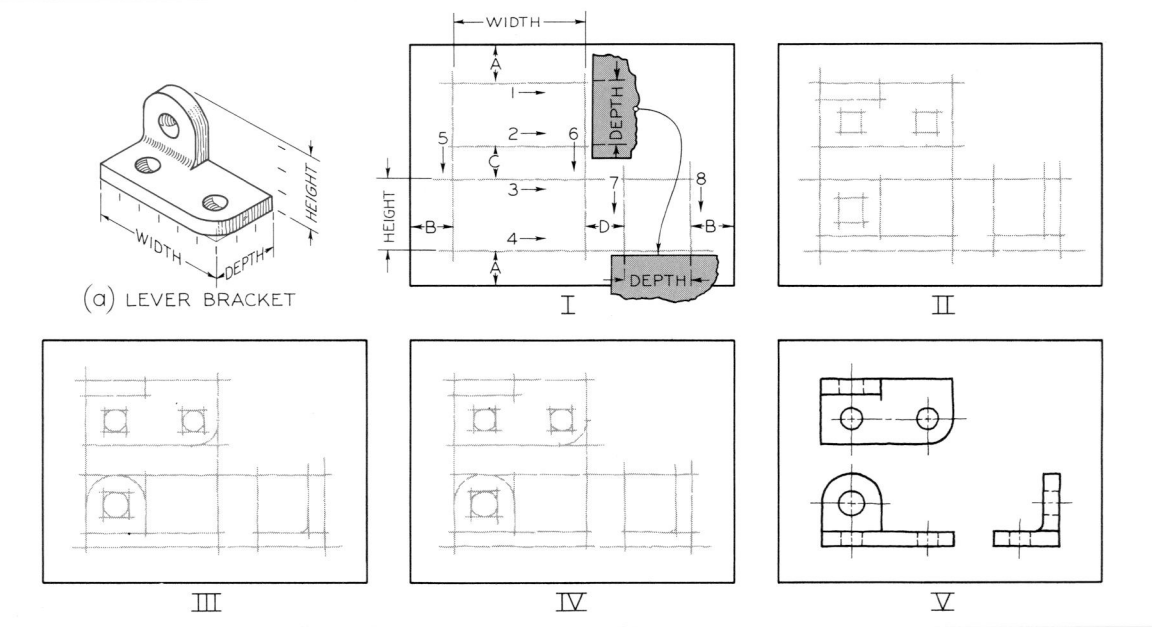

Fig. 6.46 Sketching Three Views of a Lever Bracket.

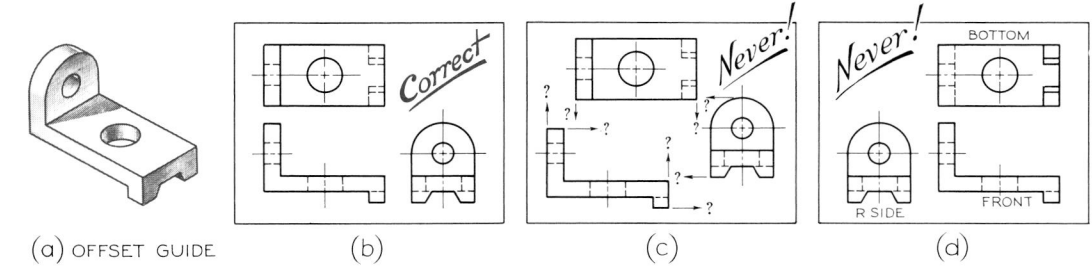

(a) OFFSET GUIDE   (b)   (c)   (d)

Fig. 6.47   Position of Views.

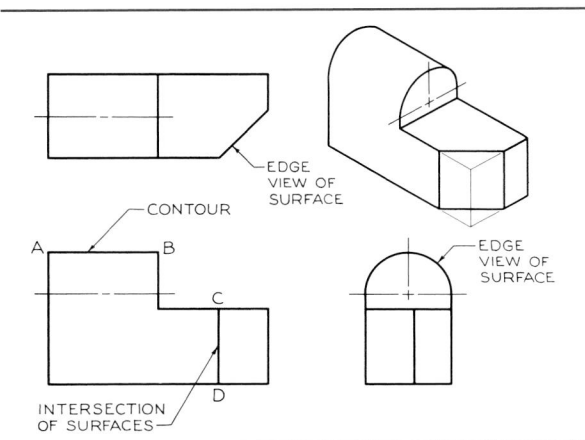

Fig. 6.48   Meaning of Lines.

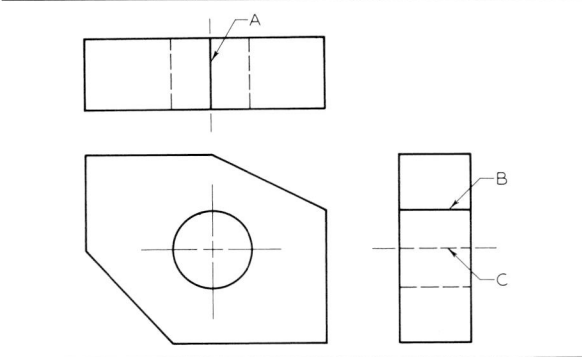

Fig. 6.49   Precedence of Lines.

Fig. 6.47 (a) an Offset Guide is shown that requires three views. These three views, correctly arranged, are shown at (b). The top view must be directly above the front view, and the right-side view di-

rectly to the right of the front view—not out of alignment, as at (c). Also, never draw the views in reversed positions, with the bottom over the front view, or the right-side to the left of the front view, as shown at (d), even though the views do line up with the front view.

6.30 Meaning of Lines

A visible line or a hidden line has three possible meanings, Fig. 6.48: (1) intersection of two surfaces, (2) edge view of a surface, and (3) contour view of a curved surface. Since *no shading is used on a working drawing*, it is necessary to examine all the views to determine the meaning of the lines. For example, the line AB at the top of the front view might be regarded as the edge view of a flat surface if we look at only the front and top views and do not observe the curved surface on top of the object as shown in the right-side view. Similarly, the vertical line CD in the front view might be regarded as the edge view of a plane surface if we look at only the front and side views. However, the top view shows that the line represents the intersection of an inclined surface.

6.31 Precedence of Lines

Visible lines, hidden lines, and center lines often coincide on a drawing, and it is necessary for the drafter to know which line to show. A visible line always takes precedence over (covers up) a center line or a hidden line, as shown at A and B in Fig. 6.49. A hidden line always takes precedence over a center line, as at C. Note that at A and C the ends of the center line are shown, but are separated from the view by short gaps.

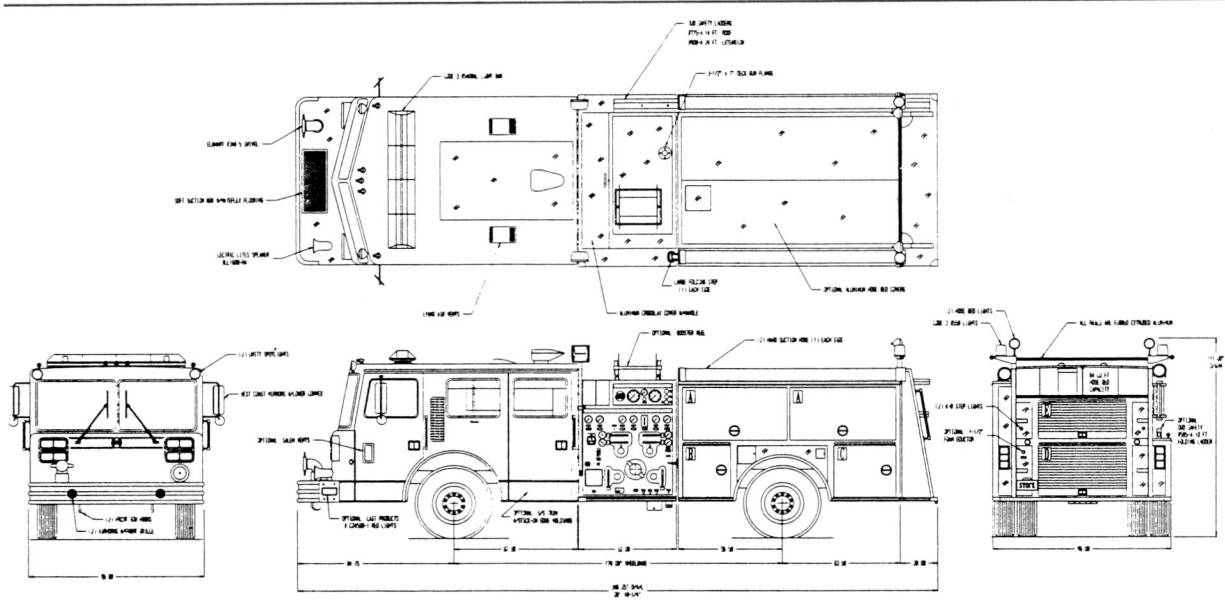

Fig. 6.50   Multiview CAD Assembly Drawing of a MAXIM Fire Truck. *Courtesy of CADKEY.*

6.32 Computer Graphics

Most preliminary sketches are done on paper with a pencil or pen, but once the user understands how a drawing is made through proper orientation of the object to be depicted and choice of views to be used, CAD programs can be used effectively to easily create pictorials or multiview drawings that can be rapidly modified, Fig. 6.50.

Sketching Problems

Figures 6.52 and 6.53 present a variety of objects from which the student is to sketch the necessary views. Using 8.5″ × 11.0″ graph paper, sketch a border and title strip and divide the sheet into two parts as shown in Fig. 6.51. Sketch two assigned problems per sheet, as shown. On the problems in Fig. 6.52, "ticks" are given that indicate .50″ or .25″ spaces. Thus, measurements may be easily spaced off on graph paper having .12″ or .25″ grid spacings.

If desired, the "ticks" on the problems in Fig. 6.52 may be used to indicate 10 mm and 5 mm spaces. Thus, metric measurements may be easily utilized on appropriate metric-grid graph paper.

On the problems in Fig. 6.53 no indications of size are given. The student is to sketch the necessary views of assigned problems to fit the spaces comfortably, as shown in Fig. 6.51. It is suggested that the student prepare a small paper scale, making the divisions equal to those on the paper scale in Prob. 1. This scale can be used to determine the approximate sizes. Let each division equal either .50″ or 10 mm on your sketch.

Missing-line and missing-view problems are given in Figs. 6.54 and 6.55, respectively. These are to be sketched, two problems per sheet, in the arrangement shown in Fig. 6.51. If the instructor so assigns, the missing lines or views may be sketched with a colored pencil. The problems given in Figs. 6.54 and 6.55 may be sketched in isometric on isometric paper or in oblique on graph paper.

Since many of the problems in this chapter are of a general nature, they can also be solved on most computer graphics systems. If a system is available, the instructor may choose to assign specific problems to be completed by this method.

Additional problems in convenient form for solution are presented in the worksheets at the back of this book. Refer to Drawings 6-1 and 6-2 and accompanying instructions.

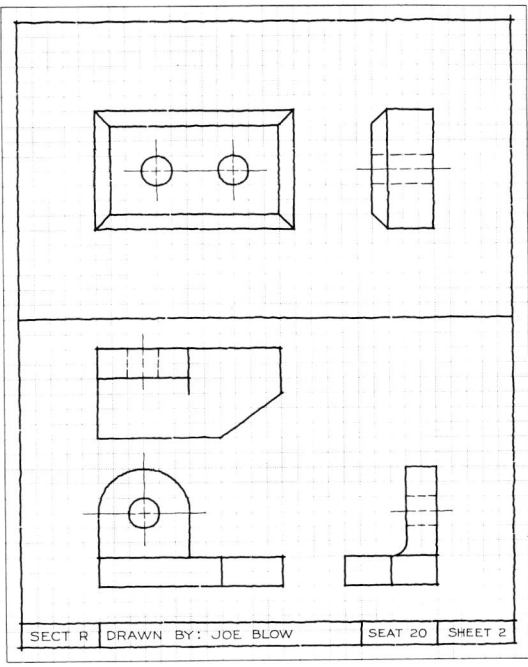

SECT R | DRAWN BY: JOE BLOW | SEAT 20 | SHEET 2

Fig. 6.51   Multiview Sketch (Layout A–1).

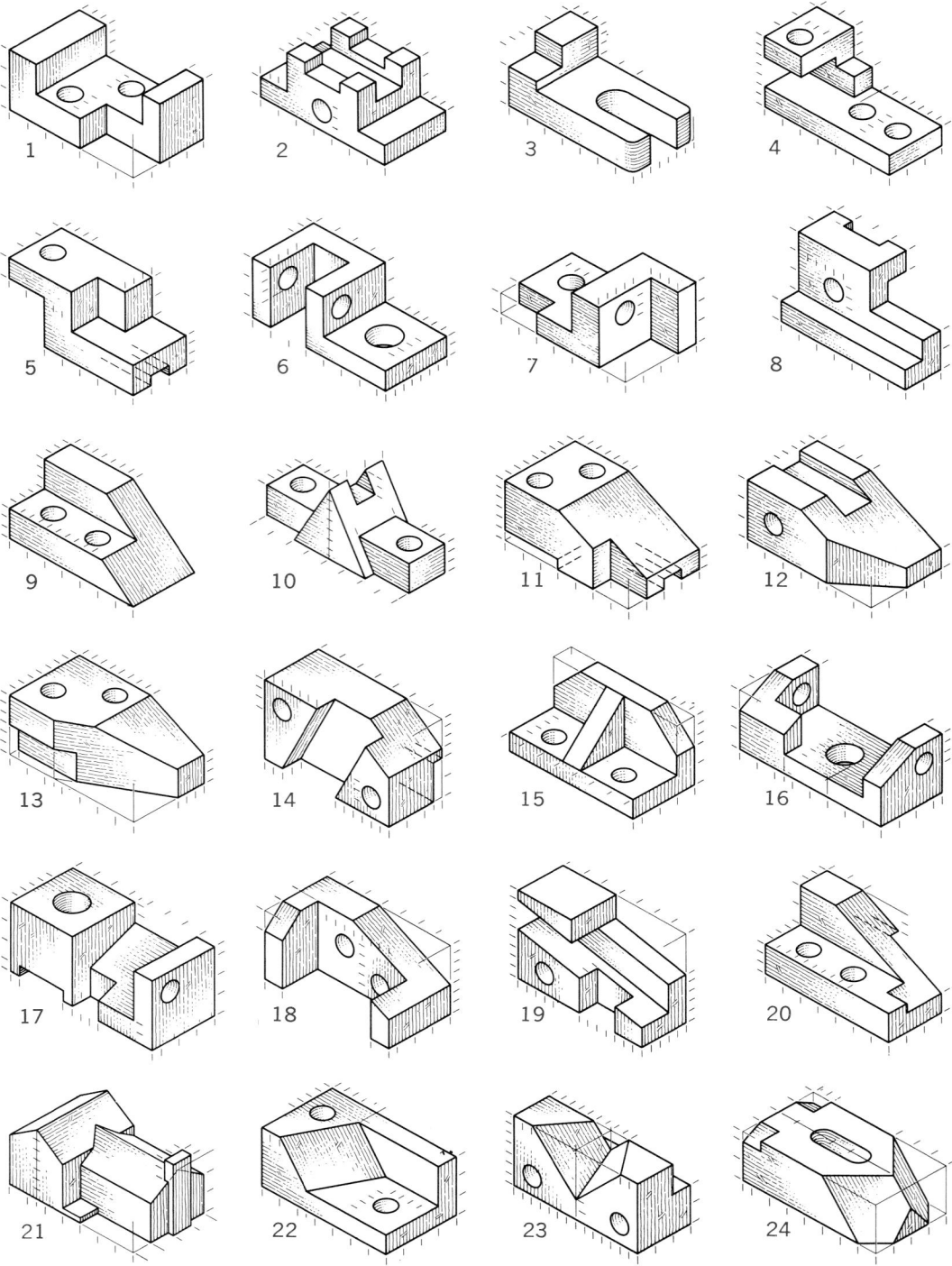

Fig. 6.52   Multiview Sketching Problems.   Sketch necessary views, using Layout A–1 or A4–1 adjusted (freehand), on graph paper or plain paper, two problems per sheet as in Fig. 6.51. The units shown may be either .50″ and .25″ or 10 mm and 5 mm. See instructions on page 173. All holes are through holes.

Fig. 6.53 Multiview Sketching Problems. Sketch necessary views, using Layout A–1 or 4A–1 adjusted (freehand), on graph paper or plain paper, two problems per sheet as in Fig. 6.51. Prepare paper scale with divisions equal to those in Prob. 1, and apply to problems to obtain approximate sizes. Let each division equal either .50″ or 10 mm on your sketch. See instructions on page 173. For Probs. 17–24, study §§7.34–7.36.

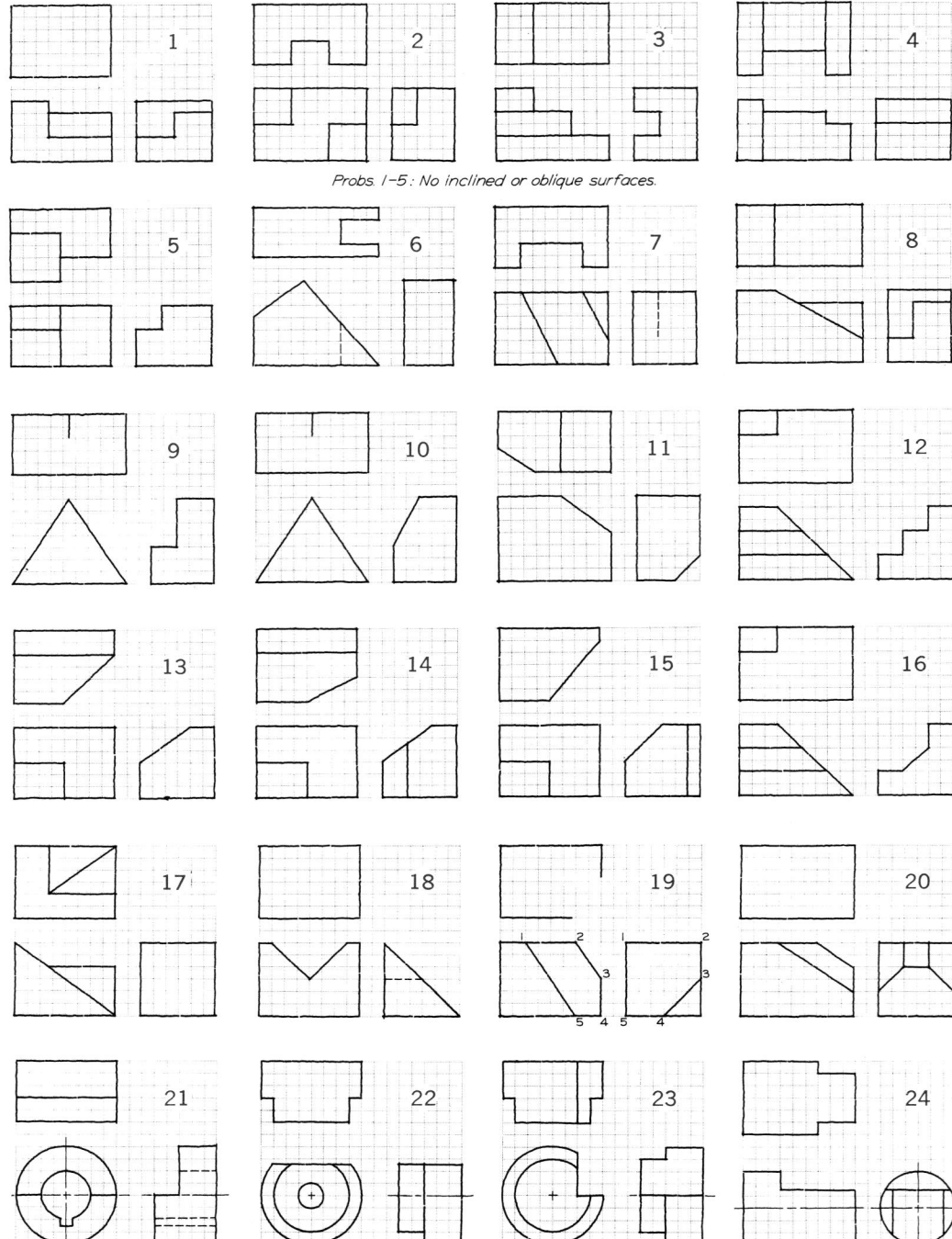

Probs. 1–5 : No inclined or oblique surfaces.

Fig. 6.54 Missing-Line Sketching Problems. (1) Sketch given views, using Layout A–1 or A4–1 adjusted (freehand), on graph paper or plain paper, two problems per sheet as in Fig. 6.51. Add missing lines. The squares may be either .25″ or 5 mm. See instructions on page 173. (2) Sketch in isometric on isometric paper or in oblique on cross-section paper.

Fig. 6.55 Third-View Sketching Problems. (1) Using Layout A–1 or A4–1 adjusted (freehand), on graph paper or plain paper, two problems per sheet as in Fig. 6.51, sketch the two given views and add the missing views, as indicated. The squares may be either .25″ or 5 mm. See instructions on page 173. The given views are either front and right-side views or front and top views. Hidden holes with center lines are drilled holes. (2) Sketch in isometric on isometric paper or in oblique on cross-section paper.

Multiview Projection

A view of a part for a design is known technically as a *projection*. A projection is a view conceived to be drawn or projected into a plane known as the *plane of projection*. A system of views of an object formed by projectors from the object perpendicular to the desired planes of projection is known as orthographic or multiview projection. See ANSI Y14.3–1975 (R1987). This system of required views provides for the shape description of the object.

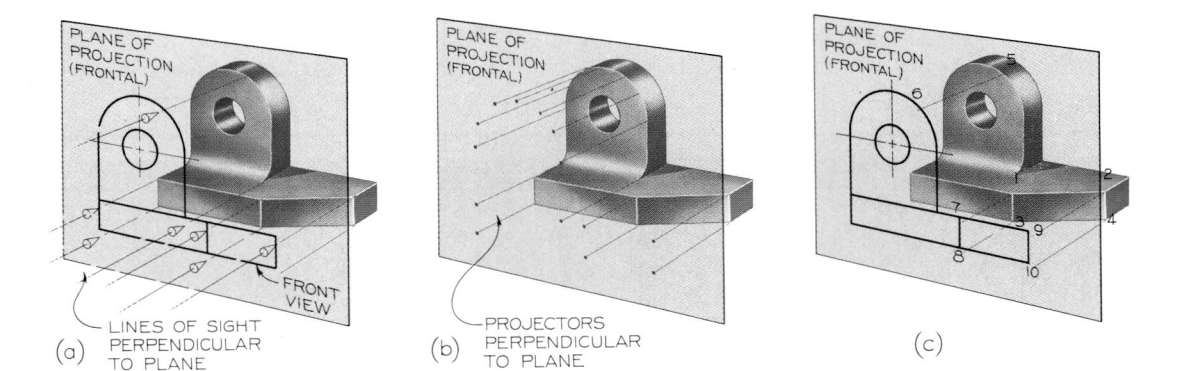

Fig. 7.1   Projection of an Object.

7.1 Projection Method

The method of viewing the part to obtain a *multi-view projection* is illustrated for a front view in Fig. 7.1 (a). Between the observer and the part, a transparent plane or pane of glass representing a plane of projection is located parallel to the front surfaces of the part. Shown on the plane of projection in outline is how the design appears to the observer. Theoretically, the observer is at an infinite distance from the part or object, so that the *lines of sight* are parallel.

In more precise terms, this view is obtained by drawing perpendiculars, called *projectors,* from all points on the edges or contours of the part or object to the plane of projection, (b). The collective piercing points of these projectors, being infinite in number, form lines on the pane of glass, as shown at (c).

Thus, as shown at (c), a projector from point **1** on the object pierces the plane of projection at point **7**, which is a view or projection of the point. The same procedure applies to point **2**, whose projection is point **9**. Since **1** and **2** are endpoints of a straight line on the object, the projections **7** and **9** are joined to give the projection of the line **7–9**. Similarly, if the projections of the four corners **1, 2, 3,** and **4** are found, the projections **7, 9, 10,** and **8** may be joined by straight lines to form the projection of the rectangular surface.

The same procedure can be applied to curved lines—for example, the top curved contour of the object. A point, **5,** on the curve is projected to the plane at **6.** The projection of an infinite number of such points, a few of which are shown at (b), on the plane of projection results in the projection of the

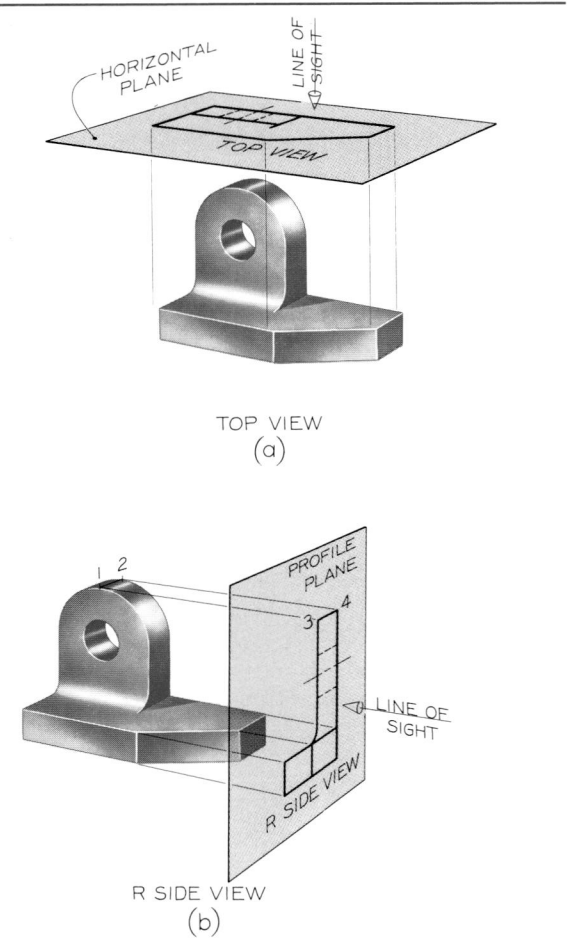

TOP VIEW
(a)

R SIDE VIEW
(b)

Fig. 7.2   Top and Right-Side Views.

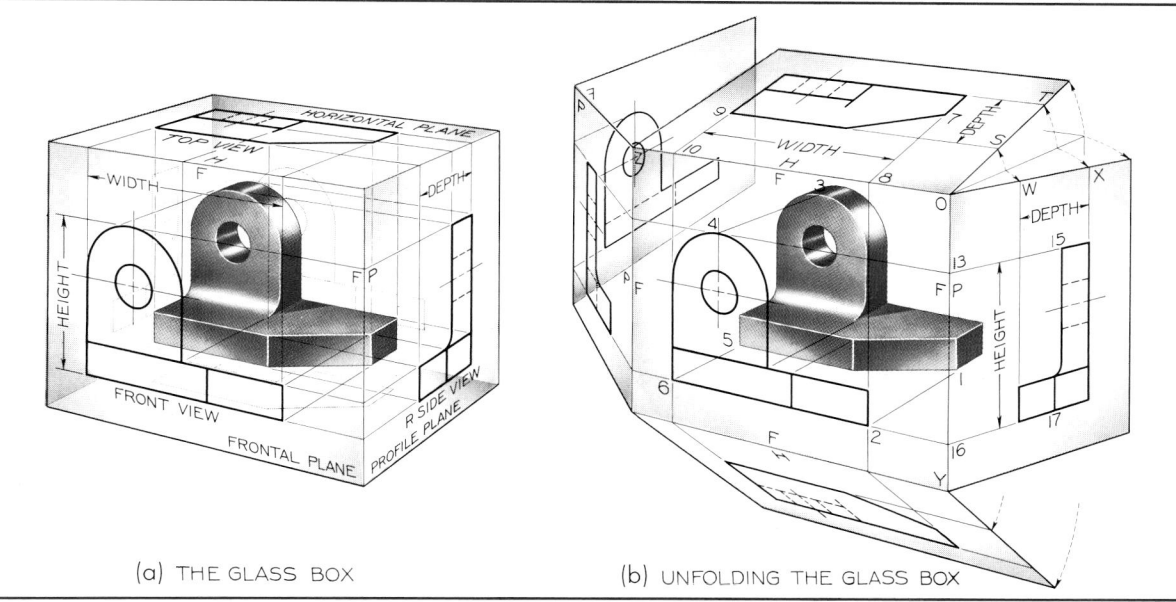

(a) THE GLASS BOX   (b) UNFOLDING THE GLASS BOX

Fig. 7.3   The Glass Box.

curve. If this procedure of projecting points is applied to all edges and contours of the object, a complete view or projection of the object results. This view is necessary in the shape description because it shows the true curvature of the top and the true shape of the hole.

A similar procedure may be used to obtain the top view, Fig. 7.2 (a). This view is necessary in the shape description because it shows the true angle of the inclined surface. In this view, the hole is invisible and its extreme contours are represented by hidden lines, as shown.

The right-side view, (b), is necessary because it shows the right-angled characteristic shape of the object and shows the true shape of the curved intersection. Note how the cylindrical contour on top of the object appears when viewed from the side. The extreme or contour element **1–2** on the object is projected to give the line **3–4** on the view. The hidden hole is also represented by projecting the extreme elements.

The plane of projection upon which the front view is projected is called the *frontal plane*, that upon which the top view is projected, the *horizontal plane,* and that upon which the side view is projected, the *profile plane.*

7.2 The Glass Box

If planes of projection are placed parallel to the principal faces of the object, they form a "glass box," as shown in Fig. 7.3 (a). Notice that the observer is always *on the outside looking in,* so that the object is seen through the planes of projection. Since the glass box has six sides, six views of the object can be obtained.

Note that the object has three principal dimensions: *width, height,* and *depth.* These are fixed terms used for dimensions in these directions, regardless of the shape of the object. See §6.18.

Since it is required to show the views of a solid or three-dimensional object on a flat sheet of paper, it is necessary to unfold the planes so that they will all lie in the same plane, Fig. 7.3 (b). All planes except the rear plane are hinged upon the frontal plane, the rear plane being hinged to the left-side plane, except as explained in §7.8. Each plane revolves outwardly from the original box position until it lies in the frontal plane, which remains stationary. The hinge lines of the glass box are known as *folding lines.*

The positions of these six planes, after they have been revolved, are shown in Fig. 7.4. Carefully identify each of these planes and corresponding

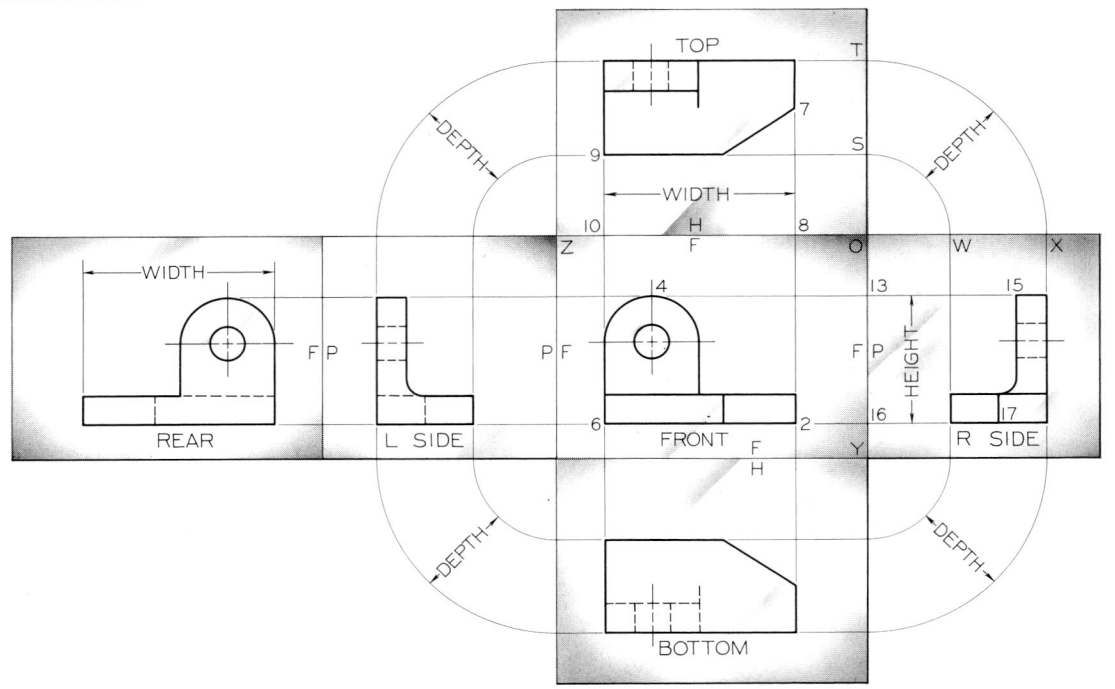

Fig. 7.4 The Glass Box Unfolded.

views with its original position in the glass box, and repeat this mental procedure, if necessary, until the revolutions are thoroughly understood.

In Fig. 7.3 (b), observe that lines extend around the glass box from one view to another upon the planes of projection. These are the *projections of the projectors* from points on the object to the views. For example, the projector **1–2** is projected on the horizontal plane at **7–8** and on the profile plane at **16–17**. When the top plane is folded up, lines **9–10** and **7–8** will become vertical and line up with **10–6** and **8–2**, respectively. Thus, **9–10** and **10–6** form a single straight line **9–6**, and **7–8** and **8–2** form a single straight line **7–2**, as shown in Fig. 7.4. This explains why the top view is the same width as the front view and why it is placed directly above the front view. The same relation exists between the front and bottom views. Therefore, *the front, top, and bottom views all line up vertically and are the same width.*

In Fig. 7.3 (b), when the profile plane is folded out, lines **4–13** and **13–15** become a single straight line **4–15**, and lines **2–16** and **16–17** become a single

straight line **2–17** as shown in Fig. 7.4. The same relation exists between the front, left-side, and rear views. Therefore, *the rear, left-side, front, and right-side views all line up horizontally and are the same height.*

In Fig. 7.3 (b), note that lines **OS** and **OW** and lines **ST** and **WX** are respectively equal. These lines of equal length are shown in the unfolded position in Fig. 7.4. Thus, it is seen that the top view must be the same distance from the folding line **OZ** as the right-side view is from the folding line **OY**. Similarly, the bottom view and the left-side view are the same distance from their respective folding lines as are the right-side view and the top view. Therefore, *the top, right-side, bottom, and left-side views are all equidistant from the respective folding lines, and are the same depth.* Note that in these four views that surround the front view, the front surfaces of the object are faced inward, or toward the front view. Observe also that the left-side and right-side views and the top and bottom views are the reverse of each other in outline shape. Similarly, the rear and front views are the reverse of each other.

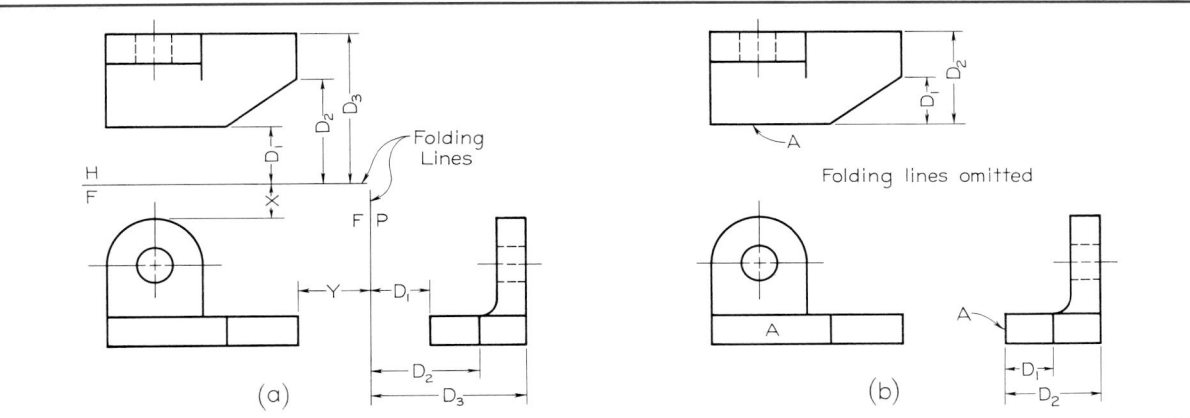

Fig. 7.5 Folding Lines.

7.3 Folding Lines

The three views of the object just discussed are shown in Fig. 7.5 (a), with folding lines between the views. These folding lines correspond to the hinge lines of the glass box, as we have seen. The H/F folding line, between the top and front views, is the intersection of the horizontal and frontal planes. The F/P folding line, between the front and side views, is the intersection of the frontal and profile planes. See Figs. 7.3 and 7.4.

The distances X and Y, from the front view to the respective folding lines, are not necessarily equal, since they depend upon the relative distances of the object from the horizontal and profile planes. However, as explained in §7.2, distances D_1, from the top and side views to the respective folding lines, must always be equal. Therefore, the views may be any desired distance apart, and the folding lines may be drawn anywhere between them, as long as distances D_1 are kept equal and the folding lines are at right angles to the projection lines between the views.

It will be seen that distances D_2 and D_3, respectively, are also equal and that the folding lines H/F and F/P are in reality reference lines for making equal *depth* measurements in the top and side views. Thus, any point in the top view is the same distance from H/F as the corresponding point in the side view is from F/P.

While it is necessary to understand the folding lines, particularly because they are useful in solving graphical problems in descriptive geometry, they are as a rule omitted in industrial drafting. The three views, with the folding lines omitted, are shown in Fig. 7.5 (b). Again, the distances between the top and front views and between the side and front views are not necessarily equal. Instead of using the folding lines as reference lines for setting off depth measurements in the top and side views, we may use the front surface A of the object as a reference line. In this way, D_1, D_2, and all other depth measurements are made to correspond in the two views in the same manner as if folding lines were used.

7.4 Two-View Instrumental Drawing

Let it be required to draw, full size with instruments on Layout A–2 (inside back cover), the necessary views of the Operating Arm shown in Fig. 7.6 (a). In this case, as shown by the arrows, only the front and top views are needed.

I. Determine the spacing of the views. The width of the front and top views is approximately 152 mm (6″; 25.4 mm = 1″) and the width of the working space is approximately 266 mm (10½″). As shown at (b), subtract 152 mm from 266 mm and divide the result by 2 to get the value of space A. To set off the spaces, place the scale horizontally along the bottom of the sheet and make short vertical marks.

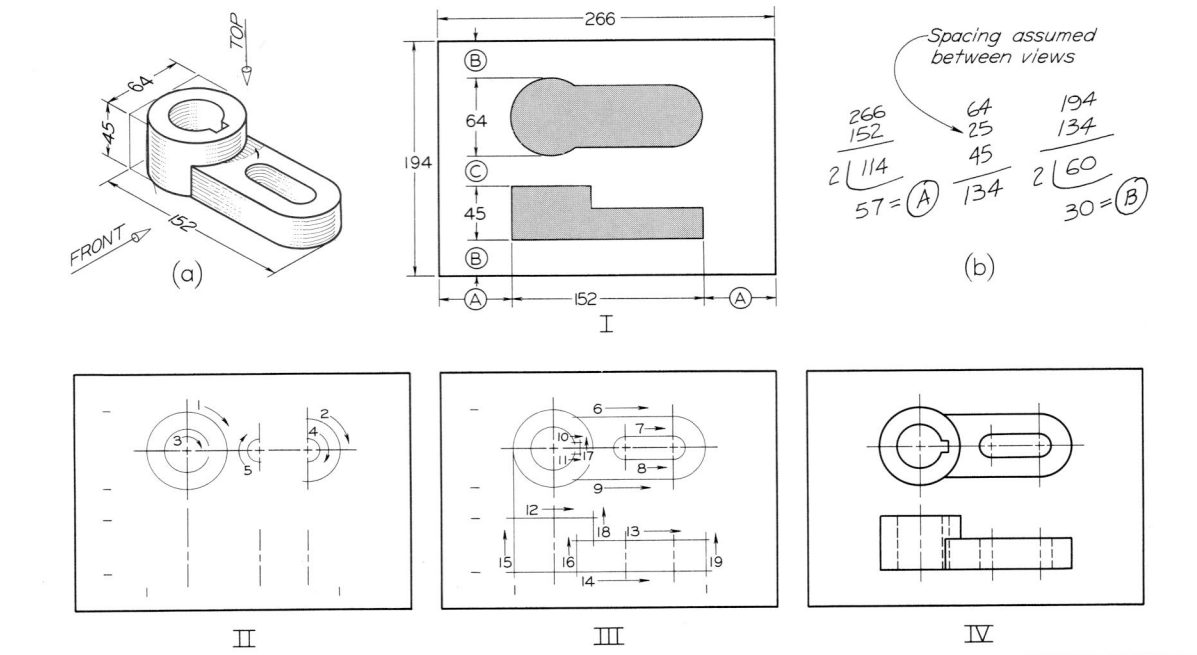

Fig. 7.6   Two-View Instrumental Drawing (dimensions in millimeters).

The depth of the top view is approximately 64 mm ($2\frac{1}{2}''$) and the height of the front view is 45 mm ($1\frac{3}{4}''$), while the height of the working space is 194 mm ($7\frac{5}{8}''$). Assume a space **C**, say 25 mm (1″), between views that will look well and that will provide sufficient space for dimensions, if any.

As shown at (b), add 64 mm, 25 mm, and 45 mm, subtract the total from 194 mm, and divide the result by 2 to get the value of space **B**. To set off the spaces, place the scale vertically along the left side of the sheet with the full-size scale on the left, and make short marks perpendicular to the scale. See Fig. 2.54 (III).

II.   Locate center lines from spacing marks. Construct arcs and circles lightly.

III.   Draw horizontal and then vertical construction lines in the order shown. Allow construction lines to cross at corners.

IV.   Add hidden lines and heavy in all final lines, clean-cut and dark. The visible lines should be heavy enough to make the views stand out. The hid-

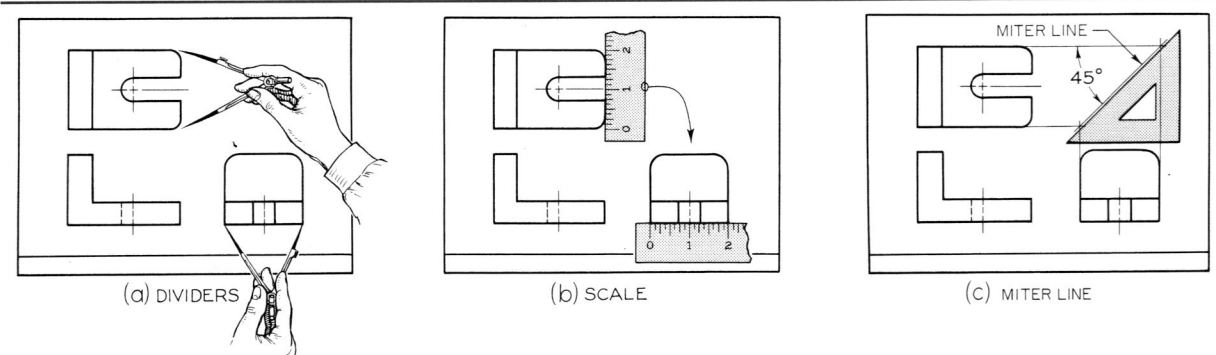

Fig. 7.7   Transferring Depth Dimensions.

den lines and center lines should be sharp in contrast to the visible lines, but dark enough to reproduce well. See §2.46 for technique of pencil drawing. Construction lines need not be erased if drawn lightly. If you are working on tracing paper, hold the sheet up to the light to see if the density of your lines is sufficient to reproduce well.

7.5 Transferring Depth Dimensions

Since all depth dimensions in the top and side views must correspond point for point, accurate methods of transferring these distances, such as D_1 and D_2, Fig. 7.5 (b), must be used.

Professional drafters transfer dimensions between the top and side views either by dividers or scale, as shown in Fig. 7.7 (a) and (b). The scale method is especially convenient when the drafting machine, Fig. 2.70, is used because both vertical and horizontal scales are readily available. Beginners might find it convenient to use a 45° miter line to project dimensions between top and side views, as in Fig. 7.7 (c). Note that the right-side view may be moved to the right or left, or the top view may be moved upward or downward, by shifting the 45° line accordingly. It is not necessary to draw continuous lines between the top and side views via the miter line. Instead, make short dashes across the miter line and project from these.

The 45° miter-line method, Fig. 7.7 (c) is also convenient for transferring a large number of points, as when plotting a curve, Fig. 7.35.

7.6 Projecting a Third View

In Fig. 7.8 (top) is a pictorial drawing of a given object, three views of which are required. Each corner of the object is given a number, as shown. At I, the top and front views are shown, with each corner properly numbered in both views. Each number appears twice, once in the top view and once again in the front view.

If a point is *visible* in a given view, the number is placed *outside* the corner, but if the point is hidden, the numeral is placed *inside* the corner. For example, at I point 1 is visible in both views, and is therefore placed outside the corners in both views. However, point 2 is visible in the top view and the number is placed outside, while in the front view it is hidden and is placed inside.

This numbering system, in which points are

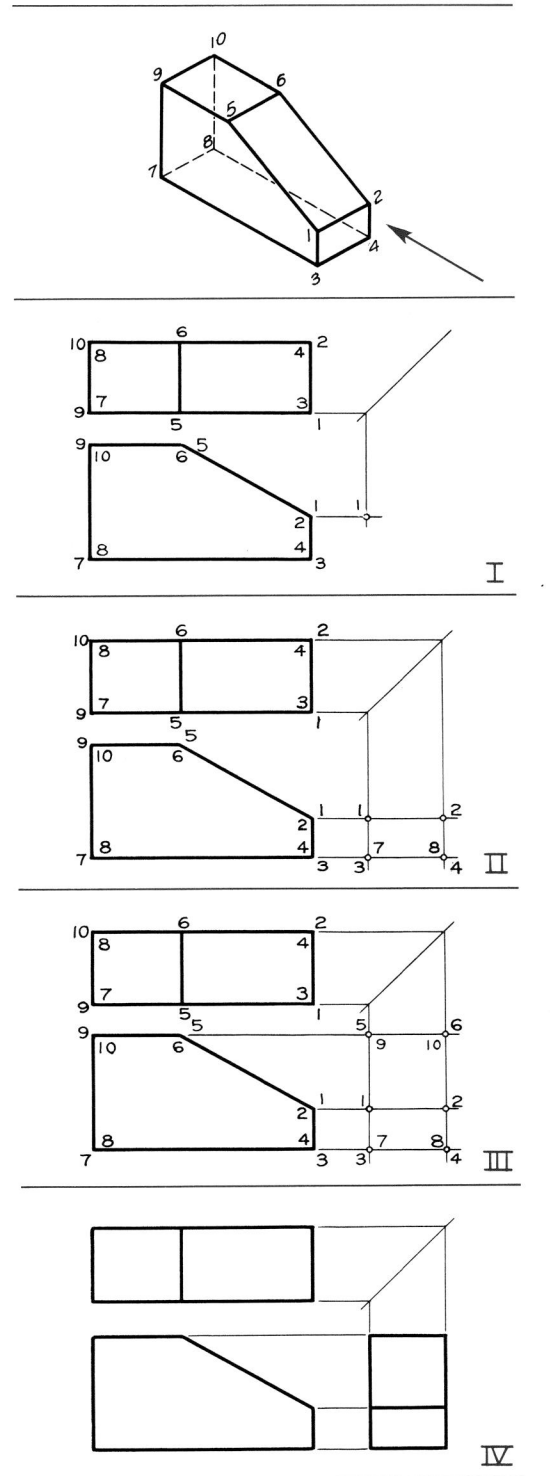

Fig. 7.8   Use of Numbers.

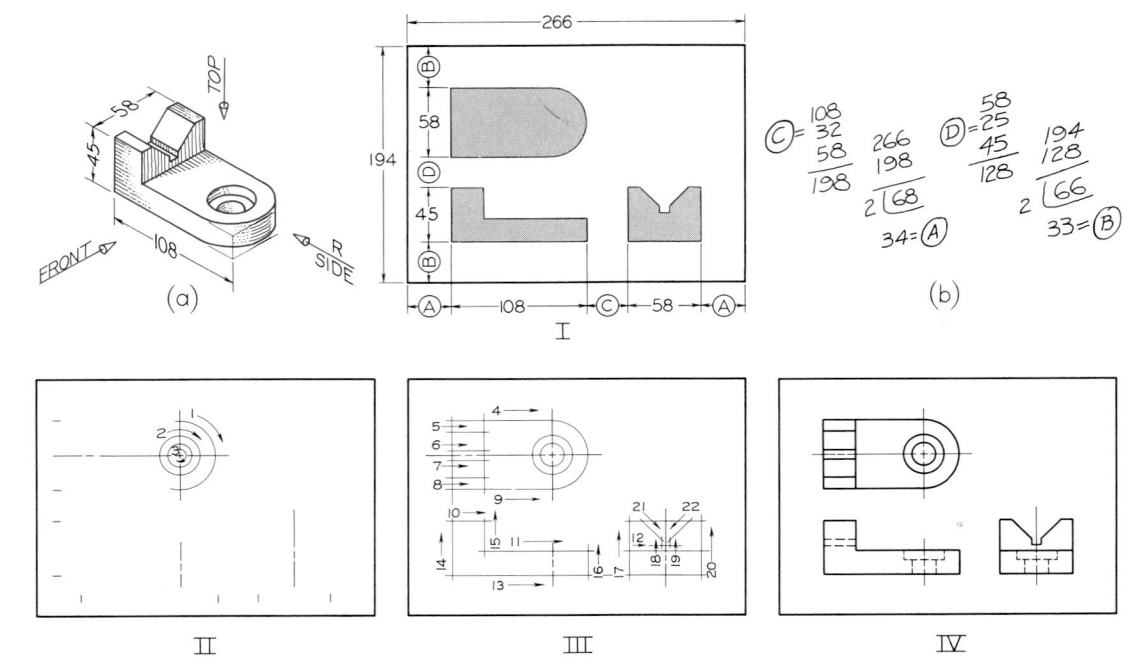

Fig. 7.9   Three-View Instrumental Drawing (dimensions in millimeters).

7.7 Three-View Instrumental Drawing

identified by the same numbers in all views, is useful in projecting known points in two views to unknown positions in a third view. Note that this numbering system assigns the same number to a given point in all views and should not be confused with the numbering system, used in Fig. 7.23 and others, in which a point has different numbers in each view.

Before starting to project the right-side view in Fig. 7.8, try to visualize the view as seen in the direction of the arrow (see pictorial drawing). Then construct the right-side view point by point, using a hard pencil and very light lines.

As shown at I, locate point 1 in the side view by projecting from point 1 in the top view and point 1 in the front view. In space II, project points 2, 3, and 4 in a similar manner to complete the vertical end surface of the object. In space III, project points 5 and 6 to complete the side view of the inclined surface 5–6–2–1. This completes the right-side view, since invisible points 9, 10, 8, and 7 are directly behind visible corners 5, 6, 4, and 3, respectively. Note that in the side view the invisible points are lettered *inside* and the visible points *outside*.

As shown in space IV, the drawing is completed by heavying in the lines in the right-side view.

Let it be required to draw, full size with instruments on Layout A–2, the necessary views of the V-block in Fig. 7.9 (a). In this case, as shown by the arrows, three views are needed.

I.   Determine the spacing of the views. The width of the front view is 108 mm, and the depth of the side view is 58 mm, while the width of the working space is 266 mm. Assume a space C between views, say, 32 mm, that will look well and will allow sufficient space for dimensions, if any.

As shown at (b), add 108 mm, 32 mm, and 58 mm, subtract the total from 266 mm, and divide the result by 2 to get the value of space A. To set off these horizontal spacing measurements, place the scale along the bottom of the sheet and make short vertical marks.

The depth of the top view is 58 mm and the height of the front view is 45 mm, while the height of the working space if 194 mm. Assume a space D between views, say, 25 mm. As shown in §7.3, space D need not be the same as space C. As shown at (b), add 58 mm, 25 mm, and 45 mm, subtract the total from 194 mm, and divide the result by 2 to get the

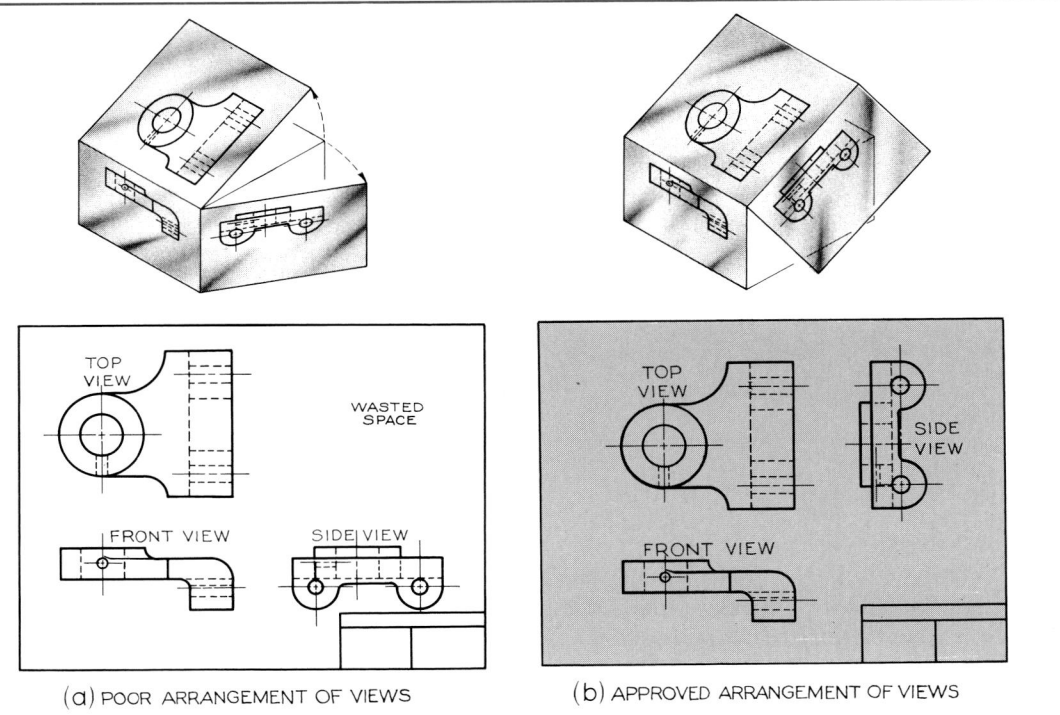

(a) POOR ARRANGEMENT OF VIEWS   (b) APPROVED ARRANGEMENT OF VIEWS

Fig. 7.10 Position of Side View.

value of space **B**. To set off these vertical spacing measurements, place the scale along the left side of the sheet with the scale used on the left, and make short marks perpendicular to the scale. Allow for dimensions, if any.

II. Locate the center lines from the spacing marks. Construct lightly the arcs and circles.

III. Draw horizontal, then vertical, then inclined construction lines, in the order shown. Allow construction lines to cross at the corners. Do not complete one view at a time; construct the views simultaneously.

IV. Add hidden lines and heavy in all final lines, clean-cut and dark. A convenient method of transferring a hole diameter from the top view to the side view is to use the compass with the same setting used for drawing the hole. The visible lines should be heavy enough to make the views stand out. The hidden lines and center lines should be in sharp contrast to the visible lines, but dark enough to reproduce well. Construction lines need not be erased if they are drawn lightly. If you are working on tracing paper, hold the sheet up to the light to see if the density of your lines is sufficient to reproduce well. See §2.46.

7.8 Alternate Positions of Views

If three views of a wide flat object are drawn, using the conventional arrangement of views, Fig. 7.10 (a), a large wasted space is left on the paper, as shown. In such cases, the profile plane may be considered hinged to the horizontal plane instead of the frontal plane, as shown at (b). This places the side view beside the top view, which results in better spacing and sometimes makes the use of a reduced scale unnecessary.

It is also permissible in extreme circumstances to place the side view across horizontally from the bottom view. In this case the profile plane is considered hinged to the bottom plane of projection. Similarly, the rear view may be placed directly above the top view or under the bottom view, if necessary, the rear plane being considered hinged to the horizontal or bottom plane, as the case may be, and then rotated into coincidence with the frontal plane.

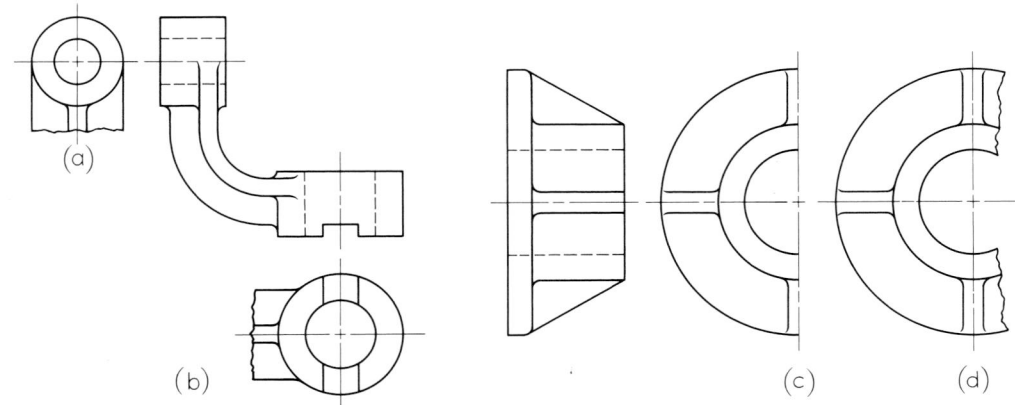

Fig. 7.11   Partial Views.

7.9 Partial Views

A view may not need to be complete but may show only what is necessary in the clear description of the object. Such a view is a partial view, Fig. 7.11. A break line, (a), may be used to limit the partial view; the contour of the part shown may limit the view, (b); or if symmetrical, a half-view may be drawn on one side of the center line, (c), or a partial view, "broken out," may be drawn as at (d). The half shown at (c) and (d) should be the near side, as shown. For half-views in connection with sections, see Fig. 9.33.

Do not place a break line where it will coincide with a visible or hidden line.

Occasionally the distinctive features of an object are on opposite sides, so that in either complete side view there would be a considerable overlapping of shapes, resulting in an unintelligible view. In such cases two side views are often the best solution, Fig. 7.12. Observe that the views are partial views, in both of which certain visible and invisible lines have been omitted for clearness.

7.10 Revolution Conventions

Regular multiview projections are sometimes awkward, confusing, or actually misleading. For example, Fig. 7.13 (a) shows an object that has three triangular ribs, three holes equally spaced in the base, and a keyway. The right-side view at (b) is a regular projection and is not recommended. The lower ribs appear in a foreshortened position, the holes do not appear in their true relation to the rim of the base, and the keyway is projected as a confusion of hidden lines.

The conventional method shown at (c) is preferred, not only because it is simpler to read, but also because it requires less drafting time. Each of the features mentioned has been revolved in the front view to lie along the vertical center line from where it is projected to the correct side view at (c).

At (d) and (e) are shown regular views of a flange with many small holes. The hidden holes at (e) are confusing and take unnecessary time to draw. The preferred representation at (f) shows the holes revolved, and the drawing is clear.

Fig. 7.12   Incomplete Side Views.

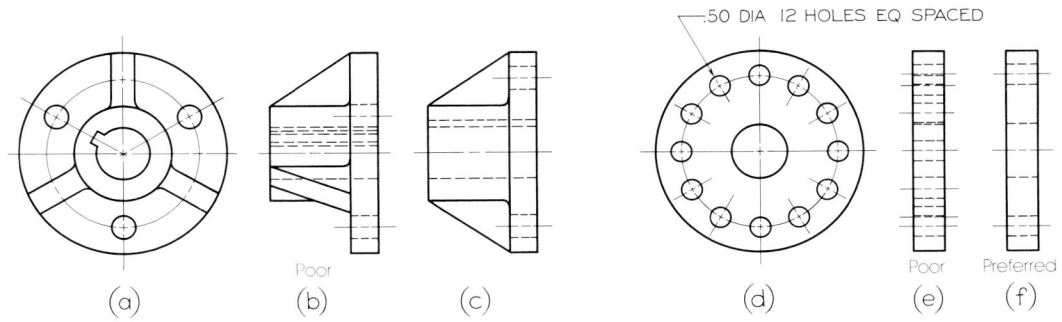

Fig. 7.13 Revolution Conventions.

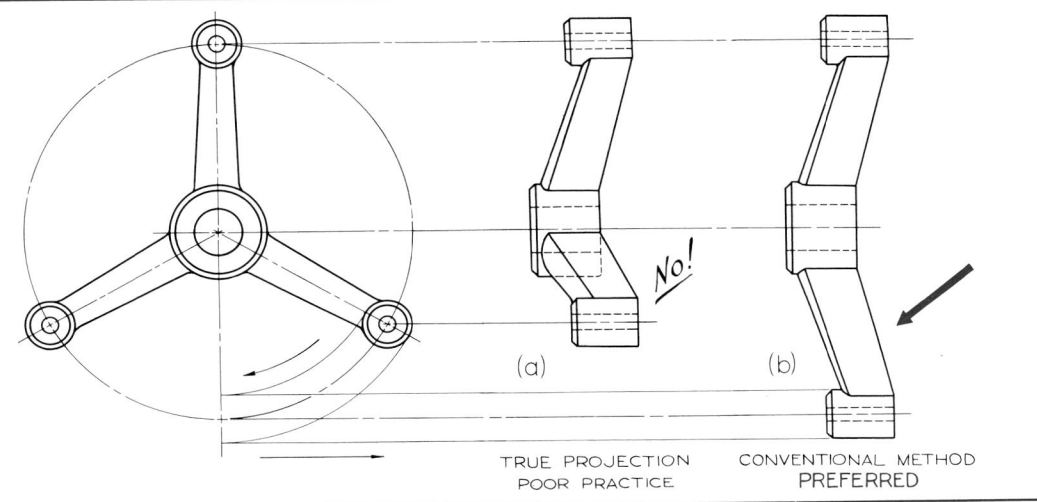

Fig. 7.14 Revolution Conventions.

Another example is shown in Fig. 7.14. As shown at (a), a regular projection results in a confusing foreshortening of an inclined arm. In order to preserve the appearance of symmetry about the common center, the lower arm is revolved to line up vertically in the front view so that it projects true length in the side view at (b).

Revolutions of the type discussed here are frequently used in connection with sectioning. Such sectional views are called *aligned sections*, §9.13.

7.11 Removed Views Fig. 7.15
A removed view is a complete or partial view removed to another place on the sheet so that it no longer is in direct projection with any other view. Such a view may be used to show some feature of the object more clearly, possibly to a larger scale, or to

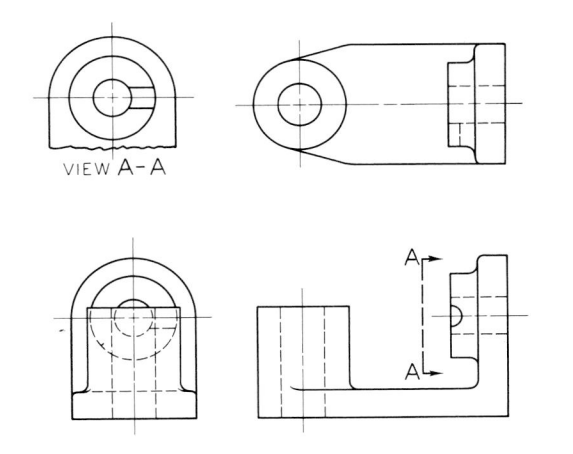

Fig. 7.15 Removed View.

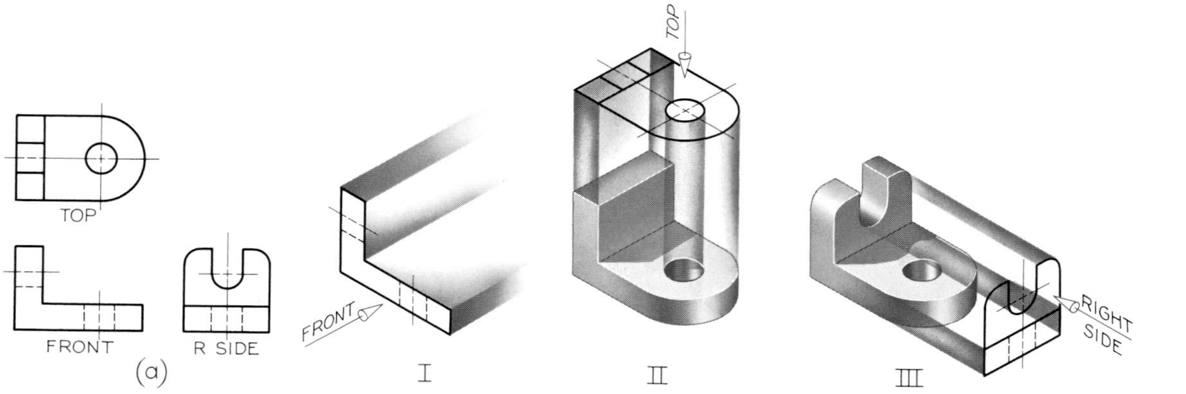

Fig. 7.16 Visualizing from Given Views.

save drawing a complete regular view. A viewing-plane line is used to indicate the part being viewed, the arrows at the corners showing the direction of sight. See §9.5. The removed view should be labeled VIEW A–A or VIEW B–B and so on, the letters referring to those placed at the corners of the viewing-plane line.

7.12 Visualization

As stated in §1.9, the ability to *visualize* or *think in three dimensions* is one of the most important requisites of the successful engineer or scientist. In practice, this means the ability to study the views of an object and to form a mental picture of it—to *visualize* its three-dimensional shape. To the designer it means the ability to *synthesize* or form a mental picture before the object even exists and the ability to express this image in terms of views. The engineer is the master planner in the construction of new machines, structures, or processes. The ability to visualize, and to use the language of drawing as a means of communication or recording of mental images, is indispensable.

Even the experienced engineer or designer cannot look at a multiview drawing and instantly visualize the object represented (except for the simplest shapes) any more than we can grasp the ideas on a book page merely at a glance. It is necessary to *study* the drawing, to read the lines in a logical way, to piece together the little things until a clear idea of the whole emerges. How this is done is described in §§7.13–7.32.

7.13 Visualizing the Views

A method of reading drawings that is essentially the reverse mental process to that of obtaining the views by projection is illustrated in Fig. 7.16. The given views of an Angle Bracket are shown at (a).

I. The front view shows that the object is L-shaped, the height and width of the object, and the thickness of the members. The meaning of the hidden and center lines is not yet clear, nor do we yet know the depth of the object.

II. The top view tells us that the horizontal member is rounded on the end and has a round hole. Some kind of slot is indicated at the left end. The depth and width of the object are shown.

III. The right-side view tells us that the left end of the object has rounded corners at the top and has an open-end slot in a vertical position. The height and depth of the object are shown.

Thus, each view provides certain definite information regarding the shape of the object. All views must be considered in order to visualize the object completely.

7.14 Models

One of the best aids to visualization is an actual model of the object. Such a model need not be made accurately to scale and may be made of any convenient material, such as modeling clay, soap, wood, styrofoam, or any material that can be easily carved or cut.

A typical example of the use of soap or clay

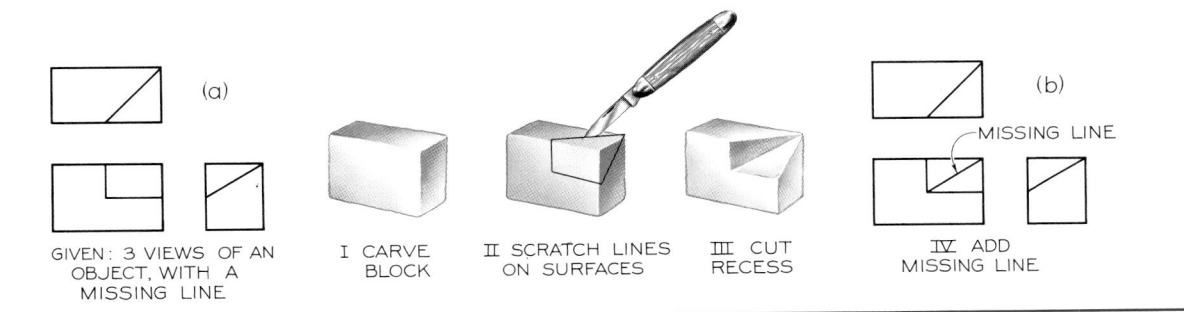

Fig. 7.17   Use of Model to Aid Visualization.

Fig. 7.18   Soap Models.

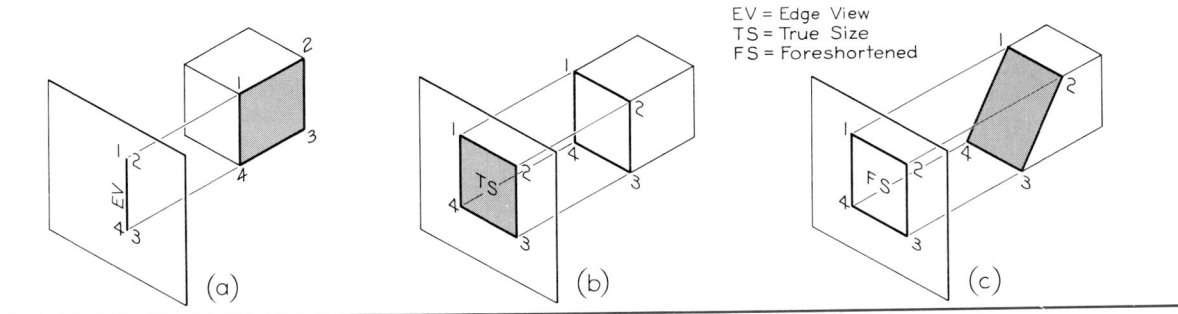

Fig. 7.19   Projections of Surfaces.

models is shown in Fig. 7.17, in which three views of an object are given, (a), and the student is to supply a missing line. The model is carved as shown in I, II, and III, and the "missing" line, discovered in the process, is added to the drawing as shown at (b).

Some typical examples of soap models are shown in Fig. 7.18.

7.15 Surfaces, Edges, and Corners

In order to analyze and synthesize multiview projections, it is necessary to consider the component elements that make up most solids. A *surface* (plane)

may be bounded by straight lines or curves, or a combination of them. A surface may be *frontal, horizontal,* or *profile,* according to the plane of projection to which it is parallel. See §7.1.

If a plane surface is perpendicular to a plane of projection, it appears as a line, *edge view* (EV), Fig. 7.19 (a). If it is parallel, it appears as a surface, *true size* (TS), (b). If it is situated at an angle, it appears as a surface, *foreshortened* (FS), (c). Thus, *a plane surface always projects as a line or a surface.*

The intersection of two plane surfaces produces an *edge,* or a straight line. Such a line is common to both surfaces and forms a boundary line for each. If an edge is perpendicular to a plane of projection, it

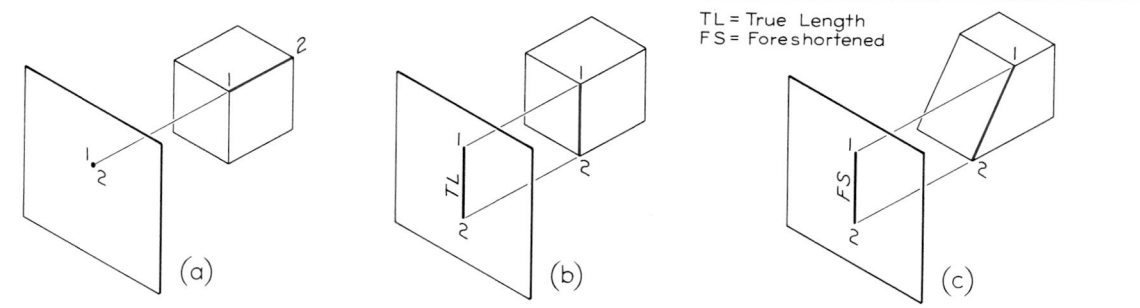

Fig. 7.20   Projections of Lines.

appears as a point, Fig. 7.20 (a); otherwise it appears as a line, (b) and (c). If it is parallel to the plane of projection, it shows true length, (b); if not parallel, it appears foreshortened, (c). Thus, a *straight line always projects as a straight line or as a point.* A line may be *frontal, horizontal,* or *profile,* according to the plane of projection to which it is parallel.

A *corner,* or point, is the common intersection of three or more surfaces or edges. A point always appears as a point in every view.

7.16 Adjacent Areas

Consider a given top view, as shown at Fig. 7.21 (a). Lines divide the view into three areas. Each of these must represent a surface *at a different level.* Surface A may be high and surfaces B and C lower, as shown at (b). Or B may be lower than C, as shown at (c). Or B may be highest, with C and A each lower, (d). Or one or more surfaces may be inclined, as at (e). Or one or more surfaces may be cylindrical, as at (f), and so on. Hence the rule: *No two adjacent areas can lie in the same plane.*

The same reasoning can apply, of course, to the adjacent areas in any given view. Since an area (surface) on a view can be interpreted in several

different ways, it is necessary to observe other views also in order to determine which interpretation is correct.

7.17 Similar Shapes of Surfaces

If a surface is viewed from several different positions, it will in each case be seen to have a certain number of sides and to have a certain characteristic shape. An L-shaped surface, Fig. 7.22(a), will appear as an L-shaped figure in every view in which it does not appear as a line. A T-shaped surface, (b), a U-shaped surface, (c), or a hexagonal surface, (d), will in each case have the same number of sides and the same characteristic shape in every view in which it appears as a surface.

This repetition of shapes is one of our best means for analyzing views.

7.18 Reading a Drawing

Let it be required to read or visualize the object shown by three views in Fig. 7.23. Since no lines are curved, the object is made up of plane surfaces.

Surface 2–3–10–9–6–5 in the top view is an L-

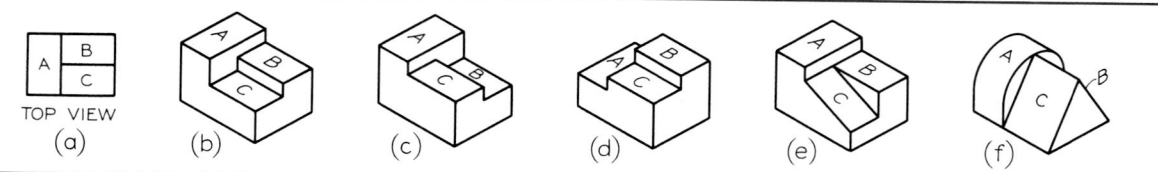

Fig. 7.21   Adjacent Areas.

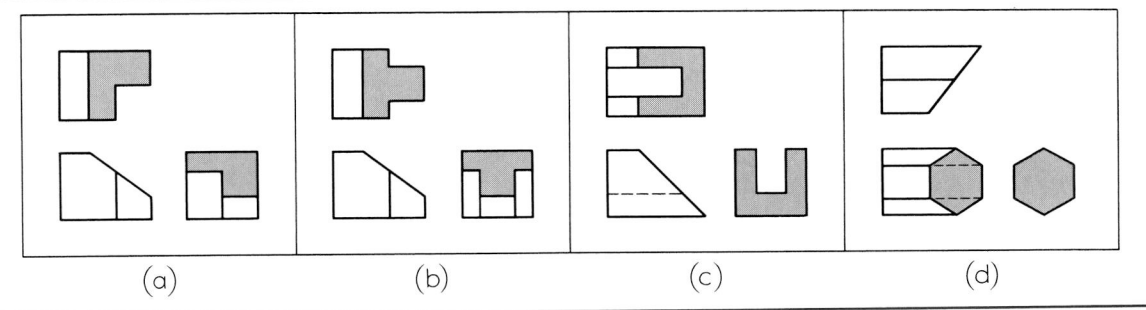

Fig. 7.22 Similar Shapes.

shaped surface of six sides. It appears in the side view at 16–17–21–20–18–19 and is L-shaped and six-sided. No such shape appears in the front view, but we note that points **2** and **5** line up with **11** in the front view, points **6** and **9** line up with **13**, and points **3** and **10** line up with **15**. Evidently line **11–15** in the front view is the edge view of the L-shaped surface.

Surface **11–13–12** in the front view is triangular in shape, but no corresponding triangles appear in either the top or the side view. We note that point **12** lines up with **8** and **4** and that point **13** lines up with **6** and **9**. However, surface **11–13–12** of the front view cannot be the same as surface **4–6–9–8** in the top view because the former has three sides and the latter has four. Obviously, the triangular surface appears as a line **4–6** in the top view and as a line **16–19** in the side view.

Surface **12–13–15–14** in the front view is trapezoidal in shape. But there are no trapezoids in the top and side views, so the surface evidently appears

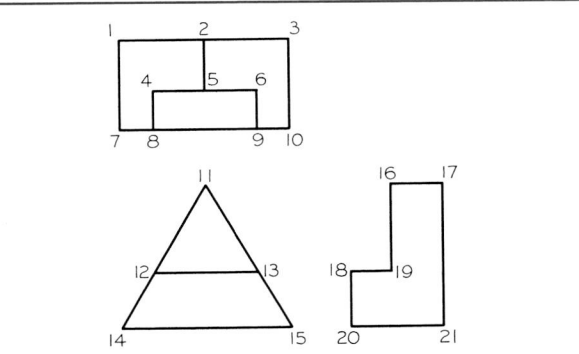

Fig. 7.23 Reading a Drawing.

in the top view as line **7–10** and in the side view as line **18–20**.

The remaining surfaces can be identified in the same manner, whence it will be seen that the object is bounded by seven plane surfaces, two of which are rectangular, two triangular, two L-shaped, and one trapezoidal.

Note that the numbering system used in Fig. 7.23 is different from that in Fig. 7.8 in that different numbers are used for all points and there is no significance in a point being inside or outside a corner.

7.19 Normal Surfaces

A normal surface is *a plane surface that is parallel to a plane of projection*. It appears in true size and shape on the plane to which it is parallel, and as a vertical or a horizontal line on adjacent planes of projection.

In Fig. 7.24 four stages in machining a block of steel to produce the final Tool Block in space IV are shown. All surfaces are normal surfaces. In space I, normal surface **A** is parallel to the horizontal plane and appears true size in the top view at **2–3–7–6**, as line **9–10** in the front view, and as line **17–18** in the side view. Normal surface **B** is parallel to the profile plane and appears true size in the side view at **17–18–20–19**, as line **3–7** in the top view, and as line **10–13** in the front view. Normal surface **C**, an inverted T-shaped surface, is parallel to the frontal plane and appears true size in the front view at **9–10–13–14–16–15–11–12**, as line **5–8** in the top view, and as line **17–21** in the side view.

All other surfaces of the object may be visualized in a similar manner. In the four stages of Fig. 7.24, observe carefully the changes in the views produced by the machining operations, including the introduction of new surfaces, new visible edges and hid-

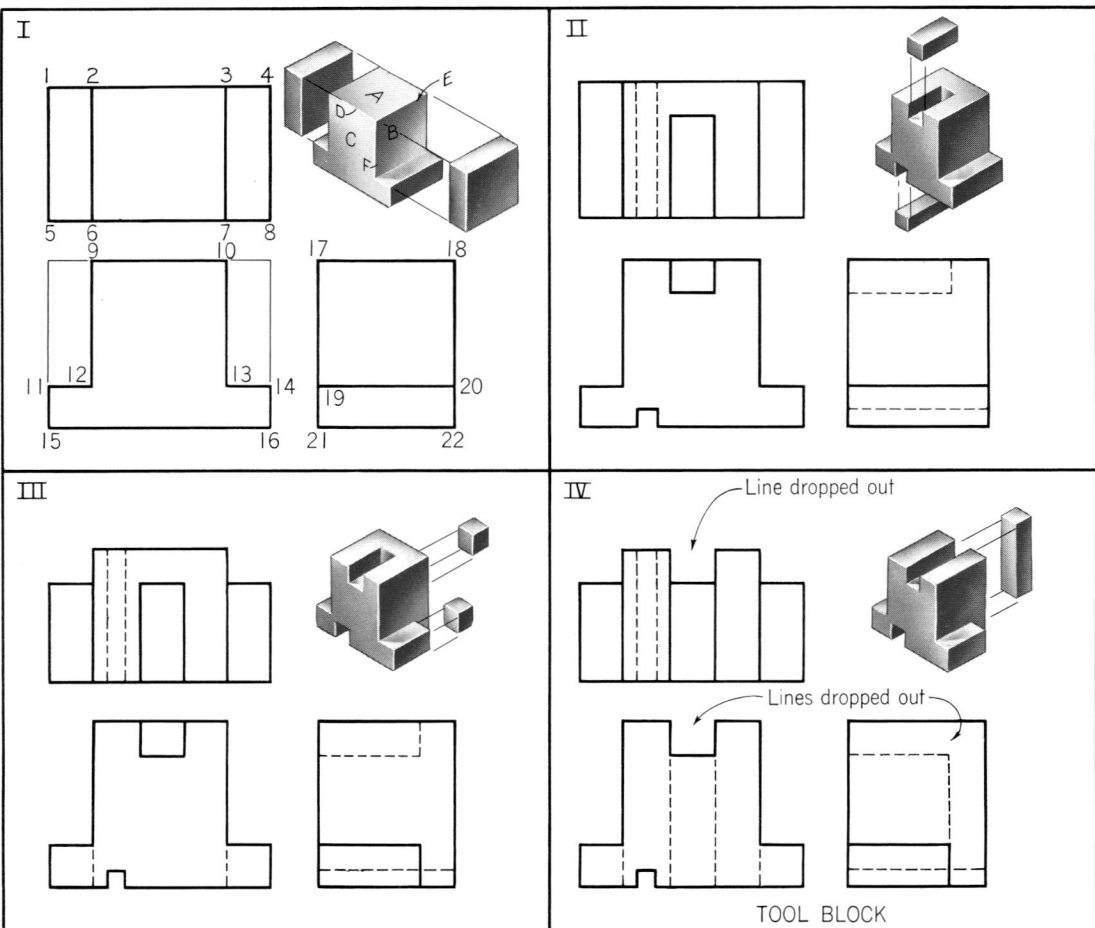

Fig. 7.24 Machining a Tool Block—Normal Surfaces and Edges.

den edges, and the dropping out of certain lines as the result of a new cut.

The top view in space I is cut by lines **2–6** and **3–7**, which means that there are three surfaces, **1–2–6–5**, **2–3–7–6**, and **3–4–8–7**. In the front view, surface **9–10** is seen to be the highest, and surfaces **11–12** and **13–14** are at the same lower level. In the side view both of these latter surfaces appear as one line **19–20**. Surface **11–12** might appear as a hidden line in the side view, but surface **13–14** appears as a visible line **19–20**, which covers up the hidden line and takes precedence over it. See §6.31.

7.20 Normal Edges

A normal edge is *a line that is perpendicular to a plane of projection*. It will appear as a point on the

plane of projection to which it is perpendicular and as a line in true length on adjacent planes of projection. In space I of Fig. 7.24, edge **D** is perpendicular to the profile plane of projection and appears as point **17** in the side view. It is parallel to the frontal and horizontal planes of projection, and is shown true length at **9–10** in the front view and **6–7** in the top view. Edges **E** and **F** are perpendicular, respectively, to the frontal and horizontal planes of projection, and their views may be similarly analyzed.

7.21 Inclined Surfaces

An inclined surface is *a plane surface that is perpendicular to one plane of projection but inclined to adjacent planes*. An inclined surface will project

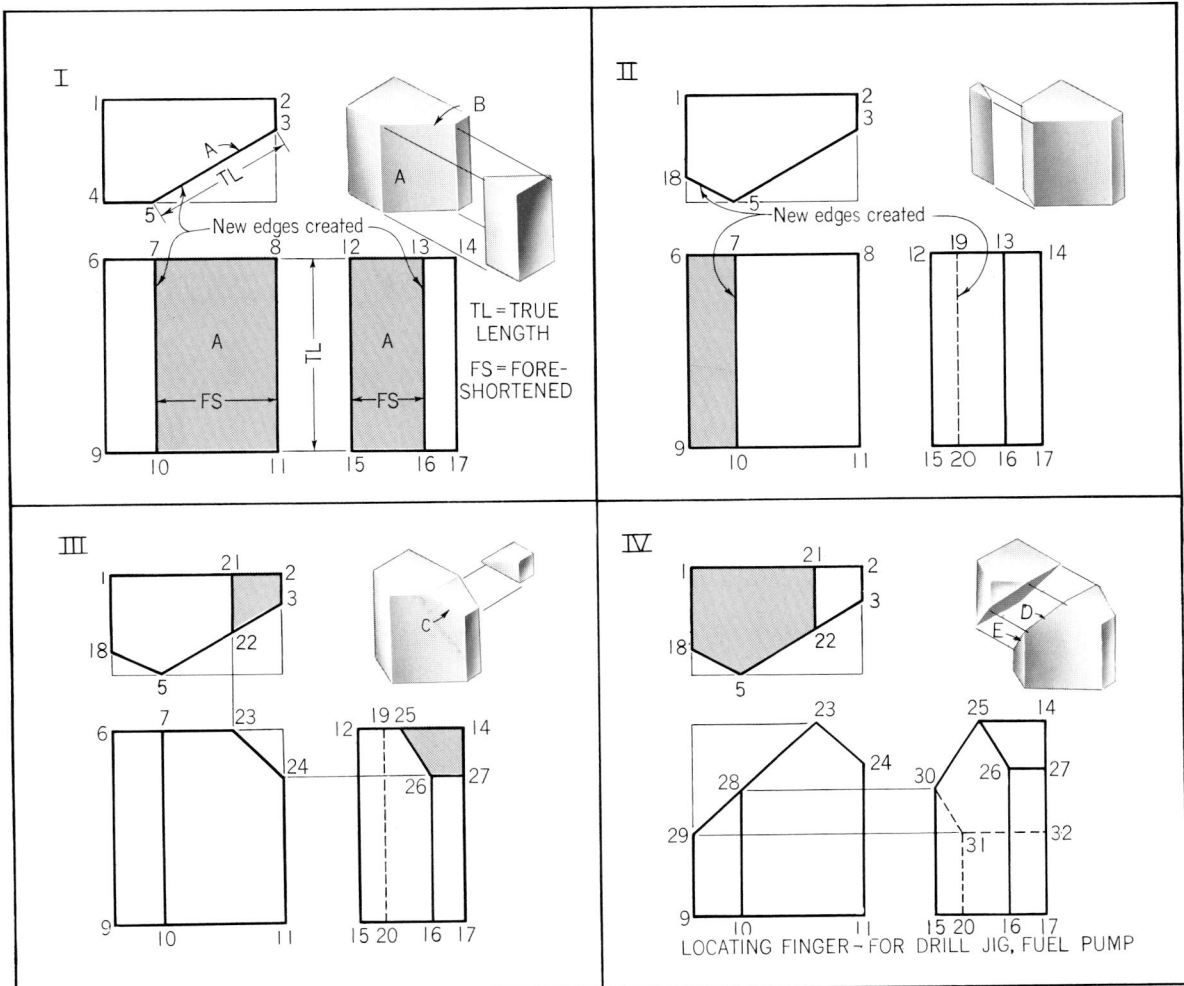

Fig. 7.25 Machining a Locating Finger—Inclined Surfaces.

as a straight line on the plane to which it is perpendicular, and it will appear foreshortened (**FS**) on planes to which it is inclined, the degree of foreshortening being proportional to the angle of inclination.

In Fig. 7.25 four stages in machining a Locating Finger are shown, producing several inclined surfaces. In space I, inclined surface **A** is perpendicular to the horizontal plane of projection and appears as line 5–3 in the top view. It is shown as a foreshortened surface in the front view at **7–8–11–10** and in the side view at **12–13–16–15**. Note that the surface is more foreshortened in the side view than in the front view because the plane makes a greater angle

with the profile plane of projection than with the frontal plane of projection.

In space III, edge **23–24** in the front view is the edge view of an inclined surface that appears in the top view as **21–2–3–22** and in the side view as **25–14–27–26**. Note that **25–14** is equal in length to **21–22** and that the surface has the same number of sides (four) in both views in which it appears as a surface.

In space IV, edge **29–23** in the front view is the edge view of an inclined surface that appears in the top view as visible surface **1–21–22–5–18** and in the side view as invisible surface **25–14–32–31–30**. While the surface does not appear true size in any

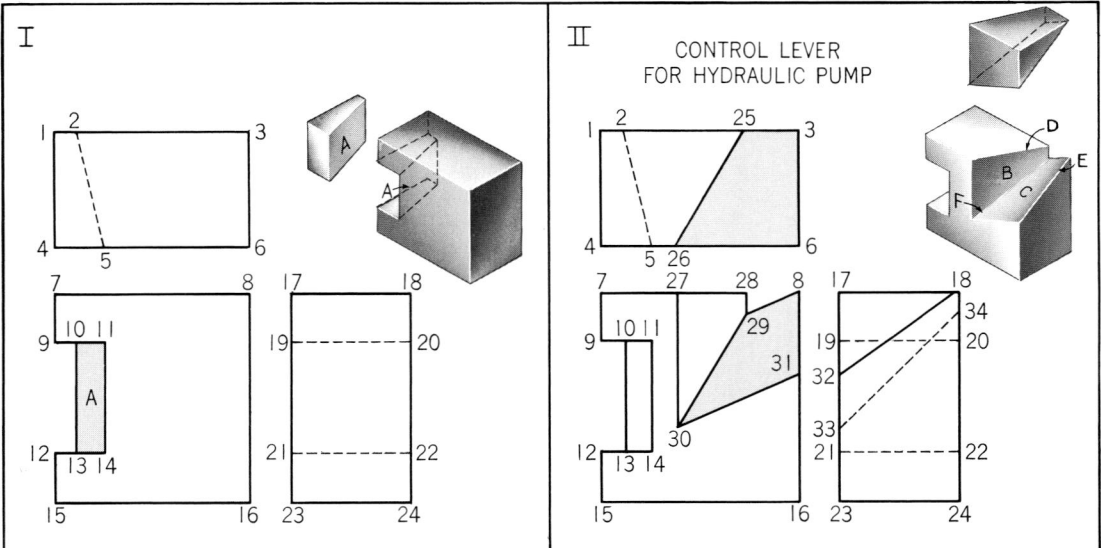

Fig. 7.26 Machining a Control Lever—Inclined and Oblique Surfaces.

view, it does have the same characteristic shape and the same number of sides (five) in the views in which it appears as a surface.

In order to obtain the true size of an inclined surface, it is necessary to construct an auxiliary view (Chapter 10) or to revolve the surface until it is parallel to a plane of projection (Chapter 11).

7.22 Inclined Edges

An inclined edge is *a line that is parallel to a plane of projection but inclined to adjacent planes.* It will appear true length on the plane to which it is parallel and foreshortened on adjacent planes, the degree of foreshortening being proportional to the angle of inclination. The true-length view of an inclined line is always inclined, while the foreshortened views are either vertical or horizontal lines.

In space I of Fig. 7.25, inclined edge B is parallel to the horizontal plane of projection, and appears true length in the top view at **5–3**. It is foreshortened in the front view at **7–8** and in the side view at **12–13**. Note that plane A produces two normal edges and two inclined edges.

In spaces III and IV, some of the sloping lines are not inclined lines. In space III, the edge that appears in the top view at **21–2**, in the front view at **23–24**, and in the side view at **14–27** is an inclined line. However, the edge that appears in the top view at **22–23**, in the front view at **23–24**, and in the side

view at **25–26** is not an inclined line by the definition given here. Actually, it is an oblique line, §7.24.

7.23 Oblique Surfaces

An oblique surface is *a plane that is oblique to all planes of projection.* Since it is not perpendicular to any plane, it cannot appear as a line in any view. Since it is not parallel to any plane, it cannot appear true size in any view. Thus, an oblique surface always appears as a foreshortened surface in all three views.

In space II of Fig. 7.26, oblique surface C appears in the top view at **25–3–6–26** and in the front view at **29–8–31–30**. What are its numbers in the side view? Note that any surface appearing as a line in any view cannot be an oblique surface. How many inclined surfaces are there? How many normal surfaces?

To obtain the true size of an oblique surface, it is necessary to construct a secondary auxiliary view, §§10.21 and 10.22, or to revolve the surface until it is parallel to a plane of projection, §11.11.

7.24 Oblique Edges

An oblique edge is *a line that is oblique to all planes of projection.* Since it is not perpendicular to any plane, it cannot appear as a point in any view. Since it is not parallel to any plane, it cannot appear true length in any view. An oblique edge appears foreshortened and in an inclined position in every view.

In space II of Fig. 7.26, oblique edge **F** appears in the top view at 26–25, in the front view at 30–29, and in the side view at 33–34.

7.25 Parallel Edges

If a series of parallel planes is intersected by another plane, the resulting lines of intersection will be parallel, Fig. 7.27 (a). At (b) the top plane of the object intersects the front and rear planes, producing the parallel edges 1–2 and 3–4. If two lines are parallel in space, their projections in any view are parallel. The example in (b) is a special case in which the two lines appear as points in one view and coincide as a single line in another and should not be regarded as an exception to the rule. Note that even in the pictorial drawings the lines are shown parallel.

Parallel inclined lines are shown in (c), and parallel oblique lines in (d).

In Fig. 7.28 it is required to draw three views of the object after a plane has been passed through the points **A**, **B**, and **C**. As shown at (b), only points that lie in the same plane are joined. In the front view, join points **A** and **C**, which are in the same plane, extending the line to P on the vertical front edge of the block extended. In the side view, join P to B, and in the top view, join B to A. Complete the draw-

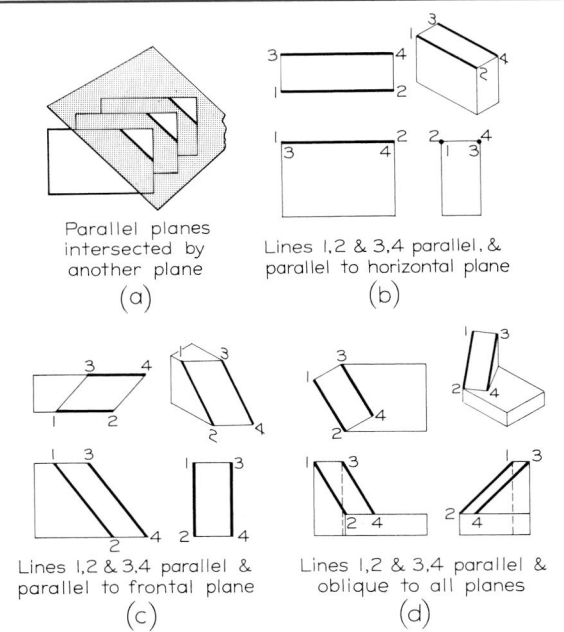

Fig. 7.27   Parallel Lines.

ing by applying the rule: *Parallel lines in space will be projected as parallel lines in any view.* The remaining lines are thus drawn parallel to lines **AP**, **PB**, and **BA**.

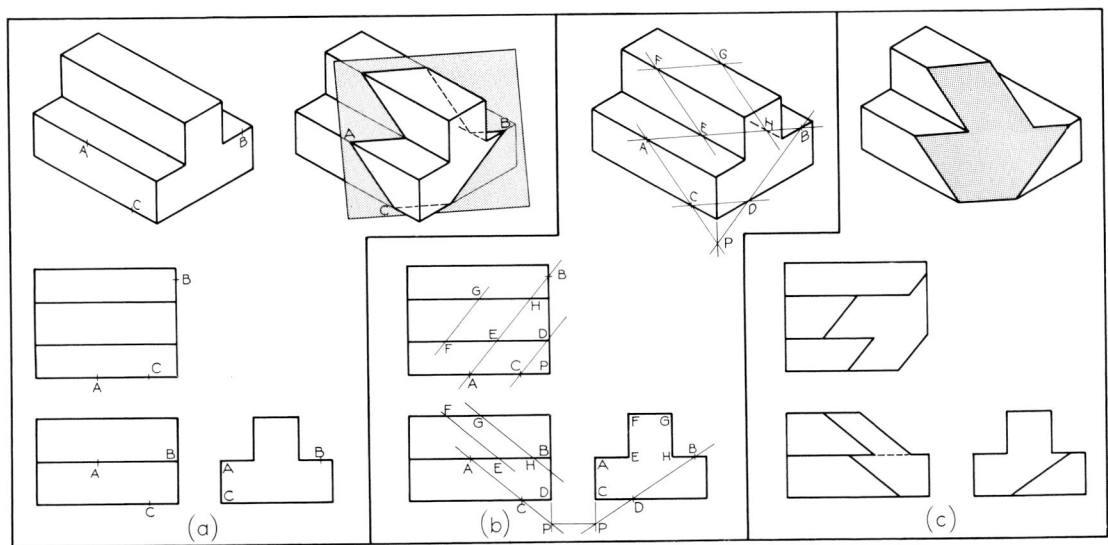

Fig. 7.28   Oblique Surface.

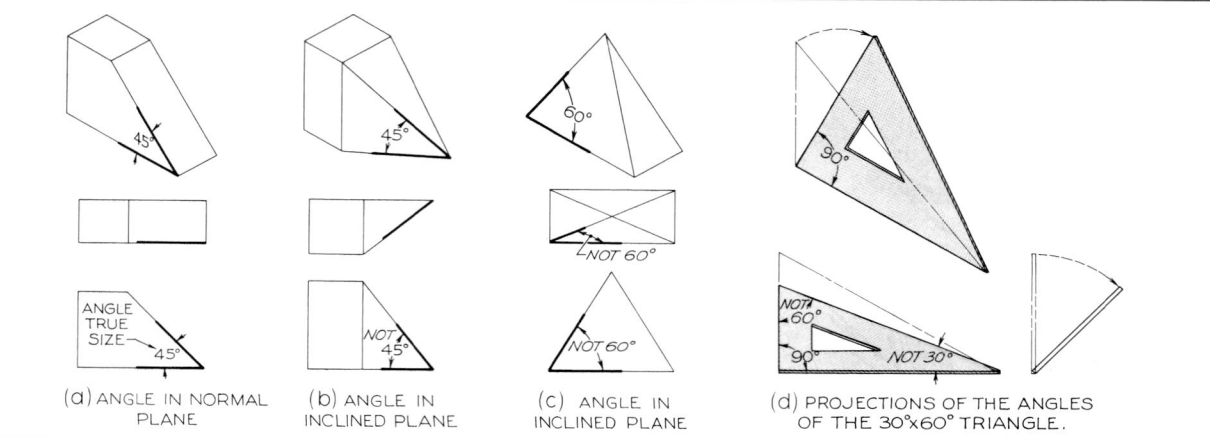

Fig. 7.29   Angles.

7.26 Angles

If an angle is in a normal plane—that is, parallel to a plane of projection—the angle will be shown true size on the plane of projection to which it is parallel, Fig. 7.29 (a).

If the angle is in an inclined plane, (b) and (c), the angle may be projected either larger or smaller than the true angle, depending upon its position. At (b) the 45° angle is shown *oversize* in the front view, and at (c) the 60° angle is shown *undersize* in both views.

A 90° angle will be projected true size, even though it is in an inclined plane, provided one leg

of the angle is a normal line, as shown at (d). In this figure, the 60° angle is projected *oversize* and the 30° angle *undersize*. Study these relations, using your own 30° × 60° triangle as a model.

7.27 Curved Surfaces

Rounded surfaces are common in engineering practice because they are easily formed on the lathe, the drill press, and other machines using the principle of rotation either of the "work" or of the cutting tool. The most common are the cylinder, cone, and

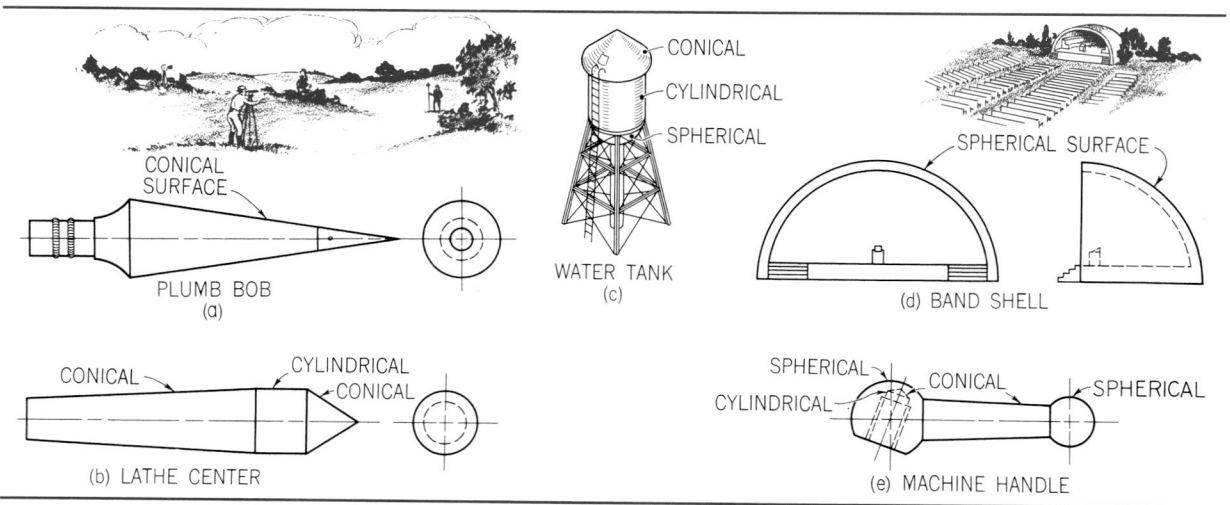

Fig. 7.30   Curved Surfaces.

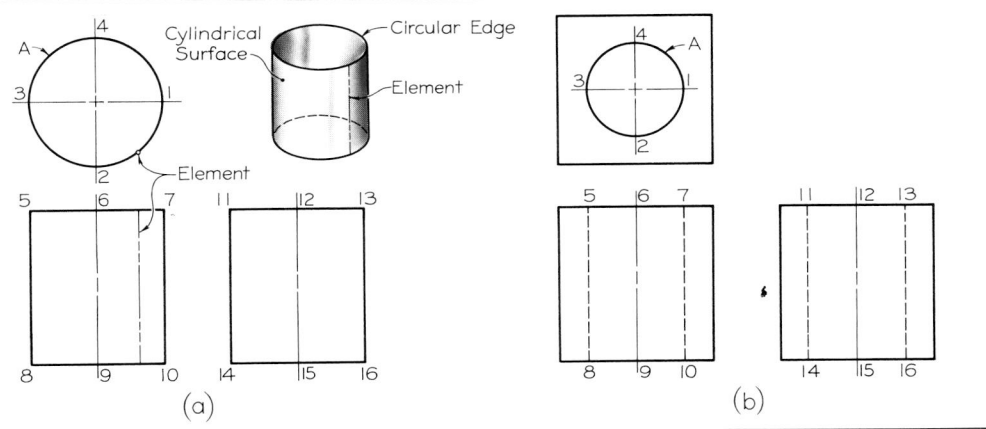

Fig. 7.31 Cylindrical Surfaces.

sphere, a few of whose applications are shown in Fig. 7.30. For other geometric solids, see Fig. 5.7.

7.28 Cylindrical Surfaces

Three views of a *right-circular cylinder*, the most common type, are shown in Fig. 7.31 (a). The single cylindrical surface is intersected by two plane (normal) surfaces, forming two curved lines of intersection or *circular edges* (the bases of the cylinder). These circular edges are the only actual edges on the cylinder. Fig. 7.31 (b) shows a cylindrical hole in a right square prism.

The cylinder is represented on a drawing by its circular edges and the contour elements. An *element* is a straight line on the cylindrical surface, parallel to the axis, as shown in the pictorial view of the cylinder at (a). In this figure, at both (a) and (b), the circular edges appear in the top views as circles A, in the front views as horizontal lines 5–7 and 8–10, and in the side views as horizontal lines 11–13 and 14–16.

The contour elements 5–8 and 7–10 in the front views appear as points 3 and 1 in the top views. The contour elements 11–14 and 13–16 in the side views appear as points 2 and 4 in the top views.

In Fig. 7.32 four possible stages in machining a Cap are shown, producing several cylindrical surfaces. In space I, the removal of the two upper corners forms cylindrical surface A which appears in the top view as surface 1–2–4–3, in the front view as arc 5, and in the side view as surface 8–9–Y–X.

In space II, a large reamed hole shows in the front view as circle 16, in the top view as cylindrical surface 12–13–15–14, and in the side view as cylindrical surface 17–18–20–19.

In space III, two drilled and counterbored holes are added, producing four more cylindrical surfaces and two normal surfaces. The two normal surfaces are those at the bottoms of the counterbores.

In space IV, a cylindrical cut is added, producing two cylindrical surfaces that appear edgewise in the front view as arcs 30 and 33, in the top view as surfaces 21–22–26–25 and 23–24–28–27 and in the side view as surfaces 36–37–40–38 and 41–42–44–43.

7.29 Deformities of Cylinders

In shop practice, cylinders are usually machined or formed so as to introduce other surfaces, usually plane surfaces. In Fig. 7.33 (a) is shown a cut that introduces two normal surfaces. One surface appears as line 3–4 in the top view, as surface 6–7–10–9 in the front view, and as line 13–16 in the side view. The other appears as line 15–16 in the side view, as line 9–10 in the front view, and as surface 3–4, arc 2 in the top view.

All elements touching arc 2, between 3 and 4 in the top view, become shorter as a result of the cut. For example, element A, which shows as a point in the top view, now becomes CD in the front view, and 15–17 in the side view. As a result of the cut, the front half of the cylindrical surface has changed

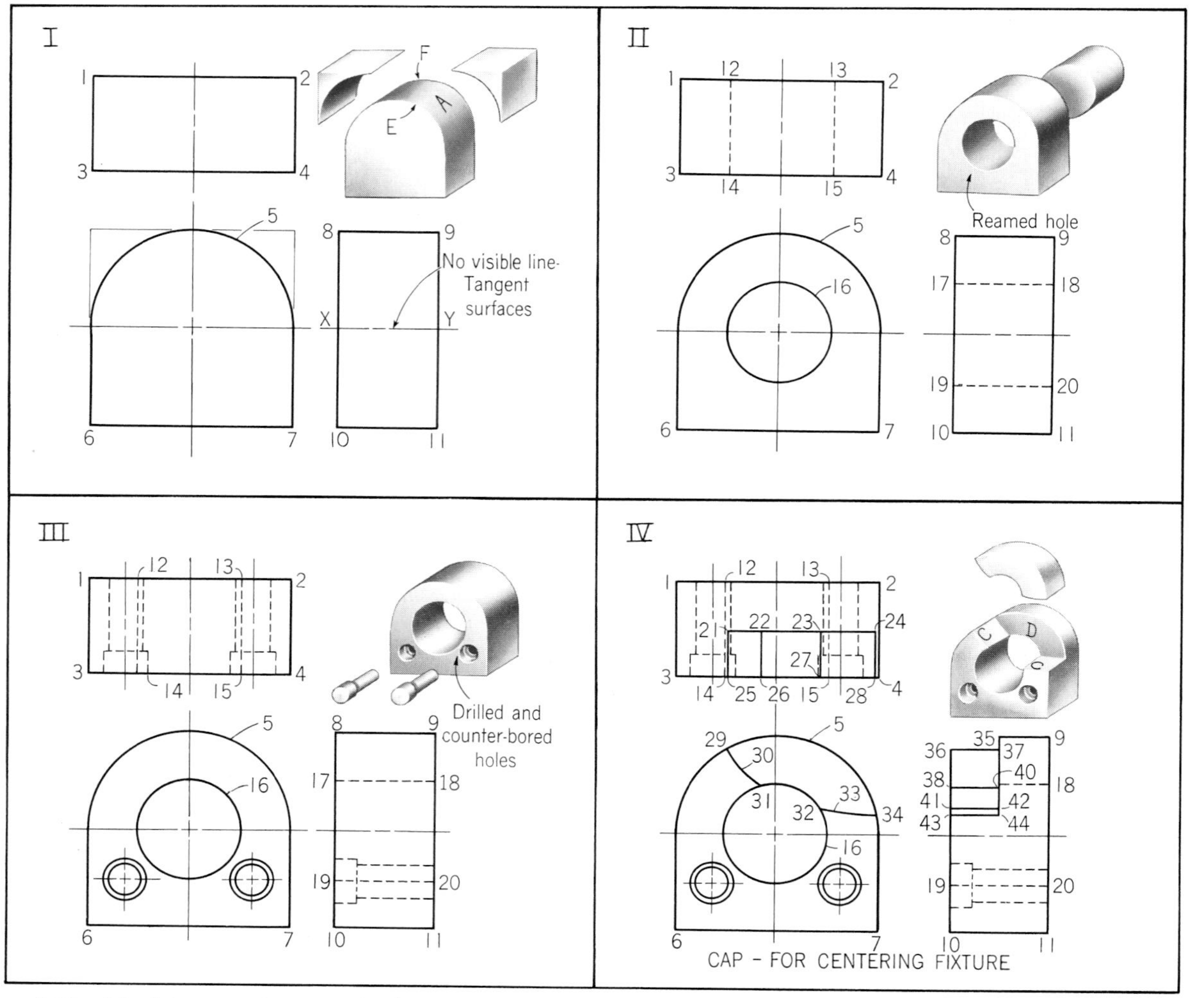

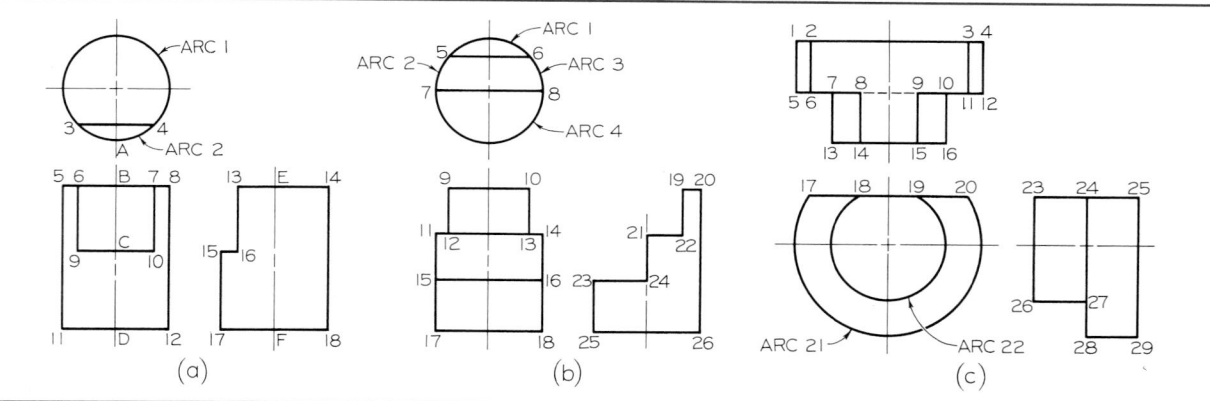

Fig. 7.32   Machining a Cap—Cylindrical Surfaces.

Fig. 7.33   Deformities of Cylinders.

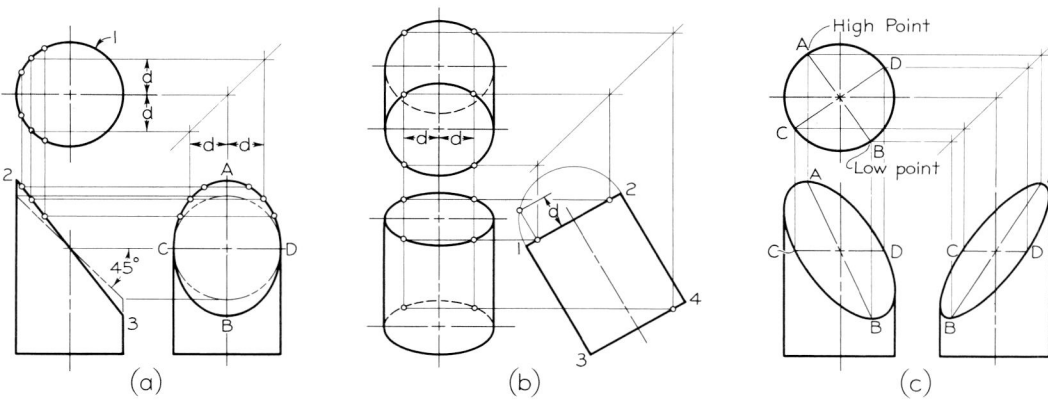

Fig. 7.34 Cylinders and Ellipses.

from 5–8–12–11 to 5–6–9–10–7–8–12–11 (front view). The back half remains unchanged.

At (b) two cuts introduce four normal surfaces. Note that surface 7–8 (top view) is through the center of the cylinder, producing in the side view line 21–24 and in the front view surface 11–14–16–15 equal in width to the diameter of the cylinder. Surface 15–16 (front view) is read in the top view as 7–8–ARC 4. Surface 11–14 (front view) is read in the top view as 5–6–ARC 3–8–7–ARC 2.

At (c) two cylinders on the same axis are shown, intersected by a normal surface parallel to the axis. Surface 17–20 (front view) is 23–25 in the side view, and 2–3–11–9–15–14–8–6 in the top view. A common error is to draw a visible line in the top view between 8 and 9. However, this would produce two surfaces 2–3–11–6 and 8–9–15–14 not in the same plane. In the front view, the larger surface appears as line 17–20 and the smaller as line 18–19. These lines coincide; hence, they are all one surface, and there can be no visible line joining 8 and 9 in the top view.

The vertical surface that appears in the front view at 17–18–ARC 22–19–20–ARC 21 appears as a line in the top view at 5–12, which explains the hidden line 8–9 in the top view.

7.30 Cylinders and Ellipses

If a cylinder is cut by an inclined plane, as in Fig. 7.34 (a), the inclined surface is bounded by an ellipse. The ellipse appears as circle 1 in the top view, as straight line 2–3 in the front view, and as ellipse ADBC in the side view. Note that circle 1 in the top view would remain a circle regardless of the angle

of the cut. If the cut is 45° with horizontal, the ellipse will appear as a circle in the side view (see phantom lines) since the major and minor axes in that view would be equal. To find the true size and shape of the ellipse, an auxiliary view will be required, with the line of sight perpendicular to surface 2–3 in the front view, §10.12.

Since the major and minor axes AB and CD are known, the ellipse can be drawn by any of the methods in Figs. 5.48–5.50 and 5.52 (a) (true ellipses) or by the aid of an ellipse template, Fig. 5.55.

If the cylinder is tilted forward, (b), the bases or circular edges 1–2 and 3–4 (side view) become ellipses in the front and top views. Points on the ellipses can be plotted from the semicircular end view of the cylinder, as shown, distances d being equal. Since the major and minor axes for each ellipse are known, the ellipses can be drawn with the aid of an ellipse template, or by any of the true ellipse methods, or by the approximate method.

If the cylinder is cut by an oblique plane, (c), the elliptical surface appears as an ellipse in two views. In the top view, points A and B are selected, diametrically opposite, as the high and low points in the ellipse, and CD is drawn perpendicular to AB. These are the projections of the major and minor axes, respectively, of the actual ellipse in space. In the front and side views, points A and B are assumed at the desired altitudes. Since CD appears true length in the top view, it will appear horizontal in the front and side views, as shown. These axes in the front and side views are the conjugate axes of the ellipses. The ellipses may be drawn upon these axes by the method of Fig. 5.51 or 5.52 (b) or by trial with the aid of an ellipse template, Fig. 5.55.

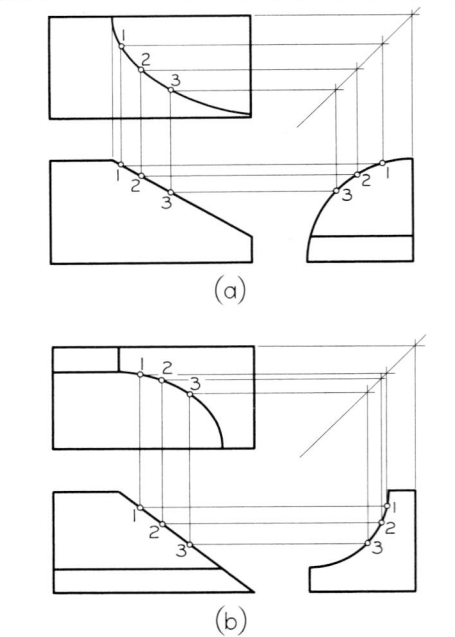

(a)

(b)

Fig. 7.35 Plotting Elliptical Curves.

In Fig. 7.35, the intersection of a plane and a quarter-round molding is shown at (a), and with a cove molding at (b). In both figures, assume points 1, 2, 3, . . , at random in the side views in which the cylindrical surfaces appear as curved lines, and project the points to the front and top views, as shown. A sufficient number of points should be used to insure smooth curves. Draw the final curves through the points with the aid of the irregular curve, §2.54.

7.31 Space Curves

The views of a space curve are established by the projections of points along the curve, Fig. 7.36. In this figure any points 1, 2, 3, . . ., are selected along the curve in the top view and then projected to the side view (or the reverse), and points are located in the front view by projecting downward from the top view and across from the side view. The resulting curve in the front view is drawn with the aid of the irregular curve, §2.54.

7.32 Intersections and Tangencies

No line should be drawn where a curved surface is tangent to a plane surface, Fig. 7.37 (a), but when a curved surface *intersects* a plane surface, a definite

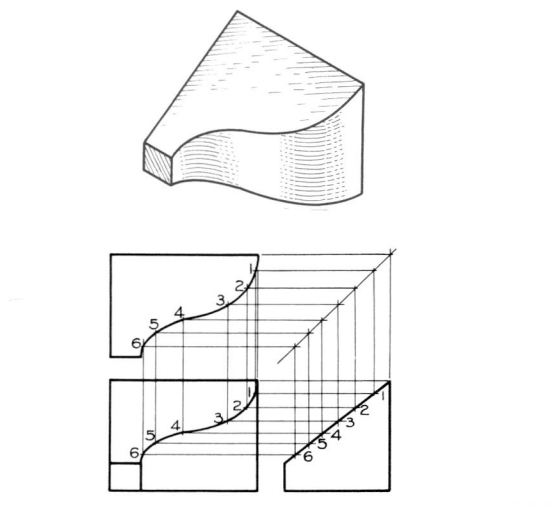

Fig. 7.36 Space Curve.

edge is formed, (b). If curved surfaces are arranged as at (c), no lines appear in the top view, as shown. If the surfaces are arranged as at (d), a vertical surface in the front view produces a line in the top view. Other typical intersections and tangencies of surfaces are shown from (e) to (h). To locate the point of tangency A in (g), refer to Fig. 5.34 (b).

The intersection of a small cylinder with a large cylinder is shown in Fig. 7.38 (a). The intersection is so small that it is not plotted, a straight line being used instead. At (b) the intersection is larger, but still not large enough to justify plotting the curve. The curve is approximated by drawing an arc whose radius r is the same as radius R of the large cylinder.

The intersection at (c) is significant enough to justify constructing the true curve. Points are selected at random in the circle in the side or top view, and these are then projected to the other two views to locate points on the curve in the front view, as shown. A sufficient number of points should be used, depending upon the size of the intersection, to insure a smooth and accurate curve. Draw the final curve with the aid of the irregular curve, §2.54.

At (d), the cylinders are the same diameter. The figure of intersection consists of two semiellipses that appear as straight lines in the front view.

If the intersecting cylinders are holes, the intersections will be similar to those for the external cylinders in Fig. 7.38. See also Fig. 9.34 (d).

In Fig. 7.39 (a), a narrow prism intersects a cylinder, but the intersection is insignificant and is ignored. At (b) the prism is larger and the intersection

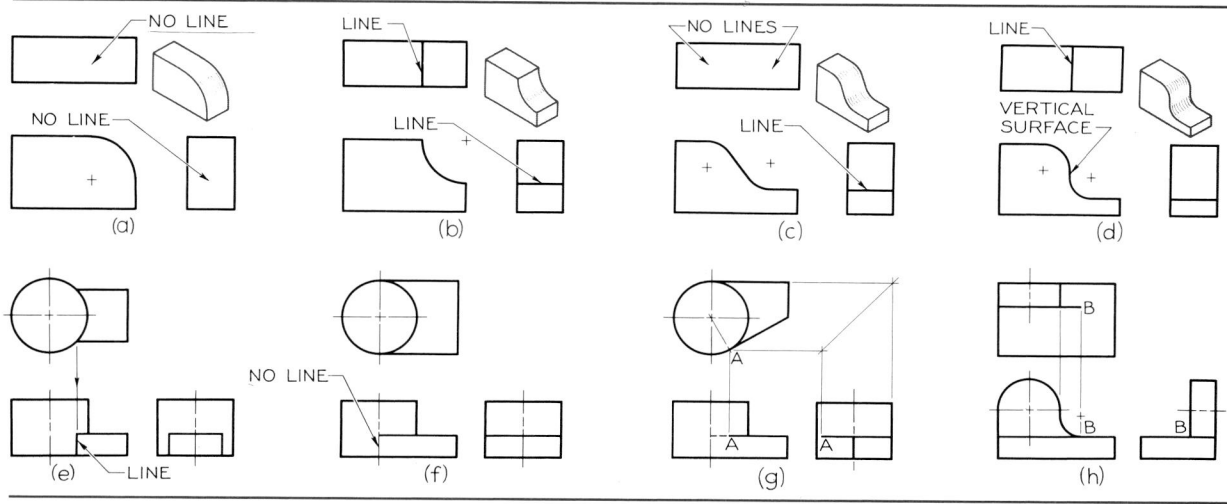

Fig. 7.37 Intersections and Tangencies.

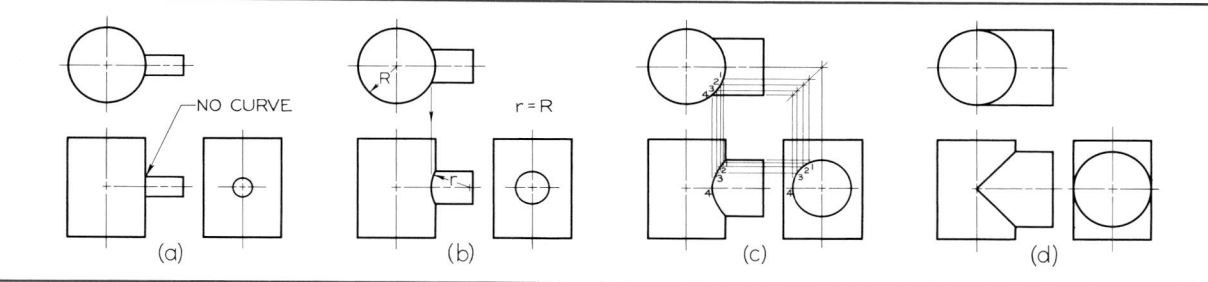

Fig. 7.38 Intersections of Cylinders.

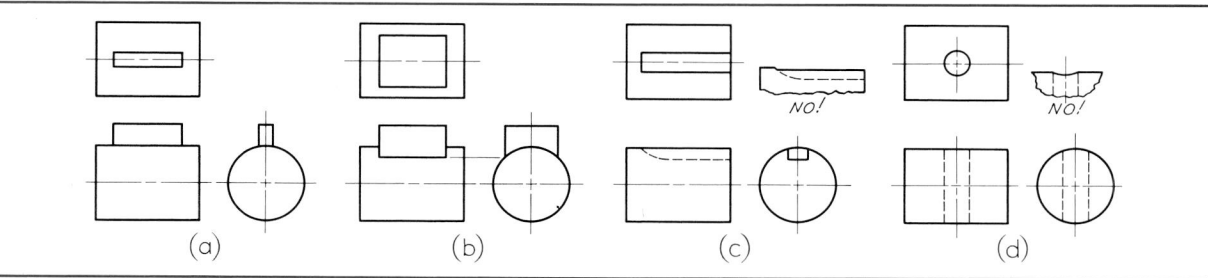

Fig. 7.39 Intersections.

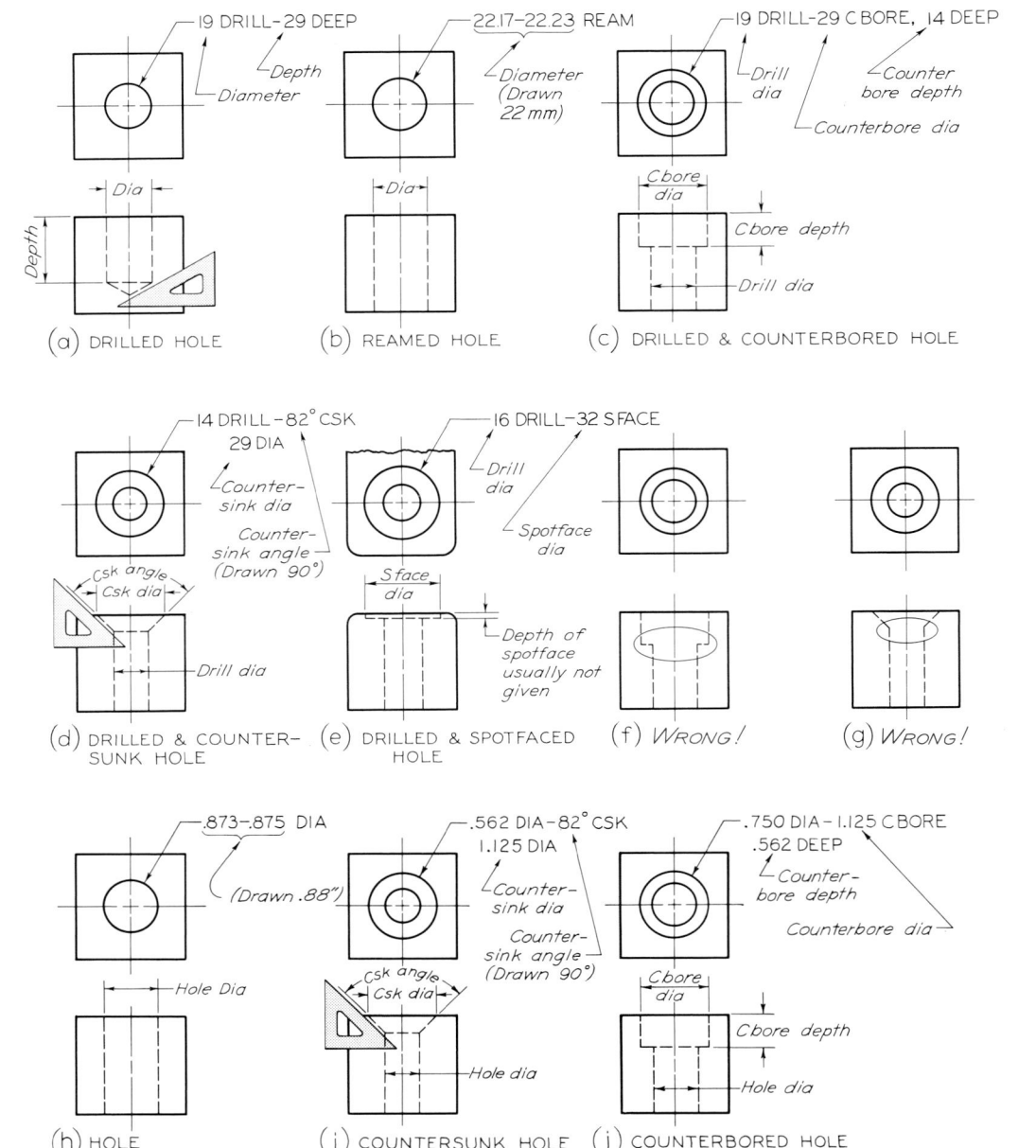

Fig. 7.40 How to Represent Holes.   Dimensions for (a)–(e) in metric. For threaded holes, see §15.24.

is noticeable enough to warrant construction, as shown. At (c) and (d) a keyseat and a small drilled hole, respectively, are shown; in both cases the intersection is not important enough to construct.

7.33 How to Represent Holes

The correct methods of representing most common types of machined holes are shown in Fig. 7.40. Instructions to the machinist are given in the form of notes, and the drafter represents the holes in con-

formity with these specifications. In general, the notes tell the machine operator what to do and in which order it is to be done. Hole sizes are always specified by diameter—never by radius. For each operation specified, the diameter is given first, followed by the method such as drill, ream, and so on, as shown in (a) and (b).

The size of the hole may be specified as a diameter without the specific method such as drill, ream, and so on, since the selection of the method

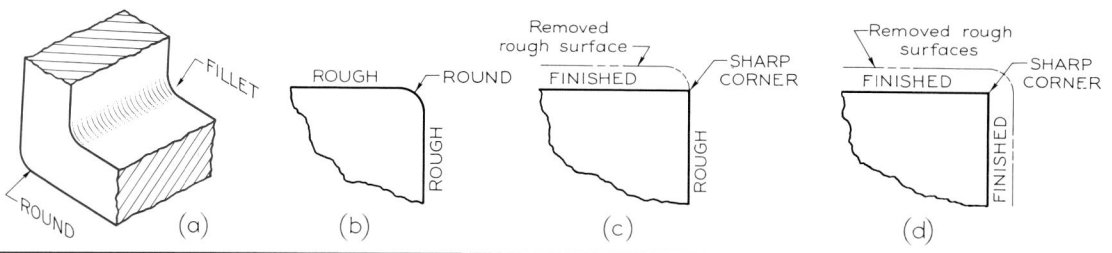

Fig. 7.41 Rough and Finished Surfaces.

will depend upon available production facilities. See (h) to (j).

A drilled hole is a *through* hole if it goes through a member. If the hole has a specified depth, as shown at (a), the hole is called a *blind* hole. The depth includes the cylindrical portion of the hole only. The point of the drill leaves a conical bottom in the hole, drawn approximately with the 30° × 60° triangle, as shown. For drill sizes, see Appendix 16 (Twist Drill Sizes). For abbreviations, see Appendix 4.

A through-drilled or reamed hole is drawn as shown at (b). The note tells how the hole is to be produced—in this case by reaming. Note that tolerances are ignored in actually laying out the diameter of a hole.

At (c) a hole is drilled and then the upper part is enlarged cylindrically to a specified diameter and depth.

At (d) a hole is drilled and then the upper part is enlarged conically to a specified angle and diameter. The angle is commonly 82° but is drawn 90° for simplicity.

At (e) a hole is drilled and then the upper part is enlarged cylindrically to a specified diameter. The depth usually is not specified, but is left to the shop to determine. For average cases, the depth is drawn 1.5 mm ($\frac{1}{16}$″).

For complete information about how holes are

made in the shop, see §12.16. For further information on notes, see §13.24.

7.34 Fillets and Rounds

A rounded interior corner is called a fillet, and a rounded exterior corner a round, Fig. 7.41 (a). Sharp corners should be avoided in designing parts to be cast or forged not only because they are difficult to produce but also because, in the case of interior corners, they are a source of weakness and failure. See §12.5 for shop processes involved.

Two intersecting rough surfaces produce a rounded corner, (b). If one of these surfaces is machined, (c), or if both surfaces are machined, (d), the corner becomes sharp. Therefore, on drawing a rounded corner means that both intersecting surfaces are rough, and a sharp corner means that one or both surfaces are machined. On working drawings, fillets and rounds are never shaded. The presence of the curved surfaces is indicated only where they appear as arcs, except as shown in Fig. 7.45.

Fillets and rounds should be drawn with the filleted corners of the triangle, a special fillets and rounds template, or a circle template.

7.35 Runouts

The correct method of representing fillets in connection with plane surfaces tangent to cylinders is shown in Fig. 7.42. These small curves are called

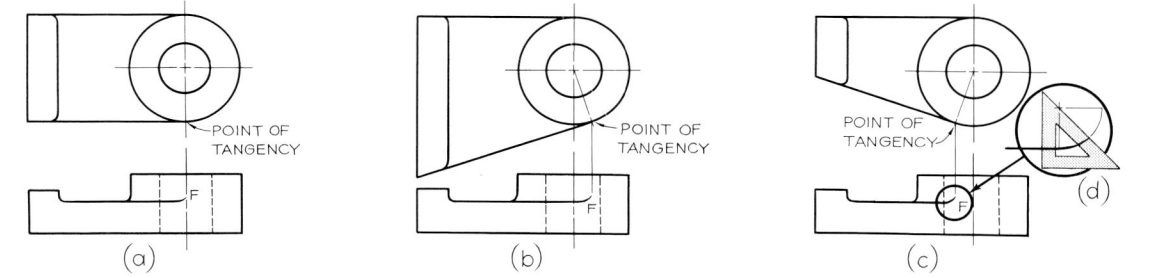

Fig. 7.42 Runouts.

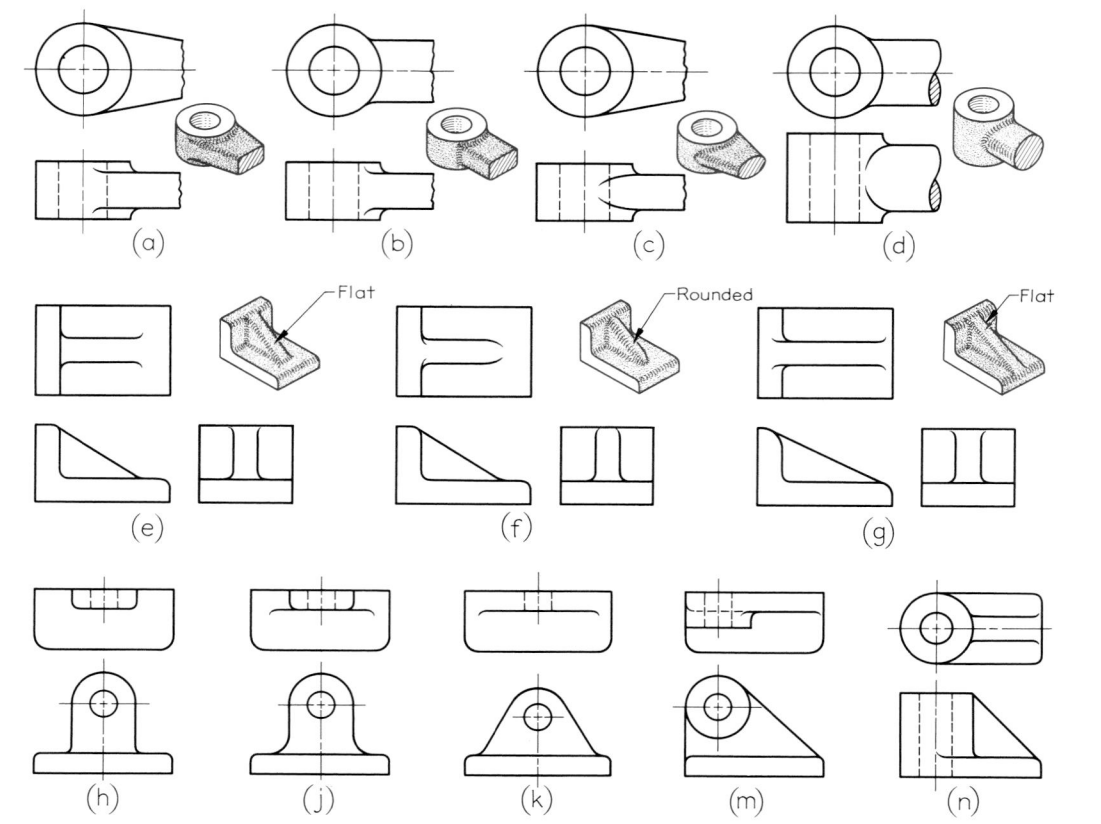

Fig. 7.43   Conventional Fillets, Rounds, and Runouts.

runouts. Note that the runouts **F** have a radius equal to that of the fillet and a curvature of about one-eighth of a circle, (d).

Typical filleted intersections are shown in Fig. 7.43. The runouts from (a) to (d) differ because of the different shapes of the horizontal intersecting members. At (e) and (f) the runouts differ because the top surface of the web at (e) is flat, with only slight rounds along the edge, while the top surface of the web at (f) is considerably rounded. When two different sizes of fillets intersect, as at (g) and (j), the direction of the runout is dictated by the larger fillet, as shown.

7.36 Conventional Edges
Rounded and filleted intersections eliminate sharp edges and sometimes make it difficult to present a clear shape description. In fact, true projection in some cases may be actually misleading, as in Fig. 7.44 (a), in which the side view of the railroad rail

is quite blank. A more clear representation results if lines are added for rounded and filleted edges, as shown at (b) and (c). The added lines are projected from the actual intersections of the surfaces as if the fillets and rounds were not present.

In Fig. 7.45, two top views are shown for each given front view. The upper top views are nearly devoid of lines that contribute to the shape descriptions, while the lower top views, in which lines are used to represent the rounded and filleted edges, are quite clear. Note, in the lower top views at (a) and (c), the use of small **Y**s where rounded or filleted edges meet a rough surface. If such an edge intersects a finished surface, no **Y** is shown.

7.37 Right-Hand and Left-Hand Parts
In industry many individual parts are located symmetrically so as to function in pairs. These opposite parts are often exactly alike, as for example, the hub caps used on the left and right sides of the auto-

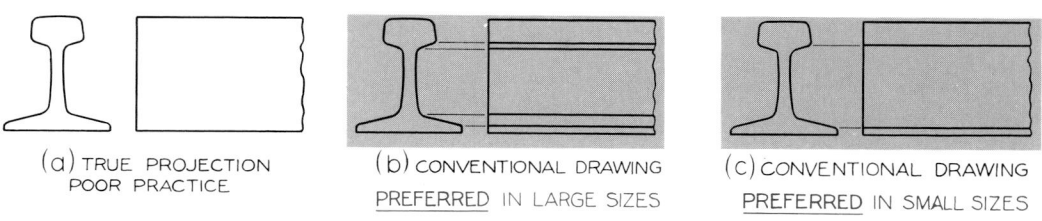

Fig. 7.44 Conventional Repression of a Rail.

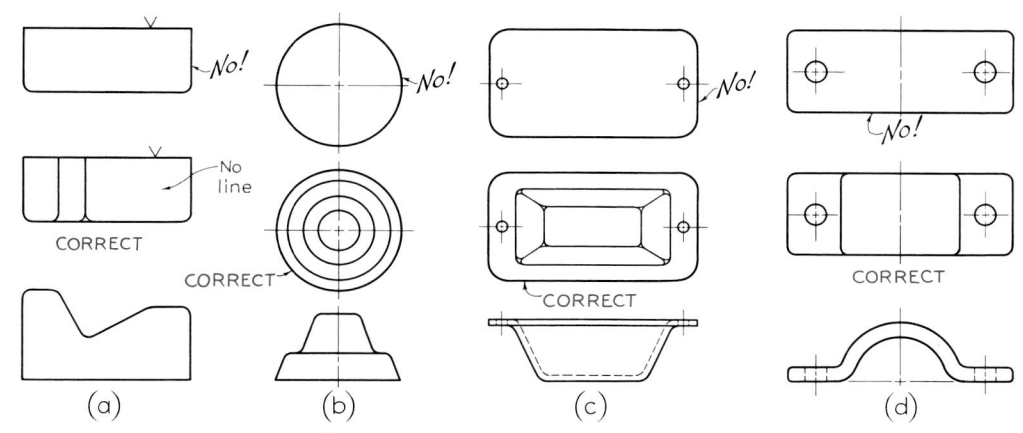

Fig. 7.45 Conventional Edges.

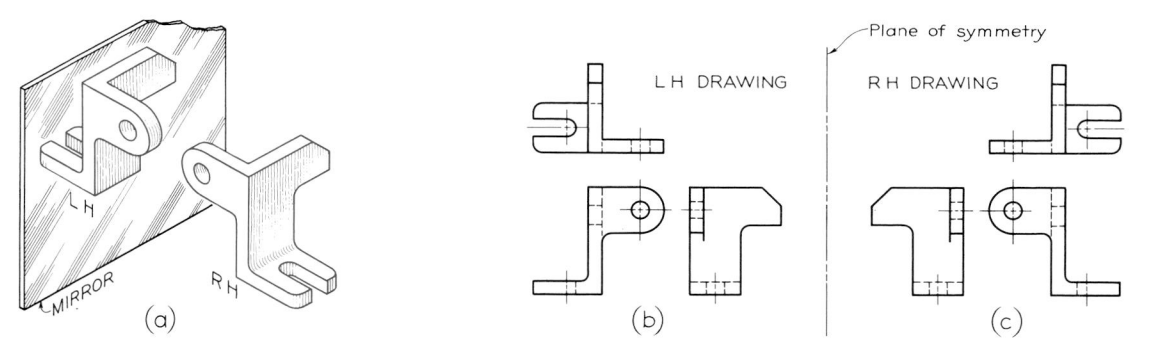

Fig. 7.46 Right-Hand and Left-Hand Parts.

mobile. In fact, whenever possible, for economy's sake the designer will design identical parts for use on both the right and left. But opposite parts often cannot be exactly alike, such as a pair of gloves or a pair of shoes. Similarly, the right-front fender of an automobile cannot be the same shape as the left-front fender. Therefore, a left-hand part is not sim-

ply a right-hand part turned around; the two parts will be opposite and not interchangeable.

A left-hand part is referred to as an LH part, and a right-hand part as an RH part. In Fig. 7.46 (a), the image in the mirror is the "other hand" of the part shown. If the part in front of the mirror is an RH part, the image shows the LH part. No matter how

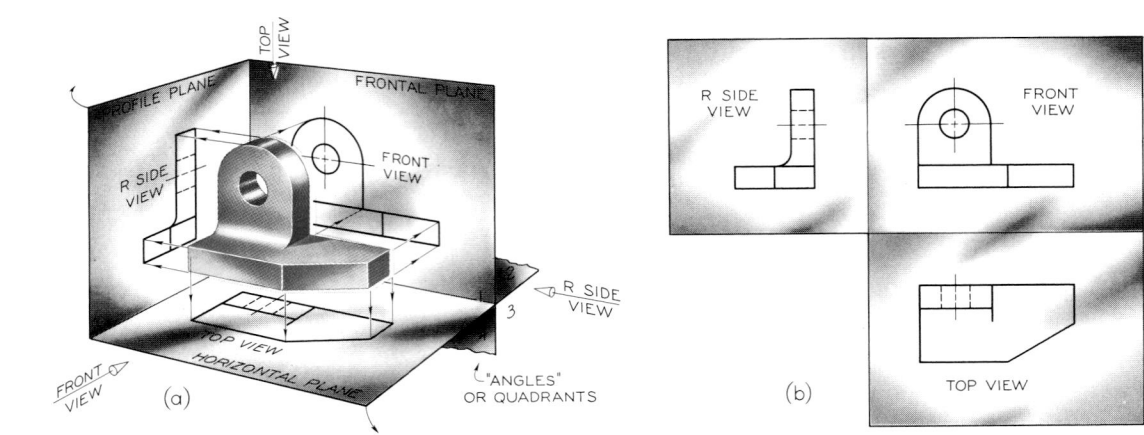

Fig. 7.47   First-Angle Projection.

the object is turned, the image will show the LH part. At (b) and (c) are shown LH and RH drawings of the same object, and it will be seen that the drawings are also symmetrical with respect to a reference-plane line between them.

If you hold a drawing faced against a windowpane or a light table so that the lines can be seen through the paper, you can trace the reverse image of the part on the back or on tracing paper, which will be a drawing of the opposite part.

It is customary to draw only one of two opposite parts and to label the one that is drawn with a note, such as **LH PART SHOWN, RH OPPOSITE**. If the opposite-hand shape is not clear, a separate drawing must be made for it and properly identified.

7.38 First-Angle Projection

If the vertical and horizontal planes of projection are considered indefinite in extent and intersecting at 90° with each other, the four dihedral angles produced are the *first, second, third,* and *fourth* angles, Fig. 7.47 (a). The profile plane intersects these two planes and may extend into all angles. If the object is placed below the horizontal plane and behind the vertical plane as in the glass box, Fig. 7.3, the object is said to be in the third angle. In this case, as we have seen, the observer is always "outside, looking in," so that for all views the lines of sight proceed from the eye *through the planes of projection and to the object.*

If the object is placed above the horizontal plane and in front of the vertical plane, the object is in the

first angle. In this case, the observer always looks *through the object and to the planes of projection.* Thus, the right-side view is still obtained by looking toward the right side of the object, the front by looking toward the front, and the top by looking down toward the top; but the views are projected from the object onto a plane in each case. When the planes are unfolded, as at (b), the right-side view falls at the left of the front view, and the top view falls below the front view, as shown. A comparison between first-angle orthographic projection and third-angle orthographic projection is shown in Fig. 7.48. The front, top, and right-side views shown in Fig. 7.47 (b) for first-angle projection are repeated in Fig. 7.48 (a). The front, top, and right-side views for third-angle projection of Fig. 7.4 are repeated at (b). Ultimately, the only difference between third-angle and first-angle projection is in the arrangement of the views. Still, confusion and possibly manufacturing errors may result when the user reading a first-angle drawing thinks it is a third-angle drawing, or vice versa. To avoid misunderstanding, international projection symbols, shown in Fig. 7.48, have been developed to distinguish between first-angle and third-angle projections on drawings. On drawings where the possibility of confusion is anticipated, these symbols may appear in or near the title box.

In the United States and Canada, and to some extent in England, third-angle projection is standard, while in most of the rest of the world, first-angle projection is used. First-angle projection was originally used all over the world, including the United States, but in this country it was abandoned around 1890.

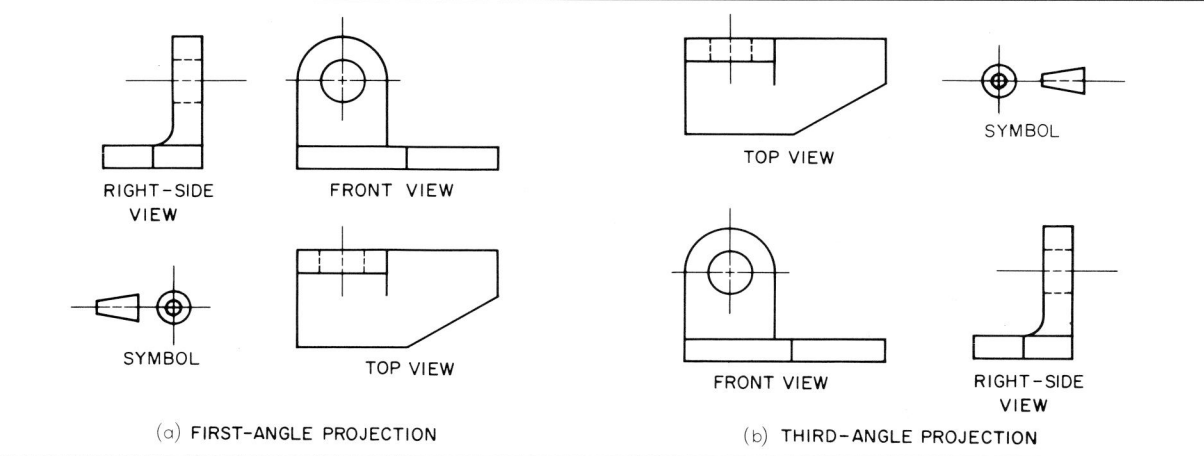

Fig. 7.48   First-Angle Projection Compared to Third-Angle Projection.

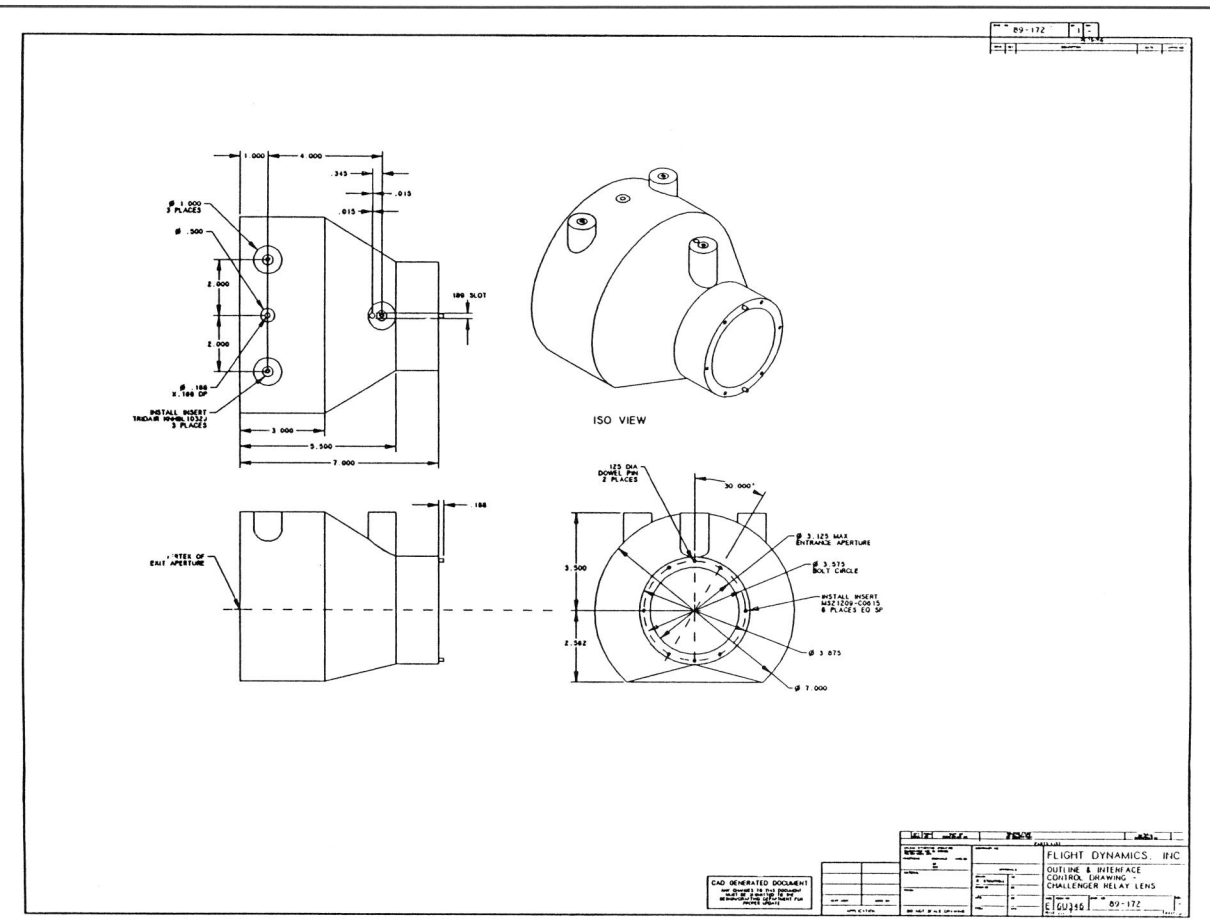

Fig. 7.49   Computer-Generated Multiview and Pictorial Drawing. *Courtesy of Computervision Corporation, a subsidiary of Prime Computer, Inc.*

7.39 Computer Graphics

CAD programs allow the drafter to rapidly create multiview drawings with a minimum amount of effort, Fig. 7.49. Symmetrical features and "mirror image" parts, §7.37, need only be drawn once and can be duplicated as many times as needed and moved around anywhere on the drawing. Features such as fillets, rounds, and runouts, tangencies, and complex curves can be added, changed or removed as desired by the CAD operator.

Multiview Projection Problems

The following problems are intended primarily to afford practice in instrumental drawing, but any of them may be sketched freehand on graph paper or plain paper. Sheet layouts, Figs. 7.50 and 7.51, or inside back cover, are suggested, but the instructor may prefer a different sheet size or arrangement.

Dimensions may or may not be required by the instructor. If they are assigned, the student should study §§13.1–13.25. In the given problems, whether in multiview or in pictorial form, it is often not possible to give dimensions in the preferred places or, occasionally, in the standard manner. The student is expected to move dimensions to the preferred locations and otherwise to conform to the dimensioning practices recommended in Chapter 13.

For the problems in Figs. 7.55–7.90, it is suggested that the student make a thumbnail sketch of the necessary views, in each case, and obtain the instructor's approval before starting the mechanical drawing.

For additional problems, see Fig. 10.29. Draw top views instead of auxiliary views.

Since many of the problems in this chapter are of a general nature, they can also be solved on most computer graphics systems. If a system is available, the instructor may choose to assign specific problems to be completed by this method.

Additional problems in convenient form for solution are presented in the worksheets at the back of this book. Refer to Drawings 7-1 to 7-5 and accompanying instructions.

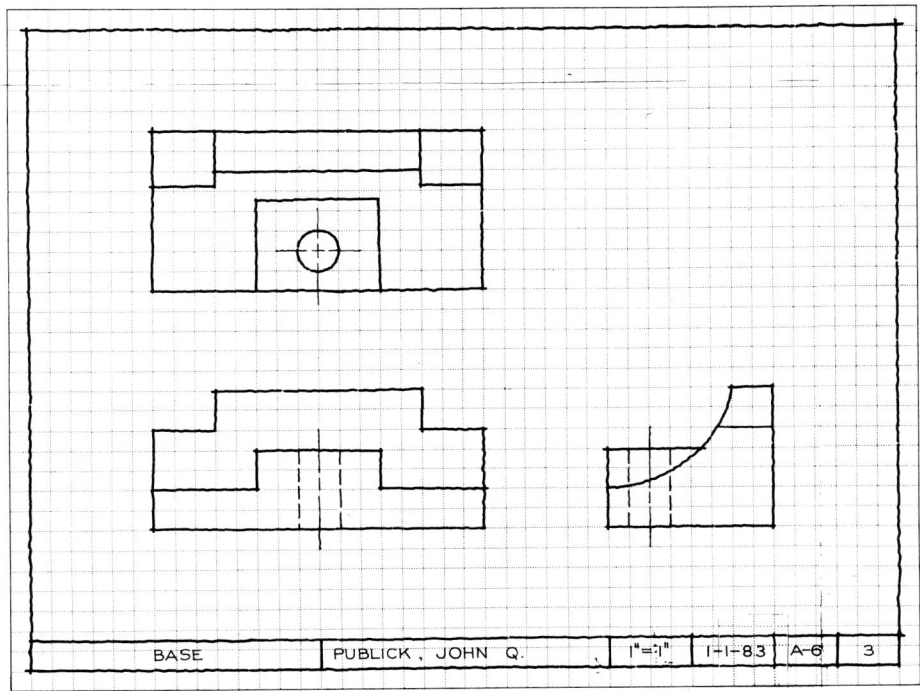

Fig. 7.50 Freehand Sketch (Layout A–2 or A4–2 adjusted).

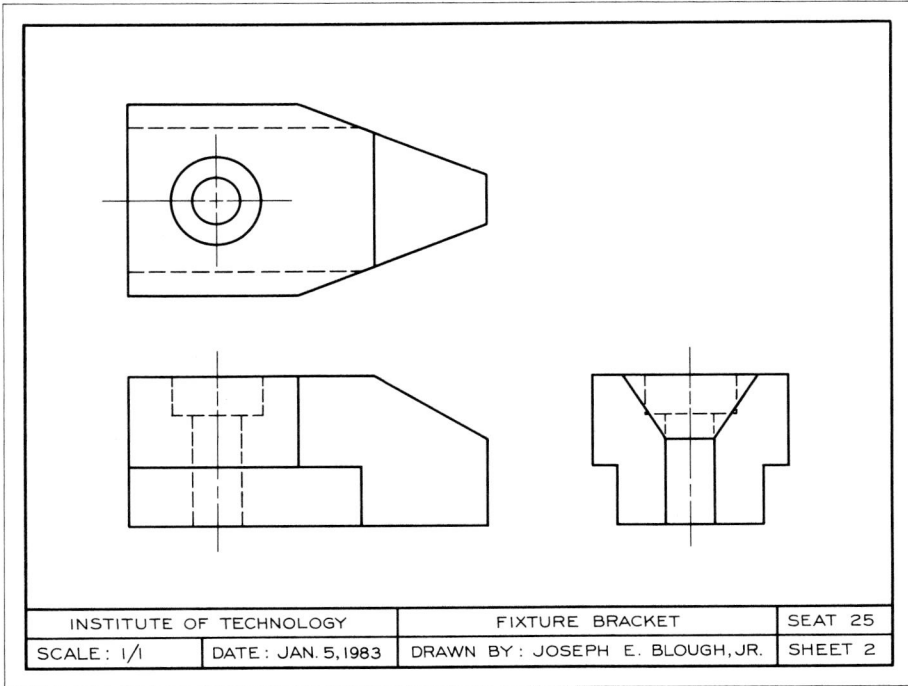

Fig. 7.51 Mechanical Drawing (Layout A–3 or A4–3 adjusted).

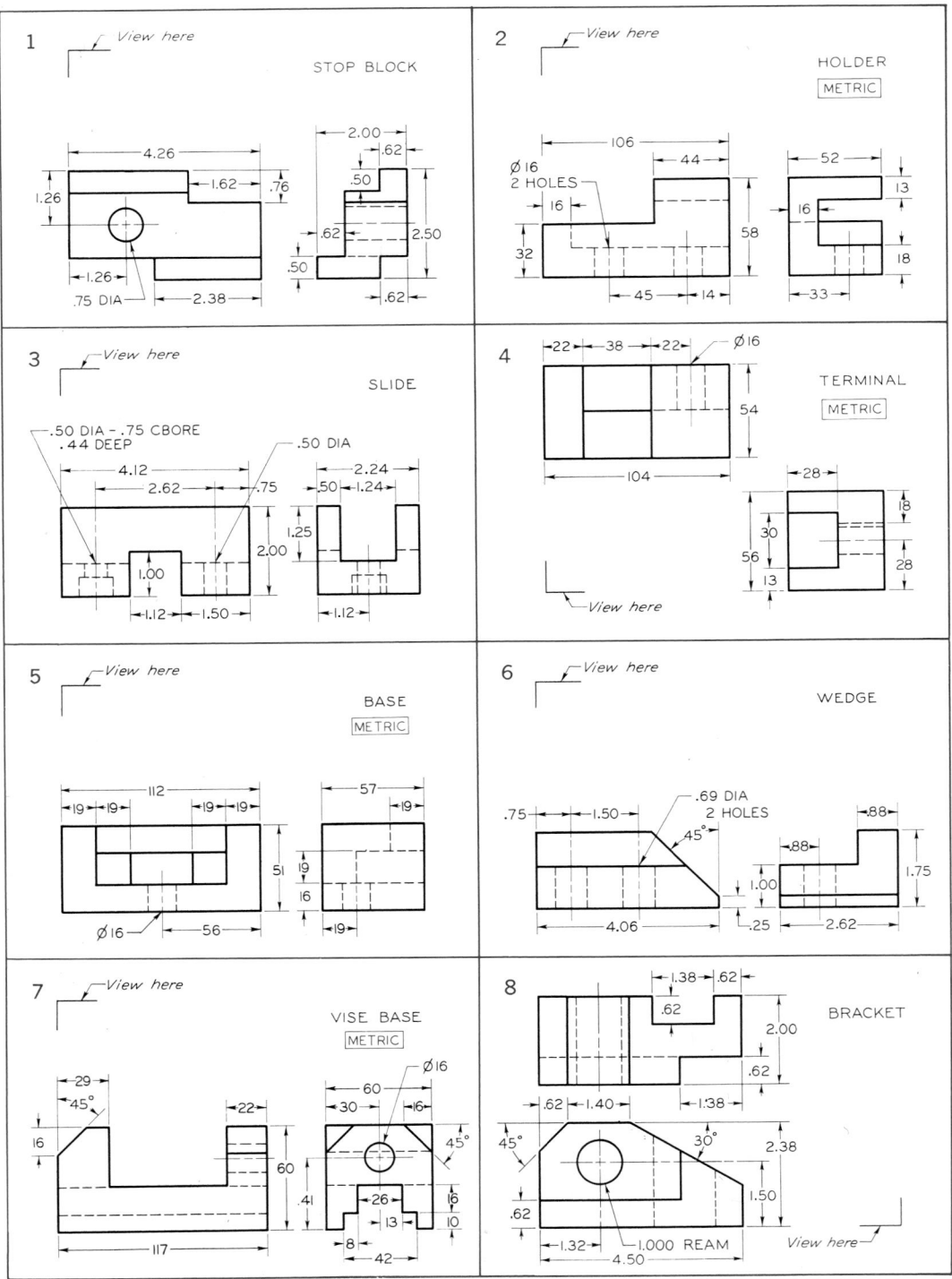

Fig. 7.52 Missing-View Problems.   Using Layout A–2 or 3 or Layout A4–2 or 3 (adjusted), sketch or draw with instruments the given views, and add the missing view, as shown in Figs. 7.50 and 7.51. If dimensions are required, study §§13.1–13.25. Use metric or decimal-inch dimensions as assigned by the instructor. Move dimensions to better locations where possible. In Probs. 1–5, all surfaces are normal surfaces.

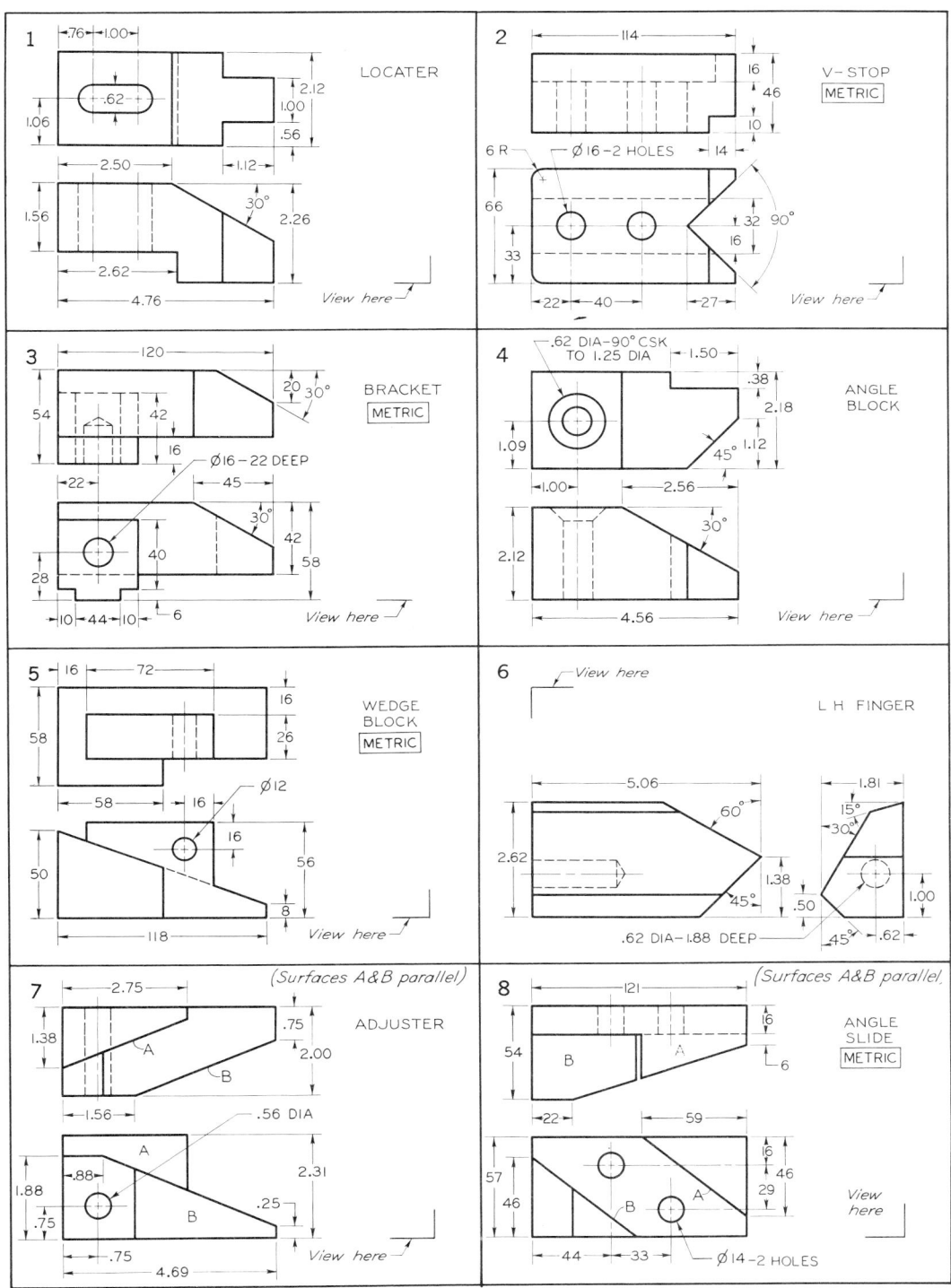

Fig. 7.53 Missing-View Problems.   Using Layout A–2 or 3 or Layout A4–2 or 3 (adjusted), sketch or draw with instruments the given views, and add the missing view, as shown in Figs. 7.50 and 7.51. If dimensions are required, study §§13.1–13.25. Use metric or decimal-inch dimensions as assigned by the instructor. Move dimensions to better locations where possible.

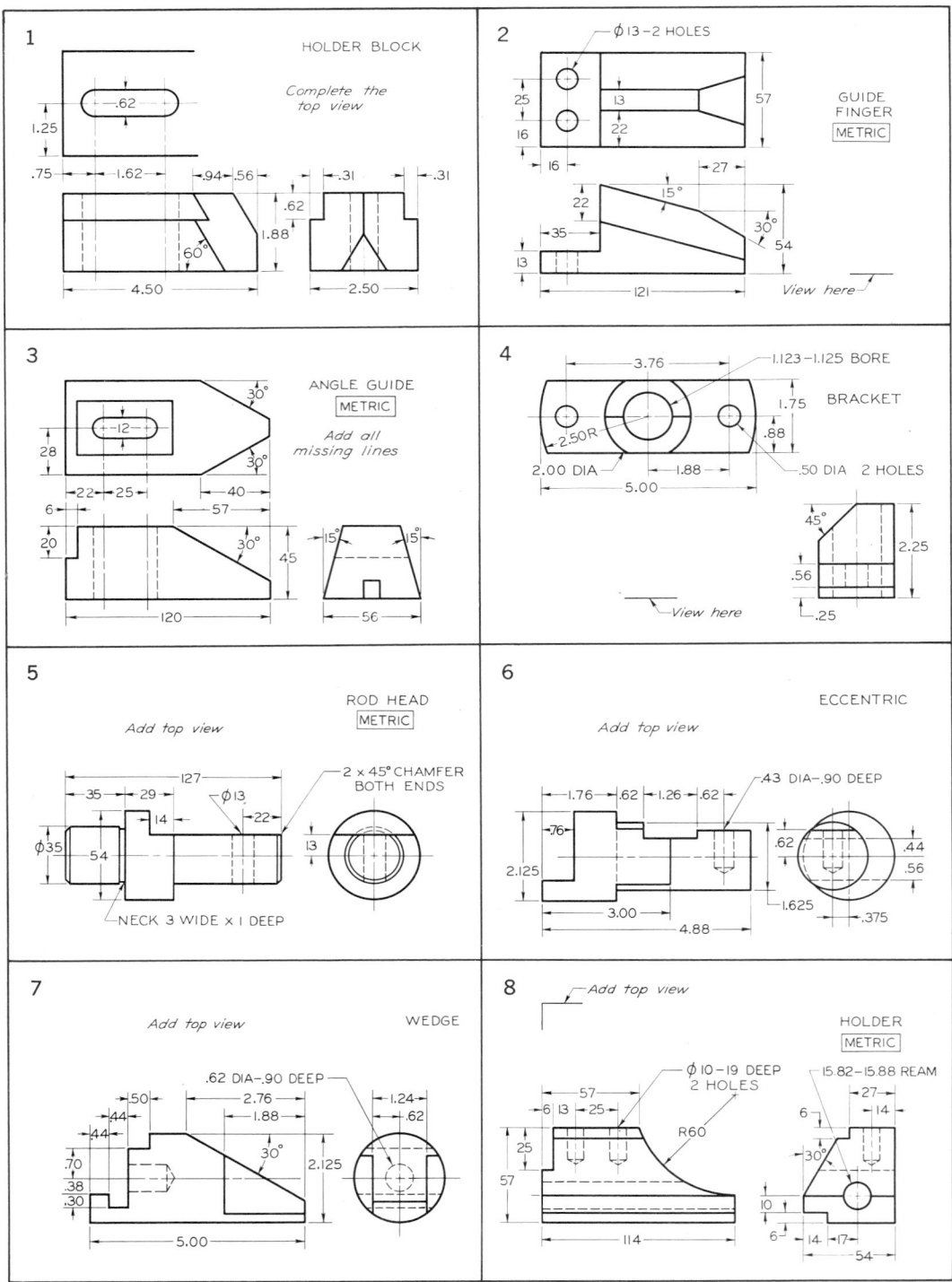

Fig. 7.54 Missing-View Problems.   Using Layout A–2 or 3 or Layout A4–2 or 3 (adjusted), sketch or draw with instruments the given views, and add the missing view, as shown in Figs. 7.50 and 7.51. If dimensions are required, study §§13.1–13.25. Use metric or decimal-inch dimensions as assigned by the instructor. Move dimensions to better locations where possible.

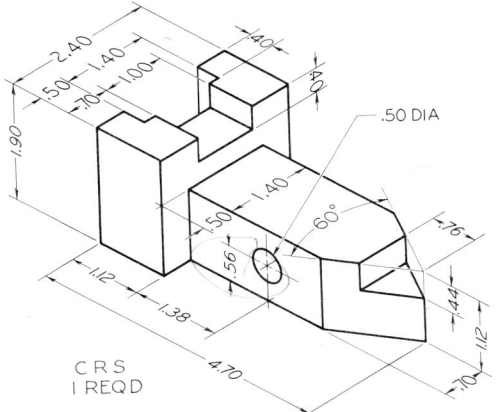

Fig. 7.55 Safety Key. Using Layout A–3 or A4–3 (adjusted), draw or sketch necessary views.*

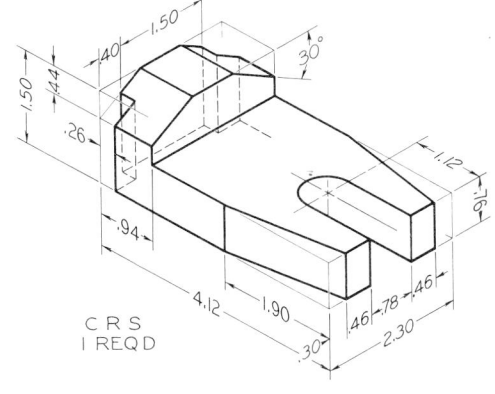

Fig. 7.56 Finger Guide. Using Layout A–3 or A4–3 (adjusted), draw or sketch necessary views.*

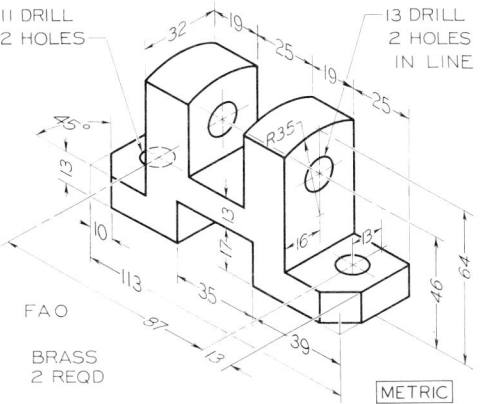

Fig. 7.57 Rod Support. Using Layout A–3 or A4–3 (adjusted), draw or sketch necessary views.*

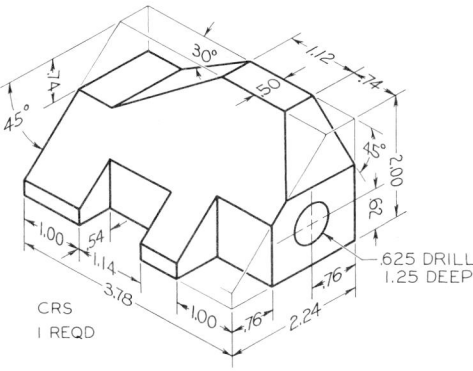

Fig. 7.58 Tool Holder. Using Layout A–3 or A4–3 (adjusted), draw or sketch necessary views.*

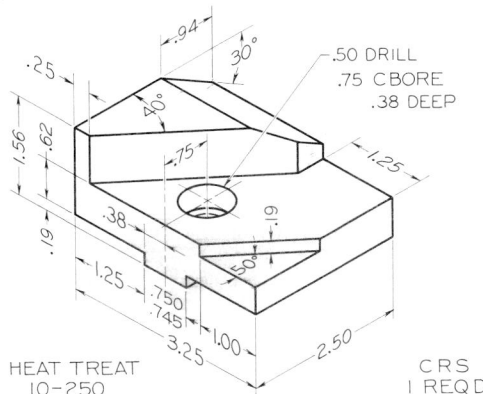

Fig. 7.59 Index Feed. Using Layout A–3 or A4–3 (adjusted), draw or sketch necessary views.*

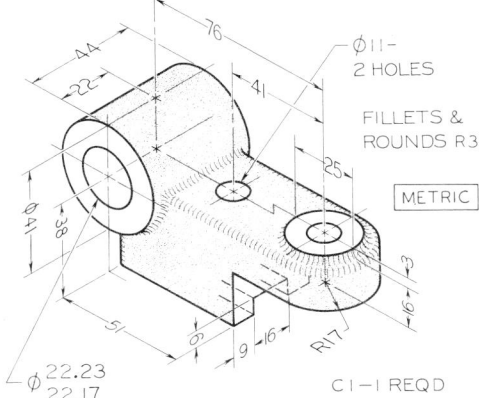

Fig. 7.60 Index Arm. Using Layout A–3 or A4–3 (adjusted), draw or sketch necessary views.*

*If dimensions are required, study §§13.1–13.25. Use metric or decimal-inch dimensions as assigned by the instructor.

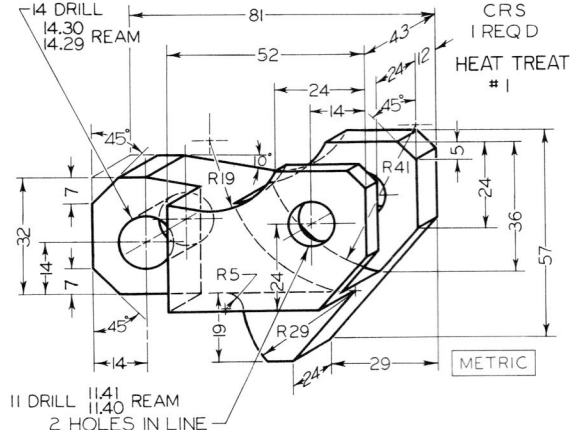

Fig. 7.61 Roller Lever. Using Layout A–3 or A4–3 (adjusted), draw or sketch necessary views.*

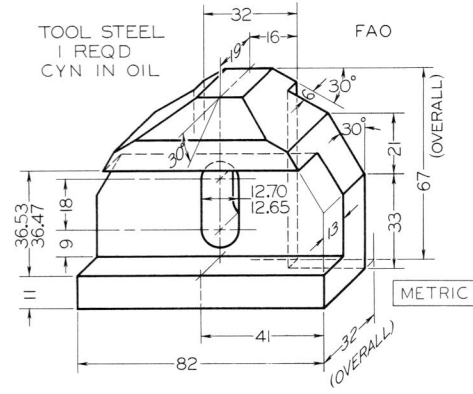

Fig. 7.62 Support. Using Layout A–3 or A4–3 (adjusted), draw or sketch necessary views.*

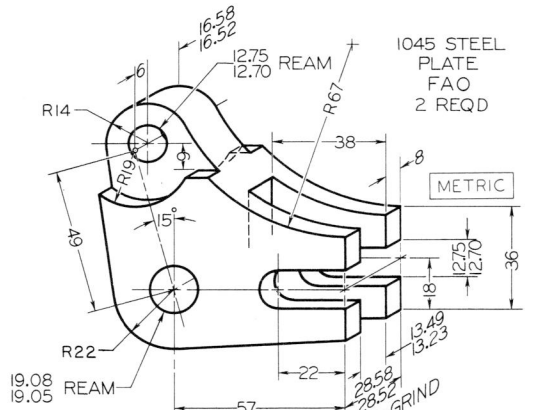

Fig. 7.63 Toggle Lever. Using Layout A–3 or A4–3 (adjusted), draw or sketch necessary views.*

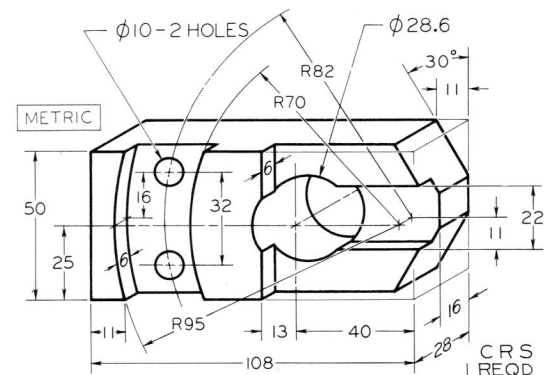

Fig. 7.64 Index Slide. Using Layout A–3 or A4–3 (adjusted), draw or sketch necessary views.*

*If dimensions are required, study §§13.1–13.25. Use metric or decimal-inch dimensions as assigned by the instructor.

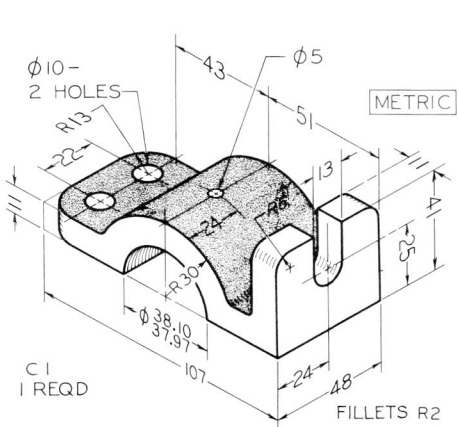

Fig. 7.65 Frame Guide. Using Layout A–3 or A4–3 (adjusted), draw or sketch necessary views.*

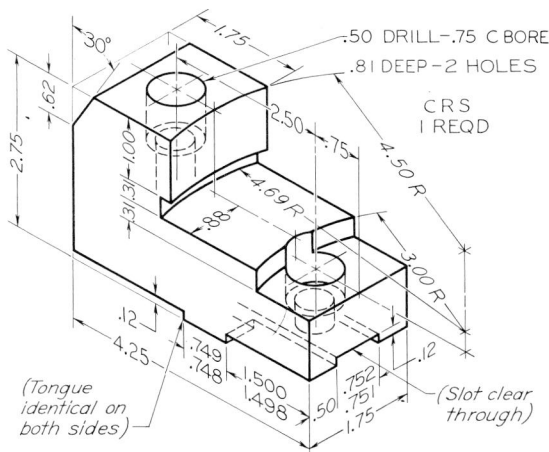

Fig. 7.66 Chuck Jaw. Using Layout A–3 or A4–3 (adjusted), draw or sketch necessary views.*

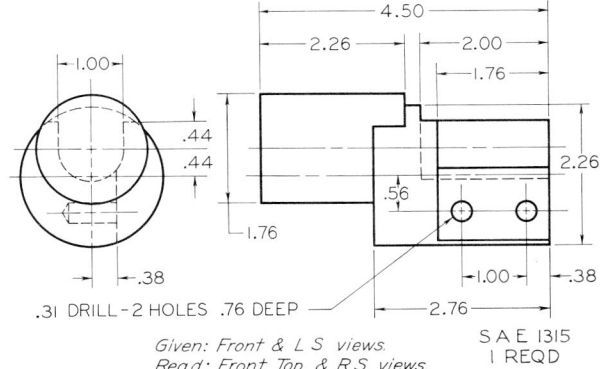

Given: Front & L S views.
Reqd: Front, Top, & R S views.

SAE 1315
1 REQD

Fig. 7.67 Tool Holder. Using Layout A–3 or A4–3 (adjusted), draw or sketch necessary views.*

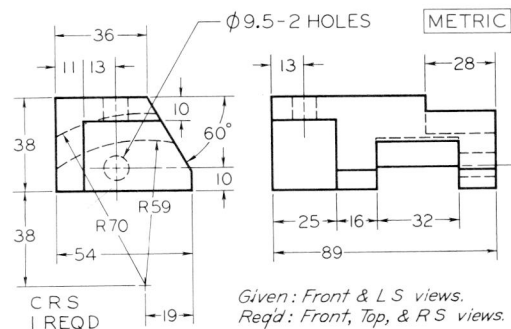

Given: Front & L S views.
Reqd: Front, Top, & R S views.

CRS
1 REQD

Fig. 7.68 Shifter Block. Using Layout A–3 or A4–3 (adjusted), draw or sketch necessary views.*

*If dimensions are required, study §§13.1–13.25. Use metric or decimal-inch dimensions as assigned by the instructor.

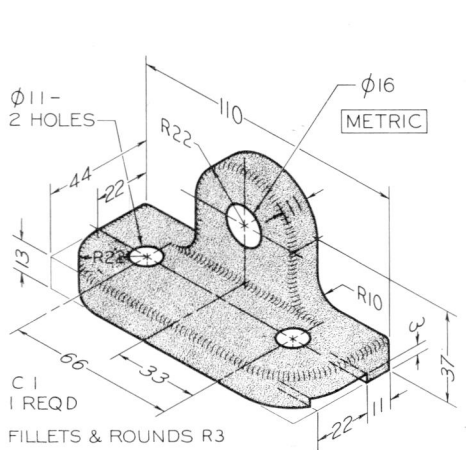

Fig. 7.69 Cross-Feed Stop. Using Layout A–3 or A4–3 (adjusted), draw or sketch necessary views.*

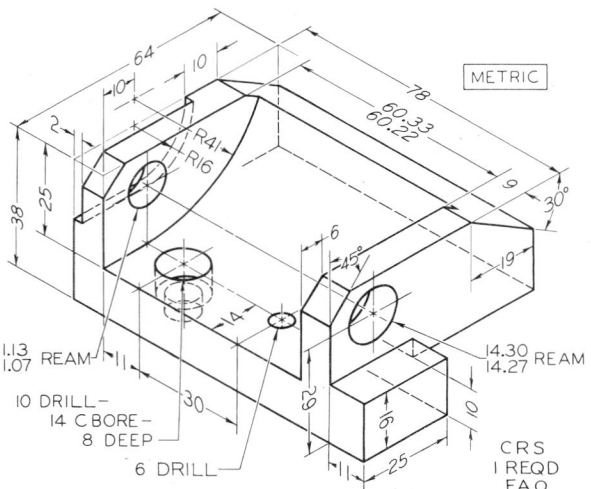

Fig. 7.70 Hinge Block. Using Layout A–3 or A4–3 (adjusted), draw or sketch necessary views.*

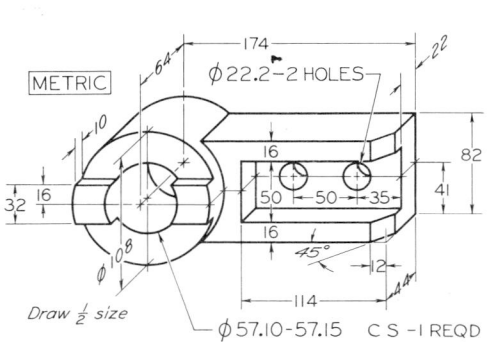

Fig. 7.71 Lever Hub. Using Layout A–3 or A4–3 (adjusted), draw or sketch necessary views.*

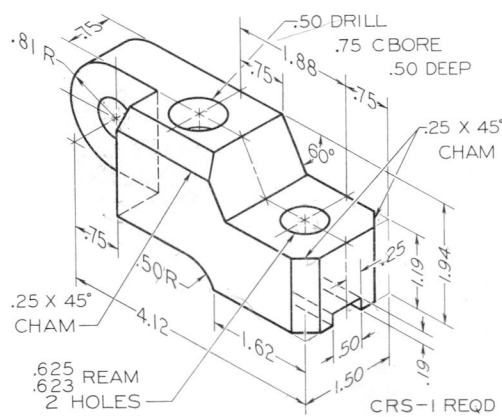

Fig. 7.72 Vibrator Arm. Using Layout A–3 or A4–3 (adjusted), draw or sketch necessary views.*

*If dimensions are required, study §§13.1–13.25. Use metric or decimal-inch dimensions as assigned by the instructor.

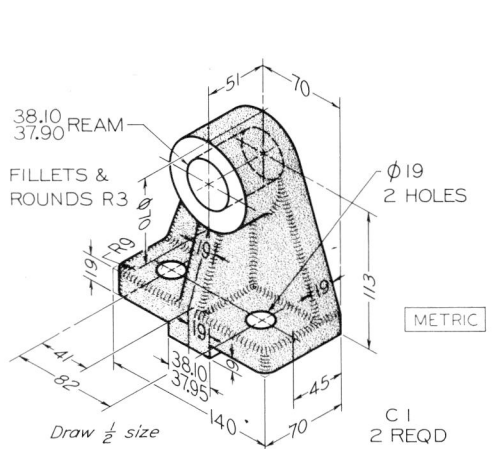

Fig. 7.73 Counter Bearing Bracket. Using Layout A–3 or A4–3 (adjusted), draw or sketch necessary views.*

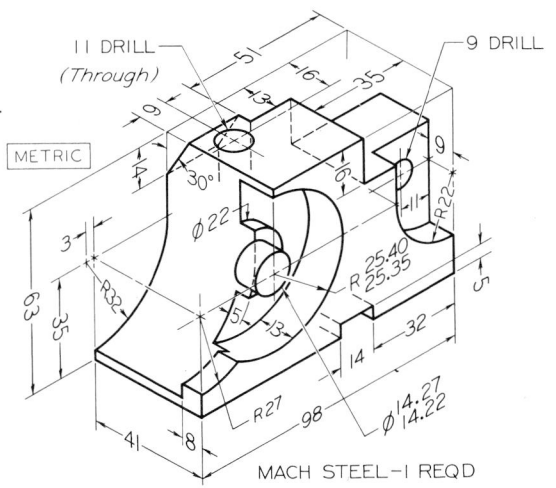

Fig. 7.74 Tool Holder. Using Layout A–3 or A4–3 (adjusted), draw or sketch necessary views.*

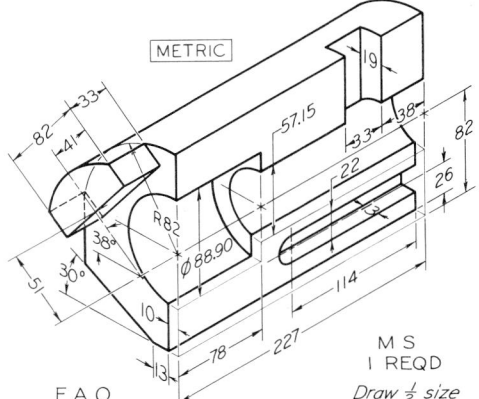

Fig. 7.75 Control Block. Using Layout A–3 or A4–3 (adjusted), draw or sketch necessary views.*

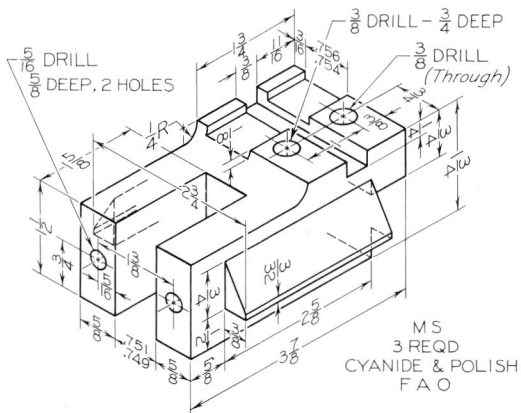

Fig. 7.76 Tool Holder. Using Layout A–3 or A4–3 (adjusted), draw or sketch necessary views.*

*If dimensions are required, study §§13.1–13.25. Use metric or decimal-inch dimensions as assigned by the instructor.

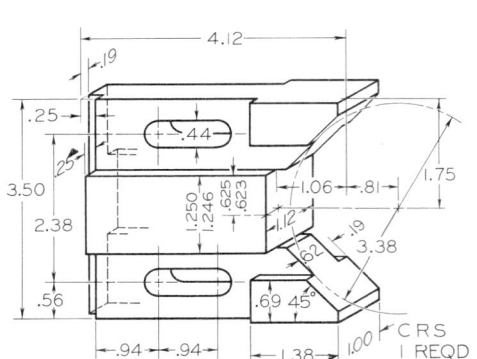

Fig. 7.77 Locating V-Block.   Using Layout A–3 or A4–3 (adjusted), draw or sketch necessary views.*

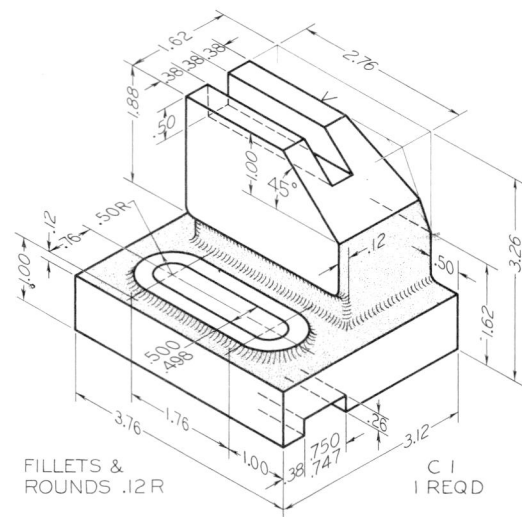

Fig. 7.78 Door Bearing.   Using Layout B–3 or A4–3 (adjusted), draw or sketch necessary views.*

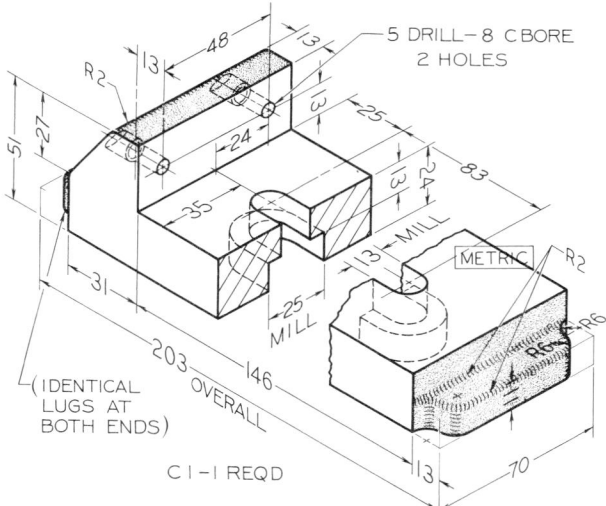

Fig. 7.79 Vise Base.   Using Layout B–3 or A3–3 (adjusted), draw or sketch necessary views.*

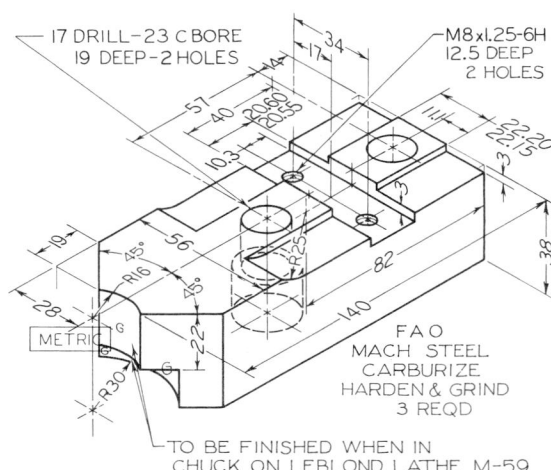

Fig. 7.80 Chuck Jaw.   Using Layout B–3 or A3–3 (adjusted), draw or sketch necessary views.*

*If dimensions are required, study §§13.1–13.25. Use metric or decimal-inch dimensions as assigned by the instructor.

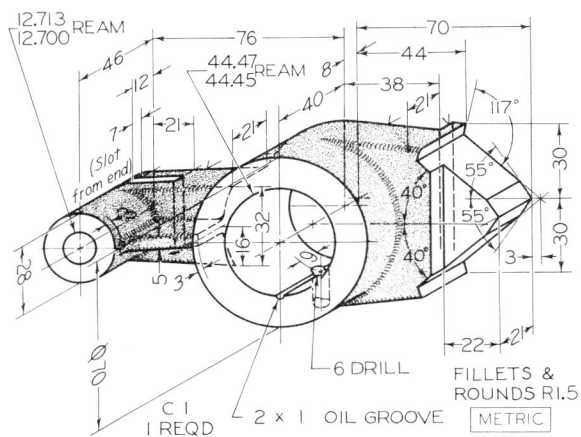

Fig. 7.81 Motor Switch Lever. Using Layout B–3 or A3–3 (adjusted), draw or sketch necessary views.*

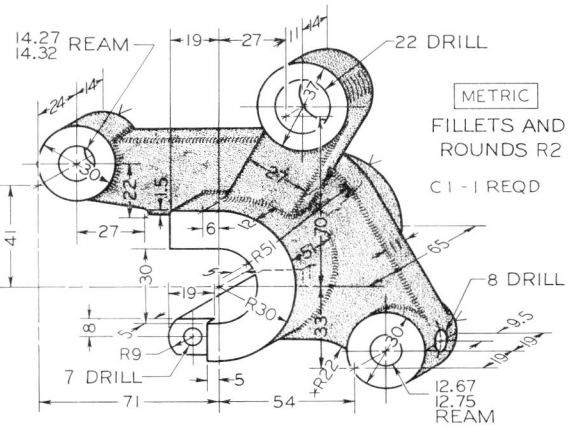

Fig. 7.82 Socket Form Roller—LH. Using Layout B–4 or A3–3 (adjusted), draw or sketch necessary views.*

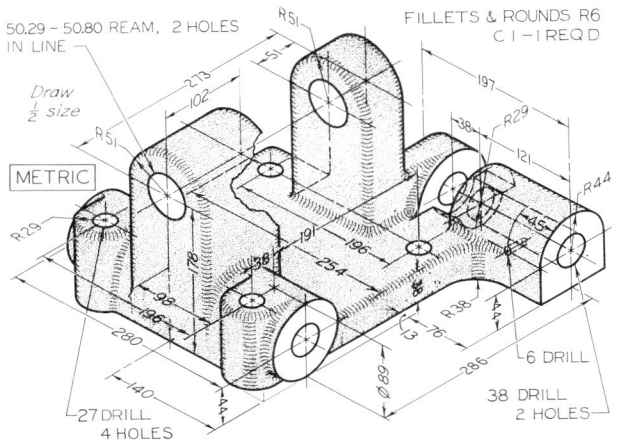

Fig. 7.83 Automatic Stop Base. Using Layout C–3 or A2–3, draw or sketch necessary views.*

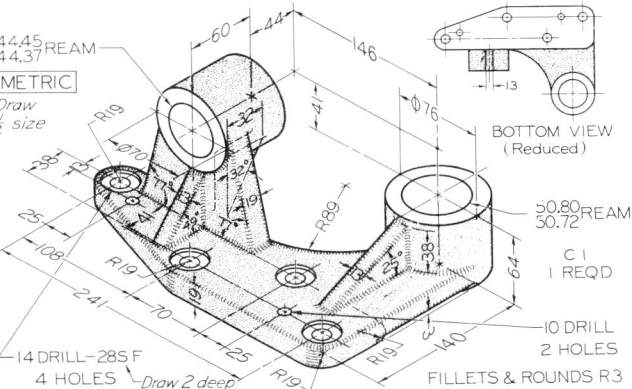

Fig. 7.84 Lever Bracket. Using Layout C–3 or A2–3, draw or sketch necessary views.*

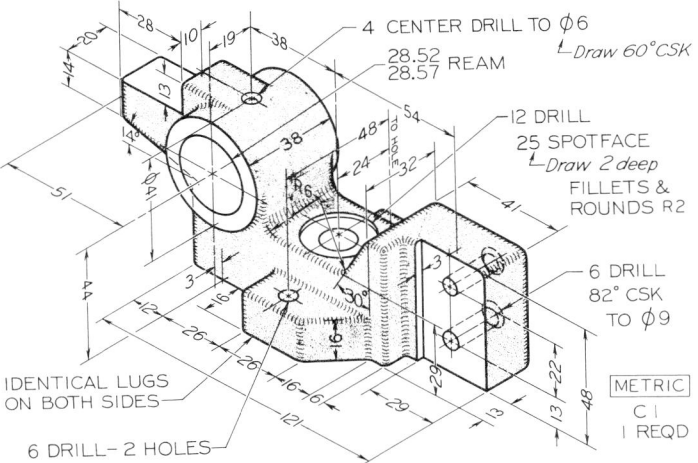

Fig. 7.85 Gripper Rod Center. Using Layout B–3 or A3–3, draw or sketch necessary views.*

*If dimensions are required, study §§13.1–13.25. Use metric or decimal-inch dimensions as assigned by the instructor.

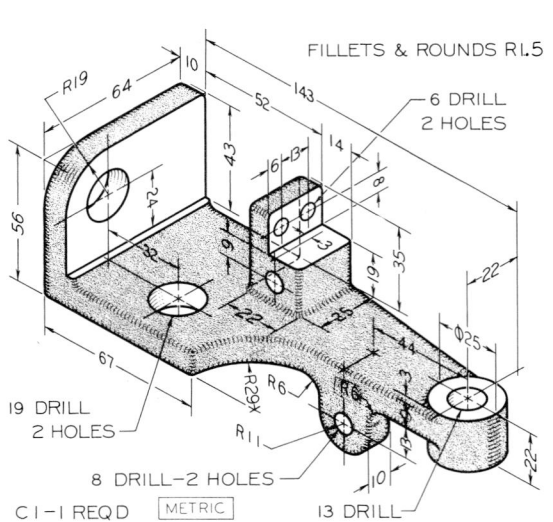

Fig. 7.86 Mounting Bracket. Using Layout B–3 or A3–3, draw or sketch necessary views.*

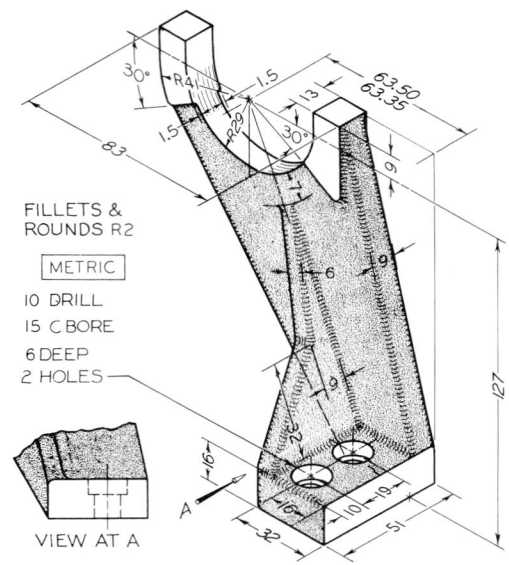

Fig. 7.87 LH Shifter Fork. Using Layout B–3 or A3–3, draw or sketch necessary views.*

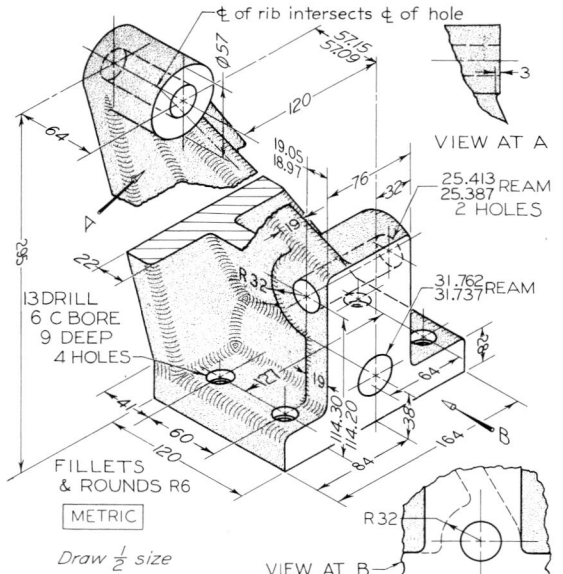

Fig. 7.88 Ejector Base. Using Layout C–4 or A2–4, draw or sketch necessary views.*

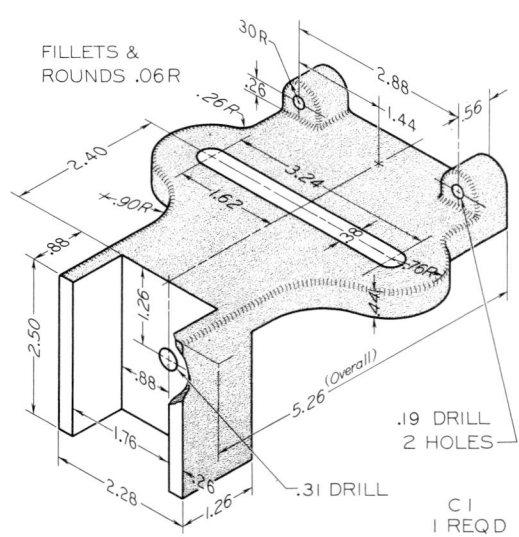

Fig. 7.89 Tension Bracket. Using Layout C–4 or A2–4, draw or sketch necessary views.*

*If dimensions are required, study §§13.1–13.25. Use metric or decimal-inch dimensions as assigned by the instructor.

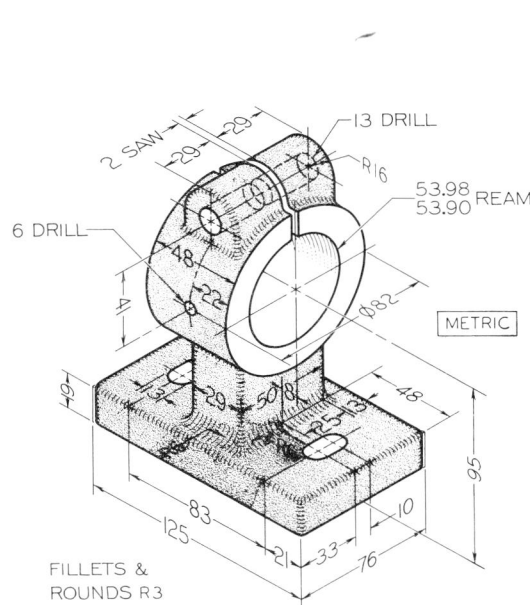

Fig. 7.90 Feed Guide. Using Layout C–4 or A2–4, draw or sketch necessary views.*

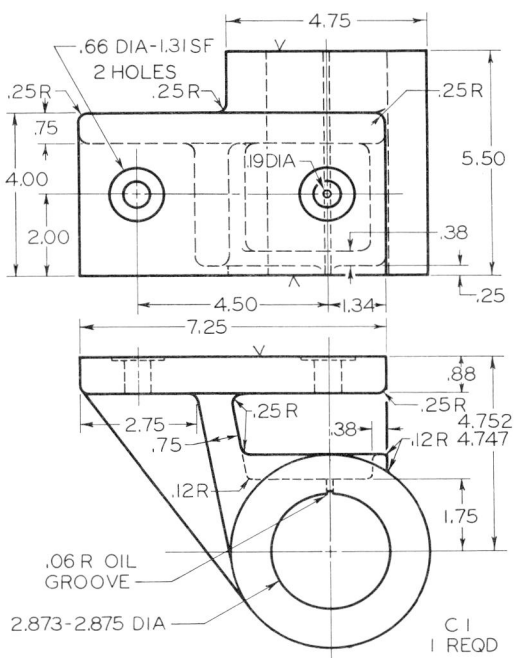

Fig. 7.91 Feed Shaft Bracket.
Given: Front and top views.
Required: Front, top, and right-side views, half size (Layout B–3 or A3–3).†

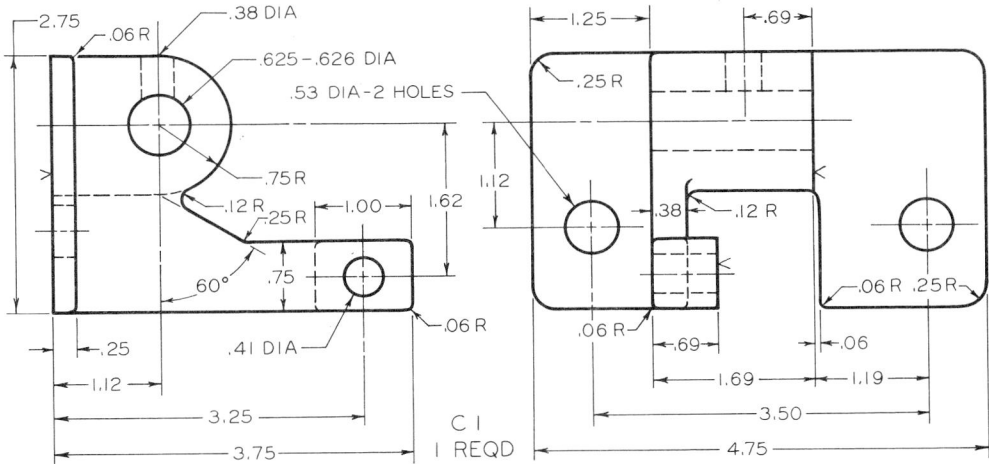

Fig. 7.92 Knurl Bracket Bearing.
Given: Front and left-side views.
Required: Take front as top view on new drawing, and add front and right-side views (Layout B–3 or A3–3).†

*If dimensions are required, study §§13.1–13.25. Use metric or decimal-inch dimensions as assigned by the instructor.

†Draw or sketch necessary views. If dimensions are required, study §§13.1–13.25. Use metric or decimal-inch dimensions as assigned by the instructor.

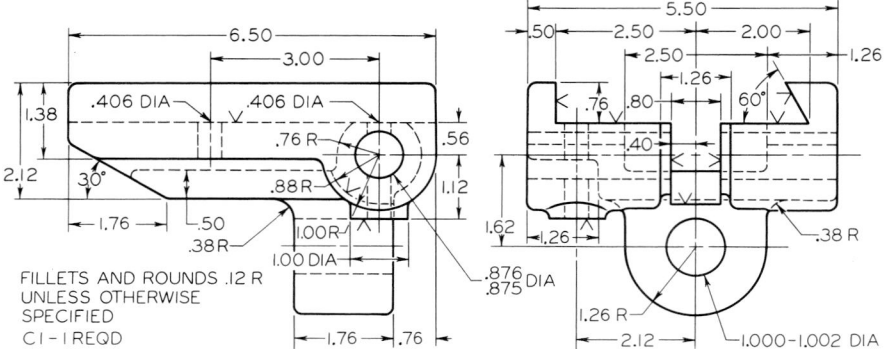

Fig. 7.93 Sliding Nut for Mortiser.
Given: Top and right-side views.
Required: Front, top, and left-side views, full size (Layout C–4 or A2–4).*

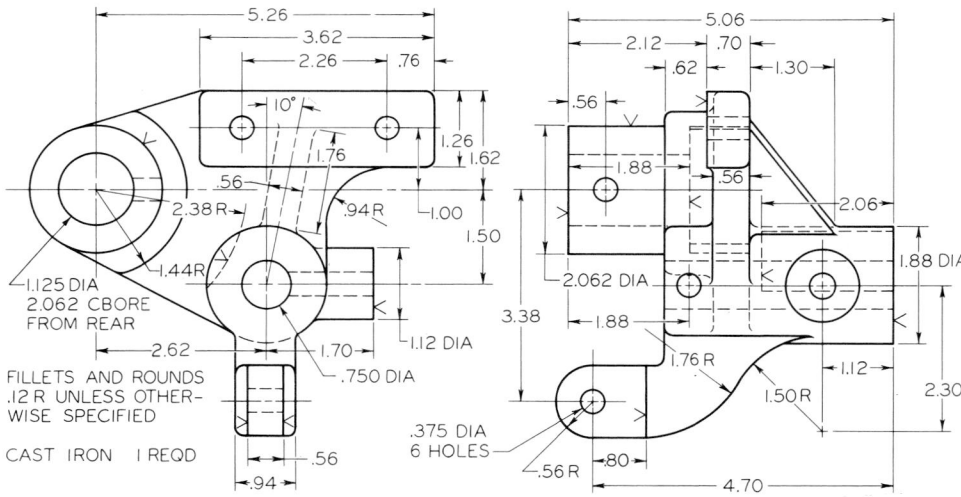

Fig. 7.94 Power Feed Bracket for Universal Grinder.
Given: Front and right-side views.
Required: Front, top, and left-side views, full size (Layout C–4 or A2–4).*

*Draw or sketch necessary views. If dimensions are required, study §§13.1–13.25. Use metric or decimal-inch dimensions as assigned by the instructor.

CHAPTER

8

Using a CAD System

By Byron W. Urbanick*

Computer-aided drafting (CAD) is a practical interactive tool, operable by the senior designer on the engineering team and every member of the staff. It is a useful tool that performs work in the engineering design office or in the manufacturing plant. The software programs for CAD and computer-aided manufacturing (CAM) can interact with the full engineering scheme of concept development to integrate manufacturing and the delivery of a product. The practical applications of such a tool may never be exhausted, for they are limited only by the imagination and creativity of the user.

Interactive CAD is a human-oriented tool. The images and details projected on the computer's monitor are visual evidence to the design engineer or CAD drafter that the all-important CAD database understands the operator's instruction, design, or input request. CAD is a practical and powerful tool because of the almost instant response to the operator's input or request for stored information. It is a high-tech system for creating new designs, developing technical documents, and managing documentation—it is more than a simple electronic drafting machine. The development of networked CAD systems has unleashed the creative imagination and design interaction ability of every individual on the engineering design team.

*Design Consultant & Vice President, Paneltech LTD., Lombard, IL 60148.

It is the purpose of this chapter to show that at any moment in the creation of CAD images, the CAD user is building a detailed graphic document using what the computer knows. That is, the CAD software allows you to work sequentially with the programs stored in the central processing unit (CPU). The potential CAD user is introduced to several CAD software "working procedures" and can examine the basic interactive screen formats presented by AutoCAD, CADKEY, and FastCAD. The text describes typical procedures for selecting a drawing command and reviews the menu options available for geometric constructions and detailing on the display screen of the CAD system. These somewhat generic descriptions of CAD functions presented on a personal computer can provide an introduction to the interaction and operations of the CAD user. More specific software instruction is available from individual CAD software developers and of course is more complete and extensive in the instructional format.

The CAD system on the personal computer as an automation tool is replacing many of the drafting instruments, drafting tables, and drafting files. But, like no other drafting tool before, it raises engineering productivity without replacing the basic functions of the designer, engineer, and drafting technician. CAD developers, in their quest to harness computer technologies, have had a profound impact on the high-tech teams as they resolve problems in research, development, design, production, and operation (the five basic engineering functions).

8.1 CAD Compatibility

How does a CAD system store your current drawing? What is RAM? CAD software stores your drawing in your computer's random access memory (RAM). In Chapter 3 the CAD system is illustrated and the various input and output devices (called hardware) are presented as the tools for the CAD user. The CAD software programs have to be compatible with specific hardware, and the CAD software programmer wants the software "commands and menus" to be compatible in ways that are similar to patterns of manual drafting work. The skills learned "on the board" are related and complementary to those needed by the CAD user. To learn the performance skills needed for creating drawings with CAD tools is time consuming and requires practice and manual dexterity, Fig. 8.1. Both methods of drafting use simple and familiar geometric

Fig. 8.1   As a human-oriented tool the CAD system is a "hands-on" high-tech feature of Electronic Interaction. *Courtesy of Computervision.*

terminology for structuring the graphic production of technical documents, and both have the same goal—drawings that will meet industry standards.

The basic principles of drafting are common to traditional drafting and computer-aided drafting. The American National Standards Institute (ANSI) has well-established standards for shaping engineering drawings. The knowledge of drafting principles from the alphabet of lines to dimensioning and sectioning procedures continues to be essential in shaping CAD documents. CAD is compatible because it can produce consistent lettering and regulates line work to improve the production of working drawings better than any other tool. Drafting continues to be a "hands on" system with CAD software serving as the main form of communication between networked CAD workstations and plotter or printers, Fig. 8.2.

8.2 Software—Invisible

Though invisible to the eye, software is the prerecorded instruction that makes the hardware operate. Today, most CAD software is stored on floppy disks, or transferred from floppy disks ($5\frac{1}{4}''$ or $3\frac{1}{2}''$) to the hard disk within the computer where it becomes quickly accessible. Software tells the computer to direct the flow of data entered by the CAD user either to working storage memory or to the disk for instant recall. Software has the ability to "remember" formulas, for example, the center of gravity for a truncated cone. As shown in Fig. 8.3, software can

Fig. 8.2 This is a high-tech system for developing technical documents. Networked personal computer systems are emerging in the classrooms. *Courtesy of Moraine Valley Community College Technical Center.*

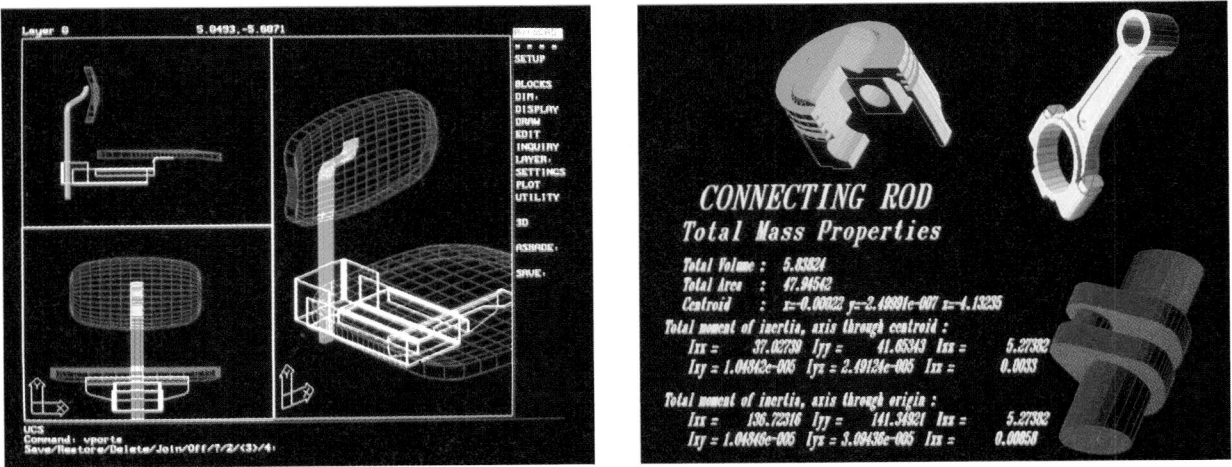

Fig. 8.3 The CAD software increases visualization through wireframe models, (a), and solids modeling, (b), to enhance pictorials. *Courtesy of AutoDesk, Inc., and CADKEY.*

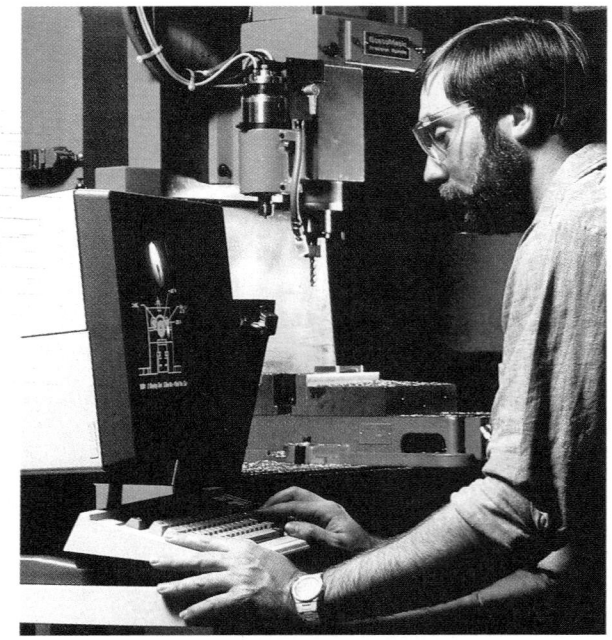

Fig. 8.4 The CAD software interacts with manufacturing processes and the engineered product has been improved through quality control of computer-aided manufacturing (CAM). *Courtesy of Computervision.*

create a wire-frame model, (a), or a shaded solid model, (b). Software helps the computer find symbols stored for use in creating or drawing and will help you create symbols for storage to be retrieved

for specific types of drawings. Software can be programmed to exchange files with other software programs.

The invisible software helps the computer compile data and arrange it on various drawing layers or levels. The invisible software can remember CAD user passwords for security and controls input of specific data and regulates output of specific data when charged (programmed) with that responsibility. Software can also count, measure, and direct devices to print or plot drawings or to create a bill of materials. CAD software has been designed to serve all the major branches of engineering and manufacturing, Fig. 8.4. The CAD user must understand how the basic software information is installed, stored, transferred, and exchanged.

8.3 CAD Software

All CAD software generates familiar geometric terminology for creating drawings. But even though the geometry is common and the procedures for construction are similar, every CAD software program will vary in operational procedures, Fig. 8.5. The variations may be considered a hierarchy of command structure and may be reviewed with AutoCAD, CADKEY, and FastCAD screens used in this chapter.

Three features are found in all CAD software, and the programmer creates these so they work interactively with basic commands and menu options.

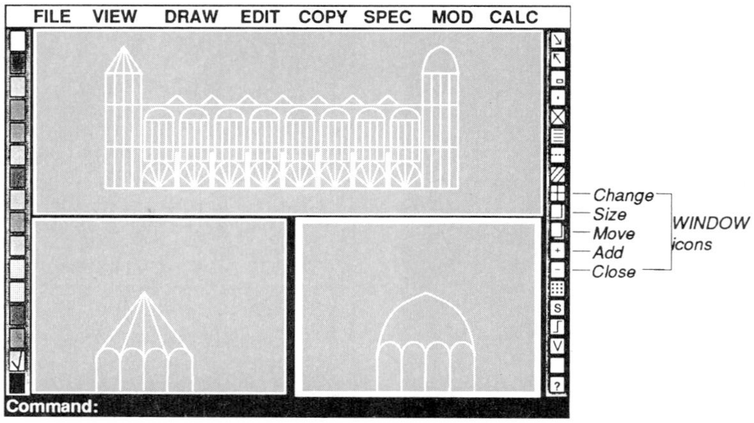

Take a moment to find the five window icons:

FILE VIEW DRAW EDIT COPY SPEC MOD CALC

—Change
—Size
—Move   WINDOW
—Add   icons
—Close

Command:

Fig. 8.5 The CAD screen display provides selection procedures that vary with each software program. FastCAD has an icon bar for use of multiple windows. *Courtesy of Evolution Computing.*

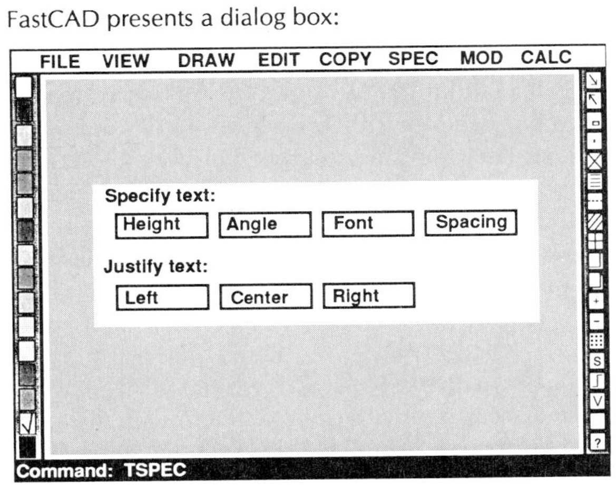

FastCAD presents a dialog box:

```
FILE  VIEW  DRAW  EDIT  COPY  SPEC  MOD  CALC

        Specify text:
        [Height]  [Angle]  [Font]  [Spacing]

        Justify text:
        [Left]  [Center]  [Right]

Command: TSPEC
```

Fig. 8.6 What do you want to do and how do you want to do it? The text specifications are generated for selection in a "how to" dialog box. *Courtesy of Evolution Computing.*

1. Commands for geometry generators (basic geometric construction).

2. Functions to control the size of generators (scale of the drawing, paper size, etc.).

3. Modifiers for changing the drawing or editing variations in the drawing (rotate, mirror, delete, group, etc.).

The normal text specification command is structured to two questions for the FastCAD user, Fig. 8.6.

1. What do you want to do?

2. How do you want to do it? For example, in the CADKEY structure, CREATE (the command), LINE (an option), ENDPOINTS (an option) assists the CAD user in creating a line.

The commands and menu options may be selected in two basic ways: the function keys (F1–F10 and PageUp and PageDown keys), and the tablet (digitizer) or mouse. With the tablet or mouse, specific areas on the monitor screen can be quickly selected, Fig. 8.7. The Cartesian coordinates may be accessed with the keyboard or the mouse. You may switch between these function keys and input devices at any time to issue commands and selected options. In the CADKEY software example cited earlier, the CAD user would press the F1 function key to obtain

Fig. 8.7 The digitizer or mouse can select the step-by-step process rather quickly with reasonable practice. *Courtesy of Tektronix.*

the command: F1 to create, then F1 to select the line option, then F1 again to select endpoints. The sequence of selection is called the hierarchy of command structure and provides an ease of operation that is the basis for selecting one software program over another.

8.4 CAD Capability Checklist

The software can offer the following characteristics required for creating technical documents.

1. Draw construction lines at any convenient spacing through any points, at any angles, and create tangent lines to one or more arcs.

2. Draw any type of line such as visible, center, hidden, or section.

3. Draw circles and arcs of any size with given data.

4. Perform cross-hatching within specified boundaries.

5. Establish a scale or set a new scale within a drawing for various drawings within a document.

6. Calculate or list pertinent data of graphic construction such as actual distances or angles.

7. Create a group of geometric figures for editing or copying.

8. Relocate a drawing to any new position. Correct or change additions in stored document.

9. Edit all or erase (delete) any part of a line, arc, or any geometric form on a drawing. Correct dimensions.

10. Make a mirrored image or create symmetrical forms.

11. Perform associative or datum unit dimensioning, Fig. 8.8.

12. Label drawings with notes and create title blocks and bills of material.

13. Save the entire drawing or any part for use on other documents.

14. Create pictorials from three-view drawings, Fig. 8.9.

15. Retrieve and use stored drawings.

List additional capabilities of your system or think of one more you need. Software programmers are constantly adding new capabilities and options to CAD software.

AutoCAD has extensive capabilities built into over 125 commands, and many commands have more than one complementary option. This CAD software has more than 20 ways to edit a drawing and over 12 dimension options. After reviewing the checklist above, you realize that the list can be expanded when you have over 125 commands in one interactive program.

8.5 Microcomputer Operations
Begin by turning on the computer and all the peripheral tools, including the monitor, digitizer/

mouse, and plotter/printer. In order to run your CAD programs on the microcomputer you must have a copy of the disk operating system (DOS) already loaded into it. System software is used to control the operation of the microcomputer, and it will manage data input and output between the microcomputer and other hardware such as disk drives. In order to operate the CAD software programs on the PC workstation, the system must first be under control of the system software.

8.6 Loading System Software
The following steps are used for booting up the operating system. Every CAD user should be well acquainted with the disk operating system (DOS) used on the computer. The ability to interact with major commands of the system software enables the CAD user to become interactive with CAD software changes.

1. For floppy disk systems (no hard disk), open the latch for the diskette drive A, and carefully insert the DOS system disk into the drive slot with the label up or facing you, Fig. 8.10. Close the drive latch. (*Note:* The A drive is usually on the left side or on top.) Diskettes should only be inserted or removed when the drive indicator light is not lit. Always wait until the light goes off, indicating that the drive is not reading or writing data.

2. Turn on the PC (floppy and hard disk systems). If the PC is already turned on, you can boot the DOS operating system by holding down the

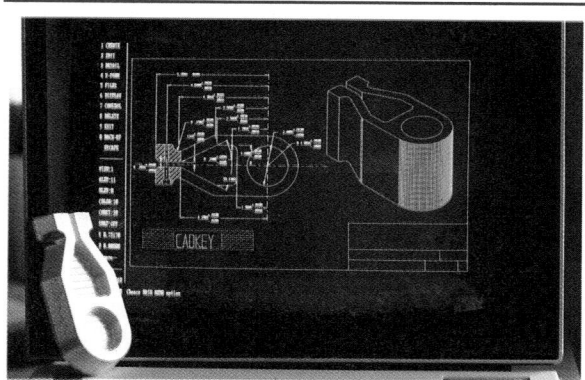

Fig. 8.8 A Casting Profile. As a high-tech tool, CAD enhances the production of design and detailing in all branches of engineering. *Courtesy of CAD-KEY.*

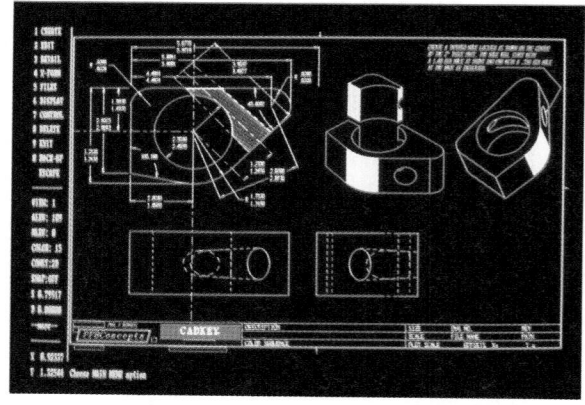

Fig. 8.9 Isometrics–Pictorials–Advanced programs generate 3D graphics. *Courtesy of CADKEY.*

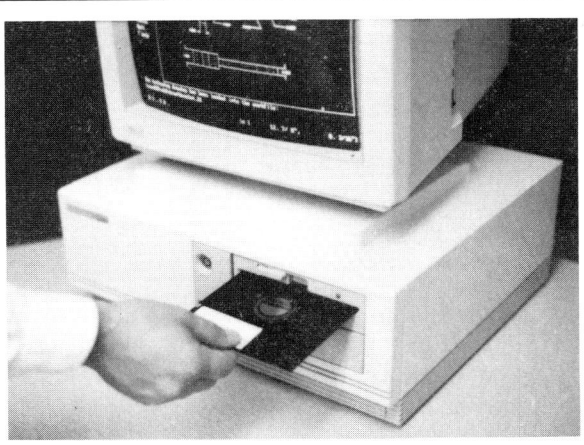

Fig. 8.10 The floppy disk should be handled carefully with the label side up when it is inserted into the computer drive opening. *Courtesy of Michael Eleder Associates.*

Ctrl and Alt keys, and then pressing the Del key.

3. After DOS has been loaded into the computer memory, the system monitor will prompt you for the DATE and TIME. Type the correct month, day, and year (for example, 10-30-92) and press RETURN. Then type the correct time (for example, 9:00) and press RETURN. Some systems have a battery clock and will not require you to enter the time and date.

4. DOS has been successfully loaded when the DOS command prompt appears on the monitor as
A:>   (for non-hard drive systems) or
C:>   (for hard drive systems).

5. You can type any DOS command or software program name at this time.

8.7 The Floppy Drives
When you are using a dual floppy drive computer, generally, DOS must be loaded each time the computer is turned on. The original DOS diskette should be stored in a safe place, and should not be used for daily operations. You should make a backup copy for daily use. You can make a backup copy using the following steps.

1. Start up DOS. The system is ready when you see the DOS prompt A:> or C:> on the monitor.

2. Type

FORMAT B: /S   <return> (press RETURN key)

3. The monitor will respond with

Insert new diskette in drive B
and strike any key when ready.

Place a new blank diskette into the B drive, close the latch, and press any key. The diskette light will go on, and the blank diskette in drive B will be formatted so it can receive data. When the light goes off, the monitor message will read

Format another (Y/N)?

Type

N

4. The A:> or C:> prompt will be displayed. Now type

COPY A:*.* B: <return>

(Be sure to leave a space before the letter A and before the letter B.)

5. The program files that are copied from the diskette in drive A and transferred to drive B will be displayed on the monitor. After the copy is complete, store the original DOS diskette in a safe place, and use the new copy for daily operations. (Hard disk systems have their working copy on drive C.)

The CAD program needs a place to store the drawings. Blank diskettes without programs may be used. They need to be formatted before drawings can be stored on them. When a previously used diskette is formatted, any information that was on the diskette will be erased. Some new diskettes can be purchased that are preformatted for DOS and do not require formatting before they can be used.

8.8 Access to Drive Commands
When the computer is turned on, the default drive is A for dual floppy systems or C for hard disk systems. When it is necessary to access a diskette drive other than the current drive, type the drive name, colon, and press return. For example, to change from drive A to drive B, type

B: <return>

at the A:> prompt. The prompt on the monitor changes to B:>. To change from the B drive to the C drive, type

C: <return>

at the B:> prompt. The prompt on the monitor changes to C:>. Whatever letter is displayed at the prompt is the current drive you will access for disk operations. Hard disk systems may also have drives D and E depending how the hard disk is partitioned and how large the hard disk is. The prompt, whether it is A:>, B:>, or C:>, is commonly called the DOS prompt.

8.9 Access to Directory Display

CAD drawing files that are stored on diskette can be viewed alphabetically on the monitor using the directory command. The directory for the current drive may be displayed by typing

DIR   <return>

at the DOS prompt. The directory that is displayed lists the files that reside on the current drive, Fig. 8.11. To see the directory of another drive, drive B for example, type

DIR B: <return>

Sometimes, the list of files is so long that it scrolls vertically off the screen and cannot be read. You can pause the scrolling by typing a modified command for directory. Type

DIR B:

then

DIR /P   <return>

at the DOS prompt and the list will pause. Press any key to view the next group of file names.

When the directory is displayed, the left column is always the file name, which may be up to eight letters, numbers, or symbols long. The next three letters are called the file extension and describe the type of file. The file name and file extension are separated by a period. Some common file extension abbreviations are

com	command file
exe	executable file
drv	driver file for peripheral device
ovl	overlay file for software program
dwg	drawing file
bak	backup file
mnu	menu file (common to AutoCAD)
doc	word processing file
txt	text file

Files are the management system common to most CAD software programs.

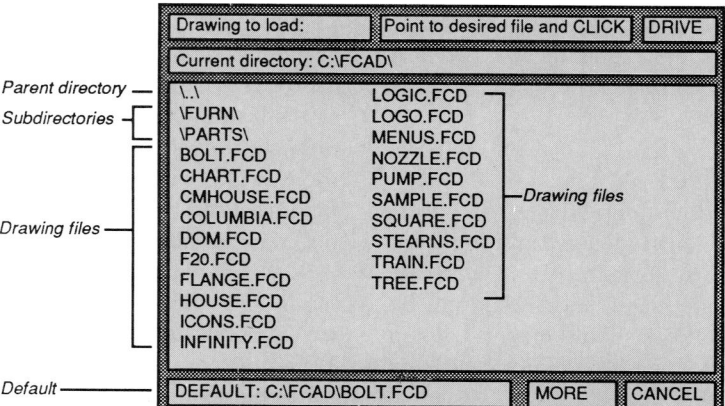

Fig. 8.11   When you access the CAD software directory, you will be able to examine the files that are created to serve the CAD user. *Courtesy of Evolution Computing.*

8.10 Deleting CAD Files

The DOS system allows CAD files to be deleted by entering the command DEL or ERASE at the DOS prompt, followed by the complete name of the file to be deleted. For example, if you type

DEL BEARING.BAK <return>

at the A:> prompt, the file bearing.bak will be erased from the diskette in drive A. If you have limited storage space on a diskette or hard drive, you may need to delete backup files one at a time as shown above. The reason for a backup file is to keep up to date with the latest copy of a drawing and provide a backup in case the current version is damaged or inadvertently erased. If a problem occurs with the current version, you have access to the backup file. To delete all of the backup files in drive B in one step, type

DEL B:*.BAK <return>

at the DOS prompt. Any file on drive B with a file extension bak will be erased with this command. Then the current drawing is loaded as an updated document in storage.

8.11 Copying CAD Files

In order to copy a drawing file from one disk to another, use the COPY command, followed by the drive and complete file name. For example, to copy the bearing.dwg file from the diskette in drive A to the diskette in drive B, type

COPY A:BEARING.DWG B: <return>

at the DOS prompt.

If you want to change the name of a file, you can use the copy command. For example, to retrieve a backup drawing called bearing.bak, you would rename it by typing

COPY A:BEARING.BAK BRG1.DWG B:
<return>

at the DOS prompt. This would copy the bearing backup file on drive A, change the name to BRG1, change the extension to DWG so the file could be read, and put the copy on drive B. This is typical of AutoCAD retrieval. The new drawing may be accessed now as BRG1.

8.12 CAD Files on the Hard Disk

The student of CAD is generally instructed to save drawings on a personal floppy diskette. The following procedure should be used to run the CAD program (AutoCAD in this example) and load or save drawings on diskette.

1. Type

CD\ACAD <return>

at the C:> prompt.

2. Type

ACAD <return>

at the C:> prompt to load the AutoCAD program.

The CAD program is now loaded and ready for use. Drawing names that students use should be preceded with B: or A: (when two drives are available for $5\frac{1}{4}''$ or $3\frac{1}{2}''$ floppy diskettes).

The CAD files stored on the hard disk can be viewed using the directory (DIR) command mentioned earlier. Students should keep their personal files on floppy diskettes (drive A or B), and not on the hard disk (drive C). When saving personal files, precede your file name with the drive letter A: or B: when beginning the CAD experience, and save your work on your personal floppy diskette.

8.13 Loading CAD Software

To install or load an additional CAD software program onto a computer's hard disk (you must have adequate storage), it must be compatible or configured with the DOS of the computer work-station. The peripheral input devices, such as the mouse, tablet with puck or cursor, must be specified or selected when the CAD software is configured during the installation of these "input tools," Fig. 8.12.

The "output tools" such as the monitor (CRT), printer, and plotter, are also specified and selected when the devices are configured for the system. CAD software is generally programmed to work with a variety of input and output devices available to the design team. CAD software is designed to work with various disk operating systems such as MS-DOS (Microsoft DOS) and UNIX. A typical example of software configuration options would list

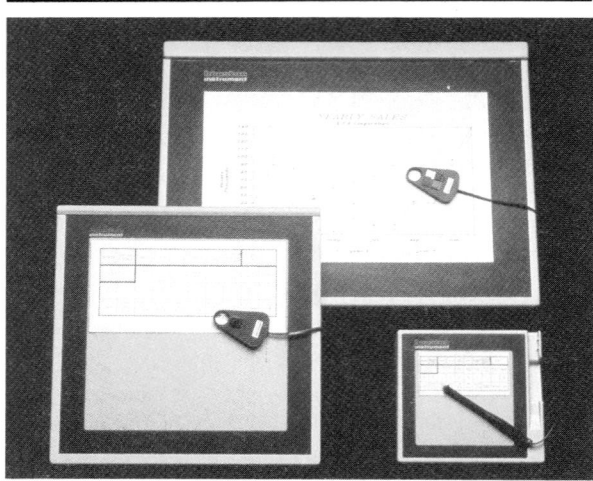

Fig. 8.12 Various input tools and output devices are configured into the CAD program before systems can start up. *Courtesy of Houston Instruments, Division of AMETEK.*

five or more plotters that would be compatible with a specific CAD software program (called environment) and ten or more different types of monitors.

Versatility and compatibility in CAD tools are needed for varying performance standards that bring high quality to drawing documents. One typical configuration might include a high resolution monitor and a high speed E size (36″ × 48″) plotter.

8.14 Software—Startup

Three CAD startup displays are now reviewed for three common software programs. After the CAD software is loaded and all peripheral devices have been installed and configured, the operation of the CAD program must be addressed. The CAD software can be loaded from sophisticated program management systems, or it may simply be loaded with keyed-in commands at the DOS system prompt.

AutoCAD Display

To load and start AutoCAD, type the symbol of the AutoCAD program at the DOS prompt

C:> ACAD

and then press the RETURN key to bring up the AutoCAD options, Fig. 8.13. This may be referred

to as "boot-up" of the program, and marks the beginning of the hands-on operation. If you select the appropriate number for a new or existing drawing, you will be viewing the program's display screen, Fig. 8.14. Examine the specific areas of the screen and note the drawing area limits.

CADKEY Display

In a like manner, you can call up the CADKEY software program by typing CADKEY at the C:> prompt and pressing the ENTER key. When you are prompted for a part name, type in the name blank and press ENTER again to start a new drawing, or you can recall an existing drawing from the disk file. When the CADKEY screen display becomes available, you can compare the initial features for the two CAD programs, AutoCAD, Fig. 8.14, and CADKEY, Fig. 8.15.

Note that the menu area for CADKEY is on the left side of the screen and dotted lines separate menu options from the status window (referred to as the intermediate modes). Another dotted line separates the status from the cursor tracking.

FastCAD Display

After your FastCAD software program has been installed, the DOS prompt will appear. To load the FastCAD program, type

FCAD   <return>

```
             A U T O C A D
Copyright (C) 1982,83,84,85,86,87 Autodesk, Inc.
Release 9.0 (9/17/87) IBM PC
Advanced Drafting Extensions 3
Serial Number:

Main Menu

   0.  Exit AutoCAD
   1.  Begin a NEW drawing +————————START HERE
   2.  Edit an EXISTING drawing
   3.  Plot a drawing
   4.  Printer Plot a drawing

   5.  Configure AutoCAD
   6.  File Utilities
   7.  Compile shape/font description file
   8.  Convert old drawing file

Enter selection: _
```

THE MAIN MENU

Fig. 8.13 AutoCAD screens allow you to start a new drawing or select a drawing from the file. *Courtesy of AutoDesk, Inc.*

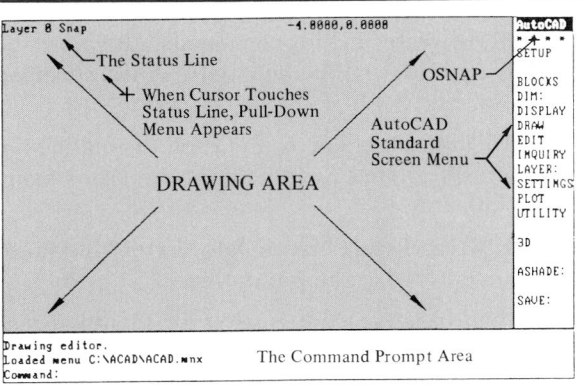

FOUR AREAS OF SCREEN

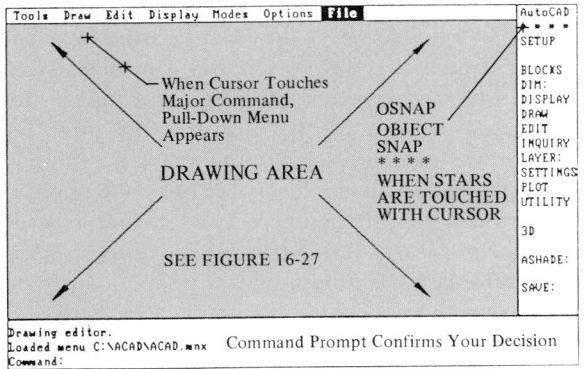

Fig. 8.14 The display screen of AutoCAD has a fixed menu area and a pull-down menu bar. Note the specific area of current info and prompt area. *Courtesy of AutoDesk, Inc.*

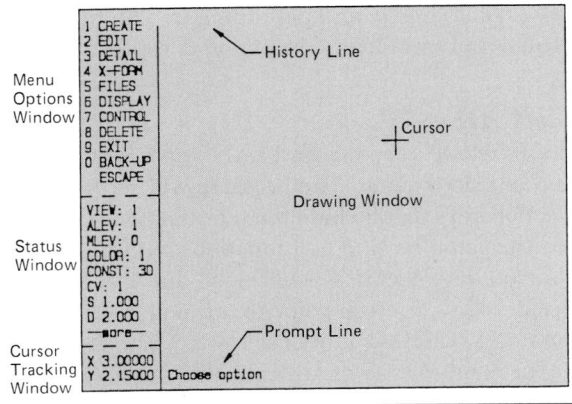

Fig. 8.15 The CADKEY display screen functions from left to right with menus located on the left. *Courtesy of CADKEY.*

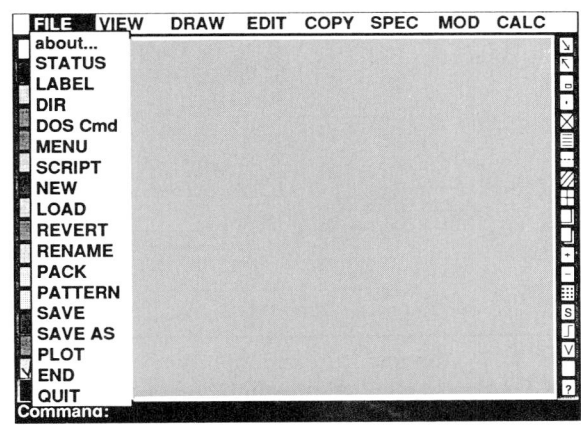

Fig. 8.16 The FastCAD display screen provides the user with a main menu bar across the top of the screen that has pull-down menus and functional icons on the right side. *Courtesy of Evolution Computing.*

at the DOS prompt. The software package will generate a display screen as shown in Fig. 8.16. This display screen has a color palette on the left margin of the screen, and the right margin contains icons for intermediate functions available while using the main menu. Now you can access these functions from the icon bar while working any of the drop down menus available from the top of the screen. Note the draw menu for geometric generators and the file menu at the upper left in Fig. 8.16. FastCAD uses an arrow for a cursor point and also has long Cartesian coordinates that serve as a cursor. (AutoCAD and CADKEY use a small cross cursor and also have a long horizontal and vertical line that serve as a Cartesian cursor.)

8.15 CAD Functions: Input

The three CAD displays reviewed have unique features for moving from one command to another and all have specific functions that may be selected with minimal effort. The keyboard of any computer contains the letters of the alphabet, numbers, the function keys (labeled F1–F10), and cursor keys labeled with arrows, Fig. 8.17. They are called cursor keys because they can move the cursor to specified locations on the computer display. The backspace key is useful for changing typed-in commands, altering the text composed for notes on a drawing, undoing characters, or erasing a whole line of text.

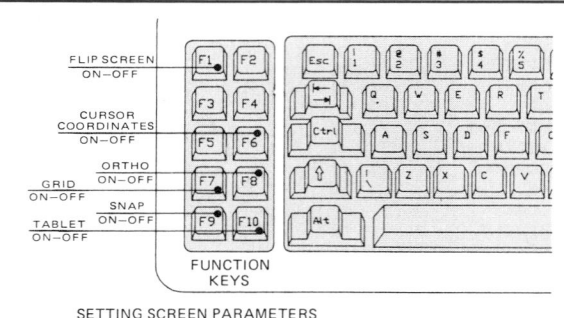

Fig. 8.17 Review the function keys used with AutoCAD. They speed up command changes.

The RETURN key is generally a larger key, and is used frequently for entering information that serves as a decision maker. Know your keyboard for effective control of the CAD software design program.

AutoCAD

Some of the AutoCAD functions are noted in Fig. 8.17 and are effective in setting up the working conditions of the screen work area for construction of geometric features. Note that F6 controls the cursor coordinates and F7 is able to turn the grid on and off. The control key can also manipulate functions when used with other specified keys. The AutoCAD user must know the following key combinations: CTRL-B for snap features that allows the cursor to move to units of measure (e.g., every quarter-inch), CTRL-C (to cancel), CTRL-D (coordinate display), CTRL-E (toggle crosshairs—the toggle acts as an on-off switch), CTRL-Q ("printer echo," which prints text only), CTRL-S (stop scrolling), and CTRL-O (ortho on or off—controls horizontal and vertical lines). The control key and the letter key have to be pressed simultaneously to effect a response. An example is pressing CTRL and Q at the same time for the text to echo to the printer. These combinations, when pressed, act as toggles, turning features on and off. AutoCAD has a user coordinate system (UCS) for 30 axes input.

CADKEY

This software program uses the keyboard for special descriptive functions.

1. ESC (escape) key will allow you to exit any function and return to the main menu.

2. CTRL (control) key is used to move into the intermediate mode commands. It must be pressed in combination with other specified keys, Fig. 8.18.

3. ALT (alternate) key is also used in conjunction with other keys to initiate intermediate mode commands.

4. BKSP (backspace) key deletes letters and numbers entered at the prompt line.

5. Space bar <space> is used for identifying or designating locations for general entry functions. The space bar can serve as a cursor button for entry.

The function keys F1–F10 can be used to select menus displayed on the screen. The successive changes of menu options are aligned numerically from top to bottom. With F1 on the top, press F1 three times, and successively, CREATE F1, LINE F1, and ENDPOINTS you can locate for lines will appear. This is only one of the three ways to enter commands. F10 returns you to the previous command or cancels the last selection mode.

Review the CADKEY display in Fig. 8.15 and note the optional control and alternate keys in Fig. 8.19 that allow the user to exercise specific functions. With the keyed-in responses, the user quickly modifies the CAD drafting tasks. The views in the intermediate mode are uniquely numbered: View 1 = top, 2 = front, 3 = back, 4 = bottom, 5 = right side, 6 = left side, 7 = isometric, and 8 = axonometric. The status window has three pages (which moves three options), and controls many performance features called attributes, such as layer, line style, color choice, and pen number. The VIEW and WORLD option allows 3D pictorial representation.

FastCAD

The function keys for FastCAD serve as a special kind of macro name. The program will recognize 40 function keys that include the ten standard (F1–F10) and the same keys in combinations with the CTRL (control) key, the SHF (shift) key, and the ALT (alternate) key. You can refer to a function key by its name (F1, CTRL-F1, ALT-F1, etc.) or just press a key or combination of keys. In the standard macro file FCAD.MAC, several function keys have been defined to select modifiers. For example, F1 enters the CEN (center) modifier; the function key F3 will

KEYS WITH SPECIAL FUNCTIONS

There are a number of assigned keys that will increase your productivity within the system. Keep in mind that some keyboards may have different names or symbols assigned to these keys (e.g. Carriage Return may appear as RETURN, ENTER, or <--). Take some time to review the following keys and their functions, and locate them on the keyboard.

ALT KEY - invokes Immediate Mode functions. When using this key, remember that it must be held down while the assigned mode key is pressed.

BKSP (<--) - deletes values entered on the prompt line before the RETURN key is pressed.

CTRL - invokes Immediate Mode functions. When using this key, remember that it must be held down while the assigned mode key is pressed.

ESCAPE (ESC) - returns you to the Main Menu without performing any functions.

FUNCTION KEYS:

F1-F9 - selects menu options displayed on the screen.

F10 - returns you to the previous menu or cancels the last entry or selection made.

The function keys usually are found to the left of, or above the main keyboard:

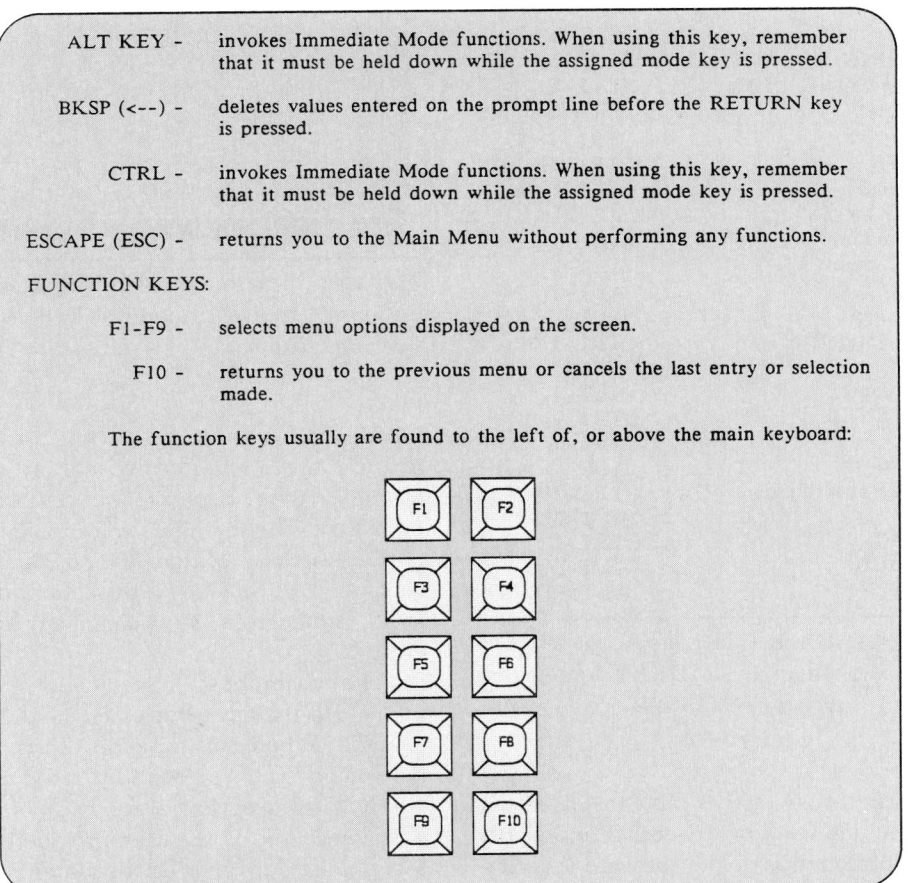

Fig. 8.18 Function keys F1–F10 are related to the menus in CADKEY and move quickly to process commands. *Courtesy of CADKEY.*

locate the midpoint, and F5 will locate the endpoint, of entities.

Note from the main menu bar across the top of the screen that the pull down option MOD (modify) was selected with a cursor arrow touching and lighting up the MOD portion of the bar, Fig. 8.20. The control keys serve to support the user as follows: CTRL-R, reenter or get cursor back; CTRL-S, scroll lock; CTRL-C, cancel current command; CTRL-D,

pause a macro program for direct input; and CTRL-A, pause macro for input with optional prompt.

FastCAD software has pull down menus, icons, and dialog boxes or the normal type-in keyboard equivalents. The CAD user can select drawing locations with a mouse or digitizer, or type the numeric coordinates, mixing methods at any time. New menus can be customized and scripts and macro libraries developed for repetitive tasks. The four win-

FUNCTION	IMMEDIATE MODE COMMAND
ARROWS IN/OUT	CTRL-A
AUTO scale	ALT-A
BACK-1 window	ALT-B
change DEPTH	CTRL-D
change VIEW	ALT-V
COLOR bar	ALT-X
cursor SNAPPING on/off	CTRL-X
CURSOR TRACKING display	CTRL-T
DELETE (single)	CTRL-Q
FILE PART (save)	CTRL-F
GRID ON/OFF	CTRL-G
LEVEL masking	ALT-N
LINE LIMITS switch	ALT-L
LINE TYPE menu	ALT-T
LINE WIDTH menu	ALT-Y
PAN	ALT-P
PEN # assignment	ALT-Z
RECALL last (undelete)	CTRL-U
REDRAW	CTRL-R
SCALE with center	ALT-S
set working LEVEL	CTRL-L
2D/3D switch	CTRL-W
type MASKING	ALT-M
VIEW/WORLD coordinates	CTRL-V
WINDOW	ALT-W
WITNESS LINE	CTRL-B
ZOOM-DOUBLE	ALT-D
ZOOM-HALF	ALT-H

Fig. 8.19 The ALT and CTRL keys are used to access functional changes in CADKEY screen display interaction. *Courtesy of CADKEY.*

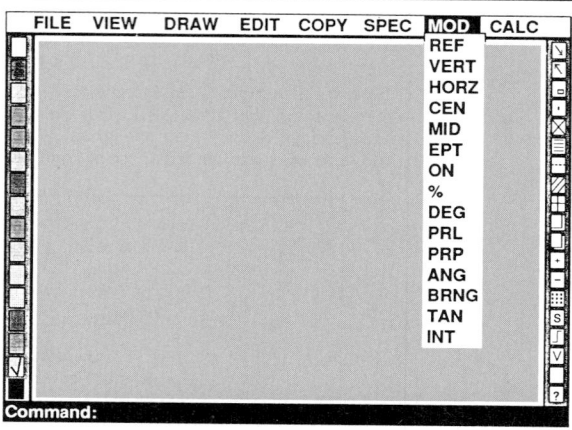

Fig. 8.20 The function keys are used to modify the options in the MOD menu of FastCAD. *Courtesy of Evolution Computing.*

mands such as ERASE, MOVE, SCALE, ROTATE, MIRROR (any angle), COPY, ROTATE COPY, MIRROR COPY, BREAK, TRIM, BEND, STRETCH, and CONNECT. The modifiers refer to specific points on entities such as center, Fig. 8.20, endpoint, percent, degree, tangent, intersection, or perpendicular to, parallel to, or any point at any angle to existing entities.

The capabilities of a specific software are numerous and cannot be addressed in the limits of one chapter. When you examine the commands available on any CAD screen illustrated in this chapter, you have an overview of the work of a programmer who keeps the CAD user provided with drawing techniques for graphic document development. FastCAD has produced 3D generated programs that produce wire-frame solids and modeling.

8.16 Drawing with CAD Software

The geometry that is created, drawn, or generated with CAD programs is generally referred to as entities or elements. The geometric elements (or bits and pieces) are individually constructed figures or groups of elements that consist of points, lines, arcs, circles, rectangles, polygons, splines, cross-hatching, dimensions, and notes. These basic building units are selected from the menu and constructed on specific graphic locations of the monitor screen by the CAD user. Many CAD users can store standard drawing symbols (called blocks) and use overlays on the digitizer for retrieval, Fig. 8.21.

dows are simultaneously active, and the user can draw a line from one window to another and watch the effects in both windows. The software is an object-oriented system. When you draw a circle on the screen, it stores the mathematical definition of a circle rather than just the screen image. When you are ready to change the circle after drawing it, simply touch a point on the circle and the software knows exactly what object to change. The programmer uses floating point numbers to represent entities (any geometric form) and their exact placement. Therefore, the largest entity on your drawing can be at least a million times larger than your smallest. The CAD user can zoom in or out at any selected multiple and place entities with precision.

Dimensioning is truly associative, so when you stretch or shrink a part of your drawing with editing commands, dimensions are automatically updated. No erasing is necessary to reenter the descriptive new dimensions. The CAD user has editing com-

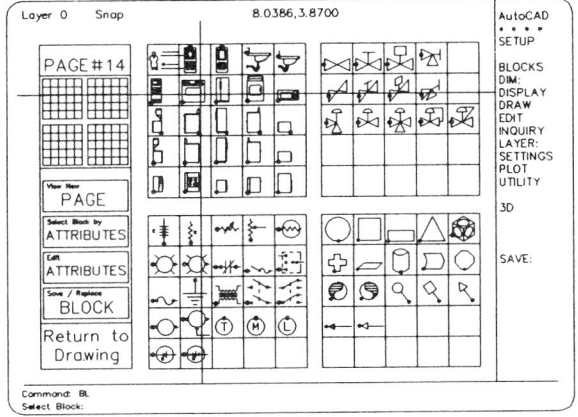

Fig. 8.21 CAD users can develop library symbols for their own software program or use software libraries available from software developers. *Courtesy of Softsource.*

8.17 Typical CAD Construction

The following sequential experiences will introduce the CAD user to the basic interaction necessary for constructing a CAD drawing.

Typical constructions
 Creating line and point.
 Creating arc and circle.
 Creating polygons and splines.
 Creating dimensions.
 Creating text and notes.
 Creating data definition with LIST or STATUS
  commands.
 Creating cross-hatching

 The CAD user will learn how to manipulate the features of screen display.

Typical screen display features
 Cursor control.
 Windows.
 Zoom.
 Ortho-Cartesian layout.
 Grid–snap.
 Command prompts.
 Layers–redraw.

The CAD user will learn how to change graphic documents.

Typical modifying (editing) tasks
 Delete.
 Trim–extend.
 Move–scale.
 Copy–mirror.
 Rotate.

Typical utilities
 Print/Plot (creates a hard copy).

 The examples that follow are considered typical, although each CAD program will use its own selective terminology and sequences for execution.

8.18 Drawing a Line

The simplest entity to construct is a line. The techniques for construction are similar for all CAD software. Choose the command LINE from the DRAW menu. FastCAD uses a pointer cursor (other CAD software uses a crosshair cursor) to select the pull down DRAW menu.

1. Move the mouse or digitizer stylus until the pointer on the screen is over the word DRAW in the menu bar at the top of the screen. Press the left mouse button, then release the button. A new column of words drops down on the screen, Fig. 8.22. Note that the top word is POINT, and

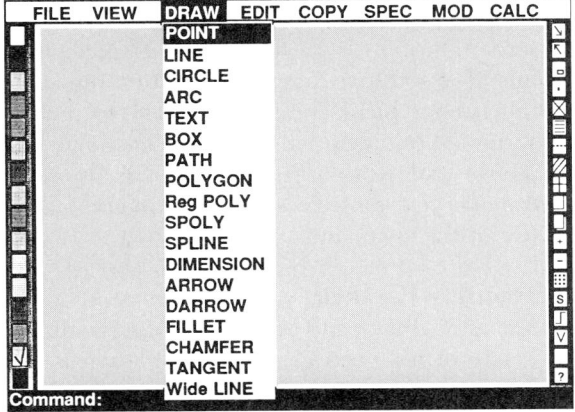

Fig. 8.22 The pull-down menu provides access to 18 DRAW features. *Courtesy of Evolution Computing.*

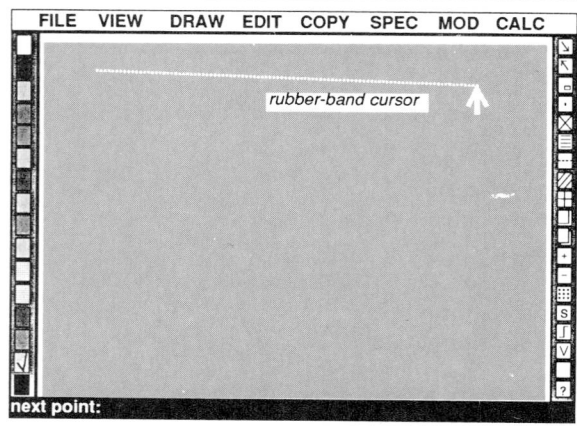

Fig. 8.23   The creation of a line can be sequentially developed with prompts "next point." *Courtesy of Evolution Computing.*

it is highlighted. You have just "pulled down" the DRAW menu. If an error occurs, press the right mouse button and try again. As you pull the mouse toward you, FastCAD highlights each option as you move down the menu.

2.   Choose the command LINE from the DRAW menu. The prompt reads "1st point" and displays a crosshairs cursor.

3.   Select a point near the upper left corner of the drawing window by moving the crosshairs there, and press the left mouse button.

4.   The prompt changes to "Next point," Fig. 8.23. The arrow pointer is now back. Move the arrow to the right. The line stretches to follow the mouse movement. Select a second endpoint by moving the mouse to the right side of the screen, and press the left button to accept the line. The software draws a line entity, replacing the rubber band cursor. It is easy to draw a series of connected lines. You can move the mouse and repeat the line process as many times as you want. Press the right mouse button to exit the command.

Horizontal–Vertical

Lines may be drawn and controlled as horizontal in the *x*-axis or as vertical lines in the *y*-axis. In AutoCAD it is the ORTHO option that controls these lines; in CADKEY it is the LINE option HRZ/VRT; and in FastCAD the icon bar for ORTHO switch is touched with the cursor.

8.19 Line Types

There are generally six or more line styles on a CAD drawing, and they can be changed by selecting one of the options. The CAD designer can change line styles, colors, and line widths. The designer can also create those lines at various levels for various pen widths in the plotter. Construction lines may be used on a specific level and masked or erased before plotting the drawing. Therefore, the layout makes it easier to assemble the graphic geometry in a technical document.

8.20 Drawing Points

This option is selected from the DRAW menu and is the first option.

1.   Select POINT.

2.   The software response is "Point at."

3.   Move the crosshairs anywhere within the drawing area and press left mouse button.

4.   The program draws the point. You can draw as many points (often called pixels) as you need without reselecting the command.

5.   Press the right mouse button to stop drawing points.

COMMAND EXAMPLES

NOTE: Commands are followed with a colon (:).

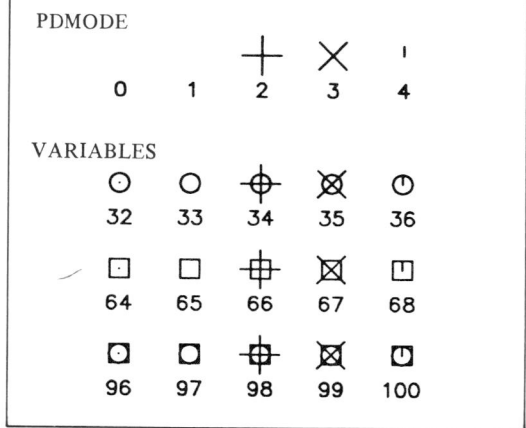

Fig. 8.24   The CAD designer has a variety of ways to represent a point with AutoCAD software. *Courtesy of AutoDesk, Inc.*

Some software programs allow you to select various types of points. AutoCAD has an assortment of points you can select as you create your graphic communication, Fig. 8.24.

8.21 Drawing Circles

Software programs allow you to choose among five methods for entering or creating circles. Three ways are illustrated in the dialog box in Fig. 8.25. This is a typical construction procedure for the CAD user.

1. Select CIRCLE from the DRAW menu and the dialog box appears.

2. Select P|Center & Point from dialog box. The prompt will read "Center point (prior)." FastCAD remembers the x and y coordinates of the last circle drawn, and will offer it as the default (suggested) center for this circle.

3. Press the right mouse button to accept the default instead of a new center. The prompt reads "Point on circle," Fig. 8.26, and then you rubber band the cursor from the center to the new location.

4. Select a point inside the existing circle. The circles can be concentric with the same circle.

5. The prompt may read "center point," but you may exit by pressing the right mouse button twice to cancel the command.

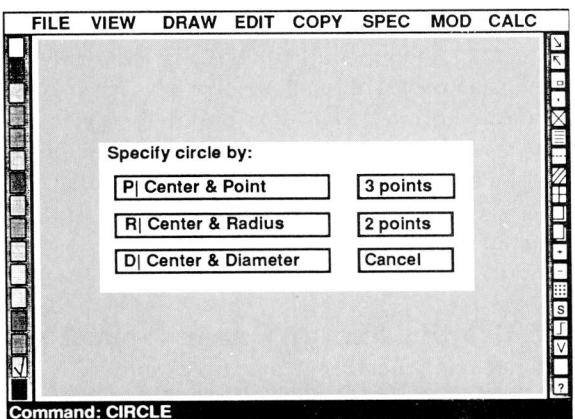

Fig. 8.25 The designer is able to respond to the construction techniques of a circle through the dialog box. *Courtesy of Evolution Computing.*

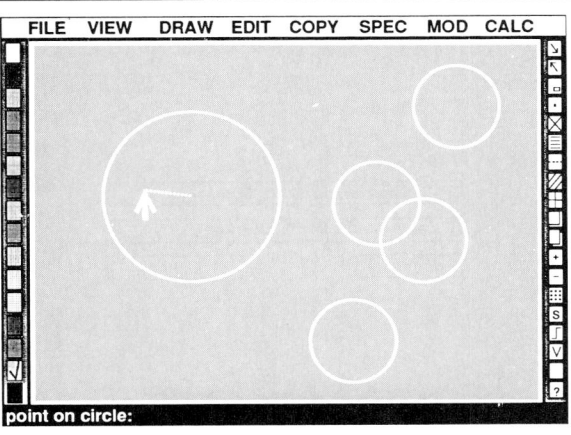

Fig. 8.26 CAD offers visual control to designers as they move the cursor around the display area to create circles. *Courtesy of Evolution Computing.*

8.22 Drawing Arcs

CAD software allows you to draw arcs by

1. Specifying the center, radius, and the starting and ending angles.

2. Specifying the center, start point, and end angle.

3. Selecting three points on the arc.

Three Point Arc

This method is used as a typical example.

1. Select ARC from the DRAW menu. A dialog box is displayed with options, Fig. 8.27.

2. Select 3 points from the lower left corner of the screen.

3. The CAD program displays crosshairs and prompts "1st point."

4. Select the points as noted in Fig. 8.28. The program will mark the 3 points you locate "2nd point" and "3rd point." The prompt will initiate "1st point" again, and you can draw a series of arcs.

5. Press the right mouse button to leave the ARC command.

8.23 Drawing Polygons

A polygon is a closed many-sided geometric figure. The simplest or base polygon is a triangle, and the

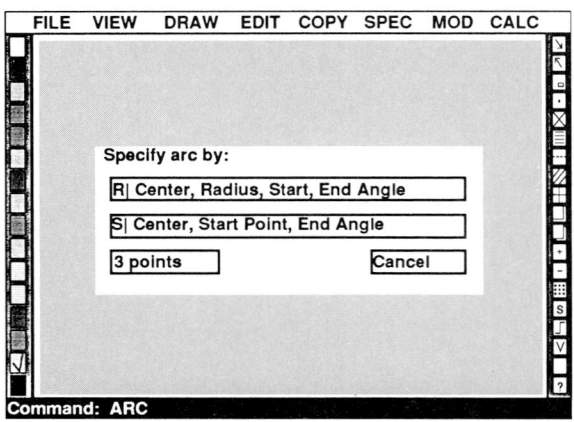

Fig. 8.27 The construction of arcs is easily controlled through CAD software options. *Courtesy of Evolution Computing.*

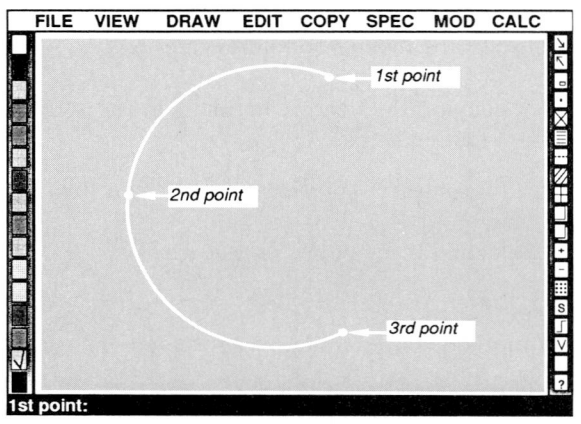

Fig. 8.28 Interactive CAD is prompting decisions for geometric construction. *Courtesy of Evolution Computing.*

system shown can create figures with up to 126 sides.

1. Select POLYGON from the DRAW menu. The prompt reads "1st point."

2. Use the crosshairs to locate a point near the lower left corner of the window. The CAD program replaces the crosshairs with a rubber band cursor, Fig. 8.29.

3. Use the cursor to locate node points 2 and 3. When the cursor is moved back to point 1, the prompt "next point" is displayed. The CAD pro-

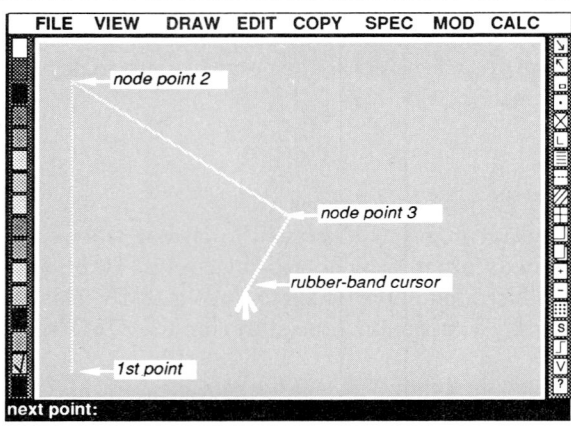

Fig. 8.29 The software allows screen display to move from crosshairs to a pointed cursor that can rubber band (move a line) to form a polygon. *Courtesy of Evolution Computing.*

gram closes the polygon automatically when the right mouse button is pressed.

There are other ways to create a polygon, and CAD programs vary in the specific methods that are available. Specifying the center, a specified radius, and the number of sides is another common construction method.

8.24 The LIST Command

CAD software can generate data that provides the designer with information about the geometry created. The LIST command in this program is located in the EDIT menu. Mathematical data is stored to define the entities of the geometry formed. It is automatically printed out. For example, select any point on a circle. The circle, layer, center point, radius, circumference, and area are printed. The STATUS command also provides current working data, Fig. 8.30.

8.25 Drawing Smooth Curves (Splines)

Drawing smooth and regular curves (splines) is like drawing smooth polygons. You can enter a series of node points, making a frame for the curve. This CAD program, shown in Figs. 8.31 and 8.32, calculates and draws a curve that goes through specified points.

```
Command: STATUS

49 entities in SAMPLE
Limits are        X:    0.0000    11.0000   (Off)
                  Y:    0.0000     8.5000
Drawing uses      X:    3.1250    12.5000   ** Over
                  Y:    1.3333     7.4500
Display shows     X:    2.0000     7.3333
                  Y:    4.0000     8.0000
Insertion base is X:    5.0000   Y:   6.0000   Z:   0.0000
Snap resolution is X:   0.2500   Y:   0.2500
Grid spacing is   X:    0.5000   Y:   0.5000

Current layer:      FOUNDATION
Current color:      BYLAYER -- 1 (red)
Current linetype: CONTINUOUS
Current elevation:     0.0000   thickness:     0.0000
Axis off    Fill on    Grid on    Ortho off   Qtext off    Snap off    Tablet off
Object snap modes:  Endpoint, Midpoint
Free RAM: 13283 bytes        Free disk: 867584 bytes
I/O page space: 124K bytes    Extended I/O page space: 1024K bytes
```

Fig. 8.30 Computers track the graphic information displayed on the screen (STATUS) and can provide data resulting from construction. AutoCAD, CAD-KEY, and FastCAD are capable of providing calculations to the designer. *Courtesy of AutoDesk, Inc.*

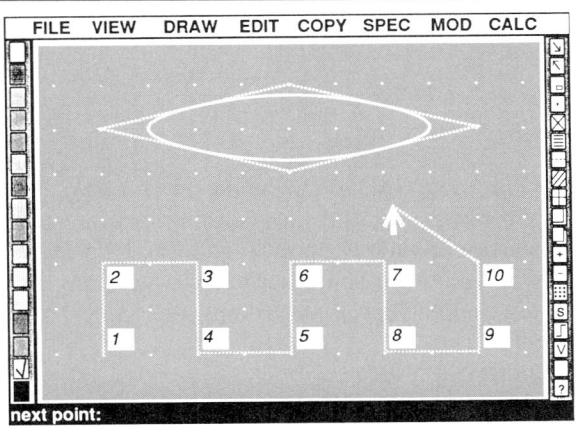

Fig. 8.31 The computer is capable of generating smooth curves from data points provided on the screen. *Courtesy of Evolution Computing.*

1. Select SPOLY from the DRAW menu. The screen prompts you to locate "1st point."

2. Use the crosshairs to select the first grid point. Use the rubber band cursor to locate the "next point." Form the diamond shape for the ellipse and the square units to form the spline curve. A smooth spline must have at least 3 points, but no more than 126 node points in this program.

8.26 Creating Text

1. From the DRAW menu select TEXT. The prompt reads "Text." Type the words "Concentric Arcs"

FastCAD draws the spline curve:

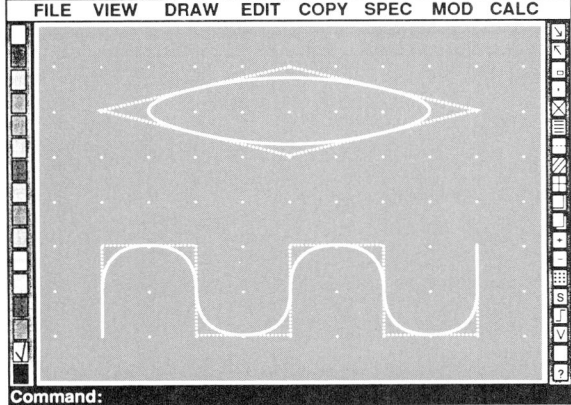

Fig. 8.32 The spline or smooth curve polygon provides a method of drawing irregular curves. *Courtesy of Evolution Computing.*

and press RETURN to end the line. The prompt reads "Text origin [next]:."

2. Select origin (below "Concentric Arcs"), Fig. 8.33. The CAD program draws the text at the point selected.

3. Press the left mouse button to repeat the text command. The prompt reads "Text."

4. Type "This is more text" and press RETURN. The prompt reads "Text origin [next]:"; again, locate a starting point. Press RETURN to accept the location of the text.

Setting Text Properties

The text selected in the previous figure was horizontal and left justified (aligned). You can use the SPEC (specifications) menu to set these properties for the text you want to create.

1. Select TEXT SPECS from the SPEC menu.

2. Review Specify text: and Justify text:, and select the appropriate features for your design as you are prompted by the dialog box.

Other CAD programs offer various font types and sizes, and provide the user with other interactive alternatives.

8.27 Dimensioning

CAD automatically calculates linear and angular dimensions and can provide the DIM FORMAT from

The prompt reads "text: ".

Type **This is more text** and press **RETURN**.

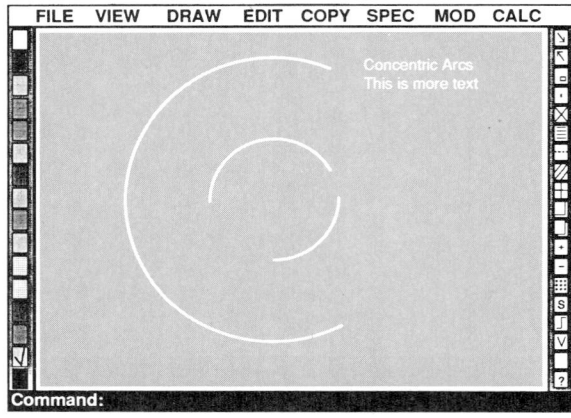

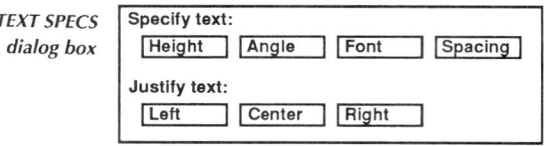

TEXT SPECS dialog box

Fig. 8.33 The TEXT menu provides options for placement of notes and has a choice of sizes. *Courtesy of Evolution Computing.*

the SPEC menu. You can select the Dimension Format from a dialog box. For example, you may choose inches for this experience and move to the next dialog box for Dimension Properties. This will allow you to set the new properties.

Linear Dimensions
You may select Horizontal, Vertical, or Parallel dimensioning. Fig. 8.34 illustrates the typical results from the placement of these dimensions. Horizontal dimensioning measures only the distance along the x-axis between two fixed points. It ignores any vertical distance between the points. Vertical dimensions can only be measured along the y-axis between two fixed points. The parallel dimension can measure actual distances at any given angle between two fixed points.

Angular Dimensions
CAD software can provide information that measures angles (in degrees) and locates dimensions when prompts are entered with Center, Start Point, and End Angle ARC. This is similar to creating arcs. You can edit the location of an angular dimension

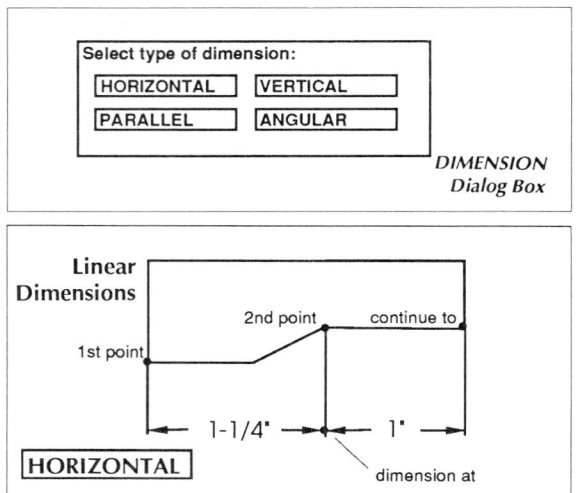

Fig. 8.34 The placement of dimensions is entirely up to CAD operators and they must know how to describe the detailed design. *Courtesy of Evolution Computing.*

with the STRETCH option in the EDIT menu. The angular dimension is drawn counterclockwise from the starting to ending point (Fig. 8.35). Other CAD programs offer similar dimension routines from their menus, and each program has specific options.

Drawing Arrows
The leader line common to machine operations or notes is created in this FastCAD program with the location of three points, as illustrated in Fig. 8.36.

8.28 Overview
There are many pages written on CAD instruction for creating the geometry of a technical document. This chapter has attempted to deliver several of the basic offerings of some of the leading CAD programs available for the microcomputer workstation. Among other important features of CAD programs is their ability to maneuver and display features on the screen for easier construction, some of which are

1. Digitizing overlay–tablet menu.
2. Pan.
3. Redraw.
4. Snap–grid–object.

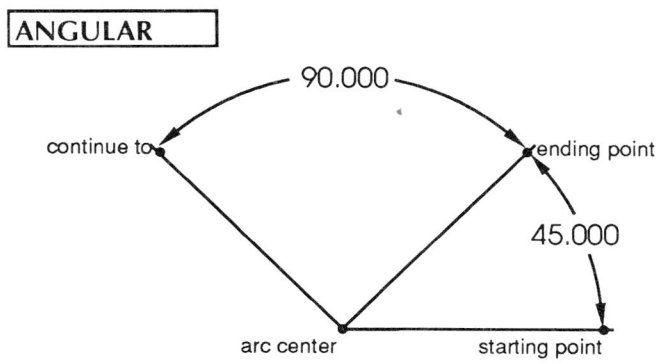

Fig. 8.35 Angular features are easily measured and described with the dimension menus. *Courtesy of Evolution Computing.*

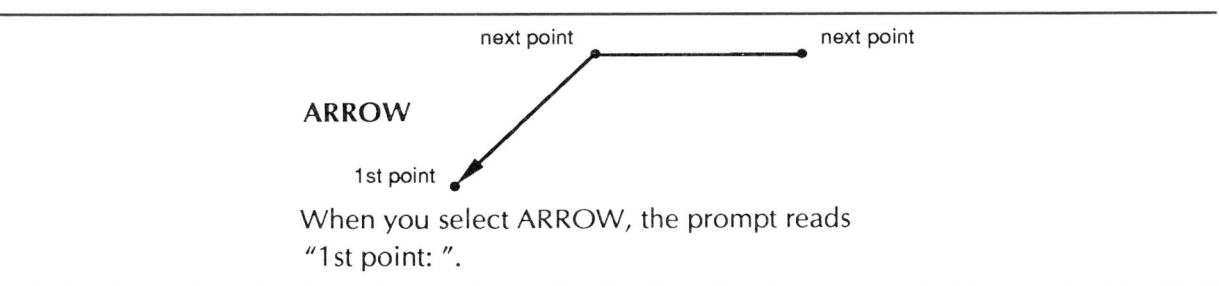

When you select ARROW, the prompt reads "1st point: ".

Fig. 8.36 Leader lines take information to specific features of a design drawing. *Courtesy of Evolution Computing.*

5. Build layers.

6. Move.

7. Scale.

8. Copy.

9. Mirror.

10. Rotate.

11. Mask.

12. Zoom.

There also are several modifying or editing features, for example,

1. Fillets.

2. Trim and extend (sketch).

3. Break.

4. Group.

5. Create segments.

6. Recall.

7. Chamfer.

8. Stretch.

The illustrations for some of these display screen features and modifying or editing capabilities are shown in Figs. 8.37–8.45.

The CAD user is responsible for preparing engineering documents that are an integral part of the total manufacturing process, Fig. 8.46. The ability to interact with all forms of technical information increases the significant role of the drafting technician.

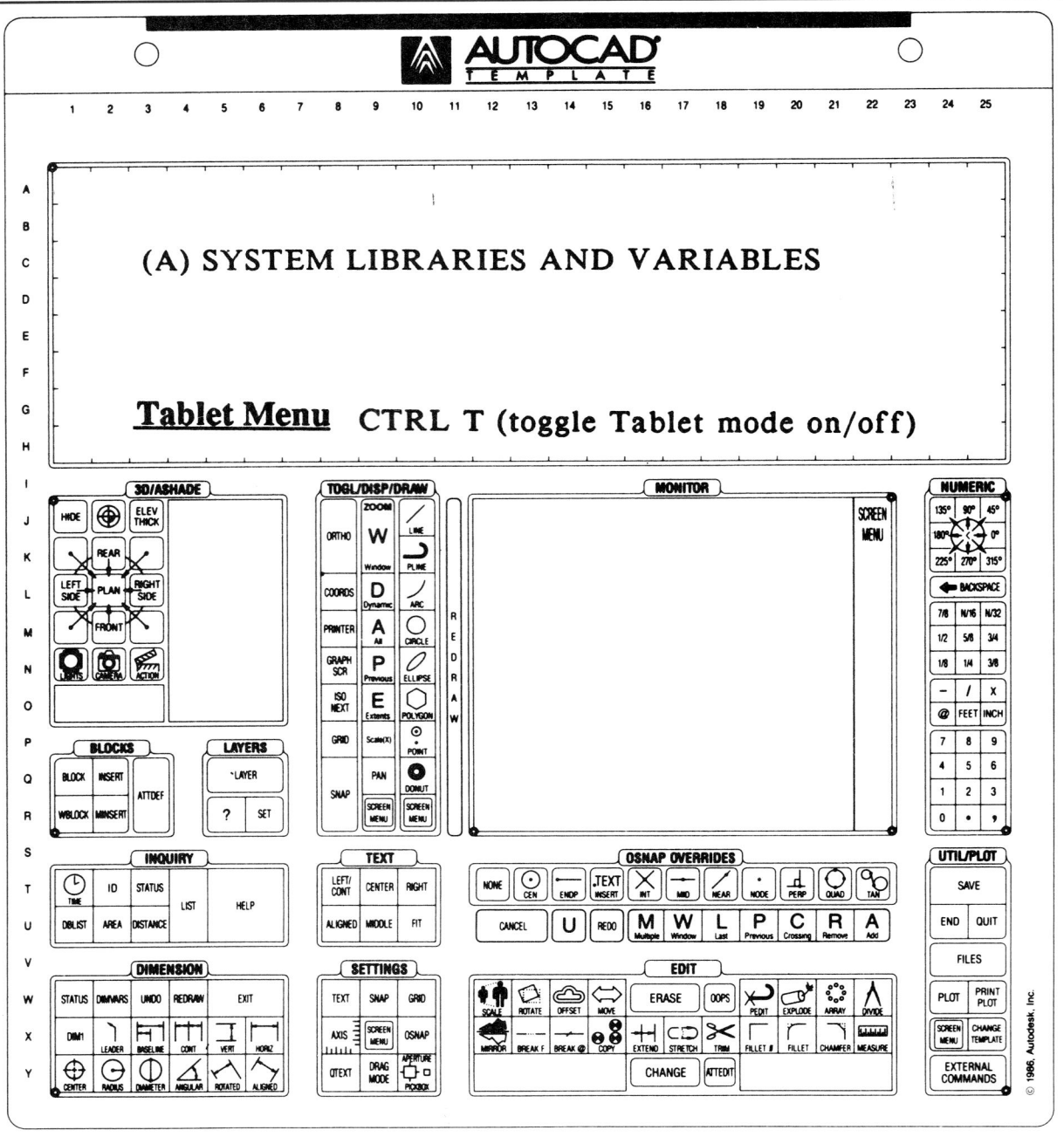

Fig. 8.37 The tablet menu for use with AutoCAD's standard tablet template uses four menu areas. It operates in conjunction with the screen menu to provide easy access to all AutoCAD facilities. *Courtesy of AutoDesk, Inc.*

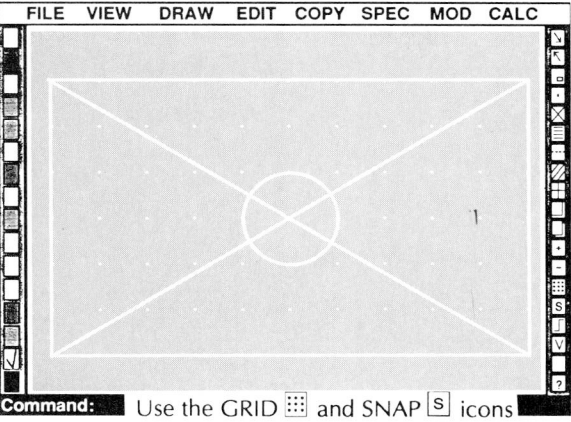

Draw a box, two lines, and a center & point circle, like the illustration. (Make the box 10 units wide and 6 units high. Put the circle's center where the lines cross, and the "point on circle" one unit to the right.)

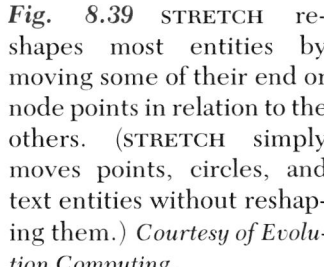

Fig. 8.38 The grid features are used for layout and snap grid for control of input. *Courtesy of Evolution Computing.*

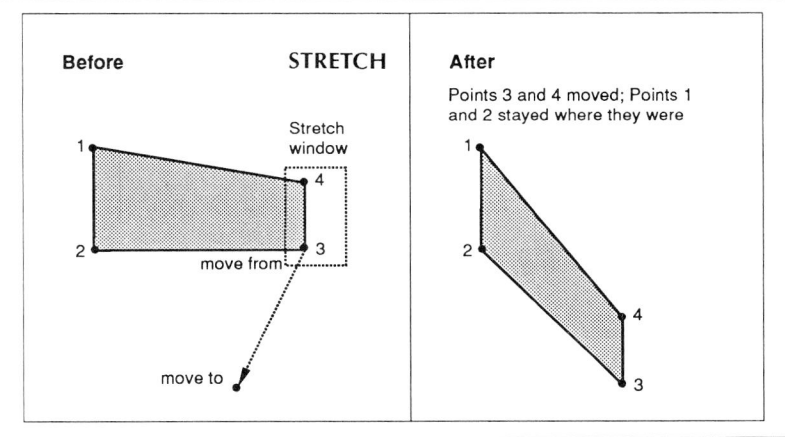

Fig. 8.39 STRETCH reshapes most entities by moving some of their end or node points in relation to the others. (STRETCH simply moves points, circles, and text entities without reshaping them.) *Courtesy of Evolution Computing.*

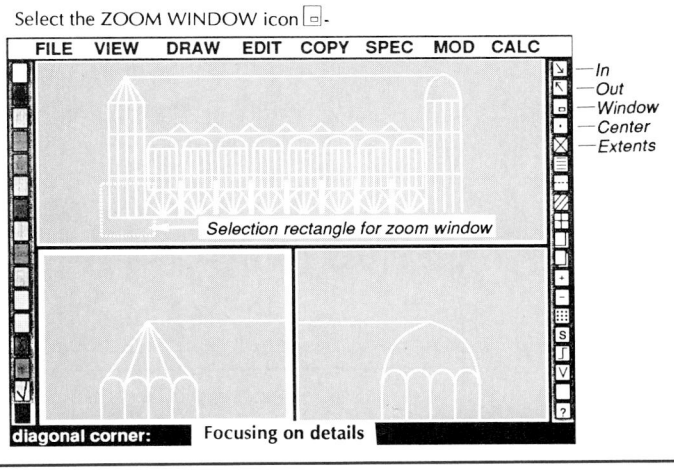

Fig. 8.40 The zoom option is capable of moving in and out and facilitates a close-up view of small details. Windows can be created and are edited interactively as shown. *Courtesy of Evolution Computing.*

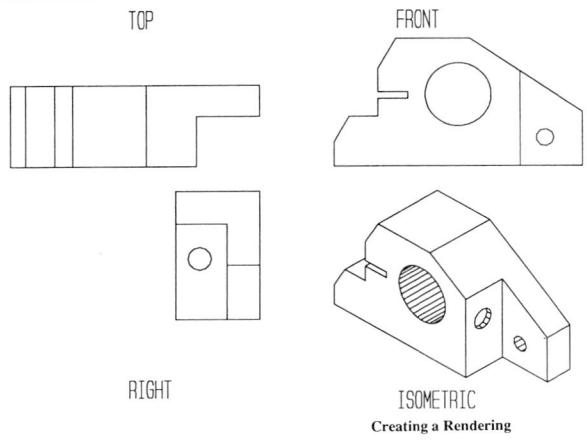

TOP   FRONT

RIGHT   ISOMETRIC

Creating a Rendering

Fig. 8.41 The three-dimensional drawing is achieved with the three-axes development in CAD software. *Courtesy of CADKEY.*

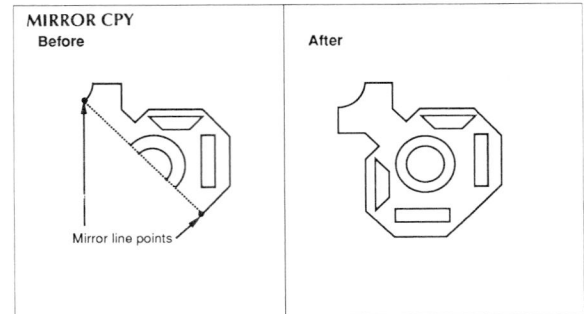

MIRROR CPY
Before   After

Mirror line points

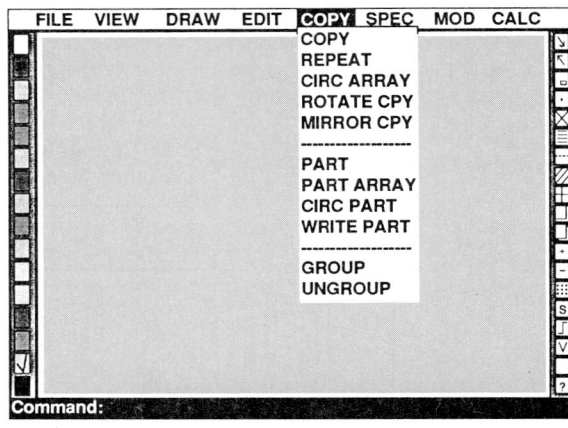

FILE   VIEW   DRAW   EDIT   COPY   SPEC   MOD   CALC

COPY
REPEAT
CIRC ARRAY
ROTATE CPY
MIRROR CPY

PART
PART ARRAY
CIRC PART
WRITE PART

GROUP
UNGROUP

Command:

Fig. 8.42 (a) The mirror imaging of a design is simply developed for accurate layout of symmetrical designs. (b) Commands in the COPY menu add new entities to your drawing by duplicating existing entities. *Courtesy of Evolution Computing.*

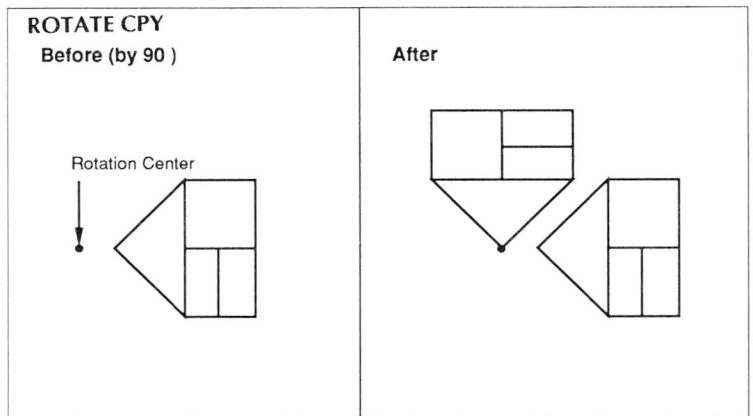

ROTATE CPY
Before (by 90)   After

Rotation Center

Fig. 8.43 The copy and rotate modifiers are capable of providing easy repetitive images.

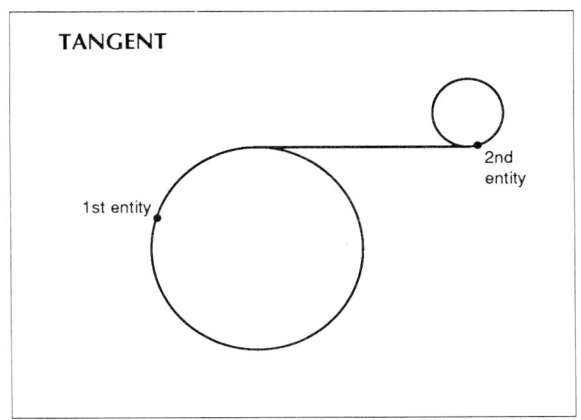

Fig. 8.44 When you select TANGENT, FastCAD prompts you for "1st entity:" and "2nd entity:". Use the crosshairs and left button to select two circles or arcs. FastCAD draws the tangent line (on the side of the circle or arc that you selected). *Courtesy of Evolution Computing.*

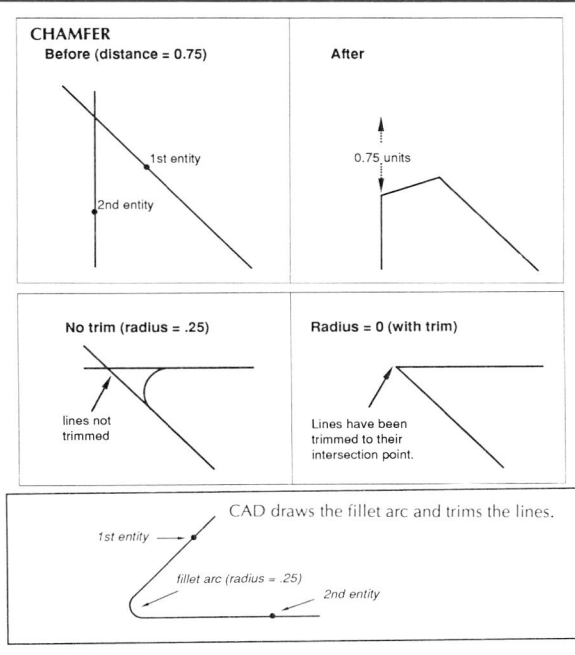

Fig. 8.45 The modifiers of software can create chamfers and fillets. *Courtesy of Evolution Computing.*

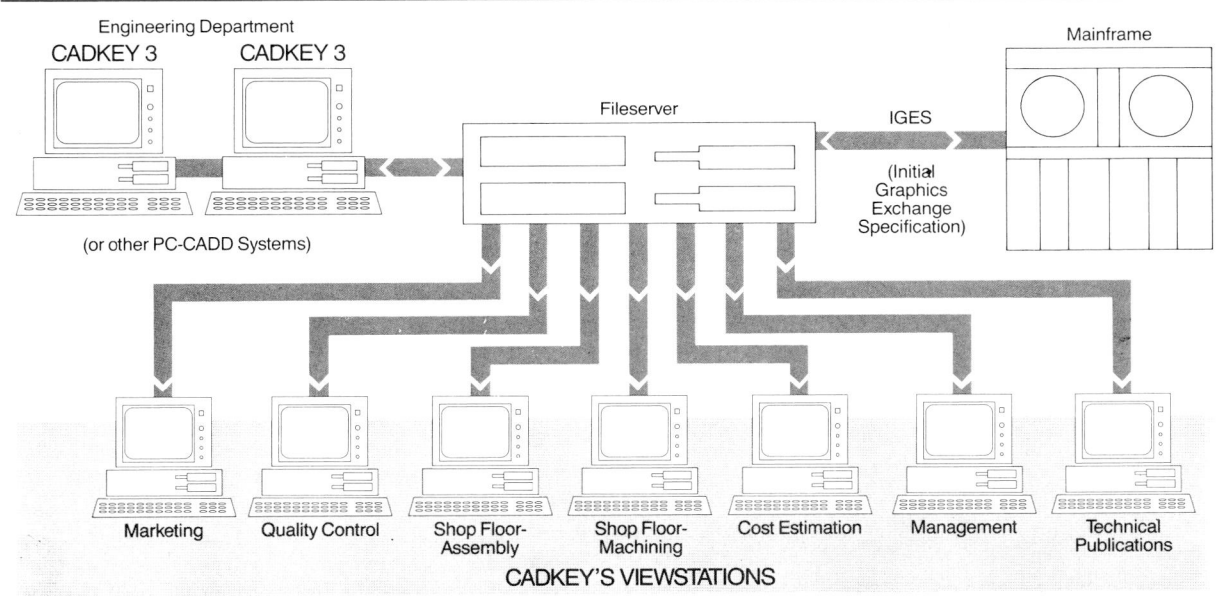

Fig. 8.46 Information is accessed from mainframes or workstations using IGES and a fileserver. Then View-stations in key departments allow for design input. This is an overview of the total Engineering Team at work. *Courtesy of CADKEY.*

CAD Problems

The problems in this chapter will allow the future CAD system user to become aware of the way CAD software solves some typical geometric construction that is similar from one software program to another. However, these problems are included for the student who is prepared to solve some problems of change. All the problems illustrated have been prepared on a CAD system. Prepare the required CAD drawing problems as shown with your CAD system and produce a hard copy with a printer or plotter for approval.

Additional problems in convenient form for solution are presented in the worksheets at the back of this book. Refer to Drawings 8-1 to 8-5 and accompanying instructions.

Prob. 8.1   Prepare a list of the software commands illustrated in this chapter. Each CAD software program is different. How many commands have been created for the AutoCAD user?

Prob. 8.2   Prepare a list of modifying (or editing) illustrations shown in this chapter. How many editing features are listed on the AutoCAD template illustrated in this chapter?

Prob. 8.3   The unknown distance KA in Fig. 8.47 has been determined and the angle measured with the use of AutoCAD. You are to recreate this problem with your CAD system, changing the 90° angle at H to 75°, and then determine the angles at K and A and length of line KA.

Prob. 8.4   Prepare a revised version of the CAD drawing, Fig. 8.48, by increasing the radius 0.40 to 0.4375 and changing the slot dimension 1.60 to 1.70.

Prob. 8.5   Prepare a detailed CAD drawing of the Safety Key, Fig. 8.49, with the following changes. Correct the right-side view and add the missing dimension 0.40. Examine the placement of dimensions and relocate where necessary. Change 1.12 to 1.25 and add the difference to dimension 4.70.

Prob. 8.6   Revise Fig. 8.50 using the "F" notation for the frontal projections instead of the V as shown. Change the 45° angle to 40°, and determine how much the dimension 2.121 changes.

Prob. 8.7   Using a CAD system, determine the true length of lines AD and CD, Fig. 8.51, when the horizontal projection of point A is relocated to a new coordinate reading of (0, 3.125) and the horizontal projection of point D is relocated to a Cartesian coordinate of (1.75, 1.625). Revise the drawing using the "F" notation for the frontal projections instead of the V notation as shown. What is the new slope of line CD?

Prob. 8.8   Create a revised CAD drawing from Fig. 8.52, stretching the 5.5000 inch dimension to 5.75 and adjusting dimensions as necessary.

Prob. 8.9   Develop a CAD working drawing of the 2″ thick Cam Lock, Fig. 8.53, and create necessary views to clarify the detailing (pictorial, sections, or auxiliary views).

Prob. 8.10   Using a CAD system, create the profile of the Swivel Joint, Fig. 8.54. Examine the proportions of the drawing and develop alternative dimensions if a three-view drawing is assigned. A pictorial is optional.

Prob. 8.11   Using a CAD system, produce a hard copy drawing of the Plastics Molder Plate shown in Fig. 2.77. Omit all dimensions on the final drawing.

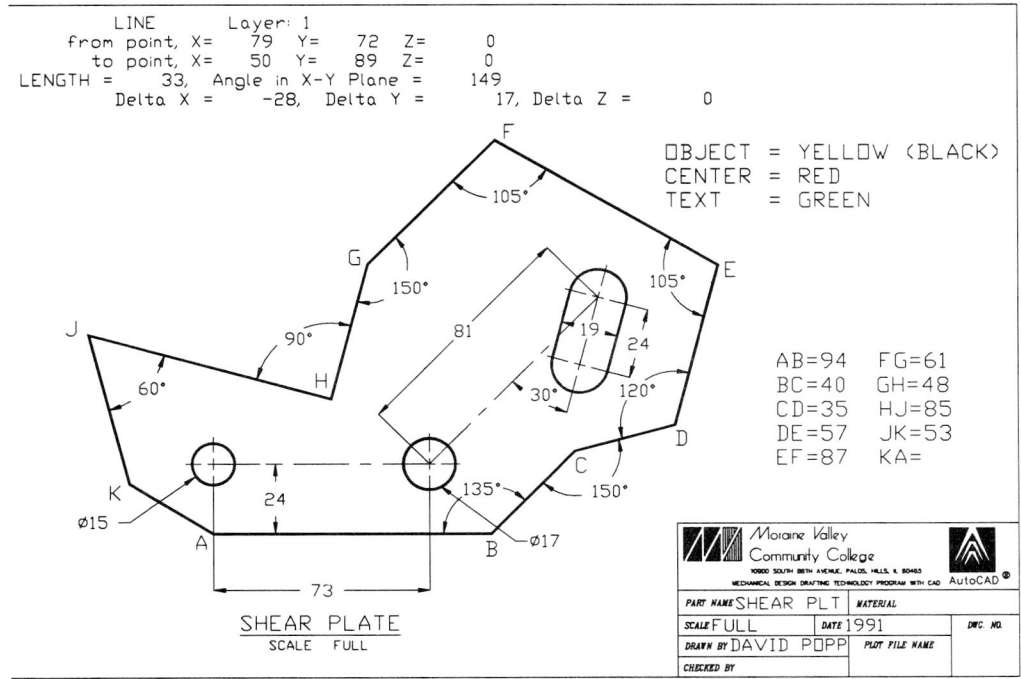

Fig. 8.47 Shear Plate (Prob. 8.3). *Courtesy of Moraine Valley Community College, David Popp.*

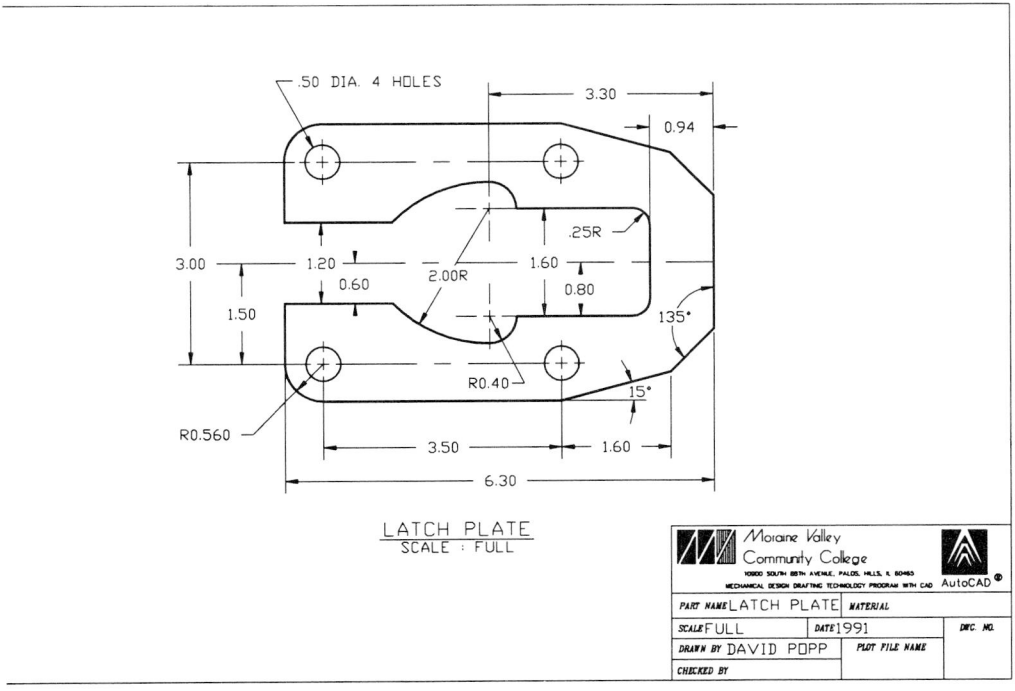

Fig. 8.48 Latch Plate (Prob. 8.4). *Courtesy of Moraine Valley Community College, David Popp.*

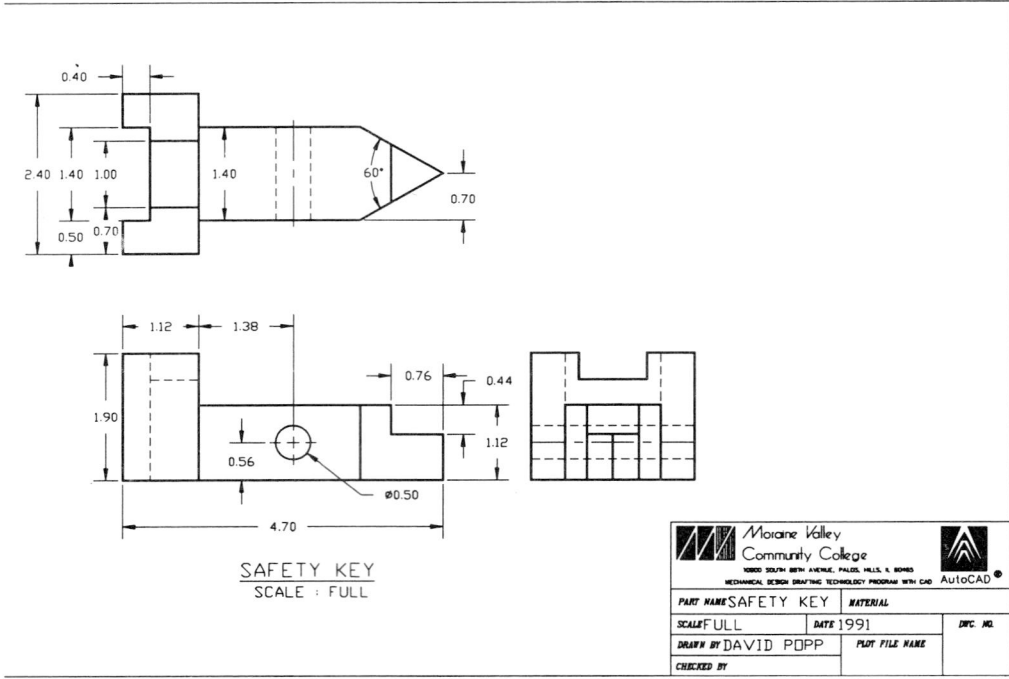

Fig. 8.49   Safety Key (Prob. 8.5). *Courtesy of Moraine Valley Community College, David Popp.*

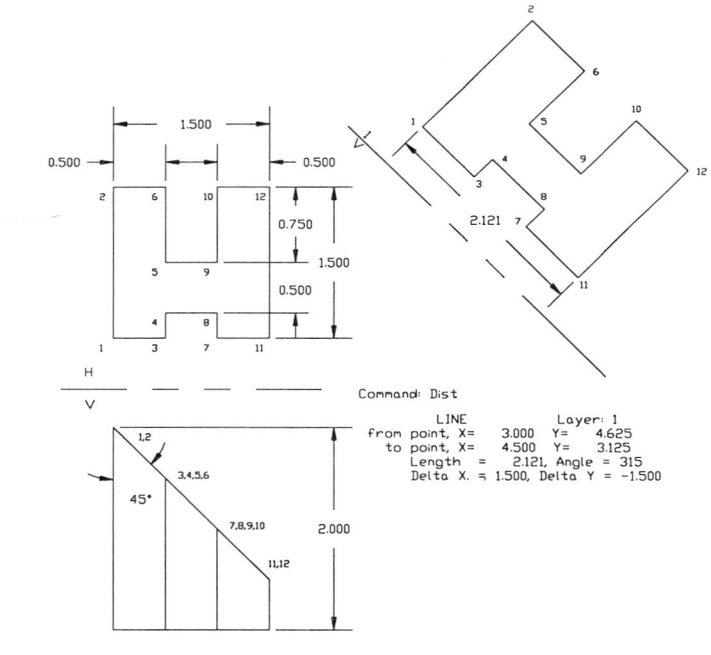

Created with AutoCAD

Fig. 8.50   H-Block (Prob. 8.6).

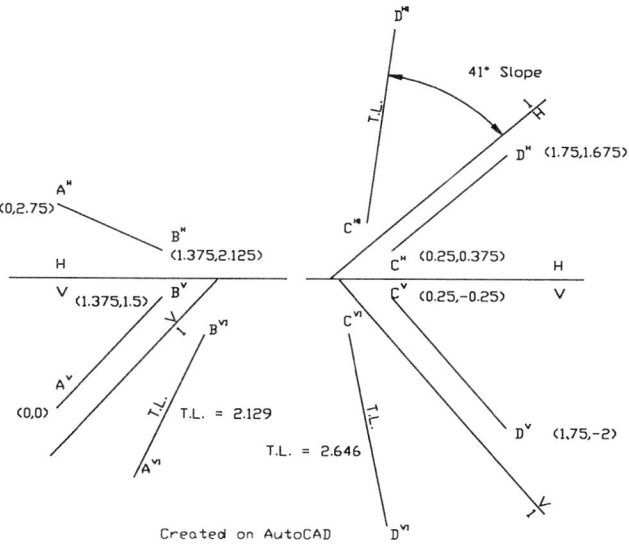

Fig. 8.51   (Prob. 8.7).

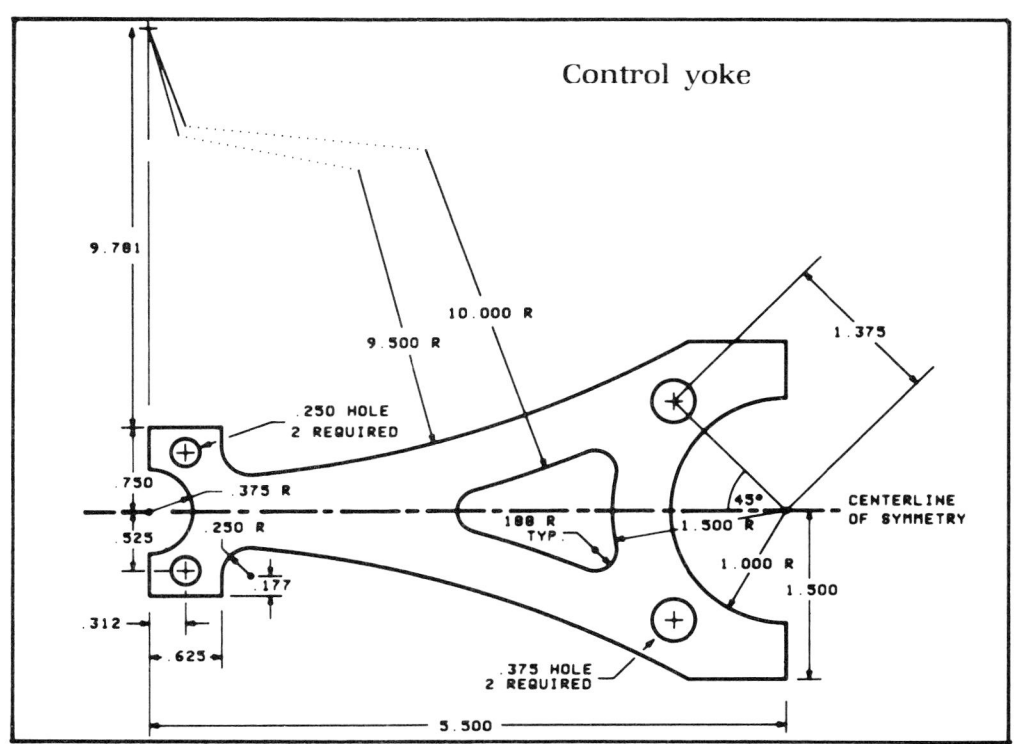

Fig. 8.52   Control Yoke (Prob. 8.8).

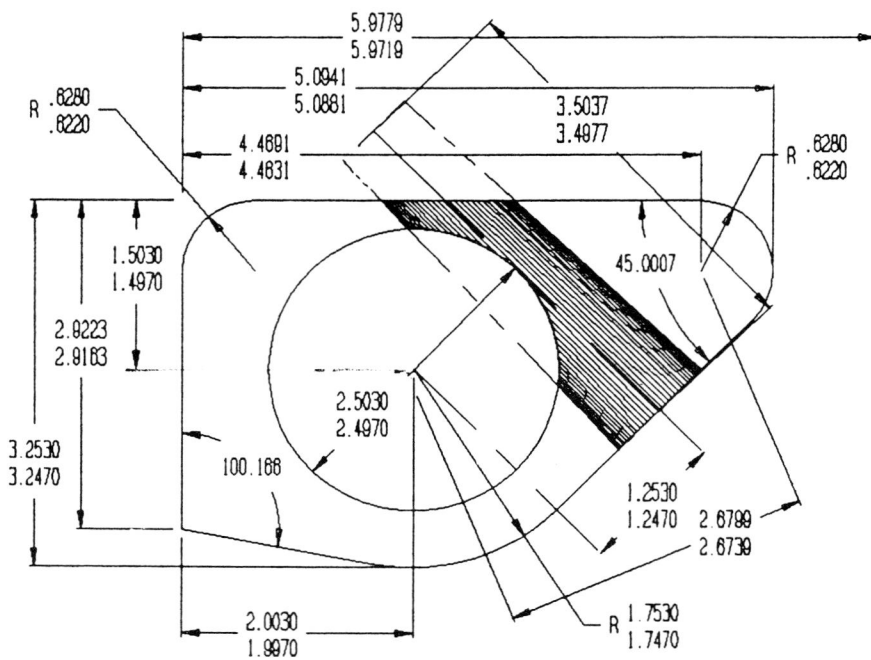

CREATE A TAPERED HOLE LOCATED AS SHOWN ON THE CENTER
OF THE 2" THICK PART. THE HOLE WILL START WITH
A 1.00 DIA HOLE AT FRONT AND END WITH A .750 DIA HOLE
AT THE BACK AS INDICATED.

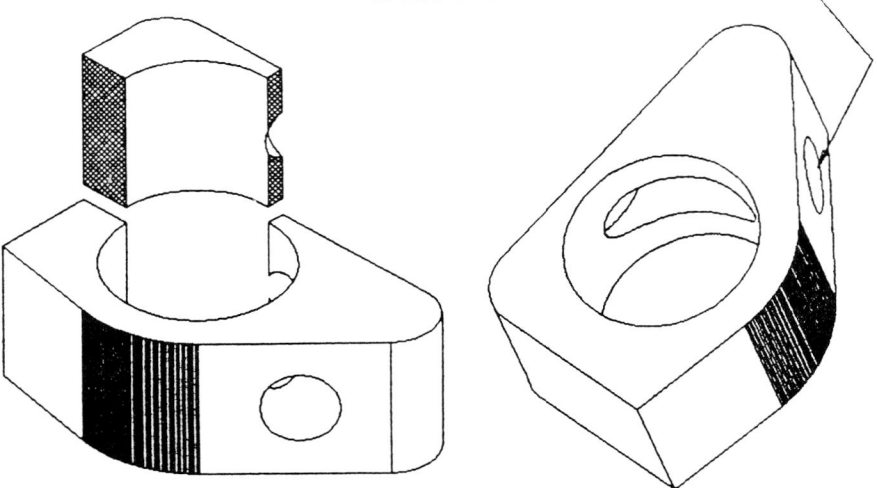

Fig. 8.53   Cam Lock (Prob. 8.9). *Courtesy of PFB Concepts*

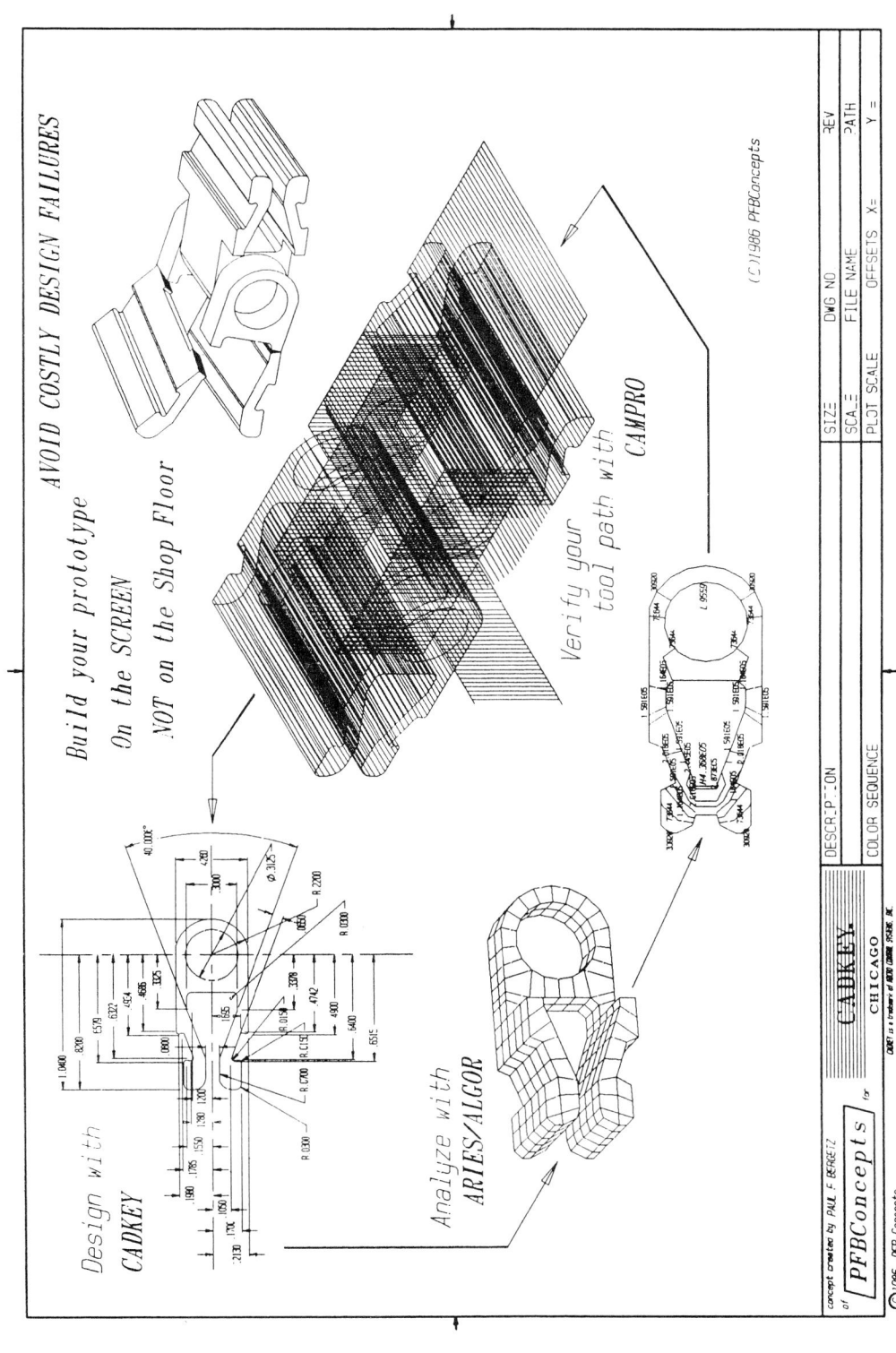

Fig. 8.54 Swivel Joint (Prob. 8.10).

CHAPTER

9

Sectional Views

The basic method of representing parts for designs by views, or projections, has been explained in previous chapters. By means of a limited number of carefully selected views, the external features of the most complicated designs can be fully described.

However, we are frequently confronted with the necessity of showing more or less complicated interiors of parts that cannot be shown clearly by means of hidden lines. We accomplish this by slicing through the part much as one would cut through an apple or a melon. A cutaway view of the part is then drawn; it is called a *sectional view*, a *cross section*, or simply a *section*. See ANSI Y14.2M–1979 (R1987) and Y14.3–1975 (R1987) for complete standards for multiview and sectional-view drawings.

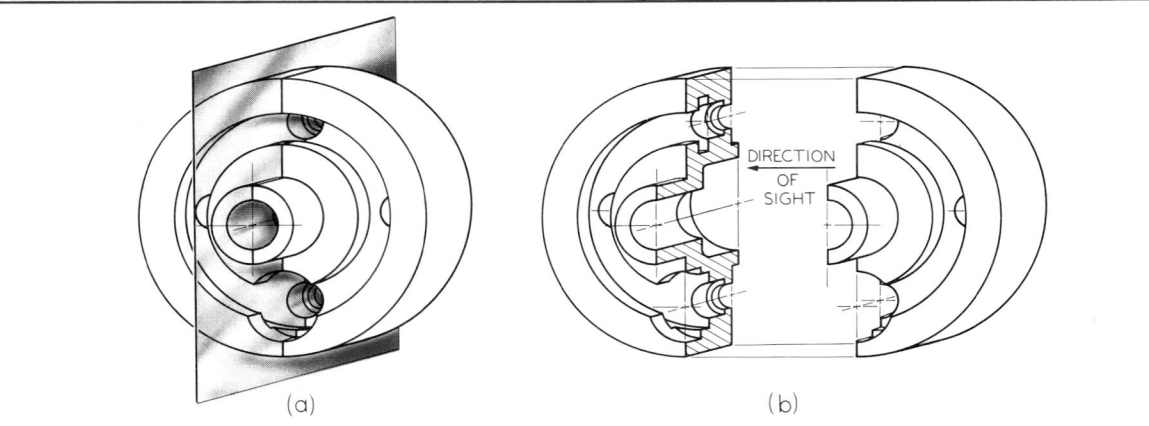

Fig. 9.1 A Section.

9.1 Sectioning

To produce a sectional view, a *cutting plane,* §9.5, is assumed to be passed through the part for the design, as shown in Fig. 9.1 (a). Then, at (b) the cutting plane is removed and the two halves drawn apart, exposing the interior construction. In this case, the direction of sight is toward the left half, as shown, and for purposes of the section the right half

is mentally discarded. The sectional view will be in the position of a right-side view.

9.2 Full Sections

The sectional view obtained by passing the cutting plane fully through the object is called a *full section,* Fig. 9.2 (c). A comparison of this sectional view with the left-side view, (a), emphasizes the advantage in

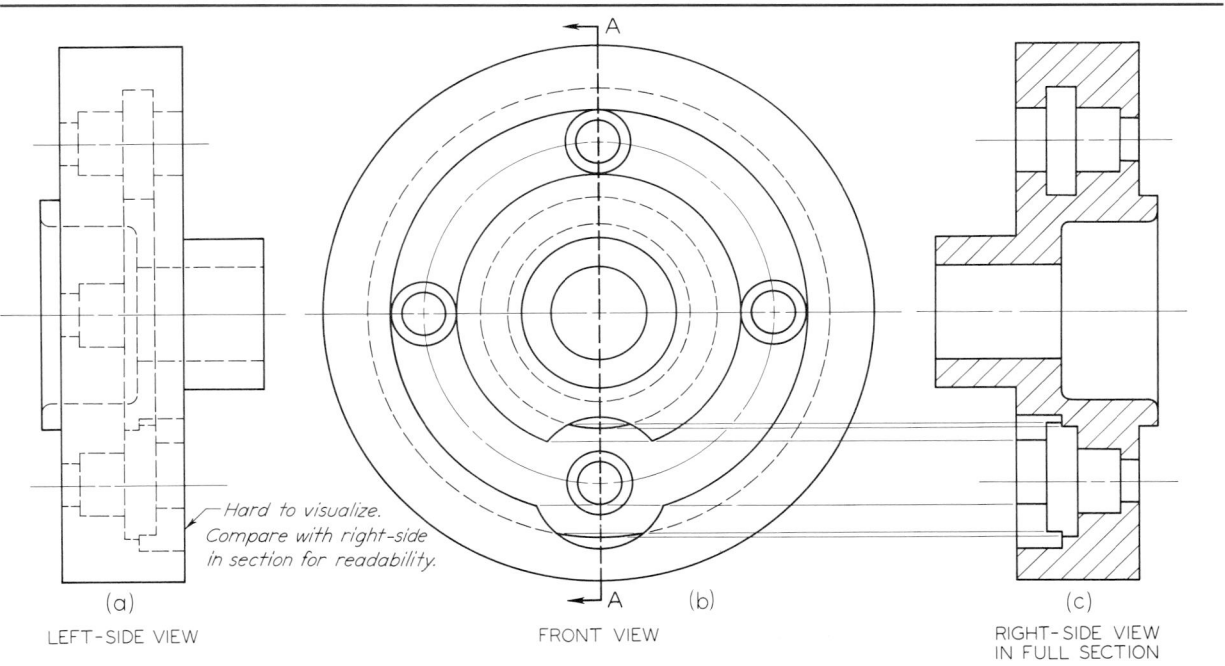

Fig. 9.2 Full Section.

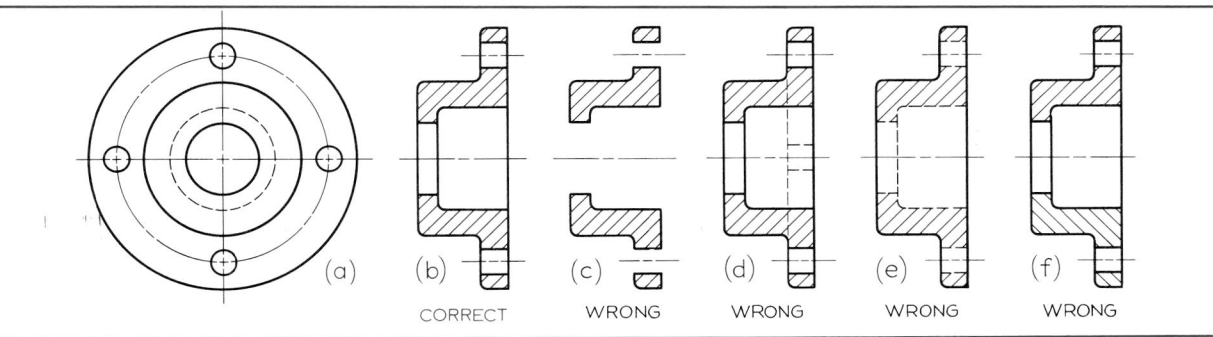

Fig. 9.3   Lines in Sectioning.

clearness of the former. The left-side view would naturally be omitted. In the front view, the cutting plane appears as a line, called a *cutting-plane line*, §9.5. The arrows at the ends of the cutting-plane line indicate the direction of sight for the sectional view.

Note that in order to obtain the sectional view, the right half is only *imagined* to be removed and not actually shown removed anywhere except in the sectional view itself. In the sectional view, the section-lined areas are those portions that have been in actual contact with the cutting plane. Those areas are *crosshatched* with thin parallel section lines spaced carefully by eye. In addition, the visible parts behind the cutting plane are shown but not crosshatched.

As a rule, the location of the cutting plane is obvious from the section itself, and, therefore, the cutting-plane line is omitted. It is shown in Fig. 9.2 for illustration only. Cutting-plane lines should, of course, be used wherever necessary for clearness, as in Figs. 9.21, 9.22, 9.24, and 9.25.

9.3 Lines in Sectioning

A correct front view and sectional view are shown in Fig. 9.3 (a) and (b). In general, *all visible edges and contours behind the cutting plane should be shown;* otherwise a section will appear to be made up of disconnected and unrelated parts, as shown in (c). Occasionally, however, visible lines behind the cutting plane are not necessary for clearness and should be omitted.

Sections are used primarily to replace hidden-line representation; hence, as a rule, *hidden lines should be omitted in sectional views.* As shown in Fig. 9.3 (d), the hidden lines do not clarify the drawing; they tend to confuse, and they take unnecessary time to draw. Sometimes hidden lines are necessary for clearness and should be used in such cases, especially if their use will make it possible to omit a view, Fig. 9.4.

A section-lined area is always completely bounded by a visible outline—never by a hidden line as in Fig. 9.3 (e), since in every case the cut surfaces and their boundary lines will be visible.

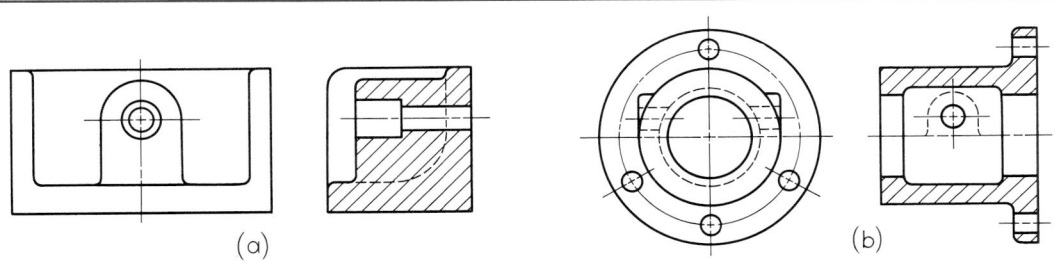

Fig. 9.4   Hidden Lines in Sections.

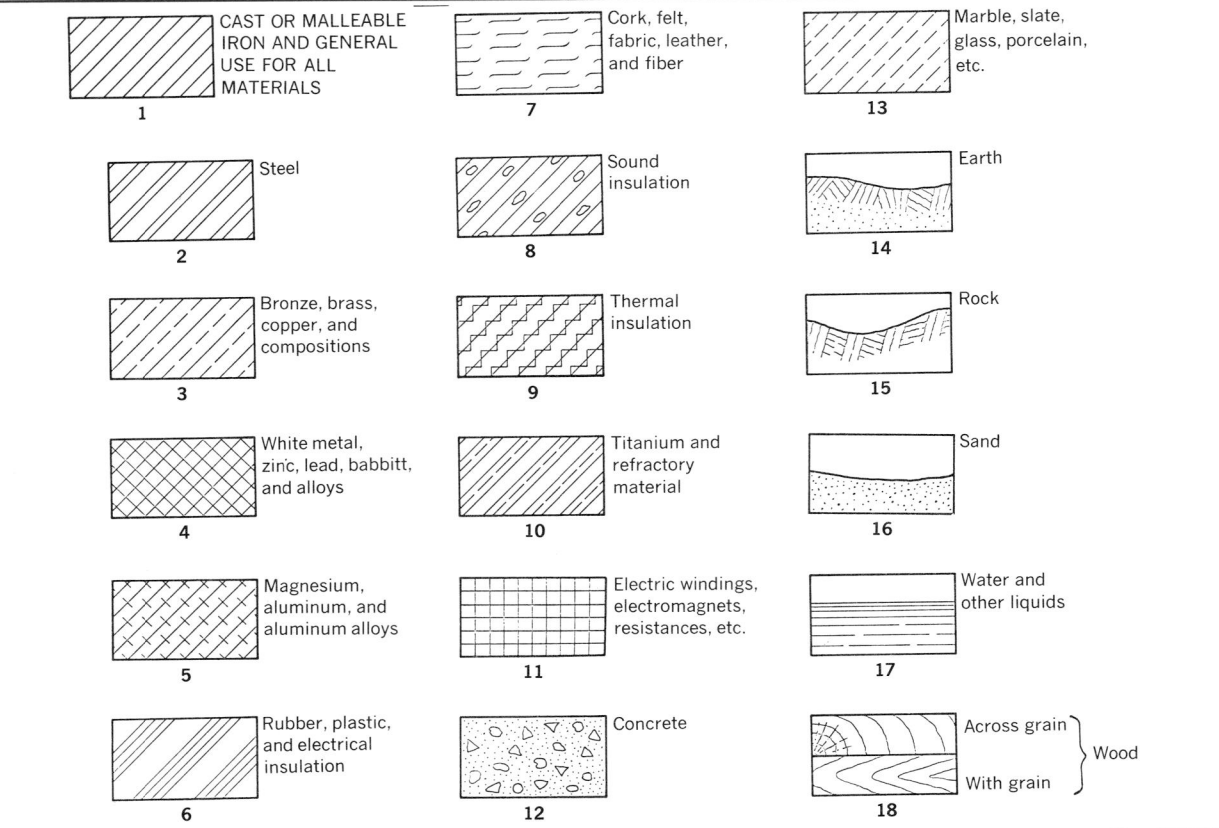

Fig. 9.5   Symbols for Section Lining.

Also, a visible line can never cut across a section-lined area.

In a sectional view of a part, alone or in assembly, the section lines in all sectioned areas must be parallel, not as shown in Fig. 9.3 (f). The use of section lining in opposite directions is an indication of different parts, as when two or more parts are adjacent in an assembly drawing, Fig. 16.35.

9.4 Section Lining

Symbolic section-lining symbols, Fig. 9.5, have been used to indicate the material to be used in producing the object. These symbols represented the general types only, such as cast-iron, brass, and steel. Now, however, there are so many different materials, and each general type has so many subtypes, that a general name or symbol is not enough. For example, there are hundreds of different kinds of steel alone. Since detailed specifications of material must be lettered in the form of a note or in the title strip, the general-purpose (cast-iron) section lining is used for all materials on detail drawings (single parts).

Symbolic section lining may be used in assembly drawings in cases where it is desirable to distinguish the different materials; otherwise, the general-purpose symbol is used for all parts. For assembly sections, see §16.21.

The correct method of drawing section lines is shown in Fig. 9.6 (a). Draw the section lines with a sharp medium-grade pencil (H or 2H) with a conical point as shown in Fig. 2.11 (c). Always draw the lines at 45° with horizontal as shown, unless there is some advantage in using a different angle. Space the section lines as uniformly as possible by eye from about approximately 1.5 mm ($\frac{1}{16}''$) to 3 mm ($\frac{1}{8}''$) or more apart, depending on the size of the drawing or of the sectioned area. *For average drawings, space the lines about 2.5 mm ($\frac{3}{32}''$) or more apart*. As a rule, space the lines as generously as possible and yet close enough to distinguish clearly the sectioned areas.

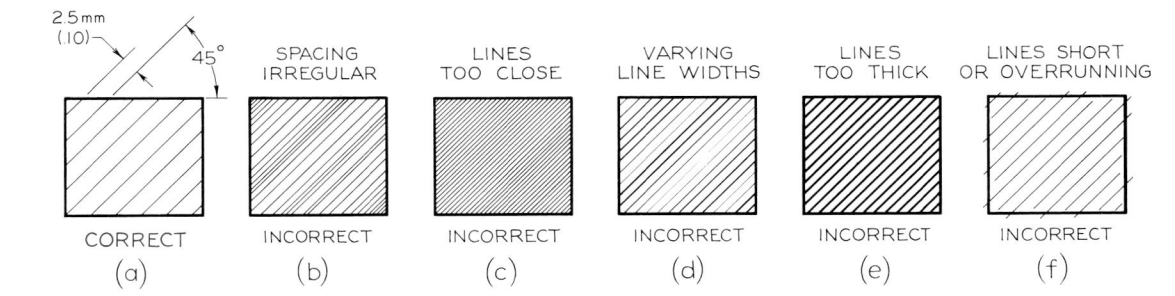

Fig. 9.6 Section-Lining Technique.

After the first few lines have been drawn, look back repeatedly at the original spacing to avoid gradually increasing or decreasing the intervals, Fig. 9.6 (b). Beginners almost invariably draw section lines too close together, (c). This is very tedious because with small spacing the least inaccuracy in spacing is conspicuous.

Section lines should be uniformly thin, never varying in thickness, as in (d). There should be a marked contrast in thickness of the visible outlines and the section lines. Section lines should not be too thick, as in (e). Also avoid running section lines beyond the visible outlines or stopping the lines too short, as in (f).

If section lines drawn at 45° with horizontal would be parallel or perpendicular (or nearly so) to a prominent visible outline, the angle should be changed to 30°, 60°, or some other angle, Fig. 9.7.

Dimensions should be kept off sectioned areas, but when this is unavoidable the section lines should be omitted where the dimension figure is placed. See Fig. 13.13.

Section lines may be drawn adjacent to the boundaries of the sectioned areas (outline sectioning) providing that clarity is not sacrificed. See Fig. 16.6.

9.5 The Cutting Plane

The cutting plane is indicated in a view adjacent to the sectional view, Fig. 9.8. In this view, the cutting plane appears edgewise, as a line called the *cutting-plane line*. Alternate styles of cutting-plane lines are shown in Fig. 9.9. See also Fig. 2.14. The first form, Fig. 9.9 (a), composed of equal dashes each about 6 mm ($\frac{1}{4}''$) or more long plus the arrowheads, is the standard in the automotive industry. This form without the dashes between the ends is especially desirable on complicated drawings. The form shown in (b), composed of alternate long dashes and pairs of short dashes plus the arrowheads, has been in general use for a long time. Both lines are drawn the same thickness as visible lines. Arrowheads indicate the direction in which the cutaway object is viewed.

Capital letters are used at the ends of the cutting-plane line when necessary to identify the cutting-plane line with the indicated section. This most often occurs in the case of multiple sections, Fig. 9.25, or removed sections, Fig. 9.21.

As shown in Fig. 9.8, sectional views occupy normal projected positions in the standard arrangement of views. At (a) the cutting plane is a frontal plane, §7.15, and appears as a line in the top view. The

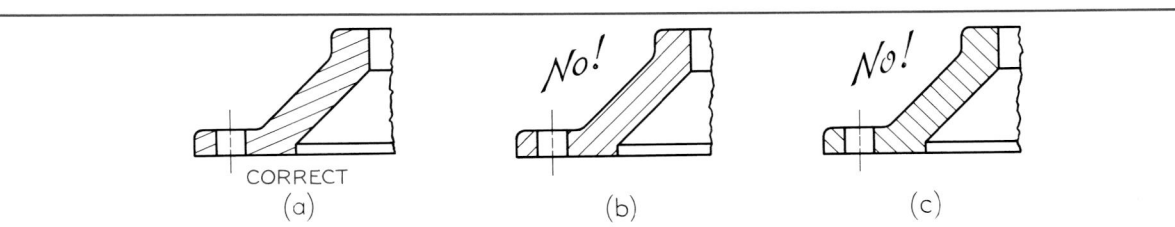

Fig. 9.7 Direction of Section Lines.

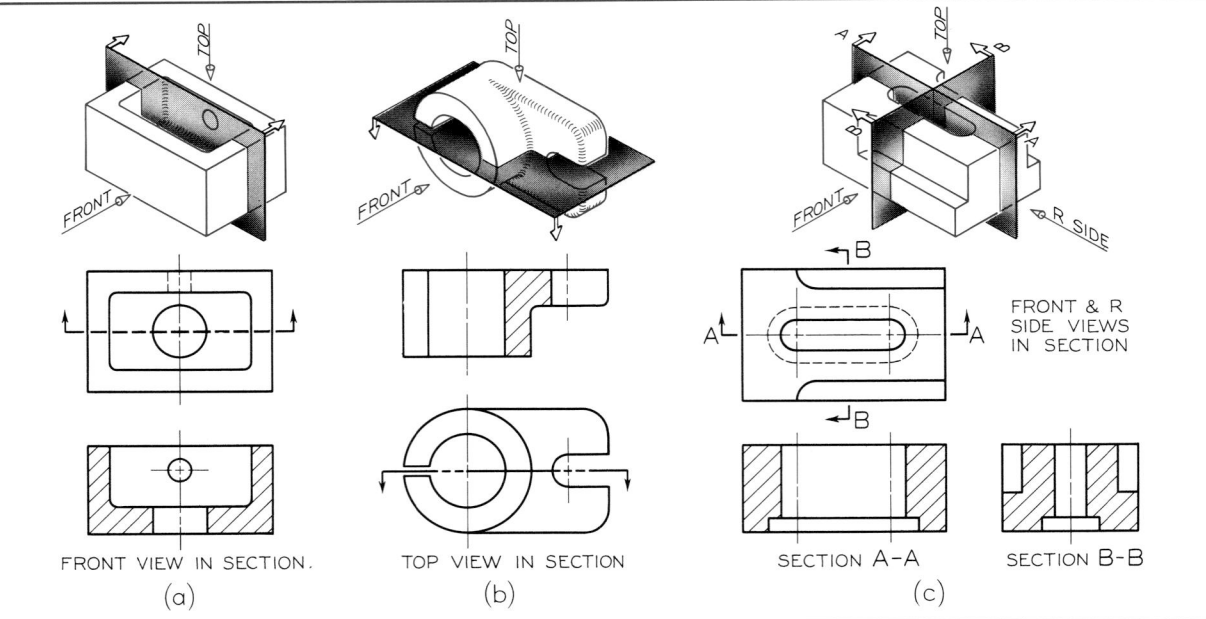

Fig. 9.8   Cutting Planes and Sections.

front half of the object (lower half in the top view) is imagined removed. The arrows at the ends of the cutting-plane line point in the direction of sight for a front view, that is, away from the front view or section. Note that the arrows do not point in the direction of withdrawal of the removed portion. The resulting full section may be referred to as the "front view in section," since it occupies the front view position.

In Fig. 9.8 (b), the cutting plane is a horizontal plane, §7.15, and appears as a line in the front view. The upper half of the object is imagined removed. The arrows point toward the lower half in the same direction of sight as for a top view, and the resulting full section is a "top view in section."

In Fig. 9.8 (c), two cutting planes are shown, one a frontal plane and the other a profile plane, §7.15, both of which appear edgewise in the top view. Each section is completely independent of the other and drawn as if the other were not present. For section

A–A, the front half of the object is imagined removed. The back half is then viewed in the direction of the arrows for a front view, and the resulting section is a "front view in section." For section B–B, the right half of the object is imagined removed. The left half then is viewed in the direction of the arrows for a right-side view, and the resulting section is a "right-side view in section." The cutting-plane lines are preferably drawn through an exterior view, in this case the top view, as shown, instead of a sectional view.

The cutting-plane lines in Fig. 9.8 are shown for purposes of illustration only. They are generally omitted in cases such as these, in which the location of the cutting plane is obvious. When a cutting-plane line coincides with a center line, the cutting-plane line takes precedence.

Correct and incorrect relations between cutting-plane lines and corresponding sectional views are shown in Fig. 9.10.

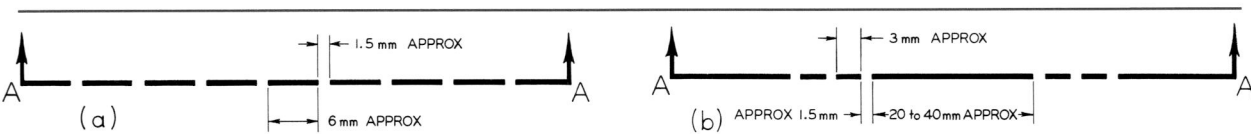

Fig. 9.9   Cutting-Plane Lines (Full Size).

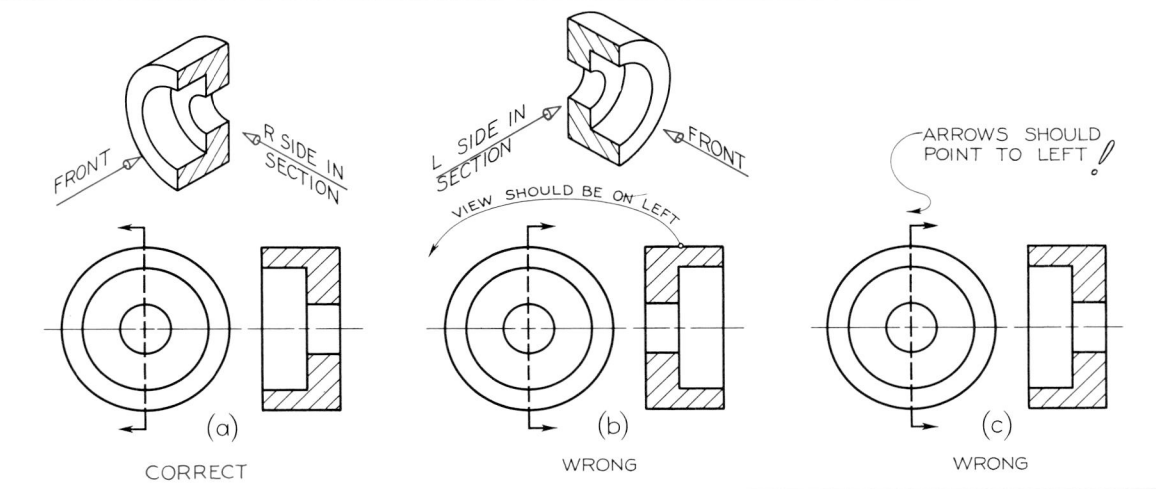

Fig. 9.10   Cutting Planes and Sections.

9.6 Visualizing a Section

Two views of an object to be sectioned, having a drilled and counterbored hole, are shown in Fig. 9.11 (a). The cutting plane is assumed along the horizontal center line in the top view, and the front half of the object (lower half of the top view) is imagined removed. A pictorial drawing of the remaining back half is shown at (b). The two cut surfaces produced by the cutting plane are 1–2–5–6–10–9 and 3–4–12–11–7–8. However, the corresponding section at (c) is incomplete because certain visible lines are missing.

If the section is viewed in the direction of sight, as shown at (b), arcs A, B, C, and D will be visible. As shown at (d), these arcs will appear as straight lines 2–3, 6–7, 5–8, and 10–11. These lines may also be accounted for in other ways. The top and bottom surfaces of the object appear in the section as lines 1–4 and 9–12. The bottom surface of the counterbore appears in the section as line 5–8. Also, the semicylindrical surfaces for the back half of the counterbore and of the drilled hole will appear as rectangles in the section at 2–3–8–5 and 6–7–11–10.

The front and top views of a Collar are shown in Fig. 9.12 (a), and a right-side view in full section is required. The cutting plane is understood to pass along the center lines AD and EL. If the cutting plane were drawn, the arrows would point to the left in conformity with the direction of sight (see arrow) for the right-side view. The right side of the object is

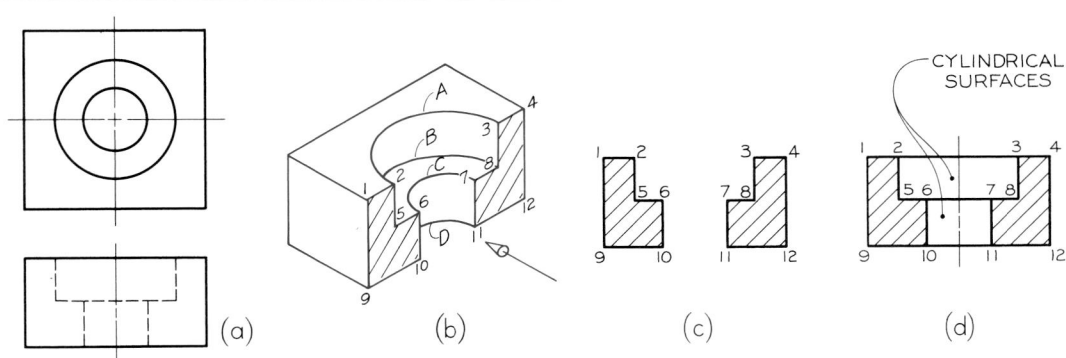

Fig. 9.11   Visualizing a Section.

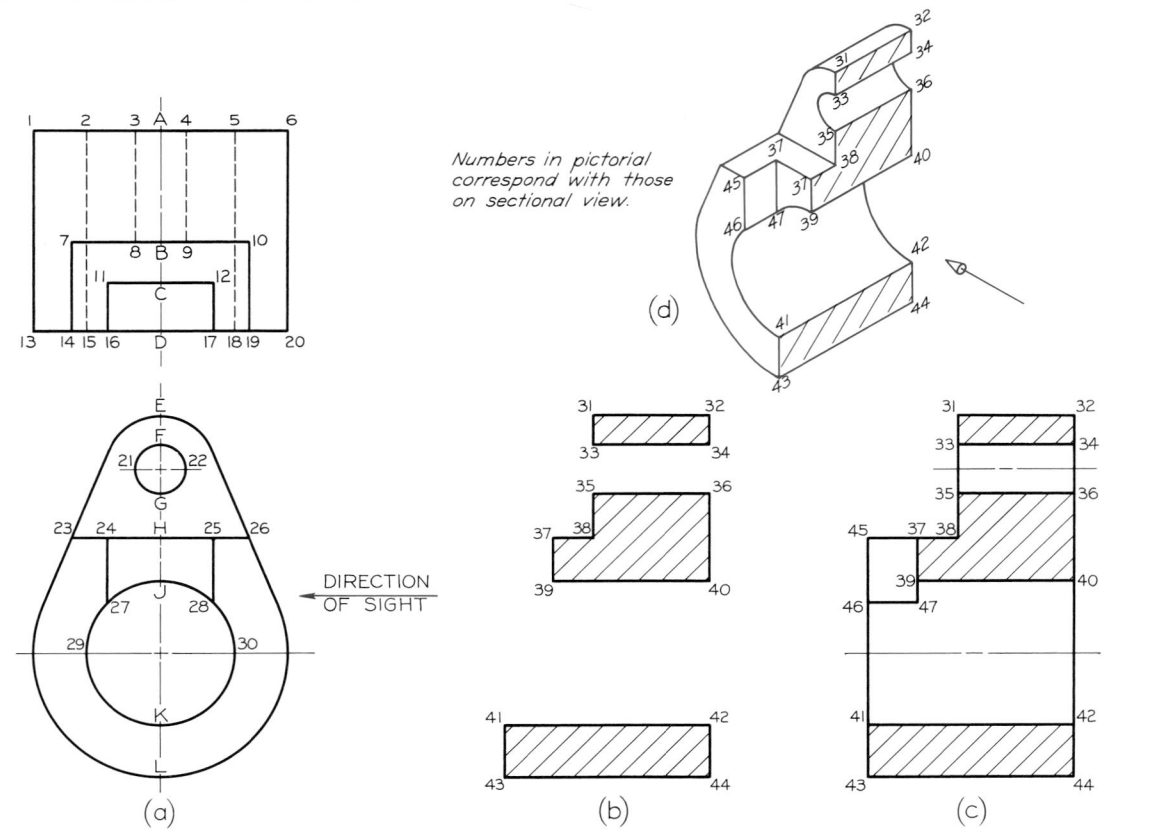

Fig. 9.12   Drawing a Full Section.

imagined removed, and the left half will be viewed in the direction of the arrow, as shown pictorially at (d). The cut surfaces will appear edgewise in the top and front views along **AD** and **EL**; and since the direction of sight for the section is at right angles to them, they will appear in true size and shape in the sectional view. Each sectioned area will be completely enclosed by a boundary of visible lines. The sectional view will show, in addition to the cut surfaces, all visible parts behind the cutting plane. No hidden lines will be shown.

Whenever a surface of the object (plane or cylindrical) appears as a line and is intersected by a cutting plane that also appears as a line, a new edge (line of intersection) is created that will appear as a *point* in that view. Thus, in the front view, the cutting plane creates new edges appearing as points at **E, F, G, H, J, K,** and **L**. In the sectional view, (b), these are horizontal lines **31–32, 33–34, 35–36, 37–38, 39–40, 41–42,** and **43–44**.

Whenever a surface of the object appears as a surface (that is, not as a line) and is cut by a cutting

plane that appears as a line, a new edge is created that will appear as a line in the view, coinciding with the cutting-plane line, and as a line in the section.

In the top view, **D** is the *point view* of a vertical line **KL** in the front view and **41–43** in the section at (b). Point **C** is the point view of a vertical line **HJ** in the front view and **37–39** in the section. Point **B** is the point view of two vertical lines **EF** and **GH** in the front view, and **31–33** and **35–38** in the section. Point **A** is the point view of three vertical lines **EF, GJ,** and **KL** in the front view, and **32–34, 36–40,** and **42–44** in the section. This completes the boundaries of three sectioned areas **31–32–34–33, 35–36–40–39–37–38,** and **41–42–44–43**. It is only necessary now to add the visible lines beyond the cutting plane.

The semicylindrical left half **F–21–G** of the small hole (front view) will be visible as a rectangle in the sections at **33–34–36–35,** as shown at (c). The two semicircular arcs will appear as straight lines in the section at **33–35** and **34–36**.

Surface **24–27,** appearing as a line in the front

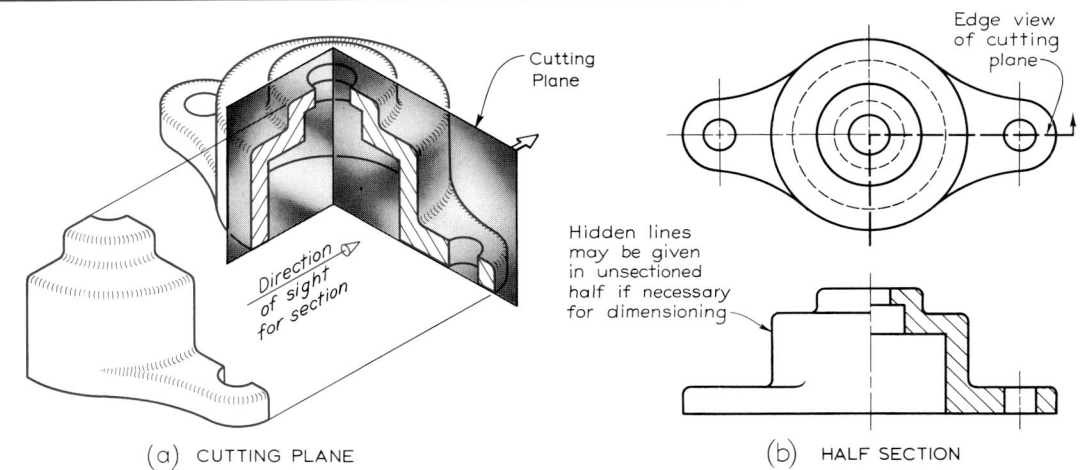

Fig. 9.13   Half Section.

view, appears as a line **11–16** in the top view and as surface **45–37–47–46**, true size, in the section at (c).

Cylindrical surface **J–29–K**, appearing as an arc in the front view, appears in the top view as **2–A–C–11–16–15**, and in the section as **46–47–39–40–42–41**. Thus, arc **27–29–K** (front view) appears in the section, (c), as straight lines **46–41**; and arc **J–29–K** appears as straight line **40–42**.

All cut surfaces here are part of the same object; hence, the section lines must all run in the same direction, as shown.

9.7 Half Sections

If the cutting plane passes halfway through the object, the result is a half section, Fig. 9.13. A half section has the advantage of exposing the interior of one half of the object and retaining the exterior of the other half. Its usefulness is, therefore, largely limited to symmetrical objects. It is not widely used in detail drawings (single parts) because of this limitation of symmetry and also because of difficulties in dimensioning internal shapes that are shown in part only in the sectioned half, Fig. 9.13 (b).

In general, hidden lines should be omitted from both halves of a half section. However, they may be used in the unsectioned half if necessary for dimensioning.

The greatest usefulness of the half section is in assembly drawing, Fig. 16.34, in which it is often necessary to show both internal and external construction on the same view, but without the necessity of dimensioning.

As shown in Fig. 9.13 (b), a center line is used to separate the halves of the half section. The American National Standards Institute recommends a center line for the division line between the sectioned half and the unsectioned half of a half-sectional view, although in some cases the same overlap of the exterior portion, as in a broken-out section, is preferred. See Fig. 9.33 (b). Either form is acceptable.

9.8 Broken-Out Sections

It often happens that only a partial section of a view is needed to expose interior shapes. Such a section, limited by a break line, Fig. 2.14, is called a broken-out section. In Fig. 9.14, a full or half section is not necessary, a small broken-out section being suffi-

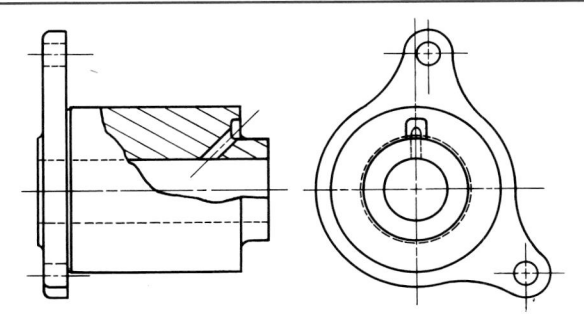

Fig. 9.14   Broken-Out Section.

cient to explain the construction. In Fig. 9.15, a half section would have caused the removal of half the keyway. The keyway is preserved by breaking out around it. Note that in this case the section is limited partly by a break line and partly by a center line.

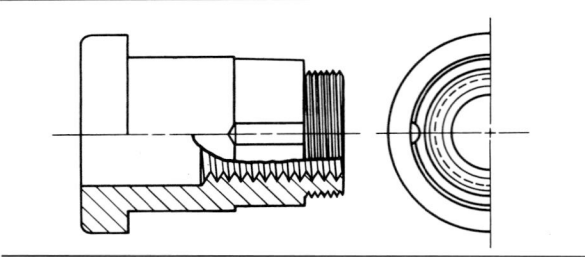

Fig. 9.15   Break Around Keyway.

9.9 Revolved Sections

The shape of the cross section of a bar, arm, spoke, or other elongated object may be shown in the longitudinal view by means of a revolved section, Fig. 9.16. Such sections are made by assuming a plane perpendicular to the center line or axis of the bar or other object, as shown in Fig. 9.17 (a), then revolving the plane through 90° about a center line at right angles to the axis, as at (b) and (c).

The visible lines adjacent to a revolved section may be broken out if desired, as shown in Figs. 9.16 (k) and 9.18.

The superimposition of the revolved section requires the removal of all original lines covered by it, Fig. 9.19. The true shape of a revolved section should be retained after the revolution of the cutting plane, regardless of the direction of the lines in the view, Fig. 9.20.

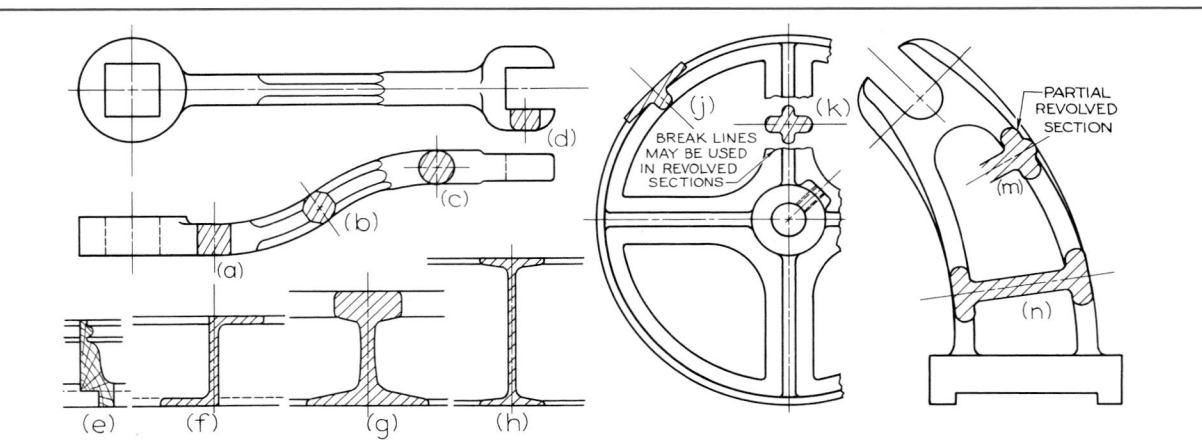

Fig. 9.16   Revolved Sections.

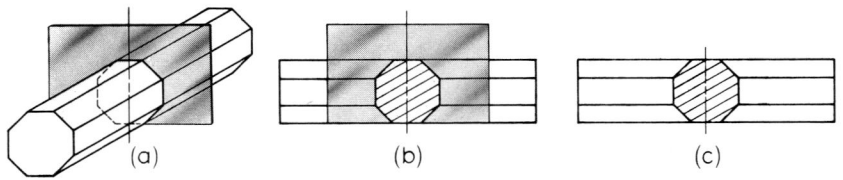

Fig. 9.17   Use of the Cutting Plane in Revolved Sections.

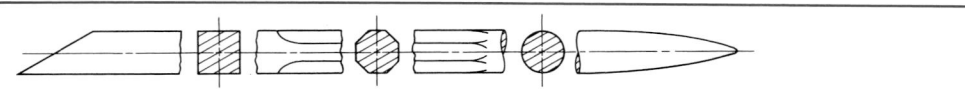

Fig. 9.18   Conventional Breaks Used with Revolved Sections.

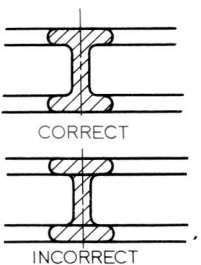

Fig. 9.19 A Common Error in Drawing Revolved Sections.

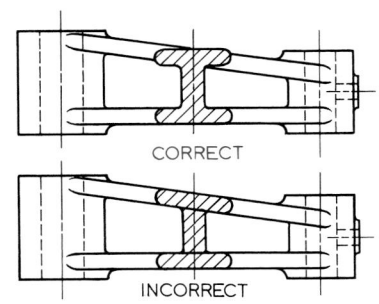

Fig. 9.20 A Common Error in Drawing Revolved Sections.

9.10 Removed Sections

A removed section is one not in direct projection from the view containing the cutting plane—that is, it is not positioned in agreement with the standard arrangement of views. This displacement from the normal projection position should be made without turning the section from its normal orientation.

Removed sections, Fig. 9.21, should be labeled, such as SECTION A–A and SECTION B–B, corresponding to the letters at the ends of the cutting-plane line.

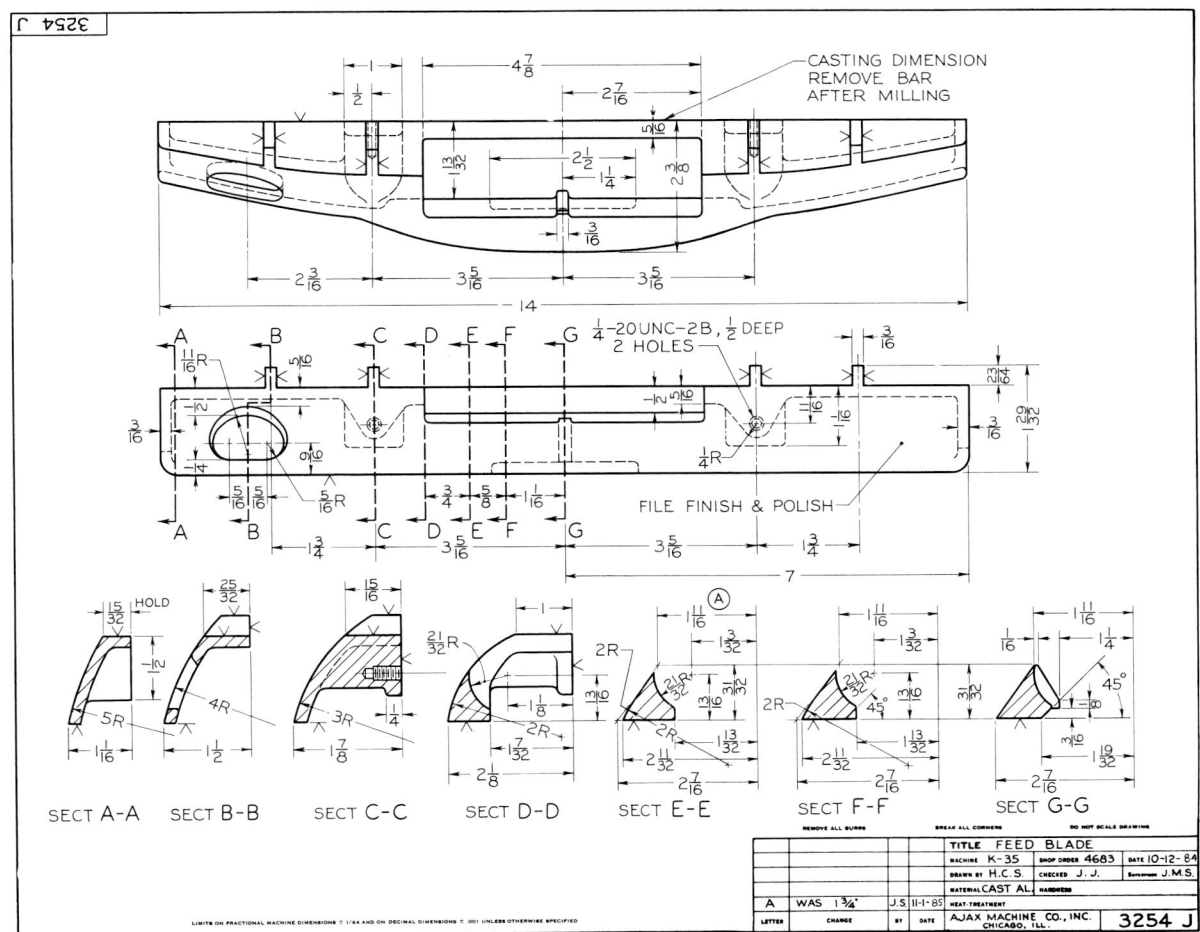

Fig. 9.21 Removed Sections.

They should be arranged in alphabetical order from left to right on the sheet. Section letters should be used in alphabetical order, but letters I, O, and Q should not be used because they are easily confused with the numeral 1 or the zero.

A removed section is often a partial section. Such a removed section, Fig. 9.22, is frequently drawn to an enlarged scale, as shown. This is often desirable in order to show clear delineation of some small detail and to provide sufficient space for dimensioning. In such a case the enlarged scale should be indicated beneath the section title.

A removed section should be placed so that it no longer lines up in projection with any other view. It should be separated clearly from the standard arrangement of views. See Fig. 14.9.

Whenever possible removed sections should be on the same sheet with the regular views. If a section must be placed on a different sheet, cross-references should be given on the related sheets. A

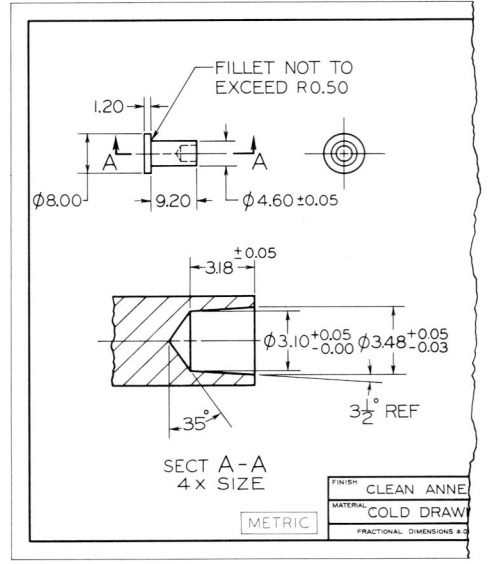

Fig. 9.22 Removed Section.

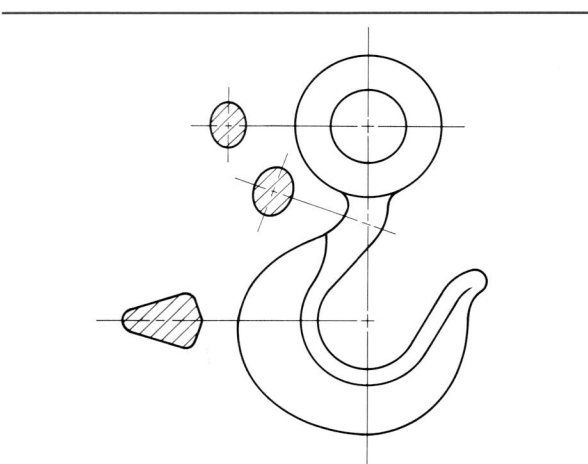

Fig. 9.23 Removed Sections.

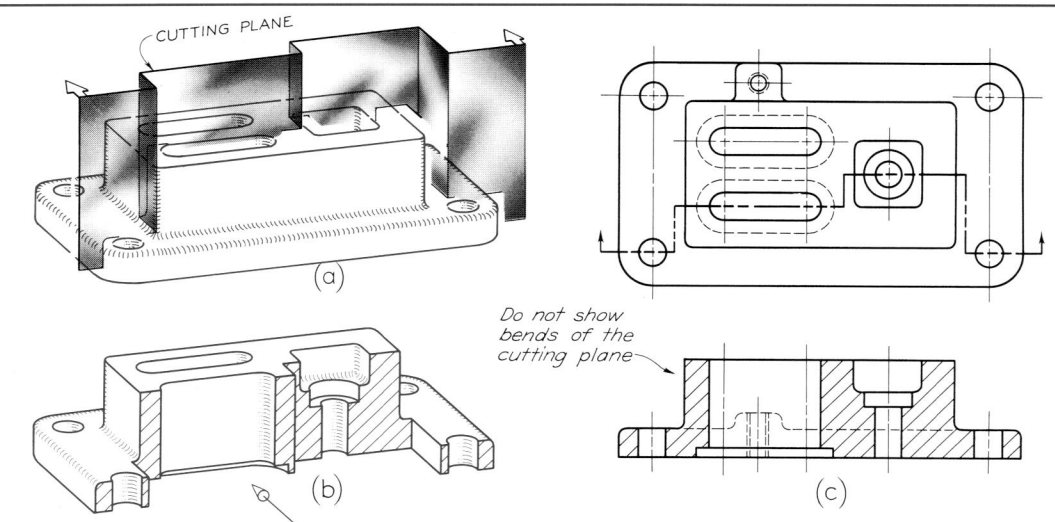

Fig. 9.24 Offset Section.

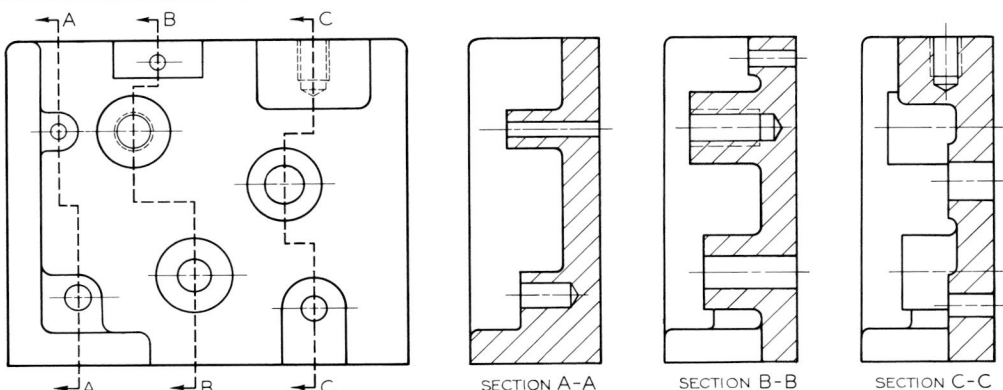

Fig. 9.25 Three Offset Sections.

note should be given below the section title, such as

SECTION B–B ON SHEET 4, ZONE A3

A similar note should be placed on the sheet on which the cutting-plane line is shown, with a leader pointing to the cutting-plane line and referring to the sheet on which the section will be found.

Sometimes it is convenient to place removed sections on center lines extended from the section cuts, Fig. 9.23.

9.11 Offset Sections

In sectioning through irregular objects, it is often desirable to show several features that do not lie in a straight line, by "offsetting" or bending the cutting plane. Such a section is called an offset section. In Fig. 9.24 (a) the cutting plane is offset in several places in order to include the hole at the left end, one of the parallel slots, the rectangular recess, and one of the holes at the right end. The front portion of the object is then imagined to be removed, (b). The path of the cutting plane is shown by the cutting-plane line in the top view at (c), and the resulting offset section is shown in the front view. The offsets or bends in the cutting plane are all 90° and are *never shown in the sectional view*.

Figure 9.24 also illustrates how hidden lines in a section eliminate the need for an additional view. In this case, an extra view would be needed to show the small boss on the back if hidden lines were not shown.

An example of multiple offset sections is shown in Fig. 9.25. Notice that the visible background

shapes without hidden lines appear in each sectional view.

9.12 Ribs in Section

To avoid a false impression of thickness and solidity, ribs, webs, gear teeth, and other similar flat features are not sectioned even though the cutting plane passes along the center plane of the feature. For example, in Fig. 9.26, the cutting plane A–A passes flatwise through the vertical web, or rib, and the

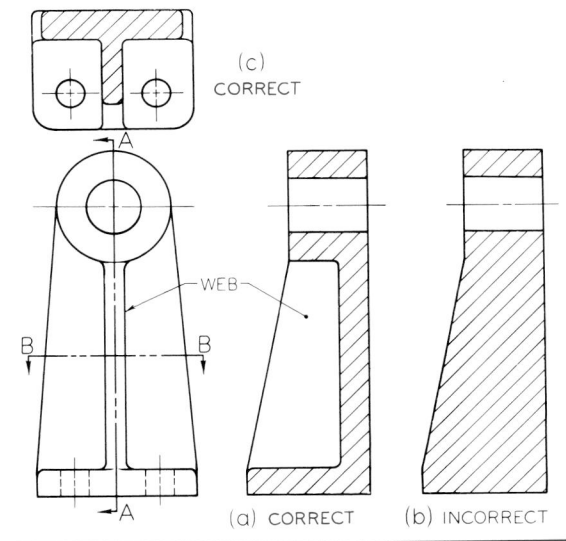

Fig. 9.26 Webs in Section.

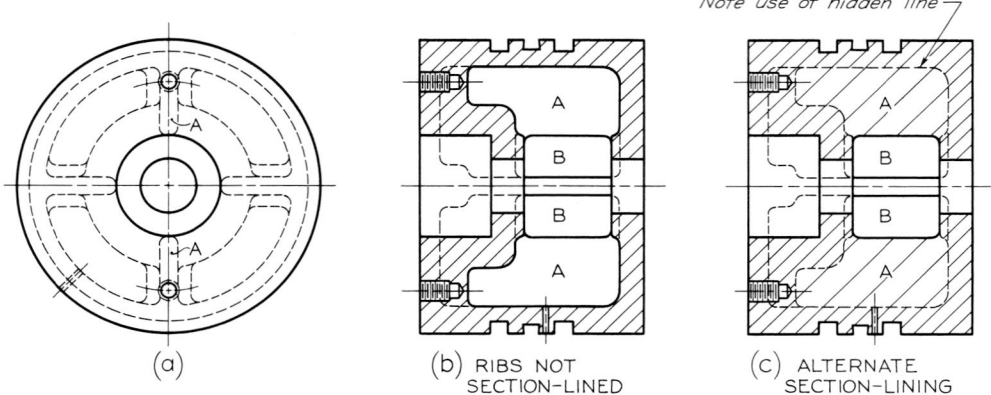

Fig. 9.27   Alternate Section Lining.

web is not section-lined, (a). *Such thin features should not be section-lined, even though the cutting plane passes through them.* The incorrect section is shown at (b). Note the false impression of thickness or solidity resulting from section lining the rib.

If the cutting plane passes *crosswise* through a rib or any thin member, as does the plane **B–B** in Fig. 9.26, the member should be section-lined in the usual manner, as shown in the top view at (c).

In some cases, if a rib is not section-lined when the cutting plane passes through it flatwise, it is difficult to tell whether the rib is actually present, as, for example, ribs **A** in Fig. 9.27 (a) and (b). It is difficult to distinguish spaces **B** as open spaces and spaces **A** as ribs. In such cases, double-spaced *section lining* of the ribs should be used, (c). This consists simply in continuing alternate section lines through the ribbed areas, as shown.

9.13 Aligned Sections

In order to include in a section certain angled elements, the cutting plane may be bent so as to pass through those features. The plane and feature are then imagined to be revolved into the original plane. For example, in Fig. 9.28, the cutting plane was bent to pass through the angled arm and then revolved to a vertical position (aligned), from where it was projected across to the sectional view.

In Fig. 9.29 the cutting plane is bent so as to include one of the drilled and counterbored holes in the sectional view. The correct section view at (b) gives a clearer and more complete description than does the section at (c), which was taken along the vertical center line of the front view—that is, without any bend in the cutting plane.

In such cases, the angle of revolution should always be less than 90°.

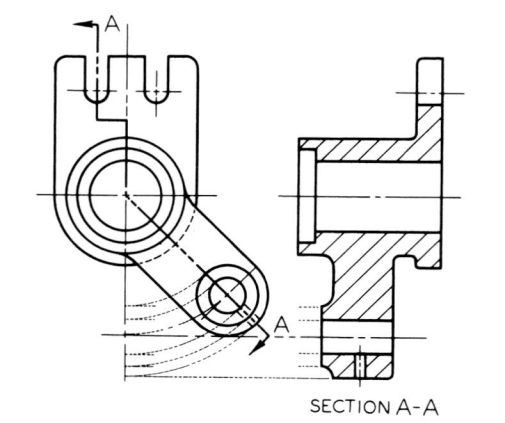

Fig. 9.28   Aligned Section.

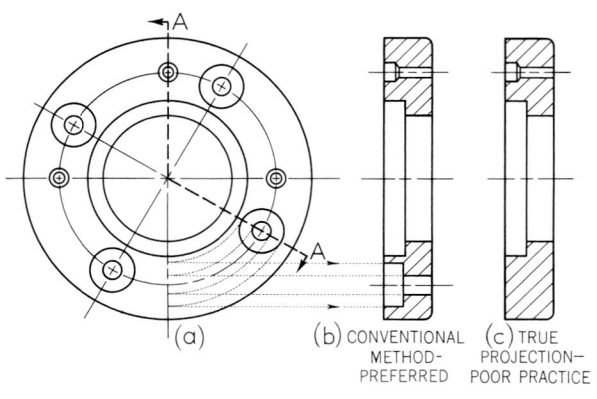

Fig. 9.29   Aligned Section.

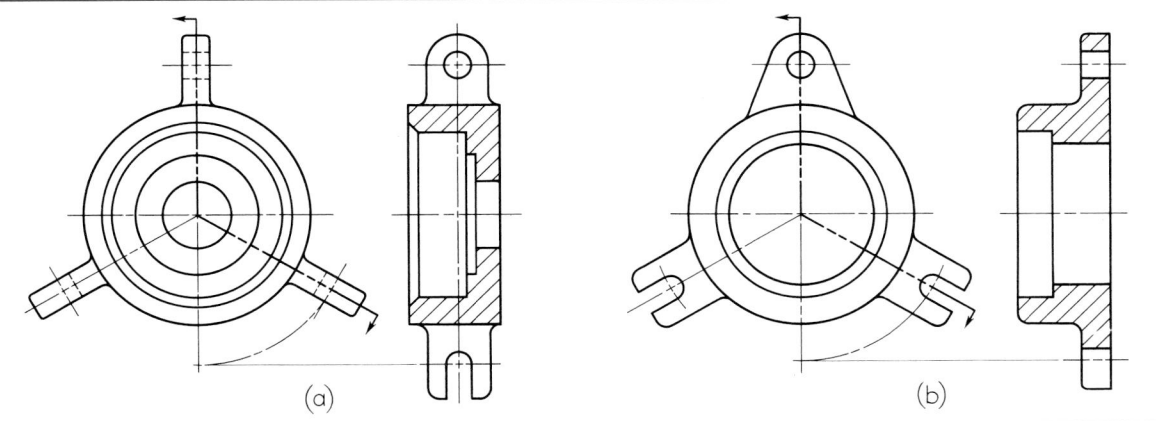

Fig. 9.30 Aligned Sections.

The student is cautioned *not to revolve* features when clearness is not gained. In some cases the revolving features will result in a loss of clarity. Examples in which revolution should not be used are Fig. 9.40, Probs. 17 and 18.

In Fig. 9.30 (a) is an example in which the projecting lugs were not sectioned on the same basis that ribs are not sectioned. At (b) the projecting lugs are located so that the cutting plane would pass through them crosswise; hence, they are sectioned.

Another example involving rib sectioning and also aligned sectioning is shown in Fig. 9.31. In the circular view, the cutting plane is offset in circular-arc bends to include the upper hole and upper rib, the keyway and center hole, the lower rib, and one of the lower holes. These features are imagined to be revolved until they line up vertically and are then projected from that position to obtain the section at (b). Note that the ribs are not sectioned. If a regular full section of the object were drawn, without the use of conventions discussed here, the resulting section, (c), would be both incomplete and confusing and, in addition, would take more time to draw.

In sectioning a pulley or any spoked wheel, it is standard practice to revolve the spokes if necessary (if there is an odd number) and not to section-line

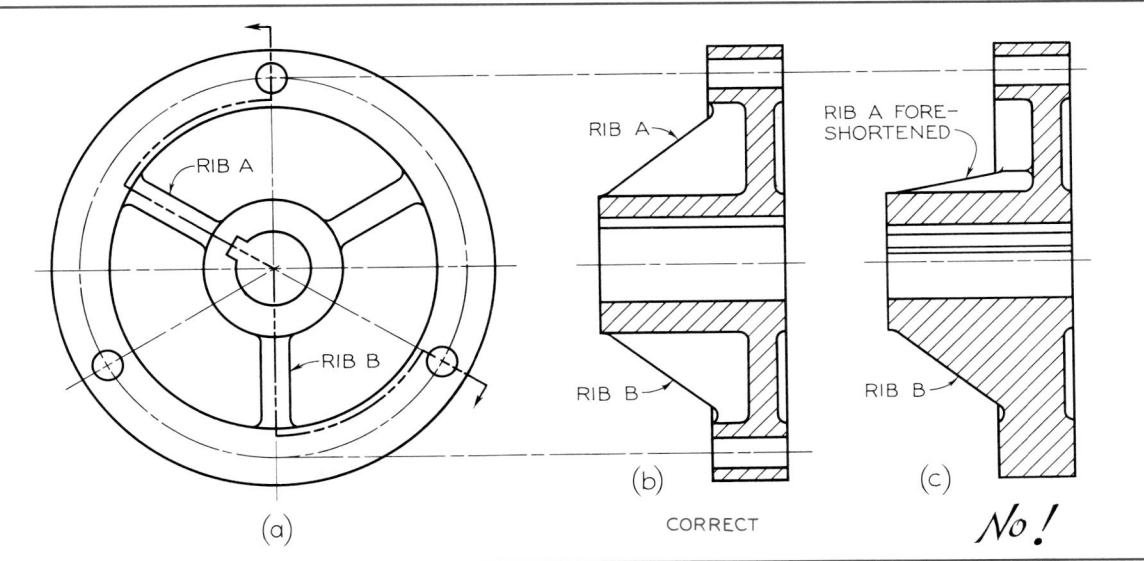

Fig. 9.31 Symmetry of Ribs.

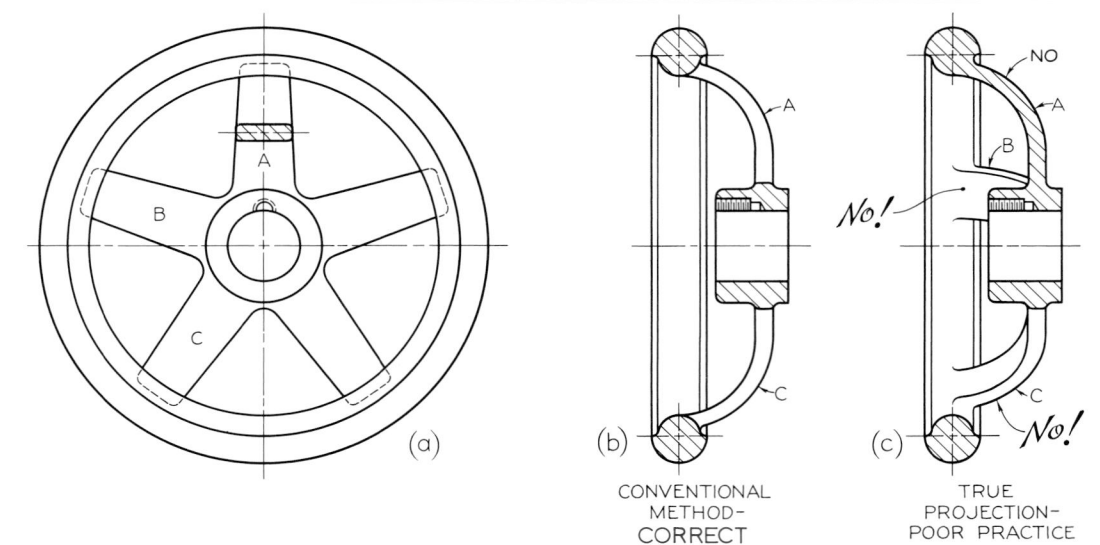

Fig. 9.32   Spokes in Section.

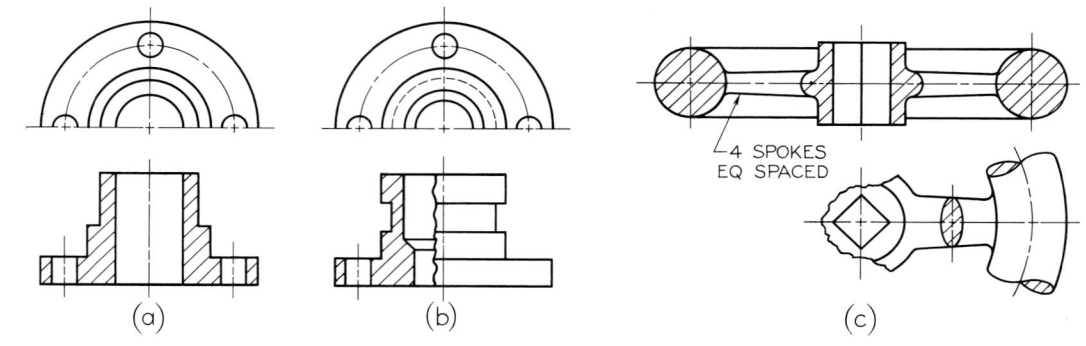

Fig. 9.33   Partial Views.

the spokes, Fig. 9.32 (b). If the spoke is sectioned, as shown at (c), the section gives a false impression of continuous metal. If the lower spoke is not revolved, it will be foreshortened in the sectional view in which it presents an "amputated" and wholly misleading appearance.

Figure 9.32 also illustrates correct practice in omitting visible lines in a sectional view. Notice that spoke B is omitted at (b). If it were included, (c), the spoke would be foreshortened, difficult and time consuming to draw, and confusing to the reader of the drawing.

9.14 Partial Views

If space is limited on the paper or if it is necessary to save drafting time, *partial views* may be used in connection with sectioning, Fig. 9.33. *Half views* are shown at (a) and (b) in connection with a full section and a half section, respectively. Note that in each case the back half of the object in the circular view is shown, in conformity with the idea of removing the front portion of the object in order to expose the back portion for viewing in section. See also §7.9.

Another method of drawing a partial view is to break out much of the circular view, retaining only those features that are needed for minimum representation, Fig. 9.33 (c).

9.15 Intersections in Sectioning

Where an intersection is small or unimportant in a section, it is standard practice to disregard the true projection of the figure of intersection, as shown in Fig. 9.34 (a) and (c). Larger figures of intersection

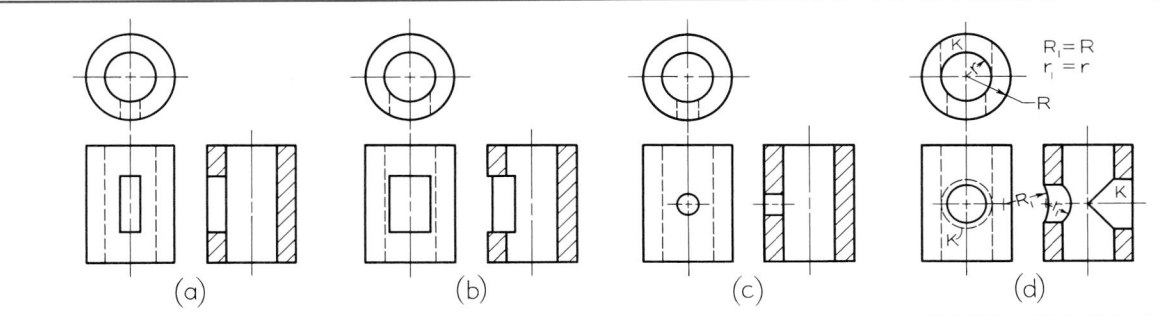

Fig. 9.34 Intersections.

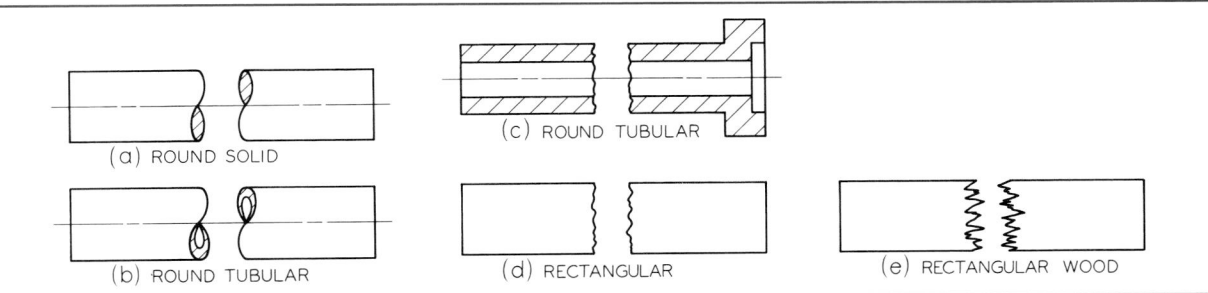

Fig. 9.35 Conventional Breaks.

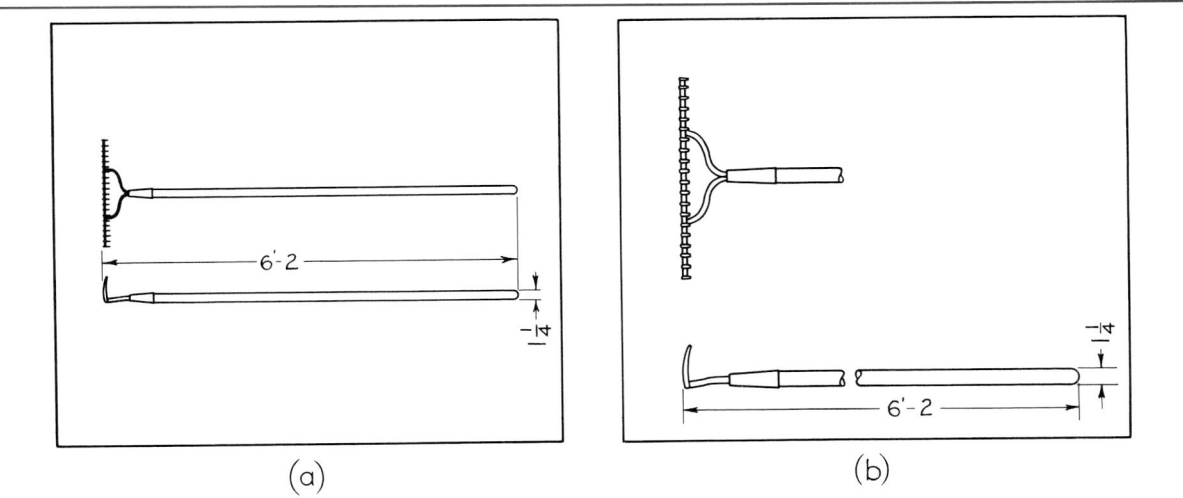

Fig. 9.36 Use of Conventional Breaks.

may be projected, as shown at (b), or approximated by circular arcs, as shown for the smaller hole at (d). Note that the larger hole K is the same diameter as the vertical hole. In such cases the curves of intersection (ellipses) appear as straight lines, as shown. See also Figs. 7.38 and 7.39.

9.16 Conventional Breaks

In order to shorten a view of an elongated object, conventional breaks are recommended, as shown in Fig. 9.35. For example, the two views of a garden rake are shown in Fig. 9.36 (a), drawn to a small scale to get it on the paper. At (b) the handle was

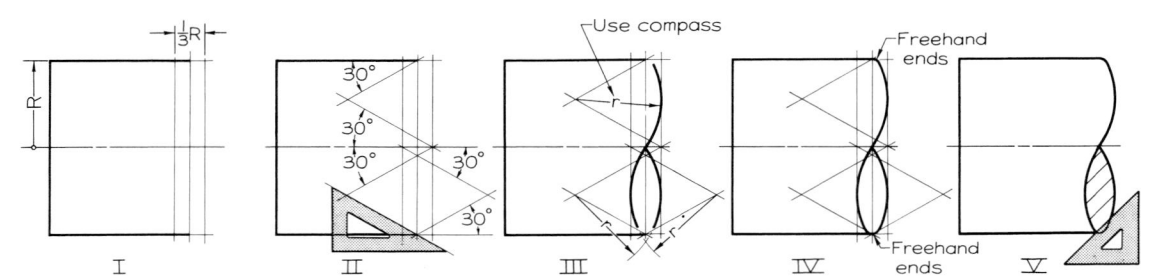

Fig. 9.37   Steps in Drawing **S**-Break for Solid Shaft.

"broken," a long central portion removed, and the rake then drawn to a larger scale, producing a much more clear delineation.

Parts thus broken must have the same section throughout, or if tapered they must have a uniform taper. Note at (b) the full-length dimension is given, just as if the entire rake were shown.

The breaks used on cylindrical shafts or tubes are often referred to as "**S**-breaks" and in the industrial drafting room are usually drawn entirely freehand or partly freehand and partly with the irregular curve or the compass. By these methods, the result is often very crude, especially when attempted by beginners. Simple methods of construction for use by the student or the industrial drafter are shown in Figs. 9.37 and 9.38 and will always produce a professional result. Excellent **S**-breaks are also obtained with an **S**-break template.

Breaks for rectangular metal and wood sections are always drawn freehand, as shown in Fig. 9.35. See also Fig. 9.18 which illustrates the use of breaks in connection with the revolved sections.

9.17 Computer Graphics

Sectioning of even the most complex objects can be readily accomplished with CAD, providing its user understands the theory of sectioning and how it is to be applied. Using computer graphics, one can quickly and efficiently explore a variety of possible solutions to a sectioning problem and choose the best representation without making tedious changes to a paper drawing. With CAD, it is relatively simple to examine various cross-sections of an object, depict removed sections, and add appropriate section lining, Fig. 9.39.

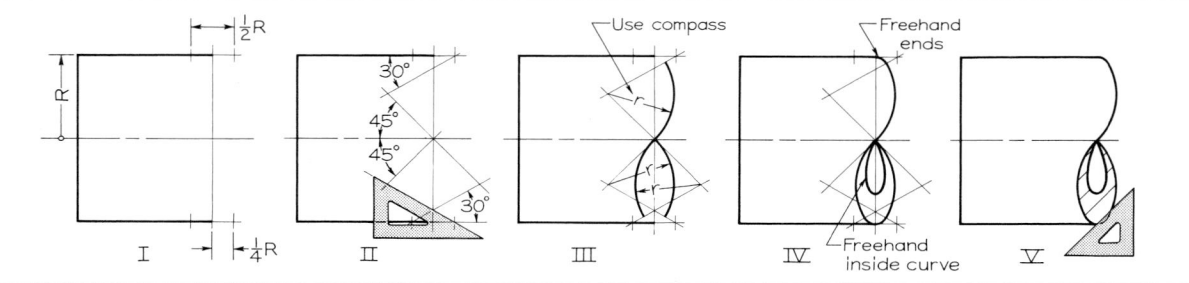

Fig. 9.38   Steps in Drawing **S**-Breaks for Tubing.

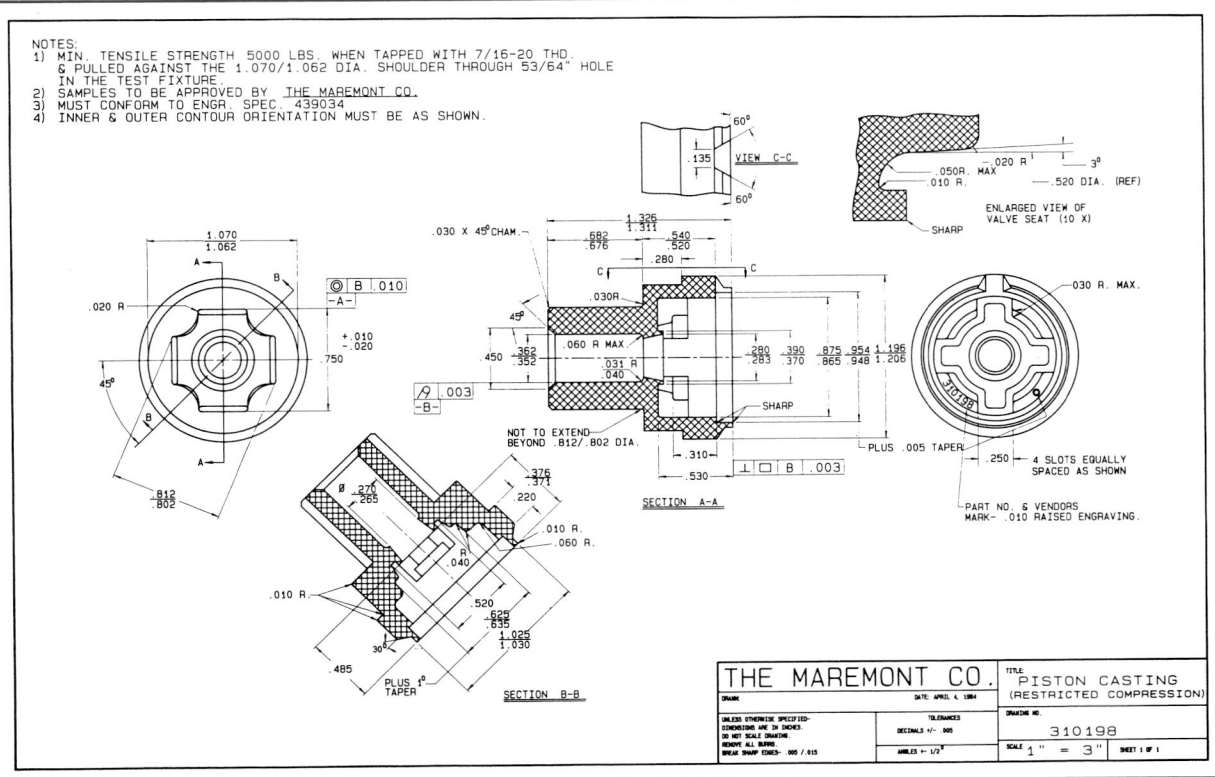

Fig. 9.39 Detail Drawing Produced by Using the VersaCAD Advanced System. *Courtesy of VersaCAD.*

Sectioning Problems

Any of the following problems, Figs. 9.40–9.58, may be drawn freehand or with instruments, as assigned by the instructor. However, the problems in Fig. 9.40 are especially suitable for sketching on 8.5″ × 11.0″ graph paper with appropriate grid squares. Two problems can be drawn on one sheet, using Layout A–1 similar to Fig. 6.51, with borders drawn freehand. If desired, the problems may be sketched on plain drawing paper. Before making any sketches, the student should study carefully §§6.1–6.10.

The problems in Figs. 9.41–9.52 are intended to be drawn with instruments, but may be drawn freehand, if desired. If metric or decimal dimensions are required, the student should first study §§13.1–13.25. If an ink tracing is required, the student is referred to §§2.50–2.52.

Since many of the problems in this chapter are of a general nature, they can also be solved on most computer graphics systems. If a system is available, the instructor may choose to assign specific problems to be completed by this method.

Additional problems in convenient form for solution are presented in the worksheets at the back of this book. Refer to Drawings 9-1 to 9-5 and accompanying instructions.

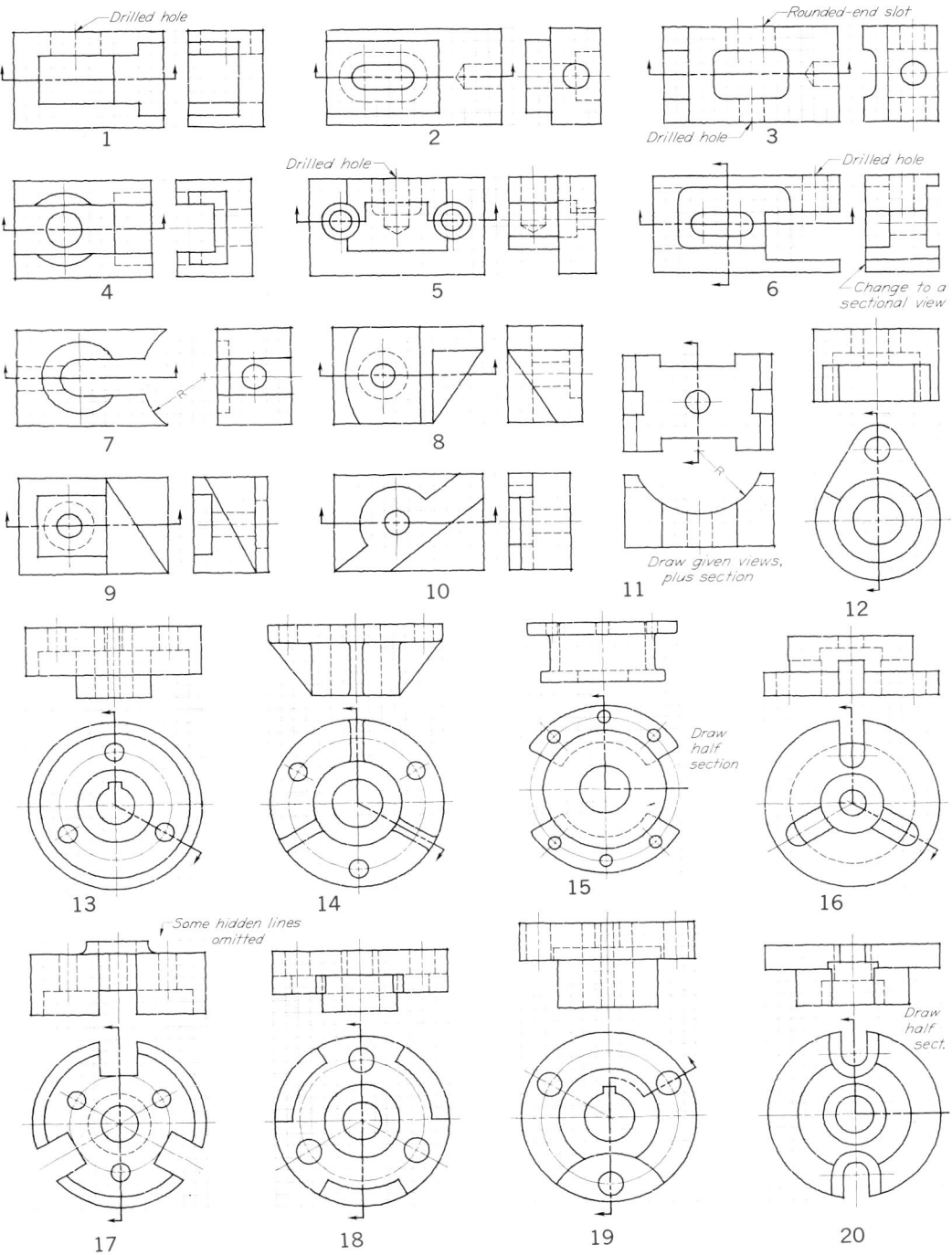

Fig. 9.40 Freehand Sectioning Problems. Using Layout A–1 or A4–1 adjusted (freehand) on graph paper or plain paper, two problems per sheet as in Fig. 6.51, sketch views with sections as indicated. Each grid square = 6 mm (¼"). In Probs. 1 to 10, top and right-side views are given. Sketch front sectional views and then move right-side views to line up horizontally with front sectional views. Omit cutting planes except in Probs. 5 and 6.

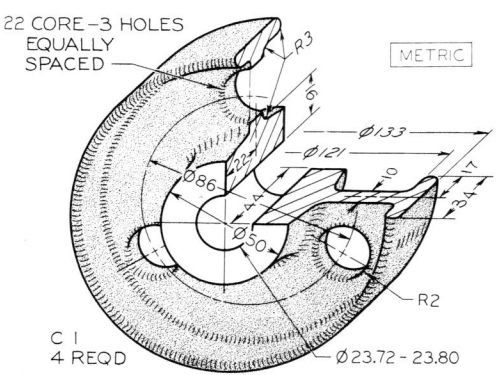

Fig. 9.41 Truck Wheel. Using Layout A–3 or A4–3 (adjusted), draw necessary views, with half section.*

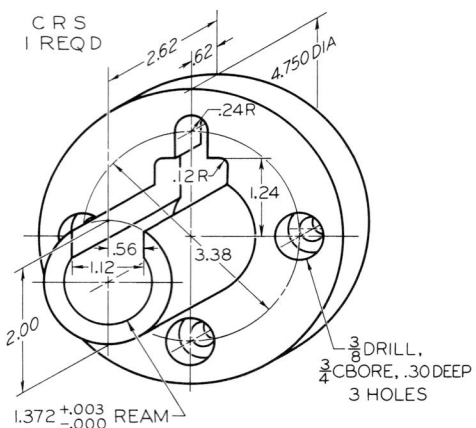

Fig. 9.42 Centering Bushing. Using Layout A–3 or A4–3 (adjusted), draw necessary views, with full section.*

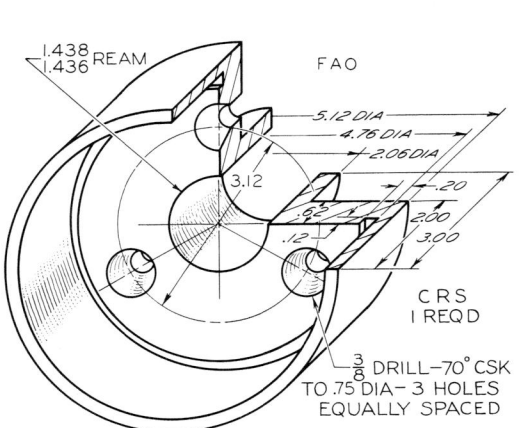

Fig. 9.43 Special Bearing. Using Layout A–3 or A4–3 (adjusted), draw necessary views, with full section.*

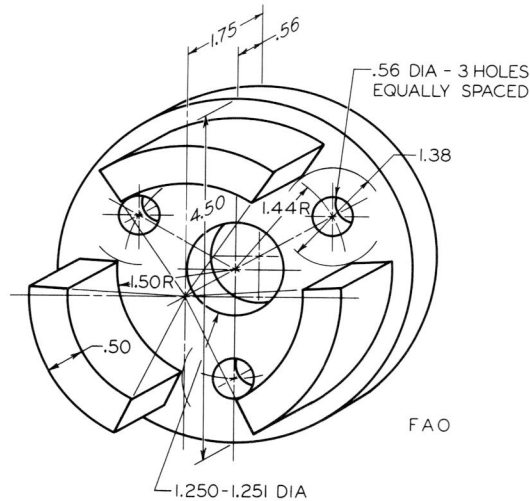

Fig. 9.44 Cup Washer. Using Layout A–3 or A4–3 (adjusted), draw necessary views, with full section.*

*If dimensions are required, study §§13.1–13.25. Use metric or decimal-inch dimensions as assigned by the instructor.

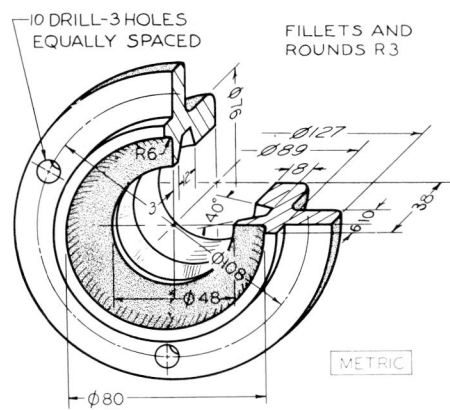

Fig. 9.45 Fixed Bearing Cup. Using Layout A–3 or A4–3 (adjusted), draw necessary views, with full section.*

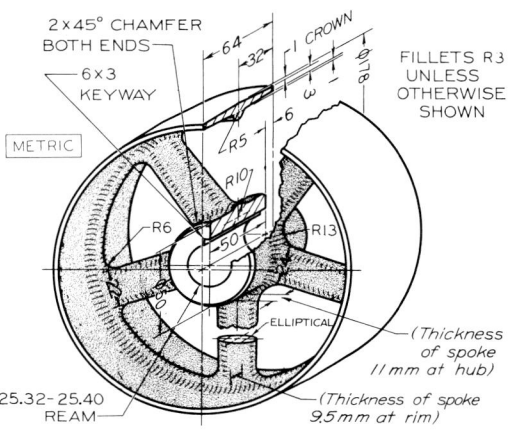

Fig. 9.46 Pulley. Using Layout B–4 or A3–4 (adjusted), draw necessary views, with full section, and revolved section of spoke.*

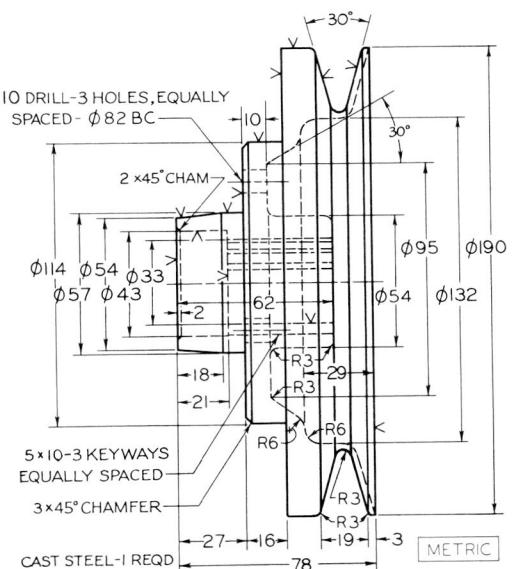

Fig. 9.47 Sheave. Using Layout B–4 or A3–4 (adjusted), draw two views, including half section.*

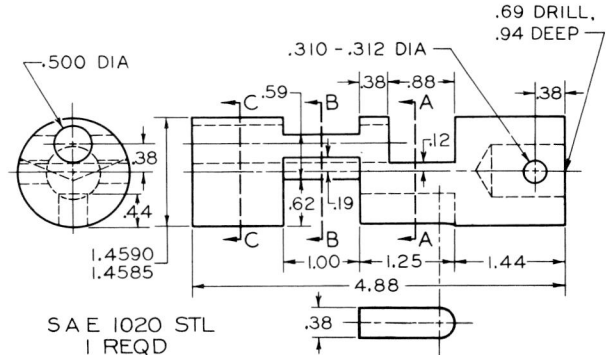

Fig. 9.48 Operating Valve.
Given: Front, left-side, and partial bottom views. Required: Front, right-side, and full bottom view, plus indicated removed sections [Layout B–4 or A3–4 (adjusted)].*

*If dimensions are required, study §§13.1–13.25. Use metric or decimal-inch dimensions as assigned by the instructor.

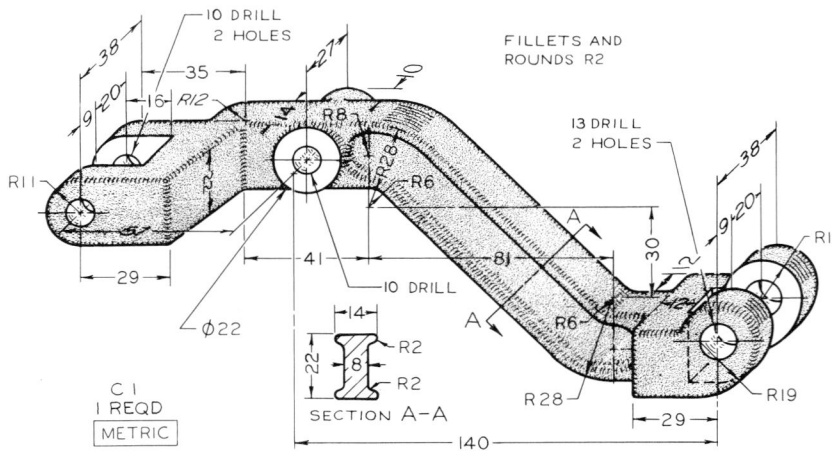

Fig. 9.49 Dash Pot Lifter. Using Layout B–4 or A3–4 (adjusted), draw necessary views, with revolved section instead of removed section.*

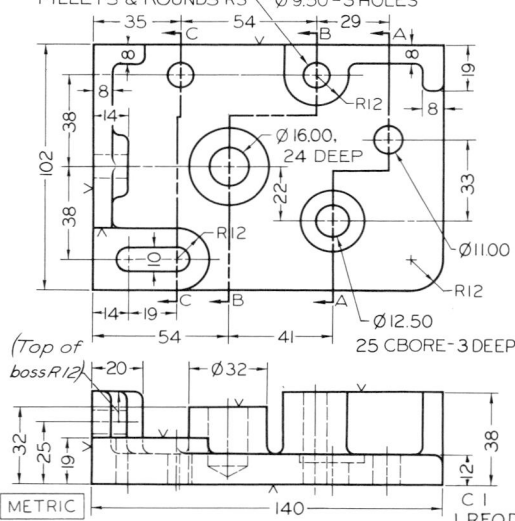

Fig. 9.50 Adjuster Base.
Given: Front and top views.
Required: Front and top views and sections A–A, B–B, and C–C. Show all visible lines. [Layout B–4 or A3–4 (adjusted)].*

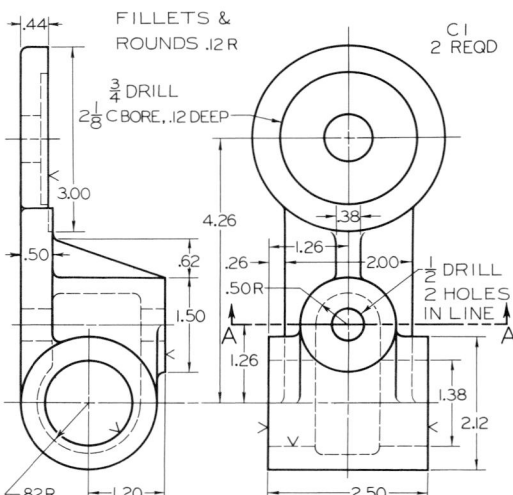

Fig. 9.51 Mobile Housing.
Given: Front and left-side views.
Required: Front view, right-side view in full section, and removed section A–A [Layout B–4 or A3–4 (adjusted)].*

*If dimensions are required, study §§13.1–13.25. Use metric or decimal-inch dimensions as assigned by the instructor.

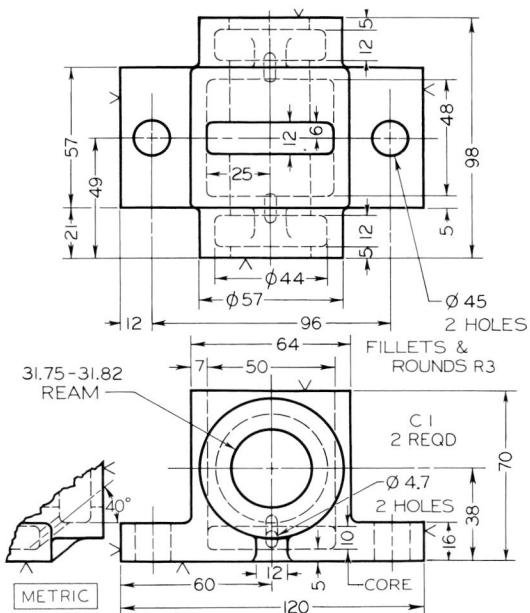

Fig. 9.52 Auxiliary Shaft Bearing.
Given: Front and top views.
Required: Front and top views and right-side view
in full section [Layout B–4 or A3–4 (adjusted)].*

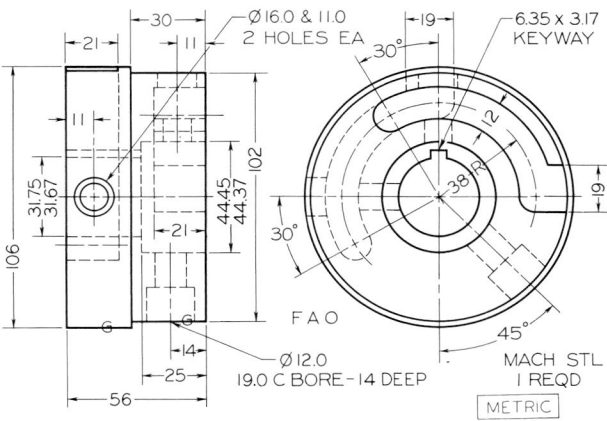

Fig. 9.53 Traverse Spider.
Given: Front and left-side views.
Required: Front and right-side views and top view
in full section [Layout B–4 or A3–4 (adjusted)].*

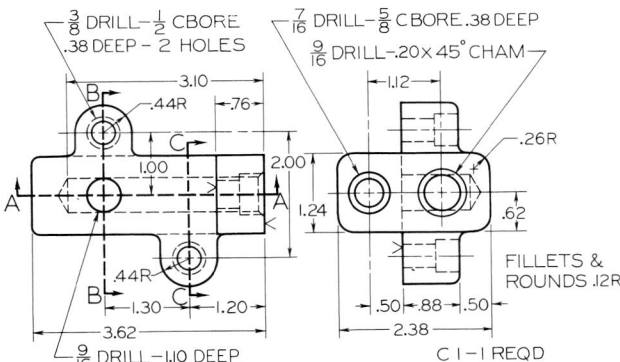

Fig. 9.54 Bracket.
Given: Front and right-side views.
Required: Take front as new top; then add right-
side view, front view in full section A–A, and sections
B–B and C–C [Layout B–4 or A3–4 (adjusted)].*

*If dimensions are required, study §§13.1–13.25. Use metric or decimal-inch dimensions as assigned by the
instructor.

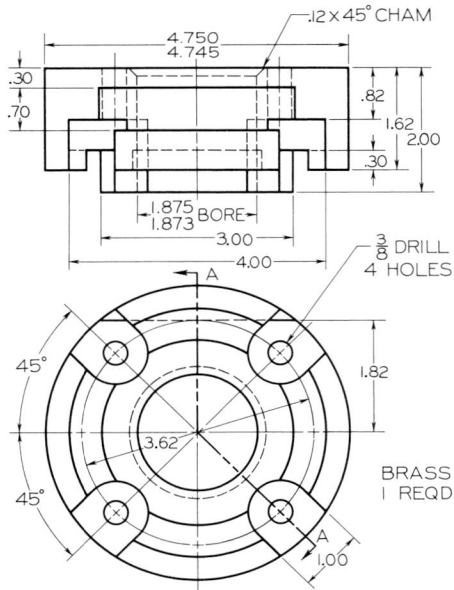

Fig. 9.55 Oil Retainer.
Given: Front and top views.
Required: Front view and section **A–A** [Layout B–4 or A3–4 (adjusted)].*

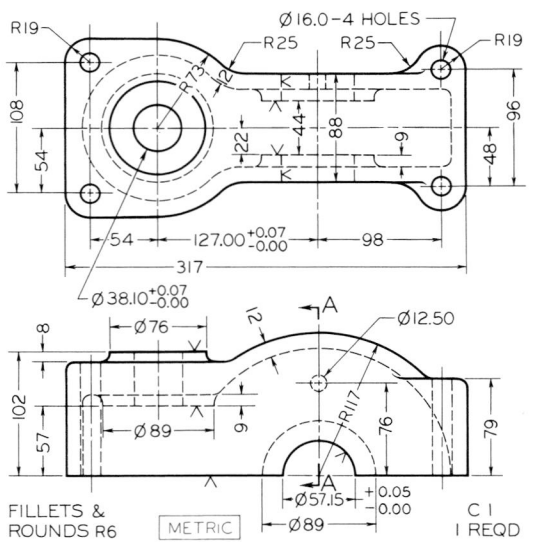

Fig. 9.56 Gear Box.
Given: Front and top views.
Required: Front in full section, bottom view, and right-side section **A–A**; half size [Layout B–4 or A3–4 (adjusted)].*

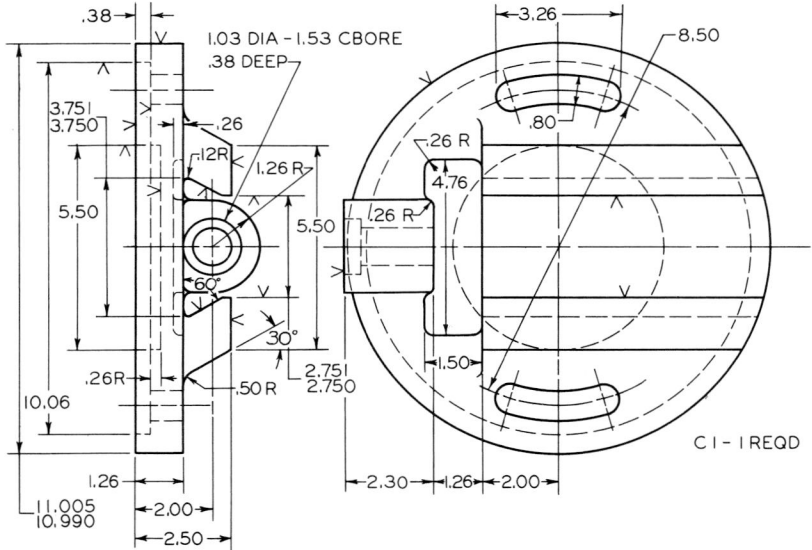

Fig. 9.57 Slotted Disk for Threading Machine.
Given: Front and left-side views.
Required: Front and right-side views and top full-section view; half size [Layout B–4 or A3–4 (adjusted)].*

*If dimensions are required, study §§13.1–13.25. Use metric or decimal-inch dimensions as assigned by the instructor.

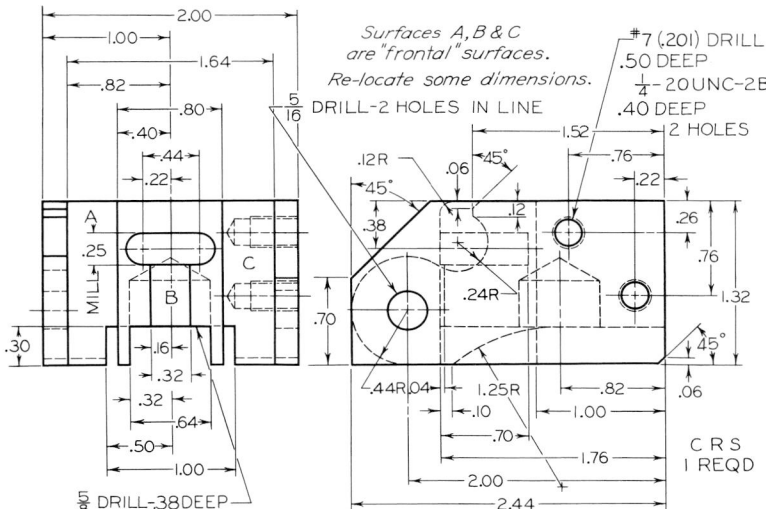

Fig. 9.58 Cocking Block.

Given: Front and right-side views.

Required: Take front as new top view; then add new front view, and right-side view in full section. Draw double size on Layout C–4 or A2–4.*

*If dimensions are required, study §§13.1–13.25. Use metric or decimal-inch dimensions as assigned by the instructor.

Auxiliary Views

Many objects are of such shape that their principal faces cannot always be assumed parallel to the regular planes of projection. For example, in Fig. 10.1 (a), the base of the design for the bearing is shown in its true size and shape, but the rounded upper portion is situated at an angle with the planes of projection and does not appear in its true size and shape in any of the three regular views.

In order to show the true circular shapes, it is necessary to assume a direction of sight perpendicular to the planes of those curves, as shown at (b). The resulting view is known as an *auxiliary view*. This view, together with the top view, completely describes the object. The front and right-side views are not necessary.

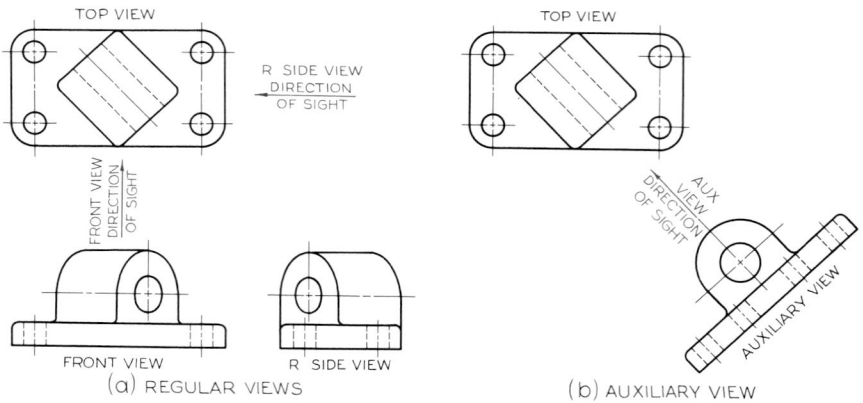

Fig. 10.1   Regular Views and Auxiliary Views.

10.1 Definitions

A view obtained by a projection on any plane other than the horizontal, frontal, and profile projection planes is called an *auxiliary view*. A *primary* auxiliary view is projected on a plane that is perpendicular to one of the principal planes of projection and is inclined to the other two. A *secondary* auxiliary view is projected from a primary auxiliary view and on a plane inclined to all three principal projection planes. See §10.19.

10.2 The Auxiliary Plane

In Fig. 10.2 (a), the object shown has an inclined surface that does not appear in its true size and shape in any regular view. The auxiliary plane is assumed parallel to the inclined surface P, that is,

perpendicular to the line of sight, which is at right angles to that surface. The auxiliary plane is then perpendicular to the frontal plane of projection and hinged to it.

When the horizontal and auxiliary planes are unfolded to appear in the plane of the front view, as shown at (b), the *folding lines* represent the hinge lines joining the planes. The drawing is simplified, as shown at (c), by retaining the folding lines, H/F and F/1, and omitting the planes. As will be shown later, the folding lines may themselves be omitted in the actual drawing. The inclined surface P is shown in its true size and shape in the auxiliary view, the long dimension of the surface being projected directly from the front view and the *depth* from the top view.

It should be observed that the positions of the

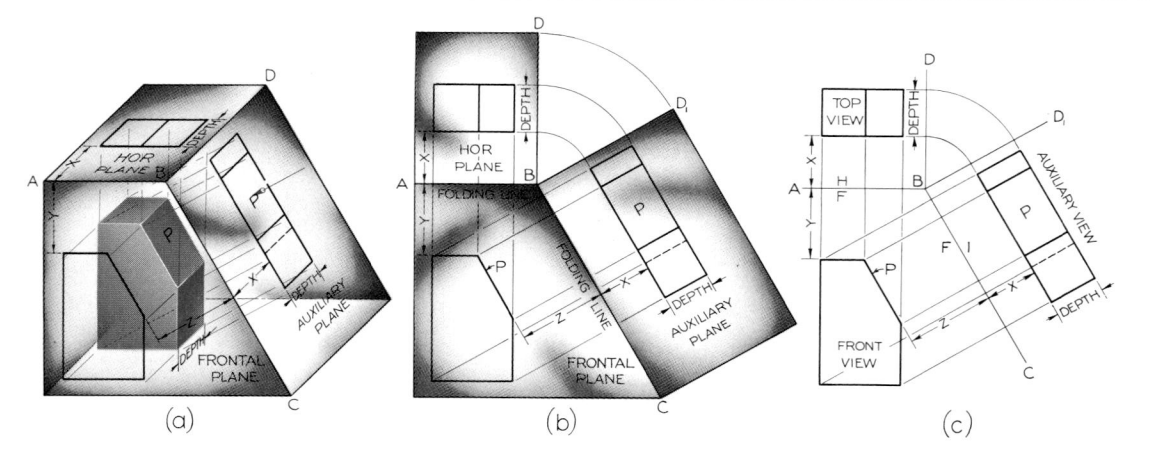

Fig. 10.2   An Auxiliary View.

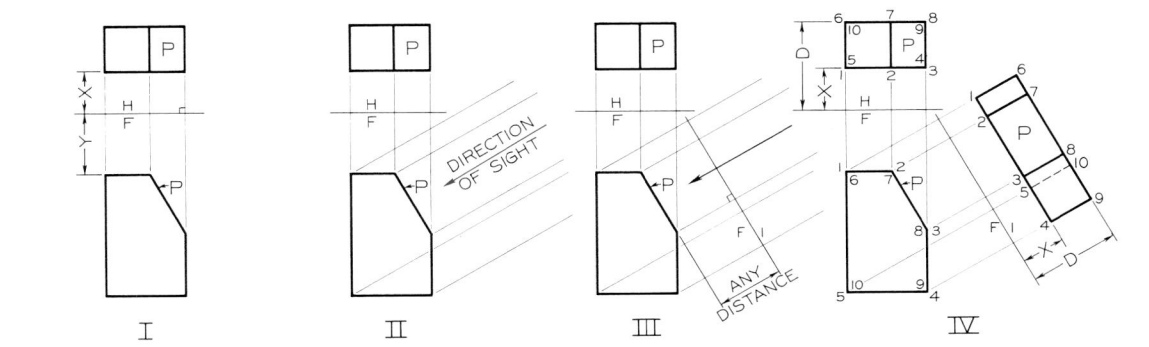

Fig. 10.3   To Draw an Auxiliary View—Folding-Line Method.

folding lines depend upon the relative positions of the planes of the glass box at (a). If the horizontal plane is moved upward, the distance Y is increased. If the frontal plane is brought forward, the distances X are increased but remain *equal*. If the auxiliary plane is moved to the right, the distance Z is increased. Note that both the top and auxiliary views show the *depth* of the object.

10.3 To Draw an Auxiliary View—Folding-Line Method

As shown in Fig. 10.2 (c), the folding lines are the hinge lines of the glass box. Distances X must be equal, since they both represent the distance of the front surface of the object from the frontal plane of projection.

Although distances X must remain equal, distances Y and Z, from the front view to the respective folding lines, may or may not be equal.

The steps in drawing an auxiliary view with the aid of the folding lines, shown in Fig. 10.3, are described as follows:

I.   The front and top views are given. It is required to draw an auxiliary view showing the true size and shape of inclined surface P. Draw the folding line H/F between the views at right angles to the projection lines. Distances X and Y may or may not be equal, as desired.

NOTE   In the following steps, manipulate the triangle (either triangle) as shown in Fig. 10.4 to draw lines parallel or perpendicular to the inclined face.

II.   Assume arrow, indicating direction of sight,

perpendicular to surface P. Draw light projection lines from the front view parallel to the arrow, or perpendicular to surface P.

III.   Draw folding line F/1 for the auxiliary view at right angles to the projection lines and at any convenient distance from the front view.

IV.   Draw the auxiliary view, using the numbering system explained in §7.6. Locate all points the same distances from folding line F/1 as they are from folding line H/F in the top view. For example, points 1 to 5 are distance X from the folding lines in both the top and auxiliary views, and points 6 to 10 are distance D from the corresponding folding lines. Since the object is viewed in the direction of the arrow, it will be seen that edge 5–10 will be hidden in the auxiliary view.

10.4 Reference Planes

In the auxiliary views shown in Figs. 10.2 (c) and 10.3, the folding lines represent the edge views of the front plane of projection. In effect, the frontal

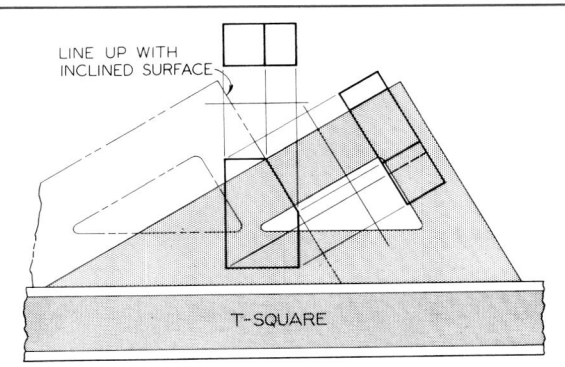

Fig. 10.4   Drawing Parallel or Perpendicular Lines.

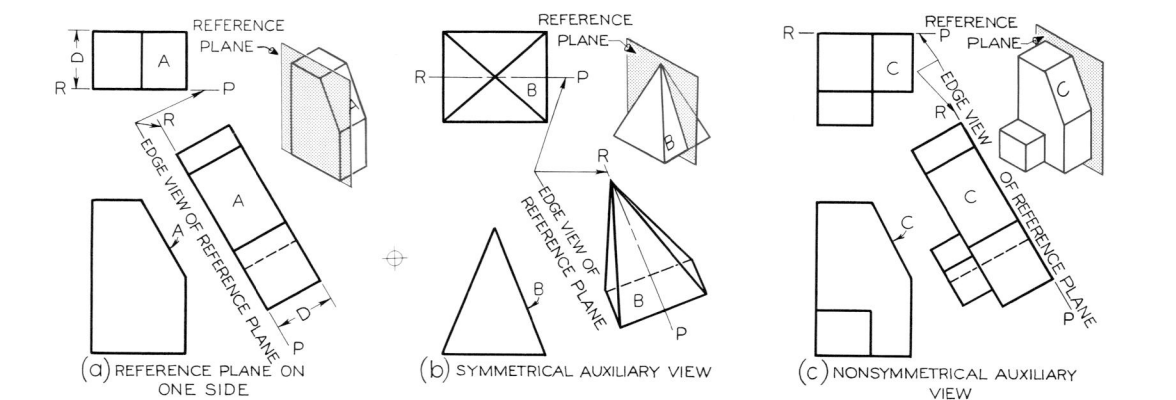

Fig. 10.5 Position of the Reference Plane.

plane is used as a *reference plane*, or *datum plane*, for transferring distances (*depth measurements*) from the top view to the auxiliary view.

Instead of using one of the planes of projection as a reference plane, it is often more convenient to assume a reference plane inside the glass box parallel to the plane of projection and touching or cutting through the object. For example, Fig. 10.5 (a), a reference plane is assumed to coincide with the front surface of the object. This plane appears edgewise in the top and auxiliary views, and the two reference lines are then used in the same manner as folding lines. Dimensions D, to the reference lines, are equal. The advantage of the reference-plane method is that fewer measurements are required, since some points of the object lie in the reference plane.

The reference plane may coincide with the front surface of the object as at (a), or it may cut through the object as at (b) if the object is symmetrical, or the reference plane may coincide with the back surface of the object as at (c), or through any intermediate point of the object.

The reference plane should be assumed in the position most convenient for transferring distances with respect to it. Remember the following:

1. Reference lines, like folding lines, are always at right angles to the projection lines between the views.

2. A reference plane appears as a line in two alternate views, never in adjacent views.

3. Measurements are always made at right angles to the reference lines or parallel to the projection lines.

4. In the auxiliary view, all points are at the same distances from the reference line as the corresponding points are from the reference line in the *second previous view*, or alternate view.

10.5 To Draw an Auxiliary View—Reference-Plane Method

The object shown in Fig. 10.6 (a) is numbered as explained in §7.6. To draw the auxiliary view, proceed as follows:

I. Draw two views of the object, and assume an arrow indicating the direction of sight for the auxiliary view of surface A.

II. Draw projection lines parallel to the arrow.

III. Assume reference plane coinciding with back surface of object as shown at (a). Draw reference lines in the top and auxiliary views at right angles to the projection lines: *these are the edge views of the reference plane.*

IV. Draw auxiliary view of surface A. It will be true size and shape because the direction of sight was taken perpendicular to that surface. Transfer depth measurements from the top view to the auxiliary view with dividers or scale. Each point in the auxiliary view will be on its projection line from the front view and the same distance from the reference line as it is in the top view to the corresponding reference line.

V. Complete the auxiliary view by adding other visible edges and surfaces of the object. Each numbered point in the auxiliary view lies on its projection line from the front view and is the same dis-

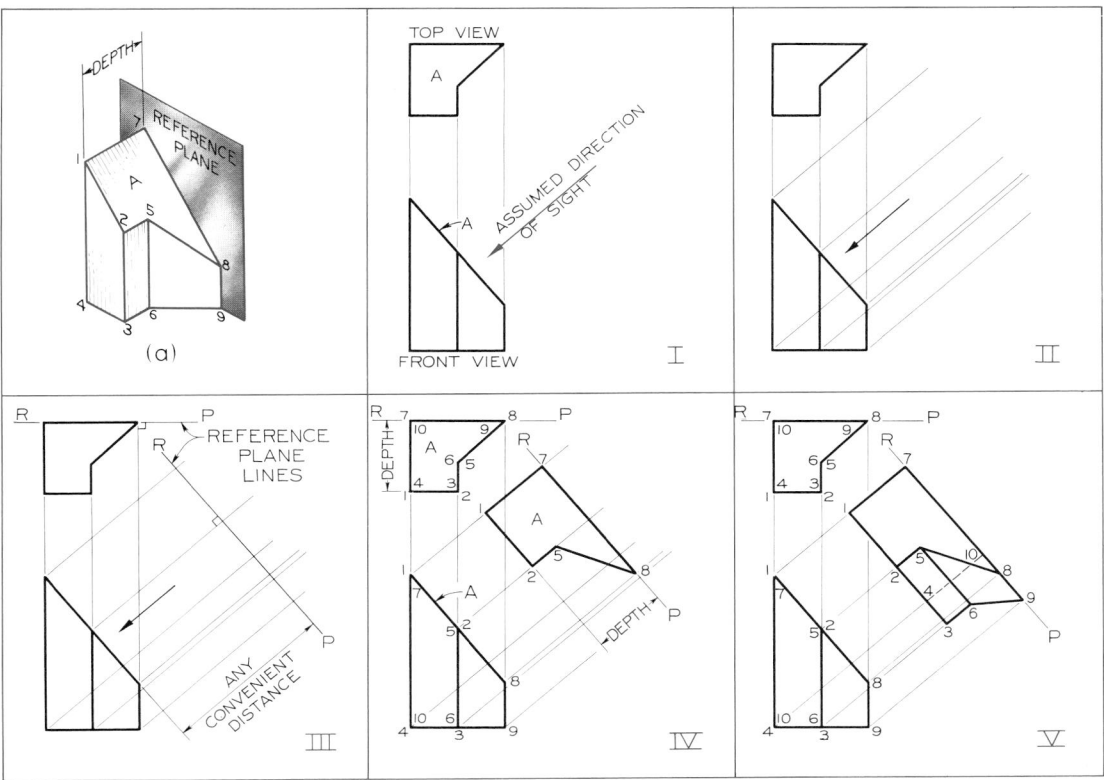

Fig. 10.6   To Draw an Auxiliary View—Reference-Plane Method.

tance from the reference line as it is in the top view. Note that two surfaces of the object appear as lines in the auxiliary view.

10.6 Classification of Auxiliary Views

Auxiliary views are classified and named according to the principal dimensions of the object shown in the auxiliary view. For example, the auxiliary view in Fig. 10.6 is a *depth auxiliary view* because it shows the principal dimension of the object, *depth*. Any auxiliary view projected from the front view, also known as front adjacent view, will show the depth of the object and is a depth auxiliary view.

Similarly, any auxiliary view projected from the top view, also known as top-adjacent view, is a height auxiliary view, and any auxiliary view projected from the side view (either side), also known as side adjacent view, is a width-auxiliary view. For examples of height auxiliary views, see Figs. 10.1 (b) and 10.13 (b). Depth auxiliary views are illustrated in Figs. 10.27 and 10.33.

10.7 Depth Auxiliary Views

An infinite number of auxiliary planes can be assumed perpendicular to, and hinged to, the frontal plane (**F**) of projection. Five such planes are shown in Fig. 10.7 (a), the horizontal plane being included to show that it is similar to the others. In all of these views the principal dimension, *depth*, is shown; hence all of the auxiliary views are depth auxiliary views.

The unfolded auxiliary planes are shown in (b), which also shows how the depth dimension may be projected from the top view to all auxiliary views. The arrows indicate the directions of sight for the several views, and the projection lines are respectively parallel to these arrows. The arrows may be assumed but need not be actually drawn, since the projection lines determine the direction of sight. The folding lines are perpendicular to the arrows and the corresponding projection lines. Since the auxiliary planes can be assumed at any distance from the object, it follows that the folding lines may be any distance from the front view.

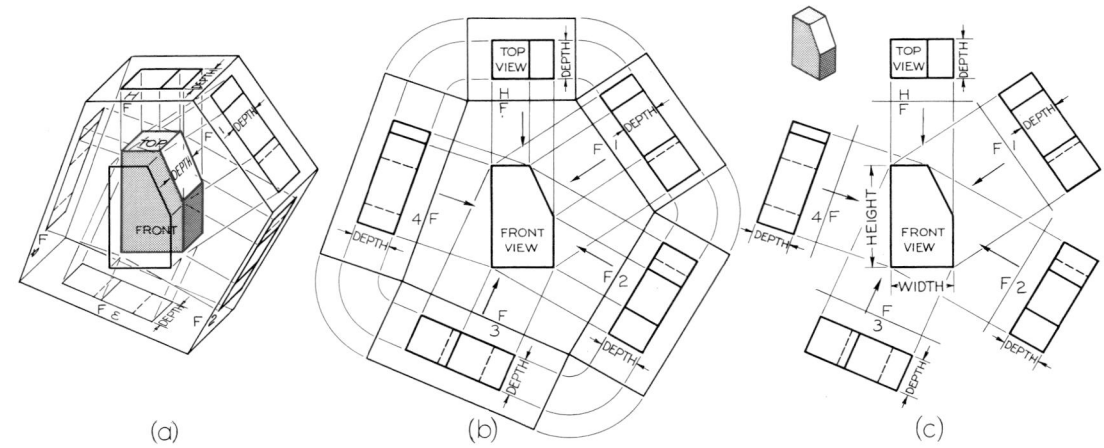

Fig. 10.7   Depth Auxiliary Views.

The complete drawing, with the outlines of the planes of projection omitted, is shown at (c). This shows the drawing as it would appear on paper, in which use is made of reference planes as described in §10.4, all depth dimensions being measured perpendicular to the reference line in each view.

Note that the front view shows the *height* and the *width* of the object, *but not the depth*. The depth is shown in all views that are projected from the front view; hence, this rule: *The principal dimension shown in an auxiliary view is that one which is not shown in the adjacent view from which the auxiliary view was projected.*

10.8 Height Auxiliary Views

An infinite number of auxiliary planes can be assumed perpendicular to, and hinged to, the horizontal plane (H) of projection, several of which are shown in Fig. 10.8 (a). The front view and all of the auxiliary views show the principal dimension, *height*. Hence, all of the auxiliary views are height auxiliary views.

The unfolded projection planes are shown at (b), and the complete drawing, with the outlines of the planes of projection omitted, is shown at (c). All reference lines are perpendicular to the corresponding projection lines, and all height dimensions are

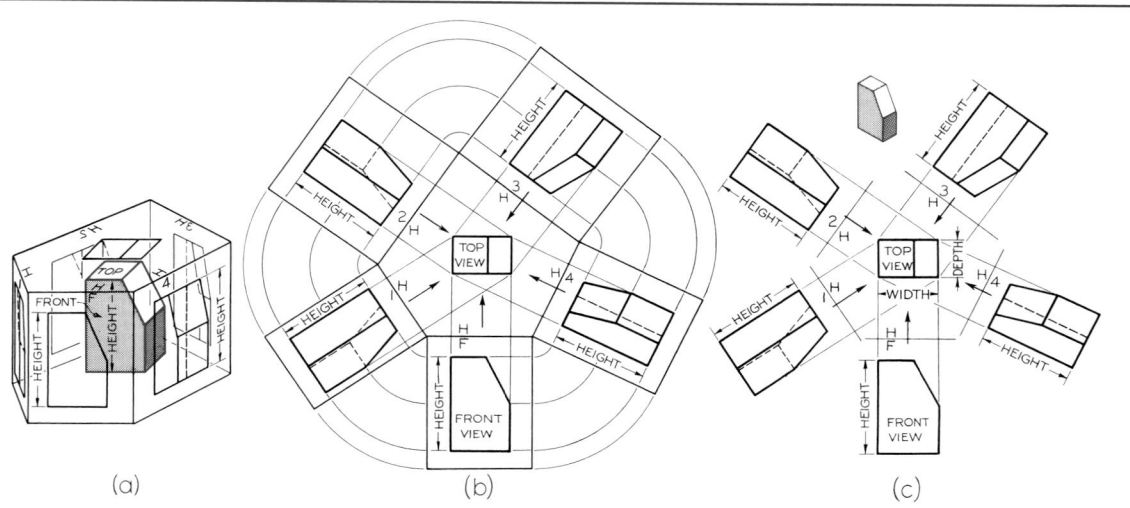

Fig. 10.8   Height Auxiliary Views.

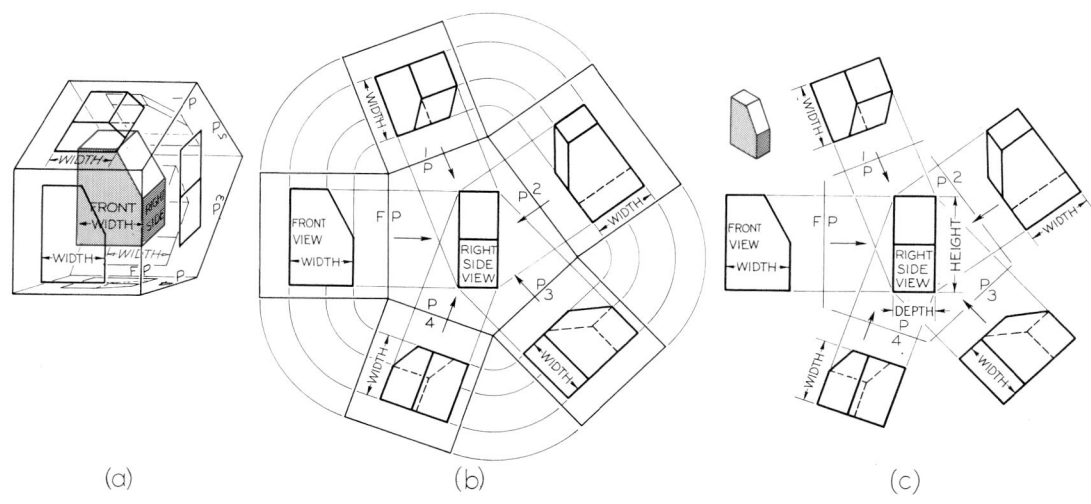

Fig. 10.9   Width Auxiliary Views.

measured parallel to the projection lines, or perpendicular to the reference lines, in each view. Note that in the view projected from, which is the top view, the only dimension *not shown* is height.

10.9 Width Auxiliary Views

An infinite number of auxiliary planes can be assumed perpendicular to, and hinged to, the profile plane (P) of projection, several of which are shown in Fig. 10.9 (a). The front view and all of the auxiliary views show the principal dimension, *width*. Hence, all of the auxiliary views are width auxiliary views.

The unfolded planes are shown at (b), and the complete drawing, with the outlines of the planes of projection omitted, is shown at (c). All reference lines are perpendicular to the corresponding projection lines, and all width dimensions are measured parallel to the projection lines, or perpendicular to the reference lines, in each view. Note that in the right-side view, from which the auxiliary views are projected, the only dimension *not shown* is width.

10.10 Revolving a Drawing

In Fig. 10.10 (a) is a drawing showing top, front, and auxiliary views. At (b) the drawing is shown revolved, as indicated by the arrows, until the auxiliary view and the front view line up horizontally. Although the views remain exactly the same, the

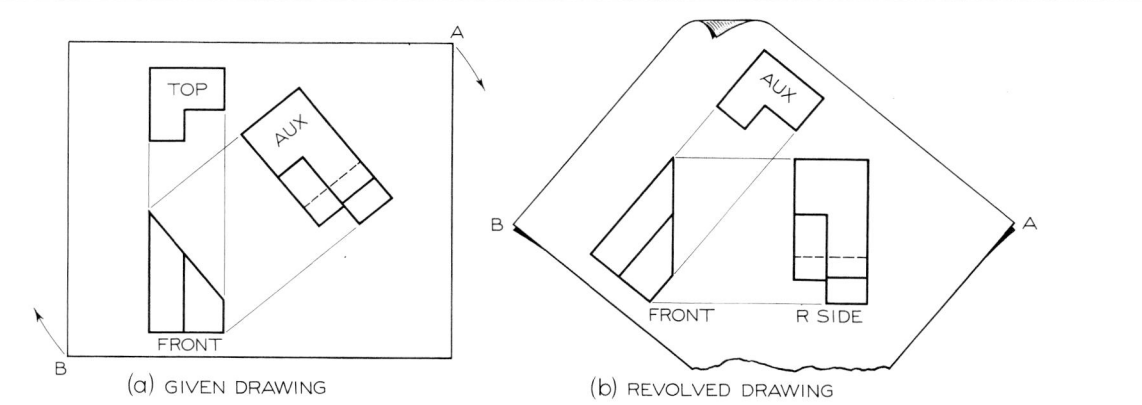

Fig. 10.10   Revolving a Drawing.

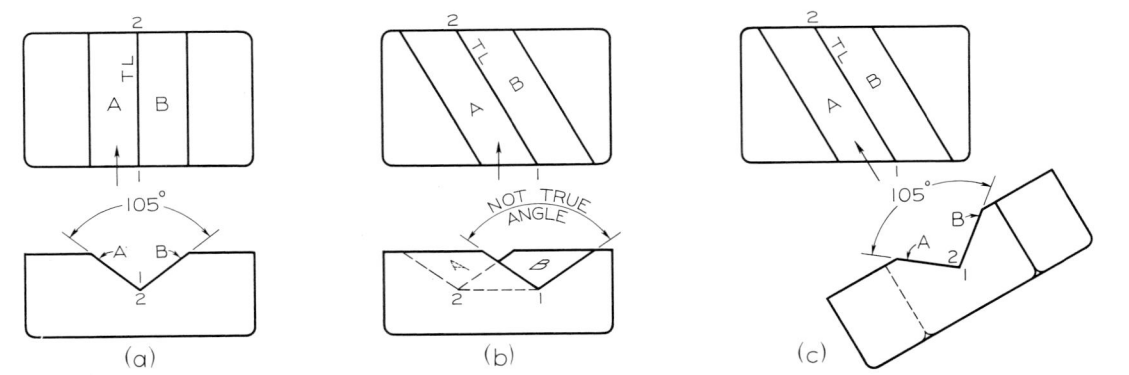

Fig. 10.11   Dihedral Angles.

names of the views are changed if drawn in this position. The auxiliary view now becomes a right-side view, and the top view becomes an auxiliary view. Some students find it easier to visualize and draw an auxiliary view when revolved to the position of a regular view in this manner. In any case, it should be understood that an auxiliary view basically is like any other view.

10.11 Dihedral Angles

The angle between two planes is a dihedral angle. One of the principal uses of auxiliary views is to show dihedral angles in true size, mainly for dimensioning purposes. In Fig. 10.11 (a) a block is shown with a V-groove situated so that the true dihedral angle between inclined surfaces **A** and **B** is shown in the front view.

Assume a line in a plane. For example, draw a straight line on a sheet of paper; then hold the paper so as to view the line as a point. You will observe that when the line appears as a point, the plane containing the line appears as a line. Hence, this rule: *To get the edge view of a plane, find the point view of any line in that plane.*

In Fig. 10.11 (a), line 1–2 is the line of intersection of planes **A** and **B**. Now, line 1–2 lies in both planes at the same time; therefore, a point view of this line will show both planes as lines, and the angle between them is the dihedral angle between the planes. Hence, this rule: *To get the true angle between two planes, find the point view of the line of intersection of the planes.*

At (b), the line of intersection 1–2 does not appear as a point in the front view; hence, planes **A** and **B** do not appear as lines, and the true dihedral

angle is not shown. Assuming that the actual angle is the same as at (a), does the angle show larger or smaller than at (a)? The drawing at (b) is unsatisfactory. The true angle does not appear because the direction of sight (see arrow) is not parallel to the line of intersection 1–2.

At (c) the direction of sight arrow is taken parallel to the line 1–2, producing an auxiliary view in which line 1–2 appears as a point, planes **A** and **B** appear as lines, and the true dihedral angle is shown. *To draw a view showing a true dihedral angle, assume the direction of sight parallel to the line of intersection between the planes of the angle.*

10.12 Plotted Curves

As shown in §7.30, if a cylinder is cut by an inclined plane, the inclined surface is elliptical in shape. In Fig. 7.34 (a), such a surface is produced, but the ellipse does not show true size and shape because the plane of the ellipse is not seen at right angles in any view.

In Fig. 10.12 (a), the line of sight is taken perpendicular to the edge view of the inclined surface, and the resulting ellipse is shown in true size and shape in the auxiliary view. The major axis is found by direct projection from the front view, and the minor axis is equal to the diameter of the cylinder. The left end of the cylinder (a circle) will appear as an ellipse in the auxiliary view, the major axis of which is equal to the diameter of the cylinder.

Since this is a symmetrical object, the reference plane is assumed to be located through the center, as shown. To plot points on the ellipses, select points on the circle of the side view, and project them across to the inclined surface or to the left-end sur-

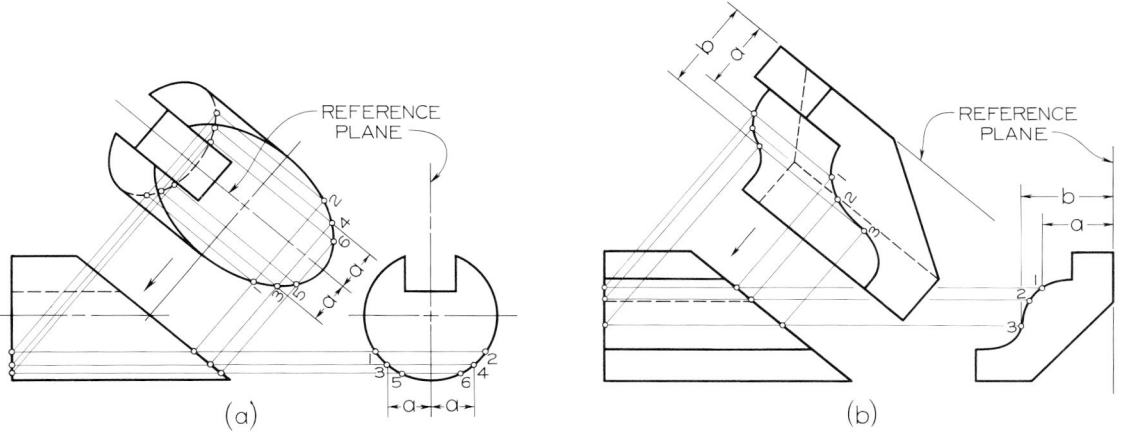

Fig. 10.12   Plotted Curves.

face, and then upward to the auxiliary view. In this manner, two points can be projected each time, as shown for points 1–2, 3–4, and 5–6. Distances *a* are equal and are transferred from the side view to the auxiliary view with the aid of dividers. A sufficient number of points must be projected to establish the curves accurately. Use the irregular curve as described in §2.54.

Since the major and minor axes are known, any of the true ellipse methods of Figs. 5.48–5.50 and 5.52 (a) may be used. If an approximate ellipse is adequate for the job in hand, the method of Fig. 5.56 can be used. But the quickest and easiest method is to use an ellipse template, as explained in §5.56.

In Fig. 10.12 (b), the auxiliary view shows the true size and shape of the inclined cut through a piece of molding. The method of plotting points is similar to that explained for the ellipse in Fig. 10.12 (a).

10.13 Reverse Construction

In order to complete the regular views, it is often necessary to construct an auxiliary view first. For example, in Fig. 10.13 (a) the upper portion of the right-side view cannot be constructed until the auxiliary view is drawn and points established on the curves and then projected back to the front view as shown.

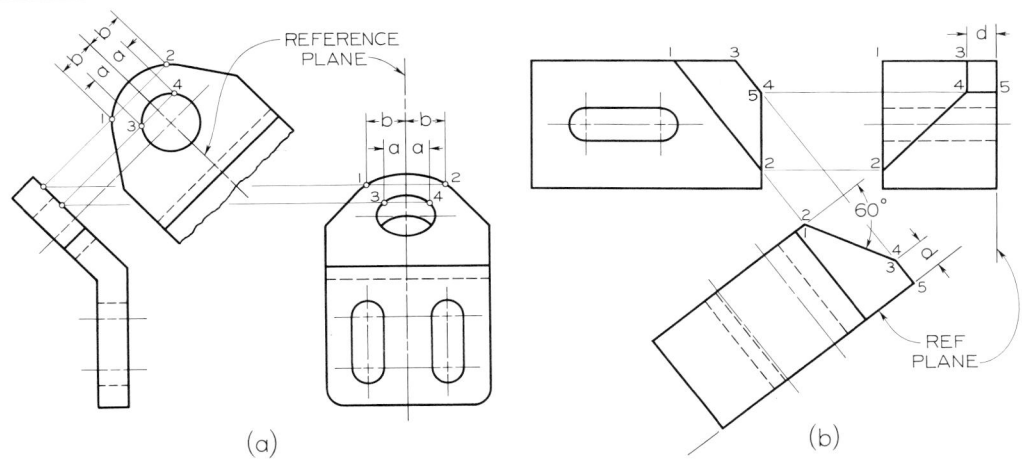

Fig. 10.13   Reverse Construction.

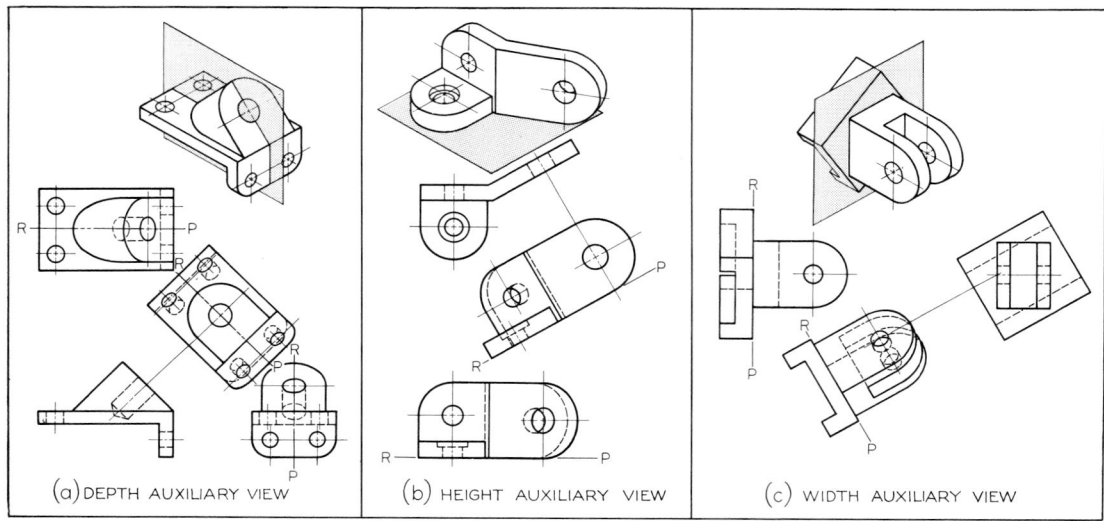

Fig. 10.14   Primary Auxiliary Views.

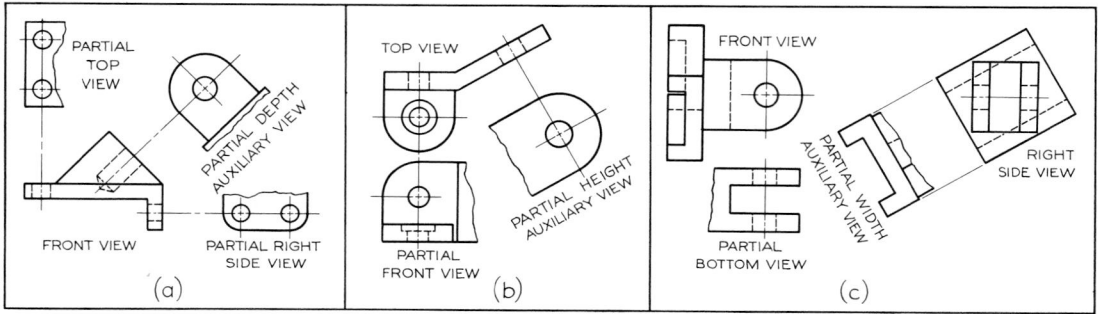

Fig. 10.15   Partial Views.

At (b), the 60° angle and the location of line 1–2 in the front view are given. In order to locate line 3–4 in the front view, the lines 2–4, 3–4, and 4–5 in the side view, it is necessary first to construct the 60° angle in the auxiliary view and project back to the front and side views, as shown.

10.14 Partial Auxiliary Views

The use of an auxiliary view often makes it possible to omit one or more regular views and thus to simplify the shape description, as shown in Fig. 10.1 (b). In Fig. 10.14 three complete auxiliary-view drawings are shown. Such drawings take a great deal of time to draw, particularly when ellipses are involved, as is so often the case, and the completeness of detail may add nothing to clearness or may even detract from it because of the clutter of lines. However, in these cases some portion of every view is needed—no view can be completely eliminated, as was done in Fig. 10.1 (b).

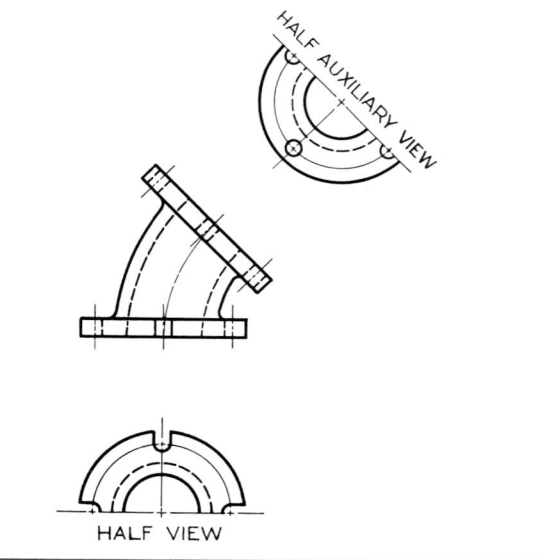

Fig. 10.16   Half Views.

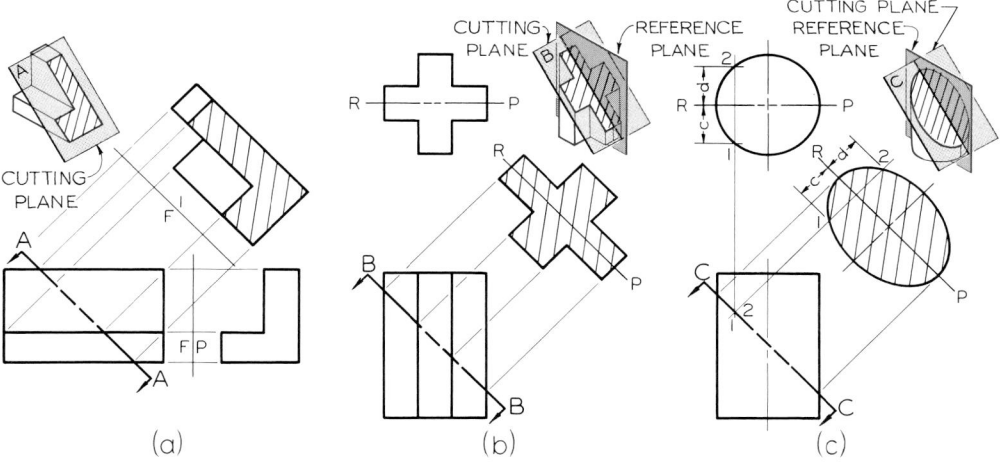

Fig. 10.17   Auxiliary Sections.

As described in §7.9, *partial views* are often sufficient, and the resulting drawings are considerably simplified and easier to read. Similarly, as shown in Fig. 10.15, partial regular views and partial auxiliary views are used with the same result. Usually a break line is used to indicate the imaginary break in the views. *Do not draw a break line coinciding with a visible line or a hidden line.*

In order to clarify the relationship of views, the auxiliary views should be connected to the views from which they are projected, either with a center line or with one or two projection lines. This is particularly important with regard to partial views that often are small and easily appear to be "lost" and not related to any view.

10.15 Half Auxiliary Views

If an auxiliary view is symmetrical, and if it is necessary to save space on the drawing or to save time in drafting, only half of the auxiliary view need be drawn, as shown in Fig. 10.16. In this case, half of a regular view is also shown, since the bottom flange is also symmetrical. See §§7.9 and 9.14. Note that in each case the *near half* is shown.

10.16 Hidden Lines in Auxiliary Views

In practice, hidden lines should be omitted in auxiliary views, as in ordinary views, §6.25, unless they are needed for clearness. The beginner, however, should show all hidden lines, especially if the auxiliary view of the entire object is shown. Later, in advanced work, it will become clearer as to when hidden lines can be omitted.

10.17 Auxiliary Sections

An auxiliary section is simply an auxiliary view in section. In Fig. 10.17 (a), note the cutting-plane line and the terminating arrows that indicate the direction of sight for the auxiliary section. Observe that the section lines are drawn at approximately 45° with visible outlines. In an auxiliary section drawing, the entire portion of the object behind the cutting plane may be shown, as at (a), or the cut surface alone, as at (b) and (c).

An auxiliary section through a cone is shown in Fig. 10.18. This is one of the conic sections, §5.47, in this case a parabola. The parabola may be drawn by other methods, Figs. 5.57 and 5.58, but the

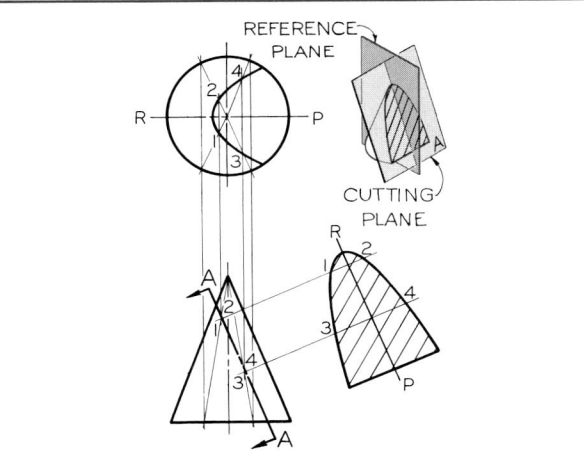

Fig. 10.18   Auxiliary Section.

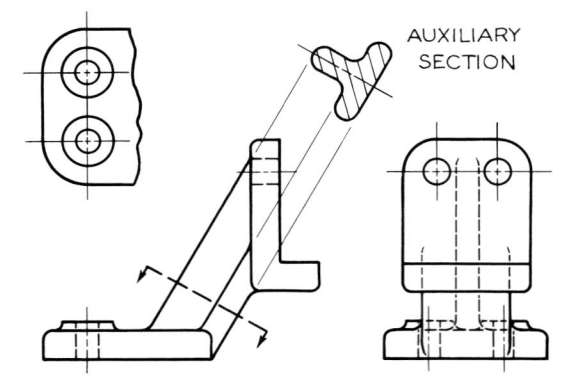

Fig. 10.19 Auxiliary Section.

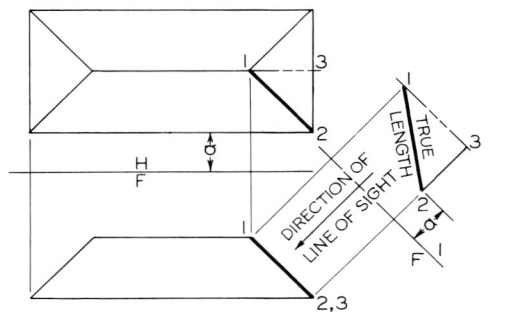

Fig. 10.20 True Length of a Line by Means of an Auxiliary View.

method shown here is by projection. In Fig. 10.18, elements of the cone are drawn in the front and top views. These intersect the cutting plane at points **1, 2, 3**, and so on. These points are established in the top view by projecting upward to the top views of the corresponding elements. In the auxiliary section, all points on the parabola are the same distance from the reference plane **RP** as they are in the top view.

A typical example of an auxiliary section in machine drawing is shown in Fig. 10.19. Here, there is not sufficient space for a revolved section, §9.9, although a removed section, §9.10, could have been used instead of an auxiliary section.

10.18 True Length of Line — Auxiliary-View Method

A line will show in true length when projected to a projection plane parallel to the line.

In Fig. 10.20, let it be required to find the true length of the hip rafter **1–2** by means of a depth auxiliary view.

I.　Assume an arrow perpendicular to **1–2** (front view) indicating the direction of sight, and place the **H/F** folding line as shown.

II.　Draw the **F/1** folding line perpendicular to the arrow and at any convenient distance from **1–2** (front view), and project the points **1** and **3** toward it.

III.　Set off the points **1** and **2** in the auxiliary view at the same distance from the folding line as they are in the top view. The triangle **1–2–3** in the auxiliary view shows the true size and shape of the roof section **1–2–3**, and the distance **1–2** in the auxiliary view is the true length of the hip rafter **1–2**.

To find the true length of a line by revolution, see §11.10.

10.19 Successive Auxiliary Views

Up to this point we have dealt with *primary* auxiliary views, that is, single auxiliary views projected from one of the regular views. In Fig. 10.21, auxiliary view **1** is a primary auxiliary view, projected from the top view.

From primary auxiliary view **1**, a *secondary* auxiliary view **2** can be drawn; then from it a third auxiliary view **3**, and so on. An infinite number of such successive auxiliary views may be drawn, a process that may be likened to the "chain reaction" in a nuclear explosion.

However, secondary auxiliary view **2** is not the only one that can be projected from primary auxiliary view **1** and thus start an independent "chain reaction." As shown by the arrows around view **1**, an infinite number of secondary auxiliary views, with different lines of sight, may be projected. *Any auxiliary view projected from a primary auxiliary view is a secondary auxiliary view.* Furthermore, any succeeding auxiliary view may be used to project an infinite number of "chains" of views from it.

In this example, folding lines are more convenient than reference-plane lines. In auxiliary view **1**, all numbered points of the object are the same distance from folding line **H/1** as they are in the front view from folding line **H/F**. These distances, such as distance **a**, are transferred from the front view to the auxiliary view with the aid of dividers.

To draw the secondary auxiliary view **2**, drop the front view from consideration, and center attention

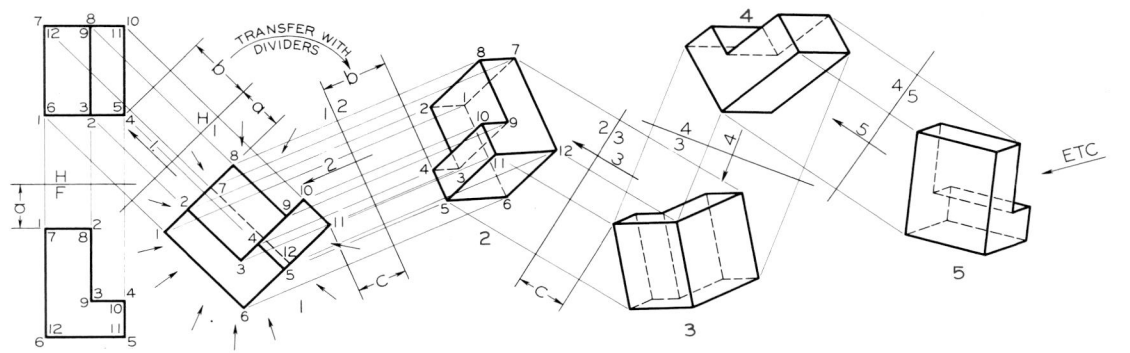

Fig. 10.21 Successive Auxiliary Views.

on the sequence of three views: the top view, view 1, and view 2. Draw arrow 2 toward view 1 in the direction desired for view 2, and draw light projection lines parallel to the arrow. Draw folding line 1/2 perpendicular to the projection lines and at any convenient distance from view 1. Locate all numbered points in view 2 from folding line 1/2 at the same distances they are in the top view from folding line H/1, using the dividers to transfer distances. For example, transfer distance b to locate points 4 and 5. Connect points with straight lines, and determine visibility. The corner nearest the observer (11) for view 2 will be visible, and the one farthest away (1) will be hidden, as shown.

To draw views 3, 4, and so on, repeat this procedure, remembering that each time we will be concerned only with a sequence of three views. In drawing any auxiliary view, the paper may be revolved so as to make the last two views line up as regular views.

10.20 Uses of Auxiliary Views
Generally, auxiliary views are used to show the true shape or true angle of features that appear distorted in the regular views. Basically, auxiliary views have the following four uses.

1. True length of line (TL), §10.18.
2. Point view of line, §10.11.
3. Edge view of plane (EV), §10.21.
4. True size of plane (TS), §10.21.

10.21 True Size of an Oblique Surface—Folding-Line Method
A typical requirement of a secondary auxiliary view is to show the true size and shape of an oblique surface, such as surface 1–2–3–4 in Fig. 10.22. In this case folding lines are used, but the same results can be obtained with reference lines. Proceed as follows.

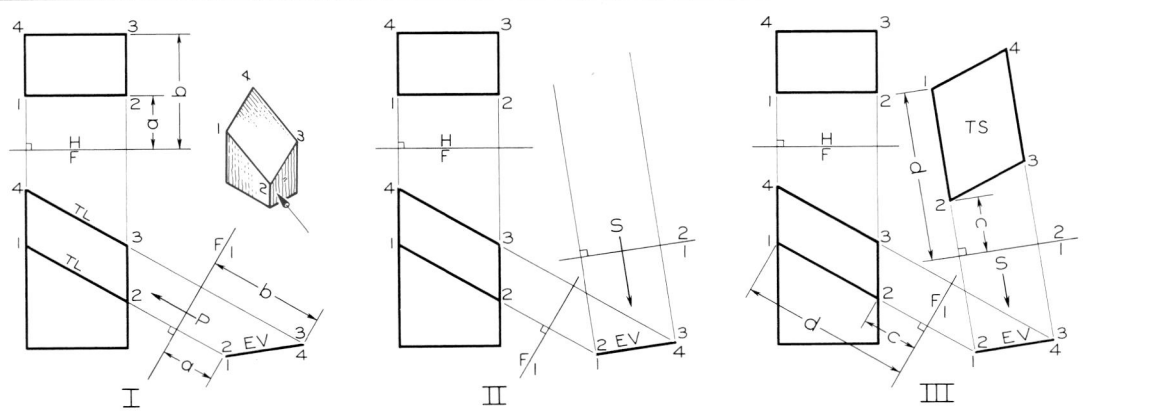

Fig. 10.22 True Size of Oblique Surface—Folding-Line Method.

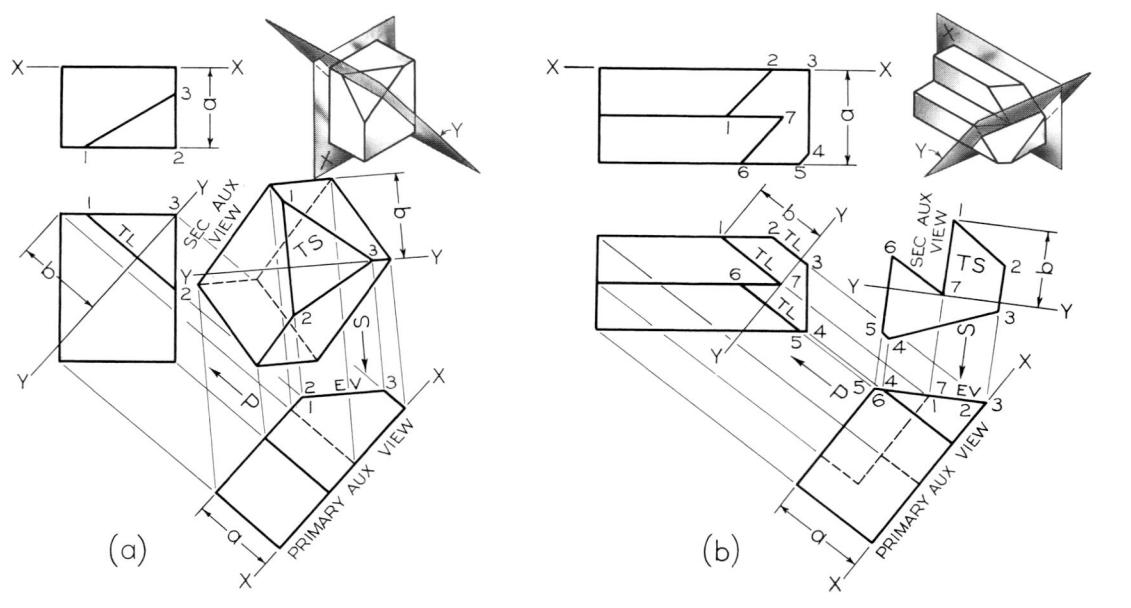

Fig. 10.23 True Size of an Oblique Surface—Reference-Plane Method.

I.   Draw primary auxiliary view showing surface 1–2–3–4 as a line. As explained in §10.11, the edge view (EV) of a plane is found by getting the point view of a line in that plane. To get the point view of a line, the line of sight must be assumed parallel to the line. Therefore, draw arrow P parallel to lines 1–2 and 3–4, which are true length (TL) in the front view, and draw projection lines parallel to the arrow. Draw folding line H/F between the top and front views and F/1 between the front and auxiliary views, perpendicular to the respective projection lines. All points in the auxiliary view will be the same distance from the folding line F/1 as they are in the top view from folding line H/F. Lines 1–2 and 3–4 will appear as points in the auxiliary view, and plane 1–2–3–4 will therefore appear *edgewise*, that is, as a line.

II.   Draw arrow S perpendicular to the edge view of plane 1–2–3–4 in the primary auxiliary view, and draw projection lines parallel to the arrow. Draw folding line 1/2 perpendicular to these projection lines and at a convenient distance from the primary auxiliary view.

III.   Draw secondary auxiliary view. Locate each point (transfer with dividers) the same distance from the folding line 1/2 as it is in the front view to the folding line F/1, as for example, dimensions c and d. The true size (TS) of the surface 1–2–3–4 will be shown in the secondary auxiliary view, since the di-

rection of sight, arrow S, was taken perpendicular to it.

10.22 True Size of an Oblique Surface— Reference-Plane Method

In Fig. 10.23 (a), it is required to draw an auxiliary view in which triangular surface 1–2–3 will appear in true size and shape. In order for the true size of the surface to appear in the secondary auxiliary view, arrow S must be assumed perpendicular to the edge view of that surface; so it is necessary to have the edge view of surface 1–2–3 in the primary auxiliary view first. In order to do this, the direction of sight, arrow P, must be parallel to a line in surface 1–2–3 that appears true length (TL) in the front view. Hence, arrow P is drawn parallel to line 1–2 of the front view, line 1–2 will appear as a point in the primary auxiliary view, and surface 1–2–3 must therefore appear edgewise in that view.

In this case it is convenient to use reference lines and to assume the reference plane X (for drawing the primary auxiliary view) coinciding with the back surface of the object, as shown. For the primary auxiliary view, all depth measurements, as a in the figure, are transferred with dividers from the top view with respect to the reference line X–X.

For the secondary auxiliary view, reference plane Y is assumed cutting through the object for

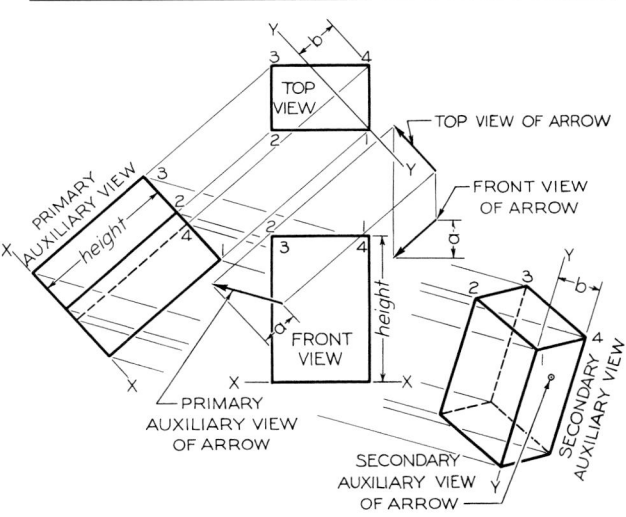

Fig. 10.24   Secondary Auxiliary View with Oblique Direction of Sight Given.

convenience in transferring measurements. All measurements perpendicular to Y–Y in the secondary auxiliary view are the same as between the reference plane and the corresponding points in the front view. Note that corresponding measurements must be *inside* (toward the central view in the sequence of three views) or *outside* (away from the central view). For example, dimension **b** is on the side of Y–Y *away* from the primary auxiliary view in both places.

In Fig. 10.23 (b) it is required to find the true size and shape of surface 1–2–3–4–5–6–7 and not to draw the complete secondary auxiliary view. The method is similar to that just described.

10.23 Secondary Auxiliary View, Oblique Direction of Sight Given

In Fig. 10.24 two views of a block are given, with two views of an arrow indicating the direction in which it is desired to look at the object to obtain a view. Proceed as follows.

I.   *Draw primary auxiliary view of both the object and the assumed arrow,* which will show the true length *of the arrow.* In order to do this, assume a horizontal reference plane X–X in the front and auxiliary views, as shown. Then assume a direction of sight perpendicular to the given arrow. In the front view, the butt end of the arrow is a distance **a** higher than the arrow point, and this distance is

transferred to the primary auxiliary view as shown. All *height* measurements in the auxiliary view correspond to those in the front view.

II.   *Draw secondary auxiliary view,* which will show the arrow as a point. This can be done because the arrow shows in true length in the primary auxiliary view, and projection lines for the secondary auxiliary view are drawn parallel to it. Draw reference line Y–Y, for the secondary auxiliary view perpendicular to these projection lines. In the top view, draw Y–Y perpendicular to the projection lines to the primary auxiliary view. All measurements, such as **b**, with respect to Y–Y correspond in the secondary auxiliary view and the top view.

It will be observed that the secondary auxiliary views of Figs. 10.23 (a) and 10.24 have considerable pictorial value. These are trimetric projections, §17.30. However, the direction of sight could be assumed, in the manner of Fig. 10.24, to produce either isometric or dimetric projections. If the direction of sight is assumed parallel to the diagonal of a cube, the resulting view is an *isometric projection,* §17.3.

A typical application of a secondary auxiliary view in machine drawing is shown in Fig. 10.25. All

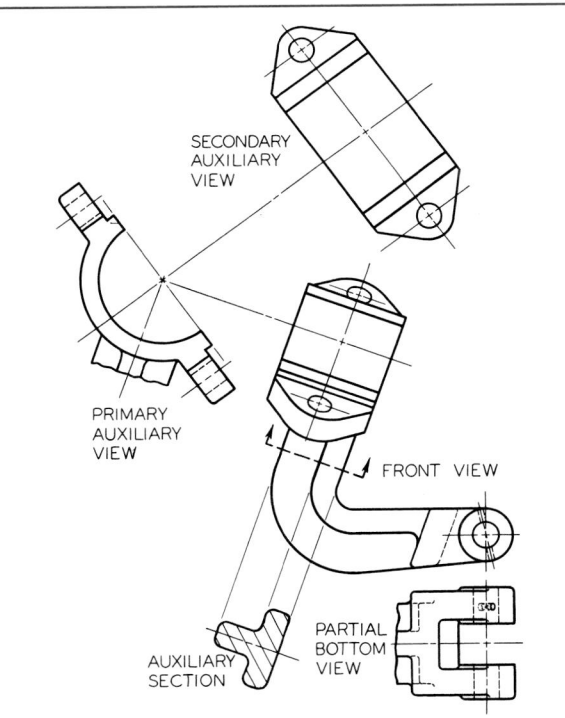

Fig. 10.25   Secondary Auxiliary View—Partial Views.

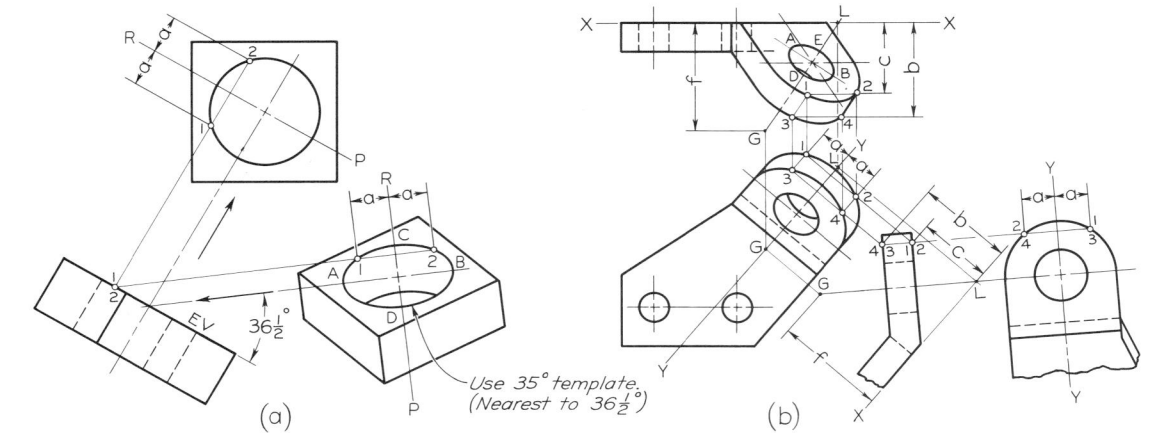

Fig. 10.26 Ellipses.

views are partial views, except the front view. The partial secondary auxiliary view illustrates a case in which break lines are not needed. Note the use of an auxiliary section to show the true shape of the arm.

10.24 Ellipses

As shown in §7.30, if a circle is viewed obliquely, the result is an ellipse. This often occurs in successive auxiliary views, because of the variety of directions of sight. In Fig. 10.26 (a) the hole appears as a true circle in the top view. The circles appear as straight lines in the primary auxiliary view and as ellipses in the secondary auxiliary view. In the latter, the major axis **AB** of the ellipse is parallel to the projection lines and equal in length to the true diameter of the circle as shown in the top view. The minor axis **CD** is perpendicular to the major axis, and its foreshortened length is projected from the primary auxiliary view.

The ellipse can be completed by projecting points, such as **1** and **2**, symmetrically located about the reference plane **RP** coinciding with **CD** with distances **a** equal in the top and secondary auxiliary views as shown, and finally, after a sufficient number of points have been plotted, by applying the irregular curve, §2.54

Since the major and minor axes are easily found, any of the true-ellipse methods of Figs. 5.48–5.50 and 5.52 (a) may be used, or an approximate ellipse, Fig. 5.56, may be found sufficiently accurate for a

particular drawing. Or the ellipses may be easily and rapidly drawn with the aid of an ellipse template, §5.56. The "angle" of ellipse to use is the one that most closely matches the angle between the direction of sight arrow and the plane (**EV**) containing the circle, as seen in this case in the primary auxiliary view. Here the angle is $36\frac{1}{2}°$, so a 35° ellipse is selected.

At (b) successive auxiliary views are shown in which the true circular shapes appear in the secondary auxiliary view, and the elliptical projections in the front and top views. It is necessary to construct the circular shapes in the secondary auxiliary view, then to project plotted points back to the primary auxiliary view, the front view, and finally to the top view, as shown in the figure for points **1**, **2**, **3**, and **4**. The final curves are then drawn with the aid of the irregular curve.

If the major and minor axes are found, any of the true-ellipse methods may be used; or better still, an ellipse template, §5.56, may be employed. The major and minor axes are easily established in the front view, but in the top view, they are more difficult to find. The major axis **AB** is at right angles to the center line **GL** of the hole, and equal in length to the true diameter of the hole. The minor axis **ED** is at right angles to the major axis. Its length is found by plotting several points in the vicinity of one end of the minor axis, or by using descriptive geometry to find the angle between the line of sight and the inclined surface, and by this angle selecting the ellipse guide required.

10.25 Computer Graphics

If the user has a thorough working knowledge of the principles of projection and can visualize which views of an object are required to best depict it in a drawing, computer graphics can provide a powerful tool allowing the operator to quickly manipulate the views of a drawing to show any desired viewing orientation.

CAD programs make it easy to create secondary auxiliary views, partial views, and auxiliary sections, Fig. 10.25.

Auxiliary View Problems

The problems in Figs. 10.27–10.49 are to be drawn with instruments or freehand. If partial auxiliary views are not assigned, the auxiliary views are to be complete views of the entire object, including all necessary hidden lines.

It is often difficult to space properly the views of an auxiliary view drawing. In some cases it may be necessary to make a trial blocking out on a preliminary sheet before starting the actual drawing. Allowances for dimensions must be made if metric or decimal dimensions are to be included. In such case, the student should study §§13.1–13.25.

Since many of the problems in this chapter are of a general nature, they can also be solved on most computer graphics systems. If a system is available, the instructor may choose to assign specific problems to be completed by this method.

Additional problems in convenient form for solution are presented in the worksheets at the back of this book. Refer to Drawings 10-1 to 10-4 and accompanying instructions.

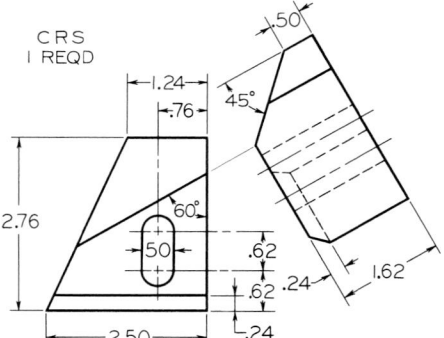

Fig. 10.27 RH Finger.
Given: Front and auxiliary views.
Required: Complete front, auxiliary, left-side, and top views [Layout A–3 or A4–3 (adjusted)].

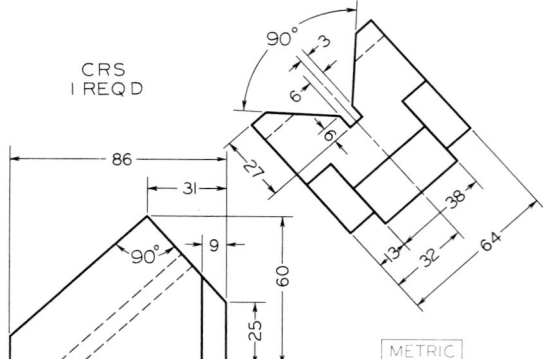

Fig. 10.28 V-Block.
Given: Front and auxiliary views.
Required: Complete front, top, and auxiliary views [Layout A–3 or A4–3 (adjusted)].

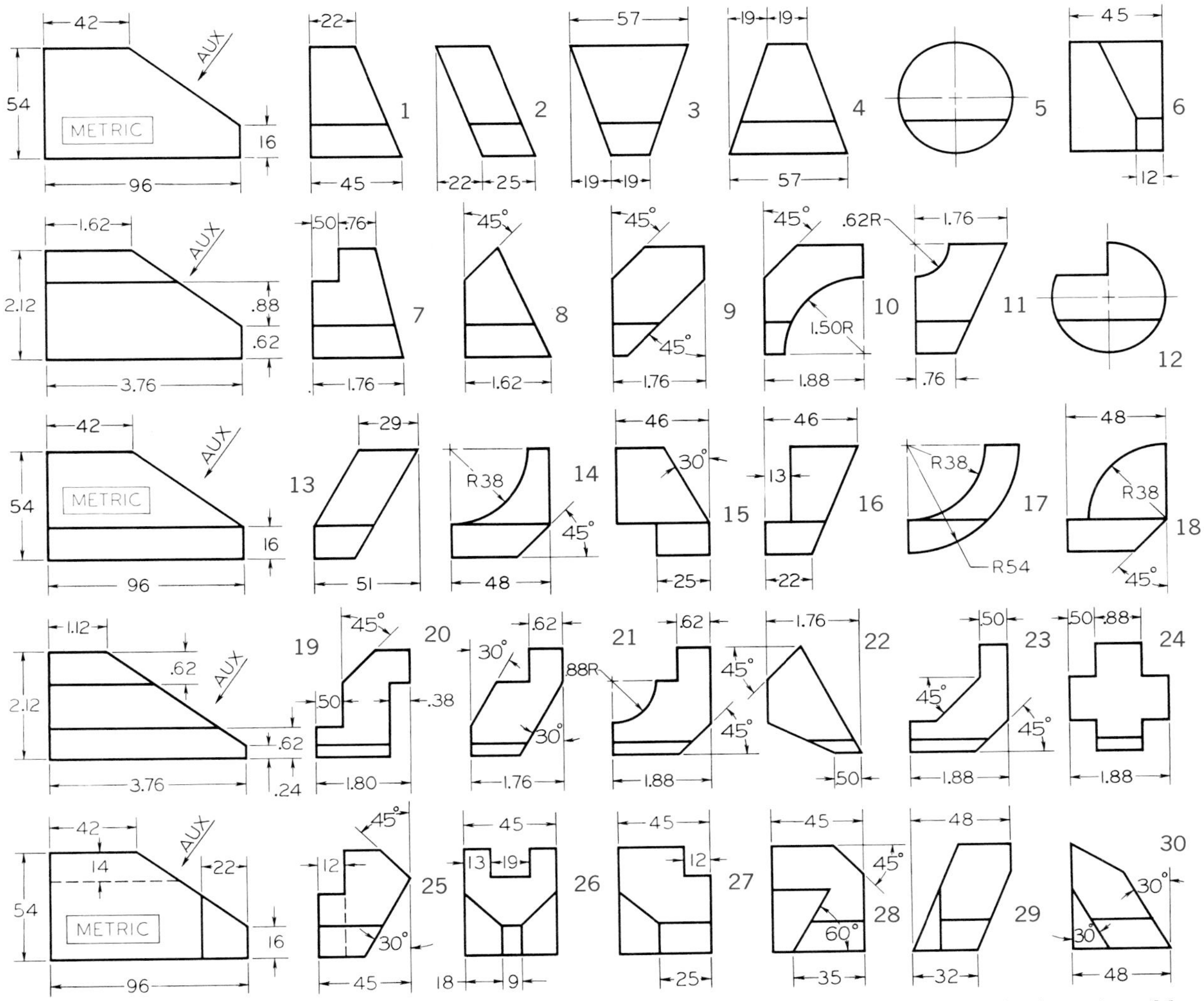

Problems 1 through 30 (Fig. 10.29), with dimensions as shown on the figures:

1 · 2 · 3 · 4 · 5 · 6
7 · 8 · 9 · 10 · 11 · 12
13 · 14 · 15 · 16 · 17 · 18
19 · 20 · 21 · 22 · 23 · 24
25 · 26 · 27 · 28 · 29 · 30

Fig. 10.29 Auxiliary View Problems. Make freehand sketch or instrument drawing of selected problem as assigned by instructor. Draw given front and right-side views, and add incomplete auxiliary view, including all hidden lines [Layout A–3 or A4–3 (adjusted)]. If assigned, design your own right-side view consistent with given front view, and then add complete auxiliary view. Problems 1 to 6, 13 to 18, and 25 to 30 are given in metric dimensions. Problems 7 to 12 and 19 to 24 are given in decimal-inch dimensions.

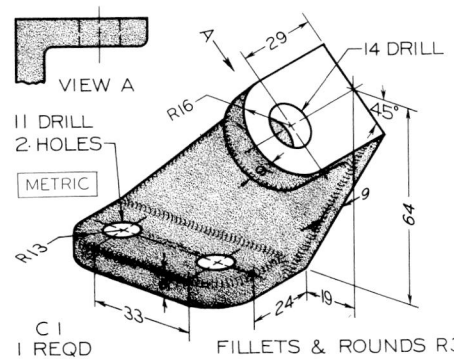

VIEW A

II DRILL
2 HOLES

METRIC

A   29   14 DRILL   45°

R16   R13   9   64   19   24   33

C I
I REQD   FILLETS & ROUNDS R3

Fig. 10.30 Anchor Bracket. Draw necessary views or partial views [Layout A–3 or A4–3 (adjusted)].*

*If dimensions are required, study §§13.1 to 13.25. Use metric or decimal-inch dimensions as assigned by the instructor.

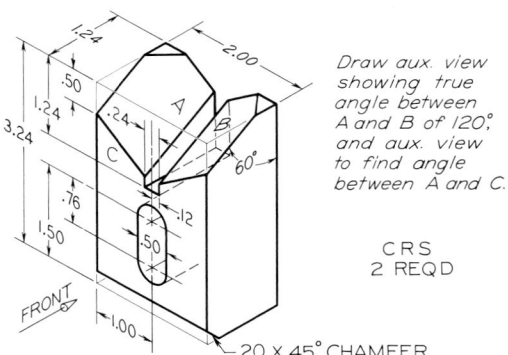

Fig. 10.31 Centering Block. Draw complete front, top, and right-side views, plus indicated auxiliary views (Layout B–3 or A3–3).*

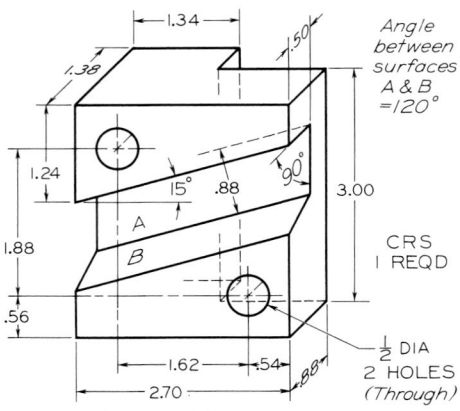

Fig. 10.32 Clamp Slide. Draw necessary views completely (Layout B–3 or A3–3).*

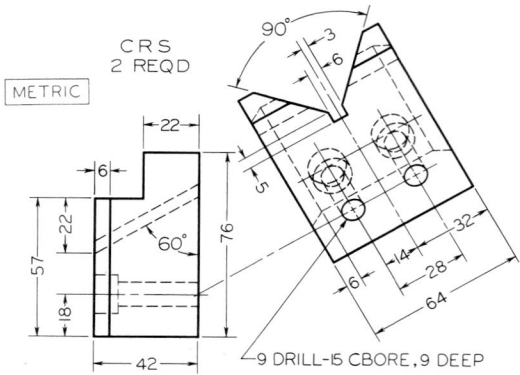

Fig. 10.33 Guide Block.
Given: Right-side and auxiliary views.
Required: Right-side, auxiliary, plus front and top views—all complete (Layout B–3 or A3–3).*

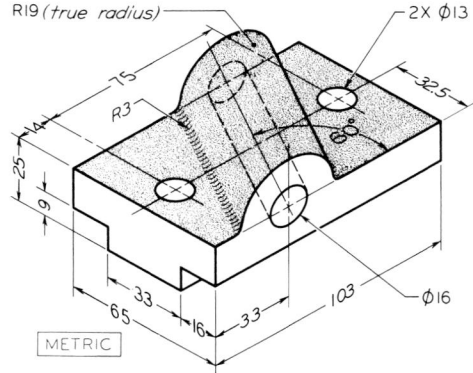

Fig. 10.34 Angle Bearing. Draw necessary views, including a complete auxiliary view [Layout A–3 or A4–3 (adjusted)].*

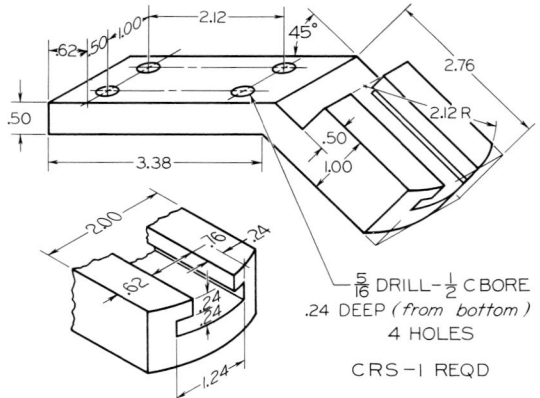

Fig. 10.35 Guide Bracket. Draw necessary views or partial views (Layout B–3 or A3–3).*

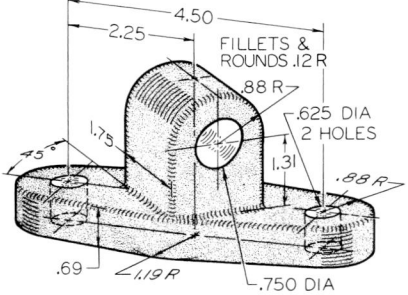

Fig. 10.36 Rod Guide. Draw necessary views, including complete auxiliary view showing true shape of upper rounded portion [Layout B–4 or A3–4 (adjusted)].*

*If dimensions are required, study §§13.1 to 13.25. Use metric or decimal-inch dimensions as assigned by the instructor.

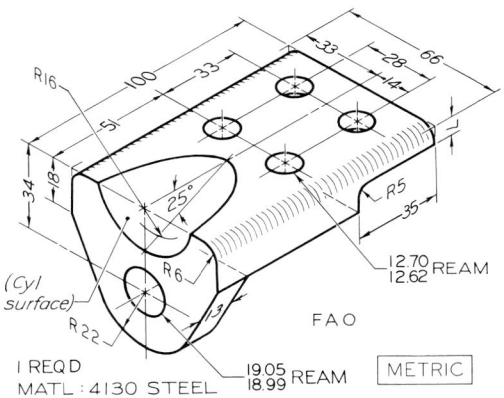

Fig. 10.37 Angle Guide. Draw necessary views, including a partial auxiliary view of cylindrical recess [Layout B–4 or A3–4 (adjusted)].*

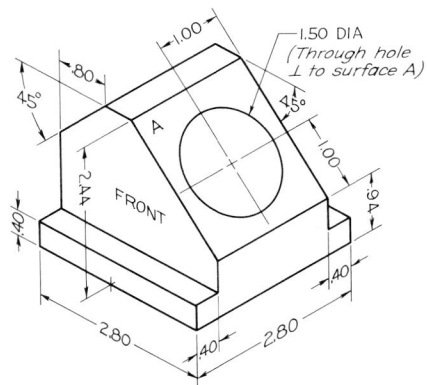

Fig. 10.38 Holder Block. Draw front and right-side views (2.80″ apart) and complete auxiliary view of entire object showing true shape of surface **A** and all hidden lines [Layout A–3 or A4–3 (adjusted)].*

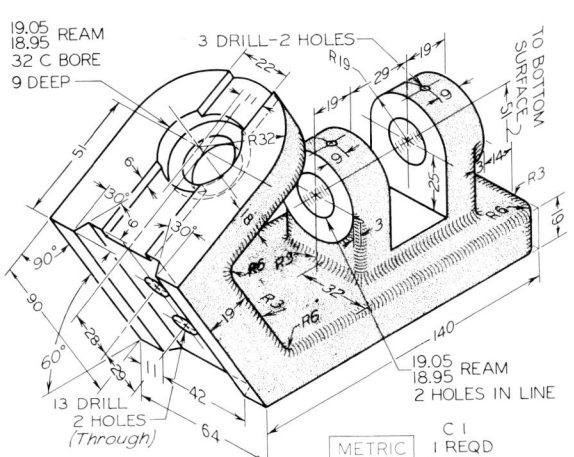

Fig. 10.39 Control Bracket. Draw necessary views, including partial auxiliary views and regular views (Layout C–4 or A2–4).*

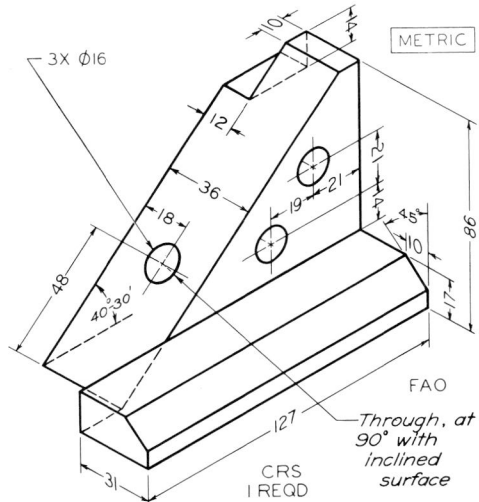

Fig. 10.40 Adjuster Block. Draw necessary views, including complete auxiliary view showing true shape of inclined surface [Layout B–4 or A3–4 (adjusted)].*

*If dimensions are required, study §§13.1 to 13.25. Use metric or decimal-inch dimensions as assigned by the instructor.

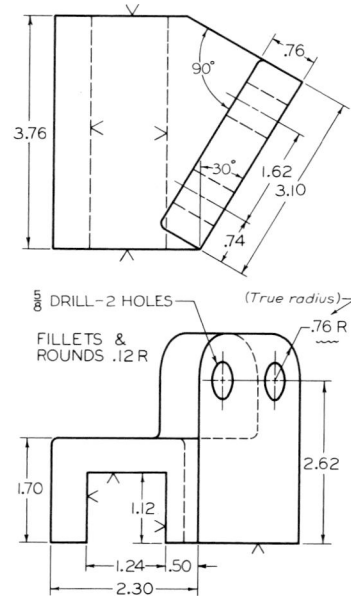

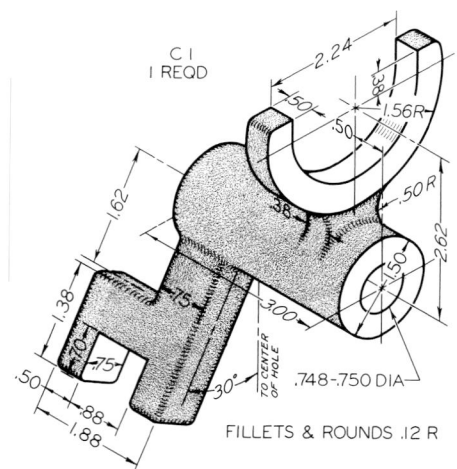

Fig. 10.41 Drill Press Bracket. Draw given views and add complete auxiliary view showing true shape of inclined face [Layout B–4 or A3–4 (adjusted)].*

Fig. 10.42 Shifter Fork. Draw necessary views, including partial auxiliary view showing true shape of inclined arm [Layout B–4 or A3–4 (adjusted)].*

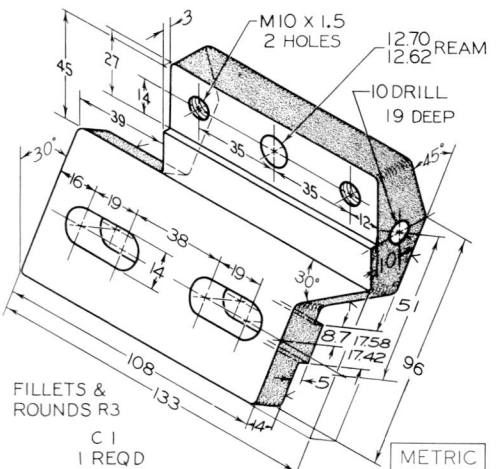

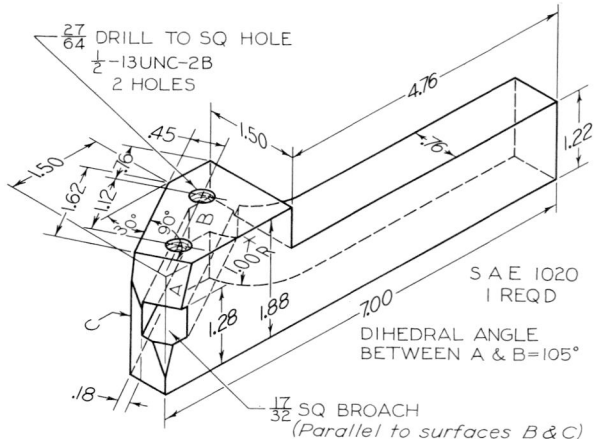

Fig. 10.43 Cam Bracket. Draw necessary views or partial views as needed. For threads, see §§15.9 and 15.10 [Layout B–4 or A3–4 (adjusted)].*

Fig. 10.44 RH Tool Holder. Draw necessary views, including partial auxiliary views showing 105° angle and square hole true size. For threads, see §§15.9 and 15.10 [Layout B–4 or A3–4 (adjusted)].*

*If dimensions are required, study §§13.1 to 13.25. Use metric or decimal-inch dimensions as assigned by the instructor.

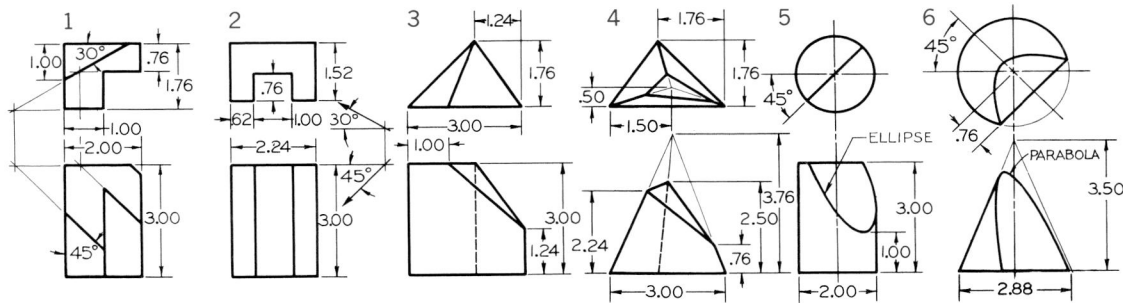

Fig. 10.45 Draw secondary auxiliary views, complete, which (except Prob. 2) will show the true sizes of the inclined surfaces. In Prob. 2, draw secondary auxiliary view as seen in direction of arrow (Layout B–3 or A3–3).*

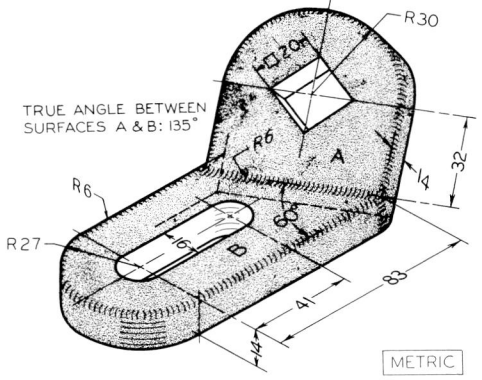

Fig. 10.46 Control Bracket. Draw necessary views including primary and secondary auxiliary views so that the latter shows true shape of oblique surface A [(Layout B–4 or A3–4 (adjusted)].*

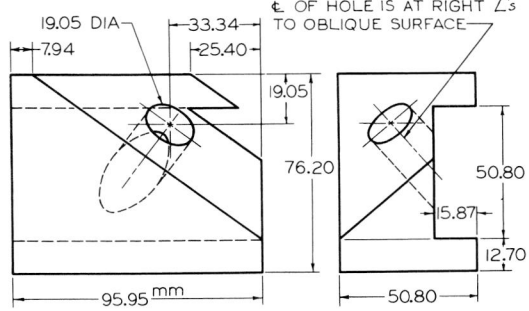

Fig. 10.47 Holder Block. Draw given views and primary and secondary auxiliary views so that the latter shows true shape of oblique surface [Layout B–4 or A3–4 (adjusted)].*

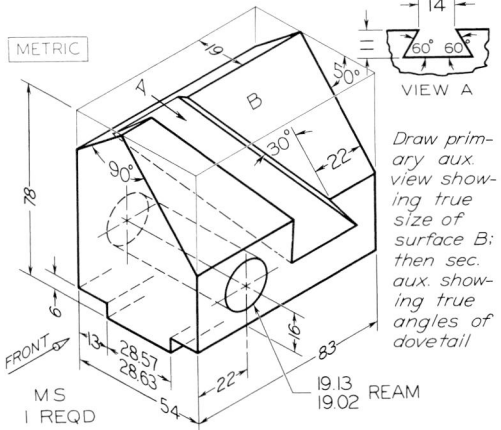

Fig. 10.48 Adjustable Stop. Draw complete front and auxiliary views plus partial right-side view. Show all hidden lines (Layout C–4 or A2–4).*

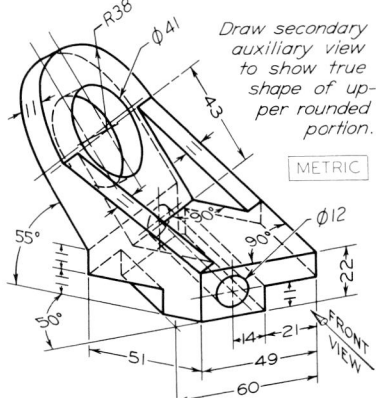

Fig. 10.49 Tool Holder. Draw complete front view, and primary and secondary auxiliary views as indicated [Layout B–4 or A3–4 (adjusted)].*

*If dimensions are required, study §§13.1 to 13.25. Use metric or decimal-inch dimensions as assigned by the instructor.

Revolutions

To obtain an auxiliary view, the observer changes position with respect to the object, as shown by the arrow in Fig. 11.1 (a). The auxiliary view shows the true size and shape of surface A. Exactly the same view of the object also can be obtained by moving the object with respect to the observer, as shown at (b). Here the object is revolved until surface A appears in its true size and shape in the right-side view.

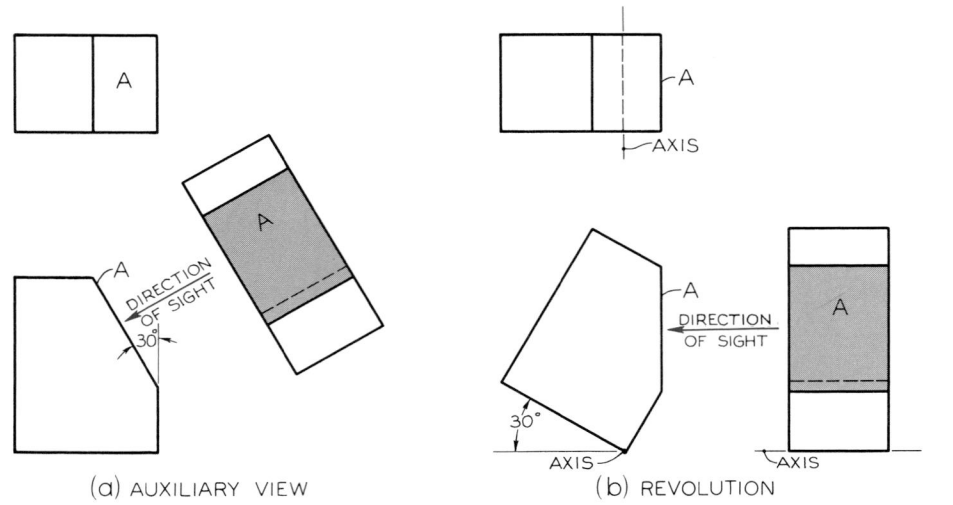

Fig. 11.1 Auxiliary View and Revolution Compared.

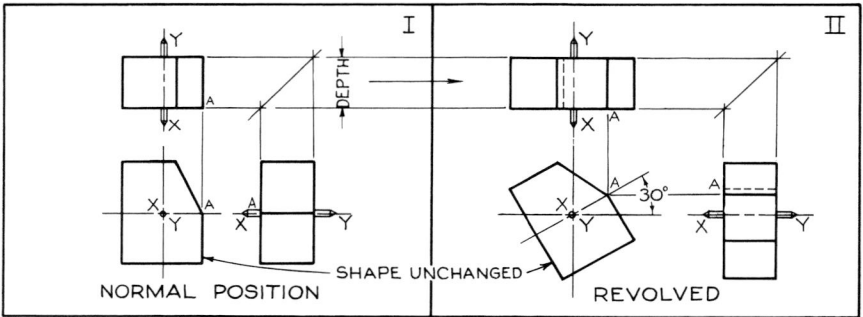

Fig. 11.2 Primary Revolution About an Axis Perpendicular to Frontal Plane.

11.1 Axis of Revolution

In Fig. 11.1 (b) the axis of revolution is assumed perpendicular to the frontal plane of projection. Note that the view in which the axis of revolution appears as a point (in this case the front view) *revolves but does not change shape* and that in the views in which the axis is shown as a line in true length the *dimensions of the object parallel to the axis do not change.*

To make a revolution drawing, the view on the plane of projection that is perpendicular to the axis of revolution is drawn first, since it is the only view that remains unchanged in size and shape. This view is drawn revolved either *clockwise* or *counterclockwise* about a point that is the end view, or point view, of the axis of revolution. This point may be assumed at any convenient point on or outside the view. The other views are then projected from this view.

The axis of revolution is usually considered perpendicular to one of the three principal planes of projection. Thus, an object may be revolved about an axis perpendicular to the horizontal, frontal, or profile planes of projection, and the views drawn in the new positions. Such a process is called a *primary revolution.* If this drawing is then used as a basis for another revolution, the operation is called *successive revolutions.* Obviously, this process may be continued indefinitely, which reminds us of the "chain reaction" in successive auxiliary views, Fig. 10.21.

11.2 Revolution About Axis Perpendicular to Frontal Plane

A primary revolution is illustrated in Fig. 11.2. An imaginary axis XY is assumed, about which the object is to revolve to the desired position. In this case the axis is selected perpendicular to the frontal

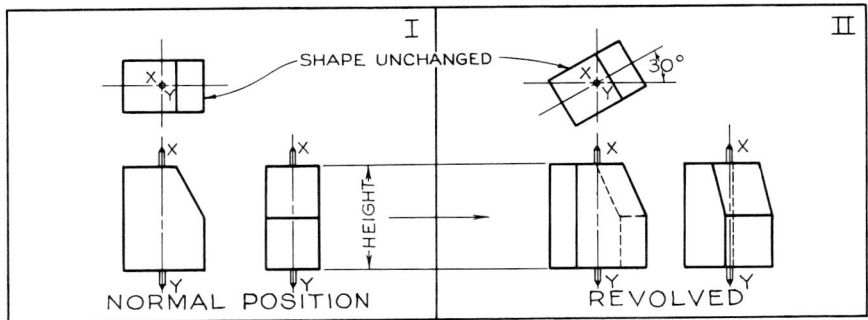

Fig. 11.3   Primary Revolution About an Axis Perpendicular to Horizontal Plane.

plane of projection, and during the revolution all points of the object describe circular arcs parallel to that plane. The axis may pierce the object at any point or may be exterior to it. In space II, the front view is drawn *revolved* (but not changed in shape) through the angle desired (30° in this case), and the top and side views are obtained by projecting from the front view. The *depth* of the top view and the side view is found by projecting from the top view of the first unrevolved position (space I) *because the depth, since it is parallel to the axis, remains unchanged.* If the front view of the revolved position is drawn directly without first drawing the normal unrevolved position, the depth of the object, as shown in the revolved top and side views, may be drawn to known dimensions. No difficulty should be encountered by the student who understands how to obtain projections of points and lines, §7.6.

Note the similarity between the top and side views in space II of Fig. 11.2 and some of the auxiliary views of Fig. 10.7 (c).

11.3 Revolution About Axis Perpendicular to Horizontal Plane

A revolution about an axis perpendicular to the horizontal plane of projection is shown in Fig. 11.3. An imaginary axis XY is assumed perpendicular to the top plane of projection, the top view is drawn revolved (but not changed in shape) to the desired position (30° in this case), and the other views are obtained by projecting from this view. During the revolution, all points of the object describe circular arcs parallel to the horizontal plane. The *heights* of all points in the front and side views in the revolved position remain unchanged, since they are measured parallel to the axis, and may be drawn by projecting from the initial front and side views of space I.

Note the similarity between the front and side views in space II of Fig. 11.3 and some of the auxiliary views of Fig. 10.8 (c).

11.4 Revolution About Axis Perpendicular to Profile Plane

A revolution about an axis XY perpendicular to the profile plane of projection is illustrated in Fig. 11.4. During the revolution, all points of the object describe circular arcs parallel to the profile plane of projection. The widths of the top and front views in the revolved position remain unchanged, since they

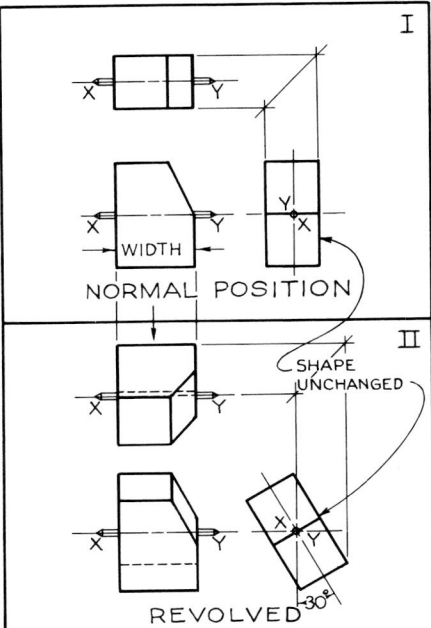

Fig. 11.4   Primary Revolution About an Axis Perpendicular to Profile Plane.

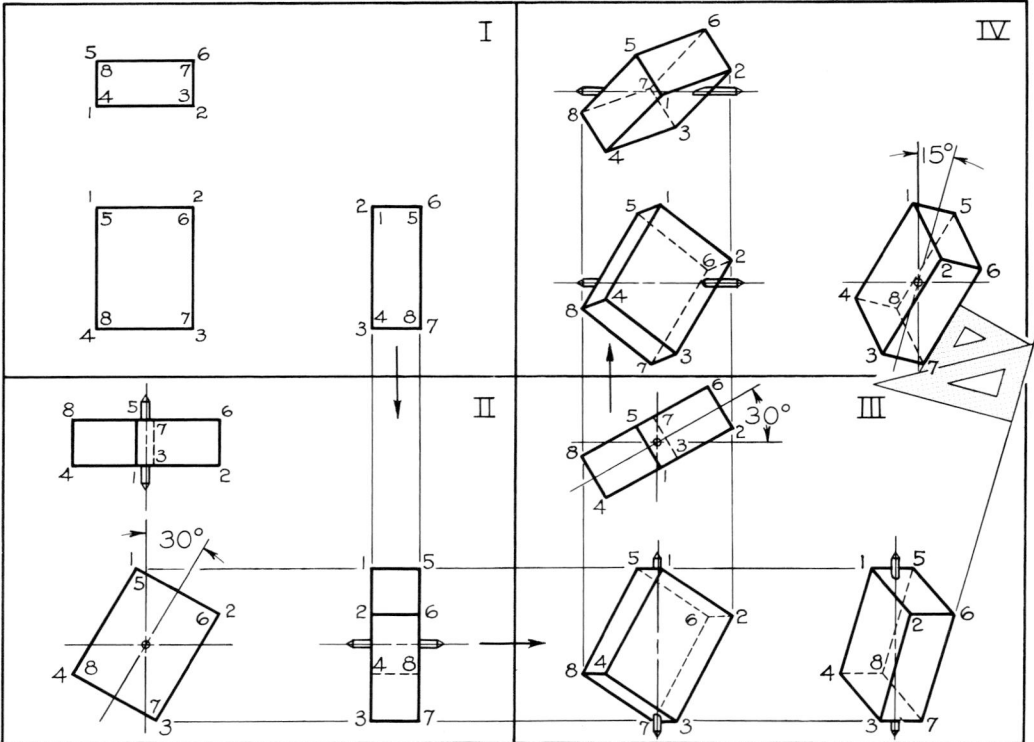

Fig. 11.5   Successive Revolutions of a Prism.

are measured parallel to the axis, and may be obtained by projection from the top and front views of space I, or may be set off by direct measurement.

Note the similarity between the top and front views in space II of Fig. 11.4 and some of the auxiliary views of Fig. 10.9 (c).

11.5 Successive Revolutions
It is possible to draw an object in an infinite number of revolved positions by making successive revolutions. Such a procedure, Fig. 11.5, limited to three or four stages, offers excellent practice in multiview projection. While it is possible to make several revolutions of a simple object without the aid of a system of numbers, it is absolutely necessary in successive revolutions to assign a number or a letter to every corner of the object. See §7.6.

The numbering or lettering must be consistent in the various views of the several stages of revolution. Figure 11.5 shows four sets of multiview drawings numbered I, II, III, and IV, respectively. These represent the same object in different positions with reference to the planes of projection.

In space I, the object is represented in its normal position, with its faces parallel to the planes of projection. In space II, the object is represented after it has been revolved clockwise through an angle of 30° about an axis perpendicular to the frontal plane. The drawing in space II is placed under space I so that the side view, whose width remains unchanged, can be projected from space I to space II as shown.

During the revolution, all points of the object describe circular arcs parallel to the frontal plane of projection and remain at the same distance from that plane. The side view, therefore, may be projected from the side view of space I and the front view of space II. The top view may be projected in the usual manner from the front and side views of space II.

In space III, the object is taken as represented in space II and is revolved counterclockwise through an angle of 30° about an axis perpendicular to the horizontal plane of projection. During the revolution, all points describe *horizontal* circular arcs and remain at the same distance from the horizontal plane of projection. The top view is copied from space II but is revolved through 30°. The front and side views are obtained by projecting from the front

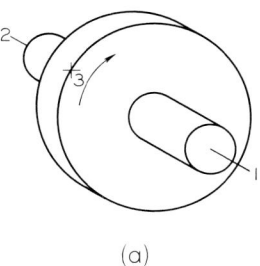

(a)

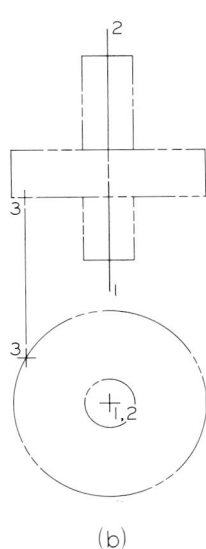

(b)

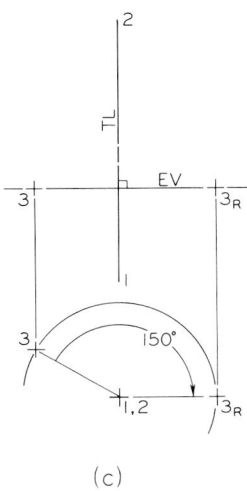

(c)

Fig. 11.6 Revolution of a Point About a Normal Axis.

and side views of space II and from the top view of space III.

In space IV, the object is taken as represented in space III and is revolved clockwise through 15° about an axis perpendicular to the profile plane of projection. During the revolution, all points of the object describe circular arcs parallel to the profile plane of projection and remain at the same distance from that plane. The side view is copied, §5.28, from the side view of space III but revolved through 15°. The front and top views are projected from the side view of space IV and from the top and front views of space III.

Another convenient method of copying a view in a new revolved position is to use tracing paper as described in §5.29. Either a tracing can be made and transferred by rubbing, or the prick points may be made and transferred, as shown.

In spaces III and IV of Fig. 11.5, each view is an axonometric projection, §17.2. An isometric projection can be obtained by revolution, as shown in Fig. 17.3, and a dimetric projection, §17.28, can be constructed in a similar manner. If neither an isometric nor a dimetric projection is specifically sought, the successive revolution will produce a trimetric projection, §17.30, as shown in Fig. 11.5.

11.6 Revolution of a Point—Normal Axis

Examples of the revolution of a point about a straight-line axis are often found in design problems that involve pulleys, gears, cranks, linkages, and so on. For example, in Fig. 11.6 (a), as the disk is revolved, point 3 moves in a circular path lying in a plane perpendicular to the axis 1–2. This relationship is represented in the two views at (b). Note in this instance that the axis is normal or perpendicular to the frontal plane of projection, resulting in a front view that shows a point view of the axis and a true-size view of the circular path of revolution for point 3. The top view shows the path of revolution in edge view and perpendicular to the true-length view of the axis. Similar two-view relationships would occur if the axis were perpendicular or normal to either the horizontal or profile planes of projection.

The clockwise revolution through 150° for point 3 is illustrated at (c).

11.7 Revolution of a Point—Inclined Axis

In Fig. 11.7 (a) the axis of revolution for point 3 is positioned parallel to the frontal plane and inclined to the horizontal and profile projection planes. Since the axis 1–2 is true length in the front view, the

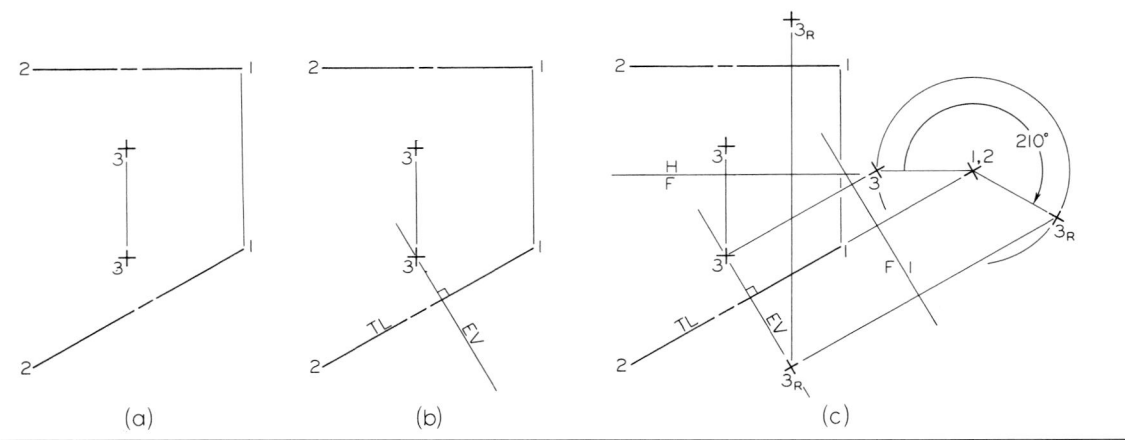

Fig. 11.7   Revolution of a Point About an Inclined Axis.

edge view of the path of revolution can be located as at (b). In order to establish the circular path of revolution for point **3**, an auxiliary view showing the axis in point view is required as at (c). The required revolution of point **3** (in this case, **210°**) is now performed in this circular view. The revolved position of the point is projected to the given front and top views, as shown.

Note the similarity of the relationships of the front view and auxiliary view and the constructions shown in Fig. 11.6 (c).

11.8 Revolution of a Point—Oblique Axis

In Fig. 11.8 (a), the axis of revolution for point **3** is oblique to all principal planes of projection and, therefore, is shown neither in true length nor as a point view in the top, front, or profile views. To establish the necessary true length and point view of the axis **1–2** in adjacent views, two successive auxiliary views are required, as shown at (b). The required revolved position of point **3** can now be located and then projected back to complete the given front and top views.

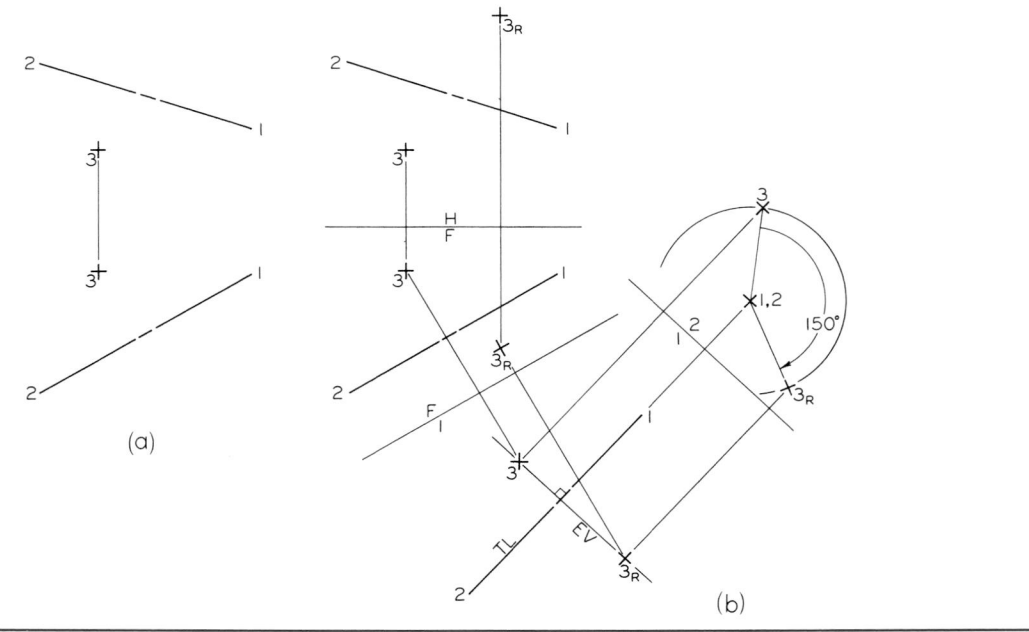

Fig. 11.8   Revolution of a Point About an Oblique Axis.

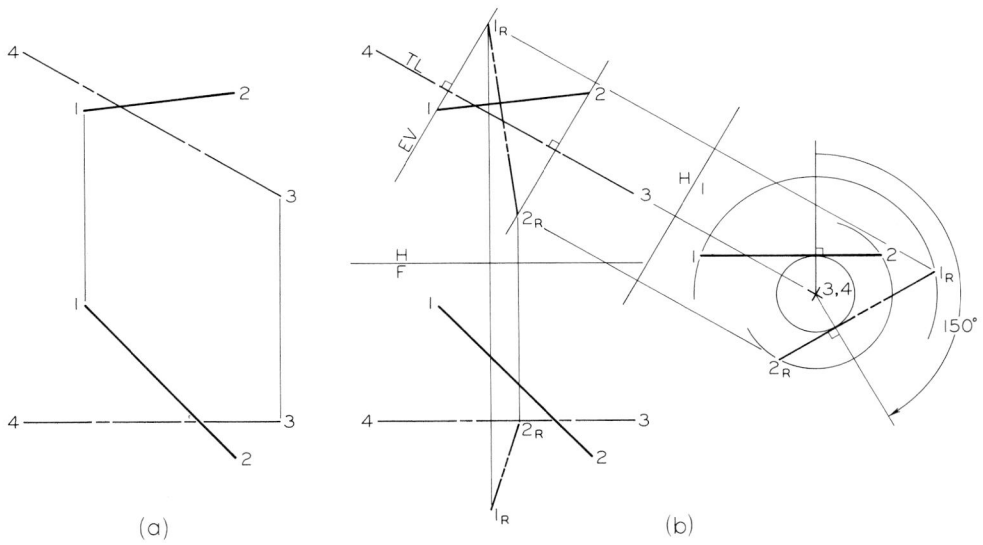

Fig. 11.9   Revolution of a Line About an Inclined Axis.

11.9 Revolution of a Line

The procedure for the revolution of a line about an axis is very similar to that required for the revolution of a point, §11.6. All points on a line must revolve through the same angle, or the revolved line becomes altered.

In Fig. 11.9 (a), the line **1–2** is to be revolved through **150°** about the inclined axis **3–4**.

Since the axis **3–4** is given in true length in the top view, an auxiliary view is required to provide a point view of the axis, as shown in Fig. 11.9 (b). The necessary revolution can then be made about point view **3–4**. In order to insure that all points on the line rotate through the same number of degrees, note that a construction circle tangent to line **1–2** is

drawn and that a perpendicular through the tangency point becomes the reference for measuring the angle of rotation. The circular arc paths for points **1** and **2** locate the points **1**$_R$ and **2**$_R$, as the revolved position of the line is drawn perpendicular to the radial line subtending the 150° arc of revolution, and tangent to the smaller circle. The alternate-position line is used to distinguish the revolved-position line from the original given line.

11.10 True Length of a Line — Revolution Method

If a line is parallel to one of the planes of projection, its projection on that plane is equal in length to the line, Fig. 7.20. In Fig. 11.10 (a), the element **AB** of

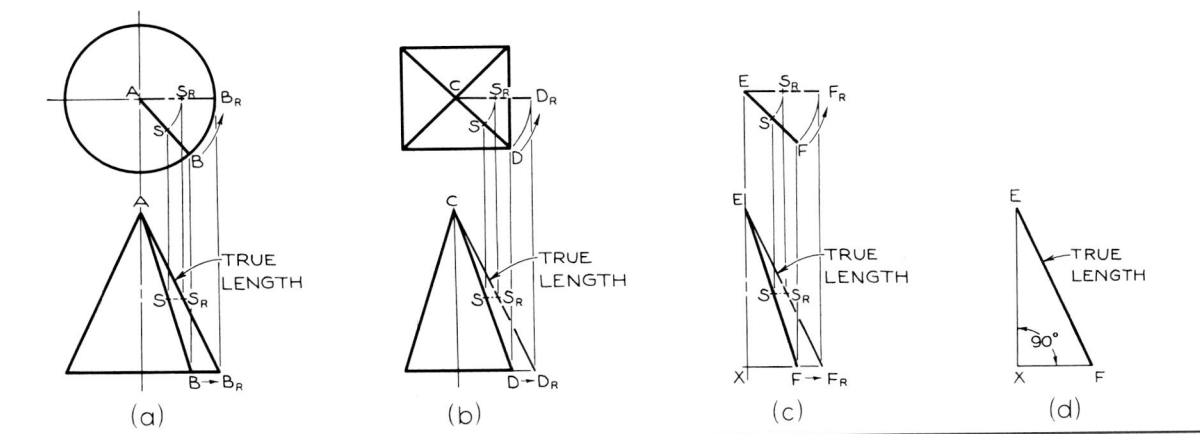

Fig. 11.10   True Length of a Line—Revolution Method.

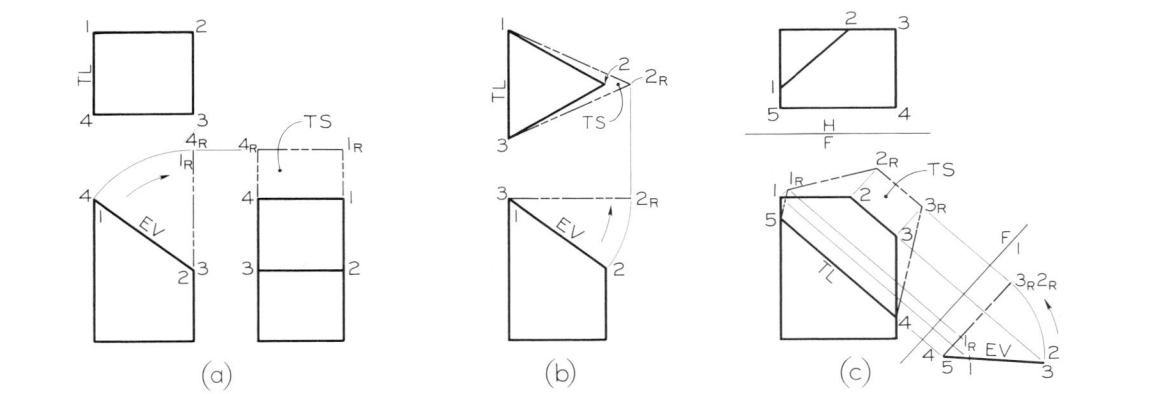

Fig. 11.11   True Size of Plane Surface—Revolution Method.

the cone is oblique to the planes of projection; hence its projections are foreshortened. If **AB** is revolved about the axis of the cone until it coincides with either of the contour elements, for example **AB**_R, it will be shown in its true length in the front view for it will then be parallel to the frontal plane of projection.

Likewise, at (b), the edge of the pyramid **CD** is shown in its true length **CD**_R when it has been revolved about the axis of the pyramid until it is parallel to the frontal plane of projection. At (c), the line **EF** is shown in its true length at **EF**_R when it has been revolved about a vertical axis until it is parallel to the frontal plane of projection.

The true length of a line may also be found by constructing a right triangle or a true-length diagram, as shown at (d), whose base is equal to the top view of the line and whose altitude is the difference in elevation of the ends. The hypotenuse of the triangle is equal to the true length of the line.

In these cases the lines are revolved until parallel to a plane of projection. The true length of a line may also be found by leaving the line stationary but shifting the position of the observer—that is, the method of auxiliary views, §10.18.

11.11 True Size of a Plane Surface— Revolution Method

If a surface is parallel to one of the planes of projection, its projection on that plane is true size, Fig. 7.19. In Fig. 11.11 (a), the inclined surface 1–2–3–4 is foreshortened in the top and side views and appears as a line in the front view. Line **2–3** is taken as the axis of revolution, and the surface is revolved

clockwise in the front view to the position 4_R–3 and projected to the side view at 4_R–1_R–2–3, which is the true size of the surface. In this case the surface was revolved until parallel to the profile plane of projection.

At (b), triangular surface 1–2–3 is revolved until parallel to the horizontal plane of projection so that the surface appears true size in the top view, as shown.

At (c), the true size of the oblique surface 1–2–3–4–5 cannot be found by a simple primary revolution. The true size can be found by two successive revolutions or by a combination of an auxiliary view and a primary revolution. The latter is shown at (c). First, draw an auxiliary view that will show the edge view (EV) of the plane. See Fig. 10.22. Second, revolve the edge view of the surface until it is parallel to the folding line **F/1**, as shown. All points in the front view, except those in the axis of revolution line 4–5, will describe circular arcs parallel to the reference plane F/1. These arcs will appear in the front view as lines parallel to the folding line, such as 2–2_R and 3–3_R. The true size of the surface is found by connecting the points with straight lines.

11.12 Revolution of Circles

As shown in Fig. 5.50 (a) to (c), a circle, when viewed obliquely, appears as an ellipse. In that case the coin is revolved by the fingers. The geometric construction of this revolution is shown in Fig. 11.12 (a). In the front view the circle appears as **ACBD**, and in the side view as line **CD**, which is really the edge view of the plane containing the circle. In the side

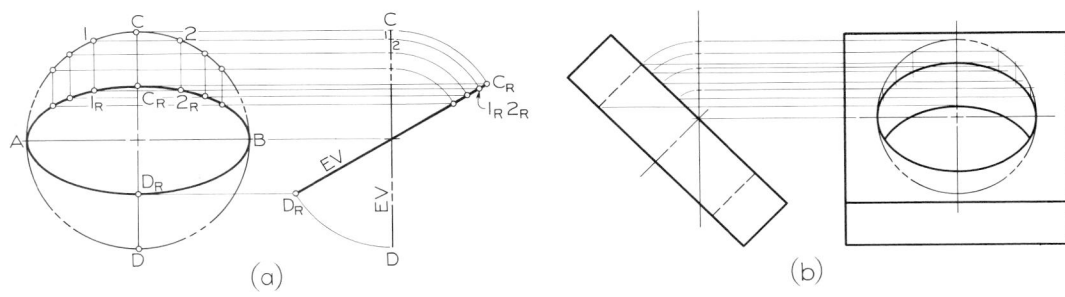

Fig. 11.12 Revolution of a Circle.

view, CD (the side view of the circle) is revolved through any desired acute angle to $C_R D_R$.

To find points on the ellipse, draw a series of horizontal lines across the circle in the front view. Each line will cut the circle at two points, as 1 and 2. Project these points across to the vertical line representing the unrevolved circle; then, revolve each point and project horizontally to the front view to establish points on the ellipse. Plot as many points as necessary to secure a smooth curve.

An application of this construction to the representation of a revolved object with a large hole is shown at (b).

11.13 Counterrevolution

The reverse procedure to revolution is *counterrevolution*. For example, if the three views of space II in Fig. 11.2 are given, the object can be drawn in the unrevolved position of space I by counterrevolution. The front view is simply counterrevolved back to its normal upright position, and the top and side views are drawn as shown. Similarly, in Fig. 11.5, the object may be counterrevolved from its position of space IV to its unrevolved position of space I by simply reversing the process.

In practice, it sometimes becomes necessary to draw the views of an object located on or parallel to a given oblique surface. In such an oblique position, it is very difficult to draw the views of the object because of the foreshortening of lines. The work is greatly simplified by counterrevolving the oblique surface to a simple position, completing the drawing, and then revolving to the original given position.

An example is shown in Fig. 11.13. Assume that the oblique surface 8–4–3–7 (three views in space I) is given and that it is required to draw the three views of a prism 13 mm high, having the given oblique surface as its base. Revolve the surface

about any horizontal axis XX, perpendicular to the side view, until the edges 8–4 and 3–7 are horizontal, as shown in space II. Then revolve the surface about any vertical axis YY, which appears as a point in the top view, until the edges 8–7 and 4–3 are parallel to the frontal plane, as shown in space III. In this position the given surface is perpendicular to the frontal plane, and the front and top views of the required prism can be drawn, as shown by phantom lines in the figure, because the edges 4–1 and 3–2, for example, are parallel to the frontal plane and, therefore, are shown in their true lengths, 13 mm. When the two views in space III have been drawn, counterrevolve the object from III to II and then from II to I to find the required views of the given object in space I.

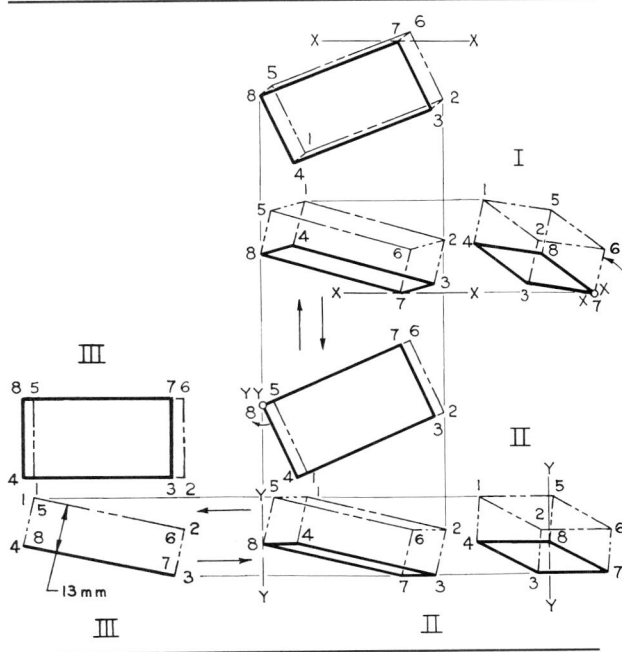

Fig. 11.13 Counterrevolution of a Prism.

11.14 Computer Graphics

Computer graphics programs provide the user with simple and fast ways of revolving objects about any desired axis. Successive revolutions can be easily accomplished using CAD. Computer-generated revolutions also enable a drafter to readily depict circular features, which appear elliptical when viewed obliquely, Fig. 11.14.

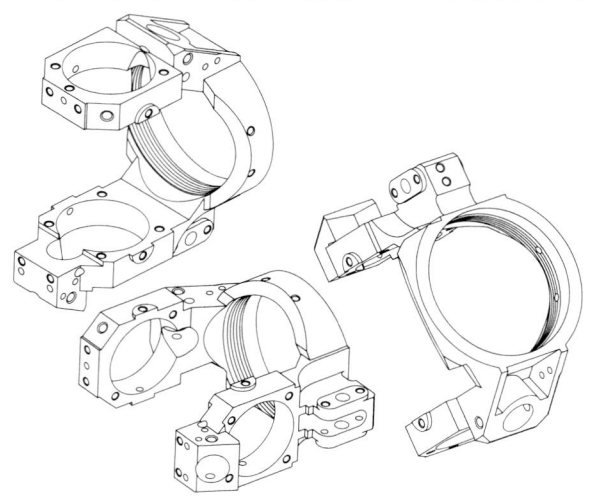

Fig. 11.14 **Pictorial Drawings With Different Viewing Angles Created by Using Computervision Designer System** The system provides complete flexibility to manipulate the original illustration to display any desired viewing orientation. *Courtesy of Computervision Corporation, a subsidiary of Prime Computer, Inc.*

Revolution Problems

In Figs. 11.15–11.19 are problems covering primary revolutions, successive revolutions, and counterrevolutions.

Since many of the problems in this chapter are of a general nature, they can also be solved on most computer graphics systems. If a system is available, the instructor may choose to assign specific problems to be completed by this method.

Additional problems in convenient form for solution are presented in the worksheets at the back of this book. Refer to Drawing 11-1 and accompanying instructions.

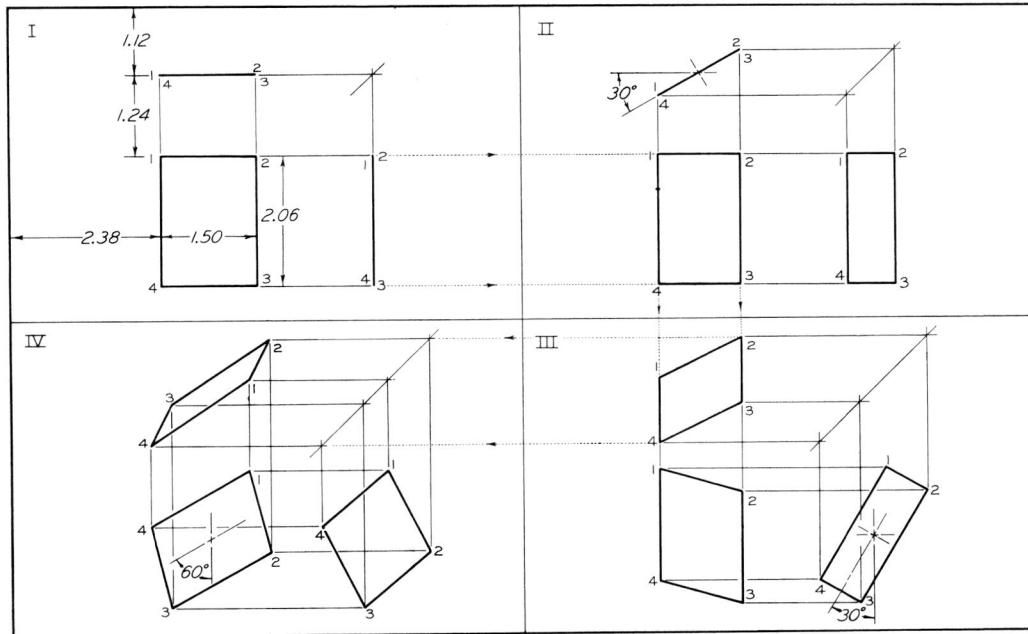

Fig. 11.15 Using size B or A3 sheet, divide working area into four equal parts, as shown. Draw given views of rectangle, and then the primary revolution in space II, followed by successive revolutions in spaces III and IV. Number points as shown. Omit dimensions. Use Form 3 title box.

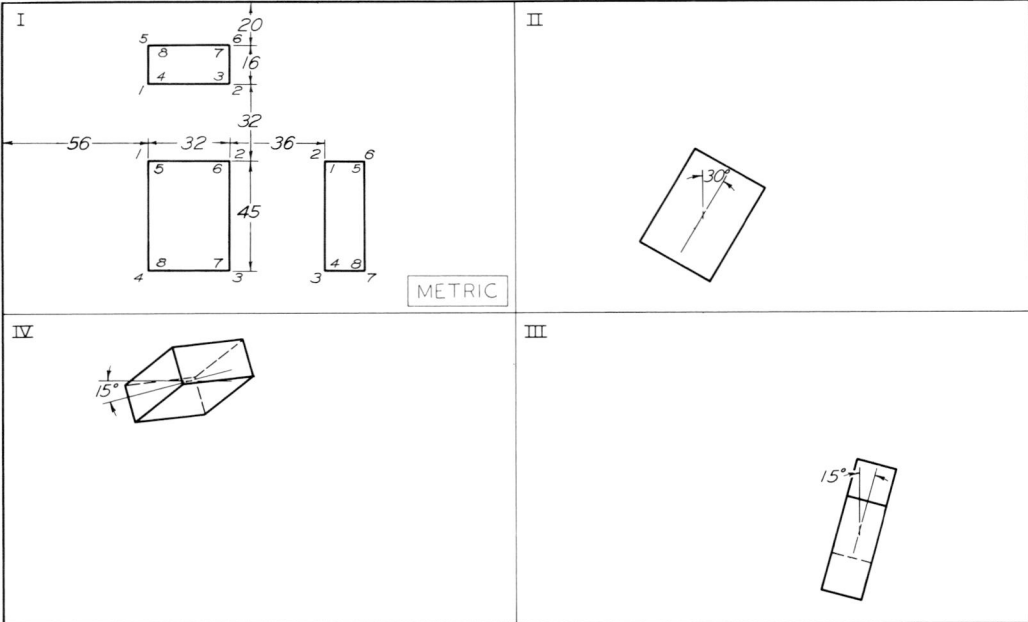

Fig. 11.16 Using size B or A3 sheet, divide working area into four equal parts, as shown. Draw given views of prism as shown in space I; then draw three views of the revolved prism in each succeeding space, as indicated. Number all corners. Omit dimensions. Use Form 3 title box.

Fig. 11.17 opposite Use Layout A–1 or A4–1 (adjusted), and divide the working area into four equal areas for four problems per sheet to be assigned by the instructor. Data for the layout of each problem are given by a coordinate system in metric dimensions. For example, in Prob. 1, point **1** is located by the scale coordinates (**28 mm, 38 mm, 76 mm**). The first coordinate locates the front view of the point from the left edge of the problem area. The second one locates the front view of the point from the bottom edge of the problem area. The third one locates either the top view of the point from the bottom edge of the problem area or the side view of the point from the left edge of the problem area. Inspection of the given problem layout will determine which application to use.

1. Revolve clockwise point 1(28, 38, 76) through 210° about the axis 2(51, 58, 94) – 3(51, 8, 94).
2. Revolve point 3(41, 38, 53) about the axis 1(28, 64, 74) – 2(28, 8, 74) until point **3** is at the farthest distance behind the axis.
3. Revolve point 3(20, 8, 84) about the axis 1(10, 18, 122) – 2(56, 18, 76) through 210° and to the rear of line 1–2.
4. Revolve point 3(5, 53, 53) about the axis 1(10, 13, 71) – 2(23, 66, 71) to its extreme position to the left in the front view.
5. Revolve point 3(15, 8, 99) about the axis 1(8, 10, 61) – 2(33, 25, 104) through 180°.
6. By revolution find the true length of line 1(8, 48, 64) – 2(79, 8, 119). Scale: 1:100.
7. Revolve line 3(30, 38, 81) – 4(76, 51, 114) about axis 1(51, 33, 69) – 2(51, 33, 122) until line **3–4** is shown true length and below the axis **1–2**. Scale: 1:20.
8. Revolve line 3(53, 8, 97) – 4(94, 28, 91) about the axis 1(48, 23, 81) – 2(91, 23, 122) until line **3–4** is in true length and above the axis.
9. Revolve line 3(28, 15, 99) – 4(13, 30, 84) about the axis 1(20, 20, 97) – 2(43, 33, 58) until line **3–4** is level and above the axis.

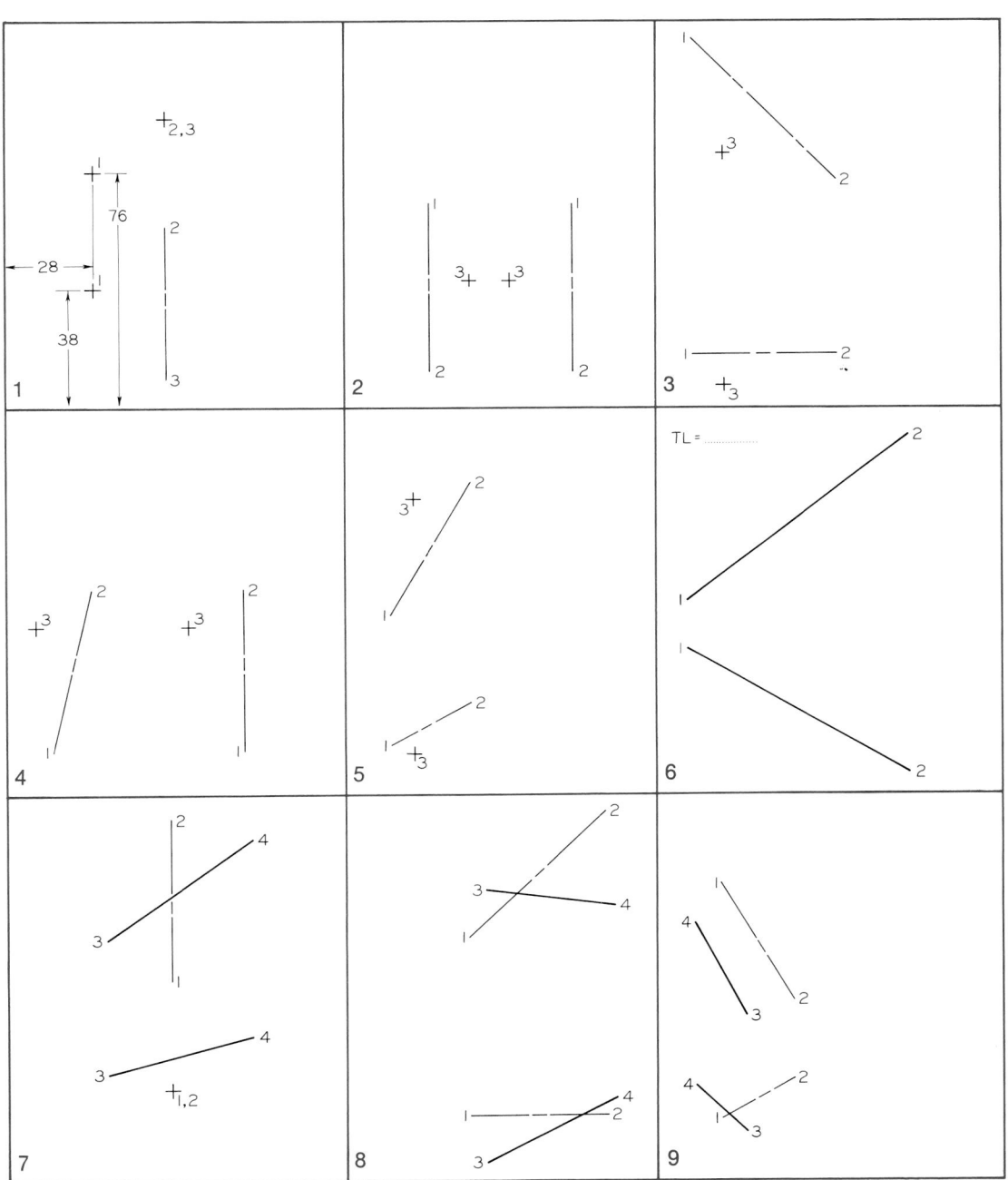

Fig. 11.17

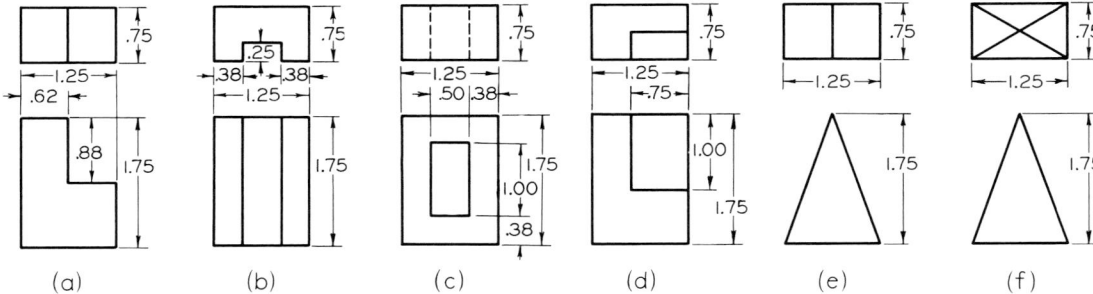

(a) (b) (c) (d) (e) (f)

Fig. 11.18 Using Layout B–4 or A3–4 (adjusted) sheet, divide into four equal parts as in Fig. 11.15. In the upper two spaces, draw a simple revolution as in Fig. 11.2, and in the lower two spaces, draw a simple revolution as in Fig. 11.3, but for each problem use a block assigned from Fig. 11.17.

Alternative Assignment: Using Layout B–4 or A3–4 (adjusted) sheet, divide into four equal parts as in Fig. 11.15. In the two left-hand spaces, draw a simple revolution as in Fig. 11.4, but use an object assigned from Fig. 11.17. In the two right-hand spaces, draw another simple revolution as in Fig. 11.4, but use a different object taken from Fig. 11.17 and revolve through 45° instead of 30°.

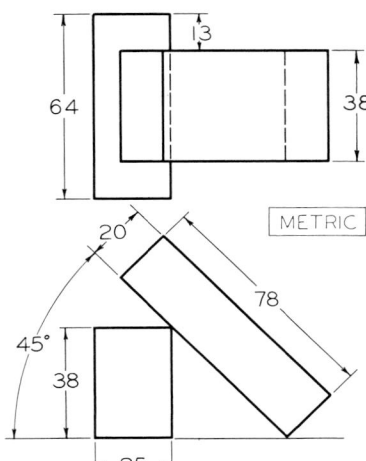

Fig. 11.19 Using Layout A–2 or A–3 or Layout A4–2 or A4–3 (adjusted), draw three views of the blocks but revolved 30° clockwise about an axis perpendicular to the top plane of projection. Do not change the relative positions of the blocks.

Manufacturing Processes

by J. George H. Thompson*
and John Gilbert McGuire†
Revised by Stephen A. Smith‡

The test of the usefulness of any working drawing is whether the object described can be satisfactorily produced without further information than that furnished on the drawing. The drawing must give information as to shape, size, material, and finish and, where necessary, indicate the manufacturing processes required to produce the desired object.

It is the purpose of this chapter to provide beginning engineers with some information about certain fundamental terms and processes and to assist them in using this information on their drawings. The drafter and engineer in any organization must have a thorough knowledge of manufacturing processes and methods before they can properly indicate on drawings the machining operations, heat-treatment, finish, and the accuracy desired on each part.

*Late Professor Emeritus of Mechanical Engineering, Texas A&M University.
†Assistant Dean of Engineering Emeritus, Texas A&M University.
‡Manager, Product Design and Development, Packaging Corporation of America, A Tenneco Company.

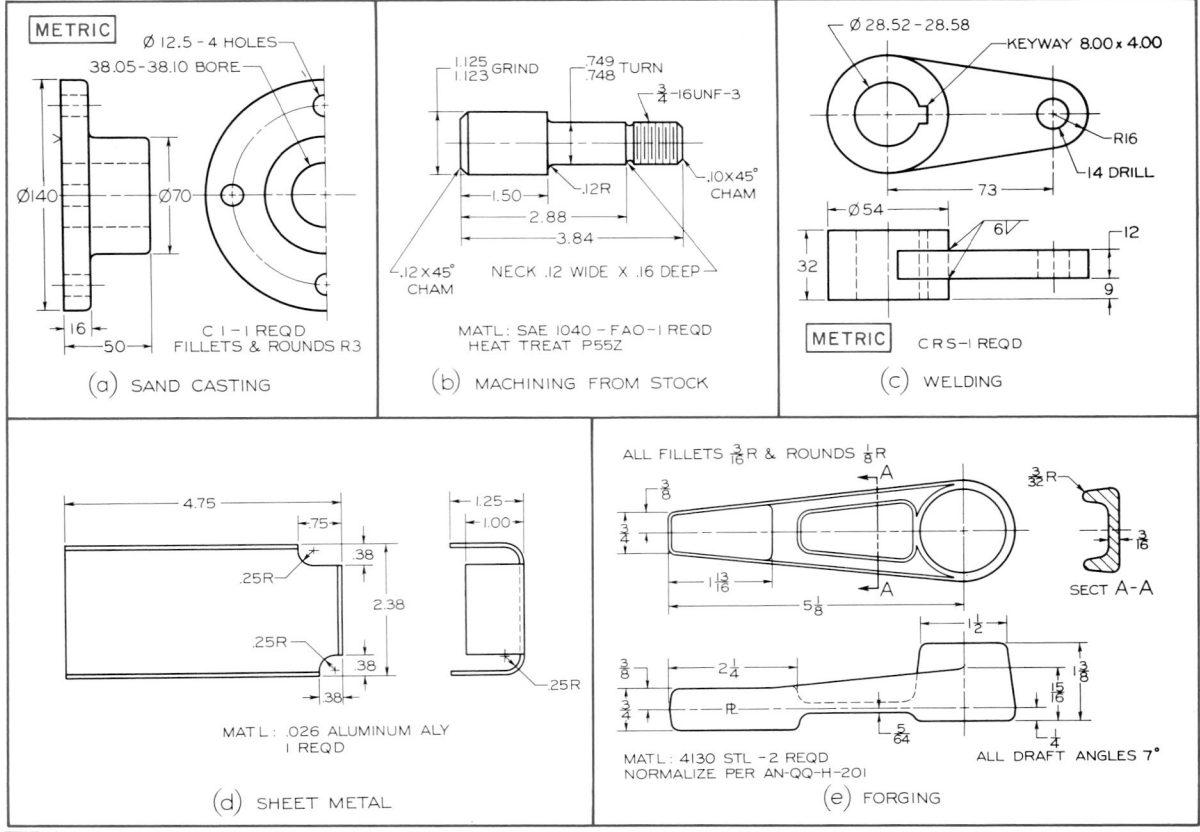

Fig. 12.1   Comparison of Drawings for Different Manufacturing Processes.

12.1 Production Processes

A manufacturing department starts with what might be called *raw stock* and modifies this until it agrees with the detail drawing. The shape of raw stock usually has to be altered.

Changing the shape and size of the material of which a part is being made requires one or more of the following processes: (1) removing part of the original material, (2) adding more material, and (3) redistributing original material. Cutting, such as turning on a lathe, punching holes by means of a power press, or cutting with a laser system, removes material. Welding, brazing, soldering, metal spraying, and electrochemical plating add material. Forging, pressing, drawing, extruding, spinning, and plastics processing redistribute material.

12.2 Manufacturing Methods and the Drawing

Before preparing a drawing for the production of a part, the drafter should consider what manufacturing processes are to be used. These processes will determine the representation of the detailed features of the part, the choice of dimensions, and the machining or processing accuracy. Principal types of metal forming are (1) casting, (2) machining from standard stock, (3) welding, (4) forming from sheet stock, and (5) forging. A knowledge of these processes, along with a thorough understanding of the intended use of the part, will help determine some basic manufacturing processes. Drawings that reflect these manufacturing methods are shown in Fig. 12.1.

In sand casting, Fig. 12.1 (a), all cast surfaces remain rough textured, with all corners filleted or rounded. Sharp corners indicate at least one of the surfaces is finished, §7.34, and finish marks are shown on the edge view of the finished surface. See §§13.16 and 13.17.

In drawings of parts machined from standard stock, Fig. 12.1 (b), most surfaces are represented as machined. In some cases, as on shafting, the surface existing on the raw stock is often accurate enough without further finishing. Corners are usually sharp, but fillets and rounds are machined when

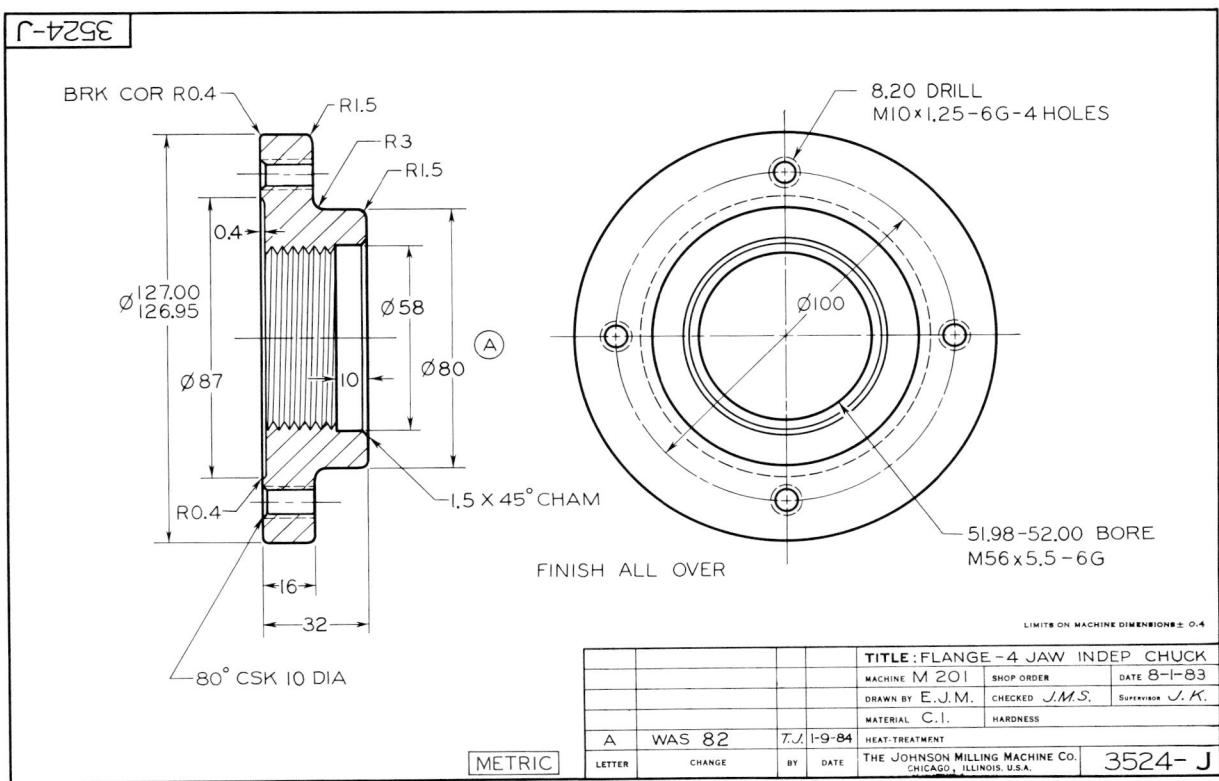

Fig. 12.2 A Detail Working Drawing.

necessary. For example, an interior corner may be machined with a radius to provide greater strength.

On welding drawings, (c), the several pieces are cut to size, brought together, and then welded. Notice that lines are shown where the separate pieces are joined.

On sheet-metal drawings, (d), the thickness of material is uniform and is usually given in the material specification note rather than by a dimension on the drawing. Bend radii and bend reliefs at corners are specified according to standard practice.

For forged parts, §12.21, separate drawings are usually made for the diemaker and for the machinist. All corners are rounded and filleted and are so shown on the drawing. The draft is drawn to scale, and is usually specified by degrees in a note.

12.3 Sand Casting

Although a number of different casting processes are used, sand molds are the most common. Sand molds are made by ramming sand around a pattern, and then carefully removing it, leaving a cavity that ex-

actly matches the pattern to receive the molten metal. The pattern must be of such a shape that it will "pull away" from the sand. The plane of separation of the two mold halves is the *parting line* on the pattern.

Since shrinkage occurs when metal cools, patterns are made slightly oversize. The patternmaker accomplishes this by increasing the pattern size by predetermined amounts, dependent upon the kind of metal being used in the casting. Due to shrinkage and draft, small holes are better drilled in the casting, and large holes are better cored (cast-in) and then bored.

12.4 The Patternmaker and the Drawing

The patternmaker receives the working drawing showing the object in its completed state, including all dimensions and finish marks. Usually the same drawing is used by the patternmaker and the machinist; hence, it should contain all dimensions and notes needed by both, as shown in Fig. 12.2. Some companies follow the practice of dimensioning a

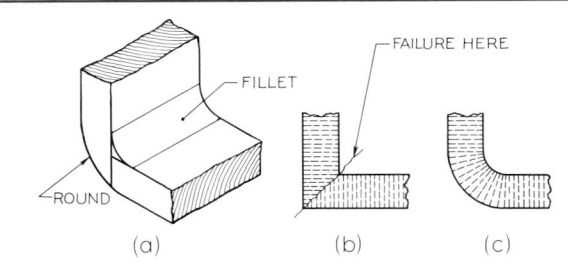

Fig. 12.3   Fillets and Rounds.

copy of the drawing in colored pencil with the patternmaker's information. Pattern dimensions, §13.27, typically need to be accurate only to within $\frac{1}{32}''$ or $\frac{1}{16}''$. More critical tolerances are required for machining however.

Finish marks, §13.17, are as important to the patternmaker as to the machinist because additional material must be provided on each surface that will eventually be machined. For small and medium-sized castings, 1.5 mm ($\frac{1}{16}''$ approximate) to 3 mm ($\frac{1}{8}''$ approximate) is usually sufficient; larger allowances are made if there is probability of distortion or warping. On the flange, Fig. 12.2, it is necessary for the patternmaker to provide material for finish on all surfaces, since the note indicates finish all over (FAO).

12.5 Fillets and Rounds

Fillets (inside rounded corners) and rounds (outside rounded corners) must be included in the pattern,

in order to provide for maximum strength as well as a pleasing appearance in the finished casting, Fig. 12.3. Crystals of cooling metal tend to arrange themselves perpendicular to the exterior surfaces as indicated at (b) and (c). If the corners of a casting are rounded as shown at (c), a much stronger casting results.

Rounds are constructed by rounding off the corners of the pattern by sanding, planing, or turning, while fillets are constructed of preformed leather, wax, or wood.

For some cylindrical patterns it is possible to form on the lathe the proper radius for the fillets and rounds as an integral part of the wood pattern.

All fillets and rounds should be shown on the drawing, either freehand or drawn to scale with the use of a compass or with a circle template. For a general discussion of fillets and rounds from the standpoint of representation on the drawing, see §§7.34 to 7.36. For dimensioning of fillets and rounds, see §13.16.

12.6 Machine Tools

Some of the more common machine tools are the engine lathe, drill press, milling machine, shaper, planer, grinding machine, and boring mill. Brief descriptions of these machines follow. See also §12.23 for examples of how these machine tools can be blended into automated processing.

12.7 Engine Lathe

The engine lathe, Fig. 12.4, is one of the most versatile machines used in the machine shop, and on it

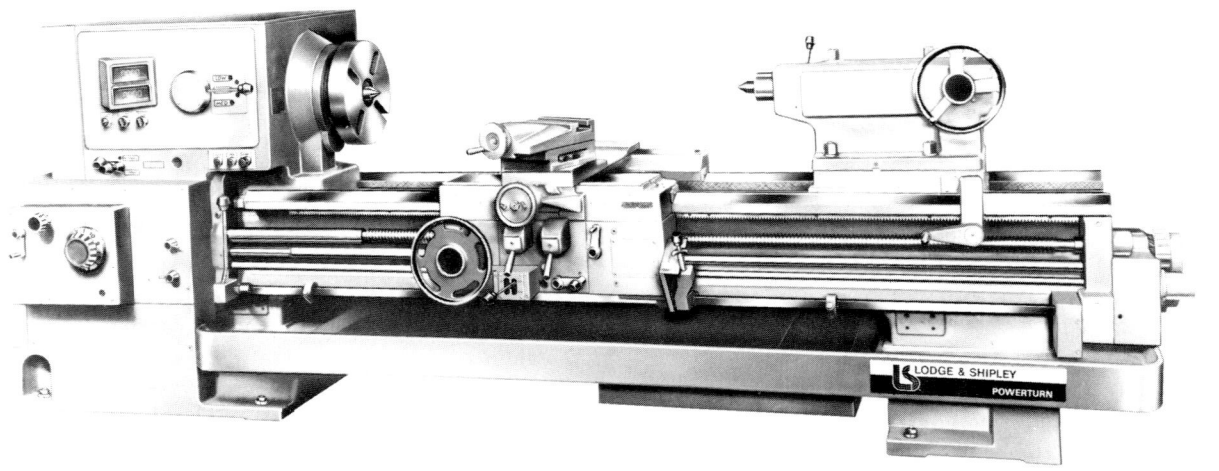

Fig. 12.4   Engine Lathe. *Courtesy of Lodge & Shipley*

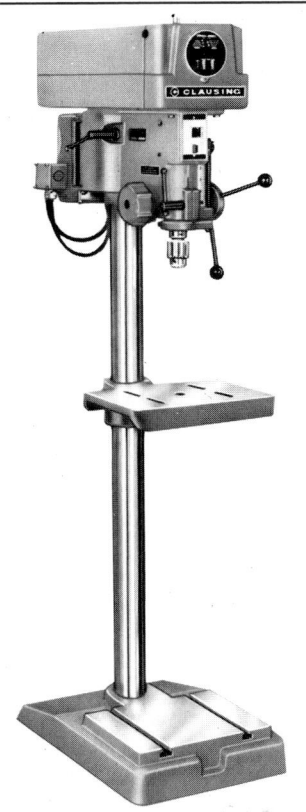

Fig. 12.5 Drill Press. *Courtesy of Clausing Machine Tools*

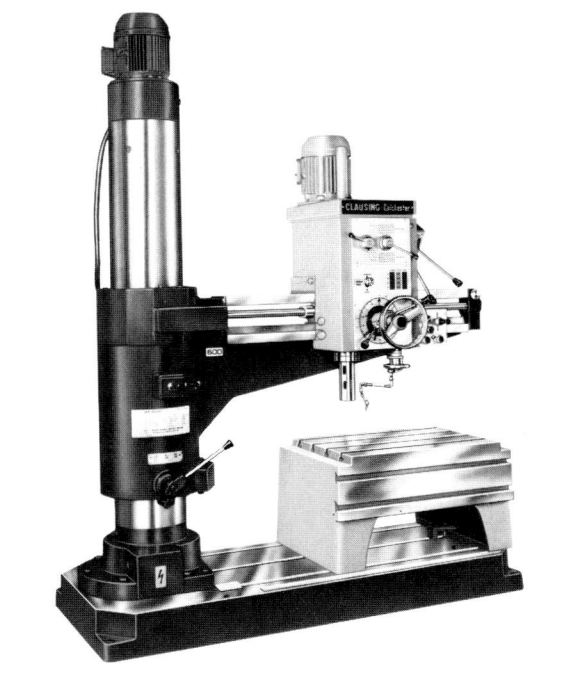

Fig. 12.6 Radial Drill Press. *Courtesy of Clausing Machine Tools*

are performed such operations as turning, boring, reaming, facing, threading, and knurling.

The workpiece is held in the lathe in a chuck (essentially a rotating vise). The cutting tool is fastened in the tool holder of the lathe and fed mechanically into the work as required.

12.8 Drill Press

The drill press, Fig. 12.5, is one of the most frequently used machine tools. Some of the operations that may be performed on this machine are drilling, reaming, boring, tapping, spot facing, counterboring, and countersinking.

The *radial* drill press, shown in Fig. 12.6, with its adjustable head and spindle, is very versatile and is especially suitable for large work.

12.9 Milling Machine

On the milling machine, Fig. 12.7, cutting is accomplished by feeding the work into a rotating cutter. Large plane milling machines, similar to the planer

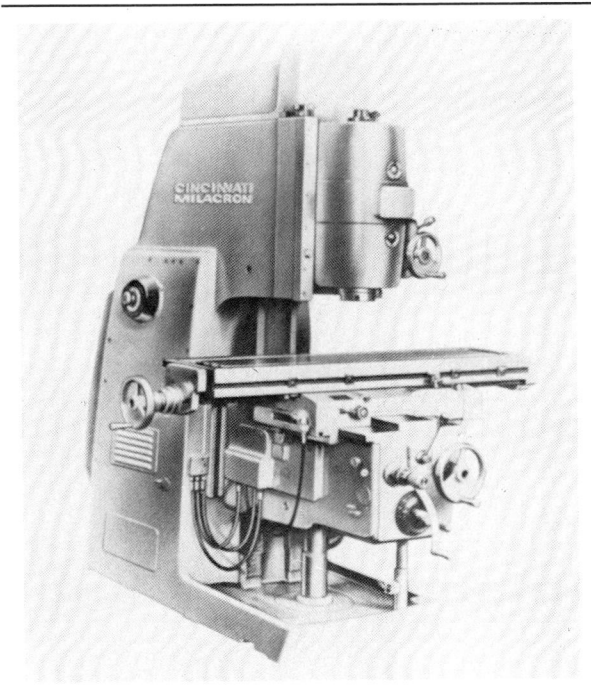

Fig. 12.7 Milling Machine. *Courtesy of Cincinnati Milacron*

The accuracy of many types of machine tools is dependent on the degree of accuracy to which the machine is set up and maintained. A laser-based measurement system, Fig. 12.9, is used in the calibration of the positioning accuracy of numerically controlled machine tools such as milling machines.

12.10 Shaper

On the shaper, Fig. 12.10, work is held in a vise while a single-pointed nonrotating cutting tool mounted in a reciprocating head is forced to move in a straight line past the stationary work. Between succeeding strokes of the tool, the vise that holds the work is fed mechanically into the path of the tool for the next cut alongside the one just completed. Shapers are often used to cut external and internal keyways, gear racks, dovetails, and T-slots.

12.11 Planer

On the planer, Fig. 12.11, work is fixed to a table that is moved mechanically so that the cutting takes place between stationary tools and moving work. This machine, with its reciprocating bed, and a tool head that is adjustable both horizontally and vertically, is used principally for machining large plane surfaces, or surfaces on a large number of pieces, as shown. In extremely large planers, the table is sta-

Fig. 12.8 Typical Milling Cutters. *Courtesy of Sharpaloy Division, Precision Industries, Inc.*

shown in Fig. 12.11, are also important production machines. In such plane mills, rotating milling cutters, Fig. 12.8, are used. In addition, it is practical to drill, ream, and bore on the milling machine.

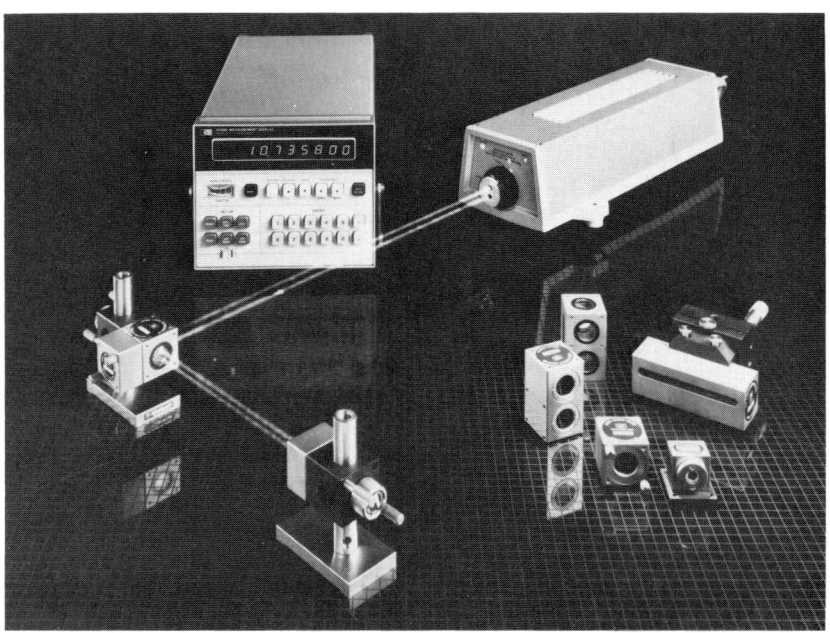

Fig. 12.9 Laser Machine Tool Calibration System. *Courtesy of Hewlett Packard.*

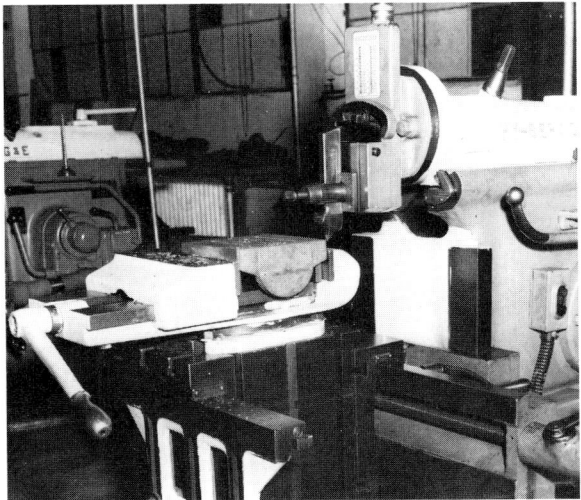

Fig. 12.10   Machining Plane Surface on Shaper.

tionary and the cutting tool is carried along a track past the work.

12.12 Boring Mill

The vertical boring mill, Fig. 12.12, is used for facing, turning, and boring heavy work weighing up to 20 tons. The vertical boring mill has a large rotating table and a nonrotating cutting tool that moves mechanically into the work.

The horizontal boring machine is suitable for

Fig. 12.12   Vertical Boring Mill.

accurate boring, reaming, facing, counterboring, and milling of pieces larger than could be handled on the typical milling machine.

The jig borer is a precision machine that somewhat resembles a drill press in its basic features of

Fig. 12.11   Planer.

Fig. 12.13   Vertical and Horizontal Turning Center. *Courtesy of Ingersoll Milling Machine Co.*

a rotating vertical spindle supporting a cutting tool and a stationary horizontal table for holding the work.

12.13 Vertical and Horizontal Turning Center

Vertical and horizontal turning centers, Fig. 12.13, eliminate the need for individual shaping, planing, and boring machines as previously described. These computer-driven machining centers not only replace planer mills, but they also do away with the need for moving a machined part from a milling machine to a drilling machine to a boring machine, and so on. The automatic tool changer on this machine stores 48 different cutters weighing up to 120 pounds each.

12.14 Grinding Machine

A grinding machine is used for removing a relatively small amount of material to bring the work to a very fine and accurate finish. In grinding, the work is fed mechanically against the rapidly rotating grinding wheel, and the depth of cut may be varied from 0.03 mm (.001″) to 0.0064 mm (.00025″).

Surface grinders, Fig. 12.14, reciprocate the work on a table that is simultaneously fed transverse to the grinding wheel. The unit shown lets the operator dial into the electronic memory the precise amount of metal to be removed during each of the roughing and finishing cuts and the amount of metal to be removed with each pass and even allows the

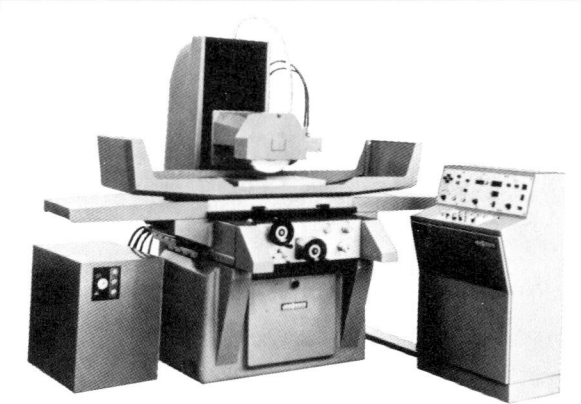

Fig. 12.14   Electronic Sequence-Controlled Surface Grinder. *Courtesy of Clausing/Jakobsen*

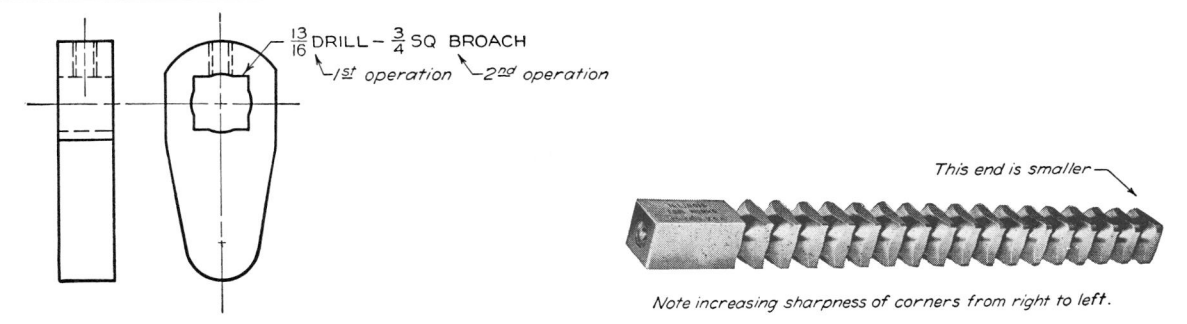

Fig. 12.15 Broaching.

operator to dial in the amount of wheel dressing to be done each cycle. The electronic memory automatically compensates for the loss of abrasive on the grinding wheel as the work proceeds.

metal, thus enlarging and forming the keyway as the broach passes through the hole.

A typical broach, along with the corresponding drawing calling for its use, is shown in Fig. 12.15.

12.15 Broaching

Broaching is similar to a single-stroke filing operation. As the broach is forced through the work, each succeeding tooth bites deeper and deeper into the

12.16 Holes

Rough holes are produced in metal by coring, piercing (punching), and flame cutting. Drilling, Fig. 12.16 (a), although superior, does not produce a hole

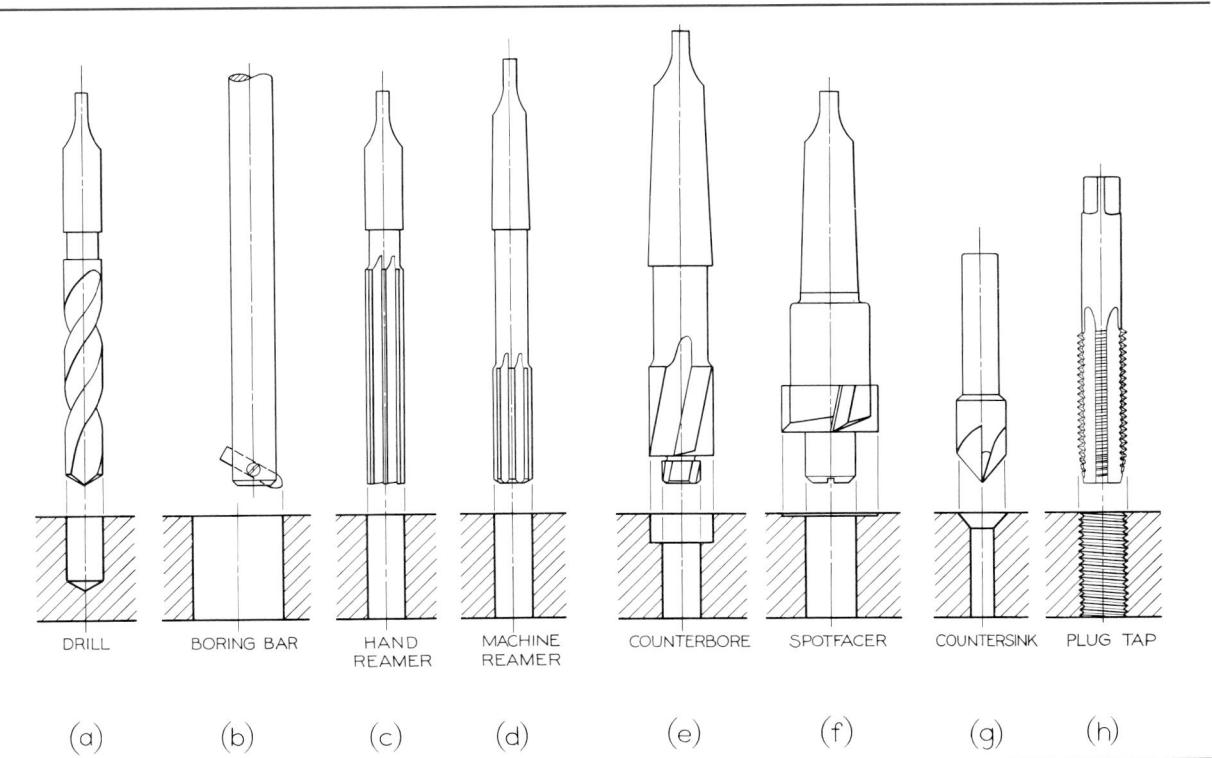

Fig. 12.16 Types of Machined Holes.

of extreme accuracy in roundness, straightness, or size.

Drills frequently cut holes slightly larger than their nominal size. A twist drill (Appendix 16) is somewhat flexible, which makes it tend to follow a path of least resistance. For work that demands greater accuracy, drilling is followed by boring, Fig. 12.16 (b), or by reaming, (c) or (d). When a drilled hole is to be finished by boring, it is drilled slightly undersize and the boring tool, which is supported by a relatively rigid bar, generates a hole that is round and straight. Reaming is also used for enlarging and improving the surface quality of a drilled or bored hole. Reamers are a finishing tool, and best results are achieved by limiting the material removed to .004″ to .012″ on the diameter.

Counterboring, Fig. 12.16 (e), is the cutting of an enlarged cylindrical portion of a previously pro-

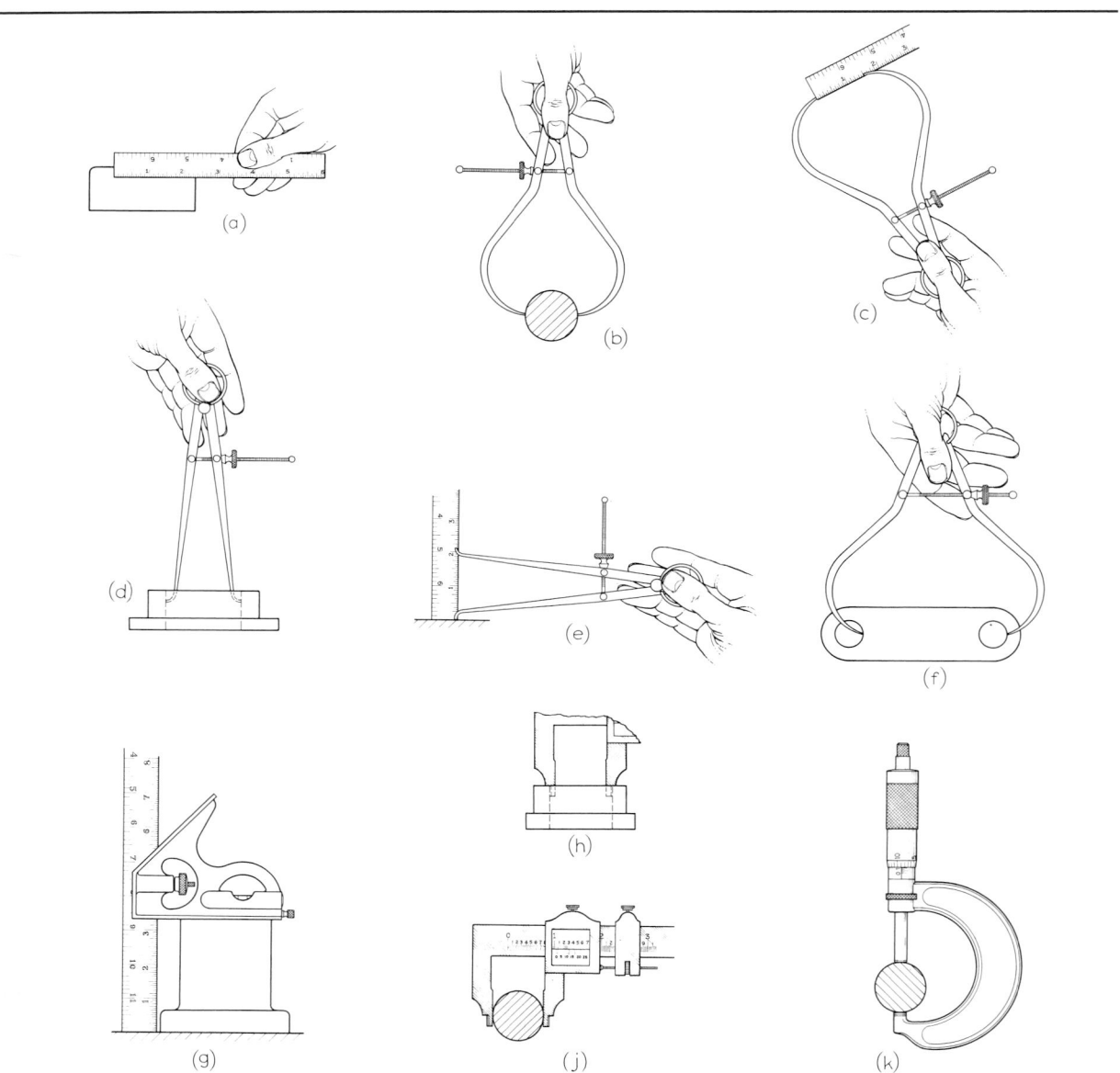

Fig. 12.17　Measuring Devices Used by the Machinist.

duced hole, usually to receive the head of a fillister-head or socket-head screw, Figs. 15.33 and 15.34.

Spotfacing is similar to counterboring, but is quite shallow, usually about 1.5 mm ($\frac{1}{16}$″) deep or just deep enough to clean a rough surface, Fig. 12.16 (f), or to finish the top of a boss to form a bearing surface. Although the depth of a spotface is commonly drawn 1.5 mm ($\frac{1}{16}$″) deep, the actual depth is usually left up to the machinist.

Countersinking, Fig. 12.16 (g), is the process of cutting a conical taper at one end of a hole, usually to receive the head of a flat-head screw, Figs. 15.32 and 15.33.

Tapping is the threading of previously drilled small holes by the use of one or more styles of taps, Fig. 12.16 (h).

12.17 Measuring Devices Used in Manufacturing

Although the machinist uses various measuring devices depending upon the kind of dimensions (fractional, decimal, or metric) shown on the drawing, it is evident that to dimension correctly, the engineering designer must have at least a working knowledge of the common measuring tools. The machinists' steel rule, or scale, is a commonly used measuring tool in the shop, Fig. 12.17 (a). The smallest division on one scale of this rule is $\frac{1}{64}$″, and such a scale is used for common fractional dimensions. Also, many machinists' rules have a decimal scale with the smallest division of .01″, which is used for dimensions given on the drawing by the decimal system, §13.10. For checking the nominal size of outside diameters, the outside spring caliper and steel scale are used as shown at (b) and (c). Likewise, the inside spring caliper is used for checking nominal dimensions, as shown at (d) and (e). Another use for the outside caliper, (f), is to check the nominal distance between holes (center-to-center). The combination square may be used for checking height, as shown at (g), and for a variety of other measurements. Measuring devices are also available that have metric scales.

For dimensions that require more precise measurements, the vernier caliper, (h) and (j), or the micrometer caliper, (k), may be used. It is common practice to check measurements to 0.025 mm (.001″) with these instruments and in some instances they are used to measure directly to 0.0025 mm (.0001″).

Computerized measuring devices have broadened the range of accuracy previously attainable.

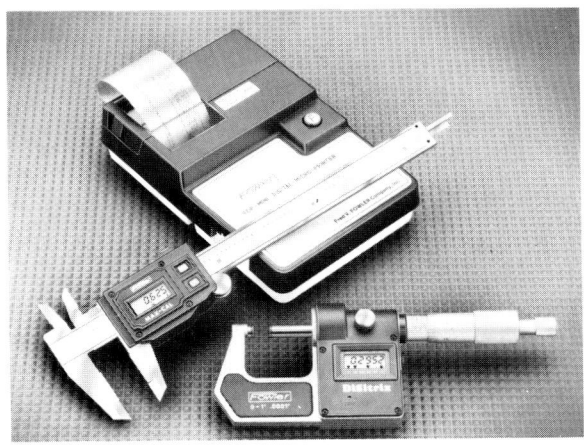

Fig. 12.18 Computerized Measurement System. *Courtesy of Fred V. Fowler Co., Inc.*

Figure 12.18 illustrates an ultraprecision electronic digital readout micrometer and caliper that contain integral microprocessors. In addition to the hand-held printer/recorder providing a hard-copy output of measurements, the printer also calculates and lists statistical mean, minimum, and maximum values as well as standard deviation.

12.18 Chipless Machining

Several manufacturing processes do not employ the cutting action described in most of the previous sections.

Chemical milling removes material through chemical reactions at the surface of the work piece. An etchant, acidic or basic, is agitated over an immersed workpiece that is masked where no metal removal is desired. For a material with high homogeneity, the tolerances obtainable in such an operation are ±0.08 mm (±.003″).

Electrodischarge machining (EDM) utilizes high-energy electric sparks that build up high charge densities on the surface of the work material. Thermal stresses, exceeding the strength of the work material, cause minute particles to break away from the work. Though this process is slow, it allows intricate shapes to be cut in hard materials, such as tungsten carbides.

Laser machine tools are helping designers and manufacturing engineers increase productivity over a wide range of machine applications. Laser systems reduce costs and improve the quality of many manufactured products that require cutting, engraving,

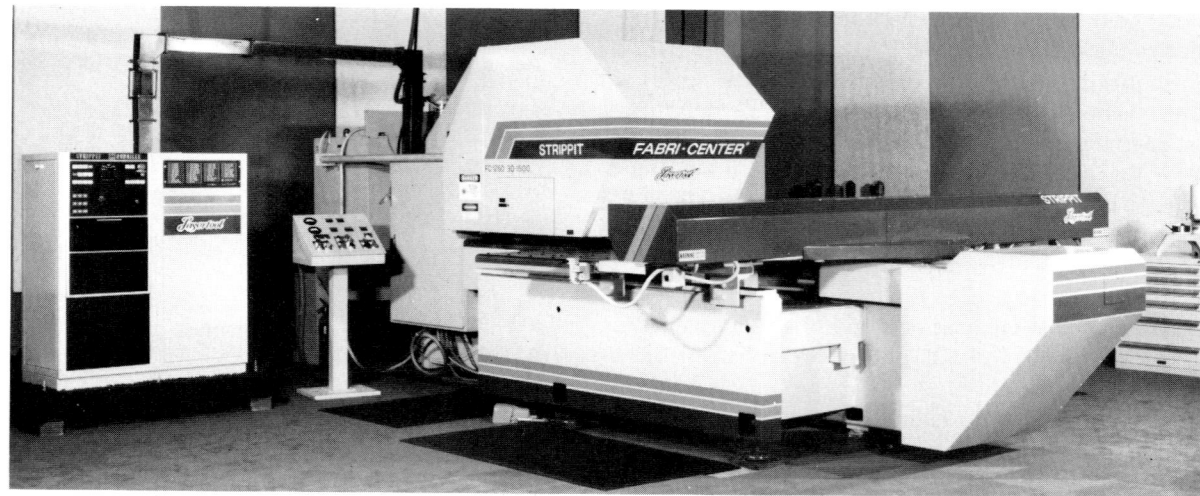

Fig. 12.19 Numerically Controlled Hole Punching and Laser Cutting System. *Courtesy of Strippit/Di-Acro Houdaille*

scribing, drilling, welding, perforating, or heat treating.

Metal cutting is the single largest application for most lasers. Laser processing offers several advantages over typical cutting processes, including greater accuracy and flexibility, reduced costs, and higher material throughput.

The computerized holemaking system shown in Fig. 12.19 combines a precision punching machine to produce conventional round and shaped holes using punch and die tooling, with a laser beam. Linear cutting rates range from 200 IPM (inches per minute) for .125″ acrylic and 160 IPM for .039″ low-carbon steel to 20 IPM for .250″ low-carbon steel.

12.19 Welding

Welding is a process of joining metals by fusion. Although welding by lasers is becoming popular in sophisticated plants, arc welding, gas welding, re-

sistance welding, and atomic hydrogen welding of stock plates, tubing, and angles are more commonly used.

12.20 Stock Forms

Many standardized structural shapes are available in stock sizes for the fabrication of parts or structures. Among these are bars of various shapes, flat stock, rolled structural shapes, and extrusions, Fig. 12.20. The tube shown at (e) is often round, square, or rectangular in shape.

12.21 Forging

Forging is the process of shaping metal to a desired form by means of pressing or hammering. Generally, forging is hot forging, Fig. 12.21, in which the metal is heated to a required temperature before forging. Some softer metals can be forged without

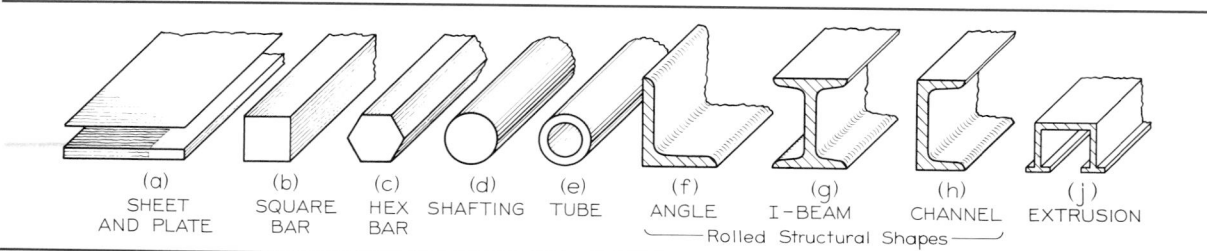

(a) SHEET AND PLATE   (b) SQUARE BAR   (c) HEX BAR   (d) SHAFTING   (e) TUBE   (f) ANGLE   (g) I-BEAM   (h) CHANNEL   (j) EXTRUSION
Rolled Structural Shapes

Fig. 12.20 Common Stock Forms.

Fig. 12.21 Drop Forging. *Courtesy of Jervis B. Webb Co.*

heating, and this is cold forging. *Draft*, or taper, must be provided on all forgings.

12.22 Heat-Treating

Heat-treating is when heat is used to alter the properties of metal. Different procedures affect metal in different ways. Annealing and normalizing involve heating to a critical temperature range, and then slowly cooling to soften the metal, thereby releasing internal stresses developed in previous manufacturing processes.

Hardening requires heating to above the critical temperature followed by rapid cooling—quenching in oil, water, brine, or in some instances in air. *Tempering* reduces internal stresses caused by hardening and also improves the toughness and ductility. *Surface hardening* is a way of hardening the surface of a steel part while leaving the inside of the piece soft. Surface hardening is accomplished by *carburizing*, followed by heat-treatment; by *cyaniding*, followed by heat-treatment; by *nitriding*; by *induction hardening*; and by *flame hardening*.

Lasers are widely used for transformation hardening of selected surface areas of metal parts. Laser hardening applies less heat to the part than do tra-ditional methods, and thermal distortion is greatly reduced.

12.23 Automation

Automation is the term applied to systems of automatic machines and processes. These machines and processes are essentially the same as previously discussed, with the addition of mechanisms to control the sequence of operation, movement of tool, flow, and so forth. Little, if any, operator interaction is required once the equipment has been "set up."

Most contain built-in computers to control all of their functions, such as the surface grinder in Fig. 12.14. Some machines are used in combination with an industrial robot, Fig. 12.22, where the robot takes the place of an operator for the load and unload functions for the machine. Robots are also used extensively for spray painting and welding applications as well as for around-the-clock performance in environments where a human operator could not exist.

When a machine's cycle is relatively long and the robot is underutilized, two or more machines can be grouped together in such a fashion that the

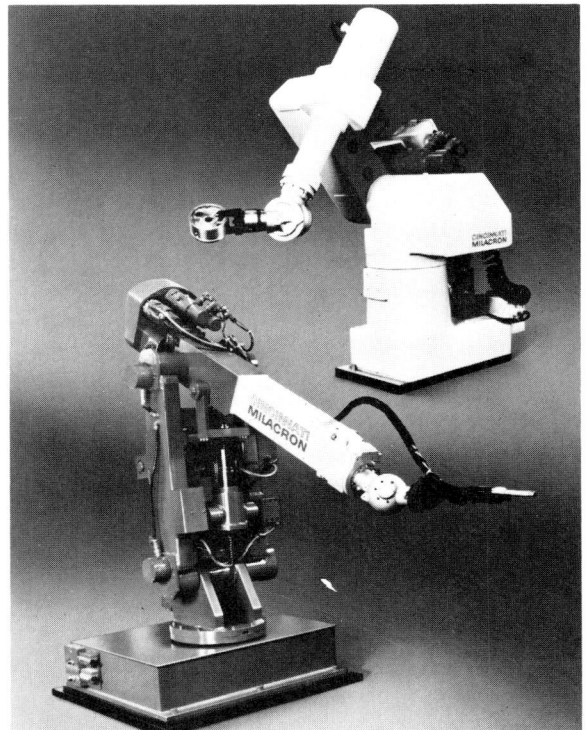

Fig. 12.22 Industrial Robots. *Courtesy of Cincinnati Milacron*

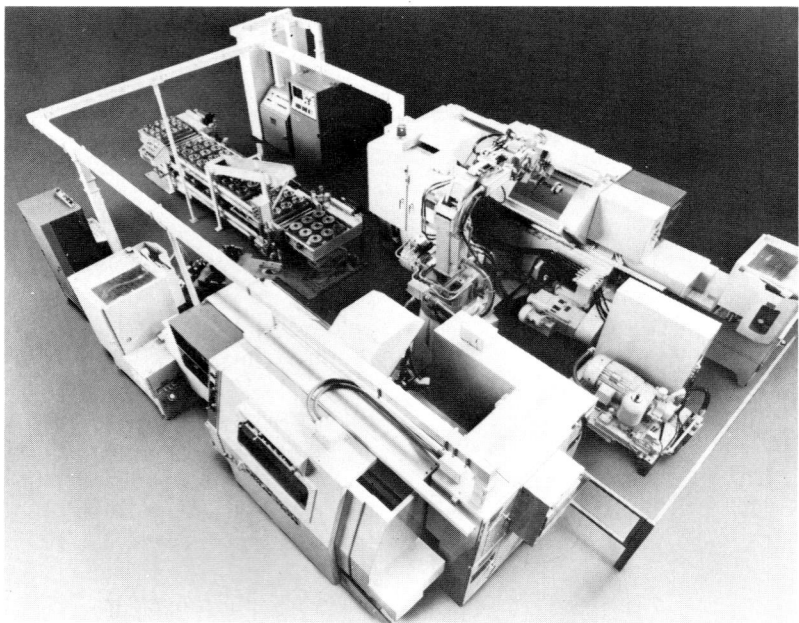

Fig. 12.23 Flexible Manufacturing System. *Courtesy of Cincinnati Milacron*

robot can service each. The flexible manufacturing system in Fig. 12.23 consists of a unique computer numerically controlled (CNC) turning system equipped with fully automated features, designed for reliable batch manufacturing of quality parts while virtually unattended. The two turning centers are rear loaded by a heavy-duty industrial robot. The system also features automatic tool changing from an 84-tool storage magazine as well as automatic postprocess gaging and a take-away parts conveyor.

The manufacturing system in Fig. 12.24 is based on a different concept. The parts being produced are the front- and rear-end housings for automotive air-conditioning compressors. A conveyor system circulates the housing parts throughout the 20-station system, where various facing, boring, drilling, chamfering, probing, reaming, gaging, wirebrushing, washing, blow drying, and unloading and reject-diverting operations are performed. The disadvantage of a system such as this is that it is usually custom-made for the specific application and, therefore, is not considered flexible enough for most smaller manufacturing operations.

Large-scale manufacturing operations such as automotive plants must be automated to remain competitive. Figure 12.25 shows Pontiac Fiero bod-ies being carried on a conveyor into a one-of-a-kind milling and drilling machine.

12.24 Plastics Processing
The growth of the plastics industry has expanded in recent decades to the point that the domestic demand for plastics reached approximately 50 billion pounds in 1990. Plastic resins used in motor vehicle production alone accounted for about 2.0 billion pounds. As an example of this tremendous increase, the 3000-pound Chevrolet Corvette contains about 580 pounds of various plastic parts.

The two main families of plastics are known as *thermosetting* and *thermoplastic*. The thermosetting plastics will take a set and will not soften when reheated, whereas thermoplastics will soften whenever heat is applied.

Typical plastic processing operations include extrusion, blow molding, compression molding, transfer molding, injection molding, and thermoforming.

12.25 Extrusion Molding
An extrusion-molding machine transfers solid plastic particles, additives, colorants, and regrinds from a feed hopper into a heating chamber. The extruder screw conveys the material forward through the bar-

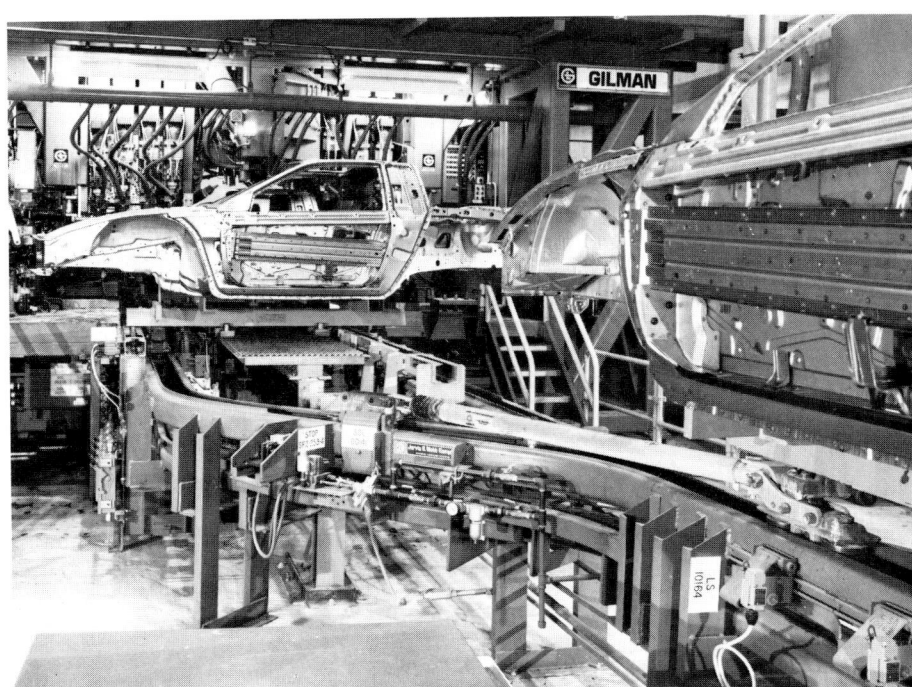

Fig. 12.24 Automated Manufacturing System. *Courtesy of Cargill Detroit*

Fig. 12.25 Automated Material Conveying. *Courtesy of Jervis B. Webb Co.*

rel toward a die. The contour of the die will determine the cross-sectional shape of the extruded member. Typical uses of the extrusion process are in compounding and pelletizing of bulk plastics, pipe and profile extrusion, blown film and sheet manufacturing, and blow molding.

12.26 Blow Molding

Blow-molding operations are classified as *extrusion*, *injection*, and *stretch* blow molding. In extrusion blow-molding, an open-ended parison (hollow tube) is extruded, and the mold is closed on the parison, thus closing the bottom of the tube. When compressed air is introduced through the blow pin or blow needles, the parison expands to take the shape of the mold. The part is cooled by being in contact with the cooler mold surface and then is removed from the mold. Automotive coolant reservoirs, seat backs, ductwork, wheels, toy parts, juice and handled bottles are common extrusion blow-molded shapes.

In injection blow molding, the parison is formed by injection molding a test-tube-shaped preform on a core pin and is then transferred to the blow-molding station. An advantage of the injection blow-molding process is that there is no flash to trim and any thread detail on the neck is of injection-molding quality.

In stretch blow molding, also called orientation blow molding, a parison is formed by either an extrusion or injection-molding operation and is subsequently stretched and blown in both an axial and radial direction. Advantages of this process are greater strength, better clarity, improved impact strength, and increased stiffness.

12.27 Compression Molding

In compression molding, a charge of plastic material, usually thermosetting, is placed into a mold, the mold is closed, and a plunger compresses the material so that heat and pressure modifies the plastic to take the shape of the mold cavity. The pressure is maintained during the curing cycle, after which the plunger is removed and the part is ejected. Preformed, preheated discs are often used for better control of the volume of material, thereby reducing variations in part thickness or part density.

12.28 Transfer Molding

In the transfer-molding process, an amount of thermosetting material is placed in a chamber (usually referred to as a pot) and then is forced out of the pot and into the closed cavities where polymerization takes place. The plastics formulations used are generally of a softer plastic than those that are used in compression molding. This enables the design of the part to include ribs and thin sections that are not formable in compression molding.

12.29 Injection Molding

Injection molding, Fig. 12.26, is primarily used to manufacture thermoplastic products.

Fig. 12.26 Injection-Molding Machine. *Courtesy of Reed Prentice*

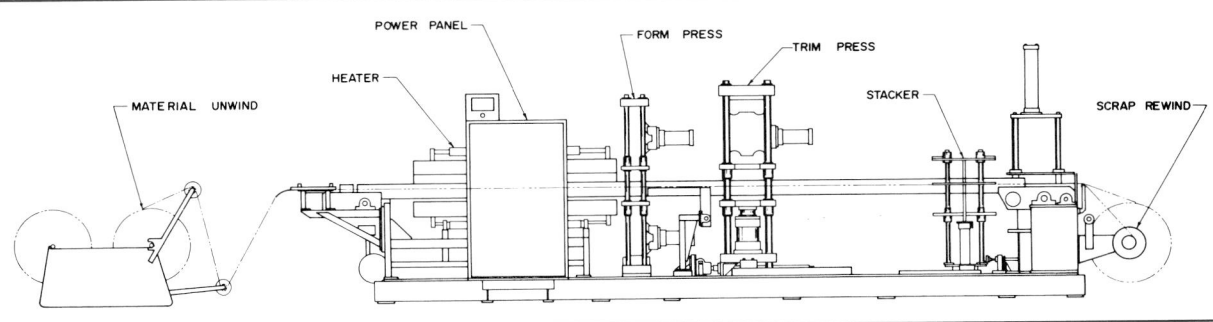

Fig. 12.27   Thermoforming Machine. *Courtesy of Sencorp Systems, Inc.*

Materials are melted and fed through the machine and injected into the mold where the plastic solidifies into the shape of the mold cavities. The press is opened after the plastic has sufficiently cooled and the parts are then ejected. Owing to the relatively high costs of tooling, the process is typically and only economically suited for mass production.

12.30 Thermoforming

Thermoforming is a process in which one or both sides of a thermoplastic sheet are heated so that it can be formed into various products. Figure 12.27 represents a thermoformer that feeds roll stock up to .050″ through the heater zone and into a form area. Once the heated sheet is clamped in place over

the mold (some machines have a form area of up to 50″ wide by 50″ long), pressure is exerted on the outside of the sheet, and a vacuum is drawn to evacuate the air that is trapped between the sheet and the mold. The sheet is held in place on the mold until the plastic is cooled sufficiently to maintain the part shape, and compressed air is then introduced through the vacuum holes to lift the parts off the mold. The sheet is then indexed to the die cutting and stack stations.

Figure 12.28 shows a machine that is geared toward high-volume production runs. The parts being molded are high-impact foam polystyrene egg cartons and are being formed at about 200 cartons per minute, cut on a matched metal punch press, and then stacked automatically for packing and shipping.

Fig. 12.28   Thermoforming Machine. *Courtesy of Brown Machine Division, John Brown Plastics Machinery.*

CHAPTER

13

Dimensioning

We have all heard of "rule of thumb." Actually, at one time an inch was defined as the width of a thumb, and a foot was simply the length of a man's foot. In old England, an inch used to be "three barley corns, round and dry." In the time of Noah and the Ark, the *cubit* was the length of a man's forearm, or about 18″.

In 1791, France adopted the *meter** (1 meter = 39.37″; 1″ = 25.4 mm), from which the decimalized metric system evolved. In the meantime England was setting up a more accurate determination of the *yard*, which was legally defined in 1824 by act of Parliament. A foot was $\frac{1}{3}$ yard, and an inch was $\frac{1}{36}$ yard. From these specifications, graduated rulers, scales, and many types of measuring devices have been developed to achieve even more accuracy of measurement and inspection.

Until this century, common fractions were considered adequate for dimensions, but as designs became more complicated, and as it became necessary to have interchangeable parts in order to support mass production, more accurate specifications were required and it became necessary to turn to the decimal-inch system or the SI system. See §§13.9 and 13.10.

*In the SI system the meter is now defined as a length equal to the distance traveled by light in a vacuum during a time interval of $\dfrac{1}{299\ 792\ 458}$ second.

13.1 Metric Units

The current rapid growth of worldwide science and commerce has fostered an international system of units (SI), based on the meter and suitable for measurements in physical science and engineering. The seven basic units of measure are the meter (length), kilogram (mass), second (time), ampere (electric current), kelvin (thermodynamic temperature), mole (amount of substance), and candela (luminous intensity).

The SI system is gradually coming into use in the United States, especially by the many multinational companies in the chemical, electronic, and mechanical industries. A tremendous effort is now under way to convert all standards of the American National Standards Institute (ANSI) to the SI units in conformity with the International Standards Organization (ISO) standards.

See inside the front cover of this book for a table for converting fractional inches to decimal inches or millimeters. For the International System of Units and their United States equivalents, see Appendix 31.

13.2 Size Description

In addition to a complete *shape description* of an object, as discussed in previous chapters, a drawing of the design must also give a complete *size description*; that is, it must be *dimensioned*. See ANSI Y14.5M–1982 (R1988).

The need for *interchangeability* of parts is the basis for the development of modern methods of size description. Drawings today must be dimensioned so that production personnel in widely separated places can make mating parts that will fit properly when brought together for final assembly or when used as repair or replacement parts by the customer, §13.26.

The increasing need for precision manufacturing and the necessity to control sizes for interchangeability has shifted responsibility for size control to the designing engineer and the drafter. The production worker no longer exercises judgment in engineering matters, but only on the proper execution of instructions given on the drawings. Therefore, it is necessary for engineers and designers to be familiar with materials and methods of construction and with production requirements. The engineering student or designer should seize every opportunity to become familiar with the fundamental manufacturing processes, especially *patternmaking, foundry, forging*, and *machine shop practice.*

The drawing should show the object in its completed condition and should contain all necessary information to bring it to that final state. Therefore, in dimensioning a drawing, the designer and the drafter should keep in mind the finished piece, the production processes required, and above all the function of the part in the total assembly. Whenever possible—that is, when there is no conflict with functional dimensioning, §13.4—dimensions should be given that are convenient for the individual worker or the production engineer. These dimensions should be given so that it will not be necessary to scale or assume any dimensions. Do not give dimensions to points or surfaces that are not accessible to the worker.

Dimensions should not be duplicated or superfluous, §13.30. Only those dimensions should be given that are needed to produce and inspect the part exactly as intended by the designer. The student often makes the mistake of giving the dimensions that are used *to make the drawing*. These are not necessarily the dimensions required. There is much more to the theory of dimensioning, as we shall see.

13.3 Scale of Drawing

Drawings should be made to scale, and the scale should be indicated in the title block even though the worker is never expected to scale the drawing or print for a needed dimension. See §2.31 for indications of scales.

A heavy straight line should be drawn under any dimension that is not to scale, Fig. 13.15, or the abbreviation *NTS* (not to scale) should be indicated. This procedure may be necessary when a change is made in the drawing that is not important enough to justify making an entirely new drawing.

13.4 Learning to Dimension

Dimensions are given in the form of linear distances, angles, or notes irrespective of the dimensioning units being used. The ability to dimension properly in millimeters, decimal inch, or fractional inch requires the following:

1. The student must learn the *technique of dimensioning:* the character of the lines, the spacing of dimensions, the making of arrowheads, and so forth. A typical dimensioned drawing is shown in Fig. 13.1. Note the strong contrast between the visible lines of the object and the thin lines used for the dimensions.

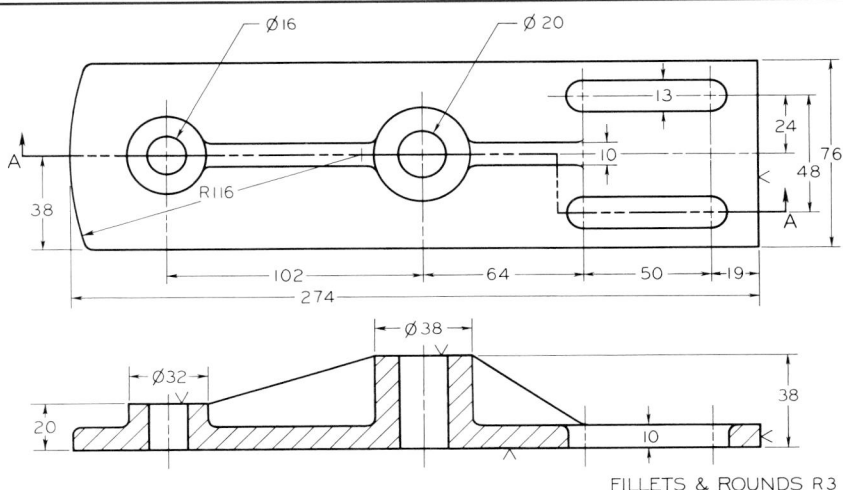

Fig. 13.1 Dimensioning Technique.   Dimensions in millimeters.

2. The student must learn the rules of *placement of dimensions* on the drawing. These practices assure a logical and practical arrangement with maximum legibility.

3. The student should learn the *choice of dimensions*. Formerly, manufacturing processes were considered the governing factor in dimensioning. Now function is considered first and the manufacturing processes second. The proper procedure is to dimension tentatively for function and then review the dimensioning to see if any improvements from the standpoint of production can be made without adversely affecting the functional dimensioning. A "geometric breakdown," §13.20, will assist the beginner in selecting dimensions. In most cases dimensions thus determined will be functional, but this method should be accompanied by a logical analysis of the functional requirements.

13.5 Lines Used in Dimensioning

A dimension line, Fig. 13.2 (a), is a thin, dark, solid line terminated by arrowheads, which indicates the direction and extent of a dimension. In machine drawing, the dimension line is broken, usually near the middle, to provide an open space for the dimension figure. In structural and architectural drawing, it is customary to place the dimension figure above an unbroken dimension line.

As shown in Fig. 13.2 (b), the dimension line nearest the object outline should be spaced at least 10 mm ($\frac{3}{8}''$) away. All other parallel dimension lines should be at least 6 mm ($\frac{1}{4}''$) apart, and more if space is available. *The spacing of dimension lines should be uniform throughout the drawing.*

An *extension line*, (a), is a thin, dark, solid line that "extends" from a point on the drawing to which a dimension refers. The dimension line meets the extension lines at right angles except in special cases, as in Fig. 13.6 (a). A gap of about 1.5 mm

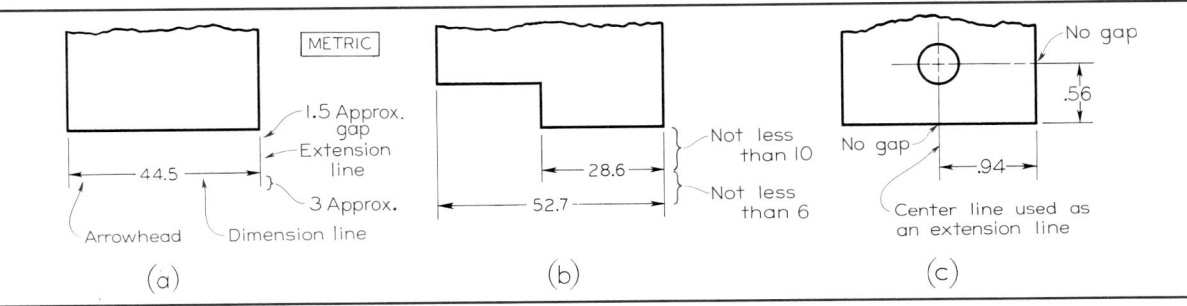

Fig. 13.2 Dimensioning Technique.

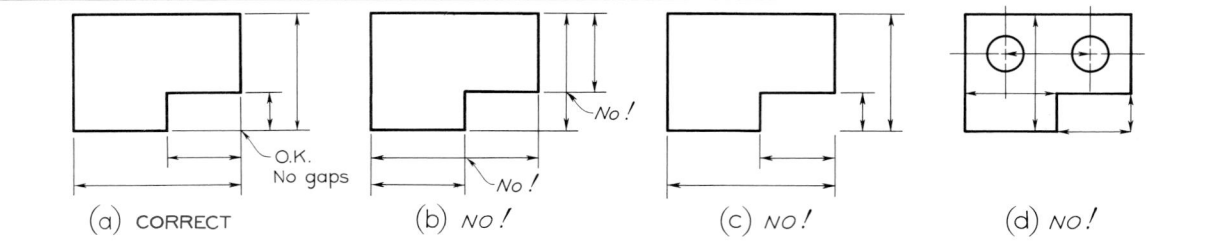

Fig. 13.3 Dimension and Extension Lines.

($\frac{1}{16}$″) should be left where the extension line would join the object outline. The extension line should extend about 3 mm ($\frac{1}{8}$″) beyond the outermost arrowhead, (a) and (b).

The foregoing dimensions for lettering height, spacing, and so on should be increased approximately 50 percent for drawings that are to be microfilmed and blown back to one-half size for the working print. Otherwise the lettering and dimensioning often are not legible.

A *center line* is a thin, dark line composed of alternate long and short dashes and is used to represent axes of symmetrical parts and to denote centers. As shown in Fig. 13.2 (c), center lines are commonly used as extension lines in locating holes and other features. When so used, the center line crosses over other lines of the drawing without gaps. A center line should always end in a long dash.

13.6 Placement of Dimension and Extension Lines

A correct example of the placement of dimension lines and extension lines is shown in Fig. 13.3 (a). The shorter dimensions are nearest to the object outline. Dimension lines should not cross extension lines as at (b), which results from placing the shorter dimensions outside. Note that it is perfectly satisfactory to cross extension lines, as shown at (a). They

should never be shortened, as at (c). A dimension line should never coincide with, or form a continuation of, any line of the drawing, as shown at (d). Avoid crossing dimension lines wherever possible.

Dimensions should be lined up and grouped together as much as possible, as shown in Fig. 13.4 (a), and not as at (b).

In many cases, extension lines and center lines must cross visible lines of the object, Fig. 13.5 (a). When this occurs, gaps should not be left in the lines, as at (b).

Dimension lines are normally drawn at right angles to extension lines, but an exception may be made in the interest of clearness, as shown in Fig. 13.6 (a). In crowded conditions, gaps in extension lines near arrowheads may be left, in order to clarify the dimensions, as shown at (b). In general, avoid dimensioning to hidden lines, as shown at (c).

13.7 Arrowheads

Arrowheads, Fig. 13.7, indicate the extent of dimensions. They should be uniform in size and style throughout the drawing and not varied according to the size of the drawing or the length of dimensions. Arrowheads should be drawn freehand and the length and width should be in a ratio of 3:1. The length of the arrowhead should be equal to the height of the dimension whole numbers. For average use, make arrowheads about 3 mm ($\frac{1}{8}$″) long and

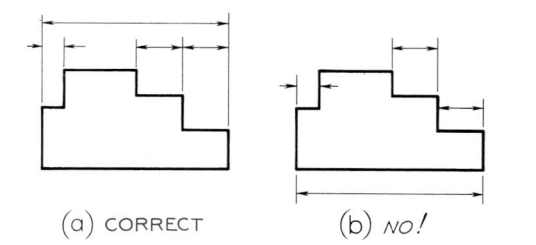

Fig. 13.4 Grouped Dimensions.

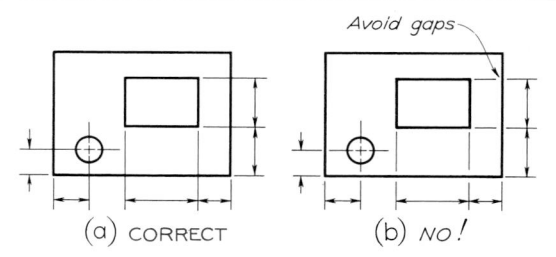

Fig. 13.5 Crossing Lines.

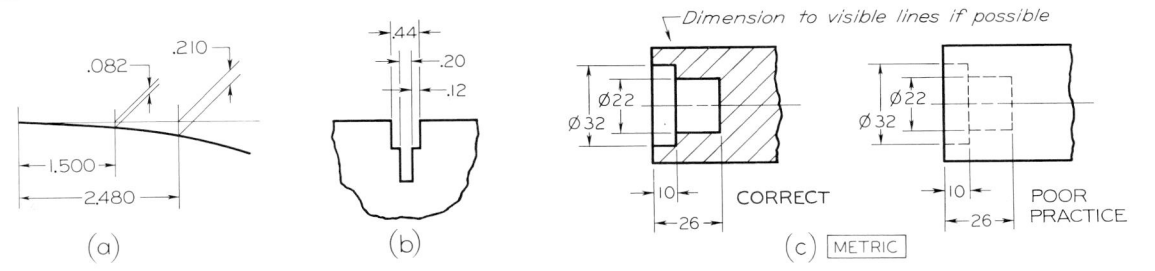

Fig. 13.6 Placement of Dimensions.

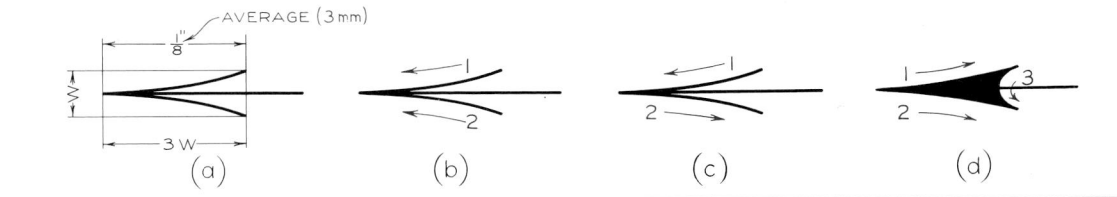

Fig. 13.7 Arrowheads.

very narrow, (a). Use strokes toward the point or away from the point desired, (b) to (d). The method at (b) is easier when the strokes are drawn toward the drafter. For best appearance, fill in the arrowhead as at (d).

13.8 Leaders

A leader, Fig. 13.8, is a thin solid line leading from a note or dimension, and terminated by an arrowhead or a dot touching the part to which attention is directed. Arrowheads should always terminate on a line such as the edge of a hole; dots should be within the outline of the object. A leader should generally be an inclined straight line, if possible, except for the short horizontal shoulder (6 mm or $\frac{1}{4}''$, approx.) extending from midheight of the lettering *at the beginning or end of a note.*

A leader to a circle should be radial; that is, if extended, it would pass through the center. A draw-

ing presents a more pleasing appearance if leaders near each other are drawn parallel. Leaders should cross as few lines as possible and should never cross each other. They should not be drawn parallel to nearby lines of the drawing, allowed to pass through a corner of the view, drawn unnecessarily long, or drawn horizontally or vertically on the sheet. A leader should be drawn at a large angle and terminate with the appropriate arrowhead, or with a dot, as shown in Fig. 13.8 (f).

13.9 Fractional, Decimal, and Metric Dimensions

In the early days of machine manufacturing in this country, the worker would scale the undimensioned design drawing to obtain any needed dimensions, and it was the worker's responsibility to see to it that the parts fitted together properly. Workers were skilled, and it should not be thought that very

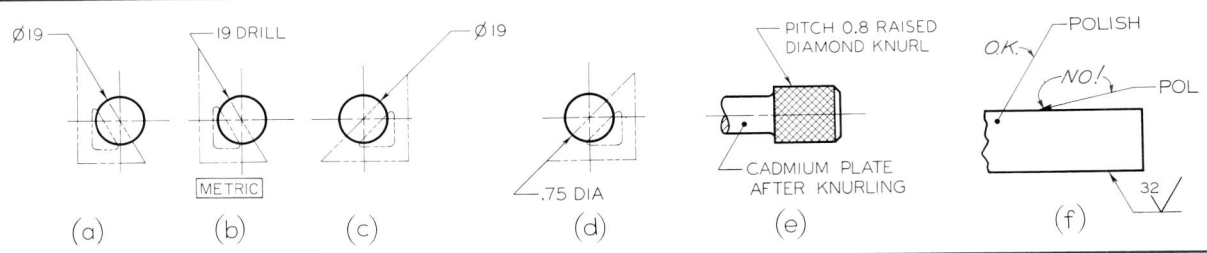

Fig. 13.8 Leaders.

accurate and excellent fits were not obtained. Hand-built machines were often beautiful examples of precision craftsmanship.

The system of units and common fractions is still used in architectural and structural work where close accuracy is relatively unimportant and where the steel tape or framing square is used to set off measurements. Architectural and structural drawings are therefore often dimensioned in this manner. Also, certain commercial commodities, such as pipe and lumber, are identified by standard nominal designations that are close approximations of actual dimensions.

As industry has progressed, there has been greater and greater demand for more accurate specifications of the important functional dimensions—more accurate than the $\frac{1}{64}''$ permitted by the engineers', architects', and machinists' scale. Since it was cumbersome to use still smaller fractions, such as $\frac{1}{128}$ or $\frac{1}{256}$, it became the practice to give decimal dimensions, such as 4.2340 and 3.815, for the dimensions requiring accuracy. However, some dimensions, such as standard nominal sizes of materials, punched holes, drilled holes, threads, keyways, and other features produced by tools that are so designated are still expressed in whole numbers and common fractions.

Thus, drawings may be dimensioned entirely with whole numbers and common fractions, or entirely with decimals, or with a combination of the two. However, more recent practice adopted the decimal-inch system and current practice also utilizes the metric system as recommended by ANSI. Millimeters and inches in the decimal form can be added, subtracted, multiplied, and divided more easily than can fractions.

Also the decimal system is compatible with the calibrations of machine tool controls, the requirements for numerically controlled machine tools, and for computer-programmed digital plotting. For examples of computer-made drawings, see Figs. 8.47–8.54.

For inch–millimeter equivalents of decimal and common fractions, see inside the front cover of this book. For additional metric equivalents, see Appendix 31. For rounding off decimals, see §13.10.

13.10 Decimal Systems

A decimal system, based upon the decimal inch or the millimeter as a linear unit of measure, has many advantages and is compatible with most measuring devices and machine tools. Metric measurement is based on the meter as a linear unit of measure, but the millimeter is used on most engineering drawings. To facilitate the changeover to metric dimensions during the transition, some drawings are dual-dimensioned in millimeters and decimal inches. See §13.11.

Total decimal dimensioning is *preferred* by the American National Standard Institute.

Complete decimal dimensioning employs decimals for all dimensions and designations except where certain commercial commodities, such as pipe and lumber, are identified by standardized nominal designations. *Combination dimensioning* employs decimals for all dimensions except the designations of nominal sizes of parts or features such as bolts, screw threads, keyseats, or other standardized fractional designations. [ANSI Y14.5M–1982 (R1988)].

In these systems, two-place inch or one-place millimeter decimals are used when a common fraction has been regarded as sufficiently accurate.

In the combination dimensioning system, common fractions may continue to be used to indicate nominal sizes of materials, drilled holes, punched holes, threads, keyways, and other standard features.

One-place millimeter decimals are used when tolerance limits of ±0.1 mm or more can be permitted. Two (or more)-place millimeter decimals are used for tolerance limits less than ±0.1 mm. Fractions are considered to have the same tolerance as two-place decimal-inch dimensions when determining the number of places to retain in the conversion to millimeters. Keep in mind that 0.1 mm is approximately equal to .004 inch.

Two-place inch decimals are used when tolerance limits of ±.01″, or more, can be permitted. Three or more decimal places are used for tolerance limits less than ±.01″. In two-place decimals, the second place preferably should be an even digit (for example, .02, .04, and .06 are preferred to .01, .03, or .05) so that when the dimension is divided by 2, as is necessary in determining the radius from a diameter, the result will be a decimal of two places. However, odd two-place decimals are used when required for design purposes, such as in dimensioning points on a smooth curve or when strength or clearance is a factor.

A typical example of the use of the complete decimal-inch system is shown in Fig. 13.9. The use of the preferred decimal-millimeter system is shown in Fig. 13.10.

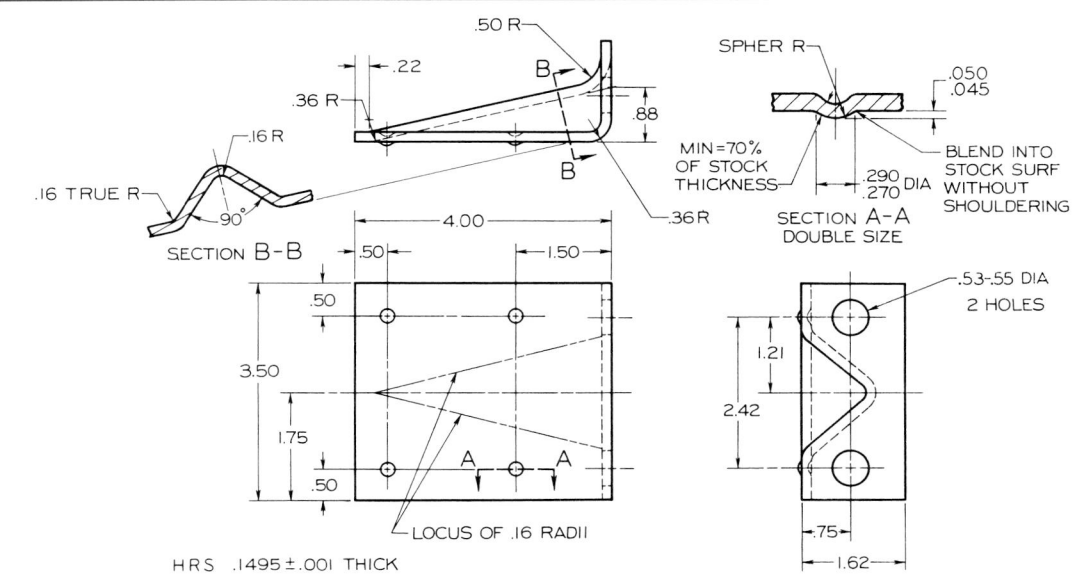

Fig. 13.9 Complete Decimal Dimensioning.

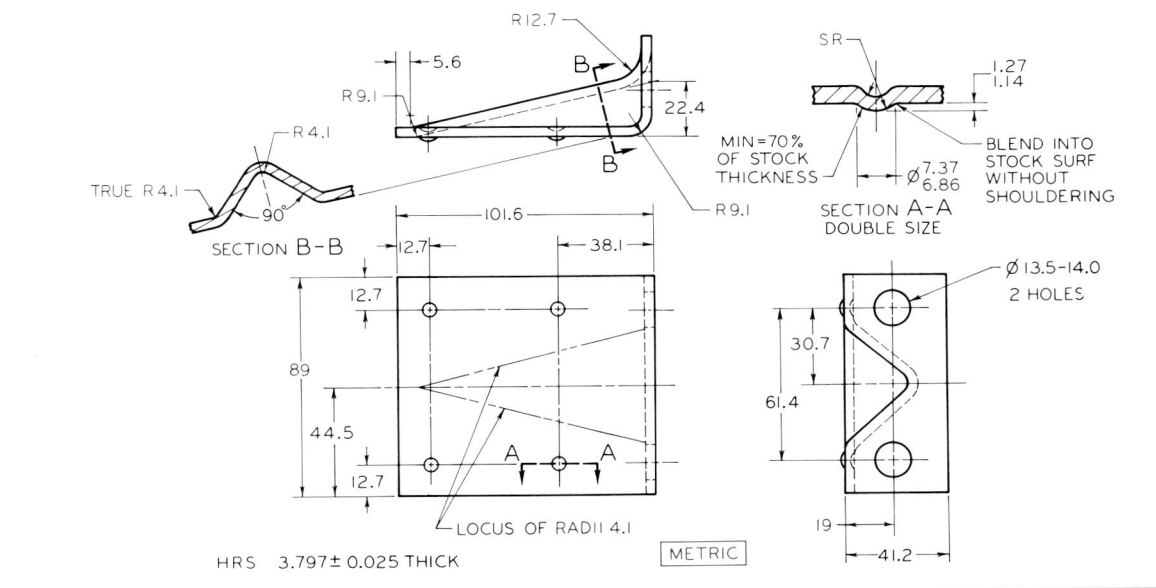

Fig. 13.10 Complete Metric Dimensioning.

When a decimal value is to be rounded off to fewer places than the calculated number, regardless of the unit of measurement involved, the method prescribed is as follows.

The last figure to be retained should not be changed when the figure beyond the last figure to be retained is less than 5.

EXAMPLE 3.46325, if rounded off to three places, should be 3.463.

The last figure to be retained should be increased by 1 when the figure beyond the last figure to be retained is greater than 5 (or two figures are greater than 50).

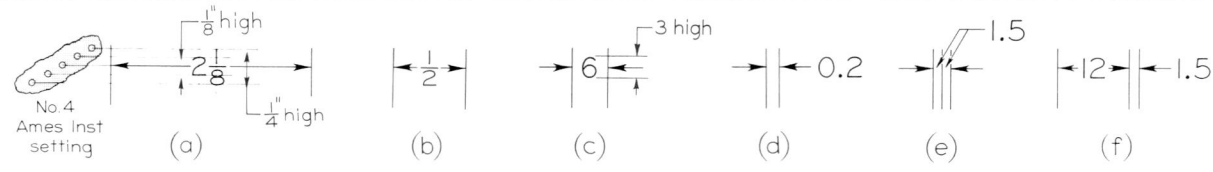

Fig. 13.11   Dimension Figures.   Metric dimensions (c) through (f).

EXAMPLE   8.37652, if rounded off to three places, should be 8.377.

The last figure to be retained should be unchanged if it is even, or increased by 1 if odd, when followed by exactly 5.

EXAMPLE   4.365 becomes 4.36 when rounded off to two places. Also 4.355 becomes 4.36 when cut off to two places.

The use of the metric system means not only a changeover of measuring equipment but also a changeover in thinking on the part of drafters and designers. They must stop thinking in terms of inches and common fractions and think in terms of millimeters and other SI units. Dimensioning practices remain essentially the same; only the units are changed. Compare Figs. 13.9 and 13.10.

Shop scales and drafting scales for use in the decimal systems are available in a variety of forms. The drafting scale is known as the *decimal scale*, and is discussed in §2.29. See inside the front cover for two-, three-, and four-place decimal equivalent table.

Once the metric system is installed, the advantages in computation, in checking, and in simplified dimensioning techniques are considerable.

13.11 Dimension Figures

The importance of good lettering of dimension figures cannot be overstated. The shop produces according to the directions on the drawing, and to save time and prevent costly mistakes, all lettering should be perfectly legible. A complete discussion of numerals is given in §§4.18–4.20. The standard height for whole numbers is $\frac{1}{8}''$ (3 mm), and for fractions double that, or $\frac{1}{4}''$ (6 mm). Beginners should use guide lines, as shown in Figs. 4.27 and 4.28. The numerator and denominator of a fraction should be clearly separated from the fraction bar, and the fraction bar should always be horizontal, as in Fig. 4.29 (c). An exception to this may be made in crowded

places, such as parts lists, but never in dimensioning.

Legibility should never be sacrificed by crowding dimension figures into limited spaces. For every such case there is a practical and effective method, as shown in Fig. 13.11. At (a) and (b) there is enough space for the dimension line, the numeral, and the arrowheads. At (c) there is only enough room for the figure, and the arrowheads are placed outside. At (d) both the arrowheads and the figure are placed outside. Other methods are shown at (e) and (f).

If necessary, a removed partial view may be drawn to an enlarged scale to provide the space needed for clear dimensioning, Fig. 9.22.

Methods of lettering and displaying decimal dimension figures are shown in Fig. 13.12. All numerals are 3 mm ($\frac{1}{8}''$) high whether on one or two lines. The space between lines of numerals is 1.5 mm ($\frac{1}{16}''$) or 0.8 mm ($\frac{1}{32}''$) on each side of a dimension line. To draw guide lines with the Ames Lettering Guide, Fig. 4.24, use the No. 4 setting or appropriate metric setting and the center column of holes.

Make all decimal points bold, allowing ample space. Where the metric dimension is a whole number, neither a decimal point nor a zero is given, Fig. 13.11 (c) and (f). Where the metric dimension is less than 1 millimeter, a zero precedes the decimal point, as at (d). Where the dimension exceeds a whole number by a fraction of 1 millimeter, the last digit to the right of the decimal point is not followed by a zero, (e) and (f), except when expressing tolerances.

Where the decimal-inch dimension is used on drawings, a zero is not used before the decimal point of values less than 1 inch, Fig. 13.12 (f)–(j). The decimal-inch dimension is expressed to the same number of decimal places as its tolerance. Thus, zeros are added to the right of the decimal point as necessary, as at (e).

Never letter a dimension figure over any line on the drawing, but break the line if necessary. Place dimension figures outside a sectioned area if possible, Fig. 13.13 (a). When a dimension must be

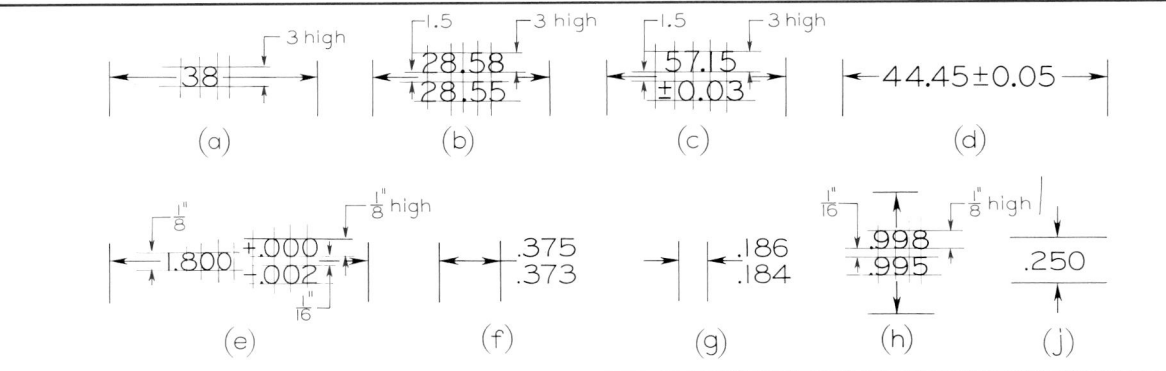

Fig. 13.12 Decimal Dimension Figures. Metric dimensions (a) through (d).

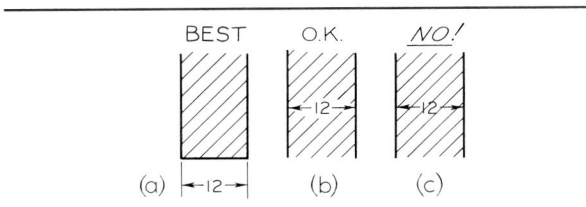

Fig. 13.13 Dimensions and Section Lines. Metric.

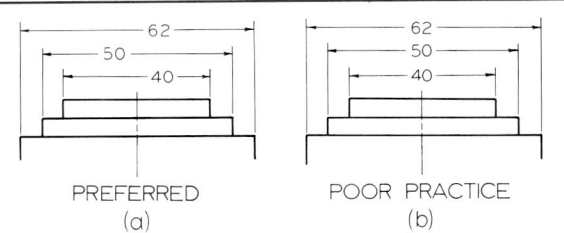

Fig. 13.14 Staggered Numerals. Metric

placed on a sectioned area, leave an opening in the section lining for the dimension figure, (b).

In a group of parallel dimension lines, the numerals should be staggered, as in Fig. 13.14 (a), and not stacked up one above the other, as at (b).

Dual dimensioning, though not recommended, is used to show metric and decimal-inch dimensions on the same drawing. Two methods of displaying the dual dimensions are as follows.

Position Method
The millimeter value is placed above the inch dimension and is separated by a dimension line or an added line for some dimensions when the unidirectional system of dimensioning is used. An alternative arrangement in a single line places the millimeter dimension to the left of the inch dimension, separated by a slash line (virgule). Each drawing should illustrate the dimension identification as $\frac{\text{MILLIMETER}}{\text{INCH}}$ or MILLIMETER/INCH. (Placement of the inch dimension above or to the left of the millimeter is also acceptable.)

EXAMPLES

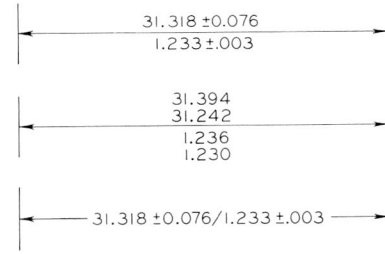

Bracket Method
The millimeter dimension is enclosed in square brackets, [ ]. The location of this dimension is optional but should be uniform on any drawing, that is, above or below or to the left or right of the inch dimension. Each drawing should include a note to identify the dimension values as DIMENSIONS IN [ ] ARE MILLIMETERS.

EXAMPLES

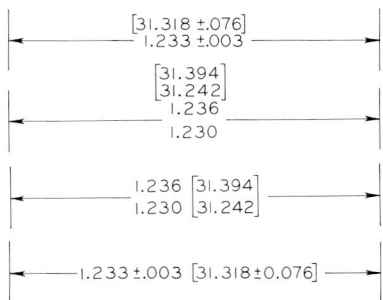

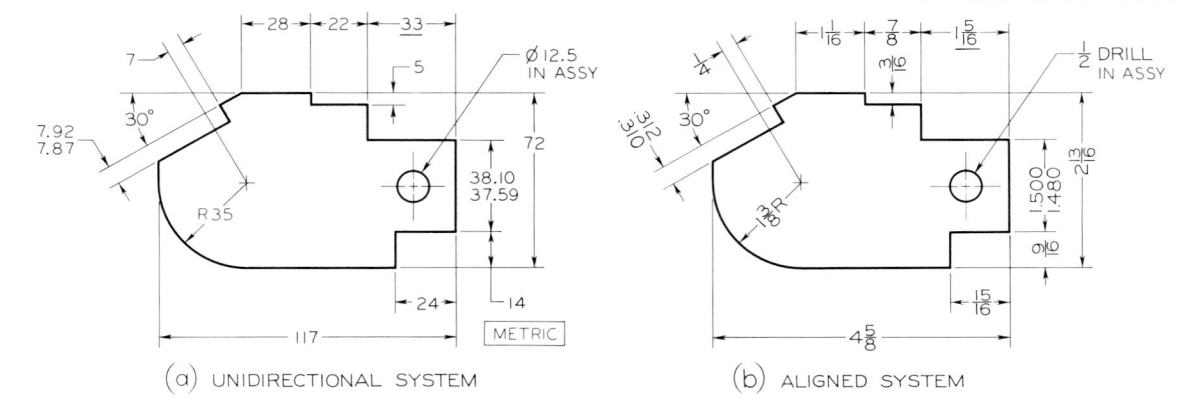

Fig. 13.15   Directions of Dimension Figures.

When converting a decimal-inch dimension to millimeters, multiply the inch dimension by 25.4 and round off to one less digit to the right of the decimal point than for the inch value (see §13.10). When converting a millimeter dimension to inches, divide the millimeter dimension by 25.4 and round off to one more digit to the right of the decimal point than for the millimeter value.

13.12 Direction of Dimension Figures

Two systems of reading direction for dimension figures are available. In the preferred *unidirectional system*, approved by ANSI, Fig. 13.15 (a), all dimension figures and notes are lettered horizontally on the sheet and are read from the bottom of the drawing. The unidirectional system has been extensively adopted in the aircraft, automotive, and other industries because it is easier to use and read, especially on large drawings. In the *aligned system*, Fig. 13.15 (b), all dimension figures are aligned with the

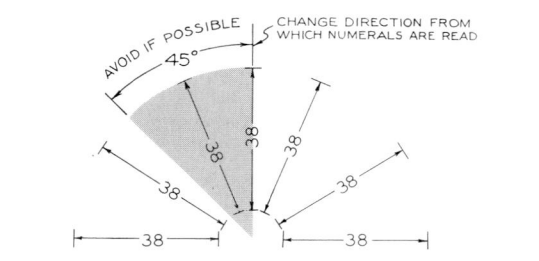

Fig. 13.16   Directions of Dimensions.

dimension lines so that they may be read from the right side of the sheet. Dimension lines in this system should not run in the directions included in the shaded area of Fig. 13.16, if avoidable.

In both systems, dimensions and notes shown with leaders are aligned with the bottom of the drawing. Notes without leaders should also be aligned with the bottom of the drawing.

13.13 Millimeters and Inches

Millimeters are indicated by the lowercase letters mm placed one space to the right of the numeral; thus, 12.5 mm. *Meters* are indicated by the lowercase letter m placed similarly; thus, 50.6 m. *Inches* are indicated by the symbol ″ placed slightly above and to the right of the numeral; thus, $2\frac{1}{2}''$. *Feet* are indicated by the symbol ′ similarly placed; thus, 3′–0, 5′–6, 10′–0$\frac{1}{4}$. It is customary in such expressions to omit the inch marks.

It is standard practice to omit mm designations and inch marks on a drawing except when there is a possibility of misunderstanding. For example, 1 VALVE should be 1″ VALVE, and 1 DRILL should be 1″ DRILL or 1 mm DRILL. Where some inch dimensions are shown on a millimeter-dimensioned drawing, the abbreviation IN. follows the inch values.

In some industries all dimensions, regardless of size, are given in inches; in others dimensions up to 72″ inclusive are given in inches, and those greater are given in feet and inches. In structural and architectural drafting, all dimensions of 1′ or over are usually expressed in feet and inches.

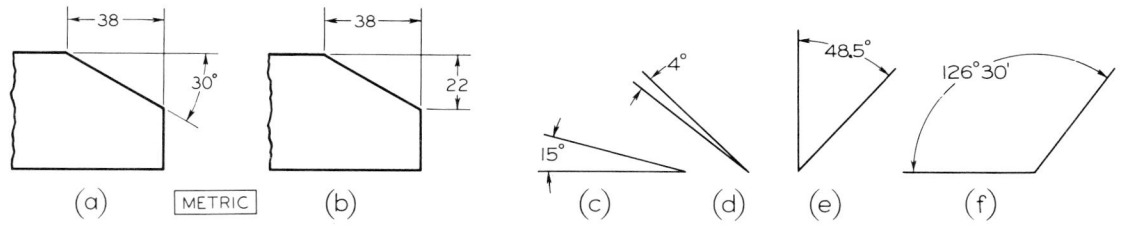

Fig. 13.17 Angles.

13.14 Dimensioning Angles

Angles are dimensioned, preferably, by means of an angle in degrees and a linear dimension, Fig. 13.17 (a), or by means of coordinate dimensions of the two legs of a right triangle, (b). The coordinate method is more suitable for work requiring a high degree of accuracy. Variations of angle (in degrees) are hard to control because the amount of variation increases with the distance from the vertex of the angle. Methods of indicating various angles are shown from (c) to (f). Tolerances of angles are discussed in §14.18.

When degrees alone are indicated, the symbol ° is used. When minutes alone are given, the number should be preceded by 0°.

EXAMPLE   0° 23′.

In all cases, whether in the unidirectional system or in the aligned system, the dimension figures for an-gles are lettered on horizontal guide lines. For a general discussion of angles, see §5.2.

In civil engineering drawings, *slope* represents the angle with the horizontal, while *batter* is the angle referred to the vertical. Both are expressed by making one member of the ratio equal to 1, as shown in Fig. 13.18. *Grade*, as of a highway, is similar to slope but is expressed in percentage of rise per 100′ of run. Thus a 20′ rise in a 100′ run is a grade of 20 percent.

In structural drawings, angular measurements are made by giving the ratio of "run" to "rise," with the larger size being 12″. These right triangles are referred to as *bevels*.

13.15 Dimensioning Arcs

A circular arc is dimensioned in the view in which its true shape is shown by giving the numerical denoting its radius, preceded by the abbreviation R, as shown in Fig. 13.19. The centers may be indicated by small crosses to clarify the drawing but not for small or unimportant radii. Crosses should not be shown for undimensioned arcs. As shown at (a) and (b), when there is room enough, both the numeral and the arrowhead are placed inside the arc. At (c) the arrowhead is left inside, but the numeral had to be moved outside. At (d) both the arrowhead and the numeral had to be moved outside. At (e) is

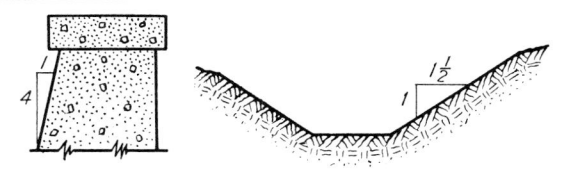

Fig. 13.18   Angles in Civil Engineering Projects.

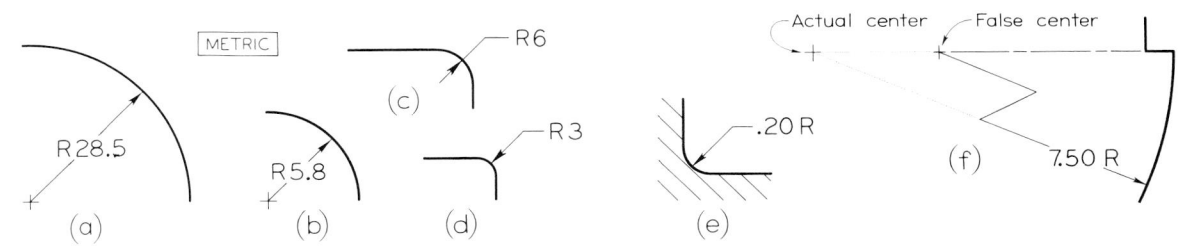

Fig. 13.19   Dimensioning Arcs.

shown an alternate method to (c) or (d) to be used when section lines or other lines are in the way. Note that in the unidirectional system, all of these numerals are lettered horizontally on the sheet.

For a long radius, as shown at (f), when the center falls outside the available space, the dimension line is drawn toward the actual center; but a false center may be indicated and dimension line "jogged" to it, as shown.

13.16 Fillets and Rounds

Individual fillets and rounds are dimensioned as any arc, as shown in Fig. 13.19 (c), (d), and (e). If there are only a few and they are obviously the same size, as in Fig. 13.43 (5), one typical radius is sufficient. However, fillets and rounds are often quite numerous on a drawing and most of them are likely to be some standard size, as R3 and R6 when dimensioning in metric or .125R and .250R when using the decimal-inch system.

In such cases it is customary to give a note in the lower portion of the drawing to cover all uniform fillets and rounds, thus,

FILLETS R6 AND ROUNDS R3 UNLESS
OTHERWISE SPECIFIED

or

ALL CASTING RADII R6 UNLESS NOTED

or simply

ALL FILLETS AND ROUNDS R6.

For a discussion of fillets and rounds in the shop, see §12.5.

13.17 Finish Marks

A *finish mark* is used to indicate that a surface is to be machined, or finished, as on a rough casting or forging. To the patternmaker or diemaker, a finish mark means that allowance of extra metal in the rough workpiece must be provided for the machining. See §12.4. On drawings of parts to be machined from rolled stock, finish marks are generally unnecessary, for it is obvious that the surfaces are finished. Similarly, it is not necessary to show finish marks when an operation is specified in a note that indicates machining, such as drilling, reaming, boring, countersinking, counterboring, and broaching, or when the dimension implies a finished surface, such as ⌀6.22–6.35 (metric) or 2.45–2.50 DIA (decimal-inch).

Three styles of finish marks, the general ∨ symbol, the new basic √ symbol, and the traditional ✗ symbol, are used to indicate an ordinary smooth machined surface. The ∨ symbol, Fig. 13.20 (a), is like a capital V, made about 3 mm ($\frac{1}{8}$″) high in conformity with the height of dimensioning lettering. The extended √ symbol, preferred by ANSI, Fig. 13.20 (b), is like a larger capital with the right leg extended. The short leg is made about 5 mm ($\frac{3}{16}$″) high and the height of the long leg is about 10 mm ($\frac{3}{8}$″). The basic symbol may be altered for more elaborate surface texture specifications; see §14.22.

For best results all finished marks should be drawn with the aid of a template or the 30° × 60° triangle. The point of the ∨ symbol should be directed inward toward the body of metal in a manner similar to that of a tool bit. The √ symbol is not shown upside down; see Figs. 13.35 and 14.45.

The preferred form and placement for the ✗ symbol are described and given in Fig. 13.20 (e). The ✗ symbol is in limited use and found mainly

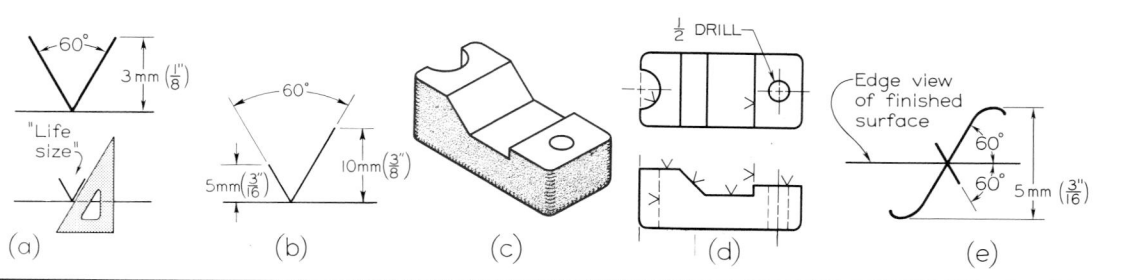

Fig. 13.20 Finish Marks.

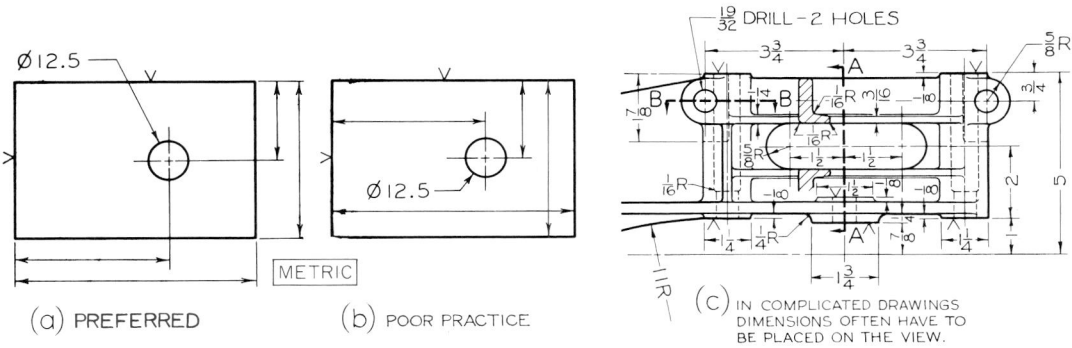

Fig. 13.21 Dimensions On or Off the Views.

on drawings made in accordance with earlier drafting standards.

At (c) is shown a simple casting having several finished surfaces, and at (d) are shown two views of the same casting, showing how the finish marks are indicated on a drawing. *The finish mark is shown only on the edge view of a finished surface and is repeated in any other view in which the surface appears as a line, even if the line is a hidden line.*

The several kinds of finishes are detailed in machine shop practice manuals. The following terms are commonly used: *finish all over, rough finish, file finish, sand blast, pickle, scrape, lap, hone, grind, polish, burnish, buff, chip, spotface, countersink, counterbore, core, drill, ream, bore, tap, broach, knurl,* and so on. When it is necessary to control the surface texture of finished surfaces beyond that of an ordinary machine finish, the new basic √ symbol is used as a base for the more elaborate surface quality symbols as discussed in §14.22.

If a part is to be finished all over, finish marks should be omitted, and a general note, such as FINISH ALL OVER or FAO, should be lettered on the lower portion of the sheet.

13.18 Dimensions On or Off Views

Dimensions should not be placed upon a view unless doing so promotes the clearness of the drawing. The ideal form is shown in Fig. 13.21 (a), in which all dimensions are placed outside the view. Compare this with the evidently poor practice shown at (b). This is not to say that a dimension should never be

placed on a view, for in many cases, particularly in complicated drawings, this is necessary, as shown at (c). Certain radii and other dimensions are given on the views, but in each case investigation will reveal a good reason for placing the dimension on the view. *Place dimensions outside of views, except where directness of application and clarity are gained by placing them on the views where they will be closer to the features dimensioned.* When a dimension must be placed in a sectioned area or on the view, leave an opening in the sectioned area or a break in the lines for the dimension figures, Figs. 13.13 (b) and 13.21 (c).

13.19 Contour Dimensioning

Views are drawn to describe the shapes of the various features of the object, and dimensions are given to define exact sizes and locations of those shapes. It follows that *dimensions should be given where the shapes are shown,* that is, in the views where the contours are delineated, as shown in Fig. 13.22 (a). Incorrect placement of the dimensions is shown at (b).

If individual dimensions are attached directly to the contours that show the shapes being dimensioned, this will automatically prevent the attachment of dimensions to hidden lines, as shown for the depth 10 of the slot at (b). It will also prevent the attachment of dimensions to a visible line, the meaning of which is not clear in a particular view, such as dimension 20 for the height of the base at (b).

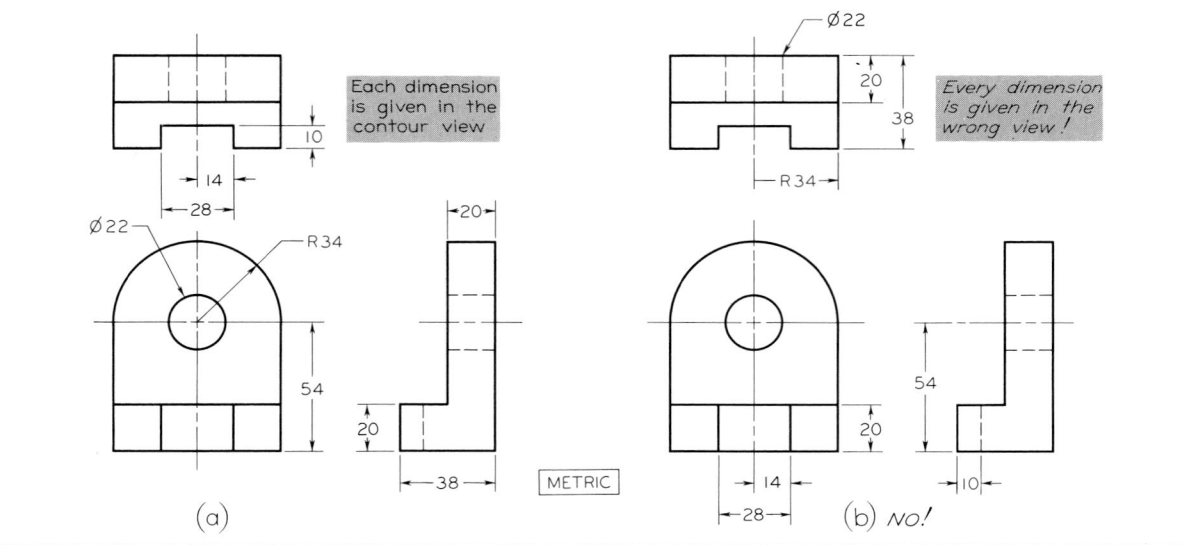

Fig. 13.22   Contour Dimensioning.

Although the placement of notes for holes follows the contour rule wherever possible, as shown at (a), the diameter of an external cylindrical shape is preferably given in the rectangular view where it can be readily found near the dimension for the length of the cylinder, as shown in Figs. 13.23 (b), 13.26, and 13.27.

13.20 Geometric Breakdown

Engineering structures are composed largely of simple geometric shapes, such as the prism, cylinder, pyramid, cone, and sphere, as shown in Fig. 13.23 (a). They may be exterior (positive) or interior (negative) forms. For example, a steel shaft is a positive cylinder, and a round hole is a negative cylinder.

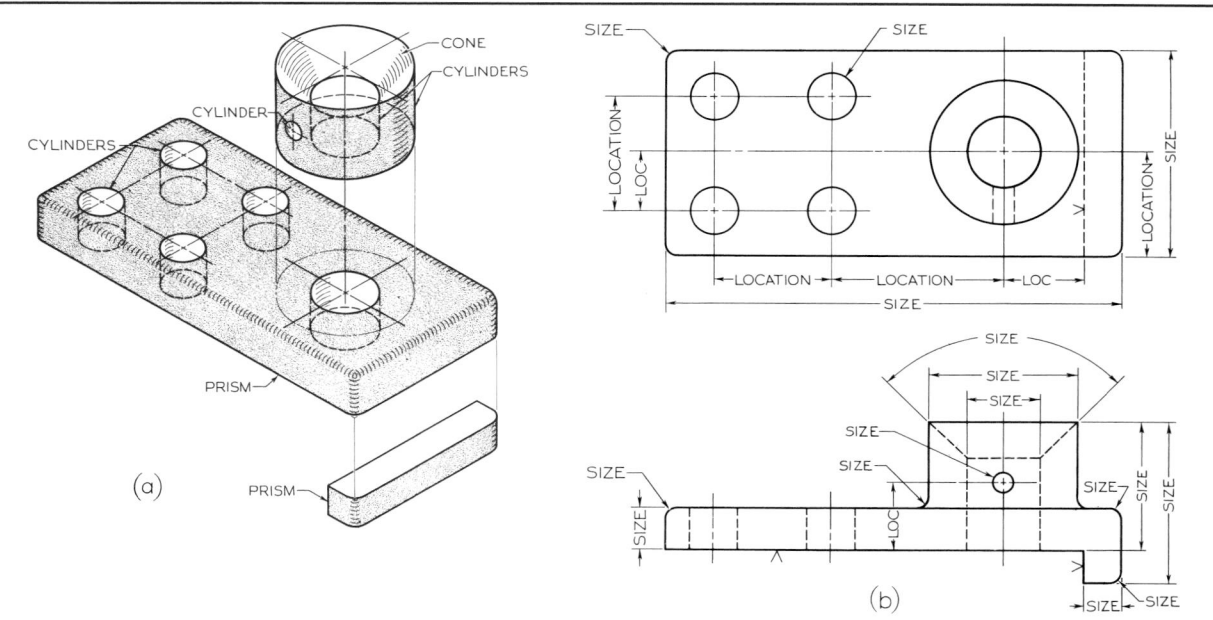

Fig. 13.23   Geometric Breakdown.

These shapes result directly from the design necessity to keep forms as simple as possible and from the requirements of the fundamental manufacturing operations. Forms having plane surfaces are produced by planing, shaping, milling, and so forth, while forms having cylindrical, conical, or spherical surfaces are produced by turning, drilling, reaming, boring, countersinking, and other rotary operations. See Chapter 12, "Manufacturing Processes."

The dimensioning of engineering structures involves two basic steps:

1. Give the dimensions showing the *sizes* of the simple geometric shapes, called *size dimensions*.

2. Give the dimensions *locating* these elements with respect to each other, called *location dimensions*.

The process of geometric analysis is very helpful in dimensioning any object, but must be modified when there is a conflict with either the function of the part in the assembly or with the manufacturing requirements in the shop.

Figure 13.23 (b) is a multiview drawing of the object shown in isometric at (a). Here it will be seen that each geometric shape is dimensioned with size dimensions and that these shapes are then located with respect to each other with location dimensions. Note that a *location dimension locates a three-dimensional geometric element* and not just a surface; otherwise, all dimensions would have to be classified as location dimensions.

13.21 Size Dimensions—Prisms

The right rectangular prism, Fig. 5.7, is probably the most common geometric shape. Front and top views are dimensioned as shown in Fig. 13.24 (a) or (b). The height and width are given in the front view and the depth in the top view. The vertical dimensions can be placed on the left or right provided both of them are placed in line. The horizontal dimension applies to both the front and top views and should be placed between them, as shown, and not above the top or below the front view.

Front and side views should be dimensioned as at (c) or (d). The horizontal dimensions can be placed above or below the views, provided both are placed in line. The dimension between views applies to both views and should not be placed elsewhere without a special reason.

An application of size dimensions to a machine

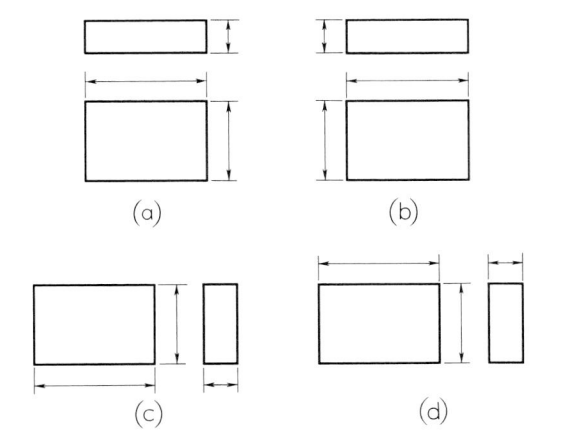

Fig. 13.24 Dimensioning Rectangular Prisms.

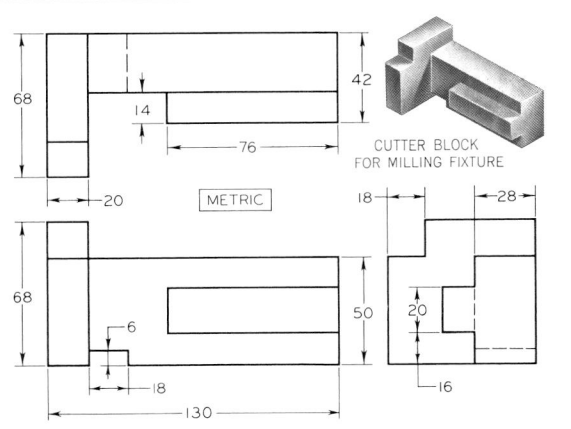

Fig. 13.25 Dimensioning a Machine Part That is Composed of Prismatic Shapes.

part composed entirely of rectangular prisms is shown in Fig. 13.25.

13.22 Size Dimensions—Cylinders

The right circular cylinder is the next most common geometric shape and is commonly seen as a shaft or a hole. The general method of dimensioning a cylinder is to give both its diameter and its length in the rectangular view, Fig. 13.26. If the cylinder is drawn in a vertical position, the length or altitude of the cylinder may be given at the right as at (a), or on the left as at (b). If the cylinder is drawn in a

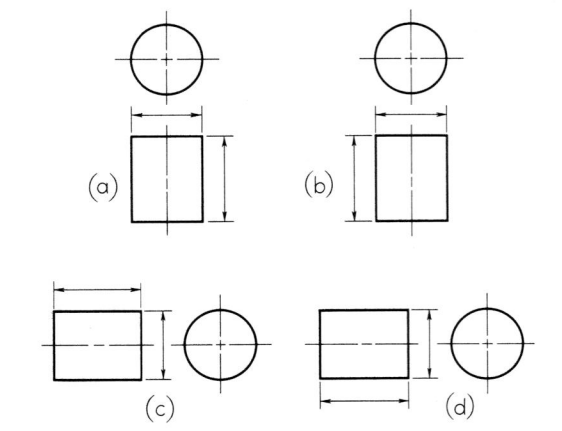

Fig. 13.26 Dimensioning Cylinders.

horizontal position, the length may be given above the rectangular view as at (c) or below as at (d). An application showing the dimensioning of cylindrical shapes is shown in Fig. 13.27. The use of a diagonal diameter in the circular view, in addition to the method shown in Fig. 13.26, is not recommended except in special cases when clearness is gained thereby. The use of several diagonal diameters on the same center is definitely to be discouraged, since the result is usually confusing.

The radius of a cylinder should never be given, since measuring tools, such as the micrometer caliper, are designed to check diameters.

Small cylindrical holes, such as drilled, reamed, or bored holes, are usually dimensioned by means of notes specifying the diameter and the depth, with or without manufacturing operations, Figs. 13.27 and 13.32.

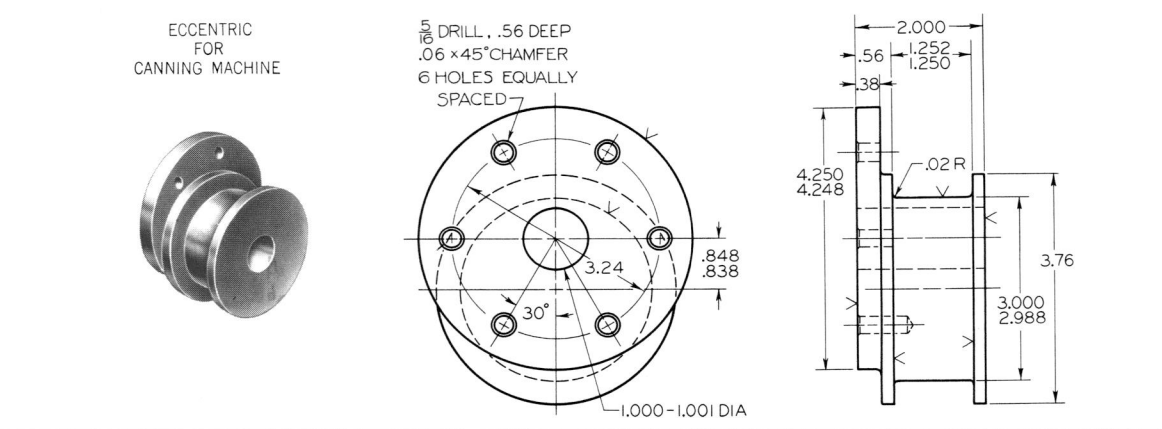

Fig. 13.27 Dimensioning a Machine Part That Is Composed of Cylindrical Shapes.

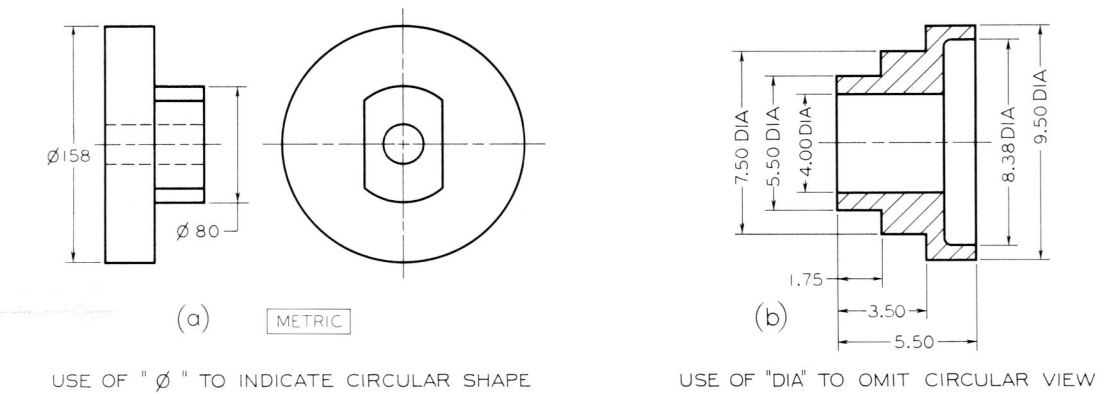

Fig. 13.28 Use of ∅ or DIA in Dimensioning Cylinders.

The diameter symbol ⌀ should be given before all diametral dimensions on metric drawings rather than the abbreviation DIA following the dimension that is used on decimal-inch drawings, Fig. 13.28 (a) [ANSI Y14.5M–1982 (R1988)]. In some cases, the symbol on metric drawings or the abbreviation on decimal-inch drawings may be used to eliminate the circular view, as in (b).

13.23 Symbols and Size Dimensions—Miscellaneous Shapes

Traditional terms and abbreviations used to describe various shapes and manufacturing processes, in addition to size specifications, are employed throughout this text. A variety of dimensioning symbols, introduced by ANSI [Y14.5M–1982 (R1988)] to replace traditional terms or abbreviations, are given with construction details in Fig. 13.29. Traditional terms and abbreviations are suitable for use where the symbols are not desired. Typical applications of some of these symbols are given in Fig. 13.30.

A triangular prism is dimensioned, Fig. 13.31 (a) by giving the height, width, and displacement of the top edge in the front view and the depth in the top view.

A rectangular pyramid is dimensioned, (b), by giving the heights in the front view, and the dimen-

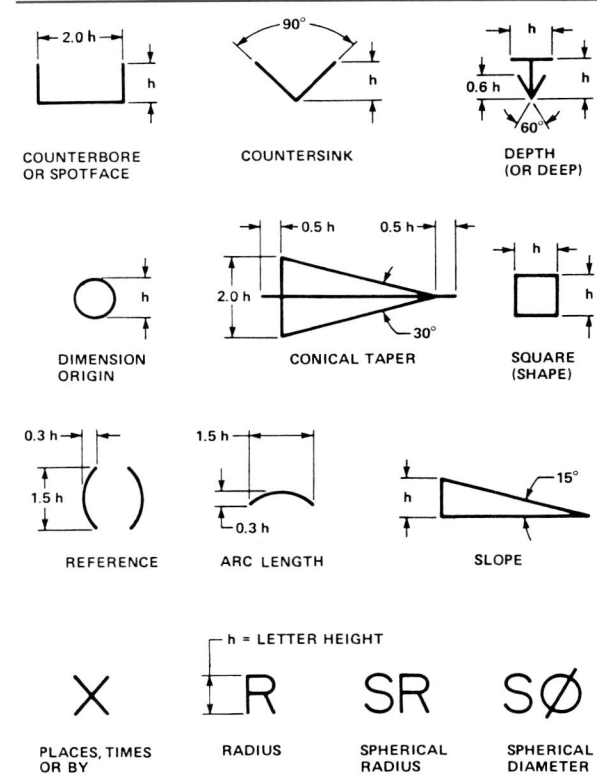

Fig. 13.29 Form and Proportion of Dimensioning Symbols [ANSI Y14.5M–1982 (R1988)].

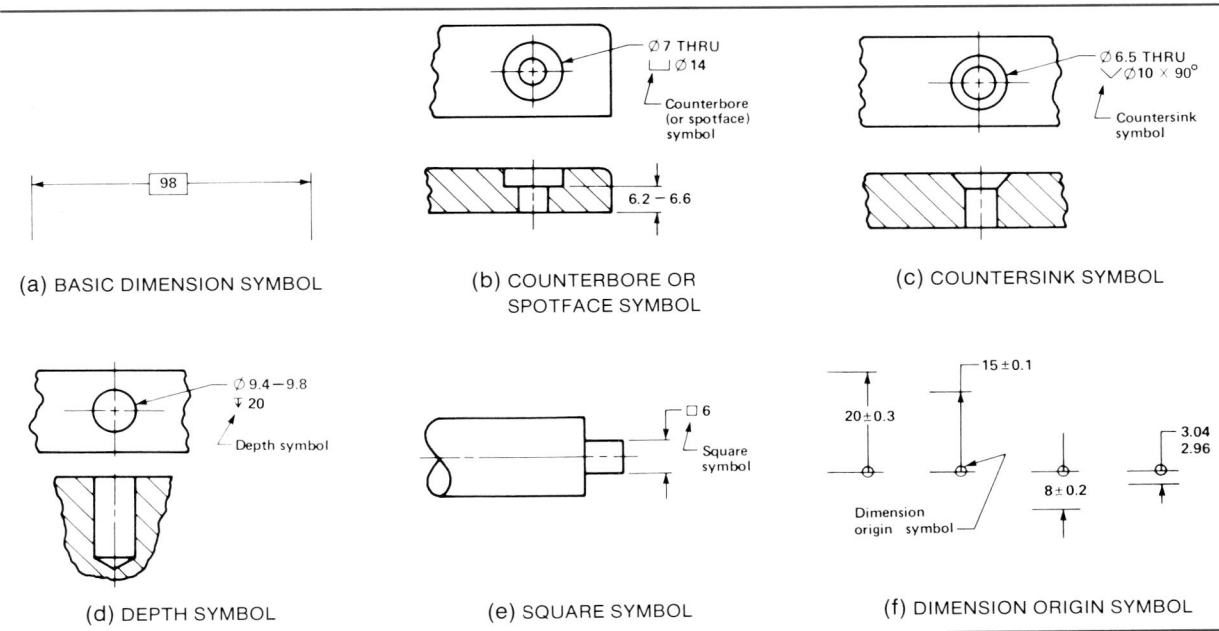

Fig. 13.30 Use of Dimensioning Symbols [ANSI Y14.5M–1982 (R1988)].

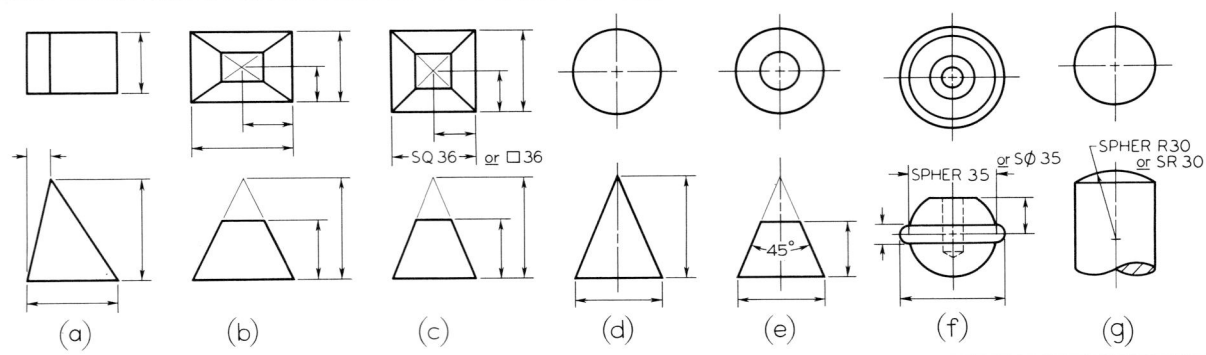

Fig. 13.31   Dimensioning Various Shapes.

sions of the base and the centering of the vertex in the top view. If the base is square, (c), it is necessary to give the dimensions for only one side of the base, provided it is labeled **SQ** as shown or preceded by the square symbol □. See Fig. 13.29 for form and proportions of dimensioning symbols.

A cone is dimensioned, (d), by giving its altitude and diameter of the base in the triangular view. A frustum of a cone may be dimensioned, (e), by giving the vertical angle and the diameter of one of the bases. Another method is to give the length and the diameters of both ends in the front view. Still another is to give the diameter at one end and the amount of taper per foot in a note, §13.33.

In Figure 13.31 (f) is shown a two-view drawing of a plastic knob. The main body is spherical and is dimensioned by giving its diameter preceded by the abbreviation and symbol for spherical diameter **SØ** or followed by the abbreviation **SPHER**. A bead around the knob is in the shape of a torus, Fig. 5.7, and it is dimensioned by giving the thickness of the ring and the outside diameter, as shown. At (g) a

spherical end is dimensioned by a radius preceded by the abbreviation SR or followed by **SPHER R**.

Internal shapes corresponding to the external shapes in Fig. 13.31 would be dimensioned in a similar manner.

13.24 Size Dimensioning of Holes

Holes that are to be drilled, bored, reamed, punched, cored, and so on are usually specified by standard notes, as shown in Figs. 7.40, 13.32 (a), and 13.44. The order of items in a note corresponds to the order of procedure in the shop in producing the hole. Two or more holes are dimensioned by a single note, the leader pointing to one of the holes, as shown at the top of Fig. 13.32.

As illustrated in Figs. 7.40 and 13.32, the leader of a note should, as a rule, point to the circular view of the hole. It should point to the rectangular view only when clearness is promoted thereby. When the circular view of the hole has two or more concentric circles, as for counterbored, countersunk, or tapped

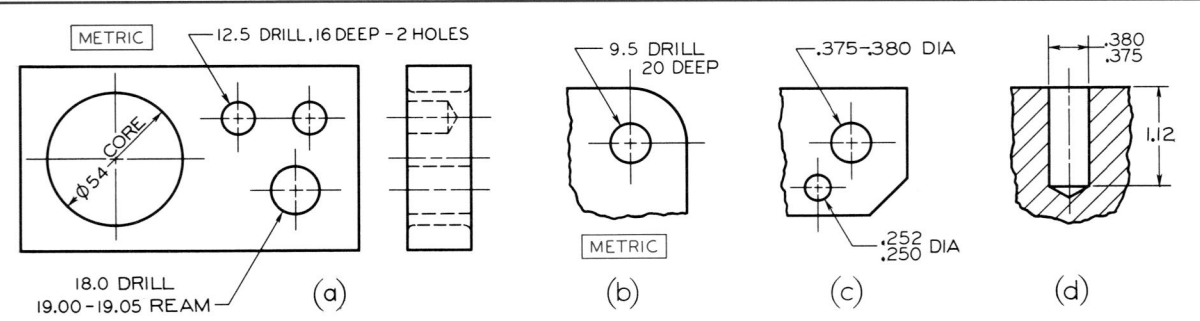

Fig. 13.32   Dimensioning Holes.

holes, the arrowhead should touch the outer circle, Fig. 13.44 (b), (c), and (e)–(j).

Notes should always be lettered horizontally on the drawing paper, and guide lines should always be used.

The use of decimal fractions to designate metric or inch drill sizes has gained wide acceptance,* Fig. 13.32 (b). For numbered or letter-size drills, Appendix 16, it is recommended that the decimal size be given in this manner, or given in parentheses; thus, #28 (.1405) DRILL, or "P" (.3230) DRILL. Metric drills are all decimal size and are not designated by number or letter.

On drawings of parts to be produced in large quantity for interchangeable assembly, dimensions and notes may be given without specification of the manufacturing process to be used. Only the dimensions of the holes are given, without reference to whether the holes are to be drilled, reamed, or punched, as in Fig. 13.32 (c) and (d). It should be realized that even though manufacturing operations are omitted from a note, the tolerances indicated would tend to dictate the manufacturing processes required.

13.25 Location Dimensions

After the geometric shapes composing a structure have been dimensioned for *size,* as discussed, *location dimensions* must be given to show the relative positions of these geometric shapes, as shown in Fig. 13.23. Fig. 13.33 (a) shows that rectangular shapes, whether in the form of solids or of recesses, are located with reference to their faces. At (b), cylindrical or conical holes or bosses, or other symmetrical shapes, are located with reference to their center lines.

As shown in Fig. 13.34, location dimensions for holes are preferably given in the circular view of the holes.

Location dimensions should lead to finished surfaces wherever possible, Fig. 13.35, because rough castings and forgings vary in size, and unfinished surfaces cannot be relied upon for accurate measurements. Of course, the *starting dimension,* used in locating the first machined surface on a rough casting or forging, must necessarily lead from a rough

*Although drills are still listed fractionally in manufacturers' catalogs, many companies have supplemented drill and wire sizes with a decimal value. In many cases the number, letter, or common fraction has been replaced by the decimal-inch size. Metric drills are usually listed separately with a decimal-millimeter value.

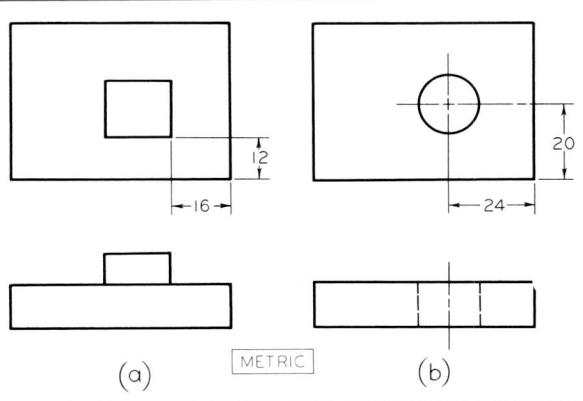

Fig. 13.33 Location Dimensions.

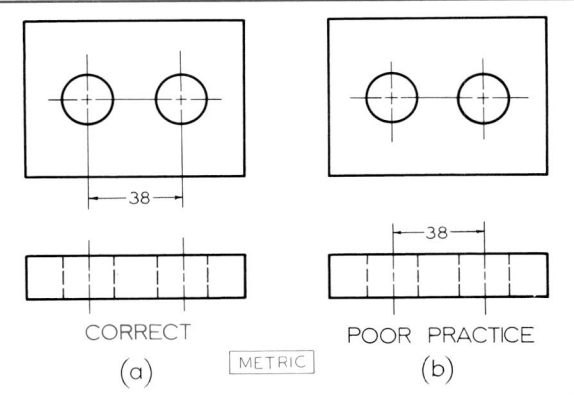

Fig. 13.34 Locating Holes.

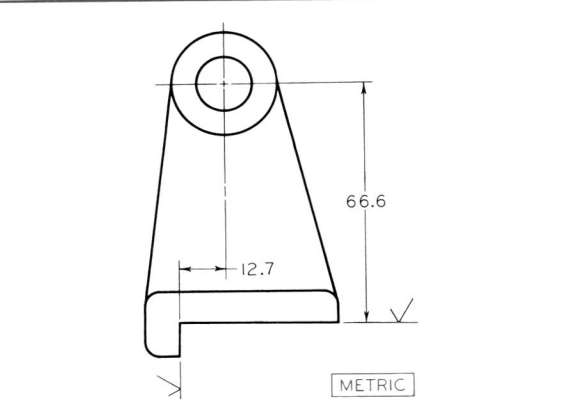

Fig. 13.35 Dimensions to Finished Surfaces.

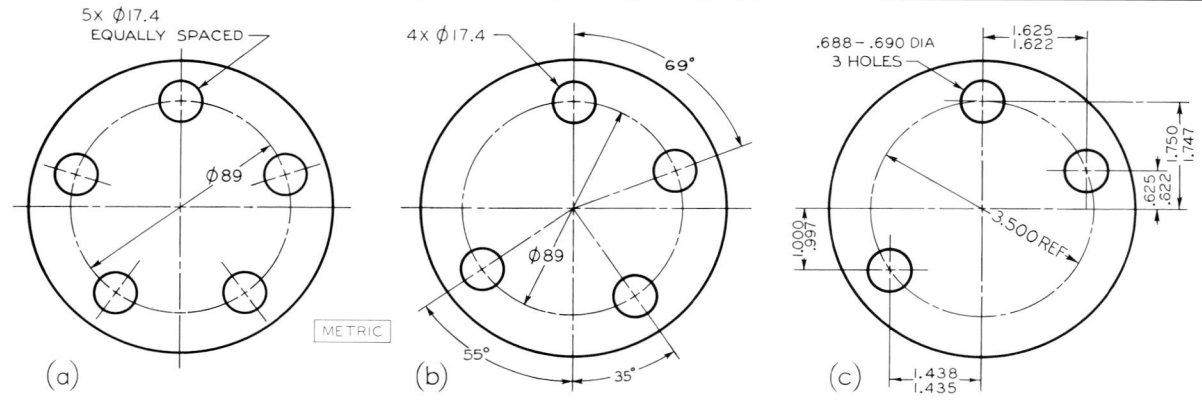

Fig. 13.36   Locating Holes About a Center.

surface, or from a center or a center line of the rough piece. See Figs. 16.74 and 16.76.

In general, location dimensions should be built from a finished surface as a datum plane, or from an important center or center line.

When several cylindrical surfaces have the same center line, as in Fig. 13.28 (b), it is not necessary to locate them with respect to each other.

Holes equally spaced about a common center may be dimensioned, Fig. 13.36 (a), by giving the diameter (diagonally) of the *circle of centers*, or *bolt circle*, and specifying "equally spaced" in the note. Repetitive features or dimensions may be specified by the use of an **X** preceded with a numeral to indicate the number of times or places the feature is required. Allow a space between the letter **X** and the dimension as at (a) and (b).

Holes unequally spaced, (b), are located by means of the bolt circle diameter plus angular measurements with reference to *only one* of the center lines, as shown.

Where greater accuracy is required, coordinate dimensions should be given, as at (c). In this case, the diameter of the bolt circle is marked **REF**, or enclosed in parentheses, ( ), Fig. 13.29, to indicate that it is to be used only as a *reference dimension*. Reference dimensions are given for information only. They are not intended to be measured and do not govern the manufacturing operations. They represent calculated dimensions and are often useful in showing the intended design sizes. See Fig. 13.36 (c).

When several nonprecision holes are located on a common arc, they are dimensioned, Fig. 13.37 (a), by giving the radius and the angular measurements from a *base line*, as shown. In this case, the base line is the horizontal center line.

At (b) the three holes are on a common center line. One dimension locates one small hole from the center; the other gives the distance between the small holes. Note the omission of a dimension at **X**. This method is used when (as is usually the case) the distance between the small holes is the important consideration. If the relation between the center hole and each of the small holes is more important, then include the distance at **X**, and mark the overall dimension **REF**.

At (c) is another example of coordinate dimensioning. The three small holes are on a bolt circle whose diameter is marked **REF** for reference purposes only. From the main center, the small holes are located in two mutually perpendicular directions.

Another example of locating holes by means of linear measurements is shown at (d). In this case, one such measurement is made at an angle to the coordinate dimensions because of the direct functional relationship of the two holes.

At (e) the holes are located from two *base lines* or *datums*. When all holes are located from a common datum, the sequence of measuring and machining operations is controlled, overall tolerance accumulations are avoided, and proper functioning of the finished part is assured as intended by the designer. The datum surfaces selected must be more accurate than any measurement made from them, must be accessible during manufacture, and must be arranged so as to facilitate tool and fixture design. Thus it may be necessary to specify accuracy of the datum surfaces in terms of straightness, roundness, flatness, and so forth. See §14.16.

At (f) is shown a method of giving, in a single line, all of the dimensions from a common datum.

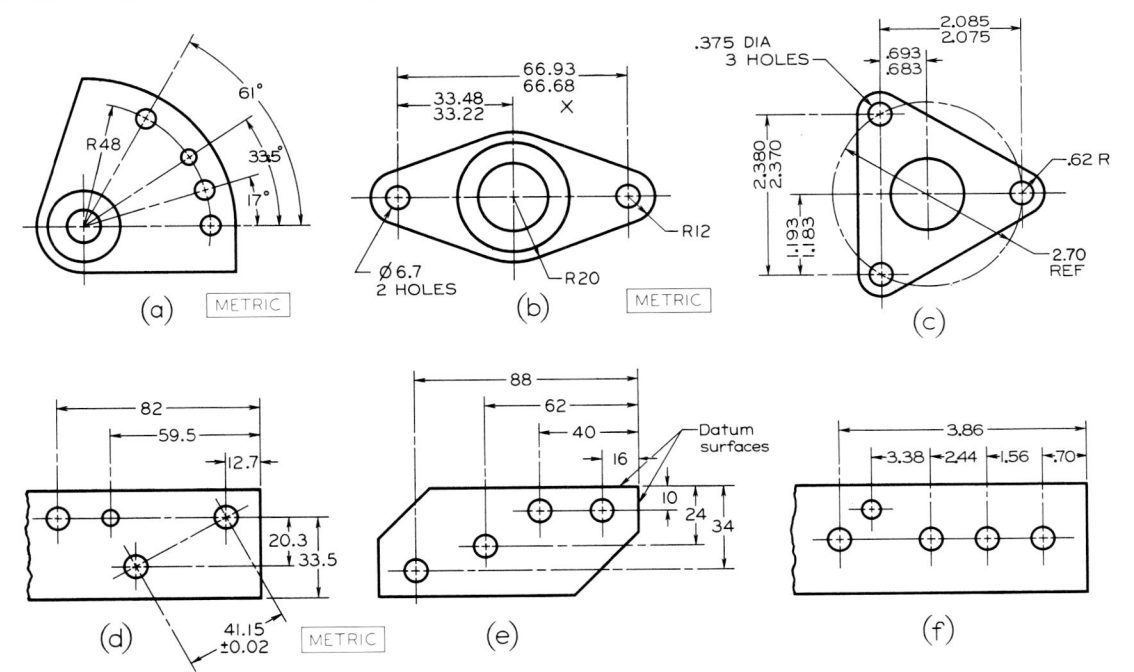

Fig. 13.37   Locating Holes.

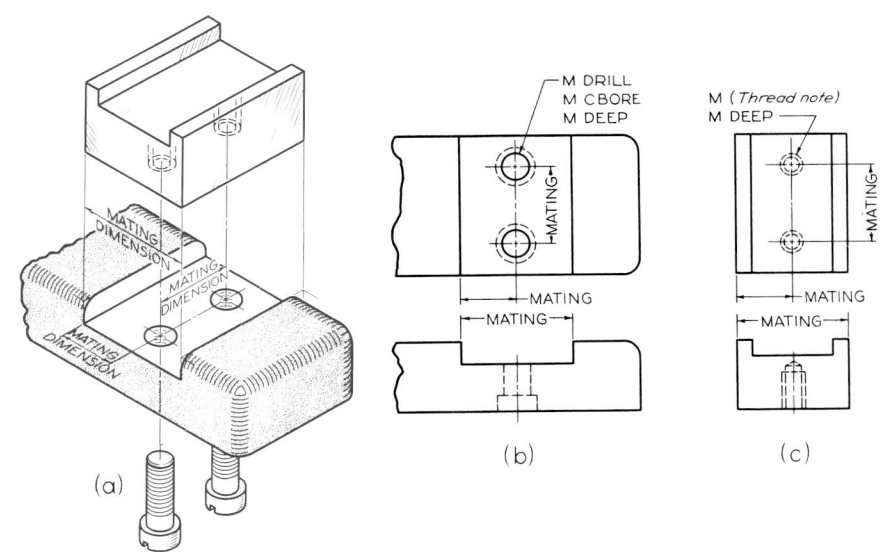

Fig. 13.38   Mating Dimensions.

Each dimension except the first has a single arrow-head and is accumulative in value. The final and longest dimension is separate and complete.

These methods of locating holes are equally applicable to locating pins or other symmetrical features.

13.26 Mating Dimensions

In dimensioning a single part, its relation to mating parts must be taken into consideration. For example, in Fig. 13.38 (a), a guide block fits into a slot in a base. Those dimensions common to both parts are *mating dimensions,* as indicated.

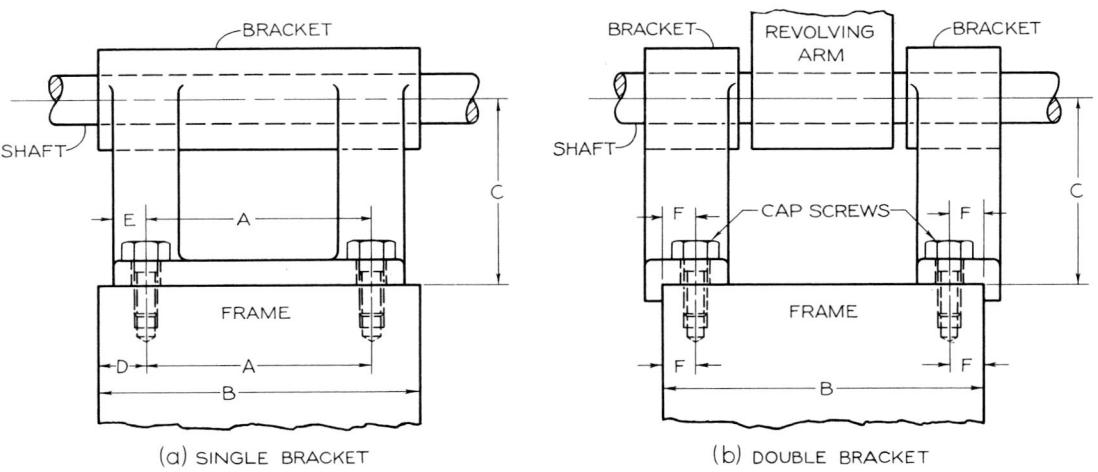

Fig. 13.39   Bracket Assembly.

These mating dimensions should be given on the multiview drawings in the corresponding locations, as shown at (b) and (c). Other dimensions are not mating dimensions since they do not control the accurate fitting together of two parts. The actual *values* of two corresponding mating dimensions may not be exactly the same. For example, the width of the slot at (b) may be dimensioned $\frac{1}{32}''$ (0.8 mm) or several thousandths of an inch larger than the width of the block at (c), but these are mating dimensions figured from a single basic width. It will be seen that the mating dimensions shown might have been arrived at from a geometric breakdown, §13.20. However, the mating dimensions need to be identified so that they can be specified in the corresponding locations on the two parts and so that they can be given with the degree of accuracy commensurate with the proper fitting of the parts.

In Fig. 13.39 (a) the dimension A should appear on both the drawings of the bracket and of the frame and, therefore, is a necessary mating dimension. At (b), which shows a redesign of the bracket into two parts, dimension A is not used on either part, as it is not necessary to control closely the distance between the cap screws. But dimensions F are now essential mating dimensions and should appear correspondingly on the drawings of both parts. The remaining dimensions E, D, B, and C, at (a) are not considered to be mating dimensions, since they do not directly affect the mating of the parts.

13.27 Machine, Pattern, and Forging Dimensions

In Fig. 13.38 (a), the base is machined from a rough casting; the patternmaker needs certain dimensions to make the pattern, and the machinist needs certain dimensions for the machining. In some cases one dimension will be used by both. Again, in most cases, these dimensions will be the same as those resulting from a geometric breakdown, §13.20, but it is important to identify them in order to assign values to them.

The same part is shown in Fig. 13.40, with the machine dimensions and pattern dimensions identified by the letters M and P. The patternmaker is interested only in the dimensions required to make the pattern, and the machinist, in general, is concerned only with the dimensions needed to machine

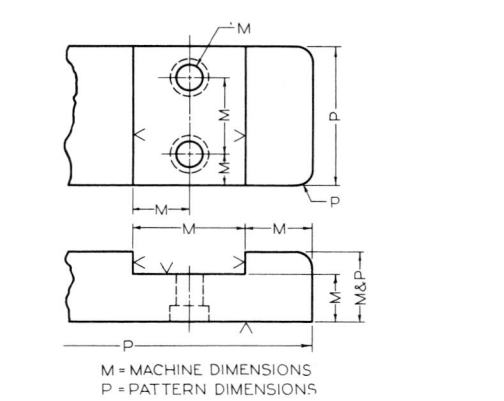

M = MACHINE DIMENSIONS
P = PATTERN DIMENSIONS

Fig. 13.40   Machine and Pattern Dimensions.

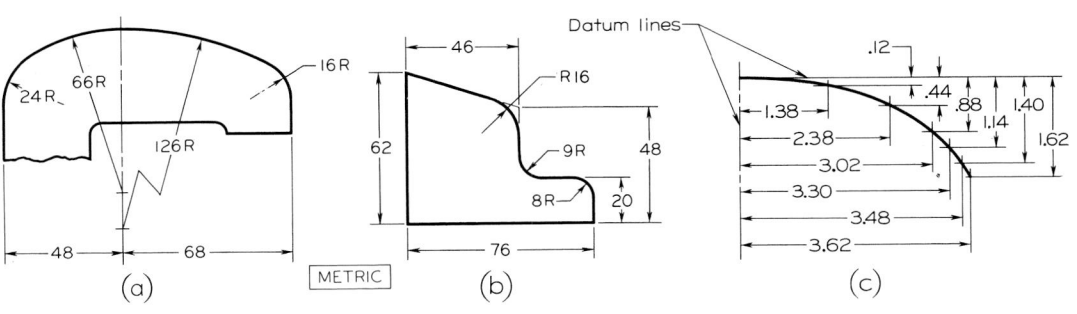

Fig. 13.41 Dimensioning Curves.

the part. Frequently, a dimension that is convenient for the machinist is not convenient for the pattern-maker, or vice versa. Since the patternmaker uses the drawing only once, while making the pattern, and the machinist refers to it continuously, the dimensions should be given primarily for the convenience of the machinist.

If the part is large and complicated, two separate drawings are sometimes made, one showing the pattern dimensions and the other the machine dimensions. The usual practice, however, is to prepare one drawing for both the patternmaker and the machinist. See §12.4.

For forgings, it is common practice to make separate forging drawings and machining drawings. A forging drawing of a connecting rod, showing only the dimensions needed in the forge shop, is shown in Fig. 16.29. A machining drawing of the same part, but containing only the dimensions needed in the machine shop, is shown in Fig. 16.30.

Unless a decimal system is used, §13.10, the pattern dimensions are nominal, usually to the nearest $\frac{1}{16}''$, and given in whole numbers and common fractions. If a machine dimension is given in whole numbers and common fractions, the machinist is usually allowed a tolerance (permissible in variation in size) of $\pm\frac{1}{64}''$. Some companies specify a tolerance of $\pm.010''$ on all common fractions. If greater accuracy is required, the dimensions are given in decimal form. Metric dimensions are given to one or more places and decimal-inch dimensions are given to three or more places, §§13.10 and 14.1. Remember that 0.1 mm is approximately .004 inch.

13.28 Dimensioning of Curves

Curved shapes may be dimensioned by giving a group of radii, as shown in Fig. 13.41 (a). Note that in dimensioning the R126 arc whose center is in-

accessible, the center may be moved inward along a center line, and a jog made in the dimension line. See also Fig. 13.19 (f). Another method is to dimension the outline envelope of a curved shape so that the various radii are self-locating from "floating centers," as at (b). Either a circular or a noncircular curve may be dimensioned by means of coordinate dimensions referred to datums, as shown at (c). See also Fig. 13.6 (a).

13.29 Dimensioning of Rounded-End Shapes

The method used for dimensioning rounded-end shapes depends upon the degree of accuracy required, Fig. 13.42. When precision is not necessary, the methods used are those that are convenient for manufacturing, as at (a), (b), and (c).

At (a) the link, to be cast or to be cut from sheet metal or plate, is dimensioned as it would be laid out for manufacture, by giving the center-to-center distance and the radii of the ends. Note that only one such radius dimension is necessary, but that the number of places may be included with the size dimension.

At (b) the pad on a casting, with a milled slot, is dimensioned from center to center for the convenience of both the patternmaker and the machinist in layout. An additional reason for the center-to-center distance is that it gives the total travel of the milling cutter, which can be easily controlled by the machinist. The width dimension indicates the diameter of the milling cutter; hence, it is incorrect to give the radius of a machined slot. On the other hand, a cored slot (see §12.3) should be dimensioned by radius in conformity with the patternmaker's layout procedure.

At (c) the semicircular pad is laid out in a similar

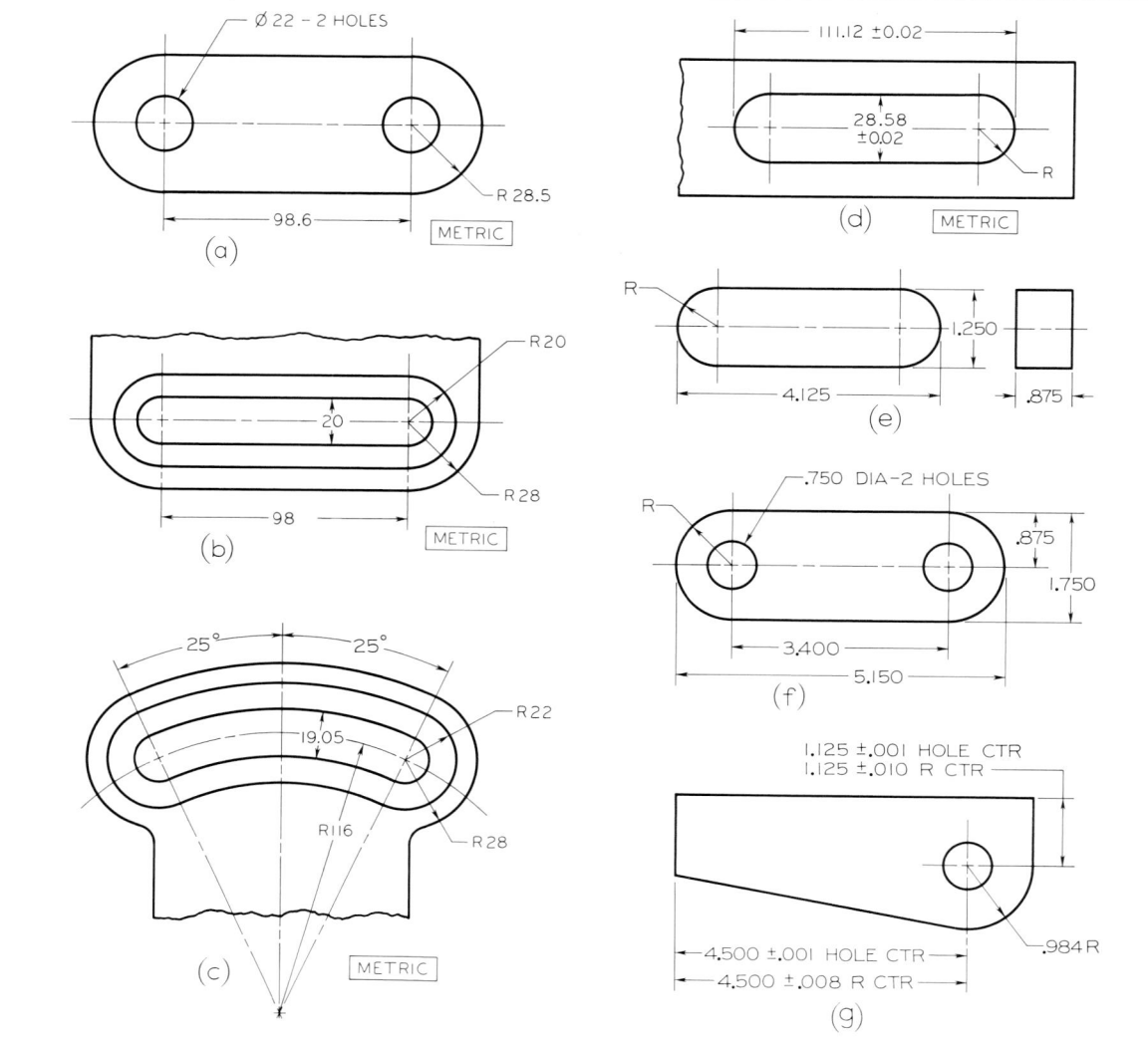

Fig. 13.42 Dimensioning Rounded-End Shapes.

manner to the pad at (b), except that angular dimensions are used. Angular tolerances, §14.18, can be used if necessary.

When accuracy is required, the methods shown at (d) to (g) are recommended. Overall lengths of rounded-end shapes are given in each case, and radii are indicated, but without specific values. In the example at (f), the center-to-center distance is required for accurate location of the holes.

At (g) the hole location is more critical than the location of the radius; hence, the two are located independently, as shown.

13.30 Superfluous Dimensions
All necessary dimensions must be shown, but the

designer should avoid giving unnecessary or superfluous dimensions, Fig. 13.43. Dimensions should not be repeated on the same view or on different views, nor should the same information be given in two different ways.

Figure 13.43 (2) illustrates a type of superfluous dimensioning that should generally be avoided, especially in machine drawing where accuracy is important. The production personnel should not be allowed a choice between two dimensions. *Avoid "chain" dimensioning*, in which a complete series of detail dimensions is given, together with an overall dimension. In such cases, one dimension of the chain should be omitted, as shown, so that the machinist is obliged to work from one surface only. This

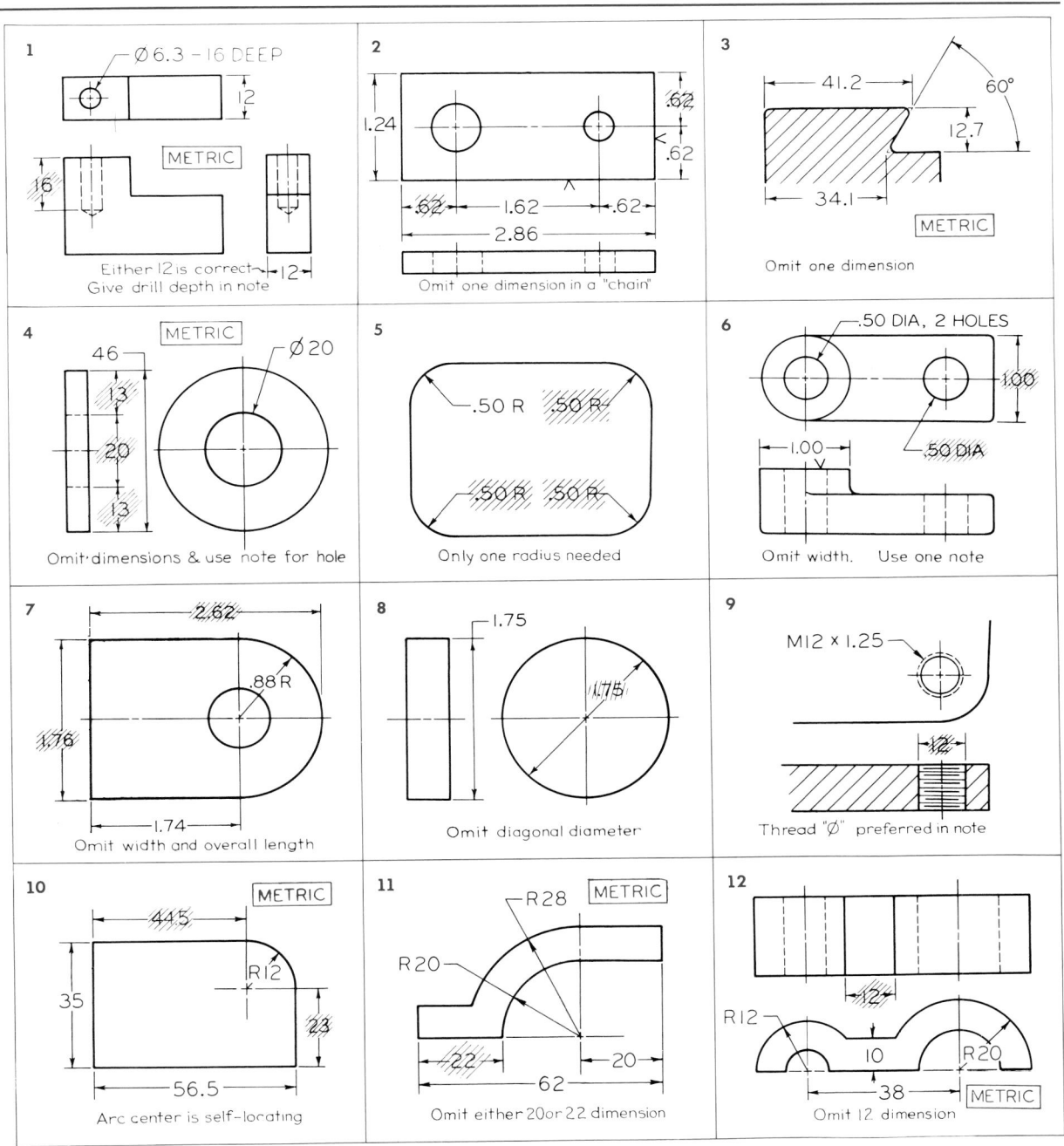

Fig. 13.43 Superfluous Dimensions.

is particularly important in tolerance dimensioning, §14.1, where an accumulation of tolerances can cause serious difficulties. See also §14.9.

Some inexperienced detailers have the habit of omitting both dimensions, such as those at the right at (2), on the theory that the holes are symmetrically located and will be understood to be centered. One of the two location dimensions should be given.

As shown at (5), when one dimension clearly applies to several identical features, it need not be repeated, but the number of places should be indicated. Dimensions for fillets and rounds and other

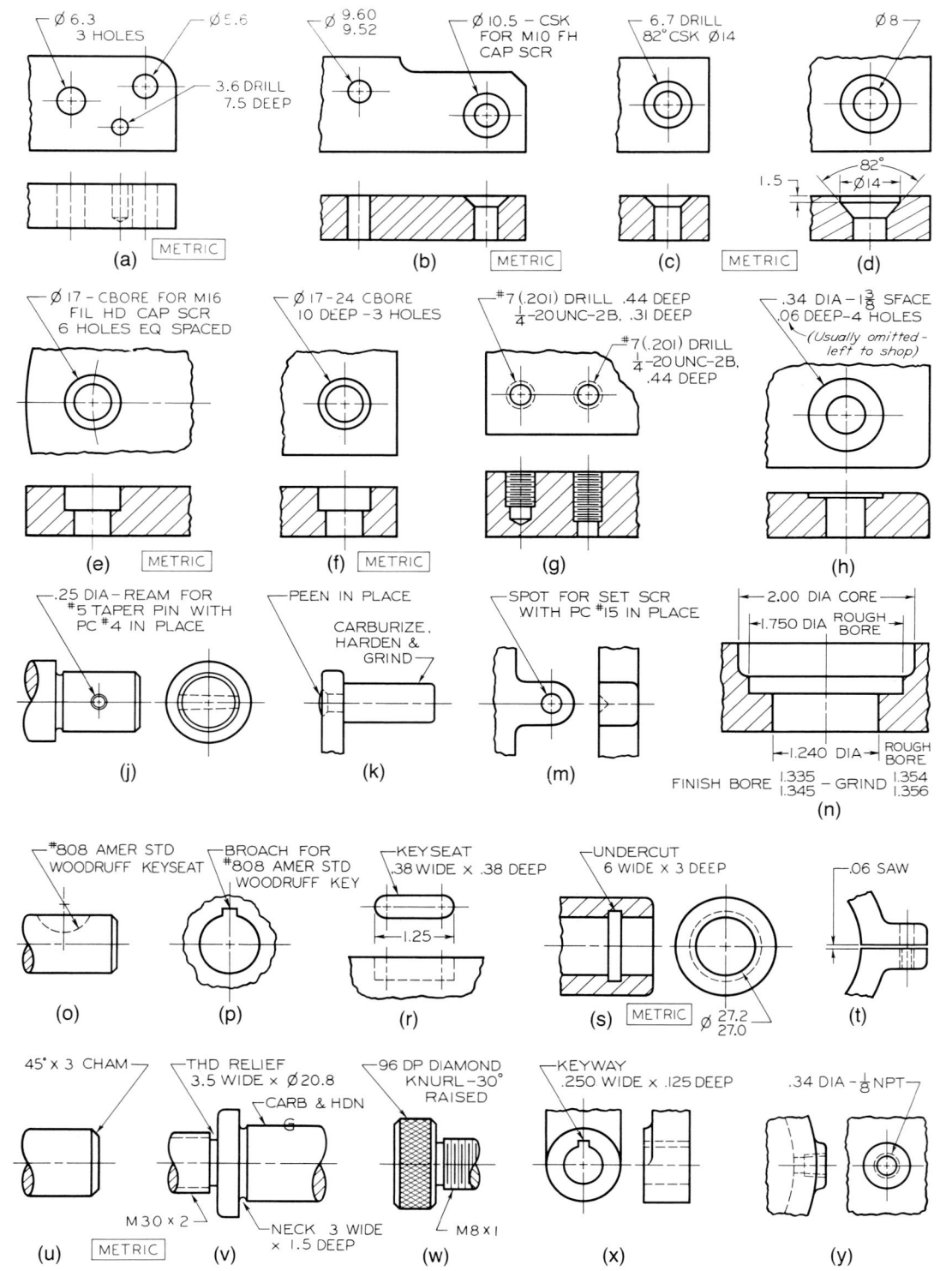

Fig. 13.44 Local Notes.   See also Figs. 7.40 and 13.32.

noncritical features need not be repeated nor number of places specified, as at (5).

For example, the radii of the rounded ends in Fig. 13.42 (a)–(f) need not be repeated, and in Fig. 13.1 both ribs are obviously the same thickness so it is unnecessary to repeat the 10 mm dimension.

13.31 Notes

It is usually necessary to supplement the direct dimensions with notes, Fig. 13.44. They should be brief and should be carefully worded so as to be capable of only one interpretation. *Notes should always be lettered horizontally on the sheet, with guide lines, and arranged in a systematic manner.* They should not be lettered in crowded places. Avoid placing notes between views, if possible. They should not be lettered closely enough to each other to confuse the reader or close enough to another view or detail to suggest application to the wrong view. Leaders should be as short as possible and cross as few lines as possible. They should never run through a corner of a view or through any specific points or intersections.

Notes are classified as *general notes* when they apply to an entire drawing and as *local notes* when they apply to specific items.

General Notes

General notes should be lettered in the lower right-hand corner of the drawing, above or to the left of the title block, or in a central position below the view to which they apply.

EXAMPLES

FINISH ALL OVER (FAO)

BREAK SHARP EDGES TO R0.8

G33106 ALLOY STEEL–BRINELL 340–380

ALL DRAFT ANGLES 3° UNLESS OTHERWISE SPECIFIED

DIMENSIONS APPLY AFTER PLATING

In machine drawings, the title strip or title block will carry many general notes, including material, general tolerances, heat treatment, and pattern information. See Fig. 16.25.

Local Notes

Local notes apply to specific operations only and are connected by a leader to the point at which such operations are performed.

EXAMPLES

6.30 DRILL–4 HOLES

45°x1.6 CHAMFER

96 DP DIAMOND KNURL, RAISED

The leader should be attached at the front of the first word of a note, or just after the last word, and not at any intermediate place.

For information on notes applied to holes, see §13.24.

Certain commonly used abbreviations may be used freely in notes, such as THD, DIA, MAX. The less common abbreviations should be avoided as much as possible. All abbreviations should conform to ANSI Y1.1–1972 (R1984). See Appendix 4 for American National Standard abbreviations. See Figs. 13.29 and 13.30 for form and use of alternative dimensioning symbols.

In general, leaders and notes should not be placed on the drawing until the dimensioning is substantially completed. If notes are lettered first, almost invariably they will be in the way of necessary dimensions and will have to be moved.

13.32 Dimensioning of Threads

Local notes are used to specify dimensions of threads. For tapped holes the notes should, if possible, be attached to the circular views of the holes, as shown in Fig. 13.44 (g). For external threads, the notes are usually placed in the longitudinal views where the threads are more easily recognized, as at (v) and (w). For a detailed discussion of thread notes, see §15.21.

13.33 Dimensioning of Tapers

A *taper* is a conical surface on a shaft or in a hole. The usual method of dimensioning a taper is to give the amount of taper in a note such as TAPER 0.167 ON DIA (often TO GAGE added), and then give the diameter at one end, plus the length, or give the diameter at both ends and omit the length. *Taper on diameter means the difference in diameter per unit of length.*

Standard machine tapers are used on machine spindles, shanks of tools, pins, for example, and are described in "Machine Tapers," ANSI B5.10–1981 (R1987). Such standard tapers are dimensioned on a drawing by giving the diameter, usually at the large end, the length, and a note, such as NO. 4 AMERICAN NATIONAL STANDARD TAPER. See Fig. 13.45 (a).

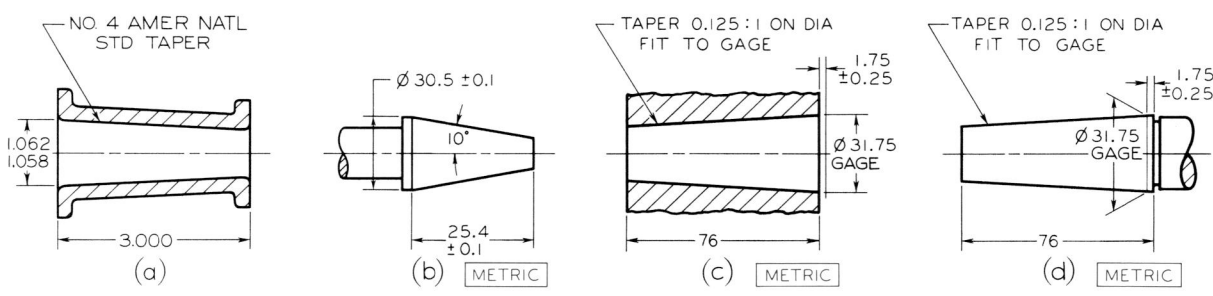

Fig. 13.45   Dimensioning Tapers.

For not-too-critical requirements, a taper may be dimensioned by giving the diameter at the large end, the length, and the included angle, all with proper tolerances, (b). Or the diameters of both ends, plus the length, may be given with necessary tolerances.

For close-fitting tapers, the amount of *taper per unit on diameter* is indicated as shown at (c) and (d).

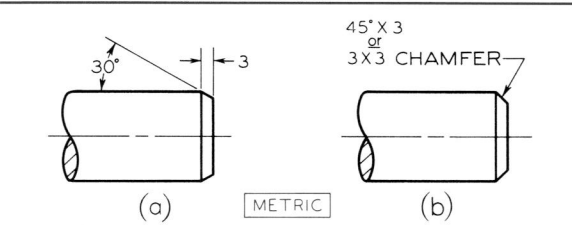

Fig. 13.46   Dimensioning Chamfers.

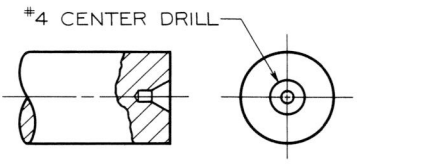

Fig. 13.47   Shaft Center.

A gage line is selected and located by a comparatively generous tolerance, while other dimensions are given appropriate tolerances as required.

13.34 Dimensioning of Chamfers
A *chamfer* is a beveled or sloping edge, and it is dimensioned by giving the length of the offset and the angle, as in Fig. 13.46 (a). A 45° chamfer also may be dimensioned in a manner similar to that shown at (a), but usually it is dimensioned by note without or with the word **CHAMFER** as at (b).

13.35 Shaft Centers
Shaft centers are required on shafts, spindles, and other conical or cylindrical parts for turning, grinding, and other operations. Such a center may be dimensioned as shown in Fig. 13.47. Normally the centers are produced by a combined drill and countersink.

13.36 Dimensioning Keyways
Methods of dimensioning keyways for Woodruff keys and stock keys are shown in Fig. 13.48. Note in both cases, the use of a dimension to center the keyway in the shaft or collar. The preferred method of dimensioning the depth of a keyway is to give the

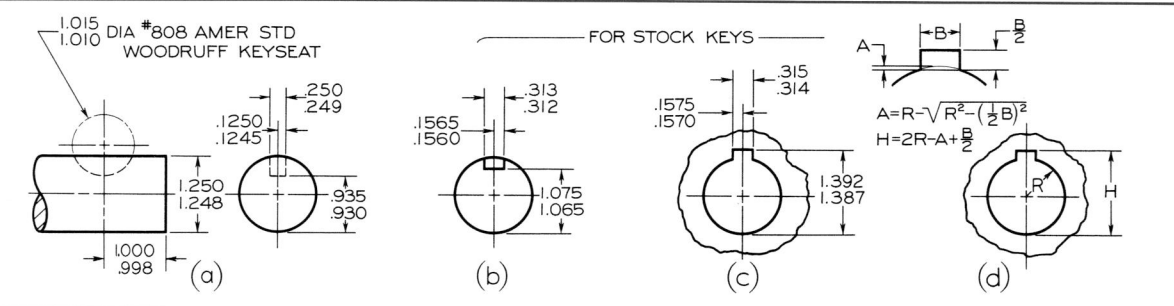

Fig. 13.48   Dimensioning Keyways.

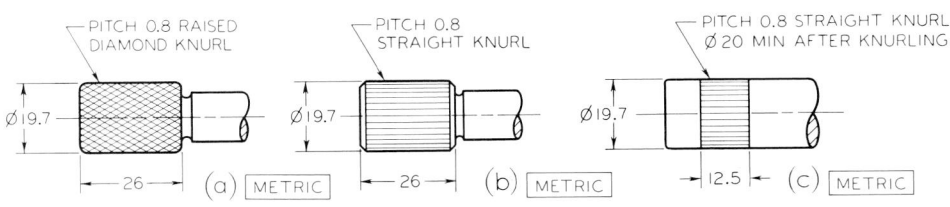

Fig. 13.49 Dimensioning Knurls.

dimension from the bottom of the keyway to the opposite side of the shaft or hole, as shown. The method of computing such a dimension is shown at (d). Values for **A** may be found in machinists' handbooks.

For general information about keys and keyways, see §15.34.

13.37 Dimensioning of Knurls

A *knurl* is a roughened surface to provide a better handgrip or to be used for a press fit between two parts. For handgripping purposes, it is necessary only to give the pitch of the knurl, the type of knurling, and the length of the knurled area, Fig. 13.49 (a) and (b). To dimension a knurl for a press fit, the toleranced diameter before knurling should be given, (c). A note should be added giving the pitch and type of knurl and the minimum diameter after knurling. See ANSI B94.6–1984.

13.38 Dimensioning Along Curved Surfaces

When angular measurements are unsatisfactory, chordal dimensions, Fig. 13.50 (a), or linear dimensions upon the curved surfaces, as shown at (b), may be given.

13.39 Sheet-Metal Bends

In sheet-metal dimensioning, allowance must be made for bends. The intersection of the plane surfaces adjacent to a bend is called the *mold line,* and this line, rather than the center of the arc, is used to determine dimensions, Fig. 13.51. The following procedure for calculating bends is typical. If the two inner plane surfaces of an angle are extended, their line of intersection is called the **IML** or *inside mold line,* Fig. 13.52 (a) to (c). Similarly, if the two outer plane surfaces are extended, they produce the **OML** or *outside mold line.* The *center line of bend* (₵B) refers primarily to the machine on which the bend is made and is at the center of the bend radius.

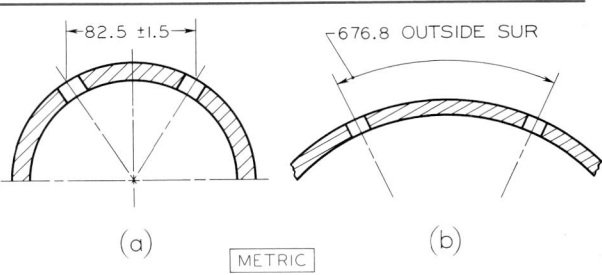

Fig. 13.50 Dimensioning Along Curved Surfaces.

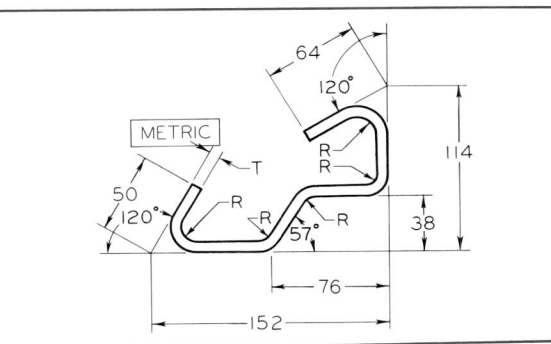

Fig. 13.51 Profile Dimensioning.

The length, or *stretchout,* of the pattern equals the sum of the flat sides of the angle plus the distance around the bend measured along the *neutral axis.* The distance around the bend is called the *bend allowance.* When metal bends, it compresses on the inside and stretches on the outside. At a certain zone in between, the metal is neither compressed nor stretched. This is called the neutral axis. See Fig. 13.52 (d). The neutral axis is usually assumed to be 0.44 of the thickness from the inside surface of the metal.

The developed length of material, or bend allowance (**BA**), to make the bend is computed from the empirical formula

$$BA = (0.017453R + 0.0078T)N$$

where R = radius of bend, T = metal thickness, and N = number of degrees of bend. See Fig. 13.52 (c).

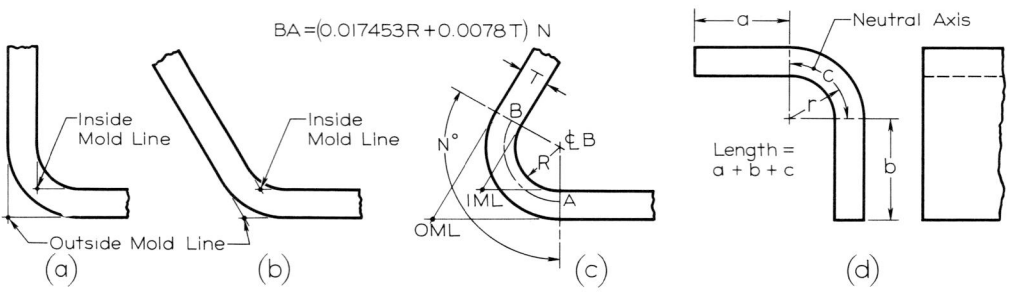

$$BA = (0.017453R + 0.0078T)N$$

Fig. 13.52   Bends.

13.40 Tabular Dimensions

A series of objects having like features but varying in dimensions may be represented by one drawing, Fig. 13.53. Letters are substituted for dimension figures on the drawing, and the varying dimensions are given in tabular form. The dimensions of many standard parts are given in this manner in the various catalogs and handbooks.

13.41 Standards

Dimensions should be given, wherever possible, to make use of readily available materials, tools, parts, and gages. The dimensions for many commonly used machine elements, such as bolts, screws, nails, keys, tapers, wire, pipes, sheet metal, chains, belts, ropes, pins, and rolled metal shapes, have been standardized, and the drafter must obtain these sizes from company standards manuals, from published handbooks, from American National Standards, or from manufacturers' catalogs. Tables of some of the more common items are given in the Appendix of this text.

Such standard parts are not delineated on detail drawings unless they are to be altered for use, but are drawn conventionally on assembly drawings and

are listed in parts lists, §16.14. Common fractions are often used to indicate the nominal sizes of standard parts or tools. If the complete decimal-inch system is used, all such sizes ordinarily are expressed by decimals; for example, .250 DRILL instead of $\frac{1}{4}$ DRILL. If the all-metric system of dimensioning is used, then the *preferred* metric drill of the approximate same size (.2480″) would be indicated as a 6.30 DRILL.

13.42 Coordinate Dimensioning

In general, the basic coordinate dimensioning practices are compatible with the data requirements for tape or computer-controlled automatic production machines. However, to design for automated production, the designer and/or drafter should first consult the manufacturing machine manuals before making the drawings for production. Certain considerations should be noted:

1. A set of three mutually perpendicular datum or reference planes is usually required for coordinate dimensioning. These planes either must be obvious or clearly identified. See Fig. 13.54.

2. The designer selects as origins for dimensions those surfaces or other features most important to the functioning of the part. Enough of these

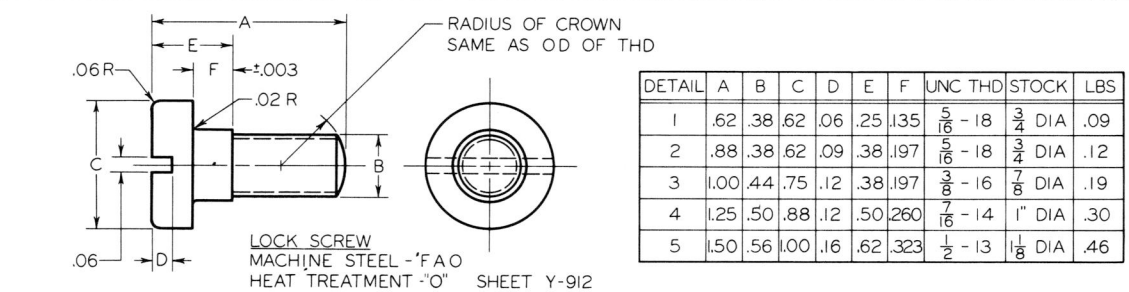

DETAIL	A	B	C	D	E	F	UNC THD	STOCK	LBS
1	.62	.38	.62	.06	.25	.135	$\frac{5}{16}$ – 18	$\frac{3}{4}$ DIA	.09
2	.88	.38	.62	.09	.38	.197	$\frac{5}{16}$ – 18	$\frac{3}{4}$ DIA	.12
3	1.00	.44	.75	.12	.38	.197	$\frac{3}{8}$ – 16	$\frac{7}{8}$ DIA	.19
4	1.25	.50	.88	.12	.50	.260	$\frac{7}{16}$ – 14	1″ DIA	.30
5	1.50	.56	1.00	.16	.62	.323	$\frac{1}{2}$ – 13	$1\frac{1}{8}$ DIA	.46

Fig. 13.53   Tabular Dimensioning.

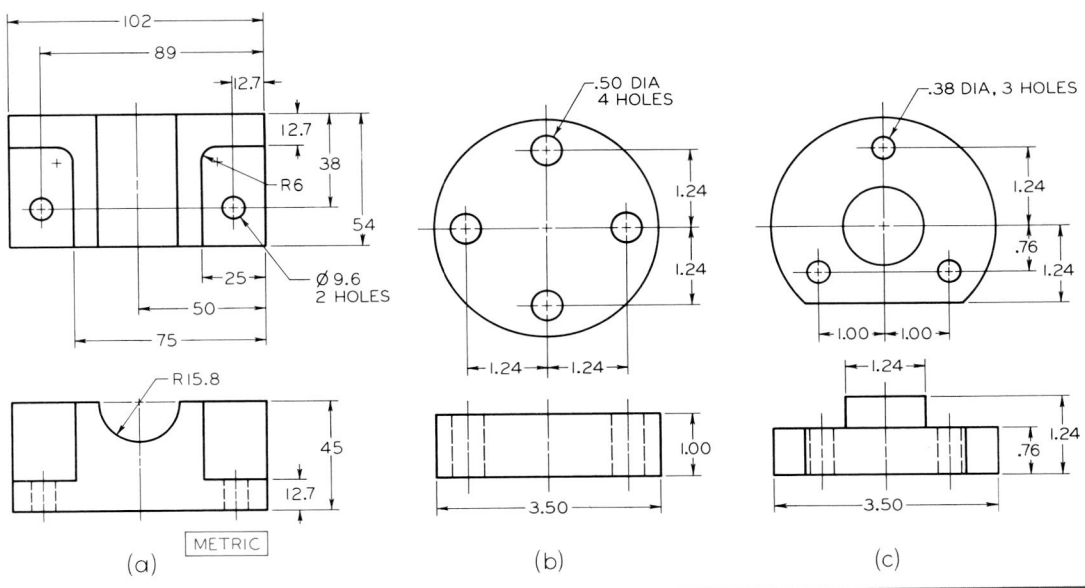

Fig. 13.54   Coordinate Dimensioning.

features are selected to position the part in relation to the set of mutually perpendicular planes. All related dimensions on the part are then made from these planes.

3.   All dimensions should be in decimals.

4.   Angles should be given, where possible, in degrees and decimal parts of degrees.

5.   Standard tools, such as drills, reamers, and taps, should be specifed wherever possible.

6.   All tolerances should be determined by the design requirements of the part, not by the capability of the manufacturing machine.

13.43 Do's and Don'ts of Dimensioning

The following checklist summarizes briefly most of the situations in which a beginning designer is likely to make a mistake in dimensioning. The student should check the drawing by this list before submitting it to the instructor.

1.   Each dimension should be given clearly, so that it can be interpreted in only one way.

2.   Dimensions should not be duplicated or the same information be given in two different ways—dual dimensioning excluded—and no dimensions should be given except those needed to produce or inspect the part.

3.   Dimensions should be given between points or surfaces that have a functional relation to each other or that control the location of mating parts.

4.   Dimensions should be given to finished surfaces or important center lines in preference to rough surfaces wherever possible.

5.   Dimensions should be so given that it will not be necessary for the machinist to calculate, scale, or assume any dimension.

6.   Dimensions should be attached to the view where the shape is best shown (contour rule).

7.   Dimensions should be placed in the views where the features dimensioned are shown true shape.

8.   Avoid dimensioning to hidden lines wherever possible.

9.   Dimensions should not be placed upon a view unless clearness is promoted and long extension lines are avoided.

10.   Dimensions applying to two adjacent views should be placed between views, unless clearness is promoted by placing some of them outside.

11.   The longer dimensions should be placed outside all intermediate dimensions, so that dimension lines will not cross extension lines.

12. In machine drawing, omit all unit marks, except when necessary for clearness; for example, 1″ VALVE or 1 mm DRILL.

13. Do not expect production personnel to assume that a feature is centered (as a hole on a plate), but give a location dimension from one side. However, if a hole is to be centered on a symmetrical rough casting, mark the center line and omit the locating dimension from the center line.

14. A dimension should be attached to only one view, not to extension lines connecting two views.

15. Detail dimensions should "line up" in chain fashion.

16. Avoid a complete chain of detail dimensions; better omit one, otherwise add REF (reference) to one detail dimension or the overall dimension or enclose the dimension within parentheses, ( ).

17. A dimension line should never be drawn through a dimension figure. A figure should never be lettered over any line of the drawing. Break the line if necessary.

18. Dimension lines should be spaced uniformly throughout the drawing. They should be at least 10 mm ($\frac{3}{8}$″) from the object outline and 6 mm ($\frac{1}{4}$″) apart.

19. No line of the drawing should be used as a dimension line or coincide with a dimension line.

20. A dimension line should never be joined end to end (chain fashion) with any line of the drawing.

21. Dimension lines should not cross, if avoidable.

22. Dimension lines and extension lines should not cross, if avoidable (extension lines may cross each other).

23. When extension lines cross extension lines or visible lines, no break in either line should be made.

24. A center line may be extended and used as an extension line, in which case it is still drawn like a center line.

25. Center lines should generally not extend from view to view.

26. Leaders for notes should be straight, not curved, and pointing to the center of circular views of holes wherever possible.

27. Leaders should slope at 45°, or 30°, or 60° with horizontal but may be made at any convenient angle except vertical or horizontal.

28. Leaders should extend from the beginning or from the end of a note, the horizontal "shoulder" extending from midheight of the lettering.

29. Dimension figures should be approximately centered between the arrowheads, except that in a "stack" of dimensions, the figures should be "staggered."

30. Dimension figures should be about 3 mm ($\frac{1}{8}$″) high for whole numbers and 6 mm ($\frac{1}{4}$″) high for fractions.

31. Dimension figures should never be crowded or in any way made difficult to read.

32. Dimension figures should not be lettered over lines or sectioned areas unless necessary, in which case a clear space should be reserved for the dimension figures.

33. Dimension figures for angles should generally be lettered horizontally.

34. Fraction bars should never be inclined except in confined areas, such as in tables.

35. The numerator and denominator of a fraction should never touch the fraction bar.

36. Notes should always be lettered horizontally on the sheet.

37. Notes should be brief and clear, and the wording should be standard in form, Fig. 13.44.

38. Finish marks should be placed on the edge views of all finished surfaces, including hidden edges and the contour and circular views of cylindrical surfaces.

39. Finish marks should be omitted on holes or other features where a note specifies a machining operation.

40. Finish marks should be omitted on parts made from rolled stock.

41. If a part is finished all over, omit all finish marks, and use the general note FINISH ALL OVER, or FAO.

42. A cylinder is dimensioned by giving both its diameter and length in the rectangular view, except when notes are used for holes. A diagonal diameter in the circular view may be used in cases where clearness is gained thereby.

43. Holes to be bored, drilled, reamed, and so on are size-dimensioned by notes in which the leaders preferably point toward the center of the circular views of the holes. Indications of manufacturing processes may be omitted from notes.

44. Drill sizes are preferably expressed in decimals. For drills designated by number or letter, the decimal size must also be given.

45. In general, a circle is dimensioned by its diameter, an arc by its radius.

46. Diagonal diameters should be avoided, except for very large holes and for circles of centers. They may be used on positive cylinders when clearness is gained thereby.

47. A metric diameter dimension value should always be preceded by the symbol ∅, and the diameter dimension value in inches should be followed by DIA.

48. A metric radius dimension should always be preceded by the letter R and the radius value in inches should be followed by the letter R. The radial dimension line should have only one arrowhead, and it should pass through or point through the arc center and touch the arc.

49. Cylinders should be located by their center lines.

50. Cylinders should be located in the circular views, if possible.

51. Cylinders should be located by coordinate dimensions in preference to angular dimensions where accuracy is important.

52. When there are several rough, noncritical features obviously the same size (fillets, rounds, ribs, etc.), it is necessary to give only typical (abbreviation TYP) dimensions, or to use a note.

53. When a dimension is not to scale, it should be underscored with a heavy straight line or marked NTS or NOT TO SCALE.

54. Mating dimensions should be given correspondingly on drawings of mating parts.

55. Pattern dimensions should be given in two-place decimals or in common whole numbers and fractions to the nearest $\frac{1}{16}''$.

56. Decimal dimensions should be used for all machining dimensions.

57. Cumulative tolerances should be avoided, especially in limit dimensioning, described in §14.9.

13.44 Computer Graphics

A drafter with thorough knowledge of the principles and practices of dimensioning will find that modern CAD software provides an easy means of applying the desired dimensional data to a drawing, Fig. 13.55. Linear dimensions in either the metric or inch systems can be shown in either a horizontal, vertical, or parallel dimensioning format. Angles, in degrees, can be calculated and displayed. Other dimensioning requirements such as arrows, leaders, extension lines, etc. are standard features of CAD dimensioning programs.

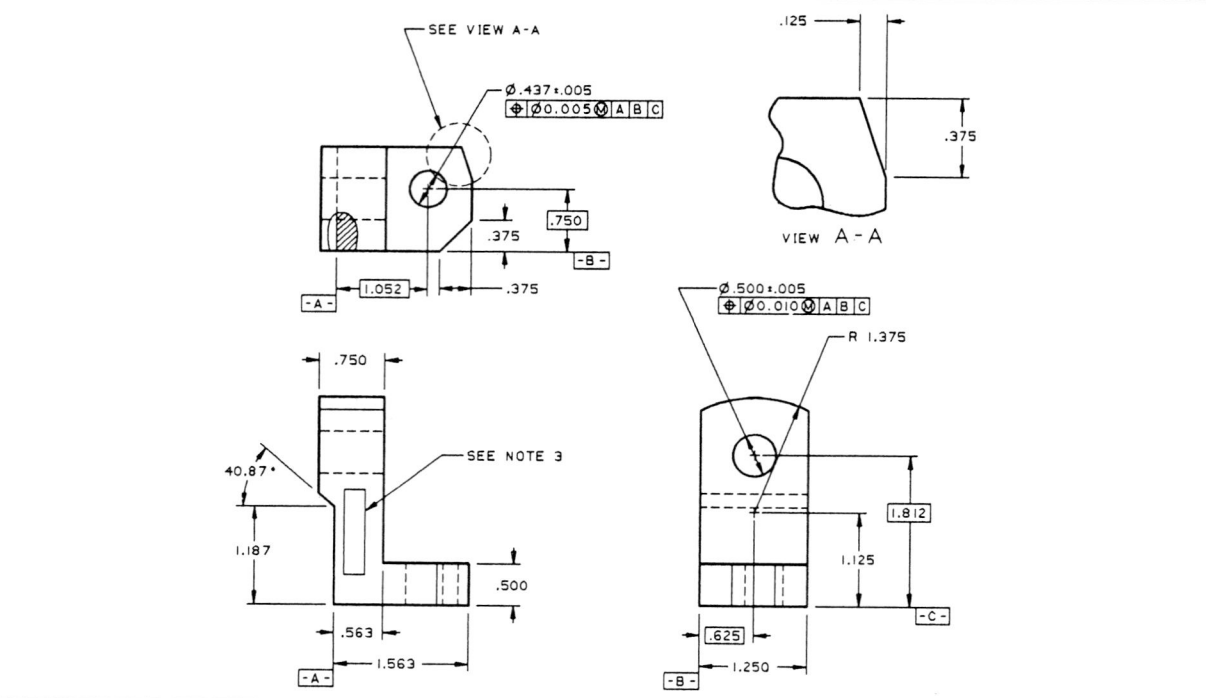

Fig. 13.55   Dimensioned Detail Drawing Produced by the Computervision CADDS 4X Production Drafting System. *Courtesy of Computervision Corporation, a subsidiary of Prime Computer, Inc.*

Dimensioning Problems

It is expected that most of the student's practice in dimensioning will be in connection with working drawings assigned from other chapters. However, a limited number of special dimensioning problems are available here in Figs. 13.56 and 13.57. The problems are designed for Layout A–3 (8.5″ × 11.0″) and are to be drawn with instruments and dimensioned to a full-size scale. Layout A4–3 (297 mm × 420 mm) may be used with appropriate adjustments in the title strip layout.

Since many of the problems in this chapter are of a general nature, they can also be solved on most computer graphics systems. If a system is available, the instructor may choose to assign specific problems to be completed by this method.

Additional problems in convenient form for solution are presented in the worksheets at the back of this book. Refer to Drawings 13-1 to 13-4 and accompanying instructions.

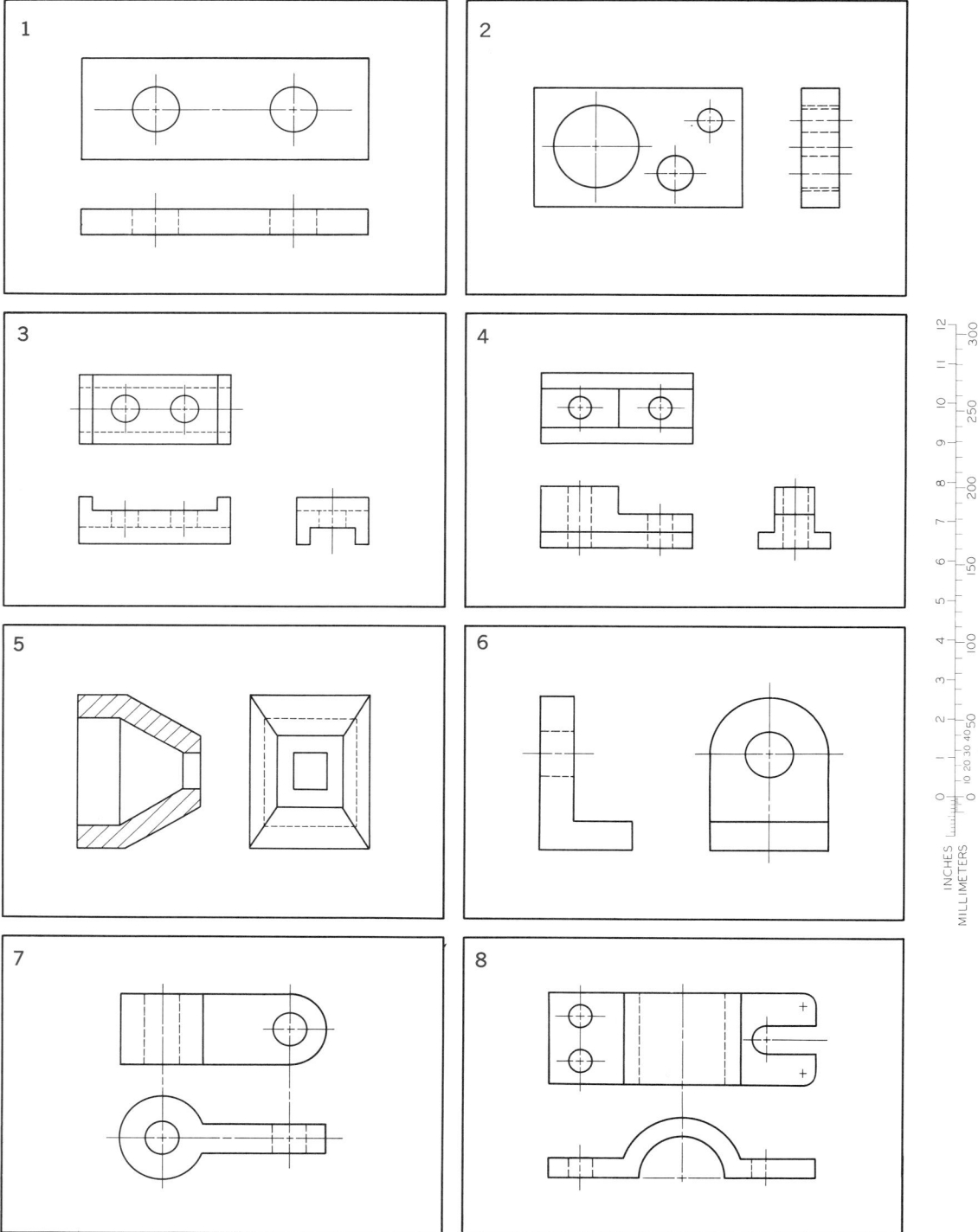

Fig. 13.56 Using Layout A–3 or A4–3 (adjusted), draw assigned problem with instruments. To obtain sizes, place bow dividers on the views on this page and transfer to scale at the side to obtain values. Dimension drawing completely in one-place millimeters or two-place inches as assigned, full size. See inside front cover for decimal-inch and millimeter equivalents.

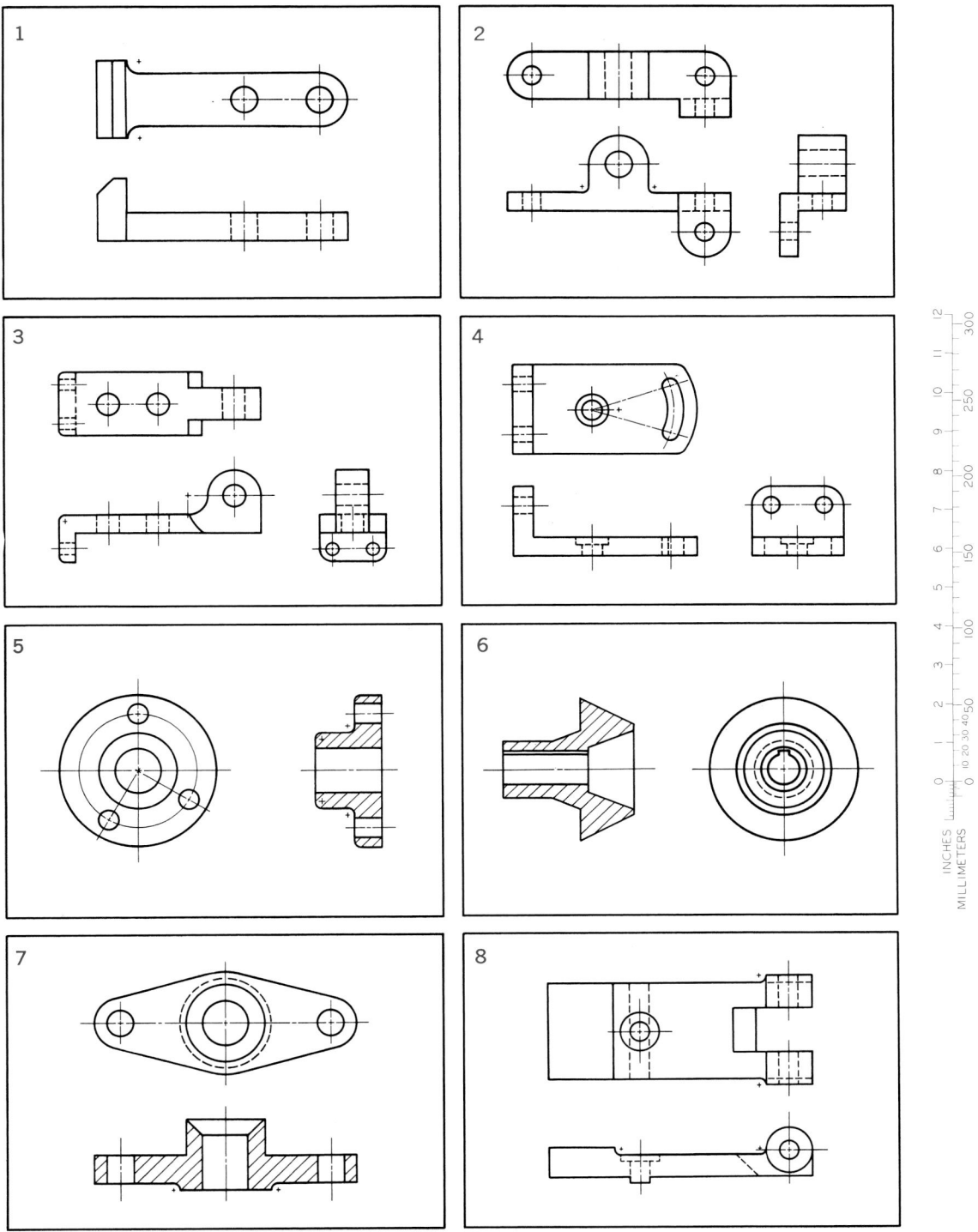

Fig. 13.57 Using Layout A–3 or A4–3 (adjusted), draw assigned problem with instruments. To obtain sizes, place bow dividers on the views on this page and transfer to scale at the side to obtain values. Dimension drawing completely in one-place millimeters or two-place inches as assigned, full size. See inside front cover for decimal-inch and millimeter equivalents.

CHAPTER
14

Tolerancing

Interchangeable manufacturing, by means of which parts can be made in widely separated localities and then be brought together for assembly, where the parts will all fit together properly, is an essential element of mass production. Without interchangeable manufacturing, modern industry could not exist, and without effective size control by the engineer, interchangeable manufacturing could not be achieved.

For example, an automobile manufacturer not only subcontracts the manufacture of many parts of a design to other companies but also must make provision for replacement parts. All parts in each category must be near enough alike so that any one of them will fit properly in any assembly. Unfortunately, *it is impossible to make anything to exact size*. Parts can be made to very close dimensions, even to a few millionths of an inch or thousandths of a millimeter (e.g., gage blocks), but such accuracy is extremely expensive.

However, exact sizes are not needed, only varying degrees of accuracy according to functional requirements. A manufacturer of children's tricycles would soon go out of business if the parts were made with jet-engine accuracy, as no one would be willing to pay the price. So what is needed is a means of specifying dimensions with whatever degree of accuracy may be required. The answer to the problem is the specification of a *tolerance* on each dimension.

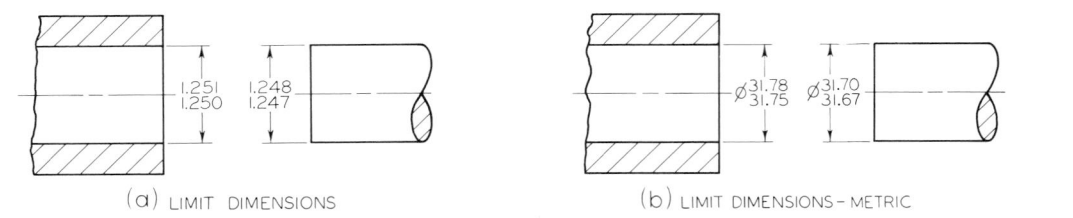

Fig. 14.1 Fits Between Mating Parts.

14.1 Tolerance Dimensioning

Tolerance is the total amount a specific dimension is permitted to vary, which is the difference between the maximum and the minimum limits [ANSI Y14.5M–1982 (R1988)]. For example, a dimension given as 1.625 ± .002 means that it may be (on the manufactured part) 1.627″ or 1.623″, or anywhere between these *limit dimensions*. The tolerance, or total amount of variation "tolerated," is .004″. Thus, it becomes the function of the detailer or designer to specify the allowable error that may be tolerated for a given dimension and still permit the satisfactory functioning of the part. Since greater accuracy costs more money, the detailer or designer will not specify the closest tolerance, but instead will specify as generous a tolerance as possible.

In order to control the dimensions of quantities of the two parts so that any two mating parts will be interchangeable, it is necessary to assign tolerances to the dimensions of the parts, as shown in Fig. 14.1 (a). The diameter of the hole may be machined not less than 1.250″ and not more than 1.251″, these two figures representing the *limits* and the difference between them, .001″, being the *tolerance*. Likewise, the shaft must be produced between the limits of 1.248″ and 1.247″, the tolerance on the shaft being the difference between these, or .001″. The metric

versions for these limit dimensions for the hole and shaft are shown at (b). The difference in the dimensions for either the hole or shaft is 0.03 mm, the total *tolerance*.

A pictorial illustration of the dimensions in Fig. 14.1 (a) is shown in Fig. 14.2 (a). The maximum shaft is shown solid, and the minimum shaft is shown in phantom. The difference in diameters, .001″, is the tolerance on the shaft. Similarly, the tolerance on the hole is the difference between the two limits shown, or .001″. The loosest fit, or maximum clearance, occurs when the smallest shaft is in the largest hole, as shown at (b). The tightest fit, or minimum clearance, occurs when the largest shaft is in the smallest hole, as shown at (c). The difference between these, .002″, is the *allowance*. The average clearance is .003″, which is the same difference as allowed in the example of Fig. 14.1 (a); thus, any shaft will fit any hole interchangeably.

When expressed in metric dimensions, the limits for the hole are 31.75 mm and 31.78 mm, the difference between them, 0.03 mm, being the tolerance. Similarly, the limits for the shaft are 31.70 mm and 31.67 mm, the tolerance on the shaft being the difference between them, or 0.03 mm.

When parts are required to fit properly in assembly but not to be interchangeable, the size of

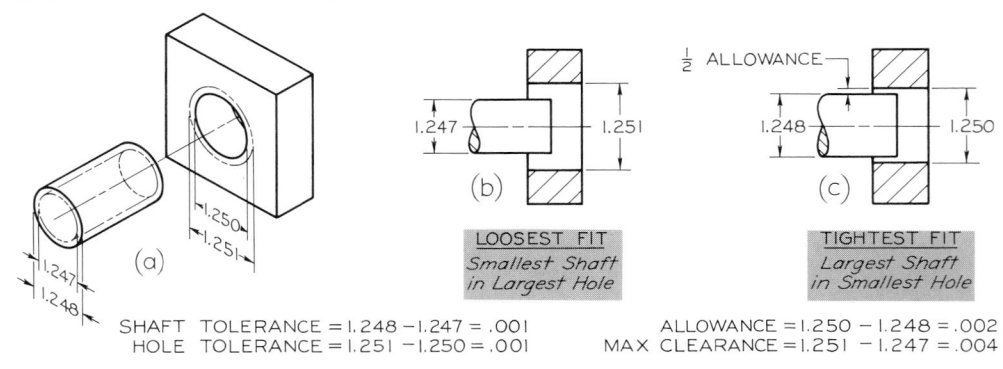

Fig. 14.2 Limit Dimensions.

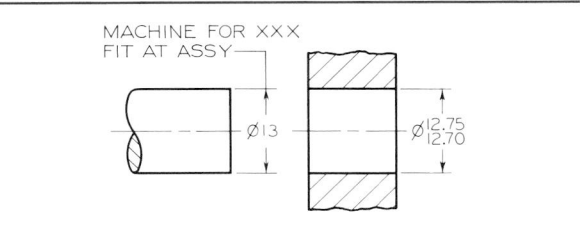

Fig. 14.3 Noninterchangeable Fit.

one part need not be toleranced, but indicated to be made to fit at assembly, Fig. 14.3.

14.2 Definitions of Terms

At this point, it is well to fix in mind the definitions of certain terms [ANSI Y14.5M–1982 (R1988)].

Nominal size The designation that is used for the purpose of general identification is usually expressed in common fractions. In Fig. 14.1, the nominal size of both hole and shaft, which is $1\frac{1}{4}''$, would be 1.25″ or 31.75 mm in a decimal system of dimensioning.

Basic size or dimension The theoretical size from which limits of size are derived by the application of allowances and tolerances. It is the size from which limits are determined for the size, shape, or location of a feature. In Fig. 14.1 (a), the basic size is the decimal equivalent of the nominal size $1\frac{1}{4}''$, or 1.250″ or 31.75 mm at (b).

Actual size The measured size of the finished part.

Tolerance The total amount by which a given dimension may vary, or the difference between the limits. In Fig. 14.2 (a) the tolerance on either the shaft or hole is the difference between the limits, or .001″.

Limits The maximum and minimum sizes indicated by a toleranced dimension. In Fig. 14.2 (a) the limits for the hole are 1.250″ and 1.251″, and for the shaft are 1.248″ and 1.247″.

Allowance The minimum clearance space (or maximum interference) intended between the maximum material condition (MMC) of mating parts. In Fig. 14.2 (c) the allowance is the difference between the smallest hole, 1.250″, and the largest shaft, 1.248″, or .002″. Allowance, then, represents the tightest permissible fit and is simply the smallest hole minus the largest shaft. For clearance fits, this difference will be positive, while for interference fits it will be negative.

14.3 Fits Between Mating Parts

"Fit is the general term used to signify the range of tightness or looseness that may result from the application of a specific combination of allowances and tolerances in mating parts." [ANSI Y14.5M–1982 (R1988)]. There are four general types of fits between parts.

Clearance fit In which an internal member fits in an external member (as a shaft in a hole), and always leaves a space or clearance between the parts. In Fig. 14.2 (c) the largest shaft is 1.248″ and the smallest hole is 1.250″, which permits a minimum air space of .002″ between the parts. This space is the allowance, and in a clearance fit it is always positive.

Interference fit In which the internal member is larger than the external member such that there is always an actual interference of metal. In Fig. 14.4 (a) the smallest shaft is 1.2513″, and the largest hole is 1.2506″, so that there is an actual interference of metal amounting to at least .0007″. Under maximum material conditions the interference would be .0019″. This interference is the allowance, and in an interference fit it is always negative.

Transition fit In which the fit might result in either a clearance or interference condition. In Fig. 14.4 (b) the smallest shaft, 1.2503″, will fit in the largest hole, 1.2506″, with .0003″ to spare. But the largest

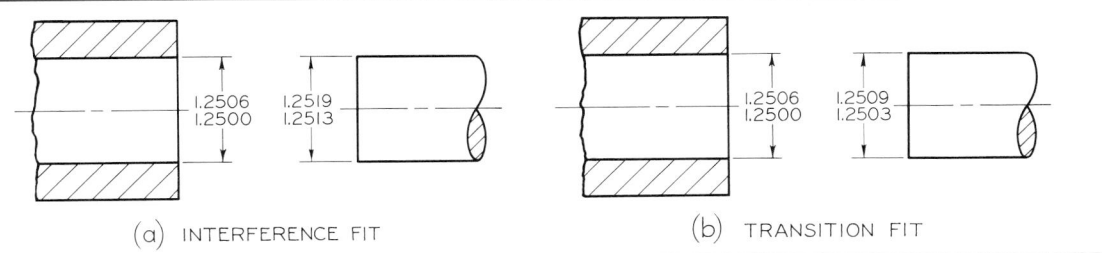

Fig. 14.4 Fits Between Parts.

shaft, 1.2509″, will have to be forced into the smallest hole, 1.2500″, with an interference of metal (negative allowance) of .0009″.

Line fit In which limits of size are so specified that a clearance or surface contact may result when mating parts are assembled.

14.4 Selective Assembly

If allowances and tolerances are properly given, mating parts can be completely interchangeable. But for close fits, it is necessary to specify very small allowances and tolerances, and the cost may be very high. In order to avoid this expense, either manual or computer controlled *selective assembly* is often used. In selective assembly, all parts are inspected and classified into several grades according to actual sizes, so that "small" shafts can be matched with "small" holes, "medium" shafts with "medium" holes, and so on. In this way, very satisfactory fits may be obtained at much less expense than by machining all mating parts to very accurate dimensions. Since a transition fit may or may not represent an interference of metal, interchangeable assembly generally is not as satisfactory as selective assembly.

14.5 Basic Hole System

Standard reamers, broaches, and other standard tools are often used to produce holes, and standard plug gages are used to check the actual sizes. On the other hand, shafting can easily be machined to any size desired. Therefore, toleranced dimensions are commonly figured on the so-called *basic hole system*. In this system, the *minimum hole is taken as the basic size*, an allowance is assigned, and tolerances are applied on both sides of, and away from, this allowance.

In Fig. 14.5 (a) the minimum size of the hole, .500″, is taken as the basic size. An allowance of .002″, is decided upon and subtracted from the basic hole size, giving the maximum shaft, .498″. Tolerances of .002″ and .003″, respectively, are applied to the hole and shaft to obtain the maximum hole of .502″ and the minimum shaft of .495″. Thus the minimum clearance between the parts becomes .500″ − .498″ = .002″ (smallest hole minus largest shaft), and the maximum clearance is .502″ − .495″ = .007″ (largest hole minus smallest shaft).

In the case of an interference fit, the maximum shaft size would be found by *adding the desired allowance* (maximum interference) to the basic hole

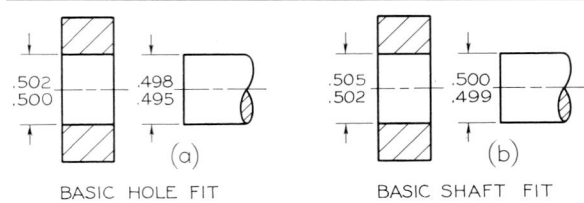

Fig. 14.5 Basic Hole and Basic Shaft Systems.

size. In Fig. 14.4 (a), the basic size is 1.2500″. The maximum interference decided upon was .0019″, which added to the basic size gives 1.2519″, the largest shaft size.

The basic hole size can be changed to the basic shaft size by subtracting the allowance for a clearance fit, or adding it for an interference fit. The result is the largest shaft size, which is the new basic size.

14.6 Basic Shaft System

In some branches of industry, such as textile machinery manufacturing, in which use is made of a great deal of cold-finished shafting, the *basic shaft system* is often used. This system should be used only when there is a reason for it. For example, it is advantageous when several parts having different fits, but one nominal size, are required on a single shaft. In this system, *the maximum shaft is taken as the basic size*, an allowance for each mating part is assigned, and tolerances are applied on both sides of, and away from, this allowance.

In Fig. 14.5 (b) the maximum size of the shaft, .500″, is taken as the basic size. An allowance of .002″ is decided upon and added to the basic shaft size, giving the minimum hole, .502″. Tolerances of .003″ and .001″, respectively, are applied to the hole and shaft to obtain the maximum hole .505″ and the minimum shaft .499″. Thus the minimum clearance between the parts is .502″ − .500″ = .002″ (smallest hole minus largest shaft), and the maximum clearance is .505″ − .499″ = .006″ (largest hole minus smallest shaft).

In the case of an interference fit, the minimum hole size would be found by *subtracting the desired allowance from the basic shaft size*.

The basic shaft size may be changed to the basic hole size by adding the allowance for a clearance fit or by subtracting it for an interference fit. The result is the smallest hole size, which is the new basic size.

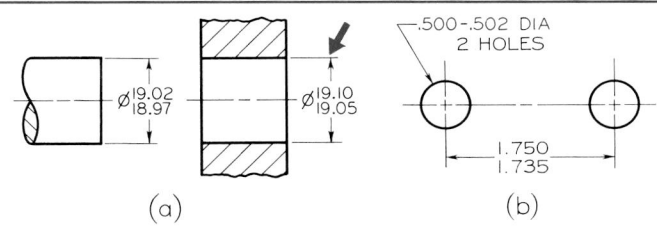

Fig. 14.6   Method of Giving Limits.

14.7 Specification of Tolerances

A tolerance of a decimal dimension must be given in decimal form to the same number of places. See Fig. 14.8.

General tolerances on decimal dimensions in which tolerances are not given may also be covered in a printed note, such as

DECIMAL DIMENSIONS TO BE HELD TO ±.001.

Thus if a dimension **3.250** is given, the worker machines between the limits **3.249** and **3.251**. See Fig. 14.9.

Tolerances for metric dimensions may be covered in a note, such as the commonly used

METRIC DIMENSIONS TO BE HELD TO ±0.08.

Thus, when the given dimension of **3.250″** is converted to millimeters, the worker machines between the limits of **82.63 mm** and **82.47 mm**.

Every dimension on a drawing should have a tolerance, either direct or by general tolerance note, except that commercial material is often assumed to have the tolerances set by commercial standards.

It is customary to indicate an overall general tolerance for all common fraction dimensions by means of a printed note in or just above the title block.

EXAMPLES

ALL FRACTIONAL DIMENSIONS ±$\frac{1}{64}$″
UNLESS OTHERWISE SPECIFIED.

HOLD FRACTIONAL DIMENSIONS TO ±$\frac{1}{64}$″
UNLESS OTHERWISE NOTED.

See Fig. 14.9. General angular tolerances also may be given as

ANGULAR TOLERANCE ±1°

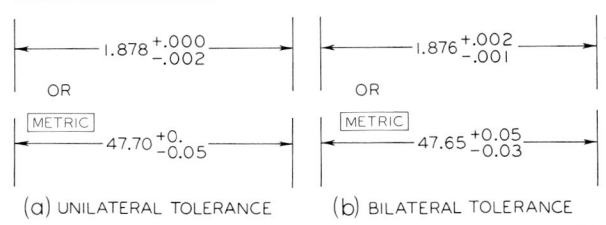

Fig. 14.7   Tolerance Expression.

Several methods of expressing tolerances in dimensions are approved by ANSI [Y14.5M–1982 (R1988)] as follows.

1. *Limit Dimensioning.* In this preferred method, the maximum and minimum limits of size and location are specified, as shown in Fig. 14.6. The high limit (maximum value) is placed above the low limit (minimum value). See Fig. 14.6 (a). In single-line note form, the low limit precedes the high limit separated by a dash, Fig. 14.6 (b).

2. *Plus and Minus Dimensioning.* In this method the basic size is followed by a plus and minus expression of tolerance resulting in either a unilateral or bilateral tolerance as in Fig. 14.7. If two unequal tolerance numbers are given, one plus and one minus, the plus is placed above the minus. One of the numbers may be zero, if desired. If a single tolerance value is given, it is preceded by the plus-or-minus symbol (±), Fig. 14.8. This method should be used when the plus and minus values are equal.

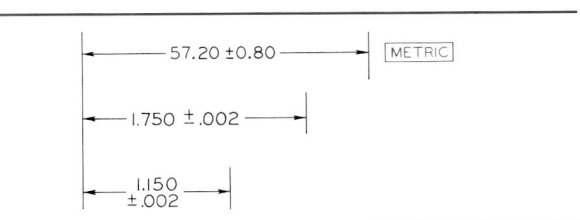

Fig. 14.8   Bilateral Tolerances.

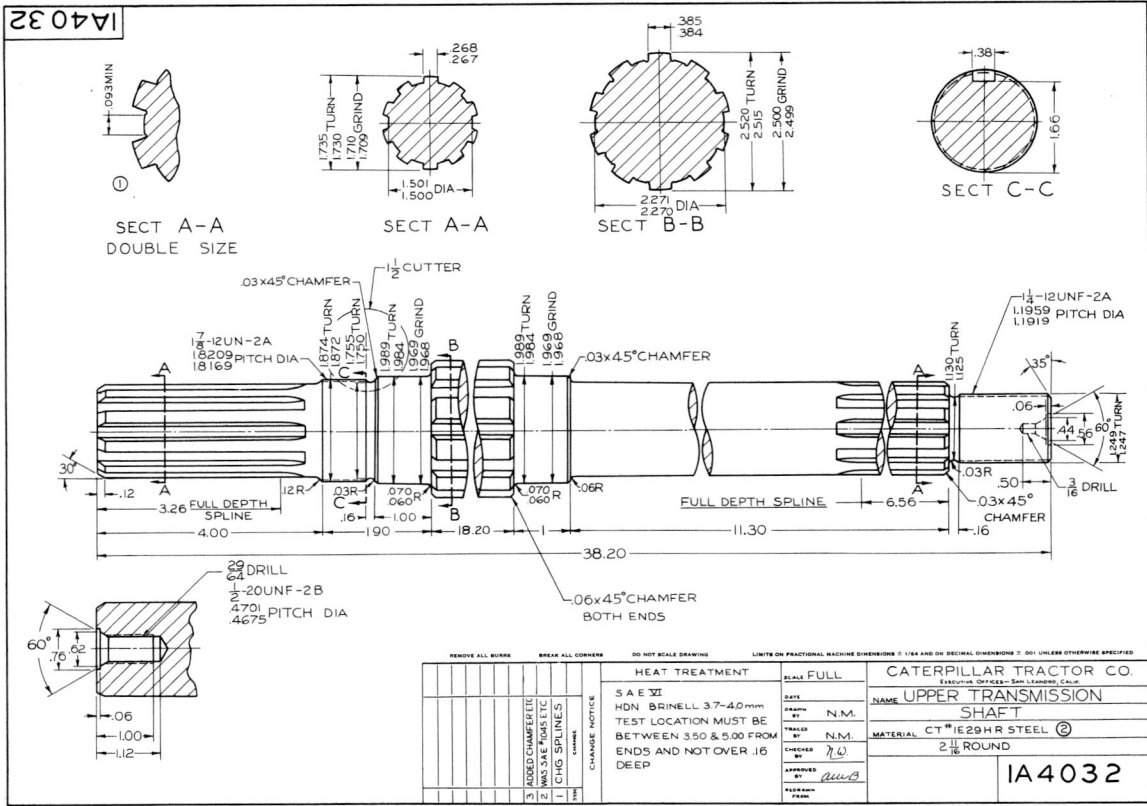

Fig. 14.9   Limit Dimensions.

The *unilateral system* of tolerances allows variations in only one direction from the basic size. This method is advantageous when a critical size is approached as material is removed during manufacture, as in the case of close-fitting holes and shafts. In Fig. 14.7 (a) the basic size is 1.878″ (47.70 mm). The tolerance .002″ (0.05 mm) is all in one direction—toward the smaller size. If this is a shaft diameter, the basic size 1.878″ (47.70 mm) is the size nearest the critical size because it is nearest to the tolerance zone; hence, the tolerance is taken *away* from the critical size. A unilateral tolerance is always all plus or all minus; that is, either the plus or the minus value must be zero. However, the zeros should be given as shown at (a).

The *bilateral system* of tolerances allows variations in both directions from the basic size. Bilateral tolerances are usually given with location dimensions or with any dimensions that can be allowed to vary in either direction. In Fig. 14.7 (b) the basic size is 1.876″ (47.65 mm), and the actual size may be larger by .002″ (0.05

mm) or smaller by .001″ (0.03 mm). If it is desired to specify an equal variation in both directions, the combined plus or minus symbol (±) is used with a single value, as shown in Fig. 14.8.

A typical example of limit dimensioning is given in Fig. 14.9.

3. *Single-Limit Dimensioning*. It is not always necessary to specify both limits. MIN or MAX is often placed after a number to indicate minimum or maximum dimensions desired where other elements of design determine the other unspecified limit. For example, a thread length may be dimensioned thus: |———1.500———| MIN FULL THD or a radius dimensioned: .05 R MAX—— Other applications include depths of holes, chamfers, and so on.

4. *Angular tolerances* are usually bilateral and in terms of degrees, minutes, and seconds.

EXAMPLES   25° ± 1°, 25° 0′ ± 0° 15′, or 25° ± 0.25°. See also §14.18.

14.8 American National Standard Limits and Fits

The American National Standards Institute has issued the ANSI B4.1–1967 (R1987), "Preferred Limits and Fits for Cylindrical Parts," defining terms and recommending preferred standard sizes, allowances, tolerances, and fits in terms of the decimal inch. This standard gives

a series of standard types and classes of fits on a unilateral hole basis such that the fit produced by mating parts in any one class will produce approximately similar performance throughout the range of sizes. These tables prescribe the fit for any given size, or type of fit; they also prescribe the standard limits for the mating parts which will produce the fit.

The tables are designed for the basic hole system, §14.5. See Appendixes 5–9. For coverage of the metric system of tolerances and fits see §§14.11–14.13, and Appendixes 11–14.

Letter symbols to identify the five types of fits are

RC   Running or Sliding Clearance Fits
LC   Locational Clearance Fits
LT   Transition Clearance or Interference Fits
LN   Locational Interference Fits
FN   Force or Shrink Fits

These letter symbols, plus a number indicating the class of fit within each type, are used to indicate a complete fit. Thus, FN 4 means a Class 4 Force Fit. The fits are described [ANSI B4.1–1967 (R1987)] as follows.

RUNNING AND SLIDING FITS

Running and sliding fits, for which description of classes of fits and limits of clearance are given [Appendix 5], are intended to provide a similar running performance, with suitable lubrication allowance, throughout the range of sizes. The clearances for the first two classes, used chiefly as slide fits, increase more slowly with diameter than the other classes, so that accurate location is maintained even at the expense of free relative motion.

LOCATIONAL FITS

Locational fits [Appendixes 6–8] are fits intended to determine only the location of the mating parts; they may provide rigid or accurate location, as with interference fits, or provide some freedom of location, as with clearance fits. Accordingly they are divided into three groups: clearance fits, transition fits, and interference fits.

FORCE FITS

Force or shrink fits [Appendix 9] constitute a special type of interference fit, normally characterized by maintenance of constant bore pressures throughout the range of sizes. The interference therefore varies almost directly with diameter, and the difference between its minimum and maximum value is small, to maintain the resulting pressures within reasonable limits.

In the tables for each class of fit, the range of nominal sizes of shafts or holes is given in inches. To simplify the tables and reduce the space required to present them, the other values are given in thousandths of an inch. Minimum and maximum limits of clearance are given, the top number being the least clearance, or the allowance, and the lower number the maximum clearance, or the greatest looseness of fit. Then, under the heading "Standard Limits" are given the limits for the hole and for the shaft that are to be applied algebraically to the basic size to obtain the limits of size for the parts, using the basic hole system.

For example, take a 2.0000″ basic diameter with a Class RC 1 fit. This fit is given in Appendix 5. In the column headed "Nominal Size Range, Inches," find 1.97–3.15, which embraces the 2.0000″ basic size. Reading to the right we find under "Limits of Clearance" the values 0.4 and 1.2, representing the maximum and minimum clearance between the parts *in thousandths of an inch*. To get these values in inches, simply multiply by one thousandth; thus, $\frac{4}{10} \times \frac{1}{1000} = .0004″$. To convert 0.4 thousandths to inches, simply move the decimal point three places to the left; thus: .0004″. Therefore, for this 2.0000″ diameter, with a Class RC 1 fit, the minimum clearance, or allowance, is .0004″, and the maximum clearance, representing the greatest looseness, is .0012″.

Reading farther to the right, we find under "Standard Limits" the value +0.5, which converted to inches is .0005″. Add this to the basic size thus: 2.0000″ + .0005″ = 2.0005″, the upper limit of the hole. Since the other value given for the hole is zero, the lower limit of the hole is the basic size of the hole, or 2.0000″. The hole would then be dimensioned as

$$\begin{matrix}2.0005\\2.0000\end{matrix}\quad or \quad 2.0000\ \begin{matrix}+.0005\\-.0000\end{matrix}$$

The limits for the shaft are read as $-.0004''$ and $-.0007''$. To get the limits of the shaft, subtract these values from the basic size; thus,

$$2.0000'' - .0004'' = 1.9996'' \text{ (upper limit)}$$
$$2.0000'' - .0007'' = 1.9993'' \text{ (lower limit)}$$

The shaft would then be dimensioned in inches as follows.

$$\begin{matrix}1.9996\\1.9993\end{matrix}\quad or \quad 1.9996\ \begin{matrix}+.0000\\-.0003\end{matrix}$$

14.9 Accumulation of Tolerances

In tolerance dimensioning, it is very important to consider the effect of one tolerance on another. When the location of a surface in a given direction is affected by more than one tolerance figure, the tolerances are *cumulative*. For example, in Fig. 14.10 (a), if dimension Z is omitted, surface A will be controlled by both dimensions X and Y, and there could be a total variation of .010″ instead of the variation of .005″ permitted by dimension Y, which is the dimension directly applied to surface A. Further, if the part is made to all the minimum tolerances of X, Y, and Z, the total variation in the length of the part will be .015″, and the part can be as short as 2.985″. However, the tolerance on the overall dimension W is only .005″, permitting the part to be only as short as 2.995″. The part is superfluously dimensioned.

In some cases, for functional reasons, it may be desired to hold all three small dimensions X, Y, and Z closely without regard to the overall length. In

such a case the overall dimension is just a *reference dimension* and should be marked REF. In other cases it may be desired to hold two small dimensions X and Y and the overall closely without regard to dimension Z. In that case, dimension Z should be omitted, or marked REF.

As a rule, it is best to dimension each surface so that it is affected by only one dimension. This can be done by referring all dimensions to a single datum surface, such as B, as shown at (b). See also Fig. 13.37 (d), (e), and (f).

14.10 Tolerances and Machining Processes

As has been repeatedly stated in this chapter, tolerances should be as coarse as possible and still permit satisfactory use of the part. If this is done, great savings can be effected as a result of the use of less expensive tools, lower labor and inspection costs, and reduced scrapping of material.

Figure 14.11 shows a chart of tolerance grades obtainable in relation to the accuracy of machining processes that may be used as a guide by the designer. Metric values may be ascertained by multiplying the given decimal-inch values by 25.4 and rounding off the product to one less place to the right of the decimal point than given for the decimal-inch value. See §13.10. For detailed information on manufacturing processes and measuring devices see Chapter 12.

14.11 Metric System of Tolerances and Fits

The preceding material on limits and fits between mating parts is suitable, without need of conversion, for the decimal-inch system of measurement. A sys-

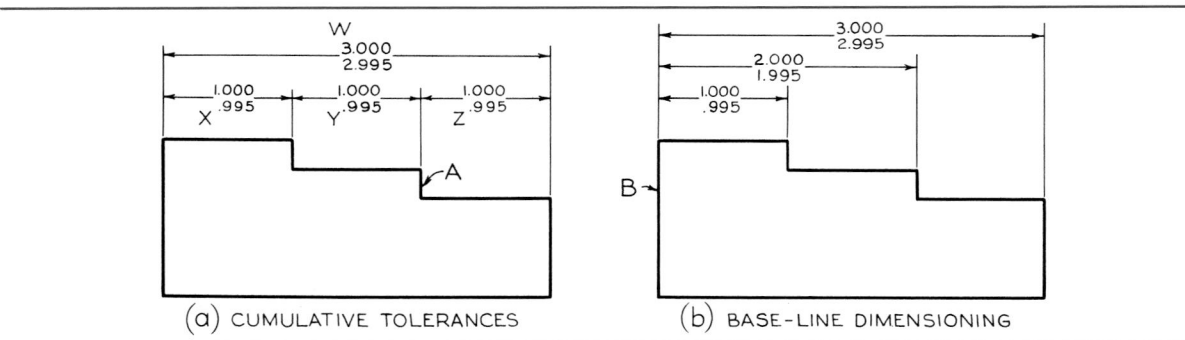

Fig. 14.10 Cumulative Tolerances.

Range of Sizes		Tolerances								
From	To & Incl.									
.000	.599	.00015	.0002	.0003	.0005	.0008	.0012	.002	.003	.005
.600	.999	.00015	.00025	.0004	.0006	.001	.0015	.0025	.004	.006
1.000	1.499	.0002	.0003	.0005	.0008	.0012	.002	.003	.005	.008
1.500	2.799	.00025	.0004	.0006	.001	.0015	.0025	.004	.006	.010
2.800	4.499	.0003	.0005	.0008	.0012	.002	.003	.005	.008	.012
4.500	7.799	.0004	.0006	.001	.0015	.0025	.004	.006	.010	.015
7.800	13.599	.0005	.0008	.0012	.002	.003	.005	.008	.012	.020
13.600	20.999	.0006	.001	.0015	.0025	.004	.006	.010	.015	.025

| Lapping & Honing |
| Grinding, Diamond Turning & Boring |
| Broaching |
| Reaming |
| Turning, Boring, Slotting, Planing & Shaping |
| Milling |
| Drilling |

Fig. 14.11 Tolerances Related to Machining Processes.

tem of preferred metric limits and fits by the International Organization for Standardization (ISO) is in the ANSI B4.2 standard. The system is specified for holes, cylinders, and shafts, but it is also adaptable to fits between parallel surfaces of such features as keys and slots. The following terms for metric fits, although somewhat similar to those for decimal-inch fits, are illustrated in Fig. 14.12.

Basic size The size from which limits or deviations are assigned. Basic sizes, usually diameters, should be selected from a table of preferred sizes. See Fig. 14.17.

Deviation The difference between the basic size and the hole or shaft size. (This is equivalent to the tolerance in the decimal-inch system.)

Upper deviation The difference between the basic size and the permitted maximum size of the part. (This compares with the maximum tolerance in the decimal-inch system.)

Lower deviation The difference between the basic size and the minimum permitted size of the part. (This compares with the minimum tolerance in the decimal-inch system.)

Fundamental deviation The deviation closest to the basic size. (This compares with the minimum allowance in the decimal-inch system.)

Tolerance The difference between the permitted minimum and maximum size of a part.

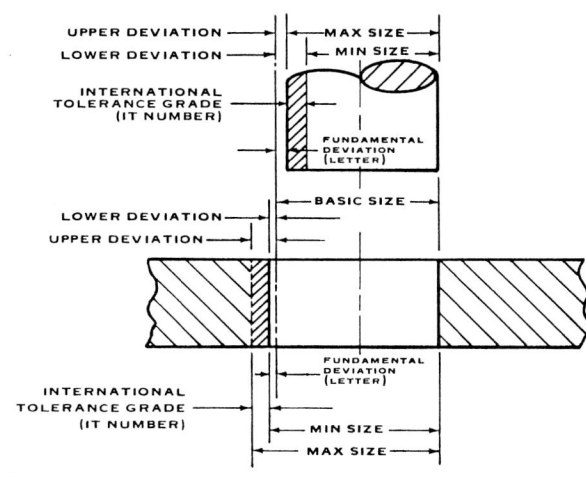

Fig. 14.12 Terms Related to Metric Limits and Fits [ANSI B4.2–1978 (R1984)].

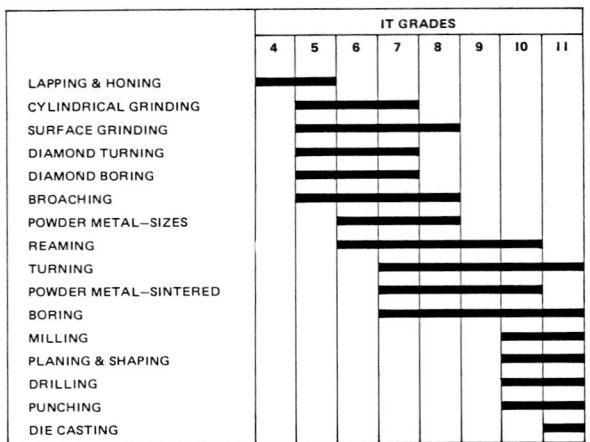

Fig. 14.13 International Tolerance Grades Related to Machining Processes [ANSI B4.2–1978 (R1984)].

International tolerance grade (IT) A set of tolerances that varies according to the basic size and provides a uniform level of accuracy within the grade. For example, in the dimension 50 H8 for a close-running fit, the IT grade is indicated by the numeral 8. (The letter H indicates the tolerance is on the hole for the 50 mm dimension.) In all, there are 18 IT grades—IT01, IT0, and IT1 through IT16. See Figs. 14.13 and 14.14 for IT grades related to machining processes and the practical use of the IT grades. See also Appendix 10.

Tolerance zone The tolerance and its position in relation to basic size. It is established by a combination of the fundamental deviation indicated by a letter and the IT grade number. In the dimension of 50 H8, for the close running fit, the H8 specifies the tolerance zone. See Fig. 14.14.

Hole-basis system of preferred fits A system based upon the basic diameter as the minimum size. For the generally preferred hole-basis system, the fundamental deviation is specified by the uppercase letter H. See Fig. 14.15 (a).

Shaft-basis system of preferred fits A system based upon the basic diameter as the maximum size of the shaft. The fundamental deviation is given by the lowercase letter f. See Fig. 14.15 (b).

Interference fit A fit that results in an interference fit between two mating parts under *all* tolerance conditions.

Transition fit A fit that results in either a clearance or an interference condition between two assembled parts.

Tolerance symbols Symbols used to specify the tolerances and fits for mating parts. See Fig. 14.15 (c). For the hole-basis system, the **50** indicates the diameter in millimeters; the fundamental deviation for the hole is indicated by the capital letter H and for the shaft it is indicated by the lowercase letter f. The numbers following the letters indicate this IT grade. Note that the symbols for the hole and shaft are separated by the slash (slanting

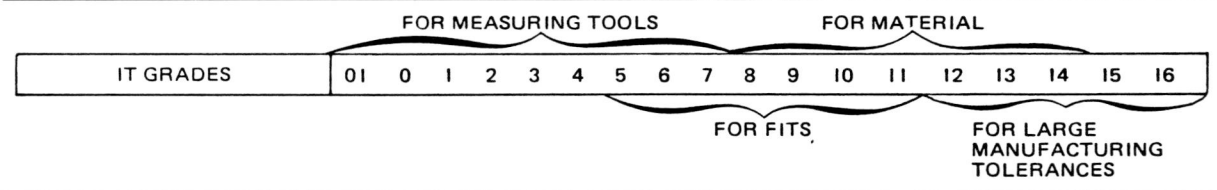

Fig. 14.14 Practical Use of International Tolerance Grades.

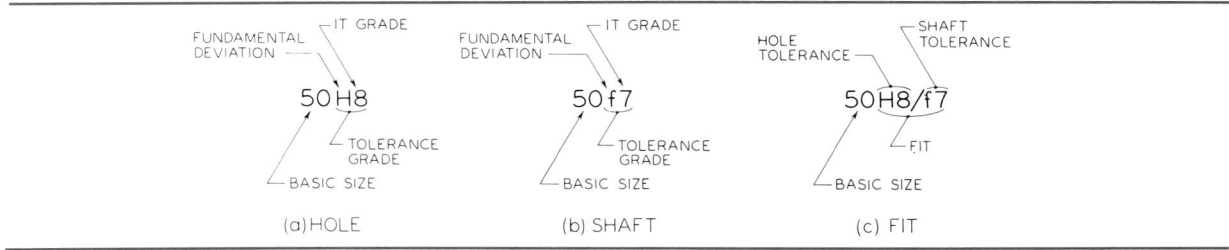

Fig. 14.15 Application of Definitions and Symbols to Holes and Shafts [ANSI B4.2–1978 (R1984)].

50 H8	50H8$\left(\dfrac{50.039}{50.000}\right)$	$\dfrac{50.039}{50.000}$(50H8)
(a) PREFERRED	(b)	(c)

Fig. 14.16 Acceptable Methods of Giving Tolerance Symbols [ANSI Y14.5M–1982 (R1988)].

line). Tolerance symbols may be given in several acceptable forms as in Fig. 14.16 for a 50 mm diameter hole. The values in parentheses are for reference only and may be omitted. The upper and lower limit values may be found in Appendix 11.

14.12 Preferred Sizes
The preferred basic sizes for computing tolerances are given in Table 14.1. Basic diameters should be selected from the first choice column since these are readily available stock sizes for round, square, and hexagonal products.

14.13 Preferred Fits
The symbols for either the hole-basis or shaft-basis preferred fits (clearance, transition, and interference) are given in Table 14.2. Fits should be selected from this table for mating parts where possible.

The values corresponding to the fits are found in Appendixes 11–14. Although second and third choice basic size diameters are possible, they must be calculated from tables not included in this text. For the generally preferred hole-basis system, note that the ISO symbols range from H11/c11 (loose running) to H7/u6 (force fit). For the shaft-basis system, the preferred symbols range from C11/h11 (loose fit) to U7/h6 (force fit).

Assume that it is desired to use the symbols to specify the dimensions for a free-running fit (hole basis) for a proposed diameter of 48 mm. Since 48 mm is not listed as a preferred size in Table 14.1, the design is altered to use the acceptable 50 mm diameter. From the preferred fits descriptions in Table 14.2, the free-running fit (hole-basis) is H9/d9. To determine the upper and lower deviation

Table 14.1 *Preferred Sizes* [ANSI B4.2–1978 (R1984)]

Basic Size, mm		Basic Size, mm		Basic Size, mm	
First Choice	Second Choice	First Choice	Second Choice	First Choice	Second Choice
1		10		100	
	1.1		11		110
1.2		12		120	
	1.4		14		140
1.6		16		160	
	1.8		18		180
2		20		200	
	2.2		22		220
2.5		25		250	
	2.8		28		280
3		30		300	
	3.5		35		350
4		40		400	
	4.5		45		450
5		50		500	
	5.5		55		550
6		60		600	
	7		70		700
8		80		800	
	9		90		900
				1000	

Table 14.2 *Preferred Fits* [ANSI B4.2–1978 (R1984)]

Hole Basis	Shaft[a] Basis	Description	
	ISO Symbol		
Hole Basis	**Shaft[a] Basis**	**Description**	
Clearance Fits			More clearance
H11/c11	C11/h11	**Loose running** fit for wide commercial tolerances or allowances on external members.	
H9/d9	D9/h9	**Free running** fit not for use where accuracy is essential, but good for large temperature variations, high running speeds, or heavy journal pressures.	
H8/f7	F8/h7	**Close running** fit for running on accurate machines and for accurate location at moderate speeds and journal pressures.	
H7/g6	G7/h6	**Sliding** fit not intended to run freely, but to move and turn freely and locate accurately.	
Transition Fits			
H7/h6	H7/h6	**Locational clearance** fit provides snug fit for locating stationary parts; but can be freely assembled and disassembled.	
H7/k6	K7/h6	**Locational transition** fit for accurate location, a compromise between clearance and interference.	
H7/n6	N7/h6	**Locational transition** fit for more accurate location where greater interference is permissible.	
Interference Fits			More interference
H7/p6	P7/h6	**Locational interference** fit for parts requiring rigidity and alignment with prime accuracy of location but without special bore pressure requirements.	
H7/s6	S7/h6	**Medium drive** fit for ordinary steel parts or shrink fits on light sections, the tightest fit usable with cast iron.	
H7/u6	U7/h6	**Force** fit suitable for parts which can be highly stressed or for shrink fits where the heavy pressing forces required are impractical.	

[a]The transition and interference shaft basis fits shown do not convert to exactly the same hole basis fit conditions for basic sizes in range from Q through 3 mm. Interference fit P7/h6 converts to a transition fit H7/p6 in the above size range.

limits of the hole as given in the preferred hole-basis table, Appendix 11, follow across from the basic size of 50 to H9 under "Free running." The limits for the hole are 50.000 and 50.062 mm. Then, the upper and lower limits of deviation for the shaft are found in the d9 column under "Free running." They are 49.920 and 49.858 mm, respectively. Limits for other fits are established in a similar manner.

The limits for the shaft basis dimensioning are determined similarly from the preferred shaft basis table in Appendix 13. See Figs. 14.16 and 14.17 for acceptable methods of specifying tolerances by symbols on drawings. A single note for the mating parts (free-running fit, hole basis) would be ⌀50 H9/d9, Fig. 14.17.

14.14 Geometric Tolerancing

Geometric tolerances state the maximum allowable variations of a form or its position from the perfect geometry implied on the drawing. The term "geo-metric" refers to various forms, such as a plane, a cylinder, a cone, a square, a hexagon. Theoretically these are perfect forms, but, because it is impossible to produce perfect forms, it may be necessary to specify the amount of variation permitted. These tolerances specify either the diameter or the width of a tolerance zone within which a surface or the axis of a cylinder or a hole must be if the part is to meet the required accuracy for proper function and fit. When tolerances of form are not given on a drawing, it is customary to assume that, regardless of form variations, the part will fit and function satisfactorily.

Tolerances of form and position or location control such characteristics as straightness, flatness, parallelism, perpendicularity (squareness), concentricity, roundness, angular displacement, and so on.

Methods of indicating geometric tolerances by means of *geometric characteristic symbols*, as recommended by ANSI, rather than by traditional notes, are discussed and illustrated subsequently.

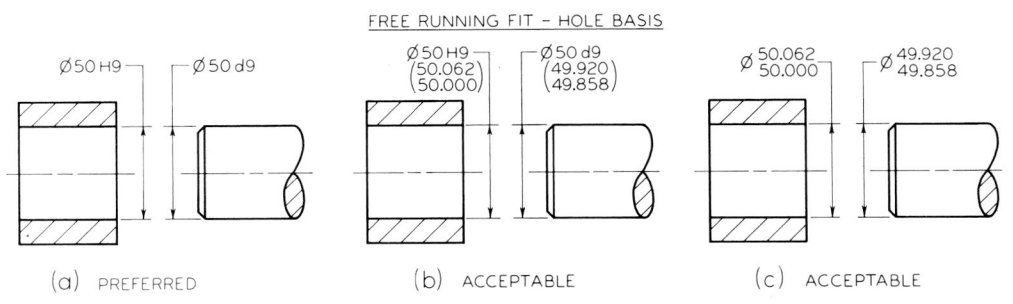

FREE RUNNING FIT – HOLE BASIS

(a) PREFERRED (b) ACCEPTABLE (c) ACCEPTABLE

Fig. 14.17 Methods of Specifying Tolerances with Symbols for Mating Parts.

See the latest Dimensioning and Tolerancing Standard [Y14.5M–1982 (R1988)] for more complete coverage.

14.15 Symbols for Tolerances of Position and Form

Since traditional narrative notes for specifying tolerances of *position* (location) and *form* (shape) may be confusing or not clear, may require much of the space available on the drawing, and often may not be understood internationally, most multinational companies have adopted symbols for such specifi-

cations [ANSI Y14.5M–1982 (R1988)]. These ANSI symbols provide an accurate and concise means of specifying geometric characteristics and tolerances in a minimum of space, Table 14.3. The symbols may be supplemented by notes if the precise geometric requirements cannot be conveyed by the symbols. For construction details of the geometric tolerancing symbols, see Appendix 32.

Combinations of the various symbols and their meanings are given in Fig. 14.18. Application of the symbols to a drawing are illustrated in Fig. 14.43.

The geometric characteristic symbols plus the

Table 14.3 *Geometric Characteristics and Modifying Symbols* [ANSI Y14.5M–1982 (R1988)]

Geometric characteristic symbols

Type of Tolerance		Characteristic	Symbol
For individual features	Form	Straightness	—
		Flatness	▱
		Circularity (roundness)	○
		Cylindricity	/○/
For individual or related features	Profile	Profile of a line	⌒
		Profile of a surface	⌓
For related features	Orientation	Angularity	∠
		Perpendicularity	⊥
		Parallelism	//
	Location	Position	⊕
		Concentricity	◎
	Runout	Circular runout	↗
		Total runout	↗↗ [a]

Modifying symbols

Term	Symbol
At maximum material condition	Ⓜ
Regardless of feature size	Ⓢ
At least material condition	Ⓛ
Projected tolerance zone	Ⓟ
Diameter	⌀
Spherical diameter	S⌀
Radius	R
Spherical radius	SR
Reference	( )
Arc length	⌒

[a]Arrowhead(s) may be filled in.

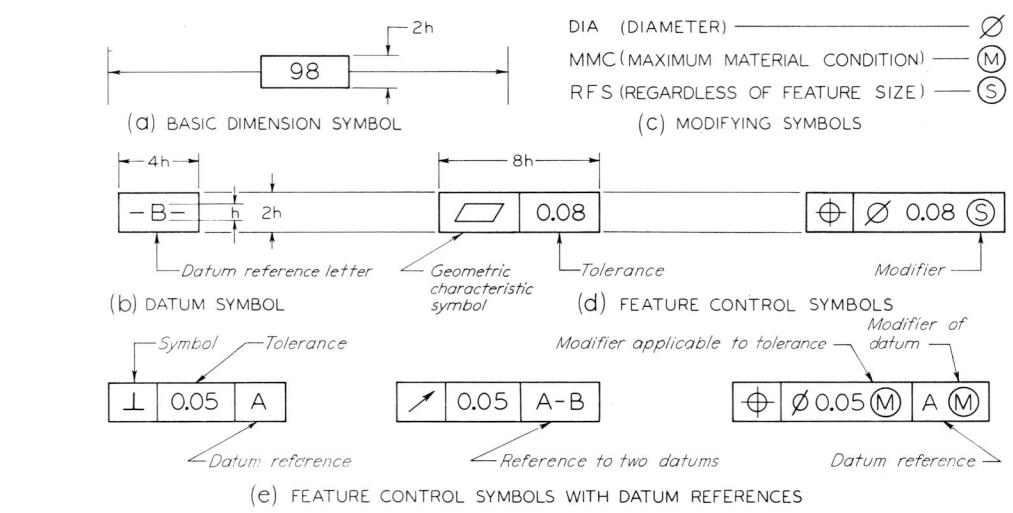

Fig. 14.18 Use of Symbols for Tolerance of Position and Form   [ANSI Y14.5M–1982 (R1988)].

supplementary symbols are further explained and illustrated with material adapted from ANSI Y14.5M–1982 (R1988), as follows.

Basic Dimension Symbol

The basic dimension is identified by the enclosing frame symbol, Fig. 14.18 (a). The basic dimension (size) is the value used to describe the theoretically exact size, shape, or location of a feature. It is the basis from which permissible variations are established by tolerances on other dimensions in notes, or in feature control frames.

Datum Identifying Symbol

The datum identifying symbol consists of frame containing a reference letter preceded and followed by a dash, Fig. 14.18 (b). A point, line, plane, cylinder, or other geometric form assumed to be exact for purposes of computation may serve as a datum from which the location or geometric relationship of features of a part may be established.

Supplementary Symbols

The symbols for MMC (maximum material condition, i.e., minimum hole diameter, maximum shaft diameter) and RFS (regardless of feature size—the tolerance applies to any size of the feature within its size tolerance and or the actual size of a datum feature) are illustrated in Fig. 14.18 (c). The abbreviations MMC and RFS are also used in notes. See also Table 14.3.

The symbol for diameter is used instead of the abbreviation DIA to indicate a diameter, and it precedes the specified tolerance in a feature control symbol, Fig. 14.18 (d). This symbol for diameter instead of the abbreviation DIA may be used on a drawing, and it should precede the dimension. For narrative notes, the abbreviation DIA is preferred.

Combined Symbols

Individual symbols, datum reference letters, needed tolerances, and so on may be combined in a single frame, Fig. 14.18 (e).

A position of form tolerance is given by a feature control symbol made up of a frame about the appropriate geometric characteristic symbol plus the allowable tolerance. A vertical line separates the symbol and the tolerance, Fig. 14.18 (d). Where needed, the tolerance should be preceded by the symbol for diameter and followed by the symbol for MMC or RFS.

A tolerance of position or form related to a datum is so indicated in the feature control symbol by placing the datum reference letter following either the geometric characteristic symbol or the tolerance. Vertical lines separate the entries, and, where applicable, the datum reference letter entry includes the symbol for MMC or RFS. See Fig. 14.18.

14.16 Positional Tolerances

In §13.25 are shown a number of examples of the traditional methods of locating holes, that is, by means of rectangular coordinates or angular dimen-

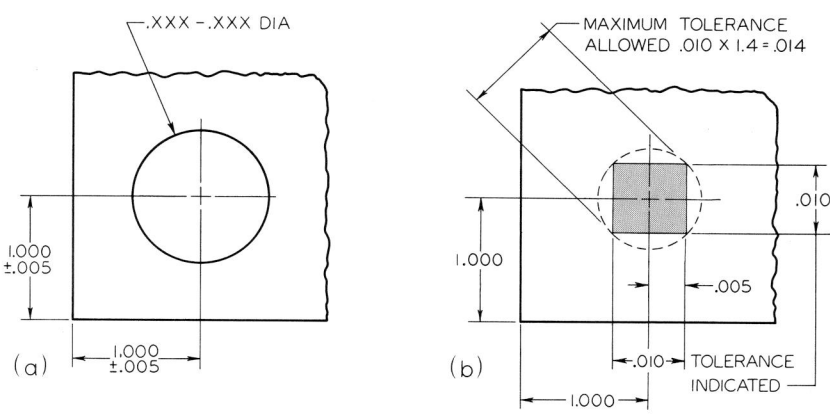

Fig. 14.19   Tolerance Zones.

sions. Each dimension has a tolerance, either given directly or indicated on the completed drawing by a general note.

For example, in Fig. 14.19 (a) is shown a hole located from two surfaces at right angles to each other. As shown at (b), the center may lie anywhere within a square tolerance zone, the sides of which are equal to the tolerances. Thus, the total variations along either diagonal of the square by the coordinate method of dimensioning will be 1.4 times greater than the indicated tolerance. Hence, a .014 diameter tolerance zone would increase the square tolerance zone area 57 percent without exceeding the tolerance permitted along the diagonal of the square tolerance zone.

Features located by toleranced angular and radial dimensions will have a wedge-shaped tolerance zone. See Fig. 14.28.

If four holes are dimensioned with rectangular coordinates as in Fig. 14.20 (a), acceptable patterns for the square tolerance zones for the holes are shown at (b) and (c). The locational tolerances are actually greater than indicated by the dimensions.

Feature control symbols are related to the feature by one of several methods illustrated in Fig. 14.43. The following methods are preferred.

1. Adding the symbol to a note or dimension pertaining to the feature.

2. Running a leader from the symbol to the feature.

3. Attaching the side, end, or corner of the symbol frame to an extension line from the feature.

4. Attaching a side or end of the symbol frame to the dimension line pertaining to the feature.

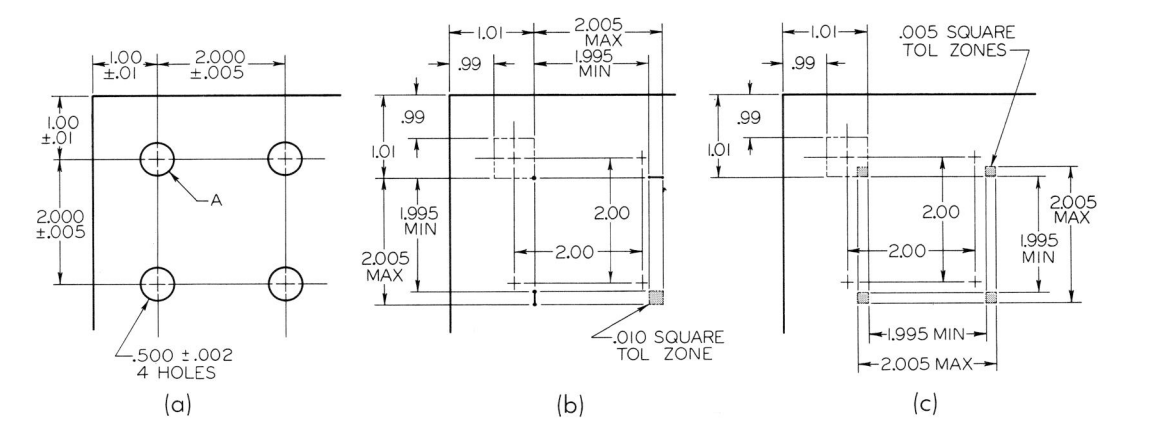

Fig. 14.20   Tolerance Zones.

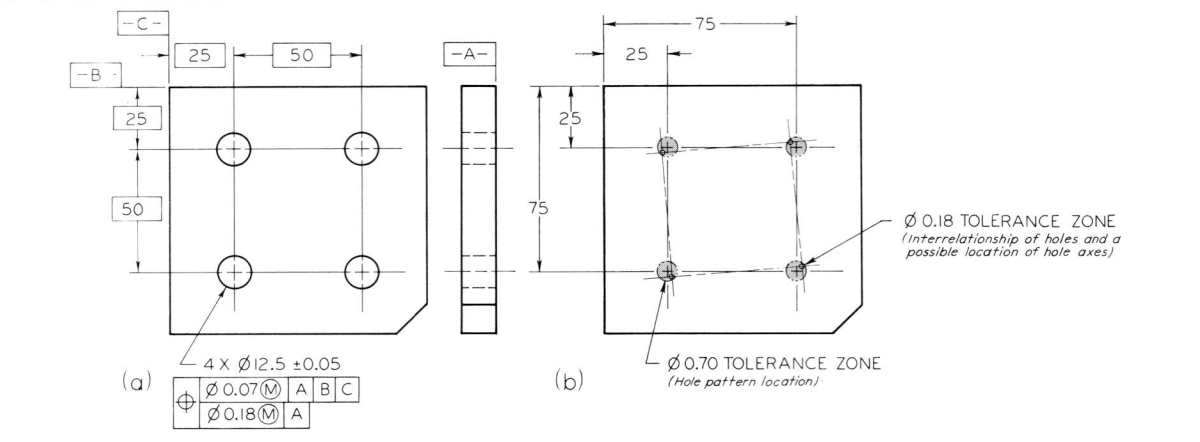

Fig. 14.21   True-Position Dimensioning   [ANSI Y14.5M–1982 (R1988)].

In Fig. 14.20 (a), hole **A** is selected as a datum, and the other three are located from it. The square tolerance zone for hole **A** results from the tolerances on the two rectangular coordinate dimensions locating hole **A**. The sizes of the tolerance zones for the other three holes result from the tolerances between the holes, while their locations will vary according to the actual location of the datum hole **A**. Two of the many possible zone patterns are shown at (b) and (c).

Thus, with the dimensions shown at (a), it is difficult to say whether the resulting parts will actually fit the mating parts satisfactorily even though they conform to the tolerances shown on the drawing.

These disadvantages are overcome by giving exact theoretical locations by untoleranced dimensions and then specifying by a note how far actual positions may be displaced from these locations. This is

called *true-position dimensioning*. It will be seen that the tolerance zone for each hole will be a circle, the size of the circle depending upon the amount of variation permitted from "true position."

A true-position dimension denotes the theoretically exact position of a feature. The location of each feature such as a hole, slot, stud, and so on, is given by untoleranced basic dimensions identified by the enclosing frame or symbol. To prevent misunderstandings, true position should be established with respect to a datum.

In simple arrangements, the choice of a datum may be obvious and not require identification.

Positional tolerancing is identified by a characteristic symbol directed to a feature, which establishes a circular tolerance zone, Fig. 14.21.

Actually, the "circular tolerance zone" is a cylindrical tolerance zone (the diameter of which is equal

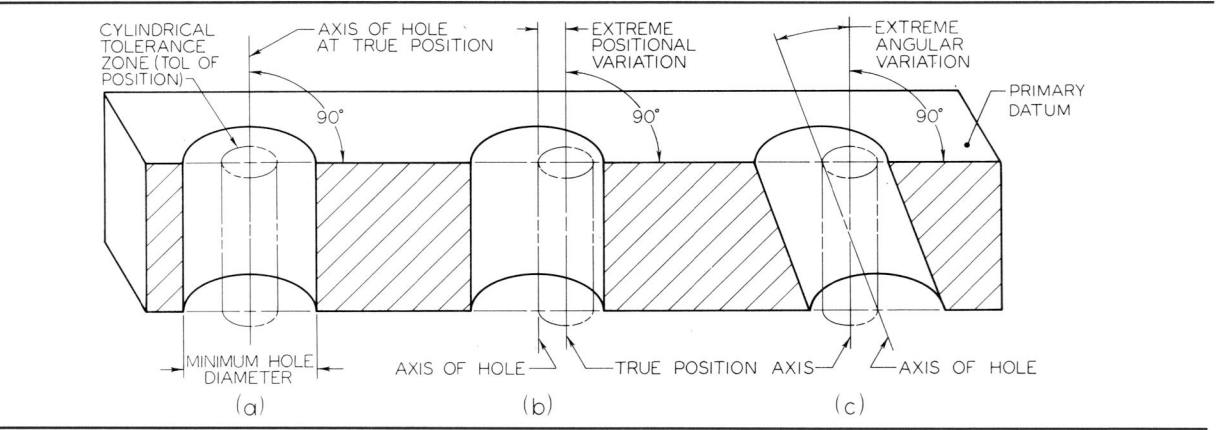

Fig. 14.22   Cylindrical Tolerance Zone   [ANSI Y14.5M–1982 (R1988)].

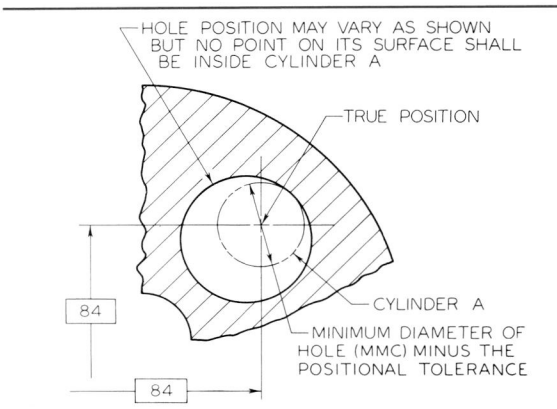

Fig. 14.23 True Position Interpretation [ANSI Y14.5M–1982 (R1988)].

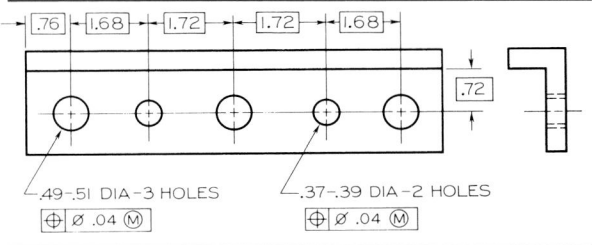

Fig. 14.24 No Tolerance Accumulation.

to the positional tolerance and its length is equal to the length of the feature unless otherwise specified), and its axis must be within this cylinder, Fig. 14.22.

The center line of the hole may coincide with the center line of the cylindrical tolerance zone, (a), or it may be parallel to it but displaced so as to remain within the tolerance cylinder, (b), or it may be inclined while remaining within the tolerance cylinder, (c). In this last case we see that the positional tolerance also defines the limits of squareness variation.

In terms of the cylindrical surface of the hole, the positional tolerance specification indicates that all elements on the hole surface must be on or outside a cylinder whose diameter is equal to the minimum diameter (MMC; §14.17) or the maximum diameter of the hole minus the positional tolerance (diameter, or twice the radius), with the center line of the cylinder located at true position, Fig. 14.23.

The use of basic untoleranced dimensions to locate features at true position avoids one of the chief difficulties in tolerancing—the accumulation of tol-

erances, §14.9, even in a chain of dimensions. Fig. 14.24.

While features, such as holes and bosses, may vary in any direction from the true-position axis, other features, such as slots, may vary on either side of a true-position plane, Fig. 14.25.

Since the exact locations of the true positions are given by untoleranced dimensions, it is important to prevent the application of general tolerances to these. A note should be added to the drawing such as

GENERAL TOLERANCES DO NOT APPLY TO
BASIC TRUE–POSITION DIMENSIONS.

14.17 Maximum Material Condition

Maximum material condition, usually abbreviated to MMC, means that a feature of a finished product contains the maximum amount of material permitted by the toleranced size dimensions shown for that feature. Thus, we have MMC when holes, slots, or other internal features are at minimum size, or when shafts, pads, bosses, and other external features are at their maximum size. We have MMC for both mating parts when the largest shaft is in the smallest hole and there is the least clearance between the parts.

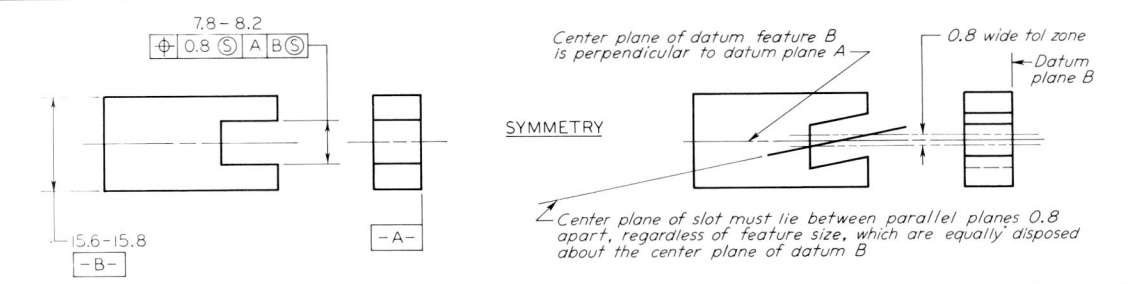

Fig. 14.25 Positional Tolerancing for Symmetry [ANSI Y14.5M–1982 (R1988)].

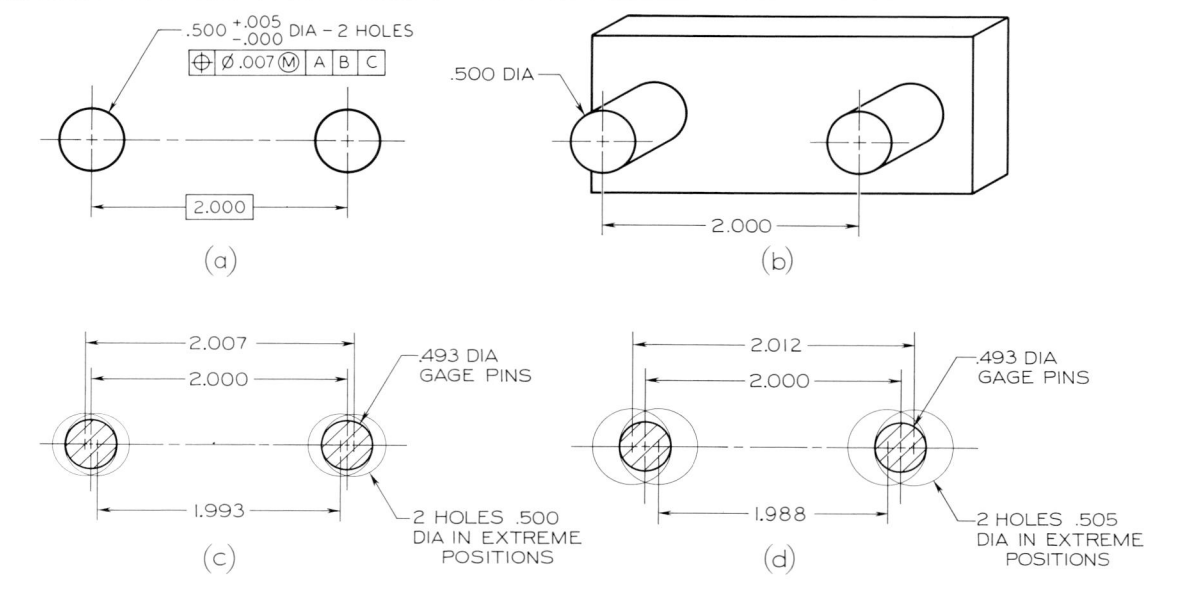

Fig. 14.26   Maximum and Minimum Material Conditions—Two-Hole Pattern   [ANSI   Y14.5M–1982 (R1988)].

In assigning positional tolerance to a hole, it is necessary to consider the size limits of the hole. If the hole is at MMC (smallest size), the positional tolerance is not affected, but if the hole is larger, the available positional tolerance is greater. In Fig. 14.26 (a) two half-inch holes are shown. If they are exactly .500″ in diameter (MMC, or smallest size) and are exactly 2.000″ apart, they should receive a gage, (b), made of two round pins .500″ in diameter fixed in a plate 2.000″ apart. However, the center-to-center distance between the holes may vary from 1.993″ to 2.007″.

If the .500″ diameter holes are at their extreme positions, (c), the pins in the gage would have to be .007″ smaller, or .493″ diameter, to enter the holes. Thus, if the .500″ diameter holes are located at the maximum distance apart, the .493″ diameter gage pins would contact the inner sides of the holes; and if the holes are located at the minimum distance apart, the .493″ diameter pins would contact the outer surfaces of the holes, as shown. If gagemakers' tolerances are not considered, the gage pins would have to be .493″ diameter and exactly 2.000 apart if the holes are .500 diameter, or MMC.

If the holes are .505″ diameter—that is, at maximum size, as at (d)—they will be accepted by the same .493″ diameter gage pins at 2.000″ apart if the inner sides of the holes contact the inner sides of the gage pins and the outer sides of the holes contact the outer sides of the gage pins, as shown. Thus the holes may be 2.012″ apart, which is beyond the tolerance permitted for the center-to-center distance between the holes. Similarly, the holes may be as close together as 1.988″ from center to center, which again is outside the specified positional tolerance.

Thus, when the holes are not at MCC—that is, when they are at maximum size—a greater positional tolerance becomes available. Since all features may vary in size, it is necessary to make clear on the drawing at what basic dimension the true position applies. In all but a few exceptional cases, the additional positional tolerance available, when holes are larger than minimum size, is acceptable and desirable. Parts thus accepted can be freely assembled whether or not the holes or other features are within the specified positional tolerance. This practice has been recognized and used in manufacturing for years, as is evident from the use of fixed-pin gages, which have been commonly used to inspect parts and control the least favorable condition of assembly. Thus it has become common practice for both manufacturing and inspection to assume that positional tolerance applies to MMC and that greater positional tolerance becomes permissible when the part is not at MMC.

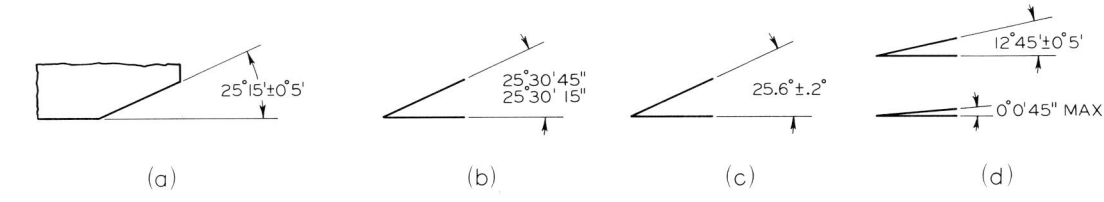

Fig. 14.27 Tolerances of Angles.

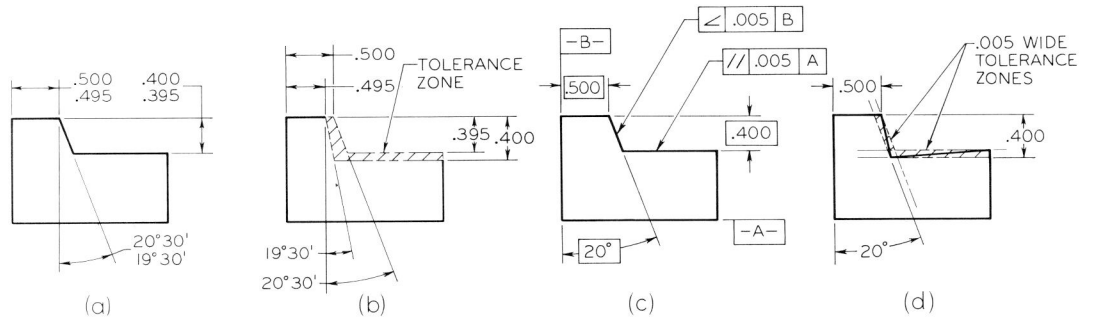

Fig. 14.28 Angular Tolerance Zones [ANSI Y14.5M–1982 (R1988)].

To avoid possible misinterpretation as to whether maximum material condition (MMC) or regardless of feature size (RFS) applies, it should be clearly stated on the drawing by the addition of MMC or RFS symbols to each applicable tolerance or by suitable coverage in a document referenced on the drawing.

When MMC or RFS is not specified on the drawing with respect to an individual tolerance, datum reference, or both, the following rules shall apply.

1. True-position tolerances and related datum references apply at MMC.

2. Angularity, parallelism, perpendicularity, concentricity, and symmetry tolerances, including related datum references, apply at RFS. No element of the actual feature is to extend beyond the envelope of the perfect form at MMC.

the tolerance had to be figured after considering the total displacement at the point farthest from the vertex of the angle before a tolerance could be specified that would not exceed the allowable displacement. The use of angular tolerances may be avoided by using gages. Taper turning is often handled by machining to fit a gage or by fitting to the mating part.

If an angular surface is located by a linear and an angular dimension, Fig. 14.28 (a), the surface must lie within a tolerance zone as shown at (b). The angular zone will be wider as the distance from the vertex increases. In order to avoid the accumulation of tolerances, that is, to decrease the tolerance zone, the *basic angle* tolerancing method of (c) is recommended [ANSI Y14.5M–1982 (R1988)]. The angle is indicated as basic with the proper symbol and no angular tolerance is specified. The tolerance zone is now defined by two parallel planes, resulting in improved angular control, (d).

14.18 Tolerances of Angles

Bilateral tolerances have traditionally been given on angles as illustrated in Fig. 14.27. Consequently, the wedge-shaped tolerance zone increases as the distance from the vertex of the angle increases. Thus,

14.19 Form Tolerances for Single Features

Straightness, flatness, roundness, cylindricity, and, in some instances, profile are form tolerances applicable to single features.

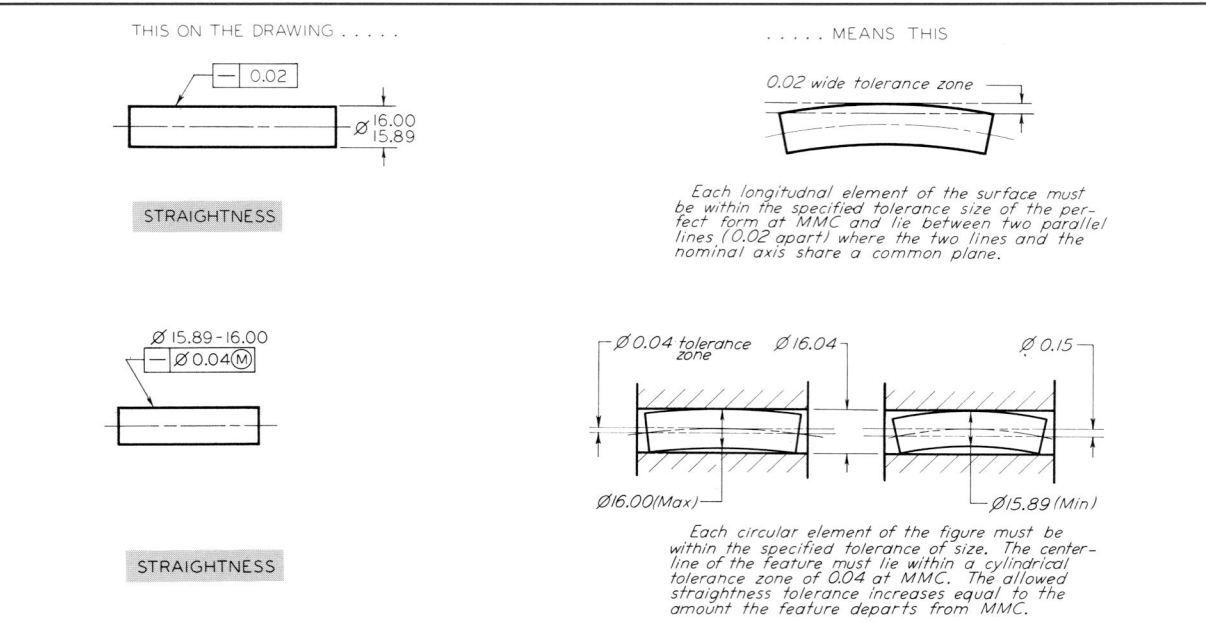

Fig. 14.29 Specifying Straightness [ANSI Y14.5M–1982 (R1988)].

Straightness Tolerance

A straightness tolerance specifies a tolerance zone within which an axis or all points of the considered element must lie, Fig. 14.29. Straightness is a condition where an element of a surface or an axis is a straight line.

Flatness Tolerance

A flatness tolerance specifies a tolerance zone defined by two parallel planes within which the surface must lie, Fig. 14.30. Flatness is the condition of a surface having all elements in one plane.

Roundness (Circularity) Tolerance

A roundness tolerance specifies a tolerance zone bounded by two concentric circles within which each circular element of the surface must lie, Fig.

14.31. Roundness is a condition of a surface of revolution where, for a cone or cylinder, all points of the surface intersected by any plane perpendicular to a common axis are equidistant from that axis. For a sphere, all points of the surface intersected by any plane passing through a common center are equidistant from that center.

Cylindricity Tolerance

A cylindricity tolerance specifies a tolerance zone bounded by two concentric cylinders within which the surface must lie, Fig. 14.32. This tolerance applies to both circular and longitudinal elements of the entire surface. Cylindricity is a condition of a surface of revolution in which all points of the surface are equidistant from a common axis. When no tolerance of form is given, many possible shapes may

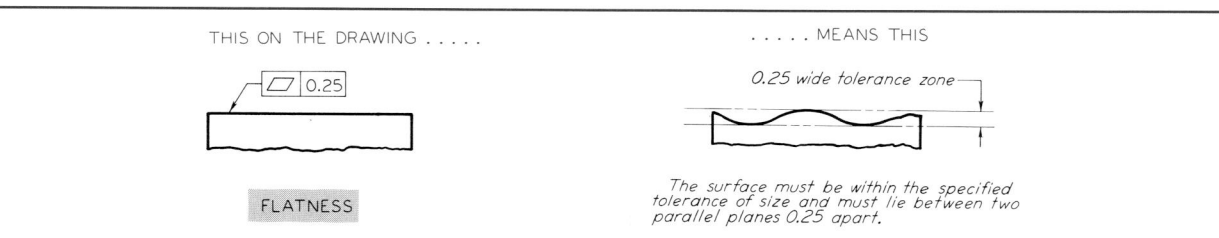

Fig. 14.30 Specifying Flatness [ANSI Y14.5M–1982 (R1988)].

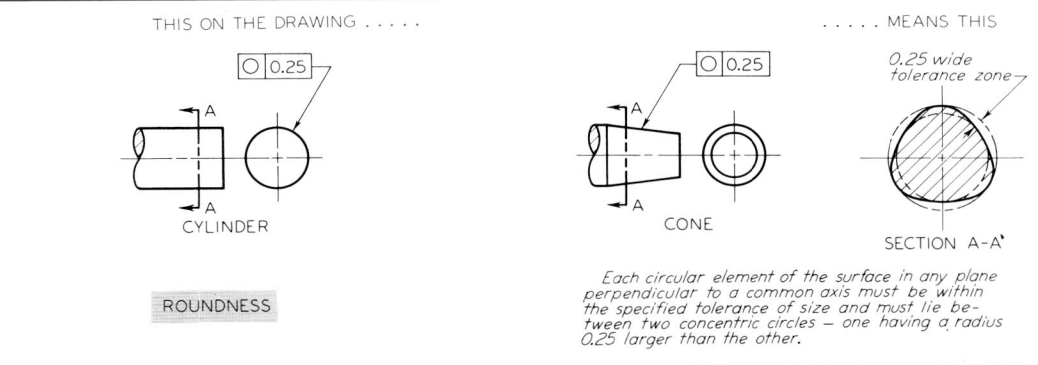

Fig. 14.31 Specifying Roundness for a Cylinder or Cone   [ANSI Y14.5M–1982 (R1988)].

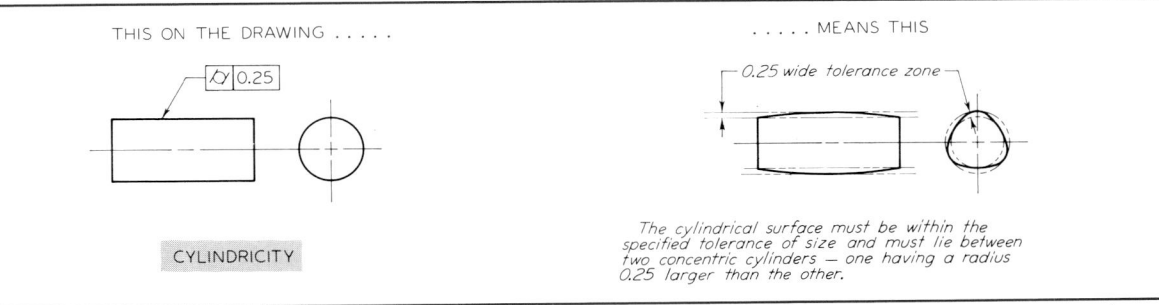

Fig. 14.32 Specifying Cylindricity   [ANSI Y14.5M–1982 (R1988)].

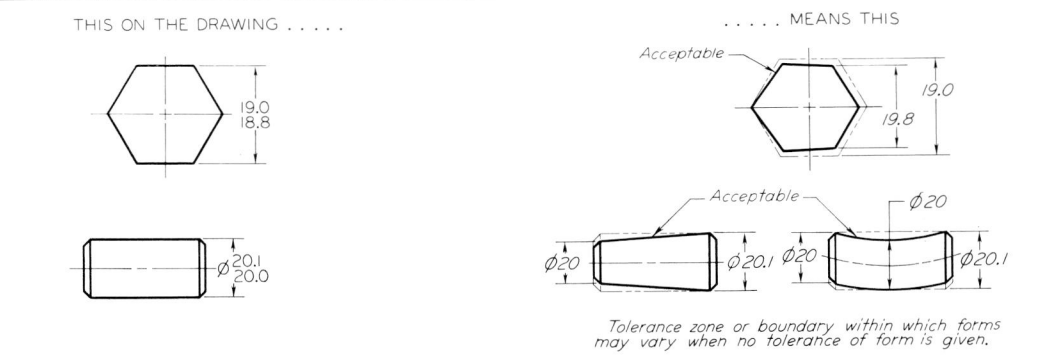

Fig. 14.33 Acceptable Variations of Form—No Specified Tolerance of Form.

exist within a tolerance zone, as illustrated in Fig. 14.33.

Profile Tolerance

A profile tolerance specifies a uniform boundary or zone along the true profile within which all elements of the surface must lie, Figs. 14.34 and 14.35. A profile is the outline of an object in a given plane (two-dimensional) figure. Profiles are formed by projecting a three-dimensional figure onto a plane or by taking cross sections through the figure with

the resulting profile composed of such elements as straight lines, arcs, or other curved lines.

14.20 Form Tolerances for Related Features

Angularity, parallelism, perpendicularity, and, in some instances, profile are form tolerances applicable to related features. These tolerances control the attitude of features to one another [ANSI Y14.5M–1982 (R1988)].

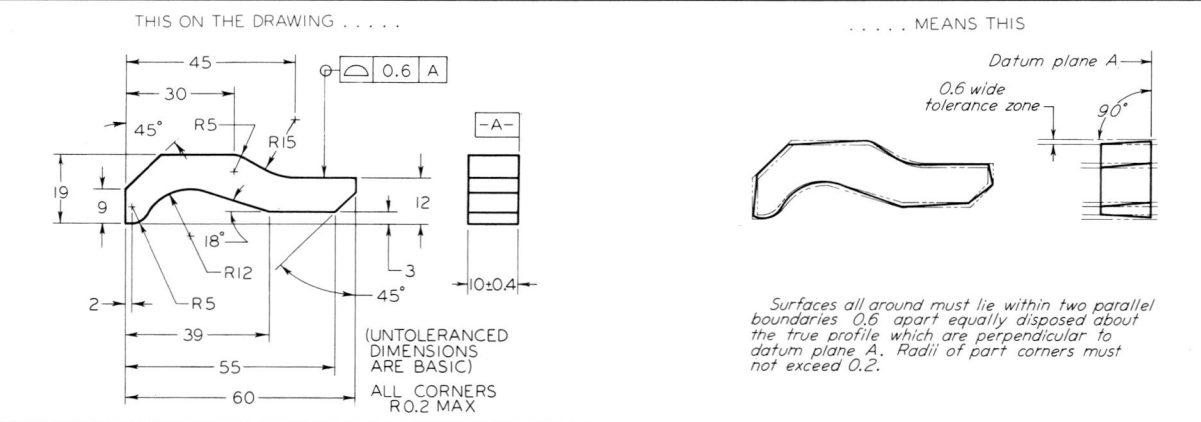

Fig. 14.34   Specifying Profile of a Surface All Around   [ANSI Y14.5M–1982 (R1988)].

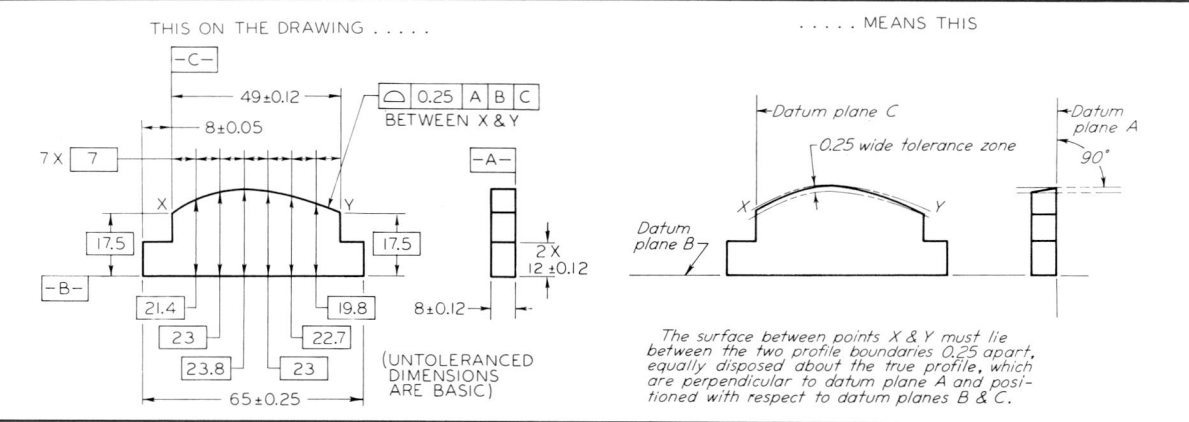

Fig. 14.35   Specifying Profile of a Surface Between Points   [ANSI Y14.5M–1982 (R1988)].

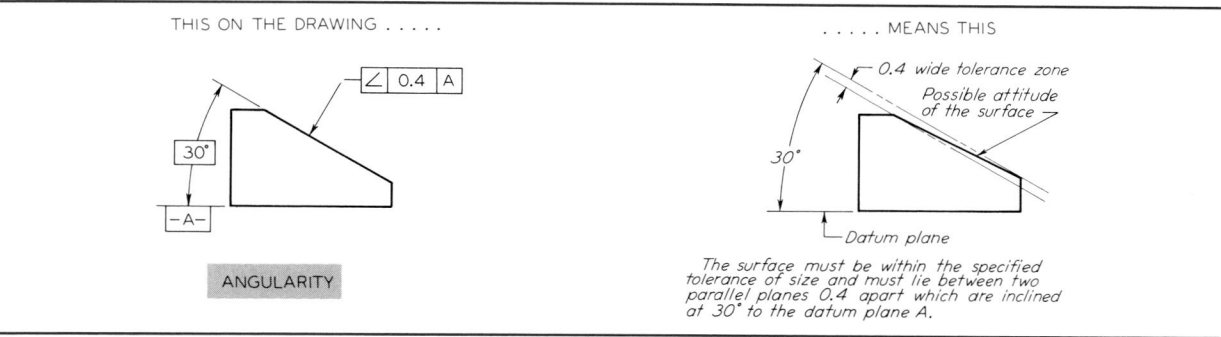

Fig. 14.36   Specifying Angularity for a Plane Surface   [ANSI Y14.5M–1982 (R1988)].

Angularity Tolerance

An angularity tolerance specifies a tolerance zone defined by two parallel planes at the specified basic angle (other than 90°) from a datum plane or axis within which the surface or the axis of the feature must lie, Fig. 14.36.

Parallelism Tolerance

A parallelism tolerance specifies a tolerance zone defined by two parallel planes or lines parallel to a datum plane or axis within which the surface or axis of the feature must lie or the parallelism tolerance may specify a cylindrical tolerance zone parallel to

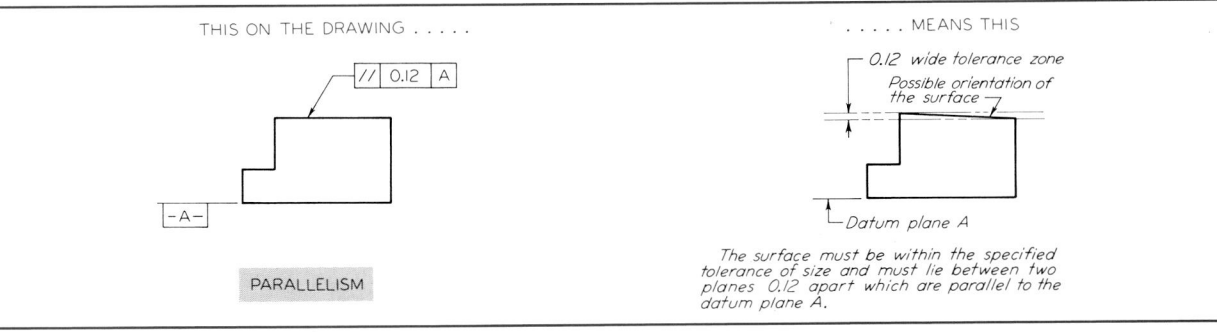

Fig. 14.37 Specifying Parallelism for a Plane Surface [ANSI Y14.5M–1982 (R1988)].

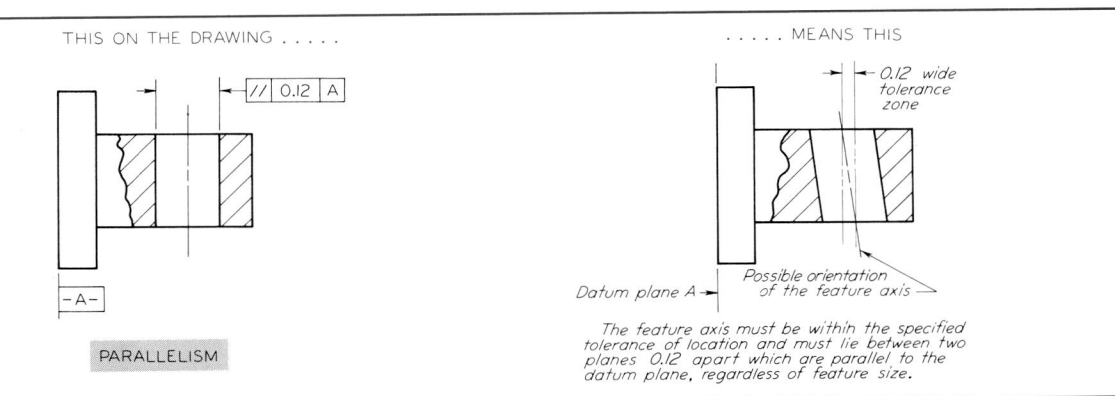

Fig. 14.38 Specifying Parallelism for an Axis Feature RFS [ANSI Y14.5M–1982 (R1988)].

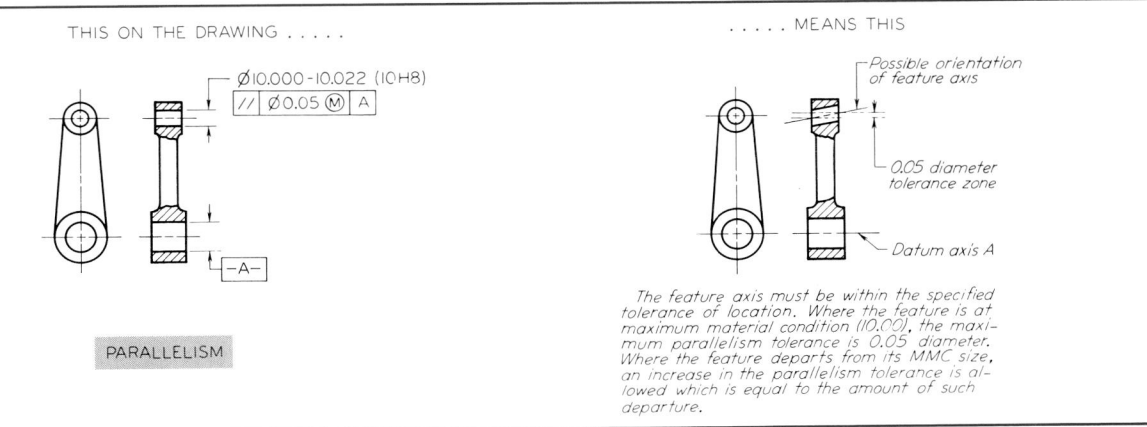

Fig. 14.39 Specifying Parallelism for an Axis Feature at MMC [ANSI Y14.5M–1982 (R1988)].

a datum axis within which the axis of the feature must lie, Figs. 14.37–14.39.

Perpendicularity Tolerance

Perpendicularity is a condition of a surface, median plane, or axis at 90° to a datum plane or axis. A perpendicularity tolerance specifies one of the following:

1. A tolerance zone defined by two parallel planes perpendicular to a datum plane, datum axis, or axis within which the surface of the feature must lie, Fig. 14.40.

2. A cylindrical tolerance zone perpendicular to a datum plane within which the axis of the feature must lie, Fig. 14.41.

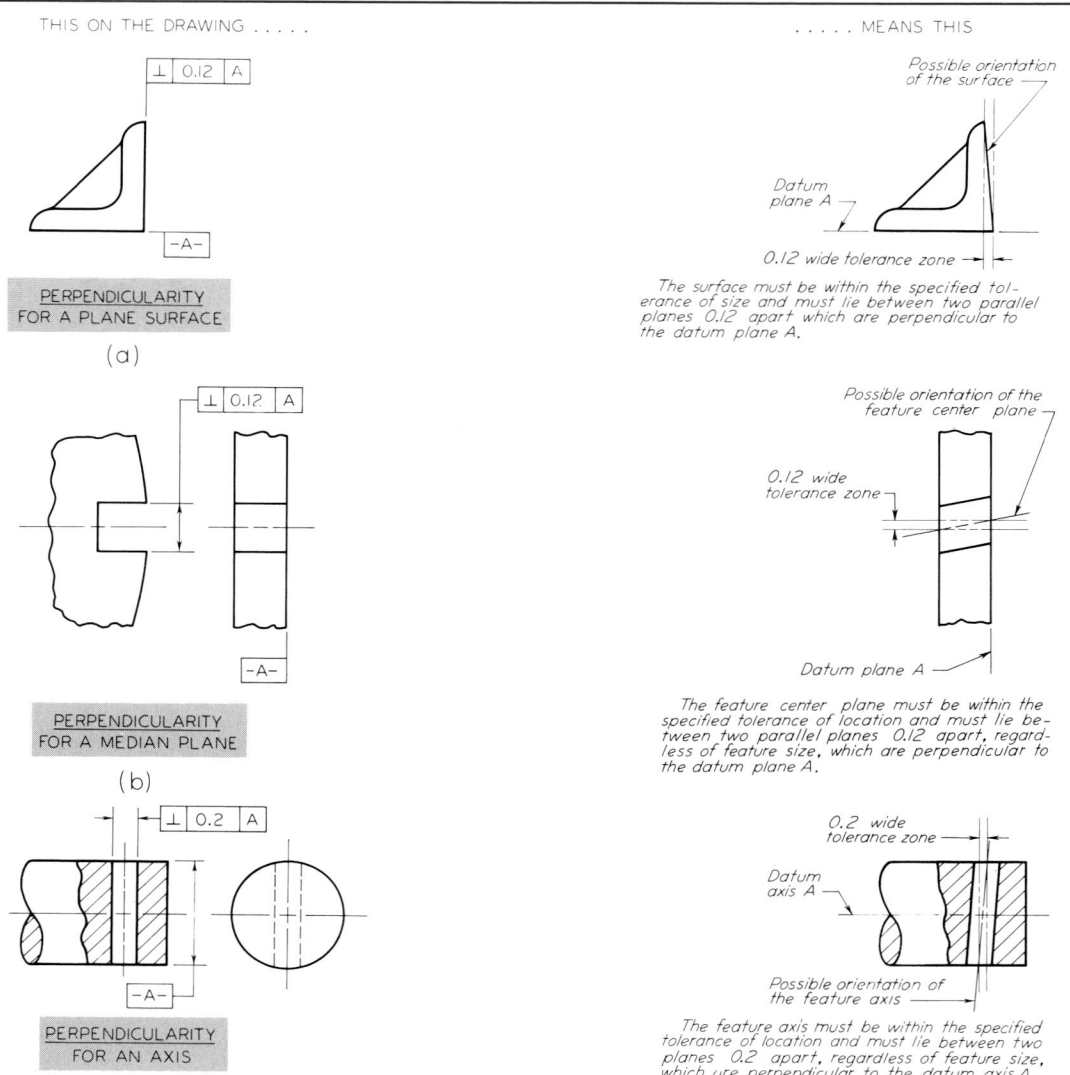

THIS ON THE DRAWING . . . . MEANS THIS

PERPENDICULARITY
FOR A PLANE SURFACE

(a)

Possible orientation of the surface

Datum plane A

0.12 wide tolerance zone

The surface must be within the specified tolerance of size and must lie between two parallel planes 0.12 apart which are perpendicular to the datum plane A.

PERPENDICULARITY
FOR A MEDIAN PLANE

(b)

Possible orientation of the feature center plane

0.12 wide tolerance zone

Datum plane A

The feature center plane must be within the specified tolerance of location and must lie between two parallel planes 0.12 apart, regardless of feature size, which are perpendicular to the datum plane A.

PERPENDICULARITY
FOR AN AXIS

(c)

0.2 wide tolerance zone

Datum axis A

Possible orientation of the feature axis

The feature axis must be within the specified tolerance of location and must lie between two planes 0.2 apart, regardless of feature size, which are perpendicular to the datum axis A.

Fig. 14.40   Specifying Perpendicularity   [ANSI Y14.5M–1982 (R1988)].

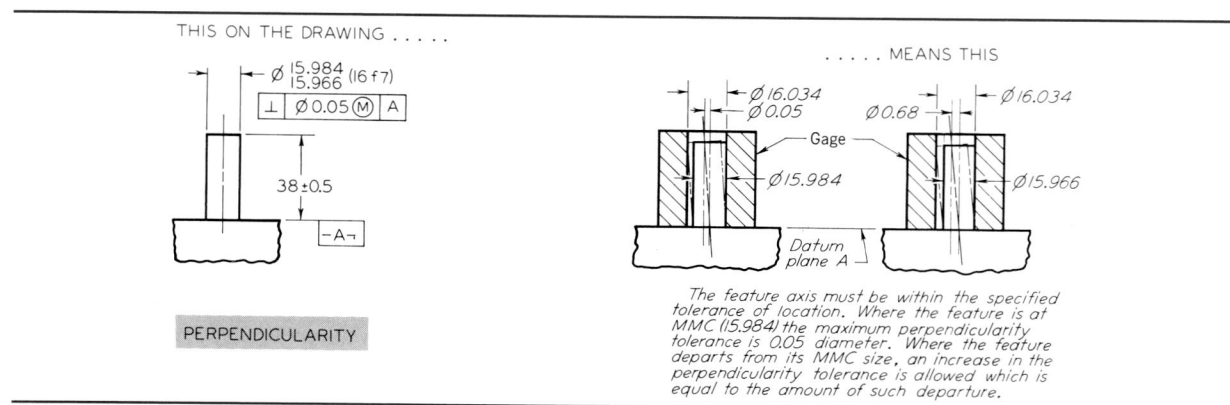

THIS ON THE DRAWING . . . . MEANS THIS

PERPENDICULARITY

Gage

The feature axis must be within the specified tolerance of location. Where the feature is at MMC (15.984) the maximum perpendicularity tolerance is 0.05 diameter. Where the feature departs from its MMC size, an increase in the perpendicularity tolerance is allowed which is equal to the amount of such departure.

Fig. 14.41   Specifying Perpendicularity for an Axis, Pin, or Boss   [ANSI Y14.5M–1982 (R1988)].

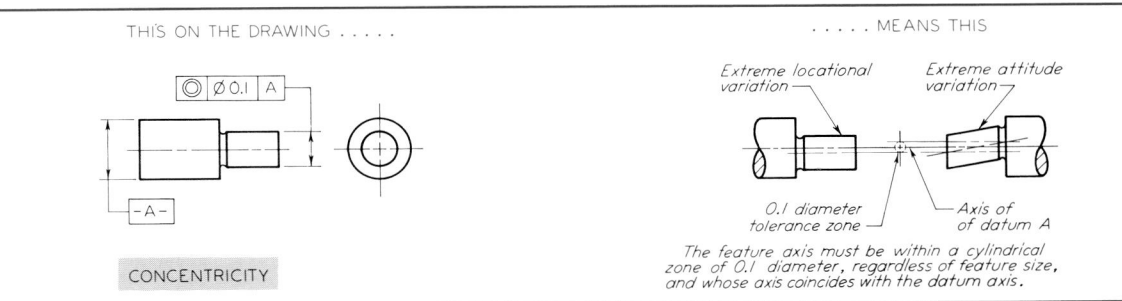

Fig. 14.42 Specifying Concentricity [ANSI Y14.5M–1982 (R1988)].

Concentricity Tolerance

Concentricity is the condition where the axes of all cross-sectional elements of a feature's surface of revolution are common to the axis of a datum feature. A concentricity tolerance specifies a cylindrical tolerance zone whose axis coincides with a datum axis and within which all cross sectional axes of the feature being controlled must lie, Fig. 14.42.

14.21 Application of Geometric Tolerancing

The use of various feature control symbols in lieu of notes for position and form tolerance dimensions as abstracted from ANSI Y14.5M–1982 (R1988) is il-

lustrated in Fig. 14.43. For a more detailed treatment of geometric tolerancing, consult the latest ANSI Y14.5 Dimensioning and Tolerancing standard.

14.22 Surface Roughness, Waviness, and Lay

The modern demands of the automobile, the airplane, and other machines that can stand heavier loads and higher speeds with less friction and wear have increased the need for accurate control of surface quality by the designer regardless of the size of the feature. Simple finish marks are not adequate to specify surface finish on such parts.

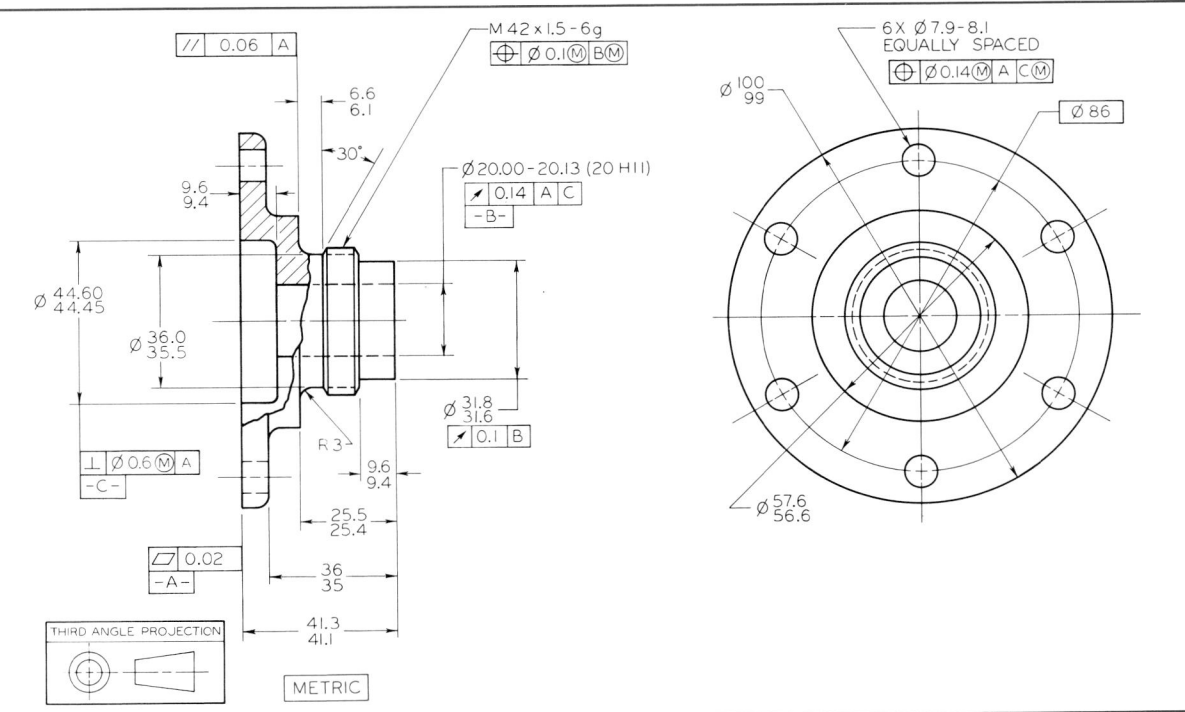

Fig. 14.43 Application of Symbols to Position and Form Tolerance Dimensions [ANSI Y14.5M–1982 (R1988)].

	Symbol	Meaning
(a)	√	Basic Surface Texture Symbol. Surface may be produced by any method except when the bar or circle, (b) or (d), is specified.
(b)	⩗	Material Removal By Machining Is Required. The horizontal bar indicates that material removal by machining is required to produce the surface and that material must be provided for that purpose.
(c)	3.5 ⩗	Material Removal Allowance. The number indicates the amount of stock to be removed by machining in millimeters (or inches). Tolerances may be added to the basic value shown or in a general note.
(d)	⊘	Material Removal Prohibited. The circle in the vee indicates that the surface must be produced by processes such as casting, forging, hot finishing, cold finishing, die casting, powder metallurgy or injection molding without subsequent removal of material.
(e)	√—	Surface Texture Symbol. To be used when any surface characteristics are specified above the horizontal line or to the right of the symbol. Surface may be produced by any method except when the bar or circle, (b) or (d), is specified.

(f)

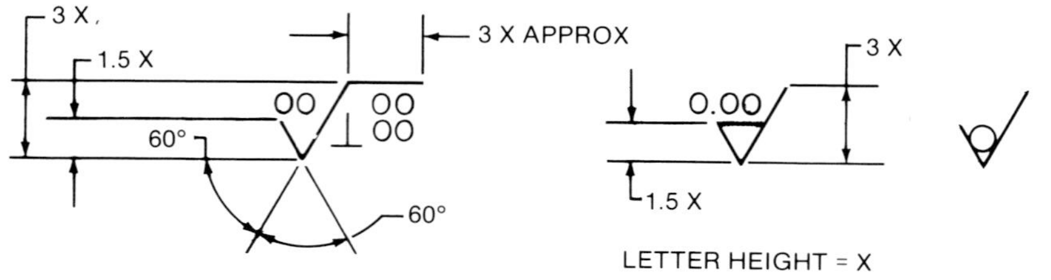

Fig. 14.44 Surface Texture Symbols and Construction   [ANSI Y14.36–1978 (R1987)].

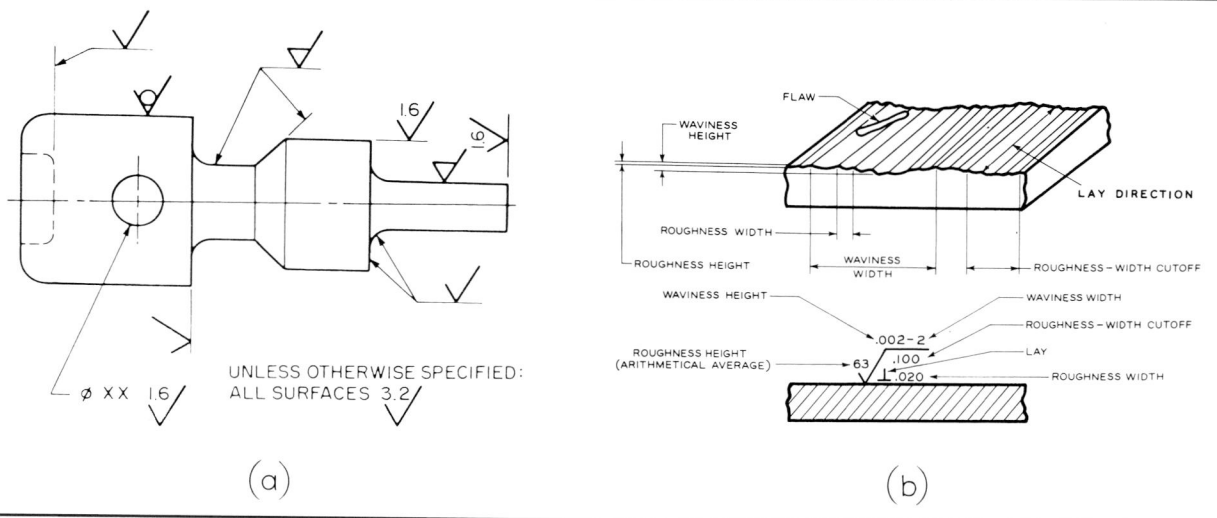

Fig. 14.45 Application of Surface Texture Symbols and Surface Characteristics   [ANSI Y14.36–1978 (R1987)].

Table 14.4 *Preferred Series Roughness Average Values*
(R_a) [ANSI Y14.36–1978 (R1987)]
Recommended values are in color.

Micrometers[a] (μm)	Microinches (μin.)	Micrometers[a] (μm)	Microinches (μin.)
0.012	0.5	1.25	50
0.025	1	1.60	63
0.050	2	2.0	80
0.075	3	2.5	100
0.10	4	3.2	125
0.125	5	4.0	180
0.15	6	5.0	200
0.20	8	6.3	250
0.25	10	8.0	320
0.32	13	10.0	400
0.40	16	12.5	500
0.50	20	15	600
0.63	25	20	800
0.80	32	25	1000
1.00	40		

[a]Micrometers are the same as thousandths of a millimeter (1 μm = 0.001 mm).

Surface finish is intimately related to the functioning of a surface, and proper specification of finish of such surfaces as bearings and seals is necessary. Surface quality specifications should be used only where needed, since the cost of producing a finished surface becomes greater as the quality of the surface called for is increased. Generally, the ideal surface finish is the roughest one that will do the job satisfactorily.

The system of surface texture symbols recommended by ANSI [Y14.36–1978 (R1987)] for use on drawings, regardless of the system of measurement used, is now broadly accepted by American industry. These symbols are used to define *surface texture, roughness,* and *lay.* See Fig. 14.44 for meaning and construction of these symbols. The basic surface texture symbol in Fig. 14.45 (a) indicates a finished or machined surface by any method just as does the general V symbol, Fig. 13.20 (a). Modifications to the basic surface texture symbol, Fig. 14.44 (b), (c), and (d), define restrictions on material removal for the finished surface. Where surface texture values other than roughness average (R_a) are specified, the symbol must be drawn with the horizontal extension as shown in (e). Construction details for the symbols are given in (f).

Applications of the surface texture symbols are given in Fig. 14.45 (a). Note that the symbols read from the bottom and/or the right side of the drawing and that they are not drawn at any angle or upside down.

Measurements for roughness and waviness, unless otherwise specified, apply in the direction that gives the maximum reading, usually across the lay. See Fig. 14.45 (b). The recommended roughness height values are given in Table 14.4.

When it is necessary to indicate the roughness-width cutoff values, the standard values to be used are listed in Table 14.5. If no value is specified, the 0.80 value is assumed.

Table 14.5 *Standard Roughness Sampling Length (Cutoff) Values* [ANSI Y14.36–1978 (R1987)]

Millimeters (mm)	Inches (in.)	Millimeters (mm)	Inches (in.)
0.08	.003	2.5	.1
0.25	.010	8.0	.3
0.80	.030	25.0	1.0

When maximum waviness height values are required, the recommended values to be used are as given in Table 14.6.

When it is desired to indicate lay, the lay symbols in Fig. 14.46 are added to the surface texture symbol as per the examples given. Selected applications of the surface texture values to the symbol are given and explained in Fig. 14.47.

A typical range of surface roughness values that may be obtained from various production methods is shown in Fig. 14.48. Preferred roughness-height values are shown at the top of the chart.

Table 14.6 *Preferred Series Maximum Waviness Height Values* [ANSI Y14.36–1978 (R1987)]

Millimeters (mm)	Inches (in.)	Millimeters (mm)	Inches (in.)
0.0005	.00002	0.025	.001
0.0008	.00003	0.05	.002
0.0012	.00005	0.08	.003
0.0020	.00008	0.12	.005
0.0025	.0001	0.20	.008
0.005	.0002	0.25	.010
0.008	.0003	0.38	.015
0.012	.0005	0.50	.020
0.020	.0008	0.80	.030

LAY SYMBOLS

SYM	DESIGNATION	EXAMPLE	SYM	DESIGNATION	EXAMPLE
—	Lay parallel to the line representing the surface to which the symbol is applied.	DIRECTION OF TOOL MARKS	X	Lay angular in both directions to line representing the surface to which symbol is applied.	DIRECTION OF TOOL MARKS
⊥	Lay perpendicular to the line representing the surface to which the symbol is applied.	DIRECTION OF TOOL MARKS	M	Lay multidirectional	
C	Lay approximately circular relative to the center of the surface to which the symbol is applied.		R	Lay approximately radial relative to the center of the surface to which the symbol is applied.	

Fig. 14.46   Lay Symbols   [ANSI Y14.36–1978 (R1987)].

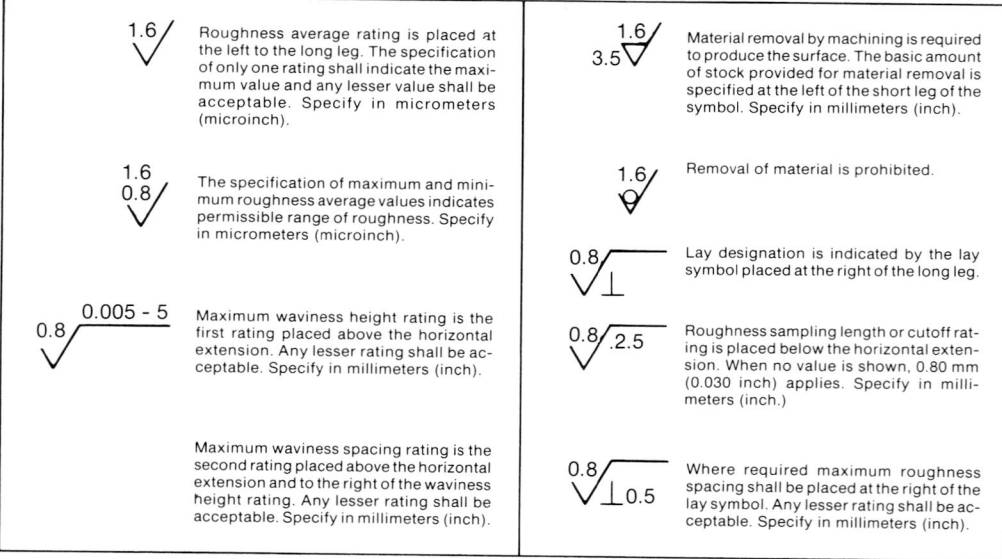

Fig. 14.47   Application of Surface Texture Values to Symbol   [ANSI Y14.36–1978 (R1987)].

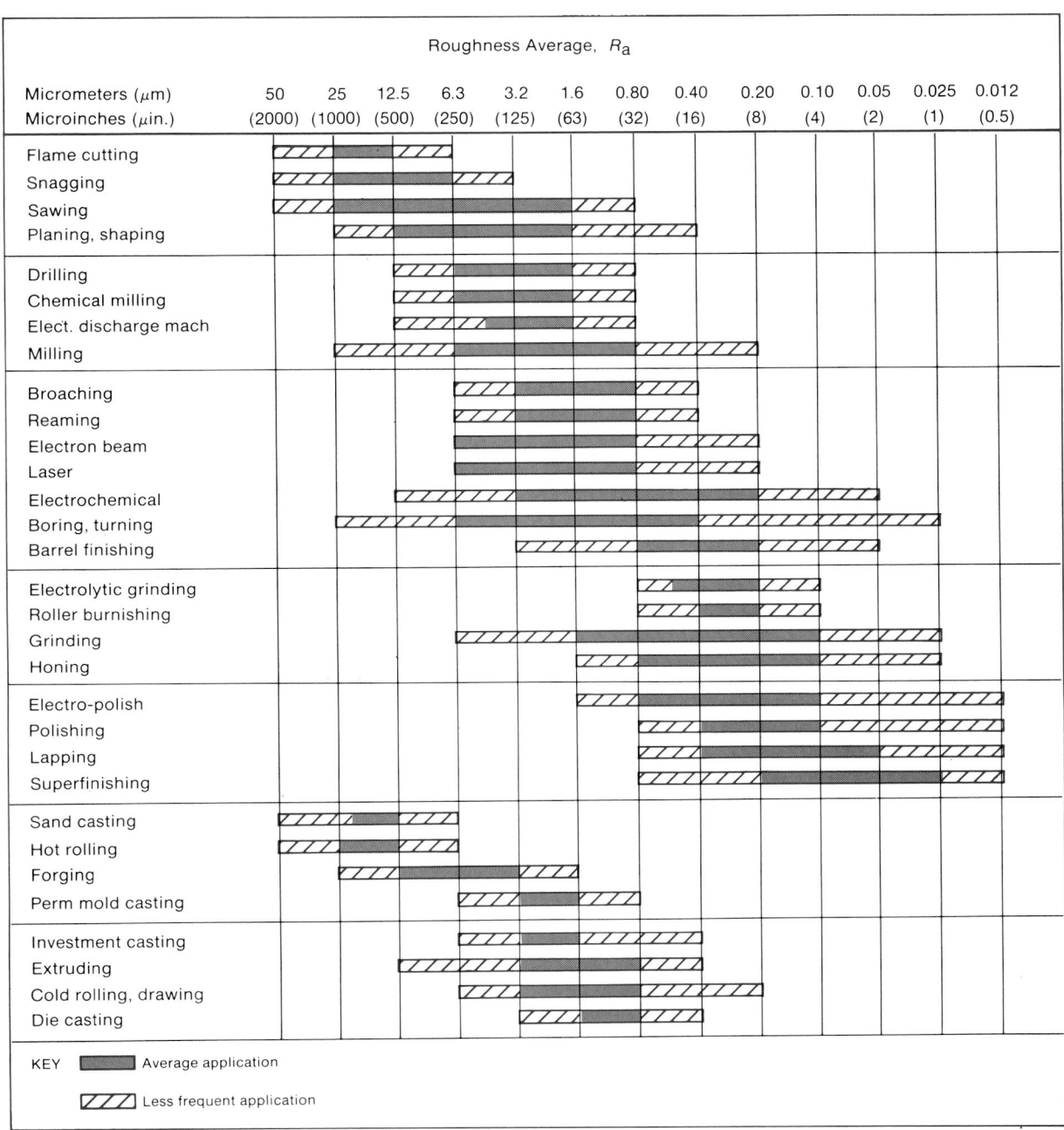

Fig. 14.48 Surface Roughness Produced by Common Production Methods [ANSI/ASME B46.1–1985]. The ranges shown are typical of the processes listed. Higher or lower values may be obtained under special conditions.

14.23 Computer Graphics

Computer graphics programs are available that allow the user to add surface finish symbols by inputting a few keystrokes, Fig. 14.49. Geometric tolerancing can be applied to a drawing with the CAD system supplying standard ANSI symbols, Fig. 14.50, as well as user-defined custom symbols.

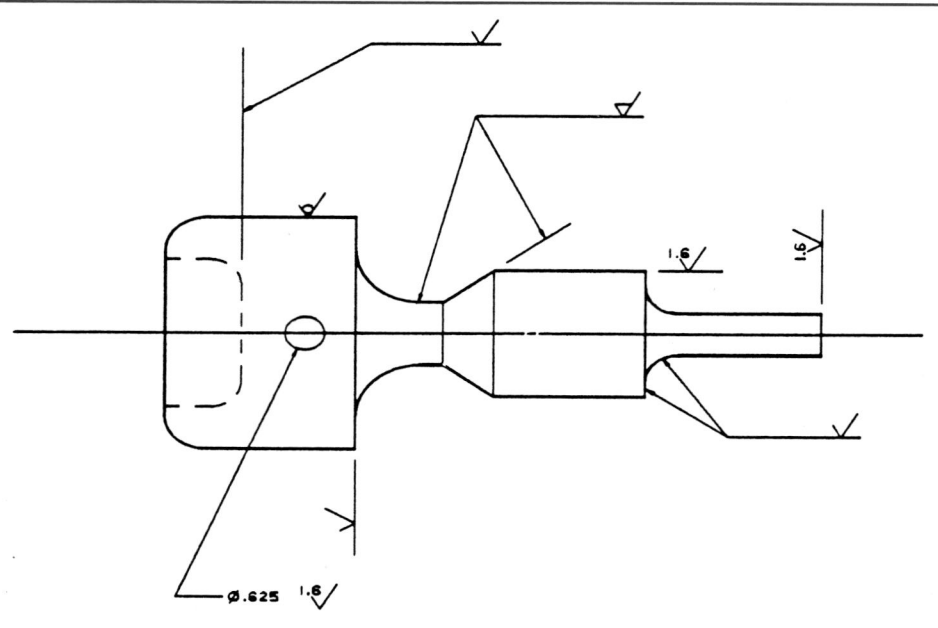

UNLESS OTHERWISE SPECIFIED: ALL SURFACES 3.2

Fig. 14.49 Application of Surface Finish Symbols with Computervision CADDS 4X Production Drafting System. *Courtesy of Computervision Corporation, a subsidiary of Prime Computer, Inc.*

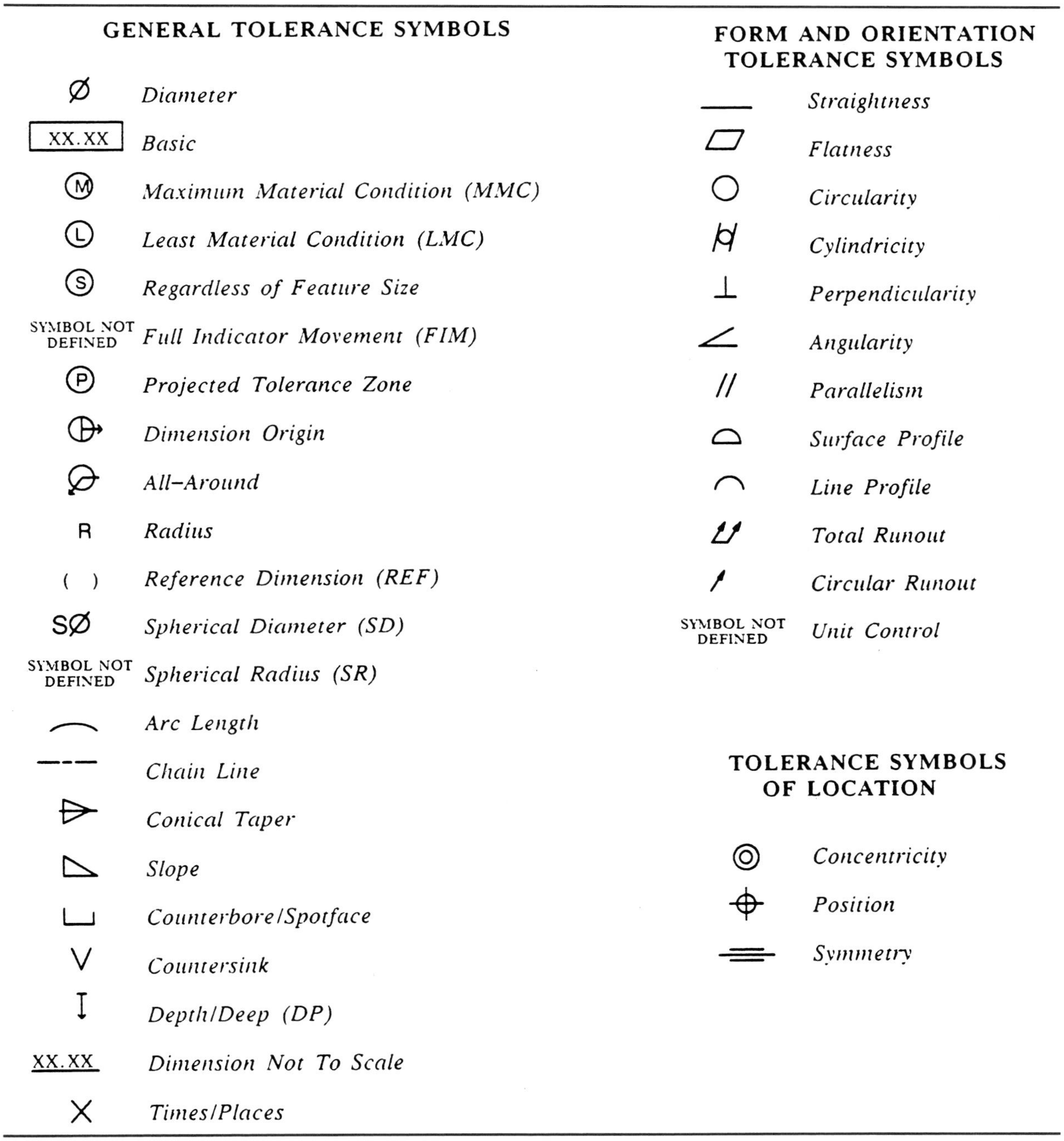

GENERAL TOLERANCE SYMBOLS

⌀	Diameter
XX.XX	Basic
Ⓜ	Maximum Material Condition (MMC)
Ⓛ	Least Material Condition (LMC)
Ⓢ	Regardless of Feature Size
SYMBOL NOT DEFINED	Full Indicator Movement (FIM)
Ⓟ	Projected Tolerance Zone
⌖➔	Dimension Origin
⌀	All–Around
R	Radius
( )	Reference Dimension (REF)
S⌀	Spherical Diameter (SD)
SYMBOL NOT DEFINED	Spherical Radius (SR)
⌒	Arc Length
---	Chain Line
▷	Conical Taper
◿	Slope
⊔	Counterbore/Spotface
∨	Countersink
↧	Depth/Deep (DP)
XX.XX	Dimension Not To Scale
✕	Times/Places

FORM AND ORIENTATION TOLERANCE SYMBOLS

—	Straightness
▱	Flatness
○	Circularity
⌭	Cylindricity
⊥	Perpendicularity
∠	Angularity
//	Parallelism
⌒	Surface Profile
⌒	Line Profile
⌰	Total Runout
↗	Circular Runout
SYMBOL NOT DEFINED	Unit Control

TOLERANCE SYMBOLS OF LOCATION

◎	Concentricity
⊕	Position
⩵	Symmetry

Fig. 14.50 Geometric Dimensioning and Tolerancing Symbols Available in Computervision's CADDS 4X Production Drafting System. *Courtesy of Computervision Corporation, a subsidiary of Prime Computer, Inc.*

CHAPTER
15

Threads, Fasteners, and Springs*

The concept of the screw thread seems to have occurred first to Archimedes, the third-century B.C. mathematician, who wrote briefly on spirals and invented or designed several simple devices applying the screw principle. By the first century B.C. the screw was a familiar element, but was crudely cut from wood or filed by hand on a metal shaft. Nothing more was heard of the screw thread in Europe until the fifteenth century.

Leonardo da Vinci understood the screw principle, and he has left sketches showing how to cut screw threads by machine. In the sixteenth century, screws appeared in German watches, and screws were used to fasten suits of armour. In 1569 the screw-cutting lathe was invented by the Frenchman Besson, but the method did not take hold for another century and a half; nuts and bolts continued to be made largely by hand. In the eighteenth century, screw manufacturing got started in England during the Industrial Revolution.

*For a listing of American National Standards Institute (ANSI) standards for threads, fasteners, and springs, see Appendix 1.

411

15.1 Standardized Screw Threads

In early times, there was no such thing as standardization. Nuts made by one manufacturer would not fit the bolts of another. In 1841 Sir Joseph Whitworth started crusading for a standard screw thread, and soon the Whitworth thread was accepted throughout England.

In 1864, the United States adopted a thread proposed by William Sellers of Philadelphia, but the Sellers' nuts would not screw on a Whitworth bolt, or vice versa. In 1935 the American Standard thread, with the same 60° V form of the old Sellers' thread, was adopted in the United States. Still there was no standardization among countries. In peacetime it was a nuisance; in World War I it was a serious inconvenience; and in World War II the obstacle was so great that the Allies decided to do something about it. Talks began among the Americans, British, and the Canadians, and in 1948 an agreement was reached on the unification of American and British screw threads. The new thread was called the *Unified screw thread*, and it represents a compromise between the American Standard and Whitworth systems, allowing complete interchangeability of threads in the three countries.

In 1946 an International Organization for Standardization (ISO) committee was formed to establish a single international system of metric screw threads. Consequently, through the cooperative efforts of the Industrial Fasteners Institute (IFI), several committees of the American National Standards Institute, and the ISO representatives, a metric fastener standard (IFI-500–1975) was prepared.

Today screw threads are vital to our industrial life. They are designed for hundreds of different purposes, the three basic applications being (1) to *hold parts* together, (2) to *adjust parts* with reference to each other, and (3) to *transmit power.*

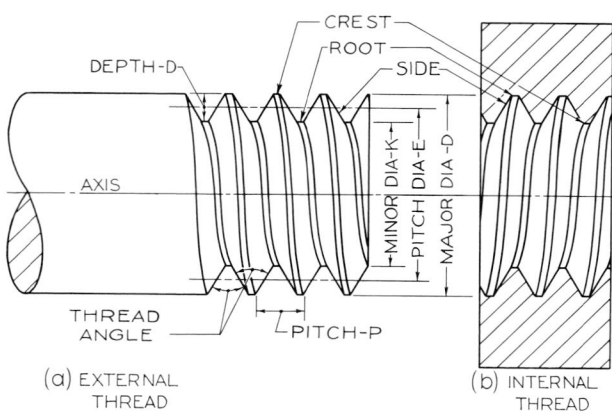

(a) EXTERNAL THREAD   **(b)** INTERNAL THREAD

Fig. 15.1   Screw-Thread Nomenclature.

15.2 Definitions of Terms

The following definitions apply to screw threads in general, Fig. 15.1.

Screw thread   A ridge of uniform section in the form of a helix, §5.63, on the external or internal surface of a cylinder.

External thread   A thread on the outside of a member, as on a shaft.

Internal thread   A thread on the inside of a member, as in a hole.

Major diameter   The largest diameter of a screw thread (applies to both internal and external threads).

Minor diameter   The smallest diameter of a screw thread (applies to both internal and external threads).

Pitch   The distance from a point on a screw thread to a corresponding point on the next thread measured parallel to the axis. The pitch P is equal to 1 divided by the number of threads per inch.

Pitch diameter   The diameter of an imaginary cylinder passing through the threads so as to make equal the widths of the threads and the widths of the spaces cut by the cylinder.

Lead   The distance a screw thread advances axially in one turn.

Angle of thread   The angle included between the sides of the thread measured in a plane through the axis of the screw.

Crest   The top surface joining the two sides of a thread.

Root   The bottom surface joining the sides of two adjacent threads.

Side   The surface of the thread that connects the crest with the root.

Axis of screw   The longitudinal center line through the screw.

Depth of thread   The distance between the crest and the root of the thread measured normal to the axis.

Form of thread   The cross section of thread cut by a plane containing the axis.

Series of thread   Standard number of threads per inch for various diameters.

15.3 Screw-Thread Forms

Various forms of threads, Fig. 15.2, are used to hold parts together, to adjust parts with reference to each other, or to transmit power. The 60° *Sharp-V thread*

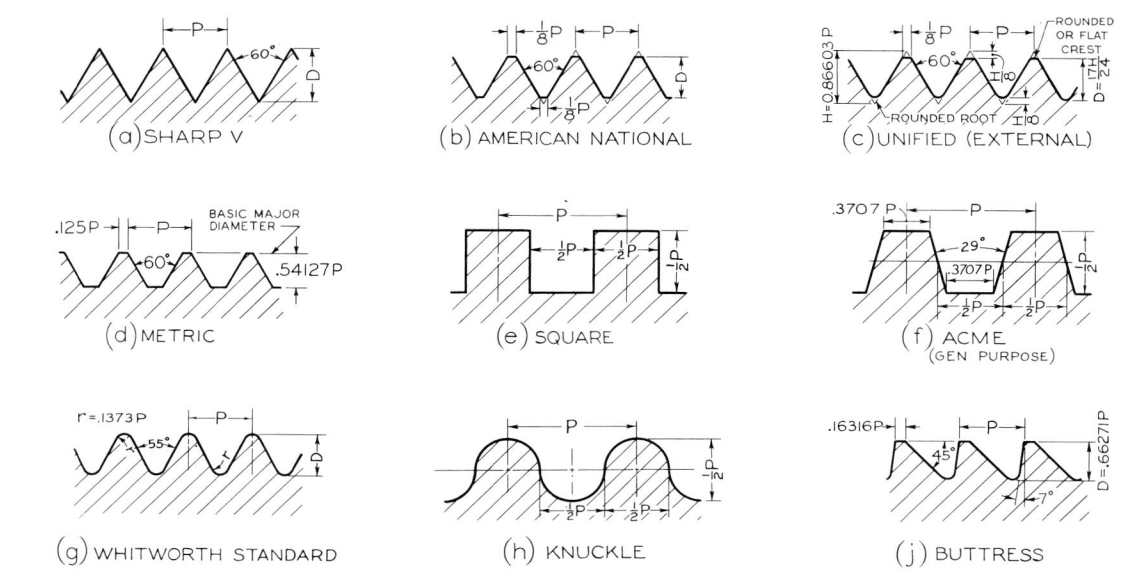

Fig. 15.2 Screw-Thread Forms.

was originally called the United States Standard thread, or the Sellers' thread. For purposes of certain adjustments, the Sharp-V thread is useful with the increased friction resulting from the full thread face. It is also used on brass pipe work.

The *American National thread* with flattened roots and crests is a stronger thread. This form replaced the Sharp-V thread for general use.

The *Unified thread* is the standard thread agreed upon by the United States, Canada, and Great Britain in 1948, and is gradually replacing the American National form. The crest of the external thread may be flat or rounded, and the root is rounded; otherwise, the thread form is essentially the same as the American National.

The *metric thread* is the standard screw thread agreed upon for international screw thread fasteners. The crest and root are flat, but the external thread is often rounded if formed by a rolling process. The form is similar to the American National and the Unified threads but with less depth of thread.

The *square thread* is theoretically the ideal thread for power transmission, since its face is nearly at right angles to the axis, but due to the difficulty of cutting it with dies and because of other inherent disadvantages, such as the fact that split nuts will not readily disengage, the square thread has been displaced to a large extent by the Acme thread. The square thread is not standardized.

The *Acme thread* is a modification of the square

thread and has largely replaced it. It is stronger than the square thread, is easier to cut, and has the advantage of easy disengagement from a split nut, as on the lead screw of a lathe.

The *standard worm thread* (not shown) is similar to the Acme thread, but is deeper. It is used on shafts to carry power to worm wheels.

The *Whitworth thread* has been the British standard and is being replaced by the Unified thread. Its uses correspond to those of the American National thread.

The *knuckle thread* is usually rolled from sheet metal but is sometimes cast, and is used in modified forms in electric bulbs and sockets, bottle tops, and the like.

The *buttress thread* is designed to transmit power in one direction only and is used in large guns, in jacks, and in other mechanisms of similarly high strength requirements.

15.4 Thread Pitch

The *pitch* of any thread form is the distance parallel to the axis between corresponding points on adjacent threads, Figs. 15.1 (a) and 15.2. For metric threads, this distance is specified in millimeters.

The pitch for a metric thread that is included with the major diameter in the thread designation determines the size of the thread, as shown in Fig. 15.3 (b). For example, M10 × 1.5. See also §15.21, or Appendix 15, for more information.

For threads dimensioned in inches, the pitch is

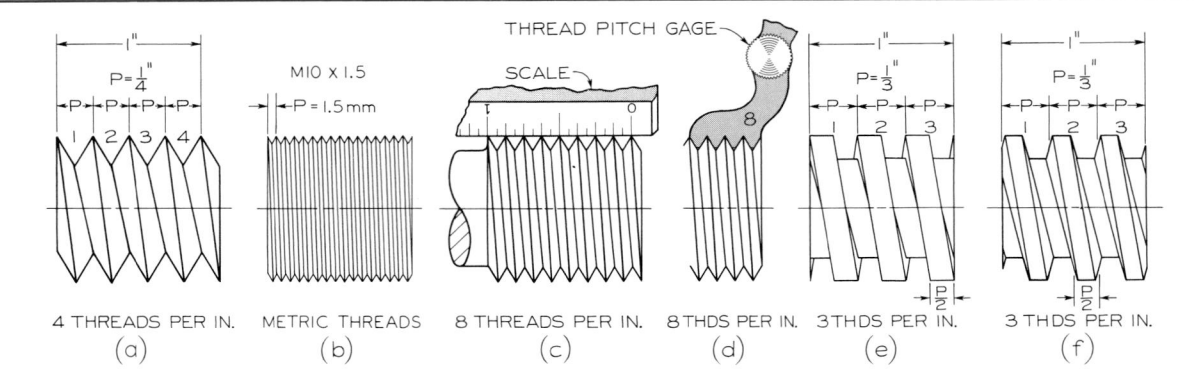

Fig. 15.3   Pitch of Threads.

equal to 1 divided by the number of threads per inch. The thread tables give the number of threads per inch for each standard diameter. Thus, a Unified coarse thread, Appendix 15, of 1″ diameter, has eight threads per inch, and the pitch P equals $\frac{1}{8}″$.

As shown in Fig. 15.3 (a), if a thread has only four threads per inch, the pitch and the threads themselves are quite large. If there are, say, sixteen threads per inch, the pitch is only $\frac{1}{16}″$, and the threads are relatively small, similar to the threads shown at (b).

The pitch or the number of threads per inch can easily be measured with a scale, (c), or with a *thread-pitch gage*, (d).

15.5 Right-Hand and Left-Hand Threads
A right-hand thread is one that advances into a nut when turned clockwise, and a left-hand thread is one that advances into a nut when turned counterclockwise, Fig. 15.4. A thread is always considered to be right-hand (RH) unless otherwise specified. A left-hand thread is always labeled **LH** on a drawing. See Fig. 15.19 (a).

15.6 Single and Multiple Threads
A *single* thread, as the name implies, is composed of one ridge, and the lead is therefore equal to the pitch. *Multiple* threads are composed of two or more ridges running side by side. As shown in Fig. 15.5 (a), (b), and (c), the *slope line* is the hypotenuse of a right triangle whose short side equals $\frac{1}{2}P$ for single threads, P for double threads, $1\frac{1}{2}P$ for triple threads, and so on. This applies to all forms of threads. In *double* threads, the lead is twice the pitch; in *triple* threads the lead is three times the pitch, and so on. On a drawing of a single or triple thread, a root is opposite a crest; in the case of a double or quadruple thread, a root is drawn opposite a root. Therefore, in one turn, a double thread advances twice as far as a single thread, and a triple thread advances three times as far.

RH double square and RH triple Acme threads are shown at (d) and (e), respectively.

Multiple threads are used wherever quick motion, but not great power, is desired, as on fountain pens, toothpaste caps, valve stems, and the like. The threads on a valve stem are frequently multiple threads, to impart quick action in opening and clos-

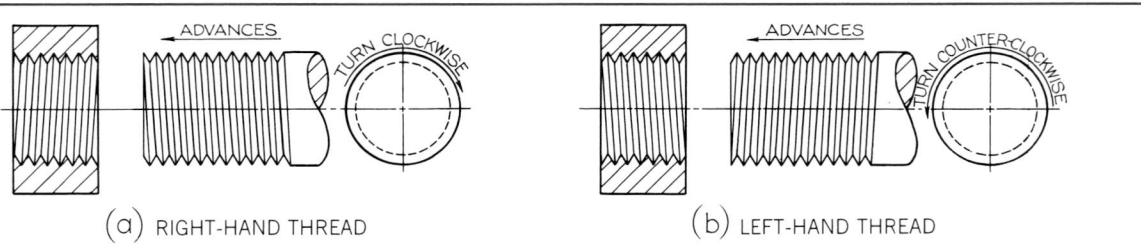

Fig. 15.4   Right-Hand and Left-Hand Threads.

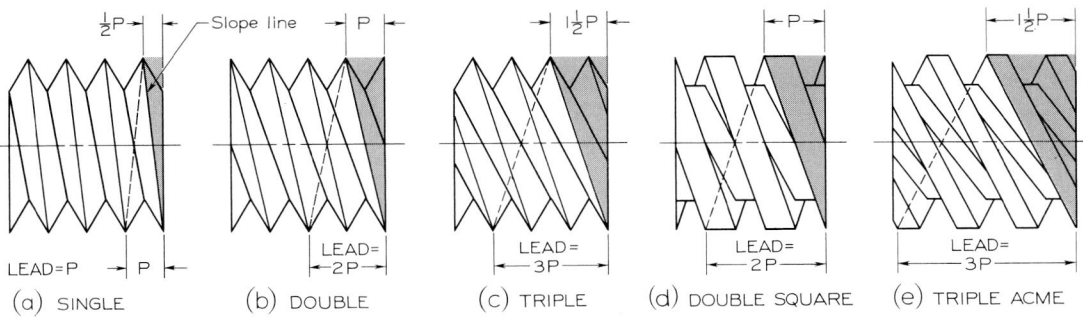

Fig. 15.5 Multiple Threads.

ing the valve. Multiple threads on a shaft can be recognized and counted by observing the number of thread endings on the end of the screw.

15.7 Thread Symbols

There are three methods of representation for showing screw threads on drawings—the *schematic*, the *simplified*, and the *detailed*. For clarity of representation and where good judgment dictates, schematic, simplified, and detailed thread symbols may be combined on a single drawing.

Two sets of thread symbols, the schematic and the more common simplified, are used to represent threads of small diameter, under approximately 1″ or 25 mm diameter on the drawing. The symbols are the same for all forms of threads, such as metric, Unified, square, and Acme.

The detailed representation is a close approximation of the exact appearance of a screw thread. The true projection of the helical curves of a screw thread, Fig. 15.1, presents a pleasing appearance, but this does not compensate for the laborious task of plotting the helices, §5.63. Consequently, the true projection is rarely used in practice.

When the diameter of the thread on the drawing is over approximately 1″ or 25 mm, a pleasing drawing may be made by the *detailed representation* method, in which the true profiles of the threads (any form of thread) are drawn; but the helical curves are replaced by straight lines, as shown in Fig. 15.6.* Whether the crests or roots are flat or rounded, they are represented by single lines and not double lines as in Fig. 15.1; consequently, American National and Unified threads are drawn in exactly the same way.

15.8 External Thread Symbols

Simplified external thread symbols are shown in Fig. 15.7 (a) and (b). The threaded portions are indicated by hidden lines parallel to the axis at the approximate depth of the thread, whether in section or in elevation. Use the schematic depth of thread

*A thread 42 mm or 1⅝″ diameter, if drawn half size, would be less than 25 mm or 1″ diameter on the drawing and hence would be too small for this method of representation.

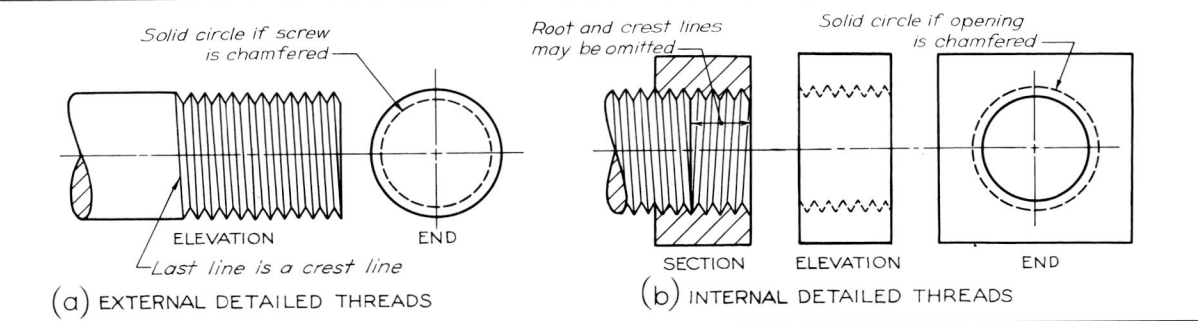

Fig. 15.6 Detailed Metric, American National, and Unified Threads.

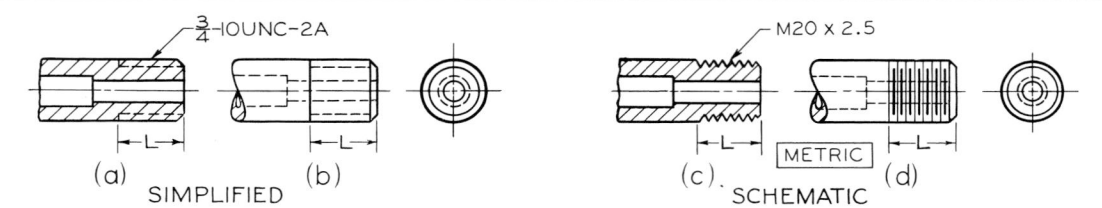

Fig. 15.7   External Thread Symbols.

as given in the table in Fig. 15.9 (a), to draw these lines, (d).

When the schematic form is shown in section, (c), it is necessary to show the V's; otherwise no threads would be evident. However, it is not necessary to show the V's to scale or according to the actual slope of the crest lines. To draw the V's, use the schematic thread depth, Fig. 15.9 (a), and let the pitch be determined by the 60° V's.

Schematic threads in elevation, Fig. 15.7 (d), are indicated by alternate long and short lines at right angles to the center line, the root lines being preferably thicker than the crest lines. Although theoretically the crest lines would be spaced according to actual pitch, the lines would often be very crowded and tedious to draw, thus defeating the purpose of the symbol, to save drafting time. In practice, the experienced drafter spaces the crest lines carefully by eye, and then adds the heavy root lines spaced by eye halfway between the crest lines. In general, the spacing should be proportionate for all diameters. For convenience in drawing, proportions for the schematic symbol are given in Fig. 15.9.

15.9 Internal Thread Symbols

Internal thread symbols are shown in Fig. 15.8. Note that the only differences between the schematic and simplified internal thread symbols occur in the sectional views. The representation of the schematic thread in section, Fig. 15.8 (m), (o), and (r), is exactly the same as the external symbol in Fig. 15.7 (d). Hidden threads, by either method, are represented by pairs of hidden lines. The hidden dashes should be staggered, as shown.

In the case of blind tapped holes, the drill depth normally is drawn at least three schematic pitches beyond the thread length, as shown in Fig. 15.8 (d), (e), (n), and (o). The symbols at (f) and (p) are used to represent the use of a bottoming tap, when the length of thread is the same as the depth of drill. See also §15.24.

15.10 To Draw Thread Symbols

Fig. 15.9 (a) shows a table of values of depth and pitch to use in drawing thread symbols. These values are selected to produce a well-proportioned

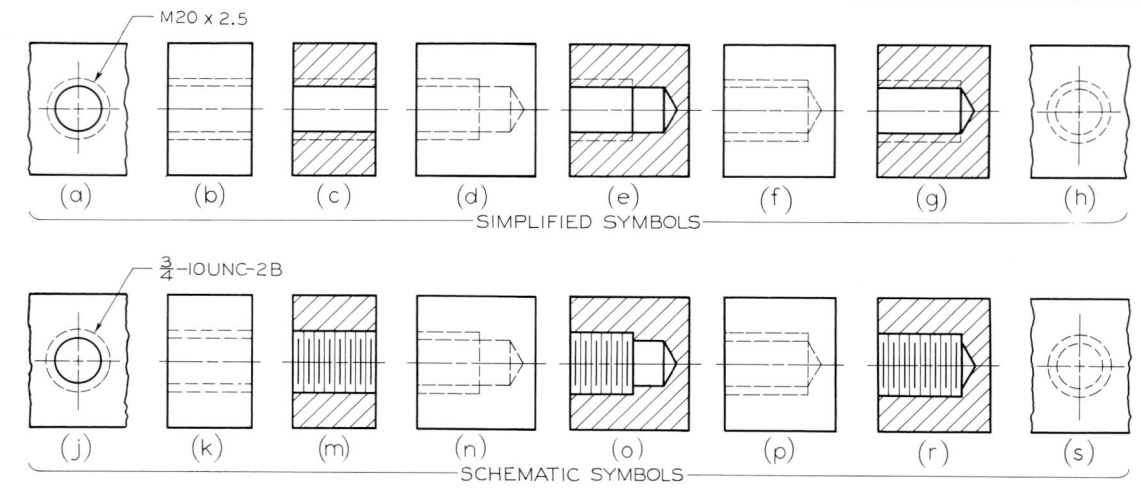

Fig. 15.8   Internal Thread Symbols.

MAJOR DIAMETER	#5 (125) TO #12 (216)	$\frac{1}{4}$	$\frac{5}{16}$	$\frac{3}{8}$	$\frac{7}{16}$	$\frac{1}{2}$	$\frac{9}{16}$	$\frac{5}{8}$	$\frac{11}{16}$	$\frac{3}{4}$	$\frac{13}{16}$	$\frac{7}{8}$	$\frac{15}{16}$	1
(a) DEPTH, D	$\frac{1}{32}$	$\frac{1}{32}$	$\frac{1}{32}$	$\frac{3}{64}$	$\frac{3}{64}$	$\frac{1}{16}$	$\frac{1}{16}$	$\frac{1}{16}$	$\frac{1}{16}$	$\frac{5}{64}$	$\frac{3}{32}$	$\frac{3}{32}$	$\frac{3}{32}$	$\frac{3}{32}$
PITCH, P	$\frac{3}{64}$	$\frac{1}{16}$	$\frac{1}{16}$	$\frac{1}{16}$	$\frac{1}{16}$	$\frac{3}{32}$	$\frac{3}{32}$	$\frac{3}{32}$	$\frac{3}{32}$	$\frac{1}{8}$	$\frac{1}{8}$	$\frac{1}{8}$	$\frac{1}{8}$	$\frac{1}{8}$

(For metric values: 1" = 25.4 mm or see inside front cover.)

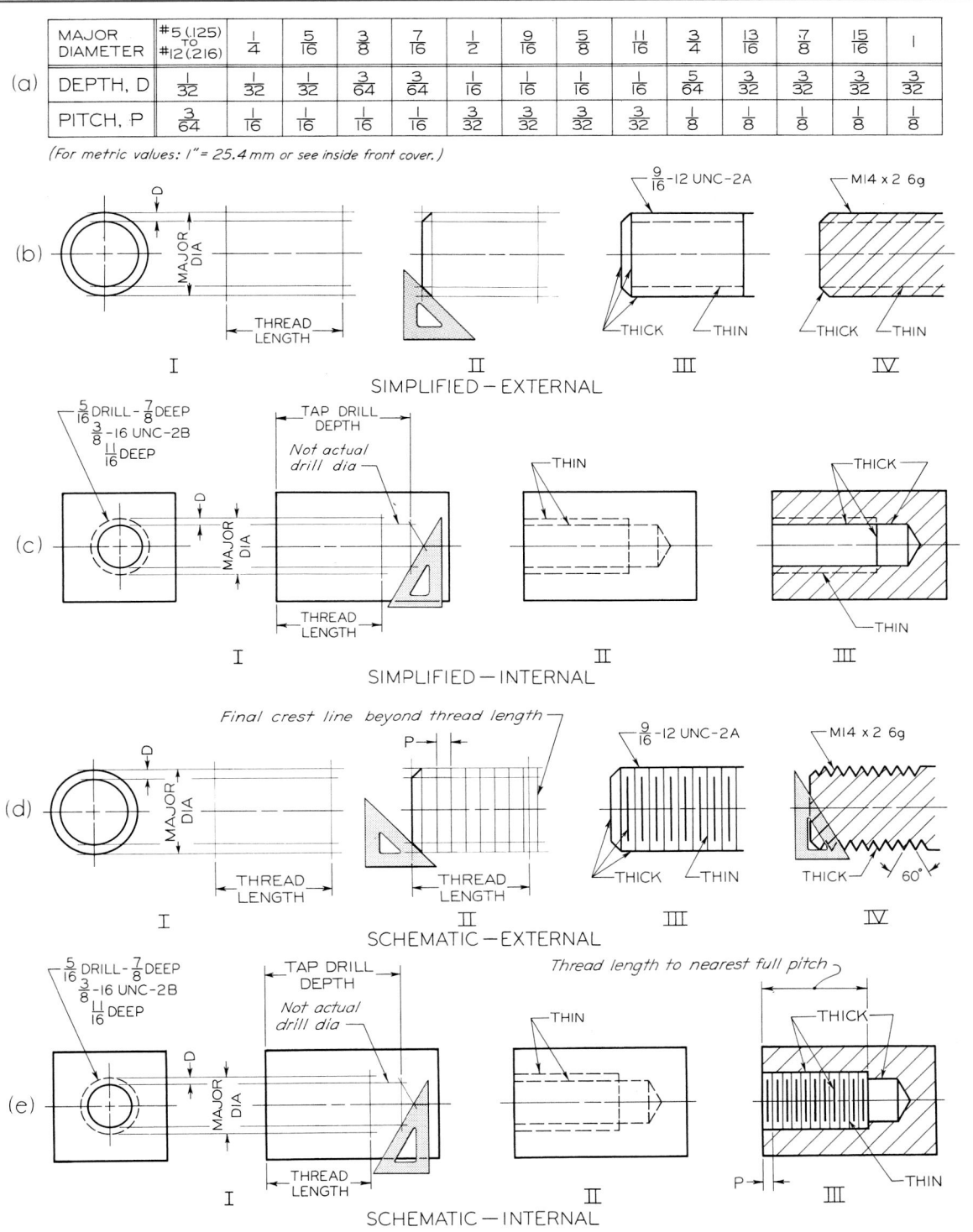

Fig. 15.9 To Draw Thread Symbols—Simplified and Schematic.

symbol and to be convenient to set off with the scale. The experienced drafter will carefully space the lines by eye, but the student should use the scale. Note that the values of D and P are for the diameter *on the drawing.* Thus a 1½″ diameter thread at half-scale would be ¾″ diameter on the drawing, and values of D and P for a ¾″ major diameter would be used. Nominal diameters for metric threads are treated in a similar manner.

Simplified Symbols

The steps for drawing the simplified symbols for an external thread in elevation and in section are shown in Fig. 15.9 (b). The thread depth from the table at (a) is used for establishing the pairs of hidden lines that represent the threads in elevation and in section. No pitch measurement is needed. The completed symbols are shown at III and IV.

The steps for drawing the simplified symbol for an internal thread in section are shown in Fig. 15.9 (c). The simplified representation for the internal thread in elevation is identical to that used for schematic representation, as the threads are indicated by pairs of hidden lines as shown at II. The simplified symbol for an internal thread in section is shown at III. The major diameter of the thread is represented by hidden lines across the sectioned area.

Schematic Symbols

The steps for drawing the schematic symbols for an external thread in elevation and in section are shown in Fig. 15.9 (d). Note that when the pitches P are set off in II, the final crest line for a full pitch may fall beyond the actual thread length as shown. The completed schematic symbol for an external thread in elevation is shown at III. The completed schematic symbol for an external thread in section is shown at IV. The schematic thread depth is used for drawing the V s, and the pitch is established by the 60° V s.

The steps for drawing the schematic symbols for an internal thread in elevation and in section are shown at (e). Here again the symbol thread length may be slightly longer than the actual given thread length. If the tap drill depth is known or given, the drill is drawn to that depth, as shown. If the thread note omits this information, as is often done in practice, the drafter merely draws the hole three thread pitches (schematic) beyond the thread length. The tap drill diameter is represented approximately, as shown, and not to actual size. The completed schematic symbol for an internal thread in elevation is

shown at II. Pairs of hidden lines represent the threads, and the hidden-line dashes are staggered. The completed schematic symbol for an internal thread in section is shown at III. The schematic internal thread in section is represented in the same manner as for the schematic external thread.

15.11 Detailed Representation—Metric, Unified, and American National Threads
The detailed representation for metric, unified, and American National threads is the same, since the flats, if any, are disregarded. The steps in drawing these threads are shown in Fig. 15.10.

I.   Draw center line and lay out length and major diameter.

II.   Find the number of threads per inch in Appendix 15 for American National and Unified threads. This number depends upon the major diameter of the thread, whether the thread is internal or external. Find P (pitch) by dividing 1 by the number of threads per inch, §15.4. The pitch for metric threads is given directly in the thread designation. For example the M14 × 2 thread has a pitch of 2 mm. See Appendix 15. Establish the slope of the thread by offsetting the slope line ½P for single threads, P for double threads, 1½P for triple threads, and so on.* For right-hand external threads, the slope line slopes upward to the left; for left-hand external threads, the slope line slopes upward to the right. If the numbers of threads per inch conforms to the scale, the pitch can be set off directly. For example, eight threads per inch can easily be set off with the architects' scale, and ten threads per inch with the engineers' scale. Otherwise, use the bow dividers or use the parallel-line method shown in Fig. 15.10 (II).

III.   From the pitch points, draw crest lines parallel to slope line. These should be dark thin lines. Slide triangle on T-square (or another triangle) to make lines parallel. Draw two V s to establish depth of thread, and draw guide lines for root of thread, as shown.

IV.   Draw 60° V s finished weight. These V s should stand vertically; that is, they should not "lean" with the thread.

*These offsets are the same in terms of P for any form of thread.

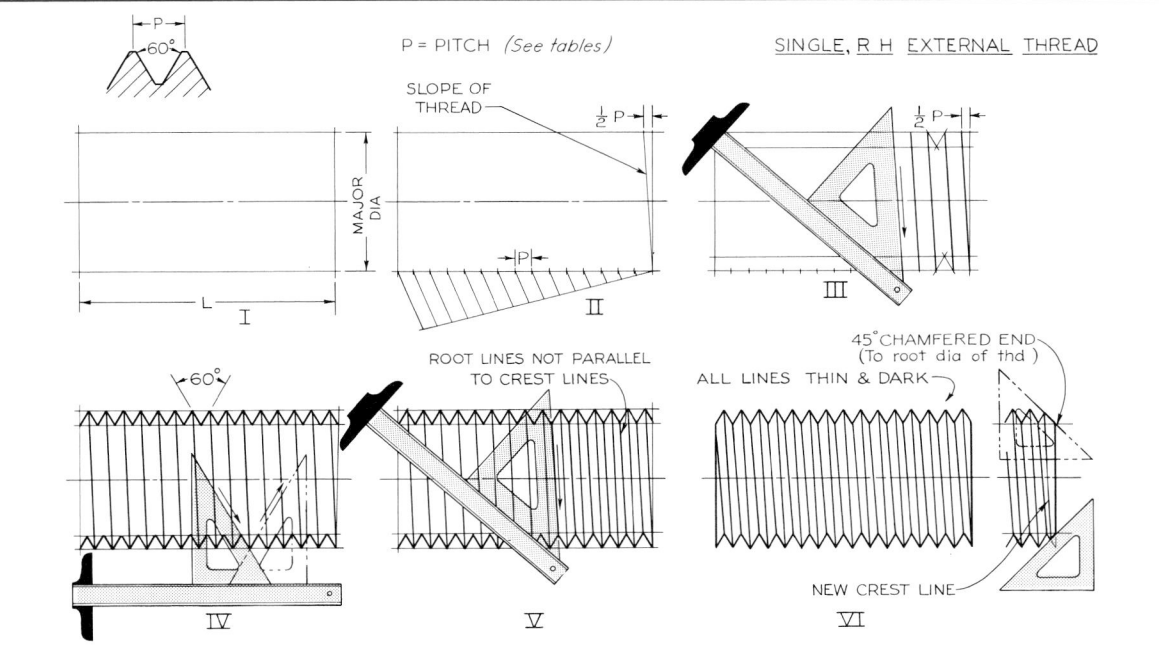

Fig. 15.10 Detailed Representation—External Metric, Unified, and American National Threads.

V. Draw root lines dark at once. Root lines will *not* be parallel to crest lines. Slide triangle on straightedge to make root lines parallel.

VI. When the end is chamfered (usually 45° with end of shaft, sometimes 30°), the chamfer extends to the thread depth. The chamfer creates a new crest line, which is then drawn between the two new crest points. It is not parallel to the other crest lines. In the final drawing, all thread lines should be approximately the same weight—thin, but dark.

The corresponding internal detailed threads, in section, are drawn as shown in Fig. 15.11. Notice that for LH threads the lines slope upward to the

left, as shown at (a), while for RH threads the lines slope upward to the right, as at (b). Make all final thread lines medium-thin but dark.

15.12 Detailed Representation of Square Threads
The steps in drawing the detailed representation of an external square thread when the major diameter is over 1″ or 25 mm (approx.) on the drawing are shown in Fig. 15.12.

I. Draw center line, and lay out length and major diameter of thread. Determine P by dividing 1 by

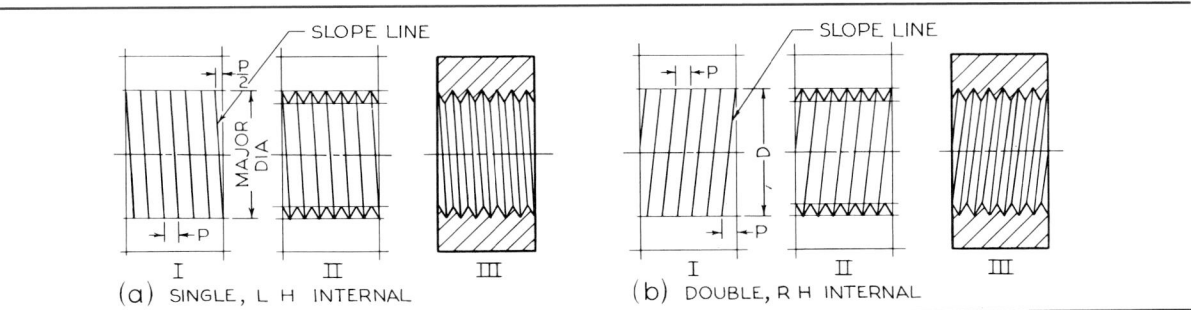

Fig. 15.11 Detailed Representation—Internal Metric, Unified, and American National Threads.

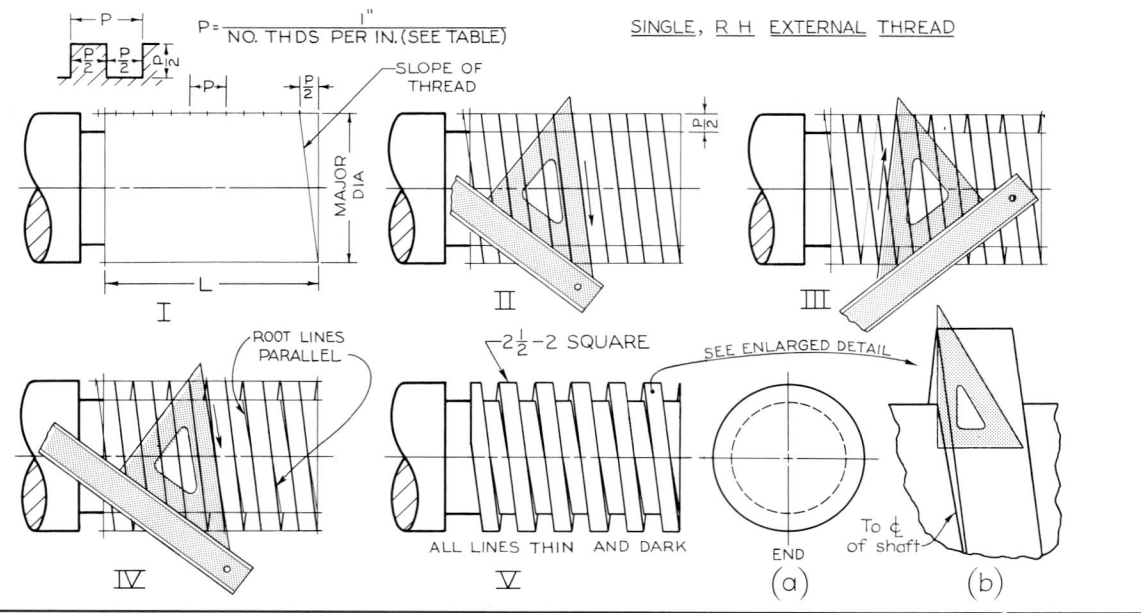

Fig. 15.12 Detailed Representation—External Square Threads.

the number of threads per inch. See Appendix 22. For a single RH thread, the lines slope upward to the left, and the slope line is offset *as for all single threads of any form.* On the upper line, set off spaces equal to $\frac{P}{2}$, as shown, using a scale if possible; otherwise, use the bow dividers or the parallel-line method to space the points.

II.   From the $\frac{P}{2}$ points on the upper line, draw fairly thin lines. Draw guide lines for root of thread, making the depth $\frac{P}{2}$ as shown.

III.   Draw parallel visible back edges of threads.

IV.   Draw parallel visible root lines. Note enlarged detail at (b).

V.   Accent the lines. All lines should be thin and dark.

Note the end view of the shaft at (a). The root circle is hidden; no attempt is made to show the true projection. If the end is chamfered, a solid circle would be drawn instead of the hidden circle.

An assembly drawing, showing an external square thread partly screwed into the nut, is shown in Fig. 15.13. The detail of the square thread at **A** is the same as shown in Fig. 15.12. But when the external and internal threads are assembled, the

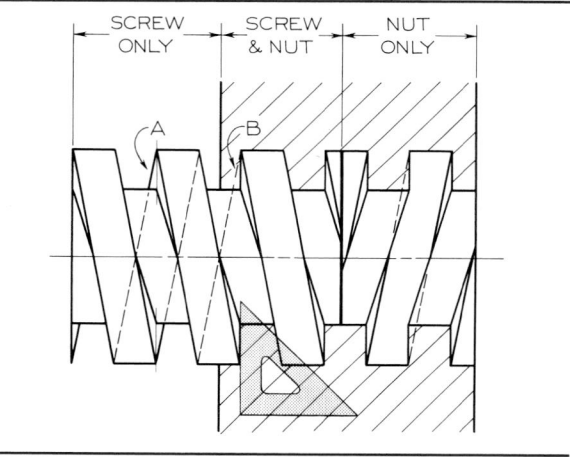

Fig. 15.13 Square Threads in Assembly.

thread in the nut overlaps and covers up half of the V, as shown at **B**.

The internal thread construction is the same as in Fig. 15.14. Note that the thread lines representing the back half of the internal threads (since the thread is in section) slope in the opposite direction from those on the front side of the screw.

Steps in drawing a single internal square thread in section are shown in Fig. 15.14. Note in step II that a crest is drawn opposite a root. This is the case

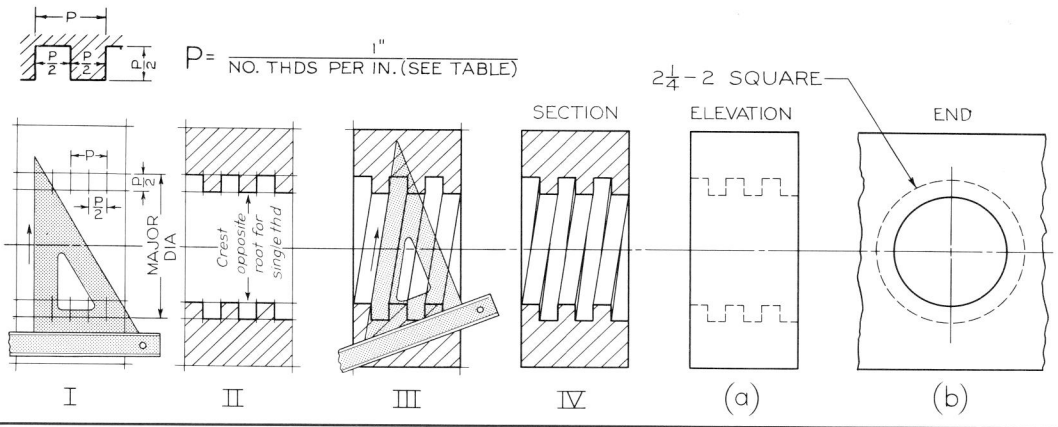

Fig. 15.14 Detailed Representation—Internal Square Threads.

for both single and triple threads. For double or quadruple threads, a crest is opposite a crest. Thus, the construction in steps I and II is the same for any multiple of thread. The differences are developed in step III where the threads and spaces are distinguished and outlined.

The same internal thread is shown in elevation (external view) in Fig. 15.14 (a). The profiles of the threads are drawn in their normal position, but with hidden lines, and the sloping lines are omitted for simplicity. The end view of the same internal thread is shown at (b). Note that the hidden and solid circles are opposite those for the end view of the shaft. See Fig. 15.12 (a).

15.13 Detailed Representation of Acme Thread

The steps in drawing the detailed representation of Acme threads when the major diameter is over 1″ or 25 mm (approx.) on the drawing are shown in Fig. 15.15.

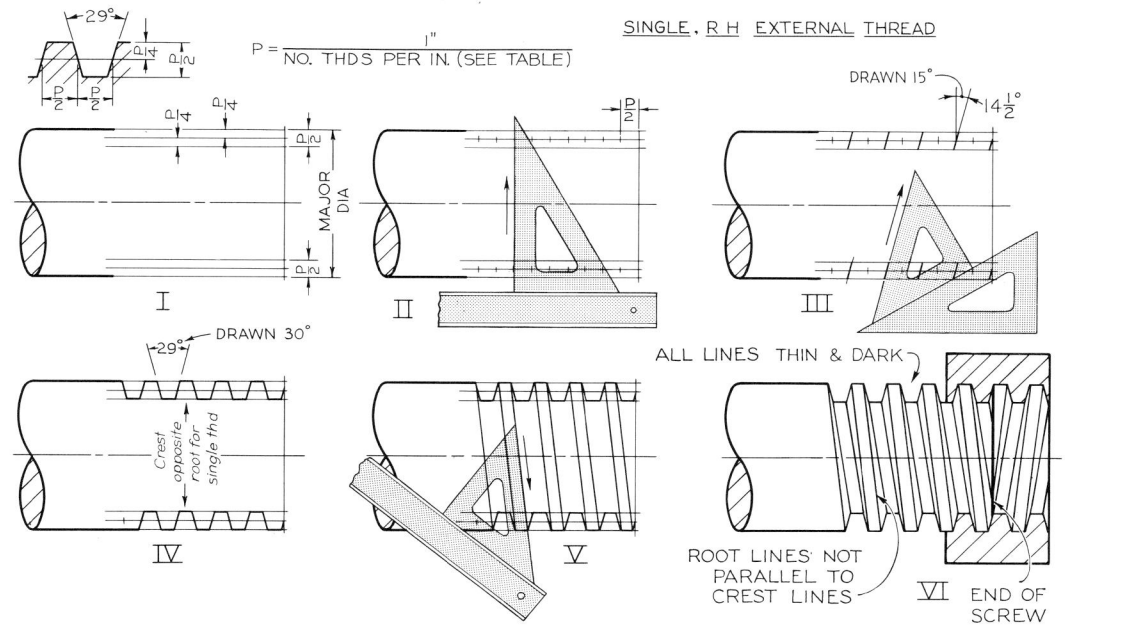

Fig. 15.15 Detailed Representation—Acme Threads.

I. Draw center line, and lay out length and major diameter of thread. Determine P by dividing 1 by the number of threads per inch. See Appendix 22. Draw construction lines for the root diameter, making the thread depth $\frac{P}{2}$. Draw construction lines halfway between crest and root guide lines.

II. On the intermediate construction lines, lay off $\frac{P}{2}$ spaces, as shown. Setting off spaces directly with a scale is possible (for example, if $\frac{P}{2} = \frac{1}{10}''$, use the engineers' scale); otherwise, use bow dividers or parallel-line method.

III. Through alternate points, draw construction lines for sides of threads (draw 15° instead of $14\frac{1}{2}°$).

IV. Draw construction lines for other sides of threads. Note that for single and triple threads, a crest is opposite a root, while for double and quadruple threads, a crest is opposite a crest. Heavy in tops and bottoms of threads.

V. Draw parallel crest lines, final weight at once.

VI. Draw parallel root lines, final weight at once, and heavy in the thread profiles. All lines should be thin and dark. Note that the internal threads in the back of the nut slope in the opposite direction to the external threads on the front side of the screw.

End views of Acme threaded shafts and holes are drawn exactly like those for the square thread, Figs. 15.12 and 15.14.

15.14 Use of Phantom Lines

In representing objects having a series of identical features, phantom lines, Fig. 15.16, may be used to save time. Threaded shafts and springs thus represented may be shortened without the use of conventional breaks, but must be correctly dimensioned. The use of phantom lines is limited almost entirely to detailed drawings.

15.15 Threads in Section

Detailed representations of large threads in section are shown in Figs. 15.6 and 15.10–15.15. As indicated by the note in Fig. 15.6 (b), the root lines and crest lines may be omitted in internal sectional views, if desired.

External thread symbols are shown in section in Fig. 15.7. Note that in the schematic symbol, the V s must be drawn. Internal thread symbols in section are shown in Fig. 15.8.

Threads in an assembly drawing are shown in Fig. 15.17. It is customary not to section a stud or a nut, or any solid part, unless necessary to show some internal shapes. See §15.23. Note that when external and internal threads are sectioned in assembly, the V s are required to show the threaded connection.

15.16 American National Thread

The old American National thread was adopted in 1935. The *form,* or profile, Fig. 15.2 (b), is the same as the old Sellers' profile, or U.S. Standard, and is known as the *National form.* The methods of representation are the same as for the Unified and metric threads. Although American National threads are being replaced by the Unified and metric threads, they may still be encountered on earlier drawings. Five *series* of threads were embraced in the old ANSI standards.

1. *Coarse thread*—A general-purpose thread for holding purposes. Designated NC (National Coarse).
2. *Fine thread*—A greater number of threads per inch; used extensively in automotive and aircraft construction. Designated NF (National Fine).
3. *8-pitch thread*—All diameters have 8 threads per inch. Used on bolts for high-pressure pipe flanges, cylinder-head studs, and similar fasteners. Designated 8N (National form, 8 threads per inch).

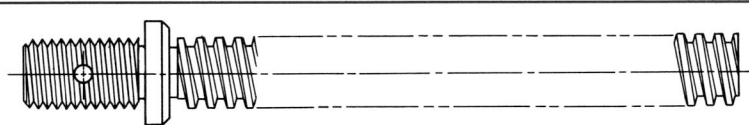

Fig. 15.16   Use of Phantom Lines.

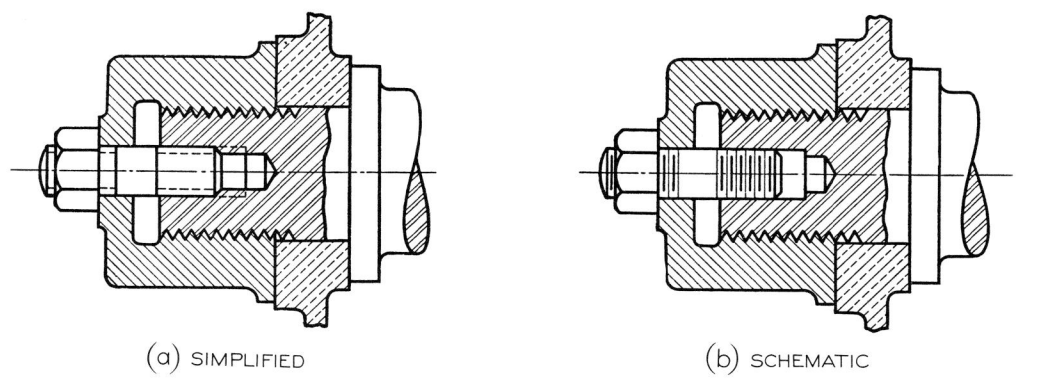

(a) SIMPLIFIED   (b) SCHEMATIC

Fig. 15.17 Threads in Assembly.

4. *12-pitch thread*—All diameters have 12 threads per inch; used in boiler work and for thin nuts on shafts and sleeves in machine construction. Designated 12N (National form, 12 threads per inch).

5. *16-pitch thread*—All diameters have 16 threads per inch; used where necessary to have a fine thread regardless of diameter, as on adjusting collars and bearing retaining nuts. Designated 16N (National form, 16 threads per inch).

15.17 Unified Extra Fine Threads

The Unified extra fine thread series has many more threads per inch for given diameters than any series of the American National or Unified.

The form of thread is the same as the American National. These small threads are used in thin metal where the length of thread engagement is small, in cases where close adjustment is required, and where vibration is great. It is designated **UNEF** (extra fine).

15.18 American National Thread Fits

For general use, three classes of screw thread fits between mating threads (as between bolt and nut) have been established by ANSI.

These fits are produced by the application of tolerances listed in the standard and are described as follows:

Class 1 fit—Recommended only for screw-thread work where clearance between mating parts is essential for rapid assembly and where shake or play is not objectionable.

Class 2 fit—Represents a high quality of commercial thread product and is recommended for the great bulk of interchangeable screw thread work.

Class 3 fit—Represents an exceptionally high quality of commercially threaded product and is recommended only in cases where the high cost of precision tools and continual checking are warranted.

The class of fit desired on a thread is indicated in the thread note, as shown in §15.21.

15.19 Metric and Unified Threads

The preferred metric thread for commercial purposes conforms to the International Organization for Standardization publication [ISO 68] basic profile M for metric threads. This M profile design is comparable to the Unified inch profile, but they are not interchangeable. For commercial purposes, two series of metric threads are preferred—coarse (general purpose) and fine—thus drastically reducing the number of previously used thread series. See Appendix 15.

The Unified thread constitutes the present American National Standard. Some of the earlier American National threads are still included in the new standard. See Appendix 15. The standard lists eleven different series of numbers of threads per inch for the various standard diameters, together with selected combinations of special diameters and pitches.

The eleven series are the *coarse thread series* (UNC or NC) recommended for general use corresponding to the old National coarse thread; the *fine*

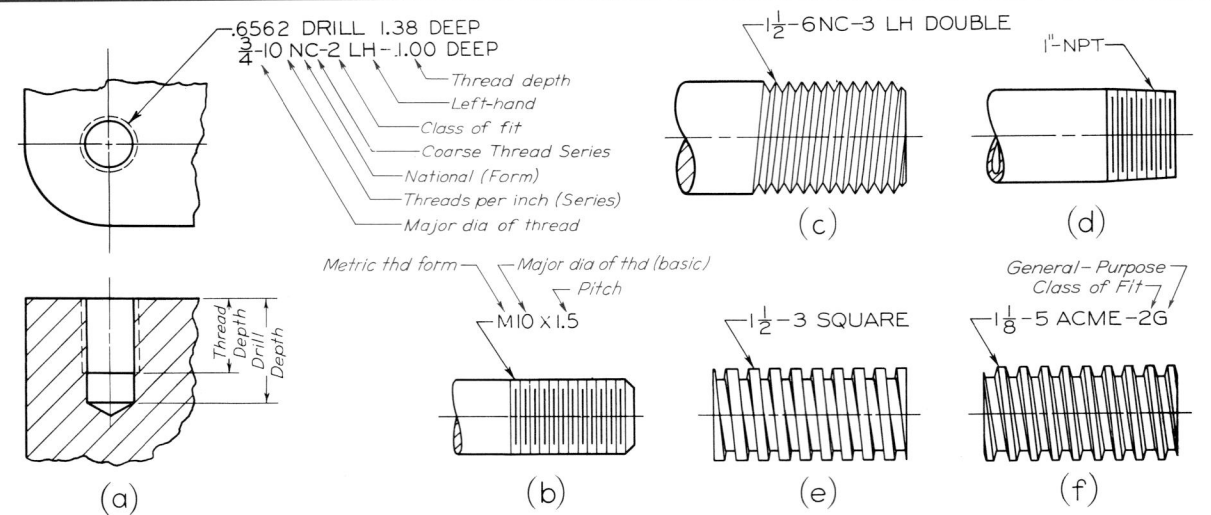

Fig. 15.18   Thread Notes.

thread series (UNF or NF), for general use in automotive and aircraft work and in applications where a finer thread is required; the *extra fine series* (UNEF or NEF), which is the same as the SAE extra fine series, used particularly in aircraft and aeronautical equipment and generally for threads in thin walls; and the eight series of 4, 6, 8, 12, 16, 20, 28, and 32 threads with constant pitch. The 8UN or 8N, 12UN or 12N, and 16UN or 16N series are recommended for the uses corresponding to the old 8-, 12-, and 16-pitch American National threads. In addition, there are three special thread series—UNS, NS, and UN—that involve special combinations of diameter, pitch, and length of engagement.

15.20 Thread Fits, Metric and Unified

For some specialized metric thread applications, the tolerances and deviations are specified by tolerance grade, tolerance position, class, and length of engagement.* Two classes of metric thread fits are generally recognized. The first class of fits is for general-purpose applications and has a tolerance class of **6H** for internal threads and a class **6g** for external threads. The second class of fits is used where closer fits are necessary and has a tolerance of class of **6H** for internal threads and a class of **5g6g** for external threads. Metric thread tolerance classes of **6H/6g** are generally assumed if not otherwise designated and

*ISO Standards Handbook No. 18, 1984.

are used in applications comparable to the **2A/2B** inch classes of fits.

The single-tolerance designation of **6H** refers to both the tolerance grade and position for the pitch diameter and the minor diameter for an internal thread. The single tolerance designation of **6g** refers to both the tolerance grade and position for the pitch diameter and the major diameter of the external thread. A double designation **5g6g** indicates separate tolerance grades for the pitch diameter and for the major diameter of the external thread.

The standard for Unified screw threads specifies tolerances and allowances defining the several classes of fit (degree of looseness or tightness) between mating threads. In the symbols for fit, the letter A refers to external threads and B to internal threads. There are three classes of fit each for external threads (1A, 2A, 3A) and internal threads (1B, 2B, 3B). Classes 1A and 1B have generous tolerances, facilitating rapid assembly and disassembly. Classes 2A and 2B are used in the normal production of screws, bolts, and nuts, as well as a variety of general applications. Classes 3A and 3B provide for applications needing highly accurate and close-fitting threads.

15.21 Thread Notes

Thread notes for metric, Unified, and American National screw threads are shown in Figs. 15.18 and 15.19. These same notes or symbols are used in correspondence, on shop and storeroom records, and

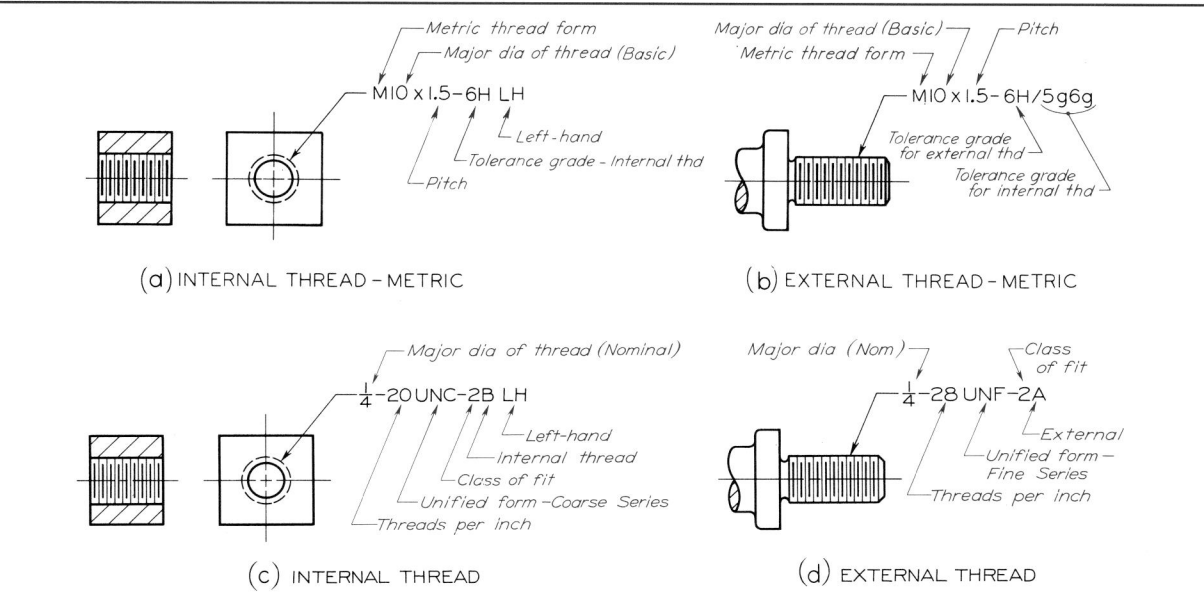

Fig. 15.19 Metric and Unified Thread Notes.

in specifications for parts, taps, dies, tools, and gages.

Metric screw threads are designated basically by the letter M for metric profile followed by the nominal size (basic major diameter) and the pitch, both in millimeters and separated by the symbol ×. For example, the basic thread note M10 × 1.5 is adequate for most commercial purposes, Fig. 15.18 (b). If the generally understood tolerances need to be specified, the tolerance class of 6H for the internal thread or the tolerance class of 6g for the external thread is added to the basic note, Fig. 15.19 (a). Where closer mating threads are desired, a tolerance of 6H for the internal thread and tolerance classes of 5g6g for the external thread are added to the basic note. When the thread note refers to mating parts, a single basic note is adequate with the addition of the internal and external thread tolerance classes separated by the slash. The basic note for mating threads now becomes M10 × 1.5–6H/6g for the general-purpose thread or M10 × 1.5–6H/5g6g for the close-fitting thread, Fig. 15.19 (b). Should the thread be left-hand, LH is added to the thread note. (Absence of LH indicates an RH thread.) If it is necessary to indicate the length of the thread engagement, the letter S (short), N (normal), or L (long) is added to the thread note. For example, the single note M10 × 1.5–6H/6g–N–LH combines the specifications for internal and external mating

left-hand metric threads of 10 mm diameter and 1.5 mm pitch with general-purpose tolerances and normal length of engagement.

A thread note for a blind tapped hole is shown in Fig. 15.18 (a). In a complete note, the tap drill and depth should be given, though in practice they are often omitted and left to the shop. For tap drill sizes, see Appendix 15. If the LH symbol is omitted, the thread is understood to be RH. If the thread is a multiple thread, the word DOUBLE, TRIPLE, or QUADRUPLE should precede the thread depth; otherwise, the thread is understood to be single. Thread notes for holes are perferably attached to the circular views of the holes, as shown.

Thread notes for external threads are preferably given in the longitudinal view of the threaded shaft, as shown in Fig. 15.18 (b)–(f). Examples of 8-, 12-, and 16-pitch threads, not shown in the figure, are 2–8N–2, 2–12N–2, and 2–16N–2. A sample special thread designation is 1½–7N–LH.

General-purpose Acme threads are indicated by the letter G, and centralizing Acme threads by the letter C. Typical thread notes are 1¾–4 ACME–2G or 1¾–6 ACME–4C.

Thread notes for Unified threads are shown in Fig. 15.19 (c) and (d). Unified threads are distinguished from American National threads by the insertion of the letter U before the series letters, and by the letters A or B (for external or internal, re-

---

spectively) after the numeral designating the class of fit. If the letters LH are omitted, the thread is understood to be RH. Some typical thread notes are

$$\tfrac{1}{4}\text{–20 UNC–2A TRIPLE}$$

$$\tfrac{9}{16}\text{–18 UNF–2B}$$

$$1\tfrac{3}{4}\text{–16 UN–2A}$$

15.22 American National Standard Pipe Threads

The American National Standard for pipe threads, originally known as the Briggs standard, was formulated by Robert Briggs in 1882. Two general types of pipe threads have been approved as American National Standard: *taper pipe threads* and *straight pipe threads*.

The profile of the taper pipe thread is illustrated in Fig. 15.20. The taper of the standard tapered pipe thread is 1 in 16 or .75″ per foot measured on the diameter and along the axis. The angle between the sides of the thread is 60°. The depth of the sharp V is .8660p, and the basic maximum depth of the truncated thread is .800p, where p = pitch. The basic pitch diameters, E_0 and E_1, and the basic length of the effective external taper thread, L_2, are determined by the formulas

$$E_0 = D - (.050D + 1.1)\tfrac{1}{n}$$
$$E_1 = E + .0625L_1$$
$$L_2 = (.80D + 6.8)\tfrac{1}{n}$$

where D = basic O.D. of pipe, E_0 = pitch diameter of thread at end of pipe, E_1 = pitch diameter of

thread at large end of internal thread, L_1 = normal engagement by hand, and n = number of threads per inch.

The ANSI also recommended two modified taper pipe threads for (1) dryseal pressure-tight joints (.88″ per foot taper) and (2) rail fitting joints. The former is used to provide a metal-to-metal joint, eliminating the need for a sealer, and is used in refrigeration, marine, automotive, aircraft, and ordnance work. The latter is used to provide a rigid mechanical thread joint as required in rail fitting joints.

While taper pipe threads are recommended for general use, there are certain types of joints where straight pipe threads are used to advantage. The number of threads per inch, the angle, and the depth of thread are the same as on the taper pipe thread, but the threads are cut parallel to the axis. Straight pipe threads are used for pressure-tight joints for pipe couplings, fuel and oil line fittings, drain plugs, free-fitting mechanical joints for fixtures, loose-fitting mechanical joints for locknuts, and loose-fitting mechanical joints for hose couplings.

Pipe threads are represented by detailed or symbolic methods in a manner similar to the representation of Unified and American National threads. The symbolic representation (schematic or simplified) is recommended for general use regardless of diameter, Fig. 15.21. The detailed method is recommended only when the threads are large and when it is desired to show the profile of the thread as, for example, in a sectional view of an assembly.

As shown in Fig. 15.21, it is not necessary to draw the taper on the threads unless there is some reason to emphasize it, since the thread note indicates whether the thread is straight or tapered. If it

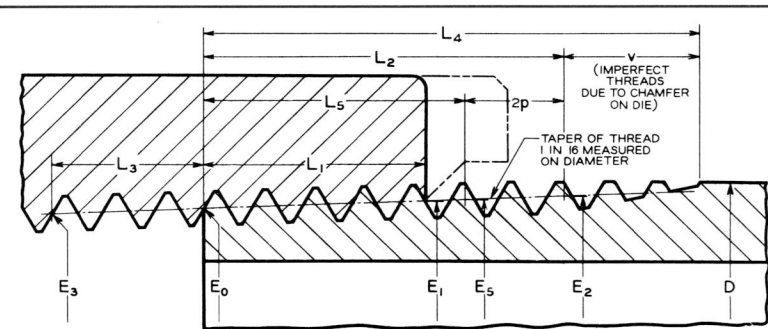

Fig. 15.20 American National Standard Taper Pipe Thread [ANSI B2.1–1968].

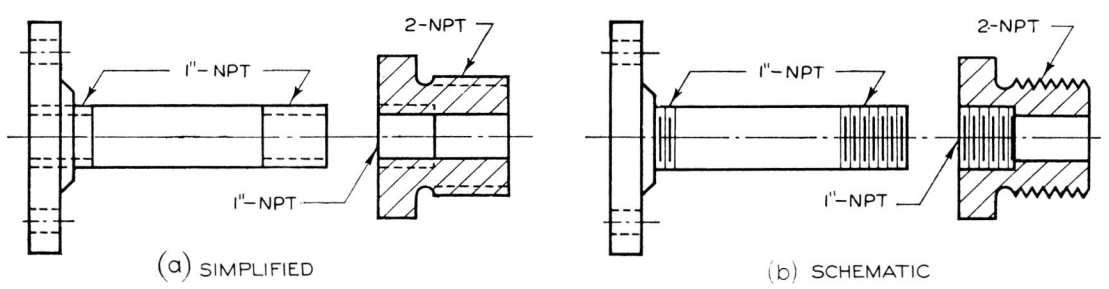

Fig. 15.21 Conventional Representation of Pipe Threads.

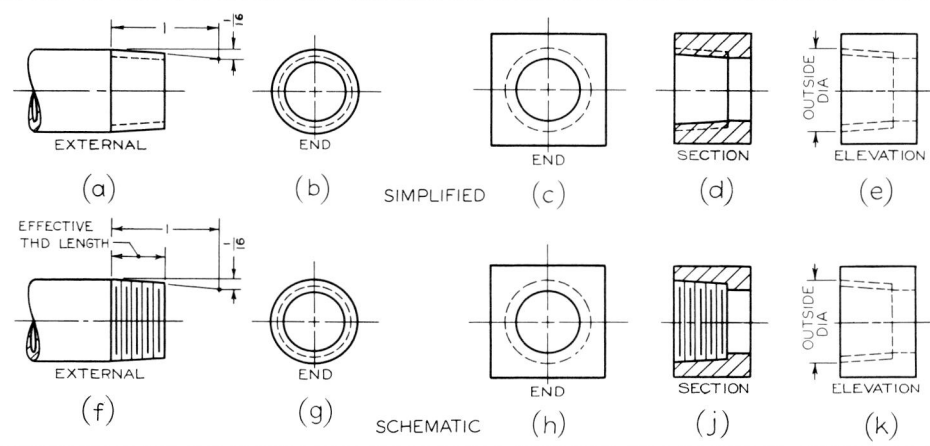

Fig. 15.22 Conventional Pipe Thread Representation.

is desired to show the taper, it should be exaggerated, as shown in Fig. 15.22, where the taper is drawn $\frac{1}{16}''$ per $1''$ *on radius* (or 6.75″ per 1′ *on diameter*) instead of the actual taper of $\frac{1}{16}''$ *on diameter*. American National Standard taper pipe threads are indicated by a note giving the nominal diameter followed by the letters NPT (National pipe taper), as shown in Fig. 15.21. When straight pipe threads are specified, the letters NPS (National pipe straight) are used. In practice, the tap drill size is normally not given in the thread note.

15.23 Bolts, Studs, and Screws

The term *bolt* is generally used to denote a "through bolt" that has a head on one end and is passed through clearance holes in two or more aligned parts and is threaded on the other end to receive a nut to tighten and hold the parts together, Fig. 15.23 (a). See also §§15.25 and 15.26.

A hexagon head *cap screw*, (b), is similar to a bolt, except that it generally has greater length of

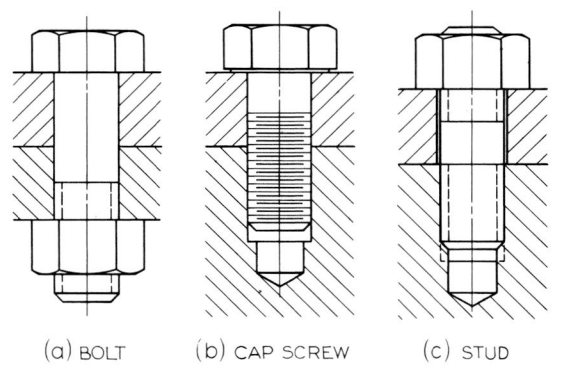

Fig. 15.23 Bolt, Cap Screw, and Stud.

thread, for when it is used without a nut, one of the members being held together is threaded to act as a nut. It is screwed on with a wrench. Cap screws are not screwed into thin materials if strength is desired. See §15.29.

A *stud*, (c), is a steel rod threaded on both ends. It is screwed into place with a pipe wrench or, pref-

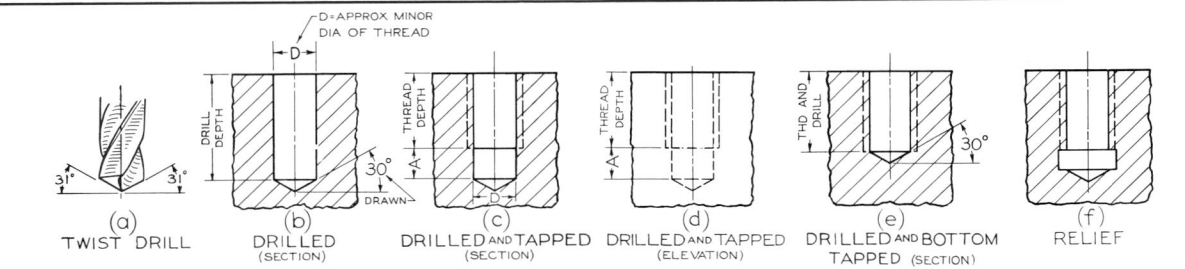

Fig. 15.24   Drilled and Tapped Holes.

erably, with a stud driver. As a rule, a stud is passed through a clearance hole in one member and screwed into another member, and a nut is used on the free end, as shown.

A *machine screw*, Fig. 15.33, is similar to the slotted-head cap screws but, in general, is smaller. It may be used with or without a nut.

A *set screw*, Fig. 15.34, is a screw with or without a head that is screwed through one member and whose special point is forced against another member to prevent relative motion between the two parts.

It is not customary to section bolts, nuts, screws, and similar parts when drawn in assembly, as shown in Figs. 15.23 and 15.32, because they do not themselves require sectioning for clearness. See §16.21.

15.24 Tapped Holes

The bottom of a drilled hole is conical in shape, as formed by the point of the twist drill, Fig. 15.24 (a) and (b). When an ordinary drill is used in connection with tapping, it is referred to as a *tap drill*. On drawings, an angle of 30° is used to approximate the actual 31°.

The thread length is the length of full or perfect threads. The tap drill depth is the depth of the cylindrical portion of the hole and does not include the cone point, (b). The portion A of the drill depth shown beyond the threads at (c) and (d) includes the several imperfect threads produced by the chamfered end of the tap. This distance A varies according to drill size and whether a plug tap, Fig. 12.16 (h), or a bottoming tap is used to finish the hole. For drawing purposes, when the tap drill depth is not specified, the distance A may be drawn equal to three schematic thread pitches, Fig. 15.9.

A tapped hole finished with a bottoming tap is drawn as shown in Fig. 15.24 (e). Blind bottoming holes should be avoided wherever possible. A better procedure is to cut a relief with its diameter slightly

greater than the major diameter of the thread, Fig. 15.24 (f).

One of the chief causes of tap breakage is insufficient tap drill depth, in which the tap is forced against a bed of chips in the bottom of the hole. Therefore, the drafter should never draw a blind hole when a through hole of not much greater length can be used. When a blind hole is necessary however, the tap drill depth should be generous. Tap drill sizes for Unified, American National, and metric threads are given in Appendix 15. It is good practice to give the tap drill size in the thread note, §15.21.

The thread length in a tapped hole depends upon the major diameter and the material being tapped. In Fig. 15.25, the minimum engagement length X, when both parts are steel, is equal to the diameter D of the thread. When a steel screw is screwed into cast iron, brass, or bronze, X = $1\frac{1}{2}$D; when screwed into aluminum, zinc, or plastic, X = 2D.

Since the tapped thread length contains only full threads, it is necessary to make this length only one or two pitches beyond the end of the engaging screw. In simplified or schematic representation, the threads are omitted in the bottoms of tapped

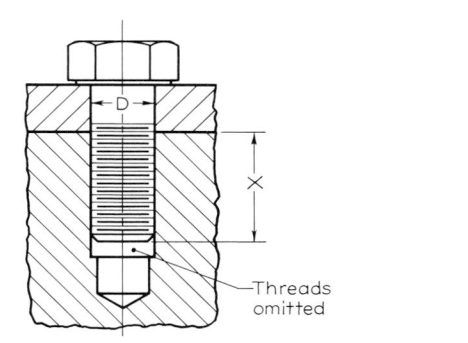

Fig. 15.25   Tapped Holes.

holes so as to show the ends of the screws clearly, Fig. 15.25.

When a bolt or a screw is passed through a clearance hole in one member, the hole may be drilled 0.8 mm ($\frac{1}{32}$″) larger than the screw up to $\frac{3}{8}$″ or 10 mm diameter and 1.5 mm ($\frac{1}{16}$″) larger for larger diameters. For more precise work, the clearance hole may be only 0.4 mm ($\frac{1}{64}$″) larger than the screw up to $\frac{3}{8}$″ or 10 mm diameter and 0.8 mm ($\frac{1}{32}$″) larger for larger diameters. Closer fits may be specified for special conditions.

The clearance spaces on each side of a screw or bolt need not be shown on a drawing unless it is necessary to show that there is no thread engagement, in which case the clearance spaces are drawn about 1.2 mm ($\frac{3}{64}$″) wide for clarity.

15.25 Standard Bolts and Nuts

American National Standard bolts and nuts,* metric and inch series, are produced in the hexagon form, and the square form is only produced in the inch series, Fig. 15.26. Square heads and nuts are chamfered at 30°, and hexagon heads and nuts are chamfered at 15° to 30°. Both are drawn at 30° for simplicity.

Bolt Types

Bolts are grouped according to use: *regular* bolts for general service, and *heavy* bolts for heavier service or easier wrenching. Square bolts come only in the regular type; hexagon bolts, screws, and nuts and square nuts are standard in both types.

Finish

Square bolts and nuts, hexagon bolts, and hexagon flat nuts are *unfinished.* Unfinished bolts and nuts are not machined on any surface except for the threads. Traditionally, hexagon bolts and hexagon nuts have been available as unfinished, semifinished, or finished. According to the latest standards, hexagon cap screws and finished hexagon bolts have been consolidated into a single product—*hex cap screws*—thus eliminating the regular semifinished hexagon bolt classification. Heavy semifinished hexagon bolts and heavy finished hexagon bolts also have been combined into a single product called *heavy hex screws.* Hexagon cap screws, heavy hexagon screws, and all hexagon nuts, except hexagon flat nuts, are considered *finished* to some degree and are characterized by a "washer face" machined or

*The ANSI standards cover several bolts and nuts. For complete details, see the standards.

otherwise formed on the bearing surface. The washer face is $\frac{1}{64}$″ thick (drawn $\frac{1}{32}$″), and its diameter is equal to $1\frac{1}{2}$ times the body diameter D for the inch series.

For nuts the bearing surface also may be a circular surface produced by chamfering. Hexagon screws and hexagon nuts have closer tolerances and may have a more finished appearance, but are not completely machined. There is no difference in the drawing for the degree of finish on finished screws and nuts.

Metric bolts, cap screws, and nuts are produced in the hexagon form, Fig. 15.26 (a). The hexagon heads and nuts are chamfered 15° to 30°. Both are drawn at 30° for simplicity.

Bolt Types

Metric hexagon bolts are grouped according to use: *regular* and *heavy* bolts and nuts for general service and *high-strength* bolts and nuts for structural bolting.

Finish

Hexagon cap screws, hexagon bolts, and hexagon nuts (including metric) are considered finished to some degree and are usually characterized by a "washer face" machined or otherwise formed on the bearing surface. The washer face is approximately 0.5 mm thick (drawn 1 mm) and its diameter is equal to $1\frac{1}{2}$ times the body diameter D.

For hexagon nuts the circular bearing surface may be produced by chamfering. Hexagon head bolts (usually the larger sizes) are available without the washer-face bearing surface.

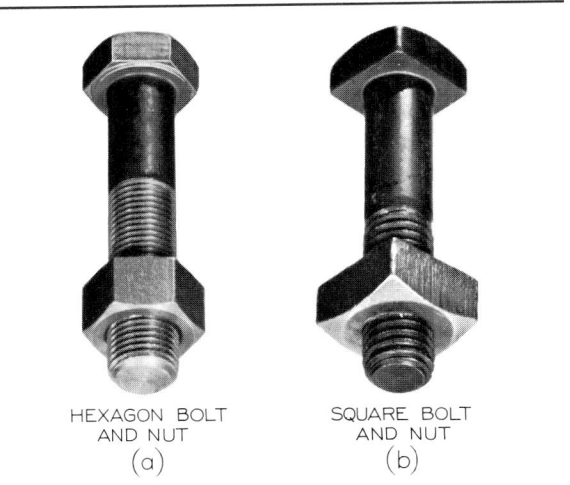

HEXAGON BOLT AND NUT

(a)

SQUARE BOLT AND NUT

(b)

Fig. 15.26 Standard Bolts and Nuts.

Proportions

Sizes based on diameter D of the bolt body (including metric), Fig. 15.27, which are either exact formula proportions or close approximations for drawing purposes, are as follows.

Regular hexagon and square bolts and nuts:

$$W = 1\tfrac{1}{2}D \qquad H = \tfrac{2}{3}D \qquad T = \tfrac{7}{8}D$$

where W = width across flats, H = head height, and T = nut height.

Heavy hexagon bolts and nuts and square nuts:

$$W = 1\tfrac{1}{2}D + \tfrac{1}{8}'' \text{ (or } + 3 \text{ mm)}$$
$$H = \tfrac{2}{3}D \qquad T = D$$

The washer face is always included in the head or nut height for finished hexagon screw heads and nuts.

Threads

Square and hex bolts, hex cap screws, and finished nuts in the inch series are usually Class 2 and may have coarse, fine, or 8-pitch threads. Unfinished nuts have coarse threads, Class 2B. For diameter and pitch specifications for metric threads, see Appendix 18.

Thread Lengths

For bolts or screws up to 6" (150 mm) in length:

$$\text{Thread length} = 2D + \tfrac{1}{4}'' \text{ (or } + 6 \text{ mm)}$$

For bolts or screws over 6" in length,

$$\text{Thread length} = 2D + \tfrac{1}{2}'' \text{ (or } + 12 \text{ mm)}$$

Fasteners too short for these formulas are threaded as close to the head as practicable. For drawing purposes, this may be taken as three pitches, approximately. The threaded end may be rounded or chamfered, but is usually drawn with a 45° chamfer from the thread depth, Fig. 15.27.

Bolt Lengths

Lengths of bolts have not been standardized because of the endless variety required by industry. Short bolts are typically available in standard length

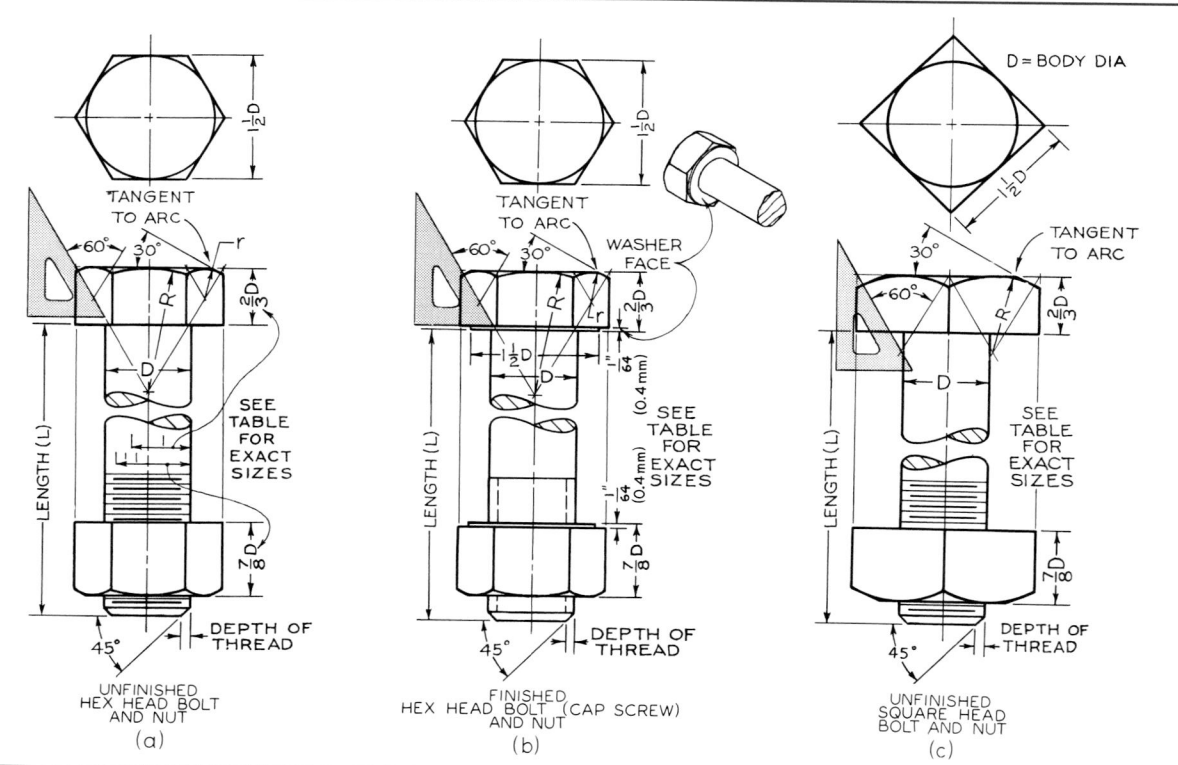

Fig. 15.27 Bolt Proportions (Regular).

increments of $\frac{1}{4}''$ (6 mm), while long bolts come in increments of $\frac{1}{2}$ to $1''$ (12 to 25 mm). For dimensions of standard bolts and nuts, see Appendix 18.

15.26 To Draw Standard Bolts

In practice, standard bolts and nuts are not shown on detail drawings unless they are to be altered, but they appear so frequently on assembly drawings that a suitable but rapid method of drawing them must be used. Time-saving templates are available, or they may be drawn from exact dimensions taken from tables (see Appendix 18) if accuracy is important, as in figuring clearances, but in the great majority of cases the conventional representation, in which proportions based upon the body diameter are used, will be sufficient, and a considerable amount of time may be saved. Three typical bolts illustrating the use of these proportions for the regular bolts are shown in Fig. 15.27.

Although the curves produced by the chamfer on the bolt heads and nuts are hyperbolas, in practice these curves are always represented approximately by means of circular arcs, as shown in Fig. 15.27.

Generally, bolt heads and nuts should be drawn "across corners" in all views, regardless of projection. This conventional violation of projection is used to prevent confusion between the square and hexagon heads and nuts and to show actual clearances. Only when there is a special reason should bolt heads and nuts be drawn across flats. In such cases, the conventional proportions shown in Fig. 15.28 are used.

Steps in drawing hexagon bolts, cap screws, and nuts are illustrated in Fig. 15.29, and those for square bolts and nuts in Fig. 15.30. Before drawing a bolt, the diameter of the bolt, the length (from the

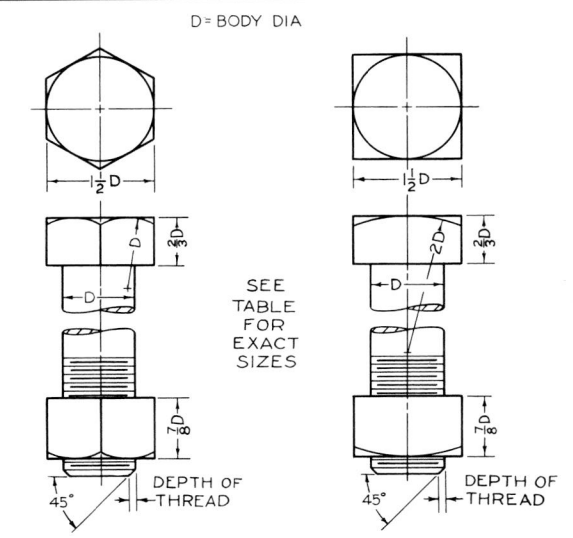

Fig. 15.28 Bolts "Across Flats."

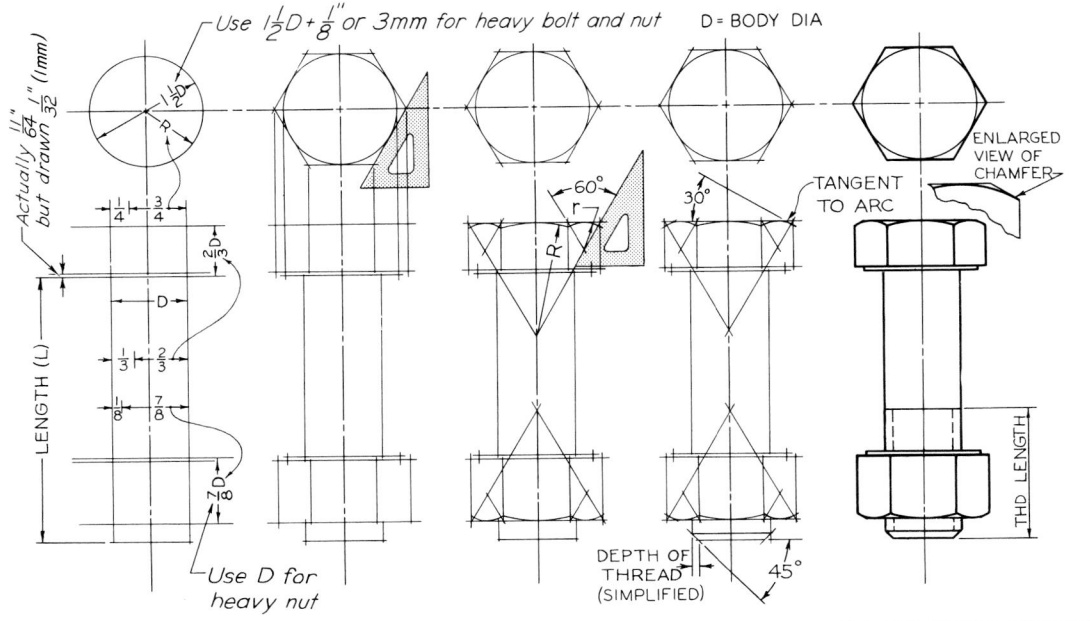

Fig. 15.29 Steps in Drawing a Finished Hexagon Head Bolt (Cap Screw) and Hexagon Nut.

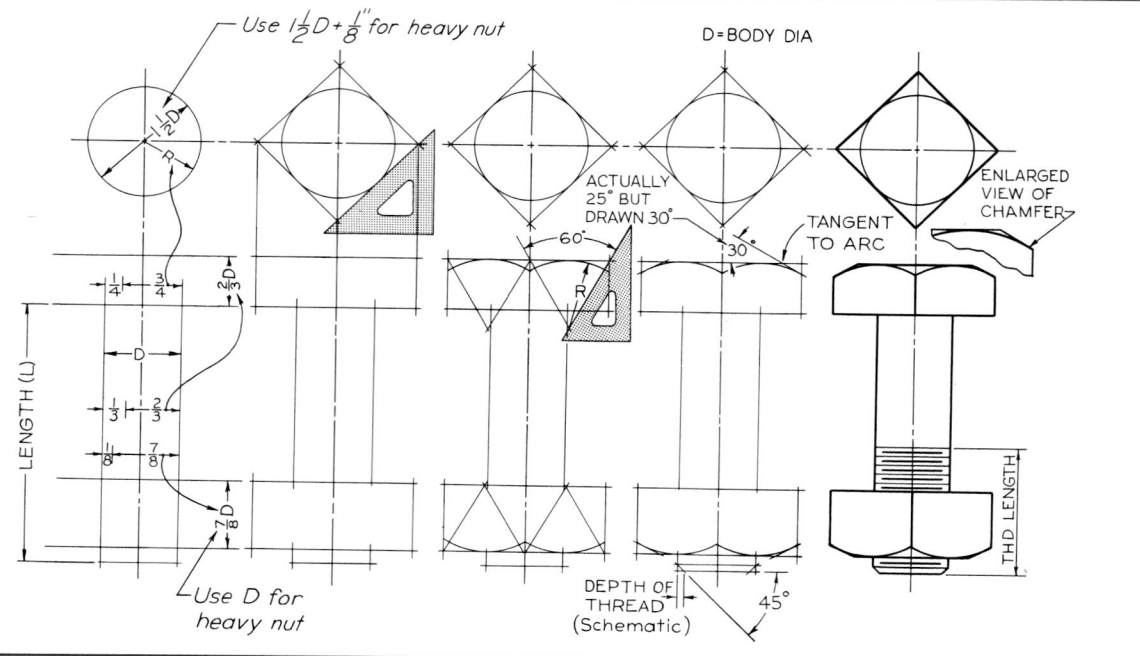

Fig. 15.30 Steps in Drawing Square-Head Bolt and Square Nut.

underside of the bearing surface to the tip), the style of head (square or hexagon), and the type (regular or heavy), as well as the finish, must be known.

If only the longitudinal view of a bolt is needed, it is necessary to draw only the lower half of the top views in Figs. 15.29 and 15.30 *with light construction lines* in order to project the corners of the hexagon or square to the front view. These construction lines may then be erased if desired.

The head and nut heights can be spaced off with the dividers on the shaft diameter and then transferred as shown in both figures, or the scale may be used as in Fig. 5.15. The heights should not be determined by arithmetic.

The $\frac{1}{64}''$ (0.4 mm) washer face has a diameter equal to the distance across flats of the bolt head or nut. It appears only on the metric and finished hexagon screws or nuts, the washer face thickness being drawn at $\frac{1}{32}''$ (1 mm) for clearness. The $\frac{1}{32}''$ (1 mm) is included in the head or nut height.

Threads should be drawn in simplified or schematic form for body diameters of 1″ (25 mm) or less on the drawing, Fig. 15.9 (b) or (d), and by detailed representation for larger diameters, §§15.7 and 15.8. The threaded end of the screw should be chamfered at 45° from the schematic thread depth, Fig. 15.9 (a).

On drawings of small bolts or nuts under approximately $\frac{1}{2}''$ diameter (12 mm), where the cham-

fer is hardly noticeable, the chamfer on the head or nut may be omitted in the longitudinal view.

Many styles of templates are available for saving time in drawing bolt heads and nuts. One of these, the Draftsquare, is illustrated in Fig. 2.68 (b).

15.27 Specifications for Bolts and Nuts

In specifying bolts in parts lists, in correspondence, or elsewhere, the following information must be covered in order:

1. Nominal size of bolt body

2. Thread specification or thread note (see §15.21)

3. Length of bolt

4. Finish of bolt

5. Style of head

6. Name

EXAMPLE (Complete)

$$\frac{3}{4}\text{–10 UNC–2A} \times 2\frac{1}{2} \text{ HEXAGON CAP SCREW}$$

EXAMPLE (Abbreviated)

$$\frac{3}{4} \times 2\frac{1}{2} \text{ HEX CAP SCR}$$

EXAMPLE (Metric)

M8 × 1.25–40, HEX CAP SCR

Nuts may be specified as follows:

EXAMPLE (Complete)

$\frac{5}{8}$–11 UNC–2B SQUARE NUT

EXAMPLE (Abbreviated) $\frac{5}{8}$ SQ NUT

EXAMPLE (Metric) M8 × 1.25 HEX NUT

For either bolts or nuts, the words REGULAR or GENERAL PURPOSE are assumed if omitted from the specification. If the heavy series is intended, the word HEAVY should appear as the first word in the name of the fastener. Likewise, HIGH STRENGTH STRUCTURAL should be indicated for such metric fasteners. However, the number of the specific ISO standard is often included in the metric specifications; for example, HEXAGON NUT ISO 4032 M12

× 1.75. Similarly, finish need not be mentioned if the fastener or nut is correctly named. See §15.25.

15.28 Locknuts and Locking Devices

Many types of special nuts and devices to prevent nuts from unscrewing are available, some of the most common of which are illustrated in Fig. 15.31. The American National Standard *jam nuts*, (a) and (b), are the same as the hexagon or hexagon flat nuts, except that they are thinner. The application at (b), where the larger nut is on top and is screwed on more tightly, is recommended. They are the same distance across flats as the corresponding hexagon nuts ($1\frac{1}{2}D$ or $1\frac{1}{2}D + \frac{1}{8}''$). They are slightly over $\frac{1}{2}D$ in thickness, but are drawn $\frac{1}{2}D$ for simplicity. They are available with or without the washer face in the regular and heavy types. The tops of all are flat and chamfered at 30°, and the finished forms have either a washer face or a chamfered bearing surface.

The lock washer, shown at (c), and the cotter pin, (e), (g), and (h), are very common. See Appendixes 27 and 30. The set screw, (f), is often made to press against a plug of softer material, such as brass, which in turn presses against the threads without deforming them.

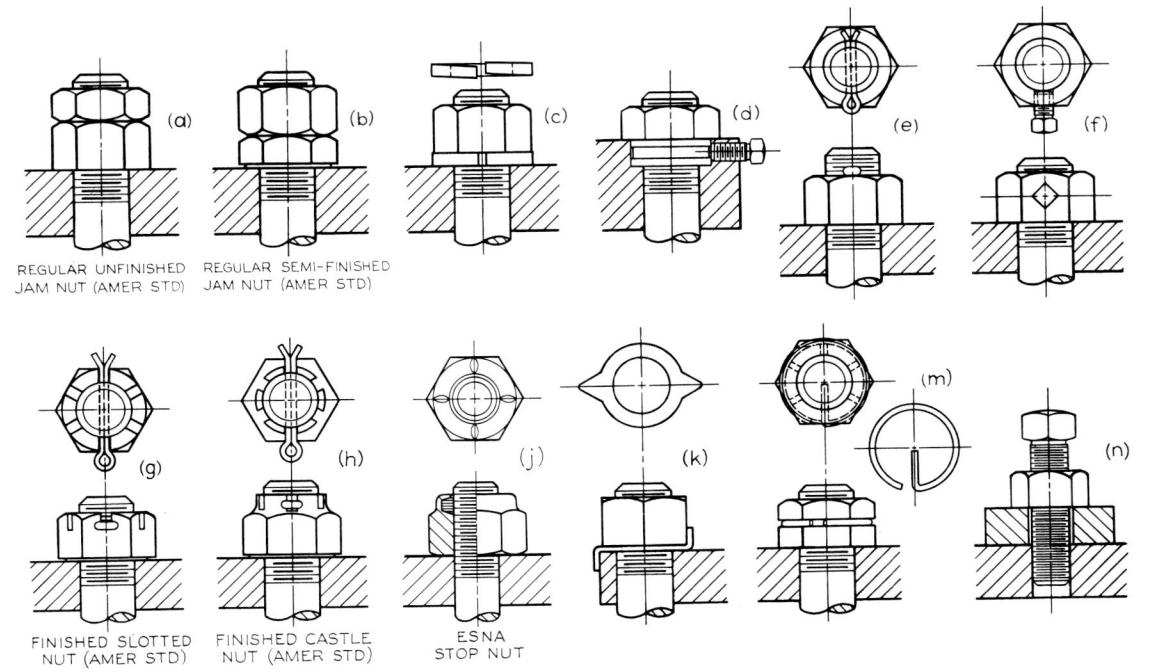

Fig. 15.31 Locknuts and Locking Devices.

For use with cotter pins (see Appendix 30), a hex slotted nut, (g), and a hex castle nut, (h), as well as a hex thick slotted nut and a heavy hex thick slotted nut are recommended.

Similar metric locknuts and locking devices are available. See fastener catalogs for details.

15.29 Standard Cap Screws

Five types of American National Standard cap screws are shown in Fig. 15.32. The first four of these have standard heads, while the socket head cap screws, (e), have several different shapes of round heads and sockets. Cap screws are regularly produced in finished form and are used on machine tools and other machines, for which accuracy and appearance are important. The ranges of sizes and exact dimensions are given in Appendixes 18 and 19. The hexagon head cap screw and hex socket head

cap screw in several forms are available in metric. See Appendix 18.

Cap screws ordinarily pass through a clearance hole in one member, as explained in §15.24, and screw into another. The clearance hole need not be shown on the drawing when the presence of the unthreaded clearance hole is obvious.

Cap screws are inferior to studs if frequent removal is necessary; hence, they are used on machines requiring few adjustments. The slotted or socket-type heads are best under crowded conditions.

The actual standard dimensions may be used in drawing the cap screws whenever exact sizes are necessary, but this is seldom the case. In Fig. 15.32 the dimensions are given in terms of body diameter D, and they closely conform to the actual dimensions. The resulting drawings are almost exact reproductions and are easy to draw. The hexagonal

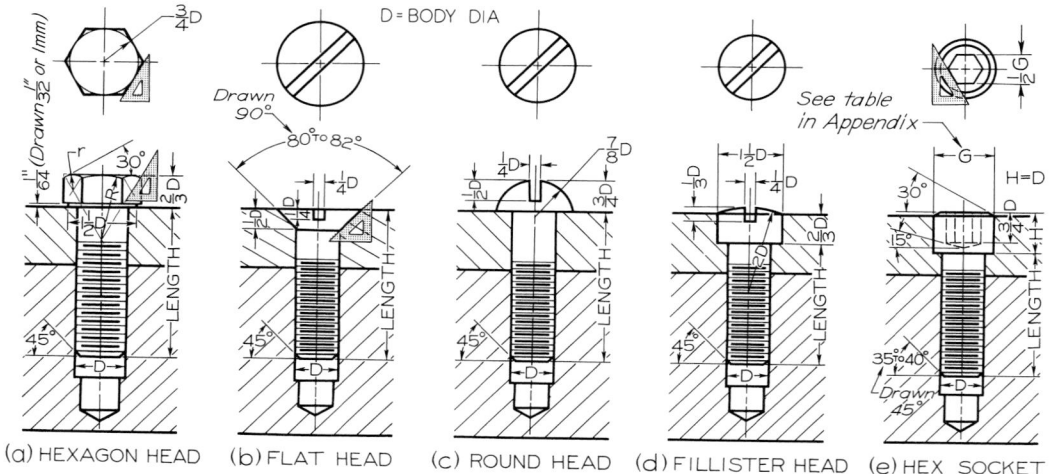

(a) HEXAGON HEAD   (b) FLAT HEAD   (c) ROUND HEAD   (d) FILLISTER HEAD   (e) HEX SOCKET

Hexagon Head Screws: Coarse, Fine, or 8-Thread Series, 2A. Thread length = $2D + \frac{1}{4}''$ up to 6″ long and $2D + \frac{1}{2}''$ if over 6″ long. For screws too short for formula, threads extend to within $2\frac{1}{2}$ threads of the head for diameters up to 1″. Screw lengths not standardized. For suggested lengths for metric Hexagon Head Screws, see Appendix 15.

Slotted Head Screws: Coarse, Fine, or 8-Thread Series, 2A. Thread length = $2D + \frac{1}{4}''$. Screw lengths not standardized. For screws too short for formula, threads extend to within $2\frac{1}{2}$ threads of the head.

Hexagon Socket Screws: Coarse or Fine Threads, 3A. Coarse thread length = $2D + \frac{1}{2}''$ where this would be over $\frac{1}{2}L$; otherwise thread length = $\frac{1}{2}L$. Fine thread length = $1\frac{1}{2}D + \frac{1}{2}''$ where this would be over $\frac{3}{8}L$; otherwise thread length = $\frac{3}{8}L$. Increments in screw lengths = $\frac{1}{8}''$ for screws $\frac{1}{4}''$ to 1″ long, $\frac{1}{4}''$ for screws 1″ to 3″ long, and $\frac{1}{2}''$ for screws $3\frac{1}{2}''$ to 6″ long.

Fig. 15.32 Standard Cap Screws. See Appendixes 18 and 19.

head cap screw is drawn in the manner shown in Fig. 15.29. The points are drawn chamfered at 45° from the schematic thread depth.

For correct representation of tapped holes, see §15.24. For information on drilled, countersunk, or counterbored holes, see §§7.33 and 12.16.

In an assembly section, it is customary not to section screws, bolts, shafts, or other solid parts whose center lines lie in the cutting plane. Such parts in themselves do not require sectioning and are, therefore, shown "in the round," Fig. 15.32 and §16.21.

Note that screwdriver slots are drawn at 45° in the circular views of the heads, without regard to true projection, and that threads in the bottom of the tapped holes are omitted so that the ends of the screws may be clearly seen. A typical cap screw note is as follows:

EXAMPLE (Complete)

$\frac{3}{8}$–16 UNC–2A $\times$ $2\frac{1}{2}$ HEXAGON HEAD CAP SCREW

EXAMPLE (Abbreviated)

$\frac{3}{8}$ $\times$ $2\frac{1}{2}$ HEX HD CAP SCR

EXAMPLE (Metric)

M20 $\times$ 2.5 $\times$ 80 HEX HD CAP SCR

15.30 Standard Machine Screws

Machine screws are similar to cap screws but are in general smaller (.060″ to .750″ dia). There are eight ANSI-approved forms of heads shown in Appendix 20. The hexagonal head may be slotted if desired. All others are available in either slotted or recessed-head forms. Standard machine screws are regularly produced with a naturally bright finish, not heat treated, and are regularly supplied with plain-sheared ends, not chamfered. For similar metric machine screw forms and specifications, see Appendix 20.

Machine screws are particularly adapted to screwing into thin materials, and all the smaller-numbered screws are threaded nearly to the head. They are used extensively in firearms, jigs, fixtures, and dies. Machine screw nuts are used mainly on the round head, pan head, and flat head types, and are usually hexagonal in form.

Exact dimensions of machine screws are given in Appendix 20, but they are seldom needed for drawing purposes. The four most common types of machine screws are shown in Fig. 15.33, where proportions based on diameter D conform closely to the actual dimensions and produce almost exact drawings. Clearance holes and counterbores should be made slightly larger than the screws, as explained in §15.24.

Note that the threads in the bottom of the tapped holes are omitted so that the ends of the screws will be clearly seen. Observe also that it is conventional practice to draw the screwdriver slots at 45° in the circular view without regard to true projection.

A typical machine screw note is as follows:

EXAMPLE (Complete)

No. 10 (.1900)–32 NF–3 $\times$ $\frac{5}{8}$ FILLISTER HEAD

MACHINE SCREW

EXAMPLE (Abbreviated)

No. 10 (.1900) $\times$ $\frac{5}{8}$ FILL HD MACH SCR

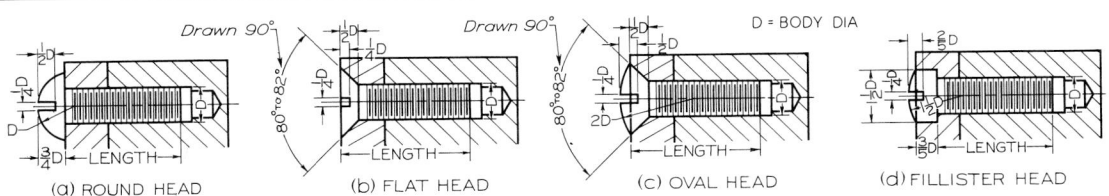

Threads: National Coarse or Fine, Class 2 fit. On Screws 2″ long or less, threads extend to within 2 threads of head; on longer screws thread length = $1\frac{3}{4}$″. Screw lengths not standardized.

Fig. 15.33 Standard Machine Screws. See Appendix 20.

EXAMPLE (Metric)

M8 × 1.25 × 30 SLOTTED PAN HEAD
MACHINE SCREW

15.31 Standard Set Screws

The function of set screws, Fig. 15.34 (a), is to prevent relative motion, usually rotary, between two parts, such as the movement of the hub of a pulley on a shaft. A set screw is screwed into one part so that its point bears firmly against another part. If the point of the set screw is cupped, (e), or if a flat is milled on the shaft, (a), the screw will hold much more firmly. Obviously, set screws are not efficient when the load is heavy or is suddenly applied. Usually they are manufactured of steel and case hardened.

The American National Standard square head set screw and slotted headless set screw are shown in Fig. 15.34 (a) and (b). Two American National Standard socket set screws are illustrated at (c) and (d). American National Standard set screw points are shown from (e) to (k). The headless set screws have come into greater use because the projecting head of headed set screws has caused many industrial casualties; this has resulted in legislation prohibiting their use in many states.

Most of the dimensions in Fig. 15.34 are American National Standard formula dimensions, and the resulting drawings are almost exact representations.

Metric hexagon socket headless set screws with the full range of points are available and are represented in the same manner as given in Fig. 15.34. Nominal diameters of metric hex socket set screws are 1.6, 2, 2.5, 3, 4, 5, 6, 8, 10, 12, 16, 20, and 24 mm.

Square head set screws have coarse, fine, or 8-pitch threads, Class 2A, but are usually furnished with coarse threads, since the square head set screw is generally used on the rougher grades of work. Slotted headless and socket set screws have coarse or fine threads, Class 3A.

Nominal diameters of set screws range from number 0 up through 2″, set screw lengths are standardized in increments of $\frac{1}{32}$″ to 1″ depending upon the overall length of the set screw.

Metric set screw length increments range from 0.5 to 4 mm, again depending upon overall screw length.

Set screws are specified as follows:

EXAMPLE (Complete)

$$\frac{3}{8}\text{–16 UNC–2a} \times \frac{3}{4} \text{ SQUARE HEAD}$$
$$\text{FLAT POINT SET SCREW}$$

EXAMPLES (Abbreviated)

$$\frac{3}{8} \times 1\frac{1}{4} \text{ SQ HD FL PT SS}$$

$$\frac{7}{16} \times \frac{3}{4} \text{ HEX SOC CUP PT SS}$$

$$\frac{1}{4}\text{–20 UNC 2A} \times \frac{5}{8} \text{ SLOT. HDLS CONE PT SS}$$

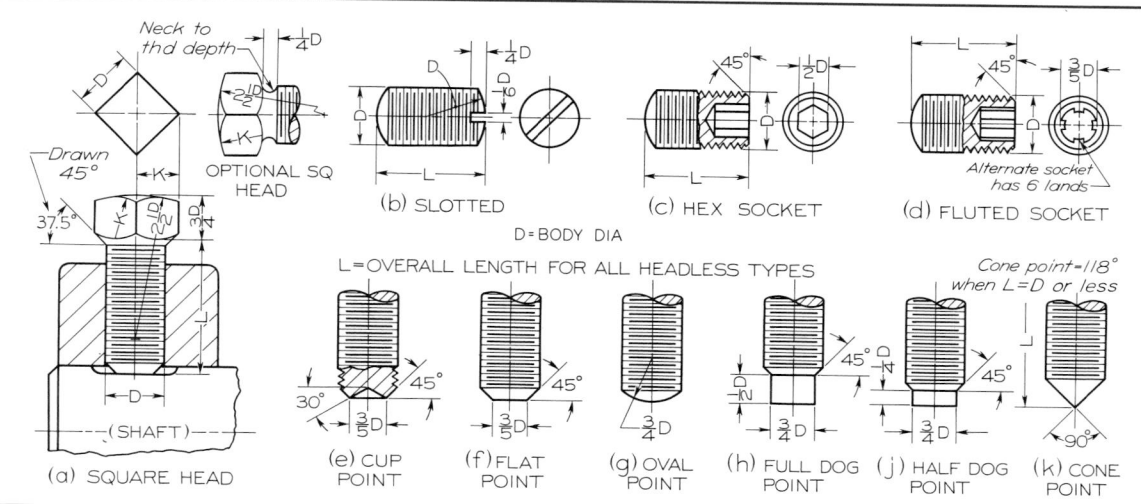

Fig. 15.34　American National Standard Set Screws.

EXAMPLE (Metric)

M10 × 1.5 × 12 HEX SOCKET HEAD SET SCREW

15.32 American National Standard Wood Screws

Wood screws with three types of heads—flat, round, and oval—have been standardized, Fig. 15.35. The dimensions shown closely approximate the actual dimensions and are more than sufficiently accurate for use on drawings.

The Phillips style recessed head is also available on several types of fasteners as well as wood screws. Three styles of cross recesses have been standardized by the ANSI. Many examples may be seen on the automobile. A special screwdriver is used, as

shown in Fig. 15.36 (q), and results in rapid assembly without damage to the head.

15.33 Miscellaneous Fasteners

Many other types of fasteners have been devised for specialized uses. Some of the more common types are shown in Fig. 15.36. A number of these are American National Standard round head bolts including carriage, button head, step, and countersunk bolts.

Aero-thread inserts, or heli-coil inserts, as shown at (p), are shaped like a spring except that the cross section of the wire conforms to threads on the screw and in the hole. These are made of phosphor bronze or stainless steel, and they provide a hard, smooth protective lining for tapped threads in soft metals and in plastics.

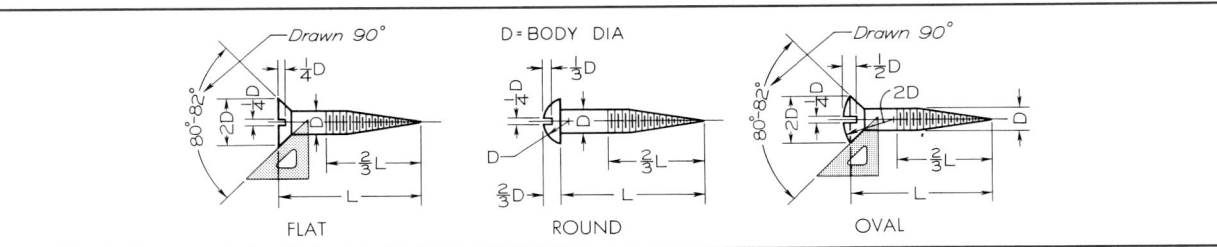

Fig. 15.35   American National Standard Wood Screws.

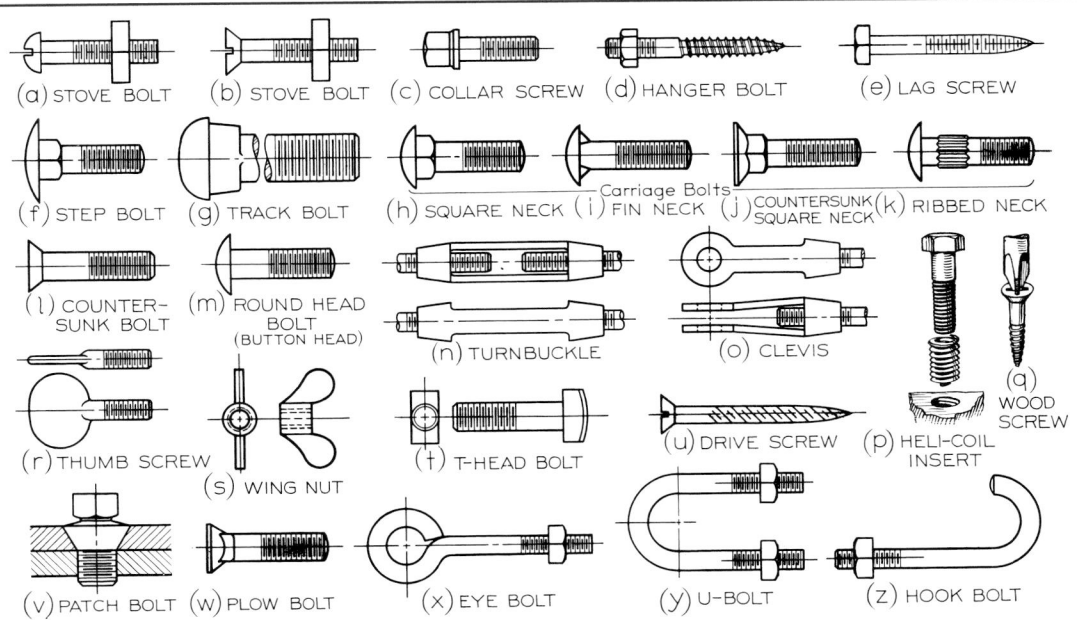

Fig. 15.36   Miscellaneous Bolts and Screws.

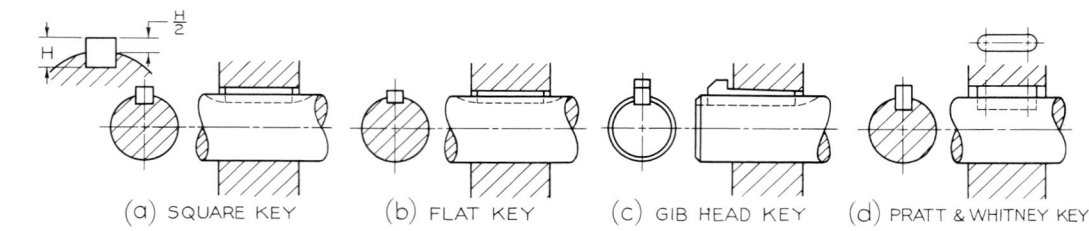

Fig. 15.37   Square and Flat Keys.

15.34 Keys

Keys are used to prevent relative movement between shafts and wheels, couplings, cranks, and similar machine parts attached to or supported by shafts, Fig. 15.37.

For heavy duty, rectangular keys (flat or square) are suitable, and sometimes two rectangular keys are necessary for one connection. For even stronger connections, interlocking *splines* may be machined on the shaft and in the hole. See Fig. 14.9.

A *square key* is shown in Fig. 15.37 (a) and a *flat key* in (b). The widths of keys generally used are about one-fourth the shaft diameter. In either case, one-half the key is sunk into the shaft. The depth of the keyway or the keyseat is measured on the side—not the center, (a). Square and flat keys may have the top surface tapered $\frac{1}{8}''$ per foot, in which case they become square taper or flat taper keys.

A rectangular key that prevents rotary motion but permits relative longitudinal motion is a *feather key,* and is usually provided with *gib heads,* or otherwise fastened so it cannot slip out of the keyway. A *gib head key* is shown at (c). It is exactly the same as the square taper or flat taper key, except that a gib head, which provides for easy removal, is added. Square and flat keys are made from cold-finished stock and are not machined. For dimensions, see Appendix 21.

The *Pratt & Whitney key,* (d), is rectangular in shape, with semicylindrical ends. Two-thirds of the height of the P & W key is sunk into the shaft keyseat. See Appendix 25.

The *Woodruff key* is semicircular in shape, Fig. 15.38. The key fits into a semicircular key slot cut with a Woodruff cutter, as shown, and the top of the key fits into a plain rectangular keyway. Sizes of keys for given shaft diameters are not standardized, but for average conditions it will be found satisfactory to select a key whose diameter is approximately equal to the shaft diameter. For dimensions, see Appendix 23.

A *keyseat* is in a shaft; a *keyway* is in the hub or surrounding part.

Typical specifications for keys are

$$\frac{1}{4} \times 1\frac{1}{2} \text{ SQ KEY}$$

No. 204 WOODRUFF KEY

$$\frac{1}{4} \times \frac{1}{16} \times 1\frac{1}{2} \text{ FLAT KEY}$$

No. 10 P & W KEY

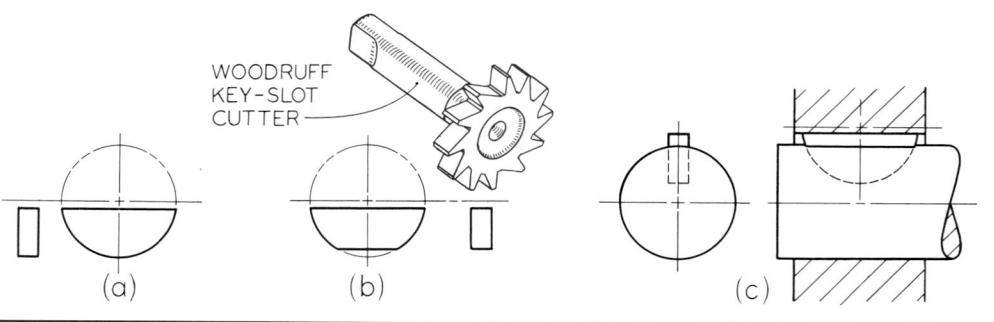

Fig. 15.38   Woodruff Keys and Key-Slot Cutter.

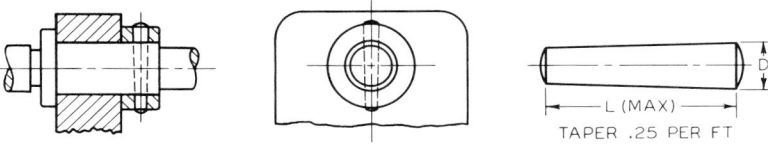

Fig. 15.39   Taper Pin.

Notes for nominal specifications of keyways and keyseats are shown in Fig. 13.44 (o), (p), (r), and (x). For production work, keyways and keyseats should be dimensioned as shown in Fig. 13.48. See manufacturers' catalogs for specifications for metric counterparts.

15.35 Machine Pins
Machine pins include taper pins, straight pins, dowel pins, clevis pins, and cotter pins. For light work, the taper pin is effective for fastening hubs or collars to shafts, as shown in Fig. 15.39, in which the hole through the collar and shaft is drilled and reamed when the parts are assembled. For slightly heavier duty, the taper pin may be used parallel to the shaft as for square keys. See Appendix 29.

Dowel pins are cylindrical or conical in shape and are used for a variety of purposes, chief of which is to keep two parts in a fixed position or to preserve alignment. The dowel pin is most commonly used and is recommended where accurate alignment is essential. Dowel pins are usually made of steel and are hardened and ground in a centerless grinder.

15.36 Rivets
Rivets are regarded as permanent fastenings as distinguished from removable fastenings, such as bolts and screws. They are generally used to hold sheet metal or rolled steel shapes together and are made of wrought iron, carbon steel, copper, or occasionally other metals.

15.37 Springs
A *spring* is a mechanical device designed to store energy when deflected and to return the equivalent amount of energy when released. Springs are classified as *helical springs*, Fig. 15.40, or *flat springs*, Fig. 15.44.

There are three types of helical springs: *compression springs*, which offer resistance to a compressive force, Fig. 15.40 (a) to (e), *extension*

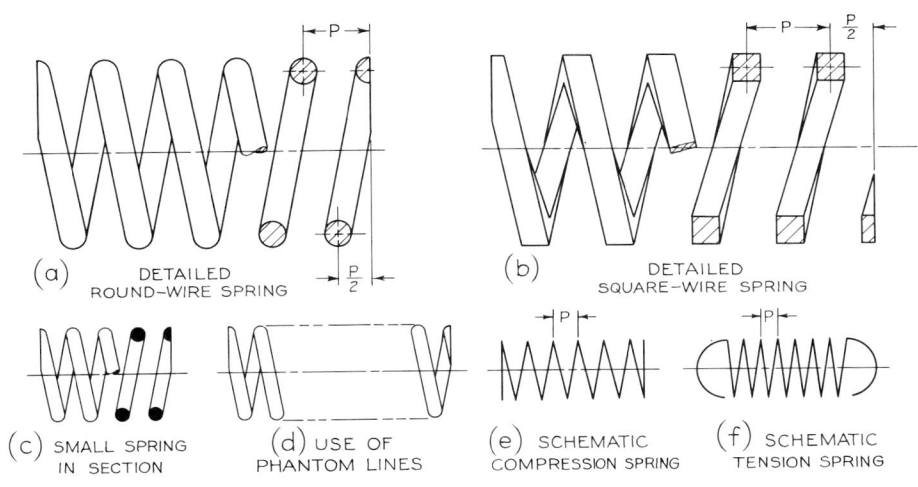

Fig. 15.40   Helical Springs.

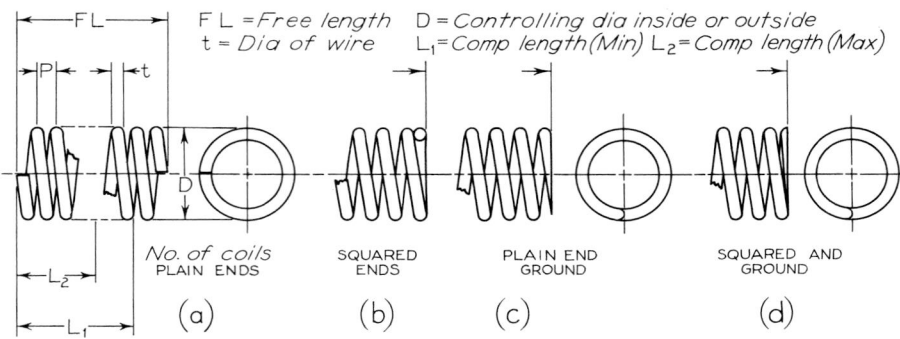

Fig. 15.41   Compression Springs.

springs, which offer resistance to a pulling force, Fig. 15.42, and *torsion springs,* which offer resistance to a torque load or twisting force, Fig. 15.43.

On working drawings, true projections of helical springs are never drawn because of the labor involved. As in the drawing of screw threads, the detailed and schematic methods, employing straight lines in place of helical curves, are used as shown in Fig. 15.40.

The elevation view of the square-wire spring is similar to the square thread with the core of the shaft removed, Fig. 15.12. Standard section lining is used if the areas in section are large, as shown in Fig. 15.40 (a) and (b). If these areas are small, the sectioned areas may be made solid black, (c). In cases where a complete picture of the spring is not necessary, phantom lines may be used to save time

in drawing the coils, (d). If the drawing of the spring is too small to be represented by the outlines of the wire, it may be drawn by the schematic method, in which single lines are used, (e) and (f).

Compression springs have *plain ends,* Fig. 15.41 (a), or *squared (closed) ends,* (b). The ends may be *ground* as at (c), or both *squared and ground* as at (d). Required dimensions are indicated in the figure. When required, RH or LH is specified.

An extension spring may have any one of many types of ends, and it is therefore necessary to draw the spring or at least the ends and a few adjacent coils, Fig. 15.42. Note the use of phantom lines to show the continuity of coils.

A typical torsion spring drawing is shown in Fig.

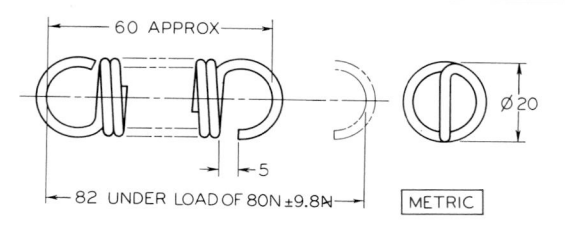

MATERIAL: 2.00 OIL TEMPERED SPRING STEEL WIRE
           14.5 COILS RIGHT HAND
           MACHINE LOOP AND HOOK IN LINE
           SPRING MUST EXTEND TO 110 WITHOUT SET
FINISH: BLACK JAPAN

Fig. 15.42   Extension Spring Drawing.

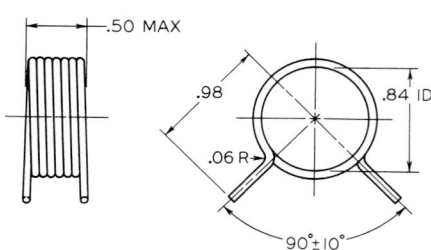

MATERIAL: .059 MUSIC WIRE
           6.75 COILS RIGHT HAND NO INITIAL TENSION
TORQUE: 2.50 INCH LB AT 155° DEFLECTION SPRING MUST
           DEFLECT 180° WITHOUT PERMANENT SET AND
           MUST OPERATE FREELY ON .75 DIAMETER SHAFT
FINISH: CADMIUM OR ZINC PLATE

Fig. 15.43   Torsion Spring Drawing.

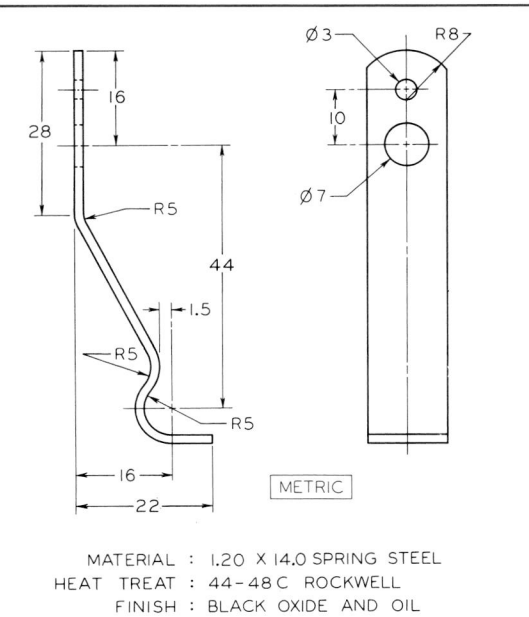

MATERIAL : 1.20 X 14.0 SPRING STEEL
HEAT TREAT : 44-48C ROCKWELL
FINISH : BLACK OXIDE AND OIL

Fig. 15.44   Flat Spring Drawing.

15.43, and a typical flat spring drawing is shown in Fig. 15.44. Other types of flat springs are *power springs* (or flat coil springs), *Belleville springs* (like spring washers), and *leaf springs* (commonly used in automobiles).

15.38 To Draw Helical Springs
The construction for a schematic elevation view of a compression spring having six total coils is shown in Fig. 15.45 (a). Since the ends are closed, or squared, two of the six coils are "dead" coils, leaving only four full pitches to be set off along the top of the spring, as shown.

If there are $6\frac{1}{2}$ total coils, as at (b), the $\frac{P}{2}$ spacings will be on opposite sides of the spring. The construction of an extension spring with six active coils and loop ends is shown at (c).

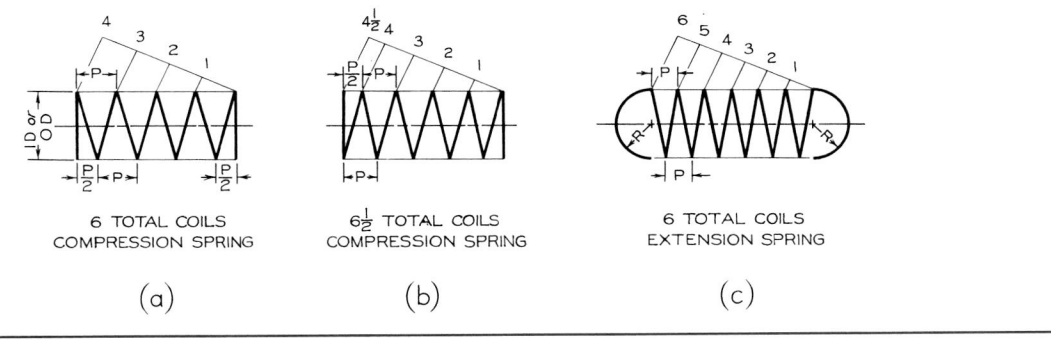

6 TOTAL COILS	$6\frac{1}{2}$ TOTAL COILS	6 TOTAL COILS
COMPRESSION SPRING	COMPRESSION SPRING	EXTENSION SPRING
(a)	(b)	(c)

Fig. 15.45   Schematic Spring Representation.

15.39 Computer Graphics
Standard representations of threaded fasteners and springs, in both detailed and schematic forms, are available in CAD program symbol libraries. Use of computer graphics frees the drafter from the need to draw time-consuming re-petitive features by hand, Fig. 15.46, and also makes it easy to modify a drawing if required. It is still necessary, however, for the CAD user to have a thorough familiarity with the various types of fasteners and springs available, and their relative usefulness in a particular application.

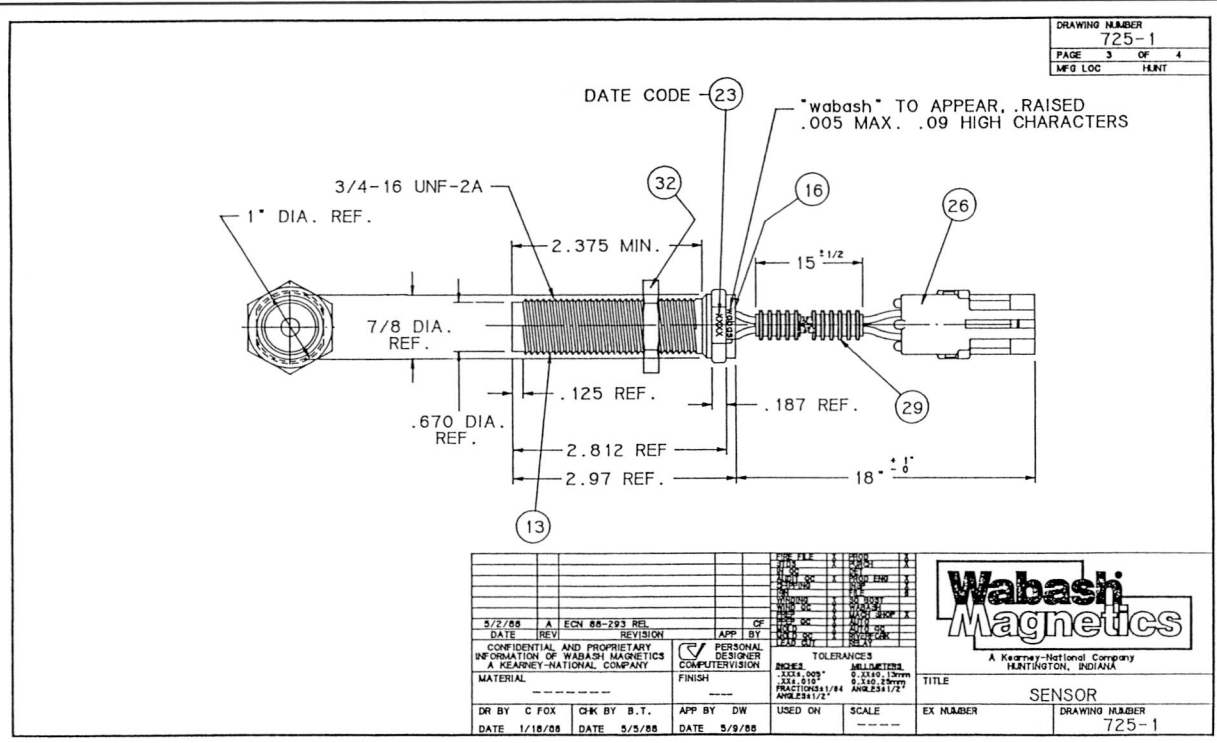

Fig. 15.46 CAD-Generated Drawing Showing Detailed Thread Representation. *Courtesy of Computervision Corporation, a Subsidiary of Prime Computer, Inc.*

Thread and Fastener Problems

It is expected that the student will make use of the information in this chapter and in various manufacturers' catalogs in connection with the working drawings at the end of the next chapter, where many different kinds of threads and fasteners are required. However, several problems are included here for specific assignment in this area, Figs. 15.47–15.50. All are to be drawn on tracing paper or detail paper, size B or A3 sheet (see inside back cover).

Additional problems in convenient form for solution are presented in the worksheets at the back of this book. Refer to Drawings 15-1 to 15-4 and accompanying instructions.

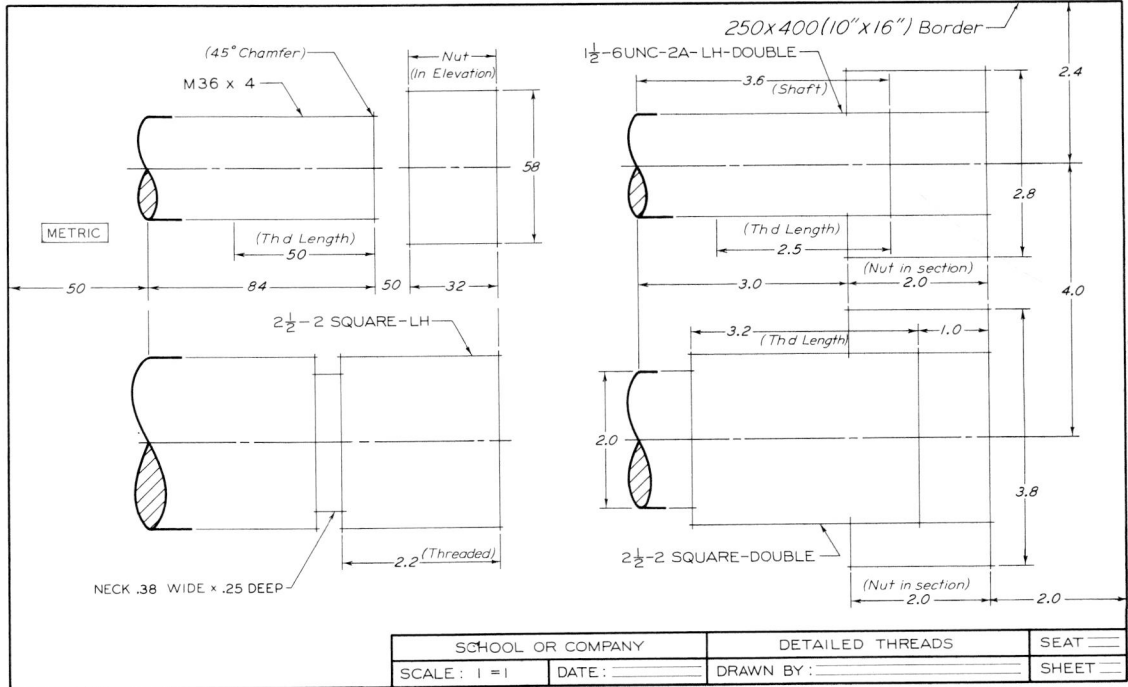

Fig. 15.47 Draw specified detailed threads arranged as shown, Layout B–3 or A3–3. Omit all dimensions and notes given in inclined letters. Letter only the thread notes and the title strip.

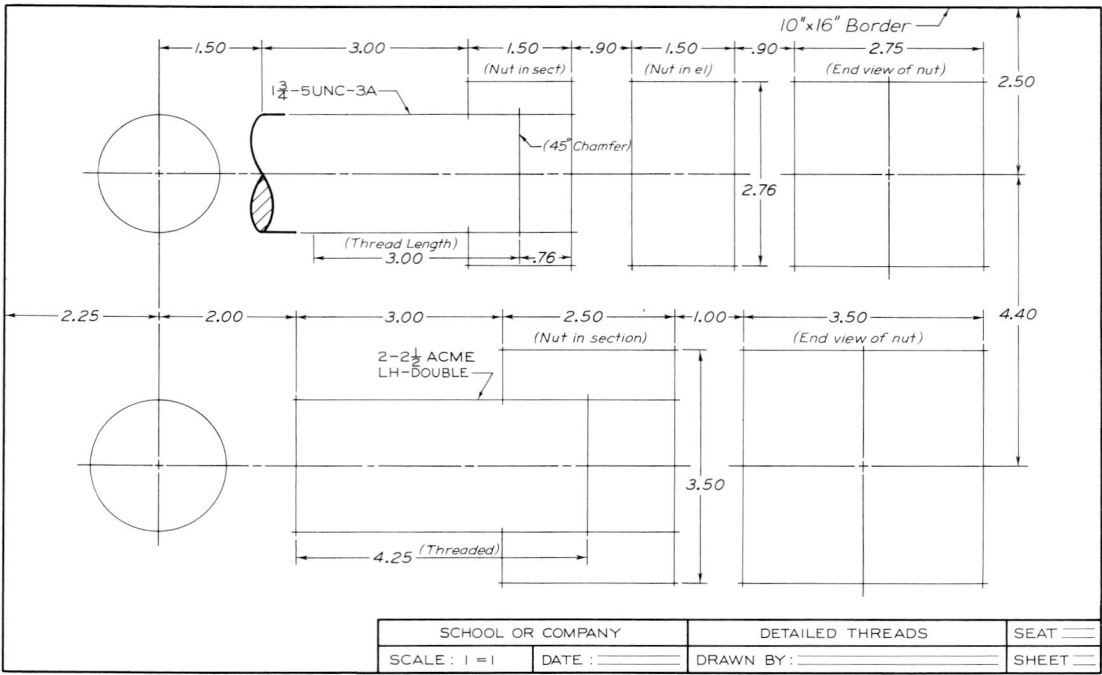

Fig. 15.48 Draw specified detailed threads, arranged as shown, Layout B–3 or A3–3. Omit all dimensions and notes given in inclined letters. Letter only the thread notes and the title strip.

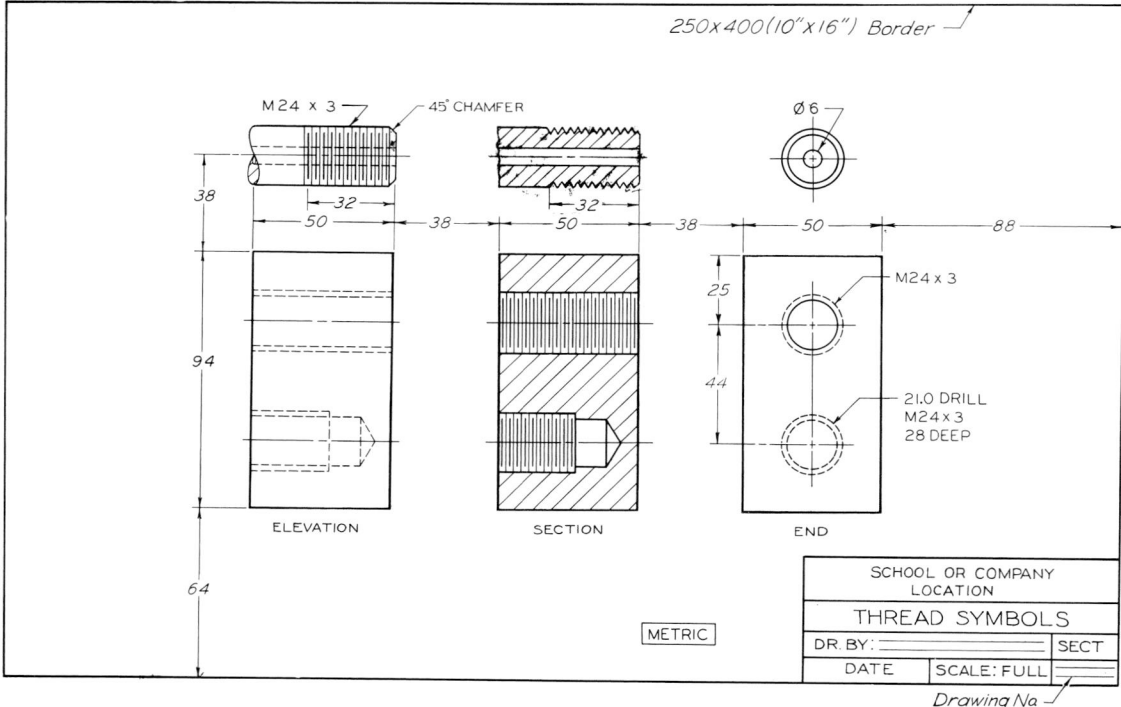

Fig. 15.49 Draw specified thread symbols, arranged as shown. Draw simplified or schematic symbols, as assigned by instructor (Layout B–5 or A3–5). Omit all dimensions and notes given in inclined letters. Letter only the drill and thread notes, the titles of the views, and the title strip.

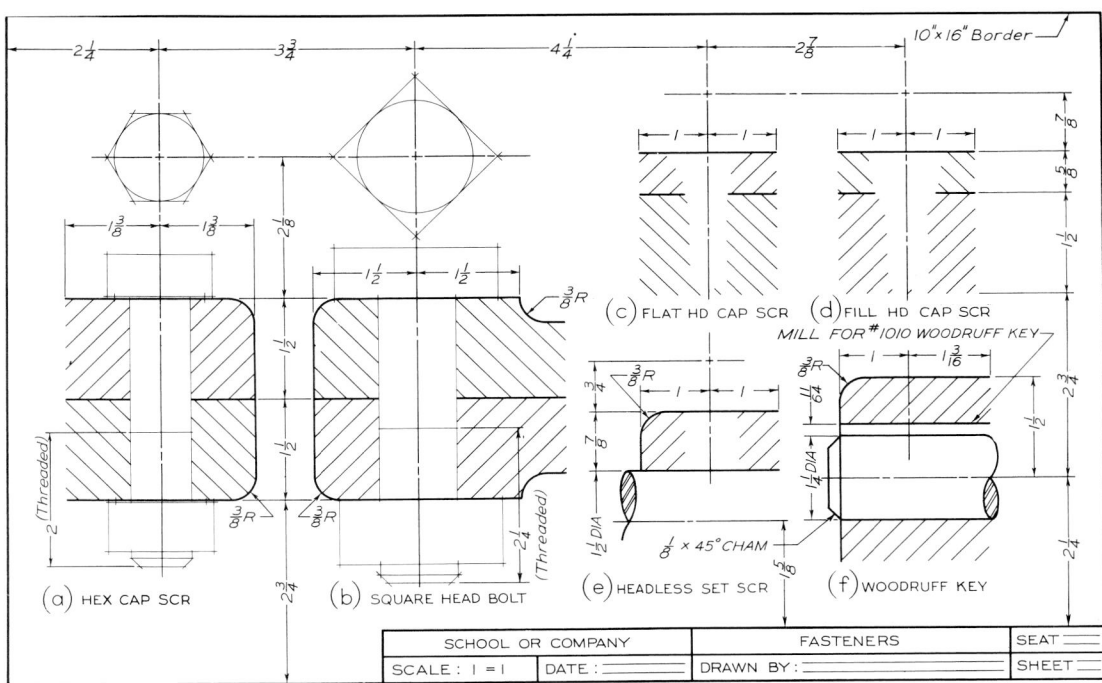

Fig. 15.50 Draw fasteners, arranged as shown (Layout B–3 or A3–3). At (a) draw $\frac{7}{8}$–9 UNC–2A × 4 Hex Cap Screw. At (b) draw $1\frac{1}{8}$–7 UNC–2A × $4\frac{1}{4}$ Sq Hd Bolt. At (c) draw $\frac{3}{8}$–16 UNC–2A × $1\frac{1}{2}$ Flat Hd Cap Screw. At (d) draw $\frac{7}{16}$–14 UNC–2A × 1 Fill Hd Cap Screw. At (e) draw $\frac{1}{2}$ × 1 Headless Slotted Set Screw. At (f) draw front view of No. 1010 Woodruff Key. Draw simplified or schematic thread symbols as assigned. Letter titles under each figure as shown.

CHAPTER

16

Design and
Working Drawings

The many products, systems, and services that enrich our standard of living are largely the result of the design activities of engineers. It is principally this design activity that distinguishes engineering from science and research; the engineer is a designer, a creator, or a "builder."

The design process is an exciting and challenging effort and the engineer-designer relies heavily upon graphics as a means to create, record, analyze, and communicate to others design concepts or ideas. The ability to communicate verbally, symbolically, and graphically is essential.

16.1 Design Sources

There are two general types of design: *empirical design*, sometimes referred to as conceptual design, and *scientific design*. In scientific design, use is made of the principles of physics, mathematics, chemistry, mechanics, and other sciences in the new or revised design of devices, structures, or systems intended to function under specific conditions. In empirical design, much use is made of the information in handbooks, which in turn has been learned by experience. Nearly all technical design is a combination of scientific and empirical design. Therefore, a competent designer has both adequate engineering and scientific knowledge and access to the many handbooks related to the field.

You may not yet have acquired the necessary educational background and experience to undertake a sophisticated design. And you probably do not have access to the variety of experts on materials, production methods, business economics, legal considerations, or other vital areas that probably would be available in a large company. Nevertheless, through conscientious application of your design ability and the sources of information that are available, you can go far toward the creation or improvement of some device, system, or service that *works* and is uniquely your own. The working models of the Postal Scale and the Educational Toys in Fig. 16.1 are examples of student design efforts.

16.2 Design Concepts

New ideas or design concepts must exist initially in the mind of the designer. In order to capture, preserve, and develop these ideas, the designer makes liberal use of freehand sketches of views and pictorials, Chapter 6. These sketches are revised or redrawn as the concept is developed. All sketches should be preserved for reference and dated as a record of the development of the design.

At some point in the development of the idea, you will probably find it to your advantage to pool your ideas with those of others and begin working in a team effort; such a team may include others familiar with problems of materials, production, marketing, and so on. In industry, the project becomes a team effort long before the product is produced and marketed. Obviously, the design process is not a haphazard operation of an inventor working in a garage or basement, although it might well begin in that manner. Industry could not long survive if its products were determined in a haphazard manner. Hence, nearly all successful companies support a well-organized design effort, and the vitality of the company depends to a large extent on the *planned* output of its designers.

Since it is important for you to be able to work effectively with others in a group or team, you must be able to express yourself clearly and concisely. Do not underestimate the importance of your communication skills, your ability to express your ideas verbally (written and spoken), symbolically (equations, formulas, etc.), and *graphically*. See page 478 for suggested format of a student design report.

The graphical skills include the ability to present information and ideas clearly and effectively in the form of sketches, drawings, graphs, and so on. This textbook is dedicated to helping you develop your communication skills in graphics.

  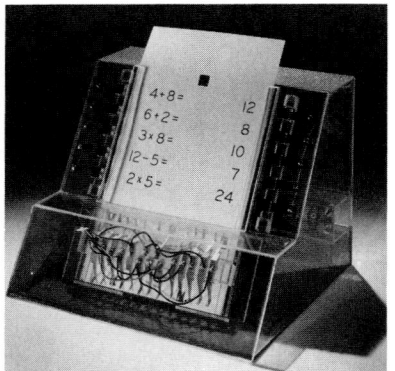

(a) POSTAL SCALE   (b) EDUCATIONAL TOYS

Fig. 16.1 Working Models of Student Designs.

16.3 The Design Process

Design is the ability to combine ideas, scientific principles, resources, and often existing products into a solution of a problem. This ability to solve problems in design is the result of an organized and orderly approach to the problem known as the *design process*.

The design process leading to manufacturing, assembly, marketing, service, and the many activities necessary for a successful product is composed of several easily recognized phases. Although many industrial groups may identify them in their own particular way, a convenient procedure for the design of a new or improved product is in five stages as follows:

1. Identification of problem.

2. Concepts and ideas.

3. Compromise solutions.

4. Models and/or prototypes.

5. Production and/or working drawings.

Ideally, the design moves through the stages as shown in Fig. 16.2, but if a particular stage proves unsatisfactory, it may be necessary to return to a previous stage and repeat the procedure as indicated by the dashed-line paths. This repetitive procedure is often referred to as *looping*.

16.4 Stage 1—Identification of Problem

The design activity begins with the recognition and determination of a need or want for a product, service, or system and the economic feasibility of fulfilling this need. Engineering design problems may range from the need for a simple and inexpensive container opener such as the pull tab commonly used on beverage cans, Fig. 16.3, to the more complex problems associated with the needs of air and ground travel, space exploration, environmental control, and so forth. Although the product may be very simple, such as the pull tab on a beverage can,

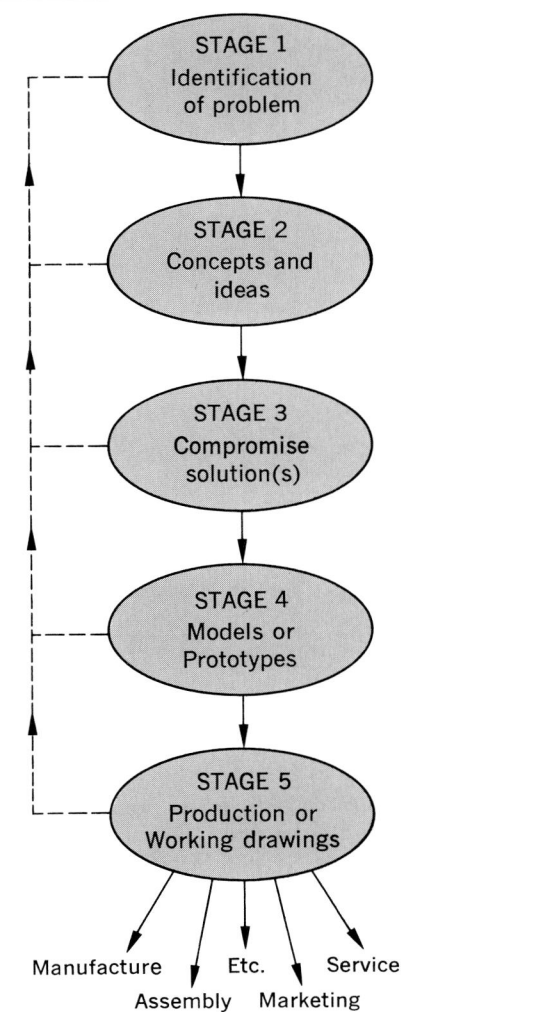

Fig. 16.2 Stages of the Design Process.

Fig. 16.3 Pull-Tab Can Opener. *John Schultz— PAR/NYC*

Fig. 16.4 Airport Transit System.
Courtesy of Westinghouse Electric Corp.

Fig. 16.5 Lunar Roving Vehicle.
Courtesy of The Boeing Co.

the production tools and dies require considerable engineering and design effort. The airport automated transit system design, Fig. 16.4, meets the need of moving people efficiently between the terminal areas. The system is capable of moving 3300 people every 10 minutes.

The Lunar Roving Vehicle, Fig. 16.5, is a solution to a need in the space program to explore larger areas of the lunar surface. This vehicle is the end result of a great deal of design work associated with the support systems and the related hardware.

At the problem identification stage, either the designer recognizes that there does exist a need requiring a design solution or, perhaps more often, a directive is received to that effect from management. No attempt is made at this time to set goals or criteria for the solution.

Information concerning the identified problem

becomes the basis for a problem proposal, which may be a paragraph or a multipage report presented for formal consideration. A proposal is a plan for action that will be followed to solve the problem. The proposal, if approved, becomes an agreement to follow the plan. In the classroom, the agreement is made between you and your instructor on the identification of the problem and your proposed plan of action.

Following approval of the proposal, further aspects of the problem are explored. Available information related to the problem is collected and parameters or guide lines for time, cost, function, and so on are defined within which you will work. For example: What is the design expected to do? What is the estimated cost limit? What is the market potential? What can it be sold for? When will the prototype be ready for testing? When must production drawings be ready? When will production begin? When will the product be available on the market?

The parameters of a design problem, including the time schedule, are established at this stage. Nearly all designs represent a compromise, and the amount of time budgeted to a project is no exception.

16.5 Stage 2—Concepts and Ideas

At this stage, many ideas are collected, "wild" or otherwise, for possible solutions to the problem. The ideas are broad and unrestricted to permit the possibility of new and unique solutions. This compilation of ideas may be from individuals, or they may come from group or team "brainstorming" sessions wherein a suggested idea often generates many more ideas from the group. As the ideas are elicited, they are written down and/or recorded in graphic form (multiview or pictorial sketches) for future consideration and refinement.

The larger the collection of ideas, the greater are the chances of finding one or more ideas suitable for further refinement. All sources of ideas such as technical literature, reports, design and trade journals, patents, and existing products are explored. The Greenfield Village Museum in Dearborn, Michigan, the Museum of Science and Industry in Chicago, trade exhibitions, large hardware and supply stores, mail order catalogs, and so on are all excellent sources for ideas. Another source is the users of an existing product, who often have suggestions for improvement. The potential user may be helpful with specific reactions to the proposed solution.

No attempt is made to evaluate ideas at this stage. All notes and sketches are signed, dated, and retained for possible patent proof.

16.6 Stage 3—Compromise Solutions

Various features of the many conceptual ideas generated in the preceding stages are selected after careful consideration and combined into one or more promising compromise solutions. At this point the best of the solutions is evaluated in detail, and attempts are made to simplify it and thereby make manufacture and performance more efficient.

The sketches of the design are often followed by a study of suitable materials and of motion problems that may be involved. What source of power is to be used—manual, electric motor, or what? What type of motion is needed? Is it necessary to translate rotary motion to linear motion or vice versa? Many of these problems are solved graphically by means of a schematic drawing in which various parts are shown in skeleton form. A pulley is represented by a circle, meshing gears by tangent pitch circles, an arm by a single line, paths of motion by center lines, and so on. At this time, too, certain basic calculations, such as those related to velocity and acceleration, may be made, if required.

These preliminary studies are followed by a *design layout*, made with instruments, or a *layout sketch* from which a drafter makes an accurate to-scale instrumental drawing so that actual sizes and proportions can be clearly visualized, Fig. 16.6. At this time all parts are carefully designed for strength and function. Costs are constantly kept in mind, for no matter how well the device performs, it must be built to sell for a profit or the time and development costs will have been a loss.

During the layout process, great reliance is placed upon what has gone on before. Experience provides a sense of proportion and size that permits the noncritical or more standard features to be designed by eye or with the aid of empirical data. Stress analysis and detailed computation may be necessary in connection with high speeds, heavy loads, or special requirements or conditions.

As shown in Fig. 16.6, the layout is an assembly showing how parts fit together and the basic proportions of the various parts. Auxiliary views or sections are used, if necessary. Section lining may be used sparingly to save time. All lines should be sharp and the drawing made as accurately as possible, since most dimensions are omitted except for a few key ones that will be used in the detail or working drawings for production. Any notes or other information related to the detail drawing should be given on the layout.

Special attention is given to clearances of moving parts, ease of assembly, and serviceability. Standard parts are used wherever possible for it is less costly to use stock items. Most companies maintain some form of an *engineering standards manual*, which contains much of the empirical data and detailed information that is regarded as "company standard." Materials and costs are carefully considered. Although functional considerations must come first, manufacturing problems must be kept constantly in mind.

A great many design problems are concerned with the improvement of an existing product or with the redesign of a device from a different approach

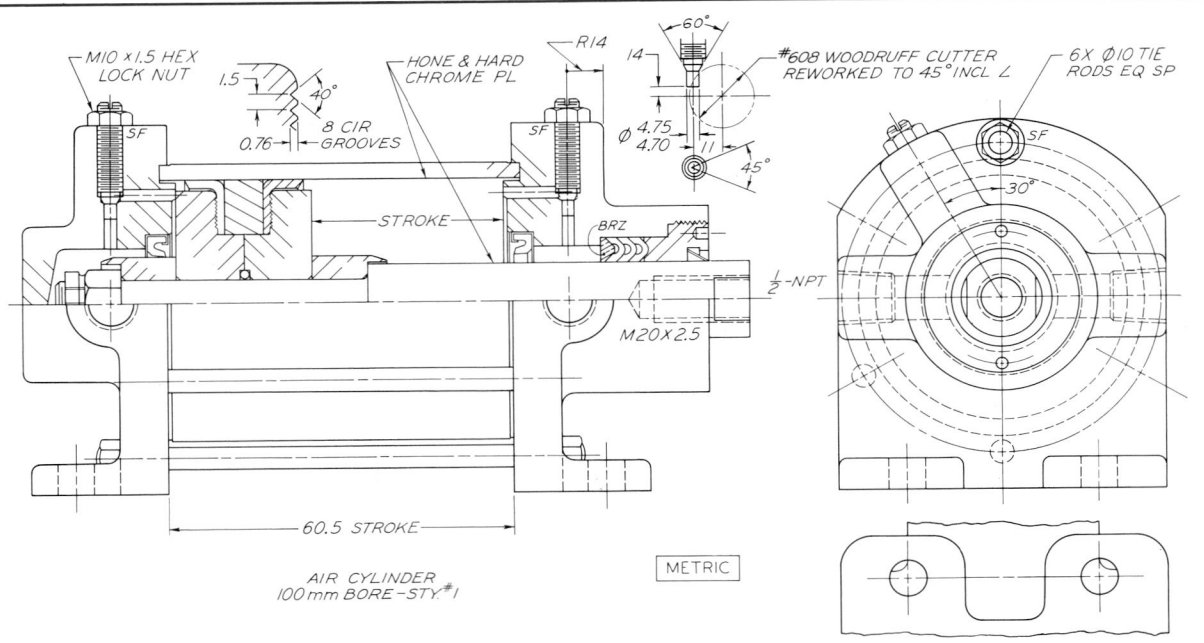

Fig. 16.6 Design Layout.

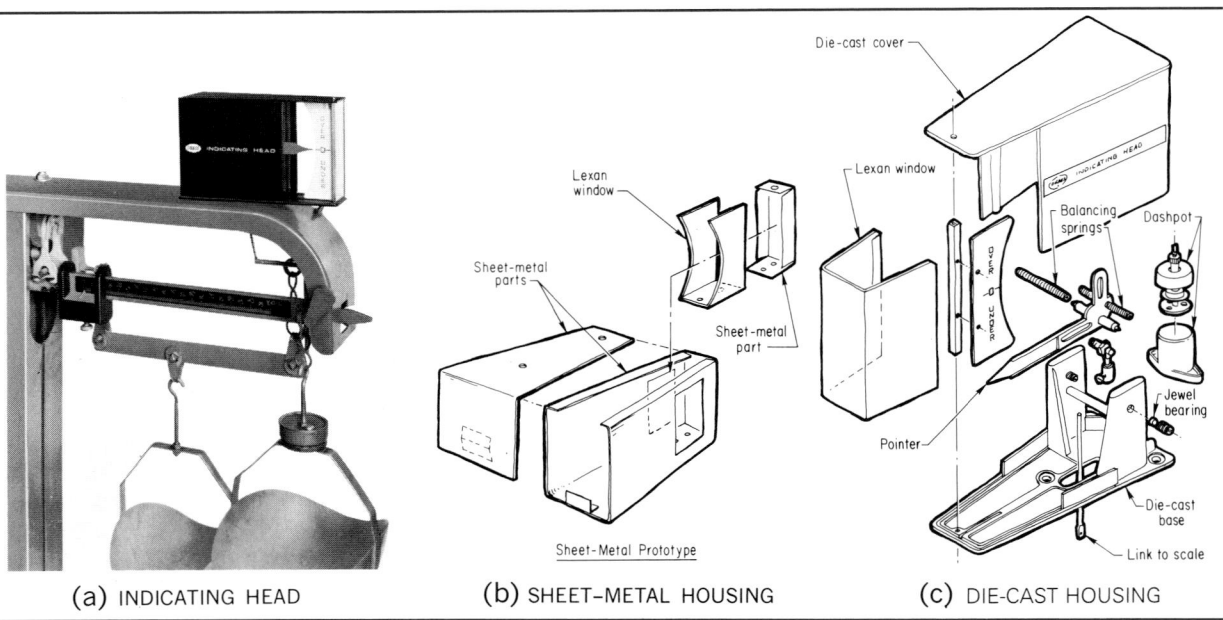

(a) INDICATING HEAD   (b) SHEET–METAL HOUSING   (c) DIE-CAST HOUSING

Fig. 16.7 Improved Design of Indicating Head. *Courtesy of Ohaus Scale Corp. and* Machine Design

in which many of the details will be similar to others previously used. For example, in Fig. 16.7, the Indicating Head is attached to a portable beam scale to add damping, sensitivity, and improved visibility to the weight readout. The original design of the housing was made of three sheet-metal parts with a plastic window, (b). The new two-piece design of a die-cast housing and larger plastic window, (c) provides more resistance to abuse and a drop in the unit cost of the housing after the first 2400 units, to less than one-third of the cost of the original sheet-metal design. Very often a change in material or a

Fig. 16.8 Redesigned Totalizer Wheel for Adding Machine. *Courtesy of Addmaster Corp. and E. I. du Pont de Nemours & Co., Inc.*

slight change in the shape of some part may be made without any loss of effectiveness and yet may save hundreds or thousands of dollars. The *ideal design* is the one that will do the job required at the lowest possible cost.

The Totalizer Wheel, Fig. 16.8, represents a cost-reducing redesign of an assembly in an adding machine. The redesigned wheel replaces an assembly of the 23 parts shown and continues to act as an indexing gear, integral bearing, integral spring, position stop, and print wheel.

An example of design from a different approach is the Electric Wheel used in heavy duty four-wheel-drive earth-moving equipment, Fig. 16.9. This self-contained wheel design eliminates the usual restrictive drive train components, such as the drive shaft, universal joints, differential gears, and transmission, and makes possible nonslip traction at each wheel. The motor in the wheel is powered by a heavy-duty diesel electric generating system aboard the equipment.

The designs for a large vacation-area complex include unique and unusual approaches or systems to the problem of housing and transportation. The 14-story A-frame hotel, as shown by the model, Fig. 16.10 (a), is serviced by water craft, surface vehicles, and special monorail trains that pass through the

Fig. 16.9 Electric Wheel. Model L-700, LeTro-Loader, manufactured by Marathon LeTourneau Co., Equipment Division, Longview, Texas. *Courtesy of Marathon LeTourneau Co.*

(a) MODEL

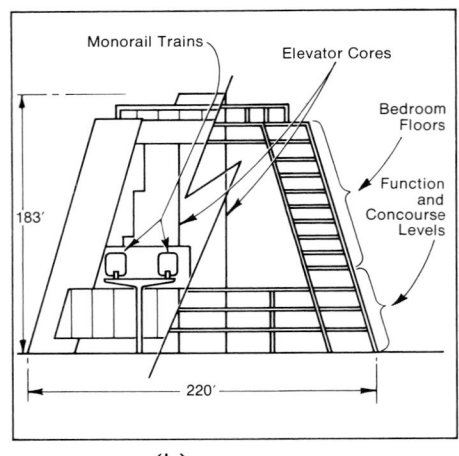

(b) ELEVATION

(c) MONORAIL TRAIN

Fig. 16.10   Recreation Park *(a, b) © Walt Disney Productions;* *(c) courtesy of* Engineering News-Record

structure as indicated in (b). A pictorial of the train is shown in (c).

In a revised electronic organ design, the room-filling pipes and bellows have been replaced by a digital musical computer composed of aerospace microelectronics that requires about 1 cubic foot, Fig. 16.11. The computer contains some 48,000 transistors and enables the organ to be played in a virtually unlimited number of voices.

An improved design of a freight handling system for the transporting of subcompact automobiles includes the unique design of a special railroad car called Vert-A-Pack, Fig. 16.12. The sides of the five compartments on each side, which hold three cars each, are hinged at the bottom for use as ramps for efficient drive-on loading and drive-away unloading. The autos lock into place as the ramps are raised, and when the compartments are closed the autos are protected from vandalism and the weather.

16.7 Stage 4—Models and Prototypes

A model to scale is often constructed to study, analyze, and refine a design, Figs. 16.1, 16.11, and 16.17. The model of the Carveyor, Fig. 16.13, shows how it works and how people may be moved in such areas as airports, shopping centers, and college campuses. It is a loop system and is designed to carry up to 22,000 people per hour.

To instruct the model shop craftsperson in the construction of the prototype or model, dimensioned sketches and/or rudimentary working drawings are required. A full-size working model made to final specifications, except possibly for materials, is known as a *prototype*. The prototype is tested, modified where necessary, and the results noted in the revision of the sketches and working drawings.

If the prototype proves to be unsatisfactory, it may be necessary to return to a previous stage in the design process and repeat the procedures. It

Fig. 16.11 Electronic Organ. *Courtesy of Allen Organ Co.*

Fig. 16.12 Railway Auto Transport System. *Courtesy of American Iron and Steel Institute.*

Fig. 16.13 Carveyor. *Courtesy of Goodyear Tire and Rubber Co.*

must be remembered that time and expense ceilings always limit the duration of this "looping." Eventually, a decision must be reached for the production model.

16.8 Stage 5—Working Drawings

To produce or manufacture a product, a final set of production or working drawings is made, checked, and approved.

In industry the approved production design layouts are turned over to the engineering department for the production drawings. The drafter, or detailers, "pick off" the details from the layouts with the aid of the scale or dividers. The necessary views, §6.22, are drawn for each part to be made and complete dimensions and notes, Chapter 13, are added

so that the drawings will describe these parts completely. These working drawings of the individual parts are also known as *detail drawings*, §16.10.

Unaltered standard parts, §13.41, do not require a detail drawing but are shown conventionally on the assembly drawing and listed with specifications in the parts list, §16.14.

A detail drawing of one of the parts from the design layout of Fig. 16.6 is shown in Fig. 16.14. For

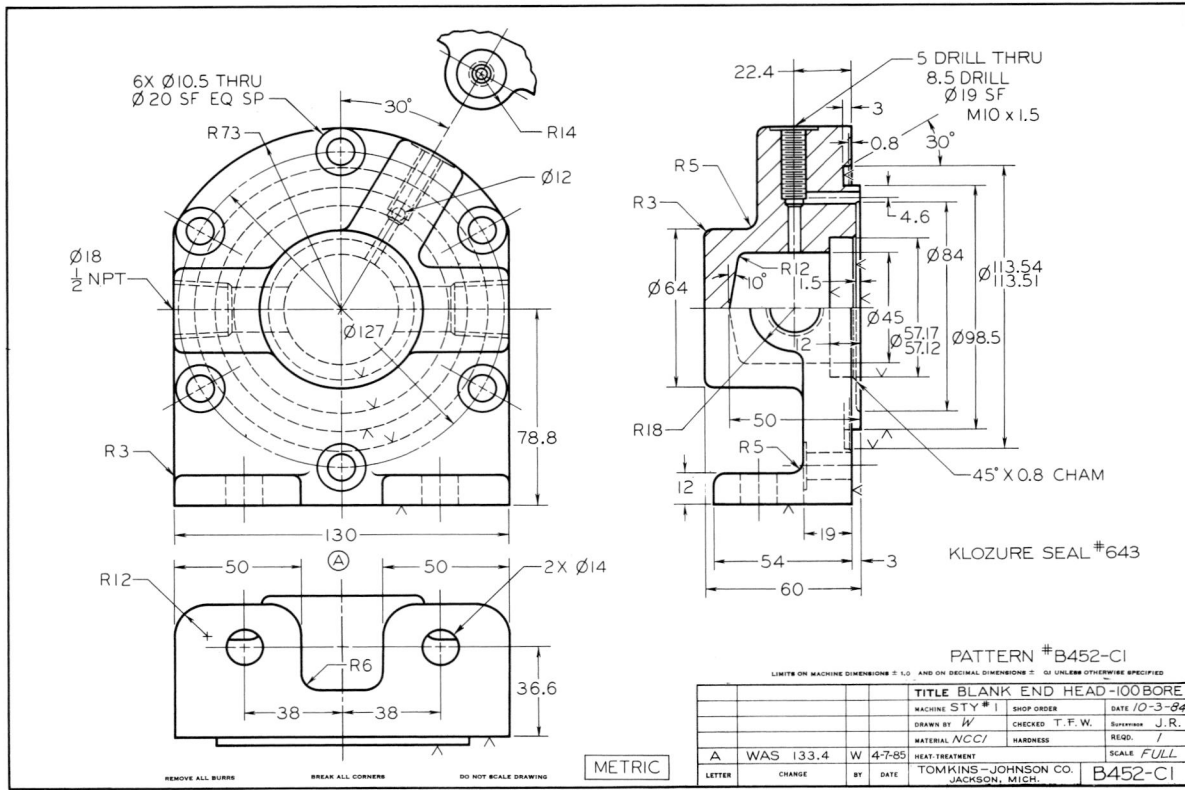

Fig. 16.14   A Detail Drawing.

details concerning working drawings, see §§16.10–16.18.

After the parts have been detailed, an *assembly drawing* is made, showing how all the parts go together in the complete product. The assembly may be made by tracing the various details in place directly from the detail drawings, or the assembly may be traced from the original design layout, but if either is done, the value of the assembly for checking purposes, §16.24, will be largely lost. The various types of assemblies are discussed in §§16.19–16.24.

Finally, in order to protect the manufacturer, a *patent drawing,* which is often a form of assembly, is prepared and filed with the U.S. Patent Office. Patent drawings are line shaded, often lettered in script, and otherwise follow rules of the Patent Office, §16.25.

16.9 Design of a New Product

An example of the design and development of a new product is that of the Cordless Electric Eraser shown in Fig. 16.15.

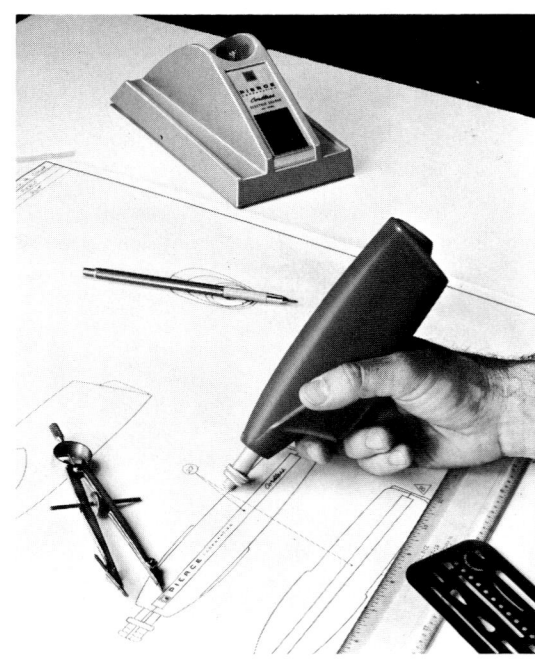

Fig. 16.15   Cordless Eraser with Recharging Console. *Courtesy of Pierce Business Products, Inc.*

Stage 1—Identification of the Problem

In order to determine the feasibility of the *first* cordless eraser, opinions and ideas were solicited from many sources, including engineers, drafters, drafting teachers, drafting supply house managers, drafting supply store owners, and others. Price ranges and estimated sales were also carefully explored. This extensive survey indicated that there was a need and a potential market for a cordless eraser, provided it was convenient to use, durable, lightweight, versatile, maintenance free, safe, and competitively priced.

Stage 2—Concepts and Ideas

Various cord erasers on the market were examined, tested, and analyzed for possible improvements. Several cordless devices on the market were also studied. Power and speed requirements for efficient erasing of pencil and/or ink lines were determined. Several methods of holding the eraser were reviewed. Various eraser refills for electric erasers were tested. With this collection of information as a background, several questions now needed to be considered. Should a direct drive and a large motor or a reduction drive and a small motor be used? What power source should be used—replaceable or rechargeable batteries? What recharging arrange-

ments are necessary for rechargeable battery power? What about safety precautions with 110 volt power for the charger? What materials are suitable? What bearings are available? What is a suitable way to chuck the eraser? Should long or short eraser plugs or only short ones be used? What standard parts are available for such items as the motor, bearings, batteries, recharging unit, and power cord?

How many ways can these components be arranged for the solution?

Stage 3—Compromise Solution

The cordless version of the eraser with a charging unit in a separate stand or console was selected as the preferred goal. The power train of a small battery-driven motor with a pinion gear meshed with a larger spur gear on the main shaft provided adequate power and speed for the eraser chuck. The batteries provided power long enough for normal usage. Recharging would occur while the eraser was at rest on the charging console. Careful selection of components and materials could lead to a durable and lightweight unit.

The few simple components of the system could be arranged in several ways. Thus, some flexibility in the final design was possible. Pictorials of several concepts, Fig. 16.16, were made and evaluated for balance, handling qualities, and appearance.

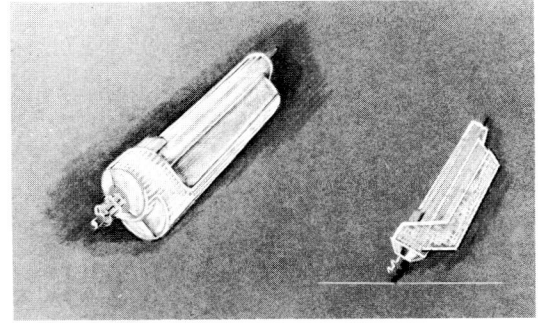
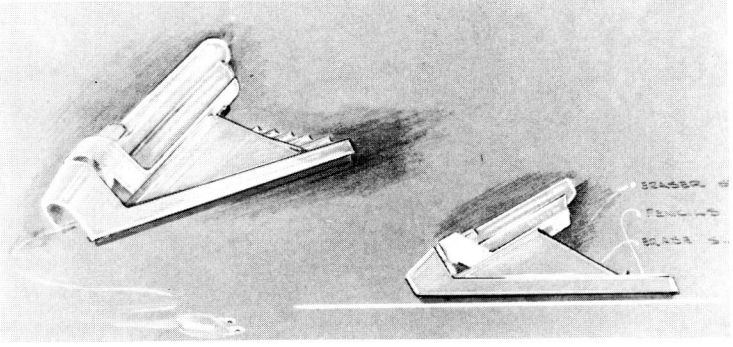

Fig. 16.16 Preliminary Design Pictorials of Cordless Eraser.
Courtesy of Pierce Business Products, Inc.

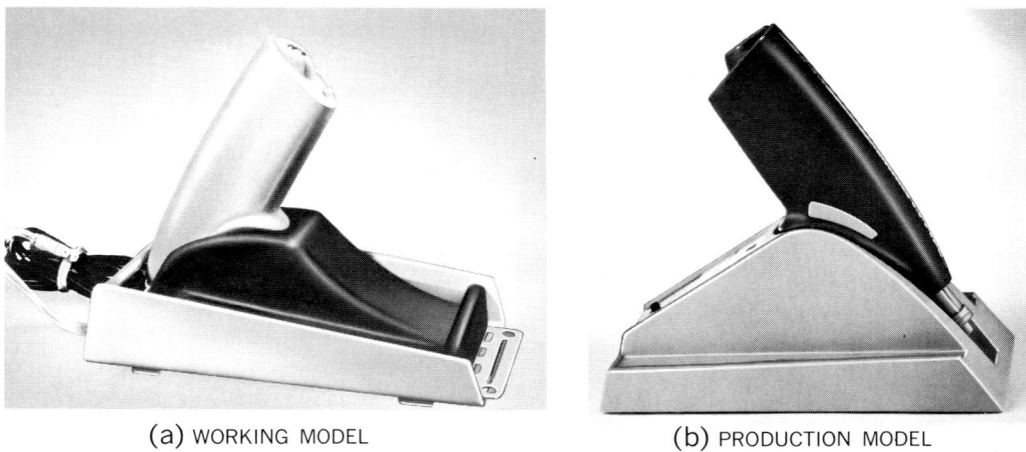

(a) WORKING MODEL   (b) PRODUCTION MODEL

Fig. 16.17 Models of Cordless Eraser. *Courtesy of Pierce Business Products, Inc.*

Stage 4—Prototype

A Prototype or working model, Fig. 16.17 (a), was built, tested, refined, and restyled into the final production design, (b). The section of the production model, Fig. 16.18, shows the selected arrangements of components; note that all the components are held in place in one half of the molded shell without additional parts or fasteners. The main shaft assembly is shown in Fig. 16.19. To achieve the goals of lightweight durability and a competitive selling price, the engineers selected a molding of reinforced nylon resin rather than a metal tubing. A manufac-

turing cost saving of over 50 percent for the main shaft alone was made possible by the elimination of several secondary operations. For example, in Fig. 16.19 note the following features.

1. No thread cutting required—threads are molded.

2. No groove cutting—molded hubs locate the bearings and also eliminate the need for retaining rings.

3. No slot cutting for chuck removal slot—slot is molded.

Fig. 16.18 Section of Cordless Eraser Production Model. *Courtesy of Pierce Business Products, Inc.*

Fig. 16.19 Main Shaft Assembly. *Courtesy of Pierce Business Products, Inc.*

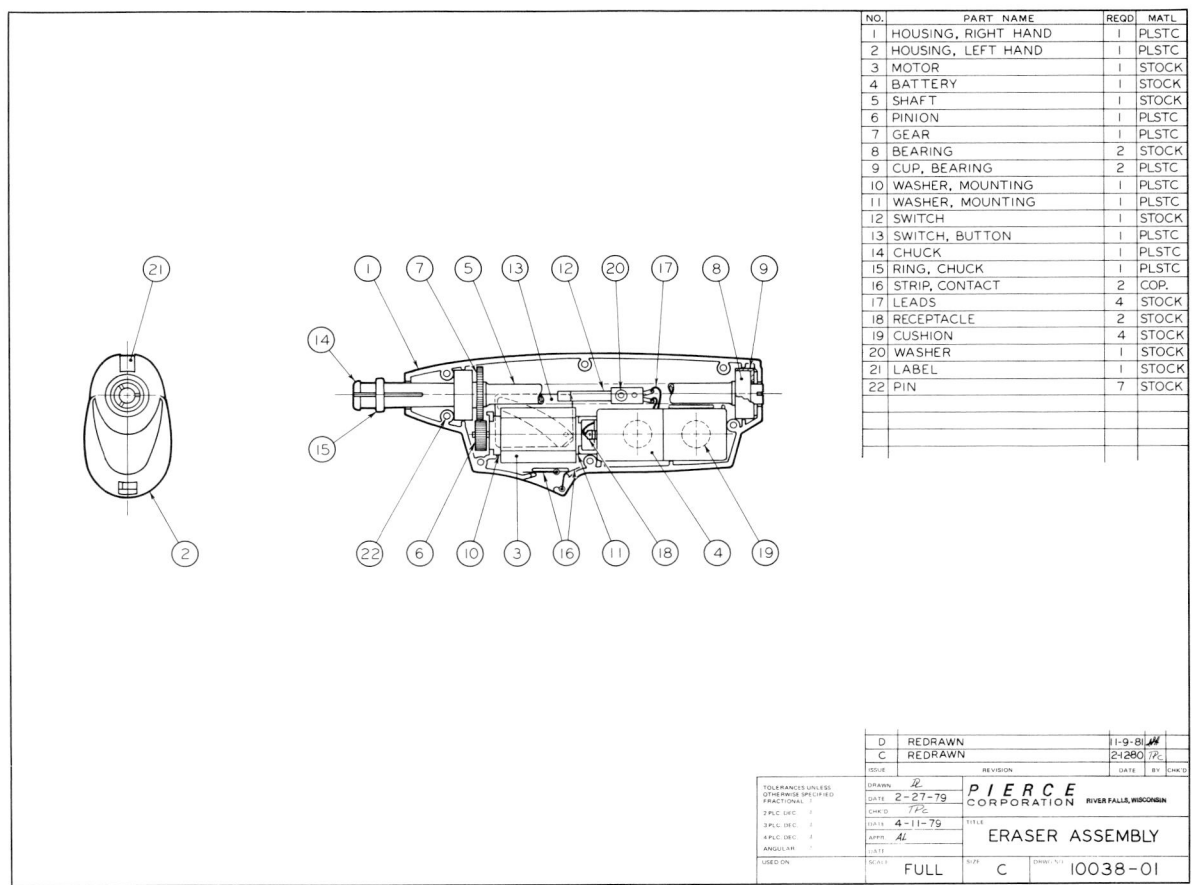

NO.	PART NAME	REQD	MATL
1	HOUSING, RIGHT HAND	1	PLSTC
2	HOUSING, LEFT HAND	1	PLSTC
3	MOTOR	1	STOCK
4	BATTERY	1	STOCK
5	SHAFT	1	STOCK
6	PINION	1	PLSTC
7	GEAR	1	PLSTC
8	BEARING	2	STOCK
9	CUP, BEARING	2	PLSTC
10	WASHER, MOUNTING	1	PLSTC
11	WASHER, MOUNTING	1	PLSTC
12	SWITCH	1	STOCK
13	SWITCH, BUTTON	1	PLSTC
14	CHUCK	1	PLSTC
15	RING, CHUCK	1	PLSTC
16	STRIP, CONTACT	2	COP.
17	LEADS	4	STOCK
18	RECEPTACLE	2	STOCK
19	CUSHION	4	STOCK
20	WASHER	1	STOCK
21	LABEL	1	STOCK
22	PIN	7	STOCK

D	REDRAWN	11-9-81	
C	REDRAWN	24280	
ISSUE	REVISION	DATE	BY CHK'D

TOLERANCES UNLESS OTHERWISE SPECIFIED
FRACTIONAL ±
2 PLC DEC ±
3 PLC DEC ±
4 PLC DEC ±
ANGULAR ±
USED ON

DRAWN _R_ DATE 2-27-79
CHK'D _TPc_ DATE 4-11-79
APPR _AL_ DATE

PIERCE CORPORATION RIVER FALLS, WISCONSIN

TITLE **ERASER ASSEMBLY**

SCALE FULL SIZE C DWG NO 10038-01

Fig. 16.20 Assembly Drawing of Cordless Eraser. *Courtesy of Pierce Business Products, Inc.*

4. No external grinding of shaft is necessary—precision molding gives a diameter suitable for installation of the high-speed bearings.

5. No keyseat required—molded-in key eliminates need for a key.

6. No keyway required on gear—molded-in keyway. No key or retaining ring installations facilitate more simplified assembly.

The foregoing considerations are typical of the attention given all components in the design.

Stage 5—Production Drawings

Complete sets of detail and assembly drawings were made for the eraser and the charging console. The assembly drawing for the eraser is shown in Fig. 16.20 and the assembly drawing of the charger base is shown in Fig. 16.21. A detail of the shaft is given in Fig. 16.22. Standard parts were specified on separate sheets or in a parts list. (Space limitations do not permit including more of the drawings necessary for the product.)

16.10 Working Drawings

Working drawings, which normally include assembly and details, are the specifications for the manufacture of a design. Therefore, they must be neatly made and carefully checked. The working drawings of the individual parts are also referred to as *detail drawings*. See §§16.11 to 16.18.

16.11 Number of Details per Sheet

Two general methods are followed in industry regarding the grouping of details on sheets. If the machine or structure is small or composed of few parts, all the details may be shown on one large sheet, Fig. 16.23.

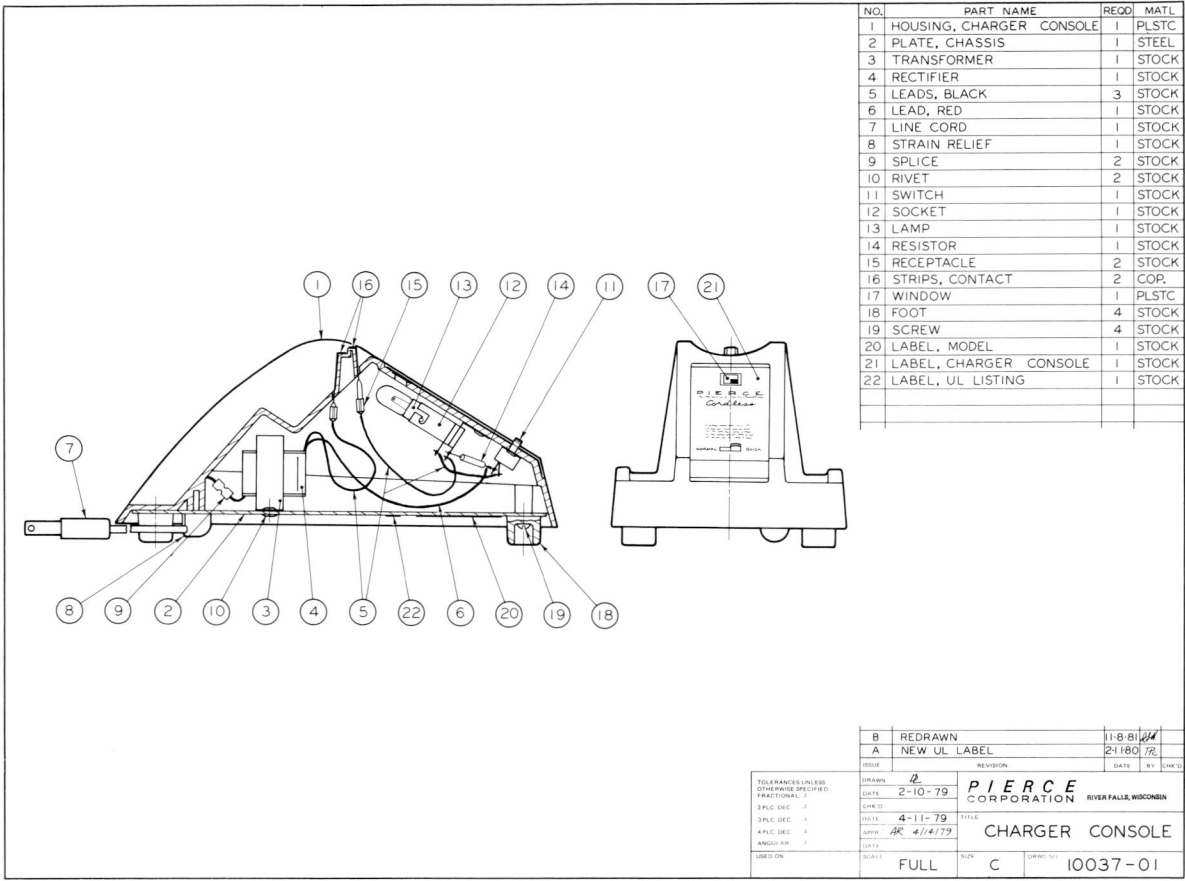

NO.	PART NAME	REQD	MATL
1	HOUSING, CHARGER CONSOLE	1	PLSTC
2	PLATE, CHASSIS	1	STEEL
3	TRANSFORMER	1	STOCK
4	RECTIFIER	1	STOCK
5	LEADS, BLACK	3	STOCK
6	LEAD, RED	1	STOCK
7	LINE CORD	1	STOCK
8	STRAIN RELIEF	1	STOCK
9	SPLICE	2	STOCK
10	RIVET	2	STOCK
11	SWITCH	1	STOCK
12	SOCKET	1	STOCK
13	LAMP	1	STOCK
14	RESISTOR	1	STOCK
15	RECEPTACLE	2	STOCK
16	STRIPS, CONTACT	2	COP.
17	WINDOW	1	PLSTC
18	FOOT	4	STOCK
19	SCREW	4	STOCK
20	LABEL, MODEL	1	STOCK
21	LABEL, CHARGER CONSOLE	1	STOCK
22	LABEL, UL LISTING	1	STOCK

| B | REDRAWN | 11-8-81 |
| A | NEW UL LABEL | 2-1-80 |

PIERCE CORPORATION RIVER FALLS, WISCONSIN

DRAWN 2-10-79
DATE 4-11-79

TITLE CHARGER CONSOLE

SCALE FULL   SIZE C   DRWG NO. 10037-01

Fig. 16.21   Assembly Drawing of Charger Console. *Courtesy of Pierce Business Products, Inc.*

When larger or more complicated mechanisms are represented, the details may be drawn on several large sheets, several details to the sheet, and the assembly drawn on a separate sheet. Most companies have now adopted the practice of drawing only one detail per sheet, however simple or small, Fig. 16.22. The basic 8.5″ × 11.0″ or 210 mm × 297 mm sheet is most commonly used for details, multiples of these sizes being used for larger details or the assembly. For standard sheet sizes, see §2.62.

When several details are drawn on one sheet, careful consideration must be given to spacing. The drafter should determine the necessary views for each detail, and *block in all views lightly before beginning to draw any view*, as shown in Fig. 16.23. Ample space should be allowed for dimensions and notes. A simple method to space the views is to cut out rectangular scraps of paper roughly equal to the sizes of the views and to move these around on the sheet until a suitable spacing is determined. The

corner locations are then marked on the sheet, and the scraps of paper are discarded.

The same scale should be used for all details on a single sheet, if possible. When this is not possible, the scales for the dissimilar details should be clearly noted under each.

16.12 Title and Record Strips

The function of the title and record strip is to show, in an organized manner, all necessary information not given directly on the drawing with its dimensions and notes. Obviously, the type of title used depends upon the filing system in use, the processes of manufacture, and the requirements of the product. The following information should generally be given in the title form:

1.   Name of the object represented.

2.   Name and address of the manufacturer.

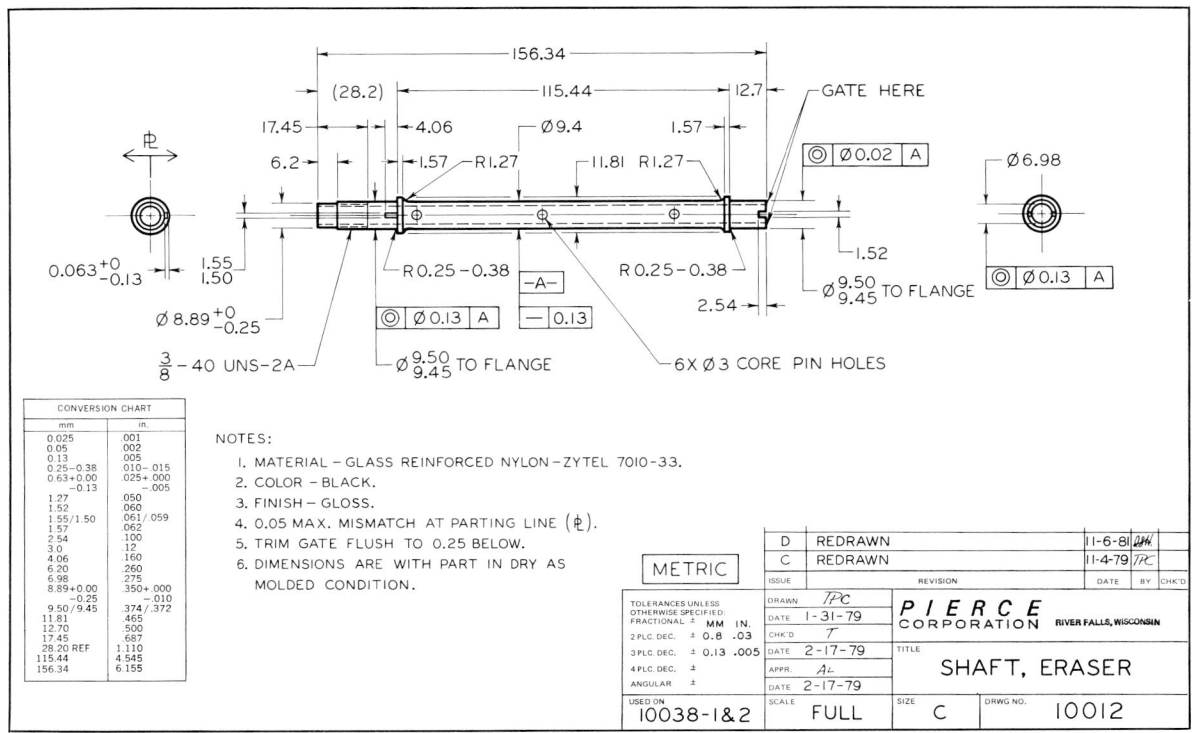

Fig. 16.22 Detail Drawing of Main Shaft. *Courtesy of Pierce Business Products, Inc.*

NOTES:
1. MATERIAL – GLASS REINFORCED NYLON – ZYTEL 7010-33.
2. COLOR – BLACK.
3. FINISH – GLOSS.
4. 0.05 MAX. MISMATCH AT PARTING LINE (℄).
5. TRIM GATE FLUSH TO 0.25 BELOW.
6. DIMENSIONS ARE WITH PART IN DRY AS MOLDED CONDITION.

CONVERSION CHART

mm	in.
0.025	.001
0.05	.002
0.13	.005
0.25-0.38	.010-.015
0.63+0.00	.025+.000
-0.13	-.005
1.27	.050
1.52	.060
1.55/1.50	.061/.059
1.57	.062
2.54	.100
3.0	.12
4.06	.160
6.20	.260
6.98	.275
8.89+0.00	.350+.000
-0.25	-.010
9.50/9.45	.374/.372
11.81	.465
12.70	.500
17.45	.687
28.20 REF	1.110
115.44	4.545
156.34	6.155

METRIC

ISSUE		REVISION	DATE	BY	CHK'D
D	REDRAWN		11-6-81		
C	REDRAWN		11-4-79	TPC	

TOLERANCES UNLESS OTHERWISE SPECIFIED:
FRACTIONAL ± — MM IN.
2 PLC. DEC. ± 0.8 .03
3 PLC. DEC. ± 0.13 .005
4 PLC. DEC. ±
ANGULAR ±

DRAWN TPC DATE 1-31-79
CHK'D T
DATE 2-17-79
APPR. AL
DATE 2-17-79

PIERCE CORPORATION RIVER FALLS, WISCONSIN

TITLE SHAFT, ERASER

USED ON 10038-1&2 | SCALE FULL | SIZE C | DRWG NO. 10012

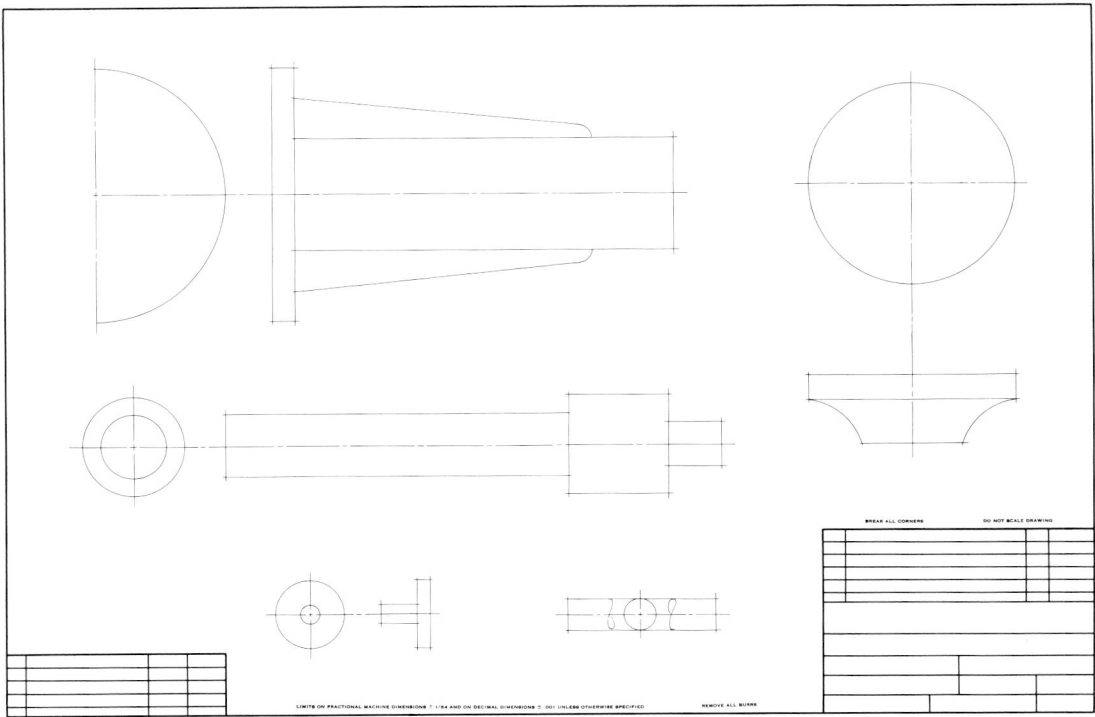

Fig. 16.23 Blocking In the Views

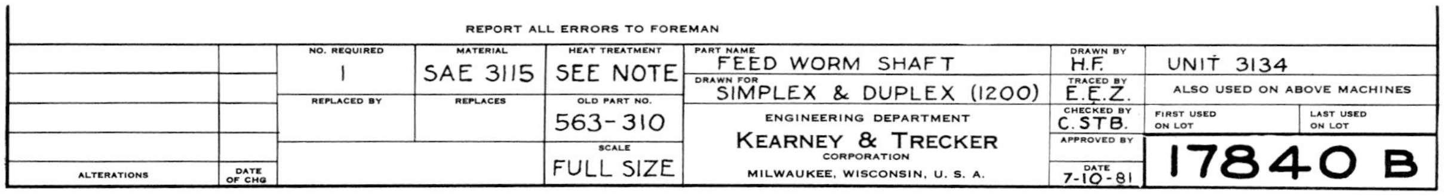

		NO. REQUIRED	MATERIAL	HEAT TREATMENT	PART NAME FEED WORM SHAFT	DRAWN BY H.F.	UNIT 3134	
		1	SAE 3115	SEE NOTE	DRAWN FOR SIMPLEX & DUPLEX (1200)	TRACED BY E.E.Z.	ALSO USED ON ABOVE MACHINES	
		REPLACED BY	REPLACES	OLD PART NO. 563-310	ENGINEERING DEPARTMENT	CHECKED BY C.STB.	FIRST USED ON LOT	LAST USED ON LOT
				SCALE FULL SIZE	**KEARNEY & TRECKER** CORPORATION	APPROVED BY	17840 B	
ALTERATIONS	DATE OF CHG				MILWAUKEE, WISCONSIN, U. S. A.	DATE 7-10-81		

REPORT ALL ERRORS TO FOREMAN

Fig. 16.24 Title Strip.

3. Name and address of the purchasing company, if any.

4. Signature of the drafter who made the drawing, and the date of completion.

5. Signature of the checker, and the date of completion.

6. Signature of the chief drafter, chief engineer, or other official, and the date of approval.

7. Scale of the drawing.

8. Number of the drawing.

Other information may be given, such as material, quantity, heat treatment, finish, hardness, pattern number, estimated weight, superseding and superseded drawing numbers, symbol of machine, and many other items, depending upon the plant organization and the peculiarities of the product. Some typical commercial titles are shown in Figs. 16.24, 16.25, and 16.26. See inside back cover for traditional title forms and ANSI-approved sheet sizes.

The title form is usually placed along the bottom of the sheet, Fig. 16.24, or in the lower right-hand corner of the sheet, Fig. 16.26, because drawings are often filed in flat, horizontal drawers, and the title must be easily found. However, many filing systems are in use, and the location of the title form is governed by the system employed.

Lettering should be single-stroke vertical or inclined Gothic capitals, Figs. 4.25 and 4.26. The items in the title form should be lettered in accordance with their relative importance. The drawing number should receive greatest emphasis, closely followed by the name of the object and the name of the company. The date, scale, and drafter's and checker's names are important, but they do not deserve prominence. Greater importance of items is indicated by heavier lettering, larger lettering, wider spacing of letters, or by a combination of these methods. See Table 16.1 for recommended letter heights.

Many companies have adopted their own title forms or those preferred by ANSI and have them printed on standard-size sheets, so that the drafters need merely fill in the blank spaces.

Drawings constitute important and valuable information regarding the products of a manufacturer. Hence, carefully designed, well-kept, systematic files are generally maintained for the filing of drawings.

16.13 Drawing Numbers

Every drawing should be numbered. Some companies use serial numbers, such as 60412, or a number with a prefix or suffix letter to indicate the sheet size, as A60412 or 60412–A. The size A sheet would probably be the standard 8.5″ × 11.0″ or 9.0″ × 12.0″, and the B size a multiple thereof. Many different numbering schemes are in use in which various parts of the drawing number indicate different things, such as model number of the machine and the general nature or use of the part. In general, it

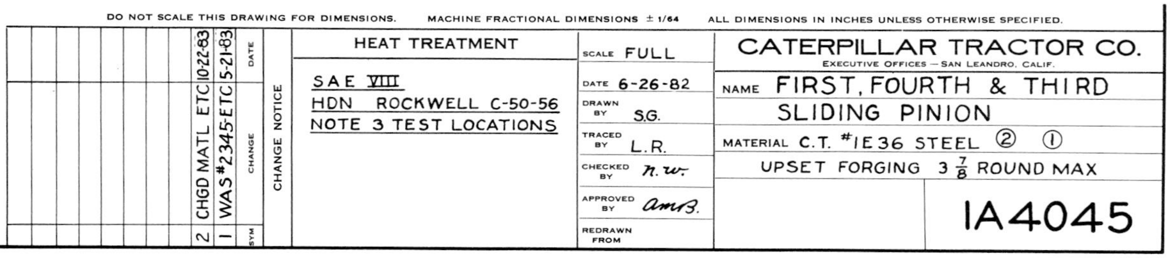

DO NOT SCALE THIS DRAWING FOR DIMENSIONS.   MACHINE FRACTIONAL DIMENSIONS ± 1/64   ALL DIMENSIONS IN INCHES UNLESS OTHERWISE SPECIFIED.

						2 CHGD MATL ETC 10.22-83	1 WAS #2345 ETC 5-21-83	DATE	CHANGE NOTICE	HEAT TREATMENT SAE VIII HDN ROCKWELL C-50-56 NOTE 3 TEST LOCATIONS	SCALE FULL	CATERPILLAR TRACTOR CO. EXECUTIVE OFFICES — SAN LEANDRO, CALIF.
											DATE 6-26-82	NAME FIRST, FOURTH & THIRD
											DRAWN BY S.G.	SLIDING PINION
											TRACED BY L.R.	MATERIAL C.T. #1E36 STEEL ② ①
											CHECKED BY n.w.	UPSET FORGING 3 7/8 ROUND MAX
										SYM	APPROVED BY amB.	1A4045
											REDRAWN FROM	

Fig. 16.25 Title Strip.

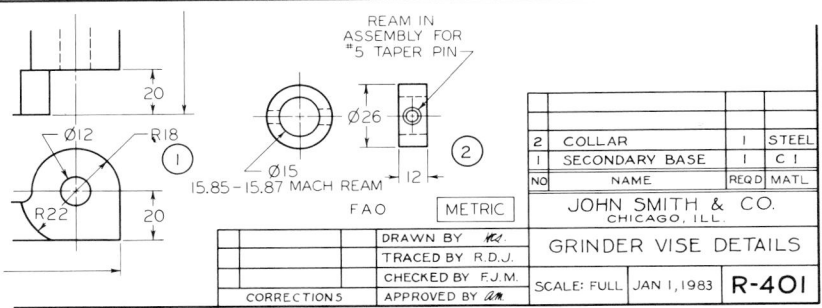

Fig. 16.26 Identification of Details with Parts List.

is best to use a simple numbering system and not to load the number with too many indications.

The drawing number should be lettered 7 mm (.250″) high in the lower-right and upper-left corners of the sheet, Fig. 16.33.

16.14 Parts Lists

A bill of material, or *parts list*, consists of an itemized list of the several parts of a structure shown on a detail drawing or an assembly drawing [ANSI Y14.34M–1982 (R1988)]. This list is often given on a separate sheet, but is frequently lettered directly on the drawing, Fig. 16.32. The title strip alone is

sufficient on detail drawings of only one part, Fig. 16.22, but a parts list is necessary on detail drawings of several parts, Fig. 16.26.

Parts lists on machine drawings contain the part numbers or symbols, a descriptive title of each part, the number required, the material specified, and frequently other information, such as pattern numbers, stock sizes of materials, and weights of parts.

Parts are listed in general order of size or importance. The main castings or forgings are listed first, parts cut from cold-rolled stock second, and standard parts such as fasteners, bushings, and roller bearings third. If the parts list rests on top of the title box or strip, the order of items should be from

Table 16.1 *Recommended*[a] *Minimum Letter Heights*

Use	Minimum Letter Heights		Drawing Size
	Freehand	Instrumental	
Drawing number in title block	.312″ ($\frac{5}{16}$) 7 mm	.290″ 7 mm	Larger than 17″ × 22″
	.250″ ($\frac{1}{4}$) 7 mm	.240″ 7 mm	Up to and including 17″ × 22″
Drawing title	.250″ ($\frac{1}{4}$) 7 mm	.240″ 7 mm	All
Section and tabulation letters	.250″ ($\frac{1}{4}$) 7 mm	.240″ 7 mm	
Zone letters and numerals in borders	.188″ ($\frac{3}{16}$) 5 mm	.175″ 5 mm	
Dimensions, tolerances, limits, notes, subtitles for special views, tables, revisions, and zone letters for the body of the drawing	.125″ ($\frac{1}{8}$) 3.5 mm	.120″ 3.5 mm	Up to and including 17″ × 22″
	.156″ ($\frac{5}{32}$) 5 mm	.140″ 5 mm	Larger than 17″ × 22″

[a]ANSI Y14.2M–1979 (R1987).

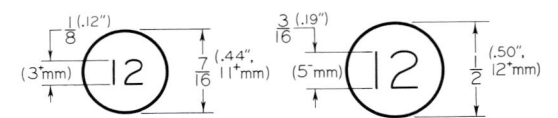

Fig. 16.27 Identification Numbers.

the bottom upward, Figs. 16.26 and 16.32, so that new items can be added later, if necessary. If the parts list is placed in the upper-right corner, the items should read downward.

Each detail on the drawing may be identified with the parts list by the use of a small circle containing the part number, placed adjacent to the detail, as in Fig. 16.26. One of the sizes in Fig. 16.27 will be found suitable, depending on the size of the drawing.

Standard parts §13.41, whether purchased or company produced, are not drawn but are included in the parts list. Bolts, screws, bearings, pins, keys, and so on are identified by the part number from the assembly drawing and are specified by name and size or number.

16.15 Zoning
To facilitate locating an item on a large or complex drawing, regular ruled intervals are labeled along the margins, often the right and lower margins only. The intervals on the horizontal margin are labeled from right to left with numerals, and the intervals on the vertical margin are labeled from bottom to top with letters. See Fig. 16.38.

16.16 Checking
The importance of accuracy in technical drawing cannot be overestimated. In commercial offices, errors sometimes cause tremendous unnecessary expenditures. *The drafter's signature on a drawing identifies who is responsible for the accuracy of the work.*

In small offices, checking is usually done by the designer or by one of the drafters. In large offices, experienced engineers are employed who devote a major part of their time to checking drawings.

The pencil drawing, upon completion, is carefully checked and signed by the drafter who made it. The drawing is then checked by the designer for function, economy, practicability, and so on. Corrections, if any, are then made by the original drafter.

The final checker should be able to discover all remaining errors, and, to be effective, the work must be done in a systematic way. The checker should study the drawing with particular attention to the following points.

1. Soundness of design, with reference to function, strength, materials, economy, manufacturability, serviceability, ease of assembly and repair, lubrication, and so on.

2. Choice of views, partial views, auxiliary views, sections, line work, lettering, and so on.

3. Dimensions, with special reference to repetition, ambiguity, legibility, omissions, errors, and finish marks. Special attention should be given to tolerances.

4. Standard parts. In the interest of economy, as many parts as possible should be standard.

5. Notes, with special reference to clear wording and legibility.

6. Clearances. Moving parts should be checked in all possible positions to assure freedom of movement.

7. Title form information.

16.17 Drawing Revisions
Changes on drawings are necessitated by changes in design, changes in tools, desires of customers, or by errors in design or in production. In order that the sources of all changes of information on drawings may be understood, verified, and accessible, an accurate record of all changes should be made on the drawings. The record should show the character of the change, by whom, when, and why made.

The changes are made by erasures directly on the original drawing or by means of erasure fluid on a reproduction print. Additions are simply drawn in on the original. The removal of information by crossing out is not recommended. If a dimension is not noticeably affected by a change, it may be underlined with a heavy line as shown in Fig. 13.15 to indicate that it is not to scale. In any case, prints of each issue or microfilms are kept on file to show how the drawing appeared before the revision. New prints are issued to supersede old ones each time a change is made.

If considerable change on a drawing is necessary, a new drawing may be made and the old one then stamped OBSOLETE and placed in the "obsolete" file. In the title block of the old drawing, the words

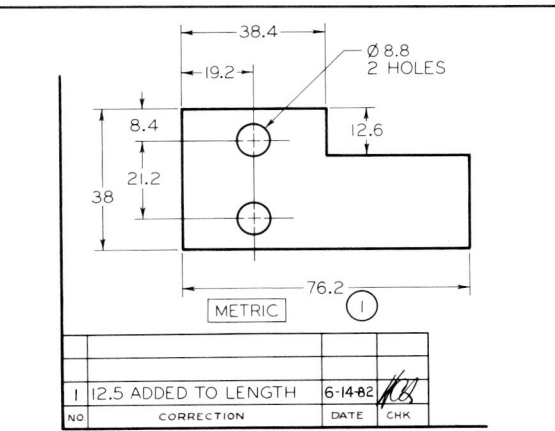

Fig. 16.28 Revisions.

"SUPERSEDED BY . . ." or "REPLACED BY . . ." are entered followed by the number of the new drawing. On the new drawing, under "SUPERSEDES . . ." or "REPLACES . . .," the number of the old drawing is entered.

Various methods are used to reference the area on a drawing where the change is made, with the entry in the revision block. The most common is to place numbers or letters in small circles near the places where the changes were made and to use the same numbers or letters in the revision block, Fig. 16.28. On zoned drawings, §16.15, the zone of the correction would be shown in the revision block. In addition, the change should be described briefly, and the date and the initials of the person making the change should be given.

16.18 Simplified Drafting

Drafting time is a considerable element of the total cost of a product. Consequently, industry attempts to reduce drawing costs by simplifying its drafting practices, but without loss of clarity to the user.

The American National Standard Drafting Manual, published by the American National Standards Institute, incorporates the best and most representative practices in this country, and the authors are in full accord with them. These standards advocate simplification in many ways, for example, partial views, half views, thread symbols, piping symbols, and single-line spring drawings. Any line or lettering on a drawing that is not needed for clarity should be omitted.

A summary of practices to simplify drafting is as follows:

1. Use word description in place of drawing wherever practicable.

2. Never draw an unnecessary view. Often a view can be eliminated by using abbreviations or symbols such as HEX, SQ, DIA, ∅, □, and ℄.

3. Draw partial views instead of full views wherever possible. Draw half views of symmetrical parts.

4. Avoid elaborate, pictorial, or repetitive detail as much as possible. Use phantom lines to avoid drawing repeated features, §15.14.

5. List rather than draw, when possible, standard parts such as bolts, nuts, keys, and pins.

6. Omit unnecessary hidden lines. See §6.25.

7. Use outline section lining in large sectioned areas wherever it can be done without loss of clarity.

8. Omit unnecessary duplication of notes and lettering.

9. Use symbolic representation wherever possible, such as piping symbols and thread symbols.

10. Draw freehand, or mechanically plus freehand, wherever practicable.

11. Avoid hand lettering as much as possible. For example, parts lists should be typed on a separate sheet.

12. Use laborsaving devices wherever feasible, such as templates and plastic overlays.

13. Use electronic devices or computer graphics systems wherever feasible for design, drawing, and repetitive work.

Some industries have attempted to simplify their drafting practices even more. Until these practices are accepted generally by industry and in time find their way into the ANSI standards, the students should follow the ANSI standards as exemplified throughout this book. Fundamentals should come first—shortcuts perhaps later.

16.19 Assembly Drawings

An assembly drawing shows the assembled machine or structure, with all detail parts in their functional positions. Assembly drawings vary in character according to use, as follows: (1) design assemblies, or layouts, discussed in §16.6, (2) general assemblies,

(3) working drawing assemblies, (4) outline or installation assemblies, and (5) check assemblies.

16.20 General Assemblies

A set of working drawings includes the *detail drawings* of the individual parts and the *assembly drawing* of the assembled unit. The detail drawings of an automobile connecting rod are shown in Figs. 16.29 and 16.30, and the corresponding assembly drawing is shown in Fig. 16.31. Such an assembly, showing only one unit of a larger machine, is often referred to as a *subassembly.*

An example of a complete general assembly appears in Fig. 16.32, which shows the assembly of a hand grinder. Another example of a subassembly is shown in Fig. 16.33.

1. Views

In selecting the views for an assembly drawing, the purpose of the drawing must be kept in mind: to show how the parts fit together in the assembly and to suggest the function of the entire unit, not to describe the shapes of the individual parts. The assembly worker receives the actual finished parts. If more information is needed about a part that cannot be obtained from the part itself, the detail drawing must be checked. Thus, the assembly drawing purports to show *relationships* of parts, *not shapes.* The view or views selected should be the minimum views or partial views that will show how the parts fit together. In Fig. 16.31, only one view is needed, while in Fig. 16.32 only two views are necessary.

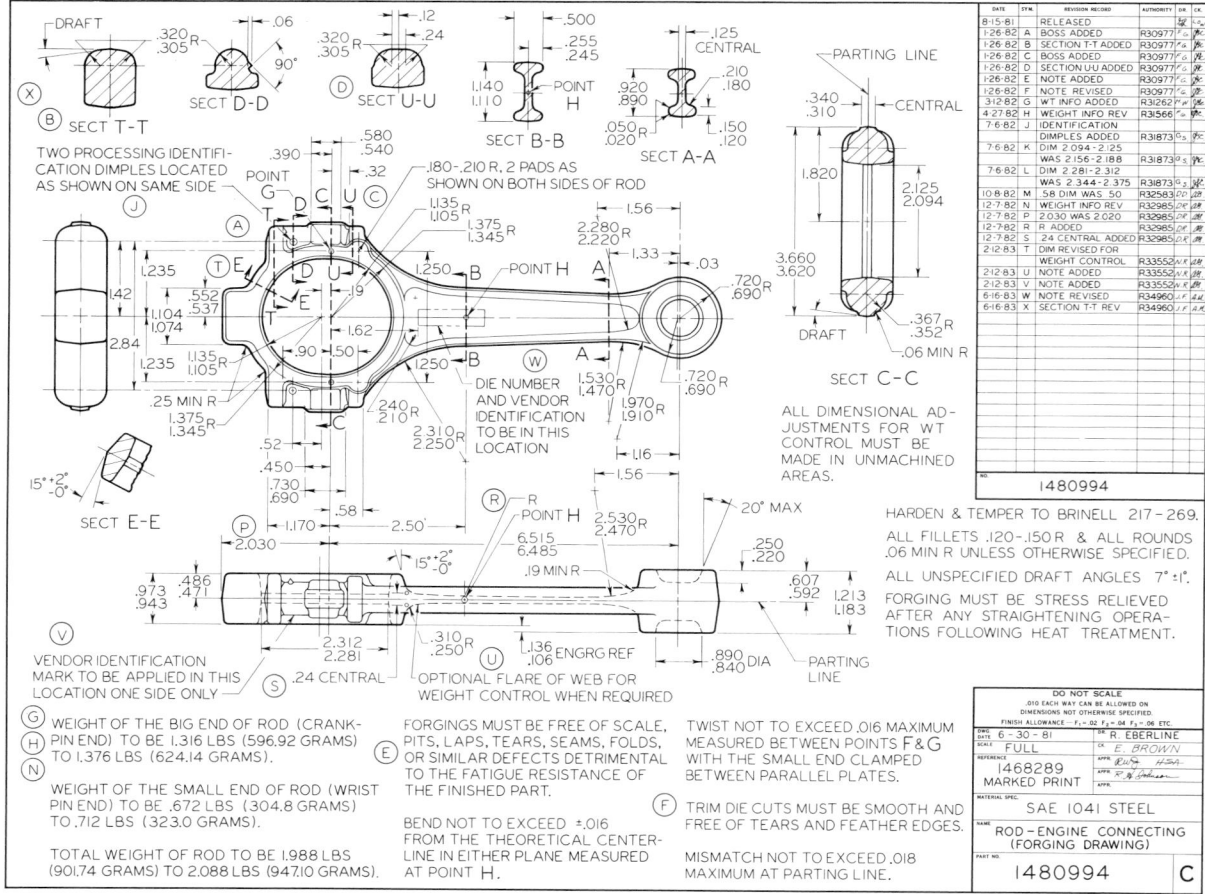

Fig. 16.29   Forging Drawing of Connecting Rod. *Courtesy of Cadillac Motor Car Division.*

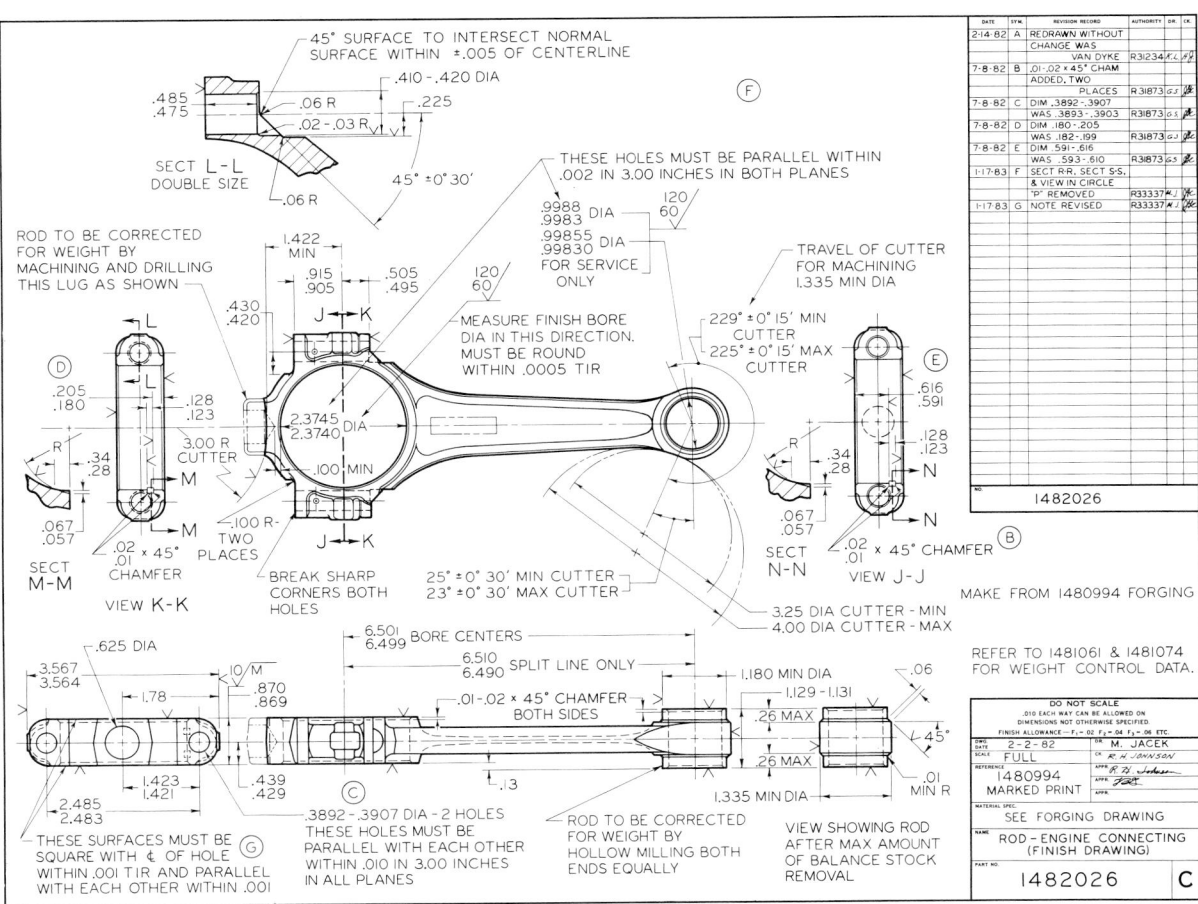

Fig. 16.30 Detail Drawing of Connecting Rod. *Courtesy of Cadillac Motor Car Division.*

2. Sections

Since assemblies often have parts fitting into or overlapping other parts, hidden-line delineation is usually out of the question. Hence, in assemblies, sectioning can be used to great advantage. For example, in Fig. 16.32, try to imagine the right-side view drawn in elevation with interior parts represented by hidden lines. The result would be completely unintelligible.

Any kind of section may be used as needed. A broken-out section is shown in Fig. 16.32, a half section in Fig. 16.33, and several removed sections are shown in Fig. 16.29. For general information on assembly sectioning, see §16.21. For methods of drawing threads in sections, see §15.15.

3. Hidden Lines

As a result of the extensive use of sectioning in assemblies, hidden lines are often not needed. However, they should be used wherever necessary for clearness.

4. Dimensions

As a rule, dimensions are not given on assembly drawings, since they are given completely on the detail drawings. If dimensions are given, they are limited to some function of the object as a whole, such as the maximum height of a jack, or the maximum opening between the jaws of a vise. Or when machining is required in the assembly operation,

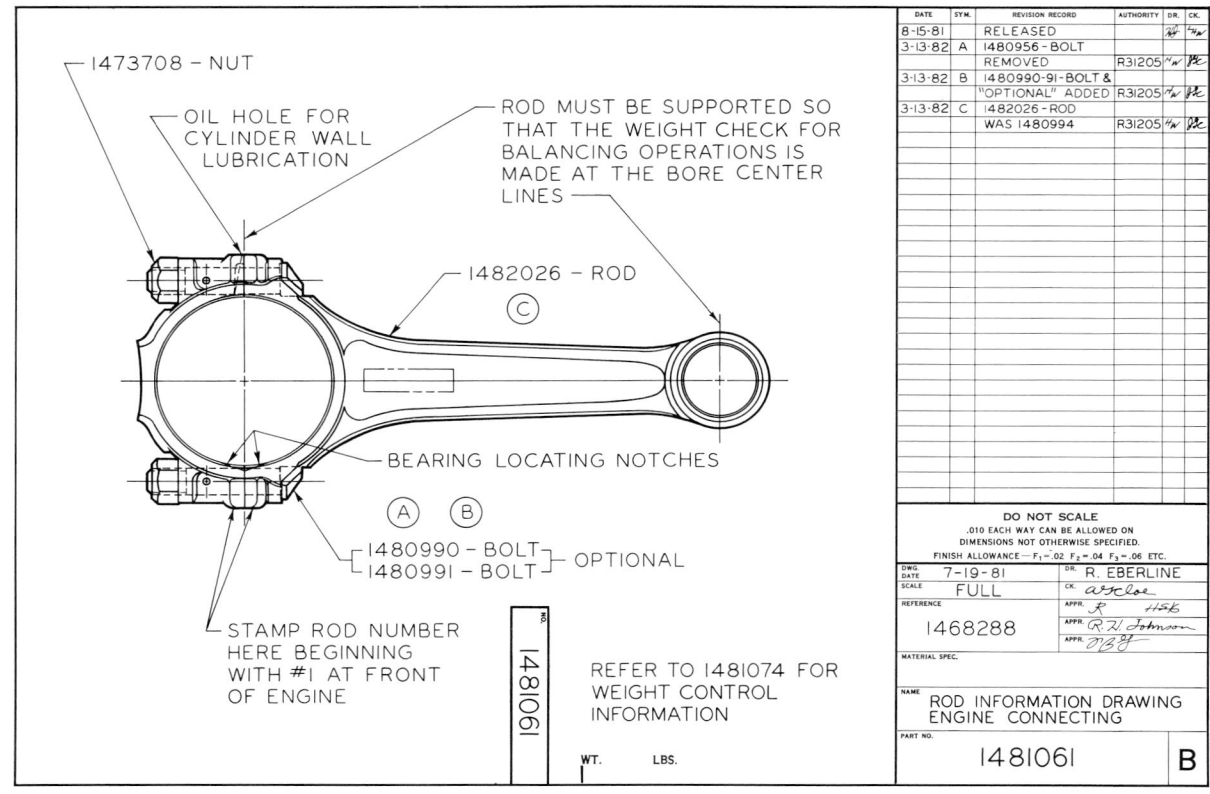

Fig. 16.31 Assembly Drawing of Connecting Rod. *Courtesy of Cadillac Motor Car Division.*

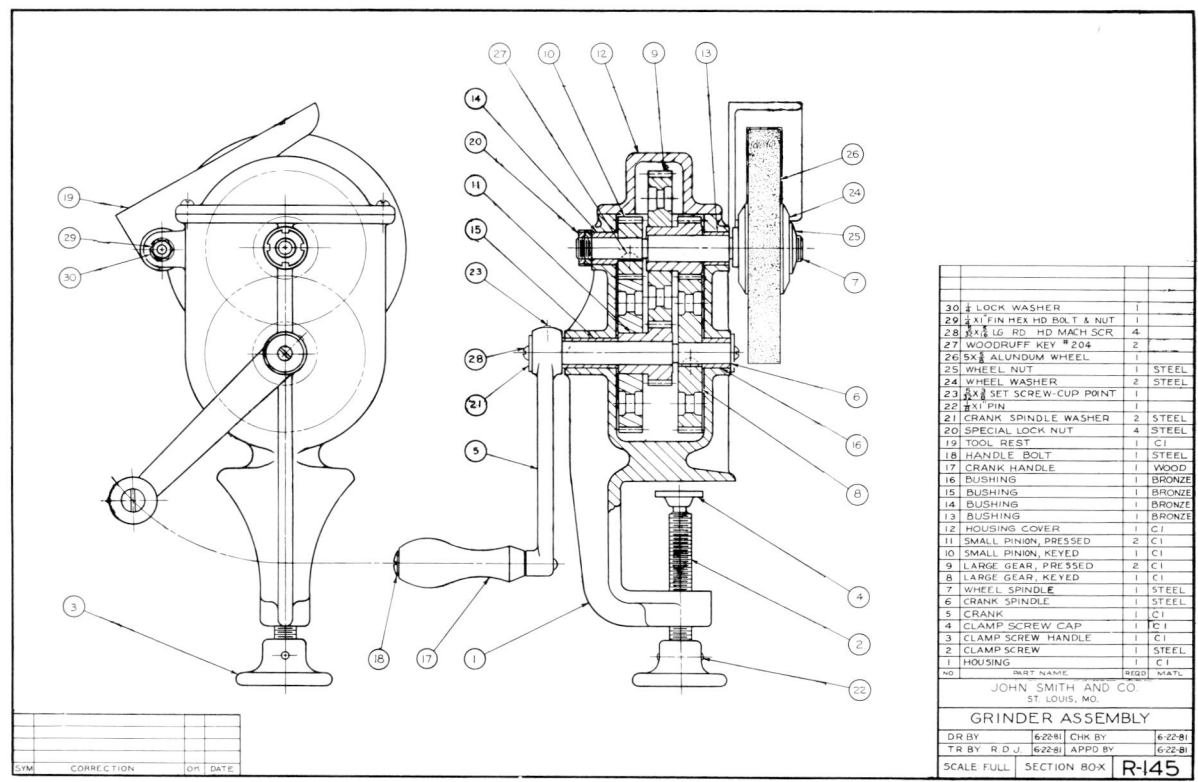

Fig. 16.32 Assembly Drawing of Grinder.

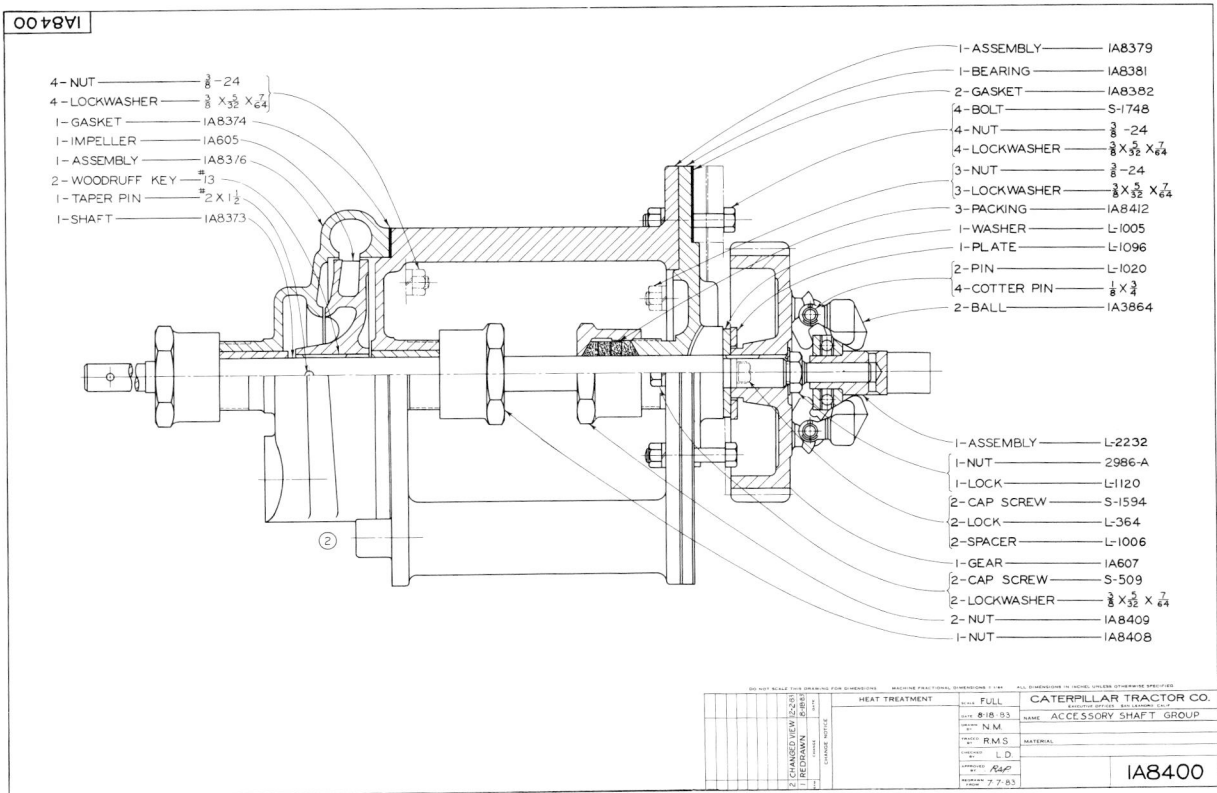

Fig. 16.33 Subassembly of Accessory Shaft Group.

the necessary dimensions and notes may be given on the assembly drawing.

5. Identification

The methods of identification of parts in an assembly are similar to those used in detail drawings where several details are shown on one sheet, as in Fig. 16.26. Circles containing the part numbers are placed adjacent to the parts, with leaders terminated by arrowheads touching the parts as in Fig. 16.32. The circles shown in Fig. 16.27 for detail drawings are, with the addition of radial leaders, satisfactory for assembly drawings. Note, in Fig. 16.32, that these circles are placed in orderly horizontal or vertical rows and not scattered over the sheet. Leaders are never allowed to cross, and adjacent leaders are parallel or nearly so.

The parts list includes the part numbers or symbols, a descriptive title of each part, the number required per machine or unit, the material specified, and frequently other information, such as pattern numbers, stock sizes, weights, and so on. Frequently the parts list is lettered or typed on a separate sheet.

Another method of identification is to letter the part names, numbers required, and part numbers, at the end of leaders as shown in Fig. 16.33. More commonly, however, only the part numbers are given, together with ANSI-approved straight-line leaders.

6. Drawing Revisions

Methods of recording changes are the same as those for detail drawings, Fig. 16.29, for example. See §16.17.

16.21 Assembly Sectioning

In assembly sections it is necessary not only to show the cut surfaces but to distinguish between adjacent parts. This is done by drawing the section lines in

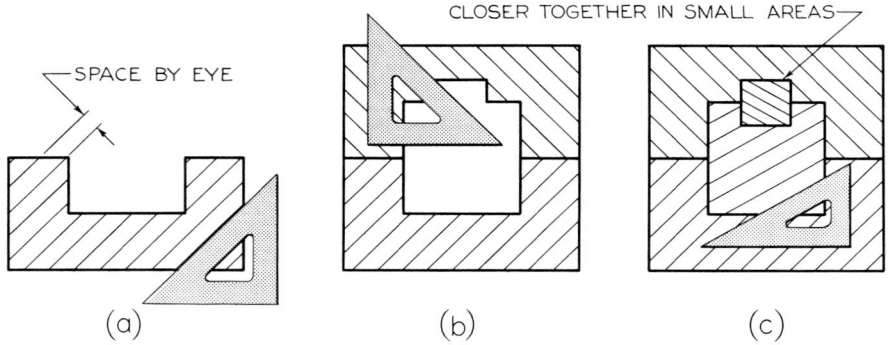

Fig. 16.34 Section Lining (Full Size).

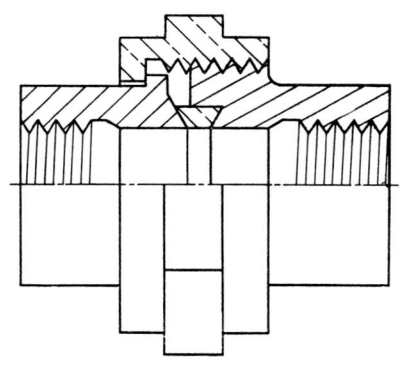

Fig. 16.35 Symbolic Section Lining.

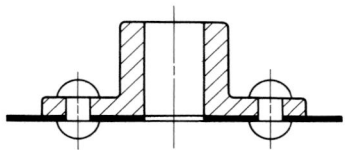

Fig. 16.36 Sectioning Thin Parts.

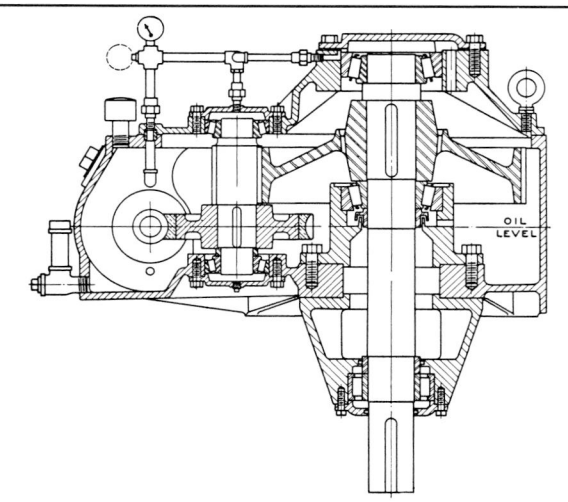

Fig. 16.37 Assembly Section. *Courtesy of Hewitt-Robins, Inc.*

opposing directions, as shown in Fig. 16.34. The first large area, (a), is section-lined at 45°. The next large area, (b), is section-lined at 45° in the opposite direction. Additional areas are then section-lined at other angles, as 30° or 60° with horizontal, as shown at (c). If necessary, "odd" angles may be used. Note at (c) that in small areas it is necessary to space the section lines closer together. The section lines in adjacent areas should not meet at the visible lines separating the areas.

For general use, the cast-iron general-purpose section lining is recommended for assemblies.

Wherever it is desired to give a general indication of the materials used, symbolic section lining may be used, as in Fig. 16.35.

In sectioning relatively thin parts in assembly, such as gaskets and sheet-metal parts, section lining is ineffective, and such parts should be shown in solid black, Fig. 16.36.

Often solid objects, or parts which themselves do not require sectioning, lie in the path of the cutting plane. It is customary and standard practice to show such parts unsectioned, or "in the round." These include bolts, nuts, shafts, keys, screws, pins,

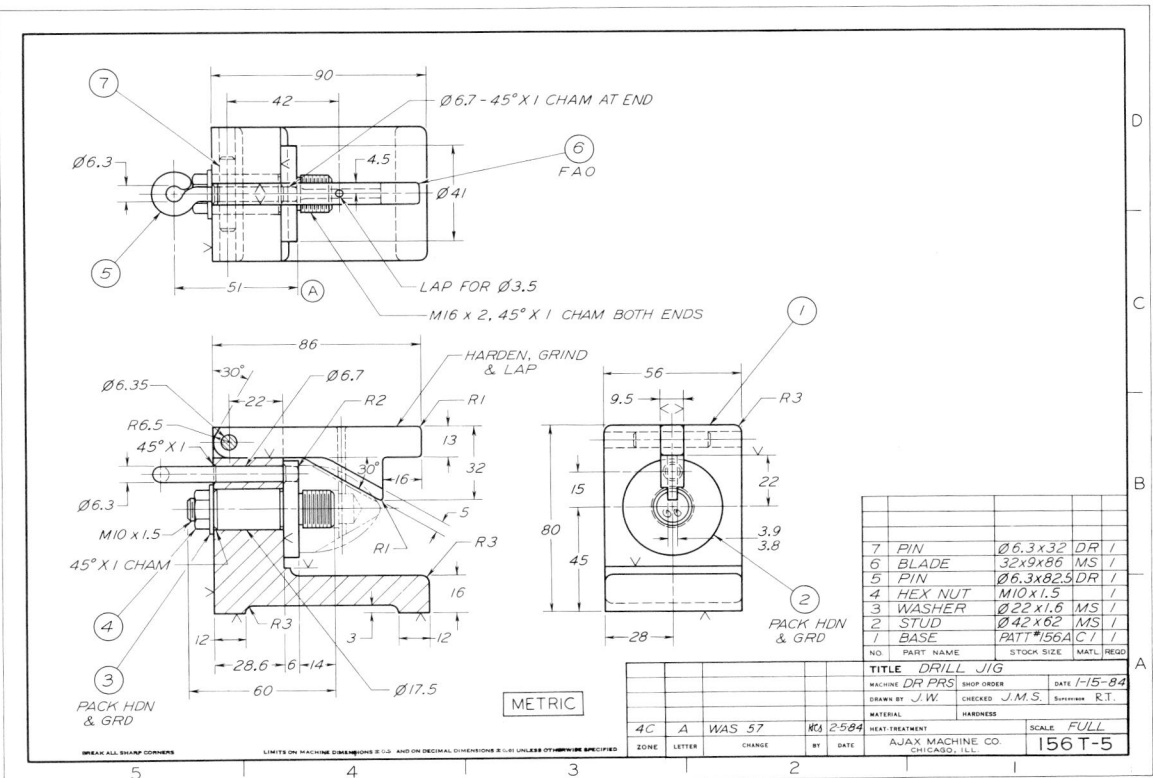

Fig. 16.38 Working Drawing Assembly of Drill Jig.

ball or roller bearings, gear teeth, spokes, and ribs among others. Many are shown in Fig. 16.37, and similar examples are shown in Figs. 16.32 and 16.33.

16.22 Working Drawing Assembly

A working drawing assembly, Fig. 16.38, is a combined detail and assembly drawing. Such drawings are often used in place of separate detail and assembly drawings when the assembly is simple enough for all of its parts to be shown clearly in the single drawing. In some cases, all but one or two parts can be drawn and dimensioned clearly in the assembly drawing, in which event these parts are detailed separately on the same sheet. This type of drawing is common in valve drawings, locomotive subassemblies, aircraft subassemblies, and in drawings of jigs and fixtures.

16.23 Installation Assemblies

An assembly made specifically to show how to install or erect a machine or structure is an *installation assembly.* This type of drawing is also often called an

outline assembly, because it shows only the outlines and the relationships of exterior surfaces. A typical installation assembly is shown in Fig. 16.39. In aircraft drafting, an installation drawing (assembly) gives complete information for placing details or subassemblies in their final positions in the airplane.

16.24 Check Assemblies

After all detail drawings of a unit have been made, it may be necessary to make a *check assembly,* especially if a number of changes were made in the details. Such an assembly is drawn accurately to scale in order to check graphically the correctness of the details and their relationship in assembly. After the check assembly has served its purpose, it may be converted into a general assembly drawing.

16.25 Patent Drawings

The patent application for a machine or device must include drawings to illustrate and explain the invention. It is essential that all patent drawings be me-

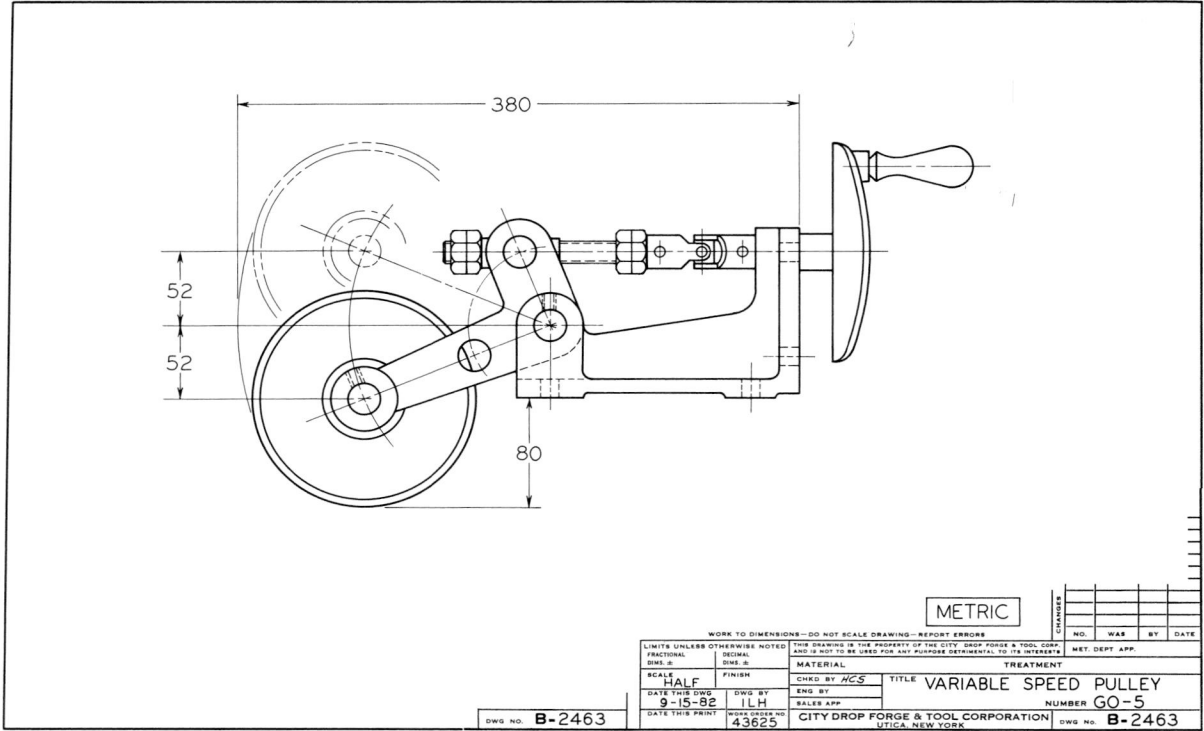

Fig. 16.39   Installation Assembly.

chanically correct and constitute complete illustrations of every feature of the invention claimed. The strict requirements of the U.S. Patent Office in this respect serve to facilitate the examination of applications and the interpretation of patents issued thereon. A typical patent drawing is shown in Fig. 16.40.

The drawings for patent applications are pictorial and explanatory in nature; hence, they are not detailed as are working drawings for production purposes. Center lines, dimensions, notes, and so forth are omitted. Views, features, and parts, for example, are identified by numbers that refer to the descriptions and explanations given in the specification section of the patent application.

Patent drawings are made with India ink on heavy, smooth, white paper, exactly 10.0″ × 15.0″ with 1.0″ borders on all sides. A space of not less than 1.25″ from the shorter border, which is the top of the drawing, is left blank for the heading of title, name, number, and other data to be added by the Patent Office.

All lines must be solid black and suitable for reproduction at a smaller size. Line shading is used whenever it improves readability.

The drawings must contain as many figures as necessary to show the invention clearly. There is no restriction on the number of sheets. The figures may be plan, elevation, section, pictorial, and detail views of portions or elements, and they may be drawn to an enlarged scale if necessary. The required signatures must be placed in the lower right-hand corner of the drawing, either inside or outside the border line.

Because of the strict requirements of the Patent Office, applicants are advised to employ competent drafters to make their drawings. To aid drafters in the preparation of drawing for submission in patent applications, the *Guide for Patent Draftsmen* was prepared and can be obtained from the Superintendent of Documents, U.S. Government Printing Office, Washington, D.C. 20402.

16.26 Reproduction and Control of Drawings

An essential part of the designer's or drafter's education is a thorough knowledge of reproduction techniques and processes. Specifically, they should be familiar with the various processes available for

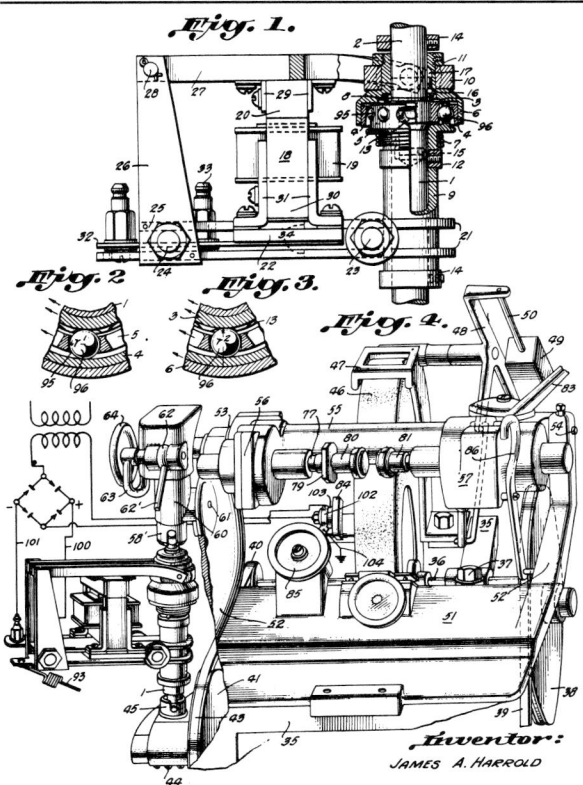

Fig. 16.40 A Well-Executed Patent Drawing.

the reproduction of drawings: *blueprint, diazo, microfilm, microfiche,* etc. Equally important is a knowledge of industrial printing and duplicating methods: *letterpress, lithography, xerography,* and so on.

Each of these processes has very definite advantages and disadvantages. In some, such as blueprinting, the original must be transparent, while in others, such as xerography, opaque or translucent originals may be used. In addition to copies, some reproducing equipment can make enlargements or reductions of the original, which often are extremely useful. A general familiarity with all of these reproduction processes is therefore absolutely necessary, since the reproduction method selected for a specific project will be dependent on the type of original used, number of copies required, size and appearance of copy desired, and the cost.

For a detailed explanation of these processes, we suggest that you consult your school or public library.

The average engineering drawing requires a considerable economic investment; therefore, adequate

control and protection of the original drawing are mandatory. Such items as drawing numbers, methods of filing, microfilming, security files, print making and distribution, drawing changes, and retrieval of drawings are all inherent in proper drawing control.

A proper drawing-control system will enable those in charge of drawings (1) to know the location and status of the drawing at all times; (2) to minimize the damage to original drawings from the handling required for revisions, printing, and so on; and (3) to provide distribution of prints to proper persons.

Those organizations with large computer-aided design (CAD) systems use computer storage of finished drawings. In addition, digitized drawing information about frequently required components and elements, such as standard bolts, nuts, screws, pins, and piping valves, is stored in the computer for recall and placement on drawings as needed. CAD systems of this type are very expensive to purchase and maintain, but they have obvious advantages for production, storage, control, and recall of drawings. Most small and medium-size companies and a substantial number of large firms may not be able to justify the acquisition of high-capacity CAD systems and thus will continue to use the conventional methods of reproduction, storage, retrieval, and control of drawings described in this chapter. But CAD systems are becoming more compact and less expensive, and as advancing technology makes such systems more affordable, it is expected that many companies will make the change to computer graphics systems.

16.27 Computer Graphics

A computer is an electronic machine that is capable of performing specific tasks at incredibly high speeds. The use of the computer today in various business and industrial operations is very well known. Engineers and scientists have used computers for many years to perform the mathematical calculations required in their work. In recent years, new and innovative technological developments in computer applications have expanded the versatility of the computer into a still more useful engineering and design tool.

Computer graphics is a general term used to define any procedure that uses computers to generate, process, and display graphic images. *Computer-aided design* or *computer-aided drafting (CAD)* and *computer-aided design and drafting (CADD),* or

Fig. 16.41   Bausch & Lomb Producer Electronic/CAD System. *Courtesy of Bausch & Lomb.*

Fig. 16.42   Prime CAD Workstation. *Courtesy of Prime Computer, Inc.*

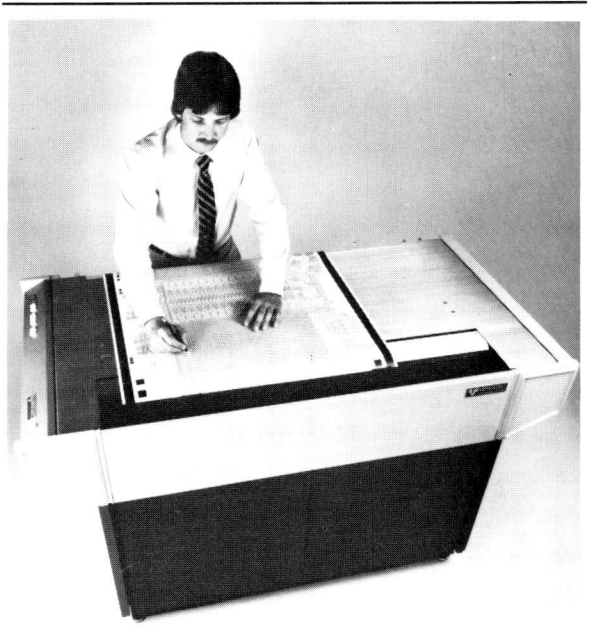

Fig. 16.43 Plotter. *Courtesy of Versatec, Inc.*

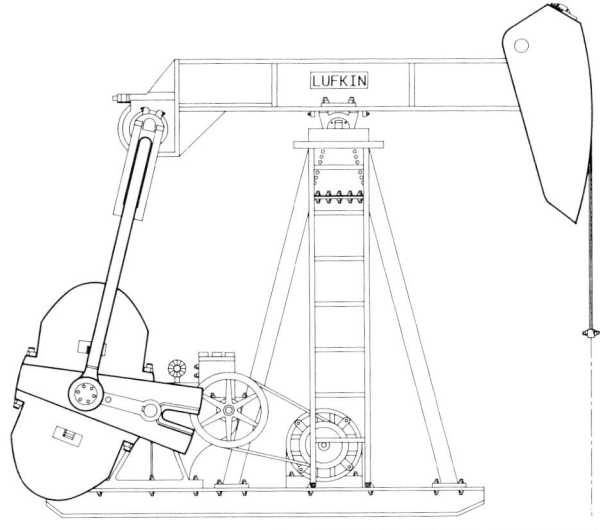

Fig. 16.44 Assembly Drawing Produced with the VersaCAD Advanced System. *Courtesy of VersaCAD.*

other comparable terms, are used synonymously and refer to a specific process that uses a computer system to assist in the creation, modification, and display of a drawing or design.

All CAD systems have similar hardware components that include input devices, a central processing unit, data storage devices, and output devices. A typical CAD system is shown in Fig. 16.41. All CAD systems must also have software, which are the programs and instructions that permit the computer system to operate.

The designer or drafter can create a drawing by first entering the appropriate data into the system at a CAD workstation, Fig. 16.42, using any one of several different input devices. The immediate result of the input is a graphic display on the screen of a cathode-ray tube (CRT). The designer can then view and analyze the drawing, make changes, delete sections, and "think out" the design on the tube much the same way as would be done on a drawing board. The final drawing displayed on the tube may then be stored in memory, or a permanent hard-copy drawing may be made using an output device such as the plotter shown in Fig. 16.43. Thus, by means of programmed data supplied to the computer, the de-

signer or drafter is able to secure from a plotter an assembly drawing, Fig. 16.44, or a detail drawing complete with all required lines, lettering, dimensions, and so forth, Fig. 16.45.

The term *computer-aided design/computer-aided manufacturing (CAD/CAM)* refers to the integration of computers into the entire design-to-manufacturing process of a product or plant. In this method, the data are transmitted directly from the CAD system to the manufacturing plant to manage and control operations. The CAD/CAM system shown in Fig. 16.46 is used to cut seat patterns for Chrysler cars and trucks. A computer-controlled trim cutter in Chrysler's trim plant, (a), makes precision cuts in bolts of material according to directions given by the CAD terminal operator, (b), located in the company's corporate engineering complex. Before CAD/CAM the cutting of seat patterns was a painstaking manual job, requires a worker to climb on top of layers of cloth and jigsaw through them following paper patterns the same way a seamstress follows a dress pattern.

The procedure for the design and preparation of engineering drawings and the production of machine parts by computer for the development of a

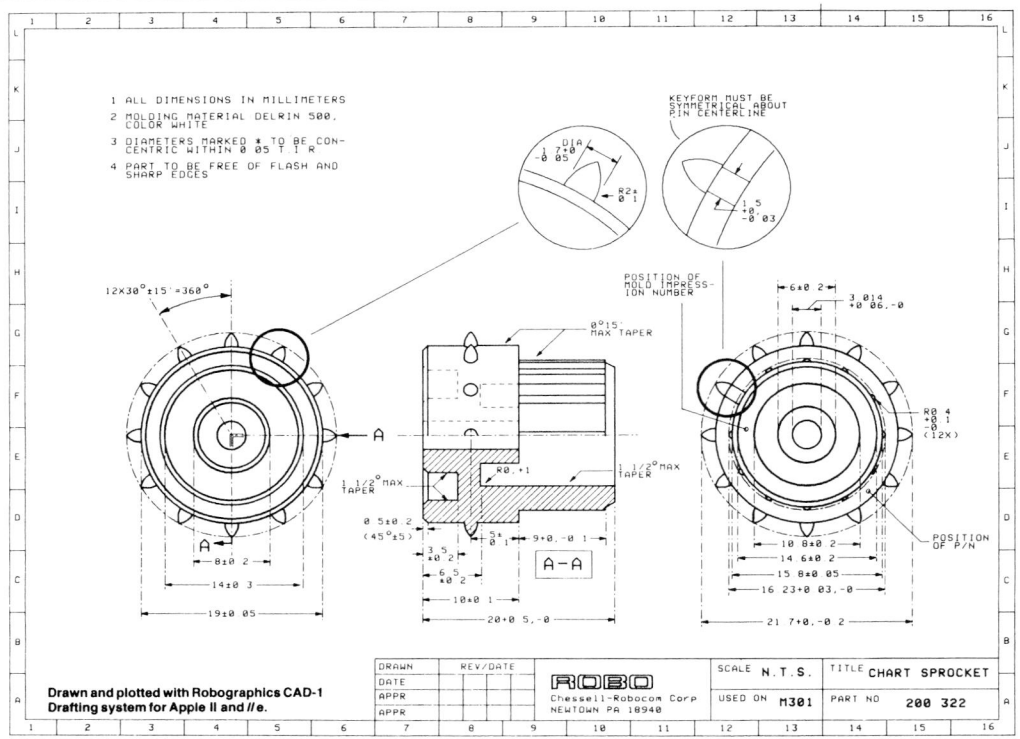

Fig. 16.45 Computer-Generated Drawing. *Courtesy of Chessell-Robocom Corp.*

Fig. 16.46 CAD/CAM System. *Courtesy of Control Data Corporation*

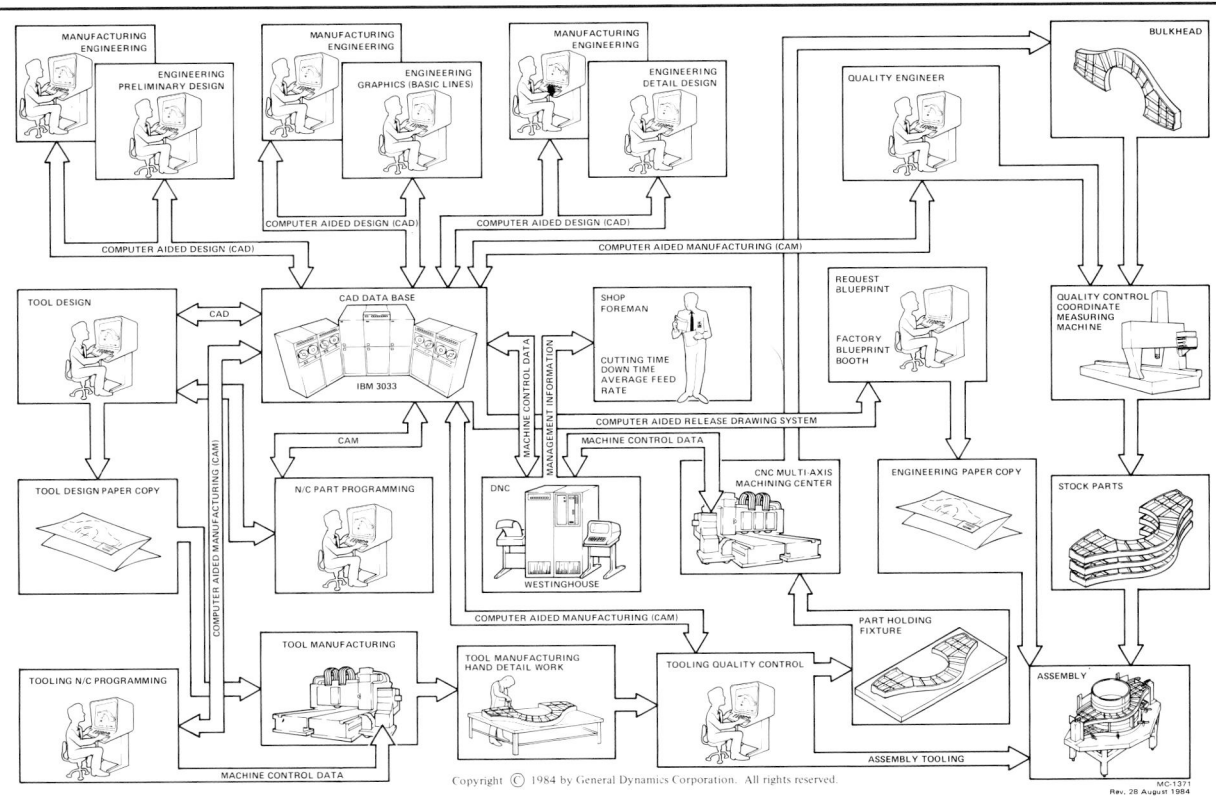

Fig. 16.47 Work Flow Diagram for Producing Detail and Assembly Drawings, and Machine Parts by Numerical Control. *Courtesy of Fort Worth Division of General Dynamics Corporation*

new aircraft is shown in the work flow diagram, Fig. 16.47. Each of the operations from design to manufacture is systematically monitored and controlled by a CAD/CAM system.

The engineers and drafters must have a thorough understanding of the graphic language in order to prepare the correct input data for the computer and to evaluate the output of the plotter. The computer will do only what it is programmed to do. Regardless of how complex or automated the method of making a drawing becomes, the time-proven mode of graphic expression is indispensable for purposes of communication, specifications, records, and so on.

For additional information about computer-aided design and drafting, see Chapters 3 and 8.

Design and Working Drawing Problems

Design Problems

The following suggestions for project assignments are of a general and very broad nature and it is expected that they will help generate many ideas for specific design projects. Much design work is undertaken to improve an existing product or system by utilization of new materials, new techniques, or new systems or procedures. In addition to the design of the product itself, another large amount of design work is essential for the tooling, production, and handling of the product. You are encouraged to discuss with your instructor any ideas you may have for a project.

1. Design new or improved playground, recreational, or sporting equipment. For example, a new child's toy could be both recreational and educational.
2. Design new or improved health equipment. For example, the physically handicapped have need for special equipment.
3. Design security or safety devices. Fire, theft, or poisonous gases are a threat to life and property.
4. Design devices and/or systems for waste handling. Home and factory waste disposal needs serious consideration.
5. Design new or improved educational equipment. Both teacher and student would welcome more efficient educational aids.
6. Design improvements in our land, sea, and air transportation systems. Vehicles, controls, highways, and airports need further refinement.
7. Design new or improved devices for material handling. A dispensing device for a powdered product is an example.
8. Improve the design of an existing device or system.
9. Design or redesign devices for improved portability.

Each solution to a design problem, whether prepared by an individual student or formulated by a group, should be in the form of a _report_, which should be typed or carefully lettered, assembled, and bound. Suitable folders or binders are usually available at the local school supply store. It is suggested that the report contain the following (or variations of them, as specified by your instructor):

1. A title sheet. The title of the design project should be placed in approximately the center of the sheet and in the lower right-hand corner place your name or the names of those in the group. The symbol PL should follow the name of the project leader.
2. Table of contents with page numbers.
3. Statement of the purpose of project with appropriate comments.
4. Preliminary design sketches, with comments on advantages and disadvantages of each, leading to the final selection of the _best_ solution. All work should be signed and dated.
5. An accurately made pictorial and/or assembly drawing(s), if more than one part is involved in the design.
6. Detail working drawings, freehand or mechanical as assigned. The 8.5″ × 11.0″ sheet size is preferred for convenient insertion in the report. Larger sizes may be bound in the report with appropriate folding.
7. A bibliography or credit for important sources of information, if applicable.

Working Drawing Problems

The problems in Figs. 16.48 to 16.77 are presented to provide practice in making regular working drawings of the type used in industry. Many problems, especially those of the assemblies, offer an excellent opportunity for you to exercise your ability to redesign or improve upon the existing design. Owing to the variations in sizes and in scales that may be used, you are required to select the sheet sizes and scales, when these are not specified, subject to the approval of the instructor. Standard sheet layouts are shown inside the back cover of this book. See also §2.63.

The statements for each problem are intentionally brief, so that the instructor may amplify or vary the requirements when making assignments. Many problems lend themselves to the preferred metric system or the acceptable complete decimal-inch system, while others may be more suitable for a combination of fractional and decimal dimensions. Either the preferred unidirectional or acceptable aligned dimensioning may be assigned.

It should be clearly understood that in problems presented in pictorial form, the placement of dimensions and finish marks cannot always be followed in the drawing. *The dimensions given are in most cases those needed to make the parts, but owing to the limitations of pictorial drawings they are not in all cases the dimensions that should be shown on the working drawing.* In the pictorial problems the rough and finished surfaces are shown, but finish marks are usually omitted. You should add all necessary finish marks and place all dimensions in the preferred places in the final drawings.

Each problem should be preceded by a thumbnail sketch or a complete technical sketch, fully dimensioned. Any of the title blocks shown inside the back cover of this book may be used, with modification if desired, or you may design the title block if so assigned by the instructor.

Since many of the problems in this chapter are of a general nature, they can also be solved on most computer graphics systems. If a system is available, the instructor may choose to assign specific problems to be completed by this method.

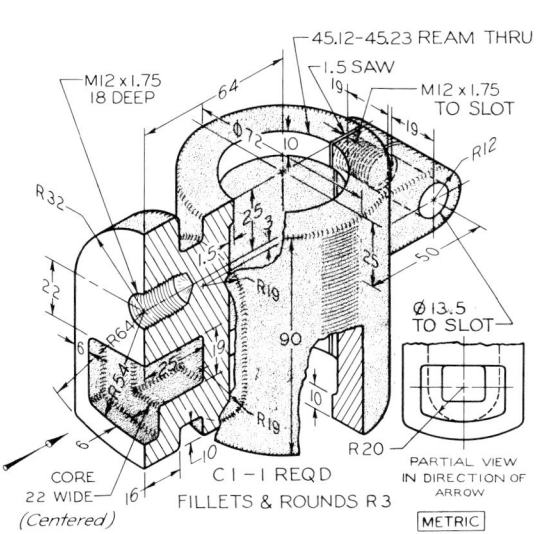

Fig. 16.48 Table Bracket. Make detail drawing. Use Size B or A3 sheet.

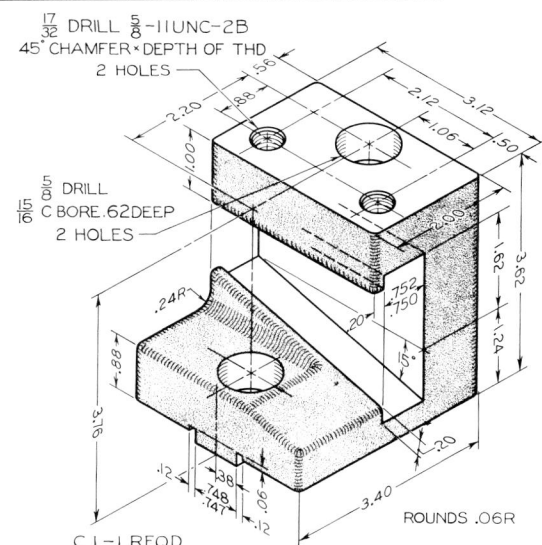

Fig. 16.49 RH Tool Post. Make detail drawing. Use Size B or A3 sheet. If assigned, convert dimensions to metric system.

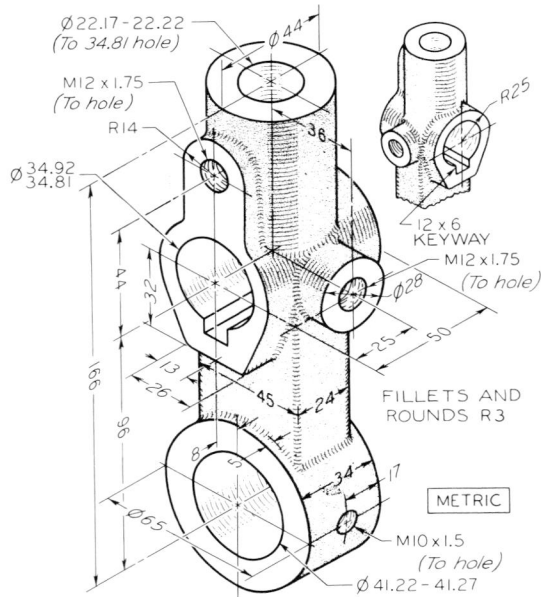

Fig. 16.50   Idler Arm.   Make detail drawing. Use Size B or A3 sheet. If assigned, convert dimensions to metric system.

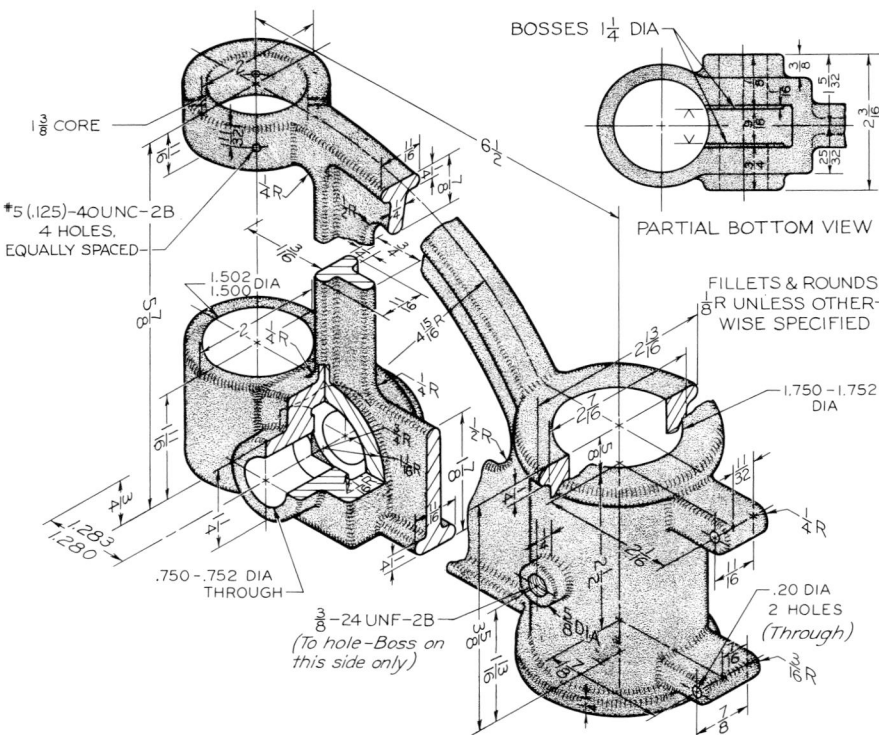

Fig. 16.51   Drill Press Bracket.   Make detail drawing. Use Size C or A2 sheet. If assigned, convert dimensions to decimal inches or redesign the part with metric dimensions.

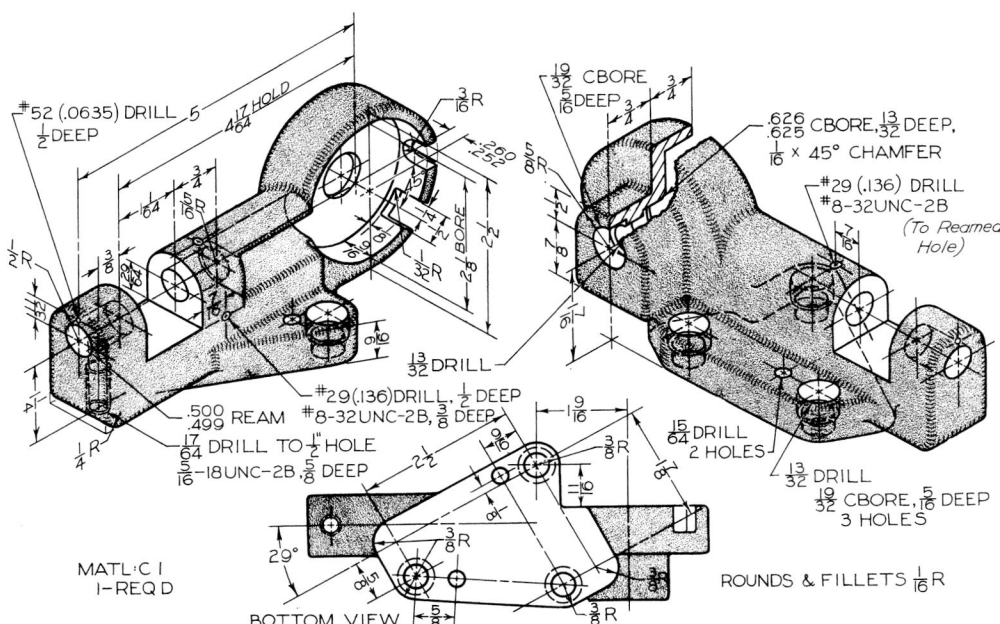

Fig. 16.52   Dial Holder.   Make detail drawing. Use Size C or A2 sheet. If assigned, convert dimensions to decimal inches or redesign the part with metric dimensions.

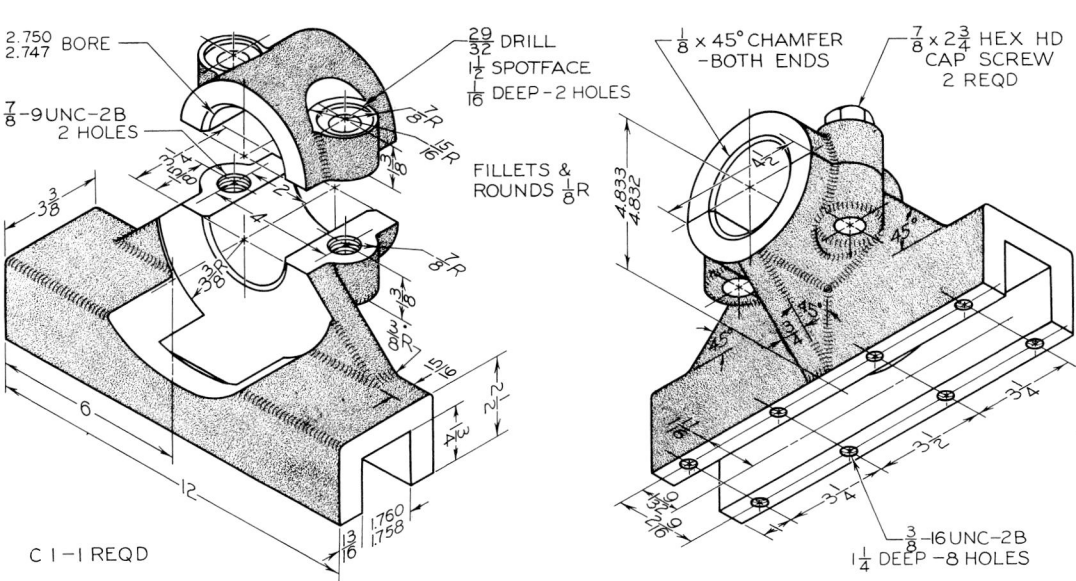

Fig. 16.53   Rack Slide.   Make detail drawings. Draw half size on Size B or A3 sheet. If assigned, convert dimensions to decimal inches or redesign the part with metric dimensions.

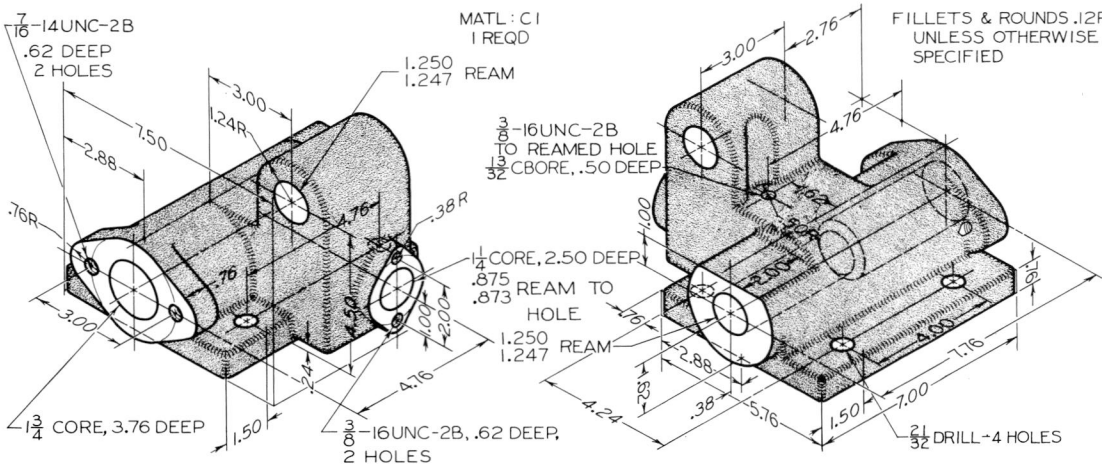

Fig. 16.54 Automatic Stop Box.   Make detail drawing. Draw half size on Size B or A3 sheet. If assigned, redesign the part with metric dimensions.

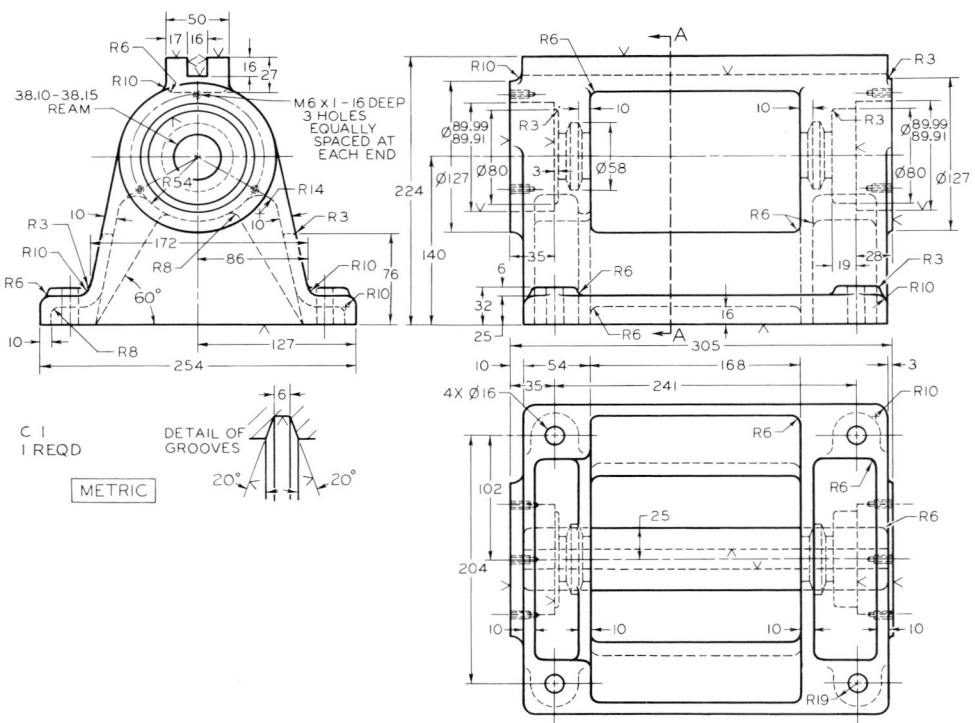

Fig. 16.55 Spindle Housing.
Given: Front, left-side, and bottom views, and partial removed section.
Required: Front view in full section, top view, and right-side view in half section on A–A. Draw half size on Size C or A2 sheet. If assigned, dimension fully.

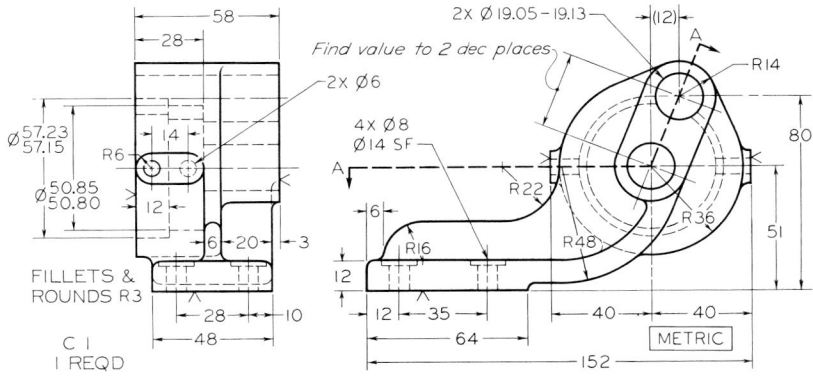

Fig. 16.56 Pump Bracket for a Thread Milling Machine.
Given: Front and left-side views.
Required: Front and right-side views, and top view in section on **A–A**. Draw full size on Size B or A3 sheet.
If assigned, dimension fully.

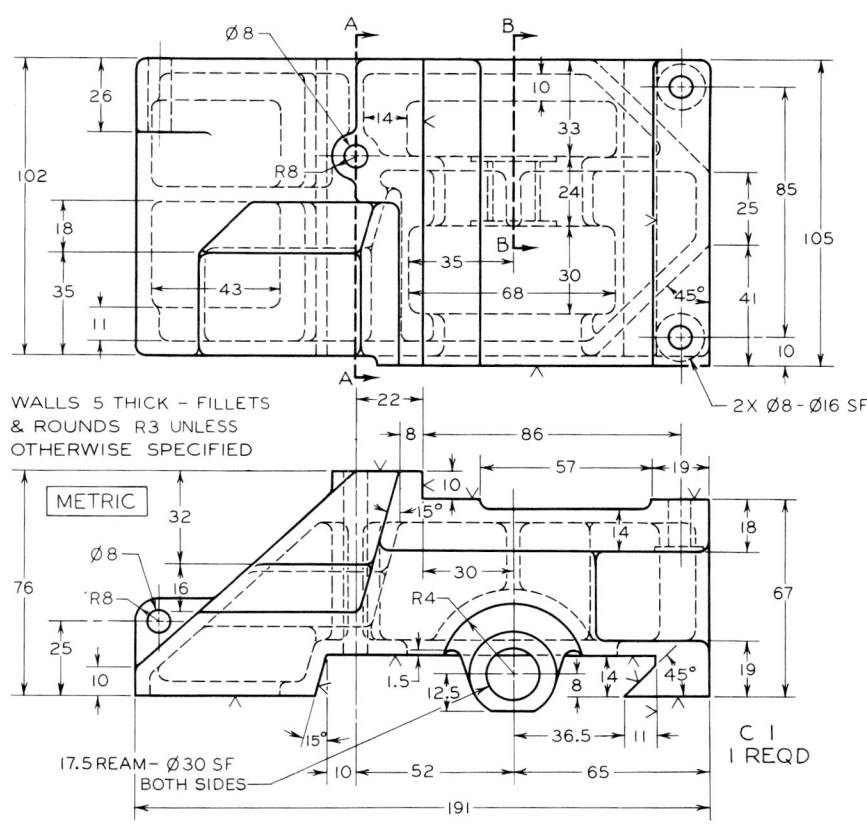

Fig. 16.57 Support Base for Planer.
Given: Front and top views.
Required: Front and top views, left-side view in full section **A–A**, and removed section **B–B**. Draw full size
on Size C or A2 sheet. If assigned, dimension fully.

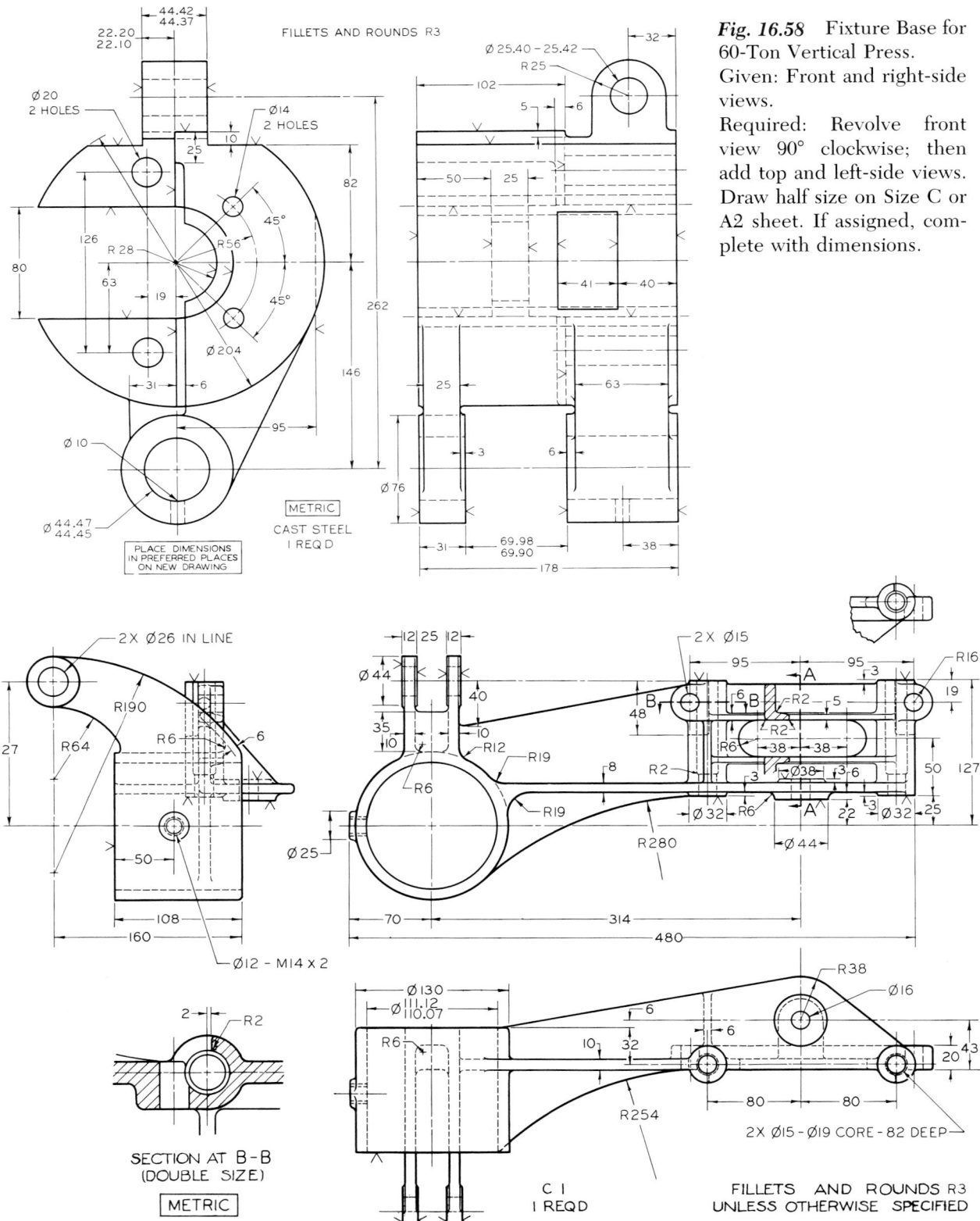

Fig. 16.58 Fixture Base for 60-Ton Vertical Press.
Given: Front and right-side views.
Required: Revolve front view 90° clockwise; then add top and left-side views. Draw half size on Size C or A2 sheet. If assigned, complete with dimensions.

Fig. 16.59 Bracket.
Given: Front, left-side, and bottom views, and partial removed section.
Required: Make detail drawing. Draw front, top, and right-side views, and removed sections A–A and B–B. Draw half size on size C or A2 sheet. Draw section B–B full size. If assigned, complete with dimensions.

484

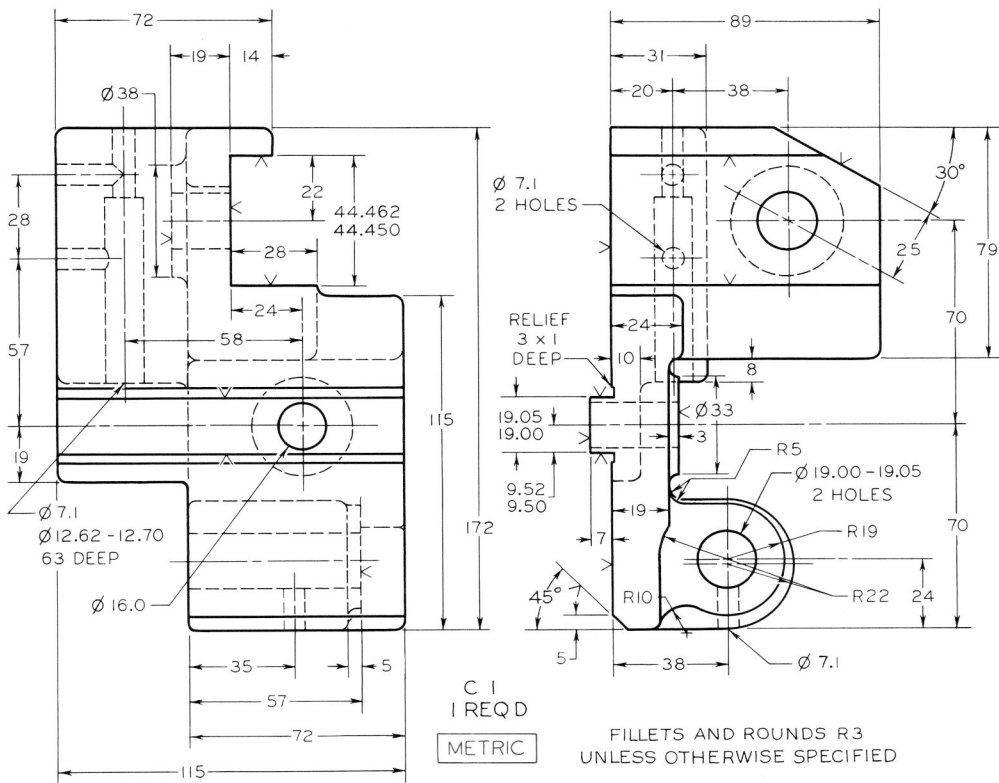

Fig. 16.60 Roller Rest Bracket for Automatic Screw Machine.
Given: Front and left-side views.
Required: Revolve front view 90° clockwise; then add top and left-side views. Draw half size on Size C or A2 sheet. If assigned, complete with dimensions.

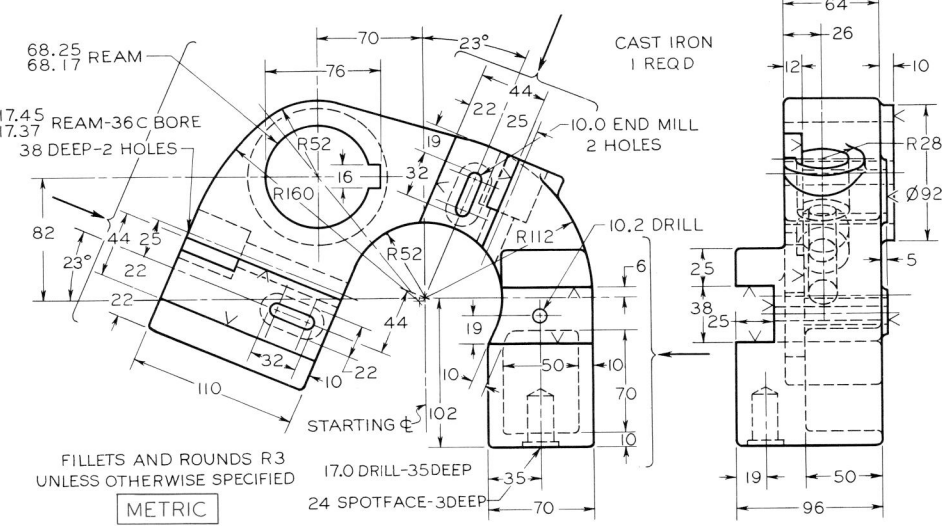

Fig. 16.61 Guide Bracket for Gear Shaper.
Given: Front and right-side views.
Required: Front view, a partial right-side view, and two partial auxiliary views taken in direction of arrows. Draw half size on Size C or A2 sheet. If assigned, complete with unidirectional dimensions.

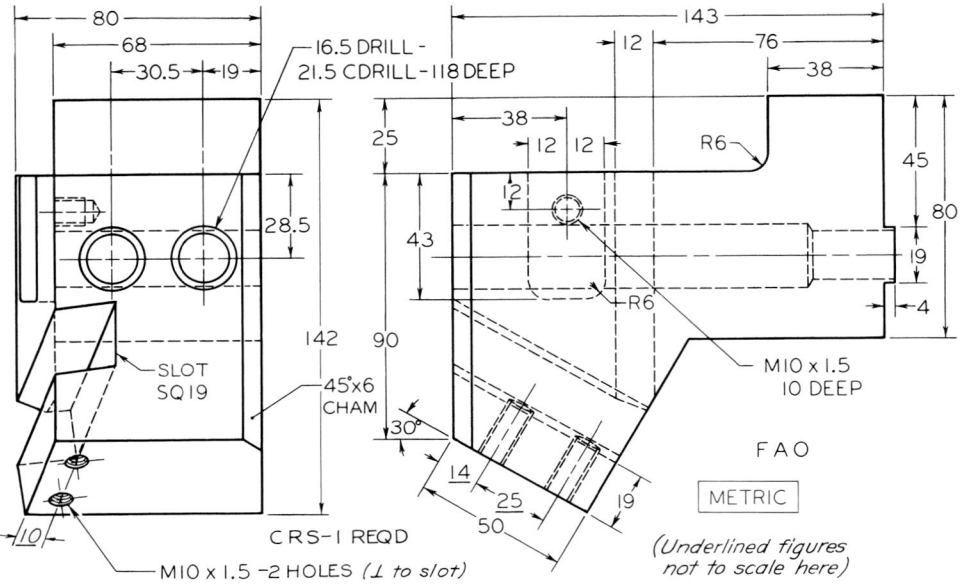

Fig. 16.62   Rear Tool Post.
Given: Front and left-side views.
Required: Take left-side view as new top view; add front and left-side views, approx. 215 mm apart, a primary auxiliary view, then a secondary view taken so as to show true end view of 19 mm slot. Complete all views, except show only necessary hidden lines in auxiliary views. Draw full size on Size C or A2 sheet. If assigned, complete with dimensions.

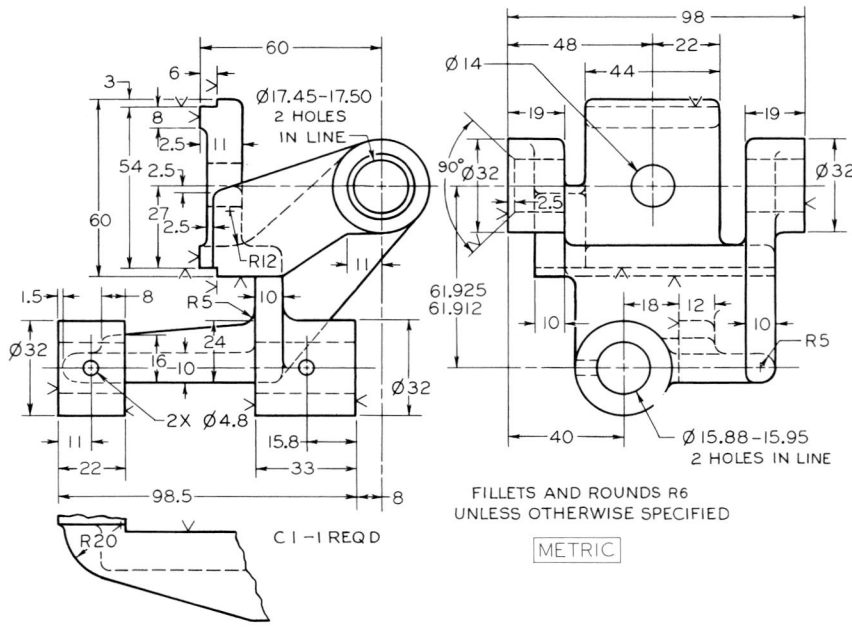

Fig. 16.63   Bearing for a Worm Gear.
Given: Front and right-side views.
Required: Front, top, and left-side views. Draw full size on Size C or A2 sheet. If assigned, complete with dimensions.

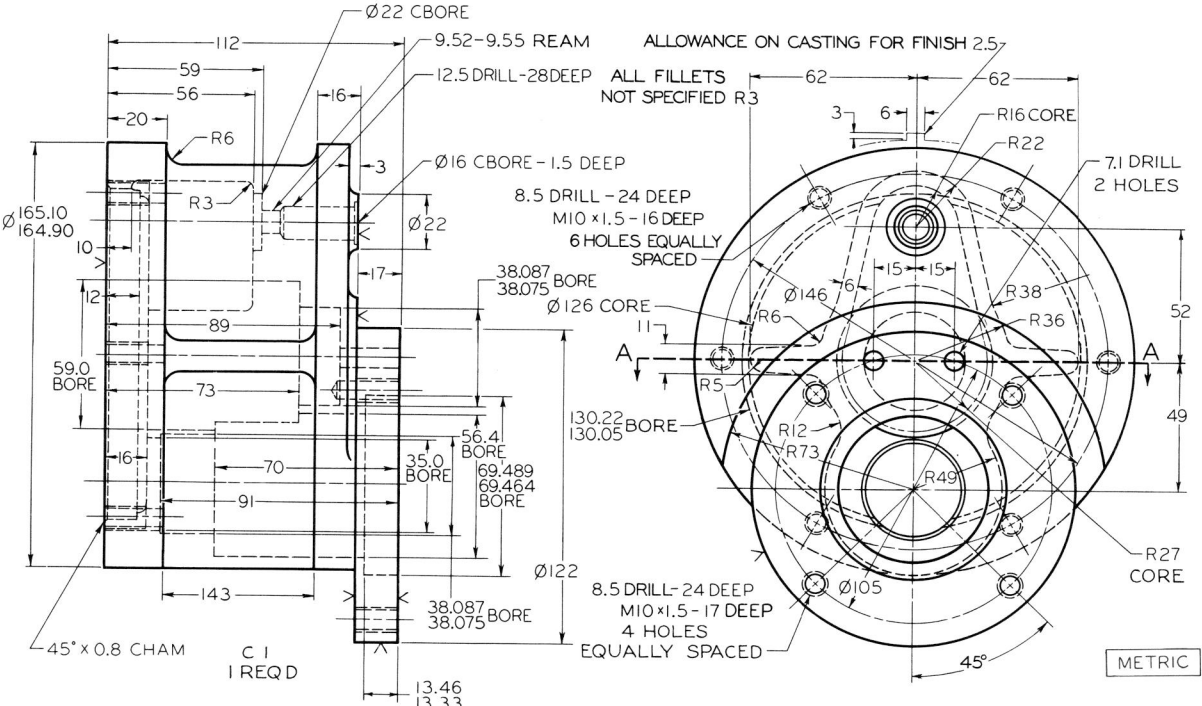

Fig. 16.64 Generator Drive Housing.
Given: Front and left-side views.
Required: Front view, right-side in full section, and top view in full section on A–A. Draw full size on Size C or A2 sheet. If assigned, complete with dimensions.

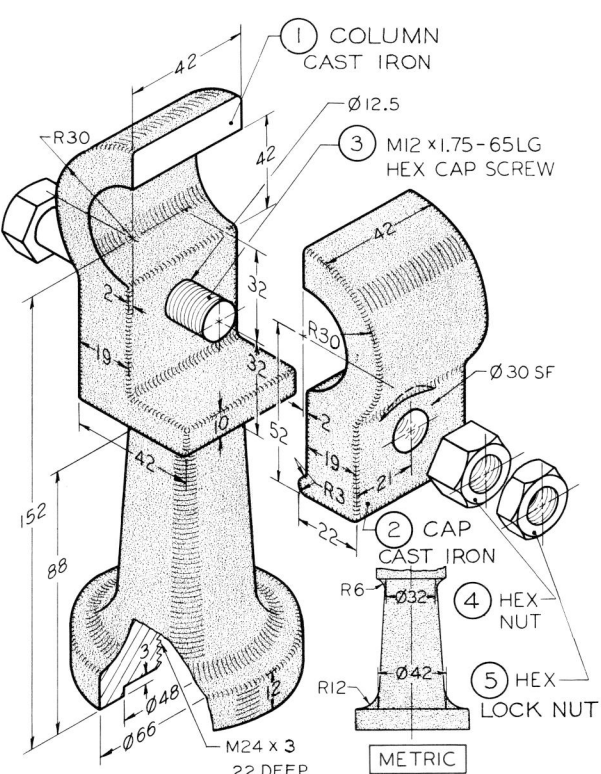

Fig. 16.65 Hand Rail Column. (1) Draw details. If assigned, complete with dimensions. (2) Draw assembly.

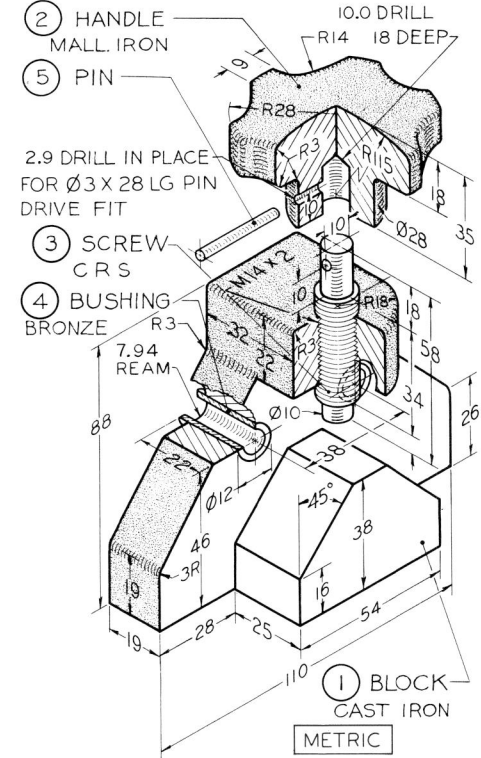

Fig. 16.66 Drill Jig (1) Draw details. If assigned, complete with dimensions. (2) Draw assembly.

487

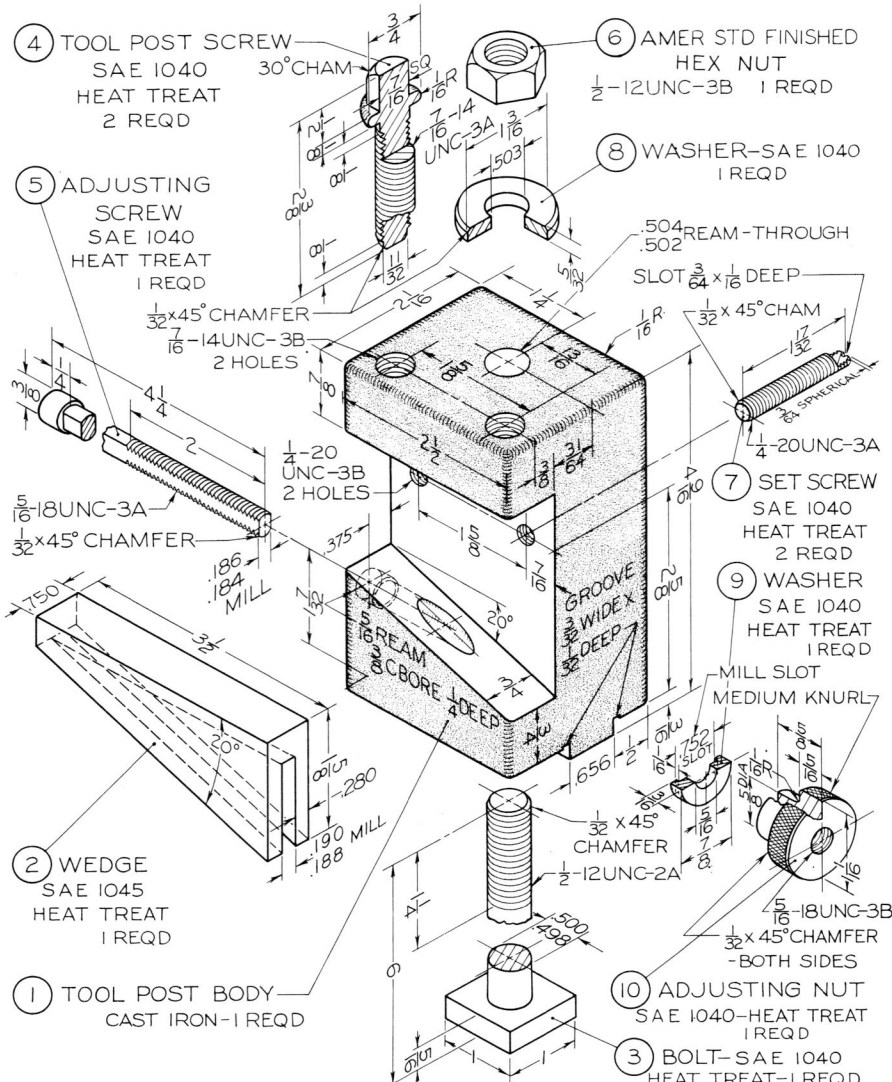

Fig. 16.67   Tool Post.   (1) Draw details. (2) Draw assembly. If assigned, use unidirectional two-place decimals for all fractional dimensions or redesign for all metric dimensions.

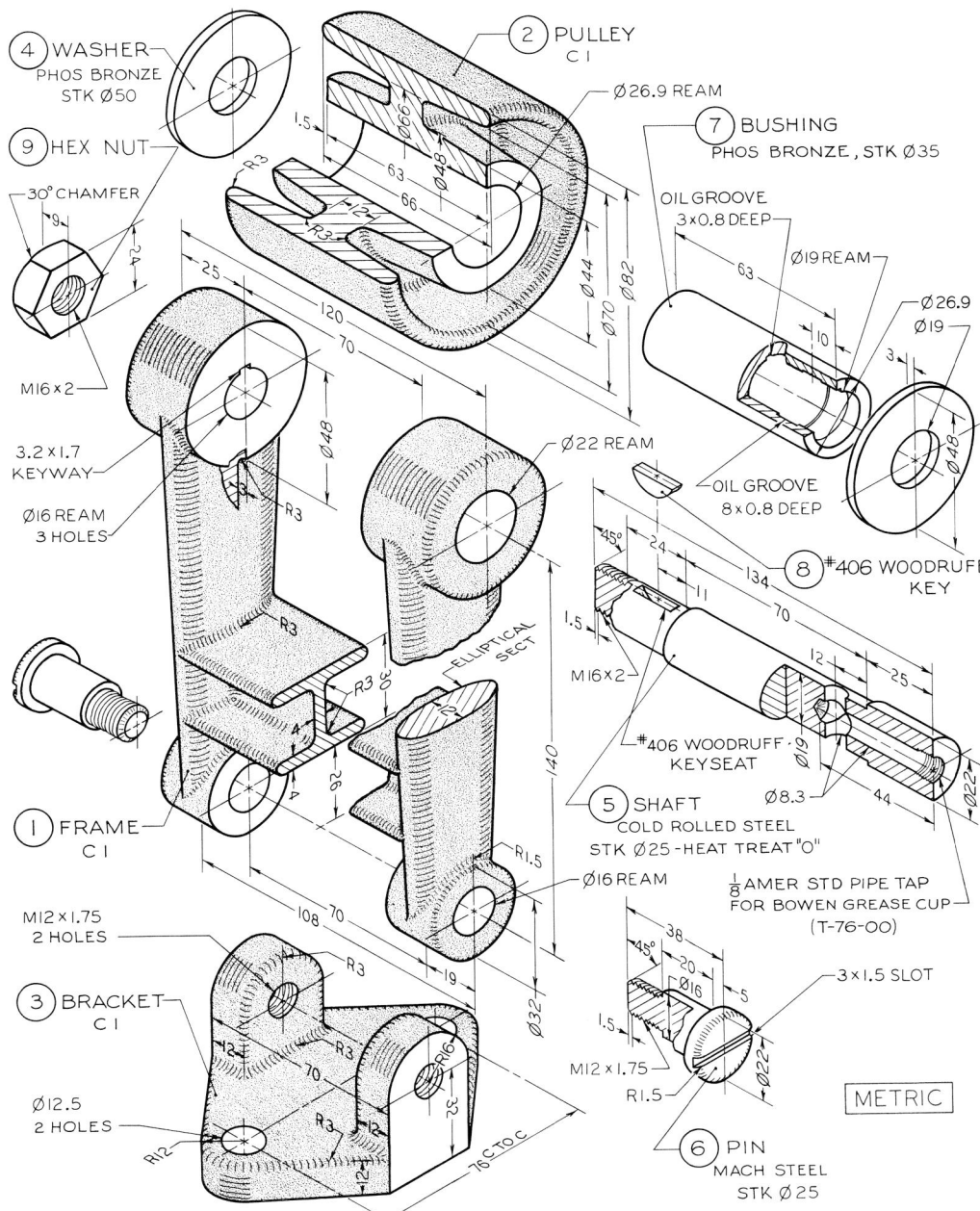

④ WASHER
PHOS BRONZE
STK Ø50

⑨ HEX NUT

30° CHAMFER

M16×2

3.2×1.7
KEYWAY

Ø16 REAM
3 HOLES

① FRAME
C1

M12×1.75
2 HOLES

③ BRACKET
C1

Ø12.5
2 HOLES

② PULLEY
C1

Ø26.9 REAM

⑦ BUSHING
PHOS BRONZE, STK Ø35

OIL GROOVE
3×0.8 DEEP

Ø19 REAM

Ø26.9
Ø19

OIL GROOVE
8×0.8 DEEP

Ø22 REAM

⑧ #406 WOODRUFF
KEY

ELLIPTICAL
SECT

#406 WOODRUFF
KEYSEAT

⑤ SHAFT
COLD ROLLED STEEL
STK Ø25 - HEAT TREAT "O"

Ø8.3

M16×2

Ø16 REAM

⅛ AMER STD PIPE TAP
FOR BOWEN GREASE CUP
(T-76-00)

3×1.5 SLOT

M12×1.75

R1.5

METRIC

⑥ PIN
MACH STEEL
STK Ø25

Fig. 16.68 Belt Tightener. (1) Draw details. (2) Draw assembly. It is assumed that the parts are to be made in quantity and they are to be dimensioned for interchangeability on the detail drawings. Use tables in Appendixes 11 to 14 for limit values. Design as follows.

a. Bushing fit in pulley: Locational interference fit.
b. Shaft fit in bushing: Free running fit.
c. Shaft fits in frame: Sliding fit.
d. Pin fit in frame: Free running fit.

e. Pulley hub length plus washers fit in frame: Allowance 0.13 and tolerances 0.10.
f. Make bushing 0.25mm shorter than pulley hub.
g. Bracket fit in frame: Same as e above.

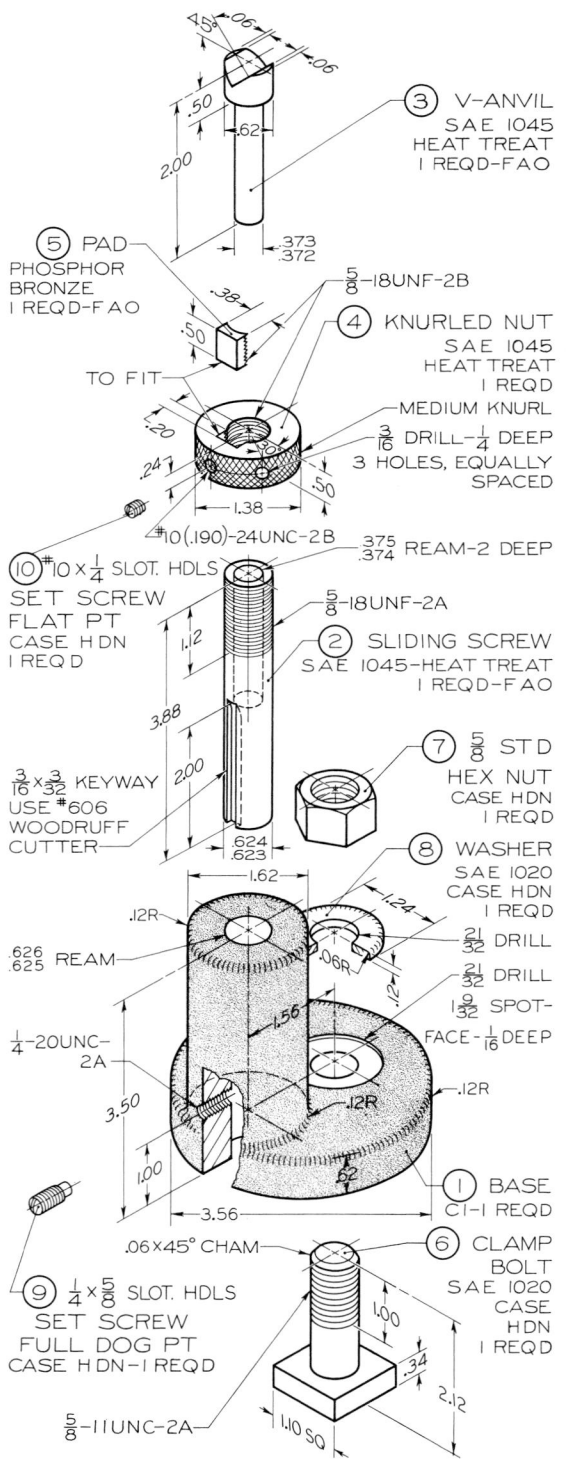

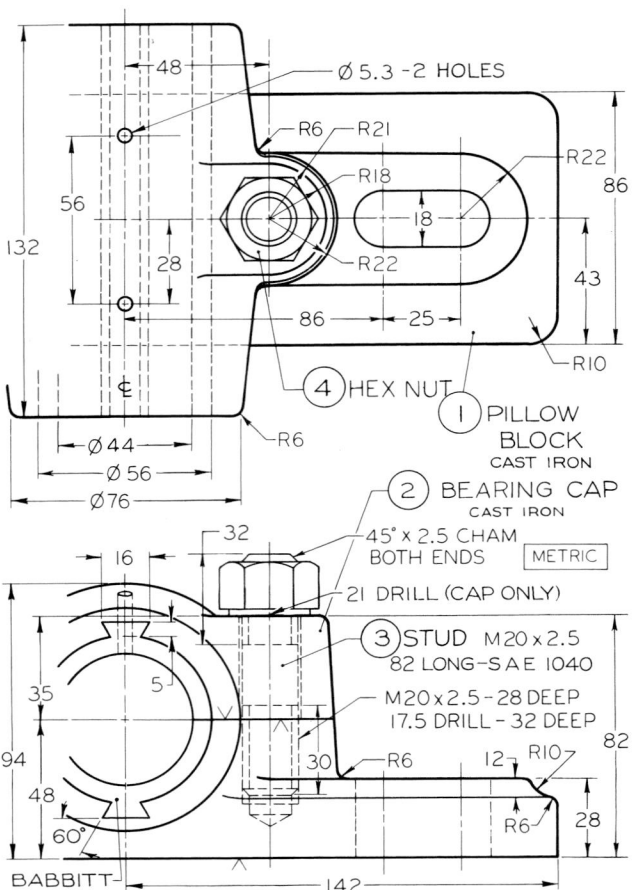

Fig. 16.70 Pillow Block Bearing. (1) Draw details. (2) Draw assembly. If assigned, complete with dimensions.

Fig. 16.69 Milling Jack. (1) Draw details. (2) Draw assembly. If assigned, convert dimensions to metric or decimal-inch system.

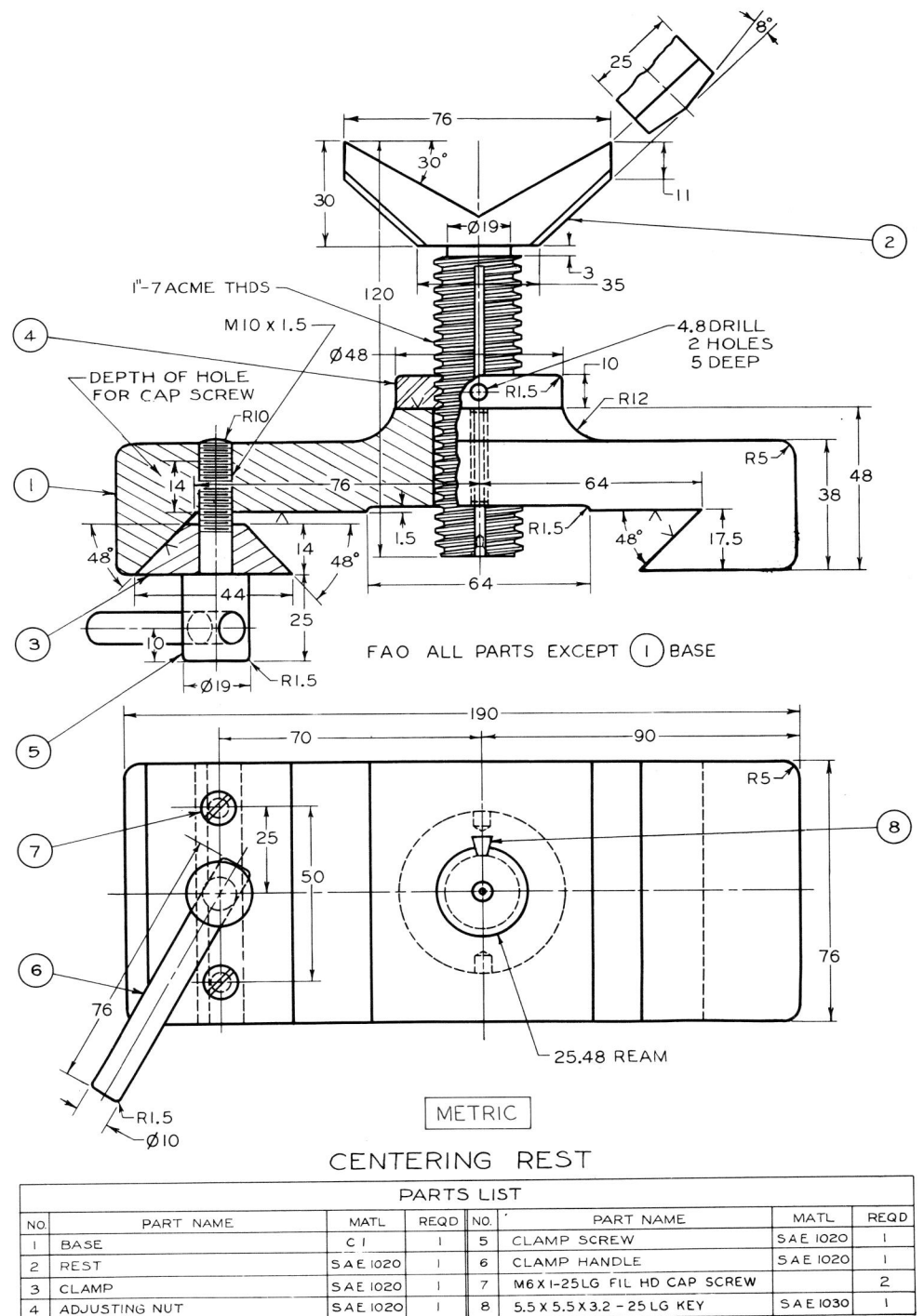

FAO ALL PARTS EXCEPT (1) BASE

METRIC

CENTERING REST

NO.	PART NAME	MATL	REQD	NO.	PART NAME	MATL	REQD
					PARTS LIST		
1	BASE	C I	1	5	CLAMP SCREW	SAE 1020	1
2	REST	SAE 1020	1	6	CLAMP HANDLE	SAE 1020	1
3	CLAMP	SAE 1020	1	7	M6 X 1-25 LG FIL HD CAP SCREW		2
4	ADJUSTING NUT	SAE 1020	1	8	5.5 X 5.5 X 3.2 – 25 LG KEY	SAE 1030	1

Fig. 16.71 Centering Rest. (1) Draw details. (2) Draw assembly. If assigned, complete with dimensions.

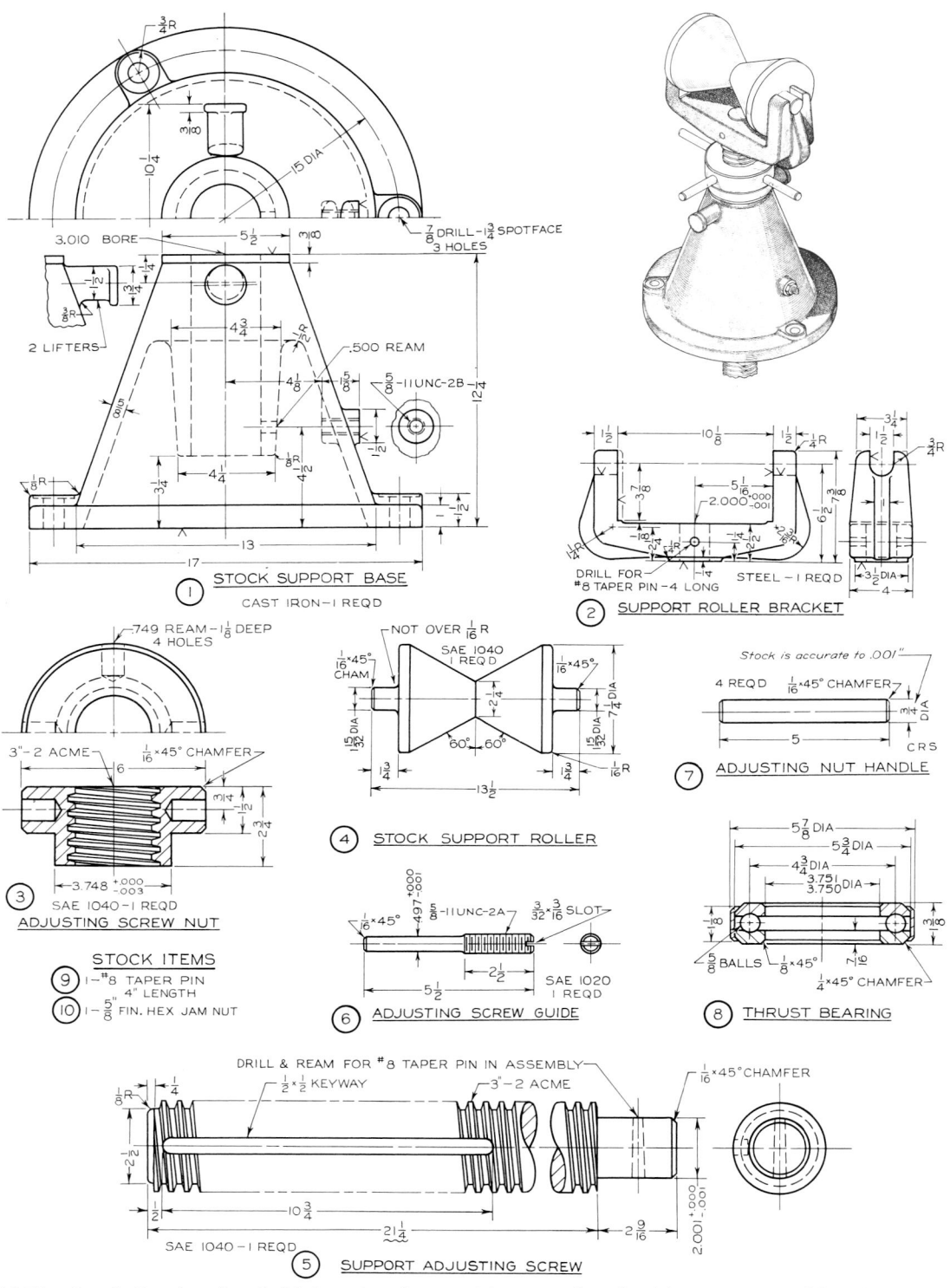

Fig. 16.72 Stock Bracket for Cold Saw Machine. (1) Draw details. (2) Draw assembly. If assigned, use unidirectional decimal-inch dimensions or redesign for metric dimensions.

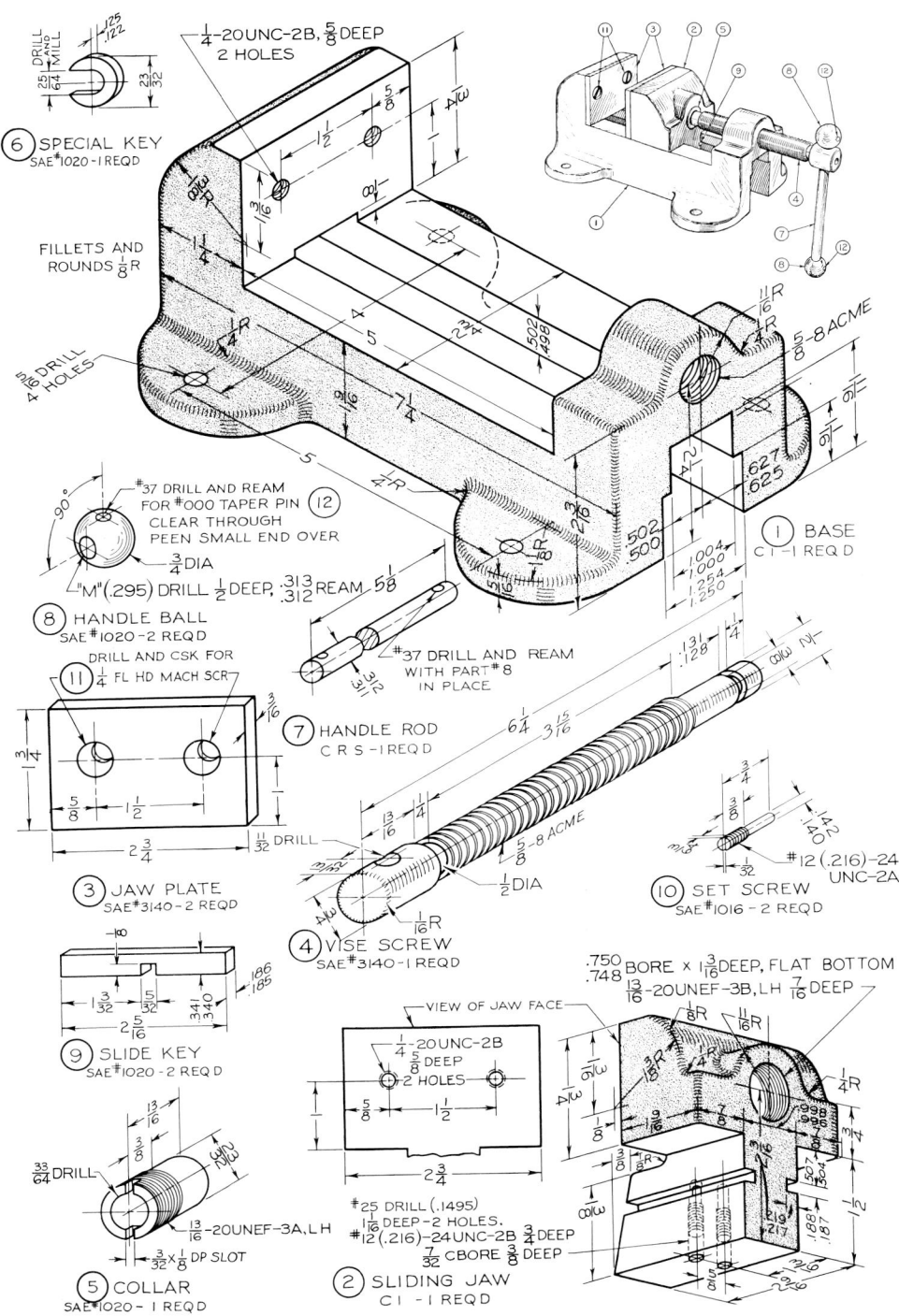

Fig. 16.73 Machine Vise. (1) Draw details. (2) Draw assembly. If assigned, convert dimensions to the decimal-inch system or redesign with metric dimensions.

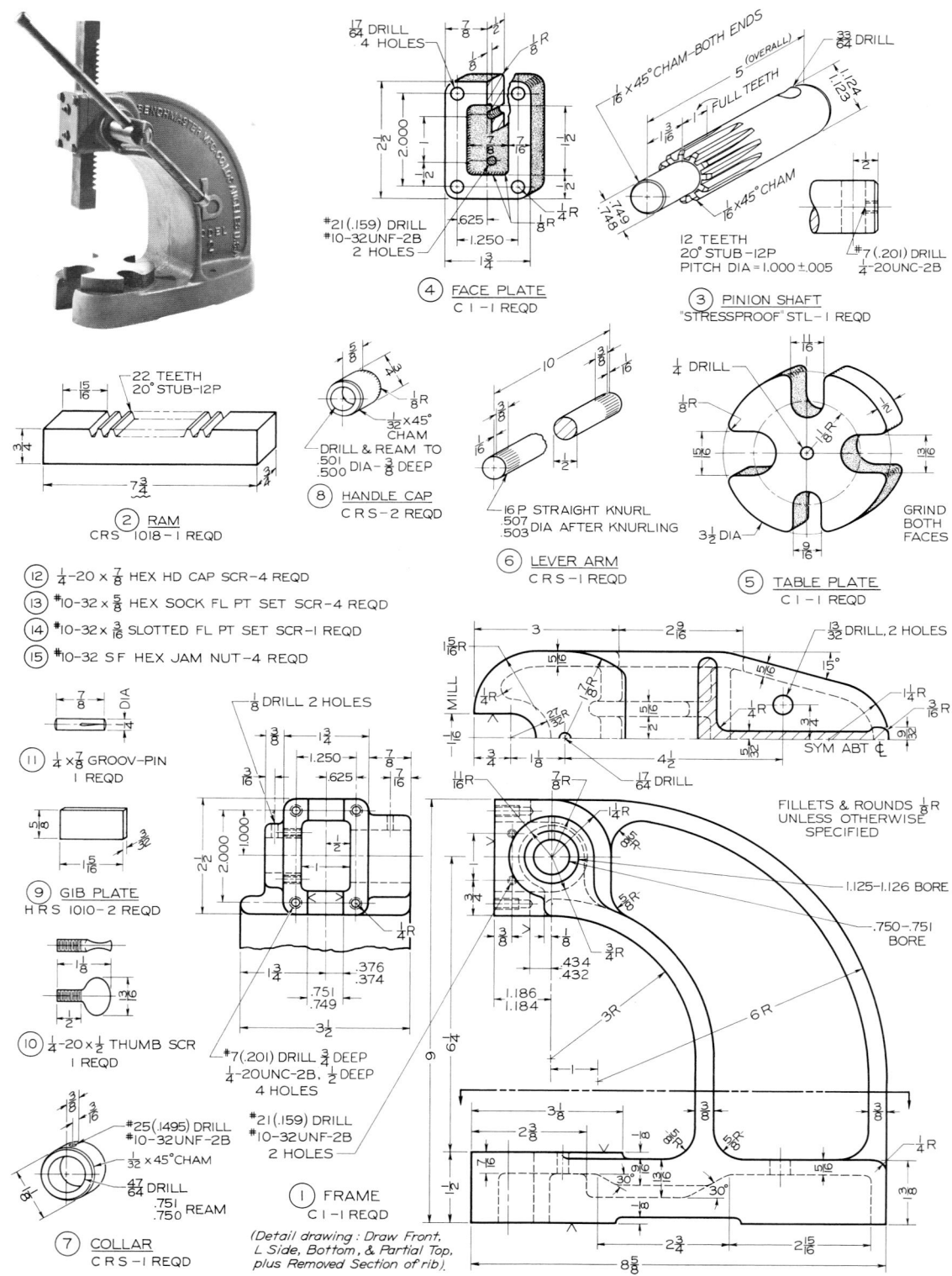

Fig. 16.74   Arbor Press.   (1) Draw details. (2) Draw assembly. If assigned, convert dimensions to decimal inches or redesign for metric dimensions.

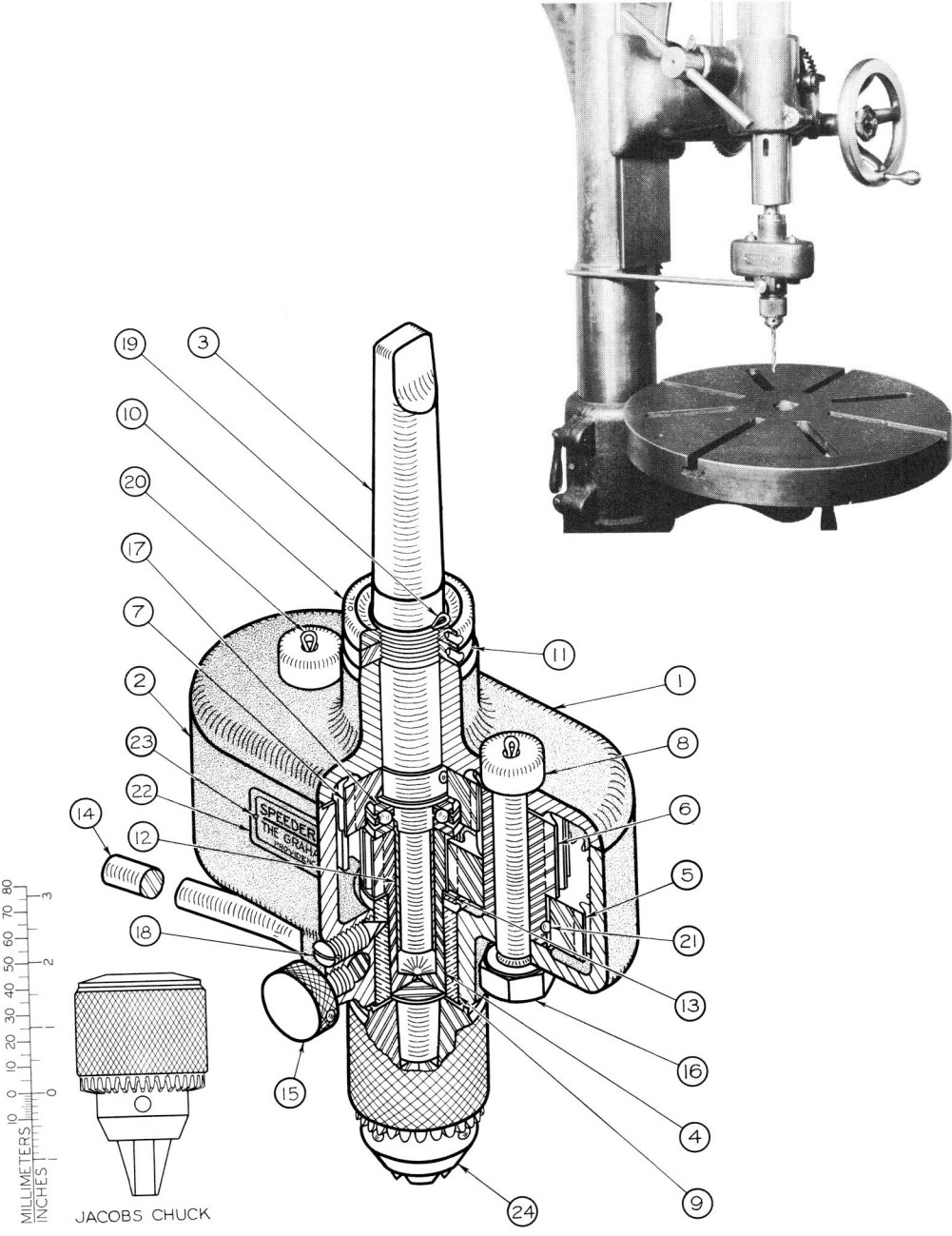

Fig. 16.75 Drill Speeder. See Figs. 16.76 and 16.77.

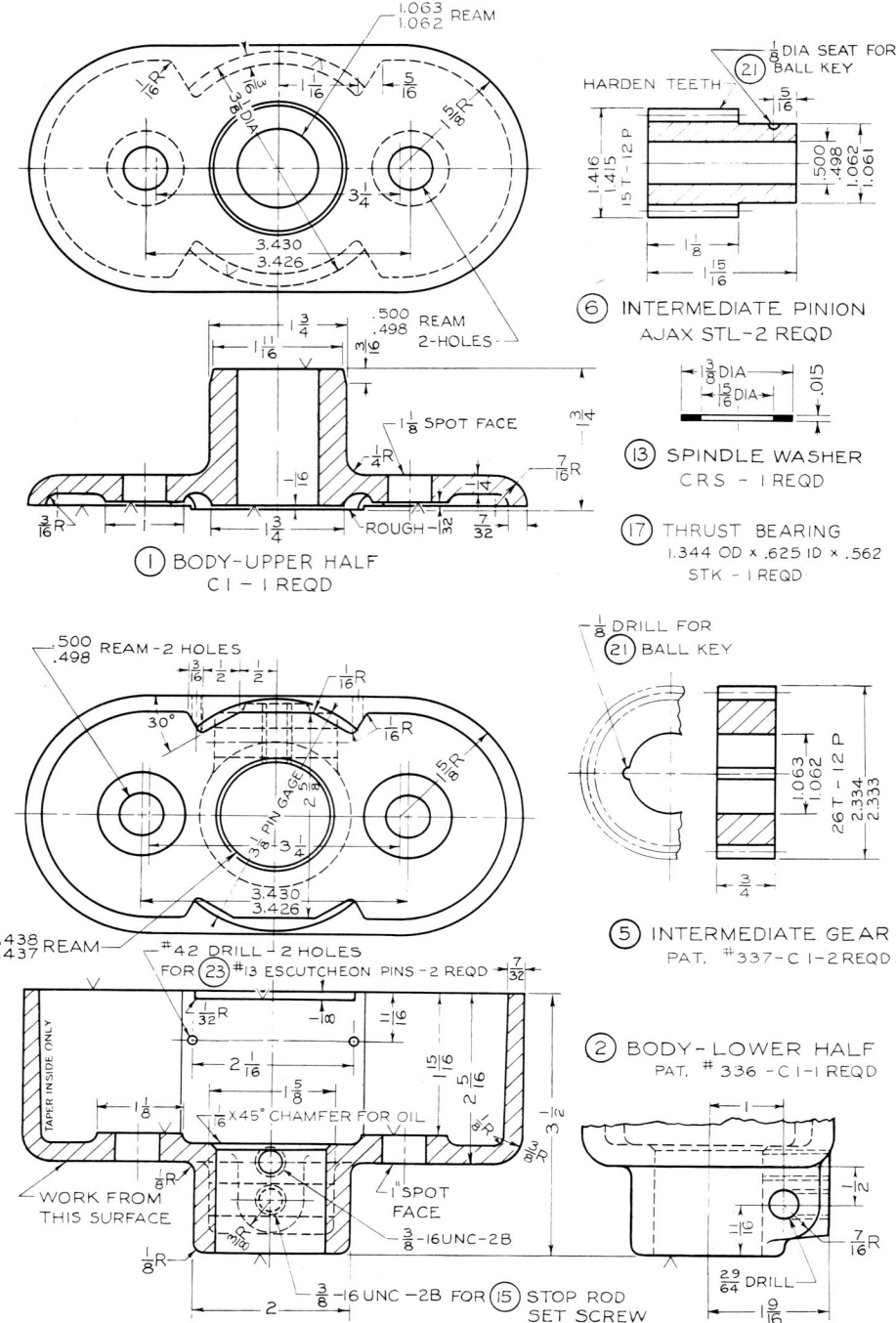

Fig. 16.76 Drill Speeder (Continued). (1) Draw details. (2) Draw assembly. See Fig. 16.75. If assigned, convert dimensions to decimal inches or redesign with metric dimensions.

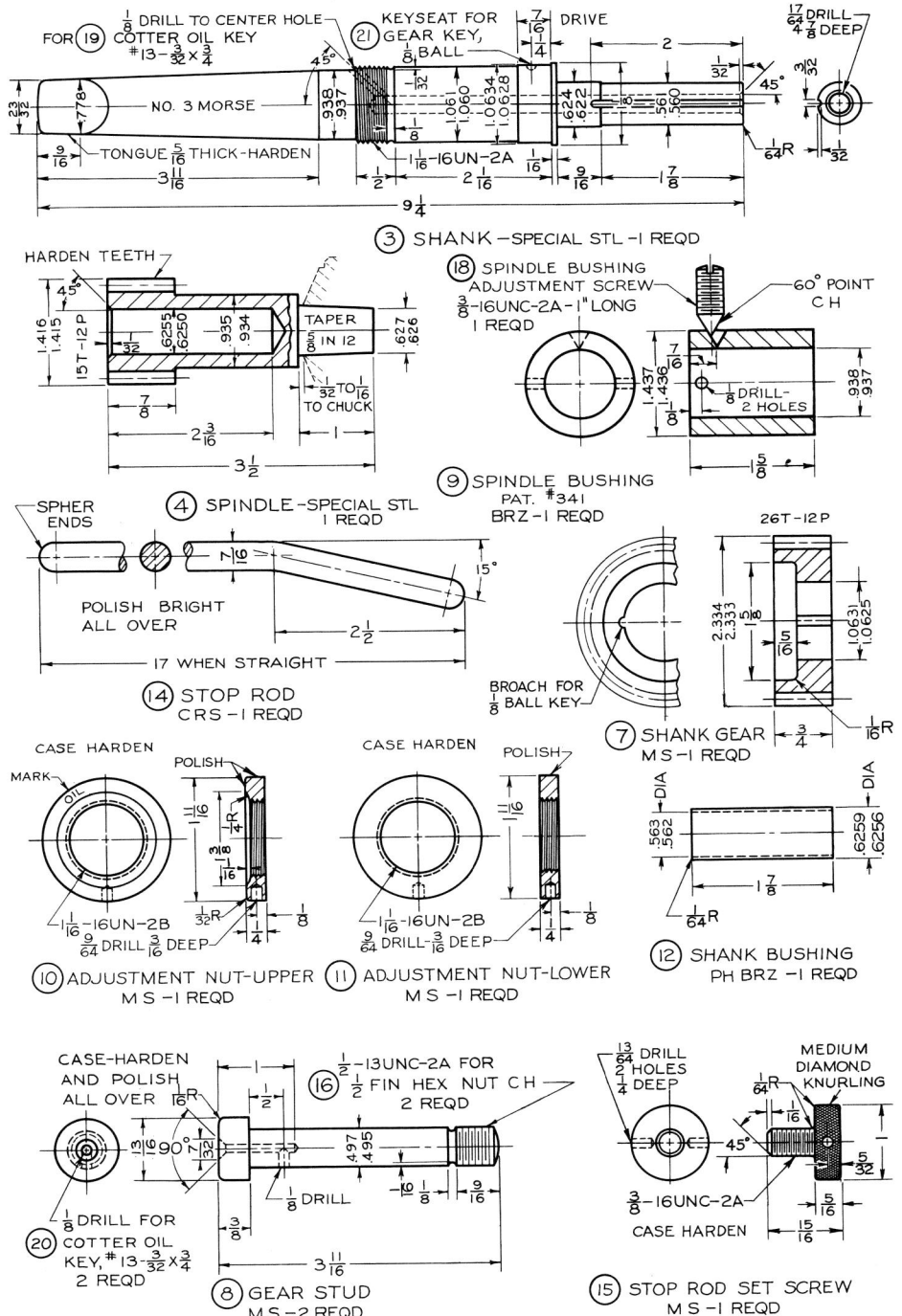

Fig. 16.77 Drill Speeder (Continued). See Fig. 16.76 for instructions.

CHAPTER

17

Axonometric Projection

As described in Chapter 7, multiview drawing makes it possible to represent accurately the most complex forms of a design by showing a series of exterior views and sections. This type of representation has two limitations, however: its execution requires a thorough understanding of the principles of multiview projection, and its reading requires a definite exercise of the constructive imagination.

Frequently, it is necessary to prepare drawings for the presentation of a design idea that are accurate and scientifically correct and can be easily understood by persons without technical training. Such drawings show several faces of an object at once, approximately as they appear to the observer. This type of drawing is called a *pictorial drawing* [ANSI Y14.4–1957 (R1987)]. Since pictorial drawing shows only the appearances of parts or devices, it is not satisfactory for completely describing complex or detailed forms.

Pictorial drawing enables the person without technical training to visualize the design represented. It also enables the designer to visualize the successive stages of the design and to develop it in a satisfactory manner.

Various types of pictorial drawing are used extensively in catalogs, in general sales literature, and also in technical work,* to supplement and amplify multiview drawings. For example, pictorial drawing is used in Patent Office drawings, in piping diagrams, in machine, structural, and architectural designs, and in furniture design.

---

*Practically all of the pictorial drawings in this book were drawn by the methods described in Chapters 17 and 18. See especially Figs. 7.55–7.94 for examples.

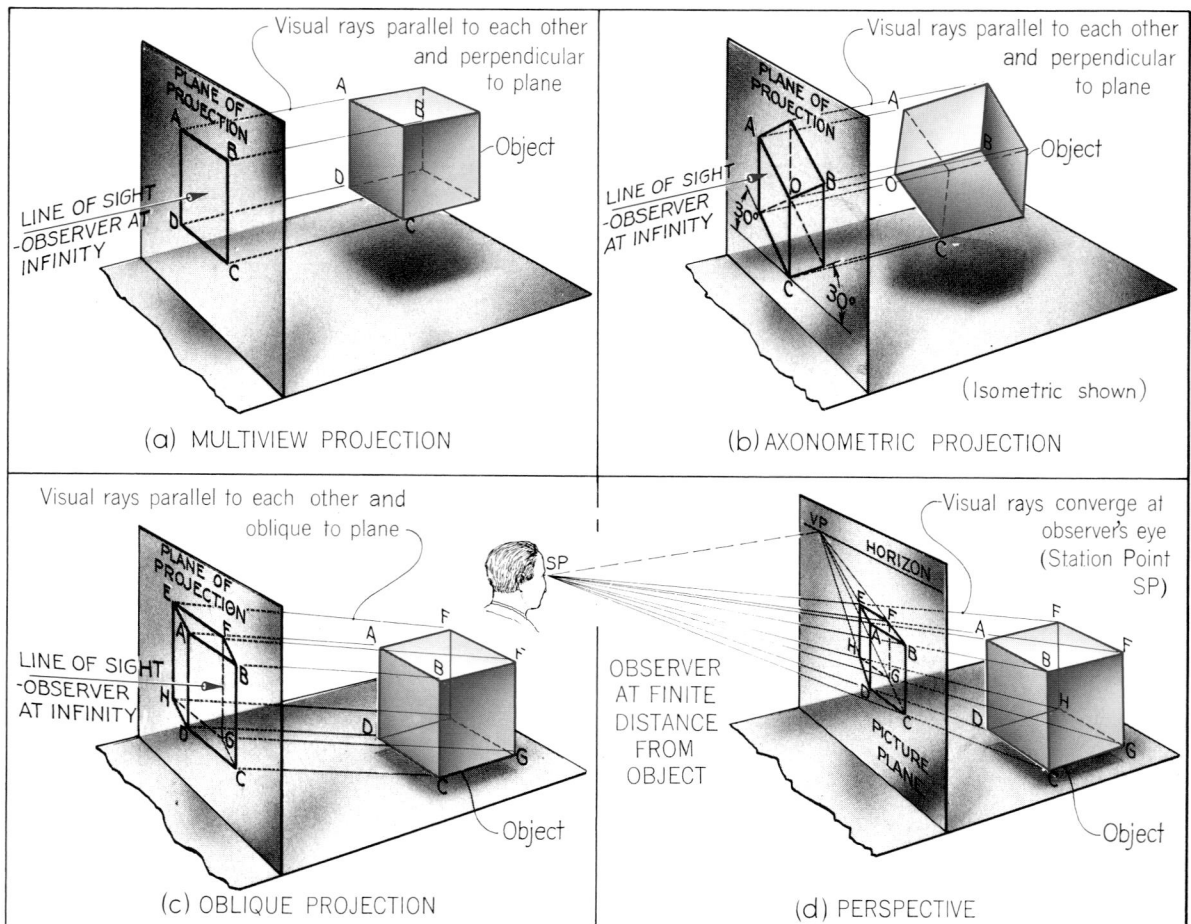

Fig. 17.1   Four Types of Projection.

17.1 Methods of Projection

The four principal types of projection are illustrated in Fig. 17.1, and all except the regular multiview projection, (a), are pictorial types since they show several sides of the object in a single view. In all cases the views, or projections, are formed by the piercing points in the plane of projection of an infinite number of visual rays or projectors.

In both multiview projection, (a), and *axonometric projection*, (b), the observer is considered to be at infinity, and the visual rays are parallel to each other and perpendicular to the plane of projection. Therefore, both are classified as *orthographic projections*, §1.10.

In *oblique projection*, (c) the observer is considered to be at infinity, and the visual rays are parallel to each other but oblique to the plane of projection. See Chapter 18.

In *perspective*, (d), the observer is considered to be at a finite distance from the object, and the visual

rays extend from the observer's eye, or the station point (**SP**), to all points of the object to form a "cone of rays." See Fig. 1.10.

17.2 Types of Axonometric Projection

The distinguishing feature of axonometric projection, as compared to multiview projection, is the inclined position of the object with respect to the plane of projection. Since the principal edges and surfaces of the object are inclined to the plane of projection, the lengths of the lines, the sizes of the angles, and the general proportions of the object vary with the infinite number of possible positions in which the object may be placed with respect to the plane of projection. Three of these are shown in Fig. 17.2.

In these cases the edges of the cube are inclined to the plane of projection and are therefore foreshortened. See Fig. 7.20 (c). The degree of fore-

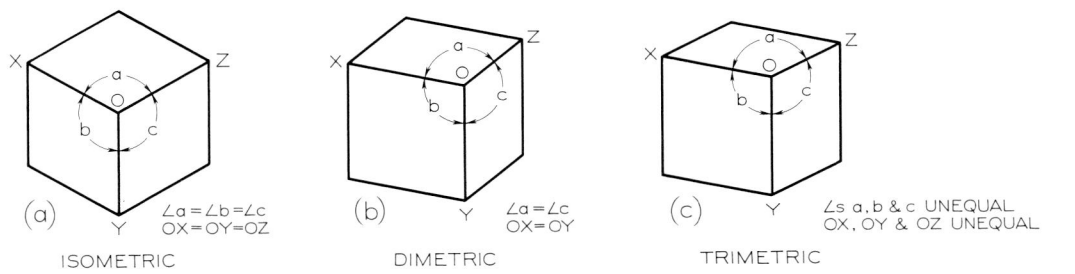

Fig. 17.2 Axonometric Projections.

shortening of any line depends on its angle with the plane of projection; the greater the angle, the greater the foreshortening. If the degree of fore-shortening is determined for each of the three edges of the cube that meet at one corner, scales can be easily constructed for measuring along these edges or any other edges parallel to them. See Figs. 17.41 (a) and 17.46.

It is customary to consider three edges of the cube that meet at the corner nearest the observer, as the *axonometric axes*. In Fig. 17.1 (b), the axon-ometric axes, or simply the *axes*, are **OA**, **OB**, and **OC**. As shown in Fig. 17.2, axonometric projections are classified as (a) *isometric projection*, (b) *dimetric projection*, and (c) *trimetric projection*, depending upon the number of scales of reduction required.

Isometric Projection

17.3 The Isometric Method of Projection

To produce an isometric projection (isometric means "equal measure"), it is necessary to place the object so that its principal edges, or axes, make equal an-gles with the plane of projection and are therefore foreshortened equally. See Fig. 6.24. In this position the edges of a cube would be projected equally and

would make equal angles with each other (**120°**), as shown in Fig. 17.2 (a).

In Fig. 17.3 (a) is shown a multiview drawing of a cube. At (b) the cube is shown revolved through 45° about an imaginary vertical axis. Now an auxil-iary view in the direction of the arrow will show the cube diagonal **ZW** as a point, and the cube appears

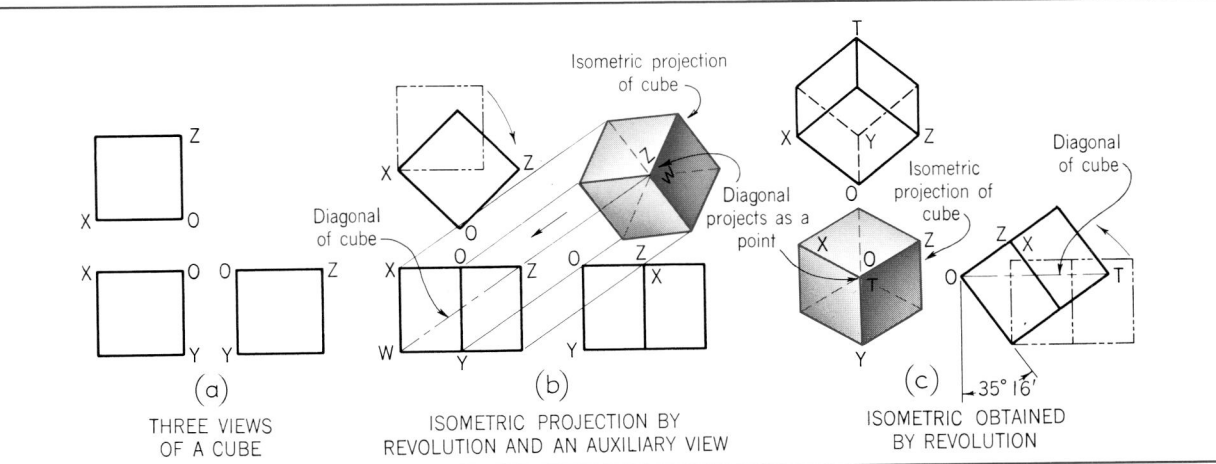

Fig. 17.3 Isometric Projection.

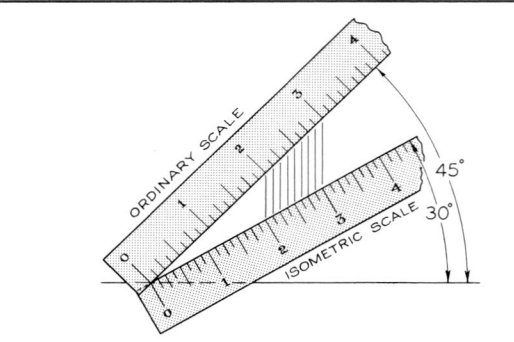

Fig. 17.4 Isometric Scale.

as a true isometric projection. However, instead of the auxiliary view at (b) being drawn, the cube may be further revolved as shown at (c), this time the cube being tilted forward about an imaginary horizontal axis until the three edges OX, OY, and OZ make equal angles with the frontal plane of projection and are therefore foreshortened equally. Here again, a diagonal of the cube, in this case OT, appears as a point in the isometric view. The front view thus obtained is a true isometric projection. In this projection the twelve edges of the cube make angles of about 35° 16′ with the frontal plane of projection. The lengths of their projections are equal to the lengths of the edges multiplied by $\sqrt{\frac{2}{3}}$, or by 0.816, approximately. Thus the projected lengths are about 80 percent of the true lengths, or still more roughly, about three-fourths of the true lengths. The projections of the axes OX, OY, and OZ make angles of 120° with each other and are called the *isometric axes*. Any line parallel to one of these is called an *isometric line*; a line that is not parallel

is called a *nonisometric line*. It should be noted that the angles in the isometric projection of the cube are either 120° or 60° and that all are projections of 90° angles. In an isometric projection of a cube, the faces of the cube, and any planes parallel to them, are called *isometric planes*.

17.4 The Isometric Scale
A correct isometric projection may be drawn with the use of a special isometric scale, prepared on a strip of paper or cardboard, Fig. 17.4. All distances in the isometric scale are $\sqrt{\frac{2}{3}}$ times true size, or approximately 80 percent of true size. The use of the isometric scale is illustrated in Fig. 17.5 (a). A scale of 9″ = 1′-0, or $\frac{3}{4}$-size scale (or metric equivalent), could be used to approximate the isometric scale.

17.5 Isometric Drawing
When a drawing is prepared with an isometric scale, or otherwise as the object is actually *projected* on a plane of projection, it is an *isometric projection*, as illustrated in Fig. 17.5 (a). When it is prepared with an ordinary scale, it is an *isometric drawing*, illustrated at (b). The isometric drawing, (b), is about 25 percent larger than the isometric projection (a), but the pictorial value is obviously the same in both.

Since the isometric projection is foreshortened and an isometric drawing is full-scale size, it is usually advantageous to make an isometric drawing rather than an isometric projection. The drawing is much easier to execute and, for all practical purposes, is just as satisfactory as the isometric projection.

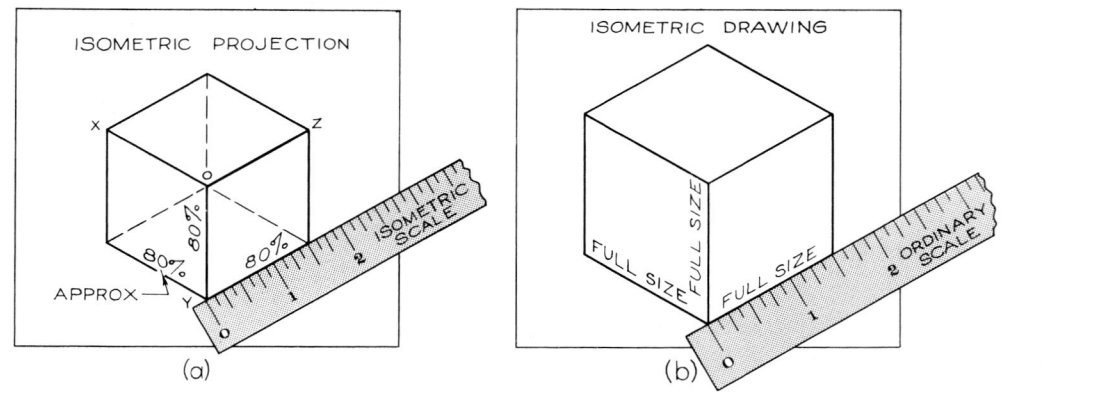

Fig. 17.5 Isometric and Ordinary Scales.

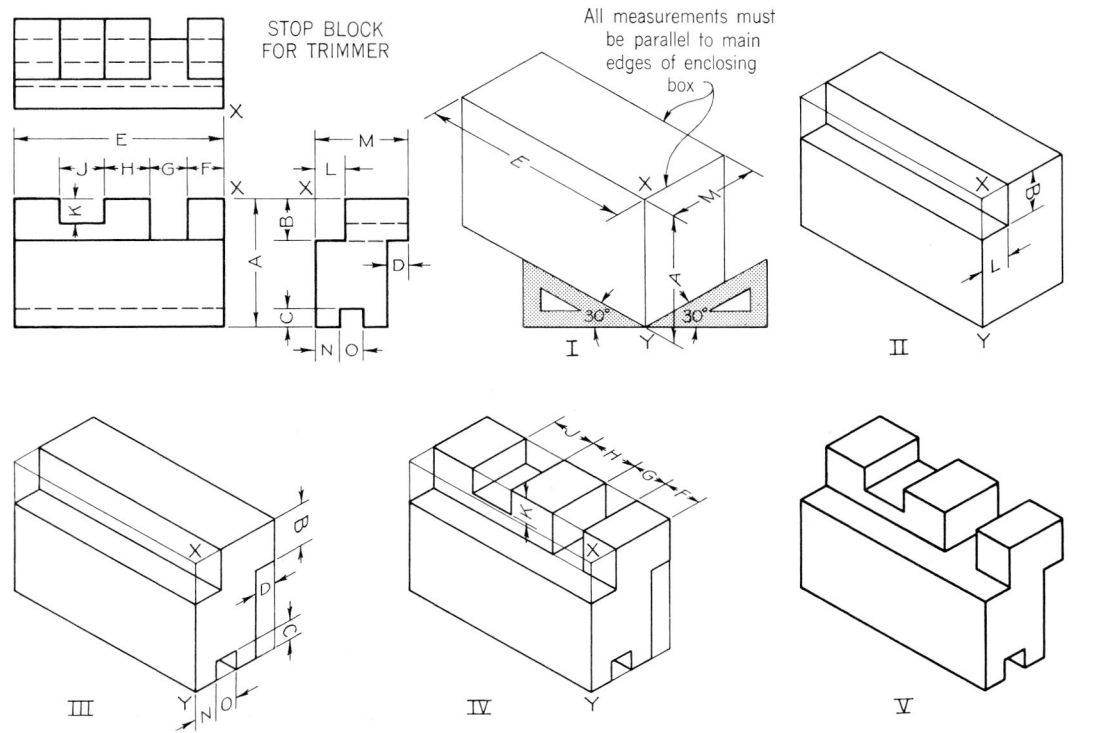

Fig. 17.6 Isometric Drawing of Normal Surfaces.

17.6 Steps in Making an Isometric Drawing

The steps in constructing an isometric drawing of an object composed only of normal surfaces, §7.19, are illustrated in Fig. 17.6. Notice that all measurements are made parallel to the main edges of the enclosing box, that is, parallel to the isometric axes. No measurement along a diagonal (nonisometric line) on any surface or through the object can be set off directly with the scale. The object may be drawn in the same position by beginning at the corner Y, or any other corner, instead of at the corner X.

The method of constructing an isometric drawing of an object composed partly of inclined surfaces (and oblique edges) is shown in Fig. 17.7. Notice that inclined surfaces are located by *offset* or *coordinate measurements* along the isometric lines. For example, dimensions E and F are set off to locate

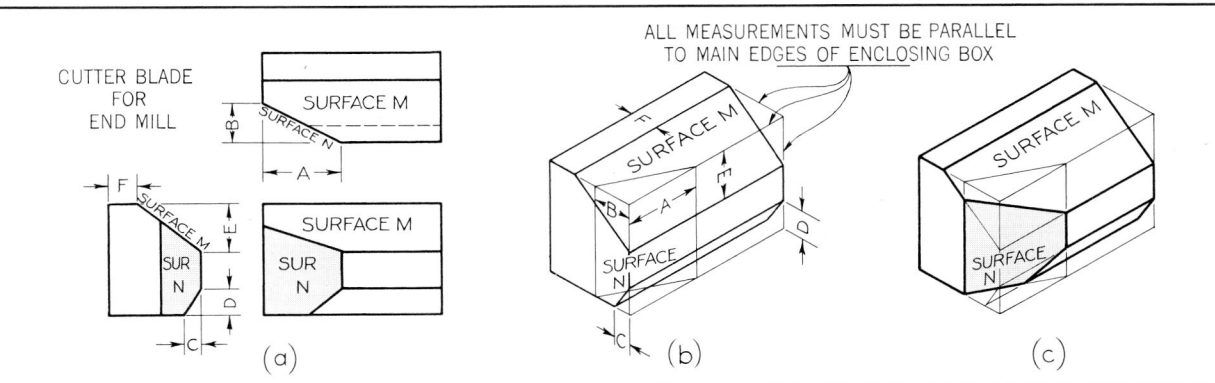

Fig. 17.7 Inclined Surfaces in Isometric.

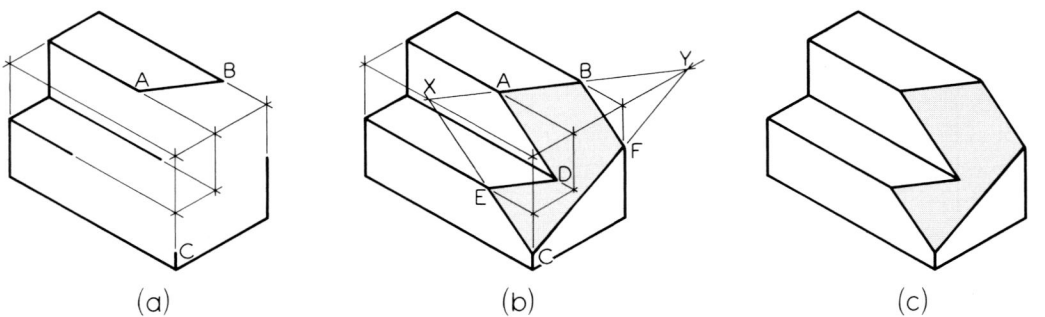

Fig. 17.8   Oblique Surfaces in Isometric.

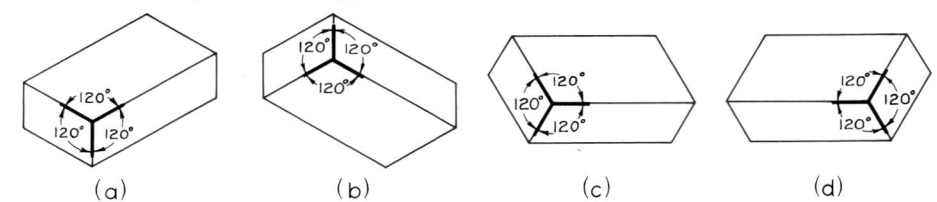

Fig. 17.9   Positions of Isometric Axes.

the inclined surface **M**, and dimensions **A** and **B** are used to locate surface **N**.

For sketching in isometric, see §§6.12–6.14.

17.7 Oblique Surfaces in Isometric

Oblique surfaces in isometric may be drawn by establishing the intersections of the oblique surface with the isometric planes. For example, in Fig. 17.8 (a), the oblique plane is known to contain points **A**, **B**, and **C**. To establish the plane, (b), line **AB** is extended to **X** and **Y**, which are in the same isometric planes as **C**. Lines **XC** and **YC** locate points **E** and **F**. Finally **AD** and **ED** are drawn, using the rule of parallelism of lines. The completed drawing is shown at (c).

17.8 Other Positions of the Isometric Axes

The isometric axes may be placed in any desired position according to the requirements of the problem, as shown in Fig. 17.9, but the angle between the axes must remain 120°. The choice of the directions of the axes is determined by the position from which the object is usually viewed, Fig. 17.10, or by the position that best describes the shape of the

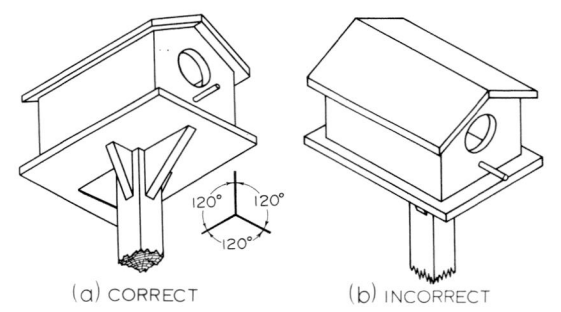

Fig. 17.10   An Object Naturally Viewed from Below.

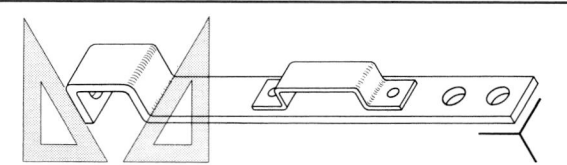

Fig. 17.11   Long Axis Horizontal.

object. If possible, both requirements should be met.

If the object is characterized by considerable length, the long axis may be placed horizontally for best effect, as shown in Fig. 17.11.

17.9 Offset Location Measurements

The method of locating one point with respect to another is illustrated in Figs. 17.12 and 17.13. In each case, after the main block has been drawn, the

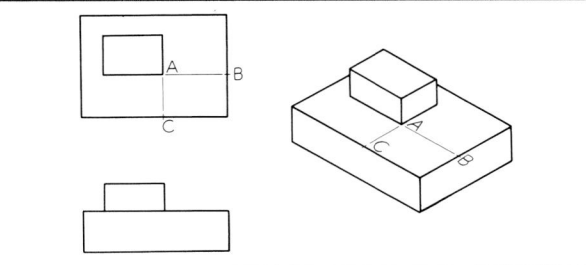

Fig. 17.12   Offset Location Measurements.

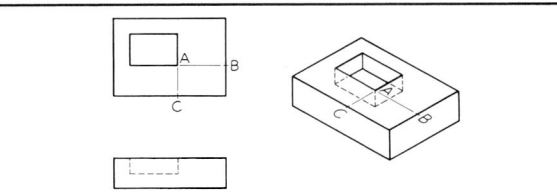

Fig. 17.13   Offset Location Measurements.

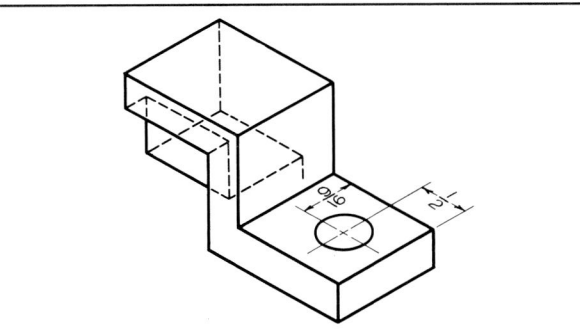

Fig. 17.14   Use of Hidden Lines.

offset lines CA and BA in the multiview drawing are drawn full size in the isometric drawing, thus, locating corner A of the small block or rectangular recess. These measurements are called *offset measurements*, and since they are parallel to certain edges of the main block in the multiview drawings, they will be parallel, respectively, to the same edges in the isometric drawings, §7.25.

17.10 Hidden Lines

The use of hidden lines in isometric drawing is governed by the same rules as in all other types of projection: *Hidden lines are omitted unless they are needed to make the drawing clear.* A case in which hidden lines are needed is illustrated in Fig. 17.14, in which a projecting part cannot be clearly shown without the use of hidden lines.

17.11 Center Lines

The use of center lines in isometric drawing is governed by the same rules as in multiview drawing: *Center lines are drawn if they are needed to indicate symmetry or if they are needed for dimensioning,* Fig. 17.14. In general, center lines should be used sparingly and omitted in cases of doubt. The use of too many center lines may produce a confusion of lines, which diminishes the clearness of the drawing. Examples in which center lines are not needed are shown in Figs. 17.10 and 17.11. Examples in which they are needed are seen in Figs. 17.14 and 17.39 (a).

17.12 Box Construction

Objects of rectangular shape may be more easily drawn by means of *box construction*, which consists simply in imagining the object to be enclosed in a rectangular box whose sides coincide with the main faces of the object. For example, in Fig. 17.15

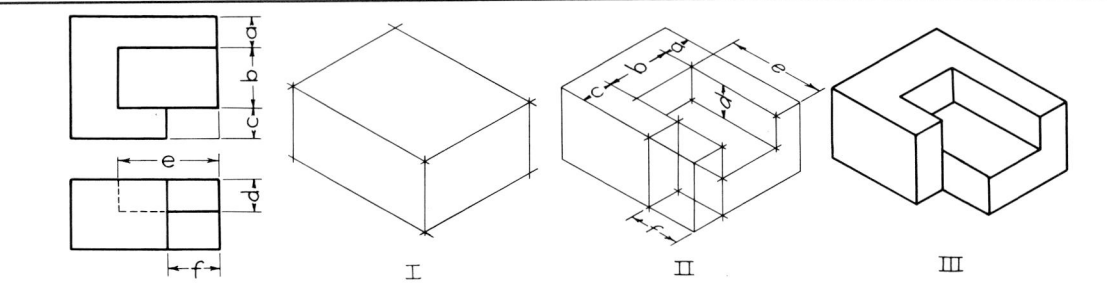

Fig. 17.15   Box Construction.

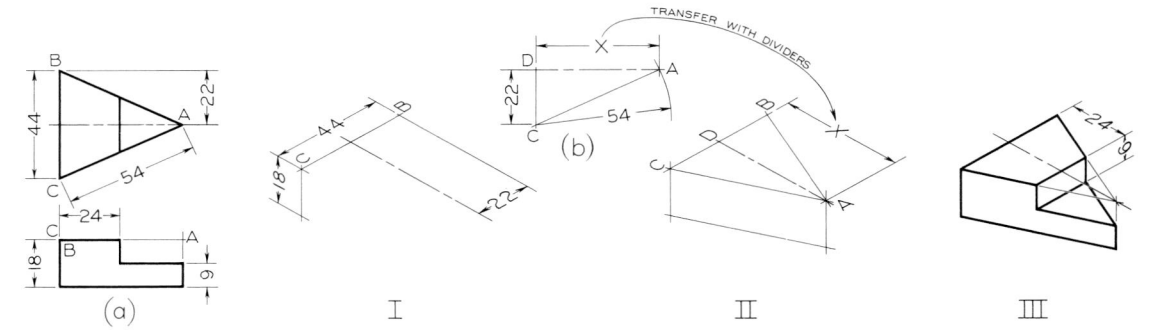

Fig. 17.16   Nonisometric Lines   (metric dimensions).

the object shown in two views is imagined to be enclosed in a construction box. This box is then drawn lightly with construction lines, as shown at I, the irregular features are then constructed as shown at II, and finally, as shown at III, the required lines are made heavy.

17.13 Nonisometric Lines

Since the only lines of an object that are drawn true length in an isometric drawing are the isometric axes or lines parallel to them, *nonisometric* lines cannot be set off directly with the scale. For example, in Fig. 17.16 (a), the inclined lines BA and CA are shown in their true lengths 54 mm in the top view, but since they are not parallel to the isometric axes, they will not be true length in the isometric. Such lines are drawn in isometric by means of box construction and offset measurements. First, as shown at I, the measurements 44 mm, 18 mm, and 22 mm can be set off directly since they are made along isometric lines. The nonisometric 54 mm dimension cannot be set off directly, but if one-half of the given top view is constructed full size to scale as shown at

(b), the dimension X can be determined. This dimension is parallel to an isometric axis and can be transferred with dividers to the isometric at II. The dimensions 24 mm and 9 mm are parallel to isometric lines and can be set off directly, as shown at III.

To realize the fact that nonisometric lines will not be true length in the isometric drawing, set your dividers on BA of II and then compare with BA on the given top view at (a). Do the same for line CA. It will be seen that BA is shorter and CA is longer in the isometric than the corresponding lines in the given views.

17.14 Angles in Isometric

As shown in §7.26, angles project true size only when the plane of the angle is parallel to the plane of projection. An angle may project larger or smaller than true size, depending upon its position. Since in isometric the various surfaces of the object are usually inclined to the plane of projection, it follows that angles generally will not be projected true size. For example, in the multiview drawing in Fig. 17.17

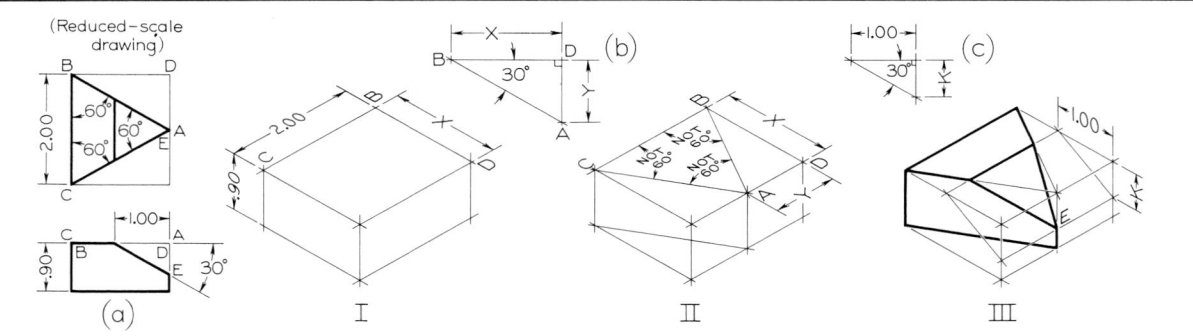

Fig. 17.17   Angles in Isometric.

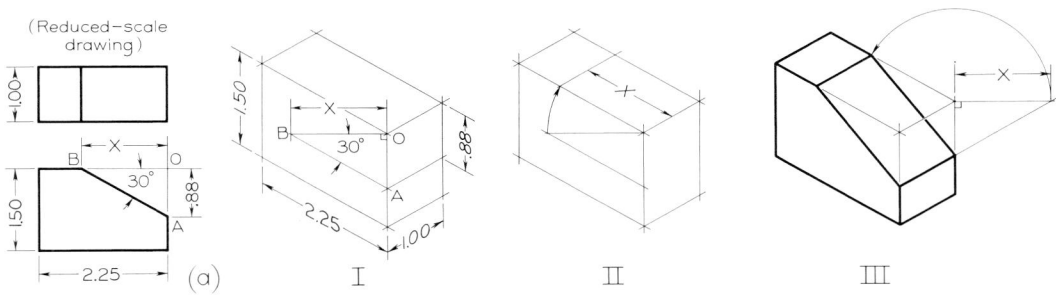

Fig. 17.18   Angle in Isometric.

(a), none of the three 60° angles will be 60° in the isometric drawing. To realize this fact, measure each angle in the isometric of II with the protractor and note the number of degrees compared to the true 60°. No two angles are the same; two are smaller and one larger than 60°.

As shown in I, the enclosing box can be drawn from the given dimensions, except for dimension X, which is not given. To find dimension X, draw triangle BDA from the top view full size, as shown at (b). Transfer dimension X to the isometric in I, to complete the enclosing box.

In order to locate point A in II, dimension Y must be used, but this is not given in the top view, (a). Dimension Y is found by the same construction, (b), and then transferred to the isometric, as shown. The completed isometric is shown at III where point E is located by using dimension K, as shown.

Thus, in order to set off angles in isometric, the regular protractor cannot be used.* *Angular measurements must be converted to linear measurements along isometric lines.*

In Fig. 17.18 (a) are two views of an object to be

*Isometric protractors for setting off angles on isometric surfaces are available from drafting supplies dealers.

drawn in isometric. Point A can easily be located in the isometric, step I, by measuring .88″ down from point O. However, in the given drawing at (a) the location of point B depends upon the 30° angle, and to locate B in the isometric linear dimension X must be known. This distance can be found graphically by drawing the right triangle BOA attached to the isometric, as shown. The distance X is then transferred to the isometric with the compass or dividers, as shown at II. Actually, the triangle could be attached in several different positions. One of these is shown at III.

When angles are given in degrees, it is necessary to convert the angular measurements into linear measurements. This is best done by drawing a right triangle separately, as in Fig. 17.17 (b), or attached to the isometric, as in Fig. 17.18.

17.15 Irregular Objects

If the general shape of an object does not conform somewhat to a rectangular pattern, as shown in Fig. 17.19, it may be drawn as shown at (a) by using the box construction discussed previously. Various points of the triangular base are located by means of offsets a and b along the edges of the bottom of

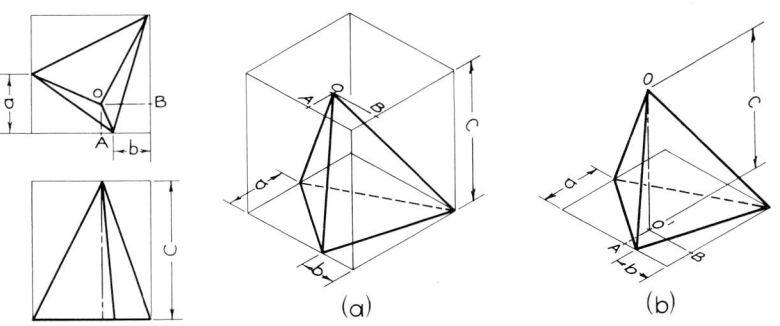

Fig. 17.19   Irregular Object in Isometric.

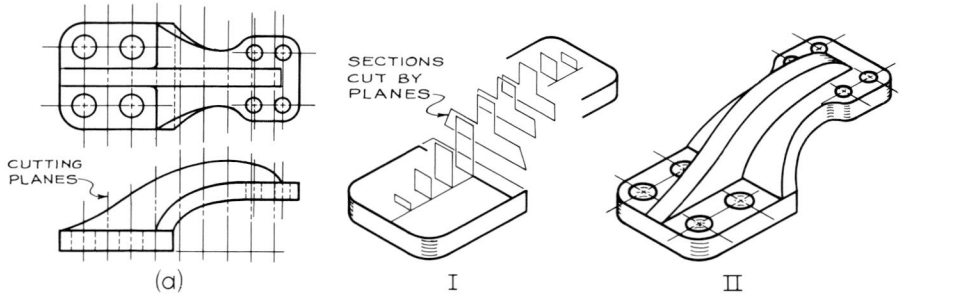

Fig. 17.20   Use of Sections in Isometric.

the construction box. The vertex is located by means of offsets **OA** and **OB** on the top of the construction box.

However, it is not necessary to draw the complete construction box. If only the bottom of the box is drawn, as shown at (b), the triangular base can be constructed as before. The orthographic projection of the vertex O′ on the base can then be located by offsets O′A and O′B, as shown, and from this point, the vertical center line O′O can be erected, using measurement C.

An irregular object may be drawn by means of a series of sections, as illustrated in Fig. 17.20. The edge views of a series of imaginary cutting planes are shown in the top and front views of the multiview drawing at (a). At I the various sections are constructed in isometric, and at II the object is completed by drawing lines through the corners of the sections. In the isometric at I, all height dimensions are taken from the front view at (a), and all depth dimensions from the top view.

17.16 Curves in Isometric

Curves may be drawn in isometric by means of a series of offset measurements similar to those discussed in §17.9. In Fig. 17.21 any desired number of points, such as A, B, and C, are selected at random along the curve in the given top view at (a). Enough points should be chosen to fix accurately the path of the curve; the more points used, the greater the accuracy. Offset grid lines are then drawn from each point parallel to the isometric axes.

As shown at I, offset measurements **a** and **b** are laid off in the isometric to locate point **A** on the curve. Points **B**, **C**, and **D** are located in a similar manner, as shown at II. A light freehand curve is sketched smoothly through the points as shown at III. Points A′, B′, C′, and D′ are located directly under points A, B, C, and D, as shown at IV, by drawing vertical lines downward, making all equal to dimension C, the height of the block. A light freehand curve is then drawn through the points. The final curve is heavied in with the aid of the

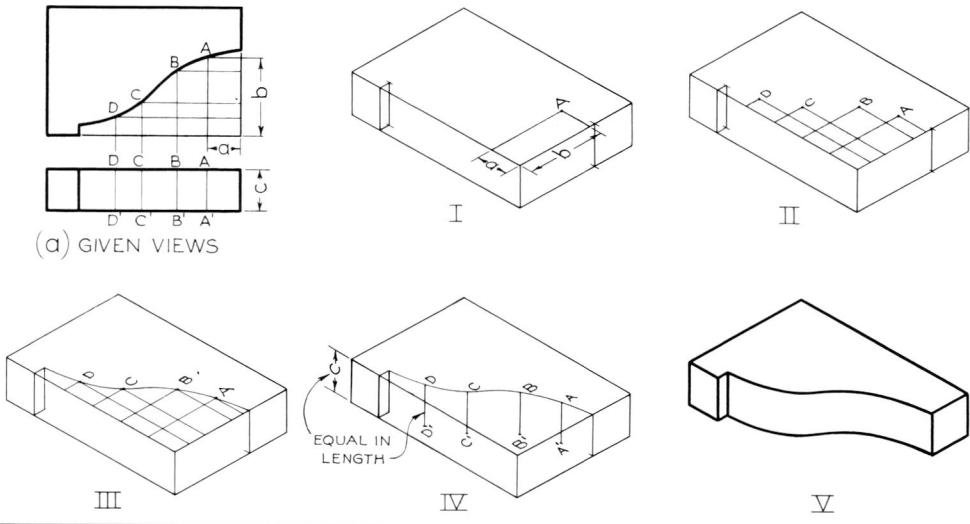

Fig. 17.21   Curves in Isometric.

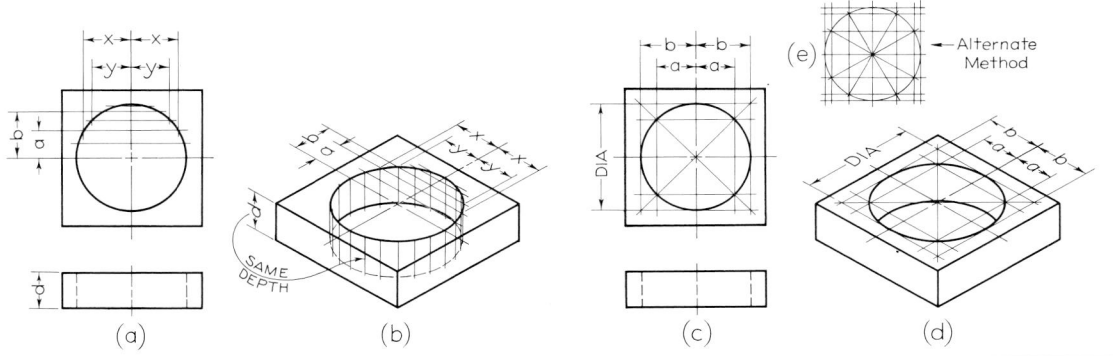

Fig. 17.22 True Isometric Ellipse Construction.

irregular curve, §2.54, and all straight lines are darkened to complete the isometric at V.

17.17 True Ellipses in Isometric

As shown in §§5.51, 6.13, and 7.30, if a circle lies in a plane that is not parallel to the plane of projection, the circle will be projected as a true ellipse. The ellipse can be constructed by the method of offsets, §17.16. As shown in Fig. 17.22 (a), draw parallel lines, spaced at random, across the circle; then transfer these lines to the isometric as shown at (b), with the aid of the dividers. To locate points in the lower ellipse, transfer points of the upper ellipse down a distance equal to the height d of the block and draw the ellipse, part of which will be hidden, through these points. Draw the final ellipses with the aid of the irregular curve §2.54.

A variation of the method of offsets, which provides eight points on the ellipse, is illustrated at (c) and (d). If more points are desired, parallel lines, as at (a), can be added. As shown at (c), circumscribe a square around the given circle, and draw diagonals. Through the points of intersection of the diagonals and the circle, draw another square, as shown. Draw this construction in the isometric, as shown at (d), transferring distances a and b with the dividers.

A similar method that provides twelve points on the ellipse is shown at (e). The given circle is divided into twelve equal parts, using the 30° × 60° triangle, Fig. 2.23. Lines parallel to the sides of the square are drawn through these points. The entire construction is then drawn in isometric, and the ellipse is drawn through the points of intersection.

When the center lines shown in the top view at

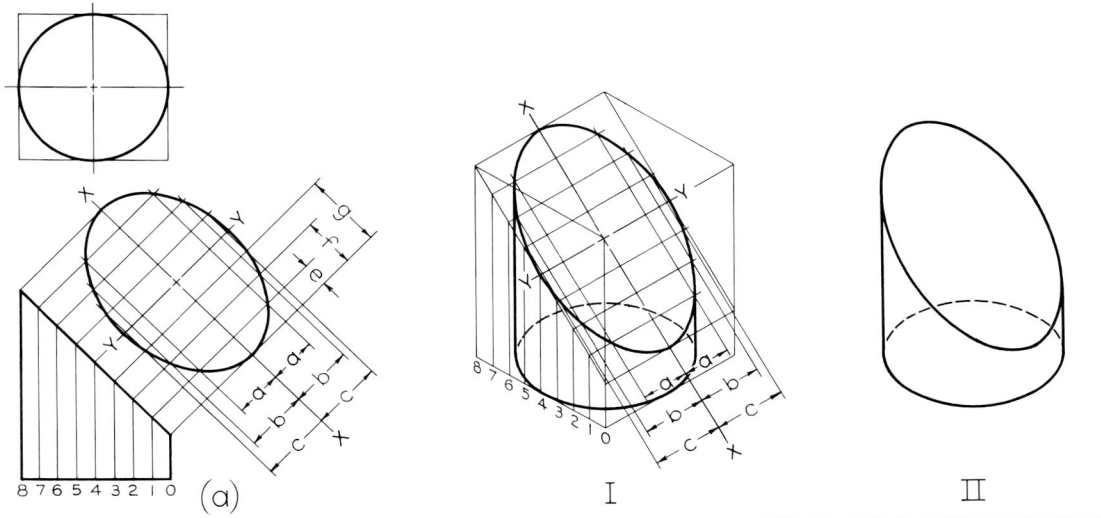

Fig. 17.23 Ellipse in Inclined Plane.

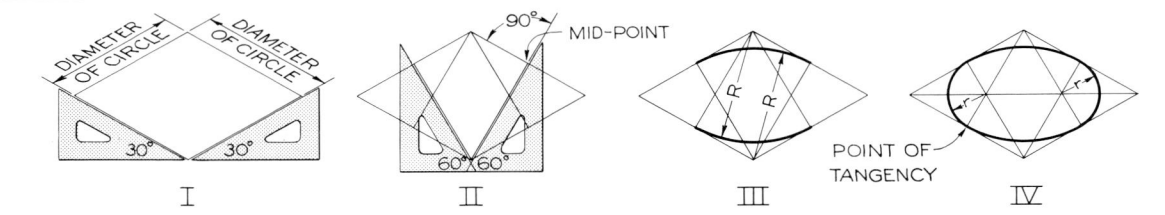

Fig. 17.24 Steps in Drawing Four-Center Ellipse.

(a) are drawn in isometric, (b), they become the *conjugate diameters* of the ellipse. The ellipse can then be constructed on the conjugate diameters by the methods of Figs. 5.51 and 5.52 (b).

When the 45° diagonals at (c) are drawn in isometric at (d), they coincide with the major and minor axes of the ellipse, respectively. Note that the minor axis is equal in length to the sides of the inscribed square at (c). The ellipse can be constructed upon the major and minor axes by any of the methods in §§5.48 and 5.51.

Remember the rule: *The major axis of the ellipse is always at right angles to the center line of the cylinder, and the minor axis is at right angles to the major axis and coincides with the center line.*

Accurate ellipses may be drawn with the aid of ellipse guides, §§5.56 and 17.21, or with a special *ellipsograph*.

If the curve lies in a nonisometric plane, not all offset measurements can be applied directly. For example, in Fig. 17.23 (a) the elliptical face shown in the auxiliary view lies in an inclined nonisometric plane. The cylinder is enclosed in a construction box, and the box is then drawn in isometric, as shown at I. The base is drawn by the method of offsets, as shown in Fig. 17.22. The inclined ellipse is constructed by locating a number of points on the ellipse in the isometric and drawing the final curve by means of the irregular curve, §2.54.

Measurements a, b, c, and so on, are parallel to an isometric axis and can be set off in the isometric at I on each side of the center line X–X, as shown. Measurements e, f, g, and so on, are not parallel to any isometric axis and cannot be set off directly in isometric. However, when these measurements are projected to the front view and down to the base, as shown at (a), they can then be set off along the lower edge of the construction box, as shown at I. The completed isometric is shown at II.

The ellipse may also be drawn with the aid of an appropriate ellipse template selected to fit the major and minor axes established along X–X and Y–Y, respectively. See Fig. 5.55.

17.18 Approximate Four-Center Ellipse

An approximate ellipse is sufficiently accurate for nearly all isometric drawings. The method commonly used, called the *four-center ellipse*, is illustrated in Figs. 17.24, 17.25, and 17.26. It can be used only for ellipses in isometric planes.

To apply this method, Fig. 17.24, draw, or conceive to be drawn, a square around the given circle in the multiview drawing; then

I.   Draw the isometric of the square, which is an equilateral parallelogram whose sides are equal to the diameter of the circle.

II.   Erect perpendicular bisectors to each side, using the 30° × 60° triangle as shown. These perpendiculars will intersect at four points, which will be centers for the four circular arcs.

III.   Draw the two large arcs, with radius R, from the intersections of the perpendiculars in the two closest corners of the parallelogram, as shown.

IV.   Draw the two small arcs, with radius r, from the intersections of the perpendiculars within the parallelogram, to complete the ellipse. As a check on the accurate location of these centers, a long diagonal of the parallelogram may be drawn, as shown. The midpoints of the sides of the parallelogram are points of tangency for the four arcs.

A typical drawing with cylindrical shapes is illustrated in Fig. 17.25. Note that the centers of the larger ellipse cannot be used for the smaller ellipse, though the ellipses represent concentric circles. Each ellipse has its own parallelogram and its own centers. Observe also that the centers of the lower ellipse are obtained by projecting the centers of the upper large ellipse down a distance equal to the height of the cylinder.

The construction of the four-center ellipse upon the three visible faces of a cube is shown in Fig. 17.26, a study of which shows that all diagonals are horizontal or 60° with horizontal; hence, the entire construction is made with the T-square and 30° × 60° triangle.

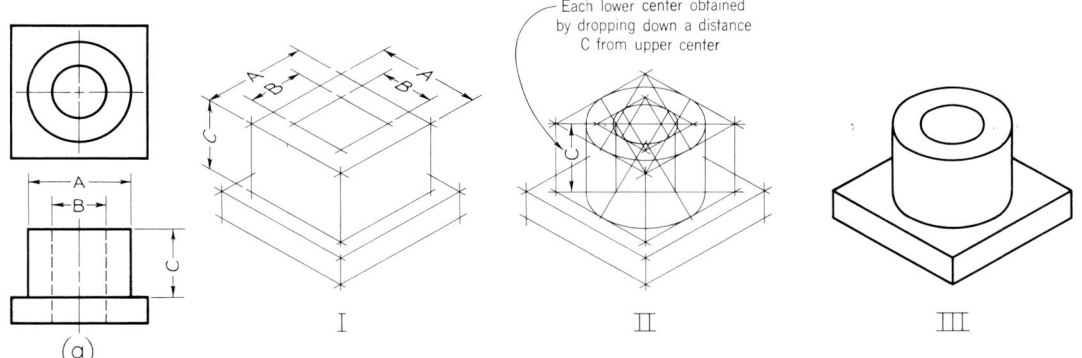

Fig. 17.25 Isometric Drawing of a Bearing.

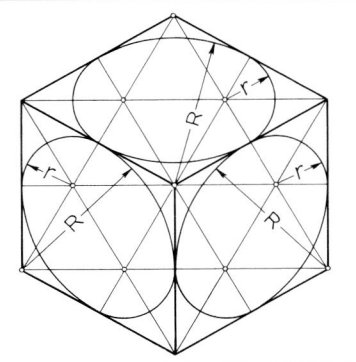

Fig. 17.26 Four-Center Ellipses.

Actually the four-center ellipse deviates considerably from the true ellipse. As shown in Fig. 17.27 (a), the four-center ellipse is somewhat shorter and "fatter" than the true ellipse. In constructions where tangencies or intersections with the four-center ellipse occur in the zones of error, the four-center ellipse is unsatisfactory, as shown at (b) and (c).

For a much closer approximation to the true ellipse, the Orth four-center ellipse, Fig. 17.28, which requires only one more step than the regular four-center ellipse, will be found sufficiently accurate for almost any problem.

When it is more convenient to start with the

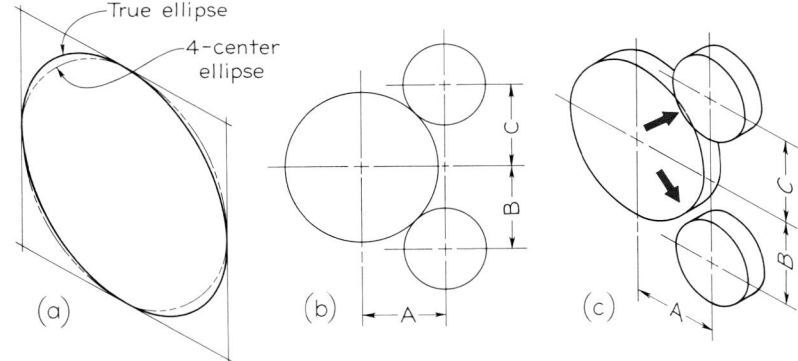

Fig. 17.27 Faults of Four-Center Ellipse.

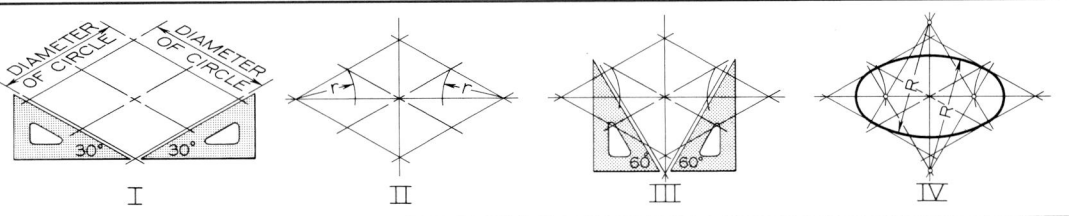

Fig. 17.28 Orth Four-Center Ellipse. *Courtesy of Professor H. D. Orth*

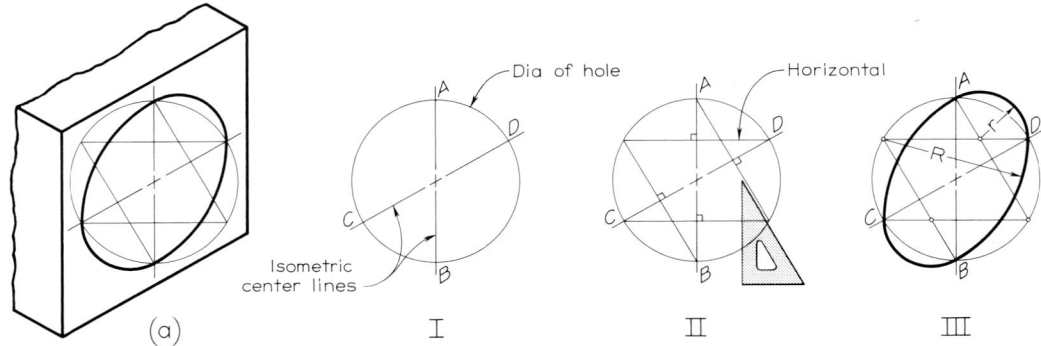

Fig. 17.29   Alternate Four-Center Ellipse.

isometric center lines of a hole or cylinder in drawing the ellipse, rather than the enclosing parallelogram, the *alternate four-center ellipse* is recommended, Fig. 17.29. A completely constructed ellipse is shown at (a), and the steps followed are shown at the right in the figure.

I.   Draw the isometric center lines. From the center, draw a construction circle equal to the actual diameter of the hole or cylinder. The circle will intersect the center lines at four points A, B, C, and D.

II.   From the two intersection points on one center line, erect perpendiculars to the other center line; then from the two intersection points on the other center line, erect perpendiculars to the first center line.

III.   With the intersections of the perpendiculars as centers, draw two small arcs and two large arcs, as shown.

NOTE   The above steps are exactly the same as for the regular four-center ellipse of Fig. 17.24 except for the use of the isometric center lines instead of the enclosing parallelogram.

17.19 Screw Threads in Isometric

Parallel partial ellipses spaced equal to the symbolic thread pitch, Fig. 15.9 (a), are used to represent the crests only of a screw thread in isometric, Fig. 17.30. The ellipses may be drawn by the four-center method of §17.18, or with the ellipse template, which is much more convenient, §§5.56 and 17.21.

17.20 Arcs in Isometric

The four-center ellipse construction is used in drawing circular arcs in isometric, as shown in Fig. 17.31. At (a) the complete construction is shown. However, it is not necessary to draw the complete constructions for arcs, as shown at (b) and (c). In each case the radius R is set off from the construction corner; then at each point, perpendiculars to the lines are erected, their intersection being the center of the arc. Note that the R distances are equal in both cases, (b) and (c), but that the actual radii used are quite different.

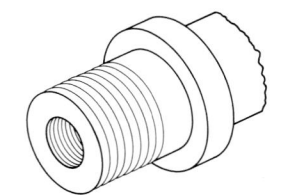

Fig. 17.30   Screw Threads in Isometric.

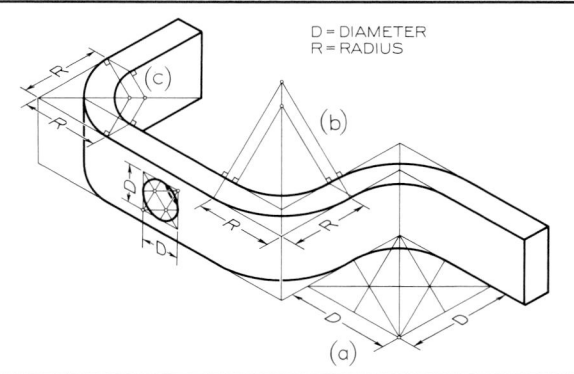

Fig. 17.31   Arcs in Isometric.

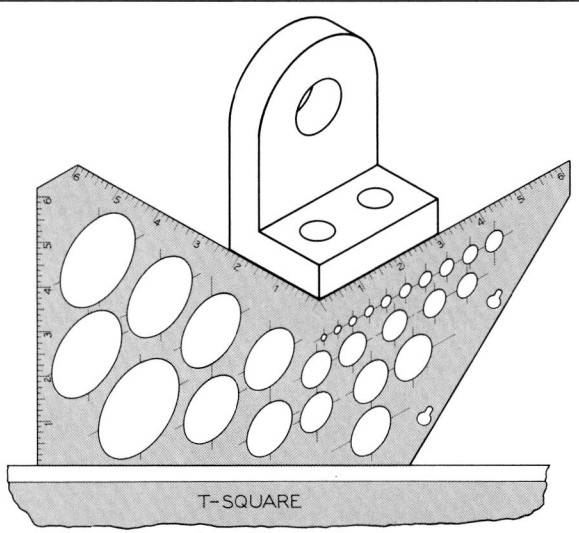

Fig. 17.32 Instrumaster Isometric Template.

If a truer elliptic arc is required, the Orth construction, Fig. 17.28, can be used. Or a true elliptic arc may be drawn by the method of offsets, §17.17, or with the aid of an ellipse guide, §17.21.

17.21 Ellipse Guides

One of the principal time-consuming elements in pictorial drawing is the construction of ellipses. A wide variety of ellipse guides, or templates, is available for ellipses of various sizes and proportions. See §5.56. They are not available in every possible size, of course, and it may be necessary to "use the fudge factor," such as leaning the pencil or pen when inscribing the ellipse, or shifting the template slightly for drawing each quadrant of the ellipse.

The design of the ellipse template, Fig. 17.32, combines the angles, scales, and ellipses on the same instrument. The ellipses are provided with markings to coincide with the isometric center lines of the holes—a convenient feature in isometric drawing.

17.22 Intersections

To draw the elliptical intersection of a cylindrical hole in an oblique plane in isometric, Fig. 17.33, draw the ellipse in the isometric plane on top of the construction box, (b); then project points down to the oblique plane as shown. It will be seen that the construction for each point forms a trapezoid, which

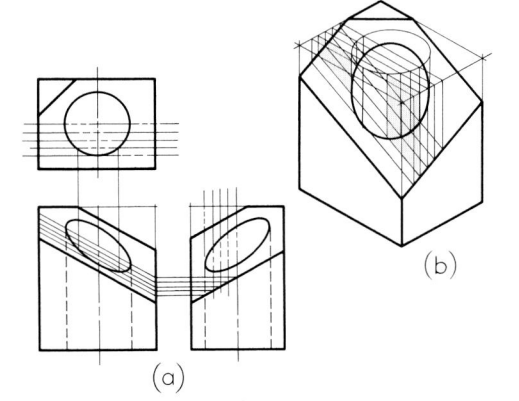

Fig. 17.33 Oblique Plane and Cylinder.

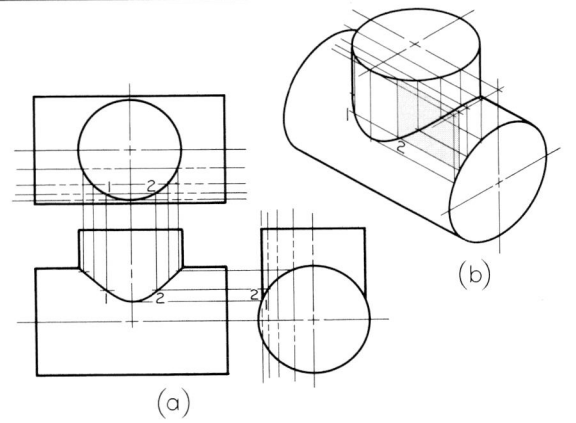

Fig. 17.34 Intersection of Cylinders.

is produced by a slicing plane parallel to a lateral surface of the block.

To draw the curve of intersection between two cylinders, Fig. 17.34, pass a series of imaginary cutting planes through the cylinders parallel to their axes, as shown. Each plane will cut elements on both cylinders that intersect at points on the curve of intersection, as shown at (b). As many points should be plotted as necessary to assure a smooth curve. For most accurate work, the ends of the cylinders should be drawn by the Orth construction, or with ellipse guides, or by one of the true-ellipse constructions.

17.23 The Sphere in Isometric

The isometric drawing of any curved surface is evidently the envelope of all lines that can be drawn on that surface. For the sphere, the great circles

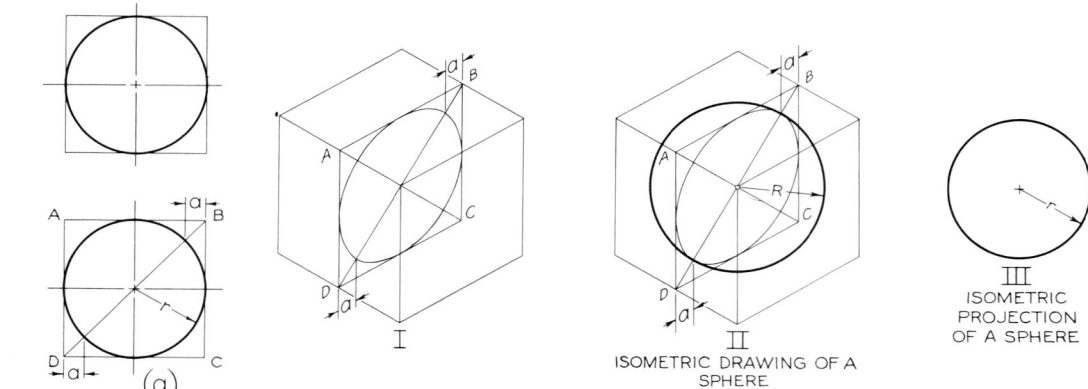

Fig. 17.35   Isometric of a Sphere.

(circles cut by any plane through the center) may be selected as the lines on the surface. Since all great circles, except those that are perpendicular or parallel to the plane of projection, are shown as ellipses having equal major axes, it follows that their envelope is a circle whose diameter is the major axis of the ellipses.

In Fig. 17.35 (a) two views of a sphere enclosed in a construction cube are shown. The cube is drawn at I, together with the isometric of a great circle that lies in a plane parallel to one face of the cube. Actually, the ellipse need not be drawn, for only the points on the diagonal located by measurements **a** are needed. These points establish the ends of the major axis from which the radius **R** of the sphere is determined. The resulting drawing shown at II is an *isometric drawing*, and its diameter is, therefore, $\sqrt{\frac{3}{2}}$ times the actual diameter of the sphere. The *isometric projection* of the sphere is simply a circle whose diameter is equal to the true diameter of the sphere, as shown at III.

17.24 Isometric Sectioning

In drawing objects characterized by open or irregular interior shapes, isometric sectioning is as appropriate as in multiview drawing. An *isometric full section* is shown in Fig. 17.36. In such cases it is usually best to draw the cut surface first and then to draw the portion of the object that lies behind the cutting plane. Other examples of isometric full sections are shown in Figs. 7.91, 9.11 (b), and 9.12 (d).

An *isometric half section* is shown in Fig. 17.37. The simplest procedure in this case is to make an isometric drawing of the entire object and then the cut surfaces. Since only a quarter of the object is

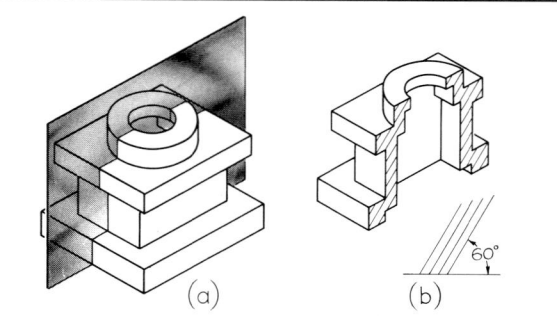

Fig. 17.36   Isometric Full Section.

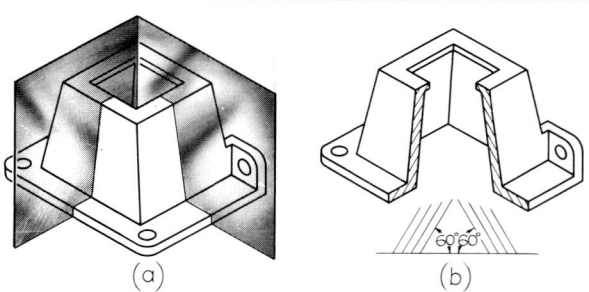

Fig. 17.37   Isometric Half Section.

removed in a half section, the resulting pictorial drawing is more useful than full sections in describing both exterior and interior shapes together. Other typical isometric half sections are shown in Figs. 9.13, 9.41, and 9.42.

Isometric broken-out sections are also sometimes used. Examples are shown in Figs. 7.98, 9.50, and 16.48.

Section lining in isometric drawing is similar to that in multiview drawing. Section lining at an angle

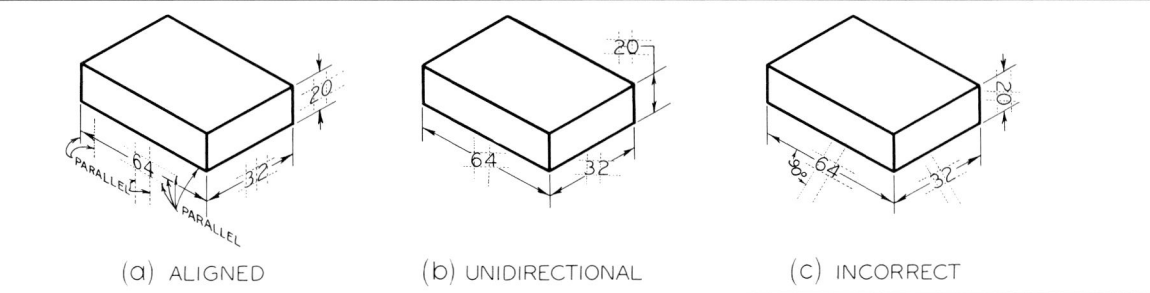

Fig. 17.38 Numerals and Arrowheads in Isometric (metric dimensions).

of 60° with horizontal, Figs. 17.36 and 17.37, is recommended, but the direction should be changed if at this angle the lines would be parallel to a prominent visible line bounding the cut surface, or to other adjacent lines of the drawing.

17.25 Isometric Dimensioning

Isometric dimensions are similar to ordinary dimensions used on multiview drawings, but are expressed in pictorial form. Two methods of dimensioning are approved by ANSI, namely, the pictorial plane (aligned) system and the unidirectional system, Fig. 17.38. Note that *vertical lettering* is used for either system of dimensioning. Inclined lettering is not recommended for pictorial dimensioning. The method of drawing numerals and arrowheads for the two systems is shown at (a) and (b). For the 64 mm dimension in the aligned system at (a), the extension lines, dimension lines, and lettering are all drawn in the isometric plane of one face of the object. The "horizontal" guide lines for the lettering are drawn parallel to the dimension line, and the "vertical" guide lines are drawn parallel to the extension lines.

The barbs of the arrowheads should line up parallel to the extension lines.

For the 64 mm dimension in the unidirectional system at (b), the extension lines and dimension lines are all drawn in the isometric plane of one face of the object and the barbs of the arrowheads should line up parallel to the extension lines, all exactly the same as at (a). However, the lettering for the dimensions is vertical and reads from the bottom of the drawing. This simpler system of dimensioning is often used on pictorials for production purposes.

As shown at (c), the vertical guide lines for the letters should not be perpendicular to the dimension lines. The example at (c) is incorrect because the 64 mm and 32 mm dimensions are lettered neither in the plane of the corresponding dimension and extension lines nor in a vertical position to read from the bottom of the drawing. The 20 mm dimension is awkward to read because of its position.

Correct and incorrect practice in isometric dimensioning using the aligned system of dimensioning is shown in Fig. 17.39. At (b) the $3\frac{1}{8}''$ dimension runs to a wrong extension line at the right, and con-

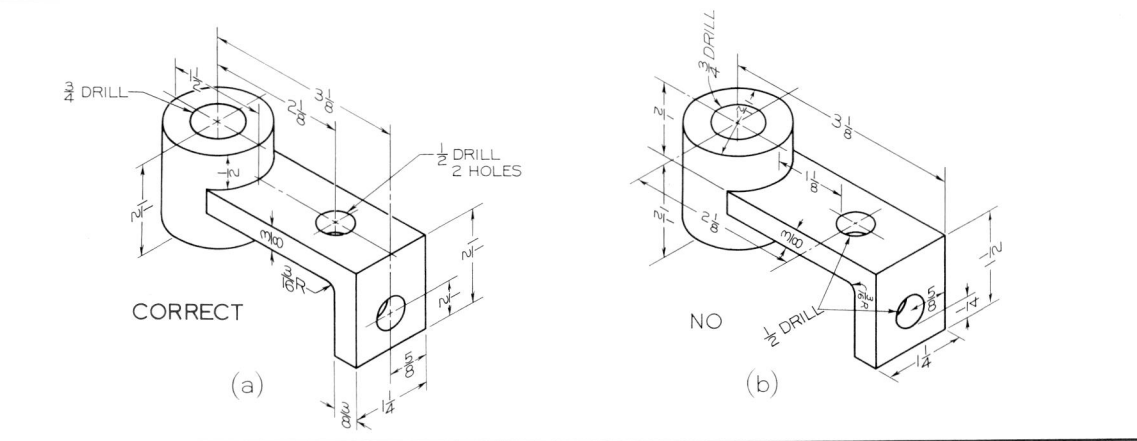

Fig. 17.39 Correct and Incorrect Isometric Dimensioning (Aligned System).

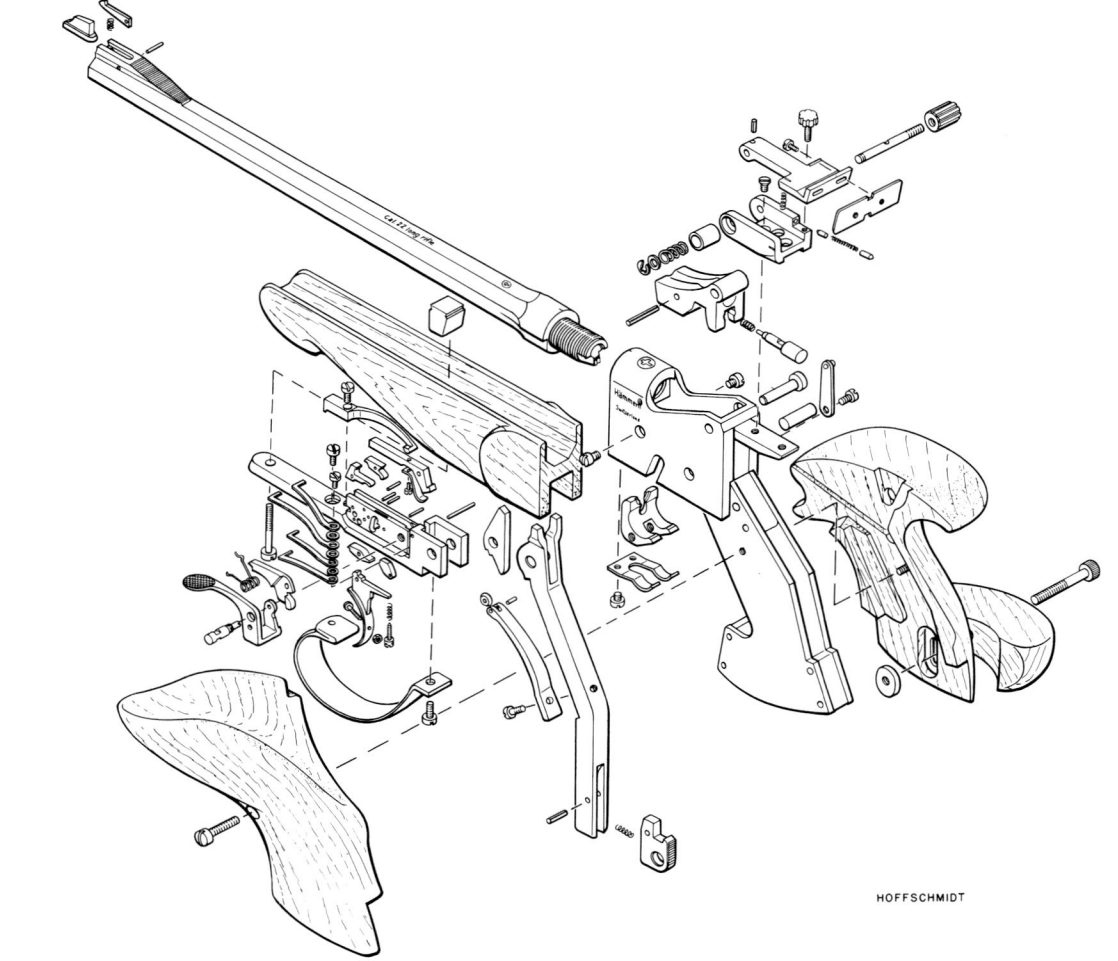

HOFFSCHMIDT

Fig. 17.40   Isometric Exploded Assembly of Hammerli Match Pistol. *Courtesy of True Magazine, Fawcett Publications*

sequently the dimension does not lie in an isometric plane. Near the left side, a number of lines cross one another unnecessarily and terminate on the wrong lines. The upper $\frac{1}{2}''$ drill hole is located from the edge of the cylinder when it should be dimensioned from its center line. Study these two drawings carefully to discover additional mistakes at (b).

The dimensioning methods described apply equally to fractional, decimal, and metric dimensions.

Many examples of isometric dimensioning are given in the problems at the end of Chapters 7, 9, 10, and 16, and you should study these to find samples of almost any special case you may encounter.

17.26 Exploded Assemblies
Exploded assemblies are often used in design presentations, catalogs, sales literature, and in the shop, to show all of the parts of an assembly and how they fit together. They may be drawn by any of the pictorial methods, including isometric, Fig. 17.40. Other isometric exploded assemblies are shown in Chapter 16.

17.27 Piping Diagrams
Isometric and oblique drawings are well suited for representation of piping layouts, as well as for all other structural work to be represented pictorially.

Dimetric Projection

17.28 The Dimetric Method of Projection

A *dimetric projection* is an axonometric projection of an object so placed that two of its axes make equal angles with the plane of projection and the third axis makes either a smaller or a greater angle. Hence, the two axes making equal angles with the plane of projection are foreshortened equally, while the third axis is foreshortened in a different ratio.

Generally, the object is so placed that one axis will be projected in a vertical position. However, if the relative positions of the axes have been determined, the projection may be drawn in any revolved position, as in isometric drawing. See §17.8.

The angles between the *projection of the axes* must not be confused with the angles the *axes themselves* make with the plane projection.

The positions of the axes may be assumed such that any two angles between the axes are equal and over 90°, and the scales determined graphically, as shown in Fig. 17.41 (a), in which OP, OL, and OS are the projections of the axes or converging edges of a cube. In this case, angle POS = angle LOS. Lines PL, LS, and SP are the lines of intersection of the plane of projection with the three visible faces of the cube. From descriptive geometry we know that since line LO is perpendicular to the plane POS, in space, its projection LO is perpendicular to PS, the intersection of the plane POS and the plane of

projection. Similarly, OP is perpendicular to SL, and OS is perpendicular to PL.

If the triangle POS is revolved about the line PS as an axis into the plane of projection, it will be shown in its true size and shape as PO'S. If regular full-size scales are marked along the lines O'P and O'S, and the triangle is counterrevolved to its original position, the dimetric scales may be laid off on the axes OP and OS, as shown.

In order to avoid the preparation of special scales, use can be made of available scales on the architects' scale by assuming the scales and calculating the positions of the axes, as follows:

$$\cos a = -\frac{\sqrt{2h^2v^2 - v^4}}{2hv}$$

where a is one of the two equal angles between the projections of the axes, h is one of the two equal scales, and v is the third scale.

Examples are shown in the upper row of Fig. 17.42, in which the assumed scales, shown encircled, are taken from the architects' scale. One of these three positions of the axes will be found suitable for almost any practical drawing.

The Instrumaster Dimetric Template, Fig. 17.41 (b), has angles of approximately 11° and 39° with

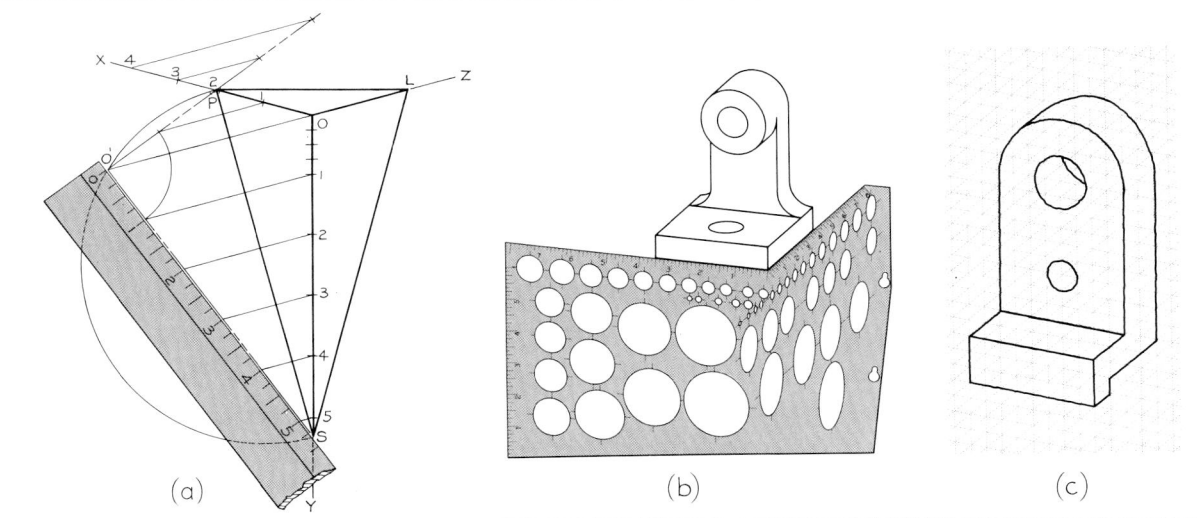

(a)   (b)   (c)

Fig. 17.41   Dimetric Projection.

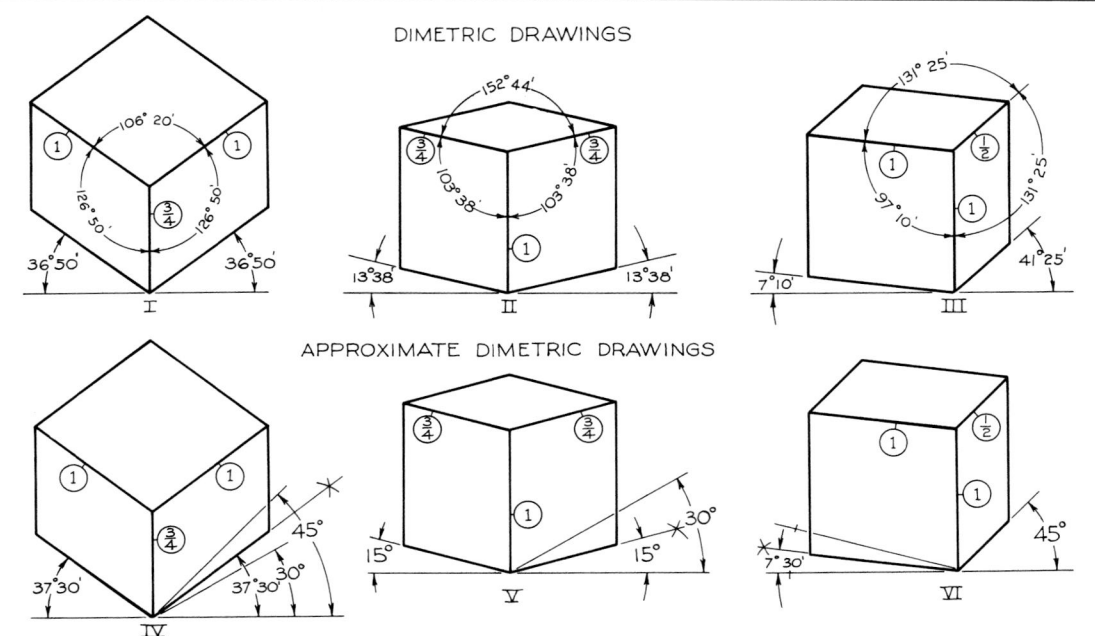

Fig. 17.42   Angles of Axes Determined by Assumed Scales.

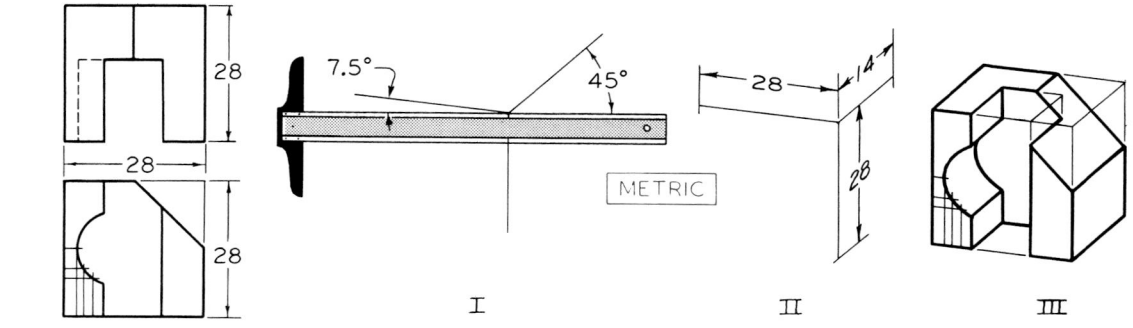

Fig. 17.43   Steps in Dimetric Drawing.

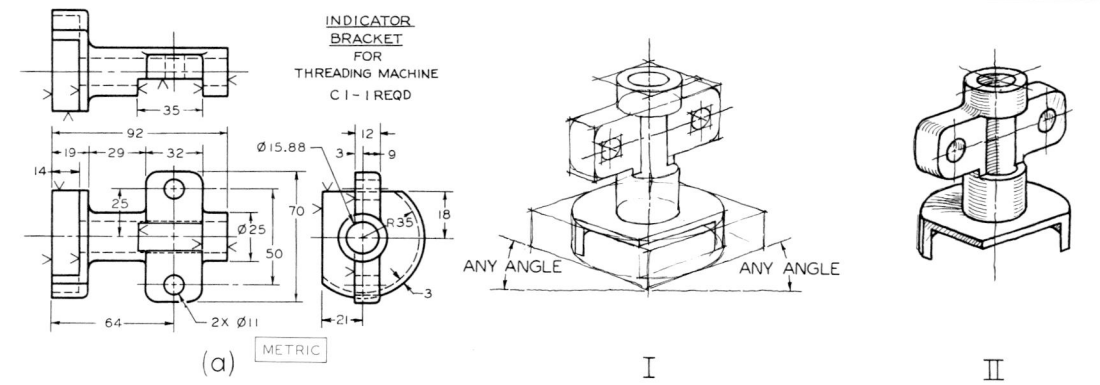

Fig. 17.44   Steps in Dimetric Sketching.

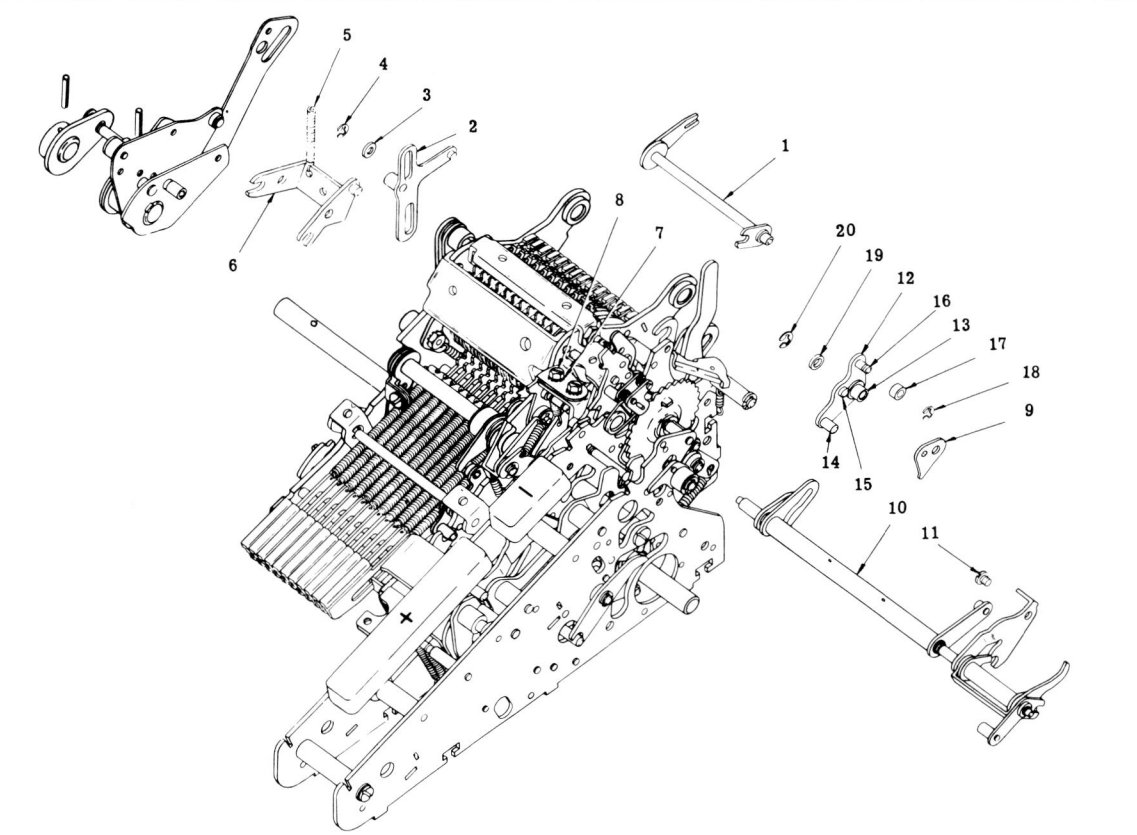

Fig. 17.45   Exploded Dimetric of an Adding Machine. *Courtesy of Victor Adding Machine Co.*

horizontal, which provides a picture similar to that in Fig. 17.42 (III). In addition, the template has ellipses corresponding to the axes and accurate scales along the edges.

For other information on drawing of ellipses, see §17.32.

The Instrumaster Dimetric Graph paper, Fig. 17.41 (c), can be used to sketch in dimetric as easily as to sketch isometrics on isometric paper. The grid lines slope in conformity to the angles on the Dimetric Template at (b) and, when printed on vellum, the grid lines do not reproduce on prints.

17.29 Approximate Dimetric Drawing

Approximate dimetric drawings, which closely resemble true dimetrics, can be constructed by substituting for the true angles shown in the upper half

of Fig. 17.42, angles that can be obtained with the ordinary triangles and compass, as shown in the lower half of the figure. The resulting drawings will be sufficiently accurate for all practical purposes.

The procedure in preparing an approximate dimetric drawing, using the position of VI in Fig. 17.42, is shown in Fig. 17.43. The offset method of drawing a curve is shown in the figure. Other methods for drawing ellipses are the same as in trimetric drawing, §17.32.

The steps in making a dimetric sketch, using a position similar to that in Fig. 17.42 (V), are shown in Fig. 17.44. The two angles are equal and about 20° with horizontal for the most pleasing effect.

An exploded approximate dimetric drawing of an adding machine is shown in Fig. 17.45. The dimetric axes used are those in Fig. 17.42 (IV). Pictorials such as this are often used in service manuals.

Trimetric Projection

17.30 The Trimetric Method of Projection

A *trimetric projection* is an axonometric projection of an object so placed that no two axes make equal angles with the plane of projection. In other words, each of the three axes and the lines parallel to them, respectively, have different ratios of foreshortening when projected to the plane of projection. If the three axes are assumed in any position on paper such that none of the angles is less than 90°, and if neither an isometric nor a dimetric position is deliberately arranged, the result will be a trimetric projection.

17.31 Trimetric Scales

Since the three axes are foreshortened differently, three different trimetric scales must be prepared and used. The scales are determined as shown in Fig. 17.46 (a), the method being the same as explained for the dimetric scales in §17.28. As shown at (a), any two of the three triangular faces can be revolved into the plane of projection to show the true lengths of the three axes. In the revolved position, the regular scale is used to set off inches or fractions thereof. When the axes have been counterrevolved to their original positions, the scales will

be correctly foreshortened, as shown. These dimensions should be transferred to the edges of three thin cards and marked OX, OZ, and OY for easy reference.

A special trimetric angle may be prepared from Bristol Board or plastic, as shown at (b). Perhaps six or seven such guides, using angles for a variety of positions of the axes, would be sufficient for all practical requirements.*

17.32 Trimetric Ellipses

The trimetric center lines of a hole, or on the end of a cylinder, become the conjugate diameters of the ellipse when drawn in trimetric. The ellipse may be drawn upon the conjugate diameters by the methods of Fig. 5.51 or 5.52 (b). Or the major and minor axes may be determined from the conjugate diameters, Fig. 5.53 (c), and the ellipse constructed on them by any of the methods of Figs. 5.48–5.50, and 5.52 (a), or with the aid of an ellipse guide, Fig. 5.55.

One advantage of trimetric projection is the infinite number of positions of the object available. The angles and scales can be handled without too much

*Plastic templates of this type are available from drafting supplies dealers.

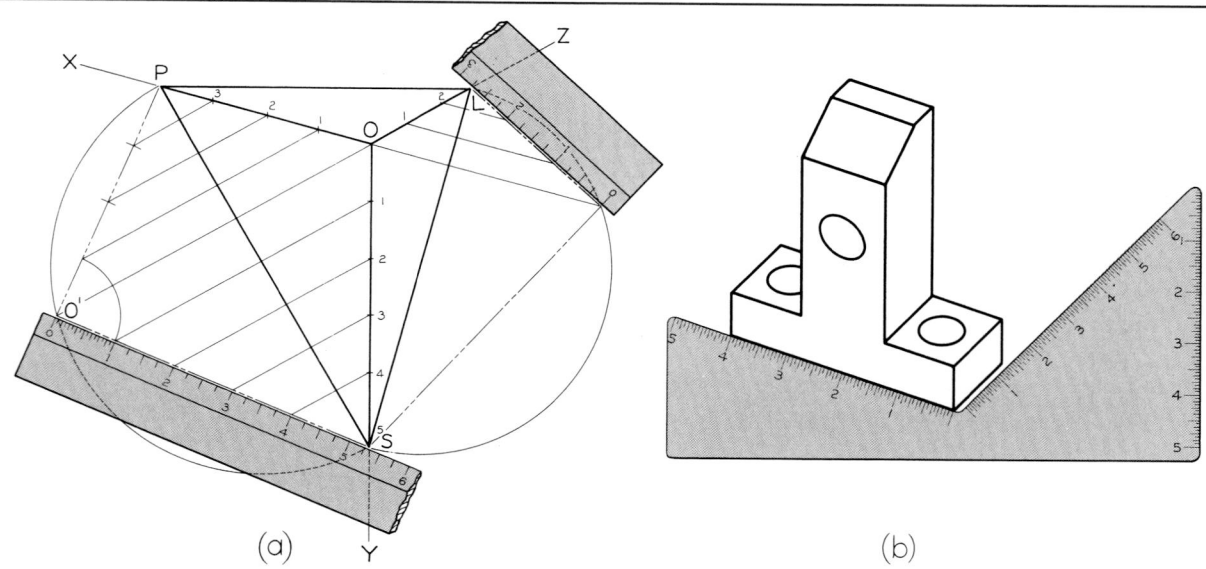

(a)   (b)

Fig. 17.46   Trimetric Scales.

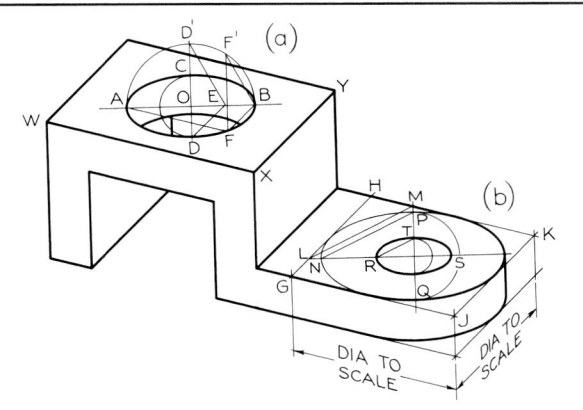

Fig. 17.47 Ellipses in Trimetric. *Method (b) courtesy of Professor H. E. Grant*

difficulty, as shown in §17.31. However, the infinite variety of ellipses has been a discouraging factor.

In drawing any axonometric ellipse, keep the following in mind:

1. On the drawing, the major axis is always perpendicular to the center line, or axis, of the cylinder.

2. The minor axis is always perpendicular to the major axis; that is, on the paper it coincides with the axis of the cylinder.

3. The length of the major axis is equal to the actual diameter of the cylinder.

Thus we know at once the directions of both the major and minor axes, and the length of the major axis. *We do not know the length of the minor axis.* If we can find it, we can easily construct the ellipse with the aid of an ellipse guide or any of a number of ellipse constructions mentioned earlier.

In Fig. 17.47 (a), center O is located as desired, and horizontal and vertical construction lines that will contain the major and minor axes are drawn through O. Note that the major axis will be on the horizontal line perpendicular to the axis of the hole, and the minor axis will be perpendicular to it, or vertical.

Set the compass for the actual radius of the hole and draw the semicircle, as shown, to establish the ends A and B of the major axis. Draw AF and BF parallel to the axonometric edges WX and YX, respectively, to locate F, which lies on the ellipse.

Draw a vertical line through F to intersect the semicircle at F′ and join F′ to B as shown. From D′ where the minor axis, extended, intersects the semicircle, draw D′E and ED parallel to F′B and BF, respectively. Point D is one end of the minor axis. From center O, strike arc DC to locate C, the other end of the minor axis. Upon these axes, a true ellipse can be constructed, or drawn with the aid of an ellipse guide. A simple method for finding the "angle" of ellipse guide to use is shown in Fig. 5.55 (c). If an ellipse guide is not available, an approximate four-center ellipse, Fig. 5.56, will be found satisfactory in most cases.

In constructions where the enclosing parallelogram for an ellipse is available or easily constructed, the major and minor axes can be readily determined as shown in Fig. 17.47 (b). The directions of both axes, and the length of the major axis, are known. Extend the axes to intersect the sides of the parallelogram at L and M, and join the points with a straight line. From one end N of the major axis, draw a line NP parallel to LM. The point P is one end of the minor axis. To find one end T of the minor axis of the smaller ellipse, it is only necessary to draw RT parallel to LM or NP.

The method of constructing an ellipse on an oblique plane in trimetric is similar to that shown for isometric in Fig. 17.33.

17.33 Axonometric Projection by the Method of Intersections

Instead of constructing axonometric projections with the aid of specially prepared scales, as explained in the preceding paragraphs, an axonometric projection can be obtained directly by projection from two orthographic views of the object. This method is called the *method of intersections;* it was developed by Profs. L. Eckhart and T. Schmid of the Vienna College of Engineering and was published in 1937.

To understand this method, let us assume Fig. 17.48, that the axonometric projection of a rectangular object is given, and it is required to find its three orthographic projections: the top view, front view, and side view.

Assume that the object is placed so that its principal edges coincide with the coordinate axes, and assume that the plane of projection (the plane upon which the axonometric projection is drawn) intersects the three coordinate planes in the triangle ABC. From descriptive geometry, we know that lines BC, CA, and AB will be perpendicular, respec-

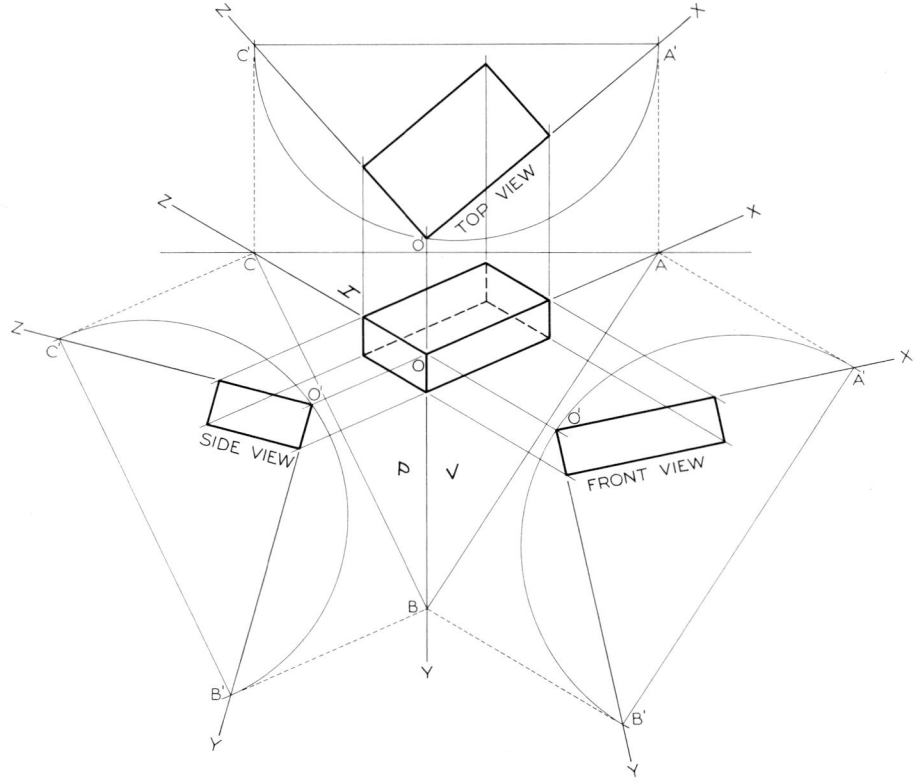

Fig. 17.48   Views from an Axonometric Projection.

tively, to axes **OX**, **OY**, and **OZ**. Any one of the three points **A**, **B**, or **C** may be assumed anywhere on one of the axes, and the triangle **ABC** drawn.

To find the true size and shape of the top view, revolve the triangular portion of the horizontal plane **AOC**, which is in front of the plane of projection, about its base **CA**, into the plane of projection. In this case, the triangle is revolved *inward* to the plane of projection through the smallest angle made with it. The triangle will then be shown in its true size and shape, and the top view of the object can be drawn in the triangle by projection from the axonometric projection, as shown, since all width dimensions remain the same. In the figure, the base **CA** of the triangle has been moved upward to **C'A'** so that the revolved position of the triangle will not overlap its projection.

In the same manner, the true sizes and shapes of the front view and side view can be found, as shown.

It is evident that if the three orthographic projections, or in most cases any two of them, are given

in their relative positions, as shown in Fig. 17.48, the directions of the projections could be reversed so that the intersections of the projecting lines would determine the required axonometric projection.

In order to draw an axonometric projection by the method of intersections, it is well to make a sketch, Fig. 17.49, of the desired general appearance of the projection. Even if the object is a complicated one, this sketch need not be complete, but may be only a sketch of an enclosing box. Draw the projections of the coordinate axes **OX**, **OY**, and **OZ**, parallel to the principal edges of the object as shown in the sketch, and the triangle **ABC** to represent the intersection of the three coordinate planes with the plane of projection.

Revolve the triangle **ABO** about its base **AB** as the axis into the plane of projection. Line **OA** will revolve to **O'A**, and this line, or one parallel to it, must be used as the base line of the front view of the object. The projecting lines from the front view to the axonometric must be drawn parallel to the

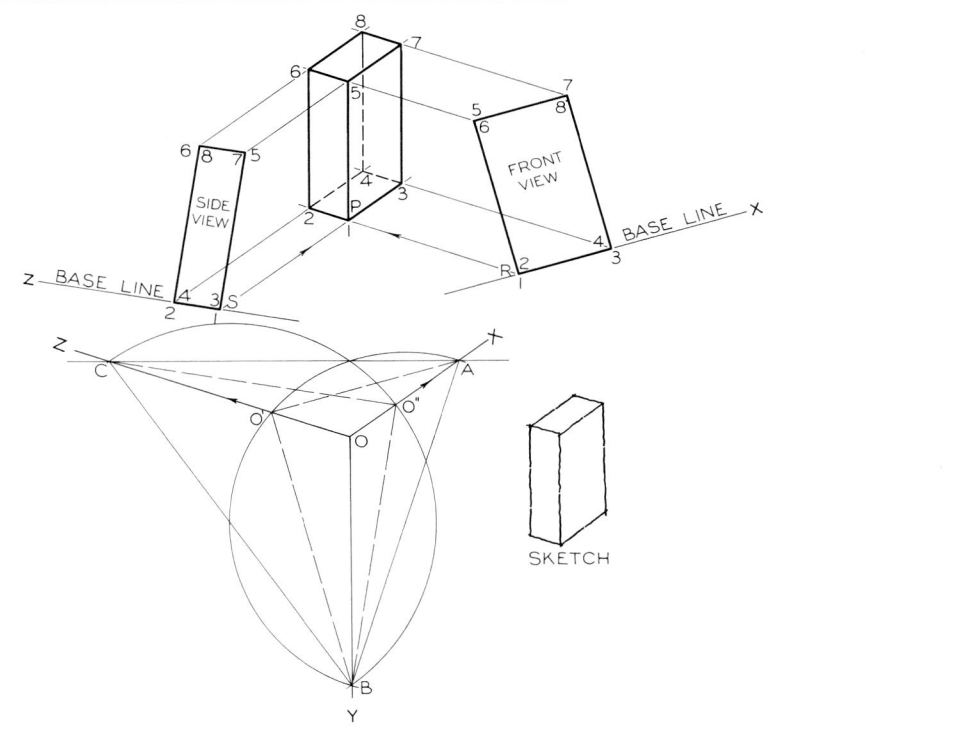

Fig. 17.49   Axonometric Projection.

projection of the unrevolved Z-axis, as indicated in the figure.

Similarly, revolve the triangle COB about its base CB as the axis into the plane of projection. Line CO will revolve to CO″, and this line, or one parallel to it, must be used as the base line of the side view. The direction of the projecting lines must be parallel to the projection of the unrevolved X-axis, as shown.

Draw the front-view base line at a convenient location, but parallel to O′X, and with it as the base, draw the front view of the object. Draw the side-view base line also at a convenient location, but parallel to O″C, and with it as the base, draw the side view of the object, as shown. From the corners of the front view, draw projecting lines parallel to OZ, and from the corners of the side view, draw projecting lines parallel to OX. The intersections of these two sets of projecting lines determine the desired axonometric projection. It will be an isometric, a dimetric, or a trimetric projection, depending upon the form of the sketch used as the basis for the projections, §17.2. If the sketch is drawn so that the three angles formed by the three coordinate axes are equal, the resulting projection will be an isometric projection;

if two of the three angles are equal, the resulting projection will be a dimetric projection; and if no two of the three angles are equal, the resulting projection will be a trimetric projection.

In order to place the desired projection on a specific location on the drawing, Fig. 17.49, select the desired projection P of the point 1, for example, and draw two projecting lines PR and PS to intersect the two base lines and thereby to determine the locations of the two views on their base lines.

Another example of this method of axonometric projection is shown in Fig. 17.50. In this case, it was deemed necessary only to draw a sketch of the plan or base of the object in the desired position, as shown. The axes are then drawn with OX and OZ parallel, respectively, to the sides of the sketch plan, and the remaining axis OY is assumed in a vertical position. The triangles COB and AOB are revolved, and the two base lines drawn parallel to O″C and O′A as shown. Point P, the lower front corner of the axonometric drawing, was then chosen at a convenient place, and projecting lines drawn toward the base lines parallel to axes OX and OZ to locate the positions of the views on the base lines. The views

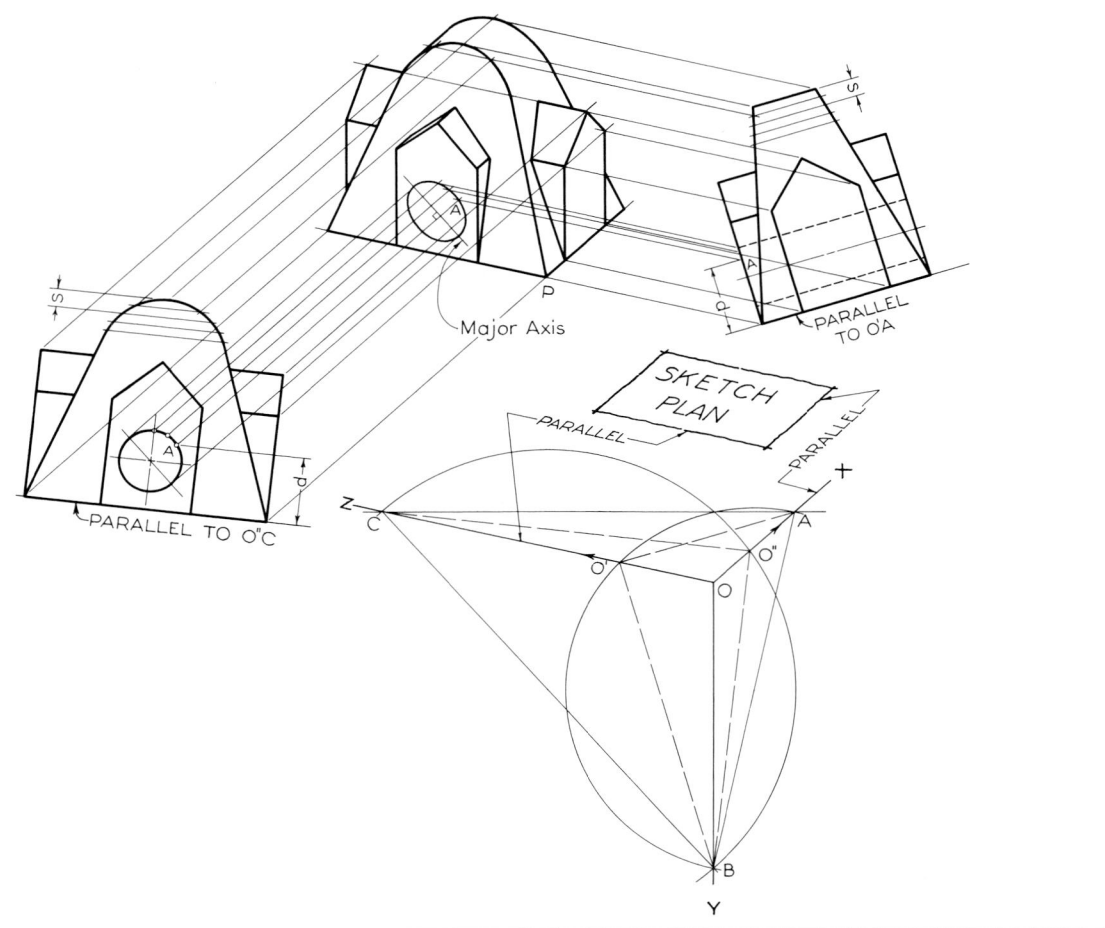

Fig. 17.50   Axonometric Projection.

are drawn upon the base lines or cut apart from another drawing and fastened in place with drafting tape.

To draw the elliptical projection of the circle, assume any points, such as A, on the circle in both front and side views. Note that point A is the same altitude d above the base line in both views. The axonometric projection of point A is found simply by drawing the projecting lines from the two views. The major and minor axes may be easily found by projecting in this manner or by methods shown in Fig. 17.47, and the true ellipse drawn by any of the methods of Figs. 5.48–5.50 and 5.52 (a), or with the aid of an ellipse guide, §§5.56 and 17.21. Or an ap-

proximate ellipse, which is satisfactory for most drawings, may be used, Fig. 5.56.

17.34 Computer Graphics

Complex pictorial illustrations can be among the most time-comsuming tasks faced by the drafter. Modern computer graphics software, however, provides relief to the knowledgeable user. Orthographic-to-axonometric programs are available that can easily convert a multiview drawing to an isometric with the user's choice of alignment, Fig. 17.51. Isometric assembly drawings, Fig. 17.52, exploded assembly drawings, Fig. 17.53, and pictorial sections can also be readily generated.

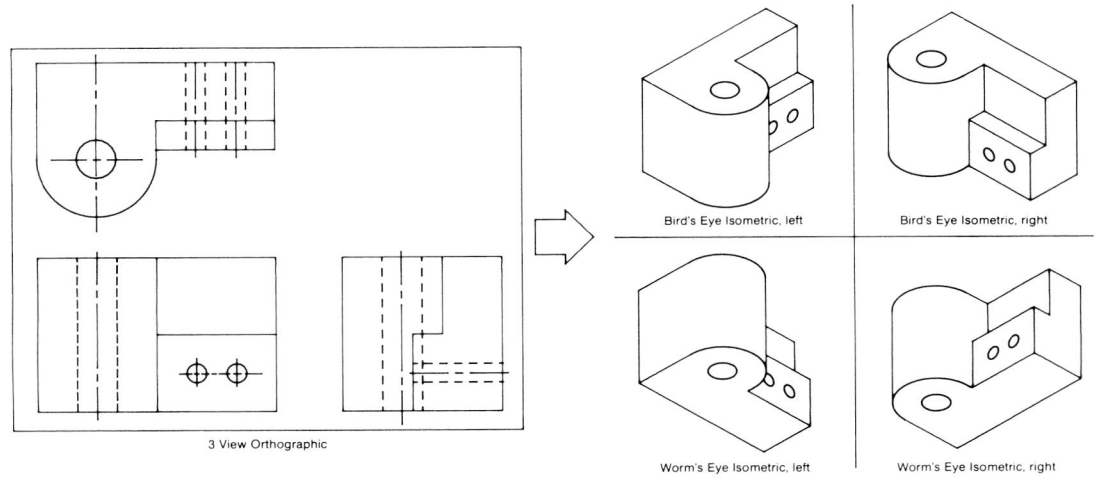

Bird's Eye Isometric, left   Bird's Eye Isometric, right

Worm's Eye Isometric, left   Worm's Eye Isometric, right

3 View Orthographic

Fig. 17.51   Orthographic to Isometric Conversion.   The Auto-trol Orthographic to Axonometric Package (OTAP) system can be used to convert an orthographic drawing to axonometric. *Courtesy of Auto-trol Technology Corporation.*

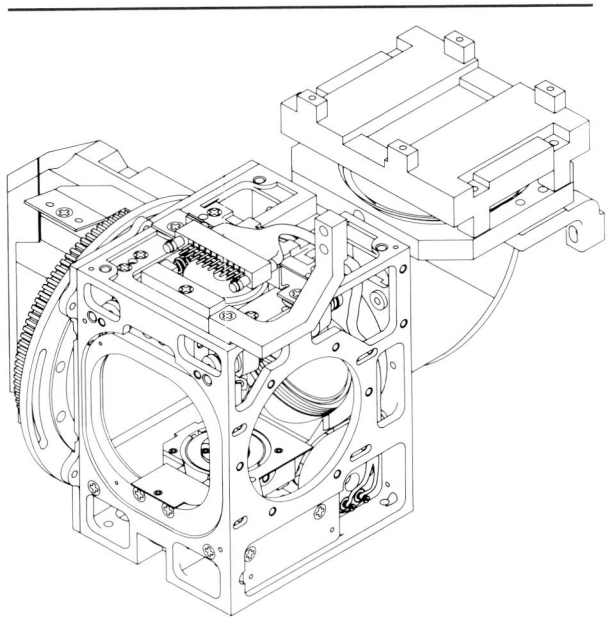

Fig. 17.52 Isometric Assembly Drawing Produced by Using the Computervision Designer System. *Courtesy of Computervision Corporation, a subsidiary of Prime Computer, Inc.*

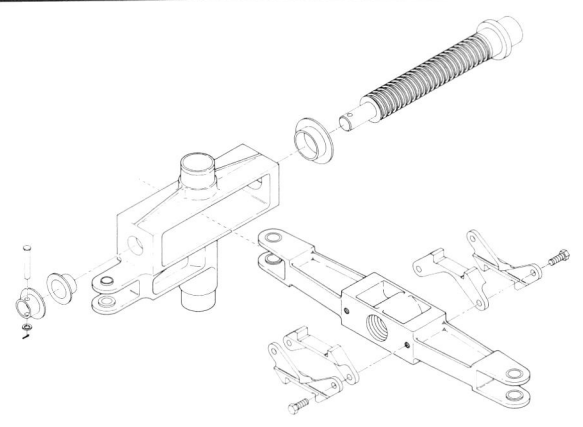

Fig. 17.53 Exploded Assembly Drawing Produced from Engineering Data by Using the Auto-trol Orthographic to Axonometric Package (OTAP) System. *Courtesy of Auto-trol Technology Corporation.*

Axonometric Problems

A large number of problems to be drawn axonometrically are given in Figs. 17.54–17.57. The earlier isometric sketches may be drawn on isometric paper, §6.14; later sketches should be made on plain drawing paper. On drawings to be executed with instruments, show all construction lines required in the solutions.

For additional problems, see Figs. 7.52–7.54 and 18.23–18.25.

Since many of the problems in this chapter are of a general nature, they can also be solved on most computer graphics systems. If a system is available, the instructor may choose to assign specific problems to be completed by this method.

Additional problems in convenient form for solution are presented in the worksheets at the back of this book. Refer to Drawings 17-1 to 17-3 and accompanying instructions.

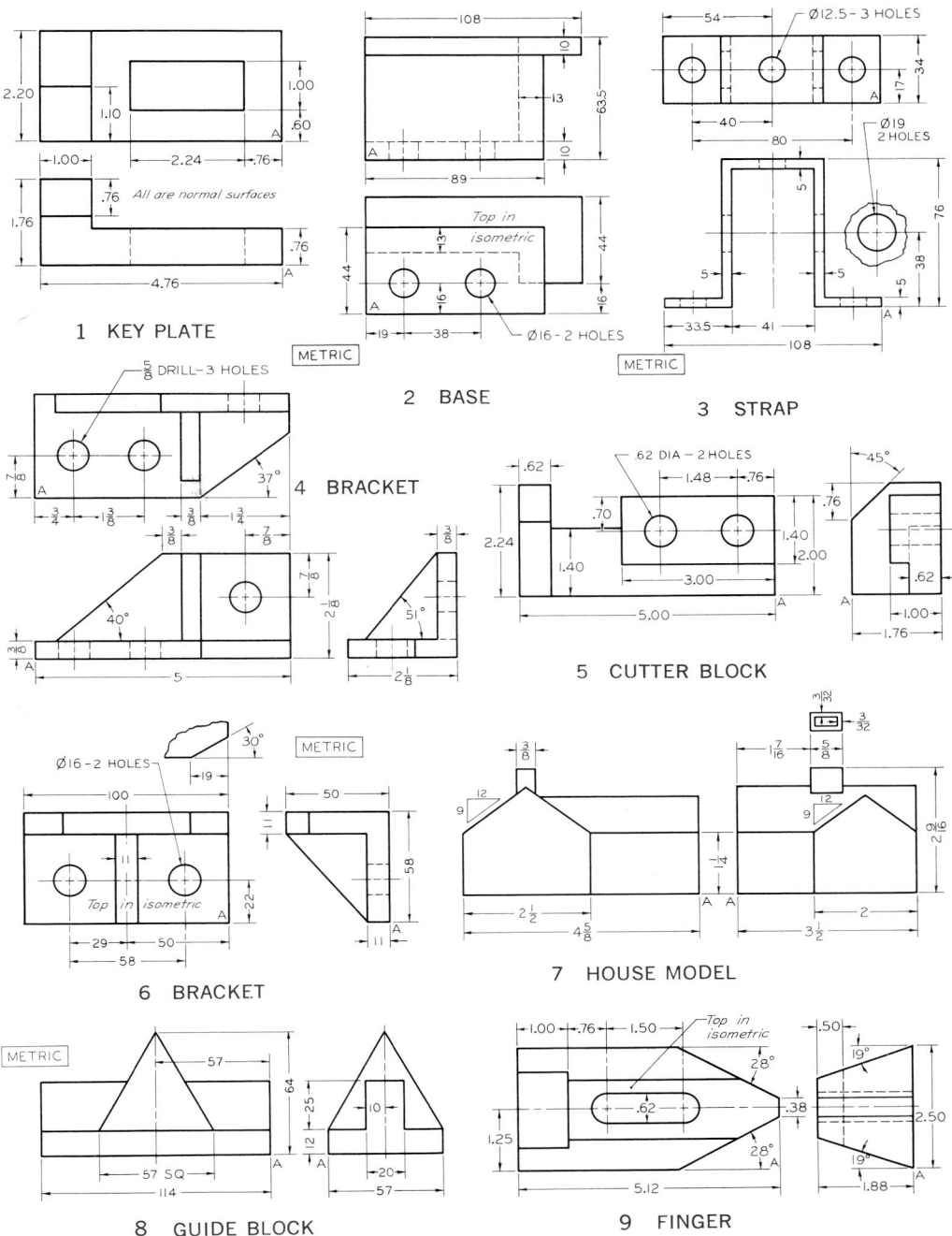

1 KEY PLATE

2 BASE

3 STRAP

4 BRACKET

5 CUTTER BLOCK

6 BRACKET

7 HOUSE MODEL

8 GUIDE BLOCK

9 FINGER

Fig. 17.54 (1) Make freehand isometric sketches. (2) Make isometric drawings with instruments on Layout A–2 or A4–2 (adjusted). (3) Make dimetric drawings with instruments, using Layout A–2 or A4–2 (adjusted), and position assigned from Fig. 17.42. (4) Make trimetric drawings, using instruments, with axes chosen to show the objects to best advantage. If dimensions are required, study §17.25.

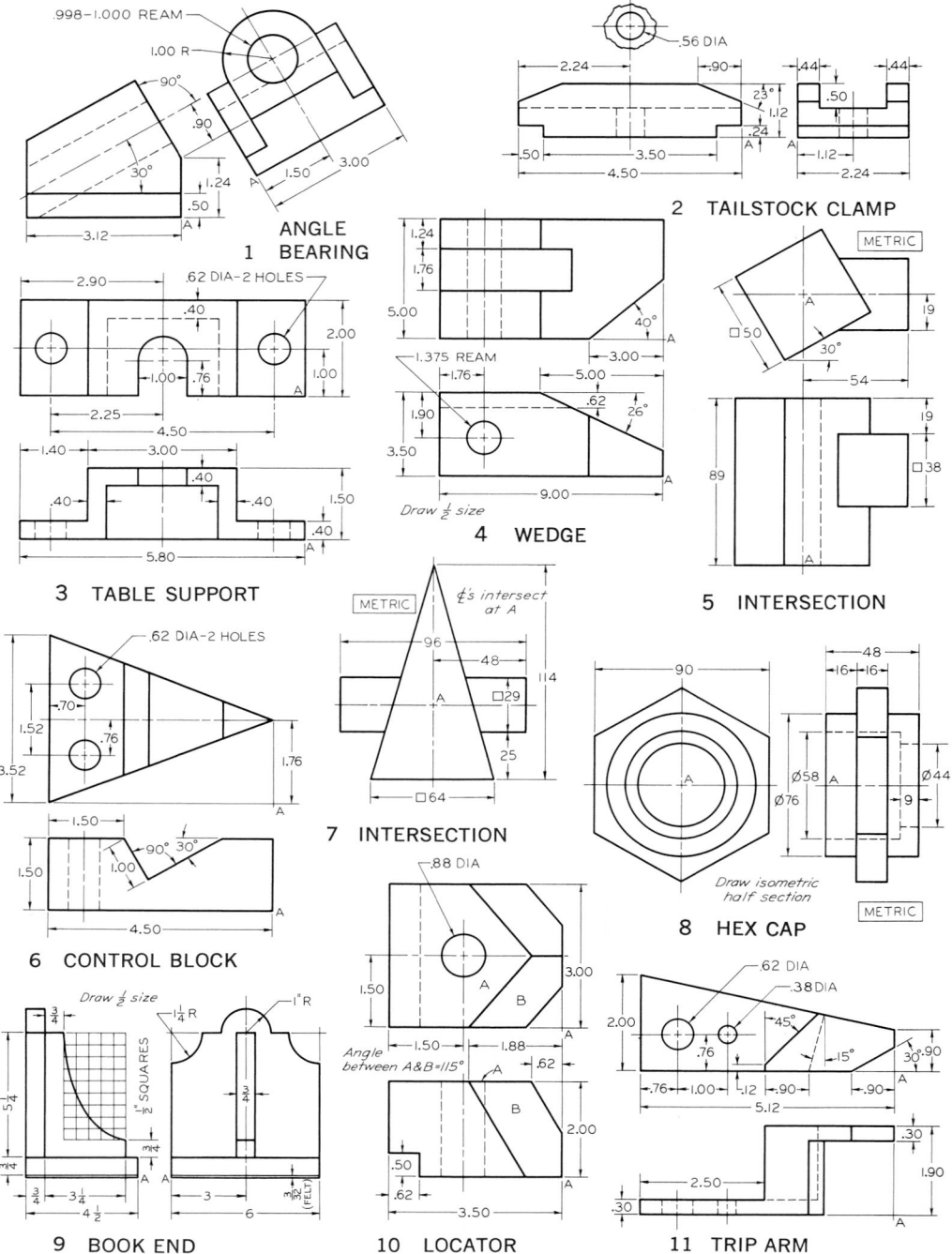

Fig. 17.55 (1) Make freehand isometric sketches. (2) Make isometric drawings with instruments on Layout A–2 or A4–2 (adjusted). (3) Make dimetric drawings with instruments, using Layout A–2 or A4–2 (adjusted), and position assigned from Fig. 17.42. (4) Make trimetric drawings, using instruments, with axes chosen to show the objects to best advantage. If dimensions are required, study §17.25.

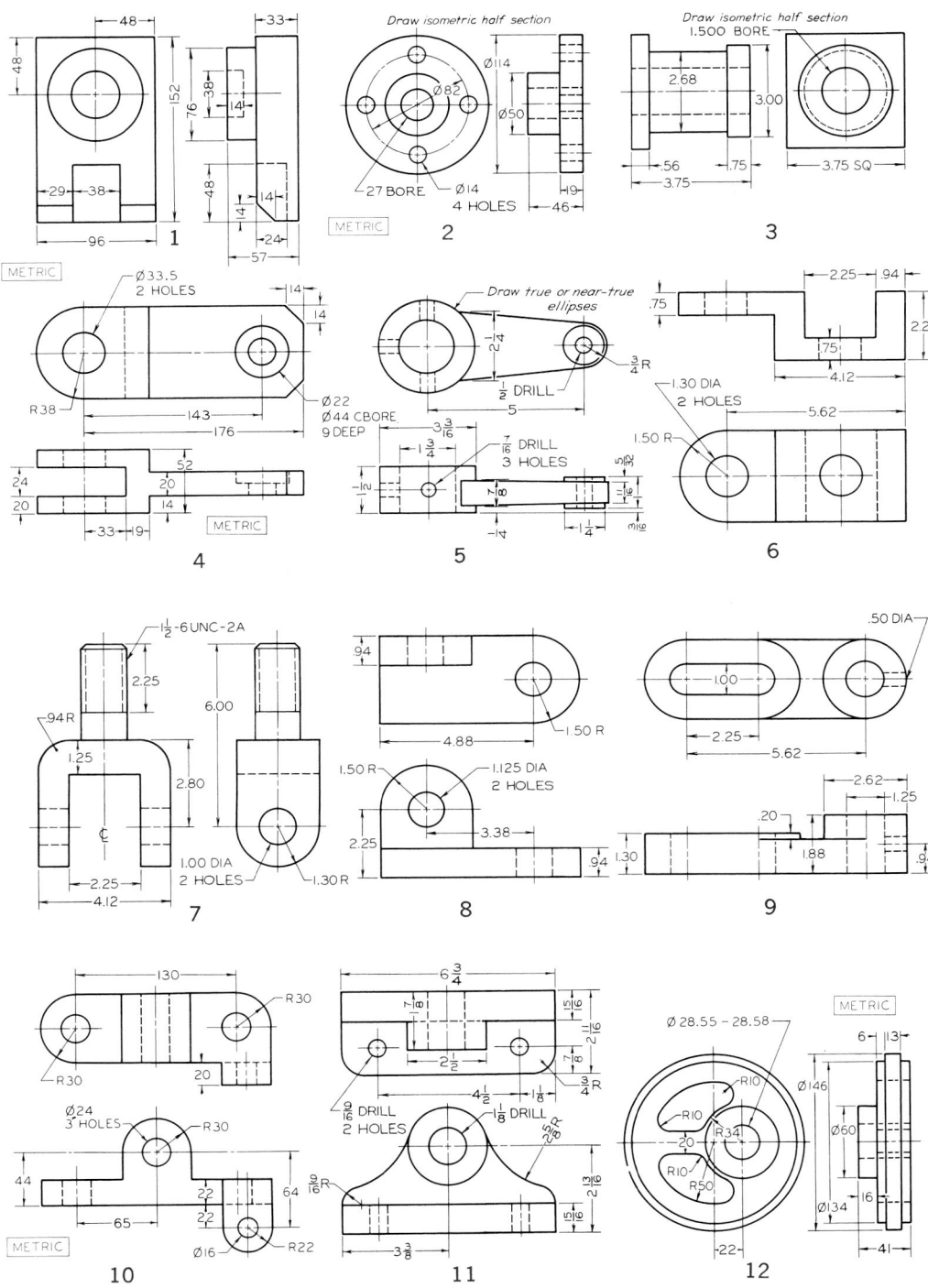

Fig. 17.56 (1) Make isometric freehand sketches. (2) Make isometric drawings with instruments, using Size A or A4 sheet or Size B or A3 sheet, as assigned. (3) Make dimetric drawings with instruments, using Size A or A4 sheet or Size B or A3 sheet, as assigned, and position assigned from Fig. 17.42. (4) Make trimetric drawings, using instruments, with axes chosen to show the objects to best advantage. If dimensions are required, study §17.25.

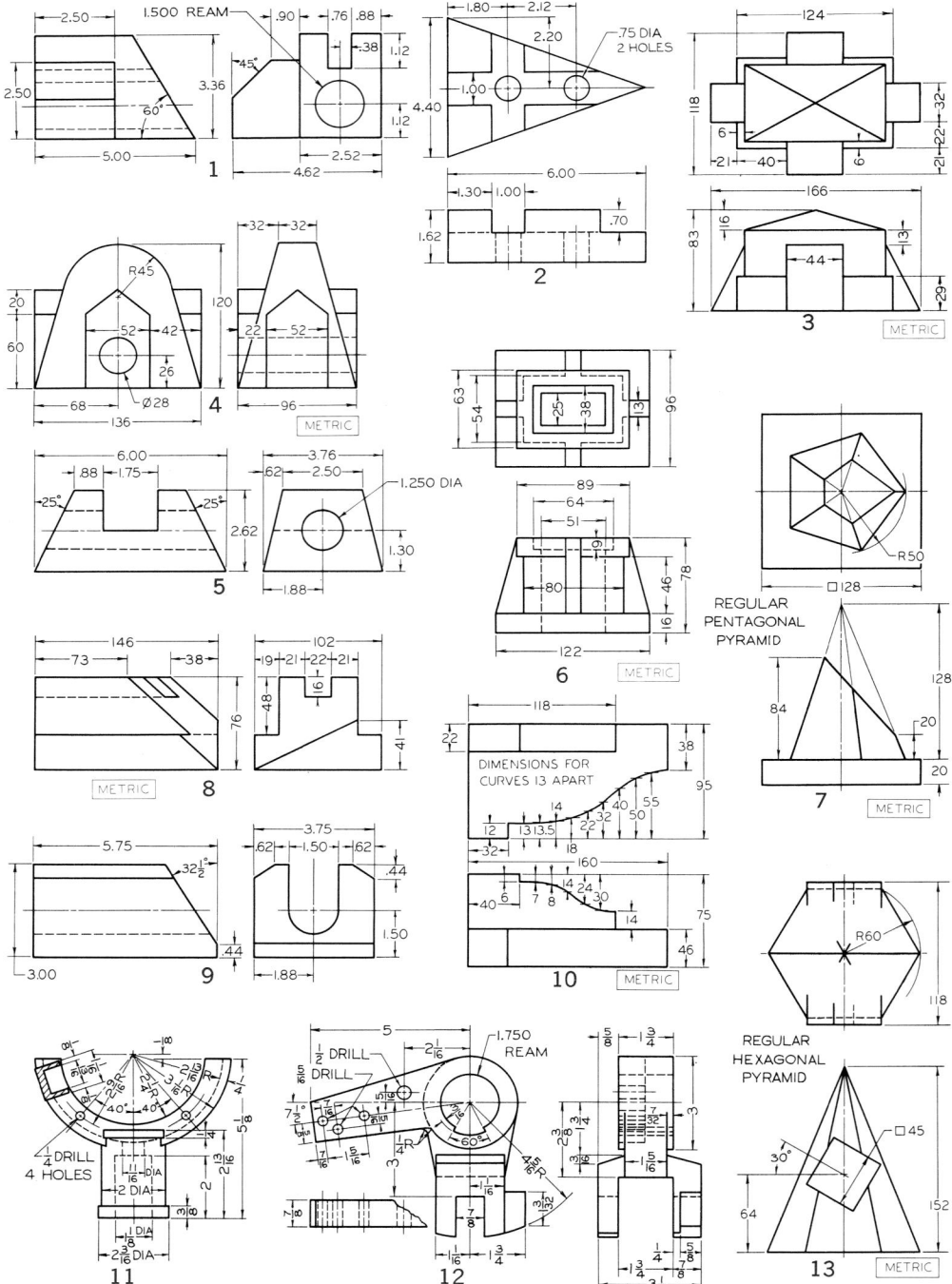

Fig. 17.57 (1) Make isometric freehand sketches. (2) Make isometric drawings with instruments, using Size A or A4 sheet or Size B or A3 sheet, as assigned. (3) Make dimetric drawings with instruments, using Size A or A4 sheet or Size B or A3 sheet, as assigned, and position assigned from Fig. 17.42 (4) Make trimetric drawings, using instruments, with axes chosen to show the objects to best advantage. If dimensions are required, study §17.25.

Oblique
Projection

If the observer is considered to be stationed at an infinite distance from the object, Fig. 17.1 (c), and looking toward the object so that the projectors are parallel to each other and oblique to the plane of projection, the resulting drawing is an *oblique projection*. As a rule, the object is placed with one of its principal faces parallel to the plane of projection. This is equivalent to holding the object in the hand and viewing it approximately as shown in Fig. 6.27.

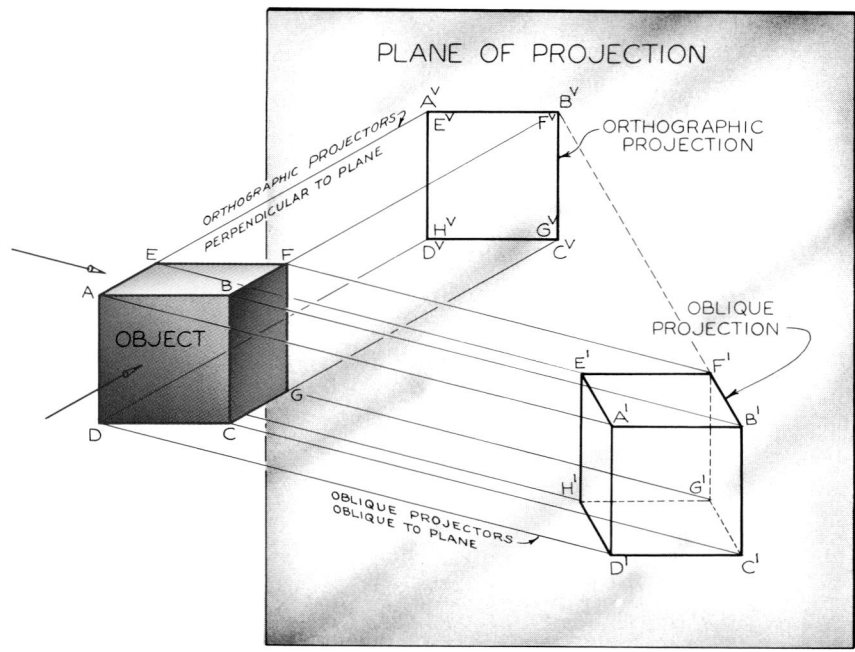

Fig. 18.1   Comparison of Oblique and Orthographic Projections.

18.1 Oblique and Other Projections Compared

A comparison of oblique projection and orthographic projection is shown in Fig. 18.1. The front face A′B′C′D′ in the oblique projection is identical with the front view, or orthographic projection, $A^VB^VC^VD^V$. Thus, if an object is placed with one of its faces parallel to the plane of projection, that face will be projected true size and shape in oblique projection as well as in orthographic or multiview projection. This is the reason why oblique projection is preferable to axonometric projection in representing certain objects pictorially. Note that surfaces of the object that are not parallel to the plane of projection will not project in true size and shape. For example, surface ABFE on the object (a square) projects as a parallelogram A′B′F′E′ in the oblique projection.

In axonometric projection, circles on the object nearly always lie in surfaces inclined to the plane of projection and project as ellipses. In oblique projection, the object may be positioned so that those surfaces are parallel to the plane of projection, in which case the circles will project as true circles, and can be easily drawn with the compass.

A comparison of the oblique and orthographic projections of a cylindrical object is shown in Fig. 18.2. In both cases, the circular shapes project as true circles. Note that although the observer, looking in the direction of the oblique arrow, does see these shapes as ellipses, the drawing, or projection, represents not what is seen but what is projected upon the plane of projection. This curious situation is peculiar to oblique projection.

Observe that the axis AB of the cylinder projects as a point A^VB^V in the orthographic projection, since the line of sight is parallel to AB. But in the oblique projection, the axis projects as a line A′B′. The more nearly the direction of sight approaches the perpendicular with respect to the plane of projection—that is, the larger the angle between the projectors and the plane—the closer the oblique projection moves toward the orthographic projection, and the shorter A′B′ becomes.

18.2 Directions of Projectors

In Fig. 18.3, the projectors make an angle of 45° with the plane of projection; hence, the line CD′, which is perpendicular to the plane, projects true length at C′D′. If the projectors make a greater angle with the plane of projection, the oblique projection is shorter, and if the projectors make a smaller angle with the plane of projection, the oblique projection is longer. Theoretically, CD′ could project in any

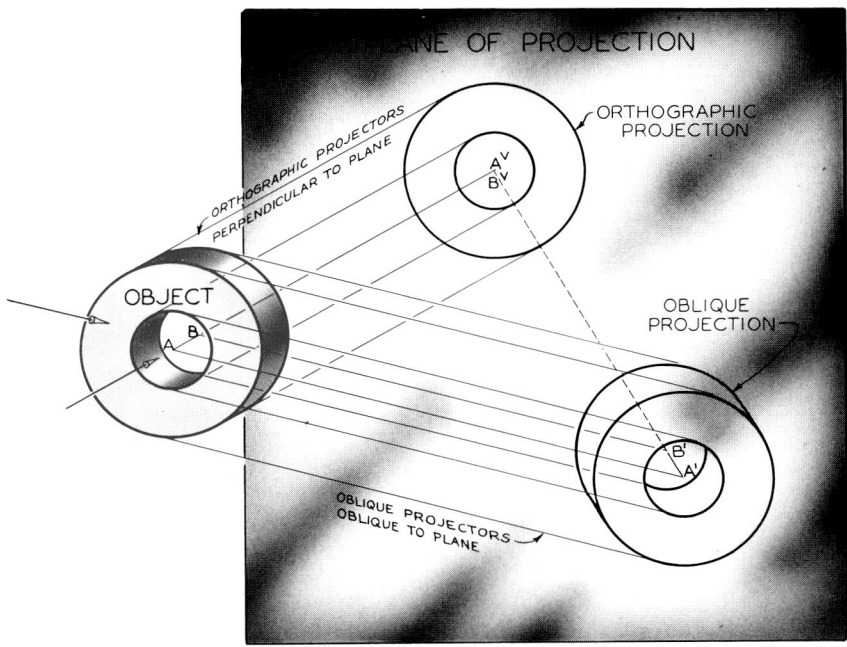

Fig. 18.2   Circles Parallel to Plane of Projection.

length from zero to infinity. However, the line **AB** is parallel to the plane and will project in true length regardless of the angle the projectors make with the plane of projection.

In Fig. 18.1 the lines **AE, BF, CG,** and **DH** are perpendicular to the plane of projection, and project as parallel inclined lines **A'E', B'F', C'G',** and **D'H'** in the oblique projection. These lines on the drawing are called the *receding lines*. As we have seen,

they may be any length, from zero to infinity, depending upon the direction of the line of sight. Our next concern is: What angle do these lines make on paper with respect to horizontal?

In Fig. 18.4, the line **AO** is perpendicular to the plane of projection, and all the projectors make angles of **45°** with it; therefore, all of the oblique projections **BO, CO, DO,** and so on, are equal in length to the line **AO.** It can be seen from the figure that

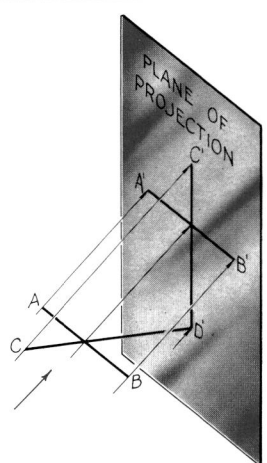

Fig. 18.3   Lengths of Projections.

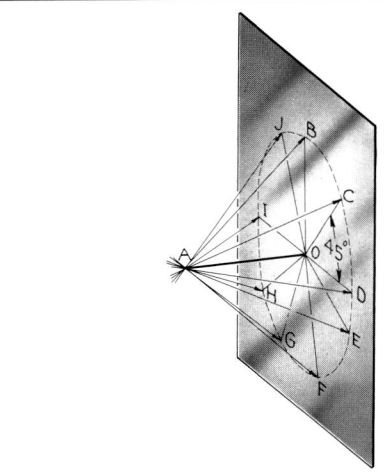

Fig. 18.4   Directions of Projections.

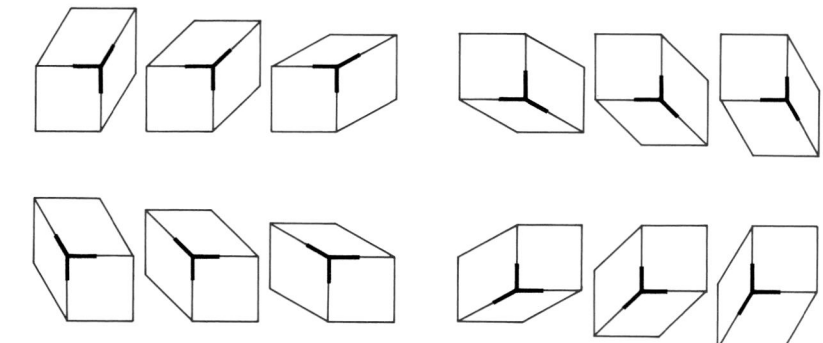

Fig. 18.5 Variation in Direction of Receding Axis.

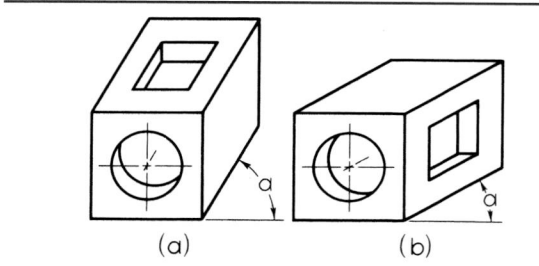

(a)   (b)

Fig. 18.6 Angle of Receding Axis.

18.3 Angles of Receding Lines

The receding lines may be drawn at any convenient angle. Some typical drawings with the receding lines in various directions are shown in Fig. 18.5. The angle that should be used in an oblique drawing depends upon the shape of the object and the location of its significant features. For example, in Fig. 18.6 (a) a large angle was used in order to obtain a better view of the rectangular recess on the top, while at (b) a small angle was chosen to show a similar feature on the side.

18.4 Length of Receding Lines

Since the eye is accustomed to seeing objects with all receding parallel lines appearing to converge, an oblique projection presents an unnatural appearance, with more or less serious distortion depending upon the object shown. For example, the object shown in Fig. 18.7 (a) is a cube, the receding lines being full length, but the receding lines appear to be too long and to diverge toward the rear of the block. A striking example of the unnatural appearance of an oblique drawing when compared with the natural appearance of a perspective is shown in Fig.

the projectors may be selected in any one of an infinite number of directions and yet maintain any desired angle with the plane of projection. It is also evident that the directions of the projections **BO**, **CO**, **DO**, and so on, are independent of the angles the projectors make with the plane of projection. Ordinarily, this inclination of the projection is **45°** (**CO** in the figure), **30°**, or **60°** with horizontal, since these angles may be easily drawn with the triangles.

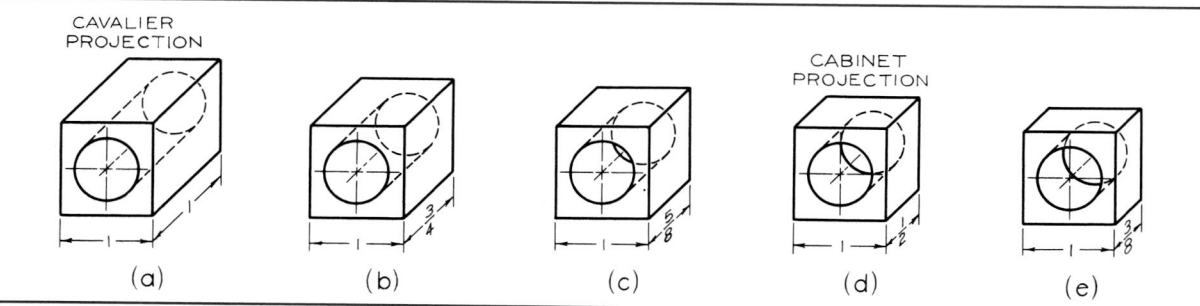

(a)   (b)   (c)   (d)   (e)

Fig. 18.7 Foreshortening of Receding Lines.

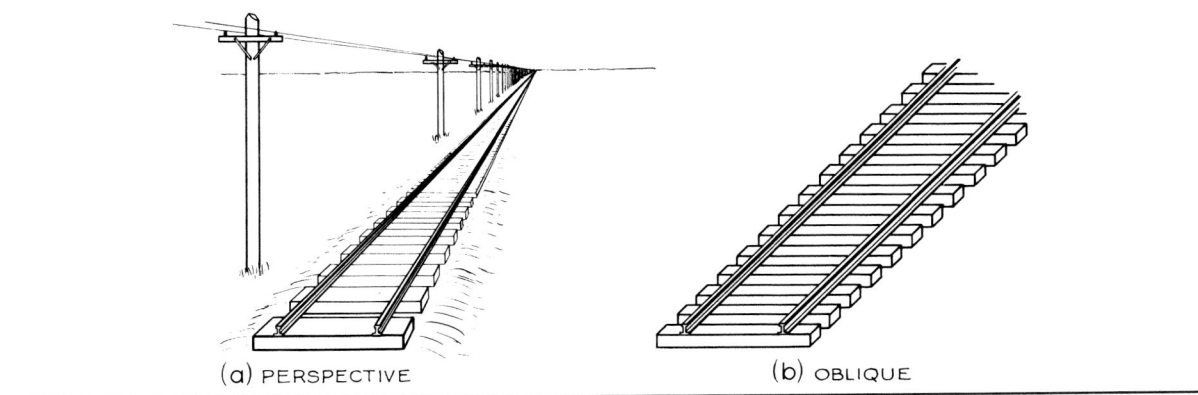

(a) PERSPECTIVE   (b) OBLIQUE

Fig. 18.8   Unnatural Appearance of Oblique Drawing.

18.8. This example points up one of the chief limitations of oblique projection: objects characterized by great length should not be drawn in oblique with the long dimension perpendicular to the plane of projection.

The appearance of distortion may be materially lessened by decreasing the length of the receding lines (remember, we established in §18.2 that they could be any length). In Fig. 18.7 a cube is shown in five oblique drawings with varying degrees of foreshortening of the receding lines. The range of scales chosen is sufficient for almost all problems, and most of the scales are available on the architects', engineers', or metric scales.

When the receding lines are true length—that is, when the projectors make an angle of 45° with the plane of projection—the oblique drawing is called a *cavalier projection*, Fig. 18.7 (a). Cavalier projections originated in the drawing of medieval fortifications and were made upon horizontal planes of projection. On these fortifications the central portion was higher than the rest and it was called *cavalier* because of its dominating and commanding position.

When the receding lines are drawn to half size, as at (d), the drawing is commonly known as a *cabinet projection*. The term is attributed to the early use of this type of oblique drawing in the furniture industries. A comparison of cavalier projection and cabinet projection is shown in Fig. 18.9.

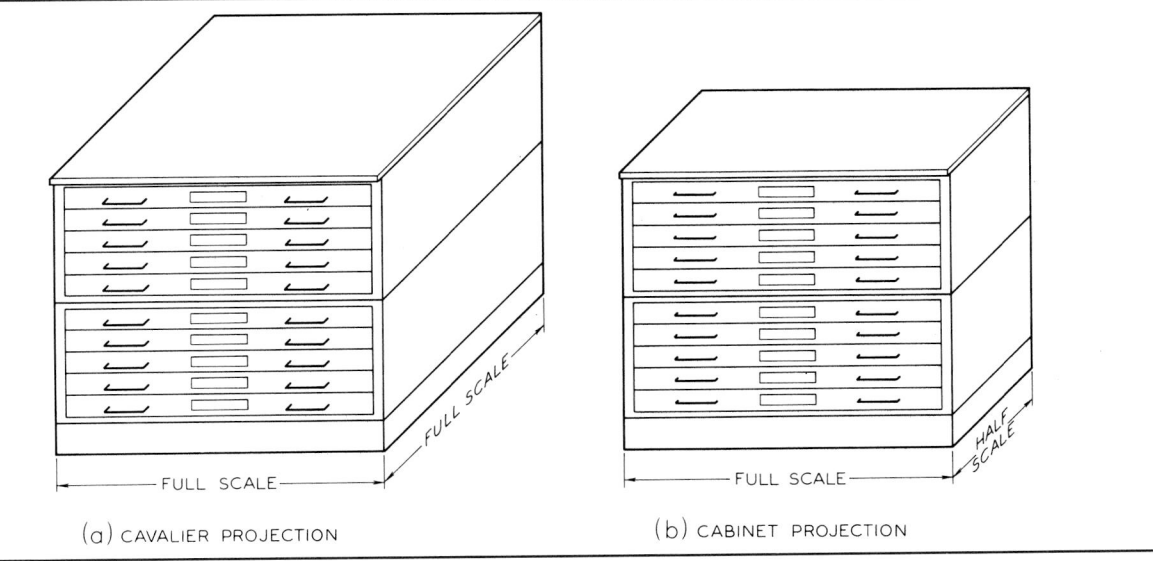

(a) CAVALIER PROJECTION   (b) CABINET PROJECTION

Fig. 18.9   Comparison of Cavalier and Cabinet Projections.

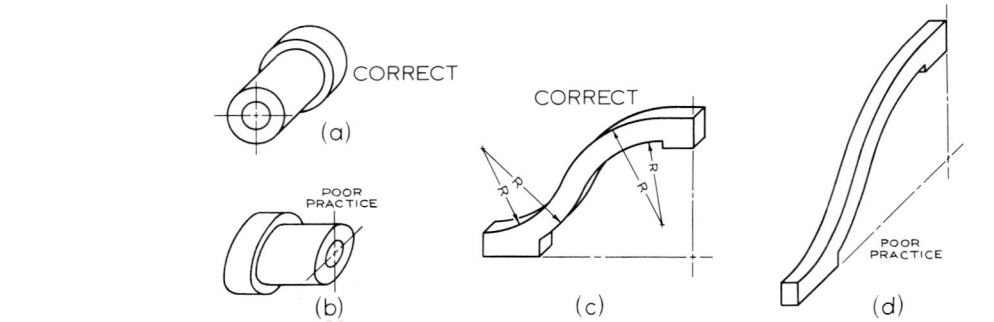

Fig. 18.10   Essential Contours Parallel to Plane of Projection.

18.5 Choice of Position

The face of an object showing the essential contours should generally be placed parallel to the plane of projection, Fig. 18.10. If this is done, distortion will be kept at a minimum and labor reduced. For example, at (a) and (c) the circles and circular arcs are shown in their true shapes and may be quickly

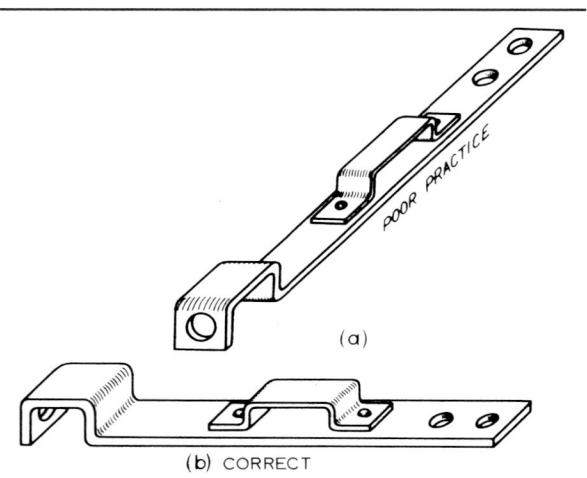

Fig. 18.11   Long Axis Parallel to Plane of Projection.

drawn with the compass, while at (b) and (d) these curves are not shown in their true shapes and must be plotted as free curves or in the form of ellipses.

The longest dimension of an object should generally be placed parallel to the plane of projection, as shown in Fig. 18.11 (b).

18.6 Steps in Oblique Drawing

The steps in drawing a cavalier drawing of a rectangular object are shown in Fig. 18.12. As shown in step I, draw the axes **OX** and **OY** perpendicular to each other and the receding axis **OZ** at any desired angle with horizontal. Upon these axes, construct an enclosing box, using the overall dimensions of the object.

As shown at II, block in the various shapes in detail, and as indicated at III, heavy in all final lines.

Many objects most adaptable to oblique representation are composed of cylindrical shapes built upon axes or center lines. In such cases, the oblique drawing is best constructed upon the projected center lines, as shown in Fig. 18.13. The object is positioned so that the circles shown in the given top view are parallel to the plane of projection and, hence, can be readily drawn with the compass in their true shapes. The general procedure is to draw

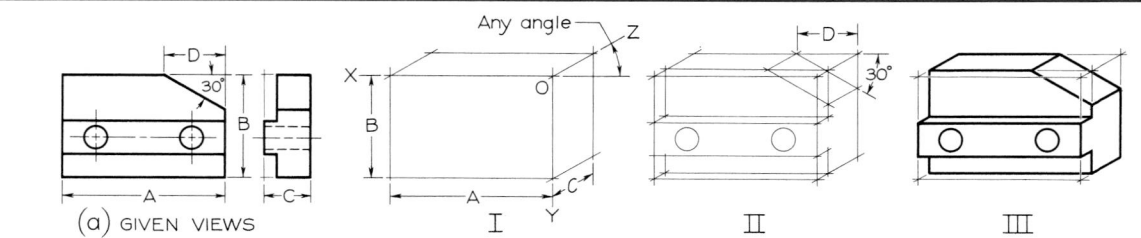

Fig. 18.12   Steps in Oblique Drawing—Box Construction.

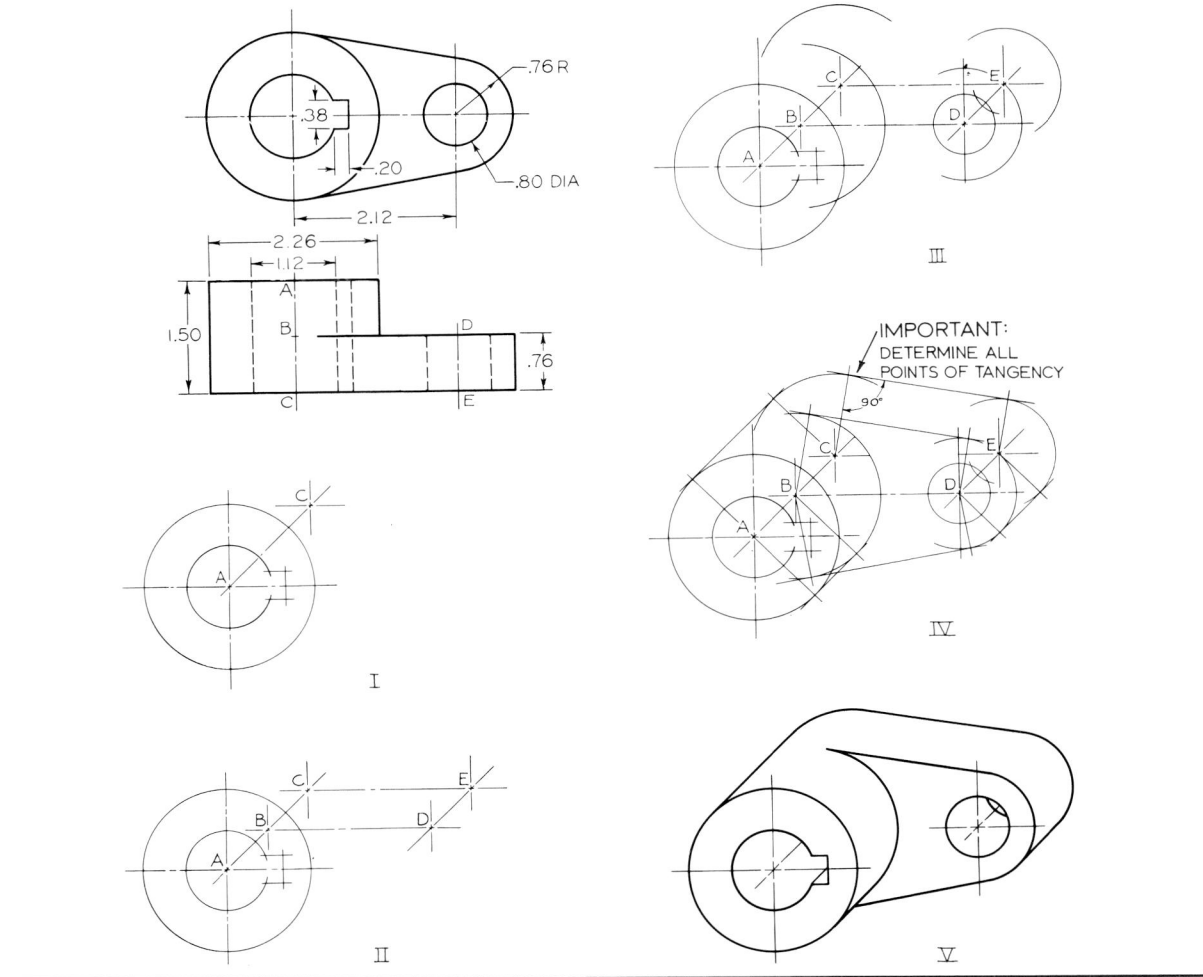

Fig. 18.13   Steps in Oblique Drawing—Skeleton Construction.

the center-line skeleton, as shown in steps I and II, and then to build the drawing on these center lines.

It is very important to construct all points of tangency, as shown in step IV, especially if the drawing is to be inked. For a review of tangencies, see §§5.33–5.41. The final cavalier drawing is shown in step V.

18.7 Four-Center Ellipse

It is not always possible to place an object so that all of its significant contours are parallel to the plane of projection. For example, the object shown in Fig. 18.14 (a) has two sets of circular contours in different

planes, and both cannot be placed parallel to the plane of projection.

In the oblique drawing at (b), the regular four-center method of Fig. 17.24 was used to construct ellipses representing circular curves not parallel to the plane of projection. This method can be used only in cavalier drawing in which case the enclosing parallelogram is equilateral—that is, the receding axis is drawn to full scale. The method is the same as in isometric: erect perpendicular bisectors to the four sides of the parallelogram; their intersections will be centers for the four circular arcs. If the angle of the receding lines is other than 30° with horizontal, as in this case, the centers of the two large arcs will not fall in the corners of the parallelogram.

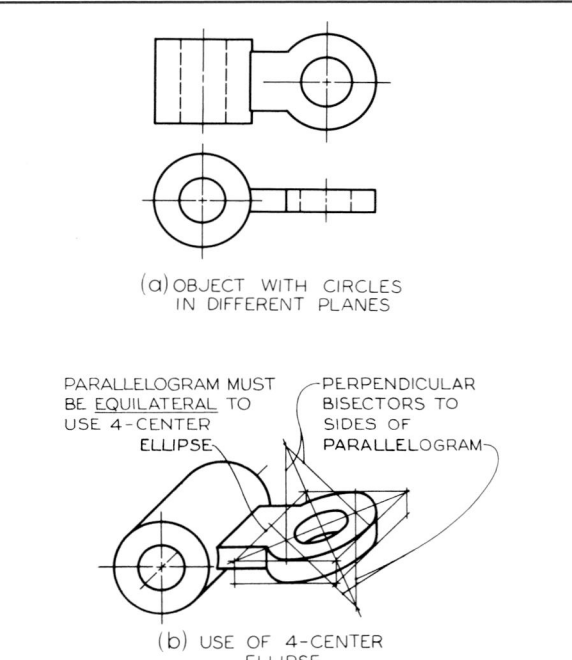

(a) OBJECT WITH CIRCLES
IN DIFFERENT PLANES

PARALLELOGRAM MUST
BE EQUILATERAL TO
USE 4-CENTER
ELLIPSE

PERPENDICULAR
BISECTORS TO
SIDES OF
PARALLELOGRAM

(b) USE OF 4-CENTER
ELLIPSE

Fig. 18.14 Circles and Arcs Not Parallel to Plane of Projection.

The regular four-center method is not convenient in oblique drawing unless the receding lines make 30° with horizontal so that the perpendicular bisectors may be drawn easily with the 30° × 60° triangle and the T-square, parallel rule, or drafting machine without the necessity of first finding the midpoints of the sides. A more convenient method is the alternate four-center ellipse drawn upon the two center lines, as shown in Fig. 18.15. This is the same method as used in isometric, Fig. 17.29, but in oblique drawing it varies slightly in appearance according to the different angles of the receding lines.

First, draw the two center lines. Then, from the center, draw a construction circle equal in diameter to the actual hole or cylinder. The circle will intersect each center line at two points. From the two points on one center line, erect perpendiculars to the other center line, then, from the two points on the other center line, erect perpendiculars to the first center line. From the intersections of the perpendiculars, draw four circular arcs, as shown.

It must be remembered that the four-center ellipse can be inscribed only in an *equilateral* parallelogram; hence, it cannot be used in any oblique drawing in which the receding axis is foreshortened. Its use is limited, therefore, to cavalier drawing.

18.8 Offset Measurements

Circles, circular arcs, and other curved or irregular lines may be drawn by means of offset measurements, as shown in Fig. 18.16. The offsets are first drawn on the multiview drawing of the curve, as shown at (a), and these are transferred to the oblique drawing, as shown at (b). In this case, the receding axis is full scale, and therefore all offsets can be drawn full scale. The four-center ellipse could be used, but the method here is more accurate. The final curve is drawn with the aid of the irregular curve, §2.54.

If the oblique drawing is a cabinet drawing, as shown at (c), or any oblique drawing in which the

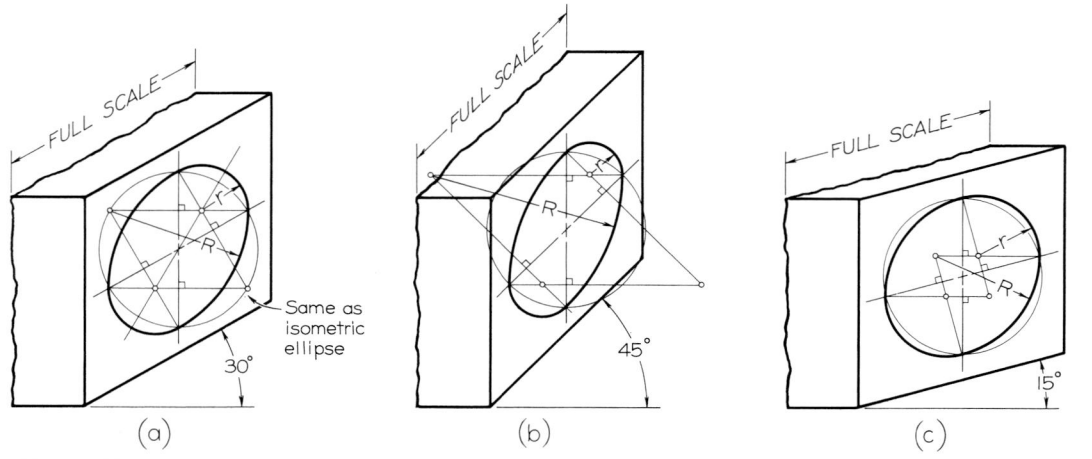

(a)   (b)   (c)

Fig. 18.15 Alternate Four-Center Ellipse.

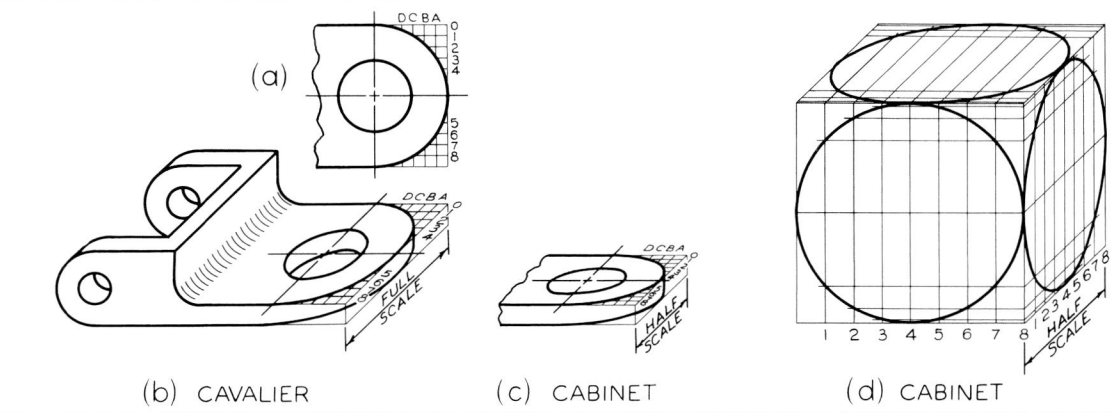

Fig. 18.16 Use of Offset Measurements.

receding axis is drawn to a reduced scale, the offset measurements parallel to the receding axis must be drawn to the same reduced scale. In this case, there is no choice of methods, since the four-center ellipse could not be used. A method of drawing ellipses in a cabinet drawing of a cube is shown at (d).

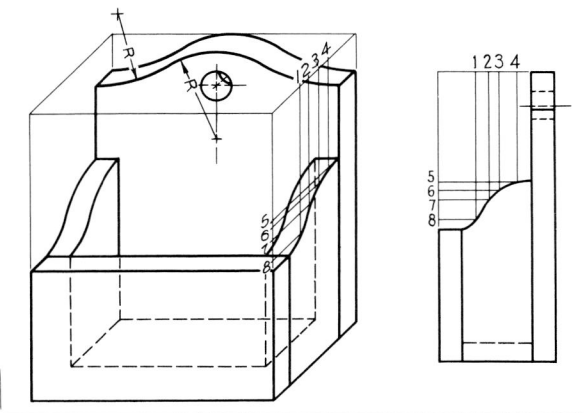

Fig. 18.17 Use of Offset Measurements.

As shown in Fig. 18.17, a free curve may be drawn in oblique by means of offset measurements. This figure also illustrates a case in which hidden lines are used to make the drawing clearer.

The use of offset measurements in drawing an ellipse in a plane inclined to the plane of projection is shown in Fig. 18.18. At (a) a number of parallel lines are drawn to represent imaginary cutting planes. Each plane will cut a rectangular surface between the front end of the cylinder and the inclined surface. These rectangles are drawn in oblique, as shown at (b), and the curve is drawn through corner points, as indicated. The final cavalier drawing is shown at (c).

18.9 Angles in Oblique Projection

If an angle that is specified in degrees lies in a receding plane, it is necessary to convert the angle into linear measurements in order to draw the angle in oblique. For example, in Fig. 18.19 (a) an angle of 30° is given. In order to draw the angle in oblique, we need to know dimensions AB and BC. The dis-

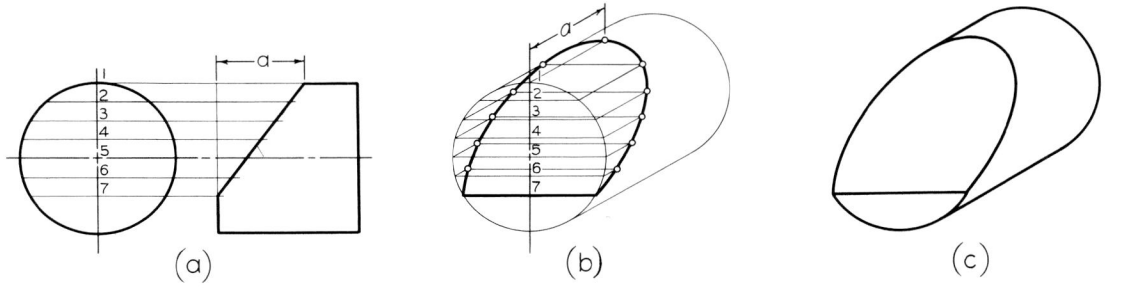

Fig. 18.18 Use of Offset Measurements.

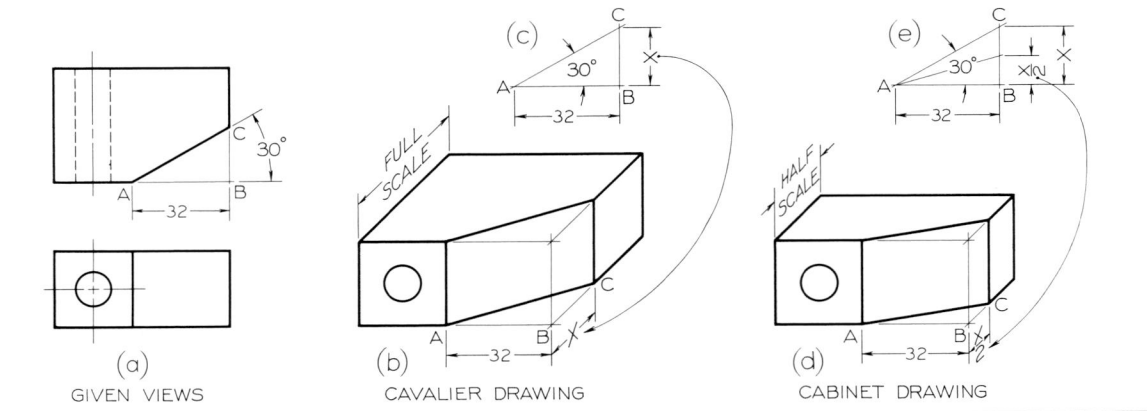

Fig. 18.19   Angles in Oblique Projection.

Fig. 18.20   Oblique Half Section.

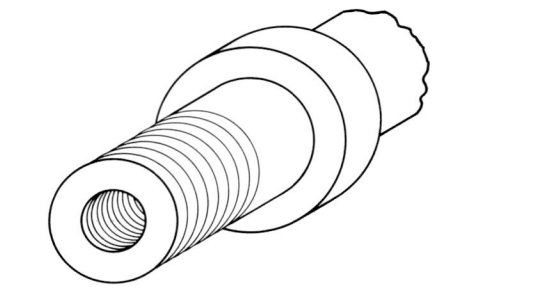

Fig. 18.21   Screw Threads in Oblique.

tance **AB** is given as $1\frac{1}{4}''$ and can be set off directly in the cavalier drawing, as shown at (b). Distance **BC** is not known, but can easily be found by constructing the right triangle **ABC** at (c) from the given dimensions in the top view at (a). The length **BC** is then transferred with the dividers to the cavalier drawing, as shown.

In cabinet drawing, it must be remembered that *all receding dimensions* must be reduced to half size. Thus, in the cabinet drawing at (d), the distance **BC** must be half the side **BC** of the right triangle at (e), as shown.

18.10 Oblique Sections
Sections are often useful in oblique drawing, especially in the representation of interior shapes. An *oblique half section* is shown in Fig. 18.20. Other examples are shown in Figs. 9.41, 9.43 and 9.45. *Oblique full sections*, in which the plane passes completely through the object, are seldom used because

they do not show enough of the exterior shapes. In general, all the types of sections discussed in §17.24 for isometric drawing may be applied equally to oblique drawing.

18.11 Screw Threads in Oblique
Parallel partial circles spaced equal to the symbolic thread pitch, Fig. 15-9 (b), are used to represent the crests only of a screw thread in a cavalier oblique, Fig. 18.21. For cabinet oblique the space would be one-half of the symbolic pitch. If the thread is so positioned to require ellipses, they may be drawn by the four-center method of §18.7.

18.12 Oblique Dimensioning
An oblique drawing may be dimensioned in a similar manner to that described in §17.25 for isometric drawing, as shown in Fig. 18.22. The general principles of dimensioning, as outlined in Chapter 13,

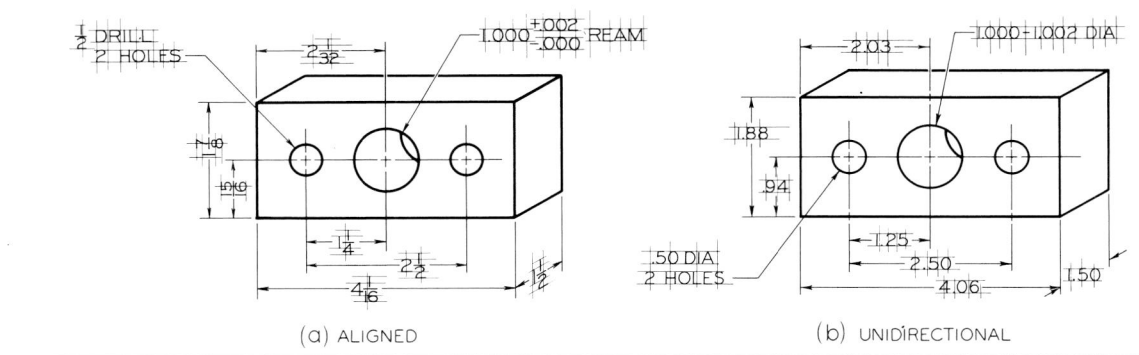

Fig. 18.22   Oblique Dimensioning.

must be followed. As shown in the figure, all dimension lines, extension lines, and arrowheads must lie in the planes of the object to which they apply. The dimension figures also will lie in the plane when the aligned dimensioning system is used as shown at (a). For the unidirectional system of dimensioning, (b), all dimension figures are set horizontal and read from the bottom of the drawing. This simpler system is often used on pictorials for production purposes. *Vertical lettering* should be used for all pictorial dimensioning.

Dimensions should be placed outside the outlines of the drawing except when greater clearness or directness of application results from placing the dimensions directly on the view. The dimensioning methods described apply equally to fractional, decimal, and metric dimensions. For many other examples of oblique dimensioning, see Figs. 7.61, 7.65, 7.66, and others on following pages.

18.13 Oblique Sketching

Methods of sketching in oblique on plain paper are illustrated in Fig. 6.27. Ordinary graph paper is very

useful in oblique sketching, Fig. 6.28. The height and width proportions can be easily controlled by simply counting the squares. A very pleasing depth proportion can be obtained by sketching the receding lines at 45° diagonally through the squares and through half as many squares as the actual depth would indicate.

18.14 Computer Graphics

Using computer graphics, the drafter can easily create an oblique drawing that will provide the desired amount of foreshortening along the receding axis as well as the preferred direction of the axis. CAD programs also permit curves and circular features, which are not parallel to the frontal plane, to be readily shown on the drawing. Oblique sections, §18.10, and repeitive features such as screw threads, §18.11, may be quickly and accurately depicted.

Oblique Projection Problems

A large number of problems to be drawn in oblique—either cavalier or cabinet—are given in Figs. 18.23–18.25. They may be drawn freehand, §6.15, using graph paper or plain drawing paper as assigned by the instructor, or they may be drawn with instruments. In the latter case, all construction lines should be shown on the completed drawing.

Many additional problems suitable for oblique projection will be found in Figs. 7.52–7.54, 10.27–10.29, and 17.54–17.57.

Since many of the problems in this chapter are of a general nature, they can also be solved on most computer graphics systems. If a system is available, the instructor may choose to assign specific problems to be completed by this method.

Additional problems in convenient form for solution are presented in the worksheets at the back of this book. Refer to Drawings 18-1 and 18-2 and accompanying instructions.

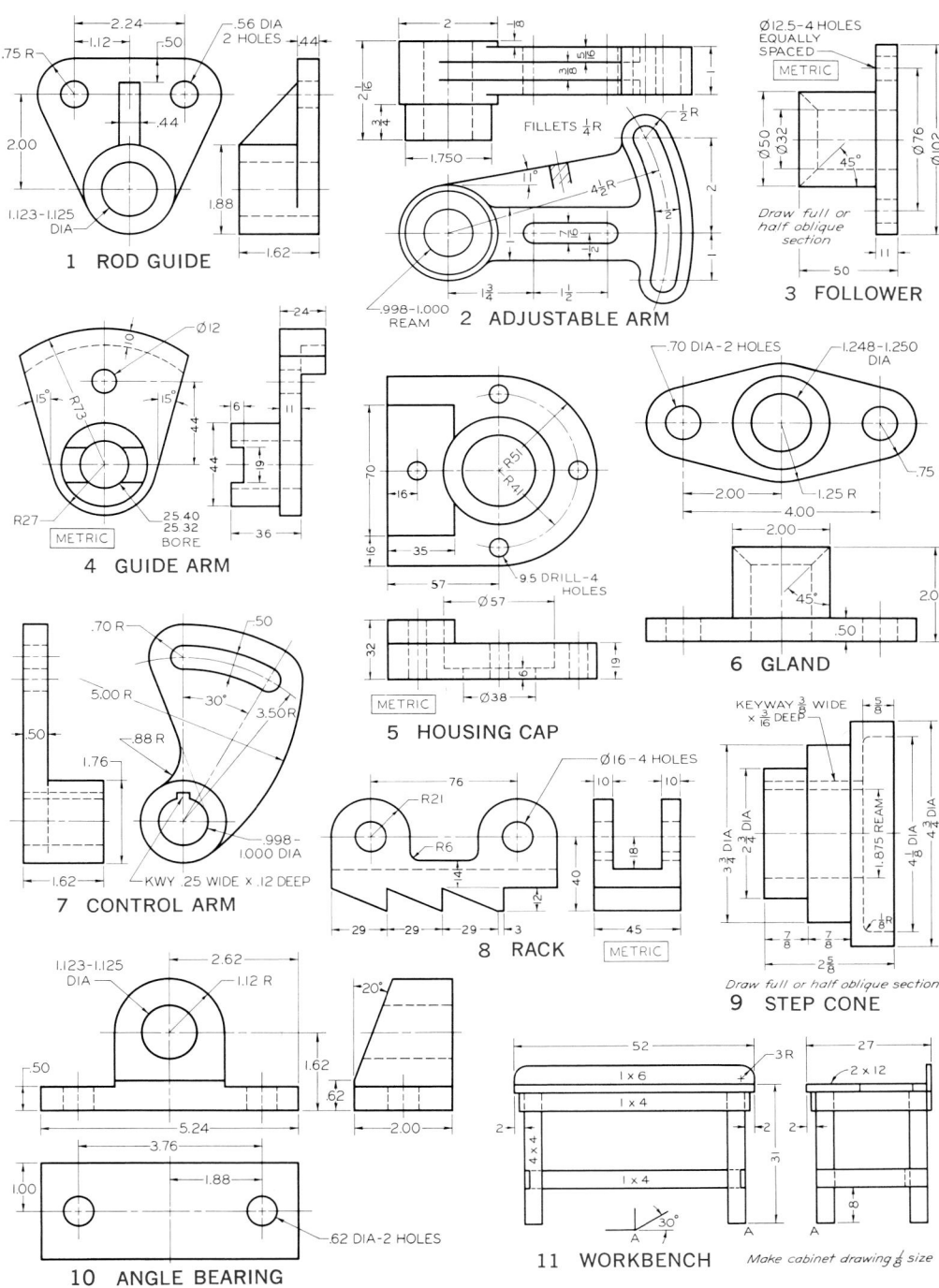

Fig. 18.23 (1) Make freehand oblique sketches. (2) Make oblique drawings with instruments, using Size A or A4 sheet or Size B or A3 sheet, as assigned. If dimensions are required, study §18.12.

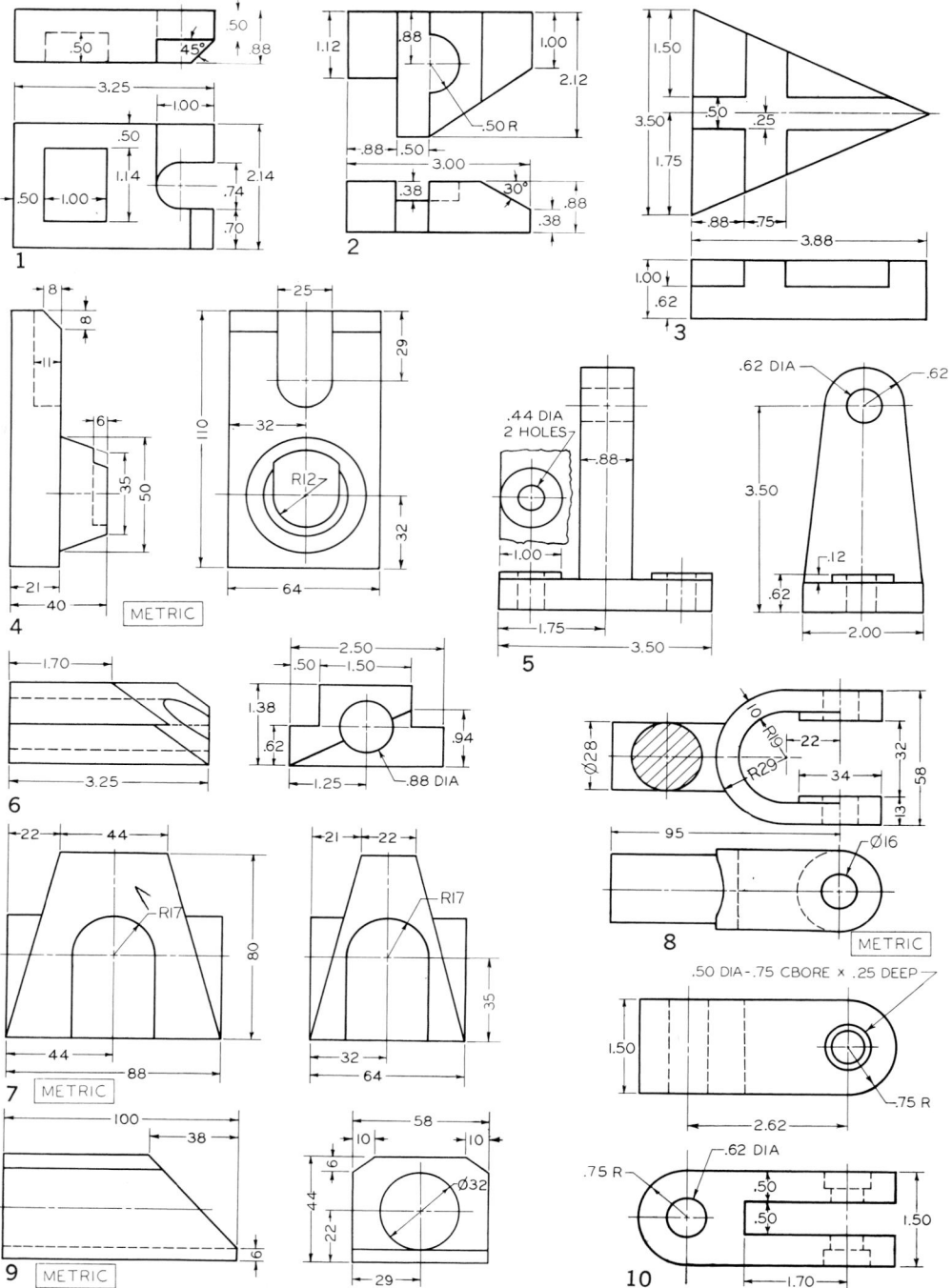

Fig. 18.24   Make oblique drawings with instruments, using Size A or A4 sheet or Size B or A3 sheet, as assigned. If dimensions are required, study §18.12.

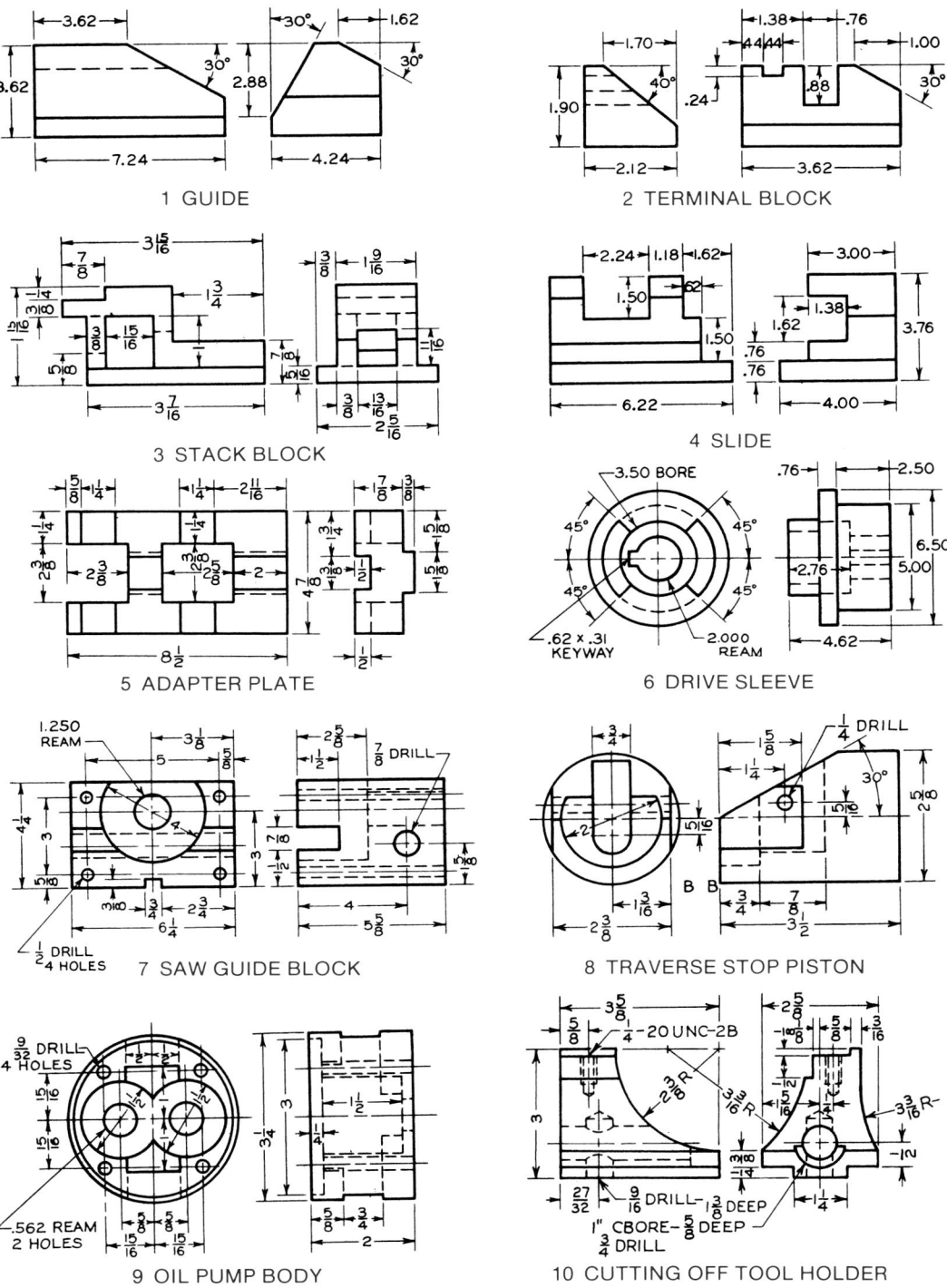

Fig. 18.25 Make oblique drawings with instruments, using Size A or A4 sheet or Size B or A3 sheet, as assigned. If dimensions are required, study §18.12. For additional problems, see Figs 7.50 to 7.53, 10.27 to 10.29, and 17.51 to 17.54.

Points, Lines, and Planes

The science of graphical representation and the solution of spatial relationships of points, lines, and planes by means of projections are the concerns of *descriptive geometry*. The methods of representation of solid objects, wherein the planes of projection of the "glass box" and views of the object were projected upon the planes, have been discussed in §§7.1, 7.2, 7.19–7.25. The elements of the objects—points, lines, and planes—now will be discussed and explained.

During the latter part of the eighteenth century the French mathematician Gaspard Monge developed the principles of descriptive geometry to solve spatial problems related to military structures. In France and Germany, Monge's descriptive geometry soon became a part of national education. In 1816 Claude Crozet introduced descriptive geometry into the curriculum of the United States Military Academy at West Point. In 1821 Crozet published his *Treatise on Descriptive Geometry*, the first important English work on descriptive geometry published in this country. Since then descriptive geometry has been taught in many engineering colleges, and today no study of engineering graphics is considered complete without a detailed study of descriptive geometry.

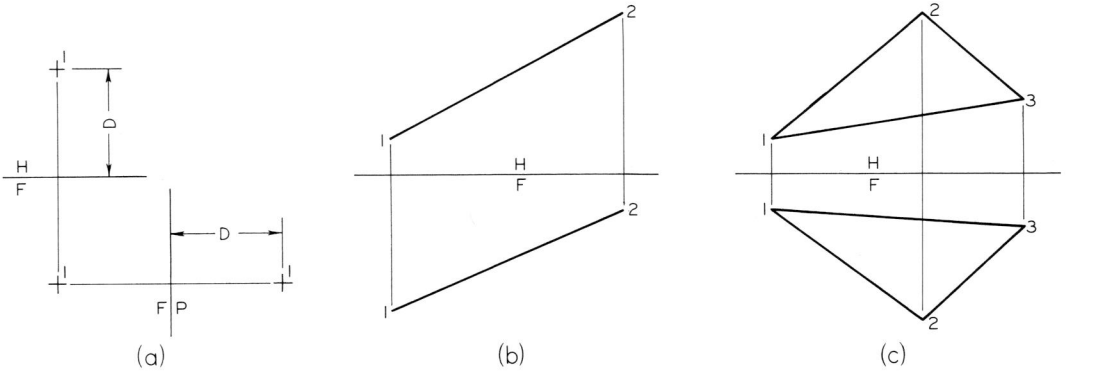

Fig. 19.1   Points, Lines, and Planes Individually Represented.

19.1 Basic Geometric Elements

We start with the representation of a single point. In Fig. 19.1(a) the front, top, and right-side views of point 1 are shown. The projections of the point are indicated by a small cross and the number 1. The folding line H/F is shown between the front and top views, and the folding line F/P is shown between the front and side views. Thus the names of the views are indicated by the letters H, F, and P (for horizontal, frontal, and profile planes of projection). See §7.3. As indicated by the dimensions D, the distance of the top view to the H/F folding line is equal to the distance of the side view to the F/P folding line.

In Fig. 19.1 (b) the front and top views, or projections, of two connected points (line 1–2) are shown. Note the thin projection lines between the views. (Projection lines are usually drawn in pencil as very light construction lines.) At (c) are shown the front and top views of three connected points, or

plane 1–2–3. Again, note the projection lines between the views.

In order to describe an object, lay out a mechanism, or begin the graphical solution of an engineering problem, the relative positions of two or more points must be specified. For example, in Fig. 19.2(a), the relative positions of points 1 and 2 could be described as follows: point 2 is 32 mm to the right of point 1, 12 mm below (or lower than) point 1, and 16 mm behind (or to the rear of) point 1.

When points 1 and 2 are connected, as at (b), observe that the preceding specifications have placed point 2 at a definite distance from point 1 along line 1–2 (more properly line *segment* 1–2, since line 1–2 could be extended).

When point 3 is introduced, as at (c), and is connected to point 2, line 2–3 is established. Since lines 1–2 and 2–3 have point 2 in common, they are *intersecting* lines.

If line 2–3 of Fig. 19.2 (c) is altered to position

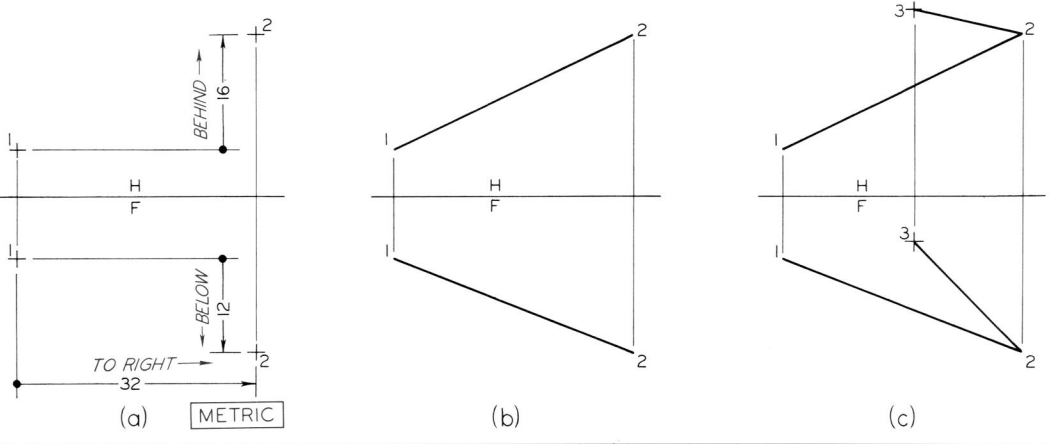

Fig. 19.2   Views of Points and Lines.

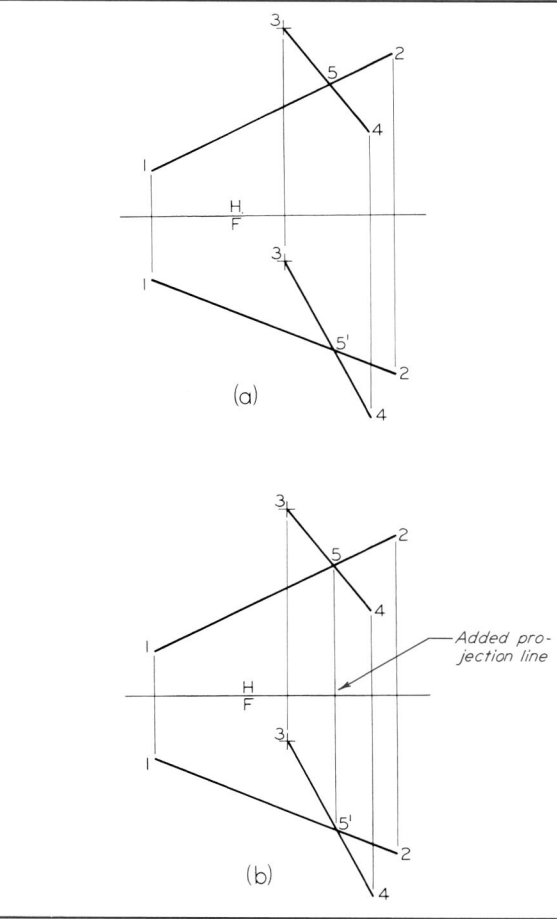

(a)

(b)

Added pro-
jection line

Fig. 19.3 Intersecting Lines.

3–4, Fig. 19.3 (a), do we still have intersecting lines? The possible point in common could only be at **5** in the top view and **5′** in the front view. The question then becomes "Are **5** and **5′** in fact views of the same point?" Since adjacent views of a point must be aligned, §7.2, a vertical projection line is added at (b), and, since this line connects **5** and **5′**, it is evident that lines **1–2** and **3–4** are actually intersecting lines.

In Fig. 19.4 (a) another pair of lines, **1–2** and **3–4** is shown. In this case apparent points of intersection **5** and **5′** are not aligned with the projection lines between views and hence do not represent views of the same point. Therefore, these two lines do not intersect. Such nonintersecting, nonparallel lines are called *skew* lines. The relationship of these skew lines will now be considered in more detail.

Since the lines do not intersect, one must be above the other in the region of point **5**. At (b) this region has been assigned two numbers, **5** and **6**, in the top view, and it is arbitrarily decided that **5** is a point on line **1–2** and **6** is on line **3–4**. These points are then projected to the front view as shown. The direction of sight for the top view is downward toward the front view of the pair of points **5** and **6**. It is observed that point **5** on line **1–2** is *higher* in space or *nearer* to the observer than is point **6** on line **3–4**. Line **1–2** thus passes above line **3–4** close to point **5**.

In like manner, at (c), numbers **7** and **8** are assigned to the apparent crossing point in the front view and projected to the top view, with **8** assigned to line **1–2** and **7** to line **3–4**. It is now noted that

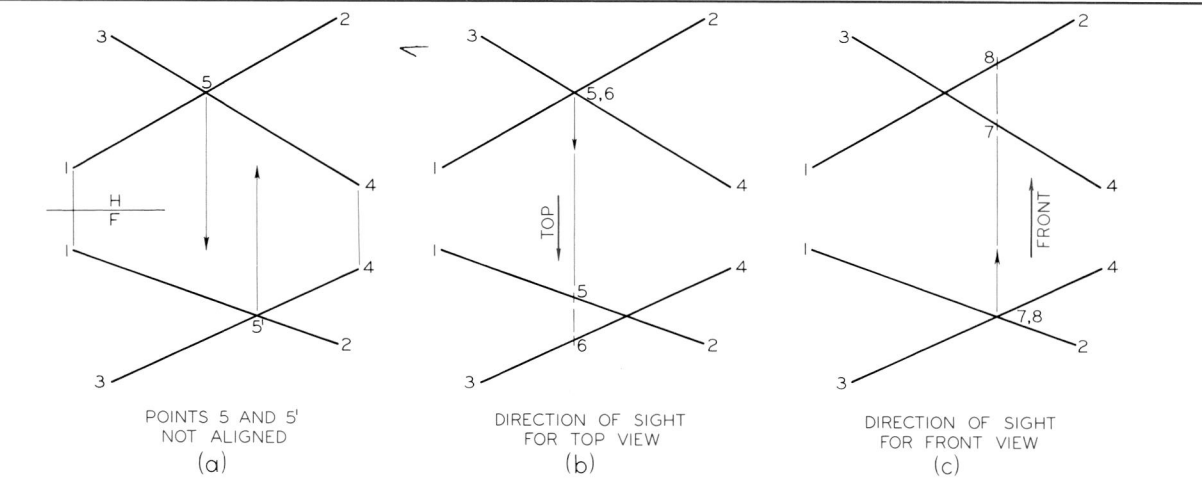

POINTS 5 AND 5′
NOT ALIGNED
(a)

DIRECTION OF SIGHT
FOR TOP VIEW
(b)

DIRECTION OF SIGHT
FOR FRONT VIEW
(c)

Fig. 19.4 Nonintersecting Lines.

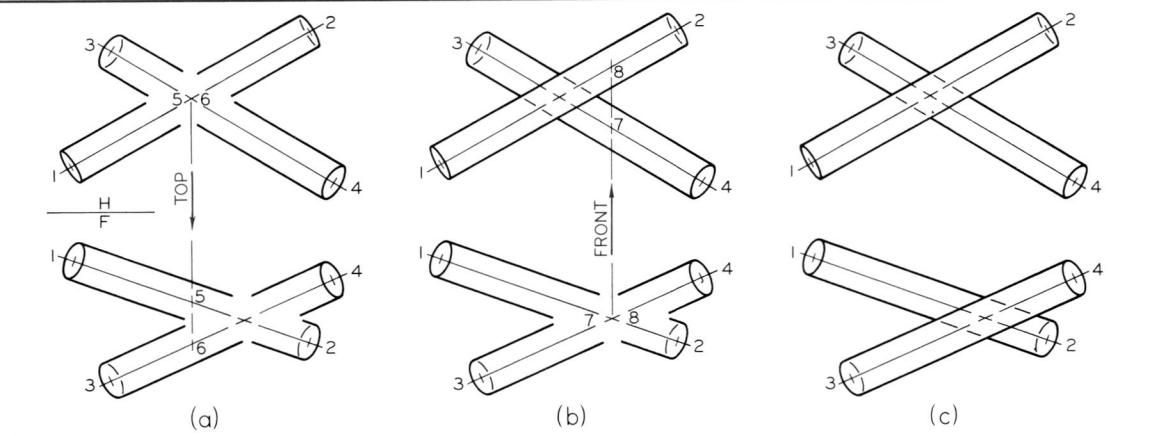

Fig. 19.5 Visibility of Nonintersecting Rods.

the direction of sight for a front view is upward (on the paper) toward the top view. With this in mind, it is observed that point 7, and therefore line 3–4, are *nearer* to the observer (in the front view) than are point 8 and line 1–2. Line 3–4 thus passes in front of line 1–2 in the vicinity of point 7.

The foregoing is useful in determining the visibility of nonintersecting members of a structure or of pipes and tubes, Fig. 19.5. At (a) the views are incomplete because it has not been determined which of the two rods is visible at the apparent crossover in each view. Only the relative positions of the center lines need be investigated. As before, concentration is limited temporarily to the apparent crossing point in the top view, with numbers 5 and 6 assigned to the region. Point 5 is projected to line 1–2 and point 6 to line 3–4 in the front view, where it is discovered that point 5 is above point 6. Line 1–2 therefore passes above line 3–4 and rod 1–2 is visible at the crossover in the top view, as shown at (b). Rod 3–4 is, of course, hidden where it passes below rod 1–2 and is completed accordingly, as shown.

Attention is now directed to the apparent crossing in the front view, Fig. 19.5 (b), and numbers 7 and 8 are assigned. Projected to the top view, these reveal that point 7 on line 3–4 is in front of point 8 on line 1–2. Rod 3–4 is therefore visible in the front view and rod 1–2 is hidden. The completed views are shown at (c).

This discussion has been in terms of front and top views, but it should be realized that the principle applies to *any pair of adjacent views* of the same structure. For example, study Figs. 19.4 and 19.5 with this book held upside down. Observe that the top views become the front views and vice versa but that the visibility is not altered.

Observe finally that *any* two adjacent views, Fig. 19.6, have this same fundamental relationship. The direction of sight for either view is always directed *toward* the adjacent view. Hence at (a), in view B, it is observed that point 5 on edge 1–3 is the nearer of the two assigned points 5 and 6. Thus edge 1–3 is visible in view B, and it follows that edge 2–4 is hidden. Note that this procedure reveals nothing about the visibility of the interior lines of view A of the tetrahedron. At (b), the positions of points 7 and 8 relative to the direction of sight for view A reveal that edge 1–3 is visible in view A.

19.2 Inclined Line and Angle with Plane of Projection

By definition, an inclined line appears true length on the plane to which it is parallel, §7.22. For convenience or precision, inclined lines are frequently classified as *frontal, horizontal,* or *profile,* Fig. 19.7.

Observe that the true-length view of an inclined line is always in an inclined position, while the foreshortened views are in either vertical or horizontal positions.

Note that additional information is available in the true-length views. The true angle between a line and a plane may be measured when the line is true length and the plane is in edge view in a single view. For example, in Fig. 19.7 (a), the horizontal and profile surfaces of the cube appear as lines (in edge

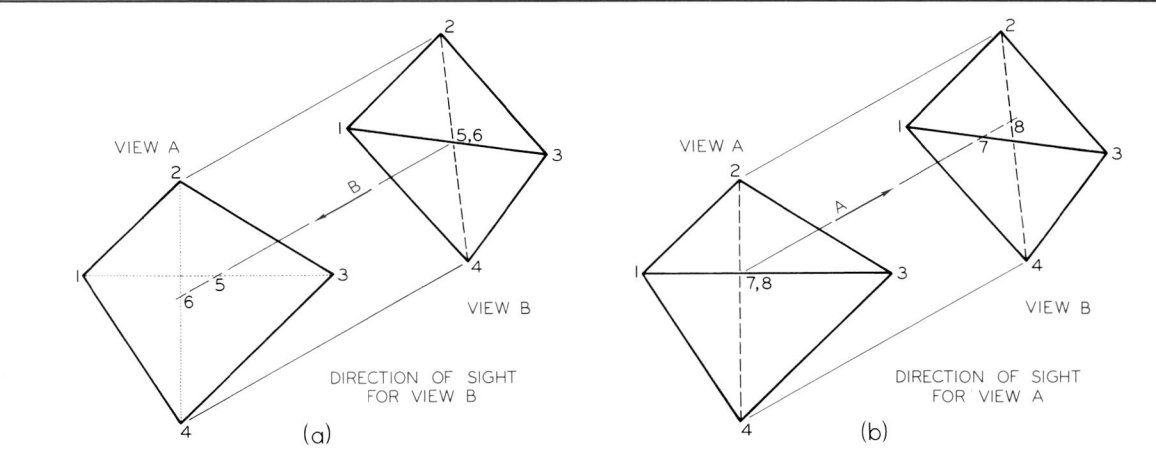

Fig. 19.6 Visibility of Nonintersecting Lines of a Tetrahedron.

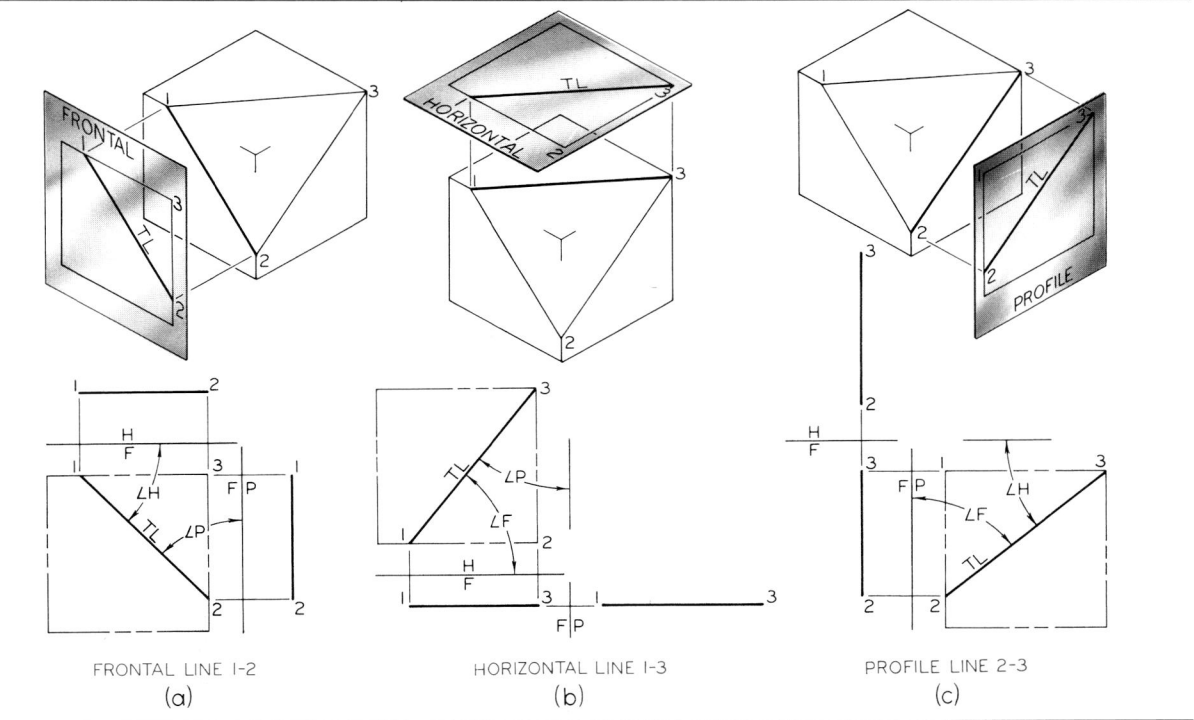

FRONTAL LINE 1-2
(a)

HORIZONTAL LINE 1-3
(b)

PROFILE LINE 2-3
(c)

Fig. 19.7 Frontal, Horizontal, and Profile Lines.

view) in the front view, where edge 1–2 is true length. Thus the angles between edge 1–2 and the horizontal plane (∠H) and between edge 1–2 and the profile plane (∠P) may be measured in the front view. Similarly, ∠F and ∠P for edge 1–3 are measured in the top view, Fig. 19.7 (b), while ∠F and ∠H for edge 2–3 appear in the side view at (c).

19.3 True Length of Oblique Line and Angle with Plane of Projection

By definition, an oblique line does not appear true length in any principal view—front, top, or side, §7.24. It follows that the angles formed with the planes of projection also cannot be measured in the principal views.

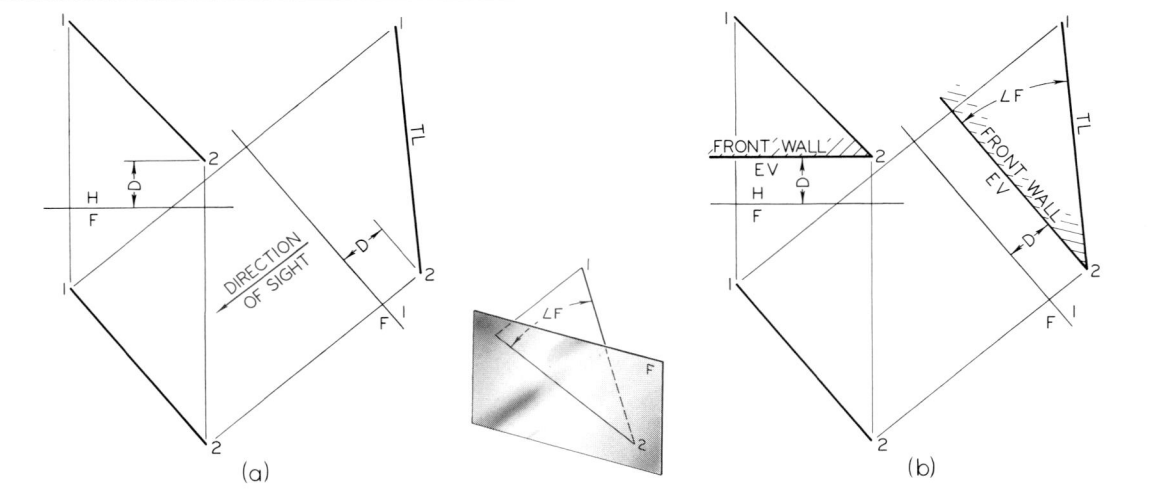

Fig. 19.8   True Length of Line and Angle with Frontal Plane (∠**F**).

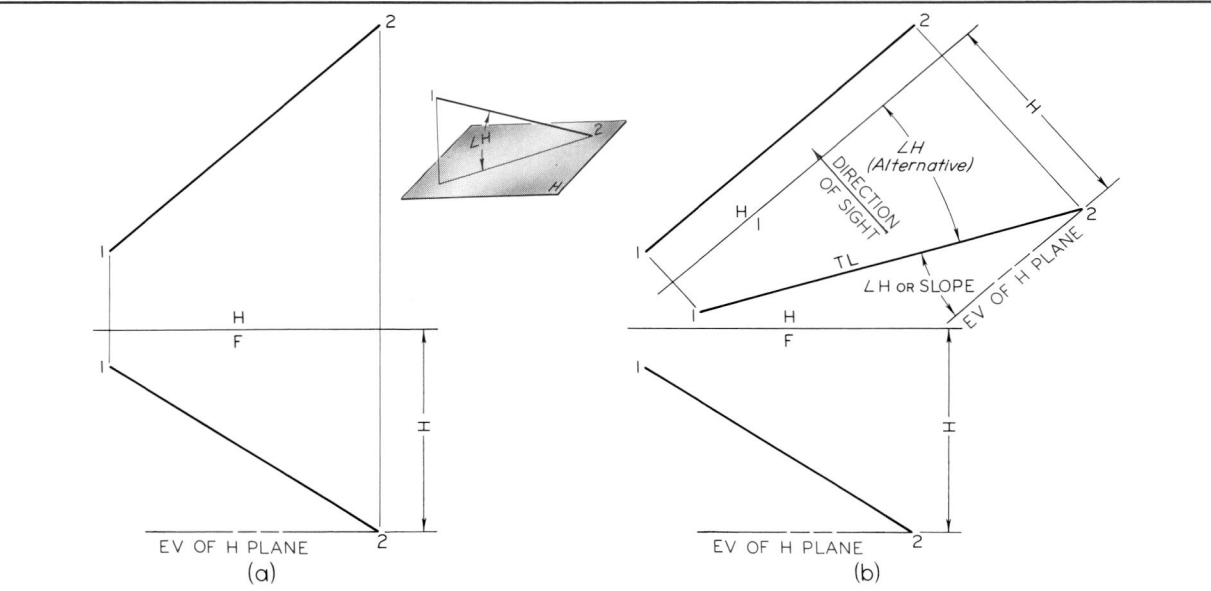

Fig. 19.9   True Length and Slope (∠**H**) of Line.

In §10.18, the true length (**TL**) of hip rafter **1–2** was obtained by assuming a direction of sight perpendicular to the front view of rafter **1–2** and constructing a depth auxiliary view. In Fig. 19.8 (a) this construction is repeated with the remainder of the roof omitted. At (b) a portion of the front wall of the building has been added, passing through point **2**. Note that, because every point of the wall is at distance **D** from the folding line **H/F** in the top view, all points of the wall are at this same distance **D** from folding line **F/1** in the auxiliary view. The entire wall

thus appears as a line (in edge view) in these views. Since line **1–2** appears true length in auxiliary view 1, the angle between line **1–2** and the edge view of the front wall, ∠**F**, can be measured.

In civil engineering, mining, and geology the most important principal plane is the horizontal plane because a map (of a relatively small area) is a horizontal projection and thus corresponds to a top view. The angle between a line, such as the center line of a highway, and a horizontal plane is a very important factor in the engineering description of

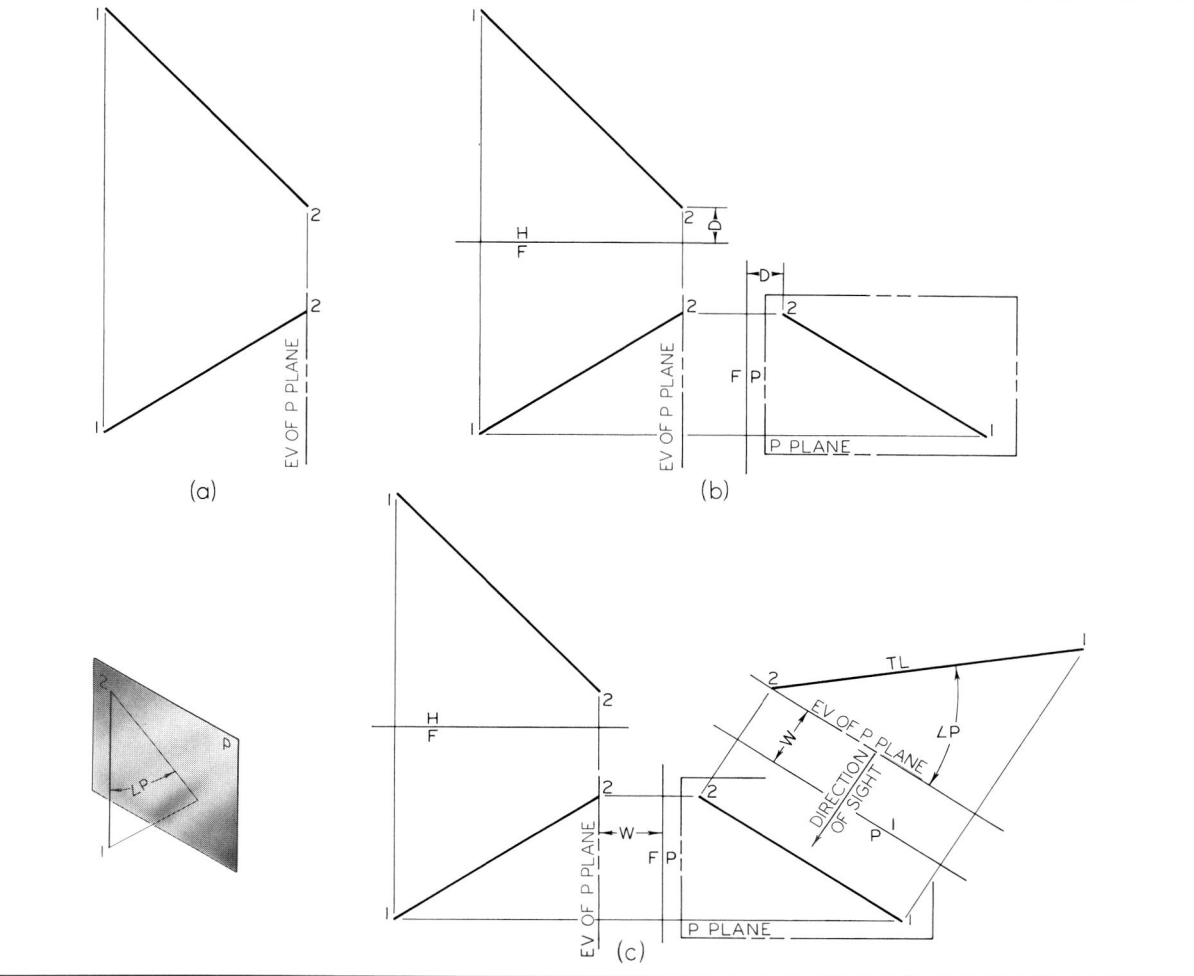

Fig. 19.10   True Length and Angle with Profile Plane (∠P).

the highway. If the angle (∠H) is measured in degrees, it is sometimes called the *slope* of the highway. More commonly it is measured by the ratio between the horizontal and vertical displacements and is called the *grade*. See §19.5.

To measure the slope (∠H) of line 1–2 in Fig. 19.9 (a), a view must be obtained in which line 1–2 appears true length and a horizontal plane appears in edge view. Any horizontal plane appears in edge view in the front view (parallel to the H/F folding line). Thus every point of a particular horizontal plane is at distance H (height) from H/F and any height auxiliary view, §10.8, will show the horizontal plane in edge view. At (b) a direction of sight perpendicular to the top view is chosen to obtain a true-length view of line 1–2. The resulting auxiliary view then shows the slope of line 1–2.

The observant student has probably noted that the angle could just as well be measured with respect to folding line H/1 in the auxiliary view. There is actually no need to introduce a special horizontal plane, providing the working space is suitable, since the H/F and H/1 folding lines represent edge views of the horizontal plane in the front view and in any height auxiliary view.

To obtain ∠P of line 1–2 in Fig. 19.10 (a), a view must be obtained in which line 1–2 appears true length and a profile plane appears in edge view.

At (b) side view P is constructed, which shows line 1–2 as it appears projected on a profile plane. At (c) the direction of sight is established perpendicular to the side view of line 1–2. The resulting auxiliary view shows a true-length view of line 1–2 and any profile plane in edge view and parallel to

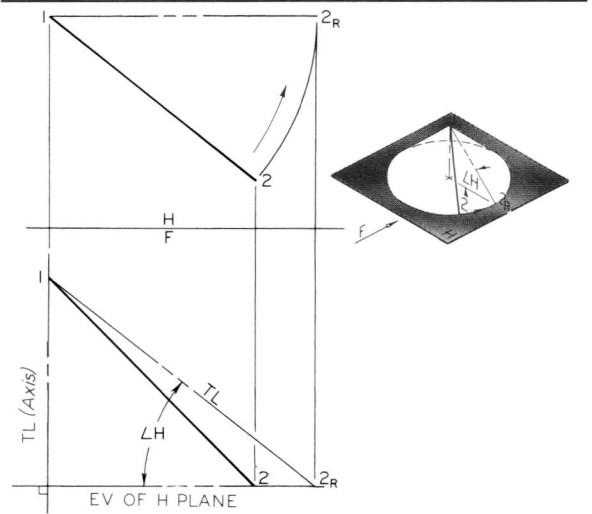

Fig. 19.11 True Length and Angle with Horizontal Plane by Revolution.

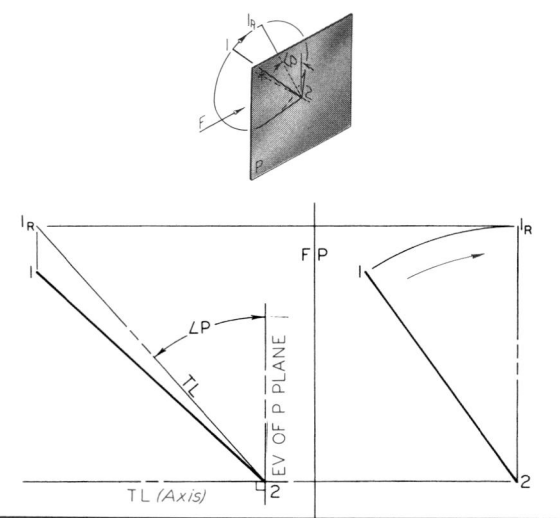

Fig. 19.12 True Length and Angle with Profile Plane by Revolution.

folding line P/1. The ∠P may then be measured with respect to the edge view of the profile plane, as indicated.

In summary, note that each of the angles ∠F, ∠H (slope), and ∠P is obtained by a separate auxiliary view, Figs. 19.8, 19.9, and 19.10, respectively; that is, an auxiliary view can show no more than one of these angles of an oblique line.

19.4 True Length and Angle with Plane of Projection by Revolution

The true length of a line may also be obtained by revolution, §11.10. In Fig. 19.11 a vertical axis of revolution is employed to find the true length of line 1–2. The path of revolution lies in a horizontal plane seen edgewise in the front view, as indicated. As the line revolves, its angle with horizontal (∠H) remains unchanged in space. Thus, in the true-length position this angle may be measured as indicated.

Note that as line 1–2 revolves about the chosen axis, its angles with the other two planes, frontal and profile, continually change. Hence this particular revolution, Fig. 19.11, cannot be used to find the angle the line forms with these planes.

The axis of revolution in Fig. 19.12 is perpendicular to a profile plane. Hence the angle revealed at the true-length position is ∠P.

To determine ∠F for line 1–2, it is necessary to establish the axis of revolution perpendicular to a frontal plane, Fig. 19.13. In practice, it is not necessary to show the axis of revolution, since the re-

maining construction makes the position of the axis obvious. Note that a separate revolution is needed for each angle of an oblique line with a projection plane.

19.5 Bearing and Grade

The position of a line in space, as is often found in geology, mining, and navigation, is described by its *bearing* and *grade* or by its bearing and slope. The

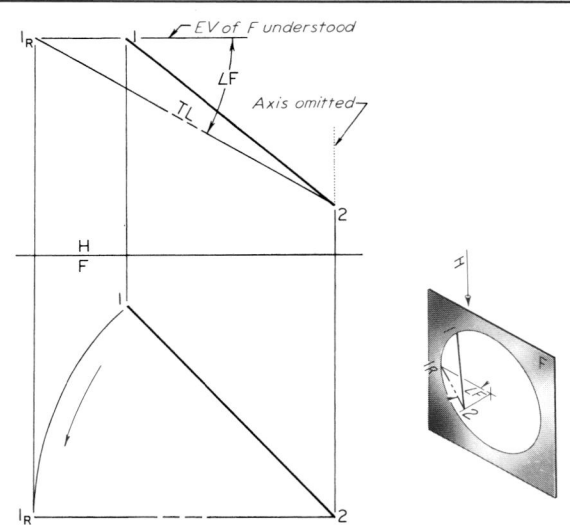

Fig. 19.13 True Length and Angle with Frontal Plane by Revolution.

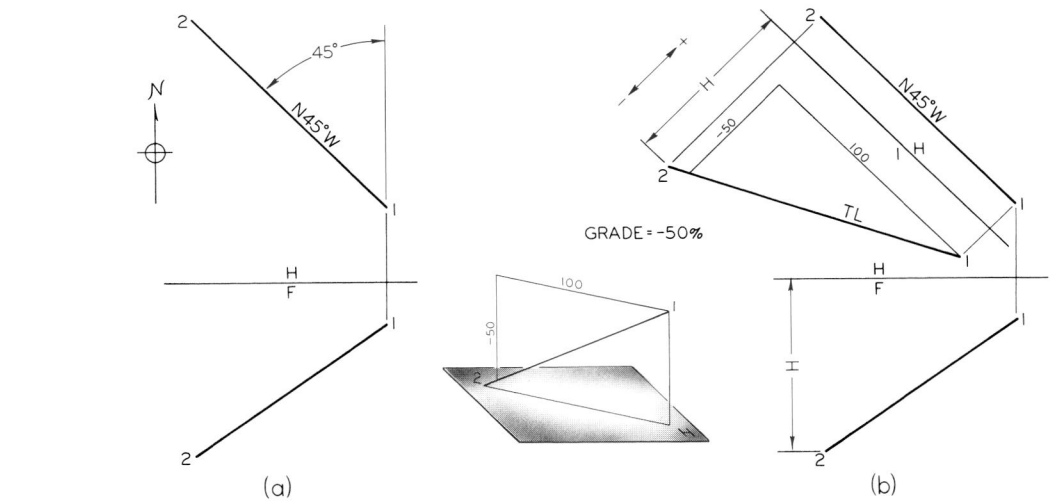

Fig. 19.14   Bearing and Percent Grade.

bearing of a line is the direction of a line on a map or horizontal projection. Since for practical purposes a limited area of the earth's surface may be considered a horizontal plane, a map is a top view of the area. Thus the bearing of a line is measured in degrees with respect to north or south in the *top view* of the line, Fig. 19.14 (a).

It is customary to consider north as being toward the top of the map unless information to the contrary is given. Hence the small symbol showing the directions of north, east, south, and west is not usually needed. These are the directions assumed in the absence of the symbol. Note that the bearing indicated, N 45° W, is that of line 1–2 (from 1 toward 2). The conventional practice is to give either the abbreviation for north or south first, chosen so that the angle is less than 90°, and then the angle, followed by the abbreviation for east or west, as appropriate. For example: N 45° W, as shown in the figure.*

At (b) a true-length auxiliary view is added, projected from the top view. As discussed in §19.3 this is the auxiliary view appropriate for measuring the slope of line 1–2 or ∠H. However, in this case another method, known as *grade*, is used to measure the inclination. The grade is the ratio of the vertical displacement (rise) to the horizonal displacement (run) expressed as a percentage.

A construction line horizontal in space (parallel to H/1) is drawn through a point of the line—point 1 in this example. Along this horizontal line 100 units of any appropriate scale are set off. In this

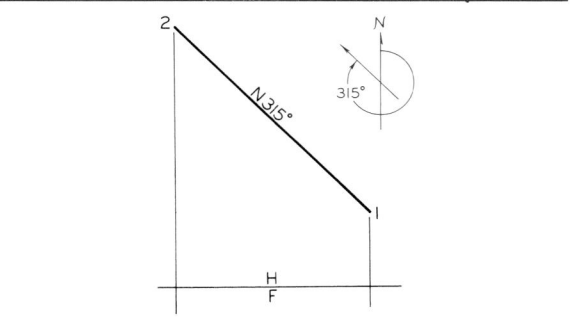

Fig. 19.15   Azimuth Bearing.

instance the 1/20 scale was used. At the 100th division a line is drawn perpendicular to the folding line H/1 and extended to intersect line 1–2 as shown. The length of this line, as measured by the previously used scale, becomes a numerical description of the inclination of line 1–2 expressed as −50%,* because

$$\frac{-50 \text{ units vertically}}{100 \text{ units horizontally}} \times 100 = -50\%\dagger$$

This is the *percent grade*, or simply the *grade*, of line 1–2.

Another means of describing the bearing of a line is by its *azimuth* bearing, Fig. 19.15. Here the total

*Special cases are "Due north," "Due south," "Due east," and "Due west."

*It is common practice to designate a vertical distance as positive or negative according to whether it is measured upward or downward, respectively.
†The student familiar with trigonometry will recognize the ratio 50:100 as the *tangent* of ∠H.

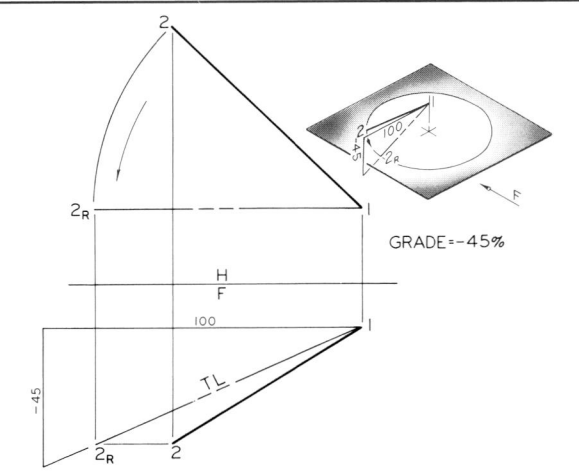

Fig. 19.16 Grade by Revolution.

clockwise angle from the base direction, usually north, is given. Line **1–2** here has the same direction as line **1–2** of Fig. 19.14 (point **1** toward **2**) so that the clockwise angle is 360° − 45° or 315°. If it is understood by all concerned that north is the base direction, the **N** may be omitted. Thus it is common for an aircraft pilot to describe his or her flight direction as "a course of 315°." On a drawing or map, however, it is best to retain the **N** to avoid possible confusion.

Grade may also be obtained by revolution. In Fig. 19.16, since the top view is revolved, the axis of revolution (not shown) projects as a point coincident with the top view of point **1**. Hence the axis is vertical, and point **2** moves horizontally to the front view to **2ᵣ**. In the true-length position, the grade of − 45% can be measured as shown.

19.6 Point View of Line

If a direction of sight for a view is parallel to a true-length view of a line, that line will appear as a point in the resulting view. See §7.15. In Fig. 19.17 (a) the vertical line **1–2** appears as a point in the top view, since a vertical line is true length in any height view.

At (b) line **3–4** appears true length in the front view. A direction of sight is chosen, as indicated by arrow **1**, parallel to the true-length view. The resulting auxiliary view **1** is a point view, since all points of line **3–4** are the same distance **D** from the folding lines.

In Fig. 19.17 (c) auxiliary view **1** is necessary to show line **5–6** in true length. Direction of sight **2** is then introduced parallel to the true-length view. The resulting view **2**, which is a secondary auxiliary view, shows the point view of line **5–6**, §10.19.

Figure 19.17 (c) illustrates an important use of point views: finding the shortest distance from a point to a line. Since the shortest distance is measured along a perpendicular from the point to the line, the perpendicular will appear true length when the given line appears in point view. Observe point **7** in the illustration. An even more important use of the point view of a line is in obtaining an edge view of plane, §§10.11 and 19.9.

19.7 Representation of Planes

We have discussed planes as surfaces of objects, §7.15, bounded by straight lines or curves. Planes can be established or represented even more simply, Fig. 19.18, by intersecting lines, (a), parallel lines, (b), three points not in a straight line, (c), or a line and a point not on the line, (d). Careful study

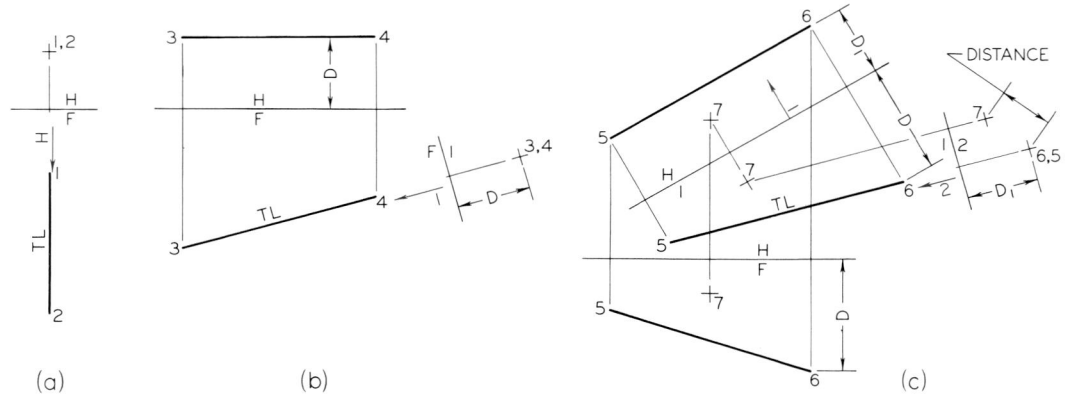

(a)   (b)   (c)

Fig. 19.17 Point View of Line.

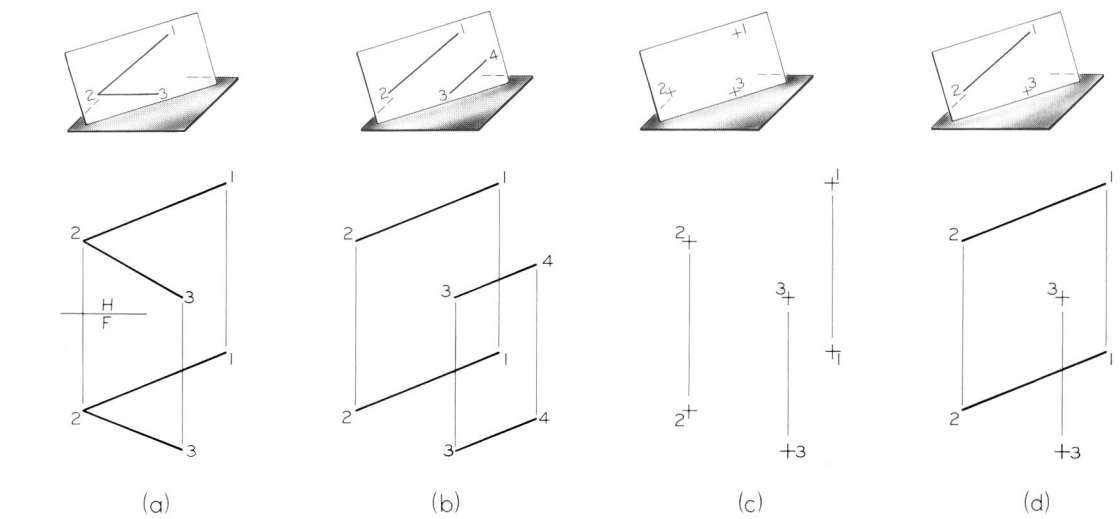

Fig. 19.18   Representation of a Plane.

of Fig. 19.18 will reveal that the same plane 1–2–3 is represented in all four examples. One method can be converted to another by adding or deleting appropriate lines without changing the position of the plane. Most problem solutions involving planes require adding lines at one stage or another, so that in practice the plane, regardless of its original representation, is in the end represented by intersecting lines.

19.8 Points and Lines in Planes

One formal definition of a plane is that it is a surface such that a straight line joining any two points of the surface lies in the surface. It follows that two straight lines in the same plane must intersect, unless the lines are parallel. These concepts are used constantly in working with points and lines in planes.

Figure 19.19 (a) shows a typical elementary problem of this nature. The top view of a line 4–5 is given. The problem is to find the front view of line 4–5 that lies in plane 1–2–3. Since lines 4–5 and 1–2 are obviously not parallel, they must intersect at point 6 as shown at (b). Point 6 is then located by projecting vertically to the front view of line 1–2. Line 4–5 extended (top view) intersects line 2–3 at 7, which is projected to line 2–3 in the front view. Line segment 4–5 in the front view then lies along a construction line through points 6 and 7, and

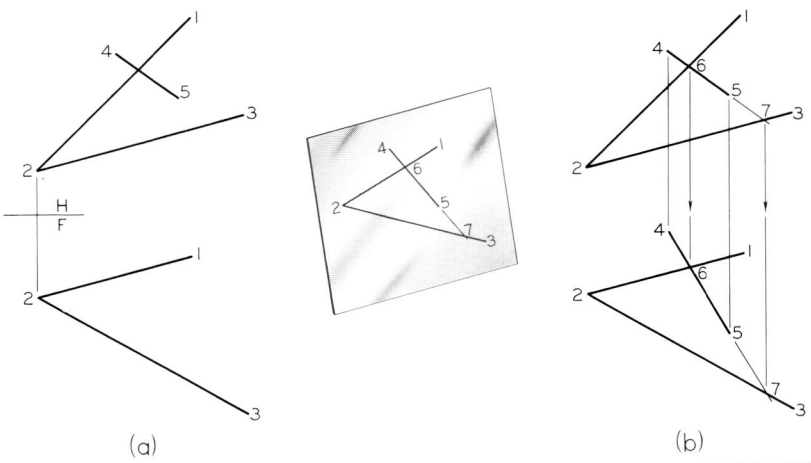

Fig. 19.19   Straight Line in a Plane.

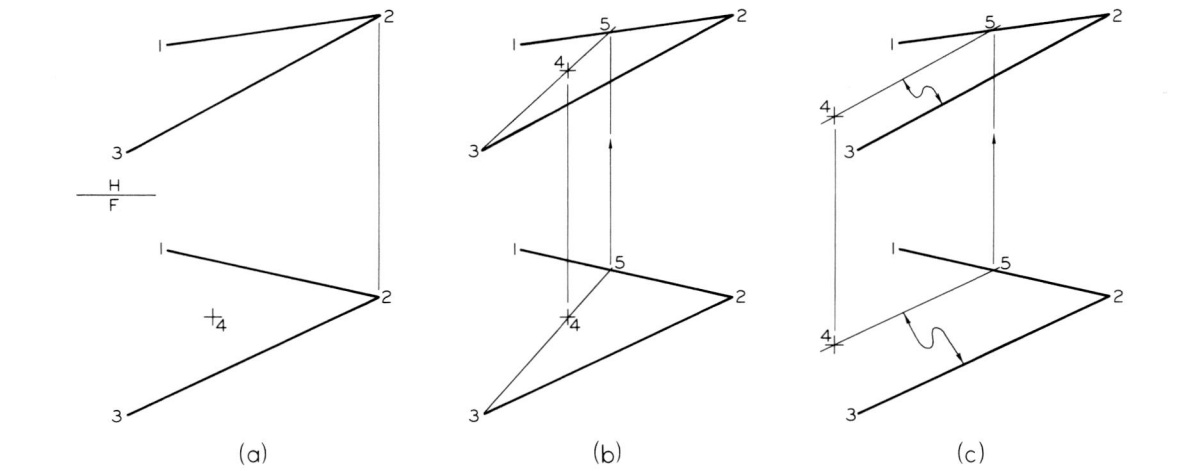

Fig. 19.20 Point in a Plane.

points 4 and 5 are established by projection from the top view as shown.

A point may be placed in a plane by locating it on a line known to be in the plane. In Fig. 19.20 (a) we are given the front view of a point 4 in plane 1–2–3 and desire to find the top view. At (b) a line is introduced through points 3 and 4 and, when extended, intersects line 1–2 at point 5. Point 5 is projected to the top view, establishing line 3–5 in that view. Point 4 is then projected from the front view to the top view of line 3–5. Theoretically, any line could be drawn through point 4 to solve this problem. However, lines approaching parallel to the projection lines between views should be avoided as they may lead to significantly inaccurate results.

A different solution of a similar problem—using the principle of parallelism*—is shown in Fig. 19.20 (c). Here lines drawn through point 1 or point 3 and given point 4 lead to inconvenient intersections. If a line is drawn through point 4 in the front view parallel to line 2–3 and intersecting line 1–2 at point 5 as shown, it will not intersect line 2–3. Therefore, according to the principles stated at the beginning of this section, the line must be parallel to line 2–3. Thus, after intersection point 5 is projected to the top view, the new line through point 5 is drawn parallel to the top view of line 2–3, and point 4 is projected to it to complete the top view. Use of this parallelism principle requires minimum construction.

*Parallelism is discussed in more detail in Chapter 20.

Another example of locating a point on a plane is shown in Fig. 19.21. Here it is desired to locate in plane 1–2–3 a point P that is 10 mm above point 2 and 12 mm behind point 3.

At (a) a horizontal line 10 mm above (higher than) point 2 is added to the front view of plane 1–2–3. Its intersection points 4 and 5 with lines 1–2 and 2–3 are projected to the top view as shown. Any point along line 4–5 lies in plane 1–2–3 and is 10 mm above point 2. Line 4–5 is said to be the *locus* of such points.

At (b) a frontal line 12 mm behind (to the rear of) point 3 is added to the top view of the plane. Its front view is obtained by projection of intersection points 6 and 7. (Note the addition of line 1–3 to secure point 7.) Line 6–7 is the locus of points in plane 1–2–3 that are 12 mm behind point 3.

The intersection point of lines 4–5 and 6–7 is the required point P. The views of P at (b) are checked with a vertical projection line, as shown, to make sure that they are views of the same point.

19.9 Edge Views of Planes

In order to get the edge view of a plane, we must get the point view of a line in the plane, §10.11. For Fig. 19.22 (a) the edge view of plane 1–2–3 could be obtained by getting the true-length view and then the point view of any one of the three given lines of the plane. Since these lines are all oblique lines, obtaining their point views would each entail two successive auxiliary views, §19.6. It is easier to add a line that appears true length in one of the principal

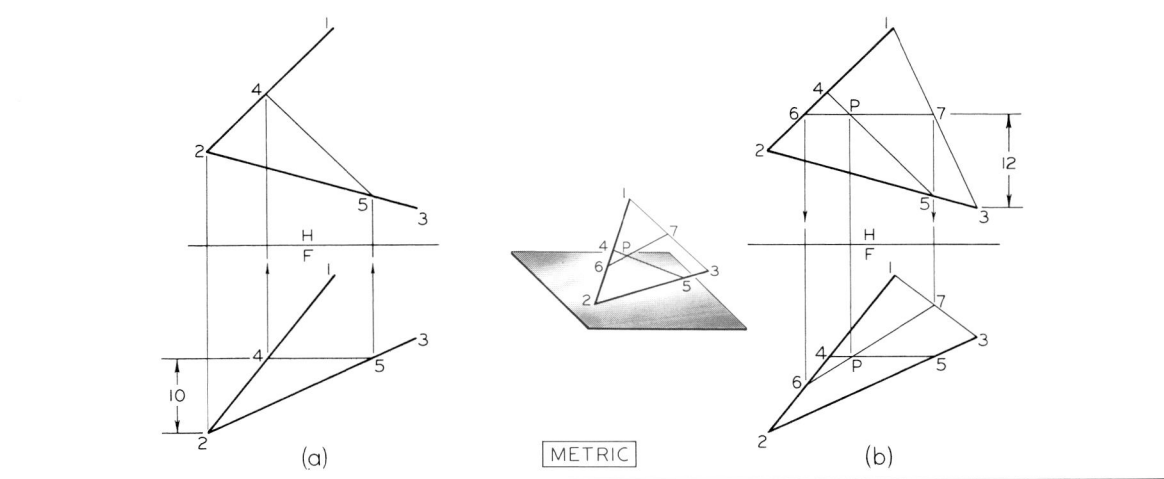

Fig. 19.21   Locus Problem.

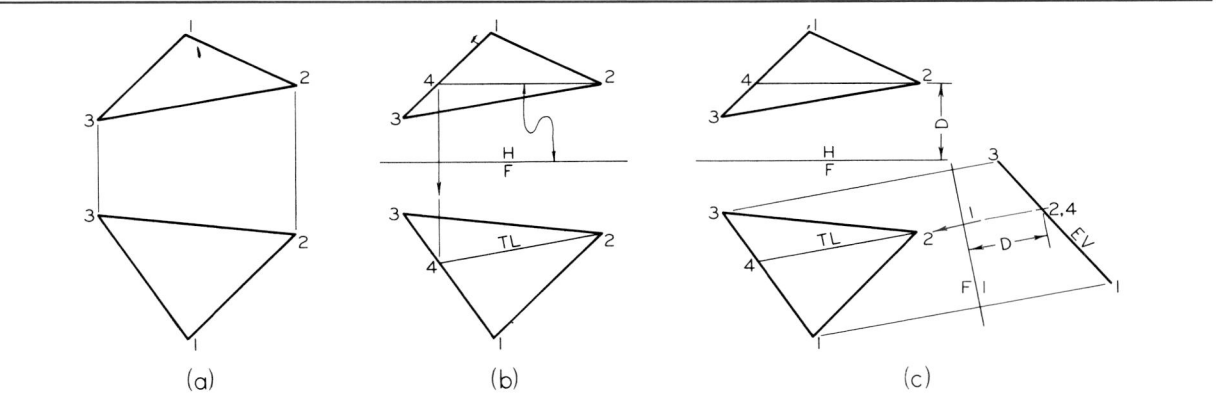

Fig. 19.22   Edge View of Plane.

views, thus eliminating the need of a second auxiliary view.

At (b) line **2–4** is drawn parallel to the **H/F** folding line (horizontal on the paper) in the top view.
Thus it is a frontal line, §19.2, and its front view,
obtained by projecting point **4** to the front view of
line **1–3**, is true length, as indicated.

Thus a true-length line in plane **1–2–3** has been
established without drawing an auxiliary view, and
we may now proceed as at (c) by assuming a direction of sight **1** parallel to the true-length view of
2–4. The resulting auxiliary view is the desired edge
view. Note that all points of the plane, not just a
minimum two points, are actually projected to the
auxiliary view. This provides a convenient check on

accuracy, since obviously the points must lie on a
straight line in the auxiliary view.

Edge views are useful as the first step in obtaining the true-size view of an oblique plane, §§10.21
and 19.10. They are also employed in showing dihedral angles, §10.11. In Fig. 10.11 (c) it was possible
to show the true angle by drawing a primary auxiliary view, since the line of intersection of the planes
appeared in true length in the top view. In Fig.
19.23 (a) the line of intersection **1–2** between surfaces **A** and **B** is not shown true length in either view.
Accordingly, at (b) auxiliary view **1** is constructed,
with the direction of sight **1** perpendicular to line
1–2. At (c) secondary auxiliary view **2** is then added,
with direction of sight **2** parallel to the true-length

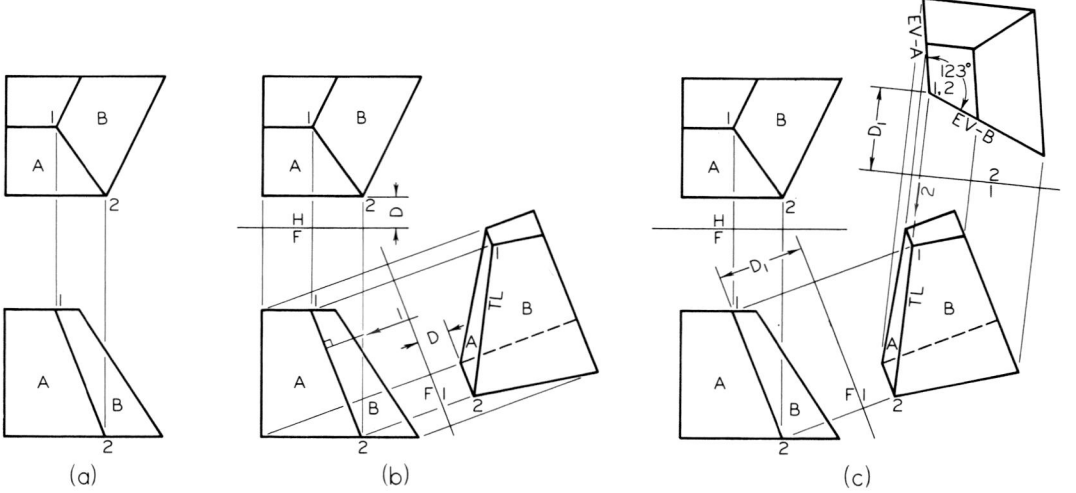

Fig. 19.23   Dihedral Angle with Oblique Line of Intersection.

view of line **1–2**. As a check, all points of the planes are located in the auxiliary views. When they fall on the respective straight-line (edge) views of the surfaces **A** and **B**, confidence in accuracy is established.

19.10 True-Size Views of Oblique Planes
The procedure for obtaining the true size of an oblique surface of an object is treated in §10.21. Many problems of a more abstract nature are also

solved through obtaining true-size views of oblique planes.

For example, let it be required to find the center of the circle passing through points **1**, **2**, and **3** of Fig. 19.24. The plane geometry construction is that of §5.31. However, the construction illustrated in that section took place in the plane of the paper, which we now recognize as a form of a true-size view. Since this is not the situation at (a), it is necessary to proceed as at (b) with the edge view and

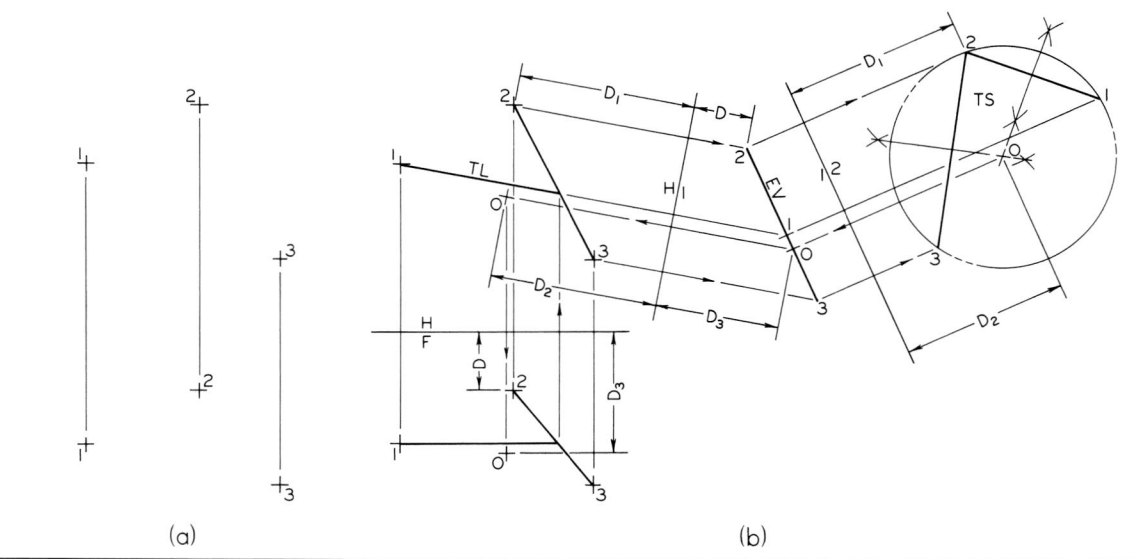

Fig. 19.24   Center of Circle in Oblique Plane.

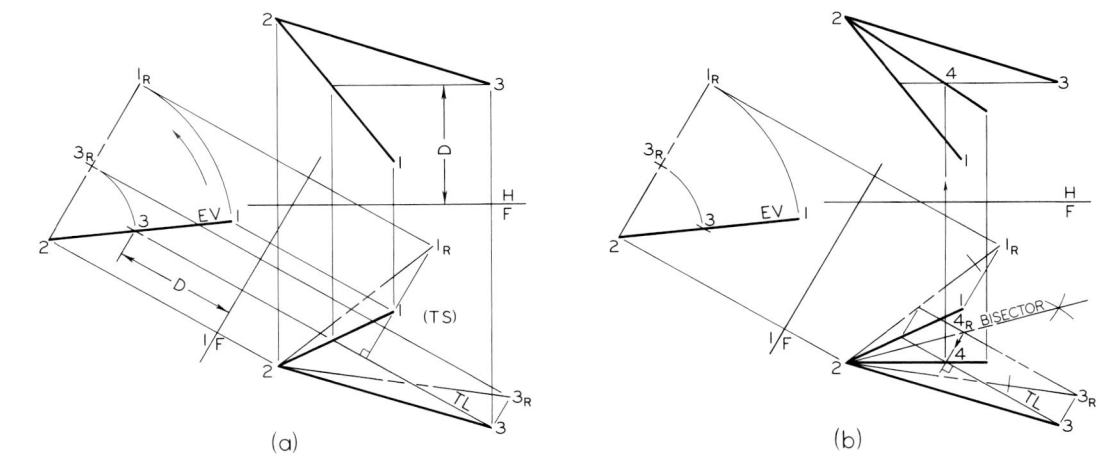

Fig. 19.25 True Size of Oblique Plane—Revolution Method.

true-size views of plane **1–2–3**. In auxiliary view **2** the construction shown in §5.31 is performed, locating center **O** for a circle through points **1**, **2**, and **3**. If desired, point **O** can be located in the divider distances D_2 and D_3 as shown. The circle, if drawn, would appear elliptical in the front and top views, §10.24.

The revolution method explained in §11.11 may also be applied to finding the true-size view of an oblique surface for geometric construction. In Fig. 19.25, the problem is to bisect the plane angle **1–2–3**. The true bisector of a plane angle lies in the same plane as the angle, and only under special circumstances when the plane of the angle is not in true size will a view of the bisector actually bisect the corresponding view of the angle. To solve this problem, the edge view of plane **1–2–3** is first constructed at (a) and then is revolved until it is parallel to folding line **F/1**. The revolved front view is then true size and angle 1_R–**2**–3_R is bisected as shown at (b). The revolution thus takes the place of a secondary auxiliary view. This has the major advantage of compactness of construction, but the overlapping front views may in some cases be confusing.

The front and top views of the bisector are obtained by selecting an additional point on the bisector in the true-size view and reversing the whole process—*counterrevolving*. Point 4_R on the true-length line through point 3_R is particularly convenient in this case because it will counterrevolve to the true-length line through point **3** and can then be projected to the top view, bypassing the auxiliary view. If desired, however, the selected point can be

projected to the revolved edge view, counter-revolved to the original edge view, and then returned to the front and top views by the usual methods.

19.11 Piercing Points

If a straight line is not parallel to a plane, it must intersect that plane in a single point called a *piercing point*. It may be necessary to extend the line, the plane, or both; this is permissible, since the abstract terms *line* and *plane* do not imply any limits on their extent. There are two recommended methods for finding piercing points.

Edge-View Method

All points of a plane are shown along its edge view. These, of course, include the piercing point of any lines that happen to be present. In Fig. 19.26 (a) the frontal line through point **3** is introduced to get a true-length line and thus the edge view of plane **1–2–3**. In this case it is necessary to extend line **4–5** to find the piercing point (encircled). At (b) the piercing point is projected first to the front view and then to the top view. Note the use of divider distance D_1 to check the accuracy of location of the top view. This procedure, under some circumstances, is more accurate than direct projection.

Note that a horizontal line could have been introduced into plane **1–2–3**, thereby establishing a different true-length line. This would have produced a different edge view, but would not give a different piercing point, as there is only one piercing

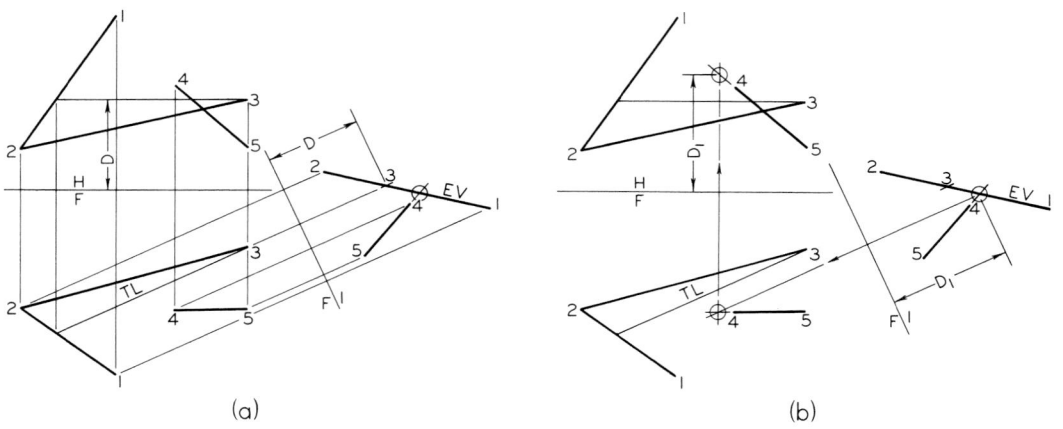

Fig. 19.26   Piercing Point—Edge-View Method.

point for a particular straight line and plane. This procedure would not be considered a different method but merely an alternative approach.

Cutting-Plane Method or Given-View Method

If a cutting plane A–A containing line 4–5 is introduced, Fig. 19.27 (a), it will cut line 6–7 from given plane 1–2–3. Lines 6–7 and 4–5, being in the same plane A–A, must intersect at the piercing point (encircled). To make the method practical, an edge-view cutting plane is used, as shown at (b). To contain line 4–5, the cutting plane must coincide with a view of the line. At (b) it was chosen to have plane

A–A coincide with the top view of 4–5. The line cut from plane 1–2–3 is line 6–7. Projected to the front view, line 6–7 locates the front view of the piercing point, which is then projected to the top view as shown.

Actually, there is no need for some of the lettering shown at (b). At (c) the symbol EV adequately identifies the cutting plane, and the numbers 6 and 7 may be omitted as being of little value other than for purposes of discussion.

Note that this illustration is similar to Fig. 19.26, except that (1) the piercing point is within the line segment 4–5 and (2) the plane is *limited* or completely bounded. It is then feasible to consider the

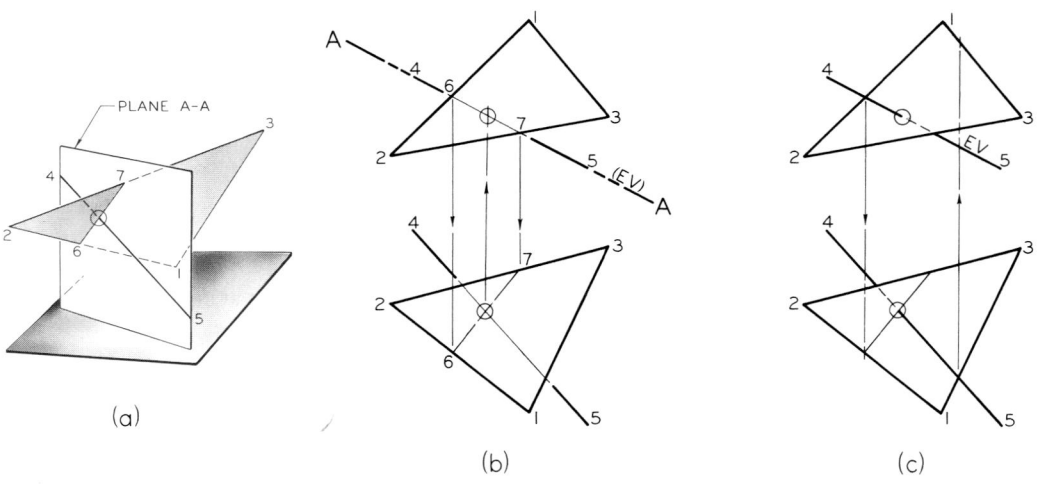

Fig. 19.27   Piercing Point—Cutting-Plane Method.

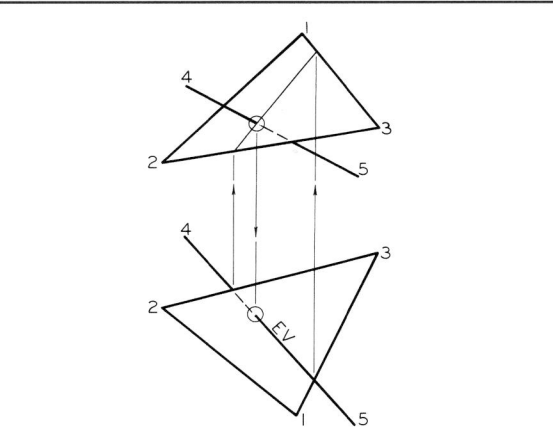

Fig. 19.28 Piercing Point—Cutting-Plane Method (alternative solution).

19.12 Intersections of Planes

The intersection of two planes is a straight line containing all points common to the two planes. Since planes are themselves represented by straight lines, §19.7, points common to two intersecting planes may be located by finding piercing points of lines of one plane with the other plane, by the use of edge-view method or the cutting-plane method of §19.11.

Edge-View Method

In Fig. 19.29, two planes are given: 1–2–3 and 4–5–6. If the edge view of either plane is constructed, the piercing points of the lines of the other plane will lie along the edge view. At (a) a horizontal line is introduced through point 3 of plane 1–2–3 in order to secure a true-length line in the top view. (A horizontal line in plane 4–5–6 or frontal lines in either plane would serve just as well in this problem.) Auxiliary view 1 is then constructed with its direction of sight parallel to the true-length view of the line. The completed auxiliary view 1 shows the edge view of plane 1–2–3 and the piercing points of lines 4–5 and 5–6 as indicated by the encircled points.

At (b) the piercing points are projected to the top view and then to the front view. (It is good practice to check accuracy by divider distances, as indicated by dimension D₁). Since the given planes are not completely bounded, there is no reason to restrict the drawn length of the segment of the line of intersection (LI). However, the views of the line of intersection should be compatible from view to view.

Since the LI is common to both planes, it must

bounded area to be opaque. The line then becomes hidden after it pierces the plane. The visibility displayed at (c) was determined by the methods of §19.1, investigating in each view any convenient point where line 4–5 crosses one of the boundary lines of the plane.

The problem in Fig. 19.27 is shown again in Fig. 19.28, this time with the edge view of the cutting plane introduced coincident with the front view of line 4–5. Of course, the same answer is obtained, and it is a matter of personal choice and convenience as to which view is chosen for introduction of the edge-view cutting plane. For the convenience of the reader, always include the letters EV as shown when the problem solutions involve such cutting planes.

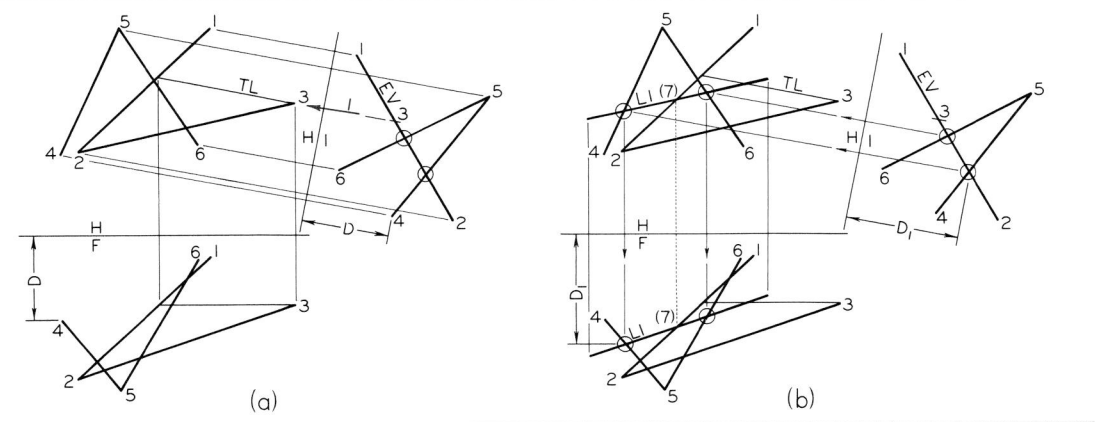

Fig. 19.29 Intersection of Two Planes—Edge-View Method.

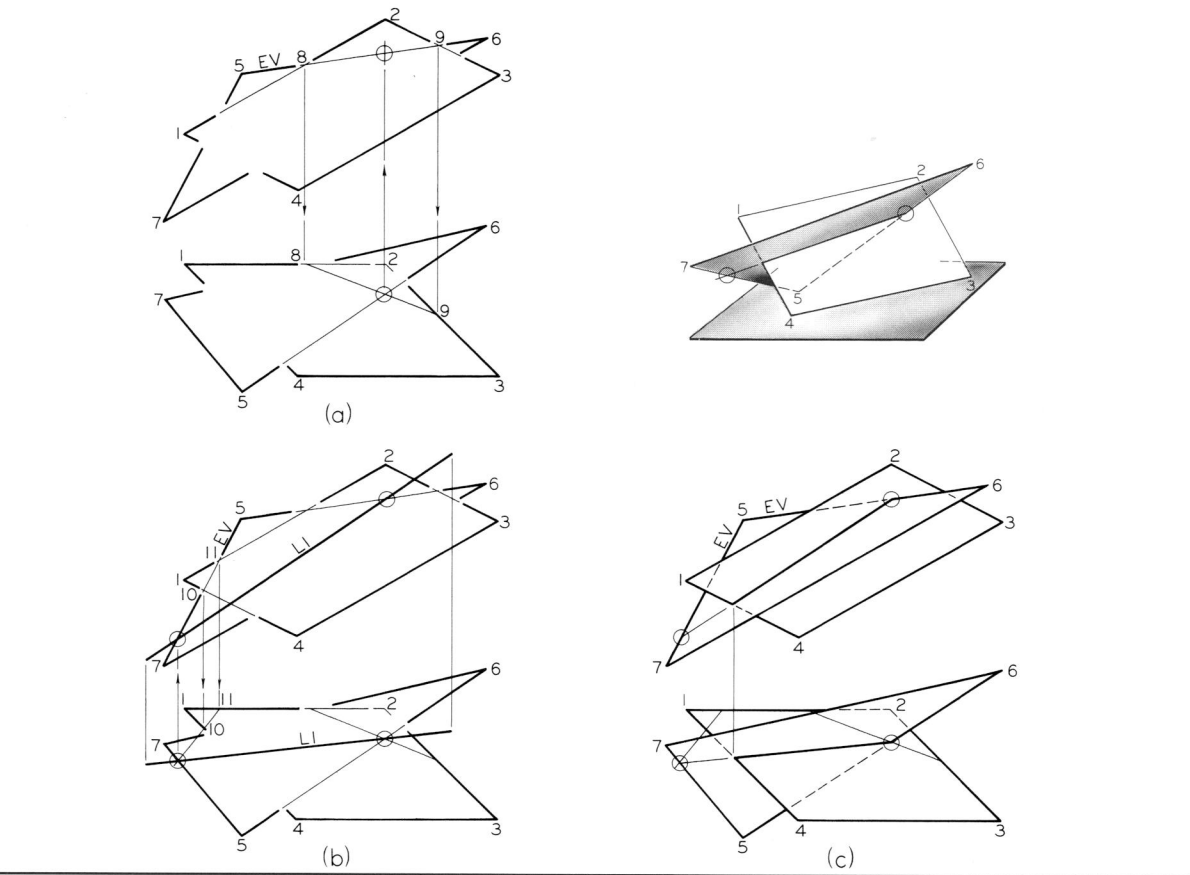

Fig. 19.30   Intersection of Two Planes—Cutting-Plane Method.

intersect or be parallel to each line of both planes. As a check on accuracy, observe in this case that the LI intersects line **1–2** at **7** and is parallel to line **2–3**.

Cutting-Plane Method

Because it requires no additional views, the cutting-plane method is frequently used to find the intersection of two planes, Fig. 19.30. At (a) it is arbitrarily decided to introduce an edge-view cutting plane coinciding with the top view of line **5–6**, with the intention of finding the piercing point of line **5–6** in plane **1–2–3–4**. The student should realize that one could introduce cutting planes in either view coinciding with any of the lines of the planes. With so many possibilities it is imperative that the choice be indicated with proper use of the symbol EV, both to avoid confusion on the student's part and as a courtesy to the person who must read the drawing.

In this case the introduced plane cuts line **8–9** from plane **1–2–3–4**. Point **8** is on line **1–2** and point **9** is on line **2–3**. Observe this carefully so as to avoid mistakes in projecting to the front view. The front view of line **8–9** intersects line **5–6** at the encircled piercing point which, after projection to the top view, represents one point common to the given planes.

At (b) another piercing point is located by introducing an edge-view cutting plane along line **5–7**. The line of intersection, LI, passes through the two piercing points as shown.

In this illustration the given planes are bounded and can therefore be considered limited as at (c). The piercing point of line **5–7** falls outside plane **1–2–3–4** and is therefore not on the "real" portion of the line of intersection, which is drawn as a visible line only in the area common to the views of both planes. The termination of this segment is at the

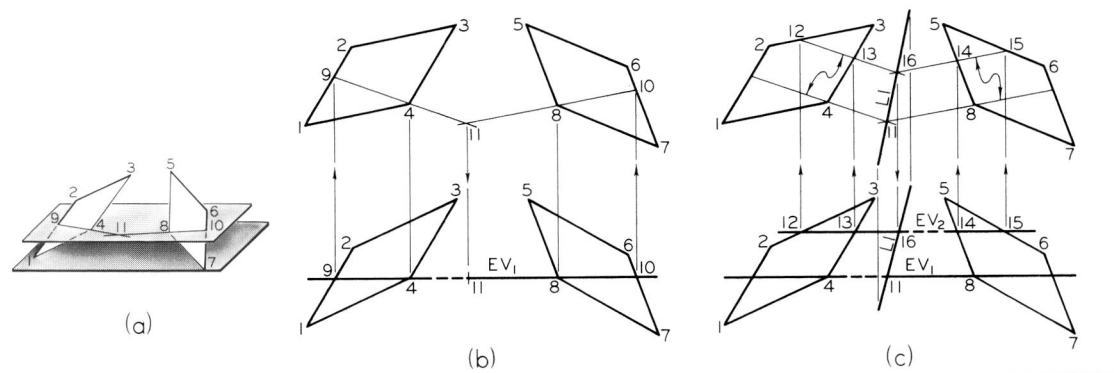

Fig. 19.31   Intersection of Two Planes—Special Cutting-Plane Method.

point that is actually the piercing point of line 1–4 in plane 5–6–7. However, this result was not obvious at the start of the construction. Visibility was determined by the method of §19.1. Usually it is necessary to examine only one apparent crossing point in each view. After visibility is established in one such region, the spatial relations of the remaining lines of that view are evident, since each boundary line in turn can change visibility only where it meets a piercing point or a boundary line of the other given plane.

Special Cutting-Plane Method

The line of intersection of two planes also may be found through the use of cutting planes that do not coincide with the views of given lines. Any plane cutting the two given planes, Fig. 19.31 (a), cuts one line from each. Since these lines lie in the cutting plane as well as in the given planes, they will intersect at a point common to the given planes. A second cutting plane will establish a second common point, giving two points on the line of intersection. For convenience, the edge-view cutting planes employed are usually drawn parallel to a regular coordinate plane, but this is not necessary. It is suggested that the two planes be introduced in the same view for more control of the distance between the points secured.

At (b) horizontal plane EV₁ cuts lines 9–4 and 8–10 from the given planes. When these lines are projected to the top view, they intersect at point 11, which is then one point on the required line of intersection. The front view of point 11 is on line EV₁ as shown. At (c) a second horizontal plane EV₂ is introduced, cutting lines 12–13 and 14–15, which intersect in the top view at point 16. After point 16

is projected to line EV₂ the line of intersection 11–16 (LI) is drawn to any desired length. Note carefully the parallelism of the lines in the top view at (c). This affords a convenient and a very desirable check on accuracy.

This method involves more construction than did the previous methods and can be confusing when the given views occupy overlapping areas, as in Figs. 19.29 and 19.30. This particular method is therefore recommended primarily for problems in which the given views of the planes are separated.

19.13 Angle Between Line and Oblique Plane

The true angle between a line and a plane of projection (frontal, horizontal, or profile) is seen in the view in which the given line is true length and the plane in question is in edge view, §19.3. This is a general principle that applies to any plane: normal, inclined, or oblique.

In Fig. 19.32 (a) two views of a plane 1–2–3 and a line 5–6 are given. One cannot expect a primary auxiliary view to show plane 1–2–3 in edge view and also line 5–6 in true length, for generally the directions of sight for these two purposes will not be parallel. Note that in Fig. 19.8 the direction of sight for the auxiliary view is toward the front view, which shows the true-size view of all frontal planes. In Fig. 19.9 the direction of sight is toward the top view, which shows the true-size view of all horizontal planes. In summary, *any view projected from a true-size view of a plane shows an edge view of that plane.*

In Fig. 19.32 (a) frontal line 2–4 is added to given plane 1–2–3. We thus now have a true-length line

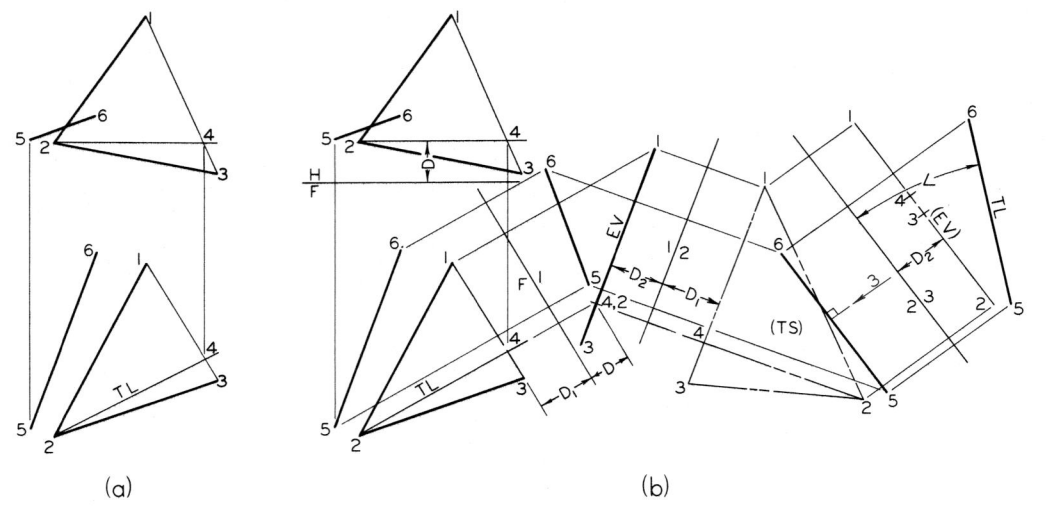

Fig. 19.32   Angle Between Line and Plane—True-Size Method.

in the front view and edge-view auxiliary view 1 is projected from it. The true-size secondary auxiliary view 2 is then constructed in the customary manner.

Any view projected from view 2 will show plane 1–2–3 in edge view. Therefore to show the true angle between line 5–6 and the plane, direction of sight 3 is established at right angles to view 2 of line 5–6. View 3 then shows the required angle ($\angle$). Be-

cause in this chain of views the edge view of the plane in view 3 is always parallel to folding line 2/3 (note divider distance D_2), the construction can be simplified if desired by omitting plane 1–2–3 from auxiliary views 2 and 3. The required angle is then measured between line 4–5 and the folding line 2/3.

Point, Line, and Plane Problems

The problems in Figs. 19.33–19.44 cover points and lines, intersecting and non-intersecting lines, visibility, true length and angles with principal planes, auxiliary-view method and revolution method, point views, points and lines in planes, dihedral angles, edge view and true size of planes, piercing points, intersection of planes, and angle between line and oblique plane.

Use Layout A–1 or A4–1 (adjusted) and divide the working area into four equal areas for problems to be assigned by the instructor. Some problems will require a single problem area, and others will require two problem areas (half the sheet). See §2.63. Data for the layout for each problem are given by a coordinate system. For example, in Fig. 19.33, Prob. 1, point 1 is located by the full-scale coordinates, **25, 38**, and **75 mm**. The first coordinate locates the front view of the point from the left edge of the problem area. The second coordinate locates the front view of the point from the bottom edge of the problem area. The third coordinate locates either the top view of the point from the bottom edge of the problem area or the side view of the point from the left edge of the problem area. Inspection of the given problem layout will determine which application to use.

Since many of the problems in this chapter are of a general nature, they can also be solved on most computer graphics systems. If a system is available, the instructor may choose to assign specific problems to be completed by this method.

Additional problems in convenient form for solution are presented in the worksheets at the back of this book. Refer to Drawings 19-1 to 19-13 and accompanying instructions.

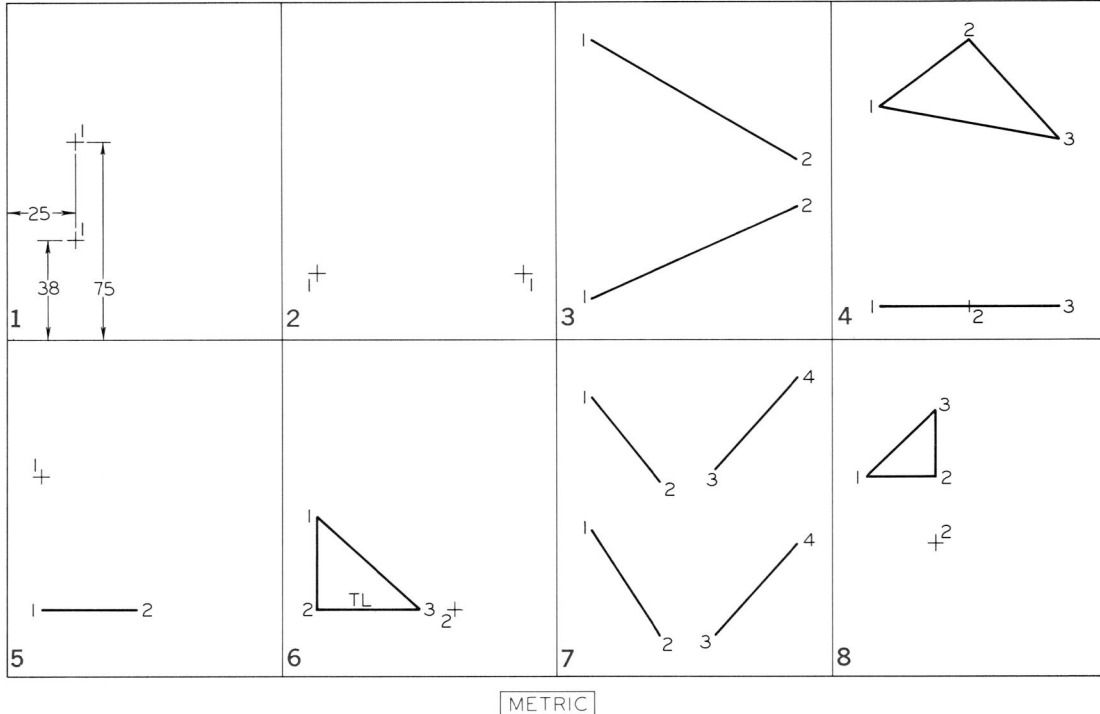

METRIC

Fig. 19.33 Lay out and solve four problems per sheet as assigned. Use Layout A–1 or A4–1 (adjusted) divided into four equal areas.

1. Given point 1(25, 38, 75), locate the front and top views of point 2, which is 50 mm to the right of point 1, 25 mm below point 1, and 30 mm behind point 1.
2. Given point 1(12, 25, 90), locate the front and side views of line 1–2 such that point 2 is 38 mm to the right of point 1, 45 mm above point 1, and 25 mm in front of point 1. Add the top view of line 1–2.
3. Find the views of points 3, 4, and 5 on line 1(12, 15, 115)–2(90, 50, 70) that fit the following descriptions: point 3, 20 mm above point 1; point 4, 65 mm to the left of point 2; and point 5, 25 mm in front of point 1.
4. Triangle 1(18, 12, 90)–2(50, 12, 115)–3(85, 12, 75) is the base of a pyramid. The vertex V is 8 mm behind point 1, 8 mm to the left of point 2, and 45 mm above point 3. Complete the front and top views of the pyramid.
5. Line 1(12, 25, 75)–2(48, 25, ?) is 43 mm long (2 behind 1). Line 1–3 is a 50 mm frontal line, and line 2–3 is a profile line. Find the true length of line 2–3.
6. Line 1(12, 60, ?)–2(12, 25, 64) is 45 mm long. The front view of line 2–3(50, 25, ?) is true length as indicated. Complete the front and side views and add a top view of triangle 1–2–3.
7. Point 5 is on line 1(12, 56, 106)–2(38, 15, 74), 18 mm below point 1. Point 6 is on line 3(58, 15, 80)–4(90, 50, 115). Line 5–6 is frontal. Find the true length of line 5–6.
8. Line 2(38, 50, 75)–3(38, ?, 100) is 38 mm long. Line 3–1(12, ?, 75) is horizontal. How long is line 1–2?

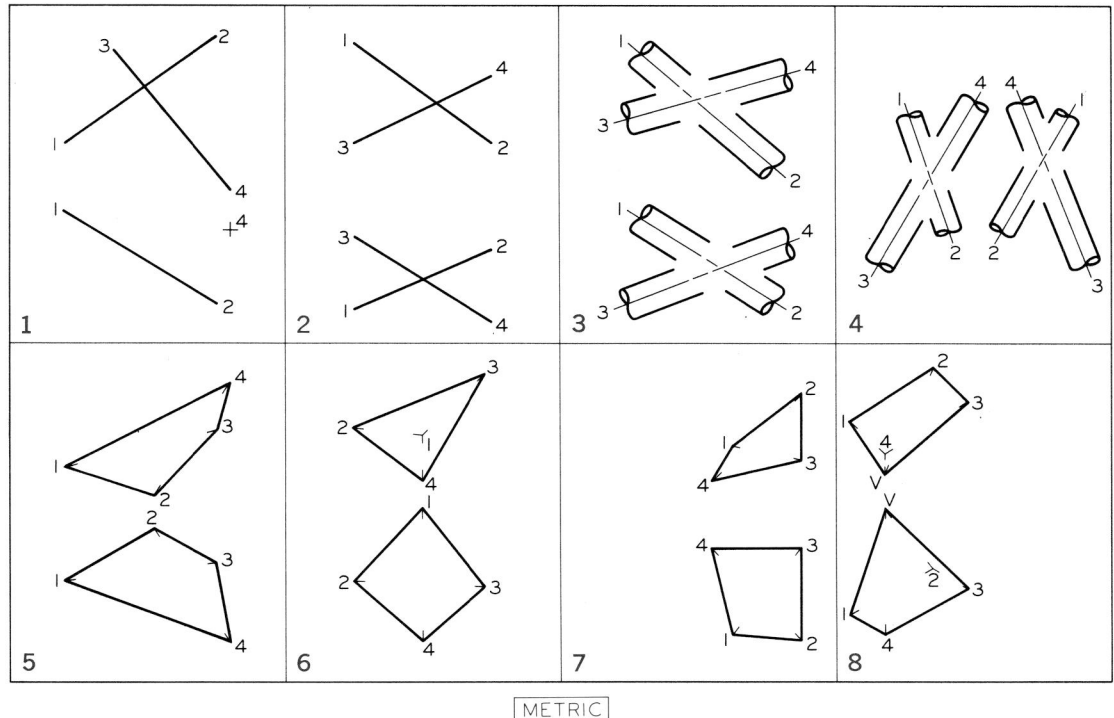

METRIC

Fig. 19.34 Lay out and solve problems as assigned. Use Layout A–1 or A4–1 (adjusted) divided into four equal areas.

1. Lines 1(20, 50, 75)–2(75, 15, 117) and 3(48, ?, 112)–4(82, 43, 58) are intersecting lines. Complete the front view.

2. Demonstrate that lines 1(25, 12, 114)–2(75, 48, 75) and 3(25, 40, 75)–4(75, 8, 100) do not intersect. Then move point 4 *vertically* in space to a new position 4′ such that line 3–4′ intersects line 1–2.

3. Lines 1(25, 50, 114)–2(84, 12, 64) and 3(20, 12, 84)–4(90, 40, 104) are the center lines of two nonintersecting cylindrical tubes, each of which has a diameter of 200 mm. Scale: 1/20. Complete the views including correct visibility.

4. Rod 1(12, 92, 90)–2(43, 38, 58) has a diameter of 10 mm. Rod 3(12, 25, 94)–4(53, 96, 66) has a diameter of 12 mm. Complete the views including correct visibility.

5. Points 1(20, 38, 80), 2(53, 58, 70), 3(75, 46, 96), and 4(90, 15, 115) are the vertices of a tetrahedron. Complete the given views with proper visibility.

6. Points 1(50, 65, 94), 2(25, 38, 96), 3(73, 35, 116), and 4(50, 15, 75) are the vertices of a tetrahedron. Complete the given views with proper visibility.

7. Points 1(63, 17, 88), 2(88, 15, 118), 3(88, 50, 83), and 4(55, 50, 75) are the vertices of a tetrahedron. Complete the given views and add a left-side view, all with proper visibility.

8. Points 1(5, 25, 98), 2(35, 43, 118), 3(48, 35, 116), and 4(18, 18, 86) are corners of the base of a pyramid. Point V(18, 66, 78) is the vertex. Complete the views and add a right-side view, including proper visibility.

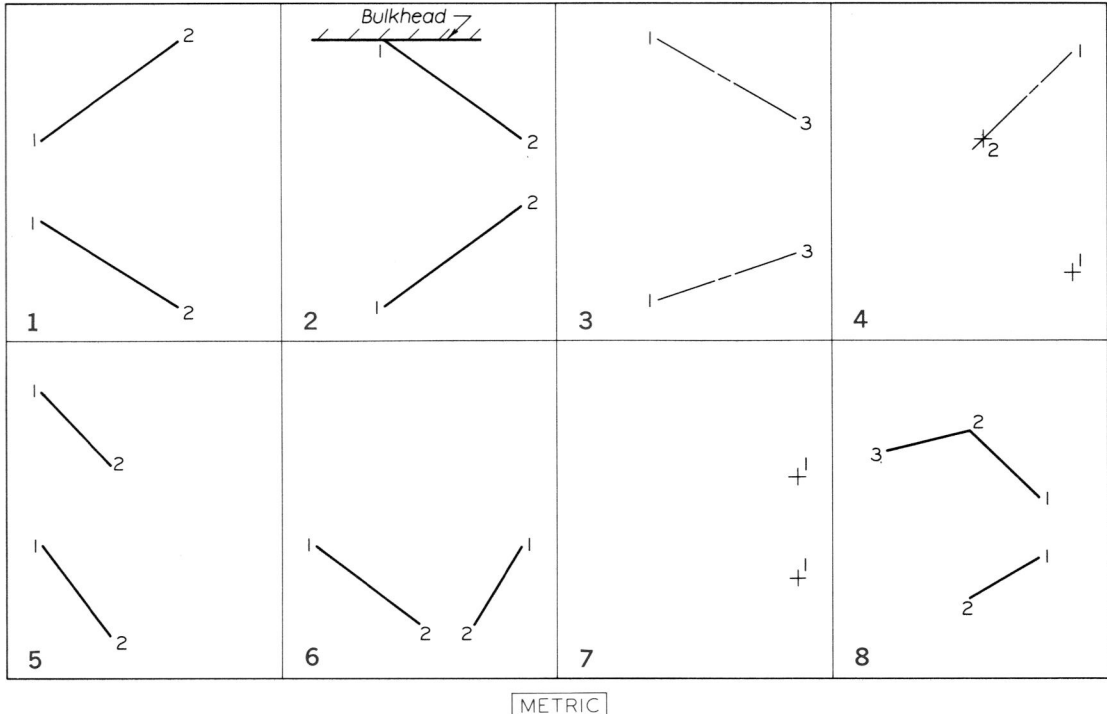

METRIC

Fig. 19.35 Lay out and solve problems as assigned. Use Layout A–1 or A4–1 (adjusted) divided into four equal areas.

1. Find and measure the true length of line 1(12, 46, 75)–2(63, 12, 114) and the angle it forms with a horizontal plane (∠H).
2. Find and dimension the true length of and the angle formed by control cable 1 (38, 12, 114)–2(80, 50, 75) and the frontal bulkhead. Scale: 1/10.
3. Measure the bearing and slope (∠H) of pipe center line 1(38, 15, 114)–3(88, 33, 83).
4. The center line of a segment of a highway runs from point 1(88, 25, 110) through point 2(56, ?, 75) to a point 3. The line slopes downward from point 1 at an angle of 15°. The length of segment 1–3 is 350 m. Scale: 1/5000. Find the top and front views of point 3.
5. Find and measure the true length of line 1 (12, 50, 110)–2(38, 15, 80) and the true angle it forms with a profile plane (∠P).
6. Find and measure the bearing and percent grade of line 1(12, 50, 88)–2(50, 20, 70).
7. A tunnel bears N 40° W from point 1(88, 38, 75) on a downgrade of 30% to point 2 at a distance of 230 m along the tunnel. Scale: 1/4000. Find the front and top views of tunnel 1–2.
8. If segments 1(75, 45, 68)–2(50, 30, 94) and 2–3(20, ?, 86) of pipeline 1–2–3 have the same grade, find the front view of 2–3.

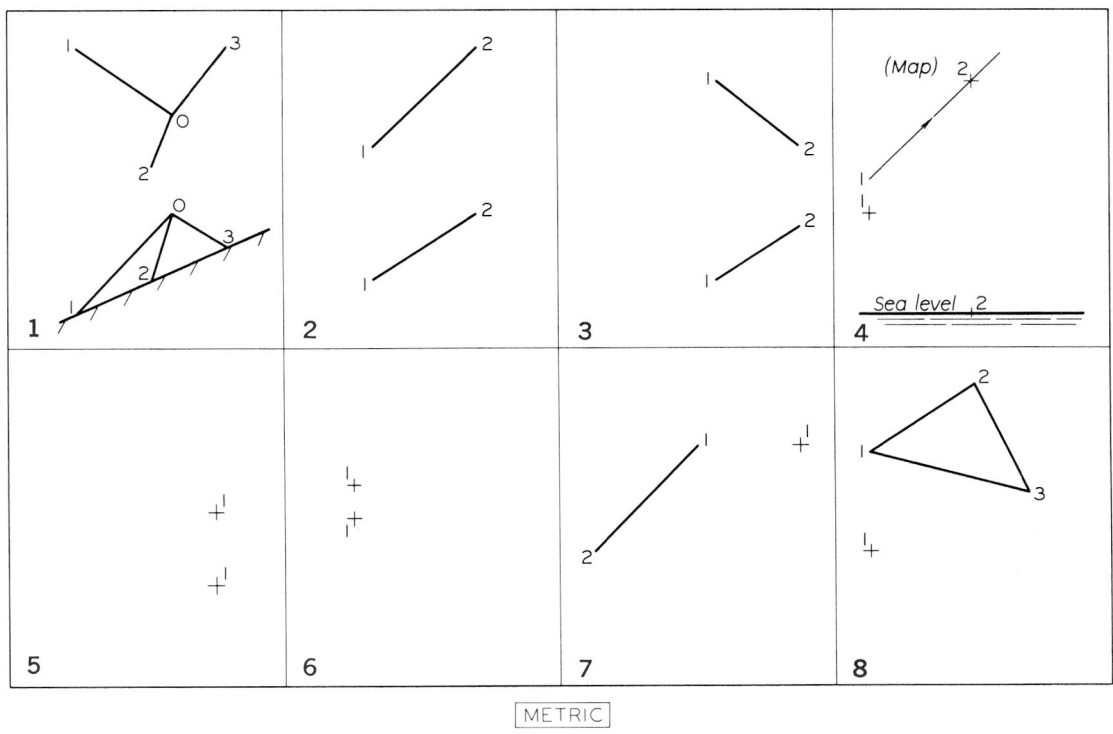

Fig. 19.36 Lay out and solve four problems per sheet, as assigned. Note: Use revolution for these problems. Use Layout A–1 or A4–1 (adjusted) divided into four equal areas.

1. Find the true lengths of the tripod legs O(60, 50, 88)–1(25, 12, 114), O–2(53, 25, 68), and O–3(80, 38, 114). Scale: 1/20.
2. Find and measure the true length and angles with H and F for line 1(33, 25, 75)–2(70, 50, 114).
3. Find the true length and angle with P of line 1(58, 25, 100)–2(88, 46, 75). Scale: 1/200.
4. An aircraft flies from position 1(12, 50, 63) toward point 2(50, 12, 100). If the craft is losing altitude at the rate of 500 m in each 1000 m (map distance), at what altitude will it pass over point 2? Scale: 1/20 000. If the aircraft fails to pull out of the dive, show the front and top views of the point of impact.
5. Pipe center line 1(75, 38, 65)–2(?, ?, ?) has an azimuth bearing of N 310°, a downgrade of 30%, and a true length of 240 m. Scale: 1/4000. Find the front and top views of line 1–2.
6. Line 1(25, 64, 75)–2(?, ?, ?) has a bearing of N 40° E, is 60 mm in length, makes an angle of 30° with a horizontal plane, and slopes downward. Complete the front and top views of 1–2.
7. Line 1(50, 90, 88)–2(12, 50, ?) forms an angle of 35° with a frontal plane. The line slopes forward. Complete the side view.
8. Line 1(12, 50, 88)–2(50, ?, 114) has a downward slope of 40°. Line 2–3(70, ?, 74) has an upward slope of 20°. What is the slope of line 1–3?

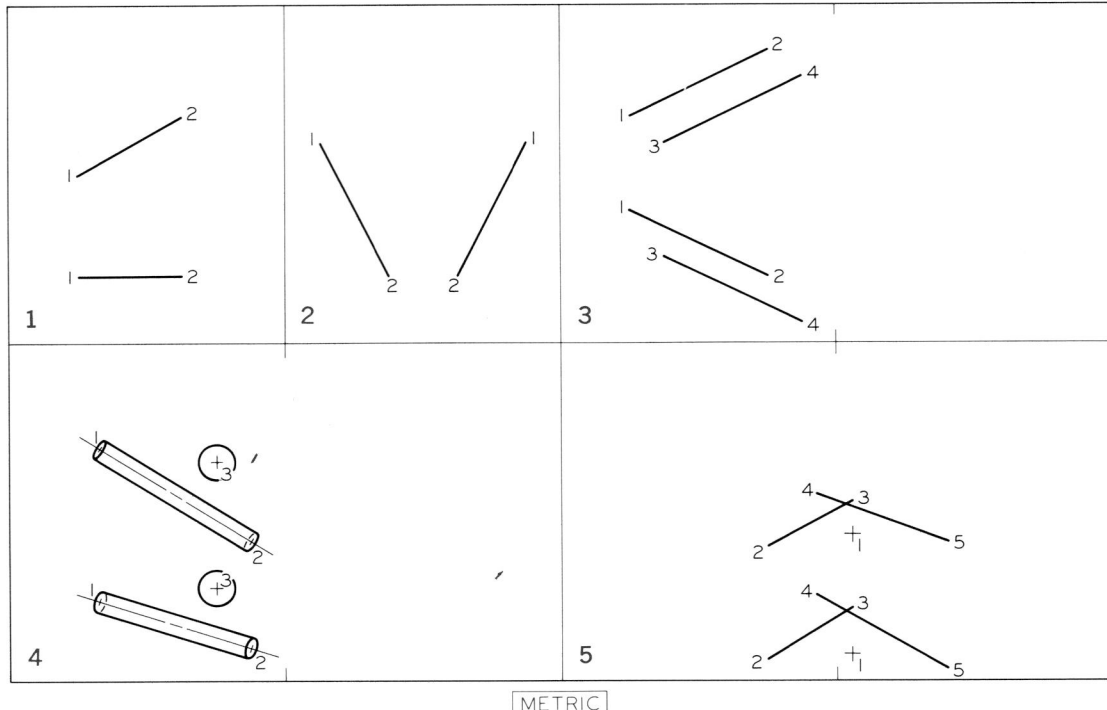

METRIC

Fig. 19.37   Lay out and solve problems as assigned. Use Layout A–1 or A4–1 (adjusted) divided into four equal areas.

1.   Find a point view of line 1(25, 25, 63)–2(63, 25, 86).
2.   Find a point view of line 1(12, 75, 88)–2(38, 25, 63).
3.   Find the true distance between parallel lines 1(25, 50, 86)–2(75, 25, 112) and 3(38, 33, 75)–4(88, ?, ?).
4.   Find the clearance between 0.8 m diameter cylinder 1(32, 30, 88)–2(88, 12, 53) and 1.25 m diameter sphere 3(75, 35, 83). Scale: 1/100.
5.   Determine if point 1(106, 10, 55) is nearer to line 2(75, 7, 50)–3(106, 28, 68) or to line 4(94, 33, 70)–5(142, 5, 53).

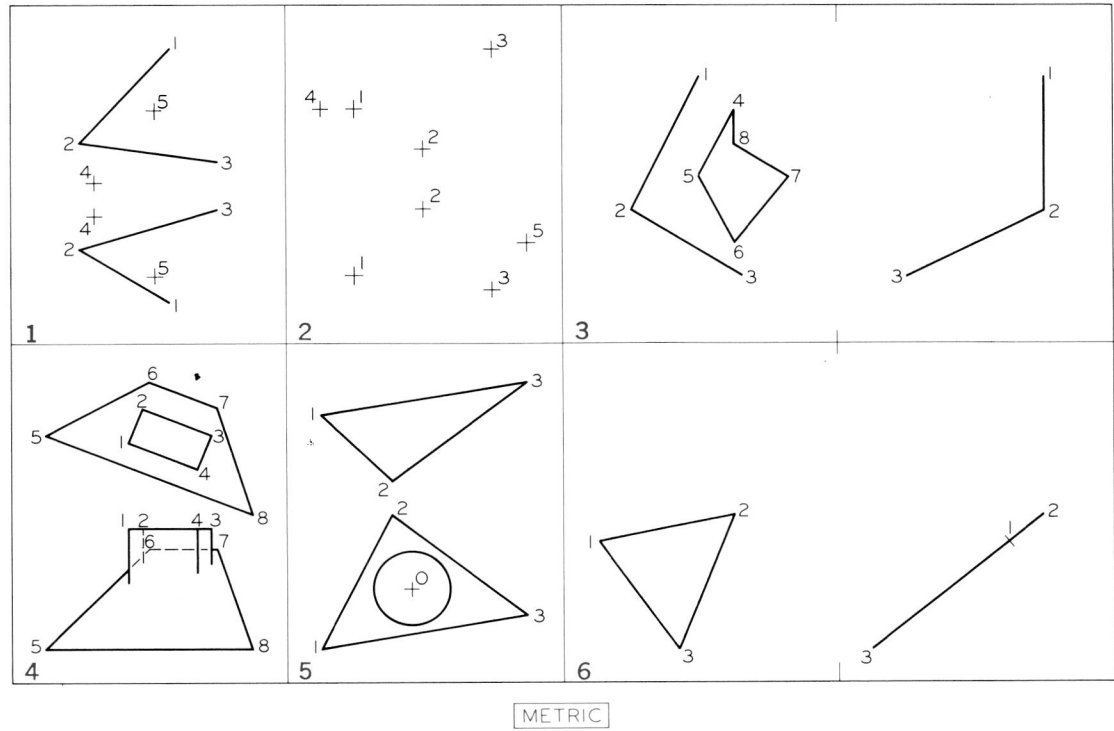

METRIC

Fig. 19.38   Lay out and solve problems as assigned. Use Layout A–1 or A4–1 (adjusted) divided into four equal areas.

1. Determine if either (or both) of points 4(30, 48, 60) and 5(53, 25, 88) lies in plane 1(58, 15, 112)–2(25, 35, 75)–3(75, 50, 68).

2. Line 4(12, ?, 88)–5(88, 38, ?) lies in plane 1(25, 25, 88)–2(50, 50, 74)–3(75, 20, 112). Complete the views of line 4–5.

3. Pentagon 4(63, 88, ?)–5(50, 63, ?)–6(63, 38, ?)–7(84, 63, ?)–8(63, 75, ?) lies in plane 1(50, 102, 178)–2(25, 50, 178)–3(65, 25, 126). Complete the side view of the pentagon.

4. Complete the front view including the opening in roof plane 5(12, 12, 94)–6(50, 50, 114)–7(75, 50, –) –8(88, 12, 63) for vertical chimney 1(43, 58, 90)–2(48, 58, 104)–3(73, 58, –)–4(68, 58, –).

5. Plot the top view of the curve centered at O(46, 35, ?) and lying in plane 1(12, 12, 100)–2(38, 63, 75)–3(88, 25, 114). The circular front view of the curve has a diameter of 28 mm.

6. Find the front and side views of the center of the circle inscribed in triangle 1(12, 53, –)–2(63, 63, 178)–3(43, 12, 114). Also locate the views of the points of tangency of the circle with the sides of the triangle. If assigned, plot the views of the circle.

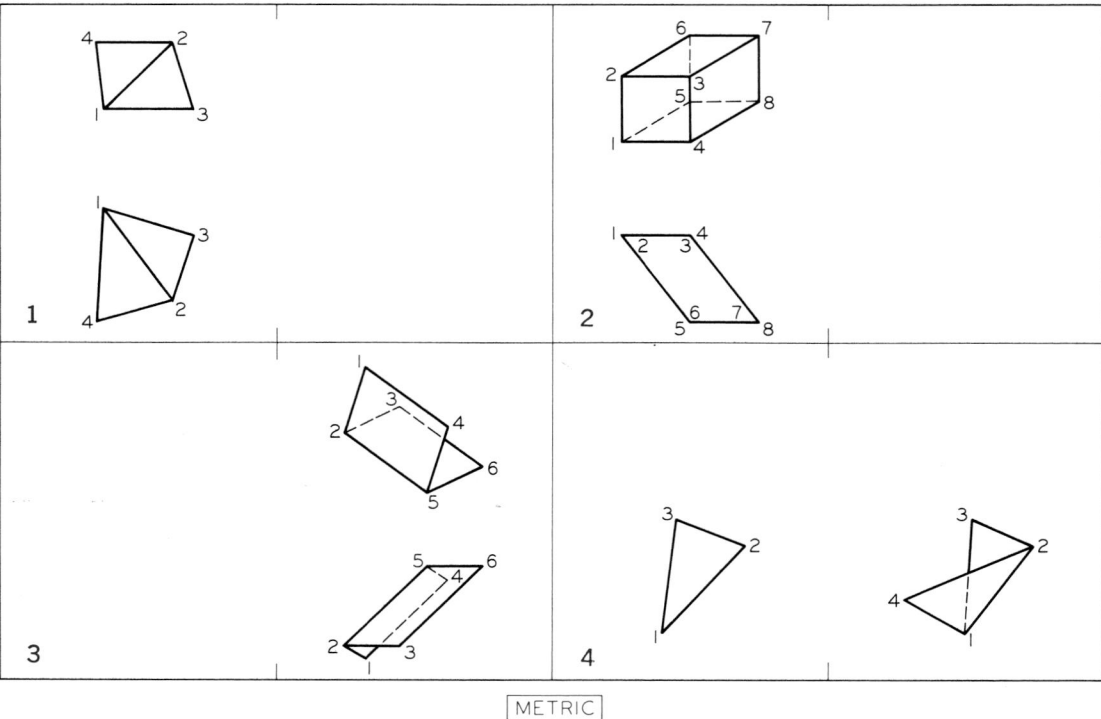

METRIC

Fig. 19.39   Lay out and solve problems as assigned. Use Layout A–1 or A4–1 (adjusted) divided into four equal areas.

1. Find the true size of the dihedral angle formed by plane 1(38, 50, 88)–2(63, 15, 114)–3(70, 40, 88) and plane 1–2–4(35, 7, 114).
2. Find the dihedral angles between the lateral faces of the prism. Bases 1(25, 40, 75)–2–3–4 and 5(50, 7, 90)–6–7–8 are 25 mm square.
3. Determine the dihedral angle of clip angle 1(134, 7, 119)–2(126, 12, 94)–3(147, 12, 104)–4(165, 38, 147)–5(–, 43, –)–6(–, 43, –).
4. Plane 1(40, 18, 152)–2(70, 50, 178)–3(45, 60, 175) and plane 1–2–4(?, 30, 130) form a dihedral angle of 60°. Complete the views.

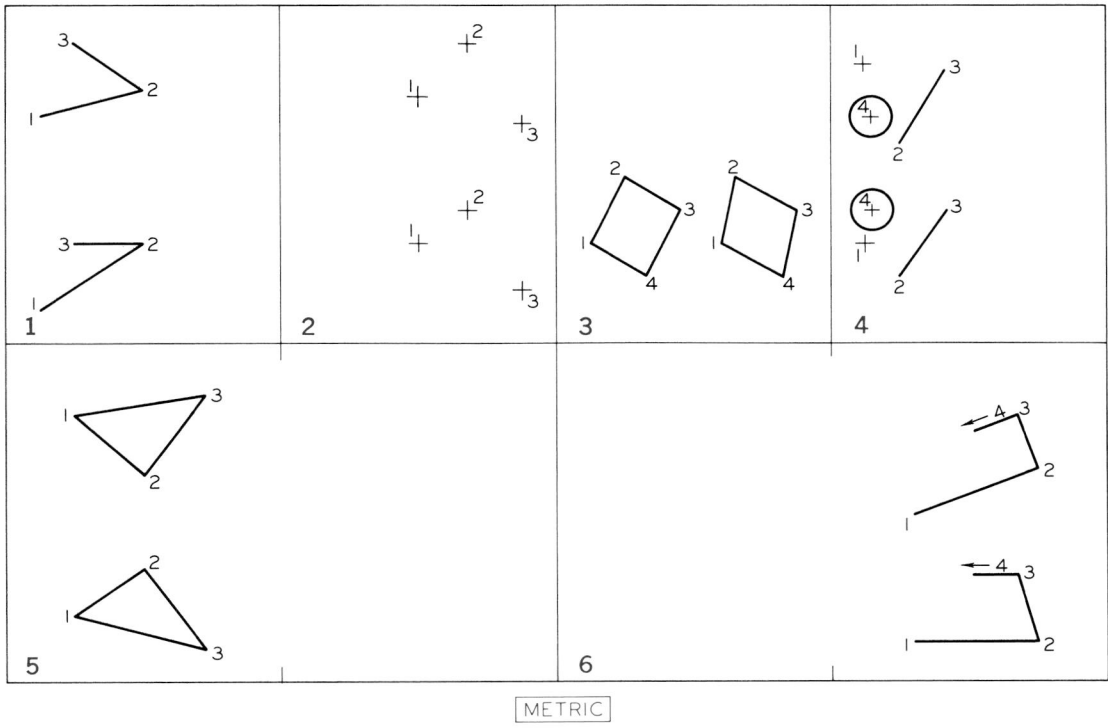

METRIC

Fig. 19.40 Lay out and solve problems as assigned. Use Layout A–1 or A4–1 (adjusted) divided into four equal areas.

1. Obtain an edge view of plane 1(12, 12, 86)–2(50, 38, 96)–3(25, 38, 114).
2. Obtain an edge view of plane 1(50, 38, 94)–2(68, 50, 114)–3(88, 20, 84).
3. Obtain an edge view of plane 1(12, 38, 60)–2(25, 62, 66)–3(45, 50, 88)–4(–, –, –).
4. Find the clearance between plane 1(12, 38, 76)–2(25, 25, 75)–3(43, 50, 104) and 300 mm diameter sphere 4(15, 50, 86) by obtaining an edge view of plane 1–2–3. Scale: 1/20.
5. Obtain a true-size view of triangle 1(25, 25, 100)–2(50, 42, 78)–3(73, 12, 118) and calculate its area. Scale: 1/1.
6. Trapezoid 1(132, 15, 63)–2(178, 15, 80)–3(170, 40, 100)–4(?, 40, ?) has an area of 175 m². Complete the front and top views of the trapezoid. Scale: 1/400.

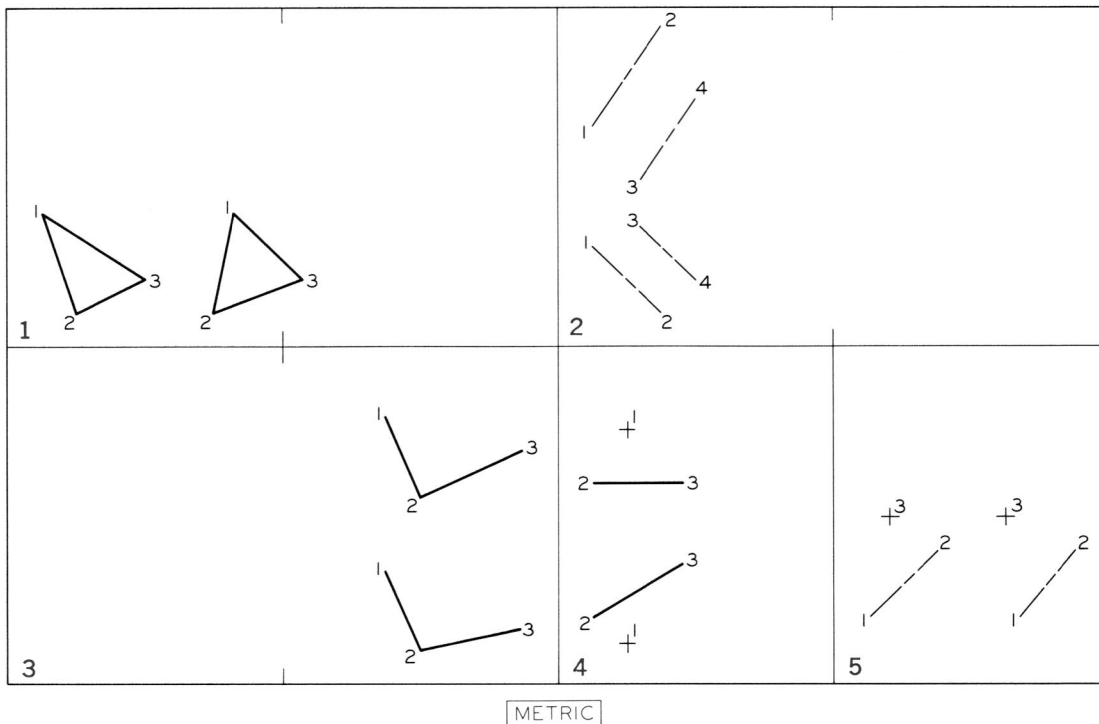

METRIC

Fig. 19.41 Lay out and solve problems as assigned. Use Layout A–1 or A4–1 (adjusted) divided into four equal areas.

1. Find the front and side views of the center of the cirlce inscribed in triangle 1(12, 50, 84)–2(25, 12, 75)–3(50, 25, 118). If assigned, find the views of the points of tangency. Also, if assigned, plot the views of the circle.
2. Pipe center lines 1(12, 38, 84)–2(38, 12, 122) and 3(30, 45, 63)–4(50, –, –) are to be connected with a feeder branch, using 45° lateral fittings. One fitting is to be located at the midpoint of pipe 1–2. Find the front and top views of the center line of the feeder branch.
3. Find the front and top views of the bisector of angle 1(140, 43, 100)–2(152, 12, 70)–3(190, 20, 88).
4. Join point 1(25, 15, 96) to line 2(12, 25, 75)–3(45, 45, 75) with a line forming an angle of 45° with line 1–2. Use revolution instead of a secondary auxiliary view.
5. Structural member 1(12, 25, 68)–2(38, 58, 88) is connected to point 3(20, 63, 63) with another structural member that is 1.8 m in length. Find the front and side views of the center line of the connecting member. Use revolution instead of a secondary auxiliary view. Scale: 1/50.

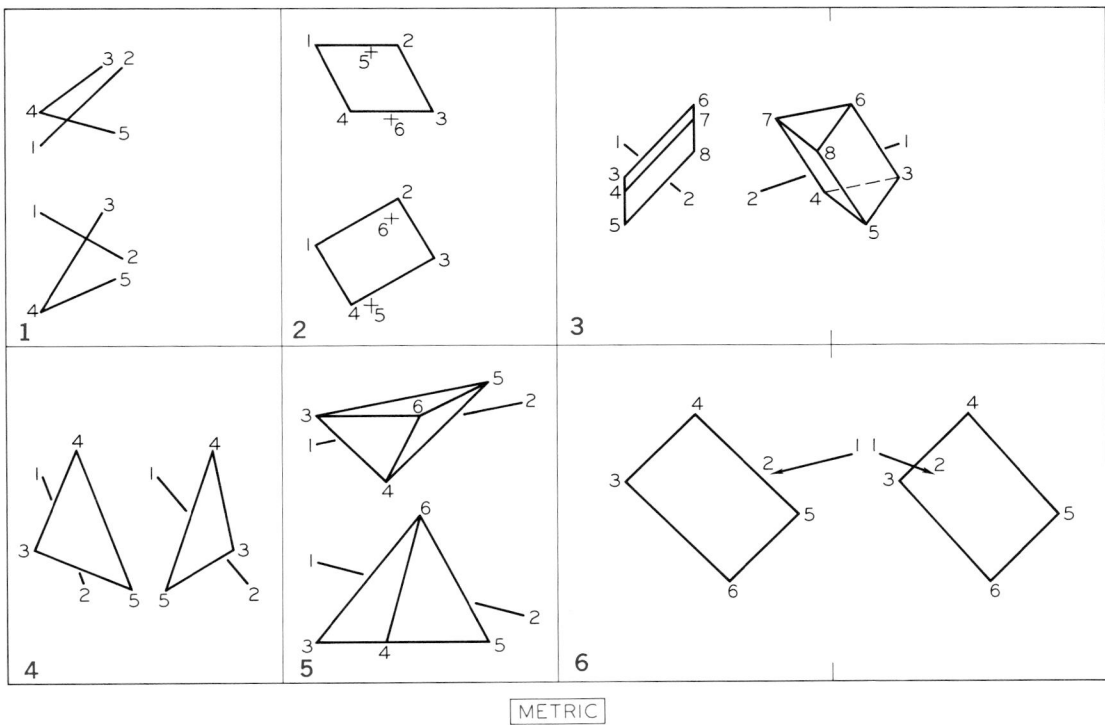

Fig. 19.42 Lay out and solve problems as assigned. Use Layout A–1 or A4–1 (adjusted) divided into four equal areas.

1. By the edge-view method, find the piercing point of line 1(12, 50, 75)–2(45, 32, 106) in plane 3(35, 50, 106)–4(12, 12, 88)–5(40, 25, 80).

2. By the edge-view method, complete the views of bulkhead 1(12, 38, 114)–2(43, 55, 114)–3(55, 33, 88)–4(–, –, –) and intersecting cable 5(33, 15, 112)–6(40, 48, 86). Show visibility.

3. Find the piercing points of line 1(25, 75, 127)–2(46, 58, 75) with the surfaces of prism 3(25, 63, 127)–4(25, 58, 98)–5(25, 45, 114)–6(50, 90, 108)–7(50, –, –)–8(50, –, –). Omit that portion of line 1–2 within the prism.

4. By the cutting-plane method, find the piercing point of line 1(12, 78, 55)–2(28, 38, 114) with plane 3(10, 50, 83)–4(25, 88, 75)–5(45, 35, 58). Show visibility.

5. By the cutting-plane method, find the piercing points of line 1(12, 45, 91)–2(88, 25, 106) with the surfaces of pyramid 3(12, 15, 100)–4(38, 15, 75)–5(75, 15, 114)–6(50, 63, 100). Omit that portion of line 1–2 within the pyramid, but show visibility otherwise.

6. Find the point at which light ray 1(109, 86, 119)–2(78, 78, 134) strikes mirror 3(25, 75, 127)–4(50, 100, 152)–5(88, 63, 185)–6(–, –, –).

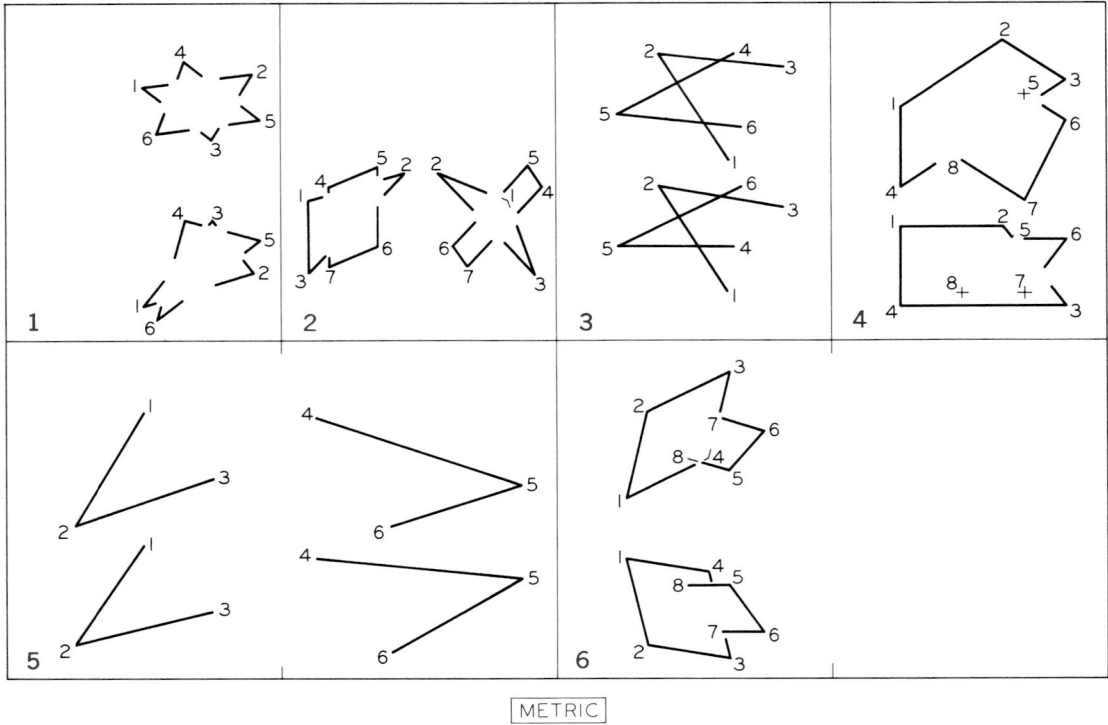

METRIC

Fig. 19.43 Lay out and solve problems as assigned. Use Layout A–1 or A4–1 (adjusted) divided into four equal areas.

1. By the edge-view method, find the intersection of planes 1(50, 12, 96)–2(91, 25, 100)–3(75, 45, 75) and 4(66, 45, 106)–5(94, 38, 83)–6(55, 7, 78). Show complete visibility.
2. By the edge-view method, find the intersection of planes 1(10, 53, 83)–2(45, 63, 58)–3(10, 25, 94) and 4(17, 58, 96)–5(35, 65, 91)–6(35, –, –)–7(17, 28, 68) Show complete visibility.
3. By the cutting-plane method, find the intersection of planes 1(63, 17, 68)–2(38, 58, 109)–3(83, 50, 104) and 4(66, 35, 109)–5(23, 35, 86)–6(68, 58, 81).
4. By the cutting-plane method, find the intersection of roof planes 1(25, 43, 88)–2(60, 43, 114)–3(86, 12, –)–4(25, 12, 58) and 5(71, 38, –)–6(86, 38, 84)–7(71, 17, 53)–8(48, 17, 68) and complete the views.
5. By the special cutting-plane method, find the intersection of planes 1(50, 50, 100)–2(25, 12, 58)–3(75, 25, 75) and 4(114, 48, 99)–5(190, 38, 73)–6(142, 10, 58).
6. Find and measure the dihedral angle between planes 1(25, 46, 68)–2(33, 12, 100)–3(63, 8, 117)–4(–, –, –) and 5(63, 35, 68)–6(75, 17, 94)–7(58, 17, –)–8(48, 35, 84).

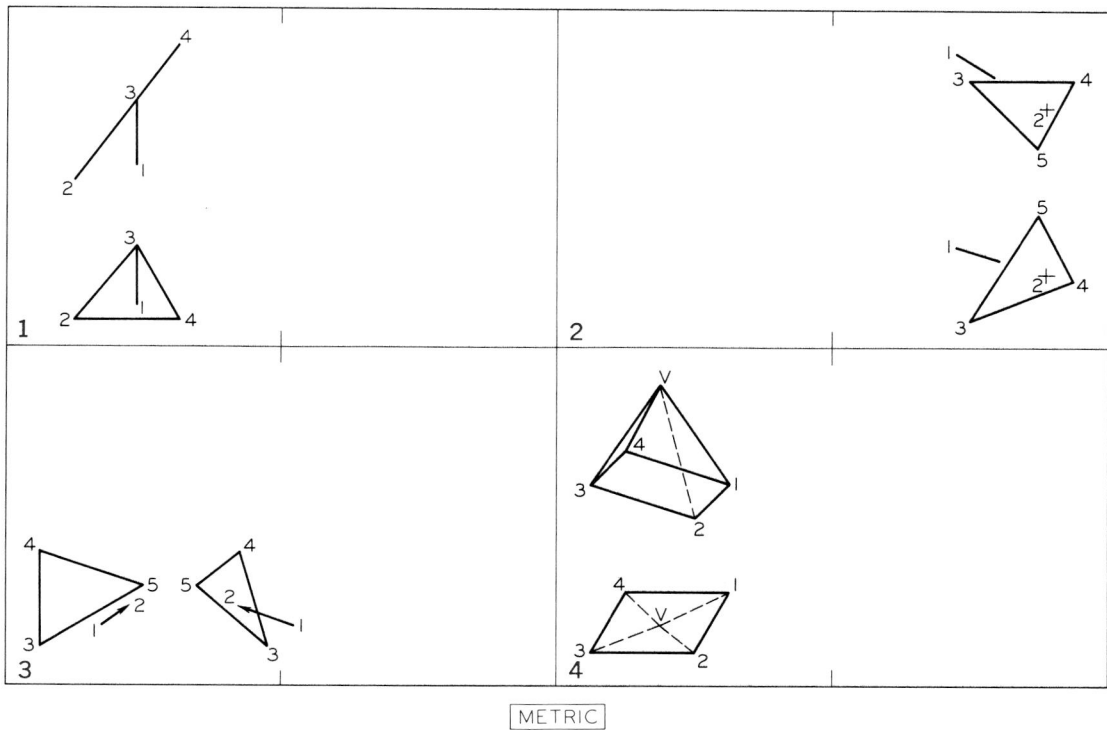

METRIC

Fig. 19.44 Lay out and solve problems as assigned. Use Layout A–1 or A4–1 (adjusted) divided into four equal areas.

1. Find the angle between line 1(48, 15, 68)–3(48, 38, –) and plane 2(50, 10, 63)–3–4(63, 10, 114).
2. Find the angle between cable 1(147, 38, 112)–2(180, 28, 91) and bulkhead 3(152, 10, 100)–4(190, 25, 100)–5(177, 50, 75). Show visibility.
3. Find the angle between force vector 1(35, 23, 106)–2(45, 30, 86) and plane 3(12, 15, 96)–4(12, 50, 86)–5(50, 38, 70).
4. Find the angle between lateral edge V(38, 23, 114)–1(63, 35, 75) and base plane 1–2(50, 12, 63)–3(12, 12, 75)–4(–, 35, –) of the pyramid.

Parallelism and Perpendicularity

The parallelism of lines is a condition that is preserved in orthographic projection, as demonstrated in §7.25. Parallel lines in space will be projected as parallel lines in any view. Although the parallel lines may appear as points or coincide as a single line in a view, these special cases are not regarded as exceptions to the rule.

The perpendicularity relationship of a line to a plane includes all lines in the plane through the foot of the perpendicular in addition to any other lines in the plane. If two lines are perpendicular in space, they will appear perpendicular in any view that shows at least one of the lines in true length, except if one of the lines appears as a point.

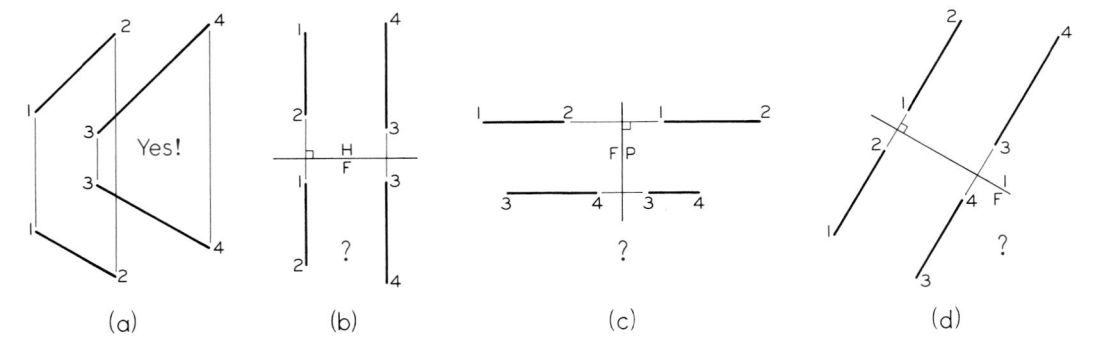

Fig. 20.1   Parallel Views: *Are the Lines Parallel in Space?*

20.1 Parallel Lines

In most situations it is valid to state that two lines drawn parallel in two adjacent views are parallel in space, Fig. 20.1 (a). However, there is an important exception: If the two adjacent views of two lines are perpendicular to the folding line between them, the lines are parallel in the views, but the lines may or may not be parallel in space, Fig. 20.1 (b), (c), and (d).

Let us study further the case of Fig. 20.1 (c). When the top view is constructed, Fig. 20.2 (a), it becomes obvious that the lines are not parallel.

If it is desired to make lines 1–2 and 3–4 parallel in space, one given view may be left incomplete, for example, the side view of line 3–4 at (b)—that is, one end point (point 4) is not immediately located. The top view is then constructed, with the top view of line 3–4 drawn parallel to line 1–2, point 4 being located by the vertical projection line from its front view. Divider distance D_1 is then used as shown at (c) to locate the side view of point 4. Thus when two or more lines in adjacent views appear perpendicular to the folding line between the views, the test

for parallelism is the construction of a third view whose direction of sight is other than parallel to the given views.

20.2 Parallel Planes

Planes may be established parallel to each other by drawing their edge views parallel, Fig. 20.3. Let it be assumed, as at (a), that plane 1–2–3 and point 4 are given, and it is desired to establish a plane 4–5–6 parallel to plane 1–2–3. First, the edge view of plane 1–2–3 is constructed as shown. Then the edge view of the other plane is drawn through point 4 parallel to the first edge view.

Because no further information about points 5 and 6 is given, points 5 and 6 are assumed at any random locations along the edge view of plane 4–5–6, as at (b). However, it is known that to represent a plane in space, three points must not be in a straight line, §19.7. Accordingly, projection lines are drawn from point 5 and 6 in the auxiliary view to the top view, and points 5 and 6 are placed arbitrarily in the top view along the respective pro-

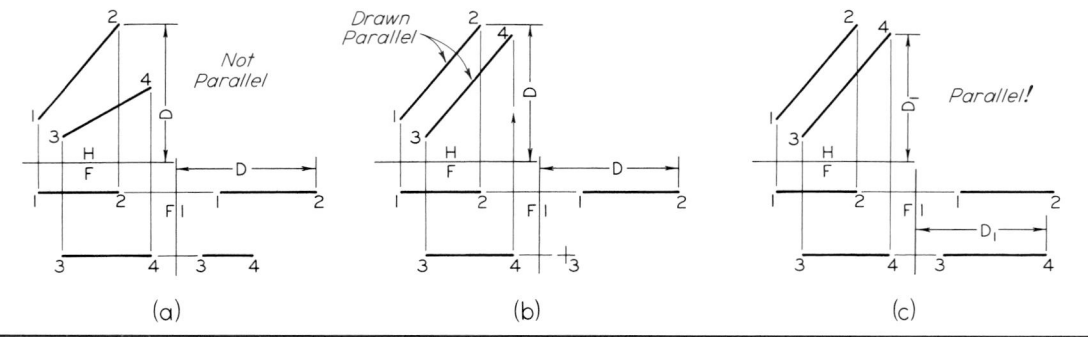

Fig. 20.2   Construction of Parallel Horizontal Lines.

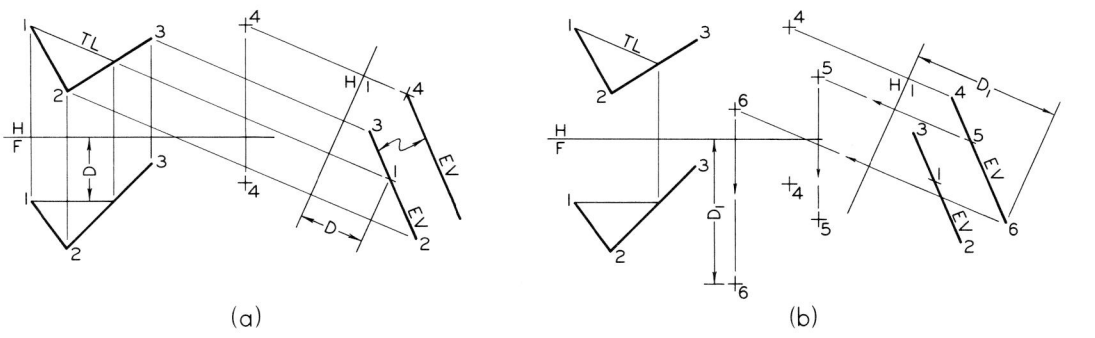

Fig. 20.3 Parallel Planes by Parallel Edge Views.

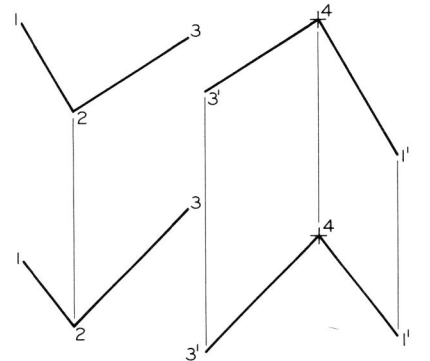

Fig. 20.4 Parallel Planes by Parallel Lines.

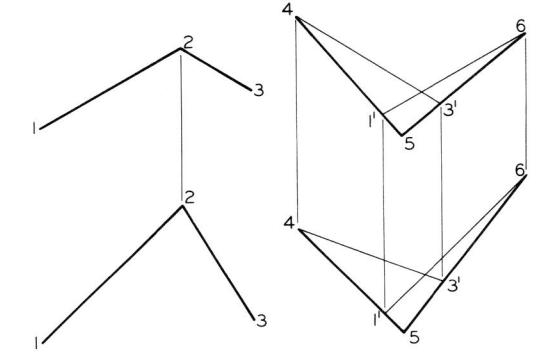

Fig. 20.5 Checking Parallelism of Planes with Intersecting Lines.

jection lines. The front views are then located by projection from the top view and transfer of distances such as D_1.

A somewhat simpler and more commonly used procedure for drawing parallel planes is shown in Fig. 20.4. The method depends on this principle: *If a pair of intersecting lines in one plane is parallel to a pair of intersecting lines in a second plane, the planes are parallel.* Thus the preceding problem, Fig. 20.3 (a), is readily solved as in Fig. 20.4. Line 4–3′ is drawn parallel to line 2–3 in both views, and line 4–1′ is drawn parallel to line 1–2. Plane 3–4–1′ is parallel to plane 1–2–3. The lines 4–3′ and 4–1′ may be of any desired length.

The intersecting-line principle can also be used to check for parallelism. In Fig. 20.5, line 6–1′ was added in the top view of plane 4–5–6 and parallel to line 1–2 of plane 1–2–3. When the front view of point 1′ is located, line 6–1′ is found to be parallel to line 1–2. Continuing the investigation: In the top view of plane 4–5–6, line 4–3′ is added parallel to line 2–3. When the front view of line 4–3′ is located,

however, it is seen that it is *not* parallel to the front view of line 2–3. Hence planes 1–2–3 and 4–5–6 are *not* parallel in space.

20.3 Line Parallel to Plane

A line is parallel to a plane if it is parallel to a line in the plane. To establish line 4–5′ parallel to the plane 1–2–3, Fig. 20.6, line 3–5 is arbitrarily se-

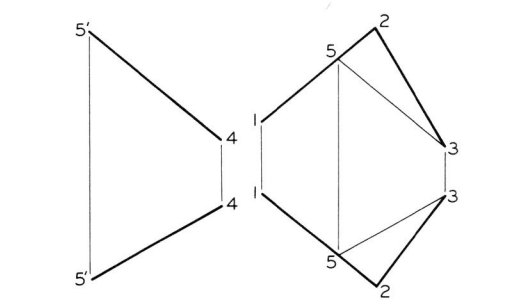

Fig. 20.6 Line Parallel to Plane.

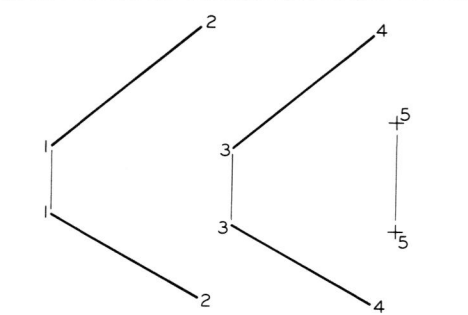

Fig. 20.7 Plane Parallel to Line.

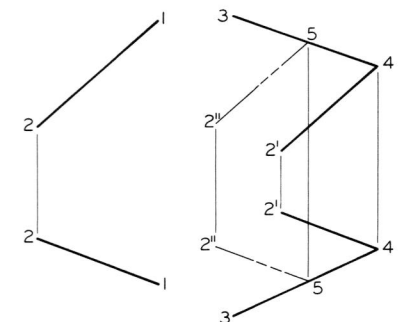

Fig. 20.8 Plane Through One or Two Skew Lines and Parallel to the Other.

lected and added to the plane 1–2–3. Line 4–5′ is then drawn parallel to line 3–5 in the plane. It is possible that line 4–5′ is *in* plane 1–2–3 (if extended). Even if true, this is not considered an exception to the general principle.

20.4 Plane Parallel to Line

A plane is parallel to a line if it contains a line that is parallel to the given line. Thus, if plane 1–2–3 is parallel to line 4–5′, Fig. 20.6, line 3–5 added to the plane 1–2–3 and parallel to line 4–5 will be parallel to line 4–5′ in all views. This is the converse of the principle of §20.3. Logically, if line 4–5′ in Fig. 20.6 is parallel to plane 1–2–3, it follows that plane 1–2–3 is parallel to line 4–5′.

Suppose we are given two parallel lines 1–2 and 3–4, Fig. 20.7. How many planes can be "passed through" line 3–4 parallel to line 1–2? If any random point 5 is added (not on 3–4), a plane 3–4–5 is established, §19.7. The plane is parallel to line 1–2 because it contains line 3–4. Thus it is seen that an infinite number of planes can be passed through one of two parallel lines and parallel to the other.

On the other hand, Fig. 20.8, let two *skew* lines 1–2 and 3–4 be given, and let it be required to pass a plane through line 3–4 and parallel to line 1–2. If a line is added, such as 4–2′, parallel to line 1–2, plane 3–4–2′ is parallel to line 1–2. Note that the added line could be made to intersect line 3–4 at any point, such as 5, resulting in plane 3–5–2″. However, this is merely a revised representation of plane 3–4–2′. It is evident, then, that through one of two skew lines only one plane can be passed parallel to the other line.

In Fig. 20.9, let skew lines 1–2 and 3–4 and point

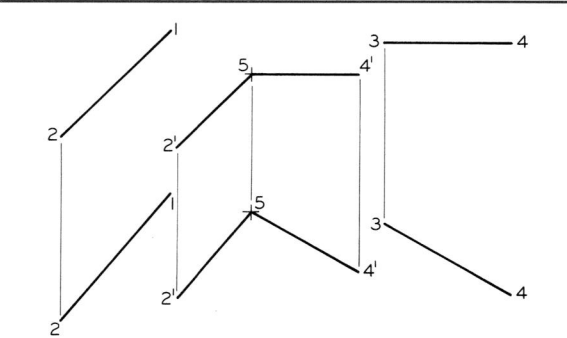

Fig. 20.9 Plane Through Point Parallel to Skew Lines.

5 be given, and let a plane be required through the point and parallel to the skew lines. If line 5–2′ is drawn parallel to line 1–2, and line 5–4′ is drawn parallel to line 3–4, plane 2′–5–4′ is parallel to both lines 1–2 and 3–4, even though nonintersecting lines 1–2 and 3–4 do not represent a plane.

20.5 Perpendicular Lines

In §7.26 it was observed that a 90° angle is projected in true size, even though it is in an inclined plane, provided one leg of the angle is a *normal* line, Fig. 7.29 (d). This principle can be restated in broader terms: *A 90° angle appears in true size in any view showing one leg true length,* provided the other leg does not appear as a point in the same view. Thus, in Fig. 20.10, lines 2–3, 2–4, 2–5, and 2–6 are all perpendicular to line 1–2, and they appear at 90° to the true-length front view of line 1–2. Note that the 90° angle is not observed in the top view where none of the lines is true length.

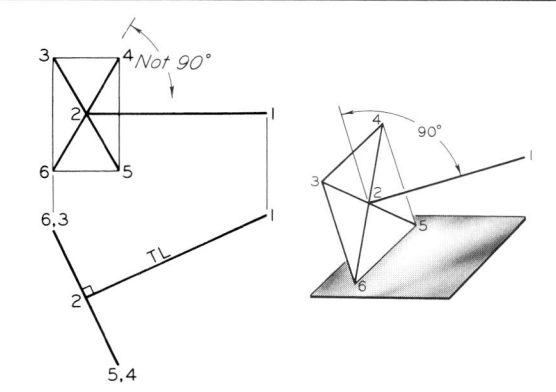

Fig. 20.10 Lines Perpendicular to True-Length Line.

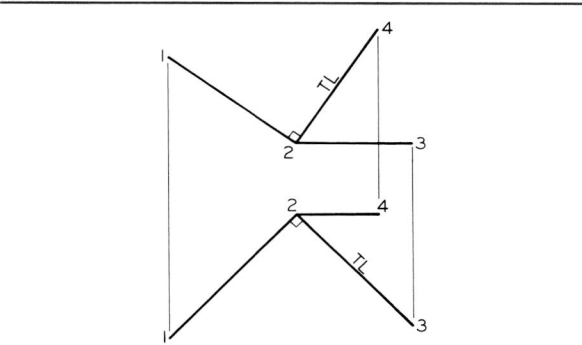

Fig. 20.11 True-Length Lines Perpendicular to Oblique Line.

In Fig. 20.11 each of the lines 2–3 and 2–4 is perpendicular to oblique line 1–2 because their true-length views are perpendicular to the corresponding views of line 1–2. (Note that line 2–3 is a frontal line and line 2–4 is a horizontal line, §19.2.)

20.6 Plane Perpendicular to Line
Given-View Method

To establish a plane perpendicular to a line, Fig. 20.12 (a), true-length lines are drawn perpendicular to given line 1–2 in the same manner as in Fig. 20.11. Now consider plane 3–2–4 in Fig. 20.12 (a). Since it is represented by intersecting lines, each of which is perpendicular to line 1–2, the plane is perpendicular to line 1–2.

Then consider the case at (b) where a plane through given point 5 and perpendicular to line 1–2 is desired. If plane 3′–5–4′ is constructed parallel to plane 3–2–4 of part (a), plane 3′–5–4′ will also be perpendicular to line 1–2. However, plane 3′–5–4′ could be drawn directly—without the use of plane 3–2–4—merely by drawing the true-length views of lines 3′–5 and 5–4′, respectively, perpendicular to the corresponding views of line 1–2, as indicated at (b).

Note that lines 3′–5 and 5–4′ do *not* intersect line 1–2. (You may prove this for yourself by extending the lines and checking vertical alignment of crossing points.) Thus, for present purposes, it is useful to regard the perpendicular true-length view *position principle* as indicating perpendicular lines, without regard to whether the lines intersect.

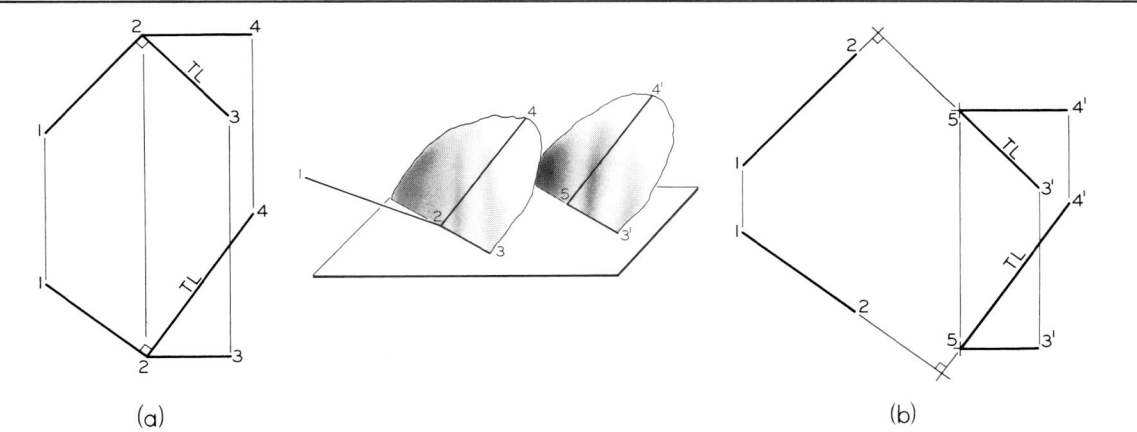

(a)   (b)

Fig. 20.12 Plane Perpendicular to Line—Given-View Method.

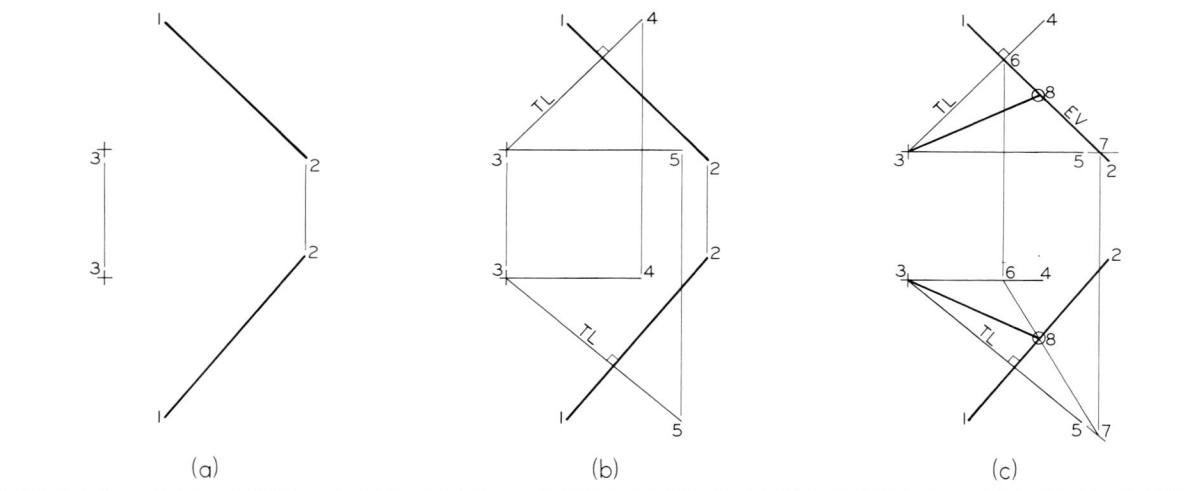

Fig. 20.13   Plane Perpendicular to Line—Application.

APPLICATION OF GIVEN-VIEW METHOD

Given: Views of a line 1–2 and a point 3, Fig. 20.13 (a).

Req'd: Find a line from point 3 perpendicular to and intersecting line 1–2. Use only the given views.

Analysis and Procedure: If a horizontal line 3–4 is drawn through point 3 with its true-length view perpendicular to the top view of 1–2 as at (b), it does not intersect line 1–2. Similarly, if a frontal line 3–5 is drawn perpendicular to line 1–2, it also does not intersect line 1–2. Neither of these lines is the required line. We conclude that the required line will not appear perpendicular in the given views. However, 4–3–5 represents a *plane* perpendicular to line 1–2, and all lines in the plane are perpendicular to line 1–2. Plane 4–3–5 is the locus of all lines through point 3 perpendicular to line 1–2. The required line belongs to this locus or family of lines.

By the cutting-plane method of §19.11, the piercing point 8 of line 1–2 in plane 4–3–5 is found, Fig. 20.13 (c). This is the only point on line 1–2 that is in the plane, and thus line 3–8 is the only possible solution to the problem.

Auxiliary-View Method

A plane also may be constructed perpendicular to a line by drawing its edge view perpendicular to the true-length view of the line, Fig. 20.14. At (a) given line 1–2 and point 3 are projected to the true-length auxiliary view, where the edge view of the required plane is drawn through point 3 and perpendicular to the true-length view as indicated. If it is desired

to represent the perpendicular plane in the top and front views, as at (b), any convenient pair of points, such as 4 and 5, is selected on the edge view. In the top view points 4 and 5 may be placed at any desired locations along the projection line from view 1. Points 4 and 5 are then located in the front view by the divider distances as indicated.

APPLICATION OF AUXILIARY-VIEW METHOD

Given: A right square prism, Fig. 5.7 (6), has its axis along line 1–2 and one corner at point 3, Fig. 20.15 (a). The other base is centered at point 4.

Req'd: Find the views of the prism.

Analysis and Procedure: Auxiliary view 1 is added showing axis 1–2 in true length. Because a *right* prism is required, the bases must be perpendicular to axis 1–2 and appear in view 1 in edge view and perpendicular to axis 1–2. At (b) the point view of axis 1–2 is added. This view shows the true shape of the square bases and the size of the square is established by the position of corner 3. By the method of Fig. 5.23 (c), the square is constructed.

The projection process is now reversed. The corners are projected from view 2 to view 1, which is then completed. Next, the corners are projected to the top view and located with divider distances such as D_2. Observe that a square prism is composed of three sets of parallel lines. Check the view for parallelism and correct any errors before proceeding.

Finally, the front view is projected in similar fashion. Again, the construction work should be

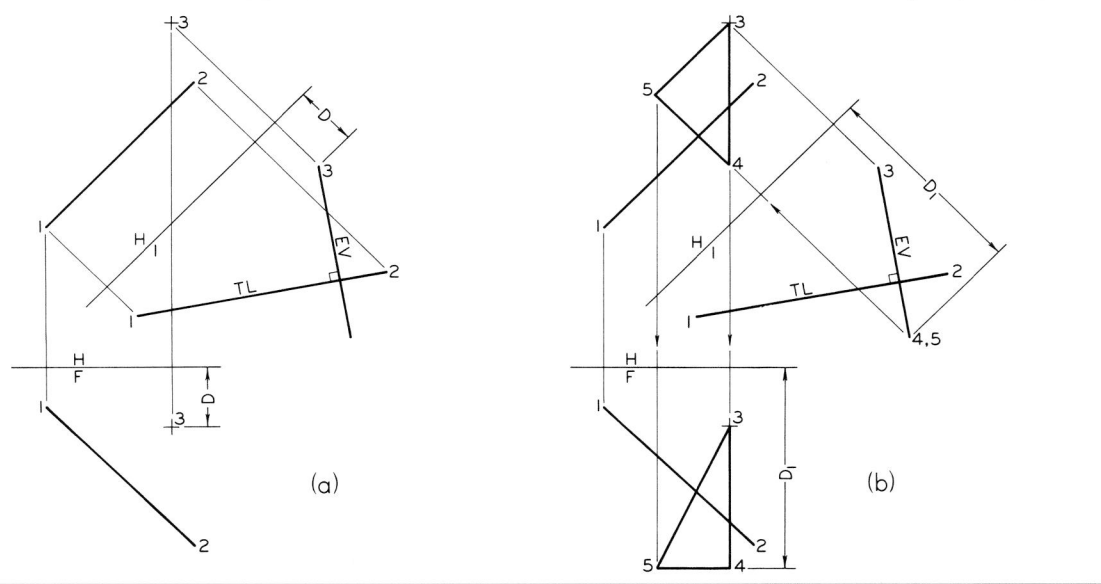

Fig. 20.14 Plane Perpendicular to Line—Auxiliary-View Method.

checked for accurate parallelism before the views are completed.

20.7 Line Perpendicular to Plane

A line perpendicular to a plane is perpendicular to all lines in the plane. In practice, it is sufficient to state that a line is perpendicular to a plane if it is perpendicular to at least two nonparallel lines in the

plane. This line will also appear perpendicular (and in true length) to the edge view of the plane. Either principle may be used in the construction of a line perpendicular to a plane.

It is desired to construct by the given-view method, Fig. 20.16, a line from point **4** perpendicular to plane **1–2–3**. Since the plane is oblique, the perpendicular line will be oblique and will not appear in true length. Although the required line will

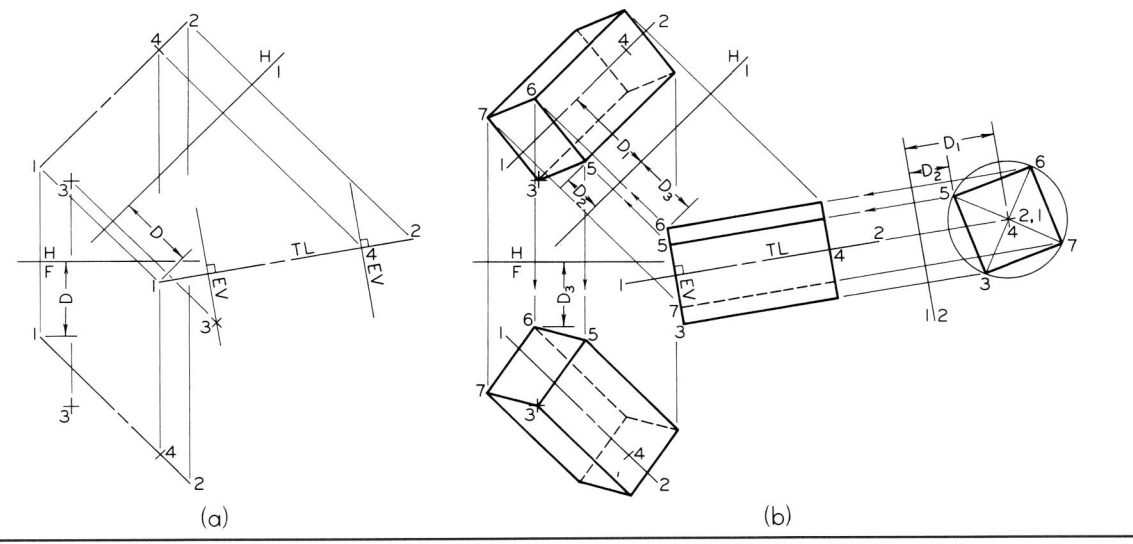

Fig. 20.15 Plane Perpendicular to Line—Application.

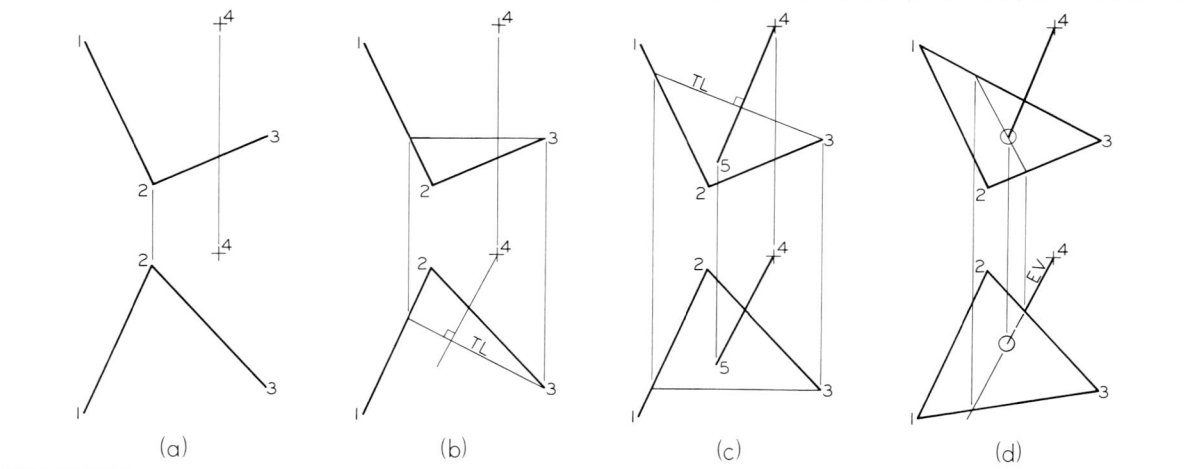

Fig. 20.16   Line Perpendicular to Plane—Given-View Method.

be perpendicular in space to lines 1–2 and 2–3, the 90° angles between the given lines 1–2 and 2–3 and the required line will not appear in the given views because lines 1–2 and 2–3 are not shown in true length.

If a frontal line is added to plane 1–2–3, as at (b), its front view is true length, and the front view of the required line will be perpendicular to the true-length view of the frontal line as shown. It must be realized that at this stage nothing has been determined about the direction of the perpendicular in the top view. Nor is the point at which the perpendicular strikes the plane—its piercing point—known. (Frequently the location of the piercing point is of no interest.)

At (c) a horizontal line is added. The true-length view of the horizontal line determines the direction of the top view of the required perpendicular. Again, the piercing point has not been determined, but two views have been established and thus a space description of the required perpendicular from point 4 with plane 1–2–3 has been constructed. Point 5 is arbitrarily selected as an end point of the line, not necessarily in the plane.

If it is desired to terminate the perpendicular in plane 1–2–3, it will be necessary to find the piercing point by one of the methods of §19.11. At (d) the cutting-plane method was used to minimize construction.

20.8 Perpendicular Planes

If a line is perpendicular to a given plane, any plane containing the line is perpendicular to the given plane. Since an infinite number of planes can be

passed through such a perpendicular, it was chosen in Fig. 20.17 to illustrate perpendicular planes by a more restricted example: How to pass a plane through given line 4–5 and perpendicular to given plane 1–2–3.

At (a) a horizontal line is added to the plane. Since a horizontal line appears true length in the top view, it determines the direction of the required perpendicular in that view (but, remember, not in the front view). Point 5 is selected as being convenient for the origin of the perpendicular.

At (b) a frontal line is added to plane 1–2–3 to establish a true-length line in the front view, which is needed to determine the direction of the front view of the required perpendicular. It is assumed that the piercing point of the perpendicular is of no interest here. Accordingly, any arbitrary point, such as 6, is used to terminate the perpendicular and complete the representation of the required perpendicular plane 4–5–6.

20.9 Common Perpendicular Between Skew Lines

The shortest distance, or clearance, between any two lines is measured along a line perpendicular to both lines. Study Fig. 20.18. Suppose line 5–6 to be perpendicular to line 1–2, intersecting line 3–4 at 6. Now let line 5–6 move to position 5′–6′, still perpendicular to line 1–2 and intersecting line 3–4 at point 6′. Continue the process of moving line 5–6 upward along line 1–2. Note that it will gradually shorten until eventually it reaches a minimum length and will begin to lengthen if moved further. At its minimum length it will be perpendicular to

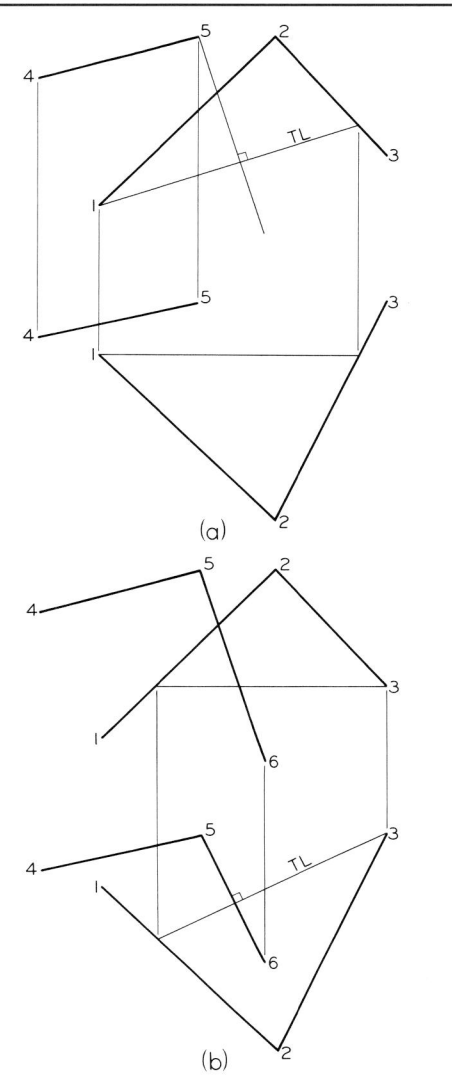

(a)

(b)

Fig. 20.17   Perpendicular Planes.

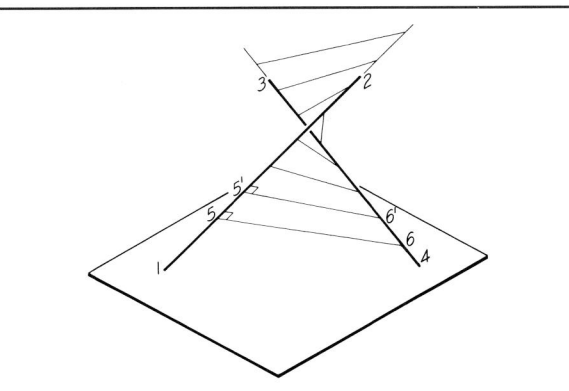

Fig. 20.18   Common Perpendicular.

line **3–4** also. This is the common perpendicular representing the shortest distance between the skew lines **1–2** and **3–4**. Several procedures are available for locating the views of the common perpendicular in multiview projection, two of which will be discussed here.

Point-View Method

If a point view of any given line is constructed, a line that is perpendicular to the given line will show in true length in the view showing the given line as a point. As noted in §19.6, a point view of a line must be preceded by a true-length view of the line. Accordingly, in Fig. 20.19 (a) line **3–4** is arbitrarily chosen to be shown in true length and view **1** is projected. As shown at (b), view **2** is then constructed showing line **3–4** as a point. In this view, any line perpendicular to line **3–4** (including the shortest connector) must appear in true length. Since the shortest connector is also perpendicular to line **1–2**, it must appear at 90° to line **1–2** as shown, even though line **1–2** is not true length. If only the shortest distance is required, it is measured in view **2** and the construction is complete.

If, in addition, the views of the common perpendicular are required, we proceed as shown at (b). Point **5** is projected to line **1–2** in view **1**. In this view the common perpendicular is not true length. Line **3–4** *is* true length, however, so line **5–6** is drawn perpendicular to line **3–4** in view **1** as shown. It is then routine to project line **5–6** to the top view and then to the front view. Divider distances such as D_2 and D_3 are used to check the accuracy of the construction.

Plane Method

If a plane containing one of two skew lines is parallel to the second line, the perpendicular distance from the second line to the plane is the shortest distance between the two lines.

In Fig. 20.20 (a) a line is drawn through point **2** parallel to line **3–4**, thus establishing a plane containing line **1–2** and parallel to line **3–4**, §20.4. The edge view of the plane is then established in auxiliary view **1**. In this view the shortest distance is measured as shown. The shortest distance being obtained in only one additional view is an advantage of the plane method over the point-view method.

If, in addition, the views of the common perpendicular are required, a second auxiliary view is necessary and the total amount of construction is slightly more than in the point-view method. At (b)

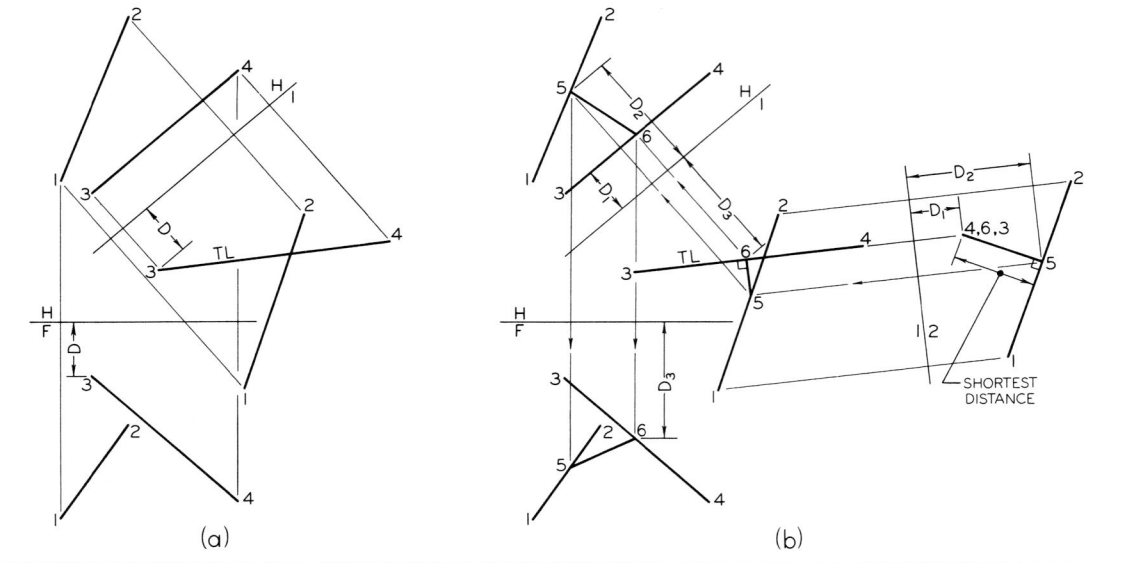

Fig. 20.19 Common Perpendicular—Point-View Method.

the second auxiliary view is constructed with its direction of sight parallel to the shortest distance (or perpendicular to the edge-view plane). In this view the shortest distance or common perpendicular must appear as a point. This can be only at the apparent crossing point **5, 6** of lines **1–2** and **3–4**. This locates the common perpendicular, which is then projected back to the other views as shown.

20.10 Shortest Horizontal Line Connecting Skew Lines

Related to the preceding plane method is the problem of finding the shortest line at zero slope or grade, the shortest horizontal line connecting two skew lines.

In Fig. 20.21 (a) a plane is constructed containing line **1–2** and parallel to line **3–4**. The edge view of

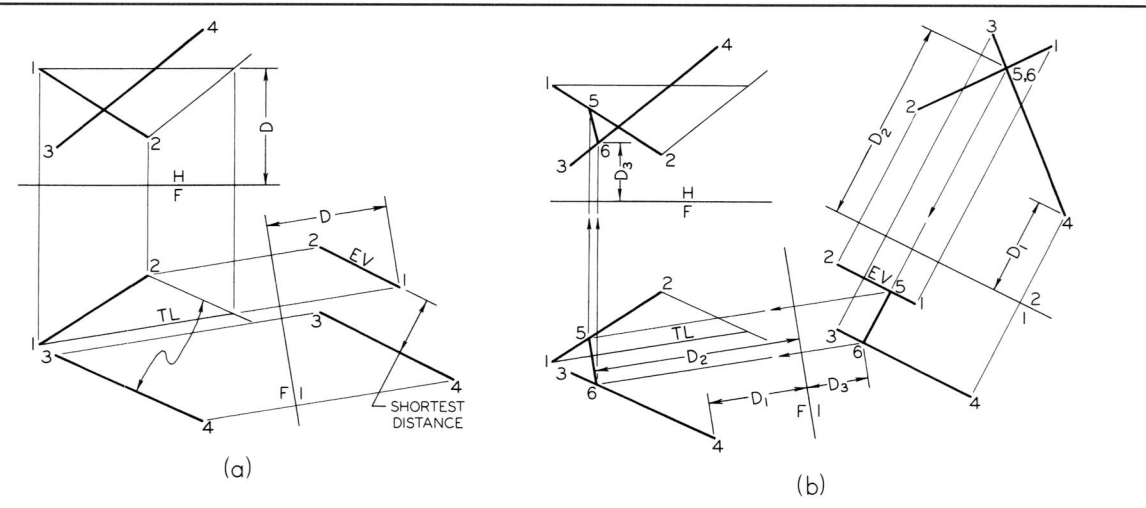

Fig. 20.20 Common Perpendicular—Plane Method.

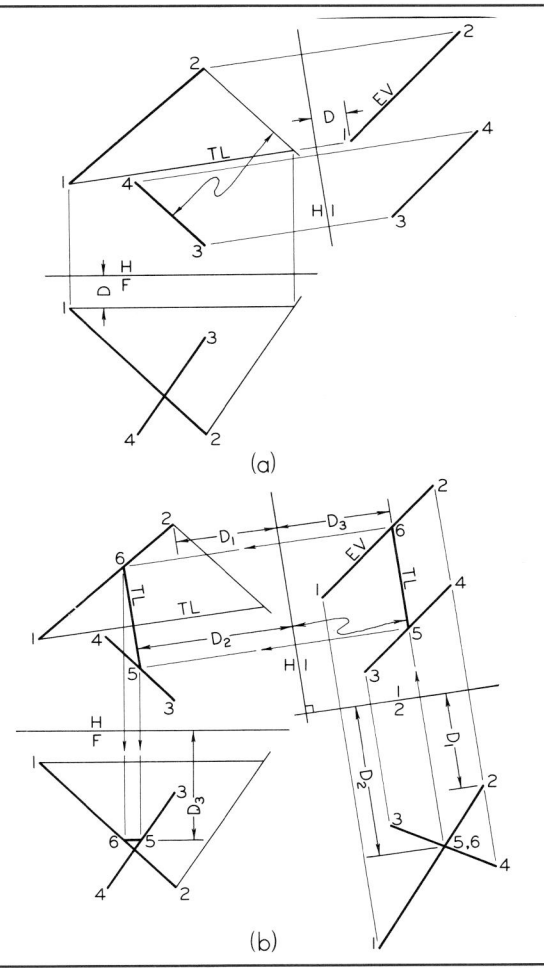

(a)

(b)

Fig. 20.21 Shortest Horizontal Line Connecting Two Skew Lines.

the plane is constructed through the use of a *horizontal* line added to the plane because in the auxiliary view **1** any horizontal connecting line will be parallel to folding line H/1.

Auxiliary view **2** is then constructed at (b) with its direction of sight parallel to folding line H/1. The shortest connector **5–6** appears in point view in view **2** at the apparent crossing point of lines **1–2** and **3–4**. It is then projected back to the other views.

20.11 Shortest Line at Specified Slope Connecting Skew Lines

For a specified slope other than zero (horizontal), the method of §20.10 requires only slight modification. In this example, it is assumed that **38°** is specified for the slope of the connecting line. The first portion of the construction is the same, Fig. 20.22 (a): A plane is passed through line **1–2** and parallel to line **3–4**, and an edge view of the plane is constructed, as shown, in an auxiliary view adjacent to the top view.

At (b) projection lines for view **2** are drawn at the prescribed slope angle with folding line H/1. In view **2**, the apparent crossing point **5, 6** of lines **1–2** and **3–4** is the point view of the shortest connector **5–6** at the specified slope of **38°**. The other views of line **5–6** are then completed by projection as before.

It should be noted that the general procedure illustrated could be readily modified for other specifications, such as the shortest connecting line at a prescribed grade or the shortest frontal line connecting two skew lines.

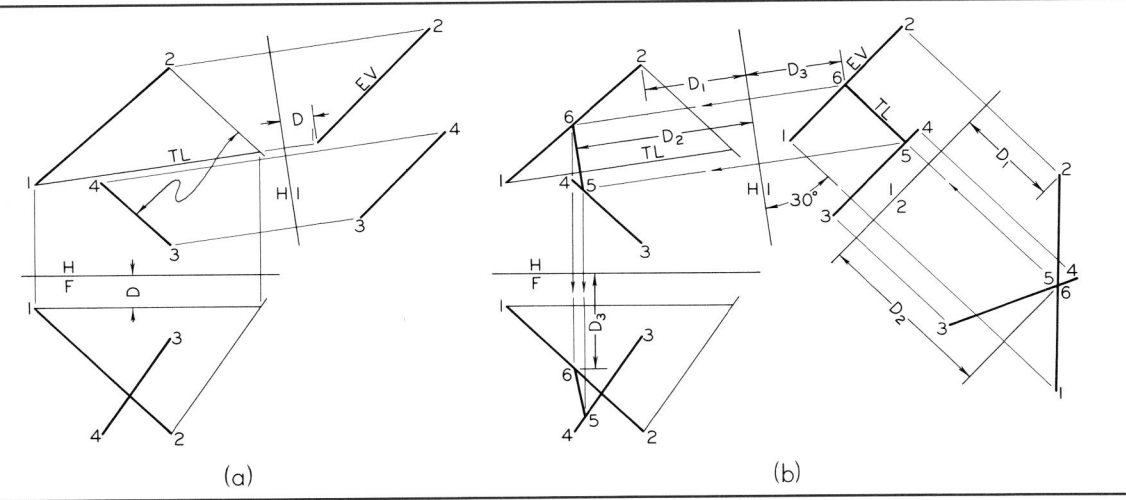

(a)   (b)

Fig. 20.22 Shortest Line at Specified Slope Connecting Two Skew Lines.

Problems in Parallelism and Perpendicularity

In Figs. 20.23–20.26 are problems covering parallel lines, lines parallel to a plane, plane parallel to a line, plane parallel to a plane or skew lines, perpendicular lines, lines perpendicular to planes, common perpendicular, and shortest line at specified angle.

Use Layout A–1 or A4–1 (adjusted) and divide the working area into four equal areas for problems to be assigned by the instructor. Some problems will require a single problem area, and others will require two problem areas or one-half sheet. Data for the layout for each problem are given by a coordinate system using metric dimensions. For example, in Fig. 20.23, Prob. 1, point **6** is located by the full-scale coordinates (**35, 20, 50**). The first coordinate locates the front view of the point from the left edge of the problem area. The second coordinate locates the front view of the point from the bottom edge of the problem area. The third coordinate locates either the top view of the point from the bottom edge of the problem area or the side view of the point from the left edge of the problem area. Inspection of the given problem layout will determine which application to use.

Since many of the problems in this chapter are of a general nature, they can also be solved on most computer graphics systems. If a system is available, the instructor may choose to assign specific problems to be completed by this method.

Additional problems in convenient form for solution are presented in the worksheets at the back of this book. Refer to Drawings 20-1 to 20-6 and accompanying instructions.

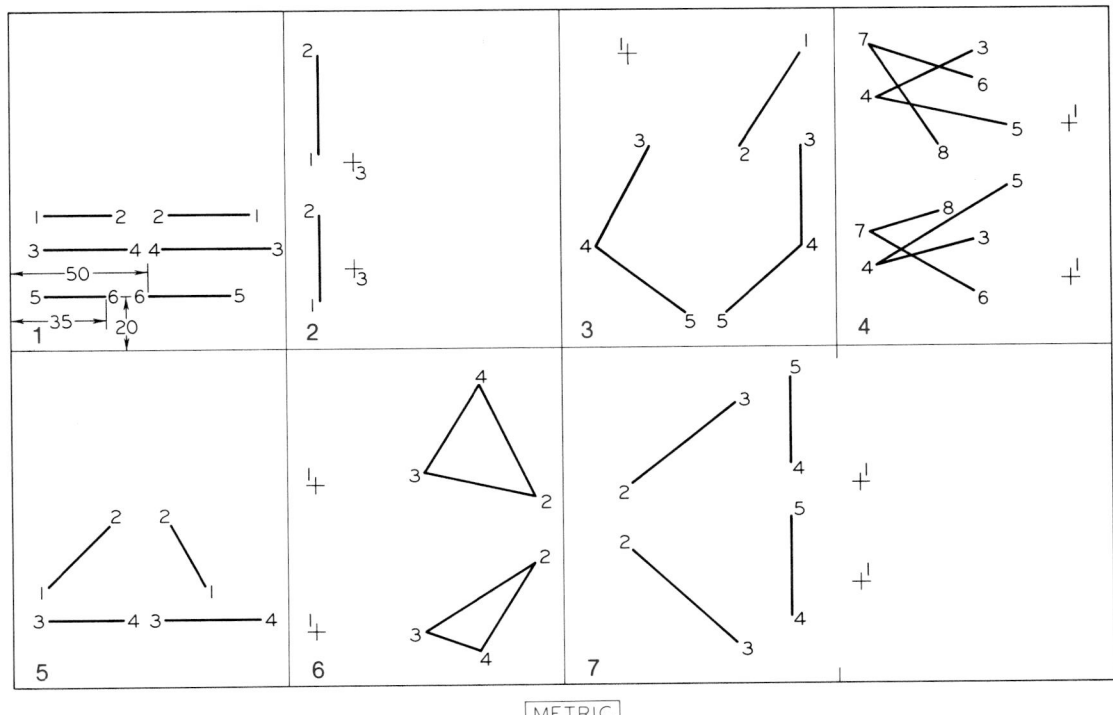

METRIC

Fig. 20.23 Lay out and solve problems as assigned. Use Layout A–1 or A4–1 (adjusted) divided into four equal areas.

1. Determine which, if any, of the lines 1(12, 50, 88)–2(38, 50, 58), 3(12, 38, 96)–4(43, 38, 55), or 5(12, 20, 81)–6(35, 20, 50) are parallel.
2. Draw a line 3(25, 30, 71)–4, 25 mm in length and parallel to line 1(12, 18, 73)–2(12, 50, 112).
3. Complete the side view of line 1(25, 112, 88)–2(?, 75, 65) that is parallel to plane 3(33, 75, 88)–4(12, 38, 88)–5(45, 12, 60).
4. Through point 1(86, 25, 83) draw a line 1–2 parallel to planes 3(50, 40, 112)–4(15, 30, 94)–5(63, 60, 84) and 6(50, 20, 100)–7(12, 43, 114)–8(38, 50, 75).
5. Pass a plane through line 1(12, 38, 70)–2(35, 60, 58) parallel to line 3(12, 25, 56)–4(40, 25, 91). Add the top view.
6. By means of a horizontal line and a frontal line represent a plane containing point 1(10, 20, 75) and parallel to plane 2(91, 45, 70)–3(50, 20, 81)–4(70, 12, 114).
7. Pass a plane through point 1(109, 38, 75) parallel to lines 2(25, 50, 75)–3(63, 15, 108) and 4(85, 25, 84)–5(85, 63, 107).

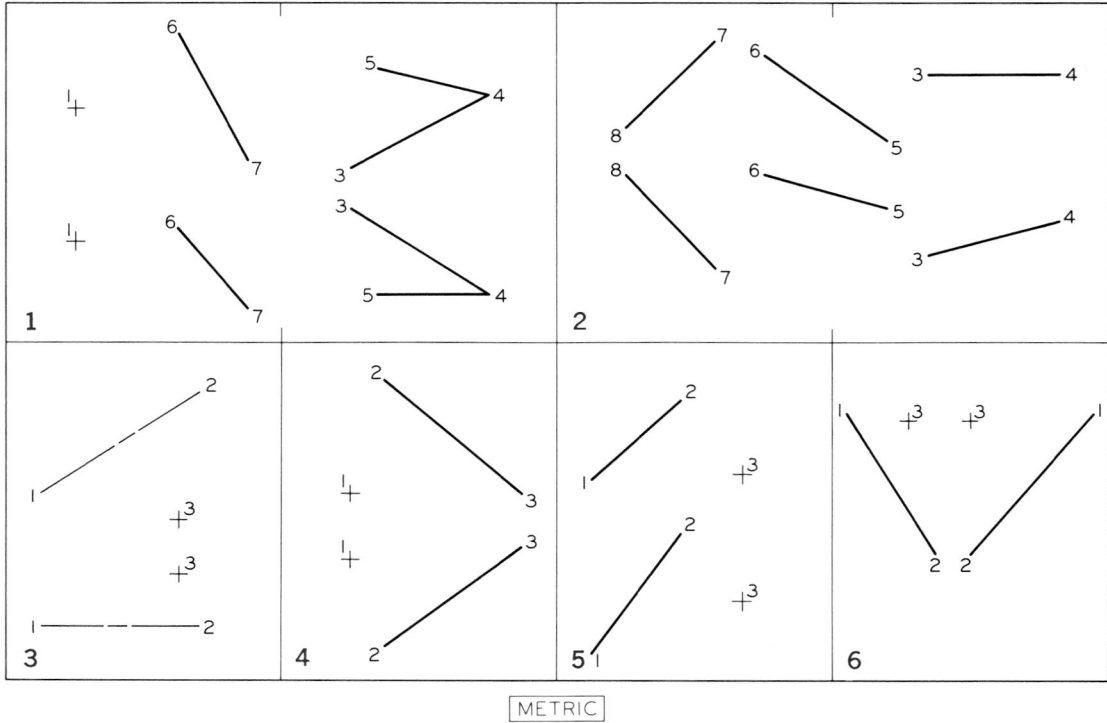

METRIC

Fig. 20.24 Lay out and solve problems as assigned. Use Layout A–1 or A4–1 (adjusted) divided into four equal areas.

1. Find a line 1(25, 38, 88)–2 that is parallel to plane 3(127, 50, 66)–4(178, 17, 94)–5(137, 17, 104) and intersects line 6(63, 43, 117)–7(88, 12, 60).

2. Establish a line 1–2 that is parallel to line 3(137, 33, 100)–4(185, 45, 100) and intersects lines 5(122, 50, 75)–6(75, 63, 109) and 7(58, 28, 114)–8(25, 63, 81).

3. Line 1(12, 20, 70)–2(70, 20, 109) is the center line of a pipe. Connect this pipe to point 3(63, 40, 60) with a 90° elbow (pipe fitting) at the juncture on 1–2. Find the true length of the center line of the connecting pipe. Scale: 1/10.

4. Draw a 50 mm frontal line from point 1(25, 45, 70) perpendicular to line 2(38, 12, 115)–3(88, 50, 70). Also draw a 50 mm horizontal line from point 1 perpendicular to line 2–3. Use only the given views. (Note that these lines do not intersect line 2–3.)

5. Using only the given views, find a line 3(68, 30, 78)–4 that is perpendicular to line 1(12, 10, 75)–2(45, 55, 106) and also intersects line 1–2.

6. Find the center of the smallest sphere that has its center on line 1(5, 100, 96)–2(38, 48, 50) and has point 3(28, 88, 50) on its surface. Use only the given views. If assigned, find the diameter of the sphere.

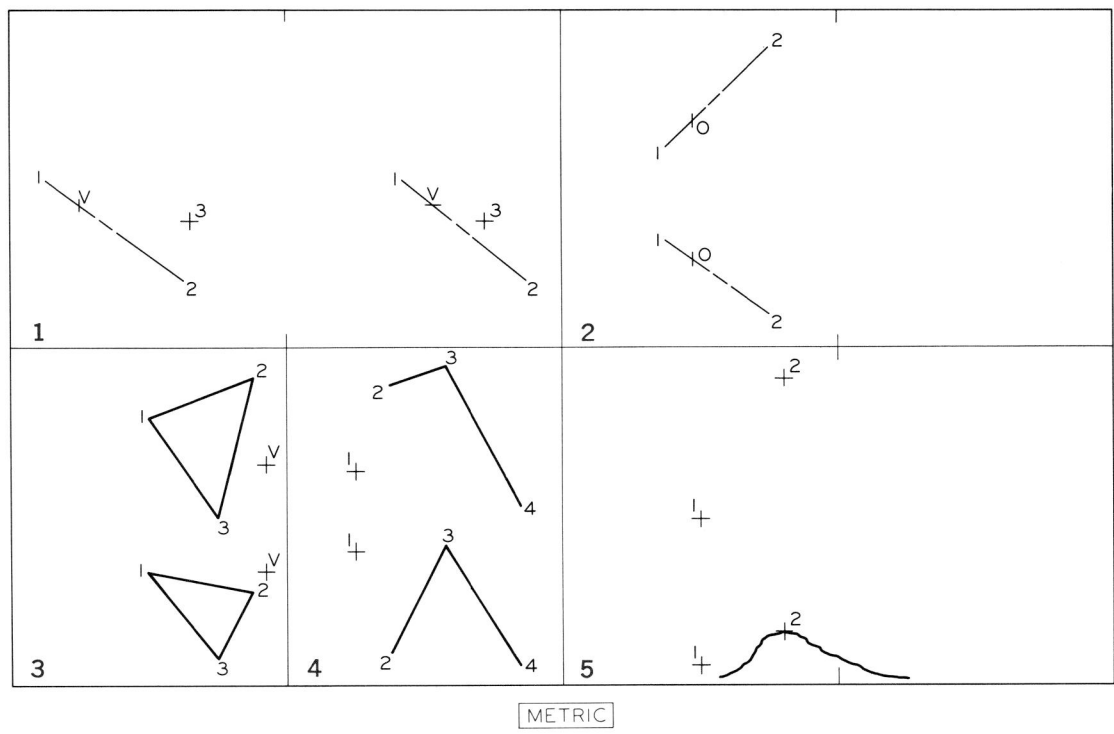

METRIC

Fig. 20.25 Lay out and solve problems as assigned. Use Layout A–1 or A4–1 (adjusted) divided into four equal areas.

1. The axis of a right square pyramid lies along center line 1(12, 63, 144)–2(63, 25, 190). One corner of the base is at point 3(66, 48, 175). The vertex is at point V(25, –, –). Find the front and side views of the pyramid.

2. The axis of a right prism lies along center line 1(38, 40, 75)–2(75, 12, 114). One base is centered at O(48, –, –). The bases are equilateral triangles inscribed in 36 mm diameter circles. The lowest side of each base is a horizontal line. The altitude of the prism is 35 mm. Complete the views.

3. If an oblique cone is drawn with its vertex at V(94, 43, 84) and its base in plane 1(50, 43, 100)–2(88, 35, 116)–3(75, 10, 63), what is its altitude in millimeters? Use an auxiliary view to solve this problem. Show the front and top views of the altitude.

4. Find the shadow of point 1(25, 50, 80) on plane 2(38, 12, 114)–3(57, 53, 122)–4(84, 7, 68) if light rays are perpendicular to the plane.

5. An aircraft on a landing approach course of N 45° passes 300 m above point 1(50, 7, 63). It is losing altitude at the rate of 200 m in 1000 m. Point 2(80, 20, 116) represents the peak of a hill. How close to point 2 does the aircraft pass? Scale: 1/10 000.

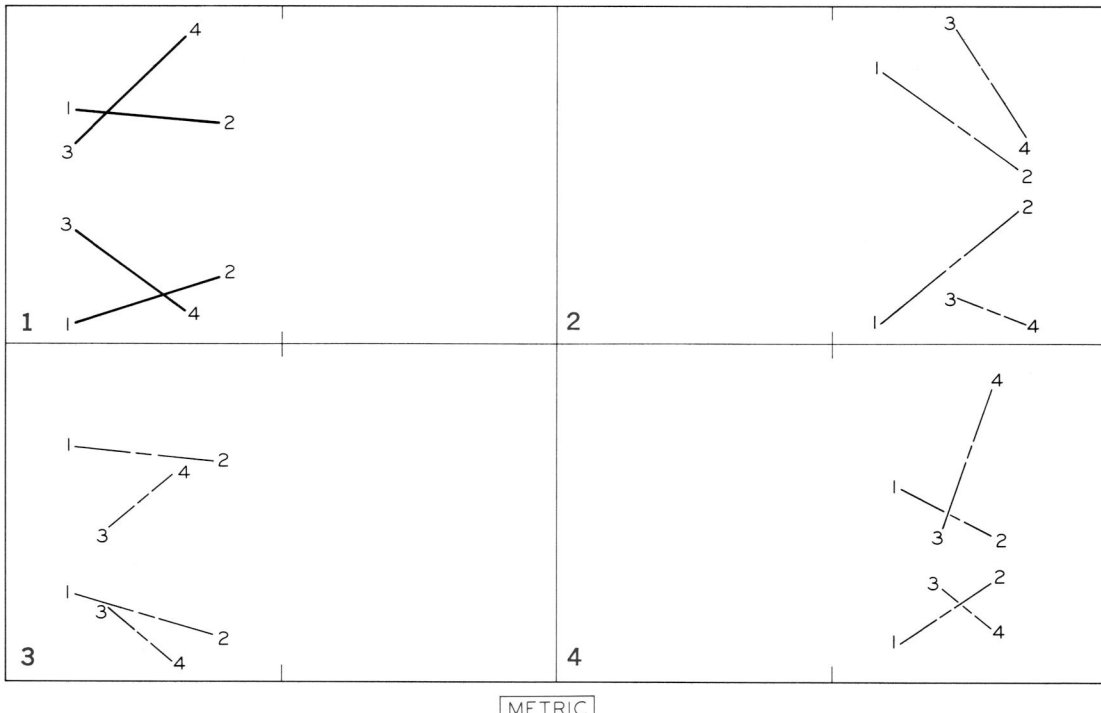

METRIC

Fig. 20.26 Lay out and solve problems as assigned. Use Layout A–1 or A4–1 (adjusted) divided into four equal areas.

1. Find the clearance between high-voltage lines 1(25, 7, 88)–2(78, 25, 84) and 3(25, 43, 75)–4(66, 12, 117). Show the views of a line representing this clearance. Scale: 1/40.
2. Determine the bearing, grade, and length of the shortest shaft connecting tunnels 1(120, 7, 104)–2(170, 50, 65) and 3(147, 18, 120)–4(172, 7, 78). Scale: 1/80.
3. Ski slopes represented by lines 1(25, 33, 88)–2(75, 18, 84) and 3(38, 28, 58)–4(61, 7, 78) are to be connected by the shortest possible horizontal path. Find the views and measure the length of this path. Scale: 1/4000.
4. Tunnel 1(127, 15, 73)–2(160, 38, 56) is to be connected to tunnel 3(142, 35, 58)–4(162, 20, 112) with the shortest tunnel at a downgrade of 10%. Find the length and bearing of this connector. Scale: 1/2000.

Intersections and Developments

A machine part or structure often consists of a number of geometric shapes so arranged as to produce the required form. Easily represented geometric forms frequently meet in lines of intersection that require knowledge and skill to produce in multiview projection. Accurate representation of the intersecting surfaces therefore becomes very important since precision fit is necessary for function and appearance. The development of these surfaces, such as those found in sheet-metal fabrication, is a flat pattern that represents the unfolded or unrolled surface of the form. The resulting plane figure gives the true size of each area of the form so connected that when fabricated the desired part or structure is produced.

21.1 Surfaces

A *surface* is a geometric magnitude having two dimensions. A surface may be generated by a line, called the *generatrix* of the surface. Any position of the generatrix is an *element* of the surface, Fig. 7.31 (a).

A *ruled surface* is one that may be generated by a straight line and may be a *plane*, a *single-curved surface*, or a *warped surface*.

A *plane* is a ruled surface that may be generated by a straight line one point of which moves along another straight line, while the generatrix remains parallel to its original position. Many of the geometric solids are bounded by plane surfaces, Fig. 5.7.

A *single-curved surface* is a developable ruled surface; that is, it can be unrolled to coincide with a plane. Any two adjacent positions of the generatrix lie in the same plane. Examples are the cylinder and the cone, Fig. 5.7.

A *warped surface* is a ruled surface that is not developable, Fig. 21.1. No two adjacent positions of the generatrix lie in the same plane. Many exterior surfaces on an airplane or automobile are warped surfaces.

A double-curved surface may be generated only by a curved line and has no straight-line elements. Such a surface, generated by revolving a curved line about a straight line in the plane of the curve, is called a *double-curved surface of revolution*. Common examples are the *sphere*, *torus*, *ellipsoid*, Fig. 5.7, and the *hyperboloid*, Fig. 21.1 (d).

A *developable surface* is one that may be unfolded or unrolled so as to coincide with a plane,

§21.4. Surfaces composed of single-curved surfaces, or of planes, or of combinations of these types, are developable. Warped surfaces and double-curved surfaces are not developable. They may be developed approximately by dividing them into sections and substituting for each section a developable surface, that is, a plane or a single-curved surface. If the material used is sufficiently pliable, the flat sheets may be stretched, pressed, stamped, spun, or otherwise forced to assume the desired shape. Nondevelopable surfaces are often produced by a combination of developable surfaces, which are then formed slightly to produce the required shape.

21.2 Solids

Solids bounded by plane surfaces are *polyhedra*, the most common of which are the pyramid and prism, Fig. 5.7. Convex solids whose faces are all equal regular polygons are *regular polyhedra*. The simple regular polyhedra are the *tetrahedron, cube, octahedron, dodecahedron,* and *icosahedron,* known as the five *Platonic solids.*

Plane surfaces that bound polyhedra are *faces* of the solids. Lines of intersection of faces are *edges* of the solids.

A solid generated by revolving a plane figure about an axis in the plane of the figure is a *solid of revolution.*

Solids bounded by warped surfaces have no group name. The most common example of such solids is the screw thread.

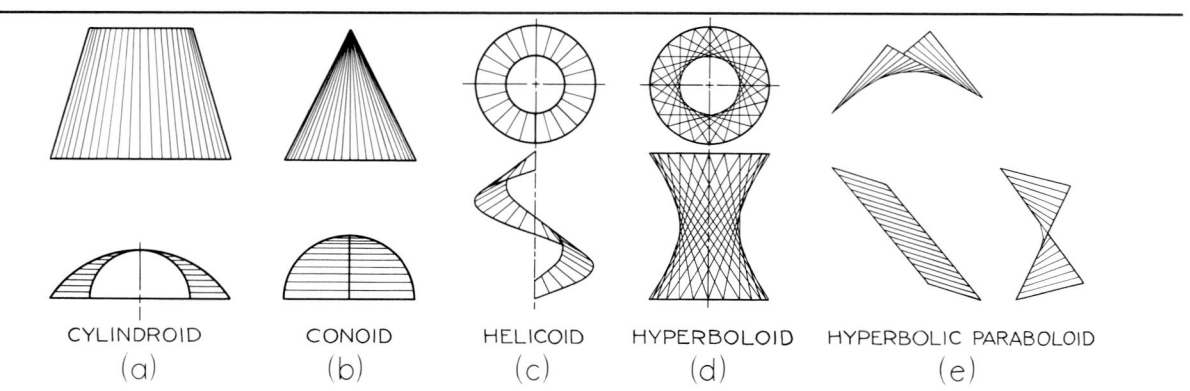

|| CYLINDROID | CONOID | HELICOID | HYPERBOLOID | HYPERBOLIC PARABOLOID |
||(a)|(b)|(c)|(d)|(e)|

Fig. 21.1　Warped Surfaces.

Intersections and Developments of Planes and Solids

21.3 Principles of Intersections

The principles involved in intersections of planes and solids have their practical application in the cutting of openings in roof surfaces for flues and stacks and in wall surfaces for pipes and chutes, and so on, and in the building of sheet-metal structures (tanks, boilers, etc.).

In such cases, the problem is generally one of determining the true size and shape of the intersection of a plane and one of the more common geometric solids. The intersection of a plane and a solid is the locus of the points of intersection of the elements of the solid with the plane. For solids bounded by plane surfaces, it is necessary only to find the points of intersection of the edges of the solid with the plane and to join these points, in consecutive order, with straight lines. For solids bounded by curved surfaces, it is necessary to find the points of intersection of several elements of the solid with the plane and to trace a smooth curve through these points. The curve of intersection of a plane and a circular cone is a *conic section*. The various conic sections are defined and illustrated in §5.47 and Fig. 5.46.

21.4 Developments

The *development* of a surface is that surface laid out on a plane, Fig. 21.2. Practical applications of developments occur in sheet-metal work, stone cutting, pattern making, packaging, and package design.

Single-curved surfaces and the surfaces of polyhedra can be developed. Warped surfaces and double-curved surfaces can be developed only approximately. See §21.1.

In sheet-metal layout, extra material must be provided for laps or seams. If the material is heavy, the thickness may be a factor, and the crowding of metal in bends must be considered. See §13.39. The drafter must also take stock sizes into account and should make layouts so as to economize in the use of material and of labor. In preparing developments, it is best to put the seam at the shortest edge and to attach the bases at edges where they match, to economize in soldering, welding, or riveting.

It is common practice to draw development layouts with the *inside surfaces up*. In this way, all fold lines and other markings are related directly to inside measurements, which are the important di-

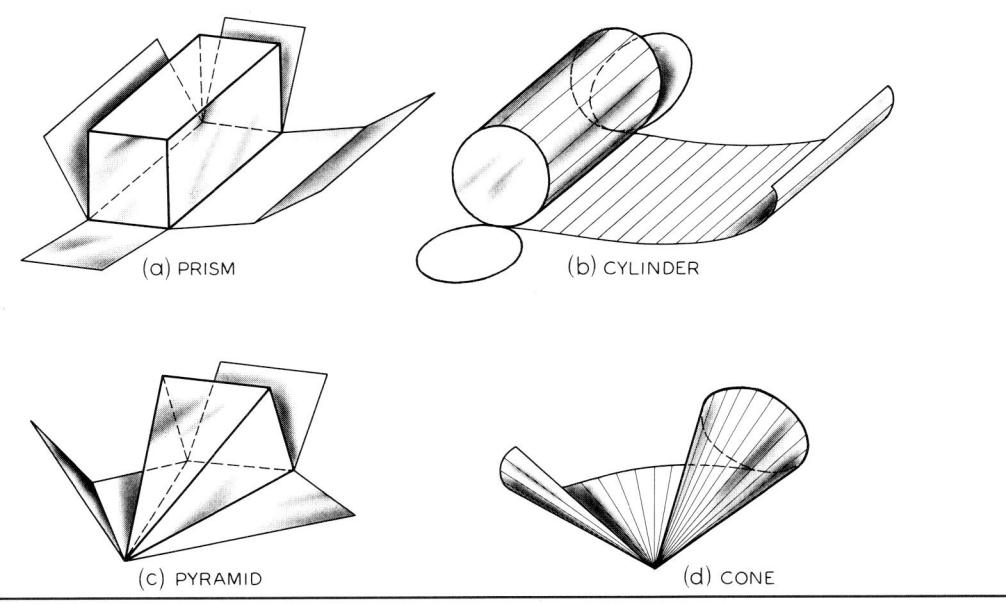

(a) PRISM   (b) CYLINDER   (c) PYRAMID   (d) CONE

Fig. 21.2   Development of Surfaces.

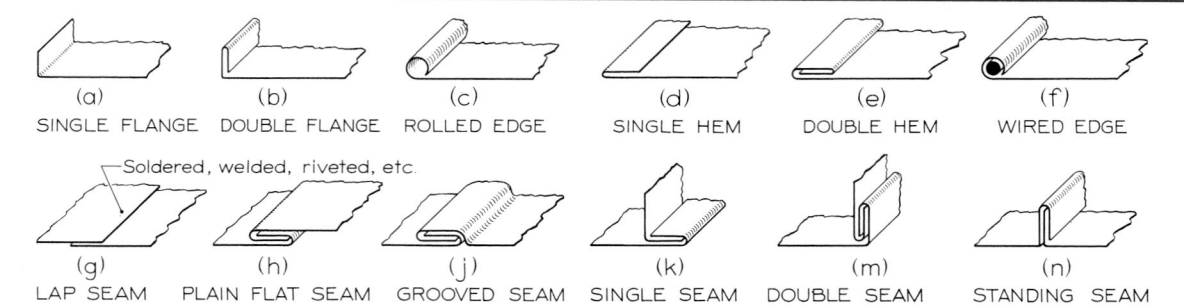

Fig. 21.3   Sheet-Metal Hems and Joints.

mensions in all ducts, pipes, tanks, and other vessels, and in this position they are also convenient for use in the fabricating shop.

21.5 Hems and Joints for Sheet Metal and Other Materials

A wide variety of hems and joints are used in the fabrication of sheet-metal developments and other materials, Fig. 21.3. Hems are used to eliminate the raw edge and also to stiffen the material. Joints and seams may be made for sheet metal by bending, welding, riveting, and soldering and by glueing and stapling for package materials.

Sufficient material as required for hems and

joints must be added to the layout or development. The amount of allowance depends on the thickness of the material and the production equipment; therefore, no specific dimensions for allowances are given in this chapter. See §13.39.

21.6 To Find the Intersection of a Plane and a Prism and the Development of the Prism Fig. 21.4

Intersection Fig. 21.4 (a)

The true size and shape of the intersection is shown in the auxiliary view. See Chapter 10. The length AB is the same as AB in the front view, and the width AD is the same as AD in the top view.

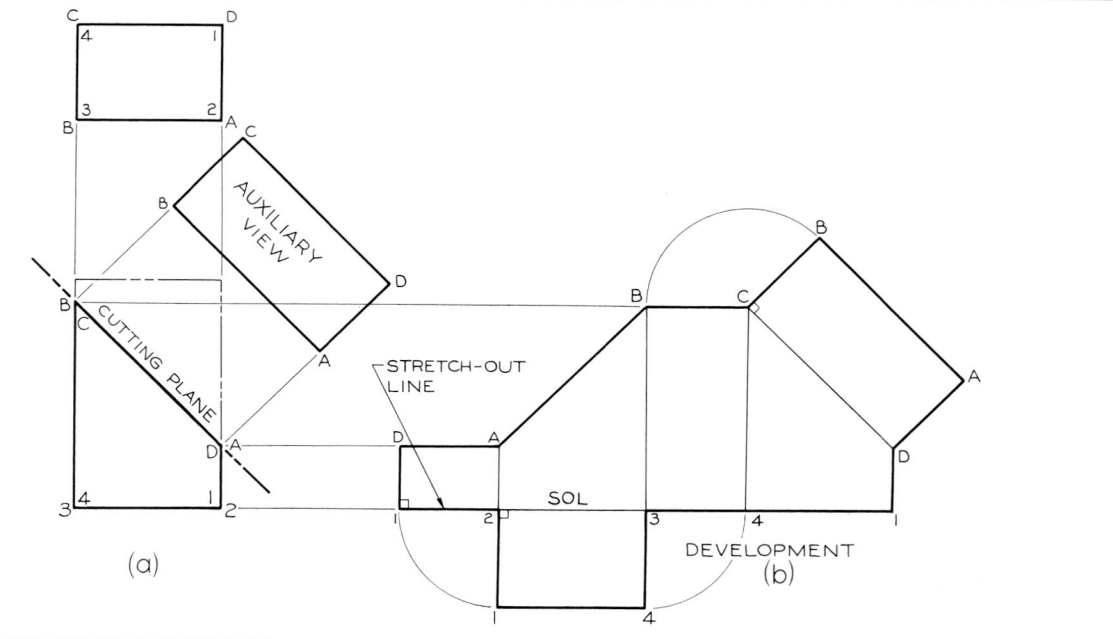

Fig. 21.4   Plane and Prism.

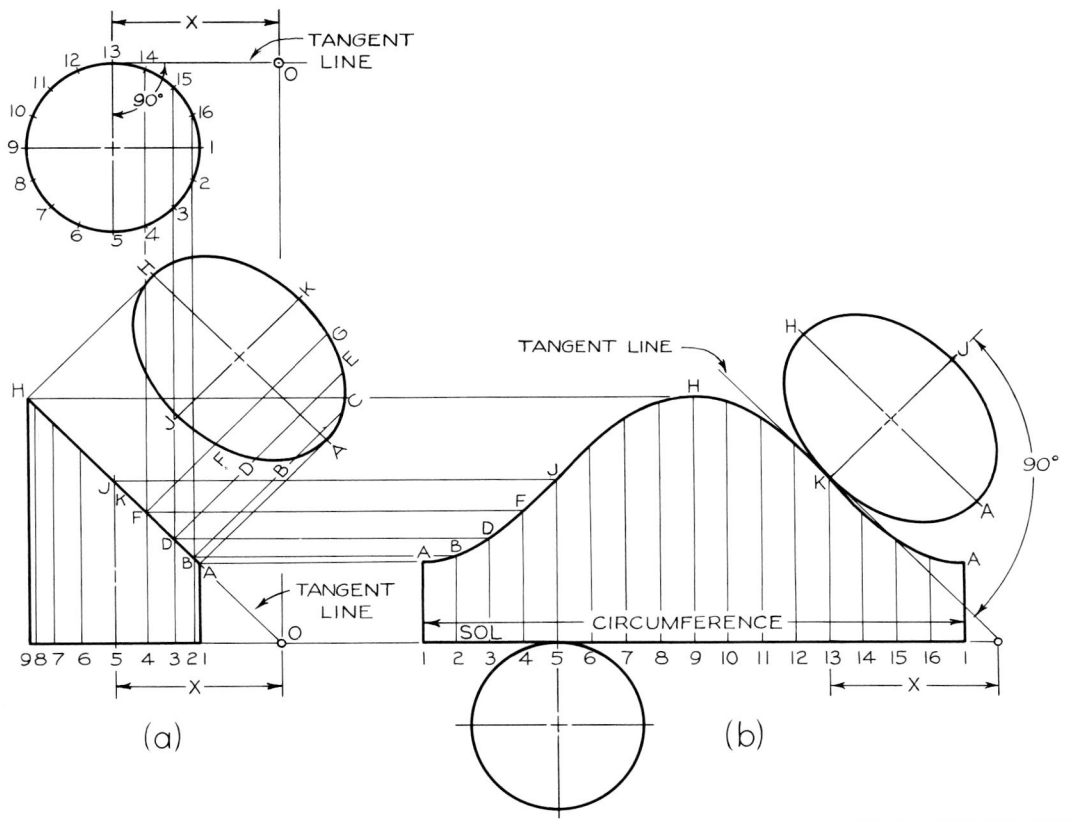

Fig. 21.5   Plane and Cylinder.

Development Fig. 21.4 (b)

On the straight line **1–1**, called the *stretchout line* (**SOL**), set off the widths of the faces **1–2, 2–3, . . .**, taken from the top view. At the division points, erect perpendiculars to **1–1**, and set off on each the length of the respective edge, taken from the front view. The lengths can be projected across from the front view, as shown. Join the points thus found by straight lines to complete the development of the lateral surface. Attach to this development the lower base and the upper base, or auxiliary view, to obtain the development of the entire surface of the frustum of the prism.

21.7 To Find the Intersection of a Plane and a Cylinder and the Development of the Cylinder Fig. 21.5

Intersection Fig. 21.5 (a)

The intersection is an ellipse whose points are the piercing points in the secant plane of the elements of the cylinder. In spacing the elements, it is best,

though not necessary, to divide the circumference of the base into *equal* parts and to draw an element at each division point. In the auxiliary view, the widths **BC, DE, . . .**, are taken from the top view at **2–16, 3–15, . . .**, respectively, and the curve is traced through the points thus determined, with the aid of the irregular curve, §2.54.

The major axis **AH** and the minor axis **JK** are shown true length in the front view and the top view, respectively; therefore, the ellipse may also be constructed as explained in §§5.48–5.51 or with the aid of an ellipse template, §5.56.

Development Fig. 21.5 (b)

The base of the cylinder develops into a straight line **1–1**, the stretchout line (**SOL**), equal to the circumference of the base, whose length may be determined by calculation (πd), by setting off with the bow dividers, or by rectifying the arcs of the base **1–2, 2–3, . . .**, §5.45. Divide the stretchout line into the same number of equal parts as the circumference of the base, and draw an element through each

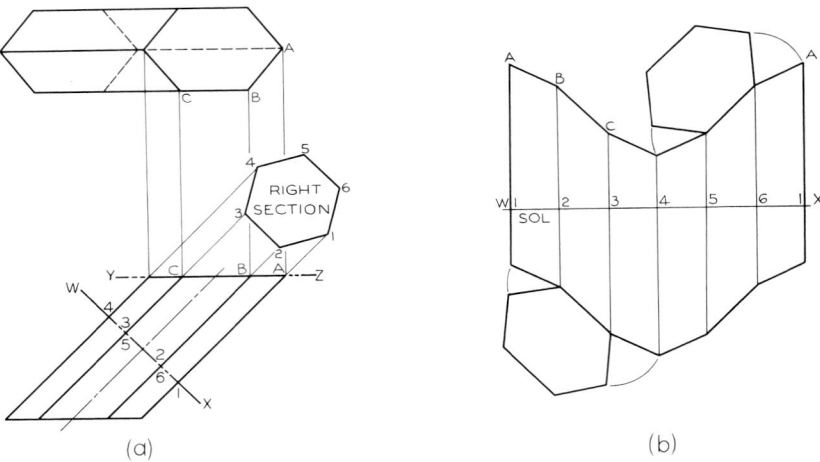

Fig. 21.6   Plane and Oblique Prism.

division perpendicular to the line. Set off on each element its length, projected from the front view, as shown; then trace a smooth curve through the points A, B, D, . . ., §2.54, and attach the bases.

21.8 To Find the Intersection of a Plane and an Oblique Prism and the Development of the Prism Fig. 21.6

Intersection Fig. 21.6 (a)

The right section cut by the plane WX is a regular hexagon, as shown in the auxiliary view; the oblique section, cut by the horizontal plane YZ, is shown in the top view.

Development Fig. 21.6 (b)

The right section develops into the straight line WX, the stretchout line (SOL). Set off, on the stretchout line, the widths of the faces 1–2, 2–3, . . ., taken from the auxiliary view, and draw a line through each division perpendicular to the line. Set off, from the stretchout line, the lengths of the respective edges measured from WX in the front view. Join the points A,B,C, . . ., with straight lines, and attach the bases, which are shown in their true sizes in the top view.

21.9 To Find the Intersection of a Plane and an Oblique Cylinder Fig. 21.7

Intersection Fig. 21.7 (a)

The right section cut by the plane WX is a circle, shown in the auxiliary view. The intersection of the horizontal plane YZ with the cylinder is an ellipse

shown in the top view, whose points are found as explained for the auxiliary view in Fig. 21.5 (a), §21.7. The major axis AH is shown true length in the top view, and the minor axis JK is equal to the diameter of the cylinder; therefore, the ellipse may be constructed as explained in §§5.48–5.51, or with the aid of an ellipse template, §5.56.

Development Fig. 21.7 (b)

The cylinder may be considered as a prism having an infinite number of edges; therefore, the development is found in a manner similar to that of the oblique prism shown in Fig. 21.6.

The circle of the right section cut by plane WX develops into a straight line 1–1, the stretchout line (SOL), equal in length to the circumference of the circle (πd). Divide the stretchout line into the same number of equal parts as the circumference of the circle as shown in the auxiliary view, and draw elements through these points perpendicular to the line. Set off on each element its length, taken from the front view with dividers, as shown; then trace a smooth curve through the points A, B, D, . . ., §2.54, and attach the bases.

21.10 To Find the Intersection of a Plane and a Pyramid and to Develop the Resulting Truncated Pyramid Fig. 21.8

Intersection Fig. 21.8 (a)

The intersection is a trapezoid whose vertices are the points in which the edges of the pyramid pierce the secant plane. In the auxiliary view, the altitude

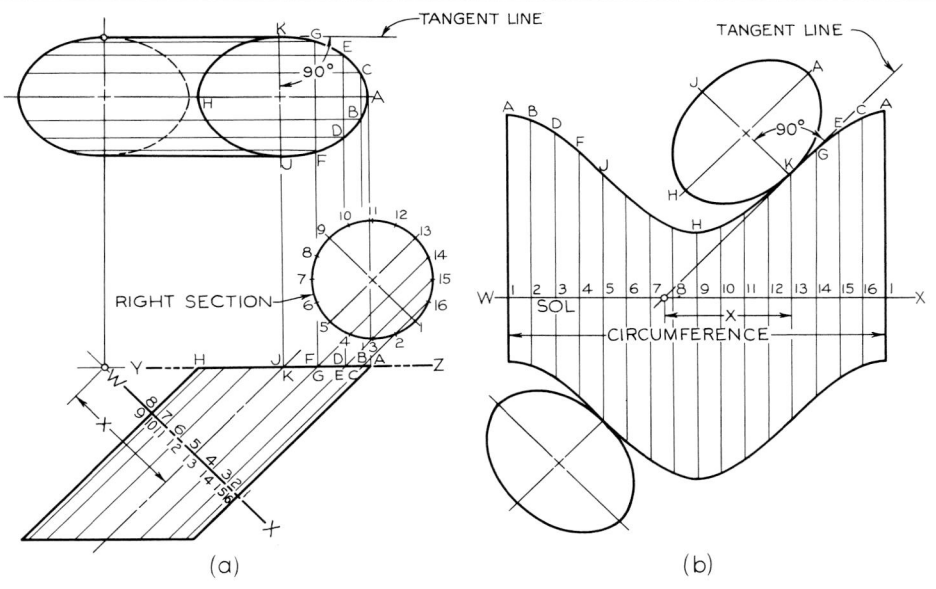

Fig. 21.7 Plane and Oblique Circular Cylinder.

of the trapezoid is projected from the front view, and the widths AD and BC are transferred from the top view with dividers.

Development Fig. 21.8 (b)

With O in the development as center and O–1′ in the front view (the true length of one of the edges) as radius, draw the arc 1′–2′–3′. . . . Inscribe the cords 1′–2′, 2′–3′, . . ., equal, respectively, to the sides of the base, as shown in the top view. Draw the lines 1′–O, 2′–O, . . ., and set off the true lengths of the lines OD′, OA′, OB′, . . ., respectively, taken from the true lengths in the front view, §11.10.

To complete the development, join the points D′, A′, B′, . . ., by straight lines, and attach the bases to their corresponding edges. To transfer an irregular figure, such as the trapezoid shown here, refer to §§5.28 and 5.29.

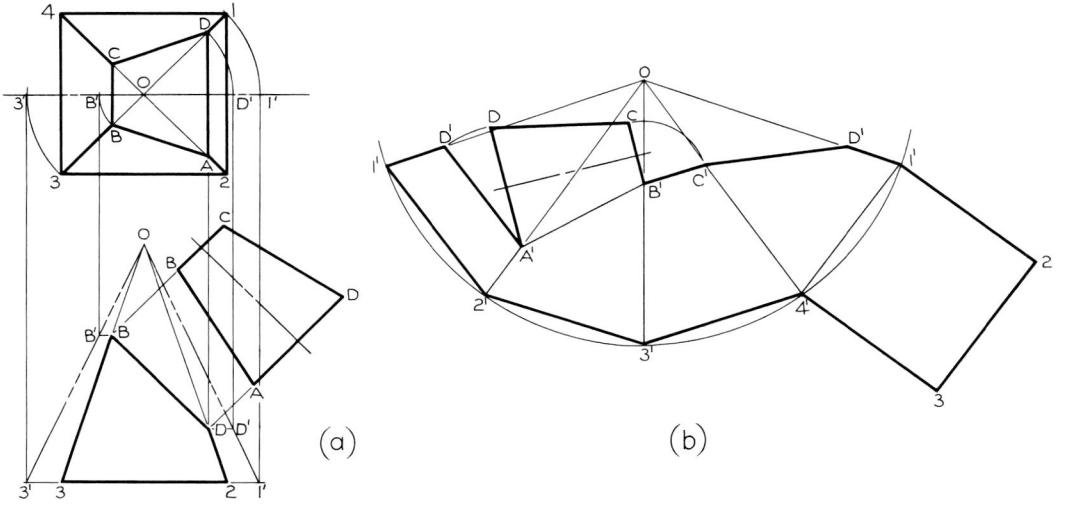

Fig. 21.8 Plane and Pyramid.

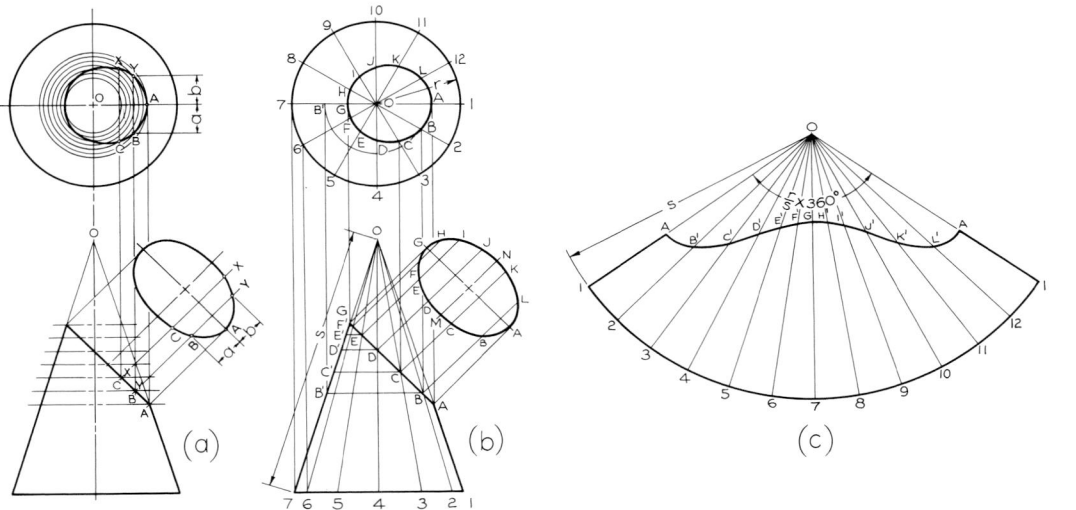

Fig. 21.9 Plane and Cone.

21.11 To Find the Intersection of a Plane and a Cone and to Develop the Lateral Surface of the Cone Fig. 21.9

Intersection Fig. 21.9 (a)

The intersection is an ellipse. If a series of horizontal cutting planes is passed perpendicular to the axis, as shown, each plane will cut a circle from the cone that will show in true size and shape in the top view. Points in which these circles intersect the original secant plane are points on the ellipse. Since the secant plane is shown edgewise in the front view, all of these piercing points may be found in that view and projected to the others, as shown.

Fig. 21.9 (b)   This method is most suitable when a development also is required, since it utilizes elements that are also needed in the development. The piercing points of these elements in the secant plane are points on the intersection. Divide the base into any number of equal parts, and draw an element at each division point. These elements pierce the secant plane in points **A, B, C, ...** The top views of these points are found by projecting upward from the front view, as shown. In the auxiliary view, the widths **BL, CK,** . . ., are taken from the top view. The ellipse is then drawn with the aid of the irregular curve, §2.54.

The major axis of the ellipse, shown in the auxiliary view, is equal to **AG** in the front view. The minor axis **MN** bisects the major axis and is equal to the minor axis of the ellipse in the top view. With these axes, the ellipse may also be constructed as explained in §§5.48–5.51 or with the aid of an ellipse template, §5.56.

Development Fig. 21.9 (c)

The cone may be considered as a pyramid having an infinite number of edges; hence, the development is found in a manner similar to that explained for the pyramid in §21.10. The base of the cone develops into a circular arc, with the slant height of the cone as its radius and the circumference of the base as its length, §5.45. The lengths of the elements in the development are taken from the element **O–7** or **O–1** in the front view, (b). Instead of our finding the true circumference of the base, the vertical angle **1–O–1** in the development can be set off equal to $\frac{r}{s}$ 360° (where **r** is the radius of the base and **s** is the slant height of the cone).

21.12 To Find the Development of a Hood and Flue Fig. 21.10

Since the hood is a conical surface, it may be developed as described in §21.11. The two end sections of the elbow are cylindrical surfaces and may be developed as described in §21.7. The two middle sections of the elbow are cylindrical surfaces, but since their bases are not perpendicular to the axes,

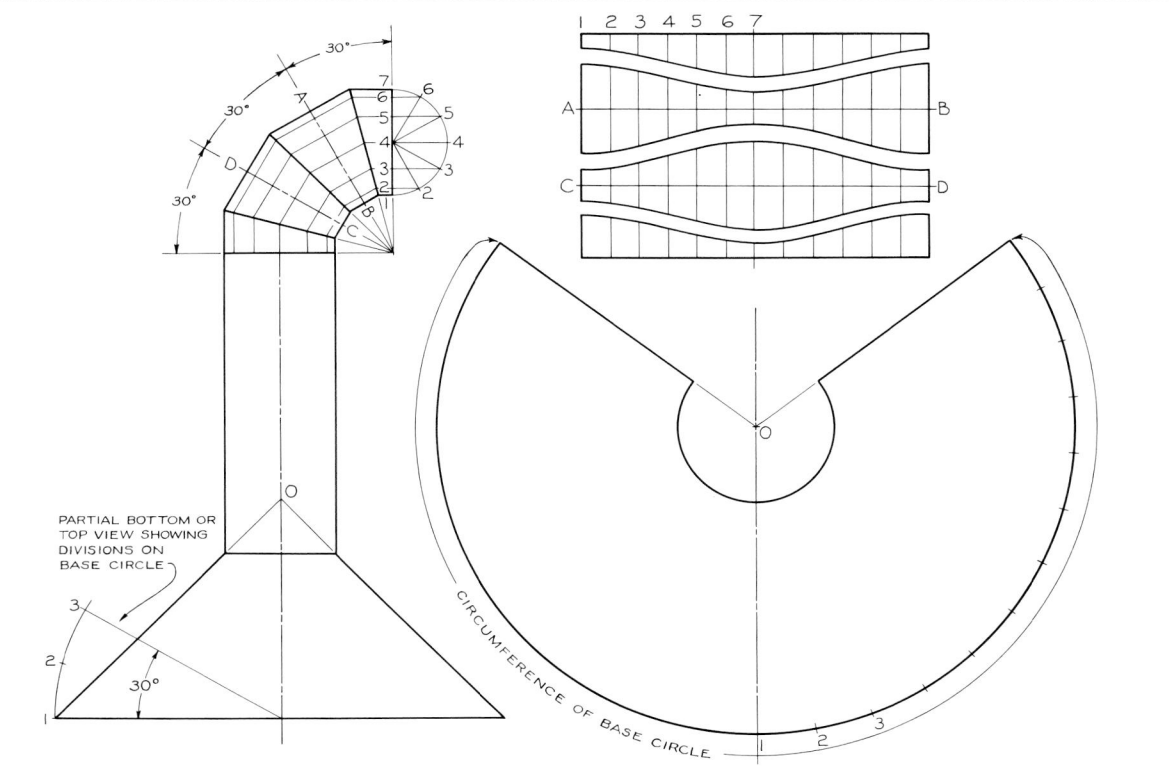

Fig. 21.10   A Hood and Flue.

they will not develop into straight lines. They will be developed in a manner similar to that for an oblique cylinder, §21.9, Fig. 21.7 (b). If the auxiliary planes AB and DC are passed perpendicular to the axes, they will cut right sections from the cylinders, which will develop into the straight lines AB and CD in the developments.

If the developments are arranged as shown in Fig. 21.10, the elbow can be constructed from a rectangular sheet of metal without wasting material. The patterns are shown separated after cutting. Before cutting, the adjacent curves coincided.

21.13 To Find the Development of a Truncated Oblique Rectangular Pyramid Fig. 21.11

None of the four lateral surfaces is shown in the multiview drawing in true size and shape. Using the method of §11.10, revolve each edge until it appears in true length in the front view, as shown. Thus, O–2 revolves to O–2', O–3 revolves to O–3', and so

on. These true lengths are transferred from the front view to the development with the compass, as shown. Notice that true lengths OD', OA', OB', . . ., are found and transferred. The true lengths of the edges of the bases are given in the top view and are transferred directly to the development.

21.14 Triangulation

Triangulation is simply a method of dividing a surface into a number of triangles and transferring them to the development. A triangle is said to be "indestructible," because if its sides are of given lengths, it can be only one shape. A triangle can be easily transferred by transferring the sides with the aid of the compass, §5.28.

21.15 To Find the Development of an Oblique Cone by Triangulation Fig. 21.12

Divide the base, in the top view, into any number of equal parts, and draw an element at each division point. Find the true length of each element, §11.10.

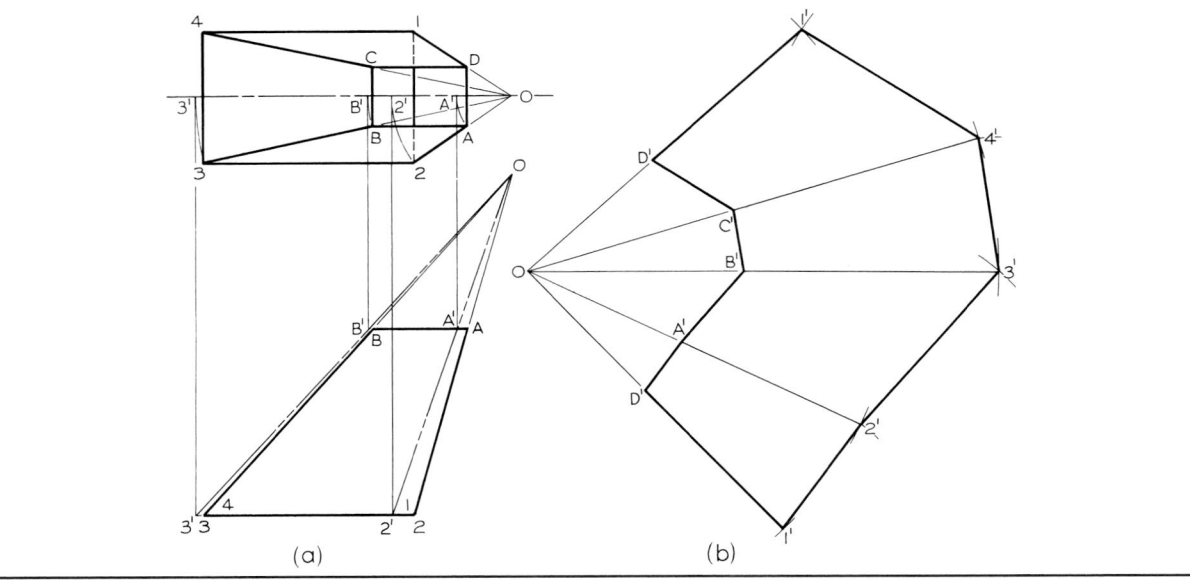

(a)   (b)

Fig. 21.11   Development of a Transition Piece.

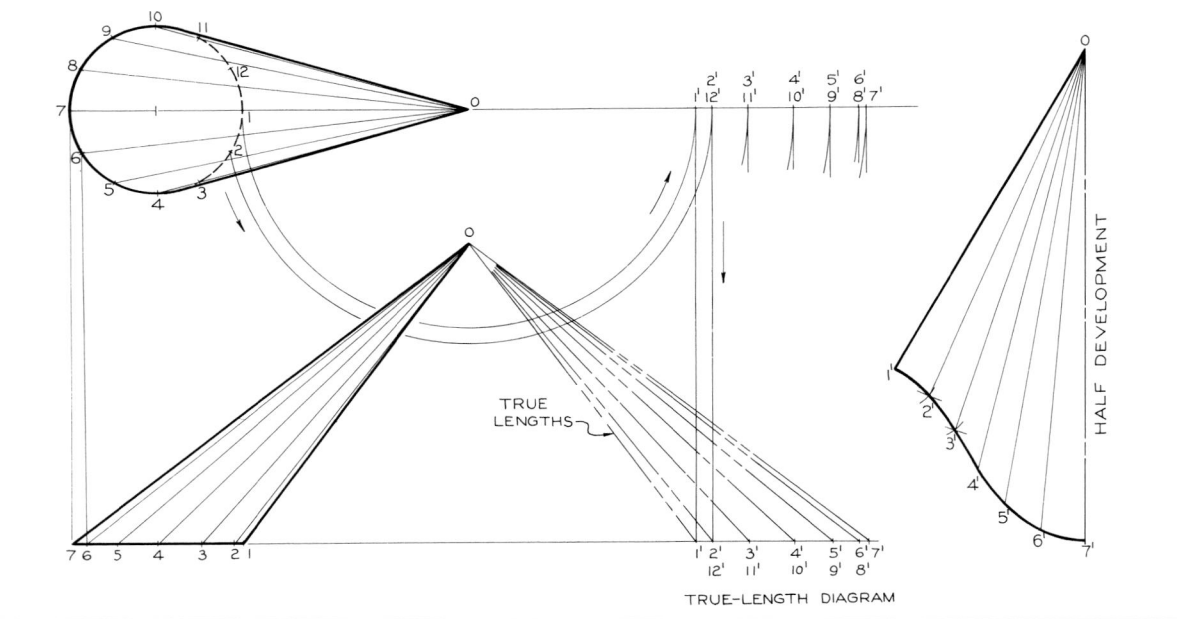

TRUE-LENGTH DIAGRAM

Fig. 21.12   Development of an Oblique Cone by Triangulation.

If the divisions of the base are comparatively small, the lengths of the chords may be set off in the development as representing the lengths of the respective subtending arcs. In the development, set off O–1′ equal to O–1 in the front view where it is shown true length. With 1′ in the development as center, and the chord 1–2 taken from the top view as radius, strike an arc at 2′. With O as center, and O–2′, the true-length of the element O–2 from the "true-length" diagram, as radius, draw the arc at 2′. The intersection of these arcs is a point on the development of the base of the cone. The points 3′, 4′,

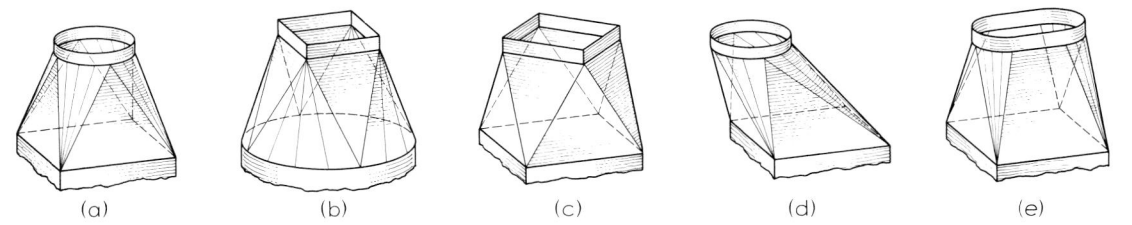

Fig. 21.13   Transition Pieces.

. . ., in the curve are found in a similar manner, and the curve is traced through these points with the aid of the irregular curve, §2.54.

Since the development is symmetrical about element O–7′, it is necessary to lay out only half the development, as shown.

21.16 Transition Pieces

A *transition piece* is one that connects two differently shaped, differently sized, or skewed-position openings, Fig. 21.13. In most cases, transition pieces are composed of plane surfaces and conical surfaces, the latter being developed by triangulation. Triangulation can also be used to develop, approximately, certain warped surfaces. Transition pieces are extensively used in air conditioning, heating, ventilating, and similar construction.

21.17 To Find the Development of a Transition Piece Connecting Rectangular Pipes on the Same Axis

The transition piece is a frustum of a pyramid, Fig. 21.14 (a). Find the vertex O of the pyramid by extending its edges to their intersection. Find the true lengths of the edges by any one of the methods explained in §11.10. The development can then be found as explained in §21.10.

If the transition piece is not a frustum of a pyramid, as in Fig. 21.14 (b), it can best be developed by triangulation, §21.14, as shown for the faces 1–5–8–4 and 2–6–7–3, or by extending the sides to form triangles, as shown for faces 1–2–6–5 and 3–4–8–7, and then finding the true lengths of the sides of the triangles, §11.10, and setting them off as shown.

As a check on the development, lines parallel on

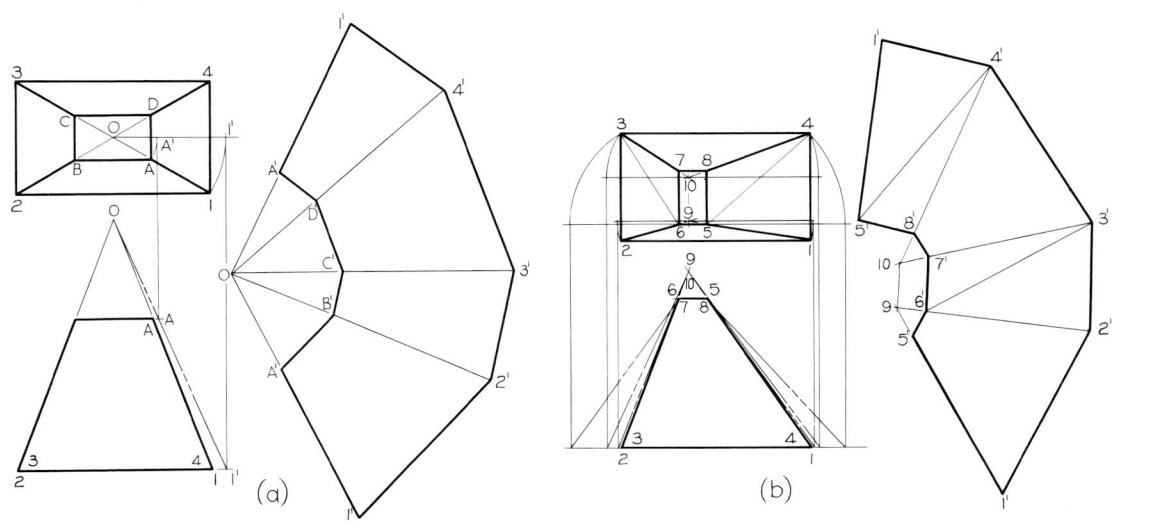

Fig. 21.14   Development of a Transition Piece.

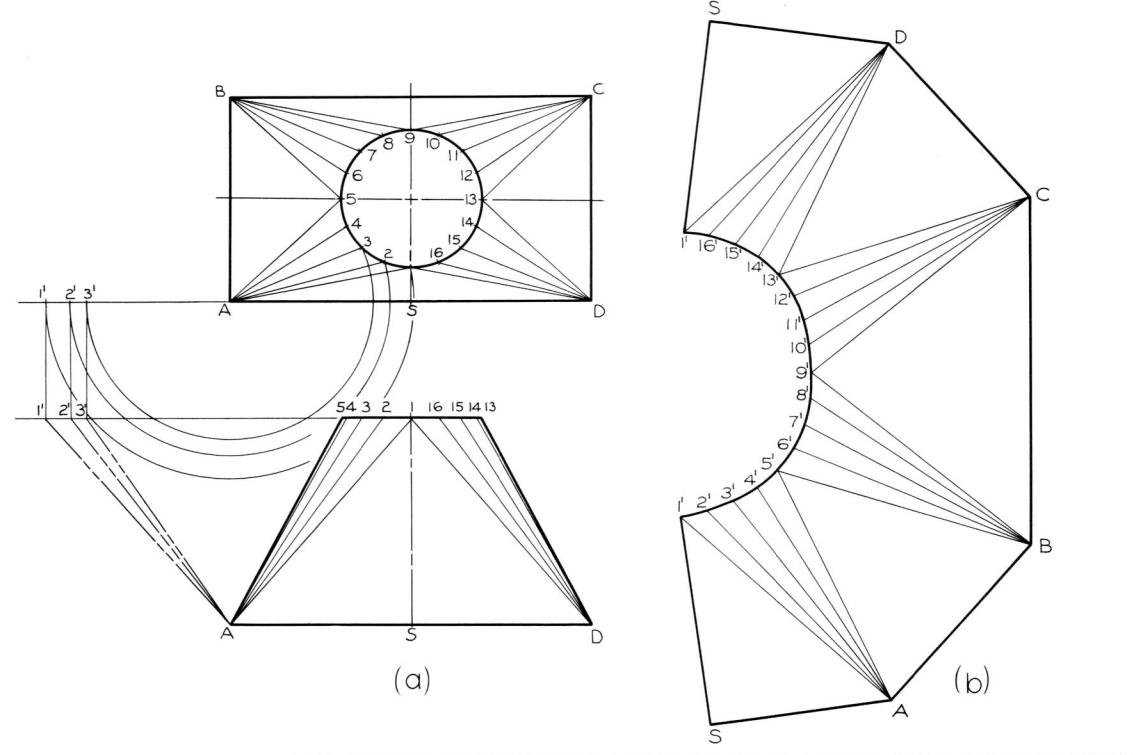

Fig. 21.15 Development of a Transition Piece.

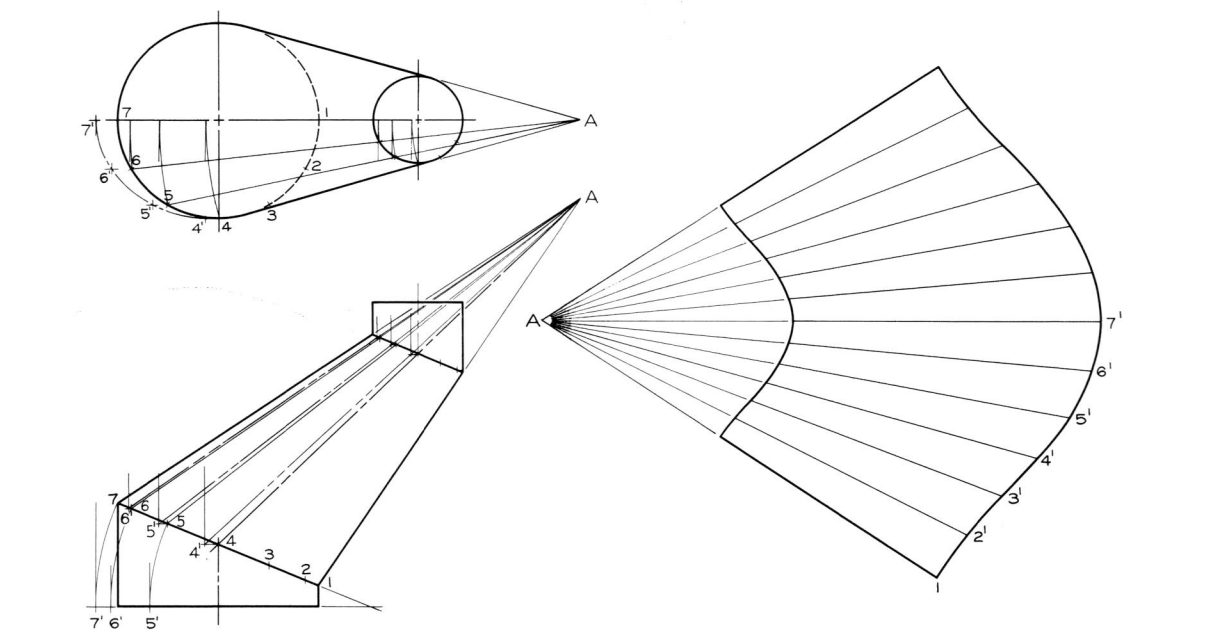

Fig. 21.16 Development of a Transition Piece.

the surface must also be parallel on the development; for example, 8′–5′ must be parallel to 4′–1′ on the development.

21.18 To Find the Development of a Transition Piece Connecting a Circular Pipe and a Rectangular Pipe on the Same Axis Fig. 21.15

The transition piece is composed of four isosceles triangles and four conical surfaces. The seam is along line S–1. Begin the development on the line 1′–S, and draw the right triangle 1′–S–A, whose base SA is equal to half the side AD and whose hypotenuse A–1′ is equal to the true length of side A–1.

The conical surfaces are developed by triangulation as explained in §§21.14 and 21.15.

21.19 To Find the Development of a Transition Piece Connecting Two Cylindrical Pipes on Different Axes Fig. 21.16

The transition piece is a frustum of a cone, the vertex of which may be found by extending the contour elements to their intersection A.

The development can be found by triangulation, as explained in §§21.14 and 21.15. The sides of each triangle are the true lengths of two adjacent elements of the cone, and the base is the true length of the curve of the base of the cone between the two elements. This curve is not shown in its true length in either view, and the plane of the base of the frustum must therefore be revolved until it is horizontal in order to find the distance from the foot of one element to the foot of the next. When the plane of the base is thus revolved, the foot of any element, such as 7, revolves to 7′, and the curve 6′–7′ (top view) is the true length of the curve of the base between the elements 6 and 7. In practice, the chord distances between these points are generally used to approximate the curved distances.

After the conical surface has been developed, the true lengths of the elements on the truncated section of the cone are set off from the vertex A of the development to secure points on the upper curve of the development.

If the transition piece is not a frustum of a cone, its development is found by another variation of triangulation, as shown in Fig. 21.17. The circular intersection with the large vertical pipe is shown

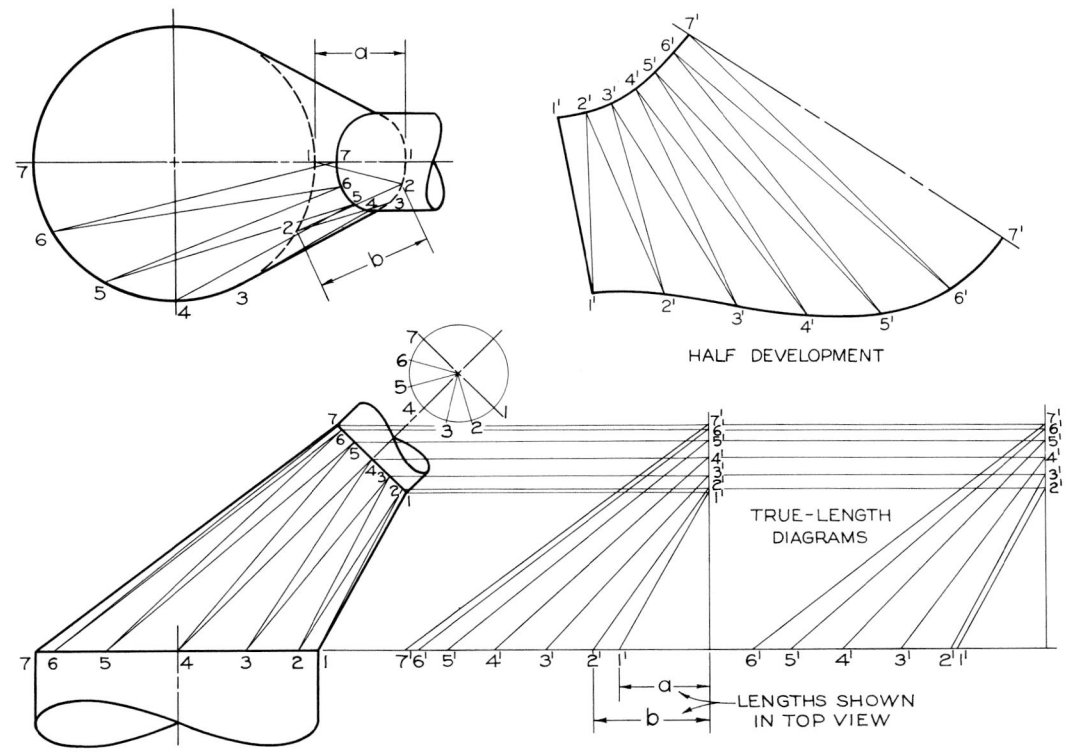

HALF DEVELOPMENT

TRUE-LENGTH DIAGRAMS

LENGTHS SHOWN IN TOP VIEW

Fig. 21.17 Development of a Transition Piece.

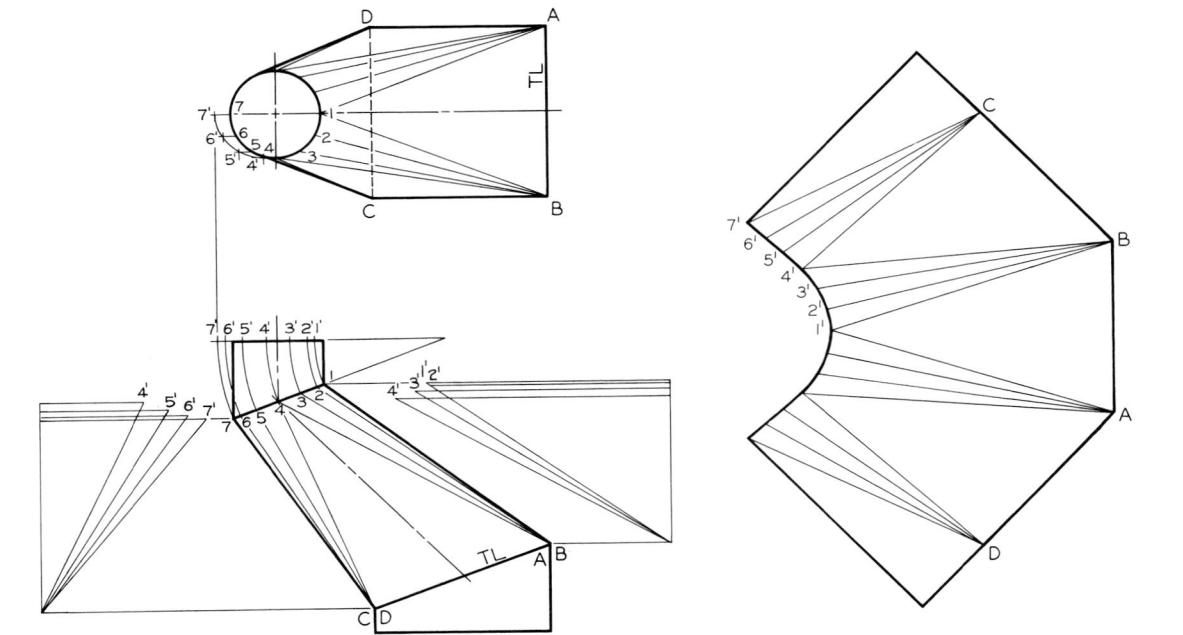

Fig. 21.18   Development of a Transition Piece.

true size in the top view, and the circular intersection with the small inclined pipe is shown true size in the auxiliary view. Since both intersections are true circles, and the planes containing them are not parallel, the lateral surface of the transition piece is a warped surface and not conical (single-curved). It is theoretically nondevelopable, but may be approximately developed by considering it to be made up of plane triangles, alternate ones of which are inverted, as shown in the development. The true lengths of the sides of the triangles are found by the method of Fig. 11.10 (d), but in a systematic manner so as to form true-length diagrams, as shown in Fig. 21.17.

21.20 To Find the Development of a Transition Piece Connecting a Square Pipe and a Cylindrical Pipe on Different Axes Fig. 21.18

The development of the transition piece is made up of five plane triangular surfaces and four triangular conical surfaces similar to those in Fig. 21.15. The development is made in a similar manner to those described in §§21.15 and 21.18.

21.21 To Find the Intersection of a Plane and a Sphere and to Find the Approximate Development of the Sphere Fig. 21.19

Intersection Fig. 21.19 (a)

The intersection of a plane and a sphere is a circle, as shown in the top views in Fig. 21.19, the diameter of the circle depending upon where the plane is passed. Any circle cut by a plane through the center of the sphere is called a *great circle*. If a plane passes through the center and perpendicular to the axis, the resulting great circle is called the *equator*. If a plane contains the axis, it will cut a great circle called a *meridian*.

Development Fig. 21.19 (a)

The surface of a sphere is a double-curved surface and is not developable, §21.1. The surface may be developed approximately by dividing it into a series of zones and substituting for each zone a frustum of a right-circular cone. The development of the conical surfaces is an approximate development of the spherical surface. If the conical surfaces are inscribed within the sphere, the development will be smaller than the spherical surface, while if the con-

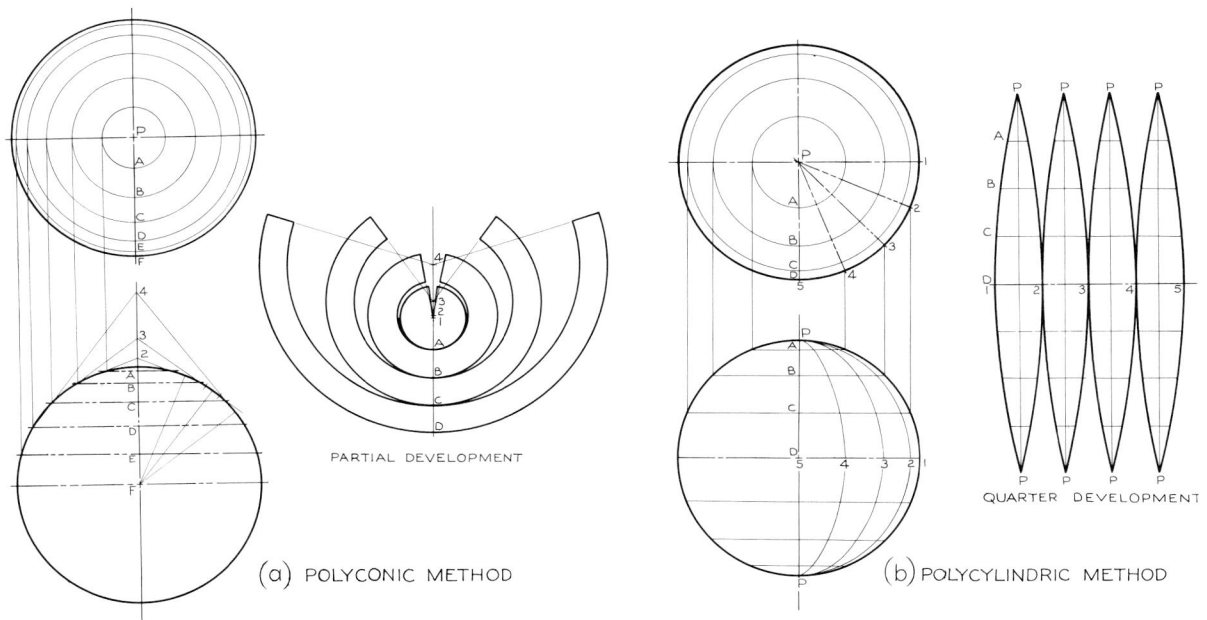

Fig. 21.19   Approximate Development of a Sphere.

ical surfaces are circumscribed about the sphere, the development will be larger. If the conical surfaces are partly within and partly without the sphere, as indicated in the figure, the resulting development very closely approximates the spherical surface.

This method of developing a spherical surface is the *polyconic* method. It is used on all government maps of the United States.

Fig. 21.19 (b)   Another method of making an approximate development of the double-curved sur-

face of a sphere is to divide the surface into equal sections with meridian planes and substitute cylindrical surfaces for the spherical sections. The cylindrical surfaces may be inscribed within the sphere, or circumscribed about it, or located partly within and partly without. The development of the series of cylindrical surfaces is an approximate development of the spherical surface. This method is the *polycylindric* method, sometimes designated as the *gore* method.

Intersections and Developments of Solids

21.22 Principles of Intersections

Intersections of solids are generally regarded as in the province of descriptive geometry, and for information on the more complicated intersections the student is referred to any standard text on that subject. However, most of the intersections encountered in drafting practice do not require a knowledge of descriptive geometry, and some of the more common solutions may be found in the paragraphs that follow.

An intersection of two solids is referred to as a *figure of intersection*. Two plane surfaces intersect in a straight line; hence, if two solids that are composed of plane surfaces intersect, the figure of intersection will be composed of straight lines, as shown in Figs. 21.20–21.23. The method generally consists of finding the piercing points of the edges of one solid in the surfaces of the other solid and joining these points with straight lines.

If curved surfaces intersect, or if curved surfaces

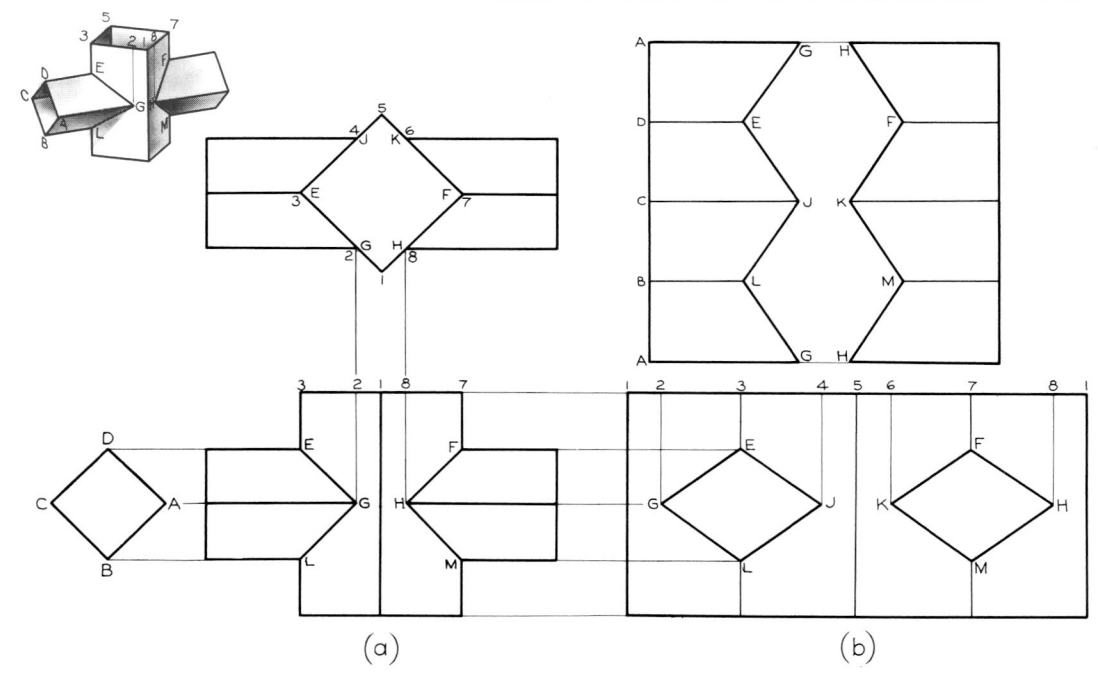

Fig. 21.20 Two Prisms at Right Angles to Each Other.

and plane surfaces intersect, the figure of intersection will be composed of curves, as shown in Figs. 21.5, 21.9, and 21.24–21.29. The method generally consists of finding the piercing points of *elements* of one solid in the surfaces of the other. A smooth curve is then traced through these points, with the aid of the irregular curve, §2.54.

21.23 To Find the Intersection and Developments of Two Prisms Fig. 21.20

Intersection Fig. 21.20 (a)

The points in which the edges A, B, C, and D of the horizontal prism pierce the vertical prism are vertices of the intersection. The edges D and B of the horizontal prism intersect the edges 3 and 7 of the vertical prism at the points E, F, L, and M. The edges A and C of the horizontal prism intersect the faces of the vertical prism at the points G, H, J, and K. The intersection is completed by joining these points in order by straight lines.

Developments Fig. 21.20 (b)

To develop the lateral surface of the horizontal prism, set off on the vertical stretchout line A–A the widths of the faces AB, BC, . . ., taken from the end

view, and draw the edges through these points, as shown. Set off, from the stretchout line, the lengths of the edges AG, BL, . . ., taken from the front view or from the top view, and join the points G, L, J, . . ., by straight lines.

To develop the lateral surface of the vertical prism, set off on the stretchout line 1–1 the widths of the faces 1–2, 3–5, . . ., taken from the top view, and draw the edges through these points, as shown. Set off on the stretchout line the distances 1–2, 5–4, 5–6, and 1–8, taken from the top view, and draw the intermediate elements parallel to the principal edges. Take the lengths of the principal edges and of the intermediate elements from the front view, and join the points E, G, L, . . ., in order with straight lines, to complete the development.

21.24 To Find the Intersection and Developments of Two Prisms Fig. 21.21

Intersection Fig. 21.21 (a)

The points in which the edges ACEH of the horizontal prism pierce the surfaces of the vertical prism are found in the top view and are projected downward to the corresponding edges ACEH in the front view. The points in which the edges 5 and 11 of the

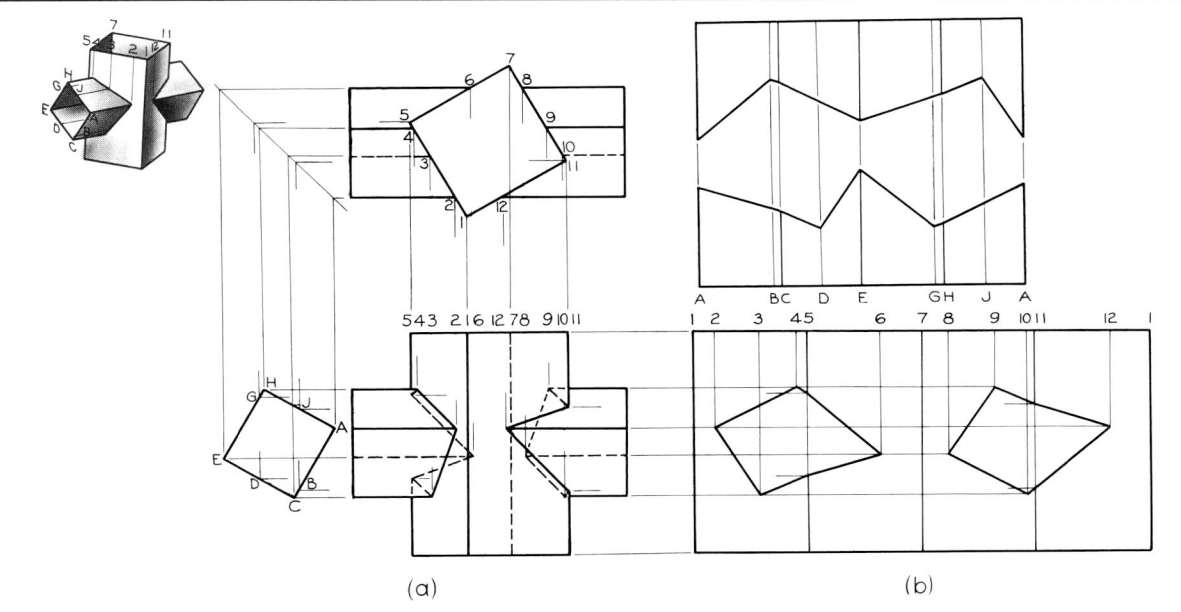

Fig. 21.21 Two Prisms at Right Angles to Each Other.

vertical prism pierce the surfaces of the horizontal prism are found in the left-side view at G, D, J, and B and are projected horizontally to the front view, intersecting the corresponding edges as shown. The intersection is completed by joining these points in order by straight lines.

Developments Fig. 21.21 (b)
The lateral surfaces of the two prisms are developed as explained in §21.23. True lengths of all lateral edges and lines parallel to them are shown in the front view of Fig. 21.21 at (a).

21.25 To Find the Intersection and Developments of Two Prisms Fig. 21.22

Intersection Fig. 21.22 (a)
The points in which edges 1–2–3–4 of the inclined prism pierce the surfaces of the vertical prism are vertices of the intersection. These points, found in the top view, are projected downward to the corresponding edges 1–2–3–4 in the front view, as shown. The intersection is completed by joining these points in order by straight lines.

Developments Fig. 21.22 (b)
The lateral surfaces of the two prisms are developed as explained in §21.23. True lengths of all edges of

both prisms are shown in the front view of Fig. 21.22 at (a).

21.26 To Find the Intersection and the Developments of Two Prisms Fig. 21.23

In this case the edges of the oblique prism are oblique to the planes of projection, and in the front and top views none of the edges is shown true length, §7.24, and none of the faces is shown true size, §7.23. Furthermore, none of the angles, including the angle of inclination, is shown true size, §7.26. Therefore, it is necessary to draw a secondary auxiliary view, §10.19, to obtain the true size and shape of the right section of the oblique prism.

The direction of sight, indicated by arrow A, is assumed perpendicular to the end face 1–2–3, that is, parallel to the principal edges of the prism. The primary auxiliary view, taken in the direction of arrow B, shows the true lengths of the edges, the true inclination of the prism with respect to the horizontal and, incidentally, the true length and inclination of arrow A. In the secondary auxiliary view, arrow A is shown as a point, and the end face 1–2–3 is shown in its true size.

Intersection Fig. 21.23 (a)
The points in which the edges 1–2–3 of the oblique prism pierce the surfaces of the vertical prism are

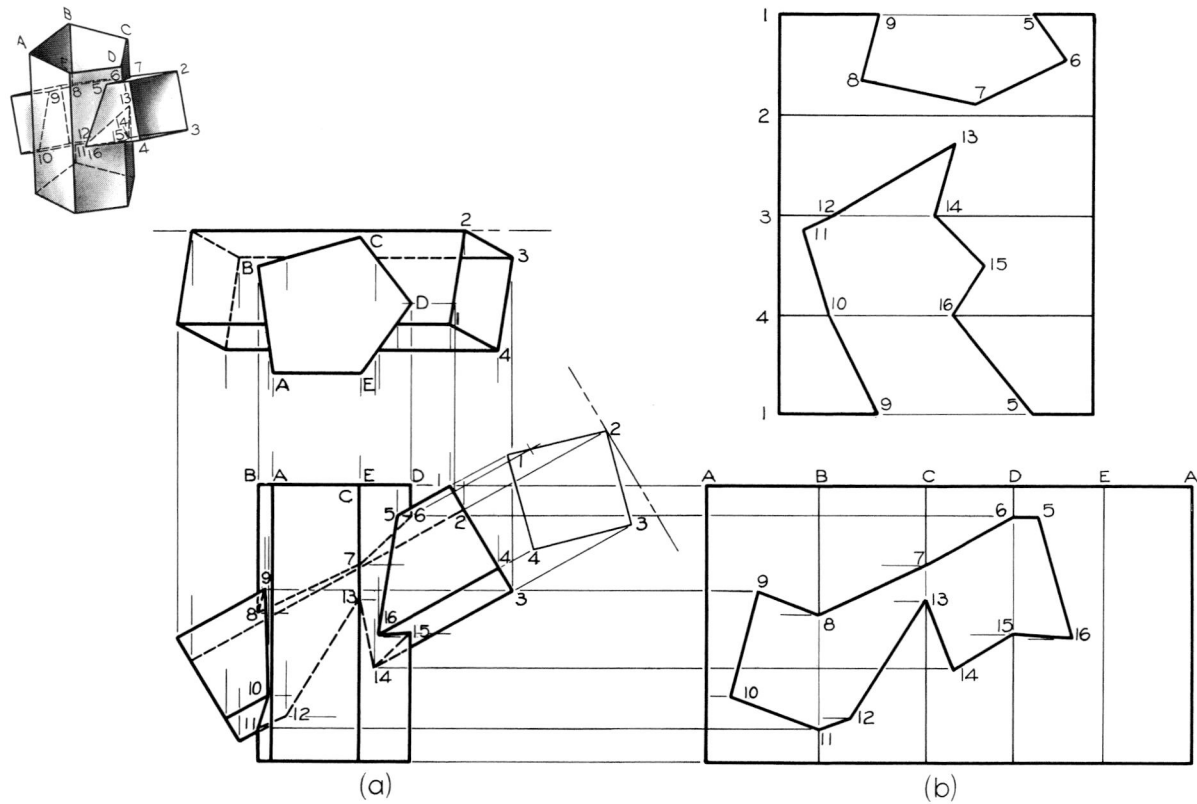

Fig. 21.22 Two Prisms Oblique to Each Other.

vertices of the intersection, found first in the top view and then projected downward to the front view.

Developments Fig. 21.23 (b)
The lateral surfaces of the two prisms are developed as explained in §21.23. True lengths of the edges of the vertical prism are shown in the front view. True lengths of the edges of the oblique prism can be shown in the primary auxiliary view; true lengths to the vertices of the intersection may be found in this view, as shown for line **X–5**.

21.27 To Find the Intersection and Developments of Two Cylinders Fig. 21.24

Intersection Fig. 21.24 (a)
Assume a series of elements (preferably equally spaced) on the horizontal cylinder, numbered 1, 2, 3, . . ., in the side view, and draw their top and front views. Their points of intersection with the surface

of the vertical cylinder are shown in the top view at A, B, C, . . ., and may be found in the front view by projecting downward to their intersections with the corresponding elements 1, 2, 3, . . ., in the front view. When a sufficient number of points have been found to determine the intersection, the curve is traced through the points with the aid of the irregular curve, §2.54. See also Fig. 7.38 (c).

Developments Fig. 21.24 (b)
The lateral surfaces of the two cylinders are developed as explained in §21.7. True lengths of all elements of both cylinders are shown in the front view. Since both cylinders have bases at right angles to the center lines, the circles will develop as straight lines, and the developments will be rectangular, as shown. The length **XY** of the stretchout line for the development of the vertical cylinder, is equal to the circumference of the cylinder, or πd, and the length 1–1 of the stretchout line for the development of the horizontal cylinder is determined in the same way. Those elements of the large cylinder that pierce the small cylinder can be identified in the top view as

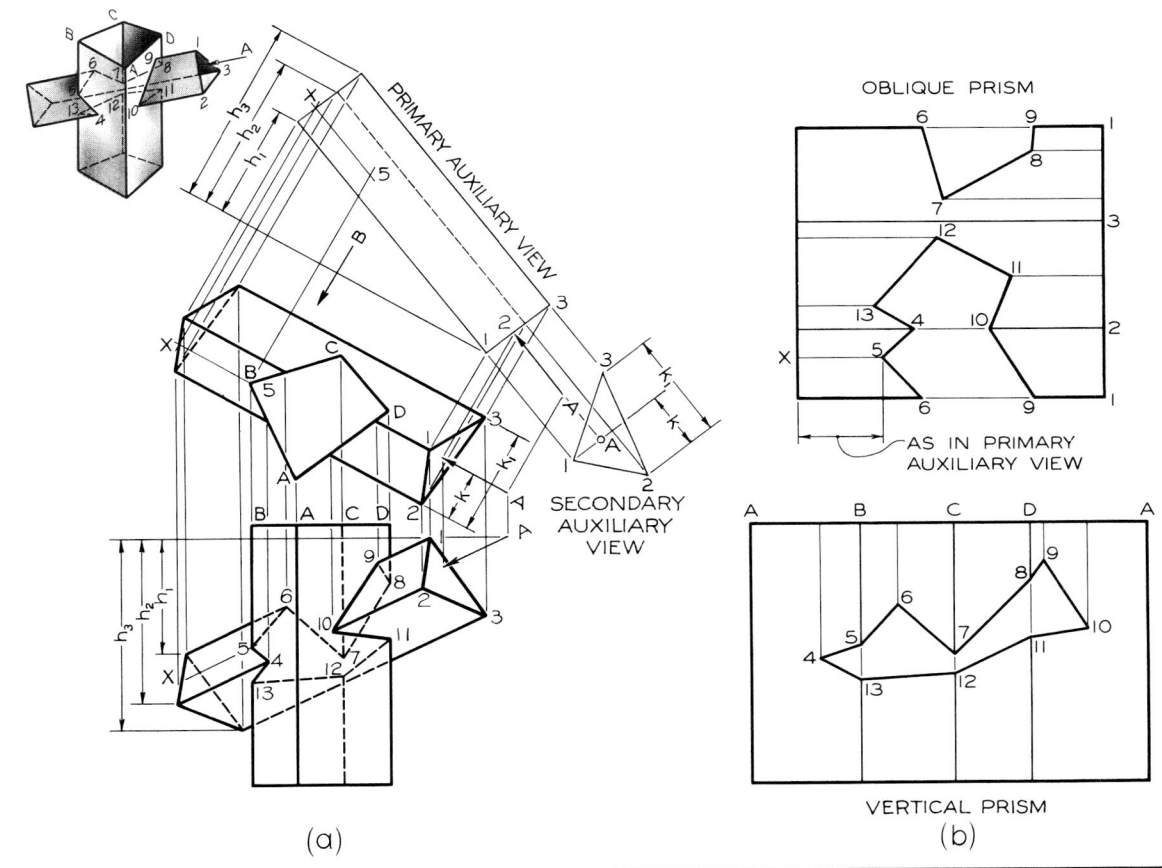

Fig. 21.23 Two Prisms Oblique to Each Other.

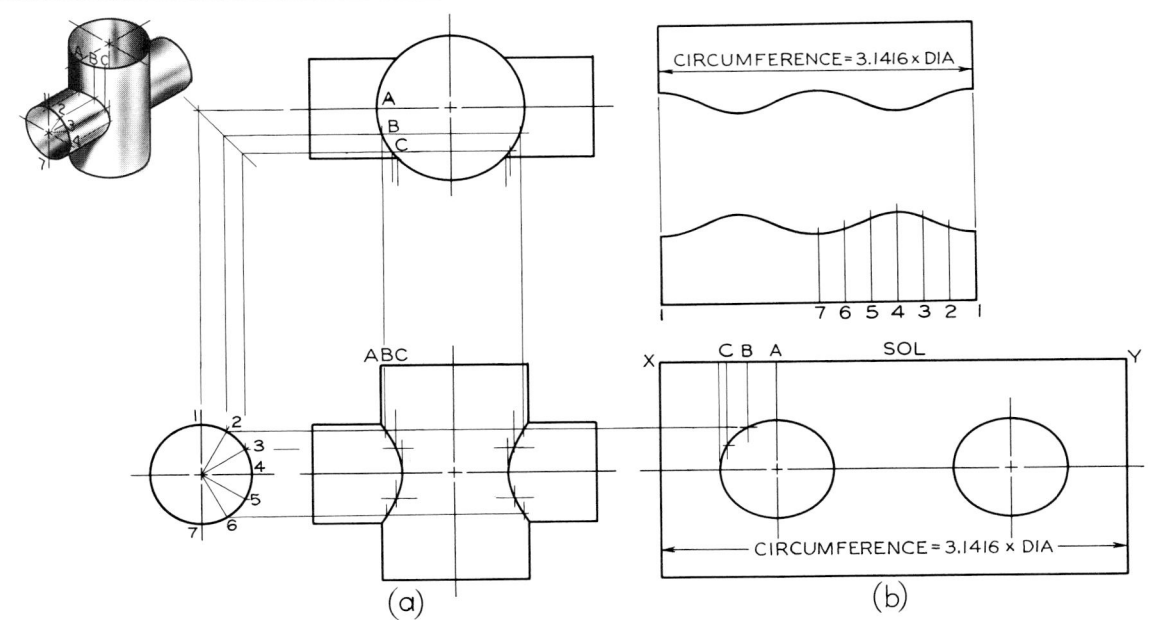

Fig. 21.24 Two Cylinders at Right Angles to Each Other.

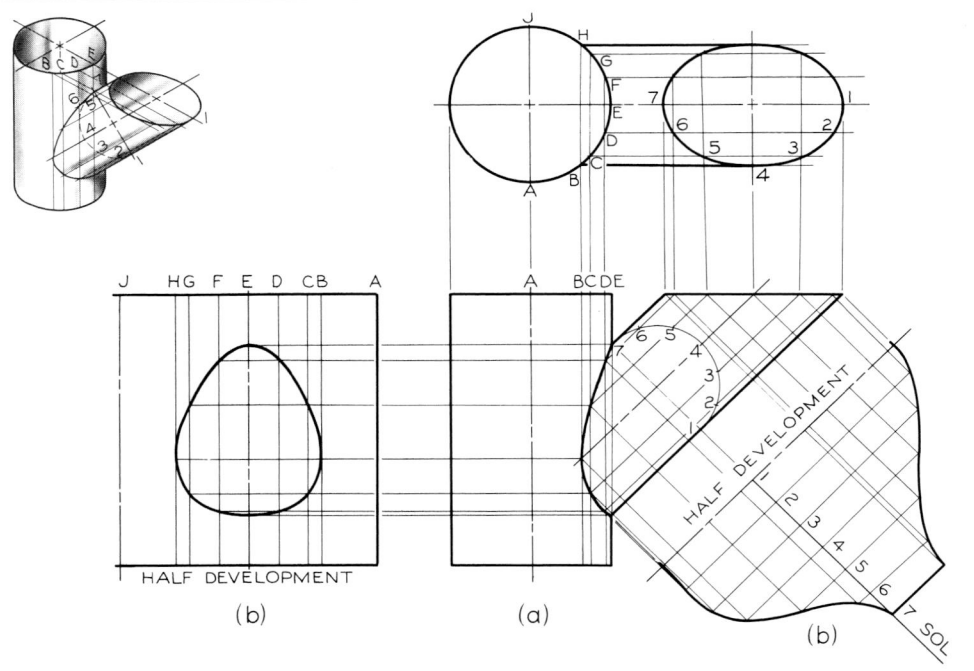

Fig. 21.25 Two Cylinders Oblique to Each Other.

elements A, B, C, ... When these are drawn in the development, the points of intersections are found at their intersections with the corresponding elements of the horizontal cylinder taken from the front view, thus determining one of the figures of intersection, as shown in Fig. 21.24 (b).

21.28 To Find the Intersection and Developments of Two Cylinders Fig. 21.25

Intersection Fig. 21.25 (a)

A revolved right section of the inclined cylinder is divided into a number of equal parts, and an element is drawn at each of the division points, 1, 2, 3, ... The points of intersection of these elements with the surface of the vertical cylinder are shown in the top view at B, C, D, . . ., and are found in the front view by projecting downward to intersect the corresponding elements 1, 2, 3, ... The curve is traced through these points with the aid of the irregular curve, §2.54.

Developments Fig. 21.25 (b)

The lateral surfaces of the two cylinders are developed as explained in §§21.7 and 21.9. True lengths

of all elements of both cylinders are shown in the front view.

21.29 To Find the Intersection and Developments of a Prism and a Cone Fig. 21.26

Intersection Fig. 21.26 (a)

Points in which the edges of the prism intersect the surface of the cone are shown in the side view at A, C, and F. Intermediate points such as B, D, E, and G are piercing points of any lines on the lateral surface of the prism parallel to the edges. Through all of the piercing points in the side view, elements of the cone are drawn and then drawn in the top and front views. The intersections of the elements of the cone with the edges of the prism (and lines along the prism drawn parallel thereto) are points of the intersections. The figures of intersections are traced through these points with the aid of the irregular curve, §2.54.

The elements 6, 5, 4, . . ., in the side view of the cone may be regarded as the edge views of cutting planes that cut these elements on the cone and edges or elements on the prism. The intersection of

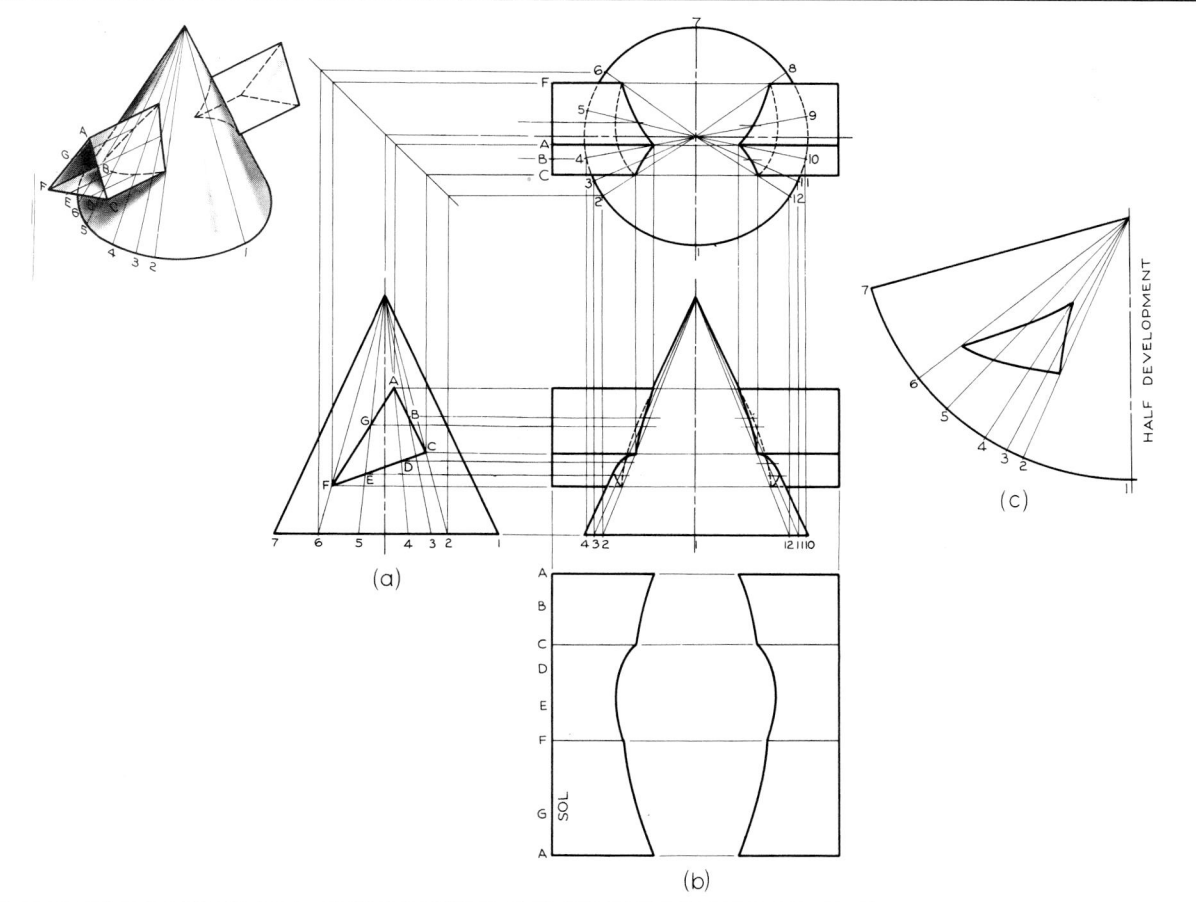

Fig. 21.26   Prism and Cone.

corresponding edges or elements on the two solids are points on the figure of intersection.

Another method of finding the figure of intersection is to pass a series of horizontal parallel planes through the solids in the manner of Fig. 21.9 (a). The plane will cut circles on the cone and straight lines on the prism, and their intersections will be points on the figure of intersection. See also Fig. 21.27 (b).

Developments Fig. 21.26 (b)

The lateral surface of the prism is developed as explained in §21.23. True lengths of all edges and lines parallel thereto are shown in both the front and top views.

The lateral surface of the cone, Fig. 21.26 (c), is developed as explained in §21.11. True lengths of elements from the vertex to points on the intersections are found as shown in Fig. 11.10 (a).

21.30 To Find the Intersection of a Prism and a Cone with Edges of Prism Parallel to Axis of Cone Fig. 21.27

Fig. 21.27 (a)   Since the lateral surfaces of the prism are parallel to the axis of the cone, the figure of intersection will be composed of a series of hyperbolas, §§5.47 and 5.60. If a series of planes is assumed containing the axis of the cone, each plane will contain edges of the prism, or will cut lines parallel to them along the prism, and will cut elements on the cone that intersect these at points on the figure of intersection.

Fig. 21.27 (b)   The intersection is the same as at (a), but it is found in a different manner. Here a series of parallel planes perpendicular to the axis of the cone cut circles of varying diameters on the cone. These circles are shown true size in the top

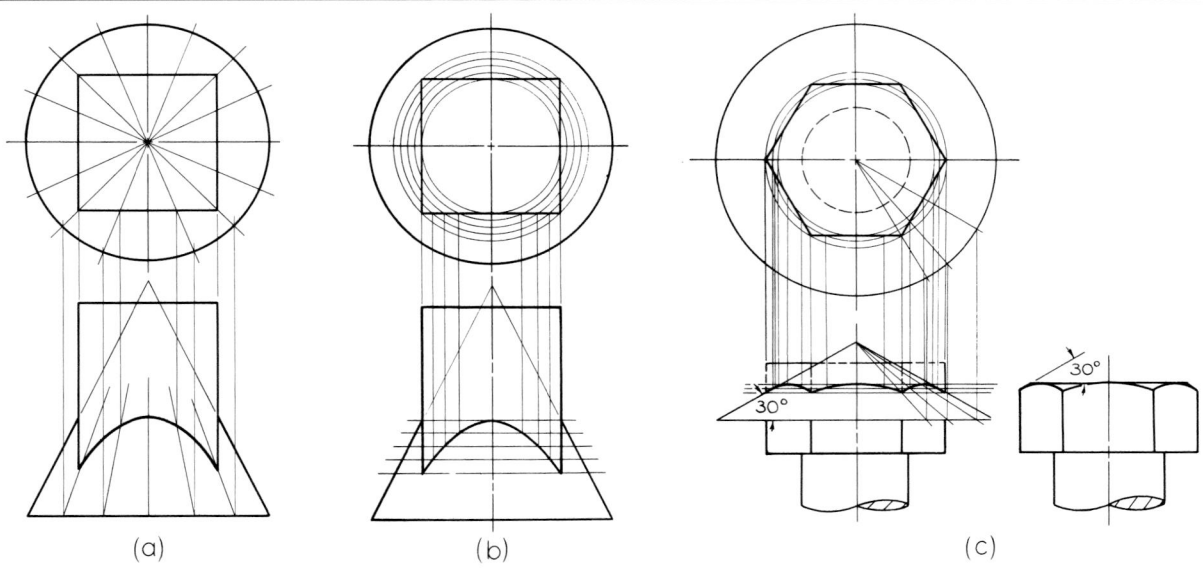

Fig. 21.27 Prisms and Cones.

view, where the piercing points of these circles in the vertical plane surfaces of the prism are also shown. The front views of these piercing points are found by projecting downward to the corresponding cutting-plane lines.

Fig. 21.27 (c) The chamfer of an ordinary hexagon bolt head or hexagon nut is actually a conical surface that intersects the six vertical sides of a hexagonal prism to form hyperbolas. At (c) the methods of both (a) and (b) are shown to illustrate how points may be found by either method.

In machine drawings of bolts and nuts, these hyperbolic curves are approximated by means of circular arcs, as shown in Fig. 15.27.

21.31 To Find the Intersections and the Developments of a Cylinder and a Cone Fig. 21.28

Intersections Fig. 21.28 (a)
Points in which elements of the cylinder (preferably equally spaced to facilitate the development) intersect the surface of the cone are shown in the side view at A, B, C, ... The elements of the cylinder are here shown as points. Elements of the cone are then drawn from the vertex through each of these points, and then drawn in their correct locations in the top and front views. The intersections of these elements with the elements A, B, C, . . ., of the cylinder are points on the figures of intersection. The

curves are then traced through these points with the aid of the irregular curve, §2.54.

As explained in §21.29, the elements 5, 6, 7, . . ., in the side view of Fig. 21.28 (a) could be regarded as edge views of cutting planes that cut elements from both the cone and the cylinder, the elements meeting at points on the figure of intersection. Or a series of horizontal parallel planes can be passed through the solids that will cut circles from the cone and elements from the cylinder that intersect at points on the figure of intersection.

Developments Fig. 21.28 (b)
The lateral surface of the cylinder is developed as explained in §21.7. True lengths of all elements are shown in both the front and top views. The lateral surface of the cone is developed as explained in §21.11. True lengths of elements from the vertex to points on the intersections are found as shown in Fig. 11.10 (a).

21.32 To Find the Intersection of a Cylinder and a Sphere Fig. 21.29

Horizontal planes 1, 2, 3, . . ., which appear edgewise in the front and side views, cut elements A, B, C, . . ., from the cylinder and circular arcs 1′, 2′, 3′, . . ., from the sphere. The intersections of the elements with the arcs produced by the corresponding planes are points on the figure of intersection. Join the points with a smooth curve, §2.54.

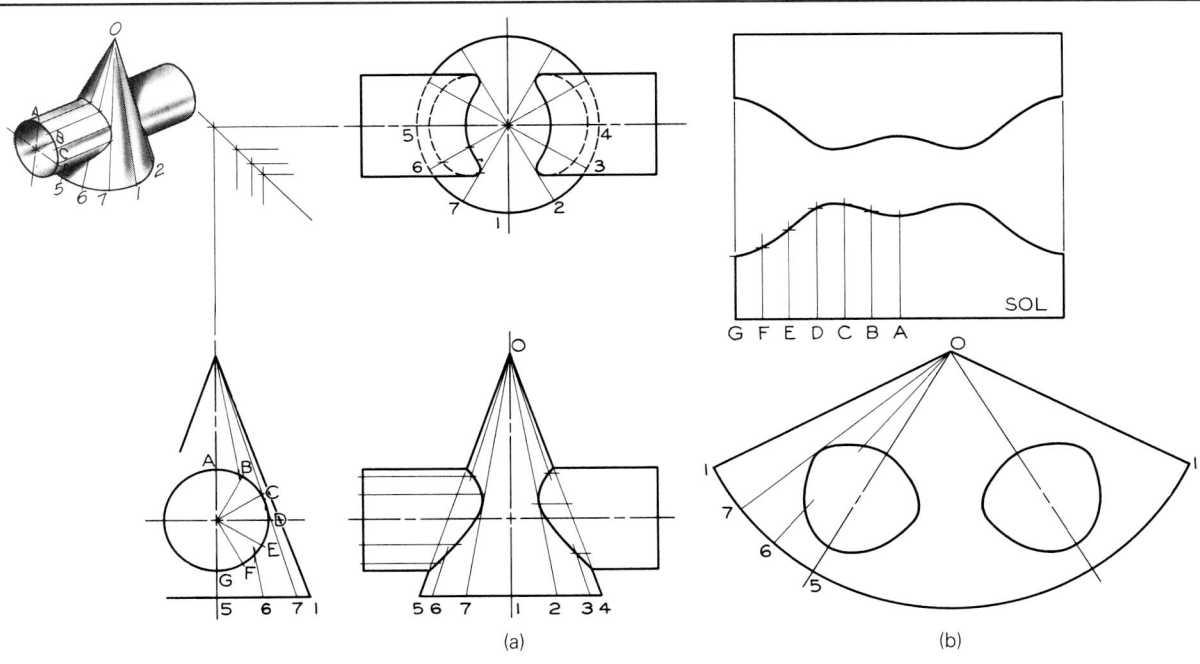

Fig. 21.28 Cone and Cylinder.

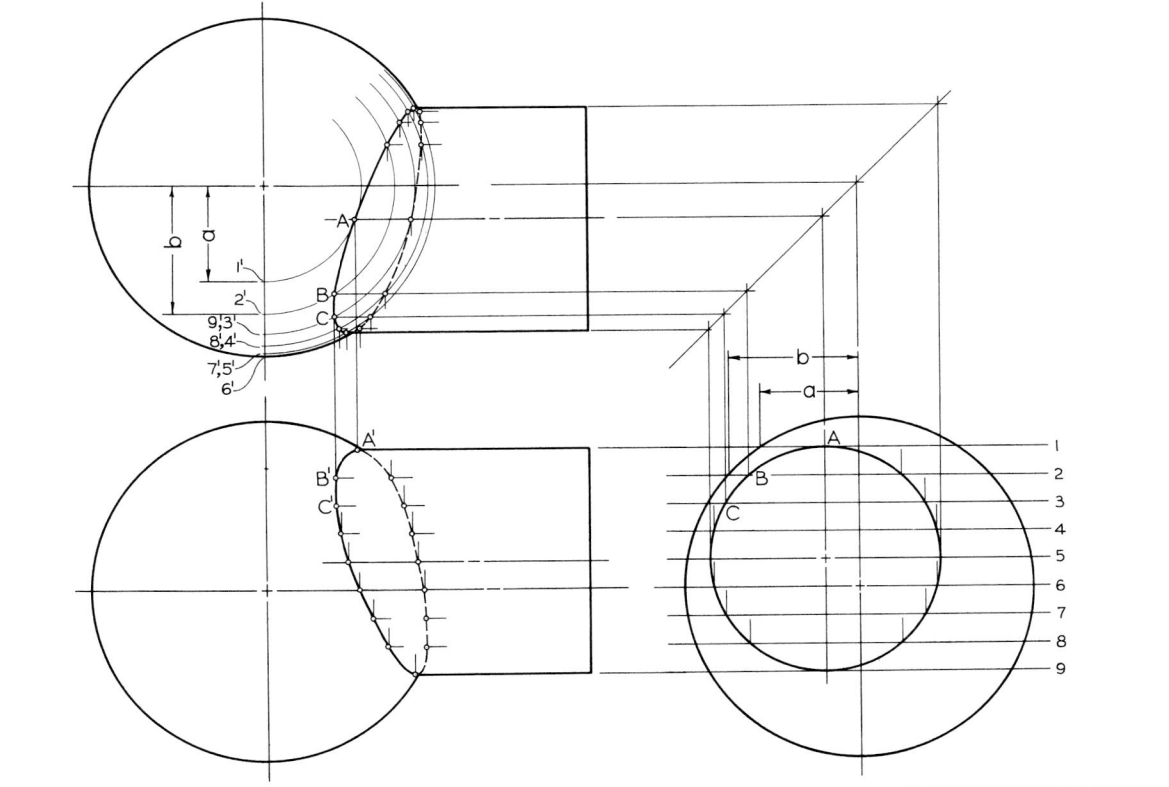

Fig. 21.29 Intersection of Sphere and Cylinder.

Intersection and Development Problems

A wide selection of intersection and development problems is provided in Figs. 21.30 to 21.37. These problems are designed to fit size B (11.0″ × 17.0″) or A3 (297 mm × 420 mm) sheets. Dimensions should be included on the given views. The student is cautioned to take special pains to obtain accuracy in these drawings and to draw smooth curves as required.

Since many of the problems in this chapter are of a general nature, they can also be solved on most computer graphics systems. If a system is available, the instructor may choose to assign specific problems to be completed by this method.

Additional problems in convenient form for solution are presented in the worksheets at the back of this book. Refer to Drawings 21-1 to 21-6 and accompanying instructions.

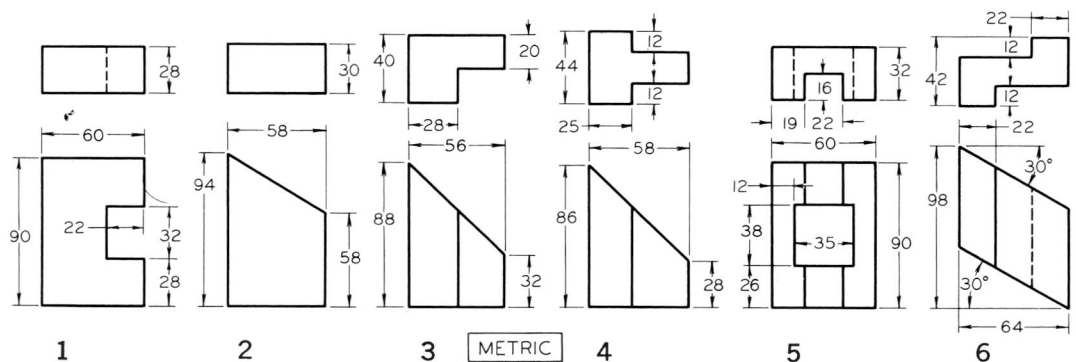

Fig. 21.30 Draw given views and develop lateral surface (Layout A3–3 or B–3).

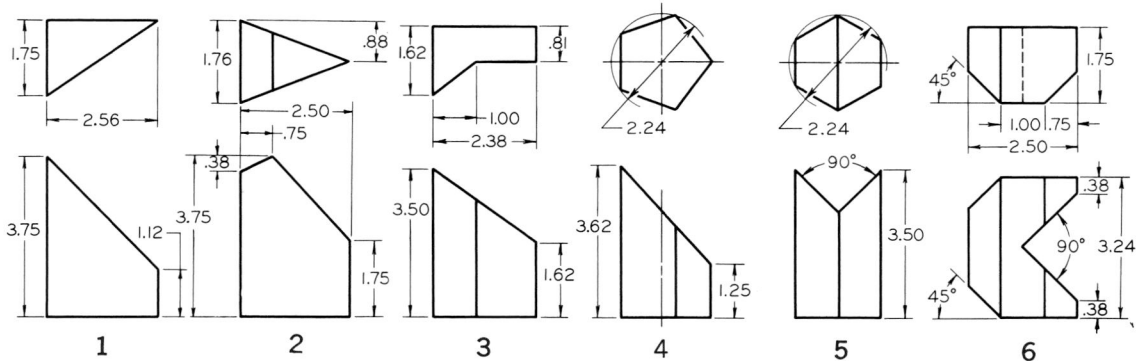

Fig. 21.31 Draw given views and develop lateral surface (Layout A3–3 or B–3).

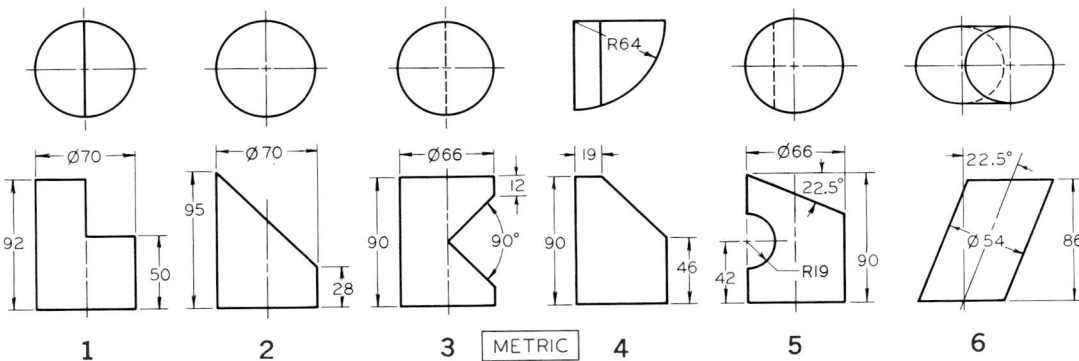

Fig. 21.32 Draw given views and develop lateral surface (Layout A3–3 or B–3).

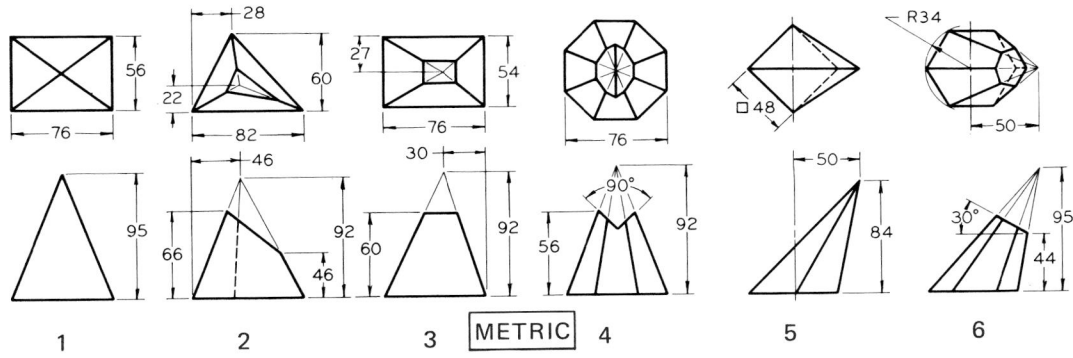

Fig. 21.33 Draw given views and develop lateral surface (Layout A3–3 or B–3).

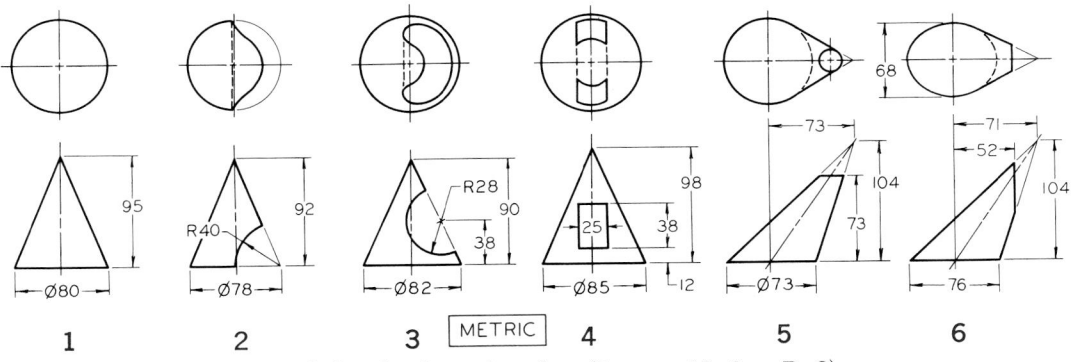

Fig. 21.34 Draw given views and develop lateral surface (Layout A3–3 or B–3).

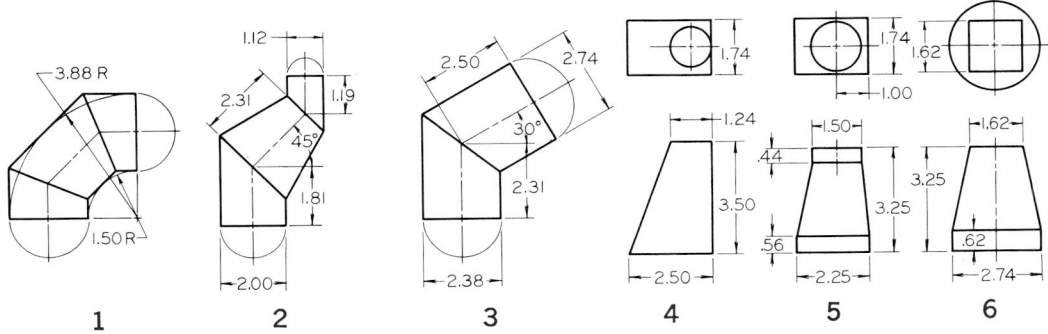

Fig. 21.35 Draw given views of the forms and develop lateral surfaces (Layout A3–3 or B–3).

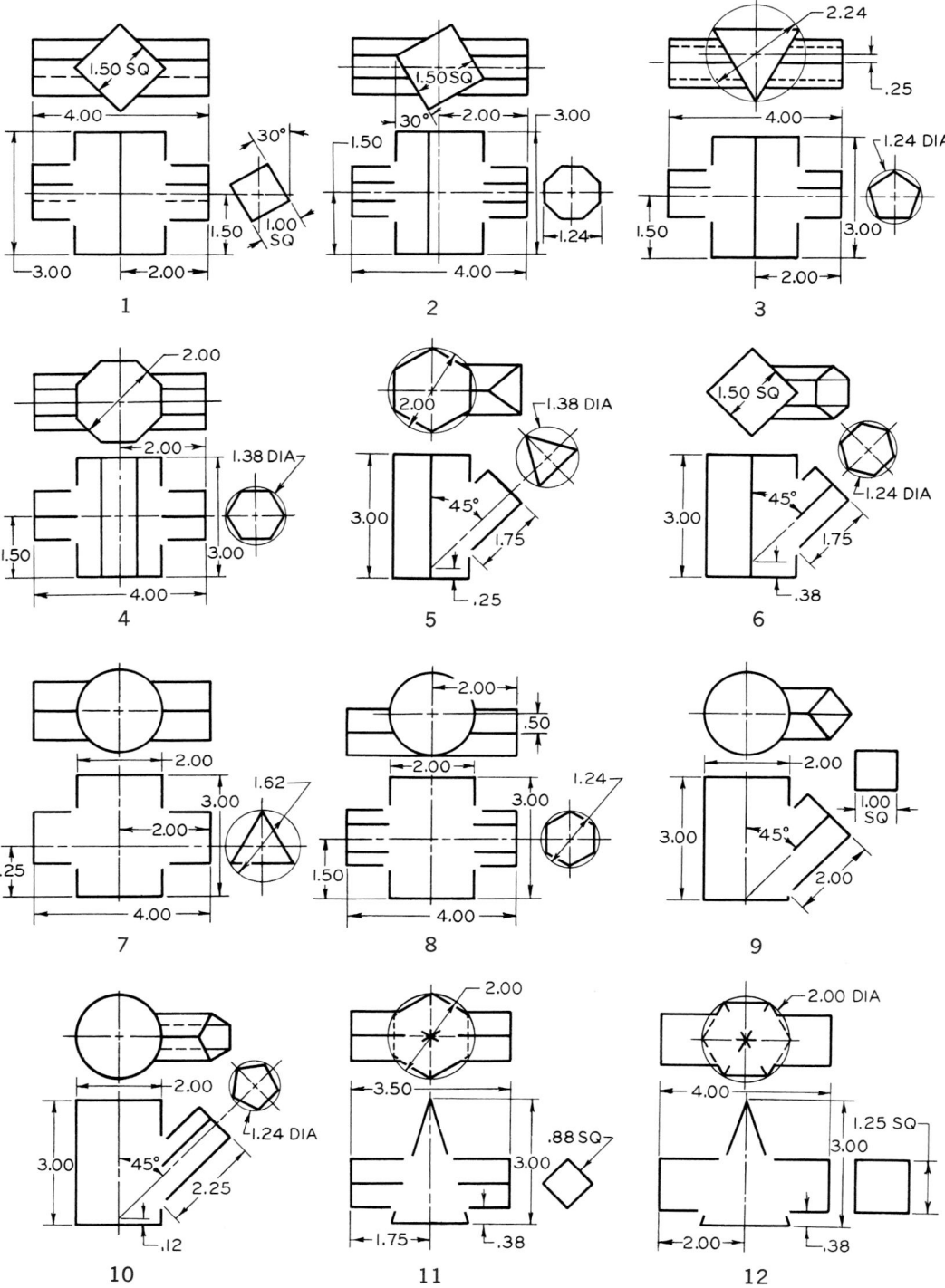

Fig. 21.36 Draw the given views of assigned form and complete the intersection. Then develop lateral surfaces (Layout A3–3 or B–3).

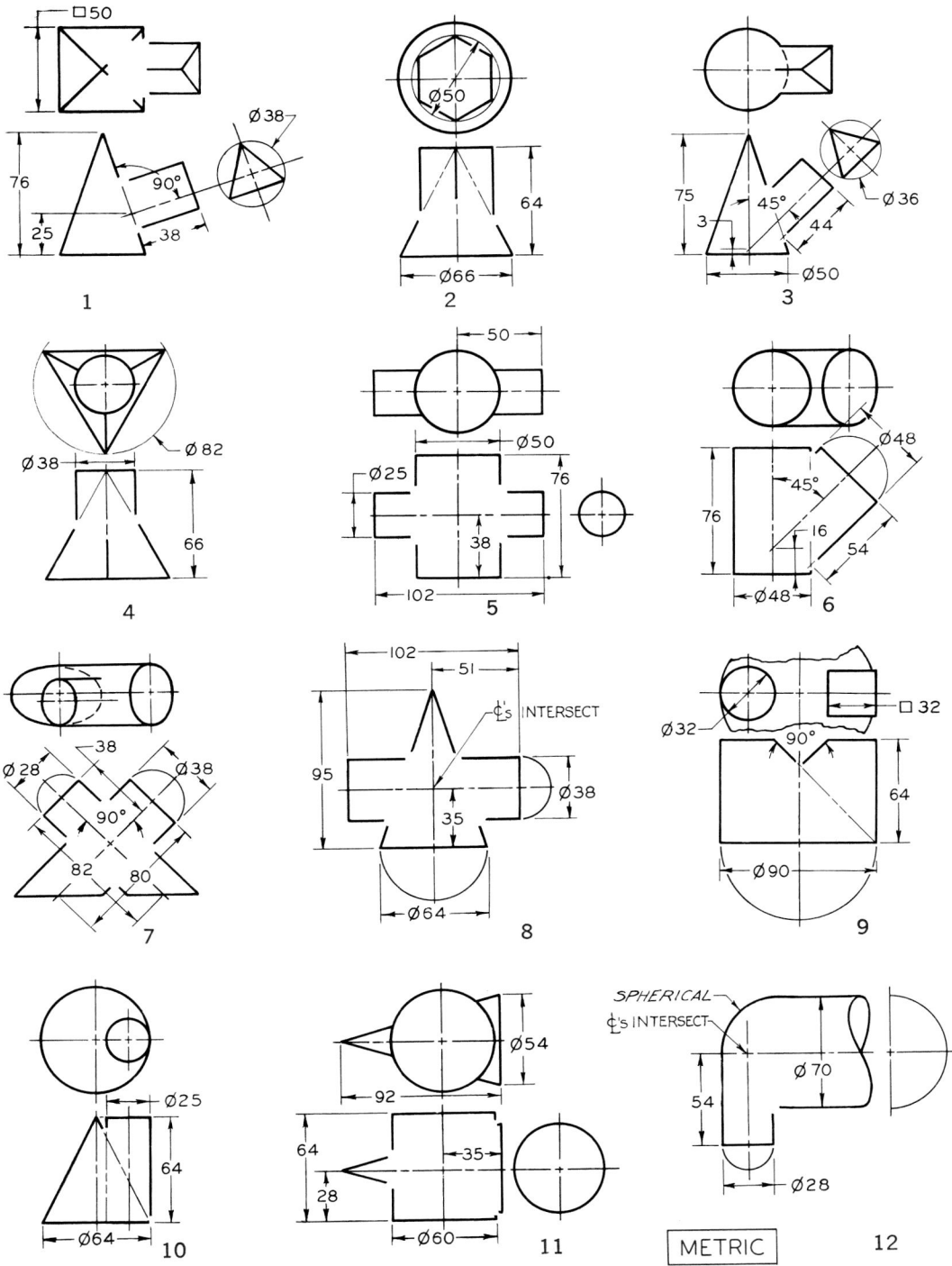

Fig. 21.37 Draw the given views of assigned form and complete the intersection. Then develop lateral surfaces (Layout A3–3 or B–3).

Line and Plane Tangencies

A plane tangent to a ruled surface such as a cone or cylinder contains only one straight-line element of that surface. A plane tangent to a double-curved surface such as a sphere contains only one point in that surface. All lines tangent to a curved surface at a particular point or at points along the same straight-line element lie in a plane tangent at the point or element. A plane tangent to a ruled surface is conveniently represented by two straight lines, one an element and the other line tangent to the surface at a point on the element. For double-curved surfaces the plane is represented by two straight lines, both tangent at the same point on the double-curved surface.

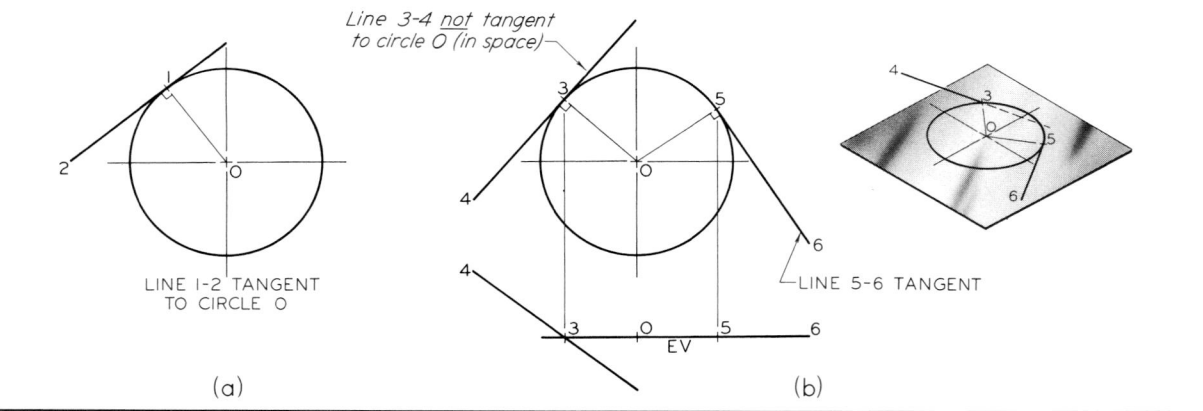

Fig. 22.1   Line Tangencies.

22.1 Line and Plane Tangencies

Line tangencies as encountered in plane geometry are discussed in Chapter 5, "Geometric Constructions." Methods such as those of §§5.33–5.35 are based on the principle that a line tangent to a circle is perpendicular to the radius drawn to the point of tangency. Thus in Fig. 22.1 (a) line 1–2 is perpendicular to radius O–1 at point 1 and is tangent to the circle O. If the assumption is made that line 1–2 and circle O are in the plane of the paper, a plane geometry construction suffices.

At (b) is given a multiview (or three-dimensional) drawing. Although the top view of line 3–4 appears to be tangent to the top view of the circle, line 3–4 is *not* tangent to the circle *in space* because line 3–4 is not in the plane of the circle, as is evident in the front view. By contrast, line 5–6 lies in the plane of the circle and *is* tangent in space to the given circle.

Because planes are easily represented by lines, §19.7, planes tangent to curved surfaces are often represented by suitable pairs of tangent lines, or by one tangent line and a line lying in the curved surface (a straight-line *element*, §7.28). It is sometimes convenient to represent a tangent plane by a tangent edge view of the plane, Fig. 22.10 (b).

22.2 Planes Tangent to Cones

Plane Tangent to a Right-Circular Cone Through Point on Surface Fig. 22.2

Let the cone and the top view of point 1 on the surface of the cone be given as at (a).

At (b) the element through point 1 is drawn in the top view, establishing point 2 on the circular base. Point 2 is then projected to the front view, and point 1 is projected to the now-established front view of the element.

If the view of element O–2 is nearly parallel to the projectors, more dependable accuracy may be secured through the use of revolution, as at (c), which is an application of §11.6

At (d) line 2–3 is drawn tangent to the circular base by drawing its top view perpendicular to element O–2 at point 2 and by drawing its front view coinciding with the edge view of the base. Plane O–1–2–3 is the required tangent plane.

Plane Tangent to Oblique Cone Through Point Outside Its Surface Fig. 22.3

Let the cone and point be given as at (a).

Because all elements of a cone pass through its vertex, a tangent plane, which must contain an element, will contain the vertex also. Hence line V–1 lies in the tangent plane. Any line tangent to the base circle lies in the plane of the base, §22.1, and thus can intersect line V–1 only at point 2, shown in the front view at (b).

At (c) point 2 is projected to the top view of line V–1, and from the top view of point 2 line 2–3 and 2–3′ may be drawn tangent to the base circle as shown. Either plane V–2–3 or V–2–3′ meets the requirements of the problem. In practice, it is usually evident which of two optional solutions is compatible with other features of the design.

Plane Tangent to Cone and Parallel to Given Line Fig. 22.4

With the given cone and line 1–2 as shown at (a), a line is drawn through vertex V of the cone, parallel to the given line and intersecting the plane of the

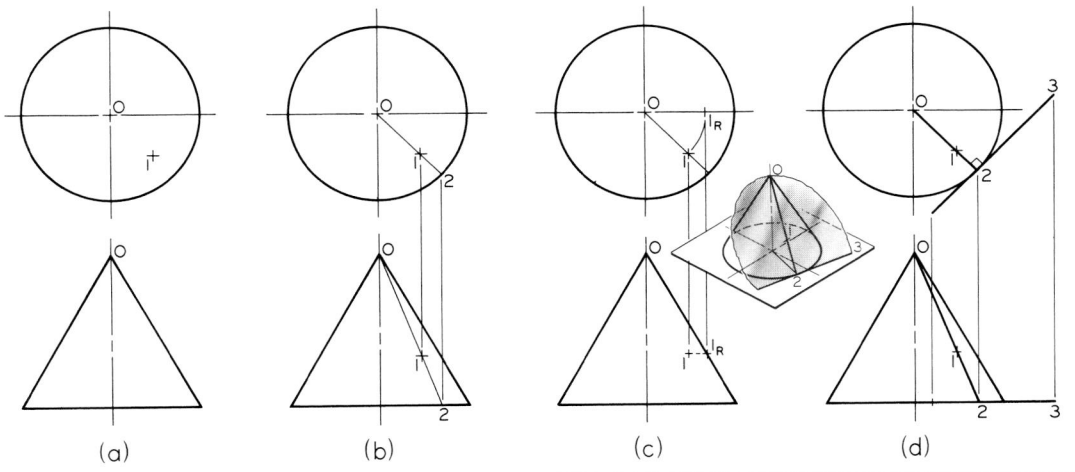

Fig. 22.2   Plane Tangent to Right-Circular Cone Through Point on Surface.

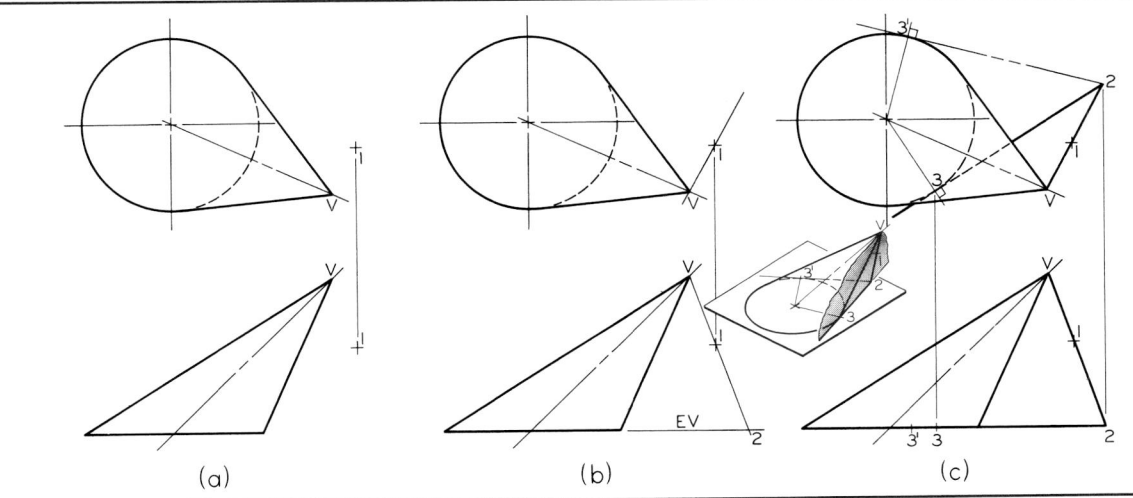

Fig. 22.3   Plane Tangent to Oblique Cone Through Point Outside Cone.

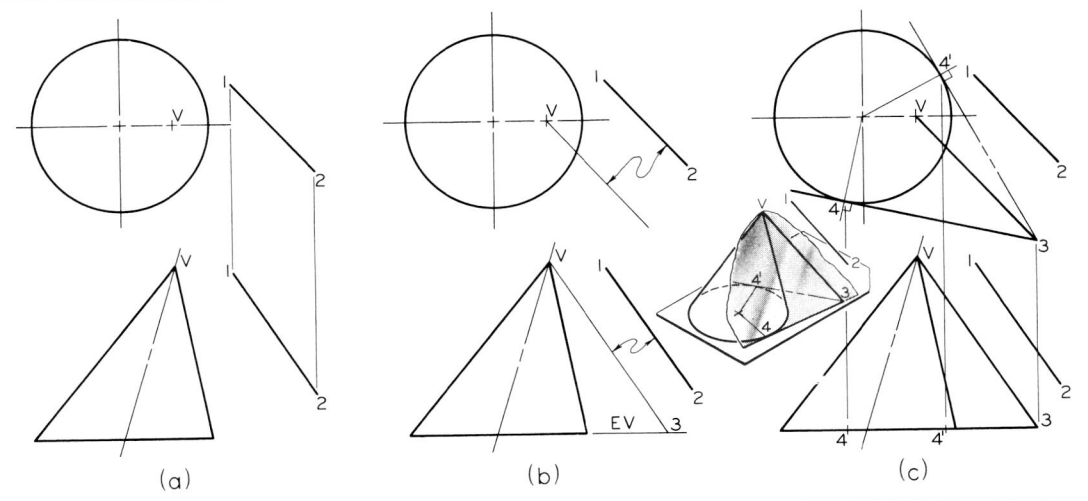

Fig. 22.4   Plane Tangent to Cone and Parallel to Given Line.

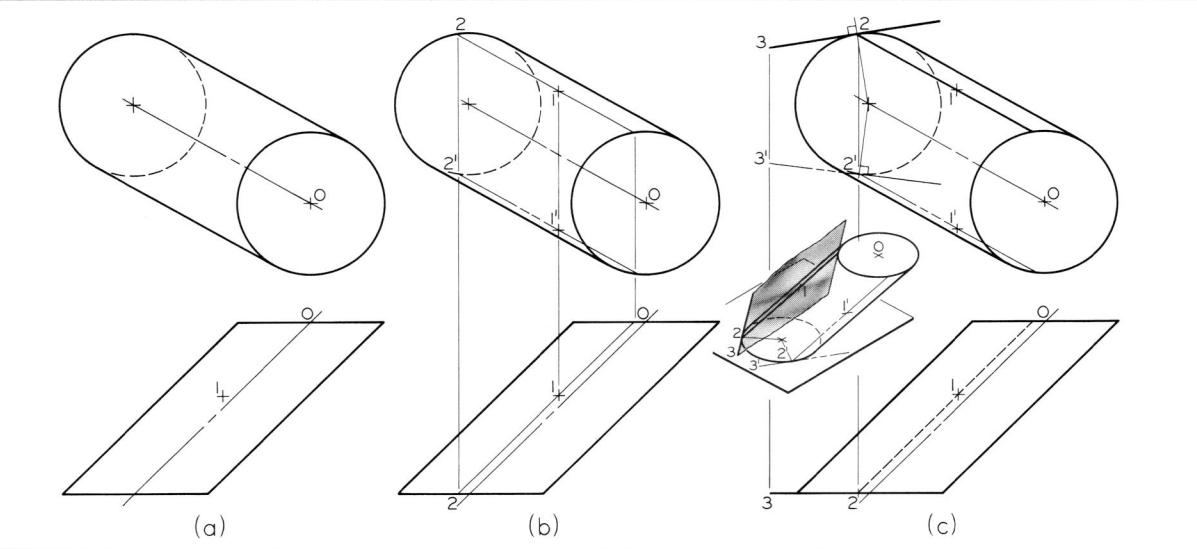

Fig. 22.5   Plane Tangent to Cylinder Through Point on Surface.

base at point **3**, as at (b), thus establishing a line in the required tangent plane. (Also see §20.4.)

At (c) point **3** is projected to the top view of the line through **V** and parallel to line **1–2**. From the top view of point **3** lines **3–4** and **3–4′** may be drawn tangent to the base circle as shown. Either plane **V–3–4** or **V–3–4′** satisfies the requirements of the problem.

22.3 Planes Tangent to Cylinders

By definition, §5.7, all elements of a cylinder are parallel to each other and to the axis of the cylinder. It follows from §20.4 that any plane tangent to a cylinder, and thus containing one element, is parallel to the remaining elements and to the axis.

Plane Tangent to Cylinder Through Point on Surface Fig. 22.5.

With one view given of point **1** on the surface of an oblique cylinder as at (a), element **1–2** is introduced as at (b). When point **2** is projected to the top view, it is observed that point **2** may fall at either position **2** or position **2′**. There are thus alternative solutions, and point **1** may be at either of the locations **1** and **1′**, as shown. Addition of line **2–3** tangent to the base of the cylinder at point **2** (or line **2′–3′** at point **2′**) completes the representation of the required tangent plane.

Plane Tangent to Cylinder Through Point Outside Its Surface Fig. 22.6

The cylinder and point **1** are given as at (a). As previously noted, any plane tangent to a cylinder must be parallel to the elements. Hence a line **1–2** drawn through point **1** and parallel to the elements, as at (b), must be common to all planes containing point **1** and parallel to the elements, §20.4. The representation of a tangent plane is completed by the addition of a line tangent to one base of the cylinder. As observed earlier, such a tangent line must lie in the same plane as the chosen base—in this example the lower base, (c). Therefore the tangent line could intersect line **1–2** only at point **2** located in the front view at the intersection of the (extended) edge view of the base plane with line **1–2**. Observe that lines could be drawn from point **2** tangent to the lower base at either point **3** or point **3′**, so that again there are alternative solutions, and in an application it would normally be apparent which solution is practical.

Plane Tangent to Cylinder and Parallel to Given Line Outside the Cylinder Fig. 22.7

Let the cylinder and line **1–2** be given as at (a). A plane is constructed parallel to a given line by the method of §20.4. However, at this stage it is not known which element will be the line of tangency.

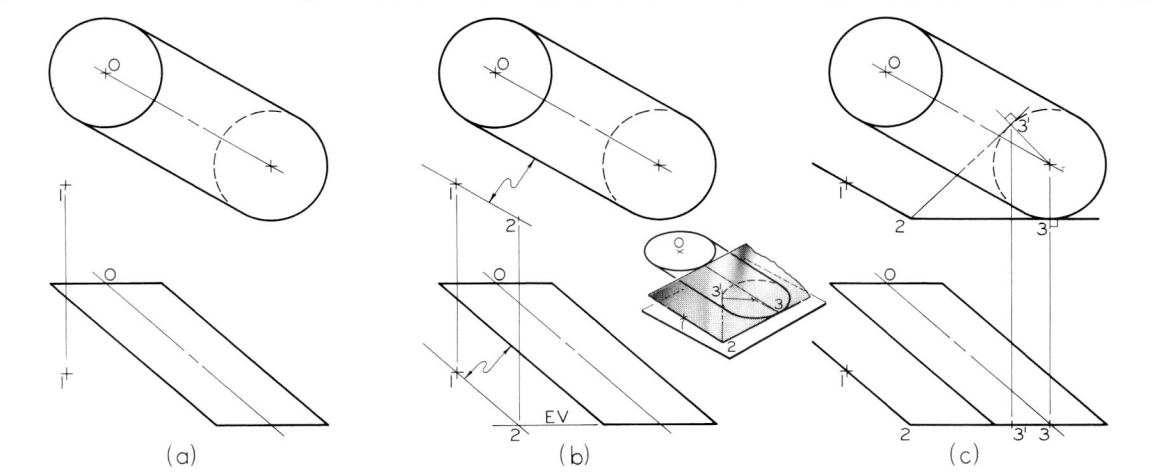

Fig. 22.6 Plane Tangent to Cylinder Through Point Outside Surface.

The tangent plane must be parallel to all elements of the cylinder as well as to line 1–2. By the method of §20.4 a plane can be constructed at any convenient location and parallel both to the elements and to line 1–2. The required tangent plane will then be parallel to this plane.

A convenient representation for this preliminary plane includes the given line 1–2, as at (b). With line 1–3 drawn parallel to the cylinder as shown, plane 2–1–3 is established parallel to the cylinder.

Any line tangent to either given cylinder base must be a horizontal line, §22.1. Since all horizontal

lines in the same oblique plane are parallel to each other, §19.8, it follows that horizontal lines in parallel oblique planes are likewise parallel to each other. Thus, if the direction of one such horizontal line is established, such as line 2–4 at (b), the direction of horizontal lines in planes parallel to plane 2–1–3, including the required plane, is also established.

At (c) line 2_1–4_1 is drawn parallel to the top view of line 2–4 and tangent to either base—in this case the lower base—of the cylinder. The point of tangency is 5, and line 5–6 is the element of tangency.

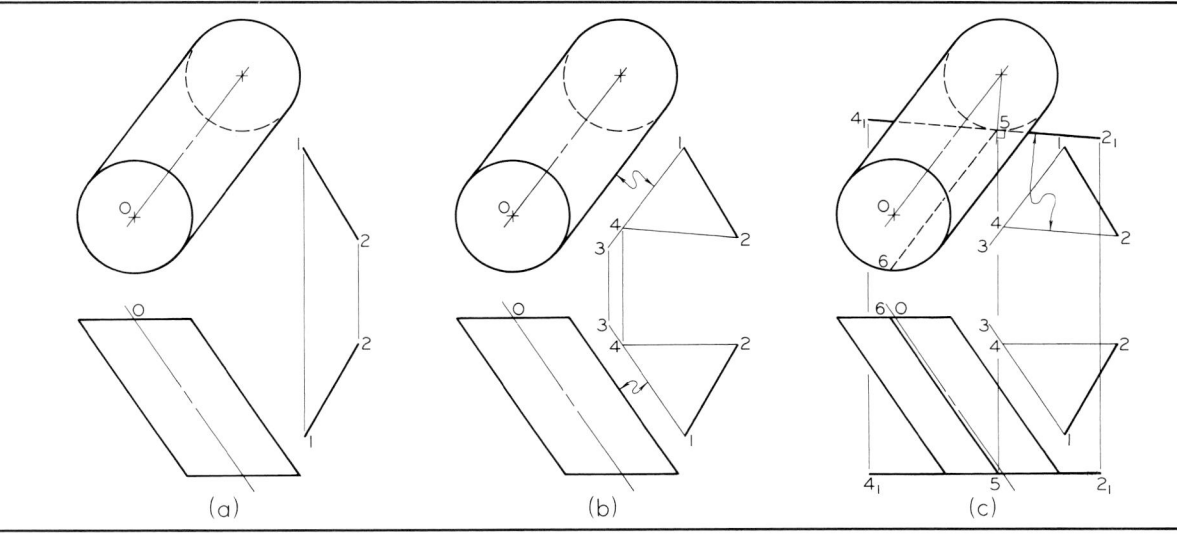

Fig. 22.7 Plane Tangent to Cylinder and Parallel to Given Line Outside the Cylinder.

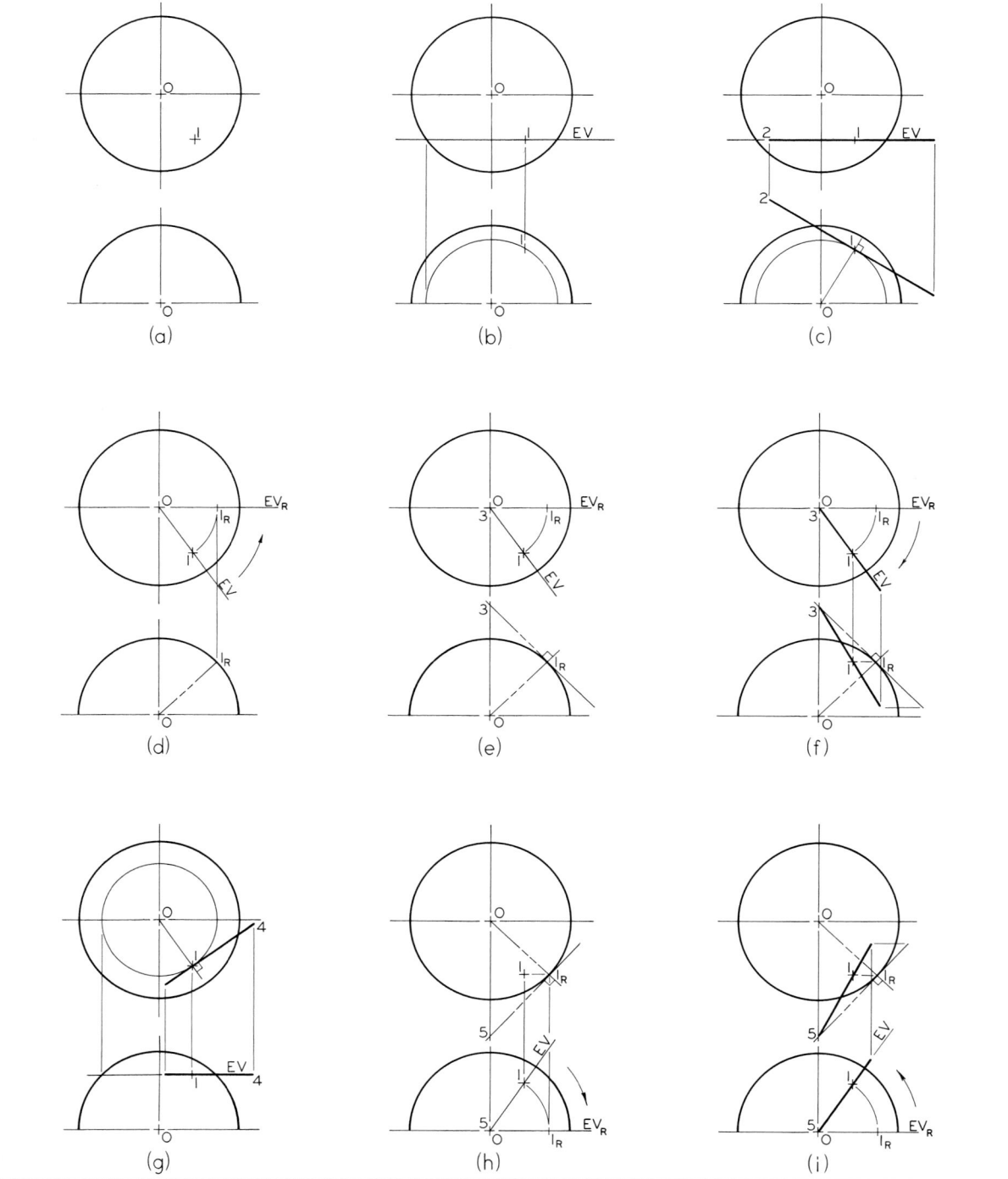

Fig. 22.8   Lines Tangent to Spherical Surface at a Point on the Surface.

Construction of the front view completes the representation of the required tangent plane parallel to given line 1–2.

Since tangent line 2_1–4_1 could have been drawn on the opposite side of the base, there is an alternative tangent plane, which is not shown here.

22.4 Planes Tangent to Spheres

A plane tangent to a *double-curved surface*, §21.1, contains one and only one point of that surface, since it follows from the definition of such a surface that it contains no straight-line elements. Hence planes tangent to double-curved surfaces are represented by appropriate combinations of lines tangent at the desired point or points of tangency. Under suitable circumstances such a tangent line may represent an edge view of the required tangent plane. An example of this appears later in this section.

The sphere, §5.7, is by far the most practical, hence most common, form of the double-curved surface. This discussion will be limited to spherical surfaces.

Lines Tangent to a Sphere at a Given Point on Its Surface Fig. 22.8

Let the front and top views of a hemisphere be given, as at (a), and let the top view of a point 1 on its surface be given also. The front view of point 1 can be located by passing a convenient cutting plane through the point and finding another view of the line (circle) of intersection. It follows that a "convenient" cutting plane is one in such position that the circle appears in one of the given views as a circle and not as an ellipse. As an example, at (b) a frontal, edge-view plane is introduced. The circle is located and constructed in the front view as shown, and point 1 is projected to it. A line tangent to this circle is tangent to the spherical surface. At (c) line 1–2 is constructed tangent to the circle at point 1 by drawing the front view of the tangent line perpendicular to radius O–1 and then drawing the top view coincident with the edge view of the cutting plane, §22.1.

At (d) point 1 is revolved, in the top view, to the frontal plane through center O. See §11.6. This amounts to revolving the edge view of a vertical cutting plane (EV), as indicated. The revolved view of the circle of intersection coincides with the circular front view of the sphere, and the revolved position 1_R of point 1 is projected to it. As shown at (e), line 1_R–3 is now drawn tangent to this circle,

intersecting the vertical center line of the sphere at point 3. Since this vertical center line is also the axis of revolution, point 3 will not move as the cutting plane counterrevolves, as at (f). Line 1–3 is thus another line tangent to the spherical surface at given point 1.

At (g) a horizontal cutting plane is introduced by first drawing the top view of the circle of intersection passing through the top view of point 1. This in turn projects to the front view as shown, locating the edge of the cutting plane, to which point 1 is projected. Line 1–4, constructed tangent to the circle of intersection at point 1, is also tangent to the spherical surface.

Finally, at (h) and (i), line 1–5 is constructed tangent to the spherical surface in a variation of the method shown at (d) to (f). An edge-view cutting plane is introduced in the front view, through points 1 and O. After it revolves to horizontal, the circle of intersection coincides with the top view of the sphere, and line 1_R–5 is drawn tangent to the cut circle of intersection. Counterrevolution establishes the views of the tangent line 1–5, as shown at (i).

Plane Tangent to a Sphere at a Given Point on Its Surface Fig. 22.9

In Fig. 22.8 four lines, 1–2, 1–3, 1–4, and 1–5, were constructed tangent to the spherical surface at point 1. Any two of these constitute intersecting tangent lines and thus establish the plane tangent at point 1. As an example, tangent lines 1–2 and 1–4 are

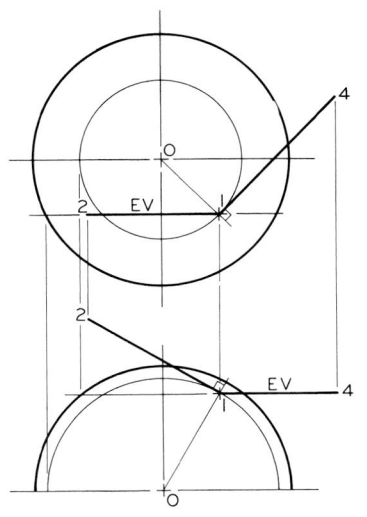

Fig. 22.9 Plane Tangent to Sphere at Given Point on Surface.

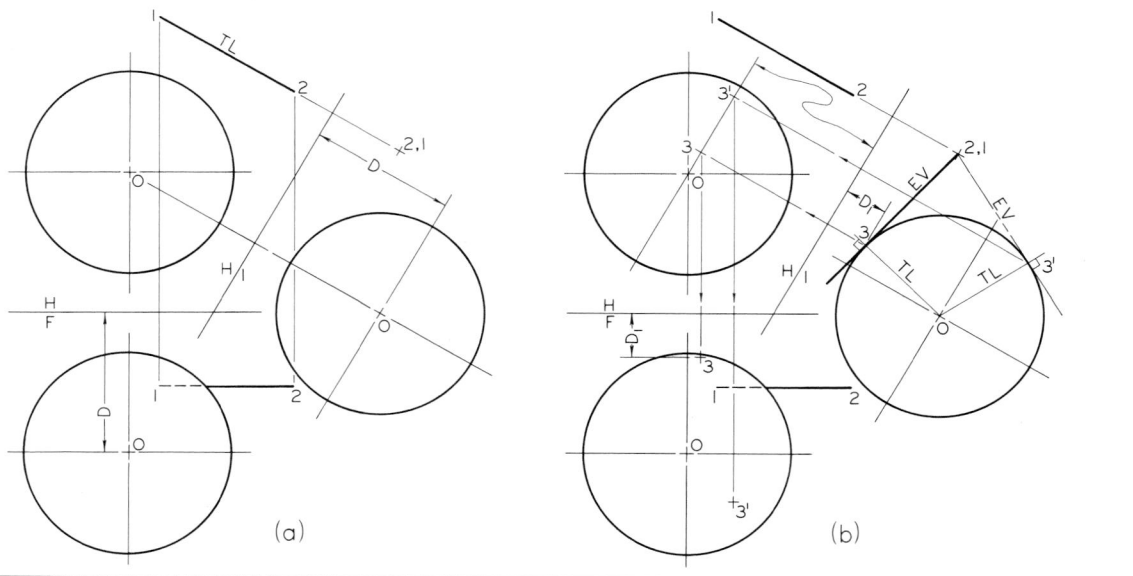

Fig. 22.10 Plane Tangent to Sphere and Containing Line Outside Sphere.

shown in Fig. 22.9. Plane **2–1–4** is one representation of the plane tangent to the spherical surface at point **1**. Incidentally, study reveals that this is simply the construction of a plane perpendicular to radius **O–1** at point **1** by the given-view method of §20.6. Analogous to the plane geometry description of a line tangent to a circle, §22.1, a plane tangent to a sphere may be defined as a plane perpendicular to the radius of the sphere drawn to the point of tangency.

A Plane Tangent to a Sphere and Containing a Given Line That Does Not Intersect the Sphere Fig. 22.10

Let sphere **O** and line **1–2** be given in the front and top views, as at (a). If a point view of a line is constructed, any plane containing the line appears in edge view, §19.9. Also any orthographic projection of a sphere shows the true diameter of the sphere. Hence in the given problem, if a point view of line **1–2** is constructed, the required tangent plane will appear in edge view and tangent to the corresponding view of the sphere. Since line **1–2** appears in true length in the top view at (a), its point view may be constructed in primary auxiliary view **1** as shown.

At (b) alternative edge views of planes are drawn through point view **2, 1** and tangent to the sphere at point **3** or point **3'** as preferred. The front and top

views of point **3** or **3'** are then projected as shown, completing the representation of the tangent plane. In practice, other lines of the tangent plane could, and probably would, be drawn to establish a recognizable configuration. Theoretically, however, additional lines are not needed.

22.5 Applications of Right-Circular Cones

As pointed out in §19.3, all elements of a right-circular cone form the same angle with the base plane of the cone. This feature is the basis for the revolution constructions of §19.3 and for the constructions following.

A Plane Containing an Oblique Line and Making a Specified Angle with Horizontal Fig. 22.11

Let line **1–2** be given, as at (a), and let it be required to construct a plane containing line **1–2** and forming an angle of 45° (or 135°) with horizontal.

A plane tangent to a right-circular cone contains one element and forms the same angle as does any element with the base plane of the cone. Because the vertex is common to all elements, it must lie in any tangent plane. Hence at (b) the vertex of a cone of suitable dimensions is placed at some chosen point **3** along given line **1–2**. In this case the re-

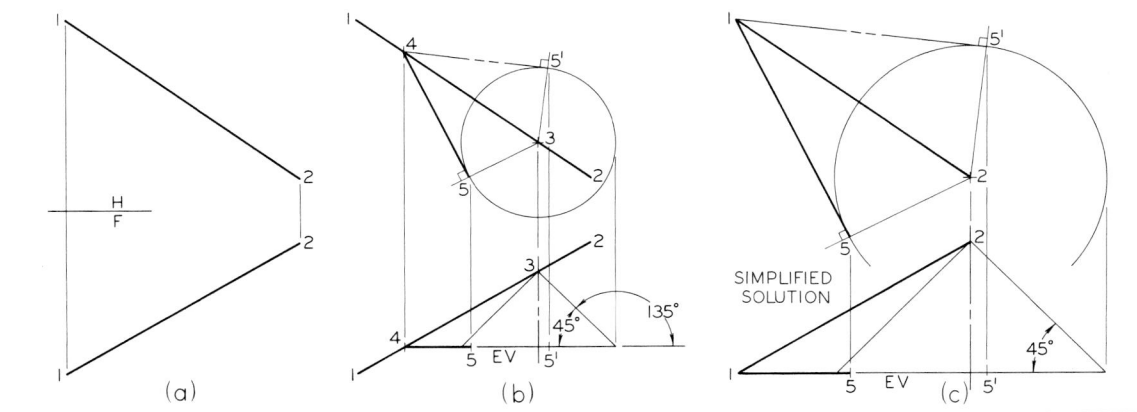

Fig. 22.11   Plane Containing Line and Forming Specified Angle with Horizontal.

quired angle is 45° with horizontal, so the cone is placed with its base horizontal (axis vertical) and with its elements at 45° with the base. This same construction is used for a specified angle of 135°, the supplement of 45°. Line 1–2 pierces the extended edge view of the base plane at point 4. See Fig. 22.3. Lines tangent to the base may be drawn alternatively from point 4 to point 5 or from point 4 to point 5'. Either of the two resulting tangent planes may be selected according to additional specifications, if any.

As shown at (c), the foregoing construction could be somewhat simplified in detail, not in principle, by placing the cone vertex at point 2 and the base plane at the same elevation as point 1.

Line at Specified Angles with Given Planes Fig. 22.12

If two right-circular cones with the same vertex intersect, the common element or elements of the two cones form the same angles with the two base planes as do the respective sets of elements. To simplify determining which elements are common, the two cones should have elements of the same length so that their base lines intersect, as exemplified by points 1 and 2 in Fig. 22.12.

As an example of an application of the foregoing, Fig. 22.13, let it be required to construct a line 1–2, with point 1 given, such that line 1–2 forms an angle of 30° with a horizontal plane and an angle of 50° with a frontal plane. At (a) a right-circular cone is constructed with its vertex at point 1 and with its

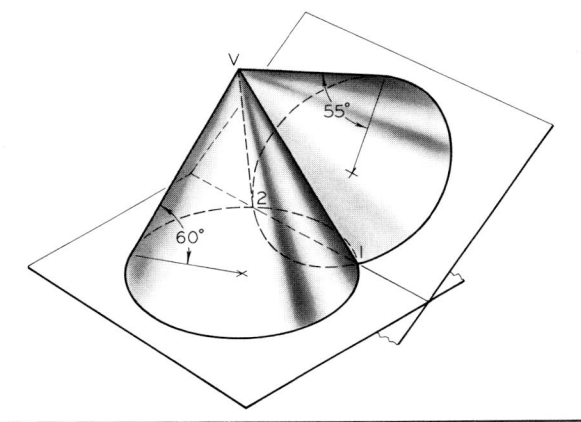

Fig. 22.12   Line at Specified Angles with Two Given Planes.

elements at 30° with horizontal. The length S of the elements can be any convenient or specified length.

At (b) a second cone is introduced with its vertex at point 1 but with its elements at 50° with a frontal plane. Note that the previously selected length S must also be used for the elements of the second cone. This selection results in the intersection of two base circles at points 2 and 2'. Thus the requirements of the problems are fulfilled by either line 1–2 or line 1–2'. There are additional alternative solutions. If we choose to reverse either cone, we find two more solutions. At (c) the cone with the 30° angle is drawn sloping upward from point 1. The two additional solutions are lines 1–3 and 1–3'.

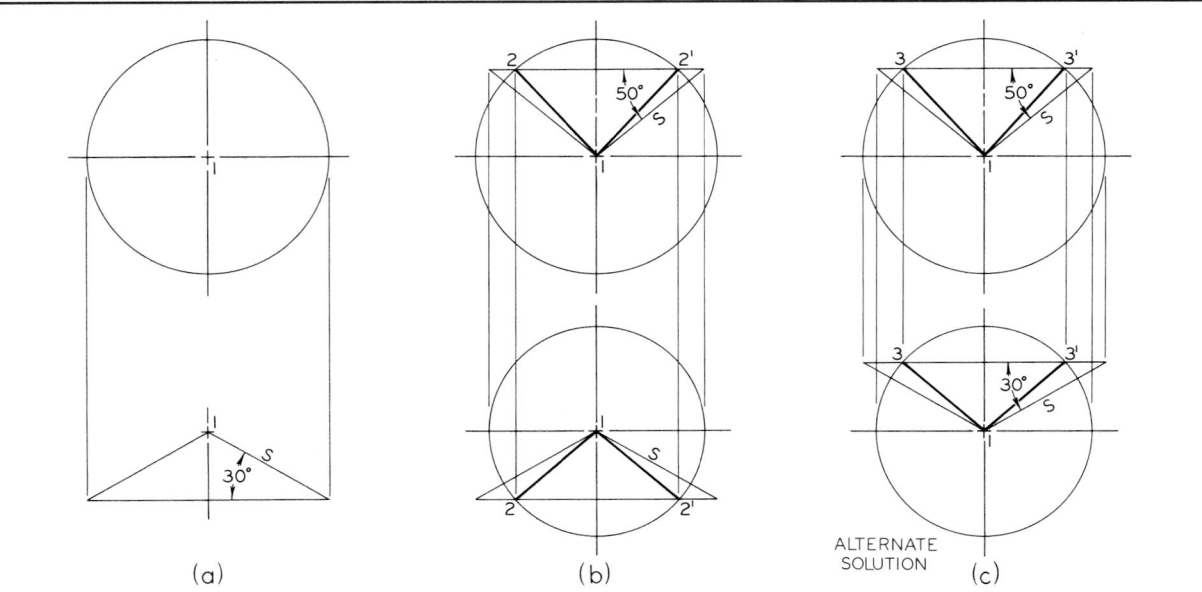

Fig. 22.13   Line at Specified Angles with Horizontal and Frontal Planes.

Additional reversals of the cones produce line-segment extensions of lines 1–2 and 1–2′ or 1–3 and 1–3′—not additional alternative solutions.

It is important to realize that there are limitations on the selection of the two angles. If their sum is greater than 90°, the cones do not intersect, and there is no solution.* If the sum equals 90°, the

*Assuming both specified angles are acute, or using supplements of obtuse angles.

cones are tangent and the element of tangency is the solution. (Two such single-element solutions are possible.) Only when the sum of the required angles is less than 90° do we have the four alternative possibilities shown in Fig. 22.13. For given planes that are not perpendicular, there are different but similar limitations dependent upon the dihedral angle, §10.11, between the two planes. In general, the sum of the required angles must be equal to or less than the dihedral angle between the given planes.

Line and Plane Tangency Problems

In Figs. 22.14–22.16 are problems involving planes tangent to cones, cylinders, and spheres, and applications of right-circular cones.

Use Layout A–1 or A4–1 (adjusted) and divide the working area into four equal areas for problems to be assigned by the instructor. Some problems require two problem areas or one-half sheet. Data for most problems are given by a coordinate system using metric dimensions. For example, in Fig. 22.14. Prob. 1, point O is located by the full-scale coordinates (60, 50, and 90 mm). The first coordinate locates the front view from the left edge of the problem area. The second coordinate locates the front view of the point from the bottom edge of the problem area. The third coordinate locates either the top view of the point from the bottom edge of the problem area or the side view of the point from the left edge of the problem area. Inspection of the given problem layout will determine which application to use.

Since many of the problems in this chapter are of a general nature, they can also be solved on most computer graphics systems. If a system is available, the instructor may choose to assign specific problems to be completed by this method.

Additional problems in convenient form for solution are presented in the worksheets at the back of this book. Refer to Drawings 22-1 and 22-2 and accompanying instructions.

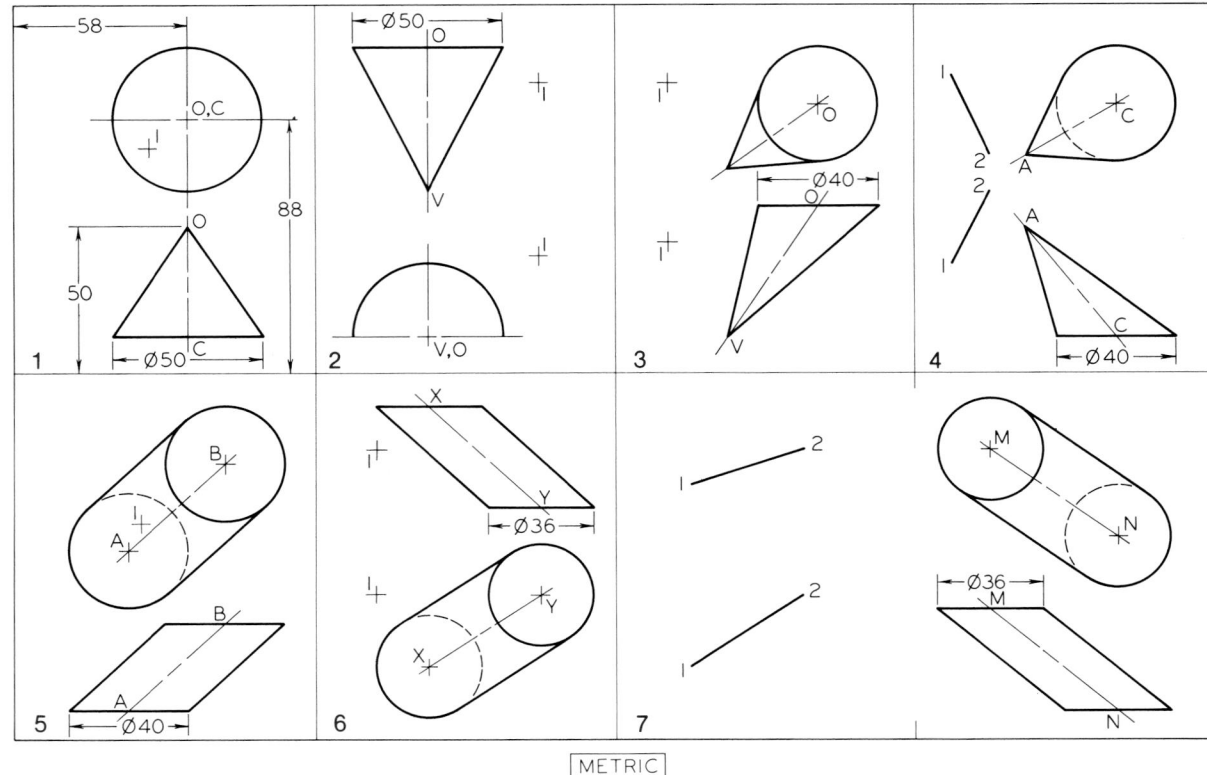

METRIC

Fig. 22.14 Lay out and solve problems as assigned. Use Layout A–1 or A4–1 (adjusted) divided into four equal areas.

1. Point 1(46, –, 79) is on the surface of cone O(58, 30, 88)–C(58, 12, 88). Pass a plane tangent to the cone and containing point 1.
2. Pass a plane through point 1(75, 40, 100) and tangent to cone V(38, 12, 63)–O(38, 12, 114).
3. Pass a plane through point 1(18, 46, 100) and tangent to cone V(38, 12, 71)–O(69, 61, 94).
4. Pass a plane tangent to cone A(38, 50, 75)–C(68, 12, 94) and parallel to line 1(12, 38, 104)–2(25, 63, 75).
5. Pass a plane tangent to cylinder A(38, 10, 66)–B(71, 40, 96) and containing point 1(43, –, 75) on the surface of the cylinder.
6. Pass a plane through point 1(20, 50, 100) and tangent to cylinder X(38, 25, 117)–Y(75, 50, 81).
7. Pass a plane tangent to cylinder M(127, 46, 100)–N(170, 10, 70) and parallel to line 1(25, 25, 88)–2(63, 50, 100).

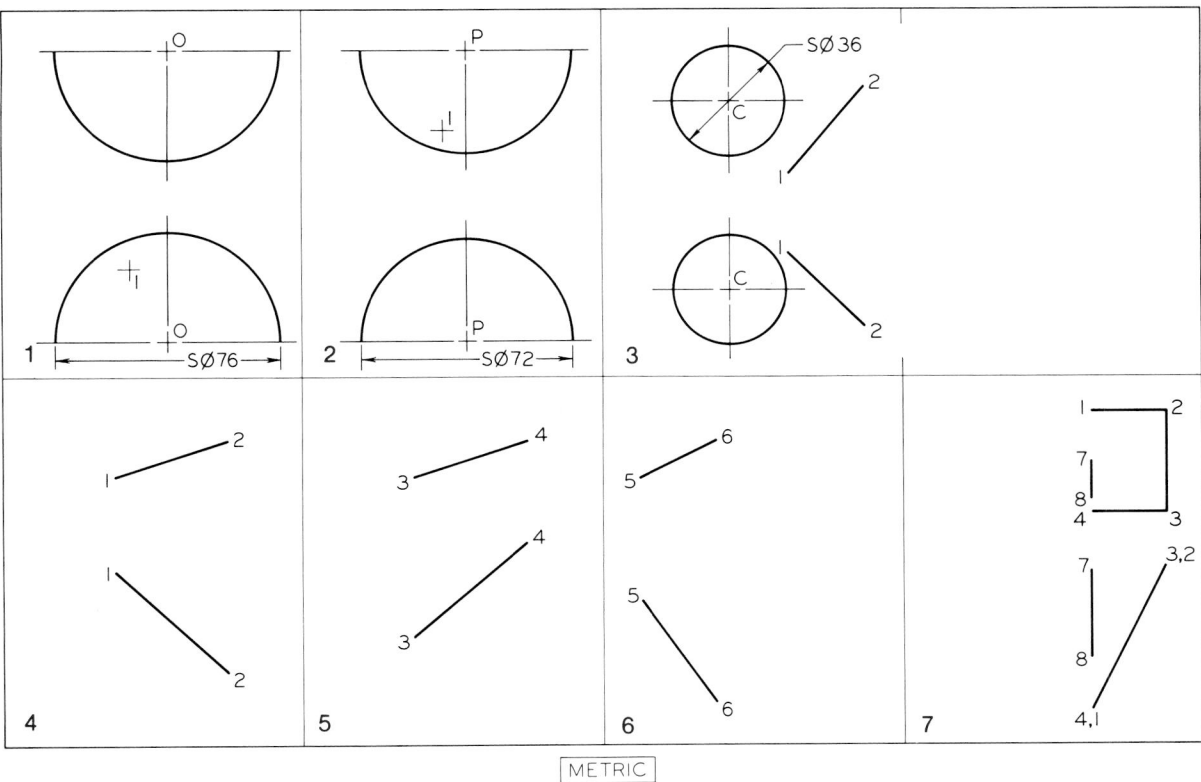

METRIC

Fig. 22.15 Lay out and solve problems as assigned. Use Layout A–1 or A4–1 (adjusted) divided into four equal areas.

1. Pass a plane tangent to sphere O(56, 12, 114) and containing point 1(43, 38, –) on the surface of the sphere.
2. Draw three lines tangent to sphere P(56, 12, 114) and containing point 1(48, –, 86) on the surface of the sphere.
3. Pass a plane tangent to sphere C(43, 30, 96) and containing line 1(63, 43, 70)–2(88, 18, 100). Show the point of tangency in all views.
4. Pass a plane through line 1(38, 61, 94)–2(75, 25, 107) and making an angle of 30° with a frontal plane.
5. Pass a plane through line 3(38, 38, 94)–4(75, 71, 107) and making an angle of 60° with horizontal.
6. Pass a plane through line 5(12, 50, 94)–6(38, 15, 107) and making an angle of 135° with a profile plane.
7. Pass a plane through line 7(63, 61, 99)–8(63, 30, 86) and making an angle of 60° with plane 1(63, 12, 117)–2(88, 63, 117)–3(88, 63, 81)–4(63, 12, 81).

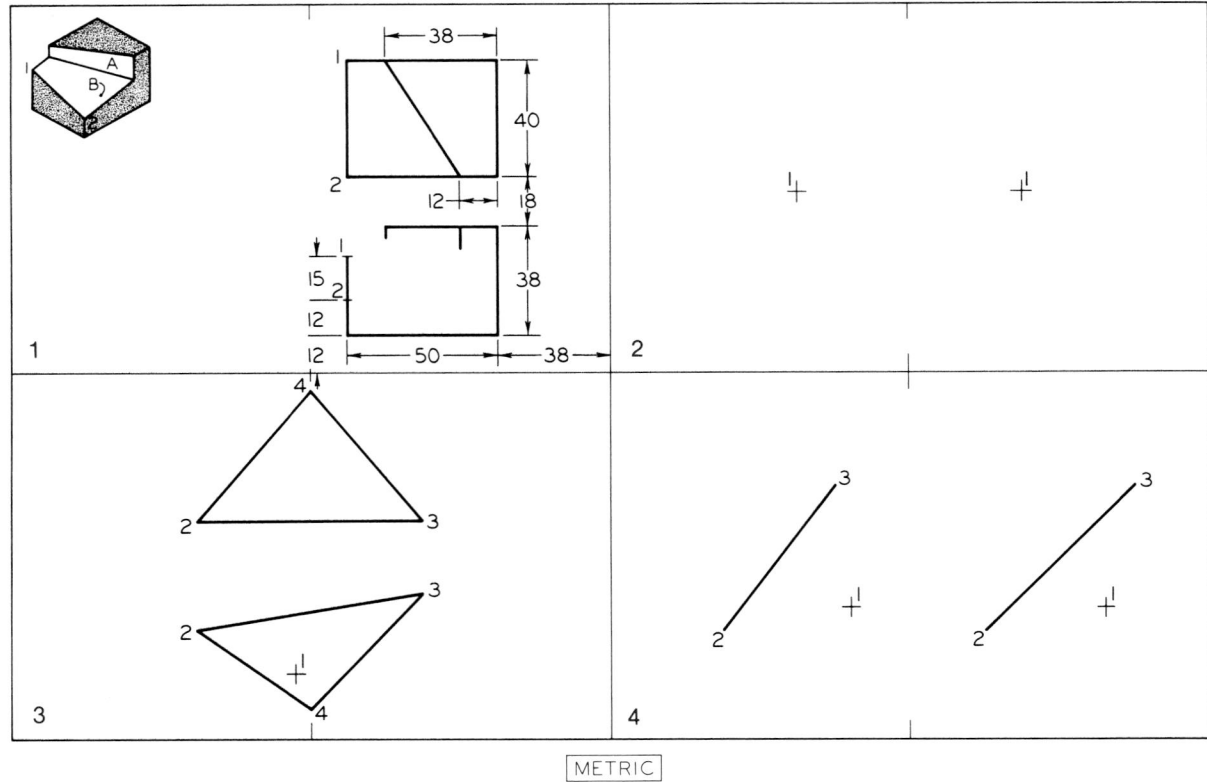

METRIC

Fig. 22.16 Lay out and solve problems as assigned. Use Layout A–1 or A4–1 (adjusted) divided into four equal areas.

1. Surfaces **A** and **B** form a dihedral angle of 130°. Complete the front view. Omit the pictorial in the layout.
2. Complete the views of a line 1(63, 63, 140)–2, which is 50 mm in length and forms angles of 45° with a profile plane and 35° with a frontal plane.
3. Point 1(96, 23, –) is in plane 2(63, 38, 75)–3(140, 50, 75)–4(100, 10, 122). Find in plane 2–3–4 a line 1–5 that forms an angle of 25° with a horizontal plane.
4. Find a line 1(81, 45, 167)–4 that is 40 mm in length, is perpendicular to line 2(38, 38, 127)–3(75, 88, 178), and makes an angle of 40° with a frontal plane.

CHAPTER

23

Graphs
and Diagrams

by E. J. Mysiak*

In previous chapters we have seen how graphical representation is used instead of words to describe the size, shape, material, and fabrication methods for the manufacture of actual objects. Graphical representation is also used extensively to present and analyze data and to solve technical problems. A pictorial or graphical presentation is much more impressive and easier to understand than a numerical tabulation or a verbal description. These graphical descriptions are synonymously termed *graphs, charts,* or *diagrams.*

The term *chart* has two meanings. It is associated with maps and also describes any of the forms of graphical presentation described in this chapter. Therefore, the term *chart* includes all graphs and diagrams. A *graph* is a special form of *chart* with data plotted on some type of grid. A *diagram* is a *chart* without the use of a grid.

Tabulated data in Fig. 23.1 (a), showing the average weekly earnings of United States manufacturing workers for the years 1974–1984, are presented as a line graph at (b) and a bar graph at (c). The greater effectiveness of graphical representation is evident.

*Engineering Manager, Phoenix Company of Chicago, Wood Dale, IL.

Year	Current Dollars	1977 Dollars
1974	176.80	217.20
1975	190.79	214.85
1976	209.32	222.92
1977	228.90	228.90
1978	249.27	231.66
1979	268.94	224.64
1980	288.62	212.64
1981	318.00	212.00
1982	330.65	207.96
1983	354.08	216.03
1984	372.91	221.05

(a)

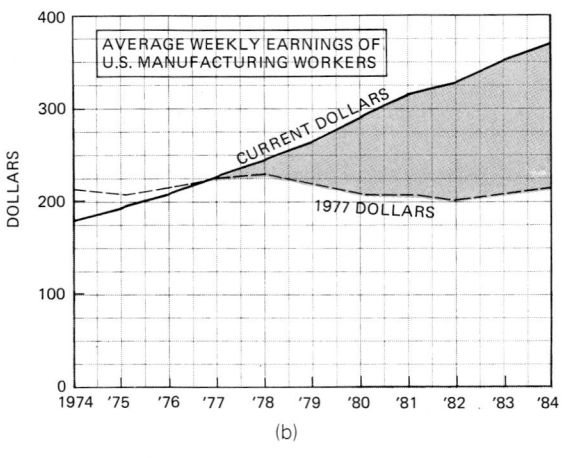

(b)

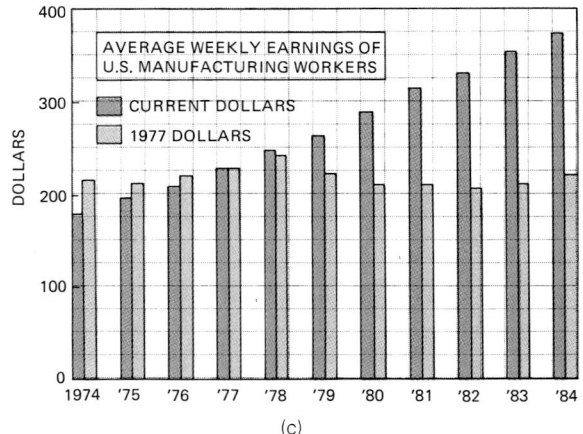

(c)

Fig. 23.1 Comparison of Tabulated and Graphical Presentations.

23.1 Uses of Graphical Representation

Graphs and diagrams can be classified into two broad categories depending upon whether their application or use is for technical purposes or for popular appeal.

Technically trained personnel communicate by means of graphs similar to Fig. 23.1 (b). When graphs are used to present data to lay personnel, a form similar to Fig. 23.1 (c) is preferred.

Scientific or technical personnel use graphs and diagrams to (a) present results of experimental investigations, (b) represent phenomena that follow natural laws, (c) represent equations for further computational purposes, and (d) derive equations to represent empirical test data. The forms of graphical representation most commonly used are

1. Rectangular coordinate line charts.
2. Semilogarithmic coordinate line charts.
3. Logarithmic coordinate line charts.
4. Trilinear coordinate line charts.
5. Polar coordinate line charts.
6. Nomographs or alignment charts.
7. Volume charts.
8. Rectangular coordinate distribution charts.
9. Flowcharts.

Often information and ideas must be presented in a way understandable to the layperson in order to have the information or idea accepted. For popular appeal, graphs and diagrams frequently used are

1. Rectangular coordinate line charts.
2. Bar or column charts.
3. Rectangular coordinate surface or area charts.
4. Pie charts.
5. Volume (map) charts.
6. Flowcharts.
7. Map distribution charts.

23.2 Rectangular Coordinate Line Graphs

The rectangular coordinate line graph is the type in which values of two related variables are plotted on coordinate paper, and the points, joined together successively, form a continuous line or "curve."

The following are some of the purposes for which a line graph can be used to advantage.

1. Comparison of a large number of plotted values in a compact space.
2. Comparison of the relative movements (trends) of more than one set of data on the same graph. There should not be more than two or three curves on the same graph, and there should be some definite relationship among them.
3. Interpolation of intermediate values.

4. Representation of movement or overall trend (relative change) of a series of values rather than the difference between values (absolute amounts).

Line graphs are *not* well suited for (1) presenting relatively few plotted values in a series, (2) emphasizing changes or difference in absolute amounts, or (3) showing extreme or irregular movement of data.

Rectangular line graphs may be classified as (1) *mathematical graphs*, (2) *time-series charts*, or (3) *engineering graphs*. Any of these may have one or more curves on the same graph. If the values plotted along the axes are pure numbers (positive and negative), showing the relationship of an equation, the plot is commonly called a mathematical graph, Fig. 23.2 (a). When one of the variables is any unit of time, the chart is known as a time-series chart, (b). This is one of the most common forms, since time is frequently one of the variables. Line, bar, or surface chart forms may be used for time-series charts, line charts being the most widely used in engineering practice. The plotting of values of any two related physical variables on a rectangular coordinate grid is referred to as an engineering chart, graph, or diagram, (c).

Line curves are generally presented for any of three types of relationships.

1. Observed relationships, usually plotted with observed data points connected by straight, irregular lines, Fig. 23.3 (a).

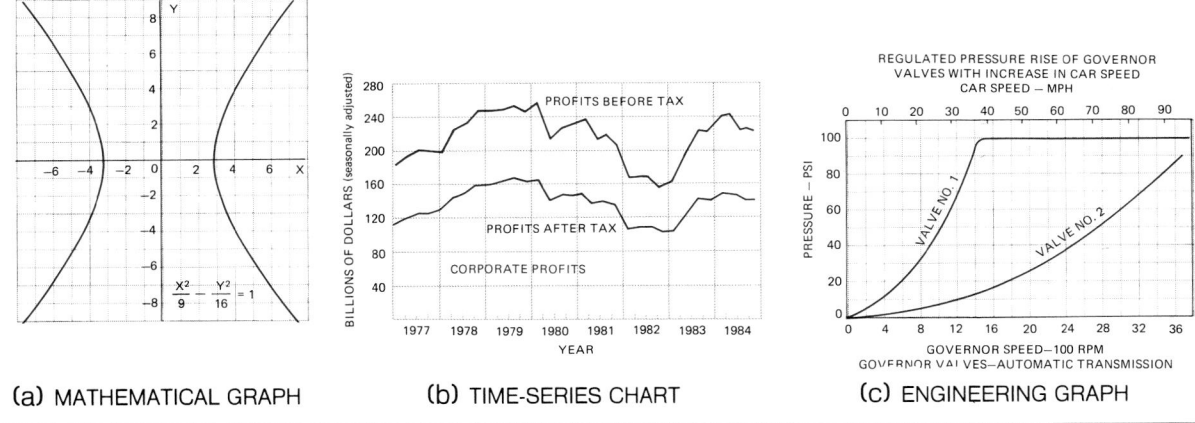

(a) MATHEMATICAL GRAPH   (b) TIME-SERIES CHART   (c) ENGINEERING GRAPH

Fig. 23.2   Rectangular Line Chart Classification.

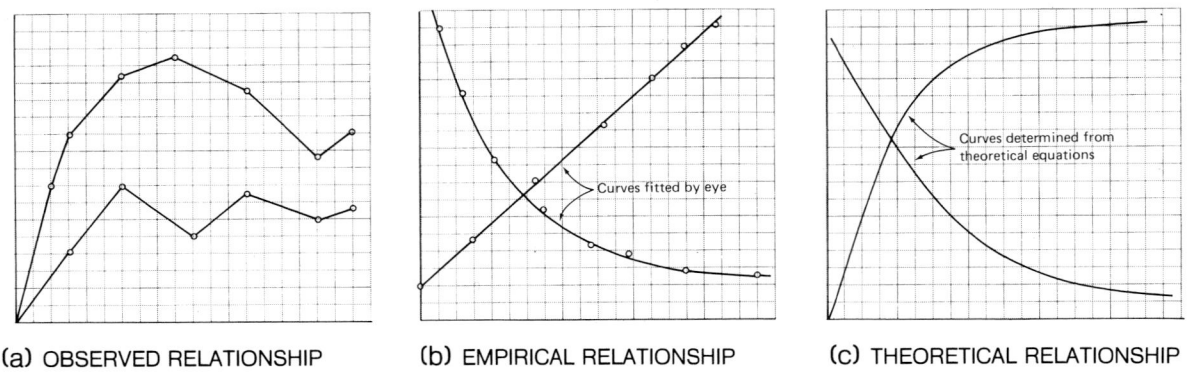

Fig. 23.3 Curve Fitting.

2. Empirical relationships, (b), normally reflecting the author's interpretation of his series of observations, represented as smooth curves or straight lines fitted to the data by eye or by formulas chosen empirically.

3. Theoretical relationships, (c), in which the curves are smooth and without point designations, though observed values may be plotted to compare them with a theoretical curve if desired. The curve thus drawn is based on theoretical considerations only, in which a theoretical function (equation) is used to compute values for the curve.

23.3 Design and Layout of Rectangular Coordinate Line Graphs

The steps in drawing a typical coordinate line graph are shown in Fig. 23.4.

I. a. Compute and/or assemble data in a convenient arrangement.

b. Select the type of graph and coordinate paper most suitable, §23.4.

c. Determine the size of the paper and locate the axes.

d. Determine the variable for each axis and choose the appropriate scales, §23.5. Letter the unit values along the axes, §23.5.

II. Plot the points representing the data and draw the curve or curves, §23.6.

III. Identify the curves by lettering names or symbols, §23.6. Letter the title, §23.7. Ink in the graph, if desired.

The completed graph, which includes the curves, captions, and designations, should have a balanced arrangement relative to the axes. Much of the foregoing procedure is also applicable to the other forms of charts, graphs, and diagrams discussed in this chapter.

23.4 Grids and Composition

To simplify the plotting of values along the perpendicular axes and to eliminate the use of a special scale to locate them, *coordinate paper*, or "graph paper," ruled with grids, is generally used and can

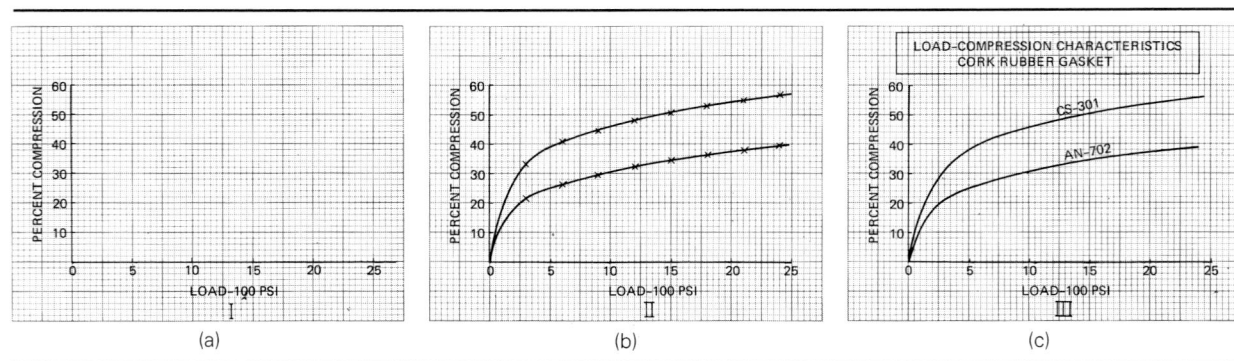

Fig. 23.4 Steps in Drawing a Graph.

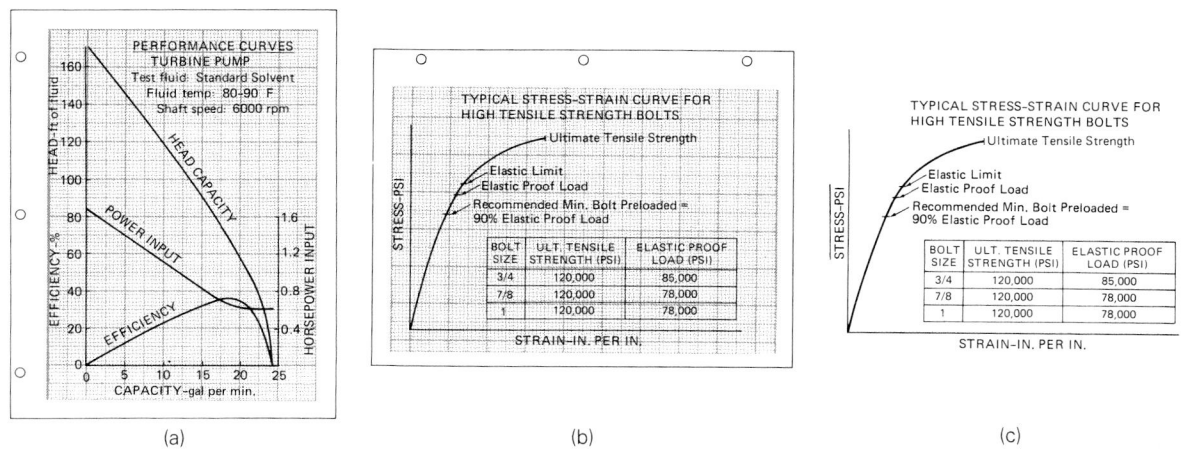

Fig. 23.5 Printed and Prepared Coordinate Paper.

be purchased already printed. Alternatively, the grids can be drawn on blank paper.

Printed coordinate papers are available in various sizes and spacings of grids, $8\frac{1}{2}'' \times 11''$ being the most common paper size. The spacing of grid lines may be $\frac{1}{10}''$, $\frac{1}{20}''$, or multiples of $\frac{1}{16}''$. A spacing of $\frac{1}{8}''$ to $\frac{1}{4}''$ is preferred. Closely spaced coordinate ruling is generally avoided for publications, charts reduced in size, and charts used for slides. Much of engineering graphical analysis, however, requires (1) close study, (2) interpolation, and (3) only one copy, with possibly a few prints that can be readily prepared with little effort. Therefore, engineering graphs are usually plotted on the closely spaced, printed coordinate paper. Printed papers can be obtained in several colors of lines and in various weights and grades. A thin, translucent paper may also be used when prints are required. A special nonreproducible-grid coordinate paper is available for use when reproductions without visible grids are desired.

Scale values and captions should be placed outside the grid axes, if possible. Since printed papers do not have sufficient margins to accommodate the axes and nomenclature, the axes should be placed far enough inside the grid area to permit sufficient space for axes and lettering, as shown in Fig. 23.5 (a) and (b). As much of the remaining grid space as possible should be used for the curve—that is, the scale should be such as to spread the curve out over the available space. A title block (and tabular data, if any) should be placed in an open space on the chart, as shown. If only one copy of the chart is

required, tabular data may be placed on the back of the graph or on a separate sheet.

Charts prepared for printed publications, conferences, or projection (slides) generally do not require accurate or detailed interpolation and should emphasize the major facts presented. For such graphs, coordinate grids drawn or traced on blank paper, cloth, or film have definite advantages when compared to printed paper. The charts in Fig. 23.5 (b) and (c) show the same information plotted on printed coordinate paper and plain paper, respectively. The specially prepared sheet should have as few grid rulings as necessary—or none, as at (c)—to allow a clear interpretation of the curve. For ease of reading, lettering is not placed upon grid lines. The title and other data can be lettered in open areas, completely free of grid lines.

The layout of specially prepared grids is restricted by the overall paper size required, or space limitations for slides and other considerations. Space is first provided for margins and for axes nomenclature; the remaining space is then divided into the number of grid spaces needed for the range of values to be plotted. Another important consideration of composition that affects the spacing of grids is the slope or trend of the curve, as discussed in §23.5.

Since independent variable values are generally placed along the horizontal axis, especially in time-series charts, vertical rulings can be made for each value plotted, if uniformly spaced, Fig. 23.6 (a). If there are many values to plot, intermediate values can be designated by *ticks* on the curves or along the axis, (b) and (c), with the grid rulings omitted.

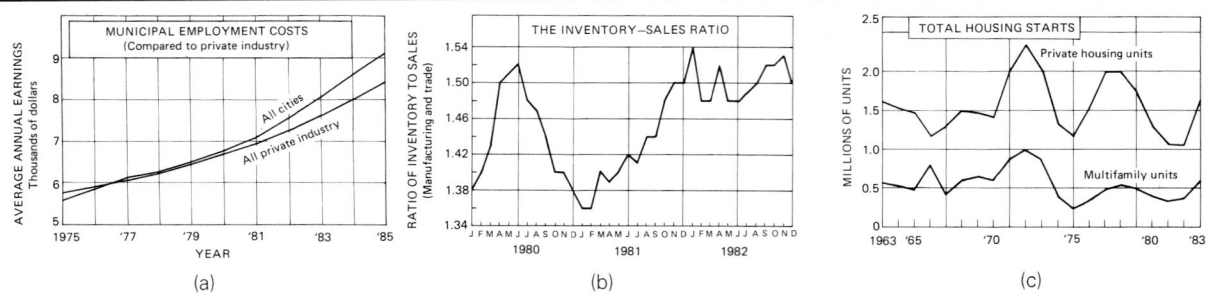

Fig. 23.6 Vertical Rulings—Specially Prepared Grids.

The horizontal lines are generally spaced according to the available space and the range of values.

The weight of the grid rulings should be thick enough to guide the eye in reading the values, but thin enough to provide contrast and emphasize the curve. The thickness of the lines generally should decrease as the number of rulings increases. As a general rule, as few rulings should be used as possible, but if a large number of rulings is necessary, major divisions should be drawn heavier than the subdivision rulings, for ease of reading.

23.5 Scales and Scale Designation

The choice of scale is the most important factor of composition and curve significance. Rectangular coordinate line graphs have values of the two related variables plotted with reference to two mutually perpendicular coordinate axes, meeting at a zero point or origin, Fig. 23.7 (a). The horizontal axis, normally designated as an *x*-axis, is called the *ab-*

scissa. The vertical axis is denoted a *y*-axis and is called the *ordinate*. It is common practice to place independent values along the abscissa and the dependent values along the ordinate. For example, if in an experiment at certain time intervals, related values are observed, recorded, or determined, the amount of these values is dependent upon the time intervals (independent or controlled) chosen. The values increase from the point of origin toward the right on the *x*-axis and upward on the *y*-axis.

Mathematical graphs, (b), quite often contain positive and negative values, which necessitates the division of the coordinate field into four quadrants, numbered counterclockwise as shown. Positive values increase toward the right on the *x*-axis and upward on the *y*-axis, from the origin. Negative values increase (negatively) to the left on the *x*-axis and downward on the *y*-axis.

Generally, a full range of values is desirable, beginning at zero and extending slightly beyond the largest value, to avoid crowding. The available co-

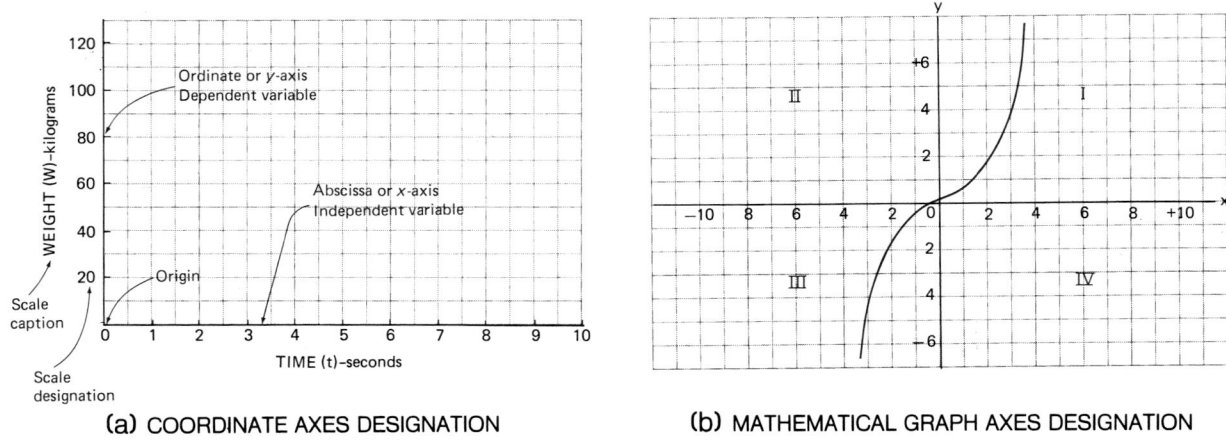

Fig. 23.7 Axes Designation.

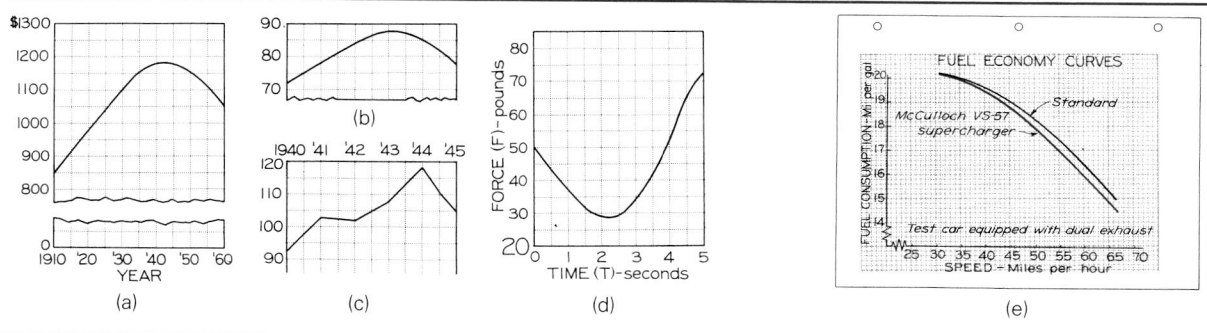

Fig. 23.8 Axes Scale "Breaks."

ordinate area should be used as completely as possible. However, certain circumstances require special consideration to avoid wasted space. For example, if the values to be plotted along one of the axes do not range near zero, a "break" in the grid may be shown, as in Fig. 23.8 (a). However, when relative amount of change is required, as it is in Fig. 23.5 (a), the axes or grid should not be broken, and the zero line should not be omitted. If the absolute amount is the important consideration, the zero line may be omitted, as in Fig. 23.8 (b), (c), and (d). Time designations of years naturally are fixed and have no relation to zero.

If a few given values to be plotted are widely separated in amount from the others, the total range may be very great, and when this is compressed to fit on the sheet, the resulting curve will tend to be "flat," as shown in Fig. 23.9 (a). It is best to arrange for such values to fall off the sheet and to indicate them as "freak" values. The curve may then be drawn much more satisfactorily, as shown at (b).

A convenient manner in which to show related

curves having the same units along the abscissa, but different ordinate units, is to place one or more sets of ordinate units along the left margin and another set of ordinate values along the right margin, as shown in Fig. 23.5 (a), using the same rulings. Multiple scales are also sometimes established along the abscissa, such as for time units of months covering multiple years, as in Fig. 23.6 (b). A more compact arrangement for the curve is shown in Fig. 23.9 (c), where the purpose is to compare the inventory/sales ratios for 1981 and 1982 on a monthly basis.

The choice of scales deserves careful consideration, since it has a controlling influence on the depicted rate of change of the dependent variable. The *slope* of the curve (trend) should be chosen to represent a true picture of the data or a correct impression of the trend.

The slope of a curve is affected by the spacing of the rulings and their designations. A slope or trend can be made to appear "steeper" by increasing the ordinate scale or decreasing the abscissa scale, Fig. 23.10 (a), and "flatter" by increasing the abscissa

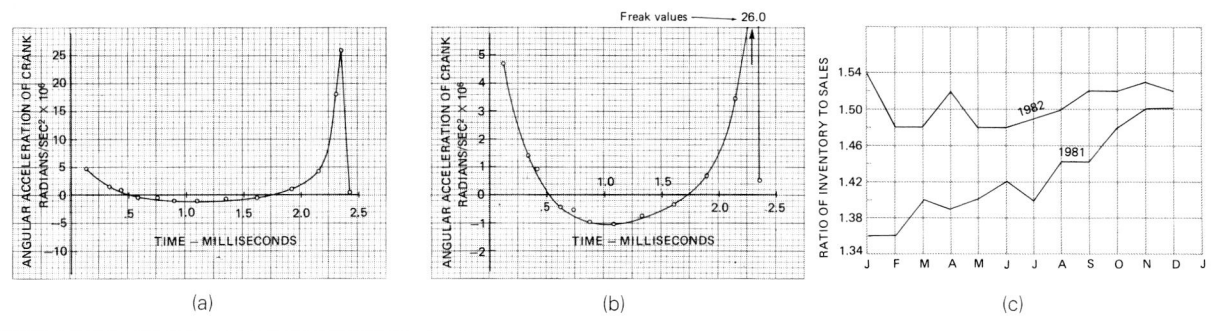

Fig. 23.9 "Freak" Values and Combined Curves.

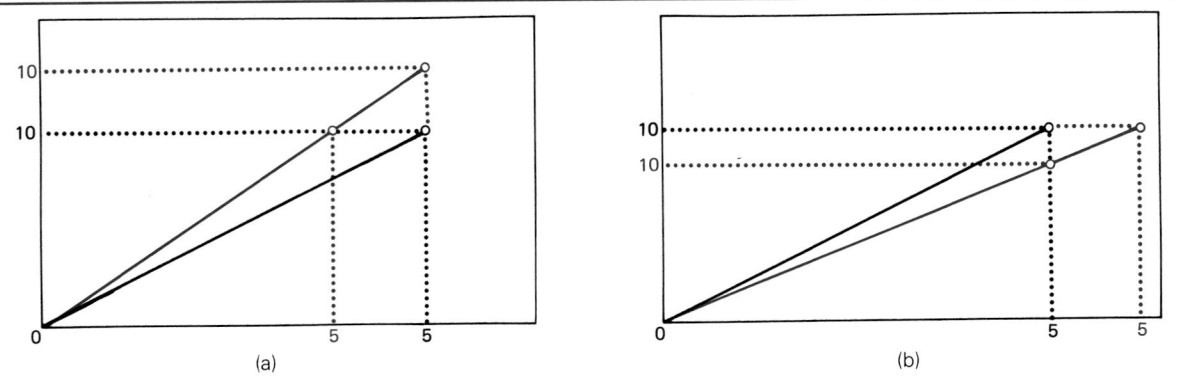

Fig. 23.10   Slopes.

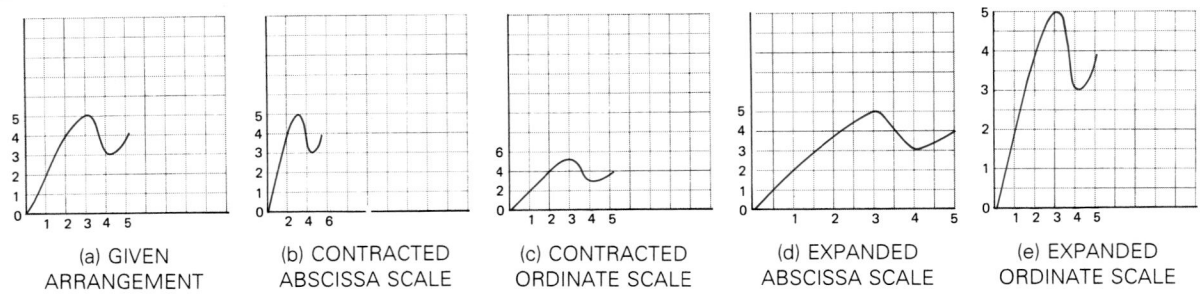

Fig. 23.11   Effects of Scale Designation.

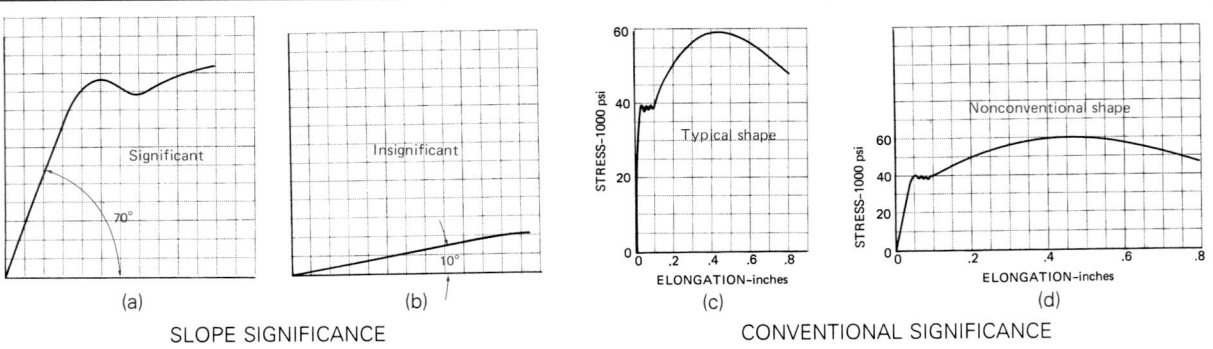

Fig. 23.12   Curve Shapes.

scale or decreasing the ordinate scale, (b). As shown in Fig. 23.11, a variety of slopes or shapes can be obtained by expanding or contracting the scales. A deciding factor is the impression desired to be conveyed graphically.

Normally, an angle greater than 40° with the horizontal gives an impression of a significant rise or increase of ordinate values, while an angle of 10° or less suggests an insignificant trend, Fig. 23.12 (a)

and (b). *The slope chosen should emphasize the significance of the data plotted.* Some relationships are customarily presented in a conventional shape, as shown at (c) and (d). In this case, an expanded abscissa scale, as shown at (d), should be avoided.

Scale designations should be placed outside the axes, where they can be shown clearly. Abscissa nomenclature is placed along the axis so that it can be read from the bottom of the graph. Ordinate values

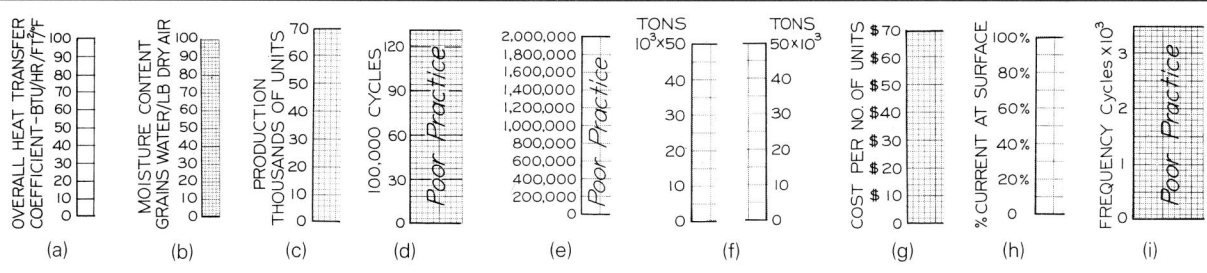

Fig. 23.13   Scale Designations.

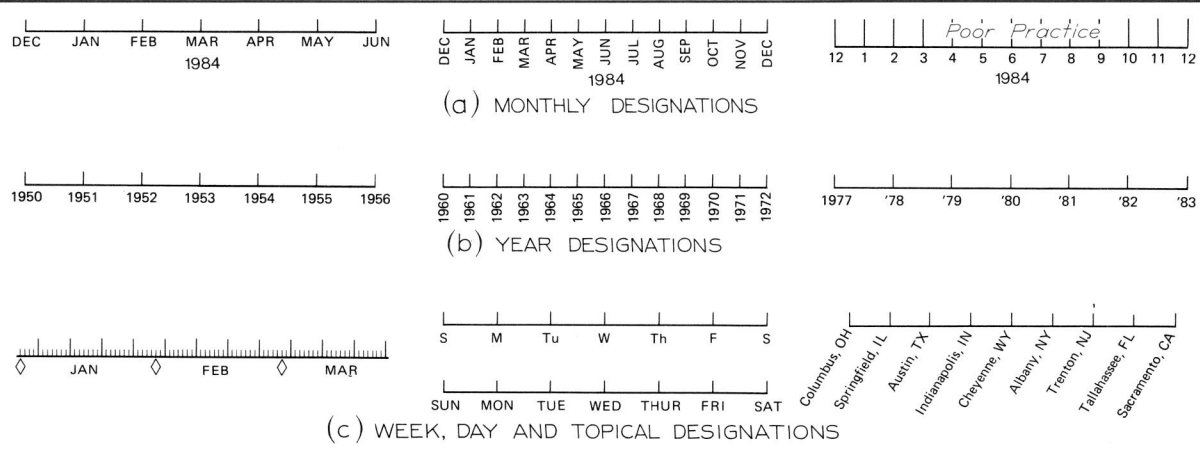

Fig. 23.14   Nonnumerical Designations.

are generally lettered so that they can also be read from the bottom; but ordinate captions, if lengthy, are lettered to be read from the right. The values can be shown on both the right and left sides of the graph, or along the top and bottom, if necessary for clearness, as when the graph is exceptionally wide or tall or when the rulings are closely spaced and hard to follow. When the major interest (e.g., maximum or minimum values) is situated at the right, the ordinate designations may be placed along the right, Fig. 23.33 (e). This arrangement also encourages reading the chart first and then the scale magnitudes.

When grid rulings are specially prepared on blank paper, every major division ruling should have its value designated, Fig. 23.13 (a). The labeled divisions should not be closer than .25″ and rarely more than 1″ apart. Intermediate values (rulings or ticks) should not be identified and should be spaced no closer than .05″. If the rulings are numerous and close together, as on printed graph paper, only the major values are noted, (b) and (c). The assigned

values should be consistent with the minor divisions. For example, major divisions designated as 0, 5, 10, . . ., should not have 2 or 4 minor intervals, since resulting values of 1.25, 2.5, 3.75, . . ., are undesirable. Similarly, odd-numbered major divisions of 3, 5, 7, . . ., or multiples of odd numbers with an even number of minor divisions, should be avoided, as (d) indicates. The numbers, if three digits or smaller, can be fully given. If the numbers are larger than three digits, (e), dropping the ciphers is recommended, if the omission is indicated in the scale caption, as at (c). Values are shortened to even hundreds, thousands, or millions, in preference to tens of thousands, for example. Graphs for technical use can have the values shortened by indicating the shortened number times some power of 10, as at (f). In special cases, such as when giving values in dollars or percent, the symbols may be given adjacent to the numbers, as at (g) and (h).

Designations other than numbers usually require additional space; therefore, standard abbreviations should be used when available, Fig. 23.14.

These abscissa values may be lettered vertically, as in the center at (a) and (b), or inclined, as at the right in (c), to fit the designations along the axes.

Scale captions (or titles) should be placed along the scales so that they can be read from the bottom for the abscissa, and from the right for the ordinate. Captions include the name of the variable, symbol (if any), units of measurement, and any explanation of digit omission in the values. If space permits, the designations are lettered completely, but if necessary, standard abbreviations may be used for the units of measurement. Notations such as shown in Fig. 23.13 (i) should be avoided, since it is not clear whether the values shown are to be multiplied by the power of 10 or already have been. Short captions may be placed above the values, Fig. 23.13 (f), especially when graphs are prepared for projection slides, since reading from the right is difficult.

23.6 Points, Curves, and Curve Designations

In mathematical and popular-appeal graphs, curves without designated points are commonly used, since the purpose is to emphasize the general significance of the curves. On graphs prepared from observed data, as in laboratory experiments, points are usually designated by various symbols, Fig. 23.15. If more than one curve is plotted on the same grid, a combination of these symbols may be used, one type for each curve, although labels are preferable if clear. The use of open-point symbols is recommended, except in cases of "scatter" diagrams, Fig. 23.39, where the filled-in points are more visible. In general, filled-in symbols should be used only when more than three curves are plotted on the same graph and a different identification is required for each curve.

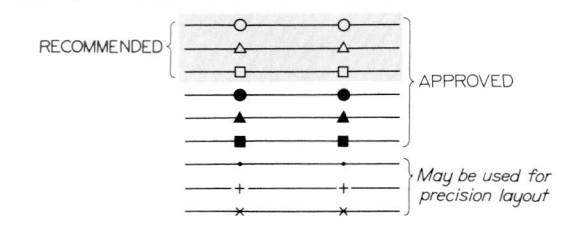

Fig. 23.15   Point Symbols.

The curve should not be drawn through the point symbols as they may be needed for reference later for additional information.

When several curves are to be plotted on the same grid, they can be distinguished by the use of various types of lines, Fig. 23.16 (a). However, solid lines are used for the curves wherever possible, while the dashed line is commonly used for *projections* (estimated values, such as future expectations), as shown at (b). The curve should be heavier in weight than the grid rulings, but a difference in weight can also be made between various curves to emphasize a preferred curve or a total value curve (sum of two or more curves), as shown at (c). A *key*, or *legend*, should be placed in an isolated portion of the grid, preferably enclosed by a border, to denote point symbols or line types that are used for the curves. If the grid lines are drawn on blank paper, a space should be left vacant for this information, Fig. 23.17. Keys may be placed off the grids below the title, if space permits. However, it is preferable to designate curves with labels, if possible, rather than letters, numbers, or keys, Fig. 23.2 (c). Colored lines are very effective for distinguishing the various curves on a grid, but they may not be suitable for multiple copies.

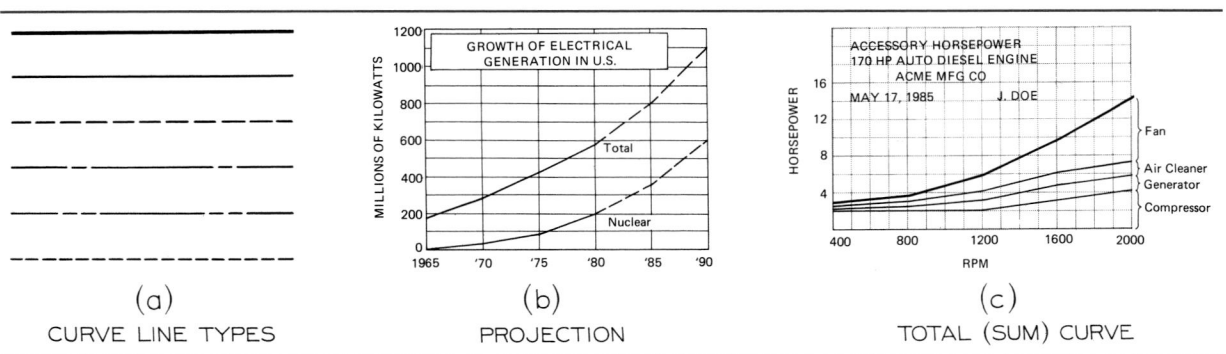

Fig. 23.16   Curve Lines.

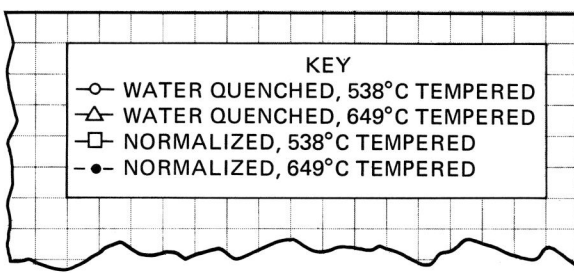

Fig. 23.17 Keys.

23.7 Titles

Titles for a graph may be placed on or off the grid surface. If placed on the grid, white space should be left for the title block, but if printed coordinate paper is used, a heavy border should enclose the title block. If further emphasis is desired, the title may be underlined. The contents of title blocks vary according to method of presentation. Typical title blocks include title, subtitle, institution or company, date of preparation, and name of the author, Fig. 23.16 (c). Some relationships may be given an appropriate name. For example, a number of curves showing the performance of an engine are commonly entitled "Performance Characteristics." If two variables plotted do not have a suitable title, "Dependent variable (name) vs. independent variable (name)" will suffice. For example, GOVERNOR PRESSURE vs SPEED.

Notes, when required, may be placed under the title for general information, Fig. 23.18 (a); labeled adjacent to the curve, (b), or along the curve, Fig. 23.20 (a); or referred to by means of reference symbols, Fig. 23.18 (c) and (d).

Any chart can be made more effective, whether it is drawn on blank paper or upon printed paper, if it is inked. For reproduction purposes, as for slides or for publications, inking is necessary.

23.8 Semilogarithmic Coordinate Line Charts

A semilog chart, also known as a *rate-of-change* or *ratio chart*, is a type in which two variables are plotted on semilogarithmic coordinate paper to form a continuous straight line or curve. Semilog paper contains uniformly spaced vertical rulings and logarithmically spaced horizontal rulings.

Semilog charts have the same advantages as rectangular coordinate line charts (arithmetic charts), §23.2. When rectangular coordinate line charts give a false impression of the trend of a curve, the semilog charts would be more effective in revealing whether the rate of change is increasing, decreasing, or constant. Semilog charts are also useful in the derivation of empirical equations.

Semilog charts, like rectangular coordinate line graphs, are not recommended for presenting only a few plotted values in a series, for emphasizing change in absolute amounts, or for showing extreme or irregular movement or trend of data.

In Fig. 23.19 (a) and (b), data are plotted on rectangular coordinate grids (arithmetic) and on semilogarithmic coordinate grids, respectively. The same data, which produce curves on the arithmetic graph, produce straight lines on the semilog grid. The straight lines permit an easier analysis of the trend or movements of the variables. If the logarithms of the ordinate values are plotted on a rectangular coordinate grid, instead of the actual values, straight lines will result on the arithmetic graph, as shown at (c). The straight lines produced on semilog grid provide a simple means of deriving empirical equations. Straight lines are not necessarily obtained on a semilog grid, but if they do occur, it means that the rate of change is constant, Fig. 23.20 (a). Irregular curves can be compared to constant-rate scales individually or between a series of curves, as shown at (b).

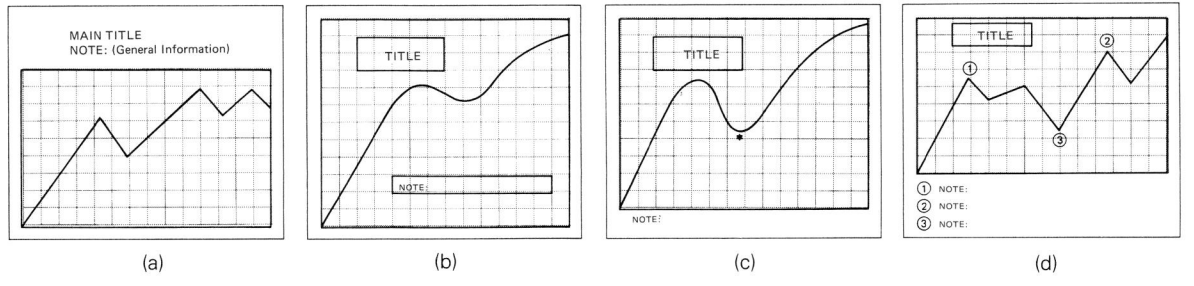

Fig. 23.18 Notes.

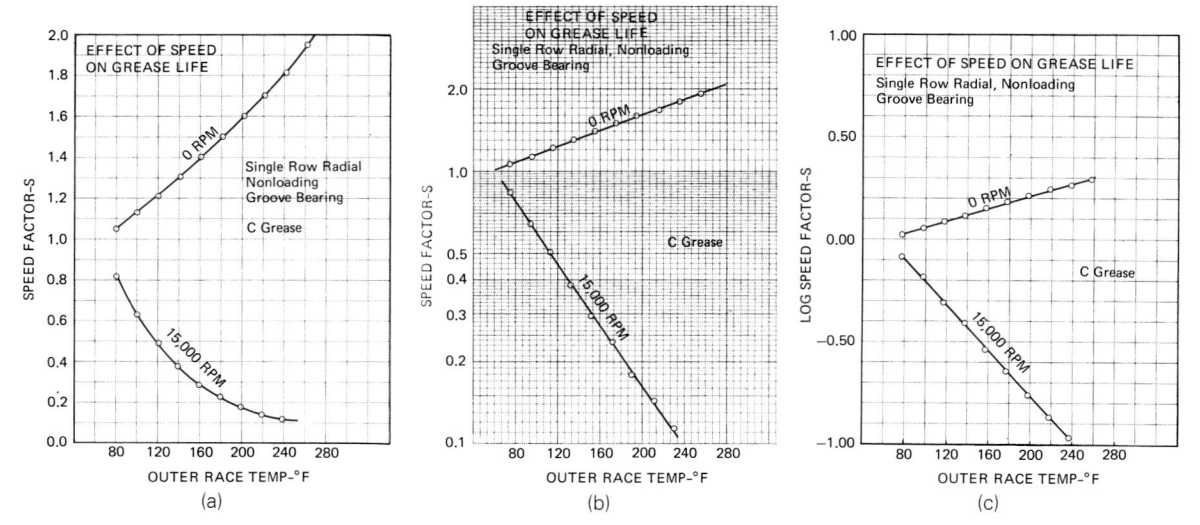

Fig. 23.19   Arithmetic and Semilogarithmic Plottings.

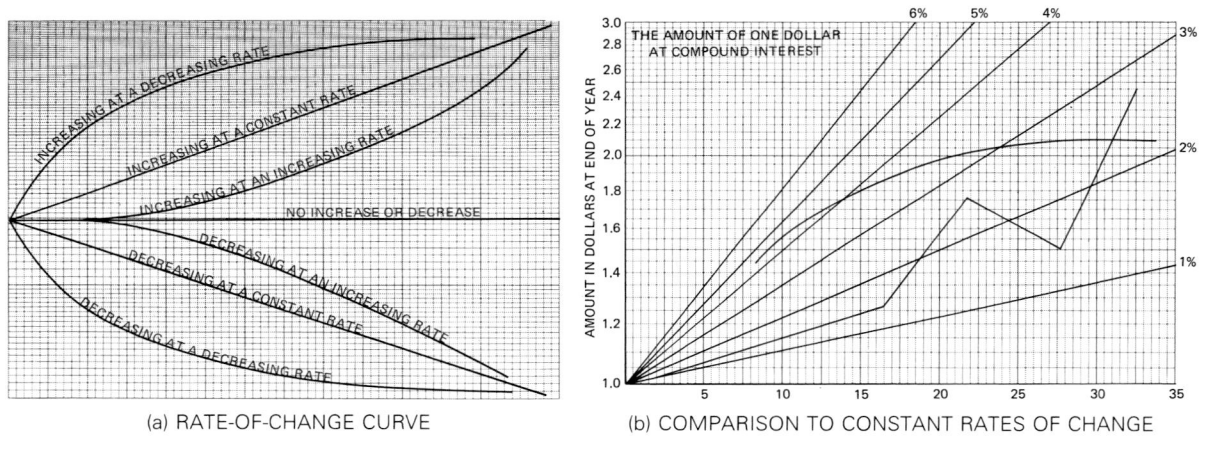

Fig. 23.20   Rates of Change.

23.9 Logarithmic Coordinate Line Charts

Logarithmic charts have two variables plotted on a logarithmic coordinate grid to form a continuous line or a "curve." Printed logarithmic paper contains logarithmically spaced horizontal and vertical rulings. As in the case of semilog charts, paper containing as many as five cycles on an axis can be purchased.

Log charts are applicable for the comparison of a large number of plotted values in a compact space and for the comparison of the relative trends of sev-

eral curves on the same chart. This form of graph is not the best form for presentation of relatively few plotted values in a series or for emphasizing change in absolute amounts. The designation of log cycles, however, permits the plotting of very extensive ranges of values.

Logarithmic charts are primarily used to determine empirical equations by fitting a single straight line to a series of plotted points. They are also used to obtain straight-line relationships when the data are suitable, as in Fig. 23.21.

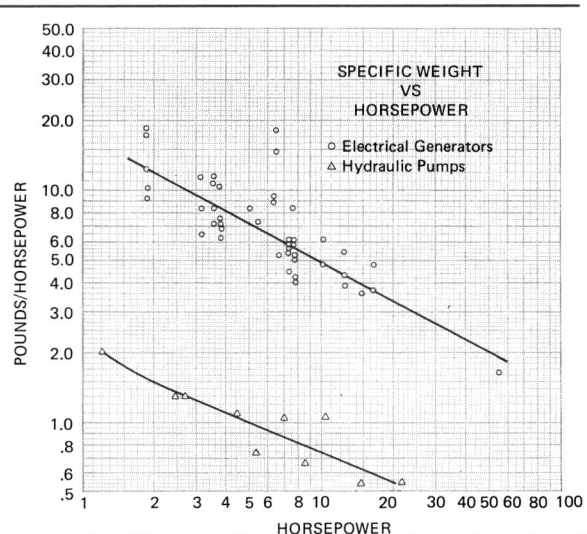

Fig. 23.21 Logarithmic Chart.

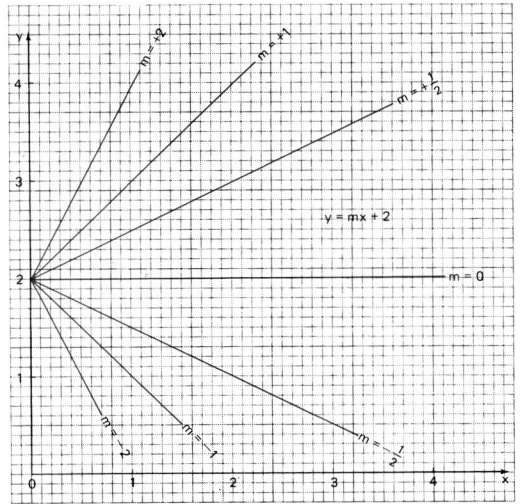

Fig. 23.22 Equation of Straight Lines on Rectangular Grid.

23.10 Empirical Equations

Empirical equations by definition are equations derived from experimental data or experience, as distinguished from equations derived from logical reasoning or hypothesis (rational equations). At times, tabulated data or the analysis of a graph is inadequate, and an equation for the data is required. A graphical plot shows the trend of the data and the value of one variable relative to the corresponding second variable. The derivation of empirical equations is a more comprehensive method of analysis and can be used to calculate additional data not obtained in experimentation.

The derivations of equations are varied in methods. A basic procedure is to plot the data on rectangular, semilogarithmic, or logarithmic coordinate graph paper in an attempt to obtain a straight line. If the plot results in a reasonably straight line on one of these papers, an approximate (empirical) equation can be derived by geometric and algebraic methods. The reader is referred to texts in the school or local library for methods of derivation and forms of empirical equations.

23.11 Empirical Equations—Solution by Rectangular Coordinates

The equation for a straight line on a rectangular coordinate grid is $y = mx + b$. As shown in Fig. 23.22, m represents the slope of the line (the tangent of the angle between the line and the x-axis) and b is the intercept on the y-axis (when $x = 0$). A negative slope is inclined downward to the right. A positive slope has an upward trend to the right. The intercept may be positive or negative.

23.12 Empirical Equations—Semilog Coordinates: $y = b(10^{mx})$ or $y = be^{mx}$

Data plotted on rectangular coordinate paper, which do not result in a straight line, may rectify to an approximate straight-line graph on a semilogarithmic coordinate grid, if the rectangular coordinate curve resembles an exponential curve, as shown in Fig. 23.23 (a) or (b). The base of the exponent may be either e ($e = 2.718$) or 10. An exponential curve intersects one of the axes at a steep angle and is asymptotic to the other axis. The same data used to plot some of the curves in Fig. 23.23 (b), when plotted on semilog coordinate paper, rectify to straight lines, as shown in Fig. 23.24.

Since semilog paper has logarithmic divisions along one of the axes (normally designated the y-axis), the equation for a straight line on this type of graph paper is

$$\log y = mx + \log b$$

or

$$\ln y = mx + \ln b$$

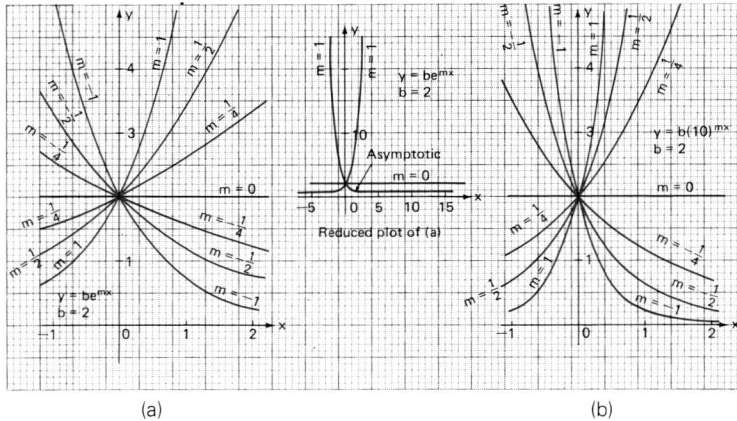

(a)   (b)

Fig. 23.23   Exponential Curves.

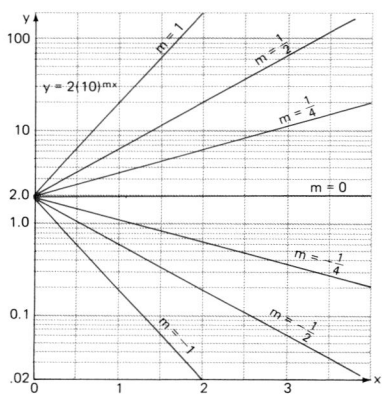

Fig. 23.24   Semilog Plot.

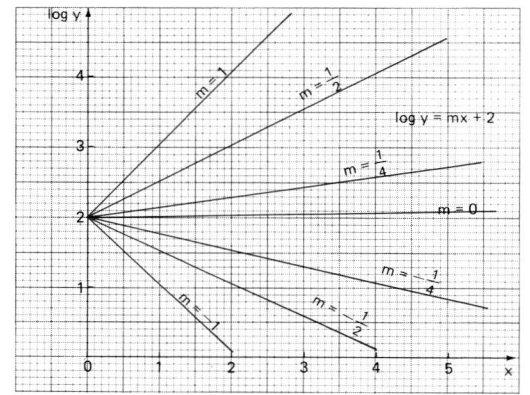

Fig. 23.25   Rectangular Grid Solution.

therefore,

$$y = b(10^{mx}) \quad \text{or} \quad y = be^{mx}$$

The derivation of the empirical equation requires the solution for the values b (y-axis intercept, when $x = 0$) and m (the slope of the straight line to the x-axis).

An alternate method is to plot log y values on rectangular coordinate graph paper, if semilog coordinate paper is not readily available, Fig. 23.25.

When a rectangular coordinate plot results in an x-axis intercept and a curve appearing asymptotic to the y-axis, Fig. 23.26, the semilog plotting may rectify to a straight line if the logarithmic scale is placed on the x-axis. The equation becomes

$$x = a(10^{my}) \quad \text{or} \quad x = ae^{my}$$

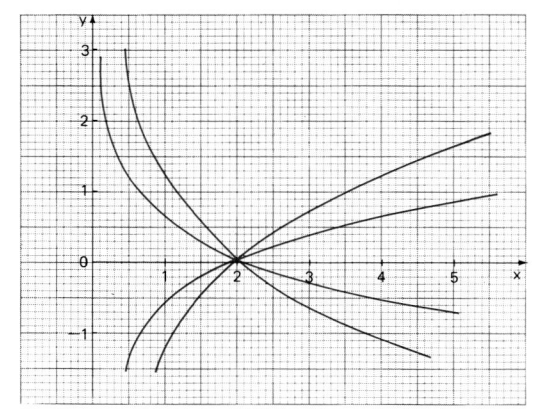

Fig. 23.26   Reverse Plot.

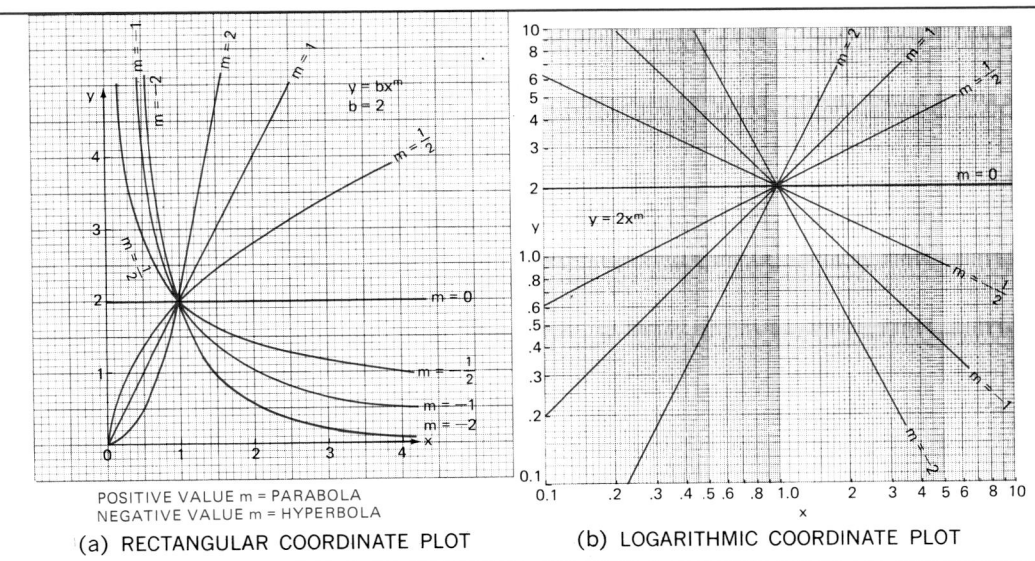

Fig. 23.27   Power Curves.

23.13 Empirical Equations—Logarithmic Coordinates: $y = bx^m$

Curves that plot as a parabola through the origin or a hyperbola asymptotic to the *x*- and *y*-axes are known as power curves, Fig. 23.27 (a), and can be rectified to a straight line by plotting the same data on logarithmic coordinate paper, as shown at (b). The equation for a straight line on logarithmic paper is

$$\log y = m \log x + \log b$$

or

$$y = bx^m$$

The derivation of an empirical equation requires the determination of the values for the slope *m* of the line and the intercept value *b* (*y* intercept when $x = 1$). The intercept is at the axis value of 1.0 since $\log 1.0 = 0$.

23.14 Trilinear Coordinate Line Charts
(Fig. 23.28)
Trilinear charts have three related variables plotted on a coordinate paper in the form of an equilateral triangle. The points joined together successively form a continuous straight line or "curve."

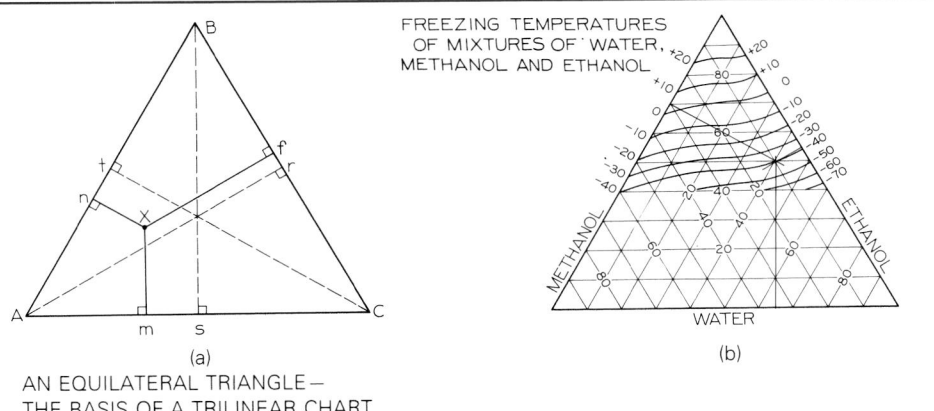

(a)
AN EQUILATERAL TRIANGLE—
THE BASIS OF A TRILINEAR CHART

(b)

Fig. 23.28   Trilinear Coordinate Line Charts.

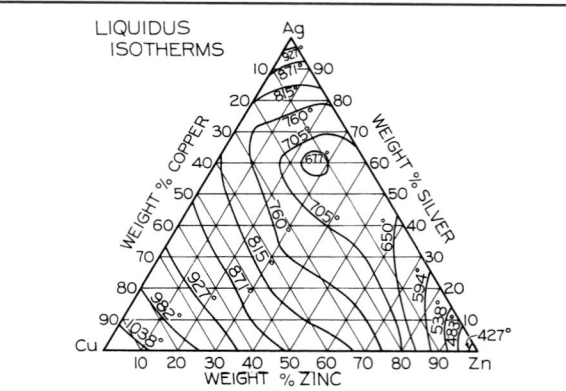

Fig 23.29   Metallurgical Trilinear Chart.

Trilinear charts are particularly suited for the following uses.

1. Comparing three related variables relative to their total composition (100 percent).

2. Analyzing the composition structure by a combination of curves—for example, metallic microstructure of trinary alloys, Fig. 23.39.

3. Emphasizing change in amount or differences between values.

The trilinear chart is *not* recommended for (1) emphasizing movement or trend of data or (2) comparing three related but dissimilar physical quantities— for example, force, acceleration, and time.

Trilinear charts are widely applied in the metallurgical and chemical fields because of the frequency of three variables in metallurgical and chemical composition. The basis of application is the geometric principle that the sum of the perpendiculars to the three sides from any point within an equilateral triangle is equal to the altitude of the triangle.

In an equilateral triangle ABC, Fig. 23.28 (a), the sum of the distances X–f, X–m, and X–n from the point X within the triangle is equal to the altitude A–r, B–s, or C–t of the triangle. For example, if the distances X–f, X–m, and X–n are, respectively, 50, 30, and 20 units, the altitude of the triangle is 100 units, and the point X will represent a quantity composed of 50, 30, and 20 parts of the three variables. At (b) is shown a chart for various freezing temperatures, with the mixture proportions by volume of water, methanol, and ethanol required. For example, a freezing temperature of $-40°F$ can be established by mixing 50 parts of water with 10 parts of ethanol and 40 parts of methanol.

23.15 Polar Coordinate Line Charts

Polar charts have two variables, one a *linear* magnitude and the other an *angular* quantity, plotted on a polar coordinate grid with respect to a pole (origin) to form a continuous line or "curve."

Polar charts are particularly applicable to

1. Comparing two related variables, one being a linear magnitude (called a *radius vector*) and the second an angular value

2. Indicating movement or trend or location with respect to a pole point

Polar charts are *not* suited for (1) emphasizing changes in amounts or differences between values or (2) interpolating intermediate values.

As shown in Fig. 23.30 (a), the zero degree line is the horizontal right axis. To locate a point P, it is necessary to know the radius vector r, and an angle

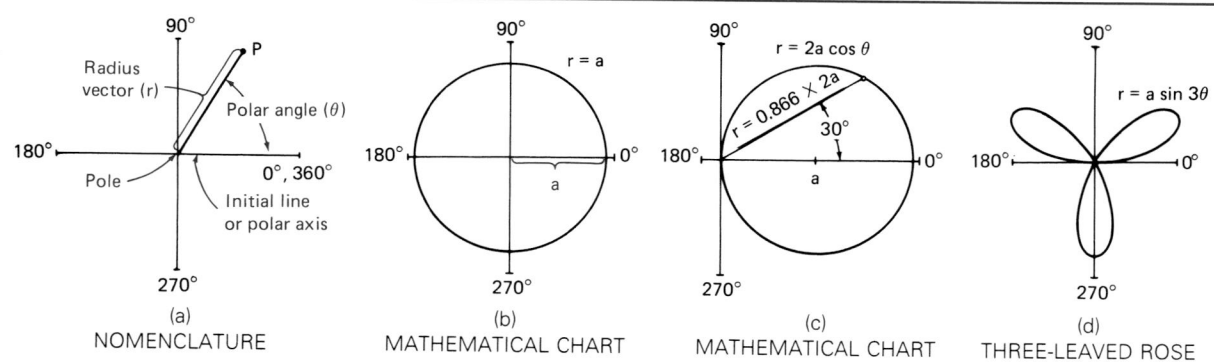

Fig. 23.30   Polar Coordinate Charts.

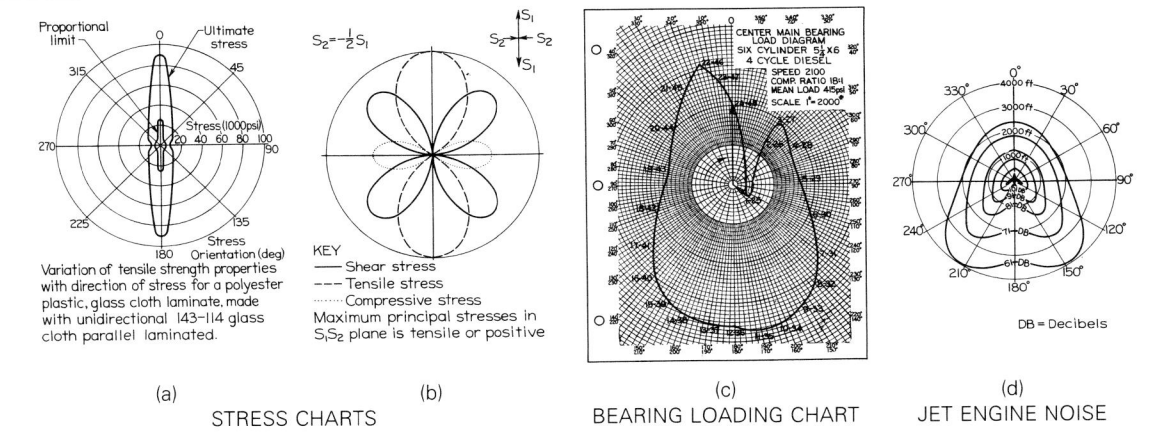

Fig. 23.31 Polar Coordinate Charts. *(a) and (b) adapted from Charts by Robert L. Stedfield and F. W. Kinsman, respectively, with permission of* Machine Design. *(c) adapted from R. R. Slaymaker,* Bearing Lubrication Analysis, *copyright 1955 by John Wiley and Sons, with permission of the publisher and Clevite Corporation. (d) adapted from chart by G. S. Schairer, with permission of author and Society of Automotive Engineers.*

θ (e.g., 5, 70°). The point P could also be denoted as (5, 430°), (5, −290°), (−5, 250°), and (−5, −110°), for example. If we plot the equation r = a (no angular designation), we will obtain a circle with the center at the pole, as shown at (b). The value a is a constant value, which determines the relative size of the radius vector and the curve. The equation r = 2a cos θ produces a circle going through the pole point, with its center on the polar axis, (c). The plot of r = a sin 3θ produces a "three-leaved rose," as shown at (d). Polar charts also have many practical applications concerned with the magnitude of some values and their location with respect to a pole point. For example, Fig. 23.31 (a) and (b) illustrate stress charts from experimentation and for stress visualization, respectively. At (c) is shown a polar chart of a bearing load diagram, and the graph at (d) indicates the noise distribution from a jet engine.

23.16 Nomographs or Alignment Charts
Nomographs or alignment charts consist of straight or curved scales, arranged in various configurations so that a straight line drawn across the scales intersects them at values satisfying the equation represented.

Alignment charts can be used for analysis, but the predominant application is for computation.

Some of the more common forms of nomographs

are shown in Fig. 23.32. Basically, a nomograph is used to solve a three-variable equation. A straight line (*isopleth*) joining known or given values of two of the variables intersects the scale of the third variable at a value that satisfies the equation represented, as at (a), (c), (f), (g), and (h). For this reason they are also called *alignment charts*. All alignment charts are nomographs, but not all nomographs are alignment charts; a rectangular coordinate graph can be classified as a nomograph. Two or more such charts can sometimes be combined to solve an equation containing more than three variables as at (b), (d), and (e). The forms shown have fixed scales and a movable alignment line. However, movable-scale nomographs can be designed with a fixed direction alignment line, the slide rule being an example of this form.

Although alignment charts require time to construct, they have considerable popular appeal for the following reasons.

1. They save time when it is necessary to make repeated calculations of certain numerical relationships (equations).

2. They enable one unskilled or lacking a background in mathematics to handle analytical solutions.

3. When constructed properly, they are limited to the scale values for which the equation is valid.

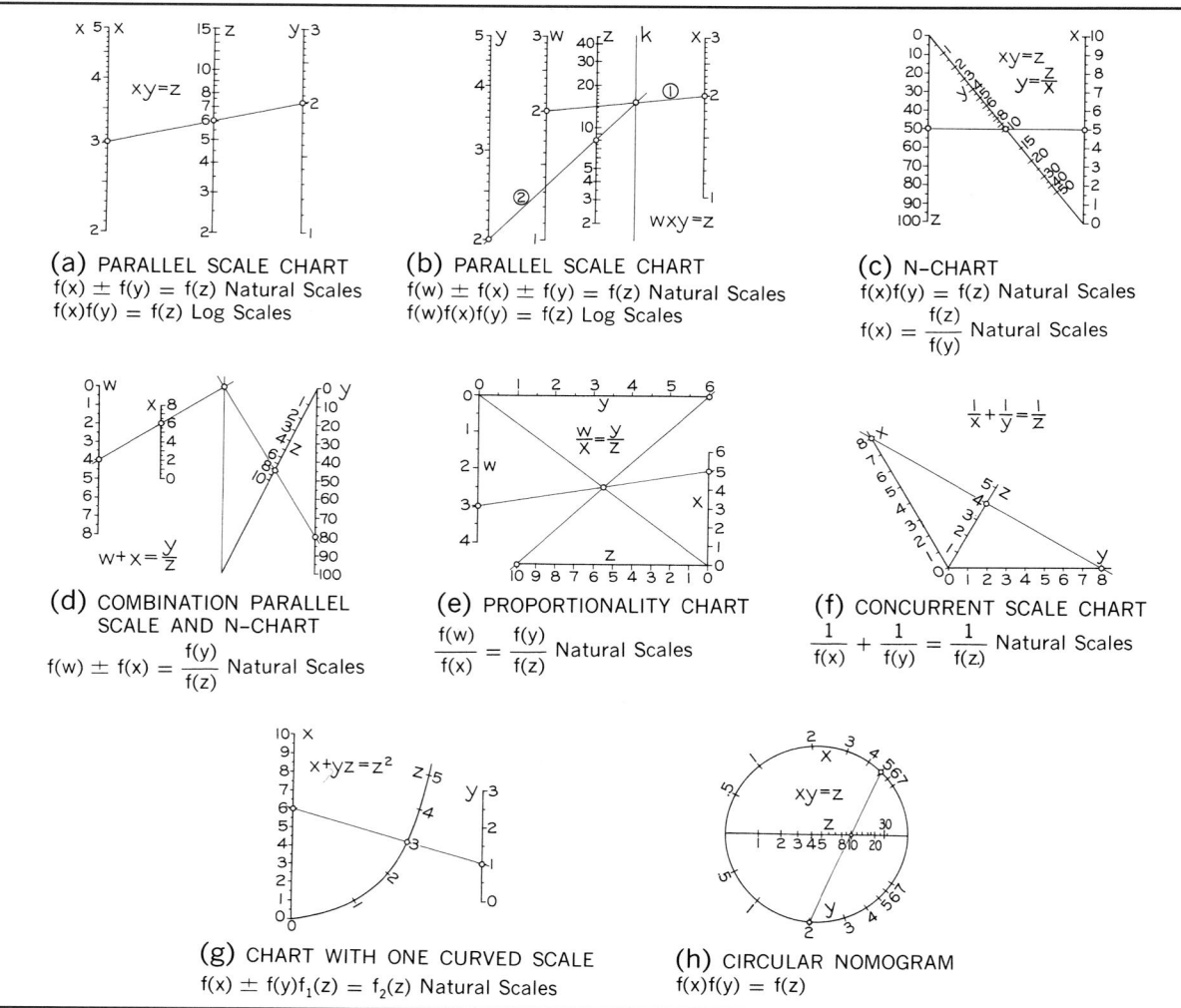

(a) PARALLEL SCALE CHART
$f(x) \pm f(y) = f(z)$ Natural Scales
$f(x)f(y) = f(z)$ Log Scales

(b) PARALLEL SCALE CHART
$f(w) \pm f(x) \pm f(y) = f(z)$ Natural Scales
$f(w)f(x)f(y) = f(z)$ Log Scales

(c) N–CHART
$f(x)f(y) = f(z)$ Natural Scales
$f(x) = \dfrac{f(z)}{f(y)}$ Natural Scales

(d) COMBINATION PARALLEL SCALE AND N–CHART
$f(w) \pm f(x) = \dfrac{f(y)}{f(z)}$ Natural Scales

(e) PROPORTIONALITY CHART
$\dfrac{f(w)}{f(x)} = \dfrac{f(y)}{f(z)}$ Natural Scales

(f) CONCURRENT SCALE CHART
$\dfrac{1}{f(x)} + \dfrac{1}{f(y)} = \dfrac{1}{f(z)}$ Natural Scales

(g) CHART WITH ONE CURVED SCALE
$f(x) \pm f(y)f_1(z) = f_2(z)$ Natural Scales

(h) CIRCULAR NOMOGRAM
$f(x)f(y) = f(z)$

Fig. 23.32   Common Forms of Nomographs or Alignment Charts.

This prevents the use of the equation with values that are not applicable.

23.17 Bar or Column Charts

Bar charts are graphic representations of numerical values by lengths of bars, beginning at a base line, indicating the relationship between two or more related variables.

Bar charts are particularly suited for the following purposes.

1. Presentation for the nontechnical reader.

2. A simple comparison of two values along two axes.

3. Illustration of relatively few plotted values.

4. Representation of data for a total period of time in comparison to point data.

Bar or column charts are *not* recommended for (1) comparing several series of data or (2) plotting a comparatively large number of values.

The bar chart is effective for nontechnical use because it is most easily read and understood. Therefore, it is used extensively by newspapers, magazines, and similar publications. The bars may be placed horizontally or vertically; when they are placed vertically, the presentation is sometimes called a column chart.

Bar charts are plotted with reference to two mutually perpendicular coordinate axes, similar to those in rectangular coordinate line charts. The graph may be a simple bar chart with two related

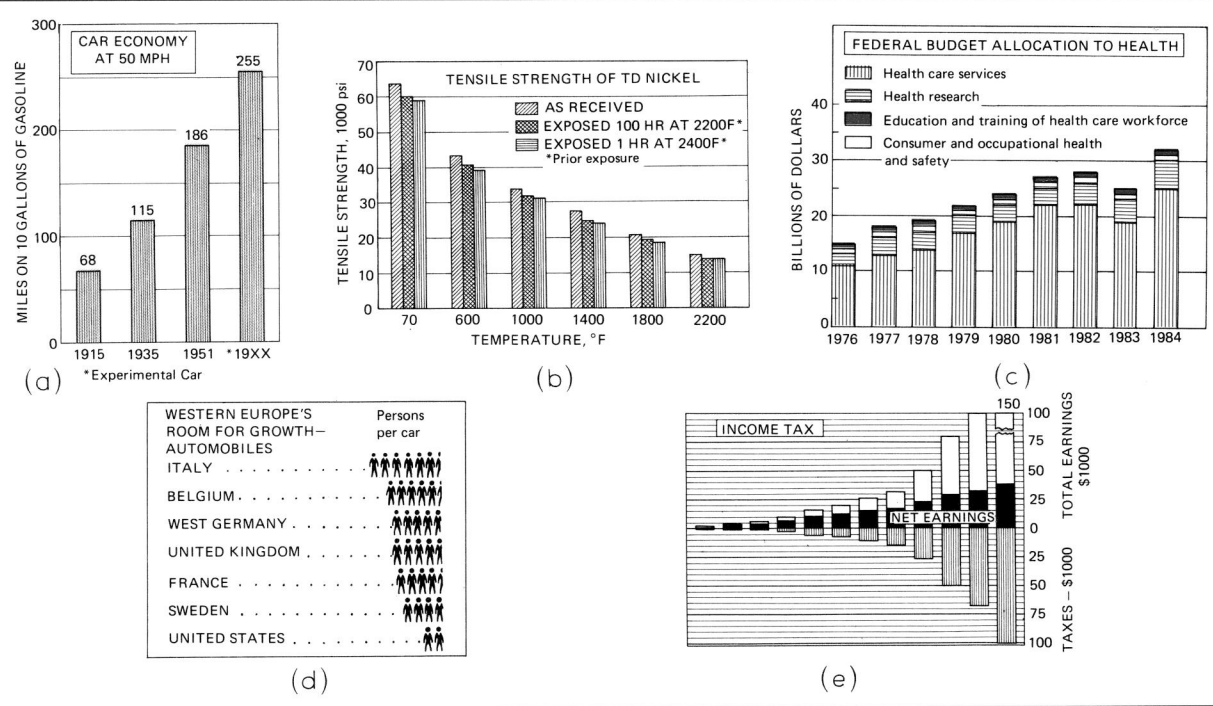

Fig. 23.33 Bar or Column Charts.

variables, Fig. 23.33 (a); a grouped bar chart (three or more related variables), (b); or a combined bar chart (three or more related variables), (c). Another type of bar graph employs pictorial symbols, composed to form bars, as shown at (d). Bar charts can also effectively indicate a "deviation" or difference between values, (e).

23.18 Design and Layout of Bar Charts
If only a few values are to be represented by vertical bars, the chart should be higher than wide, Fig. 23.33 (a). When a relatively large number of values

are plotted, a chart wider than high is preferred, (b) and (c). Composition is dictated by the number of bars used, whether they are to be vertical or horizontal, and the available space.

A convenient method of spacing bars is to divide the available space into twice as many equal spaces as bars are required, Fig. 23.34 (a). Center the bars on every other division mark, beginning with the first division at each end, as shown at (b). When the series of data is incomplete, the missing bars should be indicated by the use of ticks, (c), indicating the lack of data. The bars should be spaced uniformly when the data used are distributed. When irregu-

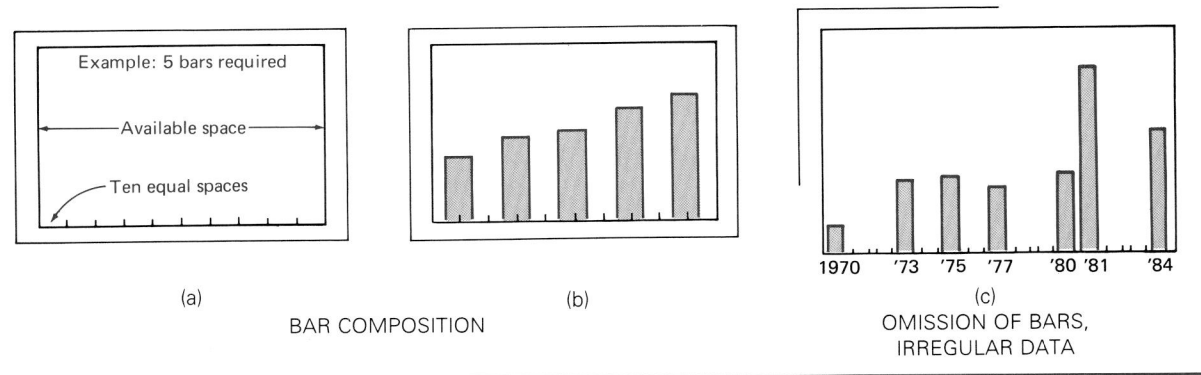

Fig. 23.34 Bar Composition.

larities in data exist, the bars should be spaced accordingly, as shown.

Bar charts may be drawn on printed coordinate paper; however, clarity for popular use is promoted by the use of blank paper and the designation of only the major rulings perpendicular to the bars. If the values of bars are individually noted, the perpendicular rulings may be omitted completely.

Since bar charts are used extensively to show differences in values for given periods of time, the values or amounts should be proportionate to the heights or lengths of the bars. The zero or principal line of reference should never be omitted. Normally, the full length of the bars should be shown to the scale chosen. When a few exceptionally large values exist, the columns may be broken as shown in Fig. 23.33 (e), with a notation included indicating the full value of the bar.

Scale designations are normally placed along the base line of the bars and adjacent to the rulings.

Standard abbreviations may be used for bar designations. The techniques of scale designations used for line curves, §23.5, are also applicable to bar charts. The values of the bars may be designated above the bars for simple and grouped bar charts, Fig. 23.33 (a). Spaces between bars should be wider than the bars when there are relatively few bars. Spaces between bars should be narrower than the bars when there are many bars, as at (b) and (c).

Bars are normally emphasized by shading or by filling in solid. Some of the common forms of shading are shown in the figure. Weight and spacing of shading depend upon the amount of area to be shaded and the final size of the chart and are therefore a matter of judgment.

Bar designations may be placed across several bars when possible, as shown at (e). Other methods include the use of notes with leaders and arrowheads and the use of keys.

As in the case of line graphs, §23.7, titles for bar charts are placed where space permits and contain similar information.

23.19 Rectangular Coordinate Surface or Area Charts

A surface chart, or area chart, is a line or bar chart with ordinate values accentuated by shading the entire area between the outlining curve and the abscissa axis, Fig. 23.35 (a).

A surface or area chart can be a simple chart (called a staircase chart), (b); a multiple surface or "strata" chart with one surface or layer on top of another, (c); or a combined surface chart indicating the distribution of components in relation to their total, (d).

Surface charts are used effectively to

1. Accentuate or emphasize data that appear weak as a line chart.

2. Emphasize amount or ordinate values.

3. Represent the components of a total, usually expressed as a percent of a total, or compared to 100 percent.

4. Present a general picture.

Surface charts are *not* recommended for (1) emphasizing accurate reading of values of charts containing more than one curve or (2) showing line curves that intersect or cross one another.

A map of terrestrial or geographic features is a form of area or surface chart. It represents a graphic picture of areas, surfaces, or the relationship of their component parts to the total configuration.

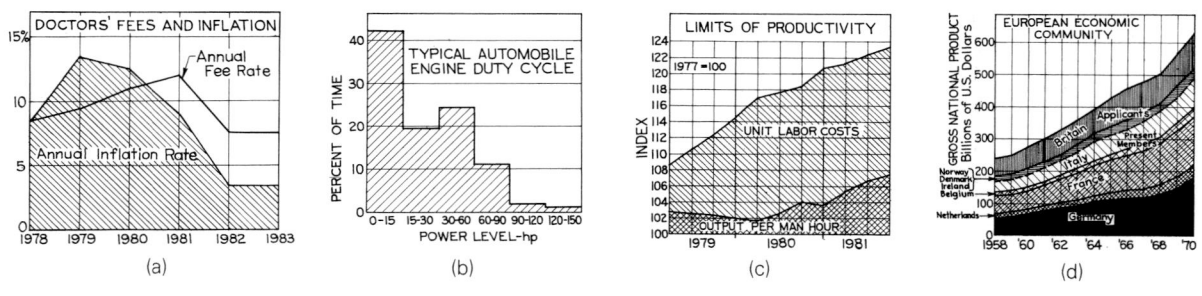

Fig. 23.35 Surface or Area Charts.

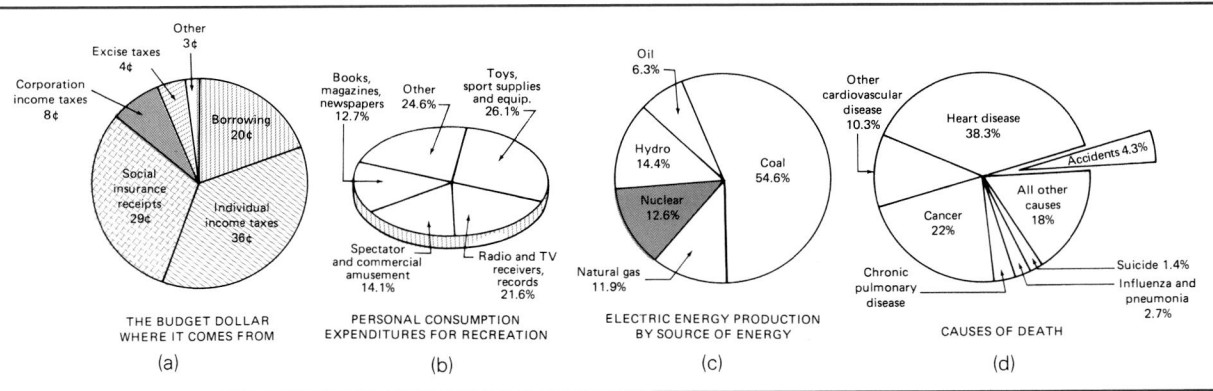

Fig. 23.36 Pie or Sector Charts.

23.20 Pie Charts

Pie charts, or sector charts, are used to compare component parts in relation to their total by the use of circular areas.

Pie charts are effective for

1. Representing data on a percentage basis.

2. Presenting a general picture.

3. Showing relatively few plotted values.

4. Emphasizing amounts rather than the trend of data.

A pie chart is normally presented as a true circular area, Fig. 23.36 (a), or in pictorial form, (b). Since most applications are concerned with monetary values, a disk or "coin" is commonly used for the circular area.

23.21 Design and Layout of Pie Charts

Grids are not used for pie charts. The circular area is drawn to a desired size, within a permissible space. The determination of the various sizes of the sectors is based upon 360° being equivalent to 100 percent. Therefore, the following relationship exists;

$$\frac{100\%}{360°} = \frac{x\%}{\theta°}$$

or

$$\theta° = \frac{x\%(360°)}{100\%} = 3.6°(x\%)$$

and 1 percent is represented by 3.6°, 2 percent by 7.2°, and so on.

Sector values (percent and amount) are placed within the sectors where possible. If a sector is small, a note with a leader and arrowhead will suffice. Labels should be clear of any shading and lettered to read from the bottom of the chart, where possible, Fig. 23.36 (c) and (d). Another technique of sector designation is to shade the areas, (a). If one of the parts is to be emphasized and compared with the other parts, it can be shaded a different tone from the others, (c), or separated from the circular area, as shown at (d).

The title should be placed above or below the figure.

23.22 Volume Charts

A volume chart is the graphic representation of three related variables with respect to three mutually perpendicular axes in space. Volume charts are generally difficult to prepare, so they are not often used. The method of construction is not discussed in detail, but some of the forms are shown.

Figure 23.37 illustrates line volume charts plotted with respect to three axes (Cartesian coordinates), in isometric and oblique projections at (a) and (b), respectively. Bar graphs can be similarly presented in three dimensions on an isometric grid.

A combination of bars and maps may be used to represent related variables, Fig. 23.38 (a). Topographic map construction also is a graphic representation of three related variables (two dimensions in a horizontal plane and one dimension in a vertical

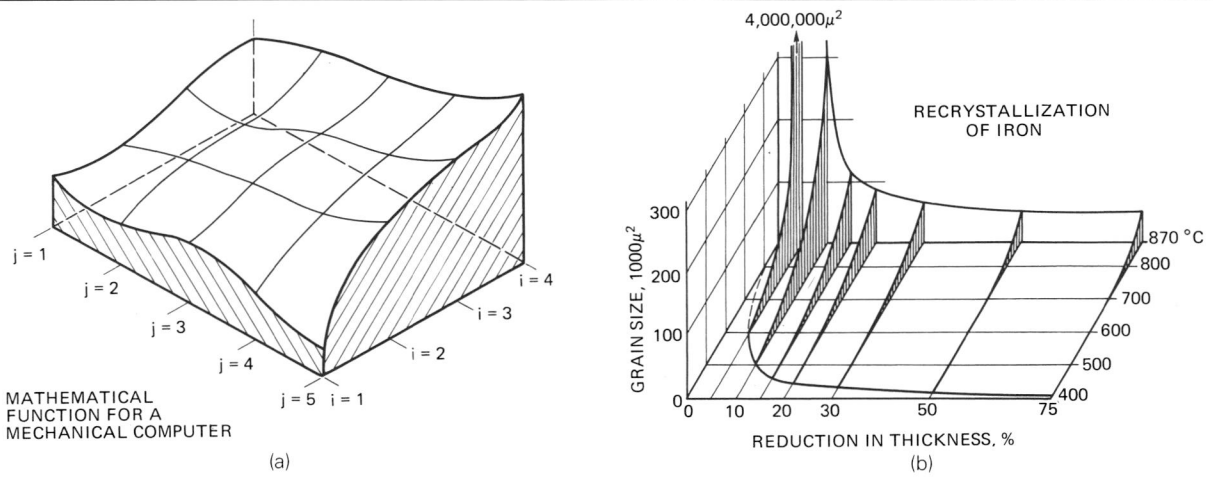

Fig. 23.37 Volume Charts. *(a) adapted from drawing by Eugene W. Pike and Thomas R. Silverberg, with permission of* Machine Design.

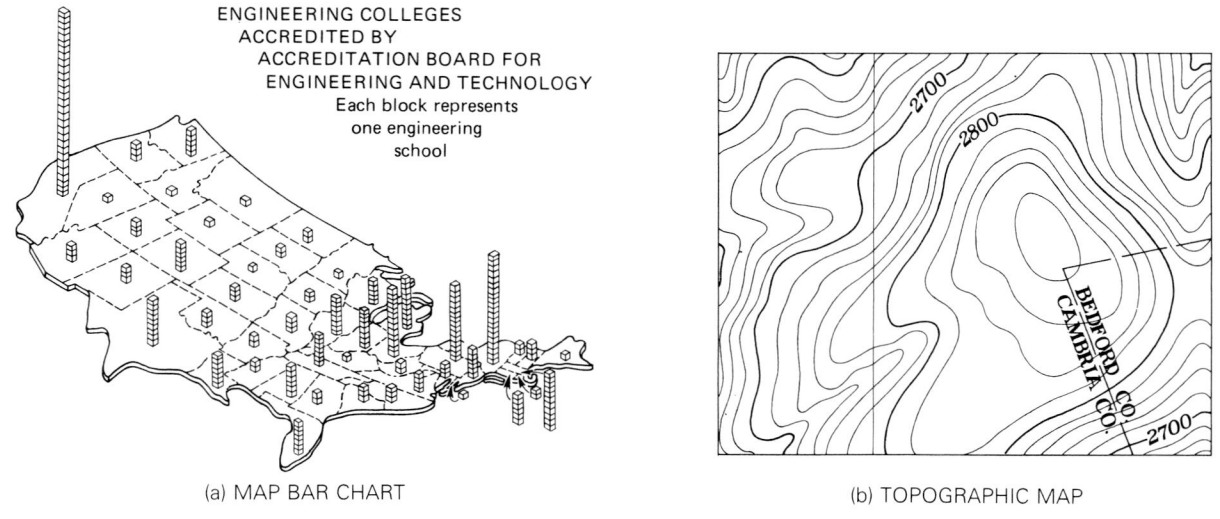

Fig. 23.38 Map Charts.

direction), all drawn in one plane of the drawing paper, as shown at (b).

23.23 Rectangular Coordinate Distribution Charts

When the data observed or obtained vary greatly, they can be plotted on a rectangular coordinate grid for the purpose of observing the distribution or areas of major concentration, with no attempt to fit a curve, Fig. 23.39. Charts of this nature are commonly called *scatter diagrams*.

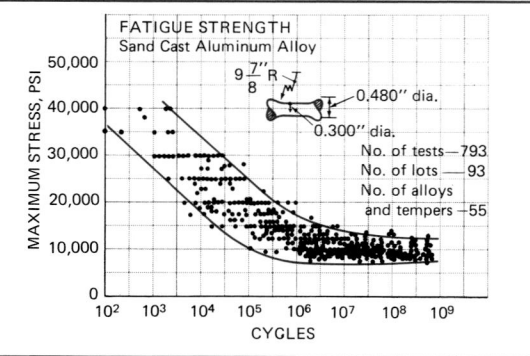

Fig. 23.39 "Scatter" Diagram. *Courtesy of Product Engineering*

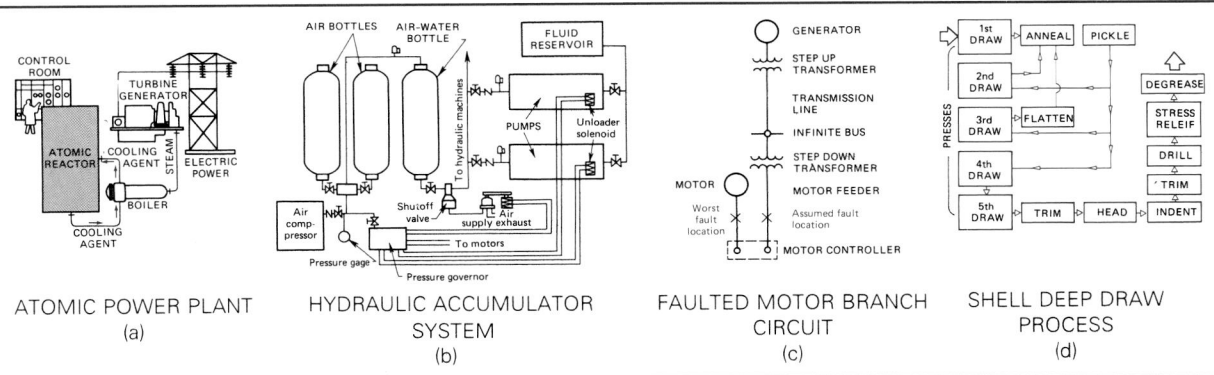

Fig. 23.40 Flowcharts. *(b) adapted from chart by A. F. Welsh, with permission of* Machine Design.

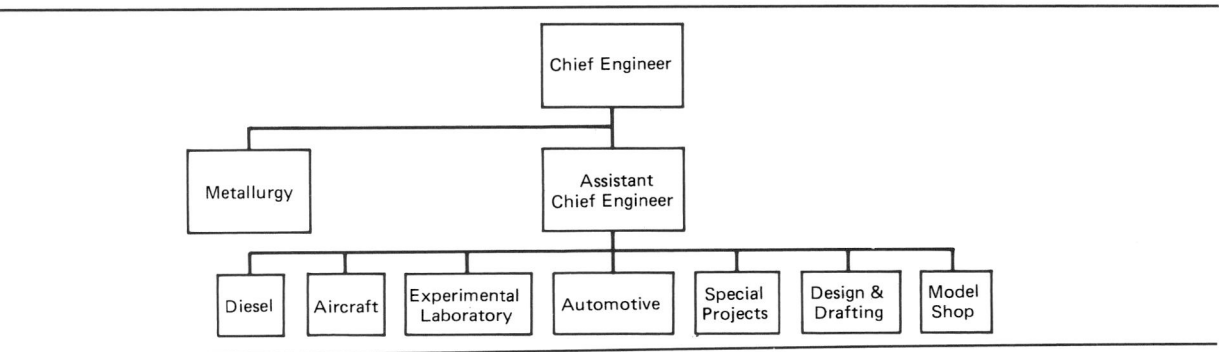

Fig. 23.41 Organization Chart.

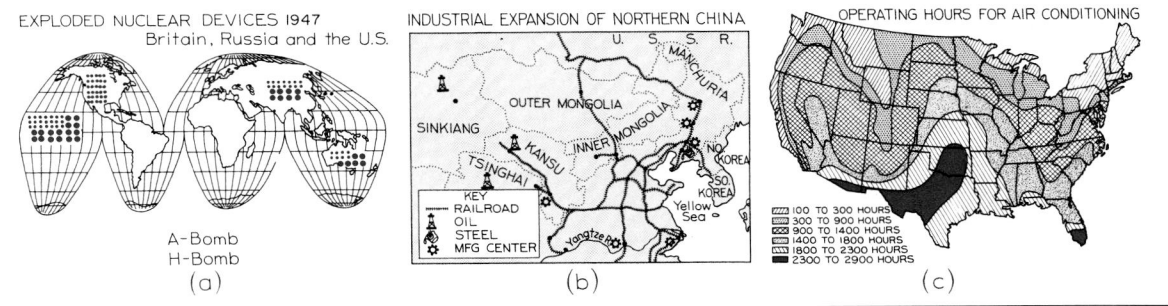

Fig. 23.42 Map Distribution Charts. *(a), (b), and (c) courtesy of* Look *Magazine,* Life *Magazine, and* Heating, Piping and Air Conditioning, *respectively.*

23.24 Flowcharts

Flowcharts are predominantly schematic representations of the flow of a process—for example, manufacturing production processes and electric or hydraulic circuits, Fig. 23.40. Pictorial forms may be used as shown at (a). Schematic symbols are also used, if applicable, (b) and (c). Blocks with captions are used in the simplest form of flowchart, as illustrated at (d).

Organization charts are similar to flowcharts, except that they are usually representations of the arrangement of personnel and physical items of specific organizations, Fig. 23.41.

23.25 Map Distribution Charts

When it is desired to present data according to geographical distribution, maps are commonly used. Locations and emphasis of data can be shown by dots of various sizes, Fig. 23.42 (a); by the use of symbols, (b); by shading of areas, (c); and by the use of numbers or colors.

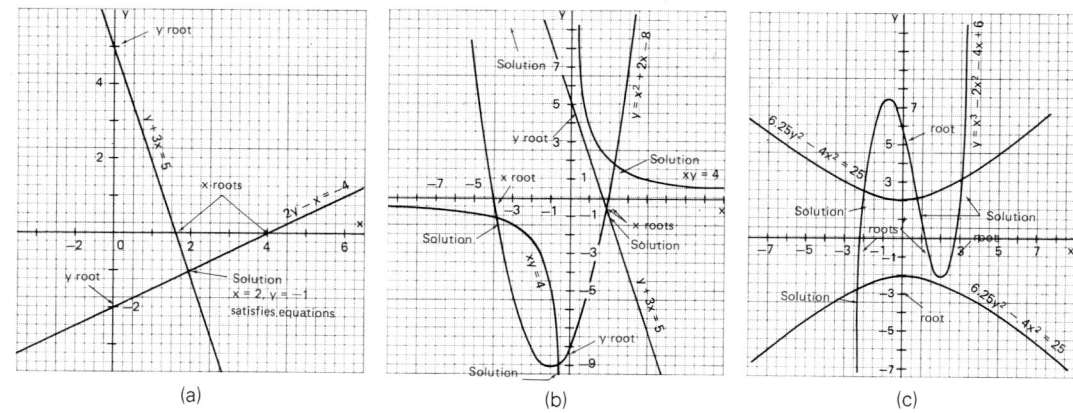

Fig. 23.43   Rectangular Coordinate Graphs—Algebraic Solutions.

23.26 Graphical Mathematics

In general, mathematical problems may be solved *algebraically* (using numerical and mathematical symbols) or *graphically* (using drawing techniques). The algebraic method is predominantly a verbal approach in comparison to the visual methods of graphics; therefore, errors and discrepancies are more evident and subject to detection in a graphical presentation. The advantages of graphics are quite evident in any mathematics text, since most writers in the field of mathematics supplement their algebraic notations with graphical illustrations to illuminate their writings and improve the visualization of the solutions.

The graphical methods cannot be used exclusively, but neither can the algebraic methods be used to the fullest degree of effectiveness without the use of graphics. Engineers should be familiar with both methods in order to convey a clearer understanding of their analyses and designs.

Since equations are mathematical expressions, mathematical operations can be (1) computations with equations, (2) derivation of equations, and (3) solutions of particular equations.

The reader is referred to texts in the school or local library for detailed methods of graphic solutions of particular equations for algebraic and calculus problems.

23.27 Rectangular Coordinate Algebraic Solution Graphs

Rectangular coordinate paper can be effectively used to visualize algebraic solutions. A common application is to solve two simultaneous polynomial equations with two unknowns. A graph of two linear equations, Fig. 23.43 (a), gives the solution at the intersection of the two lines. Linear equations are simple to solve algebraically; however, a graphical approach is advantageous in the solution of a quadratic equation for a parabola ($y = x^2 + 2x - 8$) with a linear equation for a straight line ($y + 3x = 5$) or an equation for an equilateral hyperbola ($xy = 4$), Fig. 23.43 (b). The graphical plot can also be used for further analysis. Note that the linear equation and the equation for the equilateral hyperbola do not have a real simultaneous equation solution. The ease of visualization and solution is evident as the equations become more complex. Figure 23.43 (c) is a graphical solution for the cubic equation $y = x^3 - 2x^2 - 4x + 6$ and the equation for a hyperbola $6.25y^2 - 4x^2 = 25$. If the data were empirical, without an equation, the graphical solution would be necessary.

Another graphic application to algebraic problems is the determination of the roots for the equations. The roots of the equation are determined by the intersection of the curve and the corresponding axis. The linear equation of Fig. 23.43 (a) has one root per variable, as denoted. The highest power of the quadratic equation for the x term of Fig. 23.43 (b) being 2, there are two roots on the x-axis. The y term has only one root. The equilateral hyperbola, in the same graph, is asymptotic to both axes and therefore has no real roots. The symmetrical hyperbola of Fig. 23.43 (c) has one plus and one minus root. A cubic equation can have one or three real roots, depending on the location of the curve relative to the axes. The cubic equation of Fig. 23.43 (c) has three roots.

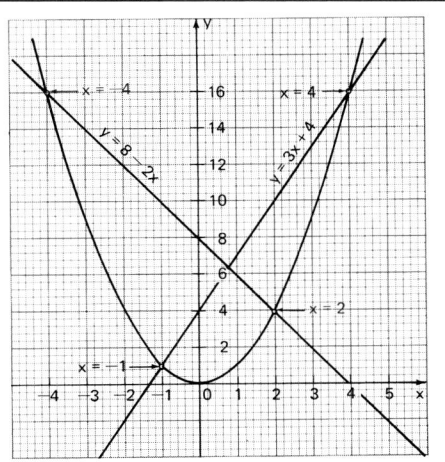

Fig. 23.44   Graphic Algebra Solutions.

A more convenient procedure to determine roots of an equation is to separate the equation and plot two separate curves. The quadratic equation of Fig. 23.43 (b), $y = x^2 + 2x - 8$, was separated to $y = x^2 = 8 - 2x$. The equation $y = x^2$ results in a symmetrical parabola, Fig. 23.44. The remaining portion of the quadratic equation, $y = 8 - 2x$, is a linear equation. The intersection of the parabola and the straight line provides the same root solution for the quadratic equation as in Fig. 23.43 (b). The parabolic curve can be used with other linear portions of similar quadratic equations to provide the respective root solutions on the same plot, (i.e., $y = 3x + 4$).

23.28 The Graphical Calculus

If two variables are so related that the value of one of them depends on the value assigned the other, then the first variable is said to be a function of the second. For example, the area of a circle is a function of the radius. *The calculus* is that branch of mathematics pertaining to the change of values of functions due to finite changes in the variables involved. It is a method of analysis called the *differential calculus* when concerned with the determination of the *rate of change* of one variable of a function with respect to a related variable of the same function. A second principal operation, called *the integral calculus*, is the inverse of the differential calculus and is defined as a *process of summation* (finding the total change).

23.29 The Differential Calculus

Fundamentally, the differential calculus is a means of determining for a given function the limit of the ratio of change in the dependent variable to the corresponding change in the independent variable, as this change approaches zero. This limit is the *derivative* of the function with respect to the independent variable. The derivative of a function $y = f(x)$ may be denoted by dy/dx, $f'(x)$, y', or $D_x y$.

23.30 Geometric Interpretation of the Derivative

As illustrated in Fig. 23.45,

1. The symbol $f(x)$ is used to denote a function of a single variable x and is read "f of x."

2. The value of the function when x has the value x_0 may be denoted by $f(x_0)$ or $F(x_0)$.

3. The increment Δy (read: "delta y") is the change in y produced by increasing x from x_0 to $x_0 + \Delta x$; therefore, $\Delta y = f(x_0 + \Delta x) - f(x_0)$.

4. The differential, dy, of y is the value that Δy would have if the curve coincided with its tangent. The differential, dx, of x is the same as Δx, when x is the independent variable.

5. The slope of the secant line is represented by the ratio $\Delta y/\Delta x$.

6. Ratio dy/dx represents the slope of the tangent line.

Draw a secant through A (coordinates x, y) and a neighboring point B on the curve (coordinates

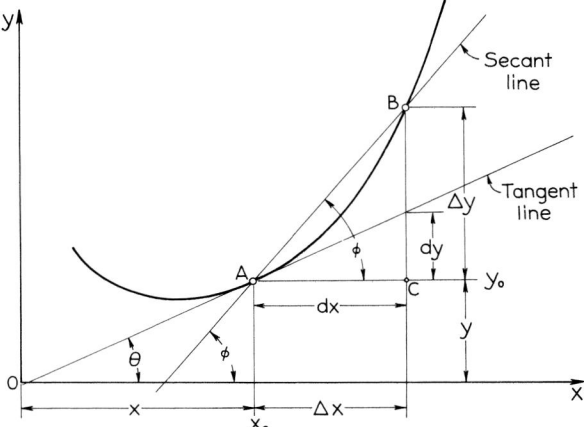

Fig. 23.45   Geometric Interpretation of the Derivative.

$x + \Delta x, y + \Delta y$). The slope of the secant line through A and B is

$$\frac{BC}{AC} = \frac{(y + \Delta y) - y}{(x + \Delta x) - x} = \frac{\Delta y}{\Delta x}$$

$$= \text{tangent of angle } BAC = \text{tangent } \phi$$

Let point B move along the curve and approach point A indefinitely. The secant line will revolve about point A, and its limiting position is the tangent line at A, when Δx, varying, approaches zero as a limit. The angle of inclination, θ, of the tangent line at A becomes the limit of the angle ϕ when Δx approaches zero. Therefore,

$$\tan \phi = \tan \theta = \frac{dy}{dx}$$

$$= \text{slope of tangent line at } A$$

The result of this analysis is the following theorem:

> The value of the derivative at any point of a curve is equal to the slope of the tangent line to the curve at that point.

Accordingly, graphical differentiation is a process of drawing tangents or the equivalent (chords parallel to tangents) to a curve at any point and determining the value of a differential (value of the slope of the tangent line to the curve or to a parallel chord, at the point selected). The value of the slope is the corresponding ordinate value on the derived curve.

23.31 Graphical Differentiation—The Slope Law

The slope of the curve at any point is the tangent of the angle (θ) between the x-axis of the graph and the tangent line to the curve at the selected point, Fig. 23.46. The slope is also the rise or fall of the tangent line in the y direction per one unit of travel in the x direction, the value of the slope being calculated in terms of the scale units of the x- and y-axes.

The *slope law* as applied to differentiation may be stated as follows.

> The slope at any point on a given curve is equal to the ordinate of the corresponding point on the next lower derived curve.

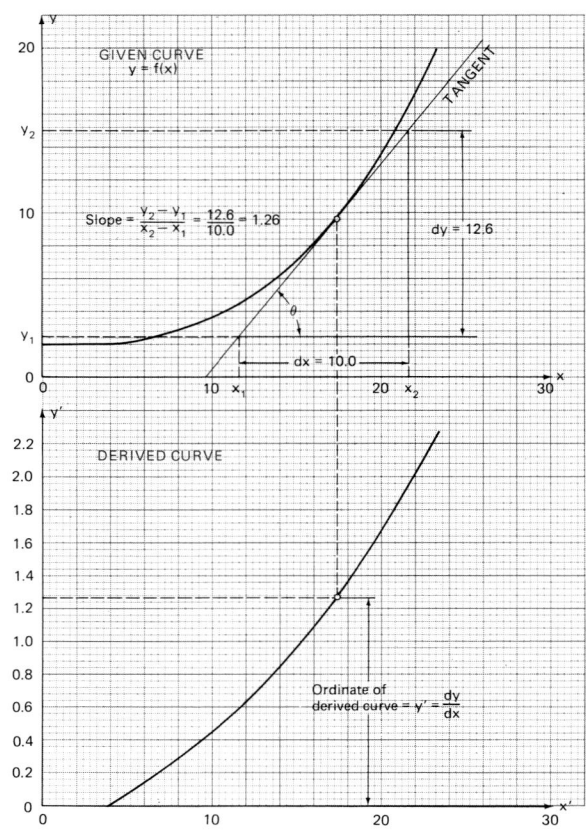

Fig. 23.46   Graphical Differentiation.

The slope law is the graphical equivalent of differentiation of the calculus.

23.32 Area Law

Given a curve, Fig. 23.47 (upper portion), a tangent to the arc is to be constructed at T. A length of arc AB is chosen so that T is at the midpoint of the length of arc. A chord is constructed through A and B, and the tangent is drawn through T parallel to the chord. The coordinates of A are x_1, y_1, and of B are x_2, y_2. Since the chord and tangent are parallel, their slopes are equal. The slope of the tangent line at T is equal to the mean ordinate y'_m of T' in the derived curve

$$y'_m = \frac{y_2 - y_1}{x_2 - x_1}$$

and

$$y_2 - y_1 = y'_m(x_2 - x_1)$$

but

$$y'_m(x_2 - x_1) = \text{area of rectangle } CDx_2x_1$$

Therefore

$$y_2 - y_1 = \text{area of rectangle } CDx_2x_1$$

The law derived from this analysis, the *area law*, may be stated as follows:

> The difference in the length of any two ordinates to a continuous curve equals the total net area between the corresponding ordinates of the next lower curve.

The application of the area law as stated, which provides for dividing the given curve into short arcs, permits the determination of the derivative curve for the given curve. The law is also applicable to the process of integration, as discussed in §23.35.

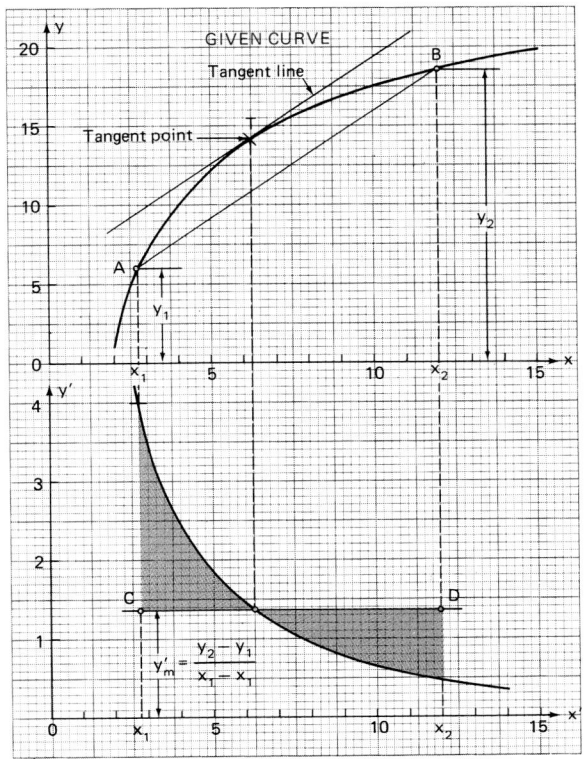

Fig. 23.47 Area Law.

23.33 Practical Applications— Differentiation

The application of the calculus, especially by graphical methods, is based on the practicality and knowledge of the subject matter. Table 23.1 summarizes only a few of the practical applications for the differential calculus. The derived curve also shows maximum and minimum values for the derivative and whether the rate is constant, variable, or zero.

Table 23.1 *Differentiation Applications*

Plotted Data		Derivative of Derived Curve
Independent	**Dependent**	
Time	Displacement	Velocity
Time	Velocity	Acceleration
Time	Amount of	Rate of
	Population	Growth
	Inches	Growth
	Volume	Flow
	Temperature	Cooling, heating
Time	Energy or work	Power
Displacement	Energy or work	Force
Quantity	Cost	Rate of cost
Variable #2	Related variable #1	Rate of change of variable #1 as variable #2 changes

23.34 The Integral Calculus

Integration is a process of summation, the integral calculus having been devised for the purpose of calculating the areas bounded by curves. If the given area is assumed to be divided into an infinite number of infinitesimal parts called *elements*, the sum of all these elements is the total area required. The integral sign ∫, the long S, was used by early writers and is still used in calculations to indicate "sum."

One of the most important applications of the integral calculus is the determination of a function from a given derivative, the inverse of differentiation. The process of determining such a function is *integration*, and the resulting function is called the *integral* of the given derivative or *integrand*. In many cases, however, graphical integration is used to determine the area bounded by curves, in which case the expression of the function is not necessary.

Graphical solutions may be classified into three general groups: graphical, semigraphical, and mechanical methods.

23.35 Graphical Solution—Area Law

Since integration is the inverse of differentiation, the area law as analyzed for differentiation, §23.32, is applicable to integration, but in reverse. The area law as applied to integration may be stated as follows.

> The area between any two ordinates of a given curve is equal to the difference in length between the corresponding ordinates of the next higher curve.

If an $\frac{acceleration}{time}$ curve were given, the integral of this derivative curve would be the $\frac{velocity}{time}$ curve. If the $\frac{velocity}{time}$ curve is integrated as shown in Fig. 23.48, the $\frac{displacement}{time}$ curve is obtained (the next higher curve).

23.36 Semigraphical Integration

When it becomes necessary to determine only an area and not an integral curve, many semigraphical methods are applicable, some of which are the rectangular rule, trapezoid rule, Simpson's rule, Durand's rule, Weddle's rule, method of Gauss, and the method of parabolas. All of these rules and methods may be found in texts at the school or local library. Simpson's rule is one of the more accurate methods. The solutions from these methods become

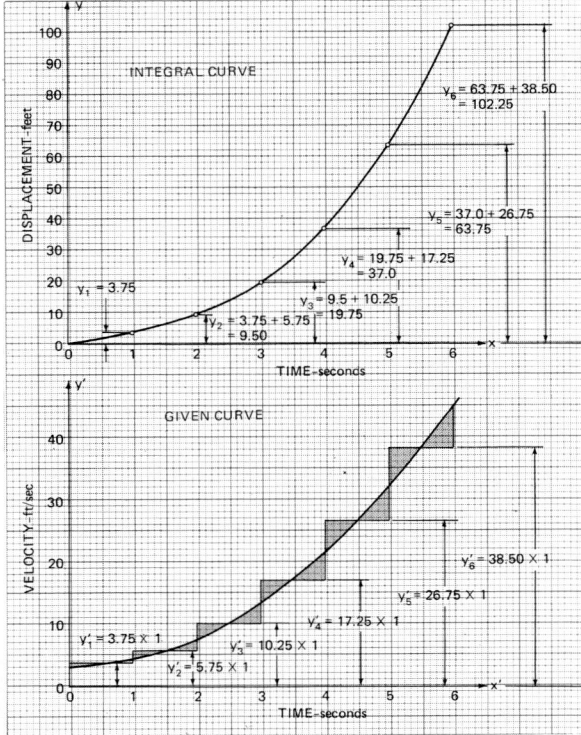

Fig. 23.48   Integration—Area Law.

partly graphical, since the data used are measured from the graphical plot.

23.37 Integration—Mechanical Methods

When the requirement for integration is the determination of the area, mechanical integrators called *planimeters* may be used. The operator manually traces the outline of the area, and the instrument automatically records on a dial the area circumnavigated.

A common type of planimeter is the polar planimeter, Fig. 23.49 (b). As illustrated at (a), by means of the polar arm OM, one end M of the tracer arm is caused to move in a circle, and the other end N is guided around a closed curve bounding the area measured. The area $M_1N_1NN_2M_2MM_1$ is "swept out" twice, but in opposite directions. The resulting displacement reading (difference in the two sweeps) on the integrating wheel indicates the amount of the area. The circumference of the wheel is graduated

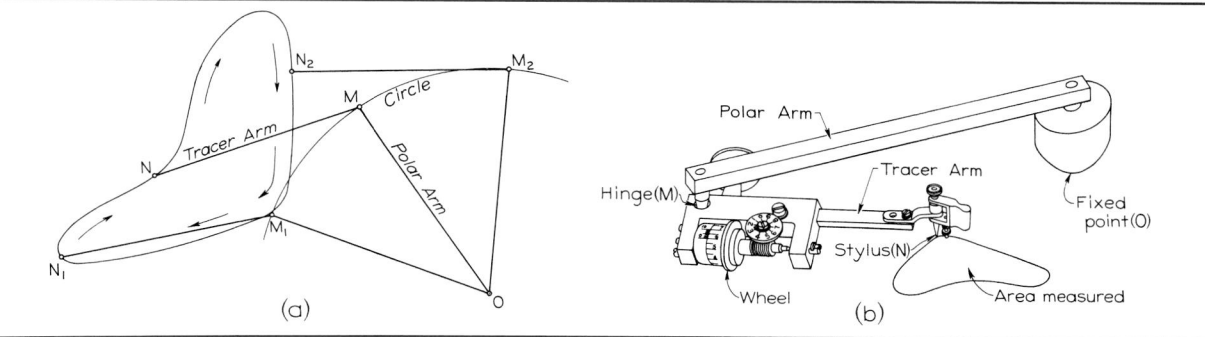

Fig. 23.49 Polar Planimeter.

so that one revolution corresponds to a definite number of square units of area.

The ordinary planimeter used to measure indicator diagrams has a length $L = 4''$, and a wheel circumference of $2.5''$, so that one revolution of the wheel is $4 \times 2.5'' = 10$ sq in. The wheel is graduated into ten parts, each part being further subdivided into ten parts, and a vernier scale facilitates a further subdivision into ten parts, enabling a reading to the nearest hundredth of a square inch.

This same operation of mechanical integration can be performed on a typical CAD software program. Any geometric shape (closed configuration) entered into a computer will compute the area of that configuration, which will be presented upon the proper command.

23.38 Practical Applications of Integration

The definition of integration as being a summation process and the reverse operation of differentiation is not sufficient for a working knowledge of the subject matter. Table 23.2 summarizes a few of the practical applications for the integral calculus.

Table 23.2 *Integration Applications*

Plotted Data		Integral of Integration Curve
Independent	**Dependent**	
Time	Acceleration	Velocity
Time	Velocity	Displacement
y values	x values	Area of X–Y plot enclosed by X-axis and/or Y-axis and the curve
Area	Pressure	Force
Displacement	Force	Work or energy
Time	Power	Work or energy
Volume	Pressure	Work or energy
Time	Force	Momentum
Velocity	Momentum	Impulse
Time	Rate based on time	Total change or cumulative change
Quantity #2	Rate of change of quantity #1 based on change of quantity #2	Max. or min. quantity #1 for values of quantity #2

23.39 Computer Graphics

The graphic presentations discussed in this chapter have all been constructed using conventional drafting equipment. Graphs, charts, and diagrams can also be produced by using a computer graphics system. Graphics software packages intended for use with PCs make it possible to store information and data that can be accessed when needed to create drawings and other graphic images in black and white or color. Text material can be incorporated with the graphics so that reports can be quickly prepared, revised, and published. The images created may be viewed on a graphic display device or monitor, Fig. 23.50. A record or copy of these images may then be produced using an output device such as a dot-matrix or laser printer. Examples of graphs and charts produced in this manner are shown in Figs. 23.51–23.54. For additional information, see Chapters 3 and 8.

Fig. 23.50 Graphic Display Device. *Courtesy of AT&T.*

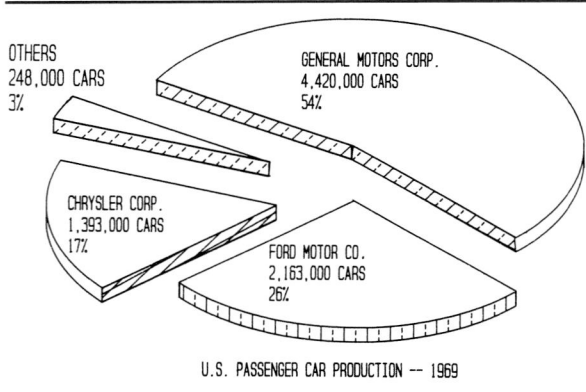

U.S. PASSENGER CAR PRODUCTION -- 1969

Fig. 23.51 Computer-Generated Pictorial Pie Chart. *Courtesy of Department of Engineering Graphics, Illinois Institute of Technology.*

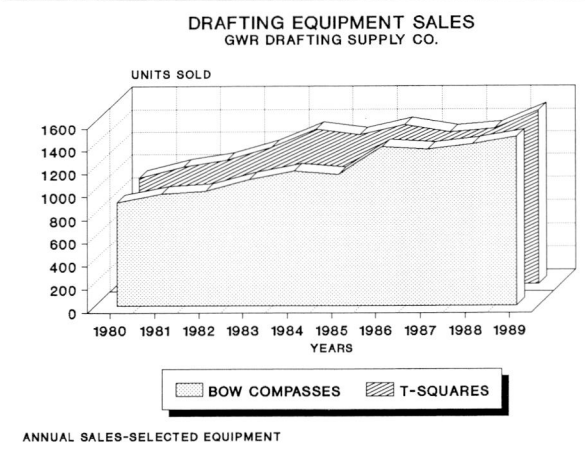

ANNUAL SALES-SELECTED EQUIPMENT

Fig. 23.52 Computer-Generated Pictorial Line Graph. *Courtesy of Department of Engineering Graphics, Illinois Institute of Technology.*

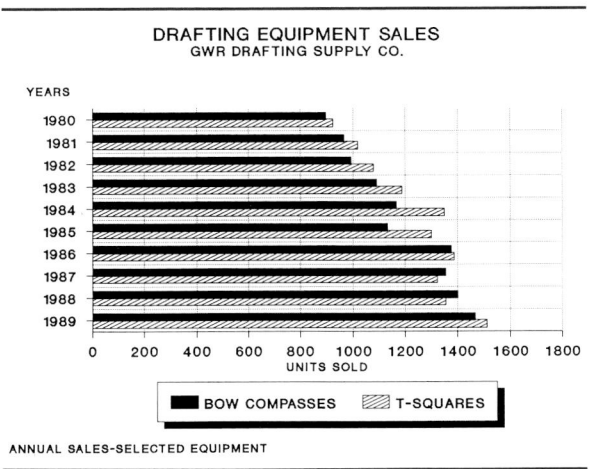

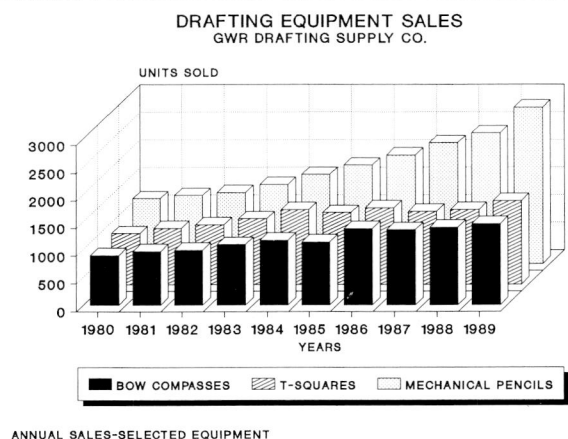

Fig. 23.53 Computer-Generated Horizontal Bar Graph. *Courtesy of Department of Engineering Graphics, Illinois Institute of Technology.*

Fig. 23.54 Computer-Generated Pictorial Vertical Bar Graph. *Courtesy of Department of Engineering Graphics, Illinois Institute of Technology.*

Graph Problems

Construct an appropriate form of graph for each set of data listed. The determination of graph form (line, bar, surface, etc.) is left to the discretion of the instructor or the student and should be based on the nature of the data or the form of presentation desired. In some cases, more than one curve or more than one series of bars are required.

Since many of the problems in this chapter are of a general nature, they can also be solved in most computer graphics systems. If a system is available, the instructor may choose to assign specific problems to be completed by this method.

Additional problems in convenient form for solution are presented in the worksheets at the back of this book. Refer to Drawings 23-1 and 23-2 and accompanying instructions.

Prob. 23.1   Medicine for Profit: A Healthy Market (revenues generated by for-profit acute-care hospitals)

Year	Gross Revenue (billions of dollars)
1969	0.75
1970	1.00
1971	1.25
1972	1.60
1973	2.00
1974	2.50
1975	3.00
1976	3.50
1977	4.00
1978	4.50
1979	5.25
1980	6.25
1981	7.30
1982	9.00
1983	10.50[a]
1984	13.00[a]

Prob. 23.2   Metal Hardness Comparison (Mohs' hardness scale)

Metal	Comparative Degree of Hardness (diamond = 10)
Lead	1.5
Tin	1.8
Cadmium	2.0
Zinc	2.5
Gold	2.5
Silver	2.7
Aluminum	2.9
Copper	3.0
Nickel	3.5
Platinum	4.3
Iron	4.5
Cobalt	5.5
Tungsten	7.5
Chromium	9.0
Diamond	10.0

Prob. 23.3   Effect of Accuracy of Gear Manufacture on Available Strength in Terms of Horsepower (60 teeth gear and 30 teeth pinion of 6 diametral pitch, 1.5″ face width, $14\frac{1}{2}°$ pressure angle; 500 Brinell Case hardness)

Pitch Line Velocity, ft/min	Horsepower			
	Perfect Gear	Aircraft Quality Gear	Accurate Quality Gear	Commercial Quality Gear
0	0	0	0	0
1000	140	100	75	50
2000	290	180	105	60
3000	Straight-line	250	120	70
4000	curve through	320	130	72
5000	two points	380	140	72

Noise limit: 2750 ft/min—accurate quality gear; 1400 ft/min—commercial quality gear.

Prob. 23.4 U.S. Population

Year	Population
1800	5,308,483
1810	7,239,881
1820	9,638,453
1830	12,866,020
1840	17,069,453
1850	23,191,876
1860	31,443,321
1870	38,558,371
1880	56,155,783
1890	62,947,714
1900	75,994,575
1910	96,977,266
1920	105,710,620
1930	122,775,046
1940	131,669,275
1950	151,325,798
1960	179,323,175
1970	203,302,031
1980	226,545,805
1990	248,709,873
2000	268,000,000[a]

[a]Estimated.

Prob. 23.6 World Population

Year	Population (billions)
1950	2.51
1960	3.03
1970	3.63
1980	4.42
1990	5.33
2000	6.13[a]

[a]Projection.

Prob. 23.8 Lumber Prices—Softwoods

Year	Index (1967 = 100)			
	Mar.	June	Sept.	Dec.
1980	362.4	328.6	349.4	355.7
1981	346.0	357.0	335.3	321.8
1982	318.9	328.1	320.9	322.7
1983	369.4	397.9	361.4	360.3

Prob. 23.5 U.S. Pedestrian Deaths, 1975–1979

Age	Number of Deaths		Age	Number of Deaths	
	Female	Male		Female	Male
1	500	800	47	225	600
3	575	1000	50	225	600
5	600	1040	52	225	575
7	400	800	55	250	500
8	300	625	57	250	550
10	325	500	60	225	575
12	425	625	62	275	575
15	400	1100	65	250	500
17	375	1075	67	290	525
20	300	1000	70	300	525
22	275	900	72	350	475
25	200	750	75	340	450
27	225	700	77	300	475
30	200	600	80	300	400
32	175	500	82	225	375
35	150	450	85	150	300
37	160	475	87	100	200
40	175	475	90	50	150
42	200	500	92	25	50
45	175	500	95	0	0

Prob. 23.7 Worldwide Growth of Engineering Periodicals

Years	Number of Periodicals
1921–1930	166
1931–1940	215
1941–1950	301
1951–1960	485
1961–1970	705
1971–1980	927
1981–1985	991

Prob. 23.9 U.S. Personal Consumption Expenditures

Year	Billions of Dollars		
	Durables	Nondurables	Services
1965	63.0	188.6	178.7
1970	85.2	265.7	270.8
1975	132.2	407.3	437.0
1980	214.7	668.8	784.5

Prob. 23.10   Industrial Energy Sources

Year	Percent of Total U.S. Industrial Use of Energy			
	Coal	Oil	Natural Gas	Electricity
1969	23	23	45	9
1971	20	24	46	10
1973	17	36	39	8
1975	16	36	38	10
1977	15	39	35	11
1979	14	41	33	12
1981	15	37	35	13
1983	12	40	35	13
1985	13	38	35	14
1987	13	39	34	14

Prob. 23.11   Psychological Analysis of Work Efficiency and Fatigue

Hours of Work	Relative Production Index	
	Heavy Work	Light Work
9–10 A.M.	100	96
10–11 A.M.	108	104
11–12 A.M.	104	104
12–1 P.M.	98	103
Lunch		
2–3 P.M.	103	100
3–4 P.M.	99	102
4–5 P.M.	98	101
After 8-hour day		
5–6 P.M.	91	94
6–7 P.M.	86	93
7–8 P.M.	68	83

Prob. 23.12   The World Economy—Industrial Production

Year	Index (1980 = 100)					
	United Kingdom	France	U.S.	West Germany	Italy	Japan
1976	94	90	86	89	80	77
1977	100	96	90	94	92	84
1978	101	94	94	95	85	85
1979	104	99	103	98	95	92
1980	106	102	103	102	102	100
1981	96	98	102	98	99	99
1982	98	97	98	97	98	102
1983	100	95	93	93	94	101
1984	105	99	108	99	95	112

Plot on semilog shows rate of change of index.

Prob. 23.13   Essential Qualities of a Successful Engineer (average estimate based on 1500 questionnaires from practicing engineers)

Quality	Percent
Character	41
Judgment	$17\frac{1}{2}$
Efficiency	$14\frac{1}{2}$
Understanding human nature	14
Technical knowledge	13
Total	100

Prob. 23.14   Automobile Accident Analysis

Type of Accident	Percent
Cross traffic (grade crossing, highway, railway)	21
Same direction	30
Head-on	21
Fixed object	11
Pedestrian	10
Miscellaneous	7
Total	100

Prob. 23.15 Comparison of Horsepower at the Rear Wheels (as shown by dynamometer tests)

	Horsepower at Rear Wheels			
Engine rpm	McCulloch Supercharged with Dual Exhausts	McCulloch Supercharged	Unsupercharged —Dual Exhausts	Unsupercharged
2000	77.0	73.0	64.5	59.5
2200	82.0	77.5	70.5	65.0
2400	88.0	83.5	75.0	69.0
2600	95.5	91.5	79.0	73.5
2800	105.0	99.0	82.5	76.5
3000	112.5	105.5	84.5	78.5
3200	117.0	109.5	85.5	79.5
3400	119.0	111.5	83.5	77.0
3600	118.5	111.5		

Prob. 23.16 How the World Uses Its Work Force: Employment by Economic Sector, 1980

	Percent of Workers			
Country	Agriculture[a]	Mining and Construction	Manufacturing	Services[b]
United States	3.6	7.2	22.1	67.1
Canada	5.4	7.7	19.7	67.2
Australia	6.5	9.1	19.9	64.5
Japan	10.1	10.1	25.0	54.8
France	8.7	9.3	25.8	56.2
Great Britain	2.7	8.3	28.4	60.6
Italy	14.2	11.2	26.9	47.7
Netherlands	6.0	9.6	21.3	63.1
Sweden	5.6	7.2	24.3	62.9

[a]Agriculture, forestry, hunting, and fishing.
[b]Transportation, communication, public utilities, trade, finance, public administration, private household services, and miscellaneous services.

Plot the data for Problems 23.17 and 23.18 on rectangular coordinate paper and on semilog paper.

Prob. 23.17 Rupture Strength of T. D. Nickel—High-Temperature Alloy

Temperature (T),°F	100-hr Rupture Stress (s_r), psi × 1000 (log scale)
1200	24
1400	17
1600	12.5
1800	9
2000	6.5
2200	4.75
2400	3.5

Prob. 23.18   Nuisance Noise

Frequency (*f*), cps (log scale)	Octave Band Level, db			
	Hearing Loss Risk Region		Power Lawn Mower at 3 ft	5-hp Chainsaw at 3 ft
	Negligible	Serious		
53	104	122	84	93
106	93	113	93	103
220	87	107	94	103
425	85	105	90	111
850	85	105	84	112
1700	85	105	84	107
3400	85	105	82	104
6800	85	105	75	98

Plot the data for the following problems on rectangular coordinate paper and on logarithmic paper.

Prob. 23.19   Loss of Head for Water Flowing in Iron Pipes

Velocity (*v*), ft/sec	Loss of Head, ft/1000 ft			
	1″ Pipe	2″ Pipe	4″ Pipe	6″ Pipe
0	0	0	0	0
1	6.0	2.9	1.6	.7
2	23.5	9.5	4.2	2.4
3	50	20	8.2	4.7
4		34	13.5	7.7
5		51	20	11.4
6			28	15.5
7			37	20

Prob. 23.20   Material and Process Economics

Weight of Steel Forging (*W*), lb	Unit Cost (*C*) for Forging, $		
	Simple	Average	Complex
0.1	0.22		
0.2	0.38		
0.4	0.67		
1.0	1.4		
2.0	2.5	2.75	4.5
4.0	4.4	5.0	8.5
10.0	9.2	11.0	19.5
20.0	16.0	20.0	37.0
40.0	28.5	36.5	70.0
100	60.0	80.0	165.0

Prob. 23.21   Pressurized Square Tubing, Fig. 23.55.

Orientation, degrees	Stress Ratio (σ_1/P)	
	D/a = 0.80	*D/a* = 0.86
0	2.0	2.6
15	3.2	4.3
30	4.2	6.3
45	4.3	5.0
60	4.2	6.3
75	3.2	4.3
90	2.0	2.6

Data are given for one quadrant; quadrants are identical.

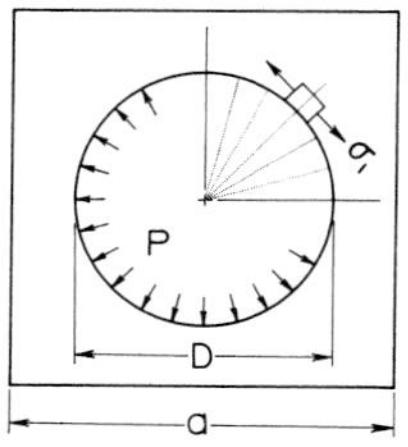

Fig. 23.55   (Prob. 23.21).

Prob. 23.22 Variation of Modulus of Elasticity (E) with Direction in Copper

	$E \times 10^6$ psi	
Orientation, degrees	As Rolled	Annealed
0	20.0	9.5
15	18.5	11.0
30	16.5	14.5
45	15.0	17.5
60	16.5	14.5
75	18.5	11.0
90	20.0	9.5
105	18.5	11.0
120	16.5	14.5
135	15.0	17.5
150	16.5	14.5
165	18.5	11.0
180	20.0	9.5

Direction of rolling is from 0° to 180°.

Prob. 23.23 Light Distribution in a Vertical Plane for a Bulb Suspended from the Ceiling with the Filament at the Origin of the Polar Chart

Orientation, degrees	Candle Power
0	140
10	210
20	310
30	320
40	310
50	310
60	300
70	290
80	280
90	250
100	270
110	290
120	295
130	300
140	315
150	330
160	340
170	350
180	340

Prob. 23.24 Main Bearing Load Diagram (4000 rpm, no counterweight)

	Load			Load	
Orientation, degrees	1000 lb	(1000 kg)	Orientation, degrees	1000 lb	(1000 kg)
0	6.6	(3.0)	190	5.3	(2.4)
10	4.8	(2.2)	200	5.2	(2.4)
20	4.2	(1.9)	210	4.9	(2.2)
30	3.7	(1.7)	220	4.5	(2.1)
40	3.2	(1.5)	230	4.2	(1.9)
50	3.0	(1.4)	240	3.7	(1.7)
60	2.8	(1.3)	250	3.3	(1.5)
70	2.7	(1.2)	260	3.1	(1.4)
80	2.7	(1.2)	270	2.9	(1.3)
90	2.8	(1.3)	280	2.8	(1.3)
100	2.9	(1.3)	290	2.7	(1.2)
110	3.3	(1.5)	300	2.8	(1.3)
120	3.6	(1.6)	310	3.0	(1.4)
130	4.1	(1.9)	320	3.2	(1.5)
140	4.6	(2.1)	330	3.7	(1.7)
150	4.9	(2.2)	340	4.4	(2.0)
160	5.0	(2.3)	350	5.3	(2.4)
170	5.2	(2.4)	360	6.6	(3.0)
180	5.3	(2.4)			

Max. load = 6600 lb (3000 kg); mean load = 4530 lb (2059 kg).

Appendix

Contents of Appendix

1   Bibliography of American National
    Standards   A•2
2   Technical Terms   A•4
3   CAD/CAM Glossary   A•8
4   Abbreviations for Use on Drawings and in
    Text—American National Standard   A•20
5   Running and Sliding Fits—American National
    Standard   A•25
6   Clearance Locational Fits—American
    National Standard   A•27
7   Transition Locational Fits—American
    National Standard   A•29
8   Interference Locational Fits—American
    National Standard   A•30
9   Force and Shrink Fits—American National
    Standard   A•31
10 International Tolerance Grades   A•33
11 Preferred Metric Hole Basis Clearance Fits—
    American National Standard   A•34
12 Preferred Metric Hole Basis Transition and
    Interference Fits—American National
    Standard   A•36
13 Preferred Metric Shaft Basis Clearance Fits—
    American National Standard   A•38
14 Preferred Metric Shaft Basis Transition and
    Interference Fits—American National
    Standard   A•40
15 Screw Threads, American National, Unified,
    and Metric   A•42

16 Twist Drill Sizes—American National
    Standard and Metric   A•45
17 Acme Threads, General Purpose   A•46
18 Bolts, Nuts, and Cap Screws—Square and
    Hexagon—American National Standard and
    Metric   A•47
19 Cap Screws, Slotted and Socket Head—
    American National Standard and
    Metric   A•50
20 Machine Screws—American National
    Standard and Metric   A•52
21 Keys—Square, Flat, Plain Taper, and Gib
    Head   A•54
22 Screw Threads—Square and Acme   A•54
23 Woodruff Keys—American National
    Standard   A•55
24 Woodruff Key Sizes for Different Shaft
    Diameters   A•55
25 Pratt and Whitney Round-End Keys   A•56
26 Washers, Plain—American National
    Standard   A•57
27 Washers, Lock—American National
    Standard   A•58
28 Wire Gage Standards   A•59
29 Taper Pins—American National
    Standard   A•60
30 Cotter Pins—American National
    Standard   A•61
31 Metric Equivalents   A•62
32 Form and Proportion of Geometric
    Tolerancing Symbols   A•63

1 Bibliography of American National Standards

American National Standards Institute, 11 West 42nd Street, New York, N.Y. 10036. For complete listing of standards, see ANSI catalog of American National Standards.

Abbreviations

Abbreviations for Use on Drawings and in Text, ANSI Y1.1–1989

Bolts, Screws, and Nuts

Bolts, Metric Heavy Hex, ANSI B18.2.3.6M–1979 (R1989)

Bolts, Metric Heavy Hex Structural, ANSI B18.2.3.7M–1979 (R1989)

Bolts, Metric Hex, ANSI B18.2.3.5M–1979 (R1989)

Bolts, Metric Round Head Short Square Neck, ANSI B18.5.2.1M–1989

Bolts, Metric Round Head Square Neck, ANSI/ASME B18.5.2.2M–1982

Hex Jam Nuts, Metric, ANSI B18.2.4.5M–1979 (R1990)

Hex Nuts, Heavy, Metric, ANSI B18.2.465M–1979, (R1990)

Hex Nuts, Slotted, Metric, ANSI B18.2.4.3M–1979 (R1989)

Hex Nuts, Style 1, Metric, ANSI B18.2.4.1M–1979 (R1989)

Hex Nuts, Style 2, Metric, ANSI B18.2.4.2M–1979 (R1989)

Hexagon Socket Flat Countersunk Head Cap Screws (Metric Series), ANSI/ASME B18.3.5M–1986

Mechanical Fasteners, Glossary of Terms, ANSI B18.12–1962 (R1981)

Miniature Screws, ANSI B18.11–1961 (R1983)

Nuts, Metric Hex Flange, ANSI B18.2.4.4M–1982

Plow Bolts, ANSI B18.9–1958 (R1989)

Round Head Bolts, Metric Round Head Short Square Neck, ANSI B18.5.2.1M–1989

Screws, Hexagon Socket Button Head Cap, Metric Series, ANSI/ASME B18.3.4M–1986

Screws, Hexagon Socket Head Shoulder, Metric Series, ANSI/ASME B18.3.3M–1986

Screws, Hexagon Socket Set, Metric Series, ANSI/ASME B18.3.6M–1986

Screws, Metric Formed Hex, ANSI B18.2.3.2M–1979 (R1989)

Screws, Metric Heavy Hex, ANSI B18.2.3.3M–1979 (R1989)

Screws, Metric Hex Cap, ANSI B18.2.3.1M–1979 (R1989)

Screws, Metric Hex Flange, ANSI/ASME B18.2.3.4M–1984

Screws, Metric Hex Lag, ANSI B18.2.3.8M–1981

Screws, Metric Machine, ANSI/ASME B18.6.7M–1985

Screws, Socket Head Cap, Metric Series, ANSI/ASME B18.3.1M–1986

Screws, Tapping and Metallic Drive, Inch Series, Thread Forming and Cutting, ANSI B18.6.4–1981

Slotted and Recessed Head Machine Screws and Machine Screw Nuts, ANSI B18.6.3–1972 (R1991)

Slotted Head Cap Screws, Square Head Set Screws, and Slotted Headless Set Screws, ANSI B18.6.2–1972 (R1983)

Socket Cap, Shoulder, and Set Screws (Inch Series) ANSI/ASME B18.3–1986

Square and Hex Bolts and Screws, Inch Series, ANSI B18.2.1–1981

Square and Hex Nuts (Inch Series) ANSI/ASME B18.2.2–1987

Track Bolts and Nuts, ANSI/ASME B18.10–1982

Wing Nuts, Thumb Screws, and Wing Screws, ANSI B18.17–1968 (R1983)

Wood Screws, Inch Series, ANSI B18.6.1–1981

Charts and Graphs

Illustrations for Publication and Projection, ANSI Y15.1M–1979 (R1986)

Process Charts, ANSI Y15.3M–1979 (R1986)

Time Series Charts, ANSI Y15.2M–1979 (R1986)

Dimensioning and Surface Finish

General Tolerances for Metric Dimensioned Products, ANSI B4.3–1978 (R1984)

Preferred Limits and Fits for Cylindrical Parts, ANSI B4.1–1967 (R1987)

Preferred Metric Limits and Fits, ANSI B4.2–1978 (R1984)

Surface Texture, ANSI/ASME B46.1–1985

Drafting Manual (Y14)

Sect. 1 Drawing Sheet Size and Format, ANSI Y14.1–1980 (R1987)

Sect. 2 Line Conventions and Lettering, ANSI Y14.2M–1979 (R1987)

Sect. 3 Multi and Sectional View Drawings, ANSI Y14.3–1975 (R1987)

Sect. 4 Pictorial Drawing, ANSI/ASME Y14.4M–1989

Sect. 5 Dimensioning and Tolerancing, ANSI Y14.5M–1982 (R1988)

Sect. 6 Screw Thread Representation, ANSI Y14.6–1978 (R1987)

Sect. 6a Screw Thread Representation, Metric, ANSI Y14.6aM–1981 (R1987)

Sect. 7.1 Gear Drawing Standards—Part 1, for Spur, Helical, Double Helical, and Rack, ANSI Y14.7.1–1971 (R1988)

Sect. 7.2 Gear and Spline Drawing Standards—Part 2, Bevel and Hypoid Gears, ANSI Y14.7.2–1978 (R1984)

Sect. 13 Mechanical Spring Representation, ANSI Y14.13M–1981 (R1987)

Sect. 15 Electrical and Electronics Diagrams, ANSI Y14.15–1966 (R1988)

Sect. 15a Electrical and Electronics Diagrams—Supplement, ANSI Y14.15a–1971 (R1988)

Sect. 15b Electrical and Electronics Diagrams—Supplement, ANSI Y14.15b–1973 (R1988)

Sect. 17 Fluid Power Diagrams, ANSI Y14.17–1966 (R1987)

Sect. 34 Parts Lists, Data Lists, and Index Lists, ANSI Y14.34M–1982 (R1988)

Sect. 36 Surface Texture Symbols, ANSI Y14.36–1978 (R1987)

Gears

Design for Fine-Pitch Worm Gearings, ANSI/AGMA 374.04–1977

Gear Nomenclature—Terms, Definitions, Symbols, and Abbreviations, ANSI/AGMA 112.05–1976

Nomenclature of Gear-Tooth Failure Modes, ANSI/AGMA 110.04–1980 (R1989)

System for Straight Bevel Gears, ANSI/AGMA 208.03–1979

Tooth Proportions for Coarse-Pitch Involute Spur Gears, ANSI/AGMA 201.02

Tooth Proportions for Fine-Pitch Involute Spur and Helical Gears, ANSI/AGMA 207.06–1977

Graphic Symbols (Y32)

Fire-Protection Symbols for Architectural and Engineering Drawings, ANSI/NFPA 172–1986

Fire-Protection Symbols for Risk Analysis Diagrams, ANSI/NFPA 174–1986

Graphic Symbols for Electrical and Electronics Diagrams (Including 1986 Supplement) ANSI/IEEE 315–1975 (R1989)

Graphic Symbols for Electrical Wiring and Layout Diagrams Used in Architecture and Building Construction, ANSI Y32.9–1972 (R1989)

Graphic Symbols for Fluid Power Diagrams, ANSI Y32.10–1967 (R1987)

Graphic Symbols for Grid and Mapping Used in Cable Television Systems, ANSE/IEEE 623–1976 (R1989)

Graphic Symbols for Heat-Power Apparatus, ANSI Y32.2.6M–1950 (R1984)

Graphic Symbols for Heating, Ventilating and Air Conditioning, ANSI Y32.2.4–1949 (R1984)

Graphic Symbols for Logic Functions, ANSI/IEEE 91–1984

Graphic Symbols for Pipe Fittings, Valves, and Piping, ANSI/ASME Y32.2.3–1949 (R1988)

Graphic Symbols for Plumbing Fixtures for Diagrams Used in Architecture and Building Construction, ANSI Y32.4–1977 (R1987)

Graphic Symbols for Process Flow Diagrams in the Petroleum and Chemical Industries, ANSI Y32.11–1961 (R1985)

Graphic Symbols for Railroad Maps and Profiles, ANSI Y32.7–1972 (R1987)

Instrumentation Symbols and Identification, ANSI/ISA S5.1–1984

Reference Designations for Electrical and Electronics Parts and Equipment, ANSI/IEEE 200–1975 (R1989)

Symbols for Fire Fighting Operations, ANSI/NFPA 178–1986

Symbols for Mechanical and Acoustical Elements as Used in Schematic Diagrams, ANSI Y32.18–1972 (R1985)

Symbols for Welding and Nondestructive Testing, Including Brazing, ANSI/AWS A2.4–86

Keys and Pins

Clevis Pins and Cotter Pins, ANSI B18.8.1–1972 (R1983)

Hexagon Keys and Bits (Metric Series), ANSI B18.3.2M–1979 (R1990)

Keys and Keyseats, ANSI B17.1–1967 (R1989)

Pins-Taper Pins, Dowel Pins, Straight Pins, Grooved Pins and Spring Pins (Inch Series), ANSI B18.8.2–1978 (R1989)

Woodruff Keys and Keyseats, ANSI B17.2–1967 (R1990)

Piping

Bronze Pipe Flanges and Flanged Fittings, Class 150 and 300, ANSI B16.24–1979

Cast Bronze Threaded Fittings, Class 125 and 250, ANSI/ASME B16.15–1985

Cast Iron Pipe Flanged and Flanged Fittings, Class 25, 125, 250 and 800, ANSI/ASME B16.1–1989

Cast Iron Threaded Fittings, Class 125 and 250, ANSI/ASME B16.4–1985

Ductile Iron Pipe, Centrifugally Cast, in Metal Molds or Sand-Lined Molds for Water or Other Liquids, ANSI/AWWA C151/A21.51–1986

Factory-Made Wrought Steel Buttwelding Fittings, ANSI/ASME B16.9–1986

Ferrous Pipe Plugs, Bushings, and Locknuts with Pipe Threads, ANSI B16.14–1991

Flanged Ductile-Iron and Gray Iron Pipe with Threaded Flanges, ANSI/AWWA C115/A21.15–88

Malleable-Iron Threaded Fittings, Class 150 and 300, ANSI/ASME B16.3–1985

Pipe Flanges and Flanged Fittings, Steel Nickel Alloy and Other Special Alloys, ANSI/ASME B16.5–1988

Stainless Steel Pipe, ANSI/ASME B36.19M–1985

Welded and Seamless Wrought Steel Pipe, ANSI/ASME B36.10M–1985

Rivets

Large Rivets ($\frac{1}{2}$ Inch Nominal Diameter and Larger) ANSI B18.1.2–1972 (R1989)

Small Solid Rivets ($\frac{7}{16}$ Inch Nominal Diameter and

Smaller) ANSI B18.1.1–1972 (R1989)
Small Solid Rivets, Metric, ANSI/ASME B18.1.3M–1983 (R1989)

Small Tools and Machine Tool Elements

Jig Bushings, ANSI B94.33–1974 (R1986)
Machine Tapers, ANSI B5.10–1981 (R1987)
Milling Cutters and End Mills, ANSI/ASME B94.19–1985
Reamers, ANSI B94.2–1983 (R1988)
T-Slots—Their Bolts, Nuts and Tongues, ANSI/ASME B5.1M–1985
Twist Drills, Straight Shank and Taper Shank Combined Drills and Countersinks, ANSI B94.11M–1979 (R1987)

Threads

Acme Screw Threads, ANSI/ASME B1.5–1988
Buttress Inch Screw Threads, ANSI B1.9–1973 (R1985)
Class 5 Interference-Fit Thread, ANSI/ASME B1.12–1987
Dryseal Pipe Threads (Inch), ANSI B1.20.3–1976 (R1982)
Dryseal Pipe Threads (Metric), ANSI B1.20.4–1976 (R1982)
Hose Coupling Screw Threads, ANSI/ASME B1.20.7–1966 (R1983)
Metric Screw Threads for Commercial Mechanical Fasteners—Boundary Profile Defined, ANSI B1.18M–1982 (R1987)
Metric Screw Threads—M Profile, ANSI/ASME B1.13M–1983 (R1989)
Metric Screw Threads—MJ Profile, ANSI B1.21M–1978
Nomenclature, Definitions and Letter Symbols for Screw Threads, ANSI/ASME B1.7M–1984
Pipe Threads, General Purpose (Inch), ANSI/ASME B1.20.1–1983
Stub Acme Threads, ANSI/ASME B1.8–1988
Unified Screw Threads (UN and UNR Thread Form), ANSI/ASME B1.1–1989
Unified Miniature Screw Threads, ANSI B1.10–1958 (R1988)

Washers

Lock Washers, ANSI/ASME B18.21.1–1990
Lock Washers, Metric, ANSI/ASME B18.21.2M–1990
Plain Washers, ANSI B18.22.1–1965 (R1981)
Plain Washers, Metric, ANSI B18.22M–1981

Miscellaneous

Knurling, ANSI/ASME B94.6–1984
Preferred Metric Sizes for Flat Metal Products, ANSI/ASME B32.3M–1984
Preferred Metric Equivalents of Inch Sizes for Tubular Metal Products Other Than Pipe, ANSI/ASME B32.6M–1984
Preferred Metric Sizes for Tubular Metal Products Other Than Pipe, ANSI B32.5–1977 (R1988)
Preferred Thickness for Uncoated Thin Flat Metals (Under 0.250 in.), ANSI B32.1–1952 (R1988)
Preferred Thickness for Uncoated Thin Flat Metals (Under 0.250 in.), ANSI B32.1–1952 (R1983)
Surface Texture (Surface Roughness, Waviness and Lay), ANSI/ASME B46.1–1985

2   Technical Terms

"The beginning of wisdom is to call things by their right names."
—CHINESE PROVERB

n *means a* noun; v *means a* verb

acme (*n*)   Screw thread form, §§15.3 and 15.13
addendum (*n*)   Radial distance from pitch circle to top of gear tooth.
allen screw (*n*)   Special set screw or cap screw with hexagon socket in head, §15.31.
allowance (*n*)   Minimum clearance between mating parts, §14.1.
alloy (*n*)   Two or more metals in combination, usually a fine metal with a baser metal.
aluminum (*n*)   A lightweight but relatively strong metal. Often alloyed with copper to increase hardness and strength.
angle iron (*n*)   A structural shape whose section is a right angle, §12.20.
anneal (*v*)   To heat and cool gradually, to reduce brittleness and increase ductility, §12.22.
arc-weld (*v*)   To weld by electric arc. The work is usually the positive terminal.

babbitt (*n*)   A soft alloy for bearings, mostly of tin with small amounts of copper and antimony.
bearing (*n*)   A supporting member for a rotating shaft.
bevel (*n*)   An inclined edge, not at right angle to joining surface.
bolt circle (*n*)   A circular center line on a drawing, containing the centers of holes about a common center, §13.25.
bore (*v*)   To enlarge a hole with a boring mill, Figs. 12.16 (b).
boss (*n*)   A cylindrical projection on a casting or a forging.

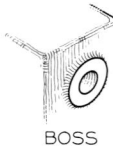

BOSS

brass (*n*)   An alloy of copper and zinc.

braze (*v*) To join with hard solder of brass or zinc.

Brinell (*n*) A method of testing hardness of metal.

broach (*n*) A long cutting tool with a series of teeth that gradually increase in size which is forced through a hole or over a surface to produce a desired shape, §12.15.

bronze (*n*) An alloy of eight or nine parts of copper and one part of tin.

buff (*v*) To finish or polish on a buffing wheel composed of fabric with abrasive powders.

burnish (*v*) To finish or polish by pressure upon a smooth rolling or sliding tool.

burr (*n*) A jagged edge on metal resulting from punching or cutting.

bushing (*n*) A replaceable lining or sleeve for a bearing.

calipers (*n*) Instrument (of several types) for measuring diameters, §12.17.

cam (*n*) A rotating member for changing circular motion to reciprocating motion.

carburize (*v*) To heat a low-carbon steel to approximately 2000°F in contact with material which adds carbon to the surface of the steel, and to cool slowly in preparation for heat treatment, §12.22.

caseharden (*v*) To harden the outer surface of a carburized steel by heating and then quenching.

castellate (*v*) To form like a castle, as a castellated shaft or nut.

casting (*n*) A metal object produced by pouring molten metal into a mold.

cast iron (*n*) Iron melted and poured into molds.

center drill (*n*) A special drill to produce bearing holes in the ends of a workpiece to be mounted between centers. Also called a "combined drill and countersink," §13.35.

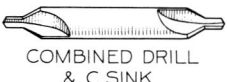

COMBINED DRILL
& C SINK

chamfer (*n*) A narrow inclined surface along the intersection of two surfaces.

CHAMFER

chase (*v*) To cut threads with an external cutting tool.

cheek (*n*) The middle portion of a three-piece flask used in molding.

chill (*v*) To harden the outer surface of cast iron by quick cooling, as in a metal mold.

chip (*v*) to cut away metal with a cold chisel.

chuck (*n*) A mechanism for holding a rotating tool or workpiece.

coin (*v*) To form a part in one stamping operation.

cold-rolled steel (CRS) (*n*) Open hearth or Bessemer steel containing 0.12–0.20% carbon that has been rolled while cold to produce a smooth, quite accurate stock.

collar (*n*) A round flange or ring fitted on a shaft to prevent sliding.

COLLAR

colorharden (*v*) Same as *caseharden*, except that it is done to a shallower depth, usually for appearance only.

cope (*n*) The upper portion of a flash used in molding.

core (*v*) To form a hollow portion in a casting by using a dry-sand core or a green-sand core in a mold.

coreprint (*n*) A projection on a pattern which forms an opening in the sand to hold the end of a core.

cotter pin (*n*) A split pin used as a fastener, usually to prevent a nut from unscrewing, Fig. 15.31 (e), (g), and (h) and Appendix 30.

counterbore (*v*) To enlarge an end of a hole cylindrically with a *counterbore*. §12.16.

COUNTERBORE

countersink (*v*) To enlarge an end of a hole conically, usually with a *countersink*, §12.16.

COUNTERSINK

crown (*n*) A raised contour, as on the surface of a pulley.

cyanide (*v*) To surface-harden steel by heating in contact with a cyanide salt, followed by quenching.

dedendum (*n*) Distance from pitch circle to bottom of tooth space.

development (*n*) Drawing of the surface of an object unfolded or rolled out on a plane.

diametral pitch (*n*) Number of gear teeth per inch of pitch diameter.

die (*n*) (1) Hardened metal piece shaped to cut or form a required shape in a sheet of metal by pressing it against a mating die. (2) Also used for cutting small male threads. In a sense is opposite to a tap.

die casting (*n*) Process of forcing molten metal under pressure into metal dies or molds, producing a very accurate and smooth casting.

die stamping (*n*) Process of cutting or forming a piece of sheet metal with a die.

dog (*n*) A small auxiliary clamp for preventing work from rotating in relation to the face plate of a lathe.

dowel (*n*) A cylindrical pin, commonly used to prevent sliding between two contacting flat surfaces.

DOWEL

draft (*n*)   The tapered shape of the parts of a pattern to permit it to be easily withdrawn from the sand or, on a forging, to permit it to be easily withdrawn from the dies, §12.21.

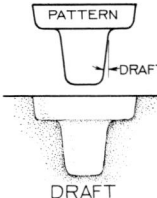

PATTERN
DRAFT
DRAFT

drag (*n*)   Lower portion of a flask used in molding.

draw (*v*)   To stretch or otherwise to deform metal. Also to temper steel.

drill (*v*)   To cut a cylindrical hole with a drill. A *blind hole* does not go through the piece, §12.16.

drill press (*n*)   A machine for drilling and other hole-forming operations, §12.8.

drop forge (*v*)   To form a piece while hot between dies in a drop hammer or with great pressure, §12.21.

face (*v*)   To finish a surface at right angles, or nearly so, to the center line of rotation on a lathe.

FAO   Finish all over, §13.17.

feather key (*n*)   A flat key, which is partly sunk in a shaft and partly in a hub, permitting the hub to slide lengthwise of the shaft, §15.34.

file (*v*)   To finish or smooth with a file.

fillet (*n*)   An interior rounded intersection between two surfaces, §§7.34 and 12.5.

fin (*n*)   A thin extrusion of metal at the intersection of dies or sand molds.

fit (*n*)   Degree of tightness or looseness between two mating parts, as a *loose fit*, a *snug fit*, or a *tight fit*. §§13.9 and 14.1–14.3.

fixture (*n*)   A special device for holding the work in a machine tool, *but not for guiding the cutting tool.*

flange (*n*)   A relatively thin rim around a piece.

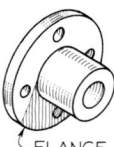

FLANGE

flash (*n*)   Same as *fin.*

flask (*n*)   A box made of two or more parts for holding the sand in sand molding.

flute (*n*)   Groove, as on twist drills, reamers, and taps.

forge (*v*)   To force metal while it is hot to take on a desired shape by hammering or pressing, §12.21.

galvanize (*v*)   To cover a surface with a thin layer of molten alloy, composed mainly of zinc, to prevent rusting.

gasket (*n*)   A thin piece of rubber, metal, or some other material, placed between surfaces to make a tight joint.

gate (*n*)   The opening in a sand mold at the bottom of the *sprue* through which the molten metal passes to enter the cavity or mold.

graduate (*v*)   To set off accurate divisions on a scale or dial.

grind (*v*)   To remove metal by means of an abrasive wheel, often made of carborundum. Use chiefly where accuracy is required, §12.14.

harden (*v*)   To heat steel above a critical temperature and then quench in water or oil, §12.22.

heat-treat (*v*)   To change the properties of metals by heating and then cooling, §12.22.

interchangeable (*adj.*)   Refers to a part made to limit dimensions so that it will fit any mating part similarly manufactured, §14.1.

jig (*n*)   A device *for guiding a tool* in cutting a piece. Usually it holds the work in position.

journal (*n*)   Portion of a rotating shaft supported by a bearing.

kerf (*n*)   Groove or cut made by a saw.

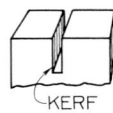

KERF

key (*n*)   A small piece of metal sunk partly into both shaft and hub to prevent rotation, §15.34.

keyseat (*n*)   A slot or recess in a shaft to hold a key, §15.34.

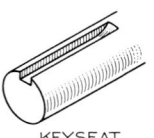

KEYSEAT

keyway (*n*)   A slot in a hub or portion surrounding a shaft to receive a key. §15.34.

KEYWAY

knurl (*v*)   To impress a pattern of dents in a turned surface with a knurling tool to produce a better hand grip, §13.37.

lap (*v*)   To produce a very accurate finish by sliding contact with a *lap*, or piece of wood, leather, or soft metal impregnated with abrasive powder.

lathe (*n*)   A machine used to shape metal or other materials by rotating against a tool, §12.7.

lug (*n*)   An irregular projection of metal, but not round as in the case of a *boss*, usually with a hole in it for a bolt or screw.

malleable casting (*n*)   A casting that has been made less brittle and tougher by annealing.

mill (*v*)   To remove material by means of a rotating cutter on a milling machine, §12.9.

mold (*n*)   The mass of sand or other material that forms the cavity into which molten metal is poured.

MS (*n*)   Machinery steel, sometimes called *mild steel* with a small percentage of carbon. Cannot be hardened.

neck (*v*)   To cut a groove called a *neck* around a cylindrical piece.

NECK

normalize (*v*)   To heat steel above its critical temperature and then to cool it in air, §12.22.

pack-harden (*v*)   To *carburize*, then to *case-harden*. §12.22.

pad (*n*)   A slight projection, usually to provide a bearing surface around one or more holes.

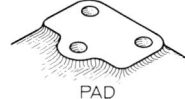

PAD

pattern (*n*)   A model, usually of wood, used in forming a mold for a casting. In sheet metal work a pattern is called a *development*.

peen (*v*)   To hammer into shape with a ballpeen hammer.

pickle (*v*)   To clean forgings or castings in dilute sulfuric acid.

pinion (*n*)   The smaller of two mating gears.

pitch circle (*n*)   An imaginary circle corresponding to the circumference of the friction gear from which the spur gear was derived.

plane (*v*)   To remove material by means of the *planer*, §12.11.

planish (*v*)   To impart a planished surface to sheet metal by hammering with a smooth-surfaced hammer.

plate (*v*)   To coat a metal piece with another metal, such as chrome or nickel, by electrochemical methods.

polish (*v*)   To produce a highly finished or polished surface by friction, using a very fine abrasive.

profile (*v*)   To cut any desired outline by moving a small rotating cutter, usually with a master template as a guide.

punch (*v*)   To cut an opening of a desired shape with a rigid tool having the same shape, by pressing the tool through the work.

quench (*v*)   To immerse a heated piece of metal in water or oil in order to harden it.

rack (*n*)   A flat bar with gear teeth in a straight line to engage with teeth in a gear.

ream (*v*)   To enlarge a finished hole slightly to give it greater accuracy, with a *reamer*, §12.16.

relief (*n*)   An offset of surfaces to provide clearance for machining.

RELIEF

rib (*n*)   A relatively thin flat member acting as a brace or support.

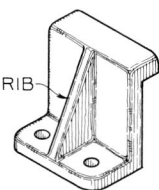

RIB

rivet (*v*)   To connect with rivets or to clench over the end of a pin by hammering, §15.36.

round (*n*)   An exterior rounded intersection of two surfaces, §§7.34 and 12.5.

SAE   Society of Automotive Engineers.

sandblast (*v*)   To blow sand at high velocity with compressed air against castings or forgings to clean them.

scleroscope (*n*)   An instrument for measuring hardness of metals.

scrape (*v*)   To remove metal by scraping with a hand scraper, usually to fit a bearing.

shape (*v*)   To remove metal from a piece with a *shaper*, §12.10.

shear (*v*)   To cut metal by means of shearing with two blades in sliding contact.

sherardize (*v*)   To galvanize a piece with a coating of zinc by heating it in a drum with zinc powder, to a temperature of 575–850 °F.

shim (*n*)   A thin piece of metal or other material used as a spacer in adjusting two parts.

solder (*v*)   To join with solder, usually composed of lead and tin.

spin (*v*)   To form a rotating piece of sheet metal into a desired shape by pressing it with a smooth tool against a rotating form.

spline (*n*)   A keyway, usually one of a series cut around a shaft or hole.

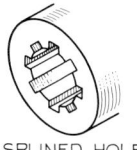

SPLINED HOLE

spotface (*v*)   To produce a round *spot* or bearing surface around a hole, usually with a *spotfacer*. The spotface may be on top of a boss or it may be sunk into the surface, §§7.33 and 12.16.

SPOTFACE

sprue (*n*)   A hole in the sand leading to the *gate* which leads to the mold, through which the metal enters.

steel casting (*n*)   Like cast-iron casting except that in the furnace scrap steel has been added to the casting.

swage (*v*) To hammer metal into shape while it is held over a *swage*, or die, which fits in a hole in the *swage block*, or anvil.

sweat (*v*) To fasten metal together by the use of solder between the pieces and by the application of heat and pressure.

tap (*v*) To cut relatively small internal threads with a *tap*. §12.16.

taper (*n*) Conical form given to a shaft or a hole. Also refers to the slope of a plane surface, §13.33.

taper pin (*n*) A small tapered pin for fastening, usually to prevent a collar or hub from rotating on a shaft.

TAPER PIN

taper reamer (*n*) A tapered reamer for producing accurate tapered holes, as for a taper pin. §§13.33 and 15.35.

temper (*v*) To reheat hardened steel to bring it to a desired degree of hardness, §12.22.

template or **templet** (*n*) A guide or pattern used to mark out the work, guide the tool in cutting it, or check the finished product.

tin (*n*) A silvery metal used in alloys and for coating other metals, such as tin plate.

tolerance (*n*) Total amount of variation permitted in limit dimension of a part, §14.2.

trepan (*v*) To cut a circular groove in the flat surface at one end of a hole.

tumble (*v*) To clean rough castings or forgings in a revolving drum filled with scrap metal.

turn (*v*) To produce, on a lathe, a cylindrical surface parallel to the center line, §12.7.

twist drill (*n*) A drill for use in a drill press, §12.16.

undercut (*n*) A recessed cut or a cut with inwardly sloping sides.

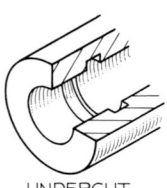
UNDERCUT

upset (*v*) To form a head or enlarged end on a bar or rod by pressure or by hammering between dies.

web (*n*) A thin flat part joining larger parts. Also known as a *rib*.

weld (*v*) Uniting metal pieces by pressure or fusion welding processes, §12.19.

Woodruff key (*n*) A semicircular flat key, §15.34.

WOODRUFF KEYS

wrought iron (*n*) Iron of low carbon content useful because of its toughness, ductility, and malleability.

3 CAD/CAM Glossary*

access time (or disk access time) One measure of system response. The time interval between the instant that data is called for from storage and the instant that delivery is completed—i.e., read time. See also *response time*.

alphanumeric (or alphameric) A term that encompasses letters, digits, and special characters that are machine-processable.

alphanumeric display (or alphameric display) A work-station device consisting of a CRT on which text can be viewed. An alphanumeric display is capable of showing a fixed set of letters, digits, and special characters. It allows the designer to observe entered commands and to receive messages from the system.

alphanumeric keyboard (or alphameric keyboard) A work-station device consisting of a typewriter-like keyboard that allows the designer to communicate with the system using an English-like command language.

*Extracted from *The CAD/CAM Glossary*, 1983 edition, published by the Computervision Corporation, Bedford, MA 01730; reproduced with permission of the publisher.

American Standard Code for Information Interchange (ASCII) An industry-standard character code widely used for information interchange among data processing systems, communications systems, and associated equipment.

analog Applied to an electrical or computer system, this denotes the capability to represent data in continuously varying physical quantities.

annotation Process of inserting text or a special note or identification (such as a flag) on a drawing, map, or diagram constructed on a CAD/CAM system. The text can be generated and positioned on the drawing using the system.

application program (or package) A computer program or collection of programs to perform a task or tasks specific to a particular user's need or class of needs.

archival storage Refers to memory (on magnetic tape, disks, printouts, or drums) used to store data on completed designs or elements outside of main memory.

array (*v*) To create automatically on a CAD system an arrangement of identical elements or components. The designer defines the element once, then indicates the starting location and spacing for automatic generation of the array. (*n*) An arrangement created in the above manner. A series of elements or sets of elements arranged in a pattern—i.e., matrix.

ASCII See *American National Standard Code for Information Exchange.*

assembler A computer program that converts (i.e., translates) programmer-written symbolic instructions, usually in mnemonic form, into machine-executable (computer or binary-coded) instructions. This conversion is typically one-to-one (one symbolic instruction converts to one machine-executable instruction). A software programming aid.

associative dimensioning A CAD capabililty that links dimension entities to geometric entities being dimensioned. This allows the value of a dimension to be automatically updated as the geometry changes.

attribute A nongraphic characteristic of a part, component, or entity under design on a CAD system. Examples include: dimension entities associated with geometry, text with text nodes, and nodal lines with connect nodes. Changing one entity in an association can produce automatic changes by the system in the associated entity; e.g., moving one entity can cause moving or stretching of the other entity.

automatic dimensioning A CAD capability that computes the dimensions in a displayed design, or in a designated section, and automatically places dimensions, dimensional lines, and arrowheads where required. In the case of mapping, this capability labels the linear feature with length and azimuth.

auxiliary storage Storage that supplements main memory devices such as disk or drum storage. Contrast with *archival storage.*

benchmark The program(s) used to test, compare, and evaluate in real time the performance of various CAD/CAM systems prior to selection and purchase. A *synthetic* benchmark has preestablished parameters designed to exercise a set of system features and resources. A *live* benchmark is drawn from the prospective user's workload as a model of the entire workload.

bit The smallest unit of information that can be stored and processed by a digital computer. A bit may assume only one of two values: 0 or 1 (i.e., ON/OFF or YES/NO). Bits are organized into larger units called *words* for access by computer instructions.

Computers are often categorized by word size in bits, i.e., the maximum word size that can be processed as a unit during an instruction cycle (e.g., 16-bit computers or 32-bit computers). The number of bits in a word is an indication of the processing power of the system, especially for calculations or for high-precision data.

bit rate The speed at which bits are transmitted, usually expressed in bits per second.

bits per inch (bpi) The number of bits that can be stored per inch of a magnetic tape. A measure of the data storage capacity of a magnetic tape.

blank A CAD command that causes a predefined entity to go temporarily blank on the CRT. The reversing command is *unblank.*

blinking A CAD design aid that makes a predefined graphic entity blink on the CRT to attract the attention of the designer.

boot up Start up (a system).

B-spline A sequence of parametric polynomial curves (typically quadratic or cubic polynomials) forming a smooth fit between a sequence of points in 3D space. The piece-wise defined curve maintains a level of mathematical continuity dependent upon the polynomial degree chosen. It is used extensively in mechanical design applications in the automotive and aerospace industries.

bug A flaw in the design or implementation of a software program or hardware design that causes erroneous results or malfunctions.

bulk memory A memory device for storing a large amount of data, e.g., disk, drum, or magnetic tape. It is not randomly accessible as main memory is.

byte A sequence of adjacent bits, usually eight, representing a character that is operated on as a unit. Usually shorter than a word. A measure of the memory capacity of a system, or of an individual storage unit (as a 300-million-byte disk).

CAD See *computer-aided design.*

CAD/CAM See *computer-aided design/computer-aided manufacturing.*

CADDS® Computervision Corporation's registered trademark for its prerecorded software programs.

CAE See *computer-aided engineering.*

CAM See *computer-aided manufacturing.*

CAMACS™ (CAM Asynchronous Communications Software) Computervision's communications link, which enables users to exchange machine control data with other automation systems and devices, or to interact directly with local or remote manufacturing systems and machines. CAMACS tailors CAD/CAM data automatically for a wide range of machine tools, robots, coordinate measurement systems, and off-line storage devices.

cathode ray tube (CRT) The principal component in a CAD display device. A CRT displays graphic representations of geometric entities and designs and can be of various types: storage tube, raster scan, or refresh. These tubes create images by means of a controllable beam of electrons striking a screen. The term *CRT* is often used to denote the entire display device.

central processing unit (CPU) The computer brain of a CAD/CAM system that controls the retrieval, decoding, and processing of information, as well as the interpretation and execution of operating instructions—the building blocks of application and other computer programs. A CPU comprises arithmetic, control, and logic elements.

character   An alphabetical, numerical, or special graphic symbol used as part of the organization, control, or representation of CAD/CAM data.

characters per second (cps)   A measure of the speed with which an alphanumeric terminal can process data.

chip   See *integrated circuit*.

code   A set of specific symbols and rules for representing data (usually instructions) so that the data can be understood and executed by a computer. A code can be in binary (machine) language, assembly language, or a high-level language. Frequently refers to an industry-standard code such as ANSI, ASCII, IPC, or Standard Code for Information Exchange. Many application codes for CAD/CAM are written in FORTRAN.

color display   A CAD/CAM display device. Color raster-scan displays offer a variety of user-selectable, contrasting colors to make it easier to discriminate among various groups of design elements on different layers of a large, complex design. Color speeds up the recognition of specific areas and subassemblies, helps the designer interpret complex surfaces, and highlights interference problems. Color displays can be of the penetration type, in which various phosphor layers give off different colors (refresh display) or the TV-type with red, blue, and green electron guns (raster-scan display).

command   A control signal or instruction to a CPU or graphics processor, commonly initiated by means of a menu/tablet and electronic pen or by an alphanumeric keyboard.

command language   A language for communicating with a CAD/CAM system in order to perform specific functions or tasks.

communication link   The physical means, such as a telephone line, for connecting one system module or peripheral to another in a different location in order to transmit and receive data. See also *data link*.

compatibility   The ability of a particular hardware module or software program, code, or language to be used in a CAD/CAM system without prior modification or special interfaces. *Upward compatible* denotes the ability of a system to interface with new hardware or software modules or enhancements (i.e., the system vendor provides with each new module a reasonable means of transferring data, programs, and operator skills from the user's present system to the new enhancements).

compiler   A computer program that converts or translates a high-level, user-written language (e.g., PASCAL, COBOL, VARPRO, or FORTRAN) or source, into a language that a computer can understand. The conversion is typically one to many (i.e., one user instruction to many machine-executable instructions). A software programming aid, the compiler allows the designer to write programs in an English-like language with relatively few statements, thus saving program development time.

component   A physical entity, or a symbol used in CAD to denote such an entity. Depending on the application, a component might refer to an IC or part of a wiring circuit (e.g., a resistor), or a valve, elbow, or vee in a plant layout, or a substation or cable in a utility map. Also applies to a subassembly or part that goes into higher level assemblies.

computer-aided design (CAD)   A process that uses a computer system to assist in the creation, modification, and display of a design.

computer-aided design/computer-aided manufacturing (CAD/CAM)   Refers to the integration of computers into the entire design-to-fabrication cycle of a product or plant.

computer-aided engineering (CAE)   Analysis of a design for basic error checking, or to optimize manufacturability, performance, and economy (for example, by comparing various possible materials or designs). Information drawn from the CAD/CAM design data base is used to analyze the functional characteristics of a part, product, or system under design and to simulate its performance under various conditions. In electronic design, CAE enables users of the Computervision Designer system to detect and correct potentially costly design flaws. CAE permits the execution of complex circuit loading analyses and simulation during the circuit definition stage. CAE can be used to determine section properties, moments of inertia, shear and bending moments, weight, volume, surface area, and center of gravity. CAE can precisely determine loads, vibration, noise, and service life early in the design cycle so that components can be optimized to meet those criteria. Perhaps the most powerful CAE technique is finite element modeling. See also *kinematics*.

computer-aided manufacturing (CAM)   The use of computer and digital technology to generate manufacturing-oriented data. Data drawn from a CAD/CAM data base can assist in or control a portion or all of a manufacturing process, including numerically controlled machines, computer-assisted parts programming, computer-assisted process planning, robotics, and programmable logic controllers, CAM can involve production programming, manufacturing engineering, industrial engineering, facilities engineering, and reliability engineering (quality control). CAM techniques can be used to produce process plans for fabricating a complete assembly, to program robots, and to coordinate plant operation.

computer graphics   A general term encompassing any discipline or activity that uses computers to generate, process and display graphic images. The essential technology of CAD/CAM systems. See also *computer-aided design*.

computer network   An interconnected complex (arrangement, or configuration) of two or more systems. See also *network*.

computer program   A specific set of software commands

in a form acceptable to a computer and used to achieve a desired result. Often called a *software program* or *package*.

configuration A particular combination of a computer, software and hardware modules, and peripherals at a single installation and interconnected in such a way as to support certain application(s).

connector A termination point for a signal entering or leaving a PC board or a cabling system.

convention Standardized methodology or accepted procedure for executing a computer program. In CAD, the term denotes a standard rule or mode of execution undertaken to provide consistency. For example, a drafting convention might require all dimensions to be in metric units.

core (core memory) A largely obsolete term for *main storage*.

CPU See *central processing unit*.

CRT See *cathode ray tube*.

cursor A visual tracking symbol, usually an underline or cross hairs, for indicating a location or entity selection on the CRT display. A text cursor indicates the alphanumeric input; a graphics cursor indicates the next geometric input. A cursor is guided by an electronic or light pen, joystick, keyboard, etc., and follows every movement of the input device.

cycle A preset sequence of events (hardware or software) initiated by a single command.

data base A comprehensive collection of interrelated information stored on some kind of mass data storage device, usually a disk. Generally consists of information organized into a number of fixed-format record types with logical links between associated records. Typically includes operating systems instructions, standard parts libraries, completed designs and documentation, source code, graphic and application programs, as well as current user tasks in progress.

data communication The transmission of data (usually digital) from one point (such as a CAD/CAM workstation or CPU) to another point via communication channels such as telephone lines.

data link The communication line(s), related controls, and interface(s) for the transmission of data between two or more computer systems. Can include modems, telephone lines, or dedicated transmission media such as cable or optical fiber.

data tablet A CAD/CAM input device that allows the designer to communicate with the system by placing an electronic pen or stylus on the tablet surface. There is a direct correspondence between positions on the tablet and addressable points on the display surface of the CRT. Typically used for indicating positions on the CRT, for digitizing input of drawings, or for menu selection. See also *graphic tablet*.

debug To detect, locate, and correct any bugs in a system's software or hardware.

dedicated Designed or intended for a single function or use. For example, a dedicated work station might be used exclusively for engineering calculations or plotting.

default The predetermined value of a parameter required in a CAD/CAM task or operation. It is automatically supplied by the system whenever that value (e.g., text, height, or grid size) is not specified.

density (1) A measure of the complexity of an electronic design. For example, IC density can be measured by the number of gates or transistors per unit area or by the number of square inches per component. (2) Magnetic tape storage capacity. High capacity might be 1600 bits/inch; low, 800 bits/inch.

device A system hardware module external to the CPU and designed to perform a specific function—i.e., a CRT, plotter, printer, hard-copy unit, etc. See also *peripheral*.

diagnostics Computer programs designed to test the status of a system or its key components and to detect and isolate malfunctions.

dial up To initiate station-to-station communication with a computer via a dial telephone, usually from a workstation to a computer.

digital Applied to an electrical or computer system, this denotes the capability to represent data in the form of digits.

digitize (1) General description: to convert a drawing into digital form (i.e., coordinate locations) so that it can be entered into the data base for later processing. A digitizer, available with many CAD systems, implements the conversion process. This is one of the primary ways of entering existing drawings, crude graphics, lines, and shapes into the system. (2) Computervision usage: to specify a coordinate location or entity using an electronic pen or other device; or a single coordinate value or entity pointer generated by a digitizing operation.

digitizer A CAD input device consisting of a data tablet on which is mounted the drawing or design to be digitized into the system. The designer moves a puck or electronic pen to selected points on the drawing and enters coordinate data for lines and shapes by simply pressing down the digitize button with the puck or pen.

dimensioning, automatic A CAD capability that will automatically compute and insert the dimensions of a design or drawing, or a designated section of it.

direct access (linkage) Retrieval or storage of data in the system by reference to its location on a tape, disk, or cartridge, without the need for processing on a CPU.

direct-view storage tube (DVST) One of the most widely used graphics display devices, DVST generates a long-lasting, flicker-tree image with high resolution and no refreshing. It handles an almost unlimited amount of data. However, display dynamics are limited since DVSTs do not permit selective erase. The image is not as bright as with refresh or raster. Also called *storage tube*.

directory   A named space on the disk or other mass storage device in which are stored the names of files and some summary information about them.

discrete components   Components with a single functional capability per package—for example, transistors and diodes.

disk (storage)   A device on which large amounts of information can be stored in the data base. Synonymous with *magnetic disk storage* or *magnetic disk memory*.

display   A CAD/CAM work station device for rapidly presenting a graphic image so that the designer can react to it, making changes interactively in real time. Usually refers to a CRT.

dot-matrix plotter   A CAD peripheral device for generating graphic plots. Consists of a combination of wire nibs (styli) spaced 100 to 200 styli per inch, which place dots where needed to generate a drawing. Because of its high speed, it is typically used in electronic design applications. Accuracy and resolution are not as great as with pen plotters. Also known as *electrostatic plotter*.

drum plotter   An electromechanical pen plotter that draws an image on paper or film mounted on a rotatable drum. In this CAD peripheral device a combination of plotting-head movement and drum rotation provides the motion.

dynamic (motion)   Simulation of movement using CAD software, so that the designer can see on the CRT screen 3D representations of the parts in a piece of machinery as they interact dynamically. Thus, any collision or interference problems are revealed at a glance.

dynamic menuing   This feature of Computervision's Instaview terminal allows a particular function or command to be initiated by touching an electronic pen to the appropriate key word displayed in the status text area on the screen.

dynamics   The capability of a CAD system to zoom, scroll, and rotate.

edit   To modify, refine, or update an emerging design or text on a CAD system. This can be done on-line interactively.

electrostatic plotter   See *dot-matrix plotter*.

element   The basic design entity in computer-aided design whose logical, positional, electrical, or mechanical function is identifiable.

enhancements   Software or hardware improvements, additions, or updates to a CAD/CAM system.

entity   A geometric primitive—the fundamental building block used in constructing a design or drawing, such as an arc, circle, line, text, point, spline, figure, or nodal line. Or a group of primitives processed as an identifiable unit. Thus, a square may be defined as a discrete entity consisting of four primitives (vectors), although each side of the square could be defined as an entity in its own right. See also *primitive*.

feedback   (1) The ability of a system to respond to an operator command in real time either visually or with a message on the alphanumeric display or CRT. This message registers the command, indicates any possible errors, and simultaneously displays the updated design on the CRT. (2) The signal or data fed back to a commanding unit from a controlled machine or process to denote its response to a command. (3) The signal representing the difference between actual response and desired response and used by the commanding unit to improve performance of the controlled machine or process. See also *prompt*.

figure   A symbol or a part that may contain primitive entities, other figures, nongraphic properties, and associations. A figure can be incorporated into other parts or figures.

file   A collection of related information in the system that may be accessed by a unique name. May be stored on a disk, tape, or other mass storage media.

file protection   A technique for preventing access to or accidental erasure of data within a file on the system.

firmware   Computer programs, instructions, or functions implemented in user-modifiable hardware, i.e., a microprocessor with read-only memory. Such programs or instructions, stored permanently in programmable read-only memories, constitute a fundamental part of system hardware. The advantage is that a frequently used program or routine can be invoked by a single command instead of multiple commands as in a software program.

flatbed plotter   A CAD/CAM peripheral device that draws an image on paper, glass, or film mounted on a flat table. The plotting head provides all the motion.

flat-pattern generation   A CAD/CAM capability for automatically unfolding a 3D design of a sheet metal part into its corresponding flat-pattern design. Calculations for material bending and stretching are performed automatically for any specified material. The reverse flat-pattern generation package automatically folds a flat-pattern design into its 3D version. Flat-pattern generation eliminates major bottlenecks for sheet metal fabricators.

flicker   An undesired visual effect on a CRT when the refresh rate is low.

font, line   Repetitive pattern used in CAD to give a displayed line appearance characteristics that make it more easily distinguishable, such as a solid, dashed, or dotted line. A line font can be applied to graphic images in order to provide meaning, either graphic (e.g., hidden lines) or functional (roads, tracks, wires, pipes, etc.). It can help a designer to identify and define specific graphic representations of entities that are view-dependent. For example, a line may be solid when drawn in the top view of an object but, when a line font is used, becomes dotted in the side view where it is not normally visible.

font, text   Sets of type faces of various styles and sizes.

In CAD, fonts are used to create text for drawings, special characters such as Greek letters, and mathematical symbols.

FORTRAN *FOR*mula *TRAN*slation, a high-level programming language used primarily for scientific or engineering applications.

fracturing The division of IC graphics by CAD into simple trapezoidal or rectangular areas for pattern-generation purposes.

function key A specific square on a data tablet, or a key on a function key box, used by the designer to enter a particular command or other input. See also *data tablet.*

function keyboard An input device located at a CAD/CAM workstation and containing a number of function keys.

gap The gap between two entities on a computer-aided design is the length of the shortest line segment that can be drawn from the boundary of one entity to the other without intersecting the boundary of the other. CAD/CAM design-rules checking programs can automatically perform gap checks.

graphic tablet A CAD/CAM input device that enables graphic and location instruments to be entered into the system using an electronic pen on the tablet. See also *data tablet.*

gray scales In CAD systems with a monochromatic display, variations in brightness level (gray scale) are employed to enhance the contrast among various design elements. This feature is very useful in helping the designer discriminate among complex entities on different layers displayed concurrently on the CRT.

grid A network of uniformly spaced points or crosshatch optionally displayed on the CRT and used for exactly locating and digitizing a position, inputting components to assist in the creation of a design layout, or constructing precise angles. For example, the coordinate data supplied by digitizers is automatically calculated by the CPU from the closest grid point. The grid determines the minimum accuracy with which design entities are described or connected. In the mapping environment, a grid is used to describe the distribution network of utility resources.

hard copy A copy on paper of an image displayed on the CRT—for example, a drawing, printed report, plot, listing, or summary. Most CAD/CAM systems can automatically generate hard copy through an on-line printer or plotter.

hardware The physical components, modules, and peripherals comprising a system—computer disk, magnetic tape, CRT terminal(s), plotter(s), etc.

hard-wired link A technique of physically connecting two systems by fixed circuit interconnections using digital signals.

high-level language A problem-oriented programming language using words, symbols, and command statements that closely resemble English-language statements. Each statement typically represents a series of computer instructions. Relatively easy to learn and use, a high-level language permits the execution of a number of subroutines through a simple command. Examples are BASIC, FORTRAN, PL/I, PASCAL, and COBOL.

A high-level language must be translated or compiled into machine language before it can be understood and processed by a computer. See also *assembler; low-level language.*

host computer The primary or controlling computer in a multicomputer network. Large-scale host computers typically are equipped with mass memory and a variety of peripheral devices, including magnetic tape, line printers, card readers, and possibly hard-copy devices. Host computers may be used to support, with their own memory and processing capabilities, not only graphics programs running on a CAD/CAM system but also related engineering analysis.

host-satellite system A CAD/CAM system configuration characterized by a graphic workstation with its own computer (typically holding the display file) that is connected to another, usually larger, computer for more extensive computation or data manipulation. The computer local to the display is a satellite to the larger host computer, and the two comprise a host-satellite system.

IC See *integrated circuit.*

IGES See *Initial Graphics Exchange Specification.*

inches per second (ips) Measure of the speed of a device (i.e., the number of inches of magnetic tape that can be processed per second, or the speed of a pen plotter).

Initial Graphics Exchange Specification (IGES) An interim CAD/CAM data base specification until the American National Standards Institute develops its own specification. IGES attempts to standardize communication of drawing and geometric product information between computer systems.

initialize To set counters, switches, and addresses on a computer to zero or to other starting values at the beginning of, or at predetermined stages in, a program or routine.

input (data) (1) The data supplied to a computer program for processing by the system. (2) The process of entering such data into the system.

input devices A variety of devices (such as data tablets or keyboard devices) that allow the user to communicate with the CAD/CAM system, for example, to pick a function from many presented, to enter text and/or numerical data, to modify the picture shown on the CRT, or to construct the desired design.

input/output (I/O) A term used to describe a CAD/CAM communications device as well as the process by which communications take place in a CAD/CAM system. An I/O device is one that makes possible communications between a device and a workstation operator or between devices on the system (such as workstations or controllers). By extension, input/output also denotes the process by which communications takes place. Input refers to the data transmitted to the processor for manipulation, and output refers to the data transmitted from the processor to the workstation operator or to another device (i.e., the results). Contrast with the other major parts of a CAD/CAM system: the CPU or central processing unit, which performs arithmetic and logical operations, and data storage devices (such as memories, disks, or tapes).

insert   To create and place entities, figures, or information on a CRT or into an emerging design on the display.

instruction set   *(1)* All the commands to which a CAD/CAM computer will respond. *(2)* The repertoire of functions the computer can perform.

integrated circuit (IC)   A tiny complex of electronic components and interconnections comprising a circuit that may vary in functional complexity from a simple logic gate to a microprocessor. An IC is usually packaged in a single substrate such as a slice of silicon. The complexity of most IC designs and the many repetitive elements have made computer-aided design an economic necessity. Also called a *chip*.

integrated system   A CAD/CAM system that integrates the entire product development cycle—analysis, design, and fabrication—so that all processes flow smoothly from concept to production.

intelligent work station/terminal   A workstation in a system that can perform certain data processing functions in a stand-alone mode, independent of another computer. Contains a built-in computer, usually a microprocessor or minicomputer, and dedicated memory.

interactive   Denotes two-way communications between a CAD/CAM system or workstation and its operators. An operator can modify or terminate a program and receive feedback from the system for guidance and verification. See also *feedback*.

interactive graphics system (IGS) or interactive computer graphics (ICG)   A CAD/CAM system in which the workstations are used interactively for computer-aided design and/or drafting, as well as for CAM, all under full operator control, and possibly also for text-processing, generation of charts and graphs, or computer-aided engineering. The designer (operator) can intervene to enter data and direct the course of any program, receiving immediate visual feedback via the CRT. Bilateral communication is provided between the system and the designer(s). Often used synonymously with *CAD*.

interface *(n)*   (1) A hardware and/or software link that enables two systems, or a system and its peripherals, to operate as a single, integrated system (2) The input devices and visual feedback capabilities that allow bilateral communication between the designer and the system. The interface to a large computer can be a communi-

cations link (hardware) or a combination of software and hard-wired connections. An interface might be a portion of storage accessed by two or more programs or a link between two subroutines in a program.

I/O   See *input/output*.

ips   See *inches per second*.

jaggies   A CAD jargon term used to refer to straight or curved lines that appear to be jagged or saw-toothed on the CRT screen.

joystick   A CAD data-entering device employing a hand-controlled lever to manually enter the coordinates of various points on a design being digitized into the system.

key file   A disk file that provides user-defined definitions for a tablet menu. See *menu*.

kinematics   A computer-aided engineering (CAE) process for plotting or animating the motion of parts in a machine or a structure under design on the system. CAE simulation programs allow the motion of mechanisms to be studied for interference, acceleration, and force determinations while still in the design stage.

layering   A method of logically organizing data in a CAD/CAM data base. Functionally different classes of data (e.g., various graphic/geometric entities) are segregated on separate layers, each of which can be displayed individually or in any desired combination. Layering helps the designer distinguish among different kinds of data in creating a complex product such as a multilayered PC board or IC.

layers   User-defined logical subdivisions of data in a CAD/CAM data base that may be viewed on the CRT individually or overlaid and viewed in groups.

learning curve   A concept that projects the expected improvement in operator productivity over a period of time. Usually applied in the first 1 to $1\frac{1}{2}$ years of a new CAD/CAM facility as part of a cost-justification study, or when new operators are introduced. An accepted tool of management for predicting manpower requirements and evaluating training programs.

library, graphics (or parts library)   A collection of standard, often-used symbols, components, shapes, or parts stored in the CAD data base as templates or building blocks to speed up future design work on the system. Generally an organization of files under a common library name.

light pen   A hand-held photosensitive CAD input device used on a refreshed CRT screen for identifying display elements, or for designating a location on the screen where an action is to take place.

line font   See *font, line*.

line printer   A CAD/CAM peripheral device used for rapid printing of data.

line smoothing   An automated mapping capability for the interpolation and insertion of additional points along a linear entity yielding a series of shorter linear segments to generate a smooth curved appearance to the original linear component. The additional points or segments are created only for display purposes and are interpolated from a relatively small set of stored representative points. Thus, data storage space is minimized.

low-level language A programming language in which statements translate on a one-for-one basis. See also *machine language.*

machine A computer, CPU, or other processor.

machine instruction An instruction that a machine (computer) can recognize and execute.

machine language The complete set of command instructions understandable to and used directly by a computer when it performs operations.

macro (1) A sequence of computer instructions executable as a single command. A frequently used, multistep operation can be organized into a macro, given a new name, and remain in the system for easy use, thus shortening program development time. (2) In Computervision's IC design system, macro refers to macroexpansion of a cell. This system capability enables the designer to replicate the contents of a cell as primitives without the original cell grouping.

magnetic disk A flat circular plate with a magnetic surface on which information can be stored by selective magnetization of portions of the flat surface. Commonly used for temporary working storage during computer-aided design. See also *disk.*

magnetic tape A tape with a magnetic surface on which information can be stored by selective polarization of portions of the surface. Commonly used in CAD/CAM for off-line storage of completed design files and other archival material.

mainframe (computer) A large central computer facility.

main memory/storage The computer's general-purpose storage from which instructions may be executed and data loaded directly into operating registers.

mass storage Auxiliary large-capacity memory for storing large amounts of data readily accessible by the computer. Commonly a disk or magnetic tape.

matrix A 2D or 3D rectangular array (arrangement) of identical geometric or symbolic entities. A matrix can be generated automatically on a CAD system by specifying the building block entity and the desired locations. This process is used extensively in computer-aided electrical/electronic design.

memory Any form of data storage where information can be read and written. Standard memories include RAM, ROM, and PROM. See also *programmable read-only memory; random access memory; read-only memory; storage.*

menu A common CAD/CAM input device consisting of a checkerboard pattern of squares printed on a sheet of paper or plastic placed over a data tablet. These squares have been preprogrammed to represent a part of a command, a command, or a series of commands. Each square, when touched by an electronic pen, initiates the particular function or command indicated on that square. See also *data tablet, dynamic menuing.*

merge To combine two or more sets of related data into one, usually in a specified sequence. This can be done automatically on a CAD/CAM system to generate lists and reports.

microcomputer A smaller, lower-cost equivalent of a full-scale minicomputer. Includes a microprocessor (CPU), memory, and necessary interface circuits. Consists of one or more ICs (chips) comprising a chip set.

microprocessor The central control element of a microcomputer, implemented in a single integrated circuit. It performs instruction sequencing and processing, as well as all required computations. It requires additional circuits to function as a microcomputer. See *microcomputer.*

minicomputer A general-purpose, single processor computer of limited flexibility and memory performance.

mirroring A CAD design aid that automatically creates a mirror image of a graphic entity on the CRT by flipping the entity or drawing on its x or y axis.

mnemonic symbol An easily remembered symbol that assists the designer in communicating with the system (e.g., an abbreviation such as MPY for *multiply*).

model, geometric A complete, geometrically accurate 3D or 2D representation of a shape, a part, a geographic area, a plant or any part of it, designed on a CAD system and stored in the data base. A mathematical or analytic model of a physical system used to determine the response of that system to a stimulus or load. See *modeling, geometric.*

modeling, geometric Constructing a mathematical or analytic model of a physical object or system for the purpose of determining the response of that object or system to a stimulus or load. First, the designer describes the shape under design using a geometric model constructed on the system. The computer then converts this pictorial representation on the CRT into a mathematical model later used for other CAD functions such as design optimization.

modeling, solid A type of 3D modeling in which the solid characteristics of an object under design are built into the data base so that complex internal structures and external shapes can be realistically represented. This makes computer-aided design and analysis of solid objects easier, clearer, and more accurate than with wireframe graphics.

modem MOdulator-DEModulator, a device that converts digital signals to analog signals, and vice versa, for long-distance transmission over communications circuits such as telephone lines, dedicated wires, optical fiber, or microwave.

module A separate and distinct unit of hardware or software that is part of a system.

mouse A hand-held data-entering device used to position a cursor on a data tablet. See *cursor.*

multiprocessor A computer whose architecture consists of more than one processing unit. See *central processing unit; microcomputer.*

network An arrangement of two or more interconnected computer systems to facilitate the exchange of information in order to perform a specific function. For example, a CAD/CAM system might be connected to a mainframe computer to off-load heavy analytic tasks. Also refers to a piping network in computer-aided plant design.

numerical control (NC) A technique of operating machine tools or similar equipment in which motion is developed in response to numerically coded commands. These commands may be generated by a CAD/CAM system on punched tapes or other communications media. Also, the processes involved in generating the data or tapes necessary to guide a machine tool in the manufacture of a part.

off-line Refers to peripheral devices not currently connected to and under the direct control of the system's computer.

on-line Refers to peripheral devices connected to and under the direct control of the system's computer, so that operator-system interaction, feedback, and output are all in real time.

operating system A structured set of software programs that control the operation of the computer and associated peripheral devices in a CAD/CAM system, as well as the execution of computer programs and data flow to and from peripheral devices. May provide support for activities and programs such as scheduling, debugging, input/output control, accounting, editing, assembly, compilation, storage assignment, data management, and diagnostics. An operating system may assign task priority levels, support a file system, provide drives for I/O devices, support standard system commands or utilities for on-line programming, process commands, and support both networking and diagnostics.

output The end result of a particular CAD/CAM process or series of processes. The output of a CAD cycle can be artwork and hard-copy lists and reports. The output of a total design-to-manufacturing CAD/CAM system can also include numerical control tapes for manufacturing.

overlay A segment of code or data to be brought into the memory of a computer to replace existing code or data.

paint To fill in a bounded graphic figure on a raster display using a combination of repetitive patterns or line fonts to add meaning or clarity. See *font, line.*

paper-tape punch/reader A peripheral device that can read as well as punch a perforated paper tape generated by a CAD/CAM system. These tapes are the principal means of supplying/data to an NC machine.

parallel processing Executing more than one element of a single process concurrently on multiple processors in a computer system.

password protection A security feature of certain CAD/CAM systems that prevents access to the system or to files within the system without first entering a password, i.e., a special sequence of characters.

PC board See *printed circuit board.*

pen plotter An electromechanical CAD output device that generates hard copy of displayed graphic data by means of a ballpoint pen or liquid ink. Used when a very accurate final drawing is required. Provides exceptional uniformity and density of lines, precise positional accuracy, as well as various user-selectable colors.

peripheral (device) Any device, distinct from the basic system modules, that provides input to and/or output from the CPU. May include printers, keyboards, plotters, graphics display terminals, paper-tape reader/punches, analog-to-digital converters, disks, and tape drives.

permanent storage A method or device for storing the results of a completed program outside the CPU—usually in the form of magnetic tape or punched cards.

photo plotter A CAD output device that generates high-precision artwork masters photographically for PC board design and IC masks.

pixel The smallest portion of a CRT screen that can be individually referenced. An individual dot on a display image. Typically, pixels are evenly spaced, horizontally and vertically, on the display.

plotter A CAD peripheral device used to output for external use the image stored in the data base. Generally makes large, accurate drawings substantially better than what is displayed. Plotter types include pen, drum, electrostatic, and flatbed.

postprocessor A software program or procedure that formats graphic or other data processed on the system for some other purpose. For example, a postprocessor might format cutter centerline data into a form that a machine controller can interpret.

precision The degree of accuracy. Generally refers to the number of significant digits of information to the right of the decimal point for data represented within a computer system. Thus, the term denotes the degree of discrimination with which a design or design element can be described in the data base.

preplaced line (or bus) A run (or line) between a set of points on a PC board layout that has been predefined by the designer and must be avoided by a CAD automatic routing program.

preprocessor A computer program that takes a specific set of instructions from an external source and translates it into the format required by the system.

primitive A design element at the lowest stage of complexity. A fundamental graphic entity. It can be a vector, a point, or a text string. The smallest definable object in a display processor's instruction set.

printed circuit (PC) board A baseboard made of insulating materials and an etched copper-foil circuit pattern on which are mounted ICs and other components required to implement one or more electronic functions. PC boards plug into a rack or subassembly of electronic equipment to provide the brains or logic to control the operation of a computer, or a communications system, instrumentation, or other electronic systems. The name derives from the fact that the circuitry is connected not by wires but by copper-foil lines, paths, or traces actually etched onto the board surface. CAD/CAM is used extensively in PC board design, testing, and manufacture.

process simulation   A program utilizing a mathematical model created on the system to try out numerous process design iterations with real-time visual and numerical feedback. Designers can see on the CRT what is taking place at every stage in the manufacturing process. They can therefore optimize a process and correct problems that could affect the actual manufacturing process downstream.

processor   In CAD/CAM system hardware, any device that performs a specific function. Most often used to refer to the CPU. In software, it refers to a complex set of instructions to perform a general function. See also *central processing unit.*

productivity ratio   A widely accepted means of measuring CAD/CAM productivity (throughput per hour) by comparing the productivity of a design/engineering group before and after installation of the system or relative to some standard norm or potential maximum. The most common way of recording productivity is Actual Manual Hours/Actual CAD Hours, expressed as 4:1, 6:1, etc.

program   (*n*) A precise sequential set of instructions that direct a computer to perform a particular task or action or to solve a problem. A complete program includes plans for the transcription of data, coding for the computer, and plans for the absorption of the results into the system. (*v*) To develop a program. See also *computer program.*

Programmable Read-Only Memory (PROM)   A memory that, once programmed with permanent data or instructions, becomes a ROM. See *read-only memory.*

PROM   See *programmable read-only memory.*

prompt   A message or symbol generated automatically by the system, and appearing on the CRT, to inform the user of (a) a procedural error or incorrect input to the program being executed or (b) the next expected action, option(s), or input. See also *tutorial.*

puck   A hand-held, manually controlled input device that allows coordinate data to be digitized into the system from a drawing placed on the data tablet or digitizer surface. A puck has a transparent window containing cross hairs.

RAM   See *random access memory.*

random access memory (RAM)   A main memory read/write storage unit that provides the CAD/CAM operator direct access to the stored information. The time

required to access any word stored in the memory is the same as for any other word.

raster display   A CAD workstation display in which the entire CRT surface is scanned at a constant refresh rate. The bright, flicker-free image can be selectively written and erased. Also called a digital TV display.

raster scan (video)   Currently, the dominant technology in CAD graphic displays. Similar to conventional television, it involves a line-by-line sweep across the entire CRT surface to generate the image. Raster-scan features include good brightness, accuracy, selective erase, dynamic motion capabilities, and the opportunity for unlimited color. The device can display a large amount of information without flicker, although resolution is not as good as with storage-tube displays.

read-only memory (ROM)   A memory that cannot be modified or reprogrammed. Typically used for control and execute programs. See also *programmable read-only memory.*

real time   Refers to tasks or functions executed so rapidly by a CAD/CAM system that the feedback at various stages in the process can be used to guide the designer in completing the task. Immediate visual feedback through the CRT makes possible real time, interactive operation of a CAD/CAM system.

rectangular array   Insertion of the same entity at multiple locations on a CRT using the system's ability to copy design elements and place them at user-specified intervals to create a rectangular arrangement or matrix. A feature of PC and IC design systems.

refresh (or vector refresh)   A CAD display technology that involves frequent redrawing of an image displayed on the CRT to keep it bright, crisp, and clear. Refresh permits a high degree of movement in the displayed image as well as high resolution. Selective erase or editing is possible at any time without erasing and repainting the entire image. Although substantial amounts of high-speed memory are required, large, complex images may flicker.

refresh rate   The rate at which the graphic image on a CRT is redrawn in a refresh display, i.e., the time needed for one refresh of the displayed image.

registration   The degree of accuracy in the positioning of one layer or overlay in a CAD display or artwork, relative to another layer, as reflected by the clarity and sharpness of the resulting image.

repaint   A CAD feature that automatically redraws a design displayed on the CRT.

resolution   The smallest spacing between two display elements that will allow the elements to be distinguished visually on the CRT. The ability to define very minute detail. For example, the resolution of Computervision's IC design system is one part in 33.5 million. As applied to an electrostatic plotter, resolution means the number of dots per square inch.

response time   The elapsed time from initiation of an operation at a workstation to the receipt of the results at that workstation. Includes transmission of data to the CPU, processing, file access, and transmission of results back to the initiating workstation.

restart To resume a computer program interrupted by operator intervention.

restore To bring back to its original state a design currently being worked on in a CAD/CAM system after editing or modification that the designer now wants to cancel or rescind.

resume A feature of some application programs that allows the designer to suspend the data-processing operation at some logical break point and restart it later from that point.

reticle The photographic plate used to create an IC mask. See also *photo plotter*.

rotate To turn a displayed 2D or 3D construction about an axis through a predefined angle relative to the original position.

robotics The use of computer-controlled manipulators or arms to automate a variety of manufacturing processes such as welding, material handling, painting and assembly.

ROM See *read-only memory*.

routine A computer program, or a subroutine in the main program. The smallest separately compilable source code unit. See *computer program; source*.

rubber banding A CAD capability that allows a component to be tracked (dragged) across the CRT screen, by means of an electronic pen, to a desired location, while simultaneously stretching all related interconnections to maintain signal continuity. During tracking the interconnections associated with the component stretch and bend, providing an excellent visual guide for optimizing the location of a component to best fit into the flow of the PC board, or other entity, minimizing total interconnect length and avoiding areas of congestion.

satellite A remote system connected to another, usually larger, host system. A satellite differs from a remote intelligent work station in that it contains a full set of processors, memory, and mass storage resources to operate independently of the host. See *host-satellite system*.

scale (*v*) To enlarge or diminish the size of a displayed entity without changing its shape, i.e., to bring it into a user-specified ratio to its original dimensions. Scaling can be done automatically by a CAD system. (*n*) Denotes the coordinate system for representing an object.

scissoring The automatic erasing of all portions of a design on the CRT that lie outside user-specified boundaries.

scroll To automatically roll up, as on a spool, a design or text message on a CRT to permit the sequential viewing of a message or drawing too large to be displayed all at once on the screen. New data appear on the CRT at one edge as other data disappear at the opposite edge. Graphics can be scrolled up, down, left, or right.

selective erase A CAD feature for deleting portions of a display without affecting the remainder or having to repaint the entire CRT display.

shape fill The automatic painting-in of an area, defined by user-specified boundaries, on an IC or PC board layout, for example, the area to be filled by copper when the PC board is manufactured. Can be done on-line by CAD.

smoothing Fitting together curves and surfaces so that a smooth, continuous geometry results.

software The collection of executable computer programs including application programs, operating systems, and languages.

source A text file written in a high-level language and containing a computer program. It is easily read and understood by people but must be compiled or assembled to generate machine-recognizable instructions. Also known as *source code*. See also *high-level language*.

source language A symbolic language comprised of statements and formulas used in computer processing. It is translated into object language (object code) by an assembler or compiler for execution by a computer.

spline A subset of a B-spline where in a sequence of curves is restricted to a plane. An interpolation routine executed on a CAD/CAM system automatically adjusts a curve by design iteration until the curvature is continuous over the length of the curve. See also *B-spline*.

storage The physical repository of all information relating to products designed on a CAD/CAM system. It is typically in the form of a magnetic tape or disk. Also called *memory*.

storage tube A common type of CRT that retains an image continuously for a considerable period of time without redrawing (refreshing). The image will not flicker regardless of the amount of information displayed. However, the display tends to be slow relative to raster scan, the image is rather dim, and no single element by itself can be modified or deleted without redrawing. See also *direct view storage tube*.

stretch A CAD design/editing aid that enables the designer to automatically expand a displayed entity beyond its original dimensions.

string A linear sequence of entities, such as characters or physical elements, in a computer-aided design.

stylus A hand-held pen used in conjunction with a data table to enter commands and coordinate input into the system. Also called an *electronic pen*.

subfigure A part or a design element that may be extracted from a CAD library and inserted intact into another part displayed on the CRT.

surface machining Automatic generation of NC tool paths to cut 3D shapes. Both the tool paths and the shapes may be constructed using the mechanical design capabilities of a CAD/CAM system.

symbol Any recognizable sign, mark, shape or pattern

used as a building block for designing meaningful structures. A set of primitive graphic entities (line, point, arc, circle, text, etc.) that form a construction that can be expressed as one unit and assigned a meaning. Symbols may be combined or nested to form larger symbols and/or drawings. They can be as complex as an entire PC board or as simple as a single element, such as a pad. Symbols are commonly used to represent physical things. For example, a particular graphic shape may be used to represent a complete device or a certain kind of electrical component in a schematic. To simplify the preparation of drawings of piping systems and flow diagrams, standard symbols are used to represent various types of fittings and components in common use. Symbols are also basic units in a language. The recognizable sequence of characters END may inform a compiler that the routine it is compiling is completed. In computer-aided mapping, a symbol can be a diagram, design, letter, character, or abbreviation placed on maps and charts, that, by convention or reference to a legend, is understood to stand for or represent a specific characteristic or feature. In a CAD environment, symbol libraries contribute to the quick maintenance, placement, and interpretation of symbols.

syntax   (1) A set of rules describing the structure of statements allowed in a computer language. To make grammatical sense, commands and routines must be written in conformity to these rules. (2) The structure of a computer command language, i.e., the English-sentence structure of a CAD/CAM command language, e.g., verb, noun, modifiers.

system   An arrangement of CAD/CAM dataprocessing, memory, display, and plotting modules—coupled with appropriate software—to achieve specific objectives. The term CAD/CAM system implies both hardware and software. See also *operating system* (a purely software term).

tablet   An input device on which a designer can digitize coordinate data or enter commands into a CAD/CAM system by means of an electronic pen. See also *data tablet.*

task   (1) A specific project that can be executed by a CAD/CAM software program. (2) A specific portion of memory assigned to the user for executing that project.

template   the pattern of a standard, commonly used component or part that serves as a design aid. Once created, it can be subsequently traced instead of redrawn whenever needed. The CAD equivalent of a designer's template might be a standard part in the data-base library that can be retrieved and inserted intact into an emerging drawing on the CRT.

temporary storage   Memory locations for storing immediate and partial results obtained during the execution of a program on the system.

terminal   See *workstation.*

text editor   An operating system program used to create and modify text files on the system.

text file   A file stored in the system in text format that can be printed and edited on-line as required.

throughput   The number of units of work performed by a CAD/CAM system or a work station during a given period of time. A quantitative measure of system productivity.

time-sharing   The use of a common CPU memory and processing capabilities by two or more CAD/CAM terminals to execute different tasks simultaneously.

tool path   Centerline of the tip of an NC cutting tool as it moves over a part produced on a CAD/CAM system. Tool paths can be created and displayed interactively or automatically by a CAD/CAM system, and reformatted into NC tapes, by means of postprocessor, to guide or control machining equipment. See also *surface machining.*

track ball   A CAD graphics input device consisting of a ball recessed into a surface. The designer can rotate it in any direction to control the position of the cursor used for entering coordinate data into the system.

tracking   Moving a predefined (tracking) symbol across the surface of the CRT with a light pen or an electronic pen.

transform   To change an image displayed on the CRT by, for example, scaling, rotating, translating, or mirroring.

transformation   The process of transforming a CAD display image. Also the matrix representation of a geometric space.

translate   (1) To convert CAD/CAM output from one language to another, for example, by means of a postprocessor such as Computervision's IPC-to-Numerics Translator program. (2) Also, by an editing command, to move a CAD display entity a specified distance in a specified direction.

trap   The area that is searched around each digitize to find a hit on a graphics entity to be edited. See also *digitize.*

turnaround time   The elapsed time between the moment a task or project is input into the CAD/CAM system and the moment the required output is obtained.

turnkey   A CAD/CAM system for which the supplier/vendor assumes total responsibility for building, installing, and testing both hardware and software, and the training of user personnel. Also, loosely, a system that comes equipped with all the hardware and software required for a specific application or applications. Usually implies a commitment by the vendor to make the system work and to provide preventive and remedial maintenance of both hardware and software. Sometimes used interchangeably with stand-alone, although stand-alone applies more to system architecture than to terms of purchase.

tutorial   A characteristic of CAD/CAM systems. If the

user is not sure how to execute a task, the system will show how. A message is displayed to provide information and guidance.

utilities   Another term for system capabilities and/or features that enable the user to perform certain processes.

vector   A quantity that has magnitude and direction and that, in CAD, is commonly represented by a directed line segment.

verification   (1) A system-generated message to a work station acknowledging that a valid instruction or input has been received. (2) The process of checking the accuracy, viability, and/or manufacturability of an emerging design on the system.

view port   A user-selected, rectangular view of a part, assembly, etc., that presents the contents of a window on the CRT. See also *window*.

window   A temporary, usually rectangular, bounded area on the CRT that is user-specified to include particular entities for modification, editing, or deletion.

wire-frame graphics   A computer-aided design technique for displaying a 3D object on the CRT screen as a series of lines outlining its surface.

wiring diagram   (1) Graphic representation of all circuits and device elements of an electrical system and its associated apparatus or any clearly defined functional portion of that system. A wiring diagram may contain not only wiring system components and wires but also nongraphic information such as wire number, wire size, color, function, component label, and pin number. (2) Illustration of device elements and their interconnectivity as distinguished from their physical arrangement. (3) Drawing that shows how to hook things up.

Wiring diagrams can be constructed, annotated, and documented on a CAD system.

word   A set of bits (typically 16 to 32) that occupies a single storage location and is treated by the computer as a unit. See also *bit*.

working storage   That part of the system's internal storage reserved for intermediate results (i.e., while a computer program is still in progress). Also called *temporary storage*.

workstation   The work area and equipment used for CAD/CAM operations. It is where the designer interacts (communicates) with the computer. Frequently consists of a CRT display and an input device as well as, possibly, a digitizer and a hard-copy device. In a distributed processing system, a work station would have local processing and mass storage capabilities. Also called a *terminal* or *design terminal*.

write   To transfer information from CPU main memory to a peripheral device, such as a mass storage device.

write-protect   A security feature in a CAD/CAM data storage device that prevents new data from being written over existing data.

zero   The origin of all coordinate dimensions defined in an absolute system as the intersection of the baselines of the x, y, and z axes.

zero offset   On an NC unit, this features allows the zero point on an axis to be relocated anywhere within a specified range, thus temporarily redefining the coordinate frame of reference.

zoom   A CAD capability that proportionately enlarges or reduces a figure displayed on a CRT screen.

4   Abbreviations for Use on Drawings and in Text— American National Standard

[Selected from ANSI Y1.1–1972 (R1984)]

A					
		after	AFT.	American wire gage	AWG
		aggregate	AGGR	amount	AMT
absolute	ABS	air condition	AIR COND	ampere	AMP
accelerate	ACCEL	airplane	APL	amplifier	AMPL
accessory	ACCESS.	allowance	ALLOW	anneal	ANL
account	ACCT	alloy	ALY	antenna	ANT.
accumulate	ACCUM	alteration	ALT	apartment	APT.
actual	ACT.	alternate	ALT	apparatus	APP
adapter	ADPT	alternating current	AC	appendix	APPX
addendum	ADD.	altitude	ALT	approved	APPD
addition	ADD.	aluminum	AL	approximate	APPROX
adjust	ADJ	American National		arc weld	ARC/W
advance	ADV	Standard	AMER NATL STD	area	A

armature	ARM.	bolt circle	BC
armor plate	ARM-PL	both faces	BF
army navy	AN	both sides	BS
arrange	ARR.	both ways	BW
artificial	ART.	bottom	BOT
asbestos	ASB	bottom chord	BC
asphalt	ASPH	bottom face	BF
assemble	ASSEM	bracket	BRKT
assembly	ASSY	brake	BK
assistant	ASST	brake horsepower	BHP
associate	ASSOC	brass	BRS
association	ASSN	brazing	BRZG
atomic	AT	break	BRK
audible	AUD	Brinell hardness	BH
audio frequency	AF	British Standard	BR STD
authorized	AUTH	British thermal unit	BTU
automatic	AUTO	broach	BRO
auto-transformer	AUTO TR	bronze	BRZ
auxiliary	AUX	Brown & Sharpe (wire gage,	
avenue	AVE	same as AWG)	B&S
average	AVG	building	BLDG
aviation	AVI	bulkhead	BHD
azimuth	AZ	burnish	BNH
		bushing	BUSH.
		button	BUT.

B

Babbitt	BAB	**C**	
back feed	BF		
back pressure	BP	cabinet	CAB.
back to back	B to B	calculate	CALC
backface	BF	calibrate	CAL
balance	BAL	cap screw	CAP SCR
ball bearing	BB	capacity	CAP
barometer	BAR	carburetor	CARB
base line	BL	carburize	CARB
base plate	BP	carriage	CRG
bearing	BRG	case harden	CH
bench mark	BM	cast iron	CI
bending moment	M	cast steel	CS
bent	BT	casting	CSTG
bessemer	BESS	castle nut	CAS NUT
between	BET.	catalogue	CAT.
between centers	BC	cement	CEM
between perpendiculars	BP	center	CTR
bevel	BEV	center line	CL
bill of material	B/M	center of gravity	CG
Birmingham wire gage	BWG	center of pressure	CP
blank	BLK	center to center	C to C
block	BLK	centering	CTR
blueprint	BP	chamfer	CHAM
board	BD	change	CHG
boiler	BLR	channel	CHAN
boiler feed	BF	check	CHK
boiler horsepower	BHP	check valve	CV
boiling point	BP	chord	CHD

circle	CIR
circular	CIR
circular pitch	CP
circumference	CIRC
clear	CLR
clearance	CL
clockwise	CW
coated	CTD
cold drawn	CD
cold-drawn steel	CDS
cold finish	CF
cold punched	CP
cold rolled	CR
cold-rolled steel	CRS
combination	COMB.
combustion	COMB
commercial	COML
company	CO
complete	COMPL
compress	COMP
concentric	CONC
concrete	CONC
condition	COND
connect	CONN
constant	CONST
construction	CONST
contact	CONT
continue	CONT
copper	COP.
corner	COR
corporation	CORP
correct	CORR
corrugate	CORR
cotter	COT
counter	CTR
counterbore	CBORE
counter clockwise	CCW
counterdrill	CDRILL
counterpunch	CPUNCH
countersink	CSK
coupling	CPLG
cover	COV
cross section	XSECT
cubic	CU
cubic foot	CU FT
cubic inch	CU IN.
current	CUR
customer	CUST
cyanide	CYN

D

decimal	DEC
dedendum	DED
deflect	DEFL

degree	(°) DEG	**F**		hard	H
density	D			harden	HDN
department	DEPT	fabricate	FAB	hardware	HDW
design	DSGN	face to face	F to F	head	HD
detail	DET	Fahrenheit	F	headless	HDLS
develop	DEV	far side	FS	heat	HT
diagonal	DIAG	federal	FED.	heat-treat	HT TR
diagram	DIAG	feed	FD	heavy	HVY
diameter	DIA	feet	(') FT	hexagon	HEX
diametral pitch	DP	figure	FIG.	high-pressure	HP
dimension	DIM.	fillet	FIL	high-speed	HS
discharge	DISCH	fillister	FIL	horizontal	HOR
distance	DIST	finish	FIN.	horsepower	HP
division	DIV	finish all over	FAO	hot rolled	HR
double	DBL	flange	FLG	hot-rolled steel	HRS
dovetail	DVTL	flat	F	hour	HR
dowel	DWL	flat head	FH	housing	HSG
down	DN	floor	FL	hydraulic	HYD
dozen	DOZ	fluid	FL		
drafting	DFTG	focus	FOC		
drawing	DWG	foot	(') FT	**I**	
drill or drill rod	DR	force	F		
drive	DR	forged steel	FST	illustrate	ILLUS
drive fit	DF	forging	FORG	inboard	INBD
drop	D	forward	FWD	inch	(") IN.
drop forge	DF	foundry	FDRY	inches per second	IPS
duplicate	DUP	frequency	FREQ	inclosure	INCL
		front	FR	include	INCL
		furnish	FURN	inside diameter	ID
				instrument	INST
E				interior	INT
				internal	INT
each	EA	**G**		intersect	INT
east	E			iron	I
eccentric	ECC	gage or gauge	GA	irregular	IREG
effective	EFF	gallon	GAL		
elbow	ELL	galvanize	GALV		
electric	ELEC	galvanized iron	GI		
elementary	ELEM	galvanized steel	GS	**J**	
elevate	ELEV	gasket	GSKT		
elevation	EL	general	GEN	joint	JT
engine	ENG	glass	GL	joint army-navy	JAN
engineer	ENGR	government	GOVT	journal	JNL
engineering	ENGRG	governor	GOV	junction	JCT
entrance	ENT	grade	GR		
equal	EQ	graduation	GRAD		
equation	EQ	graphite	GPH	**K**	
equipment	EQUIP	grind	GRD		
equivalent	EQUIV	groove	GRV	key	K
estimate	EST	ground	GRD	keyseat	KST
exchange	EXCH			Keyway	KWY
exhaust	EXH				
existing	EXIST.	**H**			
exterior	EXT			**L**	
extra heavy	X HVY	half-round	½RD		
extra strong	X STR	handle	HDL		
extrude	EXTR	hanger	HGR	laboratory	LAB

laminate	LAM	neutral	NEUT	prepare	PREP
lateral	LAT	nominal	NOM	pressure	PRESS.
left	L	normal	NOR	process	PROC
left hand	LH	north	N	production	PROD
length	LG	not to scale	NTS	profile	PF
length over all	LOA	number	NO.	propeller	PROP
letter	LTR			publication	PUB
light	LT			push button	PB
line	L				
locate	LOC	**O**			
logarithm	LOG.				
long	LG	obsolete	OBS	**Q**	
lubricate	LUB	octagon	OCT		
lumber	LBR	office	OFF.	quadrant	QUAD
		on center	OC	quality	QUAL
		opposite	OPP	quarter	QTR
		optical	OPT		
M		original	ORIG		
		outlet	OUT.	**R**	
machine	MACH	outside diameter	OD		
machine steel	MS	outside face	OF	radial	RAD
maintenance	MAINT	outside radius	OR	radius	R
malleable	MALL	overall	OA	railroad	RR
malleable iron	MI			ream	RM
manual	MAN.			received	RECD
manufacture	MFR	**P**		record	REC
manufactured	MFD			rectangle	RECT
manufacturing	MFG	pack	PK	reduce	RED.
material	MATL	packing	PKG	reference line	REF L
maximum	MAX	page	P	reinforce	REINF
mechanical	MECH	paragraph	PAR.	release	REL
mechanism	MECH	part	PT	relief	REL
median	MED	patent	PAT.	remove	REM
metal	MET.	pattern	PATT	require	REQ
meter	M	permanent	PERM	required	REQD
miles	MI	perpendicular	PERP	return	RET.
miles per hour	MPH	piece	PC	reverse	REV
millimeter	MM	piece mark	PC MK	revolution	REV
minimum	MIN	pint	PT	revolutions per minute	RPM
minute	(') MIN	pitch	P	right	R
miscellaneous	MISC	pitch circle	PC	right hand	RH
month	MO	pitch diameter	PD	rivet	RIV
Morse taper	MOR T	plastic	PLSTC	Rockwell hardness	RH
motor	MOT	plate	PL	roller bearing	RB
mounted	MTD	plumbing	PLMB	room	RM
mounting	MTG	point	PT	root diameter	RD
multiple	MULT	point of curve	PC	root mean square	RMS
music wire gage	MWG	point of intersection	PI	rough	RGH
		point of tangent	PT	round	RD
		polish	POL		
		position	POS		
		potential	POT.		
N		pound	LB	**S**	
		pounds per square inch	PSI		
national	NATL	power	PWR	schedule	SCH
natural	NAT	prefabricated	PREFAB	schematic	SCHEM
near face	NF	preferred	PFD	scleroscope hardness	SH
near side	NS				
negative	NEG				

screw	SCR	symbol	SYM	**V**	
second	SEC	system	SYS		
section	SECT			vacuum	VAC
semi-steel	SS			valve	V
separate	SEP	**T**		variable	VAR
set screw	SS			versus	VS
shaft	SFT	tangent	TAN.	vertical	VERT
sheet	SH	taper	TPR	volt	V
shoulder	SHLD	technical	TECH	volume	VOL
side	S	template	TEMP		
single	S	tension	TENS.		
sketch	SK	terminal	TERM.	**W**	
sleeve	SLV	thick	THK		
slide	SL	thousand	M	wall	W
slotted	SLOT.	thread	THD	washer	WASH.
small	SM	threads per inch	TPI	watt	W
socket	SOC	through	THRU	week	WK
space	SP	time	T	weight	WT
special	SPL	tolerance	TOL	west	W
specific	SP	tongue & groove	T & G	width	W
spot faced	SF	tool steel	TS	wood	WD
spring	SPG	tooth	T	Woodruff	WDF
square	SQ	total	TOT	working point	WP
standard	STD	transfer	TRANS	working pressure	WP
station	STA	typical	TYP	wrought	WRT
stationary	STA			wrought iron	WI
steel	STL				
stock	STK				
straight	STR	**U**			
street	ST			**X, Y, Z**	
structural	STR	ultimate	ULT		
substitute	SUB	unit	U	yard	YD
summary	SUM.	universal	UNIV	year	YR
support	SUP.				
surface	SUR				

5 Running and Sliding Fits[a]—American National Standard

RC 1 *Close sliding fits* are intended for the accurate location of parts which must assemble without perceptible play.

RC 2 *Sliding fits* are intended for accurate location, but with greater maximum clearance than class RC 1. Parts made to this fit move and turn easily but are not intended to run freely, and in the larger sizes may seize with small temperature changes.

RC 3 *Precision running fits* are about the closest fits which can be expected to run freely, and are intended for precision work at slow speeds and light journal pressures, but are not suitable where appreciable temperature differences are likely to be encountered.

RC 4 *Close running fits* are intended chiefly for running fits on accurate machinery with moderate surface speeds and journal pressures, where accurate location and minimum play are desired.

Basic hole system. Limits are in thousandths of an inch. See §14.8.
Limits for hole and shaft are applied algebraically to the basic size to obtain the limits of size for the parts.
Data in **boldface** are in accordance with ABC agreements.
Symbols H5, g5, etc., are hole and shaft designations used in ABC System.

Nominal Size Range, inches Over To	Class RC 1			Class RC 2			Class RC 3			Class RC 4		
	Limits of Clearance	Standard Limits		Limits of Clearance	Standard Limits		Limits of Clearance	Standard Limits		Limits of Clearance	Standard Limits	
		Hole H5	Shaft g4		Hole H6	Shaft g5		Hole H7	Shaft f6		Hole H8	Shaft f7
0 - 0.12	0.1 0.45	+0.2 -0	-0.1 -0.25	0.1 0.55	+0.25 -0	-0.1 -0.3	0.3 0.95	+0.4 -0	-0.3 -0.55	0.3 1.3	+0.6 -0	-0.3 -0.7
0.12- 0.24	0.15 0.5	+0.2 -0	-0.15 -0.3	0.15 0.65	+0.3 -0	-0.15 -0.35	0.4 1.12	+0.5 -0	-0.4 -0.7	0.4 1.6	+0.7 -0	-0.4 -0.9
0.24- 0.40	0.2 0.6	+0.25 -0	-0.2 -0.35	0.2 0.85	+0.4 -0	-0.2 -0.45	0.5 1.5	+0.6 -0	-0.5 -0.9	0.5 2.0	+0.9 -0	-0.5 -1.1
0.40- 0.71	0.25 0.75	+0.3 -0	-0.25 -0.45	0.25 0.95	+0.4 -0	-0.25 -0.55	0.6 1.7	+0.7 -0	-0.6 -1.0	0.6 2.3	+1.0 -0	-0.6 -1.3
0.71- 1.19	0.3 0.95	+0.4 -0	-0.3 -0.55	0.3 1.2	+0.5 -0	-0.3 -0.7	0.8 2.1	+0.8 -0	-0.8 -1.3	0.8 2.8	+1.2 -0	-0.8 -1.6
1.19- 1.97	0.4 1.1	+0.4 -0	-0.4 -0.7	0.4 1.4	+0.6 -0	-0.4 -0.8	1.0 2.6	+1.0 -0	-1.0 -1.6	1.0 3.6	+1.6 -0	-1.0 -2.0
1.97- 3.15	0.4 1.2	+0.5 -0	-0.4 -0.7	0.4 1.6	+0.7 -0	-0.4 -0.9	1.2 3.1	+1.2 -0	-1.2 -1.9	1.2 4.2	+1.8 -0	-1.2 -2.4
3.15- 4.73	0.5 1.5	+0.6 -0	-0.5 -0.9	0.5 2.0	+0.9 -0	-0.5 -1.1	1.4 3.7	+1.4 -0	-1.4 -2.3	1.4 5.0	+2.2 -0	-1.4 -2.8
4.73- 7.09	0.6 1.8	+0.7 -0	-0.6 -1.1	0.6 2.3	+1.0 -0	-0.6 -1.3	1.6 4.2	+1.6 -0	-1.6 -2.6	1.6 5.7	+2.5 -0	-1.6 -3.2
7.09- 9.85	0.6 2.0	+0.8 -0	-0.6 -1.2	0.6 2.6	+1.2 -0	-0.6 -1.4	2.0 5.0	+1.8 -0	-2.0 -3.2	2.0 6.6	+2.8 -0	-2.0 -3.8
9.85-12.41	0.8 2.3	+0.9 -0	-0.8 -1.4	0.8 2.9	+1.2 -0	-0.8 -1.7	2.5 5.7	+2.0 -0	-2.5 -3.7	2.5 7.5	+3.0 -0	-2.5 -4.5
12.41-15.75	1.0 2.7	+1.0 -0	-1.0 -1.7	1.0 3.4	+1.4 -0	-1.0 -2.0	3.0 6.6	+2.2 -0	-3.0 -4.4	3.0 8.7	+3.5 -0	-3.0 -5.2

[a]From ANSI B4.1—1967 (R1987). For larger diameters, see the standard.

5 Running and Sliding Fits[a]—American National Standard (continued)

RC 5⎫
RC 6⎭ *Medium running fits* are intended for higher running speeds, or heavy journal pressures, or both.

RC 7   *Free running fits* are intended for use where accuracy is not essential, or where large temperature variations are likely to be encountered, or under both these conditions.

RC 8⎫ *Loose running fits* are intended for use where wide commercial tolerances may be necessary, together with an
RC 9⎭ allowance, on the external member.

Nominal Size Range, inches Over — To	Class RC 5			Class RC 6			Class RC 7			Class RC 8			Class RC 9		
	Limits of Clearance	Standard Limits		Limits of Clearance	Standard Limits		Limits of Clearance	Standard Limits		Limits of Clearance	Standard Limits		Limits of Clearance	Standard Limits	
		Hole H8	Shaft e7		Hole H9	Shaft e8		Hole H9	Shaft d8		Hole H10	Shaft c9		Hole H11	Shaft
0 – 0.12	0.6 1.6	+0.6 −0	−0.6 −1.0	0.6 2.2	+1.0 −0	−0.6 −1.2	1.0 2.6	+1.0 −0	−1.0 −1.6	2.5 5.1	+1.6 −0	−2.5 −3.5	4.0 8.1	+2.5 −0	−4.0 −5.6
0.12– 0.24	0.8 2.0	+0.7 −0	−0.8 −1.3	0.8 2.7	+1.2 −0	−0.8 −1.5	1.2 3.1	+1.2 −0	−1.2 −1.9	2.8 5.8	+1.8 −0	−2.8 −4.0	4.5 9.0	+3.0 −0	−4.5 −6.0
0.24– 0.40	1.0 2.5	+0.9 −0	−1.0 −1.6	1.0 3.3	+1.4 −0	−1.0 −1.9	1.6 3.9	+1.4 −0	−1.6 −2.5	3.0 6.6	+2.2 −0	−3.0 −4.4	5.0 10.7	+3.5 −0	−5.0 −7.2
0.40– 0.71	1.2 2.9	+1.0 −0	−1.2 −1.9	1.2 3.8	+1.6 −0	−1.2 −2.2	2.0 4.6	+1.6 −0	−2.0 −3.0	3.5 7.9	+2.8 −0	−3.5 −5.1	6.0 12.8	+4.0 −0	−6.0 −8.8
0.71– 1.19	1.6 3.6	+1.2 −0	−1.6 −2.4	1.6 4.8	+2.0 −0	−1.6 −2.8	2.5 5.7	+2.0 −0	−2.5 −3.7	4.5 10.0	+3.5 −0	−4.5 −6.5	7.0 15.5	+5.0 −0	−7.0 −10.5
1.19– 1.97	2.0 4.6	+1.6 −0	−2.0 −3.0	2.0 6.1	+2.5 −0	−2.0 −3.6	3.0 7.1	+2.5 −0	−3.0 −4.6	5.0 11.5	+4.0 −0	−5.0 −7.5	8.0 18.0	+6.0 −0	−8.0 −12.0
1.97– 3.15	2.5 5.5	+1.8 −0	−2.5 −3.7	2.5 7.3	+3.0 −0	−2.5 −4.3	4.0 8.8	+3.0 −0	−4.0 −5.8	6.0 13.5	+4.5 −0	−6.0 −9.0	9.0 20.5	+7.0 −0	−9.0 −13.5
3.15– 4.73	3.0 6.6	+2.2 −0	−3.0 −4.4	3.0 8.7	+3.5 −0	−3.0 −5.2	5.0 10.7	+3.5 −0	−5.0 −7.2	7.0 15.5	+5.0 −0	−7.0 −10.5	10.0 24.0	+9.0 −0	−10.0 −15.0
4.73– 7.09	3.5 7.6	+2.5 −0	−3.5 −5.1	3.5 10.0	+4.0 −0	−3.5 −6.0	6.0 12.5	+4.0 −0	−6.0 −8.5	8.0 18.0	+6.0 −0	−8.0 −12.0	12.0 28.0	+10.0 −0	−12.0 −18.0
7.09– 9.85	4.0 8.6	+2.8 −0	−4.0 −5.8	4.0 11.3	+4.5 −0	−4.0 −6.8	7.0 14.3	+4.5 −0	−7.0 −9.8	10.0 21.5	+7.0 −0	−10.0 −14.5	15.0 34.0	+12.0 −0	−15.0 −22.0
9.85–12.41	5.0 10.0	+3.0 −0	−5.0 −7.0	5.0 13.0	+5.0 −0	−5.0 −8.0	8.0 16.0	+5.0 −0	−8.0 −11.0	12.0 25.0	+8.0 −0	−12.0 −17.0	18.0 38.0	+12.0 −0	−18.0 −26.0
12.41–15.75	6.0 11.7	+3.5 −0	−6.0 −8.2	6.0 15.5	+6.0 −0	−6.0 −9.5	10.0 19.5	+6.0 −0	−10.0 13.5	14.0 29.0	+9.0 −0	−14.0 −20.0	22.0 45.0	+14.0 −0	−22.0 −31.0

[a]From ANSI B4.1—1967 (R1987). For larger diameters, see the standard.

6 Clearance Locational Fits[a]—American National Standard

LC *Locational clearance fits are intended for parts which are normally stationary, but which can be freely assembled or disassembled. They run from snug fits for parts requiring accuracy of location, through the medium clearance fits for parts such as spigots, to the looser fastener fits where freedom of assembly is of prime importance.*

Basic hole system. Limits are in thousandths of an inch. See §14.8.
Limits for hole and shaft are applied algebraically to the basic size to obtain the limits of size for the parts.
Data in **boldface** are in accordance with ABC agreements.
Symbols H6, h5, etc., are hole and shaft designations used in ABC System.

Nominal Size Range, inches Over To	Class LC 1 Limits of Clearance	Standard Limits Hole H6	Standard Limits Shaft h5	Class LC 2 Limits of Clearance	Standard Limits Hole H7	Standard Limits Shaft h6	Class LC 3 Limits of Clearance	Standard Limits Hole H8	Standard Limits Shaft h7	Class LC 4 Limits of Clearance	Standard Limits Hole H10	Standard Limits Shaft h9	Class LC 5 Limits of Clearance	Standard Limits Hole H7	Standard Limits Shaft g6
0 – 0.12	0 / 0.45	+0.25 / -0	+0 / -0.2	0 / 0.65	+0.4 / -0	+0 / -0.25	0 / 1	+0.6 / -0	+0 / -0.4	0 / 2.6	+1.6 / -0	+0 / -1.0	0.1 / 0.75	+0.4 / -0	-0.1 / -0.35
0.12– 0.24	0 / 0.5	+0.3 / -0	+0 / -0.2	0 / 0.8	+0.5 / -0	+0 / -0.3	0 / 1.2	+0.7 / -0	+0 / -0.5	0 / 3.0	+1.8 / -0	+0 / -1.2	0.15 / 0.95	+0.5 / -0	-0.15 / -0.45
0.24– 0.40	0 / 0.65	+0.4 / -0	+0 / -0.25	0 / 1.0	+0.6 / -0	+0 / -0.4	0 / 1.5	+0.9 / -0	+0 / -0.6	0 / 3.6	+2.2 / -0	+0 / -1.4	0.2 / 1.2	+0.6 / -0	-0.2 / -0.6
0.40– 0.71	0 / 0.7	+0.4 / -0	+0 / -0.3	0 / 1.1	+0.7 / -0	+0 / -0.4	0 / 1.7	+1.0 / -0	+0 / -0.7	0 / 4.4	+2.8 / -0	+0 / -1.6	0.25 / 1.35	+0.7 / -0	-0.25 / -0.65
0.71– 1.19	0 / 0.9	+0.5 / -0	+0 / -0.4	0 / 1.3	+0.8 / -0	+0 / -0.5	0 / 2	+1.2 / -0	+0 / -0.8	0 / 5.5	+3.5 / -0	+0 / -2.0	0.3 / 1.6	+0.8 / -0	-0.3 / -0.8
1.19– 1.97	0 / 1.0	+0.6 / -0	+0 / -0.4	0 / 1.6	+1.0 / -0	+0 / -0.6	0 / 2.6	+1.6 / -0	+0 / -1	0 / 6.5	+4.0 / -0	+0 / -2.5	0.4 / 2.0	+1.0 / -0	-0.4 / -1.0
1.97– 3.15	0 / 1.2	+0.7 / -0	+0 / -0.5	0 / 1.9	+1.2 / -0	+0 / -0.7	0 / 3	+1.8 / -0	+0 / -1.2	0 / 7.5	+4.5 / -0	+0 / -3	0.4 / 2.3	+1.2 / -0	-0.4 / -1.1
3.15– 4.73	0 / 1.5	+0.9 / -0	+0 / -0.6	0 / 2.3	+1.4 / -0	+0 / -0.9	0 / 3.6	+2.2 / -0	+0 / -1.4	0 / 8.5	+5.0 / -0	+0 / -3.5	0.5 / 2.8	+1.4 / -0	-0.5 / -1.4
4.73– 7.09	0 / 1.7	+1.0 / -0	+0 / -0.7	0 / 2.6	+1.6 / -0	+0 / -1.0	0 / 4.1	+2.5 / -0	+0 / -1.6	0 / 10	+6.0 / -0	+0 / -4	0.6 / 3.2	+1.6 / -0	-0.6 / -1.6
7.09– 9.85	0 / 2.0	+1.2 / -0	+0 / -0.8	0 / 3.0	+1.8 / -0	+0 / -1.2	0 / 4.6	+2.8 / -0	+0 / -1.8	0 / 11.5	+7.0 / -0	+0 / -4.5	0.6 / 3.6	+1.8 / -0	-0.6 / -1.8
9.85–12.41	0 / 2.1	+1.2 / -0	+0 / -0.9	0 / 3.2	+2.0 / -0	+0 / -1.2	0 / 5	+3.0 / -0	+0 / -2.0	0 / 13	+8.0 / -0	+0 / -5	0.7 / 3.9	+2.0 / -0	-0.7 / -1.9
12.41–15.75	0 / 2.4	+1.4 / -0	+0 / -1.0	0 / 3.6	+2.2 / -0	+0 / -1.4	0 / 5.7	+3.5 / -0	+0 / -2.2	0 / 15	+9.0 / -0	+0 / -6	0.7 / 4.3	+2.2 / -0	-0.7 / -2.1

[a]From ANSI B4.1—1967 (R1987). For larger diameters, see the standard.

6 Clearance Locational Fits[a]—American National Standard (continued)

Nominal Size Range, inches (Over–To)	Class LC 6 Limits of Clearance	Class LC 6 Hole H9	Class LC 6 Shaft f8	Class LC 7 Limits of Clearance	Class LC 7 Hole H10	Class LC 7 Shaft e9	Class LC 8 Limits of Clearance	Class LC 8 Hole H10	Class LC 8 Shaft d9	Class LC 9 Limits of Clearance	Class LC 9 Hole H11	Class LC 9 Shaft c10	Class LC 10 Limits of Clearance	Class LC 10 Hole H12	Class LC 10 Shaft	Class LC 11 Limits of Clearance	Class LC 11 Hole H13	Class LC 11 Shaft
0 – 0.12	0.3 / 1.9	+1.0 / −0	−0.3 / −0.9	0.6 / 3.2	+1.6 / −0	−0.6 / −1.6	1.0 / 3.6	+1.6 / −0	−1.0 / −2.0	2.5 / 6.6	+2.5 / −0	−2.5 / −4.1	4 / 12	+4 / −0	−4 / −8	5 / 17	+6 / −0	−5 / −11
0.12– 0.24	0.4 / 2.3	+1.2 / −0	−0.4 / −1.1	0.8 / 3.8	+1.8 / −0	−0.8 / −2.0	1.2 / 4.2	+1.8 / −0	−1.2 / −2.4	2.8 / 7.6	+3.0 / −0	−2.8 / −4.6	4.5 / 14.5	+5 / −0	−4.5 / −9.5	6 / 20	+7 / −0	−6 / −13
0.24– 0.40	0.5 / 2.8	+1.4 / −0	−0.5 / −1.4	1.0 / 4.6	+2.2 / −0	−1.0 / −2.4	1.6 / 5.2	+2.2 / −0	−1.6 / −3.0	3.0 / 8.7	+3.5 / −0	−3.0 / −5.2	5 / 17	+6 / −0	−5 / −11	7 / 25	+9 / −0	−7 / −16
0.40– 0.71	0.6 / 3.2	+1.6 / −0	−0.6 / −1.6	1.2 / 5.6	+2.8 / −0	−1.2 / −2.8	2.0 / 6.4	+2.8 / −0	−2.0 / −3.6	3.5 / 10.3	+4.0 / −0	−3.5 / −6.3	6 / 20	+7 / −0	−6 / −13	8 / 28	+10 / −0	−8 / −18
0.71– 1.19	0.8 / 4.0	+2.0 / −0	−0.8 / −2.0	1.6 / 7.1	+3.5 / −0	−1.6 / −3.6	2.5 / 8.0	+3.5 / −0	−2.5 / −4.5	4.5 / 13.0	+5.0 / −0	−4.5 / −8.0	7 / 23	+8 / −0	−7 / −15	10 / 34	+12 / −0	−10 / −22
1.19– 1.97	1.0 / 5.1	+2.5 / −0	−1.0 / −2.6	2.0 / 8.5	+4.0 / −0	−2.0 / −4.5	3.0 / 9.5	+4.0 / −0	−3.0 / −5.5	5 / 15	+6 / −0	−5 / −9	8 / 28	+10 / −0	−8 / −18	12 / 44	+16 / −0	−12 / −28
1.97– 3.15	1.2 / 6.0	+3.0 / −0	−1.2 / −3.0	2.5 / 10.0	+4.5 / −0	−2.5 / −5.5	4.0 / 11.5	+4.5 / −0	−4.0 / −7.0	6 / 17.5	+7 / −0	−6 / −10.5	10 / 34	+12 / −0	−10 / −22	14 / 50	+18 / −0	−14 / −32
3.15– 4.73	1.4 / 7.1	+3.5 / −0	−1.4 / −3.6	3.0 / 11.5	+5.0 / −0	−3.0 / −6.5	5.0 / 13.5	+5.0 / −0	−5.0 / −8.5	7 / 21	+9 / −0	−7 / −12	11 / 39	+14 / −0	−11 / −25	16 / 60	+22 / −0	−16 / −38
4.73– 7.09	1.6 / 8.1	+4.0 / −0	−1.6 / −4.1	3.5 / 13.5	+6.0 / −0	−3.5 / −7.5	6 / 16	+6 / −0	−6 / −10	8 / 24	+10 / −0	−8 / −14	12 / 44	+16 / −0	−12 / −28	18 / 68	+25 / −0	−18 / −43
7.09– 9.85	2.0 / 9.3	+4.5 / −0	−2.0 / −4.8	4.0 / 15.5	+7.0 / −0	−4.0 / −8.5	7 / 18.5	+7 / −0	−7 / −11.5	10 / 29	+12 / −0	−10 / −17	16 / 52	+18 / −0	−16 / −34	22 / 78	+28 / −0	−22 / −50
9.85–12.41	2.2 / 10.2	+5.0 / −0	−2.2 / −5.2	4.5 / 17.5	+8.0 / −0	−4.5 / −9.5	7 / 20	+8 / −0	−7 / −12	12 / 32	+12 / −0	−12 / −20	20 / 60	+20 / −0	−20 / −40	28 / 88	+30 / −0	−28 / −58
12.41–15.75	2.5 / 12.0	+6.0 / −0	−2.5 / −6.0	5.0 / 20.0	+9.0 / −0	−5 / −11	8 / 23	+9 / −0	−8 / −14	14 / 37	+14 / −0	−14 / −23	22 / 66	+22 / −0	−22 / −44	30 / 100	+35 / −0	−30 / −65

[a]From ANSI B4.1–1967 (R1987). For larger diameters, see the standard.

7 Transition Locational Fits[a]—American National Standard

LT Transition fits are a compromise between clearance and interference fits, for application where accuracy of location is important, but either a small amount of clearance or interference is permissible.

Basic hole system. Limits are in thousandths of an inch. See §14.8.

Limits for hole and shaft are applied algebraically to the basic size to obtain the limits of size for the mating parts.

Data in **boldface** are in accordance with ABC agreements.

"Fit" represents the maximum interference (minus values) and the maximum clearance (plus values).

Symbols H7, js6, etc., are hole and shaft designations used in ABC System.

Nominal Size Range, inches (Over–To)	Class LT 1 Fit	LT1 Hole H7	LT1 Shaft js6	Class LT 2 Fit	LT2 Hole H8	LT2 Shaft js7	Class LT 3 Fit	LT3 Hole H7	LT3 Shaft k6	Class LT 4 Fit	LT4 Hole H8	LT4 Shaft k7	Class LT 5 Fit	LT5 Hole H7	LT5 Shaft n6	Class LT 6 Fit	LT6 Hole H7	LT6 Shaft n7
0 – 0.12	−0.10 / +0.50	+0.4 / −0	+0.10 / −0.10	−0.2 / +0.8	+0.6 / −0	+0.2 / −0.2							−0.5 / +0.15	+0.4 / −0	+0.5 / +0.25	−0.65 / +0.15	+0.4 / −0	+0.65 / +0.25
0.12– 0.24	−0.15 / +0.65	+0.5 / −0	+0.15 / −0.15	−0.25 / +0.95	+0.7 / −0	+0.25 / −0.25							−0.6 / +0.2	+0.5 / −0	+0.6 / +0.3	−0.8 / +0.2	+0.5 / −0	+0.8 / +0.3
0.24– 0.40	−0.2 / +0.8	+0.6 / −0	+0.2 / −0.2	−0.3 / +1.2	+0.9 / −0	+0.3 / −0.3	−0.5 / +0.5	+0.6 / −0	+0.5 / +0.1	−0.7 / +0.8	+0.9 / −0	+0.7 / +0.1	−0.8 / +0.2	+0.6 / −0	+0.8 / +0.4	−1.0 / +0.2	+0.6 / −0	+1.0 / +0.4
0.40– 0.71	−0.2 / +0.9	+0.7 / −0	+0.2 / −0.2	−0.35 / +1.35	+1.0 / −0	+0.35 / −0.35	−0.5 / +0.6	+0.7 / −0	+0.5 / +0.1	−0.8 / +0.9	+1.0 / −0	+0.8 / +0.1	−0.9 / +0.2	+0.7 / −0	+0.9 / +0.5	−1.2 / +0.2	+0.7 / −0	+1.2 / +0.5
0.71– 1.19	−0.25 / +1.05	+0.8 / −0	+0.25 / −0.25	−0.4 / +1.6	+1.2 / −0	+0.4 / −0.4	−0.6 / +0.7	+0.8 / −0	+0.6 / +0.1	−0.9 / +1.1	+1.2 / −0	+0.9 / +0.1	−1.1 / +0.2	+0.8 / −0	+1.1 / +0.6	−1.4 / +0.2	+0.8 / −0	+1.4 / +0.6
1.19– 1.97	−0.3 / +1.3	+1.0 / −0	+0.3 / −0.3	−0.5 / +2.1	+1.6 / −0	+0.5 / −0.5	−0.7 / +0.9	+1.0 / −0	+0.7 / +0.1	−1.1 / +1.5	+1.6 / −0	+1.1 / +0.1	−1.3 / +0.3	+1.0 / −0	+1.3 / +0.7	−1.7 / +0.3	+1.0 / −0	+1.7 / +0.7
1.97– 3.15	−0.3 / +1.5	+1.2 / −0	+0.3 / −0.3	−0.6 / +2.4	+1.8 / −0	+0.6 / −0.6	−0.8 / +1.1	+1.2 / −0	+0.8 / +0.1	−1.3 / +1.7	+1.8 / −0	+1.3 / +0.1	−1.5 / +0.4	+1.2 / −0	+1.5 / +0.8	−2.0 / +0.4	+1.2 / −0	+2.0 / +0.8
3.15– 4.73	−0.4 / +1.8	+1.4 / −0	+0.4 / −0.4	−0.7 / +2.9	+2.2 / −0	+0.7 / −0.7	−1.0 / +1.3	+1.4 / −0	+1.0 / +0.1	−1.5 / +2.1	+2.2 / −0	+1.5 / +0.1	−1.9 / +0.4	+1.4 / −0	+1.9 / +1.0	−2.4 / +0.4	+1.4 / −0	+2.4 / +1.0
4.73– 7.09	−0.5 / +2.1	+1.6 / −0	+0.5 / −0.5	−0.8 / +3.3	+2.5 / −0	+0.8 / −0.8	−1.1 / +1.5	+1.6 / −0	+1.1 / +0.1	−1.7 / +2.4	+2.5 / −0	+1.7 / +0.1	−2.2 / +0.4	+1.6 / −0	+2.2 / +1.2	−2.8 / +0.4	+1.6 / −0	+2.8 / +1.2
7.09– 9.85	−0.6 / +2.4	+1.8 / −0	+0.6 / −0.6	−0.9 / +3.7	+2.8 / −0	+0.9 / −0.9	−1.4 / +1.6	+1.8 / −0	+1.4 / +0.2	−2.0 / +2.6	+2.8 / −0	+2.0 / +0.2	−2.6 / +0.4	+1.8 / −0	+2.6 / +1.4	−3.2 / +0.4	+1.8 / −0	+3.2 / +1.4
9.85–12.41	−0.6 / +2.6	+2.0 / −0	+0.6 / −0.6	−1.0 / +4.0	+3.0 / −0	+1.0 / −1.0	−1.4 / +1.8	+2.0 / −0	+1.4 / +0.2	−2.2 / +2.8	+3.0 / −0	+2.2 / +0.2	−2.6 / +0.6	+2.0 / −0	+2.6 / +1.4	−3.4 / +0.6	+2.0 / −0	+3.4 / +1.4
12.41–15.75	−0.7 / +2.9	+2.2 / −0	+0.7 / −0.7	−1.0 / +4.5	+3.5 / −0	+1.0 / −1.0	−1.6 / +2.0	+2.2 / −0	+1.6 / +0.2	−2.4 / +3.3	+3.5 / −0	+2.4 / +0.2	−3.0 / +0.6	+2.2 / −0	+3.0 / +1.6	−3.8 / +0.6	+2.2 / −0	+3.8 / +1.6

[a]From ANSI B4.1–1967 (R1987). For larger diameters, see the standard.

8   Interference Locational Fits[a]—American National Standard

LN   *Locational interference fits* are used where accuracy of location is of prime importance, and for parts requiring rigidity and alignment with no special requirements for bore pressure. Such fits are not intended for parts designed to transmit frictional loads from one part to another by virtue of the tightness of fit, as these conditions are covered by force fits.

Basic hole system. Limits are in thousandths of an inch. See §14.8.
Limits for hole and shaft are applied algebraically to the basic size to obtain the limits of size for the parts.
Data in **boldface** are in accordance with ABC agreements.
Symbols H7, p6, etc., are hole and shaft designations used in ABC System.

Nominal Size Range, inches Over To	Class LN 1			Class LN 2			Class LN 3		
	Limits of Interference	Standard Limits		Limits of Interference	Standard Limits		Limits of Interference	Standard Limits	
		Hole H6	Shaft n5		Hole H7	Shaft p6		Hole H7	Shaft r6
0 – 0.12	0 0.45	+0.25 −0	+0.45 +0.25	0 0.65	+0.4 −0	+0.65 +0.4	0.1 0.75	+0.4 −0	+0.75 +0.5
0.12– 0.24	0 0.5	+0.3 −0	+0.5 +0.3	0 0.8	+0.5 −0	+0.8 +0.5	0.1 0.9	+0.5 0	+0.9 +0.6
0.24– 0.40	0 0.65	+0.4 −0	+0.65 +0.4	0 1.0	+0.6 −0	+1.0 +0.6	0.2 1.2	+0.6 −0	+1.2 +0.8
0.40– 0.71	0 0.8	+0.4 −0	+0.8 +0.4	0 1.1	+0.7 −0	+1.1 +0.7	0.3 1.4	+0.7 −0	+1.4 +1.0
0.71– 1.19	0 1.0	+0.5 −0	+1.0 +0.5	0 1.3	+0.8 −0	+1.3 +0.8	0.4 1.7	+0.8 −0	+1.7 +1.2
1.19– 1.97	0 1.1	+0.6 −0	+1.1 +0.6	0 1.6	+1.0 −0	+1.6 +1.0	0.4 2.0	+1.0 −0	+2.0 +1.4
1.97– 3.15	0.1 1.3	+0.7 −0	+1.3 +0.7	0.2 2.1	+1.2 −0	+2.1 +1.4	0.4 2.3	+1.2 −0	+2.3 +1.6
3.15– 4.73	0.1 1.6	+0.9 −0	+1.6 +1.0	0.2 2.5	+1.4 −0	+2.5 +1.6	0.6 2.9	+1.4 −0	+2.9 +2.0
4.73– 7.09	0.2 1.9	+1.0 −0	+1.9 +1.2	0.2 2.8	+1.6 −0	+2.8 +1.8	0.9 3.5	+1.6 −0	+3.5 +2.5
7.09– 9.85	0.2 2.2	+1.2 −0	+2.2 +1.4	0.2 3.2	+1.8 −0	+3.2 +2.0	1.2 4.2	+1.8 −0	+4.2 +3.0
9.85–12.41	0.2 2.3	+1.2 −0	+2.3 +1.4	0.2 3.4	+2.0 −0	+3.4 +2.2	1.5 4.7	+2.0 −0	+4.7 +3.5

[a]From ANSI B4.1—1967 (R1987). For larger diameters, see the standard.

9 Force and Shrink Fits[a]—American National Standard

FN 1 Light drive fits are those requiring light assembly pressures, and produce more or less permanent assemblies. They are suitable for thin sections or long fits, or in cast-iron external members.

FN 2 Medium drive fits are suitable for ordinary steel parts, or for shrink fits on light sections. They are about the tightest fits that can be used with high-grade cast-iron external members.

FN 3 Heavy drive fits are suitable for heavier steel parts or for shrink fits in medium sections.

FN 4 }
FN 5 } Force fits are suitable for parts which can be highly stressed, or for shrink fits where the heavy pressing forces required are impractical.

Basic hole system. Limits are in thousandths of an inch. See §14.8.

Limits for hole and shaft are applied algebraically to the basic size to obtain the limits of size for the parts.

Data in **boldface** are in accordance with ABC agreements.

Symbols H7, s6, etc., are hole and shaft designations used in ABC System.

Nominal Size Range, inches Over — To	Class FN 1 Limits of Interference	Class FN 1 Hole H6	Class FN 1 Shaft	Class FN 2 Limits of Interference	Class FN 2 Hole H7	Class FN 2 Shaft s6	Class FN 3 Limits of Interference	Class FN 3 Hole H7	Class FN 3 Shaft t6	Class FN 4 Limits of Interference	Class FN 4 Hole H7	Class FN 4 Shaft u6	Class FN 5 Limits of Interference	Class FN 5 Hole H8	Class FN 5 Shaft x7
0 – 0.12	0.05 / 0.5	**+0.25** / –0	+0.5 / +0.3	0.2 / 0.85	+0.4 / –0	**+0.85** / +0.6				0.3 / 0.95	+0.4 / –0	+ 0.95 / + 0.7	0.3 / 1.3	+0.6 / –0	+ 1.3 / + 0.9
0.12 – 0.24	0.1 / 0.6	+0.3 / –0	+0.6 / +0.4	0.2 / 1.0	+0.5 / –0	+1.0 / +0.7				0.4 / 1.2	+0.5 / –0	+ 1.2 / + 0.9	0.5 / 1.7	+0.7 / –0	+ 1.7 / + 1.2
0.24 – 0.40	0.1 / 0.75	+0.4 / –0	+0.75 / +0.5	0.4 / 1.4	+0.6 / –0	+1.4 / +1.0				0.6 / 1.6	+0.6 / –0	+ 1.6 / + 1.2	0.5 / 2.0	+0.9 / –0	+ 2.0 / + 1.4
0.40 – 0.56	0.1 / 0.8	+0.4 / –0	+0.8 / +0.5	0.5 / 1.6	+0.7 / –0	+1.6 / +1.2				0.7 / 1.8	+0.7 / –0	+ 1.8 / + 1.4	0.6 / 2.3	+1.0 / –0	+ 2.3 / + 1.6
0.56 – 0.71	0.2 / 0.9	+0.4 / –0	+0.9 / +0.6	0.5 / 1.6	+0.7 / –0	+1.6 / +1.2				0.7 / 1.8	+0.7 / –0	+ 1.8 / + 1.4	0.8 / 2.5	+1.0 / –0	+ 2.5 / + 1.8
0.71 – 0.95	0.2 / 1.1	+0.5 / –0	+1.1 / +0.7	0.6 / 1.9	+0.8 / –0	+1.9 / +1.4				0.8 / 2.1	+0.8 / –0	+ 2.1 / + 1.6	1.0 / 3.0	+1.2 / –0	+ 3.0 / + 2.2
0.95 – 1.19	0.3 / 1.2	+0.5 / –0	+1.2 / +0.8	0.6 / 1.9	+0.8 / –0	+1.9 / +1.4	0.8 / 2.1	+0.8 / –0	+ 2.1 / + 1.6	1.0 / 2.3	+0.8 / –0	+ 2.3 / + 1.8	1.3 / 3.3	+1.2 / –0	+ 3.3 / + 2.5
1.19 – 1.58	0.3 / 1.3	+0.6 / –0	+1.3 / +0.9	0.8 / 2.4	+1.0 / –0	+2.4 / +1.8	1.0 / 2.6	+1.0 / –0	+ 2.6 / + 2.0	1.5 / 3.1	+1.0 / –0	+ 3.1 / + 2.5	1.4 / 4.0	+1.6 / –0	+ 4.0 / + 3.0

[a] ANSI B4.1-1967 (R1987).

9   Force and Shrink Fits[a]—American National Standard (continued)

Nominal Size Range, inches Over–To	FN 1 Limits of Interference	FN 1 Hole H6	FN 1 Shaft	FN 2 Limits of Interference	FN 2 Hole H7	FN 2 Shaft s6	FN 3 Limits of Interference	FN 3 Hole H7	FN 3 Shaft t6	FN 4 Limits of Interference	FN 4 Hole H7	FN 4 Shaft u6	FN 5 Limits of Interference	FN 5 Hole H8	FN 5 Shaft x7
1.58– 1.97	0.4 / 1.4	+0.6 / –0	+1.4 / +1.0	0.8 / 2.4	+1.0 / –0	+2.4 / +1.8	1.2 / 2.8	+1.0 / –0	+2.8 / +2.2	1.8 / 3.4	+1.0 / –0	+3.4 / +2.8	2.4 / 5.0	+1.6 / –0	+5.0 / +4.0
1.97– 2.56	0.6 / 1.8	+0.7 / –0	+1.8 / +1.3	0.8 / 2.7	+1.2 / –0	+2.7 / +2.0	1.3 / 3.2	+1.2 / –0	+3.2 / +2.5	2.3 / 4.2	+1.2 / –0	+4.2 / +3.5	3.2 / 6.2	+1.8 / –0	+6.2 / +5.0
2.56– 3.15	0.7 / 1.9	+0.7 / –0	+1.9 / +1.4	1.0 / 2.9	+1.2 / –0	+2.9 / +2.2	1.8 / 3.7	+1.2 / –0	+3.7 / +3.0	2.8 / 4.7	+1.2 / –0	+4.7 / +4.0	4.2 / 7.2	+1.8 / –0	+7.2 / +6.0
3.15– 3.94	0.9 / 2.4	+0.9 / –0	+2.4 / +1.8	1.4 / 3.7	+1.4 / –0	+3.7 / +2.8	2.1 / 4.4	+1.4 / –0	+4.4 / +3.5	3.6 / 5.9	+1.4 / –0	+5.9 / +5.0	4.8 / 8.4	+2.2 / –0	+8.4 / +7.0
3.94– 4.73	1.1 / 2.6	+0.9 / –0	+2.6 / +2.0	1.6 / 3.9	+1.4 / –0	+3.9 / +3.0	2.6 / 4.9	+1.4 / –0	+4.9 / +4.0	4.6 / 6.9	+1.4 / –0	+6.9 / +6.0	5.8 / 9.4	+2.2 / –0	+9.4 / +8.0
4.73– 5.52	1.2 / 2.9	+1.0 / –0	+2.9 / +2.2	1.9 / 4.5	+1.6 / –0	+4.5 / +3.5	3.4 / 6.0	+1.6 / –0	+6.0 / +5.0	5.4 / 8.0	+1.6 / –0	+8.0 / +7.0	7.5 / 11.6	+2.5 / –0	+11.6 / +10.0
5.52– 6.30	1.5 / 3.2	+1.0 / –0	+3.2 / +2.5	2.4 / 5.0	+1.6 / –0	+5.0 / +4.0	3.4 / 6.0	+1.6 / –0	+6.0 / +5.0	5.4 / 8.0	+1.6 / –0	+8.0 / +7.0	9.5 / 13.6	+2.5 / –0	+13.6 / +12.0
6.30– 7.09	1.8 / 3.5	+1.0 / –0	+3.5 / +2.8	2.9 / 5.5	+1.6 / –0	+5.5 / +4.5	4.4 / 7.0	+1.6 / –0	+7.0 / +6.0	6.4 / 9.0	+1.6 / –0	+9.0 / +8.0	9.5 / 13.6	+2.5 / –0	+13.6 / +12.0
7.09– 7.88	1.8 / 3.8	+1.2 / –0	+3.8 / +3.0	3.2 / 6.2	+1.8 / –0	+6.2 / +5.0	5.2 / 8.2	+1.8 / –0	+8.2 / +7.0	7.2 / 10.2	+1.8 / –0	+10.2 / +9.0	11.2 / 15.8	+2.8 / –0	+15.8 / +14.0
7.88– 8.86	2.3 / 4.3	+1.2 / –0	+4.3 / +3.5	3.2 / 6.2	+1.8 / –0	+6.2 / +5.0	5.2 / 8.2	+1.8 / –0	+8.2 / +7.0	8.2 / 11.2	+1.8 / –0	+11.2 / +10.0	13.2 / 17.8	+2.8 / –0	+17.8 / +16.0
8.86– 9.85	2.3 / 4.3	+1.2 / –0	+4.3 / +3.5	4.2 / 7.2	+1.8 / –0	+7.2 / +6.0	6.2 / 9.2	+1.8 / –0	+9.2 / +8.0	10.2 / 13.2	+1.8 / –0	+13.2 / +12.0	13.2 / 17.8	+2.8 / –0	+17.8 / +16.0
9.85–11.03	2.8 / 4.9	+1.2 / –0	+4.9 / +4.0	4.0 / 7.2	+2.0 / –0	+7.2 / +6.0	7.0 / 10.2	+2.0 / –0	+10.2 / +9.0	10.0 / 13.2	+2.0 / –0	+13.2 / +12.0	15.0 / 20.0	+3.0 / –0	+20.0 / +18.0
11.03–12.41	2.8 / 4.9	+1.2 / –0	+4.9 / +4.0	5.0 / 8.2	+2.0 / –0	+8.2 / +7.0	7.0 / 10.2	+2.0 / –0	+10.2 / +9.0	12.0 / 15.2	+2.0 / –0	+15.2 / +14.0	17.0 / 22.0	+3.0 / –0	+22.0 / +20.0
12.41–13.98	3.1 / 5.5	+1.4 / –0	+5.5 / +4.5	5.8 / 9.4	+2.2 / –0	+9.4 / +8.0	7.8 / 11.4	+2.2 / –0	+11.4 / +10.0	13.8 / 17.4	+2.2 / –0	+17.4 / +16.0	18.5 / 24.2	+3.5 / +0	+24.2 / +22.0

[a]From ANSI B4.1–1967 (R1987). For larger diameters, see the standard.

10   International Tolerance Grades[a]

Dimensions are in millimeters.

Basic sizes		Tolerance grades[b]																		
Over	Up to and Including	IT01	IT0	IT1	IT2	IT3	IT4	IT5	IT6	IT7	IT8	IT9	IT10	IT11	IT12	IT13	IT14	IT15	IT16
0	3	0.0003	0.0005	0.0008	0.0012	0.002	0.003	0.004	0.006	0.010	0.014	0.025	0.040	0.060	0.100	0.140	0.250	0.400	0.600
3	6	0.0004	0.0006	0.001	0.0015	0.0025	0.004	0.005	0.008	0.012	0.018	0.030	0.048	0.075	0.120	0.180	0.300	0.480	0.750
6	10	0.0004	0.0006	0.001	0.0015	0.0025	0.004	0.006	0.009	0.015	0.022	0.036	0.058	0.090	0.150	0.220	0.360	0.580	0.900
10	18	0.0005	0.0008	0.0012	0.002	0.003	0.005	0.008	0.011	0.018	0.027	0.043	0.070	0.110	0.180	0.270	0.430	0.700	1.100
18	30	0.0006	0.001	0.0015	0.0025	0.004	0.006	0.009	0.013	0.021	0.033	0.052	0.084	0.130	0.210	0.330	0.520	0.840	1.300
30	50	0.0006	0.001	0.0015	0.0025	0.004	0.007	0.011	0.016	0.025	0.039	0.062	0.100	0.160	0.250	0.390	0.620	1.000	1.600
50	80	0.0008	0.0012	0.002	0.003	0.005	0.008	0.013	0.019	0.030	0.046	0.074	0.120	0.190	0.300	0.460	0.740	1.200	1.900
80	120	0.001	0.0015	0.0025	0.004	0.006	0.010	0.015	0.022	0.035	0.054	0.087	0.140	0.220	0.350	0.540	0.870	1.400	2.200
120	180	0.0012	0.002	0.0035	0.005	0.008	0.012	0.018	0.025	0.040	0.063	0.100	0.160	0.250	0.400	0.630	1.000	1.600	2.500
180	250	0.002	0.003	0.0045	0.007	0.010	0.014	0.020	0.029	0.046	0.072	0.115	0.185	0.290	0.460	0.720	1.150	1.850	2.900
250	315	0.0025	0.004	0.006	0.008	0.012	0.016	0.023	0.032	0.052	0.081	0.130	0.210	0.320	0.520	0.810	1.300	2.100	3.200
315	400	0.003	0.005	0.007	0.009	0.013	0.018	0.025	0.036	0.057	0.089	0.140	0.230	0.360	0.570	0.890	1.400	2.300	3.600
400	500	0.004	0.006	0.008	0.010	0.015	0.020	0.027	0.040	0.063	0.097	0.155	0.250	0.400	0.630	0.970	1.550	2.500	4.000
500	630	0.0045	0.006	0.009	0.011	0.016	0.022	0.030	0.044	0.070	0.110	0.175	0.280	0.440	0.700	1.100	1.750	2.800	4.400
630	800	0.005	0.007	0.010	0.013	0.018	0.025	0.035	0.050	0.080	0.125	0.200	0.320	0.500	0.800	1.250	2.000	3.200	5.000
800	1000	0.0055	0.008	0.011	0.015	0.021	0.029	0.040	0.056	0.090	0.140	0.230	0.360	0.560	0.900	1.400	2.300	3.600	5.600
1000	1250	0.0065	0.009	0.013	0.018	0.024	0.034	0.046	0.066	0.105	0.165	0.260	0.420	0.660	1.050	1.650	2.600	4.200	6.600
1250	1600	0.008	0.011	0.015	0.021	0.029	0.040	0.054	0.078	0.125	0.195	0.310	0.500	0.780	1.250	1.950	3.100	5.000	7.800
1600	2000	0.009	0.013	0.018	0.025	0.035	0.048	0.065	0.092	0.150	0.230	0.370	0.600	0.920	1.500	2.300	3.700	6.000	9.200
2000	2500	0.011	0.015	0.022	0.030	0.041	0.057	0.077	0.110	0.175	0.280	0.440	0.700	1.100	1.750	2.800	4.400	7.000	11.000
2500	3150	0.013	0.018	0.026	0.036	0.050	0.069	0.093	0.135	0.210	0.330	0.540	0.860	1.350	2.100	3.300	5.400	8.600	13.500

[a]From ANSI B4.2—1978 (R1984).

[b]IT Values for tolerance grades larger than IT16 can be calculated by using the formulas: IT17 = IT × 10, IT18 = IT13 × 10, etc.

11 Preferred Metric Hole Basis Clearance Fits[a] — American National Standard

Dimensions are in millimeters.

Basic Size		Loose Running Hole H11	Shaft c11	Fit	Free Running Hole H9	Shaft d9	Fit	Close Running Hole H8	f7	Fit	Sliding Hole H7	Shaft g6	Fit	Locational Clearance Hole H7	Shaft h6	Fit
1	Max	1.060	0.940	0.180	1.025	0.980	0.070	1.014	0.994	0.030	1.010	0.998	0.018	1.010	1.000	0.016
	Min	1.060	0.880	0.060	1.000	0.955	0.020	1.000	0.984	0.006	1.000	0.992	0.002	1.000	0.994	0.000
1.2	Max	1.260	1.140	0.180	1.225	1.180	0.070	1.214	1.194	0.030	1.210	1.198	0.018	1.210	1.200	0.016
	Min	1.200	1.080	0.060	1.200	1.155	0.020	1.200	1.184	0.036	1.200	1.192	0.002	1.200	1.194	0.000
1.6	Max	1.660	1.540	0.180	1.625	1.580	0.070	1.614	1.594	0.030	1.610	1.598	0.018	1.610	1.600	0.016
	Min	1.600	1.480	0.060	1.600	1.555	0.020	1.600	1.584	0.006	1.600	1.592	0.002	1.600	1.594	0.000
2	Max	2.060	1.940	0.180	2.025	1.980	0.070	2.014	1.994	0.030	2.010	1.998	0.018	2.010	2.000	0.016
	Min	2.000	1.880	0.060	2.000	1.955	0.020	2.000	1.984	0.006	2.000	1.992	0.002	2.000	1.994	0.000
2.5	Max	2.560	2.440	0.180	2.525	2.480	0.070	2.514	2.494	0.030	2.510	2.498	0.018	2.510	2.500	0.016
	Min	2.500	2.380	0.060	2.500	2.455	0.020	2.500	2.484	0.006	2.500	2.492	0.002	2.500	2.494	0.000
3	Max	3.060	2.940	0.180	3.025	2.980	0.070	3.014	2.994	0.030	3.010	2.998	0.018	3.010	3.000	0.016
	Min	3.000	2.880	0.060	3.000	2.955	0.020	3.000	2.984	0.006	3.000	2.992	0.002	3.000	2.994	0.000
4	Max	4.075	3.930	0.220	4.030	3.970	0.090	4.018	3.990	0.040	4.012	3.996	0.024	4.012	4.000	0.020
	Min	4.000	3.855	0.070	4.000	3.940	0.030	4.000	3.978	0.010	4.000	3.988	0.004	4.000	3.992	0.000
5	Max	5.075	4.930	0.220	5.030	4.970	0.090	5.018	4.990	0.040	5.012	4.996	0.024	5.012	5.000	0.020
	Min	5.000	4.855	0.070	5.000	4.940	0.030	5.000	4.978	0.010	5.000	4.988	0.004	5.000	4.992	0.000
6	Max	6.075	5.930	0.220	6.030	5.970	0.090	6.018	5.990	0.040	6.012	5.996	0.024	6.012	6.000	0.020
	Min	6.000	5.855	0.070	6.000	5.940	0.030	6.000	5.978	0.010	6.000	5.988	0.004	6.000	5.992	0.000
8	Max	8.090	7.920	0.260	8.036	7.960	0.112	8.022	7.987	0.050	8.015	7.995	0.029	8.015	8.000	0.024
	Min	8.000	7.830	0.080	8.000	7.924	0.040	8.000	7.972	0.013	8.000	7.986	0.005	8.000	7.991	0.000
10	Max	10.090	9.920	0.260	10.036	9.960	0.112	10.022	9.987	0.050	10.015	9.995	0.029	10.015	10.000	0.024
	Min	10.000	9.830	0.080	10.000	9.924	0.040	10.000	9.972	0.013	10.000	9.986	0.005	10.000	9.991	0.000
12	Max	12.110	11.905	0.315	12.043	11.950	0.136	12.027	11.984	0.061	12.018	11.994	0.035	12.018	12.000	0.029
	Min	12.000	11.795	0.095	12.000	11.907	0.050	12.000	11.966	0.016	12.000	11.983	0.006	12.000	11.989	0.000
16	Max	16.110	15.905	0.315	16.043	15.950	0.136	16.027	15.984	0.061	16.018	15.994	0.035	16.018	16.000	0.029
	Min	16.000	15.795	0.095	16.000	15.907	0.050	16.000	15.966	0.016	16.000	15.983	0.006	16.000	15.989	0.000
20	Max	20.130	19.890	0.370	20.052	19.935	0.169	20.033	19.980	0.074	20.021	19.993	0.041	20.021	20.000	0.034
	Min	20.000	19.760	0.110	20.000	19.883	0.065	20.000	19.959	0.020	20.000	19.980	0.007	20.000	19.987	0.000
25	Max	25.130	24.890	0.370	25.052	24.935	0.169	25.033	24.980	0.074	25.021	24.993	0.041	25.021	25.000	0.034
	Min	25.000	24.760	0.110	25.000	24.883	0.065	25.000	24.959	0.020	25.000	24.980	0.007	25.000	24.987	0.000
30	Max	30.130	29.890	0.370	30.052	29.935	0.169	30.033	29.980	0.074	30.021	29.993	0.041	30.021	30.000	0.034
	Min	30.000	29.760	0.110	30.000	29.883	0.065	30.000	29.959	0.020	30.000	29.980	0.007	30.000	29.987	0.000

[a]From ANSI B4.2—1978 (R1984). For description of preferred fits, see Table 14.2.

11   Preferred Metric Hole Basis Clearance Fits[a]— American National Standard (continued)

Dimensions are in millimeters.

Basic Size		Loose Running			Free Running			Close Running			Sliding			Locational Clearance		
		Hole H11	Shaft. c11	Fit	Hole H9	Shaft d9	Fit	Hole H8	Shaft f7	Fit	Hole H7	Shaft g6	Fit	Hole H7	Shaft h6	Fit
40	Max	40.160	39.880	0.440	40.062	39.920	0.204	40.039	39.975	0.089	40.025	39.991	0.050	40.025	40.000	0.041
	Min	40.000	39.720	0.120	40.000	39.858	0.080	40.000	39.950	0.025	40.000	39.975	0.009	40.000	39.984	0.000
50	Max	50.160	49.870	0.450	50.062	49.920	0.204	50.039	49.975	0.089	50.025	49.991	0.050	50.025	50.000	0.041
	Min	50.000	49.710	0.130	50.000	49.858	0.080	50.000	49.950	0.025	50.000	49.975	0.009	50.000	49.984	0.000
60	Max	60.190	59.860	0.520	60.074	59.900	0.248	60.046	59.970	0.106	60.030	59.990	0.059	60.030	60.000	0.049
	Min	60.000	59.670	0.140	60.000	59.826	0.100	60.000	59.940	0.030	60.000	59.971	0.010	60.000	59.981	0.000
80	Max	80.190	79.950	0.530	80.074	79.900	0.248	80.046	79.970	0.106	80.030	79.990	0.059	80.030	80.000	0.049
	Min	80.000	79.660	0.150	80.000	79.826	0.100	80.000	79.940	0.030	80.000	79.971	0.010	80.000	79.981	0.000
100	Max	100.220	99.830	0.610	100.087	99.880	0.294	100.054	99.964	0.125	100.035	99.988	0.069	100.035	100.000	0.057
	Min	100.000	99.610	0.170	100.000	99.793	0.120	100.000	99.929	0.036	100.000	99.966	0.012	100.000	99.978	0.000
120	Max	120.220	119.820	0.620	120.087	119.880	0.294	120.054	119.964	0.125	120.035	119.988	0.069	120.035	120.000	0.057
	Min	120.000	119.600	0.180	120.000	119.793	0.120	120.000	119.929	0.036	120.000	119.966	0.012	120.000	119.978	0.000
160	Max	160.250	159.790	0.710	160.100	159.855	0.345	160.063	159.957	0.146	160.040	159.986	0.079	160.040	160.000	0.065
	Min	160.000	159.540	0.210	160.000	159.755	0.145	160.000	159.917	0.043	160.000	159.961	0.014	160.000	159.975	0.000
200	Max	200.290	199.760	0.820	200.115	199.830	0.400	200.072	199.950	0.168	200.046	199.985	0.090	200.046	200.000	0.075
	Min	200.000	199.470	0.240	200.000	199.715	0.170	200.000	199.904	0.050	200.000	199.956	0.015	200.000	199.971	0.000
250	Max	250.290	249.720	0.860	250.115	249.830	0.400	250.072	249.950	0.168	250.046	249.985	0.090	250.046	250.000	0.075
	Min	250.000	249.430	0.280	250.000	249.715	0.170	250.000	249.904	0.050	250.000	249.956	0.015	250.000	249.971	0.000
300	Max	300.320	299.670	0.970	300.130	299.810	0.450	300.081	299.944	0.189	300.052	299.983	0.101	300.052	300.000	0.084
	Min	300.000	299.350	0.330	300.000	299.680	0.190	300.000	299.892	0.056	300.000	299.951	0.017	300.000	299.968	0.000
400	Max	400.360	399.600	1.120	400.140	399.790	0.490	400.089	399.938	0.208	400.057	399.982	0.111	400.057	400.000	0.093
	Min	400.000	399.240	0.400	400.000	399.650	0.210	400.000	399.881	0.062	400.000	399.946	0.018	400.000	399.964	0.000
500	Max	500.400	499.520	1.280	500.155	499.770	0.540	500.097	499.932	0.228	500.063	499.980	0.123	500.063	500.000	0.103
	Min	500.000	499.120	0.480	500.000	499.615	0.230	500.000	499.869	0.068	500.000	499.940	0.020	500.000	499.960	0.000

[a]From ANSI B4.2—1978 (R1984). For description of preferred fits, see Table 14.2.

12   Preferred Metric Hole Basis Transition and Interference Fits[a]— American National Standard

Dimensions are in millimeters.

Basic Size		Locational Transn. Hole H7	Locational Transn. Shaft k6	Locational Transn. Fit	Locational Transn. Hole H7	Locational Transn. Shaft n6	Locational Transn. Fit	Locational Interf. Hole H7	Locational Interf. Shaft p6	Locational Interf. Fit	Medium Drive Hole H7	Medium Drive Shaft s6	Medium Drive Fit	Force Hole H7	Force Shaft u6	Force Fit
1	Max	1.010	1.006	0.010	1.010	1.010	0.006	1.010	1.012	0.004	1.010	1.020	−0.004	1.010	1.024	−0.008
	Min	1.000	1.000	−0.006	1.000	1.004	−0.010	1.000	1.006	−0.012	1.000	1.014	−0.020	1.000	1.018	−0.024
1.2	Max	1.210	1.206	0.010	1.210	1.210	0.006	1.210	1.212	0.004	1.210	1.220	−0.004	1.210	1.224	−0.008
	Min	1.200	1.200	−0.006	1.200	1.204	−0.010	1.200	1.206	−0.012	1.200	1.214	−0.020	1.200	1.218	−0.024
1.6	Max	1.610	1.606	0.010	1.610	1.610	0.006	1.610	1.612	0.004	1.610	1.620	−0.004	1.610	1.624	−0.008
	Min	1.600	1.600	−0.006	1.600	1.604	−0.010	1.600	1.606	−0.012	1.600	1.614	−0.020	1.600	1.618	−0.024
2	Max	2.010	2.006	0.010	2.010	2.010	0.006	2.010	2.012	0.004	2.010	2.020	−0.004	2.010	2.024	−0.008
	Min	2.000	2.000	−0.006	2.000	2.004	−0.010	2.000	2.006	−0.012	2.000	2.014	−0.020	2.000	2.018	−0.024
2.5	Max	2.510	2.506	0.010	2.510	2.510	0.006	2.510	2.512	0.004	2.510	2.520	−0.004	2.510	2.524	−0.008
	Min	2.500	2.500	−0.006	2.500	2.504	−0.010	2.500	2.506	−0.012	2.500	2.514	−0.020	2.500	2.518	−0.024
3	Max	3.010	3.006	0.010	3.010	3.010	0.006	3.010	3.012	0.004	3.010	3.020	−0.004	3.010	3.024	−0.008
	Min	3.000	3.000	−0.006	3.000	3.004	−0.010	3.000	3.006	−0.012	3.000	3.014	−0.020	3.000	3.018	−0.024
4	Max	4.012	4.009	0.011	4.012	4.016	0.004	4.012	4.020	0.000	4.012	4.027	−0.007	4.012	4.031	−0.011
	Min	4.000	4.001	−0.009	4.000	4.008	−0.016	4.000	4.012	−0.020	4.000	4.019	−0.027	4.000	4.023	−0.031
5	Max	5.012	5.009	0.011	5.012	5.016	0.004	5.012	5.020	0.000	5.012	5.027	−0.007	5.012	5.031	−0.011
	Min	5.000	5.001	−0.009	5.000	5.008	−0.016	5.000	5.012	−0.020	5.000	5.019	−0.027	5.000	5.023	−0.031
6	Max	6.012	6.009	0.011	6.012	6.016	0.004	6.012	6.020	0.000	6.012	6.027	−0.007	6.012	6.031	−0.011
	Min	6.000	6.001	−0.009	6.000	6.008	−0.016	6.000	6.012	−0.020	6.000	6.019	−0.027	6.000	6.023	−0.031
8	Max	8.015	8.010	0.014	8.015	8.019	0.005	8.015	8.024	0.000	8.015	8.032	−0.008	8.015	8.037	−0.013
	Min	8.000	8.001	−0.010	8.000	8.010	−0.019	8.000	8.015	−0.024	8.000	8.023	−0.032	8.000	8.028	−0.037
10	Max	10.015	10.010	0.014	10.015	10.019	0.005	10.015	10.024	0.000	10.015	10.032	−0.008	10.015	10.037	−0.013
	Min	10.000	10.001	−0.010	10.000	10.010	−0.019	10.000	10.015	−0.024	10.000	10.023	−0.032	10.000	10.028	−0.037
12	Max	12.018	12.012	0.017	12.018	12.023	0.006	12.018	12.029	0.000	12.018	12.039	−0.010	12.018	12.044	−0.015
	Min	12.000	12.001	−0.012	12.000	12.012	−0.023	12.000	12.018	−0.029	12.000	12.028	−0.039	12.000	12.033	−0.044
16	Max	16.018	16.012	0.017	16.018	16.023	0.006	16.018	16.029	0.000	16.018	16.039	−0.010	16.018	16.044	−0.015
	Min	16.000	16.001	−0.012	16.000	16.012	−0.023	16.000	16.018	−0.029	16.000	16.028	−0.039	16.000	16.033	−0.044
20	Max	20.021	20.015	0.019	20.021	20.028	0.006	20.021	20.035	−0.001	20.021	20.048	−0.014	20.021	20.054	−0.020
	Min	20.000	20.002	−0.015	20.000	20.015	−0.028	20.000	20.022	−0.035	20.000	20.035	−0.048	20.000	20.041	−0.054
25	Max	25.021	25.015	0.019	25.021	25.028	0.006	25.021	25.035	−0.001	25.021	25.048	−0.014	25.021	25.061	−0.027
	Min	25.000	25.002	−0.015	25.000	25.015	−0.028	25.000	25.022	−0.035	25.000	25.035	−0.048	25.000	25.048	−0.061
30	Max	30.021	30.015	0.019	30.021	30.028	0.006	30.021	30.035	−0.001	30.021	30.048	−0.014	30.021	30.061	−0.027
	Min	30.000	30.002	−0.015	30.000	30.015	−0.028	30.000	30.022	−0.035	30.000	30.035	−0.048	30.000	30.048	−0.061

[a]From ANSI B4.2—1978 (R1984). For description of preferred fits, see Table 14.2.

12   Preferred Metric Hole Basis Transition and Interference Fits[a]— American National Standard (continued)

Dimensions are in millimeters.

Basic Size		Locational Transn. Hole H7	Locational Transn. Shaft k6	Locational Transn. Fit	Locational Transn. Hole H7	Locational Transn. Shaft n6	Locational Transn. Fit	Locational Interf. Hole H7	Locational Interf. Shaft p6	Locational Interf. Fit	Medium Drive Hole H7	Medium Drive Shaft s6	Medium Drive Fit	Force Hole H7	Force Shaft u6	Force Fit
40	Max	40.025	40.018	0.023	40.025	40.033	0.008	40.025	40.042	−0.001	40.025	40.059	−0.018	40.025	40.076	−0.035
	Min	40.000	40.002	−0.018	40.000	40.017	−0.033	40.000	40.026	−0.042	40.000	40.043	−0.059	40.000	40.060	−0.076
50	Max	50.025	50.018	0.023	50.025	50.033	0.008	50.025	50.042	−0.001	50.025	50.059	−0.018	50.025	50.086	−0.045
	Min	50.000	50.002	−0.018	50.000	50.017	−0.033	50.000	50.026	−0.042	50.000	50.043	−0.059	50.000	50.070	−0.086
60	Max	60.030	60.021	0.028	60.030	60.039	0.010	60.030	60.051	−0.002	60.030	60.072	−0.023	60.030	60.106	−0.057
	Min	60.000	60.002	−0.021	60.000	60.020	−0.039	60.000	60.032	−0.051	60.000	60.053	−0.072	60.000	60.087	−0.106
80	Max	80.030	80.021	0.028	80.030	80.039	0.010	80.030	80.051	−0.002	80.030	80.078	−0.029	80.030	80.121	−0.072
	Min	80.000	80.002	−0.021	80.000	80.020	−0.039	80.000	80.032	−0.051	80.000	80.059	−0.078	80.000	80.102	−0.121
100	Max	100.035	100.025	0.032	100.035	100.045	0.012	100.035	100.059	−0.002	100.035	100.093	−0.036	100.035	100.146	−0.089
	Min	100.000	100.003	−0.025	100.000	100.023	−0.045	100.000	100.037	−0.059	100.000	100.071	−0.093	100.000	100.124	−0.146
120	Max	120.035	120.025	0.032	120.035	120.045	0.012	120.035	120.059	−0.002	120.035	120.101	−0.044	120.035	120.166	−0.109
	Min	120.000	120.003	−0.025	120.000	120.023	−0.045	120.000	120.037	−0.059	120.000	120.079	−0.101	120.000	120.144	−0.166
160	Max	160.040	160.028	0.037	160.040	160.052	0.013	160.040	160.068	−0.003	160.040	160.125	−0.060	160.040	160.215	−0.150
	Min	160.000	160.003	−0.028	160.000	160.027	−0.052	160.000	160.043	−0.068	160.000	160.100	−0.125	160.000	160.190	−0.215
200	Max	200.046	200.033	0.042	200.046	200.060	0.015	200.046	200.079	−0.004	200.046	200.151	−0.076	200.046	200.265	−0.190
	Min	200.000	200.004	−0.033	200.000	200.031	−0.060	200.000	200.050	−0.079	200.000	200.122	−0.151	200.000	200.236	−0.265
250	Max	250.046	250.033	0.042	250.046	250.060	0.015	250.046	250.079	−0.004	250.046	250.169	−0.094	250.046	250.313	−0.238
	Min	250.000	250.004	−0.033	250.000	250.031	−0.060	250.000	250.050	−0.079	250.000	250.140	−0.169	250.000	250.284	−0.313
300	Max	300.052	300.036	0.048	300.052	300.066	0.018	300.052	300.088	−0.004	300.052	300.202	−0.118	300.052	300.382	−0.298
	Min	300.000	300.004	−0.036	300.000	300.034	−0.066	300.000	300.056	−0.088	300.000	300.170	−0.202	300.000	300.350	−0.382
400	Max	400.057	400.040	0.053	400.057	400.073	0.020	400.057	400.098	−0.005	400.057	400.244	−0.151	400.057	400.471	−0.378
	Min	400.000	400.004	−0.040	400.000	400.037	−0.073	400.000	400.062	−0.098	400.000	400.208	−0.244	400.000	400.435	−0.471
500	Max	500.063	500.045	0.058	500.063	500.080	0.023	500.063	500.108	−0.005	500.063	500.292	−0.189	500.063	500.580	−0.477
	Min	500.000	500.005	−0.045	500.000	500.040	−0.080	500.000	500.068	−0.108	500.000	500.252	−0.292	500.000	500.540	−0.580

[a]From ANSI B4.2—1978 (R1984). For description of preferred fits, see Table 14.2.

13　Preferred Metric Shaft Basis Clearance Fits[a] — American National Standard

Dimensions are in millimeters.

Basic Size		Loose Running Hole C11	Loose Running Shaft h11	Loose Running Fit	Free Running Hole D9	Free Running Shaft h9	Free Running Fit	Close Running Hole F8	Close Running Shaft h7	Close Running Fit	Sliding Hole G7	Sliding Shaft h6	Sliding Fit	Locational Clearance Hole H7	Locational Clearance Shaft h6	Locational Clearance Fit
1	Max	1.120	1.000	0.180	1.045	1.000	0.070	1.020	1.000	0.030	1.012	1.000	0.018	1.010	1.000	0.016
	Min	1.060	0.940	0.060	1.020	0.975	0.020	1.006	0.990	0.006	1.002	0.994	0.002	1.000	0.994	0.000
1.2	Max	1.320	1.200	0.180	1.245	1.200	0.070	1.220	1.200	0.030	1.212	1.200	0.018	1.210	1.200	0.016
	Min	1.260	1.140	0.060	1.220	1.175	0.020	1.206	1.190	0.006	1.202	1.194	0.002	1.200	1.194	0.000
1.6	Max	1.720	1.600	0.180	1.645	1.600	0.070	1.620	1.600	0.030	1.612	1.600	0.018	1.610	1.600	0.016
	Min	1.660	1.540	0.060	1.620	1.575	0.020	1.606	1.590	0.006	1.602	1.594	0.002	1.600	1.594	0.000
2	Max	2.120	2.000	0.180	2.045	2.000	0.070	2.020	2.000	0.030	2.012	2.000	0.018	2.010	2.000	0.016
	Min	2.060	1.940	0.060	2.020	1.975	0.020	2.006	1.990	0.006	2.002	1.994	0.002	2.000	1.994	0.000
2.5	Max	2.620	2.500	0.180	2.545	2.500	0.070	2.520	2.500	0.030	2.512	2.500	0.018	2.510	2.500	0.016
	Min	2.560	2.440	0.060	2.520	2.475	0.020	2.506	2.490	0.006	2.502	2.494	0.002	2.500	2.494	0.000
3	Max	3.120	3.000	0.180	3.045	3.000	0.070	3.020	3.000	0.030	3.012	3.000	0.018	3.010	3.000	0.016
	Min	3.060	2.940	0.060	3.020	2.975	0.020	3.006	2.990	0.006	3.002	2.994	0.002	3.000	2.994	0.000
4	Max	4.145	4.000	0.220	4.060	4.000	0.090	4.028	4.000	0.040	4.016	4.000	0.024	4.012	4.000	0.020
	Min	4.070	3.925	0.070	4.030	3.970	0.030	4.010	3.988	0.010	4.004	3.992	0.004	4.000	3.992	0.000
5	Max	5.145	5.000	0.220	5.060	5.000	0.090	5.028	5.000	0.040	5.016	5.000	0.024	5.012	5.000	0.020
	Min	5.070	4.925	0.070	5.030	4.970	0.030	5.010	4.988	0.010	5.004	4.992	0.004	5.000	4.992	0.000
6	Max	6.145	6.000	0.220	6.060	6.000	0.090	6.028	6.000	0.040	6.016	6.000	0.024	6.012	6.000	0.020
	Min	6.070	5.925	0.070	6.030	5.970	0.030	6.010	5.988	0.010	6.004	5.992	0.004	6.000	5.992	0.000
8	Max	8.170	8.000	0.260	8.076	8.000	0.112	8.035	8.000	0.050	8.020	8.000	0.029	8.015	8.000	0.024
	Min	8.080	7.910	0.080	8.040	7.964	0.040	8.013	7.985	0.013	8.005	7.991	0.005	8.000	7.991	0.000
10	Max	10.170	10.000	0.260	10.076	10.000	0.112	10.035	10.000	0.050	10.020	10.000	0.029	10.015	10.000	0.024
	Min	10.080	9.910	0.080	10.040	9.964	0.040	10.013	9.985	0.013	10.005	9.991	0.005	10.000	9.991	0.000
12	Max	12.205	12.000	0.315	12.093	12.000	0.136	12.043	12.000	0.061	12.024	12.000	0.035	12.018	12.000	0.029
	Min	12.095	11.890	0.095	12.050	11.957	0.050	12.016	11.982	0.016	12.006	11.989	0.006	12.000	11.989	0.000
16	Max	16.205	16.000	0.315	16.093	16.000	0.136	16.043	16.000	0.061	16.024	16.000	0.035	16.018	16.000	0.029
	Min	16.095	15.890	0.095	16.050	15.957	0.050	16.016	15.982	0.016	16.006	15.989	0.006	16.000	15.989	0.000
20	Max	20.240	20.000	0.370	20.117	20.000	0.169	20.053	20.000	0.074	20.028	20.000	0.041	20.021	20.000	0.034
	Min	20.110	19.870	0.110	20.065	19.948	0.065	20.020	19.979	0.020	20.007	19.987	0.007	20.000	19.987	0.000
25	Max	25.240	25.000	0.370	25.117	25.000	0.169	25.053	25.000	0.074	25.028	25.000	0.041	25.021	25.000	0.034
	Min	25.110	24.870	0.110	25.065	24.948	0.065	25.020	24.979	0.020	25.007	24.987	0.007	25.000	24.987	0.000
30	Max	30.240	30.000	0.370	30.117	30.000	0.169	30.053	30.000	0.074	30.028	30.000	0.041	30.021	30.000	0.034
	Min	30.110	29.870	0.110	30.065	29.948	0.065	30.020	29.979	0.020	30.007	29.987	0.007	30.000	29.987	0.000

[a] From ANSI B4.2—1978 (R1984). For description of preferred fits, see Table 14.2.

13   Preferred Metric Shaft Basis Clearance Fits[a]— American National Standard (continued)

Dimensions are in millimeters.

Basic Size		Loose Running			Free Running			Close Running			Sliding			Locational Clearance		
		Hole C11	Shaft h11	Fit	Hole D9	Shaft h9	Fit	Hole F8	Shaft h7	Fit	Hole G7	Shaft h6	Fit	Hole H7	Shaft h6	Fit
40	Max	40.280	40.000	0.440	40.142	40.000	0.204	40.064	40.000	0.089	40.034	40.000	0.050	40.025	40.000	0.041
	Min	40.120	39.840	0.120	40.080	39.938	0.080	40.025	39.975	0.025	40.009	39.984	0.009	40.000	39.984	0.000
50	Max	50.290	50.000	0.450	50.142	50.000	0.204	50.064	50.000	0.089	50.034	50.000	0.050	50.025	50.000	0.041
	Min	50.130	49.840	0.130	50.080	49.938	0.080	50.025	49.975	0.025	50.009	49.984	0.009	50.000	49.984	0.000
60	Max	60.330	60.000	0.520	60.174	60.000	0.248	60.076	60.000	0.106	60.040	60.000	0.059	60.030	60.000	0.049
	Min	60.140	59.810	0.140	60.100	59.926	0.100	60.030	59.970	0.030	60.010	59.981	0.010	60.000	59.981	0.000
80	Max	80.340	80.000	0.530	80.174	80.000	0.248	80.076	80.000	0.106	80.040	80.000	0.059	80.030	80.000	0.049
	Min	80.150	79.810	0.150	80.100	79.926	0.100	80.030	79.970	0.030	80.010	79.981	0.010	80.000	79.981	0.000
100	Max	100.390	100.000	0.610	100.207	100.000	0.294	100.090	100.000	0.125	100.047	100.000	0.069	100.035	100.000	0.057
	Min	100.170	99.780	0.170	100.120	99.913	0.120	100.036	99.965	0.036	100.012	99.978	0.012	100.000	99.978	0.000
120	Max	120.400	120.000	0.620	120.207	120.000	0.294	120.090	120.000	0.125	120.047	120.000	0.069	120.035	120.000	0.057
	Min	120.180	119.780	0.180	120.120	119.913	0.120	120.036	119.965	0.036	120.012	119.978	0.012	120.000	119.978	0.000
160	Max	160.460	160.000	0.710	160.245	160.000	0.345	160.106	160.000	0.146	160.054	160.000	0.079	160.040	160.000	0.065
	Min	160.210	159.750	0.210	160.145	159.900	0.145	160.043	159.960	0.043	160.014	159.975	0.014	160.000	159.975	0.000
200	Max	200.530	200.000	0.820	200.285	200.000	0.400	200.122	200.000	0.168	200.061	200.000	0.090	200.046	200.000	0.075
	Min	200.240	199.710	0.240	200.170	199.885	0.170	200.050	199.954	0.050	200.015	199.971	0.015	200.000	199.971	0.000
250	Max	250.570	250.000	0.860	250.285	250.000	0.400	250.122	250.000	0.168	250.061	250.000	0.090	250.046	250.000	0.075
	Min	250.280	249.710	0.280	250.170	249.885	0.170	250.050	249.954	0.050	250.015	249.971	0.015	250.000	249.971	0.000
300	Max	300.650	300.000	0.970	300.320	300.000	0.450	300.137	300.000	0.189	300.069	300.000	0.101	300.052	300.000	0.084
	Min	300.330	299.680	0.330	300.190	299.870	0.190	300.056	299.948	0.056	300.017	299.968	0.017	300.000	299.968	0.000
400	Max	400.760	400.000	1.120	400.350	400.000	0.490	400.151	400.000	0.208	400.075	400.000	0.111	400.057	400.000	0.093
	Min	400.400	399.640	0.400	400.210	399.860	0.210	400.062	399.943	0.062	400.018	399.964	0.018	400.000	399.964	0.000
500	Max	500.880	500.000	1.280	500.385	500.000	0.540	500.165	500.000	0.228	500.083	500.000	0.123	500.063	500.000	0.103
	Min	500.480	499.600	0.480	500.230	499.845	0.230	500.068	499.937	0.068	500.020	499.960	5.020	500.000	499.960	0.000

[a] From ANSI B4.2—1978 (R1984). For description of preferred fits, see Table 14.2.

14   Preferred Metric Shaft Basis Transition and Interference Fits[a]— American National Standard

Dimensions are in millimeters.

Basic Size		Locational Transn. Hole K7	Locational Transn. Shaft h6	Locational Transn. Fit	Locational Transn. Hole N7	Locational Transn. Shaft h6	Locational Transn. Fit	Locational Interf. Hole P7	Locational Interf. Shaft h6	Locational Interf. Fit	Medium Drive Hole S7	Medium Drive Shaft h6	Medium Drive Fit	Force Hole U7	Force Shaft h6	Force Fit
1	Max	1.000	1.000	0.006	0.996	1.000	0.002	0.994	1.000	0.000	0.986	1.000	−0.008	0.982	1.000	−0.012
	Min	0.990	0.994	−0.010	0.986	0.994	−0.014	0.984	0.994	−0.016	0.976	0.994	−0.024	0.972	0.994	−0.028
1.2	Max	1.200	1.200	0.006	1.196	1.200	0.002	1.194	1.200	0.000	1.186	1.200	−0.008	1.182	1.200	−0.012
	Min	1.190	1.194	−0.010	1.186	1.194	−0.014	1.184	1.194	−0.016	1.176	1.194	−0.024	1.172	1.194	−0.028
1.6	Max	1.600	1.600	0.006	1.596	1.600	0.002	1.594	1.600	0.000	1.586	1.600	−0.008	1.582	1.600	−0.012
	Min	1.590	1.594	−0.010	1.586	1.594	−0.014	1.584	1.594	−0.016	1.576	1.594	−0.024	1.572	1.594	−0.028
2	Max	2.000	2.000	0.006	1.996	2.000	0.002	1.994	2.000	0.000	1.986	2.000	−0.008	1.982	2.000	−0.012
	Min	1.990	1.994	−0.010	1.986	1.994	−0.014	1.984	1.994	−0.016	1.976	1.994	−0.024	1.972	1.994	−0.028
2.5	Max	2.500	2.500	0.006	2.496	2.500	0.002	2.494	2.500	0.000	2.486	2.500	−0.008	2.482	2.500	−0.012
	Min	2.490	2.494	−0.010	2.486	2.494	−0.014	2.484	2.494	−0.016	2.476	2.494	−0.024	2.472	2.494	−0.028
3	Max	3.000	3.000	0.006	2.996	3.000	0.002	2.994	3.000	0.000	2.986	3.000	−0.008	2.982	3.000	−0.012
	Min	2.990	2.994	−0.010	2.986	2.994	−0.014	2.984	2.994	−0.016	2.976	2.994	−0.024	2.972	2.994	−0.028
4	Max	4.003	4.000	0.011	3.996	4.000	0.004	3.992	4.000	0.000	3.985	4.000	−0.007	3.981	4.000	−0.011
	Min	3.991	3.992	−0.009	3.984	3.992	−0.016	3.980	3.992	−0.020	3.973	3.992	−0.027	3.969	3.992	−0.031
5	Max	5.003	5.000	0.011	4.996	5.000	0.004	4.992	5.000	0.000	4.985	5.000	−0.007	4.981	5.000	−0.011
	Min	4.991	4.992	−0.009	4.984	4.992	−0.016	4.980	4.992	−0.020	4.973	4.992	−0.027	4.969	4.992	−0.031
6	Max	6.003	6.000	0.011	5.996	6.000	0.004	5.992	6.000	0.000	5.985	6.000	−0.007	5.981	6.000	−0.011
	Min	5.991	5.992	−0.009	5.984	5.992	−0.016	5.980	5.992	−0.020	5.973	5.992	−0.027	5.969	5.992	−0.031
8	Max	8.005	8.000	0.014	7.996	8.000	0.005	7.991	8.000	0.000	7.983	8.000	−0.008	7.978	8.000	−0.013
	Min	7.990	7.991	−0.010	7.981	7.991	−0.019	7.976	7.991	−0.024	7.968	7.991	−0.032	7.963	7.991	−0.037
10	Max	10.005	10.000	0.014	9.996	10.000	0.005	9.991	10.000	0.000	9.983	10.000	−0.008	9.978	10.000	−0.013
	Min	9.990	9.991	−0.010	9.981	9.991	−0.019	9.976	9.991	−0.024	9.968	9.991	−0.032	9.963	9.991	−0.037
12	Max	12.006	12.000	0.017	11.995	12.000	0.006	11.989	12.000	0.000	11.979	12.000	−0.010	11.974	12.000	−0.015
	Min	11.988	11.989	−0.012	11.977	11.989	−0.023	11.971	11.989	−0.029	11.961	11.989	−0.039	11.956	11.989	−0.044
16	Max	16.006	16.000	0.017	15.995	16.000	0.006	15.989	16.000	0.000	15.979	16.000	−0.010	15.974	16.000	−0.015
	Min	15.988	15.989	−0.012	15.977	15.989	−0.023	15.971	15.989	−0.029	15.961	15.989	−0.039	15.956	15.989	−0.044
20	Max	20.006	20.000	0.019	19.993	20.000	0.006	19.986	20.000	−0.001	19.973	20.000	−0.014	19.967	20.000	−0.020
	Min	19.985	19.987	−0.015	19.972	19.987	−0.028	19.965	19.987	−0.035	19.952	19.987	−0.048	19.946	19.987	−0.054
25	Max	25.006	25.000	0.019	24.993	25.000	0.006	24.986	25.000	−0.001	24.973	25.000	−0.014	24.960	25.000	−0.027
	Min	24.985	24.987	−0.015	24.972	24.987	−0.028	24.965	24.987	−0.035	24.952	24.987	−0.048	24.939	24.987	−0.061
30	Max	30.006	30.000	0.019	29.993	30.000	0.006	29.986	30.000	−0.001	29.973	30.000	−0.014	29.960	30.000	−0.027
	Min	29.985	29.987	−0.015	29.972	29.987	−0.028	29.965	29.987	−0.035	29.952	29.987	−0.048	29.939	29.987	−0.061

[a]From ANSI B4.2—1978 (R1984). For description of preferred fits, see Table 14.2.

14 Preferred Metric Basis Transition and Interference Fits[a]— American National Standard (continued)

Dimensions are in millimeters.

Basic Size		Locational Transn. Hole K7	Shaft h6	Fit	Locational Transn. Hole N7	Shaft h6	Fit	Locational Interf. Hole P7	Shaft h6	Fit	Medium Drive Hole S7	Shaft h6	Fit	Force Hole U7	Shaft h6	Fit
40	Max	40.007	40.000	0.023	39.992	40.000	0.008	39.983	40.000	-0.001	39.966	40.000	-0.018	39.949	40.000	-0.035
	Min	39.982	39.984	-0.018	39.967	39.984	-0.033	39.958	39.984	-0.042	39.941	39.984	-0.059	39.924	39.984	-0.076
50	Max	50.007	50.000	0.023	49.992	50.000	0.008	49.983	50.000	-0.001	49.966	50.000	-0.018	49.939	50.000	-0.045
	Min	49.982	49.984	-0.018	49.967	49.984	-0.033	49.958	49.984	-0.042	49.941	49.984	-0.059	49.914	49.984	-0.086
60	Max	60.009	60.000	0.028	59.991	60.000	0.010	59.979	60.000	-0.002	59.958	60.000	-0.023	59.924	60.000	-0.057
	Min	59.979	59.981	-0.021	59.961	59.981	-0.039	59.949	59.981	-0.051	59.928	59.981	-0.072	59.894	59.981	-0.106
80	Max	80.009	80.000	0.028	79.991	80.000	0.010	79.979	80.000	-0.002	79.952	80.000	-0.029	79.909	80.000	-0.072
	Min	79.979	79.981	-0.021	79.961	79.981	-0.039	79.949	79.981	-0.051	79.922	79.981	-0.078	79.879	79.981	-0.121
100	Max	100.010	100.000	0.032	99.990	100.000	0.012	99.976	100.000	-0.002	99.942	100.000	-0.036	99.889	100.000	-0.089
	Min	99.975	99.978	-0.025	99.955	99.978	-0.045	99.941	99.978	-0.059	99.907	99.978	-0.093	99.854	99.978	-0.146
120	Max	120.010	120.000	0.032	119.990	120.000	0.012	119.976	120.000	-0.002	119.934	120.000	-0.044	119.869	120.000	-0.109
	Min	119.975	119.978	-0.025	119.955	119.978	-0.045	119.941	119.978	-0.059	119.899	119.978	-0.101	119.834	119.978	-0.166
160	Max	160.012	160.000	0.037	159.988	160.000	0.013	159.972	160.000	-0.003	159.915	160.000	-0.060	159.825	160.000	-0.150
	Min	159.972	159.975	-0.028	159.948	159.975	-0.052	159.932	159.975	-0.068	159.875	159.975	-0.125	159.785	159.975	-0.215
200	Max	200.013	200.000	0.042	199.986	200.000	0.015	199.967	200.000	-0.004	199.895	200.000	-0.076	199.781	200.000	-0.190
	Min	199.967	199.971	-0.033	199.940	199.971	-0.060	199.921	199.971	-0.079	199.849	199.971	-0.151	199.735	199.971	-0.265
250	Max	250.013	250.000	0.042	249.986	250.000	0.015	249.967	250.000	-0.004	249.877	250.000	-0.094	249.733	250.000	-0.238
	Min	249.967	249.971	-0.033	249.940	249.971	-0.060	249.921	249.971	-0.079	249.831	249.971	-0.169	249.687	249.971	-0.313
300	Max	300.016	300.000	0.048	299.986	300.000	0.018	299.964	300.000	-0.004	299.850	300.000	-0.118	299.670	300.000	-0.298
	Min	299.964	299.968	-0.036	299.934	299.968	-0.066	299.912	299.968	-0.088	299.798	299.968	-0.202	299.618	299.968	-0.382
400	Max	400.017	400.000	0.053	399.984	400.000	0.020	399.959	400.000	-0.005	399.813	400.000	-0.151	399.586	400.000	-0.378
	Min	399.960	399.964	-0.040	399.927	399.964	-0.073	399.902	399.964	-0.098	399.756	399.964	-0.244	399.529	399.964	-0.471
500	Max	500.018	500.000	0.058	499.983	500.000	0.023	499.955	500.000	-0.005	499.771	500.000	-0.189	499.483	500.000	-0.477
	Min	499.955	499.960	-0.045	499.920	499.960	-0.080	499.892	499.960	-0.108	499.708	499.960	-0.292	499.420	499.960	-0.580

[a]From ANSI B4.2–1978 (R1984). For description of preferred fits, see Table 14.2.

15 Screw Threads, American National, Unified, and Metric

AMERICAN NATIONAL STANDARD UNIFIED AND AMERICAN NATIONAL SCREW THREADS[a]

Nominal Diameter	Coarse[b] NC UNC		Fine[b] NF UNF		Extra Fine[c] NEF UNEF	
	Thds. per Inch	Tap Drill[d]	Thds. per Inch	Tap Drill[d]	Thds. per Inch	Tap Drill[d]
0 (.060)			80	3/64		
1 (.073)	64	No. 53	72	No. 53	....	....
2 (.086)	56	No. 50	64	No. 50	....	....
3 (.099)	48	No. 47	56	No. 45	....	....
4 (.112)	40	No. 43	48	No. 42	....	....
5 (.125)	40	No. 38	44	No. 37	....	....
6 (.138)	32	No. 36	40	No. 33	....	....
8 (.164)	32	No. 29	36	No. 29	....	....
10 (.190)	24	No. 25	32	No. 21	....	....
12 (.216)	24	No. 16	28	No. 14	32	No. 13
1/4	20	No. 7	28	No. 3	32	7/32
5/16	18	F	24	I	32	9/32
3/8	16	5/16	24	Q	32	11/32
7/16	14	U	20	25/64	28	13/32
1/2	13	27/64	20	29/64	28	15/32
9/16	12	31/64	18	33/64	24	33/64
5/8	11	17/32	18	37/64	24	37/64
11/16	....	....	....	....	24	41/64
3/4	10	21/32	16	11/16	20	45/64
13/16	....	....	....	....	20	49/64
7/8	9	49/64	14	13/16	20	53/64
15/16	....	....	....	....	20	57/64

Nominal Diameter	Coarse[b] NC UNC		Fine[b] NF UNF		Extra Fine[c] NEF UNEF	
	Thds. per Inch	Tap Drill[d]	Thds. per Inch	Tap Drill[d]	Thds. per Inch	Tap Drill[d]
1	8	7/8	12	59/64	20	61/64
1 1/16	....	....	....	....	18	1
1 1/8	7	63/64	12	1 3/64	18	1 5/64
1 3/16	....	....	....	....	18	1 9/64
1 1/4	7	1 7/64	12	1 11/64	18	1 3/16
1 5/16	....	....	....	....	18	1 17/64
1 3/8	6	1 7/32	12	1 19/64	18	1 5/16
1 7/16	....	....	....	....	18	1 3/8
1 1/2	6	1 11/32	12	1 27/64	18	1 7/16
1 9/16	....	....	....	....	18	1 1/2
1 5/8	....	....	....	....	18	1 9/16
1 11/16	....	....	....	....	18	1 5/8
1 3/4	5	1 9/16	....	....	....	....
2	4 1/2	1 25/32	....	....	....	....
2 1/4	4 1/2	2 1/32	....	....	....	....
2 1/2	4	2 1/4	....	....	....	....
2 3/4	4	2 1/2	....	....	....	....
3	4	2 3/4	....	....	....	....
3 1/4	4	....	....	....	....	....
3 1/2	4	....	....	....	....	....
3 3/4	4	....	....	....	....	....
4	4	....	....	....	....	....

[a] ANSI B1.1–1989. For 8-, 12-, and 16-pitch thread series, see next page.

[b] Classes 1A, 2A, 3A, 1B, 2B, 3B, 2, and 3.

[c] Classes 2A, 2B, 2, and 3.

[d] For approximate 75% full depth of thread. For decimal sizes of numbered and lettered drills, see Appendix 16.

15   Screw Threads, American National, Unified, and Metric (continued)

AMERICAN NATIONAL STANDARD UNIFIED AND AMERICAN NATIONAL SCREW THREADS[a] (continued)

Nominal Diameter	8-Pitch[b] Series 8N and 8UN		12-Pitch[b] Series 12N and 12UN		16-Pitch[b] Series 16N and 16UN		Nominal Diameter	8-Pitch[b] Series 8N and 8UN		12-Pitch[b] Series 12N and 12UN		16-Pitch[b] Series 16N and 16UN	
	Thds. per Inch	Tap Drill[c]	Thds. per Inch	Tap Drill[c]	Thds. per Inch	Tap Drill[c]		Thds. per Inch	Tap Drill[c]	Thds. per Inch	Tap Drill[c]	Thds. per Inch	Tap Drill[c]
$\frac{1}{2}$	....	....	12	$\frac{27}{64}$	....	....	$2\frac{1}{16}$	....	....	....	....	**16**	2
$\frac{9}{16}$	....	....	12[e]	$\frac{31}{64}$	....	....	$2\frac{1}{8}$	....	....	12	$2\frac{3}{64}$	16	$2\frac{1}{16}$
$\frac{5}{8}$	....	....	12	$\frac{35}{64}$	....	....	$2\frac{3}{16}$	....	....	....	....	**16**	$2\frac{1}{8}$
$1\frac{1}{16}$	....	....	12	$\frac{39}{64}$	....	....	$2\frac{1}{4}$	8	$2\frac{1}{8}$	12	$2\frac{11}{64}$	16	$2\frac{3}{16}.$
$\frac{3}{4}$	....	....	12	$\frac{43}{64}$	16[e]	$1\frac{1}{16}$	$2\frac{5}{16}$	....	....	....	....	**16**	$2\frac{1}{4}$
$1\frac{3}{16}$	....	....	12	$\frac{47}{64}$	16	$\frac{3}{4}$	$2\frac{3}{8}$	....	....	12	$2\frac{19}{64}$	16	$2\frac{5}{16}$
$\frac{7}{8}$	....	....	12	$\frac{51}{64}$	16	$1\frac{3}{16}$	$2\frac{7}{16}$	....	....	....	....	**16**	$2\frac{3}{8}$
$\frac{5}{16}$	....	....	12	$\frac{55}{64}$	16	$\frac{7}{8}$	$2\frac{1}{2}$	8	$2\frac{3}{8}$	12	$2\frac{27}{64}$	16	$2\frac{7}{16}$
1	8[e]	$\frac{7}{8}$	12	$\frac{59}{64}$	16	$1\frac{5}{16}$	$2\frac{5}{8}$	....	....	12	$2\frac{35}{64}$	16	$2\frac{9}{16}$
$1\frac{1}{16}$	....	....	12	$\frac{63}{64}$	16	1	$2\frac{3}{4}$	8	$2\frac{5}{8}$	12	$2\frac{43}{64}$	16	$2\frac{11}{16}$
$1\frac{1}{8}$	8	1	12[e]	$1\frac{3}{64}$	16	$1\frac{1}{16}$	$2\frac{7}{8}$	....	....	12	....	16	....
$1\frac{3}{16}$	....	....	12	$1\frac{7}{64}$	16	$1\frac{1}{8}$	3	8	$2\frac{7}{8}$	12	....	16	....
$1\frac{1}{4}$	8	$1\frac{1}{8}$	12	$1\frac{11}{64}$	16	$1\frac{3}{16}$	$3\frac{1}{8}$	....	....	12	....	16	....
$1\frac{5}{16}$	....	....	12	$1\frac{15}{64}$	16	$1\frac{1}{4}$	$3\frac{1}{4}$	8	....	12	....	16	....
$1\frac{3}{8}$	8	$1\frac{1}{4}$	12[e]	$1\frac{19}{64}$	16	$1\frac{5}{16}$	$3\frac{3}{8}$	....	....	12	....	16	....
$1\frac{7}{16}$	....	....	12	$1\frac{23}{64}$	16	$1\frac{3}{8}$	$3\frac{1}{2}$	8	....	12	....	16	....
$1\frac{1}{2}$	8	$1\frac{3}{8}$	12[e]	$1\frac{27}{64}$	16	$1\frac{7}{16}$	$3\frac{5}{8}$	....	....	12	....	16	....
$1\frac{9}{16}$	....	....	....	....	16	$1\frac{1}{2}$	$3\frac{3}{4}$	8	....	12	....	16	....
$1\frac{5}{8}$	8	$1\frac{1}{2}$	12	$1\frac{35}{64}$	16	$1\frac{9}{16}$	$3\frac{7}{8}$	....	....	12	....	16	....
$1\frac{11}{16}$	....	....	....	....	16	$1\frac{5}{8}$	4	8	....	12	....	16	....
$1\frac{3}{4}$	8	$1\frac{5}{8}$	12	$1\frac{43}{64}$	16[e]	$1\frac{11}{16}$	$4\frac{1}{4}$	8	....	12	....	16	....
$1\frac{13}{16}$	....	....	....	....	16	$1\frac{3}{4}$	$4\frac{1}{2}$	8	....	12	....	16	....
$1\frac{7}{8}$	8	$1\frac{3}{4}$	12	$1\frac{51}{64}$	16	$1\frac{13}{16}$	$4\frac{3}{4}$	8	....	12	....	16	....
$1\frac{15}{16}$	....	....	....	....	16	$1\frac{7}{8}$	5	8	....	12	....	16	....
2	8	$1\frac{7}{8}$	12	$1\frac{59}{64}$	16[e]	$1\frac{15}{16}$	$5\frac{1}{4}$	8	....	12	....	16	....

[a] ANSI B1.1–1989.
[b] Classes 2A, 3A, 2B, 3B, 2, and 3.
[c] For approximate 75% full depth of thread.
[d] Boldface type indicates American National threads only.
[e] This is a standard size of the Unified or American National threads of the coarse, fine, or extra fine series.
  See preceding page.

15   Screw Threads, American National, Unified, and Metric (continued)

METRIC SCREW THREADS[a]

Preferred sizes for commercial threads and fasteners are shown in **boldface** type.

Coarse (general purpose)		Fine	
Nominal Size & Thd Pitch	Tap Drill Diameter, mm	Nominal Size & Thd Pitch	Tap Drill Diameter, mm
M1.6 × 0.35	1.25	—	—
M1.8 × 0.35	1.45	—	—
M2 × 0.4	1.6	—	—
M2.2 × 0.45	1.75	—	—
M2.5 × 0.45	2.05	—	—
M3 × 0.5	2.5	—	—
M3.5 × 0.6	2.9	—	—
M4 × 0.7	3.3	—	—
M4.5 × 0.75	3.75	—	—
M5 × 0.8	4.2	—	—
M6 × 1	5.0	—	—
M7 × 1	6.0	—	—
M8 × 1.25	6.8	**M8 × 1**	7.0
M9 × 1.25	7.75	—	—
M10 × 1.5	8.5	**M10 × 1.25**	8.75
M11 × 1.5	9.50	—	—
M12 × 1.75	10.30	**M12 × 1.25**	10.5
M14 × 2	12.00	**M14 × 1.5**	12.5
M16 × 2	14.00	**M16 × 1.5**	14.5
M18 × 2.5	15.50	**M18 × 1.5**	16.5
M20 × 2.5	17.5	**M20 × 1.5**	18.5
M22 × 2.5[b]	19.5	**M22 × 1.5**	20.5
M24 × 3	21.0	**M24 × 2**	22.0
M27 × 3[b]	24.0	**M27 × 2**	25.0
M30 × 3.5	26.5	**M30 × 2**	28.0
M33 × 3.5	29.5	**M30 × 2**	31.0
M36 × 4	32.0	**M36 × 2**	33.0
M39 × 4	35.0	M39 × 2	36.0
M42 × 4.5	37.5	**M42 × 2**	39.0
M45 × 4.5	40.5	M45 × 1.5	42.0
M48 × 5	43.0	**M48 × 2**	45.0
M52 × 5	47.0	M52 × 2	49.0
M56 × 5.5	50.5	**M56 × 2**	52.0
M60 × 5.5	54.5	M60 × 1.5	56.0
M64 × 6	58.0	**M64 × 2**	60.0
M68 × 6	62.0	M68 × 2	64.0
M72 × 6	66.0	**M72 × 2**	68.0
M80 × 6	74.0	**M80 × 2**	76.0
M90 × 6	84.0	**M90 × 2**	86.0
M100 × 6	94.0	**M100 × 2**	96.0

[a] Metric Fasteners Standard, IFI-500 (1983) and ANSI/ASME B1.13M–1983 (R1989).
[b] Only for high strength structural steel fasteners.

16   Twist Drill Sizes—American National Standard and Metric

AMERICAN NATIONAL STANDARD DRILL SIZES[a]

All dimensions are in inches.

Drills designated in common fractions are available in diameters 1/64″ to 1¾″ in 1/64″ increments, 1¾″ to 2¼″ in 1/32″ increments. 2¼″ to 3″ in 1/16″ increments and 3″ to 3½″ in 1/8″ increments. Drills larger than 3½″ are seldom used, and are regarded as special drills.

Size	Drill Diameter	Size	Drill Diameter	Size	Drill Diameter	Size	Drill Diameter	Size	Drill Diameter	Size	Drill Diameter
1	.2280	17	.1730	33	.1130	49	.0730	65	.0350	81	.0130
2	.2210	18	.1695	34	.1110	50	.0700	66	.0330	82	.0125
3	.2130	19	.1660	35	.1100	51	.0670	67	.0320	83	.0120
4	.2090	20	.1610	36	.1065	52	.0635	68	.0310	84	.0115
5	.2055	21	.1590	37	.1040	53	.0595	69	.0292	85	.0110
6	.2040	22	.1570	38	.1015	54	.0550	70	.0280	86	.0105
7	.2010	23	.1540	39	.0995	55	.0520	71	.0260	87	.0100
8	.1990	24	.1520	40	.0980	56	.0465	72	.0250	88	.0095
9	.1960	25	.1495	41	.0960	57	.0430	73	.0240	89	.0091
10	.1935	26	.1470	42	.0935	58	.0420	74	.0225	90	.0087
11	.1910	27	.1440	43	.0890	59	.0410	75	.0210	91	.0083
12	.1890	28	.1405	44	.0860	60	.0400	76	.0200	92	.0079
13	.1850	29	.1360	45	.0820	61	.0390	77	.0180	93	.0075
14	.1820	30	.1285	46	.0810	62	.0380	78	.0160	94	.0071
15	.1800	31	.1200	47	.0785	63	.0370	79	.0145	95	.0067
16	.1770	32	.1160	48	.0760	64	.0360	80	.0135	96	.0063
										97	.0059

LETTER SIZES

A	.234	G	.261	L	.290	Q	.332	V	.377
B	.238	H	.266	M	.295	R	.339	W	.386
C	.242	I	.272	N	.302	S	.348	X	.397
D	.246	J	.277	O	.316	T	.358	Y	.404
E	.250	K	.281	P	.323	U	.368	Z	.413
F	.257								

[a] ANSI B94.11M—1979 (R1987).

16   Twist Drill Sizes—American National Standard and Metric
(continued)

METRIC DRILL SIZES
Decimal-inch equivalents are for reference only.

Drill Diameter		Drill Diameter		Drill Diameter		Drill Diameter		Drill Diameter		Drill Diameter	
mm	in.	mm	in.	mm	in.	mm	in.	mm	in.	mm	in.
0.40	.0157	1.95	.0768	4.70	.1850	8.00	.3150	13.20	.5197	25.50	1.0039
0.42	.0165	2.00	.0787	4.80	.1890	8.10	.3189	13.50	.5315	26.00	1.0236
0.45	.0177	2.05	.0807	4.90	.1929	8.20	.3228	13.80	.5433	26.50	1.0433
0.48	.0189	2.10	.0827	5.00	.1969	8.30	.3268	14.00	.5512	27.00	1.0630
0.50	.0197	2.15	.0846	5.10	.2008	8.40	.3307	14.25	.5610	27.50	1.0827
0.55	.0217	2.20	.0866	5.20	.2047	8.50	.3346	14.50	.5709	28.00	1.1024
0.60	.0236	2.25	.0886	5.30	.2087	8.60	.3386	14.75	.5807	28.50	1.1220
0.65	.0256	2.30	.0906	5.40	.2126	8.70	.3425	15.00	.5906	29.00	1.1417
0.70	.0276	2.35	.0925	5.50	.2165	8.80	.3465	15.25	.6004	29.50	1.1614
0.75	.0295	2.40	.0945	5.60	.2205	8.90	.3504	15.50	.6102	30.00	1.1811
0.80	.0315	2.45	.0965	5.70	.2244	9.00	.3543	15.75	.6201	30.50	1.2008
0.85	.0335	2.50	.0984	5.80	.2283	9.10	.3583	16.00	.6299	31.00	1.2205
0.90	.0354	2.60	.1024	5.90	.2323	9.20	.3622	16.25	.6398	31.50	1.2402
0.95	.0374	2.70	.1063	6.00	.2362	9.30	.3661	16.50	.6496	32.00	1.2598
1.00	.0394	2.80	.1102	6.10	.2402	9.40	.3701	16.75	.6594	32.50	1.2795
1.05	.0413	2.90	.1142	6.20	.2441	9.50	.3740	17.00	.6693	33.00	1.2992
1.10	.0433	3.00	.1181	6.30	.2480	9.60	.3780	17.25	.6791	33.50	1.3189
1.15	.0453	3.10	.1220	6.40	.2520	9.70	.3819	17.50	.6890	34.00	1.3386
1.20	.0472	3.20	.1260	6.50	.2559	9.80	.3858	18.00	.7087	34.50	1.3583
1.25	.0492	3.30	.1299	6.60	.2598	9.90	.3898	18.50	.7283	35.00	1.3780
1.30	.0512	3.40	.1339	6.70	.2638	10.00	.3937	19.00	.7480	35.50	1.3976
1.35	.0531	3.50	.1378	6.80	.2677	10.20	.4016	19.50	.7677	36.00	1.4173
1.40	.0551	3.60	.1417	6.90	.2717	10.50	.4134	20.00	.7874	36.50	1.4370
1.45	.0571	3.70	.1457	7.00	.2756	10.80	.4252	20.50	.8071	37.00	1.4567
1.50	.0591	3.80	.1496	7.10	.2795	11.00	.4331	21.00	.8268	37.50	1.4764
1.55	.0610	3.90	.1535	7.20	.2835	11.20	.4409	21.50	.8465	38.00	1.4961
1.60	.0630	4.00	.1575	7.30	.2874	11.50	.4528	22.00	.8661	40.00	1.5748
1.65	.0650	4.10	.1614	7.40	.2913	11.80	.4646	22.50	.8858	42.00	1.6535
1.70	.0669	4.20	.1654	7.50	.2953	12.00	.4724	23.00	.9055	44.00	1.7323
1.75	.0689	4.30	.1693	7.60	.2992	12.20	.4803	23.50	.9252	46.00	1.8110
1.80	.0709	4.40	.1732	7.70	.3031	12.50	.4921	24.00	.9449	48.00	1.8898
1.85	.0728	4.50	.1772	7.80	.3071	12.50	.5039	24.50	.9646	50.00	1.9685
1.90	.0748	4.60	.1811	7.90	.3110	13.00	.5118	25.00	.9843		

17   Acme Threads, General-Purpose[a]

Size	Threads per Inch	Size	Threads per Inch	Size	Threads per Inch	Size	Threads per Inch
¼	16	¾	6	1½	4	3	2
⁵⁄₁₆	14	⅞	6	1¾	4	3½	2
⅜	12	1	5	2	4	4	2
⁷⁄₁₆	12	1⅛	5	2¼	3	4½	2
½	10	1¼	5	2½	3	5	2
⅝	8	1⅜	4	2¾	3	. . .	. .

[a]ANSI/ASME B1.5—1988.

18 Bolts, Nuts, and Cap Screws—Square and Hexagon— American National Standard and Metric

AMERICAN NATIONAL STANDARD SQUARE AND HEXAGON BOLTS[a] AND NUTS[b] AND HEXAGON CAP SCREWS[c]

Boldface type indicates product features unified dimensionally with British and Canadian standards.
All dimensions are in inches.
For thread series, minimum thread lengths, and bolt lengths, see §15.25.

Nominal Size D Body Diameter of Bolt		Regular Bolts					Heavy Bolts		
		Width Across Flats W		Height H			Width Across Flats W	Height H	
		Sq.	Hex.	Sq. (Unfin.)	Hex. (Unfin.)	Hex. Cap Scr.[c] (Fin.)		Hex. (Unfin.)	Hex. Screw (Fin.)
¼	0.2500	⅜	⁷⁄₁₆	¹¹⁄₆₄	¹¹⁄₆₄	⁵⁄₃₂	....	....	....
⁵⁄₁₆	0.3125	½	½	¹³⁄₆₄	⁷⁄₃₂	¹³⁄₆₄	....	....	....
⅜	0.3750	⁹⁄₁₆	⁹⁄₁₆	¼	¼	¹⁵⁄₆₄	....	....	....
⁷⁄₁₆	0.4375	⅝	⅝	¹⁹⁄₆₄	¹⁹⁄₆₄	⁹⁄₃₂	....	....	....
½	0.5000	¾	¾	²¹⁄₆₄	¹¹⁄₃₂	⁵⁄₁₆	⅞	¹¹⁄₃₂	⁵⁄₁₆
⁹⁄₁₆	0.5625	....	¹³⁄₁₆	....	....	²³⁄₆₄	....	....	....
⅝	0.6250	¹⁵⁄₁₆	¹⁵⁄₁₆	²⁷⁄₆₄	²⁷⁄₆₄	²⁵⁄₆₄	1¹⁄₁₆	²⁷⁄₆₄	²⁵⁄₆₄
¾	0.7500	1⅛	1⅛	½	½	¹⁵⁄₃₂	1¼	½	¹⁵⁄₃₂
⅞	0.8750	1⁵⁄₁₆	1⁵⁄₁₆	¹⁹⁄₃₂	³⁷⁄₆₄	³⁵⁄₆₄	1⁷⁄₁₆	³⁷⁄₆₄	³⁵⁄₆₄
1	1.000	1½	1½	²¹⁄₃₂	⁴³⁄₆₄	³⁹⁄₆₄	1⅝	⁴³⁄₆₄	³⁹⁄₆₄
1⅛	1.1250	1¹¹⁄₁₆	1¹¹⁄₁₆	¾	¾	¹¹⁄₁₆	1¹³⁄₁₆	¾	¹¹⁄₁₆
1¼	1.2500	1⅞	1⅞	²⁷⁄₃₂	²⁷⁄₃₂	²⁵⁄₃₂	2	²⁷⁄₃₂	²⁵⁄₃₂
1⅜	1.3750	2¹⁄₁₆	2¹⁄₁₆	²⁹⁄₃₂	²⁹⁄₃₂	²⁷⁄₃₂	2³⁄₁₆	²⁹⁄₃₂	²⁷⁄₃₂
1½	1.5000	2¼	2¼	1	1	¹⁵⁄₁₆	2⅜	1	¹⁵⁄₁₆
1¾	1.7500	....	2⅝	....	1⁵⁄₃₂	1³⁄₃₂	2¾	1⁵⁄₃₂	1³⁄₃₂
2	2.0000	....	3	....	1¹¹⁄₃₂	1⁷⁄₃₂	3⅛	1¹¹⁄₃₂	1⁷⁄₃₂
2¼	2.2500	....	3⅜	....	1½	1⅜	3½	1½	1⅜
2½	2.5000	....	3¾	....	1²¹⁄₃₂	1¹⁷⁄₃₂	3⅞	1²¹⁄₃₂	1¹⁷⁄₃₂
2¾	2.7500	....	4⅛	....	1¹³⁄₁₆	1¹¹⁄₁₆	4¼	1¹³⁄₁₆	1¹¹⁄₁₆
3	3.0000	....	4½	....	2	1⅞	4⅝	2	1⅞
3¼	3.2500	....	4⅞	....	2³⁄₁₆	....	....	....	....
3½	3.5000	....	5¼	....	2⁵⁄₁₆	....	....	....	....
3¾	3.7500	....	5⅝	....	2½	....	....	....	....
4	4.0000	....	6	....	2¹¹⁄₁₆	....	....	....	....

[a]ANSI B18.2.1—1981.
[b]ANSI B18.2.2—1987.
[c]Hexagon cap screws and finished hexagon bolts are combined as a single product.

18   Bolts, Nuts, and Cap Screws—Square and Hexagon— American National Standard and Metric (continued)

AMERICAN NATIONAL STANDARD SQUARE AND HEXAGON BOLTS AND NUTS
AND HEXAGON CAP SCREWS (continued)

See ANSI B18.2.2 for jam nuts, slotted nuts, thick nuts, thick slotted nuts, and castle nuts.
For methods of drawing bolts and nuts and hexagon-head cap screws, see Figs. 15.29, 15.30, and 15.32.

Nominal Size D Body Diameter of Bolt	Regular Nuts					Heavy Nuts			
	Width Across Flats W		Thickness T			Width Across Flats W	Thickness T		
	Sq.	Hex.	Sq. (Unfin.)	Hex. Flat (Unfin.)	Hex. (Fin.)		Sq. (Unfin.)	Hex. Flat (Unfin.)	Hex. (Fin.)
$\frac{1}{4}$ 0.2500	$\frac{7}{16}$	$\frac{7}{16}$	$\frac{7}{32}$	$\frac{7}{32}$	$\frac{7}{32}$	$\frac{1}{2}$	$\frac{1}{4}$	$\frac{15}{64}$	$\frac{15}{64}$
$\frac{5}{16}$ 0.3125	$\frac{9}{16}$	$\frac{1}{2}$	$\frac{17}{64}$	$\frac{17}{64}$	$\frac{17}{64}$	$\frac{9}{16}$	$\frac{5}{16}$	$\frac{19}{64}$	$\frac{19}{64}$
$\frac{3}{8}$ 0.3750	$\frac{5}{8}$	$\frac{9}{16}$	$\frac{21}{64}$	$\frac{21}{64}$	$\frac{21}{64}$	$\frac{11}{16}$	$\frac{3}{8}$	$\frac{23}{64}$	$\frac{23}{64}$
$\frac{7}{16}$ 0.4375	$\frac{3}{4}$	$\frac{11}{16}$	$\frac{3}{8}$	$\frac{3}{8}$	$\frac{3}{8}$	$\frac{3}{4}$	$\frac{7}{16}$	$\frac{27}{64}$	$\frac{27}{64}$
$\frac{1}{2}$ 0.5000	$\frac{13}{16}$	$\frac{3}{4}$	$\frac{7}{16}$	$\frac{7}{16}$	$\frac{7}{16}$	$\frac{7}{8}^a$	$\frac{1}{2}$	$\frac{31}{64}$	$\frac{31}{64}$
$\frac{9}{16}$ 0.5625	....	$\frac{7}{8}$	....	$\frac{31}{64}$	$\frac{31}{64}$	$\frac{15}{16}$	....	$\frac{35}{64}$	$\frac{35}{64}$
$\frac{5}{8}$ 0.6250	1	$\frac{15}{16}$	$\frac{35}{64}$	$\frac{35}{64}$	$\frac{35}{64}$	$1\frac{1}{16}^a$	$\frac{5}{8}$	$\frac{39}{64}$	$\frac{39}{64}$
$\frac{3}{4}$ 0.7500	$1\frac{1}{8}$	$1\frac{1}{8}$	$\frac{21}{32}$	$\frac{41}{64}$	$\frac{41}{64}$	$1\frac{1}{4}^a$	$\frac{3}{4}$	$\frac{47}{64}$	$\frac{47}{64}$
$\frac{7}{8}$ 0.8750	$1\frac{5}{16}$	$1\frac{5}{16}$	$\frac{49}{64}$	$\frac{3}{4}$	$\frac{3}{4}$	$1\frac{7}{16}^a$	$\frac{7}{8}$	$\frac{55}{64}$	$\frac{55}{64}$
1 1.0000	$1\frac{1}{2}$	$1\frac{1}{2}$	$\frac{7}{8}$	$\frac{55}{64}$	$\frac{55}{64}$	$1\frac{5}{8}^a$	1	$\frac{63}{64}$	$\frac{63}{64}$
$1\frac{1}{8}$ 1.1250	$1\frac{11}{16}$	$1\frac{11}{16}$	1	1	$\frac{31}{32}$	$1\frac{13}{16}^a$	$1\frac{1}{8}$	$1\frac{1}{8}$	$1\frac{7}{64}$
$1\frac{1}{4}$ 1.2500	$1\frac{7}{8}$	$1\frac{7}{8}$	$1\frac{3}{32}$	$1\frac{3}{32}$	$1\frac{1}{16}$	2^a	$1\frac{1}{4}$	$1\frac{1}{4}$	$1\frac{7}{32}$
$1\frac{3}{8}$ 1.3750	$2\frac{1}{16}$	$2\frac{1}{16}$	$1\frac{13}{64}$	$1\frac{13}{64}$	$1\frac{11}{64}$	$2\frac{3}{16}^a$	$1\frac{3}{8}$	$1\frac{3}{8}$	$1\frac{11}{32}$
$1\frac{1}{2}$ 1.5000	$2\frac{1}{4}$	$2\frac{1}{4}$	$1\frac{5}{16}$	$1\frac{5}{16}$	$1\frac{9}{32}$	$2\frac{3}{8}^a$	$1\frac{1}{2}$	$1\frac{1}{2}$	$1\frac{15}{32}$
$1\frac{5}{8}$ 1.6250	....	....	....	....	....	$2\frac{9}{16}$	....	....	$1\frac{19}{32}$
$1\frac{3}{4}$ 1.7500	....	....	....	....	....	$2\frac{3}{4}$	....	$1\frac{3}{4}$	$1\frac{23}{32}$
$1\frac{7}{8}$ 1.8750	....	....	....	....	....	$2\frac{15}{16}$	....	....	$1\frac{27}{32}$
2 2.0000	....	....	....	....	....	$3\frac{1}{8}$	....	2	$1\frac{31}{32}$
$2\frac{1}{4}$ 2.2500	....	....	....	....	....	$3\frac{1}{2}$	....	$2\frac{1}{4}$	$2\frac{13}{64}$
$2\frac{1}{2}$ 2.5000	....	....	....	....	....	$3\frac{7}{8}$	....	$2\frac{1}{2}$	$2\frac{29}{64}$
$2\frac{3}{4}$ 2.7500	....	....	....	....	....	$4\frac{1}{4}$	....	$2\frac{3}{4}$	$2\frac{45}{64}$
3 3.0000	....	....	....	....	....	$4\frac{5}{8}$	....	3	$2\frac{61}{64}$
$3\frac{1}{4}$ 3.2500	....	....	....	....	....	5	....	$3\frac{1}{4}$	$3\frac{3}{16}$
$3\frac{1}{2}$ 3.5000	....	....	....	....	....	$5\frac{3}{8}$	....	$3\frac{1}{2}$	$3\frac{7}{16}$
$3\frac{3}{4}$ 3.7500	....	....	....	....	....	$5\frac{3}{4}$	....	$3\frac{3}{4}$	$3\frac{11}{16}$
4 4.0000	....	....	....	....	....	$6\frac{1}{8}$	....	4	$3\frac{15}{16}$

^{a} Product feature not unified for heavy square nut.

18 Bolts, Nuts, and Cap Screws—Square and Hexagon— American National Standard and Metric (continued)

METRIC HEXAGON BOLTS, HEXAGON CAP SCREWS, HEXAGON STRUCTURAL BOLTS, AND HEXAGON NUTS

Nominal Size D, mm	Width Across Flats W (max)		Thickness T (max)			
Body Dia and Thd Pitch	Bolts,[a] Cap Screws,[b] and Nuts[c]	Heavy Hex & Hex Structural Bolts[a] & Nuts[c]	Bolts (Unfin.)	Cap Screw (Fin.)	Nut (Fin. or Unfin.)	
					Style 1	Style 2
M5 × 0.8	8.0		3.88	3.65	4.7	5.1
M6 × 1	10.0		4.38	4.47	5.2	5.7
M8 × 1.25	13.0		5.68	5.50	6.8	7.5
M10 × 1.5	16.0		6.85	6.63	8.4	9.3
M12 × 1.75	18.0	21.0	7.95	7.76	10.8	12.0
M14 × 2	21.0	24.0	9.25	9.09	12.8	14.1
M16 × 2	24.0	27.0	10.75	10.32	14.8	16.4
M20 × 2.5	30.0	34.0	13.40	12.88	18.0	20.3
M24 × 3	36.0	41.0	15.90	15.44	21.5	23.9
M30 × 3.5	46.0	50.0	19.75	19.48	25.6	28.6
M36 × 4	55.0	60.0	23.55	23.38	31.0	34.7
M42 × 4.5	65.0		27.05	26.97	....	....
M48 × 5	75.0		31.07	31.07	....	....
M56 × 5.5	85.0		36.20	36.20	....	....
M64 × 6	95.0		41.32	41.32	....	....
M72 × 6	105.0		46.45	46.45	....	....
M80 × 6	115.0		51.58	51.58	....	....
M90 × 6	130.0		57.74	57.74	....	....
M100 × 6	145.0		63.90	63.90	....	....

HIGH STRENGTH STRUCTURAL HEXAGON BOLTS[a] (Fin.) AND HEXAGON NUTS[c]

M16 × 2	27.0	....	10.75	....	....	17.1
M20 × 2.5	34.0	....	13.40	....	....	20.7
M22 × 2.5	36.0	....	14.9	....	....	23.6
M24 × 3	41.0	....	15.9	....	....	24.2
M27 × 3	46.0	....	17.9	....	....	27.6
M30 × 3.5	50.0	....	19.75	....	....	31.7
M36 × 4	60.0	....	23.55	....	....	36.6

[a]ANSI B18.2.3.5M—1979, B18.2.3.6M—1979, B18.2.3.7M—1979.
[b]ANSI B18.2.3.1M—1979.
[c]ANSI B18.2.4.1M—1979, B18.2.4.2M—1979.

19   Cap Screws, Slotted^a and Socket Head^b — American National Standard and Metric

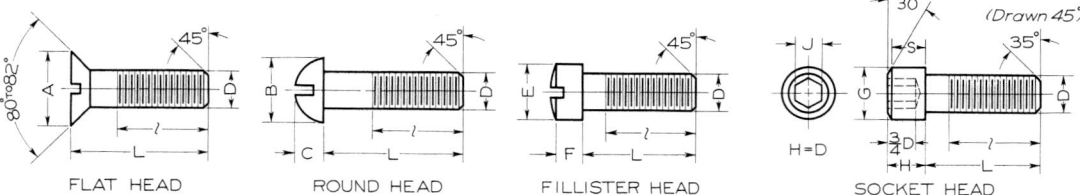

FLAT HEAD   ROUND HEAD   FILLISTER HEAD   SOCKET HEAD

For methods of drawing cap screws, screw lengths, and thread data, see Fig. 15.32.

Nominal Size D	Flat Head^a	Round Head^a		Fillister Head^a		Socket Head^b		
	A	B	C	E	F	G	J	S
0 (.060)	....	....	....	....	....	.096	.05	.054
1 (.073)	....	....	....	....	....	.118	1⁄16	.066
2 (.086)	....	....	....	....	....	.140	5⁄64	.077
3 (.099)	....	....	....	....	....	.161	5⁄64	.089
4 (.112)	....	....	....	....	....	.183	3⁄32	.101
5 (.125)	....	....	....	....	....	.205	3⁄32	.112
6 (.138)	....	....	....	....	....	.226	7⁄64	.124
8 (.164)	....	....	....	....	....	.270	9⁄64	.148
10 (.190)	....	....	....	....	....	.312	5⁄32	.171
1⁄4	.500	.437	.191	.375	.172	.375	3⁄16	.225
5⁄16	.625	.562	.245	.437	.203	.469	1⁄4	.281
3⁄8	.750	.675	.273	.562	.250	.562	5⁄16	.337
7⁄16	.812	.750	.328	.625	.297	.656	3⁄8	.394
1⁄2	.875	.812	.354	.750	.328	.750	3⁄8	.450
9⁄16	1.000	.937	.409	.812	.375	....	....	....
5⁄8	1.125	1.000	.437	.875	.422	.938	1⁄2	.562
3⁄4	1.375	1.250	.546	1.000	.500	1.125	5⁄8	.675
7⁄8	1.625	....	....	1.125	.594	1.312	3⁄4	.787
1	1.875	....	....	1.312	.656	1.500	3⁄4	.900
1 1⁄8	2.062	....	....	....	....	1.688	7⁄8	1.012
1 1⁄4	2.312	....	....	....	....	1.875	7⁄8	1.125
1 3⁄8	2.562	....	....	....	....	2.062	1	1.237
1 1⁄2	2.812	....	....	....	....	2.250	1	1.350

^{a}ANSI B18.6.2–1972 (R1983).
^{b}ANSI/ASME B18.3–1986. For hexagon-head screws, see §15.29 and Appendix 18.

19   Cap Screws, Slotted[a] and Socket Head[b]— American National Standard and Metric (continued)

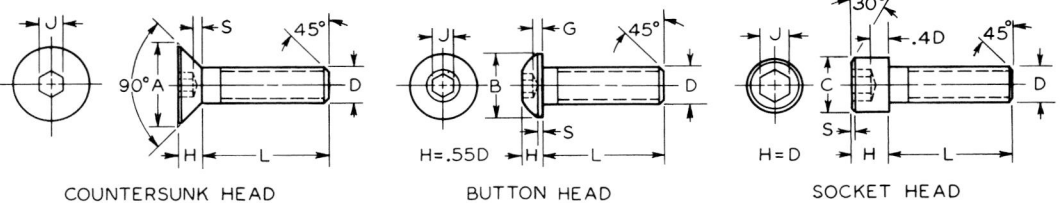

COUNTERSUNK HEAD   BUTTON HEAD   SOCKET HEAD

For methods of drawing cap screws, screw lengths, and thread data, see Fig. 15.32.

METRIC SOCKET HEAD CAP SCREWS									
Nominal Size D	Countersunk Head[a]			Button Head[b]			Socket Head[c]		Hex Socket Size
	A (max)	H	S	B	S	G	C	S	J
M1.6 × 0.35	....	....	....	....	....	....	3.0	0.16	1.5
M2 × 0.4	....	....	....	....	....	....	3.8	0.2	1.5
M2.5 × 0.45	....	....	....	....	....	....	4.5	0.25	2.0
M3 × 0.5	6.72	1.86	0.25	5.70	0.38	0.2	5.5	0.3	2.5
M4 × 0.7	8.96	2.48	0.45	7.6	0.38	0.3	7.0	0.4	3.0
M5 × 0.8	11.2	3.1	0.66	9.5	0.5	0.38	8.5	0.5	4.0
M6 × 1	13.44	3.72	0.7	10.5	0.8	0.74	10.0	0.6	5.0
M8 × 1.25	17.92	4.96	1.16	14.0	0.8	1.05	13.0	0.8	6.0
M10 × 1.5	22.4	6.2	1.62	17.5	0.8	1.45	16.0	1.0	8.0
M12 × 1.75	26.88	7.44	1.8	21.0	0.8	1.63	18.0	1.2	10.0
M14 × 2	30.24	8.12	2.0	....	....	....	21.0	1.4	12.0
M16 × 2	33.6	8.8	2.2	28.0	1.5	2.25	24.0	1.6	14.0
M20 × 2.5	19.67	10.16	2.2	....	....	....	30.0	2.0	17.0
M24 × 3	....	....	....	....	....	....	36.0	2.4	19.0
M30 × 3.5	....	....	....	....	....	....	45.0	3.0	22.0
M36 × 4	....	....	....	....	....	....	54.0	3.6	27.0
M42 × 4.5	....	....	....	....	....	....	63.0	4.2	32.0
M48 × 5	....	....	....	....	....	....	72.0	4.8	36.0

[a]IFI 535—1982.
[b]ANSI/ASME 18.3.4M—1986.
[c]ANSI/ASME 18.3.1M—1986.

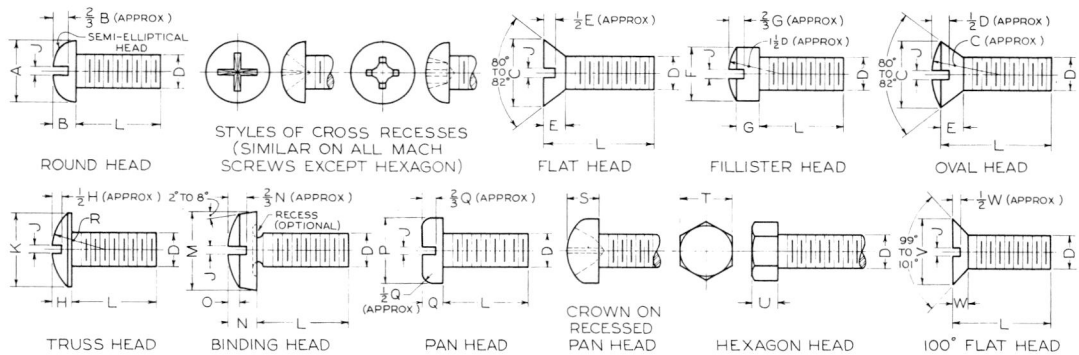

ROUND HEAD　　STYLES OF CROSS RECESSES (SIMILAR ON ALL MACH SCREWS EXCEPT HEXAGON)　　FLAT HEAD　　FILLISTER HEAD　　OVAL HEAD

TRUSS HEAD　　BINDING HEAD　　PAN HEAD　　CROWN ON RECESSED PAN HEAD　　HEXAGON HEAD　　100° FLAT HEAD

AMERICAN NATIONAL STANDARD MACHINE SCREWS[a]

Length of Thread: On screws 2″ long and shorter, the threads extend to within two threads of the head and closer if practicable; longer screws have minimum thread length of 1¾″.

Points: Machine screws are regularly made with plain sheared ends, not chamfered.

Threads: Either Coarse or Fine Thread Series, Class 2 fit.

Recessed Heads: Two styles of cross recesses are available on all screws except hexagon head.

Nominal Size	Max. Diameter D	Round Head		Flat Heads & Oval Head		Fillister Head		Truss Head			Slot Width
		A	B	C	E	F	G	K	H	R	J
0	0.060	0.113	0.053	0.119	0.035	0.096	0.045	0.131	0.037	0.087	0.023
1	0.073	0.138	0.061	0.146	0.043	0.118	0.053	0.164	0.045	0.107	0.026
2	0.086	0.162	0.069	0.172	0.051	0.140	0.062	0.194	0.053	0.129	0.031
3	0.099	0.187	0.078	0.199	0.059	0.161	0.070	0.226	0.061	0.151	0.035
4	0.112	0.211	0.086	0.225	0.067	0.183	0.079	0.257	0.069	0.169	0.039
5	0.125	0.236	0.095	0.252	0.075	0.205	0.088	0.289	0.078	0.191	0.043
6	0.138	0.260	0.103	0.279	0.083	0.226	0.096	0.321	0.086	0.211	0.048
8	0.164	0.309	0.120	0.332	0.100	0.270	0.113	0.384	0.102	0.254	0.054
10	0.190	0.359	0.137	0.385	0.116	0.313	0.130	0.448	0.118	0.283	0.060
12	0.216	0.408	0.153	0.438	0.132	0.357	0.148	0.511	0.134	0.336	0.067
¼	0.250	0.472	0.175	0.507	0.153	0.414	0.170	0.573	0.150	0.375	0.075
⁵⁄₁₆	0.3125	0.590	0.216	0.635	0.191	0.518	0.211	0.698	0.183	0.457	0.084
³⁄₈	0.375	0.708	0.256	0.762	0.230	0.622	0.253	0.823	0.215	0.538	0.094
⁷⁄₁₆	0.4375	0.750	0.328	0.812	0.223	0.625	0.265	0.948	0.248	0.619	0.094
½	0.500	0.813	0.355	0.875	0.223	0.750	0.297	1.073	0.280	0.701	0.106
⁹⁄₁₆	0.5625	0.938	0.410	1.000	0.260	0.812	0.336	1.198	0.312	0.783	0.118
⁵⁄₈	0.625	1.000	0.438	1.125	0.298	0.875	0.375	1.323	0.345	0.863	0.133
¾	0.750	1.250	0.547	1.375	0.372	1.000	0.441	1.573	0.410	1.024	0.149

Nominal Size	Max. Diameter D	Binding Head			Pan Head			Hexagon Head		100° Flat Head		Slot Width
		M	N	O	P	Q	S	T	U	V	W	J
2	0.086	0.181	0.050	0.018	0.167	0.053	0.062	0.125	0.050	....	....	0.031
3	0.099	0.208	0.059	0.022	0.193	0.060	0.071	0.187	0.055	....	....	0.035
4	0.112	0.235	0.068	0.025	0.219	0.068	0.080	0.187	0.060	0.225	0.049	0.039
5	0.125	0.263	0.078	0.029	0.245	0.075	0.089	0.187	0.070	....	....	0.043
6	0.138	0.290	0.087	0.032	0.270	0.082	0.097	0.250	0.080	0.279	0.060	0.048
8	0.164	0.344	0.105	0.039	0.322	0.096	0.115	0.250	0.110	0.332	0.072	0.054
10	0.190	0.399	0.123	0.045	0.373	0.110	0.133	0.312	0.120	0.385	0.083	0.060
12	0.216	0.454	0.141	0.052	0.425	0.125	0.151	0.312	0.155	....	....	0.067
¼	0.250	0.513	0.165	0.061	0.492	0.144	0.175	0.375	0.190	0.507	0.110	0.075
⁵⁄₁₆	0.3125	0.641	0.209	0.077	0.615	0.178	0.218	0.500	0.230	0.635	0.138	0.084
³⁄₈	0.375	0.769	0.253	0.094	0.740	0.212	0.261	0.562	0.295	0.762	0.165	0.094
⁷⁄₁₆	.4375	....	....	....	.865	.247	.305	....	....	....	....	.094
½	.500	....	....	....	.987	.281	.348	....	....	....	....	.106
⁹⁄₁₆	.5625	....	....	....	1.041	.315	.391	....	....	....	....	.118
⁵⁄₈	.625	....	....	....	1.172	.350	.434	....	....	....	....	.133
¾	.750	....	....	....	1.435	.419	.521	....	....	....	....	.149

20   Machine Screws—American National Standard and Metric
(continued)

METRIC MACHINE SCREWS[b]

Length of Thread: On screws 36 mm long or shorter, the threads extend to within one thread of the head: on longer screws the thread extends to within two threads of the head.

Points: Machine screws are regularly made with sheared ends, not chamfered.

Threads: Coarse (general-purpose) threads series are given.

Recessed Heads: Two styles of cross-recesses are available on all screws except hexagon head.

Nominal Size & Thd Pitch	Max. Dia. D, mm	Flat Heads & Oval Head		Pan Heads			Hex Head		Slot Width
		C	E	P	Q	S	T	U	J
M2 × 0.4	2.0	3.5	1.2	4.0	1.3	1.6	3.2	1.6	0.7
M2.5 × 0.45	2.5	4.4	1.5	5.0	1.5	2.1	4.0	2.1	0.8
M3 × 0.5	3.0	5.2	1.7	5.6	1.8	2.4	5.0	2.3	1.0
M3.5 × 0.6	3.5	6.9	2.3	7.0	2.1	2.6	5.5	2.6	1.2
M4 × 0.7	4.0	8.0	2.7	8.0	2.4	3.1	7.0	3.0	1.5
M5 × 0.8	5.0	8.9	2.7	9.5	3.0	3.7	8.0	3.8	1.5
M6 × 1	6.0	10.9	3.3	12.0	3.6	4.6	10.0	4.7	1.9
M8 × 1.25	8.0	15.14	4.6	16.0	4.8	6.0	13.0	6.0	2.3
M10 × 1.5	10.0	17.8	5.0	20.0	6.0	7.5	15.0	7.5	2.8
M12 × 1.75	12.0	....	....	....	....	....	18.0	9.0	....

Nominal Size	Metric Machine Screw Lengths—L[c]																				
	2.5	3	4	5	6	8	10	13	16	20	25	30	35	40	45	50	55	60	65	70	80	90
M2 × 0.4	PH	A	A	A	A	A	A	A	A	A											
M2.5 × 0.45		PH	A	A	A	A	A	A	A	A	A										
M3 × 0.5			PH	A	A	A	A	A	A	A	A	A									
M3.5 × 0.6				PH	A	A	A	A	A	A	A	A	A								
M4 × 0.7				PH	A	A	A	A	A	A	A	A	A	A							
M5 × 0.8					PH	A	A	A	A	A	A	A	A	A	A	A					
M6 × 1						A	A	A	A	A	A	A	A	A	A	A	A	A			
M8 × 1.25						A	A	A	A	A	A	A	A	A	A	A	A	A	A	A	A
M10 × 1.5							A	A	A	A	A	A	A	A	A	A	A	A	A	A	A
M12 × 1.75								A	A	A	A	A	A	A	A	A	A	A	A	A	A

Min. Thd Length—28 mm

Min. Thd Length—38 mm

[b]Metric Fasteners Standard. IFI-513 (1982).

[c]PH = recommended lengths for only pan and hex head metric screws;

   A = recommended lengths for all metric screw head-styles.

21 Keys—Square, Flat, Plain Taper,[a] and Gib Head

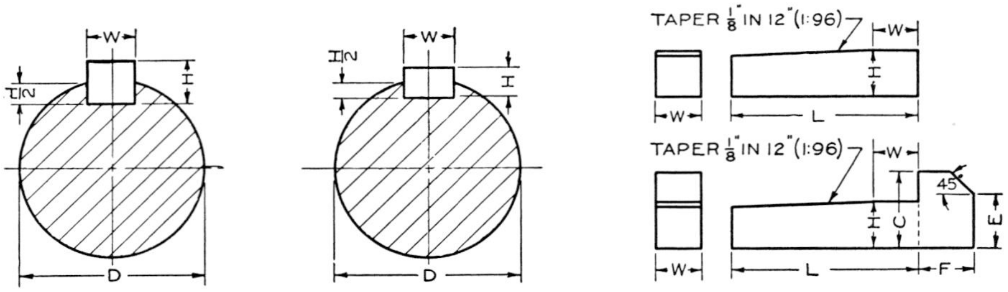

Shaft Diameters	Square Stock Key	Flat Stock Key	Gib Head Taper Stock Key					
			Square			*Flat*		
			Height	Length	Height to Chamfer	Height	Length	Height to Chamfer
D	W = H	W × H	C	F	E	C	F	E
1/2 to 9/16	1/8	1/8 × 3/32	1/4	7/32	5/32	3/16	1/8	1/8
5/8 to 7/8	3/16	3/16 × 1/8	5/16	9/32	7/32	1/4	3/16	5/32
15/16 to 1 1/4	1/4	1/4 × 3/16	7/16	11/32	11/32	5/16	1/4	3/16
1 5/16 to 1 3/8	5/16	5/16 × 1/4	9/16	13/32	13/32	3/8	5/16	1/4
1 7/16 to 1 3/4	3/8	3/8 × 1/4	11/16	15/32	15/32	7/16	3/8	5/16
1 13/16 to 2 1/4	1/2	1/2 × 3/8	7/8	19/32	5/8	5/8	1/2	7/16
2 5/16 to 2 3/4	5/8	5/8 × 7/16	1 1/16	23/32	3/4	3/4	5/8	1/2
2 7/8 to 3 1/4	3/4	3/4 × 1/2	1 1/4	7/8	7/8	7/8	3/4	5/8
3 3/8 to 3 3/4	7/8	7/8 × 5/8	1 1/2	1	1	1 1/16	7/8	3/4
3 7/8 to 4 1/2	1	1 × 3/4	1 3/4	1 3/16	1 3/16	1 1/4	1	13/16
4 3/4 to 5 1/2	1 1/4	1 1/4 × 7/8	2	1 7/16	1 7/16	1 1/2	1 1/4	1
5 3/4 to 6	1 1/2	1 1/2 × 1	2 1/2	1 3/4	1 3/4	1 3/4	1 1/2	1 1/4

[a] Plain taper square and flat keys have the same dimensions as the plain parallel stock keys, with the addition of the taper on top. Gib head taper square and flat keys have the same dimensions as the plain taper keys, with the addition of the gib head.

Stock lengths for plain taper and gib head taper keys: The minimum stock length equals 4W, and the maximum equals 16W. The increments of increase of length equal 2W.

22 Screw Threads,[a] Square and Acme

Size	Threads per Inch	Size	Threads per Inch	Size	Threads per Inch	Size	Threads per Inch
3/8	12	7/8	5	2	2 1/2	3 1/2	1 1/3
7/16	10	1	5	2 1/4	2	3 3/4	1 1/3
1/2	10	1 1/8	4	2 1/2	2	4	1 1/3
9/16	8	1 1/4	4	2 3/4	2	4 1/4	1 1/3
5/8	8	1 1/2	3	3	1 1/2	4 1/2	1
3/4	6	1 3/4	2 1/2	3 1/4	1 1/2	over 4 1/2	1

[a] See Appendix 17 for General-Purpose Acme Threads.

23   Woodruff Keys[a]—American National Standard

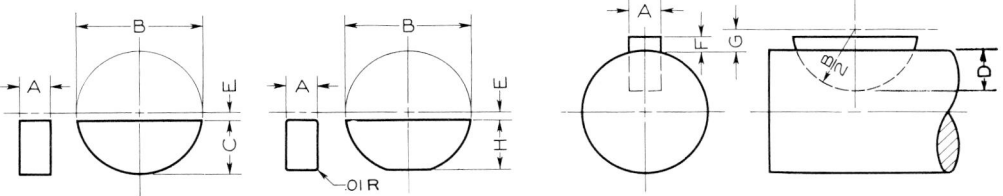

Key No.[b]	Nominal Sizes A × B	E	F	G	Max Sizes H	Max Sizes D	Max Sizes C	Key No.[b]	Nominal Sizes A × B	E	F	G	Max Sizes H	Max Sizes D	Max Sizes C
204	1/16 × 1/2	3/64	1/32	5/64	.194	.1718	.203	808	1/4 × 1	1/16	1/8	3/16	.428	.3130	.438
304	3/32 × 1/2	3/64	3/64	3/32	.194	.1561	.203	809	1/4 × 1 1/8	5/64	1/8	13/64	.475	.3590	.484
305	3/32 × 5/8	1/16	3/64	7/64	.240	.2031	.250	810	1/4 × 1 1/4	5/64	1/8	13/64	.537	.4220	.547
404	1/8 × 1/2	3/64	1/16	7/64	.194	.1405	.203	811	1/4 × 1 3/8	3/32	1/8	7/32	.584	.4690	.594
405	1/8 × 5/8	1/16	1/16	1/8	.240	.1875	.250	812	1/4 × 1 1/2	7/64	1/8	15/64	.631	.5160	.641
406	1/8 × 3/4	1/16	1/16	1/8	.303	.2505	.313	1008	5/16 × 1	1/16	5/32	7/32	.428	.2818	.438
505	5/32 × 5/8	1/16	5/64	9/64	.240	.1719	.250	1009	5/16 × 1 1/8	5/64	5/32	15/64	.475	.3278	.484
506	5/32 × 3/4	1/16	5/64	9/64	.303	.2349	.313	1010	5/16 × 1 1/4	5/64	5/32	15/64	.537	.3908	.547
507	5/32 × 7/8	1/16	5/64	9/64	.365	.2969	.375	1011	5/16 × 1 3/8	3/32	5/32	8/32	.584	.4378	.594
606	3/16 × 3/4	1/16	3/32	5/32	.303	.2193	.313	1012	5/16 × 1 1/2	7/64	5/32	17/64	.631	.4848	.641
607	3/16 × 7/8	1/16	3/32	5/32	.365	.2813	.375	1210	3/8 × 1 1/4	5/64	3/16	17/64	.537	.3595	.547
608	3/16 × 1	1/16	3/32	5/32	.428	.3443	.438	1211	3/8 × 1 3/8	3/32	3/16	9/32	.584	.4065	.594
609	3/16 × 1 1/8	5/64	3/32	11/64	.475	.3903	.484	1212	3/8 × 1 1/2	7/64	3/16	19/64	.631	.4535	.641
807	1/4 × 7/8	1/16	1/8	3/16	.365	.2500	.375	....	....	..	..	..	....	....	....

[a] ANSI B17.2–1967 (R1978).
[b] Key numbers indicate nominal key dimensions. The last two digits give the nominal diameter B in eighths of an inch, and the digits before the last two give the nominal width A in thirty-seconds of an inch.

24   Woodruff Key Sizes for Different Shaft Diameters[a]

Shaft Diameter	5/16 to 3/8	7/16 to 1/2	9/16 to 3/4	13/16 to 15/16	1 to 1 3/16	1 1/4 to 1 7/16	1 1/2 to 1 3/4	1 13/16 to 2 1/8	2 3/16 to 2 1/2
Key Numbers	204	304 305	404 405 406	505 506 507	606 607 608 609	807 808 809	810 811 812	1011 1012	1211 1212

[a] Suggested sizes; not standard.

25   Pratt and Whitney Round-End Keys

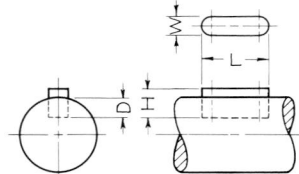

KEYS MADE WITH ROUND ENDS AND KEYWAYS CUT IN SPLINE MILLER

Maximum length of slot is 4″ + W. Note that key is sunk two-thirds into shaft in all cases.

Key No.	L^a	W or D	H	Key No.	L^a	W or D	H
1	1/2	1/16	3/32	22	1 3/8	1/4	3/8
2	1/2	3/32	9/64	23	1 3/8	5/16	15/32
3	1/2	1/8	3/16	F	1 3/8	3/8	9/16
4	5/8	3/32	9/64	24	1 1/2	1/4	3/8
5	5/8	1/8	3/16	25	1 1/2	5/16	15/32
6	5/8	5/32	15/64	G	1 1/2	3/8	9/16
7	3/4	1/8	3/16	51	1 3/4	1/4	3/8
8	3/4	5/32	15/64	52	1 3/4	5/16	15/32
9	3/4	3/16	9/32	53	1 3/4	3/8	9/16
10	7/8	5/32	15/64	26	2	3/16	9/32
11	7/8	3/16	9/32	27	2	1/4	3/8
12	7/8	7/32	21/64	28	2	5/16	15/32
A	7/8	1/4	3/8	29	2	3/8	9/16
13	1	3/16	9/32	54	2 1/4	1/4	3/8
14	1	7/32	21/64	55	2 1/4	5/16	15/32
15	1	1/4	3/8	56	2 1/4	3/8	9/16
B	1	5/16	15/32	57	2 1/4	7/16	21/32
16	1 1/8	3/16	9/32	58	2 1/2	5/16	15/32
17	1 1/8	7/32	21/64	59	2 1/2	3/8	9/16
18	1 1/8	1/4	3/8	60	2 1/2	7/16	21/32
C	1 1/8	5/16	15/32	61	2 1/2	1/2	3/4
19	1 1/4	3/16	9/32	30	3	3/8	9/16
20	1 1/4	7/32	21/64	31	3	7/16	21/32
21	1 1/4	1/4	3/8	32	3	1/2	3/4
D	1 1/4	5/16	15/32	33	3	9/16	27/32
E	1 1/4	3/8	9/16	34	3	5/8	15/16

[a]The length L may vary from the table, but equals at least 2W.

26 Washers,[a] Plain—American National Standard

For parts lists, etc., give inside diameter, outside diameter, and the thickness; for example, .344 × .688 × .065 TYPE A PLAIN WASHER.

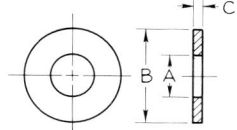

PREFERRED SIZES OF TYPE A PLAIN WASHERS[b]

Nominal Washer Size[c]			Inside Diameter	Outside Diameter	Nominal Thickness
			A	B	C
. . . .	. . . .		0.078	0.188	0.020
. . . .	. . . .		0.094	0.250	0.020
. . . .	. . . .		0.125	0.312	0.032
No. 6	0.138		0.156	0.375	0.049
No. 8	0.164		0.188	0.438	0.049
No. 10	0.190		0.219	0.500	0.049
3/16	0.188		0.250	0.562	0.049
No. 12	0.216		0.250	0.562	0.065
1/4	0.250	N	0.281	0.625	0.065
1/4	0.250	W	0.312	0.734	0.065
5/16	0.312	N	0.344	0.688	0.065
5/16	0.312	W	0.375	0.875	0.083
3/8	0.375	N	0.406	0.812	0.065
3/8	0.375	W	0.438	1.000	0.083
7/16	0.438	N	0.469	0.922	0.065
7/16	0.438	W	0.500	1.250	0.083
1/2	0.500	N	0.531	1.062	0.095
1/2	0.500	W	0.562	1.375	0.109
9/16	0.562	N	0.594	1.156	0.095
9/16	0.562	W	0.625	1.469	0.109
5/8	0.625	N	0.656	1.312	0.095
5/8	0.625	W	0.688	1.750	0.134
3/4	0.750	N	0.812	1.469	0.134
3/4	0.750	W	0.812	2.000	0.148
7/8	0.875	N	0.938	1.750	0.134
7/8	0.875	W	0.938	2.250	0.165
1	1.000	N	1.062	2.000	0.134
1	1.000	W	1.062	2.500	0.165
1 1/8	1.125	N	1.250	2.250	0.134
1 1/8	1.125	W	1.250	2.750	0.165
1 1/4	1.250	N	1.375	2.500	0.165
1 1/4	1.250	W	1.375	3.000	0.165
1 3/8	1.375	N	1.500	2.750	0.165
1 3/8	1.375	W	1.500	3.250	0.180
1 1/2	1.500	N	1.625	3.000	0.165
1 1/2	1.500	W	1.625	3.500	0.180
1 5/8	1.625		1.750	3.750	0.180
1 3/4	1.750		1.875	4.000	0.180
1 7/8	1.875		2.000	4.250	0.180
2	2.000		2.125	4.500	0.180
2 1/4	2.250		2.375	4.750	0.220
2 1/2	2.500		2.625	5.000	0.238
2 3/4	2.750		2.875	5.250	0.259
3	3.000		3.125	5.500	0.284

[a]From ANSI B18.22.1–1965 (R1981). For complete listings, see the standard.
[b]Preferred sizes are for the most part from series previously designated "Standard Plate" and "SAE." Where common sizes existed in the two series, the SAE size is designated "N" (narrow) and the Standard Plate "W" (wide).
[c]Nominal washer sizes are intended for use with comparable nominal screw or bolt sizes.

27 Washers,[a] Lock—American National Standard

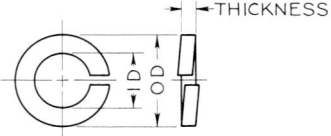

THICKNESS

For parts lists, etc., give nominal size and series; for example, ¼ REGULAR LOCK WASHER

PREFERRED SERIES

Nominal Washer Size[b]		Inside Diameter, Min.	Regular		Extra Duty		Hi-Collar	
			Outside Diameter, Max.	Thick-ness, Min.	Outside Diameter, Max.	Thick-ness, Min.	Outside Diameter, Max.	Thick-ness, Min.
No. 2	0.086	0.088	0.172	0.020	0.208	0.027	....	....
No. 3	0.099	0.101	0.195	0.025	0.239	0.034	....	....
No. 4	0.112	0.115	0.209	0.025	0.253	0.034	0.173	0.022
No. 5	0.125	0.128	0.236	0.031	0.300	0.045	0.202	0.030
No. 6	0.138	0.141	0.250	0.031	0.314	0.045	0.216	0.030
No. 8	0.164	0.168	0.293	0.040	0.375	0.057	0.267	0.047
No. 10	0.190	0.194	0.334	0.047	0.434	0.068	0.294	0.047
No. 12	0.216	0.221	0.377	0.056	0.497	0.080	....	....
¼	0.250	0.255	0.489	0.062	0.535	0.084	0.365	0.078
⁵⁄₁₆	0.312	0.318	0.586	0.078	0.622	0.108	0.460	0.093
³⁄₈	0.375	0.382	0.683	0.094	0.741	0.123	0.553	0.125
⁷⁄₁₆	0.438	0.446	0.779	0.109	0.839	0.143	0.647	0.140
½	0.500	0.509	0.873	0.125	0.939	0.162	0.737	0.172
⁹⁄₁₆	0.562	0.572	0.971	0.141	1.041	0.182	....	....
⅝	0.625	0.636	1.079	0.156	1.157	0.202	0.923	0.203
¹¹⁄₁₆	0.688	0.700	1.176	0.172	1.258	0.221	...	....
¾	0.750	0.763	1.271	0.188	1.361	0.241	1.111	0.218
¹³⁄₁₆	0.812	0.826	1.367	0.203	1.463	0.261	....	....
⅞	0.875	0.890	1.464	0.219	1.576	0.285	1.296	0.234
¹⁵⁄₁₆	0.938	0.954	1.560	0.234	1.688	0.308	....	....
1	1.000	1.017	1.661	0.250	1.799	0.330	1.483	0.250
1¹⁄₁₆	1.062	1.080	1.756	0.266	1.910	0.352	....	....
1⅛	1.125	1.144	1.853	0.281	2.019	0.375	1.669	0.313
1³⁄₁₆	1.188	1.208	1.950	0.297	2.124	0.396	....	....
1¼	1.250	1.271	2.045	0.312	2.231	0.417	1.799	0.313
1⁵⁄₁₆	1.312	1.334	2.141	0.328	2.335	0.438	....	....
1⅜	1.375	1.398	2.239	0.344	2.439	0.458	2.041	0.375
1⁷⁄₁₆	1.438	1.462	2.334	0.359	2.540	0.478	....	....
1½	1.500	1.525	2.430	0.375	2.638	0.496	2.170	0.375

[a]From ANSI B18.21.1–1972 (R1983). For complete listing, see the standard.
[b]Nominal washer sizes are intended for use with comparable nominal screw or bolt sizes.

28 Wire Gage Standards[a]

Dimensions of sizes in decimal parts of an inch.[b]

No. of Wire	American or Brown & Sharpe for Non-ferrous Metals	Birmingham, or Stubs' Iron Wire[c]	American S. & W. Co.'s (Washburn & Moen) Std. Steel Wire	American S. & W. Co.'s Music Wire	Imperial Wire	Stubs' Steel Wire[c]	Steel Manufacturers' Sheet Gage[b]	No. of Wire
7-0's	.651354	. . . .	.4900	. . . .	.500	. . . .	. . . . .	7-0's
6-0's	.580049	. . . .	.4615	.004	.464	. . . .	. . . . .	6-0's
5-0's	.516549	.500	.4305	.005	.432	. . . .	. . . . .	5-0's
4-0's	.460	.454	.3938	.006	.400	. . . .	. . . . .	4-0's
000	.40964	.425	.3625	.007	.372	. . . .	. . . . .	000
00	.3648	.380	.3310	.008	.348	. . . .	. . . . .	00
0	.32486	.340	.3065	.009	.324	. . . .	. . . . .	0
1	.2893	.300	.2830	.010	.300	.227	. . . . .	1
2	.25763	.284	.2625	.011	.276	.219	. . . . .	2
3	.22942	.259	.2437	.012	.252	.212	.2391	3
4	.20431	.238	.2253	.013	.232	.207	.2242	4
5	.18194	.220	.2070	.014	.212	.204	.2092	5
6	.16202	.203	.1920	.016	.192	.201	.1943	6
7	.14428	.180	.1770	.018	.176	.199	.1793	7
8	.12849	.165	.1620	.020	.160	.197	.1644	8
9	.11443	.148	.1483	.022	.144	.194	.1495	9
10	.10189	.134	.1350	.024	.128	.191	.1345	10
11	.090742	.120	.1205	.026	.116	.188	.1196	11
12	.080808	.109	.1055	.029	.104	.185	.1046	12
13	.071961	.095	.0915	.031	.092	.182	.0897	13
14	.064084	.083	.0800	.033	.080	.180	.0747	14
15	.057068	.072	.0720	.035	.072	.178	.0763	15
16	.05082	.065	.0625	.037	.064	.175	.0598	16
17	.045257	.058	.0540	.039	.056	.172	.0538	17
18	.040303	.049	.0475	.041	.048	.168	.0478	18
19	.03589	.042	.0410	.043	.040	.164	.0418	19
20	.031961	.035	.0348	.045	.036	.161	.0359	20
21	.028462	.032	.0317	.047	.032	.157	.0329	21
22	.025347	.028	.0286	.049	.028	.155	.0299	22
23	.022571	.025	.0258	.051	.024	.153	.0269	23
24	.0201	.022	.0230	.055	.022	.151	.0239	24
25	.0179	.020	.0204	.059	.020	.148	.0209	25
26	.01594	.018	.0181	.063	.018	.146	.0179	26
27	.014195	.016	.0173	.067	.0164	.143	.0164	27
28	.012641	.014	.0162	.071	.0149	.139	.0149	28
29	.011257	.013	.0150	.075	.0136	.134	.0135	29
30	.010025	.012	.0140	.080	.0124	.127	.0120	30
31	.008928	.010	.0132	.085	.0116	.120	.0105	31
32	.00795	.009	.0128	.090	.0108	.115	.0097	32
33	.00708	.008	.0118	.095	.0100	.112	.0090	33
34	.006304	.007	.0104	. . . .	.0092	.110	.0082	34
35	.005614	.005	.0095	. . . .	.0084	.108	.0075	35
36	.005	.004	.0090	. . . .	.0076	.106	.0067	36
37	.004453	. . . .	.0085	. . . .	.0068	.103	.0064	37
38	.003965	. . . .	.0080	. . . .	.0060	.101	.0060	38
39	.003531	. . . .	.0075	. . . .	.0052	.099	. . . . .	39
40	.003144	. . . .	.0070	. . . .	.0048	.097	. . . . .	40

[a]Courtesy Brown & Sharpe Mfg. Co.

[b]Now used by steel manufacturers in place of old U.S. Standard Gage.

[c]The difference between the Stubs' Iron Wire Gage and the Stubs' Steel Wire Gage should be noted, the first being commonly known as the English Standard Wire, or Birmingham Gage, which designates the Stubs' soft wire sizes and the second being used in measuring drawn steel wire or drill rods of Stubs' make.

29   Taper Pins[a]—American National Standard

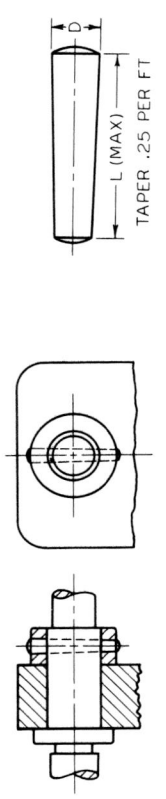

D   L (MAX)   TAPER .25 PER FT

To find small diameter of pin, multiply the length by .02083 and subtract the result from the larger diameter.
All dimensions are given in inches.
Standard reamers are available for pins given above the heavy line.

Number	7/0	6/0	5/0	4/0	3/0	2/0	0	1	2	3	4	5	6	7	8
Size (Large End)	.0625	.0780	.0940	.1090	.1250	.1410	.1560	.1720	.1930	.2190	.2500	.2890	.3410	.4090	.4920
Shaft Diameter (Approx)[b]		7/32	1/4	5/16	3/8	7/16	1/2	9/16	5/8	3/4	13/16	7/8	1	1 1/4	1 1/2
Drill Size (Before Reamer)[b]	.0312	.0312	.0625	.0625	.0781	.0938	.0938	.1094	.1250	.1250	.1562	.1562	.2188	.2344	.3125
Length L															
.250	X	X	X	X	X										
.375	X	X	X	X	X										
.500	X	X	X	X	X										
.625	X	X	X	X	X	X	X								
.750	X	X	X	X	X	X	X								
.875	X	X	X	X	X	X	X								
1.000	X	X	X	X	X	X	X	X							
1.250		X	X	X	X	X	X	X	X						
1.500				X	X	X	X	X	X	X	X				X
1.750				X	X	X	X	X	X	X	X	X	X		X
2.000					X	X	X	X	X	X	X	X	X	X	X
2.250						X	X	X	X	X	X	X	X	X	X
2.500						X	X	X	X	X	X	X	X	X	X
2.750								X	X	X	X	X	X	X	X
3.000								X	X	X	X	X	X	X	X
3.250									X	X	X	X	X	X	X
3.500										X	X	X	X	X	X
3.750										X	X	X	X	X	X
4.000											X	X	X	X	X
4.250												X	X	X	X
4.500													X	X	X

[a]ANSI B18.8.2—1978 (R1983). For Nos. 9 and 10, see the standard. Pins Nos 11 (size .8600), 12 (size 1.032), 13 (size 1.241), and 14 (size 1.523) are special sizes; hence their lengths are special.

[b]Suggested sizes; not American National Standard.

30   Cotter Pins[a]—American National Standard

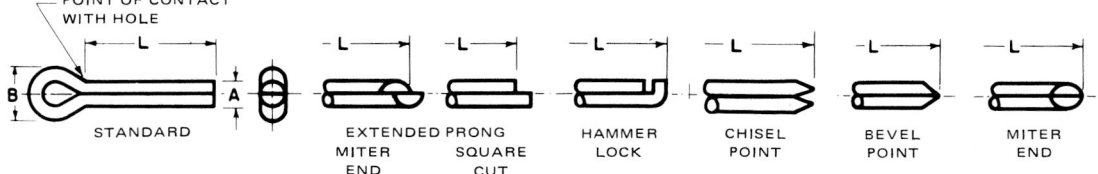

PREFERRED POINT TYPES

All dimensions are given in inches.

Nominal Size or Pin Diameter		Diameter A		Outside Eye Diameter B Min.	Extended Prong Length Min.	Hole Sizes Recommended
		Max.	Min.			
1/32	.031	.032	.028	.06	.01	.047
3/64	.047	.048	.044	.09	.02	.062
1/16	.062	.060	.056	.12	.03	.078
5/64	.078	.076	.072	.16	.04	.094
3/32	.094	.090	.086	.19	.04	.109
7/64	.109	.104	.100	.22	.05	.125
1/8	.125	.120	.116	.25	.06	.141
9/64	.141	.134	.130	.28	.06	.156
5/32	.156	.150	.146	.31	.07	.172
3/16	.188	.176	.172	.38	.09	.203
7/32	.219	.207	.202	.44	.10	.234
1/4	.250	.225	.220	.50	.11	.266
5/16	.312	.280	.275	.62	.14	.312
3/8	.375	.335	.329	.75	.16	.375
7/16	.438	.406	.400	.88	.20	.438
1/2	.500	.473	.467	1.00	.23	.500
5/8	.625	.598	.590	1.25	.30	.625
3/4	.750	.723	.715	1.50	.36	.750

[a]ANSI B18.8.1—1972 (R1983).

31   Metric Equivalents

Length

U.S. to Metric	Metric to U.S.
1 inch = 2.540 centimeters 1 foot = .305 meter 1 yard = .914 meter 1 mile = 1.609 kilometers	1 millimeter = .039 inch 1 centimeter = .394 inch 1 meter = 3.281 feet or 1.094 yards 1 kilometer = .621 mile

Area

U.S. to Metric	Metric to U.S.
$1\ inch^2 = 6.451\ centimeter^2$ $1\ foot^2 = .093\ meter^2$ $1\ yard^2 = .836\ meter^2$ $1\ acre^2 = 4{,}046.873\ meter^2$	$1\ millimeter^2 = .00155\ inch^2$ $1\ centimeter^2 = .155\ inch^2$ $1\ meter^2 = 10.764\ foot^2$ or $1.196\ yard^2$ $1\ kilometer^2 = .386\ mile^2$ or $247.04\ acre^2$

Volume

U.S. to Metric	Metric to U.S.
$1\ inch^3 = 16.387\ centimeter^3$ $1\ foot^3 = .028\ meter^3$ $1\ yard^3 = .764\ meter^3$ 1 quart = .946 liter $1\ gallon = .003785\ meter^3$	$1\ centimeter^3 = .061\ inch^3$ $1\ meter^3 = 35.314\ foot^3$ or $1.308\ yard^3$ 1 liter = .2642 gallons 1 liter = 1.057 quarts $1\ meter^3 = 264.02\ gallons$

Weight

U.S. to Metric	Metric to U.S.
1 ounce = 28.349 grams 1 pound = .454 kilogram 1 ton = .907 metric ton	1 gram = .035 ounce 1 kilogram = 2.205 pounds 1 metric ton = 1.102 tons

Velocity

U.S. to Metric	Metric to U.S.
1 foot/second = .305 meter/second 1 mile/hour = .447 meter/second	1 meter/second = 3.281 feet/second 1 kilometer/hour = .621 mile/second

Acceleration

U.S. to Metric	Metric to U.S.
$1\ inch/second^2 = .0254\ meter/second^2$ $1\ foot/second^2 = .305\ meter/second^2$	$1\ meter/second^2 = 3.278\ feet/second^2$

Force

N (newton) = basic unit of force, $kg\text{-}m/s^2$. A mass of one kilogram (1 kg) exerts a gravitational force of 9.8 N (theoretically 9.80665 N) at mean sea level.

32 Form and Proportion of Geometric Tolerancing Symbols[a]

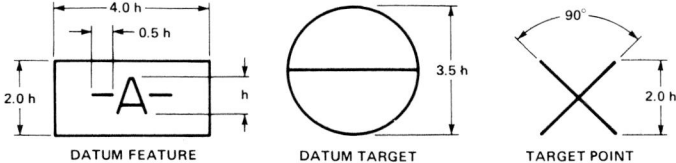

DATUM FEATURE   DATUM TARGET   TARGET POINT

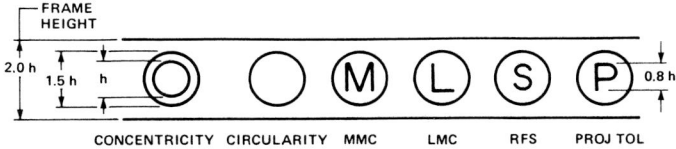

CONCENTRICITY CIRCULARITY   MMC   LMC   RFS   PROJ TOL

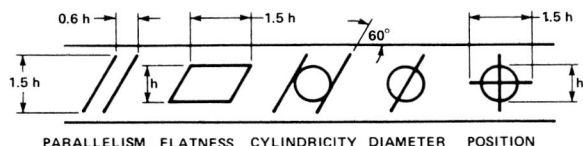

PARALLELISM FLATNESS CYLINDRICITY DIAMETER POSITION

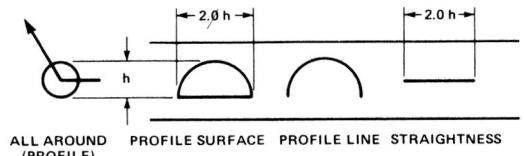

ALL AROUND   PROFILE SURFACE PROFILE LINE STRAIGHTNESS
(PROFILE)

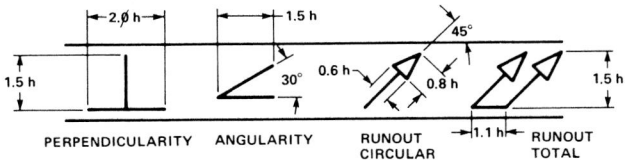

PERPENDICULARITY   ANGULARITY   RUNOUT   RUNOUT
                                   CIRCULAR   TOTAL

[a]ANSI Y14.5M—1982 (R1988).

Index

Abbreviations, American National Standard, Appx. 4
Abscissa, 644
Accuracy, 13, 346
    of measurements, 32–33
    working drawing, 464
Acme thread, 413, Appxs. 17, 22
    detailed representation, 421–22
    thread notes, 425
Actual size, definition, 381
Adjacent views, visibility of interior lines, 550
Adjustable curves, 45
Aero-thread inserts, 437
Algebraic solution graph, 662–63
Aligned sections, 189, 270–72
Alignment chart, 655–56
Allowance, definition, 381
Alternate four-center ellipse, 512
Aluminum, coated sheets, 49
American National Standard(s), Appx. 1
    abbreviations, Appx. 4
    bolts and nuts, 429–31, Appx. 18
    cap screws, 434–35, Appxs. 18–19
    conversion to SI units, 342
    cotter pins, Appx. 30
    decimal dimensioning, 346
    dimensioning, 370
    drafting, 6
    finish marks, 352–53
    geometric characteristics symbols, 390–91
    half sections, 265
    keys, Appxs. 21, 23–25
    lettering, 91
    limits and fits, 385–86, Appxs. 5–14
    lines, 19
    locknuts and locking devices, 433
    machine screws, 435–36, Appx. 20
    pipe threads, 426–27
    roughness length cutoff values, 405
    roughness width cutoff values, 405
    screw threads, Appx. 22
    set screws, 436–37
    sheet sizes, 50
    simplified drafting, 465
    slope of inclined capitals, 95
    taper dimensioning, 367–68
    taper pins, Appx. 29
    views, 164
    washers, Appxs. 26–27
    waviness height values, 406
    wire gage, Appx. 28
    wood screws, 437
American National thread, 413, 422–23, Appx. 15
    detailed representation, 418–19
    fits, 423
Ames Lettering Guide, 96–97, 99
Analog computers, 58–59
Angle, 110
    between line and oblique plane, 565–66
    bisecting, 113
    complementary, 110
    dihedral, 292, 559
    dimensioning, 351
    drafting, 24
    isometric projection, 506–507
    laying out, 117–18
    90°, 584
    oblique projection, 539–40
    plane of projection by revolution, 554
    projections, 198
    receding lines, 534
    supplementary, 110
    tolerance, 397
    transferring, 113
Angular dimensions, CAD, 244–45
Angular tolerance, 384, 400
Application programs, CAD, 73–80

Approximate dimetric drawings, 519
Approximate ellipse, 134–35
Approximate four-center ellipse, 510–12
Arc, 111
    bisecting, 112
    CAD, 241–42
    dimensioning, 351–52
    isometric projection, 512–13
    rectifying, 128–29
    series of tangent, 128
    set off length along, 129
    sketching, 154
    tangent to arc, 124–25
    tangent to line, 124
    tangent to two arcs, 126–27
    tangent to two lines, 124–26
    three-point, 241–42
Architects' scale, 30–32
    double size, 32
    eighth size, 32
    full size, 30
    half size, 31
    quarter size, 31
Architectural details, CAD, 76
Area chart, 658
Area law
    differential calculus, 664–65
    integral calculus, 666
Arrowheads, 344–45
Arrows, drawing on CAD, 244–45
Artistic drawings, 3
Ascenders, 99
Assembly drawing, 456, 465–66
    computer graphics, 525
Assembly sectioning, 469–71
Assembly views
    check, 471
    dimensions, 467, 469
    drawing revisions, 469
    hidden lines, 467
    identification of parts, 469
    installation, 471
    sections, 467–68
    view selection, 466
    working drawing, 471
AutoCAD, 234, 236
    tablet menu, 245
Automation, manufacturing processes, 335–37
Auxiliary plane, 286–87
Auxiliary sections, 295–96
Auxiliary view, 285
    auxiliary plane, 286–87
    classification, 289
    computer graphics, 301
    definitions, 286
    depth, 289–90
    dihedral angles, 292
    ellipses, 300
    folding-line method, 287, 297–98
    front adjacent, 289
    half, 295
    height, 290–91

    hidden lines in, 295
    intersection of planes, 563, 565
    partial, 294–95
    planes, 559
    plotting curves, 292–93
    primary, 286
    reference-plane method, 288–89, 298–99
    reference planes, 287–88
    reverse construction, 293–94
    secondary, 286, 296, 299–300
    side adjacent, 289
    successive, 296–97
    top-adjacent, 289
    true-length, 555
    uses, 297
    width, 291
Auxiliary-view method
    length of line, 296
    plane perpendicular to line, 586–87
Axis
    axonometric, 501
    of ellipse, 510, 521
    inclined, 313–14
    isometric, 158, 502, 504
    neutral, 369
    normal, 313
    oblique, 314
    of projection, 554
    of revolution, 310, 313, 554
    of screw, 412
Axonometric axis, 501
Axonometric projection, 151, 499
    compared to oblique projection, 532
    computer graphics, 524–25
    conversion of orthographic drawing to, 524–25
    method of intersections, 521–23, 525
    types, 500–501
    See also Dimetric projection; Isometric
        projection
Azimuth bearing, 555–56

Babbage, Charles, 55
Bar chart, 656–57
    design and layout, 657–58
    scale designation, 658
Base line, 360
Basic dimension
    definition, 381
    symbol, 392
Basic hole system, 382
Basic shaft system, 382
Basic size, definition, 381, 387
Batter, 351
Beam compass, 35–37
Bearing, 554–56
Bend allowance, 369
Bevels, 351
Bilateral tolerances, 383–84, 397
Binary coded decimal instructions, 62
Bisect angle, 113
Bisect line or arc, 112–13
Bit, 62

Blind hole, 205
Blind tapped hole, thread note, 425
Blocking in lines, 153
Blocking-in method, sketching, 157
Blow molding, 338
Blueprint reading, definition, 7
Bolt, 427
    across flats, 431
    American National Standard, 429–31, Appx.
        18
    computer graphics, 441–42
    drawing, 431–32
    finish, 429
    hexagon, 429
    lengths, 430–31
    metric, Appx. 18
    proportions, 430
    specifications, 432–33
    tapped hole, 428–29
    thread, 430
    thread lengths, 430
    types, 429
Bolt circle, 360
Boring mill, 329–30
Bottoming tap, 428
Bow instruments, 38–39
Bow pen and pencil, drop spring, 39
Box construction, 505–506
    irregular objects, 507
    oblique projection, 536
Bracket method, dimension figures, 349
Braddock-Rowe lettering triangle, 96, 99
Briggs standard, 426
Broaching, 331
Broken-out sections, 265–66
Buttress thread, 413
Byte, 62

Cabinet drawing, 538–39, 540
Cabinet projection, 535
CAD, 50, 56–58, 60–85, 225–26, 473–77
    application programs, 73–80
    applications, 60
    arc drawing, 241–42
    arrow drawing, 244–45
    capability checklist, 229–30
    central processing unit, 57, 59, 62–63, 83
    circle drawing, 241
    commands, 229
    compatibility, 226
    construction, 239
    copy and rotate features, 248
    copying files, 233
    creating text, 243
    data storage devices, 57, 59, 62, 70–73, 84
    deleting files, 233
    dimensioning, 243–44
    directory display access, 232
    display devices, 64–65, 83–84
    drawing software, 238–43
    drive command access, 231–32
    floppy drives, 231

    function keys, 229, 235–38
    glossary, Appx. 3
    hard disk, 233
    hardware, 226, 475
    horizontal-vertical controls, 240
    input, 235–38
    input devices, 56–57, 61, 65–67, 83, 233
    interactive system, 57
    lettering, 105–106
    line drawing, 239–40
    line types, 240
    linked to numerical control equipment, 60
    LIST command, 242–43
    loading software, 230–31, 233–34
    menu, 228–29
    microcomputer operations, 230
    need for, 81–82
    networks, 57, 60
    operating programs, 62, 73
    output devices, 57–58, 61–62, 67–70, 84, 233,
        475
    overview, 244–49
    passive system, 57
    point drawing, 240–41
    polygon drawing, 241–42
    software, 56, 226–29
    spline drawing, 242–43
    startup software, 234–35
    storage of finished drawings, 473
    system configurations, 57–58, 61–62
    system demonstrations, 82–84
    system selection, 81–85
    systems, 57
    three-dimensional, 60
    using, 73, 75, 81
    workstation, 57, 59, 474
CAD/CAM, 56, 475–77
    definition, 475
    glossary, Appx. 3
    work flow diagram, 477
CADD, 56, 473
CADKEY, 234, 236
Calculus, graphical, 663
    See also Differential calculus; Integral calculus
Calipers, 333
Calligraphic system, 65
CAM, 56
Capital letters
    ends of cutting-plane line, 261
    Gothic, 90
    guide lines, 94–96
    inclined, 95, 98
    Modern Roman, 89
    Old Roman, 88
    spacing, 95
    vertical, 97–98
Cap screw, 427
    American National Standard, 434–35, Appxs.
        18–19
    drawing, 431–32
    hex, 429
    metric, Appxs. 18–19

Cap screw (*Continued*)
    screwdriver slots, 435
Carveyor, 454
Cathode ray tube, 57–58
Cavalier drawing, four-center ellipse, 537
Cavalier projection, 535
CD-ROM drive, 72
Center line, 344
    of bend, 169, 369, 372
    isometric drawing, 505
    separating half sections, 265
Central processing unit, 57, 59, 62–63, 83
Chain dimensioning, 364
Chain scale, 30
Chamfer
    dimensioning, 368
    hexagon bolt, 618
    hexagon nut, 618
Chart, 639
    alignment, 655–56
    area, 658
    computer graphics, 668–69
    distribution, 660
    nomograph, 655–56
    pie, 659
    surface, 658
    volume, 659–60
    See also Bar chart; Line chart
Check assembly, 471
Chemical milling, 333
Chemistry stencil, 47
Chipless machining, 333–34
Chord method, 118
CIM, 56
Circle, 111–12
    CAD, 241
    concentric, 133
    drawing, 123
    finding center, 123
    great, 610
    involute of, 139
    leader to, 345
    rectifying quadrant, 129
    revolutions of, 316–17
    sketching, 153–54
    tangent to line, 123
    tangent to two circles, 124
    tangent through point, 123–24
Circle of centers, 360
Circular edges, 199
Circular pipe, transition piece connecting to
    rectangular pipe, 609
Circular tolerance zone, 394–95
Circularity tolerance, 398–99
Circumference, 111–112
Civil engineers' scale, 30
Clearance, 380–81, 385
    fits, Appxs. 6, 11, 13–14
    tapped holes, 429
Coated sheets, 49
Column chart, *see* Bar chart
Combination dimensioning, 346

Common perpendicular, 588–90
Compass, 33
    beam, 35–37
    lead, 36, 38
    using, 34
Compression molding, 338
Compression springs, 439
Computation sketches, 1
Computer-aided design and drafting, 56, 473
Computer-aided design/computer-aided
    manufacturing, *see* CAD/CAM
Computer-aided drafting, *see* CAD
Computer-aided manufacturing, 56
Computer graphics, 56
    axonometric projection, 524–25
    auxiliary views, 301
    definition, 7
    dimensioning, 373–74
    geometric constructions, 140–41
    graphic representations, 668–69
    image processing, 60
    lettering, 105–106
    multiview drawings, 209
    oblique projection, 541
    revolutions, 318
    sectional views, 274–75
    sketches, 172
    surface finish symbols, 408
    threaded fasteners and springs, 441–42
    tolerancing, 408–409
    working drawing, 473–77
Computer integrated manufacturing, 56
Computers, 56–63
    automated manufacturing processes, 335–37
    classes, 62–63
    components, 56–58
    as drafting tool, 50
    integrated circuit, 59–60
    measuring devices, 333
    memory, 62
    microminiaturization, 60
    printed circuit, 59–60
    systems, 56–58
    types, 58–60
    See also CAD; Computer graphics
Concentric circle, 133
    ellipse, 131–32
Concentricity tolerance, 403
Cone, 112
    development, 617
    dimensioning, 358
    intersection with cylinder, 618–19
    intersection with prism, 616–18
    line at specified angles, 633
    oblique, 605–607, 626–27
    plane containing oblique line, 632
    plane tangent to, 626–28
    right circular, 626–27, 632–34
Conical helix, 138
Conic section, 129–30, 599
Conjugate diameters, 510
Construction lines, bolt, 431

Conventional breaks, 273–75
Contour dimensioning, 353–54
Coordinate dimensioning, 370–71
Coordinate measurements, 503
Coordinate paper, 642–44
Cordless electric eraser, new product design, 457
Corner, 192
Cotter pin, 433, Appx. 30
Counterboring, 332–33
Counterrevolution, 317, 561
Countersinking, 333
Crozet, Claude, 6, 547
Cube, 598
Cursor keys, 235–36
Curve
    adjustable, 45
    dimensioning, 363
    intersections, 611–12
    irregular, 45
    isometric projection, 508–509
    line graph, 648
    plotted, 292–93
    tangent to lines, 128
Curved surfaces, 198–99, 369
Cutting plane, 258, 261–63
    offset sections, 269
    revolved sections, 266
    ribs in section, 269–70
Cutting-plane line, 259, 261
Cutting-plane method
    interaction of planes, 564–65
    piercing point, 562–63
    special, 565
Cycloid, drawing, 139–40
Cylinder, 112
    deformities, 199–201
    development, 601–602, 614
    dimensioning, 373
    intersections of, 202–203, 513, 614–15
    intersection with cone, 618–19
    intersection with plane, 601
    intersection with sphere, 618–19
    oblique, 602
    plane tangent to, 628–29, 631
    projections, 201
    S-breaks, 274–75
    size dimensions, 355–57
Cylindrical pipe, transition piece connecting, 609–10
    with square pipe, 610
Cylindrical surfaces, 199–200
Cylindrical tolerance, 398–99
    zone, 394–95

Data storage devices, CAD, 57, 59, 62, 70–73, 84
Datum, holes located from, 360
Datum identifying symbol, 392
Datum plane, 288
Decimal dimensions, 345–46, 383
Decimal scale, 32, 348

Decimal systems, 346–48
Depth
    auxiliary views, 289–90
    transferring dimensions, 185
Descriptive geometry, 547
    definition, 7
    early, 4
    See also Line; Plane; Point
Design, 447
    concepts, 448
    empirical, 448
    ideal, 453
    layout, 451
    scientific, 448
    sources, 448
    team, 448
    see also New product design
Design process
    compromise solutions, 451–54, 457
    concepts and ideas, 451, 457
    models and prototypes, 454–55, 458–59
    preliminary studies, 451
    problem identification, 449–51, 457
    working drawings, 455–56, 459–61
Detail drawings, 455–56
    grouping on sheets, 459–61
Detail paper, 48
Detail pen, 42
Developable surface, 598
Development, 597, 599–600
    cone, 617
    cylinder, 601–602, 614–16
    hood and flue, 604–605
    inclined cylinder, 616
    layouts, 599
    oblique cone, 605–607
    oblique cylinder, 602
    oblique prism, 602
    prism, 601, 612–14
    prism and cone, 617
    sphere, 610–11
    of surface, 599
    transition piece, 607–10
    triangulation, 605
    truncated oblique rectangular pyramid, 605
    truncated pyramid, 603
Deviation, definition, 387
Diagram, 639
Diameter symbol, 357
Differential calculus, 663
    applications, 665
    area law, 664–65
    geometric interpretation of derivative, 663–64
    slope law, 664
Digital computers, 58–59
Digitizing tablets, 65–67, 229
Dihedral angle, 292, 559
Dimension, basic, 392
Dimension figures, 348–50, 372
    aligned system, 350
    bracket method, 349
    direction of, 350

Dimension figures (*Continued*)
  position method, 349
  unidirectional system, 350
Dimension line, 343, 372
  placement, 344
  spacing of, 343
Dimensioning, 341
  along curved surfaces, 369
  angles, 351
  arcs, 351–52
  arrowheads, 344–45
  CAD, 238, 243–44
  chain, 364
  chamfers, 368
  combination, 346
  complete decimal, 346–47
  computer graphics, 373–74
  contour, 353–54
  coordinate, 370–71
  curves, 363
  cylinder, 373
  do's and don'ts, 371–73
  dual, 349
  of engineering structures, 355
  fillets, 352
  finish marks, 352–53
  general notes, 367
  geometric breakdown, 354–55
  holes, 373
  inches, 350
  isometric projection, 515–16, 540
  keyways, 368–69
  knurls, 369
  leaders, 345
  learning to, 342–43
  limit, 383
  lines used in, 343–44
  local notes, 366–67
  millimeters, 350
  notes, 366–67
  oblique, 540–41
  plus and minus, 383
  rounded-end shapes, 363–64
  rounds, 352
  scale of drawing, 342
  shaft centers, 368
  sheet-metal bends, 369–70
  single-limit, 384
  size, 355–59
  size description, 342
  standards, 370
  symbols, 357–58
  tabular, 370
  tapers, 367–68
  technique of, 342
  threads, 366
  tolerance, 380–81
  true-position, 394
  See also SI System
Dimensions
  assembly views, 467, 469
  choice of, 343

  decimal, 345–46
  estimating, 156
  forging, 363
  fractional, 345–46
  isometric, 515
  location, 355, 359–61
  machine, 362–63
  mating, 361–62
  metric, 27, 345–46
  on and off views, 353
  pattern, 362–63
  placement, 343, 353
  reference, 360, 386
  starting, 359–60
  superfluous, 364–65, 367
  transferring depth, 185
  untoleranced, 395
Dimetric drawing, 518–19
Dimetric projection, 501, 517–19
Direct view storage tube, 64–65
Directory display access, 232
Directrix, 135
Display monitors, CAD, 64–65, 83–84
  classification, 83–84
Disk drives, 71–72
Distribution chart, 660
  map, 661
Dividers, 37
  proportional, 38
Dodecahedron, 598
Dot matrix plotting, 69
Dot matrix printers, 70
Double-curved surface, 598, 631
Dowel pin, 439
Drafting
  accurate measurements, 32
  basics, CAD, 226
  coated sheets, 49
  cumulative errors, 33
  erasing, 44
  at home or school, 13–14
  laying out a sheet, 39
  metric scales, 27
  objectives, 12
  order of inking, 44
  paper, 48
  polyester films, 49
  protractors, 24
  simplified, 465
  standards, 6
  templates, 47
  tracing papers, 48–49
  See also CAD; Computer graphics
Drafting angles, 24
Drafting instruments, 33
  beam compass, 35–36
  bow instruments, 38
  dividers, 37–38
  early, 4
  giant bow compass, 33–34
  giant bow set, 33
  proportional dividers, 38

ruling pens, 42
technical fountain pens, 42
Drafting machine, 47–48
Drafting table, 14, 48
Drafting tape, 15
Draftsquare, 47
Drawing
  definition, 7
  equipment, 12–13
  erasing, 20–21
  ink, 42–43
  isometric, 502–504
  oblique, 536–37
  pencils, 16–17
  scale of, 26–30, 342
  technique, 40–41
  tracing, 41–42
  See also Drafting
Drawing board, 14
  placing paper on, 15–16
  working edge, 14
Drawing ink, 42–43
Drawing instruments, see Drafting instruments
Drawing papers, 48
Drawings
  abbreviations, Appx. 4
  assembly, 456, 465–66
  checking, 464
  control, 472–73
  detail, 455–56
  dimensioning, 342
  dimension line placement, 344
  dimension placement, 343
  extension line placement, 344
  keeping clean, 21–22
  one-view, 167–68
  patent, 456
  production, 459–61
  reading, 192–93
  reproduction, 472–73
  scale specification, 32
  three-view, 186–87
  transfer, 121–22
  two-view, 166–67
  two-view instrumental, 183–85
  types, 3–4
  See also Working drawing
Drill
  size dimensioning, 359
  sizes, 373, Appx. 16
Drill press, 327
Drilling, holes, 331–32
Drive command access, 231–32
Drop spring bow pencil and pen, 39
Drum plotter, 68
Dusting brush, 21

Edge, 191–92
  circular, 199
  conventional, 206–207
  inclined, 196
  normal, 194

oblique, 196–97
parallel, 197
of solid, 598
Edge view, planes, 558–60
Edge-view method
  intersection of planes, 563–64
  piercing point, 561–62
Egyptian hieroglyphics, 3
Electric Wheel, 453
Electrodischarge machining, 333
Electronic diagram, CAD, 77
Electronic organ, design, 454
Electrostatic plotters, 69
Element, 199
Elevation, 165
Ellipse
  alternate four-center, 512
  angle of, 300
  approximate, 134–35
  approximate four-center, 510–12
  auxiliary views, 300
  concentric-circle, 131–32
  conjugate diameters, 510
  construction, 130
  drawing on conjugate diameters, 132
  finding axes, 132–33
  foci, 130–31
  four-center, 510–12, 537–38
  guides, 513
  isometric, 158–59
  isometric projection, 509–10
  major axis, 130, 300, 510, 521
  method of offsets, 509
  minor axis, 130, 300, 510, 521
  parallelogram, 132
  projections, 201–202
  sketching, 154–55
  tangent to, 133
  templates, 47, 133–134, 513
  trammel, 131, 155
  trimetric projection, 520–21
  use of irregular curve, 46
Elliptical curves, plotting, 202
Empirical equations, 651
  logarithmic coordinate solution, 653
  rectangular coordinate solution, 651
  semilog coordinate solution, 651–53
Engineer, the young, 2–3
Engineering drafting and drawing, definitions, 7
Engineering graph, 641
Engineering standards manual, 451
Engineers' scale, 30, 32
Engineers' triangle, 47
Engine lathe, 326–27
Enlargement of drawing, 122–23
Epicycloid, drawing, 140
Equator, 610
Equilateral triangle, drawing, 118–19
Erasers, 20
Erasing, 20–21, 44
  machine, 21
Errors, cumulative, 33, 37

Exploded assemblies, 516, 525
Extension line, 343–44, 372
Extension springs, 439–40
External thread, 412
    symbols, 415–16
    thread notes, 425
Extrusion blow-molding, 338
Extrusion molding, 336–37

Face, of solid, 598
FastCAD, 229, 234–38
Fastener, Appxs. 18–20
    computer graphics, 441–42
    keys, 438–39
    machine pins, 439
    miscellaneous, 437
    rivets, 439
    springs, 439–41
Feather key, 438
Figure of intersection, 611
Fillets, 205
    dimensioning, 352
    sand casting, 326
Finish
    bolts and nuts, 429
    types, 353
Finish marks, 352–53, 372
First-angle projection, 6, 208–209
Fits
    American National Standard, 385–86, Appxs.
        5–14
    between mating parts, 381–82
    clearance, 381, Appxs. 6, 11, 13–14
    force, 385, Appx. 9
    interference, 381, Appxs. 8, 12
    letter symbols, 385
    line, 382
    locational, 385, Appx. 6
    metric system, 386–89
    preferred, 389–90, Appxs. 11–14
    running and sliding, 385, Appx. 5
    shrink, Appx. 9
    thread, 423–24
    transition, 381, Appx. 7
Fixed disk drive, 71–72
Flatbed plotters, 68–69
Flat key, 438, Appx. 21
Flatness tolerance, 398
Flat springs, 439
Floppy disk, 226
Floppy disk drive, 72, 231
Flowchart, 661
Flue, development, 604–605
Foci construction, 133
Folding-line method, auxiliary views, 287, 297–
    98
Folding lines, 181, 183
    auxiliary views, 286
Force fits, 385, Appx. 9
Forging, 325, 334–35
    dimensions, 363
Form tolerances

related features, 399–403
single features, 397–99
symbols, 391–92
Fountain pen, technical, 42
Four-center ellipse, 510–12, 537–38
Fractions
    combination dimensioning system, 346
    dimensioning of holes, 359
    dimensions, 345–46
    guide lines, 98–99
Freehand drawing, see Sketching
French curves, 45
Front view, orientation, 165
Frontal plane, 181
    revolutions about axis perpendicular to, 310–
        11
Full section, 258–59
    isometric, 514
    oblique, 540
Function keys, 229, 235–38
Fundamental deviation, definition, 387

General assembly, 466–69
General notes, dimensioning, 367
Geometric breakdown, 354–55
Geometric characteristic symbols, 390–91
Geometric construction, 109
    computer graphics, 140–41
Geometric elements, 548–50
Geometric tolerance, 390–91, 403, Appx. 32
Geometry, descriptive, see Descriptive
    geometry
Giant bow compass, 33–37
Giant bow set, 33–34
Gib head key, 438, Appx. 21
Given-view method
    line perpendicular to plane, 587–88
    piercing point, 562–63
    plane perpendicular to line, 585–86
Glass box, 181–82, 547
Glossary, Appx. 2
    CAD/CAM, Appx. 3
Gore method, 611
Grade, 351, 553–56
    tolerance, Appx. 10
Graph, 639
    algebraic solution, 662–63
    computer graphics, 668–69
    mathematical, 641, 644
    title, 649
    See also Line Chart
Graphic language, 1, 3
    definitions, 7
    drafting standards, 6
    what students need to know, 8
Graphical calculus, 663
Graphical differentiation, 664
Graphical mathematics, 662
Graphical representation
    computer graphics, 668–69
    forms, 640
    uses of, 640–41

See also Diagram; Graph
Graphical skills, 448
Graph paper, 150, 160–61, 642–44
Great circle, 610
Greek alphabet, 90–91
Grinding machine, 330–31
Guide lines, 94
    inclined capital letters, 95
    lowercase letters, 99–100
    spacing, 95
    vertical capital letters, 94–95
    whole numbers and fractions, 98–99

Half auxiliary view, 295
Half section, 265
    CAD drawing, 75
    isometric, 514
    oblique, 540
Half view, 272
Hard copy, 67
Hard disk, 71–72, 233
Hardening, 335
Hardware, 56
Heat-treating, 335
Heavy hex screws, 429
Height auxiliary views, 290–91
Helical springs, 439, 441
Heli-coil inserts, 437
Helix, 138
Hems, sheet metal, 600
Hexagon, drawing, 119–20
Hexagon bolt
    chamfer, 618
    drawing, 431–32
    finish, 429
    types, 429
Hexagon cap screws, 429
Hexagon head screw, 434–35
Hexagon nut
    chamfer, 618
    drawing, 431
    finish, 429
Hexagon socket screws, 434
Hidden lines, 168–69
    assembly views, 467
    auxiliary views, 295
    isometric drawing, 505
    sections, 259
Hole-basis system of preferred fits, 388
    clearance fits, Appx. 11
    transition and interference fits, Appx. 12
Holes
    basic system, 382
    blind, 205
    cylindrical surface, 395
    dimensioning, 373
    drilling, 331–32
    locating, 360
    manufacturing processes, 331–33
    maximum material condition, 396
    minimum size, 382
    representation, 204–205

size dimensioning, 358–59
through, 205
Hood, development, 604–605
Horizontal line
    drawing, 22
    shortest connecting skew lines, 590–91
Horizontal plane, 181, 552–53
    revolutions about axis perpendicular to, 311
Hyperbola, drawing, 136–37
    equilateral, 137
Hypocycloid, drawing, 140

Icosahedron, 598
Idea sketches, 1
IGES, 82
Image processing, 60
Inch, 341
    dimensioning, 350
Inch-foot scales, 30
Inclined axis, revolution of point, 313–14
Inclined cylinder, 616
Inclined edges, 196
Inclined line, 23–24, 152, 550–51
Inclined prism, intersections, 613
Inclined surface, 194–96
Initial graphics exchange specification, 82
Injection blow molding, 338
Injection molding, 338–39
Ink, drawing, 42–43
Inking, order of, 44
Ink jet printer/plotters, 70
Input, CAD, 234–38
Input devices, CAD, 56–57, 61, 65–67, 83
Installation assembly, 471
Instrumaster Dimetric Template, 517, 519
Instrumental drawing, *see* Drafting instruments
Integral calculus, 663, 666
    applications, 667
    area law, 666
    mechanical methods, 666–67
    semigraphical integration, 666
Integrated circuit, 59–60
Interchangeability, parts, 342, 379
Interference fit, 381, 388, Appxs. 8, 12, 14
Internal thread, 412, 416
International tolerance grade, definition, 388
Intersecting-line principle, 583
Intersection, 202–204, 597
    of cylinder and cone, 618–19
    of cylinder and sphere, 618–19
    of cylinders, 202–203, 614–15
    figure of, 611
    inclined cylinder, 616
    isometric projection, 513
    of plane and cylinder, 601
    of plane and oblique cylinder, 602
    of plane and oblique prism, 602
    of plane and prism, 600
    of plane and pyramid, 602–603
    of plane and solid, 599
    of plane and sphere, 610
    of planes, 563–65

Intersection (*Continued*)
  of prism and cone, 616–18
  of prisms, 612–14
  sections, 272–73
  of solids, 611–12
Involute, 139
Irregular curve, 45–47
Irregular figures, transferring, 121
Irregular objects, isometric projection, 507–508
Isometric axis, 158, 502, 504
Isometric broken-out sections, 514
Isometric dimensions, 515–16, 540
Isometric drawing, 502
  box construction, 505–506
  center lines, 505
  computer graphics, 525
  hidden lines, 505
  nonisometric lines, 506
  steps in making, 503–504
Isometric ellipse, sketching, 158–59
Isometric exploded assembly drawing, CAD, 80
Isometric full and half section, 514
Isometric line, 502
Isometric paper, sketching on, 159–60
Isometric planes, 502
Isometric projection, 299, 501–502
  angles, 506–507
  approximate four-center ellipse, 510–12
  arcs, 512–13
  curves, 508–509
  dimensioning, 540
  ellipse guides, 513
  ellipses, 509–10
  exploded assemblies, 516
  intersections, 513
  irregular objects, 507–08
  oblique surfaces, 504
  piping diagrams, 516
  scale, 502
  screw threads, 512
  sketching, 541
  sphere, 513–14
Isometric sectioning, 514–15
Isometric sketching, 157–58
Isopleth, 655

Jam nuts, 433
Jig borer, 329–30
Joints, sheet metal, 600
Joystick, 67

Key, line graph, 648
Keyboard, 65–66
Keys, 438–39, Appxs. 1, 21, 23–25
Keyseat, 438–39
Keyway, 438–39
  dimensioning, 368–69
Knuckle thread, 413
Knurls, dimensioning, 369
Kroy Lettering Machines, 103–104

Laser jet printer/plotter, 70
Laser machine tools, 333–34
Lasers, hardening with, 335
Lathe, engine, 326–27
Lay, 403–404
  symbols, 406
Layout
  bar chart, 657–58
  line graph, 642
  pie chart, 659
  sheet, 39–40
  sketch, 451
Lead
  compass, 36, 38
  grades, 16
  shaping, 18
Leaders, 345, 372
Left-handed drawing, 22
Left-handed lettering, 93–94
Left-hand parts, 206–208
Left-hand thread, 414
Legend, line graph, 648
Legibility, 13
Leroy Standard Lettering Instrument, 102–103
Lettering, 87
  American National Standards, 91
  Ames Lettering Guide, 96–97, 99
  basic strokes, 93
  Braddock-Rowe lettering triangle, 96, 99
  CAD, 105
  devices, 102–104
  dimension figures, 348–50
  dimensioning, 344
  fractions, 98–99
  Greek alphabet, 90–91
  guide lines, 94–95, 98–100
  inclined capitals, 95, 98
  Kroy Lettering Machine, 103–104
  left-handed, 93–94
  Leroy Standard Lettering Instrument, 102–103
  on maps, 104–105
  optical illusions, 91
  pencils, 92
  pens, 92–93
  spacing of letters and words, 100–101
  standardization, 91
  to a stop line, 101
  styles, 88
  technique, 93–94
  title and record strip, 462
  titles, 104–105
  triangles, 96
  uniformity, 91–92
  Varigraph, 103
  vertical, 515, 541
  vertical capital, 97–98
  Wrico Lettering Guide, 103
Letters
  CAD, 105–106
  extended and condensed, 90

filled-in, 89
Gothic, 89–90, 105
heights, title and record strips, 462
inclined capital, 95, 98
inclined lowercase, 100–101
italic, 88
large and small capital, 95–96
lightface and boldface, 90
lowercase, 99–100
microfont alphabet, 91
Modern Roman, 89, 104–105
Old English, 88
Old Roman, 88–89
Roman, 88–89
serif, 88
single-stroke Gothic, 90–91
spacing between, 100–101
stability, 92
vertical capitals, 94–95
vertical lowercase, 100
Light pen, 67
Lighting, for drafting, 14
Limit dimensioning, 380, 383
Limits
    American National Standard, 385–86
    definition, 381
Line, 110, 547
    alphabet of, 18–20
    angle with oblique plane, 565–66
    base, 360
    bearing, 554
    bisecting, 112
    blocking in, 153
    CAD drawing, 239–40
    center, 169, 344
    connecting nonparallel, 128
    contrast of, 41
    dark accented, 40–41
    dimension, 343
    dividing into equal parts, 114–15
    dividing into proportional parts, 116
    drawing through two points, 24
    extension, 343–44
    finding midpoint, 153
    folding, 181, 183
    gage, 20
    grade, 554
    hidden, 168–69
    horizontal, 22, 152
    inclined, 23–24, 152, 50–51
    intersecting, 548–49, 583
    involute, 139
    in line graphs, 648
    meaning of, 171
    nonintersecting, 549
    nonisometric, 502, 506
    oblique, 551–54
    parallel to plane, 583–84
    phantom, 422
    plane parallel to, 584
    plane perpendicular to, 585–87

in planes, 557–58
point view, 556
precedence of, 171
projection of, 191
receding, 533–35
representation, 548
revolutions of, 315
sections, 259–60
sight, 180
sketching, 152
straight, 110, 152–53
tangent, 625–26
tangent to right circular cone, 633–34
tangent to sphere, 631
technique of, 40, 151–52
thick, 20
thin, 20
at 30°, at 60°, or at 45°, 26
through point and parallel to line, 114
through point and perpendicular to line, 116–17
through two points, 24–25
true length, 296, 315–16
types, 151, 240
used in dimensioning, 343–44
vertical, 22–23, 152
width of, 20
See also Guide lines; Parallel lines;
    Perpendicular line; Skew lines
Line chart or graph, 641–42
    abscissa, 644
    axis scale break, 645
    combined curves, 645
    curve designations, 648
    curve fitting, 641
    curves, 648
    design and layout, 642
    freak values, 645
    grids, 642
    key, 648
    legend, 648
    lines in, 648
    logarithmic coordinate, 650
    ordinate, 644
    points, 648
    polar coordinate, 654–55
    scale, 644–46
    scale captions, 643, 648
    scale designation, 646–48
    scale values, 643
    semilog, 649
    specially prepared grids, 643
    trilinear coordinate, 653–54
    weight of grid rulings, 644
Line fit, 382
Linear dimensions, CAD, 244
LIST command, 242–43
Local area network, 60
Local notes, dimensioning, 366–67
Location dimensions, 355, 359–61
Locational fits, 385

Locking devices, 433–34
Locknuts, 433–34
Lock washer, 433, Appx. 27
Locus, 558
Logarithmic coordinate line chart, 650
Logarithmic coordinates, empirical equation
    solution, 653
Lowercase letters
    guide lines, 99–100
    inclined, 100–101
    spacing, 99–100
    vertical, 100
Lower deviation, definition, 387
Lunar Roving Vehicle, 450

Machine dimensions, 362–63
Machine pins, 439
Machine screw, 428, 435–36, Appx. 20
Machining from stock, 324–25
Machining processes, tolerances and, 386–87
Machinist's scale, 333
Magnetic tape storage, 71–72
Mainframe computer, 62–63
Major axis, ellipse, 130, 300, 510, 521
Manufacturing tools and processes, 323
    automation, 335–37
    blow molding, 338
    boring mill, 329–30
    broaching, 331
    chipless machining, 333–34
    compression molding, 338
    drawing, 324–25
    drill press, 327
    engine lathe, 326–27
    extrusion molding, 336–37
    fillets and rounds, 326
    forging, 334–35
    grinding machine, 330–31
    heat-treating, 335
    holes, 331–33
    injection molding, 338–39
    measuring devices used in, 332–33
    milling machine, 327–28
    patternmaker, 325–26
    planer, 328–29
    plastics, 336–37
    production processes, 324
    sand casting, 324–25
    shaper, 328–29
    stock forms, 334
    surface roughness, 407
    thermoforming, 339
    transfer molding, 338
    vertical and horizontal turning center, 330
    welding, 334
Map
    bearing and grade, 555
    distribution chart, 661
    lettering on, 104–105
    polyconic method, 611
Mathematical graph, 641, 644
Mating dimensions, 361–362

Mating parts, fits between, 381–82
Mating threads, thread notes, 425
Maximum material condition, 395–97
Measurement
    accuracy, 32–33
    devices used in manufacturing, 332–33
    offset, 121, 503, 505, 538–39
Memory, 62
Meridian, 610
Metal cutting, 334
Metal forming, types, 324
Meter, 341
Metric dimensions, 345–46, 383
Metric scales, 27–30
Metric thread, 413, 423–24, Appx. 15
    detailed representation, 418–19
    fits, 424
    thread notes, 425
    tolerance, 424
Metric units, *see* SI System
Microcomputer, 63
    CAD, 230
Microgrip plotters, 68–69
Micrometer caliper, 333
Microminiaturization, 60
Millimeters, dimensioning, 350
Milling machine, 327–28
Minicomputer, 62
Minor axis, ellipse, 130, 300, 510, 521
Model
    aiding visualization, 190–91
    design process, 454–55
    soap, 190–91
Mold line, 369
Molding
    blow, 338
    compression, 338
    extrusion, 336–37
    injection, 338–39
    transfer, 338
Monge, Gaspard, 4, 6, 547
Mouse, 67, 229
Multiple thread, 414–15
Multiview projection, 9, 151, 161, 179, 500
    adjacent areas, 192
    alternate positions of views, 187
    compared to oblique projection, 532
    computer graphics, 172, 209
    conventional edges, 206–207
    conversion to axonometric projection, 524–25
    corner, 192
    curved surfaces, 198–99
    cylinders, 201
    cylindrical surfaces, 199–200
    deformities of cylinders, 199–201
    edges, 191–92
    ellipses, 201–202
    fillets, 205
    first-angle projection, 208–209
    folding lines, 183
    glass box, 181–82, 547
    inclined edges, 196

inclined surfaces, 194–96
intersections, 202–204
models, 190–91
normal edges, 194
normal surface, 193–94
oblique surfaces, 196
parallel edges, 197
partial views, 188
projecting third view, 185–86
projection method, 180–81
reading a drawing, 192–93
removed views, 189–90
representation of holes, 204–205
revolution conventions, 188–89
right-hand and left-hand parts, 206–208
rounds, 205
runouts, 205–206
similar shapes, 192–93
space curve, 202
surfaces, 191–92
tangencies, 202–204
three-view instrumental drawing, 186–87
transferring depth dimensions, 185
two-view instrumental drawing, 183–85
visualization, 190

National form, thread, 422
Neatness, 13
Networks, CAD, 57, 60
Neutral axis, 369
New product design, 456–59
    compromise solution, 457
    concepts and ideas, 457
    problem identification, 457
    production drawings, 459–61
    prototype, 458–59
Nominal size, definition, 380
Nomograph, 655–56
Nonintersecting members, visibility, 550
Nonisometric line, 502, 506
Nonisometric plane, 510
Normal axis, revolution of point, 313
Normal edges, 194
Normal surface, 193–94
Notes, dimensioning, 366–67
Number system, 185–86
Numerals
    guide lines, 98–99
    inclined, 98
    microfont alphabet, 91
    Modern Roman, 89
    Old Roman, 88
    vertical, 97–98
Numerical control equipment, 60, 477
Nut
    American National Standard, 429–31, Appx.
        18
    drawing, 431–32
    finish, 429
    machine screw, 435
    metric, Appx. 18
    specifications, 432–33

Object
    revolving, 163–64
    view of, 161–63
Oblique axis, revolution of point, 314
Oblique-circle ellipse, 132
Oblique cone, 605–607, 626–27
Oblique cylinder, 602
Oblique dimensioning, 540–41
Oblique drawing
    four-center ellipse, 537
    offset measurements, 538–39
    steps in, 536–37
Oblique edge, 196–97
Oblique line, 551–54
Oblique plane
    angle with line, 565–66
    edge view, 559
    true-size views, 560–61
Oblique prism, 602, 613
Oblique projection, 9, 151, 500, 531
    angles, 539–40
    cabinet projection, 535
    cavalier projection, 535
    compared to other projections, 532
    computer graphics, 541
    directions of projectors, 532–34
    limitations, 535
    position choice, 536
    receding line angles, 534
    receding line length, 534
    screw threads, 540
Oblique sections, 540
Oblique sketching, 160–61
Oblique surfaces, 196
    isometric projection, 504
    true size, 297–99
Octagon, drawing, 120–21
Octahedron, 598
Offset measurements, 503, 505
    oblique drawing, 538–39
    transferring figures by, 121
Offset sections, 269
Ogee curve, drawing, 128
One-view drawings, 167–68
Operating system programs, 56, 62, 73
    loading, 230–31
Optical disk drives, 72
Ordinate, 644
Organization chart, 661
Orientation blow molding, 338
Orth four-center ellipse, 511
Orthographic projection, see Multiview
    projection
Outline assembly, 471
Output devices, CAD, 57–59, 61–62, 67–70, 84,
    233, 475
Outside mold line, 369

Paper
    drawing, 48
    fastening to drawing board, 15–16
    graph, 150, 160–61, 642–44

Paper (*Continued*)
  layout, 39–40
  tracing, 48–49
Parabola, drawing, 135–36
Parabolic curves, 136
Parallel edges, 197
Parallel lines, 110, 197, 582
  drawing, 25–26, 114, 582
Parallel planes, 582–83
  to line, 584
Parallel projection, 9
Parallel-ruling straightedge, 48–49
Parallelism, 558, 581
  intersecting-line principle, 583
  tolerance, 400–401
Parallelogram ellipse, drawing, 132
Partial auxiliary views, 294–95
Partial section, removed section, 268–69
Partial view, 272, 348
Parting line, 325
Parts
  clearance fit, 381, Appxs. 6, 11, 13–14
  identification in assembly views, 469
  interchangeability, 342, 379
  interference fit, 381, Appxs. 8, 12
  line fit, 382
  list, 463–64
  mating, 381
  transition fit, 381, Appx. 7
Patent drawings, 456, 471–72
  reproduction and control, 472–73
Pattern dimensions, 362–63
Patternmaker, and the drawing, 325–26
Pen, 42
  drop spring bow, 39
  lettering, 92–93
Pen plotter, 67–69
Pen points, 92
Pencil
  drawing, 16
  drop spring bow, 39
  grade choices, 16–17
  lettering, 92
  mechanical, 16
  points, 18, 152
  shaping leads, 18
  sharpeners, 18
  sharpening, 17–18, 152
  sketching, 152
Pencil tracing, 41
Pentagon, drawing, 119
Percent grade, 555
Perpendicular line, 110, 584–85
  common between skew lines, 588–90
  drawing, 26
  drawing through point, 116
  to plane, 587–88
Perpendicular planes, 588
  common, 588–89
Perpendicularity, 581
  auxiliary-view method, 586–87
  given-view method, 585–88

tolerance, 401–402
Perspective, 500
Perspective projection, 151
Perspective sketching, 161
Phantom lines, use, 422
Pictorial drawing, 499, 513
  CAD, 80
  computer graphics, 209
Pictorial plane system, 515
Pictorial sketching, 157
  computer graphics, 172
Pie chart, 659
Piercing point, 561–63
Pipes, transition piece, 607–10
Pipe threads, 426–27
Piping diagrams, 516
Pitch, screw threads, 412–14
Pitch diameter, 412
Pixels, 65
Plan, 165
Plane, 547
  cutting-plane method, 564–65
  definition, 557, 598
  edge-view method, 563–64
  edge views, 558–59
  horizontal, 181, 311, 552–53
  intersection, 563–65
  intersection with cylinder, 601
  intersection with oblique cylinder, 602
  intersection with oblique prism, 602
  intersection with prism, 600
  intersection with pyramid, 602–603
  line parallel to, 583–84
  line perpendicular to, 587–88
  nonisometric, 510
  oblique, 59–61, 565–66
  parallel, 582–83
  parallel to line, 584
  perpendicular, 588–89
  perpendicular to line, 585–86
  points and lines in, 557–58
  representation, 556–57
  special cutting-plane method, 565
  true-size views, 560–61
Plane figure, transferring, 121
Plane method, common perpendicular, 589–90
Plane of projection, 179
  inclined line angle with, 550–51
  oblique line angle with, 551–54
  true length and angle with, 554
Plane surface, true size, 316
Plane tangent, 625–26
  to cone, 626–28
  to cylinders, 628–29, 631
  to oblique cone, 626–27
  to right-circular cone, 626–27, 632–34
  to sphere, 631–32
Planer, 328–29
Planimeter, 666–67
Plastics processing, 336, 338–39
Platonic solids, 598
Plotters, 67–69, 475

Plotting curves, auxiliary views, 292–93
Plus and minus dimensioning, 383
Point, 110, 547
    CAD, 240–41
    joining with parabolic curve, 136
    line graph, 648
    line through two, 24–25
    piercing, 561–63
    in planes, 557–58
    representation, 548
    revolutions about axis, 313–14
    symbols, 648
Point view, 264, 556
Point-view method, common perpendicular, 589
Polar coordinate line chart, 654–55
Polar planimeter, 666–667
Polyconic method, 611
Polycylindric method, 611
Polyester films, 49
Polygon, 111
    CAD, 241–42
    transferring, 121
Polyhedra, 112, 598
Position method, dimension figures, 349
Positional tolerances, 391–92
Pratt & Whitney key, 438, Appx. 25
Preferred fits, 389–90, Appxs. 11–14
Preferred sizes, 389
Prick-point method, 121–22
Printed circuits, 59–60
    CAD drawing, 78
Prism, 112
    development, 601, 612–14, 617
    intersections, 612–14
    intersection with cone, 616–18
    intersection with plane, 600
    oblique, 602, 613
    size dimensions, 355
Production drawings, 459–61
Production processes, 324
Profile plane, 181, 311–12
Profile tolerance, 399–400
Projection, 8–10, 179
    classification, 9
    dimetric, 501, 517–19
    first-angle, 208–209
    history of, 4
    of projector, 182
    of surfaces, 191–92
    third-angle, 208–209
    types, 151, 500–501
    See also Axonometric projection; Isometric
        projection; Trimetric projection
Projectors, 180
    classification by, 10
    directions of, 532–34
Proportional dividers, 38
Proportions, sketching, 155–57
Prototype, 454–55, 458
Protractors, 24
Puck, 66
Pyramid, 112

intersection with plane, 602–603
truncated, 603
truncated oblique rectangular, 605

Quadrant, rectifying, 129
Quadrilaterals, 111

Radial drill press, 327
Railroad car, design, 454
RAM, 62, 70–71
Random scan system, 65
Raster scan devices, 64–65
Rate-of-change chart, 649
Ratio chart, 649
Raw stock, 324–25
Reaming, 332
Receding lines, 533–35
Record strip, working drawing, 460, 462
Rectangular coordinates
    algebraic solution graph, 662–63
    distribution chart, 660
    empirical equation solution, 651
    See also Line chart
Rectangular pipes, transition piece connecting,
        607–609
    to circular pipe, 609
Rectangular pyramid, dimensioning, 357–58
Reduction of drawings, 122–23
Reference dimension, 360, 386
Reference plane, 287–88
Reference-plane method, auxiliary views, 288–
        89, 298–99
Regardless of feature size, 397
Reinhardt, C. W., 90
Removed sections, 267–69
Removed view, 189–90
Repainting, 64
Repeatability, pen plotters, 69
Reproduction, of drawings, 472–73
Reverse construction, 293–94
Revisions, drawing, 464–65
Revolution, 309
    about axis perpendicular to frontal plane, 310–
        11
    about axis perpendicular to horizontal plane,
        311
    about axis perpendicular to profile plane, 311–
        12
    axis of, 310
    axis of projection, 554
    of circles, 316–17
    computer graphics, 318
    conventions, 188–89
    counterrevolution, 317
    of drawing, 291–92
    of line, 315
    of object, 163–64
    plane of projection, 554
    of point, 313–14
    successive, 312–13
Revolution method
    oblique plane, 561

Revolution method (*Continued*)
    true length of line, 315–16
    true size of plane surface, 316–17
Revolved sections, 266–67
Ribs, in section, 269–70
Right-circular cone, 626–27, 632–34
Right-hand parts, 206–208
Right-hand thread, 414
Right triangle, drawing, 117
Rivets, 439, Appx. 1
Robots, automated manufacturing processes,
    335–36
ROM, 62
Roughness, 405, 407
Rounded-end shapes, dimensioning, 363–64
Roundness tolerance, 398–99
Rounds, 205
    dimensioning, 352
    sand casting, 326
Ruled surface, single-curved surface, 598
Rule of thumb, 341
Ruling pen, 42–43
Running fits, 385, Appx. 5
Runouts, 205–206

Sand casting, 324–26
S-breaks, 274–75
Scale, 26–27
    architects', 30–32
    chain, 30
    civil engineers', 30
    combination, 32
    decimal, 32, 348
    designation, 646–48, 658
    of drawing, 26, 342
    engineers', 30
    inch-foot, 30
    isometric, 502
    line graph, 643–48
    machinist's, 333
    mechanical engineers', 32
    metric, 27–30
    sketching, 151
    specifying on drawing, 32
    trimetric, 520
    types, 26
Scale guard, 27
Scatter diagram, 660
Screw
    axis, 412
    computer graphics, 441–42
    machine, 428, 435–36
    wood, 437
    See also Cap screw; Set screw
Screwdriver slots, 435
Screw thread, 411, Appx. 15
    Acme, 413, 421–22, Appxs. 17, 22
    angle of, 412
    buttress, 413
    coarse thread series, 423
    crest, 412
    definition, 412

    depth, 412
    detailed representation, 415, 418–22
    drawing symbols, 416–18
    external, 412, 415–16, 425
    extra fine series, 424
    fine thread series, 423–24
    forms, 412–13
    internal, 412, 416
    isometric projection, 512
    knuckle, 413
    lead, 412
    length, 430
    major diameter, 412
    metric, *see* Metric thread
    minor diameter, 412
    multiple, 414–15
    notes, 424–26
    oblique projection, 540
    phantom lines, 422
    pitch, 412–14
    right-hand and left-hand, 414
    root, 412
    schematic symbols, 418
    in section, 422
    Sellers thread, 412–13
    series of, 412
    side, 412
    simplified symbols, 418
    single, 414
    square, 413, 419–21, Appx. 22
    standardized, 412
    standard worm, 413
    symbols, 415
    tapped hole, 428–29
    unified extra fine, 423
    Whitworth thread, 412–13
Secondary auxiliary views, 286, 296–97
    oblique direction of sight given, 299–300
Section, 257
    aligned, 189, 270–72
    assembly, 469–71
    assembly views, 467–68
    auxiliary, 295–96
    broken-out, 265–66
    CAD, 78
    conventional breaks, 273–75
    cutting plane, 261–63
    full, 258–59
    half, 265
    half views, 272
    hidden lines, 259
    intersections, 272–73
    lines, 259–60
    oblique, 540
    offset, 269
    partial views, 272
    point view, 264
    removed, 267–69
    revolved, 266–67
    ribs in, 269–70
    S-breaks, 274–75
    threads in, 422

visualization, 263–65
Section lining
    assembly views, 469–70
    double-spaced, 270
    isometric drawing, 514–15
    symbols, 260
    technique, 260–61
Sectioning, 258
    CAD, 274–75
    isometric, 514–15
Sector chart, 659
Selective assembly, tolerance, 382
Sellers thread, 412–13
Semiellipse, sketching, 159
Semigraphical integration, integral calculus, 666
Semilog chart, 649
Semilog coordinates, empirical equation
        solution, 651–653
Set screw, 428, 433
    American National Standard, 436–37
Shaft
    basic system, 382
    keyseat, 438
    maximum size, 382
    S-breaks, 274–75
Shaft-basis system of preferred fits, 388
    clearance fits, Appx. 13
Shaft centers, dimensioning, 368
Shaper, 328–29
Shapes
    description, 149
    similar, 192–93
Sharp-V thread, 412–13
Sheet
    layout, 39–40
    standard sizes, 50
Sheet metal, 325
    bends, dimensioning, 369–70
    hems and joints, 600
Shortest line, connective skew lines, 590–91
Shrink fits, 385, Appx. 9
Side view
    incomplete, 188
    position of, 187
Simplified drafting, American National
        Standards, 465
Sine method, 118
Single thread, 414
SI system, 27, 341–42
    equivalents, Appx. 31
    basic units, 342
    tolerances and fits, 386–89
Six views, 164–65
Size
    description, 342
    preferred, 389
Size dimensions, 355
    cylinders, 355–56
    holes, 358–59
    miscellaneous shapes, 357–58
    prisms, 355
Skeleton construction, oblique projection, 536

Sketching, 149
    advantages, 150
    arcs, 154
    blocking-in method, 157
    choice of views, 165–66
    circle, 153–54
    dimetric, 518–19
    ellipses, 154–55
    on graph paper, 150, 160
    isometric, 157–58
    isometric ellipses, 158–59
    on isometric paper, 159–60
    materials, 150–51
    method of squares, 156
    oblique, 160–61, 541
    one-point perspective, 161
    one-view, 167–68
    pencils, 152
    pictorial, 157
    proportions, 155–57
    revolving object, 163–64
    scale, 151
    semiellipse, 159
    six views, 164–65
    straight lines, 152
    technical, 150
    three views, 169–70
    two-point perspective, 161
    two views, 166–67, 169
    types, 151
    view of object, 161–63
"Sketch-pad," 50, 60, 65
Skew lines, 549
    common perpendicular, 588–90
    shortest horizontal line connecting, 590–91
    shortest line at specified slope connecting, 591
Sliding fits, 385, Appxs. 5, 11, 13
Slope, 351, 553, 591, 645–46
Slope law, 664
Slotted head screws, 434–35
Soap models, 190–91
Software
    CAD, 56, 226–29
    loading, 230–31, 233–34
    startup, 234–35
Solid, 112, 598
    intersection principles, 611–12
Space curve, 202
Spacing
    between views, 163
    of letters and words, 100–101
Special cutting-plane method, intersection of
        planes, 565
Sphere, 112
    development, 610–11
    intersection with cylinder, 618–19
    isometric projection, 513–14
    line tangent to, 630–31
    plane tangent to, 631–32
Spiral of Archimedes, drawing, 137–38
Splines, 438
    CAD, 242–43

Spotfacing, 333
Springs, 439–41
  computer graphics, 441–42
Square
  drawing, 118–19
  involute of, 139
Square key, 438, Appx. 21
Square pipe, transition piece connecting with
    cylindrical pipe, 610
Square thread, 413, Appx. 21
  detailed representation, 419–21
Square-wire spring, 440
Staircase chart, 658
Standards
  screw threads, 412
  See also American National Standard
Standard worm thread, 413
Starting dimension, 359
Stock forms, 334
Storage tube CAD monitor, 64–65
Straight pipe threads, 426
Straightedge, parallel-ruling, 48–49
Straightness tolerance, 398
Strata chart, 658
Stretch blow molding, 338
Stretchout, 369
Stretchout line, 601
Stroke writing system, 65
Stud, 427–28
Stylus, 66–67
Subassembly, 466
Successive auxiliary views, 296–97, 300
Superfluous dimensions, 364–65, 367
Supplementary symbols, 392
Surface, 191–92, 598
  curved, 198–99
  cylindrical, 199–200
  developable, 598
  development, 597, 599–600
  double-curved, 598
  generatrix, 598
  inclined, 194–96
  normal, 193–94
  oblique, 196
  projection of, 191–92
  rough and finished, 205
  ruled, 598
  similar shapes, 192–93
  single-curved, 598
  warped, 598
  See also Plane
Surface chart, 658
Surface finish, 403, 405, Appx. 1
  computer graphics, 408
Surface grinders, 330–31
Surface hardening, 335
Surface roughness, 403–407
Surface texture, symbols, 404–406
Sutherland, Ivan, 50, 60, 65
Symbols
  basic dimension, 392
  combined, 392

datum identifying, 392
diameter, 357
drawing thread symbols, 416–18
external thread, 415–16
geometric characteristic, 390–91
geometric dimensioning, 409
geometric tolerancing, Appx. 32
internal thread, 416
lay, 406
library, 73, 81
millimeters and inches, 350
miscellaneous shapes, 357–58
modifying, 391
points, 648
screw threads, 415
section-lining, 260
supplementary, 392
surface texture, 404–406
tolerance, 388–89, 409
tolerances of position and form, 391–92
types of fits, 385
Symmetrical figures, use of irregular curve, 46
Symmetrical half, transferring, 122
System of squares, transferring figures, 121
System software, 56, 62, 73
  loading, 230–31

Tabular dimensions, 370
Tangent, 202–204, 625
  to circle, 123–24
  to ellipse, 133
  to two circles, 124
  See also Arc; Line tangent; Plane tangent
Tangent method, 118
Tap drill, 428, Appx. 15
Taper pin, Appx. 29
Taper pipe thread, 426–27
Tapers, dimensioning, 367–68
Tapped holes, 428–29, 435
Tapping, 333
Technical drawing, 4
  definition, 7
  earliest, 4
  modern, 6
  what students need to know, 8
Technical fountain pen, 42, 92–93
Technical sketching, 7, 150
Tempering, 335
Template, 47
  ellipse, 133–34, 513
Tetrahedron, 598
Text, CAD, 243–44
Thermoforming, 339
Thermoplastic, 336
Thermosetting, 336
Third-angle projection, 6, 208–209
Threads
  bolts, 430
  dimensioning, 367
  See also Screw threads
Three regular views, 163
Three views, sketching, 169–70

Through hole, 205
Time-series charts, 641
Title
    graph, 649
    lettering, 104
Title box, 104
Title strip, working drawing, 460, 462
Tolerance, 379
    accumulation of, 386
    angles, 397
    angular, 384, 400
    ANSI limits and fits, 385–86
    basic dimension symbol, 392
    basic hole system, 382
    basic shaft system, 382
    bilateral, 383–84, 397
    combined symbols, 392
    computer graphics, 408–409
    concentricity, 403
    cylindricity, 398–99
    datum identifying symbol, 392
    definitions, 381, 387
    dimensioning, 380–81
    fits between mating parts, 381–82
    flatness, 398
    general, 383
    geometric, 390–91, 403, Appx. 32
    international grades, Appx. 10
    limit dimensioning, 383
    machining processes, 386–87
    maximum material condition, 395–397
    metric system, 386–89
    metric thread, 424
    parallelism, 400–401
    perpendicularity, 401–402
    plus and minus dimensioning, 383
    positional, 392–95
    preferred fits, 389–90
    preferred sizes, 389
    profile, 399
    regardless of feature size, 397
    roundness, 398–99
    selective assembly, 382
    single-limit dimensioning, 384
    specification of, 383–84
    straightness, 398
    supplementary symbols, 392
    surface roughness, waviness, and lay, 403–
        407
    symbols, 388–89, Appx. 32
    symbols for position and form, 391–92
    thread notes, 425
    unified thread, 424
    unilateral, 384
Tolerance zone, 388, 393
Topographic map, 659–60
Torsion springs, 440–41
Torus, 112
Totalizer Wheel, 453
Touch-panel displays, 67
Tracing, pencil, 41–42
Tracing cloth, 49

Tracing-paper methods, transferring figures, 121–
    22
Tracing papers, 48–49
Trackball, 67
Trammel ellipse, drawing, 131
Trammel method, 131, 155
Transfer molding, 338
Transition fit, 381–82, 388, Appxs. 7, 12, 14
Transition piece, 607
    connecting circular and rectangular pipes, 609
    connecting cylindrical pipes on different axes,
        609–10
    connecting rectangular pipes, 607–609
    connecting square and cylindrical pipes, 610
Triangle, 23–24, 110–11
    bisecting line with, 112–13
    drawing, 117
    involute of, 139
    lettering, 96
    transferring, 121
Triangle method, transfer polygon, 121
Triangle wheel, 24
Triangular prism, dimensioning, 357–58
Triangulation, 605–607
Trilinear coordinate line chart, 653–54
Trim line, 39–40
Trimetric projection, 501, 520
    advantages, 520–21
    ellipses, 520–21
    scales, 520
True-position dimensioning, 394
True-size view, oblique plane, 560–61
Truncated oblique rectangular pyramid,
        development, 605
Truncated pyramid, development, 603
T-square, 15
    bisecting line with, 112–13
Tubes, S-breaks, 274–75
Turnkey systems, 82
Twist drill, 332, Appx. 16
Two-view drawings, 166
Two-view instrumental drawing, 183–85
Two views, sketching, 169

Unidirectional system, 515
Unified thread, 413, 423–24, Appx. 15
    detailed representation, 418–19
    extra fine, 423
    fits, 424
    thread notes, 425–26
    tolerance, 424
Upper deviation, definition, 387
User friendly, 81

Varigraph, 103
Vector refresh monitors, 64–65
Vellums, 49
Vernier caliper, 333
Vert-A-Pack, 454
Vertical line, drawing, 22–23
Views, 161–63
    alignment, 170–71

Views (*Continued*)
  alternate positions, 187
  assembly, 466
  choice of, 165–66
  dimensions on and off, 353
  edge, 558
  front, 165
  minimum required, 167
  necessary, 165
  one, 167–68
  partial, 188
  position of, 171
  projecting a third, 185–86
  removed, 189–90
  reverse construction, 293–94
  the six, 164–65
  three, 169–70
  three regular, 163
  two, 166–67, 169
  visualizing, 190
Visualization, 190
  adjacent areas, 192
  angles, 198
  CAD, 226–28
  corners, 192
  curved surfaces, 198–99
  cylindrical surfaces, 199–200
  edges, 191–92
  inclined edges, 196
  inclined surfaces, 194–96
  models, 190–91
  normal edges, 194
  normal surfaces, 193–94
  oblique edges, 196
  oblique surfaces, 196–97
  parallel edges, 197
  reading a drawing, 192–93
  sections, 263–65
  similar shapes, 192–93
  surfaces, 191–92
  from views, 190

Voice recognition, 67
Volume chart, 659–60

Warped surface, 598
Washers, 433, Appxs. 1, 26–27
Washington, George, 4–5
Waviness, 403, 405–406
Welding, 325, 334
Whitworth thread, 412–13
Width, auxiliary views, 291
Wire gage standards, Appx. 28
Wireframe, CAD drawing, 80
Woodruff key, 438, Appxs. 23–24
Wood screws, American National Standard, 437
Words, spacing, 100–101
Work flow diagram, 477
Working drawing, 447, 455–56, 459
  assembly, 456, 465–66, 471
  checking, 464
  computer graphics, 473–77
  drawing numbers, 462–63
  general assembly, 466–69
  number of details per sheet, 459
  parts list, 463
  patent drawings, 471–72
  revisions, 464–65
  simplified drafting, 465
  title and record strips, 460, 462
  zoning, 464
  See also Detail drawings
Workstations, CAD, 50
Worm thread, 413
Wrico Lettering Guide, 103
Write once read many drive, 73
Workstation, CAD, 57, 59
WORM, 73

Yard, 341

Zoning, working drawing, 464

Worksheets

Instructions   W • 3

Topics   *Drawings*

Instrumental Drawing   2-1 and 2-2
Lettering   4-1 to 4-6
Geometric Constructions   5-1 to 5-3
Technical Sketching   6-1 and 6-2
Multiview Projection   7-1 to 7-5
Computer-Aided Drafting   8-1 to 8-5
Sectional Views   9-1 to 9-5
Auxiliary Views   10-1 to 10-4
Revolutions   11-1
Dimensioning   13-1 to 13-4
Threads and Fasteners   15-1 to 15-4
Isometric Drawing   17-1 to 17-3
Oblique Projection   18-1 and 18-2
Points, Lines, and Planes   19-1 to 19-13
Parallelism and Perpendicularity   20-1 to 20-6
Intersections and Developments   21-1 to 21-6
Tangencies   22-1 and 22-2
Graphs   23-1 and 23-2
Detail Drawings   24-1

Instructions

Worksheet drawing numbers are keyed to the corresponding chapters in this book. Alternative dimensions, often not the *exact* equivalents, are given in millimeters and inches. Although it is understood that 25.4 mm = 1.00″, it is more practical to use approximate equivalents such as 25 mm for 1.00″, 12.5 or 12 mm for .50″, 6 mm for .25″, 3 mm for .12″, and so on. Exact equivalents should be used when accurate fit or critical strength is involved.

In general, the following leads are suitable for instrumental drawing: a 4H for construction lines and guide lines for lettering; a 2H for center lines, section lines, dimension lines, and extension lines; and an HB or F for general linework and lettering. Instructions for specific drawings may suggest the use of other grades of lead as required. All construction lines on problems should be made *lightly* and *should not be erased.*

Drawing 2-1 Instrumental Drawing: Alphabet of Lines.
References: §§2.1–2.17, 2.20–2.31.
Spaces 1 and 2. Draw indicated lines full length in the given spaces.
Space 3. Section lines at 30° with horizontal upward to the right and 12.5 mm (.50″) apart are required. First find center of space by drawing diagonals in *very light* construction lines. Through center draw construction line 60° with horizontal upward to the left and, beginning at the center, set off 12.5 mm (.50″) intervals. Draw required section lines through these points to fill space.
Space 4. Using similar construction methods to those outlined for *Space 3*, draw visible lines at 75° with horizontal upward to the left at 12.5 mm (.50″) intervals.
Space 5. Draw center lines parallel to given line and at 12.5 mm (.50″) intervals to fill the space.
Space 6. Draw alternate visible and hidden lines 12.5 mm (.50″) apart and perpendicular to the given line. Arrange so that one visible line passes through center of space.

Drawing 2-2 Instrumental Drawing: Scales and Layout.
References: §§2.18, 2.24–2.43, 2.46, 2.47, 16.27.
Space 1. Use architects', engineers', or metric scales as necessary. Measure lines A, C, and F at the scales shown, and indicate the scaled lengths (L) at the right, At B, D, E, G, and H draw lines of specified lengths at scales shown. Terminate the lines in the same manner as for given lines. At J through L, determine the scales and lengths of lines and record the scales and lengths in the spaces provided.
Line J is over 500′ and under 600′ in length.
Line K is between 530 m and 550 m in length.
Line L is one twenty-fourth size.
Space 2. Draw the two views of the Anchor Bracket full size, locating the views by the starting corners indicated. Your final lines should approximate those shown in Fig. 2.15, with distinct differences in line thicknesses.

Drawing 4-1 Vertical Lettering: Capitals and Numerals.
References: §§4.1, 4.3, 4.5–4.18. Using an HB lead, letter the indicated characters in the spaces provided. These large letters and numerals may be sketched lightly first, and then corrected where necessary before being made heavy with the strokes shown. Omit the numbers and arrows from your letters. All lettering must be *clean-cut* and **black.** In the title strip, under DRAWN BY, draw light guide lines from the starting marks shown, plus random vertical guide lines, and letter your name with the last name first. Under FILE NO. letter your identification symbol as assigned by your instructor.

Drawing 4-2 Inclined Lettering: Capitals and Numerals.
References: §§4.1, 4.3, 4.5–4.17, 4.19. Using an HB lead, letter the indicated characters in the spaces provided. These large letters and numerals may be sketched lightly first, and then corrected as necessary before being made heavy with the strokes shown. Omit the numbers and arrows from your letters. All lettering must be *clean-cut* and **black.** In the title strip, under DRAWN BY, draw light guide lines from the starting marks shown, and letter your name with the last name first. Under FILE NO. letter your identification symbol as assigned by your instructor.

Drawing 4-3 Vertical Lettering: Capitals and Numerals.
References: §§4.1, 4.3, 4.5–4.18, 4.24. First draw light vertical guide lines at random from bottom to top of the sheet. Do not draw separate vertical guide lines for each line of lettering. Reproduce the lettering as exactly as you can, using an HB lead for the larger letters and a sharp F lead for the smaller letters. Note that the last line of lettering is to be lettered twice. All letters must be *clean-cut* and **black.**

Drawing 4-4 Inclined Lettering: Capitals and Numerals. References: §§4.1, 4.3, 4.5–4.17, 4.19, 4.20, 4.24. First, draw light inclined guide lines at random from bottom to top of the sheet. Do not draw separate inclined guide lines for each line of lettering. Reproduce the lettering as exactly as you can, using an HB lead for the larger letters, and a sharp F lead for the smaller letters. Note that the last line of lettering is to be lettered twice. All lettering must be *clean-cut* and **black**.

Drawing 4-5 Vertical Letter: Shop Notes and Dimensions. References: §§4.10, 4.5–4.18, 4.20, 4.24, 13.5, 13.7–13.11, 13.13–13.15, 13.17. On the left side of the sheet are shown a number of lettering applications. On the right, reproduce the lettering, arrowheads, and finish marks, using a sharp F lead. Except for the title **TOOL HOLDER** at the bottom, all lettering on the sheet is 3 mm or .12″ high. Draw all guide lines with the aid of a lettering triangle or the Ames Lettering guide, using a 4H or 6H lead. Letter, in vertical capitals, the title **TOOL HOLDER**, etc., on center as shown in Fig. 4.36 (b). Use height and spacing as specified. Underline **TOOL HOLDER**. All lettering must be *clean-cut* and **black**.

Drawing 4-6 Inclined Lettering: Shop Notes and Dimensions. References: §§4.1, 4.3, 4.5–4.17, 4.19, 4.20, 4.24, 13.5, 13.7–13.11, 13.13–13.15, 13.17. On the left side of the sheet are shown a number of lettering applications. On the right, reproduce the lettering, arrowheads, and finish marks, using a sharp F lead. Except for the title **TOOL HOLDER** at the bottom, all lettering on the sheet is 3 mm or .12″ high. Draw all guide lines with the aid of a lettering triangle or the Ames Lettering Guide, using a 4H or 6H lead. Letter the title **TOOL HOLDER**, etc., on center as shown in Fig. 4.36 (b). All lettering must be *clean-cut* and **black**.

Drawing 5-1 Geometric Construction: Drafting Geometry. References: §§5.1–5.6. Show light construction on all problems. Add center lines where necessary.
Space 1. References: §§5.8, 5.9. Locate and draw hole as indicated. Add center lines.
Space 2. Reference: Fig. 5.28 (a). Complete the view of the Special Washer.
Space 3. References: §§5.14, 5.15. Complete the view of the Rack. Start the first tooth at A as indicated.
Space 4. Reference: §5.18. Locate centers for holes as specified. Draw holes and add center lines.
Space 5. Reference: §5.19. Complete the view of the End Guide by adding the 90° tip as indicated in the given specifications.
Space 6. References: §5.36, Fig. 13.42 (b). Complete the view of the Bracket.

Drawing 5-2 Geometric Construction: Tangencies. Draw all construction lines *lightly* with a sharp 4H lead, and do not erase. Draw all required lines with a sharp F lead, **dark** and *clean* to match the given lines. *Show all points of tangency* by means of light construction lines as shown in Prob. 2.
Space 1. Reference: Fig. 5.35 (a).
Space 2. References: Figs. 5.34 (b), 5.36 (c).
Space 3. References: Figs. 5.35 (b), 5.37.
Space 4. Reference: Fig. 5.41.
Space 5. References: §§5.39 to 5.41.

Drawing 5-3 Geometric Constructions: Polygons, Ellipses, and Parabolas. Show light construction on all problems.
Space 1. Reference: Fig. 5.26 (c) and (d). Complete the end view of the 12-point (double hexagon) socket as indicated.
Space 2. Reference: Fig. 5.28 (a). Draw the view of the octagonal face only of the engineers' cross-peen hammer head, which is cut from 28 mm square stock.
Space 3. Reference: Fig. 5.32 (a). Determine diameter of milling cutter to cut true arc through points A, B, and C. Give diameter to nearest 0.5 mm.
Space 4. References: §§2.54, 5.52. Using the concentric-circle method, draw profile of 56 mm × 82 mm elliptical cam, starting at point A. Use a minimum of 16 points to establish the ellipse. Draw ellipse with the aid of the irregular curve.
Space 5. Reference: §5.58. Draw approximate ellipse as indicated.
Space 6. Reference: Fig. 5.57 (c) and (d). Draw parabola as indicated, and find focus.

Drawing 6-1 Technical Sketching: Multiview. References: §§6.1–6.10, 6.18–6.31. Sketch the views as indicated. Make all final lines *clean-cut* and **black**. In the space provided, letter the names of the necessary views.

Drawing 6-2 Technical Sketching: Multiview and Isometric. References: §§1.1–1.10, 6.1–6.31. Using an HB lead, sketch the views or isometrics as indicated. Make lines *clean-cut* and **black**. Omit hidden lines from the isometrics. Take great care to sketch isometric ellipses correctly, §6.13.

Drawing 7-1 Multiview Projection: Missing Lines. References: §§6.5, 6.18–6.20, 6.25, 6.26, 6.28–6.31. Each problem is incomplete because lines are missing from one or more views. Add all missing lines freehand, including center lines.

Drawing 7-2 Multiview Projection: Missing Views. References: §§6.25, 6.26, 7.1–7.14. In each problem two complete views are given, and a third view is missing. Add the third view in each case freehand.

Drawing 7-3 Multiview Projection: Missing Views and Lines. References: §§6.25, 6.26, 6.30, 6.31, 7.1–7.7, 7.12–7.33. For Probs. 1–3 study §5.34 and Fig. 7.37, and show constructions for the points of tangency. Draw all necessary center lines.

Drawing 7-4 Multiview Projection: Missing Views. References: §§7.1–7.30, 7.33. In each problem two complete views are given. Add the third view in each case, using instruments. For Prob. 1, study Fig. 7.35.

Drawing 7-5 Multiview Projection: Missing Views. References: §§7.27–7.31, 7.33.
Space 1. Draw freehand the top view as indicated.
Space 2. Draw with instruments the front view as indicated. Plot a sufficient number of points to define the curve accurately. Sketch the curve lightly through the points with a 4H lead; then draw the curve with the F lead and with the aid of the irregular curve. §2.54.

Drawing 8-1 Computer-Aided Drafting: Terms and Descriptions. References: Chapters 3 and 8, Appendix 3. Some terms related to computer graphics are given in the table. A list of descriptions for these terms is given on the right. Find the matching description for each term and enter its letter identifier in the table.

Drawing 8-2 Computer-Aided Drafting: Two-Dimensional Coordinate Plot. Reference: Chapter 8.
Space 1. Digitize the single view drawing by defining the X and Y coordinates of the indicated points and fill in the given table. Point A is the origin with values of X and Y equal to zero. Consider each division of the grid as 1 unit. Keep in mind that any X values to the left of the origin and any Y values below the origin are negative.
Space 2. From the X and Y coordinate data given in the table, plot all points on the grid and complete the drawing. Point A is the origin. Consider each division of the grid as 1 unit.

Drawing 8-3 Computer-Aided Drafting: Three-Dimensional Coordinate Plot. Reference: Chapter 8. In drawing an image, the actions of the pen are Move and Draw.

Move: The pen moves from its present position to new X, Y, and Z coordinates specified. A line is not drawn. Numeral 0 is used to indicate Move action.

Draw: A line is drawn from the present pen position to new X, Y, and Z coordinates specified. Numeral 1 is used to indicate Draw action.

Space 1. Determine X, Y, and Z coordinates for all the points of the object. Complete the table for drawing the object, starting with point A. Coordinates X, Y, and Z are positioned as indicated by the arrows, with point A as origin. Try to use a minimum number of Move actions.
Space 2. According to the data shown in the table, draw the object on the grids provided. Coordinates X, Y, and Z are positioned as indicated by the arrows, with point A as origin.

Drawing 8-4 Computer-Aided Drafting: Menu Usage. Reference: Chapter 8. The drawing shows the front view of a Bracket that is to be generated on a graphics terminal. The numbers 1 to 21 refer to graphic entities that make up the drawing. Available menu commands for generating entities are given on the right. Complete the table by determining the menu commands to generate the entities. Enter the letter identifiers (A, B, etc.) of menu selections in the table.

Drawing 8-5 Computer-Aided Drafting: Coordinate Systems. Reference: Chapter 8. Using the given descriptions for VIEW COORDINATES and WORLD COORDINATES, complete the tables for the front and right-side views of the object. Point number 1 is considered as the origin. Each grid division is equal to 1 unit.

Drawing 9-1 Sectional Views: Full and Half. References: §§9.1–9.7, 9.15. Sketch the sections as indicated, using an HB or F lead for visible lines a sharp F lead for section lines and center lines. Make section lines thin to contrast well with heavy visible lines. All lines should be *clean-cut* and **black**. No additional cutting planes are required.

Drawing 9-2 Sectional Views: Full and Revolved. References: §§7.34, 7.35, 9.1–9.4, 9.9, 9.12, 9.15, 12.5, 13.17. Draw the indicated sectional views, using instruments. Use an F lead for visible lines and a *very sharp* 2H lead for section lines. Add center lines. Omit finish marks unless assigned. In Space 1, include a revolved partial section in the front view to show the shape of the triangular rib. See Fig. 9.16 (m). In Space 2, fillets are 3 mm (.12″) R.

Drawing 9-3 Sectional Views: Full and Removed. References: §§7.33, 7.34, 9.1, 9.5, 9.10, 9.12, 12.5, 13.17. Draw sections as indicated, including visible lines behind the cutting planes. Add center lines. If assigned, add finish marks.

Drawing 9-4 Sectional Views: Full and Assembly. References: §§9.1–9.6, 16.22. Draw the indicated sectional views, using instruments. In Prob. 2 is shown a portion of an assembly full section with a round shaft extending through a cast-iron cover and a steel plate, which are held together by bolts. Section-line the sectioned areas, using symbolic section lining for each material.

Drawing 9-5 Sectional View: Aligned. References: §§7.33, 7.34, 9.13, 9.15, 12.4. Draw Section A—A as indicated.

Drawing 10-1 Auxiliary Views: Primary. References: §§10.1–10.10. Sketch the auxiliary views as indicated. Using an HB or F lead, make visible lines and hidden lines **black** so that the views will stand out clearly from the grids. Use a sharp F lead for center lines. Letter folding lines as shown in Fig. 10.3, and reference planes as in Fig. 10.6. In Probs. 3 and 4, include all hidden lines.

Drawing 10-2 Auxiliary Views: Primary. References: §§10.1–10.14, 10.16, 13.14. Using instruments, draw the indicated views. Use folding lines in Prob. 1 and reference-plane lines in Probs. 2–4. Prob. 3, dimension the angles between surfaces A and B, and A and C.

Drawing 10-3 Auxiliary Views: Primary. References: §§10.1–10.10, 10.14, 10.16, 10.17. Using instruments, add any missing lines in the regular views or auxiliary views.

Drawing 10-4 Auxiliary Views: Secondary. References: §§10.19–10.22. Using instruments, draw the indicated auxiliary views.
Space 1. Surface A is a normal surface, §7.19, and therefore appears true size in the given view. Use reference-plane lines. Dimension the 135° angle, Fig. 13.17.
Space 2. The height of the object is shown in the reduced-scale drawing. Draw the primary auxiliary view 22 mm from the given top view. Use folding lines. Dimension the angle between surfaces A and B in degrees, Fig. 13.17.

Drawing 11-1. Revolutions: Primary. References: §§7.10, 11.1–11.4, 11.11. Using instruments, draw the indicated constructions. In Probs. 1 and 2, use alternate position lines to show the revolved surfaces, as in Fig. 11.11.

Drawing 13-1 Dimensioning: Freehand. References: §§13.1–13.25, 13.30, 13.31. Use the complete decimal dimensioning system with metric values. If assigned, use decimal-inch equivalents. Add dimensions freehand, spacing dimension lines approximately 10 mm from the views and 10 mm apart. Include necessary finish marks in Prob. 2. Note that in Prob. 2 the drawing is half the size of the actual part. Dimension the keyway in the manner shown in Fig. 13.44 (x). The two small holes are drilled, Appendix 16, and the large hole is bored. In the bored-hole note, specify the diameter to two decimal places.

Drawing 13-2 Dimensioning: Mechanical. References: §§2.25, 2.27, 2.31, 4.15, 7.33, 7.34, 12.5, 13.1–13.25, 13.29–13.31. Measure the views (from centers of lines), and dimension completely, using the complete decimal dimensioning system with metric values to the nearest 0.5 mm (.02″). If assigned, use decimal-inch dimensions. Notice the scales in each problem. Space dimensions uniformly 10 mm (.40″) from the object and 10 mm (.40″) apart. Use the unidirectional system, Fig. 13.15 (b). Draw light guide lines for all dimension figures and notes, §4.19. Use a sharp 2H lead for dimension lines, extension lines, and center lines; a sharp F lead for arrowheads and lettering. Give radii dimensions for the larger arcs, Fig. 13.19, and give notes covering the small fillets and rounds, §13.16. Use V-type finish marks in Spaces 1 and 2, Fig. 13.20. In Space 2 give the angle in degrees, Fig. 13.17 (a). The large hole is reamed for an RC 6 fit, §14.8 and Appendix 5. Give the ream note in millimeters rounded off to two decimal places, Fig. 7.40 (b). *Caution:* Put dimensions in place before lettering notes; then choose the best open spots for the notes and letter them without crowding.

Drawing 13-3 Dimensioning: Mating Parts. References: §§13.9, 13.16, 13.17, 13.20–13.27, 13.31, 15.21. The T-Slot Clamp is a holding device used in the machine shop to hold work pieces in position. Dimension the parts completely, spacing dimension lines 10 mm from the views and 10 mm apart. Use the complete decimal dimensioning system with metric values. If assigned, use decimal-inch equivalents. Note that finish marks are not required on parts made of CRS (cold rolled steel).
Part No. 1. Frame. The hole in the base is drilled 1.5 mm (0.6″) larger than the M10 × 1.5 T-Slot Bolt. The bottom of the base is machined flat. For the tapped hole use metric coarse threads or if assigned, use Unified Coarse threads.

Drawing 13.4 Dimensioning: Mating Parts (continued). References: Same as for Drawing 42.
Part No. 2. Clamp Screw. The part is cylindrical except for the spherical ball on the end. The threads correspond to those in the Frame. The length of the threaded portion, including the chamfer and relief, is 66 mm. The drilled hole is 0.6 mm larger than the nominal size of the Handle.
Part No. 3. Pad. The drilled hole is 0.5 mm larger than

the ball of the Clamp Screw. The Pad is attached to the ball of the Clamp Screw by crimping the slit edges.

Part No. 4. Handle. The Handle is 90 mm long. The diameter is 6.375–8.385 mm.

Part No. 5. Handle Cap. The Cap is cylindrical. The hole is drilled and reamed to 6.350–6.365 mm diameter so as to fit tightly on the Handle.

Drawing 15-1 Threads and Fasteners: Nomenclature and Identification. References: §§15.1–15.21, 15.29–15.35. Draw light guide lines from the marks indicated, and letter the answers in the spaces provided. Standard abbreviations may be used to avoid crowding. See Appendix 4.

Drawing 15-2 Threads and Fasteners: Schematic Symbols. References: §§15.7–15.10, 15.23–15.28; Appendix 27. Draw specified threads and fastener details, using the schematic thread symbols unless otherwise assigned. Complete the section lining and leaders where required. Chamfer ends of threads 45° × thread depth in Probs. 1–3.

Drawing 15-3 Threads: Detailed. References: §§15.3–15.7, 15.11, 15.19–15.21, Appendix 15. Using detailed representation, show the specified threads for the given sectioned assembly of the cylindrical Coupler. The internal thread of the Core is a through thread and the stud of the Piston Rod is engaged to the depth indicated. Complete the section lining and the thread-note leaders.

Drawing 15-4 Acme and Square Threads: Detailed. References: §§15.3–15.17, 15.12, 15.13, 15.15, 15.21.

Adjusting Screw. Draw the specified Acme threads to complete the view. Complete the leaders and add arrowheads touching the threads. Construct the threads so as to be symmetrical about the central neck of the screw.

Leveling Jack. Draw the specified square threads to complete the assembly view. Note that the scale of the drawing is double size. Add necessary section lining and complete the thread-note leader.

Drawing 17-1 Isometric Drawing: Freehand. References: §§6.1–6.8, 6.12–6.14.

Spaces 1 to 6. Sketch isometrics of given objects. Note the given starting Point **A**.

Drawing 17-2 Isometric Drawing: Mechanical. References: §§17.5–17.18. Omit hidden lines in all problems. All "box construction" and other construction lines should be made lightly with a sharp 4H lead, and should not be erased. Darken all visible lines with a sharp F lead.

Spaces 1–3. Draw isometric drawings of the objects shown, locating the corners at **A** and using the dividers to transfer distances from the views to the isometrics.

Space 4. Draw isometric drawing, locating the corner **A** at the point **A**. Use the scale to set off dimensions. Do not transfer distances with dividers, as the given drawing is not to scale. Show construction for the 30° angle.

Space 5. Complete the isometric drawing, using the information supplied in the reduced-scale drawing.

Space 6. Complete the isometric drawing, transferring measurements directly from the given views to the isometric with dividers. Draw the final curves with the aid of the irregular curve, §2.54.

Drawing 17-3 Isometric Drawing: Mechanical. References: §§17.3–17.18, 17.20, 17.21. Using instruments, make isometric drawings of two assigned problems. Use the indicated starting corners. Show all construction.

Drawing 18-1 Oblique Projection: Freehand. References: §§6.3, 6.5, 6.15, 6.16. Using the method shown in Fig. 6.28, make oblique sketches of objects shown, using the starting corners indicated. Omit hidden lines and center lines. Make visible lines **black** so sketches will stand out clearly from the grids.

Drawing 18-2 Oblique Projection: Cabinet and Cavalier. References: §§18.1–18.7, 18.9. Draw assigned problem in Space 1 in cavalier projection and in Space 2 in cabinet projection. Omit hidden lines unless necessary for clearness. Show all constructions clearly, and do not erase construction lines. In Space 2, Prob. 1 (a), the ellipse construction must be drawn by means of offsets, §18.8.

Drawings 19-1 to 22-2

Accuracy. Graphic solutions to space problems require accurate measurements and clean, sharp line work. Properly sharpened F and 2H leads will be found suitable for most line work, while a sharp 4H lead is preferred for construction and guide lines for lettering. The F lead is normally used for lettering. Make all measurements from center to center of lines and when no scale is specified, measure to the nearest 0.2 mm.

Unless otherwise specified, the basic unit for the given scales is the millimeter. Hence, a scale of 1/2000 is 1 mm to 2000 mm or 2 m. For measurements equal to or greater than 1000 mm, indicate these measurements in meters.

Notation. A certain amount of lettering is necessary on all graphical solutions. A minimum amount of notation should include the following:

1. Label at least one point in each view, or label points that are mentioned in the instructions.
2. Label all folding lines employed.
3. Show the symbols for EV (edge view), TL (true length), TS (true size), and LI (line of intersection) when they are a part of the solution.
4. Show given and required information such as angles, distances, bearings, and other numerical items *on the views* where measured or set off.

Drawing 19-1 Points and Lines: Visibility. Reference: §19.1. Use standard alphabet of lines. §2.11, to complete the solutions. Change the dotted lines to standard lines in Spaces 3 and 4.

Drawing 19-2 Points and Lines: Points on Lines. References: §§7.15, 19.1, 19.2.
Space 1. Point 2 is 33 mm to the right of point 1, 25 mm below point 1, and 20 mm in front of point 1. Show these dimensions on the drawing.
Space 2. Line 1–2 is 38 mm long (2 is behind 1). Line 1–3 is a 40 mm long frontal line. Show these dimensions on the drawing. Line 2–3 is a profile line. Dimension the true length of line 2–3.
Space 3. Line 1–2 is 33 mm long. Show this on the drawing. The front view of line 2–3 is true length as indicated.
Space 4. Point 5 is on line 1–2 and is 15 mm above point 1. Point 6 is on line 3–4. Line 5–6 is a horizontal line. Dimension the length of line 5–6.
Space 5. Note that point 4 is to be moved vertically *in space*.
Space 6. Triangle 1–2–3 is the base of a pyramid. Vertix V is 5 mm behind point 1, 10 mm to the left of point 2, and 28 mm above point 3. Show these dimensions on the drawing.

Drawing 19-3 True Length of Line: Angles by Auxiliary Views. References: §§10.18, 19.3. Use auxiliary views. Dimension the required angles in degrees as in §13.14, and also dimension the true lengths in millimeters for Spaces 1–3. Show all given data on the drawing for Space 4.

Drawing 19-4 True Length of Line: Bearing and Grade. References: §§19.3, 19.5. Use auxiliary views. For all problems indicate the percent grade on the drawing, as in Figure 19.14 (b). For Spaces 1–3, also show the numerical values of the bearing and true length on the drawing.

Drawing 19-5 True Length of Line: Revolution. References: §§11.10, 19.4. Use American National Standard phantom lines for lines in alternate or revolved-position views.

Space 1. Dimension the true length, slope, and bearing on the drawing.
Space 2. Dimension ∠F, ∠P, and the true length on the drawing.
Space 3. Show the 30° angle on the drawing.
Space 4. Show all given data on the drawing.

Drawing 19-6 True Length of Line: Point View. References: §§10.11, 19.6.
Space 1. Include the minimum notation as recommended in the general instructions for Drawings 19-1 to 22-2.
Space 2. Dimension the clearance on the drawing.
Space 3. Dimension the true distances for comparison.

Drawing 19-7 Planes: Points and Lines in Planes. References: §§19.7, 19.8.
Space 1. Indicate your answer in the space provided.
Space 2. The *top* view of point 4 and the *front* view of point 5 are shown.
Space 4. See also Fig. 19.1. Show given data on the drawing.

Drawing 19-8 Planes: True Size. References: §§7.15, 10.1, 10.21, 19.9, 19.10.
Space 1. Indicate values for calculation of the area on the drawing and show your calculations. Record the area to two significant figures only, in the space provided.
Space 2. Show the connecting feeder line in the given views.

Drawing 19-9 Lines and Planes: Piercing Points—Edge-View Method. Reference: §19.11 Use the edge view method on this sheet and show proper visibility in all views. Show EV where appropriate and encircle the piercing points in all views.
Space 3. Do not show a hidden line for that segment of line 1–2 which is within the pyramid.

Drawing 19-10 Lines and Planes: Piercing Points—Cutting-Plane Method. Reference: §19.11. Use the cutting-plane method on this sheet and show proper visibility in all views. Show EV on the lines as edge-view cutting planes and encircle the views of the piercing points.
Space 3. Do not show a hidden line for that segment of line 1–2 which is completely within the pyramid. However, include any extension lines necessary to clarify the method of solution.
Space 4. Note that the given views are a front and a primary auxiliary view.

Drawing 19-11 Planes: Intersections. Reference: §19.12. Show the symbol EV wherever appropriate and label the line of intersection with the symbol LI.

Spaces 1 and 2. Show complete visibility.

Spaces 3 and 4. Visibility is of no concern in these problems, but special care is needed to insure accuracy of your solutions.

Drawing 19-12 Planes: Dihedral Angles. References: §§10.11, 19.9.

Space 1. See also §5.7. Dimension the angles on the drawing. Show complete visibility.

Space 2. See also §19.12. Special care is needed to assure accuracy in your solution of this problem. Show the angle on your drawing. Show complete visibility.

Drawing 19-13 Lines and Planes: Angle Between Line and Plane. Reference: §19.13.

Space 1. Dimension the angle on the drawing.

Space 2. This is an "open ended" problem (as are most engineering problems) in that there are many possible answers. Show use of given data on the drawing.

Drawing 20-1 Parallelism: Lines and Planes. References: §§7.25, 19.8, 20.1, 20.3, 20.4.

Space 1. Demonstrate your answer graphically and indicate it by a check mark(s) (✔) in the space provided.

Space 2. You may check vertical alignment with a T-square and a triangle, but do not perform any actual constructions. Indicate your answer(a) by a check mark (✔) in the spaces provided.

Spaces 3 and 4. Use only the given views.

Drawing 20-2 Parallelism: Lines and Planes. References: §§7.25, 19.5, 20.1 to 20.4.

Space 1. Show bearing on the drawing.

Drawing 20-3 Perpendicularity: Lines. References: §§20.5, 20.6. These problems are to be solved without the construction of auxiliary views. Use the symbol as shown in Fig. 5.1 (k) to show lines drawn perpendicular.

Drawing 20-4 Perpendicularity: Lines and Planes. References: §§20.5–20.7.

Space 1. Do not construct additional views.

Space 2. Use an auxiliary view, or only the given views, or both, as assigned. Show the length of the altitude on the drawing.

Space 3. Use auxiliary views. Show *all* views in completed form with proper visibility.

Drawing 20-5 Skew Lines: Common Perpendicular. References: §§20.5, 20.9. These problems are designed to be solved by the point-view method. Use of the plane method is not recommended because of space limitations.

Space 1. Show answers on views where measured. Be sure to check accuracy with divider distances.

Space 2. Indicate the actual clearance distances on the drawing where measured. Show the front and side views of lines representing the two distances. Indicate with a check mark (✔) in the spaces provided, the answer to the matter of inspection.

Drawing 20-6 Skew Lines: Lines Specified Angles. References: §§20.10, 20.11.

Spaces 1 and 2. Show given data on the drawing where measured.

Drawing 21-1 Intersections: Planes and Polyhedra. References: §§21.1–21.3, 21.6, 21.8, 21.10.

Space 1. The edge-view method is suggested. Be sure to check accuracy with divider distances. Show visibility.

Space 2. Use the cutting-plane method, including the EV symbols. Show complete visibility except that hidden line segments of the plane's boundaries within the prism should be omitted.

Drawing 21-2 Intersections: Prisms and Pyramids. References: §§21.22–21.26. Omit hidden line segments of lateral edges of either solid which are within the other solid.

If assigned: On a separate sheet develop the surface of one or more of the solids, including the intersections.

Drawing 21-3 Intersections: Circular Forms. References: §§21.27, 21.28, 21.31. Determine the figures of intersection and show visibility.

Drawing 21-4 Parallel-Line Development: Prism and Cylinder. References: §§21.8, 21.9. Show full developments inside up. Omit the bases.

Space 2. Calculate the length of the development for the cylinder. Start development with the shortest element.

Drawing 21-5 Radial-Line Development: Pyramid and Cone. References: §§21.10, 21.11, 21.13–21.15, 21.17. Show developments inside up. Start with shortest seam. Omit bases.

Drawing 21-6 Triangulation: Transition Piece. References: §§21.14–21.20. Show half development inside up. Omit the cylindrical and prismatic connectors at the top and bottom.

Drawing 22-1 Tangencies: Line and Plane. References: §§22.1–22.4. If assigned, where alternative solutions are possible, show the second solution with a phantom line.

Drawing 22-2 Tangencies: Specified Angles. Reference: §22.5. If assigned, show alternative solutions with phantom lines.

Drawing 23-1 Graphs: Pie Chart and Bar Graph.
Space 1. References: §§23.20, 23.21. According to the U.S. census (1970), Chicagoans age 25 and over (1,943,464) reported the following educational achievement.

Never attended school	2%
Dropped out before grade 8	18%
Dropped out before grade 9	16%
Dropped out in high school	21%
Graduated from high school	26%
Dropped out in college	9%
Graduated from college	8%

Divide the pie chart to illustrate the above data. Show and label the appropriate percentages for each category. Use 3 mm (.12″) engineering lettering throughout. Balance the largest sector symmetrically about a vertical center line in the lower area of the circle. Title the chart: EDUCATIONAL EXPERIENCE OF CHICAGO RESIDENTS AGE 25 AND OVER—1970. Underline the title only. Indicate outside the area of the pie chart the total number that reported.

Space 2. References: §§23.17, 23.18. Construct a column or bar chart on the rectangular grid to show the auto accidents experienced by drivers of various age groups. The Motor Vehicle Mfrs. Assn. of U.S., Inc., reported the following data (1972).

Age Groups	Licensed Drivers	Drivers Involved in Fatal Accidents
Under 25	21.6%	33.8%
25–44	39.3%	37.7%
45–64	30.6%	21.1%
65 and over	8.5%	7.4%

Locate the axes at the given starting corner. Place the PERCENT scale on the *y*-axis and the AGE GROUP scale along the *x*-axis. Two bars are required for each age group, similar to Fig. 23.22 (b). Cross-hatch at 45° the bars representing the licensed drivers. Indicate the percent values above all bars similar to Fig. 23.33 (a). Add border lines for the chart area and strengthen appropriate horizontal grid lines, but do not cross bar areas. Identify shading significance with key inserts similar to Fig. 23.33 (b). Title the chart: INVOLVEMENT IN FATAL ACCIDENTS, U.S. DRIVERS—1972.

Drawing 23-2 Graphs: Pie Chart and Bar Graph.
Space 1. References: §§23.20, 23.21. Worldwide production of cars, trucks, and buses for 1979 totaled 41 515 000 units. The percentage distribution was as follows.

U.S.	28%
Japan	23%
W. Germany	10%
France	9%
U.S.S.R.	5%
Italy	4%
Canada	4%
G. Britain	3.6%
All others	13.4%

Divide the pie chart to illustrate the given data. Label and show the value for each sector. Use 3 mm or 0.12″ engineering lettering. Place the sum of the two largest sectors about a vertical center line in the lower portion of the circle.

Space 2. References: §§23.17, 23.18. Construct a bar chart for the following data on nuclear power generation.

Nuclear Power Generation
(Millions of kilowatt-hours)

1973	85 000
1974	115 000
1975	170 000
1976	190 000
1977	255 000
1978	280 000
1979	260 000
1980	275 000

Use 12 mm wide vertical bars beginning at the given horizontal base line. Allow 6 mm spaces at the beginning and end and between the bars. Shade the bars as in Fig. 23.33 (a). Title the chart in 3 mm or 0.12″ letters. Draw horizontal grid lines for each 50,000 value indicated, but do not draw them across the bars.

Drawing 24-1 Detail Drawings. References: Chapters 6, 7, 9, 13, §16.8. Draw or sketch the necessary views of the object assigned. Select appropriate scale and sheet size. Dimension completely using metric or decimal-inch dimensions as assigned.

Alternate Assignment: Using a CAD system, produce a hard-copy multiview drawing of the problem assigned. Dimension completely.

1

VISIBLE LINE

HIDDEN LINE

SECTION, DIMENSION, AND EXTENSION LINE

CENTER LINE

CUTTING-PLANE LINE

PHANTOM LINE

2

VISIBLE LINE

HIDDEN LINE

SECTION, DIMENSION, AND EXTENSION LINE

CENTER LINE

CUTTING-PLANE LINE

PHANTOM LINE

SHORT-BREAK LINE

3

4

5

6

ALPHABET OF LINES	DRAWN BY	FILE NO.	DRAWING
INSTRUMENTAL DRAWING			**2-1**

I

A   SCALE : 12"= 1'- 0   L = ═══

B   SCALE : 6"= 1'- 0   L = 11 9/16"

C   SCALE : 1"= 10'   L = ═══

D   SCALE : 1"= 20'   L = 97.5'

E   SCALE : 1"= 600'   L = 3100.0'

F   SCALE : 1mm = 1mm   L = ═══

G   SCALE : 1mm = 10mm   L = 1315.0mm

H   SCALE : 1mm = 2mm   L = 286.0mm

J   SCALE : ═══   L = ═══

K   SCALE : ═══   L = ═══

L   SCALE : ═══   L = ═══

Measure or draw the above lengths as indicated and record answers in appropriate spaces.

2

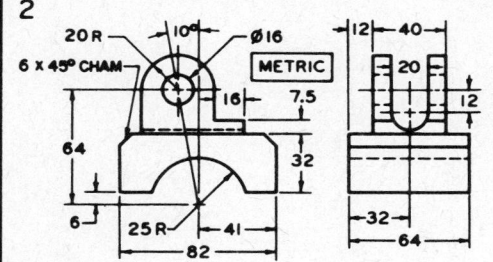

ANCHOR BRACKET

CRS—6 REQD
SCALE: 1 = 1

Draw the two views.
Omit dimensions.

SCALES AND LAYOUT	DRAWN BY	FILE NO.	DRAWING
INSTRUMENTAL DRAWING			2-2

DRAWN BY | FILE NO. | DRAWING

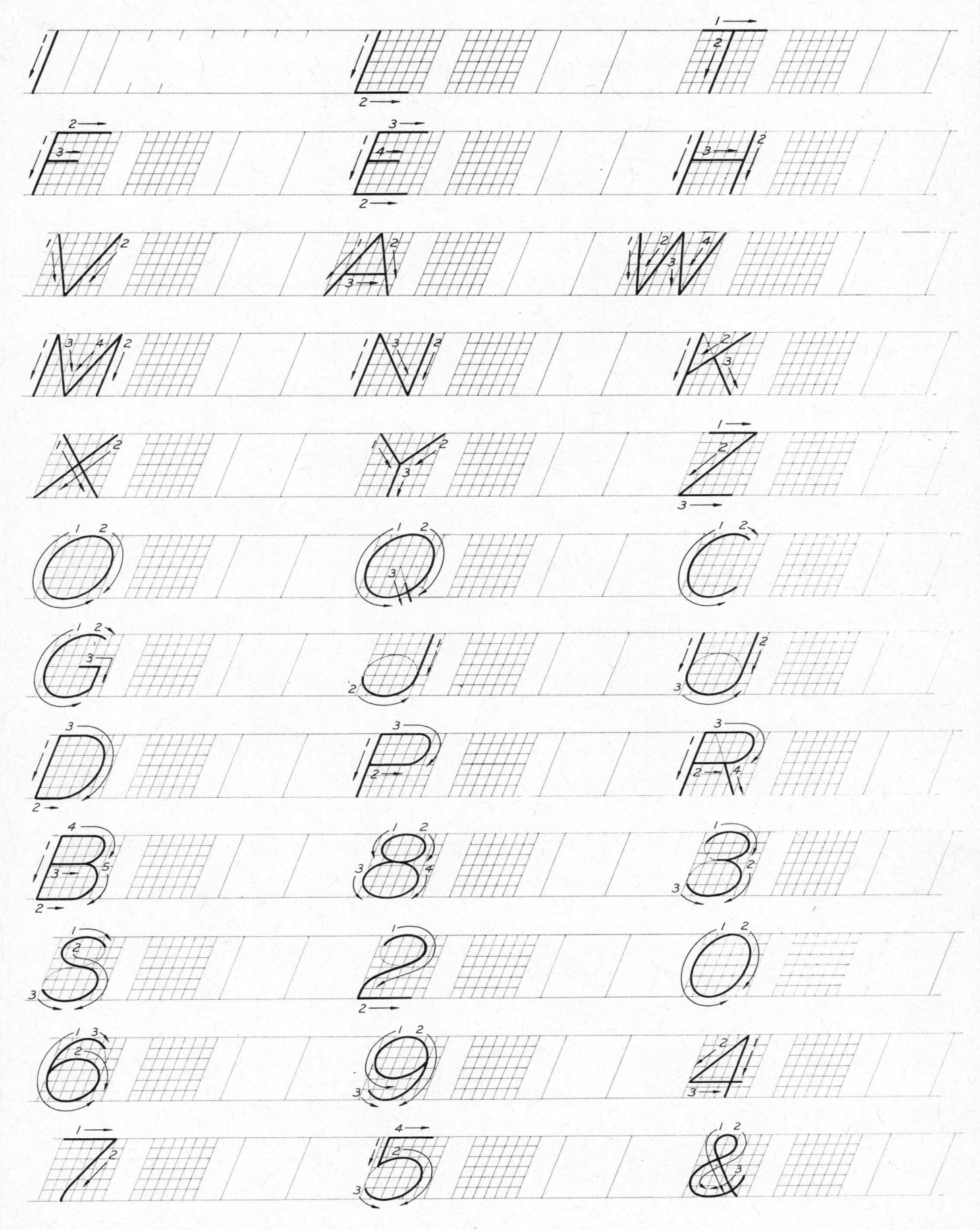

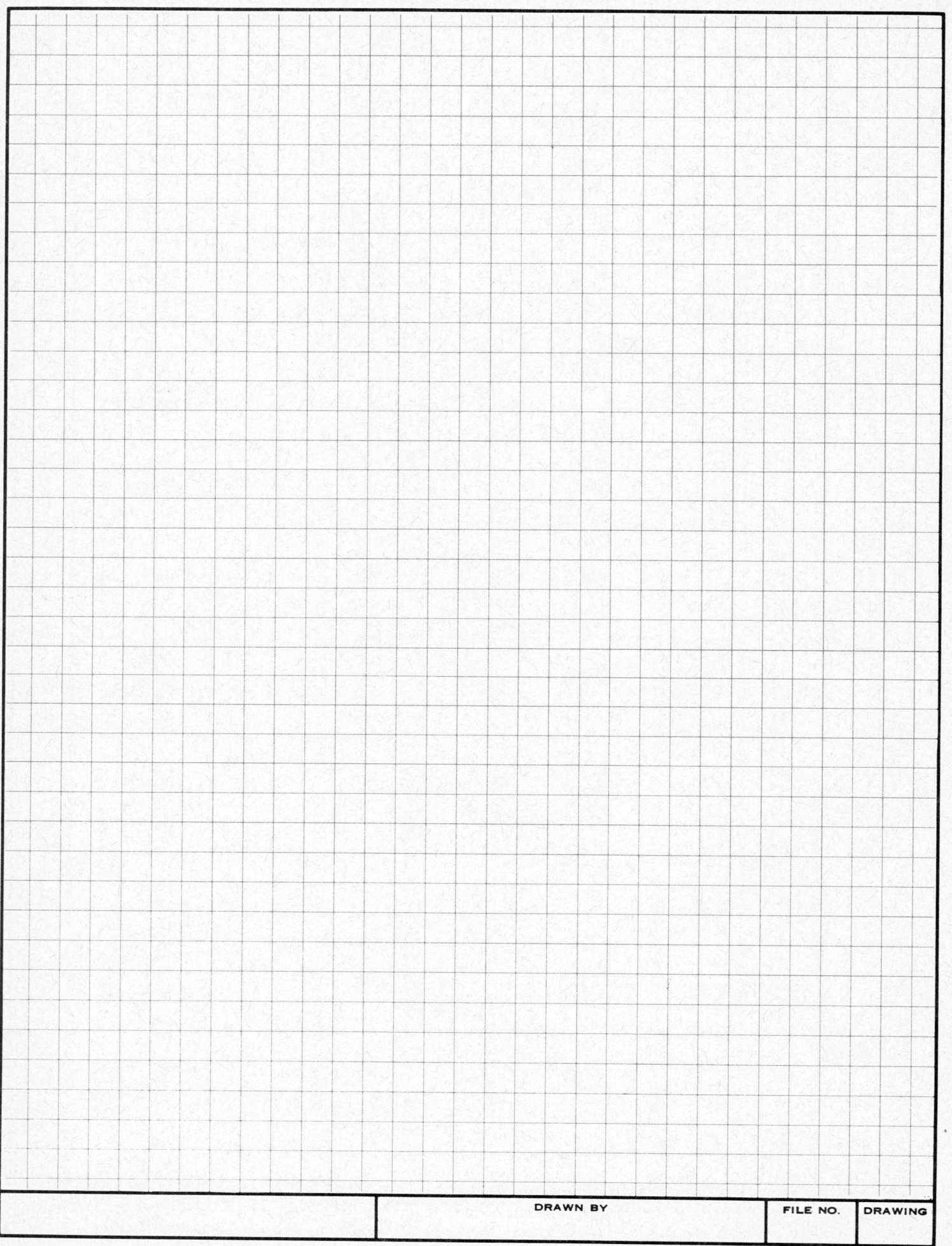

DRAWN BY   FILE NO.   DRAWING

WHILE IT IS TRUE THAT

"PRACTICE MAKES PERFECT," IT

MUST BE UNDERSTOOD THAT

PRACTICE IS NOT ENOUGH, BUT IT

MUST BE ACCOMPANIED BY A CON-

TINUOUS EFFORT TO IMPROVE. EXCEL-

LENT LETTERERS ARE OFTEN NOT GOOD

WRITERS. USE A FAIRLY SOFT PENCIL, AND AL-

WAYS KEEP IT SHARP, ESPECIALLY FOR SMALL

LETTERS. MAKE THE LETTERS CLEAN-CUT AND

DARK-NEVER FUZZY, GRAY, OR INDEFINITE. 1234

$1\frac{1}{2}$ 1.500 $\frac{3}{16}$ 45'-6 32° 15.489 $\frac{13}{64}$ 12"=1'-0 $7\frac{5}{16}$ 12.3 $\frac{1}{2}$ $2\frac{1}{4}$

ONE MUST HAVE A CLEAR MENTAL IMAGE OF THE LETTERS. 234

| CAPITALS AND NUMERALS
VERTICAL LETTERING | | DRAWN BY | FILE NO. | DRAWING
4-3 |

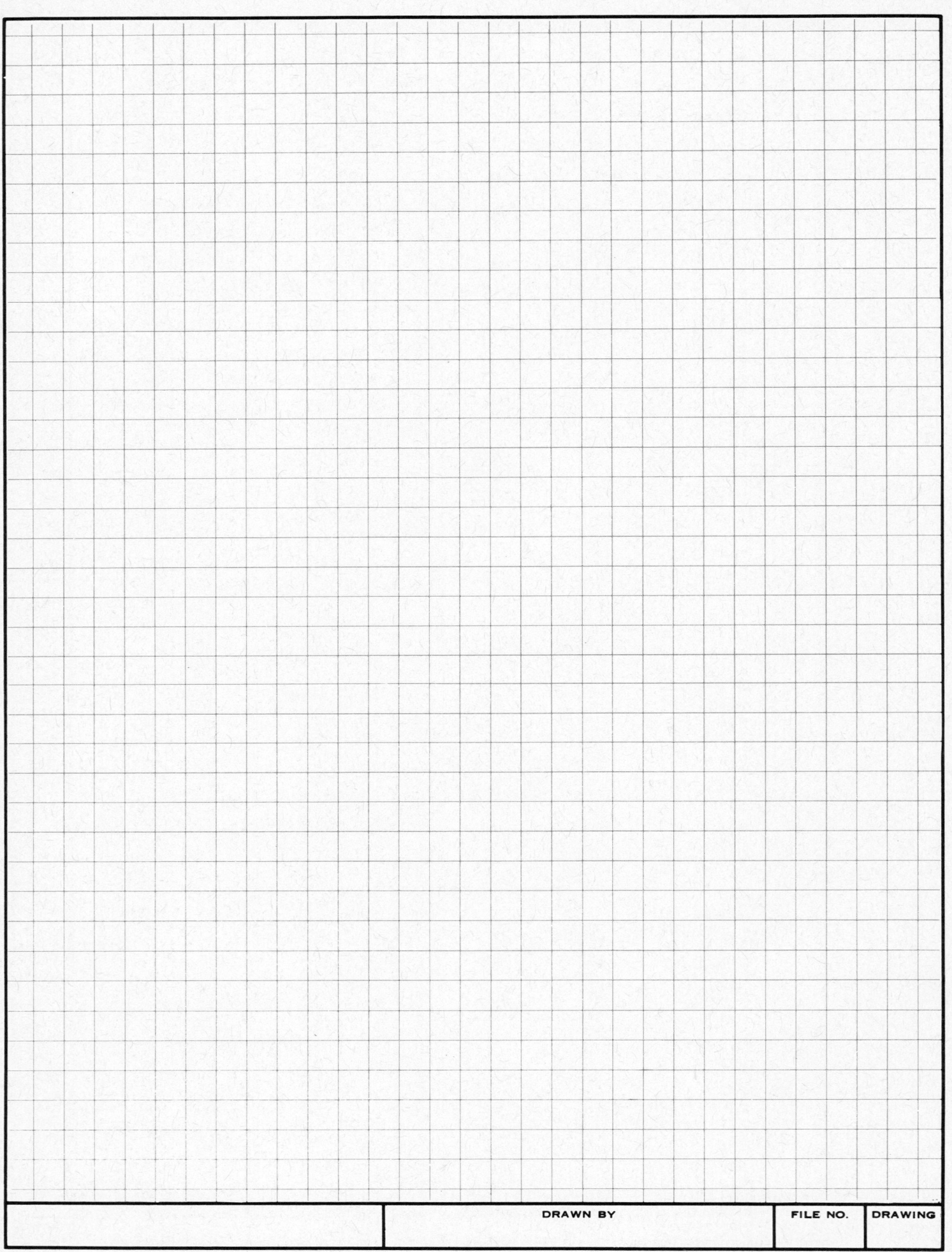

DRAWN BY   FILE NO.   DRAWING

WHILE IT IS TRUE THAT

"PRACTICE MAKES PERFECT," IT

MUST BE UNDERSTOOD THAT

PRACTICE IS NOT ENOUGH, BUT IT

MUST BE ACCOMPANIED BY A CON-

TINUOUS EFFORT TO IMPROVE. EXCEL-

LENT LETTERERS ARE OFTEN NOT GOOD

WRITERS. USE A FAIRLY SOFT PENCIL, AND AL-

WAYS KEEP IT SHARP, ESPECIALLY FOR SMALL

LETTERS. MAKE THE LETTERS CLEAN-CUT AND

DARK-NEVER FUZZY, GRAY, OR INDEFINITE. 1234

$1\frac{1}{2}$ 1.500 $\frac{3}{16}$ 45'-6 32° 15.489 $\frac{13}{64}$ 12"=1'-0 $7\frac{5}{16}$ 12.3 $\frac{1}{2}$ $2\frac{1}{4}$

ONE MUST HAVE A CLEAR MENTAL IMAGE OF THE LETTERS. 234

CAPITALS AND NUMERALS	DRAWN BY	FILE NO.	DRAWING
INCLINED LETTERING			**4-4**

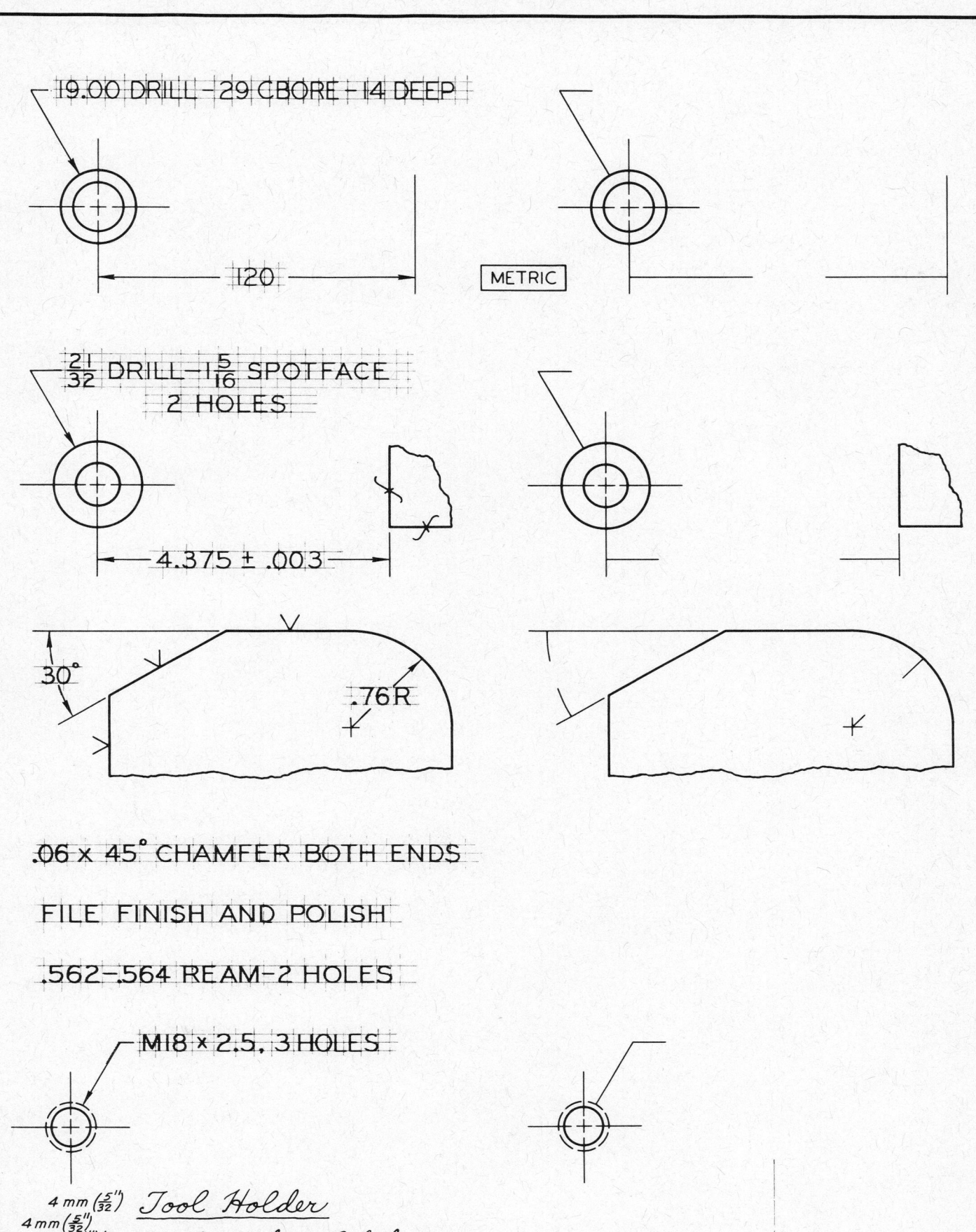

19.00 DRILL - 29 CBORE - 14 DEEP

120

METRIC

$\frac{21}{32}$ DRILL—$1\frac{5}{16}$ SPOTFACE
2 HOLES

4.375 ± .003

30°

.76R

.06 × 45° CHAMFER BOTH ENDS

FILE FINISH AND POLISH

.562–.564 REAM–2 HOLES

M18 × 2.5, 3 HOLES

4 mm ($\frac{5}{32}$") *Tool Holder*
4 mm ($\frac{5}{32}$")
3 mm ($\frac{1}{8}$") *F A O-Cyanide & Polish*
2.5mm ($\frac{3}{32}$")
3mm ($\frac{1}{8}$") *M S - 3 Reqd*

SHOP NOTES AND DIMENSIONS	DRAWN BY	FILE NO.	DRAWING
VERTICAL LETTERING			**4-5**

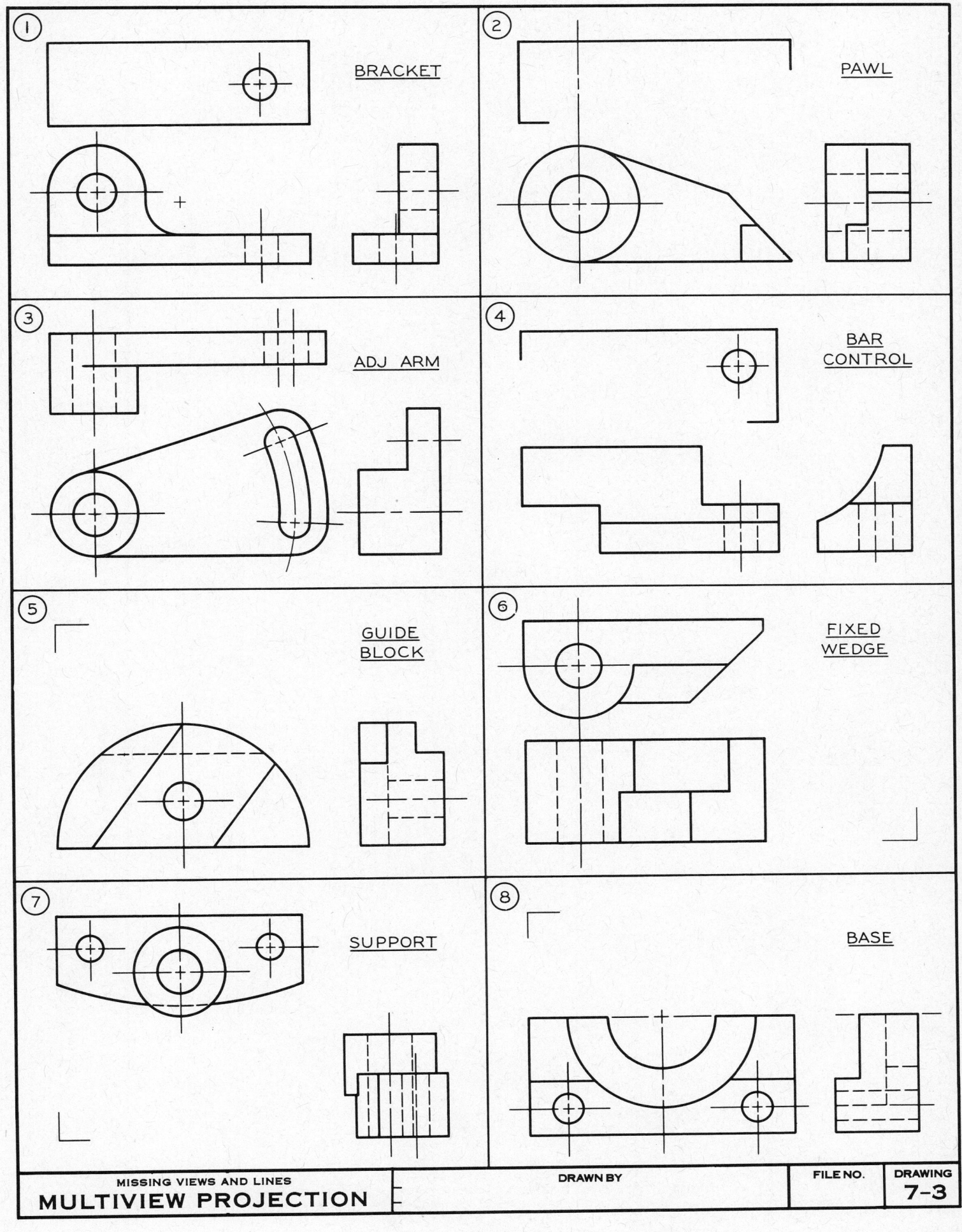

1. BRACKET
2. PAWL
3. ADJ ARM
4. BAR CONTROL
5. GUIDE BLOCK
6. FIXED WEDGE
7. SUPPORT
8. BASE

MISSING VIEWS AND LINES
MULTIVIEW PROJECTION

DRAWN BY

FILE NO.

DRAWING
7-3

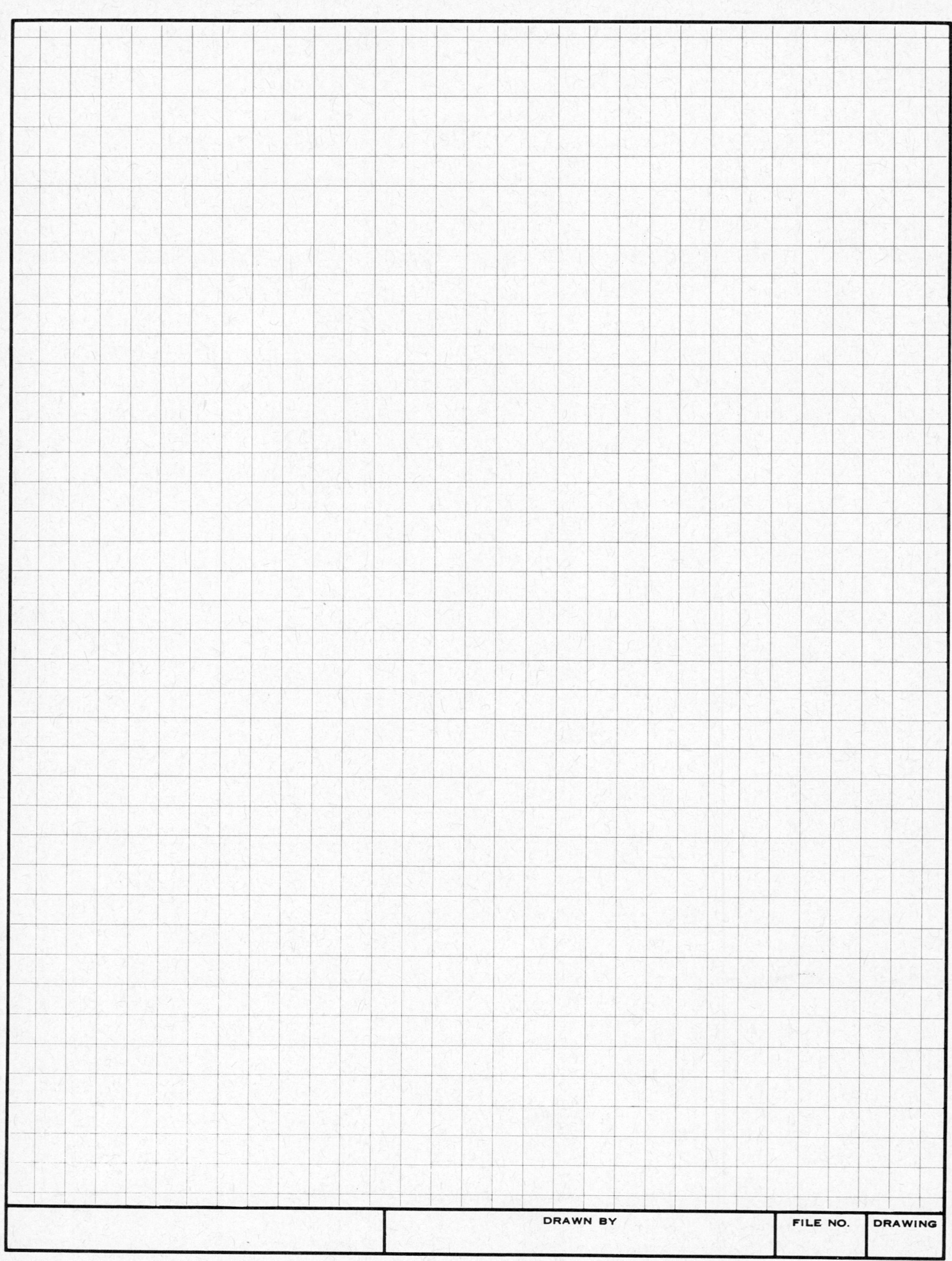

DRAWN BY   FILE NO.   DRAWING

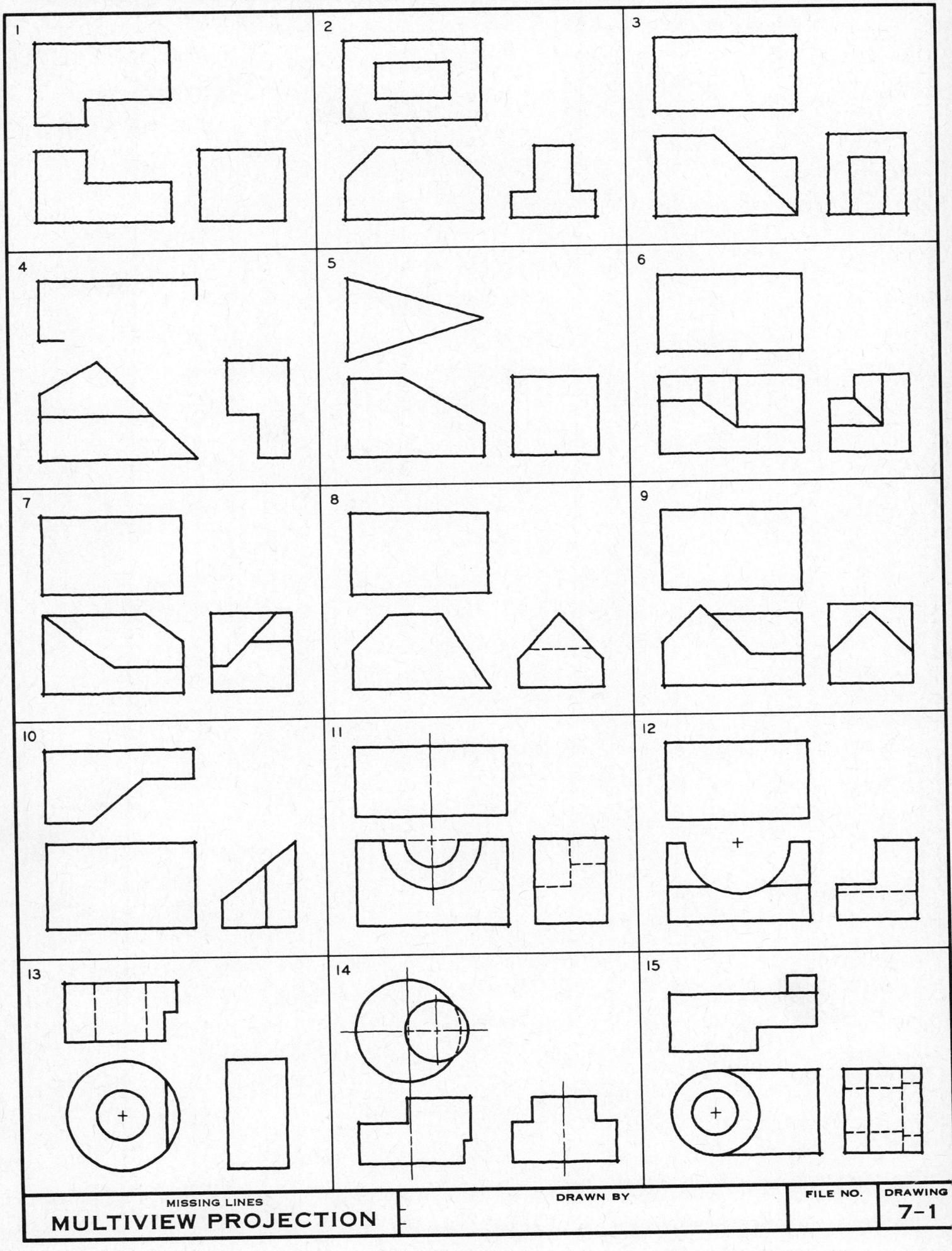

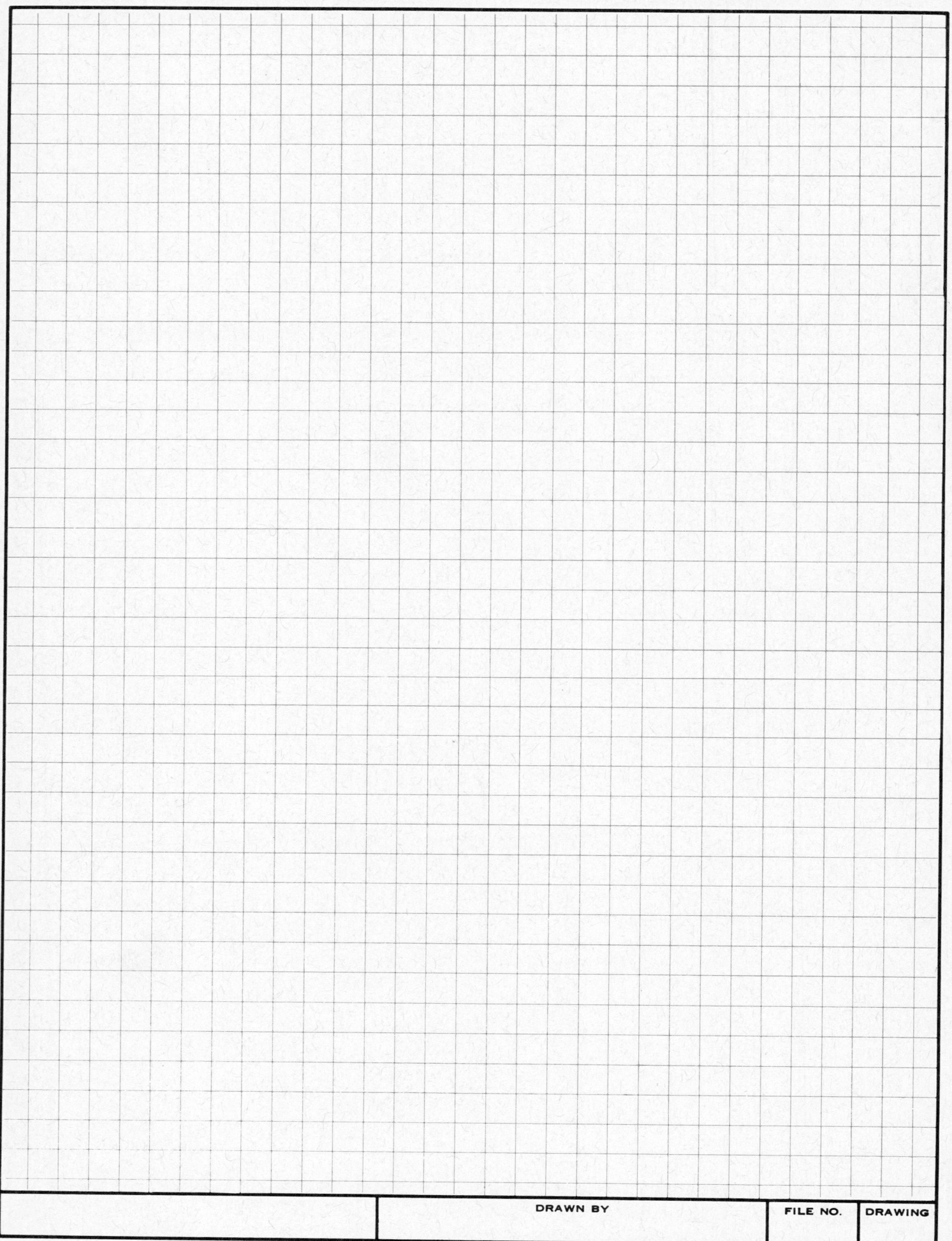

DRAWN BY

FILE NO.

DRAWING

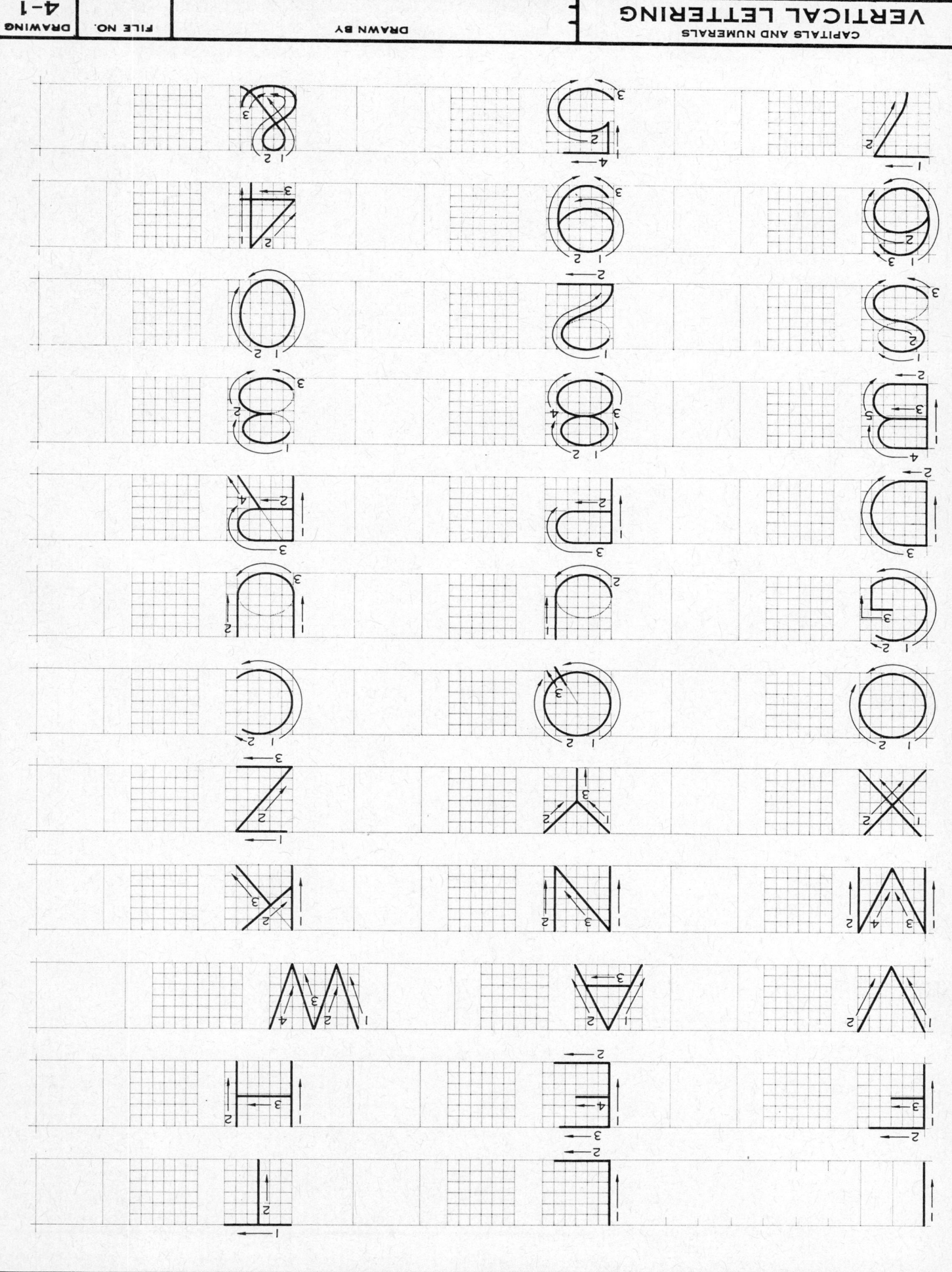

19.00 DRILL – 29 CBORE – 14 DEEP
120

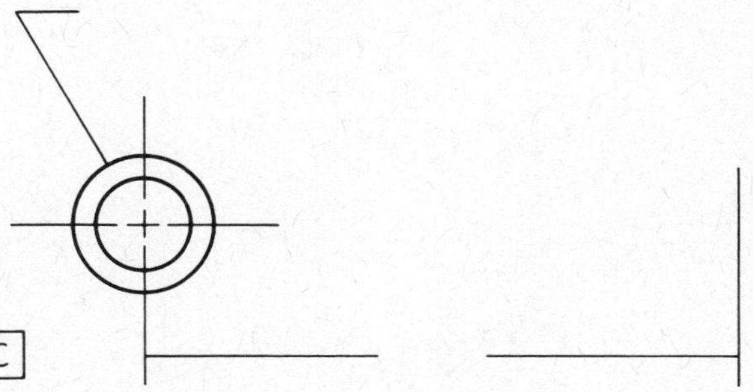

METRIC

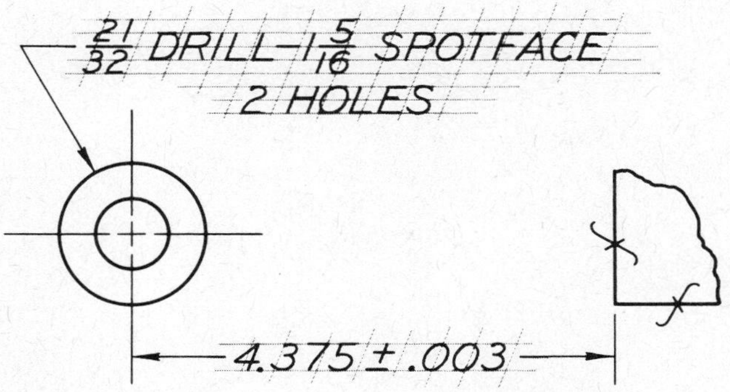

$\frac{21}{32}$ DRILL – $1\frac{5}{16}$ SPOTFACE
2 HOLES
4.375 ± .003

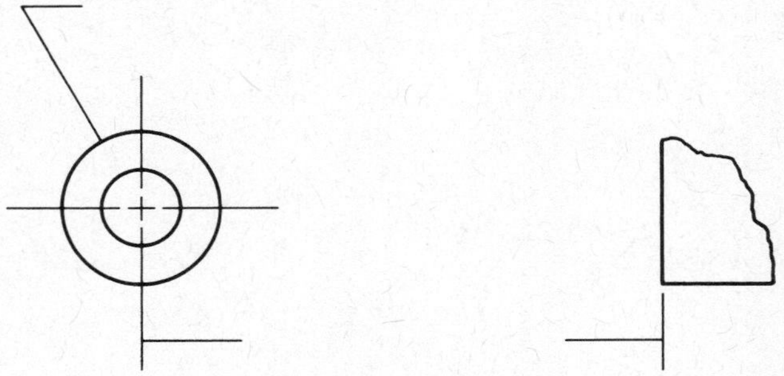

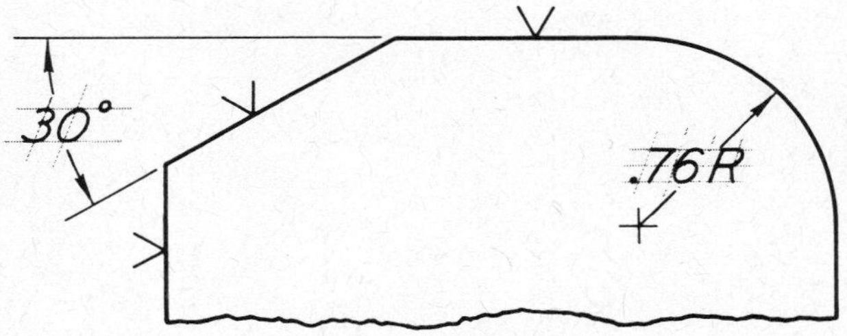

30°
.76R

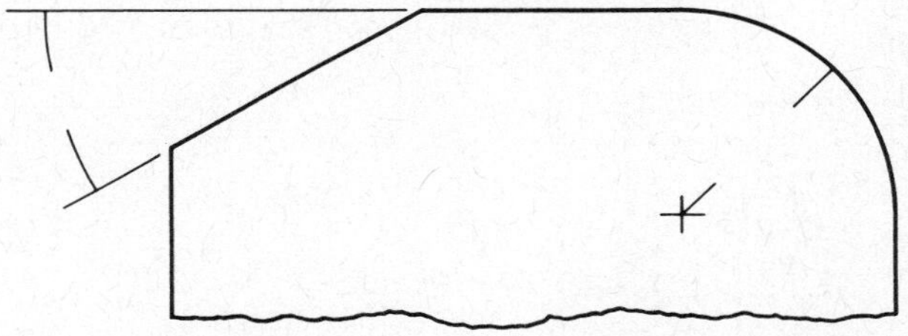

.06 × 45° CHAMFER BOTH ENDS

FILE FINISH AND POLISH

.562–.564 REAM–2 HOLES

M18 × 2.5, 3 HOLES

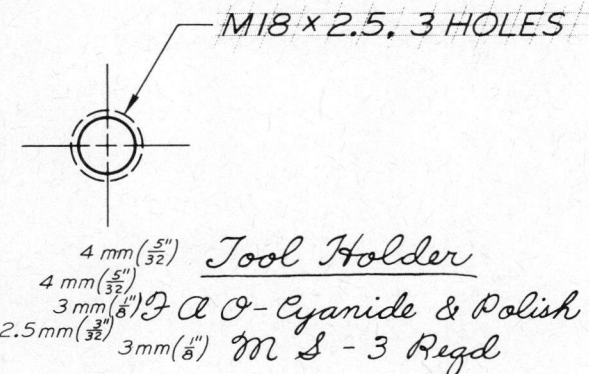

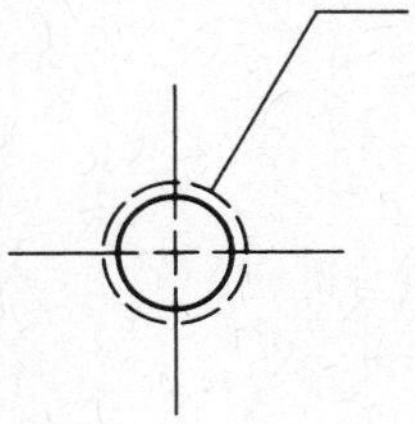

4 mm ($\frac{5}{32}$") *Tool Holder*

4 mm ($\frac{5}{32}$")

3 mm ($\frac{1}{8}$") *F A O - Cyanide & Polish*

2.5 mm ($\frac{3}{32}$")

3 mm ($\frac{1}{8}$") *M S - 3 Reqd*

SHOP NOTES AND DIMENSIONS **INCLINED LETTERING**	DRAWN BY	FILE NO.	DRAWING **4–6**

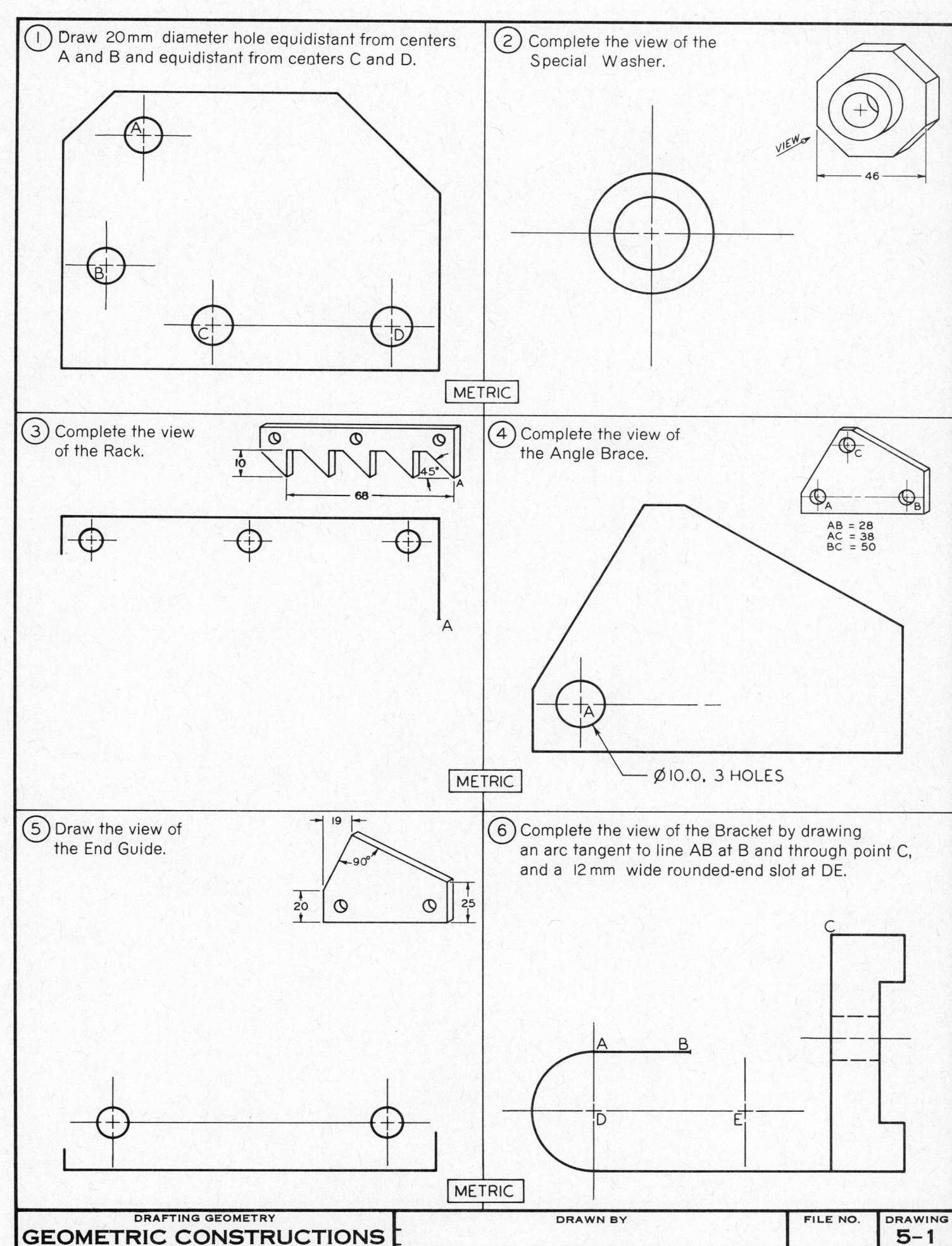

1. Draw 20mm diameter hole equidistant from centers A and B and equidistant from centers C and D.

A B C D

METRIC

2. Complete the view of the Special Washer.

VIEW

46

3. Complete the view of the Rack.

10 68 45° A

A

4. Complete the view of the Angle Brace.

C A B

AB = 28
AC = 38
BC = 50

A

Ø10.0, 3 HOLES

METRIC

5. Draw the view of the End Guide.

19 90° 20 25

6. Complete the view of the Bracket by drawing an arc tangent to line AB at B and through point C, and a 12mm wide rounded-end slot at DE.

C

A B

D E

METRIC

DRAWN BY

FILE NO.

DRAWING

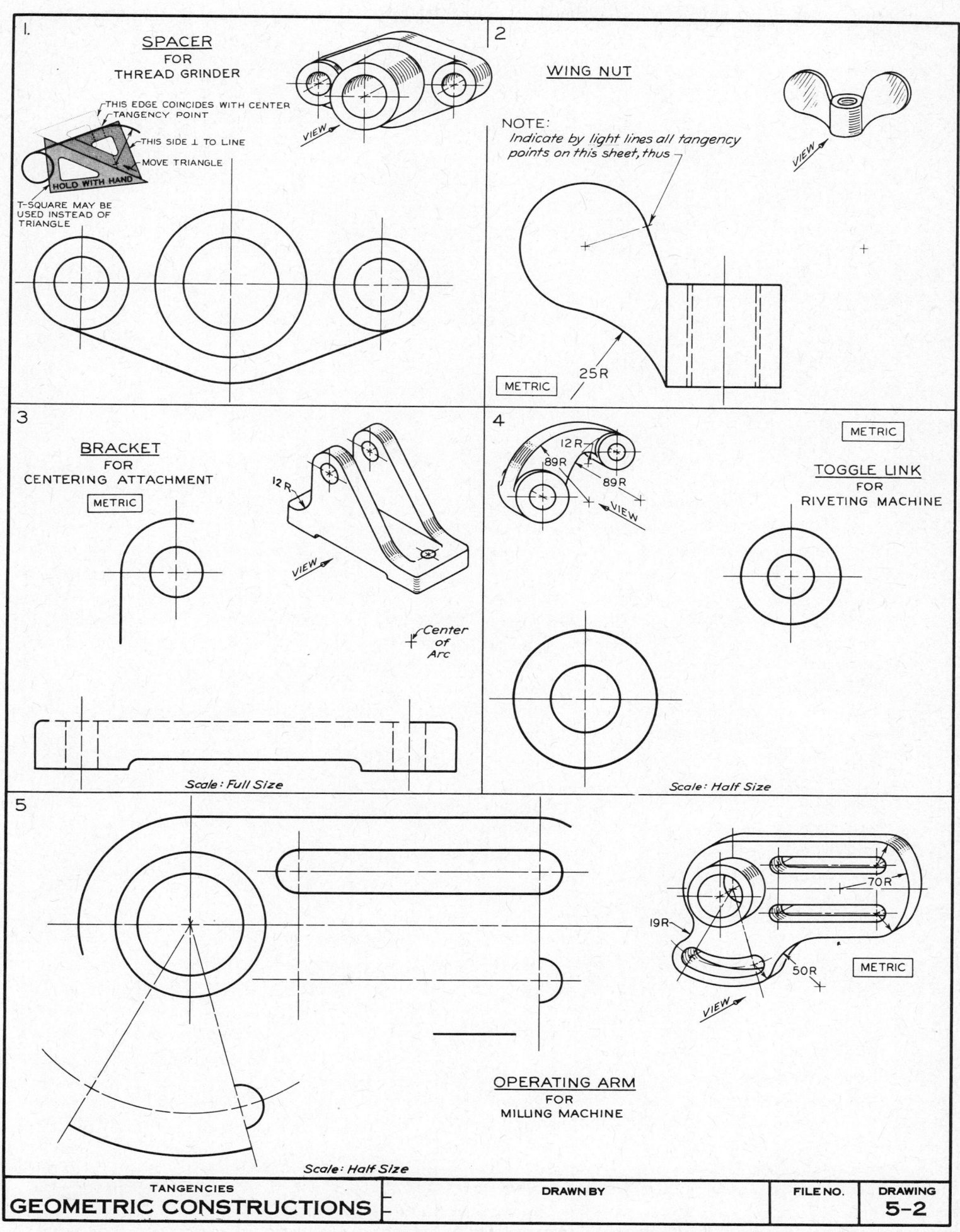

1. SPACER
FOR
THREAD GRINDER

THIS EDGE COINCIDES WITH CENTER
TANGENCY POINT

THIS SIDE ⊥ TO LINE

MOVE TRIANGLE

HOLD WITH HAND

T-SQUARE MAY BE
USED INSTEAD OF
TRIANGLE

VIEW

2. WING NUT

NOTE:
Indicate by light lines all tangency
points on this sheet, thus

VIEW

25R

METRIC

3. BRACKET
FOR
CENTERING ATTACHMENT

METRIC

12 R

VIEW

Center
of
Arc

Scale: Full Size

4. 12R

89R

89R

VIEW

METRIC

TOGGLE LINK
FOR
RIVETING MACHINE

Scale: Half Size

5.

70R

19R

50R

METRIC

VIEW

OPERATING ARM
FOR
MILLING MACHINE

Scale: Half Size

TANGENCIES
GEOMETRIC CONSTRUCTIONS

DRAWN BY

FILE NO.

DRAWING
5-2

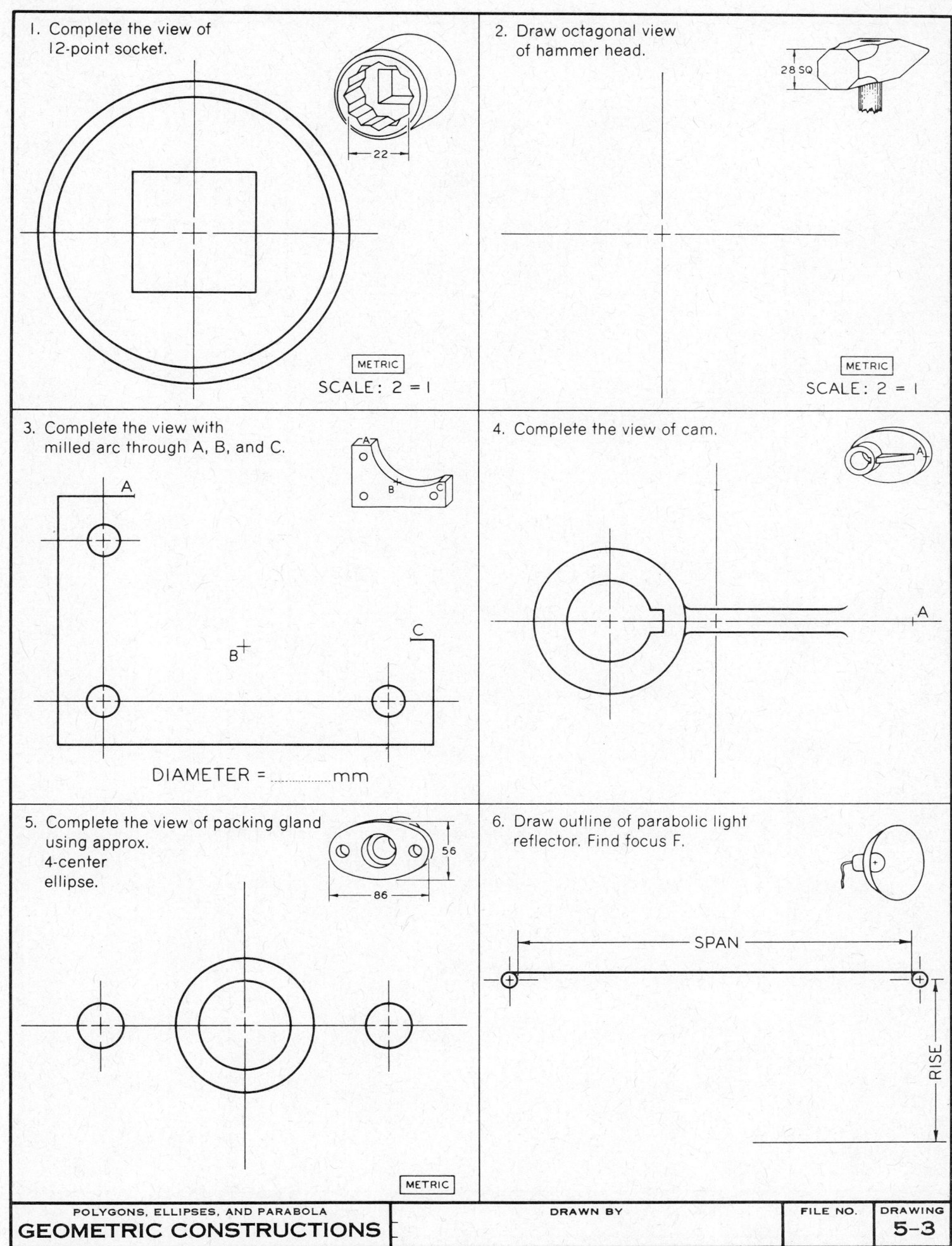

1. Complete the view of 12-point socket.

— 22 —

METRIC
SCALE: 2 = 1

2. Draw octagonal view of hammer head.

28 SQ

METRIC
SCALE: 2 = 1

3. Complete the view with milled arc through A, B, and C.

A

B

C

DIAMETER = ... mm

4. Complete the view of cam.

A

A

5. Complete the view of packing gland using approx. 4-center ellipse.

56

86

METRIC

6. Draw outline of parabolic light reflector. Find focus F.

SPAN

RISE

POLYGONS, ELLIPSES, AND PARABOLA
GEOMETRIC CONSTRUCTIONS

DRAWN BY

FILE NO.

DRAWING
5-3

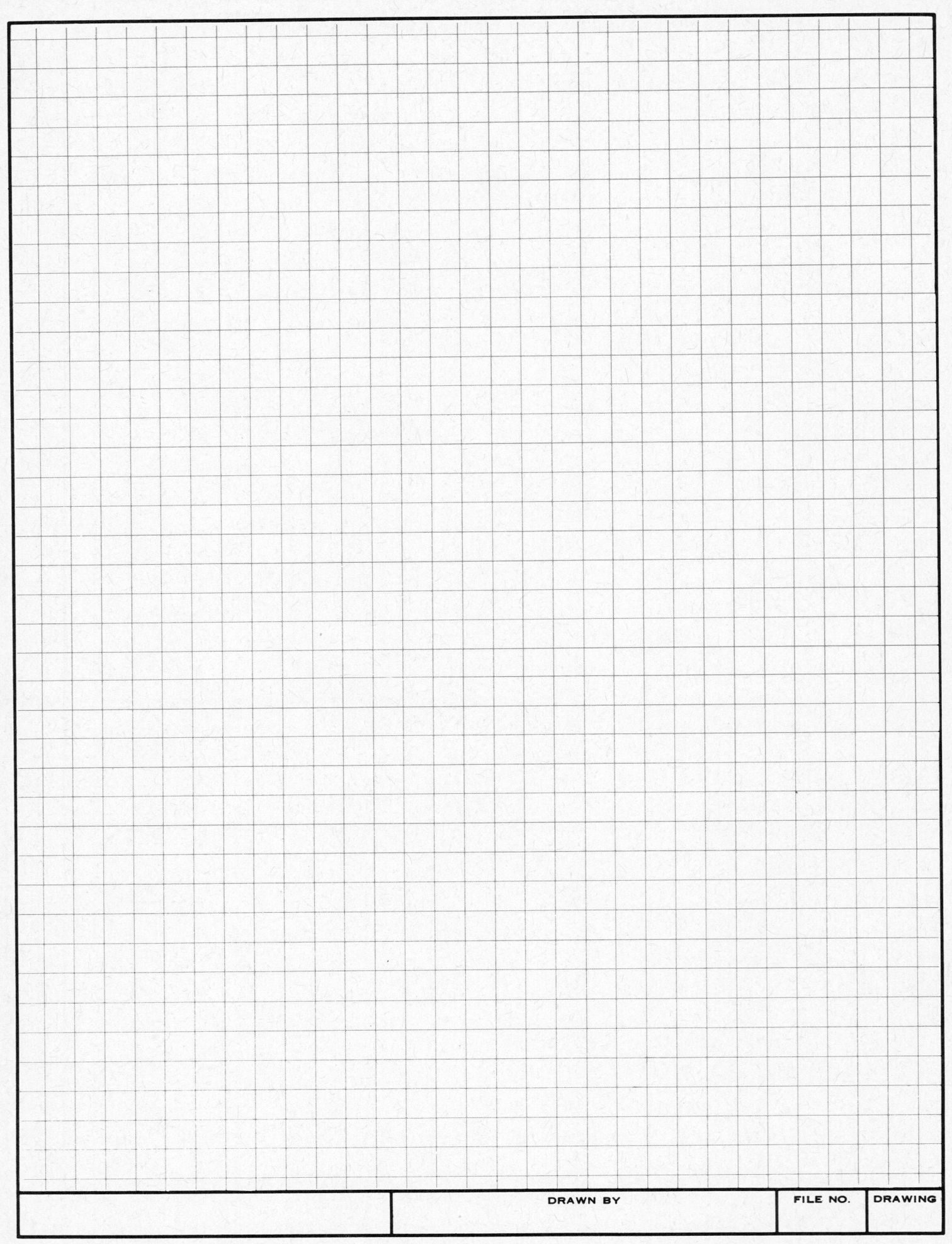

DRAWN BY   FILE NO.   DRAWING

SPECIAL BEARING

Make a full-size 6-view freehand sketch of the object, with the views in the standard arrangement. Label all views: FRONT, TOP, etc. Space the views two squares apart. Show all hidden lines and center lines.

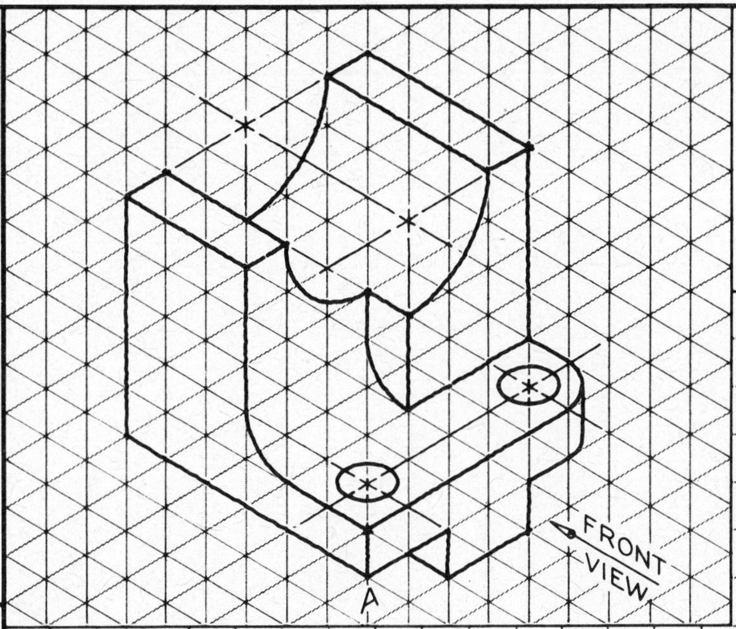

FRONT

A

FRONT
VIEW

A

The <u>necessary views</u>
for a complete shape
description are:

MULTIVIEW
TECHNICAL SKETCHING

DRAWN BY

FILE NO.

DRAWN BY   FILE NO.   DRAWING

1

BASE

Sketch front, top, and right-side views

2

BRACKET

Sketch isometric and complete the right side view

3

ANGLE BLOCK

Sketch isometric and complete the views

4

GUIDE

Sketch isometric and complete the views

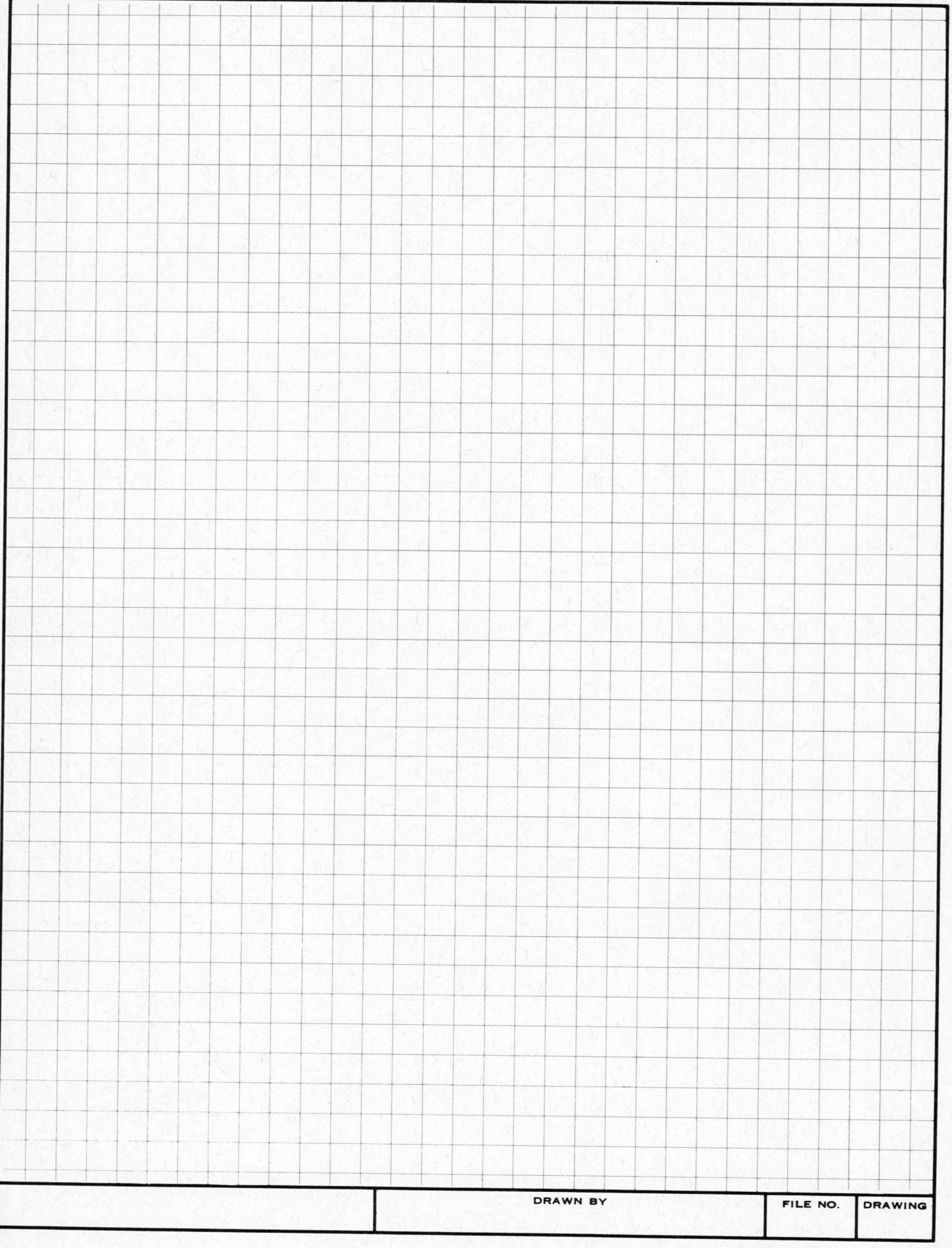

DRAWN BY

FILE NO.

DRAWING

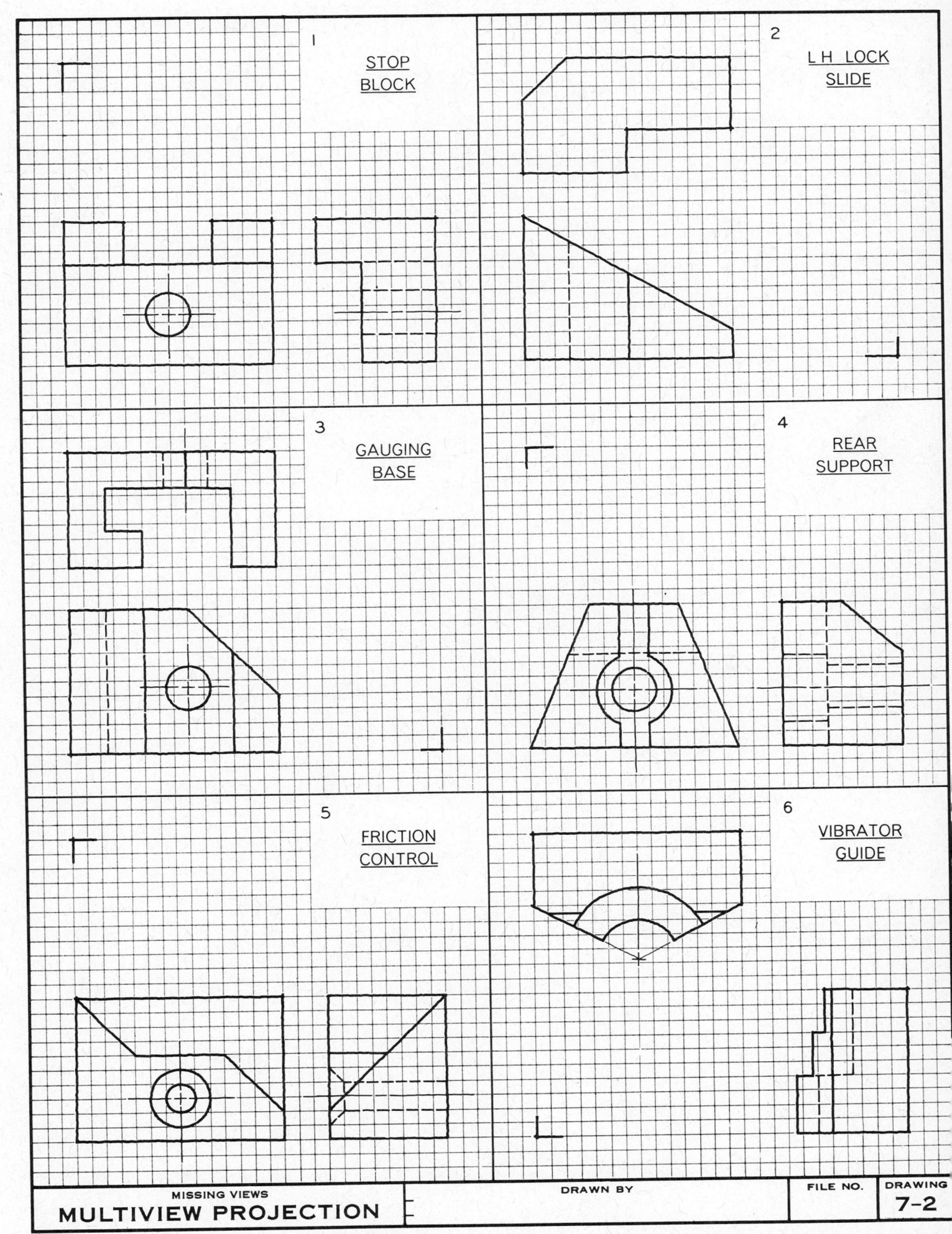

1	STOP BLOCK
2	L H LOCK SLIDE
3	GAUGING BASE
4	REAR SUPPORT
5	FRICTION CONTROL
6	VIBRATOR GUIDE

MISSING VIEWS

MULTIVIEW PROJECTION

DRAWN BY

FILE NO.

DRAWING

7-2

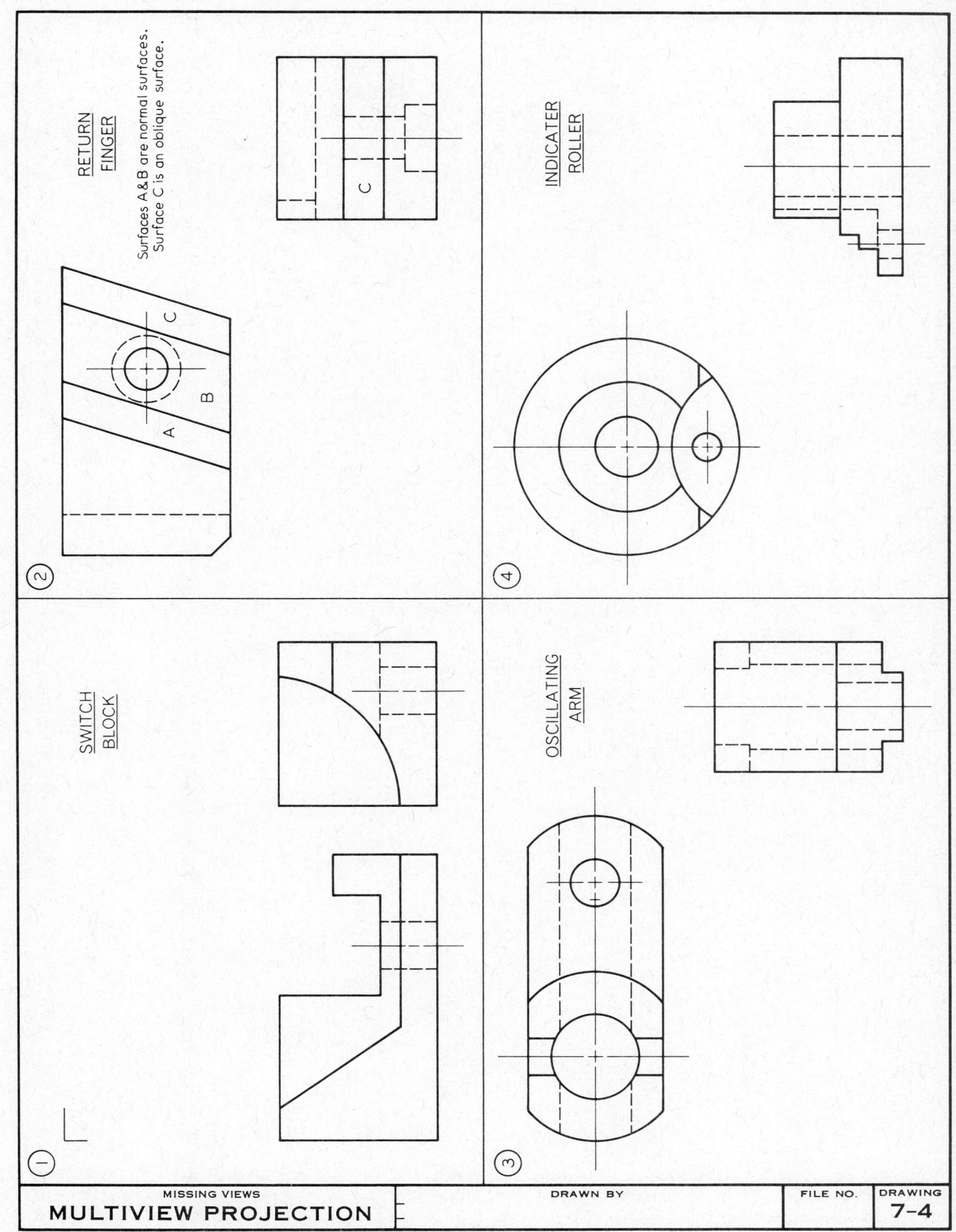

RETURN
FINGER

Surfaces A & B are normal surfaces.
Surface C is an oblique surface.

② C B A

INDICATER
ROLLER

④

SWITCH
BLOCK

①

OSCILLATING
ARM

③

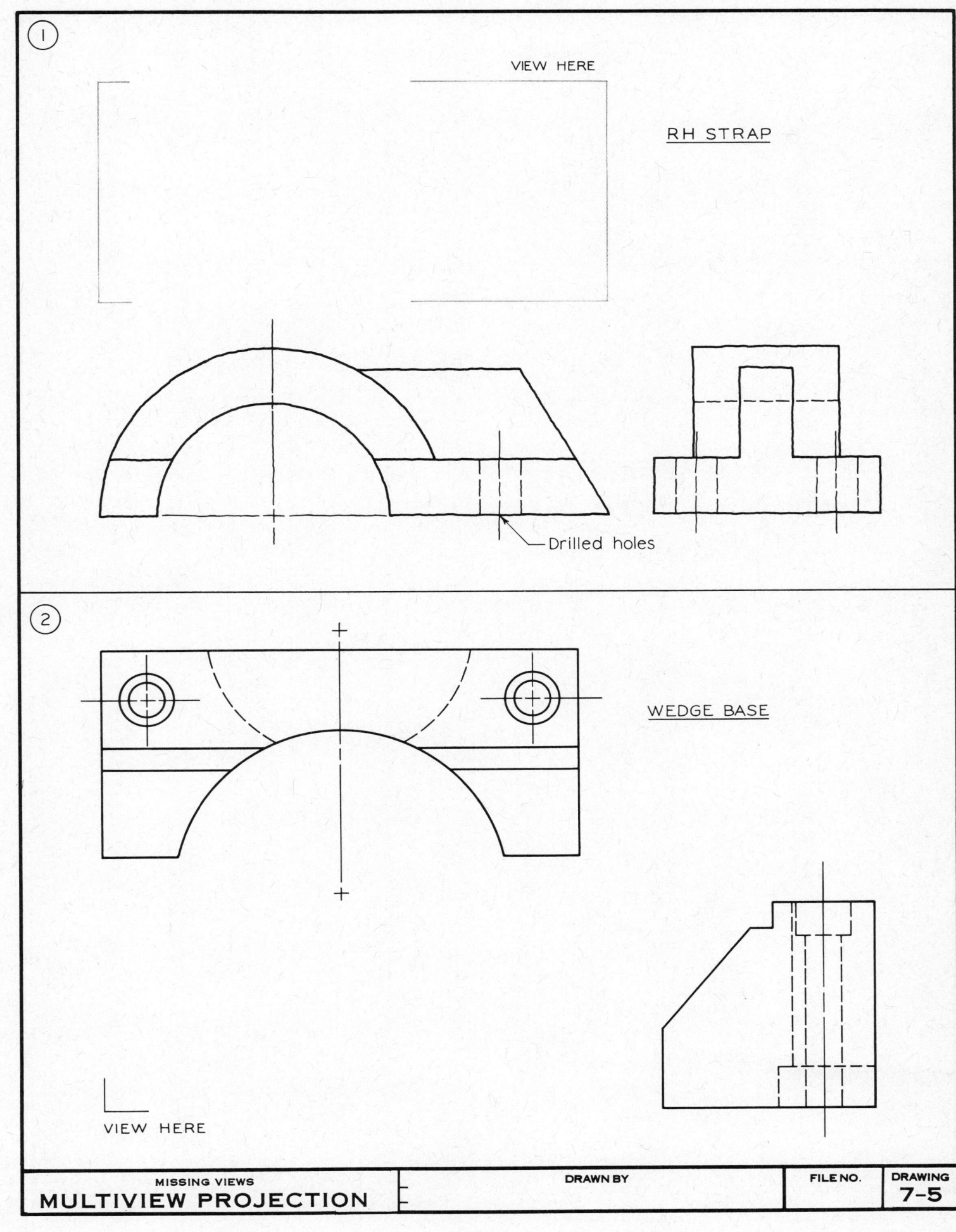

①

VIEW HERE

RH STRAP

Drilled holes

②

WEDGE BASE

VIEW HERE

DRAWN BY

FILE NO.

DRAWING

Complete the table of TERMS by entering the letter identifiers of the matching descriptions.

TERMS

Term	
CURSOR	
DIGITIZER TABLET	
GRAPHIC PRIMITIVE	
PIXEL	
RESOLUTION	
RASTER DISPLAY	
RAM	
DEBUG	
HARD COPY	
ANALOG	
DIGITAL	
CAE	
COMMAND	
PLOTTER	
HARD DISK	
VECTOR	
COORDINATE SYSTEM	
MENU	
BIT	
MOUSE	
SOFTWARE	
JOY STICK	
WINDOW	
TRANSFORM	
BYTE	
LIGHTPEN	

Descriptions

A   Handheld pointing device for pick and coordinate entry

B   Computer program to perform specific tasks

C   Counts in discrete steps or digits

D   Smallest unit of digital information

E   Collection of commands for selection

F   Device to convert analog picture to coordinate digital data

G   Fundamental drawing entity

H   Picture element dot in a display grid

I   Random Access Memory - volatile physical memory

J   Continuous measurements without steps

K   Computer assisted engineering

L   Group of 8 bits commonly used to represent a character

M   Paper printout

N   Hand controlled lever used as input device

O   Smallest spacing between CRT display elements

P   Convert an image into a proper display format

Q   Directed line segment with magnitude

R   Flicker-free scanned CRT surface

S   A bounded rectangular area on screen

T   A visual tracking symbol

U   Handheld photosensitive input device

V   Control signal

W   Correct errors

X   Non-volatile external storage device

Y   Hard copy device for vector drawing

Z   Common reference system for spatial relationships

① Complete the table by defining X and Y coordinates of the given points.

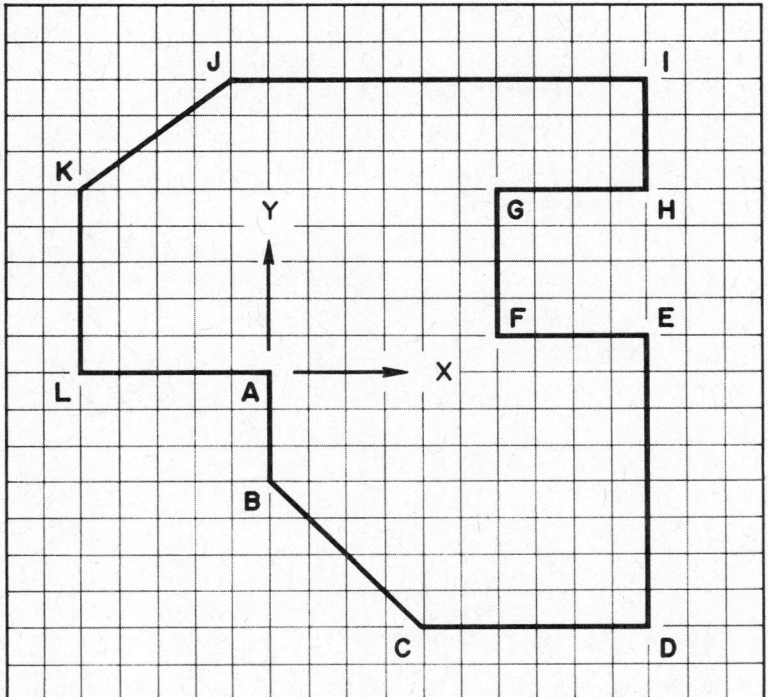

Point	Coordinate	
	X	Y
A		
B		
C		
D		
E		
F		
G		
H		
I		
J		
K		
L		

② Plot the given points on the grid and draw the view.

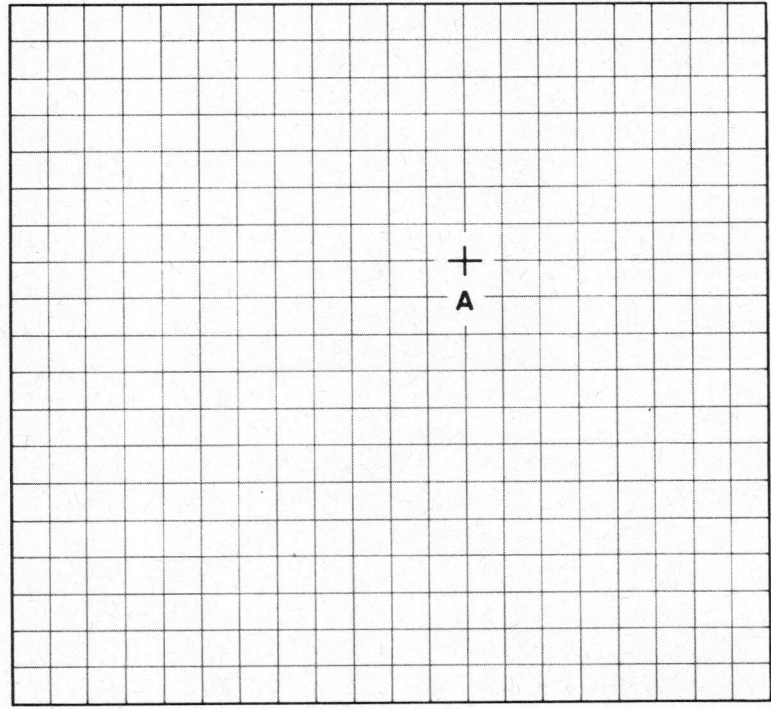

Point	Coordinate	
	X	Y
A	0	0
B	0	4
C	−5	4
D	−5	−2
E	−10	−6
F	−10	−10
G	−2	−10
H	6	−4
I	6	3
J	3	3
K	3	−2
L	0	−4

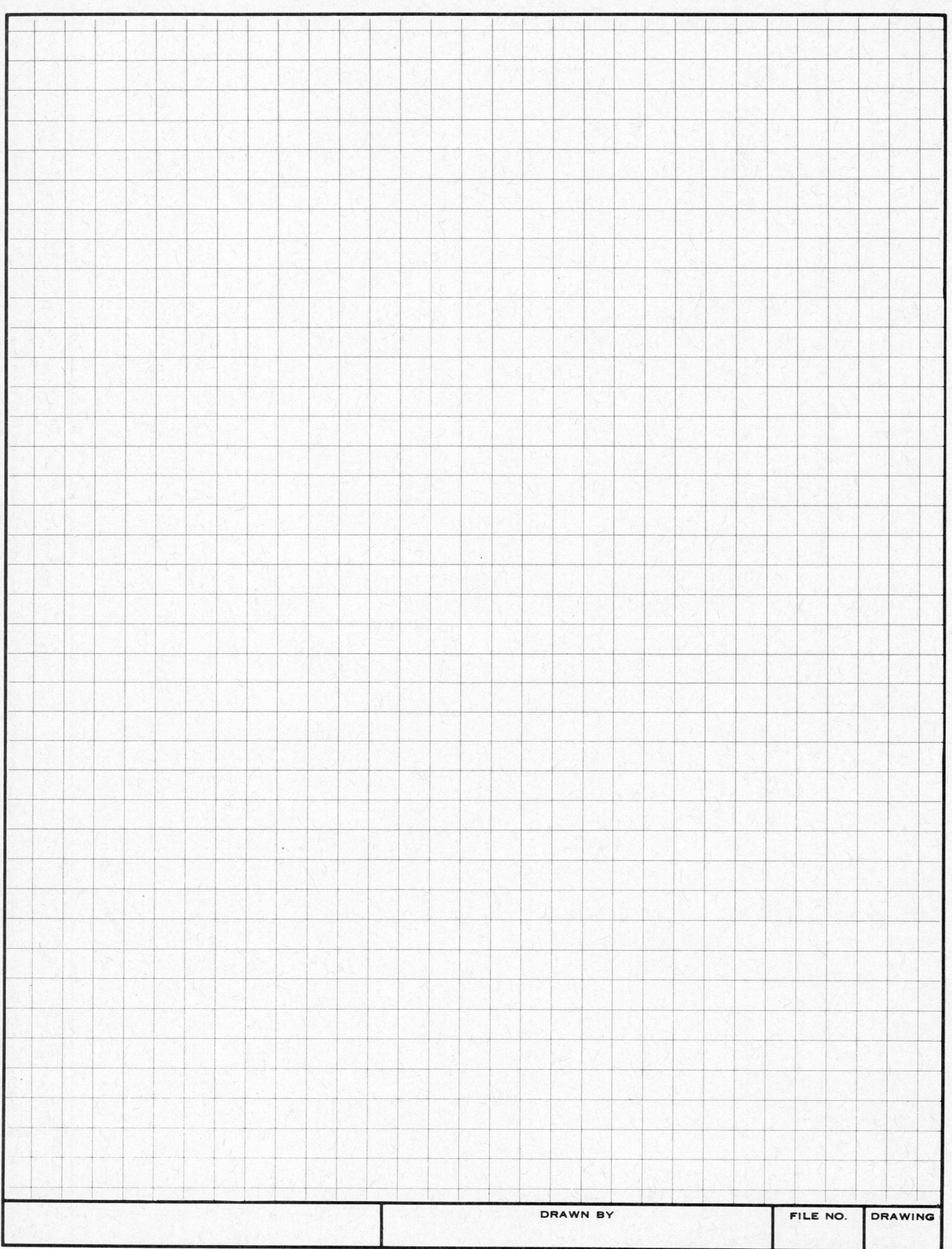

DRAWN BY   FILE NO.   DRAWING

① Complete the table for drawing the object.

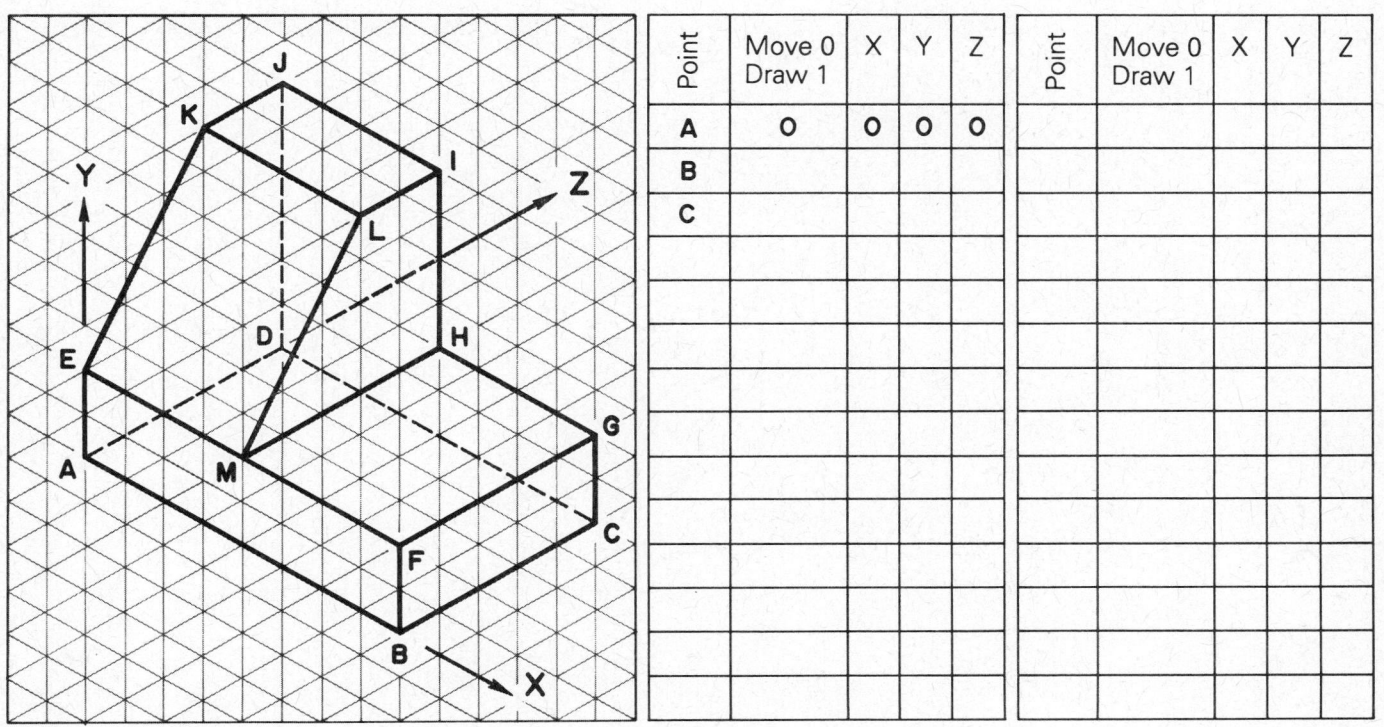

Point	Move 0 Draw 1	X	Y	Z	Point	Move 0 Draw 1	X	Y	Z
A	0	0	0	0					
B									
C									

② Draw the object based on the data given in the table.

Point	Move 0 Draw 1	X	Y	Z	Point	Move 0 Draw 1	X	Y	Z
A	0	0	0	0	G	1	-3	-4	0
B	1	0	5	0	J	1	-3	-4	5
C	1	0	5	5	L	0	-3	-1	0
D	1	0	0	5	B	1	0	5	0
E	1	6	0	5	K	0	-3	-1	5
F	1	6	0	0	C	1	0	5	5
A	1	0	0	0	H	0	0	-4	0
D	1	0	0	5	F	1	6	0	0
G	0	-3	-4	0	I	0	0	-4	5
L	1	-3	-1	0	E	1	6	0	5
K	1	-3	-1	5					
J	1	-3	-4	5					
I	1	0	-4	5					
H	1	0	-4	0					

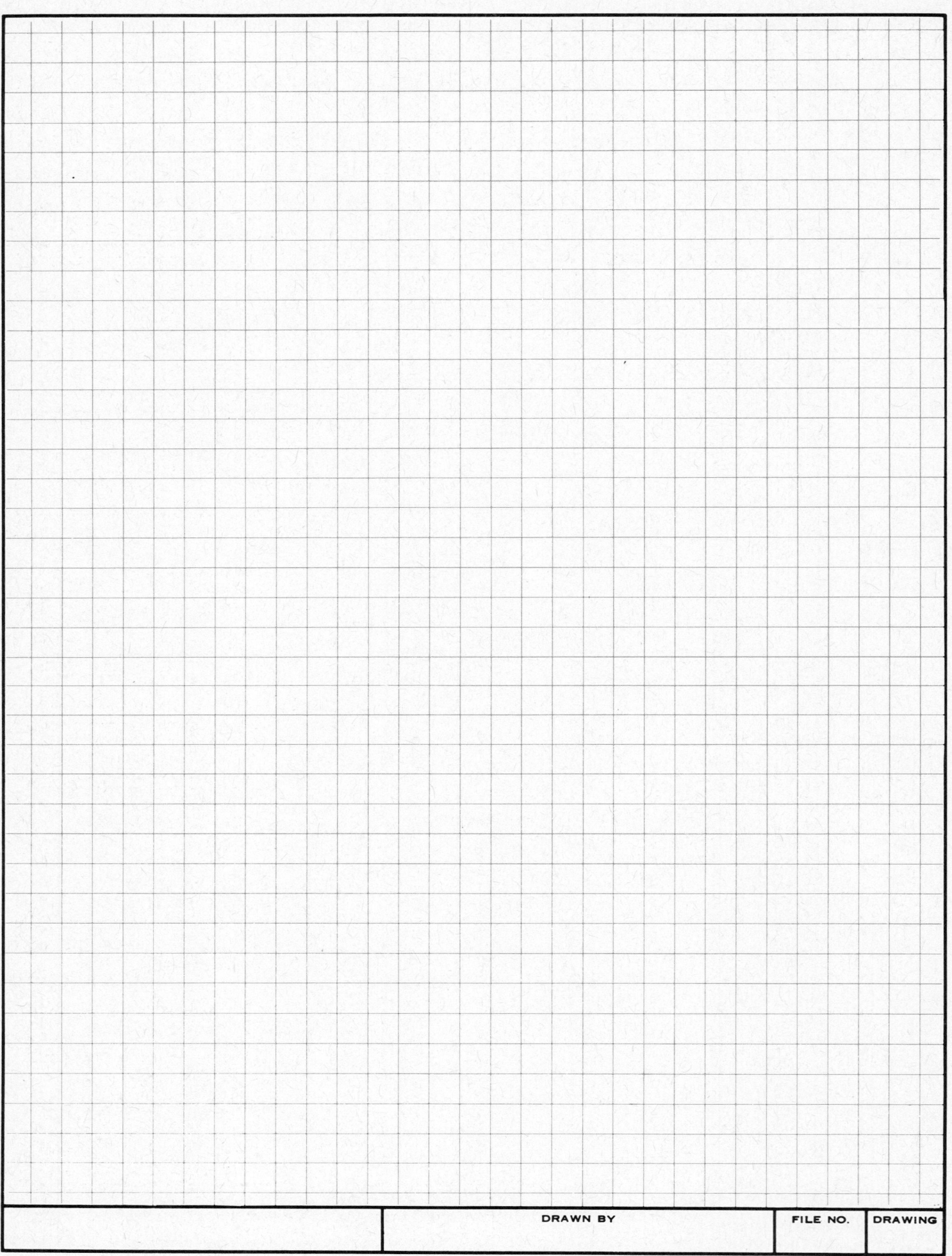

DRAWN BY

FILE NO.

DRAWING

Complete the table by entering the Menu Selections used for generating the drawing.

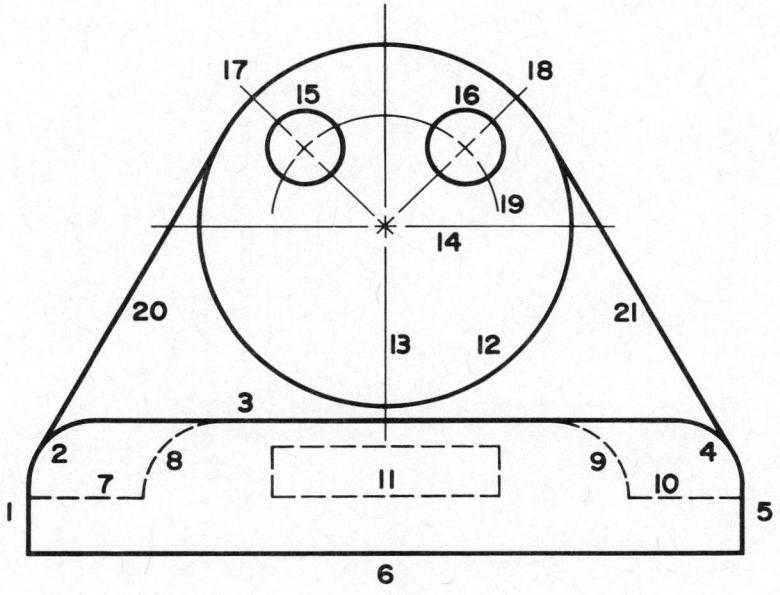

LINE TYPE MENU

A Visible
────────────

B Hidden
– – – – – – – –

C Center
──── ── ── ────

ENTITY MENU

I Line
────────────

J Circle ⭕

K Arc ◜

L Rectangle ▭

M Tangent Line

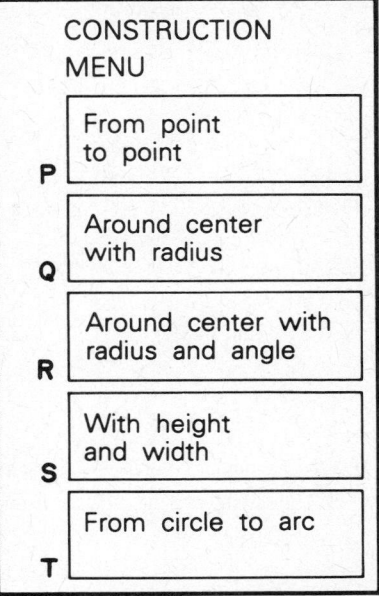

CONSTRUCTION MENU

P From point to point

Q Around center with radius

R Around center with radius and angle

S With height and width

T From circle to arc

Entity	Line type menu selection	Entity menu selection	Construction menu selection
1			
2			
3			
4			
5			
6			
7			
8			
9			
10			
11			
12			
13			
14			
15			
16			
17			
18			
19			
20			
21			

MENU USAGE
COMPUTER-AIDED DRAFTING

DRAWN BY

FILE NO.

DRAWING
8-4

Description of VIEW COORDINATES

VIEW COORDINATES are the coordinate values of the object as assigned with respect to the computer screen, with X , Y and Z axes positioned as shown below . The coordinates remain the same irrespective of the view selected on the screen .

Axis	Position	Positive Direction
X	Horizontal	To the right
Y	Vertical	Toward the top
Z	Perpendicular to the screen	Outward from the screen

Description of WORLD COORDINATES

WORLD COORDINATES are the coordinate values of the object as assigned with respect to the axes of the object . The X , Y and Z axes are positioned as shown, such that for the top view the X axis is horizontal to the right, the Y axis is vertical to the top and the Z axis is perpendicular to the screen positioned outwards . The coordinates in relation to the screen change according to the view selected on the screen.

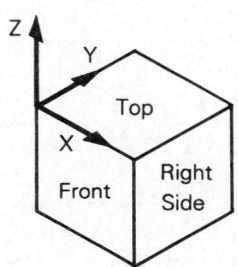

Complete the tables by entering the VIEW and WORLD COORDINATES of the given points of the object .

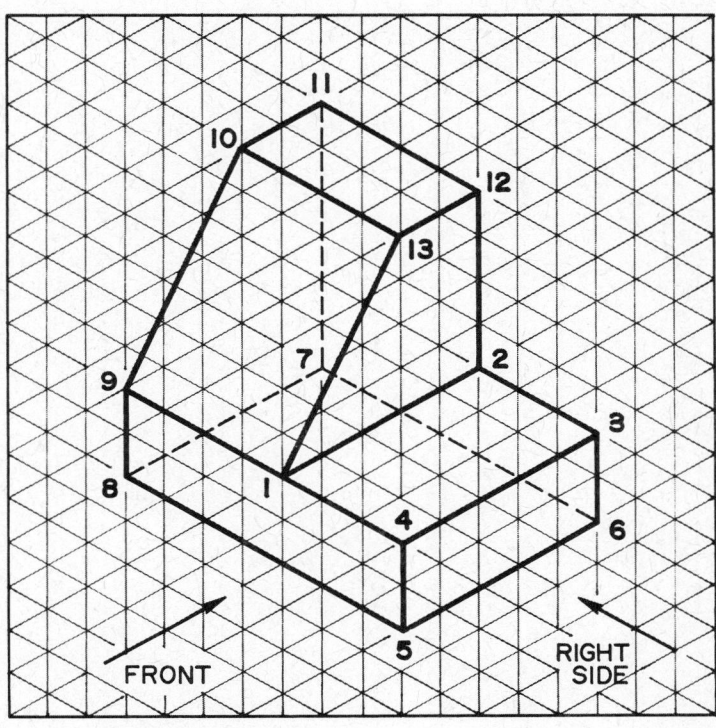

Points	View Coordinates			World Coordinates		
	X	Y	Z	X	Y	Z
FRONT VIEW						
1						
2						
3						
4						
5						
6						
7						
8						
9						
10						
11						
12						
13						

Points	View Coordinates			World Coordinates		
	X	Y	Z	X	Y	Z
RIGHT SIDE VIEW						
1						
2						
3						
4						
5						
6						
7						
8						
9						
10						
11						
12						
13						

DRAWN BY   FILE NO.   DRAWING

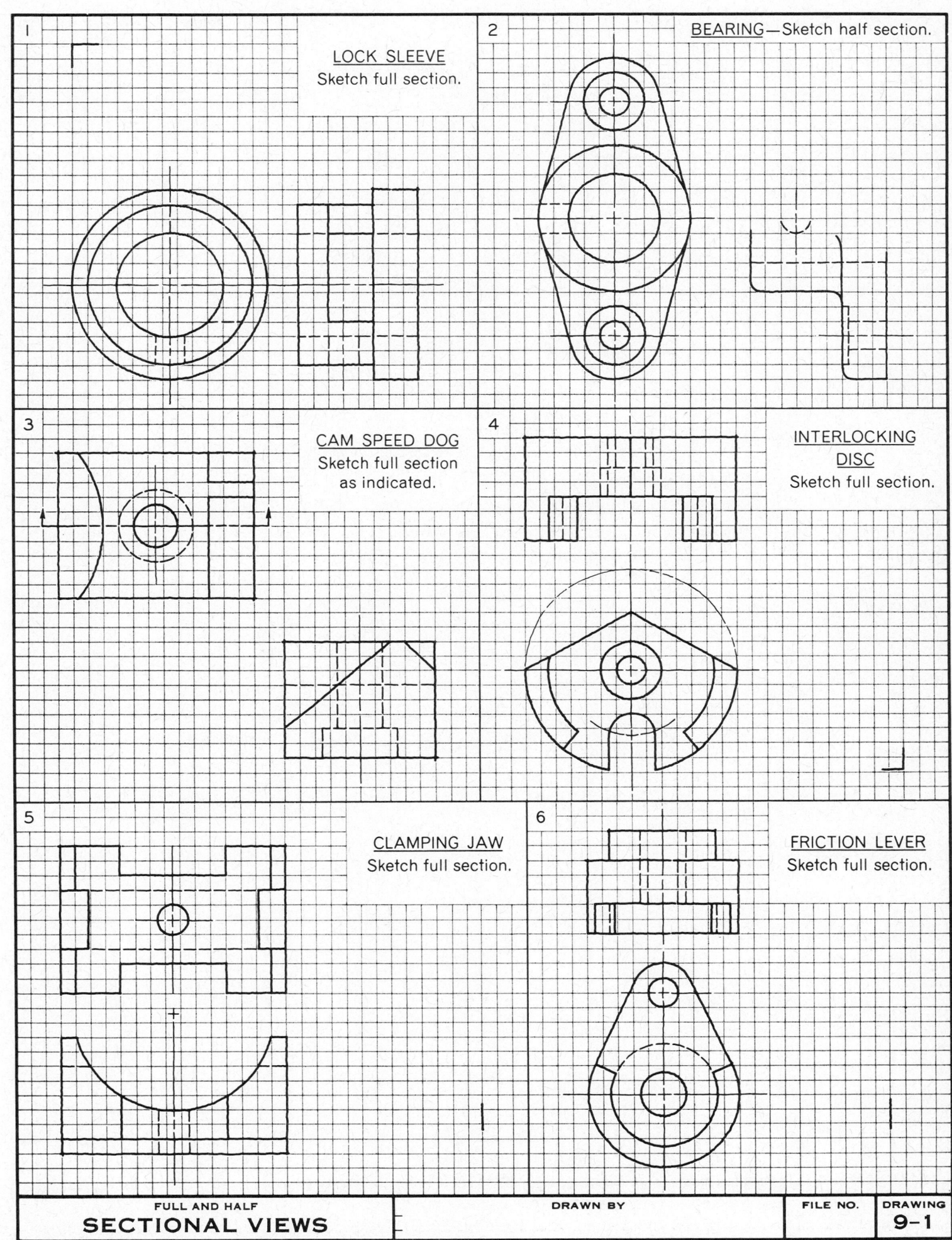

1 LOCK SLEEVE
Sketch full section.

2 BEARING—Sketch half section.

3 CAM SPEED DOG
Sketch full section
as indicated.

4 INTERLOCKING
DISC
Sketch full section.

5 CLAMPING JAW
Sketch full section.

6 FRICTION LEVER
Sketch full section.

FULL AND HALF
SECTIONAL VIEWS

DRAWN BY

FILE NO.

DRAWING
9-1

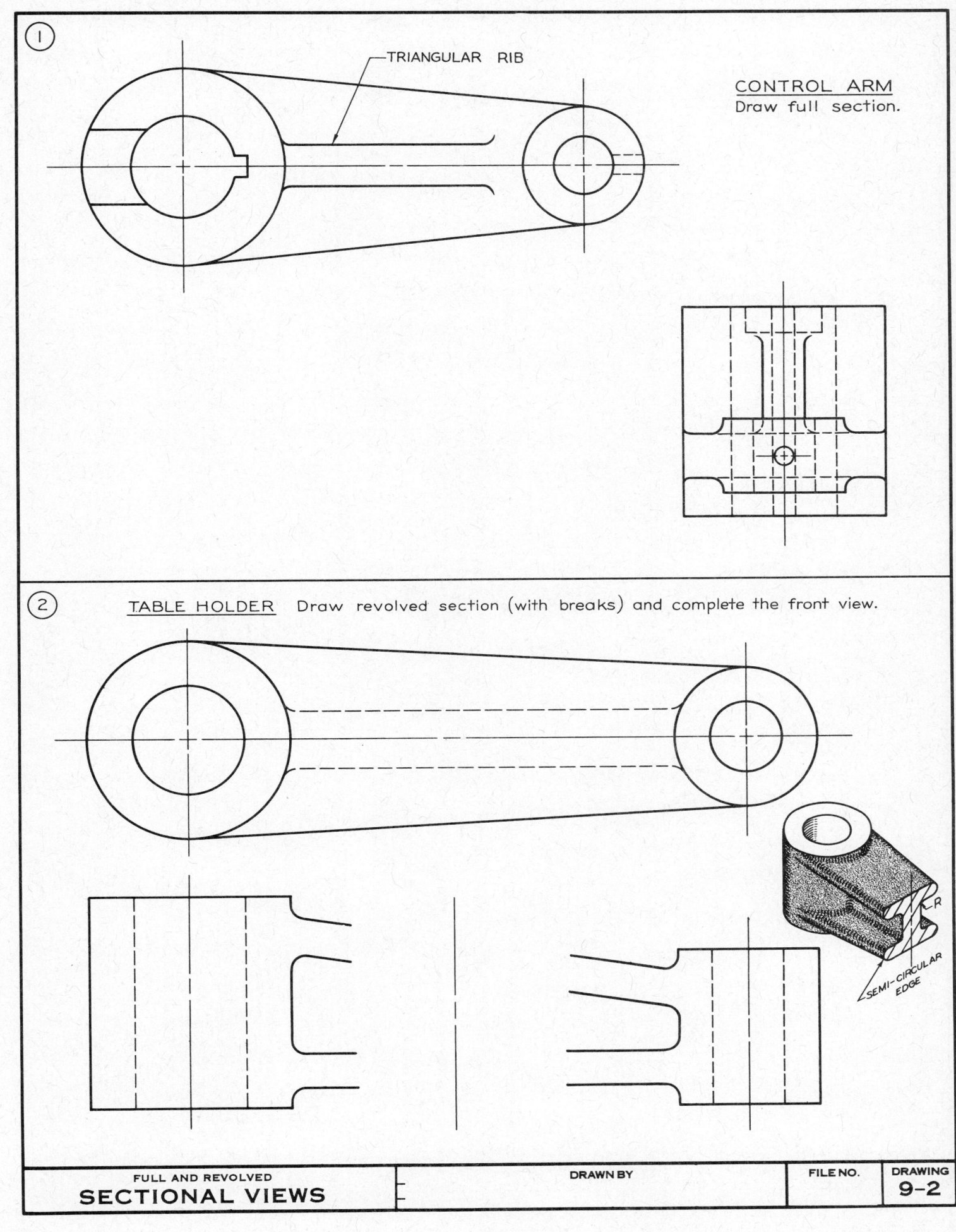

1. TRIANGULAR RIB

CONTROL ARM
Draw full section.

2. TABLE HOLDER   Draw revolved section (with breaks) and complete the front view.

R

SEMI-CIRCULAR EDGE

| FULL AND REVOLVED SECTIONAL VIEWS | DRAWN BY | FILE NO. | DRAWING 9-2 |

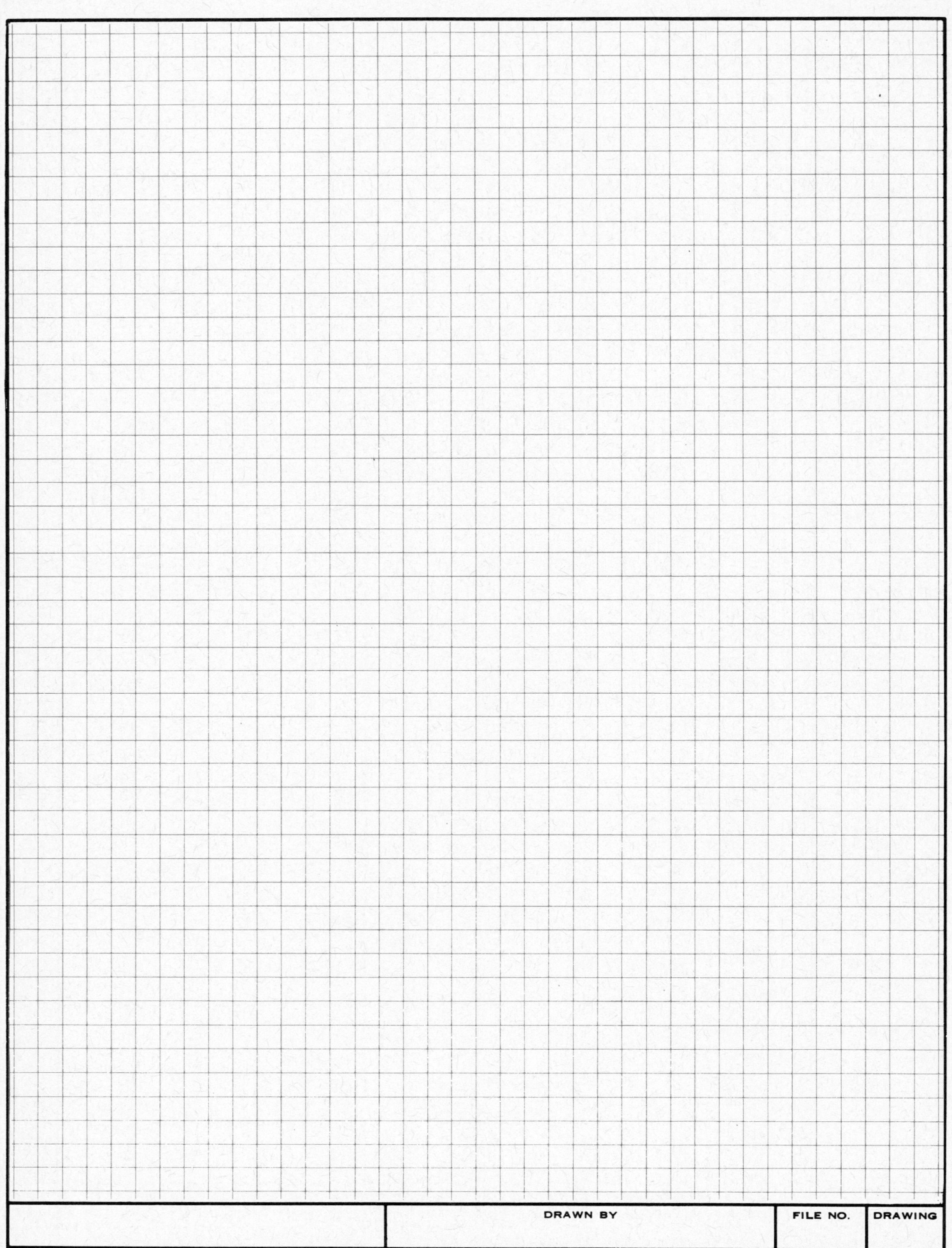

DRAWN BY

FILE NO.

DRAWING

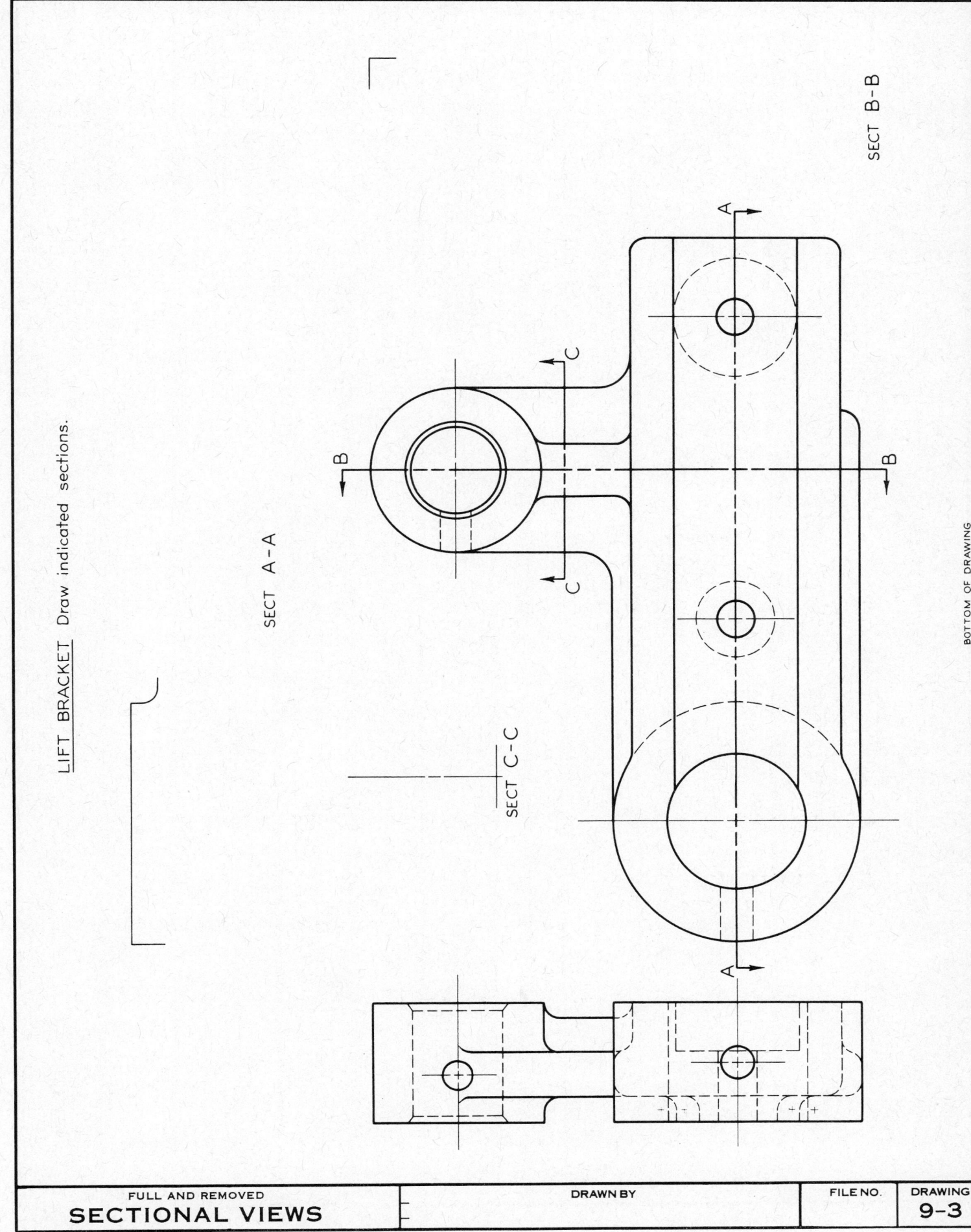

LIFT BRACKET Draw indicated sections.

SECT A-A

SECT B-B

SECT C-C

BOTTOM OF DRAWING

DRAWN BY

FILE NO.

DRAWING

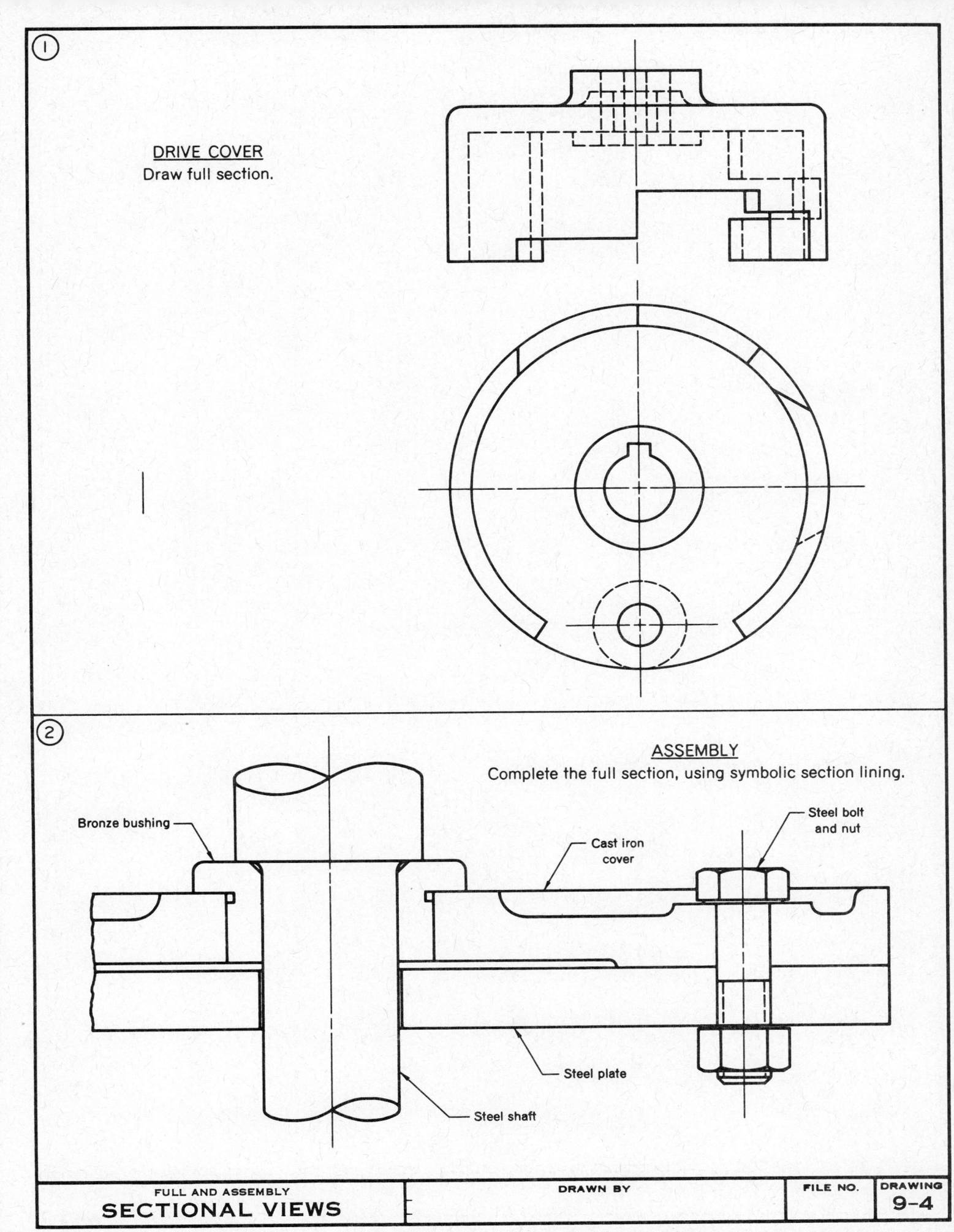

① **DRIVE COVER**
Draw full section.

② **ASSEMBLY**
Complete the full section, using symbolic section lining.

Bronze bushing

Steel bolt
and nut

Cast iron
cover

Steel plate

Steel shaft

FULL AND ASSEMBLY
SECTIONAL VIEWS

DRAWN BY

FILE NO.

DRAWING
9-4

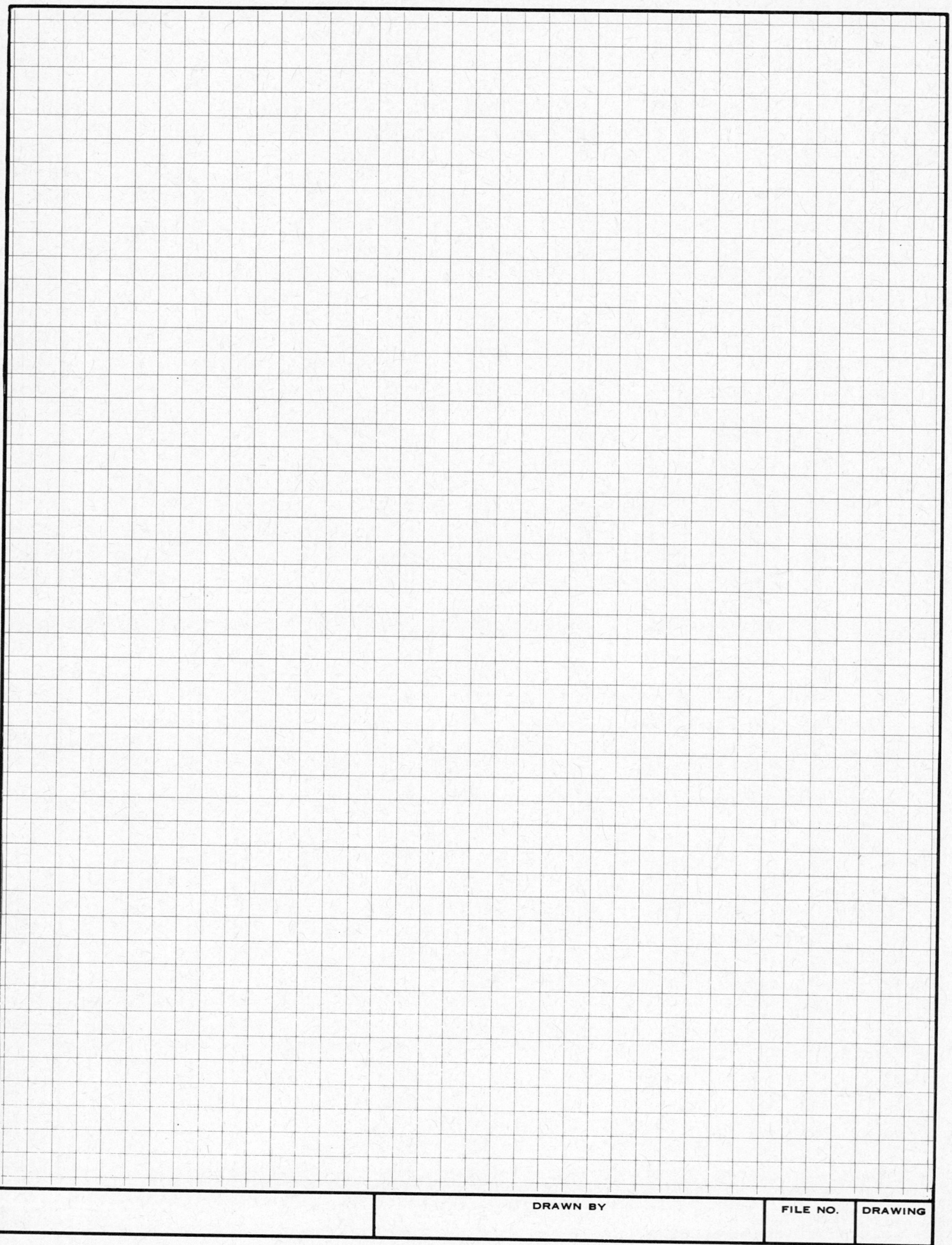

DRAWN BY   FILE NO.   DRAWING

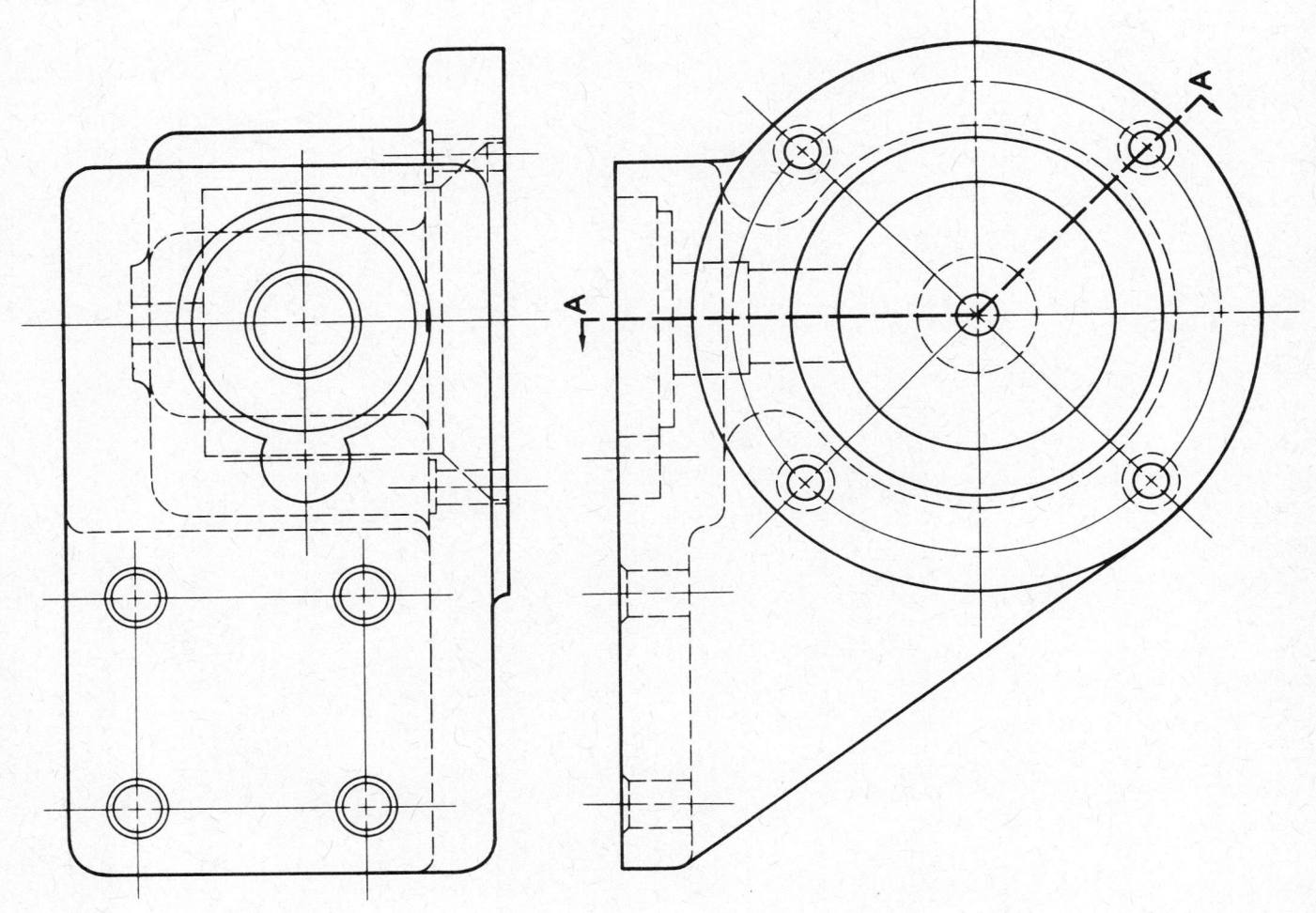

TIMER HOUSING
Draw Section A-A.

A

A

BOTTOM OF DRAWING

ALIGNED
SECTIONAL VIEW

DRAWN BY

FILE NO.

DRAWING
9-5

DRAWN BY

FILE NO.

DRAWING

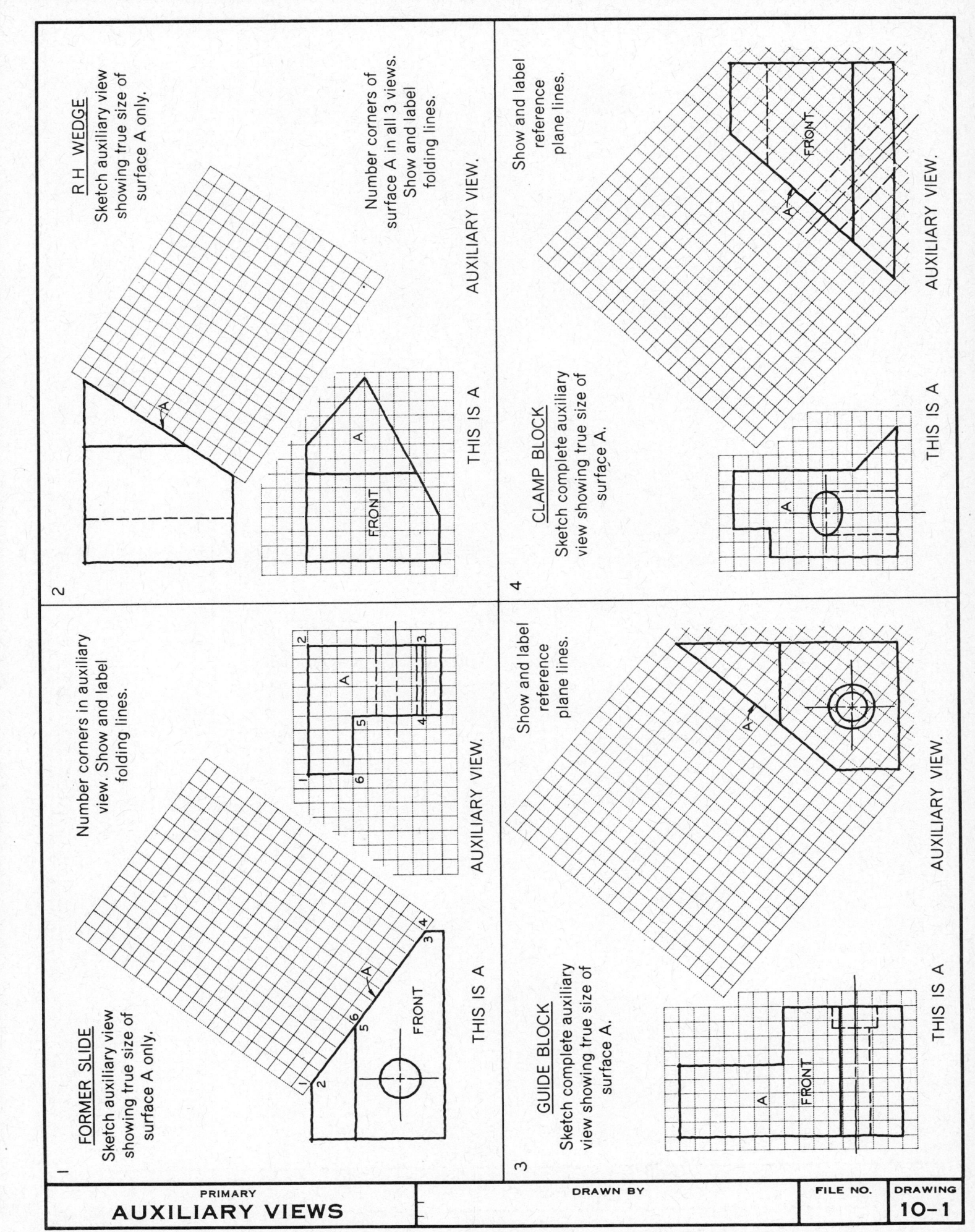

2

<u>R H WEDGE</u>
Sketch auxiliary view showing true size of surface A only.

Number corners of surface A in all 3 views. Show and label folding lines.

AUXILIARY VIEW.

THIS IS A

FRONT

A

4

Show and label reference plane lines.

FRONT

A

AUXILIARY VIEW.

<u>CLAMP BLOCK</u>
Sketch complete auxiliary view showing true size of surface A.

THIS IS A

A

1

<u>FORMER SLIDE</u>
Sketch auxiliary view showing true size of surface A only.

Number corners in auxiliary view. Show and label folding lines.

A

AUXILIARY VIEW.

FRONT

A

THIS IS A

3

Show and label reference plane lines.

A'

AUXILIARY VIEW.

<u>GUIDE BLOCK</u>
Sketch complete auxiliary view showing true size of surface A.

A

FRONT

THIS IS A

PRIMARY
AUXILIARY VIEWS

DRAWN BY

FILE NO.

DRAWING

10-1

DRAWN BY   FILE NO.   DRAWING

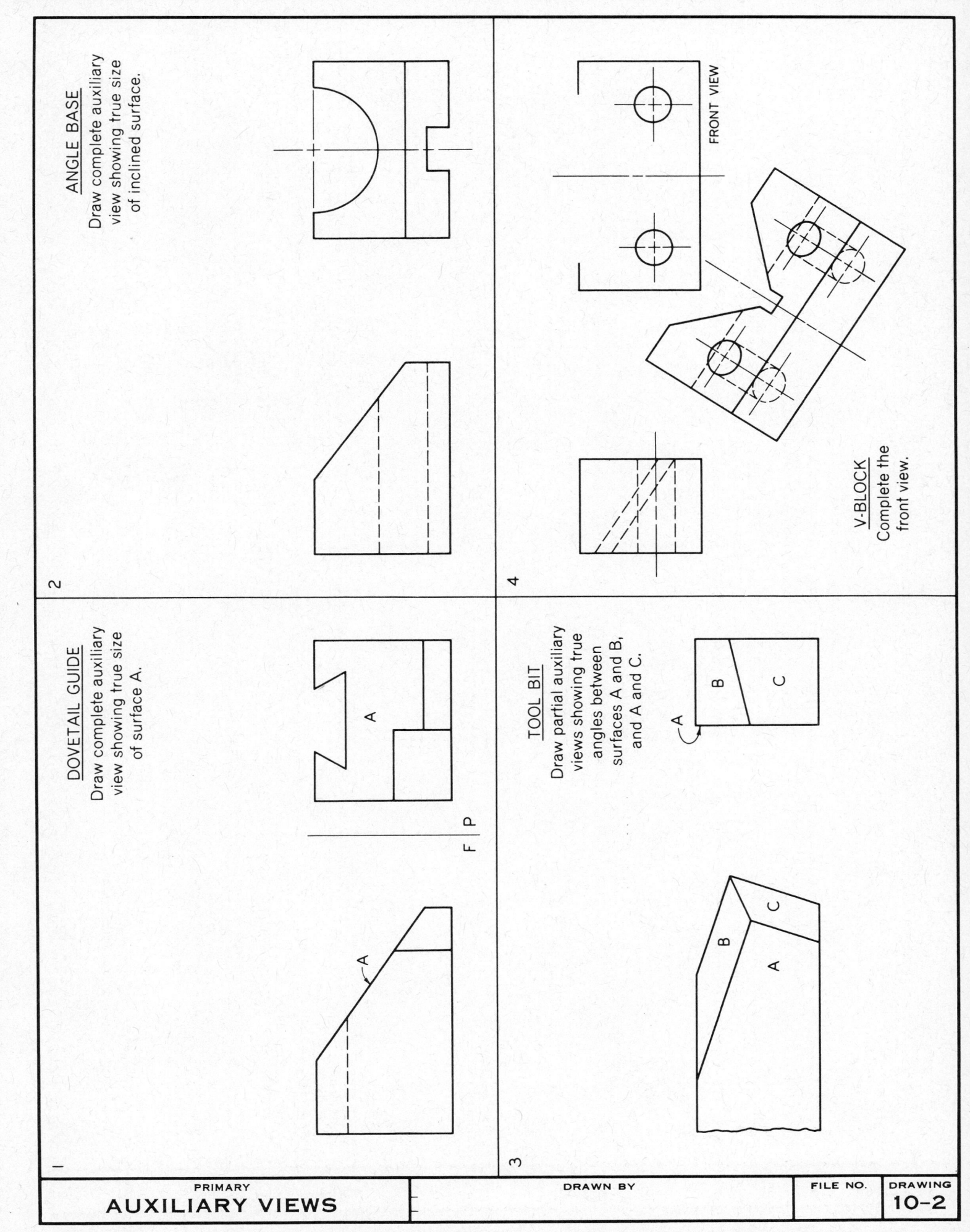

ANGLE BASE
Draw complete auxiliary view showing true size of inclined surface.

2

DOVETAIL GUIDE
Draw complete auxiliary view showing true size of surface A.

A

F P

1

TOOL BIT
Draw partial auxiliary views showing true angles between surfaces A and B, and A and C.

A
B
C

3

V-BLOCK
Complete the front view.

FRONT VIEW

4

PRIMARY
AUXILIARY VIEWS

DRAWN BY

FILE NO.

DRAWING
10-2

DRAWN BY · FILE NO. · DRAWING

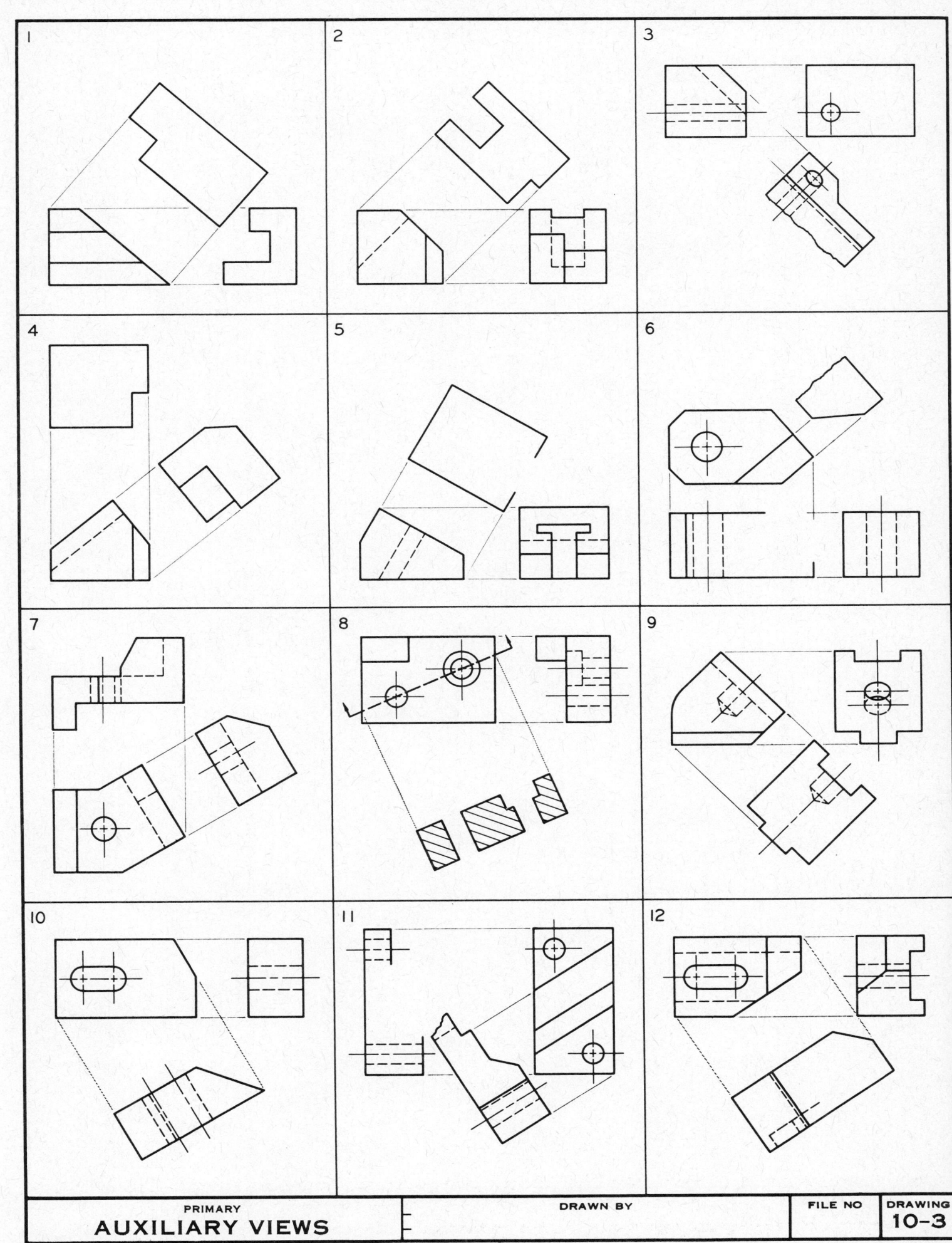

PRIMARY
AUXILIARY VIEWS

DRAWN BY

FILE NO

DRAWING
10-3

DRAWN BY

FILE NO.

DRAWING

1

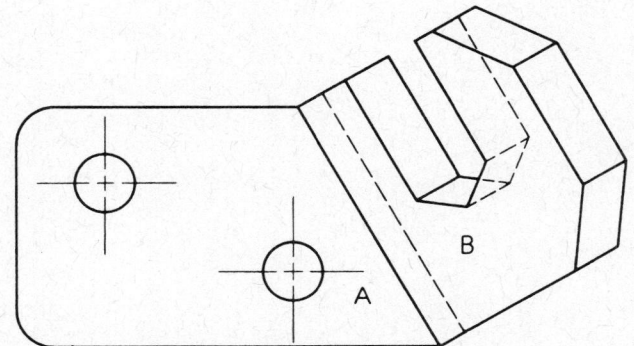

ANGLE BRACKET
Draw complete primary auxiliary view showing 135° angle between surfaces A and B; then draw partial secondary auxiliary view showing true size of member B. Thickness of members–10mm.

2

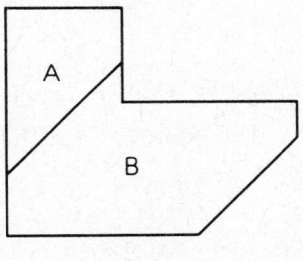

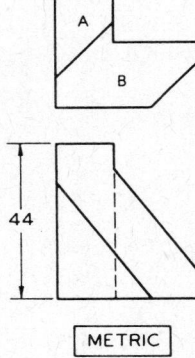

44

METRIC

STOP BLOCK
Draw complete primary auxiliary view showing angle between surfaces A and B; then draw complete secondary auxiliary view showing true size of surface B.

SECONDARY
AUXILIARY VIEWS

DRAWN BY

FILE NO.

DRAWING
10-4

DRAWN BY

FILE NO.

DRAWING

1

REGULATOR BLOCK

Revolve surface A
until it appears true
size in the top view.
Revolve surface B
until it appears true
size in the front view.

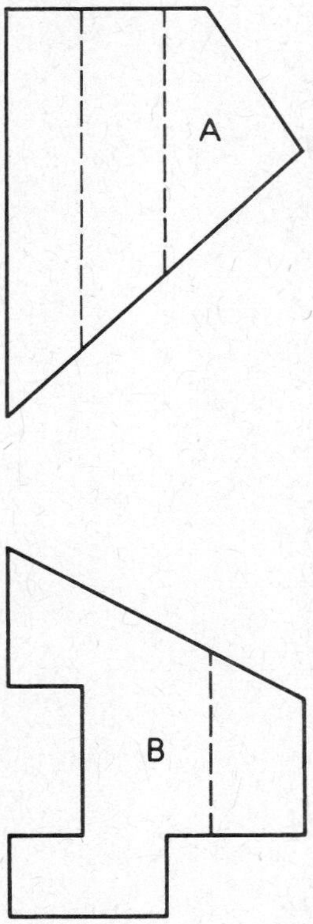

A

B

2

BEVEL CLAMP

Find true size of surface
A by means of an
auxiliary view showing
the edge view of the
surface; then by revolution
obtain true size in
front view.

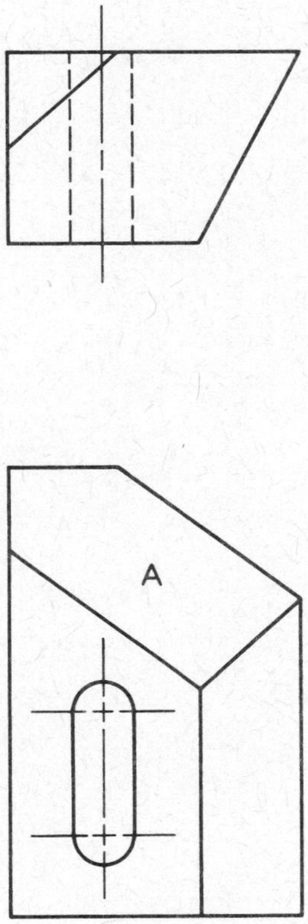

A

3

TRIP LEVER

Draw Section A-A
showing inclined
arm revolved.

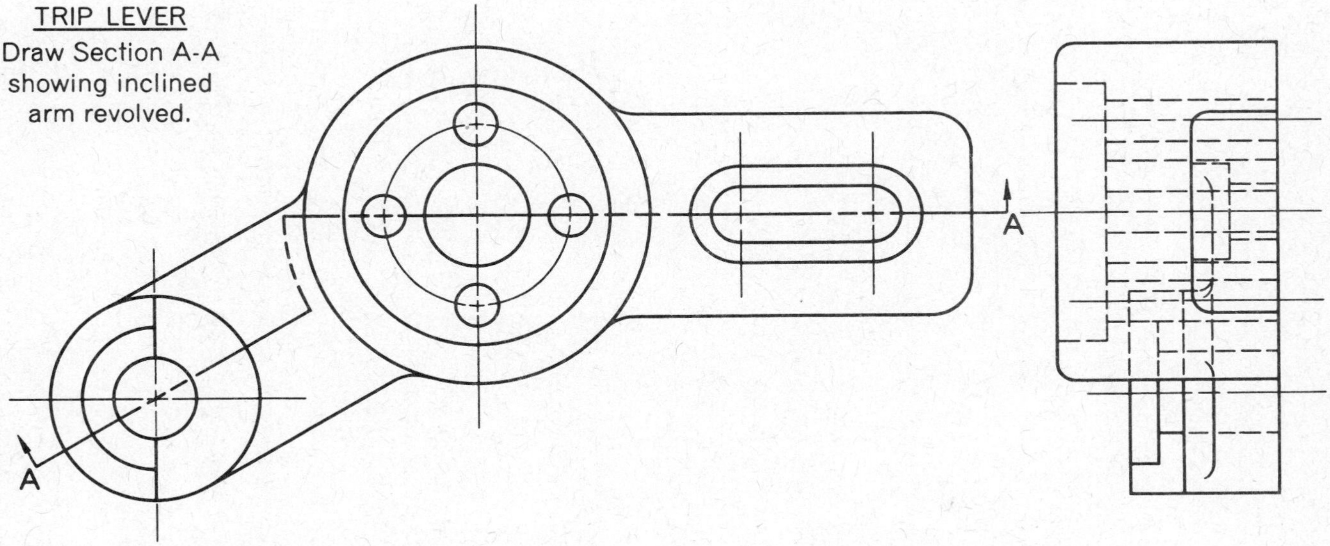

A

A

	DRAWN BY	FILE NO.	DRAWING
PRIMARY **REVOLUTIONS**			11–1

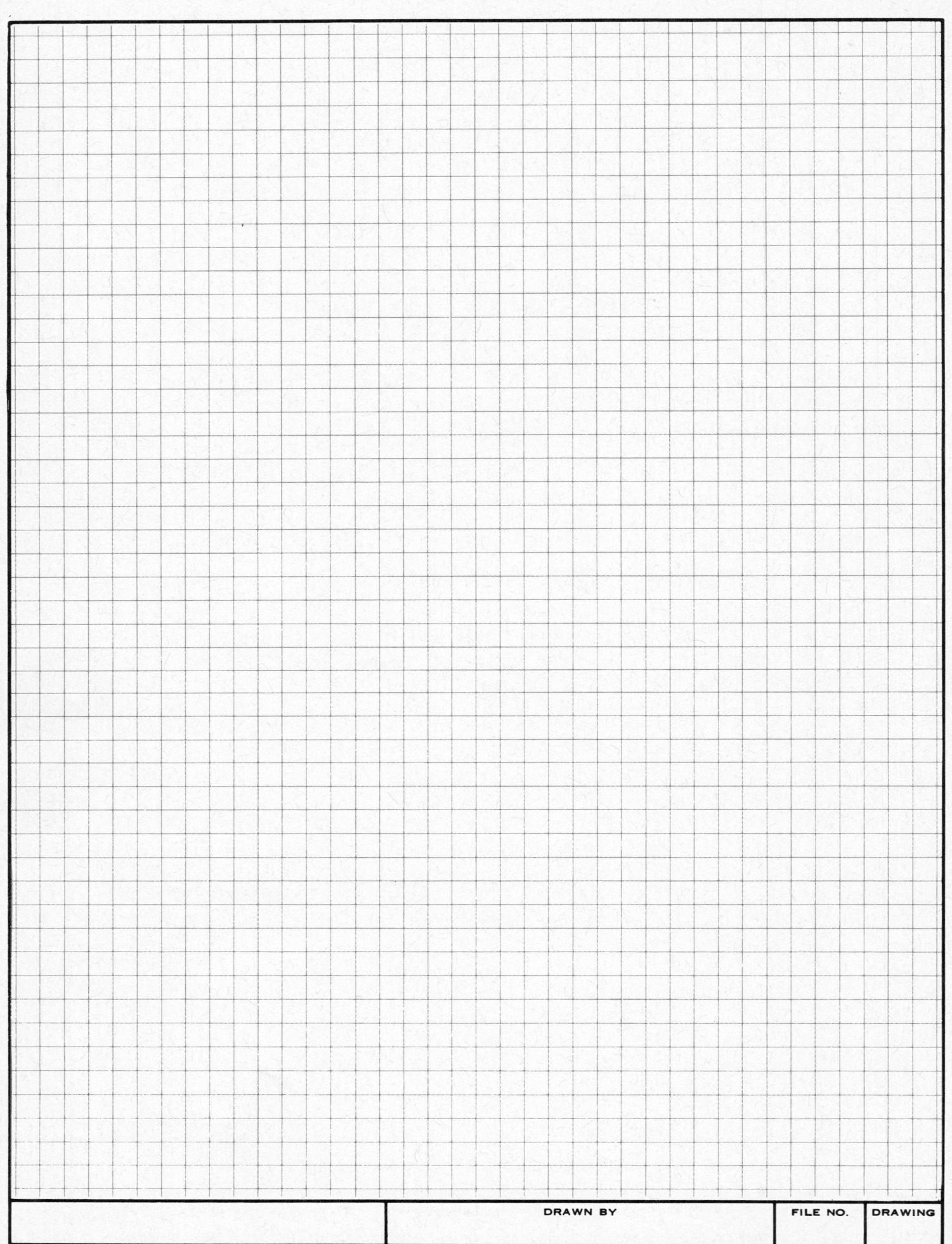

DRAWN BY | FILE NO. | DRAWING

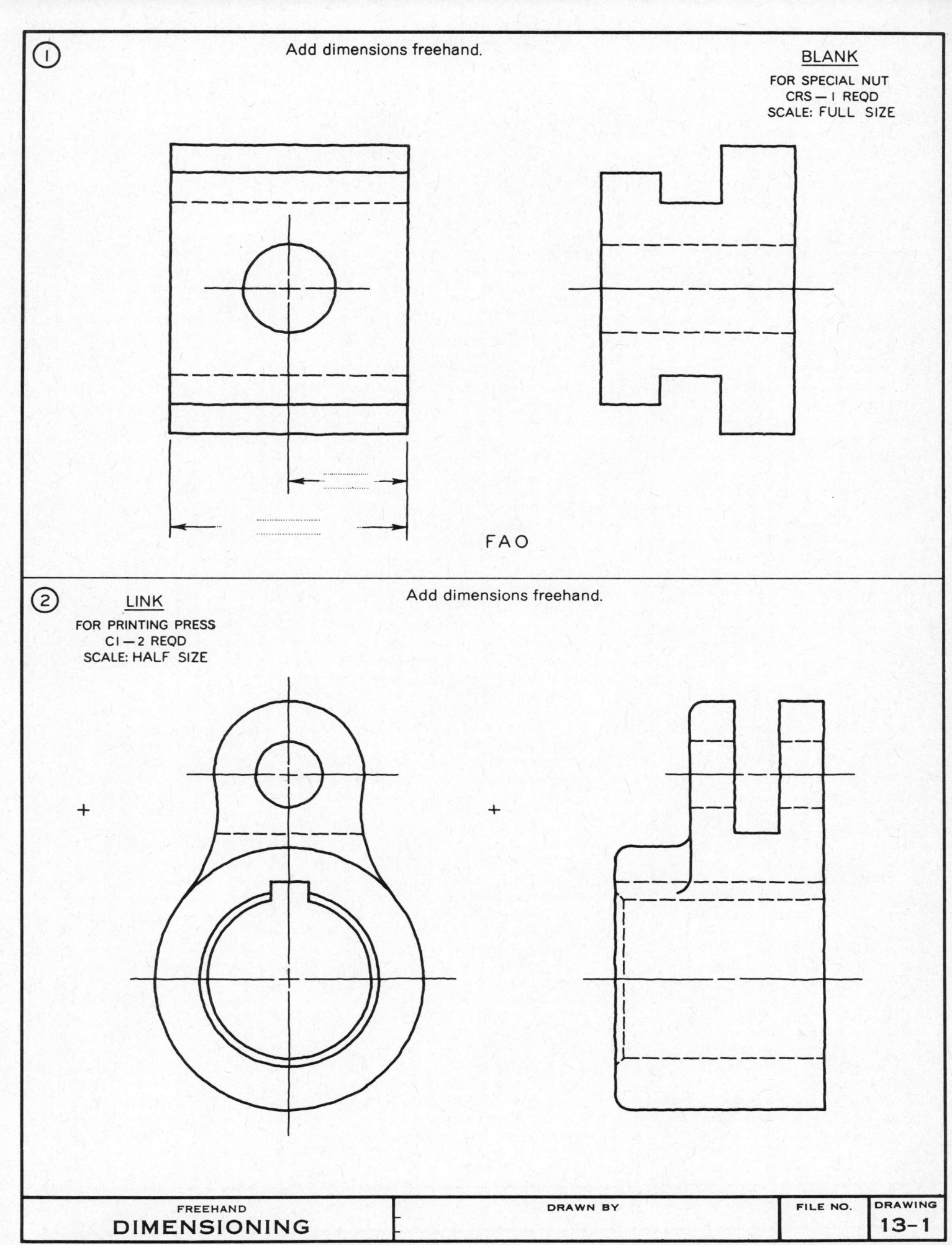

① Add dimensions freehand.

BLANK
FOR SPECIAL NUT
CRS — 1 REQD
SCALE: FULL SIZE

FAO

② LINK

FOR PRINTING PRESS
CI — 2 REQD
SCALE: HALF SIZE

Add dimensions freehand.

FREEHAND		DRAWN BY	FILE NO.	DRAWING
DIMENSIONING				13-1

DRAWN BY

FILE NO.

DRAWING

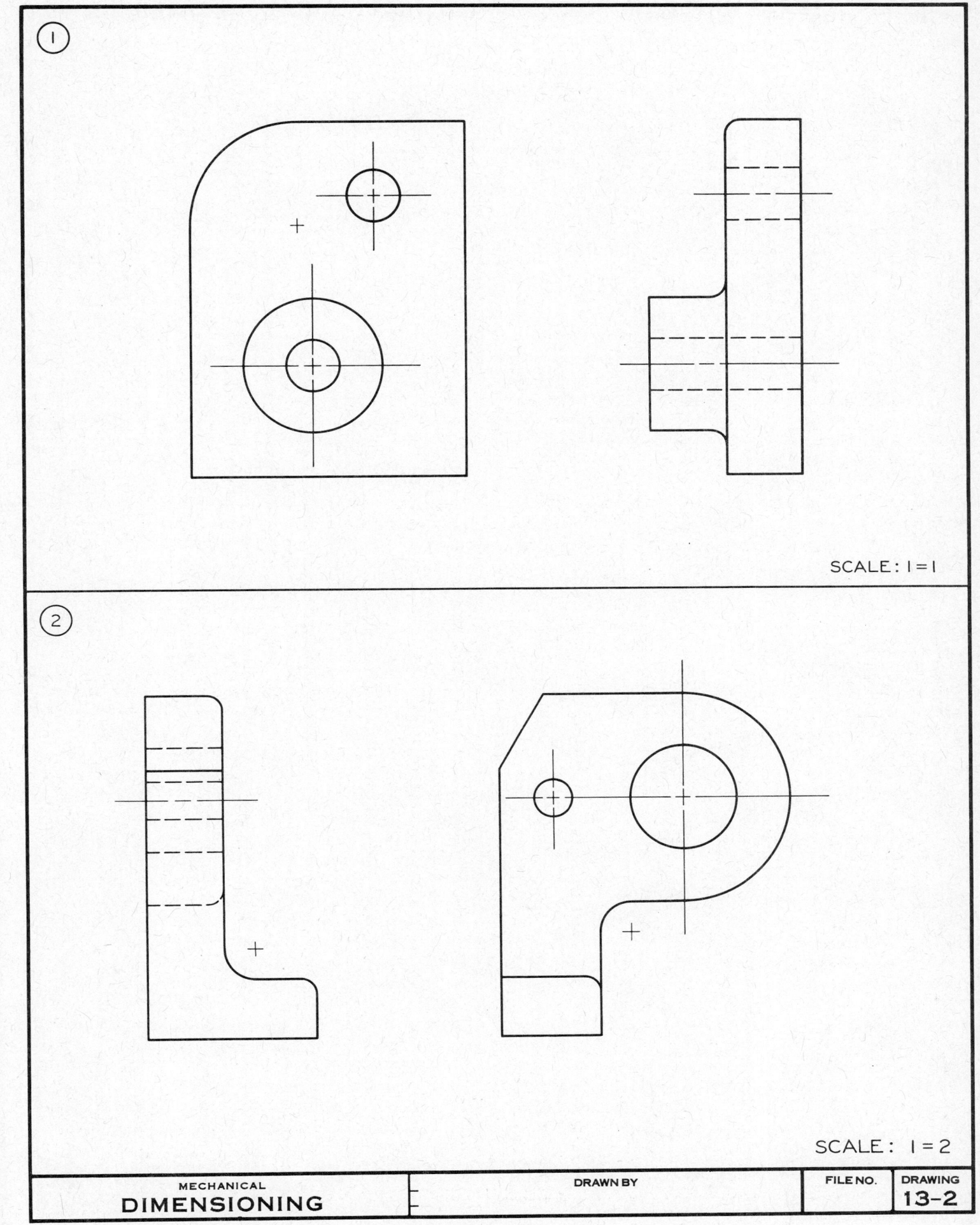

1

SCALE : 1=1

2

SCALE : 1 = 2

DRAWN BY · FILE NO. · DRAWING

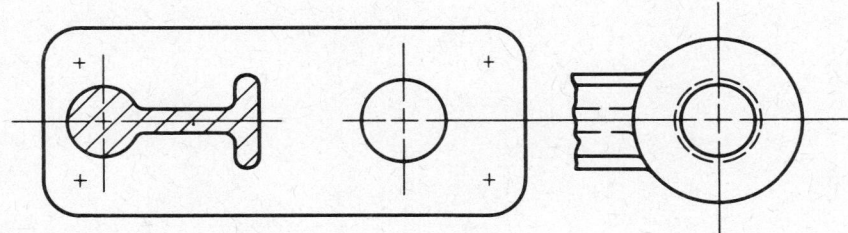

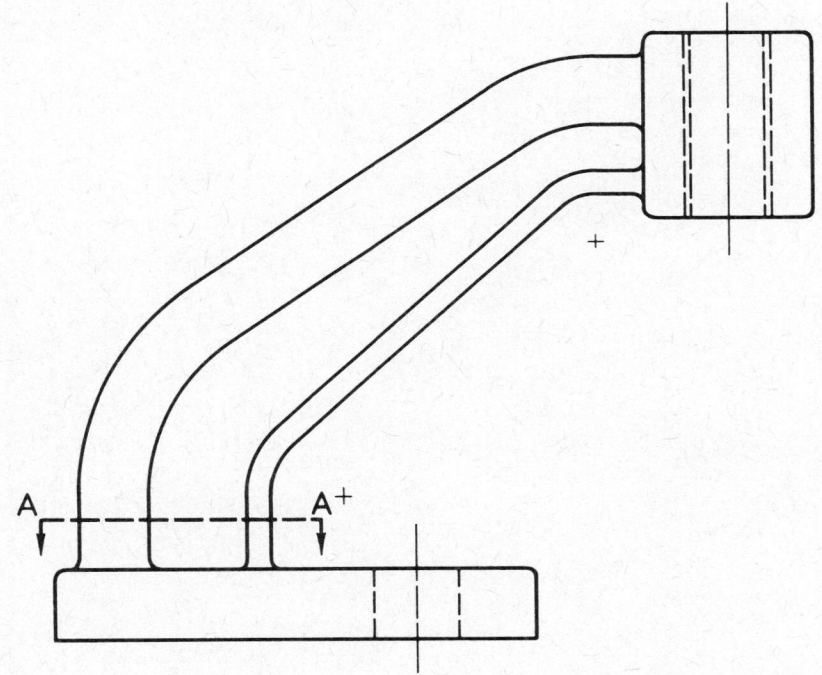

A   A +

(I) FRAME
CAST STEEL
I REQD

T-SLOT CLAMP

UNSPECIFIED FILLETS & ROUNDS .06R   FULL SIZE

MATING PARTS DIMENSIONING		DRAWN BY	FILE NO.	DRAWING 13-3

DRAWN BY

FILE NO.

DRAWING

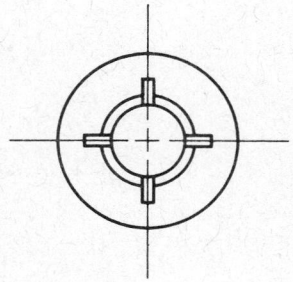

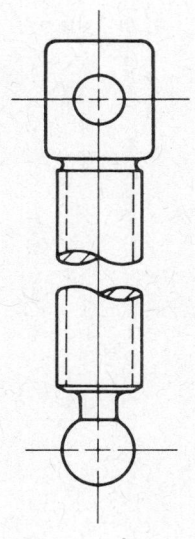

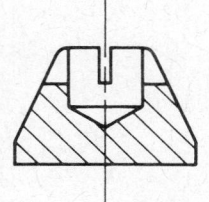

③ PAD CRS – 1 REQD

② CLAMP SCREW
CRS – 1 REQD

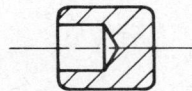

⑤ HANDLE CAP
CRS – 2 REQD

STANDARD PARTS

⑥ 1 – M10 x 1.5
HEAVY HEX NUT

⑦ 1 – 12 x 22 x 4.5 T-SLOT
WASHER

⑧ 1 – M10 x 1.5 – 50 LONG
T-SLOT BOLT

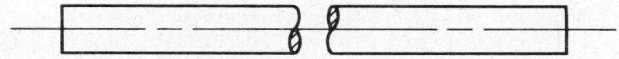

④ HANDLE CRS – 1 REQD

UNSPECIFIED FILLETS & ROUNDS 1.5 R   FULL SIZE

| MATING PARTS
DIMENSIONING | | DRAWN BY | FILE NO. | DRAWING
13-4 |

DRAWN BY · · · · · · FILE NO. · · DRAWING

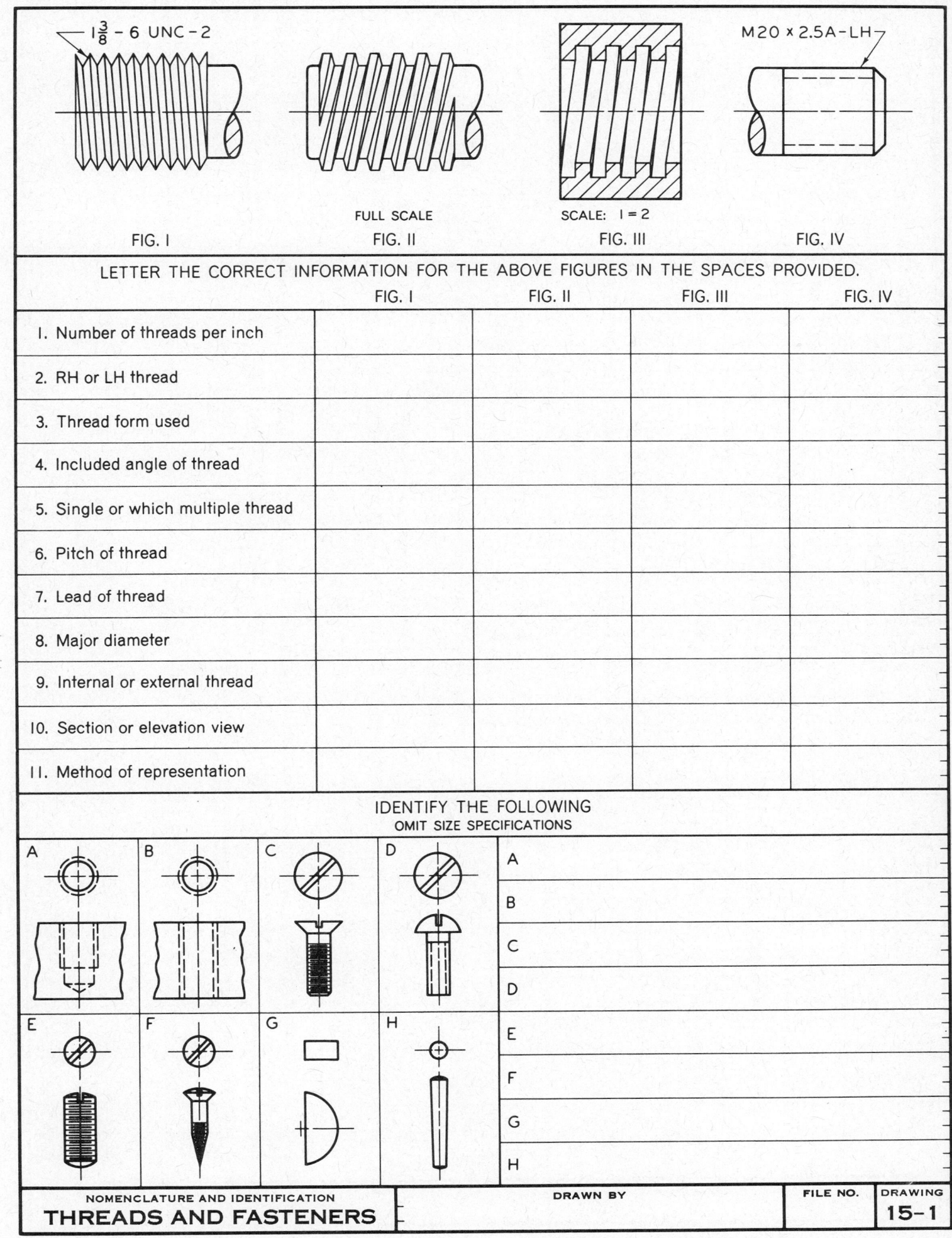

$1\frac{3}{8} - 6\ UNC - 2$

FULL SCALE

SCALE: $1 = 2$

M20 x 2.5A-LH

FIG. I   FIG. II   FIG. III   FIG. IV

LETTER THE CORRECT INFORMATION FOR THE ABOVE FIGURES IN THE SPACES PROVIDED.

	FIG. I	FIG. II	FIG. III	FIG. IV
1. Number of threads per inch				
2. RH or LH thread				
3. Thread form used				
4. Included angle of thread				
5. Single or which multiple thread				
6. Pitch of thread				
7. Lead of thread				
8. Major diameter				
9. Internal or external thread				
10. Section or elevation view				
11. Method of representation				

IDENTIFY THE FOLLOWING
OMIT SIZE SPECIFICATIONS

A

B

C

D

E

F

G

H

A

B

C

D

E

F

G

H

NOMENCLATURE AND IDENTIFICATION
THREADS AND FASTENERS

DRAWN BY

FILE NO.

DRAWING
15-1

DRAWN BY   FILE NO.   DRAWING

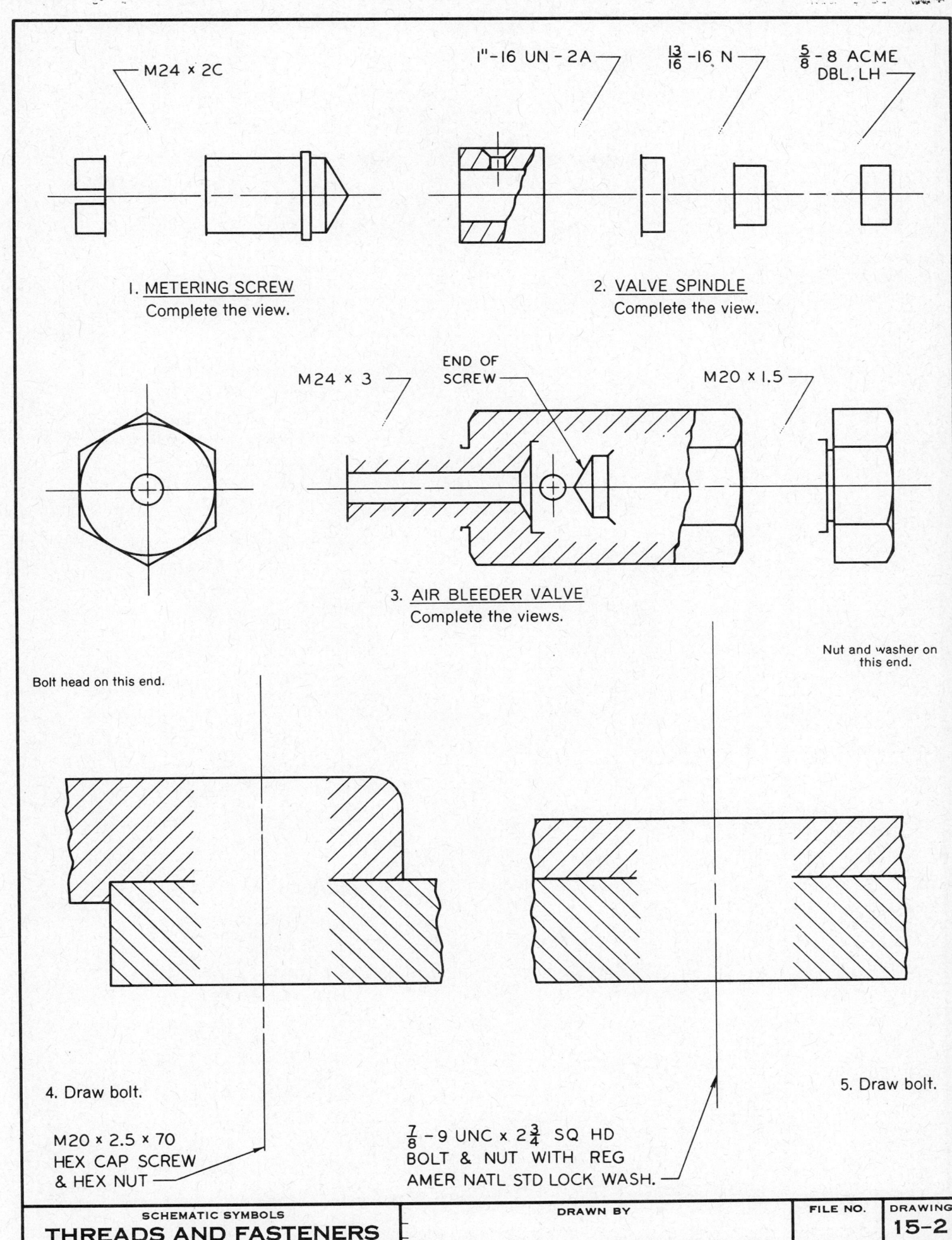

─ M24 × 2C

1. <u>METERING SCREW</u>
Complete the view.

I"−16 UN − 2A ─   ─ $\frac{13}{16}$ −16 N ─   ─ $\frac{5}{8}$ − 8 ACME
DBL, LH ─

2. <u>VALVE SPINDLE</u>
Complete the view.

M24 × 3 ─   END OF
SCREW ─   ─ M20 × 1.5

3. <u>AIR BLEEDER VALVE</u>
Complete the views.

Nut and washer on
this end.

Bolt head on this end.

4. Draw bolt.

M20 × 2.5 × 70
HEX CAP SCREW
& HEX NUT ─

5. Draw bolt.

$\frac{7}{8}$ − 9 UNC × 2$\frac{3}{4}$ SQ HD
BOLT & NUT WITH REG
AMER NATL STD LOCK WASH. ─

SCHEMATIC SYMBOLS	DRAWN BY	FILE NO.	DRAWING
THREADS AND FASTENERS			**15-2**

DRAWN BY · FILE NO. · DRAWING

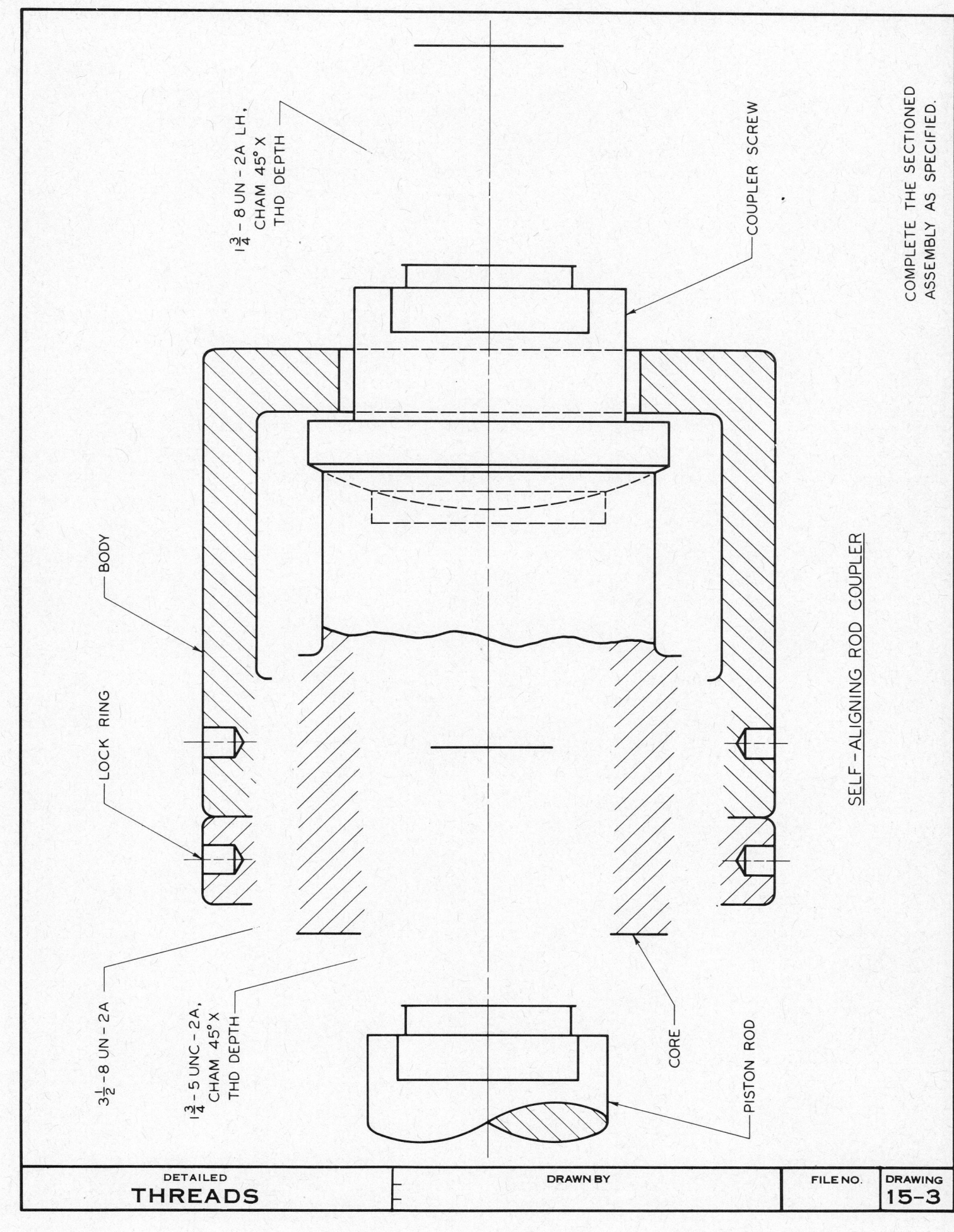

$1\frac{3}{4}$ – 8 UN – 2A LH.
CHAM 45° X
THD DEPTH

COUPLER SCREW

COMPLETE THE SECTIONED
ASSEMBLY AS SPECIFIED.

BODY

LOCK RING

$3\frac{1}{2}$ – 8 UN – 2A

$1\frac{3}{4}$ – 5 UNC – 2A,
CHAM 45° X
THD DEPTH

SELF – ALIGNING ROD COUPLER

CORE

PISTON ROD

DETAILED		DRAWN BY	FILE NO.	DRAWING
THREADS				15-3

DRAWN BY   FILE NO.   DRAWING

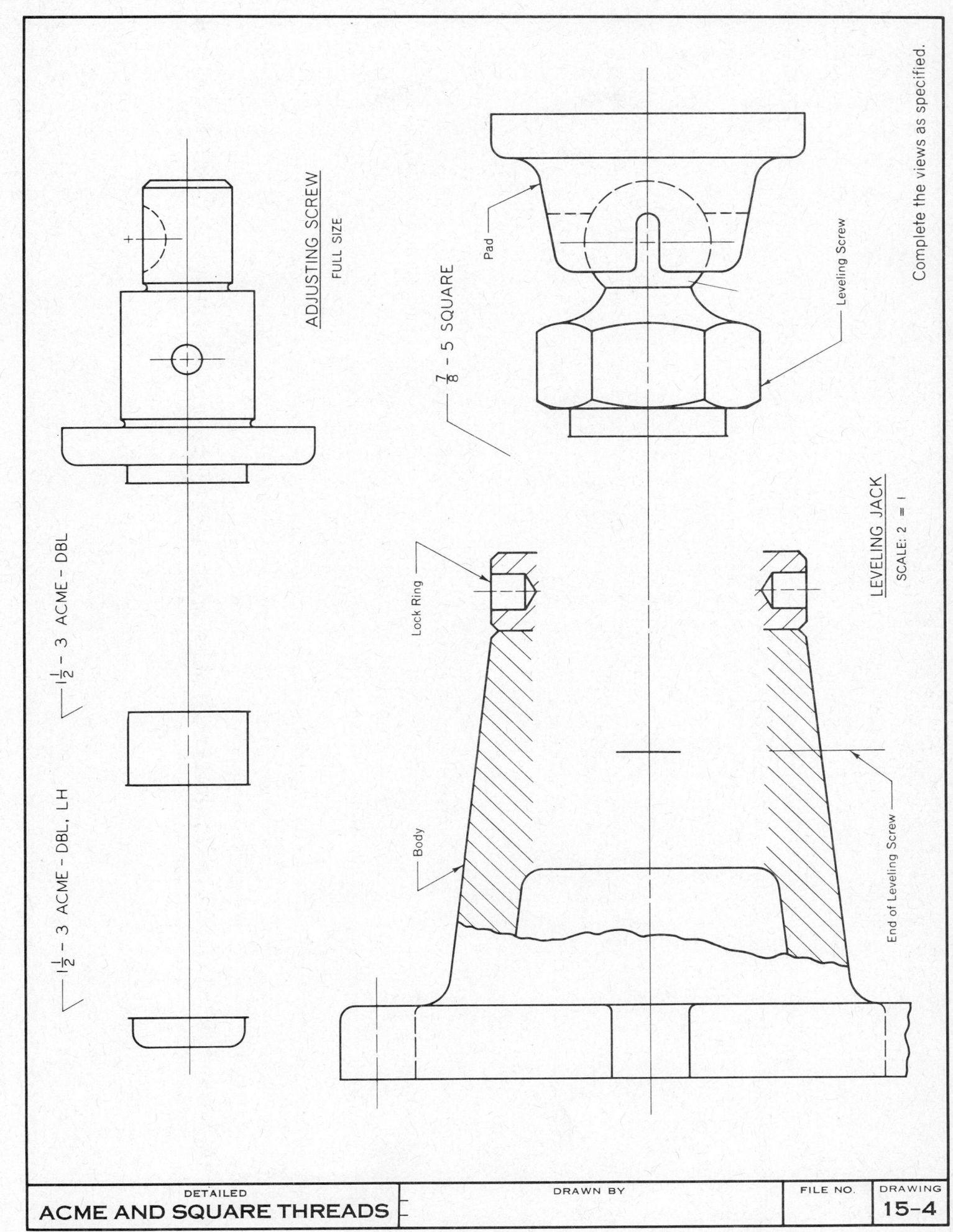

ADJUSTING SCREW

FULL SIZE

$1\frac{1}{2}$ – 3 ACME – DBL

$1\frac{1}{2}$ – 3 ACME – DBL, LH

$\frac{7}{8}$ – 5 SQUARE

Complete the views as specified.

Pad

Leveling Screw

Lock Ring

Body

End of Leveling Screw

LEVELING JACK

SCALE: 2 = 1

DETAILED

ACME AND SQUARE THREADS

DRAWN BY

FILE NO.

DRAWING

15-4

DRAWN BY   FILE NO.   DRAWING

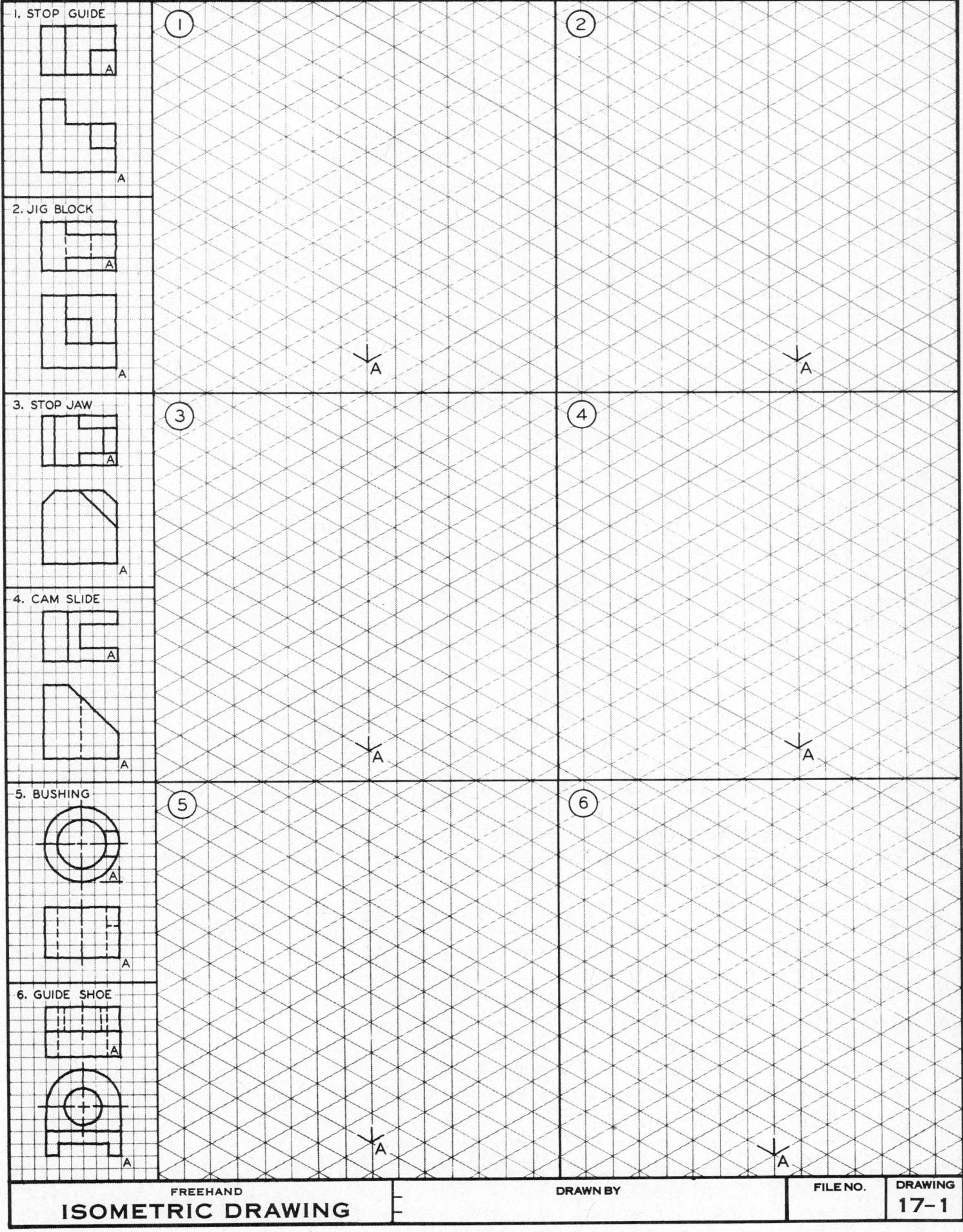

1. STOP GUIDE

A

A

2. JIG BLOCK

A

3. STOP JAW

A

4. CAM SLIDE

A

5. BUSHING

A

6. GUIDE SHOE

A

① A

② A

③ A

④ A

⑤ A

⑥ A

FREEHAND

ISOMETRIC DRAWING

DRAWN BY

FILE NO.

DRAWING

17-1

DRAWN BY | FILE NO. | DRAWING

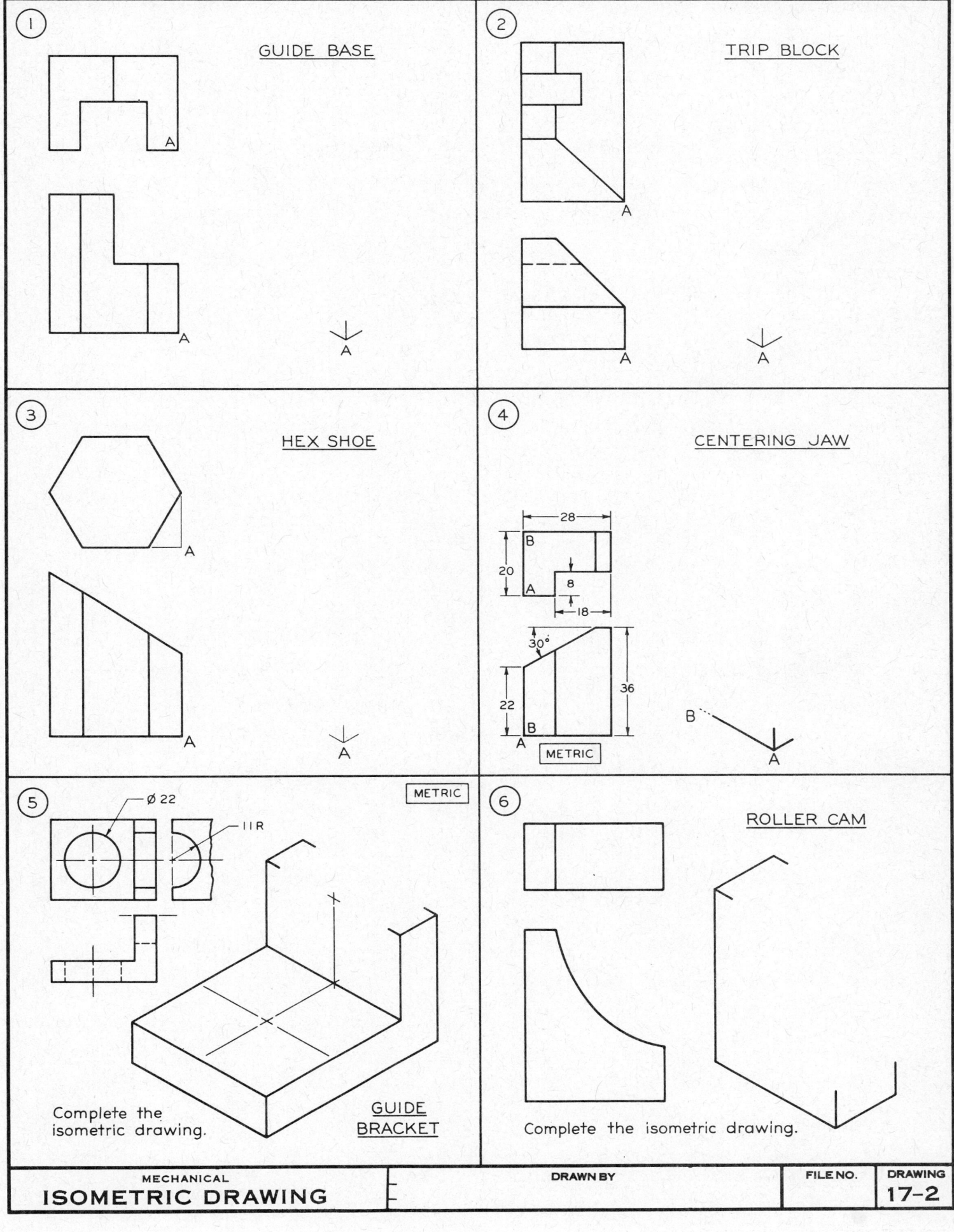

1. GUIDE BASE
2. TRIP BLOCK
3. HEX SHOE
4. CENTERING JAW

28
20
8
18
B
A
30°
22
36
B
A
METRIC

5. Ø 22
11R
METRIC
Complete the isometric drawing.
GUIDE BRACKET

6. ROLLER CAM
Complete the isometric drawing.

MECHANICAL ISOMETRIC DRAWING	DRAWN BY	FILE NO.	DRAWING 17-2

DRAWN BY   FILE NO.   DRAWING

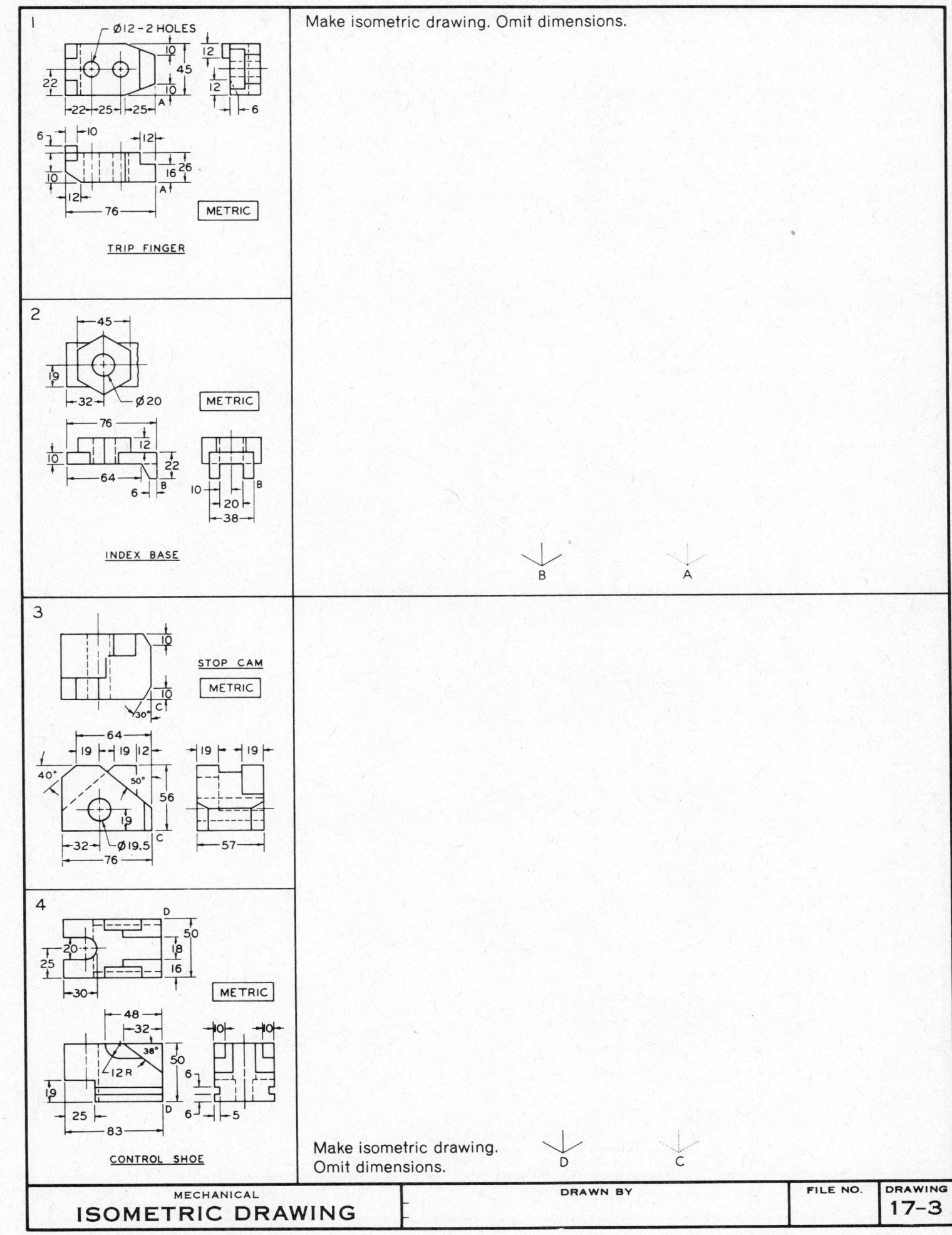

Make isometric drawing. Omit dimensions.

1

Ø12-2 HOLES

TRIP FINGER

METRIC

2

METRIC

Ø20

INDEX BASE

3

STOP CAM

METRIC

30°

40°   50°

Ø19.5

4

METRIC

12 R

38°

CONTROL SHOE

B   A

Make isometric drawing.
Omit dimensions.

D   C

DRAWN BY   FILE NO. DRAWING

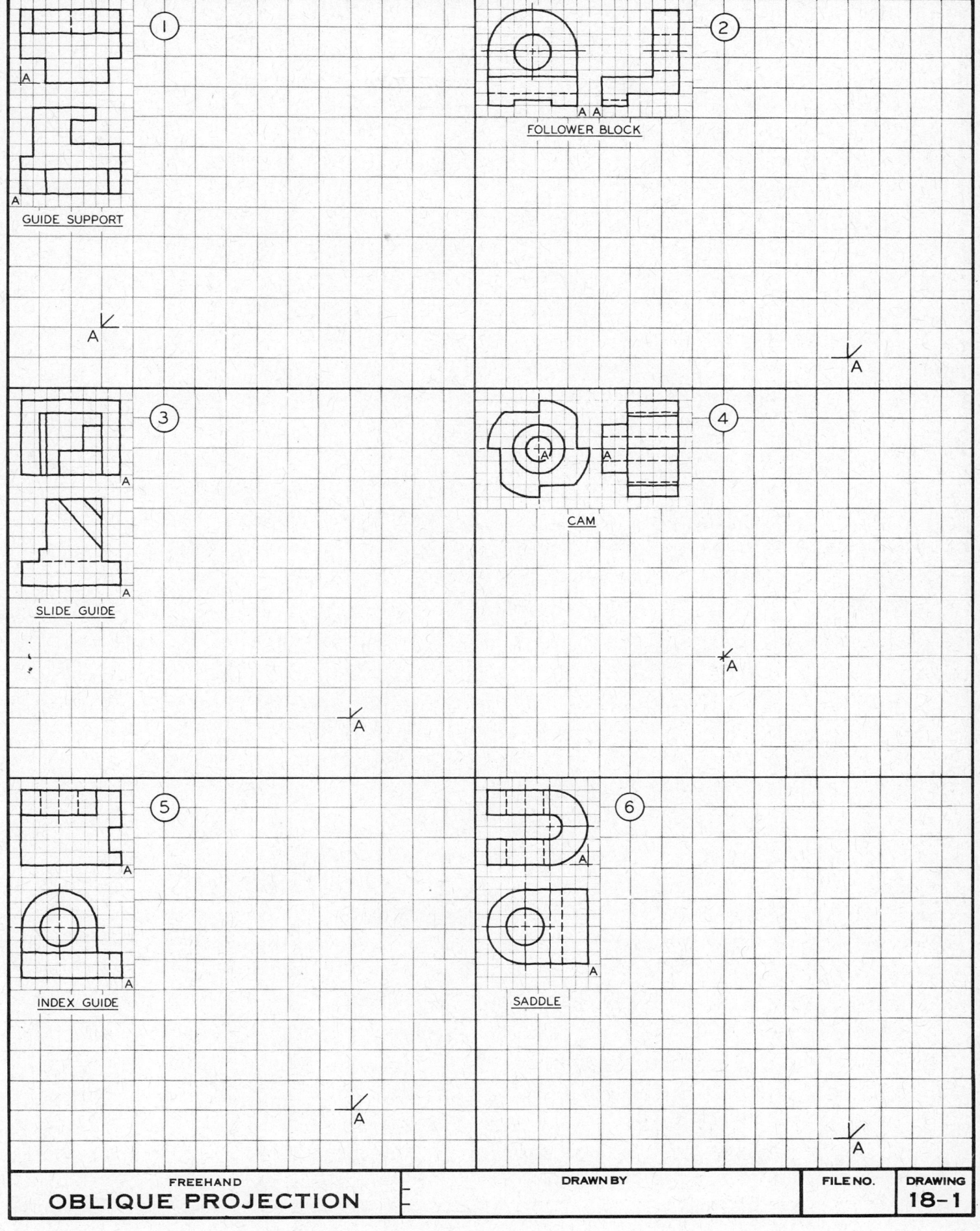

1 GUIDE SUPPORT

2 FOLLOWER BLOCK

3 SLIDE GUIDE

4 CAM

5 INDEX GUIDE

6 SADDLE

| FREEHAND **OBLIQUE PROJECTION** | DRAWN BY | FILE NO. | DRAWING **18-1** |

DRAWN BY | FILE NO. | DRAWING

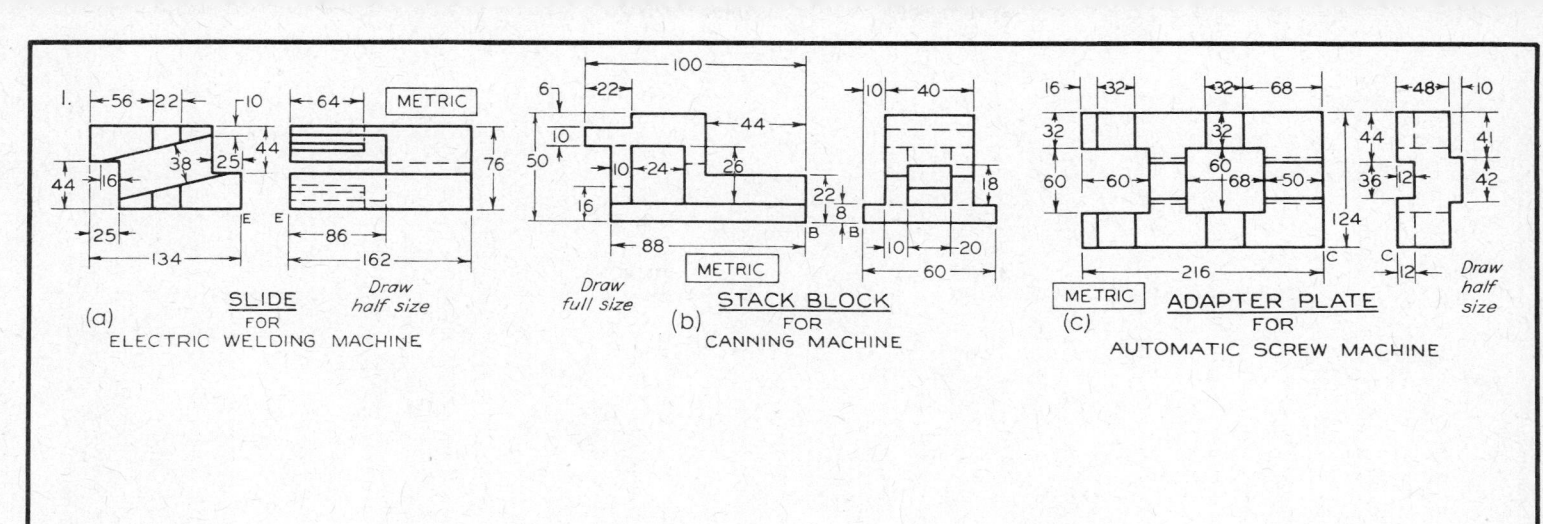

I.

56 — 22 — 10 — 64 — METRIC

SLIDE
FOR
ELECTRIC WELDING MACHINE
(a)
Draw half size

44 16 38 25 44 76
44 25 134 86 162
E E

6 22 100 10 40 METRIC
50 10 10 24 26 22 8 18
16 88 B B 10 20 60

STACK BLOCK
FOR
CANNING MACHINE
(b)
Draw full size

16 32 32 68 48 10 METRIC
32 32
60 60 60 68 50 44 36 12 41 42
124
216 C C 12

ADAPTER PLATE
FOR
AUTOMATIC SCREW MACHINE
(c)
Draw half size

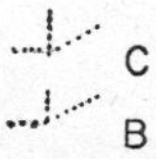

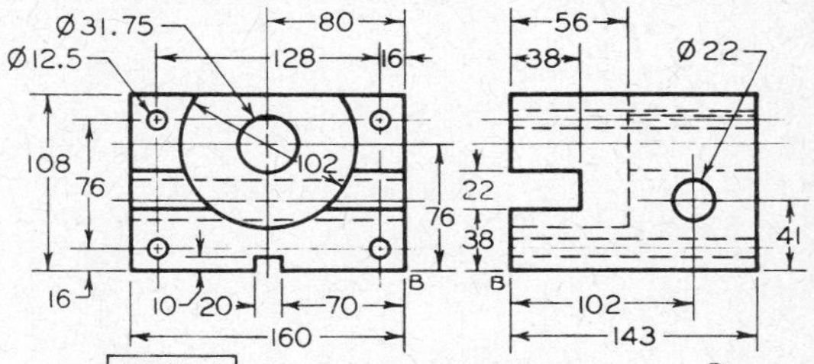

A   B   C

Ø31.75 Ø12.5 80 128 16 56 38 Ø22
108 76 102 76 22 38 41
16 10 20 70 B B 102
160 143

METRIC SAW GUIDE BLOCK
FOR
SAWING MACHINE
(a)
Draw half size

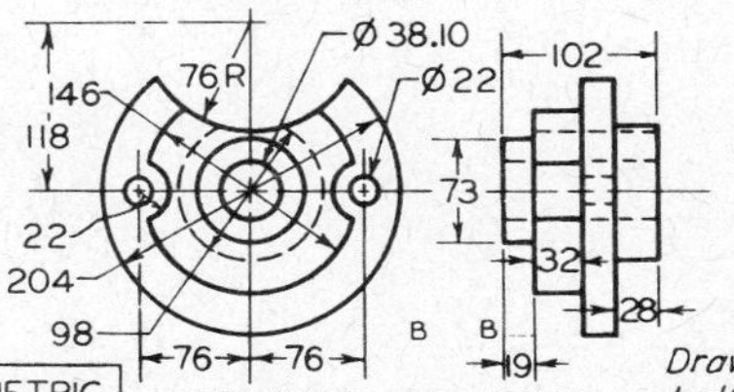

146 118 76R Ø38.10 Ø22 102
22 204 98 76 76 73 32 28 19
B B

METRIC SPINDLE BEARING
FOR
AUTOMATIC SCREW MACHINE
(b)
Draw half size

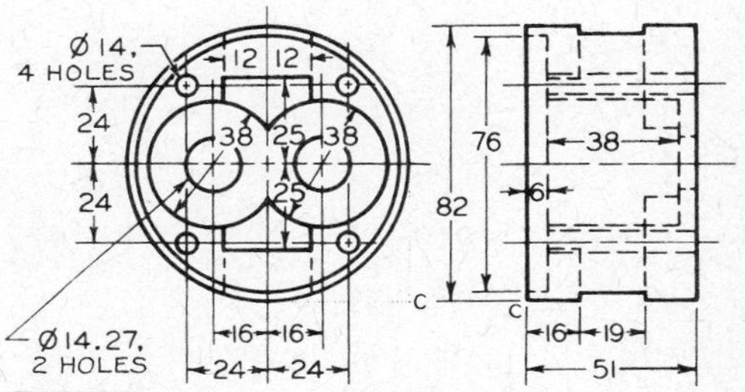

Ø14, 4 HOLES 12 12 102
24 38 25 38 76 38
24 25 82 6
Ø14.27, 2 HOLES 16 16 C C 16 19
24 24 51

METRIC OIL PUMP BODY
FOR
AIRPLANE
(c)
Draw full size

C
B

| CABINET AND CAVALIER | | DRAWN BY | FILE NO. | DRAWING |
| OBLIQUE PROJECTION | | | | 18-2 |

DRAWN BY | FILE NO. | DRAWING

① Complete the views of the nonintersecting tubes including correct visibility.

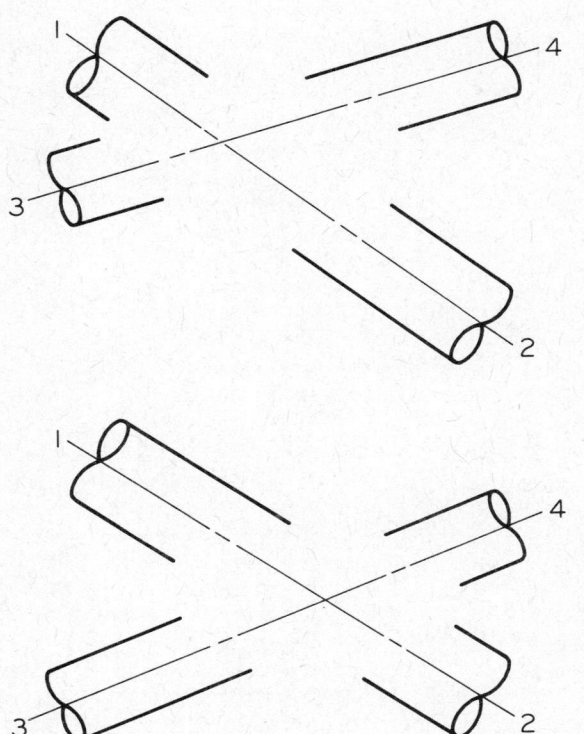

② Complete the views of the nonintersecting rods including correct visibility.

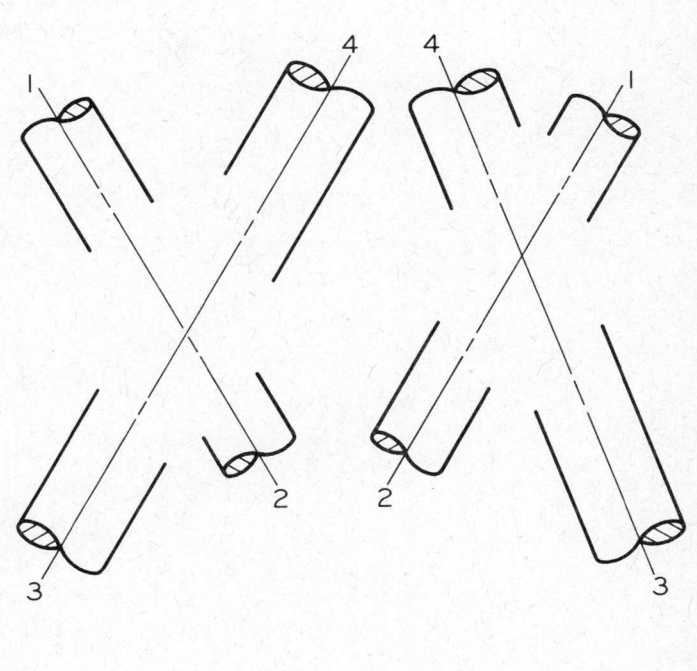

③ Points 1, 2, 3, and 4 are the vertices of a tetrahedron. Complete the views and add a left-side view, all with correct visibility.

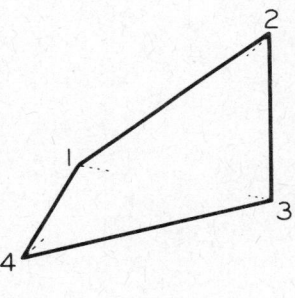

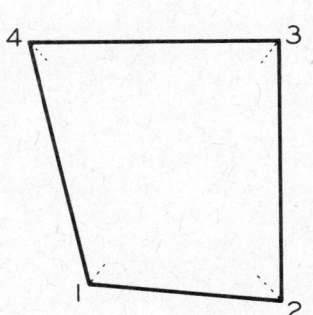

④ Parallelogram 1-2-3-4 is the base of a pyramid. Point V is the vertex. Complete the views and add a right-side view.

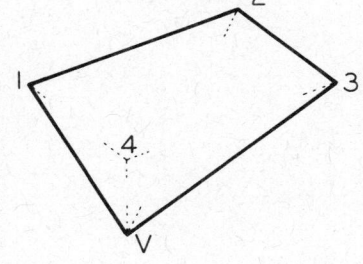

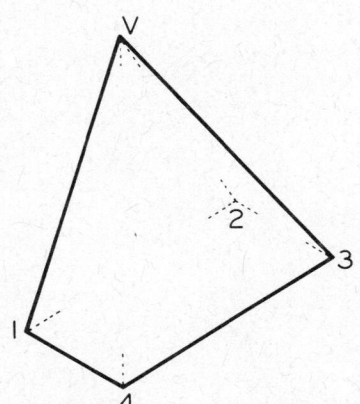

| VISIBILITY
POINTS AND LINES | | DRAWN BY | FILE NO. | DRAWING
19-1 |

DRAWN BY | FILE NO. | DRAWING

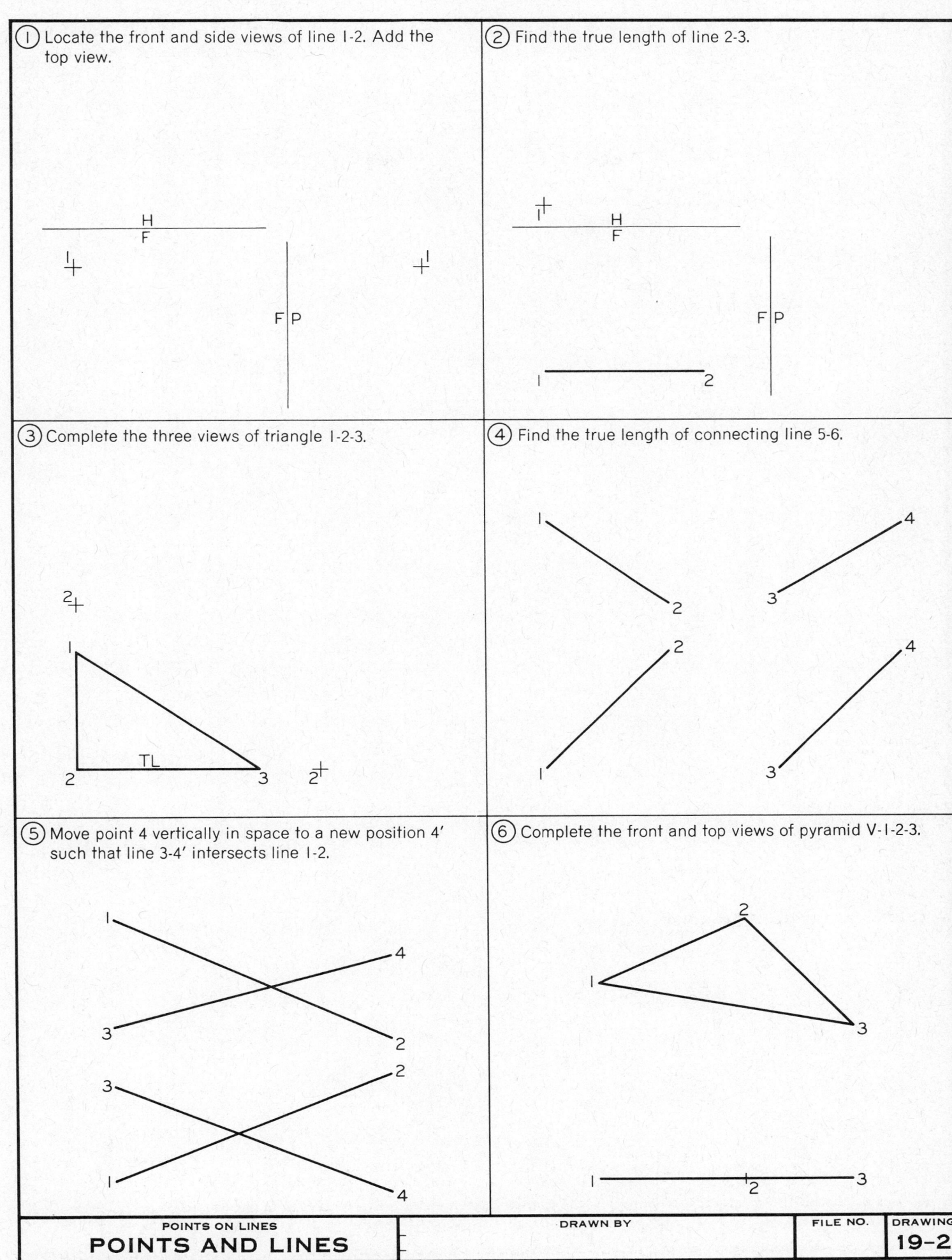

① Locate the front and side views of line 1-2. Add the top view.

② Find the true length of line 2-3.

③ Complete the three views of triangle 1-2-3.

④ Find the true length of connecting line 5-6.

⑤ Move point 4 vertically in space to a new position 4' such that line 3-4' intersects line 1-2.

⑥ Complete the front and top views of pyramid V-1-2-3.

POINTS ON LINES
POINTS AND LINES

DRAWN BY

FILE NO.

DRAWING
19-2

DRAWN BY   FILE NO.   DRAWING

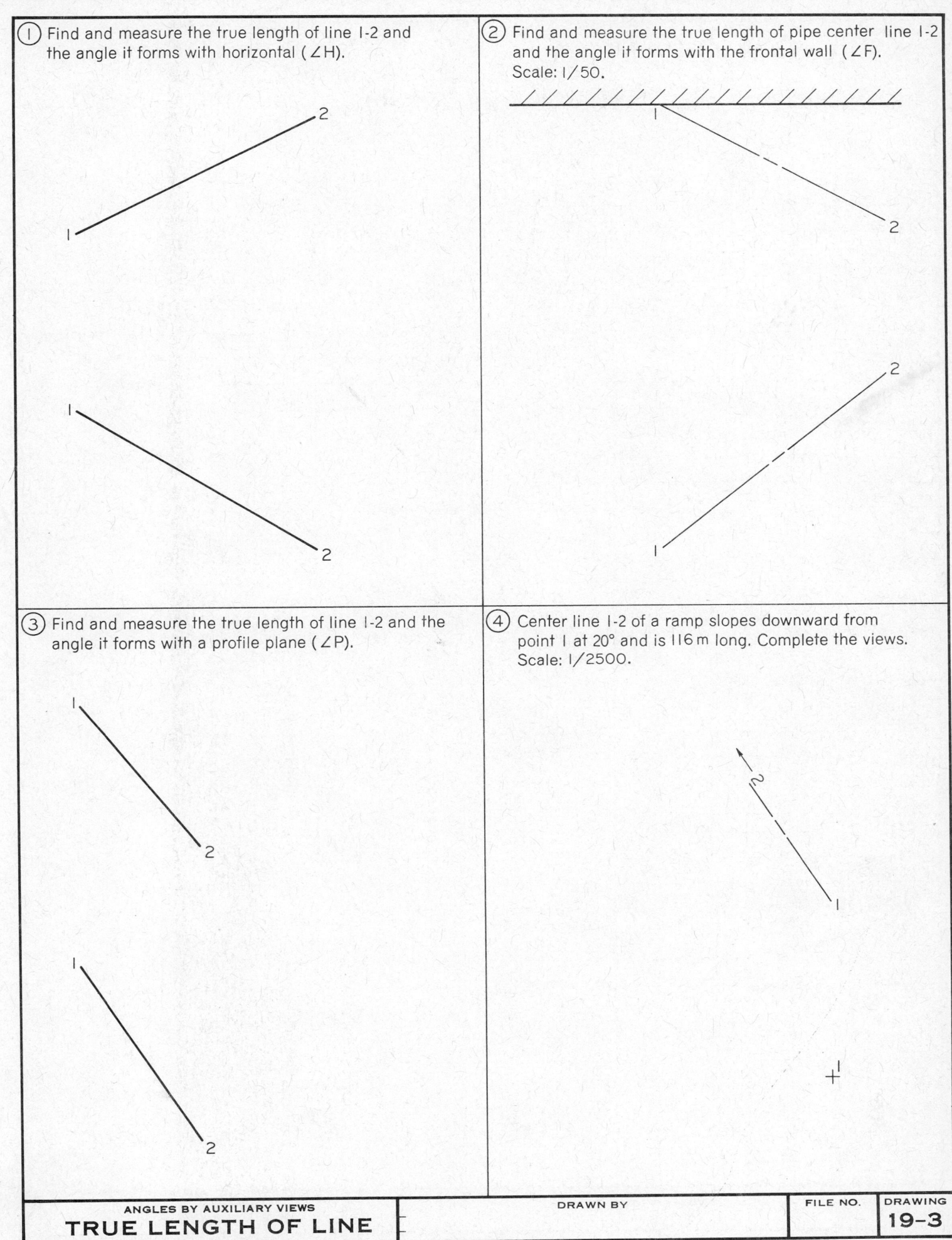

① Find and measure the true length of line 1-2 and the angle it forms with horizontal (∠H).

② Find and measure the true length of pipe center line 1-2 and the angle it forms with the frontal wall (∠F).
Scale: 1/50.

③ Find and measure the true length of line 1-2 and the angle it forms with a profile plane (∠P).

④ Center line 1-2 of a ramp slopes downward from point 1 at 20° and is 116 m long. Complete the views.
Scale: 1/2500.

ANGLES BY AUXILIARY VIEWS
TRUE LENGTH OF LINE

DRAWN BY

FILE NO.

DRAWING
19-3

DRAWN BY | FILE NO. | DRAWING

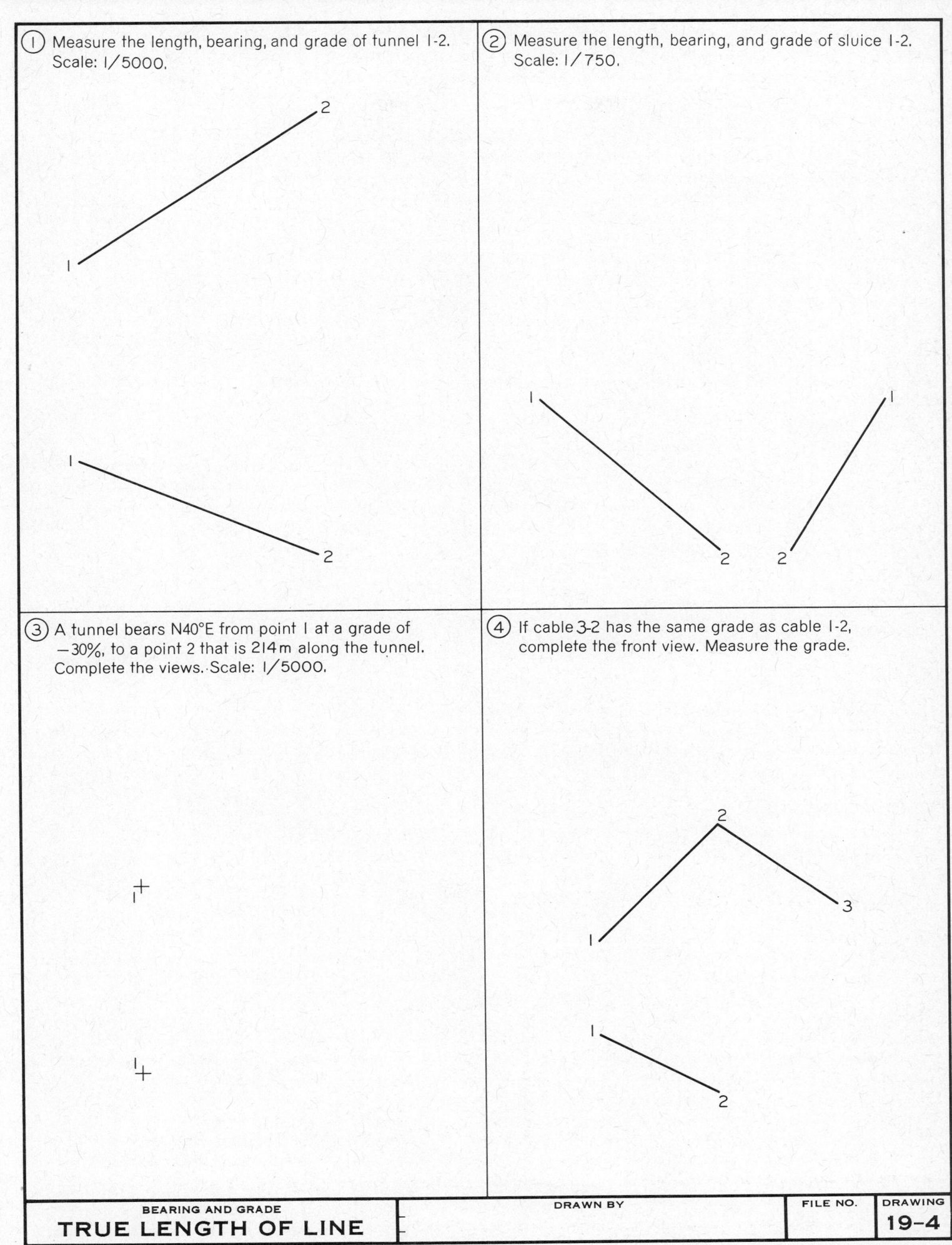

① Measure the length, bearing, and grade of tunnel 1-2.
Scale: 1/5000.

② Measure the length, bearing, and grade of sluice 1-2.
Scale: 1/750.

③ A tunnel bears N40°E from point 1 at a grade of
−30%, to a point 2 that is 214 m along the tunnel.
Complete the views. Scale: 1/5000.

④ If cable 3-2 has the same grade as cable 1-2,
complete the front view. Measure the grade.

BEARING AND GRADE
TRUE LENGTH OF LINE

DRAWN BY

FILE NO.

DRAWING
19-4

DRAWN BY   FILE NO.   DRAWING

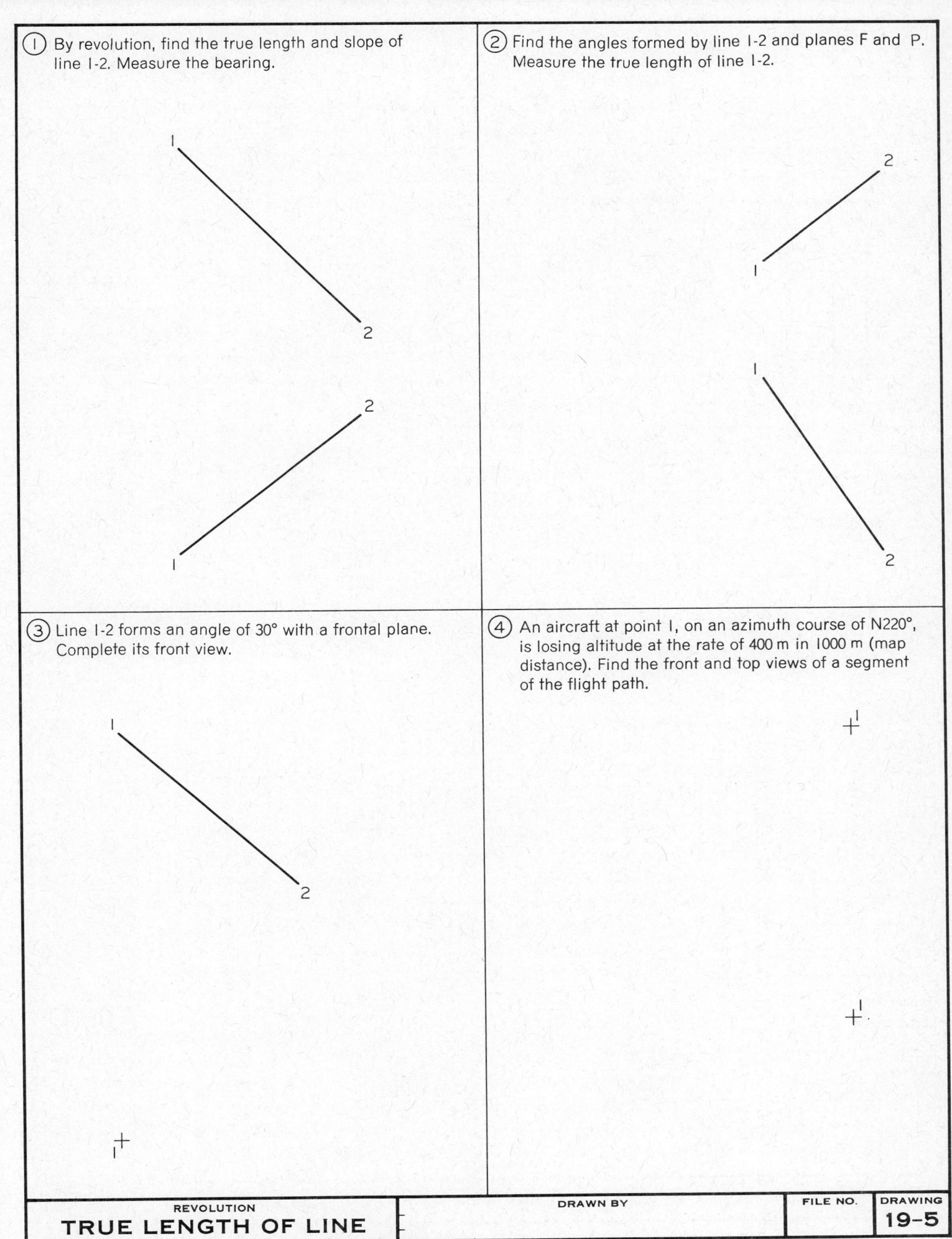

① By revolution, find the true length and slope of line 1-2. Measure the bearing.

② Find the angles formed by line 1-2 and planes F and P. Measure the true length of line 1-2.

③ Line 1-2 forms an angle of 30° with a frontal plane. Complete its front view.

④ An aircraft at point 1, on an azimuth course of N220°, is losing altitude at the rate of 400 m in 1000 m (map distance). Find the front and top views of a segment of the flight path.

REVOLUTION
TRUE LENGTH OF LINE

DRAWN BY

FILE NO.

DRAWING
19-5

DRAWN BY | FILE NO. | DRAWING

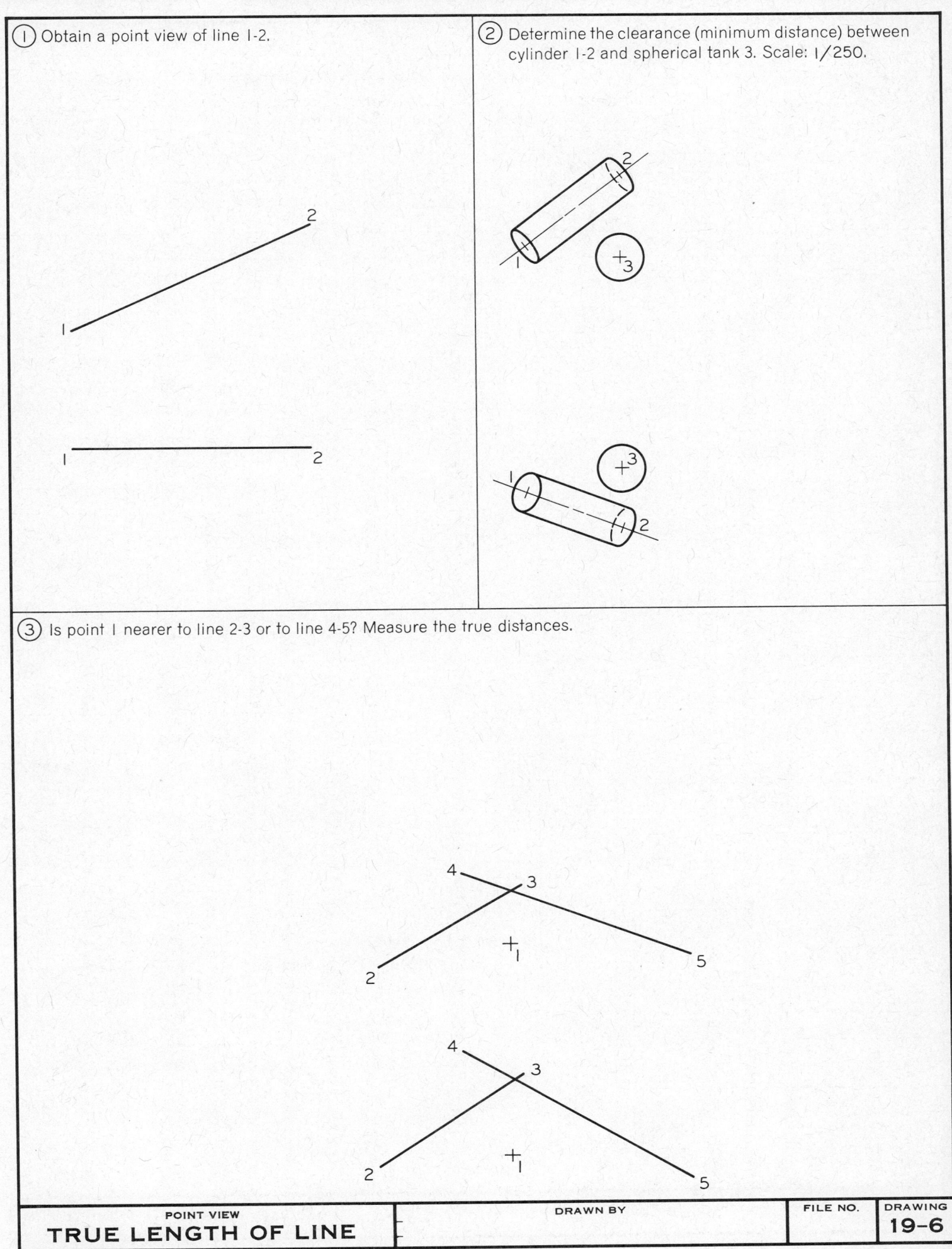

① Obtain a point view of line 1-2.

② Determine the clearance (minimum distance) between cylinder 1-2 and spherical tank 3. Scale: 1/250.

③ Is point 1 nearer to line 2-3 or to line 4-5? Measure the true distances.

POINT VIEW
TRUE LENGTH OF LINE

DRAWN BY

FILE NO.

DRAWING
19-6

DRAWN BY

FILE NO.

DRAWING

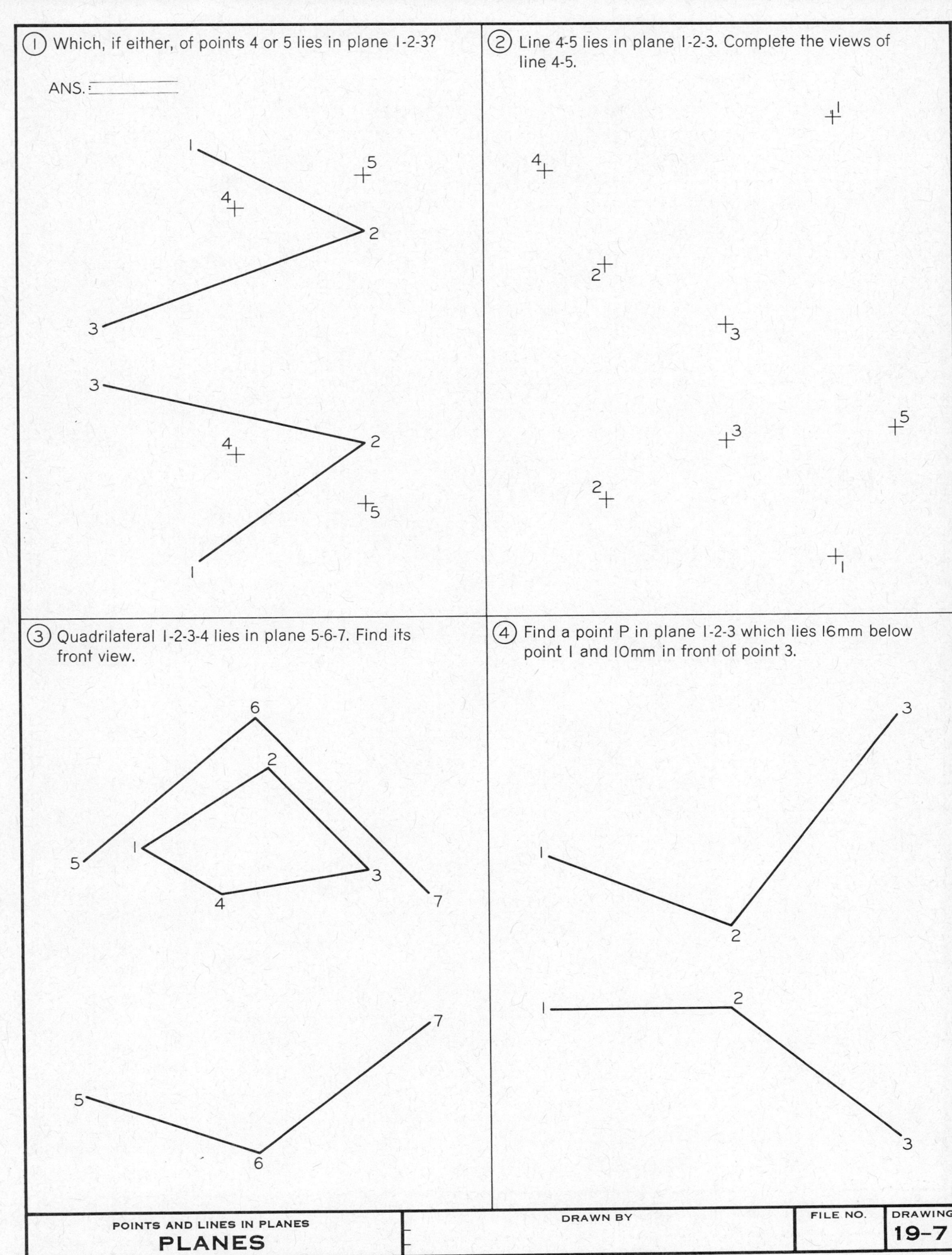

① Which, if either, of points 4 or 5 lies in plane 1-2-3?

ANS. _____

② Line 4-5 lies in plane 1-2-3. Complete the views of line 4-5.

③ Quadrilateral 1-2-3-4 lies in plane 5-6-7. Find its front view.

④ Find a point P in plane 1-2-3 which lies 16mm below point 1 and 10mm in front of point 3.

POINTS AND LINES IN PLANES
PLANES

DRAWN BY

FILE NO.

DRAWING
19-7

DRAWN BY | FILE NO. | DRAWING

① Construct a view showing the true size of triangle 1-2-3.
  Calculate the area of the triangle. Scale: 1/2500.

  AREA = _____

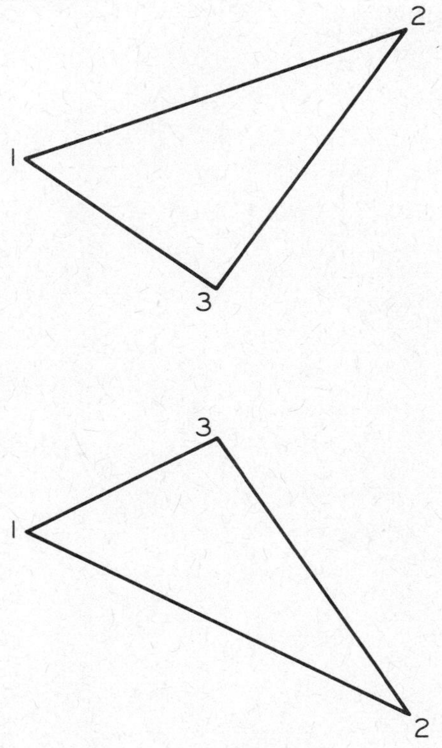

METRIC

② Pipe lines 1-2 and 3-4 are connected with a feeder branch Iusing 45° lateral
  fittings. One fitting is located at point 5 on line 3-4.
  Find the views of the feeder branch.

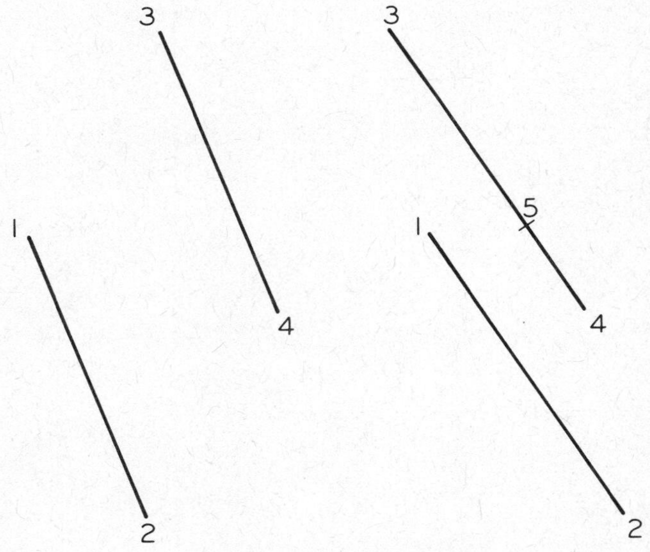

| TRUE SIZE PLANES | DRAWN BY | FILE NO. | DRAWING 19-8 |

DRAWN BY
FILE NO. DRAWING

① Find the piercing point of line 1-2 in plane 3-4-5.

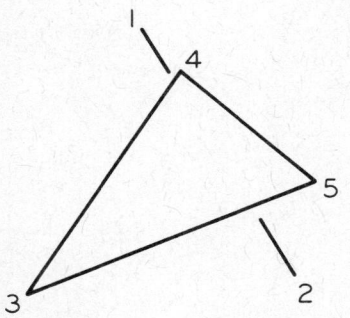

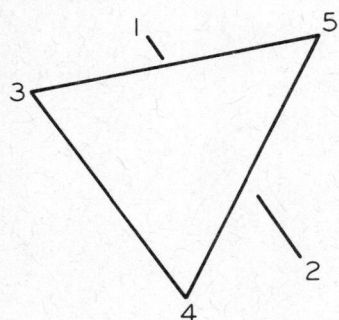

② Establish the piercing point of laser beam 1-2 in plane 3-4-5-6.

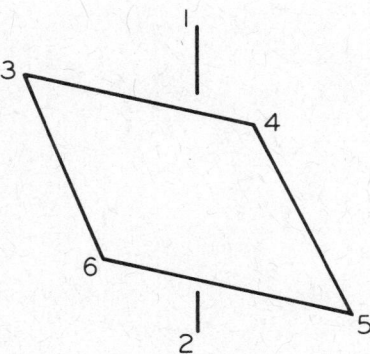

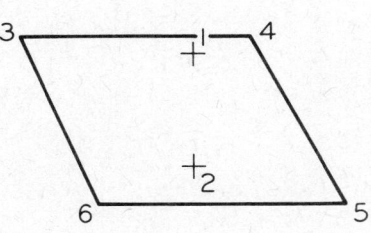

③ Show the piercing points of line 1-2 in the surfaces of the pyramid.

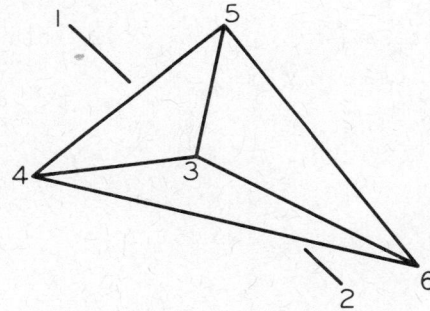

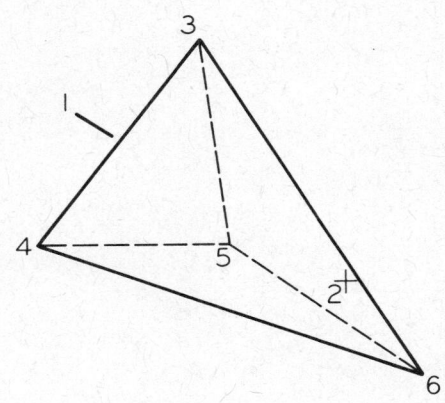

PIERCING POINTS—EDGE-VIEW METHOD
LINES AND PLANES

DRAWN BY

FILE NO.

DRAWING
19-9

DRAWN BY | FILE NO. | DRAWING

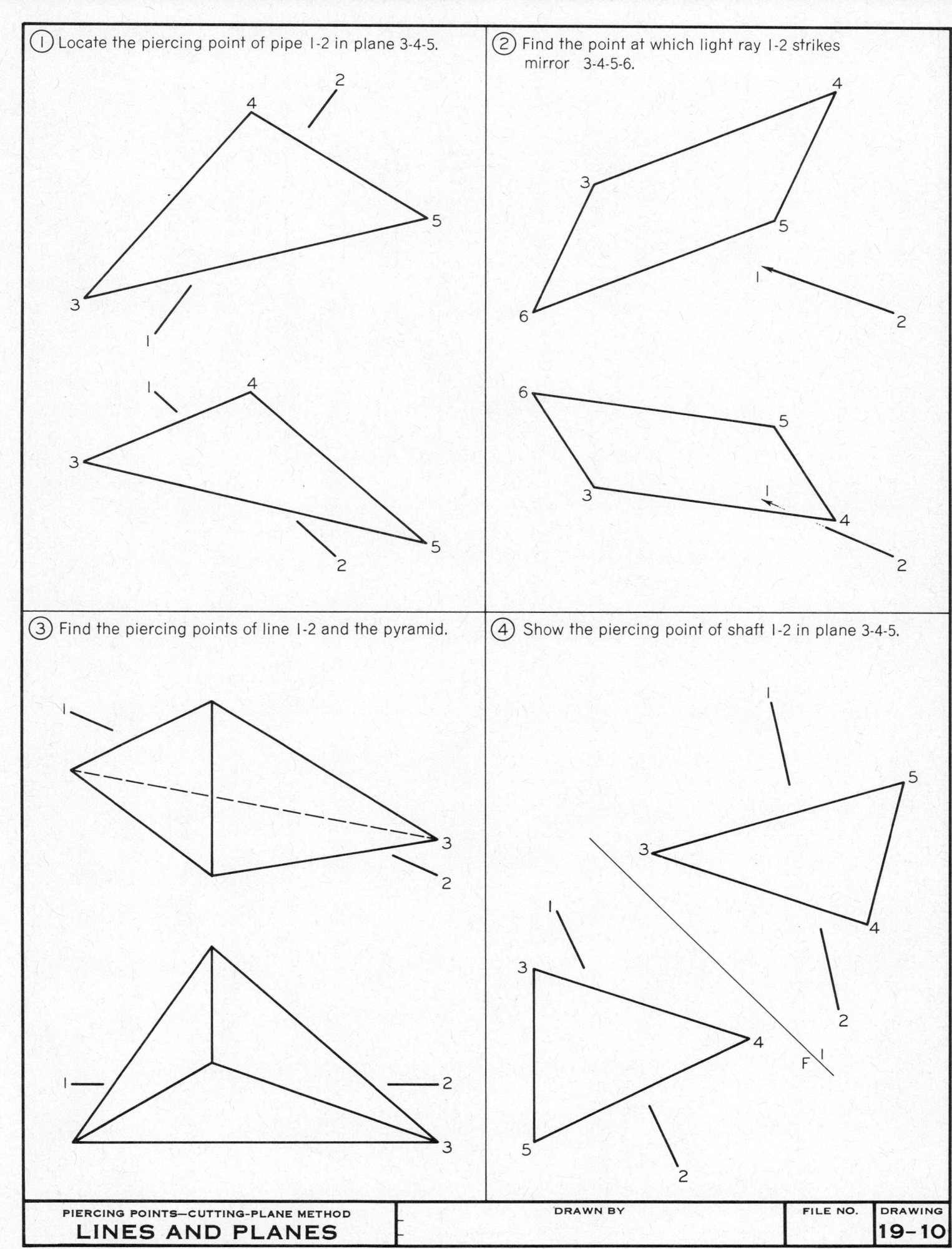

① Locate the piercing point of pipe 1-2 in plane 3-4-5.

② Find the point at which light ray 1-2 strikes mirror 3-4-5-6.

③ Find the piercing points of line 1-2 and the pyramid.

④ Show the piercing point of shaft 1-2 in plane 3-4-5.

PIERCING POINTS—CUTTING-PLANE METHOD
LINES AND PLANES

DRAWN BY

FILE NO.

DRAWING
19-10

DRAWN BY   FILE NO.   DRAWING

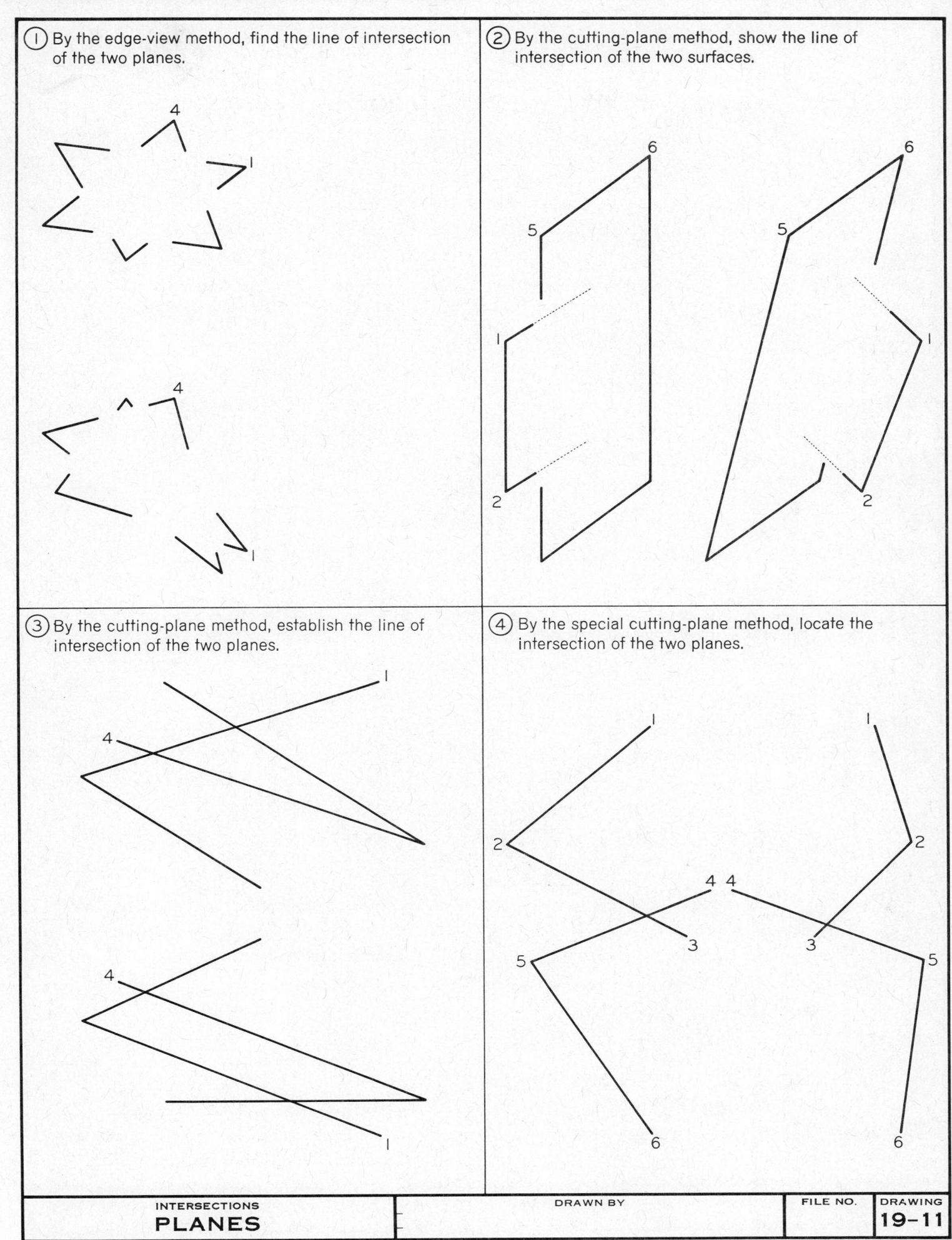

1. By the edge-view method, find the line of intersection of the two planes.

2. By the cutting-plane method, show the line of intersection of the two surfaces.

3. By the cutting-plane method, establish the line of intersection of the two planes.

4. By the special cutting-plane method, locate the intersection of the two planes.

INTERSECTIONS
PLANES

DRAWN BY

FILE NO.

DRAWING
19–11

DRAWN BY   FILE NO.   DRAWING

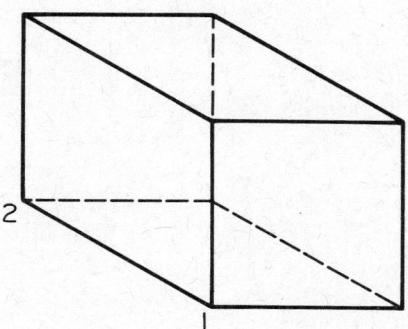

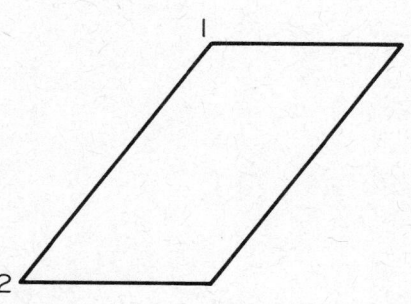

② Determine the angle between the roof planes.

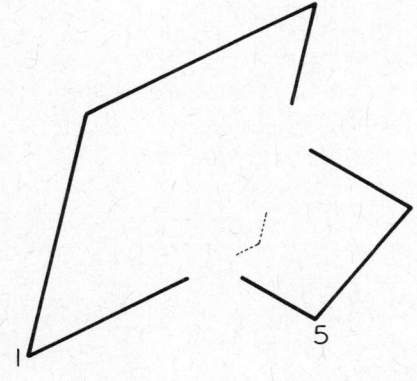

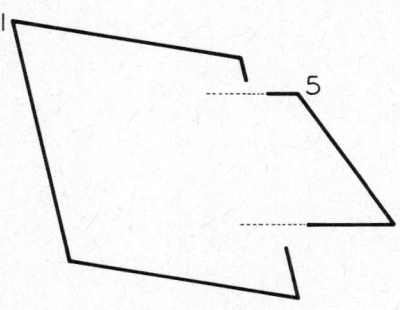

| DIHEDRAL ANGLES PLANES | DRAWN BY | FILE NO. | DRAWING 19-12 |

DRAWN BY

FILE NO.

DRAWING

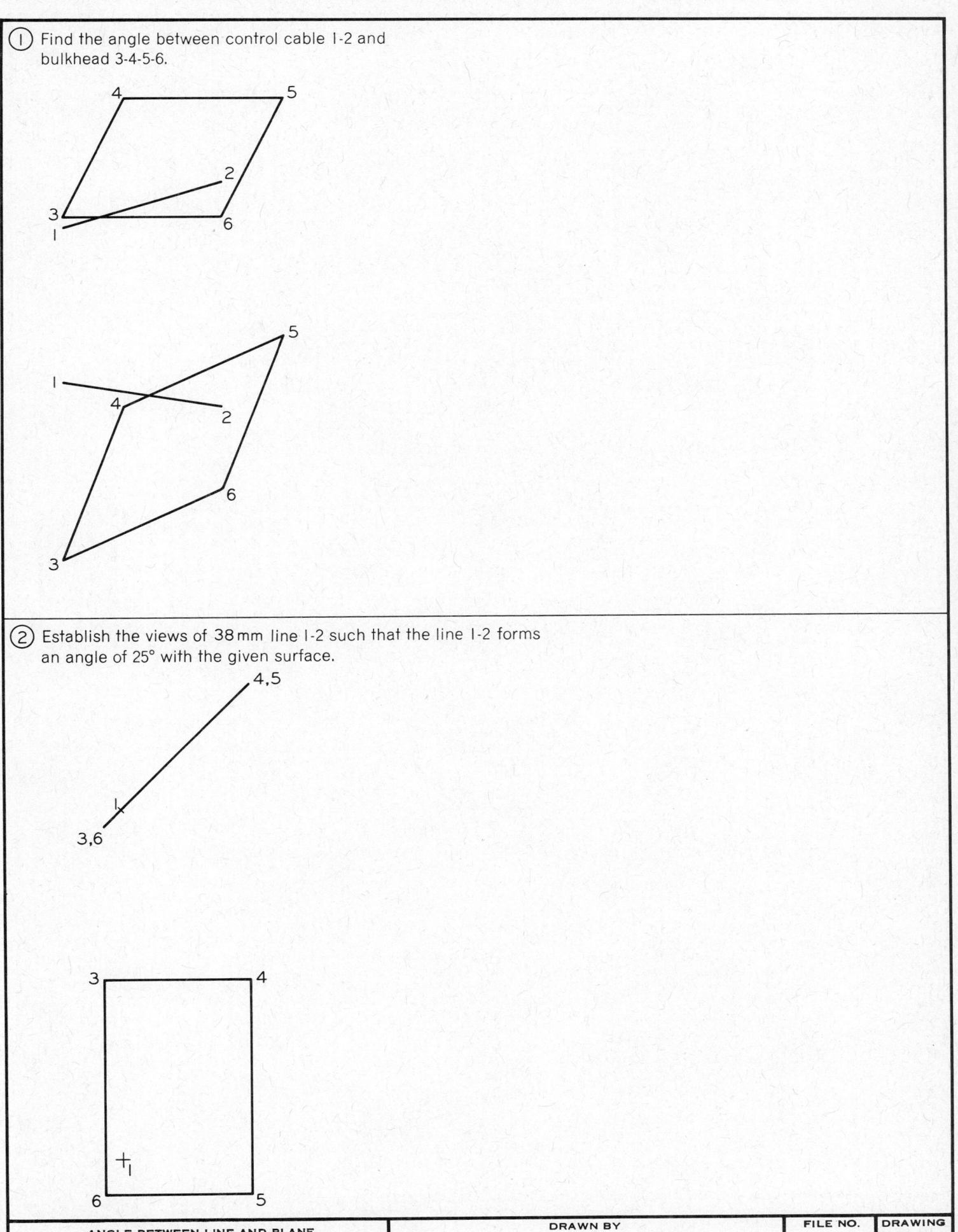

1 Find the angle between control cable 1-2 and
bulkhead 3-4-5-6.

2 Establish the views of 38 mm line 1-2 such that the line 1-2 forms
an angle of 25° with the given surface.

ANGLE BETWEEN LINE AND PLANE

LINES AND PLANES

DRAWN BY

FILE NO.

DRAWING

19-13

DRAWN BY   FILE NO.   DRAWING

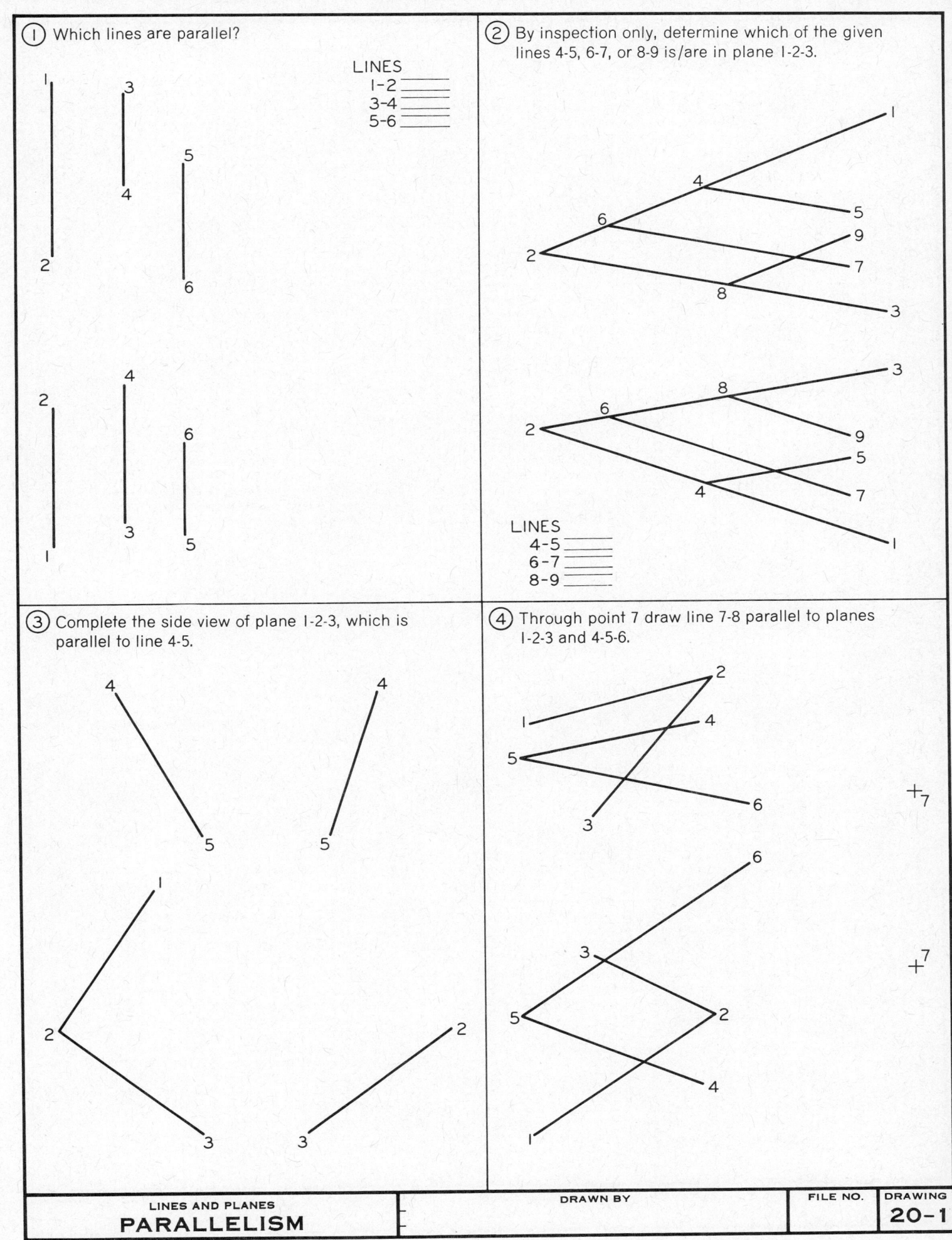

① Which lines are parallel?

LINES
1-2 _____
3-4 _____
5-6 _____

② By inspection only, determine which of the given lines 4-5, 6-7, or 8-9 is/are in plane 1-2-3.

LINES
4-5 _____
6-7 _____
8-9 _____

③ Complete the side view of plane 1-2-3, which is parallel to line 4-5.

④ Through point 7 draw line 7-8 parallel to planes 1-2-3 and 4-5-6.

LINES AND PLANES
PARALLELISM

DRAWN BY

FILE NO.

DRAWING
20-1

DRAWN BY

FILE NO.

DRAWING

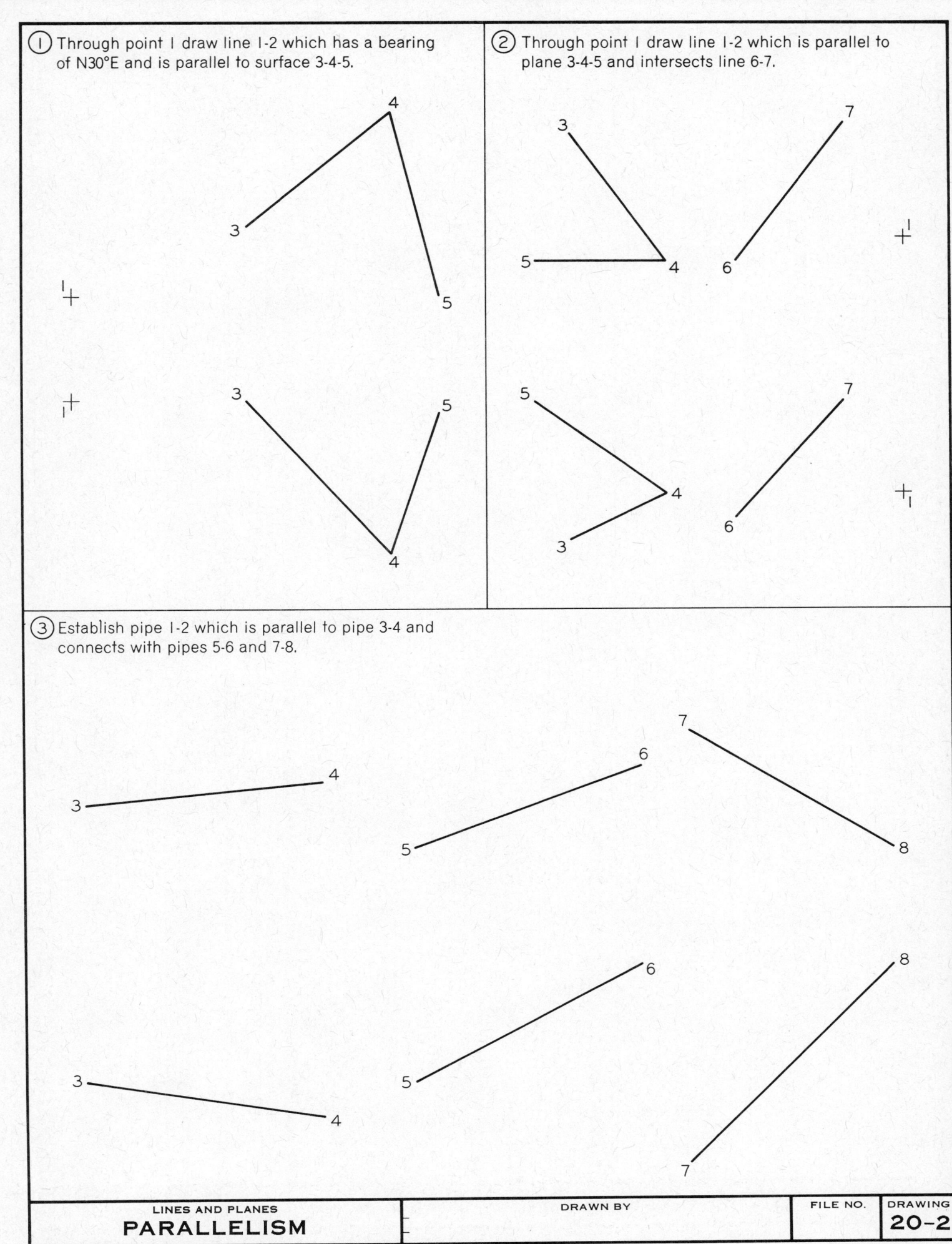

1. Through point 1 draw line 1-2 which has a bearing of N30°E and is parallel to surface 3-4-5.

2. Through point 1 draw line 1-2 which is parallel to plane 3-4-5 and intersects line 6-7.

3. Establish pipe 1-2 which is parallel to pipe 3-4 and connects with pipes 5-6 and 7-8.

LINES AND PLANES
PARALLELISM

DRAWN BY

FILE NO.

DRAWING
20-2

DRAWN BY

FILE NO. DRAWING

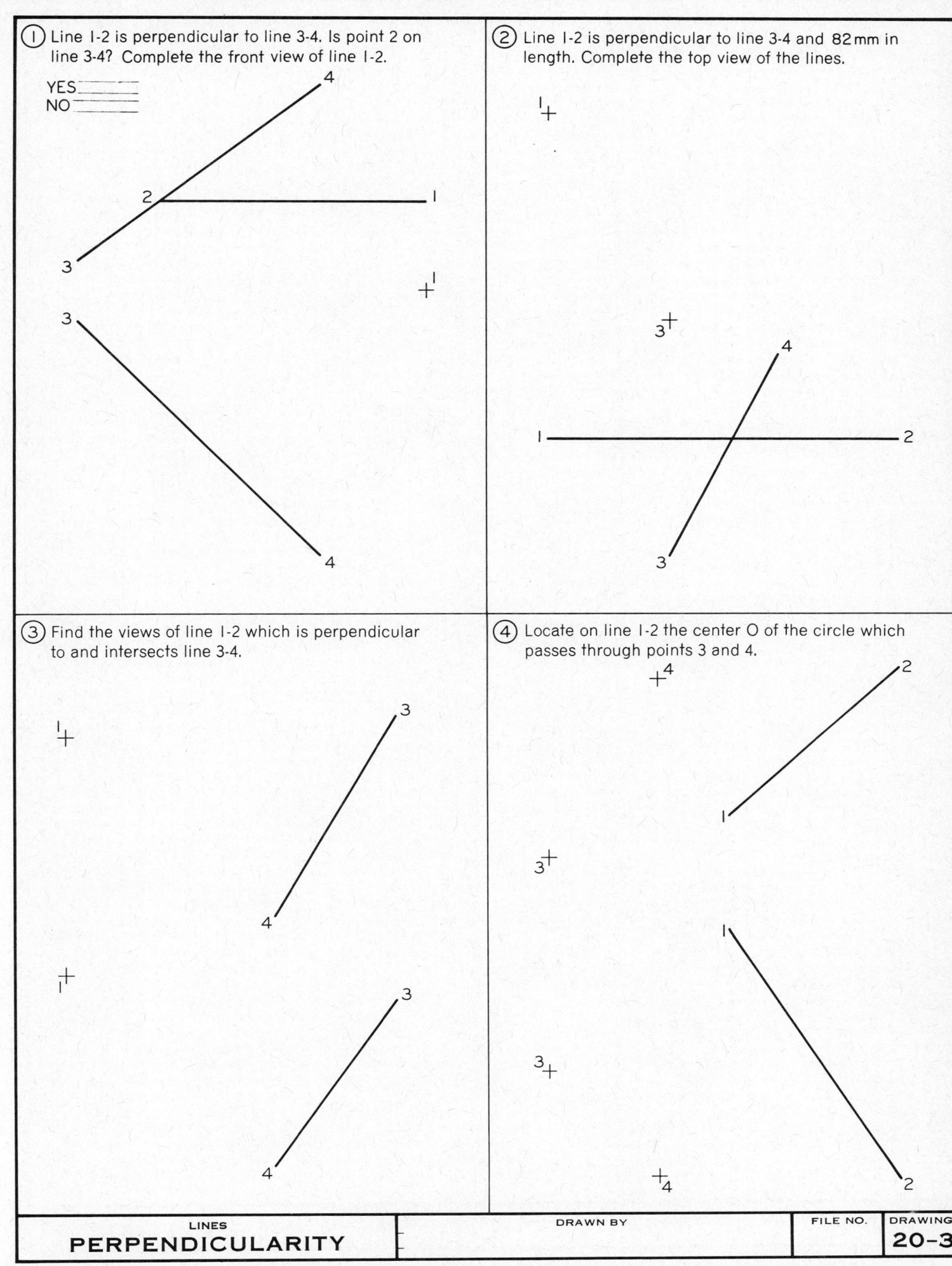

① Line 1-2 is perpendicular to line 3-4. Is point 2 on line 3-4? Complete the front view of line 1-2.

YES_____
NO_____

② Line 1-2 is perpendicular to line 3-4 and 82 mm in length. Complete the top view of the lines.

③ Find the views of line 1-2 which is perpendicular to and intersects line 3-4.

④ Locate on line 1-2 the center O of the circle which passes through points 3 and 4.

LINES
PERPENDICULARITY

DRAWN BY

FILE NO.

DRAWING
20-3

DRAWN BY

FILE NO.

DRAWING

① Locate the shadow of point 1 on surface 2-3-4-5 if the light rays are perpendicular to the surface.

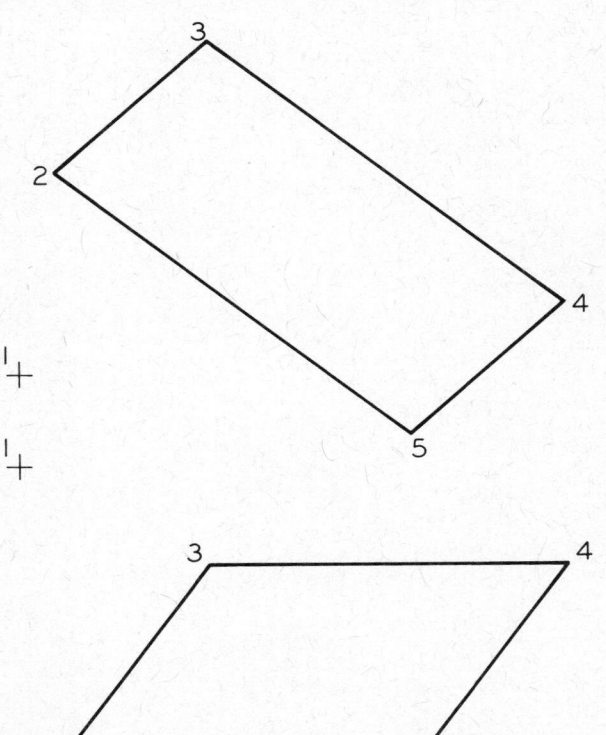

② Measure the length and show the views of the altitude of all cones having point V as the vertex and with their bases in plane 1-2-3.

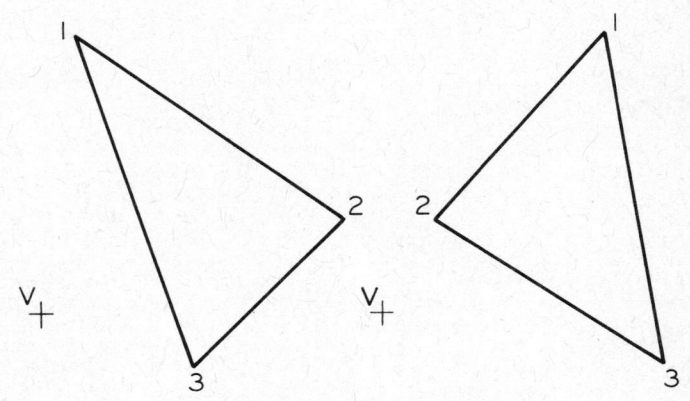

③ The axis of a right pyramid lies along line 1-2. The vertex is at point V. The base is an equilateral triangle with one corner at point 3. Complete all views.

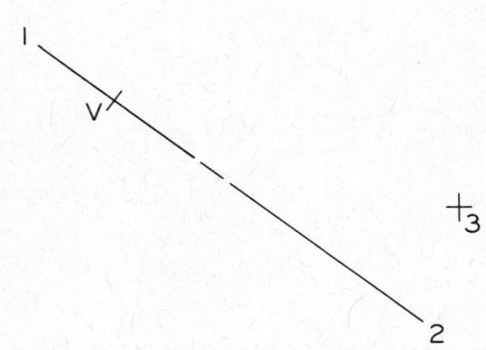

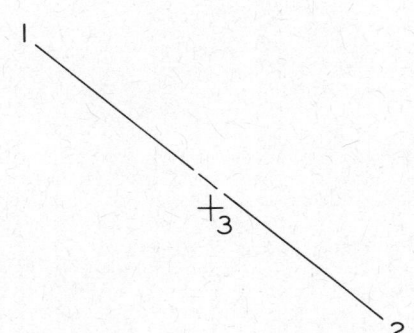

LINES AND PLANES
PERPENDICULARITY

DRAWN BY

FILE NO.

DRAWING
20-4

DRAWN BY   FILE NO.   DRAWING

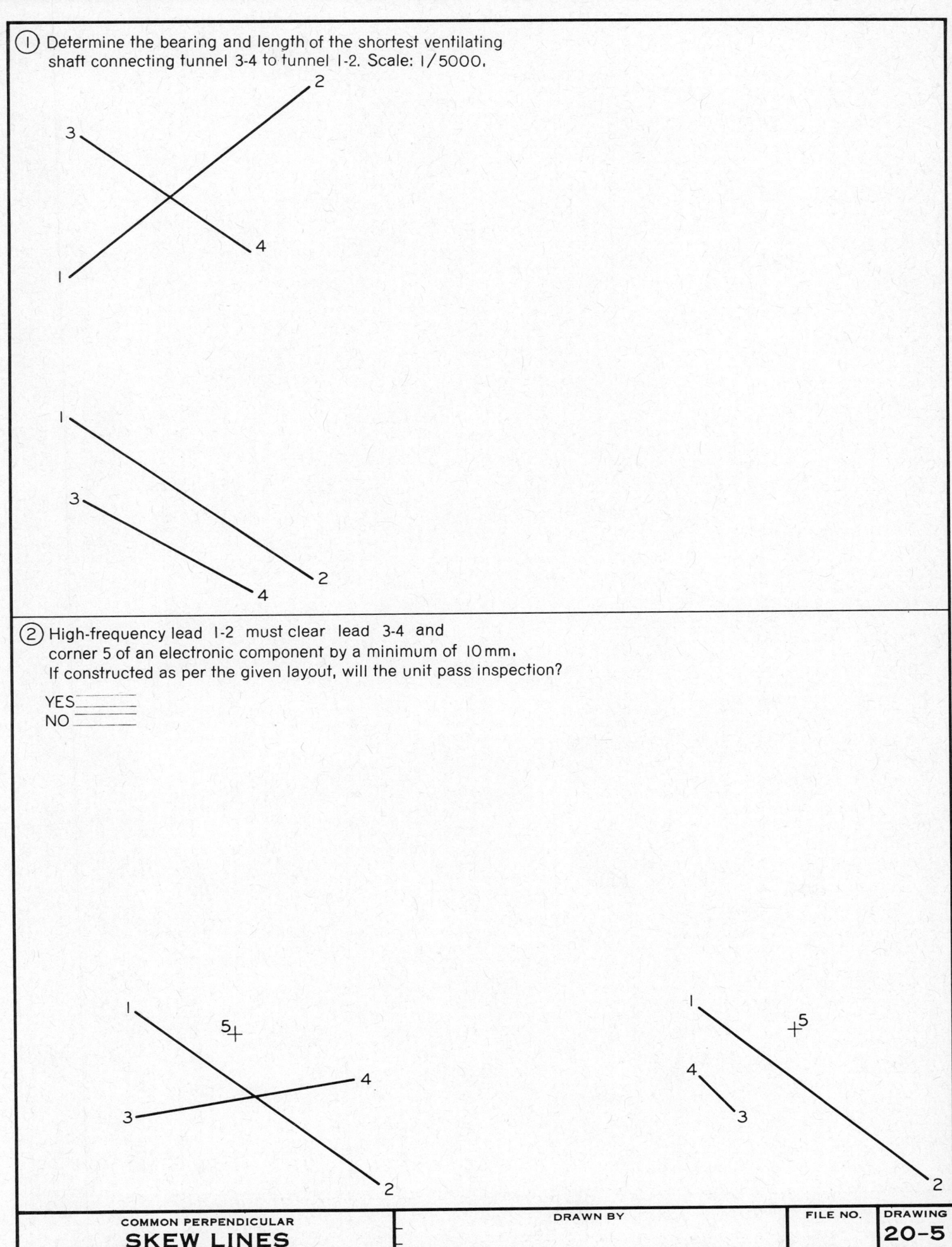

① Determine the bearing and length of the shortest ventilating shaft connecting tunnel 3-4 to tunnel 1-2. Scale: 1/5000.

② High-frequency lead 1-2 must clear lead 3-4 and corner 5 of an electronic component by a minimum of 10 mm. If constructed as per the given layout, will the unit pass inspection?

YES———
NO ———

COMMON PERPENDICULAR
SKEW LINES

DRAWN BY

FILE NO.

DRAWING
20-5

DRAWN BY

FILE NO. DRAWING

① Connect pipes 1-2 and 3-4 with the shortest branch parallel to the side (profile) wall.
Determine the length and show the views of the branch.
Scale: 1/100.

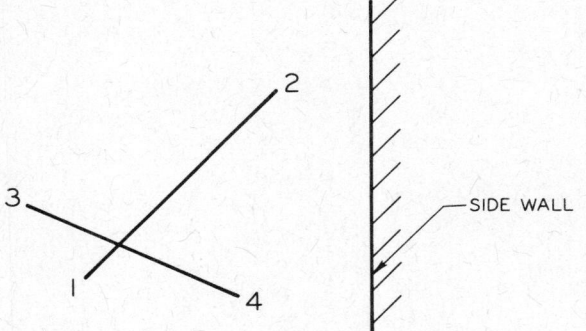

—SIDE WALL

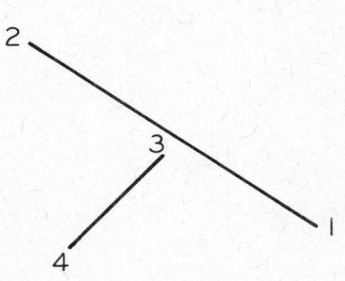

② Ski slope 1-2 is connected to ski slope 3-4 with the shortest path having a grade of − 10%.
Find the length and bearing and show the views of the path.
Scale: 1/5000.

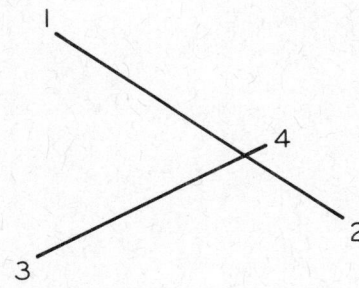

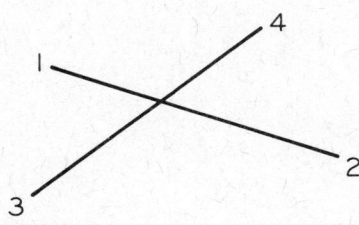

LINES AT SPECIFIED ANGLES
SKEW LINES
DRAWN BY
FILE NO.
DRAWING
20-6

DRAWN BY   FILE NO.   DRAWING

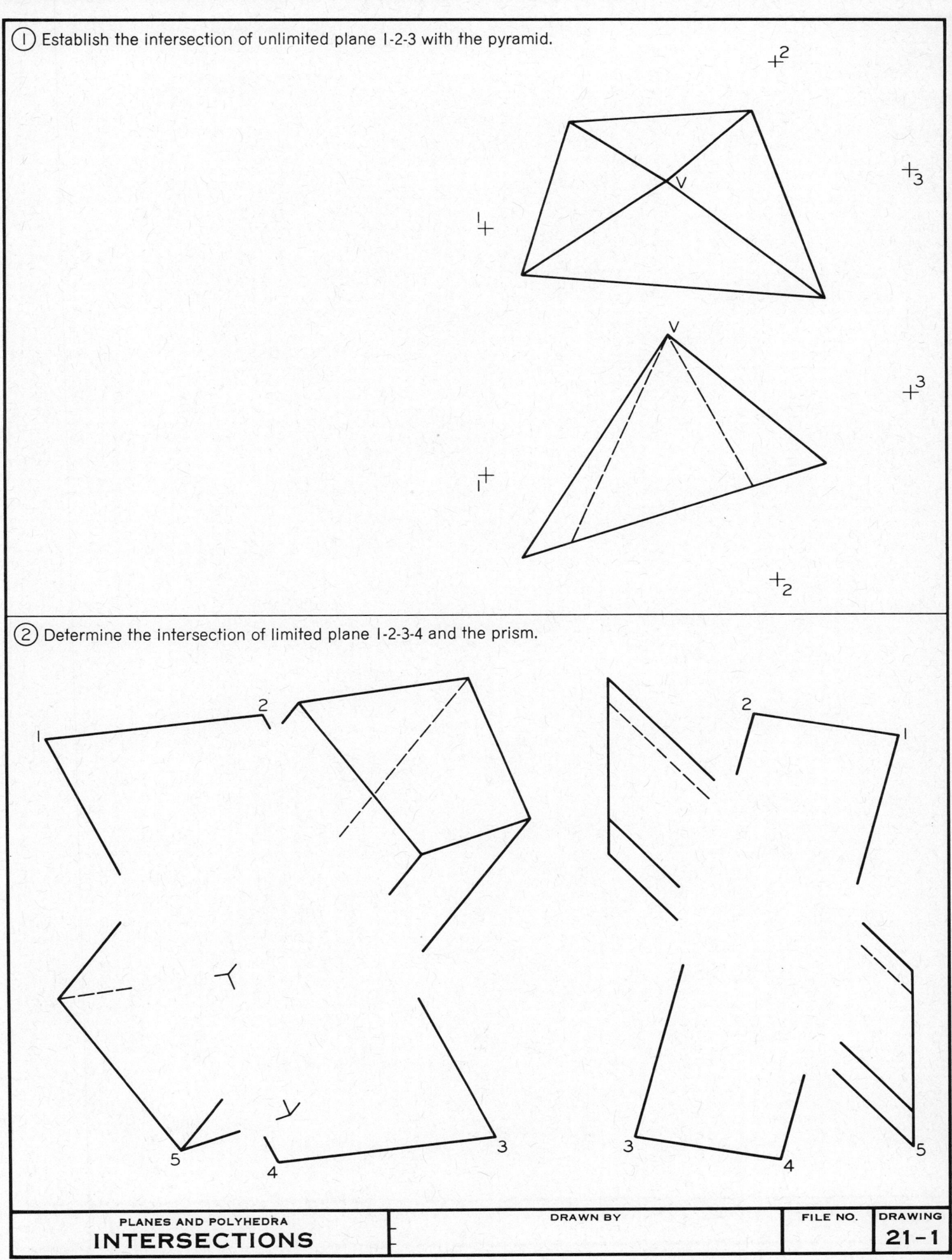

① Establish the intersection of unlimited plane 1-2-3 with the pyramid.

② Determine the intersection of limited plane 1-2-3-4 and the prism.

PLANES AND POLYHEDRA
INTERSECTIONS

DRAWN BY

FILE NO.

DRAWING
21-1

DRAWN BY | FILE NO. | DRAWING

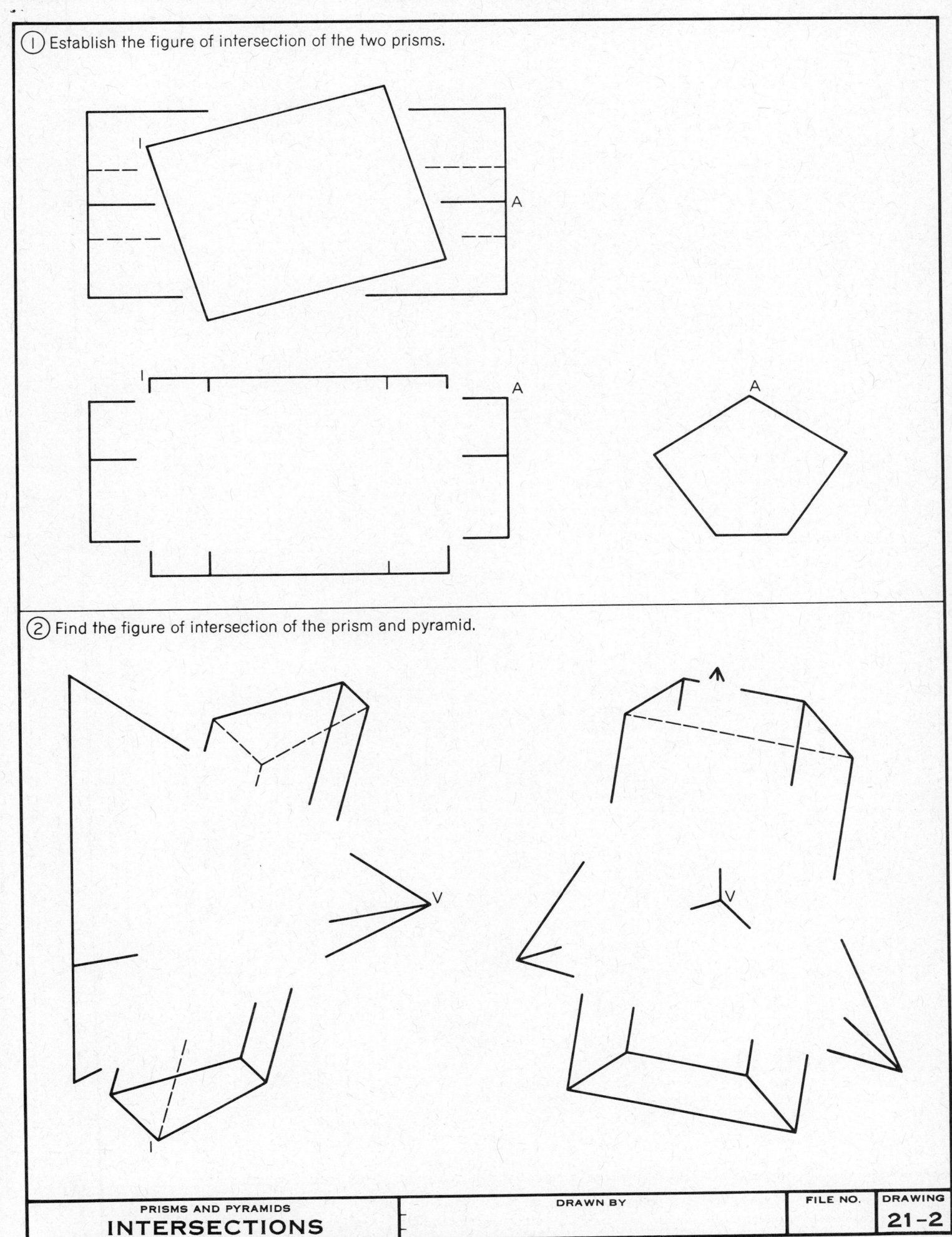

① Establish the figure of intersection of the two prisms.

A

A

A

② Find the figure of intersection of the prism and pyramid.

V

I

V

PRISMS AND PYRAMIDS
INTERSECTIONS

DRAWN BY

FILE NO.

DRAWING
21-2

DRAWN BY | FILE NO. | DRAWING

Complete the views of the intersecting forms of the Collector.

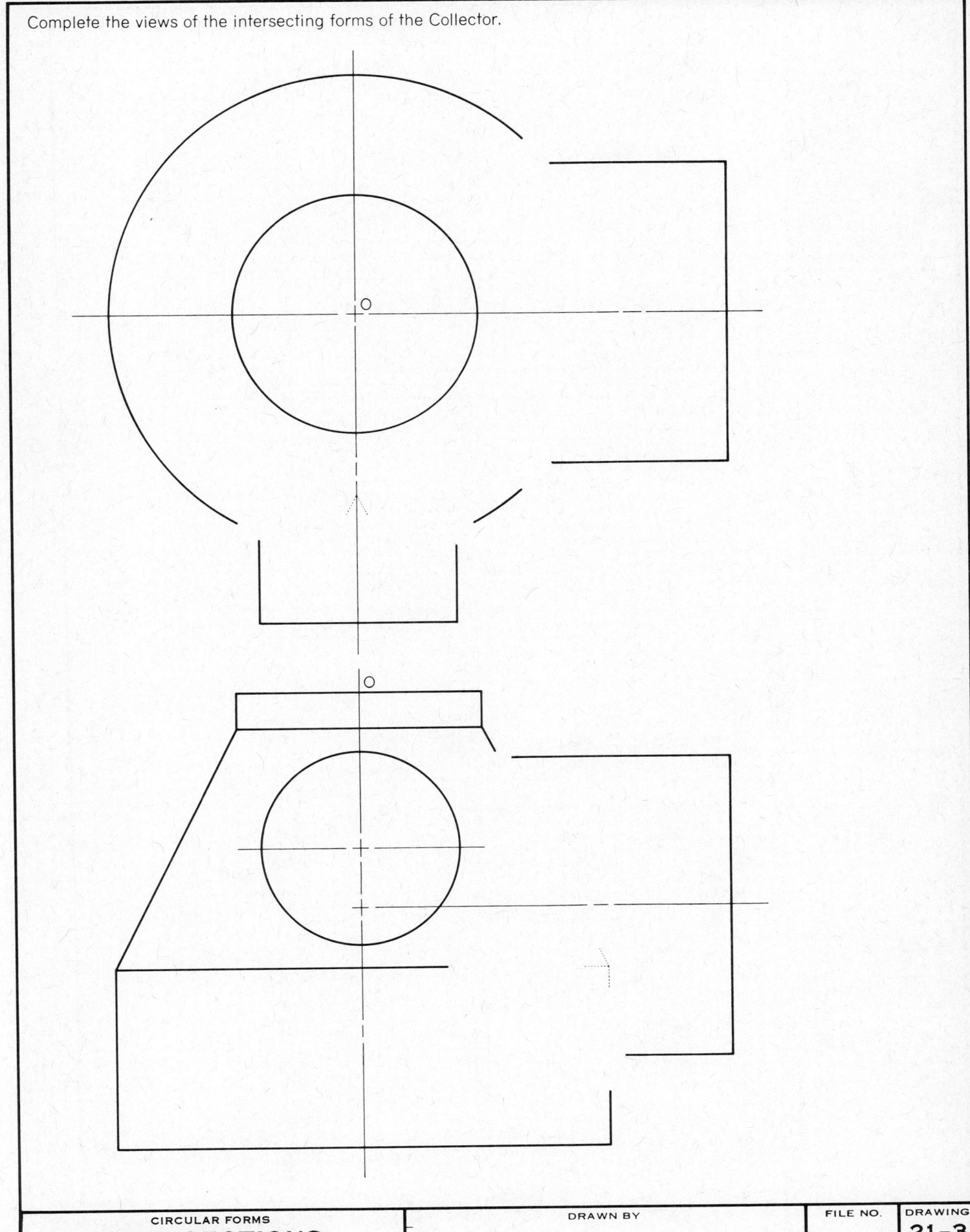

CIRCULAR FORMS
INTERSECTIONS

DRAWN BY

FILE NO.

DRAWING
21-3

DRAWN BY   FILE NO.   DRAWING

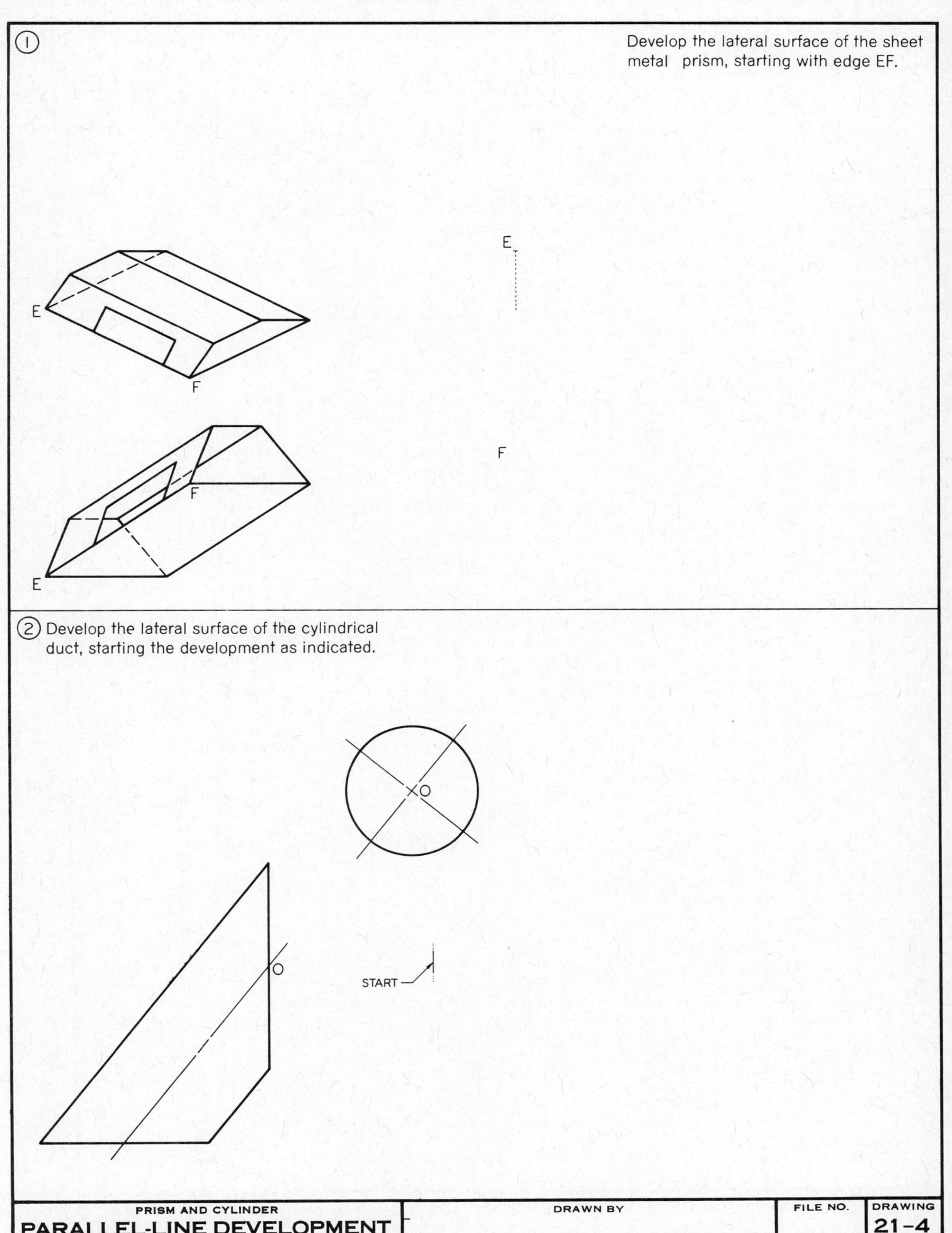

1. Develop the lateral surface of the sheet metal prism, starting with edge EF.

E

F

E
F

F
E

2. Develop the lateral surface of the cylindrical duct, starting the development as indicated.

O

O

START

PRISM AND CYLINDER
PARALLEL-LINE DEVELOPMENT

DRAWN BY

FILE NO.

DRAWING
21-4

① Develop the lateral surfaces of the pyramidal transition piece.

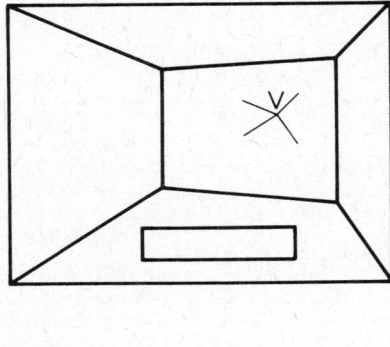

START—

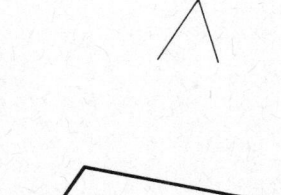

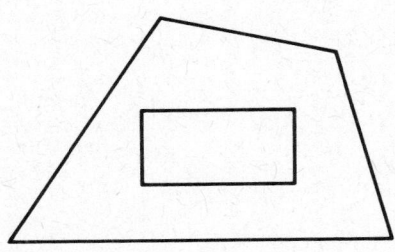

② Lay out a half development of the truncated right-circular cone.

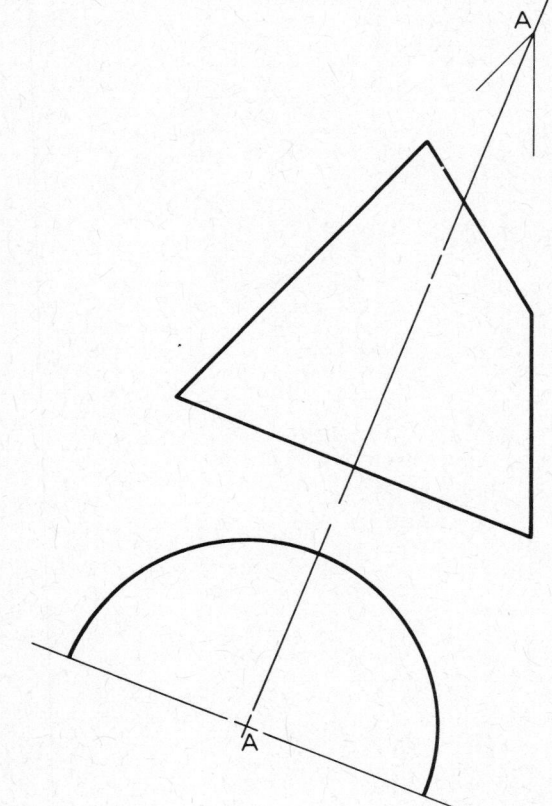

START—

PYRAMID AND CONE
RADIAL-LINE DEVELOPMENT

DRAWN BY

FILE NO.

DRAWING
21–5

DRAWN BY

FILE NO.

DRAWING

Construct a half development of the transition piece, starting with seam E-I at the indicated position and ending at the center line F-7 of panel B-C-7.

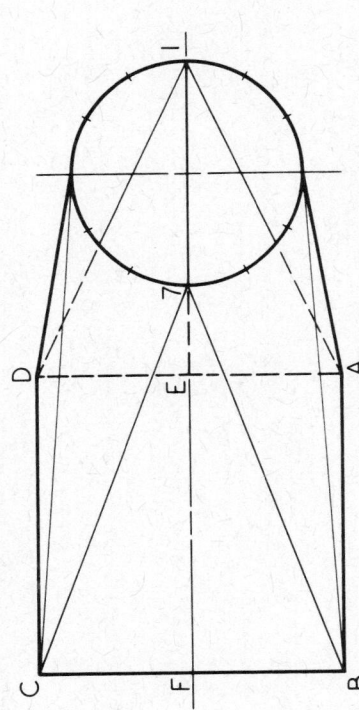

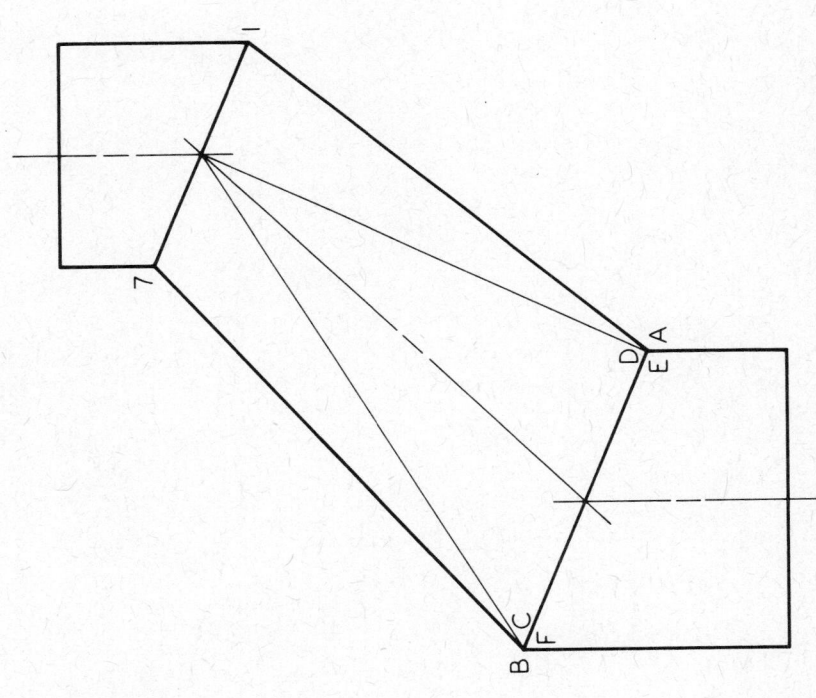

BOTTOM OF DRAWING

START

DRAWN BY

FILE NO.

DRAWING

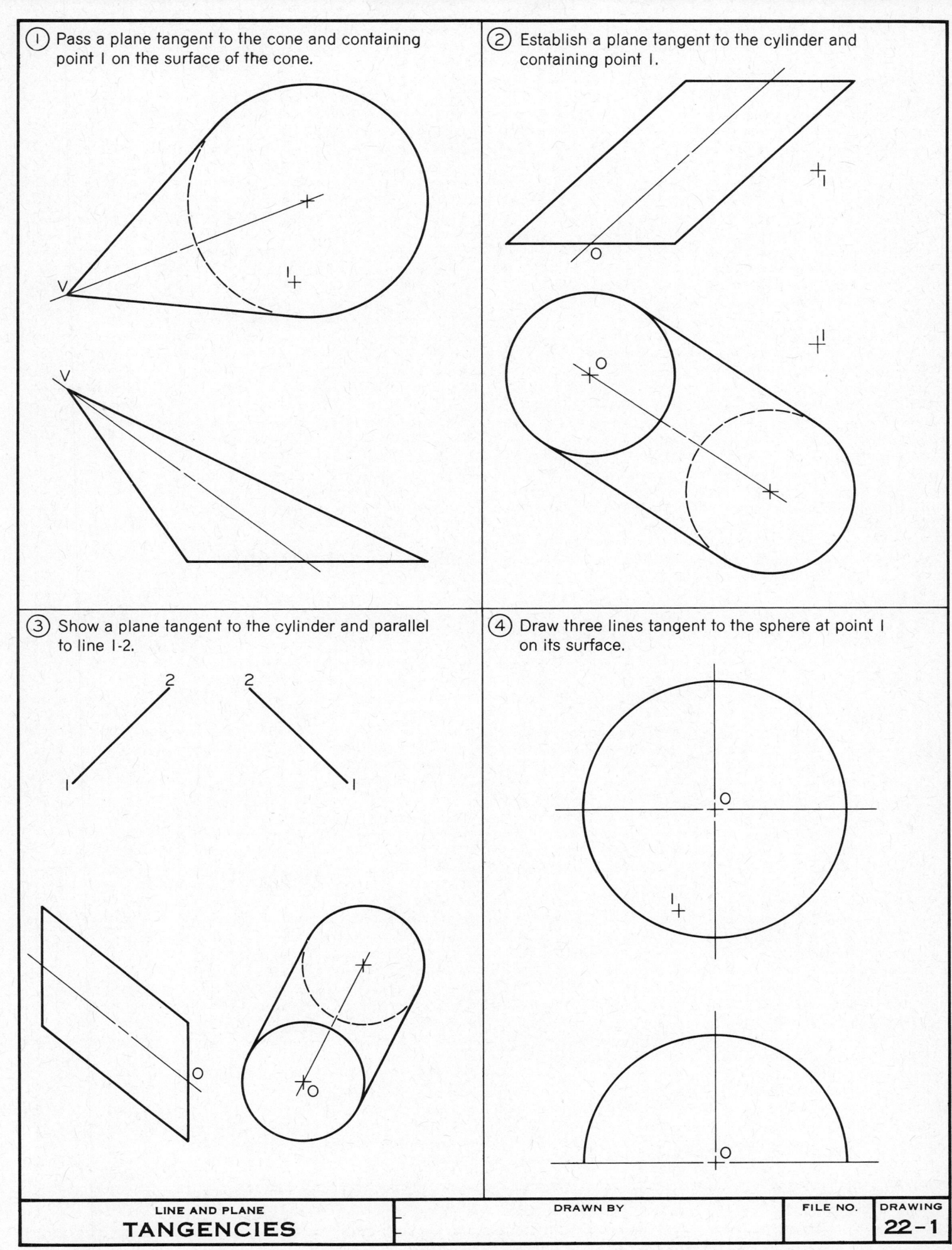

① Pass a plane tangent to the cone and containing point I on the surface of the cone.

② Establish a plane tangent to the cylinder and containing point I.

③ Show a plane tangent to the cylinder and parallel to line I-2.

④ Draw three lines tangent to the sphere at point I on its surface.

LINE AND PLANE
TANGENCIES

DRAWN BY

FILE NO.

DRAWING
22-1

DRAWN BY   FILE NO.   DRAWING

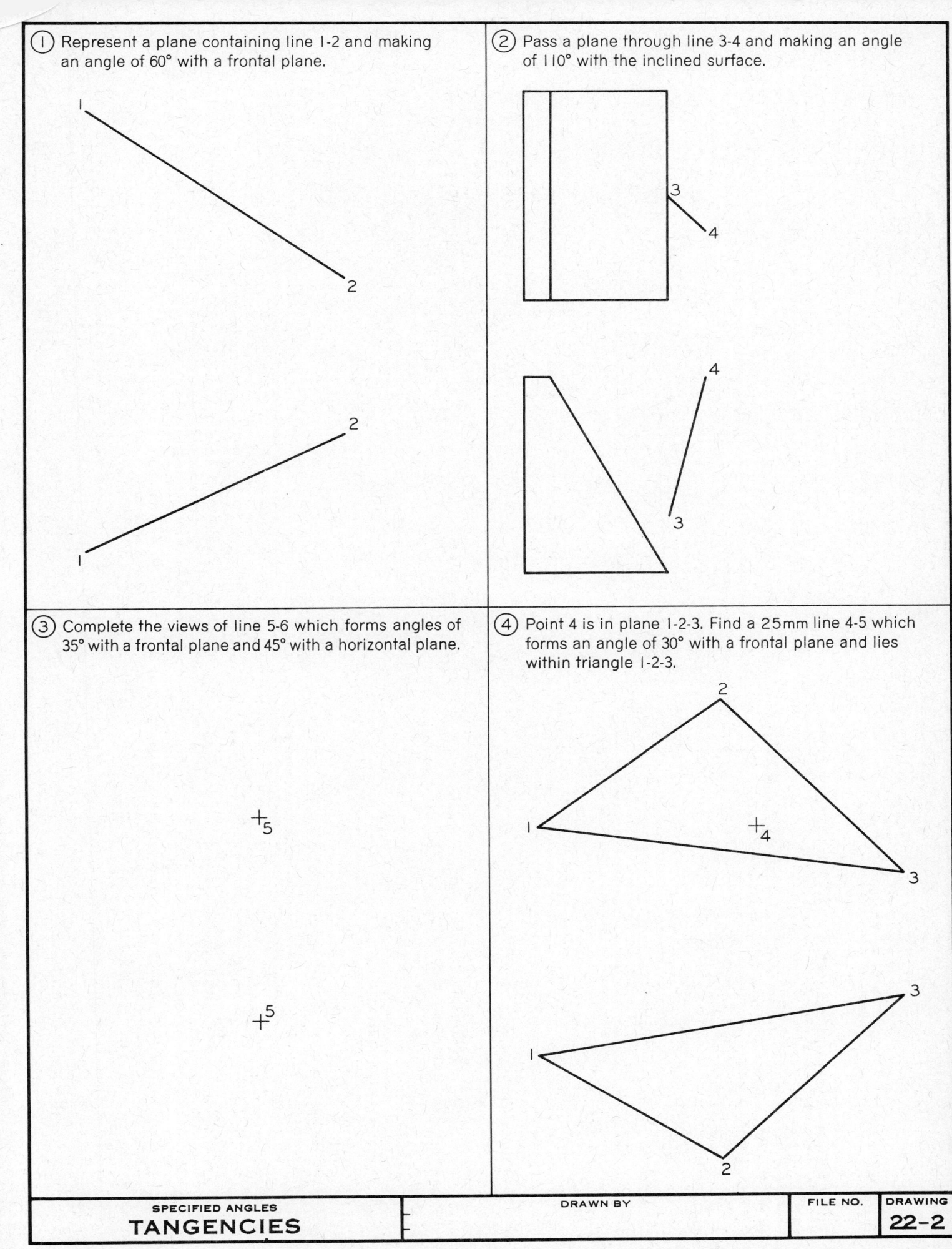

1 Represent a plane containing line 1-2 and making an angle of 60° with a frontal plane.

2 Pass a plane through line 3-4 and making an angle of 110° with the inclined surface.

3 Complete the views of line 5-6 which forms angles of 35° with a frontal plane and 45° with a horizontal plane.

4 Point 4 is in plane 1-2-3. Find a 25mm line 4-5 which forms an angle of 30° with a frontal plane and lies within triangle 1-2-3.

SPECIFIED ANGLES
TANGENCIES

DRAWN BY

FILE NO.

DRAWING
22-2

DRAWN BY   FILE NO.   DRAWING

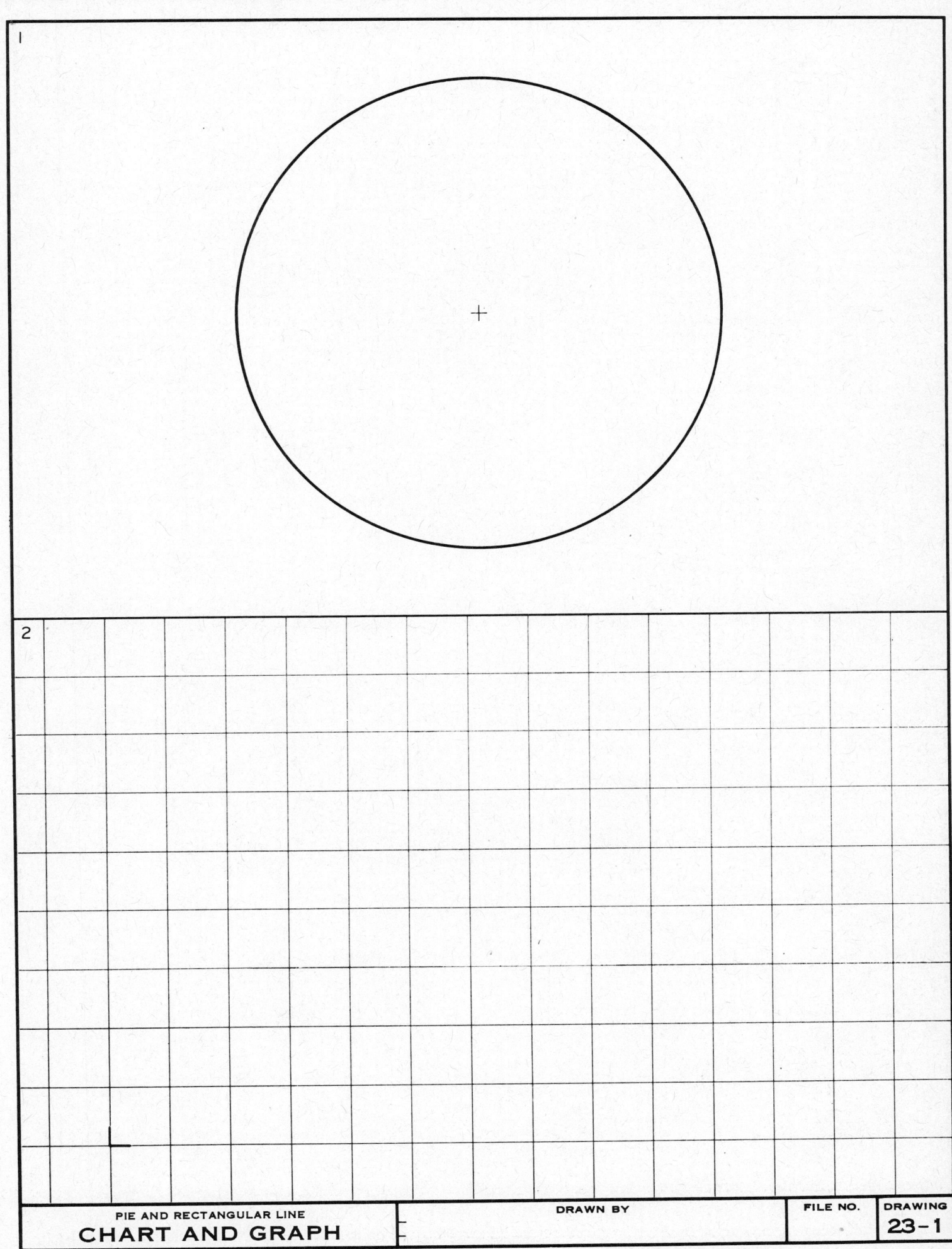

1

2

PIE AND RECTANGULAR LINE
CHART AND GRAPH

DRAWN BY

FILE NO.

DRAWING
23-1

DRAWN BY   FILE NO.   DRAWING

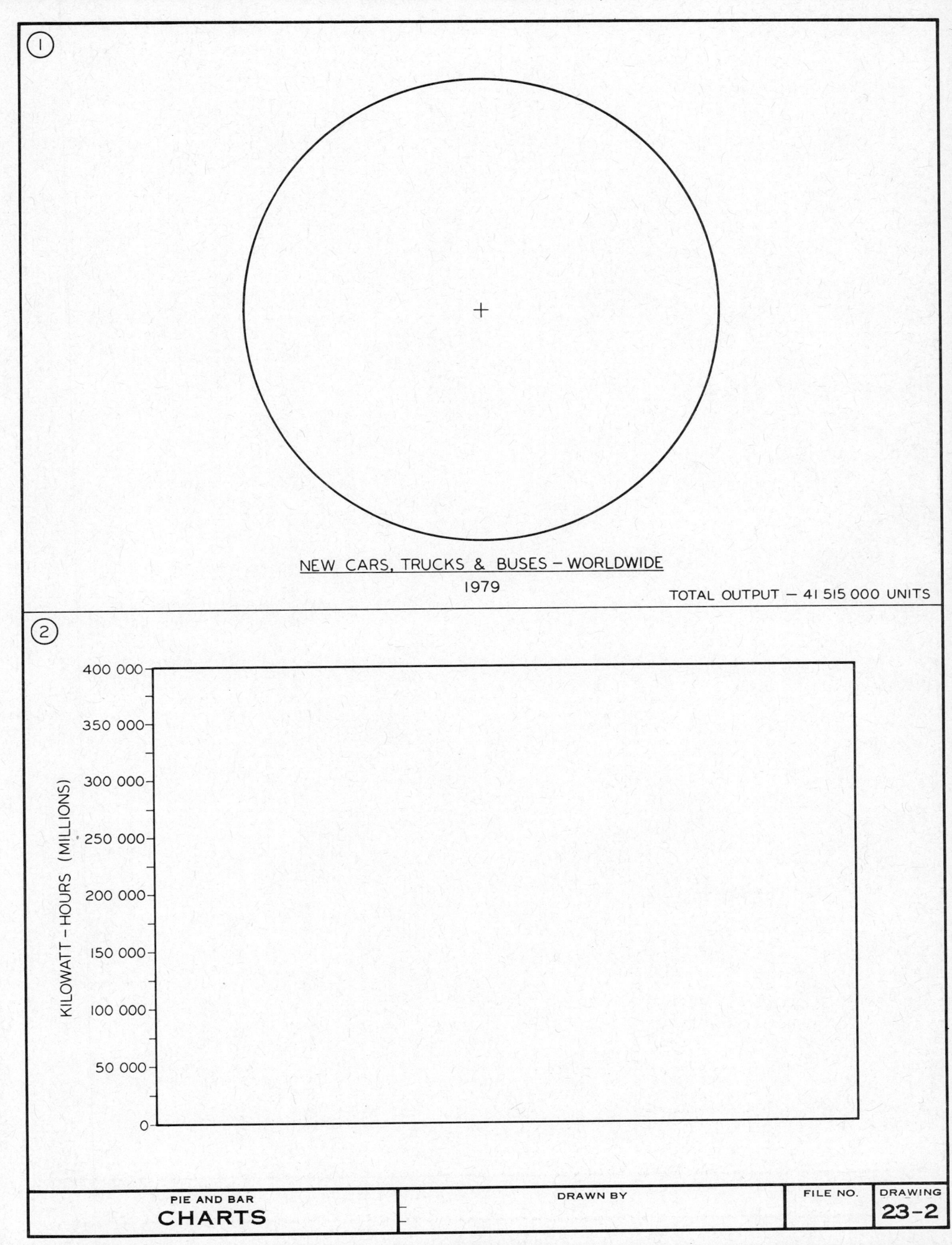

① NEW CARS, TRUCKS & BUSES — WORLDWIDE
1979
TOTAL OUTPUT — 41 515 000 UNITS

②

KILOWATT - HOURS (MILLIONS)

400 000
350 000
300 000
250 000
200 000
150 000
100 000
50 000
0

PIE AND BAR
CHARTS

DRAWN BY

FILE NO.

DRAWING
23-2

DRAWN BY   FILE NO.   DRAWING

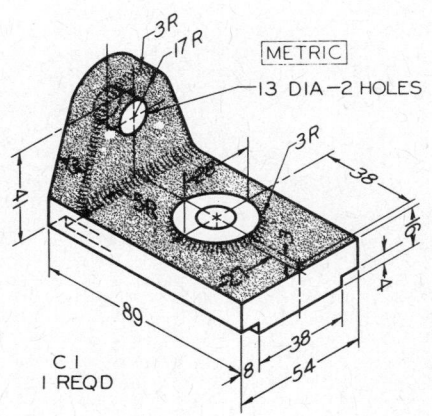

1   CUT-OFF HOLDER

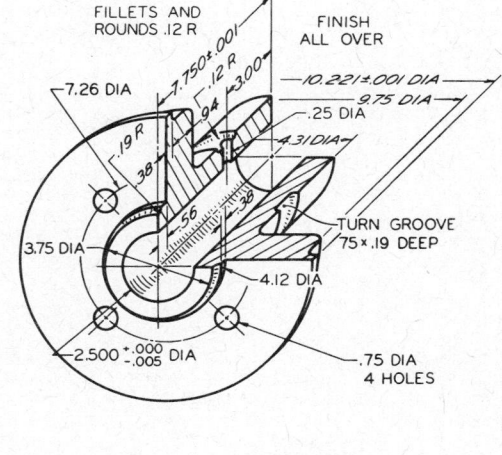

2   BEARING

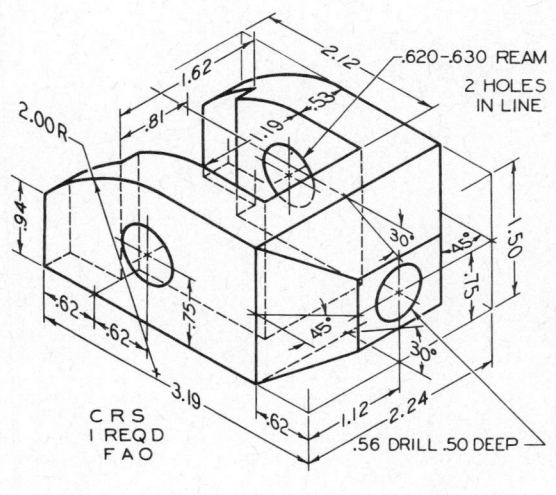

3   CAM

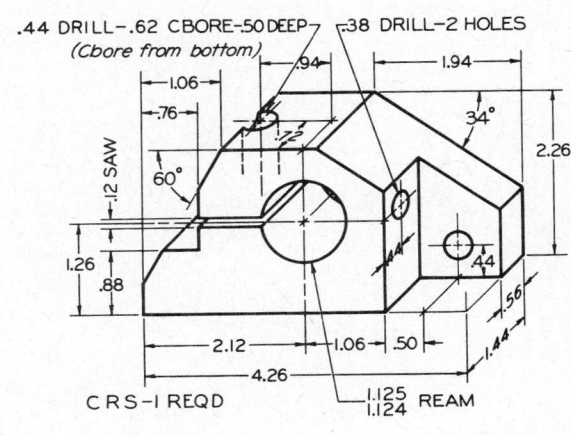

4   CLUTCH LEVER

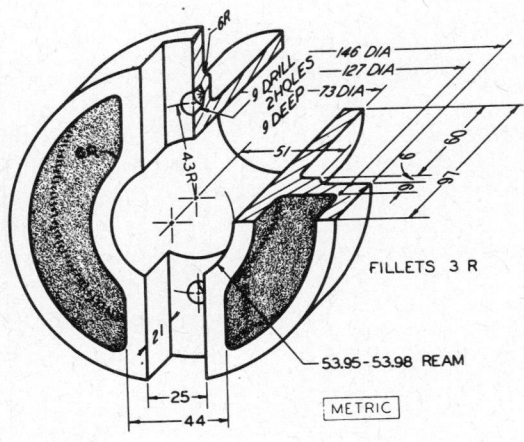

5   STOCK GUIDE

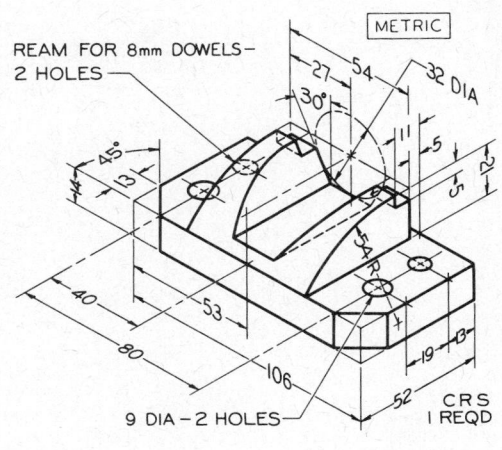

6   LOCATING FINGER

DETAIL DRAWINGS

DRAW OR SKETCH THE NECESSARY VIEWS OF THE OBJECT
ASSIGNED. DIMENSION COMPLETELY

DRAWN BY

FILE NO.

DRAWING

DRAWN BY   FILE NO.   DRAWING

DRAWN BY

FILE NO. | DRAWING

DRAWN BY

FILE NO.

DRAWING

DRAWN BY

FILE NO. DRAWING

DRAWN BY   FILE NO.   DRAWING

DRAWN BY | FILE NO. | DRAWING

DRAWN BY   FILE NO.   DRAWING

Sheet Layouts

A convenient code to identify American National Standard sheet sizes and forms suggested by the authors for title, parts or material list, and revision blocks, for use of instructors in making assignments, is shown here. All dimensions are in inches.

Three **sizes** of sheets are illustrated: **Size A**, Fig. I, **Size B**, Fig. V, and **Size C**, Fig. VI. Metric size sheets are not shown.

Eight **forms** of lettering arrangements are suggested, known as **Forms 1, 2, 3, 4, 5, 6, 7,** and **8,** as shown below and opposite. The total length of **Forms 1, 2, 3,** and **4** may be adjusted to fit **Sizes A4, A3,** and **A2**.

The term **layout** designates a sheet of certain size plus a certain arrangement of lettering. Thus **Layout A–1** is a combination of **Size A**, Fig. I, and **Form 1**, Fig. II. **Layout C–678** is a combination of **Size C**, Fig. VI, and **Forms 6, 7,** and **8**, Figs. IX, X, and XI. **Layout A4–2** (adjusted) is a combination of **Size A4** and **Form 2**, Fig. III, adjusted to fit between the borders. Other combinations may be employed as assigned by the instructor.

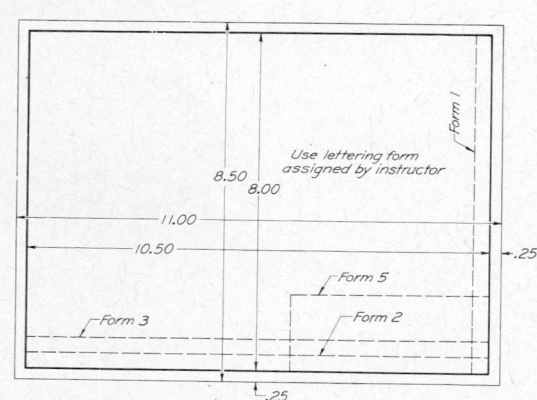

Fig. I   Size A Sheet (8.50″ × 11.00″)

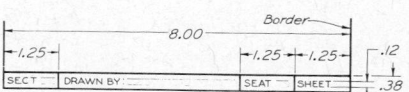

Fig. II   Form 1. Title Block

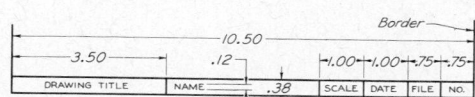

Fig. III   Form 2. Title Block

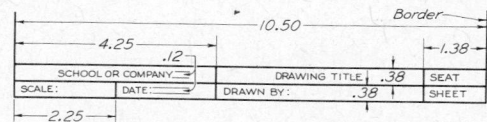

Fig. IV   Form 3. Title Block

Sheet Sizes

American National Standard

A – 8.50″ × 11.00″
B – 11.00″ × 17.00″
C – 17.00″ × 22.00″
D – 22.00″ × 34.00″
E – 34.00″ × 44.00″

International Standard

A4 – 210 mm × 297 mm
A3 – 297 mm × 420 mm
A2 – 420 mm × 594 mm
A1 – 594 mm × 841 mm
A0 – 841 mm × 1189 mm
  (25.4 mm = 1.00″)

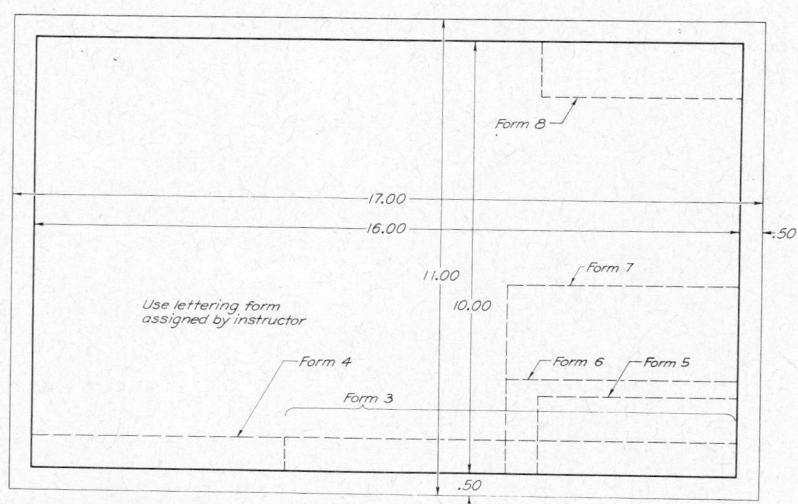

Fig. V   Size B Sheet (11.00″ × 17.00″)